Ounces	9 × 12 envelope, 9 × 12 SASE number of pages	9 × 12 SASE (for return trips) number of pages	First Class Postage	Feb. 1991	Third Class Postage **	Postage from U.S. to Canada **
under 2	...	1 to 2	$.35*	$.40	$.45*	$.40*
2	1 to 4	3 to 8	.45	.54	.45	.52
3	5 to 10	9 to 12	.65	.78	.65	.74
4	11 to 16	13 to 19	.85	1.02	.85	.96
5	17 to 21	20 to 25	1.05	1.26	1.00	1.18
6	22 to 27	26 to 30	1.25	1.50	1.00	1.40
7	28 to 32	31 to 35	1.45	1.74	1.10	1.62
8	33 to 38	36 to 41	1.65	1.98	1.10	1.84
9	39 to 44	42 to 46	1.85	2.22	1.20	2.06
10	45 to 49	47 to 52	2.05	2.46	1.20	2.28
11	50 to 55	53 to 57	2.25	2.70	1.30	2.50

* This cost includes an assessment for oversized mail that is light in weight.

** Postage to other countries and increments for Third Class had not been determined at the time we went to press. Check with your post office after February 1991.

1991 Writer's Market

Managing Editor, Market Books Department:
Constance J. Achabal

Library of Congress Catalog Number 31-20772
International Standard Serial Number 0084-2729
International Standard Book Number 0-89879-422-6

Information in U.S. Postage by the Page chart supplied by Carolyn Hardesty;
Canadian Postage by the Page by Barbara Murrin

1991
Writer's Market

*Where & How
To Sell What You Write*

Editor: Glenda Tennant Neff

Assistant Editor: Mark Kissling

Cincinnati, Ohio

The Writing Profession

The Markets

Contents

Contents

Services & Opportunities

The Writing Profession

From the Editors

You know how if feels to create, to put words to paper. It's a satisfying and fulfilling part of a writer's life.

The creative process is just one side of a writer's life, however. Getting published requires more than just good technique, and the savvy writer keeps up with the business side of the craft. At *Writer's Market* we trust that you will continue to grow as a writer, perfecting your skills and capitalizing on your strengths. Our aim is to give you the information you need to keep up with the ever-changing business side of the publishing world.

With our 62nd edition, we've included a number of new features in response to your questions and requests. Self-promotion is an area of interest to writers, ranging from those working with major publishing houses to those self-publishing their works. Elane Feldman's Self-Promotion for Writers gives you techniques for publicizing your writing, for working with the media and for promoting your work to publishers and agents.

We've expanded the First Bylines feature from last year to include two first novelists, two short story writers, and two nonfiction writers. They tell you how they work, how they earned that first byline, and they give you some advice from that experience.

This year's Writers' Roundtable deals with rights. Writers and editors both have a tough time with rights, determining what they should sell—or buy—and for what price. Three experienced writers give you tips on choosing what rights to sell, determining what the sale means to you, and then negotiating with editors. Our survey of editors also lets you know why editors buy the rights they do and how flexible they are in the rights they purchase.

New samples of magazine and book query letters provide you with examples of successful selling tools. We've also included survey information about electronic submissions in the Book Publishers, Consumer Publications and Trade Journals introductions. Find out how many editors want submission by modem or disk, as well as what methods they prefer and whether or not they'll pay extra for it. Again this year you'll find section-by-section lists of additional information about markets that have changed or no longer accept freelance submissions. In addition, the nonfiction and fiction index for Author's Agents and Book Publishers will give you a quicker method for finding agents and publishers interested in the topics on which you write.

As always, you'll find Close-up interviews with writers and editors, as well as 650 new markets for your writing.

You'll note some changes in the listing information from the 1990 edition. Because many writers want to quickly identify markets that pay on acceptance, we've put this information in bold within the listings. We've also asked for established dates on all listings because we know it's one method writers use to evaluate the stability of a market. Although photocopied and computer printout submissions were not universally accepted a few years ago, editors don't mind receiving these submissions now, so we've deleted that information from the listings.

Because the publishing industry is constantly changing, details in the market listings may change during the year. We make additions, corrections and changes in listings until the book is sent to the printer, but often publishers go out of business, editors find other jobs, and publications change policies after our press time. New markets and changes in others can be found during the year in many publishing and writers' magazines, including *Writer's Digest*, which records changes in *Writer's Market* listings.

We appreciate feedback from you, too. If you know of markets we could contact, if you have a complaint about nonpayment or lack of response from a listing, or if you have suggestions of ways we can make the book more useful to you, please write to us. Always enclose a self-addressed, stamped envelope with your letter if you expect a reply.

Whether you are a new writer or an experienced professional, working on your first or your 101st byline, we hope your use of this edition of *Writer's Market* will be the beginning of many writing opportunities in 1991.

Glenda Tennant Neff

Mark Kissling

How to Use Writer's Market

Before beginning your search for markets to send your writing to, take a moment to read this section. It will help you make full use of the individual listings and will explain the symbols and abbreviations used throughout the book.

The Table of Contents should be your next stop. That way, you'll know where to find all the publishing opportunities for your work.

Check the glossary for unfamiliar words and the addresses of certain writer's organizations. Specific symbols and abbreviations are explained in the table on page 5. The most important abbreviation is SASE—self-addressed, stamped envelope. *Always* enclose one when you send unsolicited queries or manuscripts to editors, publishers or agents. This requirement is not included in the individual market listings because it's a "given" that you must follow if you expect to receive a reply.

Review the following sample listing and the explanation section that accompanies it.

(1)‡CELEBRATE LIFE, The Magazine of Positive Living, Unimedia Corp., Suite 201, 18395 Gulf Blvd., Indian Rocks Beach FL 34635. **(2)** (813)595-4141. **(3)** Editor: Marty Johnson. **(4)** 75% freelance written. **(5)(6)** Quarterly magazine covering motivational, positive lifestyles. **(7)** Estab. 1989. **(8)** Circ. 10,000. **(9)** Pays on publication. Publishes ms an average of 3 months after acceptance. Buys first North American serial rights, all rights or makes work-for-hire assignments. **(10)** Submit seasonal/holiday material 6 months in advance. Simultaneous and previously published submissions OK "if notified." Query for electronic submissions. **(11)** Reports in 2 months. **(12)** Sample copy $2 with 9 × 12 SAE and 4 first class stamps. Writer's guidelines for #10 SASE.

(13) Nonfiction: (14) How-to (self-improvement), humor, inspirational, interview/profile, personal experience, photo feature, religious (new thought), travel, natural lifestyles (i.e. holistic health). "Each issue is thematic. This is an upbeat, positive publication." **(15)(16)** Query with or without published clips, or send complete ms. **(17)** Length: 400-2,000 words. **(18)** Pays $25-75 for assigned articles. Complimentary copies to $25 or more for unsolicited material. **(19)** "Rarely" pays expenses of writers on assignment.

(20) Photos: State availability of or send photos with submission. Reviews contact sheets, transparencies and prints. Captions, model releases and identification of subjects required. Buys one time rights.

(21) Tips: "We are very specific about what we want in each upcoming issue. Nothing outside these parameters will fit. Interviews/profiles of leaders of positive change are wanted."

(1) Symbols, names and addresses. One or more symbols (*, ‡,□) may precede the name and address of the publication or market; check the key on page 5 for their meanings. (This double dagger signifies a new listing.) This year we differentiate between post office and other boxes. Post office boxes are listed as P.O. Box.

(2) Phone and FAX numbers. A phone number or FAX number in a listing does not mean the market accepts phone queries. Make a phone query only when your story's timeliness would be lost by following the usual procedures. As a rule, don't call or FAX information unless you have been invited to do so.

(3) Contact names. In most listings, names of contact persons are given in the first paragraph or under the bold subheadings. Address your query or submission to a specific name when possible. If the name is not easily recognizable by gender, use the full name (e.g., Dear Dale Smith:). If no contact name is given, consult a sample copy. As a last resort, you can address your query to "Articles Editor" or what is appropriate. For more information, read Approaching Markets in the Business of Writing.

(4) Size of market. A market's general openness to writers is indicated by the percentage of freelance material used or by the percentage of published manuscripts from new, un-agented writers.

(5) Copyright information. Because most publications are copyrighted, the information is only given in this spot when the publication is *not* copyrighted. For information on copyrighting your own work, see Rights and the Writer in the Business of Writing.

(6) Emphasis and readership. A description of the market provides the focus and audi-ence.

(7) Established date. Beginning this year, we have attempted to include the established date for *all* listings. Book publishers, magazines and agents with older established dates tend to be more stable markets.

(8) Circulation. The figures listed are the sum of subscriptions plus shelf sales.

(9) Rights purchased. General business policies give information about rights purchased and time of payment. **Pays on acceptance** is a policy we favor, so we highlight it in the listings with bold lettering. Book publishers list average royalty and agents list commission rates. See Rights and the Writer in the Business of Writing for more information.

(10) Submission requirements. Submission requirements include how far in advance to submit seasonal material and whether or not previously published material will be consid-ered. Send manuscripts or queries to one market at a time unless it indicates simultaneous submissions are OK. If you send your manuscript to more than one market at a time, mention in your cover letter that it is a simultaneous submission. Electronic submissions are mentioned only if the market accepts them. See Writing Tools in the Business of Writing for more information.

(11) Reporting time. Reporting times indicate how soon a market will respond to your query or manuscript, but times listed are approximate. Quarterly publications, book pub-lishers, literary magazines and all new listings may be slower to respond. Wait three weeks beyond the stated reporting time before you send a polite inquiry. If no reporting time is listed, wait 2 months for a reply.

(12) Writer's guidelines and sample copies. If you're interested in writing for a particu-lar market, request the writer's guidelines and/or a sample copy if the market indicates availability. "Writer's guidelines for SASE" means that a business-size envelope (#10) with one first class stamp will be adequate. You should request a sample copy if you are unable to find the publication at a newsstand or library. A sample copy or book catalog is often available for a 9×12 self-addressed envelope with a specified number of stamps or International Reply Coupons. Most publishers will send, at no extra charge, writer's guide-lines with sample copies if you request them.

(13) Subheads. Subheads in bold (Nonfiction, Photos, etc.) guide you to requirements for those types of materials.

(14) Types of nonfiction needed. The specific material desired (and often material *not* desired) is listed. Follow the guidelines. Do not send fiction to a publication that only uses nonfiction; do not send a children's book manuscript to a publisher of men's adventure novels.

(15) Manuscripts purchased. The number of manuscripts purchased per issue or per year will give you an idea of how easy or difficult it may be to sell your work to a particular market. (This particular market did not provide us with that information.) With new list-ings, these figures may change dramatically depending on the submissions they receive or changes in policy.

(16) Submission information. If the market wants to see queries, that's what you should send. The same goes for outlines and sample chapters, etc. Don't send a complete manu-script unless the listing indicates it's acceptable.

(17) Word length. Editors know the length of most material they buy; follow their range of words or pages. If your manuscript is longer or shorter (by a wide margin) than the stated requirements, find another market.

(18) Payment rates. Payment ranges tell you what the market usually paid at the time *Writer's Market* was published.

(19) Expenses. Whether a market sometimes or usually pays expenses of writers on assignment is listed. No mention is made when a market does *not* pay expenses.

(20) Photos, columns/departments, fiction, poetry and fillers. Needs, rates and policies for specified material.

(21) Tips. Helpful suggestions are listed under the subhead Tips in many listings. They describe the best way to submit manuscripts or give special insight into needs and preferences of the market.

Key to Symbols and Abbreviations

‡ New listing in all sections

* Subsidy publisher in Book Publishers section

☐ Cable TV market in Scriptwriting section

ms-manuscript; **mss**-manuscripts

b&w-black and white (photo)

SASE-self-addressed, stamped envelope

SAE-self-addressed envelope

IRC-International Reply Coupon, for use on reply mail in Canada and foreign markets.

FAX-a communications system used to transmit documents over the telephone lines.

(See Glossary for definitions of words and expressions used in writing/publishing.)

Self-Promotion for Writers

by Elane Feldman

For many creative people the words publicity and self-promotion strike a sour note. Yet for the wise writer these are words that speak to today's realities. Submissions to magazines remain very high — *The Atlantic Monthly* estimated once that it receives about 25,000 submissions per year. And for every one of the 50,000 or so books published each year, thousands more are submitted to book publishers for consideration.

If we combine the huge number of books already in print with the number published yearly, it's obvious that lack of promotion can spell instant death to the most meritorious book. The reasons for this are multi-faceted. Frequently, publishers' publicity departments are overworked, understaffed or non-existent. This results in short-lived and less than thorough promotion of many titles. Consequently, too many writers can relate sad stories of how poorly they fared at the hands of their publishers. And too few writers in all areas of publishing are aware of how to help themselves.

In teaching writers' workshops in publicity, promotion and related areas, I am continually amazed how few creative people understand publishing realities and how many are horrified by the very thought of undertaking any self-promotion. Frequently writers think merit alone will carry them to the pinnacle of success or believe publicity is tacky, very expensive or egotistical. It is, however, just such beliefs that usually mean grave disappointment. In light of how competitive today's world is, it is patently foolish not to work to appropriately promote oneself — with appropriately being a key word.

If you are interested in doing self-promotion but are concerned that you don't know how or where to begin, there are some basic terms with which you should be familiar.

Actually, all of them — the "hook," the "pitch," and the follow-up that you've "scripted" beforehand — can be applied to many aspects of your writing career.

Start with a "hook"

Whether you will be approaching the media or other people you would like to interest in working with you, it is necessary to be able to quickly sum up who you are and what you have to say. You do this by means of "hooks," that is, statements that encapsulate your subject in an easy-to-understand manner. Hooks, also referred to as angles or "tag lines," can be used in a variety of situations.

For instance, if you are the author of a new book, a tag line will help your publisher in a myriad of ways, particularly in presenting your book to sales representatives, who in turn can use the hook to present your book to bookstore buyers.

A "hook" — especially if it promises to provide news, information or entertainment — can be used to entice electronic (TV or radio) or print media attention. This is particularly important if you plan to hold a press conference or public appearance.

Elane Feldman has been director of marketing, public relations and promotion at several New York trade book publishers and has served as a consultant in those fields for a variety of clients both in and out of publishing. Currently an adjunct assistant professor of public relations at New York University, she has had more than 150 articles published in major national magazines and regularly creates and leads seminars and workshops for publishing executives, college students and writers' organizations. Her article is excerpted from The Writer's Guide to Publicity and Self-Promotion, *available from Writer's Digest Books.*

No matter what type of writing you do, particularly in working with media, you will find it much easier to describe yourself if you have prepared an angle or tag line ahead of time. No matter how complex your subject, you must strive to reduce it to easily grasped hooks.

In the first example that follows, you can see what this writer will work from, and how he creates his tag lines. The other example is self-explanatory.

William Pickering is a retired Army officer who lives in Hilo, Hawaii. His first book is an action/adventure novel set in Hawaii (in December '41) just before the attack on Pearl Harbor. His "hook" plays up his firsthand knowledge:

Tropic Calm is a new novel by William Pickering, a retired Army officer, describing the lives of three people in the weeks and days leading up to Pearl Harbor. Mr. Pickering, a lifelong resident of the Islands, was stationed at Hickam Field in this period.

This angle summarizes who the author is and what she has to say.

Jane Goodings, who operates Middletown's "Fixit Shop," has written a new paper-back book, *Homeowners Fix It Fast*, which tells readers how to save thousands of dollars on home repair projects.

Overall, it's important that whenever you're thinking of approaching the media yourself, you understand what the media seeks. Namely, you should be able to provide news, information or entertainment—or combinations of these three. In the first example, the novel, there's an entertainment angle. The second example offers information.

Establishing a game plan

If you have not yet established a national reputation and want to generate publicity, you should establish a written plan, keeping in mind how you can supply the news, information or entertainment the media seek.

For those who have had scant publicity exposure, it is best to start modestly. If you have had little to no publicity exposure and if your subject is not one of broad general interest, rather than immediately approaching the major television and radio talk shows and the national print media, start in your own backyard. And try only those shows where your topic makes sense. (If, for instance, you specialize in cooking, don't try shows that only cover urban affairs or politics.)

To begin your written plan, draw up lists of target markets in the varied media and then build, using your successes in local and regional markets to approach the national ones.

"Pitch" letters

When you attempt to sell yourself to the media—or to other people who can help you promote yourself—you will want to create attention-getting "pitch" letters. In the parlance of public relations, the pitch letter is used to do just that. Namely, you want the recipient to "catch" your message and respond favorably.

At times you'll send your pitch with your press kit and/or a book or an article you are publicizing, and it then becomes a cover letter. Other times your pitches will go out alone. In either case you must write a focused, hard-hitting professional pitch to sell yourself and your idea. Remember that the person to whom you write probably receives hundreds of such letters monthly. You want yours to stand out.

Please note: Here we talk about pitching for publicity but, as most writers are aware, generally the same principles apply in pitching story and book ideas for publication. You can also use some of these same principles in pitching your services as a writer to a potential client.

Pitch letters — the how-to

Given the huge quantity of mail editors, news directors and others in the media receive, you must immediately gain their attention and pique interest. More importantly, you want that person to act.

In doing pitch letters, you must always include information on where and how you can be reached. It's also a good idea if you're not going to be available at all times to include information on when you will be available for interviews. (Never offer only one day.)

Clearly present the topic you are prepared to discuss. And, for general consumer media, especially the electronic media, limit yourself to one or two areas of your subject.

The following are two examples of media-oriented pitch letters. Please note that both are "provocative" pitches. Namely, they are ones that will probably gain attention and interest the recipient in setting up an interview. Use them to focus your thinking on how you can present yourself.

Pitch letter #1

This was a tough sell, as attracting attention for fiction is always difficult. This pitch was created to help publicize a novel and was sent to national and regional media — both print and electronic.

> Dear (name inserted)
>
> Picture the scene . . . as the early morning mist lifts, the city awakens . . . preparations begin. This day the city's most powerful and its most powerless will share in the excitement of the spectacle. The city itself is the world's most famous urban area . . . a magnet . . . a place where the deeds of the rich and famous are grist for gossip mills . . . one where corruption, crime and brutality vie with lavish entertainments as topics of conversation. From crowded tenements and elegant homes, the citizens take their places as thousands of naked runners set off in marathon competition.
>
> Naked marathon runners? Yes, as it is not New York City in October that we are discussing . . . it is second century Rome.
>
> It is this milieu that is the setting for *Between Eternities* by Robert H. Pilpel.
>
> This book is set for publication the week of the New York City Marathon. [here we inserted the publication date, publisher's name, etc.]
>
> We believe that the author will offer you a fresh new marathon-themed interview possibility. He will be available in your city on [we inserted dates]. Please call me at the number on this letterhead to arrange an interview.

At this point, we also sketched in the novel's story line and thus indicated its newsworthiness to the upcoming race. We also outlined the author's credentials and quoted advance favorable comments on the book. For visual media, we indicated that we had a good amount of visual material to offer.

Given the New York City Marathon's always strong media coverage, we had an excellent angle to play. We offered the by-then jaded and story-poor media an offbeat way to peg another marathon story.

We also used this same pitch in other cities holding marathons, and we skewed the letter according to the recipient's interest area — that is for radio, newspaper or magazine. We also targeted ethnic media given the Italian angle inherent in the novel's story line.

Pitch letter #2

For a magazine writer with a forthcoming article geared to radio and/or TV shows that feature such subjects.

Dear (name inserted)

Take a look at your desk or those of your colleagues, and you're likely to see what was once a forbidden substance. This item, now a virtual "must have" for millions of us, has a long and intriguing history.

It's been used by mankind for something over eleven centuries.

A 17th century English king forbade his subjects to congregate where it was sold.

Before Pope Clement VIII, it was not permissible for Christians to use it—it was deemed suitable only for "infidels."

Frederick the Great of Prussia employed a special "secret service" to root out and penalize users.

Songs (and an opera by J.S. Bach) have been written about it.

It played a special role in Revolutionary America's early history.

If you've guessed it's coffee—you're right! And, if you would like to discuss my forthcoming article in [magazine named] which details the fascinating history of coffee, I would be pleased to speak with you. I would be happy to discuss and/or demonstrate new and interesting recipes using the beverage. This is my schedule [available dates given here].

The letter went on to provide information on how, when, and where pitch letter recipients could contact the writer.

The follow-up

Successful salespeople know the importance of following up on a sales call. When you mail off a "pitch" it's important that you follow up to make sure that it's been received and determine if there's interest in what you're proposing.

When you undertake your phone follow-up to your mailings, there are several things to keep in mind:

• Wait about five to seven working days from the time you mail your pitch before you begin follow-up phone calls.

• When people you reach indicate they cannot speak with you, always ask when would be a more convenient time for you to call back. (Tip: When you call back and you reach an assistant or secretary, immediately tell that person you are calling back as you were asked to do.)

• If the person you reach says he hasn't received your material, say that you will call back in a few days to check if it's arrived. If it hasn't arrived at that point, tell him you will resubmit it.

• Write out a script—or at least the key points—for your follow-up calls. (Be sure you have the name of the person you wrote to and the date your material was mailed.)

• Professional public relations people know that they have a scant few seconds to capture the attention of the people they are calling. As a writer working on publicity or self-promotion, you should also work on these principles. If you write your script out beforehand and practice what you will say, you should be able to wind up each call within 15 to 30 seconds—leaving you more time to work on your writing.

The Business of Writing

Developments for writers in the publishing industry during the past year have been mixed. Seen as a step forward, the Authors Guild is paying for the audit each year of three randomly-selected publishers' royalty statements, and the Book Industry Systems Advisory Committee has organized a subcommittee to develop standard formats for royalty statements. In addition, the National Writers Union has met with several book publishers to seek changes in contracts.

Also two major copyright infringement lawsuits were decided in favor of the writer during the year. Margaret Mitchell's estate won a lawsuit against a French book it said was patterned after *Gone With the Wind*. And Art Buchwald won a lawsuit claiming that the movie "Coming to America" was close to a script idea he submitted to the producers.

However, on the down side, the industry continued to debate issues concerning profit, while a Columbia University survey of authors' incomes found that the great majority of fulltime authors still earn less than $25,000. Some lawsuit-wary book publishers also began issuing contracts that asked writers to pay for any possible legal costs incurred by the publisher over the manuscript. In some cases, magazine writers also claim that now up to 50% of their submissions to editors never receive a response.

Most freelance writers concentrate on their writing and overlook the business side. While writing is your main pursuit, as a writer you should also keep an eye on business developments that will affect your livelihood. Plan to invest some time in managing the business side of your writing even if you just want to make a little extra money with it. The following information will help you keep current with the industry's latest developments and help you better manage your writing.

Marketing your manuscripts

Writers often find interesting stories to write about and then begin to look for a suitable publisher or magazine. While this approach is common, it reduces your chances of success. Instead, try choosing categories that interest you and study those sections in *Writer's Market*. Select several listings that you consider good prospects for your kind of writing. Sometimes the individual listings will help you generate ideas too.

Next, make a list of the potential markets for each idea. Make the initial contact with markets using the method stated in the market listings.

If you exhaust your list of possibilities, don't give up. Reevaluate the idea, revise it, or try another angle. Continue developing ideas and approaching markets with them. Identify and rank potential markets for an idea and continue the process, but don't approach a market a second time until you've received a response to your first submission.

Prepare for rejection and the sometimes lengthy process that publishing takes. When a submission is returned, check the file folder of potential markets for that idea. Cross off the current market and immediately mail an appropriate submission to the next market on your list. If the editor has given you suggestions or reasons the manuscript was not accepted, you might want to incorporate these when revising your manuscript. In any event, remember the first editor didn't reject *you*, but simply chose not to buy your product. A rejection only means that your particular piece did not fit the needs of the publisher at that time. Veteran writers also find it helps to have several projects going at once, so you don't dwell on the one that's out for consideration.

Writing tools

Like anyone involved in a trade or business, you need certain tools and supplies to produce your product or provide your service. While writers compose their work in a variety of ways—ranging from pencil and legal pad to expensive personal computers—there are some basics you'll need for your writing business. We've also included information about some you may want in the future.

Typewriter. Many writers use electric or electronic typewriters that produce either pica or elite type. Pica type has 10 characters to a horizontal inch and elite has 12; both have six single-spaced, or three double-spaced lines to a vertical inch. The slightly larger pica type is easier to read and many editors prefer it, although they don't object to elite.

Editors do dislike, and often refuse to read, manuscripts that are single-spaced, typed in all caps or in an unusual type style like script, italic or Old English. Reading these manuscripts is hard on the eyes. You should strive for clean, easy-to-read manuscripts and correspondence that reflect a professional approach to your work and consideration for your reader.

Use a good black (never colored) typewriter ribbon and clean the keys frequently. If the enclosures of the letters a, b, d, e, g, o, etc., become inked in, a cleaning is overdue.

Even the best typists make errors. *Occasional* retyping over erasures is acceptable, but strikeovers give your manuscript a sloppy, careless appearance. Hiding typos with large splotches of correction fluid makes your work look amateurish; use it sparingly. Some writers prefer to use typing correction film for final drafts and correction fluid only for rough drafts. Better yet, a self-correcting electric typewriter with a correction tape makes typos nearly invisible. Whatever method you use, it's best to retype a page that has several noticeable corrections. Sloppy typing is taken by many editors as a sign of sloppy work habits—and the possibility of careless research and writing.

Personal computers and word processors. More and more writers are working on personal computers. A personal computer can make a writer's work much more efficient. Revising and editing are usually faster and easier on a computer than on a typewriter, and it eliminates tedious retyping. Writers also can rely on their computers to give them fresh, readable copy as they revise rough drafts into finished manuscripts. For some writers, a fairly inexpensive word processor is adequate to produce manuscripts and letters.

When a manuscript is written on a computer, it can come out of the computer in three ways: as hard copy from the computer's printer; stored on a removable 5¼" floppy disk or 3½" diskette that can be read by other computers; or as an electronic transfer over telephone lines using a modem (a device that allows one computer to transmit to another).

• Hard copy—Most editors are receptive to computer printout submissions if they look like neatly-typed manuscripts. Some older and cheaper printers produce only a low-quality dot-matrix printout with hard-to-read, poorly shaped letters and numbers. Many editors are not willing to read these manuscripts. (In addition, most editors dislike copy with even, or justified, right margins.) New dot-matrix printers, however, produce near letter-quality (NLQ) printouts that are almost indistinguishable from a typewritten manuscript. These are acceptable to editors, along with true letter-quality submissions. Remember that readability is the key. Whether you use a $100 24-pin dot-matrix printer or a $1,000 laser printer doesn't matter to the editor. He just wants to be able to read your manuscript easily.

When you submit hard copy to an editor, be sure you use quality paper. Some computer printers use standard bond paper that you'd use in a typewriter. Others are equipped with a tractor-feed that pulls continuous form paper with holes along the edges through the machine. If you use continuous form paper, be sure to remove the perforated tabs on each side and separate the pages.

• Disk—You'll find that more publishers are accepting or even requesting submissions on disk. (See section introductions in Book Publishers, Consumer Publications and Trade Journals for more detailed information from our survey on computer submissions.) A few publishers pay more for electronic submissions, and some won't accept anything but submissions on disk. Eventually, industry observers say electronic submissions will be the norm, just as typewritten submissions became the norm over handwritten manuscripts earlier in the century.

● Modem—Some publishers who accept submissions on disk also will accept electronic submissions by modem. This is the fastest method of getting your manuscript to the publisher. When you receive an assignment to send by modem, ask about the editor's computer requirements. You'll need to work out submission information before you send something by modem, but you'll probably find that even computer systems you thought were incompatible can communicate easily by modem.

Because most editors also want hard copy along with an electronic submission, you may wonder why you should even consider using a disk or modem. Editors like electronic submissions because they can revise manuscripts quickly as well as save typesetting expenses. Most want a backup hard copy in case there is a problem with a computer submission, while others prefer to edit the hard copy first and then revise the electronic version from it. If you have a particularly timely topic or a manuscript that needs to be submitted quickly, a disk or modem submission is an asset that also can save you and the editor time on deadline.

Publishers who accept submissions by disk or modem have this phrase in their listings: Query for electronic submissions. We give the information this way because you'll need to speak with someone before you send anything by these methods. Also, many magazines and publishers change system requirements each year as equipment and software is updated. Instead of listing information that you may find is outdated when you begin to send the submission, we have put just general information in the listing.

Facsimile machines and boards. This year we have added information to the listings concerning publishers' and agents' facsimile machine numbers. These machines, known commonly as fax machines, transmit copy across phone lines. Those publishers who wanted to list their facsimile machine numbers have done so.

Between businesses, the fax has come into standard daily use for materials that have to be sent quickly. In addition, some public fax machines are being installed in airports, hotels, libraries and even grocery stores. Unfortunately, the convenience of the machines has also given rise to "junk" fax transmissions, including unwanted correspondence and advertisements.

The information we have included is not to be used to transmit queries or entire manuscripts to editors, unless they specifically request it. Although some machines transmit on regular bond paper, most still use a cheaper grade that is difficult to write on, making it unsuitable for editing. In most cases, this paper also fades with time, an undesirable characteristic for a manuscript. Writers should continue to use traditional means for sending manuscripts and queries and use the fax number we list only when an editor asks to receive correspondence by this method.

Some computer owners also have fax boards installed to allow transmissions to their computer screens or computer printers. Unless the fax board can operate independently from the computer's main processor, an incoming fax forces the user to halt whatever work is in process until the transmission ends. You should never send anything by this method without calling or arranging with the editor for this type of transmission.

Types of paper. The paper you use must measure 8½×11 inches. That's a standard size and editors are adamant—they don't want unusual colors or sizes. There's a wide range of white 8½×11 papers. The cheaper ones are made from wood pulp. They will suffice, but are not recommended. Editors also discourage the use of erasable bond for manuscripts; typewriter ribbon ink on erasable bond tends to smear when handled and is difficult to write on. Don't use less than a 16 lb. bond paper; 20 lb. is preferred. Your best bet is paper with a 25% cotton fiber content. Its texture shows type neatly and it holds up under erasing and corrections.

You don't need fancy letterhead for your correspondence with editors. Plain bond paper is fine; just type your name, address, phone number and the date at the top of the page—centered or in the right-hand corner. If you want letterhead, make it as simple and business-like as possible. Many quick print shops have standard typefaces and can supply letterhead stationery at a relatively low cost. Never use letterhead for typing your manuscripts; only the first page of queries, cover letters and other correspondence should be typed on letterhead.

Photocopies. Always make copies of your manuscripts and correspondence before putting them in the mail. Don't learn the hard way, as many writers have, that manuscripts get lost in the mail and publishers sometimes go out of business without returning submissions.

You might want to make several copies of your manuscript while it is still clean and crisp. Some writers keep their original manuscript as a file copy and submit good quality photocopies. Submitting copies can save you the expense and effort of retyping a manuscript if it becomes lost in the mail. If you submit a copy, it's a good idea to explain to the editor whether or not you are making a simultaneous (or multiple) submission to several markets. Some editors will not consider material submitted simultaneously, and a few assume a photocopied submission is simultaneous. Follow the requirements in the individual listings, and see Approaching Markets later in this article for more detailed information about simultaneous submissions.

Some writers include a self-addressed postcard with a photocopied submission and suggest in their cover letter that if the editor is not interested in the manuscript, it may be tossed out and a reply returned on the postcard. This practice is recommended when dealing with foreign markets. If you find that your personal computer generates copies more cheaply than you can pay to have them returned, you might choose to send disposable manuscripts. Submitting a disposable manuscript costs the writer some photocopy or computer printer expense, but it can save on large postage bills.

The cost of personal photocopiers is coming down—some run about $500—but they remain too expensive for many writers to consider purchasing. If you need to make a large number of photocopies, you should ask your print shop about quantity discounts. One advantage of owning a personal computer and printer is that you can quickly print copies of any text you have composed and stored on it.

Assorted supplies. Where will you put all your manuscripts and correspondence? A two- or four-drawer filing cabinet with file folders is a good choice, but some writers find they can make do with manila envelopes and cardboard boxes. It's important to organize and label your correspondence, manuscripts, ideas, submission records, clippings, etc., so you can find them when you need them. See sections on Recording Submissions and Bookkeeping for other helpful hints on keeping records.

You will also need stamps and envelopes; see Mailing Submissions in this section and the U.S. and Canadian Postage by the Page tables on the inside covers of the book. If you decide to invest in a camera to increase your sales, you'll find details on submitting and mailing photos in the sections on Approaching Markets and Mailing Submissions.

Approaching markets

Before submitting a manuscript to a market, be sure you've done the following:
● Familiarize yourself with the publication or other type of market that interests you. Your first sales probably will be to markets you already know through your reading. If you find a listing in *Writer's Market* that seems a likely home for an idea you've been working on, study a sample copy or book catalog to see if your idea fits in with their current topics. If you have a magazine article idea, you may also want to check the *Reader's Guide to Periodical Literature* to be sure the idea hasn't been covered with an article in the magazine during the past year or two. For a book idea, check the *Subject Guide to Books in Print* to

see what other books have been published on the subject.

● Always request writer's guidelines if they're available. Guidelines give a publication's exact requirements for submissions and will help you focus your query letter or manuscript. If a publication has undergone editorial changes since this edition of *Writer's Market* went to press, those changes will usually be reflected in its writer's guidelines. Some publications also have theme or other special issues, or an editorial calendar planned in advance that will be included in its guidelines. The response to your request for guidelines or an editorial calendar can also let you know if a publication has folded or if it has an unreasonably long response time.

● Check submission requirements. A publication that accepts only queries may not respond at all to a writer who submits an unsolicited complete manuscript. Don't send an unpublished manuscript to a publication that publishes only reprints, and if you're submitting photos, be sure the publication reviews prints or slides, and find out if they require model releases and captions.

● Always look at the latest issues of a magazine before submitting. You'll find out about focus, article length and have a chance to double-check the editor's name and the publication's address. An editor also is impressed when a writer carefully studies a publication and its requirements before making a submission.

● With unsolicited submissions or correspondence, enclose a self-addressed, stamped envelope (SASE). Editors appreciate the convenience and the savings in postage. Some editorial offices deal with such a large volume of mail that their policies do not allow them to respond to mail that does not include a SASE. If you submit to a foreign market, enclose a self-addressed envelope (SAE) with International Reply Coupons (IRCs) purchased from the post office. (You don't need to send an SASE if you send a disposable manuscript or your manuscript is an assignment, but be sure you mention in your cover letter if it's a disposable manuscript. If it's an assignment, your cover letter should be short and should state that.)

Those are the basics; now you're ready to learn the details of what you should send when you contact an editor.

Query letters. A query letter is a brief, but detailed letter written to interest an editor in your manuscript. Some beginners are hesitant to query, thinking an editor can more fairly judge an idea by seeing the entire manuscript. Actually, most editors of nonfiction prefer to be queried.

Do your best writing when you sit down to compose your query. There is no query formula that guarantees success, but there are some points to consider when you begin:

● Queries are single-spaced business letters, usually limited to one page. Address the current editor by name, if possible. (If you cannot tell whether an editor is male or female from the name in the listing, address the editor by a full name: Dear Robin Jones:). Don't show unwarranted familiarity by immediately addressing an editor by a first name; follow the editor's lead when responding to your correspondence.

● Your major goal is to convince the editor that your idea would be interesting to the publication's readership and that you are the best writer for the job. Mention any special training or experience that qualifies you to write the article—either as an assignment or on speculation. If you have prior writing experience, you should mention it; if not there's no need to call attention to the fact. Some editors will also ask to look at clips or tearsheets—actual pages or photocopies of your published work. If possible, submit something related to your idea, either in topic or style.

● Be sure you use a strong opening to pique the editor's interest. Some queries begin with a paragraph that approximates the lead of the intended article.

● Briefly detail the structure of the article. Give some facts and perhaps an anecdote and mention people you intend to interview. Give editors enough information to make them want to know more, but don't feel the need to give them details of the whole story. You

[Address and date]

Jonathan Rosenbloom
Editor
3-2-1 Contact
Children's Television Workshop
One Lincoln Plaza
New York, NY 10023

Dear Mr. Rosenbloom:

Newspapers recently headlined the story of five-year-old Brent Meldrum, the Massachusetts boy who saved a six-year-old friend from choking on a piece of hard candy by performing the Heimlich maneuver. The boy learned the anti-choking technique, developed by Dr. Henry Heimlich of Cincinnati, on a television program.

Would *3-2-1 Contact* be interested in a story about Dr. Heimlich and his life-saving technique? Dr. Heimlich claims the procedure is simple enough to be learned by children from first grade up. Since its invention more than 12 years ago, it is estimated to have saved roughly 10,000 lives.

I have been a newspaper reporter and freelance writer for the past 16 years, specializing in consumer and human interest stories. My work has been published in the *Buffalo Evening News*, *Cincinnati Enquirer*, *Western New York* magazine, *Listen* for teens and *Writer's Digest*, among others.

My daughter, age eight, learned the Heimlich maneuver in school and tried it on me very expertly.

Thanks for considering this story idea. A self-addressed stamped envelope is included for your reply.

Sincerely,

Christine A. Dodd

Magazine query. *This sample query for a magazine article presents the author's idea and qualifications effectively. Reprinted with permission. Copyright © 1986 by Chris Dodd.*

[Address and date]

Mr. David Turner
Executive Editor
Arco Publishing Co., Inc.
219 Park Ave. S.
New York, NY 10003

Dear Mr. Turner:

Of the more than 700,000 private pilots in the U.S., half of them earn less than $10,000 a year, according to the Aircraft Owners and Pilots Association.

One thing they could use—especially the newly licensed ones—and which isn't available to them now in less than encyclopedic size and cost, is a paperback:

The Private Pilot's Dictionary and Handbook

As a recently licensed pilot myself, I've reached a hundred times for this book that isn't there. Some of the FAA handbooks and aviation books you've published have abbreviated glossaries, but there's no one book that's a handy-to-consult guide. (There are, of course, several aerospace, missile and rocketry books, but the average student pilot has less complex concerns.) The student pilot may not go into a bookstore where hardcover books are sold, but he does browse the paperback racks.

The book I'm suggesting would contain not only the expected definitions, but also some handy information on questions the pilot is sometimes seeking for himself (see Alcohol) or for others (see Airports).

I've included a few pages to show you what I mean. Would you like to see more?

I've published a number of magazine articles and am the author of four children's books for G.P. Putnam's Sons in the ''Let's Go'' series.

May I hear from you on this idea at your earliest convenience?

Sincerely,

Kirk Polking

P.S. Possibly the AOPA, Cessna, or flying schools would be interested in bulk purchases of such a book for promotion purposes.

Book query. This sample query for a book presents the author's idea, need for the book, competition, and the author's qualifications. Sample pages also give the editor a good idea of potential content. Reprinted with permission. Copyright © 1971 by Kirk Polking.

want to sell the sizzle now and save the steak for later.

● If photos are available to accompany the manuscript, let the editor know, but never send original photos, transparencies or artwork on your initial contact with a publisher. Send photocopies or contact sheets instead. You should always have duplicates, so if your material is lost, you haven't lost your only copy.

● Your closing paragraph should include a direct request to do the article; it may specify the date the manuscript can be completed and an approximate length. Don't discuss fees or request advice from the editor at this time. Editors are put off by presumption that they are beyond the point of consideration and to the point of negotiation. Treat the query like a short introductory job interview. You wouldn't presume to discuss money at this early a stage in a job interview; treat the query the same way.

● Fiction is sometimes queried but most fiction editors don't like to make a final decision until they see the complete manuscript. The majority of editors will want to see a synopsis and sample chapters. If a fiction editor does request a query, briefly describe the main theme and story line, including the conflict and resolution of your story.

● Some writers state politely in their query letters that after a specified date (slightly beyond the listed reporting time), they will assume the editor is not currently interested in their topic and will submit their query elsewhere. It's a good idea to do this only if your topic is a timely one that will suffer if not considered quickly.

For more information about writing query letters and biographical notes, read *How to Write Irresistible Query Letters*, by Lisa Collier Cool (Writer's Digest Books).

Cover letters. A brief cover letter enclosed with your manuscript is helpful in personalizing a submission. If you have previously queried the editor on the article or book, the note should be a brief reminder: "Here is the piece on changes in the Fair Housing Act, which we discussed previously. I look forward to hearing from you at your earliest convenience." Don't use the letter to make a sales pitch. Your manuscript must stand on its own at this point.

If you are submitting to a market that considers unsolicited complete manuscripts, your cover letter should tell the editor something about your manuscript and about you—your publishing history and any particular qualifications you have for writing the enclosed manuscript.

Once your manuscript has been accepted, offer to get involved in the editing process. This process varies from magazine to magazine. Most magazine editors don't send galleys to authors before publication. If the magazine regularly sends authors copies of the edited versions of their manuscripts, you should return the galleys as promptly as possible after you've reviewed them. If the editors don't regularly send galleys, you should ask to be involved in the editing process and offer to rewrite your article to the magazine's specifications. Writers almost always prefer to rework their own prose rather than have someone else do it.

Book proposals. Book proposals are some combination of a cover letter, a synopsis, an outline and/or two or three sample chapters. The exact combination of these will depend on the publisher.

Some editors use the terms synopsis and outline interchangeably. If the publisher requests only a synopsis or an outline, not both, be sure you know which format the publisher prefers. Either a synopsis or outline is appropriate for a novel, but you may find an outline is more effective for a nonfiction book.

● A synopsis is a very brief summary of your book. Cover the basic plot or theme of your book and reveal the ending. Make sure your synopsis flows well, is interesting and easy to read.

● An outline covers the highlights of your book chapter-by-chapter. If your outline is for a novel, include all major characters, the main plot, subplots and any pertinent details. An outline may run 3 to 30 pages, depending on the complexity and length of the book. Be sure your outline is clear; you will lose the reader with a tangle of ideas and events.

● Sample chapters are also requested by many editors. Most are interested in the first two or three chapters to see how well you develop your book. *How to Write a Book Proposal*, by Michael Larsen (Writer's Digest Books), also provides helpful details about submitting a book proposal.

Some writers are finding a distinct advantage in providing marketing information with their nonfiction book proposals. The marketing information tells the editor what competition there is for the potential book, who the potential audience is—including size—and any special ways the book could be marketed. An author who does this kind of homework will impress an editor with his knowledge of business considerations.

Reprints. You can get more mileage—and money—out of your research and writing time by marketing your previously published material for reprint sales. You may use a photocopy of your original manuscript and/or tearsheets from the publication in which it originally appeared. With your reprint submission, be sure to inform the editor that you are marketing the article as a reprint, especially if you send a photocopy without tearsheets. The editor will also need to know when and in what publication it appeared.

If you market for reprint an article that has not yet been published by the original purchaser, inform editors that it cannot be used before it has made its initial appearance. Give them the intended publication date and be sure to inform them if any changes take place. Note: You can only market these rights if you have not already sold them. See Rights and the Writer for more information.

Photographs and slides. The availability of good quality photos can be a deciding factor when an editor is considering a manuscript. Most publications also offer additional pay for photos accepted with a manuscript. When submitting black and white prints, editors usually want to see 8×10 glossy photos, unless they indicate another preference in the listing. The universally accepted format for transparencies is 35mm; few buyers will look at color prints.

On all your photos and slides, you should stamp or print your copyright notice and "Return to:" followed by your name, address and phone number. Rubber stamps are preferred for labeling photos since they are less likely to cause damage. You can order them from many stationery or office supply stores. If you use a pen to write this information on the back of your photos, be careful not to damage the print by pressing too hard or allowing ink to bleed through the paper. A felt tip pen is best, but you should take care not to put photos or copy together before the ink dries, or it will smear.

● Captions can be typed on a sheet of paper and taped to the back of the prints. Some writers, when submitting several transparencies or photos, number the photos and type captions (numbered accordingly) on a separate $8\frac{1}{2} \times 11$ sheet of paper.

● Submit prints rather than negatives or consider having duplicates made of your slides or transparencies. Don't risk having your original negative or slide lost or damaged when you submit it.

Manuscript mechanics

Your good writing may be hurt by your presentation if it's not done in correct form. Follow these rules of manuscript mechanics to present your work at its best.

Manuscript format. Do not use a cover sheet or title page. Use a binder only if you are submitting a play or a television or movie script. You can use a paper clip to hold pages together, but never use staples.

The upper corners of the first page contain important information about you and your manuscript. This information is always single-spaced. In the upper left corner list your name, address, phone number and Social Security number (publishers must have this to file accurate payment records with the government). If you are using a pseudonym for your byline, your legal name still must appear in this space. In the upper right corner, indicate the approximate word count of the manuscript, the rights you are offering for sale and your copyright notice (© 1991 Chris Jones). A handwritten copyright symbol is acceptable. For a book manuscript, do not specify the rights you are offering; that will be covered in your contract. Do not number the first page of your manuscript.

There is much discussion about the necessity of this information. Many writers of short fiction and poetry do not feel it necessary to put the rights or word count on manuscripts they submit to literary magazines. Some writers also consider the copyright notice unnecessary or think editors will consider it amateurish. Others use it only when they submit unsolicited complete manuscripts and not for assigned or solicited manuscripts. A copyright notice is not required to obtain copyright protection or to avoid losing it, but persons who use protected works without authorization can claim "innocent infringement" if the notice is not on the manuscript. U.S. copyright owners also must register their works with the U.S. Copyright Office before they file a copyright infringement lawsuit; otherwise, registration is not necessary.

Center the title in capital letters one-third of the way down the page. To center, set the tabulator to stop halfway between the right and left edges of the page. Count the letters in the title, including spaces and punctuation, and backspace half that number. Type the title. Set your typewriter to double-space. Type "by" centered one double-space under your title, and type your name or pseudonym centered one double-space beneath that.

After the title and byline, drop down two double-spaces, paragraph indent, and begin the body of your manuscript. Always double-space your manuscript and use standard paragraph indentations of five spaces. Margins should be about 1¼ inches on all sides of each full page of typewritten manuscript. You may lightly pencil in a line to remind you when you reach the bottom margin of your page, but be sure to erase it before submitting your manuscript.

On every page after the first, type your last name, a dash and the page number in either the upper left or right corner. (This is sometimes called the slug line.) The title of your manuscript may, but need not, be typed on this line or beneath it. Page number two would read: Jones — 2. If you are using a pseudonym, type your real name, followed by your pen name in parentheses, then a dash and the page number: Jones (Smith) — 2. Then drop down two double-spaces and continue typing. Follow this format throughout your manuscript.

If you are submitting novel chapters, leave the top one-third of the first page of each chapter blank before typing the chapter title. Subsequent pages should include the author's last name, the page number, and a shortened form of the book's title: Jones — 2 — Skating. (In a variation on this, some authors place the title before the name on the left side and put the page number on the right-hand margin.)

When submitting poetry, the poems should be typed single-spaced (double-space between stanzas), one poem per page. For a long poem requiring more than one page, paper clip the pages together.

On the final page of your manuscript, after you've typed your last word and period, skip three double-spaces and center the words "The End." Some nonfiction writers use # # # or the old newspaper symbol -30- to indicate the same thing. Further information on formats for books, articles, scripts, proposals and cover letters, with illustrated examples, is available in *The Writer's Digest Guide to Manuscript Formats*, by Dian Dincin Buchman and Seli Groves (Writer's Digest Books).

Estimating word count. To estimate word count in manuscripts, count the number of characters and spaces in an average line and divide by 6 for the average words per line. Then count the number of lines of type on a representative page. Multiply the words per line by the lines per page to find out the average number of words per page. Then count the number of manuscript pages (fractions should be counted as fractions, except in book manuscript chapter headings, which are counted as a full page). Multiply the number of pages by the number of words per page you already determined. This will give you the approximate number of words in the manuscript. For short manuscripts, it's often quicker to count each word on a representative page and multiply by the total number of pages.

Mailing submissions

No matter what size manuscript you're mailing, always include sufficient return postage and a self-addressed envelope large enough to contain your manuscript if it is returned.

A manuscript of fewer than six pages may be folded in thirds and mailed as if it were a letter using a #10 (business-size) envelope. The enclosed SASE should be a #10 folded in thirds (though these are sometimes torn when a letter opener catches in one of the folds), or a #9 envelope which will slip into the mailing envelope without being folded. Some editors also appreciate the convenience of having a manuscript folded into halves in a 6 × 9 envelope.

For larger manuscripts, use 9 × 12 envelopes for both mailing and return. The return SASE may be folded in half.

A book manuscript should be mailed in a sturdy, well-wrapped box. Your typing paper, computer paper or envelope box is a suitable mailer. Enclose a self-addressed mailing label and paper clip your return postage stamps or International Reply Coupons to the label.

Always mail photos and slides First Class. The rougher handling received by Fourth Class mail could damage them. If you are concerned about losing prints or slides, send them certified or registered mail. For any photo submission that is mailed separately from a manuscript, enclose a short cover letter of explanation, separate self-addressed label, adequate return postage, and an envelope. Never submit photos or slides mounted in glass.

To mail up to 20 prints, you can buy photo mailers that are stamped "Photos – Do Not Bend" and contain two cardboard inserts to sandwich your prints. Or use a 9 × 12 manila envelope, write "Photos – Do Not Bend" and devise your own cardboard inserts. Some photography supply shops also carry heavy cardboard envelopes that are reusable.

When mailing a number of prints, say 25 to 50 for a book with illustrations, pack them in a sturdy cardboard box. A box for typing paper or photo paper is an adequate mailer. If, after packing both manuscript and photos, there's empty space in the box, slip in enough cardboard inserts to fill the box. Wrap the box securely.

To mail transparencies, first slip them into protective vinyl sleeves, then mail as you would prints. If you're mailing a number of sheets, use a cardboard box as for photos.

Types of mail service

● First Class is the most expensive way of mailing a manuscript, but many writers prefer it. First Class mail generally receives better handling and is delivered more quickly. Mail sent First Class is forwarded for one year if the addressee has moved, and is returned automatically if it is undeliverable.

● Fourth Class rates are available for packages but you must pack materials carefully when mailing Fourth Class because they will be handled the same as Parcel Post – roughly. If a letter is enclosed with your Fourth Class package, write "First Class Letter Enclosed" on the package and add adequate First Class postage for your letter. To make sure your package will be returned to you if it is undeliverable, print "Return Postage Guaranteed" under your address.

● Certified Mail must be signed for when it reaches its destination. If requested, a signed receipt is returned to the sender. There is an 85¢ charge for this service, in addition to the required postage, and a 90¢ charge for a return receipt.

● Registered Mail is a high security method of mailing. The package is signed in and out of every office it passes through, and a receipt is returned to the sender when the package reaches its destination. This service begins at $4.40 in addition to the postage required for the item. If you obtain insurance for the package, the cost begins at $4.50.

● United Parcel Service may be slightly cheaper than First Class postage if you drop the package off at UPS yourself. UPS cannot legally carry First Class mail, so your cover letter needs to be mailed separately. Check with UPS in your area for current rates. The cost depends on the weight of your package and the distance to its destination.

● Overnight mail services are provided by both the U.S. Postal Service and several private firms. These services can be useful if your manuscript or revisions *must* be at an editor's office quickly. More information on next day service is available from the U.S. Post Office in your area, or check your Yellow Pages under "Delivery Services."

Other important details

● Money orders should be used if you are ordering sample copies or supplies and do not have checking services. You'll have a receipt and money orders are traceable. Money orders for up to $35 can be purchased from the U.S. Postal Service for a 75¢ service charge; the cost is $1 for a maximum $700 order. Banks, savings and loans, and some commercial businesses also carry money orders; their fees vary. *Never* send cash through the mail for sample copies.

● Insurance is available for items handled by the U.S. Postal Service but is payable only on typing fees or the tangible value of the item in the package—such as typing paper—so your best insurance when mailing manuscripts is to keep a copy of what you send. Insurance is 70¢ for $50 or less, and goes up to a $5 maximum charge.

● When corresponding with foreign publications and publishers, International Reply Coupons (IRCs) must be used for return postage. Surface rates in foreign countries differ from those in the U.S., and U.S. postage stamps are of no use there. Currently, one IRC costs 95¢ and is sufficient for one ounce traveling at surface rate; two must be used for airmail return. Canadian writers pay $1.50 for IRCs.

Because some post offices don't carry IRCs, many writers dealing with foreign publishers mail photocopies and tell the publisher to dispose of them if they're not appropriate. When you use this method, it's best to set a deadline for withdrawing your manuscript from consideration, so you can market it elsewhere. For the benefit of both U.S. and international writers, U.S. stamps also can be ordered by phone using a VISA credit card. Call 1-800-782-6724. If 800 service is not available in your area, you can call (816)455-4880 to place orders between 8 a.m. and 5 p.m. Central Standard Time. There is a $5 service charge for all foreign orders.

● International money orders are also available from the post office for a $3 charge.

● See U.S. and Canadian Postage by the Page on the inside covers for specific mailing costs. All charges were current at press time but subject to change during the year.

Recording submissions

A number of writers think once they've mailed a manuscript, the situation is out of their hands; all they can do is sit and wait. But submitting a manuscript doesn't mean you've lost control of it. Manage your writing business by keeping copies of all manuscripts and correspondence, and by recording the dates of submissions.

One way to keep track of your manuscripts is to use a record of submissions that includes the date sent, title, market, editor and enclosures (such as photos). You should also note the date of the editor's response, any rewrites that were done, and, if the manuscript was accepted, the publication date and payment information. You might want to keep a similar record just for queries.

Also remember to keep a separate file for each manuscript or idea along with its list of potential markets. You may want to keep track of expected reporting times on a calendar, too. Then you'll know if a market has been slow to respond and you can follow up on your query or submission.

Bookkeeping

Whether or not you are profitable in your writing, you'll need to keep accurate financial records. These records are necessary to let you know how you're doing, and, of course, the government is also interested in your financial activities.

If you have another source of income, you should plan to keep separate records for your writing expenses and income. Some writers open separate checking accounts for their writing-related expenses.

The best financial records are the ones that get used, and usually the simpler the form, the more likely it will be used regularly. Get in the habit of recording every transaction related to your writing. You can start at any time; it doesn't need to be on Jan. 1. Because you're likely to have expenses before you have income, start keeping your records whenever you make your first purchase related to writing—such as this copy of *Writer's Market*.

A simple bookkeeping system. For most freelance writers, a simple type of single-entry bookkeeping is adequate. The heart of the single-entry system is the journal, an accounting book available at any stationery or office supply store. You record all of the expenses and income of your writing business in the journal.

The single-entry journal's form is similar to a standard check register. Instead of withdrawals and deposits, you record expenses and income. You'll need to describe each transaction clearly—including the date; the source of the income (or the vendor of your purchase); a description of what was sold or bought; whether the payment was by cash, check or credit card; and the amount of the transaction.

Your receipt file. Keep all documentation pertaining to your writing expenses or income. This is true whether you have started a bookkeeping journal or not. For every payment you receive, you should have a check stub from the publisher's check, a letter of agreement or contract stating the amount of payment, or your own bank records of the deposit. For every check you write to pay business expenses, you should have a record in your check register as well as a cancelled check. Keep credit card receipts, too. And for every cash purchase, you should have a receipt from the vendor—especially if the amount is over $25. For small expenses, you can usually keep a list if you don't record them in a journal.

Tax information

Freelance writers, artists and photographers have a variety of concerns when it comes to taxes that employees don't have, including deductions, self-employment tax and home office credits. A subsection has been added to the Internal Revenue Code that exempts freelance authors, photographers and artists from having to capitalize "qualified creative expenses" incurred while in the business as a freelancer. The expenses can be allowed as deductions instead. Individuals who are involved in related but separate business and freelance activities, such as self-publishers who are writers and publishers, probably will have to keep the expenses separate and capitalize expenses related to publishing, while they deduct expenses from freelancing.

There also is a home office deduction that can be used if an area in your home is used strictly for business. Contact the IRS for information on requirements for this deduction. The deduction is limited to net income after all other deductions have been made; you cannot declare a loss on deductions from your business. The law also requires a business to be profitable three out of five years to avoid being treated as a hobby.

If your freelance income exceeds your expenses, regardless of the amount, you must declare that profit. If the profit is $400 or more, you also must pay quarterly Self-Employment Social Security Tax and fill out that self-employment form on your 1040 tax form. While we cannot offer you tax advice or interpretations, we can suggest several sources for the most current information.

• Call your local IRS office. Look in the white pages of the telephone directory under U.S. Government—Internal Revenue Service. Someone will be able to respond to your request for IRS publications and tax forms or other information. Ask about the IRS Tele-tax service, a series of recorded messages you can hear by dialing on a touch-tone phone. If you need answers to complicated questions, ask to speak with a Taxpayer Service Specialist.

• Obtain the basic IRS publications. You can order them by phone or mail from any IRS office; most are available at libraries and some post offices. Start with *Your Federal Income Tax* (Publication 17) and *Tax Guide for Small Business* (Publication 334). These are both comprehensive, detailed guides—you'll need to find the regulations that apply to you and ignore the rest. You may also want to get a copy of *Business Use of Your Home* (Publication 587) and *Self-Employment Tax* (Publication 533).

● Consider other information sources. Many public libraries have detailed tax instructions available on tape. Some colleges and universities offer free assistance in preparing tax returns. And if you decide to consult a professional tax preparer, the fee is a deductible business expense on your tax return.

Rights and the writer

We find that writers and editors sometimes define rights in different ways. To eliminate any misinterpretations, read the following definitions of each right—and you'll see the definitions upon which editors updated the information in their listings.

Occasionally, we hear from a writer who is confused because an editor claims never to acquire or buy rights. The truth is, any time an editor buys a story or asks you for permission to publish a story, even without payment, the editor is asking you for rights. In some cases, however, editors will reassign those rights to the author after publishing the story.

Sometimes people start magazines in their areas of expertise but don't have extensive knowledge of publishing terms and practices. And sometimes editors simply don't take the time to specify the rights they are buying. If you sense that an editor is interested in getting stories but doesn't seem to know what his and the writer's responsibilities are regarding rights, be wary. In such a case, you'll want to explain what rights you're offering (preferably one-time rights only) and that you expect additional payment for subsequent use of your work. Writers may also agree to sell first rights, for example to a magazine, but then never receive a check for the manuscript and subsequent inquiries bring no response. In a case like this, we recommend that the writer send a certified letter, return receipt requested, notifying the magazine that the manuscript is being withdrawn from that publication for submission elsewhere. There is no industry standard for how long a writer should wait before using this procedure. The best bet is to check the *Writer's Market* listing for what the magazine lists as its usual reporting time and then, after a reasonable wait beyond that, institute the withdrawal.

For a complete discussion about book and magazine agreements and information on rights and negotiations, see *A Writer's Guide to Contract Negotiations*, by Richard Balkin (Writer's Digest Books).

Selling rights to your writing. The Copyright Law that went into effect Jan. 1, 1978, said writers were primarily selling one-time rights to their work (plus any revision of that collective work and any later collective work in the same series) unless they—and the publisher—agreed otherwise in writing. In some cases, however, a writer may have little say in the rights sold to an editor; some companies and publications have standard rights they buy and never deviate. In this case, if negotiating isn't possible, you must decide whether selling those rights is in your best interests.

As a writer acquires skill, reliability, and professionalism on the job, he becomes more valued by editors—and rights become a more important consideration. Though a beginning writer will accept modest payment just to get in print, an experienced writer cannot afford to give away good writing just to see a byline. At this point the writer must become concerned with selling reprints of articles already sold to one market, using previously published articles as chapters in a book on the same topic, seeking markets for the same material overseas, or offering rights to TV or the movies.

You should strive to keep as many rights to your work as you can from the outset, because before you can resell any piece of writing, you must own the rights to negotiate. If you have sold all rights to an article, for instance, it can be reprinted without your permission and without additional payment to you. Some writers will not deal with editors who buy all rights. What an editor buys will determine whether you can resell your own work. Here is a list of the rights most editors and publishers seek. (Book rights will be covered by the contract submitted to the writer by a book publisher. The writer does not indicate any such rights offered.) For a more complete discussion about the sale of rights, see the Writers' Roundtable after the Business of Writing.

● First Serial Rights—First serial rights means the writer offers the newspaper or magazine the right to publish the article, story or poem for the first time in any periodical. All other rights to the material belong to the writer. Variations on this right are, for example, first North American serial rights. Some magazines use this purchasing technique to obtain the right to publish first in both the U.S. and Canada since many U.S. magazines are circulated in Canada. If an editor had purchased only first U.S. serial rights, a Canadian magazine could come out with prior or simultaneous publication of the same material. When material is excerpted from a book scheduled to be published and it appears in a magazine or newspaper prior to book publication, this is also called first serial rights.

● First North American Serial Rights—Magazine publishers that distribute in both the United States and Canada frequently buy these first rights covering publication in both countries.

● One-Time Rights—This differs from first serial rights in that the buyer has no guarantee he will be the first to publish the work. One-time rights often apply to photos, but also apply to writing sold to more than one market over a period of time. See also Simultaneous Rights.

● Second Serial (Reprint) Rights—This gives a newspaper or magazine the opportunity to print an article, poem or story after it has already appeared in another newspaper or magazine. The term is also used to refer to the sale of part of a book to a newspaper or magazine after a book has been published, whether or not there has been any first serial publication. Income derived from second serial rights to book material is often shared 50/50 by author and book publisher.

● All Rights—Some magazines buy all rights because of the top prices they pay for material or the exclusive nature of the publication; others have book publishing interests or foreign magazine connections. (Some will call this world rights.)

About 41% of the trade magazines and 29% of the consumer magazines in a *Writer's Market* survey last year bought all rights or asked for work-for-hire agreements. A writer who sells an article, story or poem to a magazine under these terms forfeits the rights to use his material in its present form elsewhere. If he signs a work-for-hire agreement, he signs away all rights and the copyright to the company making the assignment.

If the writer thinks he may want to use his material later (perhaps in book form), he must avoid submitting to such markets or refuse payment and withdraw his material if he discovers it later. Ask the editor whether he is willing to buy only first rights instead of all rights before you agree to an assignment or sale. Some editors will reassign rights to a writer after a given period, such as one year. It's worth an inquiry in writing.

● Simultaneous Rights—This term covers articles and stories sold to publications (primarily religious magazines) that do not have overlapping circulations. A Catholic publication, for example, might be willing to buy simultaneous rights to a Christmas story they like very much, even though they know a Presbyterian magazine may be publishing the same story in its Christmas issue. Publications that buy simultaneous rights indicate this fact in their listings in *Writer's Market*.

Always advise an editor when the material you are sending is a simultaneous submission to another market. Some writers put the information in their cover letters while others also add it to the upper right-hand corner of the first page of the manuscript under the word count.

● Foreign Serial Rights—Can you resell a story you had published in the U.S. or North

America to a foreign magazine? If you sold only first U.S. serial rights or first North American rights, yes, you are free to market your story abroad. Of course, you must contact a foreign magazine that buys material that has previously appeared in the U.S. or North American periodicals. Books with these markets include *International Literary Market Place*, by R.R. Bowker and *International Writers' and Artists' Yearbook*, by A&C Black Ltd.

● Syndication Rights—This is a division of serial rights. For example, a book publisher may sell the rights to a newspaper syndicate to print a book in 12 installments in each of 20 U.S. newspapers. If they did this after book publication, they would be syndicating second serial rights to the book. In either case, the syndicate would be taking a commission on the sales it made to newspapers, so the remaining percentage would split between author and publisher.

● Subsidiary Rights—The rights, other than book publication rights, that should be specified in a book contract. These may include various serial rights, dramatic rights, translation rights, etc. The contract lists what percentage of these sales goes to the author and what percentage to the publisher. Be careful when signing away these rights. If the publisher is unlikely to market them, you may be able to retain them and market them yourself or through an agent.

● Dramatic, Television and Motion Picture Rights—This means the writer is selling his material for use on the stage, in television or in the movies. Often a one-year option to buy such rights is offered (generally for 10% of the total price). The interested party then tries to sell the idea to other people—actors, directors, studios or television networks, etc.— who become part of the project, which then becomes a script. Some properties are optioned over and over again, but most fail to become dramatic productions. In such cases, the writer can sell his rights again and again—as long as there is interest in the material. Though dramatic, TV and motion picture rights are more important to the fiction writer than the nonfiction writer, producers today are increasingly interested in nonfiction material; many biographies, topical books and true stories are being dramatized.

Communicate and clarify. Before submitting material to a market, check its listing in this book to see what rights are purchased. Most editors will discuss rights they wish to purchase before any exchange of money occurs. Some buyers are adamant about what rights they will accept; others will negotiate. In any case, the rights purchased should be stated specifically in writing sometime during the course of the sale, usually in a contract, memo or letter of agreement. If the editor doesn't put this information in writing, you should. Summarize what you talked about and send a copy to the editor.

Give as much attention to the rights you haven't sold as you do to the rights you have sold. Be aware of the rights you retain, with an eye for additional sales.

Regardless of the rights you sell or keep, make sure all parties involved in any sale understand the terms of the sale. Keep in mind, too, that if there is a change in editors or publishers from the edition of *Writer's Market* you're using, the rights purchased may also change. Communication, coupled with these guidelines and some common sense, will preclude misunderstandings with editors over rights.

Copyrighting your writing

The copyright law, effective since Jan. 1, 1978, protects your writing, unequivocally recognizes the creator of the work as its owner, and grants the creator all the rights, benefits and privileges that ownership entails.

In other words, the moment you finish a piece of writing—whether it is a short story, article, novel or poem—the law recognizes that only you can decide how it is to be used.

This law gives writers power in dealing with editors and publishers, but they should understand how to use that power. They should also understand that certain circumstances can complicate and confuse the concept of ownership. Writers must be wary of these circumstances or risk losing ownership of their work. Here are answers to frequently asked questions about copyright law:

To what rights am I entitled under copyright law? The law gives you, as creator of your work, the right to print, reprint and copy the work; to sell or distribute copies of the work; to prepare "derivative works"—dramatizations, translations, musical arrangement, novelizations, etc.; to record the work; and to perform or display literary, dramatic or musical works publicly. These rights give you control over how your work is used, and assure you (in theory) that you receive payment for any use of your work.

If, however, you create the work as a "work-for-hire," you do not own any of these rights. The person or company that commissioned the work-for-hire owns the copyright.

When does copyright law take effect, and how long does it last? A piece of writing is copyrighted the moment it is put to paper and you indicate your authorship with the word Copyright or the ©, the year and your name. Protection lasts for the life of the author plus 50 years, thus allowing your heirs to benefit from your work. For material written by two or more people, protection lasts for the life of the last survivor plus 50 years. The life-plus-50 provision applies if the work was created or registered with the Copyright Office after January 1, 1978, when the updated copyright law took effect. The old law protected works for a 28-year term, and gave the copyright owner the option to renew the copyright for an additional 28 years at the end of that term. Works copyrighted under the old law that are in their second 28-year term automatically receive an additional 19 years of protection (for a total of 75 years). Works in their first term also receive the 19-year extension beyond the 28-year second term, but must still be renewed when the first term ends.

If you create a work anonymously or pseudonymously, protection lasts for 100 years after the work's creation, or 75 years after its publication, whichever is shorter. The life-plus-50 coverage takes effect, however, if you reveal your identity to the Copyright Office any time before the original term of protection runs out.

Works created on a for-hire basis are also protected for 100 years after the work's creation or 75 years after its publication, whichever is shorter. But the copyright is held by the publisher, not the writer.

Must I register my work with the Copyright Office to receive protection? No. Your work is copyrighted whether or not you register it, although registration offers certain advantages. For example, you must register the work before you can bring an infringement suit to court. You can register the work *after* an infringement has taken place, and *then* take the suit to court, but registering after the fact removes certain rights from you. You can sue for actual damages (the income or other benefits lost as a result of the infringement), but you can't sue for statutory damages and you can't recover attorney's fees unless the work has been registered with the Copyright Office *before* the infringement took place. Registering before the infringement also allows you to make a stronger case when bringing the infringement to court.

If you suspect that someone might infringe on your work, register it. If you doubt that an infringement is likely (and infringements are relatively rare), you might save yourself the time and money involved in registering the material.

I have an article that I want to protect fully. How do I register it? Request the proper form from the Copyright Office. Send the completed form, a $20 registration fee, and one copy (if the work is unpublished; two if it's published) of the work to the Register of Copyrights, Library of Congress, Washington, DC 20559. You needn't register each work individually. A group of articles can be registered simultaneously (for a single $20 fee) if they meet these requirements: They must be assembled in orderly form (simply placing them in a notebook binder is sufficient); they must bear a single title ("Works by Chris Jones," for example); they must represent the work of one person (or one set of collaborators); and they must be the subject of a single claim to copyright. No limit is placed on the number of works that can be copyrighted in a group.

If my writing is published in a "collective work"—such as a magazine—does the publication handle registration of the work? Only if the publication owns the piece of writing. Although the copyright notice carried by the magazine covers its contents, you must register any writing to which *you* own the rights if you want the additional protection registration provides.

Collective works are publications with a variety of contributors. Magazines, newspapers, encyclopedias, anthologies, etc., are considered collective works. If you sell something to a collective work, state in writing what rights you're selling. If you don't specify rights, the law allows one-time rights plus publication in any revision of the collective work and any later collective work in the same series. For example, a publishing company could reprint a contribution from one issue in a later issue of its magazine without paying you. The same is true for other collective works, so always detail in writing what rights you are selling before actually making the sale.

When contributing to a collective work, ask that your copyright notice be placed on or near your published manuscript (if you still own the manuscript's rights). Prominent display of your copyright notice on published work has two advantages: It signals to readers and potential reusers of the piece that it belongs to you, and not to the collective work in which it appears; and it allows you to register all published work bearing such notice with the Copyright Office as a group for a single $20 fee. A published work *not* bearing notice indicating you as copyright owner can't be included in a group registration.

Display of copyright notice is especially important when contributing to an uncopyrighted publication—that is, a publication that doesn't display a copyright symbol and doesn't register with the Copyright Office. When the United States joined the Berne Copyright Convention on March 1, 1989, mandatory notice of copyright was no longer required and failure to place a notice of copyright on copies no longer results in loss of copyright. It can still be important to display a copyright notice so no one will innocently infringe on your copyright, however.

Official notice of copyright consists of the symbol ©, the word "Copyright," or the abbreviation "Copr."; the name of the copyright owner or owners; and the year date of first publication (for example, "© 1991 by Chris Jones"). A hand-drawn copyright symbol is acceptable.

Under what circumstances should I place my copyright notice on unpublished works that haven't been registered? Place official copyright notice on the first page of any manuscript. This procedure is not intended to stop a buyer from stealing your material (editorial piracy is very rare, actually), but to demonstrate to the editor that you understand your rights under copyright law, that you own that particular manuscript, and that you want to retain your ownership after the manuscript is published.

How do I transfer copyright? A transfer of copyright, like the sale of any property, is simply an exchange of the property for payment. The law stipulates, however, that the transfer of any exclusive rights (and the copyright is the most exclusive of rights) must be made in writing to be valid. Various types of exclusive rights exist, as outlined above. Usually it is best not to sell your copyright. If you do, you lose control over the use of the manuscript and forfeit future income from its use.

What is a "work-for-hire assignment"? This is a work that another party commissions you to do. Two types of work-for-hire works exist: Work done as a regular employee of a company, and commissioned work that is specifically called "work for hire" in writing at the time of assignment. The phrase "work for hire" or something close must be used in the written agreement, though you should watch for similar phrasings. The work-for-hire provision was included in the new copyright law so that no writer could unwittingly sign away his copyright. The phrase "work for hire" is a bright red flag warning the writer that the agreement he is about to enter into will result in loss of rights to any material created under the agreement.

Some editors offer work-for-hire agreements when making assignments, and expect writers to sign them routinely. By signing them, you forfeit the potential for additional income from a manuscript through reprint sales, or sale of other rights. Be careful, therefore, in signing away your rights in a "work-for-hire" agreement. Many articles written as works for hire or to which all rights have been sold are never resold, but if you retain the copyright, you might try to resell the article—something you couldn't do if you forfeited your rights to the piece.

Can I get my rights back if I sell all rights to a manuscript, or if I sell the copyright itself? Yes. You or your heirs can terminate the transfer of rights 40 years after the grant was made or, in the case of publication, 35 years after publication—whichever comes first. You can do this by serving written notice, within specified time limits, to the person to whom you transferred rights. Consult the Copyright Office for the procedural details.

Must all transfers be in writing? Only work-for-hire agreements and transfers of exclusive rights *must* be in writing. However, getting any agreement in writing before the sale is wise. Beware of other statements about what rights the buyer purchases that may appear on checks, writer's guidelines or magazine mastheads. If the publisher makes such a statement elsewhere, you might insert a phrase like "No statement pertaining to purchase of rights other than the one detailed in this letter—including masthead statements or writer's guidelines—applies to this agreement" into the letter that outlines your rights agreement. Some publishers put their terms in writing on the back of a check that, when endorsed by the writer, becomes in their view a "contract." If the terms on the back of the check do not agree with the rights you are selling, then change the endorsement to match the rights you have sold before signing the check for deposit. Contact the editor to discuss this difference in rights.

Are ideas and titles copyrightable? No. Nor can facts be copyrighted. Only the actual expression of ideas or information can be copyrighted. You can't copyright the idea to do a solar energy story, and you can't copyright lists of materials for building solar energy converters. But you can copyright the article that results from that idea and that information.

Where can I get more information about copyright? Write the Copyright Office (Library of Congress, Washington, DC 20559) for a free Copyright Information Kit. Call (not collect) the Copyright Public Information Office at (202)479-0700 weekdays between 8:30 a.m. and 5 p.m. if you need forms for registration of a claim to copyright. The Copyright Office will answer specific questions but won't provide legal advice. For more information about copyright and other laws, consult the latest edition of *The Writer's Friendly Legal Guide*, edited by Kirk Polking (Writer's Digest Books).

How much should I charge?

Opportunities to sell your writing are as boundless as your imagination.

A page in a recent Sharper Image catalog offered a leather-bound, custom biography of roughly 225 pages including photographs and other documents, for $27,000. Any prospects for a handsome assignment like that with an executive in your area? Or a more modest version?

Another recent advertisement for Huggies® disposable diapers offered a Playskool® personalized cassette tape of bedtime songs with your child's name sung 68 times in the lyrics! Perhaps a variation on this idea is something you can offer proud parents in your community.

Catalog producers and diaper marketers aren't the only ones with creative ideas about how to sell the written word. Here are some other merchandising ideas for freelance writers:

Renate Burstein uses a desktop computer to produce two to eight pages of news about brides and grooms on their wedding day. The "Wedding Newspaper" might contain articles about how they met, family trees, guest lists, baby pictures, whatever the couple wants. The newspaper runs $2 to $2.80 per person on orders of 150 or more.

Michael DeWitt, on the other hand, creates "Uniquely Personalized Words of Art" including poetry for all occasions and anniversary, birthday greetings or I-love-you messages meant to be personalized alternatives to store-bought cards. Prices range from $3 to $20.

Karen Schriver, English professor at Carnegie Mellon University, says that Japan may be the world leader in the electronics industry, but it's at least 25 years behind the U.S. in writing instruction manuals. Perhaps there is a Japanese firm in your area that needs help from a freelance writer.

When setting your freelance fees, keep these factors in mind: pay rates in your area; amount of competition; how much you think the client is willing or able to pay for the job; and how much you want to earn for your time. For example, if something you write helps a businessman get a $50,000 order or a school board to get a $100,000 grant, that may influence your fees. How much you want to earn for your time should take into consideration not only an hourly rate for the time you spend writing, but also the time involved in travel, meeting with the client, doing research, rewriting and, where necessary, handling details with a printer or producer. One way to figure your hourly rate is to determine what an annual salary might be for a staff person to do the same job you are bidding on, and figure an hourly wage on that. If, for example, you think the buyer would have to pay a staff person $22,000 a year, divide that by 2,000 (approximately 40 hours per week for 50 weeks) and you will arrive at $11 an hour. Then add another 20% to cover the amount of fringe benefits that an employer normally pays (but you must now absorb) in Social Security, unemployment insurance, paid vacations, hospitalization, retirement funds, etc. Then add another dollars-per-hour figure to cover your actual overhead expense for office space, equipment, supplies; plus time spent on professional meetings, readings, and making unsuccessful proposals. (To get this figure, add up one year's expenses and divide by the number of hours per year you work on freelancing. In the beginning you may have to adjust this to avoid pricing yourself out of the market.)

Example:

$22,000 (salary) ÷ 2,000 (hours) =   per hour

                        $11
                      + 2.20 (20% to cover fringe benefits, taxes, etc.)
                      + 2   (overhead based on annual expenses of $4,000)

                     $15.20 per hour charge

Regardless of the method by which you arrive at your fee for the job, be sure to get a letter of agreement signed by both parties covering the work to be done and the fee to be paid.

If there is any question about how long the project will take you, be sure the agreement indicates that you are estimating the time and your project fee is based on X hours. If more time is required, you should be able to renegotiate with the client. This is a good reason to require partial payment as parts of the job are completed, so both you and the client have a better idea of the time involved.

You will, of course, from time to time handle certain jobs at less than desirable rates because they are for a cause you believe in, allow you to get your foot in the door, or because the job offers additional experience or exposure to some profitable client for the future. Some clients pay hourly rates; others pay flat fees for the job. Both kinds of rates are listed when the data were available so you have as many pricing options as possible.

A

Advertising copywriting: Advertising agencies and the advertising departments of large companies need part-time help in rush seasons. Newspapers, radio and TV stations also need copywriters for their small business customers who do not have agencies. Depending on the client, the locale and the job, the following rates could apply: $20-100 per hour, $250 and up per day, $500 and up per week, $1,000-2,000 as a monthly retainer. Flat-fee-per-ad rates could range from $100 and up per page depending upon size and kind of client.

Annual reports: A brief report with some economic information and an explanation of figures, $20-35 per hour; 12-page report, $600-1,500; a report that must meet Securities and Exchange Commission (SEC) standards and reports that use legal language could bill at $40-65 per hour. Some writers who provide copywriting and editing services charge flat fees ranging from $5,000-10,000.

Anthology editing: Variable advance plus 3-15% of royalties. Flat-fee-per-manuscript rates could range from $500-5,000 or more if it consists of complex, technical material.

Article manuscript critique: 3,000 words, $40.

Arts reviewing: For weekly newspapers, $15-35; for dailies, $45 and up; for Sunday supplements, $100-400; regional arts events summaries for national trade magazines, $35-100.

Associations: Miscellaneous writing projects, small associations, $15-25 per hour; larger groups, up to $85 per hour; or a flat fee per project, such as $550-900 for 10-12 page magazine articles, or $1,200-1,800 for a 10-page booklet.

Audio cassette scripts: $10-50 per scripted minute, assuming written from existing client materials, with no additional research or meetings; otherwise $75-100 per minute, $750 minimum.

Audiovisuals: For writing, $250-350 per requested scripted minute; includes rough draft, editing conference with client, and final shooting script. For consulting, research, producing, directing, soundtrack oversight, etc., $400-600 per day plus travel and expenses. Writing fee is sometimes 10% of gross production price as billed to client.

B

Book, as-told-to (ghostwriting): Author gets full advance and 50% of author's royalties; subject gets 50%. Hourly rate for subjects who are self-publishing ($25-50 per hour).

Book, ghostwritten, without as-told-to credit: For clients who are either self-publishing or have no royalty publisher lined up, $5,000 to $35,000 (plus expenses) with one-fourth down payment, one-fourth when book half finished, one-fourth at three quarters mark and last fourth of payment when manuscript completed; or chapter by chapter.

Book content editing: $12-50 per hour and up; $600-5,000 per manuscript, based on size and complexity of the project.

Book copyediting: $9-22 per hour and up.

Book indexing: $10-22.50 per hour; $25 per hour using computer indexing software programs that take fewer hours; $1.50-6 per printed book page; 40-70¢ per line of index; or flat fee of $250-500, depending on length.

Book jacket blurb writing: From $100-600 for front cover copy plus inside and back cover copy summarizing content and tone of the book.

Book manuscript criticism: $160 for outline and first 20,000 words; $300-500 for up to 100,000 words.

Book manuscript reading, nonspecialized subjects: $20-50 for a half page summary and recommendation. **Specialized subject:** $100-500 and up, depending on complexity of project.

Book proofreading: $8.50-25 per hour and up; sometimes $1.50-3 per page.

Book proposal consultation: $25-35 per hour.

Book proposal writing: $300-1,000 or more depending on length and whether client provides full information or writer must do some research.

Book query critique: $50 for letter to publisher and outline.

Book research: $5-20 per hour and up, depending on complexity.

Book reviews: For byline and the book only, on small newspapers; to $35-300 on larger publications.

Book rewriting: $18-50 per hour; sometimes $5 per page. Some writers have combination ghostwriting and rewriting short-term jobs for which the pay could be $350 per day and up. Some participate in royalties on book rewrites.

Book summaries for business people: $400 for 4-8 printed pages.

Book summaries for book clubs, film producers: $50-100/ book. Note: You must live in the area where the business is located to get this kind of work.

Brochures: $200-7,500 and up depending on client (small nonprofit organization to large corporation), length, and complexity of job.

Business booklets, announcement folders: Writing and editing, $100-1,000 depending on size, research, etc.

Business facilities brochure: 12-16 pages, $1,000-4,000.

Business letters: Such as those designed to be used as form letters to improve customer relations, $100 per letter for small businesses; $500 and up per form letter for corporations.

Business meeting guide and brochure: 4 pages, $200; 8-12 pages, $400.

Business writing: On the local or national level, this may be advertising copy, collateral materials, speechwriting, films, public relations or other jobs—see individual entries on these subjects for details. General business writing rates could range from $25-60 per hour; $100-200 per day, plus expenses.

Business writing seminars: $250 for a half-day seminar, plus travel expenses.

C

Catalogs for business: $25-40 per hour or $60-75 per printed page; more if many tables or charts must be reworked for readability and consistency.

Church history: $200-1,000 for writing 15 to 50 pages.

Collateral materials for business: See Business Booklets, Catalogs for business, etc.

Comedy writing for night club entertainers: Gags only, $2-25 each. Routines, $100-1,000 per minute. Some new comics may try to get a five-minute routine for $150; others will pay $2,500 for a five-minute bit from a top writer.

Comics writing: $35-50 per page and up for established comics writers.

Commercial reports for businesses, insurance companies, credit agencies: $6-10 per page; $5-20 per report on short reports.

Company newsletters and inhouse publications: Writing and editing 2-4 pages, $200-500; 4-8 pages, $500-1,000; 12-48 pages, $1,000-2,500. Writing, $20-60 per hour; editing, $15-40 per hour.

College/university history: $35 per hour for research through final ms.

Consultation on communications: $250 per day plus expenses for nonprofit, social service and religious organizations; $400 per day to others.

Consultation on magazine editorial: $1,000-1,500 per day plus expenses.

Consultation to business: On writing, PR, $25-50 per hour.

Consultant to publishers: $25-50 per hour.

Consumer complaint letters: $25 each.

Contest judging: Short manuscripts, $5 per entry; with one-page critique, $15-25. Overall contest judging: $100-500.

Copyediting and content editing for other writers: $10-50/hour or $2 per page. (See also Manuscript consultation and Manuscript criticism.)

Copyediting for advertising: $25 per hour.

Copyediting for book publishers: see Book copyediting.

Copyediting for nonprofit organizations: $15 per hour.

Copywriting for book club catalogs: $85-200.

Corporate comedy: Half-hour show, $300-800.

Corporate history: $1,000-20,000, depending on length, complexity and client resources.

Corporate profile: Up to 3,000 words, $1,250-2,500.

D

Dance criticism: $25-400 per article. (See also Arts reviewing.)

Direct-mail catalog copy: $75-100 per item; $400-500 per page.

Direct-mail packages: Copywriting direct mail letter, response card, etc., $1,500-10,000 depending on writer's skill, reputation, and the client.

Direct response card on a product: $250.

Drama criticism: Local, newspaper rates; non-local, $50 and up per review.

E

Editing: See Book copyediting, Company newsletters, Magazine editing, etc.

Educational consulting and educational grant and proposal writing: $250-750 per day and or $25-75 per hour.

Encyclopedia articles: Entries in some reference books, such as biographical encyclopedias, 500-2,000 words; pay ranges from $60-80 per 1,000 words. Specialists' fees vary.

Executive biography: (based on a resume, but in narrative form): $100.

English teachers—lay reading for: $6 per hour.

F

Fact checking: $17-25 per hour.

Family histories: See Histories, family.

Filmstrip script: See Audiovisuals.

Financial presentation for a corporation: 20-30 minutes, $1,500-4,500.

Flyers for tourist attractions, small museums, art shows: $50 and up for writing a brief bio, history, etc.

Fund-raising campaign brochure: $5,000 for 20 hours' research and 30 hours to write a major capital campaign brochure, get it approved, lay out and produce with a printer. For a standard fund-raising brochure, many fund-raising executives hire copywriters for $50-75 an hour to do research which takes 10-15 hours and 20-30 hours to write/produce.

G

Gags: see Comedy writing for nightclub entertainers.

Genealogical research: $25 per hour.

Ghostwriting: $25-100 per hour; $200 per day plus expenses. Ghostwritten professional and trade journal articles under someone else's byline, $400-4,000. Ghostwritten books: see Book, as-told-to (ghostwriting) and Book, ghostwritten, without as-told-to credit.

Ghostwriting a corporate book: 6 months' work, $13,000-25,000.

Ghostwriting article for a physician: $2,500-3,000.

Ghostwriting speeches: See Speechwriting.

Government public information officer: Part-time, with local governments, $25 per hour; or a retainer for so many hours per period.

Grant appeals for local non-profit organizations: $50 an hour or flat fee.

Grant proposals: $40 per hour.

H

Histories, family: Fees depend on whether the writer need only edit already prepared notes or do extensive research and writing; and the length of the work, $500-15,000.

Histories, local: Centennial history of a local church, $25 per hour for research through final manuscript for printer.

House organ editing: See Company newsletters and inhouse publications.

I

Industrial product film: $1,000 for 10-minute script.

Industrial promotions: $15-40 per hour. See also Business writing.

J

Job application letters: $10-25.

L

Lectures to local librarians or teachers: $50-100.

Lectures to school classes: $25-75; $150 per day; $250 per day if farther than 100 miles.

Lectures at national conventions by well-known authors: $2,500-20,000 and up, plus expenses; less for panel discussions.

Lectures at regional writers' conferences: $300 and up, plus expenses.

M

Magazine, city, calendar of events column: $150.

Magazine column: 200 words, $25. Larger circulation publications pay fees related to their regular word rate.

Magazine editing: Religious publications, $200-500 per month; $15-30 per hour.

Magazine stringing: 20¢-$1 per word based on circulation. Daily rate: $100-200 plus expenses; weekly rate: $750 plus expenses. Also $7.50-35 per hour plus expenses.

Manuscript consultation: $25-50 per hour.

Manuscript criticism: $25 per 16-line poem; $40 per article or short story of up to 3,000 words; book outlines and sample chapters of up to 20,000 words, $160.

Manuscript typing: Depending on ms length and delivery schedule, $1.50-2 per page with one copy; $15 per hour.

Market research survey reports: $15-30 per hour; writing results of studies or reports, $500-1,200 per day.

Medical editing: $25-65 per hour.

Medical proofreading: $12-30 per hour.

Medical writing: $25-100 per hour; manuscript for pharmeceutical company submitted to research journal, $4,500-5,000.

Movie novelization: $3,500-15,000, depending on writer's reputation, amount of work to be done, and amount of time writer is given.

N

New product release: $300-500 plus expenses.

News release: See Press release.

Newsletters: See Company newsletters and Retail business newsletters.

Newspaper column, local: 80¢ per column inch to $5-10 for a weekly; $7.50-15 for dailies of 4,000-6,000 circulation; $10-20 for 7,000-10,000 dailies; $15-20 for 11,000-25,000 dailies; and $25 and up for larger dailies.

Newspaper feature: 35¢ to $1.50 per column inch or $15-30 per article for a weekly; $70-80 for a daily.

Newspaper feature writing, part-time: $1,000 a month for an 18-hour week.

Newspaper reviews of art, music, drama: See Arts reviewing.

Newspaper stringing: 50¢-2.50 per column inch up to $7.50 per column inch for some national publications. Also publications like *National Enquirer* pay lead fees up to $250 for tips on page one story ideas.

Newspaper ads for small business: $25 for a small, one-column ad, or $10 per hour and up.

Novel synopsis for film producer: $150 for 5-10 pages typed single-spaced.

Novel synopsis for literary agent: $150 for 5-10 pages typed single-spaced.

O

Obituary copy: Where local newspapers permit lengthier than normal notices paid for by the funeral home (and charged to the family), $15. Writers are engaged by funeral homes.

Opinion research interviewing: $4-6 per hour or $15-25 per completed interview.

P

Party toasts, limericks, place card verses: $1.50 per line.

Permission fees to publishers to reprint article or story: $75-500; 10-15¢ per word; less for charitable organizations.

Photo brochures: $700-15,000 flat fee for photos and writing.

Photo research: $12-25 per hour.

Poetry criticism: $25 per 16-line poem.

Political writing: See Public relations and Speechwriting.

Press background on a company: $500-1,200 for 4-8 pages.

Press kits: $500-3,000.

Press release: 1-3 pages, $85-300.

Printers' camera-ready typewritten copy: Negotiated with individual printers, but see also Manuscript typing.

Product literature: Per page, $100-150.

Programmed instruction consultant fees: $300-700 per day; $50 per hour.

Programmed instruction materials for business: $50 per hour for inhouse writing and editing; $500-700 a day plus expenses for outside research and writing. Alternate method: $2,000-5,000 per hour of programmed training provided, depending on technicality of subject.

Proofreading: $7-12 per hour.

Public relations for business: $200-500 per day plus expenses.

Public relations for conventions: $500-1,500 flat fee.

Public relations for libraries: Small libraries, $5-10 per hour; larger cities, $35 an hour and up.

Public relations for nonprofit or proprietary organizations: Small towns, $100-500 monthly retainers.

Public relations for politicians: Small town, state campaigns, $10-50 per hour; incumbents, congressional, gubernatorial, and other national campaigns, $25-100 per hour; up to 10% of campaign budget.

Public relations for schools: $15-20 per hour and up in small districts; larger districts have full-time staff personnel.

R

Radio advertising copy: $20-65 per script; $200-225 per week for a four- to six-hour day; larger cities, $250-400 per week.

Radio continuity writing: $5 per page to $150 per week, part-time.

Radio documentaries: $200 for 60 minutes, local station.

Radio editorials: $10-30 for 90-second to two-minute spots.

Radio interviews: For National Public Radio, up to 3 minutes, $25; 3-10 minutes, $40-75; 10-60 minutes, $125 to negotiable fees. Small radio stations would pay approximately 50% of the NPR rate; large stations, double the NPR rate.

Readings by poets, fiction writers: $25-600 depending on the author.

Record album cover copy: $100-250 flat fee.

Recruiting brochure: 8-12 pages, $500-1,500.

Research for individuals: $5-20 per hour, depending on experience, geographic area and nature of the work.

Research for writers or book publishers: $15-30 an hour and up; $15-200 per day and all expenses. Some quote a flat fee of $300-500 for a complete and complicated job.

Restaurant guide features: Short article on restaurant, owner, special attractions, $15; interior, exterior photos, $15.

Résumé writing: $25-200 per résumé.

Retail business newsletters for customers: $175-300 for writing four-page publications. Some writers work with a local printer and handle production details as well, billing the client for the total package. Some writers also do their own photography.

Rewriting: Copy for a local client, $27.50 per hour.

S

Sales brochure: 12-16 pages, $750-3,000.

Sales letter for business or industry: $350-1,000 for one or two pages.

Science writing: For newspapers $150-600; magazines $2,000-5,000; encyclopedias $1 per line; textbook editing $40 per hour; professional publications $500-1,500 for 1,500-3,000 words.

Script synopsis for agent or film producer: $75 for 2-3 typed pages, single-spaced.

Scripts for nontheatrical films for education, business, industry: Prices vary among producers, clients, and sponsors and there is no standardization of rates in the field. Fees include $75-120 per minute for one reel (10 minutes) and corresponding increases with each successive reel; approximately 10% of the production cost of films that cost the producer more than $1,500 per release minute.

Services brochure: 12-18 pages, $1,250-2,000.

Shopping mall promotion: $500 monthly retainer up to 15% of promotion budget for the mall.

Short story manuscript critique: 3,000 words, $40.

Slide film script: See Audiovisuals.

Slide presentation: Including visual formats plus audio, $1,000-1,500 for 10-15 minutes.

Slide/single image photos: $75 flat fee.

Slide/tape script: $75-100 per minute, $750 minimum.

Software manual writing: $35-50 per hour for research and writing.

Special news article: For a business's submission to trade publication, $250-400 for 1,000 words.

Special occasion booklet: Family keepsake of a wedding, anniversary, Bar Mitzvah, etc., $115 and up.

Speech for government official: $4,000 for 20 minutes plus up to $1,000 travel and miscellaneous expenses.

Speech for local political candidate: $250 for 15 minutes; for statewide candidate, $375-500.

Speech for national congressional candidate: $1,000 and up.

Speech for owners of a small business: $100 for six minutes.

Speech for owners of larger businesses: $500-3,000 for 10-30 minutes.

Speech for statewide candidate: $500-800.

Speechwriting: $20-75 per hour.

Syndicated newspaper column, self-promoted: $2-8 each for weeklies; $5-25 per week for dailies, based on circulation.

T

Teaching adult education course: $10-60 per class hour.

Teaching adult seminar: $350 plus mileage and per diem for a 6- or 7-hour day; plus 40% of the tuition fee beyond the sponsor's breakeven point.

Teaching business writing to company employees: $60 per hour.

Teaching college course or seminar: $15-70 per class hour.

Teaching creative writing in school: $15-70 per hour of instruction, or $1,500-2,000 per 12-15 week semester; less in recessionary times.

Teaching elementary and middle school teachers how to teach writing to students: $75-120 for a 1-1½ hour session.

Teaching home-bound students: $5-10 per hour.

Teaching journalism in high school: Proportionate to salary scale for full-time teacher in the same school district.

Technical editing: $15-60 per hour.

Technical typing: $1-4 per double-spaced page.

Technical writing: $35 per ms page or $35-75 per hour, depending on degree of complexity and type of audience.

Textbook copyediting: $14-20 per hour, depending on el-hi, college, technical, non-technical.

Textbook editing: $15-30 per hour.

Textbook proofreading: $9-18.50 per hour.

Textbook writing: $14-50 per hour.

Trade journal ad copywriting: $250-500.

Trade journal article: For business client, $500-1,500.

Translation, commercial: Final draft from one of the common European languages, $115-120 per thousand words.

Translation for government agencies: Up to $125 per 1,000 foreign words into English.

Translation, literary: $50-100 per thousand English words.

Translation through translation agencies: Less 33⅓% (average) for agency commission.

Translation, technical: $125 per thousand words.

Tutoring: $25 per 1-1½ hour private session.

TV documentary: 30-minute 5-6 page proposal outline, $250 and up; 15-17 page treatment, $1,000 and up; less in smaller cities.

TV editorials: $35 and up for 1-minute, 45 seconds (250-300 words).

TV home shopping: Local ad copy: $6 an hour. Writing, misc. freelance: $15-85 per hour; $.50-1 per word.

TV information scripts: Short 5- to 10-minute scripts for local cable TV stations, $10-15 per hour.

TV instruction taping: $150 per 30-minute tape; $25 residual each time tape is sold.

TV news film still photo: $3-6 flat fee.

TV news story: $16-25 flat fee.

TV filmed news and features: From $10-20 per clip for 30-second spot; $15-25 for 60-second clip; more for special events.

TV, national and local public stations: $35-100 per minute down to a flat fee of $100-500 for a 30- to 60-minute script.

TV scripts: (Teleplay only), 60 minutes, prime time, Writers Guild rates: $11,780; 30 minutes, $8,733.

V

Video script: See Audiovisuals.

W

Writer-in-schools: Arts council program, $130 per day; $650 per week. Personal charges vary from $25 per day to $100 per hour depending on school's ability to pay.

Writer's workshop: Lecturing and seminar conducting, $50-150 per hour to $750 per day plus expenses; local classes, $35-50 per student for 10 sessions.

_____ *Writers' Roundtable*

Among writers, the sale of rights often raises confusion. Many don't quite understand the differences between various rights, and others feel they can't afford to jeopardize a sale by trying to negotiate different rights than those first specified by an editor.

On the other hand, editors sometimes have little control and must buy rights based on the corporation's or publisher's policy. Others buy all rights because they pay well and want exclusive material, while still others buy all rights or issue work-for-hire agreements simply because it enables them to re-use the material again and again without paying any additional fee.

The sale of rights has been a long-standing issue in publishing. Some writers refuse to work with publications that require sale of all rights or issue work-for-hire agreements. Last year, the Supreme Court considered a court case on work-for-hire, *CCNV vs. Reid*, that drew considerable attention to the issue but hasn't seemed to change much about the way the industry operates.

In a professional atmosphere, there is usually some give-and-take to the sale of rights. Editors are often willing to pay more for all rights, and some are willing to reassign rights to writers after an article has appeared in print. Writers often are unsure about negotiating the sale of rights, however. Sometimes they haven't evaluated possible resale markets so they don't know whether or not sale of all rights would greatly affect potential earnings from reprints. Others are reluctant to sell all rights with only the editor's promise of reassignment.

The listings in *Writer's Market* include the typical rights each magazine buys. We also are concerned about these industry issues, so our editorial staff conducted a survey on how the magazine industry handles rights. Among consumer publications listed in last year's *Writer's Market*, 29% bought all rights or issued work-for-hire agreements. Among trade journal editors, 41% operated this way. We noted from the survey, however, that many publications listed the purchase of more than one type of rights, meaning that many editors are open to negotiations. A full 55% of consumer publications and 52% of trade journals in the survey purchase less-restrictive first or one-time rights. The remainder of the figures are split between reprint rights or the purchase of both first and second serial rights to a piece. Explanations of each set of rights can be found in Rights and the Writer in the Business of Writing section.

Consumer magazines

In our survey we contacted 317 editors about their policies; editors from 243 consumer magazines responded. Eighty-two bought all rights or issued work-for-hire agreements for some of the following reasons:

"Because of the competitive market in arts and cultural coverage — and because we pay well for it."

"It's simpler that way."

"It's mandated by the legal department."

"To facilitate reprint by our other publications."

"We usually buy all rights because there is great enough influx of freelance material from which to choose."

"Because the publishers decided that's what they wanted to buy and changed policies."

"Many non-profit organizations request reprint rights from us and it is too much trouble to always locate the writer."

"Company policy."

"We want exclusivity and we pay well (40-75¢/word)."

"So that our licensed foreign editions can use all our material."

"We prefer to keep the option to use our material in a variety of ways."

"To simplify administrative overhead and ensure exclusivity."

"Because we want to be able to arrange reprints for publicity purposes."

A number of editors said this policy was open to negotiation or they would be willing to reassign rights after a period of time—usually three to nine months after publication. Others are perfectly willing to reassign rights to material an author may later incorporate into a book but will not reassign it for reprint in another magazine.

Magazine editors who purchased first or one-time rights had this to say:

"We publish and move on and expect the writer to do the same."

"This covers our needs and allows the writer to find additional sources of income and new audiences."

"We can't pay much and want our authors to be able to generate additional income."

"To give writers more control over their work and their careers."

"We buy the rights we need and do not believe in preventing the authors from obtaining additional income from their work."

"As a regional publication, we have no need for exclusive rights."

"We believe we get a better quality if a writer has the chance to sell his material more than once."

"We want to allow writers to market their material elsewhere. We are writers as well as editors and try to be fair to both interests."

Trade magazines

Among 74 trade magazines responding, 32 editors buy all rights. Most often they cited the need to publish exclusive material that will not appear again in competitors' magazines. But several also want the ability to reprint material without paying the author again. Of those that buy all rights, about half are willing to reassign rights later: others only want industry exclusives, freeing writers to resell to non-competing publications.

Most of the trade editors who buy one-time or first rights say they don't need to buy more extensive rights, don't mind authors reselling the work, pay too little to ask for all rights, or find their writers prefer to sell those type of rights. "We previously bought all rights," said one editor, "but most writers are protecting their work now. If the material is good, we'll buy only first rights."

In addition to responses from editors, we've also sought the experience of three writers. We asked two fulltime writers and the president of the National Writers Union a variety of questions on rights. Their answers will help you make informed decisions and show you how to negotiate sales.

Respondents are:

William Barnhill, a writer from Burdett, New York, has written for daily newspapers, a variety of national magazines and is a regular contributing author to Time-Life Books. He is the recipient of the National Media Award from the American College of Emergency Physicians, and recently worked on *Sick and Tired of Being Sick and Tired* (Wynwood Press, 1989) with medical columnist Neil Solomon. He has published in *The New York Times*, *The Washington Post*, *Good Housekeeping*, *Reader's Digest*, *Self*, *Parenting* and *Parade*, among others.

Diane Cole, a writer from New York City, is a contributing editor to *Psychology Today* and is currently at work on her second book, *After Great Pain: Coping with Loss and Change*, to be published by the Free Press. Her first book, *Hunting the Headhunters: A Woman's Guide*, was published by Fireside/Simon & Schuster in 1988. Her work has appeared in many national publications, including *The New York Times*, *The Wall Street Journal*, *The Washington Post*, *Newsweek*, *Ms.*, *Savvy* and *Redbook*, among others.

Alec Dubro began his freelance career as a rock critic with *Rolling Stone* in 1968. He has written numerous articles, TV and radio material, advertising and PR, as well as co-authoring *Yakuza*, a comprehensive study of Japanese organized crime. Elected to the executive board of the National Writers Union in 1984, he has been national president for the past three years.

About 41% of the trade publications and 29% of the consumer publications in Writer's Market *buy all rights or make work-for-hire assignments. Are there any options for freelancers other than working with at least a few of these type of publications? Do you see the situation differently for new writers versus established writers?*

WB: I see no difference between work-for-hire and all rights; either way, the writer gives up all his or her rights to the work produced. I suppose this might be acceptable, but only if the rate is much higher than that of publications willing to buy first North American publishing rights.

I have never accepted an all rights or work-for-hire arrangement, even while I was a "bright eyes," and fortunately I have encountered very few editors who demanded such concesssions. That's part luck and partly the fact I've picked some good magazines (editors) to write for — and ran like hell from those I sensed were bad news.

That's not to say I would reject such an offer out of hand. I'd want to hear the price first.

Of course there's a difference [between new and experienced writers]. Writing is a skill that must be developed, polished, and then demonstrated to editors. And experienced writers get better deals from better magazines than do newcomers to the trade.

A writer must determine his or her own immediate goals. If you are unpublished and you need a showcase for your skills, you may have to sell all rights, or take a meager fee just to show what you can do. But it appears to me that many new writers are so eager for the first few bylines that they'll accept any deal, no matter how unfair, to get them. Editors on the smaller magazines often will bend a little on rates and rights if a writer negotiates. So it never hurts to ask, and the more often you've been published, the stronger your negotiating position.

DC: I always tell writers to try to sell first North American serial rights or first serial rights only. Retaining as many rights as possible for yourself means, quite simply, that you control your article. If other magazines ask to reprint the article, the full fee is yours. If you wish to include the article or research material in a book, you need not worry about asking for permission or squabbling over copyright questions; the copyright is yours.

Beginning writers usually don't have enough experience or confidence to ask for these rights. (I know I didn't.) They also have not learned yet that many magazines issue more than one kind of contract: a "world rights" contract for writers who don't ask about rights and a first North American serial rights contract for writers who do. At the same time, some editors won't budge on the issue of certain rights even for known writers who do ask. So, depending on where you are in your career and the policies of the magazines for whom you write, you may not always be able to get the rights you want.

The question then becomes: How much do these rights mean to you *in this case*? If I'm dying to write a particular article for a particular publication, I may decide (and have) that it's worth it to me to yield on some rights. But in exchange I'd also ask for more money and try to limit the magazine's ownership of those rights to a specified amount of time (I suggest no more than a year). If you are hesitant to negotiate, remember that you won't know what the publication will say unless you ask. So ask for what you want ideally, then negotiate for the best deal possible. If you still can't live with the arrangement, you can always say "I'm sorry" and find another market.

AD: The National Writers Union believes that work for hire and all rights, as they apply to books and publications, are essentially wrong and illegal. But writers generally have more options than they think. First, and one which frequently works, is simply to strike the offending clause from your contract and return it. If this fails to work, insist that as a member of the Writers Union you cannot engage in work for hire, but offer to negotiate whatever rights the publication needs, and attempt to get additional pay for them. If all else fails, you can go elsewhere. Between 60 and 70% of publications *don't* use such contracts, and if everyone refused to sign them, work for hire would disappear.

Of course, taking a strong stand is somewhat easier for established writers, but that has as much to do with self-image as anything else. Publications buy articles because they need them, not because they respect writers, and we ought to remember that when negotiating.

In your work, do you see a method editors use to determine the rights they will buy? Does it make a difference if they work for an individual magazine or a group of magazines?

WB: If I were an editor I suspect I'd be tempted to try to buy all rights whenever I could. After-rights can be worth money and an editor's first responsibility, obligation and loyalty is to his/her publisher. Having said that, I have found that the better the magazine the more likely it is to treat its writers fairly.

If you want to see one of the fairest contracts around, try *Parade*'s standard agreement. It's simple enough for a legal illiterate like me to understand and so fair that it starts you off on an assignment with a real warm glow toward the publication, which tends to move the creative process along. I wish everyone in the business would adopt it.

Other publications are less fair. One editor, for example, recently gave me a letter of assignment that was somewhat vague. It specified length, fee, kill fee and deadline, but made no mention of rights. That came in the formal contract sent to me *after* I submitted an acceptable piece and, of course, it specified "all rights" even though my copy was marked very clearly "First North American Publishing Rights." (Unless rights are negotiated beforehand, that's something a writer always should insert at the top of every manuscript.) In this case, a polite, but very firm rejection of the contract resulted in purchase of the rights I had offered. But it'll be a long time before I offer this editor another article. Contracts always should be sent *before* a writer does the job.

I don't think [it makes a difference whether it's a single magazine or a group]. I've had editors for small publications make outrageous offers and editors with large chains (though much more rarely) suggest things that were equally outrageous. One major newspaper syndicate, for example, wrote into a contract a clause that gave it first right of refusal on everything I ever wrote for the rest of my life — if I had signed it. When I suggested to the syndicate president that Abe Lincoln had outlawed that sort of thing, he laughed and replied, "Well, we had to try, didn't we?" Maybe that's the answer: Some editors just have to try. With all that, by the way, the syndicate gave me a good deal and was great to work with. Negotiating works.

DC: Publications that have a policy of trying to buy all rights may have marketing arrangements with various syndicates or be affiliated with (or own) other publications around the world that buy reprint material from them. Other magazines may hire a special staff member to market reprint rights. All these magazines see reprint rights as a source of income for the publication. But reprint fees also are a source of income to writers, and therein lies one part of the debate over rights.

Fortunately, there are publishers and editors (some of whom were once freelancers themselves) who are quite sympathetic to questions about rights. It's not just altruism, either: The best editors understand that the better they treat their writers, the harder the writers will work for them.

AD: Owners and management make these decisions; editors are essentially foremen. And publications want copyright because they intend to re-use material for their own gain. This is easier for publication groups, but they are certainly not the only ones. *Rolling Stone*, for instance, demands all-rights agreements because they do a lot of syndication.

Do you sell the same type of rights in all situations, or do you consider this a negotiable item?

WB: To magazines I offer first North American publishing rights only; to newspapers I offer one-time rights. On the other hand, my work, any part of it, or all of it, is for sale *if the price is right*.

DC: Always try to sell first North American serial or first serial rights only. Many editors will have no problem with that; you just have to ask. In other cases you will have to negotiate, deciding what these rights mean to you in this case: Is the article so important or compelling, your career so new, the publication so prestigious, or the fee so attractive that you would be willing to compromise on the issue of rights? How much are you willing to compromise? If you compromise on some rights, will the magazine compromise on other points, such as limiting the time they own the rights and paying you a higher fee?

I'd also suggest checking *Writer's Market* and talking to other writers to find out in advance what kind of rights a particular publication usually buys and, if you do have to negotiate, the kinds of arrangements, compromises, or arguments to which the editor will best respond.

AD: The Writers Union recommends that freelancers sell only first North American serial rights and that additional rights be granted only when paid for. The U.S. is quite backward in this regard, by the way. In Britain, under the National Union of Journalists rules, all rights costs publishers 150% over fee. We have a long way to go, but it seems worth the fight.

What would you advise writers to do when magazine editors don't specify the type of rights they want to buy?

WB: I've finally learned the hard way, as I mentioned earlier. If an editor does not send me a contract that spells out our agreement very clearly, I send one to the editor. And rights are a key element. If an editor doesn't send a contract or a detailed letter of assignment, before starting work on the project a writer should fire off a letter of agreement spelling out what's being offered and what is expected in return. I've found most editors are very agreeable to this procedure.

DC: Some writers take the stance that if there is no written contract you can assume you are selling first serial rights only. I'm not entirely comfortable with that, so I recommend getting a contract that spells it out. If the publication offers no formal contract, write a letter to the editor reviewing the details of your agreement (fee, length of article, etc.) and stating that you are selling first North American serial rights. If a question ever arises, you're covered.

AD: Specify it yourself. Write them a letter of confirmation in which you state the terms. Say, "This contract is for a one-time North American use only."

Several magazines, especially literary magazines, tell us they buy all rights but are willing to reassign rights later. What's your opinion on their reasons for doing this? How do you think writers should address this?

WB: I've never had an editor offer such a deal and I have no idea why one would. But if one did, I would ask: Why? Some editors don't want a writer to resell an article for a specific period after they publish it, usually a couple of months. I think that's clear, fair and reasonable, so I always accept it.

DC: I really don't know why literary magazines follow this practice. If they have no problem reassigning rights to the writer later, why take them away to begin with? As always, writers should try to negotiate for first serial rights or the best rights possible.

AD: Given that literary magazines pay next to nothing, it's hard to countenance such behavior. Clearly they are reserving stories to re-use or resell to anthologies. If the magazine wants to undertake a joint effort to resell material, and is willing to pay for that option, then the writer can sign away those rights. But otherwise, writers are capable of deciding for themselves whether they want their work to appear in an anthology.

What's your opinion of work-for-hire assignments? Have you seen any change since CCNV v. Reid?

WB: They smell. Unless the money is right.

DC: Clearly, I don't like the idea of work-for-hire assignments. I can't say if there has been a decrease in the number of such assignments, but it seems to me that publishers can still essentially buy a "work for hire" from a freelancer by wording the contract differently and saying "all rights." To judge by the *Writer's Market* survey, far too many publications do.

AD: Work for hire is, in my mind, theft, and unconstitutional theft at that. Copyright is not some recent, contorted doctrine; it appears in Article I, Section 8 of the U.S. Constitution. It grants to authors "exclusive rights to writings," which seems pretty clear to me. The current protracted and expensive battle over work for hire is more a function of the financial power and greed of the information and publishing companies than of any ambiguity in the law.

It appears to have gotten worse since *CCNV v. Reid*. Many publications are now demanding written work-for-hire agreements. And Meredith Publications, for one, sent out a letter immediately after the *Reid* decision was rendered asking that writers agree to work for hire now and *for all future* Meredith work.

Some editors tell us they buy all rights because they pay large sums of money to get exclusive material. Others ask for all rights as a matter of course, whether or not their payment is high. How would you advise writers to deal with this?

WB: If the paycheck is large enough, the editor is welcome to exclusivity. But in my experience, what most editors really want is the first break on fresh new material. That's what I try to offer. Those who ask for all rights as a matter of course get the same stock answer: No. That's how I think all writers should handle this question.

DC: If the editor insists on buying additional or all rights, don't be afraid to negotiate for something else in exchange: Ask for more money; try to limit the time that the publication will retain world rights; arrange to split reprint fees or to retain the full amount in cases where you yourself sell reprint rights; write in a provision allowing you to use the material, in part or in full, in any future book you might write; make sure that you can base related articles or books on the research material you uncover for this project. Many editors will yield on these or other points, but you won't know if you don't ask.

AD: If the magazines are expending such huge sums on writers, why does the average freelancer make less than $10,000 a year? The fact that every writer must grasp is that fees almost *never* cover the cost of doing the work. It is *only* through subsidiary sales that we can hope to make a decent income, which is why copyright is so important. Or, as David Kline entitled an article, "If they pay you one-tenth of what it's worth, you have to sell it ten times."

Obviously, where magazines pay $2 a word, and the writer feels completely satisfied, then of course they can grant additional rights gratis. But the notion that we *owe* them all rights in exchange for their measly fees is ludicrous.

What do you think is the greatest mistake writers make in selling rights to their writing?

WB: For whatever reason, they get "the eagers." They're desperate for an addition to their resumes, frantic for a byline, or just plain hungry. Always remember that the relationship between an editor and a writer should be symbiotic: The writer needs the editor . . . the guidance, the direction, the encouragement, the soft shoulder to cry on and, of course, the check. And the editor needs writers who can produce fresh, creative, accurate, well written copy directed specifically toward that magazine's readers — and written within the deadline.

Seems to me when both approach the relationship this way, the question of rights is something that can be discussed rationally, without anger or hostility. If the deal looks good enough and the editor absolutely must have all rights, take it; if not, offer your work to some other editor.

DC: The biggest mistake writers make is being afraid to negotiate. A closely related mistake is not knowing what they *can* negotiate. Fortunately, you can learn the basics pretty quickly by reading writers' publications (like this one) and by talking to other writers. Still, when the editor says "We buy all rights," it can be scary even for experienced writers to say "Let's talk about that." That's why I highly recommend joining a writers' association like the National Writers Union. When you have a question about rights, fees or anything else related to the business of writing, you'll know where to turn and you'll also know you're not alone.

AD: Being defensive or apologetic. We are doing the essential work of the publishing industry, and we ought to act that way. You don't find printers acting apologetic when they ask publishers for a fair price to cover their costs, so why should we? Of course, isolated freelancers are in a tougher position than a big printing company, but that's why we're building a union. No worker alone is ever a match for a well-financed and organized company. And writers are no different in this respect than other workers. In short, writers should join and become active in the National Writers Union, and begin to exert their rights and their strength in this growing and lucrative industry.

Important Listing Information

Listings are based on editorial questionnaires and interviews. They are not *advertisements; publishers do not pay for their listings. The markets are* not *endorsed by* Writer's Market *editors.*

• *All listings have been verified before publication of this book. If a listing has not changed from last year, then the editor told us the market's needs have not changed and the previous listing continues to accurately reflect its policies. We require documentation in our files for each listing and never run a listing without its editorial office's approval.*

• Writer's Market *reserves the right to exclude any listing.*

• *When looking for a specific market, check the index. A market may not be listed for one of these reasons.*

  1. *It doesn't solicit freelance material.*
  2. *It doesn't pay for material.*
  3. *It has gone out of business.*
  4. *It has failed to verify or update its listing for the 1991 edition.*
  5. *It was in the middle of being sold at press time, and rather than disclose premature details, we chose not to list it.*
  6. *It hasn't answered* Writer's Market *inquiries satisfactorily. (To the best of our ability, and with our readers' help, we try to screen out fraudulent listings.)*
  7. *It buys few manuscripts, thereby constituting a very small market for freelancers.*

• *See the index of additional markets at the end of each major section for specific information on individual markets not listed.*

The Markets

_____ *Book Publishers*

Statistics from the U.S. Department of Commerce, Bureau of the Census, suggest that over the past few years, New York, Los Angeles, Boston, Chicago and Washington DC continue to lead the nation in overall sales of books. That may be no surprise, but college towns Austin, Texas; Madison, Wisconsin; and San Jose, California; ranked highest in bookstore sales per household. Clearly there is more on book publishers' minds than what will sell on the coasts. Sales have increased, in general, at a rate of 10% per year for the last five years. Bookstores, both chains and independents, are increasing their market share through book clubs, direct mail and schools. Writers looking for improved chances of selling their books to a publisher should take into consideration what's been happening in bookstores.

Before you approach a book publisher with your manuscript, you should acquaint yourself with the business of publishing. During the 1980s, many companies merged or were purchased by foreign investors. This usually resulted in staff cutbacks as firms strove to become more cost-effective. When cutbacks are made, it usually affects consideration of unsolicited manuscripts. Instead of having staff members or freelancers read stacks of over-the-transom submissions, publishers rely more on agents to screen material and submit it to them.

Submitting appropriate manuscripts also means knowing differences between publishers. Some publishers are interested only in specific areas, such as science fiction, while others consider a broad range of general interest topics. You'll find that some houses pursue mass market bestsellers only, while others want to produce literary novels or specialized books. A few publishers have started receiving submissions electronically, either by modem or computer disk, while others still prefer hard copy. Some want both. Information in the individual listings, as well as researching publisher's new titles, will help you keep up with the changing business of book publishing.

Industry trends

It's difficult to predict what topics and types of books will be strong sellers. Book publishers plan their titles months to several years in advance, and general trends such as the aging population will undoubtedly affect their choice of manuscripts. Current events and their possible future effects also influence editors' choices. Writers, especially those marketing nonfiction, should make it a practice to keep up with recent information and events to make their manuscripts as timely and salable as possible.

Here are some industry trends that may affect what editors buy in the coming year:
● A number of publishing houses have created more imprints. This has allowed increased flexibility to acquire different types of books, and has balanced out the inefficiency that often follows publishing mergers. Imprints have varying degrees of independence from the

rest of the company and may be more open to particular topics.
● Children's books remain a strong category, although the market remains soft for young adult novels. Retail sales on children's book are up from $500 million to $1 billion in the last five years. Time-Warner Inc. has started the first book club for children, entitled, appropriately enough, Children's Book-of-the-Month Club.
● Sports books are popular, particularly those about baseball, basketball and golf. Sports personalities, fitness, and instructional books all enjoy good sales.
● New Age books continue to be a strong category and have moved to an international audience. The category has pulled in psychology, philosophy, health, religion, astrology and occult titles as well. New Age is now used as a general term for titles with metaphysical, spiritual and holistic approaches. It also covers psychic phenomena, spiritual healing, UFOs and mysticism.
● True crime stories are very popular of late.
● Science fiction is enjoying a growth period.

Other strong categories include travel, gardening, the environment, parenting, cooking, business, celebrity and humor. While these categories are popular, writers should keep in mind that editors are always looking for something new and different. "The unusual new idea always attracts us if it can add something to the list and especially if it can lead to new markets for other books," says George Young, editor-in-chief of Ten Speed Press.

The markets

Give your book the best publisher possible by analyzing your manuscript and studying the market. For some writers, the best is a publisher whose books regularly appear on the bestseller lists. For others, the best is a small press where each author gets personal attention from the editor. For publishers who produce fewer than four titles per year, see the Small Press section at the end of Book Packagers and Producers. For more information on small presses, contact the Small Press Writers' and Artists' Organization, 13 Southwood Dr., Woodland CA 95695.

No matter what type of book you've written, the Book Publishers section can help you. You'll find more than 800 publishers listed. Not all of them buy the kind of work you write, but studying the listing subheads for nonfiction and fiction in the Book Publishers Subject Index will tell you which ones do.

When you read the detailed listings of publishers, choose two or three that buy what you're writing. Send for their catalogs and writer's guidelines. You'll learn the most current information about the books they've published, as well as their preferences for receiving manuscripts. Try to read a few of the publishers' books; a visit to the library is all that's necessary.

You will find publishers prefer different types of submissions. Some will read only a query letter; some want a query with an outline or synopsis; others want a one-page proposal. If editors accept submissions only through agents, don't send material directly.

Most editors like specific information in query letters. (See the Business of Writing for a sample book query letter.) Show that you understand their concerns by mentioning the audience for your book, the competition, and why your book is different. The editor also will want to know if you have previous publishing experience or special training relevant to the book's subject. Do not claim to have written the next blockbuster bestseller—even if you think you have.

Remember that only a fraction of today's writers sell a book to the first publisher to which it's submitted. Prepare a list of at least a dozen publishers that might be interested in your book. Learn more about them; send for catalogs and guidelines a few at a time. If your submission comes back with a rejection, don't lose heart. An editor who rejected the manuscript of *Lolita* was quoted in *Rotten Rejections* (Pushcart Press) as having written back to author Vladimir Nabokov, "The book would serve no purpose of any kind and should be buried under a large stone for a thousand years."

Send your work to the next publisher on your list. You may be able to speed up this process with simultaneous submissions of your query letter or manuscript. It's usually acceptable to send queries to several editors at the same time—as long as each letter is individually addressed. Never send a form letter as a query. If more than one editor responds favorably, you may be able to submit your manuscript simultaneously. Some publishers, however, refuse to consider simultaneous submissions; their *Writer's Market* listings and their guidelines will tell you their policies. Otherwise, you can send your manuscript to two or more publishers at the same time—but you should notify the editors that it's a simultaneous submission.

A number of publishers are also willing to consider electronic submissions of manuscripts. These are submissions made by modem or computer disk. A poll conducted by the editor of *Writer's Market* found that 60% of book publishers queried were open to at least a small number of these submissions. Of those that take them, 20% accept four out of five manuscripts electronically. Larger publishers are more likely to accept electronic submissions than small presses. A large portion of publishers open to electronic submissions prefer ASCii formats for its generic compatability with many word processing systems. Most, however, will still want a hard copy of the manuscript as well as the disk.

Subsidy publishing

At the *Writer's Market* office, we receive many calls and letters asking about subsidy publishing and self-publishing. As you read more about the publishing industry, you'll undoubtedly find advertisements and articles describing these alternatives. Be cautious. Know what you want from your writing.

Most writers want to make money from the books they write but don't succeed at first. Those who aspire to be professional writers know that it may take years to perfect a book, find the right publisher and receive royalty payments. They are willing to invest their time and efforts to meet that goal.

Some writers are more impatient. They've tried to sell a book and have met only rejection—encouraging rejection, maybe, but still rejection. They know they haven't written bestsellers, but they don't believe their books can be improved by further revision. They believe a specific market exists, and they want the book published.

Other writers simply write for their own satisfaction or for the pleasure of family and friends. Their writing may be just a hobby, but because of some encouragement they wonder why they can't get published. They haven't tried to market a manuscript before and are confused about the differences between royalty publishers, subsidy publishers and self-publishing.

We encourage you to work with publishers that pay writers. Most publishers do this through a royalty arrangement, paying the author 3-25% of the wholesale or retail price. These publishers actively market their books; you'll find them in bookstores and libraries, read about them in the newspaper and sometimes see their authors on TV. Whenever a copy of one of these books is sold, both the writer and the publisher make money.

Subsidy publishers, on the other hand, expect writers to pay part or all of the cost of producing a book. They may ask for $1,000 or sometimes as much as $18,000, explaining that current economic conditions in the industry necessitate authors paying the costs of publishing. Subsidy publishers rarely market books as effectively as major publishing companies. Vantage Press, a subsidy publisher, recently lost a class-action lawsuit to authors who said Vantage never promoted their books. Subsidy publishers make money by selling their services to writers, not by selling their products to bookstores and libraries. Some subsidy publishers offer royalties but expect the writer to pay for promotion expenses.

Problems can arise when writers don't understand the policies and terms of a subsidy publisher's proposal or contract. Don't sign anything unless you understand and are comfortable with the terms. If you are willing to pay to have your book published, you should be willing to hire an attorney to advise you on a contract.

Subsidy publishers are sometimes called "vanity" publishers because the companies appeal to a writer's ego in wanting to have his book published. Most subsidy publishers are offended when they are called vanity presses, but we don't distinguish between the two. Any publishing effort that asks the writer to pay all or part of the cost is identified as a subsidy publisher. Companies that ask authors to pay subsidies on more than 50% of the books they publish each year are listed in *Writer's Market* at the end of the Book Publishers section.

This doesn't mean that subsidy publishing is always a bad choice. In Canada, for example, books are often subsidized by government grants. In the U.S., a special interest book may be subsidized by the writer's friends, a foundation or church. Sometimes a royalty publisher or university press will offer a subsidy arrangement to a writer whose talent outweighs the marketing potential of the book. Companies that do this 50% of the time or less are identified with an asterisk (*) before the listings.

Self-publishing

Self-publishing is another option for writers. The successful self-published book has a potential audience and fills a need not filled by current books on the topic. If you have submitted a manuscript to a publisher and it was rejected, you should analyze the reasons for rejection. If your manuscript needs polishing, do that before you self-publish it. If a large publisher determined that it would not generate enough sales, remember that books do not have to sell in the same quantities for a self-published book to make money as for a large publisher to profit.

Your consideration of self-publishing should include answering these questions. Are you willing to pay for a few hundred to several thousand copies of your book? Can you supervise all stages of its production? Do you have the time and energy to promote and distribute the book yourself?

Writers interested in self-publishing also may approach a small press publisher and agree to split the cost of a press run. Some companies call themselves editorial services and offer a range of services to writers, from editing manuscripts to producing a book. Consider what you need, and make sure you aren't signing on for more services than you require. These agreements should be strictly on a contract basis. More often, writers contract with a local printer to produce a specific number of books for a specific price.

As with subsidy publishing, be sure you know what's involved. "Done properly, self-publishing is an exciting and viable way to get your book into print," say Marilyn and Tom Ross, authors of *The Complete Guide to Self-Publishing* (Writer's Digest Books).

Selling your work

If you receive a number of rejections, don't give up. Many successful writers submit a manuscript to dozens of publishers before finding one to publish their book. Others rely on agents to market their manuscripts. Three writers who recently published their first books all recommend having agents submit manuscripts to publishers, especially those by new writers. Refer to the First Bylines and Author's Agents sections for more information.

First, be sure you've done everything to improve your book's chances. Study writing and revision techniques and continue to study the markets. Many writers also find classes and writer's groups helpful in putting them in touch with other people who share their interest in writing.

No matter which method you choose, remember that the writing of the book comes first. Think of your book as a manuscript in transition and help it evolve into the best book it can be while you search for the best possible publisher.

For a list of publishers according to their subjects of interest, see the nonfiction and fiction sections of the Book Publishers Subject Index. Information on some book publishers and packagers not included in this edition of *Writer's Market* can be found in the Other Book Publishers and Packagers at the end of the Subsidy Publishers section.

AASLH PRESS, American Association for State and Local History, Suite 202, 172 2nd Ave. N., Nashville TN 37201. (615)255-2971. AASLH Press Director: Joanne Jaworski. Estab. 1940. Publishes hardcover and softcover originals and reprints. Averages 6 titles/year; receives 20-30 submissions annually. 50% of books from first-time authors; 100% of books from unagented writers. Pays 5-10% royalty on retail price. Publishes book an average of 1 year after acceptance. Reports in 3 months on submissions. Free book catalog.
Nonfiction: How-to, reference, self-help and textbook. "We publish books, mostly technical, that help people do effective work in historical societies, sites and museums, or do research in, or teach, history. No manuscripts on history itself—that is, on the history of specific places, events, people." Submit outline/synopsis and sample chapters. Reviews artwork/photos.
Recent Nonfiction Title: *Identifying American Furniture*, by Milo M. Naeve.
Tips: "Explain why our market will buy your book, use it, need it. The emphasis is on materials that can be practically utilized by historic preservationists."

‡ABBEY PRESS, Publishing Division, St. Meinrad IN 47577. (812)357-8011. Publisher: Keith McClellan O.S.B. Estab. 1867. Publishes mass market paperback originals. Averages 10 titles/year. Receives 200 submissions/year. 40% of books from first-time authors; 100% of books from unagented writers. Pays 10% royalty on retail price. Publishes book an average of 1 year after acceptance. Reports in 1 month on queries; 6 weeks on mss. Ms guidelines for SASE.
Nonfiction: Abbey publications focus in three general areas: marriage, parenting and family life; pastoral care and spiritual growth. These materials include inspirational, self-help, gift, and personal/professional enrichment titles. They are distinguished by a gently spiritual and religious dimension. Query with outline/synopsis and sample chapters.
Recent Nonfiction Title: *Children Facing Grief*, by Janis Romond.
Tips: "Abbey publications are designed to offer practical, supportive and uplifting materials for people challenged by the demands of vocation, career and ordinary day-to-day living."

ABBOTT, LANGER & ASSOCIATES, 548 1st St., Crete IL 60417. (312)672-4200. President: Dr. Steven Langer. Publishes trade paperback originals and loose-leaf books. Averages 14 titles/year; receives 25 submissions annually. 15% of books from first-time authors; 100% of books from unagented writers. Pays 10-15% royalty; no advance. Publishes book an average of 18 months after acceptance. Query for electronic submissions. Book catalog for 6x9 SAE with 2 first class stamps. Reports in 2 weeks on queries; 2 months on mss.
Nonfiction: How-to, reference, technical on some phase of personnel administration, industrial relations, sales management, etc. Especially needs "a very limited number (3-5) of books dealing with very specialized topics in the field of personnel management, wage and salary administration, sales compensation, training, recruitment, selection, labor relations, etc." Publishes for personnel directors, wage and salary administrators, training directors, sales/marketing managers, security directors, etc. Query with outline. Reviews artwork/photos.
Recent Nonfiction Title: *How to Build a Motivated Work Force Using Non-Monetary Incentives*, by Lynn Grensing.
Tips: "A how-to book in personnel management, sales/marketing management or security management has the best chance of selling to our firm."

ABC-CLIO, INC., 130 Cremona, Santa Barbara CA 93117 (head office). All submissions to Suite 300, 180 Cook St., Denver CO 80206. (303)333-3003. Subsidiaries include Clio Press, Ltd., Cornerstone Books. Vice President: Heather Cameron. Estab. 1955. Publishes hardcover originals. Firm averages 35 titles/year. Receives 1,000 submissions/year. 20% of books from first-time authors; 95% from unagented writers. Pays royalty on wholesale price. Publishes ms an average of 8 months after acceptance. Query for electronic submissions. Reports in 3 weeks on queries; 1 month on mss. Free book catalog and manuscript guidelines.
Nonfiction: How-to, reference. Subjects include art/architecture, education, government/politics, history, military/war, women's issues/studies. "Looking for reference books on/for older adults, current world issues, teen issues, women's issues, and for high school social studies curriculum. No monographs or textbooks." Query or submit outline/synopsis and sample chapters.
Recent Nonfiction Title: *Women Who Ruled*, by Guida Jackson.

ABINGDON PRESS, 201 8th Ave. S., P.O. Box 801, Nashville TN 37202. (615)749-6301. Editorial Director: Neil M. Alexander. Editor Trade Books: Mary Catherine Dean. Senior Editor Reference/Academic Books: Rex Mathews. Senior Editor Church Resources: Ronald P. Patterson. Editor Professional Books: Paul Franklyn. Estab. 1789. Publishes paperback originals and reprints; church supplies. Receives approximately 2,500 submissions annually. Published 100 titles last year. Few books from first-time authors; 90-95% of books from unagented writers. Average print order for a writer's first book is 4,000-5,000. Pays royalty. Publishes book an average of 18 months after acceptance. Query for electronic submissions. Ms guidelines for SASE. Reports in 2 months.
Nonfiction: Religious-lay and professional, children's religious books and academic texts. Length: 32-300 pages. Query with outline and samples only. Reviews artwork/photos.
Recent Nonfiction Title: *Last Rights*, by Joseph B. Ingle.
Fiction: Juveniles/religious.
Recent Fiction Title: *God's Love Is for Sharings*, by Helen Caswell.

‡*HARRY N. ABRAMS, INC., Subsidiary of Times Mirror Co., 100 5th Ave., New York NY 10011. (212)206-7715. President, Publisher and Editor-in-Chief: Paul Gottlieb. Publishes hardcover and "a few" paperback originals. Averages 65 titles/year; receives "thousands" of submissions annually. 5% of books from first-time authors; 25% of books from unagented writers. "We are one of the few publishers who publish almost exclusively illustrated books. We consider ourselves the leading publishers of art books and high-quality artwork in the U.S." Offers variable advance. Publishes book an average of 1-2 years after acceptance. Reports in 3 months. Free book catalog.
Nonfiction: Art, nature and science, and outdoor recreation. Needs illustrated books for art and art history, museums. Submit outline/synopsis and sample chapters and illustrations. Reviews artwork/photos as part of ms package.
Recent Nonfiction Title: *The Genius of Jacopo Bellini*, by Colin Eisler.
Tips: "We publish *only* high-quality illustrated art books, i.e., art, art history, museum exhibition catalog, written by specialists and scholars in the field. Once the author has signed a contract to write a book for our firm the author must finish the manuscript to agreed-upon high standards within the schedule agreed upon in the contract."

‡ACADEMY CHICAGO, 213 W. Institute Place, Chicago IL 60610. (312)751-7302. FAX: (312)751-7306. Editorial Director/Senior Editor: Anita Miller. Estab. 1975. Publishes hardcover and paperback originals and reprints. Averages 60 titles/year; receives approximately 2000 submissions annually. 10% of books from first-time authors; 25% of books from unagented writers. Average print order for a writer's first book 1,500-3,500. Pays 7-10% royalty; modest advances. Publishes book an average of 18 months after acceptance. Book catalog for 8½×11 SAE with 3 first class stamps; guidelines for #10 SAE with 1 first class stamp. Submit cover letter with first four chapters. Reports in 2 months.
Nonfiction: Adult, travel, true crime and historical. No how-to, cookbooks, self-help, etc. Query and submit first four consecutive chapters. Reviews artwork/photos.
Recent Nonfiction Title: *The Trial of Levi Weeks*, by Estelle Fox Kleiger.
Fiction: "Mysteries, mainstream novels." No "romantic," children's, young adult, religious or sexist fiction; nothing avant-garde.
Recent Fiction Title: *In a Dark Wood Wandering*, by Hella S. Haasse.
Tips: "The writer has the best chance of selling our firm a good mystery or true crime book, because the response to these is predictable, relatively."

ACCELERATED DEVELOPMENT INC., 3400 Kilgore Ave., Muncie IN 47304. (317)284-7511. FAX (317)284-2535. President: Dr. Joseph W. Hollis. Executive Vice President: Marcella Hollis. Estab. 1973. Publishes textbooks/paperback originals and tapes. Averages 10-15 titles/year; receives 170 submissions annually. 50% of books from first-time authors; 100% of books from unagented writers. Query for electronic submissions. Pays 6-15% royalty on net price. Publishes book an average of 1 year after acceptance. Reports in 3 months. Book catalog for 6½×9½ SAE with 3 first class stamps.
Nonfiction: Reference books and textbooks on psychology, counseling, guidance and counseling, teacher education and death education. Especially needs "psychologically-based textbook or reference materials, death education material, theories of counseling psychology, techniques of counseling, and gerontological counseling." Publishes for professors, counselors, teachers, college and secondary students, psychologists, death educators, psychological therapists, and other health-service providers. "Write for the graduate level student and at elementary and at secondary school level in the affective domain." Submit outline/synopsis, 2 sample chapters, prospectus, and author's resume. Reviews artwork/photos.
Recent Nonfiction Title: *Therapist Guide to the MMPI & MMPI-2*, by Richard Lewak, Philip Marks and Gerald Nelson.
Tips: "Freelance writers should be aware of American Psychological Association style of preparing manuscripts."

ACCENT BOOKS, A division of Accent Publications, 12100 W. 6th Ave., P.O. Box 15337, Denver CO 80215. (303)988-5300. Executive Editor: Mary B. Nelson. Estab. 1947. Publishes evangelical Christian paperbacks, the majority of which are nonfiction. Guidelines available for #10 SAE with 1 first class stamp. Averages 10-15 titles/year. 30% of books from first-time authors; 100% of books from unagented writers. Pays royalty on cover price. Publishes book an average of 1 year after acceptance. Query or submit 3 sample chapters with a brief synopsis and chapter outline. Do not submit full ms unless requested. Reports in 1-3 months. Book catalog for 9×12 SAE with 4 first class stamps.

Recent Nonfiction Title: *Running on Empty in the Fast Lane*, by Curt Dodd.

Fiction: "Fiction titles have strong evangelical message woven throughout plot. Main characters are Christians. Books are either contemporary mystery/romance or frontier romance."

Recent Fiction Title: *Dark River Legacy*, by B.J. Hoff.

Tips: "How-to books designed for personal application of biblical truth and/or dealing with problems/solutions of philosophical, societal, and personal issues from a biblical perspective have the best chance of selling to our firm. We also consider books for the professional and volunteer in church ministries."

‡ACE SCIENCE FICTION, The Berkley Publishing Group, 200 Madison Ave., New York NY 10016. (212)686-9820. Estab. 1953. Publishes paperback originals and reprints. Publishes 120 titles/year. Writer's guidelines for #10 SAE with 1 first class stamp.

Fiction: Science fiction and fantasy. Query with synopsis and first 3 chapters. Reports in 3 months.

Recent Fiction Title: *Orbital Decay*, by Allen Steele.

ACS PUBLICATIONS, INC., P.O. Box 34487, San Diego CA 92103-0802. (619)297-9203. Editorial Director: Maritha Pottenger. Estab. 1977. Publishes trade paperback originals and reprints. Averages 8 titles/year; receives 400 submissions annually. 50% of books from first-time authors; 95% of books from unagented writers. Average print order for a writer's first book is 3,000. Pays 15% royalty "on monies received through wholesale and retail sales." No advance. Publishes book an average of 2 years after acceptance. Query for electronic submissions. Reports in 1 month on queries; 2 months on mss. Book catalog and guidelines for 9×12 SAE with 3 first class stamps.

Nonfiction: Astrology and New Age. Subjects include astrology, holistic health alternatives, channeled books, numerology, and psychic understanding. "Our most important market is astrology. We are seeking pragmatic, useful, immediately applicable contributions to field; prefer psychological approach. Specific ideas and topics should enhance people's lives. Research also valued. No determinism ('Saturn made me do it.') No autobiographies. No airy-fairy 'space cadet' philosophizing. Keep it grounded, useful, opening options (not closing doors) for readers." Query or submit outline and 3 sample chapters.

Recent Nonfiction Title: *The Book of Neptune*, by Marilyn Waram.

Tips: "The most common mistake writers make when trying to get their work published is to send works to inappropriate publishers. We get too many submissions outside our field or contrary to our world view."

BOB ADAMS, INC., 260 Center St., Holbrook MA 02343. (617)767-8100. Managing Editor: Brandon Toropov. Publishes hardcover and trade paperback originals. Averages 25 titles/year. Receives 250 submissions/year. 25% of books from first-time authors; 25% of books from unagented writers. Variable royalty "determined on case-by-case basis." Publishes book an average of 12-18 months after acceptance. Reports in 6 months "if interested. We accept no responsibility for unsolicited manuscripts." Book catalog for 9×12 SAE and $2.40 postage.

Nonfiction: Reference books on careers, self-help and business. Query.

Recent Nonfiction Title: *Why Love is Not Enough*, by Sol Gordon.

‡ADDISON-WESLEY PUBLISHING CO., INC., General Books Division, Jacob Way, Reading MA 01867. Publisher: David C. Miller. Estab. 1942. Publishes hardcover and paperback originals. Publishes 125-150 titles/year. Pays royalty. Simultaneous submissions OK. Reports in 1 month. Free book catalog.

Nonfiction: Biography, history, business/economics, health, how-to, politics, psychology and science, computer books. Query, then submit outline/synopsis and 1 sample chapter.

Recent Nonfiction Title: *Nature's Thumbprint*, by Peter B. Neubauer, MD and Alexander Neubauer.

Tips: "We will accept submissions for cookbooks, computer books and general nonfiction." Queries/mss will be routed to other editors in the publishing group.

ADVOCACY PRESS, Division of The Girls Club of Greater Santa Barbara, P.O. Box 236, Santa Barbara CA 93102. (805)962-2728. Director of Operations: Kathy Araujo. Estab. 1983. Non-profit press publishes hardcover and trade paperback originals with an equity focus. Does not publish adult or young adult fiction. Children's picture books must focus on specific concepts, i.e. leadership, self-reliance, etc. Publishes average 4 titles/year. Receives 100-150 submissions/year. 25% from first-time authors; 100% from unagented writers. Publishes ms an average of 6 months after acceptance. Simultaneous submissions OK. Reports in 6 weeks.

Nonfiction: Biography, juvenile, self-help. Subjects include education, psychology and women's issues/studies. "Children's picture books needed. Non-sexist, issue-oriented adult and young adult materials." Submit outline/synopsis and sample chapters.
Recent Nonfiction Title: *More Choices*, by Bingham/Stryker (young adult self-help).
Fiction: Adventure, feminist, historical, juvenile, picture books, young adult. Submit outline/synopsis and sample chapters.
Recent Fiction Title: *Time for Horatio*, by Paine.

AFRICAN AMERICAN IMAGES, Suite 308, 9204 Commercial, Chicago IL 60617. (312)375-9682. FAX: (312)375-9349. Editor: Jawanza Kunjufu. Estab. 1983. Publishes trade paperback originals. Averages 6 titles/year. Receives 25 submissions/year. 90% of books from first-time authors. 100% from unagented writers. Pays royalty on wholesale price. Offers $500 average advance. Publishes book an average of 6-9 months after acceptance. Simultaneous submissions OK. Reports in 1 week on queries; 3 weeks on mss. Free book catalog and manuscript guidelines.
Nonfiction: Juvenile and self-help. Subjects include child guidance/parenting, education, ethnic (Black), history, psychology and sociology. Submit complete ms. Reviews artwork/photos as part of ms package.
Recent Nonfiction Title: *Color Me Light of the World*, by Sharon Carter (juvenile).
Fiction: Juvenile and young adult. "Only children's books on Black culture." Submit complete ms.
Recent Fiction Title: *Carla & Annie*, by Susan Smith.

AGLOW PUBLICATIONS, A ministry of Women's Aglow Fellowship International, P.O. Box 1548, Lynnwood WA 98046-1557. (206)775-7282. Editor: Gwen Weising. Estab. 1969. Publishes trade paperback originals. Averages 10 titles/year; receives 1,000 submissions annually. 50% of books from first-time authors; 95% of books from unagented writers. Average print order of a writer's first book is 10,000. Pays up to 10% maximum royalty on retail price. Buys some mss outright. Publishes book 18 months after acceptance. Reports in 1 month on queries; 2 months on mss. Book catalog and guidelines for 9 × 12 SAE with 3 first class stamps.
Nonfiction: Biblically-oriented support group books, self-help and inspirational. Subjects include religion (Christian only). "Familiarize yourself with our materials before submitting. Our needs and formats are very specific." Query or submit outline/synopsis and first 3 sample chapters.
Recent Nonfiction Title: *Love and Its Counterfeits*, by Barbara Cook.
Tips: "The writer has the best chance of selling our firm a book that shows some aspect of the Christian life."

ALA BOOKS, 50 East Huron St., Chicago IL 60611. (312)944-6780. Subsidiary of American Library Association. Senior Editor: Herbert Bloom. Publishes hardcover and paperback originals. Firm averages 30-35 titles/year. Receives approximately 100 submissions/year. 60% of books from first-time authors; 100% from unagented writers. Pays royalty of "not more than 15% of our receipts from sales." Publishes ms an average of 9 months after acceptance. Reports in 2 weeks on queries; 2 months on mss. Free ms guidelines.
Nonfiction: Reference. Subjects include library science, child and adult guidance, education, library service. Professional books for librarians. "We are looking for guides to information, management of information centers; and application of electronic technologies to such management particularly." Query.
Recent Nonfiction Title: *Movie Characters of Leading Performers*, by Nowlan (general reference).
Tips: "Think analytically, but write simply."

‡ALBA HOUSE, 2187 Victory Blvd., Staten Island, New York NY 10314. (212)761-0047. Estab. 1958. Publishes hardcover and paperback originals and reprints. Specializes in religious books. "We publish shorter editions than many publishers in our field." Averages 15 titles/year; receives 1,000 submissions annually. 50% of books from first-time authors; 80% of books from unagented writers. Pays 10% royalty on retail price. Publishes book an average of 9 months after acceptance. Query. State availability of photos/illustrations. Simultaneous submissions OK. Reports in 1 month. Book catalog and ms guidelines for SASE. Reviews artwork/photos.
Nonfiction: Publishes philosophy, psychology, religion, sociology, textbooks and Biblical books. Accepts nonfiction translations from French, German or Spanish. Submit outline/synopsis and 1-2 sample chapters.
Tips: "We look to new authors." Queries/mss may be routed to other editors in the publishing group.

THE ALBAN INSTITUTE, INC., 4125 Nebraska Ave. NW, Washington DC 20016. (202)244-7320. Director of Publications: Celia A. Hahn. Publishes trade paperback originals. Averages 7 titles/year; receives 100 submissions annually. 100% of books from unagented writers. Pays 7% royalty on books; $50 on publication for 2- to 8-page articles relevant to congregational life – practical – ecumenical. Publishes book an average of 1 year after acceptance. Reports in 2 months. Prefers queries. Book catalog and ms guidelines for 9 × 12 SAE and 3 first class stamps.
Nonfiction: Religious – focus on local congregation – ecumenical. Must be accessible to general reader. Research preferred. Needs mss on the task of the ordained leader in the congregation, the career path of the ordained leader in the congregation, problems and opportunities in congregational life, and ministry of the laity in the world and in the church. No sermons, devotional, children's titles, inspirational type or prayers. Query or submit outline/synopsis and sample chapters.

Recent Nonfiction Title: *Discerning the Call to Social Ministry*, by Malcolm Burson et. al.

Tips: "Our audience is intelligent, probably liberal mainline Protestant and Catholic clergy and lay leaders, executives and seminary administration/faculty—people who are concerned with the local church at a practical level and new approaches to its ministry. We are looking for titles on the ministry of the laity and how the church can empower it."

ALLEN PUBLISHING CO., 7324 Reseda Blvd., Reseda CA 91335. (818)344-6788. Owner/Publisher: Michael Wiener. Estab. 1979. Publishes mass market paperback originals. Firm averages 4 titles/year. Receives 50-100 submissions/year. 50% of books from first-time authors. 100% from unagented writers. Buys mss outright for negotiable sum. Publishes book an average of 6 months after acceptance. Simultaneous submissions OK. Reports in 2 weeks. Book catalog for #10 SAE; with 1 first class stamp.

Nonfiction: How-to and self-help. Subjects include business and economics and money/finance. "We want self-help material, 25,000 words approximately, aimed at wealth-builders, opportunity seekers, aspiring entrepreneurs. Material must be original and authoritative, not rehashed from other sources. All our books are marketed exclusively by mail, in soft-cover, 8½×11 format. We are a specialty publisher and will not consider anything that does not exactly meet our needs." Query. Reviews artwork/photos as part of ms package.

Recent Nonfiction Title: *A Consumer's Guide to Multi-Level Marketing*, by Doug Freeman.

Tips: "There are more and more people who call themselves writers but who do not have the expertise to write nonfiction books on the subjects they choose. We prefer books by people who really know their subjects. Choose a very specialized subject, learn all you can about it, and write."

‡ALMAR PRESS, 4105 Marietta Dr., Binghamton NY 13903. (607)722-0265. Editor-in-Chief: A.N. Weiner. Managing Editor: M.F. Weiner. Estab. 1977. Publishes hardcover and paperback originals and reprints. Averages 8 titles/year; receives 200 submissions annually. 75% of books from first-time authors; 100% of books from unagented writers. Average print order for a writer's first book is 2,000. Pays 10% royalty; no advance. Publishes book an average of 6 months after acceptance. Prefers exclusive submissions; however, simultaneous (if so indicated) submissions OK. Query for electronic submissions. Reports in 1 month. Book catalog for 8½×11 SAE with 2 first class stamps. *"Submissions must include SASE for reply and return of manuscript."*

Nonfiction: Publishes business, technical, regional and consumer books and reports. "These main subjects include general business, financial, travel, career, technology, personal help, North-East regional, hobbies, general medical, general legal, and how-to. *Almar Reports* are business and technology subjects published for management use and prepared in 8½×11 and book format. Publications are printed and bound in soft covers as required. Reprint publications represent a new aspect of our business." Submit outline/synopsis and sample chapters. Reviews artwork/photos as part of ms package. Looks for information in the proposed book that makes it different or unusual enough to attract book buyers. Reviews artwork/photos.

Recent Nonfiction Title: *A Postcard History of U.S. Aviation*, by Jack W. Legenfelder.

Tips: "We're adding a new series of postcard books for various topics where the postcards are illustrated and the captions describe the scene on the postcard and the history related to it. Approximately 225 illustrations per book. We are open to any suggested topic. This type of book will be important to us. We look for timely subjects. The type of book the writer has the best chance of selling to our firm is something different or unusual—*no* poetry or fiction, also *no* first-person travel or family history. The book must be complete and of good quality."

*ALPINE PUBLICATIONS, INC., 214 19th St. S.E., Loveland CO 80537. (303)667-9317. Publisher: B.J. McKinney. Estab. 1975. Publishes hardcover and trade paperback originals. Averages 6-10 titles/year. Subsidy publishes 2% of books when "book fits into our line but has a market so limited (e.g., rare dog breed) that we would not accept it on royalty terms." Occasional small advance. Pays 7-15% royalty. Publishes book an average of 1½ years after acceptance. Reports in 3 weeks on queries; 2 months on mss. Writer's guidelines for #10 SAE with 2 first class stamps.

Nonfiction: How-to books about animals. "We need comprehensive breed books on the more popular AKC breeds, books for breeders on showing, breeding, genetics, gait, new training methods, and cat and horse books. No fiction or fictionalized stories of real animals; no books on reptiles; no personal experience stories except in case of well-known professional in field." Submit outline/synopsis and sample chapters or complete ms. Reviews artwork/photos as part of manuscript package.

Recent Nonfiction Title: *The Total German Shepherd Book*, by Fred Lanting.

 The double dagger before a listing indicates that the listing is new in this edition. New markets are often the most receptive to freelance submissions.

ALYSON PUBLICATIONS, INC., 40 Plympton St., Boston MA 02118. (617)542-5679. Publisher: Sasha Alyson. Estab. 1979. Publishes trade paperback originals and reprints. Averages 20 titles/year; receives 500 submissions annually. 30% of books from first-time authors; 80% of books from unagented writers. Average print order for a writer's first book is 6,000. Pays 8-15% royalty on net price; offers $1,000-3,000 advance. Publishes book an average of 15 months after acceptance. Query for electronic submissions. Reports in 2 weeks on queries; 5 weeks on mss. Looks for "writing ability and content suitable for our house." Book catalog and ms guidelines for #10 SAE and 3 first class stamps.
Nonfiction: Gay/lesbian subjects. "We are especially interested in nonfiction providing a positive approach to gay/lesbian issues." Accepts nonfiction translations. Submit one-page synopsis. Reviews artwork/photos as part of ms package.
Recent Nonfiction Title: *In The Land of Alexander*, by Keith Hale.
Fiction: Gay novels. Accepts fiction translations. Submit one-page synopsis.
Recent Fiction Title: *Doc and Fluff*, by Pat Califia.
Tips: "We publish many books by new authors. The writer has the best chance of selling to our firm well-researched, popularly-written nonfiction on a subject (e.g., some aspect of gay history) that has not yet been written about much. With fiction, create a strong storyline that makes the reader want to find out what happens. With nonfiction, write in a popular style for a non-academic audience."

‡AMACOM BOOKS, Imprint of American Management Association, 135 W. 50th, New York NY 10020. (212)903-8081. Director, Weldon P. Rackley. Publishes hardcover and trade paperback originals and trade paperback reprints. Firm averages 50 titles/year. Receives 200 submissions/year. 50%of books from first-time authors. 90% from unagented writers. Pays 10-15% royalty on net receipts by the publisher. Publishes book an average of 10 months after acceptance. Query for electronic submissions. Reports in 2-3 weeks on queries. Free book catalog and manuscript guidelines.
Nonfiction: How-to, reference, self-help, textbook and retail bookstore market. Subjects include business, computers, education/business, business books of all types. Query. Submit outline/synopsis and sample chapters.
Tips: Our audience consists of people in the business sector looking for very applied books on business.

AMERICA WEST PUBLISHERS, P.O. Box 6451, Tehachapi CA 93582. (805)822-9655. Review Editor: George Green. Publishes hardcover and trade paperback originals and hardcover and trade paperback reprints. Averages 5 titles/year. Receives 50 submissions/year. 30% of books from first-time authors. 90% from unagented writers. Pays 10% on wholesale price. Offers $300 average advance. Publishes book an average of 6 months after acceptance. Simultaneous submissions OK. Reports in 2 weeks on queries; 3 months on mss. Free book catalog and manuscript guidelines.
Nonfiction: UFO—metaphysical. Subject includes health/medicine (holistic self-help). Submit outline/synopsis and sample chapters. Reviews artwork/photos as part of ms package.
Recent Nonfiction Title: *Conversations with Nostradamus*, by Cannon.
Tips: "We currently have materials in all bookstores that have areas of UFO's and also metaphysical information and New Age."

*AMERICAN ATHEIST PRESS, American Atheists, P.O. Box 2117, Austin TX 78768-2117. (512)458-1244. Editor: R. Murray-O'Hair. Estab. 1959. Imprints include Gusttav Broukal Press. Publishes trade paperback originals and trade paperback reprints. Averages 12 titles/year; receives 200 submissions annually. 40-50% of books from first-time authors; 100% of books from unagented writers. Pays 5-10% royalty on retail price. Publishes book an average of 1 year after acceptance. Simultaneous submissions OK. Reports in 2 months on queries; 3 months on submissions. Book catalog for 6½x9½ SAE; writer's guidelines for 9 × 12 SAE.
Nonfiction: Biography, humor, reference and general. Subjects include history (of religion and Atheism, of the effects of religion historically); philosophy and religion (from an Atheist perspective, particularly criticism of religion); politics (separation of state and church, religion and politics); Atheism (particularly the lifestyle of Atheism; the history of Atheism; applications of Atheism). "We are interested in hard-hitting and original books expounding the lifestyle of Atheism and criticizing religion. We would like to see more submissions dealing with the histories of specific religious sects, such as the L.D.S., the Worldwide Church of God, etc. We are generally not interested in biblical criticism." Submit outline/synopsis and sample chapters or complete ms. Reviews artwork/photos.
Recent Nonfiction Title: *Women, Food and Sex in History*, by Soledad de Montalvo.
Fiction: Humor (satire of religion or of current religious leaders); anything of particular interest to Atheists. "We rarely publish any fiction. But we have occasionally released a humorous book." No mainstream. "For our press to consider fiction, it would have to tie in with the general focus of our press, which is the promotion of Atheism and free thought." Submit outline/synopsis and sample chapters.
Tips: "We plan two new periodicals (start dates: 1991). This will enable us to publish a greater variety of material in regard to both length and content. We will need more how-to types of material—how to argue with creationists, how to fight for state/church separation, etc. We have an urgent need for literature for young Atheists."

‡**AMERICAN BUSINESS CONSULTANTS, INC.**, 1540 Nuthatch Lane, Sunnyvale CA 94087-4999. (408)738-3011. President: Wilfred Tetreault. Publishes trade paperback originals. Averages 30 titles/year. Receives 2 submissions/year. 100% of books from first-time authors. Buys mss outright. Publishes book an average of 1 month after acceptance. Simultaneous submissions OK. Query for electronic submissions. Reports in 1 month.
Nonfiction: Appraising, buying and selling any kind of business fraud and ripoffs. Query.
Recent Nonfiction Title: *Buying & Selling Business Opportunities*, by W. Tetreault (business how-to paperback).
Tips: "Writers have the best chance selling us books on business frauds. Our audience consists of buyers and sellers of businesses."

AMERICAN CATHOLIC PRESS, 16160 South Seton Dr., South Holland IL 60473. (312)331-5845. Editorial Director: Father Michael Gilligan, Ph.D. Estab. 1967. Publishes hardcover originals and hardcover and paperback reprints. "Most of our sales are by direct mail, although we do work through retail outlets." Averages 4 titles/year. Pays by outright purchase of $25-100; no advance. Publishes book an average of 8 months after acceptance. Simultaneous submissions OK. Reports in 2 months.
Nonfiction: "We publish books on the Roman Catholic liturgy—for the most part, books on religious music and educational books and pamphlets. We also publish religious songs for church use, including Psalms, as well as choral and instrumental arrangements. We are interested in new music, meant for use in church services. Books, or even pamphlets, on the Roman Catholic Mass are especially welcome. We have no interest in secular topics and are not interested in religious poetry of any kind." Query.
Recent Nonfiction Title: *Psalter*, by Jeanette Dandurand.

AMERICAN HOSPITAL PUBLISHING, INC., American Hospital Association, 211 East Chicago Ave., Chicago IL 60611. (312)440-6800. Vice President, Books: Brian Schenk. Estab. 1979. Publishes trade paperback originals. Firm averages 20-30 titles/year. Receives 75-100 submissions/year. 20% of books from first-time authors; 100% from unagented writers. Pays 10-12% royalty on retail price. Offers $1,000 average advance. Publishes book an average of 1 year after acceptance. Reports in 1 month on queries; 6 weeks on mss. Book catalog and manuscript guidelines for #10 SASE.
Nonfiction: Reference, technical, textbook. Subjects include business and economics (specific to health care institutions); health/medicine (never consumer oriented). Need field-based, reality-tested responses to changes in the health care field directed to hospital CEO's, planners, boards of directors, or other senior management. No personal histories, untested health care programs or clinical texts. Query.
Recent Nonfiction Title: *Restructuring for Ambulatory Care*, by Ted Matson, ed.
Tips: "The successful proposal demonstrates a clear understanding of the needs of the market and the writer's ability to succinctly present practical knowledge of demonstrable benefit that comes from genuine experience that readers will recognize, trust and accept. The audience is senior and middle management of health care institutions."

‡**AMERICAN LIBRARY ASSOCIATION**, 50 East Huron Street, Chicago IL 60611. (312)944-6780. Senior Editor-Acquisitions: Herbert Bloom. Publishes hardcover and trade paperback originals. Averages 35 titles/year. Pays royalty. Free book catalog and manuscript guidelines.
Nonfiction: Reference and library science. Query.
Recent Nonfiction Title: *Collection Management: Background & Principles*, by Wortman.

THE AMERICAN PSYCHIATRIC PRESS, INC. (associated with the American Psychiatric Association), 1400 K St. NW, Washington DC 20005. (202)682-6268. Editor-in-Chief: Carol C. Nadelson, M.D. Publishes hardcover and trade paperback originals. Averages 50 titles/year, 2-4 trade books/year; receives about 300 submissions annually. About 10% of books from first-time authors; 95% of books from unagented writers. Pays 10% minimum royalty based on all money actually received, maximum varies; offers average $3,000-5,000 advance. Publishes book an average of 9 months after acceptance. Simultaneous submissions OK (if made clear in cover letter). Query for electronic submissions. Reports in 6 weeks "in regard to an *initial* decision regarding our interest. A *final* decision requires more time." Author questionnaire and proposal guidelines available for SASE.
Nonfiction: Reference, technical, textbook and general nonfiction. Subjects include psychiatry and related subjects. Authors must be well qualified in their subject area. No first-person accounts of mental illness or anything not clearly related to psychiatry. Query with outline/synopsis and sample chapters.
Recent Nonfiction Title: *Cocaine*, by Roger D. Weiss, M.D., and Steven M. Mirin, M.D.
Tips: "Because we are a specialty publishing company, books written by or in collaboration with a psychiatrist have the best chance of acceptance. Make it authoritative and professional."

AMERICAN REFERENCES INC., 919 N. Michigan, Chicago IL 60611. (312)951-6200. President: Les Krantz. Estab. 1977. Publishes hardcover and trade paperback originals. Co-publishes some titles with Pharohs Books, World Almanac and Simon and Schuster, MacMillan and other publishers. Averages 4-10 titles/year. Payment negotiable. Simultaneous submissions OK. Reports in 6 weeks on queries.

Nonfiction: Illustrations and reference. Subjects include art and photography.
Nonfiction Title: *New York Art Review.*

‡**AMERICAN SOCIETY OF CIVIL ENGINEERS**, Book Publishing Program, 345 E. 47th St., New York NY 10017. (212)705-7689. Book Acquisitions Editor, Zoe G. Foundotos. Estab. 1988. Imprint averages 5 titles/year. 20% of books from first time authors; 100% from unagented writers. Pays 10% royalty. Advance amount is negotiable. Simultaneous submissions OK. Query for electronic submissions. Reports in 1 month on queries; 2-3 months on mss. Free book catalog and manuscript guidelines.
Nonfiction: Civil engineering. We are looking for "topics that are useful and instructive to the engineering practitioner." Query with outline/synopsis and sample chapters.
Recent Nonfiction Title: *The Colossus of 1812: An American Engineering Superlative*, by Lee H. Nelson.

AMERICAN STUDIES PRESS, INC., 13511 Palmwood Lane, Tampa FL 33624. (813)961-7200 or 974-2857. Imprints include ASP Books, Rattlesnake Books, Harvest Books and Marilu Books (Marilu imprint includes Herland—poems by women about women—and Woman). Editor-in-Chief: Donald R. Harkness. Estab. 1977. Publishes trade paperback originals. Receives 250-300 submissions/year. 80% of books from first-time authors. 100% of books from unagented writers. Averages 3-4 titles/year. Pays 10 copies plus 10% royalty on sales after printing cost is met. Publishes book an average of 6 months after acceptance. Reports in 2 weeks on queries; 2 months on mss. Book list for #10 SASE.
Nonfiction: Americana, popular (i.e. readable) scholarship, history. "I might consider a book of generalized family history, of interest to an audience wider than the immediate circle of relatives." Query (with SASE) prior to any submission.
Recent Nonfiction Title: *Affairs of My Heart*, by Elizabeth Elliott Baker.
Poetry: Submit 6 poems for a unified book or submit complete ms, after query.
Recent Poetry Title: *Poetica Erotica*, by Normajean MacLeod.
Tips: "Our audience is intelligent and appreciative college graduates, not taken in by the slick and fancy package but more concerned with content. Please don't submit anything without advance query (with SASE, of course). Sharply limiting publication in 1990."

‡**AMHERST MEDIA**, 418 Homecrest Dr., Amherst NY 14226. (716)883-9220. Publisher: Craig Alesse. Publishes hardcover and trade paperback originals and reprints. Averages 5 titles/year. Receives 20 submissions/year. 80% of books from first-time authors; 100% from unagented writers. Pays 5-8% royalty. Publishes book an average of 3-6 months after acceptance. Simultaneous submissions OK. Reports in 3 weeks. Book catalog for #10 SAE and 1 first class stamp. Manuscript guidelines free on request.
Nonfiction: How-to. Subjects include photography, astronomy and video. We are looking for well-written and illustrated photo, video and astronomy books. Query. Reviews artwork/photos as part of ms package.
Recent Nonfiction Title: *Build Your Own Home Darkroom*, by Lista Duren (how-to).
Tips: "Our audience is made up of beginning to advanced photographers. If I were a writer trying to market a book today, I would fill the need of a specific audience and edit in a tight manner."

‡**THE AMWELL PRESS**, P.O. Box 5385, Clinton NJ 08809. (201)537-6888. Editor: Robert D. Magee. Estab. 1974. Publishes hardcover originals. Averages 5-10 titles/year. Receives 10 submissions/year. 40% of books from first-time authors. 100% from unageneted writers. Pays 10% royalty on retail price. Publishes book an average of 1 year after acceptance. Reports in 1 month on queries; 3 months on mss.
Nonfiction: Hunting. Query. Reviews artwork/photos as part of ms package.
Recent Nonfiction Title: *Round The Campfire*, by Tony Henley (big game hunting).
Fiction: Hunting and fishing. Hunting and fishing books and big game hunting, safaris, professional hunter memoirs. Query.

ANCESTRY INCORPORATED, P.O. Box 476, Salt Lake City UT 84110. (801)531-1790. FAX: (801)531-1798. Managing Editor: Robert J. Welsh. Estab. 1983. Publishes hardcover and mass market paperback originals. Averages 10 titles/year; receives 10-20 submissions annually. 70% of books from first-time authors; 100% of books from unagented writers. Pays 8-12% royalty or purchases mss outright. Advances are discouraged but considered if necessary. Publishes book an average of 1 year after acceptance. Simultaneous submissions OK. Query for electronic submissions. Reports in 1 month on queries; 2 months on mss. Free book catalog and ms guidelines.
Nonfiction: How-to, reference and genealogy. Subjects include Americana; history (family and local); and hobbies (genealogy). "Our publications are aimed exclusively at the genealogist. We consider everything from short monographs to book length works on immigration, migration, record collections, etc. Good local histories and heraldic topics are considered." No mss that are not genealogical or historical. Query, or submit outline/synopsis and sample chapters, or complete ms. Reviews artwork/photos.
Recent Nonfiction Title: *The Library of Congress*, by James C. Neagles.
Tips: "Genealogical reference, how-to, and descriptions of source collections have the best chance of selling to our firm. Be precise in your description."

‡AND BOOKS, 702 S. Michigan, South Bend IN 46618. (219)219-3134. Editor: Janos Szebedinszky. Estab. 1980. Publishes trade paperback originals. Averages 10 titles/year. Receives 1,000 submissions/year. 50% of books from first-time authors. 90% of books from unagented writers. Pays 6-10% royalty on retail price. Simultaneous submissions OK. Publishes book an average of 1 year after acceptance. Query for electronic submissions. Reports in 1½ months. Book catalog for #10 SASE.
Nonfiction: Subjects include computers (consumer-level), sports, current affairs, social justice, psychology and religion, music, jazz, blues, classical. Especially needs books on computers and the law and electronic publishing. No biography, humor or diet books.
Recent Nonfiction Title: *Manhole Covers of Ft.Wayne*, by Kathryn Moore.
Tips: "Attempt to get an intro or foreword by a respected authority on your subject. Include comments by others who have reviewed your material. Research the potential market and include the results with your proposal. In other words, make every effort to communicate your knowledge of the publishing process. A little preliminary legwork and market investigation can go a long way to influence a potential publisher."

*ANDERSON PUBLISHING CO., 2035 Reading Rd., Cincinnati OH 45202. (513)421-4142. Editorial Director: Dale Hartig. Estab. 1887. Publishes hardcover, paperback originals, journals and software and reprints. Publishes 13-15 titles/year. Subsidy publishes 10% of books. Pays 15-18% royalty; "advance in selected cases." Publishes book an average of 7 months after acceptance. Simultaneous submissions OK. Reports in 2 months. Book catalog for 8½×11 SASE; guidelines for SASE.
Nonfiction: Law and law-related books, law school, paralegal and criminal justice criminology texts (justice administration legal series). Query or submit outline/chapters with vitae.
Recent Nonfiction Title: *Paralegal Resource Manual*, by Charles Nemeth.

ANDREWS AND McMEEL, 4900 Main St., Kansas City MO 64112. Editorial Director: Donna Martin. Publishes hardcover and paperback originals. Averages 30 titles/year. Pays royalty on retail price. "Query only. No unsolicited manuscripts. Areas of specialization include humor, how-to, and consumer reference books, such as *The Universal Almanac*, edited by John W. Wright."

APA PUBLICATIONS, 120 Wilton Road, London England SW1V 1JZ. Imprints include Insight Guides, Apa City Guides and Apa Short Story Guides. Editorial Director: Brian Bell. Estab. 1970. Publishes hardcover and trade paperback originals. Publishes 50 titles/year. Receives 100 submissions/year. "We assign books and parts of books, often to first-time books authors. We have a strong journalistic orientation, and apply magazine criteria to both text and photography. We pay authors outright—$7,500 for editing a book, plus expenses; 25¢/word for writing." Publishes books an average of 10 months after assignment. Query for electronic submissions. Reports on queries in 1 month. No unsolicited mss. Book catalog and ms guidelines free on request (also see *Insight Guides*, distributed by Prentice-Hall for guidance).
Nonfiction: Travel guides. "We need writers, photographers and project editors for an enormous variety of city and country books." Query along with resume, clips and statement of area of expertise. Reviews artwork/photos as part of ms package.
Recent Nonfiction Title: *Insight Guide to Bermuda*, by Zenfell, ct. al. (trade paper guidebook).
Tips: "We're embarking on an ambitious publishing program in the next two years to add to our list of travel titles."

APPALACHIAN MOUNTAIN CLUB BOOKS, 5 Joy St., Boston MA 02108. (617)523-0636. FAX: (617)523-0722. Publisher: Susan Cummings. Estab. 1897. Publishes hardcover and trade paperback originals. Averages 8 titles/year; receives 100 submissions annually. 50% of books from first-time authors; 99% of books from unagented writers. Pays 10% royalty on retail price; offers $1,000 advance. Publishes book an average of 6 months after receipt of acceptable manuscript. Simultaneous submissions OK. Query for electronic submissions. Reports in 1 month on queries; 4 months on mss. Book brochure for #10 SAE.
Nonfiction: How-to, reference, field guides and guidebooks. Subjects include history (Northeast, mountains), nature, outdoor recreation, and travel. "We want manuscripts about the environment, mountains and their history and culture, and outdoor recreation (such as hiking, climbing, skiing, canoeing, kayaking, bicycling)." No physical fitness manuals. Query or submit outline/synopsis and sample chapters.
Recent Nonfiction Title: *High Mountain Challenge: A Guide for Young Mountaineers*, by Linda Buchanan Allen.
Tips: "We are expanding into travel outside the U.S. that offers opportunities for outdoor recreation. We have also begun to publish children's books on outdoor recreation and nature."

APPLEZABA PRESS, P.O. Box 4134, Long Beach CA 90804. (213)591-0015. Publisher: D.H. Lloyd. Estab. 1977. Publishes hardcover and trade paperback originals. Firm averages 4 titles/year. Receives 1,000 submissions/year. 5% of books from first-time authors; 95% from unagented writers. Pays 8-15% royalty on retail price. Publishes book average of 3 years after acceptance. Simultaneous submissions OK. Reports in 2 weeks on queries; 3 months on mss. Free book catalog; mss guidelines for #10 SASE.

Nonfiction: Cookbook. Subjects include cooking, foods and nutrition. Query or submit complete ms. Reviews artwork/photos as part of ms package.

Recent Nonfiction Title: *College Quickies Survival Cookbook*, by Sandy Sieg.

Fiction: Literary and short story collections. Query or submit outline/synopsis and sample chapters.

Recent Fiction Title: *The Gold Rush and Other Stories*, by Gerald Locklin.

Recent Poetry Title: *Gridlock Poems about Southern California*, by Elliot Fried, ed.

THE AQUARIAN PRESS, Denington Estate, Wellingborough, Northamptonshire NN8 2RQ England. FAX: 0933-440512. Publishing Director: Eileen Campbell. Hardcover and paperback originals. Averages 70-80 titles/year. Pays 7½-10% royalty. Reports in 2 months. Free book catalog.

Nonfiction: Publishes books on all forms of divination, magic, the paranormal, personal development and general New Age topics. "Crucible is a sub-imprint of The Aquarian Press and publishes in the field of transformation—religion and spirituality, psychology and psychotherapy and philosophy and esoteric thought." Length: 50,000-100,000 words.

Tips: "We look for a clear indication that the author has thought about his market; a fundamental ability to *communicate* ideas—authority in combination with readability."

‡ARCHITECTURAL BOOK PUBLISHING CO., INC., 268 Dogwood Lane, Stamford CT 06903. (203)322-1460. Editor: Walter Frese. Estab. 1891. Averages 10 titles/year; receives 400 submissions annually. 80% of books from first-time authors; 95% of books from unagented writers. Average print order for a writer's first book is 5,000. Royalty is percentage of retail price. Publishes book an average of 10 months after acceptance. Prefers queries, outlines and 2 sample chapters with number of illustrations. Reports in 2 weeks.

Nonfiction: Publishes architecture, decoration, and reference books on city planning and industrial arts. Accepts nonfiction translations. Also interested in history, biography, and science of architecture and decoration. Reviews artwork/photos.

‡ARCHWAY/MINSTREL BOOKS, Subsidiary of Pocket Books, 1230 Avenue of the Americas, New York NY 10020. (212)698-7000. Senior Editor: Patricia MacDonald. Publishes mass market paperback originals and reprints. Averages 48 titles/year. Receives 500 submissions/year. Pays royalty. Publishes book an average of 2 years after acceptance. Reports in 1 month on queries; 2-3 months on mss.

Nonfiction: Juvenile. Subjects include animals, sports. Query. Submit outline/synopsis and sample chapters. Reviews artwork/photos as part of ms package.

Fiction: Juvenile, young adult. No heavy problem novels—quiet, boring stories. Query. Submit outline/synopsis and sample chapters.

Recent Fiction Title: *The Heart Belongs to That Boy*, by Linda Lewis (YA novel).

ARCsoft PUBLISHERS, Box 132, Woodsboro MD 21798. (301)845-8856. Publisher: Anthony R. Curtis. Publishes trade paperback originals. Averages 20 titles/year. "We now offer only 'buyout' contracts in which all rights are purchased. Typically, an advance of 20 percent is paid at contract signing and 80 percent at acceptable completion of work. Royalties are no longer offered since writers suffer under royalty contracts for small-volume technical books." Offers variable advance. Publishes book an average of 6 months after acceptance. Reports in 1 month on queries; 10 weeks on mss. Free book catalog.

Nonfiction: Technical. "We publish technical books including space science, desktop publishing, personal computers and hobby electronics, especially for beginners." Accepts nonfiction translations. Query or submit outline/synopsis and 1 sample chapter. Reviews artwork/photos as part of ms package.

Recent Nonfiction Title: *Space Almanac*, by A.R. Curtis.

Tips: "We look for the writer's ability to cover our desired subject thoroughly, writing quality and interest."

*M. ARMAN PUBLISHING, INC., 740 S. Ridgewood Ave., Ormond Beach FL 32174. (904)673-5576. FAX: (904)673-6560. Mailing address: P.O. Box 785, Ormond Beach FL 32175. Contact: Mike Arman. Estab. 1978. Publishes trade paperback originals, reprints and software. Averages 6-8 titles/year; receives 20 submissions annually. 20% of books from first-time authors; 100% of books from unagented writers. Average print order for a writer's first book is 2,500. Subsidy publishes 20% of books. Pays 10% royalty on wholesale price. No advance. Publishes book (on royalty basis) an average of 8 months after acceptance; 6 weeks on subsidy basis. Query for electronic submissions. Reports in 1 week on queries; 3 weeks on mss. Book catalog for #10 SASE.

Nonfiction: How-to, reference, technical, and textbook. "Motorcycle technical books only." Accepts nonfiction translations. Publishes for enthusiasts. Submit complete ms. Reviews artwork/photos as part of ms package.

Recent Nonfiction Title: *V-Twin Thunder*, by Carl McClanahan (motorcycle performance manual).
Tips: "The type of book a writer has the best chance of selling to our firm is how-to fix motorcycles—specifically Harley-Davidsons. We have a strong, established market for these books."

‡ART DIRECTION BOOK COMPANY, 10 E. 39th St., 6th Floor, New York NY 10016. (212)889-6500. Imprint is Infosource Publications. Editorial Director: Dan Barron. Senior Editor: Loren Bliss. Publishes hardcover and paperback originals. Publishes 10 titles/year. Pays 10% royalty on retail price; offers average $1,000 advance. Publishes book an average of 1 year after acceptance. Reports in 3 months. Book catalog for 6x9 SAE.
Nonfiction: Commercial art, ad art how-to and textbooks. "We are interested in books for the professional advertising art field—that is, books for art directors, designers, etc.; also entry level books for commercial and advertising art students in such fields as typography, photography, paste-up, illustration, clip-art, design, layout and graphic arts." Query with outline/synopsis and 1 sample chapter. Reviews artwork/photos as part of ms package.
Recent Nonfiction Title: *American Corporate Identity #4*, by D.E. Carter.

ASIAN HUMANITIES PRESS, P.O. Box 3523, Fremont CA 94539. (408)727-3151. Editor: Lew Lancaster. Publishes hardcover originals, trade paperback originals and reprints. Firm averages 8 titles/year. Receives 80 submissions/year. 100% of books from unagented authors. Pays up to 7.5% royalty on retail price. Publishes book an average of 9 months after acceptance. Query for electronic submissions. Reports on queries in 1 month; 3 months on mss. Free book catalog.
Nonfiction: Reference, textbook. Subjects include language/literature (Asian), philosophy (Asian and comparative), religion (Asian and comparative), translation (Asian religions, literature cultures and philosophy), (Asian), humanities, spiritual. "We publish books pertaining to Asian religions, literature cultures and thought directed toward scholars, students, libraries and specialty bookstores." Submit complete ms. Reviews artwork/photos as part of ms package.
Recent Nonfiction Title: *Zibo: The Last Great Zen Master of China*, by J.C. Cleary.
Tips: "Scholars and general readers interested in Asian and comparative literature religions, cultures and philosophy are our audience."

ATHENEUM CHILDREN'S BOOKS, Macmillan, Inc., 866 3rd Ave., New York NY 10022. (212)702-7894. Editorial Director: Jonathan J. Lanman or editors Marcia Marshall and Gail Paris. Publishes hardcover originals. Averages 60 titles/year; receives 7,000-8,000 submissions annually. 8-12% of books from first-time authors; 50% of books from unagented writers. Pays 10% royalty on retail price; offers average $2,000-3,000 advance. Publishes book an average of 18 months after acceptance. Reports in 2 weeks on queries; 3 months on outline and sample chapters. Book catalog and ms guidelines for 7 x 10 SAE and 2 first class stamps.
Nonfiction: Biography, how-to, humor, illustrated book, juvenile (pre-school through young adult) and self-help, all for juveniles. Subjects include: Americana, animals, art, business and economics, cooking and foods, health, history, hobbies, music, nature, philosophy, photography, politics, psychology, recreation, religion, sociology, sports, and travel, all for young readers. "Do remember, most publishers plan their lists as much as two years in advance. So if a topic is 'hot' right now, it may be 'old hat' by the time we could bring it out. It's better to steer clear of fads. Some writers assume juvenile books are for 'practice' until you get good enough to write adult books. Not so. Books for young readers demand just as much 'professionalism' in writing as adult books. So save those 'practice' manuscripts for class, or polish them before sending them." Query, submit outline/synopsis and sample chapters. Reviews artwork/photos as part of ms package; prefers photocopies of artwork.
Recent Nonfiction Title: *Dead Serious*, by Jane Mersky Leder (teenage suicide).
Fiction: Adventure, ethnic, experimental, fantasy, gothic, historical, horror, humor, mainstream, mystery, romance, science fiction, suspense, and western, all in juvenile versions. "We have few specific needs except for books that are fresh, interesting and well written. Again, fad topics are dangerous, as are works you haven't polished to the best of your ability. (The competition is fierce.) We've been inundated with dragon stories (misunderstood dragon befriends understanding child), unicorn stories (misunderstood child be-

 An asterisk preceding a listing indicates that subsidy publishing or co-publishing (where author pays part or all of publishing costs) is available. Firms whose subsidy programs comprise more than 50% of their total publishing activities are listed at the end of the Book Packagers and Producers section.

friends understanding unicorn), and variations of 'Ignatz the Egg' (Everyone laughs at Ignatz the egg [giraffe/airplane/accountant] because he's square [short/purple/stupid] until he saves them from the eggbeater [lion/storm/I.R.S. man] and becomes a hero). Other things we don't need at this time are safety pamphlets, ABC books, and rhymed narratives. In writing picture book texts, avoid the coy and 'cutesy.' " Query, submit outline/synopsis and sample chapters for novels; complete ms for picture books.

Recent Fiction Title: *The Return,* by Sonia Levitin (young adult novel).

Poetry: "At this time there is a growing market for children's poetry. However, we don't anticipate needing any for the next year or two, especially rhymed narratives."

Tips: "Our books are aimed at children from pre-school age, up through high school. Our young adult novels and much of our science fiction and fantasy also cross over into adult markets."

ATLANTIC MONTHLY PRESS, 19 Union Sq. W., New York NY 10003. (212)645-4462. FAX: (212)727-0180. Publisher: Carl Navarre. Editor-in-Chief: Ann Godoff. Averages 60 titles/year. "Advance and royalties depend on the nature of the book, the stature of the author, and the subject matter." Publishes book an average of 1 year after acceptance.

Nonfiction: Publishes general nonfiction, biography, autobiography, science, philosophy, the arts, belles lettres, history and world affairs. Length: 70,000-200,000 words. Query.

Recent Nonfiction Title: *Parting with Illusions,* by Vladimir Pozner.

Fiction: Publishes general fiction and poetry. Prefers complete fiction and poetry mss.

Recent Fiction Title: *Wild Life,* by Richard Ford.

‡**AUTO BOOK PRESS,** P.O. Bin 711, San Marcos CA 92069. (619)744-3582. Imprints include Coda Publications and Funny Farm Books. Managing Director: William Carroll. Publishes hardcover and trade paperback originals. Averages 5 titles/year. Receives 50 submissions/year. Royalties on wholesale price negotiable. Publishes book an average of 9 months after acceptance. Simultaneous submissions OK. Query for electronic submissions. Reports in 1 month on queries; 2 months on mss.

Nonfiction: Coffee table book, how-to, humor, reference and technical. Subjects include americana, business and economics, history, philosophy and automotive. No completed mss. Query with outline/synopsis and sample chapters. Reviews artwork/photos as part of ms package.

Recent Nonfiction Title: *San Marcos,* by William Carroll (history).

AVALON BOOKS, Imprint of Thomas Bouregy & Co., Inc., 401 Lafayette St., New York NY 10003. Vice President and Publisher: Barbara J. Brett. Estab. 1950. Publishes 60 titles/year. Pays $500 for first book and $600 thereafter, which is applied against sales of the first 3,500 copies of the book (initial run is 2,100 copies). Reports in 3 months. Writer's guidelines for #10 SASE.

Fiction: "We publish wholesome romances, westerns and adventure novels that are sold to libraries throughout the country. Our books are read by adults as well as teenagers, and their characters are all adults. All the romances and adventures are contemporary; all the westerns are historical." Length: 35,000 to 50,000 words. Submit first chapter and a brief, but complete summary of the book, or, if you are sure the book fits our requirements, submit the complete manuscript. Enclose manuscript size SASE.

Recent Fiction Title: *Appointment with Love,* by Sheila Fyfe.

Tips: "We do not want old-fashioned, predictable, formula-type books. We are looking for contemporary characters and fresh, contemporary plots and storylines. Every heroine should have an interesting career or profession."

‡**AVERY PUBLISHING GROUP,** 120 Old Broadway, Garden City Park NY 11040. (516)741-2155. Contact: Managing Editor. Publishes hardcover and trade paperback originals. Averages 40 titles/year. Receives 200-300 submissions/year. 90% of books from first-time authors; 95% from unagented writers. Pays 10% royalty on wholesale price. Publishes book an average of 9 months after acceptance. Simultaneous submissions OK. Reports in 1 week. Book catalog free on request.

Nonfiction: Cookbook, how-to, reference and textbook. Subjects include business and economics, child guidance/parenting, cooking, foods & nutrition, health/medicine, history, military/war, nature/environment, child birth and alternative health. Query.

Recent Nonfiction Title: *Empty Harvest,* by Dr. Bernard Jensen and Mark Anderson (ecology/health).

AVIATION BOOK CO., 1640 Victory Blvd., Glendale CA 91201-2999. (818)240-1771. FAX: (818)240-1196. Editor: Walter P. Winner. Estab. 1964. Publishes hardcover and paperback originals and reprints. Averages 5 titles/year; receives 25 submissions annually. 90% of books from first-time authors; 90% of books from unagented writers. Pays royalty on retail price. No advance. Query with outline. Publishes book an average of 9 months after acceptance. Reports in 2 months. Book catalog for 9 × 12 SAE with $1 postage.

Nonfiction: Aviation books, primarily of a technical nature and pertaining to pilot training. Young adult level and up. Also aeronautical history. Asks of ms, "Does it fill a void in available books on subject?" or "Is it better than available material?" Reviews artwork/photos as part of ms package.

Recent Nonfiction Title: *Airman's Information Manual,* by Walter Winner.

AVON BOOKS, 105 Madison, New York NY 10016. FAX: (212)532-2172. Publisher: Carolyn Reidy. Associate Publisher, Trade paperbacks: Mark Gomperk. Executive Editor: Robert Mecoy. Estab. 1942. Publishes paperback originals and paperback reprints. Averages 300 titles/year. Pay and advance are negotiable. Publishes ms an average of 2 years after acceptance. Simultaneous submissions OK. Reports in 2 months. Book catalog for SASE.
Nonfiction: How-to, popular psychology, self-help, health, history, war, sports, business/economics, biography and politics. No textbooks.
Recent Nonfiction Title: *Summer of '49*, by David Halberstam.
Fiction: Romance (contemporary), historical romance, science fiction, fantasy, men's adventure, suspense/ thriller, mystery, and western. Submit query letter only.
Recent Fiction Title: *So Worthy My Love*, by Kathleen Woodwiss.

AVON FLARE BOOKS, Young Adult Imprint of Avon Books, a division of the Hearst Corp., 105 Madison Ave., New York NY 10016. (212)481-5609. FAX (212)532-2693. Editorial Director: Ellen Krieger. Publishes mass market paperback originals and reprints. Imprint publishes 18-20 new titles annually. 25% of books from first-time authors; 15% of books from unagented writers. Pays 6-8% royalty; offers minimum $2,500 advance. Publishes book an average of 15 months after acceptance. Simultaneous submissions OK. Reports in 10 weeks. Book catalog and manuscript guidelines for 8×10 SAE and 5 first class stamps.
Nonfiction: General. Submit outline/synopsis and sample chapters. "*Very* selective with young adult nonfiction."
Fiction: Adventure, ethnic, humor, mainstream, mystery, romance, suspense and contemporary. "Very selective with mystery." Mss appropriate to ages 12-18. Query with sample chapters and synopsis.
Recent Fiction Title: *Deathtrap and Dinosaur*, by Jane McFann.
Tips: "The YA market is not as strong as it was 5 years ago. We are very selective with young adult fiction."

BACKCOUNTRY PUBLICATIONS, Imprint of The Countryman Press, Inc., Box 175, Woodstock VT 05091. (802)457-1049. Estab. 1981. Publishes trade paperback originals. Averages 12 titles/year. 50% of books from first-time authors; 95% from unagented writers. Pays 5-10% royalty on retail price. Offers $500 average advance. Publishes book average of 9 months after acceptance. Simultaneous submissions OK. Reports on queries in 2 weeks; on mss in 6 weeks. Free book catalog.
Nonfiction: Reference. Subjects include recreation. "We're looking for regional guides to hiking, bicycling, cross-country skiing, canoeing, and fishing for all parts of the country." Submit outline/synopsis and sample chapters. Reviews artwork/photos as part of ms package.
Recent Nonfiction Title: *Pennsylvania Trout Streams and Their Hatches*, by Charles Meck.

BAEN PUBLISHING ENTERPRISES, Distributed by Simon & Schuster, 260 Fifth Ave., New York NY 10001. (212)532-4111. Publisher and Editor-in-Chief: Jim Baen. Estab. 1984. Publishes mass market paperback originals and mass market paperback reprints. Averages 80-100 titles/year; receives 1,000 submissions annually. 10% of books from first-time authors; 25% of books from unagented writers. Pays 6-8% royalty on cover price. Reports in 2 weeks on queries; 1-2 months on mss. Ms guidelines for #10 SASE.
Fiction: Fantasy and science fiction. Submit outline/synopsis and sample chapters or (preferred) synopsis and complete ms.
Recent Fiction Title: *Sassinak*, by Anne McCaffrey and Elizabeth Moon.
Tips: "Our audience includes those who are interested in *hard* science fiction and quality fantasy pieces that engage the mind as well as entertain."

*BAKER BOOK HOUSE COMPANY, Box 6287, Grand Rapids MI 49516-6287. (616)676-9185. FAX: (616)676-9573. Editor, trade books: Dan Van't Kerkhoff. Editor, academic books: Allan Fisher. Publishes hardcover and trade paperback originals and reprints. Averages 120 titles/year. 25% of books from first-time authors; 85% of books from unagented writers. Subsidy publishes 1% of books. Pays 14% royalty on net receipts. Publishes book within 1 year after acceptance. Simultaneous submissions OK. Reports in 3 weeks on queries; 6 weeks on ms. Book catalog for 9×12 SAE and $1.20 postage. Manuscript guidelines for #10 SASE.
Nonfiction: Biography, juvenile, humor, reference, self-help (gift books, Bible study), Bible commentaries and textbook. Subjects include child guidance/parenting, language/literature, philosophy, psychology, religion, sociology, women's issues/studies. "We're looking for books from a religious perspective—devotional, Bible study, self-help, textbooks for Christian colleges and seminaries, counseling and humorous books." Query or submit outline/synopsis and sample chapters.
Recent Nonfiction Title: *The Courage to Go On: Life After Addiction*, by Cynthia Rowland McClure.
Tips: "Our books are sold through Christian bookstores to customers with religious background."

BALE BOOKS, Division of Bale Publications, P.O. Box 2727, New Orleans LA 70176. Editor-in-Chief: Don Bale Jr. Estab. 1963. Publishes hardcover and paperback originals and reprints. Averages 10 titles/year; receives 25 submissions annually. 50% of books from first-time authors; 90% of books from unagented writers. Average print order for a writer's first book is 1,000. Offers standard 10-12½-15% royalty contract on wholesale or retail price; sometimes purchases mss outright for $500. Offers no advance. Publishes book an average of 3 years after acceptance. Will consider photocopied submissions. "Send manuscript by registered or certified mail. Be sure copy of manuscript is retained." Book catalog for SAE and 2 first class stamps.

Nonfiction: Numismatics. "Our specialty is coin and stock market investment books; especially coin investment books and coin price guides. Most of our books are sold through publicity and ads in the coin newspapers. We are open to any new ideas in the area of numismatics. The writer should write for a teenage through adult level. Lead the reader by the hand like a teacher, building chapter by chapter. Our books sometimes have a light, humorous treatment, but not necessarily." Looks for "good English, construction and content, and sales potential." Submit outline and 3 sample chapters.

Recent Nonfiction Title: *Out of Little Coins Big Fortunes Grow*, by Bale.

BANKS-BALDWIN LAW PUBLISHING CO., 1904 Ansel Rd., Cleveland OH 44106. (216)721-7373. FAX: (216)721-8055. Editor-in-Chief: P.J. Lucier. Publishes law books and services in a variety of formats. Averages approximately 7 new titles/year; receives 7-12 submissions annually. 5% of books from first-time authors; 90% of books from unagented writers. "Most titles include material submitted by outside authors." Pays 8-16% on net revenue, or fee. Offers advance not to exceed 25% of anticipated royalty or fee. Publishes book an average of 18 months after acceptance, 3 months after receipt of ms. Query for electronic submissions. Reports in 3 weeks on queries; 6 weeks on submissions. Free book catalog; ms guidelines for SASE.

Nonfiction: Reference, law/legal. Query.

Recent Nonfiction Title: *Ohio Driving Under the Influence Law*, by Mark P. Painter and James M. Looker (handbook).

Tips: "We publish books for attorneys, government officials and professionals in allied fields. Trends in our field include more interest in handbooks, less in costly multi-volume sets; electronic publishing. Writer has the best chance of selling us a book on a hot new topic of law. Check citations and quotations carefully."

BANTAM BOOKS, Subsidiary of Bantam Doubleday Dell, 666 Fifth Ave., New York NY 10103. (212)765-6500. Imprints include Spectra, Windstone, New Age, Bantam Classics, Bantam New Fiction, Loveswept, New Sciences, Bantam Electronic Publishing, Bantam Travel Books, Peacock Press, Perigord Press, Skylark Books for Young Readers, Sweet Dreams. Publishes hardcover, trade paperback and mass market paperback originals, trade paperback, mass market paperback reprints and audio. Publishes 650 titles/year. Buys no books from unagented writers. Pays 4-15% royalty. Publishes book an average of 1 year after ms is accepted. Simultaneous submissions OK. Reports in 3 weeks on queries; 1 month on ms.

Nonfiction: Biography, coffee table book, how-to, cookbook, humor, illustrated book, juvenile and self-help. Subjects include Americana, anthropology/archaelogy, business/economics, child guidance/parenting, computers and electronics, cooking, foods and nutrition, gay/lesbian, government/politics, health/medicine, history, language/literature, military/war, money/finance, music/dance, philosophy, psychology, religion, science, sociology, sports and travel. Query or submit outline/synopsis or complete ms through agent only. All unsolicited mss are returned unopened.

Recent Nonfiction Title: *A Brief History of Time*, by Stephen Hawking.

Fiction: Adventure, fantasy, feminist, gay/lesbian, historical, horror, juvenile, literary, mainstream/contemporary, mystery, romance, science fiction, suspense, western, young adult. Query or submit outline/synopsis or complete ms through agent only. All unsolicited mss are returned unopened.

Recent Fiction Title: *The Negotiator*, by Frederick Forsythe.

BARRON'S EDUCATIONAL SERIES, INC., 250 Wireless Blvd., Hauppauge NY 11788. FAX: (516)434-3723. Publishes hardcover and paperback originals and software. Publishes 170 titles/year. 10% of books from first-time authors; 90% of books from unagented writers. Pays royalty, based on both wholesale and retail price. Publishes book an average of 9 months after acceptance. Simultaneous submissions OK. Reports in 3 months. Free catalog.

Nonfiction: Adult education, art, business, cookbooks, crafts, foreign language, review books, guidance, pet books, travel, literary guides, juvenile, young adult sports, test preparation materials and textbooks. Reviews artwork/photos as part of package. Query or submit outline/synopsis and 2-3 sample chapters. Accepts nonfiction translations.

Recent Nonfiction Title: *Working Family Cookbook*, by Irena Chalmers.

Tips: "The writer has the best chance of selling us a book that will fit into one of our series."

BEACON HILL PRESS OF KANSAS CITY, P.O. Box 419527, Kansas City MO 64141. Book division of Nazarene Publishing House. Coordinator: Betty Fuhrman. Estab. 1912. Publishes hardcover and paperback originals. Averages 65-70 titles/year. Offers "standard contract (sometimes flat rate purchase). Advance on royalty is paid on first 1,000 copies at publication date. On standard contract, pays 10% on first 10,000 copies and 12% on subsequent copies at the end of each calendar year." Publishes book an average of 2 years after acceptance. Reports in 4-8 months unless immediately returned. "Book Committee meets quarterly to select from the manuscripts which will be published."

Nonfiction: Inspirational, Bible-based. Doctrinally must conform to the evangelical, Wesleyan tradition. Conservative view of Bible. No autobiography, poetry, devotional collections, or children's picture books. Accent on holy living; encouragement in daily Christian life. Contemporary issues. Popular style books usually under 128 pages. Query. Textbooks "almost exclusively done on assignment." Full ms or outline/sample chapters. Length: 20,000-40,000 words.

Recent Nonfiction Title: *Am I My Brother's Keeper? The AIDS Crisis and the Church*, by Michael Malloy.

‡BEACON PRESS, 25 Beacon St., Boston MA 02108. (617)742-2110. Director: Wendy J. Strothman. Estab. 1902. Publishes hardcover originals and paperback reprints. Averages 60 titles/year; receives 4,000 submissions annually. 10% of books from first-time authors; 70% of books from unagented writers. Average print order for a writer's first book is 3,000. Offers royalty on net retail price; advance varies. Publishes book an average of 1 year after acceptance. Simultaneous submissions OK. Return of materials not guaranteed without SASE. Reports in 2 months. Query or submit outline/synopsis and sample chapters to Editorial Department.

Nonfiction: General nonfiction including works of original scholarship, religion, women's studies, philosophy, current affairs, literature communications, sociology, psychology, history, political science, art, anthropology, children's books, environmental concerns.

Recent Nonfiction Title: *The Global Ecology Handbook*, World Resources Institute.

Tips: "We probably accept only one or two manuscripts from an unpublished pool of 4,000 submissions per year. No fiction or poetry submissions invited. Authors should have academic affiliation."

BEAR AND CO., INC., Drawer 2860, Santa Fe NM 87504-2860. (505)983-9868. Vice President Editorial: Barbara Clow. Publishes trade paperback originals. Averages 12 titles/year. Receives 6,000 submissions/year. 20% of books from first-time authors; 80% of books from unagented writers. Pays 8-10% royalty. Publishes book an average of 18 months after acceptance. Query for electronic submissions. Reports in 1 month on queries; 3 months on mss. "No response without SASE." Free book catalog.

Nonfiction: Illustrated books, science, theology, mysticism, religion and ecology. "We publish books to 'heal and celebrate the earth.' Our interest is in New Age, western mystics, new science, ecology. We are not interested in how-to, self-help, etc. Our readers are people who are open to new ways of looking at the world. They are spiritually oriented but not necessarily religious; interested in healing of the earth, peace issues, and receptive to New Age ideas." Query or submit outline/synopsis and sample chapters. Reviews artwork/photos as part of ms package.

Recent Nonfiction Title: *Medicine Cards*, by David Carson and Jamie Sams.

BEAR FLAG BOOKS, Subsidiary of Padre Productions, P.O. Box 840, Arroyo Grande CA 93421-0840. (805)473-1947. Estab. 1974. Publisher: Lachlan P. MacDonald. Publishes hardcover and trade paperback originals and reprints. Publishes 6-8 titles/year. Receives 500 submissions/year. 80% of books from first-time authors; 90% from unagented writers. Pays 6-10% royalty on retail price; offers varying advance. Publishes book an average of 2 years after acceptance. Simultaneous submissions OK. Reports in 2 weeks on queries; 2 months on ms. Book catalog for 8½ × 11 SAE and 2 first class stamps. Manuscript guidelines for #10 SASE.

Nonfiction: Biography, illustrated book and reference. Subjects include Americana, animals, anthropology/archaeology, history (California and West), nature/environment, photography, recreation, regional and travel. "Best bet is photo-illustrated to a specific county or park or region of California. No children's picture books. We prefer adult-level material." Submit outline/synopsis and sample chapters or complete ms.

Recent Nonfiction Title: *Sierra Mountaineering*, by Leonard Daughenbaugh (history).

Fiction: "We would only consider historical fiction with a strong basis in California history and biography."

Tips: "Travelers of all ages, teachers, local residents and libraries are our audience. If I were a writer trying to market a book today, I would complete a guidebook or biography or history, then offer as many unique illustrations as possible, especially unpublished material. Try to fill a market niche."

BEAU LAC PUBLISHERS, P.O. Box 248, Chuluota FL 32766. Estab. 1968. Publishes hardcover and paperback originals.

Nonfiction: "Military subjects. Specialist in social side of service life." Query.

Recent Nonfiction Title: *The Noncommissioned Officers' Family Guide*, by Mary Preston Gross.

‡*BEAVER POND PUBLISHING & PRINTING, P.O. Box 224, Greenville PA 16125. (412)588-3492. Owner: Richard E. Faler, Jr.. Publishes trade paperback originals and reprints, 95% mass market paperback originals, 5% reprints. Averages 5 titles/year. Receives 20 submissions/year. 20% of books from first-time authors. 20% from unagented writers. Subsidy publishes 10% of books. Determines subsidy "if we don't wish to take on the book as publisher, but the author still wants us to print it." Pays 5-15% royalty on net sales. Buys mss outright for $100-1,000 on booklets. Publishes book an average of 6 months after acceptance. Simultaneous submissions OK. Reports in 1 month. Manuscript guidelines for #10 SAE and 1 first-class stamp.

Nonfiction: How-to. Subjects include animals, natural history of wildlife, hobbies particularly on exotic pets (snakes instead of dogs), nature/environment, photography especially of wildlife, recreation, hunting, fishing. "We want to see manuscripts suitable for 24 page booklets through 200 page books that are written with authority on very specific topics and that are how-to. Example: "Photographing Birds in Flight." Query. Submit outline/synopsis and sample chapters and complete ms. Reviews artwork/photos as part of ms package.

Recent Nonfiction Title: *Seining and Trapping Minnows*, by Rich Faler (booklet).

Tips: "We're looking for very specific topics in both consumptive and non-consumptive animal use that are too specific for larger publishers. There are experts out there with valuable information. We want to make that information available. Our primary audiences are hunters, fishermen and photographers. If I were a writer trying to market a book today, I would look for a niche, fill that niche, and attempt to fill it with a work that would be difficult, if not impossible, for someone to duplicate or do better."

BEHRMAN HOUSE INC., 235 Watchung Ave., W. Orange NJ 07052. (202)669-0447. FAX: (201)669-9769. Subsidiary includes Rossel Books. Managing Editor: Adam Bengal. Estab. 1921. Publishes trade-paperback originals and reprints. Averages 20 titles/year. Receives 200 submissions/year. 20% of books from first-time authors; 95% from unagented writers. Pays 2-10% on wholesale price or retail price. Buys mss outright for $500-10,000. Offers $1,000 average advance. Publishes book an average of 18 months after acceptance. Simultaneous submissions OK. Reports in 2 weeks on queries; 1 month on mss. Free book catalog and manuscript guidelines.

Nonfiction: Juvenile (1-18), reference and textbook. Subjects include religion. "We want Jewish textbooks for the El-Hi market." Query. Submit outline/synopsis and sample chapters.

THE BENJAMIN COMPANY, INC., One Westchester Plaza, Elmsford NY 10523. (914)592-8088. FAX: (914)997-7214. President: Ted Benjamin. Estab. 1953. Publishes hardcover and paperback originals. Averages 10-15 titles/year. 90-100% of books from unagented writers. "Usually commissions author to write specific book; seldom accepts proffered manuscripts." Publishes book an average of 6 months after acceptance. Buys mss by outright purchase. Offers advance. Simultaneous submissions OK. Query for electronic submissions. Reports in 2 months.

Nonfiction: Business/economics, cookbooks, cooking and foods, health, hobbies, how-to, self-help, sports and consumerism. "Ours is a very specialized kind of publishing—for clients (industrial and association) to use in promotional, PR, or educational programs. If an author has an idea for a book and close connections with a company that might be interested in using that book, we will be very interested in working together with the author to 'sell' the program and the idea of a special book for that company. Once published, our books do get trade distribution through a distributing publisher, so the author generally sees the book in regular book outlets as well as in the special programs undertaken by the sponsoring company. We do not encourage submission of manuscripts. We usually commission an author to write for us. The most helpful thing an author can do is to let us know what he or she has written, or what subjects he or she feels competent to write about. We will contact the author when our needs indicate that the author might be the right person to produce a needed manuscript." Query. Submit outline/synopsis and 1 sample chapter. Looks for "possibility of tie-in with sponsoring company or association."

Recent Nonfiction Title: *The BBB A to Z Buying Guide*.

‡BENNETT & MCKNIGHT PUBLISHING CO., Division of Glencoe Publishing Co., 809 W. Detweiller Dr., Peoria IL 61615. (309)691-4454. Vice President/Publisher: David W. Whiting. Publishes hardcover and paperback originals. Specializes in textbooks and related materials. Averages 50 titles/year. Receives 25 submissions annually. 10% of books from first-time authors; 100% of books from unagented writers. Pays up to 10% royalty for textbooks "based on cash received, less for supplements." Publishes book an average of 2 years after acceptance. Reports in 1 month. Free book catalog and ms guidelines.

Nonfiction: Publishes textbooks and related items for home economics, industrial and technology, education, career education, and art education, allied health occupations and vocational training in schools, junior high through post-secondary. Wants "content with good coverage of subject matter in a course in one of our fields; intelligent organization; and clear expression." Query "with 1-2 sample chapters that represent much of the book; not a general introduction if the ms is mostly specific 'how-to' instructions."

Recent Nonfiction Title: *Technology Today and Tomorrow*, by James Fales, Vincent Kuetemeyer and Sharon Brusic.

ROBERT BENTLEY, INC., Automotive Publishers, 1000 Massachusetts Ave., Cambridge MA 02138. (617)547-4170. Publisher: Michael Bentley. Estab. 1949. Publishes hardcover and trade paperback originals and reprints. Publishes 15-20 titles/year. 20% of books are from first-time authors; 90% from unagented writers. Pays 5-15% royalty on wholesale price; or makes outright purchase. Advances negotiable. Publishes book an average of 5 months after acceptance. Query for electronic submissions. Reports in 1 month. Book catalog and ms guidelines for SAE and 45¢ postage.

Nonfiction: How-to, technical, theory of operation, coffee/table. Automotive sugjects only; this inlcudes motor sports. Query or submit outline/synopsis and sample chapters or complete ms. Reviews artwork/photos as part of manuscript package.
Recent Nonfiction Title: *Bosch Fuel Injection and Engine Management Including High Performance Tuning*, by Charles Probst, SAE (automotive).
Tips: "We are excited about the possibilities and growth in the automobile enthusiast book market. Our audience is composed of serious and intelligent automobile, sports car, or racing enthusiasts, automotive technicians and high performance tuners."

‡**THE BERKLEY PUBLISHING GROUP**, (publishers of Berkley/Berkley Trade Paperbacks/Jove/Charter/Diamond/Pacer/ Ace Science Fiction), 200 Madison Ave., New York NY 10016. (212)951-8800. Editor-in-Chief: Leslie Gelbman. Publishes paperback originals and reprints. Publishes approximately 800 titles/year. Pays 4-10% royalty on retail price; offers advance. Publishes book an average of 18-24 months after acceptance.
Nonfiction: How-to, inspirational, family life, business, biographies, autobiographies and nutrition.
Recent Nonfiction Title: *Fatherhood*, by Bill Cosby.
Fiction: Adventure, historical, mainstream men's adventure, young adult, suspense, western, occult, romance and science fiction. Submit outline/synopsis and first 3 chapters (for Ace Science Fiction only).
Recent Fiction Title: *Playmates*, by Robert B. Parker.
Young Adult Fiction Title: *Freeway Warrior*, by Joe Dever.

BETHANY HOUSE PUBLISHERS, Subsidiary of Bethany Fellowship, Inc., 6820 Auto Club Rd., Minneapolis MN 55438. (612)944-2121. Editorial Director: Carol Johnson. Estab. 1956. Publishes hardcover and paperback originals and reprints. "Contracts negotiable." Averages 60 titles/year; receives 1,200 submissions annually. 15% of books from first-time authors; 95% of books from unagented writers. Publishes book an average of 9-18 months after acceptance. Simultaneous submissions OK. Query for electronic submissions. Reports in 2 months. Book catalog and ms guidelines for 9 × 12 SAE and 5 first class stamps.
Nonfiction: Publishes reference (lay-oriented); devotional (evangelical, charismatic); and personal growth books. Submit outline and 2-3 sample chapters. Looks for "provocative subject, quality writing style, authoritative presentation, unique approach, sound Christian truth." Reviews artwork/photos as part of ms package.
Recent Nonfiction Title: *Married Lovers, Married Friends*, by Steve and Annie Chapman.
Fiction: Well written stories with a Christian message. No poetry. Submit synopsis and 2-3 sample chapters to Acquisitions Editor. Guidelines available.
Recent Fiction Title: *Munich Signature*, by Bodie Thoene.
Tips: "The writer has the best chance of selling our firm a book that will market well in the Christian bookstore. In your query, list other books in this category (price, length, main thrust), and tell how yours is better or unique."

‡**BETHEL PUBLISHING**, Subsidiary of Missionary Church, Inc., 1819 South Main St., Elkhart IN 46516 (219)293-8585. Executive Director: Rev. Richard Oltz. Publishes trade paperback originals and reprints. Averages 5 titles/year. Receives 60 submissions/year. 10% of books from first-time authors, 100% from unagented writers. Pays 5-10% royalties. Offers $250 average advance. Publishes book an average of 1 year after acceptance. Simultaneous submissions OK. Reports in 2 weeks on queries; 3 months on mss. Free book catalog and manuscript guidelines.
Nonfiction: Reference. Subjects include religion. Reviews artwork/photos as part of ms package. Query or submit complete ms.
Recent Nonfiction Title: *We Have An Advocate*, by Ringenberg (religious).
Fiction: Adventure, religious, suspense, young adult. Books must be evangelical in approach. No occult, gay/lesbian, erotica. Query or submit complete ms.
Recent Fiction Title: *Deadline*, by Stahl (mystery).
Tips: "Our audience is made up of Christian families with children. If I were a writer trying to market a book today, I would find out what publisher specializes in the type of book I have written."

BETTER HOMES AND GARDENS BOOKS, Division of the Meredith Corporation, 1716 Locust St., Des Moines IA 50336. FAX: (515)284-2700. Managing Editor: David A. Kirchner. Estab. 1931. Publishes hardcover and trade paperback originals. Averages 40 titles/year. "The majority of our books are produced by on-staff editors, but we often use freelance writers on assignment for sections or chapters of books already in progress." Reports in 6 weeks.
Nonfiction: "We publish nonfiction in many family and home-service categories, including gardening, decorating and remodeling, crafts, money management, handyman's topics, cooking and nutrition, Christmas activities, and other subjects of home-service value. Emphasis is on how-to and on stimulating people to action. We require concise, factual writing. Audience is primarily husbands and wives with home and family as their main center of interest. Style should be informative and lively with a straightforward approach. Stress the positive. Emphasis is entirely on reader service. Because most of our books are produced by on-staff editors, we're less interested in book-length manuscripts than in hearing from freelance writers with solid

expertise in gardening, do-it-yourself, health/fitness, and home decorating. We have no need at present for cookbooks or cookbook authors. Publisher recommends careful study of specific Better Homes and Gardens Books titles before submitting material." Prefers outline and sample chapters. "Please include SASE with appropriate return postage."

Recent Nonfiction Title: *New Family Medical Guide,* by Edwin Kiester Jr.

Tips: "Writers often fail to familiarize themselves with the catalog/backlist of the publishers to whom they are submitting. We expect heavier emphasis on health/fitness, gardening and do-it-yourself titles. But, again, we're most interested in hearing from freelance writers with subject expertise in these areas than in receiving queries for book-length manuscripts. Queries/mss may be routed to other editors in the publishing group."

BETWEEN THE LINES INC., 394 Euclid Ave., Toronto, Ontario M6G 259 Canada. (416)925-8260. FAX: (416)324-8268. Editor: Sheila Nopper. Estab. 1977. Publishes trade paperback originals. Averages 9-10 titles/year. Receives 150 submissions/year. 75% of books are from first-time authors; 100% from unagented writers. Pays 8-15% royalty. Publishes ms an average of 10 months after acceptance. Simultaneous submissions OK. Query for electronic submissions. Reports in 2 months on queries; 3 months on mss. Free book catalog. Ms guidelines for #10 SASE.

Nonfiction: Subjects include agriculture/horticulture, business and economics, education, culture, ethnic, gay/lesbian, government/politics, health/medicine, women's issues/studies. Query or submit outline/synopsis and sample chapters. Reviews artwork/photos as part of ms package.

Recent Nonfiction Title: *Sultans of Sleaze,* by Joyce Nelson (culture/politics).

*BINFORD & MORT PUBLISHING, 1202 N.W. 17th Ave., Portland OR 97209. (503)221-0866. Publisher: James Gardenier. Estab. 1891. Publishes hardcover and paperback originals and reprints. Receives 500 submissions annually. 60% of books from first-time authors; 90% of books from unagented writers. Average print order for a writer's first book is 5,000. Pays 10% royalty on retail price; offers variable advance (to established authors). Publishes about 10-12 titles annually. Occasionally does some subsidy publishing (10%), at author's request. Publishes book an average of 1 year after acceptance. Reports in 4 months.

Nonfiction: Books about the Pacific Coast and the Northwest. Subjects include Western Americana, biography, history, nature, maritime, recreation, reference, and travel. Query with sample chapters and SASE. Reviews artwork/photos as part of ms package.

Recent Nonfiction Title: *We Claimed this Land: Portland's Pioneer Settlers,* by Eugene E. Snyder.

‡BLACK SPARROW PRESS, 24 Tenth St., Santa Rosa CA 95401. (707)579-4011. Imprint: Arabesque Books. Assistant to Publisher: Julie Curtiss Voss. Estab. 1966. Publishes hardcover and trade paperback originals and reprints. Averages 12 titles/year. 0% of books from first-time authors; 75% from unagented writers. Pays 5-10% royalty on retail price. Publishes book an average of 1 year after acceptance. Simultaneous submissions OK. Reports in 1 month on queries; 2 months on mss. Book catalog free on request.

Nonfiction: Subjects include language/literature. No how-to, cookbook, juvenile, self-help. Query.

Recent Nonfiction Title: *Creatures of Habit,* Wyndham Lewis (essays on art and literature).

Fiction: Literary, feminist, gay/lesbian, short story collections. We generally solicit from authors we are interested in. "We only publish 12 new books a year so our schedule is quickly filled." No genre such as romance, westerns, etc. Query.

Recent Fiction Title: *The Stone Baby,* by Laura Chester (novel). "We generally solicit from authors we are interested in." No light verse, nonsense verse, limmerick, traditional rhymed verse. Submit 5 samples.

Recent Poetry Title: *A Nation of Nothing But Poetry,* by Charles Olson (objectivist).

JOHN F. BLAIR, PUBLISHER, 1406 Plaza Dr., Winston-Salem NC 27103. (919)768-1374. Editor: Stephen Kirk. Estab. 1954. Publishes hardcover originals and trade paperbacks; receives 1,000 submissions annually. 20-30% of books from first-time authors; 90% of books from unagented writers. Average print order for a writer's first book is 3,500-5,000. Royalty to be negotiated. Publishes book an average of 1-1½ years after acceptance. Query for electronic submissions. Reports in 2-3 months. Book catalog and ms guidelines for 9 × 12 SAE and 85¢ postage.

An asterisk preceding a listing indicates that subsidy publishing or co-publishing (where author pays part or all of publishing costs) is available. Firms whose subsidy programs comprise more than 50% of their total publishing activities are listed at the end of the Book Packagers and Producers section.

Nonfiction: Especially interested in well-researched adult biography and history. Preference given to books dealing with Southeastern United States. Also interested in environment and Americana; query on other nonfiction topics. Looks for utility and significance. Submit synopsis/outline and first 3 chapters or complete ms. Reviews artwork/photos as part of ms package.
Recent Nonfiction Title: *Damn the Torpedos! Naval Incidents of the Civil War*, by A.A. Hoehling (history).
Fiction: "We are most interested in serious novels of substance and imagination. Preference given to material related to Southeastern United States." No category fiction, juvenile fiction, picture books or poetry.
Recent Fiction Title: *The Hatterask Incident*, by John D. Randall.

BLUE BIRD PUBLISHING, #306, 1713 E. Broadway, Tempe AZ 85282. (602)982-9003. Publisher: Cheryl Gorder. Publishes trade paperback originals. Firm averages 6 titles/year. 50% of books from first-time authors. 100% from unagented writers. Pays 10% royalty on wholesale price; 15% on retail price. Publishes book an average of 9 months after acceptance. Simultaneous submissions OK. Reports in 6 weeks. Book catalog and manuscript guidelines for #10 SASE.
Nonfiction: How-to, juvenile and reference. Subjects include child guidance/parenting, education (especially home education) and sociology (current social issues). "The home schooling population in the U.S. is exploding. We have a strong market for anything that can be targeted to this group: i.e., home education manuscripts; parenting guides, home business ideas. We would also like to see complete nonfiction manuscripts in current issues, how-to, and juvenile topics." Submit complete ms. Reviews artwork/photos as part of ms package.
Recent Nonfiction Title: *The Sixth Sense: Practical Tips for Everyday Safety*.
Tips: "We are interested if we see a complete manuscript that is aimed toward a general adult nonfiction audience. We are impressed if the writer has really done his homework and the manuscript includes photos, artwork, graphs, charts, and other graphics."

BLUE DOLPHIN PUBLISHING, INC., P.O. Box 1908, Nevada City CA 95959. 12380 Nevada City Hwy., Grass Valley CA 95945. (916)265-6923. (916)265-6925. President: Paul M. Clemens. Estab. 1985. Publishes hardcover and trade paperback originals. Firm averages 8 titles/year. Receives over 1,000 submissions/year. 75% of books from first-time authors. 90% from unagented writers. Pays 7.5-12.5% on wholesale price. Offers average $500 advance. Publishes book an average of 6-9 months after acceptance. Simultaneous submissions OK. Query for electronic submissions. Reports in 1 month on queries; 2-3 months on mss. Free book catalog.
Nonfiction: Biography, cookbook, how-to, humor and self-help. Subjects include anthropology/archaeology, cooking, ecology, foods and nutrition, health/medicine, psychology and comparative religion. "We are interested primarily in new age self-help psychology, and comparative spiritual traditions, including translations." Submit outline/synopsis and sample chapters. Reviews artwork as part of package.
Recent Nonfiction Title: *Do Less . . . And Be Loved More: How to Really Relate to Others*, by Peg Tompkins.
Fiction: Feminist, humor, literary, science fiction and New Age. Submit outline/synopsis and sample chapters.
Recent Fiction Title: *The Autobiography of Mary Magdalene*, by Beth Ingber-Irvin.
Poetry: "We will only consider previously published authors of some merit; translations from Japanese, Chinese, Tibetan, Sanskrit." Submit complete ms.
Recent Poetry Title: *Lightly the Harper*, by Jack Tootell (Americana).
Tips: "The new age spiritual seeker interested in self-growth and awareness for oneself and the planet is our audience."

‡BLUE HERON PUBLISHING, Rt. 3 Box 376, Hillsboro OR 97124. (503)621-3911. Imprints include Media Weavers. President: Dennis Stovall. Vice President: Linny Stovall. Publishes trade paperback originals and reprints. Firm averages 5 titles/year. Free book catalog on request.
Fiction: Juvenile, young adult. "We are only doing reprints of well known authors for 1 year. But will also consider strong ethnic multi-cultural fiction after that."
Recent Fiction Title: Reprints of 8 Walt Morey books—juvenile/YA.

BNA BOOKS, Division of The Bureau of National Affairs, Inc., 1231 25th St. NW, Washington DC 20037. (202)452-4276. FAX: (202)452-9186. Contact: Acquisitions Manager. Estab. 1929. Publishes hardcover and softcover originals. Averages 35 titles/year. Receives 200 submissions/year. 20% of books from first-time authors; 95% of books from unagented writers. Pays 5-15% royalty on net cash receipts; offers $1,000 average advance. Simultaneous submissions OK. Publishes book an average of 1 year after acceptance. Reports in 2 months on queries; 3 months on mss. Free book catalog and ms guidelines.
Nonfiction: Reference and professional/scholarly. Subjects include business law and regulation, environment and safety, legal practice, labor relations and human resource management. No biographies, bibliographies, cookbooks, religion books, humor or trade books. Submit detailed table of contents or outline.
Recent Nonfiction Title: *Supreme Court Practice*, sixth edition, by Stern, Gressman and Shapiro (law).
Tips: "Our audience is practicing lawyers and business executives; managers, federal, state, and local government administrators; unions; and libraries. We look for authoritative and comprehensive works on subjects of interest to executives, professionals, and managers, that relate to the interaction of government and business."

‡BONUS BOOKS, INC., 160 E. Illinois St., Chicago IL 60611. (312)467-0580. Assistant Editor: Sharon Turner Mulvihill. Estab. 1985. Publishes hardcover and trade paperback originals and reprints. Averages 30 titles/year. Receives 400-500 submissions/year. 40% of books from first-time authors; 60% from unagented writers. Subsidy publishes 5% of books. Determines subsidy "when some synergism exists." Pays 6-10% royalty on wholesale price. Advances are not frequent. Publishes book an average of 6 months after acceptance. Simultaneous submissions OK "if informed they are such." Query for electronic submissions. Reports in 4 weeks on queries; 5 weeks on mss. Book catalog free on request.

Nonfiction: Biography, coffee table book, how-to, self-help. Subjects include business and economics, cooking, foods and nutrition, government/politics, health/medicine, money/finance, recreation, sports and women's issues/studies. Query with outline/synopsis and sample chapters. Reviews artwork/photos as part of ms package.

Recent Nonfiction Title: *Executive's Guide to Motivating People*, by Abraham Zaleznik (business management).

BOOKCRAFT, INC., 1848 W. 2300 S., Salt Lake City UT 84119. (801)972-6180. Editorial Manager: Cory H. Maxwell. Estab. 1942. Publishes (mainly hardcover) originals and reprints. Pays standard 7½-10-12½-15% royalty on retail price; rarely gives a royalty advance. Averages 40-45 titles/year; receives 500-600 submissions annually. 20% of books from first-time authors; virtually 100% of books from unagented writers. Publishes book an average of 6 months after acceptance. Reports in about 2 months. Will send general information to prospective authors on request; ms guidelines for #10 SASE.

Nonfiction: "We publish for members of The Church of Jesus Christ of Latter-Day Saints (Mormons) and do not distribute to the national market. All our books are closely oriented to the faith and practices of the LDS church, and we will be glad to review such mss. Mss which have merely a general religious appeal are not acceptable. Ideal book lengths range from about 80 to 240 pages or so, depending on subject, presentation, and age level. We look for a fresh approach—rehashes of well-known concepts or doctrines not acceptable. Mss should be anecdotal unless truly scholarly or on a specialized subject. We do not publish anti-Mormon works. We also publish short and moderate length books for Mormon youth, about ages 14 to 19, mostly nonfiction. These reflect LDS principles without being 'preachy'; must be motivational. 30,000-45,000 words is about the right length, though good, longer mss are not entirely ruled out. This is a tough area to write in, and the mortality rate for such mss is high. We publish only 2 or 3 new juvenile titles annually." No "poetry, plays, personal philosophizings, or family histories." Query. "Include contents page with manuscript."

Recent Nonfiction Title: *A Wonderful Flood of Light*, by Neal A. Maxwell.

Fiction: Must be closely oriented to LDS faith and practices.

Recent Fiction Title: *The Falcon Heart*, by Jaroldeen Edwards.

BOOKMAKERS GUILD, INC., Subsidiary of Dakota Graphics, Inc., 9655 W. Colfax Ave., Lakewood CO 80215. (303)235-0203. Managing Editor: Leah Ann Crussell. Publisher: Barbara J. Ciletti. Estab. 1985. Publishes hardcover and trade paperback originals. Averages 10-12 titles/year; receives 700 submissions annually. 30% of books from first-time authors; 90% of books from unagented writers. Pays 10% royalty on net receipts. Publishes books an average of 12-18 months after acceptance. Mss will not be returned without SASE. Reports in 1 month on queries; 2 months on mss after query, 4 months on ms without query. Book catalog and guidelines available.

Nonfiction: Adult reference; contemporary social issues; health; natural history; and psychology (focus on children and family). "We see a continuing focus on families, children and youth, especially books on child advocacy, behavior and education. Also seeking juvenile nonfiction. No how-to, cookbooks, local history, novels, poetry, sci-fi, computers, fashion, sports or works ill-written and ill-conceived." Query or submit outline/synopsis and sample chapters. Sometimes reviews artwork/photos.

Recent Nonfiction Title: *Separate Houses*, by Roberta Shapiro, Ph.D.

Fiction: Juvenile, age 8 and up. "We seek folklore, folktale and saga along classical themes with educational and cultural merit. Primarily focus on language and literature." Query first.

Recent Fiction Title: *Death of a Stranger*, by Will Barrett.

Tips: "Current concerns regarding the family unit and adolescent growth and development have influenced the type of material that we look for. We focus on those works which seek to educate and inform. We are specifically seeking educational nonfiction in the natural sciences for young adults, as well as adult nonfiction that addresses the issues concerning the well-being of the adolescent, the aged, and the family. Books that are sensitively written, well-researched, and on topics that are not already flooding the market have the best chances of being considered for publication by our firm."

BOREALIS PRESS, LTD., 9 Ashburn Dr., Nepean, Ontario K2E 6N4 Canada. Editorial Director: Frank Tierney. Senior Editor: Glenn Clever. Publishes hardcover and paperback originals. Averages 4 titles/year; receives 400-500 submissions annually. 80% of books from first-time authors; 95% of books from unagented writers. Pays 10% royalty on retail price; no advance. Publishes book an average of 18 months after acceptance. "No multiple submissions or electronic printouts on paper more than 8½ inches wide." Reports in 8 months. Book catalog $1 with SAE and IRCs.

Nonfiction: "Only material Canadian in content." Query. Reviews artwork/photos as part of ms package. Looks for "style in tone and language, reader interest, and maturity of outlook."
Recent Nonfiction Title: *The Community Doukhsbors: A People in Transition*, by John Freisen and Michael Veregin.
Fiction: "Only material Canadian in content and dealing with significant aspects of the human situation." Query.
Recent Fiction Title: *Annie*, by Hortie (novel).
Tips: "Ensure that creative writing deals with consequential human affairs, not just action, sensation, or cutesy stuff."

THE BORGO PRESS, P.O. Box 2845, San Bernardino CA 92406. (714)884-5813. Editor: Mary A. Burgess. Estab. 1975. Publishes hardcover and paperback originals. Averages 100 titles/year; receives 1,000 submissions annually. 5% of books from first-time authors; 100% of books from unagented writers. Pays royalty on retail price: "10% of gross." No advance. Publishes book an average of 3 years after acceptance. "Virtually all of our sales are to the academic library market." Query for electronic submissions. Reports in 3 months. Book catalog and writer's guidelines for 8½ × 11 SAE and 4 first class stamps.
Nonfiction: Publishes literary critiques, bibliographies, historical research, film critiques, theatrical research, interview volumes, biographies, social studies, political science, and reference works for the academic library market. Query with letter or outline/synopsis and 1 sample chapter. "All of our books, without exception, are published in open-ended, numbered, monographic series. Do not submit proposals until you have looked at actual copies of recent Borgo Press publications. We are *not* a market for fiction, poetry, popular nonfiction, artwork, or anything else except scholarly monographs in the humanities and social sciences. We discard unsolicited manuscripts from outside of our subject fields which are not accompanied by SASEs."
Recent Nonfiction Title: *The Work of Colin Wilson: An Annotated Bibliography and Guide*, by Colin Stanley.
Tips: "We are currently buying comprehensive, annotated bibliographies of twentieth-century writers; these must be produced to a strict series format (available for SASE and 3 first class stamps)."

*DON BOSCO MULTIMEDIA, 475 N. Ave., Box T, New Rochelle NY 10802. (914)576-0122. Subsidiaries include Salesiana Publishers. Editorial Director: James Hurley. Publishes hardcover and trade paperback originals. Averages 6-10 titles/year; receives 50 submissions annually. 15% of books from first-time authors; 100% of books from unagented writers. Average print order for a writer's first book is 3,000. Subsidy publishes 10% of books. Subsidy publishes (nonauthor) 30% of books. "We judge the content of the manuscript and quality to be sure it fits the description of our house. We subsidy publish for nonprofit and religious societies." Pays 5-10% royalty on retail price; offers average $100 advance. Publishes book an average of 10 months after acceptance. Reports in 2 weeks on queries; 2 months on mss. Free book catalog.
Nonfiction: Biography, juvenile and textbook on Roman Catholic religion. "Biographies of outstanding Christian men and women of today. We are a new publisher with wide experience in school marketing, especially in religious education field." Accepts nonfiction translations from Italian and Spanish. Query or submit outline/synopsis and 2 sample chapters. Occasionally reviews artwork/photos as part of ms package.
Recent Nonfiction Title: *Access Guide to Pop Culture*, by Reynolds Ekstrom.
Tips: Queries/mss may be routed to other editors in the publishing group.

THE BOSTON MILLS PRESS, 132 Main St., Erin, Ontario N0B 1T0 Canada. (519)833-2407. FAX: (519)833-2195. President: John Denison. Estab. 1975. Publishes hardcover and trade paperback originals. Averages 16 titles/year; receives 100 submissions annually. 75% of books from first-time authors; 90% of books from unagented writers. Pays 6-10% royalty on retail price; no advance. Publishes book an average of 8 months after acceptance. Simultaneous submissions OK. Query for electronic submissions. Reports in 2 weeks on queries; 1 month on mss. Free book catalog.
Nonfiction: Illustrated book. Subjects include history. "We're interested in anything to do with Canadian or American history—especially transportation. We like books with a small, strong market." No autobiographies. Query. Reviews artwork/photos as part of ms package.
Recent Nonfiction Title: *Next Stop Grand Central*, by Stan Fischler (railway history).
Tips: "We can't compete with the big boys so we stay with short-run specific market books that bigger firms can't handle. We've done well this way so we'll continue in the same vein. We tend to accept books from completed manuscripts."

‡BOWLING GREEN STATE UNIVERSITY POPULAR PRESS, Bowling Green State University, Bowling Green OH 43403. (419)372-7866. Editor: Ms. Pat Browne. Publishes hardcover and trade paperback originals and reprints. Averages 25-30 titles/year. Receives 150-200 submissions/year. 50% of books from first-time authors; 95% from unagented writers. Pays 5-12½% royalty on wholesale price; buys mss outright. Publishes book an average of 12 months after acceptance. Reports in 1 week on queries; 3 months on mss. Book catalog and manuscript guidelines free on request.

Nonfiction: Biography, reference and textbook. Subjects include Americana, anthropology/archaeology, art/architecture, history, language/literature, photography, regional, religion, sociology, sports and women's issues/studies. Submit outline/synopsis and sample chapters.

Recent Nonfiction Title: *The Monster With a Thousand Faces*, by Brian J. Frost (reference).

Tips: "Our audience includes university professors, students, libraries."

‡*THE BOXWOOD PRESS, 183 Ocean View Blvd., Pacific Grove CA 93950. (408)375-9110. Imprints include Viewpoint Books, Free Spirit Books. Editor: Dr. Ralph Buchsbaum. Publishes hardcover and trade paperback originals. Firm averages 5 titles/year. Receives 25 submissions/year. Subsidy publishes 25% of books. Determines subsidy by high merit; low market. Pays 10% royalty. Publishes book an average of 10 months after acceptance. Query for electronic submissions. Reports in 6 weeks on queries; 2 months on mss. Book catalog free on request.

Nonfiction: Biography, technical and textbook. Subjects include biology (plants and animals), health/medicine, history, nature/environment, philosophy, psychology, regional or area studies and other science. Submit complete ms. Reviews artwork/photos as part of ms package.

Recent Nonfiction Title: *Beyond Birding*, by Grubb.

Tips: "Writers have the best chance selling us sound science and natural history books. Our audience is high school and college, general and educated. If I were a writer trying to market a book today, I would know my subject, readership and do my clearest writing."

‡BOYD & FRASER PUBLISHING COMPANY, Division of South-Western Publishing Company, Suite 1405, 20 Park Plaza, Boston MA 02116. (617)426-2292. Acquisitions Editor: James Edwards. Publishes hardcover and paperback originals primarily for the college textbook market; some trade sales of selected titles. Averages 25-30 titles/year. Receives 100 submissions/year. 50% of books from first-time authors; 100% from unagented writers. Pays 15% royalty on wholesale price. Advance is negotiated individually. Publishes book an average of 1 year after acceptance. Simultaneous submissions OK. Query for electronic submissions. Reports in 1 month on queries; 2 months on mss. Book catalog and manuscript guidelines free on request.

Nonfiction: Textbook. Subjects include computer information systems and application software. Query or submit outline/synopsis first; unsolicited mss not invited. Reviews artwork/photos as part of ms package.

Recent Nonfiction Title: *COBOL: Structured Programming Techniques for Solving Problems* by George C. Fowler (college textbook).

Tips: "Writers have the best chance sending us proposals for college-level textbooks in computer education. Our audience consists of students enrolled in business oriented courses on computers or computer application topics."

BRADBURY PRESS, Affiliate of Macmillan, Inc., 866 3rd Ave., New York NY 10022. (212)702-9809. Editorial Director: Barbara Lalicki. Publishes hardcover originals for children and young adults. Averages 30 titles/year. Pays royalty and offers advance. Reports in 3 months. Book catalog and ms guidelines for 9 × 12 SAE with 4 first class stamps.

Recent Nonfiction Title: *The Great American Gold Rush*, by Rhoda Blumburg.

Fiction: Picture books, concept books, photo essays and novels for elementary school children. Also "stories about real kids; special interest in realistic dialogue." No adult ms. No religious material. Submit complete ms.

Recent Fiction Title: *Aurora Means Dawn*, by Saunders.

Tips: "We're looking for historically accurate material that will interest kids in the past. We also look for science writers who can explain concepts of physics and biology on an elementary school level."

BRANDEN PUBLISHING CO., INC., 17 Station St., Box 843, Brookline Village MA 02147. (617)734-2045. President: Adolph Caso. Subsidiaries include International Pocket Library and Popular Technology, Four Seas and Brashear. Publishes hardcover and trade paperback originals, hardcover and trade paperback reprints and software. Averages 15 titles/year; receives 1,000 submissions annually. 80% of books from first-time authors; 90% of books from unagented writers. Average print order for a writer's first book is 3,000. Pays 5-10% royalty on net; offers $1,000 maximum advance. Publishes book an average of 10 months after acceptance. Query for electronic submissions. Reports in 1 week on queries; 2 months on mss.

Nonfiction: Biography, illustrated book, juvenile, reference, technical and textbook. Subjects include Americana, art, computers, health, history, music, photography, politics, sociology, software and classics. Especially looking for "about 10 manuscripts on national and international subjects, including biographies of well-known individuals." No religion or philosophy. Prefers paragraph query with author's vita and SASE; no unsolicited mss. Reviews artwork/photos as part of ms package.

Recent Nonfiction Title: *Barbra—An Actress Who Sings*.

Fiction: Ethnic (histories, integration); mainstream (emphasis on youth and immigrants); religious (historical-reconstructive); romance (novels with well-drawn characters). No science, mystery or pornography. Paragraph query with author's vita and SASE; no unsolicited mss.

Recent Fiction Title: *The Dance of the 12 Apostles*, by P.J. Carisella (historical novel).
Tips: "Branden publishes only manuscripts determined to have a significant impact on modern society. Our audience is a well-read general public, professionals, college students, and some high school students. If I were a writer trying to market a book today, I would thoroughly investigate the number of potential readers interested in the content of my book. We like books by or about women."

BREAKWATER BOOKS, P.O. Box 2188, St. John's Newfoundland A1C 6E6 Canada. (709)722-6680. FAX: (709)753-0708. Estab. 1973. Firm publishes hardcover and trade paperback originals. Publishes 25-30 titles/year. Pays 10% royalty on retail price. Publishes book an average of 2 years after acceptance. Letters of inquiry and manuscript summary only. Reports in 3 months. Free book catalog.
Nonfiction: Biography, coffee table book, cookbook, humor, illustrated book, juvenile, reference, textbook. Subjects include education, history, language/literature, nature/environment, photography, recreation, regional, religion, sociology and folklore. Query only. All unsolicited mss are returned unopened. Reviews artwork/photos as part of ms package.
Recent Nonfiction Title: *No Place for Fools: The Political Memoirs of Don Jamieson*, Vol I.
Fiction: Adventure, ethnic, experimental, fantasy, feminist, historical, humor, juvenile, literary, mainstream/contemporary, mystery, picture books, plays, romance, science fiction, short story collections, suspense, young adult. Query only. All unsolicited mss are returned unopened.
Recent Fiction Title: *Priest of God*, by Patrick O'Flaherty.
Poetry: Letter of inquiry and sample only.
Recent Poetry Title: *The Time of Icicles*, by Mary Dalton.

‡**BREVET PRESS, INC.**, Box 1404, Sioux Falls SD 57101. Publisher: Donald P. Mackintosh. Managing Editor: Peter E. Reid. Publishes hardcover and paperback originals and reprints. Receives 40 submissions annually. 50% of books from first-time authors; 100% of books from unagented writers. Average print order for a writer's first book is 5,000. Pays 5% royalty; advance averages $1,000. Publishes book an average of 1 year after acceptance. Simultaneous submissions OK. Reports in 2 months. Free book catalog.
Nonfiction: Specializes in business management, history, place names, and historical marker series. Americana (A. Melton, editor); business (D.P. Mackintosh, editor); history (B. Mackintosh, editor); and technical books (Peter Reid, editor). Query; "after query, detailed instructions will follow if we are interested." Reviews artwork/photos; send copies if photos/illustrations are to accompany ms.
Tips: "Write with market potential and literary excellence. Keep sexism out of the manuscripts by male authors."

*****BRIARCLIFF PRESS PUBLISHERS**, 11 Wimbledon Ct., Jericho NY 11753. Editorial Director: Trudy Settel. Senior Editor: J. Frieman. Estab. 1980. Publishes hardcover and paperback originals. Averages 5-7 titles/year; receives 250 submissions annually. 10% of books from first-time authors; 60% of books from unagented writers. Average print order for a writer's first book is 5,000. Subsidy publishes 20% of books. Pays $4,000-5,000 for outright purchase; offers average of $1,000 advance. Publishes book an average of 6 months after acceptance. "We do not use unsolicited manuscripts. Ours are custom books prepared for businesses, and assignments are initiated by us."
Nonfiction: How-to, cookbooks, sports, travel, fitness/health, business and finance, diet, gardening and crafts. "We want our books to be designed to meet the needs of specific businesses." Accepts nonfiction translations from French, German and Italian. Query. Submit outline and 2 sample chapters. Reviews artwork/photos as part of ms package.
Recent Nonfiction Title: *Nail Care*, by Kristi Wells.

BRICK HOUSE PUBLISHING CO., Box 134, 11 Thoreau Rd, Acton MA 01720. (508)635-9800. Publisher: Robert Runck. Estab. 1976. Publishes hardcover and trade paperback originals. Averages 12 titles/year; receives 500 submissions annually. 20% of books from first-time authors; 100% of books from unagented writers. Pays 10-15% royalty on wholesale price. Offers average $1,000 advance. Publishes book an average of 6 months after acceptance. Simultaneous submissions OK. Query for electronic submissions. Reports in 2 weeks on queries; 3 months on mss. Book catalog and ms guidelines for SAE with 3 first class stamps.
Nonfiction: How-to, reference, technical and textbook. Subjects include business and consumer advice. "We are looking for writers to do books in the following areas: practical guidance and information for people running small businesses, consumer trade books on money and job topics, and college business textbooks." Query with synopses.
Recent Nonfiction Title: *Planning and Financing the New Venture*, by Jeffry Timmons.
Tips: "A common mistake writers make is not addressing the following questions in their query/proposals: What are my qualifications for writing this book? Why would anyone want the book enough to pay for it in a bookstore? What can I do to help promote the book?"

BRISTOL PUBLISHING ENTERPRISES, INC., P.O. Box 1737, 14692 Wicks Blvd., San Leandro CA 94577. Imprints include Bristol Nitty Gritty Cookbooks. Chairman: Patricia J. Hall. President: Brian Hall. (415)895-4461. Publishes 12-14 titles/year. Receive 250 proposals/year. 50% of books from first-time authors; 100%

from unagented writers. Pay 6-9% royalty on wholesale price. Average advance $100. Publishes within 1 year of acceptance. Reports in 2 months. Book catalog for SAE with 2 first class stamps.

Nonfiction: Cookbooks. *Nonfiction books for readers over 50 years of age.* Submit outline/synopsis and sample chapters.

Recent Nonfiction Title: *The Encyclopedia of Grandparenting,* by Rosemary Dalton.

BROADMAN PRESS, 127 9th Ave. N, Nashville TN 37234. Editorial Director: Harold S. Smith. Publishes hardcover and paperback originals (85%) and reprints (15%). Averages 75 titles/year. Pays 10% royalty on retail price; no advance. Reports in 2 months.

Nonfiction: Religion. "We are open to freelance submissions in the children's and inspirational areas. Materials in both areas must be suited for a conservative Protestant readership. No poetry, biography, sermons, or anything outside the area of the Protestant tradition." Query, submit outline/synopsis and sample chapters, or submit complete ms. Reviews artwork/photos as part of ms package. Writer's guidelines for #10 SAE with 2 first class stamps.

Fiction: Religious. "We publish almost no fiction—less than five titles per year. For our occasional publication we want not only a very good story, but also one that sets forth Christian values. Nothing that lacks a positive Christian emphasis; nothing that fails to sustain reader interest." Submit complete ms with synopsis.

Tips: "Textbook and family material are becoming an important forum for us—Bible study is very good for us, but our publishing is largely restricted in this area to works that we enlist on the basis of specific author qualifications. Preparation for the future and living with life's stresses and complexities are trends in the subject area."

BROADWAY PRESS, Suite 407, 120 Duane St., New York NY 10007. (212)693-0570. Publisher: David Rodger. Publishes trade paperback originals. Averages 5-10 titles/year; receives 20-30 submissions annually. 50% of books from first-time authors; 75% of books from unagented writers. Pays negotiable royalty. Publishes book an average of 18 months after acceptance. Simultaneous submissions OK. Reports in 1 month on queries.

Nonfiction: Reference and technical. Subjects include theatre, film, television and the performing arts. "We're looking for professionally-oriented and authored books." Submit outline/synopsis and sample chapters.

Recent Nonfiction Title: *Professional Actor Training in New York City,* by Jim Monos.

Tips: "Our readers are primarily professionals in the entertainment industries. Submissions that really grab our attention are aimed at that market."

‡BUCKNELL UNIVERSITY PRESS, Lewisburg PA 17837. (717)524-3674. Distributed by Associated University Presses. Director: Mills F. Edgerton, Jr. Publishes hardcover originals. Averages 18-20 titles/year; receives 150 submissions annually. 20% of books from first-time authors; 99% of books from unagented writers. Pays royalty. Publishes book an average of 2 years after acceptance. Query for electronic submissions. Reports in 1 month on queries; usually 6 months on mss. Free book catalog.

Nonfiction: Subjects include scholarly art, history, literary criticism, music, philosophy, politics, psychology, religion and sociology. "In all fields, our criterion is scholarly presentation; manuscripts must be addressed to the scholarly community." Query. Reviews artwork/photos.

Recent Nonfiction Title: *Leaders in the Study of Animal Behavior,* by Donald A. Dewsbury.

Tips: "An original work of high-quality scholarship has the best chance of selling to us; we publish for the scholarly community."

‡BULL PUBLISHING CO., 110 Gilbert, Menlo Park CA 94025. (415)332-2855. Publisher: David Bull. Estab. 1974. Publishes hardcover and trade paperback originals. Averages 4-8 titles/year. Receives 100 submissions/year. 40-50% of books from first-time authors; 99% from unagented writers. Pays 14-16% royalty on wholesale price (net to publisher). Publishes ms an average of 6 months after acceptance. Simultaneous submissions OK. Query for electronic submissions. Reports in 3 weeks. Book catalog free on request.

Nonfiction: How-to, self-help. Subjects include foods and nutrition, fitness, health education, sports medicine. "We look for books that fit our area of strength: responsible books on health that fill a substantial public need, and that we can market primarily through professionals." Submit outline/synopsis and sample chapters. Reviews artwork/photos as part of ms package.

Recent Nonfiction Title: *Nutrition for the Chemotherapy Patient,* by Rosenbaum/Ramstack.

‡BUSINESS & LEGAL REPORTS, INC., 64 Wall St., Madison CT 06443. (203)245-7448. FAX: (203)245-2559. Editor: Stephen Bruce. Estab. 1978. Publishes hardcover originals. Averages 20 titles/year. Receives 100 submissions/year. Pays 2.5-5% royalty on retail price; buys mss outright for $1,000-5,000. Offers $1,500-3,000 average advance. Publishes book an average of 6 months after acceptance. Simultaneous submissions OK. Query for electronic submissions. Book catalog free on request.

Nonfiction: Reference. Subjects include business management, human resources, safety, environmental management. Query.
Recent Nonfiction Title: *Supervisor's Safety Meeting Guide*, by Barbara Kelly.

*C.S.S. PUBLISHING COMPANY, 628 South Main St., Lima OH 45804. (419)227-1818. Imprints include Fairway Press. Editorial Director: Fred Steiner. Publishes trade paperback originals. Publishes 50 titles/year. Receives 300 mss/year. 40% of books from first-time authors; 100% from unagented writers. Subsidy publishes 20%. "If books have limited market appeal and/or deal with basically same subject matter as title already on list, we will consider subsidy option." Pays 4-12% royalty on wholesale price or outright purchase of $25-250. Publishes book 2 years after acceptance. Simultaneous submissions OK. Query for electronic submissions. Reports on mss in 6 months. Book catalog free on request; ms guidelines for #10 SASE.
Nonfiction: Humor (religious) and self-help (religious). Subjects include religion: "Christian resources for mainline Protestant denominations; some Catholic resources. We are interested in sermon and worship resources, preaching illustrations, sermon seasonings, some Bible study, inspirationals, pastoral care, plays, practical theology, newsletter and bulletin board blurbs, church growth, success stories, teacher helps/training helps, church program material. Also sermon and worship resources based on the three-year lectionary; marriage helps and wedding services. We are not interested in the 'born again' movement or hellfire and brimstone stuff. No heavy theology, philosophy or scholarly themes." Reviews photos/artwork as part of ms package.
Recent Nonfiction Title: *The Greatest Passages of the Bible*, by Robert L. Allen.
Tips: "Books that sell well for us are seasonal sermon and worship resources; books aimed at clergy on professional growth and survival; also books of children's object lessons; seasonal plays (i.e. Christmas/Lent/Easter etc.). With church attendance declining, books on creative church growth will be popular. Our primary market is the clergy in all mainline denominations; others include church leaders, movers and shakers, education directors, Sunday school teachers, women's groups, youth leaders; to a certain extent we publish for the Christian layperson. Write something that makes Christianity applicable to the contemporary world, something useful to the struggling, searching Christian. The treatment might be humorous, certainly unique. We have published a few titles that other houses would not touch—with some degree of success. We are open to new ideas and would be pleased to see anything new, different, creative, and well-written that fits our traditional markets."

‡CALGRE PRESS, Subsidiary of Calgre, Inc., P.O. Box 711, Antioch CA 94509. (415)754-4916. Editor: Diane Power. Estab. 1988. Publishes hardcover and trade paperback originals. Firm averages 4 titles/ycar. 70% of books from first-time authors; 90% from unagented writers. Pays 5-15% royalty on retail price. Publishes book an average of 9 months after acceptance. Simultaneous submissions OK. Reports in 2 weeks on queries; 2 months on mss. Book catalog and manuscript guidelines for #10 SASE.
Nonfiction: How-to, reference, self-help. Subjects include child guidance/parenting, computers and electronics, education. Submit outline/synopsis and sample chapters. Reviews artwork/photos as part of ms package.
Recent Nonfiction Title: *The Defiant Ones: A Manual For Raising Kids*, by Jeffery M. Bruns.
Tips: "The writer has the best chance with how-to and self-help books, also books dealing with education and our educational system. Our audience includes adults, parents, teachers, business oriented adults in search of behavior motivation for higher productivity. If I were a writer trying to market a book today, I would contact small publishing firms specializing in the field that my book covers. An alternative is to contact literary agents hoping that they'll accept it for one of their big publishers."

CAMBRIDGE CAREER PRODUCTS, P.O. Box 2153, Charleston WV 25328-2153. (800)468-4227. FAX (304)344-5583. Subsidiaries include: Cambridge Home Economics, Cambridge Physical Education and Health. President: Edward T. Gardner, Ph.D. Estab. 1980. Publishes hardcover and trade paperback originals. Firm averages 12 titles/year. Receives 20 submissions/year. 20% of books from first-time authors. 90% from unagented writers. Pays 6-15% on wholesale price, $1,500-18,500 outright purchase. Offers $1,200 average advance. Publishes book an average of 8 months after acceptance. Simultaneous submissions OK. Reports in 2 weeks on queries; 1 month on mss. Free book catalog and manuscript guidelines.
Nonfiction: How-to, juvenile and self-help. Subjects include child guidance/parenting, cooking, foods and nutrition, education, health/medicine, money/finance, recreation and sports. "We need high quality books written for young adults (13 to 24 years old) on job search, career guidance, educational guidance, personal guidance, home economics, physical education, coaching, recreation, health, personal development, substance abuse, and sports. We only publish books written for young adults and primarily sold to libraries, schools, etc. We do not seek books targeted to adults or written at high readability levels." Query or submit outline/synopsis and sample chapters or send complete ms. Reviews artwork/photos as part of ms package.
Recent Nonfiction Title: *Job Search Guide*, by J. Lupia.
Tips: "We encourage the submission of high-quality books on timely topics written for young adult audiences at moderate to low readability levels. Call and request a copy of all our current catalogs, talk to the management about what is timely in the areas you wish to write on, thoroughly research the topic, and write a

manuscript that will be read by young adults without being overly technical. Low to moderate readibility yet entertaining, informative and accurate."

‡**CAMBRIDGE UNIVERSITY PRESS**, 40 W. 20th St., New York NY 10011. Director: Alan Winter. Estab. 1534. Publishes hardcover and paperback originals. Publishes 1,000 titles/year; receives 1,000 submissions annually. 50% of books from first-time authors; 99% of books from unagented writers. Subsidy publishes (nonauthor) 8% of books. Pays 10% royalty on receipts; 8% on paperbacks; no advance. Publishes book an average of 1 year after acceptance. Query for electronic submissions. Reports in 4 months.
Nonfiction: Anthropology, archeology, economics, life sciences, mathematics, psychology, physics, art history, upper-level textbooks, academic trade, scholarly monographs, biography, history, and music. Looking for academic excellence in all work submitted. Department Editors: Frank Smith (history, social sciences); Ellen Shaw (English as second language); Michael Agnes (reference); Lauren Cowles (mathematics, computer science); Matthew Hendryx (economics); Julia Hough (cognitive psychology); Emily Loose (politics, sociology); Beatrice Rehl (fine arts); Kathleen Zylan (life sciences); Helen Wheeler (behavioral science); Terence Moore (philosophy); and Peter-John Leone (earth sciences). Query. Reviews artwork/photos.
Recent Nonfiction Title: *Entertainment Industry Economics*, by Harold L. Vogel.

CAMELOT BOOKS, Children's Book Imprint of Avon Books, Division of the Hearst Corp., 8th Floor, 105 Madison Ave., New York NY 10016. (212)481-5609. FAX: (212)532-2172. Editorial Director: Ellen Krieger. Publishes paperback originals and reprints. Averages 60-70 titles/year; receives 1,000-1,500 submissions annually. 10-15% of books from first-time authors; 75% of books from unagented writers. Pays 6-8% royalty on retail price; offers minimum advance of $2,000. Publishes book an average of 15 months after acceptance. Simultaneous submissions OK. Reports in 10 weeks. Free book catalog and ms guidelines for 8 × 10 SAE and 5 first class stamps.
Fiction: Subjects include adventure, fantasy, humor, juvenile (Camelot, 8-12 and Young Camelot, 7-10) mainstream, mystery, ("very selective with mystery and fantasy") and suspense. Submit entire ms or 3 sample chapters and a brief "general summary of the story, chapter by chapter."
Recent Fiction Title: *Discovery at Coyote Point*, by Ann Gabhart.

‡**CAMINO BOOKS, INC.**, Box 59026, Philadelphia PA 19102. (215)732-2491. Publisher: E. Jutkowitz. Publishes hardcover and trade paperback originals. Averages 5 titles/year. Receives 100 submissions/year. 20% of books from first-time authors. Pays 6-12% royalty on net price. Offers $1,000 average advance. Publishes book an average of 12 months after acceptance. Reports in 2 weeks on queries; 1 month on mss.
Nonfiction: Biography, cookbook, how-to, humor and juvenile. Subjects include agriculture/horticulture, Americana, art/architecture, child guidance/parenting, cooking, foods and nutrition, ethnic, gardening, government/politics, history, regional and travel. Query or submit outline/synopsis and sample chapters.
Recent Nonfiction Title: *Let the Bunker Burn*, by Bowser (politics, history).
Tips: "The books must be on interest to readers in the Middle Atlantic states."

‡**CANADIAN INSTITUTE OF UKRAINIAN STUDIES PRESS**, 352 Athabasca Hall, University of Alberta, Edmonton, Alberta, T6G 2E8 Canada. (403)492-2972. Managing Editor: Myroslav Yurkevich. Publishes hardcover and trade paperback originals and reprints. Firm averages 10-15 titles/year. Receives 10 submissions/year. Subsidy publishes 20-30% of books. (Subsidies from granting agencies, not authors.) Pays 0-2% on retail price. Publishes book an average of 2 years after acceptance. Query for electronic submissions. Reports in 1 month on queries; 3 months on mss. Free book catalog and manuscript guidelines.
Nonfiction: Scholarly. Subjects include education, ethnic, government/politics, history, language/literature, religion, sociology and translation. We publish scholarly works in the humanities and social sciences dealing with Ukraine or Ukrainians in Canada. Query or submit complete ms. Reviews artwork/photos as part of ms package.
Recent Nonfiction Title: *The Ukrainian Religious Experience*, by David J. Goa (history/social science).
Fiction: Translations of Ukrainian literary works. We do not publish fiction, except translations of Ukrainian literary works that have scholarly value.
Recent Fiction Title: *Night and Day*, by Volodymyr Gzhytsky (autobiographical novel).
Tips: We are a scholarly press and do not normally pay our authors. Our audience consists of University students and teachers; general public interested in Ukrainian and Ukrainian-Canadian affairs.

*****CANADIAN PLAINS RESEARCH CENTER**, University of Regina, Regina, Saskatchewan S4S 0A2 Canada. (306)585-4795. FAX: (306)586-9862. Manager: Gillian Wadsworth Minifie. Estab. 1974. Publishes scholarly and trade paperback originals and some casebound originals. Averages 6-8 titles/year; receives 45-50 submissions annually. 35% of books from first-time authors; 90% of books from unagented writers. Subsidy publishes 80% (nonauthor) of books. Determines whether an author should be subsidy published through a scholarly peer review. Pays 5-10% royalty on retail price. "Occasionally academics will waive royalties in order to maintain lower prices." Publishes book an average of 18 months after acceptance. Query for electronic submissions. Reports in 2 months. Free book catalog and ms guidelines. Also publishes *Prairie Forum*, a scholarly journal.

Nonfiction: Biography, coffee table book, illustrated book, technical, textbook and scholarly. Subjects include animals, business and economics, history, nature, politics and sociology. "The Canadian Plains Research Center publishes the results of research on topics relating to the Canadian Plains region, although manuscripts relating to the Great Plains region will be considered. Material *must* be scholarly. Do not submit health, self-help, hobbies, music, sports, psychology, recreation or cookbooks unless they have a scholarly approach. For example, we would be interested in acquiring a pioneer manuscript cookbook, with modern ingredient equivalents, if the material relates to the Canadian Plains/Great Plains region." Submit complete ms. Reviews artwork/photos as part of ms package.

Recent Nonfiction Title: *Alvin: A Biography of the Honourable Alvin Hamilton, P.C.*, by Patrick Kyba.

Tips: "Pay great attention to manuscript preparation and accurate footnoting."

‡**C&T PUBLISHING**, 5021 Blum Rd., #1, Martinez CA 94553. (415)370-9600. Editor-in-Chief: Diane Pederson. Publishes hardcover and trade paperback originals. Publishes 6-8 titles/year; receives 24 submissions/year. Buys 10% from first-time authors; 100% from unagented writers. Pays 5-10% royalty on retail price. Offers $1,000 average advance. Publishes book an average of 9 months after acceptance. Simultaneous submissions OK. Reports in 3 weeks on queries; 2 months on mss. Free book catalog and ms guidelines.

Nonfiction: Coffee table book, how-to, technical. Subjects include art/architecture, hobbies, women's issues/studies, craft, fiber art. "Please submit typed manuscript with color snapshots of your work. Wearable art, fabric painting, fiber art, quiltmaking." No science, religion, money/finance, gay/lesbian, computers. Submit outline/synopsis and sample chapters. Reviews artwork/photos as part of ms package.

Recent Nonfiction Title: *Wearable Art for Real People*, by Mary Mashuta (quilted garments).

Tips: "In our industry, we find that how-to books have the longest selling life. The art quilt is coming into its own as an expression by women. Quiltmakers, sewing enthusiasts and fiber artists are our audience."

‡**CAPRA PRESS**, P.O. Box 2068, Santa Barbara CA 93120. (805)966-4590. Imprints include Joshua Odell Editions. Contact: Noel Young. Publishes hardcover and trade paperback originals. Firm averages 15 titles/year. Receives 4,000 submissions/year. 1% of books from first-time authors. 20% from unagented writers. Pays 10-15% royalty on wholesale price. Offers $1,000 average advance. Publishes book an average of 18 months after acceptance. Simultaneous submissions OK. Query for electronic submissions. Reports in 2 weeks on queries; 2 months on mss. Book catalog for 6×9 SAE and 2 first class stamps.

Nonfiction: Biography, how-to, self-help and natural history. Subjects include animals, art/architecture, gardening, language/literature, nature/environment, recreation, regional and sociology. We are looking for general trade titles with focus on the West. No juvenile books, code books, or poetry. Query or submit outline/synopsis and sample chapters. Reviews artwork/photos as part of ms package.

Recent Nonfiction Title: *Lawyers Are Killing America*, by Robert Wills (business).

Fiction: Historical (Western states), literary (from established authors), mainstream/contemporary and short story collections (only if stories have been in periodicals previously). No experimentals, fantasy, or genre fiction. Submit complete ms.

Recent Fiction Title: *Black Sun*, by Edward Abbey (novel).

Tips: Writers have the best chance selling us nonfiction, relating to architecture, natural history (birds, animals), or a coyote book.

‡**THE CAREER PRESS INC.**, 62 Beverly Rd., P.O. Box 34, Hawthorne NJ 07507. (201)427-0229. FAX: (201)427-2037. President: Ron Fry. Imprints include Career Directory Series and Internships Series. Estab. 1985. Publishes trade paperback originals. Averages 12-18 titles/year. Receives 50 submissions/year. 50% of books from first-time authors; 50% from unagented writers. Pays 10-15% royalty on wholesale price. Publishes book an average of 6 months after acceptance. Simultaneous submissions OK. Query for electronic submissions. Reports in 3 weeks. Book catalog free on request.

Nonfiction: How-to, reference and self-help. Subjects include business and economics, child guidance/parenting, education, money/finance and career/job search/resume. Submit complete ms. Reviews artwork/photos as part of ms package.

Recent Nonfiction Title: *How to Strengthen Your Winning Business Personality*, by B. Smith (business/management).

CAREER PUBLISHING, INC., Box 5486, Orange CA 92613-5486. (714)771-5155. FAX: (714)532-0180. Editor-in-Chief: Marilyn M. Martin. Publishes paperback originals and software. Averages 6-20 titles/year; receives 300 submissions annually. 80% of books from first-time authors; 90% of books from unagented writers. Average print order for a writer's first book is 5,000-10,000. Pays 10% royalty on actual amount received; no advance. Publishes book an average of 6 months after acceptance. Simultaneous (if so informed with names of others to whom submissions have been sent) submissions OK. Query for electronic submissions. Reports in 2 months. Book catalog for 8½×11 SAE with 2 first class stamps; ms guidelines for #10 SASE.

Nonfiction: Microcomputer material, educational software, word processing, guidance material, allied health, dictionaries, etc. "Textbooks should provide core upon which class curriculum can be based: textbook, workbook or kit with 'hands-on' activities and exercises, and teacher's guide. Should incorporate modern and effective teaching techniques. Should lead to a job objective. We also publish support materials for existing courses and are open to unique, marketable ideas with schools in mind. Reading level should be controlled appropriately—usually 8th-9th grade equivalent for vocational school and community college level courses. Any sign of sexism or racism will disqualify the work. No career awareness masquerading as career training." Submit outline/synopsis, 2 sample chapters and table of contents or complete ms. Reviews artwork/photos as part of ms package. If material is to be returned, enclose SAE and return postage.

Recent Nonfiction Title: *Desktop Publishing: PFS First Publisher*, by Richard C. Bonen, Ed. D.,.and Darla S. Babcock.

Tips: "Authors should be aware of vocational/career areas with inadequate or no training textbooks and submit ideas and samples to fill the gap. Trends in book publishing that freelance writers should be aware of include education—especially for microcomputers."

*CAROL PUBLISHING, 600 Madison Ave., New York NY 10022. (212)486-2200. Imprints include: Lyle Stuart, Birch Lane Press, Citadel Press, University Books. Publisher: Steven Schragis. Firm publishes hardcover originals, and trade paperback originals and reprints. Firm averages 100 titles/year. Receives 1,000 submissions/year. 15% of books from first-time authors; 50% from unagented writers. Subsidy publishes 5% of books. Pays 10-15% royalty on retail price. As little as $1,000, as much as $250,000 advance. Publishes book an average of 1 year after acceptance. Simultaneous submissions OK. Reports in 2 months. Free book catalog.

Nonfiction: Biography, how-to, humor, illustrated book and self-help. Subjects include Americana, animals, art/architecture, business and economics, child guidance/parenting, computers and electronics, cooking, foods and nutrition, ethnic, gay/lesbian, health/medicine, history, hobbies, money/finance, music/dance, nature/environment, philosophy, psychology, recreation, regional, science, sports, travel and women's issues/studies. Submit outline/synopsis and sample chapters.

Recent Nonfiction Title: *A Woman Named Jackie*, by C. David Heymann.

Fiction: Adventure, confession, fantasy, gay/lesbian, horror, humor, literary, mystery, science fiction and short story collections. Submit outline/synopsis and sample chapters.

Recent Fiction Title: *Earthly Remains*, by Peter Hernon.

CAROLRHODA BOOKS, INC., 241 1st Ave. N., Minneapolis MN 55401. (612)332-3344. Submissions Editor: Rebecca Poole. Publishes hardcover originals. Averages 25-35 titles/year. Receives 1,500 submissions/year. 15% of books from first-time authors; 95% of books from unagented writers. Pays 4-6% royalty on wholesale price, makes outright purchase, or negotiates cents per printed copy. Publishes book an average of 18 months after acceptance. Simultaneous submissions OK. Reports in 3 months. Book catalog and ms guidelines for 9×12 SASE.

Nonfiction: Publishes only children's books. Subjects include biography, animals, art, history, music and nature. Needs "biographies in story form on truly creative individuals—25 manuscript pages in length." Send full ms. Reviews artwork/photos as part of ms package.

Recent Nonfiction Title: *Arctic Explorer: The Story of Matthew Henson*, by Jeri Ferris.

Fiction: Children's historical. No anthropomorphized animal stories. Submit complete ms.

Recent Fiction Title: *The Stingy Baker*, retold by Janet Greeson/illustrated by David LaRochelle.

Tips: "Our audience consists of children ages four to eleven. We publish very few picture books. Nonfiction science topics, particularly nature, do well for us, as do biographies, photo essays, and easy readers. We prefer manuscripts that can fit into one of our series. Spend time developing your idea in a unique way or from a unique angle; avoid trite, hackneyed plots and ideas."

CARROLL & GRAF PUBLISHERS, INC., 260 5th Ave., New York NY 10001. (212)889-8772. Contact: Kent Carroll. Publishes hardcover, trade and mass market paperback originals, and trade and mass market paperback reprints. Averages 125 titles/year; receives 1,000 submissions annually. 10% of books from first-time authors; 10% of books from unagented writers. Pays 6-15% royalty on retail price. Publishes book an average of 9 months after acceptance. Reports in 3 weeks on queries; 1 month on mss. Book catalog for 6×9 SASE.

Nonfiction: Biography, history, psychology, current affairs. Query. Reviews artwork/photos as part of ms package.

Recent Nonfiction Title: *Personal Fouls*, by Peter Golenbock.

Fiction: Literary, erotica, mainstream, mystery and·suspense. Query with SASE.

CARSTENS PUBLICATIONS, INC., Hobby Book Division, Box 700, Newton NJ 07860. (201)383-3355. Publisher: Harold H. Carstens. Publishes paperback originals. Averages 8 titles/year. 100% of books from unagented writers. Pays 10% royalty on retail price; offers average advance. Publishes book an average of 1 year after acceptance. Query for electronic submissions. Book catalog for SASE.

Nonfiction: Model railroading, toy trains, model aviation, railroads and model hobbies. "We have scheduled or planned titles on several railroads as well as model railroad and model airplane books. Authors must know their field intimately since our readers are active modelers. Our railroad books presently are primarily photographic essays on specific railroads. Writers cannot write about somebody else's hobby, with authority. If they do, we can't use them." Query. Reviews artwork/photos as part of ms package.

Tips: "No fiction. We need lots of good b&w photos. Material must be in model, hobby, railroad transportation field only."

CASSANDRA PRESS, P.O. Box 868, San Rafael CA 94915. (415)382-8507. President: Gurudas. Estab. 1985. Publishes trade paperback originals. Averages 6 titles/year. Receives 200 submissions/year. 50% of books from first-time authors; 50% from unagented writers. About 10% agented. Pays 6-8% maximum royalty on retail price. Advance rarely offered, but to $4,000. Publishes book an average of 1 year after acceptance. Simultaneous submissions OK. Reports in 3 weeks on queries; 2 months on mss. Free book catalog and manuscript guidelines.

Nonfiction: New Age, cookbook, how-to, self-help. Subjects include cooking, foods and nutrition, health/medicine (holistic health), philosophy, psychology, religion (New Age) and metaphysical. "We like to do around six titles a year in the general New Age, metaphysical and holistic health fields so we continue to look for good material. No children's books." Submit outline/synopsis and sample chapters or complete ms. Reviews artwork/photos as part of ms package.

Recent Nonfiction Title: *Spiritual Wisdom of the Native Americans*, by John Heinerman, Ph.D.

Tips: Not accepting fiction or children's book submissions.

CASSELL PUBLICATIONS, Cassell Communications Inc., P.O. Box 9844, Ft. Lauderdale FL 33310. (305)485-0795. Executive Editor: Dana K. Cassell. Estab. 1982. Firm publishes trade paperback originals. Publishes 8 titles/year; receives 300 submissions/year. 50% from first-time authors; 100% from unagented writers. Pays 10% royalty on retail price. Pays $500 average advance. Publishes book an average of 6 months after acceptance. Simultaneous submissions OK. Query for electronic submissions. Reports in 1 month on queries; 2 months on mss. Book catalog for #10 SAE with 2 first class stamps. Ms guidelines for #10 SASE.

Nonfiction: How-to, reference. Subjects include small business, freelance writing, publishing. Wants books covering writing, advertising, promotion, marketing and how-to treatments for freelance writers, professionals and independent retailers and services businesses. Query or submit outline/synopsis and sample chapters. Reviews artwork/photos as part of ms package.

Recent Nonfiction Title: *Got A Minute? 101 Marketing Tips for Writers.*

CATHOLIC UNIVERSITY OF AMERICA PRESS, 620 Michigan Ave, NE, Washington DC 20064. (202)319-5052. Director: Dr. David J. McGonagle. Marketing Manager: Miryam B. Hirsch. Averages 15-20 titles/year; receives 100 submissions annually. 50% of books from first-time authors; 100% of books from unagented writers. Average print order for a writer's first book is 1,000. Pays variable royalty on net receipts. Publishes book an average of 1 year after acceptance. Query for electronic submissions. Reports in 2 months. Book catalog for #10 SASE.

Nonfiction: Publishes history, biography, languages and literature, philosophy, religion, church-state relations, political theory and social sciences. No unrevised doctoral dissertations. Length: 200,000-500,000 words. Query with sample chapter plus outline of entire work, along with curriculum vitae and list of previous publications. Reviews artwork/photos.

Recent Nonfiction Title: *The Italian Refuge: Rescue of Jews During the Holocaust.*

Tips: Freelancer has best chance of selling us "scholarly monographs and works suitable for adoption as supplementary reading material in courses."

‡CATO INSTITUTE, 224 2nd St. SE, Washington DC 20003. (202)546-0200. Executive Vice President: David Boaz. Estab. 1977. Publishes hardcover originals, trade paperback originals and reprints. Averages 12 titles/year. Receives 50 submissions/year. 25% of books from first-time authors; 90% from unagented writers. Buys mss by outright purchase for $1,000-10,000. Publishes book an average of 9 months after acceptance. Simultaneous submissions OK. Reports in 3 weeks on queries; 3 months on mss. Book catalog free on request.

Nonfiction: Public policy. Subjects include business and economics, education, government/politics, health/medicine, military/war, money/finance, sociology. "We want books on public policy issues from a free-market or libertarian perspective." Query.

Recent Nonfiction Title: *The Excluded Americans: Homelessness and Housing Policy*, by William Tucker.

THE CAXTON PRINTERS, LTD., 312 Main St., Caldwell ID 83605. (208)459-7421. Vice President: Gordon Gipson. Estab. 1895. Publishes hardcover and trade paperback originals. Averages 6-10 titles/year; receives 250 submissions annually. 50% of books from first-time authors; 60% of books from unagented writers. Audience includes Westerners, students, historians and researchers. Pays royalty; advance is $500-2,000. Publishes book an average of 18 months after acceptance. Simultaneous submissions OK. Reports in 2 weeks on queries; 2 months on mss. Book catalog for 9 × 12 SASE.

Nonfiction: Coffee table, Americana and Western Americana. "We need good Western Americana, especially the Northwest, preferably copiously illustrated with unpublished photos." Query. Reviews artwork/photos as part of ms package.
Recent Nonfiction Title: *Tiger on the Road: A Biography of Vardis Fisher*, by Woodward.

‡*CAY-BEL PUBLISHING COMPANY, Thompson-Lyford Bldg., 2nd Fl., 45 Center St., Brewer ME 04412. (207)989-3820. Editor-in-Chief: John E. Cayford. Estab. 1975. Imprints include C&H Publishing Co. Publishes hardcover and trade paperback originals, and reprints. Averages 8 titles/year; receives 350 submissions annually. 50% of books from first-time authors; 100% of books from unagented writers. Average print order for a writer's first book is 2,000-5,000. Subsidy publishes 2% of books when authors "want us to put their manuscript in a book form, to typeset it and print it, but want to handle their own sales." Pays 10-15% royalty on retail price. Publishes book an average of 6-8 months after acceptance. Simultaneous submissions OK. Reports in 1 month on queries; 2 months on mss. Book catalog and ms guidelines for 6½ × 9½ SAE and 2 first class stamps.
Nonfiction: Biography, cookbook, reference and maritime. Subjects include Americana, cooking and foods, history, vital records and genealogy. "Our book schedule is well filled for the next year, but we will give very careful consideration to any book about a Maine personage or to a Maine history." No poetry or pornography. Query. Reviews artwork/photos.
Recent Nonfiction Title: *Searsport Sea Captains*, by Black.

CCC PUBLICATIONS, 20306 Tau Place, Chatsworth CA 91311. (818)407-1661. Contact: Editorial Dept. Estab. 1983. Publishes trade paperback originals and mass market paperback originals. Averages 10-15 titles/year; receives 400-600 mss/year. 50% of books from first-time authors; 50% of books from unagented writers. Pays 5-10% royalty on wholesale price. Publishes book an average of 1 year after acceptance. Simultaneous submissions OK. Reports in 1 month on queries; 3 months on mss.
Nonfiction: Humorous how-to/self-help. "We are looking for *original*, *clever* and *current* humor that is not too limited in audience appeal or that will have a limited shelf life. All of our titles are as marketable 5 years from now as they are today. No rip-offs of previously published books, or too special interest mss." For best results: Query first with SASE; will review complete ms only. Reviews artwork/photos as part of ms package.
Recent Nonfiction Title: *How To Talk Your Way Out of a Traffic Ticket*, by Officer David W. Kelley.
Tips: "Humor—we specialize in the subject and have a good reputation with retailers and wholesalers for publishing super-impulse titles. SASE is a must!"

CENTER FOR APPLIED LINGUISTICS, 1118 22nd St. NW, Washington DC 20007. (202)429-9292. Publications Coordinator: Ms. Whitney Stewart. Estab. 1965. Publishes trade paperback originals. Firm averages 4 titles/year. 100% of books from unagented writers. Pays $500 maximum for outright purchase. Publishes book an average of 6 months after acceptance. Query for electronic submissions. Reports in 1 month.
Nonfiction: Textbook on language in education. Subjects include child language, literacy, computers and language, linguistics, teaching foreign languages, learning English-as-a-foreign language. "We want texts on teaching foreign languages; texts on special education; texts on bilingual education; texts on child language acquisition. NO FOREIGN LANGUAGE TEXTBOOKS. We want only theoretical information and practical methodology on language instruction." Query.
Recent Nonfiction Title: *Pigeon-birds and Rhyming Words: The Parental Role in Language Learning*, by Naomi S. Baron.
Tips: "We need manuscripts of 100-200 pages—texts on classroom theory and practice—written for the teacher, the parent, or the linguistics student. We want theory but with an emphasis on practical application."

‡CENTER FOR THANATOLOGY RESEARCH, 391 Atlantic Ave., Brooklyn NY 11217. (718)858-3026. Contact: R. Halpern. Estab. 1980. Publishes trade paperback originals. Averages 16 titles/year. Receives 10 submissions/year. 10% of books from first-time authors; 100% from unagented writers. Pays 10% royalty on wholesale price. Publishes book 1 year after acceptance. Simultaneous submissions OK. Query for electronic submissions. Reports in 1 month. Books catalog and ms guidelines free on request.
Nonfiction: Reference, self-help. Subjects include anthropology/archaelogy, education, health/medicine, philosophy, psychology, religion, sociology. Manuscript must deal with aging, dying, death or bereavement. Query.
Recent Nonfiction Title: *Gravestones of Early New England and The Men Who Made Them*, By Harriette M. Forbes.
Tips: "We are booked up now for all of 1990, but will be accepting freelance submissions in 1991."

‡CHARLESBRIDGE PUBLISHING, 85 Main St., Watertown MA 02172. (617)926-0329. Vice President: Elena Dworkin Wright. Estab. 1979. Publishes school programs and hardcover and trade paperback originals. Averages 400 titles/year. Receives 100 submissions/year. 0% of books from first-time authors; 100% from unagented writers. Buys by outright purchase. Publishes books on average of 1 year after acceptance. Query

for electronic submissions. Reports in 1 month on mss. Book catalog free on request by teacher or school; available to schools and specialty stores at museums, science centers, etc.

Nonfiction: Juvenile. "We look for books that teach about the world from a perspective that is relevant to a young child and books that use rhythm, rhyme, and repetition to entrance young children who are beginning readers." Submit outline/synopsis and sample chapter or complete ms. Reviews artwork/photos as part of ms package.

Recent Nonfiction Title: *The Yucky Reptile Book*, by Jerry Pallotta (juvenile).

Fiction: Juvenile and early readers. "We are looking for books that include good character development and plot that involves delightfully unexpected, but foreshadowed, endings. No fantasy involving witches, devils, magic. No violence, brand name products. Other types of fantasy OK, such as special powers." Submit complete ms.

*CHATHAM PRESS, Box A, Old Greenwich CT 06870. FAX: (203)622-6688. Publishes hardcover and paperback originals, reprints and anthologies relating to New England and the Atlantic coastline. Averages 15 titles/year; receives 50 submissions annually. 30% of books from first-time authors; 75% of books from unagented writers. Subsidy publishes mainly poetry or ecological topics (nonauthor) 10% of books. "Standard book contract does not always apply if the book is heavily illustrated. Average advance is low." Publishes book an average of 6 months after acceptance. Query for electronic submissions. Reports in 2 weeks. Book catalog and ms guidelines for 6×9 SAE with 10 first class stamps.

Nonfiction: Publishes mostly "regional history and natural history, involving mainly Northeast seaboard to the Carolinas, mostly illustrated, with emphasis on conservation and outdoor recreation." Accepts nonfiction translations from French and German. Query with outline and 3 sample chapters. Reviews artwork/photos as part of ms package.

Recent Nonfiction Title: *Beachcomber's Companion*, by Wesemann.

Recent Poetry Title: *Weapons Against Chaos*, by M. Ewald.

Tips: "Illustrated New England-relevant titles have the best chance of being sold to our firm. We have a slightly greater (15%) skew towards cooking and travel titles."

CHELSEA GREEN, P.O. Box 130, Post Mills VT 05058. (802)333-9073. Editor: Ian Baldwin Jr. Fiction Editor: Michael Moore. Estab. 1984. Publishes hardcover and paperback trade originals. Averages 10 titles/year.

Nonfiction: Biography, nature, politics, travel, art and history. Query only and include SASE.

Recent Nonfiction Title: *Voyage to the Whales*, by Hal Whitehead.

Fiction: Serious contemporary fiction (no genre fiction). Please submit query with SASE.

Recent Fiction Title: *The Eight Corners of the World*, by Gordon Weaver.

‡CHICAGO REVIEW PRESS, 814 N. Franklin, Chicago IL 60610. (312)337-0747. Editorial Director: Amy Teschner. Estab. 1973. Publishes hardcover and trade paperback originals. Averages 15 titles/year; receives 375 submissions annually. 60% of books from first-time authors; 90% of books from unagented writers. Pays 10-15% royalty. Offers average $1,000 advance. Publishes book an average of 1 year after acceptance. Simultaneous submissions OK. Query for electronic submissions. Reports in 2 months on queries; 3 months on mss. Book catalog free for 9×12 SAE and 7 first class stamps.

Nonfiction: Specialty cookbooks, how-to, reference and guidebooks on cooking and foods, recreation, travel, popular science, and regional. Needs regional Chicago material and how-to, travel, popular science, family, cookbooks for the national audience. Also nonfiction project books in arts and sciences for ages 10 and up. Query or submit outline/synopsis and sample chapters. Reviews artwork/photos.

Recent Nonfiction Title: *The Art of Construction: Projects & Principles for Beginning Engineers & Architects*, by Mario Salvadori.

Tips: "The audience we envision for our books is adults and young people 15 and older, educated readers with special interests, do-it-yourselfers, travellers, students."

*CHILD WELFARE LEAGUE OF AMERICA, Suite 310, 440 1st St. NW, Washington DC 20001. (202)638-2952. Director, Publications: Susan Brite. Publishes hardcover and trade paperback originals. Publishes 10-12 titles/year. Receives 60-100 submissions/year. 95% of writers are unagented. 50% of books are nonauthor subsidy published. Pays 0-10% royalty on net domestic sales. Publishes book an average of 1 year after acceptance. Query for electronic submissions. Reports on queries in 2 months; on mss in 3 months. Free book catalog and manuscript guidelines.

Nonfiction: Child welfare. Subjects include child guidance/parenting, sociology. Submit outline/synopsis and sample chapters or complete ms.

Recent Nonfiction Title: *Adoption Agency Directory*, by Julia Posner.

Recent Fiction Title: *Floating*, by Mark Krueger.

Tips: "Our audience is child welfare workers, administrators, agency executives, parents, etc."

CHILTON BOOK CO., Chilton Way, Radnor PA 19089. Editorial Director: Alan F. Turner. Publishes hardcover and trade paperback originals. Publishes 90 titles/year. Pays royalty; average advance. Simultaneous submissions OK. Query for electronic submissions. Reports in 3 weeks.

Nonfiction: Business/economics, crafts, how-to and technical. "We only want to see manuscripts with informational value." Query or submit outline/synopsis and 2-3 sample chapters. Include return postage.

Recent Nonfiction Title: *Your Home Business Can Make Dollars and Sense*, by Jo Frohbieter-Mueller.

CHOSEN BOOKS PUBLISHING CO., LTD., Imprint of Fleming H. Revell Co., 184 Central Ave., Old Tappan NJ 07675. (201)768-8060. FAX: (201)768-2749. Editor: Jane Campbell. Estab. 1971. Publishes hardcover and trade paperback originals. Averages 16 titles/year; receives 600 submissions annually. 15% of books from first-time authors; 99% of books from unagented writers. Pays royalty on retail price. Publishes book an average of 1 year after acceptance. Simultaneous submissions OK. Reports in 2 months. Manuscript guidelines for #10 SASE.

Nonfiction: How-to, self-help, and a very limited number of first-person narratives. "We publish books reflecting the current acts of the Holy Spirit in the world, books with a charismatic Christian orientation." No New Age, poetry, fiction, academic or children's books. Submit synopsis, chapter outline and SASE. No complete mss.

Recent Nonfiction Title: *Love On Its Knees*, by Dick Eastman.

Tips: "In expositional books we look for solid, practical advice for the growing and maturing Christian from authors with professional or personal experience platforms. Narratives must have a strong theme and reader benefits. No conversion accounts or chronicling of life events, please. State the topic or theme of your book clearly in your cover letter."

*THE CHRISTOPHER PUBLISHING HOUSE, 24 Rockland St., Commerce Green, Hanover MA 02339. (617)826-7474. FAX: (617)826-5556. Managing Editor: Nancy Lucas. Estab. 1910. Publishes hardcover and trade paperback originals. Averages 20-30 titles/year; receives 300-400 submissions annually. 30% of books from first-time authors; 100% of books from unagented writers. Subsidy publishes 15% of books. Pays 5-30% royalty on wholesale price; offers no advance. Publishes book an average of 18 months after acceptance. Simultaneous submissions OK. Query for electronic submissions. Reports in 1 month. Book catalog for #10 SAE with 2 first class stamps; ms guidelines for SASE.

Nonfiction: Biography, how-to, reference, self-help, textbook and religious. Subjects include Americana, animals, art, business and economics, cooking and foods (nutrition), health, history, philosophy, politics, psychology, religion, sociology and travel. "We will be glad to review all nonfiction manuscripts, particularly college textbook and religious-oriented." Submit complete ms. Reviews artwork/photos as part of ms package.

Recent Nonfiction Title: *Apostasy Within*, by Fr. Paul Trinchard.

Poetry: "We will review all forms of poetry." Submit complete ms.

Recent Poetry Title: *So Many Crossroads*, by Alannah Van Boven.

Tips: "Our books are for a general audience, slanted toward college-educated readers. There are specific books targeted toward specific audiences when appropriate."

‡CHRONICLE BOOKS, Chronicle Publishing Co., 275 Fifth St., San Francisco CA 94103. (415)777-7240. Executive Editor: Nion McEvoy. Editor, fiction: Jay Schaefer. Editor, children's: Victoria Rock. Publishes hardcover and trade paperback originals. Averages 90 titles/year; receives 1,200 submissions annually. 10% of books from first-time authors; 15% of books from unagented writers. Pays 5-10% royalty on retail price. Buys by outright purchase for $500-5,000. Publishes book an average of 1½ years after acceptance. Simultaneous submissions OK. Reports in 1 month on queries; 3 months on mss. Book catalog for 11 × 14 SAE with 5 first class stamps.

Nonfiction: Coffee table book, cookbook, and regional California on art, cooking and foods, design, gardening, health and medicine, nature, photography, recreation, and travel. Query or submit outline/synopsis and sample chapters. Reviews artwork/photos with ms. package.

Recent Nonfiction Title: *Penguins*, by Wolfgang Kaehler.

Fiction: Juvenile, picture books. Query or submit outline/synopsis and sample chapters.

Recent Fiction Title: *Lullaby*, by Jane Chelsea Aragon.

CITADEL PRESS, Subsidiary of Carol Publishing Group, 120 Enterprise, Secaucus NJ 07094. FAX: (201)866-8159. Editorial Director: Allan J. Wilson. Estab. 1944. Publishes hardcover originals and paperback reprints. Averages 60-80 titles/year. Receives 800-1,000 submissions annually. 7% of books from first-time authors; 50% of books from unagented writers. Average print order for a writer's first book is 5,000. Pays 10% royalty on hardcover, 5-7% on paperback; offers average $10,000 advance. Publishes book an average of 1 year after acceptance. Simultaneous submissions OK. Reports in 2 months. Book catalog for $1.

Nonfiction and Fiction: Biography, film, psychology, humor and history. Also seeks "off-beat material," but no "poetry, religion, politics." Accepts nonfiction and fiction translations. Query. Submit outline/synopsis and 3 sample chapters. Reviews artwork/photos as part of ms package.

Recent Nonfiction Title: *Boxing Babylon,* by Nigel Collins.
Recent Fiction Title: *The Rain Maiden,* by Jill M. Phillips.
Tips: "We concentrate on biography, popular interest, and film, with limited fiction (no romance, religion, poetry, music)."

‡CITY LIGHTS BOOKS, 261 Columbus Ave., San Francisco CA 94133. (415)362-1901. Editor and Publisher: Lawrence Ferlinghetti. Publishes trade paperback originals and reprints. Averages 15 titles/year. Receives 500 submissions/year. 25% of books from first-time authors; 75% from unagented writers. Pays 6-15% royalty on retail price. Offers $1,000 average advance. Publishes book an average of 1 year after acceptance. Simultaneous submissions OK. Reports in 1 month on queries; 2 months on mss. Free book catalog and manuscript guidelines.
Nonfiction: Subjects include anthropology/archaeology, gay/lesbian, philosophy, translation, women's issues/studies. Query.
Fiction: Ethnic, gay/lesbian, literary, mainstream/contemporary, plays. Query.

CLARION BOOKS, Houghton Mifflin Company, 215 Park Avenue South, New York NY 10003. Editor and Publisher: Dorothy Briley. Executive Editor: Dinah Stevenson. Publishes hardcover originals. Averages 30-35 titles/year. Pays 5-10% royalty on retail price; $1,000-3,000 advance, depending on whether project is a picture book or a longer work for older children. No multiple submissions. Reports in 2 months. Publishes book an average of 18 months after acceptance. Ms guidelines for #10 SASE.
Nonfiction: Americana, biography, holiday, humor, nature, photo essays and word play. Prefers books for younger children. Reviews artwork/photos as part of ms package. Query.
Recent Nonfiction Title: *Gray Wolf, Red Wolf,* by Dorothy Hinshaw Patent.
Fiction: Adventure, humor, mystery, strong character studies, and suspense. "We would like to see more humorous contemporary stories that young people of 8-12 or 10-14 can identify with readily." Accepts fiction translations. Query on ms of more than 50 pages. Looks for "freshness, enthusiasm — in short, life" (fiction and nonfiction).
Recent Fiction Title: *Come Next Spring,* by Alana White.

*ARTHUR H. CLARK CO. , P.O. Box 14707, Spokane WA 99214. (509)928-9540. Editorial Director: Robert A. Clark. Estab. 1902. Publishes hardcover originals. Averages 8 titles/year; receives 40 submissions annually. 40% of books from first-time authors; 100% of books from unagented writers. Subsidy publishes 15% of books based on whether they are "high-risk sales." Subsidy publishes (nonauthor) 5% of books. Pays 10% minimum royalty on wholesale price. Publishes book an average of 9 months after acceptance. Reports in 1 week on queries; 6 months on mss. Book catalog for 6×9 SASE.
Nonfiction: Biography, reference and historical nonfiction. Subjects include Americana and history. "We're looking for documentary source material in Western American history." Query or submit outline/synopsis with SASE. Looks for "content, form, style." Reviews artwork/photos as part of ms package.
Recent Nonfiction Title: *The Californios vs Jedediah Smith 1826-1827,* by David Weber.
Tips: "Western Americana (nonfiction) has the best chance of being sold to our firm."

CLARKSON POTTER, 201 E. 50th St., New York NY 10022. (212)572-6160. FAX: (212)572-6192. Imprint of Crown Publishers. Editor: Carol Southern, associate publisher, Crown. Publishes hardcover and trade paperback originals. Averages 55 titles/year; receives 1,500 submissions annually. 18% of books from first-time authors, but many of these first-time authors are well-known and have had media coverage. Pays 10% royalty on hardcover; 5-7½% on paperback; 5-7% on illustrated hardcover, varying escalations; advance depends on type of book and reputation or experience of author. No unagented mss can be considered. Reports in 1 month. Book catalog for 7×10 SASE.
Nonfiction: Publishes art, autobiography, biography, cooking and foods, design, how-to, humor, juvenile, nature, photography, self-help, style and annotated literature. Accepts nonfiction translations. "Manuscripts must be cleanly typed on 8½×11 nonerasable bond; double-spaced. *Chicago Manual of Style* is preferred." Query or submit outline/synopsis and sample chapters. Reviews artwork/photos as part of ms package.
Recent Nonfiction Title: *Jackson Pollock,* by Steven Naifeh and Gregory White Smith.
Fiction: Will consider "quality fiction."
Recent Fiction Title: *Doctors and Women,* by Susan Cheever.

*CLEANING CONSULTANT SERVICES, INC., 1512 Western Ave., P.O. Box 1273, Seattle WA 98101. (206)682-9748. President: William R. Griffin. Publishes trade paperback originals and reprints. Averages 4-6 titles/year; receives 15 submissions annually. 75% of books from first-time authors; 100% of books from unagented writers. Subsidy publishes 5% of books. "If they (authors) won't sell it and won't accept royalty contract, we offer our publishing services and often sell the book along with our books." Pays 5-15% royalty on retail price or outright purchase, $100-2,500, depending on negotiated agreement. Publishes book an average of 6-12 months after acceptance. Reports in 6 weeks on queries; 3 months on mss. Free book catalog; ms guidelines for SASE.

Nonfiction: How-to, illustrated book, reference, self-help, technical, textbook and directories. Subjects include business, health, and cleaning and maintenance. Needs books on anything related to cleaning, maintenance, self-employment or entrepreneurship. Query or submit outline/synopsis and sample chapters or complete ms. Reviews artwork/photos as part of ms package.

Recent Nonfiction Title: *Food Service, Health, Sanitation and Safety*, by William R. Griffin and Bruce Jackson.

Tips: "Our audience includes those involved in cleaning and maintenance service trades, opportunity seekers, schools, property managers, libraries—anyone who needs information on cleaning and maintenance. How-to and self-employment guides are doing well for us in today's market. We are now seeking books on fire damage restoration and also technical articles for *Cleaning Business Magazine*, a quarterly."

CLEIS PRESS, P.O. Box 14684, San Francisco CA 94114. Co-editor, Acquisitions Coordinator: Frederique Delacoste. Publishes trade paperback originals and reprints. Publishes 4 titles/year. 75% of books are from first-time authors; 90% from unagented writers. Royalties vary on retail price. Publishes book an average of 1 year after acceptance. Simultaneous submissions OK "only if accompanied by an original letter stating where and when ms was sent." Query for electronic submissions. Reports in 1 month. Books catalog for #10 SAE and 2 first class stamps.

Nonfiction: Human rights, feminist. Subjects include gay/lesbian, government/politics, sociology (of women), women's issues/studies. "We are interested in books that: a) will sell in feminist and progressive bookstores and b) will sell in Europe (translation rights). We are interested in books by and about women in Latin America; on lesbian and gay rights; and other feminist topics which have not already been widely documented. We do not want religious/spiritual tracts; we are not interested in books on topics which have been documented over and over, unless the author is approaching the topic from a new viewpoint." Query or submit outline/synopsis or sample chapters or complete ms.

Recent Nonfiction Title: *AIDS: The Women*, edited by Ines Rieder and Patricia Ruppelt.

Fiction: Feminist, gay/lesbian, literary. "We are looking for high quality novels by women. We are especially interested in translations of Latin American women's fiction. No romances!" Submit complete ms.

Recent Fiction Title: *Night Train to Mother*, by Ronit Lentin (novel).

Tips: "An anthology project representing the work of a very diverse group of women . . . an anthology on a very hot, very unique, risk-taking theme. These books sell well for us; they're our trademark. If I were trying to market a book today, I would become very familiar with the presses serving my market. More than reading publishers' catalogs, I think author should spend time in a bookstore whose clientele closely resembles their intended audience; be absolutely aware of her audience; have researched potential market; present fresh new ways of looking at her topic; avoid 'PR' language in query letter."

*CLEVELAND STATE UNIVERSITY POETRY CENTER, R.T. 1815, Cleveland State University, Cleveland OH 44115. (216)687-3986. Editor: Leonard M. Trawick. Estab. 1962. Publishes trade paperback and hardcover originals. Averages 5 titles/year; receives 400 queries, 700 mss annually. 60% of books from first-time authors; 100% of books from unagented writers. 30% of titles subsidized by CSU, 30% by government subsidy. CSU poetry series pays one-time, lump-sum royalty of $200-400 plus 50 copies; Cleveland Poetry Series (Ohio poets only) pays 100 copies. $1,000 prize for best manuscript each year. No advance. Publishes book an average of 1 year after acceptance. Simultaneous submissions OK. Reports in 2 weeks on queries; 6 months on mss. Book catalog for 6×9 SAE with 2 first class stamps; ms guidelines for SASE.

Poetry: No light verse, "inspirational," or greeting card verse. ("This does not mean that we do not consider poetry with humor or philosophical/religious import.") Query—ask for guidelines. Submit only December-February. Reviews artwork/photos if applicable (i.e., concrete poetry).

Recent Poetry Title: *Another Body*, by Stephen Tapscott.

Tips: "Our books are for serious readers of poetry, i.e. poets, critics, academics, students, people who read *Poetry, Field, American Poetry Review, Antaeus*, etc." Trends include "movement from 'confessional' poetry; greater attention to form and craftsmanship. Try to project an interesting, coherent personality; link poems so as to make coherent unity, not just a miscellaneous collection." Especially needs "poems with *mystery*, i.e., poems that reflect profound thought, but do not tell all—suggestive, tantalizing, enticing."

CLIFFHANGER PRESS, P.O. Box 29527, Oakland CA 94604-9527. (415)763-3510. Editor: Nancy Chirich. Estab. 1986. Publishes hardcover originals. Averages 3 titles/year. Pays 10% royalty on retail price. Publishes book an average of 1 year after acceptance. Simultaneous submissions OK. Reports in 2 weeks on 2-3 sample chapters and one-page synopsis. Do not send full ms unless requested. Book catalog for #10 SASE.

Fiction: Mystery and suspense. "Manuscripts should be about 75,000 words, heavy on American regional or foreign atmosphere. No cynical, hardboiled detectives or spies." Submit synopsis/outline and 2-3 sample chapters. "No returns without SASE."

Recent Fiction Title: *Three to Get Ready*, by Hans Ostrom.

Tips: "Mystery/suspense is our specialty. Have believable characters, a strong, uncomplicated story and heavy regional or foreign atmosphere. No justified right margins on manuscripts submitted. They're very hard to read at length. Please send SASE (#10) for writer's guidelines before submitting *anything*."

CLIFFS NOTES, INC., P.O. Box 80728, Lincoln NE 68501. (402)423-5050. General Editor: Michele Spence. Notes Editor: Gary Carey. Estab. 1958. Publishes trade paperback originals. Averages 20 titles/year. 100% of books from unagented writers. Pays royalty on wholesale price. Buys some mss outright; "full payment on acceptance of ms." Publishes book an average of 1 year after acceptance. Reports in 1 month. "We provide specific guidelines when a project is assigned."
Nonfiction: Self-help and textbook. "We publish self-help study aids directed to junior high through graduate school audience. Publications include *Cliffs Notes*, *Cliffs Test Preparation Guides*, *Cliffs Teaching Portfolios*, and other study guides. Most authors are experienced teachers, usually with advanced degrees. Some books also appeal to a general lay audience. Among these are those in a new series, *Bluffer's Guides*, published under our Centennial Press imprint. The books are both informative and humorous and cover a wide range of subject areas." Query.
Recent Nonfiction Title: *Bluff Your Way in Gourmet Cooking*, by Joseph T. Straub.

‡**COLLECTOR BOOKS**, Division of Schroeder Publishing Co., Inc., 5801 Kentucky Dam Rd., P.O. Box 3009, Paducah KY 42001. FAX: (502)898-8890. Editor: Steve Quertermous. Estab. 1974. Publishes hardcover and paperback originals. Publishes 35 titles/year. 50% of books from first-time authors; 100% of books from unagented writers. Average print order for a writer's first book is 5,000-10,000. Pays 5% royalty on retail; no advance. Publishes book an average of 8 months after acceptance. Reports in 1 month. Book catalog for 9×12 SAE and 4 first class stamps. Ms guidelines for #10 SASE.
Nonfiction: "We only publish books on antiques and collectibles. We require our authors to be very knowledgeable in their respective fields and have access to a large representative sampling of the particular subject concerned." Query. Accepts outline and 2-3 sample chapters. Reviews artwork/photos as part of ms package.
Recent Nonfiction Title: *Schroeder's Antiques Price Guide*.
Tips: Common mistakes writers make include "making phone contact instead of written contact and assuming an accurate market evaluation."

THE COLLEGE BOARD, Imprint of College Entrance Examination Board, 45 Columbus Ave., New York NY 10023-6917. (212)713-8000. Associate Director of Publications: Carolyn Trager. Publishes trade paperback originals. Firm publishes 30 titles/year; imprint publishes 12 titles/year. Receives 20-30 submissions/year. 25% of books from first-time authors; 50% from unagented writers. Pays royalty on retail price of books sold through bookstores. Offers advance based on anticipated first year's earnings. Publishes book an average of 9 months after acceptance. Reports in 2 weeks on queries; 1 month on ms. Book catalog free on request.
Nonfiction: How-to, reference, self-help. Subjects include child guidance/parenting, education, language/literature, science. "We want books to help students make a successful transition from high school to college." Query or send outline/synopsis and sample chapters. Reviews artwork/photos as part of ms package.
Recent Nonfiction Title: *Choosing a College: The Students Step-by-Step Decision-Making Workbook*, by Gordon Porter Miller.
Tips: "Our audience consists of college-bound high school students, beginning college students and/or their parents."

*****COLLEGE PRESS PUBLISHING CO., INC.**, 205 N. Main, P.O. Box 1132, Joplin MO 64802. (417)623-6280. Contact: Steven F. Jennings. Estab. 1959. Publishes hardcover and trade paperback originals and reprints. Publishes 25 titles/year. Receives 150 submissions/year. 25% of books are from first-time authors; 100% from unagented writers. Subsidy publishes 5% of books. Subsidy considered "if we really want to publish a book, but don't have room in schedule at this time or funds available." Pays 10% royalty on net receipts. Publishes book an average of 1 year after acceptance. Simultaneous submissions OK. Reports on queries in 1 month; on ms in 3 months. Free book catalog.
Nonfiction: Bible commentaries, topical Bible studies. (Christian church, Church of Christ.) Query.
Recent Nonfiction Title: *Beyond a Reasonable Doubt*, by Herbert Casteel.
Fiction: Religious. Query.
Tips: "Topical Bible study books have the best chance of being sold to our firm. Our audience consists of Christians interested in reading and studying Bible-based material."

COMPUTE! BOOKS, A Division of Chilton Book Company, 324 W. Wendover Ave., Greensboro NC 27408. (919)275-9809. Editor-in-Chief: Stephen Levy. Estab. 1979. Publishes trade paperback originals and software. Averages 20 titles/year. Pays royalties based on gross wholesale receipts. Simultaneous submissions OK if noted in cover letter. Publishes ms an average of 8 months after acceptance. Query for electronic submissions. Reports in 3 months.
Nonfiction: Books on computers. "We publish books for the home and business computer user and are always looking for game books. Writers should think of their audience as intelligent people who want their computers to improve their lives and the lives of their loved ones. We are also interested in entertainment programs and programming; home applications; educational programs; and books that teach programming at different levels — if a family or individual would find them useful and interesting." Submit outline and synopsis with sample chapters. "Writers who are known to us through articles in *COMPUTE! Magazine* and

COMPUTE!'s Gazette already have our trust—we know they can come through with the right material—but we have often bought from writers we did not know, and from writers who had never published anything before."

Recent Nonfiction Title: *COMPUTE! Guide to Nintendo Game.*

Tips: "If I were trying to create a marketable computer book today, I would become intimately familiar with one computer, then define a specific area to explain to less-familiar computer users, and write a clear, concise outline of the book I meant to write, along with a sample chapter from the working section of the book (not the introduction). Then send that proposal to a publisher whose books you believe are excellent and who targets the same audience you are aiming at. Once the proposal was in the mail, I'd forget about it. Keep learning more about the computer and develop another book proposal. *Don't write a book without a go-ahead from a publisher.* The chances are too great that you will spend 6 months writing a book, only to discover that there are nine on the market with the same concept by the time your manuscript is ready to send out."

COMPUTER SCIENCE PRESS, INC., Imprint of W.H. Freeman and Company. 41 Madison Ave., New York NY 10010. (212)576-9400. FAX: (212)689-2383. Publisher: William B. Bruener. Estab. 1974. Publishes hardcover and paperback originals and software. Averages 10 titles/year. 25% of books from first-time authors; 98% of books from unagented writers. All authors are recognized subject area experts. Pays royalty on net price. Publishes book an average of 6-9 months after acceptance. Reports ASAP.

Nonfiction: "Technical books in all aspects of computer science, computer engineering, computer chess, electrical engineering, and telecommunications. Both text and reference books. Will also consider public appeal 'trade' books in computer science, manuscripts and diskettes. Query or submit complete ms. Requires "3 copies of manuscripts." Looks for "technical accuracy of the material and the reason this approach is being taken. We would also like a covering letter stating what the author sees as the competition for this work and why this work is superior."

Recent Nonfiction Title: *Principles of Database and Knowledge Base Systems Vol. I & II*, by Ullman.

‡CONARI PRESS, 713 Euclid Ave., Berkeley CA 94708. (415)527-9915. Editor: Mary Jane Ryan. Publishes hardcover and trade paperback originals. Firm averages 4-5 titles/year. Receives 100 submissions/year. 50% of books from first-time authors. 50% from unagented writers. Pays 8-12% royalty on list price. Offers $1,500 average advance. Publishes book an average of 9 months after acceptance. Simultaneous submissions OK. Query for electronic submissions. Reports in 1 month. Free book catalog. Manuscript guidelines for #10 SASE.

Nonfiction: Self-help, consumer guides, current affairs. Subjects include business, restaurant guides, nature/environment, psychology, recreation, regional and women's issues/studies. We are looking for any well thought out and written nonfiction in areas that haven't been over done. No travel books or cookbooks. Submit outline/synopsis and sample chapters or complete ms. Reviews artwork/photos as part of ms package.

Recent Nonfiction Title: *The Civil War on Consumer Rights*, by Laurence Drivon (consumer/current affairs).

Tips: "Writers should send us well targeted, specific and focused manuscripts."

‡CONCORDIA PUBLISHING HOUSE, 3558 South Jefferson Ave., St. Louis MO 63118. (314)664-7000. Contact: Product Development. Publishes hardcover and trade paperback originals. Averages 32 titles/year. Receives 1,000 submissions/year. 10% of books from first-time authors; 100% from unagented writers. Pays royalty or buys by outright purchase. Publishes book an average of 1 year after acceptance. Simultaneous submissions OK. Query for electronic submissions. Reports in 1 month on queries; 2 months on mss. Manuscript guidelines for #10 SASE.

Nonfiction: Juvenile. Subjects include child guidance/parenting (in Christian context), religion. "We publish Protestant, inspirational, theological, family and juveniles. All manuscripts must conform to the doctrinal tenents of The Lutheran Church—Missouri Synod. Authors should query before submitting a manuscript." Query.

Recent Nonfiction Title: *Renewing the Family Spirit*, by David J. Ludwig (family relationships).

Fiction: Juvenile. "We will consider preteen and children's fiction and picture books. All books must contain Christian content. No adult Christian fiction." Query.

Recent Fiction Title: *What Happened When Grandma Died*, by Peggy Barker (picture book).

THE CONSULTANT PRESS, Subsidiary of The Photographic Arts Center, Ltd., 163 Amsterdam Ave., #201, New York NY 10023. FAX: (212)873-7065. Publisher: Bob Persky. Estab. 1980. Publishes hardcover and trade paperback originals. Firm averages 7 titles/year; Receives 10 submissions/year. 50% of books from first-time authors. 100% from unagented writers. Buys mss outright for $1,000-2,500. Publishes book an average of 6 months after acceptance. Simultaneous submissions OK. Reports in 2 weeks on queries; 1 month on mss. Free book catalog.

Nonfiction: Subjects include the business of and art, photography. "We want books filling needs of artists, photographers and galleries—business oriented. No books of pictures or books on how to take pictures or paint pictures."

Recent Nonfiction Title: *How To Publish Your Poster and Cards*, by Harold Davis.
Tips: "Artists, photographers, galleries, museums, curators and art consultants are our audience."

CONTEMPORARY BOOKS, INC., 180 N. Michigan Ave., Chicago IL 60601. (312)782-9182. Subsidiaries include Congdon & Weed. Editorial Director: Nancy J. Crossman. Publishes hardcover originals and trade paperback originals and reprints. Averages 85 titles/year; receives 2,500 submissions annually. 25% of books from first-time authors; 25% of books from unagented writers. Pays 6-15% royalty on retail price. Publishes book an average of 10 months after acceptance. Query for electronic submissions. Simultaneous and photocopied submissions OK. Reports in 3 weeks. Book catalog and ms guidelines for 9 × 12 SAE and 6 first class stamps.
Nonfiction: Biography, cookbook, how-to, humor, reference and self-help. Subjects include business, finance, cooking, health, fitness, psychology, sports, real estate, nutrition, popular culture and women's studies. Submit outline/synopsis and sample chapters. Reviews artwork/photos as part of ms package.
Recent Nonfiction Title: *Arnold, An Unauthorized Biography*, by Wendy Leigh.
Tips: "The New Age market has become saturated. Also, competition in cookbooks mean we need professional, accomplished cooks instead of amateurs to write them."

COPYRIGHT INFORMATION SERVICES, P.O. Box 1460-A, Friday Harbor WA 98250-1460. (206)378-5128. Subsidiary of Harbor View Publications Group, Inc. President: Jerome K. Miller. Publishes hardcover originals. Averages 6-8 titles/year. 50% of books from first-time authors; 100% from unagented writers. Publishes book an average of 6 months after acceptance. Simultaneous submissions OK. Reports in 6 weeks on queries. Book catalog for #10 SAE with 2 first class stamps.
Nonfiction: "Almost any topic relating to the copyright law." Query. All unsolicited mss are returned unopened.
Recent Nonfiction Title: *A Copyright Primer For Educational and Industrial Media Producers*, by E.R. Sinofsky.

CORNELL MARITIME PRESS, INC., P.O. Box 456, Centreville MD 21617. Estab. 1938. Imprint is Tidewater Publishers. Publishes hardcover originals and quality paperbacks for professional mariners and yachtsmen. Averages 15-18 titles/year; receives 150 submissions annually. 41% of books from first-time authors; 99% of books from unagented writers. Payment is negotiable but royalties do not exceed 10% for first 5,000 copies, 12½% for second 5,000 copies, 15% on all additional. Royalties for original paperbacks and regional titles are invariably lower. Revised editions revert to original royalty schedule. Publishes book an average of 10 months after acceptance. Query for electronic submissions. Send queries first, accompanied by writing samples and outlines of book ideas. Reports in 1 month. Free book catalog and ms guidelines.
Nonfiction: Marine subjects (highly technical); manuals; and how-to books on maritime subjects. Tidewater imprint publishes books on regional history, folklore and wildlife of the Chesapeake Bay and the Delmarva Peninsula.
Recent Nonfiction Title: *Charter Your Boat for Profit*, by Fred Edwards (Cornell).

COTEAU BOOKS, Imprint of Thunder Creek Publishing Cooperative, Suite 401, 2206 Dewdney Ave., Regina, Saskatchewan S4R 1H3 Canada. (306)777-0170. Subsidiaries include Coteau Books and Caragana Records. Managing Editor: Shelley Sopher. Estab. 1975. Publishes hardcover, trade paperback and mass market paperback originals. Publishes 10 titles/year; receives approximately 500 queries and mss/year. 60% of books from first-time authors; 95% from unagented writers. Pays 10% royalty on retail price or outright purchase of $50-200 for anthology contributors. Publishes book an average of 12-18 months after acceptance. Reports in 1 month on queries; 4 months on ms. Free book catalog.
Nonfiction: Humor, illustrated book, juvenile, reference, desk calendars. Subjects include art/architecture, ethnic, history, language/literature, photography, regional and women's issues/studies. "We publish only Canadian authors; we will consider NO American manuscripts. We are interested in history for our region and books on multicultural themes pertaining to our region." Reviews artwork/photos as part of ms package.
Recent Nonfiction Title: *For Love or Money: Radio in Saskatchewan*, by Wayne Schmalz.
Fiction: Ethnic, experimental, fantasy, feminist, humor, juvenile, literary, mainstream/contemporary, picture books, plays, short story collections. "No popular, mass market sort of stuff. We are a literary press." Submit complete ms. We only publish fiction and poetry from Canadian authors.
Recent Fiction Title: *The Last India Overland*, by Craig Grant.

THE COUNTRYMAN PRESS, INC., P.O. Box 175, Woodstock VT 05091. (802)457-1049. Fiction: Louis Kannenstine, president. Nonfiction: Carl Taylor, vice president. Estab. 1975. Publishes hardcover and trade paperback originals and paperback reprints. Publishes 24 titles/year. Receives 150 submissions/year. 50% of books from first-time authors; 75% from unagented writers. Pays 5-10% royalty on retail price. Offers $500 average advance. Publishes book an average of 1 year after acceptance. Simultaneous submissions OK. Reports in 1 month on queries; in 2 months on mss. Free book catalog.

Nonfiction: Cookbook, how-to, travel guides. Subjects include cooking, foods and nutrition, adult fitness, history, nature/environment, recreation, fishing, regional (New England, especially Vermont), travel. "We want good 'how-to' books, especially those related to rural life." Submit outline/synopsis and sample chapters. Review artwork/photos as part of ms package.
Recent Nonfiction Title: *Maine, An Explorer's Guide*, by Tree/Steadman (travel guide).
Fiction: Mystery. "We're looking for good mysteries of any type—new, reprint, or U.S. publication of mysteries already published abroad." Submit outline, sample chapter, and SASE.
Recent Fiction Title: *The Long Kill*, by Reginald Hill writing as Patrick Ruell (mystery).

THE COUNTRYWOMAN'S PRESS, Subsidiary of Padre Productions, P.O. Box 840, Arroyo Grande CA 93421-0840. (805)473-1947. Editor and Publisher: Karen L. Reinecke. Estab. 1974. Publishes hardcover and trade paperback originals. Firm averages 4 titles/year. Receives 100 submissions/year. 100% from first-time authors; 100% from unagented writers. Pays 6-10% royalty on retail price.
Nonfiction: Cookbook, how-to. Subjects include agriculture/horticulture, animals (domestic), cooking, foods and nutrition, gardening, nature/environment and recreation. Submit outline/synopsis and sample chapters. Reviews artwork/photos as part of ms package.
Recent Nonfiction Title: *The Complete Vegetarian Campside Cuisine*, by Carolyn Fortuna.

‡**COVENTURE PRESS,** 25 New Chardon St. #8748, Boston MA 92114. (508)281-4722. President: Sisa Sternback. Publishes hardcover and trade paperback originals and reprints. Averages 10-20 titles/year. Receives 75 submissions/year. 40% of books from first-time authors; 95% from unagented writers. Pays 5-10% royalty. Offers $1,000 average advance. Publishes book an average of 9 months after acceptance. Simultaneous submissions OK. Query for electronic submissions. Reports in 3 weeks on queries; 4 months on mss. Book catalog and manuscript guidelines free on request.
Nonfiction: Illustrated book, self-help, textbook. Subjects include child guidance/parenting, health/medicine, psychology, religion, women's issues/studies, men's studies and New Age. "Our book needs are open." Submit outline/synopsis and sample chapters or complete ms. Reviews artwork/photos as part of ms package.
Tips: "Our audience is made up of generally educated, lay or professional readers, interested in inner growth."

THE CROSSING PRESS, 97 Hangar Way, Watsonville CA 95076. (408)722-0711. Co-Publishers: Elaine Goldman Gill, John Gill. Publishes hardcover and trade paperback originals. Averages 30 titles/year; receives 1,600 submissions annually. 10% of books from first-time authors; 90% of books from unagented writers. Pays royalty. Publishes book an average of 18 months after acceptance. Simultaneous submissions OK. Reports in 6 weeks on queries; 3 months on mss. Free book catalog.
Nonfiction: Cookbook, how-to, men's studies, literary and feminist. Subjects include cooking, health, gays, mysteries, sci-fi. Submissions to be considered for the feminist series must be written by women. Submit outline and sample chapter.
Recent Nonfiction Title: *All Women Are Healers*, by Diane Stein.
Fiction: Good literary material. Submit outline and sample chapter.
Recent Fiction Title: *Married Life & Other True Adventures*, by Binnie Kirshenbaum.
Tips: "Simple intelligent query letters do best. No come-ons, no cutes. It helps if there are credentials. Authors should research the press first to see what sort of books it publishes."

CROSSWAY BOOKS, Subsidiary of Good News Publishers, 9825 W. Roosevelt Rd., Westchester IL 60154. Managing Editor: Ted Griffin. Estab. 1938. Publishes hardcover and trade paperback originals. Averages 35 titles/year; receives 2,000 submissions annually. 10% of books from first-time authors; 50% of books from unagented writers. Average print order for a writer's first book is 3,000. Pays negotiable royalty; offers negotiable advance. Publishes book an average of 1 year after acceptance. Send query and synopsis, not whole manuscript. No phone queries! Reports in 4 months. Book catalog and ms guidelines for 9 × 12 SAE and $1.05 postage.
Nonfiction: Subjects include issues on Christianity in contemporary culture, Christian doctrine, and church history. "All books must be written out of Christian perspective or world view." No unsolicited mss. Query with synopsis.
Recent Nonfiction Title: *Sanctified Through the Truth*, by Martyn Lloyd-Jones.
Fiction: Mainstream; science fiction; fantasy (genuinely creative in the tradition of C.S. Lewis, J.R.R. Tolkien and Madeleine L'Engle); and juvenile (10-14; 13-16). No formula romance. Query with synopsis. "All fiction must be written from a genuine Christian perspective."
Recent Fiction Title: *Summer of Light*, by Dennis M. Van Wey.
Tips: "The writer has the best chance of selling our firm a book which, through fiction or nonfiction, shows the practical relevance of biblical doctrine to contemporary issues and life."

CROWN PUBLISHERS, INC., 201 E. 50th St., New York NY 10022. (212)572-2568. Estab. 1933. Imprints include Clarkson N. Potter, Orion Books, and Harmony. Publishes hardcover and paperback originals. Publishes 200 titles/year. Simultaneous submissions OK. Reports in 2 months.

Nonfiction: Americana, animals, art, biography, cookbooks/cooking, health, history, hobbies, how-to, humor, military history, nature, photography, politics, psychology, recreation, reference, science, self-help and sports. Query with letter only.

Recent Nonfiction Title: *Lee Bailey's Southern Food*.

HARRY CUFF PUBLICATIONS LIMITED, 94 LeMarchant Rd., St. John's, Newfoundland A1C 2H2 Canada. (709)726-6590. Editor: Harry Cuff. Managing Editor: Douglas Cuff. Estab. 1980. Publishes hardcover and trade paperback originals. Averages 12 titles/year; receives 50 submissions annually. 50% of books from first-time authors; 100% of books from unagented writers. Pays 10% royalty on retail price. No advance. Publishes book an average of 8 months after acceptance. Reports in 6 months on mss. Book catalog for 6×9 SASE.

Nonfiction: Biography, humor, reference, technical, and textbook, all dealing with Newfoundland. Subjects include history, photography, politics and sociology. Query.

Recent Nonfiction Title: *Daughter of Labrador*, by Millicent Blake Loder.

Fiction: Ethnic, historical, humor and mainstream. Needs fiction by Newfoundlanders or about Newfoundland. Submit complete ms.

Recent Fiction Title: *The Birthing Room*, by Paddy Warrick.

Tips: "We are currently dedicated to publishing books about Newfoundland. We will return 'mainstream' manuscripts from the U.S. unread."

DANCE HORIZONS, Imprint of Princeton Book Co., Publishers, Box 57, Pennington NJ 08534. (609)737-8177. Editorial Director: Roxanne Barrett. Publishes hardcover and paperback originals and paperback reprints. Averages 10 titles/year; receives 50-75 submissions annually. 50% of books from first-time authors; 100% of books from unagented writers. Pays 10% royalty on net receipts; offers no advance. Publishes book an average of 10 months after acceptance. Simultaneous submissions OK. Reports in 3 months. Free book catalog.

Nonfiction: "Anything dealing with dance." Query first. Reviews artwork/photos.

Recent Nonfiction Title: *People Who Dance*, by John Gruen.

JOHN DANIEL AND COMPANY, PUBLISHERS, P.O. Box 21922, Santa Barbara CA 93121. (805)962-1780. Publisher: John Daniel. Estab. 1985. Publishes trade paperback originals. Averages 10 titles/year; receives 1,000 submissions annually. 50% of books from first-time authors; 100% of books from unagented writers. Pays 10% royalty on wholesale price. Publishes book an average of 8 months after acceptance. Simultaneous submissions OK. Query for electronic submissions. Reports in 3 weeks on queries; 2 months on mss. Book catalog and ms guidelines for #10 SASE.

Nonfiction: Autobiography, biography, literary memoir and essays. "We'll look at anything, but are particularly interested in books in which literary merit is foremost—as opposed to books that simply supply information. No libelous, obscene, poorly written or unintelligent manuscripts." Query or submit outline and sample chapters.

Recent Nonfiction Title: *Feminist Convert: A Portrait of Mary Ellen Chase*, by Evelyn Hyman Chase (biography).

Fiction: Novels and short story collections. "We do best with books by authors who have demonstrated a clear, honest, elegant style. No libelous, obscene, poorly written, or boring submissions." Query or submit synopsis and sample chapters.

Recent Fiction Title: *The Best of Intentions*, by Artie Shaw (short stories).

Poetry: "We're open to anything, but we're very cautious. Poetry's hard to sell." Submit complete ms.

Recent Poetry Title: *A Soldier's Time*, by R.L. Barth.

Tips: "If I were a writer trying to market a book today, I would envision my specific audience and approach publishers who demonstrate that they can reach that audience. Writing is not always a lucrative profession; almost nobody makes a living off of royalties from small press publishing houses. That's why the authors we deal with are dedicated to their art and proud of their books—but don't expect to appear on the Carson show. Small press publishers have a hard time breaking into the bookstore market. We try, but we wouldn't be able to survive without a healthy direct-mail sale."

DANTE UNIVERSITY OF AMERICA PRESS, INC., Box 843, Brookline VA 02147. Contact: Manuscripts Editor. Publishes hardcover originals and reprints, and trade paperback originals and reprints. Averages 5 titles/year; receives 50 submissions annually. 50% of books from first-time authors; 50% of books from unagented writers. Average print order for a writer's first book is 3,000. Pays royalty; offers negotiable advance. Publishes book an average of 10 months after acceptance. Simultaneous submissions OK. Query for electronic submissions. Reports in 2 weeks on queries only; 2 months on mss.

Nonfiction: Biography, reference, reprints, and nonfiction and fiction translations from Italian and Latin. Subjects include general scholarly nonfiction, Renaissance thought and letter, Italian language and linguistics, Italian-American history and culture, and bilingual education. Query first with SASE. Reviews artwork/photos as part of ms package.

Poetry: "There is a chance that we would use Renaissance poetry translations."
Recent Poetry Title: Dante *Inferno* (new translation, 34 illustrations).

MAY DAVENPORT, PUBLISHERS, 26313 Purissima Rd., Los Altos Hills CA 94022. (415)948-6499. Editor/
Publisher: May Davenport. Estab. 1975. Imprint is md Books (nonfiction and fiction). Publishes hardcover
and trade paperback originals. Averages 4 titles/year; receives 1,000-2,000 submissions annually. 95% of
books from first-time authors; 5% from professional writers. Pays 15% royalty on retail price; no advance.
Publishes book an average of 1-3 years after acceptance. Reports in 3 weeks. Ms guidelines for #10 SASE.
Nonfiction: Juvenile (13-17). Subject art, music to interest ages 13-17. "Our readers are students in elemen-
tary and secondary public school districts, as well as correctional institutes of learning, etc." No "hack
writing." Query.
Recent Nonfiction Title: *All About Turtles,* by Andrea Ross (turtles, big and small to color).
Fiction: Adventure, fantasy. "We're overstocked with picture books and first readers; prefer stage and
teleplays for TV-oriented teenagers (30 min. one act). "Be entertaining while informing." No sex or violence.
Query with SASE.
Recent Fiction Title: *Creeps,* by Shelly Fredman (young adults and cliques in school).
Tips: "If you can't entertain with words, make people laugh some other way."

DAVIS PUBLICATIONS, INC., 50 Portland St., Worcester MA 01608. (617)754-7201. Managing Editor: Wyatt
Wade. Estab. 1901. Averages 5-10 titles/year. Pays 10-15% royalty. Publishes book an average of 1 year after
acceptance. Write for copy of guidelines for authors.
Nonfiction: Publishes art, design and craft books. Accepts nonfiction translations. "Keep in mind the intended audience. Our readers are visually oriented. All illustrations should be collated separately from the
text, but keyed to the text. Photos should be good quality transparencies and black and white photographs.
Well selected illustrations should explain, amplify, and enhance the text. We average 2-4 photos/page. We
like to see technique photos as well as illustrations of finished artwork, by a variety of artists. Recent books
have been on papermaking, airbrush painting, jewelry, design, puppets, quilting, and watercolor painting."
Submit outline, sample chapters and illustrations. Reviews artwork/photos as part of ms package.
Recent Nonfiction Title: *Computers in the Artroom,* by Deborah Greh.

‡DAVIS PUBLISHING COMPANY/LAW ENFORCEMENT DIVISION, P.O. Box 17659, Montgomery AL 36117.
(205)277-4487. Editor: Carolyn Travis. Estab. 1954. Publishes trade paperback originals. Averages 10 titles/
year. Receives 5 submissions/year. 3% of books from first-time authors; 3% from unagented writers. Pays
11.5% royalty on retail price; buys mss outright for $500-1,500. Publishes book an average of 6 months after
acceptance. Reports in 4 weeks on queries; 8 weeks on mss. Book catalog free on request.
Nonfiction: Study guides on law enforcement. "Writers with test development skills develop study guides
based on existing textbook in law enforcement." Query or submit complete ms. Reviews artwork/photos as
part of ms package.
Recent Nonfiction Title: *Principles of Police Patrol,* by Sonia Livingston (law enforcement study guide).

STEVE DAVIS PUBLISHING, P.O. Box 190831, Dallas TX 75219. (214)954-4469. Publisher: Steve Davis.
Estab. 1982. Publishes hardcover and trade paperback originals. Averages 4 titles/year. Query for electronic
submissions. "Manuscripts should be professionally proofed for style, grammar and spelling before submission." Reports in 3 weeks on queries *if interested.* Not responsible for unsolicited material. Book catalog for
SASE.
Nonfiction: Books on current issues and some reference books. "We are very selective about our list. We
look for material that is professionally prepared, takes a fresh approach to a timely topic, and offers the
reader helpful information." No religious or occult topics, no sports, and no mass market material such as
diet books, joke books, exercise books, etc. Send query letter with SASE. "We can only respond to projects
that interest us."
Recent Nonfiction Title: *The Writer's Yellow Pages,* edited by Steve Davis (reference).

DAW BOOKS, INC., 1633 Broadway, New York NY 10019. Submissions Editor: Peter Stampfel. Estab. 1971.
Publishes science fiction and fantasy hardcover and paperback originals and reprints. Publishes 60-80 titles/
year. Pays in royalties with an advance that is negotiable on a book-by-book basis. Sends galleys to author.
Simultaneous submissions "returned at once, unread unless prior arrangements are made by agent." Reports
in 6 weeks "or longer, if a second reading is required." Free book catalog.
Fiction: "We are interested in science fiction and fantasy novels only. We do not publish any other category
of fiction. We accept both agented and unagented ms. We are not seeking collections of short stories or ideas
for anthologies. We do not want any nonfiction manuscripts." Submit complete ms.

‡IVAN R. DEE, INC., 1332 N. Halsted St., Chicago IL 60622. (312)787-6262. Imprints include: Elephant
Paperbacks. President: Ivan R. Dee. Estab. 1988. Publishes hardcover originals and trade paperback originals
and reprints. Averages 20 titles/year. 10% of books from first-time authors; 75% from unagented writers.

Pays royalty. Publishes book an average of 9 months after acceptance. Reports in 2 weeks on queries; 6 weeks on mss. Book catalog free on request.
Nonfiction: Biography. Subjects include anthopology/archaeology, art/architecture, business and economics, government/politics, health/medicine, history, language/literature, military/war, psychology, religion, sociology, women's issues/studies. Submit outline/synopsis and sample chapters or complete ms. Reviews artwork/photos as part of ms package.
Recent Nonfiction Title: *Culture in an Age of Money*, by Nicolaus Mills.
Tips: "We publish for an intelligent lay audience and college course adoptions."

DEL REY BOOKS, Imprint of Ballantine Books, 201 E. 50th St., New York NY 10022. (212)572-2677. Editor-in-Chief: Owen Lock. Vice President and Fantasy Editor: Lester del Rey. Estab. 1977. Publishes hardcover, trade paperback and mass market originals and mass market paperback reprints. Averages 80 titles/year; receives 1,600 submissions annually. 10% of books from first-time authors; 40% of books from unagented writers. Pays royalty on retail price. Offers competitive advance. Publishes book an average of 1 year after acceptance. Reporting time slow. Writer's guidelines for #10 SASE.
Fiction: Fantasy ("should have the practice of magic as an essential element of the plot") and science fiction ("well-plotted novels with good characterization, exotic locales, and detailed alien cultures. Novels should have a 'sense of wonder' and be designed to please readers"). Will need "80 original fiction manuscripts of science fiction and fantasy suitable for publishing over the next two years. No flying-saucers, Atlantis, or occult novels." Submit complete ms or detailed outline and first three chapters.
Recent Fiction Title: *Dragonsdawn*, by Anne McCaffrey.
Tips: "Del Rey is a reader's house. Our audience is anyone who wants to be pleased by a good entertaining novel. We do very well with original fantasy novels, in which magic is a central element, and with hard-science science fiction novels. Pay particular attention to plotting and a satisfactory conclusion. It must be/feel believable. That's what the readers like."

DELACORTE PRESS, Imprint of Dell Publishing and division of Bantam Doubleday Dell, 666 5th Ave., New York NY 10103. (212)765-6500. Editorial Director: Bob Miller. Publishes hardcover originals. Publishes 36 titles/year. Royalty and advance vary. Publishes book an average of 2 years after acceptance, but varies. Simultaneous submissions OK. Reports in 2 months. Book catalog and guidelines for SASE.
Fiction and Nonfiction: *Query, outline or brief proposal, or complete ms accepted.* No mss for children's or young adult books accepted in this division.
Recent Nonfiction Title: *Secrets About Men Every Woman Should Know*, by Barbara DeAngelis, Ph.D.
Recent Fiction Title: *Burn Marks*, by Sara Paretsky.

DELTA BOOKS, Division of Bantam Doubleday Dell Publishing Co., 666 Fifth Ave., New York NY 10103. (212)765-6500. Editorial Director: Bob Miller. Publishes trade paperback reprints and originals. Averages 20 titles/year. Pays 6-7½% royalty; offers advance. Simultaneous submissions OK. Reports in 2 months. Book catalog for 8½×11 SASE.
Nonfiction: Biography, childcare, film, music, New Age, science. "We are expanding our base of strong childcare and New Age titles, while also looking for good books on popular culture (film, music, television). Query or submit outline/synopsis and sample chapters. *Prefers submissions through agents.*"

DEMBNER BOOKS, Division of Red Dembner Enterprises, Corp., 80 8th Ave., New York NY 10011. (212)924-2525. Editor: S. Arthur Dembner. Estab. 1975. Publishes hardcover and trade paperback originals, and hardcover and trade paperback reprints. Averages 10-15 titles/year; receives 500-750 submissions annually. 20% of books from first-time authors; 75% of books from unagented writers. Pays 10-15% royalty on hardcover; 6-7½% royalty on paperback, both on retail price. Offers average $1,000-5,000 advance. Publishes book an average of 1 year after acceptance. Simultaneous submissions OK. "Include SASE with sufficient postage for return of material." Reports in 2 weeks on queries; 10 weeks on mss. Book catalog available from W.W. Norton, 500 5th Ave., New York NY 10110. Writer's guidelines available for #10 SASE.
Nonfiction: How-to, reference. Subjects include health, film, history (popular), music, sports and social causes. "We want books written by knowledgeable authors who focus on a problem area (health/home) and offer an insightful guidance toward solutions." No surveys or collections—books that do not focus on one specific, promotable topic. No first-person accounts of tragic personal events. Also, no books on heavily published topics, such as weight loss and exercise programs. Query.

Market conditions are constantly changing! If this is 1992 or later, buy the newest edition of Writer's Market at your favorite bookstore or order directly from Writer's Digest Books.

Recent Nonfiction Title: *Alfred Hitchcock and the Making of Psycho*, by Stephen Rebello.
Fiction: Mystery, suspense and literary. "We look for genre fiction (mystery, suspense, etc.), that keeps pace with the times, deals with contemporary issues, and has three-dimensional characters. Occasionally we publish literary novels, but the writing must be of excellent quality." No indulgent, self-conscious fiction. Query and two sample chapters.
Recent Fiction Title: *Haunt of the Nightingale*, by John R. Riggs.
Tips: "We take a great deal of pride in the books we publish. No humor books or fad books. We're developing a strong backlist and want to continue to do so. Small hardcover houses such as ourselves are being very careful about the books they choose for publication primarily because secondary rights sales have dropped, and the money is less. Quality is of utmost importance."

‡THE DENALI PRESS, P.O. Box 021535, Juneau AK 99802. (907)586-6014. Contact: Sally Silvas-Ottumwa. Estab. 1986. Publishes trade paperback originals. Averages 5 titles/year. Receives 10-25 submissions/year. 20% of books from first-time authors; 80% from unagented writers. Pays 10-15% royalty on wholesale price; buys mss by outright purchase. Publishes book an average of 9-12 months after acceptance. Simultaneous submissions OK. Query for electronic submissions. Reports in 1 week on queries; 1 month on mss. Book catalog free on request.
Nonfiction: Reference. Subjects include Americana, anthropology/archaeology, ethnic, government/politics, history, recreation, regional, sports and travel. "We need reference books—ethnic and minority concerns." Query with outline/synopsis and sample chapters; all unsolicited mss are returned unopened.
Recent Nonfiction Title: *Directory of Services for Refugees and Immigrants 1990-1991*, by Alan Edward Schorr.

T.S. DENISON & CO., INC., 9601 Newton Ave. S., Minneapolis MN 55431. FAX: (612)888-3831. Editor-in-Chief: Sherrill B. Flora. Acquisitions Editor: Baxter Brings. Estab. 1876. Publishes teacher aid materials; receives 500 submissions annually. 90% of books from first-time authors; 100% of books from unagented writers. Average print order for a writer's first book is 3,000. Royalty varies; no advance. Publishes book an average of 1-2 years after acceptance. Reports in 1 month. Book catalog and ms guidelines for SASE.
Nonfiction: Specializes in early childhood and elementary school teaching aids. Send prints if photos are to accompany ms. Submit complete ms. Reviews artwork/photos as part of ms package.
Recent Nonfiction Title: *Famous Children's Authors*, by Shirly Norby and Greg Ryan.
Recent Fiction Title: *Mr. Wiggle Goes to the Library*, by Paula Craig.

*DEVIN-ADAIR PUBLISHERS, INC., 6 N. Water St., Greenwich CT 06830. (203)531-7755. Editor: Jane Andrassi. Publishes hardcover and paperback originals, reprints and software. Averages 20 titles/year; receives up to 500 submissions annually. 30% of books from first-time authors; 70% of books from unagented writers. Average print order for a writer's first book is 7,500. Subsidy publishes 5% of books. Royalty on sliding scale, 5-25%; "average advance is low." Publishes book an average of 9 months after acceptance. No simultaneous submissions. Query for electronic submissions. Book catalog and guidelines for 6×9 SAE and 5 first class stamps.
Nonfiction: Publishes Americana, business, how-to, conservative politics, history, medicine, nature, economics, sports and travel books. New line: homeopathic books. Accepts translations. Query or submit outline/synopsis and sample chapters. Looks for "early interest, uniqueness, economy of expression, good style, and new information." Reviews artwork/photos as part of ms package.
Recent Nonfiction Title: *Exploring Old Block Island*, by H. Whitman and R. Fox.
Tips: "We seek to publish books of high quality manufacture. We spend 8% more on production and design than necessary to ensure a better quality book. Trends include increased specialization and a more narrow view of a subject. General overviews are now a thing of the past. Better a narrow subject in depth than a wide superficial one."

*DEVONSHIRE PUBLISHING CO., P.O. Box 85, Elgin IL 60121-0085. (312)242-3846. Vice President: Don Reynolds. Estab. 1988. Publishes hardcover and trade paperback originals. Averages 4 titles/year; receives 1,000 submissions annually. 85% of books from first-time authors; 75% of books from unagented writers. Subsidy publishes 20% of books. "Although we do not generally subsidy publish we will enter into 'cooperative publishing agreements' with an author if the subject matter is of such limited appeal that we doubt its profitability, or if the author desires a more extravagant finished product than we planned to produce." Pays 10-15% royalty on retail price. "Royalty would be higher if author engaged in cooperative venture." Offers negotiable advance. Publishes book an average of 1 year after acceptance. Simultaneous submissions OK. Reports in 1 month on queries; 2 months on submissions. Book catalog and guidelines for #10 SASE.
Nonfiction: Reference, technical and textbook. Subjects include business and economics, history, hobbies, nature, psychology, religion and sociology. "We will be looking for books that have an impact on the reader. A history or religious book will have to be more than just a recitation of past events. Our books must have some relation to today's problems or situations." No works of personal philosophy or unverifiable speculation. Query and/or submit outline/synopsis.

Recent Nonfiction Title: *The Way We Were,* by Mace Crandall Erandall (history).

Fiction: Erotica, experimental, historical, horror, religious and science fiction. "All works must have some relevance to today's reader and be well written. We hope to produce one or two titles, but our main thrust will be in the nonfiction area. However, if a work is thought-provoking and/or controversial, we may give it priority. Query and/or submit outline/synopsis."

Recent Fiction Title: *The Dew of Hermon,* by Janis Fedor (historical fiction).

Tips: "Because we are a small publishing company, we can aim for the smaller, more specialized market. We envision that the audience for our books will be well educated with a specific area of interest. We can afford to look at work that other publishers have passed over. Although we are not looking for works that are controversial just for the sake of controversy, we are looking for topics that go beyond the norm. If it is documented and has a strong basis or foundation, we will endeavor to publish it."

DIAL BOOKS FOR YOUNG READERS, Division of NAL Penguin Inc., 375 Hudson St., 3rd Floor, New York NY 10014. (212)366-2000. Submissions Editor: Phyllis J. Fogelman. Imprints include Dial Easy-to-Read Books and Dial Very First Books. Publishes hardcover originals. Averages 80 titles/year; receives 8,000 submissions annually. 10% of books from first-time authors. Pays variable royalty and advance. Simultaneous submissions OK, but not preferred. Reports in 2 weeks on queries; 4 months on mss. Book catalog and ms guidelines for 9 × 12 SASE and $1.10 postage.

Nonfiction: Juvenile picture books and young adult books. Especially looking for "quality picture books and well-researched young adult and middle-reader mss." Not interested in alphabet books, riddle and game books, and early concept books. Query with outline/synopsis and sample chapters. Reviews artwork/photos.

Recent Nonfiction Title: *The Many Lives of Benjamin Franklin,* by Mary Pope Osborne.

Fiction: Juvenile picture books and young adult books. Adventure, fantasy, historical, humor, mystery, romance (appropriate for young adults), and suspense. Especially looking for "lively and well written novels for middle grade and young adult children involving a convincing plot and believable characters. The subject matter or theme should not already be overworked in previously published books. The approach must not be demeaning to any minority group, nor should the roles of female characters (or others) be stereotyped, though we don't think books should be didactic, or in any way message-y." No "topics inappropriate for the juvenile, young adult, and middle grade audiences. No plays." Submit complete ms. Also publishes Pied Piper Book (paperback Dial reprints) and Pied Piper Giants (1½ feet tall reprints).

Recent Fiction Title: *The Road to Memphis,* by Mildred Taylor.

Tips: "Our readers are anywhere from preschool age to teenage. Picture books must have strong plots, lots of action, unusual premises, or universal themes treated with freshness and originality. Humor works well in these books. A very well thought out and intelligently presented book has the best chance of being taken on. Genre isn't as much of a factor as presentation."

*DIGITAL PRESS, Subsidiary of Digital Equipment Corp., 12 Crosby Dr., Bedford MA 01730. (617)276-4809. Executive Editor: Michael Meehan. Estab. 1979. Publishes hardcover and trade paperback originals. Firm averages 15 titles/year. Receives 75-100 submissions/year. 75% of books from first-time authors; 100% from unagented writers. Subsidy publishes 50% of books. Pays 10-18% royalty on wholesale price. Publishes book an average of 7 months after acceptance. Simultaneous submissions OK. Query for electronic submissions. Reports in 6 weeks. Free book catalog.

Nonfiction: Software and technical. Subjects include computers and electronics. "We will consider all proposed manuscripts on Digital's computer systems. VAX hardware, VMS operating system—also in the area of networking. No manuscripts based on other systems, IBM, etc." Submit outline/synopsis and sample chapters. Reviews artwork/photos as part of package.

DILLON PRESS, INC., 242 Portland Ave. S., Minneapolis MN 55415. (612)333-2691. Editorial Director: Uva Dillon. Senior Editor: Tom Schneider. Publishes hardcover originals. Averages 30-40 titles/year; receives 3,000 submissions annually. 30% of books from first-time authors; 90% of books from unagented writers. Average print order for a writer's first book is 5,000. Pays royalty or by outright purchase. Publishes book an average of 18 months after acceptance. Reports in 6 weeks. Book catalog for 10 × 12 SAE with 4 first class stamps.

Nonfiction: "We are actively seeking mss for the juvenile educational market." Subjects include world and U.S. geography, international festivals and holidays, U.S. states and cities, contemporary and historical biographies for elementary and middle grade levels, unusual approaches to science topics for primary grade readers, unusual or remarkable animals, and contemporary issues of interest and value to young people. Submit complete ms or outline and 2 sample chapters; query letters if accompanied by book proposal. Reviews artwork/photos as part of ms package.

Recent Nonfiction Title: *Those Amazing Leeches,* by Cheryl M. Halton.

Tips: "Before writing, authors should check out the existing competition for their book idea to determine if it is really needed and stands a reasonable chance for success, especially for a nonfiction proposal."

DOUBLEDAY & CO., INC., Division of Bantam Doubleday Dell, 666 5th Ave., New York NY 10103. (212)765-6500. Imprints include Dolphin Books, Double D Western, Spy Books and Zephyr Books. Publishes hardcover and paperback originals. Offers royalty on retail price; offers variable advance. Reports in 2½ months. Doubleday accepts fiction and nonfiction through agents. Will not read unsolicited material. Send proposal/synopsis to Crime Club Editor, Science Fiction Editor, or Loveswept Editor as appropriate. Sufficient postage for return via fourth class mail must accompany manuscript.

DOWN EAST BOOKS, Division of Down East Enterprise, Inc., P.O. Box 679, Camden ME 04843. (207)594-9544. Editor: Karin Womer. Estab. 1954. Publishes hardcover and trade paperback originals and trade paperback reprints. Averages 10-14 titles/year; receives 300 submissions annually. 50% of books from first-time authors; 90% of books from unagented writers. Average print order for a writer's first book is 3,000. Pays 10-15% on receipts. Offers average $200 advance. Publishes book an average of 1 year after acceptance. Simultaneous submissions OK. Reports in 2 weeks on queries; 2 months on mss. Book catalog and ms guidelines for 9 × 12 SAE with $1.05 postage.
Nonfiction: Books about the New England region, Maine in particular. Subjects include Americana, cooking and foods, history, nature, traditional crafts and recreation. "All of our books must have a Maine or New England emphasis." Query. Reviews artwork/photos as part of ms package.
Recent Nonfiction Title: *Maine's Natural Heritage: Rare Species and Unique Natural Features*, by Dean Bennett.
Fiction: "We generally publish no fiction except for an occasional juvenile title (average 1/year) but are now keeping alert for good general-audience novels—same regional criteria apply."
Recent Fiction Title: *The Amazing Marsh: Alex Discovers a Hidden World*, by Eve Knowles.

DRAMA BOOK PUBLISHERS, 260 Fifth Ave., New York NY 10001. (212)725-5377. Contact: Ralph Pine or Judith Holmes. Publishes hardcover and paperback originals and reprints. Averages 4-15 titles/year; receives 500 submissions annually. 70% of books from first-time authors; 90% of books from unagented writers. Royalty varies; advance varies; negotiable. Publishes book an average of 18 months after acceptance. Reports in 2 months.
Nonfiction: Books—texts, guides, manuals, directories, reference—for and about performing arts theory and practice: acting, directing; voice, speech, movement, music, dance, mime; makeup, masks, wigs; costumes, sets, lighting, sound; design and execution; technical theatre, stagecraft, equipment; stage management; producing; arts management, all varieties; business and legal aspects; film, radio, television, cable, video; theory, criticism, reference; playwriting; theatre and performance history. Accepts nonfiction, drama and technical works in translations also. Query; accepts 1-3 sample chapters; no complete mss. Reviews artwork/photos as part of ms package.
Fiction: Professionally produced plays and musicals.

DUNDURN PRESS LTD., 2181 Queen St. E., Toronto, Ontario M4E 1E5 Canada. (416)698-0454. Publisher: Kirk Howard. Publishes hardcover, trade paperback and hardcover reprints. Averages 15 titles/year; receives 500 submissions annually. 45% of books from first-time authors; 90% of books from unagented writers. Average print order for a writer's first book is 2,000. Pays 10% royalty on retail price; 8% royalty on some paperback children's books. Publishes book an average of 1 year after acceptance. Query for electronic submissions.
Nonfiction: Biography, coffee table books, juvenile (12 and up), literary and reference. Subjects include Canadiana, art, history, hobbies, Canadian history and literary criticism. Especially looking for Canadian biographies. No religious or soft science topics. Query with outline/synopsis and sample chapters. Reviews artwork/photos as part of ms package.
Recent Nonfiction Title: *Double Take: The Story of the Elgin & Winter Garden Theatres*, by Hilary Russell.
Tips: "Publishers want more books written in better prose styles. If I were a writer trying to market a book today, I would visit bookstores and watch what readers buy and what company publishes that type of book 'close' to my manuscript."

*DUQUESNE UNIVERSITY PRESS, 600 Forbes Ave., Pittsburgh PA 15282. (412)434-6610. FAX: (412)642-9055. Averages 9 titles/year; receives 400 submissions annually. 25% of books from first-time authors; 100% of books from unagented writers. Average print order for a writer's first book is 1,500. Subsidy publishes 20% of books. Pays 10% royalty on net sales; no advance. Publishes book an average of 1 year after acceptance. Query for electronic submissions. No unsolicited mss. Query. Reports in 3 months.
Nonfiction: Scholarly books in the humanities, social sciences for academics, libraries, college bookstores and educated laypersons. Length: open. Looks for scholarship.
Recent Nonfiction Title: *Imaginative Thinking*, by Edward L. Murray.

‡DURST PUBLICATIONS LTD., 29-28 41st Ave., Long Island City NY 11101. (718)706-0303. FAX: (718)706-0891. Owner: Sanford Durst. Publishes hardcover and trade paperback originals and reprints. Averages 20 titles/year; receives 100 submissions annually. Average print order for first book is 2,500. Pays variable royalty.

Publishes book an average of 6 months after acceptance. Reports in 1 month. Book catalog for #10 SAE and 4 first class stamps.
Nonfiction: How-to and reference. Subjects include Americana, art, business and economics, cooking and foods, hobbies-primarily coin collecting, stamp collecting, antiques and legal. Especially needs reference books and how-to on coins, medals, tokens, paper money, art, antiques-illustrated with valuations or rarities, if possible. Publishes for dealers, libraries, collectors and attorneys. Submit outline/synopsis and sample chapters. Reviews artwork/photos as part of ms package.
Recent Nonfiction Title: *Buying & Setting Country Land*, by D. Reisman (practical/legal).
Tips: "Write in simple English. Do not repeat yourself. Present matter in logical, orderly form. Try to illustrate."

DUSTBOOKS, Box 100, Paradise CA 95967. (916)877-6110. Publisher: Len Fulton. Publishes hardcover and paperback originals. Averages 7 titles/year. Offers 15% royalty. Offers average $500 advance. Simultaneous submissions OK if so informed. Reports in 2 months. Free book catalog; writer's guidelines for #10 SASE.
Nonfiction: Our specialty is directories of small presses, poetry publishers, and a monthly newsletter on small publishers (*Small Press Review*)." Submit outline/synopsis and sample chapters.

DUTTON CHILDREN'S BOOKS, Penguin Books USA Inc., 375 Hudson St., New York NY 10014. (212)366-2000. Editor-in-Chief: Lucia Monfried. Estab. 1852. Firm publishes hardcover originals. Publishes 70 titles/year. 15% from first-time authors. Pays royalty on retail price. Simultaneous submissions OK. Reports in 1 month on queries; 3 months on mss. Book catalog for 9½ × 11 SAE with $1.65 postage; ms guidelines for #10 SASE. "Please send query letter first on all except picture book manuscripts."
Nonfiction: For preschoolers to middle-graders; including animals/nature, U.S. history, general biography, sciene and photo essays.
Recent Nonfiction Title: *It's an Armadillo!*, by Bianca Lavies (photo essay).
Fiction: Dutton Children's Books has a complete publishing program that includes picture books; easy-to-read books; and fiction for all ages, from "first-chapter" books to young adult readers.
Recent Fiction Title: *Eye of the Ngedle*, by Teri Sloat (picture book).

E.P. DUTTON, Imprint of Penguin USA, 375 Hudson St., New York NY 10014 (212)366-2000. Publisher: Elaine Koster. Estab. 1852. Publishes hardcover and trade paperback originals and reprints. Firm averages 160 titles/year. Does not read unsolicited manuscripts.
Nonfiction: Biography, coffee table book, cookbook, how-to, humor, illustrated book and self-help.
Fiction: Mainstream/contemporary. "We don't publish genre romances or westerns."

*ECW PRESS, Subsidiaries include Emerson House, Essays on Canadian Writing, 307 Coxwell Ave., Toronto, Ontario M4L 3B5 Canada. (416)694-3348. President: Jack David. Estab. 1979. Publishes hardcover and trade paperback originals. Publishes 20-25 titles/year; receives 120 submissions annually. 50% of books from first-time authors; 80% of books from unagented writers. Subsidy publishes (nonauthor) up to 5% of books. Pays 10% royalty on retail price. Simultaneous submissions OK. Query for electronic submissions. Reports in 2 weeks. Free book catalog.
Nonfiction: Reference and Canadian literary criticism. "ECW is interested in all literary criticism aimed at the undergraduate and graduate university market." Query. Reviews artwork/photos as part of ms package.
Recent Nonfiction Title: *A Sense of Style*, by W.J. Keith (literary criticism).
Fiction: Humor only. Submit outline/synopsis and sample chapters.
Tips: "The writer has the best chance of selling literary criticism to our firm because that's our specialty and the only thing that makes us money."

*EDICIONES UNIVERSAL, 3090 S.W. 8th St., Miami FL 33135. (305)642-3355. FAX: (305)642-7978. Director: Juan M. Salvat. Publishes trade paperback originals in Spanish. Publishes 50 titles/year; receives 150 submissions/year. 40% of books from first-time authors. 90% of books from unagented writers. Subsidy publishes 10% of books. Pays 5-10% royalty on retail price. Publishes book an average of 9 months after acceptance. Simultaneous submissions OK. Reports in 1 month on queries; 2 months on mss. Book catalog free.
Nonfiction: Biography, cookbook, humor and reference. Subjects include cooking and foods, philosophy, politics, psychology and sociology. "We specialize in Cuban topics." All manuscripts must be in Spanish. Submit outline/synopsis and sample chapters. Reviews artwork/photos as part of ms package.
Recent Nonfiction Title: *Cuba: Destiny as Choice*, by Wilfredo del Prado.
Fiction: "We will consider everything as long as it is written in Spanish." Submit outline/synopsis and sample chapters.
Recent Fiction Title: *El Rumbo*, by Joaquin Delgado-Sanchez.
Poetry: "We will consider any Spanish-language poetry." Submit 3 or more poems.
Recent Poetry Title: *Antologia De Poesia Infantil*, by Ana Rosa Nunez.
Tips: "Our audience is composed entirely of Spanish-language readers. This is a very limited market. Books on Cuban or Latin American topics have the best chance of selling to our firm."

*EDUCATION ASSOCIATES, Division of The Daye Press, Inc., P.O. Box 8021, Athens GA 30603. (404)542-4244. Editor, Text Division: D. Keith Osborn. Estab. 1974. Publishes hardcover and trade paperback originals. Averages 2-6 titles/year; receives 300 submissions annually. 1% of books from first-time authors; 100% of books from unagented writers. Subsidy publishes 5% of books. "We may publish a textbook which has a very limited audience and is of unusual merit . . . but we still believe that the book will make a contribution to the educational field." Buys mss "on individual basis." Publishes book an average of 9 months after acceptance. Do not send ms; query first. No reponse without SASE. Reports in 1 month on queries.

Nonfiction: How-to, textbook, lab manuals. Subjects include psychology and education. "Books in the fields of early childhood and middle school education. Do not wish basic textbooks. Rather, are interested in more specific areas of interest in above fields. We are more interested in small runs on topics of more limited nature than general texts." Query only with one-page letter. If interested will request synopsis and sample chapters. Absolutely no reply unless SASE is enclosed. No phone queries.

Recent Nonfiction Title: *Observation Guide for Child Study*, by L. Paquio.

Tips: "We are not taking any unsolicited college textbook manuscripts for the year 1991. We will consider small runs of college study guides or study manuals which are used by a professor at his/her own college or university. Will consider any college academic field for a small run lab manual."

*WILLIAM B. EERDMANS PUBLISHING CO., 255 Jefferson Ave. SE, Grand Rapids MI 49503. (616)459-4591. FAX: (616)459-6540. Editor-in-Chief: Jon Pott. Managing Editor: Charles Van Hof. Publishes hardcover and paperback originals and reprints. Averages 65-70 titles/year; receives 3,000-4,000 submissions annually. 25% of books from first-time authors; 95% of books from unagented writers. Average print order for a writer's first book is 4,000. Subsidy publishes 1% of books. Pays 7½-10% royalty on retail price; usually no advance. Publishes book an average of 1 year after acceptance. Simultaneous submissions OK if noted. Reports in 3 weeks for queries; 4 months for mss. Looks for "quality and relevance." Free book catalog.

Nonfiction: Reference, textbooks and tourists guidebooks. Subjects include history, philosophy, psychology, religion, sociology, regional history and geography. "Approximately 80% of our publications are religious— specifically Protestant—and largely of the more academic or theological variety (as opposed to the devotional, inspirational or celebrity-conversion books). Our history and social studies titles aim, similarly, at an academic audience; some of them are documentary histories. We prefer that writers take the time to notice if we have published anything at all in the same category as their manuscript before sending it to us." Accepts nonfiction translations. Query. Accepts outline/synopsis and 2-3 sample chapters. Reviews artwork/photos.

Recent Nonfiction Title: *The Illuminating Icon*, by Anthony Ugolnik.

EES* PUBLICATIONS, Subsidiary of Education for Emergency Services, Inc. (EES*), 6801 Lake Worth Rd., Lake Worth FL 33467. (407)642-3340. Director: Candace Brown-Nixon. Publishes trade paperback originals. Firm averages 3-6 titles/year. 10% of books from first-time authors. Pays 10-15% royalty on retail price. Negotiable re: outright purchase. Publishes book an average of 6 months after acceptance. Reports generally in 2 weeks on queries; 1 month on mss. Free book catalog and ms guidelines, "just send legible address."

Nonfiction: How-to, reference, technical and textbook. Subjects include education (EMS field only) and health/medicine (EMS related only). "We're interested in specialized EMS, law enforcement, fire-related topics. Authors must be properly credentialed for the topic." No pictorial history, how to read an EKG, general topic initial education textbooks, or nursing topics. Query or submit outline/synopsis and sample chapters.

Recent Nonfiction Title: *How to Bitch Effectively: An Officers Guide to Selling an Idea to the Brass*, by Clarence E. Jones.

Tips: "Writers have the best chance of selling us a specialized topic about which the author is acutely knowledgeable and properly credentialed-i.e., an EMT should not attempt to write on an ALS level. EMTs, paramedics, rescue personnel, students and educators in EMS/rescue are our audience."

‡*ENGLISH MOUNTAIN PUBLISHING COMPANY, Rt. 4 Box 129, Dandridge TN 37725. (615)623-6211. Editor: Shirly Garvais. Publishes mass market paperback originals. Firm averages 8-10 titles/year. 20% of books from first-time authors. 100% from unagented writers. Subsidy publishes 5% of books. Pays 5-10% royalty on retail price. Publishes book an average of 5 months after acceptance. Simultaneous submissions OK. Query for electronic submissions. Reports in 2 weeks on queries; 2 months on mss. Book catalog for #10 SAE and 2 first class stamps. Manuscript guidelines for #10 SAE and 1 first-class stamp.

Nonfiction: Juvenile. Subjects include education (curriculum for home, school or church), religion (children's stories; Christian; ages 3-teen). "We have a need for curriculum for church or home school, Bible based Christian material suitable for ages 3-18, children's music, musicals, sing-a-long books, and secular children's stories with redeeming subject matter, ages 3-10." Query or submit complete ms. Reviews artwork/photos as part of ms package.

Recent Nonfiction Title: *How to Lead a Children's Church Choir and Not Lose Your Religion!*, by Shirly Garvais (music curriculum and methods).

Fiction: Adventure (prefer mystery for pre-teens and teens), fantasy (fun and exciting with a moral ages 8-15), juvenile (children's stories—500 words approx. for ages 3-6; 1500-2500 words for ages 8-15), mystery (ages 10-15, good plot twists, challenging and exciting, Sci-fi OK), plays (ages 6-10 and 12-15 short skits for use in church setting; also full musicals), religious (stories for 3-18 on religious topics: Christian life, growth, use in everyday life) and short story collections (ages 10-15, good moral lessons, interesting reading, helpful in pre-teen situation). "We need children's stories for ages 3-8; older children's stories for ages 9-12; short stories, collections, plays, skits, poems, musicals for church performance. All books must have a redeeming moral object lesson." Query or submit complete ms.

Recent Fiction Title: *The Adventures Mystery Series*, by Shirly Garvais (teen mystery short stories).

Poetry: Young children's poems suitable for a collection of 8-10 in a picture book. Submit complete ms.

Recent Poetry Title: *Jesus Is . . .* , by Shirly Garvais (prose).

Tips: "Our audience is made up of children, parents, grandparents, churches and church schools, home schoolers. If I were a writer trying to market a book today, I would make the book marketable in the direct sale area, something that would grab a readers attention in a mail order catalog."

ENSLOW PUBLISHERS, Bloy St. and Ramsey Ave., P.O. Box 777, Hillside NJ 07205. (201)964-4116. Editor: Ridley Enslow. Estab. 1977. Publishes hardcover and paperback originals. Averages 40 titles/year. 30% require freelance illustration. Pays royalty on net price; offers $500-5,000 advance. Publishes book an average of 8 months after acceptance. Reports in 2 weeks. Free book catalog for SASE with 25¢ postage.

Nonfiction: Interested in manuscripts for young adults and children. Some areas of special interest are science, social issues, biography, reference topics and recreation. Accepts nonfiction translations. Submit outline/synopsis and 2 sample chapters. Reviews artwork/photos as part of ms package.

Recent Nonfiction Title: *Science Fair Success*, by Ruth Bombaugh.

ENTELEK, Ward-Whidden House/The Hill, Box 1303, Portsmouth NH 03801. Editor-in-Chief: Albert E. Hickey. Publishes paperback originals. Offers royalty on retail price of 5% trade; 10% textbook. No advance. Averages 5 titles/year. Simultaneous submissions OK. Submit outline and sample chapters or submit complete ms. Reports in 1 week. Book catalog for SASE.

Nonfiction: Publishes computer books and software of special interest to educators. Length: 3,000 words minimum.

Recent Nonfiction Title: *Sail Training for Young Offenders*, edited by A. Hickey (education).

PAUL S. ERIKSSON, PUBLISHER, 208 Battell Bldg., Middlebury VT 05753. (802)388-7303; Summer: Forest Dale VT 05745. (802)247-8415. Publisher/Editor: Paul S. Eriksson. Associate Publisher/Co-Editor: Peggy Eriksson. Publishes hardcover and paperback trade originals and paperback trade reprints. Averages 5-10 titles/year; receives 1,500 submissions annually. 25% of books from first-time authors; 95% of books from unagented writers. Average print order for a writer's first book is 3,000-5,000. Pays 10-15% royalty on retail price; advance offered if necessary. Publishes book an average of 6 months after acceptance. Catalog for #10 SASE.

Nonfiction: Americana, birds (ornithology), art, biography, business/economics, cookbooks/cooking/foods, health, history, hobbies, how-to, humor, nature, politics, psychology, recreation, self-help, sociology, sports and travel. Query.

Recent Nonfiction Title: *Cocaine: The Great White Plague*, by Gabriel G. Nahas, M.D., Ph.D.

Fiction: Mainstream. Query.

Recent Fiction Title: *Norman Rockwell's Greatest Painting*, by Hollis Hodges.

Tips: "We look for intelligence, excitement and salability."

‡LAWRENCE ERLBAUM ASSOCIATES, INC., 365 Broadway, Hillsdale NJ 07642. (201)666-4110. Vice President, Editorial: Judith Amsel. Publishes hardcover originals. Firm averages 100 titles/year. Receives 300 submissions/year. 5-10% of books from first-time authors. 100% from unagented writers. Pays 10-15% royalty on net receipts. Offers $400 average advance. Publishes book an average of 9 months after acceptance. Simultaneous submissions OK. Query for electronic submissions. Reports in 2 weeks on queries; 3 months on mss. Free book catalog and manuscript guidelines.

Nonfiction: Technical, textbook and scholarly. Subjects include computers and electronics (AI, HCI), communications education, health/medicine (behaviorial), psychology, science (neuroscience), women's issues/studies and statistics. Growing lists in theoretical and applied cognitive and behavioral sciences, (monographs and some edited collections). Professional-level books, upper-level college texts and alternative media (video, software)." No trade-audience oriented. Submit outline/synopsis and sample chapters. Reviews artwork/photos as part of ms package.

Recent Nonfiction Title: *Neuroscience & Connectionist Theory*, by Gluck and Rumelhart, eds. (scholarly collection).

Tips: "Writers have the best chance with multidisciplinary titles that are appropriate for many of our markets. List increasingly includes books on applications developed from recent research, such as industrial/organizational psychology and neural networks are needed. Clean, focused writing always works better. Our audience consists of academics and professionals in the behavioral, social and cognitive sciences. If I were a writer trying to market a book today, I would go to those publishers whose books I most respect and want to have in my own library."

ETC PUBLICATIONS, 700 East Vereda Sur, Palm Springs CA 92262. (619)325-5352. Editorial Director: LeeOna S. Hostrop. Senior Editor: Dr. Richard W. Hostrop. Estab. 1972. Publishes hardcover and paperback originals. Averages 6-12 titles/year; receives 100 submissions annually. 75% of books from first-time authors; 90% of books from unagented writers. Average print order for a writer's first book is 2,500. Offers 5-15% royalty, based on wholesale and retail price. No advance. Publishes book an average of 9 months after acceptance. Reports in 3 weeks.

Nonfiction: Educational management, gifted education, futuristics and textbooks. Accepts nonfiction translations in above areas. Submit complete ms with SASE. Reviews artwork/photos as part of ms package.

Recent Nonfiction Title: *The Effective School Administrator*, by Richard W. Hostrop.

Tips: "ETC will seriously consider textbook manuscripts in any knowledge area in which the author can guarantee a first-year adoption of not less than 500 copies. Special consideration is given to those authors who are capable and willing to submit their completed work in camera-ready, typeset form."

M. EVANS AND CO., INC., 216 E. 49 St., New York NY 10017. FAX: (212)486-4544. Editor-in-Chief: George C. deKay. Publishes hardcover originals. Royalty schedule to be negotiated. Averages 30-40 titles/year. 5% of books from unagented writers. Publishes book an average of 8 months after acceptance. "No mss should be sent unsolicited. A letter of inquiry is essential." Reports in 8 weeks. SASE essential.

Nonfiction and Fiction: "We publish a general trade list of adult fiction and nonfiction, cookbooks and semireference works. The emphasis is on selectivity since we publish only 30 titles a year. Our general fiction list, which is very small, represents an attempt to combine quality with commercial potential. We also publish westerns and romance novels. Our most successful nonfiction titles have been related to health and the behavioral sciences. No limitation on subject. A writer should clearly indicate what his book is all about, frequently the task the writer performs least well. His credentials, although important, mean less than his ability to convince this company that he understands his subject and that he has the ability to communicate a message worth hearing." Reviews artwork/photos.

Tips: "Writers should review our catalog (available for 9×12 envelope with 3 first class stamps) or the *Publishers Trade List Annual* before making submissions."

‡EVERGREEN COMMUNICATIONS, INC., 2085-A Sperry Ave., Ventura CA 93003. (805)650-9248. Co-publisher/Managing Editor: Mary Beckwith. Estab. 1989. Publishes trade paperback originals. Averages 4-6 titles/year. 50% of books from first-time authors; 90% from unagented writers. Pays 12% royalty on wholesale price. Offers $500 average advance. Publishes book an average of 12 months after acceptance. Simultaneous submissions OK. Reports in 2 weeks on queries; 6-8 weeks on mss. Manuscript guidelines for #10 SAE and 2 first class stamps.

Nonfiction: Coffee table book, how-to, juvenile, reference, self-help, devotionals, personal experience. Subjects include child guidance/parenting, Christianity women's issues/studies, inspirational. Query or submit outline/synopsis and sample chapters. Reviews artwork/photos as part of ms package.

Recent Nonfiction Title: *What Christians Must Know to Grow*, by Tom Carter.

Fiction: Adventure, juvenile, mystery, Christian, romance, young adult. Query or submit outline/synopsis and sample chapters.

Tips: "We believe there's a trend to get back to the basics. We want to see manuscripts that speak to the needs of everyday people, written in a basic, easy-to-read style. Men, women, and young adults wanting to receive encouragement through solid—yet basic—teaching and good family entertainment with values based on Christian-Judeo standards. Research the market, send for publisher submission guidelines, then submit the most complete, professional proposal possible. First impressions count."

FABER & FABER, INC., Division of Faber & Faber, Ltd., London, England; 50 Cross St., Winchester MA 01890. (617)721-1427. Estab. 1976. Publishes hardcover and trade paperback originals, and trade paperback reprints. Averages 15 titles/year; receives 600 submissions annually. 10% of books from first-time authors; 25% of books from unagented writers. Pays 10% royalty on wholesale or retail price; advance varies. Publishes book an average of 1 year after acceptance. Simultaneous submissions OK. Reports in 6 weeks on queries; 2-3 months on mss. Book catalog for 9×12 SAE and 4 first class stamps; writer's guidelines for #10 SASE.

Nonfiction: Anthologies, biography, contemporary culture, film and screenplays and natural history. Subjects include Americana, animals, pop/rock music, New England, and sociology. Query with synopsis and outline with SAE. Reviews artwork/photos as part of ms package.

Recent Nonfiction Title: *Brian Eno: His Music and the Vertical Color of Sound*, by Tamm.
Fiction: Collections, ethnic, experimental, juvenile (8-12), mainstream and regional. No historical/family sagas or mysteries. Query with synopsis and outline with SAE.
Recent Fiction Title: *Cradle & All: Women Writers on Pregnancy and Birth*, by Chester (ed).
Tips: "We are concentrating on subjects that have consistently done well for us. These include popular culture; serious, intelligent rock and roll books; anthologies; and literary, somewhat quirky fiction. Please do not send entire ms; please include SASE for reply."

FACTS ON FILE, INC., 460 Park Ave. S., New York NY 10016. (212)683-2244. Associate Publisher: Gerard Helferich. Estab. 1941. Publishes hardcover originals and hardcover reprints. Averages 125 titles/year; receives approximately 1,000 submissions annually. 25% of books from unagented writers. Pays 10-15% royalty on retail price. Offers average $10,000 advance. Simultaneous submissions OK. Query for electronic submissions. Reports in 2 weeks on queries; 1 month on mss. Free book catalog.
Nonfiction: Reference and other informational books on business and economics, cooking and foods (no cookbooks), health, history, hobbies (but no how-to), music, natural history, philosophy, psychology, recreation, religion, language and sports. "We need serious, informational books for a targeted audience. All our books must have strong library interest, but we also distribute books effectively to the book trade." No cookbooks, biographies, pop psychology, humor, do-it-yourself crafts or poetry. Query or submit outline/synopsis and sample chapters. Reviews artwork/photos.
Recent Nonfiction Title: *Who Was Who in Native American History*, by Carol Waldman.
Tips: "Our audience is school and public libraries for our more reference-oriented books and libraries, schools and bookstores for our less reference-oriented informational titles."

*FAIRCHILD BOOKS & VISUALS, Book Division, Subsidiary of Capital Cities, Inc., 7 E. 12th St., New York NY 10003. FAX: (212)887-1865. Manager: E.B. Gold. Estab. 1899. Publishes hardcover and paperback originals. Offers standard minimum book contract; no advance. Pays 10% of net sales distributed twice annually. Averages 12 titles/year; receives 100 submissions annually. 50% of books from first-time authors; 99% of books from unagented writers. Subsidy publishes 2% of books—1% subsidized by authors, 1% by organizations. Publishes book an average of 1 year after acceptance. Book catalog and ms guidelines for 9×12 SASE.
Nonfiction: Publishes business books and textbooks relating to fashion, marketing, retailing, career education, advertising, home economics and management. Length: open. Query, giving subject matter, brief outline and at least 1 sample chapter. Reviews artwork/photos as part of ms package.
Recent Nonfiction Title: *Fashion Design for the Plus Size*, by Frances Zangrillo.
Tips: "The writer has the best chance of selling our firm fashion, retailing or textile related books that can be used by both the trade and schools. If possible, the writer should let us know what courses would use the book."

*FAIRLEIGH DICKINSON UNIVERSITY PRESS, 285 Madison Ave., Madison NJ 07940. (201)593-8564. Director: Harry Keyishian. Estab. 1967. Publishes hardcover originals. Averages 30 titles/year; receives 300 submissions annually. 33% of books from first-time authors; 100% of books from unagented writers. Average print order for a writer's first book is 1,000. "Contract is arranged through Associated University Presses of Cranbury, New Jersey. We are a *selection* committee only." Subsidy publishes (nonauthor) 2% of books. Publishes book an average of 18 months after acceptance. Reports in 2 weeks on queries; 4 months average on mss.
Nonfiction: Reference and scholarly books. Subjects include art, business and economics, Civil War, film, history, Jewish studies, literary criticism, music, philosophy, politics, psychology, sociology and women's studies. Looking for scholarly books in all fields. No nonscholarly books. Query with outline/synopsis and sample chapters. Reviews artwork/photos as part of ms package.
Recent Nonfiction Title: *Before Infallibility—Liberal Catholicism in Biedermeier Vienna*, by Adam Bunnell.
Tips: "Research must be up to date. Poor reviews result when authors' bibliographies and notes don't reflect current research. We follow University of Chicago style in scholarly citations."

*FALCON PRESS PUBLISHING CO., INC., P.O. Box 1718, Helena MT 59624. (406)442-6597. FAX: (406)442-2995. Publisher: Bill Schneider. Estab. 1978. Publishes hardcover and trade paperback originals. Averages 20-30 titles/year. Subsidy publishes 20% of books. Pays 8-15% royalty on net price or pays flat fee. Publishes book an average of 6 months after ms is in final form. Reports in 3 weeks on queries. Free book catalog.
Nonfiction: "We're primarily interested in ideas for recreational guidebooks and books on regional outdoor subjects for either adults or children. We can only respond to submissions that fit these categories." No fiction or poetry. Query only; do not send ms.
Recent Nonfiction Title: *Yellowstone on Fire!*, by Bob Ekey.

*THE FAMILY ALBUM, Rt. 1, Box 42, Glen Rock PA 17327. (717)235-2134. Contact: Ron Lieberman. Publishes hardcover originals and reprints and software. Averages 4 titles/year; receives 150 submissions annually. 30% of books from first-time authors; 100% of books from unagented writers. Average print order for a

writer's first book is 1,000. Subsidy publishes 20% of books. Pays royalty on wholesale price. Publishes book an average of 10 months after acceptance. Simultaneous submissions OK. Query for electronic submissions. Reports in 2 months.
Nonfiction: "Significant works in the field of (nonfiction) bibliography. Worthy submissions in the field of Pennsylvania history, biography, folk art and lore. We are also seeking materials relating to books, literacy, and national development. Special emphasis on Third World countries, and the role of printing in international development." No religious material. Submit outline/synopsis and sample chapters.

FARRAR, STRAUS AND GIROUX, INC., 19 Union Sq. W., New York NY 10003. Publisher, Books for Young Readers: Stephen Roxburgh. Editor-in-Chief, Books for Young Readers: Margaret Ferguson. Publishes hardcover originals. Receives 5,000 submissions annually. Pays royalty; advance. Publishes book an average of 18 months after acceptance. Reports in 3 months. Catalog for #10 SAE and 3 first class stamps.
Nonfiction and Fiction: "We are primarily interested in fiction picture books and novels for children and middle readers and in nonfiction—both in picture book and longer formats." Submit outline/synopsis and sample chapters. Reviews copies of artwork/photos as part of ms package.
Recent Fiction Title: *Celine*, by Brock Cole.
Recent Picture Book Title: *Carl Goes Shopping*, by Alexandra Day.
Tips: Study our style and our list.

FAWCETT JUNIPER, Imprint of Ballantine/Del Rey/Fawcett/Ivy, 201 E. 50th St., New York NY 10022. (212)751-2600. Editor-in-Chief, Vice President: Leona Nevler. Publishes 24 titles/year. Pays royalty. Publishes book an average of 1 year after acceptance. Simultaneous submissions OK. Reports in 2 months on queries; in 4 months on mss. Free book catalog.
Nonfiction: Adult books.
Recent Nonfiction Title: *All I Really Need to Know I Learned in Kindergarten*, by Robert Fulghum.
Fiction: Juvenile, mainstream/contemporary, young adult. Query.
Recent Fiction Title: *Seven Against the Dealer*, Cynthia Voigt.

FEARON EDUCATION, Subsidiary of Simon & Schuster, 500 Harbor Blvd., Belmont CA 94002. (415)592-7810. Publisher: Carol Hegarty. Averages 100-120 titles/year. Pays royalty or fee outright. Reports in 1 month. Book catalog and ms guidelines for 9 × 12 SASE.
Nonfiction: Educational. Query or submit synopsis.
Recent Nonfiction Title: *Our Century Magazine*, (social studies).
Fiction: "Fearon Education is looking for easy-to-read fiction suitable for middle school and up. We prefer the major characters to be young adults or adults. Solid plotting is essential." Length: varies with series; write for specific guidelines.
Recent Fiction Title: *An American Family*, by Bledsoe/Jones.

FIDDLEHEAD POETRY BOOKS & GOOSE LANE EDITIONS, 248 Brunswick Street, Fredericton, New Brunswick E3B 1G9 Canada. (506)454-8319. FAX: (506)453-0088. Acquisitions Editor: John Timmins. Estab. 1957. Publishes hardcover and trade paperback originals. Averages 12 titles/year; receives 350 submissions annually. 33⅓% of books from first-time authors; 75-100% of books from unagented writers. Pays royalty on retail price. Small advances. Reports in 3 weeks on queries; 2 months on mss. Book catalog free on request.
Imprints: Goose Lane Editions (nonfiction, poetry and fiction).
Nonfiction: Coffee table books and reference on Canadian and maritime provinces, history, photography, regional literature and linguistics.
Recent Nonfiction Title: *Folksongs of New Brunswick*, by Edward D. Ive.
Fiction: Experimental, mainstream, "first" novel authors and others. SASE absolutely necessary for return of manuscript. Submit complete ms. Canadian or Canadian-oriented material only.
Recent Fiction Title: *A View from the Roof*, by Helen Weinzweig (stories).
Poetry: Open to collections of poetry; modern/experimental preferable. Submit complete ms with SASE.
Tips: "Goose Lane Editions is a small Canadian-owned literary press specializing in Canadian fiction and poetry. Those few American manuscripts which we do consider for publication—3 in the last 5 years—invariably demonstrate a Canadian connection of some kind."

FINANCIAL SOURCEBOOKS, Division of Sourcebooks, Inc., P.O. Box 313, Naperville IL 60566. (312)961-2161. Publisher: Dominique Raccah. Publishes hardcover and trade paperback originals. Firm averages 7 titles/year. 50% of books from first-time authors; 100% from unagented writers. Pays 5-15% royalty on wholesale price, or buys mss outright. Publishes book an average of 6 months after acceptance. Simultaneous submissions OK. Query for electronic submissions. Reports in 1 month on queries. "We do not want to see complete manuscripts." Book catalog free for SASE.
Nonfiction: Reference, technical and textbook. Subjects include business and finance, computers, money management, small business and economics/banking. "We publish books, directories and newsletters for financial executives. We also publish more general books, particularly in business and finance. We are now

looking for additional projects. The books of interest to us will establish a standard in their domain. We look for books with a well-defined, strong market such as reference works or books with a technical, informative bent." Query or submit outline/synopsis and sample chapters (2-3 chapters, not the 1st). Reviews artwork/ photos as part of ms package.

Recent Nonfiction Title: *Outsmarting the Competition: Practical Approaches to Finding and Using Competitive Information*, by John McGonagle, Jr., and Carolyn M. Vella.

Tips: "Executives today are bombarded with information in most every form through much of their working day. Writers can easily sell us books that will help a busy professional deal with the workload more productively. That means books that 1.) compile otherwise difficult to obtain (but useful) information; or 2.) develop new concepts or ideas that will help executives "work smarter"; or 3.) reformat concepts or information executives need into some more useful or digestible form (e.g. graphics, tutorials, etc.)."

DONALD I. FINE, INC., 19 W. 21st St., New York NY 10010. (212)727-3270. Imprints include Primus Library of Contemporary Americana. Publishes hardcover originals and trade paperback originals and reprints. Firm averages 60-75 titles/year. Receives 1,000 submissions/year. 30% of books from first-time authors. Pays royalty on retail price. Advance varies. Publishes book an average of 1 year after acceptance. Book catalog for SAE.
Nonfiction: Biography, cookbook, humor, self-help. Subjects include history, military/war and sports. All unsolicited mss are returned unopened. Reviews artwork/photos as part of ms package.
Recent Nonfiction Title: *Reasonable Doubt*, by Philip Friedman.
Fiction: Adventure, ethnic, fantasy, historical, horror, humor, literary, mainstream/contemporary, mystery, science fiction, suspense and western. All unsolicited mss are returned unopened.
Recent Fiction Title: *Chained Eagle*, by Everett Alvarez Jr.

FIREBRAND BOOKS, 141 The Commons, Ithaca NY 14850. (607)272-0000. Publisher: Nancy K. Bereano. Estab. 1985. Publishes hardcover and trade paperback originals and hardcover and trade paperback reprints. Averages 6-8 titles/year; receives 200-300 submissions annually. 50% of books from first-time authors; 75% of books from unagented writers. Pays 7-9% royalty on retail price, or makes outright purchase. Publishes book an average of 18 months after acceptance. Simultaneous submissions OK "with notification." Reports in 2 weeks on queries; 2 months on mss. Free book catalog.
Nonfiction: Criticism and essays. Subjects include feminism and lesbianism. Submit complete ms.
Recent Nonfiction Title: *A Burst of Light*, by Audre Lorde.
Fiction: Will consider all types of feminist and lesbian fiction.
Recent Fiction Title: *Trash*, by Dorothy Allison.
Recent Poetry Title: *Crime Against Nature*, by Minnie Bruce Pratt.
Tips: "Our audience includes feminists, lesbians, ethnic audiences, and other progressive people."

FISHER BOOKS, P.O. Box 38040, Tucson AZ 85740-8040. (602)292-9080. Estab. 1987. Publishes trade paperback originals and trade paperback reprints. Firm averages 20 titles/year. 25% of books from first-time authors; 50% from unagented writers. Pays 10-15% royalty on wholesale price. Pays advances sometimes. Simultaneous submissions OK. Reports in 1 month. Free book catalog.
Nonfiction: Cookbook, how-to and self-help. Subjects include child guidance/parenting, cooking, foods and nutrition, gardening, health/medicine, psychology and sports. Submit outline/synopsis and sample chapters.
Recent Nonfiction Title: *Good Fat, Bad Fat, How to Lower Your Cholesterol & Beat the Odds of a Heart Attack*, by Griffin & Castelli.

FITZHENRY & WHITESIDE, LTD., 195 Allstate Parkway, Markham, Ontario L3R 4T8 Canada. (416)477-0030. FAX: (416)477-9179. Vice President: Robert Read. Estab. 1966. Publishes hardcover and paperback originals and reprints. Royalty contract varies; advance negotiable. Publishes 50 titles/year, text and trade. Reports in 3 months. Enclose return postage.
Nonfiction: "Especially interested in topics of interest to Canadians, and by Canadians." Textbooks for elementary and secondary schools, also biography, business, history, health, fine arts. Submit outline and sample chapters. Length: open.
Recent Title: *Red Arctic*.

‡FIVE STAR PUBLICATIONS, P.O. Box 3142, Scottsdale AZ 85271-3142. (602)941-0770. Publisher: Linda Foster Radke. Publishes trade paperback originals. Firm averages 4 titles/year. Pays 6-15% on wholesale price, sometimes buys by outright purchase. Simultaneous submissions OK. Reports in 3 months on queries. Book catalog for $1.65 and 3 first class stamps.
Nonfiction: Cookbook, how-to, illustrated book, juvenile and directories. Subjects include child guidance/parenting, cooking, foods and nutrition, education and women's issues/studies. Submit outline/synopsis and sample chapters. Reviews artwork/photos as part of ms package.

Recent Nonfiction Title: *Nannies, Maids & More: The Complete Guide for Hiring Household Help*, by Linda F. Radke.

Fiction: Humor, picture books. Submit outline/synopsis and sample chapters.

Recent Fiction Title: *Shakespeare for Children: The Story of Romeo & Juliet*, by Cass Foster (children's literature).

Tips: "Research your topic thoroughly and see what else has already been done. Join professional publishing associations. Select a dynamic title for your book."

‡FLOCKOPHOBIC PRESS, One Hudson Street, New York NY 10013. (212)732-4003. Contact: J. Farley Upjohn. Publishes limited editions with special bindings. Firm averages 5 titles/year. Receives 50 submissions/year. 50% of books from first-time authors. 100% from unagented writers. Publishes book an average of 1 year after acceptance. Simultaneous submissions OK. Reports in 2 weeks on queries; 1 month on mss. Book catalog free on request when available. Manuscript guidelines free on request.

Nonfiction: Illustrated book. Subjects include art. "We are only interested in original art." Query. Reviews artwork/photos as part of ms package.

Fiction: Experimental or unusual prose. Query or submit complete ms.

Recent Fiction Title: *The Red Coat*, by Jean McGarry.

Poetry: "We are looking for experimental work." Submit varied samples.

Recent Poetry Title: *You Can't Get Milk From an Earlobe*, by J. Farley Upjohn (experimental).

Tips: "We're interested in small market idiosyncratic writers and artists for fine books."

J. FLORES PUBLICATIONS, P.O. Box 163001, Miami FL 33116. Editor: Eli Flores. Estab. 1982. Publishes trade paperback originals and reprints. Averages 10 titles/year. 99% of books from unagented writers. Pays 10-15% royalty on net sales; no advance. Publishes book an average of 1 year after acceptance. Simultaneous submissions OK. Reports in 1 month on queries; 6 weeks on mss. Book catalog and ms guidelines for 6×9 SAE with 2 first class stamps.

Nonfiction: How-to, illustrated book and self-help. "We need original nonfiction manuscripts on military science, weaponry, current events, self-defense, true crime, guerrilla warfare and military history. How-to manuscripts are given priority." No pre-Vietnam material. Query with outline and 2-3 sample chapters. Reviews artwork/photos. "Photos are accepted as part of the manuscript package and are strongly encouraged."

Recent Nonfiction Title: *Mercenary's Tactical Handbook*, by Sid Campbell.

Tips: "Trends include illustrated how-to books on a specific subject. Be thoroughly informed on your subject and technically accurate."

‡FLYING PENCIL PUBLICATIONS, P.O. Box 19062, Portland OR 97219. (503)245-2314. Publisher: Madelynne Diness. Publishes trade paperback originals and reprints. Publishes 4 titles/year; receives approximately 15 submissions/year. 30% from first-time authors; 80% from unagented writers. Pays 8-15% royalty on retail price. Offers $1,200 average advance. Publishes book an average of 9 months after acceptance. Simultaneous submissions OK. Reports in 2 weeks on queries; 1 month on mss. Free book catalog and ms guidelines.

Nonfiction: How-to, humor. Subjects include history, nature/environment, recreation, regional and travel. Looking for fishing guides and fishing how-to; western U.S. Americana/guides. No hunting-related mss. Submit outline/synopsis and sample chapters. Reviews artwork/photos as part of ms package.

Recent Nonfiction Title: *Fishing in Oregon*, by Casali/Diness.

Fiction: Adventure, humor, literary, mainstream/contemporary, short story collections, young adult, women's, adventure/nature for young adults. Needs fiction firmly rooted in a place, especially the American West. Submit outline/synopsis and sample chapters.

Tips: "Our audience is comprised of literate outdoorspersons. Pay close attention to detail: Submit a complete table of contents/outline, a sample chapter or introduction. And for nonfiction especially, some evidence of having thought hard about the target audience, its size and ways of merchandising to that target group."

FOCAL PRESS, Subsidiary of Butterworth Publishers, 80 Montvale Ave., Stoneham MA 02180. (617)438-8464. Senior Editor: Karen M. Speerstra. Estab. 1972. Imprint publishes hardcover and paperback originals and reprints. Averages 20-25 UK-US titles/year; entire firm averages 50-60 titles/year; receives 500-700 submissions annually. 25% of books from first-time authors; 90% from unagented writers. Pays 10-12% royalty on wholesale price; offers $1,500 average advance. Publishes book an average of 1 year after acceptance. Simultaneous submissions OK. Reports in 3 months. Free book catalog and ms guidelines.

Nonfiction: How-to, reference, technical and textbooks in media arts: photography, film and cinematography, broadcasting and performing arts. High-level scientific/technical monographs are also considered. We generally do not publish collections of photographs or books composed primarily of photographs. Our books are text-oriented, with artwork serving to illustrate and expand on points in the text." Query preferred, or submit outline/synopsis and sample chapters or complete ms. Reviews artwork/photos as part of ms package.

Recent Nonfiction Title: *Light: Science and Magic*, by Hunter and Fuqua.

‡**FORDHAM UNIVERSITY PRESS**, University P.O. Box L, Bronx NY 10458. (212)579-2320. FAX: (212)579-2708. Director: H.G. Fletcher. Estab. 1907. Averages 24 titles/year. Subsidy publishes 0-5% of books. Pays royalty on sales income. Publishes book an average of 2 years after acceptance. Reports in 1 week. Free book catalog.
Nonfiction: Humanities. "We would like the writer to use the *MLA Style Sheet*, latest edition. We do not want dissertations or fiction material." Send written queries only; do not send unsolicited manuscripts. "We prefer abstract, description and examples."
Recent Nonfiction Title: *Over & Back: The History of Ferryboats in New York Harbor*, by Cudahy.

FORMAN PUBLISHING, Suite 201, 2932 Wilshire Blvd., Santa Monica CA 90403. FAX: (213)453-4663. President: Len Forman. Executive Vice President: Claudia Forman. Estab. 1982. Publishes hardcover and trade paperback. Averages 6 titles/year; receives 1,000 submissions/year. 100% of books from first-time authors. 90% of books from unagented writers. Pays 6-15% royalty. Simultaneous submissions OK. Publishes book an average of 18 months after acceptance. Reports in 1 month on queries; 3 months on mss. Book catalog for 9 × 12 SASE.
Nonfiction: Cookbooks, how-to and self-help. Subjects include art, business and economics, cooking and foods, health, nature and psychology. Submit outline/synopsis and sample chapters. Reviews artwork/photos as part of ms package.
Recent Nonfiction Title: *How to Save a Fortune on Your Estate Taxes*, by Barry Kaye.

‡**FOUR WALLS EIGHT WINDOWS**, P.O. Box 548, New York NY 10014. Estab. 1987. Publishes hardcover and trade paperback originals and trade papberback reprints. Averages 12-15 titles/year. Receives 500 submissions/year. 20% of books from first-time authors. 66% from unagented writers. Pays royalty (depends—negotiated contract) on retail price. Offers $2,000 average advance. Publishes book an average of 10 months after acceptance. Reports in 2 weeks on queries; 4 months on mss. Free book catalog.
Nonfiction: Political, investigative. Subjects include art/architecture, cooking, foods and nutrition, government/politics, history, language/literature, nature/environment, science, travel. We do not want New Age works. Query. Submit outline with SASE. All sent without SASE returned unopened.
Recent Nonfiction Title: *Harvey Wasserman's History of The U.S.*, by Harvey Wasserman (history).
Fiction: Erotica, ethnic, experimental, feminist, horror, literary, mystery, science fiction. "No romance, popular." Query. Submit outline with SASE.
Recent Nonfiction Title: *Man with The Golden Arm*, by Nelson Algren (novel).
Tips: "Send us something original, unusual, off-beat, possibly 'alternative.' "

*****FRANCISCAN HERALD PRESS**, Sacred Heart Province of the Order of Friars Minor, 1434 W. 51st St., Chicago IL 60609. (312)254-4462. (312)254-4854. Managing Director: Gabriel Brinkman, OFMP. Estab. 1963. Publishes hardcover originals and trade paperback originals. Firm averages 9-12 titles/year. 20% of books from first-time authors; 99% from unagented writers. Subsidy publishes 10% of books. Pays 7-10% royalty on retail price. Publishing of book varies after acceptance. Query for electronic submissions. Reports in 2 weeks on queries; 1 month on mss.
Nonfiction: Religion. Submit complete ms.
Recent Nonfiction Title: *St. Francis of Assisi*, by R. Manselli.

THE FRASER INSTITUTE, 626 Bute St., Vancouver, British Columbia V6E 3M1 Canada. (604)688-0221. FAX: (604) 688-8539. Assistant Director: Sally Pipes. Publishes trade paperback originals. Averages 4-6 titles/year; receives 30 submissions annually. Pays honorarium. Publishes book an average of 6 months after acceptance. Simultaneous submissions OK. Query for electronic submissions. Reports in 6 weeks. Free book catalog; ms guidelines for SAE and IRC.
Nonfiction: Analysis, opinion, on economics, social issues and public policy. Subjects include business and economics, politics, religion and sociology. "We will consider submissions of high-quality work on economics, social issues, economics and religion, public policy, and government intervention in the economy." Submit complete ms.
Recent Nonfiction Title: *Economics and the Environment: A Reconciliation*, edited by Walter Block.
Tips: "Our books are read by well-educated consumers, concerned about their society and the way in which it is run and are adopted as required or recommended reading at colleges and universities in Canada, the U.S. and abroad. Our readers feel they have some power to improve society and view our books as a source of the information needed to take steps to change unproductive and inefficient ways of behavior into behavior which will benefit society. Recent trends to note in book publishing include affirmative action, banking, broadcasting, insurance, health care and religion. A writer has the best chance of selling us books on government, economics, finance, or social issues."

THE FREE PRESS, Division of Macmillan Co., Inc., 866 3rd Ave., New York NY 10022. President/Publisher: Erwin A. Glikes. Averages 65 titles/year; receives 3,000 submissions annually. 15% of books from first-time authors; 50% of books from unagented writers. Royalty schedule varies. Publishes book an average of 11 months after acceptance. Reports in 6 weeks.

Nonfiction: Publishes adult nonfiction, professional books and college texts in the social sciences, humanities and business. Reviews artwork/photos as part of ms package "but we can accept no responsibility for photos or art." Looks for "identifiable target audience, evidence of writing ability." Accepts nonfiction translations. Send 1-3 sample chapters, outline, and query letter before submitting mss.

SAMUEL FRENCH, INC., 45 W. 25th St., New York NY 10010. (212)206-8990. Subsidiaries include Samuel French Ltd. (London); Samuel French (Canada) Ltd. (Toronto); Samuel French, Inc. (Hollywood); and Baker's Plays (Boston). Editor: Lawrence Harbison. Publishes paperback acting editions of plays. Averages 80-90 titles/year; receives 1,200 submissions annually, mostly from unagented playwrights. About 10% of publications are from first-time authors; 20% from unagented writers. Pays 10% book royalty on retail price. Pays 90% stock production royalty; 80% amateur production royalty. Offers variable advance. Publishes book an average of 6 months after acceptance. Simultaneous submissions OK. Reports immediately on queries; from 6 weeks to 8 months on mss. Book catalog $1.25; ms guidelines $3.
Nonfiction: Acting editions of plays.
Tips: "Broadway and Off-Broadway hit plays, light comedies and mysteries have the best chance of selling to our firm. Our market is theater producers—both professional and amateur—and actors. Read as many plays as possible of recent vintage to keep apprised of today's market; write small-cast plays with good female roles; and be one hundred percent professional in approaching publishers and producers (see guidelines)."

FULCRUM, INC., 350 Indiana St., Golden CO 80401. (303)277-1623. Contact: Submissions Editor. Estab. 1985. Publishes hardcover and trade paperback originals, and reprints. Averages 15-25 titles/year; receives up to 1,500 submissions/year. 60% of books from first-time authors; 85% of books from unagented writers. Pays royalty on retail price; offers $1,500-5,000 average advance. Average first print run is 3,000-10,000. Publishes book an average of 1 year after acceptance. Query for electronic submissions. Reports in 1 month on queries; 6 weeks on mss. Book catalog for $8 × 10$ SAE with 3 first class stamps; ms guidelines for SASE.
Nonfiction: Nature, history, biography, self-development and other subjects of general interest. No how-to, sports, cookbooks, reference. Submit outline/synopsis and sample chapters. Reviews artwork/photos as part of ms package.
Recent Nonfiction Title: *One Hundred Over One Hundred*, by Jim Hoynan and Paul Boyor.

GALLAUDET UNIVERSITY PRESS, 800 Florida Ave. NE, Washington DC 20002. (202)651-5488. Imprints include Kendall Green Publications, Clerc Books, Gallaudet University Press. Editorial Assistant: Robyn D. Twit. Publishes hardcover originals, and trade paperback and mass market paperback originals and reprints. Firm averages 15 titles/year. Receives 450 submissions/year. 50% of books from first-time authors; 95% from unagented writers. Pays 10-15% royalty on wholesale price (net). Publishes book an average of 12-18 months after acceptance. Simultaneous and photocopied submissions OK. Query for electronic submissions. Reports in 3 months. Free book catalog and manuscript guidelines.
Nonfiction: Biography, illustrated book, juvenile, reference, self-help, technical, textbook and sign language. Subjects include child guidance/parenting, education, health/medicine, history, language/literature, psychology, regional, science, sociology, sports, translation and travel. All topics must relate to hearing impairment/deafness in some way (though topic doesn't have to focus on hearing impairment/deafness). "Because of the press's mission to publish books for and about deafness/hearing impairment, we'll accept books as long as they're somehow related." Submit outline/synopsis and sample chapters or complete ms. Reviews artwork/photos as part of ms package.
Recent Nonfiction Title: *How to Survive Hearing Loss*, by Charlotte Himber.
Fiction: Adventure, ethnic, fantasy, historical, humor, literary, mainstream/contemporary, mystery, picture books, plays, science fiction, short story collections, suspense, for children/young adults only. Do not publish adult fiction. (Most categories are considered as long as they relate to hearing impairment in some way.) "We need fiction for 8 to 12-year-olds and young adults with hearing-impaired character(s), although the hearing-impairment does not need to be the focus of the story." Submit outline/synopsis and sample chapters or complete ms.
Recent Fiction Title: *Annie's World*, by Nancy Smiler Levinson.
Tips: "The market is wide open and growing for books relating to hearing impairment due especially to an increased awareness of deafness and sign language among the public. Individuals in our audience come from many walks of life and include every age group. The common denominator among them is an interest and / or openness to learn more about hearing impairment/deafness."

GARBER COMMUNICATIONS, INC., (affiliates: Steinerbooks, Spiritual Fiction Publications, Spiritual Science Library, Rudolf Steiner Publications, Freedeeds Library, Biograf Publications), 5 Garber Hill Rd., Blauvelt NY 10913. (914)359-9292. Editor: Bernard J. Garber. Estab. 1958. Publishes hardcover and paperback originals and reprints. Does not accept unsolicited submissions. "We will refuse and return unsolicited submissions at the author's expense. We are not accepting any queries until January 1991." Averages 15 titles/year; receives 250 submissions annually. 10% of books from first-time authors; 10% of books from unagented writers. Average print order for a writer's first book is 500-1,000 copies. Pays 5-7% royalty on

Close-up

Elaine Costello
Director
Gallaudet University Press

As director of the 10-year-old Gallaudet University Press, Elaine Costello sees the press as having "unlimited potential to bring out exciting new titles." In addition to publishing a number of specialized titles for deaf students and those who work with them, the press plans a book/video series and other books for the trade market.

Costello was a teacher of deaf children for 10 years when she came to Gallaudet University to work on her doctorate. While there, she wrote textbooks that attracted the interest of publishers. University officials didn't release the books to commercial publishers but asked Costello to establish a university press.

For the first nine years, the press published between five and eight books per year. This year, Costello has increased the number to 17 titles under three imprints. Gallaudet University Press is the scholarly imprint; Clerc Books covers textbooks and public service books; and Kendall Green Publications is the children's imprint. All the books are related to deafness, have a deaf author or a deaf character.

Book ideas are generated both by authors and by press staff. "Our title *The Gallaudet Survival Guide to Signing* was in response to our need to give quick sign language lessons to newly-hired staff," says Costello. "That book is in its second edition and has sold a couple hundred thousand copies. In that case, our retiring managing editor wrote the manuscript for us." Another successful book, *The Week the World Heard Gallaudet*, is a chronicle of the week Gallaudet students successfully protested the appointment of a hearing president. "The idea was also developed in-house and we went out searching for an author to put it together for us," Costello says.

In addition to these books, Gallaudet University Press also has issued a number of "crossover" books. *How to Survive Hearing Loss* "is a perfect example of the kind of contribution Gallaudet University Press can make," Costello says. "It has substance and it has trade appeal to the more than 22 million elderly people in the United States who have lost their hearing later in life." *Come Sign with Us* in particular is designed for public school teachers, Scout troop and camp leaders to teach sign language to hearing children. "Hearing children love sign language and no other book like this exists," Costello says.

As a published author with Bantam, Crown and Random House, Costello has experience on both the writing and editorial sides of the desk. "Since our editorial program is quite specific—only books related to deafness—we don't appreciate the extraneous nonsolicited manuscripts that arrive without a prior letter of inquiry," Costello says. "We prefer a letter of inquiry asking if we are interested in seeing a manuscript."

Because writing a book for the press takes specialized knowledge, Costello works with a number of first-time authors. "For a special manuscript having great potential, we have been known to go the extra mile," she says. In addition, as a part of the university's special mission, Costello says staff members of the press "feel a special commitment to deaf authors and give them special encouragement."

—Glenda Tennant Neff

retail price; offers average $500 advance. Publishes book an average of 1 year after acceptance.

Nonfiction: Spiritual sciences, occult, philosophical, metaphysical and ESP. "These are for our Steiner Books division only." Serious nonfiction. Philosophy and Spiritual Sciences: Bernard J. Garber. Query only (with SASE or no response).

Fiction: For Spiritual Fiction Publications: Patricia Abrmas, editor. "We are now looking for original manuscripts or rewrites of classics in modern terms." Query only with SASE.

*GARDNER PRESS, INC., 19 Union Square West, New York NY 10003. (212)924-8293. FAX: (212)242-6339. Publisher: Gardner Spungin. Estab. 1975. Publishes hardcover originals and reprints. Firm averages 22 titles/year. Receives 150 submissions/year. 10% of books from first-time authors; 90% from unagented writers. Subsidy publishes 10% of books. Pays 6-15% royalty on wholesale price. Publishes book an average of 8-10 months after acceptance. Simultaneous submissions OK. Reports in 3 weeks. Free book catalog.

Nonfiction: Biography, reference, self-help and textbook. Subjects include child guidance/parenting, education, ethnic, gay/lesbian, health/medicine, psychology, recreation, religion, sociology, sports, translation and women's issues/studies. Query.

Recent Nonfiction Title: *Fathers & Sons: The Most Challenging of all Family Relationships*, by Lewis Yablonsky, Ph.D.

‡GARRETT PARK PRESS, P.O. Box 190, Garret Park MD 20896. Publisher: Robert Calvert. Estab. 1967. Publishes trade paperback originals. Firm averages 6 titles/year. Receives 15 submissions/year. 20% of books from first-time authors. 100% from unagented writers. Pays 10-15% royalty on wholesale or retail price. Publishes book an average of 8 months after acceptance. Reports in 1 month on queries; 2 months on mss. Free book catalog.

Nonfiction: Reference. Subjects include education, ethnic. Query.

GASLIGHT PUBLICATIONS, 626 North College Ave., Bloomington IN 47404. (812)332-5169. Imprints include McGuffin Books. Publisher: Jack Tracy. Estab. 1979. Publishes hardcover originals. Averages 6 titles/year. Receives 15-20 submissions/year. 75% of books from first-time authors; 90% from unagented writers. Pays 10% royalty on retail price. Publishes book an average of 1 year after acceptance. Simultaneous submissions OK. Reports in 1 month. Free book catalog.

Nonfiction: "We publish specialized studies of the mystery genre and related fields: biography, criticism, analysis, reference, film. Submissions should be serious, well-researched, not necessarily for the scholar, but for readers who are already experts in their own right. 12,000 words minimum." Query, submit outline/synopsis and sample chapters or send complete ms. Reviews artwork/photos as part of ms package.

Recent Nonfiction Title: *Nova 57 Minor: The Waxing and Waning of the 61st Adventure of Sherlock Holmes*, by Jon L. Lellenberg.

Tips: "Our purchasers tend to be public libraries and knowledgeable mystery aficionados."

‡GAY SUNSHINE PRESS AND LEYLAND PUBLICATIONS, P.O. Box 40397, San Francisco CA 94140. (415)824-3184. Editor: Winston Leyland. Estab. 1970. Publishes hardcover and trade paperback originals and trade paperback reprints. Averages 10 titles/year. Pays royalty or makes outright purchase. Reports in 3 weeks on queries; 1 month on mss. Book catalog $1.

Nonfiction: How-to and gay lifestyle topics. "We're interested in innovative literary nonfiction which deals with gay lifestyles." No long personal accounts, academic or overly formal titles. Query. "After query is returned by us, submit outline/synopsis and sample chapters. All unsolicited mss are returned unopened."

Recent Nonfiction Title: *The Delight of Hearts*, by Ahmad al-Tifashi (translated by Edward Lacey).

Fiction: Erotica, ethnic, experimental, historical, mystery, science fiction and gay fiction in translation. "Interested in well-written novels on gay themes; also short story collections. We have a high literary standard for fiction." Query. "After query is returned by us, submit outline/synopsis and sample chapters. All unsolicited mss are returned unopened."

Recent Fiction Title: *Crystal Boys*, by Pai Hsien-yung (translated by Howard Goldblatt).

‡GEM GUIDES BOOK COMPANY, 3677 San Gabriel Parkway, Pico Rivera CA 90660. (213)692-5492. Imprints include Gembooks. Editor: George Wilson. Publishes trade paperback originals. Averages 6-8 titles/year. Receives 20 submissions/year. 30% of books from first-time authors. 100% from unagented writers. Pays 6-10% royalty on wholesale price. Offers $1,000 average advance. Publishes book an average of 4 months after acceptance. Simultaneous submissions OK. Reports in 2 weeks on queries; 1 month on mss.

Nonfiction: Regional books for the southwest. Subjects include cooking, foods and nutrition, hobbies, nature/environment, recreation, travel. We are looking for books on bicycling in the southwest and nature books, particularly about rocks and minerals, for young readers. Query. Submit outline/synopsis and sample chapters. Reviews artwork/photos as part of ms package.

Recent Nonfiction Title: *Discover Historic California*, by Roberts (historical sites of CA).

Tips: "Authors have the best chance selling us books about rocks, minerals, and recreational opportunities in SW. We have a general audience of people interested in recreational activities. We are building a line of natural history books for young readers. Publishers plan and have specific books lines in which they specialize.

Learn about the publisher and submit materials compatible with that publisher's product line."

*GENEALOGICAL PUBLISHING CO., INC., 1001 N. Calvert St., Baltimore MD 21202. (301)837-8271. FAX: (301)752-8492. Editor-in-Chief: Michael H. Tepper, Ph.D. Estab. 1959. Publishes hardcover originals and reprints. Subsidy publishes 10% of books. Averages 80 titles/year; receives 400 submissions annually. 50% of books from first-time authors; 100% of books from unagented writers. Average print order for a writer's first book is 2,000-3,000. Offers straight 10% royalty on retail price. Publishes book an average of 6 months after acceptance. Reports "immediately." Enclose SAE and return postage.
Nonfiction: Reference, genealogy, and immigration records. "Our requirements are unusual, so we usually treat each author and his subject in a way particularly appropriate to his special skills and subject matter. Guidelines are flexible, but it is expected that an author will consult with us in depth. Most, though not all, of our original publications are offset from camera-ready typescript. Since most genealogical reference works are compilations of vital records and similar data, tabular formats are common. We hope to receive more ms material covering vital records and ships' passenger lists. We want family history compendia, basic methodology in genealogy, heraldry, and immigration records." Prefers query first, but will look at outline and sample chapter or complete ms. Reviews artwork/photos as part of ms package.
Recent Nonfiction Title: *The Researcher's Guide to American Genealogy*, by Val Greenwood.

‡GESSLER PUBLISHING COMPANY, INC., 55 W. 13th St., New York NY 10011. (212)627-0099. Imprints include Gessler Educational Software. President: Seth Levin. Publishes hardcover and softcover originals. Averages 8 titles/year. Pays royalty. Simultaneous submissions OK. Query for electronic submissions. Reports in 2 months on queries; 3 months on mss. Free book catalog.
Nonfiction: Reference and textbooks. Subjects include education and ethnic. Gessler is looking for mss from foreign language teachers on teaching French, Spanish, German and other languages to K-12 students. Submit outline/synopsis and sample chapters.
Fiction: Ethnic, juvenile, picture books and young adult in foreign languages. Submit outline/synopsis and sample chapters.

‡THE J. PAUL GETTY MUSEUM, Subsidiary of The J. Paul Getty Museum Trust, P.O. Box 2112, Santa Monica CA 90406. (213)459-7611. FAX: (213)454-8156. Editor: Cynthia Newman Helms. Publishes hardcover and trade paperback originals and reprints. Averages 10 titles/year; receives 50 submissions annually. 10% of books from first-time authors; 100% of books from unagented writers. Average print order for a writer's first book is 3,000. Buys some mss outright; offers average $2,000 honorarium. Publishes book an average of 18 months after acceptance. Query for electronic submissions. Reports in 1 months. Book list and ms guidelines for SASE.
Nonfiction: Reference and scholarly on art and history. "Scholarly titles and well-researched general and children's titles on topics related to the museum's seven collections: Greek and Roman art and architecture (especially the Villa dei Papiri), illuminated manuscripts, drawings and paintings from the Renaissance through the nineteenth century, European sculpture and decorative arts of the Regence through Napoleonic periods, and photographs." No nonEuropean art. Query. Reviews artwork/photos as part of ms package.
Recent Nonfiction Title: *European Drawings 1: Catalogue of the Collections, the J. Paul Getty Museum*, by George Goldner.
Tips: "Art history related to museum collections has the best chance of selling to our firm."

GIFTED EDUCATION PRESS, The Reading Tutorium, 10201 Yuma Ct., P.O. Box 1586, Manassas VA 22110. (703)369-5017. Publisher: Maurice D. Fisher. Estab. 1981. Publishes paperback originals for school districts and libraries. Averages 5 titles/year; receives 50 submissions annually. 100% of books from first-time authors; 100% of books from unagented writers. Pays royalty of $1 per book. Publishes book an average of 6 months after acceptance. Simultaneous submissions OK. Reports in 4 months. Book catalog and ms guidelines for #10 SAE with 2 first class stamps. Send letter of inquiry first.
Nonfiction: How-to. Subjects include philosophy, psychology, education of the gifted; and how to teach adults to read. "Need books on how to educate gifted children—both theory and practice, and adult literacy. Also, we are searching for books on using computers with the gifted, and teaching the sciences to the gifted. Need rigorous books on procedures, methods, and specific curriculum for the gifted. Send letter of inquiry only. Do not send manuscripts or parts of manuscripts."
Recent Nonfiction Title: *Adventures in Prehistoric Archaeology*, by Robert Bleiweiss.
Tips: "If I were a writer trying to market a book today, I would develop a detailed outline based upon intensive study of my field of interest. Present creative ideas in a rigorous fashion. Be knowledgeable about and comfortable with ideas. We are looking for books on using computers with gifted students; books on science and humanities education for the gifted; and books on how to teach adults to read."

GLENBRIDGE PUBLISHING LTD., 4 Woodland Lane, Macomb IL 61455. (309)833-5104. Editor: James A. Keene. Estab. 1986. Publishes hardcover originals and reprints, and trade paperback originals. Publishes 6 titles/year. Pays 10% royalty. Publishes book an average of 1 year after acceptance. Simultaneous submissions

OK. Reports in 1 week on queries; 1 month on mss. Ms guidelines for #10 SASE.

Nonfiction: Reference and textbook. Subjects include Americana, business and economics, history, music, philosophy, politics, psychology and sociology. "Academic and scholarly" books desired. Query or submit outline/synopsis and sample chapters. Include SASE.

Recent Nonfiction Title: *Choosing Lovers*, by Martin Blindek, M.D.

*GLOBAL BUSINESS AND TRADE, Suites 209-255, 386 East "H" St., Chula Vista CA 92010. (619)421-5923. Managing Editor: Monica A. Nelson. Estab. 1987. Publishes trade paperback and video cassettes. Averages 4 titles/year. Receives 25 submissions/year. 75% of books from first-time authors; 75% from unagented writers. Subsidy publishes 25% of books. Pays 7-15% royalty on net receipts. Offers small advance. Publishes book an average of 9 months after acceptance. Simultaneous and photocopied submissions OK. Query for electronic submissions. Reports in 3 weeks on queries; 2 months on mss.

Nonfiction: We are primarily interested in international business subjects. How-to, self-help textbooks. Subjects include business and economics, education and money/finance. Submit outline/synopsis and sample chapters.

Recent Nonfiction Title: *International Marketing Manual*, by Dr. Carl A. Nelson.

‡THE GLOBE PEQUOT PRESS, INC., 138 W. Main St., Chester CT 06412. (203)526-9571. Editorial Director: Betsy Amster. Editorial Contact Person: Kathleen Gruber. Publishes hardcover and paperback originals and paperback reprints. Averages 70 titles/year; receives 2,000 submissions annually. 30% of books from first-time authors; 60% of books from unagented writers. Average print order for a writer's first book is 5,000-7,500. Offers 7½-10% royalty on net price; offers advances. Publishes book an average of 1 year after acceptance. Simultaneous submissions OK. Reports in 6-10 weeks. Book catalog for 9×12 SASE.

Nonfiction: Travel guidebooks (regional OK), natural history, outdoor recreation, gardening, carpentry, how-to, Americana, biography, and cookbooks. No doctoral theses, genealogies, or textbooks. Submit outline, table of contents, sample chapter(s), and resume/vita. Complete mss accepted. Reviews artwork/photos.

‡GLOBE PRESS BOOKS, P.O. Box 2045, Madison Sq. Station, New York NY 10159. (914)962-4614. Publisher: Joel Friedlander. Imprint includes Fourth Way Books. Estab. 1985. Publishes hardcover and trade paperback originals. Averages 4 titles/year; receives 12 submissions/year. 25% of books from first-time authors. 50% of books from unagented writers. Pays royalty on retail price. Publishes book an average of 1 year after publication. Simultaneous submissions OK. Query for electronic submissions. Reports in 6 weeks. Book catalog for #10 SASE.

Nonfiction: Self-help and esoteric psychology. Subjects include history, philosophy and psychology. "We want manuscripts on east/west psychology and esoteric thought. No economics, politics or how-to books." Query or submit outline/synopsis and sample chapters. Reviews artwork/photos as part of ms package.

Recent Nonfiction Title: *Body of Light*, by John Mann and Lar Short.

Tips: "Well written, well thought-out mss on esoteric approaches to psychology, art, literature and history are needed."

DAVID R. GODINE, PUBLISHER, INC., 300 Masachusetts Ave., Boston MA 02115. (617)536-0761. Subsidiaries: Ergo Books, Nonpareil Books. Contact: Thomas Frick, Editor. Publishes hardcover and trade paperback originals and reprints. Publishes 35 titles/year. 30% of books from first-time authors; 5-10% from unagented writers. Pays royalty on retail price. Publishes ms an average of 18 months after acceptance. Simultaneous and photocopied submissions OK. Reports in 6 weeks.

Nonfiction: Biography, cookbooks, illustrated books, juvenile. Subjects include Americana, art/architecture, cooking, foods and nutrition, gardening, history, language/literature, music/dance, nature/environment, photography, regional, translation, travel. Needs more history and biography, less photography. No genealogies, sports books, college theses, celebrity address books, or adventure/suspense. Query or submit ms. Reviews artwork/photos as part of complete ms package.

Recent Nonfiction Title: *The Complete Plain Words*, by Sir Ernest Gowers.

Fiction: Literary, mainstream/contemporary and mystery. No science fiction, fantasy, adventure, or religious books. Query or submit complete ms.

Recent Fiction Title: *Mefisto*, by John Banville.

Tips: "In fiction, literary works appeal to us the most; that is, books that are thoughtful and well written as well as original in plot and intent. We also like beautifully illustrated books."

GOLDEN WEST PUBLISHERS, 4113 N. Longview, Phoenix AZ 85014. (602)265-4392. Editor: Hal Mitchell. Publishes trade paperback originals. Averages 5-6 titles/year; receives 200 submissions annually. 50% of books from first-time authors; 100% of books from unagented writers. Average print order for a writer's first book is 5,000. Pays 6-10% royalty on retail price. No advance. Publishes book an average of 6 months after acceptance. Simultaneous submissions OK. Query for electronic submissions. Reports in 2 weeks on queries; 1 month on mss. Book catalog for #10 SASE.

Nonfiction: Cookbooks, books on the Southwest and West. Subjects include cooking and foods, southwest history and outdoors, and travel. Query or submit outline/synopsis and sample chapters. Prefers query letter first. Reviews artwork/photos as part of ms package.
Recent Title: *Mavericks: Ten Uncorralled Westerners*, by Dale Walker.
Tips: "We are primarily interested in Arizona and Southwest material and welcome material in this area."

GOSPEL PUBLISHING HOUSE, Imprint of Assemblies of God General Council, 1445 Boonville Ave., Springfield MO 65802-1894. (417)862-2781. Book Editor: Glen Ellard. Estab. 1914. Firm publishes hardcover, trade and mass market paperback originals. Publishes 18 titles/year. Receives 380 submissions/year. 90% of books from first-time authors; 90% from unagented writers. Pays 10% royalty on retail price. Publishes book an average of 18 months after acceptance. Simultaneous submissions OK. Reports in 2 weeks on queries; 2 months on mss. Free book catalog and ms guidelines.
Nonfiction: Biography and self-help. Subjects include education (Christian or deaf), history (Assemblies of God), religion (Bible study, Christian living, devotional, doctrinal, evangelism, healing, Holy Spirit, missionary, pastoral, prophecy). "Gospel Publishing House is owned and operated by the Assemblies of God. Therefore, the doctrinal viewpoint of all books published is required to be compatible with our denominational positions." Query or submit outline/synopsis and sample chapters.
Recent Nonfiction Title: *Going It Alone*, by Bette Carter.
Tips: "Not currently accepting fiction manuscripts."

GOVERNMENT INSTITUTES, INC., Suite 24, 966 Hungerford Dr., Rockville MD 20850. (301)251-9250. Vice President, Publishing: G. David Williams. Estab. 1973. Publishes hardcover and softcover originals. Averages 30 titles/year; receives 20 submissions annually. 50% of books from first-time authors; 100% of books from unagented writers. Pays variable royalty or fee. No advance. Publishes book an average of 2 months after acceptance. Simultaneous submissions OK. Reports in 1 month on queries; 2 months on mss. Book catalog available on request.
Nonfiction: Reference and technical. Subjects include environmental law, health, safety and real estate. Needs professional-level titles in environmental law, health, safety and real estate. Submit outline and sample chapters.
Recent Nonfiction Title: *Environmental Law Handbook, 10th Edition*, by J. Gordon Arbuckle, et al. (professional).

GRAPEVINE PUBLICATIONS, INC., Box 118, Corvallis OR 97339. (503)754-0583. Managing Editor: Christopher M. Coffin. Developmental Editor: Daniel R. Coffin. Publishes trade paperback originals. Averages 6-10 titles/year; receives 200-300 submissions/year. 20% of books from first-time authors; 100% of books from unagented writers. Pays 6-9% royalty on retail price. Publishes book an average of 6 months after acceptance. Simultaneous submissions OK. Query for electronic submissions. Reports in 2 weeks on queries; 1 month on mss.
Nonfiction: Tutorials on technical subjects written for the layperson, innovative curricula or resources for math and science teachers. Subjects include math, science, computers, calculators, software video, audio and other technical tools. Submit complete ms.
Recent Nonfiction Title: *Problem-Solving Situations: A Resource Book for Teachers of the 90s*, by Greenberg.
Tips: "We place heavy emphasis on readability, visual presentation, clarity, and reader participation. We will insist on numerous diagrams and illustrations, loosely-spaced text, large, easy-to-read formats, friendly, conversational writing, but tight, well-designed instruction. We disguise top-flight teaching as merely refreshing reading. The writer must be first and foremost a teacher who holds an engaging one-on-one conversation with the reader through the printed medium."

GRAPHIC ARTS CENTER PUBLISHING CO., 3019 NW Yeon Ave., P.O. Box 10306, Portland OR 97210. (503)226-2402. FAX: (503)223-1410. General Manager and Editor: Douglas Pfeiffer. Estab. 1968. Publishes hardcover originals. Averages 10 titles/year. Makes outright purchase, averaging $3,000.
Nonfiction: "All titles are pictorials with text. Text usually runs separately from the pictorial treatment. Authors must be previously published and are selected to complement the pictorial essay." Query.
Recent Nonfiction Title: *Utah*, by Ann Zwinger.

GRAPHIC ARTS TECHNICAL FOUNDATION, 4615 Forbes Ave., Pittsburgh PA 15213-3796. (412)621-6941. Editor-in-Chief: Thomas M. Destree. Estab. 1924. Publishes trade paperback originals. Firm averages 15 titles/year; imprint averages 10 titles/year. Receives 10 submissions/year. 50% of books from first-time au-

For information on book publishers' areas of interest, see the nonfiction and fiction sections in the Book Publishers Subject Index.

thors; 100% from unagented writers. Pays 5-15% royalty on member price. Publishes book an average of 1 year after acceptance. Query for electronic submissions. Reports in 1 month on queries; 2 months on mss. Free book catalog and manuscript guidelines.

Nonfiction: How-to, reference, technical and textbook. Subjects include printing/graphic arts. "We want textbook/reference relating to printing and related technologies, providing that the content does not overlap appreciably with any other GATF books in print or in production. Although original photography is related to printing, we do not anticipate publishing any books on that topic." Query or submit outline/synopsis and sample chapters. Reviews artwork/photos as part of ms package.

Recent Nonfiction Title: *Lithographers Manual*, by Ray Blair and Thomas M. Destree (textbook on lithographic printing).

Tips: "Our typical audience would be students in high schools and colleges as well as trainees in the printing industry."

GRAYWOLF PRESS, Suite 203, 2402 University Ave., St. Paul MN 55114. (612)641-0077. FAX: (612)641-0036. Assistant Editor: Rosie O'Brien. Estab. 1974. Publishes hardcover and trade paperback originals and hardcover and trade paperback reprints. Averages 12-16 titles/year. Receives 2,000 submissions/year. 20% of books from first-time authors. Pays 6-12½% royalty on retail price. Offers $2,000 average advance. Publishes book an average of 9 to 18 months after acceptance. Simultaneous submissions OK but discouraged. Reports in 1 month on queries. Free book catalog.

Nonfiction: Literary essays and memoirs. Query first.

Fiction: Literary novels and short story collections. Query first.

Recent Fiction Title: *Skywater*, by Melinda Worth Popham.

GREAT NORTHWEST PUBLISHING AND DISTRIBUTING COMPANY, INC., Box 10-3902, Anchorage AK 99510-3902. (907)373-0122. President: Marvin H. Clark Jr. Publishes hardcover and trade paperback originals. Averages 5 titles/year; receives 22-25 submissions annually. 30% of books from first-time authors; 100% of books from unagented writers. Pays 10% royalty. Publishes book an average of 1 year after acceptance. Simultaneous submissions OK. Query for electronic submissions. Reports in 2 weeks on queries; 2 months on mss. Free book catalog.

Nonfiction: Biography and how-to. Subjects include Alaska and hunting. "Alaskana and hunting books by very knowledgeable hunters and residents of the Far North interest our firm." Query.

Recent Nonfiction Title: *Alaska Safari*, by Harold Schetzle.

Tips: "Pick a target audience first, subject second. Provide crisp, clear journalistic prose."

WARREN H. GREEN, INC., 8356 Olive Blvd., St. Louis MO 63132. FAX: (314)997-1788. Editor: Warren H. Green. Estab. 1966. Imprint includes Fireside Books. Publishes hardcover originals. Offers "10-20% sliding scale of royalties based on quantity distributed. All books are short run, highly specialized, with no advance." Subsidy publishes about 1% of books, e.g., "books in philosophy and those with many color plates." Averages 30 titles/year; receives 200 submissions annually. 15% of books from first-time authors; 100% of books from unagented writers. "37% of total marketing is overseas." Catalog available on request. Publishes book an average of 10 months after acceptance. Simultaneous submissions OK. Query or submit outline and sample chapters. "Publisher requires 300- to 500-word statement of scope, plan, and purpose of book, together with curriculum vitae of author." Reports in 60-90 days.

Nonfiction: Medical and scientific. "Specialty monographs for practicing physicians and medical researchers. Books of 160 pages upward. Illustrated as required by subject. Medical books are non-textbook type, usually specialties within specialties, and no general books for a given specialty. For example, separate books on each facet of radiology, and not one complete book on radiology. Authors must be authorities in their chosen fields and accepted as such by their peers. Books should be designed for all doctors in English speaking world engaged in full or part time activity discussed in book. We would like to increase publications in the fields of radiology, anesthesiology, pathology, psychiatry, surgery and orthopedic surgery, obstetrics and gynecology, and speech and hearing." Also interested in books on health, philosophy, psychology and sociology. Reviews artwork/photos as part of ms package.

Recent Nonfiction Title: *Drug And Alcohol Abuse*, by Herrington.

GREEN TIGER PRESS INC., 435 E. Carmel St., San Marcos CA 92069-4362. (619)744-7575. FAX: (619)744-8130. Submit to Editorial Committee. Estab. 1970. Publishes picture books, greeting cards, calendars, posters and stationery. Averages 12-15 titles/year; receives 2,500 submissions annually. Pays royalty on retail price.

Recent Fiction Title: *Grandma's Scrapbook*, by Josephine Nobisso.

Tips: "We look for manuscripts containing a visionary or imaginative quality, often with a mythic feeling where fantasy and reality co-exist. We also welcome nostalgia and the world of the child themes. We do not publish science fiction. Since we are a visually-oriented house, we look for manuscripts whose texts readily conjure up visual imagery. Never send originals. Samples will be returned only if accompanied by SASE. Please allow three months before inquiring about your submission."

GREENHAVEN PRESS, INC., P.O. Box 289009, San Diego CA 92128-9009. Senior Editor: Bonnie Szumski. Estab. 1970. Publishes hard and softcover educational supplementary materials and (nontrade) juvenile nonfiction. Averages 20-30 juvenile manuscripts published/year; all are works for hire; receives 100 submissions/year. 50% of juvenile books from first-time authors; 100% of juvenile books from unagented writers. Makes outright purchase for $1,500-3,500. Publishes book an average of 1 year after acceptance. Simultaneous (if specified) submissions OK. Book catalog for 9 × 12 SAE with 2 first class stamps.

Nonfiction: Biography, illustrated book, juvenile, reference and textbook. Subjects include animals, business and economics, history, nature, philosophy, politics, psychology, religion and sociology. "We produce tightly formatted books for young people grades 4-6 and 7-9. Each series has specific requirements: Great Mysteries (5th-8th grade); Overviews (5th-8th grade); Opposing Viewpoints Juniors (5th-6th grade). Encyclopedia of Discovery and Invention (5th-8th grade). Potential writers should familiarize themselves with our catalog and senior high material. No unsolicited manuscripts." Query or submit outline/synopsis and sample chapters. Reviews artwork/photos as part of manuscript package.

Recent Nonfiction Title: *Garbage*, by Karen O'Connor.

Nonfiction Juvenile: *Pearl Harbor*, by Deborah Bacharach.

‡GROSSET & DUNLAP PUBLISHERS, 200 Madison Ave., New York NY 10016. Editor-in-Chief: Jane O'Connor. Publishes hardcover and paperback originals. Averages 75 titles/year; receives more than 3,000 submissions annually. Pays $500-2,000 in outright purchase; advance negotiable. Publishes book an average of 18 months after acceptance. Simultaneous submissions OK. Reports in 10 weeks.

Nonfiction: Juveniles. Submit proposal or query first. "Nature, science, and light technology are of interest." Looks for "new ways of looking at the world of a child."

Fiction: Juveniles, picture books for 3-7 age group and some higher. Submit proposal or query first.

Recent Fiction Title: *Whiskerville Board Books*, by Joanne Barkan.

Tips: "Nonfiction that is particularly topical or of wide interest in the mass market; a new concept for novelty format for preschoolers; and very well-written fiction on topics that appeal to parents of preschoolers have the best chance of selling to our firm. We want something new — a proposal for a new series for the ordinary picture book. You have a better chance if you have new ideas."

*GUERNICA EDITIONS, Box 633, Station N.D.G., Montreal, Quebec H4A 3R1 Canada. (514)256-5599. President/Editor: Antonio D'Alfonso. Publishes hardcover and trade paperback originals, hardcover and trade paperback reprints and software. Averages 10 titles/year; receives 1,000 submissions annually. 5% of books from first-time authors. Average print order for a writer's first book is 750-1,000. Subsidy publishes (nonauthor) 50% of titles. "Subsidy in Canada is received only when the author is established, Canadian-born and active in the country's cultural world. The others we subsidize ourselves." Pays 3-10% royalty on retail price. Makes outright purchase of $200-5,000. Offers 10¢/word advance for translators. IRCs required. "American stamps are of no use to us in Canada." Reports in 1 month on queries; 6 weeks on mss. Book catalog for SASE.

Nonfiction: Biography, humor, juvenile, reference and textbook. Subjects include art, history, music, philosophy, politics, psychology, recreation, religion and Canadiana.

Recent Nonfiction Title: *Conscience and Coercion*, by Antonio Gualtieri.

Fiction: Ethnic, historical, mystery. "We wish to open up into the fiction world. No country is a country without its fiction writers. Canada is growing some fine fiction writers. We'd like to read you. No first novels." Query.

Poetry: "We wish to have writers in translation. Any writer who has translated Italian poetry is welcomed. Full books only. Not single poems by different authors, unless modern, and used as an anthology. First books will have no place in the next couple of years." Submit samples.

Recent Poetry Title: *Positions to Pray in*, by Barry Dempster.

Tips: "We are seeking less poetry, more modern novels, and translations into the English or French."

‡*GULF PUBLISHING CO., Book Division, P.O. Box 2608, Houston TX 77252-2608. (713)529-4301. FAX: (713)520-4438. Vice President: C.A. Umbach Jr. Editor-in-Chief: William J. Lowe. Estab. 1916. Imprints include Gulf (sci-tech and business/management), Lone Star Books (regional Texas books) and Pisces Books, (travel and outdoor recreation line). Publishes hardcover and large format paperback originals and software. Averages 35 titles/year; receives 200 submissions annually. 1% of books from first-time authors; 100% of books from unagented writers. Subsidy publishes 5% of books. Pays 10% royalty on net income. Publishes book an average of 10 months after acceptance. Simultaneous submissions OK. Query for electronic submissions. Reports in 2 months. Free book catalog; ms guidelines for SASE.

Nonfiction: Popular science, business, management, reference, regional trade, scientific and technical. Submit outline/synopsis and 1-2 sample chapters. Reviews artwork/photos as part of ms package.

Recent Nonfiction Title: *Almanac of Soviet Manned Space Flight*, by Dennis Newkirk.

Tips: "Common mistakes writers make include calling first, not having a marketing plan of their own, and not matching publishers with their subject. Tell us the market, and how it can be reached at *reasonable* cost."

‡HALF HALT PRESS, INC., 6416 Burkittsville Rd., Middletown MD 21769. (301)371-9110. Publisher: Elizabeth Carnes. Publishes hardcover and trade paperback originals (90% originals, 10% reprints). Firm averages 8 titles/year. Receives 25 submissions/year. 50% of books from first-time authors. 50% from unagented authors. Pays 10-12.5% royalty on retail price. Offers advance by agreement. Publishes book an average of 1 year after acceptance. Reports in 1 month on queries; 4 months on mss. Free book catalog.
Nonfiction: Instructional: Horse and equestrian related subjects only. Subjects include horses only. We need serious instructional works by authorities in the field on horse-related topics, broadly defined. Query. Reviews artwork/photos as part of ms package.
Recent Nonfiction Title: *Dancing With Your Horse*, by Mary Campbell (freestyle dressage).
Tips: "Writers have the best chance selling us well written, unique works that teach serious horse people how to do something better. If I were a writer trying to market a book today, I would offer a straightforward presentation, letting work speak for itself, without hype or hard sell. Allow publisher to contact writer, without frequent calling to check status. They haven't forgotten the writer but may have many different proposals at hand; frequent calls to 'touch base,' multiplied by the number of submissions, become an annoyance. As the publisher/author relationship becomes close and is based on working well together, early impressions may be important, even to the point of being a consideration in acceptance for publication."

ALEXANDER HAMILTON INSTITUTE, 197 W. Spring Valley Ave., Maywood NJ 07607. (201)587-7050. Editor-in-Chief: Brian L.P. Zevnik. Estab. 1908. Publishes 3-ring binder and paperback originals. Averages 18 titles/year; receives 150 submissions annually. 40% of books from first-time authors; 90% of books from unagented writers. "We pay advance against negotiated royalty or straight fee (no royalty)." Offers average $3,000 advance. Publishes book an average of 10 months after acceptance. Simultaneous submissions OK. Reports in 1 month on queries; 2 months on mss.
Nonfiction: Executive/management books for two audiences. One is overseas, upper-level manager. "We need how-to and skills building books. *No* traditional management texts or academic treatises." The second audience is U.S. personnel executives and high-level management. Subject is legal personnel matters. "These books combine court case research and practical application of defensible programs." Query or submit outline or synopsis. Preferred form is outline, three paragraphs on each chapter, examples of lists, graphics, cases.
Recent Nonfiction Title: *Management Advancement Program*, by James M. Jenks.
Tips: "We sell exclusively by direct mail to managers and executives around the world. A writer must know his/her field and be able to communicate practical systems and programs."

HANCOCK HOUSE PUBLISHERS LTD., 1431 Harrison Ave., Blaine WA 98230. (604)538-1114. FAX: (604)538-2262. Publisher: David Hancock. Estab. 1971. Publishes hardcover and trade paperback originals, and hardcover and trade paperback reprints. Averages 12 titles/year; receives 400 submissions annually. 50% of books from first-time authors; 100% of books from unagented writers. Pays 10% maximum royalty on wholesale price. Simultaneous submissions OK. Publishes book an average of 6 months after acceptance. Reports in 6 months. Book catalog free on request. Ms guidelines for SASE.
Nonfiction: Biography, cookbook, how-to and self-help. Subject include Americana; cooking and foods; history (Northwest coast Indians); nature; recreation (sports handbooks for teachers); sports; and investment guides. Query with outline/synopsis and sample chapters. Reviews artwork/photos.
Recent Nonfiction Title: *Spirit Quest*, by Carol Batdorf.

HARBINGER HOUSE, INC., 2802 N. Alvernon Way, Tucson AZ 85712. (602)326-9595. Editor: Zdenek Gerych. Children's Book Editor: Jeffrey H. Lockridge. Publishes hardcover originals and trade paperback originals and reprints. Averages 20 titles/year. Receives 400 submissions/year. 50% of books from first-time authors. 80% from unagented writers. Pays 8-15% royalty on net receipts. Offers $1,500 average advance. Publishes book an average of 10 months after acceptance. Simultaneous submissions OK. Reports in 1 month on queries; 4 months on mss. Book catalog for 7½ × 10½ SAE and 4 first class stamps. Manuscript guidelines for #10 SASE.
Nonfiction: Personal growth, social issues. Subjects include child guidance/parenting, nature/environment, psychology, sociology and women's issues/studies. Submit outline/synopsis and 2 sample chapters, resume and SASE for return of materials.
Recent Nonfiction Title: *Corrido de Cocaine: Inside Stories of Hard Drugs, Big Money and Short Lives*, by Arturo Carrillo.
Fiction: Children's Books: picture books; stories for middle readers. For short children's books, send ms. Artwork reviewed as part of ms. package. Include SASE for return of materials.
Recent Fiction Title: *Lissa and the Moon's Sheep*, by Goldblatt, (children's book).
Tips: "We publish very few adult titles, so please submit only if you have one of the best books ever written."

HARCOURT BRACE JOVANOVICH, Children's Books Division, 1250 Sixth Ave., San Diego CA 92101. (619) 699-6810. Imprints include HBJ Children's Books, Gulliver Books, Voyager and Odyssey Paperbacks, and Jane Yolen Books. Attn: Manuscript Submissions. Publishes hardcover originals and trade paperback re-

Close-up

Lee K. Abbott
Writer

"I hope all writers are readers," says Lee K. Abbott. "There's a symbiotic relationship between the two." Reading figures heavily into a fiction writing workshop conducted by Abbott. "Fiction writing classes provide students with discipline and an audience." That audience is the writer's peer group of readers.

"Every writer needs a reader," Abbott says. "It's crucial that a writer know someone who can talk the language." These reader-writer relationships need not exist only in classroom settings or masters of fine arts programs. Abbott happened to find his peer group as a sophomore at New Mexico State University. "I hung around the creative writing ghetto," he says. "The interested students gathered around the two or three writing professors and the school literary magazine."

Abbott's first mentor was James Mealy, "an enormously accomplished pulp writer" as Abbott calls him. Mealy taught the craft of writing with drills, many of which Abbott has passed along to his students at Ohio State. "Mealy used to say that if you want to send a message, hire Western Union," Abbott says. "He accepted no excuses for writer's block or lack of inspiration. He wanted us to do a very clever thing called plain and simple writing."

With this motivation, Abbott published his first story in 1973, the same year he received his master's in English from New Mexico State. *Prism International,* a literary magazine associated with the University of British Columbia, accepted "The Next Best Thing to Being There," for which Abbott was paid $35. "I was thrilled," he recalls. He continued publishing stories in various literary magazines, and, after a brief stint teaching, returned to college for an M.F.A. from the University of Arkansas in 1979.

During this period Abbott was writing stories that were detached from his experiences of the New Mexico deserts. "They were all disengaged from me," he says. "They were well crafted, but had no guts. I was writing about New York when I should have been writing about New Mexico." He looks back on himself as a "technocrat" at that time. "I invested little of myself in the people and situations I was writing about." Gradually Abbott came around to writing from his experience again.

He hadn't given much thought to publishing a book until he had placed several stories in *North American Review.* "The editor wondered if I had a book," Abbott says, "and I didn't." Seven months later, they compiled his successful stories into *The Heart Never Fits Its Wanting,* which won the St. Lawrence Prize for best first collection of short stories.

Since then Abbott has published three more collections of short stories. His third, *Strangers in Paradise,* was nominated for a Pulitzer Prize. *Dreams of Distant Lives,* his most recent collection, was published by G.P. Putnam in 1989. His stories have appeared in *The Best American Short Stories, The O. Henry Short Story Awards* and *The Pushcart Prize.*

Abbott finds the climate for publishing short stories more conservative among book publishers than magazines, but says little/literary magazines are an excellent training ground. "Writers should disregard the trends and concentrate on their writing," he says. "Make it your challenge to put, as Perry Smith says, some hair on the walls."
—Mark Kissling

prints. Division publishes 75 hardcover originals/year and 40-50 paperback reprints/year. Royalty varies. Advance varies. Publishes ms an average of 2 years after acceptance. Reports in 6 weeks on queries; 2 months on mss. Book catalog for 9 × 12 SAE with 3 first class stamps. Manuscript guidelines for #10 SAE wth 1 first class stamp.

Nonfiction: Juvenile. Query. Reviews artwork/photos as part of ms package "but requests that no originals are sent."

Fiction: Query or submit outline/synopsis and sample chapters for middle-grade and young-adult novels; or complete ms for picture books.

Tips: "The trade division of Harcourt Brace Jovanovich does not accept any unsolicited manuscripts. The children's division is the only one open to unsolicited submissions."

MAX HARDY—PUBLISHER, P.O. Box 28219, Las Vegas NV 89126-2219. (702)368-0379. Owner: Max Hardy. Estab. 1974. Publishes trade paperback originals. Averages 5 titles/year; rccciivcs few submissions/year. Small percentage of books from first-time authors. 100% of books from unagented writers. Pays 10% royalty on retail price. Publishes book an average of 8 months after acceptance. Query for electronic submissions. Reports in 2 weeks. Book catalog free on request.

Nonfiction: Textbooks on bridge. Especially needs "quality educational material preferably from known bridge authorities. No other topics." Query.

Recent Nonfiction Title: *Better Bidding With Bergen*, by Marty Bergen.

Fiction: Bridge fiction only. Query.

Recent Fiction Title: *The Jake of Diamonds*, by Don Von Elsner (bridge novel).

HARPER & ROW, SAN FRANCISCO, Division of HarperCollins, Icehouse One #401; 151 Union St., San Francisco CA 94111-1299. (415)477-4400. Editor-in-Chief: Thomas Grady. Firm publishes hardcover and trade paperback originals and trade paperback reprints. Publishes 150 titles/year. Receives about 10,000 submissions/year. 5% of books from first-time authors; 50% from unagented writers. Pays royalty. Publishes book an average of 18 months after acceptance. Simultaneous (if notified) and photocopied submissions OK. Reports in 2 months on queries; 6 months on mss. Free book catalog and ms guidelines.

Nonfiction: Biography, how-to, reference, self-help. Subjects include addiction/recovery, philosophy, psychology, religion, women's issues/studies, theology, New Age. Query or submit outline/synopsis and sample chapters.

Recent Nonfiction Title: *Co-Dependent No More*, by Melody Beattie.

HARPER JUNIOR BOOKS GROUP, Division of HarperCollins Publishers, 10 E. 53rd St., New York NY 10022. Imprints include: Harper & Row Junior Books, including Charlotte Zolotow Books; T.Y. Crowell; Lippincott and Trophy Junior Books. Publisher: Elizabeth Gordon. Executive Editor, West Coast: Linda Zuckerman. Publishes hardcover originals. Averages 15 titles/year; receives 1500 submissions annually. 10% of books from first-time authors. 40% of books from unagented writers. Pays royalty on invoice price. Advance negotiable. Publishes book an average of 18 months after acceptance. Simultaneous and photocopied submissions OK. Computer printout submissions OK; no dot-matrix. Reports in 4 months. Book catalog and guidelines for 10 × 13 SAE with 4 first class stamps.

Nonfiction: Juvenile. Query or submit complete ms. Reviews artwork/photos as part of ms package.

Recent Nonfiction Title: *Whales*, by Seymour Simon.

Fiction: Juvenile. Submit complete ms only. No queries.

Recent Fiction Title: *The Best of Friends*, by Margaret Rostkowsbi.

Poetry: No Dr. Seuss-type verse. Submit complete ms.

Recent Poetry Title: *Under the Sunday Tree*, by Eloise Greenfield.

Tips: "Our audience is categorized into children, ages 3-6; 4-8; 8-12; 10-14; 12-16. Read contemporary children's books at all age levels; try to take some writing or children's literature courses; talk to children's librarians and booksellers in independent bookstores; read *Horn Book*, *Booklist*, *School Library Journal* and

ALWAYS submit unsolicited manuscripts or queries with a self-addressed, stamped envelope (SASE) within your country or International Reply Coupons (IRC) purchased from the post office for other countries.

Publishers Weekly; take courses in book illustration and design. West Coast office will be moving to Portland, Oregon."

HARPERCOLLINS, INC., 10 E. 53rd St., New York NY 10022. (212)207-7000. Imprints include Barnes & Noble; Harper & Row-San Francisco (religious books only); Perennial Library; and Torchbooks. Managing Editor: Helen Moore. Publishes hardcover and paperback originals, and paperback reprints. Trade publishes over 400 titles/year. Pays standard royalties; advances negotiable. No unsolicited queries or mss. Reports on solicited queries in 6 weeks.
Nonfiction: Americana, animals, art, biography, business/economics, cookbooks, health, history, how-to, humor, music, nature, philosophy, politics, psychology, reference, religion, science, self-help, sociology, sports and travel.
Recent Nonfiction Title: *The Eight-Week Cholesterol Cure* (revised edition).
Fiction: Adventure, fantasy, gothic, historical, mystery, science fiction, suspense, western and literary. "We look for a strong story line and exceptional literary talent."
Recent Fiction Title: *Family Pictures*, by Sue Miller.
Tips: "Strongly suggest that you go through a literary agent before submitting any ms. Any unsolicited query or ms will be returned unread."

HARVEST HOUSE PUBLISHERS, 1075 Arrowsmith, Eugene OR 97402. (503)343-0123. FAX: (503)342-6410. Editor-in-Chief: Eileen L. Mason. Manuscript Coordinator: LaRae Weikert. Publishes hardcover, trade paperback and mass market originals and reprints. Averages 55-60 titles/year; receives 1,200 submissions annually. 10% of books from first-time authors; 90% of books from unagented writers. Pays 14-18% royalty on wholesale price. Publishes book an average of 1 year after acceptance. Simultaneous submissions OK. Reports in 10 weeks. Book catalog for 8½ × 11 SAE with 2 first class stamps; manuscript guidelines for SASE.
Nonfiction: How-to, illustrated book, juvenile (picture books ages 2-8; ages 9-12), reference, self-help, counseling, curent issues, women's and family on Evangelical Christian religion. No cookbooks, theses, dissertations or music.
Recent Nonfiction Title: *The Culting of Christianity*, by Tim Timmons.
Fiction: Historical, mystery and religious. No short stories. Query or submit outline/synopsis and sample chapters.
Recent Fiction Title: *The Archon Conspiracy*, by Dave Hunt—evangelical Christians of all denominations.
Tips: Audience is women ages 25-40 and high school youth—evangelical Christians of all denominations.

*HAWKES PUBLISHING, INC., 1055 South 700 W., Salt Lake City UT 84104. (801)262-5555. President: John Hawkes. Publishes hardcover and trade paperback originals. Averages 24 titles/year; receives 200 submissions annually. 70% of books from first-time authors; 90% of books from unagented writers. Subsidy publishes 25-50% of books/year based on "how promising they are." Pays varying royalty of 10% on retail price to 10% on wholesale; no advance. Publishes book an average of 6 months after acceptance. Letters preferred describing book. Reports in 1 month on queries; 3 months on mss. Free book catalog.
Nonfiction: Cookbook, how-to and self-help. Subjects include cooking and foods, health, history, hobbies and psychology. Query or submit outline/synopsis and sample chapters. Reviews artwork/photos.

HAZELDEN EDUCATIONAL MATERIALS, 15251 Pleasant Valley Rd., Center City MN 55012. (612)257-4010. Imprints include Harper-Hazeldon. Publishes trade paperback originals. Averages 100 titles/year. 50% of books from first-time authors. 50% from unagented writers. Pays 7-9% royalty on retail price. Publishes ms an average of 6 months after acceptance. Simultaneous submissions OK. Reports in 6 weeks. Free book catalog and mss guidelines.
Nonfiction: Juvenile, self-help, psychology, textbook, health/medicine, eating disorders, AIDS and addictions. No autobiographies. Submit outline/synopsis sample chapters. Reviews artwork/photos as part of ms package.
Recent Nonfiction Title: *Beyond Codependency*, by Melodie Beattie.
Tips: "Common mistakes writers make include not thoroughly investigating existing works on their topic. They do not investigate the publisher's niche and submit totally inappropriate proposals."

HEALTH ADMINISTRATION PRESS, Foundation of the American College of Healthcare Executives, 1021 East Huron St., Ann Arbor MI 48104. (313)764-1380. FAX: (313)763-1105. Imprints include Health Administration Press, Health Administration Press Perspectives and ACHE Management Series. Director: Daphne M. Grew. Estab. 1972. Publishes hardcover and trade paperback originals. Publishes 12 titles/year. Pays 10-15% royalty on net revenue from sale of book. Occasionally offers small advance. Publishes book an average of 10 months after acceptance. Query for electronic submissions. Reports in 6 weeks on queries; 19 weeks on mss. Book catalog free on request.
Nonfiction: Reference or textbook. Subjects include business and economics, government/politics, health/medicine, sociology, health administration. "We are always interested in good, solid texts and references, and we are adding to our management series; books in this series offer health services CEOs and top managers

immediately useful information in an accessible format." Submit outline/synopsis and sample chapters.

Recent Nonfiction Title: *The Well-Managed Community Hospital*, by John R. Griffith.

Tips: "We publish books primarily for an audience of managers of health care institutions and researchers and scholars in health services administration. The books we like to see have something to say and say it to our audience."

‡**HEALTH COMMUNICATIONS, INC.**, 3201 SW 15th St., Deerfield Beach FL 33442. (305)360-0909. Book Editor: Marie Stilkind. Estab. 1982. Publishes trade paperback originals. Publishes 35 titles/year. Receives 520 submissions/year. 20% of books from first-time authors. 90% from unagented writers. Pays 15% royalty on wholesale price. Publishes book an average of 9 months after acceptance. Reports in 1 month on queries; 6 weeks on mss. Free book catalog and ms guidelines.

Nonfiction: Self-help recovery. Subjects include adult child and co-dependent issues, psychology and recovery/addiction. We are looking for recovery trends in self-help format. Submit outline/synopsis and sample chapters. Reviews artwork/photos as part of ms package.

Recent Nonfiction Title: *Healing the Shame That Binds You*, by John Bradshaw.

*****HEART OF THE LAKES PUBLISHING**, P.O. Box 299, Interlaken NY 14847-0299. (607)532-4997. Imprints include Empire State Books and Windswept Press. Contact: Walter Steesy. Publishes hardcover and trade paperback originals and hardcover and trade paperback reprints. Averages 20-25 titles/year; receives 200 submissions annually. 100% of books from unagented writers. Average print order for a writer's first book is 500-1,000. Subsidy publishes 10% of books, "depending on type of material and potential sales." 15% author subsidized; 35% nonauthor subsidized. Payment is "worked out individually." Publishes book an average of 1-2 years after acceptance. Simultaneous submissions OK. Query for electronic submissions. Reports in 1 week on queries; 2 weeks on mss. Current books flyer for #10 SAE and 2 first class stamps.

Nonfiction: New York state and regional, history and genealogy source materials. Query. Reviews artwork/photos.

Recent Nonfiction Title: *Cheese Making in New York State*, by Eunice Stamm.

Fiction: Will be done only at author's expense.

‡**HEINLE & HEINLE PUBLISHERS, INC.**, A division of Wadsworth, Inc., 20 Park Plaza, Boston MA 02216. (617)451-1940. FAX: (617)426-4379. Publisher: Stanley Galek. Estab. 1980. Publishes books, video and software. Averages 15-20 titles/year. 50% of books from first-time authors; 100% of books from unagented writers. Pays 6-15% royalty on net price; no advance. Publishes book an average of 18 months after acceptance. Query for electronic submissions. Reports immediately on queries; 2 weeks on mss. Free book catalog; ms guidelines for SASE.

Nonfiction: Textbook. "Foreign language and English as a second or foreign language text materials. Before writing the book, submit complete prospectus along with sample chapters, and specify market and competitive position of proposed text."

Recent Nonfiction Title: *Entradas*, by Higgs, Liskin-Gasparro, Medley.

Tips: "Introductory and intermediate college foreign language textbooks have the best chance of selling to our firm. A common mistake writers make is planning the project and/or writing the book without first reviewing the market and product concept with the publisher."

‡**HENDRICK-LONG PUBLISHING CO., INC.**, P.O. Box 25123, Dallas TX 75225. (214)358-4677. Contact: Joann Long. Publishes hardcover and trade paperback originals and hardcover reprints. Firm averages 8 titles/year. Receives 100 submissions/year. 90% from unagented writers. Pays royalty on selling price. Publishes book an agerage of 18 months after acceptance. Reports in 2 weeks on queries; 2 months on mss. Manuscript guidelines for #10 SAE and 1 first class stamp.

Nonfiction: Biography, juvenile and textbook. Subjects include history, regional, science (juvenile), and children's. Query or submit outline/synopsis and sample chapters. Reviews artwork/photos as part of ms package; copies of material are acceptable.

Recent Nonfiction Title: *Dinosaur Days in Texas*, by Tom and Jane Allen (juvenile science).

Fiction: Adventure (Texas juvenile), historical (Texas Juvenile), juvenile (Texas), mystery (Texas juvenile) and western (Texas juvenile). Query or submit outline/synopsis and sample chapters.

Recent Fiction Title: *Davy's Dawg*, by Billie Matthews and Virginia Hurlburt (juvenile).

HENDRICKSON PUBLISHERS, INC., 137 Summit St., Box 3473, Peabody MA 01961-3473. (508)532-6546. Executive Editor: Dr. Ben Aker. Publishes hardcover and trade paperback originals, and hardcover and trade paperback reprints. Averages 6-12 titles/year; receives 85 submissions annually. 5% of books from first-time authors; 100% of books from unagented writers. Pays 5-15% royalty on wholesale and retail price. Average advance depends on project. Publishes book an average of 6 months after acceptance. Simultaneous (if so notified) submissions OK. Free book catalog. Ms guidelines for SASE.

Nonfiction: Religious. "We will consider any quality manuscripts within the area of religion, specifically related to Biblical studies and related fields. Popularly written manuscripts are not acceptable." Submit outline/synopsis and sample chapters or complete ms.

Recent Nonfiction Title: *1 and 2 Timothy, Titus*, by Gordon D. Fee.

VIRGIL W. HENSLEY, INC., 6116 E. 32nd St., Tulsa OK 74135. (918)644-8520. Editor: Terri Kalfas. Estab. 1964. Publishes hardcover originals. Publishes 5 titles/year (will increase that number). Receives 100 submissions/year. 50% of books from first-time authors; 50% from unagented writers. Pays 5% minimum royalty on retail price or outright purchase of $250 minimum for study aids. Publishes ms an average of 18 months after acceptance. Reports in 6 weeks on queries; 2 months on mss. Book catalog for 9×12 SAE and $1 postage. Manuscript guidelines for #10 SAE and 1 first class stamp.

Nonfiction: Bible study curriculum. Subjects include child guidance/parenting, money/finance, religion, women's issues/studies. "We look for subjects that lend themselves to long-term Bible studies – prayer, prophecy, family, faith, etc. We do not want to see anything non-Christian." Query with brief synopsis then submit outline/sample chapters or complete ms.

Recent Nonfiction Title: *How to Reach Your Church's Financial Goals this Year*, by Virgil W. Hensley.

Tips: "Submit something that crosses denominational lines; Bible studies which are directed toward the large Christian market, not small specialized groups; heavy emphasis on student activities and student involvement. We serve an interdenominational market – churches of all sizes and Christian persuasions. Our books are used by both pastors and Christian education leaders in Bible studies, Sunday Schools, home Bible studies, and school classrooms."

‡HERALD PUBLISHING HOUSE, Division of Reorganized Church of Jesus Christ of Latter Day Saints, 3225 South Noland Rd., P.O. Box HH, Independence MO 64055. (816)252-5010. FAX: (816)252-3976. Imprints include Independence Press. Editorial Director: Roger Yarrington. Estab. 1860. Publishes hardcover and trade paperback originals and hardcover and trade paperback reprints. Averages 30 titles/year; receives 700 submissions annually. 20% of books from first-time authors; 100% of books from unagented writers. Pays 5% maximum royalty on retail price. Offers average $400 advance. Publishes book an average of 14 months after acceptance. Reports in 3 weeks on queries; 2 months on mss. Book catalog for 9×12 SASE.

Nonfiction: Self-help and religious (RLDS Church). Subjects include Americana, history and religion. Herald House focus: history and doctrine of RLDS Church. Independence Press focus: regional studies (Midwest, Missouri). No submissions unrelated to RLDS Church (Herald House) or to Midwest regional studies (Independence Press). Query. Use *Chicago Manual of Style*. Reviews artwork/photos as part of ms package.

Recent Nonfiction Title: *Missouri: Folk Heroes of the 19th Century*, by F. Mark Mokiornian and Roger D. Launius (eds).

Tips: The audience for Herald Publishing House is members of the Reorganized Church of Jesus Christ of Latter Day Saints; for Independence Press, persons living in the Midwest or interested in the Midwest.

HERE'S LIFE PUBLISHERS, INC., Subsidiary of Campus Crusade for Christ, P.O. Box 1576, San Bernardino CA 92404. (714)886-7981. FAX: (714)886-7985. President: Les Stobbe. Editorial Director: Dan Benson. Estab. 1978. Publishes hardcover and trade paperback originals. Averages 25 titles/year; receives 400 submissions annually. 40% of books from first-time authors; 100% of books from unagented writers. Average print order for a writer's first book is 5,000. Pays 15% royalty on wholesale price. Publishes book an average of 1 year after acceptance. Simultaneous proposal submissions OK. Query for electronic submissions. Reports in 1 month on queries; 3 months on mss. Ms guidelines for 8½×11 SAE with 2 first class stamps.

Nonfiction: Biography, how-to, reference and self-help. Needs "books in the areas of evangelism, Christian growth and family life; must reflect basic understanding of ministry and mission of Campus Crusade for Christ. No metaphysical or missionary biography." Query or submit outline/synopsis and sample chapters. Reviews artwork/photos.

Recent Nonfiction Title: *When Victims Marry*, by Don and Jan Frank.

Tips: "The writer has the best chance of selling our firm a sharply focused how-to book that provides a Biblical approach to a felt need."

*HERITAGE BOOKS, INC., 3602 Maureen, Bowie MD 20715. (301)464-1159. Editorial Director: Laird C. Towle. Estab. 1978. Publishes hardcover and paperback originals and reprints. Averages 100 titles/year; receives 100 submissions annually. 25% of books from first-time authors; 100% of books from unagented writers. Subsidy publishes 5% or less of books. Pays 10% royalty on retail price; no advance. Publishes book an average of 6 months after acceptance. Simultaneous submissions OK. Reports in 1 month. Book catalog for SAE.

Nonfiction: "We particularly desire nonfiction titles dealing with history and genealogy including how-to and reference works, as well as conventional histories and genealogies. Ancestries of contemporary people are not of interest. The titles should be either of general interest or restricted to Eastern U.S. Material dealing with the present century is usually not of interest. We prefer writers to query or submit an outline/synopsis." Reviews artwork/photos.

Recent Nonfiction Title: *Missouri: Genealogical Records and Abstracts, Vol. 1: 1766-1839*, by Sherida K. Eddlemon.

Tips: "The quality of the book is of prime importance; next is its relevance to our fields of interest."

HERMES HOUSE PRESS, 39 Adare Place, Northampton MA 01060. (413)584-8402. General Editor: Richard Mandell. Publishes trade paperback originals. Averages 8 titles/year; receives 45 submissions annually. 50% of books from first-time authors. "Pays in copies; after cost of publication is covered by income, pays small royalty." Publishes book an average of 8 months after acceptance. Query for electronic submissions. Reports in 2 weeks on queries; 2 months on mss. Book catalog for #10 SAE.

Fiction: Ethnic, experimental, feminist, historical, mainstream and science fiction. "We are presently backed up with submissions and therefore not accepting new submissions. Literary fiction, with some attention made to language, has the best chance of selling to our firm."

Recent Fiction Title: *Crossings*, by Marie Diamond.

Poetry: "We are not currently accepting poetry submissions."

Recent Poetry Title: *Going West*, by Stanley Diamond (narrative).

HEYDAY BOOKS, Box 9145, Berkeley CA 94709. (415)549-3564. Publisher: Malcolm Margolin. Publishes hardcover and trade paperback originals, trade paperback reprints. Averages 4-9 titles/year; receives 200 submissions annually. 50% of books from first-time authors; 75% of books from unagented writers. Pays 8-10% royalty on retail price; offers average $1,000 advance. Publishes book an average of 8 months after acceptance. Reports in 1 week on queries; up to 5 weeks on mss. Book catalog for 7×9 SAE and 2 first class stamps.

Nonfiction: Books about California only; how-to and reference. Subjects include Americana, history, nature and travel. "We publish books about native Americans, natural history, history, and recreation, with a strong California focus." Query with outline and synopsis. Reviews artwork/photos.

Recent Nonfiction Title: *Jack London and His Daughters*, by Joan London.

Tips: "Give good value, and avoid gimmicks. We are accepting *only* nonfiction books with a California focus."

HIPPOCRENE BOOKS INC.,171 Madison Ave., New York NY 10016. (212)685-4371. President: George Blagowidow. Estab. 1971. Publishes hardcover originals and trade paperback originals and reprints. Averages 100 titles/year. Receives 250 submissions annually. 25% of books from first-time authors; 50% of books from unagented writers. Pays 6-15% royalty on retail price. Offers "few thousand" dollar advance. Publishes book an average of 11 months after acceptance. Simultaneous submissions OK. Ms guidelines for SASE.

Nonfiction: Biography, how-to, reference, self-help, travel guides. Subjects include history, recreation and travel. Submit outline/synopsis and 2 sample chapters. Reviews artwork/photos as part of ms package.

Recent Nonfiction Titles: *The Elephant & the Tiger: The Full Story of the Vietnam War*, by Wilbur H. Morrison, Peter Deriabin and T.H. Bagley.

Tips: "Our recent successes in publishing general books considered midlist by larger publishers is making us more of a general trade publisher. We continue to do well with travel books and reference books like dictionaries, atlases and language studies."

HOLLOWAY HOUSE PUBLISHING CO., 8060 Melrose Ave., Los Angeles CA 90046. (213)653-8060. Estab. 1960. Publishes paperback originals (60-75%) and reprints (25-40%). Averages 30 titles/year; receives 300-500 submissions annually. 50% of books from first-time authors; 60% of books from unagented writers. Average print order for a writer's first book is 15,000-20,000. Pays royalty based on retail price. Publishes book an average of 6 months after acceptance. Query for electronic submissions. Submit outline and 3 sample chapters. Reports in 9 weeks. Free book catalog and ms guidelines for SASE. Unsolicited manuscripts without SASE will not be returned or acknowledged.

Nonfiction: Gambling and game books—from time to time publishes gambling books along the line of *How to Win, World's Greatest Winning Systems, Backgammon, How to Play and Win at Gin Rummy*, etc. Send query letter and/or outline with one sample chapter. Length: 60,000 words. Reviews artwork/photos as part of ms package.

Recent Nonfiction Title: *A Boot Courage*, by Mickey Fleming.

Fiction: "Holloway House is the largest publisher of Black Experience literature. We are in the market for easily identifiable characters and locations. Dialogue must be realistic. Some sex is acceptable but not essential (refer to writer's guidelines). Action, people and places must be thoroughly depicted and graphically presented."

Recent Fiction Title: *Chester L. Simmons*, by Odie Hawkins.

Tips: "Sixteen bios of famous Black Americans were published in 1989-90; eight more are planned. We publish history and Americana under The Mankind imprint."

HOLMES & MEIER PUBLISHERS, INC., 30 Irving Place, New York NY 10003. (212)254-4100. FAX: (212)254-4104. Publisher: Max J. Holmes. Editor: Sheila Friedling. Managing Editor: Katharine Turok. Estab. 1965. Publishes hardcover and paperback originals. Publishes 60 titles/year. Pays variable royalty. Publishes book

an average of 9 months after acceptance. Reports in 3 months. Free book catalog.
Nonfiction: Africana, art, biography, business/economics, education, history, Judaica, Latin American studies, literary criticism, music, politics, reference, sociology, and women's studies. Accepts translations. "We are noted as an academic publishing house and are pleased with our reputation of excellence in the field. However, we are also expanding our list to include books of more general interest." Query first and submit outline/synopsis, sample chapters, curriculum vitae and idea of intended market/audience.
Recent Nonfiction Title: *Memoirs*, by Raymond Aron.

HOMESTEAD PUBLISHING, Box 193, Moose WY 83102. Editor: Carl Schreier. Publishes hardcover and trade paperback originals and trade paperback reprints. Averages 5 titles/year; receives 100 submissions annually. 60% of books from first-time authors. 90% of books from unagented writers. Pays 8-12% royalty on net receipts; offers $1,000 average advance. Publishes book an average of 1 year after acceptance. Simultaneous submissions OK. Query for electronic submissions. Reports in 2 weeks on queries; 2 months on submissions. Book catalog for #10 SAE with 2 first class stamps.
Nonfiction: Biography, coffee table book, illustrated book, juvenile and reference. Subjects include animals, art, history, nature, photography and travel. Especially needs natural history and nature books for children. No textbooks. Query; or submit outline, synopsis and sample chapters or complete ms. Reviews artwork/photos as part of ms package.
Recent Nonfiction Title: *Yellowstone: Selected Photographs 1870-1960.*
Tips: "Illustrated books on natural history are our specialty. Our audiences include professional, educated people with an interest in natural history, conservation, national parks, and western art. Underneath the visual aspects, a book should be well written, with a good grasp of the English language. We are looking for professional work and top quality publications."

HORIZON PUBLISHERS & DISTRIBUTORS, P.O. Box 490, Bountiful UT 84011-0490. (801)295-9451. President/Sr. Editor: Duane S. Crowther. Estab. 1971. Publishes hardcover and trade paperback originals and reprints. Averages 30 titles/year. Receives 800-1,500 submissions/year. Pays 8-14% on wholesale price or $500 maximum outright purchase. Reports on queries in 1 month. Free manuscript guidelines with SASE.
Nonfiction: Biography, cookbook, how-to, humor, illustrated book, juvenile, self-help and textbook. Subjects include anthropology/archaeology, child guidance/parenting, cooking, foods and nutrition, education, gardening, health/medicine, history, hobbies, money/finance, music/dance, nature/environment, psychology, recreation, business management, outdoor life, scouting, emergency readiness, writing, book publishing, religion and women's issues/studies. Query only. Queries should be addressed to: Editorial Assistant: New manuscript processing.
Recent Nonfiction Title: *The Berlin Candy Bomber*, by Gail Halverson.
Fiction: At present Horizon Publishers is not accepting unsolicited manuscripts or queries for juvenile, young-adult or adult fiction. All fiction published is by company soliciation.

HOUGHTON MIFFLIN CO., Adult Trade Division, 2 Park St., Boston MA 02108. (617)725-5000. Submissions Editor: Janice Harvey. Hardcover and paperback originals and paperback reprints. Royalty of 6-7½% on retail price for paperbacks; 10-15% on sliding scale for standard fiction and nonfiction; advance varies widely. Publishes book an average of 18 months after acceptance. Publishes 100 titles/year. Simultaneous submissions OK. SASE required with all submissions. Reports in 2 months. Book catalog for 8½×11 SAE.
Nonfiction: Natural history, biography, health, history, current affairs, psychology and science. Query.
Recent Nonfiction Title: *The Bear Flag*, by Cecilia Holland.
Fiction: Historical, mainstream and literary. Query.
Recent Fiction Title: *Among School Children*, by Tracy Kidder.
Tips: "No unsolicited manuscripts will be read. Submit query letter and outline or synopsis to Submissions Editor. (Include one sample chapter for fiction.) The query letter should be short and to the point—that is, it should *not* incorporate the book's synopsis. The letter should say who the writer is (including information on previous publications in magazines or wherever) and the subject of the book."

HOUGHTON MIFFLIN CO., Children's Trade Books, 2 Park St., Boston MA 02108. Editor: Mary DeMarle. Publishes hardcover originals and trade paperback reprints (some simultaneous hard/soft). Averages 45-50 titles/year. Pays standard royalty; offers advance. Reports in 1 month on queries; 2 months on mss. Free book catalog.
Nonfiction: Submit outline/synopsis and sample chapters. Reviews artwork/photos as part of ms package.
Recent Nonfiction Title: *Who's to Know*, by Ann Weiss.
Fiction: Submit complete ms.
Recent Fiction Title: *Number the Stars*, by Lois Lowry.

‡**HOUNSLOW PRESS**, Subsidiary of Anthony R. Hawke Limited, 124 Parkview Ave., Willowdale, Ontario M2N 3Y5 Canada. (416)225-9176. President: Tony Hawke. Publishes hardcover and trade paperback originals. Firm averages 8 titles/year. Receives 250 submissions/year. 10% of books from first-time authors. 95%

from unagented writers. Pays 10-12½% royalty on retail price. Offers $500 average advance. Publishes book an average of 1 year after acceptance. Reports in 1 month on queries; 2 months on mss. Free book catalog.

Nonfiction: Biography, coffee-table book, cookbook, how-to, humor, illustrated book and self-help. Subjects include animals, art/architecture, business and economics, child guidance/parenting, cooking, foods and nutrition, health/medicine, history, money/finance, photography, translation and travel. "We are looking for controversial manuscripts and business books." Query.

Recent Nonfiction Title: *Holy Grail Across the Atlantic*, by Michael Bradley (history).

Fiction: Literary and suspense. "We really don't need any fiction for the next year or so." Query.

Poetry: "We do not need any poetry in the next few years."

Tips: "If I were a writer trying to market a book today, I would try to get a good literary agent to handle it."

HOWELL PRESS, INC., Suite B, 700 Harris St., Charlottesville, VA 22901. (804)977-4006. FAX: (804)296-5505. Senior Editor: Kathleen D. Valenzi. Estab. 1985. Publishes hardcover originals. Firm averages 8 titles/year. Receives 120 submissions/year. 30% of books from first-time authors. 80% from unagented writers. Pays 5-10% on net retail price. "We generally offer an advance, but amount differs with each project and is generally negotiated with authors on a case-by-case basis." Publishes book an average of 2 years after acceptance. Reports in 2 months. Book catalog for 9 × 12 SAE with 4 first class stamps.

Nonfiction: Coffee table book, illustrated book. Subjects include art, aviation, military history, maritime history, motorsports, gardening, sports history, fine photography, regional travel. "Generally open to most ideas, as long as writing is not scholarly (easily accessible to average adult reader) and can be illustrated in some fashion with photography or art. While our line is esoteric, it would be advisable to look over our catalog before querying to better understand what Howell Press does." Query. Submit outline/synopsis and sample chapters. Reviews artwork/photos as part of ms package.

Recent Nonfiction Title: *Special Forces at War: An Illustrated History, Southeast Asia 1959-1975*, by Shelby L. Stanton.

Tips: "We're looking for books with built-in buyers (aviation enthusiasts, motorsports fans, etc.); books that can be beautifully illustrated with four-color art/photography."

‡HRD PRESS, INC., 22 Amherst Rd., Amherst MA 01002. (413)253-3488. Subsidiaries include HRD Software. Publisher: Robert W. Carkhuff. Publishes hardcover and trade paperback originals. Averages 15-20 titles/year. Receives 30-40 submissions/year. 25% of books from first-time authors. 100% from unagented writers. Pays 10-15% royalty on wholesale price. Offers $1,000 average advance. Publishes book an average of 6 months after acceptance. Simultaneous submissions OK. Reports in 1-2 weeks on queries; 1 week to 2 months on mss. Free book catalog and ms guidelines.

Nonfiction: Juvenile, reference, self-help, software, technical. Subjects include business and economics, child guidance/parenting, psychology, sports. We are looking for mostly business oriented titles; we will consider child guidance/parenting, psychology, sports. Submit outline/synopsis and samples chapters.

Recent Nonfiction Title: *Too Smart For Trouble*, by Sharon Scott (child guidance/parenting).

Tips: Business—must be practical and useful.

HUDSON HILLS PRESS, INC., Suite 1308, 230 5th Ave., New York NY 10001-7704. (212)889-3090. President/Editorial Director: Paul Anbinder. Estab. 1978. Publishes hardcover and paperback originals. Averages 10 titles/year; receives 50-100 submissions annually. 15% of books from first-time authors; 90% of books from unagented writers. Average print order for a writer's first book is 3,000. Offers royalties of 5-8% on retail price. Average advance: $5,000. Publishes book an average of 1 year after acceptance. Simultaneous submissions OK. Reports in 1 month. Book catalog for SAE with 2 first class stamps.

Nonfiction: Art and photography. "We are only interested in publishing books about art and photography, including monographs." Query first, then submit outline/synopsis and sample chapters. Reviews artwork/photos as part of ms package.

Recent Nonfiction Title: *Impressionism*, by Gerstein.

HUMAN KINETICS PUBLISHERS, INC., P.O. Box 5076, Champaign IL 61825-5076. (217)351-5076. FAX: (217)351-2674. Publisher: Rainer Martens. Imprints include Leisure Press and Human Kinetics Books. Publishes hardcover and paperback text and reference books and trade paperback originals. Averages 80 titles/year; receives 300 submissions annually. 50% of books from first-time authors; 97% of books from unagented writers. Pays 10-15% royalty on net income. Publishes book an average of 18 months after acceptance. Simultaneous submissions OK. Query for electronic submissions. Reports in 2 months. Free book catalog.

Nonfiction: How-to, reference, self-help, technical and textbook. Subjects include health, recreation, sports, sport sciences and sports medicine, and physical education. Especially interested in books on wellness, including stress management, weight management, leisure management, and fitness; books on all aspects of sports technique or how-to books and coaching books; books which interpret the sport sciences and sports medicine, including sport physiology, sport psychology, sport pedagogy and sport biomechanics. No sport biographies, sport record or statistics books or regional books. Submit outline/synopsis and sample chapters. Reviews artwork/photos as part of ms package.

Recent Nonfiction Title: *Successful Coaching*, by Rainer Martens.
Tips: "Books which accurately interpret the sport sciences and health research to coaches, athletes and fitness enthusiasts have the best chance of selling to us."

HUMANICS PUBLISHING GROUP, 1482 Mecaslin St. NW, Atlanta GA 30309. (404)874-2176. President: Gary B. Wilson. Contact: Robert Grayson Hall, Executive Editor. Estab. 1976. Publishes softcover, educational and trade paperback originals. Averages 12 titles/year; receives 500 submissions annually. 20% of books from first-time authors; 100% of books from unagented writers. Average print order for a writer's first book is 5,000. Pays average 10% royalty on net sales; buys some mss outright. Publishes book an average of 1 year after acceptance. Reports in 4 months. Book catalog and ms guidelines for SASE.
Nonfiction: Self-help, teacher resource books and psychological assessment instruments for early education. Subjects include health, psychology, sociology, education, business and New Age. Submit outline/synopsis and at least 3 sample chapters. Reviews artwork/photos as part of ms package.
Recent Nonfiction Title: *Choosing Not Cheating*, by Midge Elias.
Tips: "Be resourceful, bold and creative. But be sure to have the facts and expertise in hand to back up your work."

*HUMANITIES PRESS INTERNATIONAL, INC., 171 First Ave., Atlantic Highlands NJ 07716. (201)872-1441. President: Keith M. Ashfield. Publishes hardcover originals and trade paperback originals and trade paperback reprints. Averages 80-100 titles/year. Receives 500 submissions/year. 5% of books from first-time authors. 80% from unagented writers. Subsidy publishes 2% of books. Pays 5-12½% royalty on retail price. Offers $500 average advance. Publishes book an average of 1 year after acceptance. Reports in 3 weeks on queries; 10 weeks on mss. Free book catalog.
Nonfiction: Subjects include politics (international/theory), history (European Early Modern to Modern), language/literature, philosophy and sociology. "We want books for senior level undergraduates and upward."
Recent Nonfiction Title: *Michel Foucault's Force of Flight: Toward an Ethic for Thought*, by James Bernauer.
Tips: "We want well-written contributions to scholarly investigation or synthesis of recent thought. Serious students and scholars are our audience."

CARL HUNGNESS PUBLISHING, P.O. Box 24308, Speedway IN 46224. (317)244-4792. Editorial Director: Carl Hungness. Publishes hardcover and paperback originals. Pays "negotiable" outright purchase. Reports in 3 weeks. Free book catalog.
Nonfiction: Stories relating to professional automobile racing. No sports car racing or drag racing material. Query.

*HUNTER HOUSE, INC., PUBLISHERS, P.O. Box 847, Claremont CA 91711. FAX: (714)624-9028. Publisher: K.S. Rana. Estab. 1978. Publishes hardcover and trade paperback originals. Averages 8 titles/year; receives 200 submissions annually. 50% of books from first-time authors; 50% of books from unagented writers. Subsidy publishes 10% of books. "We determine whether an author should be subsidy published based upon subject matter, quality of the work, and if a subsidy is available." Pays 12-15% royalty on net price. Offers modest advance. Publishes book an average of 12-18 months after acceptance and receipt of final manuscript. Simultaneous submissions OK. Query for electronic submissions. Reports in 1 month on queries; 5 months on mss. Book catalog and ms guidelines for 9 × 12 SAE with 3 first class stamps.
Nonfiction: How-to, young adult, and self-help. Subjects include family, health, women's health, self-help, psychology, ecology. Needs mss on "family and health, especially emerging areas in ecological issues, women's health, older people, especially health and intergenerational concerns." No evangelical, political, Americana, esoteric or erotica. Query or submit outline/synopsis and sample chapters. Reviews artwork/photos. "Please enclose return postage for material."
Recent Nonfiction Title: *Sexual Healing*, by Barbara Keesling, Ph. D.
Recent Fiction Title: *On the Road to Baghdad*, by Güneli GünBernard Selling.
Tips: "Manuscripts on family and health, or psychology for an aware public do well for us. Write simply, with established credentials and imagination. We respect writers and do not mistreat them. We ask for the same consideration."

HUNTINGTON HOUSE, INC., P.O. Box 53788, Lafayette LA 70505.(318)237-7049. President: Richard Trosclair. Estab. 1982. Publishes hardcover, trade paperback, and mass market paperback originals, trade paperback reprints. Averages 10-20 titles/year; receives 1,500 submissions annually. 50% of books from first-time authors; 20% of books from unagented writers. Average print order for a writer's first book is 10,000. Pays 10-15% royalty on wholesale and retail price. Publishes book an average of 18 months after acceptance. Simultaneous submissions OK. Query for electronic submissions. Free book catalog and ms guidelines.
Nonfiction: Current social and political issues, biographies, self-help, inspirational and childrens' books. Query with descriptive outline or ms.
Recent Nonfiction Title: *Pornography's Target: Children and the Family*, by Dr. Judith A. Reisman.
Tips: "Write clear, crisp and exciting mss that grab the reader. The company's goal is to educate and keep readers abreast of critical current events."

‡*IEEE PRESS**, Subsidiary of The Institute of Electrical and Electronics Engineers, 445 Hoes Ln., P.O. Box 1331, Piscataway NJ 08855. (201)562-3969. Managing Editor: Dudley R. Kay. Publishes hardcover originals and reprints. Averages 15-20 titles/year. Receives 50-60 submissions/year. 70% of books from first-time authors. 100% from unagented writers. Subsidy publishes 20% of books. Pays 5-18% royalty on wholesale price. Publishes book an average of 6-9 months after acceptance. Simultaneous submissions OK. Query for electronic submissions. Reports in 3 weeks on queries; 2 months on mss. Free book catalog and ms guidelines.
Nonfiction: Technical reference and textbooks. Subjects include computers and electronics. "We need advanced texts and references in electrical engineering, especially telecommunications. *Major* push is on original, authored works rather than edited collections and reprints. No trade/consumer orientation books in electronics and computers. We publish for the professional and advanced student in engineering." Query. Submit outline/synopsis and sample chapters.
Recent Nonfiction Title: *Teleconferencing*, by Bodson & Schaphorst (professional reference).
Tips: "Professional reference books have flourished due to changing technologies and need to keep current. However, technical writers are few. Engineers and scientists should consider trained technical writers as co-authors. Our audience consists of engineers—largely at management and project leader levels. "If I were a writer trying to market a book today, I would work with a good agent or other experienced writer with contacts and knowledge of the 'system.' Authors expend too much energy, and endure unnecessary frustration, because they don't know how to match a good idea and respectable proposal with the *appropriate* publishers."

ILR PRESS, Division of The New York State School of Industrial and Labor Relations, Cornell University, Ithaca NY 14851-0952. (607)255-3061. Director: E. Benson. Estab. 1945. Publishes hardcover and trade paperback originals and reprints. Averages 5-10 titles/year. Pays royalty. Reports in 2-3 weeks on queries; 8-12 weeks on mss. Free book catalog.
Nonfiction: All titles relate to industrial and labor relations. Biography, reference, technical, and academic books. Subjects include history, sociology of work and the workplace, and business and economics. Book manuscript needs for the next year include "manuscripts on workplace problems, employment policy, women and work, personnel issues, and dispute resolution that will interest academics and practitioners." Query or submit outline/synopsis and sample chapters or complete ms.
Recent Nonfiction Title: *Holding the Line: Women in the Great Arizona Mine Strike of 1983*, by Barbara Kingsolver.
Tips: "We are interested in manuscripts that address topical issues in industrial and labor relations that concern both academics and the general public. These must be well documented to pass our editorial evaluation, which includes review by academics in the industrial and labor relations field."

IMAGINE, INC., P.O. Box 9674, Pittsburgh PA 15226. (412)571-1430. President: R.V. Michelucci. Estab. 1982. Publishes trade paperback originals. Averages 3-5 titles/year; receives 50 submissions annually. 50% of books from first-time authors; 75% of books from unagented writers. Pays 6-10% royalty on retail price. Offers average $500 advance. Publishes book an average of 1 year after acceptance. Reports in 2 weeks on queries; 2 months on mss. Book catalog for #10 SAE with 1 first class stamp.
Nonfiction: Coffee table book, how-to, illustrated book and reference. Subjects include films, science fiction, fantasy and horror films. Submit outline/synopsis and sample chapters or complete ms with illustrations and/or photos.
Recent Nonfiction Title: *Bruno Sammartino, An Autobiography of Wrestling's Living Legend*, by Bob Michelucci and Paul McCullough.
Tips: "If I were a writer trying to market a book today, I would research my subject matter completely before sending a manuscript. Our audience is between ages 18-45 and interested in film, science fiction, fantasy and the horror genre."

‡**IN DEPTH PUBLISHERS**, 3412 Milwaukee Ave., #408, Northbrook IL 60062. (708)803-1567. Publisher: Kathryn Dokas. Publishes trade paperback originals. Averages 5 titles/year. Receives 10 submissions/year. 100% of books from first-time authors; 100% from unagented writers. Pay negotiated on author by author basis, generally 5-10%, no advance. Publishes book an agerage of 6 months after acceptance. Simultaneous submissions OK. Reports in 1 month on queries; 3 months on mss.
Nonfiction: How-to. Subjects include business and economics, money/finance, senior issues, insurance and consumer-medical. "We are looking for books on retirement, medical and health care issues and insurance. Very specific, how-to books written by experts with inside information. If it isn't within the above paremeters, please don't send it!" Submit outline/synopsis and sample chapters.
Recent Nonfiction Title: *How to File Your Health Insurance Claims*, by Border (how-to, insurance).
Tips: "We are looking for experts in their field as opposed to freelance writers. We want insider, in-depth information for our books. Our audience consists of consumers, older Americans, business owners. If I were a writer trying to market a book today, I would find a niche and specialize in it. It's so expensive to publish and market a title, you must provide concrete, unavailable information. Generalists are a dying breed."

INDUSTRIAL PRESS INC., 200 Madison Ave., New York NY 10016. (212)889-6330. FAX: (212)545-8327. Editorial Director: Woodrow Chapman. Estab. 1884. Publishes hardcover originals. Averages 12 titles/year; receives 25 submissions annually. 2% of books from first-time authors; 100% of books from unagented writers. Publishes book an average of 1 year after acceptance of finished ms. Query for electronic submissions. Reports in 1 month. Free book catalog.
Nonfiction: Reference and technical. Subjects include business and economics, science and engineering. "We envision professional engineers, plant managers, on-line industrial professionals responsible for equipment operation, professors teaching manufacturing, engineering, technology related courses as our audience." Especially looking for material on manufacturing technologies and titles on specific areas in manufacturing and industry. Computers in manufacturing are a priority. No energy-related books or how-to books. Query.
Recent Nonfiction Title: *Statistical Process Control*, by Leonard A. Doty.

INFORMATION RESOURCES PRESS, A Division of Herner and Company, Suite 550, 1110 N. Glebe Rd., Arlington VA 22201. (703)558-8270. FAX: (703)558-4979. Vice President/Publisher: Ms. Gene P. Allen. Estab. 1970. Publishes hardcover originals. Averages 6 titles/year; receives 25 submissions annually. 80% of books from first-time authors; 100% of books from unagented writers. Pays 10-15% royalty on net cash receipts after returns and discounts. Publishes book an average of 1 year after acceptance. Simultaneous submissions OK. Query for electronic submissions. Reports in 2 weeks on queries; 2 months on mss. Free book catalog available.
Nonfiction: Reference, technical and textbook. Subjects include health and library and information science. Needs basic or introductory books on information science, library science, and health planning that lend themselves for use as textbooks. Preferably, the mss will have been developed from course notes. No works on narrow research topics (nonbasic or introductory works). Submit outline/synopsis and sample chapters or complete ms.
Recent Nonfiction Title: *United States Medicolegal Autopsy Laws*, compiled by Cyril Wecht.
Tips: "Our audience includes libraries (public, special, college and university); librarians, information scientists, college-level faculty; schools of library and information science; health planners, graduate-level students of health planning, and administrators; economists. Our marketing program is slanted toward library and information science and health planning, and we can do a better job of marketing in these areas."

‡INNER TRADITIONS INTERNATIONAL, One Park St., Rochester VT 05767. (802)767-3174. FAX: (802)767-3726. Imprints include Inner Traditions, Destiny Books, Healing Arts Press, Park Street Press. Managing Editor: Leslie Colket. Estab. 1975. Publishes hardcover and trade paperback originals and hardcover and trade paperback reprints. Averages 40 titles/year. Receives 300 submissions/year. 5% of books from first-time authors. 5% from unagented writers. Pays 8-10% royalty on retail price. Offers $1,000 average advance. Publishes book an average of 9 months after acceptance. Query for electronic submissions. Reports in 3 months on queries; 3 months on mss. Free book catalog and ms guidelines.
Nonfiction: Biography, coffee table book, cookbook, humor, illustrated book, self-help, textbook. Subjects include anthropology/archaeology, art/architecture, business and economics, child guidance/parenting, cooking, foods and nutrition, ethnic, health/alternative medicine, history, music/dance, nature/environment, esoteric philosophy, psychology, religion, travel, women's issues/studies, New Age. Query. Submit outline/synopsis and sample chapters. Reviews artwork/photos as part of ms package.
Recent Nonfiction Title: *The Family Herbal*, by Barbara and Peter Theiss.

‡INSIGHT BOOKS, Subsidiary of Plenum Publishing Corp., 233 Spring St., New York NY 10013. (212)620-8000. FAX: (212)463-0742. Executive Editor: Norma Fox. Estab. 1946. Publishes hardcover and trade paperback originals. Averages 12 titles/year. Receives 100 submissions/year. 80% of books from first-time authors. 90% from unagented writers. Pays royalty. Advance varies. Publishes book an average of 1 year after acceptance. Simultaneous submissions OK. Query for electronic submissions. Reports in 1 week on queries; 4-6 weeks on mss. Free book catalog and ms guidelines.
Nonfiction: Self-help, how-to, monographs, treatises, essays, biography. Subjects include anthropology/archaeology, art/architecture, business and economics, education, ethnic, government/politics, health/medicine, language/literature, money/finance, nature/environment, philosophy, psychology, religion, science, sociology and women's issues/studies. Submit outline/synopsis and sample chapters.
Recent Nonfiction Title: *Knowing Herself: Women Tell Their Stories in Psychotherapy*, by Joan Hamerman Robbins.
Tips: "Writers have the best chance selling thoughtful quality self-help offering well-written serious information in areas of health, mental health, social sciences, education and child-rearing. Our audience consists of informed general readers as well as professionals and students in human and life sciences. If I were a writer trying to market a book today, I would say something interesting, important and useful, and say it well."

‡INSTRUMENT SOCIETY OF AMERICA, 67 Alexander Dr., P.O. Box 12277, Research Triangle Park NC 27709. (919)549-8411. Manager, Publications Services: Sally L. Walter. Publishes hardcover and trade paperback originals and trade paperback reprints. Averages 37 titles/year. 10% of books from first-time authors;

100% from unagented writers. Pays 10-15% royalty. Publishes book an average of 9 months after acceptance. Simultaneous submissions OK. Query for electronic submissions. Reports in 1 month. Free book catalog and manuscript guidelines.
Nonfiction: Technical. Subjects include industrial engineering. We are looking for current applications of technologies for measurement, automation and control in industry. Query. Reviews artwork/photos as part of ms package.
Recent Nonfiction Title: *Programmable Controllers*, by T.A. Hughes (engineering).

‡**INTEGRATED PRESS**, 526 Comstock Dr., Tiburon CA 94920. (415)435-2446. Vice President: Pete Fennessey. Publishes hardcover and trade paperback originals. Averages 9 titles/year. Receives 60 submissions/year. 100% of books from first-time authors; 92% from unagented writers. Pays 20% royalty on wholesale price. Offers $1,500 average advance. Publishes book an average of 6 months after acceptance. Reports in 3 months on queries; 4 months on mss.
Nonfiction: Biography. Subjects include psychology. Query or submit outline/synopsis and sample chapters.
Fiction: Historical, humor, literary and short story collections.

INTERCULTURAL PRESS, INC., P.O. Box 700, Yarmouth ME 04096. (207)846-5168. FAX: (207)846-5181. Contact: David S. Hoopes, Editor-in-Chief, 130 North Rd., Vershire VT 05079. (802)685-4448. FAX: (802)685-4548. Estab. 1980. Publishes hardcover and trade paperback originals. Averages 5-7 titles/year; receives 50-80 submissions annually. 50% of books from first-time authors; 95% of books from unagented writers. Pays royalty; occasionally offers small advance. Publishes book an average of 2 years after acceptance. Simultaneous submissions OK. Reports in "several weeks" on queries; 2 months on mss. Free book catalog and ms guidelines.
Nonfiction: How-to, reference, self-help, textbook and theory. Subjects include business and economics, philosophy, politics, psychology, sociology, travel, or "any book with an international or domestic intercultural, multicultural or cross-cultural focus, i.e., a focus on the cultural factors in personal, social, political or economic relations. We want books with an international or domestic intercultural or multicultural focus, especially those on business operations (how to be effective in intercultural business activities) and education (textbooks for teaching intercultural subjects, for instance). Our books are published for educators in the intercultural field, business people who are engaged in international business, and anyone else who works in an international occupation or has had intercultural experience. No manuscripts that don't have an intercultural focus." Accepts nonfiction translations. Query "if there is any question of suitability (we can tell quickly from a good query)," or submit outline/synopsis. Do not submit mss unless invited.
Recent Nonfiction Title: *Understanding Cultural Differences: French, Germans and Americans*, by Edward T. and Mildred Reed Hall.

INTERGALACTIC PUBLISHING CO., 321 New Albany Rd., Moorestown NJ 08057. (609)778-8900. Contact: Samuel W. Valenza, Jr. Intergalactic is a division of Regal Communications Corporation, publishers of *Lottery Player's Magazine*. Averages 3-10 titles/year; receives 10-20 submissions annually. 80% of books from first-time authors; 100% of books from unagented writers. Average print order for a writer's first book is 1,000-5,000. Publishes book an average of 1 year after acceptance. Query for electronic submissions.
Nonfiction: The publisher invites mss dealing with lottery in general and *systems of play* in particular. The company also produces and sells lottery and gaming related products and games, and invites submissions of ideas for same. Reviews artwork/photos.
Recent Nonfiction Title: *Win Lotto and Daily Numbers Playing Techniques*, by Steve Player.

‡**INTERLINK PUBLISHING GROUP, INC.,** 99 Seventh Ave., Brooklyn NY 11215. (718)797-4292. Imprints include Interlink Books, Crocodile Books, USA, Olive Branch Press. Publisher: Michel Moushabeck. Publishes hardcover and trade paperback originals. Averages 30 titles/year. Receives 200 submissions/year. 30% of books from first-time authors; 50% from unagented writers. Pays 5-7% royalty on retail price. Publishes book an average of 18 months after acceptance. Simultaneous submissions OK. Reports in 3 weeks on queries; 3 months on mss. Free book catalog and manuscript guidelines.
Nonfiction: Coffee table book, cookbook, how-to, illustrated book and juvenile. Subjects include art/architecture, child guidance/parenting, cooking, foods and nutrition, ethnic, gardening, government/politics, history, nature/environment, religion, travel, women's issues/studies and third world literature and criticism. Submit outline/synopsis and sample chapters for adult nonfiction; complete ms for juvenile titles. Reviews artwork/photos as part of ms package.
Recent Nonfiction Title: *Serpent of the Nile*, by Wendy Buona Ventura (dance).
Fiction: Ethnic, feminist, juvenile, picture books and short story collections (only third world). Adult fiction – We are looking for translated works relating to the Middle East, Africa or Latin America. Juvenile/Picture Books – We are looking for titles with multicultural themes. No science fiction, romance, plays, erotica, fantasy, horror. Submit outline/synopsis and sample chapters.

Recent Fiction Title: *Wild Thorns*, by Sahar Khalifeh (adult fiction/translated).
Tips: "This year we are launching our International Folktale Series. Any submissions that fit well in this series will receive careful attention. Also titles on the environment as well as socially and politically relevent titles on areas of the world often ignored by the Western media. Eastern Europe is another area of interest to us. If I were a writer trying to market a book today, I would take my time and I would look hard for the right publisher who would do justice to my book."

INTERNATIONAL FOUNDATION OF EMPLOYEE BENEFIT PLANS, P.O. Box 69, Brookfield WI 53008-0069. (414)786-6700. FAX: (414)786-2990. Director of Publications: Dee Birschel. Publishes hardcover and trade paperback originals. Averages 30 titles/year; receives 10 submissions annually. 15% of books from first-time authors. 80% of books from unagented writers. Pays 5-15% royalty on wholesale and retail price. Publishes book an average of 1 year after acceptance. Reports in 3 months on queries. Book catalog free on request; ms guidelines for SASE.
Nonfiction: Reference, technical, consumer information and textbook. Subjects include health care, pensions, retirement planning, business and employee benefits. "We publish general and technical monographs on all aspects of employee benefits—pension plans, health insurance, etc." Query with outline.
Recent Nonfiction Title: *Flexible Benefits—A How-to Guide, 3rd Ed.*, by Richard E. Johnson.
Tips: Be aware of "interests of employers and the marketplace in benefits topics, i.e., how AIDS affects employers, health care cost containment."

INTERNATIONAL MARINE PUBLISHING CO., Division of TAB Books, Inc., a McGraw-Hill Company, Box 220, Camden ME 04843. Imprints include Seven Seas Press. Vice President, Editorial: Jonathan Eaton. Publishes hardcover and paperback originals. Averages 22 titles/year; receives 500-700 submissions annually. 30% of books from first-time authors; 80% of books from unagented writers. Pays standard royalties, based on net price, with advances. Publishes book an average of 8 months after acceptance. Reports in 6 weeks. Book catalog and ms guidelines for SASE.
Nonfiction: "Mostly marine nonfiction but a wide range of subjects within that category: boatbuilding, boat design, yachting, seamanship, boat maintenance, maritime history, etc." All books are illustrated. "Material in all stages welcome. We prefer queries first with outline and 2-3 sample chapters." Reviews artwork/photos as part of ms package.
Recent Nonfiction Title: *The Fiberglass Boat Repair Manual*, by Allan Vaitses.
Fiction: "Marine fiction of excellence will be considered."
Tips: "Freelance writers should be aware of the need for clarity, accuracy and interest. Many progress too far in the actual writing, with an unsalable topic."

INTERNATIONAL PUBLISHERS CO., INC., 239 W. 23rd St., New York NY 10011. (212)366-9816. President: Betty Smith. Estab. 1924. Publishes hardcover and trade paperback originals and trade paperback reprints. Averages 15-20 titles/year; receives 100 submissions annually. 10% of books from first-time authors. Pays 5-7½% royalty on paperbacks; 10% royalty on cloth. No advance. Publishes book an average of 6 months after acceptance. Simultaneous submissions OK. Reports in 1 month on queries; send SASE. 6 months on mss. Book catalog and ms guidelines for SASE with 45¢ postage.
Nonfiction: Biography, reference and textbook. Subjects include Americana, economics, history, philosophy, politics, social sciences, and Marxist-Leninist classics. "Books on labor, black studies and women's studies based on Marxist science have high priority." Query or submit outline and sample chapters. Reviews artwork/photos as part of ms package.
Recent Nonfiction Title: *American Cities: A Working-Class View*, by Morris Zeitlin.
Fiction: "We publish very little fiction." Query or submit outline and sample chapters.
Recent Fiction Title: *A Bird in Her Hair*, by Phillip Bonosky (short stories).
Poetry: "We rarely publish individual poets, usually anthologies."
Recent Poetry Title: *Let the Railsplitter Awake and Other Poems*, by Pablo Meruda.

INTERNATIONAL RESOURCES, P.O. Box 840, Arroyo Grande CA 93421-0840. (805)473-1947. Subsidiary of Padre Productions. Publisher: Lachlan P. MacDonald. Estab. 1974. Publishes hardcover and trade paperback originals. Averages 6-10 titles/year. Receives 500 submissions/year. 90% of books from first-time authors. 95% from unagented writers. Pays 6-10% on retail price. Advance varies. Publishes book an average of 3 years after acceptance. Simultaneous submissions OK. Reports in 2 weeks on queries; 2 months on mss. Book catalog for 9×12 SAE and 2 first class stamps. Manuscript guidelines for #10 SAE and 1 first class stamp.
Nonfiction: Biography, how-to, illustrated book, reference, self-help and textbook. Subjects include Americana, animals, anthropology, archaeology, history, hobbies, nature/environment, photography, travel and women's issues/studies. "We want hot business leadership and finance topics, top-level advice for corporate CEOs, management techniques. No 'how to make millions in stocks, bonds or whatever'—usually submitted by writers with modest accomplishments. We only consider such books from self-made millionaires. Financial statement will be required." No fiction or poetry. Query or submit outline/synopsis and sample chapters. Reviews artwork/photos as part of ms package.

Recent Nonfiction Title: *An Uncommon Guide to Easter Island*, by Georgia Lee, Ph.D. (travel guide).
Tips: "We prefer authorites who offer useful information to high achievers: people active in business and industry who need guidelines. Chief executives, public relations and personnel vice presidents, active traveling retirees are our audience."

INTERNATIONAL SELF-COUNSEL PRESS, LTD., 1481 Charlotte Rd., North Vancouver, British Columbia V7J 1H1 Canada. (604)986-3366. President: Diana R. Douglas. Managing Editor: Ruth Wilson. Publishes trade paperback originals. Averages 15 titles/year; receives 1,000 submissions annually. 80% of books from first-time authors; 95% of books from unagented writers. Average print order for a writer's first book is 4,000. Pays 10% royalty on wholesale price. Publishes book an average of 9 months after submission of contracted ms. Simultaneous submissions OK. Query for electronic submissions. Reports in 6 weeks on queries; 2 months on mss. Free book catalog and manuscript guidelines.
Nonfiction: Specializes in self-help and how-to books in law, business, reference, and psychology for the lay person. Query or submit outline and sample chapters. Follow Chicago *A Manual of Style*.
Recent Nonfiction Title: *Start and Run a Successful Home-Based Business*.

INTERNATIONAL WEALTH SUCCESS, Box 186, Merrick NY 11566. (516)766-5850. Editor: Tyler G. Hicks. Averages 10 titles/year; receives 100 submissions annually. 100% of books from first-time authors; 100% of books from unagented writers. Average print order for a writer's first book "varies from 500 and up, depending on the book." Pays 10% royalty on wholesale or retail price. Buys all rights. Usual advance is $1,000, but this varies, depending on author's reputation and nature of book. Publishes book 4 months after acceptance. Query for electronic submissions. Reports in 1 month. Book catalog and ms guidelines for 9 × 12 SAE with 3 first class stamps.
Nonfiction: Self-help and how-to. "Techniques, methods, sources for building wealth. Highly personal, how-to-do-it with plenty of case histories. Books are aimed at the wealth builder and are highly sympathetic to his and her problems." Financing, business success, venture capital, etc. Length: 60,000-70,000 words. Query. Reviews artwork/photos as part of ms package.
Recent Nonfiction Title: *Money Agency Planning Guide*, by Brisky.
Tips: "With the mass layoffs in large and medium-size companies there is an increasing interest in owning your own business. So we will focus on more how-to hands-on material on owning—and becoming successful in—one's own business of any kind. Our market is the BWB—Beginning Wealth Builder. This person has so little money that financial planning is something they never think of. Instead, they want to know what kind of a business they can get into to make some money without a large investment. Write for this market and you have millions of potential readers. Remember—there are a lot more people *without* money than *with* money."

*INTERSTATE PUBLISHERS, INC., 510 N. Vermilion St., P.O. Box 50, Danville IL 61834-0050. (217)446-0500. FAX: (217)446-9706. Acquisitions/Vice President-Editorial: Ronald L. McDaniel. Estab. 1914. Hardcover and paperback originals and software. Publishes about 50 titles/year. 50% of books from first-time authors; 100% of books from unagented writers. Subsidy publishes 5% of books; 3% nonauthor subsidy. Usual royalty is 10%; no advance. Markets books by mail and exhibits. Publishes book an average of 9-12 months after acceptance. Reports in 3-4 months. Book catalog for 9 × 12 SAE. "Our guidelines booklet is provided only to persons who have submitted proposals for works in which we believe we might be interested. If the booklet is sent, no self-addressed envelope or postage from the author is necessary."
Nonfiction: Publishes high school and undergraduate college-level texts and related materials in agricultural education (production agriculture, agriscience and technology, agribusiness, agrimarketing, horticulture). Also publishes items in correctional education (books for professional training and development and works for use by and with incarcerated individuals in correctional facilities). "We favor, but do not limit ourselves to, works that are designed for class-quantity rather than single-copy sale." Query or submit synopsis and 2-3 sample chapters. Reviews artwork/photos as part of ms package.
Recent Nonfiction Title: *Forests and Forestry, 4th ed.*, by I.I. Holland, G. L. Rolfe, and David A. Anderson.
Tips: "Freelance writers should be aware of strict adherence to the use of nonsexist language; fair and balanced representation of the sexes and of minorities in both text and illustrations; and discussion of computer applications and career opportunities wherever applicable. Writers commonly fail to identify publishers who specialize in the subject areas in which they are writing. For example, a publisher of textbooks isn't interested in novels, or one that specializes in elementary education materials isn't going to want a book on auto mechanics."

INTERURBAN PRESS/TRANS ANGLO BOOKS, Box 6444, Glendale CA 91205. (213)240-9130. Subsidiaries include PRN/PTJ Magazines and Interurban Films. President: Mac Sebree. Publishes hardcover and trade paperback originals. Averages 10-12 titles/year; receives 50-75 submissions yearly. 35% of books from first-time authors; 99% of books from unagented writers. Average print order for a writer's first book is 2,000. Pays 5-10% royalty on gross receipts; offers no advance. Reports in 2 weeks on queries; 2 months on mss. Free book catalog.

Nonfiction: Western Americana and transportation. Subjects include Americana, history, hobbies and travel. "We are interested mainly in manuscripts about railroads, local transit, local history, and Western Americana (gold mining, logging, early transportation, etc.). Also anything pertaining to preservation movement, nostalgia." Query. Reviews artwork/photos.

Recent Nonfiction Title: *The Surfliners—50 Years of the San Diegan*, by Dick Stephenson.

Tips: "Our audience is comprised of hobbyists in the rail transportation field ('railfans'); those interested in Western Americana (logging, mining, etc.); and students of transportation history, especially railroads and local rail transit (streetcars)."

*INTERVARSITY PRESS, Division of Intervarsity Christian Fellowship, Box 1400, Downers Grove IL 60515. (708)964-5700. Editorial Director: Andrew T. LePeau. Publishes hardcover and paperback originals and reprints. Averages 50 titles/year; receives 800 submissions annually. 25% of books from first-time authors; 95% of books from unagented writers. Subsidy publishes (nonauthor) 6% of books. Pays average 10% royalty on retail price; negotiable advance. Sometimes makes outright purchase for $600-2,500. Publishes book an average of 15 months after acceptance of final draft. "Indicate simultaneous submissions." Reports in 3 months. Writer's guidelines for SASE.

Nonfiction: "InterVarsity Press publishes books geared to the presentation of Biblical Christianity in its various relations to personal life, art, literature, sociology, psychology, philosophy, history and so forth. Though we are primarily publishers of trade books, we are cognizant of the textbook market at the college, university and seminary level within the general religious field. The audience for which the books are published is composed primarily of adult Christians. Stylistic treatment varies from topic to topic and from fairly simple popularizations to scholarly works primarily designed to be read by scholars." Accepts nonfiction translations. Query or submit outline/synopsis and 2 sample chapters.

Recent Nonfiction Title: *When Christians Clash*, by Horace L. Fenton, Jr. (Christian living).

Fiction: Fantasy, humor, mainstream, religious, science fiction. "While fiction need not be explicity Christian or religious, it should rise out of a Christian perspective." Submit outline/synopsis and sample chapters.

Recent Fiction Title: *The Toy Campaign*, by John Bibee (juvenile fantasy).

Tips: "Religious publishing has become overpublished. Books that fill niches or give a look at a specific aspect of a broad topic (such as marriage or finances or Christian growth) are doing well for us. Also, even thoughtful books need lower reading levels, more stories and illustrative materials. If I were a writer trying to market a book today, I would read William Zinsser's *On Writing Well* and do as he says. Writers commonly send us types of mss that we don't publish, and act as if we should publish their work—being too confident of their ideas and ability."

*IOWA STATE UNIVERSITY PRESS, 2121 S. State Ave., Ames IA 50010. (515)292-0140. FAX: (515)292-3348. Director: Richard Kinney. Assistant Director and Chief Editor: Bill Silag. Estab. 1934. Hardcover and paperback originals. Averages 85 titles/year; receives 450 submissions annually. 98% of books from unagented writers. Average print order for a writer's first book is 2,000. Subsidy publishes (nonauthor) 25% of titles, based on sales potential of book and contribution to scholarship. Pays 10-12½-15% royalty on wholesale price; no advance. Publishes book an average of 1 year after acceptance. Simultaneous submissions OK, if advised. Query for electronic submissions. Reports in 4 months. Free book catalog; ms guidelines for SASE.

Nonfiction: Publishes biography, history, scientific/technical textbooks, the arts and sciences, statistics and mathematics, economics, aviation, and medical and veterinary sciences. Accepts nonfiction translations. Submit outline/synopsis and several sample chapters, preferably not in sequence; must be double-spaced throughout. Looks for "unique approach to subject; clear, concise narrative; and effective integration of scholarly apparatus." Send contrasting b&w glossy prints to illustrate ms. Reviews artwork/photos.

Recent Nonfiction Title: *Roadside America: The Automobile in Design and Culture*, edited by Jan Jennings.

‡*ISHI PRESS INTERNATIONAL, 1400 N. Shoreline Blvd., Bldg. A7, Mt. View CA 94043. (415)964-7294. FAX: (415)964-7509. Subsidiaries include Ishi Press. Estab. 1968. Publishes hardcover and trade paperback originals. Firm averages 6-10 titles/year. 10% of books from first-time authors. 100% from unagented writers. Subsidy pubishes 10% of books. Pays 5-15% royalty on retail price. Publishes book an average of 6 months after acceptance. Query for electronic submission. Reports in 2 weeks on queries; 1 month on mss. Free book catalog.

Nonfiction: Self-help, software, games. Subjects include cooking, foods and nutrition, strategy games. We are looking for mss on oriental strategy games—especially:Go, Shogi, Chinese chess, Mah Jong. Query.

Recent Nonfiction Title: *Positional Judgment*, by Cho Chi Kun (game).

Tips: "Also publish quarterly magazines *Go World* and *Shogi World*."

*ISHIYAKU EUROAMERICA, INC., Subsidiary of Ishiyaku Publishers, Inc., Tokyo, Japan: 716 Hanley Industrial Court, St. Louis MO 63144. (314)644-4322. FAX: (314)644-9532. President: Manuel L. Ponte. Inquiries should be directed to Dr. Gregory Hacke, Editor-in-Chief. Estab. 1983. Publishes hardcover originals. Averages 15 titles/year; receives 50 submissions annually. Subsidy publishes (nonauthor) 100% of books. 75% of books from first-time authors; 100% of books from unagented writers. Average print order for a writer's first book is 3,000. Pays 10% minimum royalty on retail price or pays 35% of all foreign translation rights sales. Offers average $1,000 advance. Simultaneous submissions OK. Query for electronic submissions. Reports in 2 weeks on queries; 1 week on mss. Free book catalog; ms guidelines for SASE.

Nonfiction: Reference and medical/nursing textbooks. Subjects include health (medical and dental); psychology (nursing); and psychiatry. Especially looking for "all phases of nursing education, administration and clinical procedures." Query, or submit outline/synopsis and sample chapters or complete ms. Reviews artwork/photos as part of ms package.

Recent Nonfiction Title: *Emotion Buffers: Quality in Health Care*, by Larry Hynson, Jr., Ph.D. (nursing, medicine).

Tips: "Medical authors often feel that their incomplete works deserve to be published; dental authors have a tendency to overstress facts, thereby requiring considerable editing. We prefer the latter to the former."

*JALMAR PRESS, INC., Subsidiary of B.L. Winch & Associates, 45 Hitching Post Dr., Bldg. 2, Rolling Hills Estates CA 90274-4297. (213)547-1240. FAX: (213)547-1644. Editorial Director: B.L. Winch. Estab. 1973. Publishes hardcover and trade paperback originals. Averages 4-8 titles/year. Pays 5-15% royalty on net sales. Subsidy publishes 10% of books; subsidy publishes (nonauthor) 20% of books. Publishes book an average of 18 months after acceptance. Simultaneous submissions OK. Query for electronic submissions. Reports in 3 months. Book catalog for 8½ × 11 SAE with 4 first class stamps.

Nonfiction: Positive self-esteem materials for parenting and teaching; right-brain/whole-brain learning materials; peacemaking skills activities for parenting and teaching; and inspirational titles on self-concept and values. Reviews artwork/photos as part of ms package. "Prefer completed ms."

Recent Nonfiction Title: *Feel Better Now*, by Dr. Chris Schriner.

Tips: "A continuing strong effort is being made by Jalmar in the areas of self-esteem, right brain/whole brain learning, peaceful conflict resolution and drug and alcohol abuse prevention."

‡JIST WORKS, INC., 720 North Park Ave., Indianapolis IN 46202. (317)264-3720. FAX: (317)264-3709. Editor: Mike Farr. Estab. 1981. Publishes trade paperback originals and reprints. Receives 25-30 submissions/year. 60% of books from first time authors; 100% from unagented writers. Pays 5-12% royalty on wholesale price or outright purchase (negotiable). Publishes ms an average of 6 months after acceptance. Simultaneous submissions OK. Query for electronic submissions. Reports in 1 month on queries. Book catalog and ms guidelines for SASE.

Nonfiction: How-to, reference, self-help, software, textbook. Specializes in job search and career related topics. "We want text/workbook formats that would be useful in a school or other institutional setting. All reading levels. Will consider books for professional staff and educators, appropriate software and videos." Reviews artwork/photos as part of ms package. Nonfiction areas are 1) career topics: assessment, job search, resumes, job survival, etc. 2) Reference books and professional materials for career and vocational instruction. 3) Low reading, remediation, and adult education materials.

Recent Nonfiction Title: *Exploring Careers: America's Top 300 Jobs*.

Tips: "Institutions and staff who work with people making career and life decisions or who are looking for jobs are our audience as well as persons with low reading and academic skills."

‡JOHNSON BOOKS, Johnson Publishing Co., 1880 S. 57th Ct., Boulder CO 80301. (303)443-1576. FAX: (303)443-1679. Estab. 1979. Editorial Director: Rebecca L. Herr. Publishes hardcover and paperback originals and reprints. Publishes 10-12 titles/year; receives 500 submissions annually. 30% of books from first-time authors; 90% of books from unagented writers. Average print order for a writer's first book is 5,000. Royalties vary. Publishes book an average of 1 year after acceptance. Reports in 2 months. Book catalog and ms guidelines for 9 × 12 SAE with 4 first class stamps.

Nonfiction: General nonfiction, books on the West, environmental subjects, astronomy, natural history, paleontology, geology, archaeology, travel, guidebooks, and outdoor recreation. Accepts nonfiction translations. "We are primarily interested in books for the informed popular market, though we will consider vividly written scholarly works. As a small publisher, we are able to give every submission close personal attention." Query first or call. Accepts outline/synopsis and 3 sample chapters. Looks for "good writing, thorough research, professional presentation and appropriate style. Marketing suggestions from writers are helpful." Reviews artwork/photos.

Recent Nonfiction Title: *Biologic: Environmental Protection by Design*, by David Wann.

Tips: "We are looking for nature titles with broad national, not just regional, appeal."

JONATHAN DAVID PUBLISHERS, 68-22 Eliot Ave., Middle Village NY 11379. (718)456-8611. Editor-in-Chief: Alfred J. Kolatch. Publishes hardcover and paperback originals. Averages 15 titles/year; receives 750-1,000 submissions annually. 50% of books from first-time authors; 90% of books from unagented writers. Pays standard royalty. Publishes book an average of 18 months after acceptance. Reports in 2 weeks on queries; 2 months on ms.

Nonfiction: Adult nonfiction books for a general audience. Cookbooks, cooking and foods, how-to, baseball and football, reference, self-help, Judaica. Query.
Recent Nonfiction Title: *Encyclopedia of Black Folklore and Humor,* by Henry D. Spalding.

‡JUDSON PRESS, P.O. Box 851, Valley Forge PA 19482. (215)768-2117. Director: Kristy Arnesen Pullen. Estab. 1824. Publishes hardcover and paperback originals. Averages 10-15 titles/year; receives 750 queries annually. Average print order for a writer's first book is 3,500. 10% royalty on retail price or flat fee. Publishes book an average of 15 months after acceptance. Simultaneous submissions acceptable. Query with outline and 1 sample chapter. Reports in 3 months. Enclose return postage. Book catalog for 9 × 12 SASE and 4 first class stamps; ms guidelines for SASE.
Nonfiction: Adult religious nonfiction of 30,000-80,000 words. "Our audience is mostly church members who seek to have a more fulfilling personal spiritual life and want to serve Christ in their churches and other relationships."
Recent Nonfiction Title: *My Moral Odyssey,* by Samuel Proctor.
Tips: "Writers have the best chance selling us practical books assisting clergy or laypersons in their ministry and personal lives. Our audience consists of Protestant church leaders. Be sensitive to our workload and adapt to the market's needs."

KALMBACH PUBLISHING CO., 21027 Crossroads Circle, P.O. Box 1612, Waukesha WI 53187. Books Editor: Bob Hayden. Publishes hardcover and paperback originals and paperback reprints. Averages 6-8 titles/year; receives 25 submissions annually. 85% of books from first-time authors; 100% of books from unagented writers. Offers 5-8% royalty on retail price. Average advance is $1,000. Publishes book an average of 18 months after acceptance. Reports in 2 months.
Nonfiction: Hobbies, how-to, and recreation. "Our book publishing effort is in railroading and hobby how-to-do-it titles *only.*" Query first. "I welcome telephone inquiries. They save me a lot of time, and they can save an author a lot of misconceptions and wasted work." In written query, wants to see "a detailed outline of two or three pages and a complete sample chapter with photos, drawings, and how-to text." Reviews artwork/photos as part of ms package.
Recent Nonfiction Title: *Milwaukee Road Remembered,* by Jim Scribbins.
Tips: "Our books are about half text and half illustrations. Any author who wants to publish with us must be able to furnish good photographs and rough drawings before we'll consider contracting for his book."

KAR-BEN COPIES INC., 6800 Tildenwood Ln., Rockville MD 20852. (301)984-8733 or 1-800-4KARBEN. President: Judye Groner. Publishes hardcover and trade paperback originals. Averages 8-10 titles/year; receives 150 submissions annually. 25% of books from first-time authors; 100% from unagented writers. Average print order for a writer's first book is 5,000. Pays 6-8% royalty on net receipts; makes negotiable outright purchase; offers average $1,000 advance. Publishes book an average of 1 year after acceptance. Reports in 1 week on queries; 1 month on mss. Free book catalog; ms guidelines for 9 × 12 SAE with 2 first class stamps.
Nonfiction: Jewish juvenile (ages 1-12). Especially looking for books on Jewish life-cycle, holidays, and customs for children — "early childhood and elementary." Send only mss with Jewish content. Query with outline/synopsis and sample chapters or submit complete ms. Reviews artwork/photos as part of ms package.
Recent Nonfiction Title: *Bible Heroes I Can Be,* by Ann Eisenberg.
Fiction: Adventure, fantasy, historical and religious (all Jewish juvenile). Especially looking for Jewish holiday and history-related fiction for young children. Submit outline/synopsis and sample chapters or complete ms.
Recent Fiction Title: *A Holiday for Noah,* by Susan Topek.
Tips: "We envision Jewish children and their families, and juveniles interested in learning about Jewish subjects, as our audience."

*KENT STATE UNIVERSITY PRESS, Kent State University, Kent OH 44242. (216)672-7913. Director: John T. Hubbell. Editor: Julia Morton. Publishes hardcover and paperback originals and some reprints. Averages 20-25 titles/year. Subsidy publishes (nonauthor) 20% of books. Standard minimum book contract on net sales; rarely offers advance. "Always write a letter of inquiry before submitting manuscripts. We can publish only a limited number of titles each year and can frequently tell in advance whether or not we would be interested in a particular manuscript. This practice saves both our time and that of the author, not to mention postage costs. If interested we will ask for complete manuscript. Decisions based on in-house readings and two by outside scholars in the field of study." Reports in 6-10 weeks. Enclose return postage. Free book catalog.
Nonfiction: Especially interested in "scholarly works in history and literary studies of high quality, any titles of regional interest for Ohio, scholarly biographies, archaeological research, the arts, and general nonfiction."
Recent Nonfiction Title: *Requiem for Revolution: The Untied States and Brazil, 1961-1969,* by Ruth Leacock.

MICHAEL KESEND PUBLISHING, LTD., 1025 5th Ave., New York NY 10028. (212)249-5150. Director: Michael Kesend. Estab. 1979. Publishes hardcover and trade paperback originals, and hardcover and trade paperback reprints. Averages 4-6 titles/year; receives 150 submissions annually. 50% of books from first-time authors; 50% of books from unagented writers. Pays 3-12½% royalty on wholesale price or retail price, or makes outright purchase for $500 minimum. Advance varies. Publishes book an average of 18 months after acceptance. Reports in 2 months on queries; 3 months on mss. Guidelines for #10 SASE.

Nonfiction: Biography, how-to, illustrated book, self-help and sports. Subjects include animals, health, history, hobbies, nature, sports, travel, the environment, and guides to several subjects. Needs sports, health self-help and environmental awareness guides. No photography mss. Submit outline/synopsis and sample chapters. Reviews artwork/photos as part of ms package.

Recent Nonfiction Title: *Clearing the Bases, Baseball Then & Now*, by Bill Starr.

Fiction: Literary fiction only. No science fiction or romance. No simultaneous submissions. Submit outline/synopsis and 2-3 sample chapters.

Recent Fiction Title: *Dan Yack*, by Blaise Cendrars.

Tips: "We are now more interested in nature-related topics and also regional guides."

KINSEEKER PUBLICATIONS, P.O. Box 184, Grawn MI 49637. (616)276-6745. Editor: Victoria Wilson. Estab. 1986. Publishes trade paperback originals. Averages 6 titles/year. 100% of books from unagented writers. Pays 10-25% royalty on retail price. Publishes book an average of 8 months after acceptance. Simultaneous submissions OK. Reports in 2 weeks. Book catalog and manuscript guidelines for #10 SASE.

Nonfiction: Reference books. Subjects include history and genealogy. Query or submit outline/synopsis and sample chapters. Reviews artwork/photos as part of ms package.

Recent Nonfiction Title: *Yours in Love, The Birmingham Civil War Letters*, by Zoe vonEnde Lappin.

B. KLEIN PUBLICATIONS, P.O. Box 8503, Coral Springs FL 33065. (305)752-1708. FAX: (305)752-2547. Editor-in-Chief: Bernard Klein. Estab. 1946. Hardcover and paperback originals. Specializes in directories, annuals, who's who type of books, bibliography, business opportunity, reference books. Averages 5 titles/year. Pays 10% royalty on wholesale price, "but we're negotiable." Advance "depends on many factors." Markets books by direct mail and mail order. Simultaneous submissions OK. Reports in 2 weeks. Book catalog for #10 SASE.

Nonfiction: Business, hobbies, how-to, reference, self-help, directories and bibliographies. Query or submit outline/synopsis and sample chapters or complete ms.

Recent Nonfiction Title: *Mail Order Business Directory*, by Bernard Klein.

KNIGHTS PRESS, P.O. Box 6737, Stamford CT 06901. Publisher: Elizabeth G. Gershman. Estab. 1983. Publishes trade paperback originals. Averages 12 titles/year; receives 500 submissions annually. 50% of books from first-time authors; 50% of books from unagented writers. Pays average of 10% plus escalating royalty on retail price; offers average $500 advance. Publishes book an average of 18 months after acceptance. Reports in 1 month on queries; 3 months on mss. Book catalog and ms guidelines for #10 SASE.

Nonfiction "We are looking for well-written, nonfiction of interest to gay men or discussing gay lifestyles for the general public."

Fiction: Adventure, erotica (very soft-core considered), ethnic, experimental, fantasy, gothic, historical, humor, mystery, romance, science fiction, suspense and western. "We publish *only* gay men's fiction; must show a positive gay lifestyle or positive gay relationship." No young adult or children's; no pornography; no formula plots, especially no formula romances; or no hardcore S&M. No lesbian fiction. Query a must. Submit outline/synopsis and sample chapters. Do not submit complete manuscript unless requested.

Recent Fiction Title: *Some Dance to Remember*, by Jack Fritscher.

Tips: "We are interested in well-written, well-plotted gay fiction. We are looking only for the highest quality gay literature."

ALFRED A. KNOPF, INC., 201 E. 50th St., New York NY 10022. (212)751-2600. Senior Editor: Ashbel Green. Children's Book Editor: Ms. Frances Foster. Publishes hardcover and paperback originals. Averages 200 titles annually. 15% of books from first-time authors; 40% of books from unagented writers. Royalties and advance "vary." Publishes book an average of 10 months after acceptance. Simultaneous (if so informed) submissions OK. Reports in 1 month. Book catalog for 7 × 10 SAE (7 oz.).

Nonfiction: Book-length nonfiction, including books of scholarly merit. Preferred length: 40,000-150,000 words. "A good nonfiction writer should be able to follow the latest scholarship in any field of human knowledge, and fill in the abstractions of scholarship for the benefit of the general reader by means of good, concrete, sensory reporting." Query. Reviews artwork/photos as part of ms package.

Recent Nonfiction Title: *The First Salute*, by Barbara Tuchman (history).

Fiction: Publishes book-length fiction of literary merit by known or unknown writers. Length: 30,000-150,000 words. Submit complete ms.

Recent Fiction Title: *Russia House*, by John LeCarré.

‡**KNOWLEDGE BOOK PUBLISHERS**, Suite 100, 3863 SW Loop 820, Fort Worth TX 76133-2076. (817)292-4270. Editor/Publisher: Dr. O.A. Battista. Estab. 1976. Publishes hardcover, trade paperback and mass market paperback originals. Firm averages 4-6 titles/year. Receives 50-100 submissions/year. 75% of books from

first-time authors. 0% from unagented writers. Pays 10-15% royalty on wholesale price. Advance varies. Publishes book an average of 1 year after acceptance. Query for electronic submissions. Reports in 1 month on queries; 2 months on mss. Manuscript guidelines for #10 SAE and 1 first class stamp.

Nonfiction: How-to, humor, juvenile, technical. Subjects include Americana, health/medicine, science. Submit through agent only.

Recent Nonfiction Title: *The Flemish Art of Frans de Cauter*, by Maurice Boyd.

Fiction: Juvenile. Submit through agent only.

Tips: "Our audience is a general audience interested in *new* knowledge useful in everyday life. If I were a writer trying to market a book today, I would do intense research on a new knowledge data that the general public can use to their *personal* benefit in everyday life."

‡**KODANSHA INTERNATIONAL U.S.A.**, Subsidiary of Kodansha International (Tokyo). 114 Fifth Avenue, New York NY 10011. (212)727-6460. Assistant Editor: Tina Isaac. Publishes hardcover and trade paperback originals (70%); hardcover and trade paperback reprints (30%). Averages 10-20 titles/year. Receives 300 submissions/year. 10% of books from first-time authors; 70% from unagented writers. Pays 6-15% royalty on retail price. Offers $10,000 average advance. Publishes book an average of 9 months after acceptance. Simultaneous submissions OK. Reports in 1 month. Book catalog for 8×13 SAE and 6 first class stamps.

Nonfiction: Biography, topical books-current events. Subjects include anthropology/archaeology, art/architecture, business and economics, cooking, foods and nutrition, ethnic, gardening, government/politics, health/medicine, history, hobbies, language/literature, military/war, music/dance, nature/environment, philosophy, psychology, religion, science, sociology, translation, travel and Asian subjects. We are looking for distinguished critical books on international subjects; Asian-related subjects; serious new consciousness "New Age" books. No pop psychology, how-to, true crime, regional. Query. Reviews artwork/photos as part of ms package.

Recent Nonfiction Title: *Inside the Robot Kingdom: Japan, Mechatronics, and the Coming Robotopia*, by Frederik L. Schodt (science, sociology).

Tips: "Writers have the best chance selling us well-researched, well-written nonfiction about the current state of the world or a specific area of knowledge about which the author is an expert. Our audience is the intellectually-curious bookreader or student who is a bit of world traveler. If I were a writer trying to market a book today, I would spend a lot of time in bookstores checking out what is available and from whom."

‡*KUMARIAN PRESS, INC.**, Suite 119, 630 Oakwood Ave., W. Hartford CT 06110-1529. (203)953-0214. Editor-in-Chief: Jenna Dixon. Publishes hardcover and trade paperback originals and trade paperback reprints. Averages 8-12 titles/year. Receives 50-100 submissions/year. 10% of books from first-time authors. 100% from unagented writers. Subsidy publishes 25% of books. Determines subsidy by financial viability. Pays 0-10% royalty on net. Publishes book an average of 9 months after acceptance. Query for electronic submissions. Reports in 2 weeks on queries; 2 months on mss. Free book catalog and ms guidelines.

Nonfiction: Professional. Subjects include agriculture/horticulture, business and economics, government/politics, nature/environment, relition, sociology, women's issues/studies, international development. We are looking for mss that address the practical needs of international development community; specific topics include: women in development, natural resource management, private vs. voluntary organizations, and effective and accountable public service. Query. Submit outline/synopsis and sample chapters and cover letters.

Recent Nonfiction Title: *Women's Ventures: Assistance to the Informal Sector in Latin America*, by Marguerite Berger and Mayra Burinic.

Tips: "Authors have the best chance selling us well written mss that are specifically targeted to addressing the issues faced by the international development community. Our audience is the international development community."

*PETER LANG PUBLISHING**, 62 W. 45th St., New York NY 10036. (212)302-6740. FAX: (212)302-7574. Subsidiary of Verlag Peter Lang AG, Bern, Switzerland. Managing Director: Christopher S. Myers. Head of Acquisitions: Brigitte D. McDonald. New York Acquisitions Editor: Michael J. Flamini. Chicago Acquisitions Editor: Thomas Derdak. San Francisco Acquisitions Editor: Heidi Burns. Estab. 1982. Publishes mostly hardcover originals. Averages 200 titles/year. 75% of books from first-time authors; 98% of books from unagented writers. Subsidy publishes 50% of books. All subsidies are guaranteed repayment plus profit (if edition sells out) in contract. Subsidy published if ms is highly specialized and author relatively unknown. Pays 10-20% royalty on net price. Translators get flat fee plus percentage of royalties. No advance. Publishes

For explanation of symbols, see the Key to Symbols and Abbreviations on Page 5. For unfamiliar words, see the Glossary.

book an average of 1 year after acceptance. Reports in 1 month on queries; 2 months on mss. Free book catalog and ms guidelines.

Nonfiction: General nonfiction, reference works, and scholarly monographs. Subjects include literary criticism, Germanic and Romance languages, art history, business and economics, American and European political science, history, music, philosophy, psychology, religion, sociology and biography. All books are scholarly monographs, textbooks, reference books, reprints of historic texts, critical editions or translations. "We are expanding and are receptive to any scholarly project in the humanities and social sciences." No mss shorter than 200 pages. Submit complete ms.

Fiction and Poetry: "We do not publish original fiction or poetry. We seek scholarly and critical editions only. Submit complete ms."

Tips: "Besides our commitment to specialist academic monographs, we are one of the few U.S. publishers who publish books in most of the modern languages. A major advantage for Lang authors is international marketing and distribution of all titles. Translation rights sold for many titles."

‡**LARSON PUBLICATIONS/PBPF**, 4936 Rt. 414, Burdett NY 14818. (607)546-9342. Director: Paul Cash. Publishes hardcover and trade paperback originals. Averages 4-6 titles/year. Receives 700 submissions/year. 8% of books from first-time authors. Pays 7½-10% royalty on retail price; or 10% cash received. Offers $1,000 average advance. Publishes book an average of 9 months after acceptance. Simultaneous submissions OK. Reports in 6 months on queries; unsolicited mss not accepted; queries only. Free book catalog.

Nonfiction: Self-help and spiritual philosophy. Subjects include philosophy, psychology and religion. We are looking for studies of comparative spiritual philosophy or personal fruits of independent (nonsectarian viewpoint) spiritual research/practice. Query or submit outline/synopsis and sample chapters. Reviews artwork/photos as part of ms package.

Recent Nonfiction Title: *Looking Into Mind*, by Anthony Damiani.

‡**MERLOYD LAWRENCE BOOKS**, 102 Chestnut St., Boston MA 02108. Imprint of Addison Wesley. President: Merloyd Lawrence. Publishes hardcover and trade paperback originals. Averages 7-8 titles/year. Receives 400 submissions/year. 25% of books from first-time authors. 20% from unagented writers. Pays royalty on retail price. Publishes book an average of 1 year after acceptance. Simultaneous submissions OK. Reports in 3 weeks on queries; 3 months on mss. Book catalog available from Addison Wesley.

Nonfiction: Biography. Subjects include child guidance/parenting, health/medicine, nature/environment, psychology. Query with SASE.

Recent Nonfiction Title: *Mindfulness*, by Ellen Langer, Ph.D. (psychology).

‡**LEARNING PUBLICATIONS INC.**, Twining Publications Ltd., 3008 Avenue C, P.O. Box 1338, Holmes Beach FL 34218. (813)778-6651. Editor: Edsel Erickson. Publishes hardcover originals. Publishes 20 titles/year; receives 500 submissions/year. 50% from first-time authors; 95% from unagented writers. Pays 4-10% royalty on net income. Publishes book an average of 1 year after acceptance. Simultaneous submissions OK. Query for electronic submissions. Reports in 3 weeks on queries; 4 months on mss. Book catalog for 9×12 SAE with 2 first class stamps; ms guidelines for #10 SASE.

Nonfiction: Textbook. Subjects include art (education), education, health/medicine, women's issues/studies. Need resource books for art teachers (elementary level), school administrators, student assistants and counselors; human service resource books for psychologists and social workers; trade books on health and medicine. Query or submit outline/synopsis and sample chapters. Reviews artwork/photos as part of ms package.

Recent Nonfiction Title: *Cultural Journeys.*

LEISURE BOOKS, Division of Dorchester Publishing Co., Inc., Suite 1008, 276 Fifth Ave., New York NY 10001. (212)725-8811. Editor: Frank Walgren. Estab. 1970. Publishes mass market paperback originals and reprints. Averages 144 titles/year; receives thousands of submissions annually. 20% of books from first-time authors; 40% of books from unagented writers. Pays royalty on retail price. Advance negotiable. Publishes book an average of 18 months after acceptance. Reports in 1 month on queries; up to 2 months on mss. Book catalog and ms guidelines for #10 SASE.

Nonfiction: "Our needs are minimal as we publish perhaps four nonfiction titles a year." Query.

Fiction: Historical (90,000 words); Gothics (75,000 words); futuristic romance (80,000 words). "We are strongly backing historical romance." No sweet romance, science fiction, western, erotica, contemporary women's fiction, mainstream or male adventure." Query or submit outline/synopsis and sample chapters. "No material will be returned without SASE."

Recent Fiction Title: *Lacey's Way*, by Madeline Baker (historical romance).

Tips: "Historical romance is our strongest category."

LEISURE PRESS, Affiliate of Human Kinetics Publishing, P.O. Box 5076, Champaign IL 61820. (217)351-5076. FAX: (217)351-2674. Director: Brian Holding. Estab. 1974. Publishes hardcover, trade paperback and mass market paperback originals. Averages 30 titles/year; receives 200-250 submissions annually. 50% of books from first-time authors; 90% from unagented writers. Pays 10-15% royalty on wholesale price. Offers average $1,000 advance. Publishes ms an average of 9 months after acceptance. Simultaneous submissions OK. Query for electronic submissions. Reports in 2 weeks on queries; 6 weeks on ms. Free book catalog; writer's guidelines for SASE.

Nonfiction: How-to, reference, technical. Subjects include sports, fitness and wellness. "We want coaching-related books, technique books on sports and fitness. No fitness or coaching books that are not based on sound physical education principles and research." Reviews artwork/photos as part of ms package. Query or submit outline/synopsis and sample chapters.

Recent Nonfiction Title: *Sport Stretch*, by Michael Alter.

Tips: "Our audience is coaches, athletes, physical education students and fitness enthusiasts." ·

LEXIKOS, P.O. Box 296, Lagunitas CA 94938. (415)488-0401. Imprints include Don't Call It Frisco Press. Editor: Mike Witter. Estab. 1981. Publishes hardcover and trade paperback originals and trade paperback reprints. Averages 8 titles/year; receives 200 submissions annually. 50% of books from first-time authors; 90% of books from unagented writers. Average print order for a writer's first book is 5,000. Royalties vary from 8-12½% according to books sold. "Authors asked to accept lower royalty on high discount (50% plus) sales." Offers average $1,000 advance. Publishes book an average of 10 months after acceptance. Simultaneous submissions OK. Reports in 1 month. Book catalog and ms guidelines for 6×9 SAE and 2 first class stamps.

Nonfiction: Coffee table book, illustrated book. Subjects include regional, outdoors, oral histories, Americana, history and nature. Especially looking for 50,000-word "city and regional histories, anecdotal in style for a general audience; books of regional interest about *places*; adventure and wilderness books; annotated reprints of books of Americana; Americana in general." No health, sex, European travel, diet, broad humor, fiction, quickie books (we stress backlist vitality), religion, children's or nutrition. Submit outline/synopsis and sample chapters. Reviews artwork/photos as part of ms package.

Recent Nonfiction Title: *A Short History of Santa Fe*, by Hazen-Hammond.

Tips: "A regional interest or history book has the best chance of selling to Lexikos. Submit a short, cogent proposal; follow up with letter queries. Give the publisher reason to believe you will help him *sell* the book (identify the market, point out the availability of mailing lists, distinguish your book from the competition). Avoid grandiose claims."

LIBERTY HALL PRESS, Imprint of Tab Books, division of McGraw-Hill, Inc., #1101, 10 E. 21st St., New York NY 10010. (212)475-1446. Vice President/Editorial Director: David J. Conti. Estab. 1964. Publishes hardcover originals and trade paperback originals and reprints. Publishes 25 titles/year. Receives 200 submissions/year. 50% of books from first-time authors; 80% from unagented writers. Pays 5-15% royalty on wholesale price. Offers $3,000 average advance. Publishes book an average of 9 months after acceptance. Simultaneous submissions OK. Reports on queries in 2 weeks; on ms in 1 month. Book catalog free on request; writer's guidelines for #10 SASE.

Nonfiction: Subjects include investing, real estate, personal finance, small business/entrepreneurship, legal self-help. "We're engaged in a wide-ranging business publishing program. We publish how-to books for sophisticated investors, business people, professionals as well as the general public." Submit outline/synopsis and sample chapter.

Recent Nonfiction Title: *Understanding Corporate Bonds*, by Harold Kerzner.

Tips: "We publish very practical, how-to, results-oriented books. Study the competition, study the market, then submit a proposal."

‡LIBERTY PUBLISHING COMPANY, INC., 440 S. Federal Hwy., Deerfield Beach FL 33441. (305)360-9000. Subsidiaries include LPC Software, Inc. Imprints include LPC. Publisher: Jeffrey B. Little. Publishes hardcover and trade paperback originals. Averages 5-10 titles/year. Receives 300-800 submissions/year. 90% of books from first-time authors; 95% of books from unagented writers. Pays 5-12% royalty on wholesale. Buys mss outright for $300-2,000. Offers $400 average advance. Publishes book an average of 9-18 months after acceptance. Simultaneous submissions OK. Reports in 3 weeks on queries; 6-8 weeks on mss. Book catalog for 9×12 SAE with 4 first class stamps. Manuscript guidelines for #10 SAE with 1 first class stamp.

Nonfiction: Cookbook, how-to, reference, self-help. Subjects include business and economics, cooking, foods and nutrition, hobbies, money/finance, recreation, sports especially horseracing, travel. "Liberty Publishing Company seeks only titles that can become *the* leading book in its respective area. The author should have credibility in his/her field of expertise. Seeking new ideas (e.g., retirement community guides, highly specialized cooking, etc.) No mind-benders, please. No psychology, religious, or esoteric clap-trap. Prefer only useful, hands-on, practical material." Query. Submit complete ms. "We are only interested in completed mss." Reviews artwork/photos as part of ms package.

Recent Nonfiction Title: *Ten Steps to Winning*, by Danny Holmes (guide for racing fans).

Tips: We favor nonfiction books that offer the reader an immediate and obvious benefit. Books that answer the book-buyer's initial question. "Why should I buy this book? – and the price is not the major consideration. This is one reason why horse race handicapping titles do well for us. Adults seeking to learn a specific piece of information, and less concerned about the price of the book. The potential bookbuyer probably recognizes the value of the book's message before it leaves the bookstore." The message is practical and useful, and maybe profitable. "If I were a writer trying to market a book today, I would make a point of knowing the *market* for the book and know something about the expected *audience* for the work. We also favor books that can be sold in specialty markets and we are seeking tie-ins with software and videos."

*LIBRA PUBLISHERS, INC., Suite 383, 3089C Clairemont Dr., San Diego CA 92117. (619)581-9449. Contact: William Kroll. Estab. 1960. Publishes hardcover and paperback originals. Specializes in the behavioral sciences. Averages 15 titles/year; receives 300 submissions annually. 60% of books from first-time authors; 85% of books from unagented writers. 10-15% royalty on retail price; no advance. "We will also offer our services to authors who wish to publish their own works. The services include editing, proofreading, production, artwork, copyrighting, and assistance in promotion and distribution." Publishes book an average of 8 months after acceptance. Reports in 2 weeks. Free book catalog; writer's guidelines for #10 SASE.
Nonfiction: Mss in all subject areas will be given consideration, but main interest is in the behavioral sciences. Prefers complete manuscript but will consider outline/synopsis and 3 sample chapters. Reviews artwork/photos as part of ms package.
Recent Nonfiction Title: *Highway Robbery: The Truth About America's Auto Dealers*, by Sherman Ruthmay.
Recent Fiction Title: *Tarnished Hero*, by Steve Berman.

LIBRARIES UNLIMITED, P.O. Box 3988, Englewood CO 80155-3988. FAX: (303)220-8843. Imprints include Teacher Ideas Press, Ukranian Academic Press. Editor-in-Chief: Bohdan S. Wynar. Estab. 1964. Publishes hardcover and paperback originals. Averages 50 titles/year; receives 100-200 submissions annually. 10-20% of books from first-time authors. Average print order for a writer's first book is 2,000. 10% royalty on net sales; advance averages $500. Publishes book an average of 1 year after acceptance. Reports in 2 months. Free book catalog and ms guidelines.
Nonfiction: Publishes reference and library science textbooks, teacher resource and activity books also software. Looks for professional experience. Query or submit outline and sample chapters; state availability of photos/illustrations with submission. All prospective authors are required to fill out an author questionnaire.
Recent Nonfiction Title: *Handbook of Business Information*, by Diane Strauss.

LIBRARY RESEARCH ASSOCIATES, INC., Subsidiaries include Empire State Fiction, RD #5, Box 41, Dunderberg Rd., Monroe NY 10950. (914)783-1144. President: Matilda A. Gocek. Estab. 1968. Publishes hardcover and trade paperback originals. Averages 4 titles/year; receives about 300 submissions annually. 100% of books from first-time authors; 100% of books from unagented writers. Pays 10% maximum royalty on retail price. Offers 20 copies of the book as advance. Publishes book an average of 14 months after acceptance. Reports in 3 weeks on queries; 3 months on mss. Book catalog free on request.
Nonfiction: Biography, coffee table book, how-to, reference, technical and American history. Subjects include Americana, art, business and economics, history, philosophy, politics and travel. "Our nonfiction book manuscript needs for the next year or two will include books about American artists, graphics and photography, historical research of some facet of American history, and definitive works about current or past economics or politics." No astrology, occult, sex, adult humor or gay rights. Submit outline/synopsis and sample chapters.
Recent Nonfiction Title: *Washington's Last Cantonment*, by Dempsey.
Fiction: Send fiction to Empire State Fiction, Patricia E. Clyne, senior editor. Adventure (based in an authentic NY location); historical (particularly in or about New York state); mystery; and suspense. "I try to publish at least three novels per year. Characterization is so important! The development of people and plot must read well. The realism of world events (war, terrorism, catastrophes) is turning readers to a more innocent world of reading for entertainment with less shock value. Free speech (free *everything*!) is reviving old values. Explicit sex, extreme violence, vile language in any form will not be considered." Submit outline/synopsis and sample chapters.
Recent Fiction Title: *Tales from an Irish Wake*, by Armstrong.
Tips: "Our audience is adult, over age 30, literate and knowledgeable in business or professions. The writer has the best chance of selling our firm historical fiction or nonfiction and scientific texts. If I were a writer trying to market a book today, I would try to write about people in a warm human situation – the foibles, the loss of self, the unsung heroism – angels with feet of clay."

LINCH PUBLISHING, INC., Box 75, Orlando FL 32802. (407)647-3000. Vice President: Valeria Lynch. Editor: Peggy H. Maddox. Publishes hardcover and trade paperback originals. Averages 10 titles/year. Pays 6-8% royalty on retail price. Rarely pays advances. Publishes book an average of 9 months after acceptance. Simultaneous submissions OK. Reports in 6 weeks. Book catalog for $1 and #10 SAE with 2 first class stamps.
Nonfiction: Publishes books only on estate planning and legal how-to books which must be applicable in all 50 states. "We are interested in a book on getting through probate, settling an estate, and minimizing federal estate and/or state inheritance taxes." Query editor by phone before submitting mss – "we could have already accepted a manuscript and be in the process of publishing one of the above."

Recent Nonfiction Title: *Ask an Attorney*, by J. Pippen.
Tips: Currently interest is mainly estate planning and avoiding probate "how-to."

LION PUBLISHING CORPORATION, 1705 Hubbard Ave., Batavia IL 60510. (312)879-0707. Editor: Robert Bittner. Estab. 1967. Publishes hardcover and trade paperback originals. Firm averages 15 titles/year. Pays royalty. Publishes book an average of 18 months after acceptance. Reports in 1 month on queries; 2 months on mss. Book catalog for 9 × 12 SAE and $1.05 postage. Manuscript guidelines for #10 SAE and 2 first class stamps.
Nonfiction: Subjects include child guidance/parenting, biography and religion. "We are especially interested in manuscripts on relationships and on spirituality. We do not want Bible studies or sermons." Query or submit outline/synopsis and sample chapters.
Recent Nonfiction Title: *Alzheimer's: Caring for Your Loved One, Caring for Yourself*, by Sharon Fish.
Fiction: Fantasy, literary historical, juvenile (ages 8-12) and YA. "Stories that create meaty, believable characters, not puppets or simplistic representations of certain values or beliefs. Give us a story that anyone would be intrigued with—and write it from a Christian perspective." Submit complete ms.
Recent Fiction Title: *The Breaking of Ezra Riley*, by John Moore (contemporary western).
Tips: "All Lion books are written from a Christian perspective. However, they must speak to a general audience. Because Lion's approach is unique, we strongly recommend that every potential author request our guidelines."

LITTLE, BROWN AND CO., INC., 34 Beacon St., Boston MA 02108. Contact: Editorial Department, Trade Division. Estab. 1937. Publishes hardcover and paperback originals and paperback reprints. Averages 100 titles/year. "Royalty and advance agreements vary from book to book and are discussed with the author at the time an offer is made. Submissions only from authors who have had a book published or have been published in professional or literary journals, newspapers or magazines." Reports in 5 months for queries/proposals.
Nonfiction: "Some how-to books, distinctive cookbooks, biographies, history, science and sports." Query or submit outline/synopsis and sample chapters. Reviews artwork/photos as part of ms package.
Recent Nonfiction Title: *The Last Lion: Winston Spenser Churchill, Alone*, by William Manchester.
Fiction: Contemporary popular fiction as well as fiction of literary distinction. Query or submit outline/synopsis and sample chapters.
Recent Fiction Title: *Vineland*, by Thomas Pynchon.

‡LLEWELLYN PUBLICATIONS, Subsidiary of Llewellyn Worldwide, Ltd., P.O. Box 64383, St. Paul MN 55164. (612)291-1970. Acquisitions Manager: Nancy J. Mostad. Publishes trade and mass market paperback originals. Averages 60 titles/year. Receives 1,000 submissions/year. 30% of books from first-time authors; 90% from unagented writers. Pays 10% royalty on moneys received both wholesale and retail. Publishes book an average of 1 year after acceptance. Simultaneous submissions OK. Query for electronic submissions. Reports in 2 weeks on queries; 3 months on mss. Book catalog for #10 SAE and 1 first class stamp. Manuscript guidelines free on request.
Nonfiction: How-to and self-help. Subjects include nature/environment, metaphysical/magick, psychology and women's issues/studies. Submit outline/synopsis and sample chapters. Reviews artwork/photos as part of ms package.
Recent Nonfiction Title: *Goddesses and Heroines*, by Patricia Monaghan.

LODESTAR BOOKS, Affiliate of E. P. Dutton, 2 Park Ave., New York NY 10016. (212)725-1818. FAX: (212)532-6568. Editorial Director: Virginia Buckley. Senior Editor: Rosemary Brosnan. Publishes hardcover originals. Publishes juveniles, young adults, fiction and nonfiction; and picture books. Averages 30 titles/year; receives 1,000 submissions annually. 10-20% of books from first-time authors; 25-30% of books from unagented writers. Average print order for a writer's first book is 5,000-6,000. Pays royalty on invoice list price; advance offered. Publishes book an average of 18 months after acceptance. Reports in 4 months. Ms guidelines for SASE.
Nonfiction: Query or submit outline/synopsis and 2-3 sample chapters including "theme, chapter-by-chapter outline, and 1 or 2 completed chapters." State availability of photos and/or illustrations. Queries/mss may be routed to other editors in the publishing group. Reviews artwork/photos as part of ms package.
Recent Nonfiction Title: *Christopher Columbus: Voyager to the Unknown*, by Nancy Smiler Levinson.
Fiction: Publishes for young adults (middle grade) and juveniles (ages 5-17): adventure, fantasy, historical, humorous, contemporary, mystery, science fiction, suspense and western books, also picture books. Submit complete ms.
Recent Fiction Title: *The Shadow of Fomor*, by Thomas McGowen.
Tips: "A young adult or middle-grade novel that is literary, fast-paced, well-constructed (as opposed to a commercial novel); well-written nonfiction on contemporary issues, photographic essays, and nonfiction pictures have been our staples. We are now expanding into the picture book market as well."

‡LONE EAGLE PUBLISHING CO., 9903 Santa Monica Blvd., Beverly Hills CA 90212. (213)471-8066. President: Joan V. Singleton. Estab. 1982. Publishes hardcover and trade paperback originals. Averages 8 titles/year; receives 20-30 submissions annually. 100% of books from unagented writers. Pays 10% royalty minimum on net income wholesale and retail. Offers $100-250 average advance. Publishes a book an average of 1 year after acceptance. Simultaneous submissions OK. Query for electronic submissions. Reports in 1 month on queries; 3 months on mss. Book catalog for #10 SAE and 2 first class stamps.
Nonfiction: Self-help, technical, how-to, and reference. Subjects include movies. "We are looking for technical books in the motion picture and video field by professionals. No unrelated topics or biographies." Submit outline/synopsis and sample chapters. Reviews artwork/photos as part of ms package.
Recent Nonfiction Title: *The Film Editing Room Handbook*, by Norman Hollyn.
Tips: "A well-written, well-thought-out book on some technical aspect of the motion picture (or video) industry has the best chance: for example, script supervising, editing, special effects, costume design, production design. Pick a subject that has not been done to death, make sure you know what you're talking about, get someone well-known in that area to endorse the book and prepare to spend a lot of time publicizing the book."

‡LONE PINE PUBLISHING, #206 10426 81 Avenue, Edmonton, Alberta, T6E 1X5 Canada. (403)433-9333. Imprints include Pine Cone. Editor-in-Chief: Mary Walters Riskin. Publishes hardcover and trade paperback originals and hardcover and trade paperback reprints. Averages 12-20 titles/year. Receives 100 submissions/year. 45% of books from first-time authors; 95% from unagented writers. Pays royalty. Simultaneous submissions OK. Reports in 1 month on queries; 2 months on mss. Free book catalog.
Nonfiction: Biography, cookbook, how-to, juvenile and nature/recreation guide books. Subjects include animals, anthropology/archaeology, art/architecture, business and economics, cooking, foods and nutrition, gardening, government/politics, history, nature/environment (this is where most of our books fall), photography, sports, travel (another major category for us). We publish recreational and natural history titles, and some historical biographies. Most of our list is set for the next year and a half, but we are interested in seeing new material. Submit outline/synopsis and sample chapters. Reviews artwork/photos as part of ms package.
Recent Nonfiction Title: *The Prospector: North of Sixty*, by Jordan Zinovich.
Tips: "Writers have their best chance with recreational or native guidebooks. If I were a writer trying to market a book today, I would query first, to save time and money, and possibly even contact prospective publishers before the book is completed. Always send material with SASE, and make the ms clean and easy to read."

LONGMAN FINANCIAL SERVICES PUBLISHING, 520 N. Dearborn St., Chicago IL 60610. (312)836-4400. FAX: (312)836-1021. Subsidiary includes Longman, Dearborn Financial Publishing, Real Estate Education Co. Senior Vice President: Anita Constant. Estab. 1959. Publishes hardcover originals. Averages 200 titles/year. Receives 200 submissions/year. 50% of books from first-time authors. 50% from unagented writers. Pays 1-15% on wholesale price. Publishes book an average of 8 months after acceptance. Simultaneous submissions OK. Query for electronic submissions. Reports in 2 weeks; 1 month on mss. Free book catalog and manuscript guidelines.
Nonfiction: How-to, reference and textbook. Subjects include business and economics and money/finance. Query.
Recent Nonfiction Title: *Future Scope*, by Joe Cappo.
Tips: "People seeking real estate, insurance, broker's licenses are our audience; also business professionals interested in information on managing their finances, improving their business skills, broadening their knowledge of the financial services industry."

‡LONGMAN PUBLISHING GROUP, 95 Church St., White Plains NY 10601. (914)993-5000. FAX: (914)997-8115. President: Bruce S. Butterfield. Estab. 1974. Publishes hardcover and paperback originals. Publishes 200 titles/year. Pays variable royalty; offers variable advance. Reports in 6 weeks.
Nonfiction: Textbooks only (elementary/high school, college and professional): world history, political science, economics, communications, social sciences, sociology, education, English, Latin, foreign languages, English as a second language. No trade, art or juvenile.

‡LONGSTREET PRESS, INC., Suite 102, 2150 Newmarket Parkway, Marietta GA 30067. (404)980-1488. Managing Editor: Joycelyn Woolfolk. Estab. 1988. Publishes hardcover and trade paperback originals. Averages 20 titles/year. Receives 125 submissions/year. 25-30% of books from first-time authors. 60% from unagented writers. Pays royalty. Publishes book an average of 1 year after acceptance. Simultaneous submissions OK. Reports in 6 weeks on queries; 6 months on mss. No electronic submissions via disk or modem. Book catalog for 9 × 12 SAE with 85¢ postage. Manuscript guidelines for #10 SAE with 25¢ postage.
Nonfiction: Biography, coffee table book, cookbook, humor, illustrated book, reference. Subjects include Americana, cooking, foods and nutrition, gardening, history, language/literature, nature/environment, photography, regional, sports, women's issues/studies. "We want serious journalism-oriented nonfiction on subjects appealing to a broad, various audience. No poetry, how-to, religious or inspirational, scientific or highly

technical, textbooks of any kind, erotica." Query. Submit outline/synopsis and sample chapters. Reviews artwork as part of ms package.

Recent Nonfiction Title: *Broken Pledges: The Deadly Rite of Hazing*, by Hank Nuwer.

Fiction: Literary, mainstream/contemporary. "We are looking for solid literary fiction with appeal to a general reader. No juvenile or young adult literature, science fiction, mysteries, supernatural/horror, action/adventure/thriller, romance, historical fiction and romances." Query. Submit outline/synopsis and sample chapters.

Recent Fiction Title: *Crazy Ladies*, by Michael Lee West (novel).

Tips: "Midlist books have a harder time making it. The nonfiction book, serious or humorous, with a clearly defined audience has the best chance. The audience for our books has a strong sense of intellectual curiosity and a functioning sense of humor. "If I were a writer trying to market a book today, I would do thorough, professional work aimed at a clearly defined and reachable audience."

LONGWOOD ACADEMIC, P.O. Box 2069, Wolfeboro NH 03894. (603)522-6303. FAX: (207)324-0349. Editor-in-Chief: Wyatt Benner. Estab. 1981. Publishes hardcover and quality paperback originals and hardcover and trade paperback reprints. Firm averages 24 titles/year. Receives 100 submissions/year. 25% of books from first-time authors. 90% from unagented writers. Pays 5-10% on retail price. Publishes book an average of 6 months after acceptance. Simultaneous submissions OK. Reports in 1 month on queries; 2 months on mss. Free book catalog and manuscript guidelines.

Nonfiction: Scholarly works of all kinds. Subjects include education, health/medicine, history, language/literature, music/dance, philosophy, religion, science, translation, women's issues/studies, literary criticism and Asian studies. "We publish primarily scholarly books of high quality aimed at academics and college libraries. We'll consider all topics for which there is an academic audience. That eliminates coffee table books, juvenile books, cookbooks, how-to books, etc." Submit complete ms. Reviews artwork/photos as part of ms package.

Recent Nonfiction Title: *American Renaissance and the Critics*, by Jeanette Boswell.

Fiction: Literary (translations of classics). "We'll consider new translations or first translations of neglected foreign writers, usually non-contemporaries—writers like Nicholas Chamfort, Leon Bloy, Valle-Inclan. No original contemporary fiction or poetry." Query.

Recent Fiction Title: *The Campaign of the Maestrazgo*, by Benito Perez Galdes.

Poetry: "We don't accept original poetry."

LOOMPANICS UNLIMITED, P.O. Box 1197, Port Townsend WA 98368. Book Editor: Michael Hoy. Estab. 1975. Publishes trade paperback originals. Publishes 25 titles/year; receives 100 submissions annually. 40% of books from first-time authors; 100% of books from unagented writers. Average print order for a writer's first book is 1,000. Pays 7½-15% royalty on wholesale or retail price; or makes outright purchase of $100-1,200. Offers average $500 advance. Publishes book an average of 10 months after acceptance. Simultaneous submissions OK. Reports in 6 weeks. Free book catalog and author guidelines.

Nonfiction: How-to, reference and self-help. Subjects include business and economics, philosophy, politics, travel, and "beat the system" books. "We are looking for how-to books in the fields of espionage, investigation, the underground economy, police methods, how to beat the system, crime and criminal techniques. No cookbooks, inspirational, travel, or cutesy-wutesy stuff." Query, or submit outline/synopsis and sample chapters. Reviews artwork/photos.

Recent Nonfiction Title: *Building with Junk*, by Jim Bradstreet (how-to).

Tips: "Our audience is young males looking for hard-to-find information on alternatives to 'The System.'"

‡**LOS HOMBRES PRESS**, P.O. Box 15428, San Diego CA 92115. (619)576-0104. Contact: Jim Kitchen. Estab. 1989. Publishes trade paperback originals. Averages 4 titles/year. 50% of books from first-time authors. Most from unagented writers. Pays 7-10% royalty on retail price. Publishes book an average of 9 months after acceptance. Query for electronic submission.

Nonfiction: Subjects include gay/lesbian. Query. Reviews artwork/photos as part of ms package.

Recent Nonfiction Title: *Panels of Love*, by Timothy Walters Grummon (Art).

Fiction: Gay/lesbian. "We want gay oriented mystery novels, short story collections including mysteries and science fiction and "mainstream" type novels with gay characters. Emphasis on good writing, not on explicit sex. No pornography. Query.

Recent Fiction: *Triple Fiction*, by Richard L. Stone, Marsh Cassady, Stephen Richard Smith (short stories).

Poetry: "We are interested *only* in haiku."

Recent Poetry Title: *The Rise & Fall of Sparrows*, by Alexis Rotella, Ed (haiku).

‡**LOTHROP, LEE & SHEPARD BOOKS**, Division of William Morrow & Company, 105 Madison Ave., New York NY 10016. (212)889-3050. Editor-in-Chief: Susan Pearson. Hardcover original children's books only. Royalty and advance vary according to type of book. Averages 60 titles/year; receives 4,000 submissions annually. Less than 2% of books from first-time authors; 25% of books from unagented writers. Average print order for a writer's first book is 6,000. State availability of photos to accompany ms. Publishes book an

average of 2 years after acceptance. Does *not* accept unsolicitied manuscripts. No simultaneous submissions. Responds in 6 weeks. Book catalog and guidelines for 9×12 SAE with 4 first class stamps.

Fiction and Nonfiction: Publishes picture books, general nonfiction, and novels. Submit outline/synopsis and sample chapters for nonfiction. Juvenile fiction emphasis is on novels for the 8-12 age group. Looks for "organization, clarity, creativity, literary style."

Recent Nonfiction Title: *Portrait of a Tragedy: America and the Vietnam War*, by James A. Warren.

Recent Fiction Title: *The Outside Child*, by Nina Bawden.

Tips: "Trends in book publishing that freelance writers should be aware of include the demand for books for children under age three and the shrinking market for young adult books, especially novels."

‡**LOUISIANA STATE UNIVERSITY PRESS**, Baton Rouge LA 70893. (504)388-6294. Editor-in-Chief: Margaret Fisher Dalrymple. Estab. 1935. Publishes hardcover originals and hardcover and trade paperback reprints. Averages 60-70 titles/year. Receives 500 submissions/year. 33% of books from first-time authors. 90% from unagented writers. Pays royalty on wholesale price. Publishes book an average of 1 year after acceptance. Simultaneous submissions OK. Reports in 2 weeks on queries; 6 weeks on mss. Free book catalog and ms guidelines.

Nonfiction: Biography. Subjects include anthropology/archaeology, art/architecture, ethnic, government/politics, history, language/literature, military/war, music/dance, philosophy, photography, regional, sociology, women's issues/studies. Query. Submit outline/synopsis and sample chapters.

Fiction: Literary, short story collections. Query. Submit outline/synopsis and sample chapters.

Tips: "Our audience includes scholars, intelligent laymen, general audience."

*****LOYOLA UNIVERSITY PRESS**, 3441 N. Ashland Ave., Chicago IL 60657. (312)281-1818. Editorial Director: Joseph Downey. Imprints include Campion Books. Publishes hardcover and trade paperback originals, and hardcover and trade paperback reprints. Averages 12 titles/year; receives 100 submissions annually. 40% of books from first-time authors; 95% of books from unagented writers. Subsidy publishes 2% of books. Pays 10% royalty on wholesale price; offers no advance. Publishes book an average of 1 year after acceptance. Simultaneous submissions acceptable. Query for electronic submissions. Reports in 1 month. Book catalog for 6×9 SAE.

Nonfiction: Biography and textbook. Subjects include art (religious); history (church); and religion. The four subject areas of Campion Books include Jesuitica (Jesuit history, biography and spirituality); Literature-Theology interface (books dealing with theological or religious aspects of literary works or authors); contemporary Catholic concerns (books on morality, spirituality, family life, pastoral ministry, prayer, worship, etc.); and Chicago/art (books dealing with the city of Chicago from historical, artistic, architectural, or ethnic perspectives, but with religious emphases). Query before submitting ms. Reviews artwork/photos.

Recent Nonfiction Titles: *Married to a Catholic Priest*, by Mary Dolly.

Tips: "Our audience is principally the college-educated reader with religious, theological interest."

‡**LUCENT BOOKS**, P.O. Box 289011, San Diego CA 92128-9011. (619)485-7424. Managing Editor: Bonnie Szumski. Publishes hardcover originals and reprints. Publishes 50 titles/year; receives 75 submissions/year. 50% from first-time authors; 90% from unagented writers. Buys by outright purchase of $2,000-3,000. Offers average advance of 1/3 of total fee. Publishes book an average of 9 months after acceptance. Simultaneous submissions OK. Reports in 2 weeks on queries; 2 months on mss. Book catalog and ms guidelines for 9×12 SAE with 3 first class stamps.

Nonfiction: Biography, juvenile. Subjects include anthropology/archaelogy, business and economics, computers and electronics, government/politics, history, military/war, nature/environment, science, sports, women's issues/studies. All on the juvenile level. Submit outline/synopsis and sample chapters. All unsolicited mss are returned unopened. Reviews artwork/photos as part of ms package.

Recent Nonfiction Title: *AIDS*, by Jonnie Wilson.

Tips: "A well-organized book at the juvenile reading level has the best chance of being sold to our firm. The trend is toward more interesting nonfiction at the 5-9th grade level. The more you know about a publisher the better chance you have of finding a home for your book."

LURAMEDIA, P.O. Box 261668, 10227 Autumnview Lane, San Diego CA 92126. (619)578-1948. Editorial Director: Lura Jane Geiger. Estab. 1982. Publishes trade paperback originals and reprints. Averages 8 titles/year; receives 250 submissions annually. 75% of books from first-time authors. 90% of books from unagented writers. Pays 10-15% royalty on wholesale price. Publishes book an average of 9 months after acceptance. Query for electronic submissions. Reports in 1 month. Book catalog and ms guidelines for #10 SASE with 1 first class stamp.

Nonfiction: Self-help. Subjects include health, spirituality, psychology, and creativity. "Books on renewal . . . body, mind spirit . . . using the right brain and relational material. Books on creativity, journaling, women's issues, black Christian, relationships. I want well digested, thoughtful books. No 'Jesus Saves' literature; books that give all the answers; poetry; or strident politics." Submit outline/synopsis, biography and sample chapters. Reviews artwork/photos as part of ms package.

Recent Nonfiction Title: *Circle of Stones: Woman's Journey to Herself*, by Judith Duerk.
Tips: "Our audience are people who want to grow and change; who want to get in touch with their spiritual side; who want to relax; who are creative and want creative ways to live."

LYONS & BURFORD, PUBLISHERS, INC., 31 W. 21 St., New York NY 10010. (212)620-9580. Publisher: Peter Burford. Estab. 1984. Publishes hardcover and trade paperback originals and hardcover and trade paperback reprints. Averages 30-40 titles/year. 50% of books from first-time authors. 75% from unagented writers. Pays varied royalty on retail price. Publishes book an average of 1 year after acceptance. Simultaneous submissions OK. Reports in 2 weeks on queries and mss. Free book catalog.
Nonfiction: Subjects include agriculture/horticulture, Americana, animals, art/architecture, cooking, foods and nutrition, gardening, hobbies, nature/environment, science, sports and travel. Query.
Recent Nonfiction Title: *Eiger Dreams*, by Jon Krahauer (essays).
Tips: "We want practical, well written books on any aspect of the outdoors."

‡McCUTCHAN PUBLISHING CORPORATION, 2940 San Pablo Ave., Berkeley CA 94702. (415)841-8616. Editor: Kim Sharrar. Publishes 5 titles/year. Receives 60 submissions/year. 30% of books from first-time authors; 100% from unagented writers. Pays 12-15% royalty on wholesale price. Publishes book an average of 8 months after acceptance. Reports in 6 weeks. Book catalog and ms guidelines free on request.
Nonfiction: Textbook. Subjects include education, food service and criminal justice. Submit outline/synopsis and sample chapters.
Recent Nonfiction Title: *Purchasing for Food Service Managers*, by Warfel and Cremer (food service).
Tips: "Professors and instructors of education, food service and criminal justice are our audience."

MARGARET K. McELDERRY BOOKS, Macmillan Publishing Co., Inc., 866 3rd Ave., New York NY 10022. Editor: Margaret K. McElderry. Publishes hardcover originals. Publishes 20-25 titles/year; receives 3,000-3,500 submissions annually. 8% of books from first-time authors; 45% of books from unagented writers. The average print order is 6,000-7,500 for a writer's first teen book; 10,000-12,500 for a writer's first picture book. Pays royalty on retail price. Publishes book an average of 1½ years after acceptance. Reports in 3 months. Ms guidelines for #10 SASE.
Nonfiction and Fiction: Quality material for preschoolers to 16-year-olds. Looks for "originality of ideas, clarity and felicity of expression, well-organized plot (fiction) or exposition (nonfiction); quality." Reviews artwork/photos as part of ms package.
Recent Title: *We're Going on a Bear Hunt*, by Michael Rogen, illustrated by Helen Oxenbury.
Tips: "There is not a particular 'type' of book that we are interested in above others though we always look for humor; rather, we look for superior quality in both writing and illustration. Freelance writers should be aware of the swing away from teen-age novels to books for younger readers and of the growing need for beginning chapter books for children just learning to read on their own."

McFARLAND & COMPANY, INC., PUBLISHERS, P.O. Box 611, Jefferson NC 28640. (919)246-4460. President and Editor-in-Chief: Robert Franklin. Business Manager: Rhonda Herman. Estab. 1979. Publishes hardcover and "quality" paperback originals; a non-"trade" publisher. Averages 90 titles/year; receives 1000 submissions annually. 70% of books from first-time authors; 95% of books from unagented writers. Average print order for a writer's first book is 1,000. Pays 10-12½% royalty on net receipts; no advance. Publishes book an average of 11 months after acceptance. Reports in 1 week.
Nonfiction: Reference books and scholarly, technical and professional monographs. Subjects include Americana, art, business, chess, drama/theatre, health, cinema/radio/TV (very strong here), history, librarianship (very strong here), music, parapsychology, sociology, sports/recreation (very strong here), women's studies, and world affairs (very strong here). "We will consider *any* scholarly book—with authorial maturity and competent grasp of subject." Reference books are particularly wanted—fresh material (i.e., not in head-to-head competition with an established title). "We don't like manuscripts of fewer than 200 double-spaced typed pages. Our market consists mainly of libraries." No New Age material, memoirs, poetry, children's books, devotional/inspirational works or personal essays. Query or submit outline/synopsis and sample chapters. Reviews artwork/photos as part of ms package.
Recent Nonfiction Title: *3-D Movies: A History and Filmography of Stereoscopic Cinema*, by R.M. Hayes.
Tips: "We do *not* accept novels or fiction of any kind or personal Bible studies. Don't worry about writing skills—we have editors. What we want is well-organized *knowledge* of an area in which there is not good information coverage at present, plus reliability so we don't feel we have to check absolutely everything."

McGRAW HILL RYERSON, Subsidiary of McGraw-Hill, 330 Progress Ave., Scarborough, Ontario M1P 2Z5 Canada. (416)293-1911. Editorial Director: Denise Schon. Publishes hardcover originals, trade paperback originals and reprints. Firm publishes 200 titles/year; division publishes 25 titles/year. Receives 400 submissions/year. 10% of books from first-time authors; 50% from unagented writers. Pays 8-12% royalty on retail price. Publishes book an average of 12-18 months after acceptance. Simultaneous submissions OK. Query for electronic submissions. Reports in 3 months.

Nonfiction: Canadian biography, cookbook, how-to, reference, self-help. Subjects include art/architecture, aviation, business and economics, cooking, consumer guides, Canadian government/politics, Canadian history, money/finance, recreation, sports. No exercise or diet books. Submit outline/synopsis and sample chapters.
Recent Nonfiction Title: *The Art of Mary Pratt*, (Canadian art).

MACMILLAN PUBLISHING COMPANY, Children's Book Department, 866 3rd Ave., New York NY 10022. Publishes hardcover originals. Averages 65 titles/year. Will consider juvenile submissions only. Fiction and nonfiction. Enclose return postage. Imprints include Margaret McElderry Books, Charles Scribner's Sons, Four Winds Press, Atheneum and Bradbury Press.

MADISON BOOKS, 4720 Boston Way, Lanham MD 20706. (301)459-5308. FAX: (301)459-2118. Imprints include Hamilton Press. Associate Publisher: Charles Lean. Estab. 1984. Publishes hardcover originals and trade paperback originals and reprints. Averages 20 titles/year. Receives 750 submissions/year. 15% of books from first-time authors; 50% from unagented writers. Pays 10-20% royalty on wholesale price. Offers average advance of $2,500. Publishes ms an average of 1 year after acceptance. Book catalog and manuscript guidelines for 9 × 12 SAE and 4 first class stamps.
Nonfiction: History, biography, contemporary affairs, popular culture and trade reference. Query or submit outline/synopsis and sample chapter. No complete mss.
Recent Nonfiction Title: *The Hunt for Tokyo Rose*, by Russell Warren Howe (history/biography).

‡MARLOR PRESS, 4304 Brigadoon Dr., St. Paul MN 55126. (612)483-1588. Editor: Marlin Bree. Estab. 1981. Publishes trade paperback originals. Averages 6 titles/year; receives 100 submissions annually. Pays 10% royalty on net sales. Publishes book an average of 6 months after final acceptance. Reports in 3 months on queries.
Nonfiction: Travel books. Query or submit outline/synopsis and sample chapters. Reviews artwork/photos as part of ms package.
Recent Nonfiction Title: *London for the Independent Traveler*, by Ruth Humleker.
Tips: "We publish travel guidebooks, fact books and travel directories to major vacation and travel areas in the U.S., Canada and Western Europe. No advice, personal reminiscences or anecdotal manuscripts."

‡MCN PRESS, P.O. Box 702073, Tulsa OK 74170. (918)743-6048. FAX: (918)743-4616. Publisher: Jack Britton. Estab. 1970. Publishes hardcover and trade paperback originals. Averages 5-7 titles/year; receives 30-35 submissions annually. 75% of books from first-time authors; 75% of books from unagented writers. Pays 10% royalty on wholesale or retail price; offers no advance. Publishes book an average of 6 months after acceptance. Reports in 10 weeks. Free book catalog. Ms guidelines for SASE.
Nonfiction: Biography, illustrated book and reference. Subjects include history and hobbies. "Our audience includes collectors, military personnel and military fans." Submit outline/synopsis and sample chapters or complete ms.
Recent Nonfiction Title: *Medals, Military and Civilian of U.S.*, by Borthick and Britton (reference).

MEDIA FORUM INTERNATIONAL, LTD., RFD 1, Box 107, W. Danville VT 05873. (802)592-3444. Or P.O. Box 65, Peacham VT 05862. (802)592-3310. Estab. 1969. Imprint: Media Forum Books; Division: Ha' Penny Gourmet. Managing Director: D.K. Bognár. Publishes hardcover and trade paperback originals. Averages 4 titles/year. Pays 10% minimum royalty.
Nonfiction: Biography, cookbook, humor and reference. Subjects include cooking, ethnic, broadcast/film and drama. "All mss are assigned."
Recent Nonfiction Title: *The (Naughty) Little Blue Book for the Office and the Bathroom*, by G. Narbo (humor).

‡MEDICAL ECONOMICS BOOKS, Division of Medical Economics Co., 680 Kinderkamack Rd., Oradell NJ 07649. Acquisitions Editor: Terry-lynn Grayson. Publishes hardcover, paperback, and spiral bound originals. Company also publishes magazines and references for doctors, pharmacists and laboratorians. Averages 25 titles/year; receives 100 submissions annually. 95% of books from unagented writers. Pays by individual arrangement. Publishes book an average of 11 months after acceptance. Simultaneous submissions OK. Query for electronic submissions. Reports in 6 weeks. Booklist for 3 first class stamps; ms guidelines for #10 SASE. Tests freelancers for rewriting, editing, and proofreading assignments.
Nonfiction: Clinical and practice – financial management references, handbooks, and manuals. Medical – primary care – all fields; obstetrics and gynecology, opthalmology, laboratory medicine and management. Submit table of contents and prospectus. Reviews artwork/photos as part of ms package.
Recent Nonfiction Title: *Protocols for High-Risk Pregnancies*, by John T. Queenan and John C. Hobbins.
Tips: "Books addressed to and written by M.D.'s and health-care managers and financial professionals have the best chance of selling to our firm. Looking for ms concerning changes in M.D. practice and management, new trends, options, developments, and for high quality clinical text mss." Queries/mss may be routed to other editors in the publishing group.

‡**MEERAMMA PUBLICATIONS**, 26 Spruce Lane, Ithaca NY 14850. (607)257-1715. Editor: Christine Cox. Publishes hardcover and trade paperback originals. Averages 6 titles/year. 50% of books from first-time authors; 50% from unagented writers. Pays 8-10% royalty on retail price. Advance varies. Publishes book an average of 5 months after acceptance. Simultaneous submissions OK. Reports in 2 weeks on queries; 1 month on mss. Free book catalog.
Nonfiction: Self-help, philosophical, coffee table and mystical literature. Subjects include art/architecture, health/medicine, philosophy, psychology, religion and women's issues/studies. Seeking 10 high quality manuscripts on mystical, religious, or philosophical topics, per year. Submit outline/synopsis and sample chapters or complete ms. Reviews artwork/photos as part of ms package.
Recent Nonfiction Title: *Speaking Flame*, by Andrew Harvey (mystical literature).
Fiction: Mystical religious and philosophical. Seeking 3 philosophical novels per year. Submit complete ms.
Tips: Writers have the best chance selling us biography or novelization of the lives of mystics and philosophers, or self-help/psychology with spiritual outlook. Our audience has an interest in spirituality.

‡**MENASHA RIDGE PRESS, INC.**, P.O. Box 59257, Birmingham AL 35259. (205)991-0373. Publisher: R.W. Sehlinger. Estab. 1981. Publishes hardcover and trade paperback originals. Averages 10-15 titles/year; receives 600-800 submissions annually. 50% of books from first-time authors; 90% of books from unagented writers. Average print order for a writer's first book is 4,000. Pays 10% royalty on wholesale price or purchases outright; offers average $1,000 advance. Publishes book an average of 8 months after acceptance. Simultaneous submissions OK. Query for electronic submissions. Reports in 1 month. Book catalog for 9×12 SAE and 4 first class stamps; ms guidelines for SASE.
Nonfiction: How-to, reference, self-help, consumer, outdoor recreation, travel guides and small business. Subjects include business and economics, health, hobbies, recreation, sports, travel and consumer advice. No biography or religious copies. Submit outline/synopsis. Reviews artwork/photos.
Recent Nonfiction Title: *Whitewater Sourcebook*, by Richard Penny.
Tips: Audience: age 25-60, 14-18 years' education, white collar and professional, $30,000 median income, 75% male, 75% east of Mississippi River.

‡***MENNONITE PUBLISHING HOUSE, INC.**, Subsidiary of Herald Press, 616 Walnut Ave., Scottdale PA 15683. (412)887-8500. Editor: S. David Garber. Publishes hardcover and trade paperback originals and reprints. Publishes 30 titles/year; receives 800 submissions/year. 33% of books from first-time authors; 97% from unagented writers. Subsidy publishes 15% of books—"only books sponsored by an official agency of the Mennonite Church." Pays 10-12% royalty on retail price. Publishes book an average of 1 year after acceptance. Query for electronic submissions. Reports in 1 month on queries; 2 months on mss. Book catalog for 50¢; free ms guidelines.
Nonfiction: Coffee table book, cookbook, juvenile, reference (Mennonite), self-help, textbook (Christian). Subjects include business and economics, child guidance/parenting, cooking, foods and nutrition, education, ethnic (Amish, Mennonite, Pennsylvania Dutch culture), health/medicine, history, language/literature, money/finance (stewardship), nature/environment, psychology (and faith), regional, religion, sociology, travel, women's issues/studies. Needs medium-level Bible study; peace; human relations books. No technical, scientific, general textbooks, or anything on war. Submit outline/synopsis and 2 sample chapters. Reviews artwork/photos as part of ms package.
Recent Nonfiction Title: *Copper Moons*, by Ackerman (personal exprience, Africa).
Fiction: Adventure, historical, juvenile, literary, religious, romance (Christian), young adult. Needs juvenile mss on good human relationships, peace, or mystery. Needs adult mss portraying faith in life realitically, with good dialogue for characterization. No fantasy or picture books. Submit outline/synopsis and 2 sample chapters.
Recent Fiction Title: *The Christmas Surprise*, by Moore (juvenile-peace-history).
Tips: "Books must have a theme to fit our areas: peace and justice, missions, family, Bible, Christian ethics, church history. Make sure you have a theme in mind, clearly envision the audience, do sound research, have natural dialogue that supplies characterization, plausible plot or logical outline, and fresh and interesting material."

***MERCURY HOUSE INC.**, Suite 400, 201 Filbert St., San Francisco CA 94133. (415)433-7080. President: William M. Brinton. Executive Editor: Alev Lytle Croutier. Publishes hardcover and trade paperback originals. Averages 20 titles/year; receives 500 submissions annually. 20% of books come from first-time authors; 10% of books from unagented writers. Average print order for a writer's first book is 4,000. Pays standard royalties and advances. Publishes books an average of 9 months after acceptance. Simultaneous submissions OK only if publisher is informed prior to arrangement. Reports in 1 month on queries; 6 weeks on mss.
Nonfiction: Original and unusual adult nonfiction. Query with outline/synopsis and sample chapters.
Recent Nonfiction Title: *Produced and Abandoned: The National Society of Film Critics Write on the Best Films You've Never Seen*, edited by Michael Sragon.
Fiction: Original adult fiction, translations, reprints. Query with outline/synopsis and sample chapters.
Recent Fiction Title: *The Long Lost Journey*, by Jennifer Potter.

‡**THE MERCURY PRESS**, Imprint of Aya Press, Box 446, Stratford Ontario, Canada N5A 6T3. Editor: Beverley Daurio. Publishes trade paperback originals and reprints. Averages 8 titles/year. Receives 200 submissions/year. 10% of books from first-time authors; 100% from unagented writers. Pays 5-15% royalty on retail price. Publishes book an average of 1 year after acceptance. Query for electronic submissions. Reports in 2 months. Free book catalog.
Nonfiction: Biography. Subjects include art/architecture, government/politics, history, language/literature, music/dance, sociology and women's issues/studies. Query.
Recent Nonfiction Title: *City Hall & Mrs. God*, by Cary Fagan (social issues).
Fiction: Feminist, literary, mainstream/contemporary and short story collections. No genre fiction. Submit complete ms.
Recent Fiction Title: *Figures in Paper Time*, by Richard Truhlar.
Poetry: No unsolicited mss until 1992. No traditional, rhyme, confessional. Submit complete ms.
Recent Poetry Title: Sky, by Libby Scheier.
Tips: "If I were a writer trying to market a book today, I would study markets objectively, listen to feedback, present mss professionall, and use IRCs plus SAE for submissions to Canada."

METAMORPHOUS PRESS, 3249 NW 29th Ave., P.O. Box 10616, Portland OR 92710. (503)228-4972. Publisher: David Balding. Acquisitions Editor: Gene Radeka. Estab. 1982. Publishes hardcover and trade paperback originals and reprints. Averages 4-5 titles/year; receives 800 submissions annually. 90% of books from first-time authors; 90% of books from unagented writers. Average print order for a writer's first book is 2,000-5,000. Pays minimum 10% profit split on wholesale prices. No advance. Publishes book an average of 8 months after acceptance. Simultaneous submissions OK. Query for electronic submissions. Free book catalog; ms guidelines for #10 SASE.
Nonfiction: How-to, illustrated book, reference, self-help, technical and textbook—all related to behavioral science and personal growth. Subjects include business and sales, health, psychology, sociology, education, children's books, science and new ideas in behavioral science. "We are interested in any well-proven new idea or philosophy in the behavioral science areas. Our primary editorial screen is 'will this book further define, explain or support the concept that we are responsible for our reality or assist people in gaining control of their lives.'" Submit idea, outline, and table of contents only. Reviews artwork/photos as part of ms package.
Recent Nonfiction Title: *Recreating Your Self*, by Christopher Stone.

THE MGI MANAGEMENT INSTITUTE, INC., 378 Halstead Ave., Harrison NY 10528. (914)835-5790. FAX: (914)835-4824. President: Dr. Henry Oppenheimer. Estab. 1968. Averages 5-10 new titles/year; receives 40 submissions annually. 50% of books from first-time authors; 100% of those books from unagented writers. Pays 4% royalty on retail price of correspondence course or training manual (price is usually in $100 range). Does not publish conventional books. Publishes course or manual an average of 6 months after acceptance. Query for electronic submissions. Reports in 2 weeks.
Nonfiction: How-to, technical and correspondence courses. Subjects include business and economics, engineering, computer, and manufacturing-related topics. Needs correspondence courses in management, purchasing, manufacturing management, production and inventory control, quality control, computers and marketing professional services. Reviews artwork/photos.
Recent Nonfiction Title: *Space Planning for the NCIDQ Exam*, by Dr. Mark Karlen.
Tips: "Our audience includes quality and inventory control managers, purchasing managers, graduate engineers and architects, manufacturing supervisors and managers, real estate investors, and interior designers."

*****MICHIGAN STATE UNIVERSITY PRESS**, Room 25, 1405 S. Harrison Rd., East Lansing MI 48823-5202. (517)355-9543. Director: Richard Chapin. Estab. 1947. Publishes hardcover and softcover originals. Averages 15 titles annually. Receives 100 submissions/year. 95% of books from first-time writers; 100% from unagented writers. Pays 10% royalty on net sales. Publishes ms an average of 9 months after acceptance. Query for electronic submissions. Book catalog and manuscript guidelines for #10 SASE.
Nonfiction: Reference, software, technical, textbook and scholarly. Subjects include agriculture, business and economics, history, literature, philosophy, politics and religion. Looking for "scholarly publishing representing strengths of the university." Query with outline/synopsis and sample chapters. Reviews artwork/photos.
Recent Nonfiction Title: *Dangerous Society*, by Carl S. Taylor.

‡**MICROTREND BOOKS**, Subsidiary of Slawson Communications, Inc., 165 Vallecitos de Oro, San Marcos CA 92069. (619)744-2299. Editorial Director: Lance A. Leventhal, Ph.D. Publishes trade paperback originals. Firm averages 60 titles/year; imprint averages 24 titles/year. Receives 150 submissions/year. 50% of books from first-time authors; 80% from unagented writers. Pays 12-18% royalty on retail price. Advance amount determined by subject. Publishes book an average of 4 months after acceptance. Simultaneous submissions OK. Reports in 2 weeks. Book catalog for $2.

Nonfiction: Technical. Subjects include computers and electronics. No entry level computer book manuscripts. Query or submit outline/synopsis and sample chapters; all unsolicited mss are returned unopened. Reviews artwork/photos as part of ms package.
Recent Nonfiction Title: *Clipper Programming Guide*, by Rick Spence (computer).
Tips: "Our audience is make up of mid to advanced computer users. If I were a writer trying to market a book today, I would know the computer trade."

MILKWEED EDITIONS, P.O. Box 3226, Minneapolis MN 55403. (612)332-3192. Editor: Emilie Buckwald. Estab. 1980. Publishes hardcover originals and paperback originals and reprints. Averages 8-10 titles/year. Receives 1,560 submissions/year. 30% of books from first-time authors; 70% from unagented writers. Pays 8-12% royalty on wholesale price. Offers average advance of $400. Publishes work an average of 1 year after acceptance. Simultaneous submissions OK. Reports in 2 weeks on queries; 6 months on mss. Book catalog and ms guidelines for SASE.
Nonfiction: Illustrated book. Subjects include anthropology/archaeology, art/architecture, government/politics, history, language/literature, nature/environment, photography, regional, sports, women's issues/studies. Query. Reviews artwork/photos as part of ms package.
Recent Nonfiction Title: *Coming Home Crazy*, by Bill Holm (essays).
Recent Fiction Title: *Blue Taxis*, by Eileen Drew.
Tips: "We are looking for collaborative works between writers and visual artists for our 1991 list. We also want to emphasize work by visual artists. Write for our fiction contest guidelines. Two fiction collections will be chosen for our 1991 list."

MILLER BOOKS, 2908 W. Valley Blvd., Alhambra CA 91803. (818)284-7607. Subsidiaries include *San Gabriel Valley Magazine*, Miller Press and Miller Electric. Publisher: Joseph Miller. Publishes hardcover and trade paperback originals, hardcover reprints and software. Averages 4 titles/year. Pays 10-15% royalty on retail price; buys some mss outright. Simultaneous submissions OK. Reports in 2 weeks on queries; 2 months on mss. Free book catalog.
Nonfiction: Cookbook, how-to, self-help, textbook and remedial textbooks. Subjects include Americana, animals, cooking and foods, history, philosophy and politics. "Remedial manuscripts are needed in most fields." No erotica. Submit complete ms. Reviews artwork/photos as part of ms package. "Please don't send letters. Let us see your work."
Recent Nonfiction Title: *Every Feeling is Desire*, by James Smith, M.D.
Fiction: Adventure, historical, humor, mystery and western. No erotica; "no returns on erotic material." Submit complete ms.
Recent Fiction Title: *The Magic Story*, by F.V.R. Dey (positive thinking).
Tips: "Write something good about people, places and our country. Avoid the negative – it doesn't sell."

MILLS & SANDERSON, PUBLISHERS, Suite 6, 442 Marrett Rd., Lexington MA 02173. (617)861-0992. Publisher: Georgia Mills. Estab. 1986. Publishes trade paperback originals. Publishes 6-8 titles/year; receives 400 submissions annually. 50% of books from first-time authors; 75% of books from unagented writers. Pays 12½% royalty on net price; offers average $1,000 advance. Publishes book 1 year after acceptance. Simultaneous submissions OK. Reports in 6 weeks on queries; 2 months on mss. Ms guidelines for #10 SASE.
Nonfiction: Self-help. Subjects include health, travel and parenting. "All our books are aimed at improving the individual's life in some way. No religion, music, art or photography." Query.
Recent Nonfiction Title: *The Alaska Traveler*, by Steven Levi.
Tips: "We only publish nonfiction with broad general consumer appeal because it normally is less chancy than fiction. It must be an interesting subject with broad appeal by an author whose credentials indicate he/she knows a lot about the subject, be well researched and most importantly, must have a certain uniqueness about it."

MODERN LANGUAGE ASSOCIATION OF AMERICA, 10 Astor Pl., New York NY 10003. (212)475-9500. FAX: (212)477-9863. Head, Publications Division: A. Joseph Hollander. Estab. 1883. Publishes hardcover and paperback originals. Averages 20 titles/year; receives 125 submissions annually. 100% of books from unagented writers. Pays 5-10% royalty on net proceeds. Publishes book an average of 1 year after acceptance. Query for electronic submissions. Reports in 3 weeks on mss. Book catalog free on request.
Nonfiction: Reference and professional. Subjects include language and literature. Needs mss on current issues in research and teaching of language and literature. No critical monographs. Query or submit outline/synopsis and sample chapters.
Recent Nonfiction Title: *Literary Research Guide*, by James L. Horner

‡MOON PUBLICATIONS, 722 Wall St., Chico CA 95928. (916)345-5473. Contact: Mark Morris. Estab. 1973. Publishes trade paperback originals. Publishes average of 10 titles/year; receives 30-40 submissions/year. 50% of books from first-time authors; 100% from unagented writers. Pays royalty on wholesale price; offers advance of up to $7,000. Publishes book an average of 18 months after acceptance. Simultaneous submissions

OK. Query for electronic submissions. Reports in 2 weeks on queries and ms. Book catalog and ms guidelines for #10 SASE.

Nonfiction: Subjects include travel. "We specialize in travel guides to Asia and the Pacific Basin, the western United States and Canada, and favor these areas, but are open to new ideas. Our guides include in-depth cultural and historical background, as well as recreational and practical travel information. We prefer comprehensive guides to entire countries, states, and regions over more narrowly defined areas such as cities, museums, etc. Writers should write first for a copy of our guidelines. Query with outline/synopsis, table of contents, and sample chapters. Author should also be prepared to provide photos, artwork and base maps. No fictional or strictly narrative travel writing; no how-to guides." Reviews artwork/photos as part of ms package.

Recent Nonfiction Title: *Southeast Asia Handbook*, by Carl Parkes.

Tips: "Our books are aimed for the independent, budget-minded do-it-yourself traveler but appeal to all travelers because they are the comprehensive guides to the areas they cover. If I were a writer trying to market a book today, I would first study very carefully the other books produced by the publisher I intended to approach."

*MOREHOUSE PUBLISHING CO., 78 Danbury Rd., Wilton CT 06897. FAX: (203)762-0727. Publisher: E. Allen Kelley. Senior Editor: Deborah Graham-Smith. Juvenile and Academic Editor: Theodore A. McConnell. Publishes hardcover and paperback originals. Averages 45 titles/year; receives 500 submissions annually. 40% of books from first-time authors; 75% of books from unagented writers. Pays 10% royalty on retail price. Publishes book an average of 8 months after acceptance. Book catalog for 9 × 12 SAE with 4 first class stamps.

Nonfiction: Specializes in Christian publishing (with an Anglican emphasis). Theology, ethics, church history, pastoral counseling, liturgy, religious education and children's books (preschool-teen); beginning tapes and videos. No poetry or drama. Accepts outline/synopsis and 2-4 sample chapters. Reviews artwork/photos as part of ms package.

Recent Nonfiction Title: *Banners for Beginners*, by Cory Atwood (craft book—religious subjects).

WILLIAM MORROW AND CO., 105 Madison Ave., New York NY 10016. (212)889-3050. FAX: (212)689-9139. Publisher: James D. Landis. Managing Editor: Andrew Ambraziejus. Imprints include Arbor House, Greenwillow Books (juveniles), Susan Hirschman, editor. Lothrop, Lee and Shepard (juveniles), Susan Pearson, editor. Morrow Junior Books (juveniles), David Reuther, editor. Quill (trade paperback), Andrew Dutter, editor. Affiliates include Hearst Books (trade). Editorial Director: Ann Bramson. Hearst Marine Books (nautical), Connie Roosevelt, editor. Estab. 1926. Publishes 200 titles/year. Receives 10,000 submissions annually. 30% of books from first-time authors; 5% of books from unagented writers. Payment is on standard royalty basis on retail price. Advance varies. Publishes book an average of 1-2 years after acceptance. Reports in 3 months. Query letter on all books. *No* unsolicited mss or proposals.

Nonfiction and Fiction: Publishes adult fiction, nonfiction, history, biography, arts, religion, poetry, how-to books and cookbooks. Length: 50,000-100,000 words. Query only; mss and proposals should be submitted only through an agent.

Recent Nonfiction Title: *Megatrends 2000*, by John Naisbitt/Pat Aburdene.

Recent Fiction Title: *Knight, Death and the Devil*, by Ella Leffland.

MORROW JUNIOR BOOKS, Division of William Morrow & Company, Inc., 105 Madison Ave., New York NY 10016. (212)889-3050. Editor-in-Chief: David L. Reuther. Executive Editor: Meredith Charpentier. Senior Editor: Andrea Curley. Publishes hardcover originals. Publishes 50 titles/year. All contracts negotiated separately; offers variable advance. Book catalog and guidelines for 9 × 12 SAE with 2 first class stamps.

Nonfiction: Juveniles (trade books). No textbooks. Query. Reviews artwork/photos as part of ms package.

Recent Nonfiction Title: *A Girl from Yamhill*, by Beverly Cleary (autobiography).

Fiction: Juveniles (trade books).

Recent Fiction Title: *Muggie Maggie*, by Beverly Cleary.

Tips: "We are no longer accepting unsolicited manuscripts."

MOSAIC PRESS MINIATURE BOOKS, 358 Oliver Rd., Cincinnati OH 45215. (513)761-5977. Publisher: Miriam Irwin. Estab. 1977. Publishes hardcover originals. Averages 4 titles/year; receives 150-200 submissions annually. 49% of books from first-time authors. Average print order for a writer's first book is 2,000. Buys mss outright for $50. Publishes book an average of 30 months after acceptance. Reports in 2 weeks; "but our production, if manuscript is accepted, often takes 2 or 3 years." Book catalog $3. Writer's guidelines for #10 SAE and 2 first class stamps.

Nonfiction: Biography, cookbook, humor, illustrated book and satire. Subjects include Americana, animals, art, business and economics, cooking and foods, health, history, hobbies, music, nature, sports and travel. Interested in "beautifully written, delightful text. If factual, it must be extremely correct and authoritative. Our books are intended to delight, both in their miniature size, beautiful bindings and excellent writing." No occult, pornography, science fiction, fantasy, haiku, or how-to. Query or submit outline/synopsis and sample chapters or complete ms. Reviews artwork/photos as part of ms package.

Recent Nonfiction Title: *Victorian Christmas*, by Maria von Stauffer.
Tips: "I want a book to tell me something I don't know."

MOTHER COURAGE PRESS, 1533 Illinois St., Racine WI 53405. (414)634-1047. Managing Editor: Barbara Lindquist. Estab. 1981. Publishes trade paperback and hardcover originals. Averages 4 titles/year; receives 300-400 submissions annually. 100% of books from first-time authors; 100% of books from unagented writers. Pays 10-15% royalty on wholesale and retail price; offers $250 average advance. Publishes book an average of 1 year after acceptance. No unsolicited manuscripts. Simultaneous submissions OK. Query for electronic submissions. Reports in 2 weeks on queries; 6 weeks on mss. Book catalog for #10 SASE.
Nonfiction: Biography, how-to and self-help. Subjects include health, psychology and sociology. "We are looking for books on difficult subjects — teen pregnancy; sexual abuse (no personal stories); and rape, also books about courageous women." Submit outline/synopsis and sample chapters. Reviews artwork/photos as part of ms package.
Recent Nonfiction Title: *Women at the Helm*, by Jeannine Talley.
Fiction: Adventure, fantasy, historical, humor, mystery, romance, science fiction and lesbian. "We are looking for lesbian/feminist or strictly feminist themes. Don't send male-oriented fiction of any kind." Submit outline/synopsis and sample chapters or complete ms.
Recent Fiction Title: *Night Lights*, by Bonnie Arthur (lesbian romance).
Tips: "We like to do books that have 'Women of Courage' as the theme."

MOTORBOOKS INTERNATIONAL PUBLISHERS & WHOLESALERS, INC., Box 2, Osceola WI 54020. FAX: (612)439-5627. Director of Publications: Tim Parker. Managing Editor: Barbara K. Harold. Estab. 1973. Hardcover and paperback originals. Averages 60 titles/year. 90% of books from unagented writers. Offers 7-15% royalty on net receipts. Offers $4,000 average advance. Publishes book an average of 1 year after acceptance. Simultaneous submissions OK. Query for electronic submissions. Reports in 3 months. Free book catalog; ms guidelines for #10 SASE.
Nonfiction: Biography, history, how-to, photography, and motor sports (as they relate to cars, trucks, motorcycles, R/C modeling, motor sports and aviation — domestic and foreign). Accepts nonfiction translations. Submit outline/synopsis, 1-2 sample chapters and sample of illustrations. "State qualifications for doing book." Reviews artwork/photos as part of ms package.
Recent Nonfiction Title: *Corvette Grand Sport*, by Lowell C. Paddock and Dave Friedman.

THE MOUNTAINEERS BOOKS, The Mountaineers, 306-2nd Ave W., Seattle WA 98119. (206)285-2665. Director: Donna DeShazo. Publishes hardcover and trade paperback originals (95%) and reprints (5%). Averages 25 titles/year; receives 150-250 submissions annually. 25% of books from first-time authors; 98% of books from unagented writers. Average print order for a writer's first book is 5,000-7,000. Offers royalty based on net sales. Offers advance on occasion. Publishes book an average of 1 year after acceptance. Reports in 2 months. Book catalog and ms guidelines for 9×12 SAE with 2 first class stamps.
Nonfiction: Adventure travel, recreation, conservation/environment, non-competitive sports, and outdoor how-to books. "We specialize in books dealing with mountaineering, hiking, backpacking, skiing, snowshoeing, canoeing, bicycling, etc. These can be either how-to-do-it, where-to-do-it (guidebooks)." Does *not* want to see "anything dealing with hunting, fishing or motorized travel." Submit outline/synopsis and minimum of 2 sample chapters. Accepts nonfiction translations. Looks for "expert knowledge, good organization."
Recent Nonfiction Title: *Walking Austria's Alps, Hut-to-Hut*, by Jon Hurdle (guidebook).
Fiction: "We might consider an exceptionally well-done book-length manuscript on mountaineering." Does *not* want poetry or mystery. Query first.
Tips: "The type of book the writer has the best chance of selling our firm is an authoritative guidebook (*in our field*) to a specific area not otherwise covered; or a how-to that is better than existing competition (again, *in our field*)."

JOHN MUIR PUBLICATIONS, P.O. Box 613, Santa Fe NM 87504. (505)982-4078. FAX (505)988-1680. President: Steven Cary. Estab. 1969. Publishes trade paperback originals and reprints. Averages 35 titles/year. Receives 300 submissions/year. 30% of books from first-time authors. 90% of books from unagented writers. Pays 8-12% on wholesale price. Offers $750-1,000 average advance. Publishes book an average of 1 year after acceptance. Simultaneous submissions OK. Reports in 2 weeks on queries; 1 month on mss. Free book catalog.
Nonfiction: Travel and environmental topics for adults and children, parenting, and automotive. We want "unique and/or original treatments of ideas which inform, enlighten and stimulate our independent readers." Query or submit outline/synopsis and sample chapters. Reviews artwork/photos as part of ms package.
Recent Nonfiction Title: *Schooling At Home: Parents, Kids and Learning*, by *Mothering Magazine*.

MULTNOMAH PRESS, A division of Multnomah School of The Bible, 10209 SE Division St., Portland OR 97266. (503)257-0526. Senior Editors: Liz Heaney and Al Janssen. Publishes hardcover and trade paperback originals, and a limited number trade paperback reprints. Averages 30 titles/year; receives 500 submissions annually. 20% of books from first-time authors; 100% of books from unagented writers. Pays royalty on wholesale price. Publishes books an average of 9 months after acceptance. Query for electronic submissions. Reports in 6 weeks on queries; 10 weeks on mss. Book catalog and ms guidelines for SASE.

Nonfiction: Coffee table book and self-help. Subjects include religion. "We publish issue-related books linking social/ethical concerns and Christianity; books addressing the needs of women from a Christian point of view; books addressing the needs of the traditional family in today's society; illustrated books for children; and books explaining Christian theology in a very popular way to a lay audience." No daily devotional, personal experience, scripture/photo combinations or poetry. Submit outline/synopsis and sample chapters.

Recent Nonfiction Title: *Six Hours One Friday*, by Mars Lucado.

Fiction: Realistic fiction with a Christian world view for the middle reader (8-11-year-olds).

Tips: "We have a reputation for tackling tough issues from a Biblical view; we need to continue to deserve that reputation. Avoid being too scholarly or detached. Although we like well-researched books, we do direct our books to a popular market, not just to professors of theology."

*MUSEUM OF NORTHERN ARIZONA PRESS, Subsidiary of Museum of Northern Arizona, Box 720, Rt. 4, Flagstaff AZ 86001. (602)774-5211. Publisher: Diana Clark Lubick. Publishes hardcover and trade paperback originals, and also quarterly magazine. Averages 10-12 titles/year; receives 35 submissions annually. 10% of books from first-time authors; 100% of books from unagented writers. Subsidy publishes (nonauthor) 15% of books. Pays one-time fee on acceptance of ms. No advance. Publishes book an average of 1 year after acceptance. Queries only. Query for electronic submissions. Reports in 1 month. Book catalog for 9 × 12 SAE and ms guidelines for #10 SASE.

Nonfiction: Coffee table book, reference and technical. Subjects include Southwest, art, nature, science. "Especially needs manuscripts on the Colorado Plateau that are written for a well-educated general audience." Query or submit outline/synopsis and 3-4 sample chapters. Reviews artwork/photos as part of ms package.

Recent Nonfiction Title: *A Separate Vision*, by Linda Eaton (ethnology and art).

MUSTANG PUBLISHING CO., P.O. Box 3004, Memphis TN 38173. (901)521-1406. President: Rollin Riggs. Estab. 1983. Publishes nonfiction hardcover and trade paperback originals. Averages 6 titles/year; receives 1,000 submissions annually. 50% of books from first-time authors; 100% of books from unagented writers. Pays 6-9% royalty on retail price. Publishes book an average of 1 year after acceptance. Simultaneous submissions OK. No electronic submissions. No phone calls, please. Reports in 1 month. SASE a must. Book catalog available from address above—include #10 SASE for catalog.

Nonfiction: How-to, humor and self-help. Subjects include Americana, hobbies, recreation, sports and travel. "Our needs are very general—humor, travel, how-to, nonfiction, etc.—for the 18-to 40-year-old market." Query or submit synopsis and sample chapters.

Recent Nonfiction Title: *The One Hour College Applicant*, by Rochester and Mandell.

Tips: "From the proposals we receive, it seems that many writers never go to bookstores and have no idea what sells. Before you waste a lot of time on a nonfiction book idea, ask yourself, 'How often have my friends and I actually *bought* a book like this?' Know the market!"

THE MYSTERIOUS PRESS, 129 W. 56th St., New York NY 10019. (212)765-0901. FAX: (212)265-5478. Editor-in-Chief: William Malloy. Estab. 1976. Subsidiaries include Penzler Books (non-mystery fiction by mystery authors) and *The Armchair Detective* (magazine). Publishes hardcover originals, trade paperback reprints and mass market paperback reprints. Averages 40-50 titles/year; receives 750 submissions annually. 10% of books from first-time authors. 5% of books from unagented writers. Pays standard, but negotiable, royalty on retail price; amount of advance varies widely. Publishes book an average of 1 year after acceptance. Reports in 2 months. Book catalog and guidelines for 9 × 12 SAE with 4 first class stamps.

Nonfiction: Reference books on criticism and history of crime fiction. Submit complete ms. Reviews artwork/photos as part of ms package.

Recent Nonfiction Title: *Cornell Woolrich: First You Dream, Then You Die*, by Francis M. Nevins, Jr. (biography).

Fiction: Mystery, suspense and espionage. "We will consider publishing any outstanding crime/espionage/suspense/detective novel that comes our way. No short stories." Submit complete mss.

Recent Fiction Title: *Going Wrong*, by Ruth Rondell.

Tips: "We no longer read unagented material. Agents only, please."

THE NAIAD PRESS, INC., Box 10543, Tallahassee FL 32302. (904)539-5965. FAX: (904)539-9731. Editorial Director: Barbara Grier. Publishes paperback originals. Averages 24 titles/year; receives 700 submissions annually. 20% of books from first-time authors; 99% of books from unagented writers. Average print order for a writer's first book is 12,000. Pays 15% royalty on wholesale or retail price; no advance. Publishes book an average of 18 months after acceptance. Reports in 4 months. Book catalog and ms guidelines for #10 SAE and 2 first class stamps.

Fiction: "We publish lesbian fiction, preferably lesbian/feminist fiction. We are not impressed with the 'oh woe' school and prefer realistic (i.e., happy) novels. We emphasize fiction and are now heavily reading manuscripts in that area. We are working in a lot of genre fiction—mysteries, science fiction, short stories, fantasy—all with lesbian themes, of course." Query.
Recent Fiction Title: *The Beverly Malibu*, by Katherine V. Forrest.
Tips: "There is tremendous world-wide demand for lesbian mysteries from lesbian authors published by lesbian presses, and we are doing several such series. Ms under 60,000 words have twice as good a chance as over 60,000."

NATIONAL BOOK COMPANY, Division of Educational Research Associates, P.O. Box 8795, Portland OR 97207-8795. (503)228-6345. Imprints include Halcyon House. Editorial Director: Carl W. Salser. Senior Editor: John R. Kimmel. Manager of Copyrights: Shenda M. Palmer. Publishes hardcover and paperback originals, paperback reprints, and software. Averages 23 titles/year. Pays 5-15% royalty on wholesale or retail price; no advance. Publishes book an average of 9 months after acceptance. Reports in 2 months. Free catalog for 9×12 SAE with 2 first class stamps.
Nonfiction: Only materials suitable for educational uses in all categories. Art, business/economics, health, history, music, politics, psychology, reference, science, technical and textbooks. "Many titles are multimedia Individualized Instruction/Mastery Learning programs for educational consumers. Prospective authors should be aware of this and be prepared for this type of format, although content, style and appropriateness of subject matter are the major criteria by which submissions are judged. We are most interested in materials in the areas of the language arts, social studies and the sciences." Query, submit outline/synopsis and 2-5 sample chapters or complete ms. Reviews artwork/photos as part of ms package.
Recent Nonfiction Title: *Mineral Resources and the Destinies of Nations*, by Walter Youngquist.

*****NATIONAL GALLERY OF CANADA**, Publications Division, 380 Sussex Dr., Ottawa, Ontario K1N 9N4 Canada. (613)990-0540. FAX: (613)993-4385. Head: Serge Theriault. Editorial Coordinator: Irene Lillico. Estab. 1910. Publishes hardcover and paperback originals. Averages 15 titles/year. Subsidy publishes (nonauthor) 100% of books. Pays in outright purchase of $1,500-2,500; offers average $700 advance. Reports in 3 months. Free sales catalog.
Nonfiction: "In general, we publish only *solicited* manuscripts on art, particularly Canadian art, and must publish them in English and French. Exhibition catalogs are commissioned, but we are open (upon approval by Curatorial general editors) to manuscripts for the various series, monographic and otherwise, that we publish. All manuscripts should be directed to our Editorial Coordinator, who doubles as manuscript editor. Since we publish translations into French, authors have access to French Canada and the rest of Francophonia. Because our titles are distributed by the University of Chicago Press, authors have the attention of European as well as American markets."
Recent Nonfiction Title: *Karsh: The Art of Portrait*, by James Borcoman, with Estelle Jussim, Philip Pocock, Lilly Koltun.

NATIONAL TEXTBOOK CO., 4255 W. Touhy Ave., Lincolnwood IL 60646. (708)679-5500. FAX: (708)679-2494. Editorial Director: Leonard I. Fiddle. Publishes originals for education and trade market, and software. Averages 100-150 titles/year; receives 200 submissions annually. 10% of books from first-time authors; 80% of books from unagented writers. Mss purchased on either royalty or buy-out basis. Publishes book an average of 1 year after acceptance. Reports in 4 months. Book catalog and ms guidelines for SAE and 2 first class stamps.
Nonfiction: Textbook. Major emphasis being given to foreign language and language arts texts, especially secondary level material, and business and career subjects (marketing, advertising, sales, etc.). Raymond B. Walters, Language Arts Editor. Michael Ross, Foreign Language and ESL. Michael Urban, Career Guidance. Casimir Psujek, Business Books. Send sample chapter and outline or table of contents.
Recent Nonfiction Title: *Person to Person*, by Galvin and Book.

NATUREGRAPH PUBLISHERS, INC., P.O. Box 1075, Happy Camp CA 96039. (916)493-5353. Imprint, Prism Editions. Editor: Barbara Brown. Estab. 1946. Averages 5 titles/year; receives 300 submissions annually. 75% of books from first-time authors; 100% of books from unagented writers. Average print order for a writer's first book is 2,500. "We offer 10% of wholesale; 12½% after 10,000 copies are sold." Publishes book an average of 18 months after acceptance. Reports in 2 months. Book catalog and ms guidelines for #10 SAE with 3 first class stamps.

 The double dagger before a listing indicates that the listing is new in this edition. New markets are often the most receptive to freelance submissions.

Nonfiction: Primarily publishes nonfiction for the layman in 7 general areas: natural history (biology, geology, ecology, astronomy); American Indian (historical and contemporary); outdoor living (backpacking, wild edibles, etc.); land and gardening (modern homesteading); crafts and how-to; holistic health (natural foods and healing arts); and PRISM Editions (Baha'i and other New Age approaches to harmonious living). All material must be well-grounded; author must be professional, and in command of effective style. Our natural history and American Indian lines can be geared for educational markets. "To speed things up, queries should include summary, detailed outline, comparison to related books, 2 sample chapters, availability and samples of any photos or illustrations, and author background. Send manuscript only on request." Reviews artwork/photos as part of ms package.
Recent Nonfiction Title: *Give Peas a Chance*, by Peter Barbarow.

‡**THE NAUTICAL & AVIATION PUBLISHING CO.**, Suite 314, 101 West Read St., Baltimore MD 21201. (201)659-0220. President/Publisher: Jan Snouck-Hurgronje. Publishes hardcover originals and reprints. Averages 8-10 titles/year. Receives 20-25 submissions/year. Pays 10-15% royalty on net selling price. Offers $500-1,000 average advance. Publishes book an average of 6 weeks after acceptance. Simultaneous submissions OK. Free book catalog.
Nonfiction: Reference. Subjects include history, military/war. Submit complete ms. Reviews artwork/photo as part of package.
Recent Nonfiction Title: *Semper Fidel; America & Cuba, 1776-1988*, by Mike Mazarr (history of U.S.-Cuban relations).
Fiction: Historical. "No techno thrillers *a la* Clancy." Submit outline/synopsis and sample chapters or complete ms.
Recent Fiction Title: *South to Java*, by Admiral Mack.

NAVAL INSTITUTE PRESS, Annapolis MD 21402. Manager of Acquisitions: Paul Wilderson. Press Director: Thomas F. Epley. Estab. 1873. Averages 60 titles/year; receives 400-500 submissions annually. 70% of books from first-time authors; 70% of books from unagented writers. Average print order for a writer's first book is 4,000. Pays 14-21% royalty based on net sales; advance. Publishes book an average of 1 year after acceptance. Reports in 2 weeks on queries; 2 months on other submissions. Free book catalog; ms guidelines for SASE.
Nonfiction: "We are interested only in naval and maritime subjects: tactics, strategy, navigation, naval history, biographies of naval leaders and naval aviation." Reviews artwork/photos as part of ms package.
Recent Nonfiction Title: *In Love and War*, by Jim and Sybil Stockdale.
Fiction: Limited, very high quality fiction on naval and maritime themes.
Recent Fiction Title: *Flight of the Intruder*, by Stephen Coonts.

‡**THOMAS NELSON PUBLISHERS**, Nelson Place at Elm Hill Pike, P.O. Box 141000, Nashville TN 37214. (615)889-9000. FAX: (615)391-5225.Managing Editor: Bill Watkins. Publishes hardcover and paperback originals and reprints. Averages 120 titles/year. Pays royalty or makes outright purchase. Publishes book an average of 1 year after acceptance. Reports in 2 months. SASE must accompany submissions or unable to return proposals.
Nonfiction: Adult inspirational/motivational Christian trade books and reference books on the Bible and Christianity. Accepts outline/synopsis and 3 sample chapters.
Recent Nonfiction Title: *Love Hunger: Recovery from Food Addiction*, by Drs. Frank Minirth, Paul Meier, Robert Hemfelt, and Sharon Sneed.
Fiction: Seeking high quality novels with Christian themes for adults and teens.

THE NEW ENGLAND PRESS, INC., P.O. Box 575, Shelburne VT 05482. (802)863-2520. President: Alfred Rosa. Estab. 1978. Publishes hardcover and trade paperback originals and trade paperback reprints. Averages 6-12 titles/year; receives 200 submissions annually. 25% of books from first-time authors; 75% of books from unagented writers. Pays 10-15% royalty on wholesale price. Publishes ms an average of 1 year after acceptance. Reports in 2 weeks on queries; 1 month on mss.
Nonfiction: Biography, how-to, nature and illustrated book. Subjects include Americana (Vermontiana and New England); history (New England orientation); and essays (New England orientation). No juvenile or psychology. Query or submit outline/synopsis and sample chapters. Reviews artwork/photos.
Recent Nonfiction Title: *Grace & Cal: A Vermont Love Story*, by Gloria May Stoddard.
Fiction: Historical (New England orientation). No novels. Query.

NEW LEAF PRESS, INC., Box 311, Green Forest AR 72638. Publishes hardcover and paperback originals. Specializes in charismatic books. Publishes 15 titles/year; receives 236 submissions annually. 15% of books from first-time authors; 90% of books from unagented writers. Average print order for a writer's first book is 10,000. Pays 10% royalty on first 10,000 copies, paid once a year; no advance. Send photos and illustrations to accompany ms. Publishes book an average of 10 months after acceptance. Simultaneous submissions OK.

Reports in 3 months. Reviews artwork/photos as part of ms package. Book catalog and guidelines for 9×12 SAE with 5 first class stamps.
Nonfiction: Biography and self-help. Charismatic books; life stories, and how to live the Christian life. Length: 100-400 pages. Submit complete ms.
Recent Nonfiction Title: *Pentecostals In Crisis*, by Ron Aoch.
Tips: "Biographies, relevant nonfiction, and Bible-based fiction have the best chance of being sold to our firm. Honest and real-life experience help make a book or query one we can't put down."

NEW READERS PRESS, Publishing division of Laubach Literacy International, Box 131, Syracuse NY 13210. Editor-in-Chief: Laura Martin. Publishes paperback originals. Averages 30 titles/year; receives 200 submissions/year. 40% of books by first-time authors; 95% of books by unagented writers. Average print order for a writer's first book is 5,000. "Most of our sales are adult basic education programs, with some sales to volunteer literacy programs, private human services agencies, prisons, and libraries with outreach programs for poor readers." Pays royalty on retail price, or by outright purchase. Rate varies according to type of publication and length of manuscript. Advance is "different in each case, but does not exceed projected royalty for first year." Publishes book an average of 1 year after acceptance. Query for electronic submissions. Reports in 2 months. Free book catalog and authors' brochure.
Nonfiction: "Our audience is adults and older teenagers with limited reading skills (6th grade level and below). We publish basic education materials in reading and writing, math, social studies, health, science, and English as a second language for double illiterates. We are particularly interested in materials that fulfill curriculum requirements in these areas. Manuscripts must be not only easy to read (3rd-6th grade level) but mature in tone and concepts. We are not interested in poetry or anything at all written for children." Submit outline and 1-3 sample chapters.
Recent Nonfiction Title: *Patterns in Spelling*, by Tim Brown and Deborah Knight.
Fiction: Short novels (12,000-15,000 words) at third grade reading level on themes of interest to adults and older teenagers. Submit synopsis.
Recent Fiction Title: *Fitting In*, by Rosanne Keller.

NEW VICTORIA PUBLISHERS, P.O. Box 27, Norwich VT 05055. (802)649-5297. Editor: Claudia Lamperti. Estab. 1976. Publishes trade paperback originals. Averages 4 titles/year; receives 100 submissions/year. 50% of books from first-time authors; 100% of books from unagented writers. Pays 10% royalty on wholesale price. Publishes book an average of 1 year after acceptance. Query for electronic submissions. Reports on queries in 2 weeks; on mss in 1 month. Free book catalog.
Nonfiction: History. "We are interested in feminist history or biography and interviews with or topics relating to lesbians. No poetry." Submit outline/synopsis and sample chapters.
Recent Nonfiction Title: *Radical Feminists of Hetereodoxy*, by Judith Schwarz (feminist history).
Fiction: Adventure, erotica, fantasy, historical, humor, mystery, romance, science fiction and western. "We will consider most anything if it is well written and appeals to lesbian/feminist audience." Submit outline/synopsis and sample chapters.
Recent Fiction Title: *Captive in Time*, by Sarah Dreher.
Tips: "Try to appeal to a specific audience and not write for the general market."

NEWCASTLE PUBLISHING CO., INC., 13419 Saticoy, North Hollywood CA 91605. (213)873-3191. FAX: (213)780-2007. Editor-in-Chief: Alfred Saunders. Estab. 1970. Publishes trade paperback originals and reprints. Averages 10 titles/year; receives 300 submissions annually. 70% of books from first-time authors; 95% of books from unagented writers. Average print order for a writer's first book is 3,000-5,000. Pays 5-10% royalty on retail price; no advance. Publishes book an average of 8 months after acceptance. Simultaneous submissions OK. Reports in 3 weeks on queries; 6 weeks on mss. Free book catalog; ms guidelines for SASE.
Nonfiction: How-to, self-help, metaphysical and New Age. Subjects include health (physical fitness, diet and nutrition), psychology and religion. "Our audience is made up of college students and college-age nonstudents; also, adults ages 25 and up. They are of above average intelligence and are fully aware of what is available in the bookstores." No biography, travel, children's books, poetry, cookbooks or fiction. Query or submit outline/synopsis and sample chapters. Looks for "something to grab the reader so that he/she will readily remember that passage."
Recent Nonfiction Title: *Lighten Up Your Body, Lighten Up Your Life*, by Lucia Capacchione.
Tips: "Check the shelves in the larger bookstores on the subject of the manuscript being submitted. A book on life extension, holistic health, or stress management has the best chance of selling to our firm along with books geared for older adults on personal health issues, etc."

‡NEWEST PUBLISHERS LTD., #310, 10359 Whyte Ave., Edmonton, Alberta T6E 1Z9 Canada. (403)432-9427. Editorial Assistant: Carolyn Pogue. Publishes trade paperback originals. Averages 8 titles/year. Receives 100 submissions/year. 40% of books from first-time authors; 90% from unagented writers. Pays 10% royalty. Publishes book an average of 2 years after acceptance. Simultaneous submissions OK. Reports in 2 weeks on queries; 3 months on mss. Book catalog for 9×12 SAE and 4 first class stamps.

Nonfiction: Literary/essays. Subjects include art/architecture, ethnic, government/politics (Western Canada), history (Western Canada) and Canadiana. Query.
Recent Nonfiction Title: *Architecture of Douglas Cardinal*, by Trevor Boddy (architecture/biography).
Fiction: Literary and short story collections. We are looking for Western Canadian authors. Submit outline/synopsis and sample chapters.
Recent Fiction Title: *Grace Lake*, by Glen Huser.
Tips: "Our audience consists of people interested in the west and north of Canada; teachers, professors. If I were a writer trying to market a book today, I would study publisher's catalogues and their recent titles. I'd always include a SASE."

NICHOLS PUBLISHING, Box 96, New York NY 10024. (212)580-8079. Subsidiaries include GP Courseware. Vice President and Publisher: Linda Kahn. Publishes hardcover and paperback originals. Firm publishes 50 titles/year; division publishes 40 titles/year. 15% of books from first-time authors; 98% from unagented writers. Pays 5-15% royalty on wholesale price. Offers $300-500 average advance. Publishes book an average of 9 months after acceptance. Simultaneous submissions OK. Query for electronic submissions. Reports on queries in 1 week; 6 weeks on mss. Book catalog and ms guidelines free on request.
Nonfiction: Reference, technical. Subjects include architecture, business and economics, computers and electronics, education, money/finance, training, energy, engineering. Submit outline/synopsis and sample chapters or complete ms.
Recent Nonfiction Title: *Design for Hospitality*, by Davies and Beaseley.

THE NOBLE PRESS, INCOPORATED, Suite 508, 213 W. Institute Pl, Chicago IL 60610. (312)642-1168. Editor: Mark Harris. Estab. 1988. Firm publishes hardcover and trade paperback originals. Publishes 8 titles/year; receives 200 submissions/year. 50% of books from first-time authors; 80% from unagented writers. Pays 5-15% royalty on retail price. Advance varies. Publishes book an average of 6 months after acceptance. Simultaneous submissions OK. Reports in 6 weeks. Free ms guidelines.
Nonfiction: Biography, how-to, illustrated book, juvenile, reference, self-help. Subjects include education, ethnic, government/politics, history, nature/environment, philosophy, religion, sociology, women's issues/studies. No cookbooks, technical manuals, texts in full. Submit outline/synopsis and sample chapters.
Recent Nonfiction Title: *Embracing the Earth*, by Mark Harris.
Tips: "The writer has the best chance of selling us a nonfiction book that addresses contemporary issues of importance to our society."

NORTH LIGHT, Imprint of F&W Publications, 1507 Dana Ave., Cincinnati OH 45207. Editorial Director: David Lewis. Publishes hardcover and trade paperback originals. Averages 30-35 titles/year. Pays 10% royalty on net receipts. Offers $3,000 advance. Simultaneous submissions OK. Reports in 3 weeks on queries; 2 months on mss. Book catalog for 9×12 SAE with 6 first class stamps.
Nonfiction: Art and graphic design instruction books. Interested in books on watercolor painting, oil painting, basic drawing, pen and ink, airbrush, markers, basic design, computer graphics, desktop publishing, desktop design, color, illustration techniques, layout and typography. Do not submit coffee table art books without how-to art instruction. Query or submit outline/synopsis and examples of artwork (transparencies and photographs of artwork are OK).
Recent Nonfiction Title: *The Creative Artist*.

NORTHERN ILLINOIS UNIVERSITY PRESS, DeKalb IL 60115. (815)753-1826/753-1075. Director: Mary L. Lincoln. Estab. 1965. Pays 10-15% royalty on wholesale price. Free book catalog.
Nonfiction: "The NIU Press publishes mainly history, social sciences, philosophy, literary criticism and regional studies. It does not consider collections of previously published articles, essays, etc., nor do we consider unsolicited poetry." Accepts nonfiction translations. Query with outline/synopsis and 1-3 sample chapters.
Recent Nonfiction Title: *Guns for the Tsar: Technology Transfer and the Small Arms Industry in Nineteenth Century Russia*, by Joseph Bradley.

NORTHLAND PUBLISHING CO., INC., P.O. Box N, Flagstaff AZ 86002. (602)774-5251. FAX: (602)774-0592. Editorial Director: Susan McDonald. Estab. 1958. Publishes hardcover and trade paperback originals. Firm averages 20 titles/year. Receives 250 submissions/year. 30% of books from first-time authors. 75% from unagented writers. Pays 8-15% royalty (on net receipts), depending upon terms. Offers $1,000 average advance. Publishes book an average of 10 months after acceptance. Simultaneous submissions OK. Reports in 1 month on queries; 2 months on mss. Free book catalog and manuscript guidelines.
Nonfiction: Biography, coffee table, cookbook, how-to and illustrated books. Subjects include animals, anthropology/archaeology, art/architecture, history, nature/environment, photography and regional (American west/Southwest). "We are seeking authoritative, well-written manuscripts on natural history subjects. We do not want to see poetry, general fiction, or New Age/science fiction material." Query or submit outline/synopsis and sample chapters. Reviews artwork/photos as part of ms package.

Recent Nonfiction Title: *R.C. Gorman: A Retrospective*, by Doris Monthan.
Tips: "In general, our audience is composed of general interest readers and those interested in specialty subjects such as Native American culture and crafts. It is not necessarily a scholarly market, but is sophisticated."

W.W. NORTON CO., INC., 500 5th Ave., New York NY 10110. (212)354-5500. Editor: Liz Malcolm. Imprints include Norton Paperback Fiction. Publishes 300 titles/year; receives 5,000 submissions annually. Often publishes new and unagented authors. Royalty varies on retail price; advance varies. Publishes book an average of 1 year after acceptance. Simultaneous submissions OK. Submit outline and/or 2-3 sample chapters for fiction and nonfiction. Not responsible for return of material sent without return packaging and postage. Reports in 2 months. Book catalog and guidelines for 9×12 SAE with 2 first class stamps.
Nonfiction and Fiction: "General, adult fiction and nonfiction of the highest quality possible." No occult, paranormal, religion, genre fiction, formula romances, science fiction or westerns, cookbooks, arts and crafts, young adult or children's books. Last year there were 100 book club rights sales; 36 mass paperback reprint sales; and "innumerable serializations, second serial, syndication, translations, etc." Looks for "clear, intelligent, creative writing on original subjects or with original characters."
Recent Nonfiction Title: *Freud: A Life for Our Time*, by Peter Gay.
Recent Fiction Title: *The Watch*, by Rick Bass.
Tips: "Long novels are too expensive—keep them under 350 (manuscript) pages."

NOYES DATA CORP., Noyes Bldg., Park Ridge NJ 07656. FAX: (201)391-6833. Estab. 1959. Imprints include Noyes Press and Noyes Publications. Publishes hardcover originals. Averages 60 titles/year. Pays 10%-12% royalty on retail price; advance varies, depending on author's reputation and nature of book. Reports in 2 weeks. Free book catalog.
Nonfiction: Noyes Press publishes art, classical studies, archaeology, and history. "Material directed to the intelligent adult and the academic market." Noyes Publications publishes technical books on practical industrial processing, science, economic books pertaining to chemistry, chemical engineering, food, textiles, energy, electronics, pollution control—primarily of interest to the business executive. Length: 50,000-250,000 words. Query Editorial Department.

‡NTC PUBLISHING GROUP, 4255 West Touhy Ave., Lincolnwood IL 60646-1975. (708)679-5500. FAX (708)679-2494. Imprints include National Textbook Company, Passport Books. National Textbook Company, NTC Business Books, VGM Career Books. Foreign Language and English as a Second Language/Editorial Director: Michael Ross. Language Arts Editor: Raymond Walters. Passport Books Editorial Director: Michael Ross. NTC Business Books Manager: Casimir Psujek. VGM Career Books Editor: Michael Urban. Publishes hardcover and trade paperback originals and reprints. Averages 150 titles/year. Receives 800 submissions/year. 98% of books from unagented writers. Pays royalty or buys by outright purchase. Offers varying advance. Publishes book an average of 1 year after acceptance. Simultaneous submissions OK. Query for electronic submissions. Reports in 2 months. Book catalog free on request.
Nonfiction: Textbook, travel, foreign language, advertising and marketing busines books. Subjects include business, education, language/literature, photography, travel. Query. Reviews artwork/photos as part of ms package.
Recent Nonfiction Title: *New York on $1,000 a Day*, by Ferne Kadish and Shelley Clark.
Fiction: Short story collections. Query.

OCTAMERON ASSOCIATES, 820 Fontaine St., Alexandria VA 22302. (703)823-1882. Editorial Director: Karen Stokstad. Estab. 1976. Publishes trade paperback originals. Averages 15 titles/year; receives 150 submissions annually. 10% of books from first-time authors; 100% of books from unagented writers. Average print order for a writer's first book is 8,000-10,000. Pays 7½% royalty on retail price. Publishes book an average of 6 months after acceptance. Simultaneous submissions OK. Query for electronic submissions. Reports in 2 weeks. Book catalog and guidelines for 2 first class stamps.
Nonfiction: Reference, career and post-secondary education subjects. Especially interested in "paying-for-college and college admission guides." Query. Submit outline/synopsis and 2 sample chapters. Reviews artwork/photos as part of ms package.
Recent Nonfiction Title: *College Match: A Blueprint for Choosing the Best School for You*, by Steven R. Antonoff and Marie A. Friedemann.

ODDO PUBLISHING, INC., P.O. Box 68, Redwine Rd., Fayetteville GA 30214. (404)461-7627. Managing Editor: Genevieve Oddo. Estab. 1964. Publishes hardcover and paperback originals. Averages 4 titles/year; receives 300 submissions annually. 25% of books from first-time authors; 100% of books from unagented writers. Average print order for a writer's first book is 3,500. Makes outright purchase. "We judge all scripts independently." Royalty considered for special scripts only. Publishes book an average of 2-3 years after acceptance. Reports in 4 months. Book catalog for 9×12 SAE with 5 first class stamps.

Nonfiction and Fiction: Publishes juvenile books (ages 4-10) in language arts, workbooks in math, writing (English), photophonics, science (space and oceanography), and social studies for schools, libraries, and trade. Interested in children's supplementary readers in the areas of language arts, math, science, social studies, etc. "Texts run from 1,500 to 3,500 words. Ecology, space, patriotism, oceanography and pollution are subjects of interest. Manuscripts must be easy to read, general, and not set to outdated themes. They must lend themselves to full color illustration. No stories of grandmother long ago. No love angle, permissive language, or immoral words or statements." Submit complete ms. Reviews artwork/photos as part of ms package.

Recent Fiction Title: *Bobby Bear at the Circus,* by Marilue.

Tips: "We are currently expanding our line to include materials more acceptable in the trade market. To do so, we are concentrating on adding titles to our top selling series in lieu of developing new series; however, we will consider other scripts."

OHARA PUBLICATIONS, INC., 1813 Victory Place, P.O. Box 7728, Burbank CA 91510-7728. FAX: (818)953-9244. Editor: Michael Lee. Publishes trade paperback originals. Averages 12 titles/year. Pays royalty. Write for guidelines. Reports in 3 weeks on queries; 2 months on mss.

Nonfiction: Martial arts. "We decide to do a book on a specific martial art, then seek out the most qualified martial artist to author that book. 'How to' books are our mainstay, and we will accept no manuscript that does not pertain to martial arts systems (their history, techniques, philosophy, etc.)." Query first, then submit outline/synopsis and sample chapter. Include author biography and copies of credentials.

Recent Nonfiction Title: *Small-Circle Jujitsu,* by Wally Jay (how-to).

OHIO UNIVERSITY PRESS, Scott Quad, Ohio University, Athens OH 45701. (614)593-1155. FAX: (614)593-4536. Imprint includes Swallow Press. Director: Duane Schneider. Estab. 1964. Publishes hardcover and paperback originals and reprints. Averages 25-30 titles/year. No advance. Reports in 5 months. Free book catalog.

Nonfiction: "General scholarly nonfiction with particular emphasis on 19th century literature and culture. Also history, social sciences, philosophy, western regional works and miscellaneous categories." Query.

Recent Nonfiction Title: *Klondike Women: True Tales of the 1897-1898 Gold Rush,* by Melanie J. Mager.

Tips: Does not accept unsolicited mss.

THE OLD ARMY PRESS, P.O. Box 2243, Ft. Collins CO 80522. (303)484-5535. General Manager: Dee Koury. Estab. 1968. Publishes hardcover and trade paperback originals and reprints. Averages 6 titles/year; receives 30 submissions annually. 50% of books from first-time authors. 100% of books from unagented writers. Pays 5-10% royalty on wholesale price. Publishes book an average of 18 months after acceptance. Query for electronic submissions. Reports in 3 weeks on queries; 3 months on submissions.

Nonfiction: Biography and reference—all related to western military history. Especially needs mss on Indian wars and Texas history. Query. Reviews artwork/photos as part of ms package.

Recent Nonfiction Title: *A Good Day to Die,* by Utley Gray.

ONCE UPON A PLANET, INC., 65-42 Fresh Meadow Lane, Fresh Meadows NY 11365. (718)961-9240. Susidiary includes Planet Books. President: Charles Faraone. Estab. 1978. Publishes humorous, novelty 32-page books for the international gift and stationery market. Publishes 12-20 titles/year. Pays authors 5-15% royalty on wholesale price, outright $500-3,000 purchase or flat amount per book printed or per book sold. Offers average advance of $500-1,500. Publishes ms an average of 4 months after acceptance. Simultaneous submissions OK. Reports in 2 weeks on queries and 3 weeks on mss. Book catalog and ms guidelines for #10 SASE.

Nonfiction: Humor, illustrated books. Query or submit outline/synopsis and sample chapters.

Fiction: Humor. "We'd like to find 10-15 funny books each year to fit our format." Query or submit outline/synopsis and sample chapters.

Recent Fiction Title: *Golfer's Prayer Book.*

‡*OPEN COURT PUBLISHING CO., Box 599, Peru IL 61354. Publisher: M. Blouke Carus. President: Dr. André Carus. Averages 10 titles/year; receives 300 submissions annually. 20% of books from first-time authors; 80% of books from unagented writers. Subsidy publishes 15% of books; 10% nonauthor subsidy. Royalty contracts negotiable for each book. Publishes book an average of 18 months after acceptance. Query for electronic submissions. Guidelines for 9×12 SAE.

Nonfiction: Philosophy, psychology, Jungian analysis, science and history of science, mathematics, public policy, comparative religions, education, Orientalia, and related scholarly topics. Accepts nonfiction translations. "This is a publishing house run as an intellectual enterprise, to reflect the concerns of its staff and as a service to the world of learning." Query or submit outline/synopsis and 2-3 sample chapters. Reviews artwork/photos as part of ms package.

Recent Nonfiction Title: *Cosmos and Metacosmos*, by Robert Wesson.

‡*ORBIS BOOKS, Maryknoll NY 10545. (914)941-7590. Editor-in-Chief: Robert Ellsberg. Estab. 1970. Publishes cloth and paperback originals and translations. Publishes 40 titles/year. Subsidy publishes (nonauthor) 20% of books. Pays 10-12½-15% royalty on net prices; offers average $1,000 advance. Query with outline, 2 sample chapters, and prospectus. Query for electronic submissions. Reports in 6 weeks. Enclose return postage.
Nonfiction: "Religious developments in Asia, Africa and Latin America. Global justice and peace issues. Christianity and world religions."
Recent Nonfiction Title: *War Against the Poor: Low-Intensity Conflict and Christian Family*, by Jack Nelson-Pallmeyer.

‡*ORCA BOOK PUBLISHERS LTD., 1121 Vancouver St., Victoria, British Columbia V8V 3W1 Canada. (604)380-1229. Publisher: R. Tyrrell. Publishes hardcover and trade paperback originals. Publishes 15-20 titles/year; receives 200-300 submissions/year. 50% from first-time authors; 80% from unagented writers. Subsidy publishes 10% of books. "Subsidy determined by content and marketability of the ms." Pays 10-12 ½% royalty on retail price. Offers average $500 advance. Publishes ms and average of 6-9 months after acceptance. Reports in 3 weeks on queries; 2 months on mss. Book catalog for 9 × 12 SAE and $1 (Canadian) postage; ms guidelines for SASE.
Nonfiction: Biography, illustrated book, reference, travel guides, children's. Subjects include cooking, foods and nutrition, history, nature/environment, recreation, sports, and travel. Needs history (West Coast Canadian), biography, and young children's book. Query or submit outline/synopsis and sample chapters. All unsolicited mss are returned unopened. Reviews artwork/photos as part of ms package.
Recent Nonfiction Title: *Penny Candy, Bobskates and Frozen Roadapples*, by R. Thompson (memoir/biography).
Fiction: Adventure, juvenile, literary, mainstream/contemporary, short story collections. Needs West Coast Canadian contemporary fiction; illustrated children's books, 3-6-year-old range. Query or submit outline/synopsis and sample chapters. All unsolicited mss are returned unopened.
Recent Fiction Title: *Maxine's Tree*, by D. Leger-Haskell (children's).

*OREGON HISTORICAL SOCIETY PRESS, Oregon Historical Society, 1230 SW Park, Portland OR 97205. (503)222-1741. FAX: (503)221-2035. Director—Publications: Bruce Taylor Hamilton. Estab. 1973. Publishes hardcover originals, trade paperback originals and reprints and a quarterly historical journal, *Oregon Historical Quarterly*. Publishes 12-14 titles/year. Receives 300 submissions/year. 75% of books from first-time authors; 100% from unagented writers. Subsidy publishes 70% (nonauthor) of books. Pays royalty on wholesale price or makes outright purchase. Publishes book an average of 18 months after acceptance. Simultaneous and photocopied submissions OK. Query for electronic submissions. Reports in 1 week on queries; 3 months on mss. Free book catalog. Ms guidelines for #10 SASE.
Nonfiction: Subjects include Americana, art/architecture, biography, ethnic, government/politics, history, nature/environment, North Pacific Studies, photography, reference, regional juvenile, women's. Query or submit outline/synopsis and sample chapters or submit complete ms. Reviews artwork/photos as part of ms package.
Recent Nonfiction Title: *Sowing Good Seeds: The Northwest Suffrage Campaigns of Susan B. Anthony*, by G. Thomas Edwards.

*OREGON STATE UNIVERSITY PRESS, 101 Waldo Hall, Corvallis OR 97331. (503)754-3166. Publishers hardcover and paperback originals. Averages 6 titles/year; receives 100 submissions annually. 75% of books from first-time authors; 100% of books from unagented writers. Average print order for a writer's first book is 1,500. Subsidy publishes (nonauthor) 40% of books. Pays royalty on net receipts. No advance. Publishes book an average of 1 year after acceptance. Query for electronic submissions. Reports in 1 month. Book catalog for 6 × 9 SAE with 2 first class stamps.

An asterisk preceding a listing indicates that subsidy publishing or co-publishing (where author pays part or all of publishing costs) is available. Firms whose subsidy programs comprise more than 50% of their total publishing activities are listed at the end of the Book Packagers and Producers section.

Nonfiction: Publishes scholarly books in history, biography, geography, literature, life sciences and natural resource management, with strong emphasis on Pacific or Northwestern topics. Submit outline/synopsis and sample chapters.
Recent Nonfiction Title: *William L. Finley: Pioneer Wildlife Photographer*, by Worth Mathewson (biography/photos).

‡**OSBORNE/MCGRAW-HILL**, subsidiary of McGraw-Hill Inc., 2600 Tenth St., Berkeley CA 94710. (415)549-6635. Vice President/Editor-in-Chief: Cynthia Hudson. Estab. 1979. Publishes trade paperback originals. Averages 65 titles/year. Receives 120 submissions/year. 30% of books from first-time authors; 99% from unagented writers. Pays 10-15% royalty on wholesale price. Offers $5,000 average advance. Publishes book an average of 6 months after acceptance. Simultaneous submissions OK. Query for electronic submissions. Reports in 1 week on queries; 2 weeks on mss. Book catalog and manuscript free on request.
Nonfiction: Software and technical. Subjects include computers. Query with outline/synopsis and sample chapters. Reviews artwork/photos as part of ms package.
Recent Nonfiction Title: *Dvorak's Guide to PC Telecommunications*, by John C. Dvorak/Nick Anis.

OUR SUNDAY VISITOR, INC., 200 Noll Plaza, Huntington IN 46750. (219)356-8400. Director: Robert Lockwood. Publishes paperback originals and reprints. Averages 20-30 titles a year; receives 75 submissions annually. 10% of books from first-time authors; 90% of books from unagented writers. Pays variable royalty on net receipts; offers average $500 advance. Publishes book an average of 1 year after acceptance. Query for electronic submissions. Reports in 1 month on most queries and submissions. Author's guide and catalog for SASE.
Nonfiction: Catholic viewpoints on current issues, reference and guidance, Bibles and devotional books, and Catholic heritage books. Prefers to see well-developed proposals as first submission with "annotated outline, three sample chapters, and definition of intended market." Reviews artwork/photos as part of ms package.
Recent Nonfiction Title: *Cults, Sects and the New Age*, by Fr. James J. LeBar.
Tips: "Solid devotional books that are not first person, well-researched church histories or lives of the saints and self-help for those over 55 have the best chance of selling to our firm. Make it solidly Catholic, unique, without pious platitudes."

THE OVERLOOK PRESS, Distributed by Viking/Penguin, 12 W. 21st St., New York 10010. (212)337-5200. Contact: Editorial Department. Imprints include Tusk Books. Publishes hardcover and trade paperback originals and hardcover reprints. Averages 40 titles/year; receives 300 submissions annually. Pays 3-15% royalty on wholesale or retail price. Submissions accepted only through literary agents. Reports in 2 months. Free book catalog.
Nonfiction: How-to and reference. Subjects include Americana, business and economics, history, anture, film, archetecture, art, design and travel. No pornography.
Recent Nonfiction Title: *The Genius That Was China*, by John Merson.
Fiction: Literary fiction, fantasy/mystery/suspense, fiction reprints.
Recent Fiction Title: *The Universe and Other Fictions*, by Paul West.
Poetry: We like to publish poets who have a strong following—those who read in New York City regularly in periodicals regularly." No poetry from unpublished authors. Submit complete ms.
Recent Poetry Title: *Disappearances*, by Paul Auster.

PACIFIC BOOKS, PUBLISHERS, P.O. Box 558, Palo Alto CA 94302. (415)965-1980. Editor: Henry Ponleithner. Estab. 1945. Averages 6-12 titles/year. Royalty schedule varies with book. No advance. Send complete ms. Reports "promptly." Book catalog and guidelines for 9×12 SAE.
Nonfiction: General interest, professional, technical and scholarly nonfiction trade books. Specialties include western Americana and Hawaiiana. Looks for "well-written, documented material of interest to a significant audience." Also considers text and reference books; high school and college. Accepts artwork/photos and translations.
Recent Nonfiction Title: *Inventors and Their Inventions: A California Legacy*, by Paul D. Flehr.

PACIFIC PRESS PUBLISHING ASSOCIATION, Book Division, Seventh-day Adventist Church, P.O. Box 7000, Boise ID 83707. (208)465-2595. Vice President for Editorial Development: B. Russell Holt. Estab. 1874. Publishes hardcover and trade paperback originals and hardcover and trade paperback reprints. Averages 35 titles/year; receives 600 submissions and proposals annually. Up to 50% of books from first-time authors; 100% of books from unagented writers. Pays 8-14% royalty on wholesale price. Offers average $300-500 advance depending on length. Publishes books an average of 6 months after acceptance. Query for electronic submissions. Reports in 1 month on queries; 2 months on mss. Ms guidelines for #10 SASE.
Nonfiction: Biography, cookbook (vegetarian), how-to, juvenile, self-help and textbook. Subjects include cooking and foods (vegetarian only), health, nature, religion, and family living. "We are an exclusively religious publisher. We are looking for practical, how-to oriented manuscripts on religion, health, and family

life that speak to human needs, interests and problems from a Biblical perspective. We can't use anything totally secular or written from other than a Christian perspective." Query or submit outline/synopsis and sample chapters. Reviews artwork/photos as part of ms package.

Recent Nonfiction Title: *Deceived by the New Age*, by Will Baron.

Tips: "Our primary audiences are members of our own denomination (Seventh-day Adventist), the general Christian reading market, and the secular or nonreligious reader. Books that are doing well for us are those that relate the Biblical message to practical human concerns and those that focus more on the experiential rather than theoretical aspects of Christianity."

PALADIN PRESS, P.O. Box 1307, Boulder CO 80306. (303)443-7250. FAX: (303)442-8741. President/Publisher: Peder C. Lund. General Manager: Kim R. Hood. Editorial Director: Jon Ford. Estab. 1970. Publishes hardcover and paperback originals and paperback reprints. Averages 36 titles/year. 50% of books from first-time authors; 100% of books from unagented writers. Pays 10-12-15% royalty on net sales. Publishes book an average of 1 year after acceptance. Simultaneous submissions OK. Reports in 2 months. Free book catalog.

Nonfiction: "Paladin Press primarily publishes original manuscripts on martial arts, military science, weaponry, self-defense, police science, action careers, guerrilla warfare, fieldcraft and 'creative revenge' humor. How-to manuscripts are given priority. Manuals on building weapons, when technically accurate and clearly presented, are encouraged. If applicable, send sample photographs and line drawings with complete outline and sample chapters." Query or submit outline/synopsis and sample chapters.

Recent Nonfiction Title: *Powerhouse Pistols: The Colt 1911 and Browning Hi-Power Source Book*, by Duncan Long.

Tips: "We need lucid, instructive material aimed at our market and accompanied by sharp, relevant illustrations and photos. As we are primarily a publisher of 'how-to' books, a manuscript that has step-by-step instructions, written in a clear and concise manner (but not strictly outline form) is desirable. No fiction, first-person accounts, children's, religious or joke books."

*PARAGON HOUSE PUBLISHERS, 90 5th Ave., New York NY 10011. (212)620-2820. Editor-in-Chief: Ken Stuart. Publishes hardcover and trade paperback originals and reprints. Averages 100 titles/year; receives 1,000 submissions annually. 10-20% of nonfiction from first-time authors; 50% of books from unagented writers. Subsidy publishes 2% of books/year (mostly translations). Whether an author is subsidy published is determined by "how much subsidy there is, as well as how much market." Royalty and advance negotiable. Simultaneous submissions OK. Query for electronic submissions. Reports in 1 month on queries; 2 months on mss. Book catalog free on request.

Nonfiction: Biography, reference and college textbook. Subjects include Americana, history, philosophy, politics, religion. Especially needs history, biography and serious nonfiction. No diet, gardening, crafts or humor. Query or submit outline/synopsis and sample chapters. Reviews artwork/photos as part of ms package.

Recent Nonfiction Title: *Punchlines*, by Bill Keough.

Poetry: Journals and letters only. No new or unestablished writers.

Recent Poetry Title: *In the Room We Share*, by Louis Simpson.

PARKER-GRIFFIN PUBLISHING CO., P.O. Box 9050, Carlsbad CA 92008. (619)931-5979. (800)752-9796. FAX: (619)931-7877. Subsidiaries: Parker & Son Publications. Chief Executive Officer: William L. Griffin, Jr. Publishes hardcover and trade paperback originals. Averages 35 titles/year. Pays 15% royalty on retail price. Publishes book an average of 4 months after acceptance. Query with outline/synopsis and sample chapter preferred. Reports in 1 month on queries; 6 weeks on mss. Free book list and "Information for Authors" on request.

Nonfiction: Technical law books and practice guidebooks for attorneys in active practice. Submit queries, outline/synopsis and sample chapters to Maggie O'Neill, editoral director.

Recent Nonfiction Title: *Lender Liability*, by Barry Cappelo.

‡PARKSIDE PUBLISHING CORPORATION, Subsidiary of Parkside Medical Services Corp., 205 W. Touhy Ave., Park Ridge IL 60068. (708)698-4700. FAX: (708)318-0966. Subsidiaries include Parkside; Prentice Hall/Parkside. Vice President: John Small. Estab. 1986. Publishes hardcover, trade paperback and 100% mass market paperback originals. Averages 6-10 titles/year. Receives 200 submissions/year. 50% of books from first-time authors; 50% from unagented writers. Pays 7-10% royalty on retail price. Average advance varies. Publishes book an average of 12 months after acceptance. Reports in 2 months on queries; 3 months on mss. Book catalog and manuscript guidelines free on request.

Nonfiction: Self-help, addiction/recovery. Subjects include health/medicine, addiction and recovery. "We need books on addiction and recovery (alcoholism, drug abuse, eating disorders, incest, mental health) for recovering individuals and families." No fiction or poetry. Query or submit outline/synopsis and sample chapters or complete ms. Reviews artwork/photos as part of ms package.

Recent Nonfiction Title: *Growing Through the Pain: The Incest Survivor's Companion*.

Tips: "Our audience is generally people recovering from addiction, codependency, eating disorders. Try to write a high-quality book with a clearly-defined niche in the field of addiction and recovery."

PASSPORT PRESS, P.O. Box 1346, Champlain NY 12919. (514)937-8155. Publisher: Jack Levesque. Estab. 1975. Publishes trade paperback originals. Averages 4 titles/year. 25% of books from first-time writers; 100% from unagented writers. Pays 8-12% royalty on retail price. Publishes book an average of 9 months after acceptance. Send query only. Unsolicited manuscripts or samples and non-travel material will not be returned even if accompanied by postage.
Nonfiction: Travel books only. Especially looking for manuscripts on practical travel subjects and travel guides on specific countries. Query. Reviews artwork/photos as part of ms package.
Recent Nonfiction Title: *Honduras and the Bay Islands*, by J.P. Panet.

PBC INTERNATIONAL INC., Subsidiary is The Photographic Book Company, 1 School St., Glen Cove NY 11542. (516)676-2727. FAX: (516)676-2738. Managing Director: Penny Sibal-Samonte. Estab. 1980. Imprints include Library of Applied Design (nonfiction), Great Graphics Series (nonfiction) and Design In Motion Series (nonfiction). Publishes hardcover and trade paperback originals. Averages 15 titles/year; receives 100-200 submissions annually. Most of books from first-time authors and unagented writers done on assignment. Pays royalty and/or flat fees. Simultaneous submissions OK. Book catalog for 9 × 12 SASE.
Nonfiction: Subjects include design, graphic art, and photography. The Library of Applied Design needs books that show the best in current design trends in all fields. No submissions not covered in the above listed topics. Query with outline/synopsis and sample chapters. Reviews artwork/photos as part of ms package.
Recent Nonfiction Title: *CLIO Awards—A Tribute to Thirty Years of Advertising Excellence*, by The CLIO Awards.

PEACHTREE PUBLISHERS, LTD., 494 Armour Circle NE, Atlanta GA 30324. (404)876-8761. Estab. 1978. Publishes hardcover and trade paperback originals. Averages 20-25 titles/year; receives up to 2,000 submissions annually. 50% of books from first-time authors; 75% of books from unagented writers. Average print order for a writer's first book is 5,000-10,000. Publishes book an average of 1 year after acceptance. Reports in 3 weeks on queries; 5 months on mss. Book catalog for SAE with 3 first class stamps.
Nonfiction: General and humor. Subjects include cooking and foods, history, recreation and travel. No technical, reference, art, juvenile or animals. Submit outline/synopsis and sample chapters. Reviews artwork/photos as part of ms package.
Recent Nonfiction Title: *Another Field Guide to Little Known and Seldom Seen Birds of North America*, by John, Cathryn, and Ben Sill.
Fiction: Literary, humor and mainstream. "We are particularly interested in fiction with a Southern feel." No fantasy, juvenile, science fiction or romance. Submit complete manuscript.
Recent Fiction Title: *The Song of Daniel*, by Philip Lee Williams.
Tips: "We're looking for mainstream fiction and nonfiction of general interest; although our books are sold throughout North America. We consider ourselves the national publisher with a Southern accent."

‡*PEGUIS PUBLISHERS LIMITED, 520 Hargrave St., Winnipeg Manitoba, R3M 0T8 Canada. (204)956-1486. Vice President, Acquisitions: Judy Norget. Educational paperback originals. Averages 20 titles/year. Receives 50 submissions/year. 80% of books from first-time authors; 100% from unagented writers. Pays 10% average royalty on educational net (trade less 20%). Publishes book an average of 1-2 years after acceptance. Simultaneous submissions OK. Electronic submissions only if accompanied by hard copy. Reports in 2 months on queries; 1 month on mss if quick rejection, up to 1 year if serious consideration. Free book catalog.
Nonfiction: Educational (focusing on teachers' resource material for primary education, integrated whole language, guidance). Submit outline/synopsis and sample chapters or complete ms preferably.
Recent Nonfiction Title: *The Learners' Way*, by Forester/Reinhard (teacher's resource K-3).
Fiction: Children's books for whole-language classrooms only.
Recent Fiction Title: *Lion in the Lake*, by Oberman (bilingual, French/English, alphabet book).
Tips: Writers have the best chance selling us quality educational resource materials. Our audience consists of educators—(teachers, counsellors, administrators), and school children.

PELICAN PUBLISHING COMPANY, 1101 Monroe St., Box 189, Gretna LA 70053. (504)368-1175. FAX: (504)368-1195. Editor: Nina Kooij. Estab. 1926. Publishes hardcover, trade paperback and mass market paperback originals and reprints. Averages 40-50 titles/year; receives 3,000 submissions annually. 30% of books from first-time authors; 97% of books from unagented writers. Pays royalty on publisher's actual receipts. Publishes book an average of 18 months after acceptance. Reports in 1 month on queries; 4 months on mss. Writer's guidelines for SASE.
Nonfiction: Travel, biography, coffee table book (limited), cookbook, how-to, humor, illustrated book, juvenile, self-help, motivational, inspirational, and Scottish. Subjects include Americana (especially Southern regional, Ozarks, Texas and Florida); business and economics (popular how-to and motivational); cooking and food; health; history; music (American artforms: jazz, blues, Cajun, R&B); politics (special interest in conservative viewpoint); recreation; religion (for popular audience mostly, but will consider others); and travel. *Travel*: Regional and international (especially areas in Pacific). *Motivational*: with business slant. *Inspirational*: author must be someone with potential for large audience. *Cookbooks*: "We look for authors

with strong connection to restaurant industry or cooking circles, i.e. someone who can promote successfully."
How-to: will consider broad range. Query. "We require that a query be made first. This greatly expedites the review process and can save the writer additional postage expenses." Does not consider multiple queries or submissions. Reviews artwork/photos as part of ms package.

Recent Nonfiction Title: *The Dooky Chase Cookbook*, by Leah Chase.

Fiction: Historical, humor, mainstream, Southern, juvenile and young adult. "Fiction needs are *very* limited. We are most interested in Southern novels. We are also looking for good mainstream juvenile/young adult works." No romance, science fiction, fantasy, gothic, mystery, erotica, confession, horror; no sex or violence. Submit outline/synopsis and sample chapters.

Recent Fiction Title: *A Bullet for Stonewall*, by Benjamin King.

Tips: "We do extremely well with travel, motivational, cookbooks, and children's titles. We will continue to build in these areas. The writer must have a clear sense of the market and this includes knowledge of the competition. A query letter should descrive the project briefly, give the author's writing and professional credentials, and promotional ideas. Include an SASE."

‡*PENDRAGON PRESS, R.R. 1, Box 159, Ferry Rd., Stuyvesant NY 12173-9720. (518)828-3008. Managing Editor: Robert Kessler. Publishes hardcover originals and reprints. Averages 12-15 titles/year. Receives 100 submissions/year. 50% of book from first-time authors; 99.9% from unagented writers. Subsidy publishes 30% of books. "If the book is of such special interest that sales will not cover publishing expenses, we subsidy publish." Pays 8-12% royalty on retail price. Publishes book an average of 15 months after acceptance. Simultaneous submissions OK. Query for electronic submissions. Reports in 2 weeks on queries; 2 months on mss. Book catalog and manuscript guidelines free on request.

Nonfiction: Reference. Subjects include music/dance and sociology (of music). "We deal specifically with scholarly material, for study and research. Our series in dance may need a couple of titles for 1991." Submit outline/synopsis and sample chapters. Reviews artwork/photos as part of ms package.

Recent Nonfiction Title: *The History of Orchestral Conducting*, by Elliot W. Galkin (musicology).

Tips: "In our field, music history, there is a trend toward exploring the music of Eastern Europe. We have a series in this field."

PENNSYLVANIA HISTORICAL AND MUSEUM COMMISSION, The official history agency for the Commonwealth of Pennsylvania, P.O. Box 1026, Harrisburg PA 17108-1026. (717)787-8312. FAX: (717)783-1073. Chief, Marketing, Sales and Publications Division: Douglas H. West. Estab. 1913. Publishes hardcover, trade and mass market paperback originals and reprints. Averages 6 titles/year; receives 50 submissions annually. 50% of books from first-time authors; 95% of books from unagented writers. Pays 5-10% royalty on wholesale or retail price. May make outright purchase of $500-1,000; sometimes makes special assignments; offers $350 average advance. Publishes book an average of 15 months after acceptance. Simultaneous submissions OK. Query for electronic submissions. Reports in 6 weeks on queries; 3 months on mss. Manuscripts prepared according to the Chicago *Manual of Style*.

Nonfiction: All books must be related to Pennsylvania, its history and its culture, biography, coffee table book, cookbook, how-to, illustrated book, reference, technical, visitor attractions and historic travel guidebooks. "The Commission is seeking manuscripts on Pennsylvania in general, but most specifically on archaeology, history, art (decorative and fine), politics, religion, travel, photography, nature, sports history, and cooking and food." Query or submit outline/synopsis and sample chapters.

Recent Nonfiction Title: *Guide to the State Historical Markers of Pennsylvania*, by George R. Beyer.

Tips: "Our audience is diverse—professional and avocational historians, students and scholars, specialists and generalists—all of whom are interested in one or more aspects of Pennsylvania's history and culture. Manuscripts must be well researched and documented (footnotes not necessarily required depending on the nature of the manuscript) and interestingly written. Because of the expertise of our reviewers, manuscripts must be factually accurate, but in being so, writers must not sacrifice style. We have always had a tradition of publishing scholarly and reference works, and although we intend to continue doing so, we want to branch out with more popularly styled books that will reach an even broader audience."

THE PERMANENT PRESS/SECOND CHANCE PRESS, Noyac Rd., Sag Harbor NY 11963. (516)725-1101. Editor: Judith Shepard. Estab. 1978. Publishes hardcover originals and reprints. Second Chance Press devotes itself exclusively to re-publishing fine books that are out of print and deserve continued recognition. Permanent Press publishes original fiction and some books of social and/or political significance. Averages 10 titles/year; receives 1,500 submissions annually. 35% of books from first-time authors; 75% of books from unagented writers. Average print order for a writer's first book is 2,000. Pays 10-15% royalty on wholesale price; offers $1,000 advance for Permanent Press books and royalty only on Second Chance Press titles. Publishes book an average of 18 months after acceptance. Simultaneous submissions OK. Reports in 2 weeks on queries; 3 months on mss. Book catalog for $2 postage.

Nonfiction: Biography, autobiography, historical and current events. No scientific and technical material or academic studies. Query.

Recent Nonfiction Title: *City of Discontent*, by Mark Harris.

Fiction: Adventure, confession, ethnic, experimental, fantasy, historical, humor, mainstream, mystery, and suspense. Especially looking for fiction with a unique point of view—"original and arresting" suitable for college literature classes. No mass market romance. Query.

Recent Fiction Title: *Zulus*, by Percival Everett.

PERSPECTIVES PRESS, P.O. Box 90318, Indianapolis IN 46290-0318. (317)872-3055. Publisher: Pat Johnston. Estab. 1982. Publishes hardcover and trade paperback originals. Averages 4 titles/year; receives 200 queries annually. 95% of books from first-time authors. 95% of books from unagented writers. Pays 5-15% royalty on net sales. Publishes book an average of 8 months after acceptance. Simultaneous submissions OK. Reports in 2 weeks on queries. Book catalog and writer's guidelines for #10 SAE and 2 first class stamps.

Nonfiction: How-to, juvenile and self-help books on health, psychology and sociology—all related to adoption or infertility. Query.

Recent Nonfiction Title: *Sweet Grapes: How to Stop Being Infertile and Start Living Again*, by Mike and Jean Carter.

Fiction: Adoption/infertility for adults or children. Query.

Recent Fiction Title: *Where the Sun Kisses the Sea*, by Susan Gabel.

Tips: "For adults we are seeking infertility and adoption decision-making materials, books dealing with parenting issues, books to use with children, books to share with others to help explain infertility or adoption or foster care, special programming or training manuals, etc. For children we will consider adoption or foster care related manuscripts that are appropriate for preschoolers, for early elementary, for later elementary or middle school children, for high schoolers. While we would consider a manuscript from a writer who was not personally or professionally involved in these issues, we would be more inclined to accept a manuscript submitted by an infertile person, an adoptee, a birthparent, an adoptive parent, a professional working with any of these."

PETER PAUPER PRESS, INC., 202 Mamaroneck Ave., White Plains NY 10601. (914)681-0144. Co-Publisher: Nick Beilenson. Publishes hardcover originals. Averages 8 titles/year; receives 50 submissions annually. Buys some mss outright for $1,000. Offers no advance. Publishes ms an average of 9 months after acceptance. Simultaneous submissions OK. Reports in 2 weeks. Book catalog for #10 SASE.

Nonfiction: Cookbook and humor. Subjects include Americana, humor, cooking and foods, inspirational, and religion. Submit complete ms. Reviews artwork/photos as part of ms package.

Recent Nonfiction Title: *Reigning Cats and Dogs*, by L.L. Kaufman.

Tips: Books on women's subjects have done well for Peter Pauper Press.

PETERSON'S, Box 2123, Princeton NJ 08543. (609)243-9111. Publisher/President: Peter W. Hegener. Executive Vice President: Karen C. Hegener. Vice President, General Manager, Publishing Group: Wayne Anderson. Publishes paperback originals and software (for the educational/career market). Averages 55-75 titles/year. Receives 200-250 submissions annually. 30% of books from first-time authors; 90% from unagented writers. Average print order for a writer's first book is 10,000-15,000. Pays 8-10% royalty on net sales; offers advance. Publishes book an average of 1 year after acceptance. Responds in 3 weeks. Free catalog.

Nonfiction: Educational and career reference and guidance works for professionals, libraries, and trade. Submit complete ms or detailed outline and sample chapters. Looks for "appropriateness of contents to our market, accuracy of information, author's credentials, and writing style suitable for audience." Reviews artwork/photos as part of ms package.

Recent Nonfiction Title: *Who's Going to Run General Motors?*, by Daniel Seymour and Kenneth Green.

Tips: "We're expanding into educational travel."

PHAROS BOOKS, Publisher of *The World Almanac*, 200 Park Ave., New York NY 10166. (212)692-3824. Editor-in-Chief: Hana Umlauf Lane. Editor: Eileen Schlesinger. Assistant Editor: Sharilyn K. Jee. Publishes hardcover and trade paperback originals. Averages 30 titles/year. Pays 6-15% on retail price. Publishes book an average of 1 year after acceptance. Reports in 3 weeks. Free book catalog.

Nonfiction: "We look for books under three imprints: Pharos Books for nonfiction with strong consumer interest; World Almanac for innovative reference books; Topper for humor books. We expect at least a synopsis/outline and sample chapters, and would like to see the completed manuscript." Reviews artwork/photos as part of ms package.

THE PICKERING PRESS, Suite 3A, 2575 S. Bayshore Dr., Miami FL 33133. (305)858-1321. FAX: (305)856-0873. Managing Editor: Charity H. Johnson. Estab. 1986. Publishes hardcover and trade paperback originals and trade paperback reprints. Firm averages 4-5 titles/year. Receives 25 submissions/year. 45% of books from first-time authors; 100% from unagented writers. Pays 6-15% on wholesale price. Buys mss outright for

$2,500. Publishes book an average of 9 months after acceptance. Query for electronic submissions. Reports in 1 month on queries; 1 month on mss. Free book catalog.

Nonfiction: How-to, illustrated book and self-help. Subjects include art/architecture, health/medicine, history, psychology and regional. Looking for regional/Florida history; psychology/self-help; medical/self-help ms. No regional books outside of Florida. Submit query or outline/synopsis and sample chapters. Reviews artwork/photos as part of ms package.

Recent Nonficiton Title: *Public Faces, Private Lives,* by Karen Davis.

Tips: "Nonfiction, regional history, and medical self/help have the best chance of being sold to our firm. If I were a writer trying to market a book today, I would clearly define the market for my book prior to approaching publishers, and be prepared to offer non-book trade suggestions in addition to traditional techniques."

PILOT BOOKS, 103 Cooper St., Babylon NY 11702. (516)422-2225. President: Sam Small. Estab. 1959. Publishes paperback originals. Averages 20-30 titles/year; receives 300-400 submissions annually. 20% of books from first-time authors; 90% of books from unagented writers. Average print order for a writer's first book is 3,000. Offers standard royalty contract based on wholesale or retail price. Usual advance is $250, but this varies, depending on author's reputation and nature of book. Publishes book an average of 8 months after acceptance. Reports in 1 month. Book catalog and guidelines for SASE.

Nonfiction: Financial, business, travel, career, personal guides and training manuals. "Our training manuals are utilized by America's major corporations as well as the government." Directories and books on travel and moneymaking opportunities. Wants "clear, concise treatment of subject matter." Length: 8,000-30,000 words. Send outline. Reviews artwork/photos as part of ms package.

Recent Nonfiction Title: *Directory of Low-Cost Vacations With A Difference,* by J. Crawford.

PINEAPPLE PRESS, INC., Drawer 16008, Southside Station, Sarasota FL 34239. (813)952-1085. Editor: June Cussen. Estab. 1982. Publishes hardcover and trade paperback originals. Averages 12 titles/year; receives 600 submissions annually. 20% of books from first-time authors; 80% of books from unagented writers. Pays 6½-15% royalty on retail price. Seldom offers advance. Publishes book an average of 1 year after acceptance. Simultaneous submissions OK. Query for electronic submissions. Reports in 1 month on queries; 6 weeks on mss. Book catalog for 9 × 12 SAE and 2 first class stamps.

Nonfiction: Biography, how-to, reference, nature. Subjects include animals, history and nature. "We will consider most nonfiction topics. We are seeking quality nonfiction on diverse topics for the library and book trade markets." No heavily illustrated submissions, pop psychology, or autobiographies. Query or submit outline/brief synopsis and sample chapters with SASE.

Recent Nonfiction Title: *The Rivers of Florida,* by Del and Marty Marth.

Fiction: Literary, historical and mainstream. No romance, science fiction, or children's. Submit outline/brief synopsis and sample chapters.

Recent Fiction Title: *Subtropical Speculations—Anthology of Florida Science Fiction,* editors Rick Wilber and Richard Mathews.

Tips: "If I were a writer trying to market a book today, I would learn everything I could about book publishing and book publicity and agree to actively participate in promoting my book. A query on a novel without a brief sample seems useless."

PIPPIN PRESS, A children's book company, 229 E. 85th St., Gracie Station, P.O. Box 92, New York NY 10028. (212)288-4920. Publisher/President: Barbara Francis. Estab. 1987. Publishes hardcover originals. Publishes 6-8 titles/year; receives 3,000 submissions/year. 80% of books from unagented writers. Pays royalty. Publishes book an average of 9-18 months after acceptance. Simultaneous submissions OK. Reports in 3 weeks on queries; 2 months on mss. Book catalog for 6 × 9 SASE; ms guidelines for #10 SASE.

Nonfiction: Biography, humor, juvenile, picture books. Animals, history, language/literature, nature, science. General nonfiction for children ages 4-12. Query. Reviews copies of artwork/photos as part of ms package.

Recent Nonfiction Title: *Pass the Quill: I'll Write a Draft: A Story of Thomas Jefferson,* by Robert Quackenbush (humorous).

Fiction: Adventure, fantasy, historical, humor, juvenile, mystery, picture books, suspense. Wants humorous fiction for ages 7-11. Query.

Recent Fiction Title: *A Spring Story,* by David Updike, illustrated by Robert Andrew Parker.

Tips: "Read as many of the best children's books published in the last five years as you can. I would pay particular attention to children's books favorably reviewed in *School Library Journal, The Booklist, The New York Times,* and *Book Review, Publishers Weekly."*

PLAYERS PRESS, INC., P.O. Box 1132, Studio City CA 91604. (818)789-4980. Vice President, Editorial: Robert W. Gordon. Estab. 1965. Publishes hardcover and trade paperback originals, and trade paperback reprints. Averages 15-25 titles/year; receives 75-300 submissions annually. 10% of books from first-time authors; 90% of books from unagented writers. Pays royalty on retail price. Publishes book an average of 20 months after acceptance. Reports in 4 months. Book catalog and guidelines for 6×9 SAE and 3 first class stamps.

Nonfiction: Juvenile and theatrical drama/entertainment industry. Subjects include the performing arts. Needs quality plays and musicals, adult or juvenile. Send query. Reviews artwork/photos as part of package.

Recent Nonfiction Title: *Survival*, by William-Alan Landes.

Fiction: Adventure, confession, ethnic, experimental, fantasy, historical, horror, humor, mainstream, mystery, religious, romance, science fiction, suspense and western. Submit complete ms for theatrical plays only. "No novels are accepted. We publish plays only."

Recent Fiction Title: *A Dusty Echo*, by Ev Miller.

Tips: "Plays, entertainment industry texts and children's story books have the best chance of selling to our firm."

PLAYWRIGHTS CANADA PRESS, Imprint of Playwrights Union of Canada, 54 Wolseley St., 2nd floor, Toronto, Ontario M5J 1A5 Canada. (416)947-0201. Publishes paperback originals and reprints of plays by Canadian citizens or landed immigrants, which have been professionally produced on stage. Receives 100 member submissions/year. 50% of plays from first-time authors; 50% from unagented authors. Pays 10% royalty on list price. Publishes about 1 year after acceptance. Simultaneous submissions OK. Free play catalog and ms guidelines. Non-members should query. Accepts children's plays.

Recent Fiction Title: *Scientific Americans*, by John Mighton.

PLENUM PUBLISHING, 233 Spring St., New York NY 10013. (212)620-8000. Senior Editor, Trade Books: Linda Greenspan Regan. Estab. 1947. Publishes hardcover originals. Averages 350 titles/year; trade division publishes 12. Receives 250 submissions annually. 50% of books from first-time authors. 75% of books from unagented writers. Publishes book an average of 8 months after acceptance. Simultaneous submissions OK. Query for electronic submissions. Reports in several months on queries and mss.

Nonfiction: Subjects include politics, current events, sociology, psychology, and science. "We need popular books in the social sciences, sciences and the humanities." Query only.

Recent Nonfiction Title: *Global Alert: The Ozone Pollution Crisis*, by Jack Fishman and Robert Kalish.

Tips: "Our audience consists of intelligent laymen and professionals. Authors should be experts on subject matter of book. They must compare their books with competitive works, explain how theirs differs, and define the market for their books."

POCKET BOOKS, 1230 Avenue of the Americas, New York NY 10020. Imprints include Washington Square Press (high-quality mass market), Archway and Minstrel (juvenile/YA imprints). Publishes paperback originals and reprints, mass market and trade paperbacks and hardcovers. Averages 300 titles/year; receives 750 submissions annually. 15% of books from first-time authors. Pays royalty on retail price. Publishes book an average of 1 year after acceptance. *No unsolicited mss or queries.* "All submissions must go through a literary agent."

Nonfiction: History, biography, reference and general nonfiction, cookbooks, humor, calendars.

Fiction: Adult (mysteries, thriller, psychological suspense, Star Trek ® novels, romance, westerns).

*POLKA-DOT PRESS, (formerly Java Publishing Co.), P.O. Box 25203, Colorado Springs CO 80936. (719)548-1844. Publisher: Bruce Fife. Estab. 1985. Firm publishes hardcover and trade paperback originals and trade paperback reprints. Publishes 3-8 titles/year; receives 40 submissions/year. 70% of books from first-time authors; 100% from unagented writers. Subsidy publishes 10% of books. Pays 5-10% royalty on retail price, or buys ms for $250-5,000 outright. Offers $250 average advance. Publishes book an average of 9 months after acceptance. Simultaneous submissions OK. Reports in 1 month on queries; 2 months on mss. Book catalog of 6×9 SAE and 2 first class stamps; ms guidelines for #10 SASE.

Nonfiction: Biography, how-to, humor, self-help. Subjects include hobbies, recreation, sports, entertainment and performing arts. Submit complete ms. Reviews artwork/photos as part of ms package.

Recent Nonfiction Title: *Strutter's Complete Guide to Clown Makeup*, by Jim Roberts.

Fiction: Humor. Submit complete ms.

*PORCÉPIC BOOKS, 4252 Commerce Circle, Victoria, British Columbia V8Z 4M2 Canada. (604)381-5502. Estab. 1971. Imprints include Softwords and Tesseract Books. Imprint publishes hardcover and trade paperback originals. Averages 5 titles/year; receives 300 submissions annually. 20% of books from first-time authors. 90% of books from unagented writers. Subsidy publishes (nonauthor) 100% of books. Pays 10% royalty on retail price; offers $300-500 advance. Publishes ms an average of 1 year after acceptance. Simultaneous (if so advised) submissions OK. Reports in 1 month on queries; 3 months on mss.

Nonfiction: "Not actively soliciting nonfiction books."

Fiction: Experimental, science fiction and speculative fiction. "We are interested in hearing from new Canadian writers of mainstream or experimental fiction." Press publishes Canadian authors only. Prefer query first, then sample chapters."

Recent Fiction Title: *The Silent City*, edited by Elizabeth Vonarburg.
Tips: "Make sure the manuscript is well written. We see so many mss that only the unique and excellent can't be put down."

PORTER SARGENT PUBLISHERS, INC., Suite 1400, 11 Beacon St., Boston MA 02108. (617)523-1670. FAX: (617)523-1021. Estab. 1914. Publishes hardcover and paperback originals, reprints, translations and anthologies. Averages 4 titles/year. Pays royalty on retail price. "Each contract is dealt with on an individual basis with the author." Book catalog for SASE.
Nonfiction: Reference, special education and academic nonfiction. "Handbook Series and Special Education Series offer standard, definitive reference works in private education and writings and texts in special education. The Extending Horizons Series is an outspoken, unconventional series that presents topics of importance in contemporary affairs and the social sciences." This series is particularly directed to the college adoption market. Accepts nonfiction translations from French and Spanish. Contact: Heather Lane. Send query with brief description, table of contents, sample chapter and information regarding author's background.
Recent Nonfiction Title: *1990 Handbook of Private Schools.*

POTENTIALS DEVELOPMENT FOR HEALTH & AGING SERVICES, 775 Main St., Buffalo NY 14203. (716)842-2658. Publishes paperback originals. Averages 4 titles/year; receives 30-40 submissions annually. 90% of books from first-time authors; 100% of books from unagented writers. Average print order for a writer's first book is 500. Pays 5% royalty on sales of first 3,000 copies; 8% thereafter. Publishes book an average of 1 year after acceptance. Reports in 6 weeks. Book catalog and ms guidelines for #10 SASE.
Nonfiction: "We seek material of interest to those working with elderly people in the community and in institutional settings. We need tested, innovative and practical ideas." Query or submit outline/synopsis and 3 sample chapters to J.A. Elkins. Looks for "suitable subject matter, writing style and organization."
Recent Nonfiction Title: *Messages That Motivate*, by Joan Fox-Rose.
Tips: "The writer has the best chance of selling us materials of interest to those working with elderly people in nursing homes, senior and retirement centers. Our major market is activity directors. Give us good reasons why activity directors would want or need the material submitted."

POTOMAC-PACIFIC PRESS, 5120 Kenwood Drive, Annandale VA 22003. Editor: George Mair. Estab. 1988. Publishes hardcover and trade paperback originals. Firm averages 10-15 titles/year. 20% of books from first-time authors. 100% from unagented writers. Pays royalty on retail price. Simultaneous submissions OK. Reports in 2 weeks on queries.
Nonfiction: Biography, how-to, humor and self-help. Subjects include Americana, business and economics, child guidance/parenting, government/politics, health/medicine, history, psychology, sociology, self-help, and New Age. Query with outline/synopsis. No manuscripts unless invited.
Recent Nonfiction Title: *Personal Power Writing*, by George Briechle (self-improvement/business).

‡PRAEGER PUBLISHERS, Imprint of the Greenwood Publishing Group, Inc., 1 Madison Ave., New York NY 10010. (212)685-5300. FAX: (212)685-0285. General Manager: Ron Chambers. Estab. 1950. Publishes hardcover originals and reprints and trade paperback originals. Averages 240 titles/year. Receives 800 submissions/year. 5% of books from first-time authors; 95% from unagented writers. Pays 6½-15% royalty on retail price. Advance offered varies. Publishes book an average of 9 months after acceptance. Simultaneous submissions OK. Reports in 3 weeks on queries; 6 weeks on mss. Book catalog and manuscript guidelines free on request.
Nonfiction: Biography, reference and textbook. Subjects include business and economics, education, ethnic, government/politics, health/medicine, history, military/war, philosophy, psychology, sociology and women's issues/studies. "We are looking for women's studies, sociology, psychology, education, contemporary history, military studies, political science, business, economics, international relations, philosophy. No language and literature." Query or submit outline/synopsis and sample chapters.
Recent Nonfiction Title: *Panzer Commander*, by Hans VonLuck (military history).

PRAKKEN PUBLICATIONS, INC., P.O. Box 8623, Ann Arbor MI 48107. (313)769-1211. FAX: (313)769-8383. Publisher: George Kennedy. Estab. 1934. Publishes educational hardcover and paperback originals as well as educational magazines. Averages 5 titles/year; receives 50 submissions annually. 50% of books from first-time authors; 100% of books from unagented writers. Pays 10% royalty on net price of book. Publishes book an average of 6 months after acceptance. Simultaneous submissions OK. Reports in 2 weeks on queries; 1 month on mss. Book catalog for #10 SASE.
Nonfiction: General education, vocational and technical education. "We are interested in manuscripts with broad appeal in any of the specific subject areas of the industrial arts, vocational-technical education, and in the general education field." Submit outline/synopsis and sample chapters. Reviews artwork/photos as part of ms package.

Recent Nonfiction Title: *Exploring Solar Energy! Principles and Projects*, by Allan Kaufman.
Tips: "We have a continuing interest in magazine and book manuscripts which reflect emerging policy issues in the field of education, especially vocational, industrial, and technical education."

PRENTICE-HALL CANADA, INC., College Division, Subsidiary of Simon & Schuster, 1870 Birchmount Road, Scarborough, Ontario M1P 2J7 Canada. (416)293-3621. Editorial Director: Cliff Newman. Publishes hardcover and paperback originals and software. Averages 40 titles/year. Receives 200-300 submissions annually. 30-40% of books from first-time authors; 100% of books from unagented writers. Pays 10-15% royalty on net price. Publishes book an average of 14 months after acceptance. Prefer submission on disk (MS DOS) with hard copy accompanying.
Nonfiction: The College Division publishes textbooks suitable for the community college and large university market. Most submissions should be designed for existing courses in all disciplines of study. Will consider software in most disciplines, especially business and sciences. Canadian content is important. The division also publishes books in computer science, technology and mathematics.
Recent Nonfiction Title: *Investment Management in Canada*, by Hatch.
Tips: "Manuscripts of interest to Canadians and/or by authors resident in Canada should be forwarded to above address. All other manuscripts should be sent to Prentice-Hall, Inc., Englewood Office, N.J. 07632."

PRENTICE-HALL CANADA, INC., School Division, Subsidiary of Simon & Schuster, 1870 Birchmount Road, Scarborough, Ontario M1P 2J7 Canada. (416)293-3621. FAX: (416)299-2529. President: Rob Greenaway. Editorial Director: Steve Lane. Estab. 1960. Averages 30 titles annually.
Nonfiction: Publishes texts, workbooks, and instructional media including computer courseware for junior and senior high schools. Subjects include business, computer studies, geography, history, language arts, mathematics, science, social studies, technology, and French as a second language. Query.
Recent Nonfiction Title: *The Law in Canada*, by Barnhorst/Zetzl.

PRENTICE-HALL CANADA, INC., Trade Division, 1870 Birchmount Road, Scarborough, Ontario M1P 2J7 Canada. (416)293-3621. Acquisitions Editor: Tanya Long. Estab. 1960. Publishes hardcover and trade paperback originals. Averages 25-30 titles/year; receives 750-900 submissions annually. 30% of books from first-time authors; 40% of books from unagented writers. Negotiates royalty and advance. Publishes book an average of 9 months after acceptance. Query for electronic submissions. Reports in 10 weeks. Ms guidelines for #10 SAE and 1 IRC.
Nonfiction: Subjects of Canadian and international interest; art, politics and current affairs, sports, business, travel, health and food. Send outline and sample chapters. Reviews artwork/photos as part of ms package.
Recent Nonfiction Title: *The Glory Years: Memories of a Decade 1955-65*, by Billy Harris (sports).
Tips: Needs general interest nonfiction books on topical subjects. "Present a clear, concise thesis, well-argued with a thorough knowledge of existing works. We are looking for more books on social and political issues."

PRENTICE HALL PRESS, Trade Division, 15 Columbus Circle, 15th Flr., New York NY 10023. Publisher: Elizabeth Perle. Publishes nonfiction hardcover and trade paperback originals. Publishes book an average of 10 months after acceptance. Will not consider unsolicited submissions.
Nonfiction: Categories include: literary nonfiction, history, self-help, New Age, psychology, business, health, diet, fitness, cookbooks, gardening, arts, and crafts, design, art architecture, photography, performing arts, travel, sports, nature, equestrian, military and illustrated gift books. Does not publish fiction, poetry, romances, westerns or other fiction genres.
Recent Nonfiction Title: *Art of Our Century*, by Jean-Louis Ferrier.

PREVENTION HEALTH BOOKS, Subsidiary of Rodale Press, Inc., 33 E. Minor St., Emmaus PA 18098. (215)967-5171. Senior Editor: Sharon Faelten. Estab. 1940. Publishes hardcover originals and tradepaperback originals and reprints. Imprint averages 10 titles/year. Receives 300 submissions/year. 25% of books from first-time authors; 10% from unagented writers. Pays 2-15% royalty on retail price; buys mss outright for $2,000-25,000. Offers $15,000 average advance. Publishes book an average of 8 months after acceptance. Simultaneus submissions OK. Query for electronic submissions. Reports in 3 weeks on queries; 6 weeks on mss.
Nonfiction: Cookbook, how-to, self-help, health. Subjects include cooking, foods and nutrition, health/medicine, fitness. "Our needs are innovative health and nutrition books by M.D.'s or other health professionals. No child care and parenting or relationships." Submit outline/synopsis and sample chapters. Reviews artwork/photos as part of ms package.
Recent Nonfiction Title: *The Body-Signal Diet*, by Stephen Strauss, M.D. and Gail North.
Tips: "Our audience is largely women aged 45-65 who are concerned about their health and their spouse's health. Most are pretty well-informed, but not terribly active. Very interested in diet, nutrition, self-care techniques. If I were a writer trying to market a book today, I would make sure I was familiar with what's hot, what's selling well and what's passé."

PRIMA PUBLISHING AND COMMUNICATIONS, Cal Co Am., Inc., P.O. Box 1260, Rocklin CA 95677. (916)624-5718. Publisher: Ben Dominitz. Estab. 1984. Publishes hardcover and trade paperback originals and trade paperback reprints. Publishes 45 titles/year. Receives 500 queries/year. Buys 10% of books from first-time authors; 50% from unagented writers. Pays 15-20% royalty on wholesale price. Advance varies. Publishes books an average of 6-9 months after acceptance. Simultaneous submissions OK. Query for electronic submissions. Reports in 2 months. Catalog for 9 × 12 SAE with $1.25 postage; writer's guidelines for #10 SASE.
Nonfiction: Biography, cookbook, how-to, self-help. Subjects include business and economics, cooking and foods, health, music, politics and psychology. "We want books with originality, written by highly qualified individuals. No fiction at this time." Query.
Recent Nonfiction Title: *Earth Right: What You Can Do in Your Home, Workplace and Community to Save Our Environment*, by H. Patricia Hynes.
Tips: "Prima strives to reach the primary and secondary markets for each of its books. We are known for promoting our books aggressively. Books that genuinely solve problems for people will always do well if properly promoted. Try to picture the intended audience while writing the book. Too many books are written to an audience that doesn't exist."

*PRINCETON ARCHITECTURAL PRESS, 37 East 7th St., New York NY 10003. (212)995-9620. FAX: (212)995-9454. Estab. 1983. Publishes hardcover and trade paperback originals and hardcover reprints. Averages 20 titles/year; receives 50 submissions annually. 50% of books from first-time authors; 100% of books from unagented writers. Subsidy publishes 10% of books; subsidy publishes (nonauthor) 20% of books. Pays 6-10% royalty on wholesale price. Simultaneous submissions OK. Query for electronic submissions. Reports in 1 month. Book catalog and guidelines for 9 × 12 SAE with 3 first class stamps. "Manuscripts will not be returned unless SASE is enclosed."
Nonfiction: Illustrated book and textbook. Subjects include architecture, landscape architecture and design. Needs texts on architecture, landscape architecture, architectural monographs, and texts to accompany a possible reprint, architectural history and urban design. Submit outline/synopsis and sample chapters or complete ms. Reviews artwork/photos as part of ms package.
Recent Nonfiction Title: *Surface and Symbol: Giuseppe Terrazni and the Italian Rationalist Movement*, by Thomas Schumacher.
Tips: "Our audience consists of architects, designers, urban planners, architectural theorists, and architectural-urban design historians, and many academicians and practitioners. We are still focusing on architecture and architectural history but would like to increase our list of books on design."

*PRINCETON BOOK COMPANY, PUBLISHERS, Box 57, Pennington NJ 08534. (609)737-8177. Imprints include Dance Horizons. President: Charles H. Woodford. Publishes hardcover originals, trade paperback originals and reprints. Firm averages 15 titles/year. Receives 100 submissions/year. 25% of books from first-time authors. 100% from unagented writers. Pays 10% royalty on wholesale price. Publishes book an average of 10 months after acceptance. Simultaneous submissions OK. Reports in 2 weeks on queries; 1 month on mss. Free book catalog.
Nonfiction: Biography, coffee table book, how-to, reference, self-help and textbook. Subjects include education, health/medicine, dance, recreation, sociology, sports and women's issues/studies. "We're looking for textbooks in the fields of dance, physical education, and general education. No autobiographies or special-interest books in dance that have no possibility for use as college texts." Query or submit outline/synopsis and sample chapters. Reviews artwork/photos as part of manuscript package.
Recent Nonfiction Title: *People Who Dance*, by John Gruen (dance trade book).
Tips: "Books that have appeal to both trade and text markets are of most interest to us. Our audience is made up of dance professors, students and professionals. If I were a writer trying to market a book today, I would write with a clear notion of the market in mind. Don't produce a manuscript without first considering what is needed in your field."

PRINCETON UNIVERSITY PRESS, 41 William St., Princeton NJ 08540. (609)258-4900. FAX: (609)258-6305. Imprints include Bollingen Series. Editor-in-Chief: Emily Wilkinson.Estab. 1890. Publishes hardcover and trade paperback originals and reprints. Averages 265 titles/year. Receives 10,800 submissions/year. Receives 50% of books from first-time authors. 99% from unagented writers. Pays 10% of net receipts. Publishes book an average of 1 year after acceptance. Simultaneous submissions OK. Query for electronic submission. Reports in 2 weeks on queries; 1 month on mss. Book catalog and manuscript guidelines free on request.
Nonfiction: Biography, reference, technical, and scholarly works. Subjects include art/architecture, history, language/literature, music/dance, nature/environment, philosophy, religion, science, translation, and women's issues/studies. "The books we publish all undergo a process of review by scholarly experts." Query only. Reviews artwork/photos as part of ms package.
Recent Nonfiction Title: *Prospects for Faculty in the Arts and Sciences*, by William G. Bowen and Julie Ann Sosa.

PROFESSIONAL PUBLICATIONS, INC., 1250 5th Ave., Belmont CA 94002. (415)593-9119. FAX: (415)592-4519. Acquisitions Editor: Wendy Nelson. Estab. 1975. Publishes hardcover and paperback originals. Averages 6 titles/year; receives 20-50 submissions annually. Pays 8-12% royalty on wholesale price; offers $1,000 average advance. Sometimes makes outright purchase for $1,000-2,000. Publishes book an average of 6-18 months after acceptance. Simultaneous submissions OK. Query for electronic submissions. Reports in 2 weeks on queries; 1 month on mss. Free book catalog.

Nonfiction: Reference, technical and textbook. Subjects include business and economics, mathematics, engineering, accounting, architecture, contracting and building. Especially needs "licensing examination review books for general contractors and lawyers." Query or submit outline/synopsis and sample chapters or complete ms. Reviews artwork/photos as part of ms package.

Recent Nonfiction Title: *Sample Building and Site Design Exam Problems*, by David Ballast.

Tips: "We specialize in books for working professionals: engineers, architects, contractors, accountants, etc. The more technically complex the manuscript is the happier we are. We love equations, tables of data, complex illustrations, mathematics, etc. In technical/professional book publishing, it isn't always obvious to us if a market exists. We can judge the quality of a ms, but the author should make some effort to convince us that a market exists. Facts, figures, and estimates about the market—and marketing ideas from the author—will help sell us on the work. Besides our interest in highly technical materials, we will be trying to broaden our range of titles in each discipline. Specifically, we will be looking for career guides for accountants and architects, as well as for engineers."

‡PSI RESEARCH, 300 North Valley Dr., Grants Pass OR 97526. (503)479-9464. Subsidiaries include The Oasis Press. Acquisitions Editor: Phyllis Fox-Krupp. Firm publishes hardcover, trade paperback and binder originals. Publishes 20-30 books/year; receives 90 submissions/year. 25% from first-time authors; 90% from unagented writers. Pays royalty. Publishes ms an average of 6-12 months after acceptance. Simultaneous submissions OK. Reports in 2 weeks (initial feedback). Free book catalog.

Nonfiction: How-to, reference, self-help, textbook. Subjects include business and economics, computers and electronics, education, money/finance, retirement, exporting, franchise, finance, marketing and public relations, relocations. Needs information-heavy, readable manuscripts written by professionals in their subject fields. Interactive where appropriate. Authorship credentials much less important than hands-on experience qualifications. Must relate to either small business or to individuals who are entrepreneurs, owners or managers of small business (1-300 employees). Query for unwritten material or to check current interest in topic and orientation. Submit outline/synopsis and sample chapters. Reviews artwork/photos as part of freelance ms package.

Recent Nonfiction Title: *How to Write Your Own Business Contracts*, by E. Thorpe Barrett (how-to business).

Tips: "Best chance is with practical, step-by-step manuals for operating a business, with worksheets, checklists. The audience is made up of entrepreneurs of all types: small businesses and those who would like to be; attorneys, accountants and consultants who work with small businesses; college students; dreamers. Make sure your information is valid and timely for its audience, also that by virtue of either its content quality or viewpoint, it distinguishes itself from other books on the market."

PURDUE UNIVERSITY PRESS, South Campus Courts, Bldg. D, West Lafayette IN 47907. (317)494-2035. Editor: Margaret Hunt. Publishes hardcover and trade paperback originals and trade paperback reprints. Averages 6 titles/year; receives 100 submissions annually. Pays 10% royalty on retail price. No advance. Publishes book an average of 15 months after acceptance. Reports in 2 months on mss. Book catalog and ms guidelines for SASE.

Nonfiction: Biography, textbook, scholarly and regional. Subjects include Americana (especially Indiana), business and economics, history, philosophy, politics, religion, sociology, theories of biology and literary criticism. "The writer must present good credentials, demonstrate good writing skills, and above all explain how his/her work will make a significant contribution to scholarship/regional studies. Our purpose is to publish scholarly and regional books. We are looking for manuscripts on these subjects: theory of biography, Balkan and Danubian history, interdisciplinary, regional interest, horticulture, history, literature, philosophy, criticism, and effects of science and technology on society. No cookbooks, nonbooks, textbooks, theses/dissertations, manuals/pamphlets, or books on how-to, fitness/exercise or fads." Submit complete ms. Reviews artwork/photos as part of ms package.

Recent Nonfiction Title: *In a Dark Time: The Apocalyptic Temper in the American Novel of the Nuclear Age*, by Joseph Dewey.

Tips: "Scholarly publishers are gearing books in the humanities especially toward the educated layperson so as to widen their audiences, make academic knowledge more accessible, and increase sales. If I were a writer trying to market a book today, I would show a press why publishing my book would help them meet their own long-term goals."

Q.E.D. INFORMATION SCIENCES, INC., 170 Linden St., Box 181, Wellesley MA 02181. (617)237-5656. FAX: (617)235-0826. Executive Vice President: Edwin F. Kerr. Publishes computer books, reports and journals for MIS professionals. Averages 30 titles/year. Pays 10-15% royalty on net sales. Publishes book an average of

4-6 months after acceptance. Query for electronic submissions. Preliminary reports in 1 week on queries; 3 weeks on mss. Free book catalog.

Nonfiction: Technical. Subjects include computers, systems development, personal computing, and database technology. "Our books are read by data processing managers and technicians." Submit outline/synopsis and 2 sample chapters. Reviews artwork/photos as part of ms package.

Recent Nonfiction Title: *DOS/USE SP Guide for Systems Programming*, by Leo Langenin.

*Q.E.D. PRESS OF ANN ARBOR, INC., Suite 112, 1008 Island Drive Ct., Ann Arbor MI 48105-2025. (313)994-0371. Managing Editor: Dan Fox. Publishes hardcover and trade paperback originals. Publishes 7 titles/year. Receives 300 submissions/year. 60% of books from first-time authors; 75% from unagented writers. Pays 6-10% royalty on retail price. Publishes book an average of 4 months after acceptance. Simultaneous submissions OK. Query for electronic submissions. Subsidy publishes "if the book might not be easily marketable to begin with and we would like to publish it at this point in time but budgetary constraints make it difficult; the option would be we will pick up the tab for reprints." Reports in 5 months on queries.

Nonfiction: How-to. Subjects include art/architecture, music/dance (classical, how to set up a studio, piano-related topics), literary criticism, philosophy (existentialism, theory of tragedy). "Music criticism and teaching are high on the list with literary criticism following a close second. How-to and informational books are welcome as well as books about computer technology and in particular, desk-top publishing." Query or submit outline/synopsis.

Recent Nonfiction Title: *Beyond Mystery: A New Look at the Old Testament and Vice Versa*.

Fiction: Literary. Query or submit outline/synopsis.

Recent Fiction Title: *Half Dozen Dutch: Six Writers-in-Residence at American Universities*, edited by Ton Broos.

Tips: "How-to books, informational books and books about computers (desk-top publishing) technology have the best chance of being sold to us. Our audience consists of university professors, local university bookstores, college students, artists and intellectuals. We're looking for books for targeted audience where a small press can better compete with bigger, established publishers."

QUE CORPORATION, 11711 N. College Ave., Carmel IN 46032. (317)573-2500. Executive Editor/Acquisitions: Terrie Lynn Solomon. Estab. 1983. Publishes tutorials and application books on popular business software, and trade paperback originals, programming languages and systems and technical books. Receives 500 submissions/year. 80% of books from first-time authors; 90% of books from unagented writers. Pays 2-15% escalating royalty on net price. Many work-for-hire titles are paid a flat fee. Publishes book an average of 4 months after acceptance. Simultaneous (if so advised) submissions OK. Reports in 1 month. Free book catalog.

Nonfiction: How-to, technical, and reference books relating to microcomputers; textbooks on business use of microcomputers; software user's guides and tutorials; operating systems user's guides; computer programming language reference works; books on microcomputer systems, spreadsheet software business applications, word processing, data base management, time management, popular computer programs for the home, computer graphics, networking, communications, languages, educational uses of microcomputers, computer-assisted instruction in education and business and course-authoring applications. "We will consider books on specific subjects relating to microcomputers." Query or submit outline/synopsis and sample chapters. Reviews artwork/photos as part of ms package.

Recent Nonfiction Title: *Using DOS*, by QUE Corporation.

QUILL, Imprint of William Morrow and Co., Inc., Subsidiary of The Hearst Corporation, 105 Madison Ave., New York NY 10016. (212)889-3050. Editor: Andrew Dutter. Publishes trade paperback originals and reprints. Averages 40 titles/year; receives over 2,000 submissions annually. 40% of books from first-time authors; 5% of books from unagented writers. Pays royalty on retail price. Offers variable advance. Publishes ms an average of 1 year after acceptance. Simultaneous submissions OK. No unsolicited mss or proposals; mss and proposals should be submitted through a literary agent. Reports in 3 months.

Nonfiction: Biography and trade books. Subjects include history, music, psychology, science, light reference and puzzles and games. Needs nonfiction trade paperbacks with enduring importance; books that have backlist potential and appeal to educated people with broad intellectual curiosities. No fiction, poetry, fitness, diet, how-to, self-help or humor. Query.

Recent Nonfiction Title: *How to Make the World a Better Place*, by Jeffrey Hollender.

RAINBOW BOOKS, Box 1069, Moore Haven FL 33471. (813)946-0293. Associate Editor: B. A. Lampe. Publishes hardcover, trade paperback originals, video (VHS) and audio tapes. Averages 10-20 titles/year; receives 600 submissions annually. 70% of books from first-time authors; 50% of books from unagented writers. Publishes book an average of 8 months after acceptance. Reports in 2 weeks on queries. Book catalog for 6×9 SAE and 3 first class stamps; ms guidelines for #10 SAE and 2 first class stamps.

Nonfiction: Reference, self-help, how-to and resource books. Prefer query first on all books.
Recent Nonfiction Title: *The Food Bible*, by Jane Benkendorf.
Tips: "We may be interested in seeing good fiction. However, by query letter and synopsis only please. We are always interested in seeing good reference and resource books. Please query with what you have before sending it along. No materials returned without proper postage and mailer."

*R&E PUBLISHERS, P.O. Box 2008, Saratoga CA 95070. (408)866-6303. FAX: (408)866-0825. Publisher: R. Reed. Estab. 1966. Hardcover and trade paperback originals. Averages 30 titles/year. Receives 300 submissions/year. 80% of books from first-time authors. 80% from unagented writers. Subsidy publishes 5% of books. Pays 10-20% on wholesale price. Publishes book an average of 6 months after acceptance. Simultaneous submissions OK. Query for electronic submissions. Reports in 2 months. Free book catalog and manuscript guidelines.
Nonfiction: How-to, humor, illustrated book, reference, self-help, software, technical and textbook. Subjects include business and economics, child guidance/parenting, computers and electronics, cooking, foods and nutrition, education, ethnic, government/politics, health/medicine, history, money/finance, music/dance, nature/environment, philosophy, psychology, regional, science, sociology, travel and women's issues/studies. Query or submit outline/synopsis and sample chapters. Reviews artwork as part of package.
Recent Nonfiction Title: *The Mourning After: Managing Grief Wisely*, by Stanley Cornils.

RANDOM HOUSE, INC., Subsidary of Advance Publications, 201 E. 50th St., 11th Floor, New York NY 10022. (212)572-2600. Random House Trade Division publishes 120 titles/year; receives 3,000 submissions annually. Imprints include Vintage, Villard, Times, and Random House Reference. Pays royalty on retail price. Simultaneous submissions OK. Reports in 3 weeks on queries; 6 weeks on mss. Free book catalog; ms guidelines for #10 SASE.
Nonfiction: Biography, cookbook, humor, illustrated book, self-help. Subjects include Americana, art, business and economics, cooking and foods, health, history, music, nature, politics, psychology, religion, sociology and sports. No juveniles or textbooks (separate division). Query with outline/synopsis and at least 3 sample chapters.
Fiction: Adventure, confession, experimental, fantasy, historical, horror, humor, mainstream, mystery, and suspense. Submit outline/synopsis and at least 3 sample chapters. "SASE is helpful."
Tips: "If I were a writer trying to market a book today, I would get an agent."

RANDOM HOUSE, INC./ALFRED A. KNOPF, INC. JUVENILE BOOKS, 225 Park Ave. S., New York NY 10003. (212)572-2653. Subsidiaries include Knopf Children's Books, Knopf Children's Paperbacks (Bullseye Books, Dragonfly Books and Borzoi Sprinters), Random House Children's Books, Crown Children's Books. Juvenile Division: J. Schulman, Publisher. Managing Editor: R. Abend. Alfred A. Knopf: S. Spinner, Executive Editor. Random House Juvenile: S. Spinner. Kay Ross, Editor-in-Chief. Firm publishes hardcover, trade paperback and mass market paperback originals, and mass market paperback reprints. Publishes 250 titles/year. Simultaneous submissions OK.
Nonfiction: Biography, humor, illustrated book, juvenile. Subjects include animals, nature/environment, recreation, science, sports. Query or submit outline/synopsis and sample chapters. Submit ms through agent only.
Recent Nonfiction Title: *The Random House Book of 1001 Wonders of Science*, by Brian Brendan Williams.
Fiction: Adventure, confession (young adult), fantasy, historical, horror, humor, juvenile, mystery, picture books, science fiction (juvenile/young adult), suspense, young adult. Submit through agent only.
Recent Fiction Title: *Oh, the Places You'll Go!*, by Dr. Seuss.
Tips: Books for children 6 months to 15 years old.

‡REFERENCE SERVICE PRESS, Suite 9, 1100 Industrial Rd., San Carlos CA 94070. (415)594-0743. FAX: (415)594-0411. Acquisitions Editor: Stuart Hauser. Publishes hardcover originals. Firm averages 5 titles/year. 100% of books from unagented writers. Pays 10% or higher royalty. Publishes book an average of 3-6 months after acceptance. Simultaneous submissions OK. Query for electronic submissions. Reports in 1 week on queries; 3 weeks on mss. Book catalog for #10 SASE.
Nonfiction: Reference. Subjects include education, ethnic, military/war, women's issues/studies and disabled. We are interested only in directories and monographs dealing with financial aid. Submit outline/synopsis and sample chapters.
Recent Nonfiction Title: *Financial Aid for the Disabled & Their Families*, by Schlachter and Weber (directory).
Tips: Our audience consists of librarians, counselors, researchers, students, reentry women, scholars and other fundseekers.

‡REGAL BOOKS, Division of Gospel Light Publications, 2300 Knoll Dr., Ventura CA 93003. FAX: (805)644-4729. Managing Director, Acquisitions: Linda Holland. Publishes hardcover and paperback originals. Averages 25 titles/year. Receives 5,000 submissions annually. 20% of books from first-time authors; 90% of books from unagented writers. Average print order for writer's first book is 5,000. Pays 15% net royalty on paperback titles, 10% net for curriculum books. Publishes book an average of 11 months after acceptance. Buys all rights. Reports in 3 months. Book catalog and ms guidelines for 9 × 12 SAE and 8 first class stamps.

Nonfiction: Bible studies (Old and New Testament), Christian living, counseling (self-help), contemporary concerns, evangelism (church growth), marriage and family, youth, inspirational/devotional, communication resources, teaching enrichment resources, Bible commentary for Laymen Series, and missions. Query or submit detailed outline/synopsis and 2-3 sample chapters; no complete mss.

Recent Nonfiction Title: *Always Daddy's Girl*, by H. Norman Wright.

REGNERY/GATEWAY, INC., Suite 600, 1130 17th St., N.W., Washington DC 20036. Imprints/divisions include The American Citizen Reader's Catalog, Cahill and Co., Gateway Editions. Editor: Harry Crocker. Estab. 1947. Publishes hardcover and paperback originals and paperback reprints. Averages 25 titles/year. Pays royalty. "Responds only to submissions in which we have interest."

Nonfiction: Politics, classics. Queries preferred. Looks for "expertise of the author and salability of the proposed work."

Recent Nonfiction Title: *The Hollow Men: Politics 2nd Corruption in Higher Education*, by Charles J. Sykes.

RELIGIOUS EDUCATION PRESS, 5316 Meadow Brook Rd., Birmingham AL 35242. (205)991-1000. Editor: James Michael Lee. Estab. 1974. Publishes trade paperback and hardback originals. Averages 5 titles/year; receives 280 submissions annually. 40% of books from first-time authors; 100% of books from unagented writers. Pays 10% royalty on actual selling price. "Many of our books are work for hire. We do not have a subsidy option." Offers no advance. Query for electronic submissions. Reports 2 months. Free book catalog.

Nonfiction: Technical and textbook. Scholarly subjects on religion and religious education. "We publish serious, significant and scholarly books on religious education and pastoral ministry." No mss under 200 pages, no poetry, books on Biblical interpretation, or "popular" books. Query. Reviews artwork/photos as part of ms package.

Recent Nonfiction Title: *Handbook of Faith*, by James Michael Lee.

Tips: "Write clearly, reason exactly and connectively, and meet deadlines."

*RESOURCE PUBLICATIONS, INC., Suite 290, 160 E. Virginia St., San Jose CA 95112. Editorial Director: Kenneth E. Guentert. Publishes paperback originals. Publishes 14 titles/year; receives 100-200 submissions annually. 30% of books from first-time authors; 99% of books from unagented writers. Average print order for a writer's first book is 2,000. Subsidy publishes 10% of books. "If the author can present and defend a personal publicity effort or otherwise demonstrate demand and the work is in our field, we will consider it." Pays 8% royalty; occasionally offers advance in the form of books. Publishes book an average of 18 months after acceptance. Query for electronic submissions. Reports in 2 months.

Nonfiction: "We look for imaginative but practical books relating to celebration, professional growth, and spirituality. How-to books, especially for contemporary religious art forms, are of particular interest (dance, mime, drama, choral reading, singing, music, musicianship, bannermaking, statuary, or any visual art form). No heavy theoretical, philosophical, or theological tomes. Query or submit outline/synopsis and sample chapters. "Prepare a clear outline of the work and an ambitious schedule of public appearances to help make it known and present both as a proposal to the publisher. With our company a work that can be serialized or systematically excerpted in our periodicals is always given special attention." Accepts translations. Reviews artwork/photos as part of ms package.

Recent Nonfiction Title: *Symbols For All Seasons*, by Katherine Krier.

Fiction: "We are not interested in novels or collections of short stories in the usual literary sense. But we look for storytelling resources and collections of short works in the area of drama, dance, song, and visual art, especially if related to worship celebrations, festivals, or mythology." Query or submit outline/synopsis and sample chapters.

Tips: "Books that provide readers with practical, usable suggestions and ideas pertaining to worship, celebration, education, and the arts have the best chance of selling to our firm. We've moved more clearly into the celebration resources field and are looking for resources on popular—as well as little known—celebrations, feasts, and rituals to complement our strong backlist of worship resources."

REVIEW AND HERALD PUBLISHING ASSOCIATION, 55 West Oak Ridge Dr., Hagerstown MD 21740. Acquisitions Editor: Penny Estes Wheeler. Publishes hardcover and paperback originals. Specializes in religious-oriented books. Averages 30-40 titles/year; receives 300 submissions annually. 15% of books from first-time authors; 100% of books from unagented writers. Average print order for a writer's first book is 5,000-7,500. Pays 14% of retail price, hardcover; 12% of retail price, softcover; offers average $500 advance. Publishes book an average of 1 year after acceptance. Encourages computer submissions by disk. Reports in 3 months. Free brochure; ms guidelines for SASE.

Nonfiction: Juveniles (religious-oriented only), nature, and religious, all 20,000-60,000 words; 128 pages average. Query or submit outline/synopsis and 2-3 sample chapters. Prefers to do own illustrating. Looks for "literary style, constructive tone, factual accuracy, compatibility with Adventist theology and lifestyle, and length of manuscript." Reviews artwork/photos as part of ms package.

Recent Nonfiction Title: *Making of a Mother*, by Caren Spruill.
Recent Fiction Title: *Zipporah*, by Lois Erickson.
Tips: "Familiarize yourself with Adventist theology because Review and Herald Publishing Association is owned and operated by the Seventh-day Adventist Church. We are accepting fewer but better-written manuscripts."

THE RIVERDALE COMPANY, INC., PUBLISHERS, P.O. Box 10, Glenn Dale MD 20769. (301)474-0445. President: John Adams. Vice President: Adele Adams. Editor: Mary Power. Estab. 1984. Publishes hardcover originals. Averages 16-18 titles/year; receives 100 submissions annually. 20% of books from first-time authors; 100% of books from unagented writers. Pays 0-15% royalty on wholesale price. Publishes book an average of 8 months after acceptance. Reports in 1 week on queries; 2 months on mss. Book catalog for SASE.
Nonfiction: "We publish technical and social science books for scholars, students, policymakers; and tour, restaurant and recreational guides for the mass market." Subjects include economics, history, humanities, politics, psychology, sociology and travel. Especially needs social science and travel mss on South Asia or Africa. Will consider college text proposals in economics and Third World studies; travel guides of any sort. Query. Accepts outline/synopsis and 2-3 sample chapters.
Recent Nonfiction Title: *A Woman's Guide to Carefree Travel Abroad*, by Joanne Turpin.

ROCKY TOP PUBLICATIONS, Subsidiary of Rocky Top Industries, P.O. Box 33, Stamford NY 12167. President/Publisher: Joseph D. Jennings. Estab. 1982. Publishes hardcover and paperback originals. Averages 4-6 titles/year. 70% of books from first-time authors; 95% of books from unagented writers. Pays 4-10% royalty (may vary) on wholesale price. Publishes book an average of 6 months after acceptance. No unsolicited mss!
Nonfiction: How-to, reference, self-help and technical. Subjects include animal health, health, hobbies (crafts), medical, nature, philosophy (Thoreau or environmental only) and science. No autobiographies, biographies, business "get rich quick" or fad books.
Recent Nonfiction Title: *Isolation*, by Emerson Bach.
Tips: "No unsolicited manuscripts."

*RONIN PUBLISHING INC., Box 1035, Berkeley CA 94701. (415)540-6278. Publisher: Sebastian Orfal. Publishes originals and trade paperback reprints. Averages 6-8 titles/year; mostly repackaged previously published books.
Nonfiction: How-to (business), humor, 20th century visionaries. Subjects include business and psychology (psychoactive). Query.
Recent Nonfiction Title: *Drug Testing at Work: A Guide for Employers & Employees*, by Potter and Orfalé.

THE ROSEN PUBLISHING GROUP, 29 E. 21st St., New York NY 10010. (212)777-3017. President: Roger Rosen. Imprints include Pelion Press (music titles). Publishes hardcover originals. Entire firm averages 46 titles/year; young adult division averages 35 titles/year. 45% of books from first-time authors; 80% of books from unagented writers. Pays royalty or makes outright purchase. Publishes book an average of 9 months after acceptance. Simultaneous submissions OK. Reports in 1 month. Book catalog and guidelines for 9 × 12 SAE with 3 first class stamps.
Nonfiction: Young adult, reference, self-help and textbook. Subjects include art, health (coping), and music. "Our books are geared to the young adult audience whom we reach via school and public libraries. Most of the books we publish are related to career guidance and personal adjustment. We also publish material on music and art, as well as journalism for schools. Interested in supplementary material for enrichment of school curriculum. We have begun a high/low division and are interested in material that is supplementary to the curriculum written at a 4 reading level for teenagers who are reluctant readers." Mss in the young adult nonfiction areas include vocational guidance, personal and social adjustment, journalism. For Pelion Press, mss on classical music, emphasis on opera and singing. Query or submit outline/synopsis and sample chapters. Reviews artwork/photos as part of ms package.
Recent Nonfiction Title: *Coping with Sexual Abuse*, by Judith Cooney.
Tips: "The writer has the best chance of selling our firm a book on vocational guidance or personal social adjustment, or high-interest, low reading level material for teens."

ROSS BOOKS, P.O. Box 4340, Berkeley CA 94704. FAX: (415)841-2695. President: Franz Ross. Estab. 1979. Publishes hardcover and paperback originals, paperback reprints, and software. Averages 7-10 titles/year; receives 200 submissions annually. 90% of books from first-time authors; 99% of books from unagented writers. Average print order for a writer's first book is 5,000-10,000. Offers 8-12% royalty on net price.

For information on book publishers' areas of interest, see the nonfiction and fiction sections in the Book Publishers Subject Index.

Offers average advance of 2% of the first print run. Publishes book an average of 1 year after acceptance. Simultaneous submissions OK. Query for electronic submissions. Reports in 1 month. Book catalog for 6×9 SAE with 2 first class stamps.

Nonfiction: Popular how-to on science, business, general how-to. No political, religious or children's books. Accepts nonfiction translations. Submit outline or synopsis of no more than 3 pages and 1 sample chapter with SASE. Reviews artwork/photos as part of ms package.

Recent Nonfiction Title: *Holography Marketplace 2nd Edition*, edited by F. Ross, E. Yerkes.

Tips: "We are looking for books on holography and desktop publishing."

ROXBURY PUBLISHING CO., P.O. Box 491044, Los Angeles CA 90049. (213)653-1068. Executive Editor: Claude Teweles. Publishes hardcover and paperback originals and reprints. Averages 10 titles/year. Pays royalty. Simultaneous submissions OK. Reports in 2 months.

Nonfiction: College-level textbooks only. Subjects include business and economics, humanities, speech, English, developmental studies, social sciences and sociology. Query, submit outline/synopsis and sample chapters, or submit complete ms.

Recent Nonfiction Title: *The Writing Cycle*, by Clela Allphin-Hoggatt.

RUTGERS UNIVERSITY PRESS, 109 Church St., New Brunswick NJ 08901. FAX: (201)932-7039. Averages 70 titles/year; receives 600 submissions annually. 30% of books from first-time authors; 80% of books from unagented writers. Average print order for a writer's first book is 2,000. Publishes book an average of 1 year after acceptance. Query for electronic submissions. Final decision depends on time required to secure competent professional reading reports. Book catalog and ms guidelines for 9×12 SAE with 4 first class stamps.

Nonfiction: Scholarly books in history, literary criticism, film studies, art history, anthropology, sociology, science, technology, women's studies and criminal justice. Regional nonfiction must deal with mid-Atlantic region. Length: 60,000 words minimum. Query. Reviews artwork/photos as part of ms package.

Recent Nonfiction Title: *Covering the Plague: AIDS and the American Media*, by James Kinsella.

RUTLEDGE HILL PRESS, 513 Third Ave. S, Nashville TN 37210. (615)244-2700. FAX: (615)244-2978. President: Lawrence Stone. Vice President: Ron Pitkin. Estab. 1982. Publishes hardcover and trade paperback originals and reprints. Averages 25 titles/year; receives 300 submissions annually. 40% of books from first-time authors; 90% of books from unagented writers. Pays 10-20% royalty on wholesale price. Publishes book an average of 1 year after acceptance. Reports in 6 weeks on queries; 3 months on mss. Book catalog for 9×12 SAE and 3 first class stamps.

Nonfiction: Biography, coffee table, cookbook, humor, reference and self-help. "The book must have an identifiable market, preferably one that is geographically limited." Submit outline/synopsis and sample chapters. Reviews artwork/photos as part of ms package.

Recent Nonfiction Title: *Great Stories of the American Revolution*, by Webb Garrison.

ST. ANTHONY MESSENGER PRESS, 1615 Republic St., Cincinnati OH 45210. FAX: (513)241-0399. Editor-in-Chief: The Rev. Norman Perry, O.F.M. Managing Editor: Lisa Biedenbach. Estab. 1970. Publishes paperback originals. Averages 14 titles/year; receives 250 submissions annually. 10% of books from first-time authors; 100% of books from unagented writers. Pays 10-12% royalty on net receipts of sales. Offers $600 average advance. Publishes book an average of 1 year after acceptance. Books are sold in bulk to groups (study clubs, high school or college classes, and parishes) and in bookstores. No simultaneous submissions. Query for electronic submissions. Book catalog and ms guidelines for 9×12 SAE with 2 first-class stamps.

Nonfiction: Religion. "We try to reach the Catholic market with topics near the heart of the ordinary Catholic's belief. We want to offer insight and inspiration and thus give people support in living a Christian life in a pluralistic society. We are not interested in an academic or abstract approach. Our emphasis is on popular writing with examples, specifics, color and anecdotes." Length: 25,000-40,000 words. Query or submit outline and 2 sample chapters. Reviews artwork/photos as part of ms package.

Recent Nonfiction Title: *Why Be Catholic? Understanding Our Experience and Tradition*, by Richard Rohr and Joseph Martos.

Tips: "We are looking for aids to parish ministry, prayer, spirituality, scripture, liturgy and the sacraments. Also, we are seeking manuscripts that deal with the Catholic identity—explaining it, identifying it, understanding it. The book cannot be the place for the author to think through a subject. The author has to think through the subject first and then tell the reader what is important to know. Style uses anecdotes, examples, illustrations, human interest, 'colorful' quotes, fiction techniques of suspense, dialogue, characterization, etc. Address practical problems, deal in concrete situations, free of technical terms and professional jargon."

*ST. LUKE'S PRESS, Division of The Wimmer Companies, 4210 B.F. Goodrich Blvd., Memphis TN 38118. (901)362-8923. FAX: (901)795-9806. Director: Phyllis Tickle, Averages 8-10 titles/year; receives 3,000 submissions annually. 90% of books from unagented writers. Average print order for a writer's first book is 5,000.

Pays 10% minimum royalty on monies received; offers average $1,000-5,000 advance. Publishes book an average of 2 years after acceptance. Reports in 3 months. Book catalog $1.
Recent Nonfiction Title: *At the River I Stand*, by Joan Turner Beifuss.
Fiction: Submit story line and 3 sample chapters.

ST. MARTIN'S PRESS, 175 5th Ave., New York NY 10010. Averages 1,100 titles/year; receives 3,000 submissions annually. 15-20% of books from first-time authors; 30% of books from unagented writers. Query for electronic submissions. Reports "promptly."
Nonfiction and Fiction: General and textbook. Publishes general fiction and nonfiction; major interest in adult fiction and nonfiction, history, self-help, political science, popular science, biography, scholarly, popular reference, etc. Query. Reviews artwork/photos as part of ms package. "It takes very persuasive credentials to prompt us to commission a book or outline."
Recent Title: *Hot Flashes*, by Barbara Raskin.
Tips: "We do almost every kind of book there is—trade, textbooks, reference and mass market. Crime fiction has the best chance of selling to our firm—over fifteen percent of all the trade books we published are this category."

ST. PAUL BOOKS AND MEDIA, Daughters of St. Paul, 50 St. Paul's Ave., Boston MA 02130. (617)522-8911. FAX: (617)522-4081. Director, Editorial Department: Sister Christine Robert, FSP. Firm publishes hardcover, trade paperback originals, and reprints. Average 20 titles/year; receives approximately 900 proposals/year. Pays authors 7-12% royalty on net sales. Publishes ms an average of 2-3 years after acceptance. Reports in 1 month on queries; in 2 months on mss. Book catalog free; ms guidelines for #10 SASE.
Nonfiction: Biography, juvenile, self-help. Subjects include child guidance/parenting, devotionals, psychology and religion. "No strictly secular manuscripts." Query or submit outline/synopsis and 2-3 sample chapters.
Recent Nonfiction Title: *Becoming Prayer*, by J.P. Dubois-Dumee.
Fiction: Juvenile, religious, young adult. "We want books promoting moral values for children, adolescents and young adults." Query or submit outline/synopsis and 2-3 sample chapters.
Tips: "We are looking for books with a religious and/or moral orientation. No New Age."

*ST. VLADIMIR'S SEMINARY PRESS, 575 Scarsdale Rd., Crestwood NY 10707. (914)961-8313. Managing Director: Theodore Bazil. Publishes hardcover and trade paperback originals and reprints. Averages 15 titles/year. Subsidy publishes 20% of books. Market considerations determine whether an author should be subsidy published. Pays 7% royalty on retail price. Simultaneous and photocopied submissions OK. Computer printout submissions acceptable; prefers letter-quality. Reports in 3 months on queries; 9 months on mss. Free book catalog and ms guidelines.
Nonfiction: Religion dealing with Eastern Orthodox theology. Query. Reviews artwork/photos as part of ms package.
Tips: "We have an interest in books that stand on firm theological ground; careful writing and scholarship are basic."

SAN FRANCISCO PRESS, INC., Box 6800, San Francisco CA 94101-6800. (415)524-1000. President: Terry Gabriel. Publishes hardcover originals and trade paperback originals and reprints. Averages 5-10 titles/year. Receives 25-50 submissions/year. 50% of books from first-time authors. 100% from unagented writers. Pays 10-15% on wholesale price. Publishes book an average of 6 months after acceptance. Simultaneous submissions OK. Reports in 1 month on queries; 2 weeks on mss. Book catalog for #10 SAE and 1 first-class stamp.
Nonfiction: Biography, technical and college textbook. Subjects include computers and electronics, education, government/politics, history, music and science. Submit outline/synopsis and sample chapters.
Recent Nonfiction Title: *Inventing for Fun and Profit*, by Jacob Rabinow.
Tips: "Our books are aimed at specialized audiences (e.g., engineers, public health specialists, scholars, college students)."

SANDHILL CRANE PRESS, INC., P.O. Box 1702-100, Gainesville FL 32602. (904)371-9858. FAX: (904)377-7811. Imprints include Flora & Fauna Publicaltions and Natural Science Publiclations. Publisher: Ross H. Arnett, Jr. Estab. 1947. Publishes hardcover and trade paperback originals. Entire firm publishes 350 annually; imprint averages 10-12 titles/year; receives 70 submissions annually. 50% of books from first-time authors; 100% of books from unagented writers. Average print order for a writer's first book is 500. Pays 10% royalty on list price; negotiable advance. Publishes book an average of 1 year after acceptance. Query for electronic submissions. Reports in 2 weeks on queries; 3 months on mss.
Nonfiction: Reference, technical, textbook and directories. Subjects include plants and animals (for amateur and professional biologists), and natural history. Looking for "books dealing with kinds of plants and animals, new nature guide series underway. No nature stories or 'Oh My' nature books." Query with outline and 2 sample chapters. Reviews artwork/photos as part of ms package.

Recent Nonfiction Title: *Biogeography of the West Indies*, by Charles A. Woods.

Tips: "Well-documented books, especially those that fit into one of our series, have the best chance of selling to our firm—biology, natural history, no garden books."

SANDLAPPER PUBLISHING, INC., Box 1932, Orangeburg SC 29116. (803)531-1658. Acquisitions: Frank N. Handal. Publishes hardcover and trade paperback originals and reprints. Averages 6 titles/year; receives 200 submissions annually. 80% of books from first-time authors; 95% of books from unagented writers. Pays 15% maximum royalty on net receipts. Publishes book on average of 20 months after acceptance. Simultaneous submissions OK if informed. Reports in 1 month on queries; 6 months on mss. Book catalog and ms guidelines for 9 × 12 SAE with 4 first class stamps.

Nonfiction: History, biography, illustrated books, humor, cookbook, juvenile (ages 9-14), reference and textbook. Subjects are limited to history, culture and cuisine of the Southeast and especially South Carolina. "We are looking for manuscripts that reveal underappreciated or undiscovered facets of the rich heritage of our region. If a manuscript doesn't deal with South Carolina or the Southeast, the work is probably not appropriate for us. We don't do self-help books, children's books about divorce, kidnapping, etc., and absolutely no religious manuscripts." Query or submit outline synopsis and sample chapters "if you're not sure it's what we're looking for, otherwise complete ms." Reviews artwork/photos as part of ms package.

Recent Nonfiction Title: *SC in the 1880s*, by John Hammon Moore.

Fiction: We do not need fiction submissions at present, "but I will look at good strong fiction by South Carolinians and other regional writers. We will not consider any horror, romance or religious fiction." Query or submit outline/synopsis and sample chapters. "Do check with us on books dealing with regional nature, science and outdoor subjects."

Tips: "Our readers are South Carolinians, visitors to the region's tourist spots, and friends and family that live out-of-state. We are striving to be a leading regional publisher for South Carolina. We will be looking for more history and biography."

‡SAS INSTITUTE, SAS CIRCLE INC., P.O. Box 8000, Cary NC 27512-8000. (919)677-8000. Acquisitions Editor: David D. Baggett. Publishes hardcover and trade paperback originals. Firm averages 40 titles/year. Receives 10 submissions/year. 50% of books from first-time authors. 100% from unagented writers. Payment negotiable. Offers negotiable advance. Query for electronic submissions. Reports in 2 weeks on queries; 6 weeks on mss. Free book catalog and manuscript guidelines.

Nonfiction: Software, technical, textbook and statistics. "SAS Institute's Publications Division publishes books developed and written in-house. In the past, we've also worked with non-Institute authors to publish books on a variety of topics relating to SAS software, especially to supplement our statistical documentation. We want to publish more books written by non-Institute authors on an even wider range of topics. We want to provide our users with additional titles to supplement our primary documentation and to enhance the users' ability to use the SAS System effectively. We're interested in publishing manuscripts that describe or illustrate using any of SAS Institute's software products. Books must be aimed at SAS software users, either new or experienced. Tutorials are particularly attractive, as are descriptions of user-written applications for solving real-life business, industry or academic problems. Books on programming techniques using the SAS language are also desirable. Manuscripts must reflect current or upcoming software releases, and the author's writing should indicate an understanding of the SAS System and the technical aspects covered in the manuscript." Query. Submit outline/synopsis and sample chapters. Reviews artwork/photos as part of ms package.

Recent Nonfiction Title: *SAS Sytem for Elementary Statistical Analysis*, by Sandra D. Schlotzhauer and Ramon C. Littell, Ph.D.

Tips: "Our readers are SAS software users, both new and experienced. If I were a writer trying to market a book today, I would concentrate on developing a manuscript that teaches or illustrates a specific concept or application that SAS software users will find beneficial in their own environments or can adapt to their own needs."

SASQUATCH BOOKS, 1931 Second Ave., Seattle WA 98101. (206)441-5555. FAX: (206)441-6213. Managing Editor: Anne Depue. Firm publishes hardcover and trade paperback originals. Averages 6-8 titles/year. 25% of books from first-time authors; 95% from unagented writers. Pays authors 5-12% royalty on net price. Offers wide range of advances. Publishes ms an average of 6 months after acceptance. Simultaneous submissions OK. Query for electronic submissions. Reports in 1 month. Free book catalog.

Nonfiction: Subjects include regional art/architecture, business and economics, cooking, foods and nutrition, gardening, government/politics, history, language/literature, nature/environment, photography, recreation, sports and travel. "We are seeking quality nonfiction works by, about or for people of the Pacific Northwest region. In this sense we are a regional publisher, but we do distribute our books nationally, depending on the title." Submit outline/synopsis and sample chapters.

Recent Nonfiction Title: *Mount St. Helens: The Eruption and Recovery of a Volcano*, by Rob Carson.

Tips: "We sell books through a range of channels in addition to the book trade. Our audience consists of active, literate residents of the Pacific Northwest."

‡**SCARBOROUGH HOUSE/PUBLISHERS**, 901-B Taylor St., P.O. Box 459, Chelsea MI 48118. (313)475-1210. Contact: Editorial Department. Publishes hardcover and trade paperback originals and trade paperback reprints. Firm averages 35 titles/year. 20% of books are from first-time authors. 60% from unagented writers. Pays advance against standard royalty. Publishes book an average of 9-12 months after acceptance. Simultaneous submissions OK. Reports in 2 months on queries; 3 months on mss.

Nonfiction: Biography, cookbook, how-to, reference and self-help. Subject include Americana, animals, anthropology/archaeology, business and economics, child guidance/parenting, cooking, foods and nutrition, education, ethnic, gardening, government/politics, health/medicine, history, hobbies, language/literature, military/war, money/finance, psychology, recreation, popular science, sports and travel. We are looking for quality general-interest books with a clearly definable market. Query. Submit outline/synopsis and sample chapters or complete ms upon our positive response to above. Reviews artwork/photos as part of ms package.

Recent Nonfiction Title: *Sumter: The First Day of The Civil War*, by Robert Hendrickson.

Fiction: Adventure, literary and mainstream/contemporary. We publish rather more nonfiction than fiction, and with few exceptions will seriously consider only those novelists who already have a strong commerical track record. Query. Submit outline/synopsis and sample chapters, complete ms upon our positive response to above.

Recent Nonfiction Title: *Guadalajara*, by E. Howard Hunt.

SCARECROW PRESS, INC., 52 Liberty St., P.O. Box 4167, Metuchen NJ 08840. Vice President, Editorial: Norman Horrocks. Senior Editor: Barbara Lee. Estab. 1953. Publishes hardcover originals. Averages 110 titles/year; receives 600-700 submissions annually. 70% of books from first-time authors; 100% of books from unagented writers. Average print order for a writer's first book is 1,000. Pays 10% royalty on net of first 1,000 copies; 15% of net price thereafter. 15% initial royalty on camera-ready copy. Offers no advance. Publishes book 6-18 months after receipt of ms. Query for electronic submissions. Reports in 2 weeks. Free book catalog.

Nonfiction: Books about music. Needs reference books and meticulously prepared annotated bibliographies, indexes, women's studies, movies and stage. Query. Occasionally reviews artwork/photos as part of ms package.

Recent Nonfiction Title: *American Artists: Signatures and Monograms, 1800-1989*, by John Castagno.

Tips: "Essentially we consider any scholarly title likely to appeal to libraries. Emphasis is on reference material, but this can be interpreted broadly, provided author is knowledgeable in the subject field."

‡***SCHENKMAN BOOKS INC.**, Main Street, P.O. Box 119, Rochester VT 05767. Editor-in-Chief: Joseph Schenkman. Estab. 1961. Publishes hardcover and paperback originals. Specializes in textbooks and professional and technical books. Averages 5 titles/year. Subsidy publishes 3% of books. Royalty varies on net sales, but averages 10%. "In some cases, no royalties are paid on first 2,000 copies sold." No advance. State availability of photos and/or illustrations. Publishes book an average of 1 year after acceptance. Reports in 2 months. Free book catalog.

Nonfiction: Publishes economics, history, psychology, sociology, Third World, women's studies, political science, textbooks and professional and technical books. Reviews artwork/photos as part of ms package. Query.

Recent Nonfiction Title: *Bob Marley*, by Stephen Davis.

SCHIRMER BOOKS, Macmillan Publishing Co., Inc., 866 3rd Ave., New York NY 10022. FAX: (212)319-1216. Editor-in-Chief: Maribeth Anderson Payne. Publishes hardcover and paperback originals, related audio recordings, paperback reprints and some software. Averages 20 books/year; receives 250 submissions annually. 40% of books from first-time authors; 95% of books from unagented writers. Average print order for a writer's first book is 3,000-5,000. Pays royalty on wholesale or retail price; offers small advance. Submit photos and/or illustrations "if central to the book, not if decorative or tangential." Publishes book an average of 1 year after acceptance. Query for electronic submissions. Reports in 2 months. Book catalog and ms guidelines for SASE.

Nonfiction: Publishes college texts, biographies, scholarly, reference and how-to on the performing arts specializing in music, also dance and theatre. Submit outline/synopsis and sample chapters and current vita. Reviews artwork/photos as part of ms package.

Recent Nonfiction Title: *Listen to the Music*, by Jonathan Kramer.

Tips: "The writer has the best chance of selling our firm a music book with a clearly defined, reachable audience, either scholarly or trade. Must be an exceptionally well-written work of original scholarship prepared by an expert in the field who has a thorough understanding of correct manuscript style and attention to detail (see the Chicago *Manual of Style*)."

SCHOLASTIC, INC., 730 Broadway, New York NY 10003. (212)505-3000. Executive Editor: Ann Reit. Estab. 1920. Trade paperback originals and hardcovers. Pays royalty on retail price. Reports in 3 months. Ms guidelines for #10 SASE.

Nonfiction: Publishes general nonfiction.

Recent Nonfiction Title: *Jesse Jackson*, by Patricia McKissack.

Fiction: Family stories, mysteries, school, and friendships for ages 8-12, 35,000 words. YA fiction, romance, family and mystery for ages 12-15, 40,000-45,000 words for average to good readers. Query or submit entire manuscripts.

Tips: Queries/mss may be routed to other editors in the publishing group.

SCHOLASTIC PROFESSIONAL BOOKS (AND INSTRUCTOR BOOKS), 730 Broadway, New York NY 10003. Editor-in-Chief: Kate Waters. "U.S. and Canadian school supervisors, principals and teachers purchase items in our line for instructional purposes or professional development." 90% freelance written. Buys 15-20 scripts/year from published or unpublished writers. Most scripts produced are unagented submissions. Buys all rights. Writer should have "experience in preparing materials for elementary students, including suitable teaching guides to accompany them, and demonstrate knowledge of the appropriate subject areas, or demonstrate ability for accurate and efficient research and documentation." Catalog for 8½ × 11 SAE.

Needs: Elementary curriculum enrichment – all subject areas. Display material, copy and illustration should match interest and reading skills of children in grades for which material is intended. Production is limited to printed matter: resource handbooks, teaching guides, posters, learning center packs and idea books. Length: 6,000-12,000 words. Query. Standard contract, but fees vary considerably, depending on type of project.

Tips: "Writers who reflect current educational practices can expect to sell to us."

*SCIENCE TECH PUBLISHERS, INC., 701 Ridge St., Madison WI 53705. (608)238-8664. Book publisher and independent book producer/packager. Managing Editor: Katherine Brock. Estab. 1974. Publishes hardcover originals and reprints and paperback originals. Also acts as agent and production house for similar titles published by other houses. Firm averages 8-10 titles/year. Receives 20 submissions/year. 90% of books from first-time authors. 95% from unagented authors. Subsidy publishes 5-10% of books. "Subsidy used only if his book is outside our normal area, so that we can't market it well." Pays 10% on wholesale price. Offers $500-1,000 average advance. Publishes book an average of 1 year after acceptance. Simultaneous submissions OK. Query for electronic submissions. Reports in 3 weeks on queries and mss. Manuscript quidelines "available on individual basis."

Nonfiction: Biography, reference, technical and textbook. Subjects include agriculture, health/medicine, history of science and science. "We will examine high-level references or monographs in various areas of science, history of science, biographies of scientists." Query. Submit outline/synopsis and sample chapters or complete mss. Reviews artwork/photos as part of ms package.

Recent Nonfiction Title: *Autotrophic Bacteria*, by Hans Schlegel, editor.

Fiction: "Possibly YA fiction with solid *science* orientation." Query. Submit outline/synopsis and sample chapters or complete ms.

Tips: "Writers have the best chance of selling us high quality monographs in field of research specialty. Authors generally are scientists. Biographies also welcome, at high academic level in general. Research and professional scientists; university and public libraries are our audience."

CHARLES SCRIBNER'S SONS, Children's Books Department, 866 Third Ave., New York NY 10022. (212)702-7885. Editorial Director, Children's Books: Clare Costello. Estab. 1846. Publishes hardcover originals and paperback reprints of own titles. Averages 20-25 titles/year. Pays royalty on retail price; offers advance. Publishes book an average of 1 year after acceptance. Reports in 2 weeks on queries; 10 weeks on mss. Free book catalog and ms guidelines.

Nonfiction: Subjects include animals, biography, health, history, nature, science, self-help, sports for ages 3-14. Query. Reviews artwork/photos as part of ms package.

Recent Nonfiction Title: *Shifting Shores: Rising Seas, Retreating Coastlines*, by Jeff Hecht.

Fiction: Adventure, fantasy, historical, humor, mystery, picture books, science fiction and suspense. Submit outline/synopsis and sample chapters.

Recent Fiction Title: *Secret City U.S.A.*, by Felice Holman.

‡SELF-COUNSEL PRESS, Subsidiary of International Self-Counsel Press Ltd., Head and editorial office: 1481 Charlotte Rd., North Vancouver, British Columbia V7J 1H1 Canada. (604)986-3366. U.S. address: 1704 N. State Street, Bellingham WA 98225. Managing Editor: Ruth Wilson. Publishes trade paperback originals. Averages 15 titles/year. Receives 1000 submissions/year. 80% of books from first-time authors; 95% from unagented writers. Pays 10% royalty on wholesale price. Publishes book an average of 9 months after acceptance. Simultaneous submissions OK. Query for electronic submissions. Reports in 6 weeks on queries; 2 months on mss. Book catalog and manuscript guidelines free on request.

Nonfiction: How-to, reference, self-help. Subjects include business and economics, health/medicine, money/finance, psychology, law. Query or submit outline/synopsis and sample chapters.
Recent Nonfiction Title: *Preparing a Successful Business Plan* (self-help business).
Tips: "The self-counsel author is an expert in his or her field and capable of conveying practical, specific information to those who are not. We look for manuscripts full of useful information that will allow readers to take the solution to their needs or problems into their own hands and succeed."

‡**SENTINEL BOOKS**, Division of The Orlando Sentinel (newspaper), P.O. Box 1100, Orlando FL 32802. (407)420-5588. FAX: (407)420-5588. Managing Editor: George Biggers. Estab. 1987. Publishes hardcover and trade paperback originals. Averages 8 titles/year. Receives 200 submissions/year. 50% of books from first-time authors; 90% from unagented writers. Pays negotiable royalty. Advance offered is negotiable. Publishes book an average of 6 months after acceptance. Simultaneous submissions OK. Query for electronic submissions. Reports in 1 month. Book catalog free on request.
Nonfiction: Coffee table book, cookbook, how-to, humor, illustrated book, reference. Subjects include agriculture/horticulture, Americana, art/architecture, child guidance/parenting, cooking, foods and nutrition, gardening, history, hobbies, nature/environment, photography, recreation, regional, sports and travel. "We are looking for broad, general interest titles with a lasting value, particularly those of a regional nature. No academic titles with limited audience." Query or submit outline/synopsis and sample chapters.
Recent Nonfiction Title: *Southern Shores*, by Roger Bansemer (coffee table artbook).
Tips: "We have a broad-based audience."

SERVANT PUBLICATIONS, 840 Airport Blvd., Box 8617, Ann Arbor MI 48107. (313)761-8505. Editorial Director: Ann Spangler. Publishes hardcover, trade and mass market paperback originals and trade paperback reprints. Averages 35 titles/year. 5% of books from first-time authors; 95% of books from unagented writers. Pays 7-10% royalty on retail price. Publishes book an average of 1 year after acceptance. Computer printout submissions acceptable. Reports in 2 months. Free book catalog; writer's guidelines for 9 × 12 SASE.
Nonfiction: Subjects include religion. "We're looking for practical Christian teaching, biblical psychology, fiction, scripture, current problems facing the Christian church, and inspiration." No heterodox or non-Christian approaches. Query or submit brief outline/synopsis and 1 sample chapter. All unsolicited mss are returned unopened. Reviews artwork/photos as part of ms package.
Recent Nonfiction Title: *Against the Night*, by Chuck Colson.

SEVEN LOCKS PRESS, INC., P.O. Box 27, Cabin John MD 20818. (301)320-2130. Imprint is Isidore Stephanus Sons Publishing. President/Publisher: James McGrath Morris. Estab. 1975. Publishes hardcover and trade paperback originals, and reprints. Averages 6-9 titles/year; receives 100 submissions annually. 50% of books from first-time authors; 50% of books from unagented writers. Pays 8-15% royalty of retail price on hardbacks 6-12% on paperbacks. Simultaneous submissions OK. Reports in 1 month on queries; 3 months on mss. Free book catalog.
Nonfiction: Biography, reference and textbook. Subjects include Americana, business and economics, history, international relations, nature, politics, religion and sociology. Especially needs "books that promise to enlighten public policy; also, books of regional interest that are entertaining." Query or submit outline/synopsis and sample chapters. Reviews artwork/photos as part of ms package.
Recent Nonfiction Title: *Entangling Alliances: How the Third World Saves Our Lives*, by John Maxwell Hamilton.
Tips: "Literate, intelligent, socially conscious men and women are our readers."

HAROLD SHAW PUBLISHERS, 388 Gundersen Dr., P.O. Box 567, Wheaton IL 60189. (708)665-6700. Director of Editorial Services: Ramona Cramer Tucker. Estab. 1967. Publishes hardcover and trade paperback originals and reprints. Averages 32 titles/year; receives 2,000 submissions annually. 10% of books from first-time authors; 90% of books from unagented writers. Offers 5-10% royalty on retail price. Sometimes makes outright purchase for $1,000-2,500. Publishes book an average of 12-15 months after acceptance. Reports in 1 month on queries; 6 weeks on mss. Book catalog and ms guidelines for 9 × 12 SAE with 5 first class stamps.
Nonfiction and Fiction: Juvenile (13 and up), reference and self-help. Subjects include history (of religious movements/evangelical/charismatic), psychology (self-help) and religion (Bible study guides and general religion). "We are looking for general nonfiction, with different twists – self-help manuscripts on issues and topics with fresh insight and colorful, vibrant writing style. We already have how to forgive yourself and how to deal with screaming, cancer, death and handicaps. No autobiographies or biographies accepted. Must have an evangelical Christian perspective for us even to review the ms." Query. Reviews artwork/photos as part of ms package.
Recent Nonfiction Title: *Sold into Egypt*, by Madeleine L'Engle
Tips: "Get an editor who is not a friend or a spouse who will tell you honestly whether your book is marketable. It will save a lot of your time and money and effort. Then do an honest evaluation. Who would actually read the book other than yourself? If it won't sell at least 5,000 copies, it's not very marketable and most publishers wouldn't be interested."

THE SHEEP MEADOW PRESS, Box 1345, Riverdale-on-Hudson NY 10471. (212)549-3321. Publisher/Editor: Stanley Moss. Associate Editor: Rita Kieffer. Publishes trade paperback originals. Firm averages 8-9 titles/year. Receives 150 submissions/year. 75% of books from first-time authors. 100% from unagented writers. Pays royalty. Reports in 3 weeks on queries; 3 months on mss. Book catalog for 6x9 SASE.
Poetry: "We are always in the market for original manuscripts." Submit complete ms.
Recent Poetry Title: *The Center for Cold Weather*, by Cleopatra Mathis.

‡THE SHOE STRING PRESS, 925 Sherman Ave., Box 4327, Hamden CT 06514. (203)248-6307. President: James Thorpe III. Imprints include Archon, Library Professional Publications and Linnet Books. Publishes hardcover and trade paperback originals. Publishes 30 titles/year; receives 700 submissions annually. 15% of books from first-time authors; 95% of books from unagented writers. Pays escalating royalty scale. Publishes book an average of 1 year after acceptance. Query for electronic submissions. Reports in 1 month on queries; 4 months on mss. Book catalog and ms guidelines for SASE.
Nonfiction: Biography, reference and general. Subjects include Americana, children's books, history, nature, philosophy, politics, religion, literature and military. Will consider "any good scholarly or general nonfiction, reference, children's fiction or nonfiction or professional library literature." No "flying saucers, reincarnation, or inspiration." Submit outline/synopsis and sample chapters. Reviews artwork/photos as part of ms package.
Recent Nonfiction Title: *Understanding Shakespeare's England: A Companion for the American Reader*, by Jo McMurtry (reference).

SIERRA CLUB BOOKS, 100 Bush St., San Francisco CA 94104. (415)291-1600. FAX: (415)291-1602. Editor-in-Chief: Daniel Moses. Publishes hardcover and paperback originals and reprints. Averages 20 titles/year; receives 500 submissions annually. 50% of books from unagented writers. Pays 7-12½% royalty on retail price. Offers average $3,000-5,000 advance. Publishes book an average of 12-18 months after acceptance. Reports in 2 months. Free book catalog.
Nonfiction: Animals; health; history (natural); how-to (outdoors); juveniles; nature; philosophy; photography; recreation (outdoors, nonmechanical); science; sports (outdoors); and travel (by foot or bicycle). "The Sierra Club was founded to help people to explore, enjoy and preserve the nation's forests, waters, wildlife and wilderness. The books program looks to publish quality trade books about the outdoors and the protection of natural resources. Specifically, we are interested in nature, environmental issues such as nuclear power, self-sufficiency, natural history, politics and the environment, and juvenile books with an ecological theme." Does *not* want "personal, lyrical, philosophical books on the great outdoors; proposals for large color photographic books without substantial text; how-to books on building things outdoors; books on motorized travel; or any but the most professional studies of animals." Query first, submit outline/synopsis and sample chapters. Reviews artwork/photos ("duplicates, not originals") as part of ms package.
Recent Nonfiction Title: *Global Warming*, by Stephen H. Schneider.
Fiction: Adventure, historical, mainstream and ecological fiction. "We do very little fiction, but will consider a fiction manuscript if its theme fits our philosophical aims: the enjoyment and protection of the environment." Does *not* want "any manuscript with animals or plants that talk; apocalyptic plots." Query first, submit outline/synopsis and sample chapters, or submit complete ms.

‡SIGO PRESS, 25 New Chardon St., #8748, Boston MA 92114. (508)281-4722. President: Sisa Sternback. Publishes hardcover and trade paperback originals and reprints. Averages 10-20 titles/year. Receives 75 submissions/year. 40% of books from first-time authors; 95% from unagented writers. Pays 5-10% royalty. Publishes book an average of 9 months after acceptance. Simultaneous submissions OK. Query for electronic submissions. Reports in 3 weeks on queries; 4 months on mss. Book catalog and manuscript guidelines free on request.
Nonfiction: Illustrated book, self-help, textbook. Subjects include child guidance/parenting, health/medicine, psychology, religion, women's issues/studies, men's studies, New Age. Submit outline/synopsis and sample chapters or complete ms.
Tips: "Our audience is generally educated, lay or professional readers, and interested in inner growth."

SILHOUETTE BOOKS, Division of Harlequin Enterprises, 300 E. 42nd St., New York NY 10017. (212)682-6080. Editorial Manager, Silhouette Books, Harlequin historicals: Isabel Swift. Publishes mass market paperback originals. Averages 292 titles/year; receives 4,000 submissions annually. 10% of books from first-time authors; 25% of books from unagented writers. Pays royalty. Publishes book an average of 1 year after acceptance. Computer printout submissions acceptable; no dot-matrix. No unsolicited mss. Send query letter; 2 page synopsis and SASE to head of imprint. Ms guidelines for #10 SASE.
Imprints: Silhouette Romances (contemporary adult romances), Tara Gavin, Senior Editor; 53,000-58,000 words. Silhouette Special Editions (contemporary adult romances), Leslie Kazanjian, Senior Editor; 75,000-80,000 words. Silhouette Desires (contemporary adult romances), Lucia Macro, Senior Editor; 55,000-60,000 words. Silhouette Intimate Moments (contemporary adult romances), Leslie Wainger, Senior Editor and Editorial Coordinator; 80,000-85,000 words. Harlequin Historicals (adult historical romances), Tracy Farrell and Eliza Schallcross, Editors; 95-105,000 words.

Fiction: Romance (contemporary and historical romance for adults). "We are interested in seeing submissions for all our lines. No manuscripts other than the types outlined above." Ms should "follow our general format, yet have an individuality and life of its own that will make it stand out in the readers' minds."
Recent Fiction Title: *Without a Trace*, by Nora Roberts.
Tips: "The romance market is constantly changing, so when you read for research, read the latest books and those that have been recommended to you by people knowledgeable in the genre. We are actively seeking new authors for all our lines, contemporary and historical."

SILVER BURDETT PRESS, Imprint of Simon & Schuster, 190 Sylvan Ave., Englewood Cliffs NJ 07632. FAX: (201)461-8178. President: Carole Cushmore, Editor-in-Chief: Bonnie Brook. Publishes hardcover and paperback originals. Averages 65-80 titles/year; does not accept unsolicited manuscripts. Publishes book an average of one year after acceptance. Offers variable advance. Free book catalog.
Nonfiction: Juvenile and young adult reference. Subjects include Americana, science, history, nature, and geography. "We're primarily intersted in nonfiction for students on subjects which supplement the classroom curricula, but are graphically appealing and, in some instances, have commercial as well as institutional appeal."
Recent Nonfiction Title: *History of the Civil Rights Movement*, introduction by Andrew Young.
Tips: "Our books are primarily bought by school and public librarians for use by students and young readers. Virtually all are nonfiction and done as part of a series."

‡SILVER PRESS, Silver Burdett Press, 190 Sylvan Ave., Englewood Cliffs NJ 07632. (201)461-6257. Editor-in-Chief: Bonnie Brook. Publishes hardcover and trade paperback originals. Publishes 40 titles/year; receives 100 submissions/year. 10% from first-time authors; 50% from unagented writers. Pays 5-7½% royalty on retail price or assigns work-for-hire. Publishes book an average of 1 year after acceptance. Simultaneous submissions OK. Reports in 1 month on queries; 6 months on mss. Free book catalog.
Nonfiction: Juvenile. Subjects include animals, ethnic, history, hobbies, language/literature. Need good photo essays with simple science subjects. Submit complete ms.
Recent Nonfiction Title: *More than Just a Flower Garden*, by Dwight Kuhn (photo essay).
Fiction: Juvenile, picture books. Submit complete ms.
Recent Fiction Title: *Bears, Bears, Bears*, by Mary Pope Osborne (anthology of bear literature).
Tips: "Preschool and primary (ages 3-8) are our audience."

SIMON & SCHUSTER, Trade Books Division, 1230 Avenue of the Americas, New York NY 10020. "We do not accept unsolicited manuscripts. Only manuscripts submitted by agents will be considered. In such cases, our requirements are as follows: Manuscripts must be typewritten, double-spaced, on one side of the sheet only. We suggest margins of about one and one half inches all around and the standard 8½ × 11 typewriter paper."
Nonfiction and Fiction: "Simon and Schuster publishes books of general adult fiction, history, biography, science, philosophy, the arts and popular culture, running 50,000 words or more. Our program does not, however, include school textbooks, extremely technical or highly specialized works, or, as a general rule, poetry or plays. Exceptions have been made, of course, for extraordinary manuscripts of great distinction or significance."

‡SKIDMORE-ROTH PUBLISHING, 207 Cincinnati Ave., El Paso TX 79902. (915)544-3150. President: Linda Roth. Publishes trade paperback originals and reprints. Firm averages 10/year. Receives 25 submissions/year. 50% first time authors. 100% from unagented writers. Pays 5-12½% royalty on wholesale price. Publishes book an average of 9 months after acceptance. Simultaneous submissions OK. Reports in 3 weeks on queries; 2 months on mss. Free book catalog.
Nonfiction: Self-help, technical, textbook. Subject include child guidance/parenting, health/medicine and psychology. We are currently searching for manuscripts in the following areas: geriatric nursing, consumer health, self-improvement, psychology, parenting, allied health. Nothing on religion, history, music/dance, travel, sports, agriculture, computers, military, politics, gay/lesbian or literature. Query. Reviews artwork/ photos as part of ms package.
Recent Nonfiction Title: *Warm Logic: The Art of the Intuitive Lifestyle*, by Louis Wynne Ph.D., (self-help).
Tips: Anything on consumer health is more likely to be published. Our audience is largely a geriatric population, also single women with small children, professionals in the field of medicine, nursing, allied health. "If I were a writer trying to market a book today, I would look for an area that has been completely overlooked by other writers and write on that subject."

GIBBS SMITH, PUBLISHER, Peregrine Smith Books, P.O. Box 667, Layton UT 84041. (801)544-9800. Editorial Director: Madge Baird. Fiction Editor: Steve Chapman. Estab. 1969. Publishes hardcover and paperback originals and reprints. Averages 25-30 titles/year; receives 2,000 submissions annually. 25% of books from first-time authors; 40% of books from unagented writers. Average print order for a writer's first book is 4,000-5,000. Starts at 10% royalty on wholesale price. Offers average $1,000 advance. Publishes book an average of 1½ years after acceptance. Reports in 2 months. Book catalog for 6x9 SAE and 3 first class stamps; ms guidelines for #10 SASE.

Nonfiction: "Subjects include western American history, natural history, architecture, art history, and fine arts. "We consider biographical, historical, descriptive and analytical studies in all of the above. Emphasis is also placed on pictorial content." Query. Reviews artwork/photos as part of ms package.

Recent Nonfiction Title: *For Earth's Sake: The Life and Times of David Brower*, by David Brower.

Fiction: "We publish contemporary literary fiction." Looks for "style, readable, intelligent, careful writing, contribution to the social consciousness of our time." Query.

Recent Fiction Title: *The Light Possessed*, by Alan Cheuse.

Tips: "We're looking for art books (visual arts and architecture) on the leading edge of our culture. In fiction we are interested in work with literary merit, work that demonstrates a control of subject with a distinctive and original voice will be seriously considered. We are not interested in potboilers, bodice-rippers, science fiction, techno-thrillers or anything that deals with a subject that claims to be 'as current as today's headlines.' "

SOHO PRESS, INC., 1 Union Square, New York NY 10003. (212)243-1527. Editor-in-Chief: Juris Jurjevics. Publishes hardcover and trade paperback originals. Firm averages 12 titles/year. Receives 1,000 submissions/year. 75% of books from first-time authors. 50% of books from unagented writers. Pays 10-15% on retail price. Publishes book an average of 1 year after acceptance. Simultaneous submissions OK. Reports in 1 month on queries; 2 months on mss. Book catalog for SASE.

Nonfiction: Biography. "We want literary non-fiction: travel, autobiography, biography, etc. No self-help." Submit outline/synopsis and sample chapters or complete ms with SASE.

Recent Nonfiction Title *O Come Ye Back to Ireland*, by Nialll Williams and Christine Breen, (travel and biography).

Fiction: Adventure, ethnic, feminist, historical, literary, mainstream/contemporary, mystery and suspense. Submit complete ms with SASE.

Recent Fiction Title: *Me and You*, by Margaret Diehl.

‡GORDON SOULES BOOK PUBLISHERS LTD., 1352-B Marine Dr., West Vancouver, British Columbia V7T 1B5 Canada. (604)922-6588. President: Gordon Soules. Publishes trade paperback originals. Averages 4 titles/year. Receives 500 submissions/year. 90% of books from first-time authors; 100% from unagented writers. Pays 10% royalty on retail price. Publishes book an average of 6 months after acceptance. Simultaneous submissions OK. Reports in 2 weeks. Book catalog free on request.

Nonfiction: Cookbook, how-to, self-help. Subjects include animals, business and economics, cooking, foods and nutrition, government/politics, health/medicine, history, nature/environment, recreation, regional, travel and Canadiana. Query. Reviews artwork/photos as part of ms package.

Recent Nonfiction Title: *Wild & Free, Living with Wildlife in Canada's North*, by Ian and Sally Wilson (nature/wildlife).

Tips: "We want top-quality manuscripts. Must be well-researched."

SOUTHFARM PRESS, Haan Graphic Publishing Services, Ltd., P.O. Box 1296, Middletown CT 06457. (203)344-9137. Publisher: Walter J. Haan. Estab. 1983. Publishes trade paperback originals. Firm averages 5 titles/year. 100% from first-time authors; 100% from unagented writers. Pays 5-10% royalty on retail price. Offers $500 average advance. Publishes book an average of 1 year after acceptance. Simultaneous submissions OK. Reports in 1 month. Free book catalog.

Nonfiction: Subjects include history and military/war. Submit outline/synopsis and sample chapters.

Recent Nonfiction Title: *Ghost Ship: The Confederate Raider Alabama*, by Norman C. Delaney.

THE SPEECH BIN, INC., 1766 20th Avenue, Vero Beach FL 32960. (407)770-0007. FAX: (407)770-0006. Senior Editor: Jan Binney. Estab. 1984. Publishes trade paperback originals. Publishes 10-20 titles/year. Receives 200-250 manuscripts per year. 50% of books from first-time authors; 90% from unagented writers. Pays negotiable royalty on wholesale price. Publishes ms average of 6 months after acceptance. Query for electronic submissions. Reports in one month on queries, six weeks on manuscripts. Book catalog for 9 × 12 SASE.

Nonfiction: How-to, illustrated book, juvenile (preschool-teen), reference, textbook, educational material and games. Subjects include health, communication disorders and education for handicapped persons. Query or submit outline synopsis and sample chapters. Reviews artwork/photos as part of ms package. Do not send original artwork; photocopies only please.

Recent Nonfiction Title: *Spotlight on Speech-Language Services*, by Janet Shaw.

Fiction: Booklets or books "for children and adults about handicapped persons, especially with communication disorders." Query or submit outline/synopsis and sample chapters. "This is a potentially new market for The Speech Bin."

Tips: "Our audience is made up of special educators, speech-language pathologists and audiologists, parents, caregivers, and teachers of children and adults with developmental and post-trauma disabilities. Books and materials must be research-based, clearly presented, well written, competently illustrated, and unique. We'll be adding books and materials for use by occupational and physical therapists and other allied health professionals."

SPINSTERS/AUNT LUTE BOOKS, P.O. Box 410687, San Francisco CA 94141. (415)558-9655. Editors: Sherry Thomas and Joan Pinkvoss. Publishes trade paperback originals and reprints. Averages 6-8 titles/year; receives 200 submissions annually. 50% of books from first-time authors; 95% of books from unagented writers. Pays 7-11% royalty on retail price. Publishes book an average of 1 year after acceptance. Reports in 3 weeks on queries; 6 months on mss. Free book catalog; ms guidelines for SASE.

Nonfiction: Self-help and feminist analysis for positive change. Subjects include women's issues. "We are interested in books that not only name the crucial issues in women's lives, but show and encourage change and growth. We do not want to see work by men, or anything that is not specific to women's lives (ie. humor, childrens' books, etc.). We do not want genre fiction (romances, etc.)." Query. Reviews artwork/photos as part of ms package.

Recent Nonfiction Title: *Borderlands/LaFrontera*, by Gloria Anzuidua (ethnic/women's history).

Fiction: Ethnic, women's, lesbian. Submit outline/synopsis and sample chapters.

Recent Fiction Title: *Child of Her People*, by Anne Cameron.

Poetry: Minimal. Submit complete ms.

Recent Poetry Title: *We Say We Love Each Other*, by Minnie Bruce Pratt (Southern lesbian).

ST PUBLICATIONS, INC., Signs of the Times Pubishing Co., Book Division, 407 Gilbert Ave., Cincinnati OH 45202. (513)421-4050. FAX: (513)421-5144. Book Division Manager: George B. Harper. Estab. 1957. Publishes hardcover and trade paperback originals and hardcover reprints. Averages 6 titles/year; receives 15-20 submissions annually. 50% of books from first-time authors; 100% of books from unagented writers. Pays royalty on wholesale price: 10% until recovery of production costs; 12½% thereafter; and 15% on straight reprints. Publishes book an average of 9 months after acceptance. Reports in 6 weeks on queries; 2 months on mss. Free book catalog and ms guidelines.

Nonfiction: How-to, reference, technical and textbook. Subjects include art (collections of copyright-free artwork suitable for sign, display or screen printing industries). "We need technical how-to books for professionals in three specific industries: the sign industry, including outdoor advertising, electric and commercial signs; the screen printing industry, including the printing of paper products, fabrics, ceramics, glass and electronic circuits; and the visual merchandising and store design industry. We are not interested in submissions that do not relate specifically to those three fields." Submit outline/synopsis and sample chapters. Reviews artwork/photos as part of ms package.

Recent Nonfiction Title: *Screen Printing Production Management*, by Richard C. Webb, Jr.

Tips: "The writer has the best chance of selling our firm how-to books related to our industries: signs, screen printing, and visual merchandising. These are the fields our marketing and distribution channels are geared to. Request copies of, and thoroughly absorb the information presented in, our trade magazines (*Signs of the Times, Visual Merchandising*, and *Screen Printing*). Our books are permanent packages of this type of information. We are taking a closer look at submissions that we can sell outside our primary range of customers, yet still confining our subject interests to sign painting and design, visual merchandising, display and store design, and screen printing (both technical and art aspects)."

STACKPOLE BOOKS, Company of Commonwealth Communications Services, P.O. Box 1831, Harrisburg PA 17105. FAX: (717)234-1359. Editorial Director: Judith Schnell. Estab. 1930. Publishes hardcover and paperback originals. Publishes 50 titles/year. Publishes book an average of 1 year after acceptance.

Nonfiction: Outdoor-related subject areas—fishing, hunting, wildlife, adventure, outdoor skills, gardening, decoy carving/woodcarving, outdoor sports, crafts, military guides, military history. Reviews artwork/photos as part of ms package.

Recent Nonfiction Title: *Shadows on the Tundra*, by Tom Walker.

Tips: "Stackpole seeks well-written, authoritative manuscripts for specialized and general trade markets. Proposals should include chapter outline, sample chapter and illustration, and author's credentials."

STANDARD PUBLISHING, Division of Standex International Corp., 8121 Hamilton Ave., Cincinnati OH 45231. (513)931-4050. Publisher/Vice President: Eugene H. Wigginton. Estab. 1866. Publishes hardcover and paperback originals and reprints. Specializes in religious books. Averages 125 titles/year; receives 1,500 submissions annually. 25% of books from first-time authors; 90% of books from unagented writers. Average print order for a writer's first book is 5,000. Pays 8-10% royalty on wholesale price "for substantial books. Lump sum for smaller books." Publishes book an average of 18 months after acceptance. Reports in 3 months. Ms guidelines for #10 SASE.

Nonfiction: Publishes how-to; crafts (to be used in Christian education); juveniles; Christian education; quiz; puzzle. All mss must pertain to religion. Query.
Recent Nonfiction Title: *Message in Motion: Simulation Games for Teens*, by Tim Jones.
Fiction: Religious, contemporary for ages 8-11 or 12-15.
Recent Fiction Title: *Runaway*, by Janet Willig.
Tips: "Children's books (picture books, ages 4-7), juvenile fiction (8-11 and 12-15), Christian education, activity books, and helps for Christian parents and church leaders are the types of books writers have the best chance of selling to our firm."

*STANFORD UNIVERSITY PRESS, Imprint of Stanford University, Stanford CA 94305-2235. (415)723-9598. Editor: William W. Carver. Averages 65 titles/year; receives 1,200 submissions annually. 40% of books from first-time authors, 95% of books from unagented writers. Subsidy (nonauthor) publishes 65% of books. Pays up to 15% royalty ("typically 10%, often none"); sometimes offers advance. Publishes book an average of 1 year after acceptance. Query for electronic submissions. Reports in 3 weeks on queries; 5 weeks on mss. Free book catalog.
Nonfiction: Scholarly books in the humanities, social sciences, and natural sciences: history and culture of China, Japan, and Latin America; European history; biology, natural history, and taxonomy; anthropology, linguistics, and psychology; literature, criticism, and literary theory; political science and sociology; archaeology and geology; and medieval and classical studies. Also high-level textbooks and books for a more general audience. Query. "We like to see a prospectus and an outline." Reviews artwork/photos as part of ms package.
Recent Nonfiction Title: *The Butterflies of North America*, by James A. Scott.
Tips: "The writer's best chance is a work of original scholarship with an argument of some importance and an appeal to a broad audience."

‡*STARBURST PUBLISHERS, Subsidiary of Starburst Inc., P.O. Box 4123, Lancaster PA 17604. (717)293-0939. Editorial Director: Ellen Hake. Estab. 1982. Publishes hardcover and trade papterback originals and trade paperback reprints. Averages 15-20 titles/year. Receives 100 submissions/year. 75% of books by first-time authors. 75% from unagented writers. Subsidy publishes 11% of books. Pays 6-15% royalty on net price to retailer. Publishes book an average of 1 year after acceptance. Reports in 1 month on queries; 2 months on mss. Book catalog for 9×12 SAE with 2 first class stamps. Manuscript guidelines for #10 SASE.
Nonfiction: Biography, cookbook, how-to, juvenile, self-help, Christian. Subjects include business and economics, child guidance/parenting, cooking, foods and nutrition, government/politics, health/medicine, military/war, money/finance, psychology, religion, sports. We are looking for contemporary issues facing Christians. General—how-to, business, self-help and family. Submit outline/synopsis and 3 sample chapters also bio and photo. Reviews artwork/photos as part of ms package.
Recent Nonfiction Title: *Turmoil in the Toy Box II*, by Joan Hake Robie (issues).
Fiction: Adventure, historical, juvenile, mainstream/contemporary, religious, young adult. We are looking for good, wholesome fiction that could either be Christian or general. Submit outline/synopsis and 3 sample chapters also bio and photo.
Tips: 75% our line goes into the Christian marketplace; 25% into the general marketplace. Write on an issue that slots you on talk shows and thus establish your name as an expert and writer.

STARRHILL PRESS, P.O. Box 32342, Washington DC 20007. (202)686-6703. Co-presidents: Liz Hill and Marty Starr. Publishes trade paperback originals. Firm averages 4 titles/year. Receives 10 submissions/year. 90% of books from first-time authors. 100% from unagented writers. Pays 5-10% royalty on retail price. Publishes book an average of 1 year after acceptance. Simultaneous submissions OK. Reports in 2 weeks on queries. Book catalog for #10 SASE.
Nonfiction: Reference. Subjects include art/architecture, music/dance, nature/environment and travel. "American arts, decoration, literary guide books, performing arts, short nonfiction (with line drawings only) are our needs. No popular junk, coffee table books or expensive artwork." Query or submit outline/synopsis and sample chapters. Reviews artwork/photos as part of manuscript package.
Recent Nonfiction Title: *Look Again! Clues to Modern Painting*, by Sally Montanari.

STERLING PUBLISHING, 387 Park Ave. South, New York NY 10016. (212)532-7160. Acquisitions Manager: Sheila Anne Barry. Publishes hardcover and paperback originals and reprints. Averages 80 titles/year. Pays royalty; offers advance. Publishes book an average of 8 months after acceptance. Reports in 6 weeks. Guidelines for SASE.
Nonfiction: Alternative lifestyle, fiber arts, games and puzzles, health how-to, business, foods, hobbies, how-to, children's humor, science and activities, militaria, New Age, pets, recreation, reference, self-help, sports, technical, wine and woodworking. Query or submit complete chapter list, detailed outline/synopsis and 2 sample chapters with photos if necessary. Reviews artwork/photos as part of ms package.
Recent Nonfiction Title: *Comedy Writing Workbook*, by Gene Perret.

GARETH STEVENS, INC., 1555 N. Rivercenter Dr. #201, Milwaukee WI 53212-3913. (414)255-0333. Creative Director: Paul Humphrey. Estab. 1986. Publishes only children's hardcover originals. Averages 150 titles/year. Receives 1,000 submissions/year. 50% of books from first-time authors. 100% from unagented writers. Pays 5% on wholesale price or buys mss outright for $1,500. Offers $500-1,000 average advance. Publishes book average of 1 year after acceptance. Simultaneous (but limited to 2) submissions OK. Reports in 3 months on queries; 9 months on mss. Book catalog for 9 × 12 SAE and 2 first class stamps.
Nonfiction: Biography, cookbook, juvenile, reference (all children's books). Subjects include animals, anthropology/archaeology, art/architecture, history, nature/environment and sociology. "No religious." Submit outline/synopsis and sample chapters or complete ms. Reviews artwork/photos as part of ms package.
Recent Nonfiction Title: *Isaac Asimov's Library of Universe*, by Isaac Asimov (astronomy).
Fiction: Adventure, feminist, historical, humor, juvenile, mystery, picture books (all children's books). "No religious."
Recent Fiction Title: *Bully for the Beast*, by Kathleen Stevens.

‡STILLPOINT PUBLISHING, Division of Stillpoint International, Inc., P.O. Box 640, Walpole NH 03608. (603)756-9281. Senior Editor: Dorothy Seymour. Publishes hardcover originals and trade paperback originals and reprints. Averages 15-20 titles/year. Receives 500 submissions/year. 50% of books from first-time authors; 90% from unagented writers. Pays royalty. Publishes book an average of 9-15 months after acceptance. Simultaneous submissions OK. Reports in 6 weeks. Manuscript guidelines free on request.
Nonfiction: Self-help, psychology, health and healing, personal and planetary transformation. "We are looking for manuscripts that are tools for integrating spiritual values into mainstream living to produce personal and global success and well-being." Query or submit outline/synopsis and sample chapters or complete ms.
Recent Nonfiction Title: *Diet For a New America*, by John Robbins (health/food, lifestyle).
Tips: "Writers have the best chance submitting nonfiction that offers a unique perspective gained from life experience and/or personal research, that addresses a current area of social or environmental change. The work needs to be insightful, practical and reflect a level of spiritual values. If I were a writer trying to market a book today, I would choose a publisher who understands my book's unique message."

STIPES PUBLISHING CO., 10-12 Chester St., Champaign IL 61820. (217)356-8391. FAX: (217)356-5753. Contact: Robert Watts. Publishes hardcover and paperback originals. Averages 15-30 titles/year; receives 150 submissions annually. 50% of books from first-time authors; 100% of books from unagented writers. Pays 15% maximum royalty on retail price. Publishes book an average of 4 months after acceptance. Reports in 2 weeks on queries; 2 months on mss.
Nonfiction: Technical (some areas), textbooks on business and economics, music, chemistry, agriculture/horticulture, and recreation and physical education. "All of our books in the trade area are books that also have a college text market." No "books unrelated to educational fields taught at the college level." Submit outline/synopsis and 1 sample chapter.
Recent Nonfiction Title: *Discerning Art: Concepts and Issues*, by George Hardiman and Ted Zernich.

STOEGER PUBLISHING COMPANY, 55 Ruta Court, S. Hackensack NJ 07606. (201)440-2700. Subsidiary includes Stoeger Industries. Publisher: Paul G. Emberley. Estab. 1925. Publishes trade paperback originals. Averages 12-15 titles/year. Royalty varies, depending on ms. Simultaneous submissions OK. Reports in 1 month on queries; 3 months on mss. Book catalog for SASE.
Nonfiction: Specializing in reference and how-to books that pertain to hunting, fishing and appeal to gun enthusiasts. Submit outline/synopsis and sample chapters.
Recent Nonfiction Title: *The Book of the Twenty-two*, by Sam Fadala.

STORMLINE PRESS, P.O. Box 539, Urbana IL 61801. (217)328-2665. Imprints include: Blue Heron Books. Publisher: Raymond Bial. Estab. 1985. Publishes hardcover and trade paperback originals. Averages 4-5 titles/year. Receives 500 submissions/year. Pays 15% on retail price (after production costs are met). Publishes book an average of 1 year after acceptance. Book catalog for #10 SASE.
Nonfiction: Biography, humor, illustrated book and juvenile. Subjects include agriculture, Americana, art, ethnic, history, photography and regional. "We are interested in nonfiction of the highest literary quality. Do not send unsolicited manuscripts. We generally announce when we are prepared to consider manuscripts. For complete guidelines, send SASE."
Recent Nonfiction Title: *Living With Lincoln: Life and Art in the Heartland*, by Dan Guillory (essays on life in the Midwest).
Fiction: "We are interested in considering carefully-crafted manuscripts of the highest literary quality. Please query first with SASE."
Recent Fiction Title: *Dim Tales*, by John Knoepfle.
Tips: "Do not submit unsolicited manuscripts. Please query first with a brief description of your work. Writers should also study other publications of our press."

Close-up

Meredith Lady Young
President and Publisher
Stillpoint Publishing

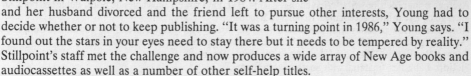

Stillpoint Publishing's titles, a mix of New Age and social issues, appeal to many people who wouldn't ordinarily buy a New Age book, says President and Publisher Meredith Young. "The books we publish are important to people. We think they can occupy a unique place in people's lives."

Young, her husband and a journalist friend started Stillpoint in Walpole, New Hampshire, in 1984. After she and her husband divorced and the friend left to pursue other interests, Young had to decide whether or not to keep publishing. "It was a turning point in 1986," Young says. "I found out the stars in your eyes need to stay there but it needs to be tempered by reality." Stillpoint's staff met the challenge and now produces a wide array of New Age books and audiocassettes as well as a number of other self-help titles.

Young's own books have played a part in Stillpoint's success. *Agartha: A Journey to the Stars* was her first book and was published in Stillpoint's first list of titles. The chronicle of her contact with "a teacher of the angelic realm" has sold more than 100,000 copies. That book was followed by *Language of the Soul*, and Young is currently working on a third book.

Because she is also a writer, Young wants Stillpoint to nurture its authors. "We try to choose authors with something important to say. We like to develop long-term relationships with authors," Young says. In addition, Young looks for authors who are "very enthusiastic about their books" and willing to promote them through workshops, lectures and the media. Young says the publishing house is open to new writers. "We look for the potential," she says. "We would spend a lot of time with the right person." Authors approaching the publishing house should send a cover letter, synopsis and several chapters of their manuscript. The cover letter should be straightforward ("not cute, no hype") but detail the potential audience, the special nature of the book, and give information about the author.

In addition to many New Age books, Stillpoint has begun publishing books on health, co-dependency and other social issues such as homelessness and extinction of animals. One of the titles, *Diet for a New America*, was a Pulitzer Prize nominee. Young believes New Age and "global ethics" are closely related. "In the beginning, I thought it was a spiritual search only, but it is much larger. It's a whole philosophy for living consciously. One very much affects the other."

Young believes the spiritual search will result in many other changes. "Readers are now ready to live their spirituality in both their personal and professional lives rather than just read about it," she says. "I believe the next ten years will see a major acceptance of spiritual values as a basis for the developing global ethics that will transform the traditional structures of society."

— Glenda Tennant Neff

‡**SUNFLOWER UNIVERSITY PRESS**, Subsidiary of Journal of the West, Inc., 1531 Yuma, Box 1009, Manhattan KS 66502-4228. (913)539-1888. Imprints include MA/AH Publishing, Wheatland Books. Associate Publisher: Carol A. Williams. Publishes trade paperback originals and reprints. Averages 15-20 titles/year. Receives 50-75 submissions/year. 75% of books from first-time authors. 80% of books from unagented writers. Pays 10% royalty after first printing. Publishes book an average of 8 months after acceptance and contract. Reports in 3 weeks on queries; 3 months on mss. Free book catalog.
Nonfiction: Biography, illustrated books, reference. Subjects include agriculture/horticulture, Americana, anthropology/archaeology, business and economics, ethnic, government/politics, health/medicine, history, language/literature, military/war, money/finance, music/dance, nature/environment, photography, recreation, regional, religion, science, sociology, sports, women's issues/studies. Our field of specialization lies in memoirs and histories of the West, and of the military, naval, and air fields; perhaps some specialized collectors' books. Query. Reviews artwork/photos as part of the ms package (photocopies acceptable).
Recent Nonfiction Title: *Harvesting Shadows: Untold Tales from the Fur Trade*, by H.D. Smiley (western history).
Fiction: Historical, western, military. We need narratives that are historically accurate and shed light on historical incidents or events. No X-rated, juvenile, stream of consciousness. Query.
Recent Fiction Title: *Tiger Tales*, by Milt Miller (military fiction).
Tips: "Our audience is the informed aviation, military, or Western American history enthusiast."

SUNSTONE PRESS, P.O. Box 2321, Santa Fe NM 87504-2321. (505)988-4418. Editor-in-Chief: James C. Smith Jr. Estab. 1971. Publishes paperback originals; few hardcover originals. Averages 20 titles/year; receives 400 submissions annually. 70% of books from first-time authors; 100% of books from unagented writers. Average print order for writer's first book is 2,000-5,000. Pays royalty on wholesale price. Publishes book an average of 1 year after acceptance. Reports in 2 months.
Nonfiction: How-to series craft books. Books on the history and architecture of the Southwest. Looks for "strong regional appeal (Southwestern)." Reviews artwork/photos as part of ms package.
Recent Nonfiction Title: *Rural Architecture*, by Myrtle Stedman.
Fiction: Publishes "material with Southwestern theme."
Recent Fiction Title: *Of Arms I Sing*, by Joseph J. Bohnaker.
Poetry: Traditional or free verse. Poetry book not exceeding 64 pages. Prefers Southwestern theme.
Recent Poetry Title: *Signature of the Spiral*, by Daniel Schreck.

‡**SURFSIDE PUBLISHING**, P.O. Box 20507, Tampa FL 33622-0507. (813)877-5555. President: J. LaFray. Publishes hardcover and trade paperback originals and reprints. Firm averages 10 titles/year. Receives 150 submissions/year. 5% of books from first-time authors. 90% from unagented writers. Pays royalty or buys mss outright. Publishes book an average of 20 months after acceptance. Reports in 1 month on queries; 6 weeks on mss. Free book catalog.
Nonfiction: "Coffee table" book, cookbook, how-to, illustrated book, reference and self-help. Subjects include agriculture/horticulture, computers and electronics, gardening, hobbies, psychology and travel. No humor or poetry. Query. Reviews artwork/photos as part of ms package.
Recent Nonfiction Title: *The Young Guide to Famous Florida Restaurants*.

SYBEX, INC., 2021 Challenger Dr., Alameda CA 94501. (415)523-8233. FAX: (415)523-2373. Editor-in-Chief: Dr. Rudolph S. Langer. Acquisitions Editor: Dianne King. Estab. 1976. Publishes paperback originals. Averages 75 titles/year. Royalty rates vary. Offers average $3,000 advance. Publishes book an average of 3 months after acceptance. Simultaneous submissions OK. Query for electronic submissions. Reports in 2 months. Free book catalog.
Nonfiction: Computers and computer software. "Manuscripts most publishable in the field of personal computers, desktop computer business applications, hardware, programming, languages, and telecommunications." Submit outline/synopsis and 2-3 sample chapters. Accepts nonfiction translations from French or German. Looks for "clear writing; technical accuracy; logical presentation of material; and good selection of material, such that the most important aspects of the subject matter are thoroughly covered; well-focused subject matter; and well-thought-out organization that helps the reader understand the material." Reviews artwork/photos as part of ms package.
Recent Nonfiction Title: *Mastering WordPerfect 5.1*.
Tips: Queries/mss may be routed to other editors in the publishing group.

‡***SYNESIS PRESS**, P.O. Box 1843-N, Bend OR 97709. (503)382-6517. FAX: (503)382-0750. Editor: Juliana Panchura. Estab. 1989. Publishes trade paperback originals. Averages 6 titles/year. Receives 30 submissions/year. 70% of books from first-time authors; 70% from unagented writers. Subsidy publishes 3% of books. Determines subsidy by subject matter, ability to communicate, and the author's ability to work. Pays 5-30% royalty on retail price. Publishes book an average of 6-9 months after acceptance. Simultaneous submissions OK. Query for electronic submissions. Reports in 3 weeks on queries; 6 weeks on mss.

Nonfiction: Cookbook, how-to, humor, illustrated book, self-help, technical, textbook. Subjects include business and economics, cooking, foods and nutrition, health/medicine, money/finance, philosophy, psychology, recreation, sports. Query. Reviews artwork/photos as part of ms package.
Recent Nonfiction Titles: *The Lean Body Promise*, by Dr. Vince Quas.
Tips: "Our audience consists of people who want more for themselves, their family and for the people around them. They are willing to participate actively, be open to possibilities and they are looking for a specific result. Be clear and concise. Know your subject and who it is intended for. The author must be the example of the material he or she is presenting."

*SYRACUSE UNIVERSITY PRESS, 1600 Jamesville Ave., Syracuse NY 13244-5160. (315)443-5534. Director: Charles Backus. Averages 40 titles/year; receives 350 submissions annually. 40% of books from first-time authors; 95% of books from unagented writers. Subsidy publishes (nonauthor) 20% of books. Pays royalty on net sales. Publishes book an average of 10 months after acceptance. Simultaneous submissions OK "if we are informed." Reports in 2 weeks on queries; "longer on submissions." Book catalog and ms guidelines for SASE.
Nonfiction: "Special opportunity in our nonfiction program for freelance writers of books on New York state. We have published regional books by people with limited formal education, but authors were thoroughly acquainted with their subjects, and they wrote simply and directly about them. Provide precise descriptions about subjects, along with background description of project. The author must make a case for the importance of his or her subject." Query. Accepts outline/synopsis and at least 2 sample chapters. Reviews artwork/photos as part of ms package.
Recent Nonfiction Title: *The Town That Started the Civil War*, by Nat Brandt (history/Civil War).

TAB BOOKS, Division of McGraw-Hill, Inc., Blue Ridge, Summit PA 17214. (717)794-2191. FAX: (717)794-2080. Director of Acquisitions: Ron Powers. Estab. 1964. Imprint is Windcrest (microcomputer books). Publishes hardcover and paperback originals and reprints. Publishes 275 titles/year; receives 600 submissions annually. 50% of books from first-time authors; 85% of books from unagented writers. Average print order for writer's first book is 10,000. Pays variable royalty; buys some mss outright for a negotiable fee. Offers advance. Query for electronic submissions. Reports in 6 weeks. Free book catalog and ms guidelines.
Nonfiction: TAB publishes titles in such fields as computer hardware, computer software, business, solar and alternate energy, marine line, aviation, automotive, music technology, consumer medicine, electronics, electrical and electronics repair, amateur radio, shortwave listening, model railroading, toys, hobbies, drawing, animals and animal power, woodworking, practical skills with projects, building furniture, basic how-to for the house, building large structures, calculators, robotics, telephones, model radio control, TV servicing, audio, recording, hi-fi and stereo, electronic music, electric motors, electrical wiring, electronic test equipment, video programming, CATV, MATV and CCTV, broadcasting, photography and film, appliance servicing and repair, advertising, antiques and restoration, bicycles, crafts, farmsteading, hobby electronics, home construction, license study guides, mathematics, metalworking, reference books, schematics and manuals, small gasoline engines, two-way radio and CB, military fiction, and woodworking. Accepts nonfiction translations. Query with outline/synopsis. Reviews artwork/photos as part of ms package.
Recent Nonfiction Title: *Abused No More*, by Robert J. Ackerman.
Tips: "Many writers believe that a cover letter alone will describe their proposed book sufficiently; it rarely does. The more details we receive, the better the chances are that the writer will get published by us. We expect a writer to tell us what the book is about, but many writers actually fail to do just that."

‡JEREMY P. TARCHER, INC., Suite 200, 5858 Wilshire Blvd., Los Angeles CA 90036. (213)935-9980. Submissions Editor: Donna Zerner. Estab. 1975. Publishes hardcover and trade paperback originals and reprints. Averages 45 titles/year; receives 2,500 submissions annually. 50% of books from first-time authors; 15% of books from unagented writers. Pays royalty with variable advance. Publishes book an average of 1 year after acceptance. Simultaneous submissions OK. Reports in 6 weeks on queries; 10 weeks on mss. Book catalog and guidelines for #10 SASE.
Nonfiction: Subjects include leading edge psychology, health, spirituality, personal and social transformation, women's and men's issues, sexuality, animals, sociology, relationships, dreams, recovery/12-step, creativity, biographies within the field of human potential enhanced performanced and amazing facts books. "We're looking for practical, self-help titles on a variety of health and psychology-related subjects. We continue to be interested in books on consciousness and creativity, science for the layperson, adult relationships, parenting, etc. No humor books, art books, fiction, poetry, esoteric or channeled material, children's books, cook-

ALWAYS submit unsolicited manuscripts or queries with a self-addressed, stamped envelope (SASE) within your country or International Reply Coupons (IRC) purchased from the post office for other countries.

books, Hollywood exposes, astrology books, textbooks, military, or game books." Submit outline/synopsis and sample chapters. "We have published books as commercial as *Women Who Love Too Much*, and as specialized as *The Possible Human*."

Tips: "It's important to us that the author has authority in his or her field and that this is conveyed in the proposal. Beginning authors, and agents representing beginning authors, should include an extensive sample chapter or other writing sample. Authors should pay particular attention to what makes their book different and exciting, and to why they're the ideal author for the book. One of the most important ingredients in a proposal, as far as we're concerned, is the market survey which lists competing books (refer to *Books in Print*) and describes the potential audience. This lets us know that the author has a clear picture of his or her audience and can deliver a saleable book."

TAYLOR PUBLISHING COMPANY, Subsidiary of Insilco, 1550 W. Mockingbird Ln., Dallas TX 75235. (214)637-2800. FAX: (214)637-2800, ext. 220. Contact: Editorial Assistant, Trade Books Division. Estab. 1981. Publishes hardcover and softcover originals. Averages 24 titles/year; receives 1,000 submissions annually. 25% of books from first-time authors; 10% of books from unagented writers. Buys some mss outright. Publishes book 1 year after acceptance. Simultaneous submissions OK. Reports in 6 weeks. Book catalog and ms guidelines for 7×9 SASE.
Nonfiction: True crime, cookbook, humor, sports, travel, self-help and trivia. Submit outline/synopsis and sample chapters. Reviews artwork/photos as part of ms package.
Recent Nonfiction Title: *The Comic Book in America*, by Mike Benton.

TEACHERS COLLEGE PRESS, 1234 Amsterdam Ave., New York NY 10027. (212)678-3929. Director: Carole P. Saltz. Publishes hardcover and paperback originals and reprints. Averages 40 titles/year. Pays royalty. Publishes book an average of 1 year after acceptance. Reports in 1 year. Free book catalog.
Nonfiction: "This university press concentrates on books in the field of education in the broadest sense, from early childhood to higher education: good classroom practices, teacher training, special education, innovative trends and issues, administration and supervision, film, continuing and adult education, all areas of the curriculum, computers, guidance and counseling and the politics, economics, philosophy, sociology and history of education. The Press also issues classroom materials for students at all levels, with a strong emphasis on reading and writing and social studies." Submit outline/synopsis and sample chapters.
Recent Nonfiction Title: *The Empowerment of Teachers*, by Gene Maeroff.

***TEXAS A&M UNIVERSITY PRESS**, Drawer C, College Station TX 77843. (409)845-1436. Director: John F. Stetter. Estab. 1974. Publishes 30 titles/year. Subsidy publishes (nonauthor) 15% of books. Pays in royalties. Publishes book an average of 1 year after acceptance. Query for electronic submissions. Reports in 1 week on queries: 1 month on submissions. Free book catalog.
Nonfiction: Natural history, American history, environmental history, military history, women's studies, economics and regional studies.
Recent Nonfiction Title: *The American Crow and the Common Raven*, by Lawrence Kilham.

***TEXAS CHRISTIAN UNIVERSITY PRESS**, P.O. Box 30783, TCU, Fort Worth TX 76129. (817)921-7822. FAX: (817)921-7333. Director: Judy Alter. Editor: A.T. Row. Estab. 1966. Publishes hardcover originals, some reprints. Averages 8 titles/year; receives 100 submissions annually. 10% of books from first-time authors; 75% of books from unagented writers. Subsidy publishes (nonauthor) 10% of books. Pays royalty. Publishes book an average of 16 months after acceptance. Reports "as soon as possible."
Nonfiction: American studies, juvenile (Chaparral Books, 10 and up), Texana, literature and criticism. "We are looking for good scholarly monographs, other serious scholarly work and regional titles of significance." Query. Reviews artwork/photos as part of ms package.
Recent Nonfiction Title: *Between the Enemy and Texas*, by Anne Bailey.
Fiction: Adult and young adult regional fiction. Query.
Recent Fiction Title: *The Heirs of Franklin Woodstock*, by Benjamin Capps.
Tips: "Regional and/or Texana nonfiction or fiction have best chance of breaking into our firm."

TEXAS WESTERN PRESS, Imprint of The University of Texas at El Paso, El Paso TX 79968-0633. (915)747-5688. Director: Dale L. Walker. Publishes hardcover and paperback originals. Publishes 7-8 titles/year. "This is a university press, 38 years old; we do offer a standard 10% royalty contract on our hardcover books and on some of our paperbacks as well. We try to treat our authors professionally, produce handsome, long-lived books and aim for quality, rather than quantity of titles carrying our imprint." Free book catalog and ms guidelines. Reports in 3 months.
Nonfiction: Scholarly books. Historic and cultural accounts of the Southwest (West Texas, New Mexico, northern Mexico and Arizona). Occasional technical titles. "Our *Southwestern Studies* use manuscripts of up to 30,000 words. Our hardback books range from 30,000 words up. The writer should use good exposition in his work. Most of our work requires documentation. We favor a scholarly, but not overly pedantic, style. We specialize in superior book design." Query with outlines. Follow Chicago *Manual of Style*.

Recent Nonfiction Title: *Literature and Landscape: Writers of the Southwest*, by Cynthia Farah.
Tips: "Texas Western Press is interested in books relating to the history of Hispanics in the U.S., will experiment with photo-documentary books, and is interested in seeing more 'popular' history and books on Southwestern culture/life."

‡**THEATRE ARTS BOOKS**, Imprint of Routledge, Chapman & Hall, Inc., 29 West 35th St., New York NY 10001. (212)244-3336. Editorial Director: William P. Germano. Publishes hardcover and trade paperback originals. Pays royalty. Publishes ms an average of 1 year after acceptance. Reports in 6 weeks. Use Chicago *Manual of Style* for ms guidelines.
Nonfiction: Drama and theater. Subjects include acting, directing, lighting, costume, dance, staging, etc. "We publish only books of broad general interest to actors, directors and theater technicians, especially books that could be useful in college classrooms. Most of our authors have had long experience in professional theater. Topics that are very narrowly focused (a costume book on women's shoes in the eighteenth century, for example) would not be acceptable. We no longer publish original plays." Query with outline, synopsis and author's qualifications.

THE THEOSOPHICAL PUBLISHING HOUSE, Subsidiary of The Theosophical Society in America, 306 W. Geneva Rd., Wheaton IL 60189. (312)665-0130. Imprint, Quest (nonfiction). Senior Editor: Shirley Nicholson. Estab. 1968. Publishes trade paperback originals. Averages 12 titles/year; receives 750-1,000 submissions annually. 50-60% of books from first-time authors; 95% of books from unagented writers. Average print order for a writer's first book is 5,000. Pays 12½% royalty on net price; offers average $1,500 advance. Publishes book an average of 9 months after acceptance. Simultaneous submissions OK. Reports in 2 weeks on queries, 2 months on mss. Free book catalog; ms guidelines for SASE.
Nonfiction: Subjects include self-development, self-help, philosophy (holistic), psychology (transpersonal), Eastern and Western religions, comparative religion, holistic implications in science, health and healing, yoga, meditation and astrology. "TPH seeks works that are compatible with the theosophical philosophy. Our audience includes the 'New Age' community, seekers in all religions, general public, professors, and health professionals. No submissions that do not fit the needs outlined above." Accepts nonfiction translations. Query or submit outline/synopsis and sample chapters. Reviews artwork/photos as part of ms package.
Recent Nonfiction Title: *Jungian Synchronicity*, by Alice O. Howell.
Tips: "The writer has the best chance of selling our firm a book that illustrates a connection between spiritually-oriented philosophy or viewpoint and some field of current interest."

*****THISTLEDOWN PRESS**, 668 East Place, Saskatoon, Saskatchewan S7J 2Z5 Canada. (306)244-1722. Editor-in-Chief: Paddy O' Rourke. Estab. 1975. Publishes hardcover and trade paperback originals by resident Canadian authors only. Averages 10-12 titles/year; receives 150 submissions annually. 50% of books from first-time authors; 100% of books from unagented writers. Average print order for a writer's first (poetry) book is 500 or (fiction) 1,000. Subsidy publishes (nonauthor) 100% of books. Pays standard royalty on retail price. Publishes book an average of 18-24 months after acceptance. Reports in 2 weeks on queries; 2 months on poetry mss; 3 months on fiction mss. Book catalog and guidelines for #10 SASE.
Fiction: Juvenile (ages 8 and up), literary. Interested in fiction mss from resident Canadian authors only. Minimum of 30,000 words. Accepts no unsolicited work. Query first.
Recent Fiction Title: *Paradise Cafe and Other Stories*, by Martha Brooks (young adult).
Poetry: "The author should make him/herself familiar with our publishing program before deciding whether or not his/her work is appropriate." No poetry by people *not* citizens and residents of Canada. Submit complete ms. Minimum of 60 pages. Prefers poetry mss that have had some previous exposure in literary magazines. Accepts no unsolicited work. Query first.
Recent Poetry Title: *Making Movies*, by Andrew Wreggitt.
Tips: "We prefer to receive a query letter first before a submission. We're looking for quality, well-written literary fiction—for children and young adults and for our adult fiction list as well."

THOMAS PUBLICATIONS, Subsidiary of Thomas Graphics, Inc., Box 33244, Austin TX 78764. (512)832-0355. Contact: Ralph D. Thomas. Publishes trade paperback originals and reprints. Averages 8-10 titles/year; receives 20-30 submissions annually. 90% of books from first-time authors; 90% of books from unagented writers. Pays 10-15% royalty on wholesale or retail price, or makes outright purchase of $500-2,000. Publishes book an average of 1 year after acceptance. Simultaneous submissions OK. Reports in 2 weeks on queries; 1 month on mss. Book catalog $1.
Nonfiction: How-to, reference and textbook. Subjects include sociology and investigation and investigative techniques. "We are looking for hardcore investigative methods books, manuals on how to make more dollars in private investigation, private investigative marketing techniques, and specialties in the investigative professions." Query or submit outline/synopsis and sample chapters. Reviews artwork/photos as part of ms package.

Recent Nonfiction Title: *How to Investigate by Computer: 1990*, by Ralph Thomas and Leroy Cook.
Tips: "Our audience includes private investigators, those wanting to break into investigation, related trades such as auto repossessors, private process servers, news reporters, and related security trades."

*THREE CONTINENTS PRESS, 1901 Pennsylvania Ave. N.W., Washington DC 20006. Publisher/Editor-in-Chief: Donald E. Herdeck. General Editor: Lyndi Schrecengost. Publishes hardcover and paperback originals and reprints. Averages 20-30 titles/year. Receives 200 submissions annually. 15% of books from first-time authors; 100% of books from unagented writers. Average print order for a writer's first book is 1,000. Subsidy publishes (nonauthor) 10% of books. Pays 10% royalty; advance "only on delivery of complete manuscript which is found acceptable; usually $300." Simultaneous submissions OK. State availability of photos/illustrations. Reports in 2 months. Book catalog and guidelines for 9×12 SAE.
Nonfiction and Fiction: Specializes in African, Caribbean and Middle Eastern (Arabic and Persian) literature and criticism and translation, Third World literature and history. Scholarly, well-prepared mss; creative writing. Fiction, poetry, criticism, history and translations of creative writing. "We search for books that will make clear the complexity and value of non-western literature and culture, including bilingual texts (Arabic language/English translations). We are always interested in genuine contributions to understanding non-western culture." Length: 50,000-125,000 words. Query. "Please do not submit manuscript unless we ask for it. We prefer an outline, and an annotated table of contents, for works of nonfiction; and a synopsis, a plot summary (one to three pages), for fiction. For poetry, send two or three sample poems." Reviews artwork/photos as part of ms package.
Recent Nonfiction Title: *The Imperishable Empire: A Study of British Fiction on India*, by Rashna B. Singh.
Recent Fiction Title: *The Fantasy Eaters, Stories from Fiji*, by Subramani.
Tips: "We need a *polished* translation, or original prose or poetry by non-Western authors *only*."

‡THUNDER'S MOUTH PRESS, #45, 54 Greene St., New York NY 10013. (212)226-0277. Publisher: Neil Ortenberg. Publishes hardcover and trade paperback originals and reprints. Averages 15 titles/year; receives 1,000 submissions annually. 10% of books from unagented writers. Average print order for a writer's first book is 5,000. Pays 5-10% royalty on retail price; offers average $1,000 advance. Publishes book an average of 8 months after acceptance. Reports in 3 months on queries. Does not consider unsolicited manuscripts.
Nonfiction: Biography, politics, popular culture. 5-10/year. Query only.
Fiction: Ethnic, experimental, historical, and political. "We are interested in doing anywhere up to 5 novels per year, particularly literary or socially relevant novels." No romance. Query only.

‡TICKNOR & FIELDS, Imprint of Houghton Mifflin, 215 Park Ave. S., New York NY 10003. (212)410-5800. Editorial Director: John Herman. Publishes hardcover originals. Firm averages 14 titles/year; imprint averages 30 titles/year. Receives 500 submissions/year. 10% of books from first-time authors. Pays royalty.
Nonfiction and Fiction: General subjects. Query.

‡TIDEWATER PUBLISHERS, Imprint of Cornell Maritime Press, Inc., P.O. Box 456, Centreville MD 21617. (301)758-1075. Contact: Editor. Publishes hardcover and paperback originals. Imprint averages 7-9 titles/year. Receives 150 submissions/year. 41% of books from first-time authors. 99% from unagented writers. Pays 7½-15% royalty on retail price. Publishes book an average of 10 months after acceptance. Simultaneous submissions OK. Query for electronic submissions. Reports in 2 weeks on queries; 1 month on mss. Free book catalog and manuscript guidelines.
Nonfiction: Coffee table books, cookbook, how-to, illustrated book, juvenile, reference, self-help, technical, textbook. Subjects include regional. Query. Submit outline/synopsis and sample chapters. Reviews artwork/photos as part of ms package.
Recent Nonfiction Title: *Smith Island, Chesapeake Bay*, by Frances Dize (history/folklore).
Fiction: Juvenile. Nothing other than juvenile fiction. Query. Submit outline/synopsis and sample chapters.
Recent Fiction Title: *Rambling Raft*, by Lynn N. Lockhart and Barbara M. Lockhart (juvenile).
Tips: "Our audience is made up of readers interested in works that are specific to the Chesapeake Bay and Delmarva Peninsula area."

TIMBER PRESS, INC., 9999 S.W. Wilshire, Portland OR 97225. (503)292-0745. FAX: (503)292-6607. Imprints include Dioscorides Press (botany), Amadeus Press (music) and Areopagitica Press (history). Editor: Richard Abel. Publishes hardcover and paperback originals. Publishes 40 titles/year; receives 300-400 submissions annually. 90% of books from first-time authors; 100% of books from unagented writers. Pays 10-20% royalty; sometimes offers advance to cover costs of artwork and final ms completion. Publishes book an average of 1 year after acceptance. Query for electronic submissions. Reports in 2 months. Book catalog for 9×12 SAE with 3 first class stamps.
Nonfiction: Horticulture (ornamental and economic), botany, plant sciences, natural history, Northwest regional material, forestry, serious music and history. Accepts nonfiction translations from all languages. Query or submit outline/synopsis and 3-4 sample chapters. Reviews artwork/photos as part of ms package.

Recent Nonfiction Title: *Foliage Plants for Decorating Indoors*, by Elbert.
Tips: "The writer has the best chance of selling our firm good books on botany, plant science, horticulture, forestry, agriculture and serious music and history."

TIME-LIFE BOOKS INC., 777 Duke St., Alexandria VA 22314. (703)838-7000. Editor: George Constable. Publishes hardcover originals. Averages 40 titles/year. Books are almost entirely staff-generated and staff-produced, and distribution is primarily through mail order sale. Query to the Director of Corporate Development.
Nonfiction: "General interest books. Most books tend to be heavily illustrated (by staff), with text written by assigned authors. We very rarely accept mss or book ideas submitted from outside our staff." Length: open.
Recent Nonfiction Title: *The Computerized Society*.

TIMES BOOKS, Division of Random House, Inc., 201 East 50 St., New York NY 10022. (212)872-8110. Vice President and Publisher: Peter Osnos. Editorial Director: Steve Wasserman. Publishes hardcover and paperback originals and reprints. Publishes 45 titles/year. Pays royalty; average advance. Publishes book an average of 1 year after acceptance. Computer printout submissions acceptable.
Nonfiction: Business/economics, science and medicine, history, biography, women's issues, the family, cookbooks, current affairs and sports. Accepts only solicited manuscripts. Reviews artwork/photos as part of ms package.
Recent Nonfiction Title: *The American Heart Association Low Fat Low Cholesterol Diet*, by Scott Grundy M.D.

TOR BOOKS, Subsidiary of St. Martin's Press, 9th Floor, 49 W. 24th St., New York NY 10010. (212)741-3100. Publisher: Tom Doherty. Publishes mass market, hardcover and trade paperback originals and reprints. Averages 300 books/year. Pays 6-8% royalty; offers negotiable advance. Book catalog for 9 × 12 SASE.
Fiction: Horror, science fiction, occult, chillers, suspense, espionage, historical and fantasy. "We prefer an extensive chapter-by-chapter synopsis and the first 3 chapters complete." Prefers agented mss or proposals.
Recent Fiction Title: *Boat of a Million Years*, by Poul Anderson (science fiction).
Tips: "We're pretty broad in the occult, horror and fantasy but more straightforward in science fiction and thrillers, tending to stay with certain authors and certain types of work."

*TRANSACTION BOOKS, Rutgers University, New Brunswick NJ 08903. (201)932-2280. FAX: (201)932-3138. President: I.L. Horowitz. Publisher: Scott Bramson. Book Division Director: Mary E. Curtis. Publishes hardcover and paperback originals and reprints. Specializes in scholarly social science books. Averages 135 titles/year; receives 800 submissions annually. 15% of books from first-time authors; 85% of books from unagented writers. Average print order for a writer's first book is 1,000. Subsidy publishes 10% of books. Royalty "depends on individual contract; we've gone anywhere from 2% edited to 15% authored." No advance. Publishes book an average of 10 months after acceptance. Electronic submissions OK, but requires hard copy also. Reports in 4 months. Book catalog and ms guidelines for SASE.
Nonfiction: Americana, biography, economics, history, law, medicine and psychiatry, music, philosophy, politics, psychology, reference, scientific, sociology, technical and textbooks. "All must be scholarly social science or related." Strong emphasis on applied social research. Query or submit outline/synopsis. "Do not submit sample chapters. We evaluate complete manuscripts only." Accepts nonfiction translations. Use Chicago *Manual of Style*. Looks for "scholarly content, presentation, methodology, and target audience." State availability of photos/illustrations and send one photocopied example. Reviews artwork/photos as part of ms package.
Recent Nonfiction Title: *Authority in Islam*, by Hamid Dabashi (religion/sociology).

TRANSNATIONAL PUBLISHERS, INC., P.O. Box 7282, Ardsley-on-Hudson NY 10503. (914)693-0089. FAX: (914)696-8776. Publisher: Ms. Heike Fenton. Estab. 1981. Publishes hardcover originals. Averages 10-15 titles/year; receives 50 submissions annually. 10% of books from first-time authors; 100% of books from unagented writers. Pays 10% royalty. Publishes book an average of 6 months after acceptance. Simultaneous submissions OK. Reports in 2 weeks on queries; 1 month on mss. Book and ms guidelines free on request.
Nonfiction: Reference, textbook and books for professionals. Subjects include politics, international law, criminal law, human rights, women's studies and political theory. Needs scholarly works in the area of international law and politics. No submissions on topics other than those listed above. Submit outline/synopsis and sample chapters.
Recent Nonfiction Title: *In Fairness to Future Generations*, by Edith Brown Weiss.
Tips: "The audience for our books includes law libraries, public libraries, universities, government personnel, military personnel, college students and women's rights groups."

TRANSPORTATION TRAILS, Subsidiary of National Bus Trader, Inc., 9698 W. Judson Road, Polo IL 61064. (815)946-2341. FAX: (815)946-2347. Editor: Larry Plachino. Estab. 1977. Publishes hardcover and trade paperback originals and mass market paperback originals. Firm averages 8 titles/year. Receives 10 submissions/year. 50% of books from first-time authors. 100% from unagented writers. Pays 10-15% on retail price. Publishes book an average of 1 year after acceptance. Simultaneous submissions OK. Reports in 2 weeks on queries; 2 months on mss. Free book catalog and manuscript guidelines.

Nonfiction: Subject includes travel. "We are only interested in transportation history—prefer electric interurban railroads or trolley lines but will consider steam locomotives, horsecars, buses, aviation and maritime." Query. Reviews artwork/photos as part of ms package.

Recent Nonfiction Title: *Sunset Lines—The Story of the Chicago Aurora and Elgin Railroads*, by Larry Plachno.

TRAVEL KEYS, P.O. Box 160691, Sacramento CA 95816. (916)452-5200. Publisher: Peter B. Manston. Estab. 1984. Publishes hardcover and trade paperback originals. Averages 4 titles/year; receives 35 submissions annually. 60% of books from first-time authors; 90% of books from unagented writers. Pays 6-15% royalty ("rarely, we mostly use work for hire"); or makes outright purchase for $500 minimum. Offers minimum $500 advance. Publishes book an average of 1 year after acceptance. Simultaneous submissions OK. Query for electronic submissions. Reports in 1 month. Book catalog for #10 SAE with 2 first class stamps.

Nonfiction: How-to on travel (mainly Europe), antiques and flea market guides and home security. "We need carefully researched, practical travel manuscripts. No science or technical submissions." Full disclosure of sponsored travel is required. Submit outline/synopsis and sample chapters. Reviews artwork/photos as part of ms package.

Recent Nonfiction Title: *Manston's Europe 90*, by Peter Manston.

Tips: "We will continue in the travel field, but we are broadening out from destination guides to more general travel topics."

TRILLIUM PRESS, Subsidiaries include Cloud 10, Box 209, Monroe NY 10950. (914)783-2999. Editor: William Neumann. Publishes hardcover and paperback originals, software, video tapes and audio tapes. Averages 150 titles/year; receives 800 submissions annually. 33% of books from first-time authors; 95% of books from unagented writers. Publishes book an average of 1 year after acceptance. Reports in 1 month on queries. Book catalog and guidelines for 9 × 12 SAE and 4 first class stamps.

Nonfiction: Self-help and textbook. Subjects include inspirational and education. Submit complete ms. Review artwork/photos as part of ms.

Recent Nonfiction Title: *Educating Children for Life*, by Annemarie Roeper.

Fiction: Children's (ages 4-17). Submit complete ms.

Recent Fiction Title: *Anna's Blanket*, by Sue Hood.

TSR, INC., Box 756, Lake Geneva WI 53147. (414)248-3625. Imprints include Dragonlance, Forgotten Realms, Greyhawk, TSR Books and Buck Rogers. Managing Editor: Mary Kirchoff. Estab. 1975. Publishes trade paperback originals. Firm averages 70-80 titles/year; imprint averages 20-25 titles/year. Receives 250 submissions/year. 30-40% of books from first-time authors. 5% from unagented authors. Pays 4% royalty on retail price. Offers $4,000 average advance. Publishes book an average of 1 year after acceptance. Simultaneous submissions OK. Reports in 1 month on queries; 6 weeks on mss.

Nonfiction: "All of our nonfiction books are generated in-house."

Fiction: Fantasy, horror, mainstream/contemporary, mystery and science fiction. "We have a very small market for good science fiction and fantasy for the TSR Book line, but also need samples from writers willing to do work-for-hire for our other lines. We do not need occult, new age, or adult theme fiction. Nor will we consider excessively violent or gory fantasy, science fiction or horror." Query. Submit outline/synopsis and sample chapters or ms.

Recent Fiction Title: *The Halfling's Gem*, by R.A. Salvatore.

Tips: Our audience is comprised of highly imaginative 12-40 year-old males.

*CHARLES E. TUTTLE PUBLISHING COMPANY, INC., 2-6 Suido 1-Chome, Tokyo 112, Japan. Managing Editor: Ray Furse. Publishes hardcover and trade paperback originals and reprints. Averages 36 titles/year. Receives 750 submissions/year. 10% of books from first-time authors; 80% from unagented writers. Subsidy publishes 5% of books. Pays 6-10% on wholesale price. Offers $1,000 average advance. Publishes book an average of 8-12 months after acceptance. Simultaneous submissions OK. Query for electronic submissions. Reports in 2 weeks on queries; 2 months on manuscripts. Free book catalog and manuscript guidelines.

Nonfiction: Cookbook, how-to, humor, illustrated book and reference. Subjects include art/architecture, business and economics, cooking, foods and nutrition, government/politics, history, language/literature, money/finance, philosophy, regional, religion, sports and travel. "We want Asia-related, but specifically Japan-related manuscripts on various topics, particularly business, martial arts, language, etc." Query with outline/synopsis and sample chapters. Reviews artwork as part of ms package.

Recent Nonfiction Title: *The Best of Tokyo*, by Don Morton and Naoko Tsuroi.
Fiction: Literature of Japan or Asia in English translation. Query with outline/synopsis and sample chapters.
Recent Fiction Title: *Crackling Mountain and Other Stories*, by Osamu Dazai.
Poetry: Submit samples.
Tips: "Readers with an interest in Japan and Asia — culture, language, business, foods, travel, etc. — are our audience."

TWIN PEAKS PRESS, P.O. Box 129, Vancouver WA 98666. (206)694-2462. President: Helen Hecker. Estab. 1984. Publishes hardcover originals and reprints and trade paperback originals and reprints. Averages 7-10 titles/year. Receives 1,000 submissions/year. 25% of books from first-time authors. 100% from unagented writers. Payment varies — individual agreement. Publishes book an average of 6 months after acceptance. Simultaneous submissions OK. Does not report unless interested. Do *not* send unsolicited mss.
Nonfiction: Cookbook, how-to, reference and self-help. Subjects include business and economics, cooking, foods and nutrition, health/medicine, hobbies, recreation, sociology, sports and travel. Query with outline in writing only.
Recent Nonfiction Title: *All About Sewing Machines*, by Robert Johanson.

TYNDALE HOUSE PUBLISHERS, INC., 351 Executive Dr., P.O. Box 80, Wheaton IL 60189. (708)668-8300. Vice President, Editorial: Ronald Beers. Publishes hardcover and trade paperback originals and hardcover and mass paperback reprints. Averages 100 titles/year; receives 3,000 submissions annually. 15% of books from first-time authors. Average print order for a writer's first book is 7,000-10,000. Royalty and advance negotiable. Publishes book an average of 18 months after acceptance. Reports in 6 weeks. Free book catalog; ms guidelines for #10 SASE.
Nonfiction: "Practical, user-friendly Christian books: home and family, Christian growth/self-help, devotional/inspirational, theology/Bible doctrine, 4 children's nonfiction, contemporary/critical issues. Submit table of contents, chapter summaries, and two sample chapters."
Fiction: "Biblical, historical and other Christian themes. No short story collections. Submit entire novel. Children's books: character building stories and nonfiction with Christian perspective. Especially interested in ages 6-12. Submit entire ms."

*UAHC PRESS, Union of American Hebrew Congregations, 838 5th Ave., New York NY 10021. (212)249-0100. Managing Director: Stuart L. Benick. Acquisitions Editor: Aron Hirt-Manheimer. Estab. 1873. Publishes hardcover and trade paperback originals. Averages 15 titles/year. 50% of books from first-time authors; 90% of books from unagented writers. Subsidy publishes 40% of books. Pays 5-15% royalty on wholesale price. Publishes book an average of 9 months after acceptance. Simultaneous submissions OK. Book catalog and ms guidelines for SASE.
Nonfiction: Illustrated, juvenile and Jewish textbooks. Subjects include Jewish religion. "We need Jewish textbooks that fit into our curriculum." Reviews artwork/photos as part of ms package.
Fiction: Jewish religion. "We publish books that teach values."

ULI, THE URBAN LAND INSTITUTE, 1090 Vermont Ave. N.W., Washington DC 20005. (202)289-8500. Staff Vice President of Publications: Frank H. Spink, Jr. Estab. 1936. Publishes hardcover and trade paperback originals. Averages 15-20 titles/year. Receives 20 submissions annually. No books from first-time authors; 100% of books from unagented writers. Pays 10% royalty on gross sales. Offers advance of $1,500-2,000. Publishes book an average of 6 months after acceptance. Query for electronic submissions. Book catalog and writer's guidelines for 9 × 12 SAE.
Nonfiction: Technical books on real estate development and land planning. "The majority of mss are created in-house by research staff. We acquire two or three outside authors to fill schedule and subject areas where our list has gaps. We are not interested in real estate sales, brokerages, appraisal, making money in real estate, opinion, personal point of view, or mss negative toward growth and development." Query. Reviews artwork/photos as part of ms package.
Recent Nonfiction Title: *Carrots and Sticks: New Downtown Zoning*, by Terry Jill Lassar.

ULTRALIGHT PUBLICATIONS, INC., Box 234, Hammelstown PA 17036. (717)566-0468. Editor: Michael A. Markowski. Imprints include Aviation Publishers and Medical Information Systems Division. Publishes hardcover and trade paperback originals. Averages 6 titles/year; receives 30 submissions annually. 50% of books from first-time authors; 100% of books from unagented writers. Average print order for a writer's first book is 5,000. Pays 10-15% royalty on wholesale price; buys some mss outright. Offers average $1,000-1,500 advance. Publishes book an average of 9 months after acceptance. Simultaneous submissions OK. Reports in 3 weeks on queries; 2 months on mss. Book catalog and ms guidelines for #10 SAE with 2 first class stamps.
Nonfiction: How-to, technical on hobbies (model airplanes, model cars, and model boats) and aviation. Publishes for "aviation buffs, dreamers and enthusiasts. We are looking for titles in the homebuilt, sport and general aviation fields. We are interested in how-to, technical and reference books of short to medium length that will serve recognized and emerging aviation needs." Also interested in popular health, medical, and

fitness for the general public, self-help, motivation and success. Query or submit outline/synopsis and 3 sample chapters. Reviews artwork/photos as part of ms package.

Recent Nonfiction Title: *Canard: A Revolution in Flight*, by Lennon (aviation history).

UMBRELLA BOOKS, Harbor View Publications Group, Inc. Box 1460-A, Friday Harbor WA 98250. (206)378-5128. Publishes 4-6 titles/year. Pays royalty on wholesale price. Advance varies. Publishes book an average of 6 months after acceptance. Simultaneous submissions OK. Query for electronic submissions. Reports in 1 month on queries. Manuscript guidelines for #10 SASE.

Nonfiction: Travel (Pacific Northwest). Query; do *not* send photos.

Recent Nonfiction Title: *Umbrella Guide to Bicycling the Oregon Coast*.

UNION SQUARE PRESS, Imprint of NJ Sambul & Co., Inc. 5 E. 16th St., New York NY 10003. (212)924-2800. FAX: (212)675-5479. Managing Editor: Karen Raugust. Estab. 1987. Publishes hardcover originals and trade paperback originals and reprints. Firm averages 7 titles/year. 50% of books from first-time authors. 90% from unagented writers. Pays 10% on list price. Offers $500-1,000 average advance. Publishes book an average of 9 months after acceptance. Simultaneous submissions OK. Query for electronic submissions. Reports in 3 months.

Nonfiction: Coffee table books, how-to, illustrated books, reference and technical. Subjects include business and economics, computers and electronics, hobbies/crafts, science (broadcast engineering) and media. Submit outline/synopsis and sample chapters. Reviews artwork/photos as part of ms package.

Recent Nonfiction Title: *Mark Schubin's HOTV Glossary*, by Mark Schubin (media, television).

*UNIVELT, INC., P.O. Box 28130, San Diego CA 92128. (619)746-4005. Publisher: H. Jacobs. Estab. 1970. Publishes hardcover originals. Averages 8 titles/year; receives 20 submissions annually. 5% of books from first-time authors; 5% of books from unagented writers. Subsidy publishes (nonauthor) 10% of books. Average print order for a writer's first book is 1,000-2,000. Pays 10% royalty on actual sales; no advance. Publishes book an average of 4 months after acceptance. Reports in 1 month. Book catalog and ms guidelines for SASE.

Nonfiction: Publishes in the field of aerospace, especially astronautics and technical communications, but including application of aerospace technology to Earth's problems, also astronomy. Submit outline/synopsis and 1-2 sample chapters. Reviews artwork/photos as part of ms package.

Recent Nonfiction Title: *To Catch a Flying Star, A Scientific Theory of UFOs*.

Tips: "Writers have the best chance of selling manuscripts on the history of astronautics (we have a history series) and astronautics/spaceflight subjects. We publish for the American Astronautical Society." Queries/mss may be routed to other editors in the publishing group.

‡UNIVERSE BOOKS, 381 Park Ave. S., New York NY 10016. (212)685-7400. Senior Editor: Adele J. Ursowe. Estab. 1956. Publishes hardcover and paperback originals and reprints. Averages 20-25 titles/year; receives 500 submissions annually. Average print order for a writer's first book is 2,000-3,000. Offers 5-10% royalty on retail price (hardbound books). Publishes book an average of 9 months after acceptance. Simultaneous submissions OK. "Will not return material without postage-paid SAE." Reports in 1 month.

Nonfiction: We publish books in the following categories: art, architecture and design. We do not publish fiction, poetry, cookbooks, criticism or belles lettres." Submit outline/synopsis and 2-3 sample chapters. Reviews artwork/photos as part of ms package.

Recent Nonfiction Title: *Africa's Mountains of the Morn*, by Guy Yeoman (illustrated travel history).

UNIVERSITY ASSOCIATES, INC., 8517 Production Ave., San Diego CA 92121. (619)578-5900. FAX: (619)578-2042. President: J. William Pfeiffer. Estab. 1968. Publishes paperback and hardback originals and reprints. Averages 12-15 titles/year. Specializes in practical materials for human resource development, consultants, etc. Pays average 10% royalty; no advance. Publishes book an average of 6 months after acceptance. Markets books by direct mail. Simultaneous submissions OK. Reports in 4 months. Book catalog and guidelines for SASE.

Nonfiction: Richard Roe, Vice President, Publications. Publishes (in order of preference) human resource development and group-oriented material, management education, personal growth, and business. No materials for grammar school or high school classroom teachers. Use *American Psychological Association Style Manual*. Query. Send prints or completed art or rough sketches to accompany ms.

Recent Nonfiction Title: *The 1990 Annual: Developing Human Resources*, J.W. Pfeiffer, editor.

UNIVERSITY OF ALABAMA PRESS, Box 870380, Tuscaloosa AL 35487. Director: Malcolm MacDonald. Estab. 1945. Publishes hardcover originals. Averages 40 titles/year; receives 200 submissions annually. 80% of books from first-time authors; 100% of books from unagented writers. "Pays maximum 10% royalty on wholesale price; no advance." Publishes book an average of 16 months after acceptance. Free book catalog; ms guidelines for SASE.

Nonfiction: Biography, history, philosophy, politics, religion, literature and anthropology. Considers upon merit almost any subject of scholarly interest, but specializes in linguistics and philology, political science and public administration, literary criticism and biography, philosophy and history. Accepts nonfiction translations. Reviews artwork/photos as part of ms package.

Recent Nonfiction Title: *Even Mississippi*, by Melany Nielson.

‡**UNIVERSITY OF ALASKA PRESS**, Signers' Hall-UAF, Fairbanks AK 99775-1580. (907)474-6389. FAX: (907)474-7225. Imprints include: Ramuson Library Historical Translation Series. Manager: Debbie Van Stone. Estab. 1927. Publishes hardcover originals and trade paperback originals and reprints. Averages 5-10 titles/year. Receives 100 submissions/year. 0% of books from first-time authors; 0% from unagented writers. Pays 10-12% royalty on net sales. Publishes book an average of 2 years after acceptance. Simultaneous submissions OK. Query for electronic submissions. Reports in 6 weeks. Book catalog free on request.

Nonfiction: Biography, reference, technical, textbook, scholarly nonfiction relating to Alaska-circumpolar north. Subjects include agriculture/horticulture, Americana (Alaskana), animals, anthropology/archaeology, art/architecture, education, ethnic, government/politics, health/medicine, history, language, military/war, nature/environment, regional, science and translation. Nothing that isn't northern or circumpolar. Query or submit outline/synopsis and sample chapters or complete ms. Reviews artwork/photos as part of ms package.

Recent Nonfiction Title: *Birds of the Seward Peninsula*, by Brina Kessel (reference).

Tips: "Writers have the best chance with scholarly, nonfiction relating to Alaska, the circumpolar north and North Pacific Rim. Our audience is made up of scholars, historians, students, libraries, universities, individuals."

THE UNIVERSITY OF ALBERTA PRESS, 141 Athabasca Hall, Edmonton, Alberta T6G 2E8 Canada. (403)492-3662. FAX: (403)492-7219. Imprint, Pica Pica Press. Director: Norma Gutteridge. Publishes hardcover and trade paperback originals, and trade paperback reprints. Averages 10 titles/year; receives 200-300 submissions annually. 60% of books from first-time authors; majority of books from unagented writers. Average print order for a writer's first book is 1,000. Pays 10% royalty on retail price. Publishes book an average of 1 year after acceptance. Query for electronic submissions. Computer printout submissions acceptable; no dot-matrix. Reports in 1 week on queries; 3 months on mss. Free book catalog and ms guidelines.

Nonfiction: Biography, how-to, reference, technical, textbook, and scholarly. Subjects include art, history, nature, philosophy, politics, and sociology. Especially looking for "biographies of Canadians in public life, and works analyzing Canada's political history and public policy, particularly in international affairs. No pioneer reminiscences, literary criticism (unless in Canadian literature), reports of narrowly focused studies, unrevised theses." Submit complete ms. Reviews artwork/photos as part of ms package.

Recent Nonfiction Title: *Nurses, Colleagues and Patients*, by Jennie Wilting.

Tips: "We are interested in original research making a significant contribution to knowledge in the subject."

UNIVERSITY OF ARIZONA PRESS, 1230 N. Park Ave., No. 102, Tucson AZ 85719. (602)621-1441. Director: Stephen Cox. Estab. 1959. Publishes hardcover and paperback originals and reprints. Averages 40 titles/year; receives 300-400 submissions annually. 30% of books from first-time authors; 90% of books from unagented writers. Average print order is 1,500. Royalty terms vary; usual starting point for scholarly monograph is after sale of first 1,000 copies. Publishes book an average of 1 year after acceptance. Query for electronic submissions. Reports in three months. Book catalog for 9×12 SAE; ms guidelines for #10 SASE.

Nonfiction: Scholarly books about anthropology, geosciences, arid lands studies, space sciences, Asian studies, Southwest Indians, and Latin America; scholarly and general nonfiction about the American West, Mexico, and natural history; creative nonfiction. Query and submit outline, list of illustrations and sample chapters. Reviews artwork/photos as part of ms package.

Recent Nonfiction Title: *Sonoran Desert Summer*, by John Alcock.

Tips: "Perhaps the most common mistake a writer might make is to offer a book manuscript or proposal to a house whose list he or she has not studied carefully. Editors rejoice in receiving material that is clearly targeted to the house's list, 'I have approached your firm because my books complement your past publications in. . .,' presented in a straightforward, businesslike manner."

‡**THE UNIVERSITY OF ARKANSAS PRESS**, Fayetteville AR 72701. (501)575-3246. Director: Miller Williams. Publishes hardcover and trade paperback originals and hardcover reprints. Averages 36 titles/year; receives 4,000 submissions annually. 30% of books from first-time authors; 90% of books from unagented writers. Pays 10% royalty on net receipts. Publishes book an average of 18 months after acceptance. Simultaneous (if so informed) submissions OK. Query for electronic submissions. Reports in 3 weeks on queries; 6 weeks on mss. Ms guidelines for #10 SAE and 2 first class stamps.

Nonfiction: Biography and literature. Subjects include Americana, history, humanities, nature, general politics and history of politics, and sociology. "Our current needs include literary criticism—especially on contemporary authors, history and biography. We won't consider manuscripts for texts, juvenile or religious studies, or anything requiring a specialized or exotic vocabulary." Query or submit outline/synopsis and sample chapters.

Recent Nonfiction Title: *Flight from Innocence*, by Judson Jerome.
Fiction: "Works of high literary merit; short stories; rarely novels. No genre fiction." Query.
Recent Fiction Title: *Power Lines*, by Jane Bradley.
Poetry: "Because of small list, query first." Arkansas Poetry Award offered for publication of first book. Write for contest rules.
Recent Poetry Title: *The Past, the Future,the Present*, by Reed Whittemore.

*THE UNIVERSITY OF CALGARY PRESS, 2500 University Drive NW, Calgary, Alberta T2N 1N4 Canada. (403)220-7578. FAX: (403)282-6837. Acting Director: L. D. Cameron. Estab. 1981. Publishes scholarly hard cover and paperback originals. Averages 12-16 titles/year; receives 120 submissions annually. 50% of books from first-time authors; 99% of books from unagented authors. Subsidy publishes (nonauthor) 100% of books. "As with all Canadian University presses, UCP does not have publication funds of its own. Money must be found to subsidize each project. We do not consider publications for which there is no possibility of subvention." Publishes book average of 1 year after acceptance. Pays negotiable royalties. "Ms must pass a two tier review system before acceptance." Query for electronic submissions. Reports on 2 weeks on queries; 2 months on mss. Free book catalog and guidelines.
Nonfiction: "The University of Calgary Press (UCP) has developed an active publishing program that includes up to 12 new scholarly titles earch year and 8 scholarly journals. (For *UCP*'s purposes works of scholarship are usually required to be analytical in nature with unity of purpose and unfolding argumentand aimed primarily at an audience of specialists.) UCP publishes in a wide variety of subject areas and is willing to consider any innovative scholarly manuscript. The intention is not to restrict the publication list to specific areas."
Recent Nonfiction Title: *Alexander Cameron Rutherford: A Gentleman of Strathcona*, by D.R. Babcock.
Tips: "If I were trying to interest a scholarly publisher, I would prepare my manuscript on a word processor and submit a completed prospectus, including projected market, to the publisher."

UNIVERSITY OF CALIFORNIA PRESS, 2120 Berkeley Way, Berkeley CA 94720. Director: James H. Clark. Assistant Director: Lynne E. Withey. Estab. 1893. Los Angeles office: Suite 613, 10995 Le Conte Ave., UCLA, Los Angeles CA 90024. New York office: Room 513, 50 E. 42 St., New York NY 10017. London office: University Presses of California, Columbia, and Princeton, Avonlea, 10 Watlington Rd., Cowley, Oxford OX4 5NF England. Publishes hardcover and paperback originals and reprints. "On books likely to do more than return their costs, a royalty contract beginning at 7% on net price is paid; on paperbacks it is less." Published 230 titles last year. Queries are always advisable, accompanied by outlines or sample material. Accepts nonfiction translations. Send to Berkeley address. Reports vary, depending on the subject. Enclose return postage.
Nonfiction: "Most of our publications are hardcover nonfiction written by scholars." Publishes scholarly books including art, literary studies, social sciences, natural sciences and some high-level popularizations. No length preferences.
Recent Nonfiction Title: *The Company We Keep*, by Wayne Booth.
Fiction and Poetry: Publishes fiction and poetry only in translation, usually in bilingual editions.

*UNIVERSITY OF ILLINOIS PRESS, 54 E. Gregory, Champaign IL 61820. (217)333-0950. FAX: (217)244-8082. Director/Editor: Richard L. Wentworth. Estab. 1918. Publishes hardcover and trade paperback originals, and reprints. Averages 90-100 titles/year. 50% of books from first-time authors; 95% of books from unagented writers. Subsidy publishes (nonauthor) 30% of books. Pays 0-10% royalty on net sales; offers average $1,000-1,500 advance (rarely). Publishes book an average of 1 year after acceptance. Query for electronic submissions. Reports in 1 week on queries; 3 months on mss. Free book catalog.
Nonfiction: Biography, reference and scholarly books. Subjects include Americana, business and economics, history (especially American history), music (especially American music), politics, sociology, sports and literature. Always looking for "solid scholarly books in American history, especially social history; books on American popular music, and books in the broad area of American studies." Query with outline/synopsis.
Recent Nonfiction Title: *Crazeology: The Autobiography of a Chicago Jazzman*, by Bud Freeman.
Fiction: Ethnic, experimental and mainstream. "We publish four collections of stories by individual writers each year. We do not publish novels." Query.
Recent Fiction Title: *Falling Free*, by Barry Targan (stories).
Tips: "Serious scholarly books that are broad enough and well-written enough to appeal to non-specialists are doing well for us in today's market. Writers of nonfiction whose primary goal is to earn money (rather than get promoted in an academic position) are advised to try at least a dozen commercial publishers before thinking about offering the work to a university press."

UNIVERSITY OF IOWA PRESS, 119 West Park Rd., Iowa City IA 52242. (319)335-2000. FAX: (319)335-2055. Director: Paul Zimmer. Estab. 1969. Publishes hardcover and paperback originals. Averages 30 titles/year; receives 300-400 submissions annually. 30% of books from first-time authors; 95% of books from unagented writers. Average print order for a writer's first book is 1,200-1,500. Pays 7-10% royalty on net price. "We market mostly by direct mailing of flyers to groups with special interests in our titles and by advertising in trade and scholarly publications." Publishes book an average of 1 year after acceptance. Query for electronic submissions. Reports within 4 months. Free book catalog and ms guidelines.

Nonfiction: Publishes anthropology, archaeology, British and American literary studies, history (Victorian, U.S., German, medieval, Latin American), aviation history, history of photography and natural history. Currently publishes the Iowa School of Letters Award for Short Fiction, and Iowa Poetry Prize selections. "Please query regarding poetry or fiction before sending manuscript." Looks for "evidence of original research; reliable sources; clarity of organization, complete development of theme with documentation and supportive footnotes and/or bibliography; and a substantive contribution to knowledge in the field treated." Query or submit outline/synopsis. Use Chicago *Manual of Style*. Reviews artwork/photos as part of ms package.

Recent Nonfiction Title: *The Lincoln Highway*.

UNIVERSITY OF MASSACHUSETTS PRESS, P.O. Box 429, Amherst MA 01004. (413)545-2217. FAX: (413)545-1226. Director: Bruce Wilcox. Estab. 1963. Publishes hardcover and paperback originals, reprints and imports. Averages 30 titles/year; receives 600 submissions annually. 20% of books from first-time authors; 90% of books from unagented writers. Average print order for a writer's first book is 1,500. Royalties generally 10% of net income. Advance rarely offered. No author subsidies accepted. Publishes book an average of 1 year after acceptance. Query for electronic submissions. Preliminary report in 1 month. Free book catalog.

Nonfiction: Publishes Afro-American studies, art and architecture, biography, criticism, history, natural history, philosophy, poetry, public policy, sociology and women's studies in original and reprint editions. Accepts nonfiction translations. Submit outline/synopsis and 1-2 sample chapters. Reviews artwork/photos as part of ms package.

Recent Nonfiction Title: *Seabrook Station: Citizen Politics and Nuclear Power*, by Henry F. Bedford.

*UNIVERSITY OF MINNESOTA PRESS, 2037 University Ave. S.E., Minneapolis MN 55414. (612)624-2516. FAX: (612)626-7313. Editor-in-Chief: Terry Cochran. Estab. 1925. Publishes hardcover and trade paperback originals and reprints. Averages 50 titles/year. Receives 500 submissions/year. 20% of books from first-time authors. 95% from unagented writers. Subsidy publishes 20% of books. Subsidies are traditionally sought for translations. Pays 4-12½% royalty on retail price. Offers $1,000 average advance. Publishes book an average of 18 months after acceptance. Simultaneous submissions OK. Query for electronic submissions. Reports in 1 month. Free book catalog and ms guidelines.

Nonfiction: Illustrated books, reference, technical and textbook. Subjects include agriculture/horticulture, Americana (popular culture), art/architecture (criticism), business and economics, child guidance/parenting (health-related), gay/lesbian, health/medicine, language/literature (literature theory), music/dance (music/criticism), nature/environment (regional geology and biology), philosophy, photography (media studics), psychology: MMPI (multi-phasic inventory), regional, and women's issues/studies. Query or submit outline/synopsis and sample chapters. Reviews artwork as part of package.

Recent Nonfiction Title: *Daring to Be Bad: A History of the Radical Feminist Movement in the United States*, by Alice Echols (history/feminism/American studies).

Fiction: Ethnic, experimental, feminist, gay/lesbian, historical, and literary. Query or submit outline/synopsis and sample chapters.

Recent Fiction Title: *Little Mountain*, by Elias Khoury (modern Arabic literature).

‡UNIVERSITY OF NEBRASKA PRESS, 901 N. 17th St., Lincoln NE 68588-0520. Editor-in-Chief: Willis G. Regier. Estab. 1941. Publishes hardcover and paperback originals and reprints. Specializes in scholarly nonfiction, some regional books; reprints of Western Americana; and natural history. Averages 50 new titles, 50 paperback reprints (*Bison Books*)/year; receives 900 submissions annually. 25% of books from first-time authors; 95% of books from unagented writers. Average print order for a writer's first book is 1,000. Royalty is usually graduated from 10% on wholesale price for original books; no advance. Reports in 4 months. Book catalog and guidelines for 9×12 SAE with 5 first class stamps.

Nonfiction: Publishes Americana, biography, history, nature, photography, psychology, sports, literature, agriculture and American Indian themes. Accepts nonfiction and fiction translations. Query. Accepts outline/synopsis, 2 sample chapters and introduction. Looks for "an indication that the author knows his subject thoroughly and interprets it intelligently." Reviews artwork/photos as part of ms package.

Recent Nonfiction Title: *Billy the Kid*, by Robert Utley.

Recent Fiction Title: *Mad Love*, by André Breton (translation).

UNIVERSITY OF NEVADA PRESS, Reno NV 89557. (702)784-6573. FAX: (702)784-1300. Director: Thomas R. Radko. Estab. 1961. Publishes hardcover and paperback originals and reprints. Averages 12 titles/year; receives 50 submissions annually. 20% of books from first-time authors; 99% of books from unagented writers. Average print order for a writer's first book is 2,000. Pays average of 10% royalty on net price. Publishes book an average of 1 year after acceptance. Preliminary report in 2 months. Free book catalog and ms guidelines.

Nonfiction: Specifically needs regional history and natural history, literature, current affairs, ethnonationalism, gambling and gaming, anthropology, biographies and Basque studies. "We are the first university press to sustain a sound series on Basque studies—New World and Old World." No juvenile books. Submit complete ms. Reviews photocopies of artwork/photos as part of ms package.

Recent Nonfiction Title: *The Last Resort: Success and Failure in Campaigns for Casinos*, by John Dombrink and William N. Thompson.

Recent Fiction Title: *The Basque Hotel*, by Robert Laxalt.

‡**THE UNIVERSITY OF NORTH CAROLINA PRESS**, P.O. Box 2288, Chapel Hill NC 27514. (919)966-3561. Editor-in-Chief: Kate Douglas Torrey. Publishes hardcover and paperback originals. Specializes in scholarly books and regional trade books. Averages 65 titles/year. 70% of books from first-time scholarly authors; 90% of books from unagented writers. Royalty schedule "varies." Occasional advances. Query for electronic submissions. Publishes book an average of 1 year after acceptance. Reports in 5 months. Free book catalog; ms guidelines for SASE.

Nonfiction: "Our major fields are American history, American studies and Southern studies." Also, scholarly books in legal history, Civil War history, literary studies, classics, oral history, folklore, political science, religious studies, historical sociology, Latin American studies. In European studies, focus is on history of the Third Reich, 20th-century Europe, and Holocaust history. Special focus on general interest books on the lore, crafts, cooking, gardening and natural history of the Southeast. Submit outline/synopsis and sample chapters; must follow Chicago *Manual of Style*. Looks for "intellectual excellence and clear writing. We do *not* publish poetry or original fiction." Reviews artwork/photos as part of ms package.

Recent Nonfiction Title: *A World Unsuspected: Portraits of Southern Childhood*, edited by Alex Harris.

UNIVERSITY OF OKLAHOMA PRESS, 1005 Asp Ave., Norman OK 73019. (405)325-5111. Editor-in-Chief: John Drayton. Estab. 1928. Publishes hardcover and paperback originals and reprints. Averages 50 titles/year. Pays royalty comparable to those paid by other publishers for comparable books. Publishes book an average of 12-18 months after acceptance. Query for electronic submissions. Reports in 4 months. Book catalog $1.

Nonfiction: Publishes American Indian studies, Western U.S. history, literary theory, and classical studies. No poetry and fiction. Query, including outline, 1-2 sample chapters and author resume. Chicago *Manual of Style* for ms guidelines. Reviews artwork/photos as part of ms package.

Recent Nonfiction Title: *Route 66: The Highway and Its People*, by Wuinta Scott and Susan Croce Kelly.

***UNIVERSITY OF PENNSYLVANIA PRESS**, University of Pennsylvania, 418 Service Dr., Philadelphia PA 19104. (215)898-6261. FAX: (215)898-0404. Director: Thomas M. Rotell. Estab. 1922. Publishes hardcover and paperback originals and reprints. Averages 70 titles/year; receives 650 submissions annually. 10-20% of books from first-time authors; 99% of books from unagented writers. Subsidy publishes (nonauthor) 4% of books. Subsidy publishing is determined by evaluation obtained by the press from outside specialists; approval by Faculty Editorial Committee and funding organization. Royalty determined on book-by-book basis. Publishes book an average of 9 months after delivery of completed ms. Query for electronic submissions. Reports in 3 months. Book catalog and ms guidelines for 9 × 12 SAE and 5 first class stamps.

Nonfiction: Publishes Americana, biography, business, economics, history, medicine, biological sciences, computer science, physical sciences, law, anthropology, folklore and literary criticism, linguistics, art history, architecture. "Serious books that serve the scholar and the professional." Follow the Chicago *Manual of Style*. Query with outline and letter describing project, state availability of photos and/or illustrations to accompany ms, with copies of illustrations. Do not send ms with query.

Recent Nonfiction Title: *Behind the Disappearances: Argentina's Dirty War Against Human Rights and the U.N.*, by Ian Guest.

Tips: Queries/mss may be routed to other editors in the publishing group.

‡**UNIVERSITY OF PITTSBURGH PRESS**, 127 N. Bellefield Ave., Pittsburgh PA 15260. (412)624-4110. FAX: (412)624-7380. Managing Editor: Catherine Marshall. Estab. 1936. Publishes hardcover and trade paperback originals and reprints. Averages 45 titles/year. 5% of books from first-time authors; 100% from unagented writers. Pays royalties on retail price (per contract). Publishes books an average of 1 year after acceptance. Query for electronic submissions. Reports in 3 weeks on queries; 2 months on mss. Book catalog free on request. Manuscript guidelines for contests for #10 SASE.

Nonfiction: Biography, coffee table book, cookbooks, reference, textbook, scholarly monographs. Subjects include anthropology/archaeology, art/architecture, business and economics, cooking, foods and nutrition, education, ethnic, government/politics, health/medicine, history, language/literature, music/dance, nature/environment, philosophy, regional, women's issues/studies, Latin American Studies. Query. Reviews artwork/photos as part of ms package.

Recent Nonfiction Title: *Creating America: George Horace Lorimer and the Saturday Evening Post*, by Jan Cohn (history).

Fiction: Literary. "One title per year, winner of the Drue Heinz Literature Prize." No novels. Submit complete ms via contest, send SASE for rules.

Recent Fiction Title: *Cartographies*, by Maya Sonenberg (short fiction collection).

Poetry: 6 titles per year; 1 from previously unpublished author. Submit complete ms via contest, send SASE for rules; authors with previous books send direct to press in Sept. and Oct.

Recent Poetry Title: *Captivity*, by Toi Derricotte (contemporary).

*THE UNIVERSITY OF TENNESSEE PRESS, 293 Communications Bldg., Knoxville TN 37996-0325. Contact: Acquisitions Editor. Averages 30 titles/year; receives 300 submissions annually. 50% of books from first-time authors; 99% of books from unagented writers. Average print order for a writer's first book is 1,250. Subsidy publishes (nonauthor) 10% of books. Pays negotiable royalty on retail price. Publishes book an average of 1 year after acceptance. Reports in 1 month. Book catalog for $1 and 12×16 SAE; ms guidelines for SASE.

Nonfiction: American history, political science, religious studies, vernacular architecture and material culture, literary criticism, Black studies, women's studies, Caribbean, anthropology, folklore and regional studies. Prefers "scholarly treatment and a readable style. Authors usually have Ph.D.s." Submit outline/synopsis, author vita, and 2 sample chapters. No fiction, poetry or plays. Reviews artwork/photos as part of ms package.

Recent Nonfiction Title: *The Feminine and Faulkner: Reading (Beyond) Sexual Differences*, by Minrose C. Gwin.

Tips: "Our market is in several groups: scholars; educated readers with special interests in given scholarly subjects; and the general educated public interested in Tennessee, Appalachia and the South. Not all our books appeal to all these groups, of course, but any given book must appeal to at least one of them."

UNIVERSITY OF TEXAS PRESS, P.O. Box 7819, Austin TX 78713-7819. Executive Editor: Theresa May. Estab. 1952. Averages 60 titles/year; receives 1,000 submissions annually. 50% of books from first-time authors; 99% of books from unagented writers. Average print order for a writer's first book is 1,000. Pays royalty usually based on net income; occasionally offers advance. Publishes book an average of 18 months after acceptance. Query for electronic submissions. Reports in 2 months. Free book catalog and writer's guidelines.

Nonfiction: General scholarly subjects: astronomy, natural history, American, Latin American and Middle Eastern studies, native Americans, classics, films, biology, contemporary architecture, archeology, anthropology, geography, ornithology, ecology, Chicano studies, linguistics, 20th-century and women's literature. Also uses specialty titles related to Texas and the Southwest, national trade titles, and regional trade titles. Accepts nonfiction and fiction translations (Middle Eastern or Latin American fiction). Query or submit outline/synopsis and 2 sample chapters. Reviews artwork/photos as part of ms package.

Recent Nonfiction Title: *Jean Stafford*, by Charlotte Goodman.

Recent Fiction Translation: *Sanitary Centennial and Selected Stories*, by Fernando Sorrentino (translated from Spanish).

Tips: "It's difficult to make a manuscript over 400 double-spaced pages into a feasible book. Authors should take special care to edit out extraneous material." Looks for sharply focused, in-depth treatments of important topics.

*UNIVERSITY OF UTAH PRESS, University of Utah, 101 University Services Bldg., Salt Lake City UT 84112. (801)581-6771. Director: David Catron. Estab. 1949. Publishes hardcover and paperback originals and reprints. Averages 25 titles/year; receives 1,000 submissions annually. 20% of books from first-time authors. Average print order for writer's first book is 2,000. Subsidy publishes (nonauthor) 10% of books. Pays 10% royalty on net sales on first 2,000 copies sold; 12% on 2,001 to 4,000 copies sold; 15% thereafter. Publishes book an average of 18 months after acceptance. Reports in 10 weeks. Free book catalog; ms guidelines for SASE.

Nonfiction: Scholarly books on Western history, philosophy, ethics, anthropology, archaeology, natural history, folklore, Mesoamerican studies, folklore, and Middle Eastern studies. Accepts nonfiction translations. Popular, well-written, carefully researched regional studies. Query with synopsis and 3 sample chapters. Author should specify ms length in query. Reviews artwork/photos as part of ms package.

Recent Nonfiction Title: *AIDS: Testing and Privacy*, by Martin Gunderson, David Mayo, and Frank Rhame.

Fiction: Regional (western) authors or subjects.

Recent Fiction Title: *The School of Love*, by Phyllis Barber.

Poetry: One volume per year selected in an annual competition (submissions in March).

Recent Poetry Title: *Against Paradise*, by Jonathan Holden.

UNIVERSITY OF WISCONSIN PRESS, 114 N. Murray St., Madison WI 53715. (608)262-4928. Director: Allen N. Fitchen. Acquisitions Editor: Barbara J. Hanrahan. Estab. 1937. Publishes hardcover and paperback originals and reprints. Averages 50 titles/year. Pays standard royalties on retail price. Reports in 3 months.

Nonfiction: Publishes general nonfiction based on scholarly research. Looks for "originality, significance, quality of the research represented, literary quality, and breadth of interest to the educated community at large." Follow Chicago *Manual of Style.* Send letter of inquiry and prospectus.
Recent Nonfiction Title: *The Hellenistic Aesthetic,* by Barbara Hughes Fowler.

UNIVERSITY PRESS OF AMERICA, INC., 4720 Boston Way, Lanham MD 20706. (301)459-3366. Publisher: James E. Lyons. Estab. 1975. Publishes hardcover and paperback originals and reprints. Averages 450 titles/year. Pays 5-15% royalty on net receipts; occasional advance. Reports in 6 weeks. Book catalog and guidelines for SASE.
Nonfiction: Scholarly monographs, college, and graduate level textbooks in history, economics, business, psychology, political science, African studies, Black studies, philosophy, religion, sociology, music, art, literature, drama and education. No juvenile, elementary or high school material. Submit outline or request proposal questionnaire.
Recent Nonfiction Title: *Thomas Jefferson: A Strange Case of Mistaken Identity,* by Alf J. Mapp Jr. (biography).

UNIVERSITY PRESS OF COLORADO, formerly Colorado Associated University Press, P.O. Box 849, Niwot CO 80544. (303)530-5337. Director: Luther Wilson. Estab. 1965. Publishes hardcover and paperback originals. Averages 25 titles/year; receives 350 submissions annually. 50% of books from first-time authors; 99% of books from unagented writers. Average print order for a writer's first book is 1,500-2,000. Pays 10-12½-15% royalty contract on net price; "no advances." Publishes book an average of 9 months after acceptance. Electronic submissions encouraged. Reports in 3 months. Free book catalog.
Nonfiction: Scholarly, regional and environmental subjects. Length: 250-500 pages. Query first with table of contents, preface or opening chapter. Reviews artwork/photos as part of ms package.
Recent Nonfiction Title: *Boomtown Blues,* by Andrew Gulliford.
Tips: "Books should be solidly researched and from a reputable scholar, because we are a university press. We have a new series on world resources and environmental issues."

UNIVERSITY PRESS OF KANSAS, 329 Carruth, Lawrence KS 66045. (913)864-4154. Editor: Cynthia Miller. Estab. 1946. Publishes hardcover and paperback originals. Averages 35 titles/year; receives 500-600 submissions annually. 25% of books from first-time authors; 95% of books from unagented writers. Royalties negotiable; occasional advances. Markets books by advertising, direct mail, publicity, and sales representation to the trade; 55% of sales to bookstores. "State availability of illustrations if they add significantly to the manuscript." Publishes book an average of 10 months after acceptance. Reports in 4 months. Free book catalog; ms guidelines for #10 SASE.
Nonfiction: Publishes biography, history, sociology, philosophy, politics, military studies, regional subjects (Kansas, Great Plains, Midwest), and scholarly. Reviews artwork/photos as part of ms package. Query first.
Recent Nonfiction Title: *A Union of Interests: Political and Economic Thought in Revolutionary America* (history).

UNIVERSITY PRESS OF KENTUCKY, 663 South Limestone, Lexington KY 40506-0336. (606)257-2951. Associate Director: Jerome Crouch. Estab. 1951. Publishes hardcover originals and hardcover and trade paperback reprints. Averages 35 titles/year; receives 200 submissions annually. 25-50% of books from first-time authors; 98% of books from unagented writers. Pays 10-15% royalty on wholesale price. "As a nonprofit press, we generally exclude the first 1,000 copies from royalty payment." No advance. Publishes ms an average of 1 year after acceptance. Reports in 1 month on queries; 3 months on mss. Free book catalog.
Nonfiction: Biography, reference and monographs. Subjects include Americana, history, politics and sociology. "We are a scholarly publisher, publishing chiefly for an academic and professional audience. Strong areas are history, literature, political science, folklore, anthropology, and sociology. Our books are expected to advance knowledge in their fields in some measure. We would be interested in the treatment of timely topics in the fields indicated, treatments that would be solid and substantial but that would be readable and capable of appealing to a general public." No "textbooks; genealogical material; lightweight popular treatments; how-to books; and generally books not related to our major areas of interest." Query. Reviews artwork/photos, but generally does not publish books with extensive number of photos.
Recent Nonfiction Title: *Hitler and Spain: The Nazi Role in the Spanish Civil War,* by Robert H. Whealey.
Tips: "Most of our authors are drawn from our primary academic and professional audience. We are probably not a good market for the usual freelance writer, unless his work fits into our special requirements. Moreover, we do not pay advances and income from our books is minimal; so we cannot offer much financial reward to a freelance writer."

UNIVERSITY PRESS OF MISSISSIPPI, 3825 Ridgewood Rd., Jackson MS 39211. (601)982-6205. FAX: (601)982-6610. Director: Richard Abel. Acquisitions Editor: Seetha Srinivasan. Estab. 1970. Publishes hardcover and paperback originals and reprints. Averages 35 titles/year; receives 300 submissions annually. 25% of books from first-time authors; 95% of books from unagented writers. "Competitive royalties and terms."

Publishes book an average of 1 year after acceptance. Reports in 2 months. Free book catalog.

Nonfiction: Americana, biography, history, politics, folklife, literary criticism, ethnic/minority studies, natural sciences and popular culture with scholarly emphasis. Interested in southern regional studies and literary studies. Submit outline/synopsis and sample chapters and curriculum vita to Acquisitions Editor. "We prefer a proposal that describes the significance of the work and a chapter outline." Reviews artwork/photos as part of ms package.

Recent Nonfiction Title: *Photographs*, by Eudora Welty.

Fiction: Commissioned trade editions by prominent writers.

Recent Fiction Title: *Homecomings*, by Willie Morris.

‡**UNIVERSITY PRESS OF NEW ENGLAND,** (Includes Wesleyan University Press), 17½ Lebanon St., Hanover NH 03755. (603)646-3349. FAX: (603)643-1540. Director: Thomas L. McFarland. Editor: Jeanne West. Estab. 1970. "University Press of New England is a consortium of university presses. Some books—those published for one of the consortium members—carry the joint imprint of New England and the member: Wesleyan, Dartmouth, Brandeis, Brown, Tufts, Clark, Universities of Connecticut, New Hampshire, Vermont and Rhode Island." Publishes hardcover and trade paperback originals and trade paperback reprints. Averages 60 titles/year. Subsidy publishes (nonauthor) 80% of books. Pays standard royalty; occasionally offers advance. Query for electronic submissions. Reports in 1 month. Book catalog and guidelines for SASE.

Nonfiction: Americana (New England), art, biography, history, music, nature, politics, psychology, reference, science, sociology, and regional (New England). No festschriften, memoirs, unrevised doctoral dissertations, or symposium collections. Submit outline/synopsis and 1-2 sample chapters.

Recent Nonfiction Title: *Witness to the Young Republic: Yankee's Journal, 1828-1870*, by Benjamin Brown French, Donald B. Cole and John J. McDonough, eds.

‡**VANCE BIBLIOGRAPHIES,** 112 N. Charter, Box 229, Monticello IL 61856. (217)762-3831. Imprints include Architecture Series (bibliography), Public Administration Series (bibliography). Publisher: Judith Vance. Publishes trade paperback originals. Averages 400 titles/year; receives 500 submissions annually. 10% of bibliographies from first-time authors; 100% of bibliographies from unagented writers. Average print order for a writer's first bibliography is 200. Pays $100 honorarium and 10-20 author's copies. Publishes bibliography an average of 4 months after acceptance. Reports in 1 week on queries; 2 weeks on mss. Free book catalog; ms guidelines for SASE.

Nonfiction: Bibliographies on public administration and/or architecture and related subject areas. Publishes for "graduate students and professionals in the field; primary customers are libraries." Query or submit complete ms.

Recent Nonfiction Title: *Housing from Redundant Buildings: A Select Bibliography*, by V.J. Nurcombe.

‡**VANWELL PUBLISHING LIMITED,** 1 Northrup Cres., P.O. Box 2131 Stn. B, St. Catharines, Ontario L2T 2C4 Canada. (416)937-3100. General Editor: Lynn J. Hunt. Publishes hardcover and trade paperback originals and reprints. Firm averages 12 titles/year. Receives 100 submissions/year. 85% of books from first-time authors. 100% from unagented writers. Pays 5-12% royalty on wholesale price. Offers $200 average advance. Publishes book an average of 18 months after acceptance. Query for electronic submissions. Reports in 2 weeks on queries; 1 month on mss. Free book catalog.

Nonfiction: Biography. Subjects include education, military/war and regional. Reviews artwork/photos as part of ms package.

Tips: The writer has the best chance of selling a manuscript to our firm which is in keeping with our publishing program, well written and organized. Our audience: Older male, history buff, war veteran; regional tourist; students.

***VESTA PUBLICATIONS, LTD.,** Box 1641, Cornwall, Ontario K6H 5V6 Canada. (613)932-2135. FAX: (613)932-1641. Editor-in-Chief: Stephen Gill. Estab. 1976. Paperback and hardcover originals. 10% minimum royalty on wholesale price. Subsidy publishes 5% of books. "We ask a writer to subsidize a part of the cost of printing; normally, it is 50%. We do so when we find that the book does not have a wide market, as in the case of university theses and the author's first collection of poems. The writer gets 25 free copies and 10% royalty on paperback editions." No advance. Publishes 16 titles/year; receives 350 submissions annually. 80% of books from first-time authors; 100% of books from unagented writers. Simultaneous submissions OK if so informed. Query for electronic submissions. Reports in 1 week on queries; 1 month on mss. Send SAE with IRCs. Free book catalog.

Nonfiction: Publishes Americana, art, biography, cookbooks, cooking and foods, history, philosophy, poetry, politics, reference, and religious books. Accepts nonfiction translations. Query or submit complete ms. Reviews artwork/photos. Looks for knowledge of the language and subject. "Query letters and mss should be accompanied by synopsis of the book and biographical notes." State availability of photos and/or illustrations to accompany ms.

Recent Nonfiction Title: *Who's Who of North American Poets*, edited by Stephen Gill.

THE VESTAL PRESS, LTD., 320 N. Jensen Rd., P.O. Box 97, Vestal NY 13851-0097. (607)797-4872. President: Grace L. Houghton. Estab. 1961. Publishes hardcover and trade paperback originals and reprints. Averages 6-8 titles/year; receives 50-75 submissions annually. 20% of books from first-time writers; 95% of books from unagented authors. Pays 10% maximum royalty on net sales. Publishes books an average of 1 year after acceptance. Simultaneous submissions OK. Usually reports in 2 weeks. Book catalog for $2.

Nonfiction: Technical antiquarian hobby topics in antique radio, mechanical music (player pianos, music boxes, etc.), reed organs, carousels, antique phonographs, early cinema history, regional history based on postcard collections. Query or submit outline/synopsis and sample chapters or submit complete ms.

Recent Nonfiction Title: *Silent Portraits: Stars of the Silent Screen in Historic Photographs*, by Anthony Slide.

VGM CAREER HORIZONS, Division of NTC Publishing Group, 4255 W. Touhy Ave., Lincolnwood IL 60646-1975. (708)679-5500. FAX: (708)679-2494. Editorial Director: Leonard Fiddle. Senior Editor: Michael Urban. Publishes hardcover and paperback originals and software. Averages 20-30 titles/year; receives 150-200 submissions annually. 10% of books from first-time authors; 95% of books from unagented writers. Pays royalty or makes outright purchase. Advance varies. Publishes book an average of 1 year after acceptance. Simultaneous submissions OK. Query for electronic submissions. Reports in 3 weeks. Book catalog and ms guidelines for 9×12 SAE with 5 first class stamps.

Nonfiction: Textbook and general trade on careers and jobs. Nonfiction book manuscript needs are for careers in eye care, performing arts, information systems, welding, etc. Query or submit outline/synopsis and sample chapters. Reviews artwork/photos as part of ms package.

Recent Nonfiction Title: *How to Make the Right Career Moves*, by Deborah Perlmutter Bloch.

Tips: "Our audience is made up of job seekers, career planners, job changers, and students and adults in education and trade markets. Study our existing line of books before sending proposals."

VICTOR BOOKS, Division of Scripture Press Publications, Inc. 1825 College Ave., Wheaton IL 60187. (708)668-6000. Address mss to Acquisitions Editor. Estab. 1934. Imprints include SonFlower, Winner, SonPower. Publishes hardcover and trade paperback originals. Firm averages 75 titles/year. Receives 1,400 submissions/year. 5% of books from first-time authors; 98% from unagented writers. Royalty negotiable on retail price. Publishes book an average of 18 months after acceptance. Simultaneous submissions OK. Reports in 1 month on queries; 2 months on mss. Ms guidelines for #10 SASE; 4 first class stamps for a catalog and guidelines.

Nonfiction: Juvenile, reference and self-help. Subjects include child guidance/parenting, psychology, life-related Bible study and women's issues/studies. "We are interested in manuscripts with a fresh approach to Bible study and Christian living/leadership topics, written from an evangelical perspective. Issues-type books are also welcome." Query or submit outline/synopsis and sample chapters.

Recent Nonfiction Title: *Parents' Most-Asked Questions About Kids and Schools*, by Cliff Schimmels.

Fiction: For ages 2-12. "We are looking for simple Bible-related stories that could be developed into picture books for the preschooler or young reader. For the 8-12-year-old, we are interested in action stories with a Christian take-away message. Fiction should also be series oriented." Submit outline/synopsis and sample chapters or submit complete ms.

Recent Fiction Title: *Lost Beneath Manhattan*, by Sigmund Brouwer.

Tips: "Too many books rehash the same topic and there are many shallow books that require no thinking. A writer has the best chance of selling Victor a well-conceived and imaginative manuscript that helps the reader apply Christianity to his/her life in practical ways. Christians active in the local church and their children are our audience."

WADSWORTH PUBLISHING COMPANY, Division of Wadsworth, Inc., 10 Davis Dr., Belmont CA 94002. (415)595-2350. Other divisions include Brooks/Cole Pub. Co., PWS/Kent Pub. Co. Editor-in-Chief for Wadsworth Publishing Company: Stephen D. Rutter. Estab. 1956. Publishes hardcover and paperback originals and software. Publishes 350 titles/year. 35% of books from first-time authors; 99% of books from unagented writers. Pays 5-15% royalty on net price. Advances not automatic policy. Publishes ms an average of 1 year after acceptance. Simultaneous submissions OK. Query for electronic submissions. Reports in 1 week. Book catalog (by subject area) and ms guidelines available.

Nonfiction: Textbook: higher education only. Subjects include mathematics, music, social sciences, economics, philosophy, religious studies, speech and mass communications, English, and other subjects in higher education. "We need books that use fresh teaching approaches to all courses taught at schools of higher education throughout the U.S. and Canada. We specifically do not publish textbooks in art and history." Query or submit outline/synopsis and sample chapters.

For information on book publishers' areas of interest, see the nonfiction and fiction sections in the Book Publishers Subject Index.

Recent Nonfiction Title: *Biology: The Unity and Diversity of Life*, by Cecie Starr and Ralph Taggart.

WAKE FOREST UNIVERSITY PRESS, Box 7333, Winston-Salem NC 27109. (919)759-5448. Director: Dillon Johnston. Manager: Guinn Batten. Publishes hardcover and trade paperback originals. Firm averages 5 titles/year. Receives 80 submissions/year. Pays 10% on retail price. Offers $500 average advance. Publishes book an average of 6 months after acceptance. Reports in 1 month on queries; 3 months on mss. Free book catalog.
Nonfiction: Subjects include language/literature and photography. "We publish exclusively poetry, photography, and criticism of the poetry of Ireland and bilingual editions of contemporary French poetry." Query.
Recent Nonfiction Title: *Selected Poems of Philippe Jaccottet*, by Jaccottet translated by Derek Mahon, (bilingual edition of the poetry).
Tips: "Readers of contemporary poetry and of books of Irish interest or French interest are our audience."

J. WESTON WALCH, PUBLISHER, P.O. Box 658, Portland ME 04104. (207)772-2846. FAX (207)772-3105. Managing Editor: Richard S. Kimball. Editor: Jane Carter. Math/Science Editor: Eric Olson. Computer Editor: Robert Crepeau. Estab. 1927. Publishes paperback originals and software. Averages 110 titles/year; receives 300 submissions annually. 10% of books from first-time authors; 95% of books from unagented writers. Average print order for a writer's first book is 700. Offers 10-15% royalty on gross receipts; buys some titles by outright purchase for $100-2,500. No advance. Publishes book an average of 18 months after acceptance. Query for electronic submissions. Reports in 6 weeks. Book catalog for 9×12 SAE with 5 first class stamps; ms guidelines for #10 SASE.
Nonfiction: Subjects include art, business, computer education, economics, English, foreign language, government, health, history, mathematics, music, physical education, psychology, science, social science, sociology and special education. "We publish only supplementary educational material for grades six to twelve in the U.S. and Canada. Formats include books, posters, master sets, card sets, cassettes, filmstrips, microcomputer courseware, video and mixed packages. Most titles are assigned by us, though we occasionally accept an author's unsolicited submission. We have a great need for author/artist teams and for authors who can write at third- to tenth-grade levels. We do *not* want basic texts, anthologies or industrial arts titles. Most of our authors—but not all—have secondary teaching experience. I cannot stress too much the advantages that an author/artist team would have in approaching us and probably other publishers." Query first. Looks for "sense of organization, writing ability, knowledge of subject, skill of communicating with intended audience." Reviews artwork/photos as part of ms package.
Recent Nonfiction Title: *Living on Your Own: An Independent Living Simulation*, by Jean Bunnell.

WALKER AND CO., Division of Walker Publishing Co., 720 5th Ave., New York NY 10019. FAX: (212)307-1764. Contact: Submissions Editor. Hardcover and trade paperback originals and reprints of British books. Averages 100 titles/year; receives 3,500 submissions annually. 50% of books from first-time authors; 50% of books from unagented writers. Pays varying royalty on retail price or makes outright purchase. Advance averages $1,000-3,000 "but could be higher or lower." Do not telephone submissions editors. Material without SASE will not be returned. Book catalog and guidelines for 8½×11 SAE with 56¢ postage.
Nonfiction: Publishes biography, business, histories, science and natural history, health, music, nature, parenting, psychology, reference, popular science, and self-help books. Query or submit outline/synopsis and sample chapter. Reviews artwork/photos as part of ms package (photographs). Do not send originals.
Recent Nonfiction Title: *Lies Your Broker Tells You*, by Thomas Saler.
Fiction: Mystery, juvenile (ages 5 and up), suspense, regency romance, western, action adventure/suspense and espionage.
Recent Fiction Title: *White Rook*, by J. Madison Davis.
Tips: "We also need preschool to young adult nonfiction, science fiction, historical novels, biographies and middle-grade novels. Query."

‡*WALL & EMERSON, INC., 6 O'Connor Dr., Toronto, Ontario M4K 2K1 Canada. (416)467-8685. FAX: (416)696-2460. Subsidiaries include Wall & Thompson and Wall Editions. President: Byron E. Wall. Publishes hardcover and trade paperback originals and reprints. Firm averages 10 titles/year. 50% of books from first-time authors. 100% from unagented writers. Subsidy publishes 10% of books. Only subsidies provided by external granting agencies accepted. Generally these are for scholarly books with a small market. Pays royalty up to 15% on wholesale price. Publishes book an average of 6-8 months after acceptance. Simultaneous submissions OK. Prefers electronic submissions. Reports in 3 weeks on queries; 2 months on mss. Free book catalog.
Nonfiction: Reference and textbook. Subjects include business and economics, computers and electronics, education, government/politics, health/medicine, history, language/literature, nature/environment, philosophy, psychology, science and mathematics. We are looking for any undergraduate college text that meets the needs of a well-defined course in colleges in the U.S. and Canada. Submit outline/synopsis and sample chapters.

Recent Nonfiction Title: *Children of Prometheus: A History of Science and Technology*, by James MacLachlan (textbook).

Tips: "We are most interested in textbooks for college courses; books that meet well defined needs and are targeted to their audiences are best. Our audience consists of college undergraduate students and college libraries. If I were a writer trying to market a book today, I would identify the audience for the book and write directly to the audience throughout the book. I would then approach a publisher that publishes books specifically for that audience."

‡**WALLACE—HOMESTEAD BOOK CO.**, Division of Chilton Book Co., 201 King of Prussia Rd., Radnor PA 19089. (215)964-4000. Publishes hardcover and trade paperback originals. Especially looking for mss on antiques, collectibles, memorabilia, quilting, and other specialty areas. Submit outline/synopsis and sample chapter with SASE. Reviews artwork/photos as part of ms package.

Recent Nonfiction Title: *Wallace-Homestead Price Guide to American Country Antiques*, 9th edition, (antiques and collectibles).

***WASHINGTON STATE UNIVERSITY PRESS**, Washington State University, Pullman WA 99164-5910. (509)335-3518. FAX: (509)335-8568. Dirctor: Thomas H. Sanders. Estab. 1928. Publishes hardcover originals, trade paperback originals and reprints. Averages 6-10 titles/year; receives 50-75 submissions annually. 50% of books from first-time writers; 100% of books from unagented authors. Subsidy publishes 20% of books. "The nature of the manuscript and the potential market for the manuscript determine whether it should be subsidy published." Pays 10% royalty. Publishes book an average of 1 year after acceptance. Simultaneous submissions OK. Query for electronic submissions. Reports on queries in 1 month; on submissions in 4 months.

Nonfiction: Biography, academic and scholarly. Subjects include Americana, art, business and economics, history (especially of the American West and the Pacific Northwest), nature, philosophy, politics, psychology, and sociology. Needs for the next year are "quality manuscripts that focus on the development of the Pacific Northwest as a region, and on the social and economic changes that have taken place and continue to take place as the region enters the 21st century. No romance novels, historical fiction, how-to books, gardening books, or books specifically written as classroom texts." Submit outline/synopsis and sample chapters. Reviews artwork/photos as part of ms package.

Recent Nonfiction Title: *Peoples of Washington*, edited by Sid White and S.E. Solberg (ethnic heritage).

Tips: "Our audience consists of scholars, specialists and informed general readers who are interested in well-documented research presented in an attractive format." Writers have the best chance of selling to our firm "completed manuscripts on regional history. We have developed our marketing in the direction of regional and local history and have attempted to use this as the base around which we hope to expand our publishing program. In regional history, the secret is to write a good narrative—a good story—that is substantiated factually. It should be told in an imaginative, clever way. Have visuals (photos, maps, etc) available to help the reader envision what has happened. Tell the local or regional history story in a way that ties it to larger, national, and even international events. Weave it into the large pattern of history."

SAMUEL WEISER, INC., Box 612, York Beach ME 03910. (207)363-4393. Editor: Susan Smithe. Publishes hardcover originals and trade paperback originals and reprints. Publishes 18-20 titles/year; receives 200 submissions annually. 50% of books from first-time authors; 98% of books from unagented writers. Pays 10% royalty on wholesale or retail price; offers average $500 advance. Publishes book an average of 1½ years after acceptance. Query for electronic submissions. Reports in 3 months. Free book catalog.

Nonfiction: How-to and self-help. Subjects include health, music, philosophy, psychology and religion. "We look for strong books in our specialty field—written by teachers and people who know the subject. Don't want a writer's rehash of all the astrology books in the library, only texts written by people with strong background in field. No poetry or novels." Submit complete ms. Reviews artwork/photos as part of ms package.

Recent Nonfiction Title: *Inner Journeys*, by Jay Earley, Ph.D.

Tips: "Most new authors do not check permissions, nor do they provide proper footnotes. If they did, it would help. We specialize in New Age material, oriental philosophy, metaphysics, esoterica of all kinds (tarot, astrology, qabalah, magic, crystals, etc.) and our emphasis is still the same. We still look at all manuscripts submitted to us. We are interested in seeing freelance art for book covers."

‡**WESTERN PRODUCER PRAIRIE BOOKS**, Division of Western Producer Publications, P.O. Box 2500, Saskatoon, Saskatchewan S7K 2C4 Canada. Publishing Director: Elizabeth Munroe. Estab. 1954. Publishes hardcover and paperback originals and reprints. Averages 20-23 titles/year; receives 400-500 submissions annually. 20% of books from first-time authors; 80% of books from unagented writers. Average print order for a writer's first book is 4,000. Pays negotiable royalty on list price. Publishes book an average of 1 year after acceptance. Query for electronic submissions. Reports in 3 months. Free book catalog; ms guidelines for SAE with IRCs.

Nonfiction: Publishes history, nature, photography, biography, reference, agriculture, economics and politics. Accepts nonfiction and fiction translations. Submit outline, synopsis and 2-3 sample chapters with contact sheets or prints if illustrations are to accompany ms.
Recent Nonfiction Title: *Frozen in Time*, by Owen Beattie and John Geiger (history).
Fiction: Young adult and juvenile novels and novels appealing to Western Canadians.
Recent Fiction Title: *Dog Runner*, by Don H. Meredith (young adult fiction).

WESTERNLORE PRESS, Box 35305, Tucson AZ 85740. Editor: Lynn R. Bailey. Publishes 6-12 titles/year. Pays standard royalties on retail price "except in special cases." Query. Reports in 2 months. Enclose return postage with query.
Nonfiction: Publishes Western Americana of a scholarly and semischolarly nature: anthropology, history, biography, historic sites, restoration, and ethnohistory pertaining to the greater American West. Re-publication of rare and out-of-print books. Length: 25,000-100,000 words.

*WESTGATE PRESS, Westgate Co., 8 Bernstein Blvd., Center Moriches NY 11934. (516)878-2901. Editor, Books: Lorraine Chandler. Estab. 1981. Publishes trade paperback originals and reprints. Firm averages 5-7 titles/year. Receives 100 submissions/year. 50% of books from first-time authors. 100% from unagented writers. Subsidy publishes 10% of books. Subsidy titles are determined by book content and author enthusiasm. Pays 10% minimum royalty on wholesale price. Outright purchase negotiable. Offers $0-1,000 average advance. Publishes book an average of 18 months after acceptance. Simultaneous submissions OK. Reports in 2 weeks on queries; 2 months on mss. Free book catalog. Ms guidelines for #10 SASE.
Nonfiction: Illustrated book. Subjects include art, metaphysics, occult/new age and related topics. "Westgate deals exclusively in the lesser known, esoteric areas of metaphysics. We'll look at mss that are not covered already by other authors and presses. Nothing already so overplayed that it's simply a rehash. No channeling, crystals, or other generic New Age material. Check what we're currently doing before submitting." Reviews artwork/photos as part of manuscript package.
Recent Nonfiction Title: *The Book of Azrael: An Intimate Encounter With the Angel of Death*, by Leilah Wendell (metaphysics).
Tips: "As many times as we ask for the *truly unusual*, we still receive repetitive topics and angles. Give us the uncommon rarity of the blockbuster status as *The Book of Azrael* is fast becoming. If I were a writer trying to market a book today, I would choose an area in which I'm comfortable, learned and sincere, find an angle not presently being used and procure a blockbuster that is timeless in its message and awesome in its impact."

‡WESTVIEW PRESS, 5500 Central Ave., Boulder CO 80301. (303)444-3541. Publisher: F.A. Praeger. Hardcover and paperback originals, lecture notes, reference books, and paperback texts. Specializes in scholarly monographs or conference reports with strong emphasis on applied science, both social and natural. Pays 0-10% royalty on net price, depending on market. Accepts subsidies for a small number of books, "but only in the case of first class scholarly material for a limited market when books need to be priced low, or when the manuscripts have unusual difficulties such as Chinese or Sanskrit characters; the usual quality standards of a top-flight university press apply, and subsidies must be furnished by institutions, not by individuals." Averages 300 titles/year. Markets books mainly by direct mail. State availability of photos and/or illustrations to accompany manuscript. Reports in 4 months. Free book catalog.
Nonfiction: Agriculture/food, agricultural economics, public policy, energy, natural resources, international economics and business, international law, international relations, area studies, development, science and technology policy, sociology, anthropology, philosophy, history, reference, military affairs, national security, health, Asia and the Pacific, comparative politics, social impact assessment, women's studies, Latin America and Caribbean, Soviet Union and Eastern Europe, Middle East, Africa, and Western Europe. Looks for "scholarly excellence and scientific relevance." Query and submit 2 sample chapters and tentative table of contents and *curriculum vitae*. Use *Chicago Manual of Style*. "Unsolicited manuscripts receive low priority; inquire before submitting projects."
Recent Nonfiction Title: *The Business of Book Publishing*, by Geiser.

‡WHITE CLIFFS MEDIA COMPANY, P.O. Box 561, Crown Point IN 46307-0561. (219)322-5537. Owner: Larry W. Smith. Estab. 1985. Publishes hardcover and trade paperback originals. Averages 5-10 titles/year. 75% of books from first-time authors; 75% from unagented writers. Pays 5-15% royalty. Publishes book an average of 1 year after acceptance. Query for electronic submissions. Reports in 3 months. Book catalog for #10 SASE.
Nonfiction: Biography, software, technical, textbook. Subjects include anthropology, education, ethnic, music/dance, sociology. "We are looking for ethnic music performance, music sociology/biography (more pop/mass oriented), books on computer/desktop publishing." Query. Reviews artwork/photos as part of ms package.

Recent Nonfiction Title: *Salsa!: The Rhythm of Latin Music*, by Charley Gerard and Marty Sheller (trade/text).

Tips: "Trend—distribution is more difficult due to the large number of publishers. Writers should send proposals that have potential for mass markets as well as college texts, and that will be submitted and completed on schedule. Our audience reads college texts, general interest trade publications. If I were a writer trying to market a book today, I would send a book on music comparable in quality, mass appeal, and readibility to a book like Stephen Hawking's *A Brief History of Time*."

WHITNEY LIBRARY OF DESIGN, Imprint of Watson-Guptill Publishers, 1515 Broadway, New York NY 10036. Senior Editor: Cornelia Guest. Publishes hardcover and trade paperback originals and reprints. Averages 10 titles/year. Receives 250 submissions/year. 30% of books from first-time authors. 100% from unagented writers. Pays 7½-15% royalty on wholesale price. Offers $3,000 average advance. Publishes book an average of 9 months after acceptance. Simultaneous submissions OK. Reports in 3 weeks on queries. Free book catalog.

Nonfiction: Subjects include architecture/interior design. "I am looking for professionally oriented titles in the fields of architecture, landscape architecture, and interior design by practitioners and teachers of these specialties." Query or submit outline/synopsis and sample chapter.

Recent Nonfiction Title: *The Design Process*, by Ellen Shoshkes.

Tips: "Writers who are well-known architects or designers or teach in these fields have the best chance of selling their books to us. Professionals and students in architecture, landscape architecture, and interior design are our audience."

THE WHITSTON PUBLISHING CO., P.O. Box 958, Troy NY 12181. (518)283-4363. Editorial Director: Jean Goode. Estab. 1969. Publishes hardcover originals. Averages 20 titles/year; receives 100 submissions annually. 50% of books from first-time authors; 100% of books from unagented writers. Pays 10% royalty on wholesale price; no advance. Publishes book an average of 30 months after acceptance. Computer printout submissions acceptable; no dot-matrix. Reports in 1 year. Book catalog for $1.

Nonfiction: "We publish scholarly and critical books in the arts, humanities and some of the social sciences. We also publish reference books, bibliographies, indexes, checklists and monographs. We do not want author bibliographies in general unless they are unusual and unusually scholarly. We are, however, much interested in catalogs and inventories of library collections of individuals, such as the catalog of the Evelyn Waugh Collection at the Humanities Research Center, the University of Texas at Austin; and collections of interest to the specific scholarly community, such as surveys of early Black newspapers in libraries in the U.S., etc." Query or submit complete ms. Reviews artwork/photos as part of ms package.

Recent Nonfiction Title: *Concrete Poetry Bibliography*, by Kathleen McCullough.

*WILDERNESS ADVENTURE BOOKS, P.O. Box 968, Fowlerville MI 48836. Editor: Clayton Klein. Estab. 1983. Publishes hardcover and trade paperback originals and reprints. Firm averages 6 titles/year. Receives 120 submissions/year. 90% of books from first-time authors. 90% from unagented writers. Subsidy publishes 25% of books. Pays 5-10% royalty on retail price. Offers $200 average advance. Publishes book an average of 10 months after acceptance. Simultaneous submissions OK. Reports in 2 weeks on queries; 6 weeks on mss. Free book catalog.

Nonfiction: Biography, how-to and illustrated book. Subjects include Americana, animals, anthropology/archaeology, history, nature/environment, regional, sports and travel. Query. Submit outline/synopsis and sample chapters or complete ms. Reviews artwork/photos as part of ms package.

Recent Nonfiction Title: *My Yellowstone Years*, by Donald C. Stewart.

Fiction: Adventure, historical and young adult. Query. Submit outline/synopsis and sample chapters or complete ms.

Recent Fiction Title: *Michilimackinac*, by David A. Turrill.

Poetry: Submit samples.

Recent Poetry Title: *Earthly Pleasures and Heavenly Treasures*, by Charles C. Myers.

WILDERNESS PRESS, 2440 Bancroft Way, Berkeley CA 94704. (415)843-8080. Editorial Director: Thomas Winnett. Estab. 1967. Publishes paperback originals. Averages 5 titles/year; receives 150 submissions annually. 20% of books from first-time authors; 95% of books from unagented writers. Average print order for a writer's first book is 5,000. Pays 8-10% royalty on retail price; offers average $1,000 advance. Publishes book an average of 6 months after acceptance. Reports in 2 weeks. Book catalog for 9×12 SASE.

Nonfiction: "We publish books about the outdoors. Most of our books are trail guides for hikers and backpackers, but we also publish how-to books about the outdoors and perhaps will publish personal adventures. The manuscript must be accurate. The author must thoroughly research an area in person. If he is writing a trail guide, he must walk all the trails in the area his book is about. The outlook must be strongly conservationist. The style must be appropriate for a highly literate audience." Query, submit outline/synopsis and sample chapters, or submit complete ms demonstrating "accuracy, literacy, and popularity of subject area." Reviews artwork/photos as part of ms package.

Recent Nonfiction Title: *Afoot and Afield in Los Angeles County*, by Jerry Schad.

WILLIAMSON PUBLISHING CO., P.O. Box 185, Church Hill Rd., Charlotte VT 05445. (802)425-2102. Editorial Director: Susan Williamson. Estab. 1983. Publishes trade paperback originals. Averages 12 titles/year; receives 450 submissions annually. 50% of books from first-time authors; 80% of books from unagented writers. Average print order for a writer's first book is 5,000-10,000. Pays 10-12% royalty on sales dollars received or makes outright purchase if favored by author. Advance negotiable. Publishes book an average of 1 year after acceptance. Simultaneous submissions OK. Reports in 1 month on queries; 3 months on mss. Book catalog for 6×9 SAE and 3 first class stamps.

Nonfiction: How-to, cookbook, illustrated book and self-help. Subjects include business, children's activity books, education, gardening, careers, home crafts, parenting, building, animals, cooking and foods, travel, hobbies, nature, landscaping, and children. "Our areas of concentration are children's activity books, people-oriented business and psychology books, women's issues, cookbooks, international marketing, gardening, small-scale livestock raising, family housing (all aspects), health and education." No children's fiction books, photography, politics, religion, history, art or biography. Query with outline/synopsis and sample chapters. Reviews photos as part of ms package.

Recent Nonfiction Title: *Doing Children's Museums: A Guide to 225 Hands-On Museums*, by Joanne Cheaver.

Tips: "We're most interested in authors who are experts in their fields—doers, not researchers. Give us a good, solid manuscript with original ideas and we'll work with you to refine the writing. We also have a highly skilled staff to develop the high quality graphics and design of our books."

WILSHIRE BOOK CO., 12015 Sherman Rd., North Hollywood CA 91605. (818)765-8579. Editorial Director: Melvin Powers. Estab. 1947. Publishes paperback originals and reprints. Publishes 50 titles/year; receives 6,000 submissions annually. 80% of books from first-time authors; 75% of books from unagented writers. Average print order for a writer's first book is 5,000. Pays standard royalty; offers variable advance. Reports in 1 month. Book catalog for SASE.

Nonfiction: Health, hobbies, how-to, psychology, recreation, self-help, entrepreneurship, how to make money, and mail order. "We are always looking for self-help and psychological books such as *Psycho-Cybernetics, The Magic of Thinking Big* and *Guide to Rational Living*. We need manuscripts teaching mail order, entrepreneur techniques, how to make money and advertising. We publish 70 horse books. All that I need is the concept of the book to determine if the project is viable. I welcome phone calls to discuss manuscripts with authors." Reviews artwork/photos as part of ms package.

Recent Nonfiction Title: *The Knight in Rusty Armor*, by Robert Fisher (adult fable).

Tips: "We are looking for such books as *Jonathan Livingston Seagull, The Little Prince*, and *The Greatest Salesman in the World*."

WINDSOR BOOKS, Subisidary of Windsor Marketing Corp., Box 280, Brightwaters NY 11718. (516)321-7830. Managing Editor: Stephen Schmidt. Estab. 1988. Publishes hardcover and trade paperback originals, reprints, and very specific software. Averages 8 titles/year; receives approximately 40 submissions annually. 60% of books from first-time authors; 90% of books from unagented writers. Pays 10% royalty on retail price; 5% on wholesale price (50% of total cost); offers variable advance. Publishes book an average of 6 months after acceptance. Simultaneous submissions OK. Reports in 2 weeks on queries; 3 weeks on mss. Free book catalog and ms guidelines.

Nonfiction: How-to and technical. Subjects include business and economics (investing in stocks and commodities). Interested in books on strategies, methods for investing in the stock market, options market, and commodity markets. Query or submit outline/synopsis and sample chapters. Reviews artwork/photos as part of ms package.

Recent Nonfiction Title: *The World's Most Valuable Investment Strategy*, by B. Becker Fisher, Jr.

Tips: "Our books are for serious investors; we sell through direct mail to our mailing list and other financial lists. Writers must keep their work original; this market tends to have a great deal of information overlap among publications."

WINE APPRECIATION GUILD LTD., 155 Connecticut St., San Francisco CA 94107. (514)864-1202. FAX: (514)864-0377. Director: Maurice Sullivan. Estab. 1973. Imprints include Vintage Image and Wine Advisory Board (nonfiction). Publishes hardcover and trade paperback originals, trade paperback reprints, and software. Averages 12 titles/year; receives 30-40 submissions annually. 30% of books from first-time authors; 100% of books from unagented writers. Pays 5-15% royalty on wholesale price or makes outright purchase. Publishes book an average of 18 months after acceptance. Simultaneous submissions OK. Query for electronic submisstions. Reports in 2 months. Book catalog for $2.

Nonfiction: Cookbook and how-to—wine related. Subjects include wine, cooking and foods and travel. Must be wine-related. Submit outline/synopsis and sample chapters. Reviews artwork/photos as part of ms package.
Recent Nonfiction Title: *Winery Technology and Operations*, by Yair Margalit, Ph.D.
Tips: "Our books are read by wine enthusiasts—from neophytes to professionals, and wine industry and food industry people. We are interested in anything of a topical and timely nature connected with wine, by a knowledgeable author. We do not deal with agents of any type. We prefer to get to know the author as a person and to work closely with him/her."

WINGBOW PRESS, Subsidiary of Bookpeople, 2929 5th St., Berkeley CA 94710. (415)549-3030. Editor: Randy Fingland. Estab. 1971. Publishes trade paperback originals. Averages 4 titles/year; receives 450 submissions annually, "mostly fiction and poetry, which we aren't even considering." 50% of books from first-time authors; 100% of books from unagented writers. Pays 7-10% royalty on retail price; offers average $250 advance. Publishes book an average of 15 months after acceptance. Query for electronic submissions. Reports in 2 weeks on queries; 2 months on mss. Book catalog for #10 SASE.
Nonfiction: Reference and self-help. Subjects include philosophy/metaphysics, psychology and women's issues. "We are currently looking most seriously at women's studies; religion/metaphysics/philosophy; psychology and personal development. Our readers are receptive to alternative/New Age ideas. No business/finance how-to." Query or submit outline/synopsis and sample chapters.
Recent Nonfiction Title: *The Heart of the Goddess*, by Hallie Islehart Austen.

*WINSTON-DEREK PUBLISHERS, INC., Pennywell Dr., Box 90883, Nashville TN 37209. (615)329-1319/321-0535. FAX: (615)329-4811. Publisher: James W. Peebles. Estab. 1976. Pubishes hardcover, trade, and mass market paperback originals. Averages 60-65 titles/year; receives 3,500 submissions annually. 60% of books from first-time authors; 75% of books from unagented authors. Average print order for writer's first book is 3,000-5,000. "We will co-publish exceptional works of quality and style only when we reach our quota in our trade book division." Subsidy publishes 20% of books; more likely to subsidy publish juvenile books. Pays 10-15% of the net amount received on sales. Advance varies. Simultaneous submissions OK. Queries and mss without SASE will be discarded. Reports in 1 month on queries; 6 weeks on mss. Book catalog and guidelines for 9×12 SASE.
Nonfiction: Biography (current or historically famous), behavioral science and health (especially interested in mss of this category for teenagers and young adults). Subjects include Americana, theology, philosophy (nontechnical with contemporary format), religion (noncultist), and inspirational. Length: 65,000-85,000 words or less. Submit outline and first 2 or 4 chapters. Reviews artwork/photos as part of ms package.
Recent Nonfiction Title: *Go Ahead—Make Your Day: The One-Shot Self Development Book*, by Jim Davidson and Gordon Shea.
Fiction: Ethnic (non-defamatory); religious (theologically sound); suspense (highly plotted); and Americana (minorities and whites in positive relationships). Length: 85,000 words or less. "We can use fiction with a semi-historical plot; it must be based or centered around actual facts and events—Americana, religion, and gothic. We are looking for juvenile books (ages 9-15) on relevant aspects of growing up and understanding life's situations. No funny animals talking." Children's/juvenile books must be of high quality. Submit complete ms for children and juvenile books with illustrations, which are optional.
Recent Fiction Title: *Sisters of A Different Dawn*, by Darcy Williamson.
Poetry: Should be inspirational and with meaning. Poetry dealing with secular life should be of excellent quality. "We will accept unusual poetry books of exceptional quality and taste. We do not publish avant-garde poetry." Submit complete ms. No single poems.
Recent Poetry Title: *Champagne Mist*, by Marla Spevak Hess.
Tips: "We do not publish material that advocates violence or is derogative of other cultures or beliefs. There is now a growing concern for books about seniors, aging, and geriatic care. Outstanding biographies are quite successful, as are books dealing with the simplicity of man and his relationship with his environment. Our imprint Scythe Books for children needs material for adolescents within the 9-13 age group. These manuscripts should help young people with motivation for learning and succeeding at an early age, goal setting and character building. Biographies of famous women and men as role models are always welcomed. Always there is a need for books about current minority, scholars, issues and concerns. Stories must have a new twist and be provocative."

WIZARDS BOOKSHELF, P.O. Box 6600, San Diego CA 92106. (619)297-9879. Contact: R.I. Robb. Estab. 1972. Publishes hardcover and trade paperback originals and reprints. Firm averages 5 titles per year. Pays royalty or buys mss outright. Publishes book an average of 1 year after acceptance. Reports in 1 month on queries; 1 month on mss. Free book catalog and manuscript guidelines.
Nonfiction: Hermetic philosophy. Subjects include translation and antiquities. Submit outline/synopsis and sample chapters.
Recent Nonfiction Title: *Books of Kiu-Te, or The Tibetan Buddhist Tantras*, by David Reigle.
Tips: "Theosophists, Masons, Rosecrusians and neoplatonists are our audience."

‡*WOOD LAKE BOOKS, INC., Box 700, Winfield, British Columbia V0H 2C0 Canada. (604)766-2778. Editor: Jim Taylor. Publishes trade paperback originals. Firm averages 6-10 titles/year. Receives 200 submissions/ year. 75% of books from first-time authors. 99% from unagented writers. Subsidy publishes 5% of books. If subsidy is available, we will accept it. But the decision is first made on the manuscript—*then* we consider additional funding. Pays 7% minimum royalty on retail price, depends on situation. Publishes book an average of 9 moths after acceptance. Simultaneous submissions OK. Query for electronic submissions. We decide on titles at editorial meetings 2 times a year, May and November. Waiting period therefore varies. Rejections take less time than acceptances. Free book catalog.

Nonfiction: We are looking for mss that approach religion from the perspective of personal experience, anecdotal style; religion that makes common sense, is open to new insights and has practical application in daily life. No academic or theoretical mss; anything based on biblical inerrancy; anything that promotes ill feeling against any race, religion, sex, etc.; anything dealing with prophecy about the future. Query. Submit outline/synopsis and sample chapters. Reviews artwork/photos as part of ms package.

Recent Nonfiction Title: *The Wanderer*, by Sangchol Lee and Erich Weingartner (autobiography).

Tips: Our audience includes people who struggle to make their beliefs relevant to daily living, without having to park their minds on a shelf. If I were a writer trying to market a book today, I would ask myself how many people I know personally who would be willing to pay to get their hands on the book. If it's less than, say, 75% of the people I know well, I would quit now.

WOODBINE HOUSE, 5615 Fishers Ln., Rockville MD 20852. (301)468-8800. FAX: (301)468-5784. Editor: Susan Stokes. Estab. 1985. Publishes hardcover and trade paperback of books from first-time authors; 80% of books from unagented writers. Pays royalty; buys some mss outright. Publishes book an average of 18 months after acceptance. Simultaneous submissions OK. Query for electronic submissions. Reports in 1 month on queries; 3 months on mss. Free book catalog; ms guidelines for #10 SAE and 3 first class stamps.

Nonfiction: Biography, reference, travel and self-help. Subjects include Americana, health, history, hobbies, natural history, science, juvenile (ages 5-18), sociology. Especially needs parents' guides for special needs children and history. No personal accounts. Submit outline/synopsis and sample chapters. Reviews artwork/ photos as part of ms.

Recent Nonfiction Title: *Saving the Neighborhood*, by Peggy Robin.

Tips: "We are always impressed by authors who can write with clarity, authority, and style and can demonstrate that their book has a clearly defined market that they know how to reach."

WOODBRIDGE PRESS, P.O. Box 6189, Santa Barbara CA 93160. (805)965-7039. Imprint includes Banquo Books. Contact: Howard Weeks. Estab. 1971. Publishes hardcover and trade paperback originals. Firm averages 4-5 titles/year. Receives 250 submissions/year. 60% of books from first-time authors. 80% from unagented writers. Pays 10-15% on wholesale price. Publishes book an average of 8 months after acceptance. Simultaneous submissions OK. Reports in 3 weeks on queries; 1 month on mss. Free book catalog.

Nonfiction: Cookbook (vegetarian) and self-help. Subjects include agriculture/horticulture, cooking, foods, and nutrition, gardening, health/medicine, nature/environment and psychology (popular). Query. Submit outline/synopsis and sample chapters or complete ms. Reviews artwork/photos as part of ms package.

Recent Nonfiction Title: *Artistically Cultivated Herbs*, by Elise Felton (gardening).

*WOODSONG GRAPHICS, INC., P.O. Box 238, New Hope PA 18938. (215)794-8321. Editor: Ellen P. Bordner. Estab. 1977. Publishes hardcover and trade paperback originals. Averages 6-8 titles/year; receives 2,500-3,000 submissions annually. 40-60% of books from first-time authors; 100% of books from unagented writers. Average print order for writer's first book is 2,500-5,000. Will occasionally consider subsidy publishing based on "quality of material, motivation of author in distributing his work, and cost factors (which depend on the type of material involved), plus our own feelings on its marketability." Subsidy publishes 50% of books. Pays royalty on net price; offers average $100 advance. Publishes book an average of 1 year after acceptance. Simultaneous submissions OK. Reports in 1 month on queries; reports on full mss *can* take several months, depending on the amount of material already in house. "We do everything possible to facilitate replies, but we have a small staff and want to give every manuscript a thoughtful reading." Book catalog for #10 SASE. "Manuscripts not returned unless SASE enclosed."

Nonfiction: Biography, cookbook, how-to, humor, illustrated book, juvenile, reference, and self-help. Subjects include cooking and foods, hobbies, philosophy and psychology. "We're happy to look at anything of good quality, but we're not equipped to handle lavish color spreads at this time. Our needs are very open, and we're interested in seeing any subject, provided it's handled with competence and style. Good writing from unknowns is also welcome." No pornography; only minimal interest in technical manuals of any kind. Query or submit outline/synopsis and at least 2 sample chapters. Reviews artwork/photos as part of ms package.

Recent Nonfiction Title: *Dogs and You*, by Doris Phillips.

Fiction: Adventure, experimental, fantasy, gothic, historical, humor, mainstream, mystery, romance, science fiction, suspense and western. "In fiction, we are simply looking for books that provide enjoyment. We want well-developed characters, creative plots, and good writing style." No pornography or "sick" material. Submit outline/synopsis and sample chapters.

Recent Fiction Title: *Snowflake Come Home*, by John A. Giegling.

Tips: "Good nonfiction with an identified target audience and a definite slant has the best chance of being sold to our firm. We rarely contract in advance of seeing the completed manuscript. We prefer a synopsis, explaining what the thrust of the book is without a chapter-by-chapter profile. If the query is interesting enough, we'll look at the full manuscript for further details. Partial subsidy program available for authors with a serious interest in promoting their own books."

‡WORD BOOKS PUBLISHER, Division of Word Inc., Subsidiary of Cap Cities/ABC, Suite 1000, 5221 North O'Connor Blvd., Irving TX 75039. (214)556-1900. Managing Editor: Al Bryant. Estab. 1965. Publishes hardcover and trade paperback originals, and hardcover, trade paperback, and mass market paperback reprints. Averages 75 titles/year; receives 2,000 submissions annually. 15% of books from first-time authors; 98% of books from unagented writers. Pays 10-15% royalty on retail price; offers average $5,000 advance. Publishes book an average of 1 year after acceptance. Query for electronic submissions. Reports in 1 month on queries; 2 months on mss. Free book catalog and ms guidelines for 9×12 SAE and 3 first class stamps.

Nonfiction: Family relationships, retirement, personal growth, how-to, reference, self-help and textbook. Subjects include health, history (church and Bible), philosophy, politics, psychology, religion, sociology, and sports. Especially looking for "religious books that help modern-day Christians cope with the stress of life in the 20th century. We welcome queries on all types of books." Query with outline/synopsis and sample chapters. Reviews artwork/photos as part of ms package.

Recent Nonfiction Title: *Grace Killers*, by Chuck Swindoll.

Fiction: No non-religious fiction. Submit outline/synopsis and sample chapters.

Recent Fiction Title: *Observers Story*, by Roger Elwood.

*WORDWARE PUBLISHING, INC., Suite 101, 1506 Capital Ave., Plano TX 75074. (214)423-0090. FAX: (214)881-9147. Publisher: Russell A. Stultz. Estab. 1982. Publishes hardcover and trade paperback originals. Averages 30-40 titles/year; receives 200 submissions annually. 40% of books from first-time authors; 95% of books from unagented writers. Subsidy publishes 5% of books. "We review manuscripts on a case-by-case basis. We are primarily a trade publisher dealing with authors on a royalty basis." Pays royalty on net price; advance varies. Publishes book an average of 6 to 9 months after acceptance. Simultaneous submissions OK. "We prefer electronic submissions." Reports in 2 weeks. Free book catalog; ms guidelines for 9×12 SAE and 5 first class stamps.

Nonfiction: Regional (Texas) 8-10 titles per year; technical. Subjects include computer, business and professional. "I am always interested in books that improve upon specific software documentation. Additionally, I am willing to consider manuscripts on any new software products or 'hot' topics in the field of computers. I do not want to see anything that is not computer or business related." Query or submit outline/synopsis and sample chapters. Reviews artwork/photos as part of ms package.

Recent Nonfiction Title: *Illustrated Lotus 1-2-3 Release 2.2*, by John Paul Mueller.

Tips: "Our audience covers the spectrum from computer novice to the professional who needs advanced reference manuals. We have very stringent deadlines that our authors must meet to access the window of opportunity for our products. So many computer books are time-sensitive and any author interested in signing with me should expect to give an all-out effort to his manuscript."

WORKMAN PUBLISHING COMPANY, INC., 708 Broadway, New York NY 10003. (212)254-5900. Estab. 1969. Publishes hardcover and trade paperback originals and reprints and calendars. Averages 25 titles (and 33 calendars)/year. Pays royalty. Simultaneous submissions OK. Reports in 6 months. Book catalog free on request.

Nonfiction: Coffee table book, cookbook, how-to, humor, illustrated book, juvenile, and self-help. Subjects include Americana, art, cooking and foods, health, history, hobbies, nature, photography, recreation, religion, sports, travel. Query or submit outline/synopsis and sample chapters.

Recent Nonfiction Titles: *The New Basics Cookbook*, by Julee Russo and Sheila Lukins.

WRITER'S DIGEST BOOKS, Imprint of F&W Publications, 1507 Dana Ave., Cincinnati OH 45207. Editorial Director: William Brohaugh. Publishes hardcover and paperback originals. Pays 10% royalty on net receipts. Simultaneous (if so advised) submissions OK. Publishes book an average of 1 year after acceptance. Enclose return postage. Book catalog for 9×12 SAE with 6 first class stamps.

Nonfiction: Writing, photography, music, and other creative pursuits, as well as general-interest subjects. "We're seeking up-to-date, how-to treatments by authors who can write from successful experience. Should be well-researched, yet lively and readable. Query or submit outline/synopsis and sample chapters. Be prepared to explain how the proposed book differs from existing books on the subject. We are also very interested in republishing self-published nonfiction books and good instructional or reference books that have gone out of print before their time. No fiction or poetry. Send sample copy, sales record, and reviews if available. If you have a good idea for a book that would be updated annually, try us. We're willing to consider freelance compilers of such works." Reviews artwork/photos as part of ms package.

Recent Nonfiction Title: *Creative Conversations: The Writer's Guide to Conducting Interviews.*

‡**WYRICK & COMPANY,** P.O. Box 89, Charleston SC 29402. (803)722-0881. FAX: (803)722-6771. Subsidiaries include Ampthill Books and Southern Images. Editor: C.L. Wyrick, Jr. Estab. 1986. Publishes hardcover and trade paperback originals. Averages 6-12 titles/year. Receives 75-100 submissions/year. 90% of books from first-time authors; 100% from unagented writers. Pays 6-10% royalty on retail price. Offers $500 average advance. Publishes book an average of 9 months after acceptance. Simultaneous submissions OK. Query for electronic submissions. Reports in 1 month on queries; 4 months on mss. Book catalog for 9 × 12 SAE and 4 first class stamps. Manuscript guidelnes for #10 SASE.

Nonfiction: Biography, humor, illustrated book and juvenile. Subjects include art/architecture, gardening, language/literature, photography, regional and travel. Submit complete ms. Reviews artwork/photos as part of ms package.

Recent Nonfiction Title: *Nets and Doors,* by Jack Leigh.

Fiction: Humor, juvenile, literary, mainstream/contemporary. Submit complete ms.

Recent Fiction Title: *Things Undone,* by Max Childers (adult).

YANKEE BOOKS, (formerly Lance Tapley, Publisher, Inc.), P.O. Box 1248, Camden ME 04843. (207)236-0933. FAX: (207)236-0941. President: Lance Tapley. Publishes hardcover and trade paperbacks of New England interest. Firm averages 20-30 titles/year. Receives over 1,000 submissions/year. 50% of books from first-time authors. 90% from unagented writers. Pays 5-15% royalty on wholesale price or retail price. Offers negotiable advance. Publishes book an average of 6 months after acceptance. Simultaneous submissions OK. Reports in 2 weeks on queries and 4 months on mss. Free book catalog.

Nonfiction: Biography, coffee table book, cookbook, how-to, humor, illustrated book, juvenile, reference, self-help. Subjects include Americana, animals, anthropology/archaeology, art/architecture, child guidance/parenting, cooking, foods and nutrition, government/politics, history, language/literature, nature/environment, photography, recreation, regional, religion and sports. Query before sending ms. Reviews artwork/photos as part of ms package.

Recent Nonfiction Title: *New England's Disastrous Weather.*

Fiction: Short stories of New England interest. No erotica. Query.

Recent Fiction Title: *Best New England Stories* (collection of stories).

YORK PRESS LTD., P.O. Box 1172, Fredericton, New Brunswick E3B 5C8 Canada. (506)458-8748. General Manager/Editor: Dr. S. Elkhadem. Estab. 1975. Publishes trade paperback originals. Averages 10 titles/year; receives 50 submissions annually. 10% of books from first-time authors; 100% of books from unagented writers. Pays 5-20% royalty on wholesale price. Publishes book an average of 6 months after acceptance. Reports in 1 week on queries; 1 month on ms. Free book catalog; ms guidelines for $2.50.

Nonfiction and Fiction: Reference, textbook and scholarly. Especially needs literary criticism, comparative literature and linguistics and fiction of an experimental nature by well-established writers. Query.

Recent Nonfiction Title: *Tennessee Williams: Life, Work and Criticism,* by F. Londré.

Recent Fiction Title: *Red White & Blue,* by Ben Stoltzfus.

Tips: "If I were a writer trying to market a book today, I would spend a considerable amount of time examining the needs of a publisher *before* sending my manuscript to him. Scholarly books and creative writing of an experimental nature are the only kinds we publish. The writer must adhere to our style manual and follow our guidelines exactly."

ZEBRA BOOKS, Subsidiary of Kensington Publishing Corp., 475 Park Ave. S., New York NY 10016. (212)889-2299. Editorial Director: Michael Seidman. Publishes mass market paperback originals and reprints. Averages 600 titles/year; receives thousands of submissions annually. 50% of books from first-time authors. Pays royalty on retail price or makes outright purchase. Publishes book an average of 12-18 months after acceptance. Simultaneous submissions OK. Reports in 3 months on queries; 4 months on mss. Book catalog for #10 SAE and 39¢ postage.

Nonfiction: Biography, how-to, humor, self-help, true crime, first-person Vietnam experience. Subjects include health, history and psychology. "We are open to many areas, especially self-help, stress, money management, child-rearing, health, war (WWII, Vietnam), and celebrity biographies." No nature, art, music,

For information on book publishers' areas of interest, see the nonfiction and fiction sections in the Book Publishers Subject Index.

photography, religion or philosophy. Query or submit outline/synopsis and sample chapters.

Recent Nonfiction Title: *Daddy's Girl*, by Clifford Irving.

Fiction: Adventure, men's action, confession, erotica, gothic, historical, horror, humor, mainstream, regencies, medical novels, romance and suspense. Tip sheet on historical romances, gothics, family sagas, adult romances and women's contemporary fiction is available. No poetry or short story collections. Query with synopsis and several sample chapters. SASE is a must.

Recent Fiction Title: *Heart of the Country*, by Gregg Matthews.

THE ZONDERVAN CORP., 1415 Lake Drive SE, Grand Rapids MI 49506. (616)698-6900. Publishes hardcover and trade paperback originals and reprints. Averages 100 titles/year; receives 3,000 submissions annually. 20% of books from first-time authors; 80% of books from unagented writers. Average print order for a writer's first book is 5,000. Pays royalty of 14% of the net amount received on sales of cloth and softcover trade editions and 12% of net amount received on sales of mass market paperbacks. Offers variable advance. Reports in 6 weeks on queries; 3 months on proposals. Book catalog for 9×12 SASE. Recommend ms guidelines for #10 SASE. Send queries, requests and proposals to Manuscript Review. To receive a recording with complete submission information call (616)698-3447.

Nonfiction and Fiction: Biography, autobiography, self-help, devotional, Bible study resources, references for lay audience; some adult fiction; youth and children's ministry, teens and children. Academic and Professional Books: college and seminary textbooks (biblical studies, theology, church history, the humanities); preaching, counseling, discipleship, worship, and church renewal for pastors, professionals, and lay leaders in ministry; theological and biblical reference books; variety of books written from the Wesleyan perspective. All from religious perspective (evangelical). Immediate needs listed in guidelines. Query or submit outline/synopsis, and 1 sample chapter.

Recent Nonfiction Title: *Honest to God?*, by Bill Hybels.

Recent Fiction Title: *The Sacred Diary of Adrian Plass (Aged 37¾)*, by Adrian Plass.

Small Presses

Following are additional listings of small presses that publish three or fewer titles per year or new presses that had not published four books by the time they completed a questionnaire for a listing in this edition of *Writer's Market*. This means the publishing opportunity is more limited, but these companies are still legitimate markets and have expressed an interest in being listed in *Writer's Market*. Writers should query for more information when first contacting a small press. Editors tell us too many writers are sending small presses complete manuscripts.

‡ACORN PUBLISHING, Box 1159W, Syracuse NY 13261. (315)689-7072. Editor: Mary O. Robb. Publishes trade paperback originals on health, recreation, sports and parenting.

AHSAHTA PRESS, Boise State University, Dept. of English, 1910 University Dr., Boise ID 83725. (208)385-1246. Co-Editor: Tom Trusky. Publishes Western poetry in trade paperback. Reads annually, January through March.

AMADEUS PUBLISHING COMPANY, P.O. Box 6141, San Jose CA 95150-6141. (408)295-6427. Proprietor: George D. Snell. Books relative to late 18th century musicians and composers.

AMERICAN SHOWCASE, INC., 724 5th Ave., New York NY 10019. (212)245-0981. FAX: (212)265-2247. Marketing Director: Ann Middlebrook. Publishes graphic design books—both trade and consumer and sourcebooks on all topics.

ANDERSON MCLEAN, INC., #508, 5 Town & Country Village, San Jose CA 95128. (408)972-0401. Sr. Editor: Jan Scott. How-to market, install, and select microcomputer accounting software.

‡BARN OWL BOOKS, P.O. Box 226, Vallecitos NM 87581. (505)582-4226. Nonfiction and fiction on women's, gay/lesbian, feminist and mainstream topics.

‡CADMUS EDITIONS, Box 687, Tiburon CA 94920. (707)431-8527. Editor: J.S. Miller. Publishes literary fiction, short story collections and poetry.

‡CAROUSEL PRESS, P.O. Box 6061, Albany CA 94706. (415)527-5849. Editor/Publisher: Carole T. Meyers. Publishes nonfiction, family-oriented travel books.

‡CHALLENGER PRESS, Wallace and Associates, Inc., Suite 8, 540 Alisal Rd., Solvang CA 93463. (805)688-2434. Project Director: Marilyn White-Munn. Publishes self-help books.

‡THE CHILE PEPPER, Out West Publishing, P.O. Box 4278, Alburquerque NM 87196. (505)889-3745. Publisher: Robert Spiegel. Publishes cookbooks, gardening and travel on specific cuisines, e.g. Asian, Cajun, Southwestern, "with an eye to the spicy."

CLARITY PRESS INC., 3277 Roswell Rd. NE, #469, Atlanta GA 30305. (404)231-0649. FAX: (306)569-8649. Editorial Committee contact: Annette Gordon. Publishes manuscripts on minorities, human rights in US, Middle East and Africa.

‡CLOTHESPIN FEVER PRESS, 5529 N. Figueroa, Los Angeles CA 90042. (213)254-1373. Contact: Jenny Wrenn. Lesbian fiction and nonfiction.

CORKSCREW PRESS, INC., 2915 Fenimore Rd., Silver Spring MD 20902. (301)933-0407. Editorial Director: J. Croker Norge. Publishes trade humorous how-to books.

‡CREATIVE WITH WORDS PUBLICATIONS, P.O. Box 223226, Carmel CA 93922. (408)649-1682. Publisher/Editor: Brigitta Geltrich. Publishes poetry and prose.

‡**DIAMOND EDITIONS**, P.O. Box 12001, Portland OR 97212. (503)287-0915. Publisher: Carolan Gladden. Publishes trade paperback fiction and nonfiction.

DIAMOND PRESS, Box 2458, Doylestown PA 18901. (215)345-6094. Marketing Director: Paul Johnson. Publishes trade paperback originals on softball and antiques.

DIMI PRESS, 3820 Oak Hollow Lane SE, Salem OR 97302. (503)364-7698. FAX: (503)769-6207. President: Dick Lutz. Trade paperback originals of health and psychology.

DRY CANYON PRESS, 914 River Hts. Blvd., Logan UT 84321. Editor: Thad Box. Publishes trade paperback originals of mainstream/contemporary fiction and poetry.

‡**FIESTA CITY PUBLISHERS**, P.O. Box 5861, Santa Barbara CA 93150-5861. (805)733-1984. President: Frank E. Cooke. Publishes how-to, health cookbooks and music books.

FREE SPIRIT PUBLISHING INC., Suite 716, 123 N. Third St., Minneapolis MN 55401. (612)338-2068. President: Judy Galbraith. Publishes psychology and self-help materials for kids, educational/parenting books for adults.

‡**FROG IN THE WELL**, P.O. Box 170052, San Francisco CA 94117. (415)431-2113. Editor: Susan Hester. Publishes fiction and nonfiction on women's issues.

FRONT ROW EXPERIENCE, 540 Discovery Bay Blvd., Byron CA 94514. (415)634-5710. Editor: Frank Alexander. Publishes teacher/educator edition paperback originals. Only wants submissions for "Movement Education" and related areas.

GREAT OCEAN PUBLISHERS, 1823 N. Lincoln St., Arlington VA 22207. President: Mark Esterman. Publishes hardcover and trade paperback originals and hardcover reprints. In nonfiction, biography, how-to, illustrated book, reference, self-help technical and educational.

GREEN TIMBER PUBLICATIONS, Box 3884, Portland ME 04104. (207)797-4180. President: Tirrell H. Kimball. Publishes trade paperback originals in juvenile nonfiction, fiction and poetry.

‡**GURZE BOOKS**, Box 2238, Carlsbad CA 92008. (619)434-7533. Editor: Lindsey Hall. "We are primarily interested in new approaches to eating disorders and related issues of self-improvement for lay readers or professional therapists (without a clinical orientation)."

HELM PUBLISHING, Subsidiary of Padre Productions, P.O. Box 840, Arroyo Grande CA 93421-0840. (805)473-1947. Editor: Louise Fox. Publishes marine or naval history dealing with California coast and including unpublished historical photos and drawings.

‡**HEMINGWAY WESTERN STUDIES SERIES**, Boise State University, 1910 University Dr., Boise ID 83725. (208)385-1999. Editor: Tom Trusky. Publishes Rocky Mountain nonfiction and popular scholarship.

‡**HIGGS PUBLISHING CORPORATION**, 2015 Grant Place, Melbourne FL 32901. (407)728-5928. Editor: Ellen Johnson. Estab. 1989. Publishes fiction for children—especially for the younger and middle-grade ranges. Seeking picturebooks, middle-grade novels and young adult novels. Holiday themes, mystery, fantasy, contemporary fiction, storybooks, some nonfiction.

‡**ILLUMINATIONS PRESS**, #B, 2110 9th St., Berkeley CA 94710-2141. (415)849-2102. Editor/Publisher: Norm Moser. Publishes poetry and plays.

JAMENAIR LTD., Box 241957, Los Angeles CA 90024-9757. (213)470-6688. Publisher: P.K. Studner. Publishes hardcover, trade paperback and mass market paperback originals and trade paperback reprints. Subjects are: business and economics, computers and electronics, education and career-advancement/job search.

‡**JASON & NORDIE PUBLISHERS**, Box 1123, Exton PA 19341. (215)363-0352. General Manager: Norma McPhee. "We want entertaining stories, well-plotted with the main character a child who is handicapped. The stories are told from this child's viewpoint. The goals must be attainable."

JONES 21ST CENTURY, INC., 9697 E. Mineral Ave., Englewood CO 80112. (303)792-3111. Editorial Director: Kim Dority. Publishes hardcover originals on reference books for cable television industry.

‡**LAHONTAN IMAGES**, P.O. Box 1093, Susanville CA 96130. (916)257-6747. Owner: Tim I. Purdy. Publishes books pertaining to Northeastern California and Western Nevada.

‡**LANDMARK EDITIONS, INC.**, 1402 Kansas Ave., P.O. Box 4469, Kansas City MO 64127. (816)241-4919. Editorial Coordinator: Nan Thatch. "We accept manuscript submissions through our contest for students aged six to nineteen."

‡**LAVENDER TAPES**, 1125 Veronica Springs Rd., Santa Barbara CA 93105. Publisher: Deby DeWeese. Produces lesbian books-on-cassette for a lesbian market. Produces approximately 10 tapes/year. Buys audio rights only.

‡**LINCOLN SPRINGS PRESS**, P.O. Box 269, Franklin Lakes NJ 07417. (201)423-5882. Contact: M. Gabrielle. Publishes nonfiction. Subjects include Americana, ethnic, government/politics, history, language/literature, military/war, sociology and women's issues/studies. Fiction: Ethnic, feminist, gothic, historical, literary, mainstream/contemporary, mystery, romance, short story collections. No erotica please.

‡**MARADIA PRESS**, 228 Evening Star Dr., Naugatuck CT 06770. (203)723-0758. Vice President: Peter A. Ciullo. Publishes well researched consumer-related issue books; especially interested in unique, balanced treatments of health topics.

‡**MERRY MEN PRESS**, 274 Roanoke Rd., El Cajon CA 92020. (619)442-5541. Contact: Robin Hood. Publishes science fiction/fantasy, erotica in a book anthology.

*****MEYERBOOKS, PUBLISHER**, Box 427, Glenwood IL 60425. (312)757-4950. Publisher: David Meyer. Publishes hardcover and trade paperback originals and reprints. History, reference and self-help works published on subjects of Americana, cooking and foods, health and nature.

MISTY HILL PRESS, 5024 Turner Rd., Sebastopol CA 95472. (415)892-0789. Managing Editor: Sally C. Karste. Estab. 1984. Publishes trade paperback originals. In nonfiction, publishes biography, in fiction, historical.

‡**MYSTIC SEAPORT MUSEUM**, 50 Greenmanville Ave., Mystic CT 06355-0990. (203)572-0711. Imprints include: American Maritime Library. Publication Director: Gerald E. Morris. "We need serious, well-documented biographics, studies of economic, social, artistic, or musical elements of American maritime (not navel) history; books on traditional boat and ship types and construction (how-to)."

‡**NAR PUBLICATIONS**, Box 233, Barryville NY 12719. (914)557-8713. Editor: Monique E. Dubacher. Publishes trade paperback originals on business and economics, child guidance/parenting, education, gardening, government/politics, health/medicine, hobbies, money/finance, recreation, sports and consumer.

NATIONAL PUBLISHING COMPANY, P.O. Box 8386, Philadelphia PA 19101-8386. (215)732-1863. Editor: Peter F. Hewitt. Publishes Bibles, New Testament and foreign language New Testaments.

‡**NATURE'S DESIGN**, P.O. Box 255, Davenport CA 95017. (408)426-8205. Publisher/Editor: Frank S. Balthis. Publishes guides to parks and books on nature and the environment.

‡**NEW SEED PRESS**, P.O. Box 9488, Berkeley CA 94709. (415)540-7576. Editor: Helen Chetin. Publishes fiction and nonfiction.

OAK TREE PUBLICATIONS, 3870 Murphy Canyon Rd., #203, San Diego CA 92123. (619)560-5163. Editor: Linda Alioto. Estab. 1976. Publishes hardcover originals for juveniles.

‡**C. OLSON & CO.**, P.O. Box 5100, Santa Cruz CA 95063-5100. (408)458-3365. Owner: C. Olson. "We are looking for nonfiction books that can be sold at natural food stores and small independent bookstores on health and on how to live a life which has less negative impact on the earth's environment."

‡**PAN-EROTIC REVIEW**, P.O. Box 2992, Santa Cruz CA 95063. (408)426-7082. Editor: David Steinberg. Publishes quality erotic books of photography and fiction.

‡**PARADISE PUBLICATIONS**, 8110 SW Wareham, Portland OR 97223. (503)246-1555. President: Christie Stilson. Publishes specific location travel guides.

PARTNERS IN PUBLISHING, P.O. Box 50374, Tulsa OK 74150. (918)584-5906. Editor: P.M. Fielding. Estab. 1976. Publishes biography, how-to, reference, self-help, technical and textbooks on learning disabilities.

‡PC PRESS, Suite 1101, 51 Monroe St., Rockville MD 20850. (301)294-7450. Publication Manager: Barbara Marsh. "We're looking for material relating to personal computers and the use of personal computers in business."

*PEACOCK BOOKS, College Square, Cuttack Orissa 753003, India. 0671-22733. Editor: Bibhu Padhi. "We are looking for 3-4 good, 56-80 page (typed, double-spaced) poetry collections from new writers, who have had at least *some* magazine publication."

‡PEEL PRODUCTIONS, P.O. Box 184-M, Molalla OR 97038. (503)829-6849. Managing Editor: S. DuBosque. Publishes how-to, picture books, juvenile books and children's plays.

THE PERFECTION FORM CO., 10520 New York Ave., Des Moines IA 50322. (515)278-0133. Publishes supplemental educational material grades K-12, including quarterly newsletter with students' responses to reading.

‡PERIVALE PRESS & AGENCY, 13830 Erwin St., VanNuys CA 91401. (818)785-4671. Managing Editor: Barbara Rhys-Davies. Publishes West Coast oriented works.

V. POLLARD PRESS, P.O. Box 19864, Jacksonville FL 32245. (904)724-8441. Owner: M.L. Lum. Publishes trade paperback and mass market paperback originals on cooking, foods and nutrition, education, hobbies, and recreation.

‡THE PRESS AT CALIFORNIA STATE UNIVERSITY, FRESNO, California State University, Fresno CA 93740. (209)278-5752. Director: Joseph Satin. "Significant books on the arts, including film, popular culture, folk arts."

THE PRESS OF MACDONALD & REINECKE, Subsidiary of Padre Productions, P.O. Box 840, Arroyo Grande CA 93421-0840. (805)473-1947. Publisher: Lachlan P. MacDonald. Publishes literary criticism, usually by invitation. Critics should submit examples of published articles devoted to a particular theme. Also publishes fiction, poetry and drama.

‡PUBLISHERS SYNDICATION INTERNATIONAL, Suite 856, 1377 K Street NW, Washington DC 20005. President: A.P. Samuels. Publishes books on military history.

PUCKERBRUSH PRESS, 76 Main St., Orono ME 04473. (207)581-3832/866-4808. Publisher/Editor: Constance Hunting. Publishes trade paperback originals of literary fiction and poetry.

‡PUMA PUBLICATIONS, 1670 Coral Dr., Santa Maria CA 93454. Manager: John Baptiste. Publishes books on small business.

‡REFERENCE PUBLICATIONS, INC., 218 St. Clair River Dr., Box 344, Algonac MI 48001. (313)794-5722. Publishes Africana, Americana, and botany reference books.

RESOLUTION BUSINESS PRESS, Suite 208, 1101 NE 8th St., Bellevue WA 98004. (206)455-4611. Contact: John Spilker. "Our focus is on books dealing with management issues related to the computer industry (hardware and software manufacturers and developers) and compiling computer industry directories emphasizing career and product development opportunities."

‡ST. JOHN'S PUBLISHING, INC., 6824 Oaklawn Ave., Edina MN 55435. (612)9044. President: Donna Montgomery. Publishes nonfiction books on parenting.

SANDPIPER PRESS, P.O. Box 286, Brookings OR 97415. (503)469-5588. Editor: Marilyn Riddle. Plans an anthology of true Native American visions and prophesies submitted by verified Native Americans only.

SOUND VIEW PRESS, 170 Boston Post Rd., Madison CT 06443. President: Peter Hastings Falk. Publishes hardcover and trade paperback originals, dictionaries, exhibition records, and price guides on 19th-mid 20th century American art.

STONE WALL PRESS, INC., 1241 30th St. NW, Washington DC 20007. President/Publisher: Henry Wheelwright. Publishes hardcover and trade paperback originals of how-to, environmental/outdoor instruction and literature.

‡TECHNICAL ANALYSIS OF STOCKS & COMMODITIES, Technical Analysis, Inc., 3517 SW Alaska St., Seattle WA 98126-2730. (206)938-0570. Editor: John Sweeney. Publishes business and economics books and software about using charts and computers to trade stocks, options, mutual funds or commodity futures.

‡TESSERA PUBLISHING, INC., 9561 Woodridge Circle, Eden Prairie MN 55347. (612)941-5053. Secretary/ Treasurer: Pat Bell. Publishes nonfiction books on "uncommon stories of common people."

TGNW PRESS, 2429 E. Aloha, Seattle WA 98112. (206)328-9656. Proprietor: Roger Herz. Estab. 1987. Publishes mass market paperback originals on baseball, and children's books with a humorous subject matter.

VICTORY PRESS, 543 Lighthouse Ave., Monterey CA 93940. (408)372-8438. Editor: Eileen Hu. Estab. 1988. Interested in topics on Chinese philosophy and medicine; martial arts books that fit in with the philosophy of Buddhism and Taoism.

VORTEX COMMUNICATIONS, Box 1008, Topanga CA 90290. (213)455-0097. President: Cynthia Riddle. Articles on health care, exercise, fitness, nutrition, spiritual well being from a holistic perspective, 1,000 to 2,500 words.

‡WATSON & DWYER PUBLISHING, 232 Academy Rd., Winnipeg, Manitoba R3M 0E7 Canada. Senior Editor: Helen Burgess. Publishes books on social history of the Northwest, North American and the Arctic.

WESTERN TANAGER PRESS, 1111 Pacific Ave., Santa Cruz CA 95060. (408)425-1111. Publisher: Hal Morris. Publishes biography, hiking and biking guides and regional history hardcover and trade paperback originals and reprints.

First Bylines

by Mark Kissling

Publishing a first book can be a very daunting task; the chances are slim for an unsolicited manuscript to rise out of the slush pile. However, historical biographer Susan Strane reminds us, "Every published writer had a first book." Three who have recently published their first books are interviewed here.

Two write fiction, the third published nonfiction. They have some tips and advice for those who would follow their lead.

To help with marketing a work, all three of our writers agree that an agent is very helpful in selling the book to a publisher. They also offer insights into methods of writing, considering trends and dealing with agents and publishers.

1990 was an especially encouraging year for new writers. Segments of the book publishing industry began to help those who published a first book. In May, B. Dalton Booksellers began promoting new literary talent in 250 stores across the nation with "Discover—Great New Writers." The *New York Times Book Review* and *Library Journal* were featuring new novelists from time to time. Still, most new writers must work hard to promote their books after meeting the challenge of getting published.

A.M. Homes
Jack (Macmillan)

A.M. Homes sees her career as a writer at a turning point, and she's only just begun. Homes realizes writing is her career, having published her first novel, *Jack*, with a collection of short stories, *The Safety of Objects*, to follow. "It's exciting and scary," she says. Given her steady work methods and continued success publishing her fiction in magazines and books, she shouldn't have to worry too much.

Photo by Willard Volz/The Washington Times

J·A·C·K

A·M·HOMES

Homes grew up in Washington D.C., and began writing at age 15. Her first serious effort was not short fiction, but rather a play that won an award in the District of Columbia. She continued to write plays at American University but took on new writing challenges with nonfiction articles and short stories for the college literary magazine.

Following her developing desire to write, Homes transferred to Sarah Lawrence College to study under Grace Paley. "Write the truth according to the character," was the advice Paley gave Homes and her other students. Homes considers this a good check. "It reminds me not to subject the character to what I as the writer think is true."

Homes started writing her novel, *Jack*, in 1982 while she was still at American University. The novel, which chronicles the difficulty a father experiences telling his son that he's gay, was influenced by the children's literature she was studying at the time. When she transferred to Sarah Lawrence, Paley did not want Homes to work on the novel, favoring newer work. "After six months she came around," says Homes, who went on to finish the novel in 1985.

Events took an unexpected turn when Homes found an agent to send out the manuscript, while she left for the Iowa Writer's Workshop. The agent died and her book was left in limbo. Homes located a new agent who promptly sold the manuscript to Macmillan for its young adult fiction line. *Jack* appeared in November 1989 and made a second appearance as a Vintage adult paperback in October 1990.

"Staying connected to your material is important," says Homes, who makes a point of writing every morning. "It keeps me on track." Despite her success with a second book on the way and short fiction placed in *Story* magazine, Homes is realistic about her writing. "You have to realize that everything you write will not be great or published," she says. "And don't send things out until they're finished," she adds. "Don't seek opinions on your writing by sending it out."

Homes recommends that all writers have an agent. "When you contact an agent," she advises, "be brief in your query letter. Don't try to set yourself apart at this stage. Then allow two months before you drop a note as a reminder." A writer should not confuse being persistent with being pushy.

The same applies to publishers. "They're aware of the proliferation of writing programs," Homes says. "As a result, bad form in first contact becomes a glaring problem." What about controversial subject matter, such as a father revealing his homosexuality to a son? "Don't tone your writing down to spare anyone's feelings or sensibilities," she says. "And don't worry about publishing trends. There's no chance to respond in time to them."

Her final advice to writers searching for role models in contemporary American fiction is to "read a lot, everything you can, and not just your subject area. Find the voice that's yours. Then *do* the writing."

Susan Strane
A Whole-Souled Woman: The Story of Prudence Crandall (W.W. Norton)

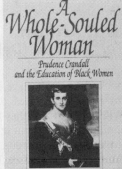

Photo by Susan Hoeltzel

A Whole-Souled Woman
Prudence Crandall
and the Education of Black Women

Susan Strane

"Research is a catalyst for writing," says Susan Strane. "I've always loved doing research, and it's given me ideas for four or five books. The next fifteen years of my writing life are already planned." Considering the ten years she put into her first book, working "in fits and starts," Strane recognizes the volume of work that faces today's writer of history and biography.

A Whole-Souled Woman: The Story of Prudence Crandall recounts the life of Prudence Crandall, a woman who shocked the town of Canterbury, Connecticut, in the 1830s by admitting black women to the boarding school she ran. After a decade of controversy, highlighted by the infamous Black Law, aimed at closing Crandall down, she left New England when her school was abandoned. For the rest of her life she remained politically active, burgeoning the women's rights movement of the late nineteenth century.

Strane did a great deal of research for *A Whole-Souled Woman*. Her primary challenge was the amount of material available. "Writers taking on major historical figures often get buried in the work already done on the person," says Strane. "The problem with minor historical figures such as Prudence Crandall is that there's too little material. I found huge gaps that are still left unknown."

She handled the problem by separating the book into three sections. Relating the parts to each other then became her task. "The sections had to be woven together to make the entire book coherent," says Strane.

Strane first had an idea of writing a screenplay about Prudence Crandall, having discovered her in research for a graduate school paper on education. Strane was studying for an M.F.A. at Columbia University at the time, and she still uses the Columbia Library for her research today.

She found a short biography on Crandall and used the bibliography to gather more material. Checking every single name she found, Strane compiled a list of all her sources. When she began to piece the material together, she found a number of contradictions. "I set out to resolve the contradictions by double checking," Strane says. "Many were merely factual errors. The biography on Crandall had given a superficial treatment to many of the important facts of her life. Then there was a bias because of her activities."

Ten years after she began her research, Strane had gotten to the bottom of Prudence Crandall's life. "There was an invisible story that had to be told," she says. "That's what kept me motivated." Up to that time, Strane had published little of her writing. "I had a couple of articles published in trade magazines while I worked in an ad agency," she says. "I really credit the crusty old newspapermen who taught me nonfiction writing at Columbia."

After she graduated, Strane worked at Macmillan as an art editor for children's books. Marriage and children followed, and her love of research carried over as she gathered a great deal of information on the history of childbirth. All the while she was sorting out the life of Prudence Crandall.

"I could never have sold the book without an agent," Strane says. "New writers have very little chance without one. Publishers are much more willing to read agented work." She worked for three months on the manuscript outline with her agent, and the book was sold to W.W. Norton in two months.

"Don't get discouraged or lose faith," she adds. "Remember that every published writer had a first book."

Will Aitken
Terre Haute (Delacorte)

"Most people have something in them that causes pain," says Will Aitken, "and they think they shouldn't write about it. I read an interview with Gordon Lish, the editor of *The Quarterly*. His advice was to find the subject you could *not* write about, then go out and write about it."

Aitken lived the first 18 years of his life in Terre Haute, Indiana. Although he now lives in Montreal, the connections he feels to his hometown are obvious. *Terre*

Photo by Robert Del Tredici

Haute, Aitken's first novel, is the story of a year in the life of a young man who comes to realize the implications and perils of his sexuality.

Publishing the novel was a bit perilous for Aitken. After finishing the manuscript, he sent it off blind to six or seven major Canadian publishing houses. He also acquired a list of five agents. *Terre Haute* was rejected by every one of the publishers. "Some of them found the content offensive," says Aitken. His luck was better with the agents. Two replies were favorable. One of the agents, Bella Pomer, liked it—with reservations. "It's a good bet," Pomer told Aitken, "but forget about getting it published in Canada. Let me take it to New York."

Discouraged by a year of having the manuscript shopped around, Aitken rewrote *Terre Haute.* His agent then took the revised work to Delacorte, a publishing company that had never handled a novel with gay themes before. They accepted it, a year and one half after he first began trying to sell the manuscript.

Aitken started writing short stories while living in Indiana. "I learned about writing from reading," he says. "My major influences have been British writers from between the World Wars: Evelyn Waugh, Christopher Isherwood, and E.M. Forster to name three." He admires the transparency of their styles, the way their writing doesn't call attention to itself.

"I didn't see much sense in studying creative writing in the university," Aitken says. "I was put off from a distance because all the students seemed to conform to the house style." Aitken graduated from the University of Missouri with a degree in English literature, and went on for a master's at Medill.

He now splits his time between fiction and journalistic writing. Devoting two or three days per week to fiction, he spends the remainder writing film criticism for the Canadian Broadcasting Corporation and the *Montreal Daily News.* He finds the nonfiction writing more a distraction from, than practice for, his fiction efforts. "It's exhausting," he says. "The articles really deplete me."

While he understands the need for models and peer groups, Aitken maintains that "in the long run, writing is solitary." His rewrite of *Terre Haute* is an example of the rewards of persistence. "That's half the battle," he says. "Other than that, you've got to believe in what you're doing. You either write or you don't write."

Book Packagers and Producers

The majority of packaged books is nonfiction, but mysteries, science fiction and picture book series have been growing among book packagers, producers and developers. Some book packagers have developed specialties; packagers listed in this section have also indicated special needs ranging from juvenile series and textbooks to books on animals.

Book packaging is a relatively new opportunity for writers. While it originated in England in the 1940s, the trend didn't pick up in the U.S. on a large scale until the 1970s. Originally known as book packagers, today many firms prefer to be called book producers or book developers. They provide a book publisher with services ranging from hiring writers, photographers or artists, to editing and delivering the finished book.

In most instances, a book packager or producer develops a book proposal, assembles the people to prepare it and submits it to a publisher. When a proposal is accepted by a publisher, the producer serves several functions. When the manuscript is in preparation, the producer is an editor. As the manuscript and illustrations or photo package are put together, the function changes to managing editor. Then the producer takes over coordination of production and may also serve as a sales consultant for the project. In other cases, a book publisher will contract with a book packager or producer to perform one or more of these functions.

The term book developer may be used to refer to a book packager or producer, or it may apply to a literary agent who joins with writers to provide writing and editorial services. An agent who functions as a book packager or developer often provides additional writing support for the author as they work together to produce a proposal. Then the agent uses his contacts within the industry to sell the work. Agents who work in book packaging have that information included in their listings in the Author's Agents section.

Speed and specialties make book packagers' and producers' services attractive to publishers. Many publishers with small editorial staffs use packagers and producers as extensions of their companies. An inhouse staff member can provide 20% of the work on the book and rely on the packager to produce the remaining 80%. This frees the staff member to move on to other projects. In some cases, publishers ask packagers to provide resources or knowledge the publisher doesn't need fulltime, but does need for a specific book. Many book packagers and producers also are experts at producing high quality illustrated books, an area where small publishers may lack inhouse expertise.

Writers who want to work in the field should be aware of differences between book publishers and book packagers. Publishers accept book proposals and ideas for books submitted to them by writers. Book packagers and agents who act as book packagers most often assign topics to writers. Occasionally, a packager will develop an idea brought in by a writer, but this is rare. When you submit material, packagers most often want to see a query with your writing credentials and list of areas of expertise. Writers who are trying to establish themselves in the industry may consider this an attractive option but should be aware that it doesn't always provide you with credit for your writing because many books require several writers. Book producers and packagers often make outright purchases of writing, contract on work-for-hire agreements or offer a large advance and low royalty percentage.

Don't expect to receive a book catalog from a book producer or book packager; they produce books for other publishers' catalogs. If you ask for a sample of titles they've produced, however, you may be surprised to find some bestsellers on the list.

More than 150 book packagers, producers and agents work in the field but most prefer to make their own contacts with writers and do not accept unsolicited queries. In this section, we've only included those who say they are interested in being contacted by writers. For a list of other book packagers and producers, see the latest edition of *Literary Market Place* in your local library.

BOOKWORKS, INC., 119 South Miami St., West Milton OH 45383. (513)698-3619. FAX: (513)698-3651. President: Nick Engler. Estab. 1984. Firm averages 6 titles/year. Receives 1-10 submissions/year. 20-40% of books from first-time authors. 100% from unagented writers. Pays 2½-5% royalty on retail price. Buys mss outright for $3,000-10,000. Offers $7,500 average advance. Publishes book an average of 8 months after acceptance. Simultaneous submissions OK. Reports in 6 weeks on queries; 2 months on mss.
Nonfiction: How-to. Subjects include hobbies, woodworking and home improvement. Nothing other than crafts/woodworking/home improvement. Query or submit outline/synopsis and sample chapters. Reviews artwork/photos as part of manuscript package.
Recent Nonfiction Title: *American Country Furniture*, by Engler.
Tips: "In the how-to field, there is more emphasis on projects, less emphasis on techniques and methods. We publish how-to books for do-it-yourselfers, hobbyists and craftsmen."

CARPENTER PUBLISHING HOUSE, Suite 4602, 175 E. Delaware Place, Chicago IL 60611. (312)787-3569. President: Allan Carpenter. Estab. 1962. Develops hardcover originals. "We develop our products or theirs on contract for major publishers. We assign work to authors and artists." Negotiates fee. Reports promptly on queries.
Nonfiction: Biography, juvenile, reference and supplementary texts. Subjects include Americana, history and directory/resource annuals. "We do not solicit mss. We specialize in books in large series." Query. All unsolicited mss are returned unopened.
Recent Nonfiction Title: *Encyclopedia of the Midwest*, by Allan Carpenter.

MICHAEL FRIEDMAN PUBLISHING GROUP, 15 W. 26th St., New York NY 10010. (212)685-6610. FAX: (212)685-1300. Subsidiaries include Friedman Group; Tern Enterprises; The Wainscott Group. Editorial Director: Karla Olson. Packages hardcover and trade paperback originals working with all major publishers. Firm averages 60 packages/year. "We work with many first-time authors and almost exclusively with un-agented authors." Buys most mss outright "under certain circumstances (when an author approaches us with an idea) we will pay a small royalty on reprints based on our price to publisher." Produces book an average of 1 year after acceptance; Friedman group responsible for all illustrative material included in book. Query for electronic submissions. Free book catalog.
Nonfiction: Coffee table book, cookbook, how-to and illustrated book. Subjects include Americana, animals, anthropology/archaeology, art/architecture, cooking, foods and nutrition, gardening, health and fitness, hobbies, nature/environment, recreation and sports. Query.
Recent Nonfiction Title: *Taking Tea*, by Angela Israel.

HELENA FROST ASSOCIATES, 117 East 24th St., New York NY 10010. (212)475-6642. FAX (212)353-2984. President: Helena Frost. Packages approximately 50 titles/year. Receives approximately 100 queries/year. Authors paid by flat or hourly fees or on freelance assignments. Query for electronic submissions. Reports in 3 weeks. Completed projects list available; ms guidelines available per project.
Nonfiction: Textbook ancillaries, some general trade titles. Subjects include business and economics, education, government/politics, health/medicine, history, language/literature, psychology. Query.
Tips: "Although we are not interested in over-the-transom mss, we do request writers' and editors' resumes and will review school-related proposals and outlines for submission to major publishers."

THE K S GINIGER COMPANY INC., Suite 519, 250 West 57th St., New York NY 10107. (212)570-7499. President: Kenneth S. Giniger. Estab. 1964. Publishes hardcover, trade paperback and mass paperback originals. Averages 8 titles/year; receives 250 submissions annually. 25% of books from first-time authors; 75% of books from unagented writers. Pays 5-15% royalty on retail price; offers $3,500 average advance. Publishes book an average of 18 months after acceptance. Reports in 2 weeks on queries.
Nonfiction: Biography, coffee table book, illustrated book, reference and self-help. Subjects include business and economics, health, history, religion and travel. "No religious books, cookbooks, personal histories or personal adventure." Query with SASE. All unsolicited mss are returned unread (if postage is enclosed for return of ms).

Recent Nonfiction Title: *The Crucible of War: Western Desert 1941*, by Barrie Pitt.
Tips: "We look for a book whose subject interests us and which we think can achieve success in the marketplace; most of our books are based on ideas originating with us by authors we commission, but we have commissioned books from queries submitted to us."

‡SUE KATZ & ASSOCIATES, INC., 211 East 51 St., New York NY 10022. (212)888-2343. FAX: (212)386-9123. President: Sue Katz. Vice President: Ms. Gareth Esersky. Book producers/agents. Estab. 1984. Firm produces hardcover and trade paperback originals. Averages 3-5 titles/year. "We have a flexible fee and royalty structure that changes to match book project." Reports in 1 month.
Nonfiction: Coffee table books, how-to, juvenile, self-help. Subjects include art/architecture, child guidance/parenting, business, gardening. Query. Reviews artwork/photos as part of freelance ms package.
Recent Nonfiction Titles: *Trade Secrets*, by James Pooley for Amacom.

‡LAING COMMUNICATIONS INC., Suite 1050, 500-108th NE, Bellevue WA 98004. (206)451-9331. FAX: (206)646-6515. Vice President/Editorial Director: Christine Laing. Estab. 1985. Firm produces hardcover and trade paperback originals. Averages 6-10 titles/year. Works with 20% first-time authors; 100% unagented writers. Payment "varies dramatically since all work is sold to publishers as royalty-inclusive package." Reports in 1 month.
Nonfiction: Biography, coffee table book, cookbook, how-to, illustrated book, juvenile, reference, software, technical, textbook. Subjects include Americana, anthropology, business and economics, computers/electronics, history, science, travel. Query. Reviews artwork/photos as part of freelance ms package.
Recent Nonfiction Titles: *A Nation Torn—How the Civil War Began*, for E.P. Dutton (juvenile, history).

‡LAMPPOST PRESS INC., 253 E. 62 St., New York NY 10021. (212)935-6030. President: Roseann Hirsch. Estab. 1988. Firm produces hardcover, trade paperback and mass market paperback originals. Averages 25 titles/year. Works with 50% first-time authors; 85% unagented writers. Pays 50% royalty or by outright purchase.
Nonfiction: Biography, cookbook, how-to, humor, illustrated book, juvenile, self-help. Subjects include child guidance/parenting, cooking, foods and nutrition, gardening, health, money/finance, women's issues. Query or submit proposal. Reviews artwork/photos as part of freelance ms package.
Recent Nonfiction Titles: *New Kids on the Block*, for Bantam.
Fiction: Gothic, historical, humor, juvenile, mainstream, mystery, picture books, romance, young adult. Query or submit proposal.
Recent Fiction Titles: *Legal Affairs*, for Simon & Schuster (modern romance).
Tips: "Call first."

LUCAS-EVANS BOOKS, 1123 Broadway, New York NY 10010. (212)929-2583. Contact: Barbara Lucas. Estab. 1984. Packages hardcover, trade paperback originals and mass market paperback originals for major publishers. Averages 10 titles/year. 20% of books from first-time authors. Pays 1-8% royalty, "depends on our contract agreement with publisher." Makes work-for-hire assignments. Offers $3,000 on up average advance. Reports in 1 month on queries; 2 months on mss.
Nonfiction: "We are looking for series proposals and selected single juvenile books: preschool through high school." Submit query letter with credentials, stating proposed subject.
Recent Nonfiction Title: *And Then There Was One*, by Margery Facklam for Crestwood House, (animal extinction).
Fiction: Preschool through high school. Prefers picture books and middle grade novels.
Recent Fiction Title: *The Glass Salamander*, by Ann Downer (novel).

MOUNT IDA PRESS, 4 Central Ave., Albany NY 12210. (518)426-5935. President: Diana S. Waite. Estab. 1984. Firm publishes hardcover and trade paperback originals. Averages 5 titles/year. Works with 50% first-time authors; 100% unagented writers. Pays royalty. Query for electronic submissions, "if hard copy also is available." Reports in 1 month. Catalog for #10 SASE.
Nonfiction: Coffee table book, illustrated book and reference. Subjects include art/architecture, history, regional and commemorative histories. Query. Reviews artwork/photos as part of freelance ms package.
Recent Nonfiction Title: *Ornamental Ironwork: Two Centuries of Craftsmanship in Albany and Troy, New York*, by Diana S. Waite.

‡NEW ENGLAND PUBLISHING ASSOCIATES, INC., P.O. Box 5, Chester CT 06412. (203)345-4976 (CT); (718)788-6641 (NY). President: Elizabeth Frost Knappman. Estab. 1983. Firm originates hardcover and trade paperback originals. Averages 1-2 titles/year. Works with 25% first-time authors; 25% unagented writers. Pays royalty. Reports in 1 month.

OTTENHEIMER PUBLISHERS, INC., 300 Reisterstown Rd., Baltimore MD 21208. (301)484-2100. FAX: (301)486-8301. Chairman of the Board: Allan T. Hirsh Jr. President: Allan T. Hirsh III. Vice President: Steven Bloom. Vice President: Edward Davis. Estab. 1890. Publishes hardcover and paperback originals and reprints. Publishes 250 titles/year; receives 500 submissions annually. 20% of books from first-time authors; 100% of books from unagented writers. Average print order for a writer's first book is 15,000. Negotiates royalty and advance, sometimes makes outright purchase for $25-3,000. Publishes book an average of 6 months after acceptance. Reports in 3 months.
Nonfiction: Cookbooks, reference, gardening, home repair and decorating, children's nonfiction activities, automotive and medical for the layperson. Submit outline/synopsis and sample chapters or complete ms. Reviews artwork/photos as part of ms package.
Recent Nonfiction Title: *The Norman Rockwell Illustrated Book.*

SCHUETTGE & CARLETON, 458 Gravatt, Berkeley CA 94705. (415)841-6962. FAX: (415)649-9271. Editor: Dick Carleton. Firm produces hardcover and trade paperback originals. Produces 10-20 titles/year. 75% from first-time authors; 100% from unagented writers. Pays 6-12% royalty on retail price. Offers average $4,000 advance. Reports in 3 weeks.
Nonfiction: Coffee table book, cookbook, how-to, illustrated book, *juvenile*. Subjects include Americana, animals, art/architecture, cooking, foods and nutrition, education, ethnic, gardening, health, history, language/literature, music, nature/environment, photography, travel. Submit proposal. Reviews artwork/photos as part of ms package.
Fiction: Fantasy, juvenile, picture books. Query or submit proposal.
Recent Fiction Title: *Peaceful Warrior,* by Millman.
Tips: "We have a specialty in children's books, with clever, special and well-prepared art. We will develop the manuscript and art if the idea is unusual and fits the surprise we put on the market."

‡TENTH AVENUE EDITIONS, 625 Broadway, New York NY 10012. (212)529-8900. FAX: (212)529-7399. Managing Editor: Rose Hass. Firm produces hardcover, trade paperback and mass market paperback originals. Averages 6 titles/year. Pays advance paid by publisher less our commission. Query for electronic submissions. Reports in 2 months.
Nonfiction: Biography, how-to, illustrated book, juvenile, catalogs. Subjects include music/dance, photography, women's issues/studies, art. Query. Reviews artwork/photos as part of freelance ms package.
Recent Nonfiction Titles: *RCA Classical Music Catalog* (music catalog).
Fiction: Historical, juvenile, literary, mainstream. Query.
Recent Fiction Titles: "We rarely publish fiction."
Tips: "Send query with publishing background."

WELCOME ENTERPRISES, INC., 164 E. 95th St., New York NY 10128. (212)722-7533. President: Lena Tabori. Agent: Richard Barber. Assistant: Hiro Clark. Estab. 1980. Firm packages 12 books per year; agents 25. Receives approximately 100-200 submissions/year. "A publisher always contractually commits to us before we package a book for them." Keeps 25% of the royalties negotiated on packaged books, 15% for agented books. Simultaneous submissions OK. Reports in 1 month on queries; 3 months on mss. Ms guidelines for #10 SAE.
Nonfiction: Coffee table book, cookbook, how-to, humor, illustrated book, reference and self-help. Subjects include animals, anthropology/archaeology, child guidance/parenting, cooking, foods and nutrition, gardening, government/politics, health/medicine, history, hobbies, literature, music/dance, nature/environment, photography, psychology, recreation, science, sociology and New Age/occult. Submit outline/synopsis, sample chapters and SASE. Reviews artwork/photos as part of ms package.
Recent Nonfiction Title: *Portrait of Great Britain and Northern Ireland,* photographs by Michael Reagan, for Turner Publishing.
Fiction: Occasionally handles fiction.

‡THE WHEETLEY COMPANY, INC., Suite 1100, 4709 Golf Rd., Skokie IL 60076. (312)675-4443. FAX: (312)675-4489. Human Resources Manager: Linda Rogers. Firm produces hardcover originals. Pays by the project. Query for electronic submissions. Does not return submissions, even those accompanied with SASE.
Nonfiction: Technical, textbook. Subjects include animals, anthropology, art/architecture, business and economics, child guidance/parenting, computers/electronics, cooking, foods and nutrition, education, government/politics, health, history, language/literature, money/finance, music/dance, nature/environment, philosophy, psychology, recreation, regional, religion, science, sociology, sports, translation. Submit resume and publishing history. Reviews artwork/photos as part of freelance ms package.
Recent Nonfiction Titles: Kept confidential.

WIESER & WIESER, INC., 118 East 25th St. New York NY 10010. (212)260-0860. FAX: (212)505-7186. Producer: George J. Wieser. Estab. 1976. Firm produces hardcover, trade paperback and mass market paperback originals. Averages 25 titles/year. Works with 10% first-time authors; 90% unagented writers. Makes outright purchase for $5,000 or other arrangement. Offers $5,000 average advance. Reports in 2 weeks.

Nonfiction: Coffee table book, cookbook, how-to, juvenile and reference. Subjects include Americana, business and economics, cooking, foods and nutrition, gardening, health, history, hobbies, military/war, money/finance, nature/environment, photography, recreation, sports and travel. Query. Reviews artwork/photos as part of freelance ms package.

Recent Nonfiction Title: *China—From the Long March to Tiananmen Square*, by the Associated Press.

Tips: "Have an original idea and pursue it completely and competently before contacting us."

WINGRA WOODS PRESS, Box 9601, Madison WI 53715. Acquisitions Editor: M.G. Mahoney. Publishes trade paperback originals. Averages 6-10 titles/year; receives 200 submissions annually. 70% of books from first-time authors; 100% of books from unagented writers. Pays 10-12% royalty on retail price, sometimes makes outright purchase of $500-10,000. Publishes book an average of 18 months after acceptance. Simultaneous submissions OK. Reports in 6 weeks.

Nonfiction: Coffee table book, cookbook, how-to, juvenile, self-help. Subjects include Americana, popular history and science, animals, art, and nature, psychology and spiritual. Especially looking for popularized book-length treatments of specialized knowledge; interested in proposals from academics and professionals. Query with outline/synopsis. Do not send complete ms. Reviews artwork/photos as part of ms package.

Recent Nonfiction Title: *The Christmas Cat.*

Tips: "Put your 'good stuff' in the very first paragraph . . . tell us why we should care. Consider page 1 of the query as distilled flap copy. Then follow up with facts and credentials."

Subsidy Publishers

The following publishers produce more than 50% of their books on a subsidy or cooperative basis. What they charge and what they offer to each writer varies, so you'll want to judge each publisher on its own merit. Because subsidy publishing can cost you several thousand dollars, make sure the number of books, the deadlines and services offered by the publisher are detailed in your contract. If you are willing to pay to have your book published, you should also be willing to hire an attorney to review the contract. This step prevents misunderstandings between you and your prospective publisher. Never agree to terms you don't understand in a contract. There are a growing number of editorial services that offer services similar to those performed by subsidy publishers. Companies offering editorial services are not listed in *Writer's Market*. Consult the Book Publishers introduction for more information on subsidy publishing.

Aegina Press, Inc.
59 Oak Lane, Spring Valley, Huntington WV 25704

American Poetry Association
Santa Cruz CA 95061

Authors' Unlimited
3324 Barham Blvd., Los Angeles CA 90068

De Young Press
P.O. Box 7252, Spencer IA 51301-7252

Eastview Editions
P.O. Box 783, Westfield NJ 07091

Fairway Press
C.S.S. Publishing Company, Inc.,
628 South Main St., Lima OH 45804

Fithian Press
P.O. Box 1525, Santa Barbara CA 93102

Nichols Publishing Co.
P.O. Box 96, New York NY 10024

Peter Randall Publisher
500 Market St., P.O. Box 4726, Portsmouth NH 03801

Rivercross Publishing, Inc.
127 East 59th St., New York NY 10022

Ronin Publishing, Inc.
P.O. Box 1035, Berkeley CA 94701

Howard W. Sams and Co., Inc.
Suite 141 11711 N. College Ave., Carmel IN 46032

San Diego Publishing Company
P.O.Box 9222, San Diego CA 92109-0060

Other Book Publishers and Packagers

The following book publishers and packagers do not have listings in this edition of *Writer's Market*. The majority did not respond to our request to update their listings or return a questionnaire for a new listing. If a reason was given for their exclusion, we have included it in parentheses after the listing name.

Acropolis Books, Ltd
American Institute of Physics
Apollo Books
Arbor House (see William Morrow listing)
Asher-Gallant Press
Augsburg Books (asked to be deleted)
Auto Book Press
Aztex Corp.
Ballentine/Epiphany Books (no longer publishing religious books)
Bart Books (out of business)
Bascom Communications
Bergh Publishing, Inc. (not accepting freelance submissions)
Berkshire Traveller Press
Betterway Publications, Inc.
Book Creations, Inc.
Allen D. Bragdon Publishers, Inc. (asked to be deleted)
Brethren Press
C Q Press
Camden House, Inc. (asked to be deleted)
Aristide D. Cartzas, Publisher
Carolina Biological Supply Co.
The Catholic Health Association of the United States (discontinued publishing)
Cheribe Publishing Company (asked to be deleted)
Cherokee Publishing Company
Chockstone Press (asked to be deleted)
Coles Publishing Co., Ltd.
Commerce Clearing House, Inc. (not accepting freelance submissions)
Communications Press
Compact Books
Compcare Publishers
Corbin House (asked to be deleted)
Craddock Publishing
Craftsman Book Company
Denlingers Publishers, Ltd.
Dimension Books, Inc.
Doll Reader
Eakin Publications, Inc.
Earth Star Publications
Elysium Growth Press
Enterprise Publishing Co., Inc.
Federal Buyers Guide, Inc.
Federal Personnel Management Institute, Inc.
Frederick Fell Publishers, Inc.
Fiction Collective (asked to be deleted)
Fleet Press Corp.
Four Winds Press (backlogged with submissions)
Garland Publishing, Inc.
Golden West Books
Gordon and Breach
Gower Publishing Company
The Stephen Greene Press/ Phelam Books
Greenleaf Classics, Inc.
Gryphon House, Inc.
Harbor House Publishers, Inc.
Harlequin Books (asked to be deleted)
Harrow and Heston (unable to contact)
Helix Press
Herald Press
Hunter Publishing, Inc.
Incentive Publications, Inc.
Indiana University Press
Institute for Policy Studies
Interweave Press
Iron Crown Enterprises
Knowledge Industry Publications, Inc.
Robert E. Krieger Publishing Co., Inc.
Laura Books, Inc.
Hal Leonard Publishing Corp.
Life Cycle Books
Liguori Publications (unable to contact)
Lintel
Liturgical Publications, Inc.
Living Flame Press
The Main Street Press (company sold)
Marathon International Publishing Co., Inc. (not accepting freelance submissions)
Maverick Publications, small press (not publishing in 1991 and 1992)
Maverick Publications, book packager
Mazda Publishers
Meadowbrook Press
Media Productions and Marketing, Inc.
Medmaster, Inc.
Melior Publications (ceased publishing)
Mercer University Press
Meriwether Publishing Ltd.
Middle Atlantic Press
Milady Publishing Company
Modern Books and Crafts, Inc.
Monitor Book Co., Inc.
Moonfall Publishing, Inc. (backlogged with submissions)
Morgan-Rand Publications, Inc.
Mott Media, Inc., Publishers
Mountain Press Publishing Company
National Association of Social Workers
Navpress
Nelson-Hall Publishers
New American Library
New Idea Press, Inc.
New York Zoetrope, Inc.
Nimbus Publishing Limited
North Point Press (no unsolicited mss)
Ohio Psychology Publishing Co.
Ohio State University Press
OISE Press
Oryx Press
Outbooks, Inc. (asked to be deleted)
P.P.I. Publishing
Parenting Press, Inc.
Pathfinder Publications
Paulist Press
Pen Dragon Publishing Co.
The Penkvill Publishing Company (asked to be deleted)
Philomel Books
Pickwick Publications
Plexus Publishing, Inc.
Pomegranate Press, Ltd. (asked to be deleted)
Poseidon Press
The Prairie Publishing Company (not publishing new titles)
Byron Preiss Visual Publications, Inc.
Price Stern Sloan Inc., Publishers
Probus Publishing Co.
Prolingua Associates
Quality Publications
Quinlan Press (complaints)
The Real Comet Press (not accepting freelance submissions)
Renaissance House Publishers (concentrating on reprints)
Fleming H. Revell Co.
Reymont Associates
Roundtable Publishing, Inc.
Routledge, Chapman & Hall, Inc.
Russell Sage, Inc.
S.C.E.-Editions L'Etincelle (unable to contact)
S.O.C.O. Publications (no longer publishing)
St. Bede's Publications
Schiffer Publishing Ltd.
Scojtia Publishing Co. (unable to contact)
Shapolsky Publishers
Shoe Tree Press

Michael Shore Associates
Signpost Press
Southern Illinois University Press
Sparrow Press (not accepting freelance submissions)
Spence Publishing
Square One Publishers (no longer publishing)
Stemmer House Publishers, Inc.
Still Point Press
Storie/McOwen Publishers, Inc.
Studio Press (not accepting freelance submissions)
Symmes Systems

T.F.H. Publications, Inc.
Tabor Publishing
Texas Monthly Press, Inc. (acquired by Gulf Publishing Co.)
Charles C. Thomas, Publisher
Trend Book Division
Troubador Press
UMI Research Press
United Resource Press (running poetry arts project contest only)
University of Michigan Press
University of Missouri Press
Unlimited Publishing Co. (investigating complaints)
Vehicule Press

Waterfront Books
Western Marine Enterprises, Inc.
Whitaker House
Whitford Press
John Wiley & Sons, Inc. (no longer publishing)
Willow Creek Press (unable to contact)
Windriver Publishing Company (no longer publishing)
Wolgemuth & Hyatt, Publishers
Worldwide Library (asked to be deleted)
Zoland Books, Inc.

Consumer Publications

The past year brought a number of changes to the consumer magazine market. As advertising sales dropped, many magazines went out of business, including _7 Days_, _Children_, _High Fidelity_ and _Modern Photography_. Other magazines dealt with the decline by dropping frequency from monthly to 10 times per year or by trimming staff. The few growing categories in the market were environmental, African-American and maturity magazines.

All of this makes the consumer magazine market an ever-changing workplace for freelancers. To keep pace with changes and startups, make regular trips to your local bookstore, newsstand or library. Read magazines like _Writer's Digest_, _Folio_ and other publications that report on magazines to learn the changes that have occurred since this edition of _Writer's Market_ went to press. Many local and national writers' publications also include information about types of contracts and experiences other writers had in working for a particular publication. These can be very valuable tools in helping you identify the best outlets for your manuscripts.

Read several copies of the publications you think would be good markets for your work and be sure to write for a sample copy if you can't locate a recent issue locally. Before you submit a manuscript, also be sure to obtain the magazine's writer's guidelines and editorial calendar. Often these items will give you information about the latest changes in staff, payment, editorial focus and manuscript needs.

In nonfiction, the trend is still toward shorter articles that can be illustrated. Writers who can provide quality photographs or suggest appropriate illustrations for their manuscripts have an advantage. Editors continue to express an interest in surveys, lists and exclusive stories.

In fiction, _Ms._ and _McCall's_ lead the way in looking for more fiction, while some new magazines such as _Wigwag_ also publish fiction. In general, however, most magazines receive far more fiction than they can possibly consider and some will send a response only if they want to accept a story for publication. Scan the categories in the Fiction subhead—science fiction, mystery, romance, men's, women's, juvenile, teen and literary—for a listing of fiction requirements for consumer magazines. You'll find complete information on the fiction field in _Novel and Short Story Writer's Market_ (Writer's Digest Books).

If you have a personal computer, you may want to consider submitting your work by disk or modem. Of 697 editors responding to our survey, 328 accept electronic submissions. Some accept a relatively low number, while others—especially computer magazines—may accept 100% of their submissions by disk or modem. While only 15% were more likely to accept an electronic submission than a typed manuscript, editors who have the equipment and staff to handle electronic submissions often appreciate the convenience and time saved with this submission method. Of those 328 that accept electronic submissions, only 19 pay more for this method, so the personal computer remains more a time-saving device for writers than one that will specifically generate more income.

Editors responding to the survey cited 14 different types of software they used, so most wanted to receive submissions in generic ASCii files they could easily convert. After ASCii, WordPerfect, Xywrite and Microsoft Word were the most frequently mentioned word processing programs used by publishers.

To make the most of your writing time, you should expand the number of publications for which you write. Magazines that buy reprints include that information in their listings.

Selling any unsold rights enables you to market your article to other magazines after it has been published the first time and allows you to make more money without investing more writing time. In addition, revising a manuscript or changing the slant to fit several publications will allow you to use material you've gathered more efficiently. Also, look for magazines that accept simultaneous submissions—this will help you decrease the amount of time it takes to sell an article. Introductions in this section and the section introductions under Trade, Technical and Professional Journals will provide you with related topics and publications for which you may write or adapt articles.

Remember to follow the requirements of the magazines listed in *Writer's Market*. If an editor specifically requests queries—and most of them do—don't send a complete manuscript. Manuscript length is also important to editors who must fit space requirements for their publications.

Information on publications not included in *Writer's Market* can be found in Other Consumer Publications at the end of this section.

Animal

The publications in this section deal with pets, racing and show horses, and other pleasure animals and wildlife. Magazines about animals bred and raised for the market are classified in the Farm category. Publications about horse racing can be found in the Sports section.

‡ANIMAL TALES, 2113 W. Bethany Home Rd., Phoenix AZ 85015. (602)246-7144. Editor: Berta Cellers. Bimonthly magazine covering animals and their relationships with humans. Estab. 1989. Pays on publication. Byline given. Buys first rights. Reports in 2 months. Writer's guidelines for #10 SASE.
Fiction: Adventure, fantasy, historical, humorous, mystery. "Animals must be the primary focus of interest." Send complete ms. Length: 2,000-6,000 words. Pays $10-50.
Poetry: Light verse and traditional. Pays $5-20.
Fillers: Facts and short humor. Pays $5-10.
Tips: "Artwork and cartoons also are accepted. All must have animal theme. Submissions should appeal to all age groups."

AQUARIUM FISH MAGAZINE, Fancy Publications, Box 6050, Mission Viejo CA 92690. (714)855-8822. FAX: (714)855-3045. Editor: Edward Bauman. 100% freelance written. Bimonthly magazine on aquariums, tropical fish, ponds and pond fish. "We need well-written feature articles, preferably with color transparencies, dealing with all aspects of the hobby and directed toward novices and experienced hobbyists." Estab. 1988. Circ. 70,000. Pays on publication. Buys first North American serial rights. ASCII files by disk or modem. Reports in 2 weeks on queries; 1 month on mss. Sample copy $3.50 Free writer's guidelines.
Nonfiction: "Articles on biology, care and breeding of aquarium and pond fish; pond and aquarium set-up and maintenance. No pet fish stories." Buys 45-60 mss/year. Query. Length: 1,500-3,500 words. Pays $100-300 for assigned articles.
Photos: Send slides with submission. Reviews contact sheets and transparencies. Offers $50-150 for color; up to $25 for b&w. Buys one-time rights.
Tips: "Know the subject; write tight, well-organized copy. Avoid 'my first aquarium' type of articles. Too many writers avoid adequate research. Many readers are knowledgeable about hobby and want solid information."

ARABIAN HORSE TIMES, Adams Corp., Rt. 3, Waseca MN 56093. (507)835-3204. FAX: (507)835-5138. Editor: Ronda Morehead. Managing Editor: Joyce Denn. 20% freelance written. Works with a small number of new/unpublished writers each year. Monthly magazine about Arabian horses. Editorial format includes hard news (veterinary, new products, book reports, etc.), lifestyle and personality pieces, and bloodline studies. Estab. 1969. Circ. 22,000. Pays on publication. Publishes ms an average of 6 months after acceptance. Byline given. Buys first serial rights. Submit seasonal/holiday material 3 months in advance. Simultaneous queries OK. Sample copy and writer's guidelines for 9×12 SAE and $6.
Nonfiction: General interest, how-to, interview/profile, new product and photo feature. Buys at least 12 mss/year. Query with published clips. Length: 1,000-5,000 words. Pays $50-350. Sometimes pays expenses of writers on assignment.

Photos: Prefers 5×7 color prints. Payment depends on circumstances. Captions and identification of subjects required. Buys one-time rights.

Fiction: Will look at anything about Arabians except erotica. Buys 1-2 mss/year. Send complete ms. Length: 1,500-5,000 words. Pays $75-250.

Tips: "As our periodical is specific to Arabian horses, we are interested in anyone who can write well and tightly about them. Send us something timely. Also, narrow your topic to a specific horse, incident, person or problem. 'Why I Love Arabians' will not work."

BIRD TALK, Dedicated to Better Care for Pet Birds, Fancy Publications, Box 6050, Mission Viejo CA 92690. (714)855-8822. FAX: (714)855-3045. Editor: Karyn New. 85% freelance written. Works with a small number of new/unpublished writers each year. Monthly magazine covering the care and training of cage birds for men and women who own any number of pet or exotic birds. Circ. 170,000. Pays latter part of month in which article appears. Publishes ms an average of 6 months after acceptance. Byline given. Buys first North American serial rights. Submit seasonal/holiday material 7 months in advance. Previously published submissions OK. No simultaneous submissions. Reports in 3 weeks on queries; 2 months on mss. Sample copy $3.50; writer's guidelines for #10 SASE.

Nonfiction: General interest (anything to do with pet birds); historical/nostalgic (of bird breeds, owners, cages); how-to (build cages, aviaries, playpens and groom, feed, breed, tame); humor; interview/profile (of bird and bird owners); new product; how-to (live with birds—compatible pets, lifestyle, apartment adaptability, etc.); personal experience (with your own bird); photo feature (humorous or informative); travel (with pet birds or to see exotic birds); and articles giving medical information, legal information, and description of breeds. No juvenile or material on wild birds not pertinent to pet care; everything should relate to *pet* birds. Buys 150 mss/year. Query or send complete ms. Length: 500-3,000 words. Pays 10-15¢/word.

Photos: State availability of photos. Reviews b&w contact sheets; prefers prints. Pays $50-150 for color transparencies; $15 minimum for 5×7 b&w prints. Model release and identification of subjects required. Buys one-time rights.

Columns/Departments: Editorial (opinion on a phase of owning pet birds) and Small Talk (short news item of general interest to bird owners). Buys 20 mss/year. Send complete ms. Length: 300-1,200 words. Pays 10-15¢/word and up.

Fiction: "Only fiction with pet birds as primary focus of interest." Adventure, fantasy, historical, humorous, mystery, suspense. No juvenile, and no birds talking unless it's their trained vocabulary. Buys 1 ms/year. Send complete ms. Length: 2,000-3,000 words. Pays 7¢/word and up.

Tips: "Send grammatical, clean copy on a human-interest story about a pet bird or about a medical or health-related topic. We also need how-tos on feather crafts; cage cover making; aviary, perch and cage building; and planting plants in aviaries safe and good for birds. Keep health, nutrition, lack of stress in mind regarding pet birds. Study back issues to learn our style."

BIRDER'S WORLD, The Magazine Exploring Wild Birds and Birding, 720 E. 8th St., Holland MI 49423. (616)396-5618. Editor: Eldon D. Greij. 80% freelance written. Bimonthly magazine on wild birds, birding and birdwatching. "*Birder's World* is designed for people with a broad interest in wild birds and birding. Readers have varying degrees of experience in the world of birds, ranging from the absolute novice to the studied ornithologist. They are well educated, curious readers." Estab. 1987. Circ. 46,000. Publishes ms an average of 1 year after acceptance. Byline given. Negotiable kill fee. Buys first North American serial rights and makes work-for-hire assignments. Submit seasonal/holiday material 8 months in advance. Query for electronic submissions. Sample copy for $3.50. Writer's guidelines for #10 SASE.

Nonfiction: Book excerpts, essays, general interest, historical/nostalgic, how-to, humor, interview/profile, opinion, personal experience, photo feature, technical and travel. Buys 40-70 mss/year. Query with or without published clips, or send complete ms. Length: 1,000-2,500 words. Pays $100-400 for assigned articles. Sometimes pays expenses of writers on assignment.

Photos: State availability of photos with submission. Reviews transparencies and prints. Offers $75-100 per inside photo; $150 for a two-page spread; and $200 for covers. Model releases and identification of subjects required. Buys one-time rights.

Columns/Departments: Buys 20 mss/year. Query with published clips. Length: 1,000-2,500 words. Pays $100-400.

Tips: "We strongly encourage interested writers to send for our writer's guidelines before submitting work."

‡CALIFORNIA HORSE REVIEW, P.O. Box 2437, Fair Oaks CA 95628. (916)638-1519. Editor: Jennifer Meyer. Managing Editor: Cleann McGuire. Monthly magazine covering equestrian interests. "*CHR* covers a wide spectrum—intensive veterinary investigation, fashion and showing trends, trainer 'how-to' tips, breeding research up-dates, personality profiles, nutritional guidance. Editorial also devotes effort to reporting news and large state and national show results." Estab. 1963. Circ. 6,500. **Pays on acceptance.** Byline given. Buys first North American serial rights. Previously published submissions OK. Free sample copy and writer's guidelines.

Nonfiction: General interest (West Coast equine emphasis), how-to (training, breeding, horse care, riding), interview/profile (West Coast horse people *only*), technical (riding, training). "No fiction or anything *without* a strong focal point of interest for *West Coast equestrians.*" Buys 25-40 mss/year. Query with published clips. Length: 500-2,500 words. Pays $50-200 for assigned articles; $25-150 for unsolicited articles. Sometimes pays expenses of writers on assignment.

Photos: Send photos with submission. Reviews 3×5 or larger prints. Offers no additional payment for photos accepted with ms. Captions required. Buys one-time rights.

Tips: "Be accurate, precise and knowledgeable about horses. Our readers are not beginners but sophisticated equestrians. Elementary, overly-basic how-tos are not appropriate for us. *See* what we publish! Personality profiles of well-known West Coast equestrians are the best way to break in. Use a lot of direct quotes; include at least one good photo. Not overly lengthy, but enough detail to provide interest."

‡**CAT COMPANION,** Quarton Group Publishers, Suite 430, 2701 Troy Center Dr., Troy MI 48084. (313)362-0044. Editor: Cynthia Kyle. 70% freelance written. Bimonthly magazine covering cats. *Cat Companion* is a magazine for people who enjoy the company of cats. Estab. 1983. Circ. 85,000. Pays on acceptance. Byline given. Offers 25% kill fee. Buys first North American serial or second serial (reprint) rights. Submit seasonal/holiday material 6 months in advance. Previously published submissions OK. Reports in 1 month on queries. Sample copy for 9×12 SAE with 8 first class stamps. Writer's guidelines for #10 SAE with 1 first class stamp.

Nonfiction: Book excerpts, general interest, historical/nostalgic, how-to (care for your cat), humor, interview/profile, photo feature and technical. Buys 20 mss/year. Query. Clips are helpful. Length: 1,000-3,000 words. Pays $50-150 for assigned articles; $25-100 for unsolicited articles. Sometimes pays expenses of writers on assignment. State availability of photos with submission.

Tips: "Be professional in your approach. Focus on subject. Be a good writer, reporter and speller. It helps to be familiar with cat issues or have a cat background. We are open to all suggestions, but they must be cat-focused. Cat ownership doesn't hurt. An enthusiasm and affection for reading about and writing about cats is a plus."

CAT FANCY, Fancy Publications, Inc., Box 6050, Mission Viejo CA 92690. (714)855-8822. Editor: K. E. Segnar. 80-90% freelance written. Monthly magazine for men and women of all ages interested in all phases of cat ownership. Estab. 1965. Circ. 280,000. Pays after publication. Publishes ms an average of 6 months after acceptance. Buys first North American serial rights. Byline given. Submit seasonal/holiday material 4 months in advance. Reports in 6 weeks. Sample copy $3.50; writer's guidelines for SASE.

Nonfiction: Historical, medical, how-to, humor, informational, personal experience, photo feature and technical. Buys 5 mss/issue. Query or send complete ms. Length: 500-3,000 words. Pays 5¢/word; special rates for photo/story packages.

Photos: Photos purchased with or without accompanying ms. Pays $15 minimum for 8×10 b&w glossy prints; $50-150 for 35mm or 2¼×2¼ color transparencies. Send prints and transparencies. Model release required.

Fiction: Adventure, fantasy, historical and humorous. Nothing written with cats speaking. Buys 1 ms/issue. Send complete ms. Length: 500-3,000 words. Pays 5¢/word.

Fillers: Newsworthy or unusual; items with photo and cartoons. Buys 10/year. Length: 100-500 words. Pays $20-35.

Tips: "We receive more filler-type articles than we can use. It's the well-researched, hard information articles we need."

CATS MAGAZINE, Cats Magazine Inc., P.O. Box 290037, Port Orange FL 32129. (904)788-2770. Editor: Linda J. Walton. 50% freelance written. A monthly magazine for cat lovers, veterinarians, breeders and show enthusiasts. Estab. 1945. Circ. 149,000. Pays on publication. Byline given. Buys one-time rights. Submit seasonal/holiday material 7 months in advance. Reports in 1 month on queries; 3 months on manuscripts (sometimes longer depending on the backlog). Sample copy and writer's guidelines with 9×12 SAE and $1.25 postage.

Nonfiction: Book excerpts; general interest (concerning cats); how-to (care for cats); humor; interview/profile (on cat owning personalities); new product; personal experience; photo feature; and technical (veterinarian writers). No talking cats. Buys 36 mss/year. Send complete ms. Length 800-2,500 words. Pays $25-300.

Photos: Send photos with submission. Reviews transparencies. Offers $5-25/photo, $150 for cover. Identification of subjects required. Buys one-time rights.

Fiction: Fantasy, historical, mystery, science fiction, slice-of-life vignettes and suspense. "We rarely use fiction, but are not averse to using it if the cat theme is handled in smooth, believable manner. All fiction must involve a cat or relationship of cat and humans, etc." No talking cats. Send complete ms. Length: 800-2,500 words. Pays $25-300.

 The double dagger before a listing indicates that the listing is new in this edition. New markets are often the most receptive to freelance submissions.

Poetry: Avant-garde, free verse, haiku, light verse and traditional. Length: 4-64 lines. Pays 50¢/line.
Tips: "Well researched articles are the freelancer's best bet. Writers must at least like cats. Writers who obviously don't miss the mark."

THE CHRONICLE OF THE HORSE, P.O. Box 46, Middleburg VA 22117. (703)687-6341. FAX: (703)687-3937. Editor: John Strassburger. Managing Editor: Nancy Comer. 80% freelance written. Weekly magazine about horses. "We cover English riding sports, including horse showing, grand prix jumping competitions, steeple-chase racing, foxhunting, dressage, endurance riding, handicapped riding and combined training. We are the official publication for the national governing bodies of many of the above sports. We feature news of the above sports, and we also publish how-to articles on equitation and horse care, and interviews with leaders in the various fields." Estab. 1937. Circ. 22,500. Pays for features on acceptance; news and other items on publication. Publishes ms an average of 3 months after acceptance. Byline given. Buys first North American rights and makes work-for-hire assignments. Submit seasonal/holiday material 3 months in advance. Reports in 3 weeks. Sample copy for 9 × 12 SAE and $2; writer's guidelines for #10 SASE.
Nonfiction: General interest; historical/nostalgic (history of breeds, use of horses in other countries and times, art, etc.); how-to (trailer, train, design a course, save money, etc.); humor (centered on living with horses or horse people); interview/profile (of nationally known horsemen or the very unusual); technical (horse care, articles on feeding, injuries, care of foals, shoeing, etc.); and news (of major competitions, clear assignment with us first). Special issues include Steeplechasing; Grand Prix Jumping; Combined Training; Dressage; Hunt Roster; Junior and Pony; and Christmas. No Q&A interviews, clinic reports, Western riding articles, personal experience, or wild horses. Buys 300 mss/year. Query or send complete ms. Length: 300-1,225 words. Pays $25-200.
Photos: State availability of photos. Only accepts prints. Accepts color for b&w reproduction. Pays $15-30. Identification of subjects required. Buys one-time rights.
Columns/Departments: Dressage, Combined Training, Horse Show, Horse Care, Racing over Fences, Young Entry (about young riders, geared for youth), Horses and Humanities, and Hunting. Query or send complete ms. Length: 300-1,225 words. Pays $25-200.
Poetry: Light verse and traditional. No free verse. Buys 30/year. Length: 5-30 lines. Pays $15.
Fillers: Anecdotes, short humor, newsbreaks and cartoons. Buys 300/year. Length: 50-175 lines. Pays $10-25.
Tips: "Get our guidelines. Our readers are sophisticated, competitive horsemen. Articles need to go beyond common knowledge. Freelancers often attempt too broad or too basic a subject. We welcome well-written news stories on major events, but clear the assignment with us."

DOG FANCY, Fancy Publications, Inc., P.O. Box 6050, Mission Viejo CA 92690. (714)855-8822. Editor: Kim Thornton . 75% freelance written. Eager to work with unpublished writers. "We'd like to see a balance of both new and established writers." Monthly magazine for men and women of all ages interested in all phases of dog ownership. Circ. 150,000. Pays after publication. Publishes ms an average of 6 months after acceptance. Buys first American serial rights. Byline given. Submit seasonal/holiday material 4 months in advance. Sample copy $3.50; writer's guidelines for #10 SASE.
Nonfiction: Historical, medical, how-to, humor, informational, interview, personal experience, photo feature, profile and technical. "We're planning one or two *major* features covering significant events in the dog world. We'll be looking for (and paying more for) high quality writing/photo packages on topics outside of our normal range of features. Interested writers should query with topics." Buys 5 mss/issue. Query or send complete ms. Length: 500-3,000 words. Pays 5/word.
Photos: Photos purchased with or without accompanying ms. Pays $15 minimum for 8 × 10 b&w glossy prints; $50-150 for 35mm or 2¼ × 2¼ color transparencies. Send prints and transparencies. Model release required.
Fillers: "Need short, punchy photo fillers and cartoons." Buys 10/year. Pays $20-35.
Tips: "We're looking for the unique experience that communicates something about the dog/owner relation-ship — with the dog as the focus of the story, not the owner. Articles that provide hard information (medical, etc.) through a personal experience are appreciated. Note that we write for a lay audience (non-technical), but we do assume a certain level of intelligence: no talking down to people. If you've never seen the type of article you're writing in *Dog Fancy*, don't expect to."

‡**THE EQUINE MARKET**, Midwest Outdoors, 111 Shore Dr., Hinsdale IL 60521. (708)887-7722. Editor: Felici-tas Camacho. 90% freelance written. Monthly tabloid covering equestrian interests. Estab. 1970. Circ. 5,000. Pays on publication. Byline given. Buys all rights or makes work-for-hire assignments. Submit seasonal/holiday material 2 months in advance. Reports in 1 month. Free sample copy and writer's guidelines.
Nonfiction: Essays, general/interest, historical/nostalgic, how-to (horse care), inspirational, interview/pro-file, new product, opinion, personal experience, photo feature, technical and travel. Special upcoming issues: holiday (November-December), farm (June) and tack shop (September). Buys 70 mss/year. Send complete ms. Length: 500-3,000 words. Pays $25-35 for assigned articles; $25 for unsolicited articles; or may trade articles for advertising. Sometimes pays expenses of writers on assignment.

Photos: Send photos with submission. Reviews negatives and 3×5 prints. Offers no additional payment for photos accepted with ms. Captions and identification of subjects required.
Fiction: Adventure, historical, humorous, mainstream and western. Buys 15/year. Send complete ms. Length 500-3,000 words. Pays $25.
Poetry: Traditional. Buys 5/year. Length: 10-20 lines. Pays $25.
Fillers: Anecdotes, facts and short humor. Buys 10/year. Length: 5-10 words. Pays $25.

EQUINEWS, All Breeds - All Disciplines, Site 15, Comp. 5, R.R. 6, Vernon, British Columbia V1T 8C3 Canada. (604)542-2002. Editor Dr. B.J. White. 50% freelance written. Monthly tabloid on horses. Serves the horse industry with current news and information. Circ. 17,492. Pays on publication. Publishes ms an average of 2 months after acceptance. Byline given. Buys first rights or second serial (reprint) rights. Submit seasonal/holiday material 2 months in advance. Simultaneous, photocopied and previously published submissions OK (if advised). Query for electronic submissions. Reports in 2 months on queries. Sample copy for 9×12 SAE and $1.50 Canadian postage; writer's guidelines for #10 SAE with 44¢ USA, 38¢ for Canada postage.
Nonfiction: General interest, humor, interview/profile (English trainers and internationally known riders) and travel. Also sponsors Christmas horse story contest for prizes. Nov. 1 deadline. "No veterinary or how-to." Buys 15 mss/year. Send complete ms. Length: 500-1,500 words. Pays $75. Pays exchange for advertising if desired at double value.
Photos: State availability of photos with submission. Reviews prints. Offers $5 per photo. Captions, model releases and identification of subjects required. Buys one-time rights.
Columns/Departments: Profiles on Trainers (background, facilities, fees, charges, successes, students philosophy), 500-1,500 words. Buys 10 mss/year. Send complete ms. Pays $25-75.
Fiction: Adventure, historical, humorous, and slice-of-life vignettes, all with equine slant. Buys 4 mms/year. Send complete mss. Length: 500-1,500 words. Pays $25-75.
Poetry: Buys 3 or 4 poems/year. Submit maximum 5 poems. Pays $10-25.
Fillers: Anecdotes, facts, gags to be illustrated by cartoonist, newsbreaks and short humor. Buys 12/year. Pays $5-25.
Tips: "Submit sample mss with introductory letter giving brief background of writer, 'horse' knowledge and any published works."

‡THE GREYHOUND REVIEW, P.O. Box 543, Abilene KS 67410. (913)263-4660. Editor: Gary Guccione. Managing Editor: Tim Horan. 20% freelance written. A monthly magazine covering greyhound breeding, training and racing. Estab. 1911. Circ. 7,000. **Pays on acceptance.** Byline given. Buys first rights. Submit seasonal/holiday material 2 months in advance. Query for electronic submissions. Reports in 2 weeks on queries; 1 month on mss. Sample copy $2.50. Free writer's guidelines.
Nonfiction: How-to, interview/profile and personal experience. "Articles must be targeted at the greyhound industry: from hard news, special events at racetracks to the latest medical discoveries." Do not submit gambling systems. Buys 24 mss/year. Query. Length: 1,000-10,000 words. Pays $85-150 for assigned articles; $85-150 for unsolicited articles. Sometimes pays the expenses of writers on assignment.
Photos: State availability of photos with submission. Reviews 35mm transparencies and 8×10 prints. Offers $10-50 per photo. Identification of subjects required. Buys one-time rights.

‡HORSE AND HORSEMAN, Gallant Charger Publications, Inc., 34249 Camino Capistrano, P.O. Box HH, Capistrano Beach CA 92624. (714)493-2101. Editor: Jack Lewis. Managing Editor: Rene E. Riley. Monthly magazine on horses. Estab. 1972. Circ. 92,000. Pays on acceptance. Publishes ms an average of 3-4 months after acceptance. Byling given. Buys first North American serial rights. Submit seasonal/holiday material 5 months in advance. Sample copy for 9x12 SAE with 6 first class stamps; writer's guidelines for #10 SASE.
Nonfiction: General interest, how-to, humor, interview/profile, personal experience, photo feature, travel. Buys 60 mss/year. Query. Length: 250-3,000 words. Pays $25-250. Sometimes pays expenses of writers on assignment.
Photos: Send photos with submission. Reviews contact sheets, transparencies, and prints. Offers no additional payment for photos accepted with ms. Captions required. Buys one-time rights.
Tips: "As our main audience is comprised of pleasure horse owners, we present material of interest to them for the most part. We do, however, cover the rest of the equine world, from rodeo to dressage, on a somewhat lesser scale. We do not publish puzzles, poems or sketches, unless the latter supports a story. The likelihood that we will purchase and use a given article is strongly affected by the amount and quality of the artwork accompanying it."

HORSE ILLUSTRATED, The Magazine for Responsible Horse Owners, Fancy Publications, Inc., P.O. Box 6050, Mission Viejo CA 92690. (714)855-8822. FAX: (714)855-3045. Managing Editor: Sharon Ralls. 90% freelance written. Prefers to work with published/established writers but eager to work with new/unpublished writers. Monthly magazine covering all aspects of horse ownership. "Our readers are adult women between the ages of 18 and 40; stories should be geared to that age group and reflect responsible horse care." Circ. 125,000. Pays on publication. Publishes ms an average of 8 months after acceptance. Byline given. Buys one-time rights. Submit seasonal/holiday material 6 months in advance. Reports in 6 weeks on queries; 2 months on mss. Sample copy $3.50. Writer's guidelines for #10 SASE.

Nonfiction: How-to (horse care, training, veterinary care), humor, personal experience and photo feature. No "little girl" horse stories, "cowboy and Indian" stories or anything not *directly* relating to horses. "We are beginning to look for longer, more in-depth features on trends and issues in the horse industry. Such articles must be queried first with a detailed outline of the article and clips." Buys 100 mss/year. Query or send complete ms. Length: 1,000-2,500 words. Pays $100-250 for assigned articles. Pays $50-200 for unsolicited articles. Sometimes pays telephone bills for writers on assignment.

Photos: Send photos with submission. Reviews contact sheet, 35mm transparencies and 5×7 prints. Occasionally offers additional payment for photos accepted with ms.

Tips: "Freelancers can break in at this publication with feature articles on Western and English training methods and trainer profiles (including training tips); veterinary and general care how-to articles; and horse sports articles. While we use personal experience articles (six to eight times a year), they must be extremely well-written and have wide appeal; humor in such stories is a bonus. Submit photos with training and how-to articles whenever possible. We have a very good record of developing new freelancers into regular contributors/columnists. We are always looking for fresh talent, but certainly enjoy working with established writers who 'know the ropes' as well."

HORSE WORLD USA, Garri Publications, Inc., 114 West Hills Rd., P.O. Box 249, Huntington Station NY 11746. (516)549-3557. FAX: (516)423-0567. Editor: Diana DeRosa. 25% freelance written. A magazine published 13 times per year about horses. Estab. 1978. Circ. 16,500. Pays on publication. Byline given. Buys first North American serial rights. Submit seasonal/holiday material 6 months in advance. Query for electronic submissions. Reports in 3 months on queries. Sample copy for 9×12 SAE, and 6 first class stamps. Writer's guidelines for #10 SASE.

Nonfiction: "Anything horse-related (see topics listed in columns/departments section below)." Buys 25 mss/year. Query with published clips. Length: 100-2,000 words. Pays $5-125 or offers complimentary ad in directory or in classifieds as payment.

Photos: State availability of photos with submission or send photos with submission. Reviews 5×7 prints. Offers $5-10 per photo. Captions, model releases and identification of subjects required. Buys one-time rights. "No name on front of photo; give credit line."

Columns/Departments: Stable Management/Horse Care, Puzzles, Equine Spotlight, Equestrian Spotlight, Celebrity Corner, Diet/Health/Fitness, Horoscopes, The Judge's Corral, From The Horse's Mouth, The Foal's Paddock (does not pay). "Remember these must all be related to horses or horse people." Features: Horse Show, Driving, Dressage, Polo, Racing, Side-Saddle, Eventing, Breeding, Gift Mart, Grand Prix, Western, Youth, Saratoga in August. Query with published clips. Length: 500-1,000 words. Pays $25-75 maximum.

Fillers: Anecdotes, facts, gags to be illustrated by cartoonist, and short humor. Buys 18/year. Length: 25 words minimum. Pays $5.

Tips: "We are an information center for horse people. Write for guidelines. We like to work with writers and artists who are new and are not necessarily looking for money but rather a chance to be published. When writing please specify whether payment is required."

HORSEMAN MAGAZINE, Horseman Publishing Corporation, Suite 390, 25025 I45 N., Spring TX 77380. (713)367-5151. FAX: (713)367-5194. Editor: Bonnie Lindsey. 60% freelance written. Monthly magazine covering the western performance horse industry. "Articles should convey quality information on western horses and horsemanship within the warmth of journalistic prose." Estab. 1956. Circ. 60,000. Publishes ms an average of 9 months after acceptance. Byline given. Pays $50 kill fee. Buys first North American serial rights. Reports in 2 weeks. Sample copy for 10×13 SAE and $1 postage; writer's guidelines for #10 SASE.

Nonfiction: How-to, general interest, interview/profile, photo feature, technical. No horse health articles. Buys 100 articles/year. Query or send complete ms. Length: 1,000-2,000 words. Pays $100-250.

Photos: Send photos with manuscript submission. Reviews transparencies (35mm) and prints (5×7). Captions required. Buys one-time rights. Rarely buys freelance photography.

Columns/Departments: "Columns are done by freelance contributors but they are assigned over a long period and are not open to other freelance writers."

HORSEMEN'S YANKEE PEDLAR NEWSPAPER, 785 Southbridge St., Auburn MA 01501. (508)832-9638. Publisher: Nancy L. Khoury. Managing Editor: Jane Sullivan. 40% freelance written. "All-breed monthly newspaper for horse enthusiasts of all ages and incomes, from one-horse owners to large commercial stables. Covers region from New Jersey to Maine." Circ. 15,000. Pays on publication. Buys all rights for one year. Submit seasonal/holiday material 3 months in advance of issue date. Query for electronic submissions. Publishes ms an average of 5 months after acceptance. Reports in 1 month. Sample copy $3.75.

Nonfiction: Humor, educational and interview about horses and the people involved with them. Pays $2/published inch. Buys 100 mss/year. Query or submit complete ms or outline. Length: 1,500 words maximum.
Photos: Purchased with ms. Captions and photo credit required. Submit b&w prints. Pays $5.
Columns/Departments: Area news column. Buys 85-95/year. Length: 1,200-1,400 words. Query.
Tips: "Query with outline of angle of story, approximate length and date when story will be submitted. Stories should be people oriented and horse focused. Send newsworthy, timely pieces, such as stories that are applicable to the season, for example: foaling in the spring or how to keep a horse healthy through the winter. We like to see how-tos, features about special horse people and anything that has to do with the preservation of horses and their rights as creatures deserving a chance to survive."

HORSEPLAY, Box 130, Gaithersburg MD 20877. (301)840-1866. FAX: (301)840-5722. Editor: Cordelia Doucet. 50% freelance written. Works with published/established writers and a small number of new/unpublished writers each year. Monthly magazine covering horses and English horse sports for a readership interested in horses, show jumping, dressage, combined training, hunting and driving. 60-80 pages. Circ. 48,000. Pays end of publication month. Buys all rights, first North American serial rights and second serial (reprint) rights. Offers kill fee. Byline given. Query first. Deadline is 2 months prior to issue date. Nothing returned without SASE. Reports within 3 weeks. Sample copy $3 with 9 × 12 SAE; writer's and photographer's guidelines for #10 SASE.
Nonfiction: Instruction (various aspects of horsemanship, course designing, stable management, putting on horse shows, etc.); competitions; interview; photo feature; profile and technical. Length: 1,000-3,000 words. Pays 10¢/word, all rights; 9¢/word, first North American serial rights; 7¢/word, second rights. Sometimes pays extra to writers on assignment.
Photos: Cathy Kuehner, art director. Purchased on assignment. Write captions on separate paper attached to photo. Query or send contact sheet, prints or transparencies. Pays $22.50 for 8 × 10 b&w glossy prints; $200 for color transparencies for cover; $45 for inside color.
Tips: Don't send fiction, Western riding, or racing articles.

HORSES WEST, The Rocky Mountain Region's Largest News Magazine Dedicated to Horses for Sport and Performance, P.O. Box 129, Castle Rock CO 80104. (303)688-1117. Editor: Phyllis Squiccimara. Tabloid published 11 times/year (Feb.-Dec.) on the horse industry. "*Horses West* is a regional magazine serving the Rocky Mountain states. Our audience includes those horsemen of English and Western riding disciplines." Estab. 1984. Pays on publication. Publishes ms an average of 3 months after acceptance. Byline given. Primarily buys second serial (reprint) rights. Submit seasonal/holiday material 5 months in advance. Photocopied and previously published submissions OK. Reports in 2 months on queries. Sample copy for 9 × 12 SAE with 5 first class stamps. Writer's guidelines for #10 SASE.
Nonfiction: Submissions sent to Articles Editor. Book excerpts, how-to (training, riding, care of the horse), humor, interview/profile, new product and photo feature. Buys 50 mss/year. Query with or without published clips, or send complete ms. Length: 250-2,500 words.
Photos: State availability of photos with submission.
Columns/Departments: Send to Column Editor. Book Review (reviews of recent high quality books on English and Western disciplines); Trainers/Judges (training and showing hints from professionals in the field), 250-1,000 words; Sports Psychologist (monthly advise on various problems in horse/rider), 250-1,000 words. Buys 20 mss/year. Query with published clips. Length: 250-1,000 words. Pays $10-75.
Poetry: Send to Poetry Editor. Free verse, haiku, light verse and traditional. "No *bad* poetry—sentimental, syrupy, abstract tributes to a favorite pony or old gray mare." Buys 6 poems/year. Submit maximum 15 poems. Length: 3-150 lines. Pays $5-20.
Fillers: Send to Fillers Editor. Facts, gags to be illustrated by cartoonist, newsbreak and short humor. Buys up to 10/year. Length: 25-250 words. *"Must be horse related"* Pays $5-20.
Tips: "Indicate photo or graphic availability in your query or ms. Querying us first saves your time and our time. *Horses West* is looking for skillfully written articles in a feature style photojournalism format. Be clear, concise and precise in your wording. We will accept profiles on trainers and how-to articles on training and showing methods for the English and Western discipline."

‡LONE STAR HORSE REPORT, P.O. Box 14767, Fort Worth TX 76117. (817)838-8642. Editor: Henry L. King. 15-20% freelance written. Monthly magazine on horses and horse people in and around Dallas/Ft. Worth metroplex. Estab. 1983. Circ. 7,500. Pays on publication. Publishes ms an average of 2 months after acceptance. Byline given. Buys first rights and second serial (reprint) rights to material originally published elsewhere. Submit seasonal/holiday material 2 months in advance. Previously published submissions OK. Reports in 2 weeks on queries; 4 weeks on mss. Sample copy $1; writer's guidelines for #10 SASE.
Nonfiction: Interview/profile (horsemen living in trade area); photo feature (horses, farms, arenas, facilities, people in trade area). Buys 30-40 mss/year. Query with published clips or send complete ms. Length: 200-2,000 words. Pays $15-60. Sometimes pays the expenses of writers on assignment.

Photos: State availability of photos. Pays $5 for 5×7 b&w or color prints. Buys one-time rights.

Tips: "We need reports of specific horse-related events in north Texas area such as trail rides, rodeos, play days, shows, etc., and also feature articles on horse farms, outstanding horses and/or horsemen. Since Texas now has pari-mutuel horse racing, more emphasis will be placed on coverage of racing and racehorse breeding. We will be reporting on the actions of the newly-appointed racing commission, locations of tracks, construction and ownership of those tracks, and the economic impact of the racing industry as new breeding farms and training facilities are established."

‡**MUSHING**, Stellar Communications, Inc., P.O. Box 149 Ester, Ester AK 99725. (907)479-0454. Editor: Richard Eathrone. Bimonthly magazine. "We cover all aspects of sleddog sport. We include information (how-to), nonfiction (entertaining), news and history stories." Estab. 1987. Circ. 5,000. Pays on publication. Publishes ms an average of 4 months after acceptance. Byline given. Buys first North American serial rights or second serial (reprint) rights. Submit seasonal/holiday material 4 months in advance. Query for electronic submissions. Reports in 3 weeks. Sample copy $3.50; free writer's guidelines.

Nonfiction: Book excerpts, general interest, historical, how-to, humor, interview/profile, new product, personal experience, photo feature, technical, travel. Themes are: December/January—Christmas, beginning race season, winter trips; February/March—travel, main race season, recreation and work season; April/May—breakup, gearing down; June/July—summer dog keep, tourists go North; August/September—Get ready for gear up; October/November—winter schedules, gear up. Query with or without published clips, or send complete ms. Length: 500-3,000 words. Pays $50-250 for articles. Sometimes pays expenses of writers on assignment.

Photos: Send photos with submission. Reviews contact sheets, transparencies, prints. Offers $10-150/photo. Captions, model releases, identification of subjects required. Buys one-time rights.

Fillers: Anecdotes, facts, gags to be illustrated by cartoonist, newsbreaks, short humor. Length: 100-250 words. Pays $25.

Tips: "Read our magazine and know something about the sport."

PAINT HORSE JOURNAL, American Paint Horse Association, P.O. Box 961023, Fort Worth TX 76161. (817)439-3412. FAX: (817)439-1509. Editor: Bill Shepard. 10% freelance written. Works with a small number of new/unpublished writers each year. For people who raise, breed and show Paint horses. Monthly magazine. Estab. 1966. Circ. 13,000. **Pays on acceptance.** Publishes ms an average of 3 months after acceptance. Buys first North American serial rights plus reprint rights occasionally. Pays negotiable kill fee. Byline given. Phone queries OK, but prefers written query. Submit seasonal/holiday material 3 months in advance. Previously published submissions OK. Reports in 1 month. Sample copy for 9×12 SAE and 5 first class stamps; writer's guidelines for #10 SASE.

Nonfiction: General interest (personality pieces on well-known owners of Paints); historical (Paint horses in the past—particular horses and the breed in general); how-to (train and show horses); photo feature (Paint horses); and articles on horse health. Now seeking informative well-written articles on recreational riding. Buys 4-5 mss/issue. Send complete ms. Pays $50-250.

Photos: Send photos with ms. Offers no additional payment for photos accepted with accompanying ms. Uses 3×5 or larger b&w glossy prints; 35mm or larger color transparencies. Captions required.

Tips: "*PHJ* needs breeder-trainer articles, Paint horse marketing and timely articles from areas throughout the U.S. and Canada. We are looking for more horse health articles, recreational and how-to articles. We are beginning to cover more equine activity outside the show ring. This can include such things as trail riding, orienteering and other outdoor events. Photos with copy are almost always essential. Well-written first person articles are welcomed. Submit well-written items that show a definite understanding of the horse business. Be sure you understand precisely what a Paint horse is as defined by the American Paint Horse Association. Use proper equine terminology and proper grounding in ability to communicate thoughts."

‡**PET HEALTH NEWS**, Fancy Publications Inc., P.O. Box 6050, Mission Viejo CA 92690. (714)855-8822. Editor: Virginia R. Parker. 50% freelance written. Monthly magazine covering pet health. *PHN* is a special-interest magazine for anyone with an interest in animals, from pet owners to veterinarians. Our main emphasis is animal health care. Estab. 1985. Controlled circulation. Pays on publication. Publishes ms an average of 2 months after acceptance. Byline given. Buys first North American serial rights. Submit seasonal/holiday material 3 months in advance. Query for electronic submissions. Reports in 2 months. Sample copy for $3.50. Writer's guidelines for #10 SAE with 1 first class stamp.

Nonfiction: "*Pet Health News* covers the gamut of the pet animal species, including dogs, cats, birds, horses, rabbits, guinea pigs, ferrets, hamsters, rats, mice, reptiles, fish and amphibians. We need informative articles geared toward educating the public about animal care in an accurate, timely and reliable manner. Topics include, but are not limited to, ongoing research in veterinary medicine, health care, training, nutrition, animal welfare legislation and grooming of pet animals." Buys 100 mss/year. Query with or without published clips, or send complete ms. Length: 1,500-3,000 words. Pays 5-10¢/word.

Photos: Offers no additional payment for photos accepted with ms. Model releases required. Buys one-time rights.

PETS MAGAZINE, Moorshead Publications, 1300 Don Mills Rd., Toronto Ontario M3B 3M8 Canada. (416)445-5600. FAX: (416)445-8149. Editor: Marie Hubbs. Editorial Director/Veterinarian: Dr. Tom Frisby. 40% freelance written. Bimonthly magazine on pets. Circ. 67,000 distributed by vet clinics; 5,500 personal subscriptions. Pays on publication. Publishes ms an average of 1 year after acceptance. Buys all rights. Submit seasonal/holiday material 4 months in advance. Previously published submissions OK (sometimes). Query for electronic submissions. Sample copy for #10 SAE with 91¢ IRC. Free writer's guidelines.

Nonfiction: General interest, historical, how-to (train, bathe/groom, build dog houses, make cat toys and photograph pets), breed profile and photo feature. No "I remember Fluffy." Buys 12-18 mss/year. Query with outline. Length: 600-1,500 words. Pays 12-18¢ (Canadian)/ word; 1-3 copies included with payment check. Pays expenses of writers on assignment only by prior agreement.

Photos: Send photos with submission. Reviews prints 3×5 and larger, b&w preferred. Offers $25 per photo. Model releases and identification of subjects required. Buys all rights.

Fillers: Facts. Query with samples. Buys 1-2/year. Length: 100-400 words. Pays 12-15¢(Canadian)/word. "Always call or send topic outline first; we always have a backlog of freelance articles waiting to be run. Prefers factual, information pieces, not anecdotal or merely humorous, but can be written with humor; we do not cover controversial areas such as product testing, vivisection, puppy mills, pound seizure."

PURE-BRED DOGS AMERICAN KENNEL GAZETTE, American Kennel Club, 51 Madison Ave., New York NY 10010. (212)696-8331. Executive Editor: Marion Lane. 80% freelance written. Monthly association publication on pure-bred dogs. "Material is slanted to interests of fanciers of pure-bred dogs as opposed to commercial interests." Circ. 58,000. **Pays on acceptance.** Publishes ms an average of 6 months after acceptance. Byline given. Offers 30% kill fee. Buys first North American serial rights. Submit seasonal/holiday material 6 months in advance. Reports in 3 weeks. Sample copy and writer's guidelines for 9×12 SAE and 11 first class stamps.

Nonfiction: General interest, historical, how-to, humor, photo feature, travel. No profiles, poetry, tributes to individual dogs, or fiction. Buys about 75 mss/year. Query with or without published clips, or send complete ms. Length: 1,000-2,500 words. Pays $100-300. Sometimes pays expenses of writers on assignment.

Photos: Send photos with submission. Reviews tranparencies and prints. Offers $25-100/photo. Captions required. Buys one-time rights. (Photo contest guidelines for #10 SASE).

Fiction: Annual short fiction contest only. Guidelines for #10 SASE. Twelve annual contest winners are anthologized in separate booklet.

Tips: "Contributors should be involved in dog fancy or be expert in the area they write about (veterinary, showing, field trialing, obedience, training, dogs in legislation, dog art or history or literature). All submissions are welcome but the author must be credible. Veterinary articles must be written by or with veterinarians. Humorous features are personal experiences relative to pure-bred dogs. For features generally, know the subject thoroughly and be conversant with jargon peculiar to dog sport."

PURRRR! THE NEWSLETTER FOR CAT LOVERS, The Meow Company, HCR 227 Rd., Islesboro ME 04848. (207)734-6745. FAX: (207)734-2262. Publisher/Editor Agatha Cabaniss. 85% freelance written. Works with a small number of new/unpublished writers each year. A bimonthly newsletter for the average cat owner. "The publication is designed to amuse while providing cat lovers with information about the care, feeding and enjoyment of house cats." Estab. 1982. Circ. 1,000. **Pays on acceptance.** Publishes ms an average of 5 months after acceptance. Byline given. Buys one time, first serial rights and second serial (reprint) rights. Submit seasonal/holiday material 6 months in advance. Previously published submissions OK unless published in a competing publication, such as *Cats* and *Cat Fancy*. Query for electronic submissions. Reports in 2 weeks. Sample copy $2; writer's guidelines for #10 SASE.

Nonfiction: General interest; historical; how-to; literary cat lovers (have featured Colette, Mark Twain and May Sarton); humor; interview/profile; new product; travel, off-beat unusual. "We want a humorous slant wherever possible; writing should be tight and professional. Avoid the first person." Special Christmas issue. No shaggy cat stories, sentimental stories, "I taught Fluffy to roll over" or no "reformed cat hater" stories. "We would like to receive articles on humane societies and animal rescue leagues." Absolutely no fiction. Buys 50/mss year. Query with published clips, or send complete ms. Length: 250-1,500 words. Pays: $15-100.

Photos: Avoid "cute" photos. State availability of photos. Pays $5-10 for 5×8 b&w prints. Buys one-time rights.

Poetry: Accepts some poetry.

Fillers: Clippings, anecdotes, short humor/cartoons and newsbreaks. Buys 20/year. Length: 25-75 words. Pays $5.

Tips: "You should know pet cats, their foibles and personalities. We are interested in good writing but also in a good story about a cat. We are interested in people who work with and for animal welfare and how-to articles on making things for cats or for people who live with cats, i.e. how to 'cat proof' a crib. We will work with a writer who has an interesting cat story. We are not interested in show cats or breeding. Query or send article and a SASE for reply."

THE QUARTER HORSE JOURNAL, Box 32470, Amarillo TX 79120. (806)376-4811. FAX: (806)372-6806. Editor-in-Chief: Audie Rackley. 10% freelance written. Prefers to work with published/established writers. Official publication of the American Quarter Horse Association. Monthly magazine. Circ. 70,000. **Pays on acceptance.** Publishes ms an average of 3 months after acceptance. Buys first North American serial rights. Submit seasonal/holiday material 2 months in advance. Reports in 2 weeks. Free sample copy and writer's guidelines.

Nonfiction: Historical ("those that retain our western heritage"); how-to (fitting, grooming, showing, or anything that relates to owning, showing, or breeding); informational (educational clinics, current news); interview (feature-type stories—must be about established horses or people who have made a contribution to the business); personal opinion; and technical (equine updates, new surgery procedures, etc.). Buys 20 mss/year. Length: 800-2,500 words. Pays $50-250.

Photos: Purchased with accompanying ms. Captions required. Send prints or transparencies. Uses 5×7 or 8×10 b&w glossy prints; 2¼×2¼ or 4×5 color transparencies. Offers no additional payment for photos accepted with accompanying ms.

Tips: "Writers must have a knowledge of the horse business. We will be purchasing more material on quarter horse racing."

‡REPTILE & AMPHIBIAN MAGAZINE, RD3 Box 3709, Pottsville PA 17901. (717)622-1098. Editor: Norman Frank, D.V.M. 80% freelance written. Bimonthly magazine covering reptiles and amphibians. Devoted to the amateur herpetologist who is generally college-educated and familiar with the basics of herpetology. Estab. 1989. Circ. 5,000. **Pays on acceptance.** Publishes ms an average of 4 months after acceptance. Byline given. Buys first North American serial, one-time and second serial (reprint) rights (occasionally). Previously published submissions OK. Reports in 6 weeks. Sample copy $4. Writer's guidelines for #10 SAE with 1 first class stamp.

Nonfiction: General interest, photo feature, technical. No first-person narrative, me-and-Joe stories or articles by writers unfamiliar with the subject matter. Buys 30 mss/year. Send complete ms. Length: 1,500-2,000 words. Pays $75-100. Sometimes pays expenses of writer on assignment.

Photos: Send photos with submission. Reviews 35mm slide transparencies, 5×7 and 8×10 glossy prints. Offers $10-25 per photo. Captions, model releases and identification of subjects required. Buys one-time rights.

Columns/Departments: Photo Dept., 750-1,000 words; Book Review, 750-1,000 words. Buys 12 mss/year. Send complete ms. Pays $50-75.

Tips: "Note your personal qualifications, such as experience in the field or advanced education. Writers have the best chance selling us feature articles—know your subject and supply high quality color photos."

TROPICAL FISH HOBBYIST, "The World's Most Widely Read Aquarium Monthly," TFH Publications, Inc., 211 W. Sylvania Ave., Neptune City NJ 07753. (201)988-8400. Editor: Ray Hunziker. Managing Editor: Neal Pronek. 75% freelance written. Monthly magazine covering the tropical fish hobby. "We favor articles well illustrated with good color slides and aimed at both the neophyte and veteran tropical fish hobbyist." Circ. 60,000. **Pays on acceptance.** Publishes ms an average of 4 months after acceptance. Byline given. Buys all rights. Submit seasonal/holiday material 4 months in advance. Reports in 2 weeks. Sample copy $3; writer's guidelines for #10 SASE.

Nonfiction: General interest, how-to, photo feature, technical, and articles dealing with beginning and advanced aspects of the aquarium hobby. No "how I got started in the hobby" articles that impart little solid information. Buys 20-30 mss/year. Length: 500-2,500 words. Pays $25-100.

Photos: State availability of photos or send photos with ms. Pays $10 for 35mm transparencies. Identification of subjects required. "Originals of photos returned to owner, who may market them elsewhere."

Fiction: "On occasion, we will review a fiction piece relevant to the aquarium hobby."

Tips: "We cater to a specialized readership—people knowledgeable in fish culture. Prospective authors should be familiar with subject; photography skills are a plus. It's a help if an author we've never dealt with queries first or submits a short item."

THE WESTERN HORSEMAN, World's Leading Horse Magazine Since 1936, Western Horseman, Inc., 3850 N. Nevada Ave., P.O. Box 7980, Colorado Springs CO 80933. (719)633-5524. Editor: Pat Close. 50% freelance written. Works with a small number of new/unpublished writers each year. Monthly magazine covering western horsemanship. Estab. 1936. Circ. 180,598. **Pays on acceptance.** Publishes ms an average of 5 months after acceptance. Buys one-time, North American serial rights or second serial (reprint) rights. Byline given. Submit seasonal/holiday material 9 months in advance. Reports in 2 weeks. Sample copy $2.25; free writer's guidelines.

Nonfiction: How-to (horse training, care of horses, tips, etc.); and informational (on rodeos, ranch life, historical articles of the West emphasizing horses). Buys 100 mss/year. Length: 500-2,000 words. Payment begins at $35-300; "sometimes higher by special arrangement."

Photos: Send photos with ms. Offers no additional payment for photos. Uses 5×7 or 8×10 b&w glossy prints and 35mm transparencies. Captions required.

Fiction: Humorous, western. Buys 2-3 mss/year. Send complete ms. Length: 1,000-1,500 words. Pays $300 maximum.

Tips: "Submit clean copy with professional quality photos. Stay away from generalities. Writing style should show a deep interest in horses coupled with a wide knowledge of the subject."

Art and Architecture

Listed here are publications about art, art history, specific art forms and architecture written for art patrons, architects and artists. Publications addressing the business and management side of the art industry are listed in the Art, Design and Collectibles category of the Trade section. Trade publications for architecture can be found in Building Interiors and Construction and Contracting sections.

ART TIMES, A Cultural and Creative Journal, P.O. Box 730, Mount Marion NY 12456. (914)246-5170. Editor: Raymond J. Steiner. 10% (just fiction and poetry) freelance written. Prefers to work with published/established writers; works with a small number of new/unpublished writers each year; and eager to work with new/unpublished writers. Monthly tabloid covering the arts (visual, theatre, dance, etc.). "*Art Times* covers the art fields and is distributed in locations most frequented by those enjoying the arts. Our 15,000 copies are distributed throughout upstate New York counties rich in the arts as well as in most of the galleries in Soho, 57th Street and Madison Avenue in the metropolitan area; locations include theaters, galleries, museums, cultural centers and the like. Subscriptions come from across U.S. and abroad. Our readers are mostly over 40, affluent, art-conscious and sophisticated." Estab. 1984. Circ. 15,000. Pays on publication. Publishes ms an average of 1 year after acceptance. Byline given. Buys first serial rights. Submit seasonal/holiday material 8 months in advance. Simultaneous queries and simultaneous submissions OK. Reports in 3 months on queries; 6 months on mss. Sample copy for 9×12 SAE and 6 first class stamps; writer's guidelines for #10 SASE.

Fiction: "We're looking for short fiction that aspires to be *literary*. No excessive violence, sexist, off-beat, erotic, sports, or juvenile fiction." Buys 8-10 mss/year. Send complete ms. Length: 1,500 words maximum. Pays $15 maximum (honorarium) and 1 year's free subscription.

Poetry: Poet's Niche. Avant-garde, free verse, haiku, light verse and traditional. "We prefer well-crafted 'literary' poems. No excessively sentimental poetry." Buys 30-35 poems/year. Submit maximum 6 poems. Length: 20 lines maximum. Offers contributor copies and 1 year's free subscription.

Tips: "Be advised that we are presently on an approximate two year lead. We are now receiving 300-400 poems and 40-50 short stories per month. We only publish 2-3 poems and one story each issue. Competition is getting very great. We only pick the best. Be familiar with *Art Times* and its special audience. *Art Times* has literary leanings with articles written by a staff of scholars knowledgeable in their respective fields. Our readers expect quality. Although an 'arts' publication, we observe no restrictions (other than noted) in accepting fiction/poetry other than a concern for quality writing—subjects can cover anything and not specifically arts."

THE ARTIST'S MAGAZINE, F&W Publications, Inc., 1507 Dana Ave., Cincinnati OH 45207. Editor: Michael Ward. 80% freelance written. Works with a small number of new/unpublished writers each year. Monthly magazine covering primarily two-dimensional art instruction for working artists. "Ours is a highly visual approach to teaching the serious amateur artist techniques that will help him improve his skills and market his work. The style should be crisp and immediately engaging." Circ. 250,000. **Pays on acceptance.** Publishes ms an average of 4 months after acceptance. Byline given; bionote given for feature material. Offers 20% kill fee. Buys first North American serial rights and second serial (reprint) rights. Simultaneous queries and previously published submissions OK "as long as noted as such." Reports in 1 month. Sample copy $2.50 with 9×12 SAE and 3 first class stamps; writer's guidelines for #10 SASE.

Nonfiction: Instructional only—how an artist uses a particular technique, how he handles a particular subject or medium, or how he markets his work. "The emphasis must be on how the reader can learn some method of improving his artwork, or the marketing of it." No unillustrated articles; no seasonal/holiday material; no travel articles; no profiles of artists (except for "Artist's Life," below). Buys 60 mss/year. Query first; all queries must be accompanied by slides, transparencies, prints or tearsheets of the artist's work as well as the artist's bio, and the writer's bio and clips. Length: 1,000-2,500 words. Pays $100-350 and up. Sometimes pays the expenses of writers on assignment.

Photos: "Transparencies are required with every accepted article since these are essential for our instructional format. Full captions must accompany these." Buys one-time rights.

Departments: Two departments are open to freelance writers: The Artist's Life and P.S. The Artist's Life (profiles and brief items about artists and their work. Also, art-related games and puzzles and art-related poetry). Query first with samples of artist's work for profiles; send complete ms for other items. Length: 600

words maximum. Pays $50 and up for profiles; up to $25 for brief items and poetry. P.S. (a humorous look at art from the artist's point of view, or at least sympathetic to the artist). Send complete ms. Pays $50 and up.

Tips: "Look at several current issues and read the author's guidelines carefully. Remember that our readers are fine and graphic artists."

‡**THE ARTS JOURNAL**, 324 Charlotte St., Asheville NC 28801. (704)255-7888. Editor: Tom Patterson. Monthly tabloid of literary, performing and visual arts. "Our purpose is to link artists with their audiences. In our reviews and interviews we try to use language that is clear to artists and non-artists." Estab. 1975. Circ. 5,000. Pays on publication. Byline given. Offers $25 kill fee. Buys one-time rights. Submit seasonal/holiday material 2 months in advance. Reports in 2 weeks. Sample copy $2 with 8×10 SAE and 4 first class stamps.

Nonfiction: Art reviews, interviews. Buys 60 mss/year. Query. Length: 500-1,500 words. Pays $25-100.

Photos: State availability of photos with submission. Offers no additional payment for photos accepted with ms.

Fiction: Fiction Editor: J.W. Bonner. Experimental, historical, mainstream, slice-of-life vignettes. Buys 12 mss/year. Send complete ms. Length: 1,400-1,600 words. Pays $50.

Poetry: Poetry Editor: J.W. Bonner. Avant-garde, free verse, traditional. Uses 45/year. Submit up to 6 poems at 1 time. Length: 40 lines maximum. Pays in copies for poetry.

Tips: "State expertise in one of the areas we cover and give evidence of writing ability."

‡**CONTEMPORANEA, International Art Magazine**, Contemporanea Ltd., 17 East 260 W. Broadway, New York NY 10013. (212)274-0730. FAX: (212)274-0737. Managing Editor: Joseph D. Watson. 80% freelance written. Magazine on contemporary visual and performing arts. Estab. 1987. Circ. 35,000. Pays ½ on acceptance and ½ on publication. Byline given. Offers 50% kill fee. Buys simultaneous rights. Simultaneous and previously published submissions OK. Query for electronic submissions.

Nonfiction: Interview/profile, reviews, and journalistic articles about contemporary art. Query with published clips. Length: 1,000-2,500 words. Payment is negotiable.

Photos: State availability of photos with submissions. Reviews transparencies (3×5). Captions, model releases and identification of subjects required. Buys one-time rights.

EQUINE IMAGES, The National Magazine of Equine Art, Equine Images Ltd., P.O. Box 916, Fort Dodge IA 50501. (800)247-2000, ext. 233. Co-Editors: Sandy Geier and Deborah Schneider. Publisher: Susan Badger. 20% freelance written. A quarterly magazine of equine art. "*Equine Images* serves artists, collectors, and equine art enthusiasts. We write for a sophisticated, culturally-oriented audience." Circ. 15,000. Pays on publication. Byline given. Offers $25 kill fee. Publication not copyrighted. Buys first rights and makes work for hire assignments. Previously published submissions OK. Reports in 2 weeks on queries; 3 weeks on mss. Sample copy for 9×12 SAE and $7.50; writer's guidelines for #10 SASE.

Nonfiction: Historical/nostalgic (history of the horse in art), how-to (art and art collections), interview/profile (equine artists, galleries, collectors), personal experience (of equine artists and collectors), photo feature (artworks or collections). "No articles about horses in general—just horse art. No casual writing style." Buys 4-8 mss/year. Query with published clips. Length: 500-3,000 words. Pays $150-500 for assigned articles; $100-350 for unsolicited articles.

Photos: State availability of photos with submission. Reviews contact sheets, transparencies, prints. Offers no additional payment for photos accepted with ms. Identification of subjects required. Buys one-time rights.

Tips: "We are interested only in art-related subjects. Writers should have an art background or be knowledgeable of the field. Experience with horses is also a plus. The most promising categories for writers are profiles of prominent artists and equine galleries or museums. If you know of a talented artist in your area, or a gallery or museum that specializes in equine art, send a good query letter with accompanying visuals, along with published clips or writing samples."

‡**METROPOLIS, The Architecture and Design Magazine of New York**, Bellerophon Publications, 177 E. 87th St., New York NY 10128. (212)722-5050. FAX: (212)427-1938. Editor: Susan S. Szenasy. Managing Editor: Eric Brand. 60% freelance written. A monthly (except bimonthly January/February and July/August) magazine for consumers interested in architecture and design. Estab. 1981. Circ. 30,000. **Pays on acceptance.** Publishes ms an average of 6 months after acceptance. Byline given. Buys first rights or makes work-for-hire assignments. Submit calendar material 6 weeks in advance. Reports in 2 weeks on queries; 1 month on mss. Sample copy $3.50 including postage.

Nonfiction: Book excerpts; essays (design, residential interiors); historical (mostly New York); opinion (design, architecture); and profile (only well-known international figures). No profiles on individuals or individual architectural practices, technical information, information from public relations firms, or fine arts. Buys approximately 30 mss/year. Query with published clips. Length: 1,500-3,000 words. Pays $500-1,000.

Photos: State availability, or send photos with submission. Reviews contact sheets, 35mm or 4×5 transparencies, or 8×10 b&w prints. Payment offered for certain photos. Captions required. Buys one-time rights.

Columns/Departments: Insites (miscellany: information on design and architecture around New York), 100-600 words; pays $150-300; In Print (book review essays), 600-750 words; Scene & Heard (NY architecture and city planning news features) 750-1,500 words; pays $300-500. Buys approximately 40 mss/year. Query with published clips.

Tips: "We're looking for ideas, what's new, the obscure or the wonderful. Keep in mind that we are interested *only* in the consumer end of architecture and design. Send query with examples of photos explaining how you see illustrations working with article. Also, be patient and don't expect an immediate answer after submission of query."

MUSEUM & ARTS/WASHINGTON, Museum & Arts/Washington, Inc., Suite 222, 1707 L St. NW, Washington D.C. 20036. (202)659-5973. Editor: Anne Abramson. 50% freelance written. Bimonthly magazine on the arts and culture. *"Museum & Arts/Washington* is a lively guide to the arts in the Washington area. It seeks to interest and enliven its readers appreciation of art and artists in the capitol city." Estab. 1985. Circ. 50,000. Pays on publication. Publishes ms an average of 2 months after acceptance. Byline given. Offers 33⅓% kill fee. Buys first North American serial rights and makes work-for-hire assignments. Submit seasonal/holiday material 4 months in advance. Query for electronic submissions. Reports in 2 weeks. Sample copy for 11×13 SAE with $2 first class postage.

Nonfiction: Submit to Mary Gabriel, executive editor. Book excerpts, essays, exposé, historical, interview/profile, opinion, personal experience and technical. Does *not* want anything that does not clearly relate to the Washington cultural scene. Length: 300-6,000 words. Pays $75-2,500 for assigned articles. Sometimes pays expenses of writers on assignment.

Photos: State availability of photos with submission or send photos with submission. Reviews transparencies. Payment negotiable. Identification of subjects required. Buys one-time rights.

THE ORIGINAL ART REPORT, P.O. Box 1641, Chicago IL 60690. Editor and Publisher: Frank Salantrie. Emphasizes "visual art conditions from the visual artists' and general public's perspectives." Newsletter; 6-8 pages. Estab. 1967. Pays on publication. Reports in 2 weeks. Sample copy $1.50 and 1 first class stamp.

Nonfiction: Expose (art galleries, government agencies ripping off artists, or ignoring them); historical (perspective pieces relating to now); humor (whenever possible); informational (material that is unavailable in other art publications); inspirational (acts and ideas of courage); interview (with artists, other experts; serious material); personal opinion; technical (brief items to recall traditional methods of producing art); travel (places in the world where artists are welcomed and honored); philosophical, economic, aesthetic, and artistic. "We would like to receive investigative articles on government and private arts agencies, and nonprofits, too, perhaps hiding behind status to carry on for business entities. Exclusive interest in visual fine art condition as it affects individuals, society and artists and as they affect it. Must take advocacy position. Prefer controversial subject matter and originality of treatment. Also artist's position on non-art topics. No vanity profiles of artists, arts organizations and arts promoters' operations." Buys 4-5 mss/year. Query or submit complete ms. Length: 1,000 words maximum. Pays ½-1¢/word.

Columns/Departments: In Back of the Individual Artist. Artists express their views about non-art topics. After all, artists are in this world, too. WOW (Worth One Wow), Worth Repeating, and Worth Repeating Again. Basically, these are reprint items with introduction to give context and source, including complete name and address of publication. Looking for insightful, succinct commentary. Submit complete ms. Length: 500 words maximum and copy of item. Pays ½-1¢/word.

Tips: "We have a stronger than ever emphasis on editorial opinion or commentary, based on fact, of the visual art condition: economics, finances, politics, and manufacture of art and the social and individual implications of and to fine art."

THEDAMU, The Black Arts Magazine, Detroit Black Arts Alliance, 13217 Livernois, Detroit MI 48238. (313)931-3427. Editor: David Rambeau. Managing Editor: Titilaya Akanke. 20% freelance written. Monthly literary magazine on the arts. "We publish Afro-American feature articles on local artists." Estab. 1965. Circ. 4,000. Pays on publication. Publishes 4 months after acceptance. Byline given. Buys one-time rights. Submit seasonal/holiday material 4 months in advance. Simultaneous and previously published submissions OK. Query for electronic submissions. Reports in 1 month on queries; 2 months on mss. Sample copy $2 with SAE and 4 first class stamps. Writer's guidelines for SAE with 1 first class stamp.

Nonfiction: Essays and interview/profile. Buys 20 mss/year. Send complete ms. Length: 500-1,500 words. Pays $10-25 for unsolicited articles. Pays with contributor copies or other premiums if writer agrees.

Photos: State availability of photos with submission. Reviews 5×7 prints. Offers no additional payment for photos accepted with ms. Captions, model releases and identification of subjects required. Buys one-time rights.

Tips: "Send a résumé and sample ms. Query for fiction, poetry, plays and film/video scenarios."

U.S. ART, The Magazine of Realism in America, Adams Publishing, Suite 400, 12 S. 6th St., Minneapolis MN 55402. (612)339-7571. FAX: (612)339-5806. Editor: Paul Froiland. Managing Editor: Laura Silver. 90% freelance written. Magazine published 9 issues/year. "We are a mainstream publication covering American realist art of all genres—wildlife, landscape, still life, Western, Americana, etc. We are directed at the consumer, and feature artist profiles and articles on historical and contemporary issues in representational art." Estab. 1982. Circ. 32,000. Pays on publication. Publishes ms an average of 3 months after acceptance. Byline given. Offers 25% kill fee. Buys first North American serial rights. Submit seasonal/holiday material 6 months in advance. Simultaneous submissions OK, if they are identified as such. Reports in 6 weeks on queries; 2 months on mss. Sample for $2.50 with 9×12 SAE and 3 first class stamps. Writer's guidelines for #10 SASE.
Nonfiction: Essays, general interest, historical, interview/profile and opinion (does not mean letters to the editor). October: Western Art theme and March: Wildlife Art theme issue. Buys 45 mss/year. Query with published clips. Length: 2,000-2,500 words. Pays $400-500 for assigned articles. Pays only telephone and mileage expenses.
Columns/Departments: Legacies (reviews of museum exhibitions, preferably traveling), 750 words; and Remarques (back-page opinion piece—humorous or serious), 500 words. Buys 23 mss/year. Query with published clips. Pays $50-200.
Tips: "Queries should be very focused, and topics should be geared toward a mainstream audience—nothing too obscure, and nothing academically written. If they are querying on a particular artist, slides or 4×5 transparencies must be submitted."

WESTART, Box 6868, Auburn CA 95604. (916)885-0969. Editor-in-Chief: Martha Garcia. Emphasizes art for practicing artists and artists/craftsmen; students of art and art patrons. Semimonthly tabloid; 20 pages. Circ. 5,000. Pays on publication. Buys all rights. Byline given. Phone queries OK. Free sample copy and writer's guidelines.
Nonfiction: Informational, photo feature and profile. No hobbies. Buys 6-8 mss/year. Query or submit complete ms. Length: 700-800 words. Pays 50¢/column inch.
Photos: Purchased with or without accompanying ms. Send b&w prints. Pays 50¢/column inch.
Tips: "We publish information which is current—that is, we will use a review of an exhibition only if exhibition is still open on the date of publication. Therefore, reviewer must be familiar with our printing deadlines and news deadlines."

WOMEN ARTISTS NEWS, Midmarch Arts Press, P.O. Box 3304, Grand Central Station, New York NY 10163. Editor: Judy Seigel. 70-90% freelance written. Works with small number of new/unpublished writers each year; eager to work with new/unpublished writers. Bimonthly magazine for "artists and art historians, museum and gallery personnel, students, teachers, crafts personnel, art critics and writers." Estab. 1975. Circ. 5,000. Buys first serial rights only when funds are available. "Token payment as funding permits." Publishes ms an average of 2 months after acceptance. Byline given. Submit seasonal material 2 months in advance. Reports in 1 month. Sample copy $3.
Nonfiction: Features, informational, historical, interview, opinion, personal experience, photo feature and technical. Query or submit complete ms. Length: 500-2,500 words.
Photos: Used with or without accompanying ms. Query or submit contact sheet or prints. Pays $5 for 5×7 b&w prints when money is available. Captions required.

Associations

Association publications allow writers to write for national audiences while covering local stories. If your town has a Kiwanis, Lions or Rotary Club chapter, one of its projects might merit a story in the club's magazine. If you are a member of the organization, find out before you write an article if the publication pays members of the organization for stories; some associations do not. In addition, some association publications gather their own club information and rely on freelancers solely for outside features. Be sure to find out what these policies are before you submit a manuscript. Club-financed magazines that carry material not directly related to the group's activities are classified by their subject matter in the Consumer and Trade sections.

CALIFORNIA HIGHWAY PATROLMAN, California Association of Highway Patrolmen, 2030 V St., Sacramento CA 95818. (916)452-6751. Editor: Carol Perri. 80% freelance written. Will work with established or new/unpublished writers. Monthly magazine. Circ. 20,000. Pays on publication. Publishes ms an average of 1 year after acceptance. Buys one-time rights. Submit seasonal/holiday material 6 months in advance. Reports in 3 months. Sample copy and writer's guidelines for 9×12 SAE and 4 first class stamps.

Nonfiction: Publishes articles on transportation safety, driver education, consumer interest, California history, humor and general interest. "Topics can include autos, boats, bicycles, motorcycles, snowmobiles, recreational vehicles and pedestrian safety. We are also in the market for California travel pieces and articles on early California. We are *not* a technical journal for teachers and traffic safety experts, but rather a general interest publication geared toward the layman." Pays 2½¢/word.

Photos: "Illustrated articles always receive preference." Pays $5/b&w photo; no transparencies. Captions required.

Tips: "If a writer feels the article idea, length and style are consistent with our magazine, submit the manuscript for me to determine if I agree. We are especially looking for articles for specific holidays."

CATHOLIC FORESTER, Catholic Order of Foresters, P.O. Box 3012, 425 W. Shuman Blvd., Naperville IL 60566-7012. (312)983-4920. Editor: Barbara Cunningham. 35% freelance written. Prefers to work with published/established writers; works with a small number of new/unpublished writers each year. A bimonthly magazine of short, general interest articles and fiction for members of the Order, which is a fraternal insurance company. Family type audience, middle class. Estab. 1983. Circ. 150,000. **Pays on acceptance.** Publishes ms an average of 6 months after acceptance. Byline given. Buys one-time rights, second serial (reprint) rights, and simultaneous rights. Submit seasonal/holiday material 6 months in advance. Simultaneous and previously published submissions OK. Reports in 6 weeks on ms. Sample copy for 9 × 12 SAE and 73¢ postage; writer's guidelines #10 SASE.

Nonfiction: General interest; historical/nostalgic; humor; inspirational; interview/profile; new product; opinion; personal experience; photo feature; technical (depends on subject); and travel. "Short feature articles are most open to freelancers." No blatant sex nor anything too violent. Send complete ms. Length: 1,000-3,000 words. Pays 5¢/word; more for excellent ms. **No queries please!**

Photos: Prefers something of unusual interest or story-telling. State availability of photos, or send photos with ms. Reviews any size b&w and color prints. Payment to be determined. Captions, model releases, and identification of subjects required. Buys one-time rights.

Columns/Departments: Needs unusual items on what is going on in the world; new, interesting products, discoveries or happenings. Would like about 800 word opinion for our View Point column. Send complete ms. Length: 1,000 words. Payment to be determined.

Fiction: No queries please! Adventure, historical, humorous, mainstream, contemporary, mystery, religious (Catholic), suspense and western. No sex or extreme violence. Length: up to 3,000 words (prefers shorter fiction). Pays 5¢/word; more for excellent ms.

Poetry: Light verse and humorous. Submit maximum 5 poems. Payment to be determined.

Fillers: Cartoons, jokes, anecdotes and short humor. Length: 300-500 words. Payment to be determined.

COMEDY WRITERS ASSOCIATION NEWSLETTER, P.O. Box 023304, Brooklyn NY 11202-0066. (718)855-5057. Editor: Robert Makinson. 10% freelance written. Quarterly newsletter on comedy writing for association members. Estab. 1989. **Pays on acceptance.** Publishes ms an average of 3 months after acceptance. Byline given. Buys all rights. Reports in 2 weeks on queries; 1 month on mss. Sample copy $4; writer's guidelines for #10 SASE.

Nonfiction: How-to, humor, opinion, personal experience. "No exaggerations about the sales that you make and what you are paid. Be accurate." Query. Length: 250-500 words. Pays 3¢/word.

Photos: State availability of photos with submission. Offers no additional payment for photos accepted with ms.

Fillers: Facts. Length: 100 words maximum. Pays 3¢/word.

Tips: "The easiest way to be mentioned in the publication is to submit short jokes. (Payment is $1-3 per joke.)"

THE ELKS MAGAZINE, 425 W. Diversey, Chicago IL 60614. Editor: Fred D. Oakes. 50% freelance written. Prefers to work with published/established writers. Emphasizes general interest with family appeal. Magazine published 10 times/year. Estab. 1922. Circ. 1.5 million. **Pays on acceptance.** Buys first North American serial rights. Reports in 6 weeks. Sample copy and writer's guidelines for 9 × 12 SAE with 85¢ postage.

Nonfiction: Articles of information, business, contemporary life problems and situations, nostalgia, or just interesting topics, ranging from medicine, science, and history, to sports. "The articles should not just be a rehash of existing material. They must be fresh, thought-provoking, well-researched and documented." No fiction, political articles, fillers or verse. Buys 2-3 mss/issue. Query; no phone queries. Length: 1,500-3,000 words. Pays from $100.

Tips: "Requirements are clearly stated in our guidelines. Loose, wordy pieces are not accepted. A submission, following a query letter go-ahead, should include several b&w prints if the piece lends itself to illustration. We offer no additional payment for photos accepted with manuscripts. We expect to continue targeting our content to an older (50+) demographic."

FEDCO REPORTER, A Publication Exclusively for FEDCO Members, Box 2605, Terminal Annex, Los Angeles CA 90051. (213)946-2511. Editor: Michele A. Brunmier-Scianna. 90% freelance written. Works with a small number of new/unpublished writers each year. A monthly catalog/magazine for FEDCO department

store members. Estab. 1940. Circ. 2 million. **Pays on acceptance.** Publishes ms an average of 4 months after acceptance. Byline given. Offers $50 kill fee. Buys first rights. Query for electronic submissions. Reports in 6 weeks. Sample copy for 9 × 12 SAE with 4 first class stamps; writer's guidelines for SASE.
Nonfiction: General interest, historical. The magazine publishes material on historical events, personalities, anecdotes and little-known happenings (especially relating to California); general interest stories on common, everyday items with an unusual background or interesting use. Seasonal stories (especially relating to California); and stories about Southern California wildlife. No first person narrative. Buys 75 mss/year. Query with or without published clips, or send complete manuscript. Length: 450 words. Pays $100.
Photos: State availability of photos. Reviews b&w and color slides. Pays $25.
Tips: "We will publish excellent writing that is well-researched regardless of prior writings. Articles should be tightly written and not stray from subject."

KIWANIS, 3636 Woodview Trace, Indianapolis IN 46268. FAX: (317)879-0204. Executive Editor: Chuck Jonak. 85% of feature articles freelance written. Buys about 50 manuscripts annually. Magazine published 10 times/year for business and professional persons and their families. Estab. 1915. Circ. 300,000. **Pays on acceptance.** Buys first serial rights. Pays 40% kill fee. Publishes ms an average of 6 months after acceptance. Byline given. Reports within 2 months. Sample copy and writer's guidelines for 9 × 12 SAE and 5 first class stamps.
Nonfiction: Articles about social and civic betterment, small-business concerns, science, education, religion, family, sports, health, recreation, etc. Emphasis on objectivity, intelligent analysis and thorough research of contemporary issues. Positive tone preferred. Concise, lively writing, absence of cliches, and impartial presentation of controversy required. When applicable, information and quotation from international sources are required. Avoid writing strictly to a U.S. audience. Especially needs articles on business and professional topics that will directly assist the readers in their own businesses (generally independent retailers and companies of less than 25 employees) or careers. "We have a continuing need for articles of international interest. In addition, we are very interested in proposals that concern helping youth, particularly prenatal through age five: infant mortality, day care, developmentally appropriate education, early intervention for at-risk children, parent education, safety and pediatric trauma." Length: 2,500-3,000 words. Pays $400-1,000. "No fiction, personal essays, profiles, travel pieces, fillers or verse of any kind. A light or humorous approach is welcomed where the subject is appropriate and all other requirements are observed." Usually pays the expenses of writers on assignment. Query first. Must include SASE for response.
Photos: "We accept photos submitted with manuscripts. Our rate for a manuscript with good photos is higher than for one without." Model release and identification of subjects required. Buys one-time rights.
Tips: "We will work with any writer who presents a strong feature article idea applicable to our magazine's audience and who will prove he or she knows the craft of writing. First, obtain writer's guidelines and a sample copy. Study for general style and content. When querying, present detailed outline of proposed manuscript's focus, direction, and editorial intent. Indicate expert sources to be used for attribution, as well as article's tone and length. Present a well-researched, smoothly written manuscript that contains a 'human quality' with the use of anecdotes, practical examples, quotations, etc."

THE LION, 300 22nd St., Oak Brook IL 60521-8842. (708)571-5466. Editor-in-Chief: Mark C. Lukas. Senior Editor: Robert Kleinfelder. 35% freelance written. Works with a small number of new/unpublished writers each year. Covers service club organization for Lions Club members and their families. Monthly magazine. Estab. 1918. Circ. 670,000. **Pays on acceptance.** Publishes ms an average of 5 months after acceptance. Buys all rights. Byline given. Phone queries OK. Reports in 2 weeks. Free sample copy and writer's guidelines.
Nonfiction: Informational (stories of interest to civic-minded individuals) and photo feature (must be of a Lions Club service project). No travel, biography, or personal experiences. No sensationalism. Prefers anecdotes in articles. Buys 4 mss/issue. Query. Length: 500-2,200. Pays $50-750. Sometimes pays the expenses of writers on assignment.
Photos: Purchased with or without accompanying ms or on assignment. Captions required. Query for photos. B&w and color glossies at least 5 × 7 or 35mm color slides. Total purchase price for ms includes payment for photos, accepted with ms. "Be sure photos are clear and as candid as possible."
Tips: "Incomplete details on how the Lions involved actually carried out a project and poor quality photos are the most frequent mistakes made by writers in completing an article assignment for us. We are geared increasingly to an international audience."

For explanation of symbols, see the Key to Symbols and Abbreviations on Page 5. For unfamiliar words, see the Glossary.

THE MODERN WOODMEN, Public Relations Department, Mississippi River at 17th St., Rock Island IL 61201. (309)786-6481. Editor: Gloria Bergh. Address manuscripts to Sandy Howell, staff writer. 5-10% freelance written. Works with both published and new writers. "Our publication is for families who are members of Modern Woodmen of America. Modern Woodmen is a fraternal life insurance society, and most of our members live in smaller communities or rural areas throughout the United States. Various age groups read the magazine." Quarterly magazine. Circ. 350,000. Not copyrighted. **Pays on acceptance.** Keeps a file of good manuscripts to meet specific future needs and to balance content. Buys one-time rights or second serial (reprint) rights to material. Simultaneous submissions OK. Reports in 1 month if SASE included. Sample copy and guidelines for 9 × 12 SAE and 2 first class stamps; writer's guidelines for #10 SASE.

Nonfiction: For children and adults. "We seek lucid style and rich content. We need manuscripts that center on family-oriented subjects, human development, and educational topics."

Fiction: "Publishes an occasional fiction story for children and teens. We stress plot and characterization. A moral is a pleasant addition, but not required." Length: about 1,200 words. Pays $50 minimum.

Tips: "We want articles that appeal to young families, emphasize family interaction, community involvement, and family life. We also consider educational, historical, patriotic, and humorous articles. We don't want religious articles, teen romances, or seasonal material. Focus on people, whether the article is about families or is educational, historical or patriotic or humorous."

MOOSE MAGAZINE, Loyal Order of Moose, Supreme Lodge Building, Mooseheart IL 60539. (708)859-2000. Managing Editor: Raymond Dickow. A monthly (10 issues/year) fraternal magazine. "Distributed to men, ages 21 and older, who are members of 2,300 Moose lodges located throughout the U.S. and Canada." Estab. 1912. Circ. 1.3 million. **Pays on acceptance.** Byline given. Buys first North American serial rights. Submit seasonal/holiday material 4 months in advance. Reports in 5 weeks on mss. Free sample copy and writer's guidelines.

Nonfiction: General interest, historical/nostalgic and sports. No politics or religion. Send complete ms. Length: 1,000-2,000 words. Pays $200-1,000 for unsolicited articles.

Photos: Send photos with submission. Offers no additional payment for photos accepted with ms.

Tips: Freelancers can best break in at this publication with "feature articles involving outdoor sports (fishing, hunting, camping) as well as golf, bowling, baseball, football, etc., and with articles of general interest reflective of community and family living in addition to those of nostalgic interest. Features should include anecdotes and provide the kind of information that is interesting, educational, and entertaining to our readers. Style of writing should show rather than tell. Submit appropriate photo(s) with manuscript whenever possible."

THE NEIGHBORHOOD WORKS, Resources for Urban Communities, Center for Neighborhood Technology, 2125 West North Ave., Chicago IL 60647. (312)278-4800. FAX: (312)278-3840. Editor: Mary O'Connell. 15-25% freelance written. A bimonthly magazine on community organizing, housing, energy, environmental and economic issues affecting city neighborhoods. "Writers must understand the importance of empowering people in low- and moderate-income city neighborhoods to solve local problems in housing, environment and local economy." Estab. 1978. Circ. 2,500. Pays on publication. Publishes ms an average of 2 months after acceptance. Byline given. Buys all rights. Submit seasonal/holiday material 2 months in advance. Previously published submissions OK. Reports in 1 month on queries; 2 months on mss. Sample copy and writer's guidelines for 9 × 12 SAE and 2 first class stamps.

Nonfiction: Exposes, historical (neighborhood history), how-to (each issue has "reproducible feature" on such topics as organizing a neighborhood block watch, a community garden, recycling, etc.), interview/profile ("of someone active on one of our issues"), personal experience ("in our issue areas, e.g, community organizing"), technical (on energy conservation and alternative energy, environmental issues). Buys 6-10 mss/year. Query with or without published clips or send complete ms. Length: 750-2,000 words. Pays $100-500. "We pay professional writers (people who make a living at it). We don't pay nonprofessionals and students but offer them a free subscription." Pays expenses of writers on assignment by previous agreement.

Photos: State availability of photos with submission. Reviews contact sheets and prints. Offers $10-35/photo. Captions and identification of subjects required. Buys one-time rights.

Columns/Departments: Reproducible features (how-to articles on issues of interest to neighborhood organizations), 1,000-2,000 words. Query with published clips. Pays $100-250.

Tips: "We are increasingly interested in stories from cities other than Chicago (our home base)."

‡**THE OPTIMIST MAGAZINE,** Optimist International, 4494 Lindell Blvd., St. Louis MO 63108. (314)371-6000. FAX: (314)371-6006. Editor: Gary S. Bradley. 10% freelance written. Monthly magazine about the work of Optimist clubs and members for the 170,000 members of the Optimist clubs in the United States and Canada. Circ. 170,000. **Pays on acceptance.** Publishes ms an average of 4 months after acceptance. Buys first North American serial rights. Submit seasonal material 3 months in advance. Reports in 1 week. Sample copy and writer's guidelines for 9 × 12 SAE and 4 first class stamps.

Nonfiction: "We want articles about the activities of local Optimist clubs. These volunteer community-service clubs are constantly involved in projects, aimed primarily at helping young people. With over 4,000 Optimist clubs in the U.S. and Canada, writers should have ample resources. Some large metropolitan areas boast several dozen clubs. We are also interested in feature articles on individual club members who have in some way distinguished themselves, either in their club work or their personal lives. Good photos for all articles are a plus and can mean a bigger check. General interest articles are also considered." Buys 1-2 mss/issue. Query. "Submit a letter that conveys your ability to turn out a well-written article and tells exactly what the scope of the article will be and whether photos are available." Length: 1,000-1,500 words. Pays $150 and up.

Photos: State availability of photos. Payment negotiated. Captions preferred. Buys all rights. "No mug shots or people lined up against the wall shaking hands."

Tips: "Find out what the Optimist clubs in your area are doing, then find out if we'd be interested in an article on a specific club project. All of our clubs are eager to talk about what they're doing. Just ask them and you'll probably have an article idea."

PERSPECTIVE, Pioneer Clubs, Division of Pioneer Ministries, Inc., P.O. Box 788, Wheaton IL 60189-0788. (312)293-1600. Editor: Rebecca Powell Parat. 15% freelance written. Works with a number of new/unpublished writers each year. "All subscribers are volunteer leaders of clubs for girls and boys in grades K-12. Clubs are sponsored by local churches throughout North America." Quarterly magazine. Circ. 24,000. **Pays on acceptance.** Publishes ms an average of 8 months after acceptance. Buys first North American serial rights and second serial (reprint) rights to material originally published elsewhere. Submit seasonal/holiday material 9 months in advance. Simultaneous submissions OK. Reports in 6 weeks. Writer's packet for 9 × 12 SAE and $1.50; includes writer's guidelines and sample magazine.

Nonfiction: Informational (relationship skills, leadership skills); inspirational (stories of leaders and children in Pioneer Clubs); interview (Christian education leaders, club leaders); personal experience (of club leaders). Buys 8-12 mss/year. Byline given. Query. Length: 500-1,500 words. Pays $25-75. Sometimes pays expenses of writers on assignment.

Columns/Departments: Storehouse (game, activity, outdoor activity, service project suggestions — all related to club projects for any age between grades K-12). Buys 4-6 mss/year. Submit complete ms. Length: 150-250 words. Pays $8-15.

Tips: "We only assign major features to writers who have proven previously that they know us and our constituency. Submit articles directly related to club work, practical in nature, i.e., ideas for leader training in communication, discipline, teaching skills. They must have practical application. We want substance — not ephemeral ideas. In addition to a summary of the article idea and evidence that the writer has knowledge of the subject, we want evidence that the author understands our purpose and philosophy."

RECREATION NEWS, Official Publication of the League of Federal Recreation Associations, Inc., Icarus Publishers, Inc., Box 32335, Washington DC 20007. (202)965-6960. Editor: Sam Polson. 85% freelance written. A monthly guide to leisure activities for federal workers covering outdoor recreation, travel, fitness and indoor pastimes. Estab. 1979. Circ. 100,000. Pays on publication. Publishes ms an average of 6 months after acceptance. Byline given. Offers 20% kill fee on 4th assignment (first 3 on speculation). Buys first rights and second serial (reprint) rights. Submit seasonal/holiday material 8 months in advance. Simultaneous queries and simultaneous and previously published submissions OK. Reports in 1 month. Sample copy and writer's guidelines for 9 × 12 SAE with $1.05 postage.

Nonfiction: Lynne Russillo, articles editor. General interest and travel (on recreation, outdoors); historical/nostalgic (Washington-related); and personal experience (with recreation, life in Washington). Special issues feature skiing (December); Chesapeake Bay (June); education (August). Buys 45 mss/year. Query with clips of published work. Length: 500-3,000 words. Pays $35-300. Sometimes pays the expenses of writers on assignment.

Photos: Photo editor. State availability of photos with query letter or ms. Reviews contact sheets, transparencies, and 5 × 7 b&w prints. Pays $25-40/b&w photo ordered from contact sheet, $50-125 for color. Captions and identification of subjects required.

Columns/Departments: Columns, departments editor. Books (recreation, outdoors, hobbies, travel); Good sport (first person sports/recreation column); Reflections (humor). Buys 15-20 mss/year. Query with clips of published work or send complete ms (on speculation only). Length: 500-1,200 words. Pays $25-75.

Tips: "Our writers generally have a few years of professional writing experience and their work runs to the lively and conversational. We'll need more manuscripts in a wider range of recreational topics, including the off-beat. The areas of our publication most open to freelancers are general articles on travel and sports, both participational and spectator, also historic in the DC area."

REVIEW, A Publication of North American Benefit Association, 1338 Military St., P.O. Box 5020, Port Huron MI 48061-5020. (313)985-5191, ext. 77. Editor: Virginia E. Farmer. Associate Editor: Patricia Pfeifer. 10-15% freelance written. Prefers to work with published/established writers, and works with a small number of new/unpublished writers each year. Quarterly trade journal on insurance/fraternal deeds. Family magazine.

Estab. 1894. Circ. 42,000. **Pays on acceptance.** Publishes ms an average of 2 years after acceptance. Byline given. Not copyrighted. Buys one-time rights, simultaneous rights, and second serial (reprint) rights. Submit seasonal/holiday material 6 months in advance. Simultaneous and previously published submissions OK. Reports in 2 months. Sample copy for 9 × 12 SAE with 4 first class stamps; writer's guidelines for #10 SASE.

Nonfiction: General interest, nature, historical/nostalgic, how-to (improve; self-help); humor; inspirational; personal experience; and photo feature. No political/controversial. Buys 4-10 mss/year. Send complete ms. Length: 600-1,500 words. Pays 3-5/word.

Photos: Prefers ms with photos if available. Send photos with ms. Reviews 5 × 7 or 8 × 10 b&w prints and color slides or prints. Pays $10-15. Model release and identification of subjects required. Buys one-time rights.

Fiction: Adventure, humorous and mainstream. Buys 2-4 mss/year. Send complete ms. Length: 600-1,500 words. Pays 3-5¢/word. "No queries please."

Tips: "We like articles with accompanying photos; articles that warm the heart; stories with gentle, happy humor. Give background of writer as to education and credits. Manuscripts and art material will be carefully considered, but received only with the understanding that North American Benefit Association shall not be responsible for loss or injury."

THE ROTARIAN, Official Magazine of Rotary International, 1560 Sherman Ave., Evanston IL 60201. (708)866-3000. FAX: (708)328-8554. Editor: Willmon L. White. 50% freelance written. Works with published and unpublished writers. For Rotarian business and professional men and women and their families; for schools, libraries, hospitals, etc. Monthly. Estab. 1911. Circ. 538,000. Usually buys all rights. **Pays on acceptance.** Query preferred. Reports in 1 month. Sample copy for SAE and 7 first class stamps; writer's guidelines for #10 SASE.

Nonfiction: "The field for freelance articles is in the general interest category. These run the gamut from guidelines for daily living to such concerns as AIDS, famine and conservation. Recent articles have dealt with high definition TV, airline terrorism, illiteracy and franchising. Articles should appeal to an international audience and should in some way help Rotarians help other people. An article may increase a readers' understanding of world affairs, thereby making them better world citizens. It may educate them in civic matters, thus helping them improve their towns. It may help them to become better employers, or better human beings. We are interested in articles on unusual Rotary club projects or really unusual Rotarians. We carry debates and symposiums, but are careful to show more than one point of view. We present arguments for effective politics and business ethics, but avoid expose and muckraking. Controversy is welcomed if it gets our readers to think but does not offend minority, ethnic or religious groups. In short, the rationale of the organization is one of hope and encouragement and belief in the power of individuals talking and working together." Query preferred. Length: 1,000-1,800 words. Payment varies. Seldom pays the expenses of writers on assignment.

Photos: Purchased with mss or with captions only. Prefers 2¼ × 2¼ or larger color transparencies, but also uses 35mm. B&w prints and photo essays. Vertical shots preferred for covers. Scenes of international interest. Color cover.

‡THE SAMPLE CASE, The Order of United Commercial Travelers of America, 632 N. Park St., Box 159019, Columbus OH 43215. (614)228-3276. Editor: Sam Perdue. Bimonthly magazine covering news for members of the United Commercial Travelers. Emphasizes fraternalism for its officers and active membership. Estab. 1889. Circ. 140,000. Pays on publication. Buys one-time rights. Submit seasonal/holiday material 6 months in advance. Simultaneous queries and submissions OK. Reports in 3 months. Free sample copy.

Nonfiction: Articles on travel destination (cities and regions in the U.S. and Canada); food/cuisine; health/fitness/safety; hobbies/entertainment; fraternal/civic activities; business finance/insurance.

Photos: David Knapp, art director. State availability of photos with ms. Pays minimum $20 for 5 × 7 b&w or larger prints; $30 for 35mm or larger transparencies used inside (more for cover). Captions required.

THE SONS OF NORWAY VIKING, Sons of Norway, 1455 W. Lake St., Minneapolis MN 55408. (612)827-3611. FAX: (612)827-0658. Editor: Gaelyn Beal. 50% freelance written. Prefers to work with published/established writers. A monthly membership magazine for the Sons of Norway, a fraternal and cultural organization, covering Norwegian culture, heritage, history, Norwegian-American topics, modern Norwegian society, genealogy and travel. "Our audience is Norwegian-Americans (middle-aged or older) with strong interest in their heritage and anything Norwegian. Many have traveled to Norway." Estab. 1903. Circ. 70,000. Pays on publication. Publishes ms an average of 8 months after acceptance. Byline given. Offers $25 kill fee. Buys first North American serial rights and second serial (reprint) rights. Submit seasonal/holiday material 6 months in advance. Previously published submissions OK. Reports in 6 weeks on queries; 8 weeks on mss. Free sample copy and writer's guidelines on request.

Nonfiction: General interest, historical/nostalgic, humor, interview/profile, and travel—all having a Norwegian angle. "Articles should not be personal impressions nor a colorless spewing of facts, but well-researched and conveyed in a warm and audience-involving manner. Does it entertain *and* inform?" Buys 30 mss/year. Query. Length: 1,500-3,000 words. Pays $75-250.

Photos: Reviews transparencies and prints. Pays $10-20/photo; pays $100 for cover color photo. Identification of subjects required. Buys one-time rights.
Tips: "Show familiarity with Norwegian culture and subject matter. Our readers are somewhat knowledgeable about Norway and quick to note misstatements. Articles about modern Norway are most open to freelancers—the society, industries—but historical periods also okay. Call before a scheduled trip to Norway to discuss subjects to research or interview while there."

THE TOASTMASTER, Toastmasters International, 23182 Arroyo Vista, Rancho Santa Margarita CA 92688 or P.O. Box 9052, Mission Viejo, CA 92690-7052. (714)858-8255. FAX: (714)858-1207. Editor: Suzanne Frey. Associate Editor: Brian Richard. 50% freelance written. A monthly magazine on public speaking, leadership and club concerns. "This magazine is sent to members of Toastmasters International, a nonprofit educational association of men and women throughout the world who are interested in developing their communication and leadership skills. Members range from novice speakers to professional orators and come from a wide variety of backgrounds." Estab. 1932. Circ. 155,000. **Pays on acceptance.** Publishes ms an average of 8 months after acceptance. Byline given. Buys second serial (reprint) rights, first-time or all rights. Simultaneous and previously published submissions OK. Query for electronic submissions. Reports in 2 weeks on queries; 3 weeks on mss. Sample copy for 9 × 12 SAE and 2 first class stamps; writer's guidelines for #10 SASE.
Nonfiction: Book excerpts, how-to (communications related), humor (only if informative; humor cannot be off-color or derogatory), interview/profile (only if of a very prominent member or former member of Toastmasters International or someone who has a valuable perspective on communication and leadership). Buys 50 mss/year. Query. Length: 1,000-2,500 words. Pays $75-250. Sometimes pays expenses of writers on assignment. "Toastmasters members are requested to view their submissions as contributions to the organization. Sometimes asks for book excerpts and reprints without payment, but original contribution from individuals outside Toastmasters will be paid for at stated rates."
Photos: Reviews b&w prints. Captions are required. Buys all rights.
Tips: "We are looking primarily for 'how-to' articles on subjects from the broad fields of communications and leadership which can be directly applied by our readers in their self-improvement and club programming efforts. Concrete examples are useful. Avoid sexist or nationalist language."

VFW MAGAZINE, Veterans of Foreign War of the United States, Suite 523, 34th and Broadway, Kansas City MO 64111. (816)968-1171. FAX: (816)968-1157. Editor: Rich Kolb. 75% freelance written. Monthly magazine on veterans' affairs. "*VFW Magazine* goes to its members worldwide, all having served honorably in the armed forces overseas during periods of conflict or war and earning a campaign medal." Circ. 2.1 million. **Pays on acceptance.** Publishes ms 6 months after acceptance. Offers 100% kill fee. Buys first rights. Submit seasonal/holiday material 6 months in advance. Query for electronic submissions. Reports in 1 month on queries; 6 weeks on mss. Free sample copy.
Nonfiction: Interview/profile and veterans' affairs. Buys 10-15 mss/year. Query. Length: 500-3,000 words. Pays $200-750.
Photos: Send photos with submission. Reviews contact sheets, negatives, transparencies and prints. Captions, model releases and identification of subjects required. Buys all rights.

WOODMEN OF THE WORLD MAGAZINE, 1700 Farnam St., Omaha NE 68102. (402)342-1890, ext. 302. Editor: Leland A. Larson. 20% freelance written. Works with a small number of new/unpublished writers each year. Published by Woodmen of the World Life Insurance Society for "people of all ages in all walks of life. We have both adult and child readers from all types of American families." Monthly. Circ. 470,000. Not copyrighted. Buys 20 mss/year. **Pays on acceptance.** Byline given. Buys one-time rights. Publishes ms an average of 2 months after acceptance. Will consider simultaneous submissions. Submit seasonal material 3 months in advance. Reports in 5 weeks. Free sample copy.Writer's guidelines for #10 SASE.
Nonfiction: "General interest articles which appeal to the American family—travel, history, art, new products, how-to, sports, hobbies, food, home decorating, family expenses, etc. Because we are a fraternal benefit society operating under a lodge system, we often carry stories on how a number of people can enjoy social or recreational activities as a group. No special approach required. We want more 'consumer type' articles, humor, historical articles, think pieces, nostalgia, photo articles." Buys 15-24 unsolicited mss/year. Submit complete ms. Length: 2,000 words or less. Pays $10 minimum, 10¢/word.
Photos: Purchased with or without mss; captions optional "but suggested." Uses 8 × 10 glossy prints, 4x5 transparencies ("and possibly down to 35mm"). Payment "depends on use." For b&w photos, pays $25 for cover, $10 for inside. Color prices vary according to use and quality. Minimum of $25 for inside use; up to $150 for covers.
Fiction: Humorous and historical short stories. Length: 1,500 words or less. Pays "$10 minimum or 10¢/word."

Astrology, Metaphysical and New Age

A number of new magazines have started publication in this category during the past few years, but many also have gone out of business. Magazines in this section carry articles ranging from the occult to holistic healing. The following publications regard astrology, psychic phenomena, metaphysical experiences and related subjects as sciences or as objects of serious study. Each has an individual personality and approach to these phenomena. If you want to write for these publications, be sure to read them carefully.

BODY, MIND & SPIRIT, Island Publishing Co. Inc., P.O. Box 701, Providence RI 02901. (401)351-4320. FAX: (401)272-5767. Publisher and Editor-in-Chief: Paul Zuromski. Editor: Carol Kramer. 75% freelance written. Prefers to work with published/established writers; works with many new/unpublished writers each year. Bimonthly magazine covering New Age, natural living, and metaphysical topics. "Our editorial is slanted toward assisting people in their self-transformation process to improve body, mind and spirit. We take a holistic approach to the subjects we present. They include spirituality, health, healing, nutrition, new ideas, interviews with new age people, travel, books and music. We avoid sensationalizing and try to present material objectively to allow the individual to decide what to accept or believe." Estab. 1982. Circ. 150,000. Pays on publication. Publishes ms an average of 6 months after acceptance. Byline given. Offers negotiable kill fee. Buys first North American serial rights. Submit seasonal/holiday material 8 months in advance. Simultaneous queries OK. Reports in 2 months on queries; 4 months on mss. Sample copy for 9 × 12 SAE and $1.45 postage; writer's guidelines for #10 SASE stamp.
Nonfiction: Book excerpts, historical/nostalgic (research on the roots of the New Age movement and related topics); how-to (develop psychic abilities, health, healing, proper nutrition, etc., based on holistic approach); inspirational; interview/profile (of New Age people); new product (or services offered in this field—must be unique and interesting); opinion (on any New Age, natural living or metaphysical topic); and travel (example: to Egypt based on past life research). Don't send "My life as a psychic" or "How I became psychic" articles. Buys 30-40 mss/year. Query with published clips. Length: 2,000-5,000 words. Pays $100-300. Sometimes pays the expenses of writers on assignment.
Photos: State availability of photos with query. Pays $10-20 for b&w contact sheets. Captions, model releases and identification of subjects required. Buys one-time rights.
Fillers: Clippings, anecdotes or newsbreaks on any interesting or unusual New Age, natural living, or metaphysical topic. Buys 10-20 fillers/year. Length: 500 words maximum. Pays $10-40.
Tips: "Examine our unique approach to the subject matter. We avoid sensationalism and overly strange or unbelievable stories. Reading an issue should give you a good idea of our approach to the subject."

FATE, Llewellyn Worlwide, Ltd., P.O. Box 64383, St. Paul MN 55164-0383. FAX: (612)291-1908. Editor: Donald Michael Kraig. 70% freelance written. Estab. 1948. Buys all rights; occasionally first serial rights only. Byline given. Pays on publication. Sample copy $3. Query. Reports in 2 months.
Nonfiction and Fillers: Personal psychic and magical experiences, 300-500 words. Pays $25. Articles on parapsychology, occultism, witchcraft, magic, spiritual healing, flying saucers, new frontiers of science, and mystical aspects of ancient civilizations, 2,000-3,000 words. *Must* include complete authenticating details. Prefers interesting accounts of single events rather than roundups. "We very frequently accept manuscripts from new writers; the majority are individual's first-person accounts of their own psychic/magical/spiritual experiences. We do need to have all details, where, when, why, who and what, included for complete documentation. We ask for a notarized statement attesting to truth of the article." Pays minimum of 5¢/word. Fillers must be be fully authenticated also, and on similar topics. Length: 100-300 words.
Photos: Buys good glossy prints with mss. Pays $10.
Tips: "For the past several years *Fate* has moved toward archeological and debunking types of articles. We will be moving back to the original concept of *Fate*—looking at the unusual in the world—the things that science doesn't like to talk about. Our focus will be more New Age-oriented, including more parapsychology, spirituality, divination, magic, UFO's, etc."

NEW AGE JOURNAL, Rising Star Associates, 342 Western Ave., Brighton MA 02135. (617)787-2005. Editor: Phillip M. Whitten. Editorial Manager: Jennifer King. 35% freelance written. Works with a small number of new/unpublished writers each year. A bimonthly magazine emphasizing "personal fulfillment and social change. The audience we reach is college-educated, social-service/hi-tech oriented, 25-45 years of age, concerned about social values, humanitarianism and balance in personal life." Payment negotiated. Publishes ms an average of 5 months after acceptance. Byline given. Offers 25% kill fee. Buys first North American serial rights and reprint rights. Submit seasonal/holiday material 6 months in advance. Simultaneous submissions OK. Reports in 2 months on queries. Sample copy for 9 × 12 SAE and $5. Writer's guidelines for letter-size SAE with 1 first class stamp.
Nonfiction: Book excerpts, exposé, general interest, how-to (travel on business, select a computer, reclaim land, plant a garden, behavior, trend pieces), humor, inspirational, interview/profile, new product, food, sci-tech, nutrition, holistic health, education and personal experience. Buys 60-80 mss/year. Query with published clips. "Written queries only—no phone calls. The process of decision making takes time and involves more than one editor. An answer cannot be given over the phone." Length: 500-4,000 words. Pays $50-2,500. Pays the expenses of writers on assignment.

Photos: State availability of photos with submission. Model releases and identification of subjects required. Buys one-time rights.
Columns/Departments: Body/Mind; Reflections; First Person. Buys 60-80 mss/year. Query with published clips. Length: 750-1,500 words. Pays $100-400.
Tips: "Submit short, specific news items to the Upfront department. Query first with clips. A query is one to two paragraphs—if you need more space than that to *present* the idea, then you don't have a clear grip on it. The next open area is columns: First Person and Reflections often take first-time contributors. Read the magazine and get a sense of type of writing run in these two columns. In particular we are interested in seeing inspirational, first-person pieces that highlight an engaging idea, experience or issue. We are also looking for new cutting edge thinking."

NEW REALITIES, Oneness of Self, Mind, and Body, Heldref Publications, 4000 Albemarle St. NW, Washington DC 20016. (202)362-6445. FAX: (202)537-0287. Editor: Neal Vahle. Assistant Editor: Mark Peters. 50% freelance written. A bimonthly magazine of new age interests. "Our emphasis is on the positive elements of life, those things that add, rather than detract, from people's lives." Estab. 1986. Circ. 23,000. Pays on publication. Byline given. Buys first North American serial rights, first rights or one-time rights. Submit seasonal/holiday material 4 months in advance. Simultaneous and previously published submissions OK. Reports in 1 month. Sample copy for $2; writer's guidelines for #10 SASE.
Nonfiction: Book excerpts, general interest, how-to, inspirational, interview/profile. No fiction, poetry, or purely reflective personal experience pieces. Buys 40 mss/year. Query with or without published clips, or send complete ms. Length: 1,000-5,000 words. Pays up to $300 for unsolicited articles. Rarely assigns articles. Sometimes pays expenses of writers on assignment.
Photos: State availability of photos with submission. Reviews contact sheets and any size prints. Offers $10-100 per photo (cover shots more). Identification of subjects required. Buys one-time rights.
Columns/Departments: Sights and Sounds (reviews of books, audio and video cassettes) 300-500 words; Tools for Transformation (experiential exercises, concrete tips on holistic living; Food for Thought (food and health, nutritional tips) 2,500 words; Vacations and Sacred Sites (holistic health spas, transformative travel) 2,500 words. Buys 30 mss/year. Send complete ms. Length: 250-2,500 words. Pays $10-100.
Tips: "We appreciate seeing the entire manuscript, along with clips of other work. We look for a journalistic, third-party, concrete approach to what usually are rather subjective topics."

RAINBOW CITY EXPRESS, Adventures on the Spiritual Path, Box 8447, Berkeley CA 94707. Editor: Helen B. Harvey. 50-75% freelance written. Quarterly magazine on "spiritual awakening and evolving consciousness, especially feminist spirituality and women's issues. We take an eclectic, mature and innovative approach to the topics of spiritual awakening and evolution of consciousness. A positive, constructive, healing tone is required, not divisive, separatist slant." Estab. 1988. Circ. 1,000. Pays on publication. Byline given. Buys first North American serial rights or second serial (reprint) rights. Submit seasonal/holiday material 4-6 months in advance. Previously published (only when full publishing information accompanies ms showing where previously published) submissions OK. Reports in 2 months on queries; 3 months on mss. Sample copy for $6; writer's guidelines for #10 SASE.
Nonfiction: Book excerpts, essays, general interest, historical/nostalgic, how-to, humor, inspirational, interview/profile, opinion, personal experience, religious, travel. "No get-rich-quick or how-to channel spirits, how-to manipulate the cosmos/others, occult/voodoo/spellcasting diatribes and no glorification of victimization/scapegoating or addictions." Buys 50-100 mss/year. Query with or without published clips, or send complete ms. Length: 250-2,000 words. Pays $5-50 per piece, negotiated individually.
Columns/Departments: Book Reviews (spirituality, goddess consciousness, New Age topics), 250-500 words; Readers' Forum. Acquires 30 mss/year. Send complete ms. Pays in contributor copies.
Fiction: Adventure, fantasy, historical, religious. "Fiction should relate directly to our slant which is about spiritual/consciousness evolution. No science fiction, thriller, sex, drugs or violence mss." Acquires about 12 mss/year. Query. Length: 500-1,000 words. Pays in contributor copies.
Poetry: Avant-garde, free verse, haiku, light verse, traditional. No rhyming poetry. Acquires about 30/year. Submit 3 poems maximum. Length: 8-30 lines.
Fillers: Anecdotes, short humor. "Fillers must relate to our spirituality slant."
Tips: "We feature true life experiences and accounts of spiritual awakenings/attendant phenomena, and consciousness evolution. Readers/writers who have experienced some of these phenomena and know what they're talking about are likely to be well received. We are particularly interested in actual experiences with Kundalini activation and archetypal stirring. We aim to demonstrate the often unsuspected connections between spiritual awakening and everyday realities. Note: *Please* obtain sample copy prior to submitting mss! No mss read or returned without SASE. Also sponsors writing contests. Send SASE for details. All material submitted on speculation."

TRANSFORMATION TIMES, Life Resources Unlimited, P.O. Box 425, Beavercreek OR 97004. (503)632-7141. Editor: Connie L. Faubel. Managing Editor: E. James Faubel. 100% freelance written. A tabloid covering new age, metaphysics, and natural health, published 10 times/year. Estab. 1983. Circ. 8,000. Pays on publication. Publishes ms an average of 2 months after acceptance. Byline given. Buys one-time rights. Submit seasonal/holiday material 2 months in advance. Simultaneous and previously published submissions OK. Query for electronic submissions. Sample copy and writer's guidelines for 9×12 SAE and 5 first class stamps.

Nonfiction: Book excerpts, inspirational, interview/profile, women's issues, metaphysical. "No articles with emphasis on negative opinions and ideas." Buys 60 mss/year. Send complete ms. Length: 500-1,000 words. Pays 1¢/word.

Photos: Send photos with submission. Reviews 3×5 prints. Offers $3/photo. Captions and identification of subjects required. Buys one-time rights.

Columns/Departments: Woman's Way (women's issues) 500-1,000 words. Buys 20 mss/year. Send complete ms. Pays 1¢/word.

Tips: "In addition to present interests, we plan on adding articles on environmental quality issues and socially responsible investing."

‡**UFO UNIVERSE**, Condor Books, 351 W. 54 St., New York NY 10019. (212)586-4432. Editor: Tim Beckley. 80% freelance written. "We want well-researched, well-thought-out stories concerning recent events of interest to UFO buffs." Estab. 1988. Pays on publication. Publishes ms an average of 6 months after acceptance. Byline given. Buys first rights and second serial (reprint) rights. Reports in 2 months. Sample copy for $4.

Nonfiction: Book excerpts, personal experience. Buys 85 mss/year. Query; send complete ms. Length: 2,000-3,500 words. Pays $50-100 for assigned article.

Photos: Send photos with submission. Reviews transparencies and prints. Offers $10-20/photo. Captions and identification of subjects required.

Columns/Departments: Asteroid Beat. Buys 10 mss/year. Send complete ms. Pays $10-15.

Automotive and Motorcycle

Publications in this section detail the maintenance, operation, performance, racing and judging of automobiles and recreational vehicles. Publications that treat vehicles as means of shelter instead of as a hobby or sport are classified in the Travel, Camping and Trailer category. Journals for service station operators and auto and motorcycle dealers are located in the Trade Auto and Truck section.

AMERICAN MOTORCYCLIST, American Motorcyclist Association, P.O. Box 6114, Westerville OH 43081-6114. (614)891-2425. Executive Editor: Greg Harrison. For "enthusiastic motorcyclists, investing considerable time and money in the sport. We emphasize the motorcyclist, not the vehicle." Monthly magazine. Circ. 140,000. Pays on publication. Rights purchased vary with author and material. Pays 25-50% kill fee. Byline given. Query with SASE. Submit seasonal/holiday material 4 months in advance. Reports in 1 month. Free sample copy and writer's guidelines.

Nonfiction: How-to (different and/or unusual ways to use a motorcycle or have fun on one); historical (the heritage of motorcycling, particularly as it relates to the AMA); interviews (with interesting personalities in the world of motorcycling); photo feature (quality work on any aspect of motorcycling); and technical or how-to articles. No product evaluations or stories on motorcycling events not sanctioned by the AMA. Buys 20-25 mss/year. Query. Length: 500 words minimum. Pays minimum $4.50/published column inch.

Photos: Purchased with or without accompanying ms, or on assignment. Captions required. Query. Pays $20 minimum per published photo.

Tips: "Accuracy and reliability are prime factors in our work with freelancers. We emphasize the rider, not the motorcycle itself. It's always best to query us first and the further in advance the better to allow for scheduling."

AMERICAN WOMAN ROAD RIDING, Ladylike Enterprises, Inc. #5, 1038 7th St., Santa Monica CA 90403. (213)395-1171. Publisher: Courtney Caldwell. Editor: Jamie Elvidge. 40% freelance written. Bimonthly magazine on women in motorcycling. "We are geared towards career, professional, and/or goal-oriented women who enjoy the sport of motorcycling. The magazine is upscale and is dedicated to image enhancement." Estab. 1988. Circ. 20,000. Pays on publication an average of 2 months after acceptance. Byline sometimes given. Buys first rights, second serial (reprint) rights or makes work-for-hire assignments. Submit seasonal/holiday material 4 months in advance. Photocopied and previously published submissions OK. Query for electronic submissions. Reports in 2 months. Free sample copy.

Nonfiction: Humor, inspirational, interview/profile, new product, photo feature, travel and biker friendly establishments, all motorcycle related. No articles depicting women in motorcycling or professions that are degrading, negative or not upscale. Buys 30 mss/year. Send complete ms. Length 250-1,000 words. Pays $30-50 for assigned articles; $20-35 for unsolicited articles. Sometimes pays expenses of writers on assignment.

Photos: Send photos with submission. Reviews contact sheets. Black and white or Kodachrome 64 preferred. Offers $10-50 per photo. Captions, model releases and identification of subjects required. Buys all rights.
Columns/Departments: Man of the Month (Highlight and profile select gentlemen who ride motorcycles and are making positive contributions to industry and community), 500-1,000 words.
Fillers: Anecdotes, facts, gags to illustrated by cartoonist, newsbreaks and short humor. Buys 12/year. Length: 25-100 words. Pays $10-25.
Tips: "It helps if the writer is into motorcycles. It is a special sport. If he/she doesn't ride, he/she should have a positive point of view of motorcycling and be willing to learn more about the subject. We are a 'people' type of publication more than a technical magazine. Positive attitudes wanted."

BRITISH CAR, P.O. Box 9099, Canoga Park CA 91309. (818)710-1234. FAX: (818)710-1877. Editor: Dave Destler. 50% freelance written. A bimonthly magazine covering British cars. "We focus upon the cars built in Britain, the people who buy them, drive them, collect them, love them. Writers must be among the aforementioned. Written by enthusiasts for enthusiasts." Estab. 1985. Circ. 30,000. Pays on publication. Publishes ms an average of 3 months after acceptance. Byline given. Buys all rights, unless other arrangements made. Submit seasonal/holiday material 4 months in advance. Query for electronic submissions. Reports in 1 month. Sample copy $2.95; writer's guidelines for #10 SASE.
Nonfiction: Historical/nostalgic; how-to (on repair or restoration of a specific model or range of models, new technique or process); humor (based upon a realistic nonfiction situation); interview/profile (famous racer, designer, engineer, etc.); photo feature and technical. "No submissions so specific as to appeal or relate to a very narrow range of readers; no submissions so general as to be out-of-place in a specialty publication. Buys 30 mss/year. Send complete ms. "Include SASE if submission is to be returned." Length: 750-4,500 words. Pays $2-5/column inch for assigned articles; pays $2-3/column inch for unsolicited articles.
Photos: Send photos with submission. Reviews transparencies and prints. Offers $15-75/photo. Captions and identification of subjects required. Buys all rights, unless otherwise arranged.
Columns/Departments: Update (newsworthy briefs of interest, not too timely for bimonthly publication), approximately 50-175 words. Buys 20 mss/year. Send complete ms.
Tips: "Thorough familiarity of subject is essential. *British Car* is read by experts and enthusiasts who can see right through superficial research. Facts are important, and must be accurate. Writers should ask themselves 'I know I'm interested in this story, but will most of *British Car's* readers appreciate it?'"

CAR AND DRIVER, 2002 Hogback Rd., Ann Arbor MI 48105. (313)971-3600. Editor: William Jeanes. For auto enthusiasts; college-educated, professional, median 24-35 years of age. Monthly magazine. Circ. 900,000. **Pays on acceptance.** Rights purchased vary with author and material. Buys all rights or first North American serial rights. "Unsolicited manuscripts are not accepted. Query letters may be addressed to the editor.
Nonfiction: Non-anecdotal articles about the more sophisticated treatment of autos and motor racing. Exciting, interesting cars. Automotive road tests, informational articles on cars and equipment; some satire and humor. Personalities, past and present, in the automotive industry and automotive sports. "Treat readers as intellectual equals. Emphasis on people as well as hardware." Informational, how-to, humor, historical, think articles, and nostalgia.
Photos: Black and white photos purchased with accompanying mss with no additional payment.
Tips: "It is best to start off with an interesting query and to stay away from nuts-and-bolts stuff since that will be handled in-house or by an acknowledged expert. Our goal is to be absolutely without flaw in our presentation of automotive facts, but we strive to be every bit as entertaining as we are informative."

CAR AUDIO AND ELECTRONICS, CurtCo Publishing, Suite 1600, 21700 Oxnard St., Woodland Hills CA 91367. (818)593-3900. FAX: (818)593-2274. Editor: William Neill. Managing Editor: Doug Newcomb. 80-90% freelance written. Monthly magazine on electronic products designed for cars. "We help people buy the best electronic products for their cars. The magazine is about electronics, how to buy, how to use, and so on: *CA&E* explains complicated things in simple ways. The articles are accurate, easy, and fun." Estab. 1988. Circ. 225,000. **Pays on acceptance.** Publishes ms an average of 3-5 months after acceptance. Byline given. Offers 50% kill fee. Buys all rights. Submit seasonal/holiday material 3-4 months in advance. Simultaneous submissions OK. Query for electronic submissions. Reports in 1 week on queries; 1 week on mss. Sample copy $3.95 with 9×12 SAE and 4 first class stamps; writer's guidelines for #10 SASE.
Nonfiction: How-to (buy electronics for your car), interview/profile, new product, opinion, photo feature and technical. Buys 60-70 mss/year. Query with or without published clips, or send complete ms. Length: 500-1,700 words. Pays $300-1,000. Sometimes pays expenses of writers on assignment.
Photos: Send photos with submission. Review transparencies, any size.
Fillers: Gags to be illustrated by cartoonist and cartoons. Pays $20-50.
Tips: "Write clearly and knowledgeably about car electronics."

CAR COLLECTOR/CAR CLASSICS, Classic Publishing, Inc., Suite 144, 8601 Dunwoody Pl., Atlanta GA 30350. Editor: Donald R. Peterson. 90% freelance written. Works with a small number of new/unpublished writers each year. Monthly magazine for people interested in all facets of collecting classic, milestone, antique, special interest and sports cars; also mascots, models, restoration, garaging, license plates and memorabilia. Estab. 1977. Circ. 35,000. Pays on cover date. Publishes ms an average of 4 months after acceptance. Buys first rights. Submit seasonal/holiday material 4 months in advance. Reports in 2 months. Sample copy for $2; writer's guidelines for #10 SASE.

Nonfiction: General interest, historical, how-to, humor, inspirational, interview, nostalgia, personal opinion, profile, photo feature, technical and travel—but must be automobile-related. Buys 50-75 mss/year; buys 24-36 unsolicited mss/year. Query with clips of published work. Length: 300-2,500 words. Pays 5¢/word minimum. Sometimes pays the expenses of writers on assignment.

Photos: "We have a continuing need for high-quality color positives (e.g., 2¼ or 35mm) *with* copy." State availability of photos with ms. Offers additional payment for photos with accompanying mss. Uses b&w glossy prints and transparencies. Pays a minimum of $75 for cover and centerfold color; $10 for inside color; $5 for inside b&w. Captions and model releases required.

Columns/Departments: "We rarely add a new columnist but we are open to suggestions." Buys 36 mss/year. Query with clips of published work. Length: 2,000 maximum; prefers 1,000-2,000 words. Pays 5¢/word minimum.

Tips: "The most frequent mistakes are made by writers who are writing to a 'Sunday supplement' audience rather than to a sophisticated audience of car collectors or who are submitting stories that are often too basic and assume no car knowledge at all on the part of the reader."

‡**CAR CRAFT**, Petersen Publishing Co., 8490 Sunset Blvd., Los Angeles CA 90069. (213)657-5100, ext. 345. Editor: Jim McGowan. For men and women, 18-34, "enthusiastic owners of 1949 and newer muscle cars." Monthly magazine. Circ. 400,000. Study past issues before making submissions or story suggestions. Pays generally on publication, on acceptance under special circumstances. Buys all rights. Buys 2-10 mss/year. Query.

Nonfiction: How-to articles ranging from the basics to fairly sophisticated automotive modifications. Drag racing feature stories and some general car features on modified late model automobiles. Especially interested in do-it-yourself automotive tips, suspension modifications, mileage improvers and even shop tips and homemade tools. Length: open. Pays $100-200/page.

Photos: Photos purchased with or without accompanying text. Captions suggested, but optional. Reviews 8×10 b&w glossy prints; 35mm or 2¼×2¼ color. Pays $30 for b&w, color negotiable. "Pay rate higher for complete story, i.e., photos, captions, headline, subtitle: the works, ready to go."

CLASSIC AUTO RESTORER, Fancy Publishing, Inc., P.O. Box 6050, Mission Viejo CA 92690. (714)855-8822. FAX: (714)855-3045. Editor: Steve Kimball. 85% freelance written. Bimonthly magazine on auto restoration. "Our readers own old cars and they work on them. We help our readers by providing as much practical, how-to information as we can about restoration and old cars." Estab. 1975. Pays on publication. Publishes an average of 3 months after acceptance. Offers $50 kill fee. Buys first North American serial rights or one-time rights. Submit seasonal/holiday material 4 months in advance. Query for electronic submissions. Reports in 2 weeks on queries. Sample copy $3.95; free writer's guidelines.

Nonfiction: How-to (auto restoration), new product, photo feature, technical and travel. Buys 60 mss/year. Query with or without published clips, or send complete ms. Length: 200-5,000 words. Pays $100-500 for assigned articles; $75-500 for unsolicited articles.

Photos: Send photos with submission. Reviews contact sheets, transparencies and 5×7 prints. Offers no additional payment for photos accepted with ms.

Columns/Departments: Buys 12 mss/year. Send complete ms. Length: 400-1,000 words. Pays $75-200.

Tips: "Send a story. Include photos. Make it something that the magazine regularly uses. Do automotive how-tos. We need lots of them. We'll help you with them."

CYCLE WORLD, DCI Communications, Inc., 853 W. 17th St., Costa Mesa CA 92627. (714)720-5300. Editor: David Edwards. 20% freelance written. For active motorcyclists, "young, affluent, educated, very perceptive." Subject matter includes "road tests (staff-written), features on special bikes, customs, racers, racing events; technical and how-to features involving mechanical modifications." Monthly. Circ. 245,000. **Pays on acceptance.** Publishes ms an average of 3 months after acceptance. Buys all rights. Query for electronic submissions. Reports in 2 weeks on queries; 1 month on mss. Sample copy $2; free writer's guidelines.

Nonfiction: Buys informative, well-researched, technical, theory and how-to articles; interviews; profiles; humor; and historical pieces. Buys 20 mss/year. Query. Length: 1,000-2,000 words. Pays variable rates. Sometimes pays the expenses of writers on assignment.

Photos: Purchased with or without ms, or on assignment. Reviews contact sheets and transparencies. Pays $75 minimum. Buys one-time rights and reprint rights.

Tips: "Area most open to freelancers is short nonfiction features. They must contain positive and fun experience regarding motorcycle travel, sport and lifestyle."

4-WHEEL & OFF-ROAD, Petersen Publishing Co., 8490 Sunset Blvd., Los Angeles CA 90069. (213)854-2360. Editor: Steve Campbell. Managing Editor: Cecily Chittick. A monthly magazine covering four-wheel-drive vehicles, "devoted to new-truck tests, buildups of custom 4×4s, coverage of 4WD racing, trail rides and other competitions." Circ. 330,000. **Pays on acceptance.** Publishes ms an average of 4 months after acceptance. Byline given. Pays 20% kill fee. Buys first North American serial rights or all rights. Submit seasonal/holiday material 4 months in advance. Reports in 3 weeks. Writer's guidelines for #10 SASE.

Nonfiction: How-to (on four-wheel-drive vehicles — engines, suspension, drive systems, etc.), new product, photo feature, technical and travel. Buys 12-16 mss/year. Send complete ms. Length: 1,000-2,500 words. Pays $200-600.

Photos: Send photos with submission. Reviews transparencies and b&w prints. Offers no additional payment for photos accepted with ms. Captions, model releases and identification of subjects required. Buys all rights.

Fillers: Anecdotes, facts, gags, newsbreaks and short humor. Buys 12-16/year. Length: 50-150 words. Pays $15-50.

Tips: "Attend 4×4 events, get to know the audience. Present material only after full research. Manuscripts should contain *all* of the facts pertinent to the story. Technical/how-to articles are most open to freelancers."

FOUR WHEELER MAGAZINE, 6728 Eton Ave., Canoga Park CA 91303. (818)992-4777. FAX: (818)992-4979. Editor: John Stewart. 20% freelance written. Works with a small number of new/unpublished writers each year. Emphasizes four-wheel-drive vehicles, competition and travel/adventure. Monthly magazine; 164 pages. Estab. 1963. Circ. 316,941. Pays on publication. Publishes ms an average of 4 months after acceptance. Buys all rights. Submit seasonal/holiday material at least 4 months in advance. Query for electronic submissions. Free sample copy; writer's guidelines for #10 SAE.

Nonfiction: 4WD competition and travel/adventure articles, technical, how-tos, and vehicle features about unique four-wheel drives. "We like the adventure stories that bring four wheeling to life in word and photo: mud-running deserted logging roads, exploring remote, isolated trails, or hunting/fishing where the 4×4 is a necessity for success." See features by Bruce Smith, Gary Wescott, Matt Conrad and Dick Stansfield for examples. Query with photos before sending complete ms. Length: 1,200-2,000 words; average 4-5 pages when published. Pays $100/page minimum for complete package. Sometimes pays the expenses of writers on assignment.

Photos: Requires professional quality color slides and b&w prints for every article. Captions required. Prefers Kodachrome 64 or Fujichrome 50 in 35mm or 2¼ formats. "Action shots a must for all vehicle features and travel articles."

Tips: "Show us you know how to use a camera as well as the written word. The easiest way for a new writer/ photographer to break in to our magazine is to read several issues of the magazine, then query with a short vehicle feature that will show his or her potential as a creative writer/photographer."

KEEPIN' TRACK OF VETTES, Box 48, Spring Valley NY 10977. (914)425-2649. Editor: Shelli Finkel. 70% freelance written. Works with a small number of new/unpublished writers each year. Monthly magazine; 74 pages. For Corvette owners and enthusiasts. Estab. 1976. Circ. 38,000. Pays on publication. Publishes ms an average of 3 months after acceptance. Buys all rights. Byline given. Submit seasonal/holiday material 3 months in advance. Reports in 1 month. Free sample copy and writer's guidelines.

Nonfiction: Expose (telling of Corvette problems with parts, etc.); historical (any and all aspects of Corvette developments); how-to (restorations, engine work, suspension, race, swapmeets); humor; informational; interview (query); nostalgia; personal experience; personal opinion; photo feature; profile (query); technical; and travel. Buys 1-2 mss/issue. Query or submit complete ms. Pays $50-200. Sometimes pays the expenses of writers on assignment.

Photos: Send photo with ms. Pays $10-35 for b&w contact sheets or negatives; $10-50 for 35mm color transparencies; offers no additional payment for photos with accompanying ms.

Tips: The writer "must have more than a passing knowledge of Corvettes specifically and automobiles in general. We're looking for more material covering '53-'67 Corvettes — as they appreciate in value, interest in those years is rising."

‡MOPAR MUSCLE, Dobbs Publishing Group, 3816 Industry Blvd., Lakeland FL 33811. (813)644-0449. Editor: Greg Rager. 25% freelance written. Quarterly magazine covering Chrysler Corp. performance vehicles. "Our audience has a knowledge of and interest in Chrysler vehicles." Estab. 1987. Circ. 75,000. Pays within 30 days of publication. Byline given. Buys first rights. Submit seasonal/holiday material 6 months in advance. Query for electronic submissions. Reports in 2 weeks. Sample copy for $3.95. Free writer's guidelines.

Nonfiction: Historical/nostalgic, how-to/technical, humor, interview/profile, new product, personal experience, photo feature, technical. Buys 20-25 mss/year. Query with published clips. Sometimes pays expenses of writers on assignment.

Photos: Send photos with submission. Reviews contact sheets and transparencies. Model release required. Buys one-time rights.

Columns/Departments: Moparts (new products), 50 words; Mopar Scene (news for Chrysler devotees), varies. Buys 20-25 mss/year. Query.

Fiction: Historical, humorous. Query.

MOTOR TREND, Petersen Publishing Co., 8490 Sunset Blvd., Los Angeles CA 90069. (213)854-2222. Editor: Jack R. Nerad. 5-10% freelance written. Prefers to work with published/established writers. For automotive enthusiasts and general interest consumers. Monthly. Circ. 800,000. Publishes ms an average of 3 months after acceptance. Buys all rights. "Fact-filled query suggested for all freelancers." Reports in 1 month.
Nonfiction: Automotive and related subjects that have national appeal. Emphasis on domestic and imported cars, roadtests, driving impressions, auto classics, auto, travel, racing, and high-performance features for the enthusiast. Packed with facts. Freelancers should confine queries to photo-illustrated exotic drives and other feature material; road tests and related activity handled inhouse.
Photos: Buys photos, particularly of prototype cars and assorted automotive matter. Pays $25-500 for transparencies.

‡**MUSTANG MONTHLY**, Dobbs Publications, Inc., P.O. Box 6320, Lakeland FL 33807. (813)646-5743. Editor: Tom Corcoran. Technical Editor: Earl Davis. 50% freelance written. A monthly magazine covering concours 1964½ through 1973 Ford Mustang, and mildly modified late-'80s Mustang. "Our average reader makes over $35,000 annually, and is 35 years of age." Circ. 75,000. Pays on publication. Publishes ms an average of 4 months after acceptance. Byline given. Buys first North American rights. No simultaneous submissions. Reports in 6 weeks on mss. Writers guidelines available.
Nonfiction: How-to and technical. Color car features. No seasonal, holiday, humor, fiction or first-person nostalgia material. Buys 35 mss/year. Query with or without published clips, or send complete ms. Freelancers should write for guidelines first. Length: 2,500 words maximum. Pays 15¢/word for first 500 words; 10¢/word to 2,500-limit. Generally uses ms within 6 months of acceptance.
Photos: Send photos with submission; photography will make or break articles. Reviews contact sheets, negatives and transparencies. No color prints. Offers $100/page color pro-rated to size, $25 minimum; $10/photo b&w, $25 minimum. Captions, model releases, (on our forms) "required."
Tips: "*Mustang Monthly* is looking for color features on trophy-winning original Mustangs and well-researched b&w how-to and technical articles. Our format rarely varies. A strong knowledge of early Mustangs is essential."

‡**NATIONAL DRAGSTER, Drag Racing's Leading News Weekly**, National Hot Rod Association, 2035 Financial Way, Glendora CA 91740. (818)963-8475. Editor: Phil Burgess. Managing Editor: Vicky Ryan. 50% freelance written. Weekly tabloid of NHRA drag racing. "Covers NHRA drag racing—race reports, news, performance industry news, hot racing rumors—for NHRA members. Membership included with subscription." Estab. 1960. Circ. 70,000. Pays on publication. Publishes ms 6 months after acceptance. Byline given. Buys all rights. Submit seasonal/holiday material 2 months in advance. Simultaneous submissions OK. Query for electronic submissions. Reports in 2 weeks. Free sample copy.
Nonfiction: General interest, historical/nostalgic, how-to, humor, interview/profile, new product, personal experience, photo feature, technical. Buys 10 mss/year. Query. Pay is negotiable. Sometimes pays expenses of writers on assignment.
Photos: State availability of photos with submission. Reviews 5×7 prints. Offers no additional payment for photos accepted with ms. Captions, model releases and identification of subjects required. Buys all rights.
Columns/Departments: On the Run (first-person written, ghost written by drag racers), 900-1,000 words. Buys 52 mss/year. Query. Pay is negotiable.
Tips: "Feature articles on interesting drag racing personalities or race cars are most open to freelancers."

NISSAN DISCOVERY, The Magazine for Nissan Owners, Donnelley Marketing, P.O. Box 4617, N. Hollywood CA 91617. (818)506-4081 Editor: Wayne Thoms. 50% freelance written. Prefers to work with published/established writers and photographers. Quarterly magazine for Nissan owners and their families. Estab. 1980. Circ. 500,000. **Pays on acceptance.** Publishes ms an average of 6 months after acceptance. Byline given. Buys first North American serial rights. Submit seasonal/holiday material 5 months in advance. Previously published submissions OK. Reports in 1 month. Sample copy 9×12 SAE and 4 first class stamps; writer's guidelines for #10 SASE.
Nonfiction: Historical/nostalgic, humor, photo feature, travel. "We need general family interest material with heavy emphasis on outstanding color photos: travel, humor, food, lifestyle, sports, entertainment." Buys 15 mss/year. Query. Length: 1,300-1,800 words. Pays $300-1,000. Sometimes pays the expenses of writers on assignment.
Photos: State availability of photos. Reviews 2¼×s¼ and 35mm color transparencies. No b&w photos. "Payment usually is part of story package—all negotiated." Captions and identification of subjects required. Buys one-time rights.
Tips: "A freelancer can best break in to our publication by submitting a brief idea query with specific information on color slides available. Offer a package of copy and art."

For information on setting your freelance fees, see How Much Should I Charge? in the Business of Writing section.

ON TRACK, The Auto Racing News Magazine, OT Publishing, Inc., Box 8509, Fountain Valley CA 92728. (714)966-1131. Editor: Craig Fischer, Andrew Crask. 90% freelance written. Biweekly magazine on auto racing (no drag racing, sprint cars, etc.). Circ. 40,000. Pays on publication. Publishes ms an average of 2 months after acceptance. Byline given. Buys first North American serial rights. Query for electronic submissions. Reports on queries. Sample copy $2. Free writer's guidelines.
Nonfiction: Interview/profile and technical. Opinions, stories about race drivers with quotes from driver. Buys 3-4 mss/year. Query with published clips, or send complete ms. Length: 800-2,000 words. Pays $5/column inch. Sometimes pays expenses of writers on assignment.
Photos: State availability of photos with submission. Review 5×7 prints. Offers $10 per photo when used. Captions and identification of subjects required. Buys one-time rights.
Columns/Departments: Inside Line (look at subjects affecting trends, safety rules, etc.), 850 words; Broadcast Booth (TV, radio), 850 words. Buys 40 mss/year. Send complete ms. Pays $5.25 per column inch.
Tips: "Show some knowledge on the subject. Our readers are very knowledgeable and are quick to spot mistakes that get by us. Most of the magazine is done by a select few, but there are openings."

OPEN WHEEL MAGAZINE, Lopez Publications, Box 715, Ipswich MA 01938. (508)356-7030. FAX: (508)356-2492. Editor: Dick Berggren. 80% freelance written. Monthly magazine. "*OW* covers sprint cars, midgets, supermodifieds and Indy cars. *OW* is an enthusiast's publication which speaks to those deeply involved in oval track automobile racing in the United States and Canada. *OW*'s primary audience is a group of men and women actively engaged in competition at the present time, those who have recently been in competition and those who plan competition soon. That audience includes drivers, car owners, sponsors and crew members who represent perhaps 50-70 percent of our readership. The rest who read the magazine are those in the racing trade (parts manufacturers, track operators and officials) and serious fans who see 30 or more races per year." Circ. 150,000. Pays on publication. Publishes ms an average of 6 months after acceptance. Byline given. Buys first rights. Submit seasonal material 2 months in advance. Reports in 3 weeks on queries. Sample copy for 9×12 SAE and $2 postage; writer's guidelines for #10 SASE.
Nonfiction: General interest, historical/nostalgic, how-to, humor, interview/profile, new product, photo feature and technical. "We don't care for features that are a blow-by-blow chronology of events. The key word is interest. We want features which allow the reader to get to know the main figure very well. Our view of racing is positive. We don't think all is lost, that the sport is about to shut down and don't want stories that claim such to be the case, but we shoot straight and avoid whitewash." Buys 125 mss/year. Query with or without published clips, or send complete ms.
Photos: State availability of photos with submission. Reviews contact sheets, negatives, transparencies and prints. Buys one-time rights.
Fillers: Anecdotes, facts and short humor. Buys 100/year. Length: 1-3 pages, double-spaced. Pays $35.
Tips: "Virtually all our features are submitted without assignment. An author knows much better what's going on in his backyard than we do. We ask that you write to us before beginning a story theme. Judging of material is always a combination of a review of the story and its support illustrations. Therefore, we ask for photography to accompany the manuscript on first submission. We've gone from bimonthly to monthly—so we are looking to use more quality material."

ROAD KING MAGAZINE, Box 250, Park Forest IL 60466. Editor-in-Chief: George Friend. 10% freelance written. Eager to work with new/unpublished writers. Truck driver leisure reading publication. Bimonthly magazine. Circ. 210,000. **Pays on acceptance.** Publishes ms an average of 2 months after acceptance. Usually buys all rights; sometimes buys first rights. Byline given "always on fiction—if requested on nonfiction." Submit seasonal/holiday material 3 months in advance. Sample copy for 7×10 SAE and 85¢ postage or get free sample copy at any Unocal 76 truck stop; writer's guidelines for #10 SASE.
Nonfiction: Trucker slant or general interest, humor, and photo feature. No articles on violence or sex. Name and quote release required. No queries. Submit complete ms. Length: 500-1,200 words. Pays $50-400.
Photos: Submit photos with accompanying ms. No additional payment for b&w contact sheets or 2¼×2¼ color transparencies. Captions preferred. Buys first rights. Model release required.
Fiction: Adventure, historical, humorous, mystery, rescue-type suspense and western. Especially about truckers. No stories on sex and violence. "We're looking for quality writing." Buys 4 mss/year. Submit complete ms. Length: approximately 1,200 words. Pays up to $400. Writer should quote selling price with submission.
Fillers: Jokes, gags, anecdotes and short humor about truckers. Buys 20-25/year. Length: 50-500 words. Pays $5-100.
Tips: "No collect phone calls or postcard requests. Never phone for free copy as we will not handle such phone calls. We don't appreciate letters we have to answer. Do not submit manuscripts, art or photos using registered mail, certified mail or insured mail. Publisher will not accept such materials from the post office. Publisher will not discuss refusal with writer. Nothing personal, just legal. Do not write and ask if we would like such and such article or outline. We buy only from original and complete manuscripts submitted on speculation. Do not ask for writer's guidelines. See above and/or get a copy of the magazine and be familiar with our format before submitting anything. We are a trucker publication whose readers are often family members and sometimes Bible Belt. We refrain from violence, sex, nudity, etc."

ROD & CUSTOM, Peterson Publishing Co., 8490 Sunset Blvd., Los Angeles CA 90069. (213)854-2250. Editor: Patrick Ganahl. Managing Editor: Kristin Kelly. 30% freelance written. Bimonthly magazine on street rods and custom cars. "*R&C* is a special interest automotive magazine covering street rods, custom cars, '50s cars and vintage race cars. All articles are photo illustrated and the slant is toward hands-on enthusiasts and how-to subjects." Estab. 1948. Circ. 102,000. **Pays on acceptance.** Byline given. Buys all rights. Reports in 2 weeks. Sample copy $3.

Nonfiction: Historical/nostalgic, how-to, interview/profile, new product, photo feature, technical. Buys 25 mss/year. Query with or without published clips, or send complete ms. Length: 250-2,000 words. Pays $150-1,000. Seldom pays expenses of writers on assignment.

Photos: Send photos with submission. Reviews contact sheets, transparencies and 5×7 or larger prints. Offers no additional payment for photos accepted with ms; pays $50-100 for photos alone. Captions and model releases required. Buys all rights.

Columns/Departments: Roddin' Around (newsy, unusual, interesting, historical short subjects on rod/custom topics), 250-500 words. Buys 20 mss/year. Query or send complete ms. Pays $50-250.

Fillers: Anecdotes, facts, newsbreaks and illustrations. Buys 25/year. Length 50-250 words. Pays $50-200.

Tips: "You must know the subject matter intimately and be able to speak the language. Professional quality photos are a must with any submission. We need technical, how-to and event articles more than we need photo features of individual cars. Other than car features, most of our photography is b&w; color features should also include b&w."

STOCK CAR RACING MAGAZINE, Box 715, Ipswich MA 01938. Editor: Dick Berggren. 80% freelance written. Eager to work with new/unpublished writers. For stock car racing fans and competitors. Monthly magazine; 120 pages. Circ. 400,000. Pays on publication. Publishes ms an average of 3 months after acceptance. Buys all rights. Byline given. Query for electronic submissions. Reports in 6 weeks. Free writer's guidelines.

Nonfiction: General interest, historical/nostalgic, how-to, humor, interviews, new product, photo features and technical. "Uses nonfiction on stock car drivers, cars, and races. We are interested in the story behind the story in stock car racing. We want interesting profiles and colorful, nationally interesting features. We are looking for more technical articles, particularly in the area of street stocks and limited sportsman." Query with or without published clips, or submit complete ms. Buys 50-200 mss/year. Length: 100-6,000 words. Pays up to $450.

Photos: State availability of photos. Pays $20 for 8×10 b&w photos; up to $250 for 35mm or larger transparencies. Captions required.

Fillers: Anecdotes and short humor. Buys 100 each year. Pays $35.

Tips: "We get more queries than stories. We just don't get as much material as we want to buy. We have more room for stories than ever before. We are an excellent market with 12 issues per year. Virtually all our features are submitted without assignment. An author knows much better what's going on in his backyard than we do. We ask that you write to us before beginning a story theme. If nobody is working on the theme you wish to pursue, we'd be glad to assign it to you if it fits our needs and you are the best person for the job. Judging of material is always a combination of a review of the story and its support illustration. Therefore, we ask for photography to accompany the manuscript on first submission."

‡SUPER FORD, Dobbs Publications, 3816 Industry Blvd., Lakeland FL 33811. (813)644-0449. Editor: Donald Farr. Managing Editor: Mike Mueller. 50% freelance written. Monthly magazine covering the Ford Motor Company automotive history and topics. Estab. 1987. Circ. 45,000. Pays on publication. Publishes ms an average of 5 months after acceptance. Byline given. Offers 50% kill fee. Buys one-time rights. Submit seasonal/holiday material 3 months in advance. Query for electronic submissions. Reports in 3 weeks. Free sample copy and writer's guidelines.

Nonfiction: Historical/nostalgic: how-to (automotive technical), interview/profile; new product; personal experience; photo features ("those on individual cars are our bread-and-butter"); and technical. Buys 48 mss/year. Send complete ms. Length: 500-2,000 words. Pays $75-500 for unsolicited articles. Sometimes pays expenses of writers on assignment.

Photos: Reviews contact sheets and negatives and 2¼×2¼ transparencies. Offers $10/b&w photo, $150/color cover. Captions and identification of subjects required. Buys one-time rights.

Columns/Departments: Keepin' Track (Ford racing coverage), 50-1,000 words; In The Fast Lane (Ford automotive news), 100-200 words. Buys 15 mss/year. Query. Pays $50-150.

VETTE MAGAZINE, CSK Publishing, Inc., 299 Market St., Saddle Brook NJ 07662. (201)712-9300. FAX: (201)712-9899. Editor: D. Randy Riggs. Managing Editor: Peter Easton. 60% freelance written. Monthly magazine. All subjects related to the Corvette automobile. "Our readership is extremely knowledgeable about the subject of Corvettes. Therefore, writers had better know the subject thoroughly and be good at fact checking." Estab. 1976. Circ. 60,000. Offers 50% kill fee. Buys first North American serial rights. Submit seasonal/holiday material 3 months in advance. Query for electronic submissions. Reports in 3 weeks on queries and mss. Sample copy for 9×12 SAE with $1.45 postage; writer's guidelines for #10 SASE.

Nonfiction: General interest, historical/nostalgic, how-to, interview/profile, new product, personal experience, photo feature, technical and travel. Buys 120 mss/year. Query with published clips. Length: 4pp-2,700 words. Pays $150-750 for assigned articles; $100-350 for unsolicited articles. Sometimes pays expenses of writers on assignment.

Photos: State availability of photos with submission. Reviews contact sheets. Offers no additional payment for photos accepted with ms. Captions and model releases are required. Buys one-time rights.

Columns/Departments: Reviews (books/videos), 400-500 words. Buys 12 mss/year. Query. Pays $50-150.

Fiction: Adventure, fantasy and slice-of-life vignettes. Buys 4 mss/year. Query with published clips. Length: 400-2,500 words. Pays $100-500.

VOLKSWAGEN WORLD, Volkswagen of America, P.O. Box 3951, 888 W. Big Beaver Rd., Troy MI 48007. Editor: Marlene Goldsmith. 75% freelance written. Magazine published 4 times/year for Volkswagen owners in the United States. Estab. 1961. Circ. 300,000. **Pays on acceptance.** Buys first North American serial rights. Byline given. Query for electronic submissions. Reports in 6 weeks. Sample copy for 9 × 12 SAE and $1.05 postage. Free writer's guidelines.

Nonfiction: "Interesting stories on people using Volkswagens; travel pieces with the emphasis on people, not places; Volkswagenmania stories; personality pieces, including celebrity interviews; and inspirational and true adventure articles. The style should be light. Our approach is subtle, however, and we try to avoid obvious product puffery, since *Volkswagen's World* is not an advertising medium. We prefer a first-person, people-oriented handling. No basic travelogues; stay away from Beetle stories. With all story ideas, query first. All unsolicited manuscripts will be returned unopened. We strongly advise writers to read at least two past issues before working on a query." Buys 10-12 mss/year. Length: 750 words maximum; "shorter pieces, some as short as 450 words, often receive closer attention." Pays minimum $150 per printed page for photographs and text; otherwise, a portion of that amount, depending on the space allotted. Most stories are 2 pages; some run 3 or 4 pages.

Photos: Submit photo samples with query. Photos purchased with ms; captions required. "We prefer transparencies, 35mm or larger. All photos should carry the photographer's name and address. If the photographer is not the author, both names should appear on the first page of the text. Where possible, we would like a selection of at least twenty transparencies. Quality photography can often sell a story that might be otherwise rejected. Every picture should be identified or explained." Model releases required. Pays $500 maximum for front cover photo.

Fillers: "Short, humorous anecdotes about current model Volkswagens." Pays $25.

Tips: "VW drivers are not the same as those who used to drive the Beetle."

Aviation

Professional and private pilots and aviation enthusiasts read the publications in this section. Editors want material for audiences knowledgable about commercial aviation. Magazines for passengers of commercial airlines are grouped in the In-flight category. Technical aviation and space journals and publications for airport operators, aircraft dealers and others in aviation businesses are listed under Aviation and Space in the Trade section.

AIR ALASKA, Pacific Rim Publishing Co., Suite 410, 900 W 5th, P.O. Box 99007, Anchorage AK 99509. (907)272-7500. FAX: (907)279-1037. Managing Editor: Gene Storm. 75% freelance written. Monthly tabloid on aviation, piloting in the far north region. "*Air Alaska* targets readers who actively use their small aircraft in recreation and business in far north regions. Writing must appeal to that audience and be good, clear and concise." Estab. 1980. Circ. 10,000. Pays within 30 days of publication. Byline given. Offers 40% kill fee. Buys first North American serial rights and second serial (reprint) rights. Submit seasonal/holiday material 6 months in advance. Simultaneous and previously published submissions OK. Query for electronic submissions. Reports in 1 month. Sample copy for 9 × 12 SAE with 5 first class stamps; free writer's guidelines.

Nonfiction: General interest, historical/nostalgic, how-to (secure floats, fly skis, winter maintenance, etc.), humor, inspirational, interview/profile, new product, personal experience, photo feature, technical, travel (to and from far north areas, far north generally means above 45°N latitude). Fly-in fishing articles - April; Fly-in hunting articles - August; Pilot's Gift guide (product description/gift ideas) - November. "If it does not relate to general aviation, it will not be considered. Exception: hang gliding, parachuting, ultralights. *No* remote control/model stuff." Buys 200 mss/year. Query. Length: 600-800 words. Pays 5-10¢/word for assigned articles; 3-8¢/word for unsolicited articles. Sometimes pays expenses of writers on assignment.

Photos: State availability of photos with submission and briefly describe. Reviews contact sheets. Offers $15-30 per photo. Captions, model releases and identification of subjects required. Buys first rights and rights to reprint. Not exclusive rights or rights to resale.

Fiction: Adventure and novel excerpts (aviation related *only*).

Fillers: Anecdotes, facts, gags, newsbreaks, and short humor. Buys 24/year. Length: 200 words. Pays 5-10¢/word.

Tips: "Limit query to one page or less. Action stopping b&w photos are paramount. People in photos necessary. We rarely use poses. We also pay more for electronic submission."

AIR & SPACE/SMITHSONIAN MAGAZINE, 370 L' Enfant Promenade S.W., 10th Floor, Washington DC 20024. (202)287-3733. Editor: George Larson. Managing Editor: Tom Huntington. 80% freelance written. Prefers to work with published/established writers. A bimonthly magazine covering aviation and aerospace for a non-technical audience. "Features are slanted to a technically curious, but not necessarily technically knowledgeable audience. We are looking for unique angles to aviation/aerospace stories, history, events, personalities, current and future technologies, that emphasize the human-interest aspect." Circ. 310,000. **Pays on acceptance.** Byline given. Offers kill fee. Buys first North American serial rights. Reports in 5 weeks. Sample copy for $3.50 plus 9½ × 13 SASE; free writer's guidelines.

Nonfiction: Book excerpts, essays, general interest (on aviation/aerospace), historical/nostalgic, how-to, humor, interview/profile, photo feature and technical. Buys 50 mss/year. Query with published clips. Length: 1,500-3,000 words. Pays $2,000 maximum. Pays the expenses of writers on assignment.

Photos: State availability of illustrations with submission. Reviews 35mm transparencies.

Columns/Departments: Above and Beyond (first person), 2,000-2,500 words; Flights and Fancy (whimsy, insight), approximately 1,200 words; Oldies & Oddities (weird, wonderful and old), 1,200 words; Groundling's Notebook (looking upward), length varies. Buys 25 mss/year. Query with published clips. Pays $1,000 maximum. Soundings (brief items, timely but not breaking news), 500-800 words. Pays $300.

Tips: "Soundings is the section most open to freelancers. We will be buying more stories about space flight than aviation now that space program is heating up again."

AIR LINE PILOT, Air Line Pilots Association, 535 Herndon Parkway, Box 1169, Herndon VA 22070. (703)689-4176. Editor: Esperison Martinez, Jr. 10% freelance written. Prefers to work with published/established writers; works with a small number of new/unpublished writers each year. A monthly magazine for airline pilots covering "commercial aviation industry information—economics, avionics, equipment, systems, safety—that affects a pilot's life in professional sense." Also includes information about management/labor relations trends, contract negotiations, etc. Estab. 1931. Circ. 60,000. **Pays on acceptance.** Publishes ms an average of 6 months after acceptance. Offers 50% kill fee. Buys all rights. Submit seasonal/holiday material 6 months in advance. Query for electronic submissions. Reports in 2 months. Sample copy $2; writer's guidelines for #10 SASE.

Nonfiction: Humor, inspirational, photo feature and technical. "We are backlogged with historical submissions and prefer not to receive unsolicited submissions at this time." Buys 20 mss/year. Query with or without published clips, or send complete ms. Length: 700-3,000 words. Pays $200-600 for assigned articles; pays $50-600 for unsolicited articles.

Photos: Send photos with submission. Reviews contact sheets, 35mm transparencies and 8 × 10 prints. Offers $10-25/photo. Identification of subjects required. Buys one-time rights.

Tips: "For our feature section, we seek aviation industry information that affects the life of a professional airline pilot from a career standpoint. We also seek material that affects his life from a job security and work environment standpoint. Any airline pilot featured in an article must be an Air Line Pilot Association member in good standing."

GENERAL AVIATION NEWS & FLYER, (formerly *Western Flyer*), N.W. Flyer, Inc., P.O. Box 98786, Tacoma WA 98498-0786. (206)588-1743. FAX: (206)588-4005. Editor: Dave Sclair. 30% freelance written. Prefers to work with published/established writers. Biweekly tabloid covering general aviation. Provides "coverage of aviation news, activities, regulations and politics of general and sport aviation with emphasis on timely features of interest to pilots and aircraft owners." Estab. 1949. Circ. 35,000. Pays 1 month after publication. Publishes ms an average of 3 months after acceptance. Byline given. Buys one-time rights and first North American serial rights, on occasion second serial (reprint) rights. Submit seasonal/holiday material 2 months in advance. Simultaneous queries and previously published submissions from noncompetitive publications OK but must be identified. Query for electronic submissions. Reports in 2 weeks on queries; 1 month on mss. Sample copy $2; writer's guidelines, style guidelines for #10 SASE.

Nonfiction: Features of current interest about aviation businesses, developments at airports, new products and services, safety, flying technique and maintenance. "Good medium-length reports on current events—controversies at airports, problems with air traffic control, FAA, etc. We want solid news coverage of breaking stories." Query first on historical, nostalgic features and profiles/interviews. Many special sections throughout the year; send SASE for list. Buys 100 mss/year. Query or send complete ms. Length: 500-2,000 words. Pays up to $3/printed column inch maximum. Rarely pays the expenses of writers on assignment.

Photos: "Good pics a must." Send photos (b&w or color prints preferred, no slides) with ms. All photos must have complete captions and carry photographer's ID. Pays $10/b&w photo used.

Tips: "We always are looking for features on places to fly and interviews or features about people and businesses using airplanes in unusual ways. Travel features must include information on what to do once you've arrived, with addresses from which readers can get more information. Get direct quotations from the principals involved in the story. We want current, first-hand information."

‡**PRIVATE PILOT,** Fancy Publications Corp., Box 6050, Mission Viejo CA 92690. (714)855-8822. Editor: Mary F. Silitch. 75% freelance written. Works with a small number of new/unpublished writers each year. For owner/pilots of private aircraft, for student pilots and others aspiring to attain additional ratings and experience. "We take a unique, but limited view within our field." Circ. 105,000. Buys first North American serial rights. Pays on publication. Publishes manuscript average of 6 months after acceptance. No simultaneous submissions. Query for electronic submissions. Reports in 2 months. Sample copy $3; writer's guidelines for SASE.

Nonfiction: Material on techniques of flying, developments in aviation, product and specific airplane test reports, travel by aircraft, development and use of airports. All must be related to general aviation field. No personal experience articles. Buys about 60-90 mss/year. Query. Length: 1,000-4,000 words. Pays $75-300.

Photos: Pays $25 for 8×10 b&w glossy prints. Pays $200 for transparencies used on cover.

Columns/Departments: Business flying, homebuilt/experimental aircraft, pilot's logbook. Length: 1,000 words. Pays $75-250.

Tips: "Writer must know the subject about which he is writing; use good grammar; know the publication for which he's writing; remember that we try to relate to the middle segment of the business/pleasure flying public. We see too many 'first flight' type of articles. Our market is more sophisticated than that. Most writers do not do enough research on their subject. We would like to see more material on business-related flying, more on people involved in flying."

‡**PROFESSIONAL PILOT,** Queensmith Communications, 3014 Colvin St., Alexandria VA 22314. (703)370-0606. FAX: (703)370-7082. Editor: Mac Tippins. 75% freelance written. A monthly magazine on major and regional airline, corporate, military and various other types of professional aviation. "Our readers are commercial pilots with highest ratings and the editorial content reflects their knowledge and experience." Estab. 1967. Circ. 32,000. Pays when accepted for publication. Publishes ms an average of 3 months after acceptance. Byline given. Kill fee negotiable. Buys all rights. Free sample copy.

Nonfiction: How-to (avionics and aircraft flight checks), humor, interview/profile, personal experience (if a lesson for professional pilots), photo feature, technical (avionics, weather, engines, aircraft). All issues have a theme such as regional airline operations, maintenance, jet aircraft, helicopters, etc. Buys 40 mss/year. Query. Length: 750-2,500. Pays $200-750. Sometimes pays expenses of writers on assignment.

Photos: Send photos with submission. Prefers transparencies. Offers no additional payment for photos accepted with ms. Captions and identification of subjects required. Buys all rights.

Columns/Departments: Pireps (aviation news), 300-500 words. Buys 12 mss/year. Query. Pays $100-250.

Tips: Query first. "Freelancer should have background in aviation that will make his articles believable to highly qualified pilots of commercial aircraft. We are placing a greater emphasis on airline operations, management and pilot concerns."

Business and Finance

Business publications give executives and consumers a range of information from local business news and trends to national overviews and laws that affect them. National and regional publications are listed below in separate categories. Magazines that have a technical slant are in the Trade section under Business Management, Finance or Management and Supervision categories.

National

BARRON'S, National Business and Financial Weekly, Dow Jones and Co. Inc., 200 Liberty St., New York NY 10281. (212)416-2759. FAX: (212)416-2829. Editor: Alan Abelson. Managing Editor: Kathryn M. Welling. 10% freelance written. Weekly tabloid covering the investment scene. "*Barron's* is written for active participants in and avid spectators of the investment scene. We require top-notch reporting *and* graceful, intelligent and irreverent writing." Circ. 244,922. Pays on publication. Byline given. Offers 25% kill fee. Buys all rights. Reports in 2 months. Writer's guidelines for SASE.

Nonfiction: Book excerpts, general interest and interview/profile. Publishes quarterly mutual fund sections. Buys 50 mss/year. Query with published clips. Length: 1,500-2,000 words. Pays $500-2,000 for assigned articles. Pays expenses of writers on assignment.

Photos: State availability of photos with submission. Reviews contact sheets, negatives and 8×10 prints. Offers $150-300/photo (day rate). Model releases and identification of subjects required. Buys one-time rights.

Columns/Departments: Richard A. Donnelly, editor. Barron's on Books (business/investment books). Buys 100 mss/year. Query with published clips. Length: 250-500 words. Pays $150.

D&B REPORTS, The Dun & Bradstreet Magazine for Small Business Management, Dun & Bradstreet, 299 Park Ave., 24th Floor, New York NY 10171. (212)593-6723. Editor: Patricia W. Hamilton. 10% freelance written. Works with a small number of new/unpublished writers each year. A bimonthly magazine for small business. "Articles should contain useful information that managers of small businesses can apply to their own companies. *D&B Reports* focuses on companies with $15 million in annual sales and under." Estab. 1954. Circ. 76,000. **Pays on acceptance.** Publishes ms an average of 2 months after acceptance. Byline given. Buys first North American serial rights. Query for electronic submissions. Reports in 3 weeks on manuscripts. Free sample copy and writer's guidelines.

Nonfiction: How-to (on management); and interview/profile (of successful entrepreneurs). Buys 5 mss/year. Query. Length: 1,500-2,500 words. Pays $500 minimum. Sometimes pays expenses of writers on assignment.

Photos: State availability of photos with submission. Identification of subjects required. Buys one-time rights.

Tips: "The area of our publication most open to freelancers is profiles of innovative companies and managers."

EXECUTIVE FEMALE, NAFE, 127 W. 24th St., 4th Fl., New York NY 10011. (212)645-0770. Editor-in-Chief: Diane P. Burley. Editor: Ingrid Eisenstadter. Emphasizes "useful career and financial information for the upwardly mobile female." 60% freelance written. Prefers to work with published/established writers; works with a small number of new/unpublished writers each year. Bimonthly magazine. Estab. 1975. Circ. 200,000. Byline given. Pays on publication. Publishes ms an average of 2 months after acceptance. Submit seasonal/holiday material 6 months in advance. Buys first rights and second serial (reprint) rights to material originally published elsewhere. Previously published submissions OK. Query for electronic submissions. Reports in 2 months. Sample copy $2.50; writer's guidelines for #10 SASE.

Nonfiction: "Articles on any aspect of career advancement and financial planning are welcomed." Needs how-tos for managers and articles about coping on the job, trends in the workplace, financial planning, trouble shooting, business communication, time and stress management, career goal-setting and get-ahead strategies. "We would also like to receive humorous essays dealing with aspects of the job/workplace." Written queries only. Submit photos with ms (b&w prints or transparencies), or include suggestions for artwork. Length: 800-1,000. words. Pays $50-400. Pays for local travel and telephone calls.

Columns/Departments: More Money (savings, financial advice, economic trends, interesting tips); Competitive Edge (tips on managing people, getting ahead); Risk (entrepreneurial stories). Buys 20 mss/year. Query with published clips or send complete ms. Department length: 500-2,000 words. Pays $50-100.

HOME BUSINESS NEWS, The Newsletter for Home-based Entrepreneurs, 12221 Beaver Pike, Jackson OH 45640. (614)988-2331. Editor: Ed Simpson. 60% freelance written. Works with a small number of new/unpublished writers each year. A bimonthly magazine covering home-based businesses and marketing. Estab. 1986. Pays on publication. Publishes ms an average of 2 months after acceptance. Byline sometimes given. Buys first North American serial rights and second serial (reprint) rights. Submit seasonal/holiday material 4 months in advance. Simultaneous and previously published submissions OK. Query for electronic submissions. Reports in 1 week on queries; 5 weeks on mss. Sample copy $2; writer's guidelines for #10 SAE with 1 first class stamp.

Nonfiction: Book excerpts, inspirational, interview/profile (of home business owners), new products, personal experience, computer-based home businesses and mail order success stories. Buys 15-20 mss/year. Query with published clips. Length: 800-3,000 words. Pays $20-100; will pay with ad space if agreed upon.

Photos: State availability of photos with submission. Offers no additional payment for photos accepted with ms. Captions and identification of subjects required. Buys one-time rights.

Columns/Departments: Home Business Profiles (profiles of home business owners), 2,000 words. Buys 15-20 mss/year. Query with published clips. Pays $20-100.

Fillers: Facts and newsbreaks. Buys 10/year. Length: 50-300 words. Pays $5-10.

‡I.B. (Independent Business), America's Small Business Magazine, F/S Publishing, #211, 875 S. Westlake Blvd., Westlake Village CA 91361. (805)496-6156. Editor: Daniel Kehrer. Editorial Director: Don Phillipson. 75% freelance written. Bimonthly magazine for small and independent business. "We publish only practical articles of interest to small business owners all across America; also some small business owner profiles." Estab. 1989. Circ. 560,000. **Pays on acceptance.** Publishes ms an average of 4 months after acceptance. Byline given. Offers 25% kill fee. First and non-exclusive reprint rights. Simultaneous queries OK. Do not send manuscripts. Reports in 2 months. Sample copy for $3. Writer's guidelines for #10 SAE and 1 first class stamp.

Nonfiction: Book excerpts, how-to, interview/profile, new product, photo feature. No "generic" business article; no articles on big business; no general articles on economic theory. Buys 80-100 mss/year. Query with bio/resume. Length: 1,000-2,000 words. Pays $500-1,500 for assigned articles. Pays expenses of writers on assignment.

Columns/Departments: Fast Track (short items on small business interests), 50-200 words. Tax Tactics, Small Business Computing, Marking Moves, Ad-visor, Managing Money, Banking & Finance, Business Cost-Savers; all 500-1,500 words. Buys 40-50 mss/year. Query with resume and published clips. Pays $100-1,500.

Fillers: Anecdotes, facts, short humor; must relate to running a small business. "Talk to small business owners anywhere in America about what they want to read, what concerns or interests them in running a business. All areas open, but we use primarily professional business writers with top credentials in the field."

‡**INDIVIDUAL INVESTOR**, Financial Data Systems, Inc., 4th Fl., 38 E. 29th St., New York NY 10016. (212)689-2777. Editor: Jonathan Steinberg. Senior Editor: Gordon T. Anderson. 60% freelance written. Monthly magazine. We publish company profiles, designed to highlight possible stock investments for individuals. Estab. 1981. Circ. 50,000. Pays on publication. Publishes ms an average of 1 month after acceptance. Byline given. Offers 40% kill fee. Buys all rights. Query for electronic submissions. Free sample copy and writer's guidelines.

Nonfiction: Financial/business. Buys 60 mss/year. Query with published clips. Length: 1,200-1,500 words. Pays $350-450 for assigned articles.

Columns/Departments: Buys 30 mss/year. Query with published clips. Length: 1,200-1,500 words. Pays $350-450.

Tips: "Because we do not accept unsolicited articles, queries are essential. We are very open to freelancers, especially those who understand the stock market."

MONEY MAKER, Your Guide to Financial Security and Wealth, Consumers Digest Inc., 5705 N. Lincoln Ave., Chicago IL 60659. (312)275-3590. Editor: Dennis Fertig. 90% freelance written. A bimonthly magazine on personal investing. "We cover the broad range of topics associated with personal finance—the strongest emphasis is on traditional investment opportunities." Estab. 1979. Circ. 165,000. **Pays on acceptance.** Publishes ms an average of 2 months after acceptance. Byline given. Offers 50% kill fee. Buys first rights and second serial (reprint) rights. Reports in 3 months on queries. Sample copy for 8½ × 11 SAE with $1 postage; writer's guidelines for #10 SASE.

Nonfiction: How-to. "No personal success stories or profiles of one company." Buys 25 mss/year. Send complete ms or query and clips. Include stamped, self-addressed postcard for more prompt response. Length: 1,500-3,000 words. Pays 25¢/word for assigned articles. Pays expenses of writers on assignment.

Tips: "Know the subject matter. Develop real sources in the investment community. Demonstrate a reader-friendly style that will help make the sometimes complicated subject of investing more accessible to the average person."

‡**NATION'S BUSINESS**, U.S. Chamber of Commerce, 1615 H. St., N.W., Washington DC 20062. (202)463-5650. Editor: Robert T. Gray. Deputy Editor: Ripley Hotch. 50% freelance written. Monthly magazine covering management of small businesses. Estab. 1912. Circ. 865,000. Pays on acceptance. Publishes ms an average of 6 months after acceptance. Byline given. Byline given. Kill fee negotiable. Buys all rights. Query for electronic submissions. Reports in 1 month. Sample copy $2.50. Free writer's guidelines.

Nonfiction: Book excerpts, how-to, new product and personal experience. No opinion or corporate personnel. Buys 100 mss/year. Query. Length: 250-3,000 words. Pays $100-2,000. Sometimes pays expenses of writers on assignment.

NEW BUSINESS OPPORTUNITIES, Entrepreneur Group, Inc., 2392 Morse Ave., Irvine CA 92714. (714)261-2083. Editor: Rieva Lesonsky. 20-25% freelance written. Monthly magazine on small business. "Provides how-to information for starting a small business and profiles of entrepreneurs who have started small businesses." Estab. 1989. Circ. 200,000. **Pays on acceptance.** Byline given. Offers 20% kill fee. Buys first time worldwide rights. Submit seasonal/holiday material 6 months in advance. Reports in 2 months on queries. Sample copy $3. Writer's guidelines for SASE.

Nonfiction: How-to-start a small business and interview/profile on entrepreneurs. Query. Length: 500-2,000 words. Pays $150-350.

Photos: State availability of photos with submission. Identification of subjects required.

TECHNICAL ANALYSIS OF STOCKS & COMMODITIES, The Trader's Magazine, 3517 S.W. Alaska St., Seattle WA 98126-2730. (206)938-0570. Publisher: Jack K. Hutson. 75% freelance written. Eager to work with new/unpublished writers. Magazine covers methods of investing and trading stocks, bonds and commodities (futures), options, mutual funds, and precious metals. Estab. 1982. Circ. 22,000. Pays on publication. Publishes ms an average of 3 months after acceptance. Byline given. Offers 50% kill fee. Buys all rights; however, second serial (reprint) rights revert to the author, provided copyright credit is given. Previously published submissions OK. Query for electronic submissions. Reports in 3 weeks on queries; 1 month on mss. Sample copy $5; detailed writer's guidelines for #10 SAE and 1 first class stamp.

Nonfiction: Melanie Bowman, managing editor. Reviews (new software or hardware that can make a trader's life easier; comparative reviews of software books, services, etc.); how-to (trade); technical (trading and software aids to trading); utilities (charting or computer programs, surveys, statistics or information to help the trader study or interpret market movements); humor (unusual incidents of market occurrences, cartoons). No newsletter-type, buy-sell recommendations. The article subject must relate to trading psychology, technical analysis, charting or a numerical technique used to trade securities or futures. Virtually requires graphics with every article. Buys 120 mss/year. Query with published clips if available, or send complete ms. Length: 1,000-4,000 words. Pays $100-500. (Applies per inch base rate and premium rate—write for information). Sometimes pays expenses of writers on assignment.

Photos: Christine M. Morrison, photo editor. State availability of photos. Pays $20-150 for 5 × 7 b&w glossy prints or color slides. Captions, model releases and identification of subjects required. Buys one-time and reprint rights.

Columns/Departments: Buys 15 mss/year. Query. Length: 800-1,600 words. Pays $50-300.

Fillers: Karen Webb, fillers editor. Jokes and cartoons on investment humor. Must relate to trading stocks, bonds, options, mutual funds or commodities. Buys 20/year. Length: 500 words. Pays $20-50.

Tips: "Describe how to use technical analysis, charting or computer work in day-to-day trading of stocks, bonds, mutual funds, options or commodities. A blow-by-blow account of how a trade was made, including the trader's thought processes, is, to our subscribers, the very best received story. One of our prime considerations is to instruct in a manner that the lay person can comprehend. We are not hyper-critical of writing style. The completeness and accuracy of submitted material are of the utmost consideration. Write for detailed writer's guidelines."

WOMAN'S ENTERPRISE for entrepreneurs, Paisano Publications Inc., 28210 Dorothy Dr., Agoura CA 91301. (818)889-8740. FAX: (818)889-4726. Editor: Caryne Brown. 40% freelance written. A bimonthly small business magazine on entrepreneurship by women. "The magazine is devoted to why and how women have created, in whole or significant part, a small business of their own. Readership comprises corporate-executive women seeking to strike out on their own, entrepreneurial homemakers, and women who are already in business." **Pays on acceptance.** Publishes ms an average of 4 months after acceptance. Byline given. Offers 15% kill fee. Buys all rights and makes work-for-hire assignments. Query for electronic submissions. Reports in 1 month on queries; 1 month on mss. Sample copy for 10 × 13 SAE with $1.50 postage. Writer's guidelines for #10 SAE with 1 first class stamp.

Nonfiction: Business features, management features and new business ideas. "Our editorial calendar is still being developed. Theme issues may appear from time to time. No personality profiles of entrepreneurs. We want to know how, why, and how much." Buys 80 mss/year. Query. Length: 1,000-2,000 words. Pays 20¢/word minimum.

Photos: State availability of photos with submission. Reviews transparencies and prints. Offers no additional payment for photos accepted with ms. Captions, model releases and subjects required. Buys all rights.

Tips: "Our readers are either in business or want to be. The more practical, how-to, specific information about what it takes for any business to succeed, the better suited it is to the magazine. A definite plus is a short, quick-hit sidebar that details key how-to information. *Woman's Enterprise* is a publication readers should be able to use to make money for themselves. When specific businesses are being profiled, specific cost, returns, and profit figures are *essential*. Otherwise we can't use the piece."

‡WOMEN'S CHRONICLE, The Business Woman's Magazine, #206-1120 Hamilton St., Vancouver, British Columbia V6B 2S2 Canada. (604)682-2242. Editor: Linda Richards-Gorowski. Executive Editor: Debra-Ann Jones. 75% freelance written. Bimonthly magazine of interest to business women. Estab. 1989. Circ. 25,000. Pays on publication. Publishes ms an average of 3 months after acceptance. Byline given. Buys first North American serial rights or second serial (reprint) rights. Submit seasonal/holiday material 5 months in advance. Simultaneous submissions OK. Query for electronic submissions. Reports in 6 weeks. Sample copy for 9 × 12 SAE.

Nonfiction: Exposé, general interest, historical/nostalgic, how-to, humor, interview/profile, new product, opinion, personal experience, photo feature, technical, travel. Buys 50 mss/year. Query with or without published clips, or send complete ms. Length: 2,000 words maximum. Pays 15-20¢/word. Sometimes pays expenses of writers on assignment.

Photos: State availability of photos with submission. Reviews contact sheets and transparencies. Offers $10-150 per photo. Captions and identification of subjects required. Buys one-time rights.

Columns/Departments: Buys 50 mss/year. Query with published clips or send complete ms. Length: 500-1,000 words. We pay 15¢/word, 20¢ if it comes on Mac disk.

Fiction: We have never published fiction, but would consider outstanding fiction written with our audience in mind. Send complete ms. Length: 1,000 words maximum. Pays $150 maximum.

Fillers: Anecdotes, facts and short humor—in sidebar format. Buys 25/year. Length: 400 words maximum. Pays 15-20¢/word.

Tips: "Query with clips. A query letter can say a lot about a person's writing style and attitudes—we need this. We are currently in the market for lengthy (1,500-2,000 words) nonfiction articles dealing with issues of importance to business women."

Regional

‡**BOSTON BUSINESS JOURNAL,** P&L Publications, 451 D. St., Boston MA 02210-1907. (617)330-1000. Editor: Rick Manning. 20% freelance written. Weekly newspaper covering business in Greater Boston. "Our audience is top managers at small, medium and Fortune 500 companies." Circ. 32,000. Pays on publication. Publishes ms an average of 2 weeks after acceptance. Byline given. Offers 50% kill fee. Buys all rights. Submit seasonal/holiday material 1 month in advance. Query for electronic submissions. Reports in 1 week on queries; in 2 weeks on mss.
Nonfiction: Expose, humor, interview/profile, opinion, and photo features. Real estate supplement (3rd week of each month); special focus on hotels, health care and the office. Buys 50 mss/year. Query with published clips. Length: 600-1,500 words. Pays $125-250 for assigned articles; $125-150 for unsolicited articles. Pays expenses of writers on assignment.
Photos: State availability of photos with submission. Reviews 8 × 10 prints. Pays $40-75 per photo. Identification of subjects required. Buys one-time rights and reprint rights.
Columns/Departments: Technology (computer and computer-related topics). Query. Length: 1,000 words. Pays $125-175.
Tips: "Read *Wall Street Journal.* Look for hard news angle versus feature angle. Use 'numbers' liberally in the story. We prefer submissions on computer disk (call for specifics)."

BOULDER COUNTY BUSINESS REPORT, 1830 N. 55th St., Boulder CO 80301. (303)440-4950. FAX: (303)440-8954. Editor: Jerry W. Lewis. 75% freelance written. Prefers to work with published/established writers; works with a small number of new/unpublished writers each year. Monthly newspaper covering Boulder County business issues. Offers "news tailored to a monthly theme and read primarily by Colorado businesspeople and by some investors nationwide. Philosophy: Descriptive, well-written articles that reach behind the scene to examine area's business activity." Estab. 1982. Circ. 16,000. Pays on publication. Publishes ms an average of 1 month after acceptance. Byline given. Buys one-time rights and second serial (reprint) rights. Simultaneous queries OK. Query for electronic submissions. Reports in 1 month on queries; 2 weeks on mss. Sample copy free on request.
Nonfiction: Interview/profile, new product, examination of competition in a particular line of business. "All our issues are written around one or two monthly themes. No articles are accepted in which the subject has not been pursued in depth and both sides of an issue presented in a writing style with flair." Buys 120 mss/year. Query with published clips. Length: 250-2,000 words. Pays $50-300.
Photos: State availability of photos with query letter. Reviews b&w contact sheets. Pays $10 maximum for b&w contact sheet. Identification of subjects required. Buys one-time rights and reprint rights.
Tips: "It would be difficult to write for this publication if a freelancer were unable to localize a subject. In-depth articles are written by assignment. The freelancer located in the Colorado area has an excellent chance here."

BUSINESS NEW HAMPSHIRE MAGAZINE, (formerly *BNH Magazine*), Suite 201, 404 Chestnut St., Manchester NH 03101-1803. Editor: Dan Wise. Managing Editor: Barbara Benham. 15% freelance written. Monthly magazine with focus on business, politics, life and people of New Hampshire. "Our audience consists of the owners and top managers of New Hampshire businesses and others interested in business and state affairs. Estab. 1985. Circ. 20,000. Pays on publication. Publishes ms an average of 2 months after acceptance. Byline given. Buys first North American serial rights. Reports in 1 month on queries. Free sample copy and writer's guidelines to likely contributors.
Nonfiction: Essays, how-to, interview/profile and opinion. Buys 14 mss/year. Query with published clips. "No unsolicited ms; interested in local writers only." Length: 500-1,800 words. $50-300 for assigned articles.
Photos: State availability of photos with submission. Reviews contact sheets. Model releases and identification of subjects required. Buys one-time rights.
Columns/Departments: Personal Business (how-to, lifestyle, health, personal finance, travel by local writers), 1,000 words. Buys 6 mss/year.
Tips: "I *always* want clips with queries. Writers must be from the area and be experienced writers. Follow up of phone call at least 3 weeks. People and how-to pieces best for new writers."

‡**CALIFORNIA BUSINESS,** Suite 400, 4221 Wilshire Blvd., Los Angeles CA 90010. (213)937-5820. Editor: Christopher Bergonzi. 50% freelance written. Monthly business publication covering California. Includes Pacific rim and Mexico. Estab. 1965. Circ. 130,000. **Pays on acceptance.** Publishes ms an average of 3 months after acceptance. Byline given. Pays 30% kill fee. Buys first North American serial rights. Submit seasonal/holiday material 6 months in advance. Query for electronic submissions. Reports in 1 month. Sample copy for 8½ × 11 SAE with 4 first class stamps. Writer's guidelines for #10 SASE.

Nonfiction: Book excerpts, expose, interview/profile. Buys 96 mss/year. Query. Length: 2,000-4,000 words. Pays $1500-4000 for assigned articles. Pays expenses of writers on assignment.

Photos: State availability of photos with submission. Reviews transparencies. Captions, model releases required. Buys one-time rights.

Tips: "Also publishes monthly business supplement titled 'LA Business,' focusing on executives' lifestyles. 80% staff written. Editor: Kristine Wyatt."

CRAIN'S DETROIT BUSINESS, Crain Communications, Inc., 1400 Woodbridge, Detroit MI 48207. (313)446-0460. FAX: (313)446-0383. Editor: Mary Kramer. Managing Editor: Dave Guilford. 20% freelance written. Weekly tabloid covering Detroit area businesses. *"Crain's Detroit Business* reports the activities of local businesses. Our readers are mostly executives; many of them own their own companies. They read us to keep track of companies not often reported about in the daily press—privately held companies and small public companies. Our slant is hard news and news features. We do not report on the auto companies, but other businesses in Wayne, Oakland, Macomb, and Washtenaw counties are part of our turf." Circ. 33,500. Pays on publication. Byline given. Offers negotiable kill fee. Buys first rights and "the right to make the story available to the other 25 Crain publications, and the right to circulate the story through the Crain News Service." Query for electronic submissions. Sample copy 50¢; writer's guidelines for SASE.

Nonfiction: Cindy Goodaker, articles editor. Book excerpts and interview/profile. No "how-tos, new product articles, or fiction." Looking for local and statewide news. Buys 200 mss/year. Query. Length: 800 words average. Pays $6/inch and expenses for assigned articles. Pays $6/inch without expenses for unsolicited articles. Pays expenses of writers on assignment.

Tips: "What we are most interested in are specific news stories about local businesses. The fact that Widget Inc. is a great company is of no interest to us. However, if Widget Inc. introduced a new product six months ago and sales have gone up from $20 million to $30 million, then that's a story. The same is true if sales went down from $20 million to $10 million. I would strongly encourage interested writers to contact me directly. Although we don't have a blanket rule against unsolicited manuscripts, they are rarely usable. We are a general circulation publication, but we are narrowly focused. A writer not familiar with us would have trouble focusing the story properly, In addition writers may not have a business relationship with the company they are writing about."

FLORIDA BUSINESS/SOUTHWEST, (formerly *Business View*), Business Journal Publishing Co., P.O. Box 9859, Naples FL 33941. (813)263-7525. FAX: (813)263-1046. Editor: Ken Gooderham. 100% freelance written. Prefers to work with published/established writers; works with a small number of new/unpublished writers each year. A monthly magazine covering business trends and issues in southwest Florida. Estab. 1982. Circ. 17,000. Pays on publication. Publishes ms an average of 6 months after acceptance. Byline given. Buys all rights or makes work-for-hire assignments. Simultaneous and previously published submissions OK. Query for electronic submissions. Reports in 2 months. Sample copy $2.95 with 8½×11 SAE and 8 first class stamps; writer's guidelines for #10 SASE.

Nonfiction: Book excerpts (business); how-to (management); humor (business); interview/profile (regional); and technical. Buys 24-36 mss/year. Query with published clips. Length: 100-3,000 words. Pays $25-350 for assigned articles; pays $15-200 for unsolicited articles. Sometimes pays the expenses of writers on assignment.

Photos: State availability of photos with submission. Reviews contact sheets and 5×7 prints. Offers $15-25/photo. Prefers color. Buys one-time rights.

Columns/Departments: Management; Technology (local manufacturers and inventors); Profiles; Viewpoint; Regional View. Buys 12-20 mss/year. Send complete ms. Length: 750-1,200 words. Pays $25-100.

Tips: "Our readers like specific answers to specific problems. Do not send generalized how-to articles that do not offer concrete solutions to management problems. Be concise, informed, and upbeat in style. Profiles of southwest Florida business leaders are most open to freelance writers. These are short (1,000 words) articles that present local, interesting personalities. How-to articles in the areas of management, personal finance, retailing, accounting, investing, personnel and stress management are also open."

INDIANA BUSINESS, 6502 Westfield Blvd., Indianapolis IN 46220. (317)252-2737. FAX: (317)252-2738. Editor: Melinda Church. 50% freelance written. Statewide publication focusing on business in Indiana. "We are a general business publication that reaches 30,000 top executives in Indiana, covering all business categories." Circ. 35,000. Pays on publication. Publishes ms an average of 2 months after acceptance. Rights negotiable. Byline given. Reports in 1 month. Sample copy $2.

Nonfiction: Expose; interview/profile; and opinion. No first person experience stories. "All articles must relate to Indiana business and must be of interest to a broad range of business and professional people. We are especially interested in profiles of Indiana executives. We would like to hear about business success stories but only as they pertain to current issues, trends (i.e., a real estate company that has made it big because they got in on the Economic Development Bonds and invested in renovation property)." Buys 60 mss/year. Submit clips with query. Length: 500-2,500 words. Pay negotiable. Pays expenses of writers on assignment.

Photos: State availability of photos. Reviews contact sheets, negatives, transparencies and 5×7 prints. Pay negotiable for b&w or color photos. Captions, model releases and identification of subjects required.
Columns/Departments: "Writers need to check with us. We may publish a column once a year or six times a year, and we will consider any business-related subject." Query. Length: 1,000-1,500 words.
Fillers: Anecdotes and newsbreaks. Length: 125-250 words.
Tips: "Give us a concise query telling us not only why we should run the article but why you should write it. Be sure to indicate available photography or subjects for photography or art. We look first for good ideas. Our readers are sophisticated business people who are interested in their peers as well as how they can run their businesses better. We will look at non-business issues if they can be related to business in some way."

MEMPHIS BUSINESS JOURNAL, Mid-South Communications, Inc., Suite 102, 88 Union, Memphis TN 38103. (901)523-0437. Editor: Barney DuBois. Weekly tabloid covering industry, trade, agribusiness and finance in west Tennessee, north Mississippi, east Arkansas, and the Missouri Bootheel. "Articles should be timely and relevant to business in our region." Estab. 1979. Circ. 12,500. **Pays on acceptance.** Byline given. Pays $50 kill fee. Buys one-time rights, and makes work-for-hire assignments. Free sample copy.
Nonfiction: Exposé, historical/nostalgic, interview/profile, business features and trends. "All must relate to business in our area." Query with or without clips of published work, or send complete ms. Length: 750-2,000 words. Pays $100-250. Sometimes pays the expenses of writers on assignment.
Photos: State availability of photos or send photos with ms. Pays $25-50 for 5×7 b&w prints. Identification of subjects required. Buys one-time rights.
Tips: "We are interested in news—and this means we can accept short, hard-hitting work more quickly. We also welcome freelancers who can do features and articles on business in the smaller cities of our region. We are a weekly, so our stories need to be timely."

NOVA SCOTIA BUSINESS JOURNAL, N S Business Publishing Limited, 2099 Gottingen St., Halifax B3K 3B2 Nova Scotia. (902)420-0437. Editor: Bette Tetreault. 25% freelance written. Monthly tabloid. "We are a business to business paper, publishing stories to keep provincial businesses aware of what is happening in the province." Circ. 26,000. Pays on publication. Publishes ms an average of 1 month after acceptance. Byline given. Buys first rights. Query for electronic submissions. Sample copy for 8½×11 SAE with $1 postage. Writer's guidelines for #10 SAE with 1 first class stamp.
Nonfiction: Interview/profile, new product and technical. "Editorial calendar available with writer's guidelines if requested." Buys 120 mss/year. Query with published clips. Length: 150-1,000 words. Pays 10¢/word. Sometimes pays expenses of writers on assignment.
Photos: State availability of photos with submission. Offers no additional payment for photos accepted with ms.

OREGON BUSINESS, Media America Publications, Suite 407, 921 SW Morrison, Portland OR 97205. (503)223-0304. Editor: Robert Hill. 60% freelance written. Works with a small number of new/unpublished writers each year. Monthly magazine covering business in Oregon. Estab. 1981. Circ. 20,000. Pays on publication. Publishes ms an average of 4 months after acceptance. Byline given. Buys first rights. Submit seasonal/holiday material 3 months in advance. Previously published submissions OK. Reports in 1 month. Sample copy for 9×12 SAE and 5 first class stamps.
Nonfiction: General interest (real estate, business, investing, small business); interview/profile (business leaders); and new products. Special issues include tourism, world trade, finance. "We need articles on real estate or small business in Oregon, outside the Portland area." Buys 50 mss/year. Query with published clips. Length: 900-2,000 words. Pays 10¢/word minimum; $200 maximum. Sometimes pays expenses of writers on assignment.

ORLANDO MAGAZINE, Orlando Media Affiliates, Box 2207, Suite 290, 341 N. Maitland Ave., Orlando FL 32802. (407)539-3939. 50% freelance written. Monthly magazine covering city growth, development and business. Circ. 35,000. Pays on publication. Publishes ms an average of 2 months after acceptance. Byline given. Offers negotiable kill fee. Submit seasonal/holiday material 3 months in advance. Simultaneous submissions OK. Reports in 3 weeks. Free sample copy and writer's guidelines.

Always check the most recent copy of a magazine for the address and editor's name before you send in a query or manuscript.

Nonfiction: Exposé, how-to (business), and interview. Buys 60 mss/year. Send complete ms. Length: 1,000-2,500 words. Pays $50-350 for assigned articles.
Photos: State availability of photos with submission. Reviews transparencies. Offers $5 per photo. Captions and identification of subjects required. Buys one-time rights.
Columns/Departments: Virtually all business topics. Length: 1,200-1,500. Buys 24 mss/year. Pays $100-200.
Fillers: Newsbreaks. "Have a well-researched query. Give me a call; I'll answer the phone, but be prepared." Buys 36/year. Length: 100-500 words. Pays $25-50.

REGARDIES: THE MAGAZINE OF WASHINGTON BUSINESS, 1010 Wisconsin Ave., NW, Washington DC 20007. (202)342-0410. Editor: Brian Kelly. 80% freelance written. Works with a small number of new/unpublished writers each year. Monthly magazine covering business and general features in the Washington DC metropolitan area for Washington business executives. Circ. 60,000. Pays within 30 days after publication. Publishes ms an average of 2 months after acceptance. Byline given. Offers variable kill fee. Buys first serial rights and second serial (reprint) rights. Submit seasonal/holiday material 3 months in advance. Reports in 3 weeks. Sample copy for $8 and 9 × 12 SAE.
Nonfiction: Profiles (of business leaders), investigative reporting, real estate, advertising, politics, lifestyle, media, retailing, communications, labor issues and financial issues—all on the Washington business scene. "If it is not the kind of story that could just as easily run in a good city magazine or a national magazine like *Harper's*, *Atlantic*, *Esquire*, etc., I don't want to see it." Also buys book mss for excerpt. No how-to. Narrative nonfiction only. Buys 90 mss/year. Length: 4,000 words average. Buys 5-6/issue. Pays negotiable rate. Pays the expenses of writers on assignment.
Columns/Departments: Length: 1,500 words average. Buys 8-12/issue. Pays negotiable rates.
Tips: "The most frequent mistake writers make is not including enough information and data about business which, with public companies, is easy enough to find. This results in flawed analysis and a willingness to accept the 'official line.'"

SAN FRANCISCO BUSINESS TIMES, 325 Fifth St., San Francisco CA 94107. (415)777-9355. Editor: Tim Clark. Managing Editor: Delbert Schafer. 10% freelance written. Weekly tabloid of Bay Area business news and issues. "The *San Francisco Business Times* is a publication targeted to small business owners, mid- and top-level managers of corporations throughout the Bay Area. The stories must be written in non-technical, jargon-free literate style." Estab. 1986. Circ. 13,000. Pays on publication. Publishes ms an average of 1 month after acceptance. Byline given. Negotiated kill fee. Query for electronic submission.
Nonfiction: "Focus" section. Length: 800-1,000 words. Pays $100.
Fillers: Facts and newsbreaks. Buys 12/year. Length: 200 words maximum. Payment negotiated.
Tips: "Become aware of the trends in the business community and prepare a brief outline of your proposed submission. Include sources that may be contacted for the story. The Focus section concentrates on issues and concerns to Bay Area business community. There is a need to relate material to local and national scene."

SOUND BUSINESS, (formerly *Seattle Business*), Vernon Publications, Suite 200, 3000 Northup Way, Bellevue WA 98004. (206)827-9900. Editorial Director: Michele Andrus Dill. 20% freelance written. Monthly magazine covering business news in Greater Seattle area. "Articles must pertain to concerns of Seattle businesses, emphasis on local, not national." Estab. 1964. Circ. 13,000. Publishes ms an average of 3 months after acceptance. Byline given. Buys all rights. Simultaneous submissions OK. Reports only on submissions used. Sample copy for 9 × 12 SAE with 54¢ postage; writer's guidelines for #10 SASE.
Nonfiction: General interest, how-to (succeed in business, be more efficient, increase profitability, etc.), humor, interview/profile, opinion, technical. Buys 5 mss/year. Query. Length: 500-2,000 words. Pays $100-250. Sometimes pays expenses of writers on assignment.
Photos: State availability of photos with submission. Reviews contact sheets, prints. Offers no additional payment for photos accepted with ms. Identification of subjects required. Buys one-time rights.
Tips: "We are interested in any feature-length (1,200-2,000 words) submission on some aspect of business in Seattle area. It is best to query in writing first."

VICTORIA'S BUSINESS REPORT, Monday Publications Ltd., 1609 Blanshard St., Victoria, British Columbia V8W 2J5 Canada. (604)382-7777. FAX: (604)381-2662. Editor: Gery Lemon. 20% freelance written. Monthly magazine that covers Vancouver Island business. "*Victoria's Business Report* is small business-oriented and focuses on Victoria and southern Vancouver Island." Pays on publication. Publishes ms an average of 2 months after acceptance. Byline given. Buys first North American serial rights. Simultaneous and previously published submissions OK. Query for electronic submissions. Reports in 3 weeks on queries. Sample copy $2.75.
Nonfiction: Length: 500-2,000 words. Pays $75-400 for assigned articles. Sometimes pays expenses of writers on assignment.
Photos: State availability of photos with submission. Offers $10-35 per photo. Captions and identification of subjects required. Buys one-time rights.

WESTERN NEW YORK MAGAZINE, Greater Buffalo Chamber Services Corporation, 107 Delaware Ave., Buffalo NY 14202. (716)852-7100. Editor: J. Patrick Donlon. 10% freelance written. Monthly magazine of the Buffalo-Niagara Falls-Southern Ontario area. "Tells the story of Buffalo and Western New York, balancing business with quality-of-life topics" Estab. 1909. Circ. 8,000. **Pays on acceptance.** Publishes ms an average of 3 months after acceptance. Byline given. Not copyrighted. Buys all rights. Submit seasonal/holiday material 3 months in advance. Simultaneous queries OK. Reports in 1 month. Sample copy for $2, 9 × 12 SAE and 3 first class stamps; writer's guidelines for #10 SASE.
Nonfiction: General interest (business, finance, commerce); historical/nostalgic (Buffalo, Niagara Falls); how-to (business management); interview/profile (community leader); and Western New York industry, quality of life. "Broad-based items preferred over single firm or organization. Submit articles that provide insight into business operations, marketing, finance, promotion and nuts-and-bolts approach to small business management. No nationwide or even New York statewide articles or pieces on specific companies, products, services." Buys 30 mss/year. Query with published clips. Length: 1,000-2,500 words. Pays $150-300. Sometimes pays the expenses of writers on assignment.
Photos: Pamela Mills, art director. State availability of photos. Reviews contact sheets. Pays $10-25 for 5 × 7 b&w prints.

Career, College and Alumni

Three types of magazines are listed in this section: university publications written for students, alumni and friends of a specific institution; publications about college life for students; and publications on career and job opportunities.

AIM, A Resource Guide for Vocational/Technical Graduates, Communications Publishing Group, 3100 Broadway, 225 PennTower, Kansas City MO 64111. (816)756-3039. FAX: (816)756-3018. Editor: Georgia Clark. 40% freelance written. A quarterly educational and career source guide "designed to assist experienced voc/tech students in their search for career opportunities and aid in improving their life survival skills. For Black and Hispanic young adults—ages 21-35." Estab. 1982. Circ. 350,000. **Pays on acceptance.** Byline sometimes given. Buys second serial (reprint) rights or makes work-for-hire assignments. Submit seasonal/holiday material 6 months in advance. Simultaneous and previously published submissions OK. Reports in 2 months. Sample copy for 9 × 10 SAE with 4 first class stamps. Writer's guidelines for #10 SASE.
Nonfiction: Book excerpts or reviews, general interest, how-to (dealing with careers or education), humor, inspirational, interview/profile (celebrity or "up and coming" young adult), new product (as it relates to young adult market), personal experience, photo feature, technical, travel. Query or send complete ms. Length: 750-3,000 words. Pays $150-400 for assigned articles; 10¢/word for unsolicited articles. Sometimes pays expenses of writers on assignment.
Photos: State availability of photos with submission. Prefers transparencies. Offers $10-50/photo. Captions, model releases and identification of subjects required. Buys all rights.
Columns/Departments: Profiles of Achievement (striving and successful minority young adult ages 21-35 in various technical careers). Buys 15 mss/year. Send complete ms. Length: 500-1,000 words. Pays $50-250.
Fiction: Adventure, ethnic, historical, humorous, mainstream, slice-of-life vignettes. Buys 3 mss/year. Send complete ms. Length: 1,000-5,000 words. Pays $100-400.
Poetry: Free verse. Buys 5 poems/year. Submit up to 5 poems at one time. Length: 10-25 lines. Pays $10-50.
Fillers: Anecdotes, facts, gags to be illustrated by cartoonist, newsbreaks, short humor. Buys 10/year. Length: 25-250 words. Pays $25-100.
Tips: "For new writers, submit full manuscript that is double spaced; clean copy only. Include on first page of manuscript your name, address, phone, Social Security Number and number of words in article. Need to have clippings of previous published works and resume. Resume should tell when available to write. Most open are profiles of successful and striving Black or Hispanic young adults (age 21-35). Include photo."

ALCALDE, P.O. Box 7278, Austin TX 78713. (512)471-3799. FAX: (512)471-8832. Editor: Ernestine Wheelock. 20% freelance written. Works with a small number of new/unpublished writers each year. Bimonthly magazine. Estab. 1913. Circ. 48,000. Pays on publication. Publishes ms an average of 6 months after acceptance. Buys all rights. Submit seasonal/holiday material 5 months in advance. Query for electronic submissions. Reports in 1 month. Sample copy 8½ × 11 and $1.10 postage. Writer's guidelines for #10 SASE.
Nonfiction: General interest; historical (University of Texas, research and faculty profile); humor (humorous Texas subjects); nostalgia (University of Texas traditions); profile (students, faculty, alumni); and technical (University of Texas research on a subject or product). No subjects lacking taste or quality, or not connected with the University of Texas. Buys 12 mss/year. Query. Length: 1,000-2,400 words. Pays according to importance of article.

THE BLACK COLLEGIAN, The Career & Self Development Magazine for African American Students, Black Collegiate Services, Inc., 1240 S. Broad St., New Orleans LA 70125. (504)821-5694. FAX: (504)821-5713. Editor: K. Kazi-Ferrouillet. 25% freelance written. Magazine for African-American college students and recent graduates with an interest in career and job information, African-American cultural awareness, sports, news, personalities, history, trends and current events. Published bimonthly during school year (4 times/year). Estab. 1970. Circ. 121,000. Buys one-time rights. Byline given. Pays on publication. Submit seasonal and special interest material 2 months in advance of issue date (Careers, September; Computers/ Grad School and Travel/Summer programs, November; Engineering and Black History programs, January; Finance and Jobs, March). Reports in 3 weeks on queries; 1 month on mss. Sample copy for 9×12 SAE and $4. Writer's guidelines for #10 SASE.

Nonfiction: Material on careers, sports, black history, news analysis. Articles on problems and opportunities confronting African-American college students and recent graduates. Book excerpts, expose, general interest, historical/nostalgic, how-to (develop employability), opinion, personal experience, profile, inspirational, humor. Buys 40 mss/year (6 unsolicited). Query with published clips or send complete ms. Length: 500-1,500 words. Pays $50-500.

Photos: State availability of photos with query or ms, or send photos with query or ms. Black and white photos or color transparencies purchased with or without ms. 8×10 prints preferred. Captions, model releases and identification of subjects required. Pays $35/b&w; $50/color.

Tips: "Career features area is most open to freelancers."

CAREER FOCUS, For Today's Professional, Communications Publishing Group, Inc., Suite 225, 3100 Broadway, Kansas City MO 64111. (816)756-3039. FAX: (816)756-3018. Editor: Georgia Clark. 40% freelance written. Bimonthly magazine "devoted to providing positive insight, information, guidance and motivation to assist Blacks and Hispanics (ages 21-35) in their career development and attainment of goals." Estab. 1988. Circ. 750,000. **Pays on acceptance.** Byline often given. Buys second serial (reprint) rights and makes work-for-hire assignments. Submit seasonal/holiday material 6 months in advance. Simultaneous and previously published submissions OK. Reports in 2 months. Sample copy for 9×12 SAE and 4 first class stamps; writer's guidelines for #10 SASE.

Nonfiction: Book excerpts, general interest, historical, how-to, humor, inspirational, interview/profile, personal experience, photo feature, technical, travel. Length: 750-3,000 words. Pays $150-400 for assigned articles; pays 10¢/word for unsolicited articles. Sometimes pays expenses of writers on assignment.

Photos: State availability of photos with submission. Reviews transparencies. Pays $10-50. Captions, model releases and identification of subjects required. Buys all rights.

Columns/Departments: Profiles (striving and successful Black and Hispanic young adult, ages 21-35). Buys 15 mss/year. Send complete ms. Length: 500-1,000 words. Pays $50-250.

Fiction: Adventure, ethnic, historical, humorous, mainstream, slice-of-life vignettes. Buys 3 mss/year. Send complete ms. Length: 1,500-5,000 words. Pays $100-400.

Poetry: Free verse. Buys 4/year. Length: 10-25 lines. Pays $10-50.

Fillers: Anecdotes, facts, gags to be illustrated by cartoonist, newsbreaks, short humor. Buys 10/year. Length: 25-250 words. Pays $25-100.

Tips: "For new writers: Submit full manuscript that is double-spaced; clean copy only. Need to have clippings and previously published works and resume. Should also tell when available to write. Most open to freelancers are profiles of successful and striving persons including photos. Profile must be of a Black or Hispanic adult living in the U.S. Include on first page of manuscript your name, address phone, Social Security number and number of words in article."

CAREER WOMAN, For Entry-Level and Professional Women, (formerly *Collegiate Career Woman*), Equal Opportunity Publications, Inc., 44 Broadway, Greenlawn NY 11740. (516)261-8917. Editor: Anne Kelly. 80% freelance written. Works with small number of new/unpublished writers each year. Magazine published 3 times/year (fall, winter, spring) covering career-guidance for college women. Strives to "aid women in developing career abilities to the fullest potential; improve job hunting skills; present career opportunities; provide personal resources; help cope with discrimination." Audience is 92% college juniors and seniors; 8% working graduates. Circ. 10,500. Controlled circulation, distributed through college guidance and placement offices. Pays on publication. Publishes ms an average of 3-12 months after acceptance. Byline given. Buys all rights. Simultaneous queries and submissions OK. Free sample copy and writer's guidelines.

Nonfiction: "We want career-related articles describing for a college-educated woman the how-tos of obtaining a professional position and advancing her career." Looks for practical features detailing self-evaluation techniques, the job-search process, and advice for succeeding on the job. Emphasizes role-model profiles of succesful career women. Needs manuscripts presenting information on professions offering opportunities to young women — especially the growth professions of the future. Special issues emphasize career opportunities for women in fields such as health care, communications, sales, marketing, banking, insurance, finance, science, engineering, and computers as well as opportunities in government, military and defense. Query first.

Photos: Send with ms. Prefers 35mm color slides, but will accept b&w prints. Captions and identification of subjects required. Buys all rights.

Tips: "Articles should focus on career-guidance, role model, and industry prospects for women and should have a snappy, down-to-earth writing style."

CARNEGIE MELLON MAGAZINE, Carnegie Mellon University, Pittsburgh PA 15213. (412)268-2900. Editor: Ann Curran. Alumni publication issued fall, winter, spring, summer covering university activities, alumni profiles, etc. Circ, 52,000. **Pays on acceptance.** Byline given. Not copyrighted. Reports in 1 month.
Nonfiction: Book reviews (faculty alumni), general interest, humor, interview/profile, photo feature. "We use general interest stories linked to CMU activities and research." No unsolicited mss. Buys 5 features and 5-10 alumni profiles/year. Query with published clips. Length: 800-2,000 words. Pays $100-400 or negotiable rate. Sample copy for 9 × 12 SAE and $2 postage.
Poetry: Avant-garde or traditional. No previously published poetry. No payment.
Tips: "Concentration is given to professional writers among alumni."

CIRCLE K MAGAZINE, 3636 Woodview Trace, Indianapolis IN 46268. FAX: (317)879-0204. Executive Editor: Nicholas K. Drake. 60% freelance written. "Our readership consists almost entirely of above-average college students interested in voluntary community service and leadership development. They are politically and socially aware and have a wide range of interests." Publishes 5 times/year. Circ. 12,000. **Pays on acceptance.** Normally buys first North American serial rights. Byline given. Submit seasonal/holiday material 6 months in advance. Reports in 1 month. Sample copy and writer's guidelines for large SAE with 3 first class stamps.
Nonfiction: Articles published in *Circle K* are of two types—serious and light nonfiction. "We are interested in general interest articles on topics concerning college students and their lifestyles, as well as articles dealing with careers, community concerns and leadership development." No "first person confessions, family histories or travel pieces." Query. Length: 2,000-2,500 words. Pays $225-350.
Photos: Purchased with accompanying ms. Captions required. Total purchase price for ms includes payment for photos.
Tips: "Query should indicate author's familiarity with the field and sources. Subject treatment must be objective and in-depth, and articles should include illustrative examples and quotes from persons involved in the subject or qualified to speak on it. We are open to working with new writers who present a good article idea and demonstrate that they've done their homework concerning the article subject itself, as well as concerning our magazine's style. We're interested in college-oriented trends, for example, entrepreneur schooling is now a major shift; more awareness of college crime; health issues."

COLLEGE MONTHLY, New England, Lapierre & Associates, Suite 805, 332 Main St., Worcester MA 01608. (508)753-2550. Editor: Maureen Castillo. Managing Editor: Randy Cohen. 25% freelance written. College lifestyle and entertainment magazine published 8 times/year. Estab. 1986. Circ. 73,000. Pays on publication. Byline given. Offers $5 kill fee. Buys one-time rights. Query for electronic submissions. Free sample copy and writer's guidelines.
Nonfiction: Humor, interview/profile, opinion, personal experience and travel. Query with published clips. Length: 500-2,000 words. Pays $25-100 for assigned articles; $5-25 for unsolicited articles. Sometimes pays the expenses of writers on assignment.
Photos: State availability of photos with submission. Offers no additional payment for photos accepted with ms. Caption required. Buys one-time rights.
Columns/Departments: Fashion (trends in the college market for clothes); Lifestyle (off-the-wall things students do); Sports (national sports and college); Politics (national level/hot social issues), all 500-750 words.
Fillers: Newsbreaks, short humor. Length: 100 words. Pays $5-25.

‡COLLEGE OUTLOOK AND CAREER OPPORTUNITIES, Townsend Outlook Publishing Company, 7007 NE Parvin Road, Kansas City, Missouri 64117. P.O. Box 34725, Kansas City, MO 64116-1125. (816)454-9660. Editor: John Hayes. 40% freelance written. Editions include Fall (Sept.) edition for high sclhool seniors and junior college transfers and spring (Feb.) edition for high school juniors. Student information publications on subjects of interest to college and career minded students. Estab. 1975. Circ. 1.3 million plus. Byline given. Generally buys all rights and second (reprint) rights. For sample copy send SAE and postage.
Nonfiction: "*College Outlook* informs students on college admissions, financial aid, career opportunities, academic options and other topics of interest to college and career bound students. We are always looking for interesting pieces."
Photos: State availability of photos. "Generally we use photos which we have found with focus on students." Model release required. Generally buys all rights.

COLLEGE PREVIEW, A Guide for College-Bound Students, Communications Publishing Group, 3100 Broadway, 225 PennTower, Kansas City MO 64111. (816)756-3039. FAX: (816)756-3018. Editor: Georgia Clark. 40% freelance written. A quarterly educational and career source guide. "Contemporary guide is designed to inform and motivate Black and Hispanic young adults, ages 16-21 years old about college preparation, career planning and life survival skills." Estab. 1982. Circ. 600,000. **Pays on acceptance.** Byline often given. Buys second serial (reprint) rights or makes work-for-hire assignments. Submit seasonal/holiday material 6 months in advance. Simultaneous and previously published submissions OK. Reports in 2 months. Sample copy for 9 × 10 SAE with 4 first class stamps. Writer's guidelines for #10 SASE.

Nonfiction: Book excerpts or reviews, general interest, how-to (dealing with careers or education), humor, inspirational, interview/profile (celebrity or "up and coming" young adult), new product (as it relates to young adult market), personal experience, photo feature, technical, travel. Send complete ms. Length: 750-3,000 words. Pays $150-400 for assigned articles; 10¢/word for unsolicited articles. Sometimes pays expenses of writers on assignment.

Photos: State availability of photos with submission. Reviews transparencies. Offers $10-$50/photo. Captions, model releases and identification of subjects required. Buys all rights.

Columns/Departments: Profiles of Achievement (striving and successful minority young adults ages 16-35 in various careers). Buys 15 mss/year. Send complete ms. Length: 500-1,500. Pays $50-250.

Fiction: Adventure, ethnic, historical, humorous, mainstream, slice-of-life vignettes. Buys 3 mss/year. Send complete ms. Length: 1,000-5,000 words. Pays $100-400.

Poetry: Free verse. Buys 5 poems/year. Submit up to 5 poems at one time. Length: 10-25 lines. Pays $10-50.

Fillers: Anecdotes, facts, gags to be illustrated by cartoonist, newsbreaks, short humor. Buys 10/year. Length: 25-250 words. Pasy $25-100.

Tips: For new writers—Send complete manuscript that is double spaced; clean copy only. If available, send clippings of previous published works and resume. Should state when available to write. Include on first page of manuscript your name, address, phone, Social Security number and word count.

‡CV, The College Magazine, Millicom Media Inc., 411 Lafayette St., New York NY 10003. (212)475-8200. Publisher: Heather Evans. 75% freelance written. Magazine on careers and college life published six times during the academic year. Estab. 1989. Circ. 1 million. **Pays on acceptance.** Publishes ms an average of 3½ months after acceptance. Byline given. Offers 25% kill fee. Buys North American rights. Submit seasonal/holiday material 5 months in advance. Query for electronic submissions. Reports in 6 weeks. Sample copy for 9 × 12 SAE with $1.35 postage; writer's guidelines for #10 SASE.

Nonfiction: Opinion (from college students), relationships, careers, issues relevant to campuses. Query with published clips. Length: 250-2,000 words. Pays $25-2,000. Pays expenses of writers on assignment.

Photos: State availability of photos with submissions. Offers no additional payment for photos accepted with ms. Buys one-time rights.

Tips: "Must be very specifically relevant to lives of college students and very informative."

EQUAL OPPORTUNITY, The Nation's Only Multi-Ethnic Recruitment Magazine for Black, Hispanic, Native American & Asian American College Grads, Equal Opportunity Publications, Inc., 44 Broadway, Greenlawn NY 11740. (516)261-8917. FAX: (516)261-8935. Executive Editor: James Schneider. 50% freelance written. Prefers to work with published/established writers. Magazine published 3 times/year (fall, winter, spring) covering career guidance for minorities. "Our audience is 90% college juniors and seniors; 10% working graduates. An understanding of educational and career problems of minorities is essential." Estab. 1967. Circ. 15,000. Controlled circulation, distributed through college guidance and placement offices. Pays on publication. Publishes ms an average of 2 months after acceptance. Byline given. Buys all rights. Deadline dates: fall, June 15; winter, August 15: spring, November 1. Simultaneous queries and previously published submissions OK. Sample copy and writer's guidelines for 9 × 12 SAE and 5 first class stamps.

Nonfiction: Book excerpts and articles (on job search techniques, role models), general interest (on specific minority concerns), how-to (on job-hunting skills, personal finance, better living, coping with discrimination); humor (student or career related), interview/profile (minority role models), opinion (problems of minorities), personal experience (professional and student study and career experiences), technical (on career fields offering opportunities for minorities), travel (on overseas job opportunities), and coverage of Black, Hispanic, Native American and Asian American interests. Special issues include career opportunities for minorities in industry and government in fields such as banking, insurance, finance, communications, sales, marketing, engineering, computers, military and defense. Query or send complete ms. Length: 1,000-1,500 words. Sometimes pays expenses of writers on assignment. Pays 10¢/word.

Photos: Prefers 35mm color slides and b&w. Captions and identification of subjects required. Buys all rights at $15 per photo use.

Tips: "Articles must be geared toward questions and answers faced by minority and women students."

ETC MAGAZINE, Student Media—University of North Carolina at Charlotte, Cone University Center UNCC, Charlotte NC 28223. (704)547-2146. Editor: Ann Larrow. A semiannual magazine on collegiate lifestyle. "*Etc. Magazine* is a student publication serving the University of North Carolina at Charlotte that features general interest articles dealing with collegiate lifestyles." Estab. 1986. Circ. 5,000. Pays on publication. Byline given. Buys one-time rights. Previously published material OK. Reports in 6 months. Free sample copy and writer's guidelines.

Nonfiction: 2,000 word general interest cover story covering topical issues in university setting and 1,000 word general interest feature articles. Magazine departments (1,000 words): Lifeline—helping students cope with stress and changes associated with college life; Skyline—highlighting university's important ties to the Charlotte community; Aspects—focusing on diverse ethnic groups which form large part of university community; Passport—interesting travel ideas for students on limited budgets. Special issues—Freshman orientation

issue and graduate section. Issue-oriented articles average 1,000 words. Pays no more than $10.
Photos: State availability of photos with submission or send photos with submission. Stipend of no more than $10 will be paid upon publication.

FLORIDA LEADER, P.O. Box 14081, Gainesville FL 32604. (904)373-6907. Publisher: W.H. "Butch" Oxendine, Jr. Editor: Christine Lenyo. Nearly 40% freelance written. "Florida's college magazine, feature oriented, especially activities, events, interests and issues pertaining to college students. Published 6 times/year. Estab. 1981. Circ. 28,000. Publishes ms an average of 6 months after acceptance. Byline given. Submit seasonal/holiday material 6 months in advance. Query for electronic submissions. Reports in 1 month on queries. Sample copy and writer's guidelines for 9×12 SAE with 5 first class stamps.
Nonfiction: How-to, humor, interview/profile, and feature—all Florida college related. Special issues include Best of Florida (February); back to school (August); careers and majors (January and June). Query. Length: 500 words or less. Payment varies; may pay writer contributor's copies or other premiums rather than cash. Sometimes pays expenses of writers on assignment.
Photos: State availability of photos with submission. Reviews negatives and transparencies. Captions, model releases and identification of subjects requested.

FORDHAM MAGAZINE, Fordham University, Suite 313, 113 West 60th St., New York NY 10023. (212)841-5360. Editor: Michael Gates. 75% freelance written. A quarterly magazine on Fordham University alumni and student life. "We are heavy on feature and personality profiles on our alumni: e.g. actor Denzel Washington, author Mary Higgins Clark, and how education influenced their careers." **Pays on acceptance.** Publishes ms an average of 8 months after acceptance. Byline given. Offers $50-100 kill fee. Makes work-for-hire assignments. Submit seasonal/holiday material 10 months in advance. Previously published submissions OK. Reports in 1 month on queries; 2 months on mss. Free sample copy; writer's guidelines for #10 SAE and 2 first class stamps.
Nonfiction: Book excerpts, essays, general interest, historical/nostalgic, humor, inspirational, interview/profile (alumni, faculty, students); photo feature. Buys 12 mss/year. Query with published clips. Length: 1,500-3,500. Pays $150-1,000 for assigned articles; $50-500 for unsolicited articles. Sometimes pays expenses of writers on assignment.
Photos: State availability of photos with submission. Reviews contact sheets, transparencies, prints. Offers additional payment for photos accepted with ms. Model releases and identification of subjects required.
Fillers: Anecdotes, facts, newsbreaks, short humor. "All must be specific to Fordham University." Buys 1-2/year. Length: 150-350 words. Pays $25-50.
Tips: "Have a good familiarity with alumni publications in general: research some of the schools and see what they use, what they look for. Research alumni of the school and see if there is a noted personality you might interview—someone who might live in your area. Be prepared to narrow the proposed idea down to the publication's very specific needs. Feature articles and personality profiles are most open to freelancers. These include interviews with famous or interesting alumni and faculty or students, as well as in-depth analytical articles on trends in university life today (pertinent to Fordham) and features on student life in New York. This includes articles on ways that our school interacts with the community around it."

‡HARVARD MAGAZINE, 7 Ware St., Cambridge MA 02138. (617)495-5746. Editor: John Bethell. Managing Editor: Christopher Reed. 50% freelance written. General interest university magazine. "Mining the resources of a great university, the magazine aims to bring the world of ideas to thoughtful readers. Articles must be of general interest but have a strong Harvard angle." Estab. 1898. Circ. 150,000. Pays on acceptance. Byline given. Offers 50% kill fee. Buys first North American serial, one-time, or second serial (reprint) rights. Query for electronic submissions. Reports in 3 weeks on queries; 6 weeks on mss.
Nonfiction: Christopher Reed, editor. Unpublished book excerpts, essays, general interest, historical/nostalgic, humor, interview/profile, opinion, personal experience, photo feature and travel. Buys 20 mss/year. Send complete ms. Length: 500-4,000 words. Pays $150-1,000. Sometimes pays expenses of writers on assignment.
Photos: State availability of photos with submission. Reviews contact sheets, transparencies and prints. Offers $25-75 per photo. Buys one-time rights.
Columns/Departments: Craig Lambert, editor. Work in Progress (reports on research in all fields at Harvard), 500 words. Buys 20 mss/year. Query. Pays $150 minimum.
Poetry: Donald Hall, Eagle Pond Farm, Danbury NH 03230. Avant-garde, free verse, haiku, light verse and traditional. Buys 25 poems/year. Pays $35 minimum.

JOURNEY, A Success Guide for College and Career Bound Students, Communications Publishing Group, 3100 Broadway, 225 PennTower, Kansas City MO 64111. (816)756-3039. FAX: (816)756-3018. Editor: Georgia Clark. 40% freelance written. A quarterly educational and career source guide for Asian-American high school and college students who have indicated a desire to pursue higher education through college, vocational and technical or proprietary schools. For students ages 16-25. Estab. 1982. Circ. 200,000. **Pays on acceptance.** Byline sometimes given. Buys second serial (reprint) rights or makes work-for-hire assignments. Submit seasonal/holiday material 6 months in advance. Simultaneous and previously published submissions

OK. Reports in 2 months. Sample copy for 9 × 12 SAE with 4 first class stamps. Writer's guidelines for #10 SASE.

Nonfiction: Book excerpts or reviews, general interest, how-to (dealing with careers or education), humor, inspirational, interview/profile (celebrity or "up and coming" young adult), new product (as it relates to young adult market), personal experience, photo feature, technical, travel and sports. First time writers with *Journey* must submit complete manuscript for consideration. Length: 750-3,000 words. Pays $150-400 for assigned articles; 10¢/word for unsolicited articles. Sometimes pays expenses of writers on assignment.

Photos: State availability of photos with submission. Prefers transparencies. Offers $10-50/photo. Captions, model releases and identification of subjects required. Buys all rights or one-time rights.

Columns/Departments: Profiles of Achievement (striving and successful minority young adult, age 16-35 in various careers). Buys 15 mss/year. Send complete ms. Length: 500-1,500. Pays $50-200.

Fiction: Adventure, ethnic, historical, humorous, mainstream, slice-of-life vignettes. Buys 3 mss/year. Send complete ms. Length: 1,000-3,000 words. Pays $100-400.

Poetry: Free verse. Buys 5/year. Submit up to 5 poems at one time. Length: 10-25 lines. Pays $10-50.

Fillers: Anecdotes, facts, gags to be illustrated by cartoonist, newsbreaks, short humor. Buys 10/year. Length: 25-250 words. Pays $25-100.

Tips: For new writers—Must submit complete manuscript that is double spaced; clean copy only. If available, send clippings of previous published works and resume. Should state when available to write. Include on first page your name, address, phone, Social Security number and number of words in article.

MISSISSIPPI STATE UNIVERSITY ALUMNUS, Mississippi State University, Alumni Association, Editorial Office, P.O. Box 5328, Mississippi State MS 39762. (601)325-3442. Editor: Mr. Linsey H. Wright. Up to 10% freelance written. Works with small number of new/unpublished writers each year. Emphasizes articles about Mississippi State graduates and former students. For well-educated and affluent audience. Quarterly magazine. Estab. 1927. Circ. 50,000. Pays on publication. Publishes ms 6 months after acceptance. Buys one-time rights. Pays 25% kill fee. Byline given. Submit seasonal/holiday material 3 months in advance. Simultaneous and previously published submissions OK. Reports in 1 month. Sample copy for 9 × 12 SAE and 5 first class stamps.

Nonfiction: Historical, humor (with strong MSU flavor; nothing risque), informational, inspirational, interview (with MSU grads), nostalgia (early days at MSU), personal experience, profile and travel (by MSU grads, but must be of wide interest to other grads). Buys 5-6 mss/years. Send complete ms. Length: 500-2,000 words. Pays $50-150 (including photos, if used).

Photos: Offers no additional payment for photos purchased with accompanying ms. Captions required. Uses 5 × 7 and 8 × 10 b&w photos and color transparencies of any size.

Columns/Departments: Statements, "a section of the *Mississippi State Alumnus* that features briefs about alumni achievements and professional or business advancement. We do not use engagements, marriages or births. There is no payment for Statements briefs."

Tips: "All stories *must* be about Mississippi State University or its alumni. We're putting more emphasis on people and events on the campus—teaching, research and public service projects. But we're still eager to receive good stories about alumni in all parts of the world. We welcome articles about MSU grads in interesting occupations and have used stories on off-shore drillers, miners, horse trainers, etc. We also want profiles on prominent MSU alumni and have carried pieces on Senator John C. Stennis, comedian Jerry Clower, professional football players and coaches, and Eugene Butler, former editor-in-chief of *Progressive Farmer* magazine. We feature two to four alumni in each issue, alumni who have risen to prominence in their fields or who are engaged in unusual occupations or who are involved in unusual hobbies. We're using more short features (500-700 words) to vary the length of our articles in each issue. We pay $50-75 for these, including one black-and-white photo."

‡NATIONAL FORUM: THE PHI KAPPA PHI JOURNAL, The Honor Society of Phi Kappa Phi, 216 Petrie Hall, Auburn University AL 36849. Editor: Stephen W. White. Managing Editor: Rose-Marie Zuk. 20% freelance written. Prefers to work with published/established writers. Quarterly interdisciplinary, scholarly journal. "We are an interdisciplinary journal that publishes crisp, nontechnical analyses of issues of social and scientific concern as well as scholarly treatments of different aspects of culture." Circ. 120,000. Pays on publication. Query first. Publishes ms an average of 6 months after acceptance. Byline given. Buys exclusive rights with exceptions. Submit seasonal/holiday material 6 months in advance. Reports in 6 weeks on queries; 2 months on mss. Sample copy $2.75; free writer's guidelines.

Nonfiction: General interest, interview/profile and opinion. No how-to or biographical articles. Each issue is devoted to the exploration of a particular theme. Upcoming theme issues: "The Human Brain," "Curricular Reform," "News and the Media." Query with clips of published work. Buys 5 unsolicited mss/year. Length: 1,500-2,000 words. Pays $50-200.

Photos: State availability of photos. Identification of subjects required. Buys all rights.

Columns/Departments: Educational Dilemmas of the 90s and Book Review section. Buys 8 mss/year for Educational Dilemmas, 40 book reviews. Length: Book reviews—400-800 words. Educational Dilemmas—1,500-1,800 words. Pays $15-25 for book reviews; $50/printed page, Educational Dilemmas.

Fiction: Humorous and short stories. No obscenity or excessive profanity. Buys 2-4 mss/year. Length: 1,500-1,800 words. Pays $50/printed page.
Poetry: No love poetry. Buys 20 mss/year. Submit 5 poems maximum. Prefers shorter poems. Prefers established poets. Include publication credentials in cover letter.

THE NEW HAMPSHIRE ALUMNUS, University Publications, Schofield House, UNH, Durham NH 03824. (603)862-1463. Editor: Drew Sanborn. 25% freelance written. *"The Alumnus* provides the alumni audience of the University of New Hampshire with features, news and notes on alumni achievements nationwide and on university people and programs two times/year." Estab. 1923. Circ. 40,000. **Pays on acceptance.** Publishes ms an average of 6 months after acceptance. Byline given. Kill fee to be negotiated. Not copyrighted. Makes work-for-hire assignments. Simultaneous and previously published submissions OK. Query for electronic submissions. Free sample copy and writer's guidelines.
Nonfiction: General interest, interview/profile, photo feature. Buys a variable number of mss/year. Query with published clips. Length: 350-1,500 words. Pays $100-400 for assigned articles; pays $50-150 for unsolicited articles. Pays the expenses of writers on assignment.
Photos: State availability of photos with submission. Reviews negatives and 5×8 prints. Identification of subjects required. Buys one-time rights.
Columns/Departments: Alumni Profile (UNH alumni achievements). Query with published clips. Length: 350-750 words. Pays $200 maximum.
Tips: "We give preference to University of New Hampshire (alumni and campus) features, articles and news briefs. We like writers to submit samples of work first with story ideas and fee requirements."

NOTRE DAME MAGAZINE, University of Notre Dame, Room 415, Administration Bldg., Notre Dame IN 46556. (219)239-5335. FAX: (219)239-6947. Editor: Walton R. Collins. Managing Editor: Kerry Temple. 75% freelance written. Quarterly magazine covering news of Notre Dame and education and issues affecting the Roman Catholic Church. "We are interested in the moral, ethical and spiritual issues of the day and how Christians live in today's world. We are universal in scope and Catholic in viewpoint and serve Notre Dame alumni, friends and other constituencies." Estab. 1972. Circ. 110,000. **Pays on acceptance.** Publishes ms an average of 1 year after acceptance. Byline given. Kill fee negotiable. Buys first rights. Simultaneous queries OK. Query for electronic submissions. Computer printout submissions acceptable; prefers letter-quality. Reports in 1 month. Free sample copy.
Nonfiction: Opinion, personal experience, religion. "All articles must be of interest to Christian/Catholic readers who are well educated and active in their communities." Buys 35 mss/year. Query with clips of published work. Length: 600-3,000 words. Pays $500-1,500. Sometimes pays the expenses of writers on assignment.
Photos: State availability of photos. Reviews b&w contact sheets, transparencies, and 8×10 prints. Model releases and identification of subjects required. Buys one-time rights.

OLD OREGON, The Magazine of the University of Oregon, University of Oregon, 101 Chapman Hall, Eugene OR 97403. (503)686-5047. Editor: Tom Hager. 50% freelance written. A quarterly university magazine of people and ideas at the University of Oregon. Circ. 90,000. **Pays on acceptance.** Publishes ms an average of 3 months after acceptance. Byline given. Offers 20% kill fee. Buys first North American serial rights. Query for electronic submissions. Computer printout submissions OK; no dot-matrix. Reports in 3 weeks. Sample copy for 9×12 SAE with 2 first class stamps.
Nonfiction: Historical/nostalgic, interview/profile, personal experience relating to U.O. issues and alumni. Buys 30 mss/year. Query with published clips. Length: 750-3,000 words. Pays $75-300. Sometimes pays expenses of writers on assignment.
Photos: State availability of photos with submission. Reviews 8×10 prints. Offers $10-25/photo. Identification of subjects required. Buys one-time rights.
Tips: "Query with strong, colorful lead; clips."

PICTURE PERFECT, formerly *IFMT Magazine*, International Fashion Model & Talent, Aquino Productions, Inc., Suite 201, 1 Bank St., Box 15760, Stamford CT 06901. (203)978-0562. Editor: Elaine Hallgren. Managing Editor: Andres Aquino. 50% freelance written. Bimonthly magazine covering fashion, photography, modeling, entertainment. Estab. 1989. Circ. 50,000. Pays on publication. Publishes ms an average of 3 months after acceptance. Offers 50% kill fee. Buys first North American serial rights or all rights. Submit seasonal/holiday material 4 months in advance. Simultaneous submissions OK. Reports in 3 weeks on queries; 6 weeks on mss. Sample copy $4. Writer's guidelines for SAE and 2 first class stamps.
Nonfiction: Book excerpts, how-to, interview/profile, new product, personal experience, photo feature and travel. Buys 36-48 mss/year. Send complete ms. Length 250-1,500 words. Pays 20¢/word for assigned articles; 15¢/word for unsolicited articles. Sometimes pays expenses of writers on assignment.
Photos: Send photos with submission. Reviews contact sheets, 2×2 transparencies and 4×6 prints. Offers $25-200 per photo. Captions, model releases and identification of subjects required. Buys one-time rights or First North American Rights.

‡**RIPON COLLEGE MAGAZINE**, Box 248, Ripon WI 54971. (414)748-8115. Editor: Loren J. Boone. 10% freelance written. *"Ripon College Magazine* is a quarterly publication that contains information relating to Ripon College. It is mailed to alumni and friends of the college." Estab. 1851. Circ. 13,000. Pays on publication. Publishes ms an average of 3 months after acceptance. Byline given. Not copyrighted. Makes work-for-hire assignments. Query for electronic submissions. Reports in 2 weeks.

Nonfiction: Historical/nostalgic and interview/profile. Buys 4 mss/year. Query with or without published clips, or send complete ms. Length: 250-1,000 words. Pays $25-500.

Photos: State availability of photos with submission. Reviews contact sheets. Offers no additional payment for photos accepted with ms. Captions and model releases are required. Buys one-time rights.

Tips: "Story ideas must have a direct connection to Ripon College."

SCORECARD, Falsoft, Inc., 9509 US Highway 42, P.O. Box 385, Prospect KY 40059. (502)228-4492. FAX: (502)228-5121. Editor: John Crawley. 50% freelance written. Prefers to work with published/established writers. A weekly sports fan tabloid covering University of Louisville sports only. Estab. 1982. Circ. 7,500. Pays on publication. Publishes ms an average of 1 month after acceptance. Byline given. Buys first rights. Submit seasonal/holiday material 1 month in advance. Previously published submissions OK "rarely." Reports in 2 weeks. Free sample copy and writer's guidelines.

Nonfiction: Assigned to contributing editors. Buys 100 mss/year. Query with published clips. Length: 750-1,500 words. Pays $20-50. Sometimes pays expenses of writers on assignment.

Photos: State availability of photos.

Columns/Departments: Notes Page (tidbits relevant to University of Louisville sports program or former players or teams). Buys 25 mss/year. Length: Approximately 100 words. Pay undetermined.

Tips: "Be very familiar with history and tradition of University of Louisville sports program. Contact us with story ideas. Know the subject."

‡**START!, Employment News**, Staats Communications, Inc., #5, 7313 Lancaster Pike, Hockessin DE 19707. (302)234-0110. Managing Editor: David Staats. 25% freelance written. Biweekly tabloid on job-hunting, career advancement, employment. "We look for practical articles on how to find a new or better job. We value new insights and information on changing conditions, especially in the Delaware Valley." Estab. 1988. Circ. 26,000. Pays on publication. Publishes ms an average of 1 month after acceptance. Byline given. Buys first North American serial rights or second serial (reprint) rights. Submit seasonal/holiday material 2 months in advance. Simultaneous and previously published submissions OK. Query for electronic submissions. Reports in 3 weeks on queries; 6 weeks on mss.

Nonfiction: Book excerpts, how-to, inspirational, interview/profile, personal experience. Buys 20 mss/year. Send complete ms. Length: 500-800 words. Pays: $25-50.

Photos: State availability of photos with submission. Offers no additional payment for photos accepted with ms. Captions and model releases required. Buys one-time rights.

THE STUDENT, 127 9th Ave. N., Nashville TN 37234. FAX: (615)251-3953. Editor: Milt Hughes. 10% freelance written. Works with a small number of new/unpublished writers each year. Publication of Student Ministry Department of the Southern Baptist Convention. For college students; focusing on freshman and sophomore levels. Published 12 times during the school year. Estab. 1922. Circ. 45,000. Buys all rights. **Payment on acceptance.** Publishes ms an average of 10 months after acceptance. Mss should be double-spaced on white paper with 50-space line, 25 lines/page. Reports usually in 6 weeks. Sample copy and guidelines for 8 × 10 SAE.

Nonfiction: Contemporary questions, problems, and issues facing college students viewed from a Christian perspective to develop high moral and ethical values. Cultivating interpersonal relationships, developing self-esteem, dealing with the academic struggle, coping with rejection, learning how to love, developing a personal relationship with Jesus Christ. Prefers complete ms rather than query. Length: 1,000 words maximum. Pays 5½¢/word after editing with reserved right to edit accepted material. Extra payment for use of computer diskette.

Fiction: Satire and parody on college life, humorous episodes; emphasize clean fun and the ability to grow and be uplifted through humor. Contemporary fiction involving student life, on campus as well as off. Length: 900 words. Pays 5½¢/word.

WPI JOURNAL, Worcester Polytechnic Institute, 100 Institute Rd., Worcester MA 01609. FAX: (508)831-5483. Editor: Michael Dorsey. 20% freelance written. A quarterly alumni magazine covering science and engineering/education/business personalities for 19,000 alumni, primarily engineers, scientists, managers, parents of students, national media. Estab. 1897. Circ. 22,500. Pays on publication. Publishes ms an average of 3 months after acceptance. Byline given. Buys one-time rights. Submit seasonal/holiday material 6 months in advance. Simultaneous queries, and simultaneous and previously published submissions OK. Query for electronic submissions. Requires hard copy also. Reports in 2 weeks on queries.

Nonfiction: Book excerpts; exposé (education, engineering, science); general interest; historical/nostalgic; humor; interview/profile (people in engineering, science); personal experience; photo feature; and technical (with personal orientation). Query with published clips. Length: 1,000-4,000 words. Pays negotiable rate. Sometimes pays the expenses of writers on assignment.

Photos: State availability of photos with query or ms. Reviews b&w contact sheets. Pays negotiable rate. Captions required.

Tips: "Submit outline of story and/or ms of story idea or published work. Features are most open to freelancers. Keep in mind that this is an alumni magazine, so most articles focus on the college and its community."

Child Care and Parental Guidance

Readers of today's parenting magazines are starting families later and having fewer children but they want more information on pregnancy, infancy, child development and parenting research. Child care magazines address these and other issues from many different perspectives: Some are general interest parenting magazines while others for child care providers combine care information with business tips. Other markets that buy articles about child care and the family are included in the Education, Religious and Women's sections.

AMERICAN BABY MAGAZINE, For Expectant and New Parents, 475 Park Ave. S., New York NY 10016. (212)689-3600. Editor: Judith Nolte. 90% freelance written. Prefers to work with published/established writers; works with a small number of new/unpublished writers each year. A monthly magazine covering pregnancy, child care and parenting. "Our readership is composed of women in late pregnancy and early new motherhood. Most readers are first-time parents; some have older children. A simple, straightforward, clear approach is mandatory." Estab. 1938. Circ. 1,150,000. **Pays on acceptance.** Publishes ms an average of 3 months after acceptance. Byline given. Buys first North American serial rights. Submit seasonal holiday material 6 months in advance. Simultaneous and previously published submissions OK. Reports in 3 weeks on queries; 2 months on mss. Sample copy for 9 × 12 SAE with 6 first class stamps. Writer's guidelines for SASE.

Nonfiction: Book excerpts, how-to (on some aspect of pregnancy or child care), humor and personal experience. "No 'hearts and flowers' or fantasy pieces." Buys 60 mss/year. Query with published clips, or send complete ms. Length: 1,500-2,500 words. Pays $350-1,000 for assigned articles; pays $300-500 for unsolicited articles. Pays the expenses of writers on assignment.

Photos: State availability of photos with submission. Reviews transparencies and prints. Model release and identification of subjects required. Buys one-time rights.

Columns/Departments: One View (an opinion or personal experience essay on some aspect of pregnancy, birth or parenting), 1,000 words. Buys 12 mss/year. Send complete ms.

Tips: "Articles should either give 'how to' information on some aspect of pregnancy or child care, cover some common problem of child raising, along with solutions, or give advice to the mother on some psychological or practical subject."

BAY AREA PARENT, The Santa Clara News Magazine, for Parents, Kids Kids Kids Publications, Inc., 455, Los Gatos Blvd. #103, Los Gatos CA 95023. FAX: (408)356-4903. Editor: Lynn Berardo. 80% freelance written. Works with locally-based published/established writers. Monthly tabloid of resource information for parents and teachers. Circ 60,000. Pays on publication. Publishes ms an average of 3 months after acceptance. Byline given. Buys one-time rights. Submit seasonal/holiday material 3 months in advance. Simultaneous and previously published submissions OK. Query for electronic submissions. Sample copy for 9 × 12 SAE and $1.75 postage; writer's guidelines for #10 SASE.

Nonfiction: Book excerpts (related to our interest group); expose (health, psychology); historical/nostalgic ("History of Diapers"); how-to (related to kids/parenting); humor; interview/profile; photo feature; and travel (with kids, family). Special issues include Music (February); Art (March); Kid's Birthdays (April); Summer Camps (May); Family Fun (June); Pregnancy and Childbirth (July); Fashion (August); Health (September); and Mental Health (October). No opinion or religious articles. Buys 36-50 mss/year. Query or send complete ms. Length: 150-1,500 words. Pays $10-50. Sometimes pays expenses of writers on assignment.

Photos: State availability of photos. Prefers b&w contact sheets and/or 3x5 b&w prints. Pays $5-25. Model release required. Buys one-time rights.

Columns/Departments: Child Care, Family Travel, Birthday Party Ideas, Baby Page, Toddler Page, Adolescent Kids. Buys 36 mss/year. Send complete ms. Length: 400-1,200 words. Pays $20-60.

Fiction: Humorous.

Tips: "Submit new, fresh information concisely written and accurately researched. Publisher also producer *Bay Area Baby Magazine* a semi-annual publication."

CENTRAL COAST PARENT, Box 12407, San Luis Obispo CA 93406. (805)544-8609. Editor: Rhonda Jones. 90% freelance written. Monthly tabloid on child-rearing, health, behavior, parenting. Readers are pregnant women and parents of children 18 and under. Estab. 1988. Circ. 20,000. Pays on publication. Publishes ms an average of 4 months after acceptance. Byline given. Buys first rights or second serial (reprint) rights. Submit seasonal/holiday material 4 months in advance. Simultaneous and previously published submissions OK. Reports in 2 months. Sample copy for 9×12 SAE with $1.25 postage; writer's guidelines and editorial calendar for #10 SASE.

Nonfiction: Book excerpts, general interest, professional, how-to, inspirational, in-depth features, religious, critical assessment of issues, personal experience and travel—all related to parenting and child development. Buys 20-40 mss/year. Send complete ms. Length: 500-1,500 words. Pays $1/column inch.

Photos: Send photos with submission. Reviews 5×7 or 3×5 prints. Pays $1. Captions required. Buys one-time rights.

Columns/Departments: Kids Korner (craft, art, educational activities for children 12 and under), 50-500 words; Family Travel (getaways, things to do with kids), 300-750 words; Babies; Expectant Parents; Teens; Growing Child; 500-1,000 words. Buys 20 mss/year. Send complete ms. Length: 300-1,000 words. Pays $1/column inch.

Fillers: Anecdotes, consumer tips, facts, newsbreaks, short humor. Buys 20/year. Length: 50-500 words. Pays $2.50.

‡CHRISTIAN PARENTING TODAY, Good Family Magazines, P.O. Box 3850, 548 Sisters Parkway, Sisters OR 97759. (503)549-8261. Editor: David Kopp. Managing Editor: Stephen T. Barclift. 50% freelance written. Bimonthly magazine covering parenting today's children. "*Christian Parenting Today* is a positive, practical magazine that targets real needs of the contemporary family with authoritative articles based on fresh research and the timeless truths of the Bible. *CPT*'s readers represent the broad spectrum of Christians who seek intelligent answers to the new demands of parenting in the 90s." Estab. 1988. Circ. 175,000. Pays on acceptance. Byline given. Buys first North American serial or second serial (reprint) rights. Submit seasonal/holiday material 6 months in advance. Query for electronic submissions. Reports in 2 months. Sample copy for 8×11 SAE with 5 first class stamps. Free writer's guidelines.

Nonfiction: Book excerpts, how-to, humor, inspirational and religious. Buys 50 mss/year. Query. Length: 750-2,000 words. Pays $175-500 for assigned articles; $115-300 for unsolicited articles. Sometimes pays expenses of writers on assignment.

Photos: State availability of photos with submission. Reviews transparencies. Model release required. Buys one-time rights.

Columns/Departments: Parent Exchange (family-tested parenting ideas from our readers), 25-100 words; Life In Our House (entertaining, true, humorous stories about your family), 25-100 words. Buys 120 mss/year. Send complete ms. Pays $25 minimum.

Poetry: Free verse. Buys 3/year. Pays $25 minimum.

Fillers: Anecdotes and short humor. Buys 75/year. Length: 25-750 words. Pays $25-175.

Tips: "Our readers are active evangelical Christians from the broad spectrum of Protestant and Roman Catholic traditions. We are *not* interested in advocating any denominational bias. Our readers want authority, conciseness, problem-solving, entertainment, encouragement and surprise. They also require a clear biblical basis for advice."

GROWING PARENT, Dunn & Hargitt, Inc., 22 N. 2nd St., P.O. Box 1100, Lafayette IN 47902. (317)423-2624. FAX: (317)423-4495. Editor: Nancy Kleckner. 40-50% freelance written. Works with a small number of new/unpublished writers each year. "We do receive a lot of unsolicited submissions but have had excellent results in working with some unpublished writers. So, we're always happy to look at material and hope to find one or two jewels each year." A monthly newsletter which focuses on parents—the issues, problems, and choices they face as their children grow. "We want to look at the parent as an adult and help encourage his or her growth not only as a parent but as an individual." Estab. 1967. **Pays on acceptance.** Publishes ms an average of 6 months after acceptance. Byline given. Buys first North American serial rights; maintains exclusive rights for three months. Submit seasonal/holiday material 6 months in advance. Previously published submissions OK. Reports in 2 weeks. Sample copy and writer's guidelines for 5×8 SAE with 2 first class stamps.

Nonfiction: "We are looking for informational articles written in an easy-to-read, concise style. We would like to see articles that help parents deal with the stresses they face in everyday life—positive, upbeat, how-to-cope suggestions. We rarely use humorous pieces, fiction or personal experience articles. Writers should keep in mind that most of our readers have children under three years of age." Buys 15-20 mss/year. Query. Length: 1,500-2,000 words; will look at shorter pieces. Pays 8-10¢/word (depends on article).

Tips: "Submit a very specific query letter with samples."

‡HEALTHY KIDS: BIRTH-3/HEALTHY KIDS: 4-10, Cahners Publishing, 475 Park Ave. S., New York NY 10016. (212)689-3600. Editor: Phyllis Steinberg. 90% freelance written. Magazine published 3 times/year covering children's health. Estab. 1989/1990. Circ. 1.5 million/2 million. **Pays on acceptance.** Byline given.

Buys first rights. Submit seasonal/holiday material 6 months in advance. Reports in 1 month on queries. Free sample copy and writer's guidelines.

Nonfiction: How-to help your child develop as a person, keep safe, keep healthy, and personal experience. No poetry, fiction, travel or product endorsement. Buys 30 mss/year. Query. Length: 1,500-2,000 words. Pays $500-1,000. Pays expenses of writers on assignment.

Columns/Departments: Buys 30 mss/year. Query. Length: 1,500-2,000 words. Pays $500-1,000.

HOME EDUCATION MAGAZINE, P.O. Box 1083, Tonasket WA 98855. Editors: Mark J. Hegener and Helen E. Hegener. 80% freelance written. Eager to work with new/unpublished writers each year. A bimonthly magazine covering home-based education. "We feature articles which address the concerns of parents who want to take a direct involvement in the education of their children—concerns such as socialization, how to find curriculums and materials, testing and evaluation, how to tell when your child is ready to begin reading, what to do when home schooling is difficult, teaching advanced subjects, etc." Estab. 1983. Circ. 5,500. Pays on publication. Publishes ms an average of 6 months after acceptance. Byline given. ("Please include a 30-50 word credit with your article.") Buys first North American serial rights, first rights, one-time rights, second serial (reprint) rights, simultaneous rights, all rights, and makes work-for-hire assignments. Submit seasonal/holiday material 6 months in advance. Simultaneous and previously published submissions OK. Query for electronic submission requirements. Reports in 2 months. Sample copy $4.50; writer's guidelines for #10 SASE.

Nonfiction: Book excerpts, essays, how-to (related to home schooling), humor, inspirational, interview/profile, personal experience, photo feature and technical. Buys 40-50 mss/year. Query with or without published clips, or send complete ms. Length: 750-3,500 words. Pays $10 per final typeset page, (about 750 words). Sometimes pays expenses of writers on assignment.

Photos: Send photos with submission. Reviews 5 × 7, 35mm prints and b&w snapshots. Write for photo rates. Identification of subjects required. Buys one-time rights.

Tips: "We would like to see how-to articles (that don't preach, just present options); articles on testing, accountability, working with the public schools, socialization, learning disabilities, resources, support groups, legislation and humor. We need answers to the questions that home schoolers ask."

HOME LIFE, Sunday School Board, 127 9th Ave. N., Nashville TN 37234. (615)251-2271. Editor-in-Chief: Charlie Warren. 60-70% freelance written. Prefers to work with published/established writers; eager to work with new/unpublished writers. Emphasizes Christian marriage and Christian family life. For married adults of all ages, but especially newlyweds and middle-aged marrieds. Monthly magazine. Estab. 1947. Circ. 700,000. **Pays on acceptance.** Publishes ms an average of 15 months after acceptance. Buys first rights, first North American serial rights and all rights. Byline given. Phone queries OK, but written queries preferred. Submit seasonal/holiday material 1 year in advance. Reports in 6 weeks. Sample copy $1; writer's guidelines for #10 SASE.

Nonfiction: How-to (good articles on marriage and family life); informational (about some current family-related issue of national significance such as "Television and the Christian Family" or "Whatever Happened to Family Worship?"); personal experience (informed articles by people who have solved marriage and family problems in healthy, constructive ways). "No column material. We are not interested in material that will not in some way enrich Christian marriage or family life." Buys 150-200 mss/year. Query or submit complete ms. Length: 600-1,800 words. Pays up to 5¢/word.

Fiction: "Fiction should be family-related and should show a strong moral about how families face and solve problems constructively." Buys 12-20 mss/year. Submit complete ms. Length: 600-1,800 words. Pays up to 5¢/word.

Tips: "Study the magazine to see our unique slant on Christian family life. We prefer a life-centered case study approach, rather than theoretical essays on family life. Our top priority is marriage enrichment material."

‡KIDS & PARENTS, Creative Consortium, Suite 108, 7115 Winding Cedar Trail, Charlotte NC 28212. (704)532-2382. Editor: Melvyn Wallace. 80% freelance written. Monthly magazine covering parental concerns. Estab. 1989. Circ. 25,000. Pays on publication. Publishes ms 3 months after acceptance. Byline given. Buys one-time rights; makes work-for-hire assignments. Submit seasonal/holiday material 3 months in advance. Previously published submissions OK. Query for electronic submissions. Reports in 1 month on queries; 6 weeks on mss. Free sample copy. Writer's guidelines for #10 SAE and 1 first class stamp.

Nonfiction: Essay, general interest, historical/nostalgic, how-to, humor, inspirational, interview/profile, personal experience, photo feature, travel. Buys 20 mss/year. Query with published clips. Length: 500-2,000 words. Pays $100-300 for assigned articles; $10-100 for unsolicited articles.

Photos: Send photos with submission. Reviews transparencies and 4 × 5 prints. Offers no additional payment for photos accepted with ms. Captions, model releases and identification of subjects required. Buys one-time rights.

Columns/Departments: Buys 24 mss/year. Query with published clips. Length: 500-1,500 words. Pays $50-200.

Fiction: Fantasy, humorous, slice-of-life vignettes. Buys 6 mss/year. Query with published clips. Length: 500-2,000 words. Pays $50-200.

Poetry: Traditional. Buys 6/year. Submit maximum 5 poems. Length: 8-30 lines. Pays $10-50.

Tips: "All areas open—must be slanted towards raising children."

L.A. PARENT, The Magazine for Parents in Southern California, P.O. Box 3204, Burbank CA 91504. (818)846-0400. FAX: (818)841-4380. Editor: Jack Bierman. 80% freelance written. Prefers to work with published/established writers, and works with a small number of new/unpublished writers each year. Monthly tabloid covering parenting. Estab. 1980. Circ. 100,000. Pays on publication. Publishes ms an average of 4 months after acceptance. Byline given. Buys first rights and reprint rights. Submit seasonal/holiday material 3 months in advance. Simultaneous queries and previously published submissions OK. Query for electronic submissions. Reports in 1 month. Sample copy and writer's guidelines for $2.

Nonfiction: David Jameison, articles editor. General interest, how-to. "We focus on southern California activities for families, and do round-up pieces, i.e., a guide to private schools, fishing spots." Buys 60-75 mss/year. Query with clips of published work. Length: 700-1,200 words. Pays $150 plus expenses.

Tips: "We will be using more contemporary articles on parenting's challenges. If you can write for a 'city magazine' in tone and accuracy, you may write for us. The 'Baby Boom' has created a need for more generic parenting material."

LIVING WITH CHILDREN, Baptist Sunday School Board, 127 9th Ave. N., Nashville TN 37234. (615)251-2229. Editor: Phillip H. Waugh. 50% freelance written. Works with a small number of new/unpublished writers each year. Quarterly magazine covering parenting issues for parents of elementary-age children (ages 6 through 11). "Written and designed from a Christian perspective." Estab. 1892. Circ. 50,000. **Pays on acceptance.** Publishes ms an average of 2 years after acceptance. Byline given. "We generally buy all rights to mss; first serial rights on a limited basis. First and reprint rights may be negotiated at a lower rate of pay." Submit seasonal/holiday material 1 year in advance. Previously published submissions (on limited basis) OK. Reports in 1 month on queries; 2 months on mss. Sample copy for 9 × 12 SASE; free writer's guidelines.

Nonfiction: How-to (parent), humor, inspirational, personal experience, and articles on child development. No highly technical material or articles containing more than 15-20 lines quoted material. Buys 60 mss/year. Query or send complete ms (queries preferred). Length: 800-1,450 words. Pays 5½¢/word.

Photos: "Submission of photos with mss is strongly discouraged."

Fiction: Humorous (parent/child relationships); and religious. "We have very limited need for fiction." Buys maximum of 4 mss/year. Length: 800-1,450 words. Pays 5½¢/word.

Poetry: Light verse and inspirational. "We have limited need for poetry and buy only all rights." Buys 15 poems/year. Submit maximum 3 poems. Length: 4-30 lines. Pays $1.75 for 1-7 lines, plus $1 for each additional line; pays $4.50 for 8 lines and more plus 65¢ each additional line.

Fillers: Jokes, anecdotes and short humor. Buys 15/year. Length: 100-400 words. Pays $5 minimum, 5¢/word.

Tips: "Articles must deal with an issue of interest to parents. A mistake some writers make in articles for us is failing to write from a uniquely Christian perspective; that is very necessary for our periodicals. Material should be 850 or 1,450 in length. All sections, particularly articles, are open to freelance writers. Only regular features are assigned."

LIVING WITH PRESCHOOLERS, Baptist Sunday School Board, 127 9th Ave. N., Nashville TN 37234. (615)251-2229. Editor: Phillip H. Waugh. 50% freelance written. Works with a small number of new/unpublished writers each year. Quarterly magazine covering parenting issues for parents of preschoolers (infants through 5-year-olds). The magazine is "written and designed from a Christian perspective." Estab. 1892. Circ. 152,000. **Pays on acceptance.** Publishes manuscript an average of 2 years after acceptance. Byline given. "We generally buy all rights to manuscripts. First and reprint rights may be negotiated at a lower rate of pay." Submit seasonal/holiday material 2 years in advance. Previously published submissions (on limited basis) OK. Reports in 1 month on queries; 2 months on mss. Sample copy for 9 × 12 SASE; free writer's guidelines.

Nonfiction: How-to (parent), humor, inspirational, personal experience and articles on child development. No highly technical material or articles containing more than 15-20 lines quoted material. Buys 60 mss/year. Query or send complete ms (queries preferred). Length: 800-1,450 words. Pays 5½¢/word for manuscripts offered on all-rights basis.

Photos: "Submission of photos with mss is strongly discouraged."

Fiction: Humorous (parent/child relationships); and religious. "We have very limited need for fiction." Buys maximum of 4 mss/year. Length: 800-1,450 words. Pays 5½¢/word.

Poetry: Light verse and inspirational. "We have limited need for poetry and buy only all rights." Buys 15 poems/year. Submit maximum 3 poems. Length: 4-30 lines. Pays $1.75 for 1-7 lines, plus $1 for each additional line; pays $4.50 for 8 lines and more plus 65¢ each additional line.

Fillers: Jokes, anecdotes and short humor. Buys 15/year. Length: 100-400 words. Pays $5 minimum, 5¢/word maximum.

Tips: "Articles must deal with an issue of interest to parents. A mistake some writers make in writing an article for us is failing to write from a uniquely Christian perspective; that is very necessary for our periodicals. Material should be 850 or 1,450 words in length. All sections, particularly articles, are open to freelance writers. Only regular features are assigned."

NANNY TIMES, The Childcare Magazine, Jack & Jill Enterprises, Inc., P.O. Box 31, Rutherford NJ 07070. (201)935-5575. FAX: (201)935-7191. 90% freelance written. Monthly magazine on childcare. "Our magazine goes to childcare providers and parents in need of childcare. We cover safety, nutrition, child psychology, health and articles on how-to fit in with family, communication, etc." Estab. 1988. Circ. 30,000. Pays on publication. Publishes ms an average of 6 months after acceptance. Byline given. Buys one-time rights. Submit seasonal/holiday material 6 months in advance. Simultaneous and previously published submissions OK. Query for electronic submissions. Reports in 6 weeks. Sample copy $1.50; free writer's guidelines for SASE.

Nonfiction: General interest, how-to and personal experience. All relating to childcare or the business of being or employing a childcare provider. Send complete ms. Length: 1,000-2,000. Pays $5-75 for features; $5-25 for fillers. Sometimes pays with advertisements.

Photos: Send photos with submissions. Reviews contact sheets, negatives, transparencies and prints. Offers no additional payment for photos accepted with ms. Model releases are required.

PARENTING MAGAZINE, 501 Second St., #110, San Francisco CA 94107. Editor: David Markus. Magazine published 10 times/year. "Edited for parents of children from birth to ten years old, with the most emphasis put on the under-sixes." Estab. 1987. **Pays on acceptance.** Byline given. Offers 25% kill fee. Buys first rights. Query for electronic submissions. Reports in 6 weeks to 3 months. Sample copy $1.95 with 9×12 SAE and $1.20 postage. Writer's guidelines for SASE.

Nonfiction: Rebecca Poole. Book excerpts, humor, investigative reports, personal experience and photo feature. Buys 20-30 mss/year. Query with or without published clips, or send complete ms. Length: 1,000-3,500 words. Pays $500-2,000. Sometimes pays expenses of writers on assignment.

Columns/Departments: Extra (news items relating to children/family), 100-400 words; Care and Feeding (health, nutrition, new products and service stories), 100-500 words; Passages (parental rites of passage), 850 words; Up in Arms (opinion, 850 words. Buys 50-60 mss/year. Pays $50-350.

PARENTS & TEENAGERS, Thom Schultz Publications, Inc., 2890 N. Monroe, Loveland CO 80539. (303)669-3836. Editorial Director: Joani Schultz. Managing Editor: Cindy Parolini. 90% freelance written. Bimonthly newsletter, practical helps for Christian parents of teenagers. Estab. 1988. Circ. 25,000. **Pays on acceptance.** Publishes ms an average of 5 months after acceptance. Byline given. Offers $25 kill fee for longer articles. Buys all rights. Submit seasonal/holiday material 6 months in advance. Reports in 3 weeks on queries; 1 month on mss. Sample copy for 9×12 SAE with $1; writer's guidelines for SASE.

Nonfiction: Barbara Beach, articles editor. How-to (ideas to build closer family; personal help ideas for marriage, single parents; understanding teenagers, self), personal experience (family success stories, parenting, family life) humor (family life); religious. Query with published clips. Length: 200-1,400 words. Pays $25-100. Sometimes pays expenses of writers on assignment.

Photos: State availability of photos with submission. Reviews 35mm transparencies and 8×10 prints. Offers $25-50/b&w photo and $50-150 for color. Model releases required.

Columns/Departments: Personal Helps for Parenting (practical ideas to help parents), 200-300 words. Query with published clips. Pays $25-75.

Tips: "Explain credentials; include writing samples, have clever, new article ideas with different slant."

‡**PARENTS CARE, PARENTS COUNT NEWSLETTER,** P.O. Box 1563, 44321 Calston Ave., Lancaster CA 93539. (805)945-2360. Editor: Marilyn Anita Dalrymple. 100% freelance written. Bimonthly newsletter for parents of addictive or disruptive children. "Writing must be done with empathy towards parents. No 'it's your fault' aimed at parent *or* child. Articles must contain message of 'I was there, and I survived,' or 'This helped me . . . .' **Pays on acceptance.** Byline given. Buys one-time rights. Submit seasonal/holiday material 4 months in advance. Simultaneous and previously published submissions OK. Reports in 2 weeks. Sample copy $1.25. Writer's guidelines for #10 SAE with 1 first class stamp.

Nonfiction: Humor, inspirational, personal experience and news updates concerning family/drugs. No how to be a "perfect" parent, or raise a "perfect child." Length: 750 words maximum. Pays $2.50-7.50 for unsolicited articles.

Columns/Departments: Have You Read (book reviews); Have You Heard (audio/visual tapes); News Reports. Buys 18 mss/year. Length: 250 words. Send complete ms. Pays $2.50.

Poetry: Avant-garde, free verse, haiku, light verse, traditional. Buys 18/year. Submit maximum 5 poems. Length: 2-16 lines. Pays $2.50.

Fillers: Anecdotes, facts and newsbreaks. Length: 250 words maximum. Pays $2.50.

Tips: "Let me know you've been there, either as the child (addict), parent or professional who works with these families. Honesty is a must. Where technical data is concerned (laws, treatments, etc.), need verification. Freelancers are welcome to contribute to all departments."

PARENTS MAGAZINE, 685 3rd Ave., New York NY 10017. Editor-in-Chief: Ann Pleshette Murphy. 25% freelance written. Monthly. Circ. 1,740,000. **Pays on acceptance.** Publishes ms an average of 8 months after acceptance. Usually buys first serial rights or first North American serial rights; sometimes buys all rights. Pays 25% kill fee. Reports in approximately 6 weeks. Writer's guidelines for #10 SASE.

Nonfiction: "We are interested in well-documented articles on the development and behavior of preschool, school-age and adolescent children and their parents; good, practical guides to the routines of baby care; articles that offer professional insights into family and marriage relationships; reports of new trends and significant research findings in education and in mental and physical health; and articles encouraging informed citizen action on matters of social concern. Especially need articles on women's issues, pregnancy, birth, baby care and early childhood. We prefer a warm, colloquial style of writing, one which avoids the extremes of either slang or technical jargon. Anecdotes and examples should be used to illustrate points which can then be summed up by straight exposition." Query. Length: 2,500 words maximum. Payment varies. Sometimes pays the expenses of writers on assignment.

PEDIATRICS FOR PARENTS, The Newsletter for Caring Parents, Pediatrics for Parents, Inc., P.O. Box 1069, Bangor ME 04401. (207)942-6212. Editor: Richard J. Sagall, M.D. 20% freelance written. Eager to work with new/unpublished writers. Monthly newsletter covering medical aspects of rearing children and educating parents about children's health. Estab. 1981. Circ. 2,000. Pays on publication. Publishes ms an average of 3-4 months after acceptance. Byline given. Buys first North American serial rights, first and second rights to the same material, and second (reprint) rights to material originally published elsewhere. Rights always include right to publish article in our books on "Best of . . ." series. Submit seasonal/holiday material 6 months in advance. Simultaneous queries and previously published submissions OK. Query for electronic submissions. Reports in 1 month on queries; 6 weeks on mss. Sample copy for $2; writer's guidelines for #10 SAE and 2 first class stamps.

Nonfiction: Book reviews; how-to (feed healthy kids, exercise, practice wellness, etc.); new product; technical (explaining medical concepts in shirtsleeve language). No general parenting articles. Query with published clips or submit complete ms. Length: 25-1,000 words. Pays 2-5¢/edited word.

Columns/Departments: Book reviews; Please Send Me (material available to parents for free or at nominal cost); Pedia-Tricks (medically-oriented parenting tips that work). Send complete ms. Pays $15-250. Pays 2¢/edited word.

Tips: "We are dedicated to taking the mystery out of medicine for young parents. Therefore, we write in clear and understandable language (but not simplistic language) to help people understand and deal intelligently with complex disease processes, treatments, prevention, wellness, etc. Our articles must be well researched and documented. Detailed references must always be attached to any article for documentation, but not for publication. We strongly urge freelancers to read one or two issues before writing."

THE SINGLE PARENT, Parents Without Partners, Inc., 8807 Colesville Rd., Silver Spring MD 20910. (301)588-9354. FAX: (301)588-9216. Editor: Allan N. Glennon. 60% freelance written. Works with small number of new/unpublished writers each year. Magazine, published 6 times/year; 48 pages. Emphasizes single parenting, family, divorce, widowhood and children. Distributed to members of Parents Without Partners, plus libraries, universities, psychologists, psychiatrists, subscribers, etc. Estab. 1957. Circ. 120,000. Pays on publication. Publishes ms an average of 9 months after acceptance. Buys one-time rights. Simultaneous and previously published submissions OK. No electronic submissions. Reports in 2 months. Sample copy $1, writer's guidelines for #10 SASE.

Nonfiction: Informational (parenting, legal issues, single parents in society, programs that work for single parents, children's problems); how-to (raise children alone, travel, take up a new career, cope with life as a new or veteran single parent; short lists of how-to tips). No first-hand accounts of bitter legal battles with former spouses. No "poor me" articles. Buys 30 unsolicited mss/year. Query not required. Mss not returned unless SASE is enclosed. Length: 1,000-3,000 words. Payment $50-150, based on content, not length.

Fiction: Publishes two short stories (800-1500 words) per issue for children. Stories may be aimed at any age group from toddlers through teens. Prefers stories about children in single parent households, coping with or learning from their situations. No anthropomorpics. Payment $35-75.

Close-up

Rebecca Poole
Articles Editor
Parenting Magazine

"We do everything our competitors do, but we do more. And we do more of it in one issue," says Rebecca Poole, articles editor of *Parenting Magazine*. *Parenting* delves into unexplored family issues, she says, an attitude that sets it apart from traditional parenting magazines.

Readers are well educated, curious and challenged by controversial topics. "We take hard-hitting issues: sex differences, day care politics, behavioral problems," Poole says. Although the publication is aimed mostly toward parents of children under age six, "We tackle issues that parents may not be dealing with now, but they should be thinking of. We look ahead."

Writer parents influenced her career. "I was offered my own column with a city paper as a freshman in high school . . . great practice and discipline," she recalls. At the University of California, Berkeley, she studied broadcasting but moved to magazine work, including stints with *California* and *Sierra*. *Parenting* offered an opportunity with a 10 times per year national publication. Poole spends 50 to 60 hours each week on the job. In the three years she's been on board, she's seen growth and change at *Parenting*. "Our circulation is now at 600,000," about triple the startup figure. The content has changed too, she says. "We have more service pieces, and they're shorter." The magazine's purchase by Time-Warner, Inc., recently boosted *Parenting* into the periodical big leagues.

Poole sometimes writes articles and sympathizes with writers. "I've been on both sides of the fence," she says. Freelancers won't find this magazine an easy market. "To be totally honest," Poole says, "there isn't much room for freelance. Our standards are very, very high. Only one out of 15 submissions is accepted."

Tactics that work with this editor include solid credentials and a dynamite query. She emphasizes published clips from high caliber markets. Stay away from the phone and exercise patience, she advises—replies take eight to 20 weeks. "We get hundreds of submissions every week, and 95% of them go to me," she says.

Best bets, Poole advises, are Parenting Extra (news items) and Care and Feeding (service articles). Pieces here run 150 to 500 words, and writers should query department editors. Writers may write on speculation, but Poole says "there's often a contract." Some writers have entered the features section through these shorter departments, she says.

Up in Arms and Passages, two essay columns, are done on speculation. "It's difficult to write a wonderful first-person essay in 850 words. Some of our best writers can't do it," Poole says.

Poole assigns features primarily to regular contributors. Determined writers can gamble with a complete manuscript, but they fare better if they "start with another magazine and work up to *Parenting*," Poole says.

Parenting's articles address mothers and fathers and leaven facts with strong viewpoints and humor. The mix, Poole says, is informative, entertaining and complex. She reminds writers that, as always, "The best guideline is the magazine itself."

—Lynn Narlesky

Columns/Departments: F.Y.I., for short news items, reports on research, tips on how to do things better, and new products, Letters to Editor column.

Photos: Purchased with accompanying ms. Also, uses freelance stock shots. Query. Pays negotiable rates. Model release required.

Tips: "Be familiar with our magazine and its readership before trying to write for us. We publish constructive, upbeat articles that present new ideas for coping with and solving the problems that confront single parents. Articles on origins of Halloween customs, tribal behavior in Ghana, or how to predict the weather have little likelihood of acceptance unless there is a clear tie-in to single parent issues."

‡THINKING FAMILIES, For Parents with Children in Elementary School, Communications Plus, Inc., 605 Worcester Rd., Towson MD 21204. (301)321-0121. Editor: Marjory Spraycar. 90% freelance written. Bimonthly magazine on schools and school kids. "We are a magazine about schools and school kids for parents with children in elementary school. Our readers are motivated to help provide the very best education possible for their children." Estab. 1988. Circ. 50,000. Pays on publication. Byline given. Offers $50 kill fee. Buys one-time rights. Submit seasonal/holiday material 4 months in advance. Query for electronic submissions. Reports in 1 month. Sample copy $2.50 with 9 × 12 SAE and 4 first class stamps. Writer's guidelines for #10 SAE with 1 first class stamp.

Nonfiction: Personal experience, photo feature, travel. Buys 15-25 mss/year. Query with published clips. Length: 1,000-3,000 words. Pays $200-1,000. Sometimes pays expenses of writers on assignment.

Photos: State availability of photos with submission. Reviews contact sheets, transparencies. Offers $10-350/photo. Captions, model releases and identification of subjects required. Buys one-time rights.

Columns/Departments: Travel Column (geared as a how-to travel with grade school kids); Electronic Home (reviews software or any technological advance that can be used by families). Buys 36-50/year. Query with published clips. Length: 1,500-2,000 words. Pays $100-350.

Tips: "Writers with good ideas and the ability to write excellent magazine articles and who have experience in the subjects we cover have an excellent chance of breaking into our pages. We write no features in-house; must rely on freelancers. We prefer writers already published in national magazines. We are a high quality publication looking for proven talent."

TWINS, The Magazine for Parents of Multiples, P.O. Box 12045, Overland Park KS 66212. (913)722-1090. FAX: (913)722-1767. Editor: Barbara C. Unell. 100% freelance written. Eager to work with new/unpublished writers. A bimonthly international magazine designed to give professional guidance to help multiples, their parents and those professionals who care for them learn about twin facts and research. Estab. 1984. Circ. 45,000. Pays on publication. Publishes ms an average of 6 months after acceptance. Byline given. Buys all rights. Submit seasonal/holiday material 10 months in advance. Simultaneous and previously published submissions OK. Reports in 6 weeks on queries; 2 months on mss. Sample copy $4.50 plus $1.50 postage and handling; writer's guidelines for #10 SASE.

Nonfiction: Book excerpts, general interest, how-to, humor, interview/profile, personal experience and photo feature. "No articles that substitute the word 'twin' for 'child'—those that simply apply the same research to twins that applies to singletons without any facts backing up the reason to do so." Buys 150 mss/year. Query with or without published clips, or send complete ms. Length: 1,250-3,000 words. Payment varies; sometimes pays in contributor copies or premiums instead of cash. Sometimes pays the expenses of writers on assignment.

Photos: Send photos with submission. Reviews contact sheets, 4 × 5 transparencies and all size prints. Captions, model releases and identification of subjects required. Buys all rights.

Columns/Departments: Resources, Supertwins, Prematurity, Family Health, Twice as Funny, Double Focus (series from pregnancy through adolescence), Personal Perspective (first-person accounts of beliefs about a certain aspect of parenting multiples), Over the Back Fence (specific tips that have worked for the writer in raising multiples), Consumer Matters, Feelings on Fatherhood, Research, On Being Twins (first-person accounts of growing up as a twin), On Being Parents of Twins (first-person accounts of the experience of parenting twins), Double Takes (fun photographs of twins), and Education Matters. Buys 70 mss/year. Query with published clips. Length: 1,250-2,000 words. Payment varies.

Fillers: Anecdotes and short humor. Length: 75-750 words. Payment varies.

Tips: "Features and columns are both open to freelancers. Columnists write for *Twins* on a continuous basis, so the column becomes their column. We are looking for a wide variety of the latest, well-researched practical information. There is no other magazine of this type directed to this market. We are interested in personal interviews with celebrity twins or celebrity parents of twins, tips on rearing twins from experienced parents and/or twins themselves, and reports on national and international research studies involving twins."

Comic Books

Comic books aren't just for kids. Today, this medium also attracts a reader who is older and wants stories presented visually on a wide variety of topics. In addition, some instruction manuals, classics and other stories are using a comic book format.

This doesn't mean you have to be an artist to write for comic books. Most of these publishers want to see a synopsis of one to two double-spaced pages. Highlight the story's beginning, middle and end, and tell how events will affect your main character emotionally. Be concise. Comics use few words and rely on graphics as well as words to forward the plot.

Once your synopsis is accepted, either an artist will draw the story from your plot, returning these pages to you for dialogue and captions, or you will be expected to write a script. Scripts run approximately 23 typewritten pages and include suggestions for artwork as well as dialogue. Try to imagine your story on actual comic book pages and divide your script accordingly. The average comic has six panels per page, with a maximum of 35 words per panel.

If you're submitting a proposal to Marvel or DC, your story should center on an already established character. If you're dealing with an independent publisher, characters are often the property of their creators. Your proposal should be for a new series. Include a background sheet for main characters who will appear regularly, listing origins, weaknesses, powers or other information that will make your character unique. Indicate an overall theme or direction for your series. Submit story ideas for the first three issues. If you're really ambitious, you may also include a script for your first issue. As with all markets, read a sample copy before making a submission. The best markets may be those you currently read, so consider submitting to them even if they aren't listed in this section. Writer's Digest Books now publishes a market book specifically for humorous writers and illustrators, *Humor and Cartoon Markets*.

AMAZING HEROES, Fantagraphics Books, 7563 Lake City Way, Seattle WA 98115. FAX: (206)524-1967. Editor: Thomas Harrington. 80% freelance written. Eager to work with new/unpublished writers. A monthly magazine for comic book fans of all ages and backgrounds. *"Amazing Heroes* focuses on both historical aspects of comics and current doings in the industry." Circ. 15,000. Pays on publication. Publishes ms an average of 2 months after acceptance. Byline given. Offers $25 kill fee on solicited ms. Buys first North American serial rights and second serial (reprint) rights. Submit seasonal/holiday material 3 months in advance. Previously published submissions OK. Reports in 2 weeks on queries; 1 month on mss. Sample copy for 7½×10½ SAE and $2.50.
Nonfiction: Essays, historical/nostalgic, interview/profile, new product. Query with published clips and interests. Length: 300-7,500 words. Pays $5-125 for assigned articles; pays $5-75 for unsolicited articles. Pays writers with double payment in Fantagraphics book merchandise if requested. Sometimes pays the expenses of writers on assignment.
Photos: State availability of photos on profile pieces and interviews.
Tips: "Recently, there has been a renaissance, though some refer to it as a glut, of new material and new publishers in the comic book industry. This has called for a greater need for more writers who are not just interested in super-heroes or just books produced by DC and Marvel. There is now, more than ever, a need to be open-minded as well as critical. Writers for *Amazing Heroes* must have a much broader knowledge of the entire, ever-widening spectrum of the comic book industry."

CARTOON WORLD, P.O. Box 30367, Dept. WM, Lincoln NE 68503. Editor: George Hartman. 100% freelance written. Works with published/established writers and a small number of new/unpublished writers each year. "Monthly newsletter for professional and amateur cartoonists who are serious and want to utilize new cartoon markets in each issue." Buys only from paid subscribers. Circ. 150-300. **Pays on acceptance.** Publishes ms an average of 2 months after acceptance. Byline given. Buys second (reprint) rights to material originally published elsewhere. Not copyrighted. Submit seasonal/holiday material 3 months in advance. Simultaneous submissions OK. Reports in 1 month. Sample copy $5.
Nonfiction: "We want only positive articles about the business of cartooning and gag writing." Buys 10 mss/year. Query. Length: 1,000 words. Pays $5/page.

COMICO THE COMIC COMPANY, 1547 DeKalb St., Norristown PA 19401. (215)277-4305. FAX: (215)277-5651. Publisher: Phil LaSorda. 100% freelance written. We work only with writers, published or unpublished, who can tell a strong, solid, and visual story." One-shot, limited and continuing series comic books. Circ. approximately 70,000 per title. Pays 1 month after acceptance. Publishes ms an average of 1 year after acceptance. Byline given. Buys first rights, makes work-for-hire assignments or offers creator ownership contracts. Simultaneous and previously published submissions OK. Reports in 1 month on queries; 2 months on mss. Sample copy for $2.50 and 7½ × 10½ SAE and 3 first class stamps; writer's guidelines for #10 SASE.

Fiction: Various genres. "We are always interested in seeing submissions of new and innovative material. Due to the words-and-pictures format of comic books, it is usually preferable, though not essential, that the writer submit material in conjunction with an artist of his or her choice." No pornography or dogma. Buys 100 mss/year. Query. Length: 24 story pages. Payment varies.

Tips: "Our industry in general and our company in particular are beginning to look more and more at the limited series format as a means of properly conveying solid stories, beautifully illustrated for the adult marketplace, as opposed to the standard continuing serials. Be familiar with comics medium and industry. Show that writer can write in script format and express intentions to artist who will create images based on writer's descriptions. The area of licensed properties is most open to freelancers. Writer must be faithful to licensed characters, to licensor's wishes, and be willing to make any requested changes."

COMICS SCENE, Starlog Group, 475 Park Ave. S., 8th Floor, New York NY 10016. (212)689-2830. FAX: (212)889-7933. Editor: David McDonnell. Bi-monthly magazine on comic books, strips, cartoons, those who create them and TV/movie adaptations of both. Estab. 1981. Pays on publication. Byline given. Offers 25% kill fee. Buys all rights or second serial (reprint) rights. Submit seasonal/holiday material 6 months in advance. Simultaneous and previously published submissions OK if noted. Reports in 6 weeks on queries; 2 months on mss. Sample copy $3.95; writer's guidelines for #10 SASE. *No* queries by phone.

Nonfiction: Book excerpts, historical/nostalgic, interview/profile, new product, personal experience. Buys 70 mss/year. Query with published clips. Length: 750-3,500 words. Pays $75-200. Does *not* publish fiction.

Photos: State availability of photos and comic strip/book/animation artwork with submission. Reviews contact sheets, transparencies, 8 × 10 prints. Offers $5-25 for original photos. Captions, model releases, identification of subjects required. Buys all rights.

Columns/Departments: The Comics Scene (interviews with comic book artists, writers and editors on upcoming projects and new developments), 100-350 words; The Comics Reporter ("newsy" interviews with writer, director, producer of TV series, or movie adaptations of comic books and strips). Buys 25 mss/year. Query with published clips. Length: 100-750 words. Pays $15-50.

Tips: "We really need small department items, re: independent comics companies' products and creators. We need interviews with specific comic strip creators. Comics are hot and comics-based movies (thanks to *Batman*) should be even hotter in '91. Most any writer can break in with interviews with hot comic book writers and artists—and with comic book creators who don't work for the big five companies. We do *not* want nostalgic items or interviews. Do not burden us with your own personal comic book stories or artwork. Get interviews we can't get or haven't thought to pursue. Out-thinking overworked editors is a certain way to sell a story."

ECLIPSE COMICS, P.O. Box 1099, Forestville CA 95436. (707)887-1521. Publisher: Dean Mullaney. Editor-in-Chief: Catherine Yronwode. 100% freelance written. Works with a small number of new/unpublished writers each year. Publishers of various four-color comic books and graphic albums. *Eclipse* publishes comic books with high-quality paper and color reproduction, geared toward the discriminating comic book fan and sold through the "direct sales" specialty store market. Estab. 1978. Circ. varies (35,000-85,000). Pays on acceptance (net 1 month). Publishes ms an average of 6 months after acceptance. Byline given. Buys first North American serial rights, second serial (reprint) rights with additional payment, and first option on collection and non-exclusive rights to sell material to South American and European markets (with additional payments). Simultaneous queries and submissions OK. Reports in 2 months. Sample copy $2; writer's guidelines for #10 SASE.

Fiction: "Most of our comics are fictional." Adventure, fantasy, mystery, science fiction, horror. "No sexually explicit material, please." Buys approximately 200 mss/year (mostly from established comics writers).

Tips: "At the present time we are publishing both adventure and super-heroic series but we are currently scheduling fewer 32-page periodical adventure comics and more 48-96 page graphic albums, some of which are nonfiction current events journalism in graphic format. We are moving into the arena of political and social commentary and current events in graphic form. We have also expanded our line of classic newspaper strip reprints. Because all of our comics are creator-owned, we do not buy fill-in plots or scripts for our periodicals. Plot synopsis less than a page can be submitted; we will select promising concepts for development into full script submissions. All full script submissions should be written in comic book or 'screenplay' form for artists to illustrate. Writers who are already teamed with artists stand a better chance of selling material to us, but if necessary we'll find an artist. Our special needs at the moment are for heroic, character-oriented series with overtones of humanism, morality, political opinion, philosophical speculation, and/or social com-

ALWAYS submit unsolicited manuscripts or queries with a self-addressed, stamped envelope (SASE) within your country or International Reply Coupons (IRC) purchased from the post office for other countries.

mentary. Comic book adaptations (by the original authors) of previously published science fiction and horror short stories are definitely encouraged. Queries about current events/nonfiction albums should be discussed with us prior to a full-blown submission."

MARVEL COMICS, 387 Park Ave. S., New York NY 10016. (212)576-9200. Editor-in-Chief: Tom DeFalco. 99% freelance written. Publishes 60 comics and magazines per month, 6-12 graphic novels per year, and specials, storybooks, industrials, and paperbacks for all ages. Over 9 million copies sold/month. Pays a flat fee for most projects, plus a royalty type incentive based upon sales. Also works on advance/royalty basis on many projects. **Pays on acceptance.** Publishes manuscript an average of 6 months after acceptance. Byline given. Offers variable kill fee. Rights purchased depend upon format and material. Submit seasonal/holiday material 1 year in advance. Simultaneous submissions OK. Reports in 6 months. Writer's guidelines for #10 SASE. Additional guidelines on request.
Fiction: Super hero, action-adventure, science fiction, fantasy, and other material. No noncomics. Buys 600-800 mss/year. Query with brief plot synopses only. Do not send scripts, short stories or long outlines. A plot synopsis should be less than two typed pages; send two synopses at most. Pays expenses of writers on assignment.

Consumer Service and Business Opportunity

Some of these magazines are geared to investing earnings or starting a new business; others show how to make economical purchases. Publications for business executives and consumers interested in business topics are listed under Business and Finance. Those on how to run specific businesses are classified by category in the Trade section.

BUSINESS TODAY, Meridian Publishing, P.O. Box 10010, Ogden UT 84409. (801)394-9446. Editor: Bryan Larsen. 40% freelance written. Monthly magazine covering all aspects of business. Particularly interested in tips to small/medium business managers. **Pays on acceptance.** Publishes ms an average of 8 months after acceptance. Byline given. Buys first rights, second serial (reprint) rights and nonexclusive reprint rights. Reports in 2 months. Sample copy for $1 and 9 × 12 SAE; writer's guidelines for #10 SASE. All requests for samples and guidelines should be addressed Attn: Editorial Assistant.
Nonfiction: General interest articles about employee relations, management principles, advertising methods and financial planning. Articles covering up-to-date practical business information are welcome. Cover stories are often profiles of people who have expertise and success in a specific aspect of business. Buys 40 mss/year. Query. Length: 1,200-1,500 words. Pays 15¢/word for first rights plus non-exclusive reprint rights. Payment for second rights is negotiable.
Photos: State availability of photos or send photos with query. Reviews 35mm or larger transparencies. Pays $35 for inside photo; pays $50 for cover photo. Captions, model releases and identification of subjects required.
Tips: "We're looking for meaty, hard-core business articles with practical applications. Profiles should be prominent business-people, preferably Fortune-500 league. The key is a well-written query letter that: 1) demonstrates that the subject of the article is tried-and-true and has national appeal, 2) shows that the article will have a clear, focused theme, 3) outlines the availability (from writer or a photographer or a PR source) of top-quality color photos and 4) gives evidence that the writer/photographer is a professional, even if a beginner."

CHANGING TIMES, The Kiplinger Magazine, 1729 H St. NW, Washington DC 20006. Editor: Ted Miller. Less than 10% freelance written. Prefers to work with published/established writers. For general, adult audience interested in personal finance and consumer information. Monthly. Estab. 1947. Circ. 1.35 million. **Pays on acceptance.** Publishes ms an average of 2 months after acceptance. Buys all rights. Reports in 1 month. Query for electronic submissions. Thorough documentation required for fact-checking.
Nonfiction: "Most material is staff-written, but we accept some freelance." Query with clips of published work. Pays expenses of writers on assignment.
Tips: "We are looking for a heavy emphasis on personal finance topics."

CONSUMER ACTION NEWS, Suite 216, 1106 E. High St., Springfield OH 45505. (513)325-2001. Editor: Victor Pence. 10% freelance written. Eager to work with new/unpublished writers. A monthly newsletter circulated in the state of Ohio for readers who are interested in knowing that problems can be solved without legal action and when other protection agencies could not solve them, or refused to handle them. "We handle consumer complaints and publish results in newsletter." Estab. 1980. **Pays on acceptance.** Byline given. Buys one-time rights. Simultaneous queries, and simultaneous and previously published submissions OK. Reports in 6 weeks.

Nonfiction: Send complete ms. Length: 1,000 words or less. Pays $10-25.

Tips: "We want only experiences with complaints that were solved when the usual protection sources couldn't solve them. Creative ways of finding solutions without legal actions. If the problem has not been solved, we will offer possible solutions to the problem anywhere in the U.S., Canada or Mexico at no charge."

CONSUMERS DIGEST MAGAZINE, for People who Demand Value, Consumers Digest, Inc., 5705 N. Lincoln Ave., Chicago IL 60201. (312)275-3590. FAX: (312)275-7273. Editor: John Manos. Executive Editor: Elliott H. McCleary. 75% freelance written. Prefers to work with published/established writers. Emphasizes anything of consumer interest. Recommends products and services for a middle-American audience, specifying brands and models as Best Buys. Bimonthly magazine. Estab. 1959. Circ. 900,000. **Pays on acceptance.** Publishes ms an average of 3 months after acceptance. Offers 50% kill fee. Buys all rights. Reports in 1 month. Free guidelines for SAE and 1 first class stamp to published writers only.

Nonfiction: Product-testing, evaluating; general interest (on advice to consumers, service, health, home, business, investments, insurance and money management); new products and travel. Query. Length: 500-3,500 words. Pays $150-1,200 for assigned articles, $150-500 for unsolicited articles. Pays expenses of writers on assignment.

Photos: State availability of photos with submission. Model releases and identification of subjects required. Buys one-time rights.

Columns/Departments: Buys 3 mss/year. Length: 100-400 words. Pays $50-200.

Tips: "Study writer's guidelines and sample copy, try for a fresh subject."

ECONOMIC FACTS, The National Research Bureau, Inc., 424 N. 3rd St., Burlington IA 52601. FAX: (319)752-3421. Editor: Rhonda Wilson. Editorial Supervisor: Doris J. Ruschill. 25% freelance written. Eager to work with new/unpublished writers; works with a small number of new/unpublished writers each year. Published 4 times/year. Estab. 1948. Pays on publication. Publishes ms an average of 1 year after acceptance. Buys all rights. Byline given. Previously published submissions OK. Reports in 1 week. Writer's guidelines for #10 SASE; sample for 6½ × 9½ envelope and 55¢ postage.

Nonfiction: General interest (private enterprise, government data, graphs, taxes and health care). Buys 3-5 mss/year. Query with outline of article. Length: 400-600 words. Pays 4¢/word.

ENTREPRENEUR MAGAZINE, 2392 Morse Ave., Box 19787, Irvine CA 92714-6234. Editor: Rieva Lesonsky. 40% freelance written. "We are eager to work with any writer who takes the time to see *Entrepreneur*'s special 'angle' and who turns in copy." For a readership looking for opportunities in small business, as owners, franchisees or seeking "tips and tactics to help them better run their existing small business." Circ. 325,000. **Pays on acceptance.** Publishes ms an average of 3-5 months after acceptance. Buys first worldwide rights. Byline given. Submit seasonal/holiday material 6 months in advance of issue date. Computer printout submissions acceptable. Reports in 2 months. Sample copy $3; writer's guidelines for #10 SASE. Please write "Attn: Writer's Guidelines" on envelope.

Nonfiction: How-to (information on running a business, profiles on unique entrepreneurs). Buys 60-70 mss/year. Query with clips of published work and SASE. Length: 750-2,000 words. Payment varies.

Photos: "We need color transparencies to illustrate articles." Offers additional payment for photos accepted with ms. Uses standard color transparencies. Captions preferred. Buys various rights. Model release required.

Tips: "It's rewarding to find a freelancer who reads the magazine *before* he/she submits a query. We get so many queries with the wrong angle. I can't stress enough the importance of reading and understanding our magazine and our audience before you write. We're looking for writers who can perceive the difference between *Entrepreneur* and other business magazines."

FDA CONSUMER, 5600 Fishers Lane, Rockville MD 20857. (301)443-3220. Editor: Judith Levine Willis. 30% freelance written. Prefers to work with experienced health and medical writers. Monthly magazine. January/February and July/August issues combined. For general public interested in health issues. A federal government publication (Food and Drug Administration). Circ. 25,000. Pays after acceptance. Publishes ms an average of 3 months after acceptance. Byline given. Not copyrighted. Pays 50% kill fee. "All purchases automatically become part of public domain." Buys 15-20 freelance mss a year. "We cannot be responsible for any work by writer not agreed upon by prior contract." Query for electronic submissions. Free sample copy.

Nonfiction: "Upbeat feature articles of an educational nature about FDA regulated products and specific FDA programs and actions to protect the consumer's health and pocketbook. Articles based on health topics with the proviso that the subjects be connected to food, drugs, medicine, medical devices, and other products regulated by FDA. All articles subject to clearance by the appropriate FDA experts as well as acceptance by the editor. All articles based on prior arrangement by contract." Query. Length: 2,000-2,500 words. Pays $800-950 for first-timers, $1,200 for those who have previously published in *FDA Consumer*. Sometimes pays the expenses of writers on assignment.

Photos: Black and white photos are purchased on assignment only.
Tips: "Besides reading the feature articles in *FDA Consumer*, a writer can best determine whether his/her style and expertise suit our needs by submitting a query letter, resume and sample clips for our review."

INCOME OPPORTUNITIES, 380 Lexington Ave., New York NY 10017. FAX: (212)986-7313. Editor: Stephen Wagner. Associate Editor: Debra Reitman. 90% freelance written. Works with a small number of new/ unpublished writers each year. Monthly magazine. For all who are seeking business opportunities, full- or part-time. Estab. 1956. Publishes ms an average of 5 months after acceptance. Buys all rights. Two special directory issues contain articles on selling techniques, mail order, import/export, franchising and home business ideas. Query for details on electronic submissions. Reports in 2 weeks. Writer's guidelines for #10 SASE.
Nonfiction and Photos: Regularly covered are such subjects as mail order, home business, direct selling, franchising, party plans, selling techniques and the marketing of handcrafted or homecrafted products. Wanted are ideas for the aspiring entrepreneur; examples of successful business methods that might be duplicated. No material that is purely inspirational. Buys 50-60 mss/year. Query with outline of article development. Length: 800 words for a short; 2,000-3,000 words for a major article. "Payment rates vary according to length and quality of the submission." Sometimes pays expenses of writers on assignment.
Tips: "Study recent issues of the magazine. Best bets for newcomers: interview-based report on a successful small business venture. Our emphasis is on home-based business."

‡**INCOME PLUS MAGAZINE,** Opportunity Associates, Suite 303, 73 Spring St., New York NY 10012. (212)925-3180. Editor: Roxane Farmanfarmaian. 33-50% freelance written. Monthly magazine on small business and money-making ideas. Provides "hands-on service to help small business owners, home office owners and entrepreneurs successfully start up and run their enterprises. Focus on francising, mail order." Estab. 1989. Circ. 200,000. Pays on publication. Byline given. Offers 20% kill fee. Buys first North American serial rights. Query for electronic submissions. Reports in 6 weeks. Sample copy $2 with 1 first class stamp; writer's guidelines for 1 first class stamp.
Nonfiction: How-to (business, finance, home office, technical start-up). Buys 48 mss/year. Query with published clips. Length: 1,500-2,500 words. Pays $200-1,000. Sometimes pays expenses of writers on assignment.
Photos: State availability of photos with submission. Offers no additional payment for photos accepted with ms.
Columns/Departments: Legal and You The Boss (original reporting with real example of business owners to back up point of story); Home Business Marketing (service with easily and immediately applicable advice. Frequent use of bullets); 1,200 words. Buys 24 mss/year. Query with published clips. Pays $200-500.

TOWERS CLUB, USA NEWSLETTER, The Original Information-By-Mail, Direct-Marketing Newsletter, Towers Club Press, P.O. Box 2038, Vancouver WA 98668. (206)574-3084. Editor: Jerry Buchanan. 5-10% freelance written. Works with a small number of new/unpublished writers each year. Newsletter published 10 times/year (not published in May or December) covering entrepreneurism (especially selling useful information by mail). Estab. 1974. Circ. 8,000. Pays on publication. Publishes ms an average of 2 months after acceptance. Byline given. Buys one-time rights. Submit seasonal/holiday material 10 weeks in advance. Simultaneous and previously published submissions OK. Query for electronic submissions. Reports in 2 weeks. Sample copy for $5 and 6×9 SAE; writer's guidelines for $1 and #10 SAE.
Nonfiction: Exposé (of mail order fraud); how-to (personal experience in self-publishing and marketing); book reviews of new self-published nonfiction how-to-do-it books (must include name and address of author). "Welcomes well-written articles of successful self-publishing/marketing ventures. Must be current, and preferably written by the person who actually did the work and reaped the rewards. There's very little we will not consider, *if* it pertains to unique money-making enterprises that can be operated from the home." Buys 10 mss/year. Send complete ms. Length: 500-1,500 words. Pays $10-35. Pays extra for b&w photo and bonus for excellence in longer manuscript.
Tips: "The most frequent mistake made by writers in completing an article for us is that they think they can simply rewrite a newspaper article and be accepted. That is only the start. We want them to find the article about a successful self-publishing enterprise, and then go out and interview the principal for a more detailed how-to article, including names and addresses. We prefer that writer actually interview a successful self-publisher. Articles should include how idea first came to subject; how they implemented and financed and promoted the project; how long it took to show a profit and some of the stumbling blocks they overcame; how many persons participated in the production and promotion; and how much money was invested (approximately) and other pertinent how-to elements of the story. Glossy photos (b&w) of principals at work in their offices will help sell article."

Contemporary Culture

These magazines combine politics, gossip, fashion and entertainment in a single package. Their approach to institutions is typically irreverent and the target is primarily a young adult audience. Although most of the magazines are centered in large metropolitan areas, some have a following throughout the country.

BOSTON REVIEW, 33 Harrison Ave., Boston MA 02111. (617)350-5353. Editor: Margaret Ann Roth. 100% freelance written. Works with a small number of new/unpublished writers each year. Bimonthly magazine of the arts, politics and culture. Estab. 1975. Circ. 10,000. **Pays on acceptance.** Publishes ms an average of 2 months after acceptance. Buys first American serial rights. Byline given. Simultaneous submissions OK. Reports in 2 months. Sample copy $4; writer's guidelines for #10 SASE.
Nonfiction: Critical essays and reviews, natural and social sciences, literature, music, painting, film, photography, dance and theatre. Buys 20 unsolicited mss/year. Length: 1,000-3,000 words. Sometimes pays expenses of writers on assignment.
Fiction: Length: 2,000-4,000 words. Pays according to length and author, ranging from $50-200.
Poetry: Pays according to length and author.
Tips: "Short (500 words) color pieces are particularly difficult to find, and so we are always on the look-out for them. We look for in-depth knowledge of an area, an original view of the material, and a presentation which makes these accessible to a sophisticated reader who will be looking for more and better articles which anticipate ideas and trends on the intellectual and cultural frontier."

FOLLOW ME , Follow Me Publications, 2nd Floor, 2-4 Bellevue St., Surry Hills, Sydney NSW Australia 2010. (2)212-5344. FAX: (02)-2126037. Editor: Deborah Bibby-Murphy. 50% freelance written. Monthly magazine "for ages 25-40 professionals, interested in fashion, art, photography, writing film etc. Circ. 51,000. **Pays on acceptance.** Publishes ms an average of 5-6 months after acceptance (long lead-time as we print overseas). Offers $100 kill fee commissioned stories only. Buys first Australian serial rights. Submit seasonal/holiday material 6 months in advance. Sample copy US $10 covers sea postage.
Nonfiction: Book excerpts, essays, historical, humor, interview/profile, photo feature and travel. Buys 30 mss/year. Query with published clips. "We will discuss individual assignments by phone, fax or mail." Length: 700-4,000 words. Pays $150-200/1,000 words.
Photos: State availability of photos with submission. Reviews 35 mm transparencies and 8 × 10 prints. Offers $50-200 per photo. Captions, model releases and identificaiton of subjects required. Buys one-time rights.
Columns/Departments: All columns currently on permanent freelance basis. Will take suggstions for new permanent columns. Buys 26 mss/year. Query with published clips. Length: 700. Pays $150-250.
Fiction: Erotica, historical, humorous, novel excerpts and slice-of-life vignettes. Buys 10 mss/year. Query with published clips. Length: 2,000-4,500 words. Pays $350 — set fee.

HIGH TIMES, Trans High Corp., Floor 20, 211 E. 43rd St., New York NY 10017. (212)972-8484. Editor: Steve Hager. Executive Editor: John Holmstrom. 75% freelance written. Monthly magazine covering marijuana. Circ. 250,000. Pays on publication. Byline given. Offers 20% kill fee. Buys one-time rights, all rights, or makes work-for-hire assignments. Submit seasonal/holiday material 6 months in advance. Simultaneous submissions OK. Reports in 1 month on queries; 2 months on mss. Sample for $5 and SASE; writer's guidelines for SASE.
Nonfiction: Book excerpts, expose, humor, interview/profile, new product, personal experience, photo feature and travel. Special issues include indoor Growers issue in September. No stories on "my drug bust." Buys 30 mss/year. Send complete ms. Length: 1,000-10,000 words. Pays $150-400. Sometimes pays in trade for advertisements. Sometimes pays expenses of writers on assignment.
Photos: Send photos with submission. Pays $50-300. Captions, model releases and identification of subjects required. Buys all rights or one-time use.
Columns/Departments: Steve Bloom, news editor. Drug related books; drug related news. Buys 10 mss/ year. Query with published clips. Length: 100-2,000 words. Pays $25-300.
Fiction: Adventure, fantasy, humorous and stories on smuggling. Buys 5 mss/year. Send complete ms. Length: 2,000-5,000 words. Pays $250-400.
Fillers: Gags to be illustrated by cartoonist, newsbreaks and short humor. Buys 10/year. Length: 100-500 words. Pays $10-50. Cartoon Editor: John Holmstrom.
Tips: "All sections are open to good, professional writers."

QUALITY LIVING, A Magazine for the Study of Values, Quality Living Publications, Inc. #16, 126 Grove St., Rutland VT 05701. (802)747-4460. Quarterly magazine. "Reflections on what deepens the best qualities in our living." Estab. 1986. Circ. 600. **Pays on acceptance.** Publishes ms an average of 6 months after acceptance. Byline given. Buys first North American serial rights. Submit seasonal/holiday material 6 months in advance. Reports in 3 weeks on queries; 2 months on mss. Writer's guidelines for #10 SASE.
Nonfiction: Essays, inspirational, interview/profile, opinion, personal experience, book reviews and movie reviews. "No pure problem-presentation, no cynicism, no highly technical, no exposé." Buys 30 mss/year. Query with or without published clips, or send complete ms. Length: 1,000-1,700 words. Pays $50 maximum.
Columns/Departments: Quality Reviews (of book or movies, from standpoint of their positive contribution to quality in life, or their exploration of this question). Buys 12 mss/year. Send complete ms. Length: 1,000 words. Pays $50 maximum.

Tips: "*Quality Living* has a subject focus for each issue. The bulk of our work is done 6 months ahead of publication date. Last minute submissions will not be read. Please note that we also accept two articles per issue that are not focus-topic articles. Write for a list of focus topics. Essays are most open to freelancers. Our audience is well educated, yet not academic. Style and vocabulary should be comfortable, not complex, highly readable. Ideas can be challenging if clearly handled. We like some sparkle!"

SPY, Spy Publishing Partners, 5 Union Sq. W., 8th Floor, New York NY 10003. (212)633-6550. Editor: K. Andersen and G. Carter. 50% freelance written. "*Spy* is a non-fiction satirical magazine published monthly." Circ. 165,000. **Pays on acceptance.** Publishes ms an average of 3 months after acceptance. Byline given. Offers 25% kill fee. Buys first and second North American serial rights, non-exclusive anthology rights. Submit seasonal/holiday material 6 months in advance. Simultaneous submissions OK. Query for electronic submissions. Reports in 2 weeks on queries; 1 month on mss. Sample copy $4.
Nonfiction: Jamie Malanowski, national editor. Book excerpts, essays, exposé, humor, interview/profile, opinion. Buys 100 mss/year. Query with published clips. Length: 200-4,000 words. Pays $50-2,000. Sometimes pays expenses of writers on assignment.
Photos: State availability of photos with submission. Reviews contact sheets. Offers $40-200/photo. Model release and identification of subjects required. Buys one-time rights.

TATTOO ADVOCATE JOURNAL, Tattoo Advocacy Inc., Box 8390, Haledon NJ 07538-0429. (201)790-0429. Editor: Tony Wang. 80% freelance written. Semiannual magazine on tattoo art. Circ. 5,000. **Pays on acceptance.** By line given. Offers $50 kill fee. Buys first North American serial rights, second serial (reprint) rights, all rights and makes work-for- hire assignments. Query for electronic submissions. Reports in 6 weeks on queries; 2 months on mss. Sample copy $5; free writer's guidelines.
Nonfiction: Shotsie Gorman, articles editor. Book excerpts, essays, general interest historical/nostalgic, humor, inspirational, interview/profile, opinion (does not mean letters to the editor), personal experience, photo feature, religious, technical and travel. "No motorcycle lifestyle, sexist, racist, or sexually oriented (unless in context)." Query with published clips or send complete ms. Length: 500-7,000. Pays $50-800 for assigned articles; $25-500 for unsolicited articles. Sometimes pays expenses of writers on assignment.
Photos: State availability of photos with submission. Reviews contact sheets, transparencies, and prints. Offers $20-300 per photo. Buys one-time rights and all rights.
Fiction: Adventure, ethnic, experimental, fantasy, historical, horror, humorous, mainstream, mystery, novel excerpts, religious, romance, science fiction, serialized novels, slice-of-life vignettes and suspense. No biker lifestyle fiction. Buys 3 mss/year. Send complete ms. Length: 1,000-7,000 words. Pays $100-700.
Poetry: Avant-garde, haiku, light verse and traditional. Buys 3 poems/year. Submit maximum 6 poems. Length: No minimum, no epics. Pays $25-400.

Detective and Crime

Fans of detective stories want to read accounts of actual criminal cases, detective work and espionage. The following magazines specialize in nonfiction, but a few buy some fiction. Markets specializing in crime fiction are listed under Mystery publications.

DETECTIVE CASES, Detective Files Group, 1350 Sherbrooke St. W., Montreal, Quebec H3G 2T4 Canada. Editor-in-Chief: Dominick A. Merle. Bimonthly magazine. See *Detective Files*.

DETECTIVE DRAGNET, Detective Files Group, 1350 Sherbrooke St. W., Montreal, Quebec H3G 2T4 Canada. Editor-in-Chief: Dominick A. Merle. Bimonthly magazine; 72 pages. See *Detective Files*.

DETECTIVE FILES, Detective Files Group, 1350 Sherbrooke St. W., Montreal, Quebec H3G 2T4 Canada. Editor-in-Chief: Dominick A. Merle. 100% freelance written. Bimonthly magazine; 72 pages. **Pays on acceptance.** Publishes ms an average of 3 months after acceptance. Buys all rights. Include International Reply Coupons. Reports in 1 month. Free sample copy and writer's guidelines.
Nonfiction: True crime stories. "Do a thorough job; don't double-sell (sell the same article to more than one market); deliver, and you can have a steady market. Neatness, clarity and pace will help you make the sale." Query. Length: 3,500-6,000 words. Pays $250-350.
Photos: Purchased with accompanying ms; no additional payment.

HEADQUARTERS DETECTIVE, Detective Files Group, 1350 Sherbrooke St. W., Montreal, Quebec H3G 2T4 Canada. Editor-in-Chief: Dominick A. Merle. Bimonthly magazine; 72 pages. See *Detective Files*.

‡INSIDE DETECTIVE, Official Detective Group, R.G.H. Publishing Corp., 460 W. 34th St., New York NY 10001. (212)947-6500. Editor-in-Chief: Rose Mandelsberg. Managing Editor: Sheila Barnes. Editor: Christos Ziros. Monthly magazine. Circ. 90,000. **Pays on acceptance.** Publishes ms an average of 3 months after acceptance. Byline given. Buys first rights and one-time world rights. Query for electronic submissions. Reports in 2 weeks. Free writer's guidelines.

Nonfiction: Buys 120 mss/year. Query. Pays $250. Length: 5,000-6,000 words (approx. 20 typed pages).

P. I. MAGAZINE, Fact and Fiction about the World of Private Investigators, 755 Bronx, Toledo OH 43609. (419)382-0967. Editor: Bob Mackowiak. 60% freelance written. "Not a trade journal. Audience includes professional investigators and mystery/private eye fans." Estab. 1988. Circ. 500. Pays on publication. Publishes ms an average of 3 months after acceptance. Buys one-time rights. Submit seasonal/holiday material 3 months in advance. Simultaneous and previously published submissions OK. Reports in 3 months on queries; 4 months on mss. Sample copy $3.75.

Nonfiction: Interview/profile, new product and personal experience (investigators only). Buys 4-10 mss/year. Send complete ms. Length: 500 words. Pays $10-25 for unsolicited articles.

Photos: Send photos with submission. Offers no additional payment for photos accepted with ms. Model releases and identification of subjects required. Buys one-time rights.

Columns/Departments: Profile (personality stories—what makes this person different from other investigators), 1,000-2,000 words. Buys 4 mss/year. Send complete ms. Pays $25.

Fiction: Adventure, humorous and mystery (Main character *must* be a private detective—not police detective, spy, or little old lady who happens to solve murders on the side. "No explicit sex.") Buys 16-20 mss/year. Length: 2,000-5,000 words. Send complete ms. Pays $25.

Tips: "The best way to get published in *P.I.* is to write a detailed story about a professional private detective's true-life case. I need much more of this."

STARTLING DETECTIVE, Detective Files Group, 1350 Sherbrooke St. W., Montreal, Quebec H3G 2T4 Canada. Editor-in-Chief: Dominick A. Merle. Bimonthly magazine; 72 pages. See *Detective Files*.

TRUE POLICE CASES, Detective Files Group, 1350 Sherbrooke St. W., Montreal, Quebec H3G 2T4 Canada. Editor-in-Chief: Dominick A. Merle. Bimonthly magazine; 72 pages. Buys all rights. See *Detective Files*.

Disabilities

These magazines are geared toward disabled persons and those who care for or teach them. A knowledge of disabilities and lifestyles is important for writers trying to break in to this field; editors regularly discard material without a realistic focus. Some of these magazines will accept manuscripts only from disabled persons or those with a background in caring for disabled persons.

ARTHRITIS TODAY, Arthritis Foundation. 1314 Spring St., N.W., Atlanta GA 30309. (404)872-7100. FAX: (404)872-0457. Editor: Cindy T. McDaniel. 70% freelance written. A bimonthly magazine about living with arthritis; latest in research/treatment. "*Arthritis Today* is written for the 37 million Americans who have arthritis and for the millions of others whose lives are touched by an arthritis-related disease. The editorial content is designed to help the person with arthritis live a more productive, independent and painfree life. The articles are upbeat and provide practical advice, information and inspiration." Estab. 1987. Circ. 600,000. Buys first North American serial rights but requires unlimited reprint rights in Arthritis Foundation publications. Submit seasonal/holiday material 6 months in advance. Simultaneous and previously published submissions OK. Reports in 1 month on queries; 6 weeks on mss. Sample copy for 9×11 SAE with 4 first class stamps. Writer's guidelines for #10 SASE.

Nonfiction: General interest, arts and entertainment, how-to (tips on any aspect of living with arthritis), humor, inspirational, interview/profile, new product, opinion, personal experience, photo feature, technical and travel. Buys 45 mss/year. Query with published clips. Length: 1,000-2,500. Pays $400-950. Sometimes pays expenses of writers on assignment.

Photos: State availability of photos with submission. Reviews 3x5 transparencies and 5×7 prints. Offers $75-200 per photo. Captions, model releases and identification of subjects required. Buys one-time rights or all rights.

Columns/Departments: Of Interest (general news and information); Personality Profiles (upbeat profiles of people living positively in spite of arthritis); Scientific Frontier (research news about arthritis) 200-600 words. Buys 16-20 mss/year. Query with published clips. Pays $250-400.

Fillers: Anecdotes, facts, gags to be illustrated by cartoonist, newsbreaks and short humor. Buys 2-4/year. Length: 75-150 words. Pays $75-200.

Tips: "In addition to articles specifically about living with arthritis, we look for articles to appeal to an older audience on subjects such as travel, history, arts and entertainment, hobbies, general health, etc."

CAREERS & THE HANDICAPPED, Equal Opportunity Publications, 44 Broadway, Greenlawn, NY 11740. (516)261-8917. Executive Editor: James Schneider. 60% freelance written. A semi-annual career guidance magazine distributed through college campuses for disabled college students and professionals. "The magazine offers role-model profiles and career guidance articles geared toward disabled college students and professionals." Pays on publication. Publishes ms an average of 6 months after acceptance. Circ. 10,000. Byline given. Buys all rights. Simultaneous and previously published submissions OK. Reports in 2 weeks. Sample copy and writer's guidelines for 7×10 SAE and $1.25 postage.

Nonfiction: General interest, interview/profile, opinion and personal experience. Buys 15 mss/year. Query. Length: 1,000-1,500 words. Pays $100-300 for assigned articles. Sometimes pays the expenses of writers on assignment.

Photos: State availability of photos with submission. Reviews prints. Offers $15 per photo. Captions. Buys one-time rights.

Tips: "Be as targeted as possible. Role model profiles which offer advice to disabled college students are most needed."

DIALOGUE, The Magazine for the Visually Impaired, Dialogue Publications, Inc., 3100 Oak Park Ave., Berwyn IL 60402. (708)749-1908. FAX: (708)749-2812. Managing Editor: Daniel Finch. 50% freelance written. Works with published/established writers and a small number of new/unpublished writers each year. Quarterly magazine of issues, topics and opportunities related to the visually impaired. Estab. 1962. **Pays on acceptance.** Publishes ms an average of 6 months after acceptance. Byline given. Buys all rights "with generous reprint rights." Submit seasonal/holiday material 6 months in advance. Reports in 2 weeks on queries; 1 month on mss. Free sample copy to visually impaired writers. Writer's guidelines in print for #10 SASE; send a 60-minute cassette for guidelines on tape.

Nonfiction: "Writers should indicate nature and severity of visual handicap." How-to (cope with various aspects of blindness); humor; interview/profile; new product (of interest to visually impaired); opinion; personal experience; technical (adaptations for use without sight); travel (personal experiences of visually impaired travelers); and first person articles about careers in which individual blind persons have succeeded. No "aren't blind people wonderful" articles; articles that are slanted towards sighted general audience. Buys 60 mss/year. Query with published clips or submit complete ms. Length: 3,000 words maximum. Prefers shorter lengths but will use longer articles if subject warrants. Pays $10-50. Sometimes pays the expenses of writers on assignment.

Columns/Departments: ABAPITA ("Ain't Blindness a Pain in the Anatomy")—short anecdotes relating to blindness; Recipe Round-Up; Around the House (household hints); Vox Pop (see magazine); Puzzle Box (see magazine and guidelines); book reviews of books written by visually impaired authors; Beyond the Armchair (travel personal experience); and Backscratcher (a column of questions, answers, hints). Buys 40 mss/year. Send complete ms. Payment varies.

Fiction: "Writers should state nature and severity of visual handicap." Adventure, fantasy, historical, humorous, mainstream, mystery, science fiction, and suspense. No plotless fiction or stories with unbelievable characters; no horror; no explicit sex and no vulgar language. Buys 12 mss/year. Send complete ms. Length: 3,000 words maximum; shorter lengths preferred. Pays $10-50.

Poetry: "Writers should state nature and severity of visual handicap." Free verse, haiku, and traditional. No religious poetry or any poetry with more than 20 lines. Buys 20/year. Submit maximum 3 poems. Pays in contributor's copies.

Fillers: Jokes, anecdotes and short humor. Buys few mss/year. Length: 100 words maximum. Payment varies.

Tips: "*Dialogue* cannot consider manuscripts from authors with 20/20 vision or those who can read regular print with ordinary glasses. Any person unable to read ordinary print who has helpful information to share with others in this category will find a ready market. We believe that blind people are capable, competent, responsible citizens, and the material we publish reflects this view. We are *not* interested in scholarly journal-type articles; 'amazing blind people I have known,' articles written by sighted writers; articles and fiction that exceed our 3,000-word maximum length; and material that is too regional to appeal to an international audience. No manuscript can be considered without a statement of visual impairment, nor can it be returned without a SASE."

INDEPENDENT LIVING, The Health Care Magazine Serving Dealers, Rehabilitation Facilities and Their Clients, Equal Opportunity Publications, Inc. 44 Broadway, Greenlawn NY 11740. (516)-261-8917. Editor: Anne Kelly. 75% freelance written. Quarterly magazine on home health care, rehabilitation and disability issues. "*Independent Living* magazine is written for persons with disabilities and the home care dealers, manufacturers, and health care professionals who serve their special needs." Circ. 35,000. Pays on publication. Byline given. Buys all rights. Simultaneous submissions OK. Reports in 1 month. Free sample copy and writer's guidelines.

Nonfiction: Essays, how-to, humor, inspirational, interview/profile, new product, opinion, personal experience, cartoons and travel. Buys 40 mss/year. Query. Length: 500-2,500 words. Pays 10¢/word.

Photos: Send photos with submission. Reviews prints. Offers $15 per photo. Prefers 35mm color slides. Captions and identification of subjects required. Buys all rights.

Tips: "The best way to have a manuscript published is to first send a detailed query on a subject related to the health care and independent lifestyles of persons who have disabilities. We need articles on innovative ways that home health care dealers are meeting their clients needs."

KALEIDOSCOPE: International Magazine of Literature, Fine Arts, and Disability, Kaleidoscope Press, 326 Locust St., Akron OH 44302. (216)762-9755. Editor: Darshan C. Perusek, Ph.D. 75% freelance written. Works with a small number of new/unpublished writers each year; eager to work with new/unpublished writers. Semiannual magazine with international collection of disability-related literature and art by disabled/nondisabled people. Estab. 1979. Circ. 1,500. Pays on publication. Publishes ms an average of 6 months after acceptance. Byline given. Buys first North American serial rights. Simultaneous queries OK. Previously published submissions "at editor's discretion." Reports in 6 months. Sample copy $2. Writer's guidelines for #10 SASE.

Nonfiction: Disability-related literary criticism, book reviews, personal experience essays, interview/profiles/photo features on literary and/or art personalities. Publishes 8-10 mss/year. Payment $25-50 for up to 2,500 words. Maximim 3,500 words. Feature length ms (15-20 pp) up to $100. All contributors receive 2 complimentary copies.

Photos: Pays up to $25/photo. Reviews 3×5, 5×7, 8×10 b&w and color prints. Captions and identification of subjects required.

Fiction: Short stories, excerpts. Traditional and experimental. Theme generally disability-related, occasional exceptions. Publishes 8-10 mss/year. Length: 5,000 words maximum. Pays $25; editor's discretion for higher payment. Two complimentary copies.

Poetry: Traditional and experimental. Theme: experience of disability. Submit up to 12 poems. Publishes 16-20/year. Payment up to $25 for multiple publication.

Tips: "Avoid the trite and sentimental. Treatment of subject should be fresh, original and imaginative. Always send photocopies. Become familiar with *Kaleidoscope* (sample copy very helpful)."

MAINSTREAM, Magazine of the Able-Disabled, Exploding Myths, Inc., 2973 Beech St., San Diego CA 92102. (619)234-3138. Editor: Cyndi Jones. 100% freelance written. Eager to develop writers who have a disability. A magazine published 10 times/year (monthly except January and June) covering disability-related topics, geared to disabled consumers. Estab. 1975. Circ. 15,500. Pays on publication. Publishes ms an average of 3 months after acceptance. Byline given. Buys all rights. Submit seasonal/holiday material 4 months in advance. Reports in 2 months. Sample copy $4.25 or 9x12 SAE with $3 and 5 first class stamps. Writer's guidelines for #10 SASE.

Nonfiction: Book excerpts, exposé, how-to (daily independent living tips), humor, interview/profile, personal experience (dealing with problems/solutions), photo feature, technical, travel, politics and legislation. "All must be disability-related, directed to disabled consumers." *NO* articles on " 'my favorite disabled character', 'my most inspirational disabled person', 'poster child stories.' " Buys 50 mss/year. Query with or without published clips, or send complete ms. Length: 6-12 pages. Pays $50-150. May pay subscription if writer requests.

Photos: State availability of photos with submission. Reviews contact sheets, $1½ \times ¾$ transparencies and 5×7 or larger prints. Offers $5-25 per b&w photo. Captions and identification of subjects required. Buys all rights.

Columns/Departments: Creative Solutions (unusual solutions to common aggravating problems); Personal Page (deals with personal relations: dating, meeting people). Buys 10 mss/year. Send complete ms. Length: 500-800 words. Pays $25-50.

Fiction: Humorous. Must be disability-related. Buys 4 mss/year. Send complete ms. Length: 800-1,200 words. Pays $50-100.

Tips: "It seems that politics and disability are becoming more important."

NEW WAYS to Bring Better Lives to People With Mental Retardation, First Publications, Inc., P.O. Box 5072, Evanston IL 60204. (312)869-7210. Editor-in-Chief/Co-Publisher: Mark Russell. 75% freelance written. A quarterly national magazine searching for excellence and innovations in areas such as housing, work, education, leisure, day programs, quality assurance, money matters, health, fitness, nutrition, psychology, guardianship and support services. Estab. 1981. Pays on publication. Publishes ms 6 months after acceptance. Byline given. Reports in 2 months. Sample copy for 9×11 SAE with 90¢ postage. Writer's guidelines for #10 SASE.

Nonfiction: Short, interesting articles slanted for readers concerned with assuring quality of life for people with mental retardation, teaching them, coping, planning for their future or increasing their integration with nondisabled people. Buys 20-30 mss/year. Query with published clips or send complete ms. Query should include the subject, proposed angle, authorities to be quoted, an example involving a person with mental retardation (if applicable) and your qualifications to write the article. Length: 700-2,000 (including sidebars). Pays $40-120 for first publication rights or reprint rights (when the writer makes extensive revisions to an article previously published). Payment usually is $20-75 for reprint rights (when the writer makes few revisions to an article published elsewhere) or one-time rights (when there's a chance the article might be published

For information on setting your freelance fees, see How Much Should I Charge? in the Business of Writing section.

elsewhere before publication in *New Ways*). Writers receive two complimentary issues containing their article. Pays some expenses of writers if approved in advance.

Photos: Pays $7.50-10 on acceptance for 5×7 or 8×10 b&w glossy print. (If possible, send contact sheets.) Buys one-time rights. Needs releases for people identifiable in photo.

Columns/Departments: Sharing (memorable moments, ironic happenings or turning points involving people with mental retardation, their relatives, caregivers, teachers or friends), 200-700 words. Buys one-time rights for 4-8 mss/year. Send complete ms. Pays $10-35 on acceptance.

Fillers: Reviews. "If you are interested in doing reviews of books or video tapes, please send the editor samples of previous reviews—even if never published—plus a summary of your qualifications, particularly those relating to the field of mental retardation. Payment for reviews varies."

Tips: "If you know at least one person with mental retardation, you have a better chance of finding a topic and approach suitable for our readers. The focus may be on autism, cerebral palsy, Down syndrome or epilepsy, as long as mental retardation is involved. For most articles, *New Ways* looks for the cutting edge combined with common sense, compassion and commitment."

Entertainment

This category's publications cover live, filmed or videotaped entertainment, including home video, TV, dance, theater and adult entertainment. Besides celebrity interviews, most publications want solid reporting on trends and upcoming productions. Magazines in the Contemporary Culture section also use articles on entertainment. For those publications with an emphasis on music and musicians, see the Music section.

‡AMERICAN FILM MAGAZINE, Billboard, Suite 1514, 6671 Sunset Blvd., Hollywood CA 90028. Editor: Wolf Schneider. Managing Editor: Randall Tierney. Senior Editor: Shawn Levy. Monthly magazine. Estab. 1975. Circ. 130,000. Pays on acceptance. Byline given. Offers 25% kill fee. Buys first North American serial rights. Submit seasonal/holiday material 6 months in advance. Query for electronic submissions. Reports in 3 months. Sample copy for $2.50 with SAE.

Nonfiction: Book excerpts, essays, exposé, general interest, historical/nostalgic, humor, interview/profile, and new product. Buys 100 mss/year. Query with published clips. Length: 300-4,000 words. Pays $100-2,500 for assigned articles. Pays expenses of writers on assignment.

Photos: State availability of photos with submission. Reviews transparencies. Payment negotiated. Identification of subjects required. Buys one-time rights and occasionally all rights for some, such as cover shots.

Columns/Departments: Illuminations (a collection of essays and issues), 200-600 words; Epilogue (last page—humorous or provocative, or both). Buys 100 mss/year. Query with published clips or send complete ms. Pays $100-750.

Tips: "Know the magazine. Know film; know good writing. We look for thinking writers who do their homework and don't take shortcuts. 'Illumination's' columns—pithy and intriguing entries, short and sweet—are the best way to break in."

AMERICAN SQUAREDANCE, Burdick Enterprises, P.O. Box 488, Huron OH 44839. (419)433-2188. Editors: Stan and Cathie Burdick. 10% freelance written. Works with a small number of new/unpublished writers each year. Monthly magazine of interviews, reviews, topics of interest to the modern square dancer. Circ. 23,000. Pays on publication. Publishes ms an average of 6 months after acceptance. Byline given. Buys all rights. Submit seasonal/holiday material 3 months in advance. Reports in 2 weeks on queries. Sample copy for 6×9 SAE with $1.05 postage; writer's guidelines for #10 SASE.

Nonfiction: General interest, historical/nostalgic, humor, inspirational, interview/profile, new product, opinion, personal experience, photo feature, travel. Must deal with square dance. Buys 6 mss/year. Send complete ms. Length: 1,000-1,500 words. Pays $2/column inch.

Photos: Send photos with ms. Reviews b&w prints. Captions and identification of subjects required.

Fiction: Subject related to square dancing only. Buys 1-2 mss/year. Send complete ms. Length: 1,500-2,000 words. Pays $2/column inch.

Poetry: Avant-garde, free verse, haiku, light verse, traditional. Square dancing subjects only. Buys 6 poems/year. Submit maximum 3 poems. Pays $2 for first 4 lines; $2/verse thereafter.

CINEASTE, America's Leading Magazine on the Art and Politics of the Cinema, Cineaste Publishers, Inc., #1320, 200 Park Ave. S., New York NY 10003. (212)982-1241. Managing Editor: Gary Crowdus. 50% freelance written. A quarterly magazine on motion pictures, offering "social and political perspective on the cinema." Circ. 7,000. Pays on publication. Publishes ms an average of 3 months after acceptance. Byline given. Offers 50% kill fee. Buys first North American serial rights. Reports in 3 weeks on queries; 1 month on mss. Sample copy $2. Writer's guidelines for #10 SASE.

Nonfiction: Essays, interview/profile, criticism. Buys 40-50 mss/year. Query with or without published clips, or send complete ms. Length: 3,000-6,000 words. Pays $20.
Photos: State availability of photos with submissions. Reviews prints. Offers no additional payment for photos accepted with ms. Identification of subjects required.

CINEFANTASTIQUE MAGAZINE, The review of horror, fantasy and science fiction films, P.O. Box 270, Oak Park IL 60303. (708)366-5566. Editor: Frederick S. Clarke. 100% freelance written. Eager to work with new/unpublished writers. A bimonthly magazine covering horror, fantasy and science fiction films. Estab. 1970. Circ. 25,000. Pays on publication. Publishes ms an average of 6 months after acceptance. Byline given. Buys all magazine rights. Simultaneous queries OK. Sample copy for $6 and 9 × 12 SAE. Reports in 2 months or longer.
Nonfiction: Historical/nostalgic (retrospects of film classics); interview/profile (film personalities); new product (new film projects); opinion (film reviews, critical essays); technical (how films are made). Buys 100-125 mss/year. Query with published clips. Length: 1,000-10,000 words. Sometimes pays the expenses of writers on assignment.
Photos: State availability of photos with query letter or ms.
Tips: "Study the magazine to see the kinds of stories we publish. Develop original story suggestions; develop access to film industry personnel; submit reviews that show a perceptive point of view."

‡COUNTRY AMERICA, Meredith Publishing Corporation, Locust at 17th, Des Moines IA 50336. (515)284-3790. Editor: Danita Allen. Managing Editor: Bill Eftink. Magazine covering country entertainment/lifestyle published 10 times/year. Estab. 1989. Circ. 500,000. **Pays on acceptance.** Byline given. Buys all rights (life-time). Submit seasonal/holiday material 8 months in advance. Previously published submissions OK "if notified." Free writer's guidelines.
Nonfiction: General interest, historical/nostalgic, how-to (home improvement), garden/food, interview/profile country music entertainers, photo feature, travel. Special Christmas, travel, wildlife/conservation, country music issues. Buys 130 mss/year. Query. Pays $100-1,000 for assigned articles. Sometimes pays expenses of writers on assignment.
Photos: State availability of photos with submission. Reviews contact sheets, negatives, 35mm transparencies. Offers $50-500/photo. Captions and identification of subjects required. Buys all rights.
Fillers: Short humor. Country curiosities that deal with animals, people, crafts, etc.
Tips: "Think visually. Our publication will be light on text and heavy on photos. Be general; this is a general interest publication meant to be read by every member of the family. We are a service-oriented publication; please stress how-to sidebars and include addresses and phone numbers to help readers find out more."

DANCE CONNECTION, Alberta Dance Alliance, 603, 815 1st St. S.W., Calgary AB T2P IN3 Canada. (403)263-3232 or 237-7327. Editor: Heather Elton. 75% freelance written. A bimonthly magazine devoted to dance with a broad editorial scope reflecting a deep commitment to a view of dance that embaces its diversity of style and fuction. Articles have ranged in subject matter from the changing role of dance in Native Indian culture from the buffalo days to the modern powwow, to the history of belly dancing, to modern dance. Estab. 1983. Circ. 5,000. Pays on publication. Byline given. Buys first rights or second serial (reprint) rights. Submit material 3 months in advance. Simultaneous and previously published submissions OK. Query for electronic submissions. Sample copy for 8½ × 11 SAE with IRCs.
Nonfiction: A variety of writing styles including criticism, essay, exposé, general interest, historical/nostalgic, humor, opinion, interview, performance review, forum debate, literature and photo feature. Query with published clips, or send complete ms. Length 800-2,500 words. Pays $5-150.
Fiction: Literature and poetry relating to dance.
Columns/Departments: Education, Children in Dance, Multiculturalism and Movement.

DANCE MAGAZINE, 33 W. 60th St., New York NY 10023. (212)245-9050. FAX: (212)956-6487. Editor-in-Chief: Richard Philp. 25% freelance written. Monthly magazine covering dance. Circ. 51,000. Pays on publication. Byline given. Offers up to $150 kill fee (varies). Makes work-for-hire assignments. Submit seasonal/holiday material 4 months in advance. Reports in "weeks." Sample copy and writer's guidelines for 8 × 10 SAE.
Nonfiction: Interview/profile. Buys 50 mss/year. Query with or without published clips, or send complete ms. Length: 300-1,500 words. Pays $15-350. Sometimes pays expenses of writers on assignment.
Photos: State availability of photos with submission. Reviews transparencies and prints. Offers $15-285/photo. Captions and identification of subjects required. Buys one-time rights.
Columns/Departments: Presstime News (topical, short articles on current dance world events) 150-400 words. Buys 40 mss/year. Query with published clips. Pays $20-75.
Tips: Writers must have "thorough knowledge of dance and take a sophisticated approach."

DRAMATICS MAGAZINE, International Thespian Society, 3368 Central Pkwy., Cincinnati OH 45225. (513)559-1996. Editor-in-Chief: Donald Corathers. 70% freelance written. Works with small number of new/unpublished writers. For theater arts students, teachers and others interested in theater arts education.

Magazine published monthly, September through May. Estab. 1929. Circ. 35,000. **Pays on acceptance.** Publishes ms an average of 3 months after acceptance. Buys first North American serial rights. Byline given. Submit seasonal/holiday material 3 months in advance. Simultaneous and previously published submissions OK. Query for electronic submissions. Reports in 1 month. Sample copy for $2 and a 9×12 SAE with 5 first class stamps; free writer's guidelines.

Nonfiction: How-to (technical theater), informational, interview, photo feature, humorous, profile and technical. Buys 30 mss/year. Submit complete ms. Length: 750-3,000 words. Pays $30-200. Rarely pays expenses of writers on assignment.

Photos: Purchased with accompanying ms. Uses b&w photos and transparencies. Query. Total purchase price for ms usually includes payment for photos.

Fiction: Drama (one-act plays). No "plays for children, Christmas plays or plays written with no attention paid to the conventions of theater." Prefers unpublished scripts that have been produced at least once. Buys 5-9 mss/year. Send complete ms. Pays $50-200.

Tips: "The best way to break in is to know our audience—drama students, teachers and others interested in theater—and to write for them. Writers who have some practical experience in theater, especially in technical areas, have a leg-up here, but we'll work with anybody who has a good idea. Some freelancers have become regular contributors. Others ignore style suggestions included in our writer's guidelines."

FANGORIA: Horror in Entertainment, Starlog Group, 475 Park Ave. S., 8th Floor, New York NY 10016. (212)689-2830. FAX: (212)889-7933. Editor: Anthony Timpone. 95% freelance written. Works with a small number of new/unpublished writers each year. Published 10 times/year. Magazine covering horror films, TV projects and literature and those who create them. Estab. 1979. Pays on publication. Publishes ms an average of 3 months after acceptance. Byline given. Buys all rights. Submit seasonal/holiday material 6 months in advance. Simultaneous queries OK. Query for electronic submissions. Reports in 6 weeks. "We provide an assignment sheet (deadlines, info) to writers, thus authorizing queried stories that we're buying." Sample copy $4.50; writers' guidelines for #10 SASE.

Nonfiction: Book excerpts, interview/profile of movie directors, makeup FX artists, screenwriters, producers, actors, noted horror novelists and others—with genre credits. No "think" pieces, opinion pieces, reviews, or sub-theme overviews (i.e., vampire in the cinema). Buys 100 mss/year. Query with published clips. Length: 1,000-3,000 words. Pays $100-225. Rarely pays the expenses of writers on assignment. Avoids articles on science fiction films—see listing for sister magazine *Starlog* in *Writer's Market* science fiction magazine section.

Photos: State availability of photos. Reviews b&w prints and transparencies. "No separate payment for photos provided by film studios." Captions and identification of subjects required. Photo credit given. Buys all rights.

Columns/Departments: Monster Invasion (news about new film productions; must be exclusive, early information; also mini-interviews with filmmakers and novelists). Query with published clips. Length: 300-500 words. Pays $25-50.

Fiction: "We do *not* publish any fiction. *Don't* send any."

Tips: "Other than recommending that you study one or several copies of *Fangoria*, we can only describe it as a horror film magazine consisting primarily of interviews with technicians and filmmakers in the field. Be sure to stress the interview subjects' words—not your own opinions as much. We're very interested in small, independent filmmakers working outside of Hollywood. These people are usually more accessible to writers, and more cooperative. *Fangoria* is also sort of a *de facto* bible for youngsters interested in movie makeup careers and for young filmmakers. We are devoted only to *reel* horrors—the fakery of films, the imagery of the horror fiction of a Stephen King or a Peter Straub—we *do not* want nor would we *ever* publish articles on real-life horrors, murders, etc. A writer must *like* and *enjoy* horror films and horror fiction to work for us. If the photos in *Fangoria* disgust you, if the sight of (*stage*) blood repels you, if you feel 'superior' to horror (and its fans), you aren't a writer for us and we certainly aren't the market for you. *Fangoria*'s frequency has increased over the last years and, with an editorial change reducing staff written articles, this has essentially doubled the number of stories we're buying. In 1991, we expect such opportunities only to increase for freelancers. *Fangoria* will try for a lighter, irreverent, more 'Gonzo' tone in the year ahead."

FILM QUARTERLY, University of California Press, Berkeley CA 94720. (415)642-6333. FAX: (415)643-7127. Editor: Ernest Callenbach. 100% freelance written. Eager to work with new/unpublished writers. Quarterly. Buys all rights. Byline given. Pays on publication. Publishes ms an average of 3 months after acceptance. Query. Sample copy and writer's guidelines for SASE.

Nonfiction: Articles on style and structure in films, articles analyzing the work of important directors, historical articles on development of the film as art, reviews of current films and detailed analyses of classics, book reviews of film books. Must be familiar with the past and present of the art; must be competently, although not necessarily breezily, written; must deal with important problems of the art. "We write for people who like to think and talk seriously about films, as well as simply view them and enjoy them. We use no personality pieces or reportage pieces. Interviews usually work for us only when conducted by someone familiar with most of a filmmaker's work. (We don't use performer interviews.)" Length: 6,000 words maximum. Pay is about 2¢/word.

Tips: *"Film Quarterly* is a specialized academic journal of film criticism, though it is also a magazine (with pictures) sold in bookstores. It is read by film teachers, students, and die-hard movie buffs, so unless you fall into one of those categories, it is very hard to write for us. Currently, we are especially looking for material on independent, documentary, etc. films not written about in the national film reviewing columns."

‡'GBH MAGAZINE, CVG Publishing Services, 332 Congress St., Boston MA 02210. (617574-9400. Editor: Jack Curtis. 50% freelance written. Monthly magazine for supporters of WGBH public TV and radio station in Boston. "*GBH* is the monthly magazine and program guide for WGBH members; it includes program-related editorial and program listings to 'complement' its broadcast partners." All editorial focuses on the full range of programming, including the performing arts, history, public affairs, science and adventure. Estab. 1987. Circ. 150,000. **Pays on acceptance.** Publishes ms an average of 2 months after acceptance. Byline given. Offers 25% kill fee. Buys first North American serial rights. Submit seasonal/holiday material 3 months in advance. Previously published submissions OK. Reports in 1 month on queries; 2 weeks on mss.

Nonfiction: Essays, expose, general interest, historical/nostalgic, humor, interview/profile, opinion, personal experience, photo feature. Buys 15-25 mss/year. Query with published clips. Length: 800-2,000 words. Pays $500-1,000.

Photos: Send photos with submission. Reviews contact sheets, negatives, transparencies. Buys one-time rights.

Columns/Departments: Interview (q and a with a local Boston or a PBS TV or NPR personality must relate to that month's WGBH programming) 500-1,000 words. Pays $250-750. Arts, etc. (essay on major local cultural event that month), 500-750 words. Pays $250-450.

Tips: "Check upcoming WGBH programming (both TV and radio) — is there an inteview worth doing with a story. Is there an essay on an issue raised by WGBH? What about examining a particularly successful PBS show? What's on WGBH that month of special interest?"

MOVIELINE MAGAZINE, 1141 S. Beverly Dr., Los Angeles CA 90035. (213)282-0711. Editors: Laurie Halpern Smith and Virginia Campbell. 10% freelance written. Monthly magazine covering motion pictures. Circ. 100,000. Pays 30 days from acceptance of ms. Publishes ms an average of 4 months after acceptance. Byline given. Offers 20% kill fee. Buys first North American serial rights. Simultaneous submissions OK. Reports in 2 months.

Nonfiction: Book excerpts, film business-oriented pieces, humor and interview/profile. No historical pieces, *please*. Buys 25-100 mss/year. Query with published clips *only*. Length: 1,000-3,000 words. Pays $200-1,000. Sometimes pays expenses of writers on assignment.

Photos: State availability of photos with submission. Reviews contact sheets, 2¼ transparencies and 5×7 photos. Offers $10-100/photo. Identification of subjects required. Buys one-time rights.

Columns/Departments: Buzz (short, funny pieces on movie-related personalities and incidents), 150-300 words. Buys 75 mss/year. Pays $100-250.

Tips: "*Movieline* is a consumer-oriented publication devoted to film. We publish interviews with actors and actresses, directors, cinematographers, producers, writers, costume designers and others with a creative involvement in motion pictures. We also seek behind-the-scenes stories relating to the movie business; fresh, insightful overviews of trends and genres; on-location pieces; and short, anecdotal items relating to any of the above. We are not, repeat not, seeking pieces on dead movie stars, like 'When Errol Flynn Came Through Town.' We consider our audience to be seasoned moviegoers, and consequently look for a knowledgeable, sophisticated approach to the subject; avoid a breathless, "fan"-like attitude, especially in star interviews. Pieces should be exciting, stylish and, because of our space limitations, tightly written."

‡NINE, St. Louis Regional Educational and Public Television Commission. 6996 Millbrook Blvd., St. Louis MO 63130. (314)725-2460. FAX: (314)726-0677. Editor: Gayle R. McIntosh. Monthly magazine of public television and related interest areas. Estab. 1977. Circ. 50,000. Pays on publication. Publishes ms an average of 2 months after acceptance. Byline given. Buys one-time rights. Submit seasonal/holiday material 4 months in advance. Simultaneous and previously published submissions OK. Query for electronic submissions. Reports in 1 month on queries. Free sample copy.

Nonfiction: Book excerpts, historical/nostalgic, how-to (garden, home, cooking), interview/profile, personal experience, travel. Buys 12 mss/year. Query with published clips. Length: 1,000-2,500 words. Pays $75-300.

Photos: State availability of photos with submission. Offers no additional payment for photos accepted with ms. Identification of subjects required. Buys one-time rights.

Columns/Departments: Business, Travel, Health (related to interests/demo profile of public television viewers). Home, books, garden and pets columns to be added. Buys 48 mss/year. Query with published clips. Length: 750-1,000 words. Pays $30-300.

‡PALMER VIDEO NEWS, 1767 Morris Ave., Union NJ 07083. (201)686-3030. Editor: Susan Baar. 50% freelance written. Monthly magazine covering video and film related topics. "*The Palmer Video News* is a 56-page magazine mailed exclusively to Palmer Video members. The magazine is both entertaining and informative as it pertains to film and video. Estab. 1981. Circ. 200,000. **Pays on acceptance.** Publishes ms 1 month

after acceptance. Makes work-for-hire assignments. Submit seasonal/holiday material 2 months in advance. Simultaneous submissions OK. Free sample copy and writer's guidelines.

Nonfiction: How-to (video related), interview/profile (must be film related) and technical (video related). Buys 40 mss/year. Query with published clips. Length: 500-2,000 words. Pays $50-200 for assigned articles.

Photos: State availability of photos with submission. Offers no additional payment for photos accepted with ms.

Columns/Departments: Video Critiques (positive reviews of films newly released on video), 50-60 words; Profile (interviews of profiles on actors/directors, etc.), 1,000 words; Cinemascope (article pertaining to film genre), 1,000-2,000 words; and Movie Motive (shorts on various movies), 500-1,000 words. Buys 40 mss/year. Query with published clips. Pays $50-200.

PERFORMING ARTS IN CANADA, 5th Fl., 263 Adelaide St. W., Toronto, Ontario M5H 1Y2 Canada. (416)971-9516. FAX: (416)971-9517. Editor: Sarah B. Hood. 80% freelance written. Prefers to work with published/established writers; works with a small number of new/unpublished writers each year. Quarterly magazine for professional performers and general readers with an interest in Canadian theater, dance, music, opera and film. Covers "modern and classical theater arts, plus articles on related subjects (government arts policy, etc.)." Estab. 1961. Pays 1 month following publication. Publishes ms an average of 3 months after acceptance. Byline given. Buys first serial rights. Query for electronic submissions. Reports in 6 weeks. Sample copy for $1 and 9×12 SAE with IRCs; writer's guidelines for #10 SASE.

Nonfiction: "Lively, stimulating, well-researched articles on Canadian performing artists or groups. Most often in need of good classical music and dance articles." No nonCanadian, nonperforming arts material. Buys 30-35 mss/year. Query preferably with an outline plus tearsheets. Writers new to this publication should include clippings. Length: 1,000-2,000 words. Pays $150-200. Sometimes pays the expenses of writers on assignment.

Tips: "We have a continuing need for articles that hale from the smaller centers in Canada. Ontario and particularly Toronto events are well covered."

‡PERFORMING ARTS MAGAZINE, 3539 Motor Ave., Los Angeles CA 90034. (213)839-8000. Managing Editor: Dana Kraft. 100% freelance written. Monthly magazine covering theater, music, dance, visual art. "We publish general pieces on the arts of a historical or 'current-events' nature." Estab. 1965. Circ. 800,000. Pays on publication. Publishes ms an average of 2 months after acceptance. Offers $150 kill fee. Buys one-time rights. Submit seasonal/holiday material 3 months in advance. Previously published submissions OK. Free sample copy.

Nonfiction: Book excerpts (on the Arts), general interest (theater, dance, opera), historical/nostalgic, interview/profile (performers, artists) and travel. No critical texts, religious, political essays or reviews. Buys 80 mss/year. Query with published clips. Length: 1,500-3,000 words. Pays $500-1,000 for assigned articles; $150-500 for unsolicited articles. Theater tickets are sometimes offered as payment if acceptable to writer. Sometimes pays expenses of writers on assignment.

Photos: State availability of photos with submission. Reviews transparencies. Offers no additional payment for photos accepted with ms. Buys one-time rights.

Tips: "Theater, dance and music on the West Coast are our main interests. Write broad information pieces or interviews."

‡THE PLAY MACHINE, P.O. Box 330507, Houston TX 77233-0507. Editor: Norman Clark Stewart Jr. 90% freelance written. Quarterly tabloid of recreation/adult play. Our publication is dedicated to reviving the spirit of playfulness in a workaholic world. Estab. 1990. Circ. 1,000. Pays on publication. Byline given. Buys first North American, one-time or second serial (reprint) rights. Submit seasonal/holiday material 8 months in advance. Simultaneous and previously published submissions OK. Reports in 8 months on mss. Sample copy with 9×12 SAE and 4 first class stamps. Writer's guidelines for #10 SAE with 2 first class stamps.

Nonfiction: How-to (play or have fun), humor (not satire—playful), interview/profile (with pranksters/jokers or genius in relation to fun), new product (recreational/hobby, etc.). Nothing that is not fun, playful or related to recreation—nothing serious. Buys 20-100 mss/year. Send complete ms. Length: 3,500 words maximum. Pays $50 maximum for unsolicited articles.

Photos: Send photos with submission. Offers no additional payment for photos accepted with ms. Model releases and identification of subjects required. Buys one-time rights.

Fillers: Anecdotes, facts, gags to be illustrated by cartoonist, short humor. Buys 200/year. Pays $5 maximum.

Tips: "Have fun writing the submissions."

PLAYBILL, Playbill Inc., Suite 320, 71 Vanderbilt Ave., New York NY 10169. (212)557-5757. Editor: Joan Alleman. 50% freelance written. Monthly magazine covering NYC, Broadway and Off-Broadway theater. Estab. 1884. Circ. 1.75 million. **Pays on acceptance.** Publishes ms an average of 2 months after acceptance. Byline given. Buys all rights. Reports in 2 months.

Nonfiction: Book excerpts, humor, interview/profile, personal experience—must all be theater related. Buys approximately 10 mss/year. Query with published clips. Length: 1,500-1,800 words. Pays $250-500.
Photos: State availability of photos with submission. Offers no additional payment for photos accepted with ms. Identification of subjects required.
Fillers: Anecdotes, facts and short humor. Buys 10 mss/year. Length: 350-700 words. Pays $50-100. Must all be theater related.

‡**PLEASURE QUEST, Your Success Guide to Sensual Adventures & Romance,** Health & Wealth Guardian, Ltd., 462 S. Gilbert Rd., Mesa AZ 85204. (602)829-8888. Editor: Phillip Fry. Executive Editor: Teresa Tokar. 50% freelance written. Quarterly magazine covering the pursuit of healthy pleasures. "P.Q. is a 'how-to' publication to help readers maximize personal pleasures such as love, romance, sex, gambling and all other healthy pleasures. Estab. 1989. Circ. 50,000. **Pays on acceptance.** Byline given. Buys first rights, second serial (reprint) rights or all rights. Submit seasonal/holiday material 6 months in advance. Simultaneous and previously published submissions OK. Reports in 2 weeks. Sample copy $3.75. Free writer's guidelines.
Nonfiction: Book excerpts, exposé, how-to, interview/profile and new product. Query with published clips. Length 500-5,000 words. Pays $250-500 for assigned articles; $75-500 for unsolicited articles.
Photos: State availability of photos with submission. Reviews 2×2 transparencies (slides) or any size prints. Offers $50-500 per photo. Captions, model releases and identification of subjects required. Buys all rights.
Columns/Departments: Gambling, massage, how-to take sexy photos of lover, romantic retreats. Buys 8 mss/year. Query with published clips. Length: 1,000-5,000 words. Pays $125-500.
Tips: "We need in-depth, 'how-to' tips for readers to maximize their personal pleasure and fun."

PREMIERE, Murdoch Publications, Inc., 2 Park Ave., 4th Fl, New York NY 10016. (212)725-7927. Editor: Susan Lyne. Monthly magazine. "Monthly magazine for young adults (18-34 years old) that takes readers behind the scenes of movies in release and in production." **Pays on acceptance.** Byline given. Offers 25% kill fee. Buys first North American serial rights and world rights for 3 months. Submit seasonal/holiday material 4 months in advance. Reports in 2-3 weeks on queries. Writer's guidelines for #10 SASE.
Nonfiction: Film. Video issue (January), Year-End Issue (February), Academy Award Issue (April), Summer Preview Issue (June), Fall Preview Issue (October). Buys 60 mss/year. Query with published clips. Maximum length 2,500 words. Pays $1/word maximum. Pays expenses of writers on assignment.
Columns/Departments: Buys 40 mss/year. Maximum length 1,000 word. Pays $1/word maximum.
Fillers: Features, columns etc. Buys 60/year. Maximum length 500 words. Pays 50¢/word maximum.
Tips: "*Premiere* looks for articles that go behind the scenes of movies in release and in production; that answer questions about creative strategy, development, financing and distribution as well as focusing on the producers, directors and stars who create the films. Feature articles include interviews, profiles and film commentary and analysis. Monthly departments look for coverage of the movie business, video technology and hardware, home video, movie music/scoring and books."

STV GUIDE, Triple D Publishing, Inc., P.O. Box 2384, Shelby NC 28151. (704)482-9673. FAX: (704)484-8558. Editor: David B. Melton. 70% freelance written. Monthly magazine covering home satellite TV. "We look for articles on satellite television entertainment, new equipment, how-to for the consumer, communications legislation, and programming for the home satellite television enthusiast." Estab. 1981. Circ. 60,000. Byline given. Pays on publication. Offers 30% kill fee. Buys all rights. Submit seasonal/holiday material 3 months in advance. Simultaneous submissions OK. Query for electronic submissions. Reports in 2 weeks. Free sample copy and writer's guidelines.
Nonfiction: How-to, interview/profile, new product, opinion, personal experience, photo feature, technical. Buys 24 mss/year. Query with or without published clips, or send complete ms. Length: 1,800-3,600 words. Pays $150-400. Sometimes pays expenses of writers on assignment.
Photos: State availability of photos with submission or send photos with submission. Reviews contact sheets, transparencies and prints. Offers $5-200 per photo. Captions, model release and identification of subjects required.
Columns/Departments: At Home (personal experiences of readers), 1,000 words. Query. Length: 1,000-1,800 words. Pays $50-100.
Tips: "A writer who is a satellite TV user or has knowledge of it would be of great help. Familiarity with television transmission and some programming knowledge would also be helpful."

‡**TDC, The Magazine of The Discovery Channel,** Cable Educational Network, Inc., Suite 1200, 8201 Corporate Dr., Landover MD 20785. (301)577-1999. Editor: Rebecca Farwell. Managing Editor: Kit Carlson. 70% freelance written. Monthly magazine for Discovery Channel viewers. "Program guide section lists TDC programs for the month. Magazine section expands on areas covered in that month's programs. Articles and channel programs cover nature, science, adventure, history, people and places." Estab. 1985. Circ. 120,000. **Pays on acceptance.** Publishes ms an average of 2 months after acceptance. Byline given. Offers 10% kill fee. Buys first and second rights or makes work-for-hire assignments. Previously published submissions OK. Query

for electronic submissions. Reports "immediately." Sample copy $2 with 10 × 12 SAE and 3 first class stamps. Writer's guidelines for #10 SASE.

Nonfiction: Book excerpt, essays, general interest, historical/nostalgic, interview/profile, personal experience, photo feature, travel. Buys 70-80 mss/year. Send letter of introduction with published clips and resume. No phone queries. Length: 750-3,500 words. Pays $350-6,000 for assigned articles. Sometimes pays expenses of writers on assignment.

Photos: State availability of photos with submission. Reviews contact sheets, transparencies, prints. Captions, model releases and identification of subjects required.

Columns/Departments: Fine Tuning (journalistic treatment/update of issue covered in a program). Length: 750-850 words. Pays $350-500.

Tips: "We assign articles based on topics being aired by The Discovery Channel. We are looking for authors with specific knowledge of nonfiction areas covered by the channel: nature, history, science, etc. If you have cable, watch the channel. We want the magazine to reflect in print the world-ranging documentary approach of The Discovery Channel. More than anything we seek fine writing a la Frances Fitzgerald, John McPhee, James Fallows, etc. Fine Tuning is the best place to start—short journalistic updates of issues being aired on the channel. We try writers out here and move them up if they merit it."

‡**TDR; The Drama Review: A Journal of Performance Studies**, New York University, 721 Broadway, 6th Floor, New York NY 10003. (212)998-1626. Editor: Richard Schechner. 95% freelance written. Works with a small number of new/unpublished writers each year. "Emphasis not only on theater but also dance, ritual, musical performance, mime, and other facets of performative behavior. For avant-garde community, students and professors of anthropology, performance studies and related fields. Political material is welcome." Quarterly magazine. Estab. 1954. Circ. 7,000. Pays on publication. Submit material 4 months in advance. Previously published (if published in another language) submissions OK. Reports in 2 months. Publishes ms an average of 6 months after acceptance. Sample copy $7 (from MIT Press); free writer's guidelines.

Nonfiction: Rebecca Schneider, managing editor. Buys 10-20 mss/issue. Query by letter only. Pays 3¢/word.

Photos: Rebecca Schneider, managing editor. State availability of photos with submission. 5 × 7 b&w photos preferred. Captions required.

Tips: "*TDR* is a place where contrasting ideas and opinions meet. A forum for writing about performances and the social, economic and political contexts in which performances happen. The editors want interdisciplinary, intercultural, multivocal, eclectic submissions."

TV ENTERTAINMENT, The Crosby Vandenburgh Group, 420 Boylston St., Boston MA 02116. Editor: Cable Neuhaus. 40% freelance written. Monthly magazine on TV and motion-picture entertainment. "We are read by U.S. cable-TV subscribers who are interested in behind-the-scenes and exclusive info about TV and motion-picture personalities as well as information about Americans whose lives are portrayed, in one way or another, on TV." Estab. 1982. Circ. 4,600,000. Pays on publication. Publishes ms an average of 2 months after acceptance. Byline given. Negotiated kill fee. Buys first North American serial rights. Submit seasonal/holiday material 4 months in advance. Reports in 1 month. Sample copy for 8 × 10 SAE with 7 first class stamps. Writer's guidelines for #10 SAE with 1 first class stamp.

Nonfiction: Book excerpts, exposé, general interest, historical/nostalgic, interview/profile, new product, personal experience, photo feature. "No stock celebrity interviews/profiles." Buys 35 mss/year. Query with published clips. Length: 100-1,800 words. Pays $50-1,500.

Photos: State availability of photos with submission. Reviews contact sheets, negatives, transparencies, prints. Payment negotiated. Captions, model releases and identification of subjects required. Rights negotiated.

Fillers: Michael Rosenstein, editor. Facts. Buys 20/year. Length: 25-300 words. Payment negotiated.

Tips: "Land exclusive interviews with difficult U.S. celebrities or have access to *verifiable* information concerning our subject matter. We are a *general interest* consumer magazine that is pegged to TV programming. All feature areas and our Talk/Show department are open to freelancers."

VIDEO, 460 W. 34th St., New York, NY 10001. (212)947-6500. FAX: (212)947-6727. Editor-in-Chief: Art Levis. Managing Editor: Stan Pinkwas. 75% freelance written. Prefers to work with published/established writers; works with a small number of new/unpublished writers each year. A monthly magazine covering home video equipment, technology and prerecorded tapes. Circ. 450,000. **Pays on acceptance.** Publishes ms an average of 2 months after acceptance. Byline given. Buys first North American serial rights. Query for electronic submissions. Requires hard copy also. Reports in 2 weeks on queries; 1 month on manuscripts. Free writer's guidelines.

Nonfiction: Buys 80 mss/year. Query with published clips. Pays $300-1,000. Sometimes pays the expenses of writers on assignment.

Tips: The entire feature area is open to freelancers. Write a brilliant query and send samples of published articles.

VIDEO MARKETPLACE MAGAZINE, World Publishing Co., 4th Floor, 990 Grove St., Evanston IL 60201. (312)491-6440. Editor: Robert Meyers. 90% freelance written. A monthly magazine on video software. "The magazine is broken down into basically two categories: movies (recent release, classic/vintage) and TV/nostalgia. Movie sub-categories include: celebrity profiles, directors chair, general theme round-ups (past or present)." Circ. 150,000. **Pays on acceptance.** Publishes ms an average of 4 months after acceptance. Byline given. Offers $75-125 kill fee. Buys one-time rights. Submit seasonal/holiday material 6 months in advance. Previously published submissions OK. Reports in 2 weeks on queries; 3 weeks on mss. Sample copy $2.50; writer's guidelines for #10 SASE.

Nonfiction: Humor (in general areas), interview/profile (celebrity, all fields), photo feature (all categories). Query with published clips or send complete ms. Feature articles: 700-900 or 1,200-1,400 words. Pays $125-350; $75-125 for reprints.

Photos: State availability of photos with submission. Black and white or color photos help overall package acceptance. Reviews transparencies. Offers no additional payment for photos accepted with ms.

Columns/Departments: Behind the Scenes (short pieces about movie/celebrity background). Length: 700-1,400 words. Pays $125-350; $75-125 for reprints.

VIDEOMANIA, "The Video Collector's Newspaper", Legs Of Stone Publishing Co., P.O. Box 47, Princeton WI 54968. Editor: Bob Katerzynske. 70% freelance written. Eager to work with new/unpublished writers. A monthly tabloid for the home video hobbyist. "Our readers are very much 'into' home video: they like reading about it—including both video hardware and software—98% also collect video (movies, vintage TV, etc.)." Estab. 1981. Circ. 5,000. Pays on publication. Publishes ms an average of 3 months after acceptance. Byline given. Buys all rights; may reassign. Submit seasonal/holiday material 6 months in advance. Reports in 3 weeks on mss. Sample copy for 9 × 12 SAE and $2.50 postage; writer's guidelines for #10 SASE .

Nonfiction: Book excerpts, videotape and book reviews, expose, general interest, historical/nostalgic, how-to, humor, interview/profile, new product, opinion, personal experience, photo feature, technical and travel. "All articles should deal with video and/or film. We always have special holiday issues in November and December." No "*complicated* technical pieces." Buys 24 mss/year. Send complete ms. Length: 500-1,000 words. Pays $2.50 maximum. "Contributor copies also used for payment."

Photos: Send photos with submissions. Reviews contact sheets and 3 × 5 prints. Offers no additional payment for photos accepted with ms. Model releases and identification of subjects required. Buys all rights; may reassign.

Fiction: Adventure, horror and humorous. "We want short, video-related fiction only on an occasional basis. Since we aim for a general readership, we do not want any pornographic material." Buys 5 mss/year. Send complete ms. Length: 500 words. Pays $2.50 maximum plus copies.

Tips: "We want to offer more reviews and articles on offbeat, obscure and rare movies, videos and stars. Write in a plain, easy-to-understand style. We're not looking for a highhanded, knock-'em-dead writing style . . . just something good! We want more short video, film and book reviews by freelancers."

‡VISIO MAGAZINE, Into the 21st Century, L.F.P. Inc., Suite 300, 9171 Wilshire Blvd., Beverly Hills CA 90210. (213)858-7100. Editor: Dean Brierly. 90% freelance written. Monthly magazine covering consumer electronics, recreation and technology. Estab. 1990. Circ. 250,000. Pays on acceptance. Byline given. Offers 20% kill fee. Buys first rights. Submit seasonal/holiday material 5 months in advance. Query for electronic submissions. Free sample copy and writer's guidelines.

Nonfiction: New product, photo feature, technical and consumer electronics. Buys 100 mss/year. Query with published clips. Length 700-2,000 words. Pays $200-500 maximum. Sometimes pays expenses of writers on assignment.

Photos: Send photos with submission.

Columns/Departments: Pageant Watch (analysis, persona experience/"hangout" type); Looking Your Best (experts in grooming/skin/hair care) 1,000-1,500 words. Buys 10-30 mss/year. Query with published clips. Pays $50-75.

Tips: "Send for guidelines; we're very picky. We don't like to see work that reads like a newspaper story. Too many writers we've worked with so far have a hard time seeing past the quotes, and too often don't get the right ones in the first place. Concentrate on what the story is about, do twice the research you think you'll need, then approach the piece like a breezily-written research paper. Writers should have a working knowledge of the entertainment industry. Unless you're an expert, or have extensive personal experience in the area you're covering, the chances are good you'll miss the mark. However, a thoughtful, well written piece will attract our attention."

Ethnic/Minority

Ethnic magazines, especially for Hispanics, have started up and done well during the past year. Some ethnic magazines seek material that unites people of all races. Ideas, interests and concerns of nationalities and religions are covered by publications in this category. General interest lifestyle magazines for these groups are also included. Many ethnic publications are locally-oriented or highly specialized and do not wish to be listed in a national publication such as *Writer's Market*. Query the editor of an ethnic publication with which you're familiar before submitting a manuscript, but do not consider these markets closed because they are not listed in this section. Additional markets for writing with an ethnic orientation are located in the following sections: Career, College and Alumni; Juvenile; Men's; Women's; and Teen and Young Adult.

‡**AFRICA ABROAD**, 1325 Crescent Hts. Rd., P.O. Box 43, Marion OH 43301-0043. (614)387-1887. Editor: Isaiah Jackson. Managing Editor: John Misha. Monthly newspaper covering news that affects Africa, Africans and the entire Black race. Estab. 1989. Circ. 200. Pays on publication. Publishes ms an average of 3 months after acceptance. Byline given. Not copyrighted. Buys all rights. Submit seasonal/holiday material 4 months in advance. Free writer's guidelines.
Nonfiction: Exposé, general interest, historical/nostalgic, humor, inspirational, interview/profile, opinion, personal experience, photo feature, travel, food, political and economy. Buys 36 mss/year. Send complete ms. Length: 500-3,000 words. Pays $20-200 for assigned articles; $20-100 for unsolicited articles. Sometimes pays expenses of writers on assignment.
Photos: State availability of photos with submission. Reviews 5×7 transparencies and prints. Offers $5 per photo. Captions, model releases and identification of subjects required. Buys all rights.
Columns/Departments: Food (cooking and review African food and restaurants), Marriage, Political and Economy, all 250-400 words. Send complete ms. Length: 250-400 words. Pays $15.
Poetry: Traditional. Submit maximum 2 poems. Pays $10.
Fillers: Facts and short humor.
Tips: "Submit with a note about interest in African affairs."

AFRICAN-AMERICAN HERITAGE, Dellco Publishing Company, Suite 103, 8443 S. Crenshaw Blvd., Inglewood CA 90305. (213)752-3706. Editor: Dennis W. DeLoach. 30% freelance written. Bimonthly magazine looking for "positive, informative, educational articles that build self-esteem, pride and an appreciation for the richness of culture and history." Estab. 1978. Circ. 25,000. Pays on publication. Publishes ms an average of 3-6 months after acceptance. Byline given. Offers 25% kill fee. Buys First North American serial rights, one-time rights or simultaneous rights. Submit seasonal/holiday material 6 months in advance. Simultaneous and previously published submissions OK. Reports in 1 month on queries; 2 months on mss. Free sample copy. Writer's guidelines for 9×12 SAE with 4 first class stamps.
Nonfiction: Book excerpts, essays, general interest, historical/nostalgic, how-to, humor, inspirational, interview/profile, new product, opinion, personal experience, photo feature, religious and travel. Black History Month (February). Buys 6 mss/year. Query. Length: 200-2,500 words. Pays $25-300 for assigned articles. Sometimes pays expenses of writers on assignment.
Photos: State availability of photos with submission. Reviews 5×7 prints. Offers no additional payment for photos accepted with ms. Identification of subject required. Buys one-time rights.
Columns/Departments: History (historical profiles); Commentary (letters to the editor) 2,500 max.; Interviews (personalities, unusual careers, positive experiences) 2,500 max.; Short Stories (well written, entertaining) 2,500 max. Buys 12 mss/year. Query. Pays $25-300.
Fiction: Adventure, ethnic, historical, humorous, mystery, religious, romance and slice-of-life vignettes. "No erotica, horror, fantasy." Buys 6 mss/year. Query. Length: 200-2,500 words. Pays $25-300.
Poetry: Avant-garde, free verse, haiku, light verse and traditional. Buys 60 poems/year. Submit maximum 5 poems. Length: 4-36 lines. Pays $10-25.
Fillers: Anecdotes and facts. Buys 12/year. Length: 10-200 words. Pays $25-100.

AIM MAGAZINE, AIM Publishing Company, 7308 S. Eberhart Ave., Chicago IL 60619. (312)874-6184. Editor: Ruth Apilado. Managing Editor: Dr. Myron Apilado. 75% freelance written. Works with a small number of new/unpublished writers each year. Quarterly magazine on social betterment that promotes racial harmony and peace for high school, college and general audience. Circ. 10,000. Pays on publication. Publishes ms an average of 3 months after acceptance. Offers 60% of contract as kill fee. Not copyrighted. Buys one-time rights. Submit seasonal/holiday material 6 months in advance. Simultaneous queries and submissions OK. Reports in 6 weeks on queries. Sample copy and writer's guidelines for $3.50, 8½×11 SAE and 4 first class stamps.
Nonfiction: Exposé (education); general interest (social significance); historical/nostalgic (Black or Indian); how-to (create a more equitable society); and profile (one who is making social contributions to community); and book reviews and reviews of plays "that reflect our ethnic/minority orientation." No religious material. Buys 16 mss/year. Send complete ms. Length: 500-800 words. Pays $25-35.

Photos: Reviews b&w prints. Captions and identification of subjects required.

Fiction: Ethnic, historical, mainstream, and suspense. Fiction that teaches the brotherhood of man. Buys 20 mss/year. Send complete ms. Length: 1,000-1,500 words. Pays $25-35.

Poetry: Avant-garde, free verse, light verse. No "preachy" poetry. Buys 20 poems/year. Submit maximum 5 poems. Length: 15-30 lines. Pays $3-5.

Fillers: Jokes, anecdotes and newsbreaks. Buys 30/year. Length: 50-100 words. Pays $5.

Tips: "Interview anyone of any age who unselfishly is making an unusual contribution to the lives of less fortunate individuals. Include photo and background of person. We look at the nations of the world as part of one family. Short stories and historical pieces about blacks and Indians are the areas most open to freelancers. Subject matter of submission is of paramount concern for us rather than writing style. Articles and stories showing the similarity in the lives of people with different racial backgrounds are desired."

THE AMERICAN CITIZEN ITALIAN PRESS, 13681 V St., Omaha NE 68137. (402)896-0403. Publisher/Editor: Diana C. Failla. 80% freelance written. Quarterly newspaper of Italian-American news/stories. Estab. 1923. Circ. 8,490. Pays on publication. Publishes ms an average of 3 months after acceptance. Byline given. Not copyrighted. Buys first North American serial rights. Submit seasonal/holiday material 2 months in advance. Previously published submissions OK. Reports in 1 month. Sample copy for 10 × 13 SAE and $1.50 postage; writer's guidelines for #10 SAE with 2 first class stamps.

Nonfiction: Book excerpts, general interest, historical/nostalgic, opinion, photo feature, celebrity pieces, travel, fashions, profiles and sports (Italian players). Query with published clips. Length: 400-600 words. Pays $15-25. Pays more for in-depth pieces.

Photos: State availability of photos. Reviews b&w prints. Pays $5. Captions and identification of subjects required. Buys all rights.

Columns/Departments: Query.

Fiction: Query. Pays $15-20.

Poetry: Submit maximum 5 poems. Pays $5-10.

Tips: "Human interest stories are the most open to freelancers. We like work dealing with current controversial issues involving those of Italian/American descent."

AMERICAN DANE, The Danish Brotherhood in America, 3717 Harney St., P.O. Box 31748, Omaha NE 68131. (402)341-5049. Editor: Jerome L. Christensen. Managing Editor: Pamela K. Dorau. 50% freelance written. Prefers to work with published/ established writers; works with a small number of new/unpublished writers each year. The monthly magazine of the Danish Brotherhood in America. All articles must have Danish ethnic flavor. Estab. 1916. Circ. 10,000. Pays on publication. Publishes ms an average of 1 year after acceptance. Byline given. Not copyrighted. Buys first rights. Submit seasonal/holiday material 1 year in advance. Reports in 2 weeks on queries. Sample copy for 9½ × 4 SAE and 3 first class stamps; writer's guidelines for #10 SASE.

Nonfiction: Historical, humor, inspirational, personal experience, photo feature and travel, all with a Danish flavor. Buys 12 mss/year. Query. Length: 1,500 words maximum. Pays $50 maximum for unsolicited articles.

Photos: Send photos with submission. Reviews prints. Offers no additional payment for photos accepted with ms. Captions and identification of subjects required. Buys one-time rights.

Fiction: Adventure, historical, humorous, mystery, romance and suspense, all with a Danish flavor. Buys 6-12 mss/year. Query with published clips. Length: 1,500 words maximum. Pays $50 maximum.

Poetry: Traditional. Buys 1-6 poems/year. Submit maximum 6 poems. Pays $35 maximum.

Fillers: Anecdotes and short humor. Buys up to 12/year. Length: 300 words maximum. Pays $15 maximum.

Tips: "Feature articles are most open to freelancers. Reviews unsolicited manuscripts in August only."

AMERICAN JEWISH WORLD, AJW Publishing Inc., 4509 Minnetonka Blvd., Minneapolis MN 55416. (612)920-7000. Managing Editor: Marshall Hoffman. 10% freelance written. Weekly Jewish newspaper covering local, national and international stories. Circ.: 6,500. Pays on publication. Publishes ms an average of 1-4 months after acceptance. Byline given. Offers 50% kill fee. Publication copyrighted. Makes work-for-hire assignments. Submit seasonal/holiday material 6 months in advance. Simultaneous and photocopied submissions OK. Free sample copy and writer's guidelines.

Nonfiction: Essays, expose, general interest, historical/nostalgic, humor, inspirational, interview/profile, opinion, personal experience, photo feature, religious, travel. Buys 30-50 mss/year. Query with or without published clips, or send complete ms. Length: 1,500-2,000 maximum. Pays $10-75. Sometimes pays expenses of writers on assignment.

Photos: State availability of photos with submission. Reviews prints. Pays $5 per photo. Identification of subjects required. Buys one-time rights.

‡AMERICAN ZIONIST, 4 E. 34th St., New York NY 10016. (212)481-1500. Editor: Jordan Malmed. 90% freelance written. Quarterly magazine on the Middle East, public affairs, Israel, Zionism, Palestinians. Estab. 1940. Circ. 45,000. Pays on publication. Publishes ms an average of 6 months after acceptance. Byline given. Buys any rights available. Submit seasonal/holiday material 6 months in advance. Simultaneous and previously published submissions OK. Query for electronic submissions. Sample copy $5 with 9 × 12 SAE.

Nonfiction: Book excerpts, essays, general interest, historical/nostalgic, photo feature, religious, travel. Buys 140 mss/year. Send complete ms. Length: 200-3,000 words. Pays $200 maximum.

Photos: State availability of send photos with submission. Reviews contact sheets. Pays $20 maximum. Captions, model releases and identification of subjects required. Buys one-time rights.

Columns/Departments: News Brief; Book Review. Buys 60 mss/year. Query with published clips or send complete ms. Length: 50-400 words. Pays $100 maximum.

Fillers: Facts, gags, newsbreaks. Buys 100/year. Length: 50-1200 words. Pays $100 maximum.

‡**THE ATHENIAN, Greece's English Language Weekly,** The Athenian Press Ltd., 4 Peta St., Athens 105 58 Greece. Editor-in-Chief: Sloane Elliott. Managing Editor: Drossoula Elliott. 50% freelance written. Monthly magazine covering Greek topics. "*The Athenian* is an English-language monthly serving the English-speaking Greek and foreign communities of Greece, and philhellenes worldwide. All articles must reflect this commitment." Estab. 1974. Circ. 17,000. Pays on publication. Publishes ms an average of 6 months after acceptance. Byline given. Buys first rights. Submit seasonal/holiday material 3 months in advance. Previously published submissions OK "if permission to republish accompanies." Query for electronic submissions. Reports in 1 month on queries. Free writer's guidelines.

Nonfiction: Deputy Editor. General interest (to Greeks); historical; humor (1,000 words maximum); interview/profile; photo feature (Greek); travel (Greece). "No first person, summer vacation or chauvinist pieces on Greece." Query with published clips. Length: 1,000-2,500 words. Pays $35-100. Pays in contributor copies or other premiums for nonprofit, service organization features.

Photos: Send photos with submission. Reviews b&w prints. Captions, model releases and identification of subjects required. Buys one-time rights.

Tips: "Please submit a short list of feature ideas, one or two clips, a SASE. Freelancers have the best chance selling us features—especially travel and historical."

‡**THE B'NAI B'RITH INTERNATIONAL, JEWISH MONTHLY,** 1640 Rhode Island Ave. NW, Washington DC 20036. (202)857-6645. 50% freelance written. Magazine covering Jewish affairs published 10 times per year. Estab. 1886. Circ. 185,000. **Pays on acceptance.** Publishes ms an average of 5 months after acceptance. Byline given. Kill fee depends on rate of payment. Buys first North American serial rights. Submit seasonal/holiday material 6 months in advance. Query for electronic submissions. Reports in 2 weeks. Sample copy $1 with 9 × 13 SAE and 2 first class stamps. Free writer's guidelines.

Nonfiction: Book excerpts, essay, exposé, general interest, historical/nostalgic, humor, inspirational, interview/profile, new product, personal experience, photo feature, travel. Buys 40-50 mss/year. Query with published clips. Length: 250-3,000 words. Pays $50-1,000 for assigned articles; $50-500 for unsolicited articles. Sometimes pays expenses of writers on assignment.

Photos: State availability of photos with submission. Reviews contact sheets, 2 × 3 transparencies and prints. Payment depends on quality and type of photograph. Identification of subjects required. Buys one-time rights.

Columns/Departments: Generations (senior citizens and parenting) and Arts (theater, movie, book reviews). Buys 10 mss/year. Query. Length: 500-750 words. Pays $60-200.

Fiction: "We publish very few works of fiction each year and strongly discourage writers from submitting such material to us. Short stories should present truly novel perspectives on Jewish life and should be of the highest caliber of writing. Fiction based on personal anecdotes or the Holocaust will not be reviewed." Buys 1-2 mss/year. Send complete ms. Length: 1,000-3,000 words. Pays $200-500.

Tips: "Writers should submit clips with their queries. The best way to break in to the *Jewish Monthly* is to submit a range of good story ideas accompanied by clips. We aim to establish relationships with writers and we tend to be loyal. All sections are equally open."

‡**CONGRESS MONTHLY,** American Jewish Congress, 15 E. 84th St., New York NY 10028. (212)879-4500. Editor: Maier Deshell. 90% freelance written. Magazine published 7 times/year covering topics of concern to the American Jewish community representing a wide range of views. Distributed mainly to the members of the American Jewish Congress; readers are intellectual, Jewish, involved. Estab. 1933. Circ. 35,000. Pays on publication. Publishes ms an average of 3 months after acceptance. Byline given. Buys one-time rights. Submit seasonal/holiday material 2 months in advance. No previously published submissions. Reports in 2 months.

Nonfiction: General interest ("current topical issues geared toward our audience"). No technical material. Send complete ms. Length: 2,000 words maximum. Pays $100-150/article.

Photos: State availability of photos. Reviews b&w prints. "Photos are paid for with payment for ms."

Columns/Departments: Book, film, art and music reviews. Send complete ms. Length: 1,000 words maximum. Pays $100-150/article.

EBONY MAGAZINE, 820 S. Michigan Ave., Chicago IL 60605. Editor: John H. Johnson. Managing Editor: Charles L. Sanders. 10% freelance written. For Black readers of the U.S., Africa, and the Caribbean. Monthly. Circ. 1.8 million. Buys first North American serial rights and all rights. Buys about 10 mss/year. Pays on publication. Publishes ms an average of 3 months after acceptance. Submit seasonal material 2 months in advance. Query. Reports in 1 month.

Nonfiction: Achievement and human interest stories about, or of concern to, Black readers. Interviews, profiles and humor pieces are bought. Length: 1,500 words maximum. "Study magazine and needs carefully. Perhaps one out of 50 submissions interests us. Most are totally irrelevant to our needs and are simply returned." Pays $200 minimum. Sometimes pays the expenses of writers on assignment.

Photos: Purchased with mss, and with captions only. Buys 8×10 glossy prints, color transparencies, 35mm color. Submit negatives and contact sheets when possible. Offers no additional payment for photos accepted with mss.

GREATER PHOENIX JEWISH NEWS, Phoenix Jewish News, Inc., P.O. Box 26590, Phoenix AZ 85068. (602)870-9470. FAX: (602)870-0426. Executive Editor: Flo Eckstein. Managing Editor: Leni Reiss. 10% freelance written. Prefers to work with published/established writers. Weekly tabloid covering subjects of interest to Jewish readers. Estab. 1948. Circ. 7,000. Publishes ms an average of 3 months after acceptance. Byline given. Submit seasonal/holiday material 3 months in advance. Simultaneous queries, and simultaneous and previously published submissions OK. Sample copy $1.

Nonfiction: General interest, issue analysis, interview/profile, opinion, personal experience, photo feature and travel. Special sections include Fashion and Health, House and Home, Back to School, Summer Camps, Party Planning, Bridal, Travel, Business and Finance, and Jewish Holidays. Send complete ms. Length: 1,000-2,500 words. Pays $15-75 for simultaneous rights; $1.50/column inch for first serial rights.

Photos: Send photos with query or ms. Pays $10 for 8×10 b&w prints. Captions required.

Tips: "We are looking for lifestyle and issue-oriented pieces of particular interest to Jewish readers. Our newspaper reaches across the religious, political, social and economic spectrum of Jewish residents in this burgeoning southwestern metropolitan area. We stay away from cute stories as well as ponderous submissions."

HADASSAH MAGAZINE, 50 W. 58th St., New York NY 10019. FAX: (212)303-8282. Executive Editor: Alan M. Tigay. 90% freelance written. Works with small number of new/unpublished writers each year. Monthly, except combined issues (June-July and August-September). Circ. 334,000. Publishes ms 18 months after acceptance. Buys first rights (with travel articles, buys all rights). Reports in 6 weeks. Free sample copy and writer's guidelines.

Nonfiction: Primarily concerned with Israel, Jewish communities around the world and American civic affairs. "We are also open to art stories that explore trends in Jewish art, literature, theater, etc." Buys 10 unsolicited mss/year. Length: 1,500-2,000 words. Pays $200-400, less for reviews. Sometimes pays the expenses of writers on assignment.

Photos: "We buy photos only to illustrate articles, with the exception of outstanding color from Israel which we use on our covers. We pay $175 and up for a suitable cover photo." Offers $50 for first photo; $35 for each additional. "Always interested in striking cover (color) photos, especially of Israel and Jerusalem."

Columns/Departments: "We have a Parenting column and a Travel column, but a query for topic or destination should be submitted first to make sure the area is of interest and the story follows our format."

Fiction: Contact Joan Michel. Short stories with strong plots and positive Jewish values. No personal memoirs, "schmaltzy" fiction, or women's magazine fiction. "We continue to buy very little fiction because of a backlog." Length: 3,000 words maximum. Pays $300 minimum.

Tips: "We are interested in reading articles that offer an American perspective on Jewish affairs (1,500 words). Send query of topic first. (For example, a look at the presidential candidates from a Jewish perspective.)"

HERITAGE FLORIDA JEWISH NEWS, 207 O'Brien Rd. P.O. Box 300742, Fern Park FL 32730. (407)834-8787. Associate Editor: Edith Schulman. Publisher/Editor: Jeffrey Gaeser. 30% freelance written. Weekly tabloid on Jewish subjects of local, national and international scope, except for special issues. "Covers news of local, national and international scope of interest to Jewish readers and not likely to be found in other publications." Estab. 1976. Circ. 10,000. Pays on publication. Publishes ms an average of 2 months after acceptance. Byline given. Buys first North American serial rights, first rights, one-time rights, second serial (reprint) rights or simultaneous rights. Submit seasonal/holiday material 2 months in advance. Photocopied and previously published submissions OK. Sample copy 50¢.

Nonfiction: General interest, interview/profile, opinion (does not mean letters to the editor), photo feature, religious and travel. "Especially needs articles for these annual issues: Rosh Hashanah, Financial, Chanukah, Celebration (wedding and bar mitzvah), Passover, Health and Fitness, Education and House and Home. No fiction, poems, first-person experiences." Buys 50 mss/year. Send complete ms. Length: 500-1,000 words. Pays $15-30. Sometimes pays expenses of writers on assignment.

Photos: State availability of photos with submission. Reviews 5×7 prints. Offers $5 per photo. Captions and identification of subjects required. Buys one-time rights.

THE HIGHLANDER, Angus J. Ray Associates, Inc., Box 397, Barrington IL 60011. (708)382-1035. Editor: Angus J. Ray. Managing Editor: Ethyl Kennedy Ray. 50% freelance written. Works with a small number of new/unpublished writers each year. Bimonthly magazine covering Scottish history, clans, genealogy, travel/history, and Scottish/American activities. Circ. 40,000. **Pays on acceptance.** Publishes ms an average of 6 months after acceptance. Byline given. Buys first North American serial rights and second serial (reprint) rights to material originally published elsewhere. Submit seasonal/holiday material 6 months in advance. Previously published submissions OK. Reports in 1 month. Sample copy for $2 and 9 × 12 SAE. Free writer's guidelines.
Nonfiction: Historical/nostalgic. "No fiction; no articles unrelated to Scotland." Buys 50 mss/year. Query. Length: 750-2,000 words. Pays $75-150. Sometimes pays the expenses of writers on assignment.
Photos: State availability of photos. Pays $5-10 for 8 × 10 b&w prints or transparencies. Reviews b&w contact sheets. Identification of subjects required. Buys one-time rights.
Tips: "Submit something that has appeared elsewhere."

‡**HISPANIC,** Hispanic Publishing Corporation, Suite 410, 111 Massachusetts Ave. NW, Washington DC 20001. (202)682-3000. FAX: (202)682-4901. Editor: Alfredo J. Estrada. Managing Editor: Liza Gross. 90% freelance written. Monthly magazine for the Hispanic community. "*HISPANIC* is a general interest, lifestyle, entertainment, upbeat, role model publication." Estab. 1987. Circ. 150,000. Pays on publication. Publishes ms an average of 4 months after acceptance. Byline given. Offers 20% kill fee. Buys all rights. Submit seasonal/holiday material 4 months in advance. Free sample copy and writer's guidelines.
Nonfiction: General interest, historical/nostalgic, humor, interview/profile, opinion, personal experience, photo feature, travel. Buys 200 mss/year. Query. Length: 50-3,000 words. Pays $50-600. Pays writers "phone, travel and lunch expenses," but these must be cleared with editors first.
Photos: State availability of photos with submission. Reviews transparencies. Offers $25-600 per photo. Captions, model releases and identification of subjects required. Buys one-time rights.
Columns/Departments: Forum (political opinion and analysis), 600 words; La Merienda (humor), 50-200 words.

INSIDE, The Jewish Exponent Magazine, Federation of Jewish Agencies of Greater Philadelphia, 226 S. 16th St., Philadelphia PA 19102. (215)893-5700. FAX: (215)546-3957. Editor: Jane Biberman. Managing Editor: Jodie Green. 95% freelance written (by assignment). Works with published/established writers and a small number of new/unpublished writers each year. Quarterly Jewish community magazine—for a general interest Jewish readership 25 years of age and older. Estab. 1979. Circ. 75,000. **Pays on acceptance.** Publishes ms an average of 2 months after acceptance. Byline given. Offers 20% kill fee. Buys first rights. Submit seasonal/holiday material 3 months in advance. Simultaneous queries OK. Reports in 2 weeks on queries; 3 weeks on mss. Sample copy for 9 × 12 SAE and $3; writer's guidelines for #10 SASE.
Nonfiction: Book excerpts, general interest, historical/nostalgic, humor, interview/profile. Philadelphia angle desirable. No personal religious experiences or trips to Israel. Buys 82 unsolicited mss/year. Query. Length: 600-3,000 words. Pays $200-1,000. Pays the expenses of writers on assignment.
Fiction: Short stories. Query.
Tips: "Personalities—very well known—and serious issues of concern to Jewish community needed."

POLISH AMERICAN JOURNAL, Polonia's Voice, Panagraphics, Inc., 774 Fillmore Ave., Buffalo NY 14212. (716)852-8211. FAX: (716)852-8230. Editor: Mark A. Kohan. Managing Editor: William Falkowski. 20% freelance written. Monthly tabloid for Polonia (Polish and Polish-American events, people, etc.). "Stories/reports should be about Polish-Americans active in their community on either a local or national level. Prefer biographies/histories of these people or essays on their accomplishments." Estab. 1911. Circ. 20,000. Pays on publication. Publishes ms an average of 2 months after acceptance. Byline given. Offers $2 kill fee. Not copyrighted. Buys one-time rights. Submit seasonal/holiday material 3 months in advance. Previously published submissions OK. Query for electronic submissions. Sample copy for 9 × 12 SAE with 3 first class stamps.
Nonfiction: Exposé (story on Polish-Americans), general interest (community news), historical/nostalgic (retrospectives on events), how-to (organize groups, etc.), interview/profile (background on local Pol-Ams), opinion (historical observations, anti-defamation, etc.), personal experience (growing up Polish). Special issues on Easter and Christmas celebrations—how practiced in other areas; travel to Poland, airfare and comparisons, etc.; salute to prominent Polish-American, business leaders, clergy, media personalities, etc. Buys 6-8 mss/year. Query. Length: 200-1,000 words. Pays $10-50. Sometimes pays expenses of writers on assignment.
Photos: State availability of photos with submission. Reviews 8½ × 11 prints. Offers $2-10 per solicited photo. Identification of subjects required. Buys one-time rights.
Columns/Departments: Forum Viewpoints (observations on recent decisions/events), 1,000 words maximum; culture (music/art developments), 1,000 words maximum; scholarships/studies (grants and programs available), 1,000 words maximum. Buys 6 mss/year. Query. Pays $10-50.

Fillers: Anecdotes, facts, gags to be illustrated by cartoonist, newsbreaks and short humor. Buys 25/year. Length: 50-200 words. Pays $2-10.

Tips: "Get a sample issue to get the feel of the paper. Best bet is to call editor to find out what stories need writers (there are, on average, One to two dozen articles/ideas 'on deck' that need writers.) Human interest stories are good but should not be run-of-the-mill. Freelancers can best break in by writing for: Cover and feature—need fresh blood, new perspectives on ethnicity, art and music reviews—need someone to cover work of Pol-Am artists. Polka music columnists are needed, also."

‡**RIGHT ON!**, Sterling's Magazines, 355 Lexington Ave., New York NY 10017. (212)949-6850. Editor: Cynthia Horner. 10% freelance written. A monthly black entertainment magazine for teenagers and young adults. Circ. 250,000. Pays on publication. Publishes ms an average of 3 months after acceptance. Byline given. Buys all rights. Submit seasonal/holiday material 4 months in advance. Reports in 1 month on queries.

Nonfiction: Interview/profile. "We only publish entertainment-oriented stories or celebrity interviews." Buys 15-20 mss/year. Query with or without published clips, or send ms. Length: 500-4,000 words. Pays $50-200. Sometimes pays the expenses of writers on assignment.

Photos: State availability of photos with submission. Reviews transparencies and 8×10 b&w prints. Offers no additional payment for photos accepted with ms. Identification of subjects required. Buys one-time rights or all rights.

THE UKRAINIAN WEEKLY, Ukrainian National Association, 30 Montgomery St., Jersey City NJ 07302. (201)434-0237. Editor: Roma Hadzewycz. 30% freelance written (mostly by a corps of regular contributors). A weekly tabloid covering news and issues of concern to Ukrainian community. Estab. 1933. Circ. 8,500. Pays on publication. Publishes ms an average of 1-2 months after acceptance. Byline given. Buys first North American serial rights, second serial (reprint) rights or makes work-for-hire assignments. Submit seasonal/ holiday material 1 month in advance. Reports in 1 month. Free sample copy.

Nonfiction: Book excerpts, essays, exposé, general interest, historical/nostalgic, interview/profile, opinion, personal experience, photo feature and news events. Special issues include Easter, Christmas, anniversary of Helsinki Accords, anniversary of Ukrainian Helsinki monitoring group, student scholarships. Buys 80 mss/ year. Query with published clips. Length: 500-2,000 words. Pays $45-100 for assigned articles. Pays $25-100 for unsolicited articles. Sometimes pays the expenses of writers on assignment.

Photos: Send photos with submission. Reviews contact sheets, negatives and 3×5, 5×7 or 8×10 prints. Offers no additional payment for photos accepted with ms.

Columns/Departments: News & Views (commentary on news events), 500-1,000 words. Buys 10 mss/year. Query. Pays $25-50.

Tips: "Become acquainted with the Ukrainian community in the U.S. and Canada. The area of our publication most open to freelancers is community news—coverage of local events. We'll put more emphasis on events in Ukraine during this period of perestroika in the USSR."

Food and Drink

Magazines appealing to gourmets are classified here. Journals aimed at food processing, manufacturing and retailing are in the Trade section. Many magazines in General Interest and Women's categories also buy articles on food topics.

‡**AMERICAN BREWER, The Micro-Brewer/Brew Pub Magazine**, Box 510, Hayward CA 94541. (415)886-9823 (mornings only). FAX: (415)537-0948. Editor: John Faulkner. 100% freelance written. Quarterly magazine covering micro beer brewing. Circ. 4,000. **Pays on acceptance.** Byline given. Buys first North American serial rights. Submit seasonal/holiday material 3 months in advance. Query for electronic submissions. Reports in 2 weeks. Sample copy $5.

Nonfiction: Book excerpts, general interest, how-to, personal experience. Plans special issue on regional breweries and beers. Buys 10 mss/year. Query. Length: 1,000-2,000 words. Pays $50-100. Pays expenses of writers on assignment.

Photos: State availability of photos with submission. Reviews contact sheets. Offers no additional payment for photos accepted with ms. Captions are required. Buys one-time rights.

COOKING LIGHT, The Magazine of Food and Fitness, Southern Living, Inc. P.O. Box 1748, Birmingham AL 35201. (205)877-6000. Editor: Katherine M. Eakin. Managing Editor: B. Ellen Templeton. 75% freelance written. Bimonthly magazine on healthy recipes and fitness information. "*Cooking Light* is a positive approach to a healthier lifestyle. It's written for healthy people on regular diets who are counting calories or trying to make calories count toward better nutrition. Moderation, balance and variety are emphasized. The writing style is fresh, upbeat and encouraging, emphasizing that eating a balanced, varied, lower-calorie diet and exercising regularly do not have to be boring." Estab. 1987. Circ. 800,000. **Pays on acceptance.** Publishes ms an average of 12 months after acceptance. Byline sometimes given. Offers 25% of original contract fee as kill fee. Buys all rights. Submit seasonal/holiday material 12 months in advance.

Nonfiction: Personal experience on nutrition, healthy recipes, fitness/exercise. Buys 150 mss/year. Query with published clips. Length: 400-2,000 words. Pays $250-2,000 for assigned articles. Pays expenses of writers on assignment.

Columns/Departments: Profile (an incident or event that occurred in one's life that resulted in a total lifestyle change), 2,000-2500 words; Children's Fitness (emphasis on prevention and intervention in regard to fitness, exercise, nutrition), 1,000-1,500 words; Taking Aim (a personal account of progression from desire to obstacle to achievement for incorporating exercise into one's routine schedule), 1,000-1,500 words and Downfall (a humorous personal account of desire to obstacle to the continuing struggle to overcome a particular food habit or addiction), 1,000-1,500 words. Buys 30 mss/year. Query. Length: 1,000-2,000 words. Pays $250-2,000.

Tips: "Emphasis should be on achieving a healthier lifestyle through food, nutrition, fitness, exercise information. In submitting queries, include information on professional background. Food writers should include examples of healthy recipes which meet the guidelines of *Cooking Light*."

COOK'S, America's Food Authority, Pennington Publishing, 2710 North Ave., Bridgeport CT 06604. (203)366-4155. Editor-in-Chief: Deborah Hartz. 50% freelance written. A magazine published 10 times/year covering food and cooking in America. "*Cook's* publishes lively informative articles that describe food and restaurant trends in the U.S. or that describe hands-on cooking techniques. Almost all of our articles include recipes." Estab. 1980. Circ. 180,000. **Pays on acceptance.** Publishes ms an average of 5 months after acceptance. Byline given. Offers 50% kill fee. Makes work-for-hire assignments. Submit seasonal/holiday material 1 year in advance. Reports in 2 months. Writer's guidelines for SASE.

Nonfiction: Food and cooking. No travel, personal experience or nostalgia pieces, history of food and cuisine, or recipes using prepared ingredients (e.g., canned soups, "instant" foods, mixes, etc.). Buys 60 mss/year. Query with clips and sample first page. Length: 1,000-2,000 words plus recipes. Pays $500-1,000. Paying of expenses. determined on a contract basis.

FOOD & WINE, American Express Publishing Corp., 1120 Avenue of the Americas, New York NY 10036. (212)382-5618. Editor: Carole Lalli. Managing Editor: Warren Picower. Monthly magazine for "active people for whom eating, drinking, entertaining, dining out, travel and all the related equipment and trappings are central to their lifestyle." Circ. 800,000. **Pays on acceptance.** Byline given. Offers 25% kill fee. Buys first world rights. Submit seasonal/holiday material 9 months in advance. Query for electronic submissions. Reports in 3 weeks on queries; 2 weeks on mss. Sample copy $3. Free writer's guidelines.

Nonfiction: Essays, how-to, humor, new product and travel. Query with published clips. Buys 125 mss/year. Length: 1,000-3,000 words. Pays $800-2,000. Pays expenses of writers on assignment.

Photos: State availability of photos with submission. No unsolicited photos or art. Offers $100-450 page rate per photo. Model releases and identification of subjects required. Buys one-time rights.

Columns/Departments: What's New, Eating Out, The Traveler, Setting the Scene. Buys 120 mss/year. Query with published clips. Length: 800-3,000 words. Pays $800-2,000.

Tips: "Good service, good writing, up-to-date information, interesting article approach and appropriate point of view for *F&W*'s audience are important elements to keep in mind. Look over several recent issues before writing query."

‡GOOD TASTE/MENUS MAGAZINES, Prestige Publications, Suite 800, 91 5th Ave., New York NY 10003. (212)929-5050. FAX: (212)633-1920. Associate Editor: Kate Krader. Managing Editor: Reg Bragonier. 50% freelance written. Quarterly magazines on food/top 35 restaurants. *Good Taste* is geared for people with no time to cook, but intentions of entertaining; *Menus* covers top restaurants in New York, Chicago, Boston, Los Angeles and San Francisco. Estab. 1983. Pays on publication. Publishes ms an average of 6 months after acceptance. Byline given. Offers 40% kill fee. Buys first North American serial rights. Submit seasonal/ holiday material 6 months in advance. Query for electronic submissions. Sample copy $4.

Nonfiction: Food/cooking. Buys 15 mss/year. Query with or without published clips, or send complete ms. Length: 1,000 words minimum. Pays $600 minimum. Sometimes pays expenses of writers on assignment.

Photos: State availability of photos with submission. Reviews contact sheets, negatives and transparencies. Model releases required. Buys one-time rights.

Tips: "If you are aware of a trend in restaurants or food, it would be good to approach us with a query for a story with that slant. For our food magazine it should fit into one of these holiday seasons—Memorial Day/ spring; 4th of July/summer; Labor Day/fall; Thanksgiving/Christmas/winter."

‡HOME & COUNTRY IDEAS HOLIDAY COOKBOOK, MSC Publishing Inc., 70 Sparta Ave., CN 1003, Sparta NJ 07442. (201)729-4477. Editor: Marion Buccieri. Managing Editor: Camille Pomaco. 10% freelance written. Bimonthly magazine of home cooking. "Each bimonthly *Homes & Country Ideas Holiday Cookbook* offers food features and collections of recipes that everyone will love to try! Practicality, fun, good health and easy-going cooking characterize this magazine. In addition to regular features each issue will host a particular seasonal/holiday theme." Estab. 1989. Pays on publication. Byline sometimes given. Buys all rights (will negotiate). Submit seasonal/holiday material 4 months in advance. Previously published submissions OK. Reports in 3 weeks on queries; 2 months on mss. Sample copy for 9 × 12 SAE with 5 first class stamps. Writer's guidelines for #10 SAE with 1 first class stamp.

Nonfiction: Essays, general interest, historical/nostalgic, how-to, humor, photo feature. Nothing unrelated to food or cooking. Buys 12-20 mss/year. Send complete ms. Length: 500-3,000 words. Pays 7-10¢/word. Pays with contributor copies if author so desires.

Photos: State availability of photos with submission. Reviews all size transparencies and prints. Offers $10-25 per photo. Captions, model releases and identification of subjects required. Buys all rights.

Columns/Departments: To Your Health (emphasis on low calorie, low sodium, low cholesterol) 500-3,000 words; International Influences (follow a particular ethnic food—include recipes and customs), 500-3,000 words; Meals In Minutes (meals that can be prepared in less than 30 minutes), 500-3,000 words; Entertaining Ideas (party and table decorating ideas pertaining to holiday theme), 500-3,000 words. Buys 12 mss/year. Query. Pays $50-200.

Fillers: Food related anecdotes, facts and short humor. Buys 6/year. Length: 50-200 words. Pays $5-20.

Tips: "We sould like to see fresh ideas and new angles relating to today's busy and health oriented lifestyles. We *will consider* all manuscripts that pertain to the theme(s) of our magazine. Including recipes and helpful hints is a plus!"

‡**INTERNATIONAL WINE REVIEW,** Beverage Testing Institute Inc., 438 W. State St., Ithaca NY 14850. (607)273-6071. 25% freelance written. Bimonthly magazine covering fine wine. Estab. 1984. Circ. 15,000. Pays on publication. Byline given. Kill fee varies. Buys first rights or second serial (reprint) rights. Previously published submissions OK. Query for electronic submission. Free sample copy.

Nonfiction: Book excerpts, essays, exposé, general interest, historical/nostalgic, how-to, humor, interview/profile, new product, opinion, personal experience, photo feature, technical and travel. Buys 25 mss/year. Query. Length: 100-5,000 words. Pays $300-700. Sometimes pays expenses of writers on assignment.

Photos: State availability of photos with submission. Reviews contact sheets, transparencies and prints. Captions, model releases and identification of subjects required. Buys one-time rights.

Fiction: Humorous. Buys 2 mss/year. Query. Length 500-2,000 words. Pays $300-700.

Fillers: Anecdotes, facts, gags to be illustrated by cartoonist and short humor. Buys 10/year. Length 25-250 words. Pays $25-100.

Tips: "Our readers are sophisticated and knowledgeable. The department most open to freelancers if 'reporting from Europe.' "

KASHRUS MAGAZINE, The Bimonthly for the Kosher Consumer, Yeshiva Birkas Reuven, P.O. Box 204, Parkville Station, Brooklyn NY 11204. (718)998-3201. Editor: Rabbi Yosef Wikler. 25% freelance written. Prefers to work with published/established writers, and is eager to work with new/unpublished writers. Bimonthly magazine covering kosher food industry. Estab. 1980. Circ. 10,000. **Pays on acceptance.** Publishes ms an average of 2 months after acceptance. Byline given. Offers 50% kill fee. Buys first or second serial (reprint) rights. Submit seasonal/holiday material 2 months in advance. Simultaneous and previously published submissions OK. Query for electronic submissions. Reports in 1 week on queries; 2 weeks on mss. Sample copy and writer's guidelines for $1.

Nonfiction: General interest, interview/profile, new product, personal experience, photo feature, religious, technical and travel. Special issues feature International Kosher Travel (October) and Passover (March). Buys 8-12 mss/year. Query with published clips. Length: 1,000-2,000 words. Pays $100-250 for assigned articles; pays up to $100 for unsolicited articles. Sometimes pays the expenses of writers on assignment.

Photos: State availability of photos with submission. Offers no additional payment for photos accepted with ms. Buys one-time rights.

Columns/Departments: Book Review (cook books, food technology, kosher food), 250-500 words; People in the News (interviews with kosher personalities), 1,000-2,000 words; Regional Kosher Supervision (report on kosher supervision in a city or community), 1,000-3,000 words; Food Technology (new technology or current technology with accompanying pictures), 1,000-2,000 words; Travel (international, national), must include Kosher information and Jewish communities, 1,000-2,000 words; Regional Kosher Cooking, 1,000-2,000 words.Buys 5 mss/year. Query with published clips. Pays $50-250.

Tips: "*Kashrus Magazine* will do more writing on general food technology, production, and merchandising as well as human interest travelogs and regional writing in 1991 than we have done in the past. Areas most open to freelancers are interviews, food technology, regional reporting and travel. We welcome stories on the availability and quality of Kosher foods and services in communities across the U.S. and throughout the world."

NATURAL FOOD & FARMING, Natural Food Associates, Highway 59, Box 210, Atlanta TX 75551. (214)796-3612. 80% freelance written. Eager to work with new/unpublished writers. Executive Director: Bill Francis. A monthly magazine covering organic gardening and natural foods, preventive medicine, and vitamins and supplements. Circ. 50,000. **Pays on acceptance.** Publishes ms an average of 3 months after acceptance. Byline given sometimes. Not copyrighted. Buys first rights or second serial (reprint) rights. Submit seasonal/holiday

Close-up

Deborah Hartz
Editor-in-Chief
Cook's

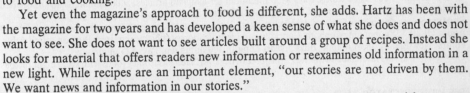

Not all food magazines are alike, says Deborah Hartz, editor-in-chief of *Cook's* magazine. In fact, many freelancers make the mistake of sending the same food article to several food-oriented publications without first determining how the editorial contents differ, she says.

Cook's is different from other consumer food magazines for several reasons. "You won't find travel articles or lifestyle material. We don't do event coverage. We're the only magazine devoted strictly to food and cooking."

Yet even the magazine's approach to food is different, she adds. Hartz has been with the magazine for two years and has developed a keen sense of what she does and does not want to see. She does not want to see articles built around a group of recipes. Instead she looks for material that offers readers new information or reexamines old information in a new light. While recipes are an important element, "our stories are not driven by them. We want news and information in our stories."

Hartz looks for topics that explore food and cooking in depth, such as articles on new food preparation or cooking methods, new varieties of foods, scientific discoveries that affect how food is used or prepared and articles that take a unique look at food. Because of the magazine's unique approach, says Hartz, some people have the mistaken impression *Cook's* is for the professional cook or chef. "We are definitely a consumer magazine. Freelancers should keep this in mind when developing recipes. We test recipes in our kitchens very carefully and we look for recipes that can be done at home. Ingredients must be easily available to the home cook." It is okay, however, to go to the experts for help in developing recipes. "We ask that when freelancers send recipes they include headnotes indicating where the recipe came from and if it was inspired by a chef's recipe."

Hartz often adds elements to freelancers' stories such as sidebars highlighting additional information. "Kitchen Reports" are close examinations of particular cooking or food preparation methods. "Science Reports" explain scientific elements in the story such as how salt affects food or why an iron knife should not be used on cabbage. "Health Reports" point out health benefits or explore current health controversies.

"We also like what we call 'fifth column material'—fun facts and bits of information." For example, with an article on using egg whites, the author added a sidebar listing five ways to use leftover egg yolks without eating them. A query that mentions sidebar possibilities not only helps Hartz see the article's potential but is also a "clear indication that the writer knows what a *Cook's* story is."

Hartz receives about four queries a day. "I do read queries. In fact, the best way to catch my eye is with a good query." Include a resume and clips with your query, she says. Write for *Cook's* readers, says Hartz. While many read other food magazines for recipes, people who read *Cook's* are interested in all aspects of food and cooking. Keep this in mind when developing a story for her magazine, she says, and it can make all the difference.

—Robin Gee

material 2-3 months in advance. Simultaneous, photocopied and previously published submissions OK. Computer printout submissions acceptable. Free sample copy and writer's guidelines.

Nonfiction: Book excerpts; exposé; how-to (gardening, recipes and canning), new product; opinion; personal experience (organic gardening) and photo feature. Buys approximately 150 mss/year. Query with or without published clips, or send complete ms. Length: 1,000-3,000 words. Pays $50-100; sometimes pays in free advertising for company, books or products. Sometimes pays the expenses of writers on assignment.

Photos: State availability or send photos with submission.

Columns/Departments: Bugs, Weeds & Free Advice (organic gardening), 800 words; Food Talk (tips on cooking and recipes), 300-1,500 words; Of Consuming Interest (shorts on new developments in field), 800-1,500 words; and The Doctor Prescribes (questions and answers on preventive medicine), 800-1,500 words. Buys 96 mss/year. Send complete ms. Pays $50-100 (negotiable).

Fillers: Facts and short humor.

Tips: "Articles on subjects concerning gardening organically or cooking with natural foods are most open to freelancers."

‡**THE WHOLE CHILE PEPPER, The Magazine of Spicy Foods**, Out West Publishing Company, 2425-C Monroe NE, P.O. Box 4278, Albuquerque NM 87196. (505)889-3745. 25-30% freelance written. Bimonthly magazine on spicy foods. "The magazine is devoted to spicy foods, and most articles include recipes. We have a very devoted readership who love their food hot!" Estab. 1986. Circ. 40,000. Pays on publication. Offers 50% kill fee. Buys first and second rights. Submit seasonal/holiday material 6 months in advance. Previously published submissions OK. Query for electronic submissions. Reports in 1 month on queries. Sample copy for 9×12 SAE with 5 first class stamps. Writer's guidelines for #10 SASE.

Nonfiction: Book excerpts (cookbooks); how-to (cooking and gardening with spicy foods), humor (having to do with spicy foods), new product (hot products), travel (having to do with spicy foods). Buys 20 mss/year. Query. Length: 1,000-3,000 words. Pays $150 minimum for assigned articles; $100 minimum for unsolicited articles. Sometimes pays expenses of writers on assignment.

Photos: State availability of photos with submission. Reviews contact sheets, negatives, transparencies and prints. Offers $25 minimum per photo. Captions and identification of subjects required. Buys one-time rights.

Fillers: Newsbreaks, short humor. Buys 5/year. Length: 100 minimum. Pays $25 minimum.

Tips: "We're always interested in queries from *food* writers. Articles about spicy foods with six to eight recipes are just right."

THE WINE SPECTATOR, M. Shanken Communications, Inc., Opera Plaza, Suite 2014, 601 Van Ness Ave., San Francisco CA 94102. (415)673-2040. Managing Editor: Jim Gordon. 20% freelance written. Prefers to work with published/established writers. Twice monthly consumer news magazine covering wine. Estab. 1976. Circ. 90,000. Pays within 30 days of publication. Publishes ms an average of 2 months after acceptance. Byline given. Buys all rights and makes work-for-hire assignments. Submit seasonal/holiday material 3 months in advance. Query for electronic submissions. Reports in 3 weeks. Sample copy $2; free writer's guidelines.

Nonfiction: General interest (news about wine or wine events); humor; interview/profile (of wine, vintners, wineries); opinion; and photo feature. No "winery promotional pieces or articles by writers who lack sufficient knowledge to write below just surface data." Query. Length: 100-2,000 words average. Pays $50-500.

Photos: Send photos with ms. Pays $75 minimum for color transparencies. Captions, model releases and identification of subjects required. Buys all rights.

Tips: "A solid knowledge of wine is a must. Query letters essential, detailing the story idea. New, refreshing ideas which have not been covered before stand a good chance of acceptance. *The Wine Spectator* is a consumer-oriented *news magazine* but we are interested in some trade stories; brevity is essential."

WINE TIDINGS, Kylix Media Inc., 5165 Sherbrooke St. W., 414, Montreal, Quebec H4A 1T6 Canada. (514)481-5892. Publisher: Judy Rochester. Editor: Barbara Leslie. 90% freelance written. Works with small number of new/unpublished writers each year. Magazine published 8 times/year primarily for men with incomes of more than $50,000. "Covers anything happening on the wine scene in Canada." Circ. 28,000. Pays on publication. Publishes ms an average of 3-4 months after acceptance. Byline given. Buys all rights. Submit seasonal/holiday material 3 months in advance. Reports in 1 month.

Nonfiction: General interest; historical; humor; interview/profile; new product (and developments in the Canadian and U.S. wine industries); opinion; personal experience; photo feature; and travel (to wine-producing countries). "All must pertain to wine or wine-related topics and should reflect author's basic knowledge of and interest in wine." Buys 20-30 mss/year. Send complete ms. Length: 500-2,000 words. Pays $35-300.

Photos: State availability of photos. Pays $20-100 for color prints; $10-25 for b&w prints. Identification of subjects required. Buys one-time rights.

Games and Puzzles

These publications are written by and for game enthusiasts interested in both traditional games and word puzzles and newer role-playing adventure, computer and video games.

Additional home video game publications are listed in the Entertainment section. Other puzzle markets may be found in the Juvenile section.

COMPUTER GAMING WORLD, The Definitive Computer Game Magazine, Golden Empire Publications, Inc., Suite B, 515 S. Harbor Blvd., Anaheim CA 92805. (714)535-4435. FAX: (714)535-1529. Editor: Johnny Wilson. 75% freelance written. Works with a small number of new/unpublished writers each year. Monthly magazine covering computer games. "*CGW* is read by an adult audience looking for detailed reviews and information on strategy, adventure and action games." Estab. 1981. Circ. 30,000. Pays on publication. Publishes ms an average of 3 months after acceptance. Byline given. Buys first rights. Submit seasonal/holiday material 4 months in advance. Query for electronic submissions; electronic submissions preferred, but not required. Reports in 1 month. Sample copy $3.50. Free writer's guidelines.
Nonfiction: Reviews, strategy tips, industry insights. Buys 60 mss/year. Query. Length: 500-3,500 words. Pays $25-200. Sometimes pays the expenses of writers on assignment.
Photos: State availability of photos with submission. Reviews contact sheets. Offers $10-50 per photo. Buys one-time rights.

DRAGON® MAGAZINE, TSR, Inc., P.O. Box 111, 201 Sheridan Springs Rd., Lake Geneva WI 53147. (414)248-3625. FAX: (414)248-0389. Editor: Roger E. Moore. Monthly magazine of fantasy and science-fiction role-playing games. 90% freelance written. Eager to work with published/established writers as well as new/unpublished writers. "Most of our readers are intelligent, imaginative teenage males." Estab. 1976. Circ. about 100,000, primarily across the United States, Canada and Great Britain. Byline given. Offers kill fee. Submit seasonal/holiday material 8 months in advance. Pays on publication for articles to which all rights are purchased; pays on acceptance for articles to which first/worldwide rights in English are purchased. Publishing dates vary from 1-24 months after acceptance. Writer's guidelines for #10 SAE and 1 first-class stamp or International Reply Coupon.
Nonfiction: Articles on the hobby of science fiction and fantasy role-playing. No general articles on gaming hobby; "our article needs are *very* specialized. Writers should be experienced in gaming hobby and role-playing. No strong sexual overtones or graphic depictions of violence." Buys 120 mss/year. Query. Length: 1,000-8,000 words. Pays $50-500 for assigned articles; pays $5-400 for unsolicited articles.
Fiction: Barbara G. Young, fiction editor. Fantasy, adventure and suspense. "No strong sexual overtones or graphic depictions of violence." Buys 12 mss/year. Send complete ms. Length: 2,000-8,000 words. Pays 6-8¢/word.
Tips: "*Dragon® Magazine* is *not* a periodical that the 'average reader' appreciates or understands. A writer must *be* a reader and must share the serious interest in gaming our readers possess."

‡GAMES SPECIAL EDITION, PSC Publications, 810 7th Ave., New York NY 10019. (212)246-4640. Editor: Will Shortz. 75% freelance written. Bimonthly puzzle magazine. "*Games* Special Edition has an educated, adult audience of both serious and casual puzzle solvers. We look for fresh, lively puzzles based on new ideas, carefully worked out for solvability. Puzzles with visual appeal and a sense of humor are especially wanted. Novelty is essential. Rough drawings or written descriptions of pictures may be submitted for visual puzzles; we can assign finished art or buy photos, as needed." Estab. 1987. Circ. 75,000. Pays 2 months before publication. Byline given. Offers 25% kill fee. Buys all rights. Submit seasonal/holiday material 6 months in advance. Reports in 1-2 weeks. Writer's guidelines for #10 SASE. "Specify puzzle type(s)."
Nonfiction: Buys 300 puzzles/year. Send complete ms. Payment is $75-200/page depending on novelty, complexity and interest. The magazine also publishes crosswords (sizes $15 \times 15 - \$60$; $17 \times 17 - \$100$; $21 \times 21 - \$200$), shaped and themed word searches ($75) and variety puzzles with novel grids (payment varies).
Tips: "Please send for specifications sheet before submitting. We do not accept freelance submissions of double-crostics, cryptograms, quizzes or types of variety puzzles found in other magazines."

GIANT CROSSWORDS, Scrambl-Gram, Inc., Puzzle Buffs International, 1772 State Road, Cuyahoga Falls OH 44223. (216)923-2397. Editors: C.J. Elum and C.R. Elum. 40% freelance written. Eager to work with new/unpublished writers. Crossword puzzle and word game magazines issued quarterly. **Pays on acceptance.** Publishes ms an average of 10 days after acceptance. No byline given. Buys all rights. Simultaneous queries OK. Reports in several weeks. "We furnish constructors' kits, master grids and clue sheets and offer a 'how-to-make-crosswords' book for $37.50 postpaid."
Nonfiction: Crosswords only. Query. Pays according to size of puzzle and/or clues.
Tips: "We are expanding our syndication of original crosswords and our publishing schedule to include new titles and extra issues of current puzzle books."

SCHOOL MATES, U.S. Chess Federation, 186 Route 9W, New Windsor NY 12553. (914)562-8350. Editor: Jennie L. Simon. 20% freelance written. Bimonthly magazine on youth chess. Estab. 1987. Circ. 5,000. Pays on publication. Publishes ms an average of 6 months after acceptance. Byline given. Buys all rights. Free sample copy and writer's guidelines.

Nonfiction: Historical/nostalgic, humor, interview/profile. Buys 4 mss/year. Query. Length: 250-800 words. Pays $40/1,000 words.
Fiction: Chess-related; should encourage good values, sportsmanship and fair play.
Photos: State availability of photos with submission. Reviews contact sheets. Pays $25 for first time rights; $12.50 for each subsequent use. Identification of subjects required.

General Interest

General interest magazines need writers who can appeal to a varied audience—teens and senior citizens, wealthy readers and the unemployed. Each magazine still has a personality that suits its audience—one that a writer should study before sending material to an editor. Other markets for general interest material are in these Consumer categories: Ethnic/Minority, In-flight, Men's, Regional and Women's.

‡**AMERICAN ATHEIST**, American Atheist Press, P.O. Box 140195, Austin TX 78714-0195. (512)458-1244. Editor: R. Murray-O'Hair. Managing Editor: Jon Garth Murray. 20-40% freelance written. Monthly magazine covering atheism and topics related to it and separation of State and Church. Estab.1959. Circ. 50,000. Publishes ms an average of 6 months after acceptance. Byline given. Buys one-time and all rights. Submit seasonal/holiday material 3 months in advance. Simultaneous queries and simultaneous and previously published submissions OK. Query for electronic submissions. Reports in 6 weeks on queries; 3 months on mss. Publishes ms an average of 4 months after acceptance. Sample copy and writer's guidelines for 9 × 12 SAE.
Nonfiction: Book excerpts, expose, general interest, historical, how-to, humor, interview/profile, opinion, personal experience and photo feature, but only as related to State/Church or atheism. "We receive a great many Bible criticism articles—and publish very few. We would advise writers not to send in such works. We are also interested in fiction with an atheistic slant." Buys 40 mss/year. Send complete ms. Length: 400-10,000 words. Pays in free subscription or 15 copies for first-time authors. Repeat authors paid $15 per 1,000 words. Sometimes pays the expenses of writers on assignment.
Columns/Departments: Atheism, Church/State separation and humor. Send complete ms. Length: 400-10,000 words.
Poetry: Avant-garde, free verse, haiku, light verse and traditional. Submit unlimited poems. Length: open. Pays $10 per thousand words maximum.
Fillers: Jokes, short humor and newsbreaks. Length: 800 words maximum, only as related to State/Church separation or atheism.
Tips: "We are primarily interested in subjects which bear directly on atheism or issues of interest and importance to atheists. This includes articles on the atheist lifestyle, on problems that confront atheists, the history of atheism, personal experiences of atheists, separation of state and church, theopolitics and critiques of atheism in general and of particular religions. We are starting to have issues which focus on lifestyle topics relevant to atheism. We would like to receive more articles on current events and lifestyle issues. Critiques of *particular* religions would also be likely candidates for acceptance."

THE AMERICAN LEGION MAGAZINE, P.O. Box 1055, Indianapolis IN 46206. (317)635-8411. Editor-in-Chief: Daniel S. Wheeler. Monthly. 95% freelance written. Prefers to work with published/established writers, eager to work with new/unpublished writers, and works with a small number of new/unpublished writers each year. Circ. 2.85 million. Buys first North American serial rights. Reports on submissions "promptly." **Pays on acceptance.** Publishes ms an average of 6 months after acceptance. Byline given. Sample copy for 9 × 12 SAE and 6 first class stamps. Writer's guidelines for #10 SASE.
Nonfiction: Query first, but will consider unsolicited mss. "Prefer an outline query. Relate your article's thesis or purpose, tell why you are qualified to write it, the approach you will take and any authorities you intend to interview. War-remembrance pieces of a personal nature (vs. historic in perspective) should be in ms form." Uses current world affairs, topics of contemporary interest, 20th century war-remembrance pieces, and 750-word commentaries on contemporary problems and points of view. No personality profiles or regional topics. Buys 75 mss/year. Length: 1,500 words maximum. Pays $300-2,000. Pays phone expenses of writers on assignment.
Photos: On assignment.
Tips: Query should include author's qualifications for writing a technical or complex article, and samples of published work. Also include thesis, length, outline and conclusion. "Send a thorough query. Submit material that is suitable for us, showing that you have read several issues. *The American Legion Magazine* considers itself '*the* magazine for a strong America.' Any query that reflects this theme (which includes strong economy, educational system, moral fiber, infrastructure and armed forces) will be given priority. No longer accepting unsolicited cartoons or jokes."

‡**THE AMERICAN SCHOLAR**, The Phi Beta Kappa Society, 1811 Q Street NW, Washington DC 20009. (202)265-3808. Editor: Joseph Epstein. Managing Editor: Jean Stipicevic. 100% freelance written. Intellectual quarterly. "Our writers are specialists writing for the college educated public." Estab. 1932. Circ. 26,000.

Pays after author has seen edited piece in galleys. Byline given. Offers ½ kill fee. Buys first rights. Submit seasonal/holiday material 6 months in advance. Reports in 2 weeks on queries; 2 months on ms. Sample copy for $5.50. Writer's guidelines for #10 SASE.
Nonfiction: Book excerpts (prior to publication only), essays, historical/nostalgic, humor. Buys 40 mss/year. Query. Length: 3,000-5,000 words. Pays $450.
Columns/Departments: Buys 16 mss/year. Query. Length: 3,000-5,000 words. Pays $450.
Poetry: Sandra Costich, poetry editor. Buys 20/year. Submit maximum 3 poems. Length: 75 lines. Pays $50. "Write for guidelines."
Tips: "The section most open to freelancers is the book review section. Query and send samples of reviews written."

ANGLO-AMERICAN SPOTLIGHT, Spotlight Verlag, Freihamer Strasse 4b (Box 1629), D-8032 Gräfelfing/Munich, Federal Republic of Germany, (049)898548221. FAX: (049)898548223. Editor: Kevin Perryman. 30% freelance written. Monthly magazine on current events, travel, personalities and history in English-speaking countries. "*Spotlight* is a general interest magazine for German-speakers who are trying to brush up and improve their English. In general we prefer an informal newsy style with relatively simple sentence structure and vocabulary." Estab. 1983. Circ. 75,000. Pays on publication. Byline given. Offers DM 150 kill fee (maximum). Buys one-time rights for West-Germany, Austria, Switzerland. Submit seasonal/holiday material 6 months in advance. Simultaneous and previously published submissions OK. Reports in 3 months. Free sample copy.
Nonfiction: General interest, historical/nostalgic, interview/profile, photo feature and travel. No pieces unrelated to the English-speaking world. Buys at least 20 mss/year. Query with published clips. Length: 1,000-2,000 words. Pays DM 105 per printed column line, (about seven words). Sometimes pays expenses of writers on assignment.
Photos: State availability of photos with submission. Reviews color transparencies and b&w prints. Offers $25-100 per photo. Buys one-time rights.
Tips: "Try a travel story (a national park, a state, an event), a city portrait (history, current problems, travel info), an article about a current issue or trend, interview or article about a well-known person. Please type flush left, 40 characters per line, triple space. It's best from an 'insiders' point of view. Tell our German readers something beyond what they can already find in travel brochures. Fill the story with anecdotes, honest information and advice about what to do and what not to do."

THE ATLANTIC MONTHLY, 745 Boylston St., Boston MA 02116. (617)536-9500. Editor: William Whitworth. Managing Editor: Cullen Murphy. Monthly magazine of arts and public affairs. Circ. 470,000. Pays on publication. Byline given. Buys first North American serial rights. Simultaneous submissions discouraged. Reporting time varies.
Nonfiction: Book excerpts, essays, general interest, humor, personal experience, religious, travel. Query with or without published clips or send complete ms. Length: 1,000-6,000 words. Payment varies. Sometimes pays expenses of writers on assignment.
Fiction: C. Michael Curtis, fiction editor. Buys 15-18 mss/year. Send complete ms. Length: 2,000-6,000 words preferred. Payment varies.
Poetry: Peter Davison, poetry editor. Buys 40-60 poems/year.

A BETTER LIFE FOR YOU, The National Research Bureau, Inc., 424 N. 3rd St., Burlington IA 52601. (319)752-5415. FAX: (319)752-3421. Editor: Rhonda Wilson. Editorial Supervisor: Doris J. Ruschill. 75% freelance written. Works with a small number of new/unpublished writers each year, eager to work with new/unpublished writers. Quarterly magazine. Estab. 1948. Pays on publication. Publishes ms an average of 1 year after acceptance. Buys all rights. Submit seasonal/holiday material 7 months in advance of issue date. Previously published submissions OK. Reports in 3 weeks. Writer's guidelines for #10 SASE; sample for 6½" × 9½" envelope with 55¢ postage.
Nonfiction: General interest (steps to better health, on-the-job attitudes); and how-to (perform better on the job, do home repair jobs, and keep up maintenance on a car). Buys 10-12 mss/year. Query or send outline. Length: 400-600 words. Pays 4¢/word.
Tips: "Writers have a better chance of breaking in at our publication with short articles."

CAPPER'S, Stauffer Communications, Inc., 616 Jefferson St., Topeka KS 66607. (913)295-1108. Editor: Nancy Peavler. 25% freelance written. Works with a small number of new/unpublished writers each year. Emphasizes home and family for readers who live in small towns and on farms. Biweekly tabloid. Estab. 1879. Circ. 385,000. Pays for poetry on acceptance; articles on publication. Publishes ms an average of 6 months after acceptance. Buys first serial rights only. Submit seasonal/holiday material at least 2 months in advance. Reports in 3 months; 8 months for serialized novels. Sample copy 85¢; writer's guidelines for #10 SASE.
Nonfiction: Historical (local museums, etc.), inspirational, nostalgia, travel (local slants) and people stories (accomplishments, collections, etc.). Buys 50 mss/year. Submit complete ms. Length: 700 words maximum. Pays $1/inch.

Photos: Purchased with accompanying ms. Submit prints. Pays $5-10 for 8×10 or 5×7 b&w glossy prints. Total purchase price for ms includes payment for photos. Limited market for color photos (35mm color slides); pays $20-25 each.

Columns/Departments: Heart of the Home (homemakers' letters, recipes, hints), and Hometown Heartbeat (descriptive). Submit complete ms. Length: 300 words maximum. Pays $1-10.

Fiction: "We have begun to buy some fiction pieces—longer than short stories, shorter than novels." Adventure and romance mss. No explicit sex, violence or profanity. Buys 4-5 mss/year. Query. Pays $75-250.

Poetry: Free verse, haiku, light verse, traditional, nature and inspiration. "The poems that appear in *Capper's* are not too difficult to read. They're easy to grasp. We're looking for everyday events, and down-to-earth themes." Buys 4-5/issue. Limit submissions to batches of 5-6. Length: 4-16 lines. Pays $3-6.

Tips: "Study a few issues of our publication. Most rejections are for material that is too long, unsuitable or out of character for our paper (too sexy, too much profanity, etc.). On occasion, we must cut material to fit column space."

THE CHRISTIAN SCIENCE MONITOR, 1 Norway St., Boston MA 02115. (617)450-2303. Contact: Submissions. International newspaper issued daily except Saturdays, Sundays and holidays in North America; weekly international edition. Circ. 150,000. Buys all newspaper rights for 3 months following publication. Buys limited number of mss, "top quality only." Publishes original (exclusive) material only. Pays on acceptance or publication, "depending on department." Reports in 1 month. Submit complete original ms or letter of inquiry. Writer's guidelines available.

Nonfiction: David Holmstrom, feature editor. In-depth features and essays. Please query by mail before sending mss. "Style should be bright but not cute, concise but thoroughly researched. Try to humanize news or feature writing so reader identifies with it. Avoid sensationalism, crime and disaster. Accent constructive, solution-oriented treatment of subjects." Home Forum page buys essays of 400-900 words. Pays $70-140. Education, people, books, food and science pages will consider articles not usually more than 800 words appropriate to respective subjects." Pays $100-150.

Poetry: Traditional, blank and free verse. Seeks non-religious poetry of high quality and of all lengths up to 75 lines. Pays $25 average.

Tips: "We prefer neatly typed originals. No handwritten copy. Enclosing an SAE and postage with ms is a must."

‡THE CONNOISSEUR, The Hearst Corp., 1790 Broadway, 18th Fl., New York NY 10019. (212)262-5595. Editor-in-Chief: Thomas Hoving. Executive Editor: Philip Herrera. Managing Editor: Sarah Scrymser. 90% freelance written. Prefers to work with published/established writers. Monthly magazine of the arts—fine, decorative and performing. "*Connoisseur* is written and designed for people who value excellence. It is informed by lively scholarship, a keen critical eye, and a civilized sense of fun. It covers a wide range of subjects and provides our audience with first-hand access to our topics and pertinent service data." Circ. 320,000. **Pays on acceptance.** Offers 33% kill fee. Buys first English language rights. Query for electronic submissions.

Nonfiction: Travel; the arts—fine, decorative, performing; food; wine; architecture; fashion and jewelry. Buys 120 mss/year. Query with published clips. Length: 500-2,500 words. Usually pays $1/word. Pays expenses of writers on assignment.

Photos: Pamela Hassell, photo editor. Captions, model releases and identification of subjects required. Buys one-time rights.

Columns/Departments: Connoisseur's World and Lively Arts. Buys 50 mss/year. Query with published clips. Length: 1,500-2,000 words. Pays $500-750.

Tips: "A freelancer can best break in to our publication with a strong, original proposal backed by good clips. Be aware of what we *have been doing*—read the magazine."

EQUINOX: THE MAGAZINE OF CANADIAN DISCOVERY, Equinox Publishing, 7 Queen Victoria Dr., Camden East, Ontario K0K 1J0 Canada. (613)378-6661. Editor: Bart Robinson. Bimonthly magazine. "We publish in-depth profiles of people, places and wildlife to show readers the real stories behind subjects of general interest in the fields of science and geography." Estab. 1982. Circ. 166,000. **Pays on acceptance.** Byline given. Offers 50% kill fee. Buys first North American serial rights only. Submit seasonal queries 1 year in advance. Reports in 6 weeks. Sample copy $5; free writer's guidelines.

Nonfiction: Book excerpts (occasionally), geography, science and art. No travel articles. Buys 40 mss/year. Query. "Our biggest need is for science stories. We do not touch unsolicited feature manuscripts." Length: 5,000-10,000 words. Pays $1,500-negotiated.

 The double dagger before a listing indicates that the listing is new in this edition. New markets are often the most receptive to freelance submissions.

Photos: Send photos with ms. Reviews color transparencies—must be of professional quality; no prints or negatives. Captions and identification of subjects required.

Columns/Departments: Nexus (current science that isn't covered by daily media) and Habitat (Canadian environmental stories not covered by daily media). Buys 80 mss/year. Query with clips of published work. Length: 200-800 words. Pays $200-500.

Tips: "Submit Habitat and Nexus ideas to us—the *only* route to a feature is through these departments if writers are untried."

FORD TIMES, 1 Illinois Center, Suite 1700, 111 E. Wacker Dr., Chicago IL 60601. Editor: Scott Powers. 85% freelance written. Works with a small number of new/unpublished writers each year. "General-interest magazine designed to attract all ages." Monthly. Circ. 1.2 million. **Pays on acceptance.** Publishes ms an average of 8-9 months after acceptance. Buys first rights only. Offers kill fee. Byline given. Submit seasonal material 6 months in advance. Reports in 1 month. Sample copy and writer's guidelines for 8½×11 SAE with 5 first class stamps.

Nonfiction: "Almost anything relating to contemporary American life that is upbeat and positive. Topics include lifestyle trends, outdoor activities and sports, profiles, food, narrow-scope destination stories, and the arts. We are especially interested in subjects that appeal to readers in the 18-35 age group. We strive to be colorful, lively and, above all, interesting. We try to avoid subjects that have appeared in other publications or in our own." Buys 100 mss/year. Length: 1,500 words maximum. Query required unless previous contributor. Pays $550-800 for full-length articles. Pays up to $200 in expenses for writers on assignment.

Photos: "Speculative submission of high-quality color transparencies and b&w photos with mss is welcomed. We need bright, graphically strong photos showing people. We need releases for people whose identity is readily apparent in photos."

FRIENDLY EXCHANGE, Meredith Publishing Services, Locust at 17th, Des Moines IA 50336. Publication Office: (515)284-2008. Editor: (702)786-7419. Editor: Adele Malott. 80% freelance written. Works with a small number of new/unpublished writers each year. Quarterly magazine exploring travel and leisure topics of interest to active Western families. For policyholders of Farmers Insurance Group of Companies. "These are traditional families (median adult age 39) who live in the area bounded by Ohio on the east and the Pacific Ocean on the west." Estab. 1981. Circ. 4.6 million. **Pays on acceptance.** Publishes ms an average of 5 months after acceptance. Offers 25% kill fee. Buys all rights. Submit seasonal/holiday material 1 year in advance. Simultaneous queries OK. Query for electronic submissions. Reports in 2 months. Sample copy for 9×12 SAE and 5 first class stamps; writer's guidelines for #10 SASE.

Nonfiction: "Travel and leisure topics of interest to the Western family can be addressed from many different perspectives, including health and safety, consumerism, heritage and education. Articles offer a service to readers and encourage them to take some positive action such as taking a trip. Style is colorful, warm, and inviting, making liberal use of anecdotes and quotes. The only first-person articles used are those assigned; all others in third person. Domestic locations in the Midwest and West are emphasized." Buys 8 mss/issue. Query. Length: 600-1,800 words. Pays $300-800/article, plus agreed-upon expenses.

Photos: Jonn Williams, art director. Pays $150-250 for 35mm color transparencies; and $50 for b&w prints. Cover photo payment negotiable. Pays on publication.

Columns/Departments: All columns and departments rely on reader-generated materials; none used from professional writers.

Tips: "We are now concentrating exclusively on the travel and leisure hours of our readers. Do not use destination approach in travel pieces—instead, for example, tell us about the people, activities, or events that make the location special. We prefer to go for a small slice rather than the whole pie, and we are just as interested in the cook who made it or the person who will be eating it as we are in the pie itself. Concentrate on what families can do together."

FUTURIFIC MAGAZINE, 280 Madison Ave., New York NY 10016. (212)684-4913. Editor-in-Chief: Balint Szent-Miklosy. 50-75% freelance written. Monthly. "Futurific, Inc. "The Foundation for Optimism," is an independent, nonprofit organization set up in 1976 to study the future, and *Futurific Magazine* is its monthly report on findings. We report on what is coming in all areas of life from international affairs to the arts and sciences. Readership cuts across all income levels and includes leadership, government, corporate and religious circles." Circ. 10,000. Pays on publication. Publishes ms an average of 1 month after acceptance. Byline given in most cases. Buys one-time rights and will negotiate reprints. Reports within 1 month. Sample copy for $5 and 9×12 SAE. Writer's guidelines for #10 SASE.

Nonfiction: All subjects must deal with the future: book, movie, theater and software reviews, general interest, how to forecast the future—seriously, humor, interview/profile, new product, photo feature and technical. No historical, opinion or gloom and doom. Send complete ms. Length: 5,000 words maximum. Payment negotiable.

Photos: Send photos with ms. Reviews b&w prints. Pay negotiable. Identification of subjects required.

Columns/Departments: Medical breakthroughs, new products, inventions, book, movie and theater reviews, etc. "Anything that is new or about to be new." Send complete ms. Length: 5,000 words maximum.

Poetry: Avant-garde, free verse, haiku, light verse and traditional. "Must deal with the future. No gloom and doom or sad poetry." Buys 6/year. Submit unlimited number of poems. Length: open. Pays in copies.

Fillers: Clippings, jokes, gags, anecdotes, short humor, and newsbreaks. "Must deal with the future." Length: open. Pays in copies.

Tips: "It's not who you are, it's what you have to say that counts with us. We seek to maintain a light-hearted, professional look at forecasting. Be upbeat and show a loving expectation for the marvels of human achievement. Take any subject or concern you find in regular news magazines and extrapolate as to what the future will be. Use imagination. Get involved in the excitement of the international developments, social interaction. Write the solution—not the problem."

‡**GLOBE,** 5401 N.W. Broken Sound Blvd., Boca Raton FL 33431. Executive Editor: Charles Montgomery. "For everyone in the family. *Globe* readers are the same people you meet on the street and in supermarket lines, average hard-working Americans who prefer easily digested tabloid news." Weekly national tabloid newspaper. Circ. 2 million. Byline given.

Nonfiction and Fillers: "We want features on well-known personalities, offbeat people, places, events and activities. No personal essays. Current issue is best guide. Stories are best that don't grow stale quickly. No padding. Remember—we are serving a family audience. All material must be in good taste. If it's been written up in a major newspaper or magazine, we already know about it." Buys informational, how-to, interview, profile, inspirational, humor, historical, exposé, photo, and spot news. Length: 1,000 words maximum; average 500-800 words. Pays $250-500(special rates for "blockbuster" material).

Photos: Ron Haines, photo editor. Photos are purchased with or without ms, and on assignment. Captions are required. Pays $50 minimum for 8 × 10 b&w glossy prints. "Competitive payment on exclusives."

Tips: "*Globe* is constantly looking for human interest subject material from throughout the United States, and much of the best comes from America's smaller cities and villages, not necessarily from the larger urban areas. Therefore, we are likely to be more responsive to an article from a new writer than many other publications. This, of course, is equally true of photographs. A major mistake of new writers is that they have failed to determine the type and style of our content, and in the ever-changing tabloid field this is a most important consideration. It is also wise to keep in mind that what is of interest to you or to the people in your area may not be of equal interest to a national readership. Determine the limits of interest first. And, importantly, the material you send us must be such that it won't be 'stale' by the time it reaches the readers."

GOOD READING, for Everyone, Henrichs Publications, Inc., P.O. Box 40, Sunshine Park, Litchfield IL 62056. (217)324-3425. Editor: Peggy Kuethe. Managing Editor: Garth Henrichs. 80% freelance written. Works with a small number of new/unpublished writers each year, and is eager to work with new/unpublished writers. A monthly general interest magazine with articles and stories based on a wide range of current or factual subjects. Estab. 1924. Circ. 7,500. **Pays on acceptance.** Publishes ms an average of 6 months after acceptance. Byline given. Buys first North American serial rights. Submit seasonal/holiday material 5 months in advance. Reports in 2 months. Sample copy for 50¢, 6 × 10 SAE and 2 first class stamps; writer's guidelines for #10 SASE.

Nonfiction: General interest, historical/nostalgic, humor, photo feature and travel. Also stories about annual festivals, trends, people who make a difference. "No material that deals with the sordid side of life, nothing about alcohol, smoking, drugs, gambling. Nothing that deals with the cost of travel, or that is too technical." Send complete ms. Length: 100-1,000 words. Pays $20-100 for unsolicited articles.

Photos: Send photos with submission. Reviews contact sheets and 3x5, 5 × 7, or 8 × 10 b&w prints. No color photos accepted. Offers additional payment for photos accepted with ms. Identification of subjects required. Buys one-time rights.

Columns/Departments: Youth Today (directed at young readers), 100 words maximum. Buys 6-9 mss/year. Send complete ms. Pays $10-50.

Poetry: Light verse. No limit to number of poems submitted at one time. Length: 4-16 lines. Pays in copies.

Fillers: Anecdotes, facts and short humor. Length: 50-150 words. Pays $10-30.

Tips: "The tone of *Good Reading* is wholesome; the articles are short. Keep writing informal but grammatically correct. *Good Reading* is general interest and directed at the entire family—so we accept only material that would be of interest to nearly every age group."

‡**GRIT, America's Family Magazine,** Grit Publishing Group, 208 W. 3rd St., Williamsport PA 17701. (717)326-1771. Editor: Michael R. Rafferty. 30% freelance written. "*Grit* is aimed at what is good about America. Its audience is generally older and conservative. We also look for stories about unusual people, places and things. Estab. 1882. Circ. 550,000. Pays on publication. Publishes ms an average of 2 months after acceptance. Byline given. Offers 15¢/word kill fee. Buys first or second rights or makes work-for-hire assignments. Submit seasonal/holiday material 8 months in advance. Simultaneous and previously published submissions OK. Query for electronic submissions. Reports in 3 weeks on queries; 1 month on mss. Sample

copy for 11×14 SAE with 4 first class stamps. Writer's guidelines for #10 SASE.

Nonfiction: General interest, how-to (car care, home and household repairs), humor, inspirational, interview/profile. "No crime, violence, alcohol, drug or tabacco uses, sex." Query. Send complete ms. Length: 600-1,500 words. 15-22¢/word for assigned articles; 12-15¢/word for unsolicited articles. Sometimes pays expenses of writers on assignment.

Photos: Send photos with submission. Reviews 35mm transparencies and 8×10 prints. Offers $40-175 per photo. Model releases and identification of subjects required. "We purchase first and subsequent-use rights."

Poetry: Joannie Decker, poetry editor. Buys 150/year. Submit maximum 20 poems. Length: 4-20 lines. Pays $6 for first four lines, 50¢ per line thereafter.

Fillers: Al Elmer, fillers editor. Short humor. Buys 150/year. Length: 50-150 words. Pays 12-15¢/word.

Tips: "Keep in mind *Grit* is looking for the uplifting and the unusual. If it might offend somebody's grandma, *don't* send it to *Grit*."

HARPER'S MAGAZINE, 666 Broadway, 11th Floor, New York NY 10012. (212)614-6500. FAX: (212)228-5889. Editor: Lewis H. Lapham. 40% freelance written. For well-educated, socially concerned, widely read men and women who value ideas and good writing. Monthly. Estab. 1850. Circ. 190,000. Rights purchased vary with author and material. Pays negotiable kill fee. **Pays on acceptance.** Reports in 2 weeks. Publishes ms an average of 3 months after acceptance. Sample copy $2.50.

Nonfiction: "For writers working with agents or who will query first only, our requirements are: public affairs, literary, international and local reporting, and humor." No interviews; no profiles. Complete mss and queries must include SASEs. No unsolicited poems will be accepted. Publishes one major report per issue. Length: 4,000-6,000 words. Publishes one major essay per issue. Length: 4,000-6,000 words. "These should be construed as topical essays on all manner of subjects (politics, the arts, crime, business, etc.) to which the author can bring the force of passionately informed statement." Publishes one short story per month. Generally pays 50¢-$1/word.

Photos: Deborah Rust, art director. Occasionally purchased with mss; others by assignment. Pays $50-500.

‡IDEALS MAGAZINE, P.O. Box 140300, Ideals Publishing, Nelson Place at Elm Hill Pike, Nashville TN 37214. (615)885-8270. Editor: Nancy Skarmeas. 95% freelance written. A magazine published eight times a year. "Our readers are generally women over 50. The magazine is mainly light poetry and short articles with a nostalgic theme. The eight issues are seasonally oriented, as well as being thematic." Pays on publication. Publishes ms an average of 1 year after acceptance. Byline given. Buys one-time North American serial and subsidiary rights. Submit seasonal/holiday material 8 months in advance. Simultaneous and previously published submissions OK. Reports in 6 months. Writer's guidelines for SAE with 1 first class stamp.

Nonfiction: Essays, historical/nostalgic, how-to (crafts), humor, inspirational and personal experience. "No down beat articles or social concerns." Buys 20 mss/year. Query with or without published clips, or send complete ms. Length: 600-1,000 words. Pays 10¢/word.

Photos: Send SASE for guidelines. Reviews transparencies and b&w prints. Offers no additional payment for photos accepted with ms. Captions, model releases, and identification of subjects required. Buys one-time rights. Payment varies.

Fiction: Slice-of-life vignettes. Buys 10 mss/year. Query. Length: 600-1,000 words. Pays 10¢/word.

Poetry: Light verse and traditional. "No erotica or depressing poetry." Buys 250/year. Submit maximum 15 poems. Pays $10.

Tips: "Poetry is the area of our publication most open to freelancers. It must be oriented around a season or theme. The basic subject of *Ideals* is nostalgia, and poetry must be optimistic (how hard work builds character—not how bad the Depression was)."

KNOWLEDGE, Official Publication of the World Olympiads of Knowledge, Knowledge, Inc., 3863 Southwest Loop 820, S 100, Ft. Worth TX 76133-2076. (817)292-4272. Editor: Dr. O.A. Battista. Managing Editor: N.L. Matous. 90% freelance written. For lay and professional audiences of all occupations. Quarterly magazine; 60 pages. Estab. 1976. Circ. 3,000. Pays on publication. Publishes ms an average of 6 months after acceptance. Buys all rights. "We will reassign rights to a writer after a given period." Byline given. Submit seasonal/holiday material 6 months in advance. Reports in 1 month. Sample copy $5; writer's guidelines for #10 SASE.

Nonfiction: Informational—original new knowledge that will prove mentally or physically beneficial to all readers. Buys 30 unsolicited mss/year. Query. Length: 1,500-2,000 words maximum. Pays $100 minimum. Sometimes pays the expenses of writers on assignment.

Columns/Departments: Journal section uses maverick and speculative ideas that other magazines will not publish and reference. Payment is made, on publication, at the following minimum rates: Why Don't They, $50; Salutes, $25; New Vignettes, $25; Quotes To Ponder, $10; and Facts, $5.

Tips: "The editors of *Knowledge* welcome submissions from contributors. Manuscripts and art material will be carefully considered but received *only* with the unequivocal understanding that the magazine will not be responsible for loss or injury. Material from a published source should have the publication's name, date and page number. Submissions cannot be acknowledged and will be returned only when accompanied by a SASE having adequate postage."

LEFTHANDER MAGAZINE, Lefthander International, Box 8249, Topeka KS 66608. (913)234-2177. Managing Editor: Suzan Ireland. 80% freelance written. Eager to work with new/unpublished writers. Bimonthly. "Our readers are lefthanded people of all ages and interests in 50 U.S. states and 12 foreign countries. The one thing they have in common is an interest in lefthandedness." Circ. 26,000. Pays on publication. Publishes ms an average of 4 months after acceptance. Byline usually given. Offers 25% kill fee. Rights negotiable. Simultaneous queries OK. Reports on queries in 6 weeks. Sample copy for 8½ × 11 SAE and $2. Writer's guidelines for #10 SASE.

Nonfiction: Interviews with famous lefthanders; features about lefthanders with interesting talents and occupations; how-to features (sports, crafts, hobbies for lefties); research on handedness and brain dominance; exposé on discrimination against lefthanders in the work world; features on occupations and careers attracting lefties; education features relating to ambidextrous right brain teaching methods. Length: Buys 50-60 mss/year. 750-1,000 words for features. Buys 6 personal experience shorts/year. Query with SASE. Length 750 words. Pays $25. Pays expenses of writer on assignment.

Photos: State availability of photos for features. Pays $10-15 for good contrast b&w glossies. Rights negotiable.

Tips: "All material must have a lefthanded hook. We prefer quick, practical, self-help and self-awareness types of editorial content; keep it brief, light and of general interest. More of our space is devoted to shorter pieces. A good short piece gives us enough evidence of writer's style, which we like to have before assigning full-length features."

LEISURE WORLD, (formerly *Leisure Ontario*), Ontario Motorist Publishing Company, 1215 Ovellette Ave., Box 580, Windsor, Ontario N9A 6N3 Canada. (519)255-1212. FAX: (519)255-7379. Editor: Douglas O'Neil. 30% freelance written. Bimonthly magazine. "*Leisure World* is distributed to members of the Canadian Automobile Association in Southwestern Ontario and the Atlantic provinces. Editorial content is focused on travel, entertainment and leisure time pursuits of interest to CAA members." Estab. 1988. Circ. 260,000. Pays on publication. Publishes ms an average of 2 months after acceptance. Buys first rights and second serial (reprint) rights. Submit seasonal/holiday material 4 months in advance. Sample copy $2. Free writer's guidelines.

Nonfiction: General interest, historical/nostalgic, humor, new product and travel. Buys 20 mss/year. Send complete ms. Length: 800-1,500 words. Pays $50-200.

Photos: Reviews negatives. Offers $15-40 per photo. Captions and model releases required. Buys one-time rights.

Columns/Departments: Query with published clips. Length: 400-800 words. Pays $40-60.

Fiction: Mainstream and slice-of-life vignettes. Buys 3-4 mss/year. Query with published clips. Length: 1,200-2,400 words. Pays $150-250.

Fillers: Carmel Ravenello. Anecdotes, facts and short humor. Buys 20/year. Length: 50-150 words. Pays $10-25.

Tips: "We are most interested in travel destination articles that offer a personal, subjective and positive point of view on international (including US) destinations. Good quality color slides are a must."

MACLEAN'S, Canada's Weekly News Magazine, Maclean Hunter Ltd., 777 Bay St., Toronto, Ontario M5W 1A7 Canada. (416)596-5386. FAX: (416)596-7730. Editor: Kevin Doyle. 15% freelance written. Works with a small number of new/unpublished writers each year. For news-oriented audience. Weekly news magazine. Estab. 1905. Circ. 615,000. Byline given. Frequently buys all rights. **Pays on acceptance.** Publishes ms "immediately" after acceptance. "Query with 200- or 300-word outline before sending material." Reports in 2 weeks. Query for electronic submissions. SAE and IRCs. Sample copy for 9 × 12 SAE.

Nonfiction: Book excerpts (nonfiction), exposé and interview/profile. "We have the conventional news magazine departments (Canada, world, business, people; also science, medicine, law, art, music, etc.) with roughly the same treatment as other news magazines. We specialize in subjects that are primarily of Canadian interest, and there is now more emphasis on international—particularly US—news. Most material is now written by staffers or retainer freelancers, but we are open to suggestions from abroad, especially in world, business and departments (medicine, lifestyles, etc.). Freelancers should write for a copy of the magazine and study the approach." Length: 350-10,000 words. Pays 40-75¢/word.

MINNESOTA INK, Minnesota Ink, Inc., P.O. Box 9148, N. St. Paul MN 55109. (612)433-3626. Publisher/Managing Editor: Valerie Hockert. Poetry Editor: Anthoney Stomski. Bimonthly. Circ. 24,000. 80% freelance written. Pays on publication. Publishes ms an average of 6 months after acceptance. Byline given. Buys first North American serial rights. Submit seasonal/holiday material 6 months in advance. Reports in 1 month on queries; 6 weeks on mss. Sample copy $3. Writer's guidelines for #10 SASE.

Nonfiction: Mechanics of writing; tips on how to get published; articles on different modes of writing (e.g. fiction, screen writing, poetry, technical writing, writing for children, etc.); motivational; interview/profile. Buys 6-12 mss/year. Prefers complete ms. Length: 500-1,500 words. Pays $5-30, sometimes subscription.
Fiction: Adventure, experimental, fantasy, historical, humorous, mainstream, mystery, romance, science fiction, suspense, western, Send complete ms. Length: 500-1,500 words. Pays $5-30, sometimes subscription.
Poetry: Open to style. Length: 25 lines maximum. Pays up to $5.
Tips: Send short (1 paragraph) biographical sketch with submission.

NATIONAL GEOGRAPHIC MAGAZINE, 17th and M Sts. NW, Washington DC 20036. Editor: William Graves. Approximately 50% freelance written. Prefers to work with published/established writers, and works with a small number of new/unpublished writers each year. For members of the National Geographic Society. Monthly. Circ. more than 10 million. Query for electronic submissions.
Nonfiction: *National Geographic* publishes first-person, general interest, heavy illustrated articles on science, natural history, exploration and geographical regions. Almost half of the articles are staff-written. Of the freelance writers assigned, most are experts in their fields; the remainder are established professionals. Fewer than one percent of unsolicited queries result in assignments. Query (500 words) by letter, not by phone, to Senior Assistant Editor Robert Poole (Contract Writers). Do not send manuscripts. Before querying, study recent issues and check a *Geographic Index* at a library since the magazine seldom returns to regions or subjects covered within the past ten years. Pays expenses of writers on assignment.
Photos: Photographers should query in care of the Illustration Division.

THE NEW YORKER, 25 W. 43rd St., New York NY 10036. Editor: Robert Gottlieb. Weekly. Circ. 600,000. Reports in 2 months. **Pays on acceptance.**
Nonfiction, Fiction, Poetry and Fillers: Long fact pieces are usually staff-written. So is "Talk of the Town," although freelance submissions are considered. Pays good rates. Uses fiction, both serious and light. About 90% of the fillers come from contributors with or without taglines (extra pay if the tagline is used).

PARADE, Parade Publications, Inc., 750 3rd Ave., New York NY 10017. (212)573-7000. Editor: Walter Anderson. Weekly magazine for a general interest audience. 90% freelance written. Circ. 37 million. **Pays on acceptance.** Publishes ms an average of 3 months after acceptance. Kill fee varies in amount. Buys first North American serial rights. Reports in 5 weeks on queries. Writer's guidelines for #10 SAE.
Nonfiction: General interest (on health, trends, social issues, business or anything of interest to a broad general audience); interview/profile (of news figures, celebrities and people of national significance); and "provocative topical pieces of news value." Spot news events are not accepted, as *Parade* has a 6-week lead time. No fiction, fashion, travel, poetry, quizzes or fillers. Address three-paragraph queries to Articles Editor. Length: 800-1,500 words. Pays $1,000 minimum. Pays expenses of writers on assignment.
Tips: "Send a well-researched, well-written query targeted to our market. Please, no phone queries. We're interested in well-written exclusive manuscripts on topics of news interest. The most frequent mistake made by writers in completing an article for us is not adhering to the suggestions made by the editor when the article was assigned."

READ ME, 1118 Hoyt Ave., Everett WA 98201. Editor-in-Cheif: Ron Fleshman. Editors: Janice Greene, Linda McMichael, Kay Nelson, Sally Taylor, Pete Young. 95% freelance written. Quarterly general interest tabloid. Estab. 1988. Circ. 2,000. Pays on publication. Publishes ms an average of 18 months after acceptance. Byline given. Buys first North American serial rights or second serial (reprint) rights. Previously published submissions (if identified) OK. Reports in 3 months. Sample copy $1.50; writer's guidelines for #10 SASE.
Nonfiction: Book excerpts, essays, general interest, humor, opinion, personal experience, travel. Buys 20 mss/year. Query with or without published clips, or send complete ms. Length: 500-2,000. Pays $20 maximum.
Columns/Departments: Outreach (first-person statements from forgotten members of society or those who work with or serve them), 1,000 words maximum; Contention (strongly expressed personal opinion on controversial issues), 1,000 words maximum; Travel (single interesting aspect of a distant place), 750 words maximum. Humor (mild to brutally sardonic, essays, short-short stories), 1,000 words maximum. Buys 40 mss/year. Send complete ms. Pays $1-20.
Fiction: Adventure, confession, ethnic, fantasy, historical, horror, humorous, mainstream, mystery, novel excerpts, romance, science fiction, suspense, western. Buys 60 mss/year. Send complete ms. Length: 100-2,500 words. Pays $1-20.
Poetry: Elizabeth Strong, editor. Free verse, traditional. No obscenity, no academic poetry. Buys 30 poems/year. Submit maximum of 6 poems at one time. Length: 50 lines maximum. Pays $1-3.
Fillers: Ellie Brauer, fillers editor. Anecdotes, facts, short humor. Buys 40/year. Length: 5-50 words. Pays $1-3.
Tips: "Reward our readers with new insight, unusual slant, fresh perspective. Material may reassure or outrage, teach or tickle. Perimeter testing is encouraged—but must be accessible. Avoid subjects quickly dated. Regarding style: less is more."

READER'S DIGEST, Pleasantville NY 10570. Monthly. Circ. 16.5 million. Publishes general interest articles "as varied as all human experience." The *Digest* does not read or return unsolicited mss. Address proposals and tearsheets of published articles to the editors. Considers only previously published articles; pays $1,200/*Digest* page for World Digest rights. (Usually split 50/50 between original publisher and writer.) Tearsheets of submitted article must include name of original publisher and date of publication.

Columns/Departments: "Original contributions become the property of *Reader's Digest* upon acceptance and payment. Life-in-these-United States contributions must be true, unpublished stories from one's own experience, revealing adult human nature, and providing appealing or humorous sidelights on the American scene. Length: 300 words maximum. Pays $400 on publication. True and unpublished stories are also solicited for Humor in Uniform, Campus Comedy and All in a Day's Work. Length: 300 words maximum. Pays $400 on publication. Towards More Picturesque Speech—the first contributor of each item used in this department is paid $50 for original material, $35 for reprints. Contributions should be dated, and the source must be given. For items used in Laughter, the Best Medicine, Personal Glimpses, Quotable Quotes, and elsewhere in the magazine payment is as follows; to the *first* contributor of each from a published source, $35. For original material, $30 per *Digest* two-column line, with a minimum payment of $50. Send complete anecdotes to excerpt editor."

READERS REVIEW, The National Research Bureau, Inc., 424 N. 3rd St., Burlington IA 52601. FAX: (319)752-3421. Editor: Rhonda Wilson. Editorial Supervisor: Doris J. Ruschill. 75% freelance written. Works with a small number of new/unpublished writers each year, and is eager to work with new/unpublished writers. Quarterly magazine. Estab. 1948. Pays on publication. Publishes ms an average of 1 year after acceptance. Buys all rights. Previously published submissions OK. Submit seasonal/holiday material 7 months in advance of issue date. Reports in 3 weeks. Writer's guidelines for #10 SASE; sample for 6½ × 9½ envelope with 55¢ postage.

Nonfiction: General interest (steps to better health, attitudes on the job); how-to (perform better on the job, do home repairs, car maintenance); and travel. Buys 10-12 mss/year. Query with outline or submit complete ms. Length: 400-600 words. Pays 4¢/word.

Tips: "Writers have a better chance of breaking in at our publication with short articles."

REAL PEOPLE, The Magazine of Celebrities and Interesting People, Main Street Publishing Co., Inc., 950 Third Ave. 16th Fl., New York NY 10022-2705. (212)371-4932. FAX: (212)838-8420. Editor: Alex Polner. 90% freelance written. Bimonthly magazine of profiles, human interest and self-help articles for audience, ages 28 and up. Estab. 1988. Circ. 165,000. Pays on publication. Byline given. Pays 33% kill fee. Buys all rights except in some specific cases. Submit seasonal/holiday material 6 months in advance. Reports in 1 month. Sample copy for $3.50 with 6x9 SAE and 65¢ postage. Writer's guidelines for #10 SASE.

Nonfiction: Book excerpts, how-to, interview/profile, photo essays. Buys 60 mss/year. Query (and SAE) with published clips. Length: 500-1,200 words. Pays $150-250 for assigned articles; $100-200 for unsolicited articles.

Photos: State availability of photos with submissions. Reviews 5 × 7 prints. Offers no additional payment for photos accepted with ms. Captions, model releases and identification of subjects required. Buys one-time rights.

SELECTED READING, The National Research Bureau, Inc., 424 N. 3rd St., Burlington IA 52601. FAX: (319)752-3421. Editor: Rhonda Wilson. Editorial Supervisor: Doris J. Ruschill. 75% freelance written. Eager to work with new/unpublished writers, works with a small number of new/unpublished writers each year. Quarterly magazine. Estab. 1948. Pays on publication. Publishes ms an average of 1 year after acceptance. Buys all rights. Previously published submissions OK. Submit seasonal/holiday material 7 months in advance of issue date. Reports in 3 weeks. Writer's guidelines for #10 SASE; sample for 6½ × 9½ envelope with 55¢ postage.

Nonfiction: General interest (economics, health, safety, working relationships); how-to; and travel (out-of-the way places). No material on car repair. Buys 10-12 mss/year. Query. A short outline or synopsis is best. Lists of titles are no help. Length: 400-600 words. Pays 4¢/word.

Tips: "Writers have a better chance of breaking in at our publication with short articles."

‡SMITHSONIAN MAGAZINE, 900 Jefferson Dr., Washington DC 20560. Articles Editor: Marlane A. Liddell. 90% freelance written. Prefers to work with published/established writers. For "associate members of the Smithsonian Institution; 85% with college education." Monthly. Circ. 3 million. Buys first North American serial rights. "Payment for each article to be negotiated depending on our needs and the article's length and excellence." **Pays on acceptance.** Publishes ms an average of 6 months after acceptance. Submit seasonal material 3 months in advance. Reports in 6 weeks. Writer's guidelines for #10 SASE.

Nonfiction: "Our mandate from the Smithsonian Institution says we are to be interested in the same things which now interest or should interest the Institution: cultural and fine arts, history, natural sciences, hard sciences, etc." Query. Length: 750-4,500 words. Payment negotiable. Pays expenses of writers on assignment.

Photos: Purchased with or without ms and on assignment. Captions required. Pays $400/full color page.

THE STAR, 660 White Plains Rd., Tarrytown NY 10591. (914)332-5000. FAX: (914)332-5043. Editor: Richard Kaplan. Executive Editors: Bill Ridley and Phil Bunton. 40% freelance written. Prefers to work with published/established writers. "For every family; all the family—kids, teenagers, young parents and grandparents." Weekly magazine; 48 pages. Estab. 1974. Circ. 3.5 million. Publishes ms an average of 1 month after acceptance. Buys first North American serial rights, occasional second serial book rights. Query for electronic submissions. Pays expenses of writers on assignment.

Nonfiction: Exposé (government waste, consumer, education, anything affecting family); general interest (human interest, consumerism, informational, family and women's interest); how-to (psychological, practical on all subjects affecting readers); interview (celebrity or human interest); new product; photo feature; profile (celebrity or national figure); health; medical; and diet. No first-person articles. Query or submit complete ms. Length: 500-1,000 words. Pays $50-1,500.

Photos: Alistair Duncan, photo editor. State availability of photos with query or ms. Pays $25-100 for 8 × 10 b&w glossy prints, contact sheets or negatives; $150-1,000 for 35mm color transparencies. Captions required. Buys one-time or all rights.

SUNSHINE MAGAZINE, Henry F. Henrichs Publications, P.O. Box 40, Sunshine Park, Litchfield IL 62056. (217)324-3425. Editor: Peggy Kuethe. Managing Editor: Garth Henrichs. 95% freelance written. Eager to work with new/unpublished writers. A monthly magazine. "Primarily human interest and inspirational in its appeal, *Sunshine Magazine* provides worthwhile reading for all the family." Estab. 1924. Circ. 70,000. **Pays on acceptance.** Publishes ms an average of 6 months after acceptance. Byline given. Buys first North American serial rights or one-time rights. Submit seasonal/holiday material 6 months in advance. Reports in 2 months. Sample copy for 50¢, 6 × 9 SAE and 2 first class stamps; writer's guidelines for #10 SASE.

Nonfiction: Essays, historical/nostalgic, inspirational and personal experience. "No material dealing with specifically religious matters or that is depressing in nature (divorce, drug abuse, alcohol abuse, death, violence, child abuse)." Send complete ms. Length: 200-1,250. Pays $10-100.

Columns/Departments: Extraordinary Experience (personal experience), 500 words; Let's Reminisce (reminiscent, nostalgia), 500 words; Guidelines (inspirational), 200 words; and Favorite Meditation (inspirational essay), 200 words. Buys 85-90 mss/year. Send complete ms. Pays $15-50.

Fiction: Inspirational and human interest. Buys 75-80 mss/year. Send complete ms.

Poetry: Light verse and traditional. No avant-garde, free verse or haiku. Buys 12-15 poems/year. No limit to the number of poems submitted at one time. Length: 4-16 lines. Pays $15-80, or may pay in copies.

Fillers: Anecdotes and short humor. Buys 1-5/year. Length: 50-150 words. Pays $10-20.

Tips: "Make a note that *Sunshine* is not religious—but it is inspirational. After reading a sample copy, you should know that we do not accept material that is very different from what we've been doing for over 60 years. Don't send a manuscript that is longer than specified or that is 'different' from anything else we've published—that's not what we're looking for. The whole magazine is written primarily by freelancers. We are just as eager to publish new writers as they are to get published."

‡TOWN AND COUNTRY, 1700 Broadway, New York NY 10019. (212)903-5000. Managing Editor: Jean Barkhorn. For upper-income Americans. Monthly. **Pays on acceptance.** Not a large market for freelancers. Always query first.

Nonfiction: Frank Zachary, department editor. "We're always trying to find ideas that can be developed into good articles that will make appealing cover lines." Wants provocative and controversial pieces. Length: 1,500-2,000 words. Pay varies. Also buys shorter pieces for which pay varies.

USA WEEKEND, Gannett Co., Inc., Box 500-W, Washington DC 20044. (703)276-6445. Managing Editor: Marcia Bullard. 70% freelance written. Weekly Sunday newspaper magazine. Circ. 15.3 million. **Pays on acceptance.** Publishes ms an average of 3 months after acceptance. Byline given. Offers 25% kill fee. Buys first North American serial rights. Submit seasonal/holiday material 5 months in advance. Query for electronic submissions. Reports in 5 weeks.

Nonfiction: Food and Family Issues, Connie Kurz; Trends, Entertainment, Mei-Mei Chan; Recreation, Tim McQuay; Cover Story Editor, Brenda Turner. Book excerpts, general interest, how-to, interview/profile, travel, food and recreation. No first-person essays, historic pieces, retrospectives. Buys 200 mss/year. Query with published clips. No unsolicited mss accepted. Length: 50-2,000 words. Pays $75-2,000. Sometimes pays expenses of writers on assignment.

Photos: State availability of photos with submission.

Columns/Departments: Food, Travel, Entertainment, Books, Recreation. "All stories must be pegged to an upcoming event, must report new and refreshing trends in the field and must include high profile people." Length: 50-1,000 words. Query with published clips. Pays $250-500.

Tips: "We are looking for authoritative, lively articles that blend the author's expertise with our style. All articles must have a broad, timely appeal. One-page query should include peg or timeliness of the subject matter. We generally look for sidebar material to accompany each article."

WHAT MAKES PEOPLE SUCCESSFUL, The National Research Bureau, Inc., 424 N. 3rd St., Burlington IA 52601. FAX: (319)752-3421. Editor: Rhonda Wilson. Editorial Supervisor: Doris J. Ruschill. 75% freelance written. Eager to work with new/unpublished writers, and works with a small number of new/unpublished writers each year. Published quarterly. Estab. 1948. Pays on publication. Publishes ms an average of 1 year after acceptance. Buys all rights. Previously published submissions OK. Submit seasonal/holiday material 8 months in advance of issue date. Reports in 3 weeks. Writer's guidelines for #10 SASE; sample for 6½ × 9½ envelope with 55¢ postage.

Nonfiction: How-to (be successful); general interest (personality, employee morale, guides to successful living, biographies of successful persons, etc.); experience; and opinion. No material on health. Buys 3-4 mss/issue. Query with outline. Length: 400-600 words. Pays 4¢/word.

Tips: Short articles (rather than major features) have a better chance of acceptance because all articles are short.

THE WORLD & I, A Chronicle of Our Changing Era, News World Communications, Inc., 2800 New York Ave., N.E. Washington DC 20002. (202)635-4000. Editor: Morton A. Kaplan. Executive Editor: Michael Marshall. 90% freelance written. Publishing more than 100 articles each month, this is a broad interest magazine for the thinking person. Estab. 1986. Circ. 30,000. Pays on acceptance. Publishes ms an average of 4 months after acceptance. Byline given. Offers 20% kill fee. Buys all rights. Submit seasonal/holiday material 5 months in advance. Query for electronic submissions. Reports in 6 weeks on queries; 10 weeks on mss. Writer's guidelines for #10 SASE. Description of Sections: Current Issues: Politics, economics and strategic trends covered in a variety of approaches, including special report, analysis, commentary and photo essay. The Arts: International coverage of music, dance, theater, film, television, design, architecture, photography, poetry, painting and sculpture – through reviews, features, essays and a 10-page Gallery of full-color reproductions. Life: Human interest section on children, family, garden, home, sports, beauty, fashion, health, adventure, humor and more. Natural Science: Covers the latest in science and technology, relating it to the social and historical context, under these headings: At the Edge, Impacts, Nature Walk, Science and Spirit, Science and Values, Scientists: Past and Present, Crucibles of Science and Science Essay. Book World: Excerpts from important, timely books (followed by commentaries) and 10-12 scholarly reviews of significant new books each month, including untranslated works from abroad. Covers current affairs, intellectual issues, contemporary fiction, history, moral/religious issues and the social sciences. Currents in Modern Thought: Examines scholarly research and theoretical debate across the wide range of disciplines in the humanities and social sciences. Featured themes are explored by several contributors. Investigates theoretical issues raised by certain current events, and offers contemporary reflection on issues drawn from the whole history of human thought. Culture: Survoyo the world's people in these subsections: Peoples (their unique characteristics and cultural symbols), Crossroads (changes brought by the meeting of cultures), Patterns (photo essay depicting the daily life of a distinct culture), Folk Wisdom (folklore and practical wisdom and their present forms), and Heritage (multicultural backgrounds of the American people and how they are bound to the world. Photo Essay: The 10-page Life and Ideals dramatizes a human story of obstacles overcome in the pursuit of an ideal. Three other photo essays appear each month: Focus (Current Issues), Gallery (The Arts), and Patterns (Culture).

Nonfiction: "No *National Enquirer*-type articles." Buys 1,200 mss/year. Query with published clips. Length: 1,000-15,000 words. Pays 10-20¢/word. Sometimes pays expenses of writers on assignment.

Fiction: Query the book editors. No erotica, confessions or UFO stories. Buys 1-5 mss/year. Query. Length: 2,000-4,000 words for reviews and commentaries. Pays 10¢/word maximum.

Poetry: Query arts editor. Avant-garde, free verse, haiku, light verse and traditional. Buys 6-12 poems/year. Submit maximum 5 poems. Pays $25-50.

Photos: State availability of photos with submission. Reivews contact sheets, transparencies and prints. Payment negotiable. Model releases and identification of subjects required. Buys one-time rights.

Tips: "Send a short query letter with a viable story idea (no unsolicited mss, please!) for a specific section and/or subsection."

WORLD'S FAIR, World's Fair, Inc., P.O. Box 339, Corte Madera CA 94925. (415)924-6035. Editor: Alfred Heller. 50% freelance written. Quarterly magazine covering fairs and expositions (past, present and future). "The people, politics and pageantry of fairs and expositions, in historical perspective; lively, good-humored articles of fact and analysis." Estab. 1981. Circ. 5,000. **Pays on acceptance.** Publishes ms an average of 3 months after acceptance. Byline given. Offers 50% kill fee. Buys all rights. Reports in 3 weeks. Free sample copy and writer's guidelines.

Nonfiction: Essays, historical/nostalgic, humor, interview/profile, personal experience and photo feature, related to international fairs and expositions. Buys 8-10 mss/year. Query with published clips. Length: 750-3,000 words. Pays $50-400. Sometimes pays expenses of writers on assignment.

Photos: State availability of photos or line drawings with submission. Reviews contact sheets and 8 × 10 b&w prints. Identification of subjects required. Buys one-time rights.

Tips: Looking for "correspondents in cities planning major expositions, in the US and abroad."

Health and Fitness

The magazines listed here specialize in covering health and fitness topics for a general audience. Many focus not as much on exercise as on general "healthy lifestyle" topics. Magazines covering health topics from a medical perspective are listed in the Medical category of Trade. Also see the Sports/Miscellaneous section where publications dealing with health and particular sports may be listed. Many general interest publications are also potential markets for health or fitness articles.

ACCENT ON LIVING, Box 700, Bloomington IL 61702. (309)378-2961. Editor: Betty Garee. 75% freelance written. Eager to work with new/unpublished writers. For physically disabled persons and rehabilitation professionals. Quarterly magazine. Circ. 20,000. Buys first rights and second (reprint) rights to material originally published elsewhere. Byline usually given. Buys 50-60 unsolicited mss/year. Pays on publication. Publishes ms an average of 6 months after acceptance. Reports in 2 weeks. Sample copy with writer's guidelines for $2.50, 6 × 8 SAE and four first class stamps; writer's guidelines alone for #10 SAE and 1 first class stamp.

Nonfiction: Articles about new devices that would make a disabled person with limited physical mobility more independent; should include description, availability, and photos. Medical breakthroughs for disabled people. Intelligent discussion articles on acceptance of physically disabled persons in normal living situations; topics may be architectural barriers, housing, transportation, educational or job opportunities, organizations, or other areas. How-to articles concerning everyday living, giving specific, helpful information so the reader can carry out the idea himself/herself. News articles about active disabled persons or groups. Good strong interviews. Vacations, accessible places to go, sports, organizations, humorous incidents, self improvement, and sexual or personal adjustment — all related to physically handicapped persons. No religious-type articles. "We are looking for upbeat material." Query. Length: 250-1,000 words. Pays 10¢/word for article as it appears in magazine (after editing and/or condensing by staff).

Photos: Pays $10 minimum for b&w photos purchased with accompanying captions. Amount will depend on quality of photos and subject matter. Pays $50 and up for four-color slides used on cover. "We need good-quality transparencies or slides with submissions — or b&w photos."

Tips: "Ask a friend who is disabled to read your article before sending it to *Accent*. Make sure that he/she understands your major points and the sequence or procedure."

‡AMERICAN FITNESS, Aerobics and Fitness Association of America, Suite 310, 15250 Ventura Blvd., Sherman Oaks CA 91403. (818)905-0040. FAX: (818)990-5468. Editor-At-Large: Peg Jordan, RN. Managing Editor: Rhonda J. Wilson. Bimonthly magazine of fitness instruction. We cover exercise trends, research, techniques; health and nutrition updates. Estab. 1983. Circ. 25,100. Pays 30 days after publication. Byline given. Buys one-time and second serial (reprint) rights. Submit seasonal/holiday material 4 months in advance. Previously published submissions OK. Reports in 1 month on queries. Sample copy $1.75 with 9 × 12 SAE and 5 first class stamps. Writer's guidelines for #10 SAE with 1 first class stamp.

Nonfiction: General interest, interview/profile, new product, travel, nutrition, humor. Women's health, outdoor/fitness-oriented sports, fitness for seniors, overweight children, disabled persons. No first person success stories! Pays $35/color slide, $10/b&w photo. Query. Length: 1,000-2,500 words. Pays $80-100 for assigned articles. Sometimes pays expense of writers on assignment.

Photos: Captions required. Buys one-time rights.

AMERICAN HEALTH MAGAZINE, Fitness of Body and Mind, Readers Digest Corp., 28 W. 23rd St., New York NY 10010. (212)242-2460. Editor-in-Chief: T. George Harris. Editor: Joel Gurin. 70% freelance written. Prefers to work with published/established writers. 10 issues/year. General interest magazine that covers both scientific and "lifestyle" aspects of health, including laboratory research, clinical advances, fitness, holistic healing and nutrition. Circ. 1 million. **Pays on acceptance.** Publishes ms an average of 4-6 months after acceptance. Byline given. Offers 25% kill fee. Buys first North American serial rights, "and certain other rights that are negotiable, in some cases." Reports in 2 months. Sample copy for $3; writer's guidelines for #10 SAE and 1 first class stamp.

Nonfiction: Mail to Editorial/Features. Book excerpts; how-to; humor; interview/profile (health or fitness related); photo feature (any solid feature or news item relating to health); and technical. No mechanical research reports, quick weight-loss plans or unproven treatments. "Stories should be written clearly, without jargon. Information should be new, authoritative and helpful to the readers." Buys 60-70 mss/year (plus many more news items). Query with 2 clips of published work. "Absolutely *no* complete mss." Length: 1,000-3,000 words. Pays $600-2,000 upon acceptance. Pays the expenses of writers on assignment.

Photos: Mail to Editorial/Photo. Send photos with query. Pays $100-600 for 35mm transparencies and 8 × 10 prints "depending on use." Captions and identification of subjects required. Buys one-time rights.

Columns/Departments: Mail to Editorial/News. Medical News, Fitness Report, Nutrition Report, Mind/ Body News, Family Report, Family Pet, Tooth Report, and Skin, Scent and Hair. Other news sections included from time to time. Buys about 300 mss/year. Query with clips of published work. Prefers 2 pages-500 words. Pays $125-375 upon acceptance.

Tips: "*American Health* has no full-time staff writers; we have chosen to rely on outside contributors for most of our articles. The magazine needs good ideas, and good articles, from professional journalists, health educators, researchers and clinicians. Queries should be short (no longer than a page), snappy and to the point. Think short; think news. Give us a good angle and a paragraph of background. Queries only. We do not take responsibility for materials not accompanied by SASE."

BETTER HEALTH, Better Health Press, 1384 Chapel St., New Haven CT 06511. (203)789-3974. Director: James F. Malerba. 75% freelance written. Prefers to work with published/established writers; will consider new/unpublished writers. A bimonthly magazine devoted to health and wellness issues, as opposed to medical issues. Estab. 1979. Circ. 110,000. Pays on publication. Byline given. Offers $50 kill fee. Buys all rights. Query. Sample copy $1.25 plus 9 × 12 SASE. Writer's guidelines for #10 SASE.

Nonfiction: Wellness/prevention issues are of prime interest. New medical techniques or similar topics are not considered. No seasonal, heavy humor, inspirational or personal experience. Length: 2,000-2,500 words. No fillers, poems or quizzes. Pays $150-400. Does not offer additional payment for photos, research costs, etc.

Tips: "Please do not submit 'how-I-overcame-my-painful-illness' articles. We look for upbeat features of interest to a general audience, particularly women. Topics range from sensible label reading on packaged foods to forms of housing available to the elderly to potential cures for baldness. Absolutely no 'cute' humor or articles that are not well-researched through medical doctors or similar authorities. Our audience demands the best wellness news available. Material not accompanied with an SASE be consigned to the wastebasket, unread."

‡BETTER NUTRITION FOR TODAY'S LIVING, Communication Channels, Inc., 6255 Barfield Rd., Atlanta GA 30328. (404)256-9800. Editor: Robert Rawls. 40% freelance written. Monthly magazine on nutrition, supplements and fitness. "*Better Nutrition* is geared toward customers of health food stores and for those who prefer natural foods and supplements. Topics covered include general health, diet, nutrition and fitness. We like to run articles on vitamins, minerals and other supplements for disease prevention and health maintenance." Circ. 540,000. Pays on publication. Publishes ms an average of 3 months after acceptance. Byline given. Buys all rights. Submit seasonal/holiday material 3 months in advance. Query for electronic submissions. Reports in 1 month. Sample copy $1 with 10 × 13 SAE and 2 first class stamps. Writer's guidelines for #10 SAE with 1 first class stamp.

Nonfiction: Exposé, interview/profile. No personal experience, articles endorsing a specific product or articles endorsing any particular diet. Buys 12 mss/year. Query with published clips. Length: 1,250-1,850 words. Pays $150-250.

Photos: Send photos with submission. Reviews contact sheets, transparencies, prints. Offers $40-100/photo. Model release required. Buys one-time rights.

Columns/Departments: News (information on newly discovered benefits of supplements, dietary habits, fitness). Buys 12 mss/year. Query with published clips. Length: 250-300 words. Pays $50-75.

Tips: "Our publication is distributed through health food stores. Our readers are most interested in reading the latest research on how specific vitamins, minerals and other nutrients help treat and prevent diseases and disorders. We speak of such supplements in the generic sense—no name brands, please. Calling us prior to submitting material is best. The type of item being written about must be currently available in health food stores."

CONCEIVE MAGAZINE, The Magazine of Infertility Issues, Knipper Publishing, Inc., P.O. Box 2047, Danville CA 94526. (415)685-9489. Editor: Catherine C. Knipper. 20% freelance written. Bimonthly magazine on infertility and alternatives. "*Conceive* is edited to support and inform infertile individuals about current medical technologies and advances in layman's terms, the emotional side of infertility and how to cope, as well as alternatives to family building such as adoption and child-free living. No special slant or philosophy." Estab. 1988. Pays on publication. Publishes ms an average of 4 months after acceptance. Byline given. Buys first North American serial rights. Simultaneous and previously published submissions OK. Reports in 2 weeks on queries; 1 month on mss. Sample copy for $5, ($6.50 foreign) and 9 × 12 SAE. Writer's guidelines for SASE.

Nonfiction: Book excerpts, general interest, historical/nostalgic, humor, inspirational, interview/profile, new product, opinion (does not mean letters to the editor), personal experience, photo feature, religious and technical. Query with or without published clips. Length: 400-4,000 words. Pays $50-175.

Photos: Send photos with submission. Reviews contact sheets, negatives and 8×10 prints. Offers $25 per photo. Buys one-time rights.
Poetry: Avant-garde, free verse, haiku, light verse and traditional. Buys 6 poems/year. No maximum number of poems. Length: 4-30 lines. Pays $1/line.
Fillers: Anecdotes, facts, gags to be illustrated by cartoonist, newsbreaks and short humor. Buys 15/year. Length: 10-250 words. Pays $10 up to 100 words.

EAST WEST, The Journal of Natural Health & Living, Auchincloss, Wadsworth & Co., 17 Station St., P.O. Box 1200, Brookline Village MA 02147. (617)232-1000. FAX: (617)232-1572. Editor: Mark Mayell. 40% freelance written. Works with a small number of new/unpublished writers each year. Monthly magazine emphasizing natural health for "people of all ages seeking balance in a world of change." Estab. 1971. Circ. 100,000. Pays on publication. Publishes ms an average of 6 months after acceptance. Buys first serial rights or second (reprint) rights. Byline given. Submit seasonal/holiday material 6 months in advance. Simultaneous submissions OK. Reports in 1 month. Sample copy $1 and 8½×11 SAE; writer's guidelines for SAE and 1 first class stamp.
Nonfiction: Major focus is on issues of natural health and diet; interviews and features (on the natural foods industry, sustainable farming and gardening, natural healing, human-potential movement, diet and fitness). No negative, politically-oriented, or New Age material. "We're looking for original, first-person articles without jargon or opinions of any particular teachings. Articles should be well documented." Buys 15-20 mss/year. Query. Length: 2,000-3,000 words. Pays 10-15¢/word. Sometimes pays expenses of writers on assignment.
Photos: Send photos with ms. Pays $15-40 for b&w prints; $15-175 for 35mm color transparencies. Captions preferred; model releases required.
Columns/Departments: Body, Whole Foods, Natural Healing, Gardening, and Cooking. Buys 15 mss/year. Submit complete ms. Length: 1,500-2,000 words. Pays 10-15¢/word.
Tips: "Read another issue. Too many freelancers don't take the time to truly understand their market and thus waste their time and ours with inappropriate submissions."

‡HEALTH & FAITH DIGEST, Center for Human Natural Nutrition, 15015 Ventura Blvd., Sherman Oaks CA 91403. (213)995-0204. Editor: Gordon Richiusa. Managing Editor: Caro Adinians. 80% freelance written. Monthly tabloid covering health—natural diet and lifestyle. "We believe in health through natural means, not promotion of the medical field." Estab. 1987. Circ. 50,000. Pays half on acceptance, half on publication. Byline given. Offers 50% kill fee. Buys all rights. Submit seasonal/holiday material 6 months in advance. Query for electronic submissions. Reports in 1 month on queries; 3 months on mss. Free sample copy; writer's guidelines for SASE.
Nonfiction: Essays, exposé, how-to, inspirational, interview/profile, opinion personal experience, photo feature, research on health. "No advertisements or public relations pieces." Buys 120 mss/year. Query with or without published clips. Pays $75-150 for assigned articles; $50-100 for unsolicited articles.
Photos: State availability of photos wtih submission. Reviews contact sheets and transparencies. Offers no additional payment for photos accepted with ms. Captions, model releases and identification of subjects required.
Fillers: Rick Burgin, fillers editor. Facts and newsbreaks. Length: 200-400 words. Pays $10-20.
Tips: "Our audience is 50 years old and up, but wanting to live to 150; they know it's possible with proper nutrition and a healthy lifestyle. We are currently looking for book-length material on the same subjects—query."

HEALTH MAGAZINE, Getting the Best From Yourself, Family Media, Inc., 3 Park Ave., New York NY 10016. (212)779-6441. Editor-in-Chief: Nan Silver. Managing Editor: Catherine Winters. 75% freelance written. A magazine covering women's health issues 10 times/year. "*Health* is a service magazine for women twenty to fifty. We run pieces on medicine and health, behavior and psychology, fitness, food, beauty and fashion." Circ. 800,000. **Pays on acceptance.** Publishes ms an average of 4 months after acceptance. Byline given. Offers 20% kill fee. Buys first North American serial rights. Submit seasonal/holiday material 6 months in advance. Reports in 2 months. Sample copy for 9×12 SAE and $1.45 postage; free writer's guidelines.
Nonfiction: Investigative, general interest, humor, interview/profile, new product and personal experience. Buys 325 mss/year. Query with published clips. Length: 175-2,500 words. Pays $150-2,000. Pays the expenses of writers on assignment.
Photos: State availability of photos with submission. Reviews transparencies.
Tips: "A freelancer's best first query to *Health* should be well researched and backed up by clips."

IN HEALTH, (formerly *Hippocrates*), Suite 225, 475 Gate 5 Rd., Sausalito CA 94965. (415)332-5866. Editor: Eric Schrier. Managing Editor: Michael Gold. 75% freelance written. A bimonthly magazine on health and medicine. "Articles should be written with wit, reflection and authority." Estab. 1986. Circ. 600,000. **Pays on acceptance.** Publishes ms an average of 6 months after acceptance. Offers 25% kill fee. Buys first North American serial rights.

Nonfiction: Essays, general interest, how-to, interview/profile, photo feature. Query with published clips. Length: 1,500-5,000 words. Pays $1,200-4,000. Pays approved expenses of writers on assignment.

Columns/Departments: Sylvia Quesada, editorial assistant. Food, Family, Fitness, Drugs, Vanities, Mind, all 800-1,200 words. Buys 12 mss/year. Query with published clips. Pays $600-850.

Fillers: Clippings: verbatim from other publications or book, $50 each *used*; nothing if unused.

Tips: "Send sharply focused queries with the proposed style and sources clearly defined. Departments are the best place to start. Queries can run to 250 words per topic and should demonstrate the finished story's structure and character. Departments are Food, Family, Fitness, Drugs, Vanities and Mind. Tightly focused stories, with real voices and touches of humor used. *Always* query first. The magazine for M.D.'s is still entitled *Hippocrates*. General public receives *In Health*."

LET'S LIVE MAGAZINE, Oxford Industries, Inc., 444 N. Larchmont Blvd., Box 74908, Los Angeles CA 90004. (213)469-8379. FAX: (213)469-9597. Editor: Debra Jenkins Robinson. Emphasizes nutrition. 10% freelance written. Works with a small number of new/unpublished writers each year. Monthly magazine. Estab. 1933. Circ. 140,000. Pays on publication. Publishes ms an average of 4 months after acceptance. Buys first North American serial rights. Byline given. Submit seasonal/holiday material 6 months in advance. Reports in 1 month on queries; 6 weeks on mss. Sample copy for $2.50 and 10 × 13 SAE with 5 first class stamps; writer's guidelines for SAE and 1 first class stamp.

Nonfiction: General interest (effects of vitamins, minerals and nutrients in improvement of health or afflictions); historical (documentation of experiments or treatment establishing value of nutrients as boon to health); how-to (acquire strength and vitality, improve health of adults and/or children and prepare tasty health-food meals); interview (benefits of research in establishing prevention as key to good health); personal opinion (views of orthomolecular doctors or their patients on value of health foods toward maintaining good health); and profile (background and/or medical history of preventive medicine, M.D.s or Ph.D.s, in advancement of nutrition). Manuscripts must be well-researched, reliably documented, and written in a clear, readable style. Buys 2-4 mss/issue. Query with published clips. Length: 1,000-1,200 words. Pays $150. Sometimes pays expenses of writers on assignment.

Photos: State availability of photos with ms. Pays $17.50 for 8 × 10 b&w glossy prints; $35 for 8 × 10 color prints and 35mm transparencies; and $150 for good cover shot. Captions and model releases required.

Tips: "We want writers with experience in researching nonsurgical medical subjects and interviewing experts with the ability to simplify technical and clinical information for the layman. A captivating lead and structural flow are essential. The most frequent mistakes made by writers are in writing articles that are too technical; in poor style; written for the wrong audience (publication not thoroughly studied), or have unreliable documentation or overzealous faith in the topic reflected by flimsy research and inappropriate tone."

LONGEVITY, General Media International, Inc., 1965 Broadway, New York NY 10023. (212)496-6100. FAX: (212)580-3693. Editor-in-Chief: Rona Cherry. A monthly magazine on medicine, health, fitness and life extension research. "*Longevity* is written for an audience with a median age of 40 who want to prolong their ability to lead a productive, vibrant, healthy life, and to look as good as they feel at their best." Estab. 1989. Circ. 300,000. **Pays on acceptance.** Publishes ms an average of 2 months after acceptance. Byline given. Offers 25% kill fee. Makes work-for-hire assignments. Query for electronic submissions.

Nonfiction: Consumer trends in anti-aging, new products, health. Query. Length: 150-950 words. Pays $100-2,500. Pays expenses of writers on assignment.

Columns/Departments: Antiaging News; Outer Limits; Looks Savers; Eat For Life; Childwise; Air, Earth & Water; Marketing Youth.

‡MEN'S FITNESS, Men's Fitness, Inc., 21100 Erwin St., Woodland Hills CA 91367. (818)884-6800. Executive Editor: Jim Rosenthal. Associate Editor: Ted Mason. 50% freelance written. Works with small number of new/unpublished writers each year. A monthly magazine for health-conscious men between the ages of 18 and 45. Provides reliable, entertaining guidance for the active male in all areas of lifestyle. Writers often share bylines with professional experts. Pays 1 month after acceptance. Publishes ms an average of 6 months after acceptance. Offers 20% kill fee. Buys all rights. Submit seasonal material 4 months in advance. Reports in 1 month. Writer's guidelines for 8½ × 11 SAE.

Nonfiction: Service, informative, inspirational, scientific studies written for men. Few interviews, regional news unless extraordinary. Query with published clips. Buys 50 mss/year. Length: 2,000-3,000 words. Pays $300-600. Occasionally buys mss devoted to specific fitness programs, including exercises, e.g. 6-week chest workout, aerobic weight-training routine. Buys 10-15 mss/year. Pays $250-300.

Columns/Departments: Nutrition, Mind Fitness, Grooming, Sex, Prevention, Health. Length: 1,250-2,000 words. Buys 40-50 mss/year. Pays $250-400.

Tips: "Articles are welcomed in all facets of men's health; they must be well-researched, entertaining and intelligent."

MEN'S HEALTH, Rodale Press, 33 E. Minor St., Emmaus PA 18098. (215)967-5171. Editor: Michael Lafavore. Managing Editor: Glenn Deutsch. 90% freelance written. Bimonthly magazine. "We publish health articles with a male slant. We take a broad view of health to encompass the physical and emotional." Circ. 250,000.

Pays on acceptance. Publishes ms an average of 2 months after acceptance. Byline given. Offers 15% kill fee. Buys first North American serial rights or second serial (reprint) rights. Submit seasonal/holiday material 6-8 months in advance. Previously published submissions OK. Query for electronic submissions. Reports in 2 weeks. Sample copy $2.95 with SAE and postage.

Nonfiction: Book excerpts, essays, exposé, interview/profile, personal experience and travel. Buys 50 mss/year. Query with published clips. Length: 100-2,000 words. Pays 25-50¢/word. Sometimes pays expenses of writers on assignment.

Photos: State availability of photos with submission. Offers no additional payment for photos accepted with ms. Model releases required. Buys one-time rights.

Columns/Departments: Eating Right (nutrition); Couples (relationships); Clinic (deals with a specific health problem) and Malegrams (short news items). Buys 10 mss/year. Query. Length: 800-1,000 words. Pays 25-60¢/word.

MUSCLE MAG INTERNATIONAL, 52 Bramsteele Rd., Unit 2, Brampton, Ontario L6W 3M5 Canada. Editor: Robert Kennedy. 80% freelance written. "We do not care if a writer is known or unknown; published or unpublished. We simply want good instructional articles on bodybuilding." For 16- to 50-year-old men and women interested in physical fitness and overall body improvement. Monthly magazine. Circ. 225,000. Buys all rights. **Pays on acceptance.** Publishes ms an average of 4 months after acceptance. Byline given. Buys 80 mss/year. Sample copy $4 and 9×12 SAE. Reports in 1 month. Submit complete ms with IRCs.

Nonfiction: Articles on ideal physical proportions and importance of supplements in the diet, training for muscle size. Should be helpful and instructional and appeal to young men and women who want to live life in a vigorous and healthy style. "We would like to see articles for the physical culturist on new muscle building techniques or an article on fitness testing." Informational, how-to, personal experience, interview, profile, inspirational, humor, historical, exposé, nostalgia, personal opinion, photo, spot news, new product, and merchandising technique articles. Length: 1,200-1,600 words. Pays 10¢/word. Sometimes pays the expenses of writers on assignment.

Columns/Departments: Nutrition Talk (eating for top results) and Shaping Up (improving fitness and stamina). Length: 1,300 words. Pays 10¢/word.

Photos: B&w and color photos are purchased with or without ms. Pays $15 for 8×10 glossy exercise photos; $15 for 8×10 b&w posing shots. Pays $100-200 for color cover and $20 for color used inside magazine (transparencies). More for "special" or "outstanding" work.

Fillers: Newsbreaks, puzzles, quotes of the champs. Length: open. Pays $5 minimum.

Tips: "The best way to break in is to seek out the muscle-building 'stars' and do in-depth interviews with biography in mind. Color training picture support essential. Writers have to make their articles informative in that readers can apply them to help gain bodybuilding success."

‡NATURAL BODY & FITNESS, P.O. Box A, New Britain PA 18901. (800)446-2060. Editor: Greta Blackburn. 100% freelance written. Bimonthly magazine of celebrity fitness. "We like anything that has to do with health and fitness, particularly if we can tie a celebrity in with it." Estab. 1988. Circ. 150,000. Pays on publication. Publishes ms an average of 3 months after acceptance. Byline given. Offers $50 kill fee. Buys first North American or second rights. Submit seasonal/holiday material 3 months in advance. Simultaneous submissions OK. Reports in 1 month on queries; 2 weeks on mss. Sample copy $3.25.

Nonfiction: How-to (exercise, diet, self-improvement), interview/profile, new product (health oriented). Special issues: holiday/ski issue, summer water sports issue. "We do not want any submission regarding health or fitness from anyone except qualified, credentialed experts." Buys 25 mss/year. Query with or without published clips, or send complete ms. Length: 800-3,500 words. Pays $100-250 for assigned articles; $50-150 for unsolicited articles. Sometimes pays expenses of writers on assignment.

Photos: State availability of photos with submission. Reviews 35mm transparencies and 3×5 prints. Offers $25-50 per photo. Identification of subjects required. Buys one-time rights.

Columns/Departments: Ya Gotta Laff (humorous/ironic slant on fitness experiences), 800-1,600 words; Experts Explain (authorities on aerobics, medicine, health write about their specialties), 1,600 words. Buys 12 mss/year. Query. Pays $50-150.

Tips: "We are open to almost anyone with something to say about health, fitness, exercise or diet, as long as he or she is well-versed in the field. Doctors, personal trainers or aerobics instructors with a good background are good writer prospects for us."

NEW BODY, The Magazine of Health & Fitness, GCR Publishing Group, Inc., 1700 Broadway, 34th Floor, New York NY 10019. (212)541-7100. Editor: Nayda Rondon. Managing Editor: Sandra Kosherick. 75% freelance written. Works with a small number of new/unpublished writers each year. A bimonthly magazine covering fitness and health for young, middle-class women. Circ. 125,000. Pays on publication. Publishes ms an average of 6 months after acceptance. Byline given. Offers negotiable kill fee. Buys all rights. Submit seasonal/holiday material 6 months in advance. Simultaneous submissions OK. Reports in 2 months.

Nonfiction: Health, exercise, psychology, relationships, diet, celebrities, and nutrition. "We do not cover bodybuilding—please no queries." No articles on "How I do exercises." Buys 75 mss/year. Query with published clips. Length: 800-1,500 words. Pays $100-300 for assigned articles; $50-150 for unsolicited articles.
Photos: Reviews contact sheets, transparencies and prints. Model releases and identification of subjects required. Buys all rights.
Tips: "We are moving toward more general interest women's material on relationships, emotional health, nutrition, etc. We look for a fresh angle—a new way to present the material. Celebrity profiles, fitness tips, and health news are good topics to consider. Make a clean statement of what your article is about, what it would cover—not why the article is important. We're interested in new ideas, new trends or new ways of looking at old topics."

SHAPE MAGAZINE, Weider Enterprises, 21100 Erwin St., Woodland Hills CA 91367. (818)595-0593. Editor: Barbara Harris. 10% freelance written. Prefers to work with published/established writers, but is eager to work with new/unpublished writers. Monthly magazine covering women's health and fitness. Circ. 785,000. Pays on publication. Publishes ms an average of 6 months after acceptance. Offers 1/3 kill fee. Buys all rights and reprint rights. Submit seasonal/holiday material 8 months in advance. Reports in 2 months.
Nonfiction: Book excerpts; expose (health, fitness related); how-to (get fit); interview/profile (of fit women); travel (spas). "We use health and fitness articles written by professionals in their specific fields. No articles which haven't been queried first." Query with clips of published work. Length: 500-2,000 words. Pays negotiable fee. Pays expenses of writers on assignment.

‡SOBER TIMES, The Recovery Magazine, Sober Times Inc., 3601 30th St., San Diego CA 92104. (619)295-5377. Editor: J.S. Rudolf, Ph.D. Managing Editor: Milt Schwartz. 70% freelance written. Monthly tabloid on recovery from addictions. "*Sober Times* provides information about recovery from drug, alcohol and other addictive behavior, and it champions sober, sane and healthy lifestyles." Estab. 1988. Circ. 42,000. Pays on publication. Publishes an average of 2 months after acceptance. Byline given. Buys all rights and makes work-for-hire assignments. Submit seasonal/holiday material 3 months in advance. Reports in 3 weeks. Free sample copy and writer's guidelines.
Nonfiction: Essays, general interest, humor, interview/profile, opinion, personal experience and photo feature. "No fiction or poetry will be considered. No medical or psychological jargon." Buys 90 mss/year. Send complete ms. Length: 900-2,000 words. Pays $100-300.
Photos: Send photos with submission. Reviews prints only. Offers no additional payment for photos accepted with ms. Identification of subjects required. Buys one-time rights.
Tips: "Send in finished ms with any prints. They will be returned if accompanied with self-addressed stamped envelope. Most accepted articles are under 1,000 words. Celebrity interviews should focus on recovery from addiction."

TOTAL HEALTH, Body, Mind and Spirit, Trio Publications, Suite 300, 6001 Topanga Cyn Blvd., Woodland Hills CA 91367. (818)887-6484. FAX: (818)887-7960. Editor: Robert L. Smith. Managing Editor: Rosemary Hofer. Prefers to work with published/established writers. 80% freelance written. A bimonthly magazine covering fitness, diet (weight loss), nutrition and mental health—"a family magazine about wholeness." Circ. 70,000. Pays on publication. Publishes ms an average of 2 months after acceptance. Byline given. Buys first rights. Submit seasonal/holiday material 4 months in advance. Reports in 1 month. Sample copy $1 with 9×12 SAE and 5 first class stamps; writer's guidelines for SAE.
Nonfiction: Exposé; how-to (pertaining to health and fitness); and religious (Judeo-Christian). Especially needs articles on skin and body care and power of positive thinking articles. No personal experience articles. Buys 48 mss/year. Send complete ms. Length: 2,000 words. Pays $50-75. Sometimes pays the expenses of writers on assignment.
Photos: State availability of photos with submission. Offers no additional payment for photos accepted with ms. Captions, model releases and identification of subjects required.
Columns/Departments: Query with or without published clips. Length: 1,000 words maximum. Pays $50-75 maximum.
Tips: "Feature-length articles are most open to freelancers. We are looking for more family fitness-exercise articles."

VEGETARIAN JOURNAL, Box 1463, Baltimore MD 21203. (301)366-VEGE. Editors: Charles Stahler/Debra Wasserman. A bimonthly journal on vegetarianism and animal rights. "*Vegetarian* issues include health, nutrition, animal rights and world hunger. Articles related to nutrition should be documented by established (mainstream) nutrition studies." Estab. 1982. Circ. 4,200. Pays on publication. Publishes ms an average of 3-5 months after acceptance. Byline given. Makes work-for-hire assignments. Submit seasonal/holiday material 6 months in advance. Reports in 1 month. Sample copy $3; writer's guidelines for SASE.
Nonfiction: Book excerpts, expose, how-to, interview/profile, new products, travel. "At present we are only looking for in-depth articles on selected nutrition subjects from registered dietitians or M.D.'s. Please query with your background. Possibly some in-depth practical and researched articles from others. No miracle cures

or use of supplements." Buys 1-5 mss/year. Query with or without published clips or send complete ms. Length: 2,500-8,250 words. Pays $10-25. Sometimes pays writers with contributor copies or other premiums "if not a specific agreed upon in-depth article." Sometimes pays the expenses of writers on assignment.

Photos: State availability of photos with submission. Reviews prints. Offers additional payment for photos accepted with ms. Identification of subjects required. Buys one-time rights.

Poetry: Avant-garde, free verse, haiku, light verse, traditional. "Poetry should be related to vegetarianism, world hunger, or animal rights. No graphic animal abuse. We do not want to see the word, blood, in any form." Pays in copies.

Tips: "We are most open to vegan-oriented medical professionals or vegetarian/animal rights activists who are new to freelancing."

VEGETARIAN TIMES, Box 570, Oak Park IL 60303. (312)848-8100. FAX: (312)848-8175. Executive Editor: Sally Cullen. 30% freelance written. Prefers to work with published/established writers; works with small number of new/unpublished writers each year. Monthly magazine. Circ. 170,000. Rights purchased vary with author and material. Buys first serial rights or all rights. Byline given unless extensive revisions are required or material is incorporated into a larger article. **Pays on acceptance.** Publishes ms an average of 6 months after acceptance. Computer printout submissions acceptable; prefers letter-quality. Submit seasonal material 6 months in advance. Reports in 1 month. Query. Sample copy $3; writer's guidelines for #10 SASE.

Nonfiction: Features articles inform readers about how vetetarianism relates to diet, cooking, lifestyle, health, consumer choices, natural foods, environmental concerns and animal welfare. "All material should be well documented and researched, and written in a sophisticated yet lively style." Informational, how-to, personal experience, interview, profile. Length: average 2,000 words. Pays 20¢/word and up, though a flat rate may be negotiated. Will also use 500-word items for new digest. Sometimes pays expenses of writers on assignment.

Photos: Pays $40 for b&w; $40 for color photos used.

Tips: "You don't have to be a vegetarian to write for *Vegetarian Times*, but it is VITAL that your article has a vegetarian slant. The best way to pick up that slant is to read several issues of the magazine (no doubt a tip you've heard over and over). We are very particular about the articles we run and thus tend to ask for rewrites. The best way to break in is by querying us on a well-defined topic that is appropriate for our news digest section. Make sure your idea is well thought out before querying."

VIBRANT LIFE, A Christian Guide for Total Health, Review and Herald Publishing Assn., 55 W. Oak Ridge Dr., Hagerstown MD 21740. (301)791-7000. 20% freelance written. Enjoys working with published/ established writers; works with a small number of new/unpublished writers each year. Bimonthly magazine covering health articles (especially from a prevention angle and with a Christian slant). Estab. 1849. Circ. 50,000. **Pays on acceptance.** "The average length of time between acceptance of a freelance-written manuscript and publication of the material depends upon the topics; some immediately used; others up to 2 years." Byline always given. Offers 25% kill fee. Buys first serial rights, first North American serial rights, or sometimes second serial (reprint) rights. Submit seasonal/holiday material 6 months in advance. Reports in 2 months. Sample copy $1; free writer's guidelines for #10 SASE.

Nonfiction: Interview/profile (with personalities on health). "We seek practical articles promoting better health and a more fulfilled life. We especially like features on breakthroughs in medicine, and most aspects of health." Buys 20-25 mss/year. Send complete ms. Length: 750-1,800 words. Pays $125-250. Pays the expenses of writers on assignment.

Photos: Send photos with ms. Needs 35mm transparencies. Not interested in b&w photos.

Tips: "*Vibrant Life* is published for the typical man/woman on the street, age 20-50. Therefore articles must be written in an interesting, easy-to-read style. Information must be reliable; no faddism. We are more conservative than other magazines in our field. Request a sample copy, and study the magazine and writer's guidelines."

WEIGHT WATCHERS MAGAZINE, 360 Lexington Ave., 11th Floor, New York NY 10017. FAX: (212)687-4398. Editor-in-Chief: Lee Haiken. Articles Editor: Ruth Papazian. 50% freelance written. Works with a small number of new/unpublished writers each year. Monthly publication for those interested in weight loss and weight maintenance through sensible eating and health/nutrition guidance. Estab. 1968. Circ. 1 million. Buys first North American serial rights only. Pays on publication. Publishes ms an average of 6 months after acceptance. Reports in 2 months. Sample copy and writer's guidelines for 8½×11 SAE and $1.75.

Nonfiction: "We are interested in general health and medical articles; nutrition pieces based on documented research results; fitness stories that feature types of exercises that don't require special skills or excessive financial costs; and weight loss stories that focus on interesting people and situations. While our articles are authoritative, they are written in a light, upbeat style; a humorous tone is acceptable as long as it is in good taste. To expedite the fact-checking process, we require a second copy of your manuscript that is annotated in the margins with the telephone numbers of all interview subjects, and with citations from such written sources as books, journal articles, magazines, newsletters, newspapers, or press releases. You must attach photocopies of these sources to the annotated manuscript with relevant passages highlighted and referenced to your margin notes. We will be happy to reimburse you for copying costs." Send detailed queries with published clips and SASE. No full-length mss; send feature ideas, as well as before-and-after weight loss story ideas dealing either with celebrities or "real people" Length: 1,000-1,200 words. Pays $250-500.

Tips: "Though we prefer working with established writers, *Weight Watchers Magazine* welcomes new writers as well. As long as your query is tightly written, shows style and attention to detail, and gives evidence that you are knowledgeable about your subject matter, we won't reject you out-of-hand just because you don't have three clips attached. When developing a story for us, keep in mind that we prefer interview subjects to be medical professionals with university appointments who have published in their field of expertise."

THE YOGA JOURNAL, California Yoga Teachers Association, 2054 University Ave., Berkeley CA 94704. (415)841-9200. FAX: (415)548-3374. Editor: Stephan Bodian. 75% freelance written. Bimonthly magazine covering yoga, holistic health, conscious living, spiritual practices, and nutrition. "We reach a middle-class, educated audience interested in self-improvement and higher consciousness." Estab. 1975. Circ. 60,000. Pays on publication. Publishes ms an average of 6 months after acceptance. Byline given. Offers $50 kill fee. Buys first North American serial rights only. Submit seasonal/holiday material 4 months in advance. Simultaneous queries OK. Reports in 6 weeks on queries; 2 months on mss. Sample copy $3; free writer's guidelines.

Nonfiction: Book excerpts; how-to (exercise, yoga, massage, etc.); inspirational (yoga or related); interview/profile; opinion; photo feature; and travel (if about yoga). "Yoga is our main concern, but our principal features in each issue highlight other New Age personalities and endeavors. Nothing too far-out and mystical. Prefer stories about Americans incorporating yoga, meditation, etc., into their normal lives." Buys 40 mss/year. Query. Length: 750-3,500 words. Pays $150-400.

Photos: Lawrence Watson, art director. Send photos with ms. Pays $200-300 for cover transparencies; $15-25 for 8×10 b&w prints. Model release (for cover only) and identification of subjects required. Buys one-time rights.

Columns/Departments: Forum; Cooking; Well-Being; Psychology; Profiles; Music (reviews of New Age music); and Book Reviews. Buys 12-15 mss/year. Pays $50-150 for columns; $35-60 for book reviews.

Tips: "We always read submissions. We are very open to freelance material and want to encourage writers to submit to our magazine. We're looking for out-of-state contributors, particularly in the Midwest and East Coast."

YOUR HEALTH, Globe Communications Corp., 5401 NW Broken Sound Blvd., Boca Raton FL 33487. (407)997-7733. Editor: Susan Gregg. Associate Editor: Lisa Rappa. 50% freelance written. Semi-monthly magazine on health and fitness. "*Your Health* is a lay-person magazine covering the entire gamut of health, fitness and medicine." Estab. 1962. Circ. 50,000. Pays on publication. Byline given. Offers $10 kill fee. Buys first North American serial rights and second serial (reprint) rights. Submit seasonal/holiday material 3 months in advance. Previously published submissions OK. Reports in 1 month on queries; 6 weeks on mss. Free sample copy and writer's guidelines.

Nonfiction: Book excerpts, exposé, general interest, how-to (on general health and fitness topics), inspirational, interview/profile, new product and personal experience. "No general articles, such as 'Why vitamins are good for you.' Give us something new and different." Buys 75-100 mss/year. Query with published clips or send complete ms. Length: 300-1,000 words. Pays $15-75. Sometimes pays expenses of writers on assignment.

Photos: Send photos with submission. Reviews contact sheets, negatives, transparencies and prints. Offers $50-100 per photo. Captions, model releases and identification of subjects required. Buys one-time rights.

Tips: "We are especially interested in profiles and features on common people and celebrities who have conquered illness or who participate in a unique physical fitness regimen. Freelancers can best break in by offering us stories of national interest that we won't find through other channels, such as wire services."

YOUR HEALTH, Meridian Publishing Inc., Box 10010, Ogden UT 84409. (801)394-9446. 65% freelance written. A monthly in-house magazine covering personal health, customized with special imprint titles for various businesses, organizations and associations. "Articles should be timeless, noncontroversial, upscale and positive, and the subject matter should have national appeal." Circ. 40,000. **Pays on acceptance.** Publishes ms an average of 8 months after acceptance. Byline given. Buys first rights and non-exclusive reprint rights. Simultaneous, photocopied, and previously published submissions OK. Computer printout submissions acceptable; prefers letter-quality. Reports in 6 weeks. Sample copy $1 with 9×12 SAE; writer's guidelines for #10 SAE with 1 first class stamp. (All requests for sample copies and guidelines should be addressed to—Attention: Editorial Assistant.)

Nonfiction: General interest stories about individual's health care needs, including preventative approaches to good health. Topics include advances in medical technology, common maladies and treatments, fitness and nutrition, hospital and home medical care, and personality profiles of both health care professionals and exceptional people coping with disability or illness. Also articles slanted to geriatric readership. "We almost never use a first person narrative. No articles about chiropractic, podiatry or lay midwifery articles." Medical pieces must be accompanied by a list of checkable resources. Buys 40 mss/year. Query. Length: 1,000-1,200 words. Pays 15¢/word for first rights plus non-exclusive reprint rights. Payment for second rights is negotiable.

Authors retain the right to resell material after it is printed by *Your Health*.

Photos: Send photos or state availability with submission. Reviews 35mm and 2¼×2¼ transparencies and 5×7 or 8×10 prints. Offers $35/inside photo and $50/cover photo. Captions, model releases and identification of subjects required.

Tips: "The key for the freelancer is a well-written query letter that demonstrates that the subject of the article has national appeal; establishes that any medical claims are based on interviews with experts and/or reliable documented sources; shows that the article will have a clear, focused theme; outlines the availability (from the writer, photographer, or a PR source) of top-quality color photos; and gives evidence that the writer/photographer is a professional, even if a beginner. The best way to get started as a contributor to *Your Health* is to prove that you can submit a well-focused article, based on facts, written clearly using AP style, along with a variety of beautiful color transparencies to illustrate the story. Material is reviewed by a medical board and must be approved by them."

YOUR HEALTH & FITNESS, General Learning Corp., 60 Revere Dr., Northbrook IL 60062-1563. (312)205-3000. Executive Editor: Laura Ruekberg. Managing Editor: Carol Lezak. 90-95% freelance written. Prefers to work with published/established writers. A bimonthly magazine covering health and fitness. Needs "general, educational material on health, fitness and safety that can be read and understood easily by the layman." Estab. 1969. Circ. 1 million. Pays within 30 days after acceptance. Publishes ms an average of 6 months after acceptance. No byline given. Offers 50% kill fee. Buys all rights. Submit seasonal/holiday material 6 months in advance.

Nonfiction: General interest. "All article topics assigned; send resumes and writing samples. All topics are determined a year in advance of publication by editors; no unsolicited manuscripts." Buys approximately 65 mss/year. Length: 350-1,400 words. Pays $100-700 for assigned articles. Sometimes pays the expenses of writers on assignment.

Photos: Offers no additional payment for photos accepted with ms.

Tips: "Write to a general audience that has only a surface knowledge of health and fitness topics. Possible subjects include exercise and fitness, psychology, nutrition, safety, disease, drug data, and health concerns."

History

Listed here are magazines and other periodicals written for historical collectors, genealogy enthusiasts, historic preservationists and researchers. Editors of history magazines look for fresh accounts of past events in a readable style. Some publications cover an era, like the Civil War, or a region while others specialize in historic preservation.

AMERICAN HERITAGE, 60 Fifth Ave., New York NY 10011. Editor: Byron Dobell. 70% freelance written. 8 times/year. Circ. 280,000. Usually buys first North American rights or all rights. Byline given. **Pays on acceptance.** Publishes ms an average of 6-12 months after acceptance. Before submitting material, "check our index to see whether we have already treated the subject." Submit seasonal material 1 year in advance. Reports in 1 month. Writer's guidelines for SAE and 1 first class stamp.

Nonfiction: Wants "historical articles by scholars or journalists intended for intelligent lay readers rather than for professional historians." Emphasis is on authenticity, accuracy and verve. "Interesting documents, photographs and drawings are always welcome. Query." Style should stress "readability and accuracy." Buys 30 unsolicited mss/year. Length: 1,500-5,000 words. Sometimes pays the expenses of writers on assignment.

Tips: "We have over the years published quite a few 'firsts' from young writers whose historical knowledge, research methods and writing skills met our standards. The scope and ambition of a new writer tell us a lot about his or her future usefulness to us. A major article gives us a better idea of the writer's value. Everything depends on the quality of the material. We don't really care whether the author is 20 and unknown, or 80 and famous, or vice versa."

AMERICAN HISTORY ILLUSTRATED, P.O. Box 8200, Harrisburg PA 17105. (717)657-9555. FAX: (717)657-9526. Editor: Ed Holm. 60% freelance written. "We are backlogged with submissions and prefer not to receive unsolicited complete manuscripts at this time." A bimonthly magazine of cultural, social, military and political history published for a general audience. Estab. 1966. Circ. 160,000. **Pays on acceptance.** Byline given. Buys all rights. Query for electronic submissions. Reports in 10 weeks on queries. Writer's guidelines for #10 SAE and 1 first class stamp; sample copy and guidelines for $3.50 (amount includes 3rd class postage) or $3 and 9×12 SAE with 4 first class stamps.

Nonfiction: Regular features include American Profiles (biographies of noteworthy historical figures); Artifacts (stories behind historical objects); Portfolio (pictorial features on artists, photographers and graphic subjects); Digging Up History (coverage of recent major archaeological and historical discoveries); and Testaments to the Past (living history articles on major restored historical sites). "Material is presented on a popular rather than a scholarly level." Writers are required to query before submitting ms. "Query letters should be limited to a concise 1-2 page proposal defining your article with an emphasis on its unique qualities." Buys 30-40 mss/year. Length: 1,000-5,000 words depending on type of article. Pays $200-1,000. Sometimes pays the expenses of writers on assignment.

Photos: Occasionally buys 8×10 glossy prints or color transparencies with mss; welcomes suggestions for illustrations. Pays for the reproduced color illustrations that the author provides.

Tips: "Key prerequisites for publication are thorough research and accurate presentation, precise English usage and sound organization, a lively style, and a high level of human interest. We are especially interested in publishing 'Testaments to the Past' articles (on significant ongoing living history sites), as well as top-quality articles on significant American women, on the Vietnam era, and on social/cultural history. Submissions received without return postage will not be considered or returned. Inappropriate materials include: fiction, book reviews, travelogues, personal/family narratives not of national significance, articles about collectibles/antiques, living artists, local/individual historic buildings/landmarks and articles of a current editorial nature."

‡AMERICANA MAGAZINE, Americana Magazine, Inc., 29 W. 38th St., New York NY 10018. (212)398-1550. Editor: Sandra Wilmot. Senior Editor: Helen Dunn. 80% freelance written. Bimonthly magazine taking a contemporary approach to American history. Estab. 1973. Circ. 300,000. Pays on publication. Byline given. Offers $150 kill fee. Buys first North American serial rights. Submit seasonal/holiday material 3 months in advance. Reports in 1 month on queries; 3 months on mss. Sample copy for 8×10 SAE and 5 first class stamps. Free writer's guidelines.

Nonfiction: Book excerpts, how-to restoration and preservation, interview/profile, photo feature, travel. No straight historical articles without a contemporary angle. Buys 20-30 mss/year. Query with published clips, or send complete ms. Length: 500-2,500 words. Pays $75-600. Pays expenses of writers on assignment. Send photos with submission. Reviews negatives and transparencies. Offers $25-300 per photo. Buys one-time rights.

Columns/Departments: Sampler (short, newsy articles), 500 words. Query with published clips. Pays $75.

Tips: "Query one idea at a time and be patient. Stress the contemporary, not historical angle. Include photographs with query."

ANCESTRY NEWSLETTER, Ancestry, Inc., P.O. Box 476, Salt Lake City UT 84110. (801)531-1790. Editor: Robb Barr. 95% freelance written. Eager to work with new/unpublished writers. A bimonthly newsletter covering genealogy and family history. "We publish practical, instructional, and informative pieces specifically applicable to the field of genealogy. Our audience is the active genealogist, both hobbyist and professional." Estab. 1984. Circ. 8,200. Pays on publication. Publishes ms an average of 9 months after acceptance. Byline given. Buys first North American serial rights or all rights. Submit seasonal/holiday material 4 months in advance. Simultaneous submissions OK. Reports in 2 weeks. Sample copy and writer's guidelines for 3 first class stamps.

Nonfiction: General interest (genealogical); historical; how-to (genealogical research techniques); instructional; and photo feature (genealogically related). No unpublished or published family histories, genealogies, the "story of my great-grandmother," or personal experiences. Buys 25-30 mss/year. Send complete ms. Length: 1,500-4,000 words. Pays $50.

Photos: Send photos with submission. Reviews contact sheets and 5×7 prints. Offers no additional payment for photos accepted with ms. Identification of subjects required. Buys one-time rights.

Tips: "You don't have to be famous, but you must know something about genealogy. Our readers crave any information which might assist them in their ancestral quest."

THE ARTILLERYMAN, Cutter & Locke, Inc., Publishers, 4 Water St., P.O. Box C, Arlington MA 02174. (617)646-2010. FAX: (617)643-1864. Editor: C. Peter Jorgensen. 60% freelance written. Quarterly magazine covering antique artillery, fortifications, and crew-served weapons 1750 to 1900 for competition shooters, collectors and living history reenactors using artillery; "emphasis on Revolutionary War and Civil War but includes everyone interested in pre-1900 artillery and fortifications, preservation, construction of replicas, etc." Estab. 1979. Circ. 2,600. Pays on publication. Publishes ms an average of 3-6 months after acceptance. Byline given. Not copyrighted. Buys one-time rights. Simultaneous queries and simultaneous and previously published submissions OK. Reports in 3 weeks. Sample copy and writer's guidelines for $8\frac{1}{2} \times 11$ SAE and 4 first class stamps.

Nonfiction: Historical; how-to (reproduce ordnance equipment/sights/implements/tools/accessories, etc.); interview/profile; new product; opinion (must be accompanied by detailed background of writer and include references); personal experience; photo feature; technical (must have footnotes); and travel (where to find interesting antique cannon). Interested in "artillery *only*, for sophisticated readers. Not interested in other weapons, battles in general." Buys 24-30 mss/year. Send complete ms. Length: 300 words minimum. Pays $20-60. Sometimes pays the expenses of writers on assignment.

Photos: Send photos with ms. Pays $5 for 5×7 and larger b&w prints. Captions and identification of subjects required.

Tips: "We regularly use freelance contributions for Places-to-Visit, Cannon Safety, The Workshop and Unit Profiles departments. Also need pieces on unusual cannon or cannon with a known and unique history. To judge whether writing style and/or expertise will suit our needs, writers should ask themselves if they could knowledgeably talk *artillery* with an expert. Subject matter is of more concern than writer's background."

CANADIAN WEST, P.O. Box 3399, Langley, British Columbia V3A 4R7 Canada. (604)534-9378. Editor-in-Chief: Garnet Basque. 80-100% freelance written. Works with a small number of new/unpublished writers each year. Emphasizes pioneer history, primarily of British Columbia, Alberta and the Yukon. Quarterly magazine. Estab. 1985. Circ. 8,000. Pays on publication. Publishes ms an average of 6 months after acceptance. Buys first North American serial rights. Phone queries OK. Query for electronic submissions. Previously published submissions OK. Reports in 2 months. Sample copy and writer's guidelines for $1.50 and 9×12 SAE.

Nonfiction: How-to (related to gold panning and dredging); historical (pioneers, shipwrecks, massacres, battles, exploration, logging, Indians, ghost towns, mining camps, gold rushes and railroads). Interested in an occasional U.S. based article from states bordering B.C. when the story also involves some aspect of Canadian history. No American locale articles. Buys 28 mss/year. Submit complete ms. Length: 2,000-3,500 words. Pays $100-300.

Photos: All mss must include photos or other artwork. Submit photos with ms. Pays $10 per b&w photo and $20 per color photo. Captions preferred. "Photographs are kept for future reference with the right to re-use. However, we do not forbid other uses, generally, as these are historical prints from archives."

Columns/Departments: Open to suggestions for new columns/departments.

‡CIVIL WAR TIMES ILLUSTRATED, 2245 Kohn Rd., P.O. Box 8200, Harrisburg PA 17105. (717)657-9555. Editor: John E. Stanchak. 90% freelance written. Works with a small number of new/unpublished writers each year. Magazine published monthly except July and August. Estab. 1961. Circ. 164,000. **Pays on acceptance.** Publishes ms an average of 12-18 months after acceptance. Buys all rights, first rights or one-time rights, or makes work-for-hire assignments. Submit seasonal/holiday material 1 year in advance. Query for electronic submissions. Reports in 2 weeks on queries; 3 months on mss. Sample copy $3; free writer's guidelines.

Nonfiction: Profile, photo feature, and Civil War historical material. "Positively no fiction or poetry." Buys 20 freelance mss/year. Length: 2,500-5,000 words. Query. Pays $75-450. Sometimes pays the expenses of writers on assignment.

Photos: W. Douglas Shirk, art director. State availability of photos. Pays $5-50 for 8×10 b&w glossy prints and copies of Civil War photos; $400-500 for 4-color cover photos; and $100-250 for color photos for interior use.

Tips: "We're very open to new submissions. Query us after reading several back issues, then submit illustration and art possibilities along with the query letter for the best 'in.' Never base the narrative solely on family stories or accounts. Submissions must be written in a popular style but based on solid academic research. Manuscripts are required to have marginal source annotations."

EL PALACIO, The Magazine of the Museum of New Mexico, Box 2087, Santa Fe NM 87504. (505)982-8594. Editor-in-Chief: Karen Meadows. 15% freelance written. Prefers to work with published/established writers. Emphasizes the collections of the Museum of New Mexico and anthropology, ethnology, history, folk and fine arts, Southwestern culture, and natural history as these topics pertain to the Museum of New Mexico and the Southwest. Quarterly magazine. Circ. 4,500. Pays on publication. We hope "to attract professional writers who can translate scholarly and complex information into material that will interest and inform a general educated readership." Acquires first North American serial rights. Byline given. Submit seasonal/holiday queries 1 year in advance. Query for electronic submissions. Reports in 6 weeks. Sample copy $6 and 9×12 SAE with $1.85 postage. Writer's guidelines for #10 SASE.

Nonfiction: Historical (on Southwest; substantive but readable — not too technical); folk art; archaeology; fine art (Southwest); photo essay; anthropology; material culture of the Southwest. Buys 3-4 unsolicited mss/year. Recent articles documented the history of Las Vegas, New Mexico; women in New Mexico; collections of the Museum of New Mexico; and contemporary photography. "Other articles that have been very successful are a photo-essay on Chaco Canyon and other archaeological spots of interest in the state and an article on Indian baskets and their function in Indian life." Query with credentials. Length: 1,750-4,000 words. Pays $50 honorarium.

Photos: Photos often purchased with accompanying ms, some on assignment. Prefers b&w prints. Informative captions required. Pays "on contract" for 5×7 (or larger) b&w photos and 5×7 or 8½×11 prints or 35mm color transparencies. Send prints and transparencies. Total purchase price for ms includes payment for photos.

Columns/Departments: Curator's Choice and Conservator's Choice.

Tips: *"El Palacio* magazine offers a unique opportunity for writers with technical ability to have their work published and seen by influential professionals as well as avidly interested lay readers. The magazine is highly regarded in its field. The writer should have strong writing skills, an understanding of the Southwest and of the field written about. Be able to communicate technical concepts to the educated reader. We like to have a bibliography, list of sources, or suggested reading list with every submission."

GHOST TOWN QUARTERLY, McLean Enterprises, P.O. Box 714, Philipsburg MT 59858. (406)859-3365. Editor: Donna B. McLean. 90% freelance written. Quarterly magazine on ghost towns and abandoned sites — U.S., Canada and Mexico. "Materials should be factual yet interesting to the general public. We want to present history in such a manner that we are a human-interest magazine yet valuable to historians." Estab. 1988. Circ. 6,000. Byline given. Offers $20 kill fee. Buys first North American serial rights, first rights, one-time rights, second serial (reprint) rights or simultaneous rights. Submit seasonal/holiday material 6 months in advance. Simultaneous and (only occasionally) previously published submissions. Reports in 3 weeks on queries; 3 months on mss. Sample copy for $3.50. Writer's guidelines for SAE with 1 first class stamp.

Nonfiction: General interest, historical/nostalgic, interview/profile, interesting, unusual up-coming events of a historical nature. Buys 80 mss/year. Send complete ms. Length: 300-6,500 words. Pays 5¢/word. Pays in contributor copies only if requested by the writer.

Photos: Send photos with submission. Reviews 5 × 7 prints, smaller or larger also OK. Also review picture postcards (old). Offers $5-50 per photo (cover photo). Captions required. Buys one-time rights.

Columns/Departments: Student's Corner (materials submitted by students from kindergarten through 12th grade. 2 pages reserved in each issue for this feature. Follow same guidelines as for adult contributors. Photos, artwork, poetry, and articles acceptable, 1,500 words maximum. Buys 30 mss/year. Send complete ms. Pays 5¢/word.

Poetry: Avant-garde, free verse, haiku, light verse and traditional. No foul language or lewdness. No extreme negativism unless it has an important purpose relevant to our themes. Buys 20 poems/year. Submit maximum 3 poems. Pays 5¢/word.

Fillers: Anecdotes, facts, short humor. Buys 20/year. Length: 30-300 words. Pays 5¢/word. Cartoons. Buys 16/year. Pays $10.

Tips: "If submitting an article, research facts and include bibliographical information. Interview people who may have first-hand knowledge, and include interesting facts you uncover, quotes from diaries, photocopies of old documents and historical photographs when available. We like to feature the unusual, things people may not have realized before—such as silver being found in petrified wood."

GOOD OLD DAYS, America's Premier Nostalgia Magazine, House of White Birches, 306 E. Parr Rd., Berne IN 46711. (219)589-8741. Editor: Rebekah Montgomery. Managing Editor: Bettina Miller. 75% freelance written. A monthly magazine of first person nostalgia, 1900-1955. "We look for strong narratives showing life as it was in the first part of this century. Our readership is nostalgia buffs, history enthusiasts, and the people who actually lived and grew up in this era." Pays on publication. Publishes ms an average of 8 months after acceptance. Byline given. Buys all rights, first North American serial rights or one-time rights. Submit seasonal/holiday material 8 months in advance. Reports in 3 weeks. Sample copy $2; writer's guidelines for #10 SASE.

Nonfiction: Historical/nostalgic, humor, interview/profile, personal experience, photo feature. Instructional (how to cane a chair, how to hand-bundle a shock of corn, etc.). Buys 300 mss/year. Query or send complete ms. Length: 4,000 words maximum. Pays 2-4¢/word or more, depending on quality and photos.

Photos: Send photos with submission. Offers $5/photo. Identification of subjects required. Buys one-time or all rights.

MEDIA HISTORY DIGEST, Media History Digest Corp., % Editor and Publisher, 11 W. 19th St., New York NY 10011. Editor: Hiley H. Ward. 100% freelance written. Semiannual (will probably return to being quarterly) magazine. Estab. 1980. Circ. 2,000. Pays on publication. Publishes ms an average of 4 months after acceptance. Byline given. Buys first or second serial (reprint) rights. Submit seasonal/holiday material 8 months in advance. Previously published submissions OK. Reports in 2 months. Sample copy $2.50.

Nonfiction: Historical/nostalgic (media); humor (media history); and puzzles (media history). Buys 15 mss/year. Query. Length: 1,500-3,000 words. Pays $125 for assigned articles; pays $100 for unsolicited articles. Pays in contributor copies for articles prepared by university graduate students. Sometimes pays the expenses of writers on assignment.

For explanation of symbols, see the Key to Symbols and Abbreviations on Page 5. For unfamiliar words, see the Glossary.

Photos: Send photos with submission. Buys first or reprint rights.

Columns/Departments: Quiz Page (media history) and "Media Hysteria" (media history humor). Query. Pays $50-125 for humor; $25 for puzzles.

Fillers: Anecdotes and short humor on topics of media history.

Tips: "Present in-depth enterprising material targeted for our specialty—media history, pre-1970."

‡**MHQ, The Quarterly Journal of Military History,** MHQ, Inc., 29 West 38th St., New York NY 10018. (212)398-1550. Editor: Robert Cowley. Managing Editor: Barbara Benton. 95% freelance written. Quarterly hardcover magazine on military history. "Our readers are people with a special interest in military history that is scholarly (well researched), yet written in a lively and imaginative style." Estab. 1988. Circ. 30,000. Pays on acceptance. Publishes ms an average of 6 months after acceptance. Byline given. Kill fee varies. Buys first rights and second serial (reprint) rights. Reports in 1 month on queries; 3 months on mss. Sample copy $20. Writer's guidelines not available.

Nonfiction: Book excerpts, essays, exposé, interview/profile and personal experience. "No articles weighted down with professional jargon." Buys 40 mss/year. Query with or without pubilshed clips, or send complete ms. Length: 2,000-4,000 words. Pays $300-1,200 for assigned articles; $200-800 for unsolicited articles. Sometimes pays expenses of writers on assignment.

Photos: State availability of photos with submission. Reviews contact sheets, negatives, transparencies and prints. Offers no additional payment for photos accepted with ms. Buys one-time rights.

Columns/Departments: Tactical Exercises (military tactics), 1,000 words; Experience of War (personal memoirs), 800-1,000 words; Arms and Men (weaponry), 1,000 words; and In Review (reviews recent publications in military history), 1,000 words. Buys 16 mss/year. Query with published clips. Pays $250-600.

Tips: "Most of our contributors are experts in the field of military history. We will consider any article on any aspect of military history that is well researched, well written, and approaches its subject from a fresh angle. Acceptance may also depend on our needs of a particular moment."

MILITARY HISTORY, Empire Press, 602 S. King St. #300, Leesburg VA 22075. (703)771-9400. Editor: C. Brian Kelly. 95% freelance written. Circ. 200,000. "We'll work with anyone, established or not, who can provide the goods and convince us as to its accuracy." Bimonthly magazine covering all military history of the world. "We strive to give the general reader accurate, highly readable, often narrative popular history, richly accompanied by period art." Pays on publication. Publishes ms 1-2 years after acceptance. Byline given. Buys all rights. Submit anniversary material 1 year in advance. Reports in 2 months on queries; 6 months on mss. Sample copy $3.95; writer's guidelines for SASE.

Nonfiction: Historical; interview (military figures of commanding interest); personal experience (only occasionally). Buys 18 mss, plus 6 interviews/year. Query with published clips. "To propose an article, submit a short, self-explanatory query summarizing the story proposed, its highlights and/or significance. State also your own expertise, access to sources or proposed means of developing the pertinent information." Length: 4,000 words. Pays $400.

Columns/Departments: Espionage, weaponry, personality, travel (with military history of the place) and books—all relating to military history. Buys 24 mss/year. Query with published clips. Length: 2,000 words. Pays $200.

Tips: "We would like journalistically 'pure' submissions that adhere to basics, such as full name at first reference, same with rank, and definition of prior or related events, issues cited as context or obscure military 'hardware.' Read the magazine, discover our style, and avoid subjects already covered. Pick stories with strong art possibilities (*real* art and photos), send photocopies, tell us where to order the art. Avoid historical overview, focus upon an event with appropriate and accurate context. Provide bibliography. Tell the story in popular but elegant style."

MILITARY IMAGES, RD2, Box 2542, East Stroudsburg PA 18301. (717)476-1388. Editor: Harry Roach. 100% freelance written. A bimonthly journal reaching a broad spectrum of military historians, antiquarians, collectors and dealers. *MI* covers American military history from 1839 to 1900, with heavy concentration on the Civil War. Circ. 3,000. Pays on publication. Byline given. Buys first North American serial rights. Submit seasonal/holiday material 2 months in advance. Query for electronic submissions. Reports in 2 weeks on queries; 1 month on mss. Sample copy for $3; free writer's guidelines.

Nonfiction: Book excerpts, historical, humor, interview/profile, photo feature and technical. No articles not tied to, or illustrated by, period photos. Buys 36 mss/year. Query. Length: 1,000-12,000 words. Pays $40-200.

Photos: State availability of photos with submission, or send photocopy with query. Reviews 5 × 7 or larger b&w prints. Offers no additional payment for photos accepted with ms. Captions required.

Columns/Departments: The Darkroom (technical, 19th-century photo processes, preservation), 1,000 words. Buys 6 mss/year. Query. Length: 1,000-3,000 words. Pays $20-75.

Tips: "Concentrate on details of the common soldier, his uniform, his equipment, his organizations. We do not publish broad-brush histories of generals and campaigns. Articles must be supported by period photos."

OLD MILL NEWS, Society for the Preservation of Old Mills, 604 Ensley Dr., Rt. 29, Knoxville TN 37920. (615)577-7757. Editor: Michael LaForest. 40% freelance written. Quarterly magazine covering "water, wind, animal, steam power mills (usually grist mills)." Estab. 1972. Circ. 2,500. **Pays on acceptance.** Byline given. Buys first North American serial rights or first rights. Simultaneous submissions OK. Reports in 2 weeks. Sample copy $3.

Nonfiction: Historical and technical. "No poetry, recipes, mills converted to houses, commercial or alternative uses, nostalgia." Buys 8 mss/year. Query with or without published clips, or send complete ms. Length: 400-1,000 words. Pays $15-50.

Photos: Send photos with submission. "At least one recent photograph of subject is highly recommended." Uses b&w or color prints only; no transparencies. Offers $5-10 per photo. Identification of subjects required. Buys one-time rights.

Fillers: Short humor. Buys 3-4/year. Length: 50-200 words. Pays $10 maximum.

Tips: "An interview with the mill owner/operator is usually necessary. Accurate presentation of the facts and good English are required."

OLD WEST, Western Periodicals, Inc., P.O. Box 2107, Stillwater OK 74076. (405)743-3370. Quarterly magazine. Byline given. See *True West*.

PERSIMMON HILL, 1700 NE 63rd St., Oklahoma City OK 73111. FAX: (405)478-4714. Editor: M.J. Van Deventer. 70% freelance written. Prefers to work with published/established writers and works with a small number of new/unpublished writers each year. For an audience interested in Western art, Western history, ranching and rodeo, including historians, artists, ranchers, art galleries, schools, and libraries. Publication of the National Cowboy Hall of Fame and Western Heritage Center. Quarterly. Estab. 1965. Circ. 15,000. Buys first rights. Byline given. Buys 12-14 mss/year. Pays on scheduling of article. Publishes ms an average of 6 months after acceptance. Reporting time on mss varies. Sample copy $5 plus 5 first class stamps; writer's guidelines for #10 SASE.

Nonfiction: Historical and contemporary articles on famous Western figures connected with pioneering the American West, Western art, rodeo, cowboys, etc. (or biographies of such people), stories of Western flora and animal life, and environmental subjects. "We want thoroughly researched and historically authentic material written in a popular style. May have a humorous approach to subject. No broad, sweeping, superficial pieces; i.e., the California Gold Rush or rehashed pieces on Billy the Kid, etc." Length: 2,000-3,000 words. Query with clips. Pays $100-250; special work negotiated.

Photos: B&w glossy prints or color transparencies purchased with ms, or on assignment. Pays according to quality and importance for b&w and color photos. Suggested captions appreciated.

Tips: "Excellent illustrations for articles essential!"

PRESERVATION NEWS, National Trust for Historic Preservation, 1785 Massachusetts Ave. NW, Washington DC 20036. (202)673-4075. Editor: Arnold M. Berke. 30% freelance written. Prefers to work with published/established writers. A monthly tabloid covering preservation of historic buildings in the U.S. "We cover proposed or completed preservation projects and controversies involving historic buildings and districts. Most entries are news stories, features or opinion pieces." Circ. 200,000. Pays on publication. Publishes ms an average of 1 month after acceptance. Byline given. Offers variable kill fee. Buys one-time rights. Simultaneous queries and previously published submissions OK. Reports in 2 months on queries. Sample copy for $1 and 10 × 14 SAE with 56¢ postage; writer's guidelines for SAE and 1 first class stamp.

Nonfiction: News, interview/profile, opinion, humor, personal experience, photo feature and travel. Buys 12 mss/year. Query with published clips. Length: 500-1,200 words. Pays $150-300. Sometimes pays the expenses of writers on assignment.

Photos: State availability of photos with query or ms. Reviews b&w contact sheet. Pays $25-100. Identification of subjects required.

Columns/Departments: "We seek an urban affairs reporter who can give a new slant on development conflict throughout the United States. We also are looking for foreign coverage, and profiles of preservation craftspersons." Buys 6 mss/year. Query with published clips. Length: 600-1,200 words. Pays $150-250.

Tips: "Do not send or propose histories of buildings, descriptive accounts of cities or towns or long-winded treatises on any subjects. This is a *newspaper*. Proposals for coverage of fast-breaking events are especially welcome."

TIMELINE, Ohio Historical Society, 1982 Velma Ave., Columbus OH 43211. (614)297-2360. Editor: Christopher S. Duckworth. 90% freelance written. Works with a small number of new/unpublished writers each year. A bimonthly magazine covering history, natural history, archaeology, and fine and decorative arts. Estab. 1984. Circ. 11,000. **Pays on acceptance.** Publishes ms an average of 1 year after acceptance. Byline given. Offers $75 minimum kill fee. Buys first North American serial rights or all rights. Submit seasonal/holiday material 6 months in advance. Query for electronic submissions. Reports in 3 weeks on queries; 6 weeks on manuscripts. Sample copy $5 and 8½ × 11 SAE. Writer's guidelines for #10 SASE.

Nonfiction: Book excerpts, essays, historical, profile (of individuals) and photo feature. Buys 22 mss/year. Query. Length: 500-6,000 words. Pays $100-900.

Photos: State availability of photos with submission. Will not consider submissions without ideas for illustration. Reviews contact sheets, transparencies, and 8×10 prints. Captions, model releases, and identification of subjects required. Buys one-time rights.

Tips: "We want crisply written, authoritative narratives for the intelligent lay reader. An Ohio slant may strengthen a submission, but it is not indispensable. Contributors must know enough about their subject to explain it clearly and in an interesting fashion. We use high-quality illustration with all features. If appropriate illustration is unavailable, we can't use the feature. The writer who sends illustration ideas with a manuscript has an advantage, but an often-published illustration won't attract us."

TRACES OF INDIANA AND MIDWESTERN HISTORY, Indiana Historical Society, 315 W Ohio St., Indianapolis IN 46202. (317)232-1884. Executive Editor: Thomas Mason. Managing Editor: Kent Calder. 100% freelance written. Quarterly magazine on Indiana and Midwestern history. Estab. 1989. Circ. 7,000. **Pays on acceptance.** Publishes ms an average of 6 months after acceptance. Byline given. Buys one-time rights. Submit seasonal/holiday material 1 year in advance. Previously published submissions OK. Reports in 3 months on mss. Sample copy $5; free writer's guidelines.

Nonfiction: Book excerpts, essays, historical/nostalgic and photo feature. Buys 20 mss/year. Send complete ms. Length: 2,000-5,000 words. Pays $100-500.

Photos: State availability of photos with submission. Reviews contact sheets, transparencies and prints. Offers $10-30 per photo. Captions, model releases and identification of subjects required. Buys one-time rights.

Columns/Departments: Profile; Midwestern Made and Now and Then (Editors seek short articles on significant people, places, and artifacts in Indiana and Midwestern history.), 750-1,500 words. Query. Pays $50-100.

Tips: "Freelancers should be aware of prerequisites for writing history in general and popular history in particular. Should have some awareness of other magazines of this type published by midwestern and western historical societies. Preference is sometimes given to subjects with an Indiana connection. Quality of potential illustration is also important. Departments are not yet fully developed. Editors will consider queries in regard to departments on any aspect of midwestern history, including art, politics, sports, industry, transportation, etc. Freelancers should submit at least 3 fully developed mss. for each department."

TRUE WEST, Western Periodicals, Inc., P.O. Box 2107, Stillwater OK 74076. (405)743-3370. Editor: John Joerschke. 100% freelance written. Works with a small number of new/unpublished writers each year. Magazine on Western American history before 1940. "We want reliable research on significant historical topics written in lively prose for an informed general audience." Circ. 30,000. **Pays on acceptance.** Publishes ms an average of 4 months after acceptance. Byline given. Buys first North American serial rights. Submit seasonal/holiday material 6 months in advance. Simultaneous queries OK. Reports in 1 month on queries; 6 weeks on mss. Sample copy for 8½×11 SAE and $2; writer's guidelines for #10 SASE.

Nonfiction: Historical/nostalgic, how-to, photo feature and travel. "We do not want rehashes of worn-out stories, historical fiction, or history written in a fictional style." Buys 150 mss/year. Query. Length: 500-4,500 words. Pays 3-6¢/word.

Photos: Send photos with accompanying query or manuscript. Pays $10 for b&w prints. Identification of subjects required. Buys one-time rights.

Columns/Departments: Western Roundup—200-300-word short articles on historically oriented places to go and things to do in the West. Should include one b&w print. Buys 12-16 mss/year. Send complete ms. Pays $35.

Tips: "Do original research on fresh topics. Stay away from controversial subjects unless you are truly knowledgeable in the field. Read our magazines and follow our guidelines. A freelancer is most likely to break in with us by submitting thoroughly researched, lively prose on relatively obscure topics. First person accounts rarely fill our needs."

VIRGINIA CAVALCADE, Virginia State Library and Archives, Richmond VA 23219-3491. (804)786-2312. Primarily for readers with an interest in Virginia history. 90% freelance written. "Both established and new writers are invited to submit articles." Quarterly magazine. Estab. 1951. Circ. 9,000. Buys all rights. Byline given. **Pays on acceptance.** Publishes ms an average of 6-12 months after acceptance. Rarely considers simultaneous submissions. Submit seasonal material 15-18 months in advance. Reports in 1-1½ months. Sample copy $2; free writer's guidelines.

Nonfiction: "We welcome readable and factually accurate articles that are relevant to some phase of Virginia history. Art, architecture, literature, education, business, technology and transportation are all acceptable subjects, as well as political and military affairs. Articles must be based on thorough, scholarly research. We require footnotes but do not publish them. Any period from the age of exploration to the mid-20th century, and any geographical section or area of the state may be represented. Must deal with subjects that will appeal to a broad readership, rather than to a very restricted group or locality. Articles must be suitable for illustration, although it is not necessary that the author provide the pictures. If the author does have pertinent illustrations or knows their location, the editor appreciates information concerning them." Buys 12-15 mss/year. Query. Length: 3,500-4,500 words. Pays $100.

Photos: Uses 8×10 b&w glossy prints; transparencies should be at least 4×5.

Tips: "*Cavalcade* employs a narrative, anecdotal style. Too many submissions are written for an academic audience or are simply not sufficiently gripping."

WILD WEST, Empire Press, 602 S. King St. #300, Leesburg VA 22075. (703)771-9400. Editor: William M. Vogt. 95% freelance written. Bimonthly magazine on history of the American West. "*Wild West* covers the popular (narrative) history of the American West—events, trends, personalities, anything of general interest." Estab. 1988. Circ. 75,000. Pays on publication. Byline given. Buys all rights. Submit seasonal/holiday material 1 year in advance. Query for electronic submissions. Sample copy $3.95; writer's guidelines for #10 SASE.

Nonfiction: Historical/nostalgic, humor, travel. No fiction or poetry—nothing current. Buys 24 mss/year. Query. Length: 4,000 words. Pays $300.

Photos: State availability of photos with submission. Captions and identification of subjects required. Buys one-time rights or all rights.

Columns/Departments: Travel; Gun Fighters & Lawmen; Personalities; Warriors & Chiefs; Books Reviews. Buys 16 mss/year. Length: 2,000. Pays $150 for departments, by the word for book reviews.

‡**YESTERDAY'S MAGAZETTE, The Magazine of Memories**, Independent Publishing Co., P.O. Box 15126, Sarasota FL 34277. (813)922-7080. Editor: Ned Burke. Managing Editor: Gail Haborak. 95% freelance written. Bimonthly magazine of nostalgia. Estab. 1973. Circ. 2,500. Pays on publication. Publishes ms an average of 6 months after acceptance. Byline given. Buys first rights. Submit seasonal/holiday material 4 months in advance. Reports in 2 weeks on queries; 2 months on mss. Sample copy for $2. Free writer's guidelines.

Nonfiction: General interest, historical/nostalgic, humor, inspirational, interview/profile ('yesterday' celebrities), opinion, personal experience, photo feature and photo. Special "Christmas" issue, deadline Nov. 15, featuring "My Favorite Christmas Memory." Plus special traditional poetry issue in May, deadline April 15. "No current topics and events." Buys 100 mss/year. Send complete ms. Length: 100-1,500 words. Pays $5-25 for unsolicited articles. Pays for most short articles, poems, etc.

Photos: Send photos with submission. Reviews 5×7 prints. Offers no additional payment for photos accepted with ms. Identification of subjects required. Buys one-time rights.

Columns/Departments: The Way We Were (a look at certain period of time—40s, 50s, etc.); When I Was a Kid (childhood memories); In A Word (objects from the past—'ice box', etc.); Yesterday Trivia (quiz on old movie stars, TV shows, etc.). All 300-750 words. Buys 12 mss/year. Send complete ms. Length: 500-750 words. Pays $5-10.

Fiction: Historical, humorous, slice-of-life vignettes. "No modern settings." Buys 4 mss/year. Send complete ms. Length: 750-2,500 words. Pays $5-25.

Poetry: Traditional. Nothing other than traditional. Buys 50 poems/year. Submit maximum 5 poems. Length: 4-32 lines. Pays $10.

Fillers: Anecdotes, short humor. Buys 5/year. Length: 50-250 words. Pays $5.

Tips: "We would like to see more 40s, 50s and 60s pieces, especially with photos. It's hard to reject any story with a good photo. All areas are open, especially 'Plain Folks Page' which uses letters, comments and opinions of readers."

Hobby and Craft

Magazines in this category range from home video to cross stitch. Craftspeople and hobbyists who read these magazines want new ideas while collectors need to know what is most valuable and why. Collectors, do-it-yourselfers and craftspeople look to these magazines for inspiration, research and information. Publications covering antiques and miniatures are also listed here, while additional publications for electronics and radio hobbyists are included in the Science classification.

‡**THE AMERICAN COLLECTORS JOURNAL**, P.O. Box 407, Kewanee IL 61443. (308)853-8441. Editor: Carol Savidge. 55% freelance written. Eager to work with new/unpublished writers. A bimonthly tabloid covering antiques and collectibles. Estab. 1963. Circ. 51,841. Pays on publication. Publishes ms an average of 4 months after acceptance. Byline given. Not copyrighted. Buys first North American serial rights. Submit seasonal/holiday material 6 months in advance. Reports in 3 weeks. Sample copy for 6×9 SAE with 4 first class stamps.

Nonfiction: Carol Harper, articles editor. General interest, interview/profile, new product, photo feature and technical. Buys 12-20 mss/year. Query or send complete ms. Pays $10-35 for unsolicited articles.

Photos: Send photos with submission. Reviews 5×7 prints. Offers no additional payment for photos accepted with ms. Captions required. Buys one-time rights.

Tips: "We are looking for submissions with photos in all areas of collecting and antiquing, unusual collections, details on a particular kind of collecting or information on antiques."

‡ANTIQUE REVIEW, P.O. Box 538, Worthington OH 43085. Editor: Charles Muller. (614)885-9757. FAX: (614)885-9762. 60% freelance written. Eager to work with new/unpublished writers. For an antique-oriented readership, "generally well-educated, interested in folk art and other early American items." Monthly tabloid. Estab. 1975. Circ. 9,500. Pays on publication date assigned at time of purchase. Publishes ms an average of 3 months after acceptance. Buys first North American serial rights, and second (reprint) rights to material originally published in dissimilar publications elsewhere. Byline given. Phone queries OK. Reports in 1 month. Free sample copy and writer's guidelines for #10 SASE.

Nonfiction: "The articles we desire concern history and production of furniture, pottery, china, and other quality Americana. In some cases, contemporary folk art items are acceptable. We are also interested in reporting on antique shows and auctions with statements on conditions and prices. We do not want articles on contemporary collectibles." Buys 5-8 mss/issue. Query with clips of published work. Query should show "author's familiarity with antiques, an interest in the historical development of artifacts relating to early America and an awareness of antiques market." Length: 200-2,000 words. Pays $80-125. Sometimes pays the expenses of writers on assignment.

Photos: State availability of photos with query. Payment included in ms price. Uses 3×5 or larger glossy b&w prints. Captions required. Articles with photographs receive preference.

Tips: "Give us a call and let us know of specific interests. We are more concerned with the background in antiques than in writing abilities. The writing can be edited, but the knowledge imparted is of primary interest. A frequent mistake is being too general, not becoming deeply involved in the topic and its research. We are interested in primary research into America's historic material culture."

THE ANTIQUE TRADER WEEKLY, P.O. Box 1050, Dubuque IA 52001. (319)588-2073. FAX: (319)588-0888. Editor: Kyle D. Husfloen. 50% freelance written. Works with a small number of new/unpublished writers each year. For collectors and dealers in antiques and collectibles. Weekly newspaper. Estab. 1957. Circ. 90,000. Publishes ms an average of 1 year after acceptance. Buys all rights. Payment at beginning of month following publication. Simultaneous submissions OK. Submit seasonal/holiday material 4 months in advance. Sample copy 50¢; free writer's guidelines.

Nonfiction: "We invite authoritative and well-researched articles on all types of antiques and collectors' items and in-depth stories on specific types of antiques and collectibles. No human interest stories. We do not pay for brief information on new shops opening or other material printed as a service to the antiques hobby." Buys about 60 mss/year. Query or submit complete ms. Pays $25-100 for feature articles; $100-200 for feature cover stories.

Photos: Submit a liberal number of good b&w photos to accompany article. Uses 35mm or larger color transparencies for cover. Offers no additional payment for photos accompanying mss.

Tips: "Send concise, polite letter stating the topic to be covered in the story and the writer's qualifications. No 'cute' letters rambling on about some 'imaginative' story idea. Writers who have a concise yet readable style and know their topic are always appreciated. I am most interested in those who have personal collecting experience or can put together a knowledgeable and informative feature after interviewing a serious collector/authority."

ANTIQUES & AUCTION NEWS, Route 230 West, Box 500, Mount Joy PA 17552. (717)653-9797, ext. 254. Editor: Doris Ann Johnson. Works with a small number of new/unpublished writers each year. A weekly tabloid for dealers and buyers of antiques, nostalgics and collectibles, and those who follow antique shows, shops and auctions. Circ. 35,000. Pays on publication. Submit seasonal/holiday material 3 months in advance. Free sample copy available if you mention *Writer's Market*. Writer's guidelines for #10 SASE.

Nonfiction: "Our readers are interested in collectibles and antiques dating approximately from the Civil War to the present, originating in the U.S. or western Europe. We normally will consider any story on a collectible or antique if it is well-written, slanted toward helping collectors, buyers and dealers learn more about the field, and is focused on the aspect of collecting. This could be an historical perspective, a specific area of collecting, an especially interesting antique or unusual collection. Issues have included material on old Christmas ornaments, antique love tokens, collections of fans, pencils and pottery, and 'The Man from U.N.C.L.E.' books and magazines. Articles may be how-to, informational research, news and reporting and even an occasional photo feature." Call or write before submitting any manuscript. Length: 1,000 words or less preferred, but will consider up to 2,000 words. Pays $12.50 for articles without photos; $15 for articles with usable photos; $20 for front page. "We also accept an occasional short article—about one typed page, with a good photo—for which we will pay $7.50, $5 without photo."

Photos: Purchased as part of ms package. "We prefer b&w photos, usually of a single item against a simple background. Color photos can be used if there is good contrast between darks and lights." Captions required. Photos are returned.

‡**BANK NOTE REPORTER**, Krause Publications, 700 E. State St., Iola WI 54990. (715)445-2214. Editor: David Harper. 30% freelance written. Works with a small number of new/unpublished writers each year, and is eager to work with new/unpublished writers. Monthly tabloid for advanced collectors of U.S. and world paper money. Circ. 4,250. Pays on publication. Publishes ms an average of 2 months after acceptance. Byline given. Buys first North American serial rights and reprint rights. Query for electronic submissions. Reports in 2 weeks. Sample copy for 8½ × 11 SAE and 3 first class stamps.

Nonfiction: "We review articles covering any phase of paper money collecting including investing, display, storage, history, art, story behind a particular piece of paper money and the business of paper money." News items not solicited. "Our staff covers the hard news." Buys 6 mss/issue. Send complete ms. Length: 500-3,000 words. Pays 3¢/word to first-time contributors; negotiates fee for later articles. Pays the expenses of writers on assignment.

Photos: Pays $5 for 5 × 7 b&w glossy prints. Captions and model releases required.

Tips: "The writer has a better chance of breaking in at our publication with short articles due to the technical nature of the subject matter and sophistication of our readers. Material about bank notes used in a writer's locale would be interesting, useful, encouraged. We like new names."

BASEBALL CARDS, Krause Publications, 700 E. State St., Iola WI 54990. (715)445-2214. FAX: (715)445-4087. Editor: Kit Kiefer. 50% freelance written. A monthly magazine covering sports memorabilia collecting. "Geared for the novice collector or general public who might become interested in the hobby." Estab. 1981. Circ. 305,000. Pays on publication. Publishes ms an average of 6 months after acceptance. Byline given. Buys first North American serial rights and second serial (reprint) rights. Submit seasonal/holiday material 6 months in advance. Reports in 2 weeks. Sample copy for 8½ × 11 SAE with 3 first class stamps. Writer's guidelines for #10 SASE.

Nonfiction: General interest, historical/nostalgic, how-to (enjoy or enhance your collection) and photo feature. No personal reminiscences of collecting baseball cards as a kid or articles that relate to baseball, rather than cards. Buys 36-50 mss/year. Query. Length: 1,000-3,000 words. Pays up to $650.

Photos: Send photos with submission. Reviews contact sheets and transparencies. Payment negotiated. Identification of subjects required.

Tips: "We would like to receive knowledgeable features on specific collectibles: card sets, team items, etc. We want to identify the collecting trends of the 90s and be the first to report on them."

BECKETT BASEBALL CARD MONTHLY, Statabase, Inc., Suite 200, 4887 Alpha Rd., Dallas TX 75244. (214)991-6657. FAX: (214)991-8930. Editor: Dr. James Beckett. Managing Editor: Fred Reed. 85% freelance written. Monthly magazine on baseball card and sports memorabilia collecting. "Our readers expect our publication to be entertaining and informative. Our slant is that hobbies are for fun and rewarding. Especially wanted are how-to collect articles." Estab. 1984. Circ. 679,000. **Pays on acceptance.** Publishes ms an average of 4 months after acceptance. Byline given. Pays $50 kill fee. Buys first North American serial rights. Submit seasonal/holiday material 6 months in advance. "No simultaneous submissions, please!" Reports in 1 month. Sample copy $2.50; free writer's guidelines.

Nonfiction: Book excerpts, historical/nostalgic, how-to, humor, interview/profile, new product, opinion, personal experience, photo feature, technical. Special issues include: March (spring training/new card sets issued); July (Hall of Fame/All Star Game issue); October (World Series issue); November (autograph special issue). No articles that emphasize speculative prices and investments. Buys 145 mss/year. Send complete ms. Length: 300-2,000 words. Pays $100-400 for assigned articles; $50-200 for unsolicited articles. Sometimes pays expenses of writers on assignment.

Photos: Send photos with submission. Reviews 35mm transparencies, 5 × 7 or larger prints. Offers $10-300 per photo. Captions, model releases and identification of subjects required. Buys one-time rights.

Columns/Departments: Pepper Hastings, editor. Autograph Experiences (memorable experience with baseball star), 50-400 words; Prospects (players on the verge of major league stardom), 300-500 words; Collecting Tips (basic but overlooked helpful hints), 300-500 words; Trivia (major league baseball odd or humorous facts), 20-50 words; Player Vignettes (general baseball articles featuring emerging or proven super-stars). Buys 60 mss/year. Send complete ms. Length: 50-400 words. Pays $25-100.

Fiction: Humorous only.

Tips: "A writer for *Becket Baseball Card Monthly* should be an avid sports fan and/or a collector with an enthusiasm for sharing his/her interests with others. Articles must be factual, but not overly statistical laden. First person (not research) articles presenting the writer's personal experiences told with wit and humor, and emphasizing the stars of the game, are *always* wanted. Acceptable articles must be of interest to our two basic reader segments: teenaged boys and their middle-aged fathers who are reexperiencing a nostalgic renaissance of their own childhoods. Prospective writers should write down to neither group!"

THE COIN ENTHUSIAST'S JOURNAL, Masongate Publishing, P.O. Box 1383, Torrance CA 90505. Editor: William J. Cook. 40% freelance written. Prefers to work with published/established writers, and works with a small number of new/unpublished writers each year. Monthly newsletter covering numismatics (coin collecting) and bullion trading. "Our purpose is to give readers information to help them make sound investment decisions in the areas we cover and to help them get more enjoyment out of their hobby." Estab. 1984. Circ. 2,000. Pays on publication. Publishes ms an average of 2 months after acceptance. Byline given. Offers $25 kill fee. Buys all rights. Submit seasonal/holiday material 3 months in advance. Simultaneous queries and submissions OK. Reports in 3 weeks. Sample copy for $1 and #10 SAE with 2 first class stamps (must mention *Writer's Market*). Guidelines sent free with sample when requested.

Nonfiction: How-to (make money from your hobby and be a better trader); opinion (what is the coin market going to do?); personal experience (insiders' "tricks of the trade"); and technical (why are coin prices going up [or down]?). No "crystal ball" predictions, i.e., "I see silver going up to to $50 per ounce by mid-1991." Query with published clips. Length: 500-2,500 words. Buys 25-36 mss/year. Pays mostly $50-150. Also looking for "staff writers" who will submit material each month or bimonthly.

Photos: State availability of photos with query. Pays $5-25 for b&w prints. Buys one-time rights.

Tips: "Occasionally we buy cartoons. We are buying a few more short articles but the majority are longer articles (i.e. 1,500 words and up). We are also buying more 'human interest' and humorous articles. More entertainment as opposed to just technical information. Try to make articles interesting—we get *too* much dry, boring stuff."

COINS, Krause Publications, 700 E. State St., Iola WI 54990. (715)445-2214. FAX: (715)445-4087. Editor: Arlyn G. Sieber. 50% freelance written. Eager to work with new/unpublished writers. Monthly magazine about U.S. and foreign coins for all levels of collectors, investors and dealers. Estab. 1952. Circ. 71,000. Free sample copy and writer's guidelines.

Nonfiction: "We're looking for stories that are going to help coin collectors pursue their hobby in today's market. Stories should include what's available in the series being discussed, its value in today's market, and tips for buying that material." Buys 2-4 mss/issue. Send complete ms. Length: 500-3,000 words. Pays 3¢/word to first-time contributors; fee negotiated for later articles. Sometimes pays the expenses of writers on assignment.

Photos: Pays $5 minimum for b&w prints. Pays $25 minimum for 35mm transparencies used. Captions and model releases required. Buys first rights.

COLLECTOR EDITIONS, (formerly *Collector Editions Quarterly*), Collector Communications Corp., 170 5th Ave., New York NY 10010. (212)989-8700. FAX: (212)645-8976. Editor: Joan Muyskens Pursley. 40% freelance written. Works with a small number of new/unpublished writers each year. Bimonthly magazine on porcelain and glass collectibles. "We specialize in contemporary (post-war ceramic and glass) collectibles, including reproductions, but also publish articles about antiques, if they are being reproduced today and are generally available." Estab. 1973. Circ. 80,000. Rights purchased vary with author and material. Buys first North American serial rights and sometimes second serial (reprint) rights. "First assignments are always done on a speculative basis." Pays within 30 days of acceptance. Publishes ms an average of 6 months after acceptance. Reports in 2 months. Sample copy $2; writer's guidelines for #10 SASE.

Nonfiction: "Short features about collecting, written in tight, newsy style. We specialize in contemporary (postwar) collectibles. Values for pieces being written about should be included." Informational, how-to, interview, profile, exposé and nostalgia. Buys 8-10 mss/year. Query with sample photos. Length: 500-2,500 words. Pays $100-300. Sometimes pays expenses of writers on assignments.

Columns/Departments: Columns cover porcelain, glass, auction reports and artist profiles. Query. Length: 750 words. Pays $75.

Photos: B&w and color photos purchased with accompanying ms with no additional payment. Captions are required. "We want clear, distinct, full-frame images that say something."

Tips: "Unfamiliarity with the field is the most frequent mistake made by writers in completing an article for us."

‡COLLECTORS' SHOWCASE, America's Premier Collecting Magazine, Sports Magazines of America, #210, 7130 S. Lewis, Tulsa OK 74136. (918)496-7405. Editorial Coordinator: Mark Owens. 90% freelance written. Collectibles magazine published nine times/year. "Our readers collect in general, but we focus editorially on antique dolls, toys, advertising and Americana." Estab. 1980. Circ. 15,000. **Pays on acceptance.** Publishes ms an average of 1-2 months after acceptance. Byline given. Buys first North American serial rights. Submit seasonal/holiday material 3 months in advance. Query for electronic submissions. Reports in 2 weeks. Sample copy for 9x12 SAE with 5 first class stamps; writer's guidelines for #10 SASE.

Nonfiction: Book excerpts, essays, general interest, how-to, interview/profile, new product, photo feature. "No modern or contemporary collectibles, no coins, no plates, no reproductions." Buys 50-70 mss/year. Query with or without published clips, or send complete ms. Length: 750-2,000 words. Pays $100-250. Sometimes pays expenses of writers on assignment.

Photos: Send photos with submission. Reviews negatives, 35mm and larger transparencies and 3×5 prints. Payment negotiable. Captions and identification of subjects required. Buys one-time rights.

Columns/Departments: Showtime (recap of show or convention), 200 words; Auction Report, 100-500 words; Museum News (museum exhibits), 100-500 words. Buys 10-15 mss/year. Send complete ms. Pays $25-100.

Tips: "Under new management, *Collectors' Showcase* is moving away from fluff and toward informative, factual and well written features. Contact in writing or over the phone with Mark Owens is encouraged. Photos are very important."

‡**CRAFTING TODAY**, MSC Publishing Co., 70 Sparta Ave., CN1003, Sparta NJ 07871. (201)729-4477. Editor: Matthew Jones. 90% freelance written. Bimonthly magazine covering crafting. The magazine publishes quick and easy crafting instructions for beginners in all craft media. Estab. 1989. Pays on publication. Publishes ms an average of 1 month after acceptance. Byline given. Buys first rights and all rights. Submit seasonal/holiday material 6 months in advance. Reports in 6 weeks on queries; 10 weeks on mss. Sample copy for 9×13 SAE with 5 first class stamps. Writer's guidelines for #10 SAE with 1 first class stamp.

Nonfiction: How-to crafts of all types. Buys 8-10 mss/year. Query. Length: 500-2,000 words. Pays 7-10¢/word. Payment in contributor copies or other premiums negotiable. Sometimes pays expenses of writers on assignment.

Photos: State availability of photos with submission. Reviews all sizes of transparencies and prints. Payment and rights negotiable. Captions, model releases and identification of subjects required.

Fillers: Buys 6-12/year. Length: 50-100 words. Pays $5-10.

Tips: "Send original designs appropriate to our subject, soft and hard crafts."

CRAFTS 'N THINGS, 14 Main St., Park Ridge IL 60068. (708)825-2161. FAX: (708)825-4806. Editor: Nancy Tosh. Associate Editor: Lois Dahlin. Published 8 times a year, covering quality crafts for today's creative woman. Estab. 1976. Circ. 320,000. Pays on publication. Byline given. Buys first North American serial rights. Submit seasonal/holiday material 6 months in advance. Reports in 1 month. Free sample copy.

Nonfiction: How-to (do a craft project). Buys 7-14 mss/issue. "Send in a photo of the item and complete directions. We will consider it and return if not accepted." Length: 1-4 magazine pages. Pays $50-200, "depending on how much staff work is required."

Photos: "Generally, we will ask that you send the item so we can photograph it ourselves."

Tips: "We're looking more for people who can craft than people who can write."

‡**CREATIVE WOODWORKS & CRAFTS**, MSC Publishing Co., 70 Sparta Ave., CN 1003, Sparta NJ 07871. (201)729-4477. Editor: Matthew Jones. 90% freelance written. Quarterly magazine on woodworking. "Simple weekend projects for the veteran woodworker and woodcrafter are presented in how-to format. For designs from fine furnishings to handpainted collectibles." Estab. 1989. Pays on publication. Publishes ms an average of 1 month after acceptance. Byline given. Buys first rights and all rights. Submit seasonal/holiday material 6 months in advance. Reports in 6 weeks on queries; 10 weeks on mss. Sample copy for 9×12 SAE with $1.05 postage. Writer's guidelines for #10 SAE with 1 first class stamp.

Nonfiction: How-to. Buys 8-10 mss/year. Query. Length: 500-2,000 words. Pays 7-10¢/word. Sometimes pays expenses of writers on assignment.

Photos: State availability of photos with submission. Reviews all sizes of transparencies and prints. Pays negotiable rates. Captions, model releases and identification of subjects required. Rights negotiable.

Fillers: Woodworking tips. Buys 6-12/year. Length: 50-100 words. Pays $5-10.

Tips: "Send original designs appropriate to our subject i.e., woodcrafts and woodworking."

‡**CROCHET FANTASY**, All American Crafts, Inc., 70 Sparta Ave., CN 1003, Sparta NJ 07871. (201)729-4477. Editorial Director: Camille Pomaco. Editor: Janice Edsall. Crochet magazine published 8 times/year. Estab. 1982. Each issue includes over 24 patterns, with a variety of sweaters, doilies, afghans and other items." Pays on publication. Publishes ms an average of 6 months after acceptance. Byline given. Buys first rights, second serial (reprint) rights or all rights. Submit seasonal/holiday material 8 months in advance. Query for electronic submissions. Reports in 2 months on queries. Sample copy for 9×12 SAE. Writer's guidelines for #10 SASE.

Nonfiction: How-to, humor, personal experience and technical. Buys 2 mss/year. Query. Length: 500-3,000 words. Pays 7-10¢/word for assigned articles.

Photos: Send photos with submission. Reviews all sizes transparencies and prints. Offers no additional payment for photos accepted with ms. Model releases required. Buys all rights.

Columns/Departments: Stitch Wit (crochet hints, crochet anecdotes, etc.), 50-500 words. Pays $5 per published hint.

DECORATIVE ARTIST'S WORKBOOK, F&W Publishing, 1507 Dana Ave., Cincinnati OH 45207. Editorial Director: Michael Ward. 50% freelance written. Bimonthly magazine covering tole and decorative painting and related art forms. Offers "straightforward, personal instruction in the techniques of tole and decorative painting." Circ. 100,000. **Pays on acceptance.** Byline given. Offers 20% kill fee. Buys first North American serial rights. Submit seasonal/holiday material 6 months in advance. Reports in 1 month. Sample copy for $2.95 with 9×12 SAE and 7 first class stamps.

Nonfiction: How-to (related to tole and decorative painting), new product and technical. No profiles and/or general interest topics. Buys 30 mss/year. Query with slides or photos. Length: 1,200-1,800 words. Pays 10-12¢/word.

Photos: State availability of photos and slides with submission or send photos with submission. Reviews 35mm, 4×5 transparencies or good quality photos. Offers no additional payment for photos accepted with ms. Captions required. Buys one-time rights.

Fillers: Anecdotes, facts and short humor. Buys 10/year. Length: 50-200 words. Pays $10-20.

Tips: "The more you know—and can prove you know—about decorative painting the better your chances. I'm looking for experts in the field who, through their own experience, can artfully describe the techniques involved. How-to articles are most open to freelancers. Be sure to query with slides or transparencies, and show that you understand the extensive graphic requirements for these pieces and are able to provide progressives—slides that show works in progress."

DOLLS, The Collector's Magazine, Collector Communications Corp., 170 5th Ave., New York NY 10010. (212)989-8700. Editor: Krystyna Poray Goddu. 75% freelance written. Works with a small number of new/unpublished writers each year. 8 times/year covering doll collecting "for collectors of antique, contemporary and reproduction dolls. We publish well-researched, professionally written articles illustrated with photographs of high quality, color or black-and-white." Estab. 1982. Circ. 85,000. Pays within 1 month of acceptance. Publishes ms an average of 6 months after acceptance. Byline given. "Almost all first manuscripts are on speculation. We rarely kill assigned stories, but fee would be about 33% of article fee." Buys first North American serial rights, second serial rights if piece has appeared in a non-competing publication. Submit seasonal/holiday material 6 months in advance. Previously published submissions OK. Reports in 2 months. Sample copy $2; writer's guidelines for #10 SASE.

Nonfiction: Book excerpts; historical (with collecting angle); interview/profile (on collectors with outstanding collections); new product (just photos and captions; "we do not pay for these, but regard them as publicity"); opinion ("A Personal Definition of Dolls"); technical (doll restoration advice by experts only); and travel (museums and collections around the world). "No sentimental, uninformed 'my doll collection' or 'my grandma's doll collection' stories or trade magazine-type stories on shops, etc. Our readers are knowledgeable collectors." Query with clips. Length: 500-2,500 words. Pays $100-350. Sometimes pays expenses of writers on assignment.

Photos: Send photos with accompanying query or ms. Reviews 4×5 transparencies; 4×5 or 8×10 b&w prints and 35mm slides. "We do not buy photographs submitted without manuscripts unless we have assigned them; we pay for the manuscript/photos package in one fee." Captions required. Buys one-time rights.

Columns/Departments: Doll Views—a miscellany of news and views of the doll world includes reports on upcoming or recently held events. "*Not* the place for new dolls, auction prices or dates; we have regular contributors or staff assigned to those columns." Query with clips if available or send complete ms. Length: 200-500 words. Pays $25-75. Doll Views items are rarely bylined.

Fillers: "We don't use fillers but would consider them if we got something good. Hints on restoring, for example, or a nice illustration." Length: 500 words maximum. Pays $25-75.

Tips: "We need experts in the field who are also good writers. The most frequent mistake made by writers in completing an article assignment for us is being unfamiliar with the field; our readers are very knowledgeable. Freelancers who are not experts should know their particular story thoroughly and do background research to get the facts correct. Well-written queries from writers outside the NYC area are especially welcomed. Non-experts should stay away from technical or specific subjects (restoration, price trends). Short profiles of unusual collectors or a story of a local museum collection, with good photos, might catch our interest. Editors want to know they are getting something from a writer they cannot get from anyone else. Good writing should be a given, a starting point. After that, it's what you know."

EARLY AMERICAN LIFE, Cowles Magazines, Inc. Box 8200, Harrisburg PA 17105. FAX: (717)657-9526. Editor: Frances Carnahan. 60-70% freelance written. Bimonthly magazine for "people who are interested in capturing the warmth and beauty of the 1600 to 1840 period and using it in their homes and lives today. They are interested in arts, crafts, travel, restoration and collecting." Estab. 1970. Circ. 200,000. Buys all rights. Buys 40 mss/year. **Pays on acceptance.** Publishes ms an average of 1 year after acceptance. Sample copy and writer's guidelines for 9×12 SAE and 4 first class stamps. Reports in 1 month. Query or submit complete ms with SASE.

Nonfiction: "Social history (the story of the people, not epic heroes and battles), travel to historic sites, country inns, antiques and reproductions, refinishing and restoration, architecture and decorating. We try to entertain as we inform. While we're always on the lookout for good pieces on any of our subjects, the 'travel to historic sites' theme is most frequently submitted. Would like to see more on how real people did something great to their homes." Buys 40 mss/year. Query or submit complete ms. Length: 750-3,000 words. Pays $100-600. Pays expenses of writers on assignment.

Photos: Pays $10 for 5×7 (and up) b&w photos used with mss, minimum of $25 for color. Prefers 2¼×2¼ and up, but can work from 35mm.

Tips: "Our readers are eager for ideas on how to bring early America into their lives. Conceive a new approach to satisfy their related interests in arts, crafts, travel to historic sites, and especially in houses decorated in the early American style. Write to entertain and inform at the same time, and be prepared to help us with illustrations, or sources for them."

FIBERARTS, The Magazine of Textiles, Nine Press, 50 College St., Asheville NC 28801. (704)253-0467. FAX: (704)253-7952. Editor: Ann Batchelder. 100% freelance written. Eager to work with new/unpublished writers. Magazine appears 5 times/year, covering textiles as art and craft (weaving, quilting, surface design, stitchery, knitting, fashion, crochet, etc.) for textile artists, craftspeople, hobbyists, teachers, museum and gallery staffs, collectors and enthusiasts. Estab. 1975. Circ. 23,000. Pays 60 days after publication. Publishes ms an average of 4 months after acceptance. Byline given. Offers 50% kill fee. Buys first rights. Submit seasonal/holiday material 8 months in advance. Editorial guidelines and style sheet available. Reports within 2 weeks. Sample copy $4 and 10×12 SAE with 2 first class stamps; writer's guidelines for #10 SAE with 2 first class stamps.

Nonfiction: Book excerpts; historical/nostalgic; how-to; humor; interview/profile; opinion; personal experience; photo feature; technical; travel (for the textile enthusiast, e.g., collecting rugs in Turkey); and education, trends, exhibition reviews and textile news. Buys 25-50 mss/year. Query. "Please be very specific about your proposal. Also an important consideration in accepting an article is the kind of photos—35mm slides and/or b&w glossies—that you can provide as illustration. We like to see photos in advance." Length: 250-1,200 words. Pays $40-300, depending on article. Rarely pays the expenses of writers on assignment.

Tips: "Our writers are very familiar with the textile field, and this is what we look for in a new writer. Familiarity with textile techniques, history or events determines clarity of an article more than a particular style of writing. The writer should also be familiar with *Fiberarts*, the magazine. We outline our upcoming issues in regular Editorial Agendas far enough in advance for a prospective writer to be aware of our future needs."

FINESCALE MODELER, Kalmbach Publishing Co., 21027 Crossroads Circle, P.O. Box 1612, Waukesha WI 53187. (414)796-8776. Editor: Bob Hayden. 80% freelance written. Eager to work with new/unpublished writers. Magazine published 8 times/year "devoted to how-to-do-it modeling information for scale model builders who build non-operating aircraft, tanks, boats, automobiles, figures, dioramas, and science fiction and fantasy models." Circ. 80,000. **Pays on acceptance.** Publishes ms an average of 14 months after acceptance. Byline given. Buys all rights. Reports in 6 weeks on queries; 3 months on mss. Sample copy for 9×12 SAE and 3 first class stamps; free writer's guidelines.

Nonfiction: How-to (build scale models); and technical (research information for building models). Query or send complete ms. Length: 750-3,000 words. Pays $30/published page minimum.

Photos: Send photos with ms. Pays $7.50 minimum for transparencies and $5 minimum for 5×7 b&w prints. Captions and identification of subjects required. Buys one-time rights.

Columns/Departments: *FSM* Showcase (photos plus description of model); and *FSM* Tips and Techniques (model building hints and tips). Buys 25-50 Tips and Techniques/year. Query or send complete ms. Length: 100-1,000 words. Pays $5-100.

Tips: "A freelancer can best break in first through hints and tips, then through feature articles. Most people who write for *FSM* are modelers first, writers second. This is a specialty magazine for a special, quite expert audience. Essentially, 99% of our writers will come from that audience."

‡THE FRANKLIN MINT ALMANAC, Franklin Center PA 19091. (215)459-7015. Publisher: Barbara Cady. Editor: Mark Mussari. 90% freelance written. Biannual magazine covering collecting, fashion, and fine and decorative arts for members of Franklin Mint Collectors Society who are regular customers and others who request. Estab. 1970. Circ. 1.2 million. **Pays on acceptance.** Publishes ms an average of 1 month after acceptance. Byline given. Pays negotiable kill fee. Buys one-time world rights. Reports in 3 weeks on queries.

Nonfiction: Profiles of collectors and their world class collections. Some celebrity/collector profiles. Query. Length: 1,000-1,200 words. Payment depends upon subject and writer. Pays expenses of writers on assignment.

Photos: State availability of photos.

Tips: "Solid writing credentials and a knowledge of collecting are a must. *Almanac* has gone through a major series of editorial changes. Each issue is now theme-specific (i.e., "The Passionate Collector," "The American Designer," "Japanese Style"). It is the collectors' magazine with the largest circulation in the world."

GEM SHOW NEWS, Shows of Integrity, Rt. #2, P.O. Box 78, Blue Ridge TX 75004. (214)752-5192. FAX: (214)752-5205. Editor: Judi Tripp. Managing Editor: Stacy Hobbs. 50% freelance written. A bimonthly newspaper on precious stones, mineral collecting and jewelry. "Slant should be gem/collectible investments including gold, gold coins, silver, silver jewelry and original silver designs." Estab. 1979. Circ. 12,000-30,000. **Pays on acceptance.** Publishes ms an average of 2 months after acceptance. Byline given. Publication not copyrighted. Buys first rights and makes work-for-hire assignments. Submit seasonal/holiday material 4 months in advance. Simultaneous and previously published submissions OK. Reports in 6 weeks. Sample copy for 9×12 SAE and 5 first class stamps. Writer's guidelines for #10 SASE.

Nonfiction: How-to (gem collecting; gem cutting/collecting), humor, interview/profile, new product, personal experience, photo feature, technical, travel. Buys 30 mss/year. Send complete ms. Length: 1,000-3,000 words. Pays $50-150.

Photos: Send photos with submission. Reviews prints (3x5). Offers $5-10/photo. Captions, model releases and identification of subjects required. Buys one-time rights.

Fillers: Anecdotes, facts, gags to be illustrated by cartoonist, newsbreaks, short humor. Buys 30 mss/year. Length: 500 words maximum. Pays $10-25.

Tips: "Attend gem and jewelry shows to see the interest in this field. The gem and mineral collecting field is the second most popular hobby (second only to coin and stamp collecting) in the U.S. All areas are open, including current fads and trends such as articles on the current quartz crystals and crystal healing craze and related subjects."

HANDWOVEN, Interweave Press, 306 N. Washington, Loveland CO 80537. (303)669-7672. FAX: (303)667-8317. Editor: Jane Patrick. 75% freelance written. Bimonthly magazine (except July) covering handweaving, spinning and dyeing. Audience includes "practicing textile craftsmen. Article should show considerable depth of knowledge of subject, although tone should be informal and accessible." Estab. 1975. Circ. 35,000. Pays on publication. Publishes ms an average of 10 months after acceptance. Byline given. Pays 50% kill fee. Buys first North American serial rights. Simultaneous queries OK. Sample copy $4.50; writer's guidelines for #10 SASE.

Nonfiction: Historical and how-to (on weaving and other craft techniques; specific items with instructions); and technical (on handweaving, spinning and dyeing technology). "All articles must contain a high level of in-depth information. Our readers are very knowledgeable about these subjects." Query. Length: 500-2,000 words. Pays $35-150.

Photos: State availability of photos. Identification of subjects required.

Tips: "We prefer work written by writers with an in-depth knowledge of weaving. We're particularly interested in articles about new weaving and spinning techniques as well as applying these techniques to finished products."

HEDDLE MAGAZINE, Muskoka Publications Group, Box 1600, Bracebridge, Ontario P0B 1C0 Canada. (705)645-4463. FAX: (705)645-3928. Editor: Verna Wilson. Managing Editor: Doug Brenner. 90% freelance written. Bimonthly magazine on weaving and spinning. "Magazine caters to skilled spinners' and weavers' designs, patterns etc." Circ. 3,500. Pays on publication. Publishes ms an average of 2 months after acceptance. Byline given. Buys second serial (reprint) rights. Submit seasonal/holiday material 2 months in advance. Simultaneous submissions OK. Reports in 2 weeks. Free sample copy and writer's guidelines.

Nonfiction: Book excerpts, general interest, how-to, humor, inspirational, interview/profile, new product, opinion, personal experience, technical and book reviews. Buys 50 mss/year. Query with or without published clips, or send complete ms. Length: 1,500-3,000 words. Pays $35-50.

Photos: Send photos with submission. Reviews 5×7 prints. Offers $10 per photo. Identification of subjects required. Buys one-time rights.

HOME MECHANIX, 2 Park Ave., New York NY 10016. (212)779-5000. Editor: Michael Morris. Executive Editor: Michael Chotiner. 50% freelance written. Prefers to work with published/established writers. "If it's good, and it fits the type of material we're currently publishing, we're interested whether writer is new or experienced." Magazine, published 10 times/year, for the active home and car owner. "Articles emphasize an active, home-oriented lifestyle. Includes information useful for maintenance, repair and renovation to the home and family car. Information on how to buy, how to select products useful to homeowners/car owners. Emphasis in home-oriented articles is on good design, inventive solutions to styling and space problems, useful home-workshop projects." Estab. 1905. Circ. 1.2 million. **Pays on acceptance.** Publishes ms an average of 6 months after acceptance. Byline given. Buys first North American serial rights. Query.

Nonfiction: Feature articles relating to homeowner/car owner, 1,500-2,500 words. "This may include personal home-renovation projects, professional advice on interior design, reports on different or unusual construction methods, energy-related subjects, outdoor/backyard projects, etc. We are no longer interested in high-tech subjects such as aerospace, electronics, photography or military hardware. Most of our automotive features are written by experts in the field, but fillers, tips, how-to repair, or modification articles on the family car are welcome. Articles on construction, tool use, refinishing techniques, etc., are also sought. Pays $300 minimum for features; fees based on number of printed pages, photos accompanying mss., etc." Pays expenses of writers on assignment.

Photos: Photos should accompany mss. Pays $600 and up for transparencies for cover. Inside color: $300/1 page, $500/2, $700/3, etc. Captions and model releases required.

Fillers: Tips and fillers useful to tool users or for general home maintenance. Pays $25 and up for illustrated and captioned fillers.

Tips: "The most frequent mistake made by writers in completing an article assignment for *Home Mechanix* is not taking the time to understand its editorial focus and special needs."

INTERNATIONAL DOLL WORLD, The doll lover's magazine, (formerly *National Doll World*), House of White Birches, 306 E. Parr Rd., Berne IN 46711. (219)589-8741. Editor: Rebekah Montgomery. Managing Editor: Läna Schurb. 90% freelance written. Bimonthly magazine covering doll collecting, restoration. "Our readers collect dolls because they enjoy them. Some do as investments, but most consider them decorative." Estab. 1970. Circ. 85,000. Pays on publication. Publishes ms an average of 8 months after acceptance. Byline given. Buys first North American serial or one-time rights. Submit seasonal/holiday material 1 year in advance. Simultaneous submissions OK. Reports in 2 weeks on queries. Sample copy $2.50. Writer's guidelines for SASE.

Nonfiction: Historical/nostalgic, how-to, interview/profile and technical. Special issue forthcoming on teddy bear and doll patterns. No articles about people and their doll collections. Buys 90 mss/year. Query with or without published clips, or send complete ms. Length: 5,000 words maximum. Pays $35-250.

Photos: Send photos with submission. Offers $5-50 per photo. Captions and identification of subjects required. Buys one-time or all rights.

Tips: "Choose a specific manufacturer and talk about his dolls or a specific doll—modern or antique—and explore its history and styles made."

INTERNATIONAL WOODWORKING, P.O. Box 706, Rt. 3 and Cummings Hill Rd., Plymouth NH 03264. (603)536-3876. Editor: Doug Werbeck. 70% freelance written. Buys first time North American serial rights. Quarterly magazine on woodworking for hobbyists and professionals. It is strongly suggested that illustrations and/or photographs accompany manuscripts. Estab. 1984. Simultaneous submissions OK. Reports in 6 weeks. Free sample copy with writer's guidelines and fact sheet for 9 × 12 SAE and postage for 5 ounces.

Nonfiction: "Articles and project plans on all aspects of woodworking, including the maintenance and repair of woodworking machinery and tools, furniture making, woodturning, antique repair, restoration, musical instrument construction, miniatures, wooden crafts, jigs and accessories. Woodworking projects plans need to be of the level that can be completed in the home shop. Readers are of the advanced amateur level." Buys 25 mss/year. Will respond to queries but mss preferred. Length 500-2,000 words. Pays $25-250 which includes illustrations.

Photos: Send photos with submission. Reviews 3 × 5 or larger prints, no transparencies. Caption, model releases and identification of subjects required. Buys first time North American serial rights.

Fillers: Anecdotes, facts, cartoons, newsbreaks and short humor. Buys 50/year. Length: 50-400 words. Pays $10-100.

Tips: "We strongly suggest prospective contributors obtain sample copy and writer's guidelines before any submission."

JUGGLER'S WORLD, International Jugglers Association, Box 443, Davidson NC 28036. (704)892-1296. FAX: (704)892-2526. Editor: Bill Giduz. 25% freelance written. A quarterly magazine on juggling. "*Juggler's World* publishes news, feature articles, fiction and poetry that relates to juggling. We also encourage 'how-to' articles describing how to learn various juggling tricks." Circ. 3,500. **Pays on acceptance.** Publishes ms an average of 6 months after acceptance. Byline given. Buys all rights. Submit seasonal/holiday material 6 months in advance. Simultaneous and previously published submissions OK. Query for electronic submissions. Reports in 1 week. Sample copy for 8½ × 11 SAE with 5 first class stamps. Writer's guidelines for #10 SASE.

Nonfiction: Essays, general interest, historical/nostalgic, how-to, humor, interview/profile, opinion, personal experience, photo feature and travel. Buys 10 mss/year. Query. Length: 500-2,000 words. Pays $50-100 for assigned articles. Pays expenses of writers on assignment.

Photos: State availability of photos with submission. Reviews contact sheets, negatives and prints. Offers no additional payment for photos accepted with ms. Captions required. Buys one-time rights.

Fiction: Ken Letko, fiction editor. Adventure, fantasy, historical, humorous, science fiction and slice-of-life vignettes. Buys 2 mss/year. Query. Length: 250-1,000 words. Pays $25-50.

Tips: "The best approach is a feature article on or an interview with a leading juggler. Article should include both human interest material to describe the performer as a individual and technical juggling information to make it clear to a knowledgeable audience the exact tricks and skits performed."

KITPLANES, For designers, builders and pilots of experimental aircraft, Fancy Publications, P.O. Box 6050, Mission Viejo CA 92690. (714)240-6001. FAX: (714)855-3045. Editor: Dave Martin. 70% freelance written. Eager to work with new/unpublished writers. Monthly magazine covering self-construction of private aircraft for pilots and builders. Estab. 1984. Circ. 52,000. Pays on publication. Publishes ms an average of 3 months after acceptance. Byline given. Offers negotiable kill fee. Buys first North American serial rights.

Submit seasonal/holiday material 6 months in advance. Query for electronic submissions. Reports in 2 weeks on queries; 6 weeks on mss. Sample copy $3; free writer's guidelines.

Nonfiction: How-to, interview/profile, new product, personal experience, photo feature, technical and general interest. "We are looking for articles on specific construction techniques, the use of tools, both hand and power, in aircraft building, the relative merits of various materials, conversions of engines from automobiles for aviation use, installation of instruments and electronics." No general-interest aviation articles, or "My First Solo" type of articles. Buys 80 mss/year. Query. Length: 500-5,000 words. Pays $100-400 including story photos.

Photos: Send photos with query or ms, or state availability of photos. Pays $250 for cover photos. Captions and identification of subjects required. Buys one-time rights.

Tips: "*Kitplanes* contains very specific information—a writer must be extremely knowledgeable in the field. Major features are entrusted only to known writers. I cannot emphasize enough that articles must be directed at the individual aircraft builder. We need more 'how-to' photo features in all areas of homebuilt aircraft."

LEGACY MAGAZINE, For the Contemporary Numismatist, Ivy Press/Heritage Capital Corp., Heritage Plaza, Highland Park Village, Dallas TX 75205. (800)527-9250. FAX: (214)520-6968. Vice President/Marketing: Budd Perlman. Editor: Mark Van Winkle. Quarterly magazine with general articles on U.S. coinage, collecting, investing, analysis of coin market. Readers are upper middle class and have about 5 years collecting experience. Estab. 1987. Circ. 12,000. Pays on publication. Byline given. Buys one-time rights. Simultaneous and previously published submissions OK. Query for electronic submissions. Reports in 2 weeks. Free sample copy.

Nonfiction: Essays, expose, historical/nostalgic, interview/profile, opinion, personal experience. Buys 15 mss/year. Query. Length: 1,500-3,000 words. Pays $50-500.

Photos: Send photos with submission. Offers no additional payment for photos accepted with ms. Identification of subjects required. Buys one-time rights.

Tips: "The magazine is aimed at intermediate to advanced coin collectors. We have features on historical, investing, collecting and analytical aspects of U.S. numismatics."

LINN'S STAMP NEWS, Amos Press, 911 Vandemark Rd., P.O. Box 29, Sidney OH 45365. (513)498-0801. FAX: (513)498-0806. Editor: Michael Laurence. Managing Editor: Elaine Boughner. 50% freelance written. Weekly tabloid on the stamp collecting hobby. "All articles must be about philatelic collectibles." Estab. 1928. Circ. 75,000. Pays on publication. Publishes an average of 1 month after acceptance. Byline given. Buys first North American serial rights. Submit seasonal/holiday material 2 months in advance. Reports on queries; 2 weeks on mss. Free sample copy. Writer's guidelines for #10 SAE with 2 first class stamps.

Nonfiction: General interest, historical/nostalgic, how-to, interview/profile and technical. "No articles merely giving information on background of stamp subject. Must have philatelic information included." Buys 300 mss/year. Send complete ms. Length: 500 words maximum. Pays $10-50. Rarely pays expenses of writers on assignment.

Photos: State availability of photos with submission. Prefers glossy b&w prints. Offers no additional payment for photos accepted with ms. Captions required. Buys all rights.

LOST TREASURE, P.O. Box 1589, Grove OK 74344. Managing Editor: Deborah Williams. 95% freelance written. For treasure hunting hobbyists, relic collectors, amateur prospectors and miners. Monthly magazine. Estab. 1966. Circ. 55,000. Buys all rights. Byline given. Buys 100 mss/year. Pays on publication. No simultaneous submissions. Reports in 2 months. Submit complete ms. Publishes an average of 2 months after acceptance. Sample copy and writer's guidelines for 9 × 12 SASE.

Nonfiction: How-to articles about treasure hunting, coinshooting, personal profiles, and stories about actual hunts, stories that give an unusual twist to treasure hunting—using detectors in an unorthodox way, odd sidelights on history, unusual finds. *Avoid* writing about the more famous treasures and lost mines. No bottle hunting stories. Length: 1,000-3,000 words. "If an article is well-written and covers its subject well, we'll buy it—regardless of length." Pays 4¢/word.

Photos: B&w glossy prints with mss help sell your story. Pays $5 for each photo published. Cover photos pay $100 each (35mm color slides). Captions required.

Tips: "Read *Lost Treasure* before submitting your stories. We are especially interested in stories that deal with the more unusual aspects of treasure hunting and metal detecting. Try to avoid the obvious—give something different. Also—good photos and graphics are a *must*."

MINIATURES SHOWCASE, Kalmbach Publishing Co., 21027 Crossroads Circle, Waukesha WI 53186. Editor: Geraldine Willems. 65% freelance written. A quarterly magazine about dollhouse miniatures. "We feature a different decorating theme each issue—our articles support the miniature room scene we focus on." Circ. 40,000. Pays on publication. Publishes an average of 3 months after acceptance. Byline given. Buys all rights. Submit seasonal/holiday material 4 months in advance. Query for electronic submissions. Reports in 1 month. Sample copy $3; writer's guidelines for SASE.

Nonfiction: Historical/social. Buys 12 mss/year. Query. Length: 100-1,500 words. Pays 10¢/word.
Photos: State availability of photos with submission. Reviews contact sheets, negatives, transparencies and 4-color prints only. Offers no additional payment for photos accepted with ms. Captions and identification of subjects required.
Tips: "Our articles are all assigned—a freelancer should query before sending in anything. Our features are open to freelancers—each issue deals with a different topic, often historical."

MODEL RAILROADER, P.O. Box 1612, Waukesha WI 53187. Editor: Russell G. Larson. For hobbyists interested in scale model railroading. Monthly. Buys exclusive rights. Study publication before submitting material. Reports on submissions within 1 month.
Nonfiction: Wants construction articles on specific model railroad projects (structures, cars, locomotives, scenery, benchwork, etc.). Also photo stories showing model railroads. Query. First-hand knowledge of subject almost always necessary for acceptable slant. Pays base rate of $75/page.
Photos: Buys photos with detailed descriptive captions only. Pays $7.50 and up, depending on size and use. Pays double b&w rate for color; full color cover earns $210.

‡MODERN GOLD MINER AND TREASURE HUNTER, Modern Gold Miner's Association, Inc., 114 Druey Rd., Box 47, Happy Camp CA 96039. (916)493-2062. FAX: (916)493-2095. Editor: Maria McCracken. Managing Editor: David McCracken. Bimonthly magazine on small-scale gold mining and treasure hunting. "We want interesting fact and fiction stories and articles about small-scale mining, treasure hunting, camping and the great outdoors." Estab. 1987. Circ. 10,000. Pays on publication. Buys all rights. Submit seasonal/holiday material 4 months in advance. Query for electronic submissions. Reports in 2 weeks on queries. Sample copy for 9 × 12 SAE with $1.35 postage. Free writer's guidelines.
Nonfiction: How-to, humor, inspirational, interview/profile, new product, personal experience, photo feature, travel. "No promotional articles concerning industry products." Buys 125 mss/year. Send complete ms. Length: 1,500-2,500 words. Pays $25-150.
Photos: Send photos with submission. Reviews any size transparencies and prints. Pays $10-50 per photo. Captions are required. Buys all rights.
Fiction: Adventure, experimental, fantasy, historical, horror, humorous, mystery, suspense, western.
Tips: "Our general readership is comprised mostly of individuals who are actively involved in gold mining and treasure hunting, or people who are interested in reading about others who are active and successful in the field. True stories of actual discoveries, along with good color photos—particularly of gold—are preferred. Also, valuable how-to information on new and workable field techniques, preferrably accompanied by supporting illustrations and/or photos."

MONITORING TIMES, Grove Enterprises Inc., P.O. Box 98, Brasstown NC 28902. (704)837-9200. Managing Editor: Larry Miller. Publisher: Robert Grove. 80% freelance written. A monthly magazine for radio hobbyists. Estab. 1982. Circ. 25,000. **Pays on acceptance.** Publishes ms an average of 2 months after acceptance. Byline given. Buys first North American serial rights. Submit seasonal/holiday material 4 months in advance. Simultaneous submissions OK. Reports in 1 month. Free sample copy for 8½ × 11 SAE and $1 postage; free writer's guidelines.
Nonfiction: General interest, how-to, humor, interview/profile, personal experience, photo feature, technical. Buys 275 mss/year. Query. Length: 1,000-2,500 words. Pays $150-200.
Photos: State availability of photos with submission. Offers $10-25/photo. Captions required. Buys one-time rights.
Columns/Departments: "Query managing editor."

MOUNTAIN STATES COLLECTOR, Spree Publishing, P.O. Box 2525, Evergreen CO 80439. FAX: (303)674-1253. Editor: Carol Rudolph. Managing Editor: Peg DeStefano. 85% freelance written. A monthly tabloid covering antiques and collectibles. Estab. 1970. Circ. 8,000. Pays on publication. Publishes ms an average of 3-6 months after acceptance. Byline given. Not copyrighted. Buys first rights, one-time rights or second serial (reprint) rights to material published elsewhere. Submit seasonal/holiday material at least 3 months in advance. Simultaneous and previously published submissions OK. Reports in 10 weeks. Sample copy for 9 × 12 SAE with 4 first class stamps; writer's guidelines for SASE.
Nonfiction: About antiques and/or collectibles—book excerpts, historical/nostalgic, how-to (collect), interview/profile (of collectors) and photo feature. Buys 75 mss/year. Query with or without published clips, or send complete ms. Length: 500-1,500 words. Pays $15. Sometimes pays the expenses of writers on assignment (mileage, phone—not long distance travel).
Photos: Send photos with submission. Reviews contact sheets, and 5 × 7 b&w prints. Offers $5/photo used. Captions preferred. Buys one-time rights.
Tips: "Writers should know their topics well or be prepared to do in-depth interviews with collectors. We prefer a down-home approach. We need articles on antiques, collectors and collections; how-to articles on collecting; how a collector can get started; or clubs for collectors. We would like to see more articles in 1991 with high-quality b&w photos."

THE NUMISMATIST, American Numismatic Association, 818 N. Cascade Ave., Colorado Springs CO 80903. (719)632-2646. FAX: (719)634-4085. Editor: Barbara Gregory. Monthly magazine "for collectors of coins, medals, tokens and paper money." Estab. 1888. Circ. 31,000. Pays on publication. Publishes ms an average of 1 year after acceptance. Byline given. Buys first North American serial rights or second serial (reprint) rights. Submit seasonal/holiday material 1 year in advance. Previously published submissions OK. Reports in 2 months. Free sample copy and writer's guidelines for #10 SASE.

Nonfiction: Essays, exposé, general interest, historical/nostalgic, humor, interview/profile, new product, opinion, personal experience, photo feature and technical. No articles that are lengthy or non-numismatic. Buys 48-60 mss/year. Send complete ms. Length: 1,000-3,500 words. Pays "on rate-per-published-page basis." Sometimes pays the expenses of writers on assignment.

Photos: Send b&w photos with submission. Reviews contact sheets and 4×5 or 5×7 prints. Offers $2.50-5/ photo. Captions and identification of subjects required. Buys one-time rights.

Columns/Departments: Buys 6 mss/year. Length: 775-2,000 words. "Pays negotiable flat fee per column."

‡NUTSHELL NEWS, For creators and collectors of scale miniatures, Kalmbach Publishing Co., 21027 Crossroads Circle, Waukesha WI 53187. (414)796-8776. Editor: Sybil Harp. 50% freelance written. Monthly magazine covering dollhouse scale miniatures. *Nutshell News* is aimed at serious, adult hobbyists. Our readers take their miniatures seriously and do not regard them as toys. "We avoid 'cutesiness' and treat our subject as a serious art form and/or an engaging leisure interest." Estab. 1971. Circ. 35,000. Pays on publication. Will occasionally pay on acceptance by special agreement. Byline given. Offers $25 kill fee. Buys all rights but will revert rights by agreement. Submit seasonal/holiday material 1 year in advance. Reports in 3 weeks on queries; 2 months on mss. Sample copy $3.50; writer's guidelines.

Nonfiction: How-to miniature projects in 1", ½", ¼" scales, interview/profile – artisans or collectors, photo feature – dollhouses, collections, museums. Upcoming special issues: May – smaller scales annual (½", ¼" or smaller scales); August – kitcrafting – customizing kits or commercial miniatures, a how-to issue. No articles on miniature shops or essays. Buys 120 mss/year. Query. Length: 1,000-2,000 words. Pays 10-12¢/word for assigned articles; 10¢/word for unsolicited articles. Sometimes pays expenses of writers on assignment.

Photos: Send photos with submission. Requires 35mm slides and larger, 3×5 prints. Pay $10-50. Captions preferred; identification of subjects required. Buys all rights.

Tips: "It is essential that writers for *Nutshell News* be active miniaturists, or at least very knowledgeable about the hobby. Our readership is intensely interested in miniatures and will discern lack of knowledge or enthusiasm on the part of an author. A writer can best break in to *Nutshell News* by convincing me that he/ she knows and is interested in miniatures, and by sending photos and/or clippings to substantiate that. Photographs are extremely important. They must be sharp and properly exposed to reveal details. A writer must convince me that he/she can provide good photos. For articles about subjects in the Chicago/Milwaukee area, we can usually send our staff photographer."

OLD CARS WEEKLY, Krause Publications, 700 E. State St., Iola WI 54990. (715)445-2214. FAX (715)445-4087. Editor: Mary Sieber. 50% freelance written. Weekly tabloid. Circ. 80,000. Pays on publication. Publishes ms an average of 2 months after acceptance. Buys all rights. Phone queries OK. Byline given. Reports in 2 weeks. Free sample copy and writer's guidelines.

Nonfiction: Short (2-3 pages) timely news reports and features on old car hobby with photos. Buys 5-10 mss/ issue. Query. Pays 3¢/word.

Photos: Pays $5 for 5×7 b&w glossy prints. Captions required. Buys all rights.

Tips: "We purchase both news and feature articles, especially interesting stories from our readers who own old cars. Will accept articles on cars, trucks, buses, toys and pedal cars, 1975 model year and older."

PAPER COLLECTORS MARKETPLACE, Watson Graphic Designs, Inc., P.O. Box 127, Scandinavia WI 54977. (715)467-2379. Editor: Doug Watson. 100% freelance written. A monthly magazine on paper collectibles. "All articles must relate to the hobby in some form. Whenever possible values should be given for the collectibles mentioned in the article." Estab. 1983. Circ. 4,000. Pays on publication. Byline given. Offers 25% kill fee on commissioned articles. Buys first North American serial rights. Submit seasonal/holiday material 2 months in advance. Reports in 2 weeks. Free sample copy; writer's guidelines for #10 SASE.

Nonfiction: Historical/nostalgic, how-to, photo feature, technical. Buys 60 mss/year. Query with published clips. Length: 1,000-2,000 words. Pays 3-5¢/words.

Photos: Send photos with submissions. Offers no additional payment for photos accepted with ms. Captions, model releases and identification of subjects required. Buys one-time rights.

Tips: "We presently publish three special issues per year: February (December 1 deadline) Mystery/Detective; April (Feb. 1 deadline), Spring Postcard Special; Oct. (Aug. 1 deadline), Fall Postcard Special."

‡THE PEN AND QUILL, Universal Autograph Collectors Club (UACC), P.O. Box 6181, Washington DC 20044-6181. (202)332-7388. Editor: Bob Erickson. 20% freelance written. Bimonthly magazine of autograph collecting. All articles must advance the hobby of autograph collecting in some manner. Estab. 1966. Circ. 1,700. Pays on publication. Publishes ms an average of 6 months after acceptance. Byline given. Buys first

North American serial rights. Submit seasonal/holiday material 4 months in advance. Sample copy $3.50.
Nonfiction: General interest, historical/nostalgic, interview/profile. Buys 4 mss/year. Send complete ms. Length: 500-2,500 words. Pays $20-100.
Photos: Send photos with submission. Offers no additional payment for photos accepted with ms. Captions and identification of subjects required. Buys one-time rights.

PLATE WORLD, The Magazine of Collector's Plates, 9200 N. Maryland Ave. Niles IL 60648. (312)763-7773. Editor-in-Chief: Alyson Wyckoff. Feature Editor: Tina Panoplos. 5% freelance written. Bimonthly magazine. "We write exclusively about limited-edition collector's plates—artists, makers, dealers and collectors. Our audience is involved in plates mostly as collectors; also dealers, makers or producers. The annual holiday issue (Nov.-Dec.) covers a variety of collectibles." Circ. 55,000. **Pays on acceptance.** Publishes ms an average of 2 months after acceptance. Byline given. Offers 50% kill fee. Buys various rights. Submit seasonal/holiday material 5 months in advance. Reports in 1 month on queries; 2 weeks on mss. Sample copy $3.50; free writer's guidelines. Pays some expenses of writers on assignment—"travel plus phone."
Nonfiction: Interview/profile (how artists create, biography or artist profile of exceptional plate collector); photo feature (about artist or plate manufacturer). "Writers can submit short profiles of interesting and exceptional plate collectors. Also, we have departments where we publish short items of interest." No critical attacks on industry. No articles on antique plates. Buys 10 mss/year. Query and send samples of work. Pays $100-500.
Photos: Albert Scharpou, art director. Human interest, technical. State availability of photos. Reviews transparencies. Pays negotiable rate. Identification of subjects required. Usually buys all rights; occasionally buys one-time rights.
Tips: Profiles of artists or collectors are the areas most open to freelancers. "The most frequent mistakes made by writers in completing an article for us are: not enough research, profiles not objective, articles too promotional. Also, writers must understand our editorial content (no antiques, etc.)."

POSTCARD COLLECTOR, Joe Jones Publishing, P.O. Box 337, Iola WI 54945. (715)445-5000. FAX: (715)445-4053. Editor: Deb Lengkeek. 70% freelance written. Monthly magazine. "Publication is for postcard collectors; all editorial content relates to postcards in some way." Estab. 1986. Circ. 6,000. Pays on publication. Publishes ms an average of 6 months after acceptance. Byline given. Buys one-time rights, first rights or second serial rights. Submit seasonal/holiday material 3 months in advance. Previously published submissions OK. Reports in 2 weeks on queries; 1 month on mss. Free sample copy and writer's guidelines.
Nonfiction: General interest, historical/nostalgic, how-to (e.g. preservatives), new product, opinion, personal experience, photo feature and travel. Buys 40 mss/year. Send complete ms. Length: 200-1,800 words. Pays 5-8¢/word for assigned articles; 3-5¢/word for unsolicited articles.
Photos: State availability of postcards with submission. Offers $1-3/photo. Captions and identification of subjects required. Buys perpetual, but nonexclusive rights.
Columns/Departments: 50-150 words. Buys 20-30 mss/year. Query. Pay is negotiable.
Tips: "We publish information about postcards written by expert topical specialists. The writer must be knowledgeable about postcards and have acquired 'expert' information. We plan more complete listings of postcard sets and series—old and new." Areas most open to freelancers are feature-length articles on specialized areas (600-1,800 words) with 1 to 10 illustrations.

THE PROFESSIONAL QUILTER, Oliver Press, P.O. Box 75277, St. Paul MN 55175-0277. (612)426-9681. Editor: Jeannie M. Spears. 80% freelance written. Works with a small number of new/unpublished writers each year. Quarterly magazine on the quilting business. Emphasis on small business, preferably quilt related. Estab. 1983. Circ. 2,000. Payment negotiated. Publishes ms an average of 6 months after acceptance. Byline given. Buys first North American serial rights, first serial rights and second serial (reprint) rights. Simultaneous queries and previously published submissions OK. Reports in 2 weeks on queries; 1 month on mss. Sample copy for 9 × 12 SAE with 4 first class stamps and $5; writer's guidelines for #10 SASE.
Nonfiction: How-to (quilting business); interview/profile; new product; opinion; and personal experience (of problems and problem-solving ideas in a quilting business). No quilting or sewing *techniques* or quilt photo spreads. Buys 20 mss/year. Query or send complete ms. Length: 500-1,500 words. Pays $25-75.
Tips: "Each issue will focus in depth on an issue of concern to the professional quilting community, such as ethics, art vs. craft, professionalism, etc. We would also like to receive articles on time and space (studio) organization, stress and family relationships. Remember that our readers already know that quilting is a time-honored tradition passed down from generation to generation, that quilts reflect the life of the maker, that quilt patterns have revealing names, etc. Ask yourself: If my grandmother had been running a quilting business for the last 5 years, would she have found this article interesting? Send a letter describing your quilt, craft or business experience with a query or manuscript."

Always check the most recent copy of a magazine for the address and editor's name before you send in a query or manuscript.

‡**QST**, American Radio Relay League, Inc., 225 Main St., Newington CT 06111. (203)666-1541. FAX: (203)665-7531. Editor: Paul L. Rinaldo. Managing Editor: Mark Wilson. 20% freelance written. Monthly magazine covering amateur radio, general interest, technical activities. "Ours are topics of interest to radio amateurs and persons in the electrical and communications fields." Estab. 1914. Circ. 160,000. Pays on publication. Publishes ms an average of 4 months after acceptance. Byline given. Buys all rights. Submit seasonal/holiday material 4-5 months in advance. Query for electronic submissions. Reports in 3 weeks on queries. Free sample copy and writer's guidelines.

Nonfiction: General interest, how-to, humor, new products, personal experience, photo feature, technical (anything to do with amateur radio). Buys 50 mss/year. Query with or without published clips, or send complete ms. Length: no minimum or maximum. Pays $50 per published page. Sometimes pays expenses of writers on assignment.

Photos: Send photos with submission. Offers no additional payment for photos accepted with ms. Captions, model releases and identification of subjects required. Buys all rights.

Columns/Departments: Hints and Kinks (hints/time saving procedures/circuits/associated with amateur radio), 50-200 words. Buys 100 mss/year. Send complete ms. Length: 50-200 words. Pays $20.

Tips: "Write with an idea, ask for sample copy and writer's guide. Technical and general interest to amateur operators, communications and electronics are most open."

‡**QUICK & EASY CRAFTS, For Today's Crafty Women**, House of White Birches, 306 E. Parr, Berne IN 46711. (219)589-8741. Editor: Rebekah Montgomery. Managing Editor: Läna Schurb. 90% freelance written. Bimonthly magazine covering crafts that are upscale but easily and quickly done. "Our audience does not mind spending money on craft items to use in their projects but they don't have lots of time to spend." Estab. 1990. Circ. 90,000. Pays on publication. Byline given. Buys first, one-time or all rights. Submit seasonal/holiday material 1 year in advance. Reports in 2 weeks on queries. Sample copy $2; free writer's guidelines.

Nonfiction: How-to. Upcoming special issue for Christmas. No profiles of other crafters. Buys 150 mss/year. Send complete ms. Pays $25-250.

Tips: "Send good, clear photo with ms. Ms should include complete instructions for project."

QUILT WORLD, House of White Birches, 306 E. Parr Rd., Berne IN 46711. (219)589-8741. Editor: Sandra L. Hatch. 100% freelance written. Works with a small number of new/unpublished writers each year. Bimonthly magazine covering quilting. "We publish articles on quilting techniques, profile of quilters and coverage of quilt shows. Reader is 50-70 years old, midwestern." Circ. 130,000. Pays on publication. Publishes ms an average of 6 months after acceptance. Byline given. Buys all rights, first rights, one-time rights and second serial (reprint) rights. Submit seasonal/holiday material 6 months in advance. Previously published submissions OK. Query for electronic submissions. Reports in 3 weeks. Sample copy $3; writer's guidelines for SASE.

Nonfiction: How-to, interview/profile (quilters), technical, new product (quilt products) and photo feature. Buys 18-24 mss/year. Query. Length: open. Pays $35-100.

Photo: Send photos with submission. Reviews transparencies and prints. Offers $15/photo (except covers). Identification of subjects required. Buys all rights or one-time rights.

Tips: "Send list of previous articles published with resume and a SASE. List ideas which you plan to base your articles around."

‡**QUILTER'S NEWSLETTER MAGAZINE**, P.O. Box 394, Wheatridge CO 80033. Editor: Bonnie Leman. Monthly. Estab. 1969. Circ. 150,000. Buys first North American serial rights or second rights. Buys about 15 mss/year. Pays on publication, sometimes on acceptance. Reports in 5 weeks. Free sample copy.

Nonfiction: "We are interested in articles on the subject of quilts and quiltmakers *only*. We are not interested in anything relating to 'Grandma's Scrap Quilts' but could use fresh material." Submit complete ms. Pays 3¢/word minimum, usually more.

Photos: Additional payment for photos depends on quality.

Fillers: Related to quilts and quiltmakers only.

Tips: "Be specific, brief, and professional in tone. Study our magazine to learn the kind of thing we like. Send us material which fits into our format but which is different enough to be interesting. Realize that we think we're the best quilt magazine on the market and that we're aspiring to be even better, then send us the cream off the top of your quilt material."

‡**QUILTING INTERNATIONAL**, All American Crafts, Inc., 70 Sparta Ave., CN 1003, Sparta NJ 07871. (201)729-4477. Editorial Director: Camille Pomaco. Editor: Mitzi Roberts. 50% freelance written. Quilts and quilting magazine published 5 times/year. "We try to offer material for every level of quilter; both inspirational and instructive." Estab. 1987. Pays on publication. Publishes ms an average of 4-6 months after acceptance. Byline given. Buys first North American serial rights or all rights. Submit seasonal/holiday material 6 months in advance. Reports in 1 month on queries; 2 months on mss. Sample copy for 9×12 SAE with $1.10 postage. Free writer's guidelines.

Nonfiction: Quilts and patterns; quilt exhibits, international and local quilt events, historical, how-to, humor, inspirational, interview/profile, new product, opinion, personal experience, photo feature, technical, travel (all as related to quilts and quilting). Buys 10-20 mss/year. Send complete ms. Length: 300-1,500 words. Pays 7-10¢/word.

Photos: Send photos with submission. Reviews 4×5 slides or transparencies. Payment negotiable. Model releases and identification of subjects required. Buys one-time rights and all rights.

Columns/Departments: Quickie (a fast project using some facet of quilting); Small Treasures (portable project). Buys 6 mss/year. Send complete ms. Length: 300-1,000 words. Pays 7-10¢/word.

Poetry: Buys 5 poems/year. Submit maximum 4 poems. Length: 2-8 lines. Pays $5-10.

Fillers: Anecdotes, gags to be illustrated by cartoonist, short humor. Buys 5/year. Length: 100-300 words. Pays 7¢/word.

Tips: "Good quality slides or chromes of beautiful quilts are highly desirable. We want articles about specific quilts and the quilters involved."

RAILROAD MODEL CRAFTSMAN, Box 700, Newton NJ 07860. (201)383-3355. Editor: William C. Schaumburg. 75% freelance written. Works with a small number of new/unpublished writers each year. For model railroad hobbyists, in all scales and gauges. Monthly. Circ. 97,000. Buys all rights. Buys 50-100 mss/year. Pays on publication. Publishes ms an average of 9 months after acceptance. Submit seasonal material 6 months in advance. Sample copy $2; writer's and photographer's guidelines for SASE.

Nonfiction: "How-to and descriptive model railroad features written by persons who did the work are preferred. Almost all our features and articles are written by active model railroaders. It is difficult for non-modelers to know how to approach writing for this field." Pays minimum of $1.75/column inch of copy ($50/page).

Photos: Purchased with or without mss. Buys sharp 8×10 glossy prints and 35mm or larger transparencies. Pays minimum of $10 for photos or $2/diagonal inch of published b&w photos, $3 for color transparencies and $100 for covers, which must tie in with article in that issue. Caption information required.

Tips: "We would like to emphasize freight car modeling based on actual prototypes, as well as major prototype studies of them."

SAGEBRUSH JOURNAL, The Best Danged Western Newspaper Going!, Allied Publishing, 430 Haywood Rd., Asheville NC 28806. Editor: Linda Hagan. Publisher: Bill Hagan. 90% freelance written. A monthly tabloid covering Western genre films and print (books and magazines). "We are oriented toward people who love the thrill of the Western genre—from the glorious B westerns of yesteryear, pulp stories and novels, to the Western revival of today." Circ. 5,000. Pays on publication. Byline given. Buys first North American serial, one-time and second serial (reprint) rights. Submit seasonal/holiday material 6 months in advance. Previously published submissions OK. Query for electronic submissions. Reports in 2 weeks on queries; 2 months on mss. Sample copy for $2.50 and SAE with $2 postage. Writer's guidelines for #10 SASE.

Nonfiction: General interest, historical/nostalgic, humor, interview/profile, personal experience, photo feature, Western convention reports, reviews of Western films and books. Buys 40-50 mss/year. Query with or without published clips, or send complete ms. Length: 200-5,000 words. Pays 25¢/column inch.

Photos: Send photos with submission. Reviews prints. Offers 25¢/column inch for photo (included with article payment); "no separate photos." Captions and identification of subjects required. Buys one-time rights.

Fillers: Unable to use slides. Western-related anecdotes, facts, newsbreaks and short humor. Buys 15-20/year. Length: 50-200 words. Pays 25¢/column inch.

SCOTT STAMP MONTHLY, P.O. Box 828, Sidney OH 45365. (513)498-0802. FAX: (513)498-0808. Editor: Richard L. Sine. 60% freelance written. Works with a small number of new/unpublished writers each year. For stamp collectors, from the beginner to the sophisticated philatelist. Monthly magazine. Estab. 1873. Circ. 22,000. Rights purchased vary with author and material; usually buys first North American serial rights. Byline given. Buys 80 unsolicited mss/year. Pays on publication. Publishes ms an average of 5 months after acceptance. Submit seasonal or holiday material at least 6 months in advance. Query for electronic submissions. Reports in 1 month. Sample copy for $1.50.

Nonfiction: "We are in the market for articles, written in an engaging fashion, concerning the remote byways and often-overlooked aspects of stamp collecting. Writing should be clear and concise, and subjects must be well-researched and documented. Illustrative material should also accompany articles whenever possible." Query. Pays about $100.

Photos: State availability of photos. Offers no additional payment for b&w photos used with mss.

Tips: "It's rewarding to find a good new writer with good new material. Because our emphasis is on lively, interesting articles about stamps, including historical perspectives and human interest slants, we are open to writers who can produce the same. Of course, if you are an experienced philatelist, so much the better. We do not want stories about the picture on a stamp taken from a history book or an encyclopedia and dressed up to look like research. If an idea is good and not a basic rehash, we are interested."

SEW NEWS, The Fashion Magazine for People Who Sew, PJS Publications, Inc., News Plaza, P.O. Box 1790, Peoria IL 61656. (309)682-6626. Editor: Linda Turner Griepentrog. 90% freelance written. Works with a small number of new/unpublished writers each year. Monthly magazine covering fashion-sewing. "Our magazine is for the beginning home sewer to the professional dressmaker. It expresses the fun, creativity and excitement of sewing." Estab. 1980. Circ. 230,000. **Pays on acceptance.** Publishes ms an average of 6 months after acceptance. Byline given. Buys all rights. Submit seasonal/holiday material 6 months in advance. Reports in 2 months. Sample copy $3; writer's guidelines for #10 SAE and 2 first class stamps.

Nonfiction: How-to (sewing techniques) and interview/profile (interesting personalities in home-sewing field). Buys 200-240 ms/year. Query with published clips. Length: 500-2,000 words. Pays $25-400. Rarely pays expenses of writers on assignment.

Photos: State availability of photos. Prefers b&w contact sheets and negatives. Payment included in ms price. Identification of subjects required. Buys all rights.

Tips: "Query first with writing sample. Areas most open to freelancers are how-to and sewing techniques; give explicit, step-by-step instructions plus rough art."

SHUTTLE SPINDLE & DYEPOT, Handweavers Guild of America, 120 Mountain Road, Bloomfield CT 06002. Editor: Judy Robbins. 60% freelance written. A quarterly magazine covering handweaving, spinning and dyeing. "We take the practical and aesthetic approach to handweaving, handspinning, and related textile arts." Estab. 1969. Pays on publication. Publishes ms 4-15 months after acceptance. Byline given. Buys first North American serial rights. Submit seasonal/holiday material 1 year in advance. Rarely accepts previously published submissions. Reports in 1 month on queries; 2 months on mss. Sample copy $6.50; free writer's guidelines.

Nonfiction: How-to, interview/profile, personal experience, photo feature and technical. "We want interesting, practical, technical information in our field." Buys 30 mss/year. Query with or without published clips, or send complete ms. Length: 500-1,500 words. Pays $25-100.

Photos: Send photos or state availability of photos with submission. Reviews contact sheets and transparencies.

Tips: "We read all submissions, especially from weavers and weaving teachers."

SUNSHINE ARTISTS USA, The Voice Of The Nation's Artists and Craftsmen, Sun Country Enterprises, 1700 Sunset Dr., Longwood FL 32750. (407)323-5937. Editor: Joan L. Wahl. Managing Editor: 'Crusty' Sy. A monthly magazine covering art and craft shows in the United States. "We are a top marketing magazine for professional artists, craftspeople and photographers working street and mall shows. We list 10,000 shows a year, critique many of them and publish articles on marketing, selling and improving arts and crafts." Circ. 16,000. Pays on publication. Publishes ms an average of 3 months after acceptance. Byline given. Buys first North American serial rights. Reports in 2 weeks on queries; 6 weeks on manuscripts. Sample copy $2.50.

Nonfiction: "We are interested in articles that relate to artists and craftsmen traveling the circuit. Although we have a permanent staff of 40 writers, we will consider well-written, thoroughly researched articles on successful artists making a living with their work, new ways to market arts and crafts. Attend some art shows. Talk to the exhibitors. Get ideas from them." No how-tos. Buys 20 mss/year. Query. Length: 550-2,000 words. Pays $15-50 for assigned articles.

Photos: State availability of photos with submission. Black & white photos only. Offers no additional payment for photos accepted with ms. Captions, model releases and identification of subjects required.

TEDDY BEAR REVIEW, Collector Communications Corp., P.O. Box 1239, Hanover PA 17331. (717)633-7333. Editor: A. Christian Revi. 40% freelance written. Works with a small number of new/unpublished writers each year. A quarterly magazine on teddy bears. Pays 30 days after acceptance. Byline given. Buys first North American serial rights. Submit seasonal/holiday material 6 months in advance. Reports in 2 months. Sample copy and writer's guidelines for $2 and 9 × 12 SAE.

Nonfiction: Book excerpts, historical, how-to and interview/profile. No nostalgia on childhood teddy bears. Buys 20 mss/year. Query with published clips. Length: 500-1,500 words. Pays $75-200. Sometimes pays the expenses of writers on assignment "if approved ahead of time."

Photos: Send photos with submission. Reviews transparencies and b&w prints. Offers no additional payment for photos accepted with ms. Captions required. Buys one-time rights.

Tips: "We are interested in good, professional writers around the country with a strong knowledge of teddy bears. Historical profile of bear companies, profiles of contemporary artists and knowledgeable reports on museum collections are of interest."

‡TRADITIONAL QUILTER, The Leading Teaching Mag for Creative Quilters, MSC Publishing Co., 70 Sparta Ave., CN 1003, Sparta NJ 07871. (201)729-4474. Editorial Director: Camille Pomaco. Editor: Phyllis Barbieri. 45% freelance written. Bimonthly magazine on quilting. Estab. 1988. Pays on publication. Byline given. Buys first rights or all rights. Submit seasonal/holiday 6 months in advance. Reports in 2 months. Sample copy for 9 × 12 SAE with $1.10 postage. Writer's guidelines for #10 SASE.

Nonfiction: Quilts and quilt patterns with instructions, quilt-related projects, historical/nostalgic, humor, interview/profile, opinion, personal experience, photo feature, travel — all quilt related. Query with published clips. Length: 350-1,000 words. Pays 7-10¢/word.

Photos: Send photos with submission. Reviews all size transparencies and prints. Offers $10-25 per photo. Captions and identification of subjects required. Buys one-time or all rights.

Columns/Departments: Finishing Touches (innovative ways to embellish or finish a quilt), 1,000 words; Quilting in Fashion (clothing and interior fashion), 1,000 words; Feature Teacher (qualified quilt teachers with teaching involved — with slides), 1,000 words; Remnants (reports on conventions, history — humor). Length: 1,000 words maximum. Pays 7-10¢/word.

Fillers: Anecdotes, facts, short humor. Buys 24/year. Length: 75-500 words. Pays 10-15¢/word.

TREASURE CHEST, The Information Source & Marketplace for Collectors and Dealers, Venture Publishing Co., Suite 211A, 253 West 72nd St., New York NY 10023. (212)496-2234. Editor: Howard E. Fischer. 60% freelance written. Monthly newspaper on antiques and collectibles. Estab. 1988. Circ. 50,000. Pays on publication. Publishes ms an average of 2 months after acceptance. Byline given. Buys first rights and second serial (reprint) rights. Previously published submissions OK. Reports in 1 month on queries; 2 months on mss. Sample copy for 9 × 12 SAE with 85¢ postage; writer's guidelines for #10 SASE.

Nonfiction: Exposé, general interest, historical/nostalgic, how-to (detect reproductions, find new sources of items, etc.), humor, interview/profile, personal experience and photo feature. Buys 20-35 mss/year. Query with published clips. Length: 700-1,000 words. Pays $20-50. Payment in contributor copies or other premiums negotiable.

Photos: State availability of photos with submission. Reviews contact sheets, 5 × 7 and 8 × 10 prints. Offers no additional payment for photos accepted with ms. Captions and identification of subjects required. Buys one-time rights.

Columns/Departments: Investing in Antiques & Collectibles (what's hot; investing tips, etc.) and Show Reviews (unusual items displayed; sales figures, etc.). Query with published clips.

Fillers: Anecdotes, facts, gags to be illustrated by cartoonist and short humor. Buys 12-30/year. Length: 30-200 words. Pays $10-25.

TREASURE SEARCH/FOUND, Jess Publishing Co., 6278 Adobe Rd., 29 Palms CA 92277. (619)367-3531. FAX: (619)367-0039. Editor: Jim Williams. 80% freelance written. Monthly magazine on treasure hunts. "We publish true stories about treasures, great and small, yet to be discovered as well as about potential coin and relic hunting sites; also product reviews, how-to articles and descriptions of both successful and unsuccessful searches. The magazine is intended to be a practical handbook for the active searcher." Estab. 1970. Pays on publication. Publishes ms an average of 2 months after acceptance. Byline given. Buys all rights. Submit seasonal/holiday material 3 months in advance. Query for electronic submissions. Reports in 2 weeks. Sample copy for 9 × 12 SAE with $1.05 in postage. Free writer's guidelines.

Nonfiction: Exposé (of treasures not worth searching), historical/nostalgic (treasures backed by history), how-to (how-to research, and search), humor (humorous experiences in the field), inspirational (accounts of treasures found), interview/profile (a treasure hunter's biography), new product (any kind of detection or recovery equipment), personal experience (accounts of searches), photo feature (showing the search for or recovery of a treasure) and technical (explaining how related equipment works). "No fiction — fabricated treasures or experiences." Buys 100 mss/year. Query. Length: 500-15,000 words. Pays $30 per magazine page. Sometimes pays expenses of writers on assignment.

Photos: Send photos with submissions. Reviews contact sheets and 2¼ or 35mm transparencies. Offers $2-75 per photo. Identification of subjects required. Buys one-time rights.

Columns/Departments: "Then And Now" (clues to treasures or sites worth exploring), 1,000 words and "The Printing Press" (reviews of books of interest to the treasure hunter), 250-400 words. Buys 24 mss/year. Query. Pays $35-45.

Tips: "Freelancers should be aware they are writing for an experienced, skeptical audience and can help themselves by being accurate in all details, getting to know treasure hunters and even practicing some of the techniques themselves. We immediately publish truthful stories of recovered treasures backed by pertinent photos and clues to previously unreported treasures yet to be found if backed by historical documentation."

THE TRUMPETER, Croatian Philatelic Society, 1512 Lancelot, Borger TX 79007. (806)273-7225. Editor: Eck Spahich. 80% freelance written. Eager to work with new/unpublished writers. A quarterly magazine covering stamps, coins, currency, military decorations and collectibles of the Balkans, and of central Europe. Circ. 800. Pays on publication. Publishes ms an average of 9 months after acceptance. Byline given. Buys first and one-time rights. Submit seasonal/holiday material 6 months in advance. Simultaneous submissions OK. Reports in 2 months on queries; 1 month on mss. Sample copy $4; free writer's guidelines with #10 SASE.

Nonfiction: Book excerpts, general interest, historical/nostalgic, how-to (on detecting forged stamps, currency etc.) interview/profile, photo feature and travel. Buys 15-20 mss/year. Send complete ms. Length: 500-1,500 words. Pays $25-50 for assigned articles; pays $5-25 for unsolicited articles. Sometimes pays the expenses of writers on assignment.

Photos: State availability of photos with submission. Reviews 3×5 prints. Offers $5-10/photo. Captions and identification of subjects required. Buys one-time rights.
Columns/Departments: Book Reviews (stamps, coins, currency of Balkans), 200-400 words; Forgeries (emphasis on pre-1945 period), 500-1,000 words. Buys 10 mss/year. Send complete ms. Length: 100-300 words. Pays $5-25.
Fillers: Facts. Buys 15-20/year. Length: 20-50 words. Pays $1-5.
Tips: "We desperately need features on Zara, Montenegro, Serbia, Bulgaria, Bosnia, Croatia, Romania and Laibach."

VIDEOMAKER™, The Video Camera User's Magazine, Videomaker Inc., P.O. Box 4591, Chico CA 95927. (916)891-8410. FAX: (916)891-8443. Editor: Bradley Kent. 75% freelance written. A monthly magazine on video production. "Our audience is a range of hobbyist and low-end professional video camera users." Editorial emphasis is on video*making* (production and exposure), *not* reviews of commercial videos. Personal video phenomenon is a young 'movement' — readership encouraged to participate — get in on the act, join the fun." Estab. 1986. Circ. 50,000. Pays on publication. Publishes ms an average of 4-6 months after acceptance. Byline given. Buys all rights. Submit seasonal/holiday material 6 months in advance. Simultaneous, and previously published submissions OK. Query for electronic submissions. Reports in 1 month. Sample copy for 9×12 SAE with 5 first-class stamps. Free writer's guidelines.
Nonfiction: How-to (tools, tips, techniques for better videomaking), interview/profile (notable videomakers), product probe (review of latest and greatest or innovative), personal experience (lessons to benefit other videomakers), technical (state-of-the-art audio/video). Articles with comprehensive coverage of product line or aspect of videomaking preferred. Buys 70 mss/year. Query with or without published clips or send complete ms. Length: open. Pays $150-300.
Photos: Send photos with submissions. Reviews contact sheets, transparencies and prints. Captions required. Payment for photos accepted with ms included as package compensation. Buys one-time rights.
Columns/Departments: Computer Video (state-of-the art products, applications, potentials for computer-video interface); Profile (highlights videomakers using medium in unique/worthwhile ways); Book/Tape Mode (brief reviews of current works pertaining to video production); Videocrafts (projects, gadgets, inventions for videomaking); Video for Hire (money-making opportunities); Edit Points (tools and techniques for successful video editing). Buys 80 mss/year. Pays $35-175.
Fillers: Anecdotes, facts, cartoons, newsbreaks, short humor. Negotiable pay.
Tips: "Comprehensiveness a must. Article on shooting tips covers *all* angles. Buyer's guide to special-effect generators cites *all* models available. Magazine strives for an 'all-or-none' approach. Most topics covered once (twice tops) per year, so we must be thorough. Manuscript/photo package submissions helpful. *Videomaker* wants videomaking to be fulfilling and fun."

WESTERN & EASTERN TREASURES, People's Publishing Co., Inc., P.O. Box 1095, Arcata CA 95521. FAX: (707)822-0973. Editor: Rosemary Anderson. Emphasizes treasure hunting and metal detecting for all ages, entire range in education, coast-to-coast readership. 90% freelance written. Monthly magazine. Estab. 1966. Circ. 70,000. Pays on publication. Publishes ms an average of 1 year after acceptance. Buys all rights. Sample copy and writer's guidelines for $2 and 8½×11 SAE.
Nonfiction: How-to "hands on" use of metal detecting equipment, how to locate coins, jewelry and relics, prospect for gold, where to look for treasures, rocks and gems, etc., "first-person" experiences. "No purely historical manuscripts or manuscripts that require two-part segments or more." Buys 200 unsolicited mss/year. Submit complete ms. Length: maximum 1,500 words. Pays 2¢/word — negotiable.
Photos: Purchased with accompanying ms. Captions required. Submit b&w prints or 35mm Kodachrome transparencies. Pays $5 maximum for 3×5 and up b&w glossy prints; $35 and up for 35mm Kodachrome cover slides. Model releases required.
Tips: "The writer has a better chance of breaking in at our publication with short articles and fillers as these give the readers a chance to respond to the writer. The publisher relies heavily on reader reaction. Not adhering to word limit is the main mistake made by writers in completing an article for us. Writers must clearly cover the subjects described above in 1,500 words or less."

WOMEN'S CIRCLE COUNTED CROSS-STITCH, House of White Birches, Inc., 4 Oak Dr., Box 158, Hampton Falls NH 03844. Editor: Anne Morgan Jefferson. 100% freelance written. Eager to work with new/unpublished writers. Bimonthly magazine featuring counted cross-stitch. Circ. 165,000. Pays on publication. Publishes ms an average of at least 6 months after acceptance. Byline given. Buys all rights. Submit seasonal/holiday material 6 months in advance. Reports in 1 month. Sample copy $3. Make checks payable to House of White Birches. Contributor tips, guidelines and deadline schedule for large SAE and 2 first class stamps.
Nonfiction: How-to, interview/profile, new product and charted designs. Buys 12-15 mss/year. Query with published clips. "Submit cross-stitch designs with cover letter, complete ms and snapshot or 35mm slide of project *or* send complete ms and finished project. Include sufficient postage for project return." Length: open. Pays $25 and up. Also publishes cross-stitch leaflets.
Tips: "We'd like larger, more complex designs using the latest techniques and products."

‡**WOODSHOP NEWS**, Soundings Publications Inc., 35 Pratt St., Essex CT 06426. (203)767-8227. Editor: Ian C. Bowen. Associate Editor: Lewis Lorini. 20% freelance written. Monthly tabloid "covering woodworking for professionals and hobbyists. Solid business news and features about woodworking companies. Feature stories about interesting amateur woodworkers. Not many how-to articles." Estab. 1986. Circ. 100,000. Pays on publication. Publishes ms an average of 2 months after acceptance. Byline given. Offers 25% kill fee. Buys first North American serial rights. Submit seasonal/holiday material 4 months in advance. Simultaneous submissions OK. Query for electronic submissions. Reports in 3 weeks on queries; 1 month on mss. Free sample copy and writer's guidelines.

Nonfiction: How-to—query first, interview/profile, new product, opinion, personal experience, photo feature. No general interest profiles of "folksy" woodworker. Buys 50-75 mss/year. Query with published clips. Length: 100-1,800 words. Pays $30-400 for assigned articles; $30-200 for unsolicited articles. Pays expenses of writers on assignment. Send photos with submission.

Photos: Reviews contact sheets and prints. Offers $20-35 per photo. Captions and identification of subjects required. Buys one-time rights.

Columns/Departments: Pro Shop (business advice, marketing, employee relations, taxes etc. for the professional written by an established professional in the field), 1,200-1,500 words; Tech Talk (technical how-to, written by experts in the topic), 1,200-1,500 words. Buys 24 mss/year. Query. Pays $200-350.

Tips: "The best way to start is a profile of a business or hobbyist woodworker in your area. Find a unique angle about the person or business and stress this as the theme of your article. Avoid a broad, general-interest theme that would be more appropriate to a daily newspaper. Our readers are woodworkers who want more depth and more specifics than would a general readership. If you are profiling a business, we need standard business information such as gross annual earnings/sales, customer base, product line and prices, marketing strategy etc. Black and white 35 mm photos are a must."

‡**WOODWORK, A magazine for all woodworkers**, Ross Periodicals, P.O. Box 1529, Ross CA 94957. (415)382-0580. Editor: Jeff Greef. Publisher: Tom Toldrian. 90% freelance written. Bimonthly magazine covering woodworking. "We are aiming at a broad audience of woodworkers, from the home enthusiast/hobbyist to more advanced." Estab. 1989. Circ. 100,000. Pays on publication. Byline given. Buys first North American serial rights and second serial (reprint) rights. Reports in 6-8 weeks. Sample copy $2 with 9×12 SAE and 6 first class stamps. Writer's guidelines for #10 SAE with 1 first class stamp.

Nonfiction: How-to (simple or complex, making attractive furniture), interview/profile (of established woodworkers that make attractive furniture), photo feature (of interest to woodworkers), technical (tools, techniques). "Do not send a how-to unless you are a woodworker." Buys 40 mss/year. Query first. Length: 1,500-3,000 words. Pays $150/published page.

Photos: Send photos with submission. Reviews 35mm slides. Offers no additional payment for photos accepted with ms. Captions and identification of subjects required. Buys one-time rights.

Columns/Departments: Feature articles (from non-woodworking freelancers, we use interview/profiles of established woodworkers. Bring out woodworker's philosophy about the craft, opinions about what is happening currently. Good photos of attractive furniture a must. Section on how-to desireable.), 1,500-3,000 words. Query with published clips. Pays $600-1,500 at $150 per published page.

Fillers: Anecdotes, facts, newsbreaks, short humor. Length: 1,000 words. Pays $150 maximum.

Tips: "If you are not a woodworker, the interview/profile is your best, really only chance. Good writing is essential as are good photos. The interview must be intertaining, but informative and pertinent to woodworkers' interests."

THE WORKBASKET, 4251 Pennsylvania Ave., Kansas City MO 64111. Editor: Roma Jean Rice. Issued monthly except bimonthly June-July and November-December. Buys first rights. **Pays on acceptance.** Reports in 6 weeks.

Nonfiction: Step-by-step directions for craft projects (400-500 words) and gardening articles (200-500 words). Query. Pays 7¢/word.

Photos: Color photos only. Pays negotiable fee.

WORKBENCH, 4251 Pennsylvania Ave., Kansas City MO 64111. (816)531-5730. Editor: Robert N. Hoffman. 75% freelance written. Prefers to work with published/established writers; works with a small number of new/unpublished writers each year. For woodworkers. Estab. 1957. Circ. 909,000. **Pays on acceptance.** Publishes ms an average of 1 year after acceptance. Byline given. Buys all rights then returns all but first rights upon request, after publication. Reports in 2 months. Sample copy for 8½×11 SAE and 6 first class stamps; free writer's guidelines.

Nonfiction: "We have continued emphasis on do-it-yourself woodworking, home improvement and home maintenance projects. We provide in-progress photos, technical drawings and how-to text for all projects. We are very strong in woodworking, cabinetmaking and classic furniture construction. Projects range from simple toys to complicated reproductions of furniture now in museums. We would like to receive contemporary and furniture items that can be duplicated by both beginning do-it-yourselfers and advanced woodworkers." Query. Pays $175/published page or more depending on quality of submission. Additional payment for good color photos. "If you can consistently provide good material, including photos, your rates will go up and you will get assignments."

Columns/Departments: Shop Tips bring $25 with a line drawing and/or b&w photo. Workbench Solver pays $75 to experts providing answers to readers' problems related to do-it-yourself projects and home repair.

Tips: "Our magazine focuses on woodworking, covering all levels of ability and home improvment projects from the do-it-yourselfer's viewpoint, emphasizing the most up-to-date materials and procedures. We would like to receive articles on indoor home improvements and remodeling, home improvement on manufactured and mobile homes, and/or simple contemporary furniture. We place a heavy emphasis on projects that are both functional and classic in design. We can photograph projects worthy for publication, so feel free to send snapshots."

WORLD COIN NEWS, Krause Publications, 700 E. State, Iola WI 54990. (715)445-2214. FAX: (715)445-4087. Editor: Roger Case. 30% freelance written. Works with a small number of new/unpublished writers each year. Weekly newsmagazine about non-U.S. coin collecting for novices and advanced collectors of foreign coins, medals, and other numismatic items. Circ. 10,000. Pays on publication. Publishes ms an average of 1 month after acceptance. Byline given. Buys first North American serial rights and reprint rights. Submit seasonal material 1 month in advance. Simultaneous submissions OK. Reports in 2 weeks. Free sample copy.

Nonfiction: "Send us timely news stories related to collecting foreign coins and current information on coin values and markets." Send complete ms. Buys 30 mss/year. Length: 500-2,000 words. Pays 3¢/word to first-time contributors; fees negotiated for later articles. Sometimes pays the expenses of writers on assignment.

Photos: Send photos with ms. Pays $5 minimum for b&w prints. Captions and model release required. Buys first rights and reprint rights.

YESTERYEAR, Yesteryear Publications, P.O. Box 2, Princeton WI 54968. (414)787-4808. Editor: Michael Jacobi. 5% freelance written. Prefers to work with published/established writers. For antique dealers and collectors, people interested in collecting just about anything, and nostalgia buffs. Monthly tabloid. Estab. 1976. Circ. 7,000. Pays on publication. Publishes ms an average of 2-3 months after acceptance. Buys one-time rights. Byline given. Submit seasonal/holiday material 3 months in advance. Simultaneous and previously published submissions OK. Reports in 1 month. Sample copy $1.

Nonfiction: General interest (basically, anything pertaining to antiques, collectible items or nostalgia in general); historical (again, pertaining to the above categories); and how-to (refinishing antiques, how to collect). The more specific and detailed, the better. "We do not want personal experience or opinion articles." Buys 10 mss/year. Send complete ms. Pays $5-25. Pays expenses of writers on assignment.

Photos: Send photos with ms. Pays $5 for 5 × 7 b&w glossy or matte prints; $5 for 5 × 7 color prints. Captions preferred.

Columns/Departments: "We will consider new column concepts as long as they fit into the general areas of antiques and collectibles." Buys 1 ms/issue. Send complete ms. Pays $5-25.

Home and Garden

Some magazines here concentrate on gardens; others on the how-to of interior design. Still others focus on homes and gardens in specific regions of the country. Be sure to read the publication to determine its focus before submitting a manuscript or query.

‡AMERICAN HORTICULTURIST, Publication of the American Horticultural Society, 7931 E. Blvd. Dr., Alexandria VA 22308. (703)768-5700. Editor: Kathleen Fisher. 90% freelance written. Bimonthly magazine covering gardening. Estab. 1922. Circ. 18,000. Pays on publication. Publishes ms an average of 6 months after acceptance. Byline given. Offers 20% kill fee. Buys first North American serial rights. Submit seasonal/holiday material 6 months in advance. Query for electronic submissions. Reports in 2 months on queries. Sample copy $2.50; free writer's guidelines.

Nonfiction: Book excerpts, historical, how-to (grow unusual plants, garden under difficult conditions), humor, interview/profile, personal experience, technical (explain science of horticulture to lay audience). Buys 40-50 mss/year. Query with published clips. Length: 1,000-2,500 words. Pays $100-400. Pays with contributor copies or other premiums when other horticultural organizations contribute articles.

Photos: Send photos with submission. Reviews transparencies. Offers $50-75 per photo. Captions required. Buys one-time rights.

Tips: "We are read by sophisticated gardeners, but also want to interest beginning gardeners. Subjects should be unusual plants, recent breakthroughs in breeding, experts in the field, translated for lay readers."

‡BACKWOODS HOME MAGAZINE, Word Publishing, P.O. Box 1624, Ventura CA 93002. (805)643-1608. Editor: Dave Duffy. 80% freelance written. Bimonthly magazine covering house building, alternate energy, gardening and health. "We write for the person who values self-independence above all else. Our readers want to build their own homes, generate their own electricity, grow their own food and in general stand on their own two feet." Estab. 1989. Circ. 6,000. Pays on publication. Publishes ms an average of 2 months after acceptance. Byline given. Offers $15 kill fee. Buys first rights and second serial (reprint) rights or makes work-for-hire assignments. Submit seasonal/holiday material 3 months in advance. Simultaneous and previously published submissions OK. Query for electronic submissions. Reports in 2 weeks. Sample copy for $1 with 9×12 SAE and $1.05 in postage. Writer's guidelines for #10 SASE.

Nonfiction: Historical/nostalgic, how-to (about country things, alternate energy), humor (country humor), interview/profile (of independent people), new product (alternate energy), personal experience, photo feature (about country things) and technical (about alternate energy production, building a house). "No opinion, exposé or religious articles." Buys 50 mss/year. Query with or without published clips, or send complete ms. Length: 300-1,800 words. Pays $15.

Photos: State availability of photos with submission. Reviews 3×5 or larger prints. Offers $5 per photo. Identification of subjects required. Buys one-time rights.

Columns/Departments: Book Review (alternate energy/house building/gardening), 300-400 words; Recipes (country cooking), 150 words; Alternate Energy (solar cells, hydro, generator), 600-1,800 words; Gardening (organic), 600-1,800 words; Home Building (do-it-yourself), 600-1,800 words. Buys 30-40 mss/year. Send complete ms. Pays $15.

Fiction: Historical, humorous, slice-of-life vignettes and western. "No erotica, confession, religious, fantasy or romance fiction." Buys 6 mss/year. Send complete ms. Length: 1,800-3,600. Pays $15.

Poetry: Free verse, haiku, light verse, traditional. Buys 15 poems/year. Length: 3-25 lines. Pays $5.

Fillers: Anecdotes, facts, short humor. Buys 9-12/year. Length: 25-150. Pays $5.

Tips: "We insist on accuracy in nonfiction articles. Writers must know the subject. We are basically a country magazine that tries to show people how to do things that make country life more pleasant."

BETTER HOMES AND GARDENS, 1716 Locust St., Des Moines IA 50336. (515)284-3000. Editor (Building): Joan McCloskey. Editor (Furnishings): Denise Caringer. Editor (Foods): Nancy Byal. Editor (Travel): (unfilled at press time). Editor (Garden Outdoor Living): Doug Jimerson. Editor (Health & Education): Paul Krantz. Editor (Money Management, Automotive, Features): Margaret Daly. 10-15% freelance written. **Pays on acceptance.** Buys all rights. "We read all freelance articles, but much prefer to see a letter of query rather than a finished manuscript."

Nonfiction: Travel, education, health, cars, money management, and home entertainment. "We do not deal with political subjects or with areas not connected with the home, community, and family." Pays rates "based on estimate of length, quality and importance."

Tips: Direct queries to the department that best suits your story line.

CANADIAN WORKSHOP, The Do-It-Yourself Magazine, Camar Publications (1984) Inc., 130 Spy Ct., Markham, Ontario L3R 5H6 Canada. (416)475-8440. Editor: Erina Kelly. 90% freelance written; half of these are assigned. Monthly magazine covering the "do-it-yourself market including woodworking projects, renovation and restoration, maintenance and decoration. Canadian writers only." Circ. 110,000. Pays on publication. Publishes ms an average of 5 months after acceptance. Byline given. Offers 75% kill fee. Rights are negotiated with the author. Submit seasonal/holiday material 6 months in advance. Simultaneous queries OK. Reports in 3 weeks. Sample copy for 8×11 SASE; free writer's guidelines with #10 SASE.

Nonfiction: How-to (home maintenance, renovation projects, woodworking projects and features). Buys 20-40 mss/year. Query with clips of published work. Length: 1,500-4,000 words. Pays $225-600. Pays expenses of writers on assignment.

Photos: Send photos with ms. Payment for photos, transparencies negotiated with the author. Captions, model releases, and identification of subjects required.

Tips: "Freelancers must be aware of our magazine format. Products used in how-to articles must be readily available across Canada. Deadlines for articles are 5 months in advance of cover date. How-tos should be detailed enough for the amateur but appealing to the experienced. A frequent mistake made by writers is not directing the copy toward our reader. Stories sometimes have a tendency to be too basic."

FINE GARDENING, Taunton Press, 63 S. Main St., P.O. Box 5506, Newtown CT 06470. 1-800-243-7252. FAX: (203)426-3434. Editor: Rita Buchanan. Bimonthly magazine on gardening. "Focus is broad subject of landscape and ornamental gardening, with secondary interest in food gardening. Articles written by avid gardeners—first person, hands-on gardening experiences." Estab. 1988. Circ. 120,000. Pays on publication. Byline given. Buys first North American serial rights. Reports in 1 month. Free writer's guidelines.

Nonfiction: Book review, essays, how-to, opinion, personal experience, photo feature. Buys 50-60 mss/year. Query. Length: 1,000-3,000 words. Pays $150/page.

Photos: Send photos with submission. Reviews 35mm transparencies. Offers some additional payment for photos accepted with ms. Buys one-time rights.

Columns/Department: Book reviews (on gardening); Gleanings (essays, stories, opinions, research); Last Word (essays/serious, humorous, fact or fiction). Query. Length: 250-1,000 words. Pays $25-150.

Tips: "It's most important to have solid first-hand experience as a gardener. Tell us what you've done with your own landscape and plants."

FLORIDA HOME & GARDEN, Suite 207, 600 Brickell Ave., Miami FL 33131. (305)374-5011. FAX: (305)374-7691. Editor: Kathryn Howard. Managing Editor: James Watson. 20% freelance written. Works with a small number of new/unpublished writers each year. Monthly magazine of Florida homes, interior design, architecture, landscape architecture, gardens, cuisine, travel, art, lifestyles and home entertainment. "We want beautiful, practical coverage of the subjects listed as they relate to Florida." Estab. 1984. Circ. 55,000. Pays on publication. Publishes ms an average of 3 months after acceptance. Byline given. Offers $25 kill fee by pre-agreement only. Buys first North American serial rights for one year, plus unlimited reuse in our magazine (no resale). Submit seasonal/holiday material 6 months in advance. Sample copy $3; writer's guidelines for #10 SASE.
Nonfiction: General interest (photos and articles about Florida homes); and travel Caribbean/Florida (home architecture or garden destinations only). Buys 36 mss/year. Query with published clips. Length: 1,000-2,000 words. Pays $200-400. Pays expenses of writers on assignment by prior agreement only.
Photos: State availability of photos or send photos with query. Reviews 35mm, 4×5 or 2″ transparencies, Polaroids and prints. Captions and identification of subjects required. Buys one-time rights plus unlimited editorial re-use of magazine's separations.
Columns/Departments: How-to (specific home how-to); Garden Care; What's Hot (Florida products); Developments; Who's Hot (Florida); Art; Cuisine; Travel (Florida, Mexico's Gulf Coast); Books (reviews); New Products (b&w photos). Buys 20 mss/year. Query with published clips. Length: 750-2,000 words. Pays $200-400.
Tips: "We're looking for stories that visually show the beauty of Florida and impart practical information to our readers. Must relate to Florida's tropicality in all subjects."

FLOWER AND GARDEN MAGAZINE, 4251 Pennsylvania, Kansas City MO 64111. Editor: Kay Melchisedech Olson. 50% freelance written. Works with a small number of new/unpublished writers each year. For home gardeners. Bimonthly picture magazine. Estab. 1955. Circ. 600,000. Buys first rights only. Byline given. **Pays on acceptance.** Publishes ms an average of 6-12 months after acceptance. Reports in 6 weeks. Sample copy $2.50 and 9½×12½ SAE; writer's guidelines for SASE.
Nonfiction: Interested in illustrated articles on how to do certain types of gardening and descriptive articles about individual plants. Flower arranging, landscape design, house plants, patio gardening are other aspects covered. "The approach we stress is practical (how-to-do-it, what-to-do-it-with). We try to stress plain talk, clarity and economy of words. An article should be tailored for a national audience." Buys 20-30 mss/year. Query. Length: 500-1,500 words. Rates vary depending on quality and kind of material.
Photos: Pays up to $12.50/5×7 or 8×10 b&w prints, depending on quality, suitability. Also buys transparencies, 35mm and larger. "We are using more four-color illustrations." Pays $30-125 for these, depending on size and use. Photos are paid for on publication.
Tips: "The prospective author needs good grounding in gardening practice and literature. Offer well-researched and well-written material appropriate to the experience level of our audience. Use botanical names as well as common. Illustrations help sell the story. Describe special qualifications for writing the particular proposed subject."

GARDEN MAGAZINE, The Garden Society, A Division of the New York Botanical Garden, Bronx Park, Bronx NY 10458. FAX: (212)220-6504. Editor: Karen Polyak. 50% freelance written. Works with a small number of new/unpublished writers each year. Bimonthly magazine, emphasizing horticulture, environment and botany for a diverse readership, largely college graduates and professionals united by a common interest in plants and the environment. Most are members of botanical gardens and arboreta. Circ. 20,000. Publishes ms an average of 1 year after acceptance. Buys first North American serial rights. Submit seasonal/holiday material 6 months in advance. Query for electronic submissions. Computer printout submissions acceptable; prefers letter-quality. Reports in 2 months. Sample copy $3.50 and 9×11 SAE; guidelines for SASE.
Nonfiction: "All articles must be of high quality, meticulously researched and botanically accurate." Exposé (environmental subjects); how-to (horticultural techniques, must be unusual and verifiable); general interest (plants in art and history, botanical news, ecology); humor (pertaining to botany and horticulture); and travel (great gardens of the world). Buys 15-20 unsolicited mss/year. Query with clips of published work. Length: 1,000-2,500 words. Pays $100-300. Sometimes pays the expenses of writers on assignment.
Photos: Pays $35-50/5×7 b&w glossy print; $40-150/4×5 or 35mm color transparency. Captions preferred. Buys one-time rights.
Tips: "We appreciate some evidence that the freelancer has studied our magazine and understands our special requirements. A writer should write from a position of authority that comes from either personal experience (horticulture); extensive research (environment, ecology, history, art); adequate scientific background; or all three. Style should be appropriate to this approach."

‡**GARDEN STATE HOME & GARDEN**, Micro Media, Inc., 50 Highway 9, Morganville NJ 07751. (201)972-1170. Editor: Donna M. Pisacano. 90% freelance written. Monthly magazine covering home and garden. Magazine devoted to New Jersey's homes, private gardens, gallery, hometown and antiques. Estab. 1986. Circ. 60,000. Pays on publication. Publishes ms an average of 3-4 months after acceptance. Byline given.

Offers 33% kill fee. Buys first North American serial rights. Submit seasonal/holiday material 6 months in advance.

Nonfiction: How-to (home/garden related), interview/profile (NJ based), new product, technical (home/garden related). "We have special issues on Kitchen and Bath, and the Great Outdoors upcoming." Query. Length: 1,200-2,000 words. Pays $400 for features.

Photos: State availability of photos with submission. Reviews transparencies and prints. Captions, model releases and identification of subjects required. Buys one-time rights.

Columns/Departments: Hometown (review of town in NJ), 1,500 words. Buys 12 mss/year. Query. Pays negotiable fee.

Tips: "Please send clips and story ideas. Most articles are assigned by editor to freelancer with a 1-month deadline."

THE HERB COMPANION, Interweave Press, 306 N. Washington, Loveland CO 80537. (303)669-7672. Editor: Linda Ligon. 80% freelance written. Bimonthly magazine about herbs: culture, history, culinary use, crafts, medicinal. Audience includes a wide range of herb enthusiasts. Circ. 30,000. Pays on publication. Byline given. Buys first North American serial rights. Sample copy $4; writer's guidelines for #10 SASE. Query. Length: 10-16 pages. Typical payment is $100 per published page.

Photos: State availability of photos.

Tips: "Articles must show depth and working knowledge of the subject, though tone should be informal and accessible."

HERB QUARTERLY, P.O. Box 548, Boiling Springs PA 17007. FAX: (717)245-2764. Publisher: Linda Sparrowe. 80% freelance written. Quarterly magazine for herb enthusiasts. Estab. 1978. Circ. 25,000. Pays on publication. Publishes ms an average of 1 year after acceptance. Buys first North American serial rights and second (reprint) rights to previously published submissions. Query for electronic submissions. Query letters recommended. Reports in 1 month. Sample copy $5 and 9 × 12 SAE; writer's guidelines for #10 SASE.

Nonfiction: Gardening (landscaping, herb garden design, propagation, harvesting); herb businesses; medicinal and cosmetic use of herbs; crafts; cooking; historical (folklore, focused piece on particular period—*not* general survey); interview of a famous person involved with herbs or folksy herbalist; personal experience; and photo essay ("cover quality" 8 × 10 b&w prints). "We are particularly interested in herb garden design, contemporary or historical." No fiction. Send double-spaced ms. Length: 1,000-3,500 words. Pays $50. Reports in 1 month.

Tips: "Our best submissions are narrowly focused on herbs with much practical information on cultivation and use for the gardener."

HOMEOWNER, Family Media Inc., 3 Park Ave., New York NY 10016. Editor-in-chief: Joe Carter. Managing Editor: Michael Hartnett. 75% freelance written. Monthly (combined Jan/Feb; July/Aug) magazine on home improvement, including remodeling, maintenance and repair. Aimed at men and women with helpful information of planning, design options, new products and do-it-yourself techniques. Circ. 775,000. **Pays on acceptance.** Publishes ms an average of 4 months after acceptance. Byline given. Offers kill fee. Buys first North American serial rights. Reports in 1 month. Sample copy on request; writer's guidelines for #10 SASE.

Nonfiction: Remodeling, home repair and maintenance, how-to; personal experience (hands-on experience with building a home, remodeling or carpentry project); and some technical information on products, materials, how things work. Length: 1,500 maximum. Rates start at $400 for short articles plus some expenses of writers on assignment.

THE ISLAND GROWER, B.C.'s Magazine of Coastal Gardening and Living, Greenheart Publications, RR4, Sooke, British Columbia V0S 1N0 Canada. (604)642-4129. Editor: Phyllis Kusch. 90% freelance written. Monthly magazine (excluding January) on gardening and outdoor coastal living. Estab. 1984. "As we have a targeted, paid readership, we address editorial to those interested in gardening with most of slant towards natural methods." Pays within three months after publication. Byline given. Buys one-time rights. Submit seasonal/holiday material 3 months in advance. Previously published submissions OK. Reports in 1 month on queries; 6 weeks on mss. Sample copy and writer's guidelines for return postage.

Nonfiction: How-to (steps to complete gardening project—comprehensive), interview/profile, new product, opinion (concerning environment), photo feature and travel (horticulture shows, events, tours, places of interest). "No general, philosophical articles that are not of practical use to readers or articles that require sources but are not included." Query with published clips. Length: 1,000-2,000 words. Pays $20-75 (Canadian) for assigned articles; $20-110 (Canadian)for unsolicited articles. Pays in contributor copies or other premiums "if known personally and can arrange agreeable payment."

Photos: Send photos with submission. Reviews 5 × 7 or 8 × 10 prints. Payment range of $10-49 for photos (prints). Model releases and identification of subjects required.

Columns/Departments: Bulbs and Vegetables (how to plant, varieties available, pertinent geographical area), 1,000-2,000 words; and New Products (of interest to environment, specifically pest control methods without chemical reliance), 500-1,000 words. Query with published clips. Pays $20-110.

Tips: "Study and observe publication to appreciate quality of publication; reflect this in query letters and submissions. We do not appreciate sloppy or poorly researched submissions. We cannot use articles not endemic to coastal South British Columbia and Pacific Northwest U.S.A. Column of quick tips, little news bits etc. pays up to $30. Greenhouse column pays a regular features rate (above). Please note: Return postage must be in Canadian stamps or cash."

METROPOLITAN HOME, Meredith Corporation, 750 Third Ave., New York NY 10017. (212)557-6600. Editor: Dorothy Kalins. Articles Editor: Barbara Graustark. 50% freelance written. Monthly magazine on home furnishings, interior design and architects. Circ. 1 million. **Pays on acceptance.** Byline given. Offers 25% kill fee. Buys all rights. Submit seasonal/holiday material 5 months in advance. Reports in 1 month on queries. Free writer's guidelines. "Encourage writers to pick up magazine on newsstand."

Nonfiction: Book excerpts, essays, interview/profile, personal experience, real estate and travel. Buys 60-100 mss/year. Query with published clips. Length: 350-2,000 words. Pays $350-2,000 for assigned articles. Pays expenses of writers on assignment if agreed in advance.

Photos: State availability of photos with submission.

Tips: "The Metro section is most open for freelancers. It provides a variety of subjects to which writers can contribute."

‡MUIR'S ORIGINAL LOG HOME GUIDE FOR BUILDERS & BUYERS, Muir Publishing Company Inc., Rt. 2, Box 581, Cosby TN 37722. (615)487-2256. FAX: (615)487-3249. Editor: Allan Muir. 65% freelance written. Quarterly magazine covering the buying and building of log homes. "We publish for persons who want to buy or build their own log home. Unlike conventional housing, it is possible for the average person to build his/her own log home. Articles should aim at providing help in this or describe the experiences of someone who has built a log home." Estab. 1917. Circ. 170,000. Pays on publication. Publishes ms an average of 6 months after acceptance. Byline given. Buys first North American rights. Submit seasonal/holiday material 4 months in advance. Simultaneous queries, and simultaneous ("writer should explain") and previously published submissions OK. Query for electronic submissions. Reports in 2 weeks. Sample copy $2.50 (postage included). Writer's guidelines for SASE.

Nonfiction: General interest; historical/nostalgic (log home historic sites, restoration of old log structures); how-to (anything to do with building log homes); inspirational (sweat equity—encouraging people that they can build their own home for less cost); interview/profile (with persons who have built their own log homes); new product (or new company manufacturing log homes—check with us first); personal experience (author's own experience with building his own log home, with photos is ideal); photo feature (on log home decor, author or anyone else building his own log home); and technical (for "Techno-log" section; specific construction details, i.e., new log buiding details, joining systems). Also, "would like photo/interview/profile stories on famous persons and their log homes—how they did it, where they got their logs, etc." Interested in log commercial structures. "Please no exaggeration—this is a truthful, back-to-basics type of magazine trying to help the person interested in log homes." Buys 25 mss/year. Query with clips of published work or send complete ms. "Prefer queries first with photo of subject house." Length: open. Pays 10-25¢/word, depending on quality.

Photos: Slides, transparencies or color prints, $5-50, depending on quality. "All payments are arranged with individual author/submitter." Captions and identification of subjects required. Buys first North American rights unless otherwise arranged.

Columns/Departments: Pro-Log (short news pieces of interest to the log-building world); Techno-Log (technical articles, i.e., solar energy systems; any illustrations welcome); Book-Log (book reviews only, on books related to log building and alternate energy; "check with us first"); Chrono-Log (features on historic log buildings); and Decor (practical information on how to finish and furnish a log house). Buys possible 50-75 mss/year. Query with clips of published work or send complete ms. Length: 100-1,000 words or more. "All payments are arranged with individual author/submitter." Enclose SASE.

Tips: "The writer may have a better chance of breaking in at our publication with short articles and fillers since writing well on log homes requires some prior knowledge of subject. The most frequent mistakes made by writers in completing an article assignment for us are not doing enough research or not having understanding of the subject; not people oriented enough; angled toward wrong audience. They don't study the publication before they submit manuscripts."

NEW HOME, Gilford Publishing, P.O. Box 2008, Village West, Laconia NH 03247. FAX: (603)524-0643. Managing Editor: Steven Maviglio. 90% freelance written. Bimonthly magazine. "*New Home* is mailed to homebuyers (new and existing within one month of filing the deed). The magazine goes to those who have purchased homes costing $85,000 or more. The first few months of living in a new house means decorating, remodeling and buying products. We show them how to make quality decisions." Estab. 1986. Circ. 300,000. **Pays on acceptance.** Publishes ms an average of 2 months after acceptance. Byline given. Kill fee varies. Buys all rights. Submit seasonal/holiday material 6 months in advance. Simultaneous submissions OK. Reports in 2 weeks. Sample copy for $5 and 8½ × 11 SAE with 6 first class stamps. Free writer's guidelines.

Nonfiction: Essays, how-to, interview/profile, new product, technical. No articles on "How I Dealt with My New Kitchen," "Why Moving Is So Terrible." Buys 50 mss/year. Query with published clips. Pays $200-3,000 words. Pays $200-1,500 for assigned articles; $200-500 for unsolicited articles. Sometimes pays expenses of writers on assignment.

Photos: State availability of photos with submission. Reviews transparencies (5×7) and slides. Offers $50-250/photo. Captions, model release and identification of subjects required. Buys all rights.

Columns/Departments: Out-of-Doors (lawn and garden, landscaping) 1,000-1,500 words; The Kitchen (kitchen cabinets, countertops, small appliances); The Bath (new tubs, working with color, Victorian baths); Details (do-it-yourself, fun projects); Back Porch (essay of a new home experience). Buys 50 mss/year. Query with published clips. Length: 250-2,000 words. Pays $200-1,500.

Fillers: "Homefront" (news and trends). Facts. Buys 20 mss/year. Length: 50-250 words. Pays up to $250.

Tips: "We assign nearly all of our stories. But it doesn't hurt for a writer to query with samples and present their idea in a one-page letter. No unsolicited manuscripts except for our Back Porch section."

1,001 HOME IDEAS, Family Media, Inc., 3 Park Ave., New York NY 10016. (212)779-6200. Editor: Ellen Frankel. Executive Editor: Errol Croft. 40% freelance written. Prefers to work with published/established writers. A monthly magazine covering home furnishings, building, remodeling and home equipment. "We are a family shelter magazine edited for young, mainstream homeowners, providing ideas for decorating, remodeling, outdoor living, and at-home entertaining. Emphasis on ideas that are do-able and affordable." Estab. 1945. Circ. 1.5 million.

Pays on acceptance. Publishes ms an average of 6 months after acceptance. Byline given. Offers 25% kill fee. Buys first North American serial rights, second serial (reprint) rights, or makes work-for-hire assignments. Submit seasonal/holiday material 12 months in advance. Reports in 1 month. Sample copy $2.50; writer's guidelines for #10 SASE.

Nonfiction: Book excerpts (on interior design and crafts only); how-to (on decorating, remodeling and home maintenance); interview/profile (of designers only); new product; photo feature (on homes only); crafts; home equipment; and home furnishings and decor. No travel, religious, technical or exposés. Buys 25 mss/year. Query with or without published clips, or send complete ms. Length: 300-2,000 words. Pays $100-750 for assigned articles; pays $100-500 for unsolicited articles. Sometimes pays the expenses of writers on assignment.

Photos: State availability of photos with submission. Reviews transparencies and prints. Offers $10-125/photo. Captions, model releases, and identification of subjects required. Buys one-time rights.

Columns/Departments: Kathie Robitz, column/department editor. 1,001 Ways to Save $$$ (consumer buymanship, housing, finance, home furnishings, products, etc.) 1,500 words. Buys 12 mss/year. Query. Pays $300-400.

Tips: "The idea is what sells an article to us ... good ideas for decorating, remodeling and improving the home, and well-researched information on how-to, with any necessary directions and patterns, to help the reader carry out the idea. The department, 1,001 Ways to Save, is the area most open to freelance writers. We also look for features which we can turn into photo features on decorating, remodeling and improving the home."

PHOENIX HOME & GARDEN, PHG, Inc., Suite A-100, 4041 N. Central Ave., Phoenix AZ 85012. (602)234-0840. Editor: Manya Winsted. Managing Editor: Nora Burba Trulsson. 50% freelance written. Works with a small number of new/unpublished writers each year. Monthly magazine covering homes, furnishings, entertainment, lifestyle and gardening for Phoenix area residents interested in better living. Estab. 1980. Circ. 38,000. Pays on publication. Publishes ms an average of 2 months after acceptance. Byline given. Buys first rights. Submit seasonal/holiday material 6 months in advance. Reports in 2 weeks on queries. Sample copy $2.50, plus 9 first class stamps.

Nonfiction: General interest (on interior decorating, architecture, regional Southwest gardening, entertainment, food); historical (Arizona history); and travel (of interest to Phoenix residents). Buys 100 or more mss/year. Query with published clips. Length: 1,200 words maximum. Pays $75-300/article. Pays expenses of writers on assignment.

Tips: "It's not a closed shop. I want the brightest, freshest, most accurate material available. Study the magazine to see our format and style. Major features are assigned to contributing editors."

PRACTICAL HOMEOWNER, Practical Homeowner Publishing Co., 27 Unquowa, Fairfield CT 06430. (203)259-9877. Editor: Joe Provey. 75% freelance written. Works with a small number of new/unpublished writers each year. Magazine published 9 times/year about well-designed remodelings, home improvements and new home construction. Estab. 1988. Circ. 760,000. **Pays on acceptance.** Publishes ms an average of 3 months after acceptance. Submit seasonal material at least 1 year in advance. Query for electronic submissions. Reports in 6 weeks.

Nonfiction: "*Practical Homeowner* is a home improvement magazine for people who want to create a safe, efficient and healthy home environment. Its aim is to put the reader in control of all decisions affecting his home, which may mean simplifying day-to-day maintenance and improving an existing structure or the more involved overseeing of new home construction." Feature articles relating to the home, including—but not limited to—remodeling, home repair, home management, improving energy efficiency, landscaping, home design, construction techniques, building materials and technology, home ownership trends, and home health issues. Length: 1,000-1,500 words. Buys all rights. Payment $400-2,500.

Photos: Horst Weber, art director. State availability of photos. Pays $35-100 for b&w; $75-400 for transparencies or 35mm slides, depending on size and use. Captions and model releases required. Buys one-time rights.

Columns/Departments: Healthy Home (maintaining a safe, healthy home environment), Financial Advisor (managing home and home improvement finances), Well-Crafted Home (projects for the intermediate to advanced do -it-yourselfer), Trade Secrets (professional tradesmen explain techniques), Practical Products (building supplies, home furnishings, tools) and Life at My House (anecdotal essays on life at home). Length: 600-1,000 words. All columns are on assignment basis. Pays: $150-600.

SOUTHERN PRESTIGIOUS HOMES & INTERIORS, BD Publishing, Inc. P.O. Box 306, Mt. Pleasant SC 29465. (803)884-0159. FAX: (803)849-6717. Editor: Bill Macchi. 80% freelance written. Bimonthly magazine on Southeastern real estate/lifestyle. "Writing for higher income residents, particularly in Northern states, interested in Southern real estate and lifestyle. Our focus is presently on the coast of NC, SC and Georgia, but we are expanding." Estab. 1980. Circ. 30,000. Pays on publication. Publishes ms an average of 3 months after acceptance. Byline given. Buys one-time rights. Reports in 1 month on queries. Sample copy $1.50.

Nonfiction: Interview, photo feature, travel and real estate development, resorts, prestigious homes and interiors. Buys 30 mss/year. Query. Length: 1,000 words maximum. Pays $50 maximum for assigned articles. Sometimes pays expenses of writers on assignment.

Photos: Send photos with submission. Reviews 3×5 prints. Offers $5 per photo. Captions and identification of subjects required. Buys one-time rights.

Tips: "We are not looking for articles on home repair, do-it-yourself decorating or profiles of realtors who had a million dollar year. Our readers are primarily affluent and in the market for a second home or a more expensive primary residence. We are interested in profiles of developers with a national reputation, prestigious homes of the rich, famous or infamous and interiors of the same, and articles targeting resorts and resort living. Unless it's about the Southeast, however, we're not interested."

SPROUTLETTER, Sprouting Publications, P.O. Box 62, Ashland OR 97520. (503)488-2326. Editor: Michael Linden. 50% freelance written. Quarterly newsletter covering sprouting, live foods and indoor food gardening. "We emphasize growing foods (especially sprouts) indoors for health, economy, nutrition and food self-sufficiency. We also cover topics related to sprouting, live foods and holistic health." Estab. 1980. Circ. 2,500. Pays on publication. Publishes ms an average of 3 months after acceptance. Byline given. Buys North American serial rights and second (reprint) rights. Submit seasonal/holiday material 4 months in advance. Previously published submissions OK. Reports in 2 weeks on queries; 3 weeks on mss. Sample copy $2.50.

Nonfiction: General interest (raw foods, sprouting, holistic health); how-to (grow sprouts, all kinds of foods indoors; build devices for sprouting or indoor gardening); personal experience (in sprouting or related areas); and technical (experiments with growing sprouts). No common health food/vitamin articles or growing ornamental plants indoors (as opposed to food producing plants). Buys 4-6 mss/year. Query. Length: 500-2,400 words. Pays $15-50. Trades for merchandise are also considered.

Columns/Departments: Book Reviews (books oriented toward sprouts, nutrition or holistic health). Reviews are short and informative. News Items (interesting news items relating to sprouts or live foods); Recipes (mostly raw foods). Buys 5-10 mss/year. Query. Length: 100-450 words. Pays $3-10.

Fillers: Short humor and newsbreaks. Buys 3-6/year. Length: 50-150 words. Pays $2-6.

Tips: "Writers should have a sincere interest in holistic health and in natural whole foods. We like tight writing which is optimistic, interesting and informative. Consumers are demanding more thorough and accurate information. Articles should cover any given subject in depth in an enjoyable and inspiring manner. A frequent mistake is that the subject matter is not appropriate. Also buys cartoon strips and singles. Will consider series."

THE WEEKEND GARDENER, Tel-A-Cast Group, P.O. Drawer Q, Griffin GA 30224. (404)229-6231. FAX: (404)229-5225. Editor: Debbie Burns. 95% freelance written. Magazine appearing 8 times/year on gardening. "The magazine is aimed at the weekend gardener and carries articles on all aspects of food and ornamental gardening, garden related crafts and projects. Articles should be accurate, well-researched, in-depth (but not *too* technical) and to the point." Estab. 1984. Pays on publication. Publishes an average of 2 months after acceptance. Buys first North American rights and will consider second serial (reprint) rights. Submit seasonal/holiday material 3 months in advance. Reports in 1 month. Sample copy $1 and 10×12½ SAE with 75¢ postage. Free writer's guidelines for #10 SASE.

Nonfiction: General garden interest, how-to (gardening and building gardening aids) and personal gardening experience. Buys 170 mss/year. Send complete ms. Length: 800-1,100 words. Pays $60-135 (occasionally higher).

Photos: Send photos with submission. Reviews transparencies. Offers $15-50 per photo. Model releases and identification of subjects required. Buys one-time rights.

Poetry: "No poetry that does not relate to gardening." Pays $30-60.

Fillers: Anecdotes, facts and short humor. Pays $10-30.

Tips: "Submit only clear concise, readable manuscripts with color photos. We work with new writers eagerly. We like to emphasize appropriate seasonal material and encourage such submissions. Where possible, make stories applicable to all parts of the U.S. Most of our features are freelance written. We prefer that these features not be too technical and that they relate to the weekend gardener. Our readers enjoy gardening as a hobby, not a career."

YOUR HOME, Meridian Publishing, Inc., Box 10010, Ogden UT 84409. (801)394-9446. 65% freelance written. A monthly in-house magazine covering home/garden subjects. **Pays on acceptance.** Publishes ms an average of 8 months after acceptance. Byline given. Buys first rights and second serial (reprint) rights. Eight-month lead time. Submit seasonal material 10 months in advance. Simultaneous and previously published submissions OK. Reports in 6 weeks. Sample copy for $1 and 9×12 SAE; writer's guidelines for #10 SASE. All requests for samples and guidelines and queries should be addressed Attn: Editor.

Nonfiction: General interest articles about fresh ideas in home decor, ranging from floor and wall coverings to home furnishings. Subject matter includes the latest in home construction (exteriors, interiors, building materials, design), the outdoors at home (landscaping, pools, patios, gardening), remodeling projects, home management and home buying and selling. "No do-it-yourself pieces." Buys 40 mss/year. Length: 1,000-1,400 words. Pays 15¢/word for first rights plus nonexclusive reprint rights. Payment for second serial rights is negotiable.

Photos: State availability of photos with query. Reviews 35mm or larger transparencies and 5×7 or 8×10 "sharp, professional-looking" color prints. Pays $35 for inside photo; pays $50 for cover photo. Captions, model releases and identification of subjects required.

Tips: "Always looking for upscale, universal pieces. No do-it-yourself articles. The key is a well-written query letter that: (1) demonstrates that the subject of the article is practical and useful and has national appeal; (2) shows that the article will have a clear, focused theme and will be based on interviews with experts; (3) outlines the availability (from the writer, a photographer or a PR source) of top-quality color photos; (4) gives evidence that the writer/photographer is a professional."

Humor

Publications listed here specialize in gaglines or prose humor, some just for readers and others for performers or speakers. Other publications that use humor can be found in nearly every category in this book. Some have special needs for major humor pieces; some use humor as fillers; many others are interested in material that meets their ordinary fiction or nonfiction requirements but also has a humorous slant. The majority of humor articles must be submitted as complete manuscripts on speculation because editors usually can't know from a query whether or not the piece will be right for them. For more information and markets for humor, see *Humor and Cartoon Markets* (Writer's Digest Books).

CURRENT COMEDY, Suite 4D, 165 West 47th St., New York NY 10036. Editor: Gary Apple. For "speakers, toastmasters, business executives, public officials, educators, public relations specialists and communication professionals." Estab. 1955. Pays on publication (at end of month material published). Buys all rights. Writer's guidelines for SASE.

Fillers: "We are looking for funny, performable one-liners and short jokes that deal with happenings in the news, fads, trends, and other topical subjects. The accent is on laugh-out-loud comedy. We are particularly interested in material that can be used by speakers and toastmasters: lines for beginning a speech, ending a speech, acknowledging an introduction, specific speaking occasions—any clever, original comments that would be of use to a person making a speech. We are also in the market for jokes used to respond to specific speaking situations (microphone feedback, broken air conditioning, hecklers). Short, sharp comment on business trends and events is also desirable. No puns, poems, sexist or stereotype jokes." Pays $12/joke.

Tips: "The material *must be original*. Do not send jokes you have heard, only those from your own creativity. We have a constant need for good comedy writers. Please send only your strongest material. We'd rather receive 5 truly funny jokes than 50 so-so ones. If you're not sure that your jokes are funny, try them out on some friends before trying them out on us. Please enclose a #10 SASE for the return of your material."

KNUCKLEHEAD PRESS, World Headquarters, 6442 West 111th St., Worth IL 60482. Editors: Chris Miksanek and Jim Riley. A quarterly humor newsletter. "We print anything that's funny." Estab. 1984. Circ. 1,000. Pays on publication. Publishes ms an average of 6 months after acceptance. "We include writer in editorial bar as Contributing Editor." Buys all rights. Submit seasonal/holiday material 6 months in advance. Simultaneous and previously published submissions OK. Query for electronic submissions. Reports in 3 weeks on mss. Sample copy for 9×12 SAE with 2 first class stamps; or $1. Free writer's guidelines with sample copy request. "Please request a sample issue before trying to write for us."

Nonfiction: Everything in Knucklehead Press is fiction in that it's not true, but we would welcome parodies of: exposé, general interest, historical/nostalgic, how-to, interview/profile, new product and technical. "We're always doing special 1 or 2 page sections. They're not planned, but based on material submitted. For example, if we have 3 or 4 food pieces, we might do a special restaurant/dining out section. Always looking for news parody. Please, no first person bits." Buys 10-15 mss/year. Send complete ms. Length: 50-300 words. Pays $5-20 for unsolicited articles. Send photos with submission. Reviews prints (b&w only). Offers no additional payment for photos accepted with ms. Captions, model releases and identification of subjects required. Buys all rights.

Columns/Departments: Newsbriefs (short news-type bits), 25-50 words. Buys 10 mss/year. Send complete ms. Length: 10-100 words. Pays $3-5.

Fiction: "Anything funny." Buys 4 mss/year. Send complete ms. Length: 250-500 words. Pays $5-20.

Fillers: Newsbreaks, short humor and gag classifieds. Buys 15/year. Length: 20-50 words. Pays $1-3.

Tips: "A comedy writer has to ask himself, 'Does my material entertain me? Can I read my own material and laugh as I would reading someone else's?' If the answer is 'yes' then we want to see your stuff. Every part of our newsletter is open to freelancers. If they can do something funnier than us, we're more than happy to step aside. Our goal is to publish a gut-busting newsletter, and any way that we accomplish that goal is OK by us. Make every word count. There's nothing more agonizing than a long not-so-funny piece; make your point and exit. Short and sweet."

LATEST JOKES, P.O. Box 3304, Brooklyn NY 11202-0066. (718)855-5057. Editor: Robert Makinson. Estab. 1974. 20% freelance written. Monthly newsletter of humor for TV and radio personalities, comedians and professional speakers. **Pays on acceptance.** Byline given. Buys all rights. Submit seasonal/holiday material 3 months in advance. Reports in 1 month. Sample copy $3 and 1 first class stamp.

Nonfiction: Humor (short jokes). No "stupid, obvious, non-funny vulgar humor. Jokes about human tragedy also unwelcome." Send complete ms. Pays $1-3 for each joke.

Fiction: Humorous jokes. Pays $1-3.

Poetry: Light verse (humorous). Submit maximum 3 poems at one time. Line length: 2-8 lines. Pays 25¢/line.

Tips: "No famous personality jokes. Clever statements are not enough. Be original and surprising."

LONE STAR HUMOR, Lone Star Publications of Humor, Suite 103, Box 29000, San Antonio TX 78229. Editor: Lauren I. Barnett. Less than 25% freelance written. Eager to work with new/unpublished writers. A humor book-by-subscription for "the general public and 'comedy connoisseur' as well as the professional humorist." Pays on publication, "but we try to pay before that." Publishes ms an average of 8 months after acceptance. Buys variable rights. Submit seasonal/holiday material 6 months in advance. Photocopied submissions and sometimes previously published work OK. Query for electronic submissions. Computer printout submission acceptable; no dot-matrix. Reports in 4 months. Inquire with SASE for prices and availability of sample copy. Writer's guidelines for #10 SASE.

Nonfiction: Humor (on anything topical/timeless); interview/profile (of anyone professionally involved in humor); and opinion (reviews of stand-up comedians, comedy plays, cartoonists, humorous books, *anything* concerned with comedy). "Inquire about possible theme issues." Buys 15 mss/year. Query with clips of published work if available. Length: 500-1,000 words; average is 700-800 words. Pays $5-30 and contributor's copy.

Fiction: Humorous. Buys variable mss/year. Send complete ms. Length: 500-1,000 words. Pays $5-30 and contributor's copy.

Poetry: Free verse, light verse, traditional, clerihews and limericks. "Nothing too 'artsy' to be funny." Buys 10-20/year. Submit maximum 5 poems. Length: 4-16 lines. Inquire for current rates.

Fillers: Clippings, jokes, gags, anecdotes, short humor and newsbreaks—"must be humorous or humor-related." Buys 20-30 mss/year. Length: 450 words maximum. Inquire for current rates.

Tips: "Our needs for freelance material will be somewhat diminished; writers should inquire (with SASE) before submitting material. We will be generating more and more of our humor inhouse, but will most likely require freelance material for books and other special projects. If the words 'wacky, zany or crazy' describe the writer's finished product, it is *not* likely that his/her piece will suit our needs. The best humor is just slightly removed from reality."

MAD MAGAZINE, 485 Madison Ave., New York NY 10022. (212)752-7685. Editors: Nick Meglin and John Ficarra. 100% freelance written. Magazine published 8 times/year. Estab. 1952. Circ. 1 million. **Pays on acceptance.** Publishes ms an average of 6 months after acceptance. Byline given. Buys all rights. Submit seasonal/holiday material 6 months in advance. Reports in 6 weeks. Writer's guidelines for #10 SASE.

Nonfiction: Satire, parody. "We're always on the lookout for new ways to spoof and to poke fun at hot trends — music, computers, fashions etc. We're *not* interested in formats we're already doing or have done to death like... 'you know you're a when....' " Buys 400 ms yearly. Submit a premise with 3 or 4 examples of how you intend to carry it through, describing the action and visual content. Rough sketches are not necessary. Pays minimum $350/*MAD* page. One-page gags: 2-8 panel cartoon continuities in the style and tradition of *MAD*. Buys 30 yearly. Pays minimum of $350/*MAD* page. Don't send riddles, advice columns, TV or movie satires, book manuscripts, articles about Alfred E. Neuman or text pieces.

Tips: "Have fun! We're interested in anything and everything that you think is funny. Remember to think visually! Freelancers can best break in with nontopical material. If we see even a germ of talent, we will work with that person. We like outrageous, silly and/or satirical humor."

NATIONAL LAMPOON, National Lampoon Inc., 155 Avenue of the Americas, New York NY 10013. (212)645-5040. FAX: (212)645-9219. Executive Editor: Larry Sloman. 50% freelance written. Works with small number of new/unpublished writers each year. A bimonthly magazine of "offbeat, irreverent satire." Circ. 250,000. **Pays on acceptance.** Publishes ms an average of 4 months after acceptance. Byline given. Offers 20% kill fee. Buys first North American serial rights. Simultaneous submissions OK. Reports in 3 months. Sample copy $3.95 with SAE.

Nonfiction: Humor. Buys 60 mss/year. Query with published clips. Length: approximately 2,000 words. Pays 20-40¢/word. Pays the expenses of writers on assignment.

Columns/Departments: John Bendel, column/department editor. True Facts (weird true-life stories). Special True Facts issue during first quarter of each year. Buys 240/year. Send complete ms. Length: 200 words maximum. Offers T-shirt for items, $10 and T-shirt for photos.

Tips: "We use very few new freelancers for major articles." True Facts section is most open to freelancers.

‡O'LINERS, Suite 1900, 11060 Cashmere St., Los Angeles CA 90049. Editor: Dan O'Day. 20% freelance written. Monthly newsletter of comedy material for radio disc jockeys. "*O'Liners* provides fresh, sharp, topical comedy one-liners for radio disc jockeys around the world. Material submitted should be appropriate for on-air use — both in content and in form." Estab. 1976. Circ. 1,000. **Pays on acceptance.** Publishes ms an average of 1 month after acceptance. Buys all rights. Submit seasonal/holiday material 2 months in advance. Reports in 1 week on queries; 2 weeks on mss. Sample copy $10 with #10 SASE. Writer's guidelines for #10 SASE.

Nonfiction: Humor. "I do not want to see anything that is not a comedy one-liner. No poems, essays, short stories, puns, limericks, philosophical musings, etc." Pays $6 for each one-liner.

Tips: "Listen to the most successful humorous radio disc jockeys in your area. Listen to recordings of good comedians (e.g. Woody Allen). Read everything you can find by Robert Benchley, James Thurber, Max Schulman."

THE ONION, Suite 270, 33 University Square, Madison WI 53715. (608)256-1372. Editor Scott Dikkers. 80% freelance written. Weekly humor-entertainment newspaper. "*The Onion* is an irreverent humor publication with witty and outrageous stories, articles and cartoons satirizing college life, or any subject of interest to a college audience." Estab. 1988. Circ. 25,000. Pays on publication. Publishes manuscript an average of 1 month after acceptance. Byline given. Buys one-time rights. Submit seasonal/holiday material 3 months in advance. No simultaneous, photocopied or previously published submissions. Reports in 1 month. Sample copy and writer's guidelines for 9 × 12 SASE.

Nonfiction: Humor, personal experience and mean-spirited parodies. Buys 20 mss/year. Send complete ms. Length: 50-400 words. Pays $10.

Photos: Send photos with submission. Offers $5. Buys one-time rights.

Columns/Departments: "We do not publish columns for which freelancers may write; we publish columns by freelancers willing to create their own column of engaging, original and humorous thoughts. Buys 2 mss/year. Send complete ms. Length: 50-300. Pays $10.

Fiction: Humorous, slice-of-life vignettes and humorous, shocking and offbeat stories. Buys 180 mss/year. Send complete ms. Length: 50-1,000. Pays $10.

Tips: "Hip, funny and unconventional submissions are always taken seriously. First-time writers are welcome. We plan to expand to other cities around the country, and we'd like creative, witty and reliable writers to expand with us. We are most interested in short short stories and satirical articles of interest to a college audience. Our tone is sharp, intelligent and irreverent, but deviations for comic effect are encouraged. We're sick of traditional comedy."

THE PUN, Play on Words, The Silly Club and Michael C. Rayner, P.O. Box 536-583, Orlando FL 32853. (407)898-3469. Editor: Danno Sullivan. 15% freelance written. Eager to work with new/unpublished writers. A bimonthly newsletter for a nonexistent organization, The Silly Club. "The P.U.N. readers enjoy humor bordering on intellectual, all the way down or up to just plain silliness. Politeness, though, above all. Despite the title, we very rarely use puns as such. *P.U.N.* is an acronym, not an indication of content." Estab. 1981. Circ. 400. **Pays on acceptance.** Publishes ms an average of 2 months after acceptance. Byline given, "listed in credits." Buys one-time rights. Submit seasonal/holiday material 1-2 months in advance. Simultaneous and previously published submissions OK. Reports in 5 weeks on mss. Sample copy for #10 SASE and $1.

Nonfiction: Humor. "Nothing rude, no foul language and no naughty things. We want *funny*. Not amusing or chuckle-worthy. Outright funny. If it doesn't make you laugh out loud, don't send it." Buys 10-15 mss/year. Send complete ms. Length: 10-1,000 words. Pays $1-10 for unsolicited articles.
Columns/Departments: Buys 10-15 mss/year. Send complete ms. Length: 10-100 words. Pays $1-25.
Fiction: Humorous. Buys 3-5 mss/year. Send complete ms. Length: 10-2,000 words. Pays $1-25. Also single panel cartoons. "Our fiction is mostly 'fictional nonfiction.'"
Poetry: Humorous poetry. Buys 5 poems/year. Submit maximum 2 poems. Pays $1-2.
Fillers: Gags and short humor. Buys 15/year. Pays $1-25.

Inflight

Most major inflight magazines cater to business travelers and vacationers who will be reading, during the flight, about the airline's destinations and other items of general interest. Airline mergers and acquisitions continue to decrease the number of magazines published in this area. The writer should watch for airline announcements in the news and in ads and read the latest sample copies and writer's guidelines for current information.

AMERICA WEST AIRLINES MAGAZINE, Skyword Marketing, Inc., Suite 240, 7500 N. Dreamy Draw Dr., Phoenix AZ 85020. (602)997-7200. Editor: Michael Derr. 80% freelance written. Works with small number of new/unpublished writers each year. A monthly "general interest magazine emphasizing the western and southwestern U.S. Some midwestern, northwestern and eastern subjects also appropriate. We look for ideas and people that celebrate opportunity, and those who put it to positive use." Estab. 1986. Query with published clips and SASE. Pays on publication. Publishes ms an average of 4 months after acceptance. Byline given. Offers 15% kill fee. Buys first North American rights. Submit seasonal/holiday material 6-8 months in advance. Simultaneous submissions OK, "if indicated as such." Query for electronic submissions. Reports in 1 month on queries; 5 weeks on mss. Sample copy for $3; writer's guidelines for 9 × 12 SAE with 3 first class stamps.
Nonfiction: General interest, creative leisure, events, profile, photo feature, science, sports, business issues, entrepreneurs, nature, health, history, arts, book excerpts, travel and trends. Also considers essays and humor. No puzzles, reviews or highly controversial features. Buys 130-140 mss/year. Query with published clips. Length: 500-2,200. Pays $200-750. Pays some expenses.
Photos: State availability of original photography. Offers $50-250/photo. Captions, model releases and identification of subjects required. Buys one-time rights.

AMERICAN WAY, Box 619640, Dallas/Fort Worth Airport TX 75261-9640. (817)967-1804. FAX: (817)967-1571. Editor: Doug Crichton. 98% freelance written. Prefers to work with published/established writers. Fortnightly inflight magazine for passengers flying with American Airlines. **Pays on acceptance.** Publishes ms an average of 4 months after acceptance. Buys first serial rights.
Nonfiction: Business and CEO profiles, the arts and entertainment, sports, personalities, technology, food, science and medicine and travel. "We are amenable to almost any subject that would be interesting, entertaining or useful to a passenger of American Airlines." Also humor, trivia, trends, and will consider a variety of ideas. Buys 450 mss/year. Query with published clips. Length: 1,000-4,000 words. Pays $750 and up. Usually pays the expenses of writers on assignment.

‡NORTHWEST AIRLINES, Compass Readings, Skies America Publishing Co., 7730 S.W. Mohawk, Tualatin OR 97062. (503)691-1955. Editor: Terri J. Wallo. Managing Editor: Kelly Kearns. 75% freelance written. Monthly magazine of business and leisure. Estab. 1969. Circ. 425,000. Pays on publication. Publishes ms an average of 2 months after acceptance. Byline given. Offers 100% kill fee. Buys first rights. Submit seasonal/holiday material 6 months in advance. Simultaneous submissions OK. Query for electronic submissions. Reports in 1 month. Sample copy $3 with 8 × 11 SAE. Writer's guidelines for #10 SAE with 1 first class stamp.
Nonfiction: General interest, interview/profile, personal experience, photo feature, travel. No poetry, new product, controversial, fiction, religious, fillers. Buys 10 mss/year. Query. Length: 2,000-3,000 words. Pays $850-1,000. Pays expenses of writers on assignment.
Photos: State availability of photos with submission. Reviews transparencies. Offers $200 maximum per photo. Captions and identification of subjects required. Buys one-time rights.
Tips: "Query letter only. No ms. No phone calls. Study structure of magazine. Freelancers have the best chance breaking in with articles on adventure sports, corporate profiles or sports profiles."

SKY, Inflight Magazine of Delta Air Lines, Halsey Publishing Co., 12955 Biscayne Blvd., N. Miami FL 33181. (305)893-1520. Editor: Lidia De Leon. 90% freelance written. Monthly magazine. "Delta *SKY* is a general interest, nationally oriented magazine with a primary editorial focus on business and management, with the main purpose to entertain and inform business travelers aboard Delta Air Lines." Circ. 410,000.

Pays on acceptance. Publishes ms an average of 2 months after acceptance. Byline given. Offers 100% kill fee when cancellation is through no fault of the writer. Buys one-time rights. Submit seasonal/holiday material 9 months in advance. Simultaneous submissions OK. Reports in 1 month. Sample copy for 9×12 SAE; free writer's guidelines for SASE.

Nonfiction: General interest and photo feature. "No excerpts, essays, personal experience, opinion, religious, reviews, poetry, fiction or fillers." Buys 200 mss/year. Query with published clips. Length: 1700-2500 words. Pays $500-700 for assigned articles; pays $300-450 for unsolicited articles. Pays expenses of writers on assignment.

Photos: State availability of photos with submission. Reviews transparencies (4×5) and prints (5×7). Offers $25-50/photo. Captions, model releases and identification of subject required. Buys one-time rights.

Columns/Departments: On Management (managerial techniques, methods of topical nature). Buys 40 mss/year. Query with published clips. Length: 1500-1800 words. Pays $400-450.

Tips: "Send a comprehensive, well detailed query tied in to one of the feature categories of the magazine along with clips of previously published work. Since our lead times call for planning of editorial content 6-9 months in advance, that should also be kept in mind when proposing story ideas. We are always open to good feature story ideas that have to do with business and technology. Next in order of priority would be leisure, sports, entertainment and consumer topics. All feature story categories (Business, Lifestyle, Sports, Arts/Entertainment, Consumer, Technology and Collectibles) are open to freelancers, with the exceptions of Travel (areas are predetermined by the airline) and the executive Profile Series (which is also predetermined)."

USAIR MAGAZINE, Pace Communications, 1301 Carolina St., Greensboro NC 27401. (919)378-6065. Editor: Maggie Oman. Assistant Editor: Terri Barnes. 95% freelance written. Prefers to work with published/established writers. A monthly general interest magazine published for airline passengers, many of whom are business travelers, male, with high incomes and college educations. Circ. 475,000. Pays before publication. Publishes ms an average of 4 months after acceptance. Buys first rights only. Submit seasonal material 4 months in advance. Computer printout submissions acceptable; prefers letter-quality. Reports in 6 weeks. Sample copy $4; free writer's guidelines with SASE.

Nonfiction: Travel, business, sports, health, food, personal finance, nature, the arts, science/technology and photography. Buys 100 mss/year. Query with clips of previously published work. Length: 1,500-2,800 words. Pays $400-800. Pays expenses of writers on assignment, if requested.

Photos: Send photos with ms. Pays $75-150/b&w print, depending on size; color from $100-250/print or slide. Captions preferred; model release required. Buys one-time rights.

Columns/Departments: Sports, food, money, health, business, living and science. Buys 8-10 mss/issue. Query. Length: 1,200-1,800 words. Pays $300-500.

Tips: "Send irresistible ideas and proof that you can write. It's great to get a clean manuscript from a good writer who has given me exactly what I asked for. Frequent mistakes are not following instructions, not delivering on time, etc."

‡VIAJANDO/TRAVELING, Global Magazines, Inc., 6355 N.W. 36 St., Virginia Gardens FL 33166. (305)871-6400. ext. 203 or 229. Editor-in-Chief: Christina Juri-Arencibia. 80% freelance written. Monthly magazine covering tourist destinations with an emphasis on Peru. *Viajando* is a bilingual (Spanish/English) magazine. Articles should be informative, entertaining and not controversial. Estab. 1989. Circ. 20,000. Pays on publication. Byline given. Buys one-time rights or all rights. Submit seasonal/holiday material 3 months in advance. Reports in 2 weeks on queries; 1 month on mss. Sample copy for 11×14 SAE with 4 first class stamps. Writer's guidelines for #10 SASE.

Nonfiction: Book excerpts, general interest, historical/nostalgic, travel tips, interview/profile, new product, health, electronics, gastronomy, sports, entertainment, fashion, photo feature, technical, travel, art. No fiction and nothing political or controversial. Query with or without published clips, or send complete ms. Length: 1,400-1,600 words. Pays $150 maximum with photos/$100 maximum without photos. Sometimes pays expenses of writers on assignment.

Photos: Send photos with submission. Reviews 35mm, 2×2 and 4×5 transparencies. Pays $25 per photo, $50 for cover shot. Captions and identification of subjects required.

‡WASHINGTON FLYER MAGAZINE, #111, 11 Canal Center Plaza, Alexandria VA 22314. (703)739-9292. Editor: Brian T. Cook. Editorial Assistant: Laurie McLaughlin. 90% freelance written. Bimonthly in-airport magazine for freelance Washington flyers. "Primarily affluent, well educated audience that flies frequently in and out of Washington, D.C." Estab. 1989. Circ. 160,000. Pays on acceptance. Byline given. Buys first North American or second serial (reprint) rights. Submit seasonal/holiday material 4 months in advance. Previously published submissions OK. Query for electronic submissions. Reports in 1 month. Free sample copy; writer's guidelines for #10 SASE.

Nonfiction: General interest, historical/nostalgic, how-to, interview/profile, personal experience, travel. Buys 30-40 mss/year. Query with published clips. Length: 500-3,500 words. Pays $100-600. Sometimes pays expenses of writers on assignment.

Close-up

Lidia de Leon
Editor
SKY

"I think one of the most obvious ways that inflight magazines differ from other consumer publications is that they are published for a client, i.e., an airline," says Lidia de Leon, editor of Delta *SKY*. "Though the extent of each corporation's involvement in its publication varies in degree, I think it's safe to say that the inflight magazine has to in some way reflect the 'image' of that airline. Also, the nature and 'mind-set' of the inflight readership is quite unique; one always has to remember that it is a magazine whose primary environment is 30,000 feet up in the air."

De Leon became editor of *SKY* in 1983. As editor she is primarily responsible for setting the editorial tone of the magazine and coordinating all the elements that go into creating an entertaining and informative publication each month. "One of the things I've found in this job is that there are few 'typical' days per se; things can change at a moment's notice and you have to be able to roll with the punches. The reality is that it is a lot of hard work; what makes it worth it is when that magazine comes out and it all comes together. I think that's where the real art of it lies—in making it look easy.

"A big challenge is to come up with topical editorial content as far as stories that haven't necessarily been featured in other media. The reader picking up the inflight magazine has already been saturated with information from numerous other sources, and it's important to present ideas that will be fresh in terms of piquing their interest," says de Leon.

She says the magazine receives about 200-300 unsolicited submissions per month. Out of those only about five to ten queries are held for future consideration. "Many of the unsolicited manuscripts/queries are clearly from writers who have not taken the time to review either our editorial guidelines or the magazine; but we do include the guidelines with all rejections so writers can review them for future reference." She says it's important to immerse oneself in the style and nature of a magazine. "It's easy to spot writers who have done their homework; their thoroughness enhances the credibility of their submissions."

De Leon initiated a policy at *SKY* to pay 100% kill fees when articles are dropped through no fault of the writer. "It just seemed to me that I couldn't think of any other situation where a job was completed entirely to the satisfaction of the 'customer,' and then adjusting an agreed upon fee due to decisions made after that person finished the work. Though I've never been a freelance writer, I do feel particularly attuned to writers' needs from a fairness basis. Perhaps policies such as these can help in promoting a more thorough industry examination of the thinking behind kill fees."

De Leon says the editor/writer relationship has long been perceived as an adversarial one—"the power-trip editor hacking away at the precious work of the inspired writer. I think this is nonsense; the writer/editor relationship has always been and will always be a symbiotic one, a learning experience that goes both ways. The most fruitful collaborations are those in which the sensitivity exists on both sides to the needs of each—with the common goal of presenting the best possible work to the readership involved."

—*Deborah Cinnamon*

Photos: State availability of photos with submission. Reviews negative and transparencies. Offers no additional payment for photos accepted with ms. Identification of subjects required. Buys one-time rights.
Tips: "Know the Washington market and issues relating to frequent business/pleasure travelers as we move toward a global economy."

Juvenile

Just as children change and grow, so do juvenile magazines. Children's magazine editors stress that writers must read recent issues. This section lists publications for children ages 2-12. Magazines for young people 13-19 appear in the Teen and Young Adult category. Many of the following publications are produced by religious groups and, where possible, the specific denomination is given. For the writer with a story or article slanted to a specific age group, the following children's index is a quick reference to markets for each age group. A book of juvenile markets, *Children's Writer's and Illustrator's Market*, is available from Writer's Digest Books.

Juvenile publications classified by age

Two- to Five-Year-Olds: *Chickadee, The Friend, Humpty Dumpty, Stone Soup, Story Friends, Turtle, Wee Wisdom.*

Six- to Eight-Year-Olds: *Boys' Life, Chickadee, Child Life, Children's Playmate, Cricket, The Dolphin Log, The Friend, Highlights for Children, Hopscotch, Humpty Dumpty, Jack and Jill, Kid City, Noah's Ark, Odyssey, Pockets, R-A-D-A-R, Ranger Rick, Shofar, Sports Illustrated for Kids, Stone Soup, Story Friends, 3-2-1 Contact, Touch, Wee Wisdom, Wonder Time, Young American.*

Nine- to Twelve-Year-Olds: *Boys' Life, Calliope, Children's Digest, Cobblestone, Cricket, Crusader, Discoveries, The Dolphin Log, The Friend, High Adventure, Highlights for Children, Hopscotch, Jack and Jill, Junior Trails, Kid City, Noah's Ark, Odyssey, On the Line, Pockets, R-A-D-A-R, Ranger Rick, Shofar, Sports Illustrated for Kids, Stone Soup, 3-2-1 Contact, Touch, Wee Wisdom, Young American, Young Soldier.*

BOYS' LIFE, Boy Scouts of America, P.O. Box 152079, 1325 Walnut Hill Lane, Irving TX 75015-2079. Editor-in-chief: William B. McMorris. 75% freelance written. Prefers to work with published/established writers; works with small number of new/unpublished writers each year. Monthly magazine covering activities of interest to all boys ages 8-18. Most readers are Scouts or Cub Scouts. Estab. 1911. Circ 1.4 million. **Pays on acceptance.** Publishes ms an average of 6-12 months after acceptance. Buys one-time rights. Reports in 2 weeks. Sample copy for 9 × 12 SAE and $2.50. Writer's guidelines for #10 SASE.
Nonfiction: Major articles run 1,000-1,200 words. Preferred length is about 1,000 words including sidebars and boxes. Pays minimum $500 for major article text. Uses strong photo features with about 500 words of text. Separate payment or assignment for photos. "Much better rates if you really know how to write for our market." Buys 60 major articles/year. Also needs how-to features and hobby and crafts ideas. "We pay top rates for ideas accompanied by sharp photos, clean diagrams, and short, clear instructions." Query first in writing. Buys 30-40 how-tos/year. Query all nonfiction ideas in writing. Pays expenses of writers on assignment. Also buys freelance comics pages and scripts. Query first.
Columns: "Food, Health, Pets, Bicycling and Magic Tricks are some of the columns for which we use 400-600 words of text. This is a good place to show us what you can do. Query first in writing." Pays $150 minimum. Buys 75-80 columns/year.
Fiction: Short stories 1,000-1,500 words; occasionally longer. Send complete ms. Pays $500 minimum. Buys 15 short stories/year.
Tips: "We strongly recommend reading at least 12 issues of the magazine and learning something about the programs of the Boy Scouts of America before you submit queries. We are a good market for any writer willing to do the necessary homework."

CALLIOPE: The World History Magazine for Young People, (formerly *Faces*), Cobblestone Publishing, Inc., 30 Grove St., Peterborough NH 03458. (603)924-7209. Editors: Rosalie and Charles Baker. 80% freelance written. Prefers to work with published/established writers. A magazine published 5 times/year covering world history through 1600 AD for 9- to 15-year-olds. Articles must relate to the issue's theme. Pays on publication. Byline given. Buys all rights. Simultaneous submissions OK. Previously published submissions rarely accepted. Sample copy (available September 1990) 7½ × 10½ SAE with 5 first class stamps and $3.95; writer's guidelines for SASE.

Nonfiction: Book excerpts, essays, expose, general interest, historical/nostalgic, how-to (activities), recipes, humor, interview/profile, personal experience, photo feature, technical and travel. Articles must relate to the theme. No religious, pornographic, biased or sophisticated submissions. Buys approximately 30-40 mss/year. Query with published clips. Length: 250-1,000 words. Pays up to 15¢/word.

Photos: State availability of photos with submission. Reviews contact sheets, color slides and b&w prints. Offers $10/photo. Buys one-time rights.

Fiction: All fiction must be theme-related. Buys 10 mss/year. Query with published clips. Length: 500-1,000 words. Pays 10-15¢/word.

Poetry: Light verse and traditional. No religious or pornographic poetry or poetry not related to the theme. Submit maximum 1 poem. Pays on individual basis.

Tips: "Writers must have an appreciation and understanding of early history. Writers must not condescend to our readers."

CHICKADEE MAGAZINE, For Young Children from *OWL*, The Young Naturalist Foundation, 56 The Esplanade, Suite 306, Toronto, Ontario M5E 1A7 Canada. (416)868-6001. Editor: Catherine Ripley. 25% freelance written. Magazine published 10 times/year (except July and August) for 4-9-year-olds. "We aim to interest young children in the world around them in an entertaining and lively way." Estab. 1979. Circ. 110,000 Canada and U.S. Pays on publication. Byline given. Buys all rights. Submit seasonal/holiday material up to 1 year in advance. Reports in 2½ months. Sample copy for $3.50 and SAE; writer's guidelines for SAE.

Nonfiction: How-to (arts and crafts, easy experiments for children); personal experience (real children in real situations); and photo feature (wildlife features). No articles for older children; no religious or moralistic features. Sometimes pays the expenses of writers on assignment.

Photos: Send photos with ms. Reviews 35mm transparencies. Identification of subjects required.

Fiction: Adventure (relating to the 4-9-year-old), humor. No science fiction, fantasy, talking animal stories or religious articles. Send complete ms with $1 money order for handling and return postage. No IRCs. Pays $100-300.

Tips: "A frequent mistake made by writers is trying to teach too much—not enough entertainment and fun."

‡CHILD LIFE, Children's Better Health Institute, 1100 Waterway Blvd., Box 567, Indianapolis IN 46206. (317)636-8881. Editor: Steve Charles. 80% freelance written. Monthly (except bimonthly Jan/Feb, Mar/Apr, May/June, July/August) magazine covering "general topics of interest to children-emphasis on health preferred but not necessary." Pays on publication. Publishes ms an average of 8 months after acceptance. Byline given. Buys all rights. Submit seasonal/holiday material 8 months in advance. Reports in 3 months. Sample copy 75¢. Writer's guidelines for SASE.

Nonfiction: How-to (simple crafts), anything children might like—health topics preferred. Buys 20 mss/year. Send complete ms. Length: 400-1,500. Pays 8¢/word (approx). "Readers chosen for Young Author Story receive copies."

Photos: Send photos with submission. Reviews transparencies and prints. Offers $10 for inside b&w; $20 for inside color photo, $50 for front cover. Captions, model releases and identification of subjects required. Buys one-time rights.

Fiction: Adventure, ethnic, fantasy, historical, humorous, mystery, science fiction and suspense. All must be geared to children. Buys 20-25 mss/year. Send complete ms. Length: 500-1,800 words. Pays 6¢/word (approx).

Poetry: Free verse, haiku, light verse and traditional. No long "deep" poetry not suited for children. Buys 8 poems/year. Submit maximum 5 poems. "We have used some verse 'stories'—500 words." Pays approx 50¢/line.

Fillers: "We do accept puzzles, games, mazes, etc." Variable pay.

Tips: "Present health-related items in an interesting, non-textbook manner. The approach to health fiction can be subtle—tell a good story first. We also consider non-health items—make them fresh and enjoyable for children."

CHILDREN'S DIGEST, Children's Better Health Institute, P.O. Box 567, Indianapolis IN 46206. (317)636-8881. Editor: Elizabeth Rinck. 85% freelance written. Works with a small number of new/unpublished writers each year. Magazine published 8 times/year covering children's health for preteen children. Estab. 1950. Pays on publication. Publishes ms an average of 1 year after acceptance. Byline given. Buys all rights. Submit seasonal/holiday material 8 months in advance. Submit *only* complete manuscripts. "No queries, please." Reports in 2 months. Sample copy for 75¢; writer's guidelines for #10 SASE.

Nonfiction: Historical, interview/profile (biographical), craft ideas, health, nutrition, hygiene, exercise and safety. "We're especially interested in factual features that teach readers about the human body or encourage them to develop better health habits. We are *not* interested in material that is simply rewritten from encyclopedias. We try to present our health material in a way that instructs *and* entertains the reader." Buys 15-20 mss/year. Send complete ms. Length: 500-1,200 words. Pays 8¢/word. Sometimes pays the expenses of writers on assignment.

Photos: State availability of full color or b&w photos. Payment varies. Model releases and identification of subjects required. Buys one-time rights.

Fiction: Adventure, humorous, mainstream and mystery. Stories should appeal to both boys and girls. "We need some stories that incorporate a health theme. However, we don't want stories that preach, preferring instead stories with implied morals. We like a light or humorous approach." Buys 15-20 mss/year. Length: 500-1,500 words. Pays 8¢/word.

Poetry: Pays $10 minimum.

Tips: "Many of our readers have working mothers and/or come from single-parent homes. We need more stories that reflect these changing times while communicating good values."

CHILDREN'S PLAYMATE, 1100 Waterway Blvd., P.O. Box 567, Indianapolis IN 46206. (317)636-8881. Editor: Elizabeth Rinck. 75% freelance written. Eager to work with new/unpublished writers. "We are looking for articles, stories, and activities with a health, safety, exercise or nutritionally oriented theme. Primarily we are concerned with preventative medicine. We try to present our material in a positive—not a negative—light, and we try to incorporate humor and a light approach wherever possible without minimizing the seriousness of what we are saying." For children ages 6-8. Magazine published 8 times/year. Estab. 1928. Buys all rights. Byline given. Pays on publication. Publishes ms an average of 1 year after acceptance. Submit seasonal material 8 months in advance. Reports in 2 months. Sometimes may hold mss for up to 1 year, with author's permission. Write for guidelines. "Material will not be returned unless accompanied by a self-addressed envelope and sufficient postage." Sample copy 75¢; free writer's guidelines with SASE.

Nonfiction: Beginning science, 600 words maximum. A feature may be an interesting presentation on animals, people, events, objects or places, especially about good health, exercise, proper nutrition and safety. Include number of words in articles. Buys 30 mss/year. "We do not consider outlines. Reading the whole manuscript is the only way to give fair consideration. The editors cannot criticize, offer suggestions, or review unsolicited material that is not accepted." No queries. Pays about 8¢/word.

Fiction: Short stories for beginning readers, not over 700 words. Seasonal stories with holiday themes. Humorous stories, unusual plots. "We are interested in stories about children in different cultures and stories about lesser-known holidays (not just Christmas, Thanksgiving, Halloween, Hanukkah)." Vocabulary suitable for ages 6-8. Submit complete ms. Pays about 8¢/word. Include number of words in stories.

Fillers: Puzzles, dot-to-dots, color-ins, hidden pictures and mazes. Buys 30 fillers/year. Payment varies.

Tips: Especially interested in stories, poems and articles about special holidays, customs and events.

CLUBHOUSE, Your Story Hour, Box 15, Berrien Springs MI 49103. (616)471-3701. Editor: Elaine Trumbo. 75% freelance written. Works with a small number of new/unpublished writers each year. Magazine published 6 times/year covering many subjects with Christian approach, though not associated with a church. "Stories and features for fun for 9-14 year-olds. Main objective: To provide a psychological 'up' magazine that lets kids know that they are acceptable, 'neat' people." Circ. 10,000. **Pays on acceptance.** Publishes ms an average of 1 year after acceptance. Byline given. Buys first serial rights or first North American serial rights, one-time rights, simultaneous rights, and second serial (reprint) rights. Simultaneous queries, and simultaneous and previously published submissions OK. Reports in 5 weeks. Sample copy for 6×9 SAE and 3 first class stamps; writer's guidelines for #10 SASE.

Nonfiction: How-to (crafts), personal experience and recipes (without sugar or artificial flavors and colors). "No stories in which kids start out 'bad' and by peer or adult pressure or circumstances are changed into 'good' people." Send complete ms. Length: 750-800 words ($25); 1,000-1,200 words ($30); feature story, 1,200 words ($35).

Photos: Send photos with ms. Pays on publication according to published size. Buys one-time rights.

Columns/Departments: Body Shop (short stories or "ad" type material that is anti-smoking, drugs and alcohol and pro-good nutrition, etc.); and Jr. Detective (secret codes, word search, deduction problems, hidden pictures, etc.). Buys 20/year. Send complete ms. Length: 400 words maximum for Jr. Detective; 1,000 maximum for Body Shop. Pays $10-30.

Fiction: Adventure, historical, humorous and mainstream. "Stories should depict bravery, kindness, etc., without a preachy attitude." No science fiction, romance, confession or mystery. Cannot use Santa-elves, Halloween or Easter Bunny material. Buys 40 mss/year. Send query or complete ms (prefers ms). Length: 750-800 words ($20); 1,000-1,200 words ($30); lead story ($35).

Poetry: Free verse, light verse and traditional. Buys 6-10/year. Submit maximum 5 poems. Length: 4-24 lines. Pays $5-20.

Fillers: Cartoons. Buys 18/year. Pay $12 maximum.

Tips: "Send all material during March or April. (Not accepting material until April 1990.) By the middle of June acceptance or rejection notices will be sent. Material chosen will appear the following year. Basically, kids are more and more informed and aware of the world around them. This means that characters in stories for *Clubhouse* should not seem too simple, yet maintain the wonder and joy of youth."

COBBLESTONE: The History Magazine for Young People, Cobblestone Publishing, Inc., 30 Grove St., Peterborough NH 03458. (603)924-7209. Associate Editor: Beth Turin Weston. 80% freelance written (approximately 2 issues/year are by assignment only). Prefers to work with published/established writers. Monthly magazine covering American history for children ages 8-14. "Each issue presents a particular theme, from different angles, making it exciting as well as informative. Half of all subscriptions are for schools." Circ. 45,000. Pays on publication. Publishes ms an average of 4 months after acceptance. Byline given. Buys all rights; makes work-for-hire assignments. All material must relate to monthly theme. Simultaneous and previously published submissions OK. Sample copy for 7½ × 10½ SAE with 5 first class stamps and $3.95; writer's guidelines for SASE.

Nonfiction: Historical/nostalgic, how-to, interview, plays, biography, recipes, activities and personal experience. "Request a copy of the writer's guidelines to find out specific issue themes in upcoming months." No material that editorializes rather than reports. Buys 5-8 mss/issue. Length: 800-1,200 words. Supplemental nonfiction 200-800 words. Query with published clips, outline and bibliography. Pays up to 15¢/word.

Fiction: Adventure, historical, humorous and biographical fiction. "Has to be very strong and accurate." Buys 1-2 mss/issue. Length: 800-1,200 words. Request free editorial guidelines that explain upcoming issue themes and give query deadlines. "Message" must be smoothly integrated with the story. Query with written samples. Pays up to 15¢/word.

Poetry: Free verse, light verse and traditional. Submit maximum 2 poems. Length: 5-100 lines. Pays on an individual basis.

Tips: "All material is considered on the basis of merit and appropriateness to theme. Query should state idea for material simply, with rationale for why material is applicable to theme. Request writer's guidelines (includes themes and query deadlines) before submitting a query. Include SASE."

CRICKET, The Magazine for Children, Carus Publishing Co., 315 5th St., P.O. Box 300, Peru IL 61354. (815)224-6643. Publisher and Editor-in-Chief: Marianne Carus. Monthly magazine. Estab. 1973. Circ. 120,000. Pays on publication. Byline given. Buys first North American serial rights. Submit seasonal/holiday material 1 year in advance. Previously published submissions OK. Reports in 3-4 months. Sample copy $2; writer's guidelines for SASE.

Nonfiction: Historical/nostalgic, lively science, personal experience and travel. Send complete ms. Length: 200-1,200 words. Pays up to 25¢/word.

Fiction: Adventure, ethnic, fantasy, historical, humorous, mystery, novel excerpts, science fiction, suspense and western. No didactic, sex, religious or horror stories. Buys 24-36 mss/year. Send complete ms. Length: 200-1,500 words. Pays up to 25¢/word.

Poetry: Buys 8-10 poems/year. Length: 100 lines maximum. Pays up to $3/line on publication.

CRUSADER MAGAZINE, P.O. Box 7259, Grand Rapids MI 49510. FAX: (616)241-5558. Editor: G. Richard Broene. 40% freelance written. Works with a small number of new/unpublished writers each year. Magazine published 7 times/year. "*Crusader Magazine* shows boys (9-14) how God is at work in their lives and in the world around them." Estab. 1958. Circ. 13,000. Buys 20-25 mss/year. **Pays on acceptance.** Byline given. Publishes ms an average of 8 months after acceptance. Rights purchased vary with author and material; buys first serial rights, one-time rights, second serial (reprint) rights, and simultaneous rights. Submit seasonal material (Christmas, Easter) at least 5 months in advance. Simultaneous submissions OK. Reports in 1 month. Free sample copy and writer's guidelines for 9 × 12 SAE and 3 first class stamps.

Nonfiction: Articles about young boys' interests: sports, outdoor activities, bike riding, science, crafts, etc., and problems. Emphasis is on a Christian multi-racial perspective, but no simplistic moralisms. Informational, how-to, personal experience, interview, profile, inspirational and humor. Submit complete ms. Length: 500-1,500 words. Pays 2-5¢/word.

Photos: Pays $4-25 for b&w photos purchased with mss.

Fiction: "Considerable fiction is used. Fast-moving stories that appeal to a boy's sense of adventure or sense of humor are welcome. Avoid preachiness. Avoid simplistic answers to complicated problems. Avoid long dialogue and little action." Length: 900-1,500 words. Pays 2¢/word minimum.

Fillers: Uses short humor and any type of puzzles as fillers.

DISCOVERIES, 6401 The Paseo, Kansas City MO 64131. Editor: Middler Editor. 75% freelance written. For boys and girls ages 9-12 in the Church of the Nazarene. Weekly. Estab. 1974. Publishes ms an average of 1 year after acceptance. Buys first serial rights and second (reprint) rights. "Minimal comments on pre-printed form are made on rejected material." Reports in 1 month. Sample copy and guidelines for #10 SASE.

Fiction: Stories with Christian emphasis on high ideals, wholesome social relationships and activities, right choices, Sabbath observance, church loyalty and missions. Informal style. Submit complete ms. Length: 500-1,000 words. Pays 3½¢/word for first serial rights and 2¢/word for second (reprint) rights.

Tips: "The freelancer needs an understanding of the doctrine of the Church of the Nazarene and the Sunday school material for third to sixth graders."

THE DOLPHIN LOG, The Cousteau Society, 8440 Santa Monica Blvd., Los Angeles CA 90069. (213)656-4422. Editor: Pamela Stacey. 30-40% freelance written. Prefers to work with published/established writers; works with a small number of new/unpublished writers each year. Bimonthly magazine covering marine biology, ecology, environment, natural history, and water-related stories. "The *Dolphin Log* is an educational publication for children ages 7-15 offered by The Cousteau Society. Subject matter encompasses all areas of science, history and the arts which can be related to our global water system. The philosophy of the magazine is to delight, instruct and instill an environmental ethic and understanding of the interconnectedness of living organisms, including people." Estab. 1981. Circ. 100,000. Pays on publication. Publishes ms an average of 1 year after acceptance. Byline given. Buys one-time and translation rights. Reports in 1 month. Sample copy for $2 with 9×12 SAE and 3 first class stamps; writer's guidelines for SASE.

Nonfiction: General interest (per guidelines); how-to (water-related crafts or science); personal experience (ocean related); and photo feature (marine subject). "Of special interest are articles on specific marine creatures, and games involving an ocean/water-related theme which develop math, reading and comprehension skills. Humorous articles and short jokes based on scientific fact are also welcome. Experiments that can be conducted at home and demonstrate a phenomenon or principle of science are wanted as are clever crafts or art projects which also can be tied to an ocean theme. Try to incorporate such activities into any articles submitted." No fiction or "talking" animals. Buys 8-12 mss/year. Query or send complete ms. Length: 500-1,000 words. Pays $50-150.

Photos: Send photos with query or ms (duplicates only). Prefers underwater animals, water photos with children, photos that explain text. Pays $25-100/photo. Identification of subjects required. Buys one-time and translation rights.

Columns/Departments: Discovery (science experiments or crafts a young person can easily do at home), 50-500 words; Creature Feature (lively article on one specific marine animal), 500-700 words. Buys 1 mss/year. Send complete ms. Pays $25-150.

Poetry: No "talking" animals. Buys 1-2 poems/year. Pays $10-100.

Tips: "Find a lively way to relate scientific facts to children without anthropomorphizing. We need to know material is accurate and current. Articles should feature an interesting marine creature and yet contain factual material that's fun to read. We will be increasingly interested in material that draws information from current scientific research."

THE FRIEND, 50 East North Temple, Salt Lake City UT 84150. Managing Editor: Vivian Paulsen. 60% freelance written. Eager to work with new/unpublished writers as well as established writers. Appeals to children ages 3-11. Monthly publication of The Church of Jesus Christ of Latter-Day Saints. Circ. 205,000. **Pays on acceptance.** Buys all rights. Submit seasonal material 8 months in advance. Sample copy and writer's guidelines for 8½×11 SAE with 4 first class stamps.

Nonfiction: Subjects of current interest, science, nature, pets, sports, foreign countries, and things to make and do. Special issues for Christmas and Easter. "Submit only complete ms—no queries, please." Length: 1,000 words maximum. Pays 8¢/word minimum.

Fiction: Seasonal and holiday stories and stories about other countries and their children. Wholesome and optimistic; high motive, plot, and action. Character-building stories preferred. Length: 1,200 words maximum. Stories for younger children should not exceed 250 words. Pays 8¢/word minimum.

Poetry: Serious, humorous and holiday. Any form with child appeal. Pays $15.

Tips: "Do you remember how it feels to be a child? Can you write stories that appeal to children ages 3-11 in today's world? We're interested in stories with an international flavor and those that focus on present-day problems. Send material of high literary quality slanted to our editorial requirements. Let the child solve the problem—not some helpful, all-wise adult. No overt moralizing. Nonfiction should be creatively presented—not an array of facts strung together. Beware of being cutesy."

HIGH ADVENTURE, Assemblies of God, 1445 Boonville, Springfield MO 65802. (417)862-2781, ext. 1497. Editor: Marshall Bruner. Eager to work with new/unpublished writers. Quarterly magazine "designed to provide boys with worthwhile, enjoyable, leisure reading; to challenge them in narrative form to higher ideals and greater spiritual dedication; and to perpetuate the spirit of the Royal Rangers program through stories, ideas and illustrations." Estab. 1971. Circ. 87,000. **Pays on acceptance.** Byline given. Buys one-time rights. Submit seasonal/holiday material 9 months in advance. Simultaneous queries, and simultaneous and previously published submissions OK. Reports in 1 month. Sample copy for 9×12 SAE with 3 first class stamps; free writer's guidelines.

Nonfiction: Historical/nostalgic, how-to, humor and inspirational. Buys 25-50 mss/year. Query or send complete ms. Length: 800-1,200 words. Pays 3¢/word.

Photos: Reviews b&w negatives, color transparencies and prints. Identification of subjects required. Buys one-time rights.

Fiction: Adventure, historical, humorous, religious and western. Buys 25-50 mss/year. Query or send complete ms. Length: 800-1,800 words maximum. Pays 3¢/word.

Fillers: Jokes, gags and short humor. Pays $2-4 for jokes; $12-20 for cartoons; others vary.

HIGHLIGHTS FOR CHILDREN, 803 Church St., Honesdale PA 18431. Editor: Kent L. Brown Jr. 80% freelance written. Magazine published 11 times/year for children ages 2-12. Estab. 1946. Circ. 2.8 million. **Pays on acceptance.** Buys all rights. Reports in about 2 months. Free sample copy; writer's guidelines for #10 SASE.
Nonfiction: "We need articles on science, technology and nature written by persons with strong backgrounds in those fields. Contributions always welcomed from new writers, especially engineers, scientists, historians, teachers, etc., who can make useful, interesting facts accessible to children. Also writers who have lived abroad and can interpret the ways of life, especially of children, in other countries in ways that will foster world brotherhood. Sports material, biographies and articles of general interest to children. Direct, original approach, simple style, interesting content, not rewritten from encyclopedias. State background and qualifications for writing factual articles submitted. Include references or sources of information. Length: 900 words maximum. Pays $75 minimum. Also buys original party plans for children ages 7-12, clearly described in 300-800 words, including drawings or samples of items to be illustrated. Also, novel but tested ideas in crafts, with clear directions and made-up models. Projects must require only free or inexpensive, easy-to-obtain materials. Especially desirable if easy enough for early primary grades. Also, fingerplays with lots of action, easy for very young children to grasp and to dramatize. Avoid wordiness. We need creative-thinking puzzles that can be illustrated, optical illusions, brain teasers, games of physical agility and other "fun" activities. Pays minimum $50 for party plans; $20 for crafts ideas; $25 for fingerplays.
Fiction: Unusual, meaningful stories appealing to both girls and boys, ages 2-12. Vivid, full of action. "Engaging plot, strong characterization, lively language." Prefers stories in which a child protagonist solves a dilemma through his or her own resources. Seeks stories that the child ages 8-12 will eagerly read, and the child ages 2-7 will begin to read and/or will like to hear when read aloud (900 words maximum). "We publish stories in the suspense/adventure/mystery, fantasy and humor category, all requiring interesting plot and a number of illustration possiblities. Also need rebuses (picture stories 150 words or under), stories with urban settings, stories for beginning readers (500 words), sports and horse stories and retold folk tales. We also would like to see more material of 1-page length (300-500 words), both fiction and factual. War, crime and violence are taboo. Pays $65 minimum.
Tips: "We are pleased that many authors of children's literature report that their first published work was in the pages of *Highlights*. It is not our policy to consider fiction on the strength of the reputation of the author. We judge each submission on its own merits. With factual material, however, we do prefer that writers be authorities in their field or people with first-hand experience. In this manner we can avoid the encyclopedic article that merely restates information readily available elsewhere. We don't make assignments. Query with simple letter to establish whether the nonfiction *subject* is likely to be of interest. A beginning writer should first become familiar with the type of material which *Highlights* publishes. Include special qualifications, if any, of author. Write for the child, not the editor."

‡**HOPSCOTCH, The Magazine for Girls**, Hopscotch, Inc., P.O. Box 1292, Saratoga Springs NY 12866. (518)587-2268. Editor: Donald P. Evans. 90% freelance written. Bimonthly magazine on basic subjects of interest to young girls. "*HOPSCOTCH* is a digest-size magazine with a four-color cover and two-color format inside. It is designed for girls ages 6 to 12 and features pets, crafts, hobbies, games, science, fiction, history, puzzles, careers, etc." Estab. 1989. Pays on publication. Publishes ms an average of 4 months after acceptance. Byline given. Offers 50% kill fee. Buys first and second rights. Submit seasonal/holiday material 6-8 months in advance. Simultaneous and previously published submissions OK. Reports in 3 weeks on queries; 1 month on mss. Sample copy $2.50. Writer's guidelines for #10 SAE with 1 first class stamp.
Nonfiction: Book excerpts, general interest, historical/nostalgic, how-to (crafts), humor, inspirational, interview/profile, personal experience, pets, games, fiction, careers, sports, cooking."No fashion, hairstyles, sex or dating articles." Buys 40 mss/year. Send complete ms. Length: 400-1,100 words. Pays $25-75. Sometimes pays expenses of writers on assignment.
Photos: Send photos with submission. Reviews negatives, transparencies and 5×7 prints. Offers $7.50-10 per photo. Captions, model releases and identification of subjects required. Buys one-time rights.
Columns/Departments: Science—nature, crafts, pets, cooking—(basic), 400-1,000 words. Send complete ms. Pays $25-60.
Fiction: Adventure, fantasy, historical, humorous, mainstream, mystery, novel excerpts, suspense. Buys 15 mss/year. Send complete ms. Length: 600-1,000 words. Pays $30-70.
Poetry: Free verse, light verse and traditional. "No experimental or obscure poetry." Submit maximum 6 poems. Pays $10-30.
Tips: "Almost all sections are open to freelancers. Freelancers should remember that *HOPSCOTCH* is a bit old fashioned, appealing to *young* girls (6 to 12). We cherish nonfiction pieces that have a young girl or young

ALWAYS submit unsolicited manuscripts or queries with a self-addressed, stamped envelope (SASE) within your country or International Reply Coupons (IRC) purchased from the post office for other countries.

girls directly involved in unusual and/or worthwhile activities. Any piece accompanied by decent photos stands an even better chance of being accepted."

HUMPTY DUMPTY'S MAGAZINE, Children's Better Health Institute, 1100 Waterway Blvd., Box 567, Indianapolis IN 46206. Editor: Christine French Clark. 90% freelance written. "We try not to be overly influenced by an author's credits, preferring instead to judge each submission on its own merit." Magazine published 8 times/year stressing health, nutrition, hygiene, exercise and safety for children ages 4-6. Combined issues: January/February, March/April, May/June, July/August. Pays on publication. Publishes ms at least 8 months after acceptance. Buys all rights. Submit seasonal material 8 months in advance. Reports in 10 weeks. Sample copy 75¢; writer's guidelines for SASE.

Nonfiction: "We are open to nonfiction on almost any age-appropriate subject, but we especially need material with a health theme—nutrition, safety, exercise, hygiene. We're looking for articles that encourage readers to develop better health habits without preaching. Very simple factual articles that creatively teach readers about their bodies. We use simple crafts, some with holiday themes. We also use several puzzles and activities in each issue—dot-to-dot, hidden pictures and other activities that promote following instructions, developing finger dexterity and working with numbers and letters. Submit complete ms. "Include number of words in manuscript and Social Security number." Length: 600 words maximum. Pays minimum 8¢/word.

Fiction: "We use some stories in rhyme and a few easy-to-read stories for the beginning reader. All stories should work well as read alouds. Currently we need seasonal stories with holiday themes. We use contemporary stories and fantasy, some employing a health theme. We try to present our health material in a positive light, incorporating humor and a light approach wherever possible. Avoid stereotyping. Characters in contemporary stories should be realistic and up-to-date. Remember, many of our readers have working mothers and/or come from single-parent homes. We need more stories that reflect these changing times but at the same time communicate good, wholesome values." Submit complete ms. "Include number of words in manuscript and Social Security number." Length: 600 words maximum. Pays about 8¢/word.

Poetry: Short, simple poems. Pays $10 minimum.

Tips: "Writing for *Humpty Dumpty* is similar to writing picture book manuscripts. There must be a great economy of words. We strive for at least 50% art per page (in stories and articles), so space for text is limited. Because the illustrations are so important, stories should lend themselves well to visual imagery."

‡JACK AND JILL, 1100 Waterway Blvd., Box 567, Indianapolis IN 46206. (317)636-8881. Editor: Steve Charles. 85% freelance written. Magazine published 8 times/year for children ages 7-10. Pays on publication. Publishes ms an average of 8 months after acceptance. Buys all rights. Byline given. Submit seasonal material 8 months in advance. Reports in 10 weeks. May hold material seriously being considered for up to 1 year. "Material will not be returned unless accompanied by self-addressed envelope with sufficient postage." Sample copy 75¢; writer's guidelines for SASE.

Nonfiction: "Because we want to encourage youngsters to read for pleasure and for information, we are interested in material that will challenge a young child's intelligence *and* be enjoyable reading. Our emphasis is on good health, and we are in particular need of articles, stories, and activities with health, safety, exercise and nutrition themes. We are looking for well-written articles that take unusual approaches to teaching better health habits and scientific facts about how the body works. We try to present our health material in a positive light—incorporating humor and a light approach wherever possible without minimizing the seriousness of what we are saying." Straight factual articles are OK if they are short and interestingly written. "We would rather see, however, more creative alternatives to the straight factual article. For instance, we'd be interested in seeing a health message or facts presented in articles featuring positive role models for readers. Many of the personalities children admire—athletes, musicians, and film or TV stars—are fitness or nutrition buffs. Many have kicked drugs, alcohol or smoking habits and are outspoken about the dangers of these vices. Color slides, transparencies, or black and white photos accompanying this type of article would greatly enhance salability." Buys 25-30 nonfiction mss/year. Length: 500-1,200 words. Pays approximately 8¢ a word.

Photos: When appropriate, photos should accompany ms. Reviews sharp, contrasting b&w glossy prints. Sometimes uses color slides, transparencies, or good color prints. Pays $10 for b&w, $20 for color, $50 for cover. Buys one-time rights.

Fiction: May include, but is not limited to, realistic stories, fantasy adventure—set in past, present or future. All stories need a well-developed plot, action and incident. Humor is highly desirable. "Currently we need stories with holiday themes. Stories that deal with a health theme need not have health as the primary subject. We would like to see more biographical fiction." Length: 500-1,500 words, short stories; 1,500 words/installment, serials of two parts. Pays approximately 8¢ a word. Buys 20-25 mss/year.

Fillers: Puzzles (including various kinds of word and crossword puzzles), poems, games, science projects, and creative craft projects. Instructions for activities should be clearly and simply written and accompanied by models or diagram sketches. "We also have a need for recipes. Ingredients should be healthful; avoid sugar, salt, chocolate, red meat, and fats as much as possible. In all material, avoid references to eating sugary foods, such as candy, cakes, cookies and soft drinks."

Tips: "We are constantly looking for new writers who can tell good stories with interesting slants—stories that are not full of out-dated and time-worn expressions. Our best authors are writers who know what today's children are like. Keep in mind that our readers are becoming 'computer literate', living in an age of rapidly developing technology. They are exploring career possibilities that may be new and unfamiliar to our generation. They are faced with tough decisions about drug and alcohol use. Many of them are latch-key children because both parents work or they come from single-parent homes. We need more stories and articles that reflect these changing times but that also communicate good, wholesome values. Obtain *current* issues of the magazines and *study* them to determine our present needs and editorial style."

JUNIOR TRAILS, Gospel Publishing House, 1445 Boonville Ave., Springfield MO 65802. (417)862-2781. Editor: Sinda S. Zinn. 100% freelance written. Eager to work with new/unpublished writers. Weekly tabloid covering religious fiction; and biographical, historical and scientific articles with a spiritual emphasis for boys and girls ages 10-11. Circ. 75,000. **Pays on acceptance.** Publishes ms an average of 9-12 months after acceptance. Byline given. Not copyrighted. Buys simultaneous rights, first rights, or second (reprint) rights to material originally published elsewhere "indicate on ms which it is." Submit seasonal/holiday material 15 months year in advance. List number of words in ms. Simultaneous and previously published submissions OK. Reports 2 months on mss. Sample copy and writer's guidelines for 9 × 12 SAE and 2 first class stamps.
Nonfiction: Biographical, historical and scientific (with spiritual lesson or emphasis). "Junior-age children need to be alerted to the dangers of drugs, alcohol, smoking, etc. They need positive guidelines and believable examples relating to living a Christian life in an ever-changing world." Buys 20-30 mss/year. Send complete ms. Length: 500-800 words. Pays 2-3¢/word.
Fiction: Adventure (with spiritual lesson or application); and religious. "We're looking for fiction that presents believable characters working out their problems according to Biblical principles. No fictionalized accounts of Bible stories or events." Buys 60-80 mss/year. Send complete ms. Length: 1,000-1,500 words. Pays 2-3¢/word.
Poetry: Free verse and light verse. Buys 6-8 mss/year. Pays 20¢/line.
Fillers: Anecdotes (with spiritual emphasis). Buys 15-20/year. Length: 200 words maximum. Pays 2-3¢/word.
Tips: "We like to receive stories showing contemporary children positively facing today's world. These stories show children who are aware of their world and who find a moral solution to their problems through the guidance of God's Word. They are not 'super children' in themselves. They are average children learning how to face life through God's help. We tend to get settings in stories that are out of step with today's society. We will tend to turn more and more to purely contemporary settings unless we are using a historical or biographical story. We will have the setting, characters and plot agree with each other in order to make it more believable to our audience."

KID CITY™, Children's Television Workshop, 1 Lincoln Plaza, New York NY 10023. (212)595-3456. Editor: Maureen Hunter-Bone. Associate Editor: Lisa Rao. 10% freelance written. Works with small number of new/unpublished writers each year. Magazine published 10 times/year. "We are a humor/reading/activity magazine for children 6-10 years old." Estab. 1969. Circ. 250,000. **Pays on acceptance.** Publishes ms an average of 8 months after acceptance. Byline given. Offers 50% kill fee. Buys all rights. Submit seasonal/ holiday material at least 6 months in advance. Simultaneous submissions OK. Reports in 6 weeks. Sample copy for 9 × 12 SAE with 6 first class stamps.
Nonfiction: General interest, humor and photo feature. Buys 3-4 mss/year. Query with or without published clips, or send complete ms. Length: 500 words maximum. Pays $25-350.
Photos: State availability of photos with submission. Reviews transparencies. Offers $75 maximum/photo. Model releases and identification of subjects required.
Fiction: Adventure, fantasy, historical, humorous, mystery and western. "No stories with heavy moral messages or those whose main focus is child abuse, saying 'no,' divorce, etc." Buys 3 mss/year. Query or send complete ms. Length: 250-700 words. Pays $400 maximum.
Tips: "Just think about what you liked to read about when you were a kid and write it down. No stories about doggies, bunnies or kitties. No stories with heavy moral message. We're looking for more interesting items about *real* kids who have done something newsworthy or exceptional."

NOAH'S ARK, A Newspaper for Jewish Children, 7726 Portal, Houston TX 77071. (713)771-7143. Editors: Debbie Israel Dubin and Linda Freedman Block. A monthly tabloid that "captures readers' interest and reinforces learning about Jewish history, holidays, laws and culture through articles, stories, recipes, games, crafts, projects, Hebrew column and more." For Jewish children, ages 6-12. Circ. 450,000. **Pays on acceptance.** Byline given. Buys first North American serial rights. Submit seasonal/holiday material 4 months in advance. Simultaneous submissions OK. Reports in 6 weeks on queries; 2 months on mss. Sample copy and writer's guidelines for #10 SASE.

Nonfiction: Historical/nostalgic, craft projects, recipes, humor, interview/profile. Send complete ms. Length: 350 words maximum. Usually pays 5¢/word.

Photos: State availability of photos with submission or send photos with submission. Offers no additional payment for photos accepted with ms. Identification of subjects required. Buys one-time rights.

Fiction: All must be of Jewish interest: Historical, humorous, religious (Jewish), slice-of-life vignettes. Any and all suitable for Jewish children. Buys 2-3 mss/year. Send complete ms. Length: 600 words maximum. Pays 5¢/word.

Poetry: Light verse and traditional. Buys 1 poem/year. Submit maximum 1 poem. Payment varies.

Fillers: All must be of Jewish interest: Anecdotes, facts, gags, short humor and games. Buys 3-5/year. Payment varies.

Tips: "We're just looking for high quality material suitable for entertainment as well as supplemental religious school use." Encourages freelancers to take an "unusual approach to writing about holidays. All submissions must have Jewish content and positive Jewish values. Content should not be exclusively for an American audience."

ODYSSEY, Kalmbach Publishing Co., 21027 Crossroads Circle, Waukesha WI 53186. (414)796-8776. FAX: (414)796-0126. Editor: Nancy Mack. 50% freelance written. Works with a small number of new/unpublished writers each year. Monthly magazine emphasizing astronomy and outer space for children ages 8-12. Estab. 1978. Circ. 100,000. Pays on publication. Publishes ms an average of 8 months after acceptance. Buys one-time rights. Submit seasonal/holiday material 4 months in advance. Previously published submissions OK. Reports in 2 months. "Material with little news connection may be held up to one year." Sample copy and writer's guidelines for 8½ × 12½ SAE and 5 first class stamps.

Nonfiction: General interest (astronomy, outer space, spacecraft, planets, stars, etc.); how-to (astronomy projects, experiments, etc.); and photo feature (spacecraft, planets, stars, etc.). "We like short, off-beat articles with some astronomy or space-science tie-in. A recent example: an article about a baseball game that ended with the explosion of a meteorite over the field. Study the styles of the monthly columnists. No general overview articles; for example, a general article on the Space Shuttle, or a general article on stars. We do not want science fiction articles." Buys 12 mss/year. Query with published clips. Length: 750-2,000 words. Pays $100-350 depending on length and type of article. Sometimes pays expenses of writers on assignment.

Photos: State availability of photos. Buys one-time rights. Captions preferred; model releases required. Payment depends upon size and placement.

Tips: "Since I am overstocked and have a stable of regular writers, a query is very important. I often get several manuscripts on the same subject and must reject them. Write a very specific proposal and indicate why it will interest kids. If the subject is very technical, indicate your qualifications to write about it. Frequent mistakes writers make are trying to fudge on material they don't understand, using outdated references, and telling me their articles are assignments for the Institute of Children's Literature."

ON THE LINE, Mennonite Publishing House, 616 Walnut Ave., Scottdale PA 15683-1999. (412)887-8500. Editor: Mary Clemens Meyer. 95% freelance written. Works with a small number of new/unpublished writers each year. Weekly magazine for children ages 10-14. Circ. 10,000. **Pays on acceptance.** Publishes ms an average of 1 year after acceptance. Byline given. Buys one-time rights. Submit seasonal/holiday material 6 months in advance. Simultaneous and previously published submissions OK. Reports in 1 month. Sample copy for 8½ × 11 SAE and 2 first class stamps.

Nonfiction: How-to (things to make with easy-to-get materials); and informational (500-word articles on wonders of nature, people who have made outstanding contributions). Buys 95 unsolicited mss/year. Send complete ms. Length: 500-900 words. Pays $10-30.

Photos: Photos purchased with or without ms. Pays $10-25 for 8 × 10 b&w photos. Total purchase price for ms includes payment for photos.

Fiction: Adventure, humorous and religious. Buys 52 mss/year. Send complete ms. Length: 800-1,200 words. Pays $15-40.

Poetry: Light verse and religious. Length: 3-12 lines. Pays $5-15.

Tips: "Study the publication first. We need short well-written how-to and craft articles. Don't send query; we prefer to see the complete manuscript."

POCKETS, The Upper Room, 1908 Grand Ave., Box 189, Nashville TN 37202. (615)340-3300. Editor: Janet M. Bugg. 50% freelance written. Eager to work with new/unpublished writers. A monthly themed magazine (except combined January and February issues) covering children's and families spiritual formation. "We are a Christian, non-denominational publication for children 6 to 12 years of age." Circ. 70,000. **Pays on acceptance.** Byline given. Offers 4¢/word kill fee. Buys first North American serial rights. Submit seasonal/holiday material 1 year in advance. Previously published submissions OK. Reports in 10 weeks on manuscripts. Sample copy for 5 × 7 SAE with 4 first class stamps; writer's guidelines and themes for #10 SASE.

Nonfiction: Learmond Chapman, articles editor. Interview/profile, religious (retold scripture stories) and personal experience. List of themes for special issues available with SASE. No violence or romance. Buys 5 mss/year. Send complete ms. Length: 600-1,500 words. Pays 7¢-10¢/word.

Photos: Send photos with submission. Reviews contact sheets, transparencies and prints. Offers $25-50/photo. Buys one-time rights.

Columns Departments: Refrigerator Door (poetry and prayer related to themes), 25 lines; Pocketsful of Love (family communications activities), 300 words; and Peacemakers at Work (profiles of people, particularly children, working for peace, justice and ecological concerns), 300-600 words. Buys 20 mss/year. Send complete ms. Pays 7¢-10¢/word; recipes $25.

Fiction: Adventure, ethnic and slice-of-life. "Stories should reflect the child's everyday experiences through a Christian approach. This is often more acceptable when stories are not preachy or overtly Christian." Buys 22 mss/year. Send complete ms. Length: 750-1,600 words. Pays 7-10¢/word.

Poetry: Buys 8 poems/year. Length: 4-25 lines. Pays $25-50.

Tips: "Theme stories, role models and retold scripture stories are most open to freelancers. Poetry is also open, but we rarely receive an acceptable poem. It's very helpful if writers send for our themes. These are *not* the same as writer's guidelines."

R-A-D-A-R, 8121 Hamilton Ave., Cincinnati OH 45231. (513)931-4050. Editor: Margaret Williams. 75% freelance written. Prefers to work with published/established writers; works with a small number of new/unpublished writers each year. Weekly for children in grades 3-6 in Christian Sunday schools. Estab. 1866 (publishing house). Rights purchased varies with author and material; prefers buying first serial rights, but will buy second (reprint) rights. Occasionally overstocked. **Pays on acceptance.** Publishes ms an average of 1 year after acceptance. Submit seasonal material 1 year in advance. Reports in 2 months. Free sample copy; writer's guidelines for #10 SASE.

Nonfiction: Articles on hobbies and handicrafts, nature, famous people, seasonal subjects, etc., written from a Christian viewpoint. No articles about historical figures with an absence of religious implication. Length: 500-1,000 words. Pays 3¢/word maximum.

Fiction: Short stories of heroism, adventure, travel, mystery, animals and biography. True or possible plots stressing clean, wholesome, Christian character-building ideas, but not preachy. Make prayer, church attendance and Christian living a natural part of the story. "We correlate our fiction and other features with a definite Bible lesson. Writers who want to meet our needs should send for a theme list." No talking animal stories, science fiction, Halloween stories or first-person stories from an adult's viewpoint. Length: up to 1,000 words. Pays 3¢/word maximum.

RANGER RICK, National Wildlife Federation, 1400 16th St. NW, Washington DC 20036. (703)790-4274. Editor: Gerald Bishop. 30% freelance written. Works with a small number of new/unpublished writers each year. Monthly magazine for children from ages 6-12, with the greatest concentration in the 7-10 age bracket. Buys all world rights unless other arrangements made. Byline given "but occasionally, for very brief pieces, we will identify author by name at the end. Contributions to regular columns usually are not bylined." Estab. 1967. **Pays on acceptance.** Publishes ms an average of 18 months after acceptance. Reports in 6 weeks. "Anything written with a specific month in mind should be in our hands at least 10 months before that issue date." Writer's guidelines for #10 SASE.

Nonfiction: "Articles may be written on anything related to nature, conservation, the outdoors, environmental problems or natural science." Buys 20-25 unsolicited mss/year. Query. Pays from $50-550, depending on length, quality and content (maximum length, 900 words).

Fiction: "Same categories as nonfiction plus fantasy and science fiction. The attributing of human qualities to animals is limited to our regular feature, 'The Adventures of Ranger Rick,' so please do not humanize wildlife. The publisher, The National Wildlife Federation, discourages keeping wildlife as pets."

Photos: "Photographs, when used, are paid for separately. It is not necessary that illustrations accompany material."

Tips: "Include in query details of what manuscript will cover; sample lead; evidence that you can write playfully and with great enthusiasm, conviction and excitement (formal, serious, dull queries indicate otherwise). Think of an exciting subject we haven't done recently, sell it effectively with query, and produce a manuscript of highest quality. Read past issues to learn successful styles and unique approaches to subjects. If your submission is commonplace, we won't want it."

SHOFAR Magazine, Senior Publications Ltd., 43 Northcote Dr., Melville NY 11747. (516)643-4598. Managing Editor: Gerald H. Grayson. 80-90% freelance written. A monthly children's magazine on Jewish subjects. Estab. 1984. Circ. 10,000. Pays on publication. Byline given. Buys one-time rights. Submit seasonal/holiday material 6 months in advance. Simultaneous and previously published submissions OK. Sample copy and writer's guidelines for 9×12 SAE and 4 first class stamps.

Nonfiction: Dr. Gerald H. Grayson, publisher. Historical/nostalgic, humor, inspirational, interview/profile, personal experience, photo feature, religious and travel. Buys 15 mss/year. Send complete ms. Length: 750-1,000 words. Pays 7-10¢/word. Sometimes pays the expenses of writers on assignment.

Photos: State availability of photos with submission or send photos with submission. Offers $10-50 per photo. Identification of subjects required. Buys one-time rights.

Fiction: Adventure, historical, humorous and religious. Buys 15 mss/year. Send complete ms. Length: 750-1,000 words. Pays 7-10¢/word.

Poetry: Free verse, light verse and traditional. Buys 4-5 poems/year. Length: 8-50 words. Pays 7-10¢/word.

Tips: "Submissions must be on a Jewish theme and should be geared to readers who are 8 to 12 years old."

SPORTS ILLUSTRATED FOR KIDS, Time-Warner, Time & Life Building, New York NY 10020. (212)522-5437. FAX: (212)522-0120. Managing Editor: John Papanek. 50% freelance written. Monthly magazine on sports for children eight years old and up. Content is divided 50/50 between sports as played by kids, and sports as played by professionals. **Pays on acceptance.** Publishes ms an average of 3 months after acceptance. Byline given. Offers 25% kill fee. Buys all rights. Sample copy $1.75. Writer's guidelines for SAE.

Nonfiction: Patricia Berry, articles editor. Games, general interest, how-to, humor, inspirational, interview/profile, photo feature and puzzles. Buys 60 mss/year. Query with published clips. Length: 100-1,500 words. Pays $75-1,000 for assigned articles; $75-800 for unsolicited articles. Pays expenses of writers on assignment.

Photos: State availability of photos with submission. Buys one-time rights.

Columns/Departments: The Worst Day I Ever Had (tells about day in pro athlete's life when all seemed hopeless), 500-600 words; Hotshots (young [8-15] athlete getting good things out of sports), 100-250 words; and Home Team (son, daughter, brother, sister of famous athlete), 500-600 words. Buys 30-40 mss/year. Query with published clips. Pays $75-600.

STONE SOUP, The Magazine by Children, Children's Art Foundation, P.O. Box 83, Santa Cruz CA 95063. (408)426-5557. Editor: Ms. Gerry Mandel. 100% freelance written. A bimonthly magazine of writing and art by children, including fiction, poetry, book reviews, and art by children through age 13. Estab. 1973. Audience is children, teachers, parents, writers, artists. "We have a preference for writing and art based on real-life experiences; no formula stories or poems." **Pays on acceptance.** Publishes ms an average of 3 months after acceptance. Buys all rights. Submit seasonal/holiday material 6 months in advance. Reports in 2 weeks on queries; 1 month on mss. Sample copy $4. Free writer's guidelines.

Nonfiction: Book reviews. Buys 10 mss/year. Query. Pays $15 for assigned articles. "We pay book reviewers (solicited writers) and illustrators (solicited artists) in cash. We pay for unsolicited fiction, poetry and art in copies."

Fiction: Adventure, ethnic, experimental, fantasy, historical, humorous, mystery, science fiction, slice-of-life vignettes and suspense. "We do not like assignments or formula stories of any kind." Accepts 35 mss/year. Send complete ms. Pays in copies only.

Poetry: Avant-garde and free verse. Accepts 20 poems/year. Pays in copies only.

Tips: "We can't emphasize enough how important it is to read a couple of issues of the magazine. We have a strong preference for writing on subjects that mean a lot to the author. If you feel strongly about something that happened to you or something you observed, use that feeling as the basis for your story or poem. Stories should have good descriptions, realistic dialogue and a point to make. In a poem, each word must be chosen carefully. Your poem should present a view of your subject and a way of using words that are special and all your own."

STORY FRIENDS, Mennonite Publishing House, 616 Walnut Ave., Scottdale PA 15683. (412)887-8500. FAX: (412)887-3111. Editor: Marjorie Waybill. 80% freelance written. Monthly story paper in weekly parts for children ages 4-9. "*Story Friends* is planned to provide wholesome Christian reading for the 4- to 9-year-old. Practical life stories are included to teach moral values and remind the children that God is at work today. Activities introduce children to the Bible and its message for them." Estab. 1905. Circ. 10,500. **Pays on acceptance.** Publishes ms an average of 1 year after acceptance. Byline given. Publication not copyrighted. Buys one-time rights and second serial (reprint) rights. Submit seasonal/holiday material 6 months in advance. Simultaneous submissions and previously published material OK. Sample copy for 8½×11 SAE with 2 first class stamps. Writer's guidelines for #10 SASE.

Nonfiction: How-to (craft ideas for young children), photo feature. Buys 20 mss/year. Send complete ms. Length: 300-500 words. Pays 3-5¢/word.

Photos: Send photos with submission. Reviews 8½×11 b&w prints. Offers $20-25/photo. Model releases required. Buys one-time rights.

Fiction: See writer's guidelines for *Story Friends*. Buys 50 mss/year. Send complete ms. Length: 300-800 words. Pays 3-5¢/word.

Poetry: Traditional. Buys 20 poems/year. Length: 4-16 lines. Pays $5-10/poem.

Tips: "Send stories that children from a variety of ethnic backgrounds can relate to; stories that deal with experiences similar to all children. For example, all children have fears but their fears may vary depending on where they live."

3-2-1 CONTACT, Children's Television Workshop, One Lincoln Plaza, New York NY 10023. (212)595-3456. FAX: (212)580-3845. Editor-in-Chief: Jonathan Rosenbloom. Senior Editor: Curtis Slepian. 40% freelance written. Magazine published 10 times/year covering science and technology for children ages 8-14. Estab.

1979. Circ. 400,000. **Pays on acceptance.** Publishes ms an average of 6 months after acceptance. Buys all rights "with some exceptions." Submit seasonal material 8 months in advance. Simultaneous and previously published submissions OK if so indicated. Reports in 1 month. Sample copy $1.75 with 8½ × 11 SAE; writer's guidelines for SASE.

Nonfiction: General interest (space exploration, the human body, animals, computers and the new technology, current science issues); profile (of interesting scientists or children involved in science or with computers); photo feature (centered around a science theme); and role models of women and minority scientists. No articles on travel not related to science. Buys 5 unsolicited mss/year. Query with published clips. Length: 700-1,000 words. Pays $150-500. Sometimes pays expenses of writers on assignment.

Photos: Do *not* send photos on spec.

Tips: "I prefer a short query, without manuscript, that makes it clear that an article is interesting. When sending an article, include your telephone number. Don't call us, we'll call you. Many submissions we receive are more like college research papers than feature stories. We like articles in which writers have interviewed kids or scientists, or discovered exciting events with a scientific angle. Library research is necessary; but if that's all you're doing, you aren't giving us anything we can't get ourselves. If your story needs a bibliography, chances are, it's not right for us."

TOUCH, Box 7259, Grand Rapids MI 49510. Editor: Joanne Ilbrink. 80% freelance written. Prefers to work with published/established writers. Monthly magazine. Purpose of publication is to show girls ages 7-14 how God is at work in their lives and in the world around them. "The May/June issue annually features the material written by our readers." Circ. 15,000. **Pays on acceptance.** Publishes ms an average of 1 year after acceptance. Byline given. Buys second serial (reprint) rights and first North American serial rights. Submit seasonal/holiday material 9 months in advance. Simultaneous and previously published submissions OK. Reports in 2 months. Free sample copy and writer's guidelines for 9 × 12 SAE and 3 first class stamps.

Nonfiction: How-to (crafts girls can make easily and inexpensively); informational (write for issue themes); humor (need much more); inspirational (seasonal and holiday); interview; multicultural materials; travel; personal experience (avoid the testimony approach); and photo feature (query first). "Because our magazine is published around a monthly theme, requesting the letter we send out twice a year to our established freelancers would be most helpful. We do not want easy solutions or quick character changes from bad to good. No pietistic characters. Constant mention of God is not necessary if the moral tone of the story is positive. We do not always want stories that have a good ending." Buys 36-45 unsolicited mss/year. Submit complete ms. Length: 100-1,000 words. Pays 2½¢/word, depending on the amount of editing.

Photos: Purchased with or without ms. Reviews 5 × 7 clear b&w (only) glossy prints. Appreciate multicultural subjects. Pays $5-25 on publication.

Fiction: Adventure (that girls could experience in their hometowns or places they might realistically visit); humorous; mystery (believable only); romance (stories that deal with awakening awareness of boys are appreciated); suspense (can be serialized); and religious (nothing preachy). Buys 20 mss/year. Submit complete ms. Length: 300-1,500 words. Pays 2½¢/word.

Poetry: Free verse, haiku, light verse and traditional. Buys 10/year. Length: 30 lines maximum. Pays $5 minimum.

Fillers: Puzzles, short humor and cartoons. Buys 3/issue. Pays $2.50-7.

Tips: "Prefers not to see anything on the adult level, secular material or violence. Writers frequently oversimplify the articles and often write with a Pollyanna attitude. An author should be able to see his/her writing style as exciting and appealing to girls ages 7-14. The style can be fun, but also teach a truth. The subject should be current and important to *Touch* readers. We would like to receive material that features a multicultural slant."

TURTLE MAGAZINE FOR PRESCHOOL KIDS, Children's Better Health Institute, Benjamin Franklin Literary & Medical Society, Inc., 1100 Waterway Blvd., Box 567, Indianapolis IN 46206. (317)636-8881. Editor: Beth Wood Thomas. 95% freelance written. Monthly magazine (bimonthly Jan/Feb, Mar/Apr, May/June, July/Aug) for preschoolers emphasizing health, safety, exercise and good nutrition. Estab. 1979. Pays on publication. Publishes ms an average of 1 year after acceptance. Byline given. Buys all rights. Submit seasonal/holiday material 8 months in advance. Reports in 10 weeks. Sample copy 75¢; writer's guidelines for #10 SASE.

Fiction: Fantasy, humorous and health-related stories. "Stories that deal with a health theme need not have health as the primary subject but should include it in some way in the course of events." No controversial material. Buys 40 mss/year. Submit complete ms. Length: 700 words maximum. Pays approximately 8¢/word.

Poetry: "We use many stories in rhyme—vocabulary should be geared to a 3- to 5-year-old. Anthropomorphic animal stories and rhymes are especially effective for this age group to emphasize a moral or lesson without 'lecturing'." Pays variable rates.

Tips: "We are primarily concerned with preventive medicine. We try to present our material in a positive— not a negative—light and to incorporate humor and a light approach wherever possible without minimizing the seriousness of what we are saying. We would like to see more stories, articles, craft ideas and activities with the following holiday themes: New Year's Day, Valentine's Day, President's Day, St. Patrick's Day, Easter, Independence Day, Thanksgiving, Christmas and Hannukah. We like new ideas that will entertain as well as teach preschoolers. Publishing a writer's first work is very gratifying to us. It is a great pleasure to receive new, fresh material."

VENTURE, Christian Service Brigade, P.O. Box 150, Wheaton IL 60189. (708)665-0630. Editor: Steven P. Neideck. 15% freelance written. Works with a small number of new/unpublished writers each year. "Venture is a bimonthly company publication published to support and compliment *CSB's* Stockade and Battalion programs. We aim to provide wholesome, entertaining reading for boys ages 10-15." Estab. 1959. Circ. 25,000. Pays on publication. Publishes ms an average of 4-6 months after acceptance. Byline given. Offers $35 kill fee. Buys first North American serial, one-time and second serial (reprint) rights. Submit seasonal/holiday material 6 months in advance. Previously published submissions OK. Reports in 2 weeks. Sample copy $1.50 with 9 × 12 SAE and 4 first class stamps; writer's guidelines for #10 SASE.
Nonfiction: Exposé, general interest, historical/nostalgic, humor, inspirational, interview/profile, personal experience, photo feature and religious. Buys 10-12 mss/year. Query. Length: 1,000-1,500 words. Pays $75-125 for assigned articles; pays $40-100 for unsolicited articles. Sometimes pays expenses of writers on assignment.
Photos: Send photos with submission. Reviews contact sheets and 5 × 7 prints. Offers $35-125/photo. Buys one-time rights.
Fiction: Adventure, humorous, mystery and religious. Buys 10-12 mss/year. Query. Length: 1,000-1,500 words. Pays $40-125.
Tips: "Talk to young boys. Find out the things that interest them and write about those things. We are looking for material relating to our theme: Building Men to Serve Christ."

WEE WISDOM, Unity Village MO 64065. Editor: Ms. Judy Gehrlein. 90% freelance written. "We are happy to work with any freelance writers whose submissions and policies match our needs." Magazine published 10 times/year "for children aged 13 and under, dedicated to the truth that each person has an inner source of wisdom, power, love and health that can be applied in a practical manner to everyday life." Estab. 1893. Circ. 175,000. Publishes ms an average of 8 months after acceptance. Submit seasonal/holiday material 10-12 months in advance. **Pays on acceptance.** Byline given. Buys first North American serial rights only. Sample copy and editorial policy for 6 × 9 SAE and 4 first class stamps.
Fiction: Character-building stories that encourage a positive self-image. Although entertaining enough to hold the interest of the older child, they should be readable by the third grader. "Characters should be appealing; plots should be imaginative but plausible, and all stories should be told without preaching. Life combines fun and humor with its more serious lessons, and our most interesting and helpful stories do the same thing. Language should be universal, avoiding the Sunday school image." Length: 500-800 words. Rates vary, depending on excellence.
Poetry: Limited. Prefers short, seasonal and general poems for children. Pays $15 minimum, 50¢ per line after 15 lines. Rhymed prose (read aloud) stories are paid at about the same rate as prose stories, depending on excellence. Poetry by children pubilshed in "Writer's Guild" section not eligible for payment.
Fillers: Pays $8-10 for puzzles and games.

WONDER TIME, 6401 The Paseo, Kansas City MO 64131. (816)333-7000. Editor: Evelyn Beals. 75% freelance written. "Willing to read and consider appropriate freelance submissions." Published weekly by Church of the Nazarene for children ages 6-8. Estab. early 1900s. **Pays on acceptance.** Publishes ms an average of 1 year after acceptance. Byline given. Buys first serial rights, second serial (reprint) rights, simultaneous rights and all rights for curriculum assignments. Sample copy and writer's guidelines for 9 × 12 SAE with 3 first class stamps.
Fiction: Buys stories portraying Christian attitudes without being preachy. Uses stories for special days— stories teaching honesty, truthfulness, kindness, helpfulness or other important spiritual truths, and avoiding symbolism. Also, stories about real life problems children face today. "God should be spoken of as our Father who loves and cares for us; Jesus, as our Lord and Savior." Buys 52/mss year. Length: 350-550 words. Pays 3½¢/word on acceptance.
Poetry: Uses verse which has seasonal or Christian emphasis. Length: 4-8 lines. Pays 25¢/line, minimum $2.50.
Tips: "Any stories that allude to church doctrine must be in keeping with Nazarene beliefs. Any type of fantasy must be in good taste and easily recognizable. We are overstocked now with poetry and stories with general themes. We plan to reprint more than before to save art costs, therefore we will be more selective and purchase fewer new manuscripts."

THE WORLD OF BUSINE$$ KIDS, Busine$$ Kids/America's Future, Lemonade Kids, Inc., Suite 330, 301 Almeria Ave., Coral Gables FL 33134. (305)445-8869. Editor: Jacky Robinson. Monthly tabloid on business, specifically young entrepreneurs. "We cover stories about young entrepreneurs, how teens and preteens can become entrepreneurs, and useful information for effective business operation and management." Estab. 1988. Circ. 75,000. **Pays on acceptance.** Publishes ms an average of 6 months after acceptance. Teens get byline; others listed as contributors. Buys all rights. Submit seasonal/holiday material 6 months in advance. Reports in 10 weeks on mss. Free sample copy and writer's guidelines.

Nonfiction: Any nonfiction pertaining to teens in the business world. How-to choose, build, improve, market or advertise a business. Profiles of successful young entrepreneurs. The latest in any field, entertainment, sports, medicine, etc., where teens are making megabucks or just movie money. Articles on the stock market, bonds, precious metals, taxes, how to invest/save money, news releases, cartoons, puzzles, games, poetry, new products and companies. "No articles with inappropriate language; any mention of alcohol, drugs or tobacco, religious articles; product advertising; inappropriate themes for teens; cheesecake; inappropriate photo backgrounds." Buys 50 mss/year. Send complete ms. Length: 200-600 words. Pays 15¢/word.

Photos: Send photos with submission. Reviews 5 × 7 b&w prints or 35mm transparencies. Offers $5-10 per photo. Captions, model releases and identification of subjects required. Buys all rights.

Columns/Departments: Corporate Champs (corporations in community affairs); News-Worthy (companies with new and innovative products or services); Klever Kids (opinion/interview); Bright Busines$ Idea; Biz Quiz (games); Biz Blasts (movie, book, TV and video reviews) Inside Fax (international business news). Parentally Speaking (book review or advice for parents, what teens should know about money). Send complete ms. Length: 200-400 words.

Poetry: Avant-garde, free verse, haiku, light verse and traditional. Nothing unrelated to business. Buys 8-10 poems/year. No limit on number of poem submissions. Length: open. Pays $15-20.

Fillers: Cartoons, puzzles and games. Buys 8-10/year. Length: 25-100 words. Pays cartoons $15-20; puzzles and games $35-50.

Tips: "Write thoroughly researched, entertaining, factual and *positive* how-tos. No sermonettes or abstract concepts. Understanding teens is a prerequisite. Study our guidelines. Use words economically, and submit clean copy with SASE."

YOUNG AMERICAN, America's Newspaper for Kids, Young American Publishing Co., Inc., P.O. Box 12409, Portland OR 97212. Editor: Kristina T. Linden. 3% freelance written. Eager to work with new/ unpublished writers. A tabloid-size newspaper supplement to suburban newspapers for children and their families. Circ. 4.8 million. Pays on publication. Publishes ms an average of 6 months after acceptance. Buys first North American serial rights. Submit seasonal/holiday material 6 months in advance. Reports in 4 months on mss. Sample copy $1.50; writer's guidelines for SASE.

Nonfiction: General interest; historical/nostalgic; how-to (crafts, fitness); humor; interview/profile (of kids, or people particularly of interest to them); and newsworthy kids. No condescending articles or articles relating to religion, sex, violence, drugs or substance abuse. Buys 30 mss/year. *No queries*; send complete ms. Length: 350 words maximum. Pays $5-75. Sometimes pays the expenses of writers on assignment.

Photos: Send photos with submission. Offers negotiable maximum/photo. Identification of subjects required. Buys one-time rights.

Columns/Departments: You and the News (stories about newsworthy kids), science (new developments, things not covered in textbooks). Length: 350 words maximum. Buys 20 mss/year. Send complete ms. Pays $5-75.

Fiction: Adventure, ethnic, fantasy, humorous, mystery, science fiction, suspense, western and lore. No condescending stories or stories relating to religion, sex, drugs or substance abuse. Buys 24 mss/year. Send complete ms. Length: 500-1,000 words. Pays $35-75.

Poetry: Light verse. No "heavy" or depressing poetry. Buys 30 poems/year. Length: 4 lines, 500 words maximum. Pays $5-35.

Fillers: Facts and short humor. Buys 20/year. Length: 30-300 words. Pays $2.10-21.

Tips: "*Young American* is particularly interested in publishing articles about newsworthy kids. These articles should be under 350 words and accompanied by photos—we prefer color to black and white. The *Young American* focus is on children—and they are taken seriously. Articles are intended to inform, entertain, stimulate and enlighten. They give children a sense of being a part of today's important events and a recognition which is often denied them because of age. If applicable, photos, diagrams or information for illustration helps tremendously as our publication is highly visual. The fiction we have been receiving is excellent. We are now distributed nationwide and have a more national perspective. Kids want to read about what other kids in different places are doing."

THE YOUNG SOLDIER, The Salvation Army, 799 Bloomfield Ave., Verona NJ 07044. Editor: Robert R. Hostetler. 75% freelance written. Monthly Christian/religious magazine for children, ages 8-12. "Only material with clear Christian or Biblical emphasis is accepted." Circ. 48,000. **Pays on acceptance.** Publishes ms an average of 6 months after acceptance. Byline given. Buys first North American serial rights, first rights, one-time rights or second serial (reprint) rights. Submit seasonal/holiday material 6 months in advance. Previously published submissions OK. Reports in 1 month. Sample copy for 8½ × 11 SAE with 3 first class stamps. Writer's guidelines for #10 SASE.

Nonfiction: How-to (craft, Bible study, etc.), religious, games, puzzles, activities. Buys 60 mss/year. Send complete ms. Length: 300-1,000 words. Pays 3-5¢/word.

Photos: State availability or send photos with submission. Reviews contact sheets, negatives, transparencies and prints. Payment varies for photos accepted with ms. Buy one-time rights.

Fiction: Adventure, religious. "Must have Christian emphasis." Buys 10-12 mss/year. Send complete ms. Length: 500-1,000 words. Pays 3-5¢/word.

Poetry: Free verse, light verse, traditional. Buys 6 poems/year. Length: 4-20 lines. Pays 5¢/word ($5 minimum).

Literary and "Little"

Literary and "little" magazines contain fiction, poetry, book reviews, essays and literary criticism. Many are published by colleges and universities and have a regional or scholarly focus.

Literary magazines launch many writers into print. Serious writers will find great opportunities here; some agents read the magazines to find promising potential clients, and many magazines also sponsor annual contests. Writers who want to get a story printed may have to be patient. Literary magazines, especially semiannuals, will buy good material and save it for future editions. When submitting work to literary magazines, the writer may encounter frequent address changes or long response times. On the other hand, some editors carefully read submissions several times and send personal notes to writers.

Many literary magazines do not pay writers or pay in contributor's copies. Only literary magazines which pay are included in *Writer's Market* listings. However, *Novel and Short Story Writer's Market*, published by Writer's Digest Books, includes nonpaying fiction markets and has indepth information about fiction techniques and markets. Literary and "little" magazine writers will notice that *Writer's Market* does not have a Poetry section, although Poetry subheads can be found in this section and in many consumer magazine listings. Writer's Digest Books also publishes *Poet's Market*, edited by Judson Jerome, with detailed information for poets.

ALASKA QUARTERLY REVIEW, College of Arts & Sciences, University of Alaska Anchorage, Dept. of English, 3221 Providence Dr., Anchorage AK 99508. (907)786-1731. Executive Editors: Ronald Spatz and James Liszka. 100% freelance written. Prefers to work with published/established writers; eager to work with new/unpublished writers. A semiannual magazine publishing fiction and poetry, both traditional and experimental styles, and literary criticism and reviews, with an emphasis on contemporary literature. Circ. 1,000. Pays honorariums on publication when funding permits. Publishes ms an average of 6 months after acceptance. Byline given. Buys first North American serial rights. Upon request, rights will be transferred back to author after publication. Reports in 4 months. Sample copy $3 and 8×10 SAE; writer's guidelines for #10 SAE.

Nonfiction: Essays, literary criticism, reviews and philosophy of literature. Buys 1-5 mss/year. Query. Length: 1,000-20,000 words. Pays $50-100 subject to funding; pays in copies when funding is limited.

Fiction: Ronald Spatz, fiction editor. Experimental and traditional literary forms. No romance, children's or inspirational/religious. Buys 10-20 mss/year. Send complete ms. Length: 500-20,000 words. Pays $50-150 subject to funding; sometimes pays in contributor's copies only.

Poetry: Thomas Sexton, poetry editor. Avant-garde, free verse, haiku and traditional. No light verse. Buys 10-30 poems/year. Submit maximum 10 poems. Pays $10-50 subject to availability of funds.

Tips: "All sections are open to freelancers. We rely exclusively on unsolicited manuscripts. *AQR* is a nonprofit literary magazine and does not always have funds to pay authors."

AMELIA MAGAZINE, Amelia Press, 329 E St., Bakersfield CA 93304. (805)323-4064. Editor: Frederick A. Raborg Jr. 100% freelance written. Eager to work with new/unpublished writers. "*Amelia* is a quarterly international magazine publishing the finest poetry and fiction available, along with expert criticism and reviews intended for all interested in contemporary literature. *Amelia* also publishes three supplements each year: *Cicada*, which publishes only high quality traditional or experimental haiku and senryu plus fiction, essays and cartoons pertaining to Japan; *SPSM&H*, which publishes the highest quality traditional and experimental sonnets available plus romantic fiction and essays pertaining to the sonnet; and the annual winner of the Charles William Duke long poem contest." Circ. 1,250. **Pays on acceptance.** Publishes ms an average of 6 months after acceptance. Byline given. Offers 50% kill fee. Buys first North American serial rights. Submit seasonal/holiday material 2 months in advance. Reports in 2 months on mss. Sample copy $7.95 (includes postage); writer's guidelines for #10 SASE. Sample copy of any supplement $4.50.

Nonfiction: Historical/nostalgic (in the form of belles lettres); humor (in fiction or belles lettres); interview/profile (poets and fiction writers); opinion (on poetry and fiction only); personal experience (as it pertains to poetry or fiction in the form of belles lettres); travel (in the form of belles lettres only); and criticism and book reviews of poetry and small press fiction titles. "Nothing overtly slick in approach. Criticism pieces must have depth; belles lettres must offer important insights into the human scene." Buys 8 mss/year. Send complete ms. Length: 1,000-2,000 words. Pays $25 or by arrangement. "Ordinarily payment for all prose is a flat rate of $25/piece, more for exceptional work." Sometimes pays the expenses of writers on assignment.

Fiction: Adventure; book excerpts (original novel excerpts only); erotica (of a quality seen in Anais Nin or Henry Miller only); ethnic; experimental; fantasy; historical; horror; humorous; mainstream; mystery; novel excerpts; science fiction; suspense; and western. "We would consider slick fiction of the quality seen in *Redbook* and more excellent submissions in the genres—science fiction, wit, Gothic horror, traditional romance, stories with complex *raisons d'être*; avant-garde ought to be truly avant-garde." No pornography ("good erotica is not the same thing"). Buys 24-36 mss/year. Send complete ms. Length: 1,000-5,000 words. Pays $35 or by arrangement for exceptional work.

Poetry: Avant-garde, free verse, haiku, light verse and traditional. "No patently religious or stereotypical newspaper poetry." Buys 100-160 poems/year depending on lengths. Prefers submission of at least 3 poems. Length: 3-100 lines. Pays $2-25; additional payment for exceptional work, usually by established professionals. *Cicada* pays $10 each to three "best of issue" poets; *SPSM&H* pays $14 to two "best of issue" sonnets; winner of the long poem contest receives $100 plus copies and publication.

Tips: "*Have something to say* and say it well. If you insist on waving flags or pushing your religion, then do it with subtlety and class. We enjoy a good cry from time to time, too, but sentimentality does not mean we want to see mush. Read our fiction carefully for depth of plot and characterization, then try very hard to improve on it. With the growth of quality in short fiction, we expect to find stories of lasting merit. I also hope to begin seeing more critical essays which, without sacrificing research, demonstrate a more entertaining obliqueness to the style sheets, more 'new journalism' than MLA. In poetry, we also often look for a good 'storyline' so to speak. Above all we want to feel a sense of honesty and value in every piece. As in the first issue of *Amelia*, 'name' writers are used, but newcomers who have done their homework suffer no disadvantage here. So often the problem seems to be that writers feel small press publications allow such a sloughing of responsibility. It is not so."

THE AMERICAN VOICE, 332 W. Broadway, Louisville KY 40202. (502)562-0045. Editors: Sallie Bingham and Frederick Smock. Works with small number of new/unpublished writers each year. A quarterly literary magazine "for readers of varying backgrounds and educational levels, though usually college-educated. Radical, feminist, unpredictable, we publish new writers' work along with the more radical work of established writers. Avant-garde, open-minded." Circ. 2,000. Pays on publication. Publishes ms an average of 4 months after acceptance. Byline given. Offers 50% kill fee. Buys first North American serial rights. Reports in 1 month on queries; 2 months on mss. Sample copy $5.

Nonfiction: Essays, opinion, and criticism. Buys 25 mss/year. Send complete ms. Length: 10,000 words maximum. Pays $400/essay; $150 to translator.

Fiction: Buys 15 mss/year. Send complete ms. Pays $400/story; $150 to translator.

Poetry: Avant-garde and free verse. Buys 35 poems/year. Submit maximum 10 poems. Pays $150/poem; $75 to translator.

Tips: "We are looking only for vigorously original fiction, poetry and essays, from new and established writers, and will consider nothing that is in any way sexist, racist or homophobic."

ANTIOCH REVIEW, P.O. Box 148, Yellow Springs OH 45387. Editor: Robert S. Fogarty. 80% freelance written. Quarterly magazine for general, literary and academic audience. Estab. 1941. Buys all rights. Byline given. Pays on publication. Publishes ms an average of 10 months after acceptance. Reports in 6 weeks. Sample copy for $5; writer's guidelines for #10 SASE.

Nonfiction: "Contemporary articles in the humanities and social sciences, politics, economics, literature and all areas of broad intellectual concern. Somewhat scholarly, but never pedantic in style, eschewing all professional jargon. Lively, distinctive prose insisted upon." Length: 2,000-8,000 words. Pays $10/published page.

Fiction: Quality fiction only, distinctive in style with fresh insights into the human condition. No science fiction, fantasy or confessions. Pays $10/published page.

Poetry: Concrete visual imagery. No light or inspirational verse. Contributors should be familiar with the magazine before submitting.

BAD HAIRCUT, 3115 SW Roxbury, Seattle WA 98126. Editors: Ray Goforth and Kim Goforth. 99% freelance written. Circ. 2,000. Pays on publication. Byline given. Buys first North American serial rights. Submit seasonal/holiday material 4 months in advance. Simultaneous and previously published submissions OK. Reports in 1 week on queries; 1 month on mss. Sample copy $4; writer's guidelines for #10 SASE.

Nonfiction: Essays, expose (government), general interest, interview/profile (political leaders, activists), opinion, photo feature. No pornography or hate-oriented articles. Buys 6 mss/year. Query with or without published clips, or send complete ms. Length: 500-5,000. Pays $50 maximum. Sometimes pays writers with contributor copies or other premiums rather than a cash payment.
Photos: Send photos with submission. Reviews 5×7 prints. Offers $5-100/photo. Model release and identification of subjects required. Buys one-time rights.
Fiction: Adventure, experimental, historical, science fiction. Buys 6 mss/year. Send complete ms. Length: 500-5,000 words. Pays $50 maximum, (usually copies).
Poetry: Avant-garde, free verse. Buys 300 poems/year. Submit up to 10 poems at one time. Length: 1-100 lines. Pays with tear sheets or copy.
Fillers: Anecdotes, facts, newsbreaks. Buys 20 mss/year. Length: 7-100 words. Pays $2.
Tips: "There is a rising tide of activism—a caring for others and the common future we all share. Tap into this—let your heart guide you along the path to peace."

‡**BLACK MOUNTAIN REVIEW**, Lorien House, P.O. Box 1112, Black Mountain NC 28711-1112. (704)669-6211. Editor: David A. Wilson. 100% freelance written. Annual magazine covering literary figures. Each issue is dedicated to a writer. For example, #6 (1990) is on Edgar Allan Poe; #7 (1992) is on Thomas Wolfe. Estab. 1987. Circ. 200. Payment is quarterly, as the magazine sells. Byline given. Buys one-time rights. Previously published submissions OK. Reports in 1 week on queries, 2 weeks on mss. Sample copy for $3.50; writer's guidelines for #10 SAE with 1 first class stamp.
Nonfiction: Essays, historical/nostalgic. Upcoming issues: #7 "On Thomas Wolfe"—printing date 3/92; #8 "On Ernest Hemingway"—printing date 10/93. No violence, sex, or general material not related to the theme. Buys 3-4 mss/year. Query. Length: 500-2,000 words. Pays $10 plus percentage of sales.
Photos: State availability of photos with submission. Reviews prints (5×7). Offers $5. Model release and identification of subjects required. Buys one-time rights.
Fiction: Historical, mainstream, slice-of-life vignettes. Buys 1-2 mss/year. Must relate to theme. Query. Length: 500-2,000 words. Pays $10 plus percentage sales.
Poetry: Free verse, traditional. Buys 2 poems/year. Submit maximum 3 poems. Length: 60 lines maximum. Pays $5.
Tips: "Each issue is a specific theme, and by getting into some aspect of the theme, a writer has a very good chance of being published. The greatest problem is receiving general material which does not relate to the theme. A query first saves everyone time, energy and postage. Nonfiction is most needed, and well-researched material has the best chance of publication."

BLACK WARRIOR REVIEW, P.O. Box 2936, Tuscaloosa AL 35486. (205)348-4518. Editor, volume 17: Alicia Griswold. Managing Editor: Dale Prince. 95% freelance written. A semiannual magazine of fiction and poetry. Estab. 1974. Circ. 2,000. Pays on publication. Publishes ms an average of 6 months after acceptance. Byline given. Buys first rights. Reports in 2 weeks on queries; 3 months on mss. Sample copy $4; writer's guidelines for #10 SASE.
Nonfiction: Interview/profile and book reviews. Buys 5 mss/year. Query or send complete ms. No limit on length. Payment varies.
Photos: State availability of photos with submission. Offers no additional payment for photos accepted with ms. Identification of subjects required. Buys one-time rights.
Fiction: J.R. Jones, fiction editor. Buys 10 mss/year.
Poetry: Glenn Mott, poetry editor. Submit 3-6 poems. Long poems encouraged. Buys 50 poems/year.
Tips: "Read the *BWR* before submitting; editor changes each year. Send us your best work. Submissions of photos and/or artwork is encouraged. We sometimes choose unsolicited photos/artwork for the cover. Address all submissions to the appropriate genre editor."

CANADIAN FICTION MAGAZINE, Box 946, Station F, Toronto, Ontario M4Y 2N9 Canada. Editor: Geoffrey Hancock. Quarterly magazine; 148 pages. Publishes only Canadian fiction, short stories and novel excerpts. Circ. 1,800. Pays on publication. Buys first North American serial rights. Byline given. Reports in 6 weeks. Back issue $6; current issue $9.95 (in Canadian funds).
Nonfiction: Interview (must have a definite purpose, both as biography and as a critical tool focusing on problems and techniques) and book reviews (Canadian fiction only). Looking for a critical series featuring speculation on the future of fiction. Buys 35 mss/year. Query. Length: 1,000-3,000 words. Pays $10/printed page plus 1-year subscription.
Photos: Purchased on assignment. Send prints. Pays $10 for 5×7 b&w glossy prints; $50 for cover. Model releases required.
Fiction: "No restrictions on subject matter or theme. We are open to experimental and speculative fiction as well as traditional forms. Style, content and form are the author's prerogative. Novellas and instant fiction also considered. We also publish self-contained sections of novel-in-progress and French-Canadian fiction in translation, as well as an annual special issue on a single author such as Mavis Gallant, Leon Rooke, Robert Harlow or Jane Rule. Please note that *CFM* is an anthology devoted *exclusively* to Canadian fiction.

We publish only the works of writers and artists residing in Canada and Canadians living abroad." Pays $10/ printed page.

Tips: "Prospective contributors must study several recent issues carefully. *CFM* is a serious professional literary magazine whose contributors include the finest writers in Canada."

CANADIAN LITERATURE, #223-2029 West Mall, University of British Columbia, Vancouver, British Columbia V6T 1W5 Canada. Editor: W.H. New. 70% freelance written. Works with "both new and established writers depending on quality." Quarterly. Estab. 1959. Circ. 2,000. Not copyrighted. Buys first Canadian rights only. Pays on publication. Publishes ms an average of 2 years after acceptance. Query "with a clear description of the project." Sample copy and writer's guidelines for $7.50 (Canadian) and 7×10 SAE with $2.50 Canadian postage.

Nonfiction: Articles of high quality only on Canadian books and writers written in French or English. Articles should be scholarly and readable. Length: 2,000-5,500 words. Pays $5/printed page.

CAROLINA QUARTERLY, University of North Carolina, Greenlaw Hall 066A, Chapel Hill NC 27514. (919)962-0244. Editor: Rebecca Barnhouse. Managing Editor: Michael Evans. 100% freelance written. Eager to work with new/unpublished writers. Literary journal published 3 times/year. Estab. 1948. Circ. 1,000. Pays on publication. Publishes ms an average of 4 months after acceptance. Byline given. Buys first North American serial rights. Reports in 6 months. Sample copy $5 (includes postage); writer's guidelines for SASE.

Photos: Publishes 12 photographs or graphics/year.

Fiction: "We are interested in maturity: control over language; command of structure and technique; understanding of the possibilities and demands of prose narrative, with respect to stylistics, characterization, and point of view. We publish a good many unsolicited stories; *CQ* is a market for newcomer and professional alike." No pornography. Buys 12-18 mss/year. Send complete ms. Length: 7,000 words maximum. Pays $15/ author per issue.

Poetry: "*CQ* places no specific restrictions on the length, form or substance of poems considered for publication." Submit 2-6 poems. Buys 60 mss/year. Pays $15/author per issue.

Tips: "Send *one* fiction manuscript at a time; no cover letter is necessary. Address to appropriate editor, not to general editor. Look at the magazine, a recent number if possible."

THE CHARITON REVIEW, Northeast Missouri State University, Kirksville MO 63501. (816)785-4499. Editor: Jim Barnes. 100% freelance written. Semiannual (fall and spring) magazine covering contemporary fiction, poetry, translation and book reviews. Circ. 600. Pays on publication. Publishes ms an average of 6 months after acceptance. Byline given. Buys first North American serial rights. Reports in 1 week on queries; 2 weeks on mss. Sample copy for $2.50, 7×10 SAE and $1 postage.

Nonfiction: Essays and essay reviews of books. Buys 2-5 mss/year. Send complete ms. Length: 1,000-5,000. Pays $15.

Fiction: Ethnic, experimental, mainstream, novel excerpts and traditional. "We are not interested in slick material." Buys 6-10 mss/year. Send complete ms. Length: 1,000-6,000 words. Pays $5/page.

Poetry: Avant-garde, free verse and traditional. Buys 50-55 poems/year. Submit maximum 10 poems. Length: open. Pays $5/page.

Tips: "Read *Chariton* and similar magazines. Know the difference between good literature and bad. Know what magazine might be interested in your work. We are not a trendy magazine. We publish only the best. All sections are open to freelancers. Know your market or you are wasting your time—and mine. Do *not* write for guidelines; the only guideline is excellence in all matters."

THE DENVER QUARTERLY, University of Denver, Denver CO 80208. (303)871-2892. Editor: Donald Revell. 100% freelance written. Works with a small number of new/unpublished writers. Quarterly magazine for generally sophisticated readership. Estab. 1966. Circ. 1,000. Pays on publication. Publishes ms an average of 6-12 months after acceptance. Buys first North American serial rights. Reports in 3 months. Sample copy $5.

Nonfiction: "Most reviews are solicited; we do publish a few literary essays in each number. Use non-sexist language, please." Send complete ms. Pays $5/printed page.

Fiction: Buys 10 mss/year. Send complete ms. Pays $5/printed page.

Poetry: Buys 50 poems/year. Send poems. Pays $5/printed page.

Tips: "We decide on the basis of quality only. Prior publication is irrelevant. Promising material, even though rejected, may receive some personal comment from the editor; some material can be revised to meet our standards through such criticism. I receive more good stuff than *DQ* can accept, so there is some subjectivity and a good deal of luck involved in any final acceptance. *DQ* is becoming interested in issues of aesthetics and *lucid* perspectives and performances of the avant-garde. We are also interested in topics and translations in the literature of Eastern Europe. Please look at a *recent* issue before submitting. Reading unsolicited mss during academic year only; we do *not* read between May 15 and Sept. 15."

EPOCH, Cornell University, 251 Goldwin Smith, Ithaca NY 14853. (607)256-3385. Editor: Michael Koch. 50-98% freelance written. Works with a small number of new/unpublished writers each year. Literary magazine of original fiction and poetry published 3 times/year. Estab. 1947. Circ. 1,000. Pays on publication. Publishes ms an average of 2-12 months after acceptance. Byline given. Buys first North American serial rights. Sample copy $4.

Fiction: "Potential contributors should *read* a copy or two. There is *no other way* for them to ascertain what we need or like." Buys 15-20 mss/year. Send complete ms. Pays $10/page.

Poetry: "Potential contributors should read magazine to see what type of poetry is used." Buys 20-30 poems/year. Pays $1/line.

Tips: Mss received over the summer (May 15 - Sept 15) will be returned unread."

‡**EROTIC FICTION QUARTERLY**, EFQ Publications, Box 4958, San Francisco CA 94101. Editor: Richard Hiller. 100% freelance written. Small literary magazine (published irregularly) for thoughtful people interested in a variety of highly original and creative short fiction with sexual themes. **Pays on acceptance.** Byline given. Buys first rights. Writer's guidelines for SASE.

Fiction: Heartfelt, intelligent erotica, any style. Also, stories—not necessarily erotic—about some aspect of authentic sexual experience. No standard pornography or men's magazine-type stories; no contrived or formula plots or gimmicks; no broad satire or parody. We do not publish poetry. Send complete ms. Length: 500-5,000 words, average 1,500 words. Pays $50 minimum.

Tips: "What we especially need and do not see enough of is truly interesting and original erotica, whether graphic or subtle, as well as literary-quality fiction that depends on sexual insight. No particular 'slant' is required. Stories should reflect real life, not media ideas."

EVENT, c/o Douglas College, Box 2503, New Westminster, British Columbia V3L 5B2 Canada. FAX: (604)527-5095. Managing Editor: Bonnie Bauder. 100% freelance written. Works with a small number of new/unpublished writers each year. Triannual magazine (March, July and November) for "those interested in literature and writing." Estab. 1970. Circ. 1,000. Uses 80-100 mss/year. Small payment and contributor's copy only. Publishes ms an average of 3 months after acceptance. Buys first North American serial rights. Byline given. Reports in 4 months. Submit complete ms with IRCs.

Nonfiction: "High quality work." Reviews of Canadian books and essays.

Fiction: Short stories and drama.

Poetry: Submit complete ms. "We are looking for high quality modern poetry."

THE FIDDLEHEAD, University of New Brunswick, Campus House, P.O. Box 4400, Fredericton, New Brunswick E3B 5A3 Canada. (506)453-3501. Editor: Michael Taylor. 90% freelance written. Eager to work with new/unpublished writers. Quarterly magazine covering poetry, short fiction, drawings and photographs and book reviews. Estab. 1945. Circ. 1,100. Pays on publication. Publishes ms an average of 6-12 months after acceptance. Not copyrighted. Buys first North American serial rights. Submit seasonal/holiday material 6 months in advance. Simultaneous queries OK. Reports in 3 weeks on queries; 2 months on mss. Sample copy $5.50.

Fiction: Michael Taylor, Anthony Boxill, Diana Austin, fiction editors. "Stories may be on any subject—acceptance is based on quality alone. Because the journal is heavily subsidized by the Canadian government, some preference is given to Canadian writers." Buys 20 mss/year. Pays $12/page.

Poetry: Robert Gibbs, Robert Hawkes, poetry editors. "Poetry may be on any subject—acceptance is based on quality alone. Because the journal is heavily subsidized by the Canadian government, some preference is given to Canadian writers." Buys average of 60 poems/year. Submit maximum 10 poems. Pays $12/page; $100 maximum.

Tips: "Quality alone is the criterion for publication. Return postage (Canadian, or IRCs) should accompany all manuscripts."

THE GAMUT, A Journal of Ideas and Information, Cleveland State University, 1218 Fenn Tower, Cleveland OH 44115. (216)687-4679. FAX: (216)687-9366. Editor: Louis T. Milic. Managing Editor: Susan Grimm Dumbrys. 50-60% freelance written. Triannual magazine. Estab. 1980. Circ. 1,000. Pays on publication. Publishes ms an average of 6 months after acceptance. Byline given. Buys one-time rights. Submit seasonal/holiday material 6 months in advance. Simultaneous submissions OK. Reports in 1 month on queries; 3 months on mss. Sample copy $2.50; writer's guidelines for #10 SASE.

Nonfiction: Essays, general interest, historic/nostalgic, humor, opinion, personal experience, photo feature and technical. Buys 15-20 mss/year. Query with or without published clips, or send complete ms. Length: 1,000-6,000 words. Pays $25-250. Pays authors associated with the university with contributor copies.

Photos: State availability of photos with submission. Offers no additional payment for photos accepted with ms. Captions, model releases and identification of subjects required. Buys one-time rights.

Columns/Departments: Languages of the World (linguistic). Length: 2,000-4,000. Buys 1-2 mss/year. Query with published clips or send complete ms. Pays $75-125.

Fiction: Ethnic, experimental, historical, humorous, mainstream, novel excerpts and science fiction. No condensed novels or genre fiction. Buys 1-2 mss/year. Send complete ms. Length: 1,000-6,000 words. Pays $25-150.

Close-up

Jim Barnes
Editor
The Chariton Review

Photo by Carolyn Barnes

"I have no problem separating what I like from what I consider to be good literature," says Jim Barnes, editor of *The Chariton Review*, a little/literary magazine published out of Northeast Missouri State University. "The canon of great literature has evaporated," he says. "We were lied to in college about what is good. I publish what I like. That's my ultimate criterion."

The Chariton Review is one of the launching pads for tomorrow's writers of fiction, poetry, essays and criticism. "The door is always open to new writers," says Barnes. "We never have theme issues and avoid slick or trendy material entirely." He believes the future of literature is in the hands of small press literary magazines such as *The Chariton Review*. "It's been that way for almost a hundred years already."

Reading the giants of the literary magazines' heyday, Faulkner and Hemingway, inspired Barnes to take up writing. His background in comparative literature landed him a professor's job at Northeast Missouri State in 1970. Together with another faculty member, he founded *The Chariton Review* in 1975, as a forum for the best literature it could publish. "It was never a money-making venture," he says. Barnes became sole editor a year later.

"I'm not so sure any literary magazine is truly unique," says Barnes, "except that they all publish different material. Perhaps *Chariton* is different because I don't solicit poems or short stories from anyone. Everything I publish was once an unsolicited manuscript." This attitude makes magazines such as *The Chariton Review* an excellent place for new and younger writers to break into print.

Barnes likes to be the first editor to publish a writer. To those seeking first publication, he suggests, as many editors do, that the writer read several copies of *The Chariton Review* before sending any work. "Don't query," he says. "That's a waste of time with this kind of magazine. Save money, save trees, just send the manuscript." He considers it naive of a writer to type "copyright" or "first North American serial rights" at the top of the page. "Every legitimate [literary] magazine is aware of those things," says Barnes.

Barnes doesn't want to see cover letters or credit sheets either. "I'm only interested in the work itself," he says. "I don't like a writer to think I'm going to be influenced by a credit page. These things have nothing to do with the story, poem or essay."

Barnes reads every manuscript sent to his office, and he tries to return rejected material in two weeks. Of course, sufficient return postage is required. "I don't use a cut system or keep a slush pile," he says. "If I like something, I'll read it again and let the writer know in about a month." Accepted work appears in *The Chariton Review* within a year.

What ultimately attracts Barnes to a piece of writing? "A strong sense of place and being is essential for good literature," he says. "The small press literary magazine is its mecca."

— Mark Kissling

Poetry: Leonard Trawick, poetry editor. Buys 6-15 poems/year. Submit up to 10 at one time. Pays $25-75.
Tips: "Get a fresh approach to an interesting idea or subject; back it up with solid facts, analysis, and/or research. Make sure you are writing for an educated, but general and not expert reader."

‡HANSON'S, A Magazine of Literary and Social Interest, CIRE Publishing, 113 Merryman Ct., Annapolis MD 21401. (301)626-1643. Editor: Eric Hanson. Managing Editor: Will McIntire. 80% freelance written. Semiannual literary magazine. "Hanson's is a magazine of literary and social interest appealing to the larger community of readers who enjoy stimulating thought communicated through excellent writing." Estab. 1988. Circ. 3,000. Pays 70% on acceptance; remainder on publication. Publishes ms an average of 4 months after acceptance. Byline given. Offers 50% kill fee. Buys first North American serial rights or one-time rights. Previously pubished submissions OK. Reports in 2 weeks on queries; 3 weeks on mss. Sample copy $2. Writer's guidelines for #10 SAE with 2 first class stamps.
Nonfiction: Book excerpt, essays, expose, general interest, historical/nostalgic, humor, interview/profile, opinion, personal experience, travel. Buys 8 mss/year. Send complete ms. Length: 1,000-5,000 words. Pays $50-200 for assigned articles; $40-100 for unsolicited articles. Sometimes pays expenses of writers on assignment.
Photos: State availability of photos with submission. Reviews 3×5 prints. Offers no additional payment for photos accepted with ms. Identification of subjects required. Buys one-time rights.
Columns/Departments: Column/Department Editor: Daniel Sentso. Wordly Wisdom (history and derivation of interesting words), 1,000 words; Ask Auntie Em (humorous parody of advice columnists), 750 words; Potable Quotes (enlightening quotes from life and literature), 750 words; Uncovered (muckracking); Other Shoes (examinations of unusual lifestyles and situations). Buys 8 mss/year. Query. Length: 750-2,000 words. Pays $40-100.
Fiction: Eric Hanson, fiction editor. Adventure, erotica, experimental, fantasy, historical, horror, humorous, mainstream, mystery, science fiction, suspense. Buys 10 mss/year. Send complete ms. Length: 1,500-5,000 words. Pays $50-200.
Poetry: Shannon Rogowski, poetry editor. Avant-garde, free verse, haiku, light verse and traditional. Buys 50 poems/year. Submit maximum 5 poems. Length: 4-100 lines. Pays $20-50.
Tips: "The most important quality in any good writing is honesty. Beyond that, we look for pieces that immediately grab the reader's attention, and from there go on to thrill, enlighten, or shock. An obvious attention to detail is your best bet. Nothing turns an editor off quicker than a messy, poorly edited manuscript. In terms of format, work received on floppy disk is greatly appreciated."

THE HUDSON REVIEW, 684 Park Ave., New York NY 10021. Managing Editor: Ronald Koury. Quarterly. Pays on publication. Buys first world serial rights in English. Reports in 2 months.
Nonfiction: Articles, translations and reviews. Length: 8,000 words maximum.
Fiction: Uses "quality fiction." Length: 10,000 words maximum. Pays 2½¢/word.
Poetry: 50¢/line for poetry.
Tips: Unsolicited mss will be read according to the following schedule: *Nonfiction:* Jan. 1-March 31, and Oct. 1-Dec. 31; *Poetry:* April 1-Sept. 30; *Fiction:* June 1-Nov. 30.

‡INDIANA REVIEW, Indiana University, 316 N. Jordan, Bloomington IN 47405. (812)855-3439. Editor: Renée Manfredi. 100% freelance written. Magazine published 3 times/year. "We publish fine innovative fiction and poetry. We're interested in energy, originality and careful attention to craft. While we publish many well-known writers, we also publish new and emerging poets and fiction writers." Circ. 500. **Pays on acceptance.** Byline given. Buys first North American serial rights. Reports in 2 weeks on queries; 3 months on mss. Sample copy $4; free writer's guidelines.
Nonfiction: Essays. No pornographic or strictly academic articles dealing with the traditional canon. Buys 3 mss/year. Query. Length: 5,000 maximum. Pays $25-200.
Fiction: Experimental and mainstream. No pornography. Buys 18 mss/year. Send complete ms. Length: 250-15,000. Pays $5/page.
Poetry: Avant-garde and free verse. "No pornography and no slavishly traditional poetry." Buys 60 mss/year. Submit up to 5 poems at one time. Length: 5 lines minimum. Pays $5/page.
Tips: "Read us before you send."

THE IOWA REVIEW, 369 EPB, The University of Iowa, Iowa City IA 52242. (319)335-0462. Editor: David Hamilton, with the help of colleagues, graduate assistants, and occasional guest editors. Magazine published 3 times/year. Buys first serial rights. Reports in 3 months.
Nonfiction, Fiction and Poetry: "We publish essays, stories and poems and would like for our essays not always to be works of academic criticism." Buys 65-85 unsolicited mss/year. Submit complete ms. Pays $1/line for verse; $10/page for prose.
Tips: Does not read mss during summer.

JAPANOPHILE, Box 223, Okemos MI 48864. Editor: Earl Snodgrass. 80% freelance written. Works with a small number of new/unpublished writers each year. Quarterly magazine for literate people who are interested in Japanese culture anywhere in the world. Pays on publication. Publishes ms an average of 5 months after acceptance. Buys first North American serial rights. Previously published submissions OK. Reports in 1 month. Sample copy $4, postpaid. Writer's guidelines with #10 SASE.

Nonfiction: "We want material on Japanese culture in *North America or anywhere in the world*, even Japan. We want articles, preferably with pictures, about persons engaged in arts of Japanese origin: a Michigan naturalist who is a haiku poet, a potter who learned raku in Japan, a vivid 'I was there' account of a Go tournament in California. We use some travel articles if exceptionally well-written, but we are *not* a regional magazine about Japan. We are a little magazine, a literary magazine. Our particular slant is a certain kind of culture wherever it is in the world: Canada, the U.S., Europe, Japan. The culture includes flower arranging, haiku, sports, religion, art, photography, fiction, etc. It is important to study the magazine." Buys 8 mss/issue. Query preferred but not required. Length: 1,600 words maximum. Pays $8-20.

Photos: State availability of photos. Pays $10-20 for 8×10 b&w glossy prints.

Fiction: Experimental, mainstream, mystery, adventure, science fiction, humorous, romance and historical. Themes should relate to Japan or Japanese culture. Length: 1,000-6,000 words. Contest each year pays $100 to best short story. (Reading fee $5.) Should include one or more Japanese and non-Japanese characters in each story.

Columns/Departments: Regular columns and features are Tokyo Scene and Profile of Artists. "We also need columns about Japanese culture in other cities." Query. Length: 1,000 words. Pays $20 maximum.

Poetry: Traditional, avant-garde and light verse related to Japanese culture or in a Japanese form such as haiku. Length: 3-50 lines. Pays $1-100.

Fillers: Newsbreaks, clippings and short humor of up to 200 words. Pays $1-5.

Tips: "We prefer to see more articles about Japanese culture in the U.S., Canada and Europe." Lack of convincing fact and detail is a frequent mistake.

LIGHTHOUSE, P.O. Box 1377, Auburn WA 98071-1377. Editor: Tim Clinton. 100% freelance written. A bimonthly literary magazine. Estab. 1986. Circ. 300. Pays on publication. Byline given. Buys first North American serial rights and first rights. Reports in 2 months. Sample copy and writer's guidelines for $2; writer's guidelines only for #10 SASE.

Fiction: Lynne Trindl, fiction editor. Adventure, humorous, mainstream, mystery, romance, science fiction, suspense, western. "No murder mysteries or anything not G-rated." Buys 66 mss/year. Send complete ms. Length: 5,000 words maximum. Pays up to $50.

Poetry: Lorraine Clinton, poetry editor. Free verse, light verse, traditional. Buys 24 poems/year. Submit up to 5 poems at one time. Pays up to $5.

Tips: "Both fiction and poetry are open to freelancers; just follow the guidelines."

LITERARY MAGAZINE REVIEW, KSU Writers Society, English Dept., Denison Hall, Kansas State University, Manhattan KS 66506. (913)532-6106. Editor: G.W. Clift. 98% freelance written. "Most of our reviewers are recommended to us by third parties." A quarterly literary magazine devoted almost exclusively to reviews of the current contents of small circulation serials publishing some fiction or poetry. Estab. 1951. Circ. 500. Pays on publication. Publishes ms an average of 1 month after acceptance. Byline given. Buys first rights. Query for electronic submissions. Reports in 2 weeks. Sample copy $4.

Nonfiction: Buys 60 mss/year. Query. Length: 1,500 words. Pays $25 maximum for assigned articles and two contributor's copies. Sometimes pays expenses of writers on assignment.

Photos: State availability of photos with submission. Identification of subjects required.

Tips: Interested in "omnibus reviews of magazines sharing some quality, editorial philosophy, or place of origin and in articles about literary magazine editing and the literary magazine scene."

LITERARY SKETCHES, P.O. Box 810571, Dallas TX 75381-0571. (214)243-8776. Editor: Olivia Murray Nichols. 33% freelance written. Willing to work with new/unpublished writers. Monthly newsletter for readers with literary interests; all ages. Estab. 1961. Circ 500. Byline given. Pays on publication. Publishes ms an average of 1 year after acceptance. Reports in 1 month. Sample copy for #10 SASE.

Nonfiction: Interviews of well-known writers and biographical material of more than common knowledge on past writers. Concise, informal style. Centennial pieces relating to a writer's birth, death or famous works. Buys 4-6 mss/year. Submit complete ms. Length: up to 1,000 words. Pays ½¢/word, plus copies.

Tips: "Articles need not be footnoted, but a list of sources should be submitted with the manuscript. We appreciate fillers of 100 words or less if they concern some little known information on an author or book."

LOS ANGELES TIMES BOOK REVIEW, Times Mirror, Times Mirror Sq., Los Angeles CA 90053. (213)237-7777. Editor: Jack Miles. 70% freelance written. Weekly tabloid reviewing current books. Circ. 1.5 million. Pays on publication. Publishes ms an average of 3 weeks after acceptance. Byline given. Offers variable kill fee. Buys first North American serial rights. Accepts no unsolicited book reviews or requests for specific titles to review. "Query with published samples—book reviews or literary features." Buys 500 mss/year. Length: 200-1,500 words. Pays approximately $260-500.

‡**LOST CREEK LETTERS**, Lost Creek Publications, Box 373A, Rushville MO 64484. Editor: Pamela Montgomery. 100% freelance written. Quarterly magazine. "We seek mature, thoughtful fiction, poetry and essays. Nothing trite or sentimental or didactic. We publish material on any subject. Our audience is generally college educated." Estab. 1988. Pays on publication. Publishes ms an average of 4 months after acceptance. Byline given. Buys one-time rights. Simultaneous and previously published submissions OK. Query for electronic submissions. Sample copy $4 with 6×9 SAE and 3 first class stamps. Writer's guidelines for #10 SAE with 1 first class stamp.
Nonfiction: Essays, humor, personal experience. "No religious or inspirational." Buys 50 mss/year. Send complete ms. Length: 500-2,500 words. Pays $5.
Fiction: Ethnic, experimental, fantasy, historical, humorous, mainstream, science fiction, slice-of-life vignettes, surrealism. "No religious or romance." Buys 8-10 mss/year. Send complete ms. Length: 200-3,000 words. Pays $5.
Poetry: Avant-garde, free verse, haiku, light verse, traditional. No "Hallmark card" poems. Buys 50-100 poems/year. Submit maximum 20 poems. Pays $2.
Tips: "Study literature which has withstood the test of time. Have something to say and say it *once very well*. Keep in mind our audience of college educated mature adults. Although we publish authors who have published before, your publication credits mean nothing here; your work must stand on its own merit."

THE MALAHAT REVIEW, The University of Victoria, P.O. Box 1700, Victoria, British Columbia V8W 2Y2 Canada. Contact: Editor. 100% freelance written. Eager to work with new/unpublished writers. Magazine published 4 times/year covering poetry, fiction, drama and criticism. Estab. 1967. Circ. 1,700. **Pays on acceptance.** Publishes ms up to 1 year after acceptance. Byline given. Offers 100% kill fee. Buys first serial rights. Reports in 2 weeks on queries; 3 months on mss. Sample copy $6.
Nonfiction: Interview/profile (literary/artistic). Buys 2 mss/year. Query first. Length: 1,000-8,000. Pays $35-175.
Photos: Pays $25-50 for b&w prints. Captions required.
Fiction: Buys 20 mss/year. Send complete ms. Length: no restriction. Pays $40/1,000 words.
Poetry: Avant-garde, free verse and traditional. Buys 100/year. Pays $20/page.

THE MASSACHUSETTS REVIEW, Memorial Hall, University of Massachusetts, Amherst MA 01003. (413)545-2689. Editors: Mary Heath and Fred Robinson. "As pleased to consider new writers as established ones." Quarterly. Pays on publication. Publishes ms 6-18 months after acceptance. Buys first North American serial rights. Reports in 3 months. Mss will not be returned unless accompanied by SASE. Sample copy for $4.50 plus 50¢ postage.
Nonfiction: Articles on literary criticism, women, public affairs, art, philosophy, music and dance. Length: 6,500 words average. Pays $50.
Fiction: Short stories or chapters from novels when suitable for independent publication. Length: max. 25 typed pages (approx.). Pays $50.
Poetry: 35¢/line or $10 minimum.
Tips: No fiction manuscripts are considered from June to October.

MICHIGAN QUARTERLY REVIEW, 3032 Rackham Bldg., University of Michigan, Ann Arbor MI 48109. Editor: Laurence Goldstein. 75% freelance written. Prefers to work with published/established writers; works with a small number of new/unpublished writers each year. Quarterly. Estab. 1962. Circ. 2,000. Publishes ms an average of 1 year after acceptance. Pays on publication. Buys first serial rights. Reports in 1 month for mss submitted in September-May; in summer, 2 months. Sample copy $2 with 2 first class stamps.
Nonfiction: "*MQR* is open to general articles directed at an intellectual audience. Essays ought to have a personal voice and engage a significant subject. Scholarship must be present as a foundation, but we are not interested in specialized essays directed only at professionals in the field. We prefer ruminative essays, written in a fresh style and which reach interesting conclusions. We also like memoirs and interviews with significant historical or cultural resonance." Length: 2,000-5,000 words. Pays $100-150, sometimes more.
Fiction and Poetry: No restrictions on subject matter or language. "We publish about 10 stories a year and are very selective. We like stories which are unusual in tone and structure, and innovative in language." Send complete ms. Pays $10/published page.
Tips: "Read the journal and assess the range of contents and the level of writing. We have no guidelines to offer or set expectations; every manuscript is judged on its unique qualities. On essays — query with a very thorough description of the argument and a copy of the first page. Watch for announcements of special issues, which are usually expanded issues and draw upon a lot of freelance writing. Be aware that this is a university quarterly that publishes a limited amount of fiction and poetry; that it is directed at an educated audience, one that has done a great deal of reading in all types of literature."

MID-AMERICAN REVIEW, Dept. of English, Bowling Green State University, Bowling Green OH 43403. (419)372-2725. Editor: Ken Letko. 100% freelance written. Eager to work with new/unpublished writers. Semiannual literary magazine of "the highest quality fiction, poetry and translations of contemporary poetry and fiction." Also publishes critical articles and book reviews of contemporary literature. Estab. 1972. Pays on publication. Publishes ms an average of 3-6 months after acceptance. Byline given. Buys one-time rights. Reports in 4 months or less. Sample copy $4.50, back issues for $3; rare back issues $10.

Fiction: Character-oriented, literary. Buys 12 mss/year. Send complete ms; do not query. Pays $7/page up to $50.

Poetry: Strong imagery, strong sense of vision. Buys 60 poems/year. Pays $7/page up to $50.

Tips: "We are seeking translations of contemporary authors from all languages into English; submissions must include the original; essays in feminist criticism."

MIDWEST POETRY REVIEW, Box 4776, Rock Island IL 61201. Editor: Hugh Ferguson. Managing Editor: Tom Tilford. 100% freelance written. Eager to work with new/unpublished writers. A quarterly magazine of poetry. **Pays on acceptance.** Publishes ms an average of 3 months after acceptance. Byline given. Buys first North American serial rights. Submit seasonal/holiday material 6 months in advance. Computer printout submissions acceptable; no dot-matrix. Reports in 2 weeks. Sample copy $3; writer's guidelines for #10 SASE.

Nonfiction: Poetry reviews and technical (on poetry). Buys 4 mss/year. Query. Length: 800-1,500 words. Pays $10 minimum. Sometimes pays expenses of writers on assignment.

Columns/Departments: Comment (poetry enhancement, improvement) 800-1,500 words. Buys 4 mss/year. Query. Pays $10 minimum.

Poetry: Avant-garde, free verse haiku, light verse and traditional. No jingles. Buys 400 poems/year. Submit maximum 5 poems; must be subscriber to submit. Pays $5 minimum.

Tips: "We would like authenticated live interviews with known poets."

MODERN SHORT STORIES, Claggk Inc., Suite 101-C, 4820 Alpine Pl., Bldg. A, Las Vegas NV 89107. (702)878-0449. FAX: (702)878-1501. Editor: Glenn Steckler. 100% freelance written. Quarterly magazine on short fiction. Estab. 1988. Circ. 40,000. **Pays on acceptance.** Publishes ms an average of 4-8 months after acceptance. Byline given. Buys first North American serial rights, first rights and second serial (reprint) rights. Submit seasonal/holiday material 6-9 months in advance. Query for electronic submissions. Reports in 1 month. Sample copy for $2.50. Free writer's guidelines.

Fiction: Adventure, confession, erotica, ethnic, experimental, fantasy, historical, horror, humorous, mainstream, mystery, religious, romance, science fiction, suspense and western. Buys 72 mss/year. Send complete ms. Length: 1,000-5,000 words. Pays $50-100.

Tips: Also runs Story Masters, an on-line marketing system, for $10 monthly fee.

NEW ENGLAND REVIEW/BREAD LOAF QUARTERLY, NER/BLQ Middlebury College, Middlebury VT 05753. (802)388-3711, Ext 5075. Editors: T.R. Hummer and Maura High. Managing Editor: Toni Best. 99% freelance written. Quarterly magazine covering contemporary literature. "We print a wide range of contemporary poetry, fiction, essays and reviews. Our readers tend to be literary and intellectual, but we're not academic, over-refined or doctrinaire." Circ. 3,200. Pays on publication. Publishes ms an average of 6 months after acceptance. Byline given. Buys first-time rights. Reports in 1 week on queries; 2 months on ms. Sample copy $4; writer's guidelines for #10 SASE.

Nonfiction: Book excerpts, essays, general interest, humor and personal experience. Buys 10 mss/year. Send complete ms. Length: 500-6,000 words. Pays $5/page, $10 minimum.

Photos: Also accepts drawings, woodcuts and etchings. Send with submission. Reviews transparencies and prints. Offers $60 minimum for cover art. Captions and identification of subjects required. Buys one-time rights.

Fiction: Ethnic, experimental, mainstream, novel excerpts, slice-of-life vignettes. Buys 18 mss/year. Send complete ms. Pays $5/page, $10 minimum.

Poetry: Avant-garde, free verse and traditional. Buys 50 poems/year. Submit up to 6 at one time. Pays $5/page, $10 minimum.

Tips: "Read at least one issue to get an idea of our range, standards and style. Don't submit simultaneously to other publications. All sections are open. We look for writing that's intelligent, well informed and well crafted."

‡THE NEW RENAISSANCE, An International Magazine of Ideas and Opinions, Emphasizing Literature and the Arts, 9 Heath Road, Arlington MA 02174. Editor: Louise T. Reynolds. 95% freelance written. Works with a small number of new/unpublished writers each year. "Not accepting ms until 1/91." International biannual literary magazine covering literature, visual arts, ideas and opinions for a general literate, sophisticated public. Estab. 1968. Circ. 1,500. Pays after publication. Publishes ms 18-25 months after acceptance. Buys all rights. Does not read any ms without SASE or IRCs. Answers no queries without SASE, IRCs or stamped postcards. Does not read mss from July 1 through December 31 of any year. Reports in 1 month on queries; 7 months on mss. Sample copy $5.45 for back issues; $4.65 recent issue; $6.30 current issue (all rates apply to U.S. submission; add 50¢ for foreign requests).

Nonfiction: Interview/profile (literary/performing artists); opinion; and literary/artistic essays. "We prefer expert opinion in a style suitable for a literary magazine (i.e., *not* journalistic). Send complete manuscript or essays. Because we are biannual, we prefer to have writers query us, with outlines, etc., on political/sociological articles and give a sample of their writing." Buys 3-6 mss/year. Query for political/sociological pieces with published clips; SASE and IRC. Length: 11-35 pages. Pays $24-95.

Photos: State availability of photos or send photos with query. Do not send slides; do not send originals without SASE. Pays $5-11 for 5×7 b&w prints. Captions, model releases and identification of subjects required, if applicable. Buys one-time rights.

Fiction: Quality fiction, well-crafted, literary and "serious"; occasionally, experimental or light. No "formula or plotted stories; no pulp or woman's magazine fiction; no academic writing. We are looking for writing with a personal voice and with something to say." Buys 5-12 mss/year. Send complete ms. Length: 2-35 pages. Send only one ms. Pays $30-70.

Poetry: James E. S. Woodbury, poetry editor. Avant-garde, free verse, light verse, traditional and translations (with originals). No heavily academic poetry; "we publish occasional light verse but do not want to see 'Hallmark Card' writing." Submit maximum 6 average length poems; 1-2 long poems. Reports in 4 months. Buys 20-49 poems/year. Pays $13-30.

Tips: "Know your markets. We still receive manuscripts that, had the writer any understanding of our publication, would have been directed elsewhere. Don't submit to independent small magazines unless you've bought and studied an issue. *tnr* is a unique litmag and should be *carefully* perused. Close reading of one or two issues will reveal that we have a classicist philosophy and want manuscripts that hold up to re-readings. Fiction and poetry are completely open to freelancers. Writers most likely to break in to *tnr* are 'serious' writers, poets, those who feel 'compelled' to write. We don't want to see 'pop' writing, trendy or formula writing. Nor do we want writing where the 'statement' is imposed on the story, or writing where the author shows off his superior knowledge or sensibility. Respect the reader and do not 'explain' the story. If we've rejected your work and our comments make some sense to you, keep on submitting to us. Always send us your best work. New writers frequently don't know how to structure or organize for greatest impact, or sometimes they attempt ambitious statements that they need more skill or expertise to bring off. Do not submit anything from July 1 through December 31. Submissions during those months will be returned unread. We now are working with a backlog of material."

THE NORTH AMERICAN REVIEW, University of Northern Iowa, Cedar Falls IA 50614. (319)273-2681. Editor: Robley Wilson. 50% freelance written. Quarterly. Circ. 5,000. Buys all rights for nonfiction and North American serial rights for fiction and poetry. Pays on publication. Publishes ms an average of 1 year after acceptance. Familiarity with magazine helpful. Reports in 10 weeks. Sample copy $3.

Nonfiction: No restrictions, but most nonfiction is commissioned by magazine. Query. Rate of payment arranged.

Fiction: No restrictions; highest quality only. Length: open. Pays minimum $10/page. Fiction department closed (no mss read) from April 1 to December 31.

Poetry: Peter Cooley, department editor. No restrictions; highest quality only. Length: open. Pays 50¢/line minimum.

THE OHIO REVIEW, Ellis Hall, Ohio University, Athens OH 45701-2979. (614)593-1900. Editor: Wayne Dodd. 40% freelance written. Published 3 times/year. "A balanced, informed engagement of contemporary American letters, with special emphasis on poetics." Circ. 2,000. Publishes ms an average of 8 months after acceptance. Rights acquired vary with author and material; usually buys first serial rights or first North American serial rights. Submit complete ms. Unsolicited material will be read only September-May. Reports in 10 weeks.

Nonfiction, Fiction and Poetry: Buys essays of general intellectual and special literary appeal. Not interested in narrowly focused scholarly articles. Seeks writing that is marked by clarity, liveliness, and perspective. Interested in the best fiction and poetry. Buys 75 unsolicited mss/year. Pays minimum $5/page, plus copies.

Tips: "Make your query very brief, not gabby—one that describes some publishing history, but no extensive bibliographies. We publish mostly poetry—short fiction, some book reviews."

THE PARIS REVIEW, 45-39 171st Place, Flushing NY 11358. Submit mss to 541 E. 72nd St., New York NY 10021. Editor: George A. Plimpton. Quarterly. Buys all rights. Pays on publication. Address submissions to proper department and address. Sample copy $6.90. Writer's guidelines for #10 SASE (from Flushing Office).

Fiction: Study publication. No length limit. Pays up to $250. Makes award of $1,000 in annual fiction contest. Awards $1,500 in John Train Humor Prize contest, and $1,000 in Bernard F. Conners, Poetry Prize contest.

Poetry: Patricia Storace, poetry editor. Study publication. Pays $35/1-24 lines; $50/25-59 lines; $75/60-99 lines; and $150-175/100 lines and over.

THE PENNSYLVANIA REVIEW, University of Pittsburgh, English Dept./526 CL, Pittsburgh PA 15260. (412)624-0026. Editor: Lori Jakiela. A semiannual magazine publishing contemporary fiction, poetry, book reviews and interviews with authors. Estab. 1984. Circ. approximately 1,200. Manuscripts accepted from

September 1 to April 1. Pays on publication. Publishes ms an average of 6-8 months after acceptance. Byline given. An SASE must accompany all submissions or manuscript will not be returned. Reports in 13 weeks. Sample copy $5; writer's guidelines for #10 SAE.

Columns/Departments: Phil Orr, editor, book reviews. Buys 5-10 reviews of contemporary work a year. Maximum 5 pages. Pays $5/page. Lori Jakiela, editor, interviews. Buys 1-2 interviews with recognizable authors a year. Send complete interview. Pays $5/page.

Fiction: Jill Weaver, fiction editor. Interested in publishing strong, mainstream fiction. Attention paid to character voice, movement and resolution. Genre discouraged. Buys 6-8 mss/year. Send complete ms. Maximum 20 pages. Pays $5/page.

Poetry: Jan Beatty, poetry editor. Buys 50-75 poems/year. Submit maximum 6 poems. Length: open. Pays $5/page.

PIG IRON MAGAZINE, Pig Iron Press, P.O. Box 237, Youngstown OH 44501. (216)783-1269. Editors-in-Chief: Jim Villani, Naton Leslie and Rose Sayre. 90% freelance written. Annual magazine emphasizing literature/art for writers, artists and intelligent lay audience interested in popular culture. Circ. 1,500. Buys one-time rights. Pays on publication. Publishes ms an average of 6-18 months after acceptance. Byline given. Photocopied and previously published submissions OK. Reports in 3 months. Sample copy $3; writer's guidelines and list of current themes with #10 SASE.

Nonfiction: General interest, personal opinion, criticism, new journalism and lifestyle. Buys 3 mss/year. Query. Length: 8,000 words maximum. Pays $3/page minimum.

Photos: Submit photo material with query. Pays $3 minimum for 5×7 or 8×10 b&w glossy prints. Buys one-time rights.

Fiction: Narrative fiction, psychological fiction, environment, avant-garde, experimental, metafiction, satire and parody. Buys 4-12 mss/issue. Submit complete ms. Length: 8,000 words maximum. Pays $3 minimum.

Poetry: Avant-garde and free verse. Buys 25-50/issue. Submit in batches of 5 or less. Length: open. Pays $3 minimum.

Tips: "Looking for fiction and poetry about the environment, about the earth and its physical dimensions for our 1991 anthology. Looking for any work that explores the significance of the 'letter' as a discourse form and its impact upon culture and the individual."

PLOUGHSHARES, Emerson College, Dept. M, 100 Beacon St., Boston MA 02116. Executive Director: De-Witt Henry. Quarterly magazine for "readers of serious contemporary literature: students, educators, adult public." Circ. 3,800. Pays on publication. Publishes ms an average of 6 months after acceptance. Buys first North American serial rights. Reports in 5 months. Sample/back issue $5; writer's guidelines for SASE.

Nonfiction: Interview and literary essays. Length: 5,000 words maximum. Pays $50. Reviews (assigned). Length: 500 words maximum. Pays $10/page, $50 maximum.

Fiction: Literary and mainstream. Buys 25-35 unsolicited mss/year. Length: 300-6,000 words. Pays $10/page, $50 maximum.

Poetry: Traditional forms, blank verse, free verse and avant-garde. Length: open. Pays $10/poem minimum, $5/page per poem over 2 printed pages, $50 maximum.

Tips: "Because of our policy of rotating editors, we suggest writers check the current issue for news of reading periods and upcoming editors and/or themes."

POETRY, The Modern Poetry Association, 60 West Walton St., Chicago IL 60610. (312)280-4870. Editor: Joseph Parisi. Managing Editor: Helen Lothrop Klaviter. 100% freelance written. A monthly poetry magazine. Estab. 1912. Circ. 7,000. Pays on publication. Byline given. Buys all rights. "Copyright assigned to author on request." Submit seasonal/holiday material 6 months in advance. Reports in 2 months. Sample copy $3.50. Writer's guidelines for #10 SASE.

Poetry: All styles and subject matter. Buys 180-250 poems/year. Submit maximum 6 poems. All lengths considered. Pays $2/line.

THE PRAIRIE JOURNAL of Canadian Literature, P.O. Box 997, Station G, Calgary, Alberta T3A 3G2 Canada. Editor: A. Burke. 100% freelance written. A semiannual magazine of Canadian literature. Estab. 1983. Circ. 400. Pays on publication; "honorarium depends on grant." Byline given. Buys first North American serial rights. Reports 1 month on queries. Sample copy $3 and IRCs.

Nonfiction: Interview/profile and scholarly. Buys 5 mss/year. Query with published clips. "Include IRC." Pays $25 maximum. Pays contributor copies or honoraria for literary work.

Photos: Send photos with submission. Offers no additional payment for photos accepted with ms. Identification of subjets required. Buys one-time rights.

Fiction: Literary. Buys 10 mss/year. Send complete ms.

Poetry: Avant-garde and free verse. Buys 10 poems/year. Submit maximum 6-10 poems.

Tips: "Commercial writers are advised to submit elsewhere. Art needed, b&w pen and ink drawings or good-quality photocopy. We are strictly small press editors interested in highly talented, serious artists. We are oversupplied with fiction but seek more high-quality poetry, especially the contemporary long poem or sequences from longer works."

392 *Writer's Market '91*

PRISM INTERNATIONAL, Department of Creative Writing, University of British Columbia, Vancouver, British Columbia V6T 1W5 Canada. Editor-in-Chief: Blair Rosser. Executive Editor: Heidi Neufeld Raine. 100% freelance written. Eager to work with new/unpublished writers. Quarterly magazine emphasizing contemporary literature, including translations. For university and public libraries, and private subscribers. Estab. 1959. Circ. 1,000. Pays on publication. Publishes ms an average of 3 months after acceptance. Buys first North American serial rights. Reports in 3 months. Sample copy $4. Writer's guidelines for #10 SAE with 1 first class Canadian stamp (Canadian entries) or 1 IRC (U.S. entries).

Nonfiction: Memoirs, belles-lettres, etc. *"Creative* nonfiction that possibly reads like fiction." No reviews, tracts or scholarly essays.

Fiction: Jim King, fiction editor. Experimental and traditional. Buys 3-5 mss/issue. Send complete ms. Length: 5,000 words maximum. Pays $30/printed page and 1-year subscription.

Poetry: Mary Cameron, poetry editor. Avant-garde and traditional. Buys 30 poems/issue. Submit maximum 6 poems. Pays $30/page printed page and 1-year subscription.

Drama: One-acts preferred. Pays $30/page printed page and 1-year subscription.

Tips: "We are looking for new and exciting fiction. Excellence is still our number one criterion. As well as poetry, imaginative nonfiction and fiction, we are especially open to translations of all kinds, very short fiction pieces and drama which works well on the page. This year we plan to publish an issue that focuses on the theme of sexuality."

QUEEN'S QUARTERLY, A Canadian Review, Queen's University, Kingston, Ontario K7L 3N6 Canada. (613)545-2667. Editors: Dr. Clive Thomson and Ms. Martha J. Bailey. Quarterly magazine covering a wide variety of subjects, including science, humanities, arts and letters, politics and history for the educated reader. 15% freelance written. Circ. 1,900. Pays on publication. Publishes ms an average of 1 year after acceptance. Byline given. Buys first North American serial rights. Requires 1 double-spaced hard copy and 1 copy on disk in WordPerfect. Reports in 3 months on mss. Sample copy $5.

Fiction: Fantasy, historical, humorous, mainstream and science fiction. Buys 8-12 mss/year. Send complete ms. Length: 5,000 words maximum. Pays $80-150.

Poetry: Avant-garde, free verse, haiku, light verse and traditional. No "sentimental, religious, or first efforts by unpublished writers." Buys 25/year. Submit maximum 6 poems. Length: open. Pays $20-35.

Tips: "Poetry and fiction are most open to freelancers. Don't send less than the best. No multiple submissions. No more than 6 poems or one story per submission. We buy very a few freelance submissions."

‡THE RENOVATED LIGHTHOUSE MAGAZINE, Renovated Lighthouse Publications, P.O. Box 21130, Columbus OH 43221. Editor: R. Allen Dodson. 90% freelance written. Monthly literary magazine covering New Age, poetry, fiction, markets and chapbooks. Our publications are intended to be entertaining, enlightening and informative to the serious freelancer: poetic, musical, artistic and writer. Estab. 1986. Circ. 200. Pays on publication. Publishes ms an average of 6-10 months after acceptance. Byline given. Buys first North American serial rights or makes work-for-hire assignments. Reports in 1 week on queries; 2 weeks on mss. Sample copy for $2.50. Chapbook guidelines for SASE.

Nonfiction: Book excerpts, essays, exposé, general interest, historical/nostalgic, how-to (related to writing), humor, inspirational (non-religious), interview/profile (query first), opinion, personal experience, photo feature, travel. Send complete ms. Length: 500-3,000 words. Pays $1 per page. Pays in contributor copies or other premiums in addition to monetary payment.

Photos: Send photos with submission. Reviews 5×7 prints. Offers $1 per photo. Identification of subjects required. Buys one-time rights.

Columns/Departments: Space Music Record Review (New Age music), 500 words; Poetry Publishers' Review (beginning or [I] markets), 500 words; Book Review (alternative lifestyles publications), 1,500 words. Buys 12 mss/year. Send complete ms. Pays $2.50 minimum.

Fiction: Adventure, social, experimental, fantasy, mainstream, novel excerpts, science fiction, slice-of-life vignettes. Buys 12 mss/year. Send complete ms. Length: 500-5,000. Pays $2.50 minimum.

Poetry: Avant-garde, free verse, haiku, light verse, traditional, prose. Buys 144/year. Pays 2¢/line and contributor copies.

Tips: "I appreciate being able to correspond in-depth with my contributors. All of my publications are for freelancers. Their comments about (what should go/what should be added) are the only editorial board I have."

ROOM OF ONE'S OWN, A Feminist Journal of Literature & Criticism, P.O. Box 46160, Station G, Vancouver, British Columbia V6R 4G5 Canada. Editors: Growing Room Collective. 100% freelance written. Eager to work with new/unpublished writers. Quarterly magazine of original fiction, poetry, literary criticism, and reviews of feminist (literary) concern. Estab. 1975. Circ 1,200. Pays on publication. Byline given. Buys first serial rights. Reports in 4 months. Sample copy $4.

Nonfiction: Interview/profile (of authors) and literary reviews. Buys 4 mss/year. Send complete ms. Length: 1,500-6,000 words. Pays $50.
Fiction: Quality short stories by women with a feminist outlook. Not interested in fiction written by men. Buys 12 mss/year. Send complete ms. Length: 1,500-6,000 words. Pays $50.
Poetry: Avant-garde, eclectic free verse and haiku. Not interested in poetry from men. Buys 32 poems/year. Submit maximum 8 poems. Length: open. Pays $10-25.

SEWANEE REVIEW, University of the South, Sewanee TN 37375. (615)598-1246. Editor: George Core. Works with a small number of new/unpublished writers each year. Quarterly magazine for audience of "variable ages and locations, mostly college-educated and with interest in literature." Estab. 1892. Circ. 3,400. Pays on publication. Publishes ms an average of 9 months after acceptance. Reports in 1 month. Sample copy $5.75, writer's guidelines for #10 SASE.
Nonfiction and Fiction: Short fiction (but not drama); essays of critical nature on literary subjects (especially modern British and American literature); and essay-reviews and reviews (books and reviewers selected by the editor). Unsolicited reviews rarely accepted. Length: 5,000-7,500 words. Payment varies: averages $12/printed page.
Poetry: Selections of 4 to 6 poems preferred. In general, light verse and translations not acceptable. Maximum payment is 70¢ per line.

‡SING HEAVENLY MUSE!, Women's Poetry and Prose, Sing Heavenly Muse! Inc., Box 13299, Minneapolis MN 55414. (612)822-8713. 100% freelance written. Prefers to work with published/established writers; eager to work with new/unpublished writers. A semi-annual journal of women's literature. Circ. 1,500. Pays on publication. Publishes ms an average of 6 months after acceptance. Byline given. Buys first North American serial rights. Reports in 3 months. Sample copy $3.50; writer's guidelines for #10 SASE.
Fiction: Women's literature, journal pieces, memoir. Buys 15-20 mss/year. Length: 5,000 words maximum. Pays $15-25; contributors receive 2 free copies.
Poetry: Avant-garde, free verse, haiku, light verse and traditional. Accepts 75-100 poems/year. No limit on length. Pays $15-25.
Tips: "To meet our needs, writing must be feminist and women-centered. We read manuscripts generally in April and September. Issues are often related to a specific theme; writer should always query for guidelines and upcoming themes before submitting manuscripts. We occasionally hold contests. Writers should query for contest guidelines."

THE SOUTH FLORIDA POETRY REVIEW, South Florida Poetry Institute, 7190 NW 21st St., Ft. Lauderdale FL 33313. (305)742-5624. Editor: S.A. Stirnemann. Assistant Editor: Virginia Wells. Managing Editor: Shirley Blum. 100% freelance written. Quarterly magazine on poetry. "*SFPR* invites submissions of contemporary poetry of the highest literary quality. We are also interested in essay-reviews of books of poetry published in previous year, Q&A interviews with established poets, and essays on current American poetry." Estab. 1983. Circ. 750. Pays on publication. Publishes ms an average of 3-12 months after acceptance. Byline given. Buys first rights. Reports in 3 months on ms. Sample copy $3.50. Writer's guidelines for #10 SASE.
Nonfiction: Essays (reviews and American poetry), interview/profile (Q&A). Do not want to see "anything that is *not* related to poetry." Buys 16 mss/year. Query. Length: 300-2,000 words. Pays $5-25 for unsolicited articles.
Poetry: Avant-garde, free verse and traditional. Buys 125 poems/year. Submit 6 maximum poems.
Tips: "All sections are open to freelancers. They should be familiar with contemporary American poetry as it is defined in most national literary journals."

‡THE SOUTHEASTERN REVIEW: A Quarterly Journal of the Humanities in the Southeastern Mediterranean, Amerikis & 18 Valaoritou Sts., Athens 106 71 Greece. Editor: Elizabeth Boleman Herring. Quarterly magazine of the humanities. Estab. 1989. Pays on publication. Publishes ms an average of 6 months after acceptance. Byline given. Buys first Greek serial rights. Query for electronic submissions. Reports in 3 months on queries. Sample copy $6.50.
Nonfiction: Book excerpts, essays, historical. Buys 4-10 mss/year. Query with publication history prior to sending complete ms. Length: 1,000-5,000 words. Pays $50-300 maximum.
Fiction: Ethnic (Greek), experimental, historical, novel excerpts, short stories. Buys 4-10 mss/year. Query with publication history. Length: 1,000-5,000 words. Pays $50-300 maximum.
Poetry: Avant-garde, free verse, haiku, traditional (Greek slant). Buys 12-20 poems/year. Submit minimum of 5 poems. Pays $25-150 maximum.
Tips: "*TSR*'s 'province' is the Southeastern Mediterranean, and we accept only material dealing with Greece, Turkey, Cyprus, classical studies and the Levant. An exception is made in the case of established writers in the region."

THE SOUTHERN REVIEW, 43 Allen Hall, Louisiana State University, Baton Rouge LA 70803. (504)388-5108. Editors: James Olney and Dave Smith. 75% freelance written. Works with a moderate number of new/unpublished writers each year. Quarterly magazine for academic, professional, literary, intellectual audience.

Estab. 1965. Circ. 3,100. Buys first serial rights only. Byline given. Pays on publication. Publishes ms an average of 18 months after acceptance. No queries. Reports in 2 to 3 months. Sample copy $5. Writer's guidelines for #10 SASE.

Nonfiction: Essays with careful attention to craftsmanship, technique and to seriousness of subject matter. "Willing to publish experimental writing if it has a valid artistic purpose. Avoid extremism and sensationalism. Essays exhibit thoughtful and sometimes severe awareness of the necessity of literary standards in our time." Emphasis on contemporary literature, especially Southern culture and history. Minimum number of footnotes. Buys 45 mss/year. Length: 4,000-10,000 words. Pays $12/page for prose.

Fiction and Poetry: Short stories of lasting literary merit, with emphasis on style and technique. Length: 4,000-8,000 words. Pays $12/page for prose; $20/page for poetry.

SPECTRUM, Spectrum/Anna Maria College, Box 72-F, Sunset Lane, Paxton MA 01612. (508)757-4586. Editor: Robert H. Goepfert. Managing Editor: Robert Lemieux. A literary magazine, "*Spectrum* is a multidisciplinary national publication aimed particularly at scholarly generalists affiliated with small liberal arts colleges." Estab. 1985. Circ. 1,000. Pays on publication. Publishes ms an average of 6 months after acceptance. Byline given. Publication copyrighted. Buys first North American serial rights. Reports in 3 weeks on queries; 6 weeks on ms. Sample copy $3. Writer's guidelines for #10 SASE.

Nonfiction: Robert H. Goepfert, articles editor. Essays, general interest, historical/nostalgic, inspirational, opinion and interdisciplinary. Buys 8 mss/year. Send complete ms. Length: 3,000-15,000 words. Pays $20 for unsolicited articles. State availability of photos with submission. Prints (8 × 10) b&w only. Offers no additional payment for photos accepted with ms. Model releases and identification of subjects required. Buys one-time rights.

Columns/Departments: Sandra Rasmussen, reviews and correspondence editor. Reviews (books/recordings/audiovisual aids), 300-500 words; (educational computer software), up to 2,000 words. Buys 2 mss/year. Send complete ms. Length: 300-2,000 words. Pays $20.

Fiction: Joseph Wilson, fiction editor. Ethnic, experimental, fantasy, historical, humorous, mainstream, romance and slice-of-life vignettes. "No erotica, mystery, western or science fiction." Buys 2 ms/year. Send complete ms. Length: 3,000 words. Pays $20.

Poetry: Joseph Wilson, poetry editor. Avant-garde, free verse, light verse and traditional. No long poems (over 100 lines). Buys 8 poems/year. Submit maximum 6 poems.

Tips: "We welcome short fiction and poetry, as well as short- to medium-length articles that are interdisciplinary or that deal with one discipline in a manner accessible to the scholarly-generalist reader. Articles referring to or quoting work of other authors should be footnoted appropriately. All areas are equally open to freelancers. In general, originality and relative brevity are paramount, although we will occasionally publish longer works (e.g., articles) that explore ideas not subject to a briefer treatment."

‡STAR*LINE, Newsletter of the Science Fiction Poetry Association, Science Fiction Poetry Association, P.O. Box 491, Nantucket MA 02254. Editor: Robert A. Frazier. 95% freelance written. Eager to work with new/unpublished writers. A bimonthly newsletter covering science fiction, fantasy, horror poetry for association members. Estab. 1978. Circ. 200. **Pays on acceptance.** Byline given. Buys one-time rights. Submit seasonal/holiday material 3 months in advance. Reports in 1 month. Sample copy for $1.50 and 5½ × 8½ SAE and 2 first class stamps; writer's guidelines for #10 SASE.

Nonfiction: Articles must display familiarity with the genre. How to (write a poem); interview/profile (of science fiction, fantasy and horror poets); opinion (science fiction and poetics); and essays. Buys 4-6 mss/year. Send complete ms. Length: 500-2,000 words. Pays $1-5 plus complimentary copy.

Columns/Department: Reviews (books, chapbooks, magazines, collections of science fiction, fantasy or horror poetry) 50-500 words; and Markets (current markets for science fiction, fantasy or horror poetry) 20-100 words. Buys 40-60 mss/year. Send complete ms. Pays 50¢-$2.

Poetry: Avant-garde, free verse, haiku, light verse and traditional. "Poetry must be related to speculative fiction subjects." Buys 60-80 poems/year. Submit maximum 3 poems. Length: 1-100 lines. Pays $1 for first 10 lines; 5¢/line thereafter plus complimentary copy.

Fillers: Speculative-oriented quotations—prose or poetic. Length: 10-50 words. Pays $1.

STORY, F&W Publications, Inc., 1507 Dana Ave., Cincinnati OH 45207. (513)531-2222. Editor: Lois Rosenthal. Associate Editor: Jack Heffron. 100% freelance written. Quarterly literary magazine of short fiction. "We want short stories and self-inclusive novel excerpts of general interest that are extremely well-written. Our audience is sophisticated and accustomed to the finest imaginative writing available by both new and established writers." Estab. 1931. Circ. 20,000. **Pays on acceptance.** Byline given. Buys first North American

The double dagger before a listing indicates that the listing is new in this edition. New markets are often the most receptive to freelance submissions.

serial rights. Reports in 1 month. Sample copy $5 with 9 × 12 SAE and $2.40 in postage. Writer's guidelines for #10 SASE.

Fiction: Novel excerpts, experimental and mainstream. No genre fiction. Buys 40-50 mss/year. Send complete ms. Length: 1,000-8,000 words. Pays $250.

‡**THE STRAIN, World's Premiere Interactive Arts Magazine**, Box 330507, Houston TX 77233. (713)733-6042. Editor: Norman Clark Stewart Jr. 80% freelance written. Monthly literary magazine. Estab. 1987. Circ. 200-1,000. Pays on publication. Publishes ms an average of 1 year after acceptance. Byline given. Buys first, one-time, or second serial rights. Makes work-for-hire assignments. Submit seasonal/holiday material 4 months in advance. Previously published submissions OK. Reports in 1-12 months. Sample copy for $5 with 9 × 12 SAE and 7 first class stamps. Writer's guidelines for #10 SAE with 2 first class stamps.

Nonfiction: Alicia Alder, articles editor. Essays, expose, how-to, humor, photo feature, technical. Buys 2-20 mss/year. Send complete ms. Pays $5 minimum.

Photos: Send photos with submissions. Reviews transparencies and prints. Model releases and identification of subjects required. Buys one-time rights.

Columns/Departments: Charlie Mainze, editor. Multi-media performance art. Send complete ms. Pays up to $500.

Fiction: John Peterson, editor. Buys 1-35 mss/year. Send complete ms. Pays $500 maximum.

Poetry: Michael Bond, editor. Avant-garde, free verse, light verse, traditional. Buys 100. Submit maximum 5 poems. Pays $50 maximum.

Tips: "Don't be too trendy. Our issues are often book-length and are designed to last."

THE SUN, A Magazine Of Ideas, The Sun Publishing Company, Inc., 107 N. Roberson St., Chapel Hill NC 27516. (919)942-5282. Editor: Sy Safransky. 75% freelance written. Monthly magazine. Circ. 15,000. Pays on publication. Publishes ms an average of 2 months after acceptance. Byline given. Buys first-rights. Previously published submissions OK. Reports in 2 months. Sample copy $3, 9 × 12 SAE and 3 first class stamps; writer's guidelines for #10 SASE.

Nonfiction: General interest. Buys 40 mss/year. Send complete ms. Length: 10,000 words maximum. Pays $100 and up plus copies and a subscription.

Photos: Send photos with submissions. Offers $25 for photos accepted with ms. Model releases required. Buys one-time rights.

Fiction: General. Buys 15 mss/year. Send complete ms. Length: 10,000 words maximum. Pays $100 and up.

Poetry: General. Buys 25 poems/year. Submit maximum 6 poems. Length: open. Pays $25.

Tips: "We're interested in any writing that makes sense and enriches our common space."

TAMPA REVIEW, Humanities Division, University of Tampa, Tampa FL 33606. (813)253-3333. Editor of Fiction: Andy Solomon, Box 135F. Editors of Poetry: Don Morrill, Box 115F; Kathy Van Spanckeren, Box 16F. 100% freelance written. Annual magazine of literary fiction and poetry. Estab. 1988. Circ. 5,000. Pays on publication. Publishes ms an average of 4 months after acceptance. Byline given. Buys first North American serial rights. Reports in 6 weeks on mss. Sample copy $9.

Fiction: Experimental, mainstream. "We are far more concerned with quality than genre." Buys 4-6 mss/year. Send complete ms. Length: 1,000-6,000 words; slight preference for mss less than 20 pp. Pays $10/printed page.

Poetry: Buys 30 poems/year. Submit up to 5 poems at one time. Pays $10/printed page.

THE THREEPENNY REVIEW, Box 9131, Berkeley CA 94709. (415)849-4545. Editor: Wendy Lesser. 100% freelance written. Works with small number of new/unpublished writers each year. A quarterly literary tabloid. "We are a general interest, national literary magazine with coverage of politics, the visual arts and the performing arts as well." Circ. 8,000. **Pays on acceptance.** Publishes ms an average of 1 year after acceptance. Byline given. Buys first North American serial rights. Reports in 1 month on queries; 2 months on mss. Sample copy for 10 × 13 SAE, 5 first class stamps and $4; writer's guidelines for SASE.

Nonfiction: Essays, exposé, historical, interview/profile, personal experience, book, film, theater, dance, music and art reviews. Buys 40 mss/year. Query with or without published clips, or send complete ms. Length: 1,500-4,000 words. Pays $100.

Fiction: No fragmentary, sentimental fiction. Buys 10 mss/year. Send complete ms. Length: 800-4,000 words. Pays $100.

Poetry: Free verse and traditional. No poems "without capital letters or poems without a discernible subject." Buys 30 poems/year. Submit maximum 10 poems. Pays $50.

Tips: Nonfiction (political articles, reviews) is most open to freelancers.

TRIQUARTERLY, 2020 Ridge Ave., Northwestern University, Evanston IL 60208. (312)491-3490. Editor: Reginald Gibbons. 70% freelance written. Eager to work with new/unpublished writers. Published 3 times/year. Publishes fiction, poetry, and essays, as well as artwork. Pays on publication. Publishes ms an average of 1 year after acceptance. Buys first serial rights and nonexclusive reprint rights. Reports in 3 months. Study magazine before submitting. Sample copy $4. Writer's guidelines for #10 SASE.

Nonfiction: Query before sending essays (no scholarly or critical essays except in special issues).

Fiction and Poetry: No prejudice against style or length of work; only seriousness and excellence are required. Buys 20-50 unsolicited mss/year. Pays $40/page.

UNIVERSITY OF TORONTO QUARTERLY, University of Toronto Press, Suite 700, 10 St. Mary St., Toronto, Ontario M4Y 2W8 Canada. Editor-in-Chief: T.H. Adamowski. 66% freelance written. Eager to work with new/unpublished writers. Quarterly magazine restricted to criticism on literature and the humanities for the university community. Estab. 1933. Pays on publication. Publishes ms an average of 1 year after acceptance. Acquires all rights. Byline given. Sample copy $8.95, SAE and IRCs.

Nonfiction: Scholarly articles on the humanities; literary criticism and intellectual discussion. Buys 12 unsolicited mss/year. Pays $50 maximum.

THE UNSPEAKABLE VISIONS OF THE INDIVIDUAL INC., P.O. Box 439, California PA 15419. Editors-in-Chief: Arthur Winfield Knight, Kit Knight. 50% freelance written. Annual magazine/book for an adult audience, generally college-educated (or substantial self-education) with an interest in Beat (generation) writing. Estab. 1971. Circ. 2,000. Payment (if made) on acceptance. Publishes ms an average of 2 months after acceptance. Buys first North American serial rights. Reports in 2 months. Sample copy $4.

Nonfiction: Interviews (with Beat writers), personal experience and photo feature. "Know who the Beat writers are—Jack Kerouac, Allen Ginsberg, William S. Burroughs, etc." Uses 20 mss/year. Query or submit complete ms. Length: 300-15,000 words. Pays 2 copies, "sometimes a small cash payment, i.e., $10."

Photos: Used with or without ms or on assignment. Send prints. Pays 2 copies to $10 for 8 × 10 b&w glossies. Uses 40-50/year. Captions required.

Fiction: Uses 10 mss/year. Submit complete ms. Pays 2 copies to $10.

Poetry: Avant-garde, free verse and traditional. Uses 10 poems/year. Submit maximum 10 poems. Length: 100 lines maximum. Pays 2 copies to $10.

THE VIRGINIA QUARTERLY REVIEW, 1 W. Range, Charlottesville VA 22903. (804)924-3124. Editor: Staige Blackford. 50% freelance written. Quarterly. Estab. 1925. Pays on publication. Publishes ms an average of 2 years after acceptance. Byline given. Buys first serial rights. Reports in 1 month. Sample copy $5.

Nonfiction: Articles on current problems, economic, historical; and literary essays. Length: 3,000-6,000 words. Pays $10/345-word page.

Fiction: Good short stories, conventional or experimental. Length: 2,000-7,000 words. Pays $10/350-word page. Prizes offered for best short stories and poems published in a calendar year.

Poetry: Generally publishes 15 pages of poetry in each issue. No length or subject restrictions. Pays $1/line.

Tips: Prefers not to see pornography, science fiction or fantasy.

WEBSTER REVIEW, Webster University, 470 E. Lockwood, Webster Groves MO 63119. (314)432-2657. Editor: Nancy Schapiro. 100% freelance written. A semiannual magazine. "*Webster Review* is an international literary magazine publishing fiction, poetry, essays and translations of writing in those categories. Our subscribers are primarily university and public libraries, and writers and readers of quality fiction and poetry." Circ. 1,000. Pays on publication. Publishes ms an average of 1 year after acceptance. Byline given. Buys first North American serial rights. Simultaneous submissions OK. Reports in 6 weeks on manuscripts. Sample copy for 9½ × 6½ SAE with 4 first class stamps.

Nonfiction: Essays. Send complete ms.

Fiction: Will consider all types of literature. Buys 6 mss/year. Send complete ms. Pays $25-50, (if funds are available).

Poetry: Pamela White Hadas, poetry editor. Buys 100 poems/year. Pays $10-50 (if funds are available).

WESTERN HUMANITIES REVIEW, University of Utah, Salt Lake City UT 84112. (801)581-6070. Managing Editor: Pamela Houston. Quarterly magazine for educated readers. Circ. 1,200. **Pays on acceptance.** Publishes ms an average of 3 months after acceptance. Buys all rights. Phone queries OK. Simultaneous submissions OK. Reports in 3 months.

Nonfiction: Barry Weller, editor-in-chief. Authoritative, readable articles on literature, art, philosophy, current events, history, religion and anything in the humanities. Interdisciplinary articles encouraged. Departments on film and books. "We commission book reviews." Buys 40 unsolicited mss/year. Pays $50-150.

Fiction: Larry Levis, fiction editor. Any type or theme. Buys 2 mss/issue. Send complete ms.

Poetry: Richard Howard, poetry editor. "See magazine. Recent contributors include Joseph Brodsky, Charles Simic, Charles Wright, Carol Muske, David St. John, Thomas Lux and Sandra McPherson."

Tips: "The change in editorial staff will probably mean a slight shift in emphasis. We will probably be soliciting more submissions and relying less on uninvited materials. More poetry and scholarly articles (and perhaps less fiction) may be included in the future."

YELLOW SILK, Journal of Erotic Arts, verygraphics, Box 6374, Albany CA 94706. (415)644-4188. Editor: Lily Pond. 90% freelance written. Prefers to work with published/established writers; works with a small number of new/unpublished writers each year. A quarterly magazine of erotic literature and visual arts. "Editorial policy: All persuasions; no brutality." Our publication is artistic and literary, not pornographic or pandering. Humans are involved: heads, hearts and bodies—not just bodies alone; and the quality of the literature is as important as the erotic content." Circ. 15,000. Pays on publication. Publishes ms an average of 6 months after acceptance. Byline given. Buys all publication rights for one year, at which time they revert to author; and reprint and anthology rights for duration of copyright. Reports in 3 months on manuscripts. Sample copy $6.

Nonfiction: Book excerpts, essays, humor and reviews. "We often have theme issues, but non-regularly and usually not announced in advance. No pornography, romance-novel type writing, sex fantasies. No first-person accounts or blow-by-blow descriptions. No articles. No novels." Buys 5-10 mss/year. Send complete ms. All submissions should be typed, double-spaced, with name, address and phone number on each page; always enclose SASE. No specified length requirements. Pays minimum $10 and 3 contributor copies and subscription.

Photos: Photos may be submitted independently, not as illustration for submission. Reviews photocopies, contact sheets, transparencies and prints. We accept 4-color and b&w artwork. Offers varying payment for series of 8-20 used, plus copies. Buys one-time rights and reprint rights.

Columns/Departments: Reviews (book, movie, art, dance, food, anything). "Erotic content and how it's handled is focus of importance. Old or new does not matter. Want to bring readers information of what's out there." Buys 8-10 mss/year. Send complete ms or query. Pays minimum of $10 plus copies.

Fiction: Erotica, including ethnic, experimental, fantasy, humorous, mainstream, novel excerpts and science fiction. See "Nonfiction." Buys 12-16 mss/year. Send complete ms. Pays $1/printed column inch, plus copies.

Poetry: Avant-garde, free verse, haiku, light verse and traditional. "No greeting-card poetry." Buys 80-100 poems/year. No limit on number of poems submitted, "but don't send book-length manuscripts." Pays .375¢/line, plus copies.

Tips: "The best way to get into *Yellow Silk* is produce excellent, well-crafted work that includes eros freshly, with strength of voice, beauty of language, and insight into character. I'll tell you what I'm sick of and have, unfortunately, been seeing more of lately: the products of 'How to Write Erotica' classes. This is not brilliant fiction; it is poorly written fantasy and not what I'm looking for."

ZYZZYVA, The Last Word: West Coast Writers and Artists, Suite 1400, 41 Sutter St., San Francisco CA 94104. (415)255-1282. Editor: Howard Junker. 100% freelance written. Works with a small number of new/unpublished writers each year. Quarterly magazine. "We feature work by West Coast writers only. We are essentially a literary magazine, but of wide-ranging interests and a strong commitment to nonfiction." Estab. 1985. Circ. 3,500. **Pays on acceptance.** Publishes ms an average of 3 months after acceptance. Byline given. Buys first North American serial rights and one-time anthology rights. Reports in 1 week on queries; 2 weeks on mss. Sample copy $8.

Nonfiction: Book excerpts, general interest, historical/nostalgic, humor and personal experience. Buys 15 mss/year. Query. Length: open. Pays $50-250.

Fiction: Ethnic, experimental, humorous, mainstream and mystery. Buys 20 mss/year. Send complete ms. Length: open. Pays $50-250.

Poetry: Buys 20 poems/year. Submit maximum 5 poems. Length: 3-200 lines. Pays $50-250.

Men's

Men's magazines have been able to stabilize the downward spiral that has affected them during the past several years, but few are prospering. Not many new magazines in this category have succeeded, but those that have are focusing either on information, service or fashion. Magazines that also use material slanted toward men can be found in Business and Finance, Relationships, Military and Sports sections.

CAVALIER, Suite 204, 2355 Salzedo St., Coral Gables FL 33134. (305)443-2378. Editor: Douglas Allen. 80% freelance written. Works with published/established and new/unpublished writers each year. Monthly magazine for "young males, ages 18-29, 80% college graduates, affluent, intelligent, interested in current events, sex, sports, adventure, travel and good fiction." Circ. 250,000. Pays on publication. Publishes ms an average of 3 months after acceptance. Byline given. Buys first serial and second serial (reprint) rights. Buys 44 or more mss/year. See past issues for general approach to take. Submit seasonal material at least 3 months in advance. Reports in 5 weeks. Writer's guidelines for #10 SAE.

Nonfiction: Personal experience, interview, humor, think pieces, exposé and new product. "Be frank—we are open to dealing with controversial issues. No timely material (have 4 month lead time). Prefers 'unusual' subject matter as well as sex-oriented (but serious) articles." Query. Length: 2,800-3,500 words. Pays maximum $500 with photos. Sometimes pays the expenses of writers on assignment.

Photos: Photos purchased with or without captions. No cheesecake.

Fiction: Nye Willden, department editor. Mystery, science fiction, humorous, adventure and contemporary problems "with at least one explicit sex scene per story." Send complete ms. Length: 2,500-3,500 words. Pays $250 maximum, higher for special.

Tips: "Our greatest interest is in originality—new ideas, new approaches; no tired, overdone stories—both feature and fiction. We do not deal in 'hack' sensationalism but in high quality pieces. Keep in mind the intelligent 18- to 29-year-old male reader. We will be putting more emphasis in articles and fiction on sexual themes. We prefer serious articles. Pornography—fiction can be very imaginative and sensational."

ESQUIRE, 1790 Broadway, New York NY 10019. (212)459-7500. Editor-in-Chief: Lee Eisenberg. 99% freelance written. Monthly. Estab. 1933. **Pays on acceptance.** Publishes ms an average of 6 months after acceptance. Usually buys first serial rights. Reports in 3 weeks. "We depend chiefly on solicited contributions and material from literary agencies. We are unable to accept responsibility for unsolicited material." Query.

Nonfiction: Articles vary in length, but features usually average 3,000-7,000 words. Articles should be slanted for sophisticated, intelligent readers; however, not highbrow in the restrictive sense. Wide range of subject matter. Rates run roughly between $300 and $3,000, depending on length, quality, etc. Sometimes pays expenses of writers on assignment.

Photos: Alison Morley, photo editor. Payment depends on how photo is used, but rates are roughly $300 for b&w; $500-750 for color. Guarantee on acceptance. Buys first periodical publication rights.

Fiction: L. Rust Hills, fiction editor. "Literary excellence is our only criterion." Discourages genre fiction (horror, science fiction, murder mystery, etc.). Length: about 1,000-6,000 words. Payment: $1,000-5,000.

Tips: The writer sometimes has a better chance of breaking in at *Esquire* with short, lesser-paying articles and fillers (rather than with major features) "because we need more short pieces."

FLING, Relim Publishing Co., Inc., 550 Miller Ave., Mill Valley CA 94941. (415)383-5464. Editor: Arv Miller. Managing Editor: Ted Albert. 30% freelance written. Prefers to work with published/established writers; works with a small number of new/unpublished writers each year. Bimonthly magazine in the men's sophisticate field. Young male audience of adults ages 18-34. Sexual-oriented field. Estab. 1957. Circ. 100,000. **Pays on acceptance.** Publishes ms an average of 3 months after acceptance. Buys first North American serial rights and second serial (reprint) rights; makes work-for-hire assignments. Submit seasonal/holiday material 8 months in advance. Does not consider multiple submissions. Reports in 1 week on queries; 2 weeks on mss. Sample copy $4; writer's guidelines for SASE.

Nonfiction: Exposé; how-to (better relationships with women, better lovers); interview/profile; personal experience; photo feature; and taboo sex articles. Buys 15 mss/year. Query. Length: 1,500-3,000 words. Pays $150-250. Sometimes pays expenses of writers on assignment.

Photos: Send photos with query. Reviews b&w contact sheets and 8×10 prints; 35mm color transparencies. Pays $10-25 for b&w; $20-35 for color. Model releases required. Buys one-time rights.

Columns/Departments: Buys 12 mss/year. Query or send complete ms. Length: 100-200 words. Pays $15-125.

Fiction: Confession, erotica and sexual. No science fiction, western, plotless, private-eye, "dated" or adventure. Buys 20 mss/year. Send complete ms. Length: 2,000-3,000 words. Pays $135-200.

Fillers: Clippings. Buys 50/year. Length: 100-500 words. Pays $5-15.

Tips: "Nonfiction and fiction are wide open areas to freelancers. Always query with one-page letter to the editor before proceeding with any writing. Also send a sample photocopy of published material, similar to suggestion."

GALLERY MAGAZINE, Montcalm Publishing Corp., 401 Park Ave. S., New York NY 10016-8802. (212)779-8900. FAX: (212)725-7215. Editorial Director: Marc Lichter. Managing Editor: Barry Janoff. 50% freelance written. Prefers to work with published/established writers. Monthly magazine "focusing on features of interest to the young American man." Estab. 1972. Circ. 500,000. Pays 50% on acceptance, 50% on publication. Byline given. Pays 25% kill fee. Buys first North American serial rights; makes work-for-hire assignments. Submit seasonal/holiday material 6 months in advance. Reports in 1 month on queries; 2 months on mss. Sample copy $3.50 plus $1.75 postage and handling. Free writer's guidelines.

Nonfiction: Investigative pieces, general interest, how-to, humor, interview, new products and profile. "We *do not* want to see pornographic articles." Buys 7-9 mss/issue. Query or send complete mss. Length: 1,000-3,000 words. Pays $300-2,000. "Special prices negotiated." Sometimes pays expenses of writers on assignment.

Photos: Send photos with accompanying mss. Pay varies for b&w or color contact sheets and negatives. Buys one-time rights. Captions preferred; model release required.

Fiction: Adventure, erotica, experimental, humorous, mainstream, mystery and suspense. Buys 1 ms/issue. Send complete ms. Length: 1,000-3,000 words. Pays $350-1,000.

GENT, Suite 204, 2355 Salzedo St., Coral Gables FL 33134. (305)443-2378. Editor: Bruce Arthur. 75% freelance written. Prefers to work with published/established writers. Monthly magazine for men from every strata of society who enjoy big breasted, full-figured females. Circ. 200,000. Buys first North American serial rights. Byline given. Pays on publication. Publishes ms an average of 2 months after acceptance. Reports in 6 weeks. Sample copy $5; writer's guidelines for #10 SASE.

Nonfiction: Looking for traditional men's subjects (cars, racing, outdoor adventure, science, gambling, etc.) as well as sex-related topics. Query first. Length: 2,000-3,500 words. Buys 70 mss/year. Pays from $200.

Photos: B&w photos and color transparencies purchased with mss. Captions (preferred).

Fiction: Erotic. "Stories should contain a huge-breasted female character, as this type of model is *Gent*'s main focus. And this character's endowments should be described in detail in the course of the story." Submit complete ms. No fiction queries. Length: 2,000-4,000 words. Pays from $200.

Tips: "Our efforts to make *Gent* acceptable to Canadian censors as a condition for exportation to that country have forced some shifting of editorial focus. Toward this end, we have de-emphasized our editorial coverage of pregnancy, lactation, anal intercourse and all forms of sadism and masochism. Study sample copies of the magazine before trying to write for it. We like custom-tailored stories and articles."

GENTLEMEN'S QUARTERLY, Condé Nast, 350 Madison Ave., New York NY 10017. (212)880-8800. Editor-in-Chief: Arthur Cooper. Managing Editor: Eliot Kaplan. 60% freelance written. Circ. 675,000. Monthly magazine emphasizing fashion, general interest and service features for men ages 25-45 with a large discretionary income. **Pays on acceptance.** Byline given. Pays 25% kill fee. Submit seasonal/holiday material 6 months in advance. Computer printout submissions acceptable; prefers letter-quality. Reports in 1 month.

Nonfiction: Politics, personality profiles, lifestyles, trends, grooming, nutrition, health and fitness, sports, travel, money, investment and business matters. Buys 4-6 mss/issue. Query with published clips. Length: 1,500-4,000 words. Pay varies.

Columns/Departments: Eliot Kaplan, managing editor. Body & Soul (fitness, nutrition and grooming); Private Lives; Health; Games (sports); All About Adam (nonfiction by women about men). Query with published clips. Length: 1,000-2,500 words. Pay varies.

Tips: "Major features are usually assigned to well-established, known writers. Pieces are almost always solicited. The best way to break in is through the columns, especially Male Animal, All About Adam, Games, Health or Humor."

‡HUSTLER BUSTY BEAUTIES, America's Breast Magazine, HG Publications, Inc., Suite 300, 9171 Wilshire Blvd., Beverly Hills CA 90210. (213)858-7100. FAX: (213)275-3857. Editor: N. Morgen Hagen. Managing Editor: Rick Woods. 40% freelance written. Men's sophisticate magazine published monthly. "*Hustler Busty Beauties* is an adult title that showcases attractive large-breasted women with accompanying erotic fiction, reader letters, humor." Estab. 1974. Circ. 180,000. Pays on publication. Publishes ms an average of 1-3 months after acceptance. Byline given. Offers 25% kill fee. Buys all rights. Reports in 2 weeks on queries; 1 month on mss. Sample copy for $3 with 9×12 SAE. Free writer's guidelines.

Columns/Departments: LewDDD Letters (erotic experiences involving large-breasted women from first-person point-of-view), 500-1,000 words. Buys 24-36 mss year. Send complete ms. Pays $50-75.

Fiction: Adventure, erotica, fantasy, humorous, mystery, science fiction, suspense. "No violent stories or stories without a bosomy female character." Buys 12 mss year. Send complete ms. Length: 750-2,500 words. Pays $250-500.

NUGGET, Suite 204, 2355 Salzedo St., Coral Gables FL 33134. (305)443-2378. Editor: Jerome Slaughter. 75% freelance written. Magazine "primarily devoted to fetishism." Pays on publication. Publishes ms an average of 2 months after acceptance. Byline given. Buys first North American serial rights. Reports in 6 weeks. Sample copy $5; writer's guidelines for SASE.

Nonfiction: Articles on fetishism—every aspect. Buys 20-30 mss/year. Submit complete ms. Length: 2,000-4,000 words. Pays from $150.

Photos: Erotic pictorials of women and couples—essay types on fetish clothing (leather, rubber, underwear, etc.) or women wrestling or boxing other women or men, preferably semi-nude or nude. Captions or short accompanying ms desirable. Reviews transparencies or b&w photos.

Fiction: Erotic and fetishistic. Should be oriented to *Nugget*'s subject matter. Length: 2,000-4,000 words. Pays from $150.

Tips: "We require queries on articles only, and the letter should be a brief synopsis of what the article is about. Originality in handling of subject is very helpful. It is almost a necessity for a freelancer to study our magazine first, be knowledgeable about the subject matter we deal with and able to write explicit and erotic fetish material."

OPTIONS, The Bi-Monthly, AJA Publishing, P.O. Box 470, Port Chester NY 10573. (914)939-2111. Editor: Don Stone. Assistant Editor: Diana Sheridan. Mostly freelance written. Sexually explicit magazine for and about bisexuals and homosexuals, published 10 times/year. "Articles, stories and letters about bisexuality. Positive approach. Safe-sex encounters unless the story clearly pre-dates the AIDS situation." Circ. 100,000. Pays on publication. Publishes ms an average of 4-10 months after acceptance. Byline given. Buys all rights. Submit seasonal/holiday material 6-8 months in advance; buys very little seasonal material. Reports in 3 weeks. Sample copy $2.95 with 6×9 SAE and 5 first class stamps. Writer's guidelines for SASE.

Nonfiction: Essays (occasional), how-to, humor, interview/profile, opinion and (especially) personal experience. All must be bisexually related. Does not want "anything not bisexually related, anything negative, anything opposed to safe sex, anything dry/boring/ponderous/pedantic; write even serious topics informally if not lightly." Buys 70 mss/year. Send complete ms. Length: 2,000-3,000. Pays $100.

Photos: Reviews transparencies and prints. Pays $10 for b&w photos; $200 for full color. Previously published photos acceptable.

Fiction: "We don't usually get enough true first-person stories and need to buy some from writers. They must be bisexual, usually man/man, hot and believable. They must not read like fiction." Buys 60 ms/year. Send complete ms. Length: 2,000-3,000. Pays $100.

Tips: "We use many more male/male pieces than female/female. Use only one serious article per issue. A serious/humorous approach is good here, but only if it's natural to you; don't make an effort for it. No longer buying 'letters'; we get enough real ones."

PLAYBOY, 680 N. Lakeshore Dr., Chicago IL 60611. 50% freelance written. Prefers to work with published/established writers; works with a small number of new/unpublished writers each year. Monthly. **Pays on acceptance.** Publishes ms an average of 6 months after acceptance. Offers 20% kill fee. Buys first serial rights and others. Computer printout submissions acceptable; prefers letter-quality. Reports in 1 month. Writer's guidelines for #10 SASE.

Nonfiction: John Rezek, articles editor. "We're looking for timely, topical pieces. Articles should be carefully researched and written with wit and insight. Little true adventure or how-to material. Check magazine for subject matter. Pieces on outstanding contemporary men, sports, politics, sociology, business and finance, music, science and technology, games, all areas of interest to the contemporary urban male." Query. Length: 3,000-5,000 words. Pays $3,000 minimum. *Playboy* interviews run between 10,000 and 15,000 words. After getting an assignment, the freelancer outlines the questions, conducts and edits the interview, and writes the introduction. Pays $5,000 minimum. For interviews contact John Rezek, Executive Editor, 747 3rd Ave., New York NY 10017. Pays expenses of writers on assignment.

Photos: Gary Cole, photography director, suggests that all photographers interested in contributing make a thorough study of the photography currently appearing in the magazine. Generally all photography is done on assignment. While much of this is assigned to *Playboy*'s staff photographers, approximately 50% of the photography is done by freelancers, and *Playboy* is in constant search of creative new talent. Qualified freelancers are encouraged to submit samples of their work and ideas. All assignments made on an all rights basis with payments scaled from $600/color page for miscellaneous features such as fashion, food and drink, etc.; $300/b&w page; $1,000/color page for girl features; cover, $1,500. Playmate photography for entire project: $10,000-13,000. Assignments and submissions handled by senior editor: Jeff Cohen and associate editors: James Larson and Michael Ann Sullivan, Chicago; Marilyn Grabowski and Linda Kenney, Los Angeles. Assignments made on a minimum guarantee basis. Film, processing, and other expenses necessitated by assignment honored.

Fiction: Alice Turner, fiction editor. Both light and serious fiction. "Entertainment pieces are clever, smoothly written stories. Serious fiction must come up to the best contemporary standards in substance, idea and style. Both, however, should be designed to appeal to the educated, well-informed male reader." General types include comedy, mystery, fantasy, horror, science fiction, adventure, social-realism, "problem" and psychological stories. Fiction lengths are 3,000-6,000 words; short-shorts of 1,000 to 1,500 words are used. Pays $2,000; $1,000 short-short. Rates rise for additional acceptances.

Fillers: Party Jokes are always welcome. Pays $100 each. Also interesting items for Playboy After Hours section (check it carefully before submitting). The After Hours front section pays $75 for humorous or unusual news items (submissions not returned). Send to After Hours editor. Has regular movie, book and record reviewers. Ideas for Playboy Potpourri pay $75. Query to John Rezek, Chicago. Games, puzzles and travel articles should be addressed to New York office.

SCREW, P.O. Box 432, Old Chelsea Station, New York NY 10113. Managing Editor: Manny Neuhaus. 95% freelance written. Eager to work with new/unpublished writers. Weekly tabloid newspaper for a predominantly male, college-educated audience; ages 21 through mid-40s. Estab. 1968. Circ. 125,000. Pays on publication. Publishes ms an average of 3 months after acceptance. Byline given. Buys all rights. Reports in 3 months. Free sample copy and writer's guidelines.

Nonfiction: "Sexually-related news, humor, how-to articles, first-person and true confessions. Frank and explicit treatment of all areas of sex; outrageous and irreverent attitudes combined with hard information, news and consumer reports. Our style is unique. Writers should check several recent issues." Buys 150-200 mss/year. Will also consider material for Letter From . . ., a consumer-oriented wrap-up of commercial sex

Always check the most recent copy of a magazine for the address and editor's name before you send in a query or manuscript.

scene in cities around the country; submit complete ms or query. Length: 1,000-3,000 words. Pays $100-250. Also, My Scene, a sexual true confession. Length: 1,000-2,500 words. Pays $40.

Photos: Reviews b&w glossy prints (8×10 or 11×14) purchased with or without manuscripts or on assignment. Pays $10-50.

Tips: "All mss get careful attention. Those written in *Screw* style on sexual topics have the best chance. I anticipate a need for more aggressive, insightful political humor."

SWANK, GCR Publishing Corp., 1700 Broadway, New York NY 10019. (212)541-7100. Editor: Michael Wilde. 75% freelance written. Works with new/unpublished writers. Monthly magazine on "sex and sensationalism, lurid. High quality adult erotic entertainment." Audience of men ages 18-38, high school and some college education, medium income, skilled blue-collar professionals, union men. Circ. 350,000. Pays on publication. Publishes ms an average of 4 months after acceptance. Byline given; pseudonym, if wanted. Buys first North American serial rights. Submit seasonal/holiday material 6 months in advance. Reports in 3 weeks on queries; 8 weeks on mss. Sample copy $5.95; writer's guidelines for SASE.

Nonfiction: Exposé (researched) and adventure must be accompanied by photographs. "We buy articles on sex-related topics, which don't need to be accompanied by photos." Interested in lifestyle (unusual) pieces. Buys photo pieces on autos, action, adventure. Buys 34 mss/year. Query with or without published clips. Pays $350-500. Sometimes pays the expenses of writers on assignment.

Photos: Bruce Perez, photo editor. State availability of photos. "If you have good photographs of an interesting adventure/lifestyle subject, the writing that accompanies is bought almost automatically." Model releases required.

Tips: "Don't even bother to send girl photos unless you are a published professional." Looks for "lifestyle and adventure pieces that are accompanied by color 35mm chromes and articles about sex-related topics. We carry one photo/journalism piece about automobiles or related subjects per issue."

TURN-ON LETTERS, AJA Publishing, P.O. Box 470, Port Chester NY 10573. Editor: Julie Silver. Magazine published 9 times/year covering sex. "Adult material, must be positive, no pain or degradations. No incest, no underage." Circ. 100,000. Pays on publication. Publishes ms an average of 4-6 months after acceptance. Buys all rights. No byline. No kill fee; "assigned mss are not killed unless they do not fulfill the assignment and/or violate censorship laws." Mss accepted by *Turn-on Letters* will also be considered for publication in *Uncensored Letters*. Submit seasonal/holiday material 6 months in advance. Reports in 3 weeks. Sample copy $2.50 with 6×9 SAE and 4 first class stamps. Writer's guidelines for #10 SASE.

Fiction: Sexually explicit material in the format of a letter. Buys 441 "letters"/year. Send complete ms. Length: 500-750 words (2-3 typed pages). Pays $15.

Photos: Reviews transparencies and prints. Buys b&w for $10 and full color for $200. Previously published pictures OK. Buys all rights.

Tips: "When you write, be different, be believable."

Military

These publications emphasize military or paramilitary subjects or other aspects of military life. Technical and semitechnical publications for military commanders, personnel and planners, as well as those for military families and civilians interested in Armed Forces activities are listed here.

‡**ACTION DIGEST**, J. Flores Publications, P.O. Box 163001, Miami FL 33116. (305)559-4652. Editor: Eli Flores. 90% freelance written. Quarterly magazine on guns, military and adventure. "We cover a wide range of action-related topics, including guns, self-defense, military history, true crime stories, outdoor adventure." Estab. 1990. Circ. 10,000. Pays on publication. Publishes ms an average of 6-12 months after acceptance. Byline given. Buys first or second serial (reprint) rights. Simultaneous and previously published submissions OK. Query for electronic submissions. Reports in 2 weeks on queries; 1 month on mss. Sample copy for $3.95; writer's guidelines for #10 SASE.

Nonfiction: Book excerpts, expose, general interest, how-to, humor, interview/profile, new product, opinion, personal experience, photo feature, technical. No book or video reviews. Buys 20-30 mss/year. Send complete ms. Length: 800-4,000 words. Pays $50-200.

Photos: Send photos with submission. Reviews contact sheets, negatives, transparencies and 4×5 prints. Offers no additional payment for photos accepted with ms. Captions, model releases and identification of subjects required. Buys one-time rights.

Columns/Departments: Viewpoint (op/ed of interest to our readership); Complaint Department (humorous column on "getting even" with big business and other bureaucracies); both 500-800 words. Buys 20 mss/year. Send complete ms. Pays $35-50.

AMERICAN SURVIVAL GUIDE, McMullen Publishing, Inc., 2145 W. La Palma Ave., Anaheim CA 92801. (714)635-9040. FAX: (714)533-9979. Editor: Jim Benson. 50% freelance written. Monthly magazine covering "self-reliance, defense, meeting day-to-day and possible future threats—survivalism for survivalists." Circ. 72,000. Pays on publication. Publishes ms up to 1 year after acceptance. Byline given. Submit seasonal/holiday material 5 months in advance. Sample copy $3.50; writer's guidelines for SASE.

Nonfiction: Expose (political); how-to; interview/profile; personal experience (how I survived); photo feature (equipment and techniques related to survival in all possible situations); emergency medical; health and fitness; communications; transportation; food preservation; water purification; self-defense; terrorism; nuclear dangers; nutrition; tools; shelter; etc. "No general articles about how to survive. We want specifics and single subjects." Buys 60-100 mss/year. Query or send complete ms. Length: 1,500-2,000 words. Pays $140-350. Sometimes pays some expenses of writers on assignment.

Photos: Send photos with ms. "One of the most frequent mistakes made by writers in completing an article assignment for us is sending photo submissions that are inadequate." Captions, model releases and identification of subjects mandatory. Buys all rights.

Tips: "Prepare material of value to individuals who wish to sustain human life no matter what the circumstance. This magazine is a text and reference."

‡**ARMY MAGAZINE**, 2425 Wilson Blvd., Arlington VA 22201. (703)841-4300. FAX: (703)525-9039. Editor-in-Chief: L. James Binder. Managing Editor: Mary Blake French. 80% freelance written. Prefers to work with published/established writers; eager to work with new/unpublished writers. Monthly magazine emphasizing military interests. Estab. 1902. Circ. 150,000. Pays on publication. Publishes ms an average of 6 months after acceptance. Buys all rights. Byline given except for back-up research. Submit seasonal/holiday material 3 months in advance. Sample copy and writer's guidelines for 8½ × 12 SAE with $1 postage.

Nonfiction: Historical (military and original); humor (military feature-length articles and anecdotes); interview; new product; nostalgia; personal experience; photo feature; profile; and technical. No rehashed history. "We would like to see more pieces about little-known episodes involving interesting military personalities. We especially want material lending itself to heavy, contributor-supplied photographic treatment. The first thing a contributor should recognize is that our readership is very savvy militarily. 'Gee-whiz' personal reminiscences get short shrift, unless they hold their own in a company in which long military service, heroism and unusual experiences are commonplace. At the same time, Army readers like a well-written story with a fresh slant, whether it is about an experience in a foxhole or the fortunes of a corps in battle." Buys 12 mss/issue. Submit complete ms. Length: 4,500 words. Pays 12-18¢/word.

Photos: Submit photo material with accompanying ms. Pays $15-50 for 8 × 10 b&w glossy prints; $35-150 for 8 × 10 color glossy prints or 2¼ × 2¼ transparencies, will also accept 35mm. Captions preferred. Buys all rights. Pays $35-50 for cartoon with strong military slant.

Columns/Departments: Military news, books, comment (*New Yorker*-type "Talk of the Town" items). Buys 8/issue. Submit complete ms. Length: 1,000 words. Pays $40-150.

‡**ASIA-PACIFIC DEFENSE FORUM**, Commander-in-Chief, U.S. Pacific Command, Box 13, Camp H.M. Smith HI 96861. (808)477-0760/1454. Editor-in-Chief: Lt. Col. Paul R. Stankiewicz. Editor: Major Robyn Blanpied. 12% (maximum) freelance written. Quarterly magazine for foreign military officers in 51 Asian-Pacific, Indian Ocean and other countries; all services—Army, Navy, Air Force and Marines. Secondary audience—government officials, media and academicians concerned with defense issues. "We seek to keep readers abreast of current status of U.S. forces and of U.S. national security policies in the Asia-Pacific area, and to enhance regional dialogue on military subjects." Estab. 1976. Circ. 34,000. **Pays on acceptance.** Publishes ms an average of 4 months after acceptance. Byline given. Buys simultaneous rights, second serial (reprint) rights or one-time rights. Simultaneous and previously published submissions OK. Requires only a self-addressed label. Reports in 3 weeks on queries; at most 10 weeks on mss. Free sample copy and writer's guidelines (send self-addressed label).

Nonfiction: General interest (strategy and tactics, current type forces and weapons systems, strategic balance and security issues and Asian-Pacific armed forces); historical (rarely used); how-to (training, leadership, force employment procedures, organization); interview and personal experience (rarely used, and only in terms of developing professional military skills). "We do not want overly technical weapons/equipment descriptions, overly scholarly articles, controversial policy, and budget matters; nor do we seek discussion of in-house problem areas. We do not deal with military social life, base activities or PR-type personalities/job descriptions." Buys 2-4 mss/year. Query or send complete ms. Length: 1,000-3,000 words. Pays $100-300.

Photos: State availability of photos with query or ms. "We provide nearly all photos; however, we will consider good quality photos with manuscripts." Reviews color, b&w glossy prints or 35mm color transparencies. Offers no additional payment for photos accompanying mss. Photo credits given. Captions required. Buys one-time rights.

Tips: "Don't write in a flashy, Sunday supplement style. Our audience is relatively staid, and fact-oriented articles requiring a newspaper/journalistic approach are used more than a normal magazine style. Provide material that is truly foreign audience-oriented and easily illustrated with photos."

FAMILY MAGAZINE, The Magazine for Military Wives, Box 4993, Walnut Creek CA 94596. (415)284-9093. Editor: Janet A. Venturino. 100% freelance written. Works with a small number of new/unpublished writers each year. A monthly magazine for military wives who are young, high school educated and move often. Circ. 545,000. Pays on publication. Publishes ms an average of 6-12 months after acceptance. Byline given. Buys first North American serial rights. Submit seasonal/holiday material 6 months in advance. Simultaneous submissions OK. Reports in 1 month. Sample copy $1.25; writer's guidelines for SASE.

Nonfiction: Humor, personal experience, photo feature and travel, of interest to military wives. No romance, anything to do with getting a man or aging. Buys 30 mss/year. Send complete ms. Length: 2,000 words maximum. Pays $75-200.

Photos: Send photos with submissions. Reviews contact sheets, transparencies and prints. Offers $25-100/photo. Identification of subjects required. Buys one-time rights.

Fiction: Humorous, mainstream and slice-of-life vignettes. No romance or novel excerpts. Buys 5 mss/year. Length: 2,000 words maximum. Pays $75-150.

‡LEATHERNECK, P.O. Box 1775, Quantico VA 22134. (703)640-3171. FAX: (703)640-0823. Editor: William V.H. White. Managing Editor: Tom Bartlett. Emphasizes all phases of Marine Corps activities. Monthly magazine. Estab. 1913. Circ. 104,000. **Pays on acceptance.** Buys first rights. Phone queries OK. Submit seasonal/holiday material 3 months in advance. Free sample copy and writer's guidelines.

Nonfiction: "All material submitted to *Leatherneck* must pertain to the U.S. Marine Corps and its members." General interest, how-to, humor, historical, interview, nostalgia, personal experience, profile, and travel. "No articles on politics, subjects not pertaining to the Marine Corps, and subjects that are not in good taste." Buys 24 mss/year. Query. Length: 1,500-3,000 words. Pays $50/magazine page.

Photos: "We like to receive a complete package when we consider a manuscript for publication." State availability of photos with query. No additional payment for 4×5 or 8×10 b&w glossy prints. Captions required. Model release required. Buys first rights.

LIFE IN THE TIMES, Times Journal Co., Springfield VA 22159-0200. (703)750-8666. FAX: (703)750-8622. Editor: Barry Robinson. Managing Editor: Roger Hyneman. 30% freelance written. Eager to work with new/unpublished writers. Weekly lifestyle section of Army, Navy and Air Force Times covering current lifestyles and problems of career military families around the world. Circ. 300,000. **Pays on acceptance.** Publishes ms an average of 2 months after acceptance. Byline given. Offers negotiable kill fee. Buys first rights. Submit seasonal/holiday material 6 months in advance. Query for electronic submissions. Reports in about 2 months. Writer's guidelines for #10 SASE.

Nonfiction: Exposé (current military); coping (families); interview/profile (military); personal experience (military only); and travel (of military interest). "We accept food articles and short items about unusual things military people and their families are doing." No poetry, cartoons or historical articles. Buys 110 mss/year. Query with published clips. Length: 750-2,000 words. Pays $75-350. Sometimes pays the expenses of writers on assignment.

Photos: State availability of photos or send photos with ms. Reviews 35mm color contact sheets and prints. Captions, model releases and identification of subjects required.

Tips: "In your query write a detailed description of story and how it will be told. A tentative lead is nice. Just one good story 'breaks in' a freelancer. Follow the outline you propose in your query letter and humanize articles with quotes and examples."

MARINE CORPS GAZETTE, Professional Magazine for United States Marines, Marine Corps Association, P.O. Box 1775, Quantico VA 22134. (703)640-6161. Editor: Col. John E. Greenwood, USMC (Ret.). FAX: (703)640-2628. Managing Editor: Joseph D. Dodd. Less than 5% freelance written. "Will continue to welcome and respond to queries, but will be selective due to large backlog from Marine authors." Monthly magazine. "*Gazette* serves as a forum in which serving Marine officers exchange ideas and viewpoints on professional military matters." Estab. 1916. Circ. 37,000. Pays on publication. Publishes ms an average of 6 months after acceptance. Byline given. Buys all rights. Reports in 3 weeks on queries; 2 months on mss. Free sample copy and writer's guidelines.

Nonfiction: Historical/nostalgic (Marine Corps operations only); and technical (Marine Corps related equipment). "The magazine is a professional journal oriented toward hard skills, factual treatment, technical detail—no market for lightweight puff pieces—analysis of doctrine, lessons learned goes well. A very strong Marine Corps background and influence are normally prerequisites for publication." Buys 4-5 mss/year from non-Marine Corps sources. Query or send complete ms. Length: 2,500-5,000 words. Pays $200-400; short features, $50-100.

Photos: "We welcome photos and charts." Payment for illustrative material included in payment forms. "Photos need not be original, nor have been taken by the author, but they must support the article."

Columns/Departments: Book Reviews (of interest and importance to Marines); and Ideas and Issues (an assortment of topical articles, e.g., opinion or argument, ideas of better ways to accomplish tasks, reports on weapons and equipment, strategies and tactics, etc., also short vignettes on history of Corps). Buys 60 book reviews and 120 Ideas and Issues mss/year, most from Marines. Query. Length: 500-1,500 words. Pays $25-50 plus book for 750-word book review; $50-100 for Ideas and Issues.

Tips: "Book reviews or short articles (500-1,500 words) on Marine Corps related hardware or technological development are the best way to break in. Sections/departments most open to freelancers are Book Reviews and Ideas & Issues sections—query first. We are not much of a market for those outside U.S. Marine Corps or who are not closely associated with current Marine activities."

MILITARY LIFESTYLE, Downey Communications, Inc., 1732 Wisconsin Ave. NW, Washington DC 20007. (202)944-4000. FAX: (202)333-0499. Editor: Hope M. Daniels. 80-90% freelance written. Works with equal balance of published and unpublished writers. For military families in the U.S. and overseas. Published 10 times a year. Magazine. Estab. 1969. Circ. 520,000. Pays on publication. Publishes ms an average of 4-6 months after acceptance. Buys first North American serial rights. Submit seasonal/holiday material at least 6 months in advance. Reports in approximately 2 months. Sample copy $1.50 and 9×12 SAE. Writer's guidelines for #10 SASE.

Nonfiction: "All articles must have special interest for military families. General interest articles are OK if they reflect situations our readers can relate to." Food, humor, profiles, childrearing, health, home decor and travel. "Query letter should name sources, describe focus of article, use a few sample quotes from sources, indicate length, and should describe writer's own qualifications for doing the piece." Length: 1,000-2,000 words. Pays $400-750/article. Negotiates expenses on a case-by-case basis.

Photos: Purchased with accompanying ms and on assignment. Uses 35mm or larger transparencies. Captions and model releases are required. Query art director Judi Connelly.

Columns/Departments: Your Point of View—personal experience pieces by military family members. Also, Your Pet, Your Money and Your Baby. Query. Length: 800-1,200 words. Rates vary.

Fiction: Slice-of-life, family situation, contemporary tableaux. "Military family life or relationship themes only." Buys 6-8 mss/year. Query. Length: 1,500-2,000 words. Pays $300-500.

Tips: "We are a magazine for military families, not just women. Our editorial attempts enthusiastically to reflect that. Our ideal contributor is a military family member who can write. However, I'm always impressed by a writer who has analyzed the market and can suggest some possible new angles for us. Sensitivity to military issues is a must for our contributors, as is the ability to write good personality profiles and/or do thorough research about military family life. We don't purchase household hints, historical articles, WW II-era material or parenting advice that is too personal and limited only to the writer's own experience."

MILITARY LIVING R&R REPORT, Box 2347, Falls Church VA 22042. (703)237-0203. Publisher: Ann Crawford. Bimonthly newsletter for "military travelers worldwide. Please state when sending submission that it is for the *R&R Report Newsletter* so as not to confuse it with our monthly magazine which has different requirements." Pays on publication. Buys first serial rights but will consider other rights. Sample copy $2.

Nonfiction: "We use information on little-known military facilities and privileges, discounts around the world and travel information. Items must be short and concise. Most reports are done by *R&R*'s subscribers on a 'sharing with others' basis with no fee paid. Used only a few freelance pieces in last year. Payment is on an honorarium basis, 1-1½¢/word."

MILITARY REVIEW, U.S. Army Command and General Staff College, Fort Leavenworth KS 66027-6910. (913)684-5642. FAX: (913)684-7671. Editor-in-Chief: Lt. Col. Steven F. Rausch. Managing Editor: Maj. Chris LeBlanc. Associate Editor: Lt. Col. Donald G. Rhodes. 75% freelance written. Eager to work with new/unpublished writers. Monthly journal (printed in three languages; English, Spanish and Brazilian Portuguese), emphasizing the military for military officers, students and scholars. Estab. 1922. Circ. 27,000. Pays on publication. Publishes ms an average of 8 months after acceptance. Byline given. Buys first serial rights and reserves right to reprint for training purpose. Phone queries OK. Query for electronic submissions. Reports in 1 month. Writer's guidelines for #10 SASE.

Nonfiction: Operational level of war, military history, international affairs, tactics, new military equipment, strategy and book reviews. Buys 100-120 mss/year. Query. Length: 2,000-3,000 words. Pays $50-200.

Tips: "We need more articles from military personnel experienced in particular specialties. Examples: Tactics from a tactician, military engineering from an engineer, etc. By reading our publication, writers will quickly recognize our magazine as a forum for any topic of general interest to the U.S. Army. They will also discover the style we prefer: concise and direct, in the active voice, with precision and clarity, and moving from the specific to the general."

OVERSEAS!, Military Consumer Today, Inc., Kolpingstr 1, 6906 Leimen, West Germany 011-49-6224-7060. FAX: 011-49-6224-70616. Editorial Director: Charles L. Kaufman. Managing Editor: Greg Ballinger. 95% freelance written. Eager to work with new/unpublished writers; "we don't get enough submissions." Monthly magazine. "*Overseas!* is aimed at the U.S. military in Europe. It is the leading military lifestyle magazine slanted toward living in Europe." Estab. 1973. Circ. 83,000. Pays on publication. Publishes ms an average of 3 months after acceptance. Byline given. Publishes photos, bio of new writers in editor's column. Offers kill fee depending on circumstances and writer. Buys one-time rights. Submit seasonal/holiday material at least

4 months in advance. Simultaneous queries and simultaneous and previously published submissions OK. Reports in 2 weeks on queries; 1 month on mss. Sample copy for SAE and 4 IRCs; writer's guidelines for SAE and 1 IRC.

Nonfiction: General interest (lifestyle for men and other topics); how-to (use camera, buy various types of video, audio, photo and computer equipment); humor ("We want travel/tourist in Europe humor like old *National Lampoon* style. Must be funny."); interview/profile (music, personality interviews; current music stars for young audience); technical (video, audio, photo, computer; how to purchase and use equipment); travel (European, first person adventure; write toward male audience); men's cooking; and men's fashion/lifestyle. Special issues include Video, Audio, Photo, and Military Shopper's Guide. Needs 250-750-word articles on video, audio, photo and computer products. Published in September every year. No articles that are drug- or sex-related. No cathedrals or museums of Europe stories. Buys 30-50 mss/year "but would buy more if we got better quality and subjects." Query with or without published clips or send complete ms. Length: 750-2,000 words. Pays 10¢/word. Usually pays expenses of writers on assignment; negotiable.

Photos: Send photos with accompanying query or ms. Pays $20 minimum, b&w; $35 transparencies, 35mm or larger. Photos must accompany travel articles—color slides.

Columns/Departments: Back Talk—potpourri page of humor, cartoons and other materials relating to tourist life in Europe and the military. Buys 20-50 mss/year. Length: 150 words maximum. Pays $25-150/piece used. "Would buy more if received more."

Tips: "We would like more submissions on travel in Europe and humor for the 'Back Talk' page. Writing should be lively, interesting, with lots of good information. We anticipate a change in the length of articles. Articles will be shorter and livelier with more sidebars because readers don't have time to read longer articles. *Overseas!* magazine is the *Travel and Leisure/GQ/Esquire* of this market; any articles that would be suitable for these magazines would probably work in *Overseas!*"

PARAMETERS: U.S. ARMY WAR COLLEGE QUARTERLY, U.S. Army War College, Carlisle Barracks PA 17013. (717)245-4943. Editor: Col. Lloyd J. Matthews, U.S. Army Retired. Quarterly. 100% freelance written. Prefers to work with published/established writers or experts in the field. Readership consists of senior leadership of U.S. defense establishment, both uniformed and civilian, plus members of the media, government, industry and academia interested in national and international security affairs, military strategy, military leadership and management, art and science of warfare, and military history (provided it has contemporary relevance). Most readers possess a graduate degree. Circ. 10,000. Not copyrighted; unless copyrighted by author, articles may be reprinted with appropriate credits. Buys first serial rights. Byline given. Pays on publication. Publishes ms an average of 6 months after acceptance. Reports in 1 month. Free writer's guidelines.

Nonfiction: Articles preferred that deal with current security issues, employ critical analysis and provide solutions or recommendations. Liveliness and verve, consistent with scholarly integrity, appreciated. Theses, studies and academic course papers should be adapted to article form prior to submission. Documentation in complete endnotes. Submit complete ms. Length: 4,500 words average, preferably less. Pays $150 average (including visuals).

Tips: "Make it short; keep it interesting; get criticism and revise accordingly. Tackle a subject only if you are an authority."

PERIODICAL, Council on America's Military Past, 4970 N. Camino Antonio, Tucson AZ 85718. Editor-in-Chief: Dan L. Thrapp. 90% freelance written. Works with a small number of new/unpublished writers each year. Quarterly magazine emphasizing old and abandoned forts, posts and military installations; military subjects for a professional, knowledgeable readership interested in one-time defense sites or other military installations. Circ. 1,500. Pays on publication. Publishes ms an average of 6 months after acceptance. Buys one-time rights. Simultaneous and previously published (if published a long time ago) submissions OK. Reports in 3 weeks. Writer's guidelines for #10 SASE.

Nonfiction: Historical, personal experience, photo feature and technical (relating to posts, their construction/operation and military matters). Buys 4-6 mss/issue. Query or send complete ms. Length: 300-4,000 words. Pays $2/page minimum.

Photos: Purchased with or without ms. Query. Reviews glossy, single-weight 8×10 b&w prints. Offers no additional payment for photos accepted with accompanying ms. Captions required.

Tips: "We plan more emphasis on appeal to professional military audience and military historians."

R&R ENTERTAINMENT DIGEST, R&R Communications GmbH, 1 Kolpingstrasse, 6906 Leimen, W. Germany 06224-7060. FAX: 06224-70616. Editor: Tory Billard. 50% freelance written. Monthly entertainment guide for military and government employees and their families stationed in Europe "specializing in travel in Europe, audio/video/photo information, music and the homemaker scene. Aimed exclusively at military/DoD based in Europe—Germany, Britain and the Mediterranean." Estab. 1969. Circ. 180,000. Pays on publication. Publishes ms an average of 2-6 months after acceptance. Byline given. "We offer 50% of payment as a kill fee, but this rarely happens—if story can't run in one issue, we try to use it in a future edition." Buys first serial rights for military market in Europe only. "We will reprint stories that have run in stateside publications if applicable to us." Submit seasonal/holiday material 3 months in advance. Simultaneous queries, and simultaneous and previously published submissions OK. Reports in 2 months. Sample copy and writer's guidelines available for #10 SAE and 5 IRCs.

Nonfiction: Travel (always looking for good travel in Europe features). "We want readers to use our travel articles as a handy guide as well as be entertained by them. We buy only articles by writers who have been to or lived in the destination on which they write. Not interested in tourist articles. Our readers live in Europe, average age 26.5, married with 2 children. Over 50% travel by car. Annual vacation is 1 week or more. Weekend trips are also popular. Should always include specific details: restaurant/clubs/hotel recommendations as well as prices. Looking for bargains." Humor (limited amount used—dealing with travel experiences in Europe) is accepted. No interviews of singers, historical pieces, album/movie/book reviews, or technical stories. Buys 15 mss/year. Query with published clips or send complete ms. Length: 600-1,000 words. Pays in Deutsche Marks—DM 90 (an estimated $45) /page; partial payment for partial page.

Photos: State availablility of photos or send photos with query or mss. Pays DM 80 for 35mm transparencies. Captions required. "We pay once for use with story but can reuse at no additional cost."

Columns/Departments: Monthly audio, video and photo stories, movie reviews and TV interviews. "We need freelancers with solid background in these areas who can write for general public on a variety of topics." Buys 10 mss/year. Query with published clips or send complete ms. Length: 1,300-1,400 words. Pays DM 90/ magazine page.

Fiction: Very little fiction accepted. Query. "It has to be exceptional to be accepted." Length: 600-1,200 words. Pays DM 90/page.

Fillers: Cartoons pertaining to television. Buys 5/year. Pays DM 80/cartoon.

Tips: "Best chance would be a tie-in travel or first-person (personalized) story with an American holiday: Mother's Day in Paris, Labor Day, Thanksgiving, St. Pat's Day in Europe, etc. Stories must be written with an American military member and family in mind—young married, 2 children with car, 2 weeks annual leave, several 3-day weekends. Sports/adventure travel stories and 'walking tours' of a city are popular with our readers."

THE RETIRED OFFICER MAGAZINE, 201 N. Washington St., Alexandria VA 22314. (800)245-8762. FAX: (703)838-8173. Editor: Col. Charles D. Cooper, USAF-Ret. 60% freelance written. Prefers to work with published/established writers. Monthly for officers of the 7 uniformed services and their families. Estab. 1929. Circ. 365,000. **Pays on acceptance.** Publishes ms an average of 9-12 months after acceptance. Byline given. Buys first serial rights. Submit seasonal material (holiday stories with a military theme) at least 9-12 months in advance. Reports on material accepted for publication within 2 months. Sample copy and writer's guidelines for 9 × 12 SAE with 5 first class stamps.

Nonfiction: Current military/political affairs, health and wellness, recent military history, humor, hobbies, travel, second-career job opportunities and military family lifestyle. Also, upbeat articles on aging, human interest and features pertinent to a retired military officer's milieu. True military experiences are also useful. "We rarely accept unsolicited mss. We look for detailed query letters with resumé and sample clips attached. We do not publish poetry or fillers." Buys 48 mss/year. Length: 750-2,000 words. Pays up to $500.

Photos: Query with list of stock photo subjects. Reviews 8 × 10 b&w photos (normal halftone). Pays $25. Original slides or transparencies must be suitable for color separation. Pays up to $175 for inside color; up to $250 for cover.

Tips: "Our readers are 55-65. We never write about them as senior citizens, yet we look for upbeat stories that take into consideration the demographic characteristics of their age group. An author who can submit a complete package of story and photos is valuable to us."

SEA POWER, 2300 Wilson Blvd., Arlington VA 22201-3308. Editor: James D. Hessman. Issued monthly by the Navy League of the U.S. for sea service personnel and civilians interested in naval maritime and defense matters. 10% freelance written. "We prefer queries from experts/specialists in maritime industry." Pays on publication. Buys all rights. Free sample copy.

Nonfiction: Factual articles on sea power and national defense in general, U.S. industrial base, mineral resources, and the U.S. Navy, U.S. Marine Corps, U.S. Coast Guard, U.S. Merchant Marine, oceanographic industries and other navies of the world. Should illustrate and expound the importance of the seas and sea power to the U.S. and its allies. Wants timely, clear, nonpedantic writing for audience that is intelligent and well-educated but not necessarily fluent in military/hi-tech terminology. No opinion pieces or "I was there" articles. Material should be presented in the third person, well documented with complete attribution. No historical articles, commentaries, critiques, abstract theories, poetry or editorials. Query first. Length: 500-2,500 words. Pays $100-500 depending upon length and research involved.

Photos: Purchased with ms.

Tips: "The writer should be invisible. Copy should be understandable without reference to charts, graphs or footnotes."

SOLDIER OF FORTUNE, The Journal of Professional Adventurers, Omega Group, Ltd., P.O. Box 693, Boulder CO 80306. (303)449-3750. FAX: (303)444-5617. Editor: Robert K. Brown. 50% freelance written. A monthly magazine covering military, paramilitary, police and combat subjects. "We are an action-oriented magazine; we cover combat hot spots around the world such as Afghanistan, Central America, Angola, etc. We also provide timely features on state-of-the-art weapons and equipment; elite military and police units; and historical military operations. Readership is primarily active-duty military, veterans and law enforcement." Estab. 1975. Circ. 175,000. **Pays on acceptance.** Publishes ms an average of 5 months after acceptance. Byline given. Offers 25% kill fee. Buys first North American serial rights. Submit seasonal/holiday material 5 months in advance. Reports in 3 weeks on queries; 1 month on mss. Sample copy $5; writer's guidelines for #10 SASE. Send ms to articles editor; queries to managing editor.

Nonfiction: Exposé; general interest; historical/nostalgic; how-to (on weapons and their skilled use); humor; profile; new product; personal experience; photo feature ("number one on our list"); technical; travel; combat reports; military unit reporters and solid Vietnam history. "No 'How I won the war' pieces; no op-ed pieces *unless* they are fully and factually backgrounded; no knife articles (staff assignments only). *All* submitted articles should have good art; art will sell us on an article." Buys 75 mss/year. Query with or without published clips, or send complete ms. Length: 2,500-5,000 words. Pays $300-1,200 for assigned articles; pays $200-1,000 for unsolicited articles. Sometimes pays the expenses of writers on assignment.

Photos: Send photos with submission (copies only, no originals). Reviews contact sheets and transparencies. Offers no additional payment for photos accepted with ms. Pays $500 for cover photo. Captions and identification of subjects required. Buys one-time rights.

Columns/Departments: Address to appropriate column editor (i.e., I Was There Editor). Combat weaponcraft (how-to military and police survival skills) and I Was There (first-person accounts of the arcane or unusual based in a combat or law enforcement environment), all 600-800 words. Buys 16 mss/year. Send complete ms. Length: 600-800 words. Combat weaponcraft pays $200; I was There pays $50.

Fillers: Bulletin Board editor. Newsbreaks; military/paramilitary related, *"has* to be documented." Length: 100-250 words. Pays $25.

Tips: "Submit a professionally prepared, complete package. All artwork with cutlines, double-spaced typed manuscript, cover letter including synopsis of article, supporting documentation where applicable, etc. Manuscript must be factual; writers have to do their homework and get all their facts straight. One error means rejection. We will work with authors over the phone or by letter, tell them if their ideas have merit for an acceptable article, and help them fine-tune their work. I Was There is a good place for freelancers to start. Vietnam features, if carefully researched and art heavy, will always get a careful look. Combat reports, again, with good art, are number one in our book and stand the best chance of being accepted. Military unit reports from around the world are well received as are law enforcement articles (units, police in action). If you write for us, be complete and factual; pros read *Soldier of Fortune,* and are *very* quick to let us know if we (and the author) err. We plan more articles on terrorism. Read the magazine before you try to write for it!"

‡VIETNAM, Empire Press, 602 S. King St., #300, Leesburg VA 22075. (703)771-9400. Editor: Colonel Harry G. Summers, Jr. Managing Editor: Kenneth Phillips. 80-90% freelance written. Quarterly magazine on military aspects of the Vietnam War. "Without debating the wisdom of U.S. involvement, pro or con, our objective is to tell the story of the military events, weaponry and personalities of the war, as it happened." Estab. 1988. Circ. 140,000. Pays on publication. Publishes ms up to 2 years after acceptance. Byline given. Buys all rights. Query for electronic submissions. Reports in 2 months on queries; 3 months on mss. Sample copy $3.95. Writer's guidelines for #10 SASE.

Nonfiction: Book excerpts (if original), historical, interview, personal/experience, military history. "Absolutely no fiction or poetry; we want straight history, as much personal narrative as possible, but not the gung-ho, shoot-em-up variety, either." Buys 30 mss/year. Query. Length: 4,000 words maximum. Pays $300 for features.

Photos: State availability of photos with submission. Pays up to $100/photo. Identification of subjects required. Buys one-time rights.

Columns/Departments: Arsenal (about weapons used, all sides); Personality (profiles of the players, all sides), Fighting Forces (about various units or types of unites: air, sea, rescue); Bases and Installations. Query. Length: 2,000 words. Pays $150.

WORLD WAR II, Empire Press, 602 S. King St. #300, Leesburg VA 22075. (703)771-9400. Editor: C. Brian Kelly. 95% freelance written. Prefers to work with published/established writers. A bimonthly magazine covering "military operations in World War II—events, personalities, strategy, national policy, etc." Estab. 1983. Circ. 200,000. Pays on publication. Publishes ms an average of 1-2 years after acceptance. Byline given. Buys all rights. Submit anniversary-related material 1 year in advance. Reports in 2 months on queries; 3 months or more on mss. Sample copy $4; writer's guidelines for #10 SASE.

Nonfiction: World War II military history. No fiction. Buys 24 mss/year. Query. Length: 4,000 words. Pays $200.

Photos: State availability of art and photos with submission. (For photos and other art, send photocopies and cite sources. "We'll order.") Sometimes offers additional payment for photos accepted with ms. Captions and identification of subjects required. Buys one-time rights.

Columns/Department: Undercover (espionage, resistance, sabotage, intelligence gathering, behind the lines, etc.); Personalities (WW II personalities of interest); and Armaments (weapons, their use and development), all 2,000 words. Book reviews, 300-750 words. Buys 18 mss/year (plus book reviews). Query. Pays $100.

Tips: "List your sources and suggest further readings in standard format at the end of your piece—as a bibliography for our files in case of factual challenge or dispute. All submissions are on speculation. When the story's right, but the writing isn't, we'll pay a small research fee for use of the information in our own style and language."

Music

Music fans follow the latest music industry news in these publications. Types of music and musicians or specific instruments are the sole focus of some magazines. Publications geared to music industry and professionals can be found in the Trade Music section. Additional music and dance markets are included in the Entertainment section.

AMERICAN SONGWRITER, 27 Music Square E, Nashville TN 37203. (615)244-6065. Editor: Vernell Hackett. Managing Editor: Deborah Price. 30% freelance written. Bimonthly magazine, educating amateur songwriters while informing professionals. Estab. 1984. Circ. 4,000. Pays on publication. Publishes ms an average of 2 months after acceptance. Offers $10 kill fee. Buys first North American serial rights. Simultaneous submissions OK. Query for electronic submissions. Reports in 2 months. Sample copy $3. Writer's guidelines for SAE.

Nonfiction: General interest, interview/profile, new product, and technical. "No fiction." Buys 20 mss/year. Query with published clips. Length: 300-1,200 words. Pays $25-50 for assigned articles.

Photos: State availability of photos with submission. Reviews 3×5 prints. Offers no additional payment for photos accepted with ms. Identification of subjects required. Buys one-time rights.

‡BAM, Rock and Video/the California Music Magazine, BAM Publications, 5951 Canning St., Oakland CA 94609. (415)652-3810. Editors: Steve Stoller and Dave Zimmer. 60% freelance written. Biweekly tabloid. Circ. 110,000. Pays on publication. Publishes ms an average of 1 month after acceptance. Byline given. Offers negotiable kill fee. Buys first North American serial rights. Submit seasonal/holiday material 3 months in advance. Reports in 3 weeks. Sample copy $2.

Nonfiction: Book excerpts, interview/profiles, record reviews and new product reviews. Buys 100 mss/year. Query with published clips. Length: 1,500-5,000 words. Pays $40-300. Sometimes pays expenses of writers on assignment.

Tips: "*BAM*'s focus is on both the personality and the craft of musicians. Writers should concentrate on bringing out their subject's special traits and avoid bland, clichéd descriptions and quotes. Clear, crisp writing is essential. Many potential *BAM* writers try to be too clever and end up sounding stupid. Also, it helps to have a clear focus. Many writers tend to ramble and simply string quotes together."

BANJO NEWSLETTER, Box 364, Greensboro MD 21639. (301)482-6278. Editor: Hub Nitchie. 10% freelance written. Monthly magazine covering the "instructional and historical treatment of the 5-string banjo. Covers all aspects of the instrument. Tablature is used for musical examples." Circ. 7,000. Pays on publication. Byline given. Buys one-time rights. Query for electronic submissions. Reports in 1 month on queries. Sample copy for $1.

Nonfiction: Interviews with 5-string banjo players, banjo builders, shop owners, etc. No humorous fiction from anyone unfamiliar with the popular music field. Buys 6 mss/year. Query. Length: 500-4,000 words. Pays $20-100. Sometimes pays writers with contributor copies or other premiums "if that is what writer wants." Very seldom pays expenses of writers on assignment. "We can arrange for press tickets to musical events."

Photos: State availability of photos with submission. Reviews b&w prints. Offers $10-40/photo. Captions and identification of subjects required whenever possible. Buys one-time rights.

Columns/Departments: Buys 60 mss/year. Query. Length: 500-750 words. Payment varies.

Poetry: Don Nitchie, poetry editor: Rt. 1, Box 289, Chilwark MA 02535. Buys 2 poems/year. Submit maximum 1 poem at one time.

Tips: "The writer should be motivated by being a student of the 5-string banjo or interested in the folk or bluegrass music fields where 5-string banjo is featured. Writers should be able to read and write banjo tablature and know various musicians or others in the field."

BLUEGRASS UNLIMITED, Bluegrass Unlimited, Inc., P.O. Box 111, Broad Run VA 22014. (703)349-8181. Editor: Peter V. Kuykendall. 80% freelance written. Prefers to work with published/established writers. Monthly magazine on bluegrass and old-time country music. Estab. 1966. Circ. 21,500. Pays on publication. Publishes ms an average of 4 months after acceptance. Byline given. Kill fee negotiated. Buys first North American serial rights, one-time rights, all rights and second serial (reprint) rights. Submit seasonal/holiday material 4 months in advance. Reports in 2 weeks on queries; 2 months on mss. Free sample copy and writer's guidelines for #10 SASE.
Nonfiction: General interest, historical/nostalgic, how-to, interview/profile, personal experience, photo feature and travel. No "fan" style articles. Buys 75-80 mss/year. Query with or without published clips. No set word length. Pays 6-8¢/word.
Photos: State availability of photos or send photos with query. Reviews 35mm transparencies and 3×5, 5×7 and 8×10 b&w and color prints. Pays $50-150 for transparencies; $25-50 for b&w prints; and $50-150 for color prints. Identification of subjects required. Buys one-time rights and all rights.
Fiction: Ethnic and humorous. Buys 3-5 mss/year. Query. No set word length. Pays 6-8¢/word.
Tips: "We would prefer that articles be informational, based on personal experience or an interview with lots of quotes from subject, profile, humor, etc."

B-SIDE, B-Side Publishing, P.O. Box 1860, Burlington NJ 08016. (609)387-9424. Editor: Carol Schutzbank. Managing Editor: Sandra Garcia. 35% freelance written. A bimonthly tabloid on entertainment. *"B-Side* offers an alternative look at alternative music. It delivers in-depth interviews and intelligent reviews. It bridges the gap between larger more 'commercial' publications and grass roots, 'gonzo-styled' home grown fanzines." Circ. 11,000. Byline given. Buys first rights. Reports in 1 month on queries; 3 months on ms. Sample copy $3. Writer's guidelines for #10 SASE.
Nonfiction: Essays, exposé, humor, interview/profile, new product, opinion, personal experience, photo feature and technical. Query with published clips. Length: 300-2,000 words. Pays up to $25 for assigned articles but pays in copies for unsolicited mss. State availability of photos with submission. Reviews contact sheets. Offers no additional payment for photos accepted with ms. Identification of subjects required. Buys one-time rights.

‡CD REVIEW, WGE Publishing, Forest Road, Box 278, Hancock NH 03449. (603)525-4201. Editorial Director: Dick Lewis. Executive Editor: Larry Canale. 50% freelance written. Monthly magazine on compact disc recordings and hardware. Estab. 1984. Circ. 120,000. Pays on publication. Publishes ms an average of 3 months after acceptance. Byline given. Offers 20% kill fee. Buys first North American serial rights. Submit seasonal/holiday material 3 months in advance. Query for electronic submissions. Reports in 2 weeks. Sample copy for 8½×11 SAE; writer's guidelines for #10 SASE.
Nonfiction: Interview/profile. Buys 50 mss/year. Query with published clips. Length: 500-2,500 words. Pays $50-600. Sometimes pays expenses of writers on assignment.
Photos: State availability of photos with submission. Reviews contact sheets and transparencies. Offers $50-100 per photo. Identification of subjects required. Buys one-time rights.
Columns/Departments: Classical Critique; Rock Report; 17th Bit. Buys 12 mss/year. Query with published clips. Length: 750-1,000 words. Pays $250-350.

GUITAR PLAYER MAGAZINE, GPI Publications, 20085 Stevens Creek, Cupertino CA 95014. (408)446-1105. Editor: Tom Wheeler. 70% freelance written. Monthly magazine for persons "interested in guitars, guitarists, manufacturers, guitar builders, bass players, equipment, careers, etc." Circ. 150,000. Buys first serial and limited reprint rights. **Pays on acceptance.** Publishes ms an average of 3 months after acceptance. Byline given. Reports in 6 weeks. Free sample copy; writer's guidelines for #10 SASE.
Nonfiction: Publishes "wide variety of articles pertaining to guitars and guitarists: interviews, guitar craftsmen profiles, how-to features—anything amateur and professional guitarists would find fascinating and/or helpful. On interviews with 'name' performers, be as technical as possible regarding strings, guitars, techniques, etc. We're not a pop culture magazine, but a magazine for musicians." Also buys features on such subjects as a guitar museum, role of the guitar in elementary education, personal reminiscences of past greats, technical gadgets and how to work them, analysis of flamenco, etc. Buys 30-40 mss/year. Query. Length: open. Pays $100-300. Sometimes pays expenses of writers on assignment.
Photos: Reviews b&w glossy prints. Pays $50-100. Buys 35mm color transparencies. Pays $250 (for cover only). Buys one time rights.

‡HIT PARADER, Charlton Publishing, 441 Lexington Ave. #900, New York NY 10017. (212)370-0986. Editor: Andy Secher. Managing Editor: Anne Leighton. 5% freelance written. Monthly magazine covering heavy metal music. "We look for writers who have access to the biggest names in heavy metal music." Estab. 1948. Circ. 100,000. Pays on publication. Publishes ms an average of 4 months after acceptance. Byline given. Negotiable kill fee. Buys all right. Submit seasonal material 4 months in advance. Reports in 1 month on queries. Sample copy for 9×12 SAE with 5 first class stamps.

Nonfiction: General interest and interview/profile. Buys 3-5 mss/year. Query with published clips. Length: 600-800 words. Pays $75-140.

Photos: Reviews transparencies, 5×7 and 8×10 b&w prints and Kodachrome 64 slides. Offers $25-200 per photo. Buys one-time rights.

Tips: "Interview big names in metal, get published in other publications. We don't take chances on new writers."

ILLINOIS ENTERTAINER, Suite 150, 2250 E. Devon, Des Plaines IL 60018. (708)298-9333. FAX: (708)298-7973. Editor: Michael C. Harris. 95% freelance written. Prefers to work with published/established writers but open to new writers with "style." Monthly tabloid covering music and entertainment for consumers within 100-mile radius of Chicago. Estab. 1975. Circ. 80,000. Pays on publication. Publishes ms an average of 2 months after acceptance. Byline given. Offers 10% kill fee. Buys one-time rights. Simultaneous queries OK. Reports in 1 month on queries; 2 months on mss. Sample copy $5.

Nonfiction: Interview/profile (of entertainment figures). No Q&A interviews. Buys 75 mss/year. Query with published clips. Length: 500-2,000 words. Pays $15-100. Sometimes pays expenses of writers on assignment.

Photos: State availability of photos. Pays $20-30 for 5×7 or 8×10 b&w prints; $125 for color cover photo, both on publication only. Captions and identification of subjects required.

Columns/Departments: Software (record reviews stress record over band or genre). Buys 50 mss/year. Query with published clips. Length: 150-250 words. Pays $6-20.

Tips: "Send clips (published or unpublished) with phone number, and be patient. Full staff has seniority, but if you know the ins and outs of the entertainment biz, and can balance that knowledge with a broad sense of humor, then you'll have a chance. Also, *IE* is more interested in alternative music than the pop-pap you can hear/read about everywhere else."

INTERNATIONAL MUSICIAN, American Federation of Musicians, Suite 600, Paramount Building, 1501 Broadway, New York NY 10036. (212)869-1330. Editor: Kelly L. Castleberry II. 10% freelance written. Prefers to work with published/established writers. Monthly for professional musicians. Estab. 1900. **Pays on acceptance.** Publishes ms an average of 3 months after acceptance. Byline given. Reports in 2 months.

Nonfiction: Articles on prominent instrumental musicians (classical, jazz, rock or country). Send complete ms. Length: 1,500 words.

THE LISTEN AGAIN MUSIC NEWSLETTER, Listen Again Music, 165 Beaver St., New Brighton PA 15066. Editor: William E. Watson. 50% freelance written. Monthly newsletter on songwriting. "The newsletter seeks to improve songwriter's and musician's understanding of how to break into the music business, how to increase their income, with specific tips." Estab. 1986. Circ. 1,100. **Pays on acceptance.** Byline sometimes given. Offers $25 kill fee. Buys one-time rights. Submit seasonal/holiday material 3 months in advance. Reports in 2 weeks on queries; 1 month on manuscripts. Sample copy $5 (note: 2 samples are sent). Free writer's guidelines.

Nonfiction: How-to (improve demos and improve songwriting), personal experience (related to music, either writing or playing) and technical (article should show how new equipment can improve a songwriter's product). "No articles about rock stars or articles that are too general." Buys 24 mss/year. Send complete ms. Length: 500-800 words. Pays $25-75.

Columns/Departments Demo Tips (specific ways to improve the sound quality of a demo tape); Writing Tips (specific ways to improve songwriting abilities). Buys 24 mss/year. Send complete ms. Length: 500-800 words. Pays $25-75.

Tips: "Writing about music can be boring. All articles submitted should have some humor to lighten things up but *must* teach our readers something about music. For the past two years all articles have been staff-written. We want to open up to outside writers but don't want to change the slant we started with. Study samples and guidelines *thoroughly*. Be open to rewriting."

THE MISSISSIPPI RAG, "The Voice of Traditional Jazz and Ragtime," 6500 Nicollet Ave. S, Minneapolis MN 55423. (612)861-2446 or (612)920-0312. Editor: Leslie Johnson. 70% freelance written. Works with small number of new/unpublished writers each year. A monthly tabloid covering traditional jazz and ragtime. Estab. 1973. Circ. 3,500. Pays on publication. Publishes ms an average of 4 months after acceptance. Byline given. Buys all rights, "but writer may negotiate if he wishes to use material later." Submit seasonal/holiday material 3 months in advance. Sample copy and writer's guidelines for 9×12 SAE with 85¢ postage.

Nonfiction: Historical, interview/profile, personal experience, photo features, current jazz and ragtime, festival coverage, book reviews and record reviews. Reviews are always assigned. No "long-winded essays on jazz or superficial pieces on local ice cream social Dixieland bands." Buys 24-30 mss/year. Query with or without published clips, or send complete ms. Length: 1,500-4,000 words. Pays 1½¢/word.

Photos: Send photos with submission. Prefers b&w 5×7 or 8×10 prints. Offers $4 minimum per photo. Identification of subjects required. Buys one-time rights.

Columns/Departments: Book and Record reviews. Buys 60 assigned mss/year. Query with published clips. Pays 1½¢/word.

Tips: "Become familiar with the jazz world. The *Rag* is read by musicians, jazz/ragtime writers, historians and jazz/ragtime buffs. We want articles that have depth—solid facts and a good basic grasp of jazz and/or ragtime history. Not for the novice jazz writer. Interviews with jazz and ragtime performers are most open to freelancers. It's wise to query first because we have already covered so many performers."

MODERN DRUMMER, 870 Pompton Ave., Cedar Grove NJ 07009. (201)239-4140. Editor-in-Chief: Ronald Spagnardi. Features Editor: William F. Miller. Managing Editor: Rick Van Horn. Monthly for "student, semi-pro and professional drummers at all ages and levels of playing ability, with varied specialized interests within the field." 60% freelance written. Circ. 85,000. Pays on publication. Publishes ms an average of 3 months after acceptance. Buys all rights. Previously published submissions OK. Reports in 1 month. Sample copy $3.95; free writer's guidelines.

Nonfiction: How-to, informational, interview, new product, personal experience and technical. "All submissions must appeal to the specialized interests of drummers." Buys 20-30 mss/year. Query or submit complete ms. Length: 5,000-8,000 words. Pays $200-500. Pays expenses of writers on assignment.

Photos: Purchased with accompanying ms. Reviews 8×10 b&w prints and color transparencies.

Columns/Departments: Jazz Drummers Workshop, Rock Perspectives, In The Studio, Show Drummers Seminar, Teachers Forum, Drum Soloist, The Jobbing Drummer, Strictly Technique, Book Reviews and Shop Talk. "Technical knowledge of area required for most columns." Buys 40-50 mss/year. Query or submit complete ms. Length: 500-2,500 words. Pays $25-150.

MUSIC EXPRESS, Rock Express Communications., 47 Jefferson Ave., Toronto, Ontario M6K 1Y3 Canada. (416)538-7500. FAX: (416)538-7503. Editor: Perry Stern. Managing Editor: Keith Sharp. 50% freelance written. Monthly magazine on contemporary music. "A contemporary consumer music magazine covering all forms of popular music slanted at a demographic between 18-25 with equal appeal for male and female readers." Estab. 1975. Circ. 678,000. Pays 30 days after publication. Byline given. Offers 20% kill fee. Buys first North American serial rights. Submit seasonal/holiday material 2 months in advance. Simultaneous submissions OK. Reports in 6 weeks on queries; 1 month on mss.

Nonfiction: Humor, interview/profile and photo feature. Spring Audio Special; Summer Special Activities; Special College Issue; and Fall Audio Special. Buys 18 mss/year. Query. Length: 500-3,000 words. Pays $75-1,000. Sometimes pays expenses of writers on assignment.

Photos: State availability of photos with submission. Reviews transparencies and 5×7 and 8×10 prints. Offers $35-500 per photo. Captions, model releases and identification of subjects required. Buys one-time rights.

Columns/Departments: Kerry Doole. Regional (local news); Video (latest releases); Specific Music Columns (jazz, country, blues, hard rock); and Film (latest movie releases). Buys 80 mss/year. Query. Length: 200-500 words. Pays $60-250.

MUSIC MAGAZINE, Future Perfect Publishing, P.O. Box 96, Station R, Toronto, Ontario M4G 3Z3 Canada. Publisher: Valerie Fletcher. 90% freelance written. Prefers to work with published/established writers; works with a small number of new/unpublished writers each year. Quarterly magazine emphasizing classical music. Estab. 1978. Circ. 10,000. Pays on publication. Publishes ms an average of 4 months after acceptance. Byline given. Buys first North American rights, one-time rights and second serial (reprint) rights. Submit seasonal/holiday material 4 months in advance. Previously published submissions (book excerpts) OK. Query for electronic submissions. Reports in 2 months. Sample copy and writer's guidelines for 9×12 SAE and $3.

Nonfiction: Interview, historical articles, photo feature and profile. "All articles should pertain to classical music and people in that world. We do not want any academic analysis or short pieces of family experiences in classical music." Query with published clips; phone queries OK. Unsolicited articles will not be returned. Length: 1,500-3,500 words. Pays $100-500 Canadian funds. Sometimes pays expenses of writers on assignment.

Photos: State availability of photos. Pays $15-25 for 8×10 b&w glossy prints or contact sheets; $100 for transparencies. No posed promotion photos. "Candid, lively material only." Captions required. Buys one-time rights.

Tips: "Send a sample of your writing with suggested subjects. Off-beat subjects are welcome but must be thoroughly interesting to be considered. A famous person or major subject in music are your best bets."

MUSICAL AMERICA, 825 7th Ave., New York NY 10019. FAX: (212)586-1364. Editor: Shirley Fleming. 50% freelance written. Bimonthly. Circ. 20,000. Pays on publication. Publishes ms an average of 3-4 months after acceptance. Buys all rights. Free sample copy and writer's guidelines.

Nonfiction: Articles on classical music and classical record reviews are generally prepared by acknowledged writers and authorities in the field, but uses freelance material. Query with published clips. Length: 2,000 words maximum. Pays $300 minimum.

Photos: New b&w and color photos of musical personalities, events, etc.

‡**MUSICIAN**, Billboard Publications, 1515 Broadway, 39th Floor, New York NY 10036. (212)536-5208. Editor: Bill Flanagan. Managing Editor: Matt Resnicoff. 85% freelance written. Monthly magazine covering contemporary music, especially rock, pop and jazz. Estab. 1976. Circ. 170,000. Pays on publication. Byline given. Offers kill fee of 25-33%. Buys first North American serial rights. Submit seasonal/holiday material 3 months in advance.

Nonfiction: All music-related: book excerpts, exposé, historical, how-to (recording and performing), humor, interview/profile, new product and technical. Buys 150 mss/year. Query with published clips. Length: 300-10,000 words. Payment negotiable. Pays expenses of writers on assignment.

Photos: Assigns photo shoots. Uses some stock. Offers $50-300 per photo.

Columns/Departments: Jazz (jazz artists or works), 1,000-5,000 words; Reviews (record reviews), 300-500 words; Faces (short, newsy stories), 300 words; and Working Musician (technical "trade" angles on musicians), 1,000-3,000 words. Query with published clips. Length 300-1,500 words.

Tips: "Be aware of special music writers' style; don't gush, be somewhat skeptical; get the best quotes you can and save the arcane criticism for reviews; know and apply Strunk and White; be interesting. Please send *published* clips; we don't want to be anyone's first publication. Our writing is considered excellent (in all modesty), even though we don't pay as much as we'd like. We recognize National Writers Union."

‡**THE NOTE, The Midwest Guide to Music and Entertainment**, Noteworthy Productions, 735½ New Hampshire, Lawrence KS 66044. (913)843-6561. Editor: Patrick Quinn. Music Editor: Steve Ozark. 50% freelance written. Monthly tabloid covering music/music industry. "The *Note* covers the entire spectrum of rock 'n' roll in the Midwest—mainstream, college, alternative, metal, rap, you name it. Our readership is composed of savvy music fans and working musicians who are interested in what's happening *right now* in the industry, with a particular emphasis on the action in the Midwest." Estab. 1985. Circ. 45,000. Pays on publication. Publishes ms an average of 3 months after acceptance. Byline given. Buys one-time rights. Submit seasonal/holiday material 3 months in advance. Reports in 1 month. Sample copy $1. Writer's guidelines for #10 SAE with 1 first class stamp.

Nonfiction: Exposé, interview/profile, new product and technical. "No 'my life on the road with the band' articles." Buys 30-40 mss/year. Query with or without published clips, or send complete ms. Length: 250-2,000 words. Pays $10-300 for assigned articles; $10-200 for unsolicited articles. Pays in contributor's copies or filler material. Sometimes pays expenses of writers on assignment.

Photos: Send photos with submission. Reviews contact sheets and 4×5 prints. Offers $5 per photo. Captions and identification of subjects required. Buys one-time rights.

Columns/Departments: Record Reviews (new releases, all formats—(CD, LP, cassette), 250-350 words; Books new (music/music industry), 250-350 words. Buys 30 mss/year. Query with published clips. Length: 300-500 words. Pays $10-50.

Fillers: Newsbreaks. Buys 20/year. Length: 250 words. Pays $5-10.

Tips: "We're particularly interested in interview/profile pieces (with art) on acts touring the Kansas/Missouri markets. We preview shows—we rarely if ever, review shows—so catch them on their way here and let us know what to look forward to. We're beginning a technical/equipment section this year, so we're interersted in consumer and commercial equipment reviews. We also run industry-related book reviews. Query first; with published clips if available. Record reviews are the best way to break in. We're interested in brand new releases. Don't be afraid to have an opinion, but don't try to sound like Robert Christgau—we're not particularly interested in the long-range sociological impact of a new album. Our readers just want to know if it bops. Reviews of demo tapes from unsigned bands are OK *as long as the act is touring this market.*"

ONE SHOT, Attentive Writing for Neglected Rock 'N' Roll, One Shot Enterprises, P.O. Box 1284, Cincinnati OH 45201. Editor: Steve Rosen. 80% freelance written. Eager to work with new/unpublished writers. "*One Shot* is a quarterly magazine dedicated to remembering now-obscure or under-appreciated performers of rock and related musics; expecially the one-hit wonders. Uses interviews, essays and journalism." Estab. 1985. Circ. 200. Pays on publication. Publishes ms up to 1 year after acceptance. Byline given. Buys one-time, second serial (reprint) or simultaneous rights, and makes work-for-hire assignments. Simultaneous and previously published submissions OK. Reports in 1 month. Sample copy $3. Writer's guidelines for #10 SASE.

Nonfiction: Book excerpts, essays, exposé, general interest, historical/nostalgic, interview/profile, opinion, personal experience and travel. No religious/inspirational articles. Buys 16 mss/year. Query. Length: 2,500 maximum words. Pays up to $100 maximum for assigned articles. Pays with copies for nonjournalism work. Sometimes pays expenses of writers on assignment.

Photos: State availability of photos with submission. Reviews contact sheets and 8½×11 prints. Offers additional payment for photos accepted with ms. Buys one-time rights.

Columns/Departments: Speak, Memory! (personal experiences with now-obscure rock, etc., performers); and Travel (update on a place that once figured in a rock song, or performer's career, such as "Hitsville USA" studios in Detroit). Buys 10 mss/year. Query with or without published clips or send complete ms. Length: 1,000 maximum words. Pays about $50.

Tips: *"One Shot* needs 'Where are They Now' articles on obscure and neglected rock performers who once were popular. Those pieces should include interviews with the performer and others; and provide a sense of 'being there'. *One Shot* will pay for such stories. Just send me a note explaining your interests, and I'll respond with detailed suggestions. I won't disqualify anyone for not following procedures; I want to encourage a body of work on this topic. Also looking for remembrances, travel pieces, concerning neglected rock."

OPERA CANADA, Suite 433, 366 Adelaide St. E., Toronto, Ontario M5A 3X9 Canada. (416)363-0395. Editor: Harvey Chusid. 80% freelance written. Prefers to work with published/established writers. Quarterly magazine for readers who are interested in serious music; specifically, opera. Estab. 1960. Circ. 7,000. Pays on publication. Byline given. Not copyrighted. Buys first serial rights. Simultaneous submissions OK. Reports on material accepted for publication within 1 year. Sample copy $4.25.

Nonfiction: "Because we are Canada's only opera magazine, we like to keep 75% of our content Canadian, i.e., by Canadians or about Canadian personalities and events. We prefer informative and/or humorous articles about any aspect of music theater, with an emphasis on opera. The relationship of the actual subject matter to opera can be direct or indirect. We accept interviews with major operatic personalities. Please, no reviews of performances; we have staff reviewers." Query or submit complete ms. Length (for all articles except reviews of books and records): 1,000-3,000 words. Pays $50-200.

Photos: Photos with cutlines (i.e. captions) to accompany mss are welcome. No additional payment for photos used with mss. Captions required.

Tips: "We are interested in articles with an emphasis on current or controversial issues in opera."

‡PULSE!, Tower Records, 2500 Del Monte, Building C W., Sacramento CA 95691. (916)373-2450. Editor: Mike Farrace. Contact: Laurie MacIntosh. 90% freelance written. Works with a small number of new/unpublished writers each year. Monthly tabloid covering recorded music. Estab. 1983. Circ. 200,000. Pays on publication. Publishes ms an average of 2 months after acceptance. Byline given. Buys first serial rights. Reports in 5 weeks. Sample copy for 12×15 SAE and 8 first class stamps; writer's guidelines for SAE.

Nonfiction: Feature stories and interview/profile (angled toward artist's taste in music, such as 10 favorite albums, first record ever bought, anecdotes about early record buying experiences). Always looking for concise news items and commentary about nonpopular musical genres. Buys 200-250 mss/year. Query or send complete ms. Length: 200-2,500 words. Pays $20-1,000. Sometimes pays expenses of writers on assignment.

Photos: State availability of photos. Transparencies preferred, but will also review b&w prints. Caption and identification of subjects required. Buys one-time rights.

Fillers: Newsbreaks.

Tips: "Break in with 200- to 400-word news-oriented stories on recording artists or on fast breaking, record-related news, personnel changes, unusual match-ups, reissues of great material. Any kind of music. The more obscure genres on independent labels are the hardest for us to cover, so they stand a good chance of being used. Remember, we are not only a magazine about records, but one that is owned by a record retailer."

RELIX MAGAZINE, Music for the Mind, Box 94, Brooklyn NY 11229. Editor: Toni A. Brown. 60% freelance written. Eager to work with new/unpublished writers. Bimonthly magazine covering rock 'n' roll music and specializing in Grateful Dead and other San Francisco and '60's related groups for readers ages 15-45. Circ. 31,000. Pays on publication. Publishes ms an average of 6 months after acceptance. Byline given. Buys all rights. Sample copy $3.

Nonfiction: Historical/nostalgic, interview/profile, new product, personal experience, photo feature and technical. Special issues include year-end special. Query with published clips if available or send complete ms. Length open. Pays $1.75/column inch.

Columns/Departments: Query with published clips, if available, or send complete ms. Length: open. Pays variable rates.

Tips: "The most rewarding aspects of working with freelance writers are fresh writing and new outlooks."

‡ROCK & ROLL DISC, TAG Enterprises, P.O. Box 17601, Memphis TN 38187-0601. Editor: Tom Graves. 20% freelance written. A monthly magazine devoted to reviews and news about compact discs. "We review current compact discs relating to rock and roll. Our market is CD buyers who listen to rock and roll primarily. *Rock & Roll Disc* wants to publish the most informed and inspired music writing possible." Estab. 1987. Circ. 5,000. Pays on publication. Publishes ms an average of 2 months after acceptance. Byline given. Buys all rights. Submis seasonal/holiday material 3 months in advance. Reports in 1 month on queries and manuscripts only if accompanied by SASE. Sample copy mailed for three first class stamps.

Nonfiction: Interviews with rock personalities and reviews of compact discs, plus special features. Buys 100 mss/year. Query with two published music-related clips. Length: 200-2,000 words. Pays $10-50 depending on assignment.

Tips: "The writer needs to know the compact disc market and know rock music intimately. Don't bother if you don't, because knowledge can't be faked. Don't overwhelm editor with too many writing samples. Send only two and make sure they are music-related. Also, many writers don't bother to include an SASE. When that happens we don't bother to reply. Including a checklist on queries is most helpful since it saves the editor valuable time."

THE ROCK HALL REPORTER, Big "O" Publications, P.O.Box 24124, Cleveland OH 44124. Editor: Professor Witt. Managing Editor: Martha L. Rutty. 50% freelance written. Bimonthly newsletter on the Rock and Roll Hall of Fame. Estab. 1989. Circ. 10,000. Pays on publication. Publishes ms an average of 1 month after acceptance. Sometimes offers byline. Offers 25% kill fee. Makes work-for-hire assignments. Submit seasonal/holiday material 3 months in advance. Reports in 6 weeks on queries; 2 months on mss. Sample copy $2 with 9 × 12 SAE and 2 first class stamps.

Nonfiction: Essays, exposé, general interest, historical/nostalgic, humor, interview/profile, new product, opinion, personal experience, photo feature, technical, travel and other—inside stories on Rock Hall of Fame. "No fiction." Buys 10 mss/year. Send complete ms. Length: 150-500 words. Pays $25-500 for assigned articles; $25-200 for unsolicited articles. Sometimes pays expenses of writers on assignments.

Photos: Send photos with submission. Offers no additional payment for photos accepted with ms. Identification of subjects required. Buys all rights.

THE $ENSIBLE SOUND, 403 Darwin Dr., Snyder NY 14226. Publisher: John A. Horan. 80% freelance written. Eager to work with new/unpublished writers. Quarterly magazine. "All readers are high fidelity enthusiasts, and many have a high fidelity industry-related job." Circ. 6,900. **Pays on acceptance.** Publishes ms an average of 3-6 months after acceptance. Byline given. Buys all rights. Simultaneous and previously published submissions OK. Reports in 2 weeks. Sample copy $2, or free with writing sample, outline, ideas.

Nonfiction: Exposé; how-to; general interest; humor; historical; interview (people in hi-fi business, manufacturers or retail); new product (all types of new audio equipment); nostalgia (articles and opinion on older equipment); personal experience (with various types of audio equipment); photo feature (on installation, or how-to tips); profile (of hi-fi equipment); and technical (pertaining to audio). "Subjective evaluations of hi-fi equipment make up 70% of our publication. We will accept 10 per issue." Buys 8 mss/year. Submit outline. Pays $25 maximum. Pays expenses of writers on assignment.

Columns/Departments: Bits & Pieces (short items of interest to hi-fi hobbyists); Ramblings (do-it-yourself tips on bettering existing systems); and Record Reviews (of records which would be of interest to audiophiles and recordings of an unusual nature). Query. Length: 25-400 words. Pays $10/page.

‡SH-BOOM, The Best of Then and Now, LFP Inc., Suite 300, 9171 Wilshire Blvd., Beverly Hills CA 90210. (213)858-7155. Editor: Jim Dawson. 90% freelance written. Bimonthly magazine covering 50s, 60s, early 70s rock 'n' roll, film and TV. "We are geared to the baby boom audience 24 to 60." Estab. 1989. Circ. 100,000. **Pays on acceptance.** Publishes ms an average of 2-4 months after acceptance. Byline given. Offers 20% kill fee. Buys first rights. Previously published submissions OK "if they appeared in small newsletters or fan club magazines." Reports in 3 weeks. Sample copy for 10 × 13 SAE.

Nonfiction: Expose, historical/nostalgic, interview/profile, photo feature. "No profiles that lack first-hand quotes from the subject. Also, we don't record collector articles." Query with published clips or send complete ms. Length: 1,000-2,000 words. Pays $200-500. Pays expenses of writers on assignment.

Photos: State availability or send photos with submission. Reviews any size transparencies or 8 × 10 prints. Offers no additional payment for photos accepted with ms. Captions required. Buys one-time rights.

Columns/Departments: One Step Beyond (profile of artist who had a great influence on rock 'n' roll, with quotes from famous people. Past profiles include T-Bone Walker, Big Joe Turner and Johnny Ace.) 1,000 words. Buys 2-3 mss/year. Query. Pays $100-200.

Tips: "We're looking for in-depth interviews with entertainment figures from the 50s, 60s, and early 70s, but we don't want fluff pieces. We want to know the nuts and bolts, how things got done, how they came up with hit songs and records, how they got ripped off and how fame and fortune can backfire. Any copy of *Sh-Boom* should give you an idea of stuff we're looking for."

SONG HITS, Charlton Publications, 60 Division St., Derby CT 06418. (203)735-3381. Editor: Mary Jane Canetti. 60% freelance written. Works with a small number of new/unpublished writers each year. A bimonthly magazine covering recording artists—rock, heavy metal. "*Song Hits* readers are between the ages of 10 and 21. Our philosophy in writing is to gear our material toward what is currently popular with our audience." Estab. 1942. Circ. 100,000. Pays on publication. Publishes ms an average of 3 months after acceptance. Byline given. Buys all rights. Simultaneous submissions OK. Reports in 2 weeks. Free sample copy.

Nonfiction: Interview/profile. Query with published clips. Length: 1,250-3,000 words.
Photos: State availability of photos with submission. Reviews 2×2 transparencies and 8×10 prints. Identification of subjects required. Buys one-time rights.
Columns/Departments: Concert Review (current reviews of popular touring groups), and Pick of the Litter (album reviews of current and/or up and coming talent; 8-10 per issue). Query with published clips. Length: 500-1,000 words.

STEREO REVIEW, Diamandis Communications, Inc., 1633 Broadway, New York NY 10019. (212)767-6000. Editor-in-Chief: Louise Boundas. Music Editor: Christie Barter. Executive Editor: Michael Smolen. 65% freelance written, almost entirely by established contributing editors, and on assignment. A monthly magazine. Circ. 600,000. **Pays on acceptance.** Publishes ms an average of 5 months after acceptance. Byline given. Buys first North American rights or all rights. Sample copy for 9×12 SAE with $1.24 postage.
Nonfiction: Equipment and music reviews, how-to-buy, how-to-use, stereo and interview/profile. Buys approximately 25 mss/year. Query with published clips. Length: 1,500-3,000 words. Pays $500-800 for assigned articles.

TRADITION, Prairie Press, Box 438, Walnut IA 51577. (712)366-1136. Editor: Robert Everhart. 20% freelance written. Bimonthly magazine emphasizing traditional country music and other aspects of pioneer living. Circ. 2,500. Pays on publication. Not copyrighted. Byline given. Buys one-time rights. Submit seasonal/holiday material 6 months in advance. Simultaneous queries, and simultaneous and previously published submissions OK. Reports in 1 month. Sample copy for $1 to cover postage and handling.
Nonfiction: Historical (relating to country music); how-to (play, write, or perform country music); inspirational (on country gospel); interview (with traditional country performers,); nostalgia (pioneer living); personal experience (country music); and travel (in connection with country music contests or festivals). Query. Length: 800-1,200 words. Pays $10-15.
Photos: State availability of photos with query. Payment included in ms price. Reviews 5×7 b&w prints. Captions and model releases required. Buys one-time rights.
Poetry: Free verse and traditional. Buys 4 poems/year. Length: 5-20 lines. Submit maximum 2 poems with SASE. Pays $2-5.
Fillers: Clippings, jokes and anecdotes. Buys 5/year. Length: 15-50 words. Pays $5-10.
Tips: "Material must be concerned with what we term 'real' country music as opposed to today's 'pop' country music. Freelancer must be knowledgable of the subject; many writers don't even know who the father of country music is, let alone write about him."

‡**THE WASHINGTON OPERA**, Kennedy Center, Washington DC 20566. (202)416-7815. Editor: Eleanor Forrer. Managing Editor: Paul Dupree. 60% freelance written. Bimonthly magazine covering opera. "Highlights opera performances in and around the Washington DC area, and specifically productions at Kennedy Center by The Washington Opera." Estab. 1974. Circ. 50,000. Pays on publication. Publishes ms an average of 2 months after acceptance. Byline given. Buys first rights, one-time rights and second serial (reprint) rights. Submit seasonal/holiday material 2 months in advance. Simultaneous and previously published submissions OK. Query for electronic submissions. Reports in 2 weeks. Sample copy for 8½×11 SAE with 2 first class stamps.
Nonfiction: Book excerpts, essays, exposé, general interest, historical/nostalgic, how-to, humor, inspirational, interview/profile, new product, opinion personal experience, photo feature, religious, technical and travel. Buys 20 mss/year. Query with published clips. Length: 500-2,500 words. Pays $200-1,500 for assigned articles; $200-1,000 for unsolicited articles. Sometimes pays in contributor's copies or other premiums. Sometimes pays expenses of writers on assignment.
Photos: State availability of photos with submission. Reviews transparencies. Offers $50-200 per photo. Captions, model releases and identification of subjects required. Buys one-time rights.

Mystery

These magazines buy fictional accounts of crime, detective work and mystery. Additional mystery markets can be found in the Literary and "Little" section. Skim through other sections to identify markets for fiction; some will consider mysteries.

ALFRED HITCHCOCK'S MYSTERY MAGAZINE, Davis Publications, Inc., 380 Lexington Ave., New York NY 10017. Editor: Cathleen Jordan. Magazine published 13 times a year emphasizing mystery fiction. Circ. 225,000. **Pays on acceptance.** Byline given. Buys first serial rights, second serial (reprint) rights and foreign rights. Submit seasonal/holiday material 7 months in advance. Reports in 2 months. Writer's guidelines for SASE.
Fiction: Original and well-written mystery and crime fiction. Length: up to 14,000 words.

ELLERY QUEEN'S MYSTERY MAGAZINE, Davis Publications, Inc., 380 Lexington Ave., New York NY 10017. Editor: Eleanor Sullivan. 100% freelance written. Magazine published 13 times/year. Estab. 1941. Circ. 375,000. **Pays on acceptance.** Publishes ms an average of 6 months after acceptance. Byline given. Buys first serial rights or second serial (reprint) rights. Submit seasonal/holiday material 7 months in advance. Simultaneous and previously published submissions OK. Reports in 1 month. Writer's guidelines for #10 SASE.

Fiction: Special consideration will be given to "anything timely and original. We publish every type of mystery: the suspense story, the psychological study, the deductive puzzle—the gamut of crime and detection from the realistic (including stories of police procedure) to the more imaginative (including 'locked rooms' and impossible crimes). We always need detective stories, and do not want sex, sadism or sensationalism-for-the-sake-of-sensationalism." No gore or horror; seldom publishes parodies or pastiches. Buys up to 13 mss/issue. Length: 6,000 words maximum; occasionally higher but not often. Pays 3-8¢/word.

Tips: "We have a Department of First Stories to encourage writers whose fiction has never before been in print. We publish an average of 13 first stories a year."

Nature, Conservation and Ecology

These publications—probably the fastest-growing category during the past year—promote reader awareness of the natural environment, wildlife, nature preserves and ecosystems. Many of these "green magazines" also concentrate on recycling and related issues. They do not publish recreation or travel articles except as they relate to conservation or nature. Other markets for this kind of material can be found in the Regional; Sports; and Travel, Camping and Trailer categories, although magazines listed there require that nature or conservation articles be slanted to their specialized subject matter and audience. Some juvenile and teen publications also buy nature-related material for young audiences.

AMERICAN FORESTS, American Forestry Association, 1516 P St. NW, Washington DC 20005. (202)667-3300. Editor: Bill Rooney. 70% freelance written. Bimonthly magazine. "The magazine of trees and forests, published by a citizens' organization for the advancement of intelligent management and use of our forests, soil, water, wildlife and all other natural resources necessary for an environment of high quality." Circ. 30,000. **Pays on acceptance.** Publishes ms an average of 8 months after acceptance. Byline given. Buys one-time rights. Phone queries OK but written queries preferred. Submit seasonal/holiday material 5 months in advance. Reports in 2 months. Sample copy $1.20; writer's guidelines for SASE.

Nonfiction: General interest, historical, how-to, humor and inspirational. All articles should emphasize trees, forests, forestry and related issues. Buys 7-10 mss/issue. Query. Length: 2,000 words. Pays $300-700.

Photos: State availability of photos. Offers no additional payment for photos accompanying ms. Uses 8×10 b&w glossy prints; 35mm or larger transparencies, originals only. Captions required. Buys one-time rights.

Tips: "Query should have honesty and information on photo support."

THE AMICUS JOURNAL, Natural Resources Defense Council, 40 N. 20th St., New York NY 10011. (212)727-2700. Editor: Peter Borrelli. 80% freelance written. Quarterly magazine covering national and international environmental policy. "*The Amicus Journal* is intended to provide the general public with a journal of thought and opinion on environmental affairs, particularly those relating to policies of national and international significance." Estab. 1979. Circ. 120,000. **Pays on acceptance.** Publishes ms an average of 6 months after acceptance. Byline given. Offers 50% kill fee. Buys first North American serial rights. Submit seasonal/holiday material 6 months in advance. Query for electronic submissions. Reports in 6 weeks. Sample copy for 9×12 SAE with 5 first class stamps. Writer's guidelines for #10 SASE.

Nonfiction: Exposé and interview/profile. No articles not concerned with environmental issues of national or international policy significance. Buys 25 mss/year. Query with published clips. Length: 200-1,500 words. Payment negotiable. Sometimes pays expenses of writers on assignment.

Photos: State availability of photos with submssion. Reviews contact sheets, negatives, transparencies and 8×10 prints. Offers negotiable payment for photos. Captions, model releases and identification of subjects required. Buys one-time rights.

Columns/Departments: News and Comment (summary reporting of environmental issues, usually tied to topical items), 200-500 words; Articles (in-depth reporting on issues and personalities), 750-1,500 words; Book Reviews (well-informed essays on books of general interest to environmentalists interested in policy and history), 500-1,000 words. Buys 25 mss/year. Query with published clips. Payment negotiable.

Poetry: Brian Swann, poetry editor. Avant-garde and free verse. All poetry should be rooted in nature. Buys 20 poems/year. Pays $25.

Tips: "Except for editorials, all departments are open to freelance writers. Queries should precede manuscripts, and manuscripts should conform to the *Chicago Manual of Style*. Writers are asked to be sensitive to tone. As a policy magazine, we do not publish articles of a personal or satirical nature."

APPALACHIAN TRAILWAY NEWS, Appalachian Trail Conference, P.O. Box 807, Harpers Ferry WV 25425. (304)535-6331. 50% freelance written. Bimonthly magazine "subject matter must relate to Appalachian Trail." Estab. 1925. Circ. 26,000. **Pays on acceptance.** Byline given. Buys first North American serial rights or second serial (reprint) rights. Previously published submissions OK. Reports in 1 month. Sample copy includes guidelines for $2.50; guidelines only for SASE.

Nonfiction: Essays, general interest, historical/nostalgic, how-to, humor, inspirational, interview/profile, photo feature, technical and travel. No poetry or religious materials. Buys 15-20 mss/year. Query with or without published clips, or send complete ms. Length: 250-3,000 words. Pays $25-300. Pays expenses of writers on assignment. Publishes, but does not pay for "hiking reflections."

Photos: State availability of b&w photos with submission. Reviews contact sheets, negatives and 5 × 7 prints. Offers $25-125 per photo. Identification of subjects required. Negotiates future use by ATC.

Tips: "Contributors should display an obvious knowledge of or interest in the Appalachian Trail. Those who live in the vicinity of the Trail may opt for an assigned story and should present credentials and subject in which interested to the editor."

THE ATLANTIC SALMON JOURNAL, The Atlantic Salmon Federation, Suite 1030, 1435 St. Alexandre, Montreal, Quebec H3A 2G4 Canada. (514)842-8059. Editor: Terry Davis. 50-68% freelance written. Works with a small number of new/unpublished writers each year. A quarterly magazine covering conservation efforts for the Atlantic salmon. Caters to "affluent and responsive audience – the dedicated angler and conservationist of the Atlantic salmon." Circ. 20,000. Pays on publication. Publishes ms an average of 3-6 months after acceptance. Byline given. Buys first serial rights to articles and one-time rights to photos. Submit seasonal/holiday material 3 months in advance. Simultaneous queries and submissions OK. Query for electronic submissions. Reports in 2 months. Sample copy for 9 × 12 SAE and $1 (Canadian), or SAE with IRC; free writer's guidelines.

Nonfiction: Exposé, historical/nostalgic, how-to, humor, interview/profile, new product, opinion, personal experience, photo feature, technical, travel, conservation, cuisine, science, research and management. "We are seeking articles that are pertinent to the focus and purpose of our magazine, which is to inform and entertain our membership on all aspects of the Atlantic salmon and its environment, preservation and conservation." Buys 15-20 mss/year. Query with published clips and state availability of photos. Length: 1,500-3,000 words. Pays $150-300. Sometimes pays the expenses of writers on assignment.

Photos: State availability of photos with query. Pays $50 for 3 × 5 or 5 × 7 b&w prints; $50-100 for 2¼ × 3¼ or 35mm color slides. Captions and identification of subjects required.

Columns/Departments: Adventure Eating (cuisine) and First Person (nonfiction, anecdotal, from first-person viewpoint, can be humorous). Buys about 6 mss/year. Length: 1,000-1,500 words. Pays $100.

Fiction: Adventure, fantasy, historical, humorous and mainstream. "We don't want to see anything that does not deal with Atlantic salmon directly or indirectly. Wilderness adventures are acceptable as long as they deal with Atlantic salmon." Buys 3 ms/year. Query with published clips. Length: 3,000 words maximum. Pays $150-300.

Fillers: Clippings, jokes, anecdotes and short humor. Length: 100-300 words average. Does not pay. Cartoons, single panel, $25-50.

Tips: "We will be buying more consumer oriented articles – travel, equipment. Articles must reflect informed and up-to-date knowledge of Atlantic salmon. Writers need not be authorities, but research must be impeccable. Clear, concise writing is a plus, and submissions must be typed. Anecdote, River Log and photo essays are most open to freelancers. The odds are that a writer without a background in outdoors writing and wildlife reporting will not have the 'informed' angle I'm looking for. Our readership is well-read and critical of simplification and generalization."

AUDUBON, The Magazine of the National Aubudon Society, National Audubon Society, 950 Third Ave., New York NY 10022. FAX: (212)755-3752. Editor: Les Line. 85% freelance written. Bimonthly magazine on conservation, environment and natural history. "We are edited for people who delight in, care about and are willing to fight for the protection of wildlife, natural resources, and the global environment." Estab. 1887. Circ. 430,000. **Pays on acceptance.** Byline given. Offers negotiable kill fee, but prefers not to use. Buys first North American serial rights; first rights and second serial (reprint) rights (rarely). Query for electronic submissions. Reports in 3 months. Sample copy $4 with 8½ × 11 SAE and $2.40 in postage. Free writer's guidelines.

Nonfiction: Book excerpts (well in advance of publication), essays, exposé, historical, humor, interview/profile, opinion and photo feature. "No poorly written, ill-researched or duplicative articles; things that sound as if they were written for a small-town newspaper or encyclopedia." Length: 250-4,000 words. Pays $250-2,500. Pays expenses of writers on assignment.

Photos: Reviews 35mm transparencies. Offers page rates per photo on publication. Caption info and identification of subjects required. Write for photo guidelines.
Fiction: Appropriate to our audience. Send complete ms. Length: 500-3,000 words. Pays $250-2,000.
Tips: "Because we are presently overstocked, we are not actively soliciting freelance submissions. However, a *good* story, *well* written, always seems to find room. But, please, study the magazine carefully before querying. And be advised that we have recently shifted the emphasis away from nature appreciation and natural history and more toward environmental issues."

BIRD WATCHER'S DIGEST, Pardson Corp., P.O. Box 110, Marietta OH 45750. Editor: Mary Beacom Bowers. 60% freelance written. Works with a small number of new/unpublished writers each year. Bimonthly magazine covering natural history—birds and bird watching. "*BWD* is a nontechnical magazine interpreting ornithological material for amateur observers, including the knowledgeable birder, the serious novice and the backyard bird watcher; we strive to provide good reading and good ornithology." Estab. 1978. Circ. 80,000. Pays on publication. Publishes ms an average of 1 year after acceptance. Byline given. Buys one-time rights, first serial rights and second serial (reprint) rights. Submit seasonal/holiday material 6 months in advance. Previously published submissions OK. Reports in 6 weeks. Sample copy $3; writer's guidelines for #10 SASE.
Nonfiction: Book excerpts, how-to (relating to birds, feeding and attracting, etc.), humor, personal experience and travel (limited—we get many). "We are especially interested in fresh, lively accounts of closely observed bird behavior and displays and of bird watching experiences and expeditions. We often need material on less common species or on unusual or previously unreported behavior of common species." No articles on pet or caged birds; none on raising a baby bird. Buys 75-90 mss/year. Send complete ms. Length: 600-3,500 words. Pays $25-50 minimum.
Photos: Send photos with ms. Pays $10 minimum for b&w prints; $25 minimum for transparencies. Buys one-time rights.
Poetry: Avant-garde, free verse, light verse and traditional. No haiku. Buys 12-18 poems/year. Submit maximum 3 poems. Length 8-20 lines. Pays $10.
Tips: "We are aimed at an audience ranging from the backyard bird watcher to the very knowledgeable birder; we include in each issue material that will appeal at various levels. We always strive for a good geographical spread, with material from every section of the country. We leave very technical matters to others, but we want facts and accuracy, depth and quality, directed at the veteran bird watcher and at the enthusiastic novice. We stress the joys and pleasures of bird watching, its environmental contribution, and its value for the individual and society."

‡**BUZZWORM, The Environmental Journal**, Buzzworm Inc., 1818 16th St., Boulder CO 80302. Editor: Joseph E. Daniel. Managing Editor: Elizabeth Darby Junkin. 75% freelance written. Bimonthly magazine. Estab. 1988. Circ. 75,000. Pays within 90 days of publication. Byline given. Buys first world serial rights, first rights or all rights. Submit seasonal/holiday material 6 months in advance. Reports in 1 month on queries; 2 months on mss. Sample copy $3.50 with 9 × 11 SAE and 6 first class stamps. Writer's guidelines for #10 SAE with 1 first class stamp.
Nonfiction: Book excerpts, essays, expose, interview/profile, photo feature, environmental. Buys 18-20 mss/ year. Query with published clips. Length: 100-3,500 words. Pays $50-1,500 for assigned articles; $25-1,500 for unsolicited articles. Sometimes pays expenses of writers on assignment.
Photos: Send photos with submission. Offers no additional payment for photos accepted with ms. Captions, model releases and identification of subjects required. Buys all rights.
Columns/Departments: Eco Voice Editor/Eco Business Editor/Recycle Primer Editor. Eco Voice (personal view), 1,250-1,700 words; Eco Business (green/environmental business column), 1,250-1,500 words; Recycle Primer (how to/inside business of recycling), 1,250-1,500 words. Buys 3-4 mss/year. Query with published clips or send complete ms. Pays $100-350.
Fiction: Fiction Editor. Environmental only. Buys 3 mss/year. Send complete ms. Length: 3,500 + words. Pays $750.
Poetry: Poetry Editor. Free verse and haiku. Buys 1-2 poems/year. Submit maximum 5 poems. Pays $25-50.
Fillers: Notes, New and Reviews Editor. Newsbreaks. Buys 10-20/year. Length: 250-750 words. Pays $25-100.
Tips: "Know what has been covered, read the magazine and read the guidelines!"

ENVIRONMENT, 4000 Albemarle St. NW, Washington DC 20016. Managing Editor: Barbara T. Richman. 2% freelance written. For citizens, scientists, business and government executives, teachers, high school and college students and teachers interested in environment or effects of technology and science in public affairs. Magazine published 10 times/year. Circ. 15,000. Buys all rights. Byline given. Pays on publication to profes-

The double dagger before a listing indicates that the listing is new in this edition. New markets are often the most receptive to freelance submissions.

sional writers. Publishes ms an average of 5 months after acceptance. Reports in 2 months. Query or submit 3 double-spaced copies of complete ms. Sample copy $4.50.

Nonfiction: Scientific and environmental material, and effects of technology on society. Preferred length: 2,500-4,500 words for full-length article. Pays $100-300, depending on material. Also accepts shorter articles (1,000-1,700 words) for "Overview" section. Pays $100. "All full-length articles must be annotated (referenced), and all conclusions must follow logically from the facts and arguments presented." Prefers articles centering around policy-oriented, public decision-making, scientific and technological issues.

ENVIRONMENTAL ACTION, 1525 New Hampshire Ave. NW, Washington DC 20036. (202)745-4870. FAX: (202)745-4880. Editor: Hawley Truax. 30% freelance written. Bimonthly magazine on environmental news and policy. "*Environmental Action* provides balanced reporting on key environmental issues facing the U.S. – particularly at a national level. Articles are written for a general audience – we don't assume any knowledge of environmental conditions or problems." Circ. 16,000. Pays on publication. Publishes ms an average of 2 months after acceptance. Kill fee negotiated. Byline given. Buys first North American serial rights or second serial (reprint) rights. Simultaneous submissions OK if noted. Reports in 4 months. Sample copy for 9 × 12 SAE with 4 first class stamps; free writer's guidelines.

Nonfiction: Exposé, profile, news feature, political analysis, book reviews. No nature appreciation, personal history, adventure in nature, academic/journal articles, or opinion articles. Buys 20 mss/year. Query with published clips and résumé, or send complete ms. Length: 250-3,000 words. Pays $50-500. Sometimes pays expenses of writers on assignment.

Photos: State availability of photos (b&w prints preferred) with submission. Reviews contact sheets, negatives and prints. Offers $25/photo, $50/cover. Captions required. Buys one-time rights.

FORESTS & PEOPLE, Official Publication of the Louisiana Forestry Association, Louisiana Forestry Association, P.O. Drawer 5067, Alexandria LA 71301. (318)443-2558. Editor: Georgiann Gullett. 50% freelance written. Works with a small number of new/unpublished writers each year. Quarterly magazine covering forests, forest industry, wood-related stories, wildlife for general readers, both in and out of the forest industry. Estab. 1951. Circ. 8,500, readership 39,000. **Pays on acceptance.** Publishes ms an average of 6 months after acceptance. Byline given. Not copyrighted. Submit seasonal/holiday material 2 months in advance. Simultaneous submissions, queries, and previously published submissions OK. Reports in 2 weeks on queries; 3 weeks on mss. Sample copy $1.75; writer's guidelines for #10 SASE.

Nonfiction: General interest (recreation, wildlife, crafts with wood, festivals); historical/nostalgic (logging towns, historical wooden buildings, forestry legends); interview/profile (of forest industry execs, foresters, loggers, wildlife managers, tree farmers); photo feature (of scenic forest, wetlands, logging operations); and technical (innovative equipment, chemicals, operations, forestland studies, or industry profiles). No research papers. Articles may cover a technical subject but must be understandable to the general public. Stories should be of interest to Louisiana readers." Buys 12 mss/year. Query with published clips. Length: open. Pays $100.

Photos: State availability of photos. Reviews b&w and color slides. Identification of subjects required.

HIGH COUNTRY NEWS, High Country Foundation, P.O. Box 1090, Paonia CO 81428. (303)527-4898. Editor: Betsy Marston. 80% freelance written. Works with a small number of new/unpublished writers each year. Biweekly tabloid covering environment and natural resource issues in the Rocky Mountain states for environmentalists, politicians, companies, college classes, government agencies, etc. Estab. 1970. Circ. 7,500. Pays on publication. Publishes ms an average of 2 months after acceptance. Byline given. Buys one-time rights. Reports in 1 month. Free sample copy and writer's guidelines.

Nonfiction: Reporting (local issues with regional importance); exposé (government, corporate); interview/profile; opinion; personal experience; and centerspread photo feature. Special issues include those on states in the region. Buys 100 mss/year. Query. Length: 3,000 words maximum. Pays 5-10¢/word. Sometimes pays the expenses of writers on assignment.

Photos: Send photos with ms. Reviews b&w prints. Captions and identification of subjects required.

Poetry: Chip Rawlins, poetry editor, 67½ S. 500 W., Logan UT 84321. Avant-garde, free verse, haiku, light verse and traditional. Pays in contributor copies.

Tips: "We use a lot of freelance material, though very little from outside the Rockies. Start by writing short, 500-word news items of timely, regional interest."

INTERNATIONAL WILDLIFE, National Wildlife Federation, 8925 Leesburg Pike, Vienna VA 22184. Editor: Jonathan Fisher. 85% freelance written. Prefers to work with published/established writers. Bimonthly for persons interested in natural history, outdoor adventure and the environment. Estab. 1971. Circ. 650,000. **Pays on acceptance.** Publishes ms an average of 4 months after acceptance. Usually buys all rights to text. "We are now assigning most articles but will consider detailed proposals for quality feature material of interest to a broad audience." Reports in 6 weeks. Writer's guidelines for #10 SASE.

Nonfiction: Focuses on world wildlife, environmental problems and man's relationship to the natural world as reflected in such issues as population control, pollution, resource utilization, food production, etc. Stories deal with non-U.S. subjects. Especially interested in articles on animal behavior and other natural history, first-person experiences by scientists in the field, well-reported coverage of wildlife-status case studies which also raise broader themes about international conservation, and timely issues. Query. Length: 2,000-2,500 words. Also in the market for short, 750-word "one pagers." Examine past issue for style and subject matter. Pays $1,200 minimum. Sometimes pays expenses of writers on assignment.

Photos: Purchases top-quality color photos; prefers packages of related photos and text, but single shots of exceptional interest and sequences also considered. Prefers Kodachrome or Fujichrome transparencies. Buys one-time rights.

MICHIGAN NATURAL RESOURCES MAGAZINE, State of Michigan Department of Natural Resources, P.O. Box 30034, Lansing MI 48909. (517)373-9267. Editor: N.R. McDowell. Managing Editor: Richard Morscheck. 60% freelance written. Works with a small number of new/unpublished writers each year. Bimonthly magazine covering natural resources in the Great Lakes area. Estab. 1931. Circ. 125,000. **Pays on acceptance.** Publishes ms an average of 6 months after acceptance. Byline given. Offers 100% kill fee. Buys first rights. Submit seasonal/holiday material 1 year in advance. Reports in 1 month. Sample copy for $2.50 and 9 × 12 SAE; writer's guidelines for #10 SASE.

Nonfiction: "All material must pertain to this region's natural resources: lakes, rivers, wildlife, flora and special features. No personal experience, domestic animal stories or animal rehabilitation." Buys 24 mss/year. Query with clips of published work. Length: 1,000-3,000 words. Pays $150-400. Sometimes pays the expenses of writers on assignment.

Photos: Gijsbert (Nick) vanFrankenhuyzen, photo editor. "Photos submitted with an article can help sell it, but they must be razor sharp in focus." Send photos with ms. Pays $50-200 for 35mm transparencies; Fuji or Kodachrome preferred. Model releases and identification of subjects required. Buys one-time rights.

Tips: "We hope to exemplify why Michigan's natural resources are valuable to people and vice versa."

‡**NATIONAL PARKS**, 1015 31st St., Washington DC 20007. (202)944-8565. Senior Editor: Michele Strutin. 75% freelance written. Prefers to work with published/established writers. Bimonthly magazine for a highly educated audience interested in preservation of National Park System units, natural areas and protection of wildlife habitat. Estab. 1917. Circ. 100,000. **Pays on acceptance.** Publishes ms an average of 6 months after acceptance. Buys first North American serial rights and second serial (reprint) rights. Submit seasonal/holiday material 5 months in advance. Query for electronic submissions. Reports in 10 weeks. Sample copy $2.50; writer's guidelines for SASE.

Nonfiction: Exposé (on threats, wildlife problems to national parks); descriptive articles about new or proposed national parks and wilderness parks; brief natural history pieces describing park geology, wildlife, or plants; "adventures" in national parks (cross country skiing, bouldering, mountain climbing, kayaking, canoeing, backpacking); and travel tips to national parks. All material must relate to national parks. No poetry or philosophical essays. Buys 6-10 unsolicited mss/year. "We prefer queries rather than unsolicited stories." Length: 1,000-1,500 words. Pays $75-400.

Photos: State availability of photos or send photos with ms. Pays $25-50 for 8 × 10 b&w glossy prints; $35-150 for transparencies. Captions required. Buys first North American serial rights.

NATIONAL WILDLIFE, National Wildlife Federation, 8925 Leesburg Pike, Vienna VA 22184. (703)790-4510. Editor-in-Chief: Bob Strohm. Editor: Mark Wexler. 90% freelance written. Works with a small number of new/unpublished writers each year. Bimonthly magazine on wildlife, natural history and environment. "Our purpose is to promote wise use of the nation's natural resources and to conserve and protect wildlife and its habitat. We reach a broad audience that is largely interested in wildlife conservation and nature photography. We avoid too much scientific detail and prefer anecdotal, natural history material." Estab. 1963. Circ. 950,000. **Pays on acceptance.** Publishes ms an average of 1 year after acceptance. Offers 25% kill fee. Buys all rights. Submit seasonal/holiday material 8 months in advance. Reports in 6 weeks. Sample copy for 9 × 12 SAE and 4 first class stamps; writer's guidelines for #10 SASE.

Nonfiction: General interest (2,500-word features on wildlife, new discoveries, behavior, or the environment); how-to (an outdoor or nature related activity); personal experience (outdoor adventure); photo feature (wildlife); and short 700-word features on an unusual individual or new scientific discovery relating to nature. Buys 50 mss/year. Query with or without published clips. Length: 750-2,500 words. Pays $500-2,000. Sometimes pays expenses of writers on assignment.

Photos: John Nuhn, photo editor. State availability of photos or send photos with query. Reviews 35mm transparencies. Pays $250-750. Buys one-time rights.

Tips: "Writers can break in with us more readily by proposing subjects (initially) that will take only one or two pages in the magazine (short features)."

‡**NATURAL HISTORY**, Natural History Magazine, 79th and Central Park W., New York NY 10024. Editor: Alan Ternes. Over 75% freelance written. Monthly magazine for well-educated, ecologically aware audience: professional people, scientists and scholars. Circ. 500,000. Pays on publication. Publishes ms an average of 3

months after acceptance. Byline given. Buys first serial rights and becomes agent for second serial (reprint) rights. Submit seasonal material 6 months in advance.

Nonfiction: Uses all types of scientific articles except chemistry and physics—emphasis is on the biological sciences and anthropology. Prefers professional scientists as authors. "We always want to see new research findings in almost all the branches of the natural sciences—anthropology, archeology, zoology and ornithology. We find that it is particularly difficult to get something new in herpetology (amphibians and reptiles) or entomology (insects), and we would like to see material in those fields. We lean heavily toward writers who are scientists. We expect high standards of writing and research. We favor an ecological slant in most of our pieces, but do not generally lobby for causes, environmental or other. The writer should have a deep knowledge of his subject, then submit original ideas either in query or by manuscript. Acceptance is more likely if article is accompanied by high-quality photographs." Buys 60 mss/year. Query or submit complete ms. Length: 2,000-4,000 words. Pays $650-1,000, plus additional payment for photos used.

Photos: Rarely uses 8×10 b&w glossy prints; pays $125/page maximum. Much color is used; pays $300 for inside and up to $500 for cover. Buys one-time rights.

Tips: "Learn about something in depth before you bother writing about it."

OCEANUS, The International Magazine of Marine Science and Policy, Woods Hole Oceanographic Institution, Woods Hole MA 02543. (508)548-1400, ext. 2386. FAX: (508)548-1400, ext. 6016. Editor: Paul R. Ryan. Assistant Editor: T.M. Hawley. 10% freelance written. "*Oceanus* is an international quarterly magazine that monitors significant trends in ocean research, technology and marine policy. Its basic purpose is to encourage wise, environmentally responsible use of the oceans. In addition, two of the magazine's main tasks are to explain the significance of present marine research to readers and to expose them to the substance of vital public policy questions." Estab. 1952. Circ. 15,000. Pays on publication. Publishes ms an average of 3 months after acceptance. Byline given. Buys all rights. Simultaneous queries OK. Reports in 2 months. Sample copy $4; free writer's guidelines.

Nonfiction: Interview/profile and technical. *Oceanus* publishes 4 thematic issues/year. Most articles are commissioned. Length: 2,500-3,500 words. Pays $300 minimum. Sometimes pays expenses of writers on assignment.

Photos: State availability of photos. Reviews b&w and color contact sheets and 8×10 prints. Pays variable rates depending on size; $125/full-page b&w print. Captions required. Buys one-time rights.

Tips: The writer has a better chance of breaking in at this publication with short articles and fillers. "Most of our writers are top scientists in their fields."

OUTDOOR AMERICA, 1401 Wilson Blvd., Level B, Arlington VA 22209. (703)528-1818. FAX: (703)528-1836. Editor: Kristin Merriman. 30% freelance written. Prefers to work with published/established writers. Quarterly magazine about natural resource conservation and outdoor recreation for sports enthusiasts and local conservationists who are members of the Izaak Walton League. Estab. 1922. Circ. 55,000. Pays half on receipt of manuscript, half on publication. Publishes ms an average of 4 months after acceptance. Byline and brief biography given. Buys one-time North American rights, depending on arrangements with author. "Considers previously published material if there's not a lot of audience overlap." Query first. Submit seasonal material 6 months in advance. Reports in 1 month. Sample copy $1.50 with 9×12 SAE; writer's guidelines for SASE.

Nonfiction: "We are interested in thoroughly researched, well-written pieces on current natural resource and recreation issues of national importance (threats to water, fisheries, wildlife habitat, air, public lands, soil, etc.); articles on wildlife management controversies, and first-person essays and humor pieces on outdoor recreation themes (fishing, hunting, camping, ethical outdoor behavior, etc.)." Length: 1,500-2,500 words. Payment: 20¢/word; 10¢/word for reprints.

Photos: Reviews 5×7 b&w glossy prints and 35mm and larger transparencies. Additional payment for photos with ms negotiated. Pays $225 for covers. Captions and model releases required. Buys one-time rights.

Columns/Departments: Interested in shorter articles for the following departments: "Closer to Home" (short articles on enviromental/consumer problems—e.g. radon, lawn chemicals, etc.); "From the Naturalist's Notebook" (pieces that give insight into the habits and behavior of animals, fish, birds). Length: 600 words. Payment: 20¢/word.

Tips: "Writers should obtain guidelines and sample issue *before* querying us. They will understand our needs and editorial focus much better if they've done this. Queries submitted without the writer having read the guidelines are *almost always* off base and almost always rejected."

PACIFIC DISCOVERY, California Academy of Sciences, Golden Gate Park, San Francisco CA 94118. (415)750-7116. Editor: Keith Howell. 100% freelance written. Prefers to work with published/established writers. "A journal of nature and culture in California, the West, the Pacific and Pacific Rim countries read by scientists, naturalists, teachers, students, and others having a keen interest in knowing the natural world more thoroughly." Published quarterly by the California Academy of Sciences. Estab. 1948. Circ. 25,000. Buys first North American serial rights on articles; one-time rights on photos. Pays on publication. Query for electronic submissions. Usually reports within 1 month. Sample copy for 9×12 SAE and $1.25 postage; writer's guidelines for #10 SASE.

Nonfiction: "Subjects of articles include behavior and natural history of animals and plants, ecology, evolution, anthropology, geology, paleontology, biogeography, taxonomy and related topics in the natural sciences. Occasional articles are published on the history of natural science, exploration, astronomy and archaeology. Emphasis is on current research findings. Authors need not be scientists; however, all articles must be based, at least in part, on firsthand fieldwork. Accuracy is crucial." Query with 100-word summary of projected article for review before preparing finished ms. Length: 800-4,000 words. Pays 25¢/word.

Photos: Send photos with submission "even if an author judges that his own photos should not be reproduced. Referrals to professional photographers with coverage of the subject will be greatly appreciated." Reviews 35mm, 4×5 or other transparencies or 8×10 b&w glossy prints. Offers $75-175 and $200 for the cover. Buys one-time rights.

SEA FRONTIERS, 4600 Rickenbacker Causeway, P.O. Box 499900, Virginia Key, Miami FL 33149. (305)361-4888. Editor: Bonnie Bilyeu Gordon. Executive Editor: Jean Bradfisch. 95% freelance written. Works with a small number of new/unpublished writers each year. Bimonthly. "For anyone interested in the sea, its conservation, and the life it contains. Our audience is professional people for the most part; people in executive positions and students." Circ. 55,000. **Pays on acceptance.** Publishes ms an average of 4-10 months after acceptance. Byline given. Buys first serial rights. Reports on submissions in 2 months. Sample copy $3; writer's guidelines for SASE.

Nonfiction: "Articles (with illustrations) covering interesting and little known facts about the sea, marine life, chemistry, geology, physics, fisheries, mining, engineering, navigation, influences on weather and climate, ecology, conservation, explorations, discoveries or advances in our knowledge of the marine sciences, or describing the activities of oceanographic laboratories or expeditions to any part of the world. Emphasis should be on research and discoveries rather than personalities involved." Buys 40-50 mss/year. Query. Length: 1,000-3,000 words. Pays 25¢/word minimum.

Photos: Reviews 8×10 b&w glossy prints and 35mm (or larger) color transparencies. Pays $125 for color used on front and $75 for the back cover.

Tips: "Query should include a paragraph or two that tells the subject, the angle or approach to be taken, and the writer's qualifications for covering this subject or the authorities with whom the facts will be checked."

SIERRA, 730 Polk St., San Francisco CA 94109. (415)923-5656. FAX: (415)776-0350. Editor-in-Chief: Jonathan F. King. Managing Editor: Annie Stine. Senior Editor: Joan Hamilton. Associate Editor: Reed McManus. 80% freelance written. Works with a small number of new/unpublished writers each year. Bimonthly magazine emphasizing conservation and environmental politics for people who are well educated, activist, outdoor-oriented and politically well informed with a dedication to conservation. Estab. 1893. Circ. 413,000. **Pays on acceptance.** Publishes ms an average of 4 months after acceptance. Byline given. Buys first North American serial rights. Query for electronic submissions. Reports in 2 months. Writer's guidelines for SAE and 2 first class stamps.

Nonfiction: Exposé (well-documented on environmental issues of national importance such as energy, wilderness, forests, etc.); general interest (well-researched nontechnical pieces on areas of particular environmental concern); historical (relevant to environmental concerns); how-to and equipment pieces (on camping, climbing, outdoor photography, etc.); profiles (of environmental activists); interview (with very prominent figures in the field); photo feature (photo essays on threatened or scenic areas); and journalistic treatments of semi-technical topics (energy sources, wildlife management, land use, waste management, etc.). No "My trip to . . ." or "why we must save wildlife/nature" articles; no poetry or general superficial essays on environmentalism and local environmental issues. Buys 10-15 mss/issue. Query with published clips. Length: 300-3,000 words. Pays $75-1,500. Sometimes pays limited expenses of writers on assignment.

Photos: Silvana Nova, art and production manager. State availability of photos. Pays $300 maximum for transparencies; more for cover photos. Buys one-time rights.

Columns/Departments: Book reviews. Buys 20-25 mss/year. Length: 750-1,000 words. Pays $100; submit queries to Mark Mardon, assistant editor. For Younger Readers, natural history and conservation topics presented for children ages 8 to 13. Pays $200-500; submit queries to Reed McManus, associate editor. Afield, short (250-300 word) punchy pieces for graphic-heavy front-of-book section.

Tips: "Queries should include an outline of how the topic would be covered and a mention of the political appropriateness and timeliness of the article. Familiarity with Sierra Club positions and policies is recommended. Statements of the writer's qualifications should be included. We don't have fillers in our format."

SNOWY EGRET, The Fair Press, RR #1, Box 354, Poland IN 47868. (812)829-4339. Editor: Karl Barnebey. 95% freelance written. Semiannual magazine of natural history from literary, artistic, philosophical and historical perspectives. "We are interested in works that celebrate the abundance and beauty of nature, encourage a love and respect for the natural world, and examine the variety of way, both positive and negative, through which human beings interact with the environment." Circ. 500. Pays on publication. Publishes ms an average of 6 months after acceptance. Buys first North American serial rights and one-time rights. Submit seasonal/holiday material 6 months in advance. Simultaneous and photocopied submissions OK. Reports in 2 weeks on queries; 1 month on mss. Sample copy $8 with 9 × 12. Prospectus with recently published work and writer's guidelines for 6 × 9 SASE.

Nonfiction: Essays, general interest, historical, how-to, humor, inspirational, interview/profile, opinion, personal experience and travel. "No topical, dated articles, highly scientific or technical pieces." Buys 20 mss/year. Send complete ms. Length: 500-10,000. Pays $2/page.

Fiction: Literary with natural history orientation. "No popular and genre fiction." Buys up to 10 mss/year. Send complete ms. Length: 500-10,000. Pays $2/page.

Poetry: Nature-oriented: avant-garde, free verse, haiku, light verse and traditional. Buys 20 poems/year. Pays $2/poem to $4/page.

Tips: "Make sure that all general points, ideas, messages, etc. are thoroughly rooted in detailed observations, shared wtih the reader through description, dialogue, and narrative. The reader needs to see what you've seen, live what you've lived. Whenever possible the subject shown should be allowed to carry its own message, to speak for itself. We look for book reviews, essays, poetry, fiction, conservation and environmental studies based on first-hand observations of plants and animals that show an awareness of detail and a thoroughgoing familiarity with the organisms or habitats in question."

‡**WILDLIFE CONSERVATION** (Incorporating *Animal Kingdom*), New York Zoological Society, 185 St. and Southern Blvd., Bronx NY 10460. (212)220-5121. Editor: Eugene J. Walter, Jr. Executive Editor: Penny O'Prey. 90% freelance written. Bimonthly magazine covering wildlife. Estab. 1895. Circ. 130,000. **Pays on acceptance.** Publishes ms an average of 1 year or more after acceptance. Byline given. Buys first North American serial rights. Submit seasonal/holiday material 1 year in advance. Simultaneous submissions OK. Reports on 1 month on queries; 3 months on mss. Sample copy $2.95 with 9 × 12 and 6 first class stamps. Free writer's guidelines.

Nonfiction: Nancy Christie, articles editor. Essays, personal experience and wildlife articles. No pet or any domestic animal stories. Buys 12 mss/year. Query. Length 1,500-2,500 words. Pays $750-3,500 for assigned articles; $750-2,000 for unsolicited articles. Sometimes pays expenses of writers on assignment.

Photos: State availability of photos with submission. Reviews transparencies. Buys one-time rights.

Personal Computers

Personal computer magazines continue to change and evolve. The most successful have a strong focus on a particular family of computers or widely-used applications and carefully target a specific type of computer use. Magazines serving MS-DOS and Macintosh families of computers are expected to grow, while new technology will also offer opportunities for new titles. Some of the magazines offer an on-line service for readers in which they can get the magazine alone or with a supplement on computer disk. Be sure you see the most recent issue of a magazine before submitting material.

AMAZING COMPUTING, PiM Publications, Inc., 1 Currant Place, Box 869, Fall River MA 02720. (508)678-4200. Submissions Editor: Elizabeth G. Fedorzyn. Managing Editor: Donald D. Hicks. 90% freelance written. Monthly magazine for the Commodore Amiga computer system user. Circ. 35,000. Pays on publication. Publishes ms an average of 1-2 months after acceptance. Byline given. Buys all rights. Query for electronic submissions. Sample copy for $5; free writer's guidelines.

Nonfiction: How-to, new product, technical, reviews and tutorials. Buys 100 mss/year. Query. Length: 1,000 words minimum. Pays $65/page. Sometimes pays the expenses of writers on assignment.

Photos: Send photos with submission. Reviews 4 × 5 prints. Offers $25 per photo. Captions required. Buys all rights.

Columns/Departments: Reviews, Programs. Buys 200 mss/year. Query. Length: 1,000-5,000 words.

BYTE MAGAZINE, 1 Phoenix Mill Lane, Peterborough NH 03458. (603)924-9281. Editor: Fred Langa. Monthly magazine covering personal computers for college-educated, professional users of computers. 50% freelance written. Circ. 461,000. **Pays on acceptance.** Byline given. Buys all rights. Reports on rejections in 6 weeks; 3 months if accepted. Electronic submissions accepted, IBM or Macintosh compatible. Sample copy $3.50; writer's guidelines for #10 SASE.

Nonfiction: News, reviews, and in-depth discussions of topics related to microcomputers or technology. Buys 160 mss/year. Query. Length: 1,500-5,000 words. Pay is $50-1,000+ for assigned articles; $500-750 for unassigned.

Tips: "Read several issues of BYTE to see what we cover, and how we cover it. Read technical journals to stay on the cutting edge of new technology and trends. Send us a proposal with a short outline of an article explaining some new technology, software trend, and the relevance to advanced business users of personal computers. Our readers want accurate, useful, technical information; not fluff and not meaningless data presented without insight or analysis."

CLOSING THE GAP, INC., P.O. Box 68, Henderson MN 56044. (612)248-3294. Managing Editor: Paul M. Malchow. 40% freelance written. Eager to work with new/unpublished writers. Bimonthly tabloid covering microcomputers for handicapped readers, special education and rehabilitation professionals. "We focus on currently available products and procedures written for the layperson that incorporate microcomputers to enhance the educational opportunities and quality of life for persons with disabilities." Estab. 1982. Circ. 10,000. Pays on publication. Publishes ms an average of 2 months after acceptance. Byline given. Buys first serial rights. Simultaneous queries and simultaneous submissions OK. Query for electronic submissions. Reports in 2 weeks. Free sample copy and writer's guidelines.

Nonfiction: How-to (simple modifications to computers or programs to aid handicapped persons); interview/profile (users or developers of computers to aid handicapped persons); new product (computer products to aid handicapped persons); personal experience (by a handicapped person or on use of microcomputer to aid a handicapped person); articles of current research on projects on microcomputers to aid persons with disabilities; and articles that examine current legislation, social trends and new projects that deal with computer technology for persons with disabilities. No highly technical "computer hobbyist" pieces. Buys 25 mss/year. Query. Length: 500-2,000 words. Pays $25 and up (negotiable). "Many authors' material runs without financial compensation." Sometimes pays expenses of writers on assignment.

Tips: "Knowledge of the subject is vital, but freelancers do not need to be computer geniuses. Clarity is essential; articles must be able to be understood by a layperson. All departments are open to freelancers. We are looking for new ideas. If you saw it in some other computer publication, don't bother submitting. *CTG*'s emphasis is on increasing computer user skills in our area of interest, not developing hobbyist or technical skills. The most frequent mistakes made by writers in completing an article for us is that their submissions are too technical—they associate 'computer' with hobbyist, often their own perspective—and don't realize our readers are not hobbyists or hackers."

COMPUTER LANGUAGE, Miller Freeman Publications, 500 Howard Street, San Francisco CA 94105. (415)397-1881. Editor: J.D. Hildebrand. Managing Editor: Brett Warren. 100% freelance written. Monthly magazine covering programming languages and software design. Estab. 1902. Circ. 65,000. Pays on publication. Byline given. Buys first rights. Query for electronic submissions. Reports in months. Free sample copy and writer's guidelines. Query author's BBS: (415)882-9915 (300/1,200 baud).

Nonfiction: Interview/profile, new product, technical how-to and product reviews. Buys 150 mss/year. Query. Length: 1,500-4,000. Pays $100-650.

Columns/Departments: Product Wrap-Up (in-depth comparative software review); Software Review. Buys 24 mss/year. Query only.

Tips: "Introduce idea for article and/or send manuscripts to editor; propose to become software reviewer. Current hot topics: object-oriented programming, OS/2, multitasking, 80386, TSRs, C, Pascal, Ada, BASIC. Communicate with editors via online edition on CompuServe. 'Go CLMFORUM' to access the Forum; address editor J.D. Hildebrand: 76701, 32."

COMPUTING NOW!, Canada's Personal Computing Magazine, Moorshead Publications, 1300 Don Mills Rd., Toronto, Ontario, M3B 3M8 Canada. (416)445-5600. FAX: (416)445-8149. Editor: Frank Lenk. 15-20% freelance written. A monthly magazine covering microcomputing, the use of microcomputers in business, software/reviews, programming. Estab. 1979. Circ. 17,000. Pays on publication. Publishes ms an average of 6 months after acceptance. Byline given. Buys all rights. Electronic submissions mandatory; whether hard copy is required depends on the article.

Nonfiction: How-to (hardware/software); new product (hardware or software review); and technical. No humor, inspirational or general/historical articles. Query. Length: 2,000-3,000 words. Pays 12¢(Canadian)/word. Sometimes pays the expenses of writers on assignment.

Photos: State availability of photos with submission. Reviews prints. Captions, model releases and identification of subjects required.

Tips: "Will work with authors knowledgeable in specific subject areas—operating systems, software applications, connectivity, hardware."

COMPUTOREDGE, San Diego's Computer Magazine, The Byte Buyer, Inc., P.O. Box 83086, San Diego CA 92138. (619)573-0315. FAX: (619)573-0205. Editors: Tina Berke and Wally Wang. 90% freelance written. A weekly magazine on computers. "We cater to the novice/beginner/first-time computer buyer. Humor is welcome. Nothing too technical." Estab. 1983. Circ. 90,000. Pays on publication. Byline given. Offers $15 kill fee. Buys first North American serial rights. Submit seasonal/holiday material 2 months in advance. Query for electronic submissions. Reports in 2 months. Writer's guidelines for #10 SASE.

Nonfiction: General interest (computer), how-to, humor and personal experience. Buys 80 mss/year. Send complete ms. Length: 300-1,200 words. Pays 10¢/word for assigned articles. Pays 5-10¢/word for unsolicited articles. State availability of photos with submission. Reviews prints (8×10). Offers $15-50 per photo. Captions and identification of subjects required. Buys one-time rights.

Columns/Departments: Beyond Personal Computing (a reader's personal experience). Buys 80 mss/year. Send complete ms. Length: 500-1,000 words. Pays $50.

Fiction: Confession, fantasy and slice-of-life vignettes. Buys 5 mss/year. Send complete ms. Length: 500-1,200 words. Pays 10¢/word.

Poetry: Light verse and traditional. "We're not big on poems, but we might find some interesting." Buys 25 poems/year. Submit maximum 20 poems. Length: 6-30 words. Pays $15.

Tips: "Be relentless. Don't be technical. We like light material, but not fluff. Write as if you're speaking with a friend. Avoid the typical 'Love at First Byte' article. Avoid the 'How My Grandmother Loves Her New Computer' article. Avoid sexual innuendoes/metaphors."

GENEALOGICAL COMPUTING, Ancestry Inc., P.O. Box 476, Salt Lake City UT 84110. (801)531-1790. FAX: (801)531-1798. Editor: Robert Passaro. 50% freelance written. Quarterly magazine on genealogy, using computers. Designed for genealogists who use computers for records management. "We publish articles on all types of computers: PC, Macintosh, Apple II, etc." Estab. 1981. Circ. 2,500. Pays on publication. Publishes ms an average of 4 months after acceptance. Byline given. Buys all rights. Query for electronic submissions. Reports in 2 months.

Nonfiction: New product, personal experience (with software), technical (telecommunications, data exchange, data base development) how-to, reviews, opinion and programming. "Articles on pure genealogy cannot be accepted; this also applies to straight computer technology." Query with outline/summary. Length: 1,300-4,000 words. Pays $100.

Tips: "We need how-to articles describing methods of managing genealogical information with your computer. We accept a *limited* number of pertinent BASIC programs or programming ideas and how-to for publication."

HOME OFFICE COMPUTING, Scholastic Inc., 730 Broadway, New York NY 10003. Editor: Claudia Cohl. Executive Editor: Bernadette Grey. 75% freelance written. Monthly magazine on home/small business and computing. Estab. 1983. Circ. 400,000. **Pays on acceptance.** Publishes ms an average of 6 weeks after acceptance. Byline given. Offers 25% kill fee. Buys all rights or makes work-for-hire assignments. Submit seasonal/holiday material 6 months in advance. Simultaneous submissions OK. Query for electronic submissions. Free sample copy and writer's guidelines for 8½ × 11 SAE.

Nonfiction: How-to, interview/profile, new product, technical, reviews. "No fiction, humor, opinion." Buys 12 mss/year. Query with published clips. Length: 200-4,000 words. Pays $100-2,000.

Photos: Sometimes pays the expenses of writers on assignment. State availability of photos with submission.

Columns/Departments: Word Processing, Desktop Publishing, Business Basics, Spreadsheets, Hardware/Software Reviews. Length: 500-1,000 words. Pays $100-2,000.

Tips: "Submission must be on disk or telecommunicated."

LINK-UP, The Newsmagazine for Users of Online Services, Learned Information, Inc., 143 Old Marlton Pike, Medford NJ 08055. (609)654-4888. FAX: (609)654-4309. Editor: Joseph A. Webb. 33% freelance written. Bimonthly tabloid. "*Link-Up* covers the dynamic new world of online services for business, personal and educational use. Our readers are executives, hobbyists, students, office workers and researchers who share a common goal: they own a computer and modem and are eager to go online." Estab. 1985. Circ. 10,000. Pays on publication. Publishes ms an average of 2 months after acceptance. Byline given. Buys first rights. Submit seasonal/holiday material 2 months in advance. Prefers electronic submissions. Reports in 3 weeks on queries; 1 month on mss. Free sample copy and writer's guidelines.

Nonfiction: General interest, how-to get the most from going online, interview/profile, new product, opinion (does not mean letters to the editor), personal experience, technical, book reviews (we pay $55 for these; length: 500-800 words). "No overly technical pieces or strictly hobbyist articles." Buys 30 mss/year. Send complete ms. Length: 500-2,000 words. Pays $90-220.

Photos: Sometimes pays the expenses of writers on assignment. Send photos with submission. Reviews negatives and prints. Offers no additional payment for photos accepted with ms. Identification of subjects required. Buys one-time rights.

Columns/Departments: Hardware Review (must write about and evaluate a specific hardware product that has something to do with telecommunications.) Length: 1,000-2,000. Buys 6 mss/year. Query. Pays $90-220.

Fillers: Cartoons. Buys 12/year. Pays $25.

Tips: "Become familiar with the online industry. Writers must know what they are talking about in order to inform our readers. We appreciate articles on new developments. Our features section is most open to freelancers. Articles should be well-structured and lively."

THE MACINTOSH BUYER'S GUIDE, Redgate Communications Corp., 660 Beachland Blvd., Vero Beach FL 32963. (407)231-6904. FAX: (407)231-6847. Managing Editor: Ron Errett. Directory Editor: Paulette Siclari. Editorial Assistant: Julie Van Gaasbeck. 80% freelance written. Quarterly magazine covering Macintosh software, hardware and peripherals. Estab. 1984. Circ. 125,000. Pays 45 days after acceptance. Publishes ms an average of 3 months after acceptance. Byline given. Buys all rights. Submit seasonal/holiday material 3 months in advance. Electronic submissions preferred. Reports in 3 weeks on queries. Sample copy $2.50 with 10×13 SAE; free writer's guidelines.

Nonfiction: General interest, how-to, new product, personal experience and technical. No humor—"we're business related." Buys 35 mss/year. Query with published clips. Length: 600-5,000 words. Pays $100-1,000. Pays expenses of writers on assignment.

Photos: State availability of photos with submission. Reviews transparencies. Offers $25-300 per photo. Buys one-time rights.

Columns/Departments: Quarterly Report (news of interest to the Macintosh computer community), 1500 words; and Reviews (software, hardware and peripherals), 1,000 words and up. Buys 40 mss/year. Query with published clips. Pays $100-800.

Tips: "Please call the editor to ascertain current business topics of interest. By far, most freelancers are users of Macintosh computers." Looking for "feature article writing and new product reviews."

MICROAGE QUARTERLY, MicroAge Computer Stores, Inc., Box 1920, Tempe AZ 85281. (602)968-3168. Managing Editor: Jay O'Callaghan. 90% freelance written. Prefers to work with published/established writers. A quarterly magazine for business users of microcomputers. Circ. 200,000. **Pays on acceptance.** Publishes ms an average of 3 months after acceptance. Byline given. Offers kill fee. Buys first North American serial rights, one-time rights and second serial (reprint) rights. Sample copy and writer's guidelines for 9×12 SAE with $1.50 postage.

Nonfiction: Query with published clips. Length: 800-2,000 words. Pays $200-1,200. Pays the phone expenses of writers on assignment.

Columns/Departments: Changing Market (changes in uses of business-oriented microcomputer equipment—what affects the market, and how it changes); Changing Technology (changes/improvements in microcomputer technology that affect the business user); and Changing Industry (adaptations in the microcomputer industry); all 1,000-2,000 words.

Tips: "We're looking for problem-solving articles on office automation and microcomputer applications oriented toward small- and medium-sized businesses. We're willing to discuss ideas with experienced business or computer-literate writers. Please, no queries on home-computer subjects."

MICROpendium, Covering the TI99/4A, Myarc 9640 compatibles, Burns-Koloen Communications Inc., P.O. Box 1343, Round Rock TX 78664. (512)255-1512. Editor: Laura Burns. 40% freelance written. Eager to work with new/unpublished writers. A monthly magazine for users of the "orphaned" TI99/4A. "We are interested in helping users get the most out of their home computers." Estab. 1984. Circ. 6,000. Pays on publication. Publishes ms an average of 2-3 months after acceptance. Byline given. Buys second serial rights. Previously published submissions OK. Query for electronic submission. Reports in 2 weeks on queries; 2 months on manuscripts. Free sample copy and writer's guidelines.

Nonfiction: Book excerpts; how-to (computer applications); interview/profile (of computer "personalities," e.g. a software developer concentrating more on "how-to" than personality); and opinion (product reviews, hardware and software). Buys 30-50 mss/year. Query with or without published clips, or send complete ms. "We can do some articles as a series if they are lengthy, yet worthwhile." Pays $10-150, depending on length. No pay for product announcements. Sometimes pays the expenses of writers on assignment.

Photos: Send photos with submission. Reviews contact sheets, negatives, transparencies, and prints (b&w preferred). Buys negotiable rights.

Columns/Departments: User Notes (tips and brief routines for the computer) 100 words and up. Buys 35-40 mss/year. Send complete ms. Pays $10.

Tips: "We have more regularly scheduled columnists, which may reduce the amount we accept from others. The area most open to freelancers is product reviews on hardware and software. The writer should be a sophisticated TI99/4A computer user. We are more interested in advising our readers of the availability of good products than in 'panning' poor ones. We are interested in coverage of the Geneve 9640 by Myarc. We are not at all interested in general computer or technology-related articles unrelated to TI or Myarc computers."

PC COMPUTING, America's Computing Magazine, Ziff-Davis Publishing Co., 4 Cambridge Ctr., Cambridge MA 02142. (617)492-7500. Editor: Preston Gralla. Monthly magazine on personal computing. Estab. 1988. Circ. 471,642. Pays on publication. Byline given. Offers negotiable kill fee. Makes work-for-hire assignments. Query for electronic submissions. Computer printout submissions OK; no dot-matrix. Reports in 1 month. Sample copy for $2.95; writer's guidelines for #10 SASE.

Nonfiction: Book excerpts, how-to, interview/profile, new product, technical. Query with published clips. Payment negotiable. Sometimes pays expenses of writers on assignment.

Photos: State availability of photos with submission. Reviews 35mm transparencies. Payment negotiable. Captions, model releases and identification of subjects required. Buys all rights.

‡PC LAPTOP COMPUTERS, LFP Inc., Suite 300, 9171 Wilshire Blvd., Beverly Hills CA 90210. (213)858-7155. Editor: Craig Patchett. 90% freelance written. Monthly magazine on laptop computers and the people who use them. "Our goal is to bring information about laptops and their uses to the general public (mostly business people) in a non-technical format." Estab. 1989. Circ. 150,000. Pays on publication. Publishes ms an average of 1 months after acceptance. Byline given. Offers $100 kill fee. Buys first and second serial (reprint) rights. Submit seasonal/holiday material 4 months in advance. Query for electronic submissions. Reports in 2 weeks on queries; 1 month on mss. Free sample copy.

Nonfiction: Michael Goldstein, articles editor. Book excerpts; how-to (applications of laptops that are of general interest); interview/profile; opinion; photo feature; reviews. No technical how-to articles. Buys 60 mss/year. Query with published clips. Length: 1,000-3,000 words. Pays $150-750. Sometimes pays expenses of writers on assignment.

Photos: Send photos with submission. Reviews 35mm and larger transparencies, 4×5 and larger prints. Offers $50 per photo. Model releases and identification of subjects required. Buys one-time rights.

Columns/Departments: Laptop People (well known or interesting people who use laptops), 2,000 words; Perspective (guest editorial for opinions or viewpoints on the industry), 1,500 words. Buys 20 mss/year. Query with published clips. Pays $225-500.

Tips: "We are looking for a rare breed of writer—someone who can communicate technical information in a non-technical, conversational style that does not talk down to our readers. Test your material on non-technical readers to make sure it is understandable."

PCM, The Personal Computing Magazine for Tandy Computer Users, Falsoft, Inc., Falsoft Bldg., 9509 U.S. Highway 42, Box 385, Prospect KY 40059. (502)228-4492. FAX: (502)228-5121. Editor: Lawrence C. Falk. Managing Editor: Judy Hutchinson. 75% freelance written. A monthly (brand specific) magazine for owners of the Tandy Model 100, 200 and 600 portable computer and the Tandy 1000, 1200, 2000 and 3000, 4000 and 5000. Estab. 1983. Circ. 54,874. Pays on publication. Publishes ms an average of 3 months after acceptance. Byline given. Buys full rights, and rights for disk service reprint. Submit seasonal/holiday material 4 months in advance. Query for electronic submissions. Reports in 2 months. Sample copy for SASE; free writer's guidelines.

Nonfiction: Tony Olive, submissions editor. How-to. "We prefer articles with programs." No general interest material. Buys 80 mss/year. Send complete ms. "Do not query." Length: 300 words minimum. Pays $40-50/page.

Photos: State availability of photos. Rarely uses photos.

Tips: "At this time we are only interested in submissions for the Tandy MS-DOS and portable computers. Strong preference is given to submissions accompanied by brief program listings. All listings must be submitted on tape or disk as well as in hard copy form."

PERSONAL COMPUTING MAGAZINE, VNU Business Publications, Inc., 999 Riverview Dr., Totowa NJ 07512. (201)812-1200. Editor: Sondra Reed. Executive Editor: Peter McKie. 15% freelance written. Monthly magazine written, edited, and illustrated for professionals and managers who use personal computers as a tool in day-to-day business tasks. *Personal Computing* is a service-oriented consumer magazine that details hands-on computing tips and techniques, personal computing management strategies, product trends, and manufacturer profiles and product analyses. Circ. 525,000. **Pays on acceptance.** Publishes ms an average of 4 months after acceptance. Byline given. Offers 30% kill fee. Buys all rights. Submit seasonal/holiday material 5 months in advance. Simultaneous submissions OK. Computer printout submissions acceptable; prefers letter-quality. Reports in 2 weeks. Sample copy and writer's guidelines for 9×12 SAE and 11 first class stamps.

Nonfiction: Peter McKie. Essays, how-to and interview/profile. "All of our articles are written from the user's perspective. We focus on ways business executives can improve the quality of their work or increase their productivity. In addition, we cover stories on the personal computing industry that we deem of merit in helping our readers develop an effective personal computing strategy. No product-based stories, computer neophyte stories or reviews." Query with published clips. Length: 2,500-3,000 words. Pays expenses of writers on assignment.

Fillers: Jack Bell, editor. Any shortcuts readers discover in using applications.

Tips: "Hands-on, applications-oriented features and relevant industry stories are most open to freelancers. We will be looking for occasional articles that target a sophisticated, corporate user involved in micro-to-mainframe communications."

PUBLISH, The Magazine for Graphic Communicators, MultiMedia Communications, Inc., 501 Second St., San Francisco CA 94107. (415)546-7722. Editor-in-Chief: Susan Gubernat. Managing Editor: Leslie Steere. 80% freelance written. Monthly magazine on desktop publishing and presentations. *"Publish!* helps communications professionals learn to effectively use desktop publishing. The emphasis is on practical hands-on advice for computer novice and publishing professional alike." Estab. 1986. Circ. 107,000. **Pays on acceptance.** Publishes ms an average of 3 months after acceptance. Byline given. Buys first international rights. Query for electronic submissions. Reports in 3 weeks. Free writer's guidelines.

Nonfiction: Book excerpts, product reviews, how-to (publishing topics), interview/profile, news, new products, technical tips. Buys 120 mss/year. Query with published clips to Leslie Steere. Length: 300-2,500 words. Pays $300-2,000. Sometimes pays expenses of writers on assignment.

Photos: State availability of photos with submission. Reviews contact sheets. Captions and identification of subjects required.

SHAREWARE MAGAZINE, Software for the IBM & Compatible, PC-SIG, Inc., 1030-D East Duane Ave., Sunnyvale CA 94086. (408)730-9291. FAX: (408)730-2107. Editor: Tracy A. Stephenson. 80% freelance written. Bimonthly magazine on shareware software. Estab. 1988. Circ. 110,000. Pays on publication. Publishes ms an average of 3-4 months after acceptance. Byline given. Buys first North American serial rights. Submit seasonal/holiday material 4 months in advance. Simultaneous and previously published submissions OK. Query for electronic submissions. Reports in 2 weeks. Sample copy and writer's guidelines for 9 × 12 SAE and 3 first class stamps.

Nonfiction: How-to (computers), humor, interview/profile, new product, personal experience, photo feature, technical. "No articles reviewing software not related to shareware." Buys 40 mss/year. Query with or without published clips, or send complete ms. Length: 1,200-6,000 words. Pays $50-400.

Photos: Send photos with submission. Reviews contact sheets. Payment for photos included in total payment for article. Captions, model releases and identification of subjects required. Buys one-time rights.

WANG IN THE NEWS, an independent newspaper for Wang Computer Users, Publications and Communications, Inc., 251 Live Oak, Marlin TX 76661. (817)883-2533. FAX: (817)883-2536. Editor: Larry Storer. 30-40% freelance written. Works with small number of new/unpublished writers each year. A monthly newspaper of technical articles relating to all Wang computer applications. Circ. 22,000. Pays on publication. Publishes ms an average of 2 months after acceptance. Byline given. Buys first North American serial rights and reprints from other PCI magazines. Submit seasonal/holiday material 5 months in advance. Simultaneous submissions OK. Query for electronic submissions. Sample copy and writer's guidelines for 9 × 12 SASE.

Nonfiction: How-to, interview/profile, new product, opinion and technical on Wang-related articles only. Query with or without published clips, or send complete ms. Length 500-1,500 words. Fees negotiable upon assignment, acceptance. Occasionally pays with subscription or other premiums; will negotiate. Sometimes pays the expenses of writers on assignment.

Photos: State availability of photos with submissions. Reviews contact sheets, transparencies, and prints. Offers $10 maximum/photo. Captions, model releases and identification of subjects required. Buys one-time rights.

Tips: "We accept submissions from Value Added Resellers of Wang and solicit material on all Wang computers and applications."

WORDPERFECT, THE MAGAZINE, WordPerfect Publishing Co., 270 W. Center St., Orem UT 84057. (801)226-5555. FAX: (801)226-8804. Editor: Clair F. Rees. 85% freelance written. Monthly magazine of "how-to" articles for users of various WordPerfect computer software. "Easy-to-understand articles written with *minimum* jargon. Articles should provide readers good, useful information about word processing and other computer functions." Estab. 1988. Circ. 100,000. Publishes ms an average of 6-8 months after acceptance. Byline given. Negotiable kill fee. Buys first world rights. Submit seasonal/holiday material 8 months in advance. Query for electronic submissions only (WordPerfect 4.2, 5.0 or 5.1). Reports in 2 months. Sample copy for 9 × 12 SAE with $1.25 postage. Free writer's guidelines.

Nonfiction: How-to, humor, interview/company profile, new product and technical. Buys 120-160 mss/year. Query with or without published clips. Length: 800-2,000 words.

Photos: State availability of photos with submission. Reviews transparencies (35mm or larger). Offers no additional payment for photos accepted with ms. Captions and identification of subjects required. Buys one-time rights.

Columns/Departments: Macro Magic (WordPerfect macros), 1,000-1,400 words; Back to Basics (tips for beginners), 1,000-1,400 words; Final Keystrokes (humor), 800 words. Buys 90-120 mss/year. Query with published clips. Pays $400-700, on acceptance.

Tips: "Studying publication provides best information. We're looking for writers who can both inform *and* entertain our specialized group of readers."

Photography

Readers of these magazines use their cameras as a hobby and for weekend assignments. Magazines geared to the professional photographer can be found in the Photography Trade section.

AMERICAN PHOTOGRAPHER, 1633 Broadway, New York NY 10019. Editor: David Schonauer. Managing Editor: Sudie Redmond. Monthly magazine for advanced amateur, sophisticated general interest and pro-photographer. **Pays on acceptance.** Byline given. Offers 25% kill fee. Buys first North American serial rights. Sample copy $2.50.

Nonfiction: Length: 2,000-2,500 words. Sometimes pays writers expenses on assignment (reasonble).
Columns/Departments: Buys 10-30 mss/year. Length: 700 words maximum.

DARKROOM & CREATIVE CAMERA TECHNIQUES, Preston Publications, Inc., P.O. Box 48312, 7800 Merrimac Ave., Niles IL 60648. (708)965-0566. FAX: (708)965-7639. Publisher: Seaton Preston. Editor: David Alan Jay. 85% freelance written. Prefers to work with experienced photographer-writers; happy to work with excellent photographers whose writing skills are lacking. "Article conclusions often require experimental support." Bimonthly publication covering the most technical aspects of photography: photochemistry, lighting, optics, processing and printing, Zone System, special effects, sensitometry, etc. Aimed at advanced workers. Estab. 1979. Circ. 45,000. Pays within about 2 weeks of publication. Publishes ms an average of 6 months after acceptance. Byline given. Buys one-time rights. Query for electronic submissions. Sample copy $4.50; writer's guidelines with #10 SASE.
Nonfiction: Special interest articles within above listed topics; how-to, technical product reviews and photo features. Query or send complete ms. Length open, but most features run approximately 2,500 words or 3-4 magazine pages. Pays $100/published page for well-researched technical articles.
Photos: "Don't send photos with ms. Will request them at a later date." Ms payment includes photo payment. Prefers transparencies and 8×10 b&w prints. Captions, model releases (where appropriate) and technical information required. Buys one-time rights.
Tips: "We like serious photographic articles with a creative or technical bent. Successful writers for our magazine are doing what they write about. Also, any ms that addresses a serious problem facing many photographers will get our immediate attention."

DARKROOM PHOTOGRAPHY MAGAZINE, Suite 300, 9171 Wilshire Blvd., Beverly Hills CA 90210. (213)858-7100. FAX: (213)274-7985. Editorial Director: Thomas Harrop. Senior Editor: Anna Ercegovac. Editorial Assistant: Maggie Devach. A photography magazine with darkroom emphasis, published 12 times/year for both professional and amateur photographers "interested in what goes on after the picture's been taken: processing, printing, manipulating, etc." Estab. 1979. Circ. 80,000. Pays on publication; pays regular writers on acceptance. Byline given. Buys one-time rights. Query for electronic submissions. Reports in 6 weeks. Sample copy and writer's guidelines for 8½×11 SASE.
Nonfiction: Historical/nostalgic (some photo-history pieces); how-to (darkroom equipment build-its); interview/profile (famous photographers); and technical (articles on darkroom techniques, tools, and tricks). No stories on shooting techniques, strobes, lighting, or in-camera image manipulation. Query or send complete ms. Length: varies. Pays $50-500, depending on project.
Photos: State availability or send photos with query or ms. Reviews transparencies and prints. "Supporting photographs arc considcrcd part of thc manuscript packagc."
Columns/Departments: Darkroom Basics, Tools & Tricks, Special Effects, Making Money and Larger Formats. Query or send complete ms. Length: 800-1,200 words. "Published darkroom-related 'tips' receive free one-year subscriptions." Length: 100-150 words.

POPULAR PHOTOGRAPHY, 1633 Broadway, New York NY 10019. Editorial Director: Jason Schneider. 20% freelance written. Monthly. "The magazine is designed for advanced amateur and professional photographers." Estab. 1937. Circ. 950,000. **Pays on acceptance.** Publishes ms an average of 4 months after acceptance. Byline given. "Rights purchased vary occasionally but are usually one-time." Submit material 4 months in advance. Reports in 1 month. SASE.
Nonfiction: "This magazine is mainly interested in instructional articles on photography that will help photographers improve their work. This includes all aspects of photography, from theory to camera use and darkroom procedures. Utter familiarity with the subject is a prerequisite to acceptance. It is best to submit article ideas in outline form since features are set up to fit the magazine's visual policies. Style should be easily readable but with plenty of factual data when a technique story is involved." Buys how-to, pictorial/technical pieces, historical articles. Query. Length: 500-2,000 words. Pays $250/page.
Photos: Jeanne Stallman, picture editor. Interested in seeing portfolios in b&w and color of highest quality in terms of creativity, imagination and technique.

WESTERN PHOTO TRAVELER, Photo Traveler Publications, P.O. Box 39912, Los Angeles CA 90039. (213)660-0473. Editor: Nadine Orabona. 40% freelance written. Bimonthly newsletter on photo travel. "Travel articles on places or events in California and the West written from a photographer's point of view. Audience is amateur and professional photographers." Estab. 1985. Circ. 2,000. Pays on publication. Publishes ms an average of 3-6 months after acceptance. Byline given. Buys first, one-time or second serial (reprint) rights. Submit seasonal/holiday material 6 months in advance. Simultaneous and previously published submissions OK. Query for electronic submissions. Reports in 1 month on queries; 6 weeks on mss. Sample copy $4.95; writer's guidelines for SASE.
Nonfiction: Travel. "No regular travel articles." Buys 18 mss/year. Query with or without published clips, or send complete ms. Length: 500-2,500 words. Pays $25 for feature articles of more than 1,500 words and $10 for short articles of under 1,500 words.

Tips: "Writer should know photography and should visit the site or event. We want specifics such as best photo spots, best time of day or year, photo tips, recommended equipment, etc., but not a lot of technical advice. We like maps showing best photo spots."

WILDLIFE PHOTOGRAPHY, P.O. Box 224, Greenville PA 16125. (412)588-3492. Editor: Rich Faler. 90% freelance written. Eager to work with new/unpublished writers. Quarterly magazine. "We are dedicated to the pursuit and capture of wildlife on film. Emphasis on how-to." Estab. 1985. Circ. 3,000. **Pays on acceptance.** Publishes ms an average of 1 year after acceptance. Byline given. Buys first rights, one-time rights or second serial (reprint) rights. Submit seasonal/holiday material 4 months in advance. Simultaneous and previously published submissions OK. Reports in 2 weeks on queries; 6 weeks on mss. Sample copy for $2 and 9×12 SAE; free writer's guidelines.

Nonfiction: Book excerpts; how-to (work with animals to take a good photo); interview/profile (of professionals); new product (of particular interest to wildlife photography); personal experience (with cameras in the field); and travel (where to find superb photo opportunities of plants and animals). No fiction or photography of pets, sports and scenery. Buys 30 mss/year. Query or send complete ms. Length: 500-3,000 words. Pays $30-100.

Photos: Send sharp photos with submission. Reviews contact sheets, negatives, transparencies and 5×7 prints as part of ms package. Photos not accepted separate from ms. Offers no additional payment for photos accepted with ms. Captions and identification of subjects required. Buys one-time rights.

Fillers: Anecdotes and facts. Buys 12/year. Length: 50-200 words. Pays $5-15.

Tips: "Give solid how-to info on how to photograph a specific species of wild animal. Send photos, not only of the subject, but of the photographer and his gear in action. The area of our publication most open to freelancers is feature articles."

Politics and World Affairs

These publications cover politics for the reader interested in current events. Other publications that will consider articles about politics and world affairs are listed under Business and Finance, Contemporary Culture, Regional and General Interest. For listings of publications geared toward the professional, see Government and Public Service and International Affairs in the Trade section.

AFRICA REPORT, 833 United Nations Plaza, New York NY 10017. (212)949-5731. FAX: (212)682-6421. Editor: Margaret A. Novicki. 60% freelance written. Prefers to work with published/established writers. A bimonthly magazine for U.S. citizens and residents with a special interest in African affairs for professional, business, academic or personal reasons. Not tourist-related. Circ. 10,500. Pays on publication. Publishes ms an average of 2 months after acceptance. Rights purchased vary with author and material; usually buys all rights, very occasionally first serial rights. Byline given unless otherwise requested. Sample copy for $4.50; free writer's guidelines.

Nonfiction: Interested in "African political, economic and cultural affairs, especially in relation to U.S. foreign policy and business objectives. Style should be journalistic but not academic or light. Articles should not be polemical or long on rhetoric but may be committed to a strong viewpoint. I do not want tourism articles." Would like to see in-depth topical analyses of lesser known African countries, based on residence or several months' stay in the country. Buys 15 unsolicited mss/year. Pays $150-250.

Photos: Photos purchased with or without accompanying mss with extra payment. Reviews b&w only. Pays $25. Submit 12×8 "half-plate."

Tips: "Read *Africa Report* and other international journals regularly. Become an expert on an African or Africa-related topic. Make sure your submissions fit the style, length and level of *Africa Report*."

ARETE, Forum for Thought, Suite 418, 405 W. Washington, San Diego CA 92103. (619)237-0074. Publisher/ Editor: Alden Mills. Managing Editor: Dana Plank. 75% freelance written. A bimonthly political/social/arts and literary magazine. "We are dedicated to presenting high-quality work of any viewpoint, providing an unbiased forum of thought-provoking ideas." Estab. 1987. Circ. 35,000. **Pays on acceptance.** Publishes ms an average of 2 months after acceptance. Byline given. Offers 15% kill fee. Not copyrighted. Buys one-time rights. Previously published submissions OK. Query for electronic submissions. Reports in 1 month. Sample copy $3.50. Free writer's/photographer's guidelines.

Nonfiction: Harlan Lewin, Doug Balding—nonfiction editors. Book excerpts, essays, exposé, general interest, historical/nostalgic, humor, interview/profile, opinion, personal experience, photo feature and travel (features on the arts). Send complete ms. Length: 1,000-9,000 words (negotiable). Pays $100-2,000 (negotiable). Sometimes pays expenses of writers on assignment.

Photos: Send photos with submission to Adrienne Hopkins. Reviews contact sheets and negatives. Pays $100 a page (negotiable). Buys one-time rights.
Fiction: Dana Plank, fiction editor. Adventure, condensed novels, ethnic, experimental, fantasy, historical, horror, humorous, mainstream, mystery, novel excerpts, science fiction, slice-of-life vignettes and suspense. No dry academic pieces. Buys 25-30 mss/year. Send complete ms. Length: 500-9,000 words. Pays $100-2,000 (negotiable).
Poetry: Dana Plank, poetry editor. Free verse, light verse and traditional. Buys 60-100 poems/year. Submit maximum 6 poems. "Prefer shorter poetry." Pays $20-200 (negotiable).

CALIFORNIA JOURNAL, 1714 Capitol Ave., Sacramento CA 95814. (916)444-2840. Editor: Richard Zeiger. Managing Editor: A.G. Block. 50% freelance written. Prefers to work with published/established writers. Monthly magazine that emphasizes analysis of California politics and government. Estab. 1970. Circ. 20,000. Pays on publication. Publishes ms an average of 2 months after acceptance. Byline given. Buys all rights. Query for electronic submissions. Writer's guidelines for #10 SASE.
Nonfiction: Profiles of state and local government and political analysis. No outright advocacy pieces. Buys 25 unsolicited mss/year. Query. Length: 900-3,000 words. Pays $150-500. Sometimes pays the expenses of writers on assignment.

‡EMPIRE STATE REPORT, The magazine of politics and public policy in New York State, State Report Network, 545 8th Ave., 16th Fl., New York NY 10018. (212)239-9797. Managing Editor: Alex Storozynski. 50% freelance written. Monthly magazine covering politics and public policy in NY State. "We provide timely political and public policy features for local and statewide public officials in New York State. Anything that would be of interest to them is of interest to us." Estab. 1983. Circ. 12,000. Pays 2 months after publication. Byline given. Buys first North American serial rights. Query for electronic submissions. Reports in 1 month on queries; 2 weeks on mss. Sample copy $3.50 with #10 SASE.
Nonfiction: Essays, exposé, interview/profile, opinion. Writers should send for our editorial calendar. Buys 48 mss/year. Query with published clips. Length: 750-3,000 words. Pays $35-400 for assigned articles. Sometimes pays expenses of writers on assignment.
Photos: State availability of photos with submission. Reviews any size prints. Offers $50-100 per photo. Identification of subjects required. Buys one-time rights.
Columns/Departments: Heard in the halls (short gossip pieces about state politics), 200 words maximum; Perspective (opinion pieces), 750-800 words. Buys 24 mss/year. Query. Length: 750-1,000 words. Pays $50-100.
Tips: Send us a query. If we are not already working on the idea, and if the query is well written, we might work something out with the writer. Writers have the best chance selling something for "Heard In The Halls."

EUROPE, 2100 M St. NW, 707, Washington DC 20037. Managing Editor: Anke Middelmann. 20% freelance written. Magazine published 10 times a year for anyone with a professional or personal interest in Western Europe and European/U.S. relations. Circ. 25,000. **Pays on acceptance.** Publishes ms an average of 2 months after acceptance. Buys first serial rights and all rights. Submit seasonal material 3 months in advance. Reports in 1 month.
Nonfiction: Interested in current affairs (with emphasis on economics and politics), the Common Market and Europe's relations with the rest of the world. Publishes occasional cultural pieces, with European angle. "High quality writing a must. We publish anything that might be useful to people with a professional interest in Europe." Query or submit complete ms or article outline. Include résumé of author's background and qualifications. Length: 500-2,000 words. Pays $75-150.
Photos: Photos purchased with or without accompanying mss. Buys b&w and color. Pays $25-35 for b&w print, any size; $100 for inside use of transparencies; $450 for color used on cover; per job negotiable.

THE FREEMAN, 30 S. Broadway, Irvington-on-Hudson NY 10533. (914)591-7230. FAX: (914)591-8910. Senior Editor: Brian Summers. 85% freelance written. Eager to work with new/unpublished writers. Monthly for "the layman and fairly advanced students of liberty." Buys all rights, including reprint rights. Byline given. Estab. 1946. Pays on publication. Publishes ms an average of 5 months after acceptance. Sample copy for 7½ × 10½ SASE with 4 first class stamps.
Nonfiction: "We want nonfiction clearly analyzing and explaining various aspects of the free market, private enterprise, limited government philosophy. Though a necessary part of the literature of freedom is the exposure of collectivistic clichés and fallacies, our aim is to emphasize and explain the positive case for individual responsibility and choice in a free economy. Especially important, we believe, is the methodology of freedom—self-improvement, offered to others who are interested. We try to avoid name-calling and personality clashes and find satire of little use as an educational device. Ours is a scholarly analysis of the principles underlying a free market economy. No political strategy or tactics." Buys 60 mss/year. Length: 3,500 words maximum. Pays 10¢/word. Sometimes pays expenses of writers on assignment.
Tips: "It's most rewarding to find freelancers with new insights, fresh points of view. Facts, figures and quotations cited should be fully documented, to their original source, if possible."

MOTHER JONES MAGAZINE, The Foundation for National Progress, 1663 Mission St., Second Floor, San Francisco CA 94103. (415)558-8881. Editor: Doug Foster. Managing Editor: Peggy Orenstein. 90% freelance written. Bimonthly magazine with focus on progressive politics and the arts. Specializes in investigative reporting. "*Mother Jones* is the largest magazine of political opinion in the United States." Estab. 1976. Circ. 200,000. **Pays on acceptance.** Byline given. Offers 25% kill fee. Buys first North American serial rights. Submit seasonal/holiday material 4 months in advance. Sample copy $5; free writer's guidelines for #10 SASE.
Nonfiction: Book excerpts, essays, exposé, interview/profile, personal experience and photo feature. Buys 35 mss/year. Query with published clips. Length: 3,000-5,000 words. Pays $1,500-2,000. Pays expenses of writers on assignment.
Photos: State availablility of photos with submission. Reviews contact sheets, negatives, transparencies and prints. Offers $75 minimum/photo. Captions, model releases and identification of subjects required. Buys one-time rights.
Columns/Departments: Latest Thinking (essays), Hot Spots (foreign coverage), Trips (travel for non-ugly American), Out of Pocket (financial). Buys 20 mss/year. Length: 1,000-2,500 words. Query with published clips. Pays $500-900.
Fiction: "Please read our magazine to get a feel for our fiction." No western, romance or confession. Buys 3 mss/year. Send complete ms. Length: 1,500-5,000 words. Pays $400-2,000.
Fillers: David Beers, fillers editor. Outfront (short profiles), Previews (reviews and arts coverage—Peggy Orenstein, editor). Buys 75 mss/year. Length: 100-600 words. Pays $75-200.
Tips: "Read an issue before you query us. We have a 3-month lead time. Think ahead."

THE NATION, 72 5th Ave., New York NY 10011. FAX: (212)463-9712. Editor: Victor Navasky. 75% freelance written. Works with a small number of new/unpublished writers each year. Weekly. Buys first serial rights. Query for electronic submissions. Free sample copy and writer's guidelines for 6×9 SASE.
Nonfiction: "We welcome all articles dealing with the social scene, from an independent perspective." Queries encouraged. Buys 100 mss/year. Length: 2,500 words maximum. Modest rates. Sometimes pays expenses of writers on assignment.
Tips: "We are firmly committed to reporting on the issues of labor, national politics, business, consumer affairs, environmental politics, civil liberties and foreign affairs."

‡NATIONAL REVIEW, National Review Inc., 150 E. 35th St., New York NY 10016. (212)679-7330. Editor: John O'Sullivan. Managing Editor: Linda Bridges. 60% freelance written. Biweekly political and cultural journal of conservative opinion. "While we sometimes publish symposia including liberal or even leftist opinion, most of what we publish has a conservative or liberatarian angle." Estab. 1955. Circ. 140,000. Pays on publication. Byline given. Offers 50% kill fee "on pieces definitely accepted." Buys first, one-time, second serial or simultaneous rights. Submit seasonal/holiday material 2 months in advance. Reports in 2 weeks on queries; 3 months on mss. Free sample copy.
Nonfiction: Mark Cunningham, assistant articles editor. Essays, expose (of government boondoggles), interview/profile, religious. No editorial-type pure opinion. Buys 130 mss/year. Query. Length: 500-3,000 words. Pays $100-1,000 for assigned articles; $100-600 for unsolicited articles. Sometimes pays expenses of writers on assignment.
Columns/Departments: Book reviews (conservative political where applicable); Arts piece. Buys 130 mss/year. Query. Length: 800-1,200 words. Pays $225-300.
Tips: "Query—although if a writer already has a manuscript ready, he may as well send it in instead. We accept phone queries. Double-space manuscripts. For the book section, always query before sending manuscript. We expect a fairly conservative point of view, but don't want a lot of editorializing. And we prefer pieces that are a bit more essayistic than a standard newspaper report."

NEWSWEEK, 444 Madison Ave., New York NY 10022. (212)350-4000. My Turn Editor. Although staff written, accepts unsolicited mss for My Turn, a column of opinion. The 1,000- to 1,100-word essays for the column must be original and contain verifiable facts. Payment is $1,000, on publication. Buys first rights. Reports in 6 weeks.

THE PRAGMATIST, A Utilitarian Approach, P.O. Box 392, Forest Grove PA 18922. Editor: Jorge Amador. Publisher: Hans G. Schroeder. 67% freelance written. Bimonthly magazine on politics and current affairs. "*The Pragmatist* is a free-market magazine with a social conscience. We explore the practical benefits of tolerance, civil liberties and the market order, with emphasis on helping the poor and the underprivileged." Estab. 1983. Circ. 1,550. Pays on publication. Publishes ms an average of 4 months after acceptance. Byline given. Publication not copyrighted "but will run copyright notice for individual author on request." Buys first rights and/or second serial (reprint) rights. Submit seasonal/holiday material 6 months in advance. Previously published submissions OK. Query for electronic submissions. Reports in 2 months. Sample copy $3; writer's guidelines for #10 SASE.

Nonfiction: Essays, humor, opinion. "*The Pragmatist* is solution-oriented. We seek facts and figures, no moralizing or abstract philosophy, and focus on the issues, not personalities. Recent articles have surveyed alternatives to government-issued money and examined how regulation hurts consumers." Buys 35 mss/year. Query with published clips or send complete ms. Length: 500-2,500 words. Pays 1¢/published word plus copies.

Columns/Departments: Book Review (history/current affairs, dealing with the dangers of power or the benefits of civil liberties and market relations). Buys 10-15 mss/year. Query with published clips or send complete ms. Length: 1,000-1,500 words. Pays 1¢/published word plus copies.

Fiction: "We use very little fiction, and then only if it makes a political point."

Tips: "We welcome new writers. Most of our authors are established, but the most important article criteria are clear writing and sound reasoning backed up by facts. Write for an educated lay audience, not first-graders or academics. Polite correspondence gets answered first. No phone calls, please. Don't get discouraged by initial rejections; keep working on your writing and your targeting."

THE PROGRESSIVE, 409 E. Main St., Madison WI 53703. (608)257-4626. FAX: (608)257-3373. Editor: Erwin Knoll. 75% freelance written. Monthly. Estab. 1909. Pays on publication. Publishes ms an average of 6 weeks after acceptance. Byline given. Buys all rights. Reports in 2 weeks. Sample copy for 8½×11 SAE and $1.05 postage. Writer's guidelines for #10 SASE.
Nonfiction: Primarily interested in articles which interpret, from a progressive point of view, domestic and world affairs. Occasional lighter features. "*The Progressive* is a *political* publication. General-interest material is inappropriate." Query. Length: 3,000 words maximum. Pays $75-250.
Tips: "Display some familiarity with our magazine, its interests and concerns, its format and style. We want query letters that fully describe the proposed article without attempting to sell it — and that give an indication of the writer's competence to deal with the subject."

REASON MAGAZINE, Suite 1062, 2716 Ocean Park Blvd., Santa Monica CA 90405. (213)392-0443. Editor: Virginia I. Postrel. 50% freelance written. "Strongly prefer experienced, published writers." A monthly public-affairs magazine with a classical liberal/libertarian perspective. Estab. 1968. Circ. 37,000. **Pays on acceptance.** Publishes ms an average of 2 months after acceptance. Rights purchased vary with author and material. Byline given. Offers kill fee by pre-arrangement. Query for electronic submissions. Reports in 2 months. Sample copy for $3 and 9×12 SAE with $1.24 postage.
Nonfiction: "*Reason* deals with social, economic and political issues, supporting both individual liberty and economic freedom. We are looking for politically sophisticated analysis, solid reporting, and excellent writing. Authors should not submit manuscripts without reviewing at least one recent issue." Query. Buys 50-70 mss/year. Length: 1,000-5,000 words. Sometimes pays expenses of writers on assignment.

RIPON FORUM, Ripon Society, 6 Library Ct. SE, Washington DC 20003. (202)546-1292. Editor: William P. McKenzie. 20% freelance written. Willing to work with new/unpublished writers. A bimonthly magazine on progressive Republicanism/GOP politics. Estab. 1962. Circ. 3,000. Pays on publication. Publishes ms an average of 2-4 months after acceptance. Byline given. Simultaneous submissions OK. Reports in 2 months. Sample copy for 9×12 SAE and 4 first class stamps. Writer's guidelines for #10 SASE.
Nonfiction: Essays and opinion. Query with published clips. Length: 800-1,500 words. Pays $80-150.

‡THIRD WORLD, Editora Terceiro Mondo, Rua da Gloria, 122 Sala 105, Rio de Janeiro CEP 20241 Brazil. (5521)222-1370. Editor: Bill Hinchberger. 25% freelance written. Bimonthly magazine covering the third world. "*Third World* attempts to present world affairs from a Third World perspective. Estab. 1986. Circ. 5,000. Pays on publication. Publishes ms an average of 2 months after acceptance. Offers 25% kill fee. Buys first rights or second serial (reprint) rights. Submit seasonal/holiday material 2 months in advance. Simultaneous and previously published submissions OK. Reports in 1 month. Please leave time for international mail. Free sample copy.
Nonfiction: Book excerpts, essays, exposé, general interest, humor, interview/profile, opinion, personal experience, photo feature, religious, politics, the economy and culture. No articles that reinforce stereotypes of the Third World. Buys 25-30 mss/year. Query with published clips. Length: 500 word minimum; no set maximum — average length is 2,000 words. Pays $10-100. Pays with contributor copies upon agreement with the writer.
Photos: State availability of photos with submission. Reviews contact sheets or 5×7 or 8×10 prints. Offers $5-10 per photo. Identification of subjects required. Buys one-time rights.
Columns/Departments: Openpage (opinion), 800 words; Continent Sections (current affairs in Latin America, Africa, Asia, the Middle East, the Caribbean) 1,000-2,000 words. Buys 15-20 mss/year. Query with published clips. Pays $25-100.

Poetry: Avant-garde, free verse, haiku, light verse and traditional. Nothing that reinforces Third World stereotypes. Buys 2-5/year. Submit maximum 10 poems. Pays $5-20.

Fillers: Anecdotes, facts and newsbreaks. Buys 10-15/year. Length: 200-700 words. Pays $5-25.

Tips: "We are interested in first-hand reporting from the Third World—especially from those who live in or are from the country about which they are writing. Tell the story from a Third World perspective. Find the angle that is missing from major newspapers and magazines. The entire publication is open—especially to beginning writers."

WASHINGTON MONTHLY, 1611 Connecticut Ave., Washington DC 20009. (202)462-0128. Editor-in-Chief: Charles Peters. 35% freelance written. Works with a small number of new/unpublished writers each year. For "well-educated, well-read people interested in politics, the press and government." Monthly. Circ. 30,000. Rights purchased depend on author and material; buys all rights, first rights, or second serial (reprint) rights. Buys 20-30 mss/year. Pays on publication. Sometimes does special topical issues. Query or submit complete ms. Computer printout submissions acceptable. Tries to report in 2 months. Publishes ms an average of 2-6 weeks after acceptance. Sample copy $4.

Nonfiction: Responsible investigative or evaluative reporting about the U.S. government, business, society, the press and politics. "No editorial comment/essays." Also no poetry, fiction or humor. Length: "average 2,000-6,000 words." Pays 4-10¢/word.

Photos: Buys b&w glossy prints.

Tips: "Best route is to send 1-2 page proposal describing article and angle. The most rewarding aspect of working with freelance writers is getting a solid piece of reporting with fresh ideas that challenge the conventional wisdom."

WORLD POLICY JOURNAL, World Policy Institute, 777 UN Plaza, New York NY 10017. (212)490-0010. Editor: Sherle Schwenninger. 20% freelance written. "We are eager to work with new or unpublished writers as well as more established writers." A quarterly magazine covering international politics, economics and security issues. "We hope to bring a new sense of imagination, principle and proportion, as well as a restored sense of reality and direction to America's discussion of its role in the world." Circ. 10,000. **Pays on acceptance.** Publishes ms an average of 3 months after acceptance. Byline given. Offers variable kill fee. Buys all rights. Reports in 2 months. Sample copy for 9×12 SAE, 10 first class stamps and $5.75.

Nonfiction: Articles that "define policies that reflect the shared needs and interests of all nations of the world." Query. Length: 30-40 pages (8,500 words maximum). Pays variable commission rate. Sometimes pays the expenses of writers on assignment.

Tips: "By providing a forum for many younger or previously unheard voices, including those from Europe, Asia, Africa and Latin America, we hope to replace lingering illusions and fears with new priorities and aspirations. Articles submitted on speculation very rarely suit our particular needs."

Psychology and Self-Improvement

These publications focus on psychological topics, how and why readers can improve their own outlooks, and how to understand people in general. Many General Interest, Men's and Women's publications also publish articles in these areas.

‡CELEBRATE LIFE, The Magazine of Positive Living, Unimedia Corp., Suite 201, 18395 Gulf Blvd., Indian Rocks Beach FL 34635. (813)595-4141. Editor: Marty Johnson. 75% freelance written. Quarterly magazine covering motivational, positive lifestyles. Estab. 1989. Circ. 10,000. Pays on publication. Publishes ms an average of 3 months after acceptance. Byline given. Buys first North American serial rights, all rights or make work-for-hire assignments. Submit seasonal/holiday material 6 months in advance. Simultaneous and previously published submissions OK "if notified." Query for electronic submissions. Reports in 2 months. Sample copy $2 with 9×12 SAE and 4 first class stamps. Writer's guidelines for #10 SAE with 1 first class stamp.

Nonfiction: How-to (self-improvement), humor, inspirational, interview/profile, personal experience, photo feature, religious (new thought), travel, natural lifestyles (i.e. holistic health). "Each issue is thematic. This is an upbeat, positive publication." Query with or without published clips, or send complete ms. Length: 400-2,000 words. Pays $25-75 for assigned articles. Complimentary copies to $25 or more for unsolicited material. "Rarely" pays expenses of writers on assignment.

Photos: State availability or send photos with submission. Reviews contact sheets, transparencies and prints. Captions, model releases and identification of subjects required. Buys one-time rights.

Columns/Departments: Books and Tapes (must be assigned), 100 words; Humor (new thought, reflections), 200 words. Query with published clips or send complete ms. Pays $10-20.

Poetry: Light verse. Submit maximum 3 poems. Length: 8-24 lines. Pays $5 maximum. "Usually for byline only."

Fillers: Anecdotes, facts, gags, newsbreaks, short humor. Length: 1-100 words. Pays $5-20.

Tips: "We are very specific about what we want in each upcoming issue. Nothing outside these parameters will fit. Interviews/profiles of leaders of positive change are wanted."

JOURNAL OF GRAPHOANALYSIS, 111 N. Canal St., Chicago IL 60606. Editor: William R. Harms. For an audience interested in self-improvement. Monthly magazine. Buys all rights. Pays negotiable kill fee. Byline given. **Pays on acceptance.** Reports on submissions in 1 month.
Nonfiction: Self-improvement material helpful for ambitious, alert, mature people. Applied psychology and personality studies, techniques of effective living, etc.; all written from intellectual approach by qualified writers in psychology, counseling and teaching, preferably with advanced degrees. Length: 2,000 words. Pays 10¢/word, minimum.

PSYCHOLOGY TODAY, P.T. Partners, L.P., 80 5th Ave., New York NY 10011. (212)886-2840. FAX: (212)727-2326. Editor: Peter Edidin. 85% freelance written. Published 10 times/year, magazine covering psychology and the social and behavioral sciences. Estab. 1968. Circ. 875,000. **Pays on acceptance.** Publishes ms an average of 5 months after acceptance. Byline given. Offers 20% kill fee. Buys first North American serial rights, one-time rights, second serial (reprint) rights or all rights. Submit seasonal/holiday material 6 months in advance. Reports in 6 weeks. Sample copy for 9 × 12 SAE with $3 postage. Writer's guidelines for #10 SASE.
Nonfiction: Book excerpts, essays, exposé, general interest, interview/profile, opinion, and technical. Buys 60 mss/year. Query with published clips. Length: 1,000-3,500 words. Pays $500-2,500. Pays expenses of writers on assignment.
Photos: State availability of photos with submission.
Columns/Departments: Covering Health (work, family matters, men and women, media, sports, brain, therapy, and some first-person articles, book reviews. Contact: Wray Herbert.) Query: Jack Horn, news editor. Length: 300-1,000 words. Pays $150-750.

Regional

Many regional publications rely on staff-written material, but others accept work from freelance writers who live in or know the region. Many of these magazines are among the bestselling magazines in a particular area and are read carefully, so writers must be able to supply accurate, up-to-date material. The best regional publication is usually the one in your hometown, whether it's a city or state magazine or a Sunday supplement in a newspaper. (Since you are familiar with the region, it is easier to propose suitable story ideas.)

Listed first are general interest magazines slanted toward residents of and visitors to a particular region. Next, regional publications are categorized alphabetically by state, followed by Canada. Publications that report on the business climate of a region are grouped in the regional division of the Business and Finance category. Recreation and travel publications specific to a geographical area are listed in the Travel, Camping and Trailer section. Regional publications are not listed if they only accept material from a select group of freelancers in their area or if they did not want to receive the number of queries and manuscripts a national listing would attract. If you know of a regional magazine that is not listed, approach it by asking for writer's guidelines before you send unsolicited material.

General

AMERICAS, Organization of American States, Editorial Offices, General Secretariat Bldg., 1889 F Street NW, Washington DC 20006. FAX: (201)458-6421. Managing Editor: Rebecca Read Medrano. 80% freelance written. Official magazine of Organization of American States. Editions published in English and Spanish. Bimonthly. Estab. 1948. Circ. 55,000. Buys first publication and reprint rights. Byline given. Pays on publication. Publishes ms an average of 6 months after acceptance. Queries preferred. Articles received on speculation only. Include cover letter with writer's background.
Nonfiction: Articles of general New World interest on history, art, literature, theatre, development, archaeology, etc. Emphasis on modern, up-to-date Latin America. Taboos are religious and political themes or articles with noninternational slant. "Photos are not required, but are a big plus." Buys 6-10 unsolicited mss/year. Length: 2,500 words maximum. Pays $400 for features.
Tips: "Send excellent photographs in both color and b&w. Address an international readership, not a local or national one. We want something insightful culturally."

BLUE RIDGE COUNTRY, Leisure Publishing, 3424 Brambleton Ave. SW, P.O. Box 21535, Roanoke VA 24018-1535. (703)989-6138. FAX: (703)989-7603. Editor: Kurt Rheinheimer. 75% freelance written. Bimonthly magazine on the Blue Ridge region from Maryland to Georgia. "The magazine is designed to celebrate the history, heritage and beauty of the Blue Ridge region. It is aimed at the adult, upscale readers who enjoy living or traveling in the mountain regions of Virginia, North Carolina, West Virginia, Kentucky, Tennessee, South Carolina and Georgia." Estab. 1972. Circ. 55,000. Pays on publication. Publishes ms an average of 6-8 months after acceptance. Byline given. Offers $50 kill fee for commissioned pieces only. Buys first and second serial (reprint) rights. Submit seasonal/holiday material 6 months in advance. Query for electronic submissions. Reports in 5 weeks. Sample copy for 9×12 SAE with $2 postage. Writer's guidelines for #10 SASE.

Nonfiction: General interest interest, historical/nostalgic, interview/profile, personal expeerience, photo feature, travel, history. Buys 25-30 mss/year. Query with or without published clips or send complete ms. Length: 500-4,000 words. Pays $50-350 for assigned articles; $25-300 for unsolicited articles.

Photos: State availability of photos with submission. Reviews transparencies. Offers $10-25 per photo and $100 for cover photo. Identification of subjects required. Buys all rights.

Columns/Departments: Country Roads (stories on people, events, ecology, history, antiques, books); Mountain Living (profiles of cooks and their recipes, garden tips, weather info); 50-300 words. Buys 12-24 mss/year. Query. Pays $10-25.

Tips: Freelancers needed for departmental shorts and "macro" issues affecting whole region. Need field reporters from all areas of Blue Ridge region. "Also, we need updates on the Blue Ridge, Appalachian trail, national forests, ecological issues, preservation movements."

COUNTRY ROADS QUARTERLY, Appalachian Life for Today, P.O. Box 479, Oakland MD 21550. Editor/Publisher: Carol L. Fox. Associate Editor: Lori Cooley. 75% freelance written. Quarterly regional magazine of Appalachia. "*CRQ* is designed to inform, interest and entertain readers about Maryland, Pennsylvania, and West Virginia people, places and things that make this area appealing." Estab. 1986. Pays on acceptance, or before publication. Byline given. Offers 20% kill fee. Buys first North American serial rights. Submit seasonal/holiday material 2 months in advance. Simultaneous and previously published submissions OK. Reports in 1 month on queries; 2 months on mss. Sample copy for $2 and 9×12 SAE with 4 first class stamps; free writer's guidelines.

Nonfiction: General interest, historical/nostalgic, humor, interview/profile, opinion, personal experience, photo features, religious, travel. "No first-person material, no fiction." Buys 40 mss/year. Query with or without published clips, or send complete ms. Length: 500-3,000 words. Pays $5-150. Sometimes pays expenses of writers on assignment.

Photos: Send photos with submission. Reviews 5×7 prints. Offers $2.50-10. Captions and identification of subjects required. Buys one-time rights.

Columns/Departments: Country Food/Cooking (homestyle cuisine/outdoor cooking), 500-2,000 words; Nostalgia (bygone days in Pennsylvania, Maryland, West Virginia portion of Appalachia), 500-3,000 words. Buys 20-30/year. Send complete ms. Length: 500-2,000 words. Pays $5-75.

Poetry: Free verse, haiku, light verse, traditional. Buys 10 poems/year. Length: 6-20 lines. Pays $5-10.

Fillers: Anecdotes, short humor. Buys 10/year. Length: 500 words maximum. Pays $5-15.

Tips: "I'm anxious to work with new writers but only if they follow my guidelines. Anyone who's lived in Appalachia would understand the uniqueness of mountains and rural living. All areas are open to freelancers—particularly profile, nostalgia, culture and history of the land. Material must have relevance to coverage area."

INLAND, The Magazine of the Middle West, Inland Steel Co., 18 S. Home Ave., Park Ridge IL 60068. Managing Editor: Sheldon A. Mix. 35-50% freelance written. Prefers to work with published/established writers, but eager to work with new/unpublished writers. Quarterly magazine that emphasizes steel products, services and company personnel. Circ. 8,000. **Pays on acceptance.** "Articles assigned are published within 4 months usually, but pieces in the inventory may remain years without being published." Buys first North American serial rights. "We have always paid the full fee on articles that have been killed." Byline given. Submit seasonal/holiday material at least 1 year in advance. Query for electronic submissions. Tries to report in 4 months. Free sample copy.

Nonfiction: Essays, humorous commentaries, profile, historical, think articles, personal opinion and photo essays. "We encourage individuality. At least half of each issue deals with staff-written steel subjects; half with widely ranging nonsteel matter. Articles and essays related somehow to the Midwest (Illinois, Wisconsin, Minnesota, Michigan, Missouri, Iowa, Nebraska, Kansas, North Dakota, South Dakota, Indiana and Ohio) in such subject areas as business, entertainment, history, folklore, sports, humor, current scene generally. But subject is less important than treatment. We like perceptive, thoughtful writing, and fresh ideas and approaches. Please don't send slight, rehashed historical pieces or any articles of purely local interest." Buys 5-10 unsolicited mss/year. Length: 1,200-5,000 words. Payment depends on individual assignment or unsolicited submission (usual range: $300-750). Sometimes pays expenses of writers on assignment.

Photos: Purchased with or without mss. Captions required. "Payment for pictorial essay same as for text feature."

Tips: "We are overstocked with nostalgia and are not looking for folksy treatments of family life and personal experiences. Our publication particularly needs humor that is neither threadbare nor in questionable taste, and shorter pieces (800-1,500 words) in which word choice and wit are especially important. The most frequent mistake made by writers in completing an article for us is untidiness in the manuscript (inattentiveness to good form, resulting in errors in spelling and facts, and in gaping holes in information). A writer who knows our needs and believes in himself or herself should keep trying. 'The Education of a Steel Hauler's Daughter'; 'How the Midwest was Won' (bicentennial of Northwest Ordinance); 'Adventures of a Young Balzac' (Vincent Starrett's early newspaper days in Chicago); articles on the gold rush to Pikes Peak in 1859; first steamboat in the Middle West; Illinois-Michigan Canal National Heritage Corridor; Jane Addams; Garrison Keillor; the birth of night baseball; pioneer women; origins of unusual place names in the Middle West; the Battle of Lake Erie (1812) are recent article examples."

INTERNATIONAL LIVING, Agora Publishing, 824 E. Baltimore St., Baltimore MD 21202. (301)234-0515. Editor: Kathleen Peddicord. 60% freelance written. "We prefer established writers and unpublished writers with original, first-hand experience." Monthly newsletter covering international lifestyles, travel, retirement, education, employment and investment for Americans. Aimed at affluent and not-so-affluent dreamers to whom the romance of living overseas has a strong appeal, especially when it involves money-saving angles. Estab. 1980. Circ. 55,000. Pays within 1 month of publication. Publishes ms an average of 6 months after acceptance. Byline given. Buys all rights. Submit seasonal/holiday material 2 months in advance. Query for electronic submissions. Reports in 1 month on queries; 6 weeks on mss. Sample copy $2.50; writer's guidelines for #10 SASE.
Nonfiction: Book excerpts (overseas, travel, retirement, investment, save money overseas, invest overseas); how-to (save money, find a job overseas); interview/profile (famous people and other Americans living abroad); personal experience; travel (unusual, imaginative destinations—give how-to's and costs); and other (humor, cuisine). "We want pithy, fact-packed articles. No vague, long-winded travel articles on well-trodden destinations. No articles on destinations in the United States." Buys 100 mss/year. Query with published clips or send complete ms. Length: 200-1,500 words. Pays $50-400.
Tips: "We are looking for writers who can combine original valuable information with a style that suggests the romance of life abroad. Break in with highly specific, well-researched material combining subjective impressions of living in a foreign country or city with information on taxes, cost of living, residency requirements, real estate, employment and entertainment possibilities. We do heavy rewrites and usually reorganize because of tight space requirements. We are moving toward more how-to and source lists."

ISLANDS, An International Magazine, Islands Publishing Company, 3886 State St., Santa Barbara CA 93105. FAX: (805)569-0349. Editor: Joan Tapper. 95% freelance written. Works with established writers. Bimonthly magazine covering islands throughout the world. "We cover accessible and once-in-a-lifetime islands from many different perspectives: travel, culture, lifestyle. We ask our authors to give us the essence of the island and do it with literary flair." Estab. 1981. Circ. 150,000. **Pays on acceptance.** Publishes ms an average of 8 months after acceptance. Byline given. Buys all rights. Query for electronic submissions. Reports in 1 month on queries; 6 weeks on ms. Sample copy for $5.25; writer's guidelines with #10 SASE.
Nonfiction: General interest, historical/nostalgic, interview/profile, personal experience, photo feature, technical, and any island-related material. "Each issue contains 3 or 4 feature articles of roughly 2,000-4,000 words, and 4 or 5 topical articles for departments, each of which runs approximately 750-1,500 words. Any authors who wish to be commissioned should send a detailed proposal for an article, an estimate of costs (if applicable) and samples of previously published work." Buys 25 mss/year. "The majority of our manuscripts are commissioned." Query with published clips or send complete ms. Length: 500-3,000 words. Pays $100-3,000. Pays expenses of writers on assignment.
Photos: State availability or send photos with query or ms. Pays $75-300 for 35mm transparencies. "Fine color photography is a special attraction of *Islands*, and we look for superb composition, technical quality and editorial applicability." Label slides with name and address, include captions, and submit in protective plastic sleeves. Identification of subjects required. Buys one-time rights.
Columns/Departments: "Columns and departments are generally assigned, but we have accepted short features for our Island Hopping department or very short items for our Logbook section. These should be highly focused on some specific aspect of islands." Buys 50 mss/year. Query with published clips. Length: 500-1,000 words. Pays $100-500.
Tips: "A freelancer can best break in to our publication with short (500-1,000 word) features or departments that are highly focused on some aspect of island life, history, people, etc. Stay away from general, sweeping articles. We are always looking for topics for our Islanders and Logbook pieces. These are a good place to break in. We will be using big name writers for major features; will continue to use newcomers and regulars for columns and departments."

For explanation of symbols, see the Key to Symbols and Abbreviations on Page 5. For unfamiliar words, see the Glossary.

‡**MAGAZINE OF THE MIDLANDS,** *Omaha World-Herald,* World-Herald Square, Omaha NE 68102. (402)444-1000. Magazine Editor: David Hendee. 10% freelance written. A Sunday newspaper magazine on people and places of the Midlands (Midwest). "We are a general interest, regional, Sunday newspaper magazine. Readership ranges from the cornfields of Iowa to the foothills of the Rocky Mountains." Estab. 1941. Circ. 288,000. Pays on publication. Byline given. Buys one-time rights. Submit seasonal/holiday material 3 months in advance. Simultaneous and previously published submissions OK. Reports in 1 month. Sample copy for 9×11 SAE with 2 first class stamps. Writer's guidelines for #10 SAE with 1 first class stamp.
Nonfiction: General interest, historical/nostalgic, humor, interview/profile, personal experience, photo feature, religious and travel. No poetry, filler or fiction. Buys 25 mss/year. Send complete ms. Length: 400-2,400 words. Pays $40-150 for unsolicited articles. Send photos with submission. Reviews contact sheets, negatives, transparencies and prints. Offers no additional payment for photos accepted with ms. Captions and identification of subjects required. Buys one-time rights.
Tips: "Articles on almost any subject—as long as there is a regional link—are in demand. Most common freelance mistakes: shallow reporting, material not geared to our audience, no sense of storytelling. Send SASE."

NORTHWEST MAGAZINE, Sunday magazine of *The Oregonian,* 1320 SW Broadway, Portland OR 97201. FAX: (503)227-5306. Editor: Ellen Heltzel. 90% freelance written. Prefers to work with published/established writers. Weekly newspaper Sunday supplement magazine. For an upscale, 25-49-year-old audience distributed throughout the Pacific Northwest. Circ. 420,000. Buys first serial rights for Oregon and Washington state. Pays mid-month in the month following acceptance. Publishes ms an average of 4 months after acceptance. Simultaneous submissions considered. Query for electronic submissions. Reports in 2 weeks. Sample copy for 11×14 SAE and 65¢ postage. Free writer's guidelines.
Nonfiction: "Contemporary, regional articles with a strong hook to concerns of the Pacific Northwest. Cover stories usually deal with regional issues and feature 'professional-level' reporting and writing. Personality profiles focus on young, Pacific Northwest movers and shakers. Short humor, personal essays, regional destination travel, entertainment, the arts and lifestyle stories also are appropriate. No history without a contemporary angle, boilerplate features of the type that are mailed out en masse with no specific hook to our local audience, poorly documented and highly opinionated issue stories that lack solid journalistic underpinnings, routine holiday features, or gushy essays that rhapsodize about daisies and rainbows. We expect top-quality writing and thorough, careful reporting. A contemporary writing style that features involving literary techniques like scenic construction stands the best chance." Buys 400 mss/year. Query much preferred, but complete ms considered. All mss on speculation. Length: 800-3,000 words. Pays $75-1,000.
Photos: Photographs should be professional quality Kodachrome slides. Pays $75-150.
Fiction: Address submissions to fiction editor. Short-short stories that reflect the culture and social structure of the Pacific Northwest in a way that relates to contemporary life in the region as well as to the magazine's target audience. New writers welcomed; Northwest writers preferred. Buys 20-24 mss/year. Length: 1,500-2,500 words. Pays $200-225.
Poetry: Paul Pintarich, book review editor. "*Northwest Magazine* seeks poetry with solid imagery, skilled use of language and having appeal to a broad and intelligent audience. We do not accept cutesy rhymes, jingles, doggeral or verse written for a specific season, i.e., Christmas, Valentine's Day, etc. We currently are accepting poems only from poets in the Pacific Northwest region (Oregon, Washington, Idaho, Montana, Northern California, British Columbia and Alaska). Poems from Nevada and Hawaii receive consideration. We are looking for a few fine and distinctive poems each week. Poems on dot-matrix printers accepted if near letter-quality only. No handwritten submissions or threats." Send at least 3 poems for consideration. Length: 23 lines maximum. Pays $10 on acceptance.
Tips: "Pay rates and editing standards are up, and this market will become far more competitive. However, new writers with talent and good basic language skills still are encouraged to try us. Printing quality and flexibility should improve, increasing the magazine's potential for good color photographers and illustrators."

NOW AND THEN, Center for Appalachian Studies and Services, East Tennessee State University, Box 19180A, Johnson City TN 37614. (615)929-5348. FAX: (615)929-5770. 80% freelance written. A tri-annual regional magazine. Estab. 1984. Circ. 1,500. Pays on publication. Publishes ms an averge of 6 months after acceptance. Byline given. Buys one-time rights. Simultaneous and previously published submissions OK. Reports in 1 month on queries; 4 months on mss. Sample copy $3.50; writer's guidelines for #10 SASE.
Nonfiction: Book excerpts, essays, historical, humor, interview/profile, personal experience, photo feature. "We do have a special focus in each issue—we've featured Appalachian Blacks, Cherokees, women, music and veterans. Write for future themes. Stereotypes (especially granny rocking on the front porch), generalizations, sentimental writing are rejected. It must have to do with Appalachia." Buys 8 mss/year. Query with or without published clips, or send complete ms. Length: 2,500 words. Pays $15-60 for assigned articles; $10-60 for unsolicited articles. Sometimes pays expenses of writers on assignment.
Photos: Send photos with submission. Reviews contact sheets and prints. Offers no additional payment for photos accepted with ms. Captions, model releases and identification of subjects required. Buys one-time rights.

Fiction: Ethnic, experimental, historical, humorous, novel excerpts, slice-of-life vignettes. "Everything we publish has to be by or about Appalachians. No stereotypes, generalizations, or sentimentality." Buys 3 mss/ year. Send complete ms. Length: 2,500 words maximum. Pays $10-50.

Poetry: Avant-garde, free verse. "Must have something to do with the Appalachian region. Avoid stereotypes, generalizations and sentimentality." Buys 30-35 poems/year. Pays 2 contributor's copies and a year subscription. Send no more than 5 poems at a time.

Tips: "Everything we publish has something to do with life in Appalachia present and past. Profiles of people living and working in the region, short stories that convey the reality of life in Appalachia (which can include malls, children who wear shoes and watch MTV) are the kinds of things we're looking for."

RURALITE, P.O. Box 558, Forest Grove OR 97116. (503)357-2105. Editor: Ken Dollinger. 50-70% freelance written. Works with new/unpublished writers each year. Monthly magazine primarily slanted toward small town and rural families, served by consumer-owned electric utilities in Washington, Oregon, Idaho, Nevada, Alaska and northern California. "Ours is an old-fashioned down-home publication, with something for all members of the family." Estab. 1954. Circ. 250,000. **Pays on acceptance.** Buys first serial rights and occasionally second serial (reprint) rights. Byline given. Submit seasonal material at least 3 months in advance. Sample copy and writer's guidelines for $1 and 10 × 13 SAE.

Nonfiction: Walter J. Wentz, nonfiction editor. Primarily human-interest stories about rural or small-town folk, preferably living in areas (Northwest states and Alaska) served by Rural Electric Cooperatives. Articles emphasize self-reliance, overcoming of obstacles, cooperative effort, hard or interesting work, unusual or interesting avocations, odd or unusual hobbies or histories, public spirit or service and humor. Also considers how-to, advice for rural folk, little-known and interesting Northwest history, people or events. Stories on economic recovery or development, or unusual small businesses in our service areas, inventors, entrepreneurs, innovators in small towns or rural areas will be carefully considered. As always, energy-related stories pertaining to publicly-owned utilities will be of interest. No "sentimental nostalgia or subjects outside the Pacific Northwest; nothing racy." Buys 15-20 mss/year. Query. Length: 500-900 words. Pays $30-140, depending upon length, quality, appropriateness and interest, number and quality of photos.

Photos: Reviews b&w negatives with contact sheets. Illustrated stories have better chance for acceptance.

Tips: "Freelance submissions are evaluated and decided upon immediately upon arrival. We need good, solid, well-illustrated 'first-feature' articles to lead off the magazine each month. These receive our best pay rate. We are overloaded with second- and third-feature stories already. We will be placing more emphasis on illustrations and layout; good, professional-quality b&w negatives will add to the appeal of any mss. Due to a loss of feature pages, we will be judging freelance submissions much more critically."

SUNDAY JOURNAL MAGAZINE, Providence Journal Co., 75 Fountain St., Providence RI 02902. (401)277-7349. Editor: Elliot Krieger. 50% freelance written. Weekly Sunday supplement magazine about news of Rhode Island and New England. Estab. 1860. Circ. 250,000. Pays on publication. Byline given. Buys first North American serial rights. Submit seasonal/holiday 3 months in advance. Simultaneous submissions OK. Query for electronic submissions. Reports in 2 weeks on queries.

Nonfiction: Book excerpts, exposé, general interest, historical/nostalgic, interview/profile and photo feature. "We are strictly a regional news magazine." No fiction, poetry or personal opinion. Buys 100 mss/year. Query. Length: 750-5,000. Pays $100-1,000.

Photos: State availability of photos with submission. Offers $25-100/photo. Captions and identification of subjects required.

Fiction: Mainstream, historical. Must relate to Rhode Island. Buys 5-10 mss/year. Send complete ms. Length: 10,000 words maximum. Pays $100-750.

Alabama

ALABAMA HERITAGE, University of Alabama, Box 870342, Tuscaloosa AL 35487-0342. (205)348-7467. Editor: Suzanne Wolfe. Managing Editor: G. Ward Hubbs. 50% freelance written. Quarterly magazine on Alabama history and culture. "*Alabama Heritage* is a nonprofit historical quarterly published by the University of Alabama for the intelligent lay reader. We are interested in lively, well written and thoroughly researched articles on Alabama/Southern history and culture. Readability and accuracy are essential." Estab. 1986. Pays on publication. Byline given. Buys first rights and second serial (reprint) rights. Query for electronic submissions. Reports in 1 month. Sample copy $3.50. Writer's guidelines for #10 SASE.

Nonfiction: Historical. "We do not want fiction, poetry, book reviews, articles on current events or living artists and personal/family reminiscences." Buys 10 mss/year. Query. Length: 1,500-5,000 words. Pays $100 minimum. Pays 10 copies to each author.

Photos: Reviews contact sheets. Identification of subjects required. Buys one-time rights.

Tips: "Authors need to remember that we regard history as a fascinating subject, not as a dry recounting of dates and facts. Articles that are lively and engaging, in addition to being well researched, will find interested readers among our editors. No term papers, please. All areas of our magazine are open to freelance writers. Best approach is a written query."

Alaska

ALASKA, The Magazine of Life on the Last Frontier, Suite 200, 808 E. St., Anchorage AK 99501. (907)272-6070. Editor: Ron Dalby. 60% freelance written. Eager to work with new/unpublished writers. A monthly magazine covering topics "uniquely Alaskan." Estab. 1935. Circ. 235,000. **Pays on acceptance.** Publishes ms an average of 6 months after acceptance. Byline given. Buys first rights or one-time rights. Submit seasonal/holiday material 1 year in advance. Query for electronic submissions. Reports in 1 month on queries; 2 months on manuscripts. Sample copy $3; writer's guidelines for #10 SASE.

Nonfiction: Historical/nostalgic, how-to (on anything Alaskan), humor, interview/profile, personal experience and photo feature. Also travel articles and Alaska destination stories. Does not accept fiction or poetry. Buys 60 mss/year. Query. Length: 100-2,500 words. Pays $100-1,250. Pays expenses of writers on assignment.

Photos: Send photos with submission. Reviews 35mm or larger transparencies. Captions and identification of subjects required.

ALASKA OUTDOORS MAGAZINE, Swensen's Alaska Outdoors Corporation, Suite 200, 400 "D" St., P.O. Box 190324, Anchorage AK 99519. (907)276-2672. FAX: (907)258-6027. Editor: Evan Swensen. Managing Editor: Diane Clawson. 90% freelance written. Monthly magazine on outdoor recreation in Alaska. Estab. 1978. Circ. 55,000. Pays 30 days after publication. Publishes ms an average of 4 months after acceptance. Byline given. Offers 50% kill fee. Buys first North American serial rights. Submit seasonal/holiday material 4 months in advance. Query for electronic submissions. Reports in 3 weeks on queries; 4 weeks on mss. Sample copy $1 with 8½×11 SAE and 3 first class stamps. Free writer's guidelines.

Nonfiction: Essays, how-to (outdoor recreation), humor, personal experience, photo feature and travel. Buys 150-175 mss/year. Query with or without published clips or send complete ms. Length: 800-2,400 words. Pays $75-200. Pays in advertising.

Photos: Send photos with submission. Reviews transparencies and prints. Offers no additional payment for photos accepted with ms (except cover). Captions, model releases and identification of subjects required. Buys one-time rights.

Arizona

ARIZONA HIGHWAYS, 2039 W. Lewis Ave., Phoenix AZ 85009. (602)258-6641. FAX: (602)254-4505. Managing Editor: Richard G. Stahl. 90% freelance written. Prefers to work with published/established writers. State-owned magazine designed to help attract tourists into and through the state. Estab. 1925. **Pays on acceptance.** Publishes ms an average of 6 months after acceptance. Writer's guidelines for SASE.

Nonfiction: Contact managing editor. Subjects include narratives and exposition dealing with contemporary events, popular geography, history, anthropology, nature, special things to see and do, outstanding arts and crafts, travel, etc.; all must be oriented toward Arizona and the Southwest. Buys 6 mss/issue. Buys first serial rights. Query with "a lead paragraph and brief outline of story. We deal with professionals only, so include list of current credits." Length: 600-2,000 words. Pays 35-50¢/word. Sometimes pays expenses of writers on assignment. Writer's guidelines available.

Photos: "We will use transparencies of 2¼, 4×5 or larger, and 35mm when it displays exceptional quality or content. We prefer Kodachrome in 35mm. Each transparency *must* be accompanied by information attached to each photograph: where, when, what. No photography will be reviewed by the editors unless the photographer's name appears on *each* and *every* transparency." Pays $80-350 for "selected" transparencies. Buys one-time rights.

Tips: "Writing must be of professional quality, warm, sincere, in-depth, well-peopled and accurate. Avoid themes that describe first trips to Arizona, the Grand Canyon, the desert, Colorado River running, etc. Emphasis is to be on Arizona adventure and romance as well as flora and fauna, when appropriate, and themes that can be photographed. Double check your manuscript for accuracy."

‡**TUCSON LIFESTYLE,** Old Pueblo Press, Suite 13, 7000 E. Tangue Verde Rd., Tucson AZ 85715. (602)721-2929. Editor-in-Chief: Sue Giles. 90% freelance written. Prefers to work with published/established writers. A monthly magazine covering city-related events and topics. Circ. 32,000. **Pays on acceptance.** Publishes ms an average of 6 months after acceptance. Byline given. Buys first rights and second serial (reprint) rights. Submit seasonal/holiday material 1 year in advance. Previously published submissions OK. Reports in 2 months. Sample copy $3; free writer's guidelines.

Nonfiction: All stories need a Tucson angle. Historical/nostalgic, humor, interview/profile, personal experience, travel and local stories. Special Christmas issue (December). "We do not accept *anything* that does not pertain to Tucson or Arizona." Buys 100 mss/year. Query. Length: open. Pays $50-300. Sometimes pays expenses of writers on assignment.

Photos: Reviews contact sheets, 2¼ × 2¼ transparencies and 5 × 7 prints. Offers $25-100/photo. Identification of subjects required. Buys one-time rights.

Columns/Departments: In Business — articles on Tucson businesses and business people; Southwest Homes (environmental living in Tucson: homes, offices). Buys 36 mss/year. Query. Length: open. Pays $100-200.

Tips: Features are most open to freelancers. " 'Style' is not of paramount importance; good, clean copy with interesting lead is a 'must.' "

Arkansas

ARKANSAS TIMES, Arkansas Writers' Project, Inc., Box 34010, Little Rock AR 72203. (501)375-2985. Editor: Richard Martin. 50% freelance written. Monthly magazine. "We are an Arkansas magazine. We seek to appreciate, enliven and, where necessary, improve the quality of life in the state." Circ. 32,000. **Pays on acceptance.** Publishes ms an average of 3 months after acceptance. Byline given. Buys first serial rights. Submit seasonal/holiday material 5 months in advance. Simultaneous and previously published submissions OK. Reports in 2 weeks on queries; 1 month on mss. Sample copy $3.50; writer's guidelines for SASE.

Nonfiction: Book excerpts; exposé (in investigative reporting vein); general interest; historical/nostalgic; humor; interview/profile; opinion; recreation; and entertainment, all relating to Arkansas. "The Arkansas angle is all-important." Buys 24 mss/year. Query. Length: 250-6,000 words. Pays $100-500. Sometimes pays the expenses of writers on assignment.

Photos: Melissa James, art director. State availability of photos. Pays $25-75. Identification of subjects required. Buys one-time rights.

Columns/Departments: Mike Trimble, column editor. In Our Times (articles on people, places and things in Arkansas or with special interest to Arkansans). "This is the department that is most open to freelancers." Buys 15 mss/year. Query. Length: 250-1,000 words. Pays $100-150.

Tips: "The frustrating aspect of freelance submissions is that so many of the writers have obviously never seen our magazine. Only writers who know something about Arkansas should send us mss."

California

CALIFORNIA MAGAZINE, 11601 Wilshire Blvd., Los Angeles CA 90025. (213)479-6511. Editor: Bob Roe. Managing Editor: Rebecca Levy. 90% freelance written. Monthly magazine about California — lifestyle, the arts, politics, business, crime, education, technology, etc. Estab. 1976. Circ. 363,000. **Pays on acceptance.** Publishes ms an average of 3 months after acceptance. Byline given. Offers variable kill fee. Buys first North American serial rights. Reports in 6 weeks on queries. Sample copy $2 and 9 × 12 SAE.

Nonfiction: Greg Critser, Susan Gordon and David Weir (San Francisco office), features editors. Exposé (environment, government, education, business), general interest, historical/nostalgic, humor, interview/profile, new product, photo feature and travel; *all* must pertain to California. Length: 800-4,000 words. Pays expenses of writers on assignment.

Photos: Assigns most photos; reviews portfolios. Captions, model releases and identification of subjects required. Buys one-time rights.

Columns/Departments: Open to freelance: Travel, New West. Query with published clips. Length: 750-2,000 words. Pays $450-1,500.

Tips: "Query first with clips. *Read* the magazine."

L.A. STYLE, 6834 Hollywood Blvd., Los Angeles CA 90028. (213)467-4244. Editor–in–Chief: Ms. Joie Davidow. Managing Editor: Jeffrey Hirsch. 80% freelance written. Monthly magazine on Los Angeles lifestyle. "Our readers are highly educated and affluent; they are involved in the artistic, social and political whirlwind of Los Angeles and they are always interested in what is new — *L.A. Style* attempts to discover and re-discover Los Angeles." Circ. 65,000. Pays within 30 days of acceptance. Byline given. Offers 25% kill fee — "one rewrite may be required before kill fee is paid." Buys first rights. Submit seasonal/holiday material 4 months in advance. Simultaneous and photocopied submissions OK. Reports in "one week to two months depending on editorial load." Sample copy $5.50; writer's guidelines for #10 SASE.

Nonfiction: Book excerpts, essays, exposé, general interest, historical/nostalgic, how-to, humor, interview/profile, opinion, personal experience, photo feature, technical, travel. No "health and beauty stereotyped women's magazine stories; any story that does not have a strong L.A. angle." Buys 100 mss/year. Query with published clips or send complete ms. Length: 1,000-5,000 words. Pays $300-1,500. Sometimes pays expenses of writers on assignment.

Photos: "We prefer to assign our own art." Buys one-time rights.

Fiction: Bob LaBrasca, senior editor. Erotica, ethnic, experimental, humorous, novel excerpts, slice-of-life vignettes. "No teen, genre, romance, devotional—what we do want is sophisticated, highly literate, innovative fiction." Buys 4-8 mss/year. Send complete ms. Length: 1,000-5,000 words. Pays $300-1,000.

Tips: "It is not impossible to write for *L.A. Style* without living in Los Angeles—it is just very unlikely that writers who do not know the evolving city intimately will be able to find the contemporary slant we require. Service pieces, how-to pieces, humor pieces and overview pieces are the hardest to come by and the most eagerly considered."

LOS ANGELES MAGAZINE, ABC/Capital Cities, 1888 Century Park East, Los Angeles CA 90067. (213)557-7569. Editor: Lew Harris. 98% freelance written. Monthly magazine about southern California. "The primary editorial role of the magazine is to aid a literate, upscale audience in getting the most out of life in the Los Angeles area." Estab. 1960. Circ. 174,000. Pays on publication. Publishes ms an average of 4 months after acceptance. Byline given. Offers 30% kill fee. Buys first North American serial rights. Submit seasonal/holiday material 3-6 months in advance. Reports in 6 weeks. Sample copy $5; writer's guidelines for #10 SASE.

Nonfiction: Rodger Claire, executive editor. Book excerpts (about L.A. or by famous L.A. author); exposé (any local issue); general interest; historical/nostalgic (about L.A. or Hollywood); and interview/profile (about L.A. person). Buys 400 mss/year. Query with published clips. Length: 250-3,500 words. Pays $50-1,200. Sometimes pays expenses of writers on assignment.

Photos: Rodger Claire, photo editor. State availability of photos.

Columns/Departments: Rodger Claire, executive editor. Buys 170 mss/year. Query with published clips. Length: 250-1,200 words. Pays $50-500.

‡LOS ANGELES READER, Suite 301, 5550 Wilshire Blvd., Los Angeles CA 90036. (213)933-0161. Editorial Director: Eric Mankin. 85% freelance written. Only serious, polished work by experienced writers should be submitted. Weekly tabloid of features and reviews for "affluent young Los Angelenos interested in the arts and popular culture." Circ. 70,000. Pays on publication. Publishes ms an average of 3 months after acceptance. Byline given. Buys one-time rights. Reports in 2 months. Sample copy $1 and 9×12 SAE; free writer's guidelines.

Nonfiction: General interest, journalism, interview/profile, personal experience and photo features—all with strong local slant. Buys "dozens" of mss/year. Send complete ms. Length: 200-2,000 words. Pays $10-250.

Tips: "Break in with submissions for our Cityside page which uses short news items on Los Angeles happenings. We only want writing about local themes, topics and people by local writers."

LOS ANGELES TIMES MAGAZINE, Los Angeles Times, Times Mirror Sq., Los Angeles CA 90053. Editorial Director: Wallace Guenther. Editor: Linda Mathews. 50% freelance written. Weekly magazine of regional general interest. Circ. 1 million. Payment schedule varies. Publishes ms an average of 2 months after acceptance. Byline given. Buys first North American serial rights. Submit seasonal/holiday material 3 months in advance. Simultaneous queries and submissions OK. Computer printout submissions acceptable; no dot-matrix. Reports in 1 month. Sample copy for 9×12 SAE and 6 first class stamps. Writer's guidelines for SAE and 2 first class stamps.

Nonfiction: General interest, historical/nostalgic, interview/profile, personal experience and photo feature. Must have California tie-in, but no need to be set in California. Query with published clips. "We welcome all queries." Length: 400-1,800 words. Pays $400-2,000. Sometimes pays the expenses of writers on assignment.

Photos: Query first. Reviews color transparencies and b&w prints. Payment varies. Captions, model releases and identification of subjects required. Buys one-time rights.

Tips: "The writer should know the subject well or have researched it adequately. As for style, the best style is when the writer goes to the trouble of employing proper English and self-edits an article prior to submission."

MONTEREY LIFE MAGAZINE, The Magazine of California's Spectacular Central Coast, P.O. Box 2107, Monterey CA 93942. (408)372-9200. FAX: (408)372-6259. Editor: Sue Sanguinetti. 50% freelance written. Prefers to work with published/established writers. Monthly magazine covering art, regional affairs, music, sports, environment and lifestyles for "a sophisticated readership in the Central California coast area." Estab. 1980. Circ. 25,000. Pays on publication. Publishes ms an average of 3 months after acceptance. Byline given. Submit seasonal/holiday material 4 months in advance. Simultaneous queries and submissions OK. Electronic submissions acceptable via IBM format but requires hard copy also. Reports in 1 month on queries; 6 weeks on mss. Sample copy for $1.85 postage and SAE.

Nonfiction: Historical/nostalgic, humor, interview/profile, photo feature and travel. No poetry. "All articles must pertain to issues and lifestyles within the counties of Monterey, Santa Cruz and San Benito." Buys 75 mss/year. Query with published clips if available. Length: 175-3,000 words. Pays 10¢/word. Sometimes pays expenses of writers on assignment.

Photos: State availability of photos. Pays $45-100 for transparencies; $15-75 for 5 × 7 and 8 × 10 b&w prints. Captions, model releases and identification of subjects required.

Columns/Departments: Community Focus. Query with published clips. Length: 150-500 words. Pays $25-100.

Tips: "Since we have a core of very capable freelance writers for longer articles, it is easier to break in with short articles and fillers. Ask probing questions."

NORTHCOAST VIEW, Blarney Publishing, P.O. Box 1374, Eureka CA 95502. (707)443-4887. Publishers/Editors: Scott K. Ryan and Damon Maguire. 95% freelance written. Works with a small number of new/unpublished writers each year. A monthly magazine covering entertainment, recreation, the arts, consumer news, in-depth news, fiction and poetry for Humboldt and Del Norte counties audience, mostly 18-50 year olds. Estab. 1982. Circ. 22,500. Pays on publication. Publishes ms an average of 1-6 months after acceptance. Byline given. Generally buys all rights, but will reassign. Submit seasonal/holiday material 6 months in advance. Simultaneous queries, and simultaneous (so long as not in our area), and previously published (so long as rights available) submissions OK. Query for electronic submissions. Reports in 2 months on queries; 6 months on mss. Sample copy $2; writer's guidelines for SASE.

Nonfiction: Book excerpts (locally written); expose (consumer, government); historical/nostalgic (local); humor; interview/profile (entertainment, recreation, arts or political people planning to visit county); new product (for arts); photo feature (local for art section); and travel (weekend and short retreats accessible from Humboldt County). "Most features need a Humboldt County slant." Special issues include Christmas (December). Buys 10-20 mss/year. Query with published clips or send complete ms. Length: 1,250-2,500 words. Pays $25-75.

Photos: State availability of photos with query letter or ms and send proof sheet, if available. Pays $5-30 for 5 × 7 b&w prints. Buys all rights but will reassign.

Columns/Departments: A La Carte (restaurant reviews of county restaurants); Ex Libris (books); Reel Views (film); Vinyl Views (albums); Cornucopia (calendar); Poetry; Rearview (art). Buys 80-100 mss/year. Send complete ms. Length: 500-750 words. Pays $25-75.

Fiction: Adventure, condensed novels, experimental, fantasy, horror, humorous, mystery, novel excerpts (local), science fiction and suspense. "We are open to most ideas and like to publish new writers. Topic and length are all very flexible—quality reading is the only criteria." No clichéd, contrived or predictable fiction." Buys 5-10 mss/year. Send complete ms. Length: 600-4,500 words; Submissions without SASE will not be returned.

Poetry: Stephen Miller, poetry editor. Avant-garde, free verse, haiku, light verse and traditional. Open to all types. No "sappy, overdone or symbolic poetry." Buys work of 12-20 poets (3-4 poems each)/year. Submit maximum 5 poems. Length: 12-48 lines. Pays $25.

Tips: "Our greatest need always seems to be for reviews—book, album and film. Films need to be current. Book and album—we're always looking for somewhat current but lesser known works that are exceptional. The most frequent mistakes made by writers are using too few quotes and too much paraphrasing."

‡**ORANGE COAST MAGAZINE, The Magazine of Orange County**, O.C.N.L., Inc., 245-D Fischer, Costa Mesa CA 92626. (714)545-1900. Editor: Palmer Thomason Jones. Managing Editor: Erik Himmelsbach. Associate Editor: Elizabeth Smith. 95% freelance written. Monthly. "*Orange Coast* is designed to inform and enlighten the educated, upscale residents of affluent Orange Country, California and is highly graphic and well-researched." Estab. 1974. Circ. 40,000. **Pays on acceptance.** Publishes ms an average of 5 months after acceptance. Byline given. Buys first serial rights. Submit seasonal/holiday material 6 months in advance. Simultaneous queries and submissions OK. Query for electronic submissions. Reports in 2 months. Sample copy $2.50 with 10 × 12 SAE and $2.25 postage; writer's guidelines for SASE.

Nonfiction: Expose (Orange Country government, refugees, politics, business, crime); general interest (with Orange County focus); historical/nostalgic; guides to activities and services; interview/profile (Orange County prominent citizens); local sports; lifestyle features and travel. Special issues include Dining (March); Health and Beauty (January); Resort Guide (October); Home and Garden (June); and Holiday (December). Buys 100 mss/year. Query or send complete ms. No phone queries. Length: 1,000-4,000 words. Pays $250 maximum.

Columns/Departments: Local Consumer, Investments, Business, Health, Profiles, Adventure, and Destination. Not open for submission are: Music, Art, Medicine, Film, Sports, Insight, Couples, Parents, Restaurant Review ("we have regular reviewers"). Buys 200 mss/year. Query or send complete ms; no phone queries. Length: 1,000-2,000 words. Pays $100 maximum.

Fiction: Buys only under rare circumstances. Send complete ms. Length: 1,000-5,000 words. Must have an Orange County setting. Pays $150 maximum.

Tips: "Most features are assigned to writers we've worked with before. Don't try to sell us 'generic' journalism. *Orange Coast* prefers well-written stories with specific and unusual angles that in some way include Orange County. Be professional and write manuscripts that present you as a stylized, creative writer. A lot of writers miss the Orange County angle. Our writers *must* concentrate on the local angle. We get far too many generalized manuscripts."

‡**PALM SPRINGS LIFE**, Desert Publications, Inc., 303 N. Indian Ave., Palm Springs CA 92262. (619)325-2333. FAX: (619)325-7008. Editor: Jamie Pricer. Estab. 1959. 30% freelance written. Monthly magazine covering "affluent resort/southern California/Coachella Valley. Printed in full color on the highest quality 70 lb. paper. *Palm Springs Life* is a luxurious magazine aimed at the 'affluence' market. Surveys show that our readership has a median age of 50.1, a median household income of $190,000, a primary home worth $275,150 and a second home worth $190,500." Circ. 75,000. Pays on publication. Publishes ms an average of 3 months after acceptance. Byline given. Buys universal (all) rights. Submit seasonal/holiday material 4 months in advance. Simultaneous and previously published submissions OK. Query for electronic submissions. Reports in 2 weeks. Sample copy $5.
Nonfiction: Book excerpts, general interest, historical/nostalgic, humor, interview/profile, new product, photo feature and travel. Special issues include Real Estate (May); Home and Garden (June); Health (July); Desert Living Animal/Coachella Valley focus (September); Desert Progress (October); Arts & Culture (November); Holiday Shopping (December). Query with published clips. Length: 700-1,200 words. Pays 15¢/word. Sometimes pays the expenses of writers on assignment.
Photos: Reviews 4×5 and 35mm transparencies. Offers $50-375 (for cover). Captions, model releases and identification of subjects required.
Tips: "*Palm Springs Life* publishes articles about dining, fashion, food, wine, beauty, health, sports (especially tennis and golf) and the lifestyle of the powerful, rich and famous. We are always interested in new ways to enjoy wealth, display luxury and consume it. We want to hear what's 'in' and what's 'out,' what's new in Palm Springs and the Coachella Valley, and how to solve problems experienced by our readers."

‡**PALO ALTO WEEKLY**, Embarcadero Publishing Co., 703 High St., P.O. Box 1610, Palo Alto CA 94301. (415)326-8210. Editor: Becky Bartindale. 5% freelance written. Weekly tabloid focusing on local issues and local sources. Estab. 1979. Circ. 48,000. Pays on publication. Publishes ms an average of 1 month after acceptance. Byline given. Offers 50% kill fee. Buys first rights. Submit seasonal/holiday material 2 months in advance. Reports in 2 weeks. Sample copy for 9×12 SAE with 2 first class stamps.
Nonfiction: General interest, historical/nostalgic, interview/profile, photo feature. Together (weddings—mid February); Interiors (May, October). Nothing that is not local; no travel. Buys 25 mss/year. Query with published clips. Length: 700-1,000 words. Pays $25-40.
Photos: State availability of photos with submission. Reviews contact sheets and 5×7 prints. Offers $10 minimum per photo. Captions, model releases and identification of subjects required. Buys one-time rights.
Tips: "Writers have the best chance if they live within circulation area and know publication and area well. DON'T send generic, broad-based pieces. The most open sections are food, interiors, sports. Keep it LOCAL."

PENINSULA MAGAZINE, 656 Bair Island Rd., 2nd Fl., Redwood City CA 94063. (415)368-8800. FAX: (415)368-6251. Editor: David Gorn. Managing Editor: Dale Conour. 50% freelance written. A monthly magazine on San Mateo and Santa Clara counties. "We have an educated and affluent readership, so we need stories with a little bite." Estab. 1985. Circ. 40,000. **Pays on acceptance.** Publishes ms an average of 2 months after acceptance. Byline given. Offers 30% kill fee. Buys first rights. Submit seasonal/holiday material 4 months in advance. Simultaneous and previously published submissions OK. Query for electronic submissions. Reports in 2 months. Sample copy for 9×12 SAE with $4 postage. Writer's guidelines for #10 SAE with 2 first class stamps.
Nonfiction: Exposé, general interest, interview/profile, photo feature, environment, innovations, power and money, the arts, history, fashion, finance, food, health, fitness and medicine. Buys 30 mss/year. Send complete ms. Length: 2,000-4,000 words. Pays $125-600 for assigned articles. Pays $75-350 for unsolicited articles. Sometimes pays the expenses of writers on assignment.
Photos: State availability of photos with submission or send photos with submission. Reviews transparencies and prints. Offers $10-100 per photo. Model releases and identification of subjects required. Buys one-time rights.

‡**RANCH & COAST**, L.A. West Media Magazine, Inc., #204, 462 Stevens Ave., Solana Beach CA 92075. (619)481-7659. FAX: (619)481-6205. Publisher/Editor-in-Chief: Hershel Sinay. Editor: Mary Shepardson. 30% freelance written. Monthly magazine targeted at a sophisticated, upper-income readership, in San Diego County and surrounding areas. Most articles have a strong San Diego County focus. Circ. 30,000. Pays on publication. The vast majority of feature articles and departments are written on assignment; very few unsolicited mss are purchased. Queries with published clips are preferred to complete mss as the magazine's needs are very specific. Sample copy $4; writer's guidelines for SASE.
Photos: Availability of top-quality photos is essential.
Tips: "Familiarity with *Ranch & Coast* in its current form is strongly advised."

SACRAMENTO MAGAZINE, P.O. Box 2424, Sacramento CA 95812-2424. Editor: Jan Haag. 60-70% freelance written. Works with a small number of new/unpublished writers each year. Monthly magazine emphasizing a strong local angle on politics, local issues, human interest and consumer items for readers in the middle to high income brackets. Estab. 1975. Pays on publication. Publishes ms an average of 3 months after acceptance. Rights vary; generally buys first North American serial rights, rarely second serial (reprint) rights. Original mss only (no previously published submissions). Reports in 2 months. Sample copy $3.50; writer's guidelines for #10 SASE.

Nonfiction: Local issues vital to Sacramento quality of life. Buys 15 unsolicited feature mss/year. Query first; no phone queries. Length: 2,000-3,000 words, depending on author, subject matter and treatment. Sometimes pays expenses of writers on assignment.

Photos: State availability of photos. Payment varies depending on photographer, subject matter and treatment. Captions (including IDs, location and date) required. Buys one-time rights.

Columns/Departments: Business, home and garden, media, parenting, first person essays, local travel, gourmet, profile, sports and city arts (850-1,250 words); City Lights (250 words).

SAN FRANCISCO BAY GUARDIAN, 520 Hampshire St., San Francisco CA 94110. (415)255-3100. Editor/Publisher: Bruce Brugmann. 60% freelance written. Works with a small number of new/unpublished writers each year. An urban newsweekly specializing in investigative, consumer and lifestyle reporting for a sophisticated, urban audience. Circ. 80,000. Pays 1 month after publication. Publishes ms an average of 2 months after acceptance. Byline given. Buys 200 mss/year. Buys first rights. No simultaneous or multiple submissions. Query for electronic submissions.

Nonfiction: Vince Bielski, city editor; Eileen Ecklund, arts and entertainment editor; also features and book editor. Publishes "incisive local news stories, investigative reports, features, analysis and interpretation, how-to, consumer and entertainment reviews. Most stories have a Bay Area angle." Freelance material should have a "public interest advocacy journalism approach." Sometimes pays the expenses of writers on assignment.

Photos: John Schmitz, photo editor. Purchased with or without mss.

Tips: "Work with our volunteer and intern projects in investigative, political and consumer reporting. We teach the techniques and send interns out to do investigative research. We like to talk to writers in our office before they begin doing a story."

THE SAN GABRIEL VALLEY MAGAZINE, Miller Books, 2908 W. Valley Blvd., Alhambra CA 91803. (213)284-7607. Editor-in-Chief: Joseph Miller. 75% freelance written. Bimonthly magazine. For middle- to upper-income people who dine out often at better restaurants in Los Angeles County. Estab. 1962. Circ. 3,400. Pays on publication. Publishes ms an average of 45 days after acceptance. Buys simultaneous rights, second serial (reprint) rights and one-time rights. Phone queries OK. Submit seasonal/holiday material 1 month in advance. Simultaneous and previously published submissions OK. Reports in 2 weeks. Sample copy $1.

Nonfiction: Exposé (political); informational (restaurants in the Valley); inspirational (success stories and positive thinking); interview (successful people and how they made it); profile (political leaders in the San Gabriel Valley); and travel (places in the Valley). Interested in 500-word humor articles. Buys 18 unsolicited mss/year. Length: 500-10,000 words. Pays 5¢/word.

Columns/Departments: Restaurants, Education, Valley News and Valley Personality. Buys 2 mss/issue. Send complete ms. Length: 500-1,500 words. Pays 5¢/word.

Fiction: Historical (successful people) and western (articles about Los Angeles County). Buys 2 mss/issue. Send complete ms. Length: 500-10,000 words. Pays 5¢/word.

Tips: "Send us a good personal success story about a Valley or a California personality. We are also interested in articles on positive thinking."

VALLEY MAGAZINE, World of Communications, Inc., Suite 275, 16800 Devonshire St., Granada Hills CA 91344. (818)368-3353. Editor: Barbara Wernik. 90% freelance written. Monthly magazine covering topics and people of interest to the San Fernando Valley. Estab. 1978. Circ. 40,000. Pays within 2 months of acceptance. Publishes ms an average of 3 months after acceptance. Byline given. Offers 20% kill fee. Buys first North American serial rights. Submit seasonal/holiday material 6 months in advance. Simultaneous and previously published submissions OK. Reports in 2 weeks. Sample copy for $3 and 10×13 SAE; writer's guidelines for #10 SASE.

Nonfiction: Book excerpts, education, business, essays, general interest, how-to, humor, interview/profile, personal experience and travel. "General interest articles range from health to business to personality profiles. There must be a Valley slant. Audience is upscale, mature professionals." Special issues include, Dining, Travel, Health and Local Business. Buys 130 mss/year. Query with published clips. Length: 750-2,000 words. Pays $50-350 for assigned articles; pays $25-250 for unsolicited articles.

Photos: State availability of photos with submission. Reviews transparencies. Captions, model releases and identification of subjects required.

VENTURA COUNTY & COAST REPORTER, VCR Inc., Suite 213, 1583 Spinnaker Dr., Ventura CA 93001. (805)658-2244; (805)656-0707. Editor: Nancy Cloutier. 12% freelance written. Works with a small number of new/unpublished writers each year. Weekly tabloid covering local news. Circ. 35,000. Pays on publication.

Publishes ms an average of 2 weeks after acceptance. Byline given. Buys first North American serial rights. Reports in 3 weeks.

Nonfiction: General interest (local slant), humor, interview/profile and travel (local—within 500 miles). Local (Ventura County) slant predominates. Length: 2-5 double-spaced typewritten pages. Pays $10-25.

Photos: State availability of photos with ms. Reviews b&w contact sheet.

Columns/Departments: Entertainment, Sports, Dining News, Real Estate and Boating Experience (Southern California). Send complete ms. Pays $10-25.

Tips: "As long as topics are up-beat with local slant, we'll consider it."

‡**WESTWAYS**, Auto Club of Southern California, 2601 S. Figueroa St., Los Angeles CA 90007. (213)741-4760. Editor: Mary Ann Fisher. Managing Editor: Eric Seyfarth. 95% freelance written. Monthly magazine covering travel (domestic and foreign), and Western states. "Our readers are upscale southern California residents who enjoy culture, leisure and outdoor recreation. We also cover art, historical and cultural topics in the West." Estab. 1909. Circ. 465,000. Pays on publication. Byline given. Offers 25% kill fee. Buys first North American serial rights. Submit seasonal/holiday material 6 months in advance. Reports in 2 weeks on queries; 3 weeks on mss. Sample copy for $2 with 9×11 SAE and 4 first class stamps. Writer's guidelines for #10 SAE with 1 first class stamp.

Nonfiction: General interest, historical/nostalgic, humor (wit and wisdom), photo feature and travel. "We avoid controversial, political and first-person articles." Buys 100-120 mss/year. Query with published clips. Length: 1,500 words. Pays $200-400. Sometimes pays expenses of writers on assignment.

Photos: Send photos with submission. Reviews 35mm transparencies. Offers $50-250 per photo. Captions and identification of subjects required. Buys one-time rights.

Columns/Departments: People, Places, Points of Interest, 500-700 words; Wit and Wisdom, 750 words. Buys 72 mss/year. Query. Length: 500-750 words. Pays $150-250.

Tips: "Let us know you are familiar with the publication. Explain why the story idea is appropriate and why you are the best person to write the proposed article."

Colorado

‡**ASPEN MAGAZINE**, Ridge Publications, P.O. Box G3, Aspen CO 81612. (303)920-4040. Editor: Janet C. O'Grady. Managing Editor: Carolyn Ely Hines. 85% freelance written. Bimonthly magazine covering Aspen and the Roaring Fork Valley. Estab. 1974. Circ. 15,000. Pays on publication. Byline given. Kill fee varies. Buys first North American serial rights. Query for electronic submissions. Sample copy for 9×12 SAE with 10 first class stamps. Free writer's guidelines.

Nonfiction: Essays, historical/nostalgic, interview/profile, new product, photo feature, travel, sports, outdoors and arts. "We do not publish general interest articles without an Aspen hook. We do not publish 'theme' (skiing in Aspen) or anniversary (40th year of Aspen Music Festival)." Buys 30-60 mss/year. Query with published clips. Length: 50-5,000 words. Pays $50-1,000. Sometimes pays expenses of writers on assignment.

Photos: State availability of photos with submission. Reviews contact sheets, negatives, transparencies and prints. ASMP standard minimum useage fees. Model release and identification of subjects required.

Columns/Departments: Discoveries (favorite spot: sense of place; enterprise: business; made in Aspen: crafts; then and now: history/present), 300-1,000. Query with published clips. Pays $50-150.

SUNDAY MAGAZINE, *Rocky Mountain News*, 400 W. Colfax Ave., Denver CO 80204. (303)892-5000. FAX: (303)892-5499. Magazine Editor: Joe Rassenfoss. Sunday supplement of daily newspaper covering general interest topics; newspaper circulates throughout Colorado and southern part of Wyoming. Estab. 1859. Circ. 410,000. Pays on publication. Byline given. Buys one-time rights. Submit seasonal/holiday material 2 months in advance. Simultaneous and previously published submissions OK ("if outside circulation area—Colorado and Southern Wyoming"). Reports in 1 month.

Nonfiction: Investigative; general interest; historical; photo feature; articles with Western angle on an out-of-the-way place; travel articles. Also looking for commentary pieces for Sunday newspapers; query Jean Otto. Buys 20 mss/year. Send complete ms. Length: 1,500-2,000 words. Pays $30-100.

Photos: State availability of photos or send photos with ms ("if article covers an event we can't cover ourselves"). Reviews color transparencies and 8×10 b&w glossy prints. Pay varies. Captions required. Buys one-time rights.

Tips: "The magazine is increasingly interested in people, events and trends that face Coloradans. We are less and less interested in personal columns."

Connecticut

‡**CONNECTICUT MAGAZINE**, Communications International, 789 Reservoir Ave., Bridgeport CT 06606. (203)374-5488. FAX: (203)371-6561. Editor: Charles Monagan. Managing Editor: Dale Salm. 80% freelance written. Prefers to work with published/established writers who know the state and live/have lived here. A

monthly magazine covering the state of Connecticut. "For an affluent, sophisticated, suburban audience. We want only articles that pertain to living in Connecticut." Estab. 1971. Circ. 90,000. Pays on publication. Publishes ms an average of 3-4 months after acceptance. Byline given. Offers 20% kill fee. Buys first North American serial rights. Submit seasonal/holiday material 4 months in advance. Reports in 6 weeks on queries. Writer's guidelines for #10 SASE.

Nonfiction: Book excerpts, expose, general interest, interview/profile and other topics of service to Connecticut readers. No personal essays. Buys 50 mss/year. Query with published clips. Length: 2,500-4,200 words. Pays $600-1,200. Sometimes pays the expenses of writers on assignment.

Photos: State availability of photos with submission. Reviews contact sheets and transparencies. Offers $50 minimum/photo. Model releases and identification of subjects required. Buys one-time rights.

Columns/Departments: Business, Health, Politics, Connecticut Guide, Lively Arts, Gardening, Environment, Education, People, Sports, Law and Courts, Media and From the Past. Buys 50 mss/year. Query with published clips. Length: 1,500-2,500 words. Pays $300-600.

Fillers: Around and About editor—Valerie Schroth, senior editor. Anecdotes and facts. Buys 50/year. Length: 150-400 words. Pays $75 maximum.

Tips: "Make certain that your idea is not something that has been covered to death by the local press and can withstand a time lag of a few months. Free-lancers can best break in with Around and About; find a Connecticut story that is offbeat and write it up in a fun, light-hearted, interesting manner. Again, we don't want something that has already gotten a lot of press."

HW, (formerly *Hartford Woman*), Gamer Publishing, 595 Franklin Ave., Hartford CT 06114. (203)278-3800. Editor: Susan Phillips Plese. Circ. 40,000. Pays on publication. Publishes ms an average of 3 months after acceptance. Byline given. Offers 50% kill fee. Buys first rights and reprint rights. Submit seasonal/holiday material 3 months in advance. Simultaneous (unless within our geographic area), and previously published submissions OK. Reports in 2 weeks on queries; 1 month on mss. Sample copy for 11×14 SAE and $1.25 postage; writer's guidelines for #10 SASE.

Nonfiction: Essays of opinion, humorous, serious or reflective. Essays: "Hers," "His" and "Ours." Buys 3/month. Length: 750 words. Pays $35-50.

Fiction: Any topic of interest to women. Buys 1/month. Length: 1,500-2,000 words. Pays $60-125 on publication.

Poetry: Any topic. No set length. Buys 1-3/month. Pays $25-50.

Tips: "Send complete manuscripts. No phone calls, please. Manuscripts must be submitted with SASE if return is requested. We are looking for fresh ideas, innovative twists on old topics."

‡NORTHEAST MAGAZINE, *The Hartford Courant*, 285 Broad St., Hartford CT 06115. (203)241-3700. FAX: (203)520-6906. Editor: Lary Bloom. 50% freelance written. Eager to work with new/unpublished writers. Weekly magazine for a Connecticut audience. Estab. 1982. Circ. 300,000. **Pays on acceptance.** Publishes ms an average of 10 month after acceptance. Byline given. Buys one-time rights. Reports in 3 months.

Nonfiction: General interest (has to have strong Connecticut tie-in); in-depth investigation of stories behind news (has to have strong Connecticut tie-in); historical/nostalgic; interview/profile (of famous or important people with Connecticut ties); and personal essays (humorous or anecdotal). No poetry. Buys 75-100 mss/year. Length: 750-2,500 words. Pays $200-1,500.

Photos: Most assigned; state availability of photos. "Do not send originals."

Fiction: Well-written, original short stories. Length: 750-1,500 words.

Tips: "Less space available for all types of writing means our standards for acceptance will be much higher. We can only print 3-4 short stories a year."

District of Columbia

THE WASHINGTON POST, 1150 15th St. NW, Washington DC 20071. (202)334-7591. Travel Editor: Linda L. Halsey. 60% freelance written. Works with small number of new/unpublished writers each year. Prefers to work with published/established writers. Weekly newspaper travel section (Sunday). Pays on publication. Publishes ms an average of 3-6 months after acceptance. Byline given. "We are now emphasizing staff-written articles as well as quality writing from other sources. Stories are rarely assigned; all material comes in on speculation; there is no fixed kill fee." Buys first North American serial rights. Query for electronic submissions. Usually reports in 3 weeks.

Nonfiction: Emphasis is on travel writing with a strong sense of place, color, anecdote and history. Query with published clips. Length: 1,500-2,500 words, plus sidebar for practical information.

Photos: State availability of photos with ms.

THE WASHINGTON POST MAGAZINE, *The Washington Post*, 1150 15th St. NW, Washington DC 20071. Managing Editor: Linton Weeks. 40% freelance written. Prefers to work with published/established writers. Weekly magazine featuring articles of interest to Washington readers. Circ. 1.2 million (Sunday). Average issue includes 2-3 feature articles and 2-3 columns. **Pays on acceptance.** Publishes ms an average of 2 months after acceptance. Byline given. Buys all rights or first North American serial rights, depending on fee. Submit seasonal material 4 months in advance. Computer printout submissions acceptable; no dot-matrix unless near letter-quality. Reports in 6 weeks on queries; 3 weeks on mss. Sample copy for 9×12 SAE and 2 first class stamps.

Nonfiction: Controversial and consequential articles with a strong Washington angle. Buys 2 mss/issue. Query with published clips. Length: 1,500-6,500 words. Pays $100-up; competitive with major national magazine rates. Pays expenses of writers on assignment.

Photos: Reviews 4x5 or larger b&w glossy prints and 35mm or larger color transparencies. Model releases required.

Tips: "Always send SASE for return of material."

THE WASHINGTONIAN MAGAZINE, 1828 L St. NW, Washington DC 20036. Editor: John A. Limpert. 20% freelance written. Prefers to work with published/established writers who live in the Washington area. For active, affluent and well-educated audience. Monthly magazine. Circ. 166,891. Buys first rights only. Pays on publication. Publishes ms an average of 2 months after acceptance. Simultaneous submissions OK. Reports in 6 weeks. Sample copy for $3 and 9×12 SAE; writer's guidelines for #10 SASE.

Nonfiction: *"The Washingtonian* is written for Washingtonians. The subject matter is anything we feel might interest people interested in the mind and manners of the city. The style, as Wolcott Gibbs said, should be the author's—if he is an author, and if he has a style. The only thing we ask is thoughtfulness and that no subject be treated too reverently. Audience is literate. We assume considerable sophistication about the city, and a sense of humor." Buys how-to, personal experience, interview/profile, humor, coverage of successful business operations, think pieces and exposes. Buys 75 mss/year. Length: 1,000-7,000 words; average feature 4,000 words. Pays 30¢/word. Sometimes pays the expenses of writers on assignment. Query or submit complete ms.

Photos: Photos rarely purchased with mss.

Fiction and Poetry: Margaret Cheney, department editor. Must be Washington-oriented. No limitations on length for fiction; poetry not to exceed 30 lines. Pays 30¢/word for fiction; $35 on acceptance for poetry.

Florida

‡BOCA RATON MAGAZINE, JES Publishing, Suite 100, 6413 Congress Ave., Boca Raton FL 33487. (407)997-8683. FAX: (407)997-8909. Editor: Darrell Hofheinz. 70% freelance written. Bimonthly magazine covering Boca Raton lifestyles. "Ours is a lifestyle magazine devoted to the residents of South Florida, featuring fashion, interior design, food, people, places and issues that shape the South Florida market." Estab. 1981. Circ. 18,000. Pays on pubication. Publishes ms an average of 2 months after acceptance. Byline given. Offers $25 kill fee. Buys second serial (reprint) rights. Submit seasonal/holiday material 7 months in advance. Simultaneous and previously published submissions OK. Query for electronic submission. Reports in 1 month. Sample copy $3.50 with 10×13 SAE and 10 first class stamps. Writer's guidelines for #10 SAE with one first class stamp.

Nonfiction: General interest, historical/nostalgic, humor, interview/profile, photo feature, travel. Query with or without published clips, or send complete ms. Length: 800-2,500 words. Pays $50-500 for assigned articles; $50-300 for unsolicited articles. Sometimes pays expenses of writers on assignment.

Photos: State availability of photos with submission.

Columns/Departments: Body & Soul (medical column, general interest), 1,000 words; Family Room (family and social interactions), 1,000 words; Humor (South Florida topics), 600-1,200 words. Buys 6 mss/year. Query with published clips or send complete ms. Length: 600-1,500 words. Pays $50-250.

Fiction: Adventure, humorous, mainstream, romance, slice-of-life vignettes. "This is still a new category for us. We especially would like submissions that have South Florida setting or theme." Buys 3 mss/year. Query with published clips or send complete ms. Length: 1,000-2,000 words. Pays $50-200.

‡CENTRAL FLORIDA MAGAZINE, P.O. Box 948439, Maitland FL 32794-8439. (407)539-3939. Editor: Nancy Long. 25% freelance written. Monthly magazine covering the lifestyle of Central Florida. Estab. 1972. Circ. 25,000. Pays on publication. Publishes ms an average of 4-5 months after acceptance. Byline given. Offers 100% kill fee (assigned mss). Buys all rights (in circulation area). Submit seasonal/holiday material 6 months in advance. Simultaneous submissions OK. Reports in 1 month. Sample copy for $2.50 with 10×13 SAE and 4 first class stamps.

Nonfiction: General interest, interview/profile, personal experience and travel. No fiction or first-person articles that do not relate to Central Florida. Buys 35 mss/year. Query with published clips. Length: 200-3,000 words. Pays $35-450 for assigned articles. Pays expenses (gas, phone) of writers on assignment.

Photos: State availability of photos with submission. Offers $50-100 per photo. Captions and identification of subjects required. Buys one-time rights.

Columns/Departments: Lunch With, Sports, Recreation, Health and Medicine, Dining In, Dining Out, Travels. Buys 15 mss/year. Query with published clips. Length: 1,000-1,500 words. Pays $200-350.

CORAL SPRINGS MONTHLY/PLANTATION MONTHLY, 7452 Wiles Rd., P.O. Box 8783, Coral Springs FL 33067. (305)344-8090. Executive Editor: Karen King. Monthly lifestyle magazines catering to residents of Coral Springs and Plantation. Residents are well-educated and interested in timely, innovative subjects. The magazines offer a variety of topics each month, among them health, fashion, classic cars, interior design, etc. Estab. 1986. Cir. 8,000. Pays on publication. Publishes ms an average of 2-3 months after acceptance. Byline given. Buys first rights and second serial (reprint) rights; all rights for an assigned story. Submit seasonal/holiday material 5-6 months in advance. Reports in 3 months. Sample copy $1.95.

Nonfiction: General interest, how-to, home decorating, gardening, fashion and beauty, humor, interview/profile, new products and travel. Buys 60 mss/year. Send complete ms; will return if unused. Length: 900-1,500 words. Pays $55-75.

Photos: Send photos with submission. Reviews transparencies (2½ × 2½ or 4 × 5); 5 × 7 b&w prints. Captions, model releases and identification of subjects required. Pay is negotiable.

Columns/Departments: On the Light Side (humorous slants on life, raising children, etc.); Classic Cars; Vital Signs (timely health news); Innovations (new consumer electronic products).

Tips: "Send completed manuscript. Any subject that might appeal to families will be considered. Our residents love to travel, like to learn about new ideas and services, and are interested in world and community issues."

FOLIO WEEKLY, Landmark Communications, Suite 14, 8101 Phillips Highway, Jacksonville FL 32256. (904)733-3103. FAX: (904)733-7431. Editor: Judy Wells. 50% freelance written. Weekly tabloid on arts, entertainment, lifestyle. "An arts and entertainment direct distribution newsprint magazine aimed at young, active affluent residents of greater Jacksonville, Florida." Estab 1987. Circ. 30,000. Pays on publication. Publishes ms an average of 1-2 months after acceptance. Byline given. Negotiable kill fee. Buys first North American serial rights, second serial (reprint) rights or makes work-for-hire assignments. Submit seasonal/holiday material 4 months in advance. Simultaneous submissions OK. Reports in 3 weeks on queries; 1 month on mss. Sample copy for 9 × 12 SAE.

Nonfiction: Humor and opinion. Buys 20-30 mss/year. Query with published clips. Length: 100-3,000 words. Pays $10-125 for assigned articles. Sometimes pays expenses of writers on assignment.

Photos: State availability of photos with submission. Offers $10 per photo. Captions, model releases and identification of subjects required.

Columns/Departments: Folio Finish (locally oriented editorials), 1,000 words; Vanities (trendy items in local market), 250 words; Habitat (new developments, resales, condos, renovation), 300 words; Preview/Reviews (theatre, movies, dance, art, music, records, sports, restaurants), 600 words; and Briefcases (news nuggets, inside stories), 100-150 words. Buys 200-250 mss/year. Query with published clips. Pays $10-70. "All but Folio Finish by assignment only."

Tips: "Currently seeking editorialists to write on issues of interest in N. Florida area every other week. Easiest way to catch my attention: write bright, hip, brief about something going on hereabouts we don't already know about, always keeping in mind that our readers are young (20-45) and affluent ($30,000 up salaries/incomes)."

GULF COAST, The Magazine of Southwest Florida, Gulfcoast Media Affiliates, 205 S. Airport Rd., Naples FL 33942. (813)643-4232. FAX: (813)643-6253. Managing Editor: Barbara Amrhein. 65% freelance written. Monthly magazine. "We reach an affluent, literate readership with information on Florida's Gulf Coast." Estab. 1987. Circ. 25,000. Pays within 30 days of acceptance. Byline given. Offers $50 kill fee. Buys first North American serial rights, one-time rights or makes work-for-hire assignments. Submit seasonal/holiday material 4 months in advance. Query for electronic submissions. Reports in 3 weeks on queries; 2 months on mss. Sample copy for 9 × 12 SAE with 6 first class stamps. Writer's guidelines for #10 SASE.

Nonfiction: General interest and interview/profile. "We are heavily regional and use very little material that is not written by area writers." Buys 75-80 mss/year. Query. Length: 800-3,000 words. Pays $200-750 for assigned articles. Pays expenses of writers on assignment.

Photos: State availability of photos with submission. Reviews contact sheets, 35mm to 4 × 5 transparencies and prints. Pays $25 minimum per photo. Captions, model releases and identification of subjects required. Buys one-time rights.

Columns/Departments: Outdoors, Business, Travel, Media, The Arts, People, and Insiders, 150-1,200 words. Buys 50 mss/year. Query. Pays $50-200.

‡GULFSHORE LIFE, 2975 S. Horseshoe Dr., Naples FL 33942. (813)643-3933. Editor: Janis Lyn Johnson. 30% freelance written. 10 times per year lifestyle magazine of southwest Florida. Estab. 1970. Circ. 20,000. Pays on publication. Publishes ms an average of 4 months after acceptance. Byline given. Offers ¼-⅓ kill fee. Buys first North American serial rights. Submit seasonal/holiday material 8 months in advance. Simultaneous and previously published submissions OK. Query for electronic submissions. Reports in 6 weeks. Sample copy for 8½ × 11 SAE with 10 first class stamps.

Nonfiction: Historical/nostalgic (SW Florida), interview/profile (SW Florida), travel/unusual Florida destinations. No articles that have absolutely nothing to do with SW Florida. Buys 30 mss/year. Query with published clips. Length: 1,200-3,000 words. Pays $150-450 for assigned articles. Sometimes pays expenses of writers.

Photos: State availability of photos with submission. Reviews 35mm transparencies and 5×7 prints. Pays $25-50. Captions, model releases and identification of subjects required. Buys one-time rights.

Fiction: SW Florida orientation. Sponsors an annual fiction contest. Deadline for entries (which can't exceed 3,000 words) is in December. Prize is $300. Buys 1 mss/year. Send complete ms. Length: 1,800-3,000 words. Pays $300.

Tips: "Send me a superb query letter offering a must-use story idea. Tell me about a SW Florida place or person we don't already know about!"

ISLAND LIFE, The Enchanting Barrier Islands of Florida's Southwest Gulf Coast, Island Life Publications, Box 929, Sanibel FL 33957. Editor: Joan Hooper. Editorial Associate: Susan Shores. 40% freelance written. Prefers to work with published/established writers, but works with a small number of new/unpublished writers each year. Quarterly magazine of the Barrier Islands from Anna Maria Island to Key West, for upper-income residents and vacationers of Florida's Gulf Coast area. Circ. 20,000. Pays on publication. Publishes ms an average of 1 year after acceptance. Byline given. Buys first serial rights and second serial (reprint) rights. Simultaneous queries and submissions OK. Reports in 1 month on queries; 3 months on mss. Sample copy and writer's guidelines for $3; writer's guidelines only for #10 SASE.

Nonfiction: General interest, historical. "Travel and interview/profile done by staff. Our past use of freelance work has been heavily on Florida wildlife (plant and animal), Florida cuisine, and Florida parks and conservancies. We are a regional magazine. No fiction or first-person experiences. No poetry. Our editorial emphasis is on the history, culture, wildlife, art, scenic, sports, social and leisure activities of the area." Buys 10-20 mss/year. Query with ms and photos. Length: 500-1,500 words. Pays 3-8¢/word.

Photos: Send photos with ms. No additional payment. Captions, model releases, and identification of subjects required.

Tips: "Submissions are rejected, most often, when writer sends other than SW Florida focus."

‡JACKSONVILLE TODAY, White Publishing Co., Suite 900, 1325 San Marco Blvd., Jacksonville FL 32207. (904)396-8666. FAX: (904)396-0926. Editor: Dale Dermott. 90% freelance written. Prefers to work with published/established writers, and works with a small number of new/unpublished writers each year. A monthly city lifestyle magazine "which explores all facets of the North Florida experience—from politics and people to recreation and leisure." Estab. 1985. Circ. 25,000. Pays on publication. Publishes ms an average of 3 months after acceptance. Byline given. Buys first North American serial rights. Submit seasonal/holiday material 3 months in advance. Reports in 3 weeks on queries; 6 weeks on manuscripts.

Nonfiction: Exposé, general interest, historical, interview, photo feature and travel. Special issue features golf-oriented material (March material due Jan. 9). No religious, non-localized features, humor, or film reviews. Buys 20 mss/year. Query with or without published clips, or send complete ms. Length: features 1,500-3,000 words. Pays $150-350. Sometimes pays the expenses of writers on assignment.

Photos: State availability of photos with submission. Reviews contact sheets. Offers $25 minimum per photo. Model releases and identification of subjects required.

Columns/Departments: Arts, controversy, health, home, reading and sports. Buys 72 mss/year. Query with published clips. Length: 1,000 words. Pays $150-200.

Tips: "All articles must be localized to the Jacksonville/North Florida area."

PALM BEACH LIFE, Palm Beach Newspapers Inc./Cox Enterprises, 265 Royal Poinciana Way, Palm Beach FL 33486. (407)837-4750. FAX: (407)655-4594. Editor: Joyce Harr. 100% freelance written. Monthly magazine, a regional publication for Palm Beach County and South Florida. Estab. 1906. Circ. 19,971. **Pays on acceptance.** Publishes ms an average of 3 months after acceptance. Byline given. Buys first North American serial rights. Submit seasonal/holiday material 6 months in advance. Query for electronic submission. Reports in 1 month.

Nonfiction: Essays, exposé, general interest, historical/nostalgic, humor, interview/profile, photo feature and travel. Buys 100 mss/year. Query with published clips. Length: 900-5,000 words. Pays $150-700 for assigned articles; $75-400 for unsolicited articles. Sometimes pays expenses of writers on assignment (depending on agreed-upon fee).

Photos: Send photos with submission. Reviews transparencies. Offers $35-200 per photo. Captions, model releases and identification of subjects required. Buys one-time rights.

Columns/Departments: Traveler's Journal (specifically focused topical travel pieces), 1,500 words; High Profile (profiles of people of interest to readers in our region), 2,500 words. Buys 36 mss/year. Query with published clips. Pays $75-300.

SOUTH FLORIDA, Florida Media Affiliates, Suite 207, 600 Brickell Ave., Miami FL 33131. (305)374-5011. FAX: (305)374-7691. Editor: Marilyn A. Moore. Managing Editor: Brian Paul Kaufman. 90% freelance written. Monthly magazine; general interest, must relate to Miami, Fort Lauderdale or Palm Beach County.

Circ. 43,000. **Pays on acceptance.** Publishes ms an average of 3 months after acceptance. Byline given. Offers 50% kill fee. Buys first North American serial rights, one-time rights or second serial (reprint) rights. Submit seasonal/holiday material 4 months in advance. Simultaneous and previously published submissions OK. Query for electronic submissions. Reports in 6 weeks on queries. Sample copy $2.65 plus $1.50 postage. Writer's guidelines for #10 SASE.

Nonfiction: Exposé, general interest, humor, interview/profile, photo feature, South Florida Lifestyles and travel. Buys 120 mss/year. Query with or without published clips, or send complete ms. Length: 3,500 words maximum. Pays $300-1,000 for assigned articles. Sometimes pays expenses of writers on assignment.

Photos: State availability of photos with submission. Identification of subjects required. Buys one-time rights.

Columns/Departments: Business, Media, Arts, Home and "Lunch With" (profile of a locally connected celebrity). Buys 12 mss/year. Query with published clips. Length: 1,200-1,500 words. Pays $300-400.

SUNSHINE: THE MAGAZINE OF SOUTH FLORIDA, The News & Sun-Sentinel Co., 101 N. New River Dr., Fort Lauderdale FL 33301-2293. (305)761-4037. Editor: John Parkyn. 50% freelance written. Prefers to work with published/established writers, and works with a small number of new/unpublished writers each year. A general interest Sunday magazine for the *Sun-Sentinel's* 750,000 readers in South Florida. Circ. 300,000. Pays within 1 month of acceptance. Publishes ms an average of 2 months after acceptance. Byline given. Offers 25% kill fee for assigned material. Buys first serial rights or one-time rights in the state of Florida. Submit seasonal/holiday material 2 months in advance. Simultaneous queries, and simultaneous and previously published submissions OK. Reports in 2 weeks on queries; 1 month on mss. Free sample copy and writer's guidelines.

Nonfiction: General interest, how-to, interview/profile and travel. "Articles must be relevant to the interests of adults living in South Florida." Buys about 100 mss/year. Query with published clips. Length: 1,000-3,000 words; preferred length 1,500-2,500 words. Pays 20-25¢/word to $1,000 maximum.

Photos: State availability of photos. Pays negotiable rate for 35mm and 2¼ color slides and 8×10 b&w prints. Captions and identification of subjects required; model releases required for sensitive material. Buys one-time rights for the state of Florida.

Tips: "Do not phone—we don't have the staff to handle calls of this type—but do include your phone number on query letter. Keep your writing tight and concise—readers don't have the time to wade through masses of 'pretty' prose. We are always in the market for first-rate profiles, human-interest stories and travel stories (which must spotlight destinations within easy access of South Florida (e.g. S.E. U.S., Caribbean, Central America.) Be as sophisticated and stylish as you can—Sunday magazines have come a long way from the Sunday supplements of yesteryear."

‡**TALLAHASSEE MAGAZINE,** Marketplace Communications, Inc., 2365 Centerville Rd., Tallahassee FL 32308. (904)385-3310. Editor: Marion McDanield. Managing Editor: W.R. Lundquist. 80% freelance written. Prefers to work with published/established writers. Quarterly magazine covering people, events and history in and around Florida's capital city. Estab. 1978. Circ. 16,000. Pays on publication. Publishes ms an average of 3 months after acceptance. Buys first North America serial rights. Submit seasonal/holiday material 6 months in advance. Simultaneous queries and previously published submissions OK. Reports in 1 month. Sample copy for 9×12 SAE. Query for list of topics.

Nonfiction: General interest (relating to Florida or Southeast); historical/nostalgic (for Tallahassee, North Florida, South Georgia); and interview/profile (related to North Florida, South Georgia). No fiction, poetry or topics unrelated to area. Buys 30 mss/year. Query. Length: 500-1,400 words. Pays 10¢/word, unsolicited; 12¢/word solicited.

Photos: State availability of photos with query. Pays $35 minimum for 35mm color transparencies; $25 minimum for b&w prints. Model releases and identification of subjects required. Buys one-time rights.

Tips: "We seek to show positive aspects of life in and around Tallahassee. Know the area. A brief author biographic note should accompany manuscripts."

‡**TAMPA BAY LIFE, The Bay Area's Magazine,** Tampa Bay Media Affiliates, Inc., Suite 990, 6200 Courtney Campbell Causeway, Tampa FL 33607. (813)281-8855. FAX: (813)281-1920. Editor: David J. Wilson. 90% freelance written. Monthly magazine on Tampa Bay area lifestyle. "All material must be relevant to Tampa Bay area readers, whether it is trendy lifestyle material or serious environmental, social or political material." Estab. 1988. Circ. 25,000. **Pays on acceptance.** Publishes ms an average of 3 months after acceptance. Offers 25% kill fee. Buys first North American serial rights. Submit seasonal/holiday material 5 months in advance. Query for electronic submissions. Sample copy $2.50 with $2.50 postage. Writer's guidelines for #10 SAE with 1 first class stamp.

Nonfiction: Exposé, general interest, historical, humor, interview/profile, travel. Buys 100 mss/year. Query with published clips. Length: 800-3,500 words. Pays $125-600. Sometimes pays expenses of writers on assignment.

Photos: State availability of photos with submission. Reviews contact sheets, transparencies and prints. Captions, model releases and identification of subjects required. Buys one-time rights.

Columns/Departments: Lively Arts (arts of all types, personalities, trends); Sporting Life (sports relevant to area, personalities, trends); Epicure (gourmet slant to anything edible, especially Florida edibles). Buys 36 mss/year. Query with published clips. Length: 1,030-1,400 words. Pays $200-300.

Fiction: Adventure, historical, mainstream, mystery, slice-of-life vignettes. "It should be noted that we have bought only one fiction piece since publication began—we are open to buying more, if it is relevant to our area and extremely well written." Buys 1 ms/year. Query with published clips. Length: 800-3,000 words. Pays $200-450.

Tips: "Most open to freelancers are: Front Pages—bright briefs about the Tampa Bay area and its people; Journal—again, relevant to the Tampa Bay area on an unlimited range of subjects, but copy must be cogent, plunge the reader immediately into the story and make its sound point within 830 words."

TROPIC MAGAZINE, Sunday Magazine of the Miami Herald, Knight Ridder, 1 Herald Plaza, Miami FL 33132. (305)376-3432. Executive Editor: Gene Weingarten. Editor: Tom Shroder. 20% freelance written. Works with small number of new/unpublished writers each year. Weekly magazine covering general interest, locally oriented topics for local readers. Circ. 500,000. Pays on publication. Publishes ms an average of 2 months after acceptance. Byline given. Buys first serial rights. Submit seasonal/holiday material 2 months in advance. Reports in 6 weeks. Sample copy for 11 × 14 SAE.

Nonfiction: General interest; interview/profile (first person); and personal experience. No fiction or poetry. Buys 20 mss/year. Query with published clips or send complete ms. Length: 1,500-3,000 words. Pays $200-1,000/article.

Photos: Philip Brooker, art director. State availability of photos.

Georgia

NORTH GEORGIA JOURNAL, Legacy Communications, Inc., 110 Hunters Mill, Woodstock GA 30188. (404)928-7739. Editor: Olin Jackson. 75% freelance written. A quarterly magazine of feature-length history articles, leisure lifestyles, and of travel opportunities to historic sites in the North Georgia area. Estab. 1984. Pays on publication. Publishes ms an average of 6 months after acceptance. Byline given. Buys first publication rights or all rights. Reports in 6 weeks. Sample copy $3.95 with 9 × 12 SAE and 8 first class stamps; free writer's guidelines.

Nonfiction: Historical/nostalgic personal experiences; photo features, travel. "I'm interested primarily in a first-person account of experiences involving the exploration of unique historic sites and travel opportunities indigenous to north Georgia and areas contiguous to north Georgia in other states." Buys 20-30 mss/year. Query. Length: 2,000-4,000 words. Pays $75-250.

Photos: Send photos with submission. "Photos are crucial to the acceptance of submissions." Reviews contact sheets and 8 × 10 and 5 × 7 prints. Offers no additional payment for photos accepted with ms. Captions and identification of subjects required. Buys first publication rights or all rights.

Tips: "We're interested in first-person accounts of experiences involving travel to and exploration of unique and interesting historic sites, travel opportunities and lifestyles indigenous to the Appalachian Mountains of north Georgia and areas contiguous to north Georgia in Tennessee, North Carolina, South Carolina and Alabama. An approach similar to that taken by submissions in *National Geographic* magazine is most desired. Subject matter of particular interest includes gold mining; pioneers in the area; Indian/early settlements/communities; catastrophic events and occurrences; and travel subject matter related to present-day opportunities at scenic and historic sites such as historic bed and breakfast/mountain inns, etc. Unique present-day mountain lifestyles features and featurettes with a historic twist are also highly desired."

Hawaii

ALOHA, THE MAGAZINE OF HAWAII AND THE PACIFIC, Davick Publishing Co., 49 S. Hotel St., #309, Honolulu HI 96813. FAX: (808)533-2055. Editor: Cheryl Tsutsumi. 50% freelance written. *Aloha* is a bimonthly regional magazine of international interest. "Most of our readers do not live in Hawaii, although most readers have been to the Islands at least once. Even given this fact, the magazine is directed primarily to residents of Hawaii in the belief that presenting material to an immediate critical audience will result in a true and accurate presentation that can be appreciated by everyone. *Aloha* is not a tourist publication and is not geared to such a readership, although travelers will find it to be of great value." Circ. 65,000. Pays on publication. Publishes ms an average of 6 months after acceptance; unsolicited ms can take a year or more. Byline given. Offers variable kill fee. Buys first-time rights. Submit seasonal/holiday material 1 year in advance. Reports in 2 months. Sample copy $2.95 with $2.75 postage; writer's guidelines for SASE.

Nonfiction: Book excerpts; historical/nostalgic (historical articles must be researched with bibliography); interview/profile; and photo features. Subjects include the arts, business, flora and fauna, people, sports, destinations, food, interiors and history of Hawaii. "We don't want stories of a tourist's experiences in Waikiki or odes to beautiful scenery. We don't want an outsider's impressions of Hawaii, written for outsiders." Buys

24 mss/year. Query with published clips. Length: 1,000-4,000 words. Pay ranges from $250-400. Sometimes pays expenses of writers on assignment.

Photos: State availability of photos with query. Pays $25 for b&w prints; prefers negatives and contact sheets. Pays $60 for 35mm (minimum size) color transparencies used inside; $125 for double-page bleeds; $175 for color transparencies used as cover art. "*Aloha* features Beautiful Hawaii, a collection of photographs illustrating that theme, in every issue. A second photo essay by a sole photographer on a theme of his/her own choosing is also run occasionally. Queries are essential for the sole photographer essay." Model releases and identification of subjects required. Buys one-time rights.

Fiction: Ethnic and historical. "Fiction depicting a tourist's adventures in Waikiki is not what we're looking for. As a general statement, we welcome material reflecting the true Hawaiian experience." Buys 2 mss/year. Send complete ms. Length: 1,000-2,500 words. Pays $300.

Poetry: Haiku, light verse and traditional. No seasonal poetry or poetry related to other areas of the world. Buys 6 poems/year. Submit maximum 6 poems. Prefers "shorter poetry." Pays $25.

Tips: "Read *Aloha*. Be meticulous in research and have good illustrative material available."

‡**HAWAII MAGAZINE**, Fancy Publications, Inc., P.O. Box 6050, Mission Viejo CA 92690. (714)855-8822. Editor: Dennis Shattuck. Managing Editor: Julie Applebaum. 60% freelance written. Bimonthly magazine covering The Islands of Hawaii. "Hawaii magazine is written for people all over the world who visit and enjoy the culture, people and places of the Hawaiian Islands." Estab. 1984. Circ. 65,000. Pays on publication. Byline given. Buys first North American serial rights. Submit seasonal/holiday material 6 months in advance. Query for electronic submissions. Reports in 4 weeks on queries; 6 weeks on mss. Sample copy for $3.95. Free writer's guidelines.

Nonfiction: General interest, historical/nostalgic, how-to, interview/profile, personal experience, photo feature and travel. "No articles on the following: first trip to Hawaii—How I discovered the Islands, the Hula, Poi, or Luaus." Buys 66 mss/year. Query with or without published clips or send complete ms. Length: 4,000 words maximum. Pays $100-500 for assigned articles.

Photos: Send photos with submission. Reviews contace sheets and transparencies. Offers $25-150 per photo. Identification of subjects preferred. Buys one-time rights.

Columns/Departments: Backdoor Hawaii (humorous look at the islands), 800-1,200 words; Hopping the Islands (news, general interest items), 100-200 words. Buys 6-12 mss/year. Query. Length: 800-1,500 words. Pays $100-200.

Tips: "Freelancers must be knowledgeable on Island subjects, virtual authorities on them. We see far too many first-person, wonderful-experience types of gushing articles. We buy articles only from people who are thoroughly grounded in the subject on which they are writing."

HONOLULU, Honolulu Publishing Co., Ltd., 36 Merchant St., Honolulu HI 96813. (808)524-7400. FAX: (808)531-2306. Editor: Brian Nicol. 20% freelance written. Prefers to work with published/established writers. Monthly magazine covering general interest topics relating to Hawaii. Estab. 1888. Circ. 75,000. **Pays on acceptance.** Publishes ms an average of 4 months after acceptance. Byline given. Offers $50 kill fee. Buys first serial rights. Submit seasonal/holiday material 5 months in advance. Simultaneous queries and simultaneous submissions OK. Sample copy $2 with 9×12 SAE and $2.40 postage; free writer's guidelines.

Nonfiction: Exposé, general interest, historical/nostalgic, and photo feature—all Hawaii-related. "We run regular features on fashion, interior design, travel, etc., plus other timely, provocative articles. No personal experience articles." Buys 10 mss/year. Query with published clips if available. Length: 2,000-4,000 words. Pays $500. Sometimes pays expenses of writers on assignment.

Photos: Teresa Black, photo editor. State availability of photos. Pays $15 maximum for b&w contact sheet; $25 maximum for 35mm transparencies. Captions and identification of subjects required. Buys one-time rights.

Columns/Departments: Calabash (light, "newsy," timely, humorous column on any Hawaii-related subject). Buys 15 mss/year. Query with published clips or send complete ms. Length: 250-1,000 words. Pays $35.

‡**KAU KAU KITCHEN NEWSLETTER**, Yuen Media Services, 372 Haili St., Hilo HI 96720. (808)961-3984. Editor: Leilehua Yuen. 50% freelance written. Quarterly newsletter on regional-Hawaii cooking, food, beverage and nutrition. "Food is meant to be enjoyed. Cooking is fun. Hawaii's food is special and deserves preservation. *Kau Kau Kitchen* gives a taste of Hawaii's culture—past and present." Estab. 1988. Circ. 100. Publishes ms an average of 3-6 months after acceptance. Byline given. Offers kill fee by arrangement with author. Buys one-time rights. Submit seasonal/holiday material 6 months in advance. Simultaneous and previously published submissions OK. Reports in 2 months. Sample copy $2. Writer's guidelines for #10 SASE with 1 first class stamp.

Nonfiction: Book excerpts, how-to (cooking techniques), humor (related to cooking), interview/profile (of interesting Hawaii cooks, not necessarily chefs) and new product. "No fiction, anything blatantly opinionated on vegetarianism or any other 'ism'." Query with or without published clips, or send complete ms. Length: 50-800 words. Pays $5 minimum for assigned articles. Pays in advertising space, subscriptions. Sometimes pays expenses of writers on assignment.

Columns/Departments: TuTu's Tips (kitchen and household tips with Hawaii slant) and Keiki Kitchen (kitchen and household with children's slant). Query or send complete ms. Length: 300-800 words. Pays $5 minimum.

Poetry: Avant-garde, free verse, haiku, light verse and traditional. Hawaii slant on food, household or family. "No erotic or non-food/household/family." Buys 30-50 poems/year. Submit maximum 10 poems. Should fit a 40 character by 20 line space. "Please, please, please stop sending poetry on rolling New England oceans, and God's glory over the Appalachians. If it doesn't touch the Pacific Ocean, we don't want it."

Fillers: Anecdotes, facts, newsbreaks and cartoons if well drawn. Length: 50 words maximum.

Tips: "Love what you write about and the people you write for. *Kau Kau Kitchen* is very informal. Technically perfect writing is not as desireable as honestly talking with the reader. Yes, I occasionally end sentences with prepositions, but my readers *know* what I'm saying. We're all sitting around the kitchen table. It's not the place for dissertations."

Idaho

OH! IDAHO, The Idaho State Magazine, Peak Media, Inc., 118 River St. N., Hailey ID 83333. (208)788-4500. FAX: (208)788-5098. Editor: Colleen Daly. 80% freelance written. Quarterly magazine on Idaho related topics. Estab. 1988. Circ. 20,000. Pays on publication. Publishes ms an average of 3 months after acceptance. Byline given. Buys first North American serial rights. Submit seasonal/holiday material 6 months in advance. Simultaneous submissions and previously published submissions (if not in an Idaho publication within same year) OK. Query for electronic submissions. Reports in 6 weeks. Sample copy $3 with 8½ × 11 SAE. Writer's guidelines for #10 SASE.

Nonfiction: Buys 15-20 mss/year. Query. Length: 1,500-2,500 words. Pays $100-250 (more for *top quality*).

Photos: Send photos in response to want list (generated 4 times/year). Reviews transparencies. Offers $25-200 per photo, more for cover shot. Captions, model releases and identification of subjects required. Buys one-time rights.

Columns/Departments: Education (exciting topics from Idaho universities or schools), food; general interest; interview/profile; new product; opinion; and travel, all Idaho related. "No descriptions of small business unless it has an Idaho base and a national impact." Buys 30-40 mss/year. Query or send complete ms. Length: 900-1,500 words. Pays $90-150, more for top quality.

Tips: "All articles must specifically be related to Idaho. Most willing to consider all queries and submissions. Writing should *sparkle* and avoid journalistic approach."

Illinois

CHICAGO MAGAZINE, 414 N. Orleans, Chicago IL 60610. Editor: Hillel Levin. Managing Editor: Joanne Trestrail. 40% freelance written. Prefers to work with published/established writers; works with a small number of new/unpublished writers each year. Monthly magazine for an audience which is "95% from Chicago area; 90% college-trained; upper income; overriding interests in the arts, politics, dining, good life in the city and suburbs. Most are in 25-50 age bracket, well-read and articulate." Circ. 210,000. Buys first serial rights. **Pays on acceptance.** Publishes ms an average of 6 months after acceptance. Submit seasonal material 4 months in advance. Computer printout submissions acceptable "if legible." Reports in 2 weeks. Query; indicate "specifics, knowledge of city and market, and demonstrable access to sources." For sample copy, send $3 to Circulation Dept.; writer's guidelines for #10 SASE.

Nonfiction: "On themes relating to the quality of life in Chicago: past, present, and future." Writers should have "a general awareness that the readers will be concerned, influential longtime Chicagoans reading what the writer has to say about their city. We generally publish material too comprehensive for daily newspapers." Personal experience and think pieces, profiles, humor, spot news, historical articles and exposés. Buys about 50 mss/year. Length: 500-6,000 words. Pays $100-$2,500. Pays expenses of writers on assignment.

Photos: Reviews b&w glossy prints, 35mm color transparencies or color prints. Usually assigned separately, not acquired from writers.

Tips: "Submit detailed queries, be business-like and avoid clichéd ideas."

THE CHICAGO TRIBUNE MAGAZINE, (formerly *Sunday*), Chicago Tribune Co., 435 N. Michigan Ave., Chicago IL 60611. Editor: Denis Gosselin. Managing Editor: Ruby Scott. 35% freelance written. A weekly Sunday magazine. "*Sunday* looks for unique, compelling, all researched, elequently written articles on subjects of general interest." Circ. 1 million. Pays on publication. Publishes ms an average of 2 months after acceptance. Offers 35-50% kill fee. Buys one-time rights. Submit seasonal/holiday material 6 months in advance. Query for electronic submissions. Reports in1 month on queries; 6 weeks on manuscripts.

Nonfiction: Book excerpts, exposé, general interest, interview/profile, photo feature, technical and travel. No humor, first person or casual essays. Buys 35 mss/year. Query or send complete ms. Length: 2,500-5,000 words. Pays $1,000. Sometimes pays the expenses of writers on assignment. State availability of photos with submission. Offer varies for photos. Captions and identification of subjects required. Buys one-time rights.

Columns/Departments: First Person (Chicago area subjects only, talking about their occupations), 1,000 words. Buys 52 mss/year. Query. Pays $250.

ILLINOIS MAGAZINE, The Magazine of the Prairie State, Sunshine Park, P.O. Box 40, Litchfield IL 62056. (217)324-3425. Editor: Peggy Kuethe. 85% freelance written. Works with a small number of new/unpublished writers each year, and is eager to work with new/unpublished writers. A bimonthly magazine devoted to the heritage of the state. Emphasizes history, current interest and travel in Illinois for historians, genealogists, students and others who are interested in the state. Estab. 1924. Circ. 16,000. Pays on publication. Publishes ms an average of 6 months after acceptance. Byline given. Buys first North American serial rights or one-time rights. Submit seasonal/holiday material 6 months in advance. Reports in 2 months on queries; 4 months on mss. Sample copy for 10 × 12 SAE and 5 first class stamps; writer's guidelines for #10 SASE.
Nonfiction: Essays, general interest, historical/nostalgic, interview/profile, photo feature and travel. Also, festivals (annual events), biography, points of interest, botany, animals, scenic areas that would be of interest to travelers. "We do not want to see family history/family tree/genealogy articles." Buys 75-85 mss/year. Send complete ms. Length: 100-1,500 words. Pays $20-200.
Photos: Send photos with submission. Reviews contact sheets, 35mm or 4 × 5 transparencies and 3 × 5, 5 × 7 and 8 × 10 b&w prints. Offers $5-50 photo. Captions, model releases, and identification of subjects required. Buys one-time rights.
Fillers: Anecdotes, facts and short humor. Buys 3-5/year. Length: 50-200 words. Pays $10-$25.
Tips: "Be sure to include a phone number where you can be reached during the day. Also, try if at all possible to obtain photographs for the article if it requires them. And don't forget to include sources or references for factual material used in the article."

‡NEAR WEST GAZETTE, Near West Gazette Publishing Co., 1335 W. Harrison St., Chicago IL 60607. (312)243-4288. Editor: Mark J. Valentino. Managing Editor: William S. Bike. 50% freelance written. Eager to work with new/unpublished writers. A monthly neighborhood newspaper covering Near West Side of Chicago. News and issues for residents, students and faculty of the neighborhood west of the University of Illinois of Chicago. Estab. 1983. Circ. 4,500. Pays on publication. Publishes ms an average of 1 month after acceptance. Byline given. Offers 15% kill fee. Not copyrighted. Buys one-time or simultaneous rights. Submit seasonal/holiday material 2 months in advance. Simultaneous and previously published submissions OK. Reports in 5 weeks. Sample copy for 11 × 14 SAE with 3 first class stamps.
Nonfiction: Essays, exposé, general interest, historical/nostalgic, humor, inspirational, interview/profile, opinion, personal experience, religious or Near West Side's sports. Publishes a special Christmas issue. Doesn't want to see product promotions. Buys 60 mss/year. Length: 300-1,800 words. Pays $30. Sometimes pays the expenses of writers on assignment.
Photos: Send photos with submission. Reviews 5 × 7 prints. Offers no additional payment for photos accepted with ms. Identification of subjects required. Buys one-time rights.
Columns/Departments: To Your Health (health/exercise tips), 600 words; Forum (opinion), 750 words; Streets (Near West Side history), 500 words. Buys 12 mss/year. Query. Pays $30.

‡ROCKFORD MAGAZINE, Northwest Publishing, 331 E. State St., Rockford IL 61103. (815)961-2400. Acting Editor: Chris Hewitt. 20% freelance written. Monthly magazine covering the city of Rockford. Stories must concern, or be of interest to, the people of the Rockford area. Estab. 1986. Circ. 22,000. Pays on publication. Publishes ms an average of 1½ months after acceptance. Byline given. Offers 3¢/word kill fee. Buys first rights. Submit seasonal/holiday material 2 months in advance. Query for electronic submissions. Sample copy for $2. Free writer's guidelines.
Nonfiction: General interest, historical/nostalgic and interview/profile. "No personal experiences, poetry or fiction." Buys 10 mss/year. Send complete ms. Length: 1,200-2,000 words. Pays $200-300 for assigned articles. Sometimes pays expenses of writers on assignment.
Photos: State availability of photos with submission. Captions and model releases required. Buys one-time rights.
Columns/Departments: Eats (food, restaurant); Nostalgia (Rockford-related historical/anecdotal stories). Buys 10 mss/year. Send complete ms. Length: 1,300-1,800 words. Pays $150-250.
Tips: "The difficulty is the freelancers pretty much have to be from this area. We're open to them in most departments of the magazine."

Indiana

ARTS INDIANA, Arts Indiana, Inc. Suite 701, 47 S. Pennsylvania, Indianapolis IN 46204-3622. (317)632-7894. Editor: Richard J. Roberts. 95% freelance written. Monthly, Sept.-June magazine on artists and arts organizations working in Indiana—literary, visual and performing. Circ. 12,000. Pays on publication. Publishes ms an average of 3-6 months after acceptance. Byline given. Offers 50% kill fee. Buys first North American serial rights. Submit seasonal/holiday material 4 months in advance. Reports in 3 months. Free sample copy and writer's guidelines.

Nonfiction: Essays, historical/nostalgic, interview/profile, opinion, photo feature and interviews with reviews; Q & A format. "No straight news reportage." Query with published clips. Length: 1,000-3,000 words. Pays $50-250 for assigned articles; $50-150 for unsolicited articles. Complimentary one-year subscription is given in addition to cash payment. Sometimes pays expenses of writer on assignment.

Photos: Send photos with submission. Reviews 5 × 7 or larger prints. Offers no additional payment for photos accepted with ms. Captions and identification of subjects required. Buys one-time rights.

Tips: "We are looking for people-oriented and issue-oriented articles. Articles about people should reveal the artist's personality as well as describe his artwork. Contributing writers must reside in Indiana."

Kansas

‡KANSAS!, Kansas Department of Economic Development, 400 W. 8th, 5th Floor, Topeka KS 66603. (913)296-3479. Editor: Andrea Glenn. 90% freelance written. Quarterly magazine. Emphasizes Kansas "people and places for all ages, occupations and interests." Estab. 1945. Circ. 54,000. **Pays on acceptance.** Publishes ms an average of 1 year after acceptance. Byline given. Buys one-time rights. Submit seasonal/holiday material 8 months in advance. Reports in 2 months. Free sample copy and writer's guidelines.

Nonfiction: "Material must be Kansas-oriented and have good potential for color photographs. We feature stories about Kansas people, places and events that can be enjoyed by the general public. In other words, events must be open to the public, places also. People featured must have interesting crafts, etc." General interest, interview, photo feature and travel. Query. "Query letter should clearly outline story in mind. I'm especially interested in Kansas freelancers who can supply their own photos." Length: 3-5 pages double-spaced, typewritten copy. Pays $75-175. Sometimes pays expenses of writers on assignment.

Photos: "We are a full-color photo/manuscript publication." State availability of photos with query. Pays $50-75 (generally included in ms rate) for 35mm or larger format transparencies. Captions required.

Tips: "History and nostalgia stories do not fit into our format because they can't be illustrated well with color photography."

Kentucky

‡BACK HOME IN KENTUCKY, Greysmith Publishing Inc., 128 Holiday Ct., P.O. Box 1627, Franklin TN 37064. (615)791-1953. Editor: Nanci P. Gregg. 90% freelance written. Bimonthly magazine covering Kentucky heritage, peoples, places, events. We publish articles about Kentucky places, heritage, people, and events. We reach Kentuckians and "displaced" Kentuckians living outside the state. Estab. 1977. Pays on publication. Publishes ms an average of 8 months after acceptance. Byline sometimes given. Buys first North American serial rights. Submit seasonal/holiday material 8 months in advance. Query for electronic submissions. Reports in 2 months. Sample copy for $1 with 9 × 12 SAE and 5 first class stamps. Writer's guidelines for #10 SAE with 1 first class stamp.

Nonfiction: Historical/nostalgic (Kentucky related), how-to (might be gardening or crafts), humor (Kentucky nostalgic humor), interview/profile (noted or unusual Kentuckians), personal experience (nostalgic, Kentucky experience), photo feature (Kentucky places and events), travel (Kentucky places). No inspirational or religion – all must be Kentucky related. Buys 50 mss/year. Query with or without published clips or send complete ms. Length: 500-1,000 words. Pays $25-100 for assigned articles; $15-50 for unsolicited articles. "In addition to normal payment writers receive 4 copies of issue containing their article and 1 year subscription." Sometimes pays expenses of writers on assignment.

Photos: Send photos with submission. Reviews transparencies and 5 × 7 prints. Offers no additional payment for photos accepted with ms. Model releases and identification of subjects required. Rights purchased depends on situation.

Columns/Departments: Kentucky travel, Kentucky Crafts and Kentucky Gardening. Buys 10-12 mss/year. Query with published clips. Length: 500-750 words. Pays $15-40.

Tips: "We recently purchased this magazine and are trying to organize and departmentalize its content. We work mostly with unpublished writers who have a feel for Kentucky – its people, places, events, etc. The areas most open to freelancers are travel – places in Kentucky, nostalgia/history, and stories about interesting, unusual Kentuckians."

KENTUCKY HAPPY HUNTING GROUND, Kentucky Dept. of Fish and Wildlife Resources, 1 Game Farm Rd., Frankfort KY 40601. (502)564-4336. Editor: John Wilson. Works with a small number of new/unpublished writers each year. A bimonthly state conservation magazine covering hunting, fishing, general outdoor recreation, conservation of wildlife and other natural resources. Estab. 1945. Circ. 35,000. Pays on publication. Publishes ms an average of 6 months-1 year after acceptance. Byline given. Buys one-time rights. Submit seasonal/holiday material 6 months in advance. Previously published submissions OK. Reports in 3 weeks on queries; 2 months on mss. Sample copy for 8½ × 11 SAE. Free sample copy and writer's guidelines.

Nonfiction: General interest, historical/nostalgic, how-to, humor, interview/profile, personal experience and photo feature. All articles should deal with some aspect of the natural world, with outdoor recreation or with natural resources conservation or management, and should relate to Kentucky. "No 'Me and Joe' stories (i.e., accounts of specific trips); nothing off-color or otherwise unsuitable for a state publication." Buys 3-6 mss/year. Query or send complete ms. Length: 500-2,000 words. Pays $75-250 (with photos).

Photos: State availability of photos with query; send photos with accompanying ms. Reviews transparencies and b&w prints (5×7 minimum). No separate payment for photos, but amount paid for article will be determined by number of photos used.

Tips: "We would be much more kindly disposed toward articles accompanied by several good photographs (or other graphic material) than to those without."

KENTUCKY LIVING, P.O. Box 32170, 4515 Bishop Lane, Louisville KY 40232. (502)451-2430. Editor: Gary W. Luhr. Mostly freelance written. Prefers to work with published/established writers. Monthly feature magazine primarily for Kentucky residents. Estab. 1948. Circ. 340,000. **Pays on acceptance.** Publishes ms on average of 2-8 months after acceptance. Byline given. Buys first serial rights for Kentucky. Submit seasonal/holiday material at least 6 months in advance. Will consider previously published and simultaneous submissions (if previously published and/or simultaneous submissions outside Kentucky). Reports in 2 weeks. Sample copy for 8½×11 SAE and 4 first class stamps.; writer's guidelines for #10 SASE.

Nonfiction: Prefers Kentucky-related profiles (people, places or events), history, biography, recreation, travel, leisure or lifestyle articles or book excerpts; articles on contemporary subjects of general public interest and general consumer-related features including service pieces. Publishes some humorous and first-person articles of exceptional quality and opinion pieces from qualified authorities. No general nostalgia. Buys 24-36 mss/year. Query or send complete ms. Length: 800-2000 words. Pays $50-$250. Sometimes pays the expenses of writers on assignment.

Photos: Send photos with submission. Reviews color slides and b&w prints. Identification of subjects required. Payment for photos included in payment for ms. Pays extra if photo used on cover.

Tips: "The quality of writing and reporting (factual, objective, thorough) is considered in setting payment price. We prefer well-documented pieces filled with quotes and anecdotes. Avoid boosterism. Well-researched, well-written feature articles, particularly on subjects of a serious nature, are given preference over light-weight material."

Louisiana

SUNDAY ADVOCATE MAGAZINE, Box 588, Baton Rouge LA 70821. (504)383-1111, ext. 319. Editor: Larry Catalanello. 5% freelance written. "We are backlogged but still welcome submissions." Byline given. Pays on publication. Publishes ms up to 1 year after acceptance. Query for electronic submissions.

Nonfiction and Photos: Well-illustrated, short articles; must have local, area or Louisiana angle, in that order of preference. Also interested in travel pieces. Photos purchased with mss. Rates vary.

Tips: Styles may vary. Subject matter may vary. Local interest is most important. No more than 4-5 typed, double-spaced pages.

Maine

GREATER PORTLAND MAGAZINE, Chamber of Commerce of the Greater Portland Region, 142 Free St., Portland ME 04101. (207)772-2811. Editor: Shirley Jacks. 75% freelance written. Works with a small number of new/unpublished writers each year. "We enjoy offering talented and enthusiastic new writers the kind of editorial guidance they need to become professional freelancers." A quarterly magazine covering metropolitan and island lifestyles of Greater Portland. "We cover the arts, night life, islands, people and progressive business in and around Greater Portland." Circ. 10,000. Pays on publication. Publishes ms an average of 2 months after acceptance. Byline given. Buys first serial rights or second serial reprint rights. Submit seasonal/holiday material 6 months in advance. Query for electronic submissions. Reports in 1 week on queries; 2 weeks on mss. Sample copy $2; writer's guidelines for #10 SASE.

Nonfiction: Articles about people, places, events, institutions and the arts in greater Portland. "*Greater Portland* is largely freelance written. We are looking for well-researched, well-focused essayistic features. First-person essays are welcome." Buys 20 mss/year. Query with published clips. Length: 1,500-3,500 words. Pays 10¢/word maximum.

Photos: Buys b&w and color slides with or without ms. Captions required.

Tips: "Send some clips with several story ideas. We're looking for informal, essayistic features structured around a well-defined point or theme. A lively, carefully crafted presentation is as important as a good subject. We enjoy working closely with talented writers of varying experience to produce a literate (as opposed to slick or newsy) magazine."

ISLESBORO ISLAND NEWS, Islesboro Publishing, HCR 227, Islesboro ME 04848. (207)734-6745. FAX: (207)734-2262. Publisher/Editor: Agatha Cabaniss. 20% freelance written. Bimonthly magazine on Penobscot Bay islands and people. Estab. 1985. **Pays on acceptance.** Byline given. Buys first rights and second serial (reprint) rights. Sample copy $2; writer's guidelines for #10 SAE with 3 first class stamps.

Nonfiction: Articles about contemporary issues on the islands, historical pieces, personality profiles, arts, lifestyles and businesses on the islands. Any story must have a definite Maine island connection. No travel pieces. Query or send complete ms. Pays $20-50.

Photos: State availability of photos with submission.

Tips: "Writers must know the Penobscot Bay Islands. We are not interested in pieces of generic island nature unless it relates to development problems, or the viability of the islands as year round communities. We do not want 'vacation on a romantic island,' but we are interested in island historical pieces."

‡**MAINE MOTORIST**, AAA Maine, P.O. Box 3544, Portland ME 04104. (207)774-6377. Editor: Ellen Kornet-sky. 5% freelance written. Bimonthly tabloid on travel, car care, AAA news. "Our readers enjoy learning about travel opportunities in the New England region and elsewhere. In addition, they enjoy topics of interest to automobile owners." Estab. 1910. Circ. 120,000. Pays on publication. Publishes ms an average of 3 months after acceptance. Byline given. Not copyrighted. Buys simultaneous rights; makes work-for-hire assignments. Submit seasonal/holiday material 4 months in advance. Simultaneous submissions OK. Free sample copy and writer's guidelines.

Nonfiction: Historical/nostalgic (travel); how-to (car care, travel); humor (travel); and travel (New England, U.S. and foreign). No exotic travel destinations that cost a great deal. Send complete ms. Length: 500-1,000 words. Pays $50-100.

Photos: State availability of photos. Reviews 5×7 transparencies. Pays $10-25 for b&w; $25-100 for color. Captions required. Buys one-time rights.

Tips: "Travel (particularly New England regional) material is most needed. Interesting travel options are appreciated. Humorous flair sometimes helps."

Maryland

CHESAPEAKE BAY MAGAZINE, Suite 157, 1819 Bay Ridge Ave., Annapolis MD 21403. (301)263-2662. Editor: Jean Waller. 40% freelance written. Works with a small number of new/unpublished writers each year. "*Chesapeake Bay Magazine* is a monthly regional publication for those who enjoy reading about the Chesapeake and its tributaries. Our readers are yachtsmen, boating families, fishermen, ecologists – anyone who is part of Chesapeake Bay life." Circ. 30,000. Pays either on acceptance or publication, depending on "type of article, timeliness and need." Publishes ms an average of 14 months after acceptance. Buys first North American serial rights and all rights. Submit seasonal/holiday material 4 months in advance. Simultaneous (if not to magazines with overlapping circulations) submissions OK. Reports in 1 month. Sample copy $2.50; writer's guidelines for SASE.

Nonfiction: "All material must be about the Chesapeake Bay area – land or water." How-to (fishing and sports pertinent to Chesapeake Bay); general interest; humor (welcomed, but don't send any "dumb boater" stories where common safety is ignored); historical; interviews (with interesting people who have contributed in some way to Chesapeake Bay life: authors, historians, sailors, oystermen, etc.); and nostalgia (accurate, informative and well-paced – no maudlin ramblings about "the good old days"); personal experience (drawn from experiences in boating situations, adventures, events in our geographical area); photo feature (with accompanying ms); profile (on natives of Chesapeake Bay); technical (relating to boating, fishing); and Chesapeake Bay folklore. "We do not want material written by those unfamiliar with the Bay area, or general sea stories. No personal opinions on environmental issues or new column (monthly) material and no rehashing of familiar ports-of-call (e.g., Oxford, St. Michaels)." Buys 25-40 unsolicited mss/year. Query or submit complete ms. Length: 1,000-2,500 words. Pays $85-100. Sometimes pays the expenses of writers on assignment.

Photos: Chris Gill, art director. Submit photo material with ms. Reviews 8×10 b&w glossy prints and color transparencies. Pays $100 for 35mm, $2\frac{1}{4} \times 2\frac{1}{4}$ or 4×5 color transparencies used for cover photos; $50, $30 or $15 for color photo used inside. Captions and model releases required. Buys one-time rights with reprint permission.

Fiction: "All fiction must deal with the Chesapeake Bay and be written by persons familiar with some facet of bay life." Adventure, fantasy, historical, humorous, mystery and suspense. "No general stories with Chesapeake Bay superimposed in an attempt to make a sale." Buys 3-4 mss/year. Query or submit complete ms. Length: 1,000-2,500 words. Pays $85-100.

Tips: "We are a regional publication entirely about the Chesapeake Bay and its tributaries. Our readers are true 'Bay' lovers, and look for stories written by others who obviously share this love. We are particularly interested in material from the Lower Bay (Virginia) area and the Upper Bay (Maryland/Delaware) area. We are looking for personal experience Chesapeake boating articles/stories, especially from power boaters."

Massachusetts

BOSTON GLOBE MAGAZINE, *Boston Globe*, Boston MA 02107. Editor-in-Chief: Ms. Ande Zellman. 50% freelance written. Weekly magazine; 72 pages. Circ. 805,099. **Pays on acceptance**. Publishes ms an average of 2 months after acceptance. No reprints of any kind. Buys first serial rights. Submit seasonal/holiday material 3 months in advance. SASE must be included with ms or queries for return. Reports in 1 month.

Nonfiction: Expose (variety of issues including political, economic, scientific, medical and the arts); interview (not Q&A); profile; and book excerpts (first serial rights only). No travelogs. Buys up to 100 mss/year. Query. Length: 3,000-5,000 words. Payment negotiable from $1,000.
Photos: Purchased with accompanying ms or on assignment. Reviews contact sheets. Pays standard rates according to size used. Captions required.

BOSTON MAGAZINE, 300 Massachusetts Ave., Boston MA 02115. (617)262-9700. FAX: (617)262-4925. Editor: David Rosenbaum. Managing Editor: Betsy Buffington. 20% freelance written. Monthly magazine. "Looks for strong reporting of locally based stories with national interest." Estab. 1963. Circ. estimated 137,000. Pays on publication. Publishes ms an average of 2 months after acceptance. Byline given. Offers 20% kill fee. Buys first North American serial rights. Submit seasonal/holiday material 3 months in advance. Query for electronic submissions. Reports in 1 month. Sample copy for 9×12 SAE with $2.40 postage; writer's guidelines for #10 SASE.
Nonfiction: General interest, investigative reports, profiles. No fiction or poetry. Buys 6 mss/year. Query with published clips or send complete ms. Length: 3,000 words maximum. Pays $500-1,500. Sometimes pays the expenses of writers on assignment.
Photos: State availability of photos with submission. Reviews transparencies and prints. Offers payment for photos accepted with ms. Captions, model releases and identification of subjects required. Buys one-time rights.
Columns/Departments: Boston Inc. (portraits of Bostonians). Send complete ms. Length: 1,500-2,500 words. Pays up to $900.
Tips: "Query should contain an outline of proposed story structure, including sources and source material. Stories should seek to be controversial. Area most open to freelancers is investigative journalism. Stories concerning newsworthy scandals that are unreported. Look for something everyone believes to be true—then question it."

BOSTONIA, The Magazine of Culture & Ideas, Boston University, 10 Lenox St., Brookline MA 02146. (617)353-3081. FAX: (617)313-6488. Publisher/Editor: Keith Botsford. 90% freelance written. Bimonthly magazine on culture and ideas in New England. Circ. 138,000. **Pays on acceptance.** Publishes ms an average of 2 months after acceptance. Byline given. Offers 20% kill fee. Buys first rights. Simultaneous submissions OK. Query for electronic submissions. Reports in 1 month.
Nonfiction: National, international issues, the arts, profiles, social issues. Primarily commissioned but will consider queries with published clips. Length: 2,000-5,000 words. Pays up to $1,250 plus expenses.
Photos: Portfolios with proposals to Art Director. All must be identified.
Columns/Departments: Commonwealth Avenue, 300-1,000 words. $150 per acceptance.
Fiction: No length restrictions, internationally-known writers are preferred; will read new writers. Pays up to $1,500.
Tips: "Freelancers' best way in is Commonwealth Avenue column."

CAPE COD HOME & GARDEN (formerly *Cape Cod Compass*), Cove Communications Corp., 60 Munson Meeting, Chatham MA 02633. (508)945-3542. Editor: John C. Whitmarsh. Managing Editor: Donald Davidson. 90% freelance written. A magazine published 5 times/year about fine homes and gardens on Cape Cod, Martha's Vineyard and Nantucket. Estab. 1989. Circ. 20,000. Pays on publication. Publishes ms an average of 2 months after acceptance. Byline given. Offers variable kill fee. Buys first North American serial rights or one-time rights. Reports in 1 month. Sample copy $4; writer's guidelines for #10 SAE.
Nonfiction: Colorful features and regular columns on interior design and architecture, art and antiques, gardening and landscaping, cooking and dining, restoration and remodelling. Articles must be of interest to primary and second homeowners in this unique geographic region. We do not publish first-person articles, poetry, fiction, history or memoirs. Buys 70 mss/year. Query with published clips or send complete ms. Length: 2,000-2,500 words. Pays $150-400 for assigned articles. Sometimes pays the expenses of writers on assignment.
Photos: Send photos with submission, if any. Reviews transparencies. Offers $70/photo. Model releases and identification of subjects required. Buys one-time rights.
Tips: "We welcome submissions from published writers who are familiar with the unique living environment on Cape Cod and the Islands. Our readers are upscale homeowners with a serious interest in their homes and an appreciation of their natural environment. Both features and columns must have a strong 'local angle.'"

‡**COAST & COUNTRY MAGAZINE**, Hastings Group, Suite 43, 644 Humphrey St., Swampscott MA 01907. (617)592-0160. Editor: Robert Hastings. 80% freelance written. Prefers to work with published/established writers. A bimonthly magazine covering topics of interest to readers residing on the North Shore of Boston. "*Coast & Country* is a controlled circulation magazine distributed to households with an income over $50,000. All of our articles have a local flavor. We publish articles on money, fashion, sports, medicine, culture, business and humor." Estab. 1984. Circ. 75,000. Pays on publication. Publishes ms an average of 4-6 months after acceptance. Byline given. Buys first rights. Submit seasonal/holiday material 6 months in advance.

Reports in 1 week on queries; 3 weeks on mss. Sample copy $2.50; free writer's guidelines.
Nonfiction: Essays, humor, opinion, personal experience. Special issues include holidays (December/January) and home guide (April/May). Buys 40 mss/year. Query with published clips. Length: 500-1,000 words. Pays $50-100.
Photos: State availability of photos with submission. Reviews contact sheets and negatives. Model releases and identification of subjects required.

Michigan

ABOVE THE BRIDGE MAGAZINE, Star Rt. 550, Box 189-C, Marquette MI 49855. Editor: Jacqueline J. Miller. Managing Editor: Judith A. Hendrickson. 100% freelance written. A quarterly magazine on the upper peninsula of Michigan. "Most material, including fiction, has an upper peninsula of Michigan slant. Our readership is past and present upper peninsula residents." Circ. 2,000. Pays on publication. Publishes ms an average of 6 months after acceptance. Byline given. Offers 50% kill fee. Buys one-time rights. Submit seasonal/holiday material 6 months in advance. Previously published submissions. Query for electronic submissions. Reports in 2 months. Sample copy for $3.50. Writer's guidelines for #10 SASE.
Nonfiction: Book excerpts (books on upper peninsula or UP writer), essays, historical/nostalgic (UP), interview/profile (UP personality or business) personal experience, photo feature (UP). Note: Travel by assignment only. "This is a family magazine; therefore, no material in poor taste." Buys 60 mss/year. Send complete ms. Length: 1,000-2,500 words. Pays 2¢/word. Send photos with submission. Reviews prints (5×7 or larger). Offers $5 ($15-20 if used for cover). Captions, model releases and identification of subjects required. Buys one-time rights.
Fiction: Ethnic (UP heritage), humorous, mainstream and mystery. No horror or erotica. "Material set in UP has preference for publication. Accepts children's fiction." Buys 12 mss/year. Send complete ms. Length: 2,000 words (1,000 maximum for children's). Pays 2¢/word.
Poetry: Free verse, haiku, light verse and traditional. No erotica. Buys 20 poems/year. Shorter poetry preferred. Pays $5.
Fillers: Anecdotes and short humor. Buys 25/year. Length: 100-500 words. Pays $5 or 2¢/word maximum.
Tips: "Material on the shorter end of our requirements has a better chance for publication. We're very well-stocked at the moment, so if we receive a submission that might not be published for a year of more, we'll pay on acceptance. As the budget allows we're attempting to eventually pay for all material on acceptance. We can't use material by out-of-state writers with content not tied to upper peninsula of Michigan. Know the area and people, read the magazine. Most material received is too long. Stick to our guidelines. We love to publish well written material by previously unpublished writers."

‡**ANN ARBOR MAGAZINE**, Arbor Publications, Suite 6, 2004 Hogback Rd., Ann Arbor MI 48105. (313)973-0602. Editor: Michael Tunison. 40% freelance written. Monthly magazine covering Ann Arbor area interests. "A monthly magazine with stories that have some connection with Ann Arbor. Our readers are cosmopolitan, educated and interested in the Ann Arbor community." Circ. 20,000. Pays on publication. Publishes ms an average of 2 months after acceptance. Byline given. Buys first North American serial rights or second serial (reprint) rights. Submit seasonal/holiday material 4 months in advance. Previously published submissions OK. Reports in 2 weeks. Sample copy $2; free writer's guidelines.
Nonfiction: General interest, historical/nostalgic, humor, interview/profile, personal experience, photo feature. Buys 15 mss/year. Send complete ms. Length: 1,000-1,500 words. Pays $50-100. Sometimes pays expenses of writers on assignment.
Photos: Send photos with submission. Reviews contact sheets, 35mm or larger transparencies and 5×7 or larger prints. Offers no additional payment for photos accepted with ms. Captions and identification of subjects required. Buys all rights.
Fiction: Historical, humorous, mainstream, slice-of-life vignettes. "No erotica, fantasy, science fiction, romance or confessional works."
Fillers: Anecdotes, facts, gags to illustrated by cartoonist, short humor. Buys 25/year. Length: 50-100 words. Pays $10.
Tips: "We're always looking for polished pieces with strong connections to the Ann Arbor area. Captioned photos and artwork are very important."

ANN ARBOR OBSERVER, Ann Arbor Observer Company, 206 S. Main, Ann Arbor MI 48104. Editor: John Hilton. 50% freelance written. Works with a small number of new/unpublished writers each year. Monthly magazine featuring stories about people and events in Ann Arbor. Estab. 1976. Circ. 52,000. Pays on publication. Publishes ms an average of 2 months after acceptance. Byline given. Buys one-time rights. Query for electronic submissions. Reports in 3 weeks on queries; 1 month on mss. Sample copy for 12½×15 SAE and $2.40 postage; free writer's guidelines.
Nonfiction: Historical, investigative features, profiles and brief vignettes. Must pertain to Ann Arbor. Buys 75 mss/year. Length: 100-7,000 words. Pays up to $1,000/article. Sometimes pays expenses of writers on assignment.

Tips: "If you have an idea for a story, write up a 100-200-word description telling us why the story is interesting. We are most open to intelligent, insightful features of up to 5,000 words about interesting aspects of life in Ann Arbor."

DETROIT MONTHLY, Crain Communications, 1400 Woodbridge, Detroit MI 48207. (313)446-0600. Editor: Brux Austin. 50% freelance written. Monthly magazine. "We are a city magazine for educated, reasonably well-to-do, intellectually curious Detroiters." Circ. 100,000. **Pays on acceptance.** Byline given. Offers negotiable kill fee. Buys first North American serial rights. Submit seasonal/holiday material 4 months in advance. Query for electronic submissions. Reports in 6 weeks.
Nonfiction: Book excerpts, exposé and travel. Buys 25 mss/year. Query with published clips. Length: 1,000-5,000 words. Pays $100-1,200. Sometimes pays the expenses of writers on assignment.
Photos: State availability of photos with submission.

GRAND RAPIDS MAGAZINE, Suite 1040, Trust Bldg., 40 Pearl St., NW, Grand Rapids MI 49503. (616)459-4545. FAX: (616)459-4800. Publisher: John H. Zwarensteyn. Editor: Carol Valade Smith. 45% freelance written. Eager to work with new/unpublished writers. Monthly general feature magazine serving western Michigan. Estab. 1964. Circ. 12,000. Pays on 15th of month of publication. Publishes ms an average of 4 months after acceptance. Buys first serial rights. Phone queries OK. Submit seasonal material 3 months in advance. Previously published submissions OK. Query for electronic submissions. Reports in 2 months. Sample copy $2 and 6 first class stamps.
Nonfiction: Western Michigan writers preferred. Western Michigan subjects only: government, labor, investigative, criminal justice, environment, health/medical, education, general interest, historical, interview/profile and nostalgia. Inspirational and personal experience pieces discouraged. No breezy, self-centered "human" pieces or "pieces not only light on style but light on hard information." Humor appreciated but must be specific to region. Buys 5-8 unsolicited mss/year. "If you live here, see the managing editor before you write. If you don't, send a query letter with published clips, or phone." Length: 500-4,000 words. Pays $25-200. Sometimes pays the expenses of writers on assignment.
Photos: State availability of photos. Pays $25 minimum for 5×7 glossy print and $35 minimum for 35 or 120mm transparency. Captions and model releases required.
Tips: "Television has forced city/regional magazines to be less provincial and more broad-based in their approach. People's interests seem to be evening out from region to region. The subject matters should remain largely local, but national trends must be recognized in style and content. And we must *entertain* as well as inform."

‡MICHIGAN COUNTRY LINES, Michigan Electric Cooperative Association, 400 North Walnut, Lansing MI 48933. (517)484-5022. Editor: Michael Buda. Managing Editor: Michelle Smith. 20% freelance written. Bimonthly magazine covering rural Michigan. Estab. 1980. Circ. 160,000. Pays on publication. Publishes ms an average of 2 months after acceptance. Byline given. Buys one-time rights and second serial (reprint) rights. Submit seasonal/holiday material 3 months in advance. Query for electronic submissions. Reports in 2 weeks. Free sample copy.
Nonfiction: Historical/nostalgic, how-to (rural living) and photo feature. No product or out-of-state. Buys 6 mss/year. Send complete ms. Length: 700-1,500 words. Pays $100-200 for assigned articles; $100-150 unsolicited articles. Pays expenses of writers on assignment.
Photos: Send photos with submission. Reviews contact sheets, 35mm transparencies and 3×5 prints. Offers $10-15 per photo. Captions, model releases and identification of subjects required. Buys one-time rights.
Tips: "Features are most open to freelancers."

Minnesota

LAKE SUPERIOR MAGAZINE, Lake Superior Port Cities, Inc., P.O. Box 16417, Duluth MN 55816-0417. (218)722-5002. FAX: (218)722-1341. Editor: Paul L. Hayden. 60% freelance written. Works with a small number of new/unpublished writers each year. A bimonthly regional magazine covering contemporary and historic people, places and current events around Lake Superior. Circ. 16,000 (subscribers in all states and 56 foreign countries). Pays on publication. Publishes ms an average of 8-10 months after acceptance. Byline given. Offers $25 kill fee. Buys first North American serial rights and some second rights. Submit seasonal/holiday material 8-12 months in advance. Query for electronic submissions. Reports in 3 months on manuscripts. Sample copy $3.95 and 6 first class stamps; writer's guidelines for #10 SASE.
Nonfiction: Book excerpts, general interest, historic/nostalgic, humor, interview/profile (local), personal experience, photo feature (local), travel (local), city profiles, regional business, some investigative. Buys 45 mss/year. Query with published clips. Length 300-3,000 words. Pays $80-400 maximum. Sometimes pays the expenses of writers if on assignment.
Photos: Quality photography is our hallmark. State availability of photos with submission. Reviews contact sheets, 2×2 transparencies and 4×5 prints. Offers $20 for b&w and $30 for color transparencies. Captions, model releases and identification of subjects required.

Columns/Departments: Current events and things to do (for Events Calendar section) short, under 300 words; Lake Watch (media reviews and short pieces on Lake Superior or Great Lakes environmental or issues themes), up to 200 words; I Remember (nostalgic lake-specific pieces), up to 700 words; Shore Lines (letters and short pieces on events and highlights of the Lake Superior Region), up to 150 words; Life Lines (single personality profile with b&w), up to 350 words. Buys 20 mss/year. Query with published clips. Pays $10-75.

Fiction: Ethnic, historic, humorous, mainstream, slice-of-life vignettes and ghost stories. Must be regionally targeted in nature. Buys 2-3 mss/year. Query with published clips. Length: 300-2,500 words. Pays $1-200.

Tips: "Well-researched queries are attended to. We actively seek queries from writers in Lake Superior communities. We prefer manuscripts to queries. Provide enough information on why the subject is important to the region and our readers, or why and how something is unique. We want details. The writer must have a thorough knowledge of the subject and how it relates to our region. We prefer a fresh, unused approach to the subject which provides the reader with an emotional involvement. Almost all of our articles feature quality photography, color or black and white. It is a prerequisite of all nonfiction. All submissions should include a *short* biography of author/photographer."

MPLS. ST. PAUL MAGAZINE, Suite 400, 12 S. 6th St., Minneapolis MN 55402. (612)339-7571. FAX: (612)339-5806. Editor: Brian Anderson. Executive Editor: Sylvia Paine. Managing Editor: Claude Peck. 90% freelance written. Monthly general interest magazine covering the metropolitan area of Minneapolis/St. Paul and aimed at college-educated professionals who enjoy living in the area and taking advantage of the cultural, entertainment and dining out opportunities. Reports on people and issues of importance to the community. Circ. 62,000. **Pays on acceptance.** Publishes ms an average of 3 months after acceptance. Byline given. Offers 25% kill fee. Buys first North American serial rights. Submit seasonal/holiday material 5 months in advance. Query for electronic submissions. Reports in 1 month. Sample copy $4.

Nonfiction: Book excerpts; general interest; historical/nostalgic; interview/profile (local); new product; photo feature (local); and travel (regional). Buys 250 mss/year. Query with published clips. Length: 1,000-4,000 words. Pays $100-1,200. Sometimes pays expenses of writers on assignment.

Photos: Chris Greco, photo editor.

Columns/Departments: Nostalgia—Minnesota historical; Home—interior design, local. Query with published clips. Length: 750-2,000 words. Pays $100-400.

Tips: People profiles (400 words) and Nostalgia are areas most open to freelancers.

Mississippi

‡MISSISSIPPI, Downhome Publications, 254 Highland Village, Box 16445, Jackson MS 39236. (601)982-8418. Editor: Ann Becker. 95% freelance written. Bimonthly magazine covering Mississippi. "Our magazine focuses almost exclusively on positive aspects of Mississippi—people, places, events." Estab. 1982. Circ. 25,000. Pays on publication. Publishes ms an average of 6 months after acceptance. Byline given. Offers $75 kill fee. Buys one-time rights. Submit seasonal/holiday material 1 year in advance. Query for electronic submissions. Reports in 3 months. Sample copy for $2.50. Free writer's guidelines.

Nonfiction: Essays, general interest, historical/nostalgic, interview/profile, personal experience, photo feature and travel. No essays on Southern accents or Southerners in the North. Buys 72 mss/year. Query with published clips. Length: 500-2,000 words. Pays $50-500.

Photos: Send photos with submission. Reviews contact sheets, 2¼ × 2¼ transparencies and 4×5 prints. Offers $25-100 per photo. Captions, model releases and identification of subjects required. Buys one-time rights.

Columns/Departments: Travel, People, Music, Heritage, Sports, Business, Art, Outdoors, Homes and Gardens (focuses on Mississippi people, places or events), 1,500 words each. Buys 35 mss/year. Query with published clips. Length: 500-1,500 words. Pays $125.

Tips: "Query by mail. Query should give some idea of how story would read. Including a lead is good. Be patient. Be aware of past articles—we only feature a subject once. All departments are good starting points. Be sure subject has *state*wide interest. Be sure subject has good reputation in field."

Missouri

‡MISSOURI MAGAZINE, 22 N. Euclid Ave., St Louis MO 63108. (314)367-0907. Editor: Jeanne Lafser. Quarterly magazine covering Missouri-oriented topics. "We prefer human-interest articles unique to Missouri—from historical pieces to profiles of people and places in Missouri today." Estab. 1974. Circ. 15,000. Pays on publication. Publishes ms an average of 6 months after acceptance. Byline given. Offers $25 kill fee. Buys first rights. Submit seasonal/holiday material 3 months in advance. Simultaneous submissions OK. Query for electronic submissions. Reports in 1 month queries; 3 months on mss. Sample copy for $4.95. Free writer's guidelines.

Nonfiction: General interest, historical/nostalgic, interview/profile, photo feature, travel, Missouri geology, natural history and wildlife. No fiction. Buys 28 mss/year. Send complete ms. Length: 1,500-3,000 words. Pays $150-300 for assigned articles; $75-200 for unsolicited articles. Sometimes pays in trade out with ads. Sometimes pays expenses of writers on assignment.

Photos: State availability of photos with submission. Reviews 2¼ × 2¼ transparencies. Offers $10-25 per photo. Captions, model releases and identification of subjects required. Buys one-time rights.

Columns/Departments: Bed & Breakfast Review (reviews B&Bs in Missouri—unique, 'quality' establishments), 300 words; Best Foot Forward (listing of exemplary establishments or services in Missouri), 50-100 words. Buys 28 mss/year. Send complete ms. Length 50-300 words. Pays $10-25.

Fillers: Facts. Buys 40/year. Length: 50-100 words. Pays $5-25.

‡**SPRINGFIELD! MAGAZINE**, Springfield Communications Inc., P.O. Box 4749, Springfield MO 65808. (417)882-4917. Editor: Robert C. Glazier. 85% freelance written. Works with a small number of new/unpublished writers each year; eager to work with new/unpublished writers. Monthly magazine. "This is an extremely local and provincial magazine. No *general* interest articles." Estab. 1979. Circ. 10,000. Pays on publication. Publishes ms an average of 6 months after acceptance. Byline given. Buys first serial rights. Submit seasonal/holiday material 6-12 months in advance. Simultaneous queries OK. Reports in 3 months on queries; 6 months on mss. Sample copy for $2.50 and 9½ × 12½ SAE.

Nonfiction: Book excerpts (by Springfield authors only); expose (local topics only); historical/nostalgic (top priority but must be local history); how-to (local interest only); humor (if local angle); interview/profile (needs more on females than on males); personal experience (local angle); photo feature (local photos); and travel (1 page per month). Buys 150 mss/year. Query with published clips or send complete ms. Length: 500-5,000 words. Pays $25-250. Sometimes pays expenses of writers on assignment.

Photos: State availability of photos or send photos with query or ms. Reviews b&w and color contact sheets; 4 × 5 color transparencies; and 5 × 7 b&w prints. Pays $5-35 for b&w; $10-50 for color. Captions, model releases, and identification of subjects required. Buys one-time rights.

Columns/Departments: Buys 250 mss/year. Query or send complete ms. Length varies widely but usually 500-2,500 words. Pays scale.

Tips: "We prefer that a writer read eight or ten copies of our magazine prior to submitting any material for our consideration. The magazine's greatest need is for features which comment on these times in Springfield. We are overstocked with nostalgic pieces right now. We also are much in need of profiles about young women and men of distinction."

Montana

MONTANA MAGAZINE, American Geographic Publishing, Box 5630, 3020 Bozeman Ave., Helena MT 59604. (406)443-2842. FAX: (406)443-5480. Editor: Carolyn Zieg Cunningham. 35% freelance written. Bimonthly magazine; "*Montana Magazine* is a strictly Montana-oriented magazine that features community profiles, personality profiles, contemporary issues, travel pieces." Circ. 72,000. Publishes ms an average of 6-8 months after acceptance. Byline given. Offers $50 kill fee on assigned stories only. Buys one-time rights. Submit seasonal material at least 6 months in advance. Simultaneous submissions OK. Reports in 6 weeks. Sample copy $2; writer's guidelines for #10 SASE.

Nonfiction: Essays, general interest, interview/profile, new product, opinion, photo feature and travel. Special features on "summer and winter destination points. Query by January for summer material; July for winter material. No 'me and Joe' hiking and hunting tales; no blood-and-guts hunting stories; no poetry; no fiction; no sentimental essays." Buys 30 mss/year. Query. Length: 300-2,500 words. Pays $75-500 for assigned articles; pays $50-350 for unsolicited articles. Sometimes pays the expenses of writers on assignment.

Photos: Send photos with submission. Reviews contact sheets, 35mm or larger format transparencies; and 5 × 7 prints. Offers no additional payment for photos accepted with ms. Captions, model releases and identification of subjects required. Buys one-time rights.

Columns/Departments: Over the Weekend (destination points of interest to travelers, family weekends and exploring trips to take), 300 words plus b&w photo; Food and Lodging (great places to eat; interesting hotels, resorts, etc.), 700-1,000 words plus b&w photo; Made in MT (successful cottage industries), 700-1,200 words plus b&w photo. Query. Pays $75-125.

Nevada

NEVADA MAGAZINE, 1800 E. Hwy. 50, Carson City NV 89710. (702)687-5416. Editor: David Moore. 50% freelance written. Works with a small number of new/unpublished writers each year. Bimonthly magazine

The double dagger before a listing indicates that the listing is new in this edition. New markets are often the most receptive to freelance submission.

published by the state of Nevada to promote tourism in the state. Circ. 80,000. Pays on publication. Publishes ms an average of 6 months after acceptance. Byline given. Buys first North American serial rights. Phone queries OK. Submit seasonal/holiday material at least 6 months in advance. Query for electronic submissions. Reports in 1 month. Sample copy $1; free writer's guidelines.

Nonfiction: Nevada topics only. Historical, nostalgia, photo feature, people profile, recreational, travel and think pieces. "We welcome stories and photos on speculation." Buys 40 unsolicited mss/year. Submit complete ms or queries to Associate Editor Cliff Glover. Length: 500-2,000 words. Pays $75-300.

Photos: Brian Buckley, art director. Send photo material with accompanying ms. Pays $10-50 for 8×10 glossy prints; $15-75 for color transparencies. Name, address and caption should appear on each photo or slide. Buys one-time rights.

Tips: "Keep in mind that the magazine's purpose is to promote tourism in Nevada. Keys to higher payments are quality and editing effort (more than length). Send cover letter, no photocopies. We look for a light, enthusiastic tone of voice without being too cute; articles bolstered by amazing facts and thorough research; and unique angles on Nevada subjects."

THE NEVADAN, *The Las Vegas Review Journal,* P.O. Box 70, Las Vegas NV 89125-0070. (702)383-0270. Editor-in-Chief: A.D. Hopkins. 75% freelance written. Works with a small number of new/unpublished writers each year. Locally-edited Sunday newspaper magazine. For Las Vegas and surrounding small town residents of all ages "who take our Sunday paper—affluent, thinking people." Estab. 1961. Circ. 160,000. Pays on publication. Publishes ms an average of 2 months after acceptance. Byline given. Buys one-time rights and simultaneous rights. Submit seasonal/holiday material 3 months in advance. Previously published submissions OK. Reports in 3 weeks. Sample copy and writer's guidelines for 9×12 SAE with 65¢ postage; mention *Writer's Market* in request. Writer's guidelines for #10 SASE.

Nonfiction: Historical, travel, always linked to Nevada, southern Utah, northern Arizona and Death Valley); personalities; personal experience (any with strong Nevada angle, current or pioneer; pioneer can be 1948 in some parts of Nevada). "We also buy contemporary pieces of about 2,400-5,000 words. An advance query is absolutely essential for these. No articles on history that are based on doubtful sources; no current show business material; and no commercial plugs." Buys 110 mss/year. Query. Phone queries OK. Length: average 1,200 words (contemporary pieces are longer). Usually pays $200-650.

Fiction: Stories set in our region and aimed at mostly adult readers. No explicit sex or foul language. Contemporary fiction needed more than historical.

Photos: State availability of photos. Pays $20 for 5×7 or 8×10 b&w glossy prints, or $25 for 35 or 120mm color transparencies. Captions required. Buys one-time rights on both photos and text. Also buys photo essays on case-by-case basis and arrangement for payment.

Tips: "We are shifting emphasis of our main pieces from people to issues. We still need strong, several-source pieces about important and interesting people with strong Las Vegas connections—investors or sport figures for example. But we need more stories relating to issues which can be national in scope, but addressed from a Nevada standpoint: for instance, what happens to couples who work different hours, particularly in Nevada where a lot of people do it. In queries, come to the point. Tell me what sort of photos are available, whether historic or contemporary, b&w or color. Be specific in talking about what you want to write."

New Hampshire

FOREST NOTES, Society for the Protection of New Hampshire Forests, 54 Portsmouth St., Concord NH 03301. (603)224-9945. Editor: Richard Ober. 25% freelance written. Works with a small number of new/ unpublished writers each year. A bimonthly non-profit journal covering forestry, conservation, wildlife and land protection. "Our readers are concerned with in-depth examinations of natural resource issues in New Hampshire." Estab. 1901. Circ. 12,000. **Pays on acceptance.** Publishes ms an average of 3 months after acceptance. Byline given. Query first. Buys first or second serial (reprint) rights; primarily makes work-for-hire assignments. Previously published submissions OK. Query for electronic submissions. Reports in 2 weeks on queries; 1 month on mss. Free sample copy.

Nonfiction: Interview/profile (on assignment only); photo feature (b&w photos of New Hampshire) and technical (on forestry). Query. Length: 500-2,000 words. Pay varies. Sometimes pays the expenses of writers on assignment.

Photos: State availability of photos with submission. Reviews 5×7 prints. Offers no additional payment for photos accepted with ms. Captions required. Buys one-time rights.

Columns/Departments: Book review. Buys 1 mss/year. Query. Length: 150-500 words. Pays $25-75.

Tips: "Live in New Hampshire or New England; know your subject."

NEW HAMPSHIRE PROFILES, Isle of Shoals Publishing, P.O. Box 370, Stratham NH 03885. (603)772-5252. Editor: Suki Cassanave. 90% freelance written. Prefers to work with published/established writers; works with small number of new/unpublished writers each year. Bimonthly magazine; articles concentrate on audience ages 25 and up, consumer-oriented readers who want to know more about the quality of life in New Hampshire. Pays on publication. Publishes ms an average of 4 months after acceptance. Offers 25% kill fee. Buys first North American serial rights. Submit seasonal/holiday material 9 months in advance. Query for electronic submissions. Reports in 2 months. Sample copy $2.50 with 9½ × 12 SAE. Writer's guidelines for #10 SASE.

Nonfiction: Interview, profile, photo feature and interesting activities for and about the state of New Hampshire and people who live in it. Buys 75 mss/year. Query with published clips or send complete ms. Length varies from 1,000-3,000 words, depending on subject matter. Pays $100-500. Sometimes pays expenses of writers on assignment.

Photos: Uses seasonal stock and makes some assignments. Pays $50-150.

Columns/Departments: Buys 40 mss/year. Query with published clips. Length: 1,000-1,500 words. Pays $100-275.

Tips: "Query before submitting manuscript, and don't send us your only copy of the manuscript—photocopy it. Familiarity with magazine is essential."

New Jersey

NEW JERSEY MONTHLY, P.O. Box 920, Morristown NJ 07963-0920. (201)539-8230. Executive Editor: Patrick Sarver. 85% freelance written. Monthly magazine covering New Jersey. "Almost anything that's New Jersey related." Estab. 1976. Circ. 106,000. **Pays on acceptance.** Byline given. Offers 33% kill fee. Buys first rights. Submit seasonal/holiday material 6 months in advance. Query for electronic submissions. Reports in 6 weeks. Sample copy $3.75; writer's guidelines for #10 SASE.

Nonfiction: Book excerpts, essays, exposé, general interest, historical, humor, interview/profile, opinion, personal experience and travel. Special issue features Dining Out and Bridal (Jan.); Real Estate (March); Home & Garden (April); Great Weekends (May); Shore Guide (June); Summer Pleasures (July); Dining Out (Aug.); Fall Getaways (Oct.); Entertaining (Nov.); Holiday Gala (Dec.). No experience pieces from people who used to live in New Jersey or general pieces that have no New Jersey angle. Buys 180 mss/year. Query with published magazine clips. Length: 2,000-3,000 words. Pays 35¢/word and up. Pays expenses of writers on assignment.

Photos: State availability of photos with submission. Payment negotiated. Identification of subjects required. Buys one-time rights.

Columns/Departments: New Jersey & Co. (company profile, trends, individual profiles); Health (trends, how-to, personal experience, service); Politics (perspective pieces from writers working the political beat in Trenton); Home & Garden (homes, gardens, how-tos, trends, profiles, etc.); Health; Media; Travel (in and out-of-state); Education. Buys 60 mss/year. Query with published clips. Length: 1,500-1,800 words. Pays 35¢ and up per word.

Tips: "Almost everything here is open to freelancers, since most of the magazine is freelance written. However, to break in, we suggest contributing short items to our front-of-the-book section, 'Upfront' (light, offbeat items, trends, people, things; short service items, such as the 10 best NJ-made ice creams; short issue-oriented items; gossip; media notes). We pay 35¢ per published word. This is the only section we pay for on publication."

NEW JERSEY REPORTER, A Journal of Public Issues, The Center for Analysis of Public Issues, 16 Vandeventer Ave., Princeton NJ 08542. (609)924-9750. FAX: (609)924-0363. Managing Editor: Alice Chason. 30% freelance written. Prefers to work with published/established writers. Magazine published 10 times/year covering New Jersey politics, public affairs and public issues. "*New Jersey Reporter* is a hard-hitting and highly respected magazine published for people who take an active interest in New Jersey politics and public affairs, and who want to know more about what's going on than what newspapers and television newscasts are able to tell them. We publish a great variety of stories ranging from analysis to exposé." Estab. 1970. Circ. 3,000. Pays on publication. Publishes ms an average of 2 months after acceptance. Byline given. Buys all rights. Simultaneous queries and submissions and previously published submissions OK. Reports in 1 month. Sample copy $3.50.

Nonfiction: Book excerpts, exposé, interview/profile and opinion. "We like articles from specialists (in planning, politics, economics, corruption, etc.), but we reject stories that do not read well because of jargon or too little attention to the actual writing of the piece. Our magazine is interesting as well as informative." Buys 10 mss/year. Query with published clips or send complete ms. Length: 2,000-6,000 words. Pays $100-350. Pays expenses of writers on assignments.

Tips: "Queries should be specific about how the prospective story represents an issue that affects or will affect the people of New Jersey. The writer's résumé should be included. Stories—unless they are specifically meant to be opinion—should come to a conclusion but avoid a 'holier than thou' or preachy tone. Allegations should be scrupulously substantiated. Our magazine represents a good opportunity for freelancers to acquire great clips. Our publication specializes in longer, more detailed, analytical features. The most frequent mistake made by writers in completing an article for us is too much personal opinion versus reasoned advocacy. We are less interested in opinion than in analysis based on sound reasoning and fact. *New Jersey Reporter* is a well-respected publication, and many of our writers go on to nationally respected newspapers and magazines."

THE SANDPAPER, Newsmagazine of the Jersey Shore, The SandPaper, Inc., 1816 Long Beach Blvd., Surf City NJ 08008. (609)494-2034. FAX: (609)494-1437. Editor: Curt Travers. Freelance Submissions Editor: Gail Travers. 20% freelance written. Weekly tabloid covering subjects of interest to Jersey shore residents and visitors. *"The SandPaper* publishes three editions covering many of the Jersey Shore's finest resort communities. Each issue includes a mix of hard news, human interest features, opinion columns and entertainment/calendar listings." Circ. 85,000. Pays on publication. Publishes ms an average of 1 month after acceptance. Byline given. Offers 100% kill fee. Buys first rights or all rights. Submit seasonal/holiday material 3 months in advance. Simultaneous and previously published submissions OK. Reports in 1 month.
Nonfiction: Essays, general interest, historical/nostalgic, humor, opinion and environmental submissions relating to the ocean, wetlands and pinelands. Must pertain to New Jersey shore locale. Also, arts and entertainment news and reviews if they have a Jersey shore angle. Buys 25 mss/year. Send complete ms. Length: 200-2,000 words. Pays $15-100. Sometimes pays the expenses of writers on assignment.
Photos: State availability of photos with submission. Offers $6-25/photo. Buys one-time rights or all rights.
Columns/Departments: SpeakEasy (opinion and slice-of-life; often humorous); and Commentary (forum for social science perspectives); all 500-1,500 words, preferably with local or Jersey shore angle. Buys 50 mss/year. Send complete ms. Pays $15-35.
Tips: "Anything of interest to sun worshippers, beach walkers, nature watchers, water sports lovers is of potential interest to us. There is an increasing coverage of environmental issues. The opinion page and columns are most open to freelancers. We are steadily increasing the amount of entertainment-related material in our publication."

New Mexico

SOUTHWEST PROFILE, Whitney Publishing Co., Suite #102, 941 Calle Mejia, P.O. Box 1236, Santa Fe NM 87504-1236. (505)984-1773. Editor: Stephen Parks. 50% freelance written. Magazine on the Southwest, published 10 times per year. *"Southwest Profile* is a guide to travel and adventure, art and culture, and living and leisure in the Southwest, with special emphasis on Arizona and New Mexico." Estab. 1978. Circ. 20,000. Pays on publication. Publishes ms an average of 2 months after acceptance. Byline given. Offers 50% kill fee. Buys first North American serial rights. Submit seasonal/holiday material 6 months in advance. Query for electronic submissions. Reports in 1 month. Sample copy for 9×12 SAE with $1.25 postage; writer's guidelines for #10 SASE.
Nonfiction: General interest, interview/profile, photo feature, travel and art. Buys 30 mss/year. Query with published clips. Length: 1,000-2,500 words. Pays $150-300. Sometimes pays expenses of writers on assignment.
Photos: Send photos with submission. Reviews 35mm or larger transparencies and 5×7 prints. Offers $25-50 per photo. Captions required. Buys one-time rights.

New York

ADIRONDACK LIFE, Route 86, P.O. Box 97, Jay NY 12941. FAX (518)946-7461. Editor: Tom Hughes. 50% freelance written. Prefers to work with published/established writers; works with a small number of new/unpublished writers each year. Emphasizes the Adirondack region and the North Country of New York State in articles concerning outdoor activities, history, and natural history directly related to the Adirondacks. Bimonthly magazine. Circ. 50,000. **Pays on acceptance.** Publishes ms an average of 6 months after acceptance. Buys one-time rights. Byline given. Submit seasonal/holiday material 1 year in advance. Reports in 1 month. Sample copy for 9×12 SAE and $1.65 postage; writer's guidelines for #10 SASE.
Nonfiction: *Adirondack Life* attempts to capture the unique flavor and ethos of the Adirondack mountains and North Country region through feature articles directly pertaining to the qualities of the area and through department articles examining specific aspects. Example: Barkeater: personal essay; Special Places: unique spots in the Adirondacks; Working: careers in the Adirondacks; Wilderness: environmental issues, personal experiences. Buys 10-16 unsolicited mss/year. Query. Length: for features, 3,000 words maximum; for departments, 1,500 words. Pays up to 25¢/word. Sometimes pays expenses of writers on assignment.
Photos: All photos must have been taken in the Adirondacks. Each issue contains a photo feature. Purchased with or without ms or on assignment. All photos must be identified as to subject or locale and must bear photographer's name. Submit color slides or b&w prints. Pays $25 for b&w prints; $50 for transparencies; $300 for cover (color only, vertical in format). Credit line given.
Tips: "We are looking for clear, concise, well-organized manuscripts, written with flair. We are continually trying to upgrade the editorial quality of our publication."

‡**BUFFALO SPREE MAGAZINE**, Spree Publishing Co., Inc., 4511 Harlem Rd., P.O. Box 38, Buffalo NY 14226. (716)839-3405. Editor: Johanna V. Shotell. 90% freelance written. A quarterly literary, consumer-oriented, city magazine. Estab. 1967. Circ. 21,000. Pays on publication. Publishes ms an average of 6-12 months after

acceptance. Byline given. Buys first North American serial rights. Submit seasonal/holiday material 9-12 months in advance. Reports in 6 months on mss. Sample copy $2 with 9×12 SAE and $2.40 postage.

Nonfiction: Essays, interview/profile, historical/nostalgic, humor, personal experience and travel. Buys 50 mss/year. Send complete ms. Length: 600-1,800 words. Pays $75-125 for unsolicited articles.

Photos: State availability of photos with submission. Reviews prints (any size). Offers no additional payment for photos accepted with ms. Captions required. Buys one-time rights.

Fiction: Experimental, mainstream. "No pornographic or religious manuscripts." Buys 60 mss/year. Send complete ms. Length: 500-2,000 words. Pays $75-100.

Poetry: Janet Goldenberg, poetry editor. Buys 24 poems/year. Submit maximum 4 poems. Length: 50 lines maximum. Pays $25.

CAPITAL MAGAZINE, Capital Region Magazine, Inc., 4 Central Ave., Albany NY 12210. (518)465-3500. Editor-in-Chief: Dardis McNamee. 20% freelance written. Prefers to work with published/established writers. A monthly city/regional magazine for New York's capital region. Circ. 35,000. Pays 30 days from acceptance. Publishes ms an average of 3 months after acceptance. Byline given. Offers 25% kill fee. Buys one-time and second serial (reprint) rights. Submit seasonal/holiday material 3 months in advance. Query for electronic submissions. Reports in 2 months. Sample copy for 9×12 SAE with $1.95; writer's guidelines for #10 SASE.

Nonfiction: Book excerpts, essays, exposé, general interest, historical/nostalgic, humor, interview/profile, arts and culture, photo feature, travel, business and politics. Buys 75 mss/year. Query with published clips (preferred) or send complete ms. Length: 1,500-3,000. Pays $120-400. Fees set at approximately 10¢/word. Pays the expenses of writers on assignment "if agreed upon in advance."

Photos: State availability of photos with submission. Pays $300 plus expenses for covers; $350 plus expenses for features. Identification of subjects required. Buys one-time rights.

Columns/Departments: Politics, Business, Culture, Food & Wine, Design, Destinations and Media, all 1,000-1,400 words. Buys 30 mss/year. Query with published clips or send complete ms. Length: 1,000-1,400 words. Pays $150 maximum.

Fiction: "One fiction issue per year, July; short stories, novel excerpts, poetry. Deadline Feburary 15. For writers with a link to the region. Professional quality only; one slot for writers previously unpublished in a general circulation magazine."

Fillers: Vignettes, short essays, newsbreaks and short humor. Buys 30/year. Length: 150-750 words. Pays $25-75.

Tips: "Exclusively local focus, although we welcome pieces seen in larger context. Investigative reporting, profiles, business stories, trend pieces, behind-the-scenes, humor, service features, arts and culture, nitty-gritty. Looking for The Great Read in every story."

CITY LIMITS, City Limits Community Information Service, Inc., 40 Prince St., New York NY 10012. (212)925-9820. FAX: (212)996-3407. Editor: Doug Turetsky. Associate Editor: Lisa Glazer. 50% freelance written. Works with a small number of new/unpublished writers each year. A monthly magazine covering housing and related urban issues. "We cover news and issues in New York City as they relate to the city's poor, moderate and middle-income residents. We are advocacy journalists with a progressive or 'left' slant." Estab. 1976. Circ. 5,000. Pays on publication. Publishes ms an average of 1-2 months after acceptance. Byline given. Buys first North American serial rights, one-time rights, or second serial (reprint) rights. Query for electronic submissions. Reports in 3 weeks. Sample copy $2.

Nonfiction: Expose, interview/profile, opinion, hard news and community profile. "No fluff, no propaganda." Length: 600-2,500 words. Pays $50-150. Sometimes pays expenses of writers on assignment.

Photos: Reviews contact sheets and 5×7 prints. Offers $10-40/photo, cover only. Identification of subjects required. Buys one-time rights.

Columns/Departments: Short Term Notes (brief descriptions of programs, policies, events, etc.), 250-400 words; Book Reviews (housing, urban development, planning, etc.), 250-600 words; Pipeline (covers community organizations, new programs, government policies, etc.), 600-800 words; People (who are active in organizations, community groups, etc.), 600-800 words; and Organize (groups involved in housing, job programs, health care, etc.), 600-800 words. Buys 50-75 mss/year. Query with published clips or send complete ms. Pays $25-35.

Tips: "We are open to a wide range of story ideas in the community development field. If you don't have particular expertise in housing, urban planning etc., start with a community profile or pertinent book or film review. Short Term Notes is also good for anyone with reporting skills. We're looking for writing that is serious and informed but not academic or heavy handed."

‡FACETS, The Unconventional guide to NYC, NYNEX Information Resources Co., Room 945, 100 Church St., New York NY 10007. (212)513-9405. Editor: Wayne J. Mitchell. 50% freelance written. Quarterly magazine on New York City culture, people and events. Estab. 1986. Pays on publication. Byline sometimes given. Offers 25% kill fee. Buys one-time rights. Submit seasonal/holiday material 6 months in advance. Simultaneous and previously published submissions OK. Query for electronic submissions. Reports in 2 weeks on queries; 1 month on mss. Free sample copy and writer's guidelines.

Nonfiction: Expose, general interest, humor, interview/profile, opinion, personal experience, photo feature, travel to New York City. No fiction or New York put-downs. Buys 20 mss/year. Query with or without published clips, or send complete ms. Length: 500-2,000 words. Pays 10-25¢/word. Sometimes pays expenses of writers on assignment.
Photos: State availability of photos with submision. Offers no additional payment for photos accepted with ms. Captions and model releases required. Buys one-time rights.
Columns/Departments: Undercover, Sports Update, Note 4 Note (music), Brushstrokes (art), Sights & Sounds (things to do in New York, odd events). Buys 20 mss/year. Query. Length: 500-1,000 words. Pays 10-25¢/word.
Tips: *"Facets* is published for the New York visitor—usually a young 40ish who visits NYC 10+ times a year. He or she is in tune with New York so don't write about the Circle Line or the Empire State Building. Delve into the more offbeat things that make New York great."

‡FINGER LAKES MAGAZINE, Grapevine Press, Inc., 108 S. Albany St., Ithaca NY 14850. (607)272-3470. Editor: Linda McCandless. 95% freelance written. A bimonthly magazine covering Finger Lakes Region of New York State. Estab. 1974. Circ. 20,000. Pays 1 month after publication. Publishes ms an average of 6-12 months after acceptance. Byline given. Offers negotiable kill fee. Buys first North American serial rights. Submit seasonal/holiday material 8 months in advance. Simultaneous submissions OK. Reports in 1 month on queries; 2 months on mss. Sample copy for 9×12 SAE and 5 first class stamps; writer's guidelines for #10 SASE.
Nonfiction: Investigative reporting, expose, general interest, historical/nostalgic, humor, interview/profile, recreation and photo feature. Buys 30 mss/year. Query with published clips. Length: 600-2,400 words. Pays $40-200.
Columns/Departments: Lake Takes (profile on person of interest). Query with published clips. Length: 100-300 words. Pays $20-40. Excursions (day trip). Query with published clips. Length: 300-400 words. Pays $30-40.
Fiction: Needs 2-3 "Fiend of The Finger Lakes" each year; one crime for the past 200 years in Central New York reconstructed in colorful detail. Buys 4 mss/year. Query with published clips or send complete ms. Length: 1,200-1,500 words. Pays $75.

‡HUDSON VALLEY MAGAZINE, Suburban Publishing, P.O. Box 429, 297 Main Mall, Poughkeepsie NY 12602. (914)485-7844. Editor: Susan Agrest. Articles Editor: Jim Defelice. Monthly magazine. Estab. 1973. Circ. 27,000. Pays on publication. Byline given. Offers 25% kill fee. Buys first North American serial rights or first rights. Submit seasonal/holiday material 6 months in advance. Query for electronic submissions. Sample copy for $1 with 11×14 SAE and 4 first class stamps.
Nonfiction: Only articles related to the Hudson Valley. Book excerpts, exposé, general interest, historical/nostalgic, how-to, humor, interview/profile, new product, opinion, photo feature, travel and business. Buys 150 mss/year. Query with published clips. Length: 300-3,500 words. Pays $25-500 for assigned articles. Sometimes pays expenses of writers on assignment.
Photos: State availability of photos with submission. Captions, model releases and identification of subjects required.
Columns/Departments: Open Season (advocacy/editorial), 1,200-1,500 words; Book Reviews, 800-1,200 words. Query with published clips. Length: 1,200-1,500 words. Pays $75-200.
Fillers: Anecdotes, facts, gags to be illustrated by cartoonist, newsbreaks, short humor. Buys 36/year. Length: 300-500 words. Pays $25-50.
Tips: "Send a letter, resume, sample of best writing and queries. No manuscripts. Factual accuracy imperative."

LONG ISLAND MONTHLY, CMP Publications, 600 Community Dr., Manhasset NY 11030. (516)562-5000. Editor: John Atwood. 75% freelance written. Monthly magazine, general interest, usually with Long Island connection. Estab. 1988. Circ. 70,000. Byline given. Offers 25% kill fee. Buys first North American serial rights. Submit seasonal/holiday material 4 months in advance. Simultaneous submissions OK. Query for electronic submissions. Reports in 6 weeks. Sample copy $3.50. Writer's guidelines for #10 SASE.
Nonfiction: Book excerpts, essays, exposé, general interest, historical/nostalgic, humor, interview/profile, personal experience and photo feature. Buys 150 mss/year. Query with published clips. Pays 10¢-$1/word for assigned articles. Pays expenses of writers on assignment.
Photos: State availability of photos with submission. Captions, model releases and identification of subjects required. Buys one-time rights.

N.Y. HABITAT, For Co-op, Condominium and Loft Living, Carol Group Ltd., Suite 1105, 928 Broadway, New York NY 10010. (212)505-2030. FAX: (212)254-6795. Editor: Carol Ott. Managing Editor: Lloyd Chrein. 75% freelance written. Publishes 8 issues/year. *"N.Y. Habitat* is a magazine directed to owners, board members, and potential owners of co-ops and condos. All articles should be instructive to these readers, offering them information in an easy-to-read and entertaining manner." Circ. 10,000. Pays on publication. Byline

given. Offers 50% kill fee. Buys one-time rights. Submit seasonal/holiday material 6 months in advance. Reports in 2 weeks on queries; 1 month on mss. Sample copy $5; writer's guidelines for #10 SASE.
Nonfiction: How-to (run a co-op); interview/profile (of co-op/condo managers, board members, etc.); personal experience; news stories on trends in co-ops and condos. Special issues include Annual Management Issue (July/August). No articles on lifestyles or apartment furnishings. Buys 30 mss/year. Query with published clips. Length: 500-2,000 words. Pays $75-800 for assigned articles. Pays expenses of writers on assignment.
Photos: State availability of photos with submission. Reviews contact sheets. Offers $50-75 per photo. Captions, model releases and identification of subjects required. Buys one-time rights.
Columns/Departments: Hotline (short, timely news items about co-op and condo living), 500 words; Finances (financial information for buyers and owners), 1000-1,500 words. Westchester Report (news, profiles, management. stories pertaining to Westchester County), 1,000-1,500 words. Buys 15 mss/year. Query with published clips. Pays $100.
Tips: "The Hotline section is the most accessible to freelancers. This calls for light (but informative) news and personality pieces pertaining to co-op/condo concerns. If you have ideas for our other columns, however, query, as most of them are completely freelance written."

NEW YORK DAILY NEWS, Travel Section, 220 E. 42 St., New York NY 10017. (212)210-1699. FAX: (212)661-4675. Travel Editor: Harry Ryan. 30% freelance written. Prefers to work with published/established writers. Weekly tabloid. Circ. 1.8 million. "We are the largest circulating newspaper travel section in the country and take all types of articles ranging from experiences to service oriented pieces that tell readers how to make a certain trip." Pays on publication. Publishes ms an average of 3 months after acceptance. Byline given. Submit seasonal/holiday material 4 months in advance. Contact first before submitting electronic submissions; requires hard copy also. Computer printout submissions acceptable "if crisp"; prefers letter-quality. Reports "as soon as possible." Writer's guidelines for #10 SASE.
Nonfiction: General interest, historical/nostalgic, humor, inspirational, personal experience and travel. "Most of our articles involve practical trips that the average family can afford—even if it's one you can't afford every year. We put heavy emphasis on budget saving tips for all trips. We also run stories now and then for the Armchair Traveler, an exotic and usually expensive trip. We are looking for professional quality work from professional writers who know what they are doing. The pieces have to give information and be entertaining at the same time. No 'How I Spent My Summer Vacation' type articles. No PR hype." Buys 60 mss/year. Query with SASE. Length: 1,500 words maximum. Pays $75-150.
Photos: "Good pictures always help sell good stories." State availability of photos with ms. Reviews contact sheets and negatives. Captions and identification of subjects required. Buys all rights.
Columns/Departments: Short Hops is based on trips to places within a 300-mile radius of New York City. Length: 800-1,000 words. Travel Watch gives practical travel advice.
Tips: "A writer might have some luck gearing a specific destination to a news event or date: In Search of Irish Crafts in March, for example, but do it well in advance."

NEW YORK MAGAZINE, News America Publishing, Inc., 755 2nd Ave., New York NY 10017. (212)880-0700. Editor: Edward Kosner. Managing Editor: Laurie Jones. 25% freelance written. Weekly magazine focusing on current events in the New York metropolitan area. Circ. 433,813. **Pays on acceptance.** Offers $150-250 kill fee. Buys first North American serial rights. Submit seasonal/holiday material 2 months in advance. Reports in 1 month. Sample copy for $3.50 if the individual has the copy mailed. Otherwise, the charge is $2. Free writer's guidelines.
Nonfiction: Exposé, general interest, profile, new product, personal experience, travel. Query. Pays 75¢-$1.25/word. Pays expenses of writers on assignment.
Tips: "Submit a detailed query to Laurie Jones, *New York*'s managing editor. If there is sufficient interest in the proposed piece, the article will be assigned."

NEW YORK'S NIGHTLIFE AND **LONG ISLAND'S NIGHTLIFE**, MJC Publications Inc., 1770 Deer Park Ave., Deer Park NY 11729. (516)242-7722. Publisher: Michael Cutino. Managing Editor: Fred Goodman. 35% freelance written. Eager to work with new/unpublished writers. A monthly entertainment magazine. Circ. 50,000. Pays on publication. Publishes ms an average of 3 months after acceptance. Byline given. Offers $15 kill fee. Buys first North American serial rights and all rights. Submit seasonal/holiday material 10 weeks in advance. Simultaneous queries OK. Query for electronic submissions. Reports in 10 weeks. Free sample copy and writer's guidelines for 8½×11 SAE and $1.25 postage.
Nonfiction: General interest, humor, inspirational, interview/profile, new product, photo feature, travel and entertainment. Length: 500-1,500 words. Pays $25-75.
Photos: Send photos with ms. Reviews b&w and color contact sheets. Pays $10 for transparencies and b&w prints. Captions and model releases required. Buys all rights.
Columns/Departments: Films, Movies, Albums, Sports, Fashion, Entertainment and Groups. Buys 150 mss/year. Send complete ms. Length: 400-600 words. Pays $25.
Fillers: Clippings, jokes, gags, anecdotes, short humor and newsbreaks. Buys 10/year. Length: 25-100 words. Pays $10.

NEWSDAY, Long Island NY 11747. Viewpoints Editor: James Lynn. Opinion section of daily newspaper. Byline given.

Nonfiction: Seeks "opinion on current events, trends, issues—whether national or local government or lifestyle. Must be timely, pertinent, articulate and opinionated. Preference for authors within the circulation area including New York City." Length: 600-2,000 words. Pays $150-400.

Tips: "The writer has a better chance of breaking in at our publication with short articles since the longer essays are commissioned from experts and well-known writers."

ROCHESTER BUSINESS MAGAZINE, Rochester Business, Inc., 1600 Lyell Ave., Rochester NY 14606. (716)458-8280. Editor: Douglas Sprei. 25% freelance written. Monthly magazine. "*RBM* is a colorful tutorial business publication targeted specifically toward business owners and upper level managers in the Rochester metropolitan area. Our audience is comprised of upscale decision-makers with keen interest in the 'how-to' of business. Some features deal with lifestyle, travel, cultural focus, etc." Circ. 17,000. Pays on publication. Publishes ms an average of 2-6 months after acceptance. Byline given. Buys all rights. Previously published submissions OK. Reports in 1 month. Sample $2.

Nonfiction: Essays, historical/nostalgic, how-to, humor, interview/profile and personal experience, all with business slant. Buys 12-24 mss/year. Query with published clips. Length: 1,500 words maximum. Pays $50-100. Pays barter (trade dollars) to interested writers.

Photos: State availability of photos with submission. Offers no additional payment for photos accepted with ms. Captions required.

North Carolina

CHARLOTTE, New South Press, Inc., P.O. Box 37208, Charlotte NC 28273. (704)332-0148. FAX: (704)332-0165. Editor: Andrea Anapol. 90% freelance written. Bimonthly magazine. "The editorial content is slanted to upscale and affluent readers within the Charlotte Metrolina region of North Carolina." Estab. 1988. Circ. 15,000. Pays on publication. Publishes ms an average of 2 months after acceptance. Byline given. Buys one-time rights. Submit seasonal/holiday material 3 months in advance. Simultaneous and previously published submissions OK. Query for electronic submission. Reports in 2 months. Sample copy $2.95; free writer's guidelines.

Nonfiction: Essays, general interest, historical/nostalgic, humor, interview/profile, photo feature, religious, travel and other consumer articles. Buys 40 mss/year. Query with published clips. "No phone calls, please." Length: 500-2,500. Pays 15¢/word. Sometimes pays expenses of writers on assignment.

Photos: State availability of photos with submission. Reviews contact sheets, negatives, up to 4 × 5 transparencies and 5 × 7 prints. Offers negotiable pay for photos. Captions, model releases and identification of subjects required. Buys one-time rights.

Columns/Departments: Random Thoughts (general interest, unique tidbits of information) 250 words; Business (trends, ideas) 250-1,000 words; The Arts (performing and visual), 250-1,000 words; Sports, 250-1,000 words. Buys 12 mss/year. Query with published clips or send complete ms. Pays 15¢/word.

Fillers: Anecdotes, facts and short humor. Buys 12/year. Length: 25-100 words. Pays 15¢/word.

SOUTHERN EXPOSURE, P.O. Box 531, Durham NC 27702. (919)688-8167. Contact: Editor. Quarterly journal for Southerners interested in "left-liberal" political perspective and the South; all ages; well-educated. Estab. 1970. Circ. 7,500. Pays on publication. Buys all rights. Offers kill fee. Byline given. Will consider simultaneous submissions. Submit seasonal material 6 months in advance. Reports in 3 months. "Query is appreciated, but not required." Sample copy $4. Writer's guidelines for #10 SASE.

Nonfiction: "Ours is one of the few publications about the South *not* aimed at business or upper-class people; it appeals to all segments of the population. *And*, it is used as a resource—sold as a magazine and then as a book—so it rarely becomes dated." Needs investigative articles about the following subjects as related to the South: politics, energy, institutional power from prisons to universities, women, labor, black people and the economy. Informational interview, profile, historical, think articles, exposé, opinion and book reviews. Length: 4,500 words maximum. Pays $50-200. Smaller fee for short items.

Photos: "Very rarely purchase photos, as we have a large number of photographers working for us." 8 × 10 b&w preferred; no color. Payment negotiable.

Tips: "Because we will be publishing shorter issues, we will be looking for clear and thoughtful writing, articles that relate specific experiences of individual Southerners or grass roots groups to larger issues."

THE STATE, Down Home in North Carolina, Suite 2200, 128 S. Tryon St., Charlotte NC 28202. Editor: Jim Duff. 70% freelance written. Publishes material from published and unpublished writers from time to time. Monthly. Buys first serial rights. Pays on publication. Deadlines 2 months in advance. Sample copy $3.

Nonfiction: General articles about places, people, events, history, nostalgia and general interest in North Carolina. Emphasis on travel in North Carolina. Will use humor if related to region. Length: 1,000-2,000 words average. Pays $15-25.

Photos: Black & white photos, color. Pays $15-25, "depending on use."

WHAT'S NEW MAGAZINE, Multicom 7 Inc., 8305 Paces Oak Blvd., Charlotte NC 28123-5142. Editor: Bob Leja. 80% freelance written. A monthly magazine covering music, entertainment, sports and lifestyles for the "baby-boom" generation. Estab. 1977. Circ. 125,000. Pays on publication. Publishes ms an average of 2 months after acceptance. Byline given. Offers 25% kill fee. Buys one-time rights. Submit seasonal/holiday material 4 months in advance. Electronic submissions OK; call system operator. Reports in 2 months. Sample copy $3 with 9 × 12 SAE and 6 first class stamps.

Nonfiction: Book excerpts, general interest, humor, new product, photo feature and travel. Special issues include motorcycle buyer's guide, consumer elect buyer's guide, and automotive buyer's guide. Buys 120 mss/ year. Query with published clips. Length: 150-3,000 words. Pays $25-250 for assigned articles. Sometimes pays the expenses of writers on assignment.

Photos: State availability of photos with submission. Reviews contact sheets. Offers $15 for first photo, $5 for each additional photo published in 1 issue. Captions, model releases and identification of subjects required. Buys one-time rights.

Columns/Departments: Great Escapes (undiscovered or under-explored vacation possibilities); Food Department (new and unusual developments in food and drink); and Fads, Follies and Trends (weird things that everyone is doing—from buying breakdancing accessories to brushing with pump toothpaste). Buys 150 mss/year. Query with published clips. Length: 150-3,000 words. Pays $25-250.

Tips: *"What's New* will remain a unique magazine by continuing to combine informative coverage of established, mainstream artists with reports on the newest bands, movies, fads or trends and by writing about them in the same snappy, witty and irreverent style that has singled it out in the past. The magazine will remain creative enough to find the angle that others fail to see. This calls for some extraordinary talent, and the magazine is fortunate to have such a resource in its national network of freelance writers."

Ohio

BEACON MAGAZINE, Akron Beacon Journal, 44 E. Exchange St., Akron OH 44328. (216)996-3586. Editor: Ann Sheldon Mezger. 25% freelance written. Eager to work with new/unpublished writers and works with a small number of new/unpublished writers each year. Sunday newspaper magazine of general interest articles with a focus on Northeast Ohio. Circ. 225,000. Pays on publication. Publishes ms an average of 2 months after acceptance. Byline given. Offers 50% kill fee. Buys one-time rights, simultaneous rights and second serial (reprint) rights. Submit seasonal/holiday material 3 months in advance. Simultaneous queries, and simultaneous and previously published submissions OK. Computer printout submissions acceptable; no dot-matrix. Reports in 1 month. Free sample copy and writer's guidelines.

Nonfiction: General interest, historical/nostalgic, short humor and interview/profile. Buys 50 mss/year. Query with or without published clips. Include Social Security number with story submission. Length: 500-3,000 words. Pays $75-450. Sometimes pays expenses of writers on assignment.

Photos: State availability of photos. Pays $25-50 for 35mm color transparencies and 8 × 10 b&w prints. Captions and identification of subjects required. Buys one-time rights.

BEND OF THE RIVER® MAGAZINE, 143 W. Third St., P.O. Box 239, Perrysburg OH 43551. (419)874-7534. FAX: (419)874-1466. Publishers: Christine Raizk Alexander or R. Lee Raizk. 90% freelance written. Works with a small number of new/unpublished writers each year, and eager to work with new/unpublished writers. "We buy material that we like whether by an experienced writer or not." Monthly magazine for readers interested in Ohio history, antiques, etc. Estab. 1972. Circ. 3,500. Pays on publication. Publishes ms an average of 6 months after acceptance. Byline given. Buys one-time rights. Submit seasonal material 2 months in advance; deadline for holiday issue is October 15. Reports in 6 weeks. Sample copy $1.

Nonfiction: "We deal heavily in Northwestern Ohio history. We are looking for well-researched articles about local history and modern day pioneers doing the unusual. We'd like to see interviews with historical (Ohio) authorities; travel sketches of little-known but interesting places in Ohio; articles about grass roots farmers, famous people from Ohio like Doris Day, Gloria Steinem, etc. and preservation. Our main interest is to give our readers happy thoughts and good reading. We strive for material that says 'yes' to life, past and present." No personal reflection or nostalgia unless you are over 65. Buys 75 unsolicited mss/year. Submit complete ms or send query. Length: 1,500 words. Pays $10-25. Sometimes pays the expenses of writers on assignment.

Photos: Purchases b&w or color photos with accompanying mss. Pays $1 minimum. Captions required.

Tips: "Any Toledo area, well-researched history will be put on top of the heap. Send us any unusual piece that is either cleverly humorous, divinely inspired or thought provoking. We like articles about historical topics treated in down-to-earth conversational tones. We pay a small amount (however, we're now paying more) but usually use our writers often and through the years. We're loyal."

‡CINCINNATI MAGAZINE, 409 Broadway, Cincinnati OH 45202. (513)421-4300. Editor: Laura Pulfer. Monthly magazine emphasizing Cincinnati living. Circ. 32,000. **Pays on acceptance.** Byline given. Offers 33% kill fee. Buys all rights. Submit seasonal/holiday material 3 months in advance. Simultaneous and previously published submissions OK. Reports in 5 weeks.
Nonfiction: How-to, informational, interview, photo feature, profile and travel. No humor. Buys 4-5 mss/issue. Query. Length: 2,000-4,000 words. Pays $150-400.
Photos: Thomas Hawley, art director. Photos purchased on assignment only. Model release required.
Columns/Departments: Travel, how-to, sports and consumer tips. Buys 5 mss/issue. Query. Length: 750-1,500 words. Pays $75-150.
Tips: "It helps to mention something you found particularly well done in our magazine. It shows you've done your homework and sets you apart from the person who clearly is not tailoring his idea to our publication. Send article ideas that probe the whys and wherefores of major issues confronting the community, making candid and in-depth appraisals of the problems and honest attempts to seek solutions. Have a clear and well defined subject about the city (the arts, politics, business, sports, government, entertainment); include a rough outline with proposed length; a brief background of writing experience and sample writing if available. We are looking for critical pieces, smoothly written, that ask and answer questions that concern our readers. We do not run features that are 'about' places or businesses simply because they exist. There should be a thesis that guides the writer and the reader. We want balanced articles about the city—the arts, politics, business, etc."

COLUMBUS MONTHLY, 171 E. Livingston Ave., Columbus OH 43215. (614)464-4567. Editor: Lenore E. Brown. 20-40% freelance written. Prefers to work with published/established writers; works with a small number of new/unpublished writers each year. Monthly magazine emphasizing subjects specifically related to Columbus and central Ohio. Pays on publication. Publishes ms an average of 2 months after acceptance. Byline given. Buys all rights. Query for electronic submissions. Reports in 1 month. Sample copy $3.57.
Nonfiction: No humor, essays or first person material. "I like query letters which are well-written, indicate the author has some familiarity with *Columbus Monthly*, give me enough detail to make a decision and include at least a basic biography of the writer." Buys 4-5 unsolicited mss/year. Query. Length: 400-4,500 words. Pays $50-400. Sometimes pays the expenses of writers on assignment.
Photos: State availability of photos. Pay varies for b&w or color prints. Model release required.
Columns/Departments: Art, business, food and drink, movies, politics, sports and theatre. Buys 2-3 columns/issue. Query. Length: 1,000-2,000 words. Pays $100-175.
Tips: "It makes sense to start small—something for our Around Columbus section, perhaps. Stories for that section run between 400-1,000 words."

OHIO MAGAZINE, Ohio Magazine, Inc., Subsidiary of Dispatch Printing Co., 40 S. 3rd St., Columbus OH 43215. Editor: Ellen Stein Burbach. 40% freelance written. Works with a small number of new/unpublished writers each year. Monthly magazine. Emphasizes news and feature material of Ohio for an educated, urban and urbane readership. Estab. 1978. Circ. 103,327. Pays on publication. Publishes ms an average of 5 months after acceptance. Buys all rights, second serial (reprint) rights, one-time rights, first North American serial rights or first serial rights. Byline given except on short articles appearing in sections. Submit seasonal/holiday material 5 months in advance. Previously published submissions OK. Reports in 2 months. Sample copy $3 and 9×12 SAE; writer's guidelines for #10 SASE.
Nonfiction: Features: 2,000-8,000 words. Pays $350-950. Cover pieces $650-1,000; Ohioana and Ohioans (should be offbeat with solid news interest; 1,000-2,000 words, pays $200-500); Ohioguide (pieces on upcoming Ohio events, must be offbeat and worth traveling for; 100-300 words, pays $10-15); Diners' Digest ("We are still looking for writers with extensive restaurant reviewing experience to do 5-10 short reviews each month in specific sections of the state on a specific topic. Fee is on a retainer basis and negotiable"); Money (covering business related news items, profiles of prominent people in business community, personal finance—all Ohio angle; 1,000 words and up, pays $200-500); and Living (embodies dining in, home furnishings, gardening and architecture; 1,000 words and up, pays $200-500). Send submissions for features to Ellen Stein Burbach, editor; Ohioguide and Diners' Digest to Lynn Campbell; and Money to Ellen Stein Burbach, editor. Buys minimum 40 unsolicited mss/year. Sometimes pays expenses of writers on assignment.
Columns/Departments: Ellen Stein Burbach, editor. Sports, Last Word, Travel.
Photos: Brooke Wenstrup, editorial designer. Rate negotiable.
Tips: "Freelancers should send a brief prospectus prior to submission of the complete article. All articles should have a definite Ohio application."

PLAIN DEALER MAGAZINE, Plain Dealer Publishing Co., 1801 Superior Ave., Cleveland OH 44114. (216)344-4546. FAX: (216)344-4122. Editor: Clint O'Connor. 50% freelance written. A general interest Sunday newspaper magazine focusing on (but not limited to) Cleveland and Ohio. Circ. 550,000. Pays on publication. Publishes ms an average of 2-3 months after acceptance. Byline given. Buys first or one-time rights. Submit seasonal/holiday material 3 months in advance. Simultaneous and previously published submissions OK. Reports in 6 weeks on queries; 3 months on mss. Sample copy $1.

Nonfiction: Profiles, in-depth features, essays, exposé, historical/nostalgic, humor, personal experience and travel. Buys 20 mss/year. Query with published clips, or send complete ms. Length: 800-5,000 words. Pays $150-500.

Photos: State availability of photos with submission. Buys one-time rights.

Fiction: Adventure, confession, fantasy, humorous, mainstream and slice-of-life vignettes. Buys 5 mss/year. Send complete ms. Length: 1,000-5,000 words. Pays $150-500.

Tips: "We're always looking for good writers and good stories."

TOLEDO MAGAZINE, The Blade, 541 Superior St., Toledo OH 43660. (419)245-6121. Editor: Sue Stankey. 60% freelance written. Prefers to work with published/established writers and works with a small number of new/unpublished writers each year. Weekly general interest magazine that appears in the Sunday newspaper. Circ. 225,000. Pays on publication. Publishes ms an average of 3 months after acceptance. Byline given. Buys one-time rights. Submit seasonal/holiday material 4-6 months in advance. Simultaneous queries and submissions OK. Reports in 2 weeks on queries; 1 month on mss. Sample copy for 9×12 SASE.

Nonfiction: General interest, historical/nostalgic, humor, interview/profile and personal experience. Buys 100-200 mss/year. Query with or without published clips. Length: 500-6,000 words. Pays $75-500.

Photos: State availability of photos. Reviews b&w and color contact sheets. Payment negotiable. Captions, model release and identification of subjects required. Buys one-time rights.

Tips: "Submit a well-organized story proposal and include copies of previously published stories."

Oklahoma

OKLAHOMA TODAY, Oklahoma Department of Tourism and Recreation, P.O. Box 53384, Oklahoma City OK 73152. Editor-in-Chief: Sue Carter. Managing Editor: Jeanne Devlin. 99% freelance written. Works with a small number of new/unpublished writers each year. Bimonthly magazine covering travel and recreation in the state of Oklahoma. "We are interested in showing off the best Oklahoma has to offer; we're pretty serious about our travel slant but will also consider history, nature and personality profiles." Estab. 1956. Circ. 45,000. **Pays on acceptance.** Publishes ms an average of 3 months after acceptance. Byline given. Buys first serial rights. Submit seasonal/holiday material 1 year in advance "depending on photographic requirements." Simultaneous queries OK. Reports in 2 months. Sample copy $2.50 with 8½×11 SASE; writer's guidelines for #10 SASE.

Nonfiction: Book excerpts (pre-publication only, on Oklahoma topics); photo feature and travel (in Oklahoma). "We are a specialized market; no first-person reminiscences or fashion, memoirs, though just about any topic can be used if given a travel slant." Buys 35-40 mss/year. Query with published clips; no phone queries. Length: 1,000-1,500 words. Pays $150-250.

Photos: High-quality transparencies, b&w prints. "We are especially interested in developing contacts with photographers who either live in Oklahoma or have shot here. Send samples and price range." Free photo guidelines with SASE. Send photos with ms. Pays $50-100 for b&w and $50-250 for color; reviews 2¼ and 35mm color transparencies. Model releases, identification of subjects and other information for captions required. Buys one-time rights plus right to use photos for promotional purposes.

Tips: "The best way to become a regular contributor to *Oklahoma Today* is to query us with one or more story ideas, each developed to give us an idea of your proposed slant. We're looking for *lively* writing, writing that doesn't need to be heavily edited and is not newspaper style. We have a two-person editorial staff, and freelancers who can write and have done their homework get called again and again."

Oregon

CASCADES EAST, 716 NE 4th St., P.O. Box 5784, Bend OR 97708. (503)382-0127. Editor: Geoff Hill. 100% freelance written. Prefers to work with published/established writers. Quarterly magazine. For "all ages as long as they are interested in outdoor recreation in central Oregon: fishing, hunting, sight-seeing, golf, tennis, hiking, bicycling, mountain climbing, backpacking, rockhounding, skiing, snowmobiling, etc." Estab. 1972. Circ. 10,000 (distributed throughout area resorts and motels and to subscribers). Pays on publication. Publishes ms an average of 6 months after acceptance. Buys all rights. Byline given. Submit seasonal/holiday material 6 months in advance. Reports in 6 weeks. Sample copy and writer's guidelines for $4 and 9×12 SAE.

ALWAYS submit unsolicited manuscripts or queries with a self-addressed, stamped envelope (SASE) within your country or International Reply Coupons (IRC) purchased from the post office for other countries.

Nonfiction: General interest (first person experiences in outdoor central Oregon—with photos, can be dramatic, humorous or factual); historical (for feature, "Little Known Tales from Oregon History," with b&w photos); and personal experience (needed on outdoor subjects: dramatic, humorous or factual). "No articles that are too general, sight-seeing articles that come from a travel folder, or outdoor articles without the first-person approach." Buys 20-30 unsolicited mss/year. Query. Length: 1,000-3,000 words. Pays 3-10¢/word.

Photos: "Old photos will greatly enhance chances of selling a historical feature. First-person articles need black and white photos, also." Pays $8-20 for b&w; $15-75 for transparencies. Captions preferred. Buys one-time rights.

Tips: "Submit stories a year or so in advance of publication. We are seasonal and must plan editorials for summer '92 in the spring of '91, etc., in case seasonal photos are needed."

‡**OREGON COAST, The Bi-Monthly Magazine of Coastal Living,** 1870 Highway 126, P.O. Box 18000, Florence OR 97439. (503)997-8401. Editor: Alicia Spooner. Managing Editor: Lynne LaReau Owens. 90% freelance written. Bimonthly magazine covering the Oregon Coast. Estab. 1982. Circ. 60,000. Pays on publication. Publishes ms an average of 6 months after accpetance. Byline given. Offers ⅓ kill fee. Buys one-time rights. Submit seasonal/holiday material 5 months in advance. Query for electronic submissions. Reports in 6 weeks. Sample copy $3.50 with 11 × 14 SAE and 8 first class stamps. Writer's guidelines for #10 SAE with 2 first class stamps.

Nonfiction: General interest, historical/nostalgic, humor, interview/profile, personal experience, photo feature, travel, nature or Coast focus. Buys 60 mss/year. Query with published clips. Length: 500-2,500 words. Pays $50-200.

Photos: Send photos with submission. Reviews 35mm or larger transparencies and 3 × 5 or larger prints. Offers no additional payment for photos accepted with ms. Captions and identification of subjects required. Buys one-time rights.

Columns/Departments: On Your Way (interesting stories from the routes to the Oregon Coast: Highway 101 in Northern California, Long Beach peninsula in Washington state and the I-5 corridor in Oregon), 1,000-1,500 words. Buys 6 mss/year. Query with published clips. Pays $50-100.

Poetry: Free verse, haiku, light verse, traditional. Nothing unrelated to the Northwest Coast. Buys 30 poems/year. Submit maximum 4 poems. Length: 60 lines maximum. Pays 5 copies in which work appears.

Fillers: Gags to be illustrated by cartoonist, newsbreaks (no-fee basis), short humor, short articles. Buys 30/year. Length: 300-1,000 words. Pays $35-50.

Tips: "Slant article for readers who do not live at the Oregon Coast. At least one historical article is used in each issues. Reminiscence articles are the most often returned. Manuscript/photo packages are preferred over manuscripts with no photos. Be sure and clearly list photo credits and captions for each print or slide. Check for spelling and grammatical errors again and again. Check all facts, proper names and numbers carefully. Fillers on places to visit and coastal happenings as well as researched historical features are the easiest to get published. Query first. After go-ahead send cover letter with manuscript/photo package. Photos often make the difference in deciding which article gets published."

Pennsylvania

PENNSYLVANIA, Pennsylvania Magazine Co., Box 576, Camp Hill PA 17011. (717)761-6620. Editor: Albert E. Holliday. Managing Editor: Joan Holliday. 90% freelance written. Bimonthly magazine. Circ. 40,000. Pays on acceptance for assigned articles. Publishes ms an average of 6 months after acceptance. Byline given. Offers 33% kill fee. Buys first North American serial rights or one-time rights. Reports in 2 weeks on queries; 3 weeks on mss. Sample copy $2.95 and 9 × 12 SAE; writer's guidelines for #10 SASE.

Nonfiction: General interest, historical/nostalgic, photo feature and travel—all dealing with or related to Pennsylvania. Nothing on Amish topics, hunting or skiing. Buys 50-75 mss/year. Query. Length: 250-2,500 words. Pays $25-250. Sometimes pays the expenses of writers on assignment. All articles must be illustrated; send photocopies of possible illustrations with query.

Photos: Reviews 35mm and 2¼ color transparencies and 5 × 7 to 8 × 10 color and b&w prints. Pays $15-50 for b&w; $15-100 for color. Captions required. Buys one-time rights.

Columns/Departments: Panorama—short items about people, unusual events; Made in Pennsylvania-short items about family and individually owned consumer-related businesses. Scrapbook (short historical items).

PENNSYLVANIA HERITAGE, Pennsylvania Historical and Museum Commission, P.O. Box 1026, Harrisburg PA 17108-1026. (717)787-7522. Editor: Michael J. O'Malley III. 90% freelance written. Prefers to work with published/established writers. Quarterly magazine. "*Pennsylvania Heritage* introduces readers to Pennsylvania's rich culture and historic legacy, educates and sensitizes them to the value of preserving that heritage

For information on setting your freelance fees, see How Much Should I Charge? in the Business of Writing section.

and entertains and involves them in such as way as to ensure that Pennsylvania's past has a future. The magazine is intended for intelligent lay readers." Circ. 10,000. **Pays on acceptance.** Publishes ms an average of 8-12 months after acceptance. Byline given. Buys all rights. Simultaneous queries and submissions OK. Reports in 6 weeks on queries; 10 weeks on mss. Sample copy for 9 × 12 SAE and $3; free writer's guidelines for #10 SASE.

Nonfiction: Art, science, biographies, industry, business, politics, transportation, military, historic preservation, archaeology, photography, etc. No articles which in no way relate to Pennsylvania history or culture. "Our format requires feature-length articles. Manuscripts with illustrations are especially sought for publication." Buys 20-24 mss/year. Query. Length: 2,000-3,500 words. Pays $300-500.

Photos: State availability or send photos with query or ms. Pays $25-100 for transparencies; $5-10 for b&w photos. Captions and identification of subjects required. Buys one-time rights.

Tips: "We are looking for well-written, interesting material that pertains to any aspect of Pennsylvania history or culture. Potential contributors should realize that, although our articles are popularly styled, they are not light, puffy or breezy; in fact they demand strident documentation and substantiation (sans footnotes). The most frequent mistake made by writers in completing articles for us is making them either too scholarly or too nostalgic. We want material which educates, but also entertains."

PHILADELPHIA MAGAZINE, 1500 Walnut St., Philadelphia PA 19102. Editor: Ron Javers. 40% freelance written. Prefers to work with published/established writers; works with a small number of new/unpublished writers each year. Monthly magazine for sophisticated middle- and upper-income people in the Greater Philadelphia/South Jersey area. Circ. 152,272. **Pays on acceptance.** Publishes ms an average of 2 months after acceptance. Buys first serial rights. Pays 20% kill fee. Byline given. Reports in 1 month. Writer's guidelines for SASE.

Nonfiction: Laurene Stains, articles editor. "Articles should have a strong Philadelphia (city and suburbs) focus but should avoid Philadelphia stereotypes—we've seen them all. Submit lifestyles, city survival, profiles of interesting people, business stories, music, the arts, sports and local politics, stressing the topical or unusual. Intelligent, entertaining essays on subjects of specific local interest. No puff pieces. We offer lots of latitude for style." Buys 50 mss/year. Length: 1,000-7,000 words. Pays $100-2,000. Sometimes pays expenses of writers on assignment.

PITTSBURGH MAGAZINE, Metropolitan Pittsburgh Public Broadcasting, Inc., 4802 5th Ave., Pittsburgh PA 15213. (412)622-1360. FAX: (412)622-1488. Editor-in-Chief: Bruce VanWyngarden. 60% freelance written. Prefers to work with published/established writers; works with a small number of new/unpublished writers each year. "The magazine is purchased on newsstands and by subscription and is given to those who contribute $35 or more a year to public TV in western Pennsylvania." Estab. 1970. Circ. 65,000. Pays on publication. Publishes ms an average of 2 months after acceptance. Buys first North American serial rights and second serial (reprint) rights. Pays kill fee. Byline given. Submit seasonal/holiday material 6 months in advance. Query for electronic submissions. Reports in 2 months. Publishes ms an average of 2 months after acceptance. Sample copy $2.

Nonfiction: Expose, lifestyle, sports, informational, service, interview, nostalgia and profile. Query or send complete ms. Length: 2,500 words. Pays $50-500. Query for photos. Model releases required. Sometimes pays the expenses of writers on assignment.

Columns/Departments: Art, books, films, dining, health, sports and theatre. "All must relate to Pittsburgh or western Pennsylvania."

Rhode Island

RHODE ISLAND MONTHLY, 60 Branch Ave., Providence RI 02904. (401)421-2552. FAX: (401)831-5624. Editor: Dan Kaplan. Managing Editor: Vicki Sanders. 90% freelance written. Estab. 1988. Circ. 26,000. Pays on publication. Publishes ms an average of 2 months after acceptance. Byline given. Kill fee varies. Buys first rights. Submit seasonal/holiday material 4 months in advance. Query for electronic submissions. Reports in 1 month. Sample copy $1.95 with 9 × 12 SAE with $1.20 postage.

Nonfiction: Profiles, human interest features, exposé, photo feature. "We do not want material unrelated to Rhode Island." Buys 48 mss/year. Query with published clips. Length: 200-6,000 words. Pays $100-1,000. Pays expenses of writers on assignment for stories over $400.

Photos: State availability of photos with submission. Reviews contact sheets and 5 × 7 prints. Offers $50-200. Captions, model releases and identification of subjects required. Buys one-time rights.

South Carolina

SANDLAPPER, The Magazine of South Carolina, RPW Publishing Corp., P.O. Box 1108, Lexington SC 29072. (803)359-9954. Editor: Robert P. Wilkins. Managing Editor: Daniel E. Harmon. 70% freelance written. A bimonthly feature magazine focusing on the positive aspects of South Carolina. Estab. 1989. Circ. 20,000. Pays during the dateline period. Publishes ms an average of 3 months after acceptance. Byline given. Buys first North American serial rights and the right to reprint. Submit seasonal material 6 months in advance. Query for electronic submissions. Reports in 1 month on queries; 2 months on mss. Current sample copy for $6.20 postpaid; free writer's guidelines.

Nonfiction: Feature articles and photo essays about South Carolina's interesting people, places, cuisine, things to do. Occasional history articles. Query. Length: 600-5,000 words. Pays $50-500. Sometimes pays the expenses of writers on assignment.

Tips: "We're not interested in articles about topical issues, politics, crime or commercial ventures. Humorous angles are encouraged. Avoid first-person nostalgia and remembrances of places that no longer exist."

South Dakota

DAKOTA OUTDOORS, South Dakota, Hipple Publishing Co., P.O. Box 669, Pierre SD 57501. (605)224-7301. FAX: (605)224-9210. Editor: Kevin Hipple. 50% freelance written. Monthly magazine on Dakota outdoor life. Estab. 1975. Circ. 4,150. Pays on publication. Publishes ms an average of 2 months after acceptance. Byline given. Submit seasonal/holiday material 3 months in advance. Simultaneous and previously published submissions (if notified) OK. Query for electronic submissions. Sample copy for 9 × 12 SAE with 2 first class stamps.

Nonfiction: General interest, how-to, humor, interview/profile, new product, opinion, personal experience, photo feature and technical (all on outdoor topics—prefer in Dakotas). Buys 50 mss/year. Query with or without published clips, or send complete ms. Length: 200-1,000 words. Pays $5-40 for assigned articles; $40 maximum for unsolicited articles. Pays in contributor copies or other premiums (inquire).

Photos: Send photos with submission. Reviews 5 × 7 prints. Offers no additional payment for photos accepted with ms. Identification of subjects preferred. Buys one-time rights.

Fillers: Anecdotes, facts, gags to be illustrated by cartoonist, newsbreaks and short humor. Buys 4/year. Also publishes line drawings of fish and game. Prefers 5 × 7.

Tips: "Submit samples of manuscript or previous works for consideration, photos or illustrations with manuscript are helpful."

Tennessee

CHATTANOOGA LIFE & LEISURE, Metro Publishing, 1085 Bailey Ave., Chattanooga TN 37404. (615)629-5375. FAX: (615)629-5379. Editor: Mark Northern. Managing Editor: Eileen Hoover. 90% freelance written. Monthly magazine on the Chattanooga region. Estab. 1977. Circ. 10,000. Pays on publication. Byline given. Offers 50% kill fee. Buys first North American serial rights or second serial (reprint) rights. Submit seasonal/holiday material 1 year in advance. Query for electronic submissions. Sample copy $1.95; writer's guidelines for SASE.

Nonfiction: Book excerpts, expose, general interest, historical, interview/profile and photo feature. Buys 120 mss/year. Query with or without published clips. Length: 150-3,000 words. Pays $20-200.

Photos: Send photos with submission. Reviews b&w contact sheets, 35mm or larger transparencies, and any size color prints. Offers $20 per photo. Captions, model releases and identification of subjects required. Buys one-time rights.

Tips: "Contributors must know their subjects. We expect all material to be in-depth and about a local subject. We present complex subjects in a clear manner so our readers can see the entire picture in perspective. I am most satisfied when my readers stop me in the street and say 'I read such-and-such article. I have lived here all my life and I didn't know that.' "

MEMPHIS, MM Corporation, P.O. Box 256, Memphis TN 38101. (901)521-9000. Editor: Larry Conley. 60% freelance written. Works with a small number of new/unpublished writers. Estab. 1976. Circ. 26,500. Pays on publication. Publishes ms an average of 3 months after acceptance. Byline given. Buys first North American serial rights. Pays $35-100 kill fee. Simultaneous and previously published submissions OK. Reports in 6 weeks. Sample copy for 9 × 12 SAE and $2.50 postage; writer's guidelines for SASE.

Nonfiction: Exposé, general interest, historical, how-to, humor, interview and profile. "Virtually all our material has strong mid-South connections." Buys 25 freelance mss/year. Query or submit complete ms or published clips. Length: 1,500-5,000 words. Pays $100-1,000. Sometimes pays expenses of writers on assignment.

Tips: "The kinds of manuscripts we most need have a sense of story (i.e., plot, suspense, character), an abundance of evocative images to bring that story alive, and a sensitivity to issues at work in Memphis. The most frequent mistakes made by writers in completing an article for us are lack of focus, lack of organization, factual gaps and failure to capture the magazine's style. Tough investigative pieces would be especially welcomed."

Texas

‡CORPUS CHRISTI MAGAZINE, Second Wind, Inc., Suite 807, 606 N. Carancahua, Corpus Christi TX 78410. (512)883-0916. Editor: Signe Tischner. 80% freelance written. Monthly magazine covering Corpus Christi area interests. "The purpose of our magazine is to inform and entertain. All submissions should be professional and upbeat in tone." Estab. 1982. Circ. 10,000. Pays 30 days after publication. Publishes ms an average of 2 months after acceptance. Byline given. Buys first North American, first, one-time, second serial (reprint) or simultaneous rights. Submit seasonal/holiday material 3 months in advance. Simultaneous and previously published submissions OK. Reports in 2 weeks. Free sample copy and writer's guidelines.

Nonfiction: Book excerpts, general interest, historical/nostalgic, how-to (remodeling, decorating), humor, interview/profile, new product, photo feature, travel. "Nothing negative or opinionated." Buys 50 mss/year. Query with or without published clips, or send complete ms. Length: 250-1,200 words. Pays $25-50. Sometimes pays the expenses of writers on assignment.

Photos: State availability of photos with submission. Offers $5-25. Model releases and identification of subjects required. Buys one-time rights.

Columns/Departments: Business (local); Real Estate (local design and home included); Health (local and special interest national); Style (national); Food (general interest). Buys 30 mss/year. Query with published clips or send complete ms. Length: 500-800 words. Pays $25-50.

Fillers: Elaine Srnka, fillers editor. Anecdotes, facts, newsbreaks, short humor. Buys 15/year. Length: 50-250 words. Pays $5-25.

"D" MAGAZINE, Southwest Media Corporation, Suite 1200, 3988 N. Central Expressway, Dallas TX 75204. (214)827-5000. FAX: (214)827-8844. Editor: Ruth Miller Fitzgibbons. 25% freelance written. Monthly magazine. "We are a general interest magazine with emphasis on events occuring in Dallas." Estab. 1974. Circ. 100,000. **Pays on acceptance.** Publishes ms an average of 3 months after acceptance. Byline given. Offers 25% kill fee. Buys first North American serial rights. Submit seasonal/holiday material 3 months in advance. Query for electronic submissions. Reports in 1 month. Sample copy $2.50 with SAE and 5 first class stamps; free writer's guidelines.

Nonfiction: Essays, exposé, general interest, historical/nostalgic, how-to, interview/profile and travel. Buys 20-30 mss/year. Query with published clips. Length: 1,000-5,000 words. Pays $75-750 for assigned articles; pays $50-500 for unsolicited articles. Pays expenses of writers on assignment.

Photos: State availability of photos with submission. Reviews transparencies and 35mm prints. Offers $50-75 per photo. Captions required. Buys one-time rights.

Columns/Departments: Business, Politics, Travel and Relationships. Query with published clips or send complete ms. Length: 1,500-2,000 words. Pays $250-350.

Tips: "Tell us something about our city that we have not written about. We realize that is very difficult for someone outside of Dallas to do—that's why 90% of our magazine is written by people who live in the North Texas area."

DENTON TODAY MAGAZINE, Community Life Publications, Inc., Suite #304, 207 W. Hickory, Denton TX 76201. (817)566-3464. Editor: Jonathan B. Cott. 100% freelance written. Quarterly magazine of news/entertainment in North Texas. Circ. 5,000. Pays on publication. Publishes ms an average of 1 month after acceptance. Byline given. Buys first North American serial rights, second serial (reprint) rights or makes work-for-hire assignments. Submit seasonal/holiday material 2 months in advance. Previously published submissions OK. Reports in 2 weeks. Sample copy $1.95 with 9 × 12 SAE and $1.50 postage; writer's guidelines for #10 SASE.

Nonfiction: Essays, general interest, historical/nostalgic, how-to, humor, inspirational, interview/profile, new product, personal experience, photo feature. No religious or controversial articles. Buys 40 mss/year. Send ocmplete ms. Length: 500-3,000. Pays $25-210 for assigned articles; $25-150 for unsolicited articles. Sometimes pays expenses of writers on assignment.

Photos: Send photos with submission. Offers $5-50 per photo. Captions, model releases and identification of subjects required. Buys one-time rights.

Columns/Departments: Business/economy, Government/services, Education, Health, Arts/entertainment. All with north Texas, positive slant. Buys 40 mss/year. Send complete ms. Length: 500-750 words. Pays $25-50.

Fiction: Historical, humorous, mainstream, slice-of-life vignettes. Buys 5 mss/year. Send complete ms. Length: 1,000-3,000 words. Pays $50-210.

HOUSTON METROPOLITAN MAGAZINE, City Home Publishing, Box 25386, Houston TX 77265. (713)524-3000. Editorial Director: Gabrielle Cosgriff. Managing Editor: Mike Peters. 85% freelance written. A monthly city magazine. Circ. 87,500. **Pays on acceptance.** Publishes ms an average of 3 months after acceptance. Byline given. Offers 25% kill fee. Buys first North American serial rights. Submit holiday/seasonal material 6 months in advance. Query for electronic submissions. Simultaneous and photocopied submissions OK. Computer printout submissions OK; no dot-matrix. Reports in 2 weeks on queries; 1 month on mss. Sample copy for 9½×12 SAE and 8 first class stamps.

Nonfiction: Issue-oriented features, profiles, lifestyle/entertainment, food features, visual stories, and humorous features. Query with published clips or send complete ms. Length: 300-2,500 words. Pays $50-1,000.

Photos: Carla Poindexter, art director. State availability of photos with submission. Buys one-time rights. "Also assigns photographers at day or job rates."

Columns/Departments: City Insight and Artbeat. All must have strong Houston-area slant. Length: 300-2,500 words. Pays $50-1,000.

Tips: "Submit clips demonstrating strong writing and reporting skills with detailed queries, bearing in mind that this is a city magazine. Our intent is to be a lively, informative city book, addressing the issues and people who affect our lives objectively and fairly. But also with affection and, where suitable, a sense of humor. Only those familiar with the Houston metropolitan area should approach us."

‡**ULTRA**, Suite 305, 1400 Post Oak Blvd., Houston TX 77056. (713)622-1967. Executive Editor: Timothy Brookover. 70% freelance written. Monthly magazine covering connoissership in the arts, architecture, design, food, fashion and letters in Texas. Estab. 1982. Circ. 100,000. Pays on publication. Publishes ms an average of 2 months after acceptance. Byline given. Offers 25% kill fee. Buys first North American serial rights. Query for electronic submissions. Reports in 1 month. Sample copy $4 with 11×14 SAE and 6 first class stamps.

Nonfiction: Book excerpts, essays, general interest, historical, photo feature and travel. Buys 100 mss/year. Query with published clips. Pays expenses of writers on assignment.

Photos: State availability of photos with submission. Reviews transparencies. Captions, model releases and identification of subjects required. Buys one-time rights.

THE WEST TEXAS SUN, NJN Inc., Box 61541, San Angelo TX 76906. (915)944-8918. Editor: Soren W. Nielsen. 95% freelance written. Monthly magazine on West Texas. "This is a chronicle of the West Texas experience. All freelance submissions should have a relevant hook or have impact on the West Texas reader." Estab. 1989. Circ. 5,000. Pays on publication. Publishes ms an average of 4 months after acceptance. Byline given. Buys one-time rights. Submit seasonal/holiday material 3 months in advance. Simultaneous and previously published submissions OK. Reports 3-4 weeks. Writer's guidelines for #10 SASE.

Nonfiction: Book excerpts, essays, exposé, general interest, historical/nostalgic, how-to, humor, inspirational, interview/profile, personal experience, photo feature, and vignettes of life in West Texas—fillers. Buys 65 mss/year. Query. Length: 40-4,000 words. Pays $5-300. Sometimes pays expenses of writers on assignment.

Photos: State availability of photos with submission. Reviews contact sheets. Offers $10-25 maximum per photo. Captions and identification of subjects required. Buys one-time rights.

Columns/Departments: The Way It Was (historical pieces, personal recollections of West Texas), 2,000 words. Query. Pays $50-200.

Fiction: Adventure, historical, humorous, mainstream, mystery, novel excerpts, science fiction, slice-of-life vignettes, Western. "No erotica." Buys 10-12 mss/year. Query. Length: 1,000-4,000. Pays $10-300.

Fillers: Anecdotes, facts, short humor. Buys 100/year. Length: 20-200 words. Pays $5-25.

Tips: "Submissions of quality ideas and writing about West Texas will always get full consideration. Well-researched historical pieces and well-written fiction stand the best chance of being published. Vignettes of the West Texas experience, even if short, are also likely candidates."

Utah

UTAH HOLIDAY MAGAZINE, Utah, Tuesday Publishing Co., 807 E. South Temple, #200, Salt Lake City UT 84102. (801)532-3737. FAX: (801)532-3742. Editor: Bruce Lee. Managing Editor: Mildred Evans. 100% freelance written. Monthly magazine on Utah oriented—subjects newspapers do not print, provocative opinion. Theatre, art, movie reviews. Estab. 1971. Circ. 10,000. Pays on 15th of month of publication. Byline given. Offers $50 kill fee. Buys first North American serial rights. Submit seasonal/holiday material 3 months in advance. Query for electronic submissions. Reports in 3 weeks on queries. Sample copy for 10×12 SAE and 5 first class stamps; writer's guidelines for #10 SASE.

For explanation of symbols, see the Key to Symbols and Abbreviations on Page 5. For unfamiliar words, see the Glossary.

Nonfiction: Essays, exposé, interview/profile, opinion and personal experience. "No travel outside Utah, humor or personal essays." Buys 1 ms/year. Query with or without published clips, or send complete ms. Length: 2,500-8,000 words. Pays $90-350 for assigned articles. Also pays in contributor copies or other premiums. Sometimes pays expenses of writers on assignment.

Photos: State availability of photos with submission. Send photos with submission. Reviews contact sheets and transparencies. Offers $15-70 per photo. Identification of subjects required. Buys one-time rights.

Columns/Departments: Movie Reviews, Opera, Theatre, Ballet and Art (all slanted to current Utah productions), 1,500 words. Buys 10 mss/year. Query with published clips. Pays $90-120.

Vermont

VERMONT LIFE MAGAZINE, 61 Elm St., Montpelier VT 05602. (802)828-3241. Editor-in-Chief: Thomas K. Slayton. 90% freelance written. Prefers to work with published/established writers. Quarterly magazine. Circ. 110,000. Publishes ms an average of 9 months after acceptance. Byline given. Offers kill fee. Buys first serial rights. Submit seasonal/holiday material 1 year in advance. Simultaneous queries, and simultaneous and previously published submissions OK. Reports in 1 month. Writer's guidelines for #10 SASE.

Nonfiction: Wants articles on today's Vermont, those which portray a typical or, if possible, unique aspect of the state or its people. Style should be literate, clear and concise. Subtle humor favored. No Vermont dialect attempts as in "Ayup," outsider's view on visiting Vermont, or "Vermont clichés" — maple syrup, town meetings or stereotyped natives. Buys 60 mss/year. Query by letter essential. Length: 1,500 words average. Pays 20¢/word. Seldom pays expenses of writers on assignment.

Photos: Buys photographs with mss; buys seasonal photographs alone. Prefers b&w contact sheets to look at first on assigned material. Color submissions must be 4×5 or 35mm transparencies. Rates on acceptance: $75-150 inside, color; $200 for cover. Gives assignments but only with experienced photographers. Query in writing. Captions, model releases, and identification of subjects required. Buys one-time rights, but often negotiates for re-use rights.

Tips: "Writers who read our magazine are given more consideration because they understand that we want authentic articles about Vermont. If a writer has a genuine working knowledge of Vermont, his or her work usually shows it. Vermont is changing and there is much concern here about what this state will be like in years ahead. It is a beautiful, environmentally sound place now and the vast majority of residents want to keep it so. Articles reflecting such concerns in an intelligent, authoritative, non-hysterical way will be given very careful consideration. The growth of tourism makes *Vermont Life* interested in intelligent articles about specific places in Vermont, their history and attractions to the traveling public."

VERMONT VANGUARD PRESS, Statewide Weekly, Vanguard Publishing, 87 College St., Burlington VT 05401. (802)864-0506. Editor: Joshua Mamis. Managing Editor: Pamela Polston. 70% freelance written. Works with a small number of new/unpublished writers each year. A weekly alternative newspaper, locally oriented, covering Vermont politics, environment, arts, etc. Estab. 1978. Circ. 25,000. Pays on publication. Byline given. Offers 50% kill fee only after written acceptance. Buys first serial rights. Submit seasonal/holiday material 1 month in advance. Simultaneous queries, simultaneous and previously published submissions OK. Query for electronic submissions. Reports in 1 month.

Nonfiction: Exposé and humor. Articles must have a Vermont angle. Buys about 12 mss/year. Query with published clips. Length: 500-2,500 words. Pays $30-150.

Photos: Barb Leslie, photo editor. State availability of photos. Pays $10-20 for b&w contact sheets and negatives. Captions, model releases and identification of subjects required. Buys one-time rights.

Tips: "Short news stories are most open to freelancers. Knowledge of Vermont politics is essential."

Virginia

NORTHERN VIRGINIAN MAGAZINE, 135 Park St., P.O. Box 1177, Vienna VA 22180. (703)938-0666. Editor: Goodie Holden. 80% freelance written. Bimonthly magazine concerning the five counties of northern Virginia. Estab. 1971. Pays first of month following publication. Publishes ms an average of 3 months after acceptance. Byline given. Buys first serial rights and second serial (reprint) rights. Submit seasonal/holiday material 3 months in advance. Simultaneous queries, and simultaneous and previously published submissions OK. "Send photocopy of manuscript as we can't guarantee its return." Reports in 2 weeks on queries; 1 month on mss. Sample copy $1; free writer's guidelines.

Nonfiction: "Freelance manuscripts welcomed on speculation. We are particularly interested in articles about or related to northern Virginia. Articles on 'the Lighter Side of Northern Virginia' preferred." Buys 75 mss/year. Query or send complete ms. Length: 2,500 words minimum. Pays 1½¢/word.

Photos: Prefers good, clear b&w glossy photos. Pays $5/photo or photo credit line. Captions, model releases and identification of subjects required.

Tips: Longer articles preferred, minimum 2,500 words. History articles accepted only if unique.

‡RICHMOND SURROUNDINGS, Target Communications Inc., Suite 110, 7814 Carousel Ln., Richmond VA 23294. (804)346-4130. Editor: Frances C. Helms. 90% freelance written. Bimonthly magazine covering the metropolitan Richmond area. *"Richmond Surroundings* is a city magazine with an editorial mix of news and features which appeal to our upscale audience, ages 30-55. We want to inform as well as entertain." Estab. 1979. Circ. 20,000. Pays on publication. Publishes ms an average of 2 months after acceptance. Negotiable kill fee. Buys first rights, one-time rights, second serial (reprint) rights and makes work-for-hire assignments. Submit seasonal/holiday material 6 months in advance. Simultaneous submissions OK. Query for electronic submissions. Reports in 2 weeks. Sample copy $2. Free writer's guidelines.

Nonfiction: Investigative, general interest, historical/nostalgic, humor, interview/profile, personal experience, photo feature and travel. Upcoming special issue: Newcomers Edition, each February. Information pertinent to newcomers to the metro Richmond area. "No articles not about Virginians or not pertinent to Virginia in general and Richmond in particular." Buys 150 mss/year. Query with published clips. Length: 250-7,000 words. Pays 10-15¢/word for assigned articles. Sometimes pays expenses of writers on assignment.

Photos: Send photos with submission. Reviews contact sheets and 5×7 prints or slides. Offers $25-75 per photo (more for special assignments). Identification of subjects required. Buys one-time rights or all rights.

Tips: "Make a personal contact by phone first, then in person; let us see your work; call and suggest a topic; write on spec. Ask for a copy of our editorial calendar and see what you can contribute. Then be able to produce on a short deadline. Our entire publication is open to freelancers. Let us know your specialty (travel, profiles, investigative, etc.)."

THE ROANOKER, Leisure Publishing Co., 3424 Brambleton Ave., P.O. Box 21535, Roanoke VA 24018. (703)989-6138. FAX: (703)989-7603. Editor: Kurt Rheinheimer. 75% freelance written. Works with a small number of new/unpublished writers each year. Monthly magazine covering people and events of Western Virginia. *"The Roanoker* is a general interest city magazine edited for the people of Roanoke, Virginia, and the surrounding area. Our readers are primarily upper-income, well-educated professionals between the ages of 35 and 60. Coverage ranges from hard news and consumer information to restaurant reviews and local history." Estab. 1974. Circ. 14,000. Pays on publication. Publishes ms an average of 4 months after acceptance. Byline given. Buys all rights; makes work-for-hire assignments. Submit seasonal/holiday material 4 months in advance. Simultaneous queries OK. Reports in 2 months. Sample copy for $2 and 9×12 SAE with $2 postage; writer's guidelines for #10 SASE.

Nonfiction: Exposé; historical/nostalgic; how-to (live better in western Virginia); interview/profile (of well-known area personalities); photo feature; and travel (Virginia and surrounding states). "We are attempting to broaden our base and provide more and more coverage of western Virginia, i.e., that part of the state west of Roanoke. We emphasize consumer-related issues and how-to articles." Periodic special sections on fashion, real estate, media, banking, investing. Buys 60 mss/year. Query with published clips or send complete ms. Length: 3,000 words maximum. Pays $35-200. Sometimes pays expenses of writers on assignment.

Photos: Send photos with ms. Reviews color transparencies. Pays $5-10 for 5×7 or 8×10 b&w prints; $10 maximum for 5×7 or 8×10 color prints. Captions and model releases required. Rights purchased vary.

Tips: "It helps if freelancer lives in the area. The most frequent mistake made by writers in completing an article for us is not having enough Roanoke area focus: use of area experts, sources, slants, etc."

Washington

‡PACIFIC NORTHWEST, Pacific Northwest Media, Inc., 222 Dexter Ave. N., Seattle WA 98109. (206)682-2704. Editor: Ann Naumann. 80% freelance written. *"Pacific Northwest* is a monthly magazine directed primarily at longtime residents of Oregon, Washington, Idaho and British Columbia." Estab. 1966. Circ. 81,300. Pays on publication. Publishes ms an average of 3 months after acceptance. Byline given. Offers kill fee. Buys first North American serial rights. Submit seasonal/holiday material 6 months in advance. Simultaneous submissions OK. Query for electronic submissions. Reports in 5 weeks on queries; 6 weeks on mss. Sample copy $3. Free writer's guidelines.

Nonfiction: Book excerpts (Northwest), essays, exposé, general interest, historical/nostalgic, humor, interview/profile, personal experience, photo feature, travel, business, arts. "No self-help or how-to." Buys 180 mss/year. Query with published clips. Length: 800-2,500 words. Pays $100-1,000 for assigned articles. Sometimes pays expenses of writers on assignment.

Photos: State availability of photos with submission. Reviews contact sheets. Offers $50-250 per photo. Identification of subjects required. Buys one-time rights.

Columns/Departments: Ventures (business/enterprise), 500-1,700 words; Health & Fitness (current health and fitness issues), 800-1,700 words; The Arts (profiles of artists and their endeavors), 800-1,700 words; Reading Matters (books/authors—not simple reviews but short features), 800-1,700 words. Buys 90 mss/year. Query with published clips. Pays $125-400.

THE SEATTLE WEEKLY, Sasquatch Publishing, 1931 2nd Ave., Seattle WA 98101. (206)441-5555. FAX: (206)441-6213. Editor: David Brewster. 20% freelance written. Eager to work with new/unpublished writers, especially those in the region. Weekly tabloid covering arts, politics, food, business, sports and books with local and regional emphasis. Estab. 1976. Circ. 33,000. Pays 1 week after publication. Publishes ms an average of 1 month after acceptance. Byline given. Offers variable kill fee. Buys first North American serial rights. Submit seasonal/holiday material minimum 2 months in advance. Simultaneous queries OK. Reports in 1 month. Sample copy $2; writer's guidelines for #10 SASE.

Nonfiction: Book excerpts; expose; general interest; historical/nostalgic (Northwest); how-to (related to food and health); humor; interview/profile; opinion; travel; and arts-related essays. Buys 6-8 cover stories/year. Query with resume and published clips. Length: 700-4,000 words. Pays $75-800. Sometimes pays the expenses of writers on assignment.

Tips: "The *Seattle Weekly* publishes stories on Northwest politics and art, usually written by regional and local writers, for a mostly upscale, urban audience; writing is high quality magazine style. We will likely publish a new regional news magazine for Seattle's suburban audience."

WASHINGTON, The Evergreen State Magazine, Evergreen Publishing Co., 200 W. Thomas, Seattle WA 98119. FAX: (206)285-3248. Managing Editor: Gail E. Hullson. Executive Editor: Judy Mills. Associate Editor: Heather M. Doran. 80% freelance written. A 10 times-per-year magazine covering all facets of life in Washington for an in-state audience. Estab. 1984. Circ. 72,000. Pays 45 days after acceptance for assigned pieces. Publishes mss an average of 4 months after acceptance. Byline given. Offers 20% kill fee on accepted stories. Submit seasonal/holiday material 6 months in advance. Query before submitting any material. Reports in 1 month on queries; 6 weeks on mss. Sample copy for $3.50; free writer's guidelines.

Nonfiction: Interview/profile; travel; historical; humor; book excerpts (unpublished Washington-related); newsfeatures; personal experience; business; food; home and garden; style. "No subjects not related specifically to Washingtonians." Query with published clips. Length: features, 1,500-3,000 words; sidebars, 200-600 words. Pays $350-800.

Photos: Karen Gutawsy, art editor. Original transparencies only. State availability of photos with query or send photos with query. Pays $50-250 for b&w; $125-325 for 35mm transparencies. Captions, model releases and identification of subjects required. Buys one-time rights.

Columns/Departments: Book of Days (a compendium of short news and insight pieces on nature or culture); Business; Sports (professional and participatory sports); The Lively Arts (arts and entertainment profiles); Reading Matters (books); Ground Rules (gardening); Appearance's Sake (fashion/health and fitness). Buys about 70 mss/year. Length: 500-1,500 words. Pays $50-$800.

Tips: "All areas are open, but the writer has a better chance of breaking in at our publication with short features and news stories. Our articles emphasize people—sometimes writers get sidetracked. We're also looking for original thinking, not tired approaches."

West Virginia

‡WONDERFUL WEST VIRGINIA, State of West Virginia Department of Natural Resources, 1900 Kanawha Blvd. E., Bldg. 3, State Capital Complex, Charleston WV 25305. (304)348-9152. Editor: Nancy Clark. 85% freelance written. Monthly magazine. "A general interest, show-piece quality, magazine portraying a positive image of West Virginia, with emphasis on outdoor/natural resources subjects." Estab. 1970. Circ. 85,000. **Pays on acceptance.** Publishes ms an average of 8 months after acceptance. Byline given. Offer 5¢/word kill fee. Buys first or second rights. Submit seasonal/holiday material 6 months in advance. Previously published submissions OK. Reports in 1 month. Sample copy $3. Free writer's guidelines.

Nonfiction: General interest, historical/nostalgic, photo feature, travel. "No outsider's views of West Virginia and its people; nothing negative or about poor, ignorant 'hillbilly' types of people or places. No Me and Joe hunting and fishing stories." Buys 50 mss/year. Query. Length: 500-3,000 words. Pays $50-300.

Photos: Photos are taken by staff photographer, if feasible. Will consider photos with submission. Reviews 35mm or larger transparencies. Offers $75 per color photo. Captions, model releases and identification of subjects required. Buys one-time rights.

Tips: "Read Guidelines for Writers. Write an article especially for readers who love West Virginia about an interesting place or event in West Virginia. Entire publication is open to freelancers. We have only recently started buying professionally written articles and welcome submissions from all writers with a personal knowledge of West Virginia subjects."

Wisconsin

MADISON MAGAZINE, P.O. Box 1604, Madison WI 53701. Editor: James Selk. 50% freelance written. Prefers to work with published/established writers. Monthly magazine. General city magazine aimed at upscale audience. Estab. 1978. Circ. 24,000. Pays on publication. Publishes ms an average of 2 months after acceptance. Buys all rights. Reports on material accepted for publication 10 days after acceptance. Returns rejected material immediately. Query. Sample copy $3 and 9×12 SAE.

Nonfiction: General human interest articles with strong local angles. Buys 100 mss/year. Length: 1,000-5,000 words. Pays $25-500. Pays the expenses of writers on assignment.

Photos: Offers no additional payment for b&w photos used with mss. Captions required.

WISCONSIN, *The Milwaukee Journal Magazine,* P.O. Box 661, Milwaukee WI 53201. (414)224-2341. FAX: (414)224-2047. Editor: Alan Borsuk. 20% freelance written. Prefers to work with published/established writers. Weekly general interest magazine appealing to readers living in Wisconsin. Estab. 1969. Circ. 520,000. Pays on publication. Publishes ms an average of 4 months after acceptance. Byline given. Buys first serial rights. Submit seasonal/holiday material 4 months in advance. Simultaneous queries OK. Reports in 1 month on queries; 6 months on mss. Free sample copy; writer's guidelines for 9×12 SASE.
Nonfiction: Expose, general interest, humor, interview/profile, opinion, personal experience and photo feature. No nostalgic reminiscences. Buys 50 mss/year. Query. Length: 150-2,500 words. Pays $75-600. Sometimes pays expenses of writers on assignment.
Photos: State availability of photos.
Columns/Departments: Opinion, Humor and Essays. Buys 50 mss/year. Length: 300-1,000 words. Pays $100-200.
Tips: "We are primarily Wisconsin-oriented and are becoming more news-oriented."

WISCONSIN VISITOR, (formerly *Indianhead Star*), Rt. 2, Box 24, Clear Lake WI 54005. (715)269-5226. Editor: Carole Inez Santoro. 75% freelance written. Weekly newspaper on small town life in Wisconsin. "Focus on people who reflect rural lifestyle. Where to visit in Wisconsin, profiles of 'ordinary' people, history, entrepreneurs, farming." Circ. 5,000. Pays on publication. Publishes ms an average of 1 month after acceptance. Buys first North American serial rights, first rights, one-time rights, second serial (reprint) rights and makes work-for-hire assignments. Submit seasonal/holiday material 2 months in advance. Simultaneous and previously published submissions OK. Reports in 1 month on mss. Sample copy for SAE with $1.50 postage. Writer's guidelines for SAE with 2 first class stamps.
Nonfiction: Book excerpts, essays (historical link to Wisconsin), general interest, historical/nostalgic, how-to (fix old houses, cooking, raising children), humor, inspirational, interview/profile, new product, opinion, personal experience, photo feature (rural life), religious, travel (what's happening in Wisconsin), nostalgia, 30's depression, growing up, grandparents. All pertaining to Wisconsin. Special issues: Spring farming issue; Auto (old car stories welcome); Christmas—growing up; Veteran rememberances, (war stories women waiting at home, child's viewpoint). Buys 200 mss/year. Send complete ms and published clips. Length: 300-2,000. Pays $20-100 for assigned articles; $10-50 for unsolicited articles. Pays with contributor's copies to new columnists (plus $5). Sometimes pays expenses of writers on assignment.
Photos: Send photos with submission. Reviews negatives and prints. Offers no additional payment for photos accepted with ms, but ms has greater chance of acceptance. Captions and identification of subjects required. Buys one-time rights.
Columns/Departments: Lest We Forget (war stories); Farming Page (farm issues); Cooking Page (recipe, hints column); Out & About (What's happening in Wisconsin). Buys 100 mss/year. Send complete ms. Length: 300 words. Pays $5-25.
Fiction: Ethnic, historical (Wisconsin or war remembrances), humorous, slice-of-life vignettes (historical, growing-up). Buys 100 mss/year. Send complete ms. Length: 300-1,500 words. Pays $10-25.
Fillers: Anecdotes, facts, gags to be illustrated by cartoonist, newsbreaks, short humor. Buys 50/year. Pays $5.
Tips: "Accept small pay now—grow with us. We need reporters to cover hard news and political news."

Canada

CANADIAN GEOGRAPHIC, 39 McArthur Ave., Ottawa, Ontario K1L 8L7 Canada. FAX: (613)744-0947. Editor: Ian Darragh. Managing Editor: Eric Harris. 90% freelance written. Works with a small number of new/unpublished writers each year. Circ. 215,000. Bimonthly magazine. **Pays on acceptance.** Publishes ms an average of 3 months after acceptance. Buys first Canadian rights; interested only in first-time publication. Sample copy for 9×12 SAE and $5; free writer's guidelines.
Nonfiction: Buys authoritative geographical articles, in the broad geographical sense, written for the average person, not for a scientific audience. Predominantly Canadian subjects by Canadian authors. Buys 30-45 mss/year. Always query first in writing. Length: 1,500-3,000 words. Pays 30¢/word minimum. Usual payment for articles ranges between $500-2,500. Higher fees reserved for commissioned articles. Sometimes pays the expenses of writers on assignment.
Photos: Reviews 35mm slides, 2¼ transparencies or 8×10 glossies. Pays $75-400 for color photos, depending on published size.

GEORGIA STRAIGHT, Vancouver Free Press Publishing Corp., 2nd Floor, 1235 W. Pender St., Vancouver, British Columbia. V6E 2V6 Canada. (604)681-2000. FAX: (604)681-0272. Managing Editor: Charles Campbell. 90% freelance written. Weekly tabloid on arts/entertainment/lifestyle/civic issues. Circ. 75,000. Pays on publication. Byline given. Offers 75-100% kill fee. Buys first North American serial rights or second serial (reprint) rights. Simultaneous and previously published submissions OK. Reports in 1 month. Sample copy for 9×12 SAE and $1.

Nonfiction: General interest, humor, interview/profile, travel, and arts and entertainment. Buys 600 mss/year. Query with published clips. Length: 250-4,000 words. Pays $20-300. Sometimes pays expenses of writers on assignment.

Photos: Send photo with submission. Reviews, contact sheets, transparencies and 8×10 prints. Offers $30-70 per photo. Captions, model releases and identification of subjects required. Buys one-time rights.

Tips: "Be aware of entertainment events in the Vancouver area and expansion of our news coverage. Most stories relate to those events."

KEY TO VICTORIA/ESSENTIAL VICTORIA, Key Pacific Publishers Co. Ltd., 3rd Fl., 1001 Wharf St., Victoria, BC V8W 1T6 Canada. (604)388-4324. FAX: (604)388-6166. Editor: Janice Strong. 40% freelance written. Monthly magazine on Victoria and Vancouver Island. Estab. 1977. Circ. 30,000. Pays on publication. Publishes ms an average of 1-2 months after acceptance. Byline given. Buys first North American serial rights and all rights. Query for electronic submissions. Reports in 3 months. Free sample copy.

Nonfiction: General interest and travel. Essential Victoria. Buys 30 mss/year. Query with published clips. Length: 500-2,500 words. Pays 20-40¢/word.

Photos: State availability of photos with submission. Reviews contact sheets, transparencies and prints. Offers $50-150 per photo. Model releases and identification of subjects required. Buys one-time rights.

THE MIRROR, The Mirror-Northern Report, P.O. Box 269, High Prairie, Alberta T0G 1E0 Canada. (403)523-3706. 25% freelance written. Weekly magazine of northern Alberta news and features. Estab. 1986. Circ. 2,000. Pays on publication. Publishes ms an average of 3 months after acceptance. Byline given. Publication not copyrighted. Buys one-time rights. Simultaneous and previously published submissions OK. Reports in 3 months. Sample copy for 9×12 SAE and $2.

Nonfiction: Buys 20 mss/year. Send complete ms. Length: 2,000 words maximum. Pays 1¢/word.

Photos: Send photos with submission. Reviews prints. Offers no additional payment for photos accepted with ms. Captions and identification of subjects required. Buys one-time rights.

Fiction: Buys 10 mss/year. Send complete ms. Length: 1,500 words.

OTTAWA MAGAZINE, Ottawa Magazine Inc., 192 Bank St., Ottawa, Ontario K2P 1W8 Canada. (613)234-7751. Editor: Louis Valenzuela. 80% freelance written. Prefers to work with published/established writers. Magazine, published 11 times/year, covering life in Ottawa and environs. "*Ottawa Magazine* reflects the interest and lifestyles of its readers who tend to be married, ages 35-55, upwardly mobile and urban." Circ. 50,000. **Pays on acceptance.** Publishes ms an average of 6 months after acceptance. Byline given. "Kill fee depends on agreed-upon fee; very seldom used." Buys first North American serial rights and second serial (reprint) rights. Simultaneous queries and previously published submissions OK. Reports in 2 months. Sample copy $1.

Nonfiction: Book excerpts (by local authors or about regional issues); exposé (federal or regional government, education); general interest; interview/profile (on Ottawans who have established national or international reputations); photo feature (for recurring section called Freezeframe); and travel (recent examples are Brazil, Trinidad & Tobago, Copenhagen). "No articles better suited to a national or special interest publication." Buys 100 mss/year. Query with published clips. Length: 2,000-3,500 words. Pays $500/1,000 (Canadian).

Tips: "A phone call to our associate editor is the best way to assure that queries receive prompt attention. Once a query interests me the writer is assigned a detailed 'treatment' of the proposed piece which is used to determine viability of story. We will be concentrating on more issue-type stories with good, solid fact-researched base, also doing more fluffy pieces—best and worst of Ottawa—that sort of stuff. Harder for out-of-town writers to furnish. The writer should strive to inject a personal style and avoid newspaper-style reportage. *Ottawa Magazine* also doesn't stoop to boosterism and points out the bad along with the good. Good prospects for U.S. writers are interiors (house and garden type), gardening (for Northern climate), leisure/lifestyles. Second rights OK."

TORONTO LIFE, 59 Front St. E., Toronto, Ontario M5E 1B3 Canada. (416)364-3333. Editor: Marq de Villiers. 95% freelance written. Prefers to work with published/established writers. Monthly magazine emphasizing local issues and social trends, short humor/satire, and service features for upper income, well educated and, for the most part, young Torontonians. Uses some fiction. **Pays on acceptance.** Publishes ms an average of 3-4 months after acceptance. Byline given. Buys first North American serial rights. Pays 50% kill fee "for commissioned articles only." Phone queries OK. Reports in 3 weeks. Sample copy $2.50 with SAE and IRCs.

Nonfiction: Uses most types of articles. Buys 17 mss/issue. Query with published clips. Buys about 40 unsolicited mss/year. Length: 1,000-5,000 words. Pays $800-3,000.

Photos: State availability of photos. Uses good color transparencies and clear, crisp b&w prints. Seldom uses submitted photos. Captions and model release required.

Columns/Departments: "We run about five columns an issue. They are all freelanced, though most are from regular contributors. They are mostly local in concern and cover politics, money, fine art, performing arts, movies and sports." Length: 1,800 words. Pays $1,500.

WESTERN PEOPLE, Supplement to the Western Producer, Western Producer Publications, Box 2500, Saskatoon, Saskatchewan S7K 2C4 Canada. (306)665-3500. Managing Editor: Liz Delahey. Weekly farm newspaper supplement covering rural Western Canada. "Our magazine reflects the life and people of rural Western Canada both in the present and historically." Circ. 135,000. **Pays on acceptance.** Publishes ms an average of 6 months after acceptance. Byline given. Buys first rights. Submit seasonal/holiday material 3 months in advance. Reports in 2 weeks on queries; 6 weeks on mss. Sample copy for 9 × 12 SAE and 3 IRC's; writer's guidelines for #10 SAE and 2 IRC's.

Nonfiction: General interest, historical/nostalgic, humor, interview/profile, personal experience and photo feature. Buys 450 mss/year. Send complete ms. Length: 500-2,500 words. Pays $80-250.

Photos: Send photos with submission. Reviews transparencies and prints. Offers $5-25 per photo. Captions and identification of subjects required. Buys one-time rights.

Fiction: Adventure, historical, humorous, mainstream, mystery, novel excerpts, romance, serialized novels, suspense and western stories reflecting life in rural Western Canada. Buys 50 mss/year. Send complete ms. Length: 1,000-2,000 words. Pays $50-200.

Poetry: Free verse, traditional, haiku and light verse. Buys 75 poems/year. Submit maximum 3 poems. Length: 4-50 lines. Pays $10-35.

Tips: "Western Canada is geographically very large. The approach for writing about an interesting individual is to introduce that person *neighbor-to-neighbor* to our readers."

THE WESTERN PRODUCER, Western Producer Publications, Box 2500, Saskatoon, Saskatchewan S7K 2C4 Canada. (306)665-3500. FAX: (306)653-1255. Editor: Keith Dryden. Managing Editor: Garry Fairbairn. 30% freelance written. Weekly newspaper covering agriculture and rural life. Publishes "informative material for 135,000 western Canadian farm familes." **Pays on acceptance.** Byline given. Kill fee varies. Not copyrighted. Buys one-time rights. Submit seasonal/holiday material 2 months in advance. Simultaneous and previously published submissions OK. Query for electronic submissions. Reports in 1 week on queries; 3 weeks on mss. Sample copy for 11 × 14 SAE with IRC; writer's guidelines for #10 SAE.

Nonfiction: General interest, historical/nostalgic, how-to (on farm machinery or construction), humor, new product, technical and rural cartoons. Special issue includes Weeds and Chemical issue (March). Nothing "non-Canadian, over 1,500 words." Buys 600 mss/year. Query. Length: 2,000 words. Pays $100-400 for assigned articles; pays $150 maximum for unsolicited articles. Sometimes pays the expenses of writers on assignment.

Photos: Send photos with submission. Reviews contact sheets, negatives, transparencies and prints. Offers $15-50 per photo. Captions required. Buys one-time rights.

Columns/Departments: Liz Delahey, editor. Western People (magazine insert focusing on Western Canadian personalities, hobbies, history, fiction), 500-2,000 words. Buys 350 mss/year. Query. Length: 500-2,000 words. Pays $50-500.

Fiction: Ethnic, historical, humorous, slice-of-life vignettes, western and rural settings. No non-western Canadian subjects. Buys 40 mss/year. Query. Length: 500-2,000. Pays $50-500.

Poetry: Free verse, light verse and traditional. Buys 20 poems/year. Length: 10-100 lines. Pays $10-100.

Tips: "Use CP/AP/UPI style and a fresh ribbon." Areas most open to freelancers are "cartoons, on-farm profiles, rural Canadian personalities."

YORK MAGAZINE, 65 Valleywood Dr., Markham, Ontario L3R 5L9 Canada. (416)474-5050. FAX: (416)474-0631. Editor: Lorie Sculthorp. 100% freelance written. Magazine appears 10 times a year, on York Region (north of Toronto). Circ. 50,000. **Pays on acceptance.** Publishes ms an average of 3 months after acceptance. Offers kill fee. Buys one-time rights or second serial (reprint) rights. Submit seasonal/holiday material 3 months in advance. Previously published submissions OK. Query for electronic submissions. Sample copy for SASE.

Nonfiction: Exposé (investigative), how-to and interview/profile (people in York region). "No fiction." Buys 50 mss/year. Length: 2,000-3,000 words. Pays up to $1,500 for assigned articles; $500-700 for unsolicited articles. Pays expenses of writers on assignments.

Photos: State availability of photos with submissions. Reviews negatives. Offers $50-200 per photo. Captions, model releases and identification of subjects required. Buys one-time rights.

Tips: "We are a small but friendly publication—give us a call with your ideas. We accept only articles about issues or people in York Region. If we like what you say we'll ask for a query. We pay promptly!"

Relationships

These publications focus on lifestyles and relationships. These magazines are read and often written by single people, gays and lesbians and those interested in these lifestyles or in alternative outlooks. They may offer writers a forum for unconventional views or serve as a voice for particular audiences or causes.

ATLANTA SINGLES MAGAZINE, Sigma Publications, Inc., Suite 320, 3423 Piedmont Rd. NE., Atlanta GA 30305 and Box 11929, Atlanta GA 30355. (404)239-0642. FAX: (404)261-2214. Editor: Margaret Anthony. Associate Editor: Sally Stephens. 10% freelance written. Works with a small number of new/unpublished writers each year. A bi-monthly magazine for single, widowed or divorced adults, medium to high income level, many business and professionally oriented; single parents, ages 25 to 55. Estab. 1977. Circ. 15,000. Pays on publication. Publishes ms an average of 6 months after acceptance. Byline given. Buys one-time rights, second serial (reprint) rights and simultaneous rights. Submit seasonal/holiday material 6 months in advance. Simultaneous and previously published submissions OK. Sample copy $2; writer's guidelines for #10 SASE.
Nonfiction: General interest, humor, personal experience, photo feature and travel. No pornography. Buys 5 mss/year. Send complete ms. Length: 600-1,200 words. Pays $100-200 for unsolicited articles; sometimes trades for personal ad.
Photos: Send photos with submission. Cover photos also considered. Reviews prints. Offers no additional payment for photos accepted with ms. Model releases and identification of subjects required. Buys one-time rights.
Columns/Departments: Will consider ideas. Query. Length: 600-800 words. Pays $100-200 per column/department.
Tips: No fiction. "We are open to articles on *any* subject that would be of interest to singles, i.e., travel, autos, movies, love stories, fashion, investments, real estate, etc. Although singles are interested in topics like self-awareness, being single again, and dating, they arc also interested in many of the same subjects that married people are, such as those listed."

BAY WINDOWS, New England's Largest Gay and Lesbian Newspaper, Bay Windows, Inc.. 1523 Washington St., Boston MA 02118. (617)266-6670. FAX: (617)266-5973. Editor: Jeff Epperly; Arts Editor: Ruby Kikel. 30-40% freelance written. A weekly newspaper of gay news and concerns. "*Bay Windows* covers predominantly news of New England, but will print non-local news and features depending on the newsworthiness of the story. We feature hard news, opinion, news analysis, arts reviews and interviews." Estab. 1981. Publishes ms within 2 months of acceptance, pays within 2 weeks of publication. Byline given. Offers 50% kill fee. Rights obtained varies, usually first serial rights. Simultaneous submissions accepted if other submissions are outside of New England. Submit seasonal-holiday material 3 months in advance. Sample copies $1; writer's guidelines for #10 SASE.
Nonfiction: Hard news, general interest with a gay slant, interview/profile, opinion and photo features. Publishes 100 mss/year. Query with published clips, or send complete ms. Length: 500-1,500 words. Pay varies: $25 100 news; $10-60 arts.
Photos: $25 per published photo, b&w photos only. Model releases and identification of subjects required.
Columns/Departments: Film, music, dance, books, art. Length: 500-1,500 words. Buys 200 mss/year. Pays $10-100.
Poetry: All varieties. Publishes 50 poems per year. Length: 10-30 lines. No payment.
Tips: "Too much gay-oriented writing is laden with the clichés and catch phrases of the movement. Writers must have intimate knowledge of gay community; however, this should not mean that standard English usage is not required. We look for writers with new—even controversial perspectives on the lives of gay men and lesbians. While we assume gay is good, we will print stories which examine problems within the community and movement. No pornography."

CHANGING MEN, Issues in Gender, Sex and Politics, Feminist Men's Publications, 306 N. Brooks St., Madison WI 53715. Editor: Rick Cote. Managing Editor: Michael Birnbaum. 80% freelance written. Works with a small number of new/unpublished writers each year. A feminist men's journal published two times a year. "We are a forum for anti-sexist men and women to explore the politics of gender, the complexities of sexual relations, and the expressions of love in a changing world." Estab. 1979. Circ. 4,000. Publishes ms an average of 1 year after acceptance. Byline given. Buys one-time rights. Simultaneous queries and simultaneous and previously published submissions OK. Reports in 2 months. Sample copy $4.50; writer's guidelines for #10 SASE.
Nonfiction: Submit nonfiction to: Rick Cote, P.O. Box 639, Durham NH 03824-0639. Book excerpts, humor, interview/profile, opinion, personal experience and photo feature. Plans special issues on male/female intimacy. Future issues expected to focus on fathering, feminism, divorce, prisons. No theoretical articles. Query with published clips. Length: 3,500 words maximum. Pays $25 maximum.
Columns/Departments: Men and War (focus on masculinity and how culture shapes male values), Sports (with a feminist slant), and Book Reviews (focus on sexuality and masculinity). Query with published clips. Length: 500-1,500 words. Pays $15 maximum.
Fiction: Submit fiction to: Jeff Kirsch, fiction editor, Department of Spanish and Portugese, Tulane University, New Orleans LA 70118. Erotica, ethnic, experimental, humorous and novel excerpts. Buys 1 ms/year. Query with published clips. Length: 3,500 words maximum. Pays $20 maximum.

Poetry: Free verse, haiku and light verse. Submit maximum 3 poems. Length: 50 lines maximum. No payment for poetry.

Fillers: Clippings, jokes and newsbreaks. Length: 300 words. No payment for fillers.

COLUMBUS BRIDE & GROOM MAGAZINE, National Bridal Publications, Inc., 303 East Livingston Ave., Columbus OH 43215. (614)224-1992. Editor: Marvin Brown. Managing Editor: Lori Meeker. 5% freelance written. Semiannual magazine on weddings. Estab. 1985. Circ. 13,000. Pays on publication. Publishes ms an average of 4 months after acceptance. Byline given. Offers 50% kill fee. Buys all rights. Submit seasonal/holiday material 6 months in advance. Reports in 1 month. Sample copy $1.50.

Nonfiction: General interest (within our specialized field), how-to (plan and execute a wedding and take up married life), humor and inspirational. "No articles promoting a specifically named product and/or service." Buys 4-5 mss/year. Query. Length: 250-1,500 words. Pays $40-250 for assigned articles; $25-150 for unsolicited articles. Sometimes pays expenses of writers on assignment.

Photos: State availability of photos with submission. Reviews contact sheets, 35mm and up transparencies and 5×7 and up prints. Captions and model releases required. Buys one-time rights.

Fillers: Anecdotes, facts, newsbreaks and short humor. Length: 40-200 words.

FIRST HAND, Experiences For Loving Men, Firsthand, Ltd., 310 Cedar Lane, Teaneck NJ 07666. (201)836-9177. Editor: Bob Harris. Publisher: Jackie Lewis. 75% freelance written. Eager to work with new/unpublished writers. Monthly magazine of homosexual erotica. Estab. 1980. Circ. 70,000. Pays 8 months after acceptance or on publication, whichever comes first. Publishes ms an average of 8 months after acceptance. Byline given. Buys all rights (exceptions made) and second serial (reprint) rights. Submit seasonal/holiday material 10 months in advance. Reports in 2 months. Sample copy $5; writer's guidelines for #10 SASE.

Nonfiction: "We seldom use nonfiction except for our 'Survival Kit' section, but will consider full-length profiles, investigative reports, and so on if they are of information/inspirational interest to gay people. Erotic safe sex stories are acceptable." Length: 3,000 words maximum. Pays $100-150. "We will consider original submissions only." Query.

Columns/Departments: Survival Kit (short nonfiction articles, up to 1,000 words, featuring practical information on safe sex practices, health, travel, books, video, psychology, law, fashion, and other advice/consumer/lifestyle topics of interest to gay or single men). "These should be written in the second or third person." Query. "For this section, we sometimes also buy reprint rights to appropriate articles previously published in local gay newspapers around the country." Pays $35 to $70, depending on length, if original; if reprint, pays half that rate.

Fiction: Erotic fiction up to 5,000 words in length, average 2,000-3,000 words. "We prefer fiction in the first person which is believable—stories based on the writer's actual experience have the best chance. We're not interested in stories which involve underage characters in sexual situations. Other taboos include bestiality, rape—except in prison stories, as rape is an unavoidable reality in prison—and heavy drug use. Writers with questions about what we can and cannot depict should write for our guidelines, which go into this in more detail. We print mostly self-contained stories; we will look at novel excerpts, but only if they stand on their own."

Poetry: Free verse and light verse. Buys 12/year. Submit maximum 5 poems. Length: 10-30 lines. Pays $25.

Tips: "*First Hand* is a very reader-oriented publication for gay men. Half of each issue is comprised by letters from our readers describing their personal experiences, fantasies and feelings. Our readers are from all walks of life, all races and ethnic backgrounds, all classes, all religious and political affiliations, and so on. They are very diverse, and many live in far-flung rural areas or small towns; for some of them, our magazines are the primary source of contact with gay life, in some cases the only support for their gay identity. Our readers are very loyal and save every issue. We return that loyalty by trying to reflect their interests—for instance, by striving to avoid the exclusively big-city bias so common to national gay publications. So bear in mind the diversity of the audience when you write."

IN TOUCH FOR MEN, In Touch Publications International, Inc., 7216 Varna, North Hollywood CA 91605. (818)764-2288. Editor-in-Chief: Tom Quinn. 80% freelance written. Works with a small number of new/unpublished writers each year. A monthly magazine covering the gay male lifestyle, gay male humor and erotica. Circ. 70,000. **Pays on acceptance.** Byline given. Buys one-time rights. Submit seasonal/holiday material 4 months in advance. Simultaneous submissions OK. Reports in 2 weeks on queries; 6 weeks on mss. Sample copy $4.95; writer's guidelines for #10 SAE.

Nonfiction: Buys 36 mss/year. Send complete ms. Length: 1,000-3,500 words. Pays $25-75.

Photos: State availability of photos with submission. Reviews contact sheets, transparencies, and prints. Offers $35/photo. Captions, model releases and identification of subjects required. Buys one-time rights.

Columns/Departments: Touch and Go (brief comments on various items or pictures that have appeared in the media), 50-500 words. Buys 12 mss/year. Send complete ms. Pays $25.

Fiction: Adventure, confession, erotica, historical, horror, humorous, mainstream, mystery, romance, science fiction, slice-of-life vignettes, suspense, and western; all must be gay male erotica. No "heterosexual, heavy stuff." Buys 36 mss/year. Send complete ms. Length: 2,500-3,500 words. Pays $75 maximum.

Fillers: Short humor. Buys 12/year. Length: 1,500-3,500 words. Pays $50-75.

Tips: "Our publication features male nude photos plus three fiction pieces, several articles, cartoons, humorous comments on items from the media, photo features, and gay travel. We try to present the positive aspects of the gay lifestyle, with an emphasis on humor. Humorous pieces may be erotic in nature. We are open to all submissions that fit our gay male format; the emphasis, however, is on humor and the upbeat. We receive many fiction manuscripts but not nearly enough articles and humor."

METRO SINGLES LIFESTYLES, Metro Publications, P.O. Box 28203, Kansas City MO 64118. (816)436-8424. Editor: Robert L. Huffstutter. 40% freelance written. Eager to work with new/unpublished writers and photographers. A tabloid appearing 6 times/year covering singles lifestyles. Estab. 1984. **Pays on acceptance.** Publishes ms an average of 2 months after acceptance. Byline given with photo optional. Buys one-time rights and second serial (reprint) rights. Submit seasonal/holiday material 3 months in advance. Reports in 6 weeks. Sample copy $2 and 9×12 SAE with 5 first class stamps.

Nonfiction: Essay, general interest, how-to (on meeting the ideal mate, recovering from divorce, etc.), inspirational, interview/profile, personal experience and photo feature. No sexually-oriented material. Buys 6-12 mss/year. Send complete ms. Length: 700-1,200 words. Pays $100 maximum for assigned articles; pays $20-50 for unsolicited articles. Will pay in copies or other if writer prefers.

Photos: Pays up to $100 for photo layouts (10-12 photos). Subject matter suggested includes swimwear fashion, recreational events, "day in the life of an American single," etc. Reviews 3×5 and 8×10 color or b&w prints. Model releases of close-up or fashion shots required. Buys one-time and reprint rights. **Pays on acceptance.**

Columns/Departments: Movie Reviews, Lifestyles, Singles Events, and Book Reviews (about singles), all 400-1,000 words. Buys 9-12 mss/year. Send complete ms. Pays $20-50.

Fiction: Confession, humorous, romance and slice-of-life vignettes. Buys 6-12 mss/year. Send complete ms. Length: 700-1,200 words. Pays $20-50.

Poetry: Free verse and light verse. Buys 40-60 poems/year. Submit maximum 3 poems. Length: 21 lines. Pays in complimentary copies and subscriptions for poetry. Byline given.

Tips: "A freelancer can best approach and break in to our publication with positive articles, photo features about singles and positive fiction about singles. Photos and short bios of singles (blue collar, white collar, and professional) at work needed. Photos and a few lines about singles enjoying recreation (swimming, sports, chess, etc.) always welcome. Color photos, close-up, are suitable."

MOM GUESS WHAT NEWSPAPER, New Helvetia Communications, 1725 L St., Sacramento CA 95814. (916)441-6397. Editor: Linda Birner. 80% freelance written. Works with small number of new/unpublished writers each year. Biweekly tabloid covering gay rights and gay lifestyles. Estab. 1978. Circ. 21,000. Publishes ms an average of 3 months after acceptance. Byline given. Buys all rights. Submit seasonal/holiday material 3 months in advance. Reports in 2 months. Sample copy $1; writer's guidelines for 8½×11 SAE with 3 first class stamps.

Nonfiction: Interview/profile and photo feature of international, national or local scope. Buys 8 mss/year. Query. Length: 200-1,500 words. Payment depends on article. Pays expenses of writers on special assignment.

Photos: State availability of photos with submission. Reviews 5×7 prints. Offers no additional payment for photos accepted with ms. Captions and identification of subjects required. Buys one-time rights.

Columns/Departments: News, Restaurants, Political, Health, and Film, Video and Book Reviews. Buys 12 mss/year. Query. Payment depends on article.

‡SINGLELIFE MAGAZINE, SingleLife Enterprises, Inc., 606 W. Wisconsin Ave., Milwaukee WI 53203. (414)271-9700. FAX: (414)271-5263. Editor: Leifa Butrick. 40% freelance written. Prefers to work with published/established writers; works with a small number of new/unpublished writers each year. Bimonthly magazine covering single lifestyles. Estab. 1982. Circ. 22,000. Pays on publication. Publishes ms an average of 4 months after acceptance. Byline given. Buys one-time rights, second serial (reprint) rights and simultaneous rights. Submit seasonal material 4 months in advance. Simultaneous and previously published submissions OK. Reports in 3 weeks. Sample copy and writer's guidelines for $3.50 and 9×11 SASE; writer's guidelines for #10 SAE with 1 first class stamp.

Nonfiction: Upbeat and in-depth articles on significant areas of interest to single people such as male/female relationships, travel, health, sports, food, single parenting, humor, finances, places to go and things to do. Prefers third person point of view and ms to query letter. Our readers are between 25 and 50. Length: 1,000-3,000 words. Pays $50-150. Sometimes pays expenses of writers on assignment.

Fiction and Poetry: Buys 3-4 stories or poems per year, which are well written and cast a new light on what being single means. Length: not over 2,500 words. Submit any number of poems that pertain to being single. Pays $25-50.

For information on setting your freelance fees, see How Much Should I Charge? in the Business of Writing section.

Tips: "The easiest way to get in is to write something light, unusual, but also well-developed."

TORSO, Varsity Communications, 462 Broadway, New York NY 10013. (212)966-8400. Editor: Stan Leventhal. 75% freelance written. Works with a small number of new/unpublished writers each year. A monthly magazine for gay men. "Divergent viewpoints are expressed in both feature articles and fiction, which examine values and behavior patterns characteristic of a gay lifestyle. *Torso* has a continuing commitment to well-documented investigative journalism in areas pertaining to the lives and well-being of homosexuals." Circ. 60,000. Pays on publication. Publishes ms an average of 5 months after acceptance. Byline given. Buys first North American serial rights. Submit seasonal/holiday material 6 months in advance. No simultaneous submissions accepted. Reports in 2 weeks on queries; 1 month on mss. Sample copy $5; writer's guidelines for #10 SASE.

Nonfiction: Exposé, general interest, humor, interview/profile, opinion, personal experience, photo feature and travel. "*Torso* also regularly reports on cultural and political trends, as well as the arts and entertainment, often profiling the people and personalities who affect them. The tone must be positive regarding the gay experience." Buys 12 mss/year. Query with or without published clips or send complete ms (typewritten and double-spaced). Length: 2,000-4,000 words. Pays $150.

Fiction: Erotica, adventure, fantasy, humorous, novel excerpts and romance. "No long, drawn-out fiction with no form, etc." Buys 35 mss/year. Query with or without published clips or send complete ms. Length: 2,000-4,000 words. Pays $100.

Tips: "Write about what is happening—what you as a gay male (if you are) would care to read."

THE WASHINGTON BLADE, Washington Blade, Inc., 8th Floor, 724 9th St. NW, Washington DC 20001. (202)347-2038. FAX: (202)393-6510. Senior Editor: Lisa M. Keen. 20% freelance written. Weekly news tabloid covering the gay/lesbian community. "Articles (subjects) should be written from or directed to a gay perspective." Estab. 1969. Circ. 27,500. Pays in 1 month. Publishes ms an average of 1 month after acceptance. Byline given. Offers $15 kill fee. Buys first North American serial rights. Submit seasonal/holiday material 1 month in advance. Sample copy and writer's guidelines for 8½×11 SASE and $1.

Nonfiction: Exposé (of government, private agency, church, etc., handling of gay-related issues); historical/nostalgic; interview/profile (of gay community/political leaders; persons, gay or nongay, in positions to affect gay issues; outstanding achievers who happen to be gay; those who incorporate the gay lifestyle into their professions); photo feature (on a nationally or internationally historic gay event); and travel (on locales that welcome or cater to the gay traveler). *The Washington Blade* basically covers two areas: news and lifestyle. News coverage of D.C. metropolitan area gay community, local and federal government actions relating to gays, as well as national news of interest to gays. Section also includes features on current events. Special issues include: Annual gay pride issue (early June). No sexually explicit material. Articles of interest to the community must include and be written for both gay men and lesbians. Buys 30 mss/year, average. Query with published clips and resume. Length: 500-1,500 words. Pays 5-10¢/word. Sometimes pays the expenses of writers on assignment.

Photos: "A photo or graphic with feature/lifestyle articles is particularly important. Photos with news stories are appreciated." State availability of photos. Reviews b&w contact sheets and 5×7 glossy prints. Pays $25 minimum. Captions preferred; model releases required. On assignment, photographer paid mutually agreed upon fee, with expenses reimbursed. Publication retains all rights.

Tips: "Send good examples of your writing and know the paper before you submit a manuscript for publication. We get a lot of submissions which are entirely inappropriate. We're looking for more features, but fewer AIDS-related features." Greatest opportunity for freelancers resides in current events, features, interviews and book reviews.

WASHINGTON JEWISH SINGLES NEWSLETTER, WJSN, Suite L, 444 N. Frederick Ave., Box 239, Gaithersburg MD 20877. (301)990-0210. Editor: Ben Levitan. Managing Editor: Ellen Caswell. 100% freelance written. Monthly newsletter for singles (unmarried professionals). "All articles should have a singles slant. Must relate to life/career/humor, etc. for singles." Estab. 1987. Pays on publication. Byline given. Buys first North American serial rights or second serial (reprint) rights. Submit seasonal/holiday material 2 months in advance. Simultaneous and previously published submissions OK. Query for electronic submissions. Query for electronic submissions. Reports in 1 week. Sample copy $1 with 9×12 SAE and 2 first class stamps.

Nonfiction Book excerpts, exposé, general interest, how-to (travel alone, manage finance/career, write "personal" ads), humor (especially dating romance), inspirational, interview/profile (new/unusual single activities in other cities), opinion personal experience, religious (Jewish only), technical and travel. Every March special "Personal Ad" issue; every May—"State of Jewish American singles" report and survey results. "We try to maintain an upbeat/light mood. We discourage negative/depressing articles." Send complete ms. Length: 300-800 words. Pays $10-35. Fillers: articles under 100 words bought are paid in copies (2).

Photos: State availability of photos with submissions. Reviews contact sheets and negatives. Offers no additional payment for photos accepted with ms. Identification of subjects required. Buys one-time rights.

Columns/Departments: Where Shall We Go? (fun/different dates in DC area), 300 words; For What It's Worth (offbeat items/fun current facts), 100 words; Dynamic People (DC area singles of special note), 400 words; The Bright Side (humor/comedy), 100-400 words; Your Money (finance for singles), 50-300 words; and Single Serving (20 min. recipes for singles). Buys 12 mss/year. Send complete ms. Pays $10-35. New columns welcome.

Fiction: Confession, historical (singles related), humorous, mystery, romance, serialized novels and slice-of-life vignettes. Buys 3 mss/year. Send complete ms.

Fillers: Anecdotes, facts, gags to be illustrated by cartoonist, newsbreaks and short humor. Length: 20-150 words. Pays 2 copies to $10.

Tips: "Short, to-the-point articles and fillers are always appreciated—especially humor. All *must* have a slant to unmarried singles. Depressing articles are tossed. Stay in touch via the electronic Bulletin Board for writers (open 24 hours at 301-963-0067)."

THE WEEKLY NEWS, The Weekly News Inc., 901 NE 79th St., Miami FL 33138. (305)757-6333. Editor: Jay Vail. Managing Editor: Bill Watson. 40% freelance written. Weekly gay tabloid. Circ. 32,000. Pays on publication. Byline given. Buys one-time rights. Submit seasonal/holiday material 2 months in advance. Simultaneous and previously published submissions OK. Sample copy for 9½ × 12½ SAE with $1.50 postage.

Nonfiction: Exposé, humor and interview/profile. Buys 8 mss/year. Send complete ms. Length: 1,000-5,000 words. Pays $25-125. Sometimes pays the expenses of writers on assignment.

Photos: State availability of photos with submission. Reviews 3 × 5 prints. Offers $5-20/photo. Buys first and future use.

Columns/Departments: Send complete ms. Length: 900 words maximum. Pays $15-30.

Religious

Religious magazines focus on a variety of subjects, styles and beliefs. Many are publishing articles relating to current affairs like AIDS, cults, or substance abuse. Fewer religious publications are considering poems and personal experience articles, but many emphasize special ministries to singles, seniors and deaf people. Such diversity makes reading each magazine essential for the writer hoping to break in. Educational and inspirational material of interest to church members, workers and leaders within a denomination or religion is needed by the publications in this category. Publications intended to assist professional religious workers in teaching and managing church affairs are classified in Church Administration and Ministry in the Trade section. Religious magazines for children and teenagers can be found in the Juvenile and Teen and Young Adult classifications.

AGLOW, For the Spirit-Renewed Christian Woman, Aglow Publications, Box 1548, Lynnwood WA 98046-1557. (206)775-7282. Editor: Gwen Weising. 66% freelance written. Works with a small number of new/unpublished writers each year. Bimonthly nondenominational Christian charismatic magazine for women. **Pays on acceptance.** Publishes ms an average of 6 months to 1 year after acceptance. Byline given. Buys first North American serial rights, and reprint rights for use in *Aglow* magazine in other countries. Submit seasonal/holiday material 8 months in advance. Simultaneous queries OK. Reports in 2 months. Sample copy for 9 × 12 SAE and 2 first class stamps; writer's guidelines for #10 SASE.

Nonfiction: Contact Gloria Chisholm, Acquisitions Editor. Christian women's spiritual experience articles (first person) and some humor. "Each article should be either a personal experience of or teaching about Jesus as Savior, as Baptizer in the Holy Spirit, or as Guide and Strength in everyday circumstances." Queries only. "We would like to see material about 'Women of Vision' who have made and are making an impact on their world for God." Length: 1,000-2,000 words. Pays up to 10¢/word. Sometimes pays expenses of writers on assignment.

THE ASSOCIATE REFORMED PRESBYTERIAN, Associate Reformed Presbyterian General Synod, 1 Cleveland St., Greenville SC 29601. (803)232-8297. Editor: Ben Johnston. 5% freelance written. Works with a small number of new/unpublished writers each year. A Christian publication serving a conservative, evangelical and Reformed denomination, most of whose members are in the Southeast U.S. Estab. 1976. Circ. 7,000. **Pays on acceptance.** Publishes ms an average of 3 months after acceptance. Byline given. Not copyrighted. Buys first rights, one-time rights, or second serial (reprint) rights. Submit seasonal/holiday material 4 months in advance. Simultaneous submissions and previously published submissions OK. Reports in 1 month. Sample copy $1.50; writer's guidelines for #10 SASE.

Nonfiction: Book excerpts, essays, inspirational, opinion, personal experience and religious. Buys 10-15 mss/year. Query. Length: 400-2,000 words. Pays $50 maximum.

Photos: State availability of photos with submission. Reviews 5×7 reprints. Offers $25 maximum per photo. Captions and identification of subjects required. Buys one-time rights. Sometimes pays expenses of writers on assignment.

Fiction: Religious and children's. Pays $50 maximum.

Tips: "Feature articles are the area of our publication most open to freelancers. Focus on a contemporary problem and offer Bible-based solutions to it. Provide information that would help a Christian struggling in his daily walk. Writers should understand that we are denominational, conservative, evangelical, Reformed and Presbyterian. A writer who appreciates these nuances would stand a much better chance of being published here than one who does not."

AXIOS, 800 S. Euclid St., Fullerton CA 92632. (714)526-4952. Computer number for Axios BBS (714)526-2387. Editor: Daniel John Gorham. 10% freelance written. Eager to work with new/unpublished writers. Monthly journal seeking spiritual articles mostly on Orthodox Christian background, either Russian, Greek, Serbian, Syrian or American. Estab. 1980. Circ. 8,789. Pays on publication. Publishes ms an average of 6 months after acceptance. Byline given. Offers 50% kill fee. Buys all rights. Submit seasonal/holiday material 4 months in advance. Simultaneous queries, and simultaneous and previously published submissions OK. Query for electronic submissions. Reports in 1 month. Sample copy for $2 and 9×12 SAE with 50¢ postage.

Nonfiction: Book excerpts; exposé (of religious figures); general interest; historical/nostalgic; interview/profile; opinion; personal experience; photo feature; and travel (shrines, pilgrimages). Special issues include the persecution of Christians in Iran, Russia, behind Iron Curtain or in Arab lands; Roman Catholic interest in the Orthodox Church. Nothing about the Pope or general "all-is-well-with-Christ" items. Buys 14 mss/year. Send complete ms. Length: 1,000-3,000 words. Pays 4¢/word minimum.

Columns/Departments: Reviews religious books and films. Buys 80 mss/year. Query.

Tips: "We need some hard hitting articles on the 'political' church—the why, how and where of it and why it lacks the timelessness of the spiritual. Here in *Axios* you can discuss your feelings, your findings, your needs, your growth; give us your outpouring. Don't mistake us for either Protestant or Roman Catholic; we are the voice of Catholics united with the Eastern Orthodox Church, also referred to as the Greek Orthodox Church. We are most interested in the western rite within eastern Orthodoxy; and the return of the Roman Catholic to the ancient universal church. Very interested in the old calendar."

BAPTIST LEADER, Valley Forge PA 19482-0851. (215)768-2153. Editor: Linda Isham. For pastors, teachers and leaders in churches. 5% freelance written. Works with several new/unpublished writers each year. Quarterly. Estab. 1939. **Pays on acceptance.** Publishes ms an average of 8 months after acceptance. Deadlines are 8 months prior to date of issue. Sample copy for $1.25; writer's guidelines for #10 SASE.

Nonfiction: Educational topics. How-to articles for local church teachers and leaders. Length: 1,500-2,000 words. Pays $25-75.

Tips: "We're planning more emphasis on Christian education administration and planning and articles for all church leaders."

THE CATHOLIC ANSWER, Our Sunday Visitor, Inc., 200 Noll Plaza, Huntington IN 46750. (219)356-8400. Editor: Father Peter M.J. Stravinskas. Managing Editor: George Foster. 50% freelance written. Bimonthly magazine on the Catholic faith. "*The Catholic Answer* seeks to inform, interpret and apply solid, fundamental Catholic belief for orthodox Catholics, converts and those wishing to learn more about the traditional Catholic faith." Circ. 100,000. Pays on publication. Publishes ms an average of 6 months after acceptance. Byline given. Buys all rights. Submit seasonal/holiday material 6 months in advance. Simultaneous submissions OK. Query for electronic submissions. Free sample copy and writer's guidelines for SASE.

Nonfiction: Essays, general interest (Catholic), historical/nostalgic, inspirational. "No superficial treatments of the Faith." Buys 80 mss/year. Query with published clips. Length: 1,200-2,200 words. Pays $100 flat payment.

Tips: "Write for guidelines and begin sending material according to those specifications. *TCA* has 3 sections that are most open to freelance writers. Two regular columnists and the remainder is freelance—average of 5-8 articles per issue."

CATHOLIC DIGEST, Box 64090, St. Paul MN 55164. Editor: Henry Lexau. Managing Editor: Richard Reece. 50% freelance written. Works with large number of new/unpublished writers each year. Monthly magazine covering the daily living of Roman Catholics for an audience that is 60% female, 40% male; 37% is college educated. Circ. 600,000. Publishes ms an average of 6 months after acceptance. Byline given. Buys first North American serial rights or one-time reprint rights. Submit seasonal material 6 months in advance. Previously published submissions OK, if so indicated. Reports in 1 month. Free sample copy and writer's guidelines.

Nonfiction: General interest (daily living and family relationships); interview (of outstanding Catholics, celebrities and locals); nostalgia (the good old days of family living); profile; religion; travel (shrines); humor; inspirational (overcoming illness, role model people); and personal experience (adventures and daily living).

Buys 30 articles/issue. No queries. Send complete ms. Length: 500-3,000 words, 2,000 average. Pays on acceptance—$200-400 for originals, $100 for reprints.

Columns/Departments: "Check a copy of the magazine in the library for a description of column needs. Payment varies and is made on publication. We buy about 5/issue."

Fillers: Jokes, anecdotes and short humor. Buys 10-15 mss/issue. Length: 10-300 words. Pays $3-50 on publication.

CATHOLIC LIFE, 35750 Moravian Dr., Fraser MI 48026. Editor-in-Chief: Fr. John J. Majka, PIME. 20% freelance written. Monthly (except July or August) magazine. Emphasizes foreign missionary activities of the Catholic Church in Burma, India, Bangladesh, the Philippines, Hong Kong, Africa, etc., for middle-aged and older audience with either middle incomes or pensions. High school educated (on the average), conservative in both religion and politics. Estab. 1954. Circ. 23,800. Pays on publication. Publishes ms an average of 3 months after acceptance. Buys all rights. Byline given. Submit seasonal/holiday material 4 months in advance. Simultaneous submissions OK. Reports in 2 weeks.

Nonfiction: Informational and inspirational foreign missionary activities of the Catholic Church. Buys 10-15 unsolicited mss/year. Query or send complete ms. Length: 1,000-1,500 words. Pays 4¢/word.

Tips: "Query with short, graphic details of what the material will cover or the personality involved in the biographical sketch. Also, we appreciate being advised on the availability of good black-and-white photos to illustrate the material."

CHICAGO STUDIES, Box 665, Mundelein IL 60060. (708)566-1462. Editor: Rev. George J. Dyer. 50% freelance written. Magazine published 3 times/year. For Roman Catholic priests and religious educators. Circ. 8,200. **Pays on acceptance.** Buys all rights. Reports in 2 months. Sample copy $5; free writer's guidelines.

Nonfiction: Nontechnical discussion of theological, Biblical and ethical topics. Articles aimed at a nontechnical presentation of the contemporary scholarship in those fields. Submit complete ms. Buys 30 mss/year. Length: 3,000-5,000 words. Pays $35-100.

‡THE CHRISTIAN CENTURY, 407 S. Dearborn St., Chicago IL 60605. (312)427-5380. Editor: James M. Wall. Senior Editors: Martin E. Marty and Dean Peerman. Managing Editor: David Heim. 70% freelance written. Eager to work with new/unpublished writers. Weekly magazine for ecumenically-minded, progressive church people, both clergy and lay. Circ. 37,000. Pays on publication. Publishes ms an average of 2 months after acceptance. Usually buys all rights. Reports in 1 month. Free sample copy.

Nonfiction: "We use articles dealing with social problems, ethical dilemmas, political issues, international affairs, and the arts, as well as with theological and ecclesiastical matters. We focus on concerns that arise at the juncture between church and society, or church and culture." Query appreciated, but not essential. Length: 2,500 words maximum. Payment varies, but averages $30/page.

‡CHRISTIAN HERALD, 40 Overlook Dr., Chappaqua NY 10514. (914)769-9000. Editor: Bob Chuvala. 50% freelance written. A monthly magazine for evangelical Protestants. Estab. 1877. Circ. 160,000. **Pays on acceptance.** Byline given. Offers ⅓ kill fee. Buys first North American serial rights or second serial (reprint) rights. Submit seasonal/holiday material 4 months in advance. Reports in 1 month. Sample copy for 9 × 12 SAE with 2 first class stamps; writer's guidelines for #10 SASE.

Nonfiction: Sandra P. Aldrich, associate editor. Humor, interview/profile, personal experience and religious. "No articles that tell the reader what to do or how to live." Buys 50 mss/year. Query with published clips, or send complete ms. Length: 100-2,500 words. Pays 10-15¢/word. Sometimes pays the expenses of writers on assignment.

Photos: Peter Gross, art director. Send photos with submission. Reviews contact sheets, transparencies and prints. Captions, model releases and identification of subjects required. Buys one-time rights.

Columns/Departments: Kids of the Kingdom (enlightening moments in the course of parenting or teaching children), up to 200 words; The Two of Us (special moments in a Christian marrriage), up to 200 words; One Last Word (personal experiences that pointed out something eternal), up to 1,000 words. Buys 30 mss/year. Send complete ms. Pays 10-15¢/word.

Tips: "Look around for people who are demonstrating their faith, not just talking about it."

CHRISTIAN HOME & SCHOOL, Christian Schools International, 3350 East Paris Ave. SE, P.O. Box 8709, Grand Rapids MI 49508. (616)957-1070. Editor: Gordon L. Bordewyk. Associate Editor: Judy Zylstra. 30% freelance written. Works with a small number of new/unpublished writers each year. Magazine published 8 times/year covering family life and Christian education. "The magazine is designed for parents who support Christian education. We feature material on a wide range of topics of interest to parents." Estab. 1922. Pays on publication. Publishes ms an average of 4 months after acceptance. Byline given. Buys first North American serial rights. Submit seasonal/holiday material 4 months in advance. Simultaneous queries OK. Reports in 3 weeks on queries; 1 month on mss. Sample copy for 9 × 12 SAE and 4 first class stamps; writer's guidelines for #10 SASE.

Nonfiction: Book excerpts, interview/profile, opinion, personal experience and articles on parenting and school life. "We publish features on issues which affect the home and school and profiles on interesting individuals, providing that the profile appeals to our readers and is not a tribute or eulogy of that person." Buys 40 mss/year. Send complete ms. Length: 500-2,000 words. Pays $25-85. Sometimes pays the expenses of writers on assignment.

Photos: "If you have any black-and-white photos appropriate for your article, send them along."

Tips: "Features are the area most open to freelancers. We are publishing articles that deal with contemporary issues which affect parents; keep that in mind. Use an informal easy-to-read style rather than a philosophical, academic tone. Try to incorporate vivid imagery and concrete, practical examples from real life."

CHRISTIAN OUTLOOK, Hutton Publications, Box 1870, Hayden ID 83835. (208)772-6184. Editor: Linda Hutton. 50% freelance written. Quarterly newsletter of inspirational material. "Send us uplifting poetry and fiction, with a subtle moral, but nothing overly religious or preachy." Estab. 1988. Circ. 200. **Pays on acceptance.** Publishes ms an average of 9 months after acceptance. Byline given. Buys one-time rights or second serial (reprint) rights. Submit seasonal/holiday material 9 months in advance. Simultaneous and previously published submissions OK. Reports in 1 month on mss. Sample copy and writer's guidelines for #10 SAE with 2 first class stamps.

Fiction: Religious. Buys 4 mss/year. Send complete ms. Length: 300-1,500 words. Pays ¼-1¢/word.

Poetry: Free verse, light verse, traditional, "Nothing overly religious, merely uplifting and inspirational." Buys 8 poems/year. Submit up to 3 poems at one time. Length: 4-8 lines. Pays 10-25¢/line.

CHRISTIAN SINGLE, Family Ministry Dept., Baptist Sunday School Board, 127 9th Ave. N., Nashville TN 37234. (615)251-2277. Editor: Cliff Allbritton. 50-70% freelance written. Prefers to work with published/established writers; works with a small number of new/unpublished writers each year. Monthly magazine covering items of special interest to Christian single adults. "*Christian Single* is a contemporary Christian magazine that seeks to give substantive information to singles for living the abundant life. It seeks to be constructive and creative in approach." Circ. 105,000. Pays on acceptance "for immediate needs"; on publication "for unsolicited manuscripts." Publishes ms 1-2 years after acceptance. Byline given. Buys all rights; makes work-for-hire assignments. Submit seasonal/holiday material 1½ years in advance. Reports in 2 months. Sample copy and writer's guidelines for 9 × 12 SASE with 85¢ postage.

Nonfiction: Humor (good, clean humor that applies to Christian singles); how-to (specific subjects which apply to singles; query needed); inspirational (of the personal experience type); high adventure personal experience (of single adults); photo feature (on outstanding Christian singles; query needed); well researched financial articles targeted to single adults (query needed). No "shallow, uninformative mouthing off. This magazine says something, and people read it cover to cover." Buys 120-150 unsolicited mss/year. Query with published clips. Length: 300-1,200 words. Pays 5¢/word.

Tips: "We look for freshness and creativity, not duplication of what we have already done. Don't write on loneliness! Need more upbeat personal experience articles written by Christian *single men*! We are backlogged with submissions by women and with poetry at this time. We give preference to Christian single adult writers but publish articles by *sensitive* and *informed* married writers also. Remember that you are talking to educated people who attend church. Study the magazine before submitting materials."

CHRISTIANITY & CRISIS, 537 W. 121st St., New York NY 10027. (212)662-5907. Editor: Leon Howell. Managing Editor: Gail Hovey. 10% freelance written. Works with a small number of new/unpublished writers each year. Biweekly Protestant journal of opinion. "We are interested in foreign affairs, domestic, economic and social policy, and theological developments with social or ethical implications, e.g., feminist, black and liberation theologies. As an independent religious journal it is part of *C&C*'s function to discuss church policies from a detached and sometimes critical perspective. We carry no 'devotional' material but welcome solid contemplative reflections. Most subscribers are highly educated, well-informed." Estab. 1941. Circ. 14,000. Pays on publication. Publishes ms an average of 2 months after acceptance. Byline given. Offers variable kill fee. Submit seasonal/holiday material 2 months in advance. Simultaneous queries OK. Reports in 1 month. Sample copy $1.75 with 9 × 12 SAE and 2 first class stamps; writer's guidelines for #10 SASE.

Nonfiction: Buys 150 mss/year. Query with or without published clips. Length: 1,000-4,000 words. Pays 3¢/word. Rarely pays expenses of writers on assignment.

Tips: "We have been publishing more international stories and need to build up reporting on U.S. issues."

CHRISTIANITY TODAY, 465 Gundersen Dr., Carol Stream IL 60188. 80% freelance written. Works with a small number of new/unpublished writers each year. Emphasizes orthodox, evangelical religion. Semimonthly magazine. Circ. 180,000. Publishes ms an average of 6 months after acceptance. Usually buys first serial rights. Submit seasonal/holiday material at least 8 months in advance. Reports in 2 months. Sample copy and writer's guidelines for 9 × 12 SAE and 3 first class stamps.

Nonfiction: Theological, ethical, historical and informational (not merely inspirational). Buys 4 mss/issue. *Query only.* Unsolicited mss not accepted and not returned. Length: 1,000-4,000 words. Pays negotiable rates. Sometimes pays the expenses of writers on assignment.

Columns/Departments: The Arts (Christian review of the arts). Buys 12 mss/year. Send complete ms. Length: 800-900 words. Pays negotiable rates.
Tips: "We are developing more of our own manuscripts and requiring a much more professional quality of others."

CHRISTMAS, The Annual of Christmas Literature and Art, Augsburg Fortress, Publishers, 426 S. 5th St., Box 1209, Minneapolis MN 55440. (612)330-3437. Editor: Gloria E. Bengtson. 100% freelance written. "An annual literary magazine that celebrates Christmas focusing on the effect of the Christmas love of God on the lives of people, and how it colors and shapes traditions and celebrations." **Pays on acceptance.** Byline given. Buys first rights, one-time rights and all rights; makes work-for-hire assignments. Submit seasonal/ holiday material 18 months in advance. Reports in 2 weeks on queries; 3 weeks on mss. Sample copy $9.95 plus postage.
Nonfiction: Historical/nostalgic (on Christmas customs); inspirational, interview/profile, personal experience and travel. Focusing on more family-oriented articles with stories for children and young adults. Articles on art and music with Christmas relationships. Buys 6-8 mss/year. Query with published clips, or send complete ms. Length: 2,500-7,500 words. Pays $200-450 for assigned articles; pays $150-300 for unsolicited articles.
Photos: State availability of photos with submission. Reviews transparencies. Offers $15-100 per photo. Captions and identification of subjects required. Buys one-time rights.
Fiction: Jennifer Huber, editor. Ethnic, historical and slice-of-life vignettes. "No stories of fictionalized characters at the Bethlehem stable. Fiction should show the effect of God's love on the lives of people." Buys 2 mss/year. Send complete ms. Length: 5,000 words maximum. Pays $150-300.
Poetry: Jennifer Huber, editor. Free verse, light verse and traditional. No poetry dealing with Santa Claus. Buys 3 poems/year. Submit maximum 30 poems. Pays $35-40.

CHRYSALIS, Journal of the Swedenborg Foundation, 139 East 23rd St., New York NY 10010. FAX: (804)983-1074. Send inquiries and manuscripts directly to the editorial office: Route 1, Box 184, Dillwyn VA 23936. Editor: Carol S. Lawson. Managing Editor: Susanna van Rensselaer. 50% freelance written. A literary magazine published 3 times per year on spiritually related topics. (*It is very important to send for writer's guidelines and sample copies before submitting.*) "Content of fiction, articles, reviews, poetry, etc., should be directly focused on that issue's theme and directed to the educated, intellectually curious reader." Estab. 1985. Circ. 1,200. Pays at page-proof stage. Publishes ms an average of 9 months after acceptance. Byline given. Buys first rights and makes work-for-hire assignments. Reports in 2 weeks on queries; 2 months on mss. Sample copy and writer's guidelines for 9 × 12 SAE and $3.50. Writer's guidelines and copy deadlines for SASE. Upcoming Themes: Spring 1991: "Cosmopolitan Connections"; Summer 1991: "Ethics"; Autumn 1991: "The Archetype of the Wise Man"; Spring 1992: "Science and Spirituality"; and Summer 1992: "The Future of Human Nature."
Nonfiction: Essays and interview/profile. Buys 15 mss/year. Query. Length: 750-2,500 words. Pays $50-250 for assigned articles. Pays $50-150 for unsolicited articles.
Photos: Send suggestions for illustrations with submission. Offers no additional payment for photos accepted with ms. Captions and identification of subjects required. Buys original artwork for cover and inside copy, $25-150. Buys one-time rights.
Columns/Departments: Vital Issues (articles and material related to practical psychology, health, healing), 750-2,000 words; Patterns (philosophical inquiry into the underlying patterns found within reality), 750-2,000 words; Currents (articles and material on the fine and visionary arts); 750-2,000 words; and Fringe Benefits (book, film, art, video reviews relevant to *Chrysalis* subject matter), 350-500 words. Buys 12 mss/year. Length: 350-2,000. Pays $50-250.
Fiction: Phoebe Loughrey, fiction editor. Adventure, experimental, historical, mainstream, mystery and science fiction, related to theme of issue. Buys 6 mss/year. Query. Length: short more likely to be published, 500-2,000 words. Pays $50-150.
Poetry: Avante-garde and traditional. Buys 10 poems/year. Pays $25. Submit maximum 6.

CHURCH & STATE, Americans United for Separation of Church and State, 8120 Fenton St., Silver Spring MD 20910. (301)589-3707. Managing Editor: Joseph Conn. 10% freelance written. Prefers to work with published/established writers. Monthly magazine. Emphasizes religious liberty and church/state relations matters. Readership "includes the whole spectrum, but is predominantly Protestant and well-educated." Estab. 1947. Circ. 33,000. **Pays on acceptance.** Publishes ms an average of 2 months after acceptance. Buys all rights. Simultaneous and previously published submissions OK. Reports in 1 month. Sample copy and writer's guidelines for 9 × 12 SAE and 3 first class stamps.
Nonfiction: Expose, general interest, historical and interview. Buys 11 mss/year. Query. Length: 3,000 words maximum. Pays negotiable fee.
Photos: State availability of photos with query. Pays negotiable fee for b&w prints. Captions preferred. Buys one-time rights.

COLUMBIA, One Columbus Plaza, New Haven CT 06507. Editor: Richard McMunn. Monthly magazine for Catholic families; caters particularly to members of the Knights of Columbus. Estab. 1921. Circ. 1.5 million. **Pays on acceptance.** Buys first time serial rights. Free sample copy and writer's guidelines.
Nonfiction: Fact articles directed to the Catholic layman and his family dealing with current events, social problems, Catholic apostolic activities, education, ecumenism, rearing a family, literature, science, arts, sports and leisure. Color glossy prints, transparencies or contact prints with negatives are required for illustration. Articles without ample illustrative material are not given consideration. Pays up to $500, including photos. Buys 30 mss/year. Query. Length: 1,000-1,500 words.

‡THE COMPANION OF ST. FRANCIS AND ST. ANTHONY, Conventual Franciscan Friars, P.O. Box 535, Postal Station F, Toronto, Ontario M4Y 2L8 Canada. (416)924-6349. Editor-in-Chief: Friar Philip Kelly, OFM Conv. 15% freelance written. Monthly magazine. Emphasizing religious and human values and stressing Franciscan virtues—peace, simplicity, joy. Estab. 1937. Circ. 10,000. Pays on publication. Publishes ms an average of 6 months after publication. Buys first North American serial rights. Phone queries OK. Submit seasonal/holiday material 6 months in advance. Reports in 6 weeks. Writer's guidelines for SAE with IRCs.
Nonfiction: Historical; how-to (medical and psychological coping); informational; inspirational; interview; nostalgia; profile; and family. No old time religion, antiCatholic or pro-abortion material. No poetry. Buys 6 mss/issue. Send complete ms. Length: 800-1,000 words. Pays 6¢/word, Canadian funds.
Photos: Photos purchased with accompanying ms. Pays $8 for 5 × 7 (but all sizes accepted) b&w glossy prints. Send prints. Total purchase price for ms includes payment for photos. Captions required.
Fiction: Adventure, humorous, mainstream and religious. Canadian settings preferred. Buys 6 mss/year. Send complete ms. Length: 800-1,000 words. Pays 6¢/word, Canadian funds.
Tips: "Manuscripts on human interest with photos are given immediate preference. In the year ahead we will be featuring shorter articles, more Canadian and Franciscan themes, and better photos. Use a good typewriter, good grammar and good sense."

CONFIDENT LIVING, P.O. Box 82808, Lincoln NE 68501. (402)474-4567. Editor: Jan Reeser. 40% freelance written. Monthly interdenominational magazine for adults, mostly age 50 and up. Estab. 1944. Circ. 85,000. **Pays on acceptance.** Buys first serial rights or first North American serial rights, or second serial (reprint) rights. Submit seasonal material at least 1 year in advance. Reports in 5 weeks. Sample copy $1.75; writer's guidelines with SASE.
Nonfiction: Jan E. Reeser, managing editor. Articles which will help the reader learn and apply Christian Biblical principles to his life from the writer's or the subject's own experience. Writers are required "to affirm agreement with our doctrinal statement. We are especially looking for true, personal experience 'salvation,' church, 'how to live the Christian life' articles, reports and interviews regarding major and interesting happenings and people in fundamental, evangelical Christian circles." Nothing rambling or sugary sweet, or without Biblical basis. Details or statistics should be authentic and verifiable. Style should be conservative but concise. Buys approximately 100 mss/year. Length: 1,500 words maximum. Pays 7-12¢/word, unassigned; 10-15¢/word, assigned; 3¢/word reprint.
Photos: Pays $25 maximum for b&w glossies; $50 maximum for transparencies inside, $85 cover. Photos paid on publication.
Tips: "The basic purpose of the magazine is to explain the Bible and how it is relevant to life because we believe this will accomplish one of two things—to present Christ as Savior to the lost or to promote the spiritual growth of believers, so don't ignore our primary purposes when writing for us. Nonfiction should be Biblical and timely; at the least Biblical in principle. Use illustrations of your own experiences or of someone else's when God solved a problem similar to the reader's. Be so specific that the meanings and significance will be crystal clear to all readers."

CONSCIENCE, A Newsjournal of Prochoice Catholic Opinion, Catholics for a Free Choice, Suite 301, 1436 U St., NW, Washington DC 20009-3916. (202)638-1706. Editor: Nancy H. Evans. 80% freelance written. Eager to work with new/unpublished writers. Bimonthly newsjournal covering reproductive rights, specifically abortion rights in area of church and church and government in U.S. and worldwide. "A feminist, prochoice perspective is a must, and knowledge of Christianity and specifically Catholicism is helpful." Circ. 10,000. Pays on publication. Publishes ms an average of 4 months after acceptance. Byline given. Buys first North American serial rights; makes work-for-hire assignments. Submit seasonal/holiday material 4 months in advance. Simultaneous queries and previously published submissions OK. Query for electronic submissions. Reports in 2 months; free sample copy for #10 SAE with 2 first class stamps; free writer's guidelines for #10 SASE.
Nonfiction: Book excerpts, interview/profile, opinion and personal experience. Especially needs "expose/refutation of antichoice misinformation and specific research into the implications of new reproductive technology and fetal personhood bills/court decisions." Buys 8-12 mss/year. Query with published clips or send complete ms. Length: 1,000-3,500 words. Pays $25-100. "Writers should be aware that we are a nonprofit organization." A substantial number of articles are contributed without payment by writers. Sometimes pays the expenses of writers on assignment.

Photos: State availability of photos with query or ms. Prefers 5×7 b&w prints. Identification of subjects required. Buys all rights.

Columns/Departments: Book reviews. Buys 6-10 mss/year. Send complete ms. Length: 1,000-2,000 words. Pays $25.

Fillers: Clippings and newsbreaks. Uses 6/year. Length: 25-100 words. No payment.

Tips: "Say something new on the abortion issue. Thoughtful, well-researched and well-argued articles needed. The most frequent mistakes made by writers in completing an article for us are untimeliness and wordiness. When you have shown you can write thoughtfully, we may hire you for other types of articles."

CORNERSTONE, Jesus People USA, 4707 N. Malden, Chicago IL 60640. Editor: Dawn Herrin. 10% freelance written. Works with a small number of new/unpublished writers each year; eager to work with new/unpublished writers. A bimonthly magazine covering contemporary issues in the light of Evangelical Christianity. Estab. 1972. Circ. 50,000. Pays after publication. Publishes ms an average of 4-6 months after acceptance. Byline given. Buys first serial rights. Submit seasonal/holiday material 6 months in advance. Simultaneous and previously published submissions OK. Reports in 1 month. Sample copy and writer's guidelines for 12×16 SAE with 6 first class stamps.

Nonfiction: Essays, personal experience, religious. Buys 3-4 mss/year. Query. Length: 2,700 words maximum. Pays negotiable rate. Sometimes pays the expenses of writers on assignment.

Photos: Send photos with accompanying ms. Reviews 8×10 b&w and color prints and 35mm slides. Identification of subjects required. Buys negotiable rights.

Columns/Departments: Music (interview with artists, mainly rock, focusing on artist's world view and value system as expressed in his/her music); Current Events; Personalities; Film and Book Reviews (focuses on meaning as compared and contrasted to Biblical values). Buys 2-6 mss/year. Query. Length: 100-2,500 words (negotiable). Pays negotiable rate.

Fiction: "Articles may express Christian world view but should not be unrealistic or 'syrupy.' Other than porn, the sky's the limit. We want fiction as creative as the Creator." Buys 1-4 mss/year. Send complete ms. Length: 250-2,500 words (negotiable). Pays negotiable rate.

Poetry: Avant-garde, free verse, haiku, light verse and traditional. No limits *except* for epic poetry ("We've not the room!"). Buys 10-50 poems/year. Submit maximum 10 poems. Payment negotiated.

Tips: "A display of creativity which expresses a biblical world view without clichés or cheap shots at non-Christians is the ideal. We are known as the most avant-garde magazine in the Christian market, yet attempt to express orthodox beliefs in language of the '80s. *Any* writer who does this may well be published by *Cornerstone.* Creative fiction is begging for more Christian participation. We anticipate such contributions gladly. Interviews where well-known personalities respond to the gospel are also strong publication possibilities. Please address all submissions to: Nanci Fahey, submissions editor."

THE COVENANT COMPANION, Covenant Publications of the Evangelical Covenant Church, 5101 N. Francisco Ave., Chicago IL 60625. (312)784-3000. Editor: James R. Hawkinson. 10-15% freelance written. "As the official monthly organ of The Evangelical Covenant Church, we seek to inform, stimulate and gather the denomination we serve by putting Covenants in touch with each other and assisting them in interpreting contemporary issues. We also seek to inform them on events in the church. Our background is evangelical and our emphasis is on Christian commitment and life." Circ. 25,000. Publishes ms an average of 2 months after acceptance. Byline given. Buys first or all rights. Submit seasonal/holiday material 4 months in advance. Simultaneous and previously published submissions OK. Query for electronic submissions. Sample copy $2; writer's guidelines for #10 SASE. Unused mss only returned if accompanied by SASE.

Nonfiction: Humor, inspirational and religious. Buys 10-15 mss/year. Send complete ms. Length: 500-2,000 words. Pays $15-50 for assigned articles; pays $15-35 for unsolicited articles.

Photos: Send photos with submissions. Reviews prints. Offers no additonal payment for photos accepted with ms. Identification of subjects required. Buys one-time rights.

Poetry: Traditional. Buys 10-15 poems/year. Submit maximum 10 poems. Pays $10-15.

Tips: "Seasonal articles related to church year and on national holidays are welcome."

DAILY MEDITATION, Box 2710, San Antonio TX 78299. Editor: Ruth S. Paterson. Quarterly. Byline given. Rights purchased vary. **Payment on acceptance.** Submit seasonal material 6 months in advance. Sample copy 50¢.

Nonfiction: "Inspirational, self-improvement and nonsectarian religious articles, 750-1,600 words, showing the path to greater spiritual growth." Pays 1½-2¢/word.

Fillers: Length: 400 words maximum.

Poetry: Inspirational. Length: 16 lines maximum. Pays 14¢/line.

Tips: "All our material is freelance submission for consideration except our meditations, which are staff written. We buy approximately 250 manuscripts a year. We must see finished manuscripts; no queries, please. Checking copy is sent upon publication."

DECISION, Billy Graham Evangelistic Association, 1300 Harmon Place, Minneapolis MN 55403-1988. (612)338-0500. Editor: Roger C. Palms. 25% freelance written. Works each year with small number of new/unpublished writers, as well as a solid stable of experienced writers. A magazine, published 11 times per year, "to set forth to every reader the Good News of salvation in Jesus Christ with such vividness and clarity that he or she will be drawn to make a commitment to Christ; to encourage, teach and strengthen Christians." Circ. 2 million. Pays on publication. Byline given. Buys first rights and assigns work-made-for-hire manuscripts, articles, projects. Include telephone number with submission. Submit seasonal/holiday material 10 months in advance; other mss published up to 1 year after acceptance. No simultaneous submissions. Reports in 2 months on mss. Sample copy for 8½ × 11 SAE and 4 first class stamps; writer's guidelines for #10 SASE.
Nonfiction: How-to, motivational, personal experience and religious. "No personality-centered articles or articles which are issue oriented or critical of denominations." Buys approximately 50 mss/year. Send complete ms. Length: 400-1,800 words. Pays $35-200. Pays expenses of writers on assignment.
Photos: State availability of photos with submission. Reviews prints. Captions, model releases and identification of subjects required. Buys one-time rights.
Tips: "We are seeking personal conversion testimonies and personal experience articles which show how God intervened in a person's daily life and the way in which Scripture was applied to the experience in helping to solve the problem. The conversion testimonies describe in first person what author's life was like before he/she became a Christian, how he/she committed one's life to Christ and what tangible difference He has made since that decision. We also are looking for vignettes on various aspects of personal evangelism. SASE required with submissions."

DISCIPLESHIP JOURNAL, NavPress, a division of The Navigators, P.O. Box 6000, Colorado Springs CO 80934. (719)528-5363 ext. 291. FAX: (719)598-7128. Editor: Susan Maycinik. 90% freelance written. Works with a small number of new/unpublished writers each year. Bimonthly magazine on Christian discipleship. "The mission of *Discipleship Journal* is to help believers develop a deeper relationship with Jesus Christ, and to provide practical help in understanding the scriptures and applying them to daily life and ministry." Estab. 1981. Circ. 90,000. **Pays on acceptance.** Publishes ms an average of 6 months after acceptance. Byline given. Buys first North American serial rights and second serial (reprint) rights. Submit seasonal/holiday material 6 months in advance. Simultaneous queries, and simultaneous and previously published submissions OK. Query for electronic submissions. Reports in 1 month on queries; 2 months on mss. Sample copy and writer's guidelines for 9 × 12 SAE and 7 first class stamps.
Nonfiction: Book excerpts (rarely); how-to (grow in Christian faith and disciplines; help others grow as Christians; serve people in need; understand and apply the Bible); inspirational; interview/profile (focusing on one aspect of discipleship); and interpretation/application of the Bible. No personal testimony; humor; anything not directly related to Christian life and faith; politically partisan articles. Buys 80 mss/year. Query with published clips or send complete ms. Length: 500-3,000 words. Pays 3¢/word reprint; 10-12¢/word first rights. Pays the expenses of writers on assignment.
Tips: "Our articles are meaty, not fluffy. Study writer's guidelines and back issues and try to use similar approaches. Don't preach. Polish before submitting. About half of the articles in each issue are related to one theme. Freelancers should write to request theme list. We are looking for more practical articles on ministering to others and more articles dealing with world missions."

EVANGEL, Free Methodist Publishing House, 999 College Ave., Winona Lake IN 46590. (219)267-7161. Editor: Vera Bethel. 100% freelance written. Weekly magazine. Audience is 65% female, 35% male; married, 25-31 years old, mostly city dwellers, high school graduates, mostly nonprofessional. Circ. 35,000. Pays on publication. Publishes ms an average of 1 year after acceptance. Buys simultaneous rights, second serial (reprint) rights or one-time rights. Submit seasonal/holiday material 3 months in advance. Reports in 1 month. Sample copy and writer's guidelines for 6 × 9 SAE with 2 first class stamps.
Nonfiction: Interview (with ordinary person who is doing something extraordinary in his community, in service to others); profile (of missionary or one from similar service profession who is contributing significantly to society); and personal experience (finding a solution to a problem common to young adults; coping with handicapped child, for instance, or with a neighborhood problem. Story of how God-given strength or insight saved a situation). Buys 100 mss/year. Submit complete ms. Length: 300-1,000 words. Pays $10-25.
Photos: Purchased with accompanying ms. Captions required. Send prints. Pays $5-10 for 8 × 10 b&w glossy prints.
Fiction: Religious themes dealing with contemporary issues dealt with from a Christian frame of reference. Story must "go somewhere." Buys 50 mss/year. Submit complete ms. Length: 1,200 words. Pays $45.
Poetry: Free verse, haiku, light verse, traditional and religious. Buys 50 poems/year. Submit maximum 6 poems. Length: 4-24 lines. Pays $10.
Tips: "Seasonal material will get a second look (won't be rejected so easily) because we get so little. Write an attention grabbing lead followed by a body of article that says something worthwhile. Relate the lead to some of the universal needs of the reader—promise in that lead to help the reader in some way. Remember that everybody is interested most in himself. Lack of SASE brands author as a nonprofessional; I seldom

even bother to read the script. If the writer doesn't want the script back, it probably has no value for me, either."

THE EVANGELICAL BEACON, 1515 E. 66th St., Minneapolis MN 55423. (612)866-3343. FAX: (612)866-7539. Editor: George Keck. 30% freelance written. Works with a small number of new/unpublished writers each year. Denominational magazine of the Evangelical Free Church of America—evangelical Protestant readership; published 17 times/year (every third Monday, except for a 4-week interval, June-August). Estab. 1931. Pays on publication. Publishes ms an average of 6 months after acceptance. Rights purchased vary with author and material. Buys first rights or all rights, and some reprints. Reports in 10 weeks. Sample copy and writer's guidelines for 75¢.
Nonfiction: Articles on the church, Christ-centered human interest and personal testimony articles, well researched on current issues of religious interest. Desires crisp, imaginative, original writing—not sermons on paper. Length: 250-2,000 words. Pays 3-4¢/word with extra payment on some articles, at discretion of editor.
Photos: Prefers 8×10 b&w photos. Pays $10 minimum.
Fiction: Not much fiction used, but will consider. Length: 100-1,500 words.
Poetry: Very little poetry used. Pays variable rate, $3.50 minimum.
Tips: "Articles need to be helpful to the average Christian—encouraging, challenging, instructive. Also needs material presenting reality of the Christian faith to nonChristians. Some tie-in with the Evangelical Free Church of America is helpful but not required."

EVANGELIZING TODAY'S CHILD, Child Evangelism Fellowship Inc., Warrenton MO 63383. (314)456-4321. Editor: Elsie Lippy. 75% freelance written. Prefers to work with published/established writers. Bimonthly magazine. "Our purpose is to equip Christians to win the world's children to Christ and disciple them. Our readership is Sunday school teachers, Christian education leaders and children's workers in every phase of Christian ministry to children up to 12 years old." Estab. 1942. Circ. 22,000. Pays within 90 days of acceptance. Publishes ms an average of 6 months after acceptance. Byline given. Pays a kill fee if assigned. Buys first serial rights. Submit seasonal/holiday material 6 months in advance. Simultaneous queries OK. Reports in 3 weeks on queries; 2 months on mss. Free sample copy; writer's guidelines with SASE.
Nonfiction: Unsolicited articles welcomed from writers with Christian education training or current experience in working with children. Buys 25 mss/year. Query. Length: 1,200-1,500. Pays 6-8¢/word.
Photos: Submissions of photos on speculation accepted. Needs photos of children or related subjects. Pays $25 for 8×10 b&w glossy prints; $100 for transparencies.

THE FAMILY, Daughters of St. Paul, 50 St. Paul's Ave., Boston MA 02130. (617)522-8911. Editor: Sr. Mary Lea Hill. Managing Editor: Sr. Donna William Giaimo. Monthly magazine on Catholic family life. "*The Family* magazine stresses the special place of the family within society as an irreplaceable center of life, love and faith. Articles on timely, pertinent issues help families approach today's challenges with a faith perspective and a spirit of commitment to the Gospel of Jesus Christ." Estab. 1953. Pays on publication. Publishes ms an average of 6 months after acceptance. Byline given. Buys first and second serial (reprint) rights. Reimbursement for reprints varies. Submit seasonal/holiday material 5 months in advance. Previously published submissions OK. Sample copy $1.75 with 8½×11 SAE with 5 first class stamps. Writer's guidelines for #10 SASE.
Nonfiction: Humor, inspirational, interview/profile, religious. Buys 70 mss/year. Send complete ms. Length: 500-1,500 words. Pays $50-150. Also may pay in contributor's copies.
Photos: Send photos with submission. Reviews 4×5 transparencies. Captions, model releases and identification of subjects required. Buys one-time rights.
Fiction: Humorous, religious, slice-of-life vignettes, family. Buys 12 mss/year. Send complete ms. Length: 1,000-2,000 words. Pays $50-150.
Fillers: Anecdotes, short humor. Buys 30/year. Length: 100-300 words. Pays $10-30.

THE GEM, Churches of God, General Conference, P.O. Box 926, Findlay OH 45839. (419)424-1961. Editor: Marilyn Rayle Kern. 98% freelance written. Works with a small number of new/unpublished writers each year. "We are backlogged with submissions but still hope to find new submissions of high quality." Weekly magazine; adult and youth church school take-home paper. "Our readers expect to find true-to-life help for daily living as growing Christians." Estab. 1866. Circ. 8,000. Pays on publication. Publishes ms an average of 9 months after acceptance. Byline given. Not copyrighted. Buys simultaneous rights, first serial rights or second serial (reprint) rights. Submit seasonal/holiday material 3 months in advance. Simultaneous and previously published submissions OK. Query for electronic submission. Reports in 6 months. Sample copy and writer's guidelines for #10 SASE (unless more than 1 copy).
Nonfiction: General interest, historical/nostalgic, humor, inspirational and personal experience. No preachy, judgmental articles, or use of quotes from other sources. Buys 50 mss/year. Send complete ms. Length: 600-1,600 words. Pays $10-15.

Fiction: Adventure, historical, humorous and religious. No mss which are preachy or inauthentic. Buys 50 mss/year. Send complete ms. Length: 1,000-1,600 words. Pays $10-15.

Fillers: Anecdotes and short humor. Buys 40/year. Length: 100-500 words. Pays $5-7.50.

Tips: "Humor, which does not put down people and leads the reader to understand a valuable lesson, is always in short supply."

‡**GROUP MAGAZINE**, 2890 N. Monroe, Box 481, Loveland CO 80539. (303)669-3836. Editor: Joani Schultz. Managing Editor: Cindy Parolini. 60% freelance written. 8 times/year magazine covering youth ministry. "Writers must be actively involved in youth ministry. Articles we accept are practical, not theoretical, and focused for local church youth workers." Estab. 1974. Circ. 57,000. **Pays on acceptance.** Publishes ms an average of 6 months after acceptance. Byline given. Offers $20 kill fee. Buys all rights. Submit seasonal/holiday material 7 months in advance. Reports in 1 month. Sample copy for 8½×11 SAE with 3 first class stamps. Writer's guidelines for 8½×11 SAE with 2 first class stamps.

Nonfiction: Rick Lawrence, articles editor. How-to (youth ministry issues). No personal testimony, theological or lecture-style articles. Buys 50-60 mss/year. Query. Length: 500-1,800 words. Pays $75-200. Sometimes pays for phone calls on agreement.

Photos: State availability of photos with submission. Model releases and identification of subjects required. Buys all rights.

GROUP'S JUNIOR HIGH MINISTRY MAGAZINE, Group Publishing, 2890 N. Monroe Ave., P.O. Box 481, Loveland CO 80539. (303)669-3836. FAX: (303)669-3269. Editorial Director: Joani Schultz. 90% freelance written (assigned). Magazine published 5 times/year for leaders of junior-high Christian youth groups. "How-to articles for junior high membership building, worship planning, handling specific group problems and improving as a leader; hints for parents of junior highers; special style-formatted junior high group meetings on topics like competition, faith in action, seasonal themes, friendship, dealing with life situations and service projects." Estab. 1974. Circ. 27,000. **Pays on acceptance.** Publishes ms an average of 3 months after acceptance. Byline given. Offer $25 kill fee. Buys all rights and makes work-for-hire assignments. Submit seasonal/holiday material 6 months in advance. Query for electronic submissions. Sample copy for 9×12 SAE with $1 postage; writer's guidelines for SASE.

Nonfiction: How-to, humor, inspirational/motivational, personal experience, religious/Bible studies, and curriculum. No fiction. Buys 65 assigned mss/year. Query. Length: 500-1,700. Pays $75-100 for assigned articles. Sometimes pays expenses of writers on assignment.

Photos: Send photos with submission. Reviews contact sheets, transparencies and prints. Offers $20-50/b&w photo; $50-150/color photo. Model releases required. Buys one-time rights (occasionally buys additional rights).

Columns/Departments: Parent's Page (brief helps for parents of junior highers; for example, tips on discipline, faith, communication, building close family, parent-self understanding, understanding junior highers and values). Buys 30 mss/year. Send complete ms. Length: 150 words. Pays $25. One Group's Success, (a one-page article on a successful junior high group). Length: 500 words. Pays $75. New Jr. High Resources, (reviews on books, curriculum and videos for junor high leaders.) 200 words. The actual resource serves as payment.

Tips: "Writers who are also successful junior high workers or teachers have the best chance of being published in *Group's Jr. High Ministry* simply because they know the kids. We need authors who can give our readers practical tips for ministry with junior highers. We need step-by-step experiential, Bible-oriented, fun meetings for leaders to do with junior high youth groups. The meetings must help the kids apply their Christian faith to life and must follow the standard format in the magazine."

‡**GROWING CHURCHES**, 127 9th Ave., N., Nashville TN 37234. (615)251-2062. Editor: Gary Hardin. 30% freelance written. Works with new/unpublished writers. Quarterly. For Southern Baptist pastors, staff and volunteer church leaders. Uses some freelance material. **Pays on acceptance.** Publishes ms an average of 1 year after acceptance. Byline given. Buys all rights. Free sample copy and writer's guidelines for SAE with 2 first class stamps.

Nonfiction: "This is a magazine that focuses on practical church growth ideas for Southern Baptists." Length: 1,200-1,800 words. Pays 5½¢/word.

Tips: "Send query letter. Articles must be targeted to Southern Baptist churches and their leaders. Type at 54 characters per line, 25 lines per page, double-spaced. Not responsible for manuscripts not accompanied by return postage."

GUIDEPOSTS MAGAZINE, 747 3rd Ave., New York NY 10017. Editor: Van Varner. 30% freelance written. "Works with a small number of new/unpublished writers each year, and reads all unsolicited manuscripts. *Guideposts* is an inspirational monthly magazine for people of all faiths, in which men and women from all walks of life tell in first-person narrative how they overcame obstacles, rose above failures, handled sorrow, learned to master themselves and became more effective people through faith in God." Estab. 1945. Publishes ms an "indefinite" number of months after acceptance. Pays 25% kill fee for assigned articles. Byline given.

"Most of our stories are ghosted articles, so the writer would not get a byline unless it was his/her own story." Buys all rights and second serial (reprint) rights.

Nonfiction and Fillers: Articles and features should be written in simple, anecdotal style with an emphasis on human interest. Short mss of approximately 250-750 words (pays $50-200) would be considered for such features as Quiet People and general one-page stories. Full-length mss, 750-1,500 words, pays $200-400. All mss should be typed, double-spaced and accompanied by a stamped, self-addressed envelope. Annually awards scholarships to high school juniors and seniors in writing contest. Buys 40-60 unsolicited mss/year. Pays expenses of writers on assignment.

Tips: "Study the magazine before you try to write for it. Each story must make a single spiritual point. The freelancer would have the best chance of breaking in by aiming for a one-page or maybe two-page article. That would be very short, say two and a half pages of typescript, but in a small magazine such things are very welcome. Sensitively written anecdotes are extremely useful. And they are much easier to just sit down and write than to have to go through the process of preparing a query. They should be warm, well written, intelligent and upbeat. We like personal narratives that are true and have some universal relevance, but the religious element does not have to be driven home with a sledge hammer. A writer succeeds with us if he or she can write a true article in short-story form with scenes, drama, tension and a resolution of the problem presented." Address short items to Rick Hamlin.

HICALL, Gospel Publishing House, 1445 Boonville Ave., Springfield MO 65802. (417)862-2781, ext. 4349. Editor: Deanna Harris. Mostly freelance written. Eager to work with new/unpublished writers. Assemblies of God (denominational) weekly magazine of Christian fiction and articles for church-oriented teenagers, 12-17. Circ. 85,000. **Pays on acceptance.** Publishes ms an average of 15 months after acceptance. Byline given. Buys first North American serial rights, one-time rights, simultaneous rights and second serial (reprint) rights. Submit seasonal/holiday material 18 months in advance. Simultaneous and previously published submissions OK—if typed, double-spaced, on 8½×11 paper. Reports in 6 weeks. Sample copy for 8×11 SAE and 2 first class stamps; writer's guidelines for SAE.

Nonfiction: Book excerpts; historical; general interest; how-to (deal with various life problems); humor; inspirational; and personal experience. Buys 80-100 mss/year. Send complete ms. Length: 500-1,500 words. Pays 2-3¢/word.

Photos: Photos purchased with or without accompanying ms. Pays $25/8×10 b&w glossy print; $30/35mm.

Fiction: Adventure, humorous, mystery, romance, suspense, western and religious. Buys 80-100 mss/year. Send complete ms. Length: 500-1,500 words. Pays 2-3¢/word.

Poetry: Free verse, light verse and traditional. Buys 30 poems/year. Length: 10-30 lines. Pays 25¢/line, minimum of $5 (first rights).

Fillers: Clippings, anecdotes, short humor and newsbreaks. Buys 30/year. Pays 2-3¢/word.

INTERLIT, David C. Cook Foundation, Cook Square, Elgin IL 60120. (708)741-2400, ext. 316. Editor: Tim Bascom. 80% freelance written on assignment. Works with a small number of new/unpublished writers each year. Quarterly journal. Emphasizes sharpening skills in Christian journalism and publishing. Especially for editors, publishers and writers in the third world (developing countries). Also goes to missionaries, broadcasters and educational personnel in the U.S. Circ. 6,000. **Pays on acceptance.** Publishes ms an average of 6 months after acceptance. Buys all rights. Reports in 6 weeks. Free sample copy.

Nonfiction: Technical and how-to articles about all aspects of publishing, writing and literacy. "Please study publication and query before submitting manuscripts." Buys 7 mss/issue, mostly on assignment. Length: 500-1,500 words. Pays 8-10¢/word.

Photos: Purchased with accompanying ms only. Uses b&w. Query or send prints. Captions required.

THE JEWISH WEEKLY NEWS, Bennett-Scott Publications Corp., 99 Mill St., P.O. Box 1569, Springfield MA 01101. (413)739-4771. 25% freelance written. Jewish news and features, secular and non-secular; World Judaism; arts (New England based). Estab. 1945. Circ. 2,500. Pays on publication. Publishes ms an average of 2 months after acceptance. Byline given. Not copyrighted. Buys first North American serial rights and second serial (reprint) rights. Submit seasonal/holiday material 2 months in advance. Simultaneous and previously published submissions OK. Query for electronic submissions. Sample copy for 9×12 SAE with 5 first class stamps.

Nonfiction: Interview/profile, religious and travel. Special issues include Jewish New Year (September); Chanukah (December); Home Issues (March); Bar/Bat Mitzvahs (May). Buys 61 mss/year. Query with published clips. Length: 300-1,000 words. Pays $5.

Photos: Send photos with submission. Reviews 5×7 prints. Offers no additional payment for photos accepted with ms. Identification of subjects required.

Columns/Departments: Jewish Kitchen (Kosher recipes), 300-500 words. Buys 10 mss/year. Query with published clips. Length: 300-5,000 words. Pays 50¢/inch.

Fiction: Sheila Thompson, editor. Slice-of-life vignettes. Buys 5 mss/year. Query with published clips. Length: 750-1,000 words. Pays 50¢/inch.

LIGHT AND LIFE, Free Methodist Church of North America, P.O. Box 535002, Indianapolis IN 46253-5002. FAX: (317)244-1247. Editor: Bob Haslam. 35% freelance written. Works with a small number of new/unpublished writers each year. Monthly magazine. Emphasizes evangelical Christianity with Wesleyan slant for a cross section of adults. Estab. 1860. Circ. 40,000. Pays on publication. Publishes ms an average of 6 months after acceptance. Byline given. Prefers first serial rights; rarely buys second serial (reprint) rights. Submit seasonal/holiday material 6 months in advance. Reports in 6 weeks. Sample copy and guidelines $1.50; writer's guidelines for SASE.

Nonfiction: "Each issue includes a mini-theme (3 or 4 articles addressing contemporary topics such as entertainment media, personal relationships, Christians as citizens), so freelancers should request our schedule of mini-theme topics. We also need fresh, upbeat articles showing the average layperson how to be Christlike at home, work and play." Submit complete ms. Buys 70-80 unsolicited ms/year. Pays 4¢/word. Sometimes pays expenses of writers on assignment.

Photos: Purchased without accompanying ms. Send prints. Pays $5-35 for b&w photos. Offers additional payment for photos accepted with accompanying ms.

LIGUORIAN, Liguori MO 63057. FAX: (314)464-8449. Editor: Rev. Allan Weinert. Managing Editor: Francine M. O'Connor. 50% freelance written. Prefers to work with published/established writers; works with a small number of new/unpublished writers each year. Monthly. For families with Catholic religious convictions. Estab. 1913. Circ. 525,000. **Pays on acceptance.** Publishes ms an average of 3-4 months after acceptance. Byline given "except on short fillers and jokes." Buys all rights but will reassign rights to author *after* publication upon written request. Submit seasonal material 6 months in advance. Query for electronic submissions. Reports in 6 weeks. Sample copy and writer's guidelines for 6×9 SAE with 3 first class stamps.

Nonfiction: "Pastoral, practical and personal approach to the problems and challenges of people today. No travelogue approach or unresearched ventures into controversial areas. Also, no material found in secular publications—fad subjects that already get enough press, pop psychology, negative or put-down articles." Buys 60 unsolicited mss/year. Length: 400-2,000 words. Pays 10-12¢/word. Sometimes pays expenses of writers on assignment.

Photos: Photographs on assignment only unless submitted with and specific to article.

LIVE, 1445 Boonville Ave., Springfield MO 65802. (417)862-2781. Editor: John T. Maempa. 100% freelance written. Works with several new/unpublished writers each year. Weekly. For adults in Assemblies of God Sunday schools. Circ. 180,000. **Pays on acceptance.** Publishes ms an average of 1 year after acceptance. Not copyrighted. Submit seasonal material 1 year in advance; do not mention Santa Claus, Halloween or Easter bunnies. Reports on material within 6 weeks. Submissions held for further consideration may require more time. Free sample copy and writer's guidelines for 7½×10½ SASE and 35¢ postage. Letters without SASE will not be answered.

Nonfiction: Articles with reader appeal emphasizing some phase of Christian living presented in a down-to-earth manner. Biography or missionary material using fiction techniques. Historical, scientific or nature material with spiritual lesson. "Be accurate in detail and factual material. Writing for Christian publications is a ministry. The spiritual emphasis must be an integral part of your material." Prefers not to see material on highly controversial subjects but would appreciate articles on contemporary issues and concerns (e.g. substance abuse, AIDS, euthanasia, cults, integrity, etc.). Buys about 120 mss/year. Length: 1,000-1,600 words. Pays 3¢/word for first serial rights; 2¢/word for second serial (reprint) rights, according to the value of the material and the amount of editorial work necessary. "Please do not send large numbers of articles at one time."

Photos: Color photos or transparencies purchased with mss, or on assignment. Pay open.

Fiction: "Present believable characters working out their problems according to Bible principles; in other words, present Christianity in action without being preachy. We use very few serials, but we will consider three- to four-part stories if each part conforms to average word length for short stories. Each part must contain a spiritual emphasis and have enough suspense to carry the reader's interest from one week to the next. Stories should be true to life but not what we would feel is bad to set before the reader as a pattern for living. Stories should not put parents, teachers, ministers or other Christian workers in a bad light. Setting, plot and action should be realistic, with strong motivation. Characterize so that the people will live in your story. Construct your plot carefully so that each incident moves naturally and sensibly toward crisis and conclusion. An element of conflict is necessary in fiction. Short stories should be written from one viewpoint only. We do not accept fiction based on incidents in the Bible." Length: 1,200-1,600 words. Pays 3¢/word for first serial rights; 2¢/word for second serial (reprint) rights. "Please do not send large numbers of articles at one time."

Poetry: Traditional, free and blank verse. Length: 12-20 lines. "Please do not send large numbers of poems at one time." Pays 20¢/line.

Fillers: Brief and purposeful, usually containing an anecdote, and always with a strong evangelical emphasis. Length: 200-600 words.

LIVING WITH TEENAGERS, Baptist Sunday School Board, 127 9th Ave. N., Nashville TN 37234. (615)251-2273. Editor: Jimmy Hester. 50-75% freelance written. Works with a small number of new/unpublished writers each year. Quarterly magazine about teenagers for Baptist parents of teenagers. Estab. 1978. Circ. 50,000. Pays within 2 months of acceptance. Publishes ms an average of 18 months after acceptance. Buys all rights. Submit seasonal material 1 year in advance. Reports in 2 months. Sample copy for 9 × 12 SAE with 4 first class stamps; writer's guidelines for #10 SASE.

Nonfiction: "We are looking for a unique Christian element. We want a genuine insight into the teen/parent relationship." General interest (on communication, emotional problems, growing up, drugs and alcohol, leisure, sex education, spiritual growth, working teens and parents, money, family relationships and church relationships); inspirational; and personal experience. Buys 60 unsolicited mss/year. Query with clips of previously published work. Length: 600-2,000 words. Pays 5½¢/published word.

Fiction: Humorous and religious, but must relate to parent/teen relationship. "No stories from the teen's point of view." Buys 2 mss/issue. Query with clips of previously published work. Length: 600-2,000 words. Pays 5½¢/published word.

Poetry: Free verse, light verse, traditional and devotional inspirational; all must relate to parent/teen relationship. Buys 3 mss/issue. Submit 5 poems maximum. Length: 35 lines maximum. Pays $2.10 plus $1.25/line for 1-7 lines; $5.40 plus 75¢/line for 8 lines minimum.

Tips: "A writer can meet our needs if they have something to say to parents of teenagers concerning an issue the parents are confronting with the teenager."

THE LOOKOUT, 8121 Hamilton Ave., Cincinnati OH 45231. (513)931-4050. Editor: Mark A. Taylor. 50-60% freelance written. Eager to work with new/unpublished writers. Weekly for adults and young adults attending Sunday schools and Christian churches. **Pays on acceptance.** Publishes ms an average of 4 months after acceptance. Byline given. Buys first serial rights, one-time rights, second serial (reprint) rights, or simultaneous rights. Simultaneous submissions OK. Reports in 2 months, sometimes longer. Sample copy and writer's guidelines 50¢. Guidelines only for #10 SASE.

Nonfiction: "Seeks stories about real people or Sunday school classes; items that shed Biblical light on matters of contemporary controversy; and items that motivate, that lead the reader to ask, 'Why shouldn't I try that?' or 'Why couldn't our Sunday school class accomplish this?' Articles should tell how real people are involved for Christ. In choosing topics, *The Lookout* considers timeliness, the church and national calendar, and the ability of the material to fit the above guidelines. Tell us about ideas that are working in your Sunday school and in the lives of its members. Remember to aim at laymen." Submit complete ms. Length: 1,200-1,800 words. Pays 4-7¢/word. We also use inspirational short pieces. "About 600-800 words is a good length for these. Relate an incident that illustrates a point without preaching." Pays 4-6¢/word.

Fiction: "A short story is printed in many issues; it is usually between 1,200-1,800 words long and should be as true to life as possible while remaining inspirational and helpful. Use familiar settings and situations. Most often we use stories with a Christian slant." Pays 5-6¢/word.

Photos: Reviews b&w prints, 4 × 6 or larger. Pays $5-35. Pays $50-75 for color transparencies for covers and inside use. Needs photos of people, especially adults in a variety of settings. Send to Photo Editor, Standard Publishing, at the above address.

‡**THE LUTHERAN, Magazine of the Evangelical Lutheran Church in America**, Evangelical Lutheran Church in America, 8765 W. Higgins Rd., Chicago IL 60631. (312)380-2540. Editor: Edgar R. Trexler. Managing Editor: Roger R. Kahle. 30% freelance written. Biweekly magazine. "Audience is lay people in church. News and activities of the Evangelical Lutheran Church in America, news of the world of religion, ethical reflections on issues in society, personal Christian experience." Estab. 1831. Circ. 1.25 million. **Pays on acceptance.** Publishes ms an average of 3 months after acceptance. Byline given. Offers kill fee of half of acceptance fee. Buys first rights. Submit seasonal/holiday material 4 months in advance. Query for electronic submissions. Reports in 3 weeks on queries; 6 weeks on mss. Free sample copy and writer's guidelines.

Nonfiction: David L. Miller. Inspirational, interview/profile, personal experience, photo feature, religious. "No articles unrelated to the world of religion." Buys 40 mss/year. Query with published clips. Length: 300-2,000 words. Pays $400-1,000 for assigned articles; $50-400 for unsolicited articles. Pays expenses of writers on assignment.

Photos: Send photos with submission. Reviews contact sheets, transparencies and prints. Offers $10-50 per photo. Captions and identification of subjects required. Buys one-time rights.

Columns/Departments: Lite Side (humor—church, religious), 25-100 words. Send complete ms. Length: 25-100 words. Pays $5.

Tips: "Writers have the best chance selling us feature articles."

LUTHERAN FORUM, at the Wartburg, Bradley Ave., Mt. Vernon NY 10552. (914)699-1226. Editor: Dr. Paul R. Hunlicky. Works with a small number of new/unpublished writers each year. Quarterly magazine. For church leadership, clerical and lay. Circ. 3,500. Pays on publication. Publishes ms an average of 6 months after acceptance. Byline given. Rights purchased vary with author and material; buys all rights, first North American serial rights, second serial (reprint) rights and simultaneous rights. Will consider simultaneous submissions. Reports in 9 weeks. Sample copy $1.50, SAE and 4 first class stamps; writer's guidelines for #10 SASE.

Nonfiction: Articles about important issues and developments in the church's institutional life and in its cultural/social setting. No purely devotional/inspirational material. Buys 2-3 mss/year. Query or submit complete ms. Length: 1,000-3,000 words. Payment varies; $30 minimum. Informational, how-to, interview, profile, think articles and exposé. Length: 500-3,000 words. Pays $25-75.

Photos: Purchased with ms and only with captions. Prefers 4×5 prints. Pays $15 minimum.

MARIAN HELPERS BULLETIN, Eden Hill, Stockbridge MA 01263. (413)298-3691. FAX: (413)298-3583. Editor: Rev. Gerald Ornowski, M.I.C. 60% freelance written. Bimonthly magazine for average Catholics of varying ages with moderate religious views and general education. Circ. 1 million. **Pays on acceptance.** Byline given. Submit seasonal material 6 months in advance. Reports in 4 months. Sample copy $1. Unsolicited mss will not be returned.

Nonfiction: "Articles on spiritual, devotional and moral topics for a Catholic audience. Use a positive, practical approach, well done without being sophisticated." Buys 18-24 mss/year. Length: 300-900 words. Pays 3-10¢/word.

Photos: Photos should be sent to complement articles.

Tips: "Human interest stories are very valuable, from which personal reflection is stimulated."

MARRIAGE & FAMILY, St. Meinrad IN 47577. (812)357-8011. Managing Editor: Kass Dotterweich. 75% freelance written. Monthly magazine. Circ. 28,000. **Pays on acceptance.** Byline given. Buys first international serial rights, first book reprint option, and control of other reprint rights. Query. Reports in 6 weeks. Sample copy $1 with 9×12 SAE; writer's guidelines for #10 SASE.

Nonfiction: Articles which affirm marriage and parenting as an awesome vocation created by God; and personal essays relating amusing, heartwarming or insightful incidents which reflect the rich human side of marriage and family life. Length: 1,500-2,000 words maximum. Pays 7¢/word. Pays expenses of writers on assignment.

Photos: Attention, art director. Reviews 8×10 b&w glossy prints and transparencies or 35mm slides. Pays $150/4-color cover or center spread photo. Uses approximately 6-8 b&w photos and an occasional illustration inside. Pays variable rate on publication. Photos of couples, families and individuals especially desirable. Model releases required.

Poetry: Short, free verse. Pays $15 on publication; please include phone number.

MENNONITE BRETHREN HERALD, 3-169 Riverton Ave., Winnipeg, Manitoba R2L 2E5 Canada. FAX: (204)667-0680. Contact: Editor. 25% freelance written. Family publication "read mainly by people of the Mennonite faith, reaching a wide cross section of professional and occupational groups, but also including many homemakers. Readership includes people from both urban and rural communities." Biweekly. Estab. 1962. Circ. 13,500. Pays on publication. Publishes ms an average of 4-6 months after acceptance. Not copyrighted. Byline given. Sample copy for $1 with 9×12 SAE and IRCs. Reports in 6 months.

Nonfiction: Articles with a Christian family orientation; youth directed, Christian faith and life, and current issues. Wants articles critiquing the values of a secular society, attempting to relate Christian living to the practical situations of daily living; showing how people have related their faith to their vocations. Length: 1,500 words. Pays $30-40. Pays the expenses of writers on assignment.

Photos: Photos purchased with mss; pays $5.

THE MESSENGER OF THE SACRED HEART, Apostleship of Prayer, 661 Greenwood Ave., Toronto, Ontario M4J 4B3 Canada. (416)466-1195. Editor: Rev. F.J. Power, S.J. For "Canadian and U.S. Catholics interested in developing a life of prayer and spirituality; stresses the great value of our ordinary actions and lives." 20% freelance written. Monthly. Estab. 1891. Circ. 16,500. Buys first rights only. Byline given. **Pays on acceptance.** Submit seasonal material 5 months in advance. Reports in 1 month. Sample copy $1 and 7½×10½ SAE; writer's guidelines for #10 SASE.

Fiction: Religious/inspirational. Stories about people, adventure, heroism, humor, drama. Buys 12 mss/year. Send complete ms with SAE and IRCs. Unsolicited manuscripts, unaccompanied by return postage, will not be returned. Length: 750-1,500 words. Pays 4¢ word.

Tips: "Develop a story that sustains interest to the end. Do not preach, but use plot and characters to convey the message or theme. Aim to move the heart as well as the mind. Before sending, cut out unnecessary or unrelated words or sentences. If you can, add a light touch or a sense of humor to the story. Your ending should have impact, leaving a moral or faith message for the reader."

MODERN LITURGY, Suite 290, 160 E. Virginia St., San Jose CA 95112. Editor: John Gallen. 80% freelance written. Magazine; 40-48 pages published 10 times/year for Roman Catholic ministers who plan group worship, services; teachers of religion. Circ. 15,000. Buys first serial rights. Pays on publication. Publishes ms an average of 6 months after acceptance. Byline given. Query for electronic submissions. Reports in 6 weeks. Sample copy $4; free writer's guidelines for SASE.

Nonfiction and Fiction: Articles (historical, theological and practical) that address special interest topics in the field of liturgy; example services; and liturgical art forms (music, poetry, stories, dances, dramatizations, etc.). Practical, creative ideas; and art forms for use in worship and/or religious education classrooms. "No material out of our field." Buys 10 mss/year. Query. Length: 750-2,000 words. Pays with subscriptions, copies, and negotiated cost stipend for regular contributors.
Tips: "Don't be preachy; use too much jargon; or make articles too long."

MOODY MONTHLY, Moody Bible Institute, 820 N. LaSalle Dr., Chicago IL 60610. (312)329-2163. FAX: (312)329-2144. Senior Editors: Andrew Scheer. 40% freelance written. A monthly magazine for evangelical Christianity. "Our readers are conservative, evangelical Christians highly active in their churches and concerned about family living." Estab. 1900. Circ. 160,000. **Pays on acceptance.** Publishes ms an average of 6-9 months after acceptance. Byline given. Offers $50 kill fee. Buys first North American serial rights. Submit seasonal/holiday material 9 months in advance. Query for electronic submissions. Reports in 1 month on queries; 2 months on mss. Sample copy for 10 × 13 SASE; writer's guidelines for #10 SASE.
Nonfiction: How-to (on living the Christian life), personal experience. Buys 60 mss/year. Query. Length: 750-2,000 words. Pays 10-15¢/word for assigned articles. Sometimes pays the expenses of writers on assignment.
Photos: State availability of photos with submission. Offers $35-50 per photo. Buys one-time rights.
Columns/Departments: First Person (the only article written for non-Christians; a personal conversion testimony written by the author [we will accept 'as told to's']; the objective is to tell a person's testimony in such a way that the reader will understand the gospel and want to receive Christ as Savior), 800-1,000 words; Just for Parents (provides practical anecdotal guidance for parents, solidly based on biblical principles), 1,300-1,500 words. Buys 30 mss/year. Query. Pays 10-15¢/word.

MY DAILY VISITOR, Our Sunday Visitor, Inc., 200 Noll Plaza, Huntington IN 46750. (219)356-8400. Editor: Jacquelyn M. Eckert. 99% freelance written. Bimonthly magazine on spirituality and scripture meditations. Circ. 30,000. **Pays on acceptance.** Publishes ms an average of 1 year after acceptance. Byline given. Not copyrighted. Buys one-time rights. Reports in 2 months. Sample copy and writer's guidelines for #10 SAE with 2 first class stamps. "Guest editors write on assignment basis only."
Nonfiction: Inspirational, personal experience, religious. Buys 12 mss/year. Query with published clips. Length: 175 words times number of days in month. Pays $100-200 for one month (28-31) of meditations. Sometimes pays writers 25 gratis copies.

NATIONAL CHRISTIAN REPORTER, Box 222198, Dallas TX 75222. (214)630-6495. Editor/General Manager: Spurgeon M. Dunnam III. Managing Editor: John A. Lovelace. 5% freelance written. Prefers to work with published/established writers. Weekly newspaper for an interdenominational national readership. Circ. 25,000. Pays on publication. Publishes ms an average of 1 month after acceptance. Byline given. Not copyrighted. Free sample copy and writer's guidelines.
Nonfiction: "We welcome short features, approximately 500 words. Articles need to have an explicit 'mainstream' Protestant angle. Write about a distinctly Christian response to human need or how a person's faith relates to a given situation. Preferably including evidence of participation in a local Protestant congregation." Send complete ms. Pays 4¢/word. Sometimes pays the expenses of writers on assignment.
Photos: Purchased with accompanying ms. "We encourage the submission of good action photos (5 × 7 or 8 × 10 b&w glossy prints) of the persons or situations in the article." Pays $10.
Poetry: "Good poetry welcomed on a religious theme." Length: 4-20 lines. Pays $2.

NORTH AMERICAN VOICE OF FATIMA, Fatima Shrine, Youngstown NY 14174. Editor: Rev. Paul M. Keeling, C.R.S.P. 40% freelance written. Works with a small number of new/unpublished writers each year. For Roman Catholic readership. Estab. 1961. Circ. 3,000. Pays on publication. Publishes ms an average of 2 months after acceptance. Not copyrighted. Buys first North American serial rights. Reports in 6 weeks. Free sample copy.
Nonfiction and Fiction: Inspirational, personal experience, historical and think articles. Religious and historical fiction. Length: 700 words. All material must have a religious slant. Pays 2¢/word.
Photos: B&w photos purchased with ms.

OBLATES, Missionary Association of Mary Immaculate, 15 S. 59th St., Belleville IL 62223-4694. (618)233-2238. Managing Editor: Jacqueline Lowery Corn. 30-50% freelance written. Prefers to work with published writers but will work with new/unpublished writers. Bimonthly inspirational magazine for Christians; audience mainly older adults. Circ. 450,000. **Pays on acceptance.** Usually publishes ms within 1 year after acceptance. Byline given. Buys first North American serial rights. Submit seasonal/holiday material 8 months in advance. Reports in 2 months. Sample copy and writer's guidelines for 6 × 9 or larger SAE with 2 first class stamps.
Nonfiction: Inspirational and personal experience with positive spiritual insights. No preachy, theological or research articles. Avoid current events and controversial topics. Send complete ms. Length: 500 words. Pays $75.

Poetry: Light verse—reverent, well written, perceptive, with traditional rhythm and rhyme. "Emphasis should be on inspiration, insight and relationship with God." Submit maximum 2 poems. Length: 8-16 lines. Pays $25.

Tips: "Our readership is made up mostly of mature Americans who are looking for comfort, encouragement, and a positive sense of applicable Christian direction to their lives. Focus on sharing of personal insight to problem (i.e. death or change), but must be positive, uplifting. We have well-defined needs for an established market, but are always on the lookout for exceptional work."

ORT REPORTER, Woman's American ORT, Inc., 315 Park Ave. So., New York NY 10010. (212)505-7700. Editor: Eve Jacobson. Assistant to the Editor: Freyda Reiss Weiss. 85% freelance written. Nonprofit journal published by Jewish women's organization. Quarterly magazine covering "Jewish topics, social issues, education, Mideast and women." Estab. 1966. Circ. 25,000. Payment time varies. Publishes ms ASAP after acceptance. Byline given. Buys first North American serial rights or second serial (reprint) rights. Submit seasonal/holiday material 6 months in advance. Reports "as soon as possible." Free sample copy with 9 × 12 SASE.

Nonfiction: Book excerpts, essays, general interest, humor, opinion. Buys approximately 40 mss/year. Send complete ms. Length: 500-3,000. Pays 15¢/word.

Photos: Send photos with submission. Reviews 5 × 7 prints. Offers $35-85 per photo. Identification of subjects required. Purchases "whatever rights photographer desires."

Columns/Departments: Books, Film, Stage, TV. Buys 4-10 mss/year. Send complete ms. Length: 200-2,000 words. Pays 15¢/word.

Fiction: Jewish novel excerpts. Buys 2 ms/year. Send complete ms. Pays 15¢/word, less for reprints.

Tips: "Simply send ms; do not call. First submission must be 'on spec.' Open Forum (opinion section) is most open to freelancers, although all are open. Looking for well-written essay on relevant topic that makes its point strongly—evokes response from reader."

THE OTHER SIDE, 1225 Dandridge St., Fredericksburg VA 22401. Editor: Mark Olson. Associate Editor: Dee Dee Risher. 50% freelance written. Prefers to work with published/established writers; works with a small number of new/unpublished writers each year. Magazine published bimonthly, focusing on "peace, justice and economic liberation from a radical Christian perspective." Circ. 15,000. **Pays on acceptance.** Publishes ms an average of 6 months after acceptance. Byline given. Buys all or first serial rights. Query for electronic submissions. Reports in 6 weeks. Sample copy $4.50; free writer's guidelines with #10 SASE.

Nonfiction: Niki Amarantides, managing editor. Current social, political and economic issues in the U.S. and around the world: personality profiles, interpretative essays, interviews, how-to's, personal experiences and investigative reporting. "Articles must be lively, vivid and down-to-earth, with a radical Christian perspective." Length: 500-6,000 words. Pays $25-300. Sometimes pays expenses of writers on assignment.

Photos: Cathleen Boint, art director. Photos or photo essays illustrating current social, political, or economic reality in the U.S. and Third World. Pays $15-75 for b&w and $50-300 for color.

Fiction: Barbara Moorman, fiction editor. "Short stories, humor and satire conveying insights and situations that will be helpful to Christians with a radical commitment to peace and justice." Length: 300-4,000 words. Pays $25-250.

Poetry: Rod Jellema, poetry editor. "Short, creative poetry that will be thought-provoking and appealing to radical Christians who have a strong commitment to spirituality, peace and justice." Length: 3-50 lines. No more than 4 poems may be submitted at one time by any one author. Pays $15-20.

Tips: "We're looking for tightly written pieces (1,000-1,500 words) on interesting and unusual Christians (or Christian groups) who are putting their commitment to peace and social justice into action in creative and useful ways. We're also looking for provocative analytical and reflective pieces dealing with contemporary social issues in the U.S. and abroad."

OUR FAMILY, Oblate Fathers of St. Mary's Province, P.O. Box 249, Battleford, Saskatchewan S0M 0E0 Canada. (306)937-7772. FAX: (306)937-7644. Editor: Nestor Gregoire. 60% freelance written. Prefers to work with published/established writers; works with a small number of new/unpublished writers each year. Monthly magazine for average family men and women with high school and early college education. Estab. 1949. Circ. 14,265. **Pays on acceptance.** Publishes ms an average of 6 months after acceptance. Byline given. Offers 100% kill fee. Generally purchases first North American serial rights; also buys all rights, simultaneous rights, second serial (reprint) rights or one-time rights. Submit seasonal/holiday material 4 months in advance. Simultaneous and previously published submissions OK. Reports in 1 month. Sample copy $2.50 in postage and 9 × 12 SAE; writer's guidelines for #10 SAE and 45¢ (Canadian funds). U.S. postage cannot be used in Canada.

Nonfiction: Humor (related to family life or husband/wife relations); inspirational (anything that depicts people responding to adverse conditions with courage, hope and love); personal experience (with religious dimensions); and photo feature (particularly in search of photo essays on human/religious themes and on persons whose lives are an inspiration to others). Phone queries OK. Buys 72-88 unsolicited mss/year. Pays expenses of writers on assignment.

Photos: Photos purchased with or without accompanying ms. Pays $35 for 5×7 or larger b&w glossy prints and color photos (which are converted into b&w). Offers additional payment for photos accepted with ms (payment for these photos varies according to their quality). Free photo spec sheet with SASE.

Poetry: Avant-garde, free verse, haiku, light verse and traditional. Buys 4-10 poems/issue. Length: 3-30 lines. Pays 75¢-$1/line.

Fillers: Jokes, gags, anecdotes and short humor. Buys 2-10/issue.

Tips: "Writers should ask themselves whether this is the kind of an article, poem, etc. that a busy housewife would pick up and read when she has a few moments of leisure. We are particularly looking for articles on the spirituality of marriage. We will be concentrating more on recent movements and developments in the church to help make people aware of the new church of which they are a part."

‡OUR SUNDAY VISITOR MAGAZINE, Noll Plaza, Huntington IN 46750. (219)356-8400. Publisher: Robert P. Lockwood. Editor: Louis F. Jacquet. 5% freelance written. Works with small number of new/unpublished writers each year. Weekly magazine for general Catholic audience. Circ. 300,000. **Pays on acceptance.** Publishes ms an average of 2 months after acceptance. Byline given. Submit seasonal material 2 months in advance. Query for electronic submissions. Reports in 3 weeks. Free sample copy with SASE.

Nonfiction: Uses articles on Catholic-related subjects. Should explain Catholic religious beliefs in articles of human interest; articles applying Catholic principles to current problems, Catholic profiles, etc. Payment varies depending on reputation of author, quality of work, and amount of research required. Buys 25 mss/year. Query. Length: 1,000-1,200 words. Minimum payment for features is $100. Pays expenses of writers on assignment.

Photos: Purchased with mss; with captions only. Reviews b&w glossy prints and transparencies. Pays minimum of $200/cover photo story; $125/b&w story; $25/color photo; $10/b&w photo.

PARISH FAMILY DIGEST, Our Sunday Visitor, Inc., 200 Noll Plaza, Huntington IN 46750. (219)356-8400. Editor: George P. Foster. 100% freelance written. Works with small number of new/unpublished writers each year. Bimonthly magazine. "*Parish Family Digest* is geared to the Catholic family and to that family as a unit of the parish." Circ. 150,000. **Pays on acceptance.** Publishes ms an average of 6 months-1 year after acceptance. Byline given. Buys first North American rights. Submit seasonal/holiday material 6 months in advance. Reports in 2 weeks on queries; 3 weeks on mss. Sample copy and writer's guidelines for 6½×9½ SAE and 2 first class stamps.

Nonfiction: General interest, historical, inspirational, interview, nostalgia (if related to overall Parish involvement) and profile. No personal essays or preachy first person "thou shalt's or shalt not's." Send complete ms. Buys 72 unsolicited mss/year. Length: 1,000 words maximum. Pays $5-50.

Photos: State availability of photos with ms. Pays $10 for 3×5 b&w prints. Buys one-time rights. Captions preferred; model releases required.

Fillers: Anecdotes and short humor. Buys 6/issue. Length: 100 words maximum.

Tips: "If an article does not deal with some angle of Catholic family life, the writer is wasting time in sending it to us. We rarely use reprints; we prefer fresh material that will hold up over time, not tied to an event in the news. We will be more oriented to families with kids and the problems such families face in the Church and society, in particular, the struggle to raise good Catholic kids in a secular society. Articles on how to overcome these problems will be welcomed."

PENTECOSTAL EVANGEL, The General Council of the Assemblies of God, 1445 Boonville, Springfield MO 65802. (417)862-2781. FAX: (417)862-8558. Editor: Richard G. Champion. 33% freelance written. Works with a small number of new/unpublished writers each year. Weekly magazine. Emphasizes news of the Assemblies of God for members of the Assemblies and other Pentecostal and charismatic Christians. Estab. 1913. Circ. 280,000. **Pays on acceptance.** Publishes ms an average of 4-6 months after acceptance. Byline given. Buys first serial rights, a few second serial (reprint) rights or one-time rights. Submit seasonal/holiday material 6 months in advance. Reports in 3 months. Free sample copy and writer's guidelines.

Nonfiction: Informational (articles on homelife that convey Christian teachings); inspirational; and personal experience. Buys 5 mss/issue. Send complete ms. Length: 500-1,500 words. Pays 5¢/word maximum. Sometimes pays the expenses of writers on assignment.

Photos: Photos purchased without accompanying ms. Pays $7.50-15 for 8×10 b&w glossy prints; $10-35 for 35mm or larger transparencies. Total purchase price for ms includes payment for photos.

Poetry: Religious and inspirational. Buys 1 poem/issue. Submit maximum 6 poems. Pays 20-40¢/line.

Tips: "Break in by writing up a personal experience. We publish first-person articles concerning spiritual experiences; that is, answers to prayer for help in a particular situation, of unusual conversions or healings through faith in Christ. All articles submitted to us should be related to religious life. We are Protestant, evangelical, Pentecostal, and any doctrines or practices portrayed should be in harmony with the official position of our denomination (Assemblies of God)."

‡PRAIRIE MESSENGER, Catholic Weekly, Benedictine Monks of St. Peter's Abbey, P.O. Box 190, Muenster, Saskatchewan S0K 2Y0 Canada. (306)682-5215. Editor-in-Chief: Andrew Britz. Editor: Art Babych. Associate Editor: Marian Noll. 10% freelance written. A weekly Catholic journal with strong emphasis on social justice, Third World and ecumenism. Circ. 11,000. Pays on publication. Publishes ms an average of 2-3 months after acceptance. Byline given. Offers 70% kill fee. Not copyrighted. Buys first North American serial rights, first rights, one-time rights, second serial (reprint) rights or simultaneous rights. Submit seasonal/holiday material 3 months in advance. Query for electronic submissions. Sample copy for 9×12 SAE with 78¢ Canadian postage; writers guidelines for 9×12 SAE with 78¢ first class Canadian stamps.

Nonfiction: Interview/profile, opinion, and religious. "No articles on abortion or homosexuality." Buys 30 mss/year. Send complete ms. Length: 250-600 words. Pays $40-60. Sometimes pays expenses of writers on assignment.

Photos: Send photos with submission. Reviews 3×5 prints. Offers $10/photo. Captions required. Buys all rights.

PRESBYTERIAN RECORD, 50 Wynford Dr., Don Mills, Ontario M3C 1J7 Canada. (416)444-1111. FAX: (416)441-2825. 50% freelance written. Eager to work with new/unpublished writers. Monthly magazine for a church-oriented, family audience. Circ. 68,000. Buys 35 mss/year. Pays on publication. Publishes ms an average of 4 months after acceptance. Buys first serial rights, one-time rights, simultaneous rights. Submit seasonal material 3 months in advance. Reports on ms accepted for publication in 2 months. Returns rejected material in 3 months. Sample copy and writer's guidelines for 9×12 SAE with $1 Canadian postage or IRCs.

Nonfiction: Material on religious themes. Check a copy of the magazine for style. Also, personal experience, interview, and inspirational material. No material solely or mainly American in context. When possible, black-and-white photos should accompany manuscript; i.e., current events, historical events and biographies. Buys 15-20 unsolicited mss/year. Query. Length: 1,000-2,000 words. Pays $45-55 (Canadian funds). Sometimes pays expenses of writers on assignment.

Photos: Pays $15-20 for b&w glossy photos. Uses positive transparencies for cover. Pays $50. Captions required.

Tips: "There is a trend away from maudlin, first-person pieces redolent with tragedy and dripping with simplistic pietistic conclusions."

PURPOSE, 616 Walnut Ave., Scottdale PA 15683-1999. (412)887-8500. Editor: James E. Horsch. 95% freelance written. Weekly magazine "for adults, young and old, general audience with interests as varied as there are people. My readership is interested in seeing how Christianity works in difficult situations." Estab. 1908. Circ. 19,250. **Pays on acceptance.** Publishes ms an average of 8 months after acceptance. Byline given, including city, state/province. Buys one-time rights. Submit seasonal material 6 months in advance. Simultaneous submissions OK. Submit complete ms. Reports in 2 months. Free sample copy and writer's guidelines for 6×9 SAE with 2 first class stamps.

Nonfiction: Inspirational articles from a Christian perspective. "I want stories that go to the core of human problems in family, business, politics, religion, sex and any other areas—and show how the Christian faith resolves them. I want material that's upbeat. *Purpose* is a story paper which conveys truth either through quality fiction or through articles that use the best story techniques. Our magazine accents Christian discipleship. Christianity affects all of life, and we expect our material to demonstrate this. I would like to see story-type articles about individuals, groups and organizations who are intelligently and effectively working at some of the great human problems such as overpopulation, hunger, poverty, international understanding, peace, justice, etc., because of their faith." Buys 175-200 mss/year. Submit complete ms. Length: 1,000 words maximum. Pays 5¢/word maximum. Buys one-time rights only.

Photos: Photos purchased with ms. Pays $5-25 for b&w (less for color), depending on quality. Must be sharp enough for reproduction; prefers prints in all cases. Can use color prints. Captions desired.

Fiction: Humorous, religious and historical fiction related to discipleship theme. "Produce the story with specificity so that it appears to take place somewhere and with real people. It should not be moralistic."

Poetry: Traditional poetry, blank verse, free verse and light verse. Length: 12 lines maximum. Pays $5-15 per poem depending on length and quality. Buys one-time rights only.

Fillers: Anecdotal items from 200-800 words. Pays 4¢/word maximum.

Tips: "We are looking for articles which show the Christian faith working at issues where people hurt; stories need to be told and presented professionally. Good photographs help place material with us."

QUEEN OF ALL HEARTS, Montfort Missionaries, 26 S. Saxon Ave., Bay Shore NY 11706. (516)665-0726. Managing Editor: Roger Charest, S.M.M. 50% freelance written. Bimonthly magazine covering Marian doctrine and devotion. "Subject: Mary, Mother of Jesus, as seen in the sacred scriptures, tradition, history of the church, the early Christian writers, lives of the saints, poetry, art, music, spiritual writers, apparitions, shrines, ecumenism, etc." Estab. 1950. Circ. approx 6,000. **Pays on acceptance.** Publishes ms an average of 6 months after acceptance. Byline given. Not copyrighted. Submit seasonal/holiday material 6 months in advance. Reports in 6 weeks. Sample copy $2.

Nonfiction: Essays, inspirational, personal experience and religious. Buys 25 ms/year. Send complete ms. Length: 750-2,500 words. Pays $40-60. Sometimes pays writers in contributor copies or other premiums "by mutual agreement. Poetry paid by contributor copies."

Photos: Send photos with submission. Reviews transparencies and prints. Offers variable payment per photo. Buys one-time rights.
Fiction: Religious. Buys 6 mss/year. Send complete ms. Length: 1,500-2,500 words. Pays $40-60.
Poetry: Joseph Tusiani, poetry editor. Free verse. Buys approximately 10 poems/year. Submit 2 poems maximum at one time. Pays in contributor copies.

REVIEW FOR RELIGIOUS, 3601 Lindell Blvd., Room 428, St. Louis MO 63108. (314)535-3048. Editor: David L. Fleming, S.J. 100% freelance written. "Each ms is judged on its own merits, without reference to author's publishing history." Bimonthly. For Roman Catholic priests, brothers and sisters. Estab. 1942. Pays on publication. Publishes ms an average of 9 months after acceptance. Byline given. Buys first North American serial rights and rarely second serial (reprint) rights. Reports in 2 months.
Nonfiction: Articles on ascetical, liturgical and canonical matters only; not for general audience. Length: 2,000-8,000 words. Pays $6/page.
Tips: "The writer must know about religious life in the Catholic Church and be familiar with prayer, vows and problems related to them."

ST. ANTHONY MESSENGER, 1615 Republic St., Cincinnati OH 45210. Editor-in-Chief: Norman Perry. 55% freelance written. "Willing to work with new/unpublished writers if their writing is of a professional caliber." Monthly magazine for a national readership of Catholic families, most of which have children in grade school, high school or college. Circ. 380,000. **Pays on acceptance.** Publishes ms an average of 9 months after acceptance. Byline given. Buys first North American serial rights. Submit seasonal/holiday material 6 months in advance. Query for electronic submissions. Sample copy and writer's guidelines for 9 × 12 SASE.
Nonfiction: How-to (on psychological and spiritual growth, problems of parenting/better parenting, marriage problems/marriage enrichment); humor; informational; inspirational; interview; personal experience (if pertinent to our purpose); personal opinion (limited use; writer must have special qualifications for topic); and profile. Buys 35-50 mss/year. Length: 1,500-3,500 words. Pays 14¢/word. Sometimes pays the expenses of writers on assignment.
Fiction: Mainstream and religious. Buys 12 mss/year. Submit complete ms. Length: 2,000-3,500 words. Pays 14¢/word.
Tips: "The freelancer should ask why his or her proposed article would be appropriate for us, rather than for *Redbook* or *Saturday Review.* We treat human problems of all kinds, but from a religious perspective. Get authoritative information (not merely library research); we want interviews with experts. Write in popular style. Word length is an important consideration."

ST. JOSEPH'S MESSENGER & ADVOCATE OF THE BLIND, Sisters of St. Joseph of Peace, St. Joseph's Home, Box 288, Jersey City NJ 07303. Editor-in-Chief: Sister Ursula Maphet. 30% freelance written. Eager to work with new/unpublished writers. Quarterly magazine. Circ. 25,000. **Pays on acceptance.** Publishes ms an average of 3 months after acceptance. Buys first serial rights and second serial (reprint) rights, but will reassign rights back to author after publication asking only that credit line be included in next publication. Submit seasonal/holiday material 3 months in advance (no Christmas issue). Simultaneous and previously published submissions OK. Reports in 3 weeks. Sample copy and writer's guidelines 8½ × 11 SAE with 45¢ postage.
Nonfiction: Humor, inspirational, nostalgia, personal opinion and personal experience. Buys 24 mss/year. Submit complete ms. Length: 300-1,500 words. Pays $3-15.
Fiction: Romance, suspense, mainstream and religious. Buys 30 mss/year. Submit complete ms. Length: 600-1,600 words. Pays $6-25.
Poetry: Light verse and traditional. Buys 25 poems/year. Submit maximum 10 poems. Length: 50-300 words. Pays $5-20.
Tips: "It's rewarding to know that someone is waiting to see freelancers' efforts rewarded by 'print'. It's annoying, however, to receive poor copy, shallow material or inane submissions. Human interest fiction, touching on current happenings, is what is most needed. We look for social issues — woven into story form. We also seek non-preaching articles that carry a message that is positive."

SCP JOURNAL AND SCP Newsletter, Spiritual Counterfeits Project, P.O. Box 4308, Berkeley CA 94704. (415)540-0300. Editor: William P. Kellogg. 5% freelance written. Prefers to work with published/established writers. "The *SCP Journal* and *SCP Newsletter* are occasional publications that analyze new religious movements and spiritual trends from a Christian perspective. Their targeted audience is the educated lay person." Estab. 1975. Circ. 16,500. Pays on publication. Publishes ms an average of 6 months after acceptance. Byline given. Simultaneous and previously published submissions OK. Sample copy for 8½ × 11 SAE and 4 first class stamps.
Nonfiction: Book excerpts, essays, exposé, interview/profile, opinion, personal experience and religious. Buys 10 mss/year. Query with published clips. Length: 2,500-3,500 words. Pays $20-35/typeset page.
Photos: State availability of photos with submission. Reviews contact sheets and prints. Offers no additional payment for photos accepted with ms. Captions, model releases and identification of subjects required. Buys one-time rights.

Tips: "The area of our publication most open to freelancers is reviews of books relevant to subjects covered by *SCP*. These should not exceed 6 typewritten, double-spaced pages, 1,500 words. Send samples of work that are relevant to the *SCP's* area of interest."

SHARING THE VICTORY, Fellowship of Christian Athletes, 8701 Leeds Rd., Kansas City MO 64129. (816)921-0909. Editor: John Dodderidge. Assistant Editor: Dana J. King. Managing Editor: Don Hilkemeir. 60% freelance written. Prefers to work with published/established writers, but works with a growing number of new/unpublished writers each year. A bimonthly magazine. "We seek to encourage and enable athletes and coaches at all levels to take their faith seriously on and off the 'field.' " Circ. 50,000. Pays on publication. Publishes ms an average of 4 months after acceptance. Byline given. Buys first rights. Submit seasonal/holiday material 3 months in advance. Reports in 1 week on queries; 2 weeks on manuscripts. Sample copy $1 with 9×12 SAE and 3 first class stamps; free writer's guidelines for #10 SASE.
Nonfiction: Humor, inspirational, interview/profile (with "name" athletes and coaches solid in their faith), personal experience, and photo feature. No "sappy articles on 'I became a Christian and now I'm a winner.' " Buys 5-20 mss/year. Query. Length: 500-1,000 words. Pays $100-200 for unsolicited articles, more for the exceptional profile.
Photos: State availability of photos with submission. Reviews contact sheets. Pay depends on quality of photo but usually a minimum $100. Model releases required for "name" individuals. Buys one-time rights.
Poetry: Free verse. Buys 3 poems/year. Pays $50.
Tips: "Profiles and interviews of particular interest to coed athlete, primarily high school and college age. Our graphics and editorial content appeal to youth. The area most open to freelancers is profiles on or interviews with well-known athletes or coaches (male, female, minorities); and offbeat but interscholastic team sports."

SISTERS TODAY, The Liturgical Press, St. John's Abbey, Collegeville MN 56321. Editor-in-Chief: Sister Mary Anthony Wagner, O.S.B. Associate Editor: Sister Mary Elizabeth Mason, O.S.B. Review Editor: Sister Stefanie Weisgram, O.S.B. 80% freelance written. Prefers to work with published/established writers; works with a small number of new/unpublished writers each year. Magazine, beginning with January 1990, will be published bimonthly, exploring the role of women and the Church, primarily. Circ. 8,000. Pays on publication. Publishes ms 1-2 years after acceptance. Byline given. Buys first rights. Submit seasonal/holiday material 4 months in advance. Reports in 3 months. Sample copy $2.
Nonfiction: How-to (pray, live in a religious community, exercise faith, hope, charity etc.); informational; and inspirational. Also articles concerning religious renewal, community life, worship, and the role of sisters in the Church and in the world today. Buys 50-60 unsolicited mss/year. Query. Length: 500-2,500 words. Pays $5/printed page.
Poetry: Free verse, haiku, light verse and traditional. Buys 3 poems/issue. Submit maximum 4 poems. Pays $10.
Tips: "Some of the freelance material evidences the lack of familiarity with *Sisters Today*. We would prefer submitted articles not to exceed eight or nine pages."

SOCIAL JUSTICE REVIEW, 3835 Westminister Place, St. Louis MO 63108. (314)371-1653. Contact: Rev. John H. Miller, C.S.C. 25% freelance written. Works with a small number of new/unpublished writers each year. Bimonthly. Estab. 1908. Publishes ms an average of 6-12 months after acceptance. Not copyrighted; "however special articles within the magazine may be copyrighted, or an occasional special issue has been copyrighted due to author's request." Buys first serial rights.
Nonfiction: Wants scholarly articles on society's economic, religious, social, intellectual and political problems with the aim of bringing Catholic social thinking to bear upon these problems. Query. Length: 2,500-3,500 words. Pays about 2¢/word.

SONLIGHT/SUN, Christian newspaper, 4118 10th Ave. N., Lake Worth FL 33461. (407)439-3509. Editor/Publisher: Dennis Lombard. 50% freelance written. Eager to work with new/unpublished writers. Biweekly tabloid distributed free to churches and the public, geared to all denominations. Circ. 10,000. Pays on publication. Publishes ms an average of 2 months after acceptance. Byline given. Buys first North American serial rights, one-time rights, second serial (reprint) rights, or simultaneous rights, and makes work-for-hire assignments (locally). Submit seasonal/holiday material 2 months in advance. Simultaneous or previously published submissions OK. Reports in 2 weeks. Sample copies and guidelines $1 with 9×12 SAE; writer's guidelines for #10 SASE.
Nonfiction: Book reviews; essays; (or "Op-Ed" pieces on current issues); general interest (Christian subjects); how-to; humor; inspirational; interview/profile; opinion; personal experience; photo feature; and religious. "All require inter-denominational, non-doctrinal viewpoint." No critical attitudes. Buys 50 mss/year. Send complete ms only. Length: 500-1,000 words. Pays $25-75 for assigned articles; pays $15-35 for unsolicited articles. Sometimes pays expenses of writers on assignment.

Photos: Send photos with submission. 4×5 b&w glossy prints preferred; can use color. Offers $3-5/photo. Captions, model releases and identification of subjects required. Buys one-time rights.
Fiction: Now buying humorous, religious, romance. Must have Christian perspective, but should not be preachy. Send complete ms. Length: 500-1,500 words.
Poetry: Light verse and traditional. Buys 3-5 poems/year. Submit maximum 3 poems. Length: 4-20 lines. Pays $5. Nothing too abstract or overly sentimental.
Tips: "We would like to receive testimonies, how-to for Christians (singles too), essays, and humor in the Christian life. New writers are welcome. How-to and personal experience articles are most open to freelancers. Testimonial articles should include an informal b&w photo of subject and subject's signed release. We're looking for the light and inspirational side. Send for samples and guidelines."

SPIRIT, Lectionary-based Weekly for Catholic Teens, Editorial Development Associates, 1884 Randolph Ave., St. Paul MN 55434. (612)690-7005. Editor: Joan Mitchell, CSJ. Managing Editor: Therese Sherlock, CSJ. 50% freelance written. Weekly newsletter for religious education of high schoolers. "We want realistic fiction and nonfiction that raises current ethical and religious questions and conflicts in multi-racial contexts." Estab. 1988. Circ. 26,000. Pays on publication. Publishes ms an average of 6 months after acceptance. Byline given. Buys all rights. Submit seasonal/holiday material 4-6 months in advance. Simultaneous submissions OK. Reports in 2 weeks on queries; 6 weeks on mss. Free sample copy and writer's guidelines.
Nonfiction: Interview/profile, personal experience, photo feature (homelessness, illiteracy), religious, Roman Catholic leaders, human interest features, social justice leaders, projects, humanitarians. "No Christian confessional pieces." Buys 12 mss/year. Query. Length: 1,100-1,200 words. Pays $135-150 for articles; $75 for one-page articles.
Photos: State availability of photos with submission. Reviews contact sheets, transparencies and prints. Offers $25-35 per photo. Identification of subjects required. Buys one-time rights.
Fiction: Fantasy and slice-of-life vignettes. "We want realistic pieces for and about teens – nonpedantic, nonpious." Buys 12 mss/year. Query. Length: 1,100-1,200 words. Pays $150.
Tips: "Query to receive call for stories, spec sheet, sample issues."

SPIRITUAL LIFE, 2131 Lincoln Rd. NE, Washington DC 20002. (202)832-6622. Editor: Rev. Steven Payne, O.C.D. 80% freelance written. Prefers to work with published/established writers; works with a small number of new/unpublished writers each year. Quarterly. "Largely Catholic, well-educated, serious readers. A few are nonCatholic or nonChristian." Circ. 14,000. **Pays on acceptance.** Publishes ms an average of 1 year after acceptance. Buys first North American serial rights. "Brief autobiographical information (present occupation, past occupations, books and articles published, etc.) should accompany article." Reports in 1 month. Sample copy and writer's guidelines for SASE (9×6 or larger) with 4 first class stamps.
Nonfiction: Serious articles of contemporary spirituality. High quality articles about our encounter with God in the present day world. Language of articles should be college level. Technical terminology, if used, should be clearly explained. Material should be presented in a positive manner. Sentimental articles or those dealing with specific devotional practices not accepted. Buys inspirational and think pieces. No fiction or poetry. Buys 20 mss/year. Length: 3,000-5,000 words. Pays $50 minimum. "Five contributor's copies are sent to author on publication of article." Book reviews should be sent to Rev. Steven Payne, O.C.D.

STANDARD, Nazarene International Headquarters, 6401 The Paseo, Kansas City MO 64131. (816)333-7000, ext. 555. Editor: Beth A. Watkins. 95% freelance written. Works with a small number of new/unpublished writers each year. Weekly inspirational paper with Christian reading for adults. Estab. 1938. Circ. 177,000. **Pays on acceptance.** Publishes ms an average of 15 months after acceptance. Byline given. Buys one-time rights and second serial (reprint) rights. Submit seasonal/holiday material 10-12 months in advance. Reports in 6 weeks. Free sample copy; writer's guidelines for SAE with 2 first class stamps.
Nonfiction: How-to (grow spiritually); inspirational; social issues; and personal experience (with an emphasis on spiritual growth). Buys 400 mss/year. Send complete ms. Length: 300-1,500 words. Pays 3½¢/word for first rights; 2¢/word for reprint rights.
Photos: Pays $25-45 for 8×10 b&w prints. Buys one-time rights. Accepts photos with ms.
Fiction: Adventure, religious, romance and suspense – all with a spiritual emphasis. Buys 400 mss/year. Send complete ms. Length: 500-1,500 words. Pays 3½¢/word for first rights; 2¢/word for reprint rights.
Poetry: Free verse, haiku, light verse and traditional. Buys 50 poems/year. Submit maximum 5 poems. Length: 50 lines maximum. Pays 25¢/line.
Fillers: Jokes, anecdotes and short humor. Buys 52/year. Length: 300 words maximum. Pays same as nonfiction and fiction.
Tips: "Articles should express Biblical principles without being preachy. Setting, plot and characterization must be realistic. Fiction articles should be labeled 'Fiction' on the manuscript. True experience articles may be first person, 'as told to,' or third person."

SUNDAY DIGEST, David C. Cook Publishing Co., 850 N. Grove Ave., Elgin IL 60120. Editor: Ronda Oosterhoff. 75% freelance written. Prefers to work with established writers. Issued weekly to Christian adults in Sunday School. "*Sunday Digest* provides a combination of original articles and reprints, selected to help adult readers better understand the Christian faith, to keep them informed of issues within the Christian community, and to challenge them to a deeper personal commitment to Christ." Estab. 1886. **Pays on acceptance.** Publishes ms an average of 15 months after acceptance. Buys first or reprint rights. Reports in 3 months. Sample copy and writer's guidelines for 6½×9½ SAE with 2 first class stamps.

Nonfiction: Needs articles applying the Christian faith to personal and social problems, articles on family life and church relationships, inspirational self-help, personal experience; how-to and interview articles preferred over fiction. Length: 400-1,700 words. Pays $40-200, less for reprints.

Tips: "It is crucial that the writer is committed to quality Christian communication with a crisp, clear writing style. Christian message should be woven in, not tacked on."

SUNDAY SCHOOL COUNSELOR, General Council of the Assemblies of God, 1445 Boonville, Springfield MO 65802. (417)862-2781. Editor: Sylvia Lee. 60% freelance written. Works with small number of new/unpublished writers each year. Monthly magazine on religious education in the local church—the official Sunday school voice of the Assemblies of God channeling programs and help to local, primarily lay, leadership. Estab. 1939. Circ. 35,000. **Pays on acceptance.** Publishes ms an average of 9 months after acceptance. Byline given. Offers variable kill fee. Buys first North American serial rights, one-time rights, all rights, simultaneous rights, first serial rights, or second serial (reprint) rights; makes work-for-hire assignments. Submit seasonal/holiday material 7 months in advance. Simultaneous and previously published submissions OK. Reports in 2 weeks on queries; 1 month on mss. Free sample copy and writer's guidelines for SASE.

Nonfiction: How-to, inspirational, interview/profile, personal experience and photo feature. All related to religious education in the local church. Buys 100 mss/year. Send complete ms. Length: 300-1,800 words. Pays $25-90. Sometimes pays expenses of writers on assignment.

Photos: Send photos with ms. Reviews b&w and color prints. Model releases and identification of subjects required. Buys one-time rights.

TEACHERS INTERACTION, A Magazine Church School Workers Grow By, Concordia Publishing House, 3558 S. Jefferson, St. Louis MO 63118. Mail submissions to LCMS, 1333 S. Kirkwood Rd., St. Louis MO 63122-7295. Editor: Martha Streufert Jander. 20% freelance written. Quarterly magazine (newsletter seven times/year) of practical, inspirational, theological articles for volunteer church school teachers. Material must be true to the doctrines of the Lutheran Church—Missouri Synod. Estab. 1960. Circ. 20,400. **Pays on acceptance.** Publishes ms an average of 1 year after acceptance. Byline given. Buys first rights. Submit seasonal/holiday material 7 months in advance. Query for electronic submissions. Reports in 3 months on queries; 6 months on mss. Sample copy $1; writer's guidelines for 9×12 SAE (with sample copy); for #10 SAE (without sample copy).

Nonfiction: How-to (practical helps/ideas used successfully in own classroom); inspirational (to the church school worker—must be in accordance with LCMS doctrine); and personal experience (of a Sunday school classroom nature—growth). No theological articles. Buys 6 mss/year. Send complete ms. Length: 750-1,500 words. Pays $35.

Fillers: Cartoons. Buys 14/year. "*Teachers Interaction* buys short items—activities and ideas planned and used successfully in a church school classroom." Buys 50/year. Length: 100 words maximum. Pays $10.

Tips: "Practical, or 'it happened to me' experiences articles would have the best chance. Also short items—ideas used in classrooms; seasonal and in conjunction with our Sunday school material; Our Life in Christ. Our format includes all volunteer church school teachers, not just Sunday school teachers. Because of backlog, accepting little freelance material."

‡THIS PEOPLE MAGAZINE, Exploring LDS issues and personalities, Utah Alliance Publishing Co., Box 2250, Salt Lake City UT 84110. (801)538-2262. Editor: William B. Smart. 75% freelance written. Quarterly magazine covering Mormon issues and personalities. "This magazine is aimed at Mormon readers and examines Mormon issues and people in an upbeat, problem-solving way." Estab. 1979. Circ. 30,000. Pays on publication. Publishes ms an average of 6 months after acceptance. Byline given. Offers 15% kill fee. Buys first rights. Submit seasonal/holiday material 6 months in advance. Query for electronic submissions. Reports in 2 months. Sample copy 8½×11 SAE with 4 first class stamps. Writer's guidelines for #10 SAE with 1 first class stamp.

Nonfiction: Essays, historical/nostalgic, humor, inspirational, interview/profile, personal experience, photo feature and travel—all Mormon oriented. No poetry, cartoons, fiction. Buys 15-20 mss/year. Query with or without published clips, or send complete ms. Length: 1,000-3,500 words. Pays $150-400 for assigned articles; $100-400 for unsolicited articles. Sometimes pays expenses of writers on assignment.

Photos: State availability of photos with submission. Model releases and identification of subjects required. Buys all rights.

Tips: "I prefer query letters that include the first 6-8 paragraphs of an article plus an outline of the article. Clips and credits of previous publications are helpful."

‡TODAY'S PARISH, Twenty-Third Publications, 185 Willow St., Box 180, Mystic CT 06355. (203)536-2611. Editor: Daniel Connors. 25% freelance written. A magazine published 7 times/year covering parish ministry. "Articles must deal with some practical aspect of parish life for parish leaders." Circ. 16,000. Pays on publication. Publishes ms an average of 6 months to 1 year after acceptance. Byline given. Buys first rights. Submit seasonal/holiday material 6 months in advance. No multiple submissions. Reports in 3 months. Sample copy and writer's guidelines for 8½ × 11 SASE.

Nonfiction: Opinion, personal experience, and photo feature all related to religion. Buys 15 mss/year. Query or send complete ms. Length: 800-1,800 words. Pays $50-100.

Photos: State availability of photos with submission or send photos. Reviews slides and prints. Offers no additional payment for photos accepted with ms. Identification of subjects required. Buys one-time rights.

THE UNITED CHURCH OBSERVER, 85 St. Clair Ave. E., Toronto, Ontario M4T 1M8 Canada. (416)960-8500. Interim Editor: Muriel Duncan. 40% freelance written. Prefers to work with published/established writers. A 60-page monthly newsmagazine for people associated with The United Church of Canada. Deals primarily with events, trends and policies having religious significance. Most coverage is Canadian, but reports on international or world concerns will be considered. Pays on publication. Publishes ms an average of 4 months after acceptance. Byline usually given. Buys first serial rights and occasionally all rights.

Nonfiction: Occasional opinion features only. Extended coverage of major issues usually assigned to known writers. No opinion pieces, poetry. Submissions should be written as news, no more than 1,200 words length, accurate and well-researched. Queries preferred. Rates depend on subject, author and work involved. Pays expenses of writers on assignment "as negotiated."

Photos: Buys photographs with mss. B&w should be 5 × 7 minimum; color 35mm or larger format. Payment varies.

Tips: "The writer has a better chance of breaking in at our publication with short articles; it also allows us to try more freelancers. Include samples of previous *news* writing with query. Indicate ability and willingness to do research, and to evaluate that research. The most frequent mistakes made by writers in completing an article for us are organizational problems, lack of polished style, short on research, and a lack of inclusive language."

UNITED EVANGELICAL ACTION, P.O. Box 28, Wheaton IL 60189. (708)665-0500. FAX: (708)665-8575. Editor: Donald R. Brown. Managing Editor: Brad Davis. 50% freelance written. Prefers to work with published/established writers. Bimonthly magazine. Offers "an objective evangelical viewpoint and interpretive analysis of specific issues of consequence and concern to the American Church and updates readers on ways evangelicals are confronting those issues at the grass roots level." Estab. 1943. Circ. 10,500. Pays on publication. Publishes ms an average of 2 months after acceptance. Buys first serial rights. Phone queries OK. Query for electronic submissions. Reports in 1 month. Sample copy for 9 × 12 SAE with 4 first class stamps. Writer's guidelines for #10 SASE.

Nonfiction: Issues and trends in the Church and society that affect the ongoing witness and outreach of evangelical Christians. Content should be well thought through, and should provide practical suggestions for dealing with these issues and trends. Buys 8-10 mss/year. "Always send a query letter before sending manuscript." Length: 900-1,000 words. Pays $50-175. Sometimes pays expenses of writers on assignment.

Tips: Editors would really like to see news (action) items that relate to the National Association of Evangelicals. "We are interested in expanding coverage of NAE activities throughout the country. Send query letter about important topics facing evangelicals or news features about local works by evangelicals. Keep writing terse, to the point, and stress practical over theoretical."

UNITED METHODIST REPORTER, Box 660275, Dallas TX 75266-0275. (214)630-6495. Editor/General Manager: Spurgeon M. Dunnam, III. Managing Editor: John A. Lovelace. Weekly newspaper for a United Methodist national readership. Circ. 475,000. Pays on publication. Byline given. Not copyrighted. Free sample copy and writer's guidelines.

Nonfiction: "We accept occasional short features, approximately 500 words. Articles need not be limited to a United Methodist angle but need to have an explicit Protestant angle, preferably with evidence of participation in a local congregation. Write about a distinctly Christian response to human need or how a person's faith relates to a given situation." Send complete ms. Pays 4¢/word.

Photos: Purchased with accompanying ms. "We encourage the submission of good action photos (5 × 7 or 8 × 10 b&w glossy prints) of the persons or situations in the article." Pays $10.

UNITY MAGAZINE, Unity School of Christianity, Unity Village MO 65065. (816)524-3550. Editor: Philip White. 90% freelance written. Monthly magazine on the metaphysical. Circ. 500,000. **Pays on acceptance.** Publishes ms an average of 7 months after acceptance. Byline given. Buys first North American serial rights. Submit seasonal/holiday material 6-7 months in advance. Reports in 3 weeks on queries; 2 months on mss. Free sample copy and writer's guidelines.

Nonfiction: Inspirational, personal experience, religious. Buys 200 mss/year. Send complete ms. Length: 2,000 words. Pays $15/page.

Photos: State availability of photos with submission. Reviews transparencies and prints. Offers $35-200/photo. Model release and identification of subjects required. Buys one-time rights.

Poetry: "Any type fitting magazine." Buys 100 poems/year. Submit maximum 10 poems. Length: 30 lines maximum. Pays $20 minimum.

VENTURE AND VISIONS, Lectionary-based weeklies for Catholic youth, Pflaum/Editorial Development Associates, 1884 Randolph Ave., St. Paul MN 55105. (612)690-7010. Editor: Joan Mitchell, CSJ. Managing Editor: Therese Sherlock, CSJ. 40% freelance written. Weekly newsletter on religious education for intermediate and junior high students. "We want realistic fiction and nonfiction that raises current ethical and religious questions and conflicts in multiracial contexts to which intermediate and junior high youth can relate." Circ. 140,000. Pays on publication. Byline given. Publishes ms an average of 6 months after acceptance. Buys all rights. Submit seasonal/holiday material 4-6 months in advance. Simultaneous submissions OK. Reports in 2 weeks on queries; 2 months on mss. Free sample copy. Writer's guidelines for #10 SASE.
Nonfiction: Marianne W. Nold. General interest (human interest features), interview/profile, personal experience, photo feature (students in other countries), religious, Roman Catholic leaders, humanitarians and social justice projects. "No Christian confessional pieces." Buys 14 mss/year. Query. Length: 900-1,100 words. Pays $100-125 for assigned articles; $75-125 for unsolicited articles.
Photos: State availability of photos with submission. Reviews contact sheets, transparencies and prints. Offers $15-50 per photo. Identification of subjects required. Buys one-time rights.
Fiction: Fantasy, religious and slice-of-life-vignettes. "No 'Christian'. We want realistic pieces for and about intermediate and junior-high aged students—non-pedantic, non-pious." Buys 30-40 mss/year. Query. Length: 900-1,100 words. Pays $100-125.
Tips: "Query to receive call for stories, spec sheet, sample issues."

VIRTUE, The Christian Magazine for Women, 548 Sisters Pkwy, P.O. Box 850, Sisters OR 97759. (503)549-8261. Editor: Becky Durost Fish. Managing Editor: Ruth Nygren Keller. 75% freelance written. Works with small number of new/unpublished writers each year. Bimonthly magazine that "encourages women in their development as individuals and provides practical help for them as they minister to their families, churches and communities." Estab. 1978. Circ. 175,000. **Pays on acceptance.** Publishes ms an average of 4 months after acceptance. Byline given. Buys first North American serial rights. Submit seasonal/holiday material 9 months in advance. Reports in 6 weeks on queries; 2 months on mss. Sample copy $3; writer's guidelines for #10 SASE.
Nonfiction: Book excerpts, how-to, humor, inspirational, interview/profile, opinion, personal experience and religious. Buys 70 mss/year. Query. Length: 600-1,800 words. Pays 15-25¢/word. Sometimes pays the expenses of writers on assignment.
Photos: State availability of photos with submission.
Columns/Departments: In My Opinion (reader editorial); One Woman's Journal (personal experience); Equipped for Ministry (practical how-to for helping others). Buys 25 mss/year. Query. Length: 1,000-1,500. Pays 15-25¢/word.
Fiction: Humorous and religious. Buys 4-6 mss/year. Send complete ms. Length: 1,500-1,800 words. Pays 15-25¢/word.
Poetry: Free verse, haiku and traditional. Buys 7-10 poems/year. Submit maximum 3 poems. Length: 3-30 lines. Pays $15-50.

VISTA, Wesleyan Publishing House, P.O. Box 50434, Indianapolis IN 46250-0434. Editor: Rebecca Higgins. 80% freelance written. Eager to work with new/unpublished writers—"quality writing a must, however." Weekly publication of The Wesleyan Church for adults. Circ. 50,000. **Pays on acceptance.** Publishes ms an average of 10 months after acceptance. Byline given. Not copyrighted. Buys first rights, simultaneous rights, second rights and reprint rights. Submit seasonal/holiday material 10 months in advance. Reports in 2 months. Sample copy for 9 × 12 SAE with 45¢ postage. Writer's guidelines for #10 SASE.
Nonfiction: Testimonies, how-to's, humor, interviews, opinion pieces from conservative Christian perspective. Length: 500-1,200 words.
Photos: Pays $15-40 for 5 × 7 or 8 × 10 b&w glossy print natural-looking close-ups of faces in various emotions, groups of people interacting. Various reader age groups should be considered.
Fiction: Believable, quality articles, no Sunday "soaps." Length: 500-1,200 words. Pays 2-4¢/word.
Tips: "Read the writer's guide carefully before submitting."

WAR CRY, The Official Organ of the Salvation Army, 799 Bloomfield Ave., Verona NJ 07044. Editor: Henry Gariepy. 10% freelance written. Prefers to work with published/established writers. Biweekly magazine for "persons with evangelical Christian background; members and friends of the Salvation Army; the 'man in the street.'" Estab. 1880. Circ. 500,000. **Pays on acceptance.** Publishes ms an average of 8 months after acceptance. Buys first serial rights and second serial (reprint) rights. Reports in 2 months. Sample copy and guidelines for 9 × 12 SAE and 65¢ postage.
Nonfiction: Inspirational and informational articles with a strong evangelical Christian slant, but not preachy. In addition to general articles, needs articles slanted toward most of the holidays including Easter, Christmas, Mother's Day, Father's Day, etc. Buys 12 mss/year. Length: approximately 700-1,400 words. Pays 10¢/word.
Photos: Pays $25-35 for b&w glossy prints; $150 for color prints.

THE WESLEYAN ADVOCATE, The Wesleyan Publishing House, P.O. Box 50434, Indianapolis IN 46250-0434. (317)576-1313. FAX: (317)842-9188. Editor: Dr. Wayne E. Caldwell. 10% freelance written. A biweekly magazine by the Wesleyan Church. Circ. 20,000. Pays on publication. Publishes ms an average of 1 year after acceptance. Byline given. Buys first rights or simultaneous rights. Submit seasonal/holiday material 1 year in advance. Simultaneous submissions OK. Query for electronic submissions. Reports in 2 weeks. Sample copy for $2; writer's guidelines for #10 SASE.

Nonfiction: Humor, inspirational and religious. Buys 5 mss/year. Send complete ms. Length: 250-650 words. Pays $10-40 for assigned articles; $5-25 for unsolicited articles.

Photos: Send photos with submission. Reviews transparencies. Buys one-time rights.

Tips: "Write for a guide."

Retirement

Retirement magazines have changed to meet the active lifestyles of their readers and dislike the kinds of stereotypes people have of retirement magazines. More people are retiring in their 50s, while others are starting a business or traveling and pursuing hobbies. These publications give readers specialized information on health and fitness, medical research, finances and other topics of interest, as well as general articles on travel destinations and recreational activities.

‡ALIVE! A Magazine for Christian Senior Adults, Christian Seniors Fellowship, P.O. Box 369, West Chester OH 45069. (513)825-3681. Editor: J. David Lang. Office Editor: A. June Lang. 60% freelance written. Quarterly magazine for senior adults ages 55 and older. "We need timely articles about Christian seniors in vital, productive lifestyles, travels or ministries." Estab. 1988. **Pays on acceptance.** Byline given. Buys first or second serial (reprint) rights. Submit seasonal/holiday material 6 months in advance. Previously published submissions OK. Reports in 6 weeks. Sample copy for 8½×11 SAE with $1 postage; writer's guidelines for #10 SASE.

Nonfiction: General interest, humor, inspirational, interview/profile, photo feature, religious, travel. Buys 25 mss/year. Send complete ms. Length: 600-1,800 words. Pays $18-75. Organization membership may be deducted from payment at writer's request.

Photos: State availability of photos with submission. Offers $10-25. Model releases and identification of subjects required. Buys one-time rights.

Columns/Departments: Heart Medicine (humorous personal anecdotes; prefer grandparent/grandchild stories or anecdotes re: over 55 persons), 10-100 words; Games n' Stuff (word games, puzzles, word search), 200-500 words. Buys 50 mss/year. Send complete ms. Pays $2-25.

Fiction: Adventure, humorous, religious, romance (if it fits age group), slice-of-life vignettes, motivational/inspirational. Buys 12 mss/year. Send complete ms. Length: 600-1,500 words. Pays $20-60.

Fillers: Anecdotes, facts, gags to be illustrated by cartoonist, short humor. Buys 15/year. Length: 50-500 words. Pays $2-15.

Tips: "Include SASE. If second rights, list where article has appeared and if ms if to be returned or tossed."

‡FIFTY-SOMETHING MAGAZINE, For the Fifty-or-Better Mature Adult, Media Trends Publications, Unit E, 8250 Tyler Blvd., Mentor OH 44060. (216)974-9594. Editor: Linda L. Lindeman. 40% freelance written. Bimonthly magazine on aging, travel, relationships, money, health, hobbies. "We are looking for a positive and upbeat attitude on aging. Proving that 50 years old is *not* over-the-hill but instead a prime time of life." Estab. 1989. Circ. 25,000. Pays on publication. Publishes ms an average of 2 months after acceptance. Byline given. Buys all rights. Submit seasonal/holiday material 4 months in advance. Simultaneous and previously published submissions OK. Query for electronic submissions. Reports in 2 months. Free sample copy and writer's guidelines.

Nonfiction: Book excerpts, essays, expose, general interest, historical/nostalgic, how-to (sports), humor, inspirational, interview/profile, opinion, personal experience, photo feature, religious, travel, health, employment. Buys 6 mss/year. Query with published clips, or send complete ms. Length: 100-1,000 words. Pays $25-500 for assigned articles; $25-100 for unsolicited articles. Sometimes pays expenses of writers on assignment.

Photos: Send photos with submission. Reviews contact sheets, negatives, transparencies, and 5×7 prints. Offers $25-100 per photo. Captions, model releases and identification of subjects required. Buys one-time or all rights.

Columns/Departments: Book Review (50 and over market); Movie/Play Review (new releases); Sports (for the mature adult); Travel (for the mature adult). Buys 50 mss/year. Send complete ms. Length: 100-1,000 words. Pays $25-500.

Fiction: Adventure, condensed novels, ethnic, experimental, fantasy, historical, humorous, mainstream, mystery, novel excerpts, religious, romance, slice-of-life vignettes, suspense. Buys 25 mss/year. Send complete ms. Length: 100-1,000 words. Pays $25-500.

Poetry: Avant-garde, free verse, light verse and traditional. Buys 15 poems/year. Length: 25-150 lines. Pays $25-100.

Fillers: Anecdotes, facts, gags to be illustrated by cartoonist, newsbreaks, short humor. Buys 100/year. Length: 25-150 words. Pays $25-100.

Tips: "We are a regional publication in northeast Ohio. All areas are open. If you are 50 or more, write as if you are addressing your peers. If you are younger, take a generic approach to age. You don't have to be 50 to address this market."

GOLDEN YEARS MAGAZINE, Golden Years Senior News, Inc., 233 E. New Haven Ave., Melbourne FL 32902-0537. (407)725-4888. FAX: (407)724-0736. Editor: Carol Brenner Hittner. 50% freelance written. Prefers to work with published/established writers. Bimonthly national magazine covering the needs and interests of our fastest growing generation. Editorial presented in a positive, uplifting, straightforward manner. Estab. 1978. Circ. 450,000. Pays on publication. Publishes ms an average of 7 months after acceptance. Byline given. Buys first serial rights and first North American serial rights. Submit seasonal/holiday material 1 year in advance. Simultaneous queries OK. SASE for return of ms *required* for acceptance. Sample copy for 9 × 12 SAE and $2; writer's guidelines for #10 SASE.

Nonfiction: Profile (senior celebrities), travel, second careers, hobbies, retirement ideas and real estate. Limited need for poetry and cartoons. Nostalgia articles generally not accepted. Buys 100 mss/year. Query with published clips or send complete ms. Length: 600 words maximum. Pays 10¢/word.

Photos: "We like to include a lot of photos." Send photos with query or ms. Pays $25 for transparencies. Captions, model releases, and identification of subjects required. Buys one-time rights. Pays $10 per each b&w photo.

Tips: "Our magazine articles are short and special—that's why we are successful."

‡GRAY PANTHER NETWORK, Gray Panthers Project Fund. 130 Glenview Ave., Wyncote PA 19095. (215)545-6555. Editor: Abby Lederman. 20% freelance written. A bimonthly tabloid covering the fight for human rights, national health system, elder advocacy issues, legislation and ageism. "Readers of *Network* are 50-plus. Most have been and continue to be active in the peace, human rights movements. Writers need to have leftist leanings and be sensitive to older people." Circ. 25,000. **Pays on acceptance.** Publishes ms an average of 6 months after acceptance. Byline given. Buys one-time rights or second serial (reprint) rights. Photocopied and previously published submissions OK. Reports in 5 weeks. Sample copy and writer's guidelines with 9 × 12 SASE and 85¢ postage.

Nonfiction: Exposé (against corporate, dehumanizing elements of society), humor (on a Gray Panther topic-i.e. ageism) and interview/profile (people active in human rights, peace struggle, older Americans). "No first-person experience. No travel, religious, how-to except when dealing with community, grass roots organizing." Buys 15-20 mss/year. Query with published clips. Length: 500-1,500 words. Pays $75-250.

Photos: State availability of photos with submission. Reviews contact sheets and prints (3 × 5). Offers $10-75 per photo. Buys one-time rights.

Columns/Departments: Book & Video Reviews (ageism in the movies, healthy view of aging, book reviews about issues of peace, human rights, economic justice), 500-1,500. Pays $50-200.

‡KEY HORIZONS, The Magazine For Your Best Years, Emmis Publishing Corp., Suite 225, 8425 Keystone Crossing, Indianapolis IN 46240. (317)259-8222. Editor: Deborah Paul. Managing Editor: Jolene Phelps Ketzenberger. 75% freelance written. Quarterly magazine for older adults, age 55 +. "*Key Horizons* takes a positive approach to life, stressing the opportunities available to older adults." Estab. 1988. Circ. 200,000 (controlled circulation—sent to certain Blue Cross/Blue Shield policy holders). Pays on publication. Publishes ms an average of 1-2 months after acceptance. Byline given. Offers 50% kill fee. Buys first North American serial rights. Submit seasonal/holiday material 4 months in advance. Query for electronic submissions. Reports in 1 month on queries; 2 months on mss. Free writer's guidelines.

Nonfiction: General interest, historical/nostalgic, interview/profile, travel. Buys 25-35 mss/year. Query with published clips or send complete ms. Length: 1,500-3,000 words. Pays $250-500.

Photos: State availability of photos with submission. Reviews 2¼ × 2¼ transparencies and 8 × 10 prints. Offers $25 per photo. Captions and identification of subjects required. Buys one-time rights. Always looking for scenic parting shot. Payment negotiable.

Columns/Departments: In the Spotlight (achievers in any field age 55 + who reside in Indiana or western Pennsylvania), 300-400 words; Wellness (upbeat health-oriented articles), 1,500-2,000 words; Generations (coping with families, children, grandchildren), 1,500-2,000 words; Nostalgia (retrospective pieces on Midwestern places, people, events), 1,500-3,000 words; Cooking (1,500 words); Personal Finance (1,500-2,000 words). Buys 12-16 mss/year. Query with published clips or send complete ms. Pays $200-300. Pays $75 for In The Spotlight.

Tips: "Take an upbeat approach. View older adults as vital, productive, active people. We appreciate detailed, well-written query letters that show some preliminary research. Currently, articles must quote Midwestern sources, specifically those in Indiana and western Pennsylvania. In The Spotlight is quite open to freelancers. Watch for older adults in Indiana and western Pennsylvania who have distinguished themselves in a specific way. We're always open to Generations ideas, articles that help seniors cope with family trends. Take a positive approach to Wellness ideas, focusing on what people can do to make their lives healthier."

MATURE LIVING, A Christian Magazine for Senior Adults, Sunday School Board of the Southern Baptist Convention, 127 9th Ave. N., Nashville TN 37234. (615)251-2274. Assistant Editor: Judy Pregel. 70% freelance written. A monthly leisure reading magazine for senior adults 60 and older. Estab. 1892. Circ. 340,000. **Pays on acceptance.** Byline given. Buys all rights and sometimes one-time rights. Submit seasonal/holiday material 18 months in advance. Reports in 3 months. Sample copy for 9 × 12 SAE with 85¢ postage; writer's guidelines for #10 SASE.
Nonfiction: General interest, historical/nostalgic, how-to, humor, inspirational, interview/profile, personal experience, photo feature, crafts, and travel. No pornography, profanity, occult; liquor, dancing, drugs, gambling; no book reviews. Buys 100 mss/year. Send complete ms. Length: 1,475 words maximum, prefers 950 words. Pays 5¢/word (accepted).
Photos: State availability of photos with submission. Offers $10-15/photo. Pays on publication. Buys one-time rights.
Fiction: Humorous, mainstream and slice-of-life vignettes. No reference to liquor, dancing, drugs, gambling; no pornography, profanity or occult. Buys 12 mss/year. Send complete ms. Length: 900-1,475 words. Pays 5¢/word.
Poetry: Light verse and traditional. Buys 50 poems/year. Submit maximum 5 poems. Length: open. Pays $5-24.
Fillers: Anecdotes, facts and short humor. Buys 15/issue. Length: 50 words maximum. Pays $5.

MATURE OUTLOOK, Meredith Corp., 1716 Locust St., Des Moines IA 50336. Editor: Marjorie P. Groves, Ph.D. 80% freelance written. A bimonthly magazine and newsletter on travel, health, nutrition, money and garden for over-50 audience. They may or may *not* be retired. Circ. 870,000. **Pays on acceptance.** Publishes ms an average 3 months after acceptance. Byline given. Offers 20% kill fee. Buys all rights or makes work-for-hire assignments. Submit seasonal/holiday material 9 months in advance. Query for electronic submissions. Reports in 2 weeks. Sample copy $1. Writer's guidelines for #10 SASE.
Nonfiction: How-to, interview/profile, technical and travel. No humor, personal experience or poetry. Buys 50-60 mss/year. Query with published clips. Length: 500-2,000 words. Pays $200-1,000 for assigned articles. Pays telephone expenses of writers on assignment.
Photos: State availability of photos with submission.
Tips: "Please query. Please don't call."

MATURE YEARS, 201 8th Ave., S., Nashville TN 37202. Editor: Donn C. Downall. 30% freelance written. Prefers to work with published/established writers; works with a small number of new/unpublished writers each year. Quarterly magazine for retired persons and those facing retirement; persons seeking help on how to handle problems and privileges of retirement. **Pays on acceptance.** Publishes ms an average of 14 months after acceptance. Rights purchased vary with author and material; usually buys first North American serial rights. Submit seasonal material 14 months in advance. Query for electronic submissions. Reports in 6 weeks. Sample copy for 9 × 12 SAE and $2; writer's guidelines for #10 SASE.
Nonfiction: *"Mature Years* is different from the secular press in that we like material with a Christian and church orientation. Usually we prefer materials that have a happy, healthy outlook regarding aging. Advocacy (for older adults) articles are at times used; some are freelance submissions. We need articles dealing with many aspects of pre-retirement and retirement living, and short stories and leisure-time hobbies related to specific seasons. Give examples of how older persons, organizations, and institutions are helping others. Writing should be of interest to older adults, with Christian emphasis, though not preachy and moralizing. No poking fun or mushy, sentimental articles. We treat retirement from the religious viewpoint. How-to, humor and travel are also considered." Buys 24 unsolicited mss/year. Submit complete ms (include SASE and Social Security number with submissions). Length: 1,200-1,500 words.
Photos: 8 × 10 b&w glossy prints, color prints or transparencies purchased with ms or on assignment.
Fiction: "We buy fiction for adults. Humor is preferred. No children's stories and no stories about depressed situations of older adults." Length: 1,000-1,500 words. Payment varies, usually 4¢/word.
Tips: "We like writing to be meaty, timely, clear and concrete."

MODERN MATURITY, American Association of Retired Persons, 3200 E. Carson, Lakewood CA 90712. Editor-in-Chief: Ian Ledgerwood. 50% freelance written. Prefers to work with published/established writers. Bimonthly magazine for readership of persons 50 years of age and over. Circ. 22 million. **Pays on acceptance.** Publishes ms an average of 4-6 months after acceptance. Byline given. Buys first North American serial rights. Submit seasonal/holiday material 6 months in advance. Query for electronic submissions. Reports in 2 months. Free sample copy and writer's guidelines.
Nonfiction: Careers, workplace, practical information in living, financial and legal matters, personal relationships, and consumerism. Query first. Length: up to 2,000 words. Pays up to $3,000. Sometimes pays expenses of writers on assignment.

Photos: Photos purchased with or without accompanying ms. Pays $250 and up for color and $150 and up for b&w.

Fiction: Very occasional short fiction.

Tips: "The most frequent mistake made by writers in completing an article for us is poor follow-through with basic research. The outline is often more interesting than the finished piece. We do not accept unsolicited manuscripts."

PRIME TIMES, Grote Deutsch & Co., Suite 120, 2802 International Ln., Madison WI 53704. Executive Editor: Rod Clark. 80% freelance written. Prefers to work with published/established writers, but "we will work at times with unpublished writers." Quarterly magazine "for people who are in prime mid-life or at the height of their careers and planning a dynamic retirement lifestyle or second career." Estab. 1980. Circ. 75,000. Pays on publication. Buys first North American serial rights and second serial (reprint) rights. Publishes ms an average of 6 months after acceptance. Submit seasonal material 6 months in advance. Previously published submissions OK as long as they were not in another national maturity-market magazine. Reports in 2 months. Sample copy for $2.50 or a 9 × 12 SAE and 5 first class stamps; writer's guidelines for #10 SASE.

Nonfiction: Investigative journalism, new research and updates (related to financial planning methods, consumer activism, preventive health and fitness, travel, and careers/dynamic lifestyle after retirement); opinion; profile; travel; popular arts; self-image; personal experience; humor; and photo feature. "No rocking-chair reminiscing." Articles on health and medical issues and research *must* be founded in sound scientific method and must include current, up-to-date data. "Health-related articles are an easy sale, but you must be able to document your research. Don't waste your time or ours on tired generalizations about how to take care of the human anatomy. If you've heard it before, so have we. We want to know who is doing new research, what the current findings may be, and what scientists on the cutting edge of new research say the future holds, preferably in the next one to five years. Give us the facts, only the facts, and all of the facts. Allow the scientists and our audience to draw their own conclusions." Buys 30-40 mss/year, about half from new talent. Query with published clips. Length: 1,000-3,000 words. Pays $50-1,000. "Be sure to keep a photocopy." Sometimes pays the expenses of writers on assignment.

Photos: Payment is based on one-time publication rights; $75 for less than ½ page, $125 for ½ page and $250 for full page. Cover photos, spreads, multiple purchases to be negotiated. Payment on publication. Photo release is necessary to prove ownership of copyright. No standard kill fee. "Do not send irreplaceable *anything.*"

Fiction: Length: 1,500-3,500 words. Pays $200-750. "If you are not sure your work is of outstanding quality, please do not submit it to us."

Tips: "Query should reflect writing style and skill of the author. Special issues requiring freelance work include publications on adult relationships and developmental transitions such as mid-life and 'empty-nest' passages and couple renewal; mid-life women's issues; health and medical research and updates; second careers; money management; continuing education; consequences of the ongoing longevity revolution; and the creation of new lifestyles for prime-life adults (ages 40-70 primarily) who are well-educated, affluent, and above all, *active*. About 55% of our readers are women. All are active and redefining the middle years with creative energy and imagination. Age-irrelevant writing is a must. The focus of *Prime Times* in 1991 will be on presenting readers with refreshing and newsworthy material for dynamic mid-lifers, people who have a forever-forty mentality."

RETIREMENT LIFESTYLES, Club 55, Suite 104, 1260 Hornby St., Vancouver, British Columbia U6Z 1W2 Canada. (604)683-4747. Editor: David Todd. Magazine published 10 times/year on retirement topics. Audience: age 40 plus. Circ. 50,000. Pays on publication. Publishes ms an average of 3 months after acceptance. Byline given. Buys one-time rights. Simultaneous and previously published submissions OK. Free sample copy.

Nonfiction: General interest, historical/nostalgic, humor, interview/profile, new product, personal experience, photo feature. Buys 50 mss/year. Send complete ms. Length: 500-2,000 words. Pays $50-300.

Photos: State availability of photos with submission. Reviews contact sheets. Captions required. Buys one-time rights.

Fillers: Anecdotes and gags illustrated by cartoonist. Buys 10/year. Pays $5-15.

SENIOR, California Senior Magazine, 3565 S. Higuera St., San Luis Obispo CA 93401. (805)544-8711. Editor: George Brand. Associate Editor: Herb Kamm, R. Judd. 90% freelance written. Monthly magazine covering senior citizens to inform and entertain the "over-50" audience. Estab. 1982. Circ. 340,000. Pays on publication. Byline given. Publishes ms an average of 1 month after acceptance. Not copyrighted. Buys first rights or second rights. Submit seasonal/holiday material 2 months in advance. Reports in 2 weeks. Sample copy for 9 × 11 SAE and 6 first class stamps; free writer's guidelines.

Nonfiction: Historical/nostalgic, humor, inspirational, personal experience and travel. Special issue features War Years (November); Christmas (December); and Travel (April). Buys 30-75 mss/year. Query. Length: 300-900 words. Pays $1.50/inch.

Photos: Send photos with submission. Reviews 8 × 10 b&w prints only. Offers $10-25 per photo. Captions and identification of subjects required. Buys one-time rights.
Columns/Departments: Finance (investment); Taxes; Auto; Medicare, Health. Length: 300-900 words. Pays $1.50/inch.

SENIOR LIFE MAGAZINE, The Magazine for Active Southern Southern California Adults, Suite 200 "L", 1420 E. Cooley Dr., Colton CA 92324. (714)824-6681. Editor: Bobbi Mason. Monthly magazine of general interest to people 50+. "Readers are 50+, mobile and active. Most live in California full or part time." Circ. 40,000. Pays on publication. Byline given. Buys first rights, second serial (reprint) rights, or simultaneous rights. Submit seasonal/holiday material 4 months in advance. Simultaneous and previously published submissions OK. Sample copy $2.50.
Nonfiction: General interest, historical/nostalgic, how-to (crafts), humor, inspirational, interview/profile, personal experience, financial, sports and photo feature. Buys 5 mss/year. Send complete ms. Length: 300-800 words. Pays up to $50 for assigned articles; $10-45 for unsolicited articles.
Photos: State availability of photos with submission. Reviews transparencies and prints. Offers no additional payment for photos accepted with ms unless negotiated in writing prior to publication. Captions, model releases and identification of subjects required. Buys one-time rights.
Columns/Departments: Special to this issue (open to stories on fashion, financial, nostalgia, or a highlight of a not-famous-but-special-senior) 500-2,500 words. Send complete ms. Length: 300-900 words. Pays $10-50.
Fiction: Adventure, fantasy, historical, humorous, mainstream, mystery, romance, slice-of-life-vignettes, westerns. Buys 6 mss/year. Send complete ms. Length: 200 words minimum. Pays $10-75.
Tips: "Write tightly: space for us is a problem. Short articles with photo(s) most likely accepted. No travel or food/recipe articles. Poetry also OK. Sports and sports-related humor and gardening most highly desired."

‡**SENIOR SPOTLITE, The Paper of Choice for People Over 50**, 55 Newspapers Inc., 8169 Webster St., Arvada CO 80003. (303)421-8171. Editor: Joann Jones. 10% freelance written. Monthly tabloid covering anything of interest to seniors—health issues, travel, legislation, etc. Estab. 1986. Circ. 200,000. Pays on publication. Byline given. Buys one-time rights. Submit seasonal/holiday material 3 months in advance. Simultaneous submissions OK. Reports in 3 months. Sample copy $1 with 9 × 12 SAE and 2 first class stamps.
Nonfiction: General interest, historical/nostalgic, humor, inspirational, interview/profile, religious, travel. No poetry. Buys 5 mss/year. Send complete ms. Length: 200-1,000 words. Pays $25-100. Pays in contributor copies or other premiums if asked.
Photos: State availability of photos with submission or send photos with submission. Offers no additional payment for photos accepted with ms. Model releases and identification of subjects required.

SENIOR WORLD OF CALIFORNIA, Californian Publishing Co., Box 1565, 1000 Pioneer Way, El Cajon CA 92022. (619)442-4404. Executive Editor: Laura Impastato. Travel Editor: Jerry Goodrum. Entertainment Editor: Iris Neal. Health Editor: Arlene Holmes. Lifestyle Editor: Sandy Pasqua. 10% freelance written. Prefers to work with published/established writers. Monthly tabloid newspaper for active older adults living in San Diego, Orange, Los Angeles, Santa Barbara, Ventura, Riverside and San Bernardino counties. Circ. 525,000. Pays on publication. Publishes ms an average of 3 months after acceptance. Buys first serial rights. Simultaneous submissions OK. Reports in 2 months. Sample copy $2; free writer's guidelines.
Nonfiction: "We are looking for stories on health, stressing wellness and prevention; travel—international, domestic and how-to; profiles of senior celebrities and remarkable seniors; finance and investment tips for seniors; and interesting hobbies." Send query or complete ms. Length: 500-1,000 words. Pays $30-100.
Photos: State availability of photos with submission. Need b&w with model release. Will pay extra for photos. Buys all rights to photos selected to run with a story.
Columns/Departments: Most of our columns are local or staff-written. We will consider a query on a column idea accompanied by a sample column.
Tips: "No pity the poor seniors material. Remember that we are primarily a news publication and that our content and style reflect that. Our readers are active, vital adults 55 years of age and older." No telephone queries.

Romance and Confession

Listed here are publications that need stories of romance ranging from ethnic and adventure to romantic intrigue and confession. Each magazine has a particular slant; some are written for young adults, others to family-oriented women. Some magazines also are interested in general interest nonfiction on related subjects.

AFFAIRE DE COEUR, Keenan Enterprises, Suite B, 1555 Washington Ave., San Leandro CA 94577. (415)357-5665. Editor: Barbara N. Keenan. 56% freelance written. Monthly magazine of book reviews, articles and information on publishing for romance readers and writers. Circ. 15,000. Pays on publication. Publishes ms an average of 6-12 months after acceptance. Byline given. Buys one-time rights. Submit seasonal/holiday material 3 months in advance. Simultaneous and previously published submissions OK. Reports in 4 months. Sample copy $10.

Nonfiction: Book excerpts, essays, general interest, historical/nostalgic, how-to, interview/profile, personal experience and photo feature. Buys 2 mss/year. Query. Length: 500-2,200 words. Pays $5-15. Sometimes pays writers with contributor copies or other premiums.

Photos: State availability of photos with submission. Review prints. Identification of subjects required. Buys one-time rights.

Columns/Departments: Reviews (book reviews). Bios and articles, 2,000 word or less.

Fiction: Historical, mainstream and romance. Pays $15.

Poetry: Light verse. Buys 2 poems/year. Submit 1 poem. Does not pay.

Fillers: Newsbreaks. Buys 2/year. Length: 50-100 words. Does not pay.

Tips: "Please send clean copy. Do not send material without SASE. Do not expect a return for 2-3 months. Type all information. Send some sample of your work."

BLACK CONFESSIONS, Lexington Library, Inc., 355 Lexington Ave., New York NY 10017. (212)949-6850. Editor: D. Boyd. See *Jive.*

BRONZE THRILLS, Lexington Library, Inc., 355 Lexington Ave., New York NY 10017. (212)949-6850. Editor: D. Boyd. See *Intimacy/Black Romance.* "Stories can be a bit more extraordinary than in the other magazines. They have to be romantic just like the other stories in the other magazines."

JIVE, Lexington Library, Inc., 355 Lexington Ave., New York NY 10017. (212)949-6850. Editor: D. Boyd. 100% freelance written. Eager to work with new/unpublished writers. A bimonthly magazine covering romance and love. Circ. 100,000. Pays on publication. Publishes ms an average of 3 months after acceptance. Byline given. Buys first and one-time rights. Submit seasonal/holiday material 6 months in advance. Reports in 2 months on queries; 3-6 months on mss. Sample copy for 9 × 12 SAE with 5 first class stamps; free writer's guidelines.

Nonfiction: How-to (relating to romance and love); personal experience (confessions); and feature articles on any aspect of love and romance. "I would not like to see any special features that are overly researched." Buys 100 mss/year. Query with published clips, or send complete ms. Length: 3-5 typed pages. Pays $100.

Columns/Departments: Beauty (Black skin, hair, foot and hand care); Fashion (any articles about current fashions that our audience may be interested in will be considered); Health (about topics that deal with issues pertaining to safe sex, birth control, etc.); how-to special features that deal with romance. Buys 50 mss/year. Query with published clips or send complete ms. Length: 3-5 typed pages. Pays $100.

Fiction: Confession and romance. "I would not like to see anything that stereotypes Black people. Stories which are too sexual in content and lack romance are unacceptable. However, all stories must contain one or two love scenes that are romantic, not lewd." All love scenes should not show the sex act, but should allude to it through the use of metaphors and tags. Buys 300 mss/year. Send complete ms (12-15 typed pages). Pays $75-100.

Tips: "We will continue to buy material that is timely and is based on contemporary themes. However, we are leaning toward more of the romantic themes as opposed to the more graphic themes of the past. We reach an audience that is comprised mostly of women who are college students, high school students, housewives, divorcees and older women. The audience is mainly Black and ethnic. Our slant is Black and should reinforce Black pride. Our philosophy is to show our experiences in as positive a light as possible without addressing any of the common stereotypes that are associated with Black men, lovemaking prowess, penile size, etc. Stereotypes of any kind are totally unacceptable. The fiction section which accepts romance stories and confession stories about love and romance are most open to freelancers. Also, our special features section is very open. We would like to see stories that are set outside the U.S. — perhaps they should be set in the Caribbean, Europe, Africa, etc. Women should be shown as being professional, assertive, independent, but should still enjoy being romanced and loved by a man. We'd like to see themes that are reflective of things happening around us in the 80's — crack, AIDS, living together, surrogate mothers, etc. The characters should be young, but not the typical 'country bumpkin girl who was turned out by a big city pimp' type story. Cosmopolitan storylines would be great too. Please, writers who are not Black, research your story to be sure that it depicts Black people in a positive manner. Do not make Black characters a caricature of a white character. This is totally unacceptable."

MODERN ROMANCES, Macfadden Women's Group, Inc., 233 Park Ave. South, New York NY 10003. Editor: Cherie Clark King. 100% freelance written. Monthly magazine for family-oriented women, ages 18-65 years old. Circ. 200,000. Pays the last week of the month of issue. Buys all rights. Submit seasonal/holiday material at least 6 months in advance. Reports in 6 months. Writer's guidelines for #10 SASE.

Nonfiction: Confession stories with reader identification and a strong emotional tone. No third-person material. Buys 12 mss/issue. Submit complete ms. Length: 2,500-12,000 words. Pays 5¢/word.

Poetry: Light, romantic poetry, and seasonal/holiday subjects. Length: 24 lines maximum. Pay depends on merit.

SECRETS, Macfadden Holdings, Inc., 233 Park Ave. S., New York NY 10003. (212)979-4898. Editorial Director: Susan Weiner. Editor: Pat Byrdsong. 100% freelance written. Monthly magazine for blue-collar black family women, ages 18-35. "*Secrets* is a woman's confession/romance magazine geared toward a black audience. We are particularly interested in seeing true to life stories that address contemporary social issues as well as light romance." Pays on publication. Publishes ms an average of 4 months after acceptance. Buys all rights. Submit seasonal material *at least* 5 months in advance. Reports in 3 months.

Nonfiction and Fiction: Wants true stories of special interest to women: family, marriage and emotional conflict themes, "woman-angle articles," or self-help or inspirational fillers. "No pornographic material; no sadistic or abnormal angles. Stories must be written in the first person." Buys about 150 mss/year. Submit complete ms. Length: 300-1,000 words for features; 2,500-7,500 words for full-length story. Occasional 10,000-worders. Greatest need: 4,500-6,000 words. Pays 3¢/word for story mss.

Columns/Departments: Woman (readers share anecdotes about their lives, loves and families); My Best Friend (photographs of pets and children with article of 50 words or less). Pays $50.

Tips: "Know our market. We are keenly aware of all contemporary lifestyles and activities that involve black women and family — i.e.; current emphasis on child abuse, or renewed interest in the image of marriage, etc."

TRUE CONFESSIONS, Macfadden Holdings, Inc., 233 Park Ave. S., New York NY 10003. (212)979-4800. Editor: H. Marie Atkocius. 90% freelance written. Eager to work with new/unpublished writers. For high-school-educated, blue-collar women, teens through maturity. Monthly magazine. Circ. 250,000. Buys all rights. Byline given on some articles. Pays during the last week of month of issue. Publishes ms an average of 4 months after acceptance. Submit seasonal material 6 months in advance. Reports in 6-8 months. Submit complete ms. Computer printout submissions acceptable; prefers letter-quality. No simultaneous submissions.

Stories, Articles, and Fillers: Timely, exciting, emotional first-person stories on the problems that face today's women. The narrators should be sympathetic, and the situations they find themselves in should be intriguing, yet realistic. Many stories may have a strong romantic interest and a high moral tone; however, personal accounts or "confessions," no matter how controversial the topic, are encouraged and accepted. Careful study of a current issue is suggested. Length: 2,000-6,000 words; 5,000-word stories preferred; also book lengths of 8,000-10,000 words. Pays 5¢/word. Also publishes articles poetry, recipes and mini-stories (1,200 words maximum).

TRUE LOVE, Macfadden Women's Group, 233 Park Ave. South, New York NY 10016. (212)979-4800. Editor: Marcia Pomcrantz. 100% freelance written. Monthly magazine. For young, blue-collar women, teens through mid-30's. Confession stories based on true happenings, with reader identification and a strong emotional tone. No third-person material; no simultaneous submissions. Circ. 200,000. Pays the last week of the month of the issue. Buys all rights. Submit seasonal material 6 months in advance. Reports within 2 months. Sample copy for 9 × 12 SAE and $2. Writer's guidelines for #10 SASE.

Nonfiction and Fiction: Confessions, true love stories; problems and solutions; health problems; marital and child-rearing difficulties. Avoid graphic sex. Stories dealing with reality, current problems, everyday events, with emphasis on emotional impact. Buys 10 stories/issue. Submit complete ms. Length: 2,000-10,000 words. Pays 3¢/word.

Columns/Departments: "The Life I Live," $100; "How I Know I'm In Love," 700 words or less; $75; "Pet Shop," $50.

Poetry: Light romantic poetry. Length: 24 lines maximum. Pay depends on merit.

Tips: "The story must appeal to the average blue-collar woman. It must deal with her problems and interests. Characters — especially the narrator — must be sympathetic. Focus is especially on teenagers, young working (or student) women."

TRUE ROMANCE, Macfadden Women's Group, 233 Park Ave. South, New York NY 10003. (212)979-4800. Editor: Jean Sharbel. Monthly magazine. 100% freelance written. Readership primarily young, blue-collar women, teens through mid-30's. Confession stories based on true happenings, with reader identification and strong emotional tone. No third-person material; no simultaneous submissions! Circ. 225,000. Pays 1 month after publication. Buys all rights. Submit seasonal/holiday material at least 5 months in advance. Reports in 3 months.

Nonfiction and Fiction: Confessions, true love stories; problems and solutions; dating and marital and child-rearing difficulties. Realistic stories dealing with current problems, everyday events, with strong emotional appeal. Buys 14 stories/issue. Submit complete ms. Length 1,500-7,500 words. Pays 3¢/word; slightly higher rates for short-shorts. Informational and how-to articles. Byline given. Length: 250-800 words. Pays 5¢/word minimum.

Poetry: Light romantic poetry. Buys 100/year. Length: 24 lines maximum. Pay depends on merit.

Tips: "A timely, well-written story that is told by a sympathetic narrator who sees the central problem through to a satisfying resolution is all important to break into *True Romance*. We are always looking for good love stories."

Rural

Readers may be conservative or liberal, but these publications draw them together with a focus on rural lifestyles. Surprisingly, many readers are from urban centers who dream of or plan to build a house in the country.

COUNTRY JOURNAL, P.O. Box 8200, Harrisburg PA 17105. FAX: (717)657-9526. Editor: Peter V. Fossel. 90% freelance written. Works with a small number of new/unpublished writers each year. Bimonthly magazine featuring country living for people who live in rural areas or who are thinking about moving there. Estab. 1974. Circ. 320,000. Average issue includes 6-8 feature articles and 10 departments. **Pays on acceptance.** Rates range from 30-50¢/word. Byline given. Buys first North American serial rights. Submit seasonal material 1 year in advance. Reports in 1 month. Sample copy $3; writer's guidelines for SASE.
Nonfiction: Book excerpts; general interest; opinion (essays); profile (people who are outstanding in terms of country living); how-to; issues affecting rural areas; and photo feature. Query with published clips. Length: 2,000-3,500 words. Pays 30-50¢/word. Pays the expenses of writers on assignment.
Photos: Sheryl O'Connell, art director. State availability of photos. Reviews b&w contact sheets, 5×7 and 8×10 b&w glossy prints and 35mm or larger transparencies. Captions, model release, and identification of subjects required. Buys one-time rights.
Columns/Departments: Listener (brief articles on country topics, how-to's, current events and updates). Buys 5 mss/issue. Query with published clips. Length: 200-400 words. Pays approximately $75.
Poetry: Free verse, light verse and traditional. Buys 1 poem/issue. Pays $50/poem. Include SASE.
Tips: "Be as specific in your query as possible and explain why you are qualified to write the piece (especially for how-to's and controversial subjects). The writer has a better chance of breaking in at our publication with short articles."

‡**ELECTRIC CONSUMER**, Indiana Statewide Assn. of Rural Electric Cooperatives, Inc., 720 N. High School Rd., Indianapolis IN 46214. (317)248-9453. Editor: Emily Born. Associate Editor: Richard G. Biever. Monthly tabloid covering rural electric cooperatives (relevant issues affecting members). News/feature format for electric cooperative members in Indiana. Among regular featured departments are: gardening, food, poetry, health and humor. Estab. 1951. Circ. 278,000. Pays on publication. Byline given. Buys one-time rights. Submit seasonal/holiday material 2 months in advance. Simultaneous submissions OK. Reports in 1 month. Free sample copy and writer's guidelines.
Nonfiction: General interest and humor. Buys 25 mss/year. Send complete ms. Considers any length. Pays $25-150. Pays expenses of writers on assignment.
Photos: State availability of photos with submission. Offers $10 per photo. Captions, model releases and identification of subjects required. Buys one-time rights.
Columns/Departments: Humor (personal experiences usually, always "clean" family-oriented), 2,000 words. Buys 10-12 mss/year. Send complete ms. Considers any length. Pays $75.
Poetry: Light verse and traditional. "We don't pay for poems we publish."
Tips: "We receive the majority of our freelance submissions for our humor department although we're happy to look at submissions of other types as well. Keep in mind that our readers are rural/suburban, generally conservative and have the common bond of electric cooperative membership."

FARM & RANCH LIVING, Reiman Publications, 5400 S. 60th St., Greendale WI 53129. (414)423-0100. Editor: Bob Ottum. 80% freelance written. Eager to work with new/unpublished writers. A bimonthly lifestyle magazine aimed at families that farm or ranch full time. "*F&RL* is *not* a 'how-to' magazine—it deals with people rather than products and profits." Estab. 1970. Circ. 380,000. **Pays on acceptance.** Publishes ms an average of 1 year after acceptance. Byline given. Offers 25% kill fee. Buys first serial rights and one-time rights. Submit seasonal/holiday material 6 months in advance. Previously published submissions OK. Reports in 6 weeks. Sample copy $2; writer's guidelines for #10 SASE.
Nonfiction: Interview/profile, photo feature, historical/nostalgic, humor, inspirational and personal experience. No how-to articles or stories about "hobby farmers" (doctors or lawyers with weekend farms); no issue-oriented stories (pollution, animal rights, etc.). Buys 50 mss/year. Query first with or without published clips; state availability of photos. Length: 1,000-3,000 words. Pays $150-500 for text-and-photos package. Pays expenses of writers on assignment.
Photos: Scenic. Pays $75-200 for 35mm color slides. Buys one-time rights.
Fillers: Jokes, anecdotes and short humor with farm or ranch slant. Buys 150/year. Length: 50-150 words. Pays $20 minimum.
Tips: "In spite of poor farm economy, most farm families are proud and optimistic, and they especially enjoy stories and features that are upbeat and positive. *F&RL*'s circulation continues to increase, providing an excellent market for freelancers. A freelancer must see *F&RL* to fully appreciate how different it is from other farm publications—ordering a sample is strongly advised (not available on newsstands). Query first— we'll give plenty of help and encouragement if story looks promising, or we'll explain why if it doesn't. Photo

features (about interesting farm or ranch families) and personality profiles are most open to freelancers. We can make separate arrangements for photography if writer is unable to provide photos."

FARM FAMILY AMERICA, Fieldhagen Publishing, Inc., Suite 121, 333 On Sibley, St. Paul MN 55101. (612)292-1747. Editor: George Ashfield. 75% freelance written. A quarterly magazine published by American Cyanamid and written to the lifestyle, activities and travel interests of American farm families. Circ. 295,000. **Pays on acceptance.** Publishes ms an average of 2 months after acceptance. Byline given. Offers 25% kill fee. Buys first or second serial (reprint) rights. Submit seasonal/holiday material 6 months in advance. Simultaneous submissions OK. Query for electronic submissions. Reports in 6 weeks. Writer's guidelines for #10 SASE.
Nonfiction: General interest and travel. Buys 24 mss/year. Query with published clips. Length: 1,000-1,800 words. Pays $300-650. Sometimes pays the expenses of writers on assignment.
Photos: State availability of photos with submission. Reviews 35mm transparencies and prints. Offers $160-700 per photo. Model releases and identification of subjects required. Buys one-time rights.

HAROWSMITH COUNTRY LIFE, Ferry Road, Charlotte VT 05445. (802)425-3961. FAX: (802)425-3307. Editor: Thomas H. Rawls. Bimonthly magazine covering country living, gardening, shelter, food, and environmental issues. "*Harrowsmith Country Life* readers are generally college educated country dwellers, looking for good information." Estab. 1986. Circ. 225,000. Pays 30-45 days after acceptance. Byline given. Offers 25% kill fee. Buys first North American periodical rights. Reports in 6 weeks. Sample copy $4; writer's guidelines for #10 SASE.
Nonfiction: Book excerpts, essays, exposé (environmental issues), how-to (gardening/building), humor, interview/profile, opinion. Buys 36 mss/year. Query with published clips. Length: 500-5,000 words. Pays $500-1,500. Pays expenses of writers on assignment.
Photos: State availability of photos with submission. Reviews 35mm transparencies. Offers $100-325/photo. Model releases and identification of subjects required. Buys one-time rights.
Columns/Departments: Sourcebank (ideas, tips, techniques relating to gardening, the environment, food, health), 50-400 words; Gazette (brief news items). Buys 30 mss/year. Query with published clips. Length: 40-400 words. Pays $25-150.
Tips: "While main feature stories are open to freelancers, a good way for us to get to know the writer is through our Screed (essays), Sourcebank (tips and ideas) and Gazette (brief news items) departments. Articles should contain examples, quotations and anecdotes. They should be fairly detailed and factual."

HARROWSMITH MAGAZINE, Camden House Publishing, Ltd., Camden East, Ontario K0K 1J0 Canada. (613)378-6661. Editor: Michael Webster. 75% freelance written. Published 6 times/year "for those interested in country life, nonchemical gardening, energy, self-sufficiency, small-stock husbandry, owner-builder architecture and alternative styles of life." Circ. 154,000. **Pays on acceptance.** Publishes ms an average of 4 months after acceptance. Byline given. Buys first North American serial rights. Submit seasonal/holiday material 6 months in advance. Reports in 6 weeks. Sample copy $5; free writer's guidelines.
Nonfiction: Exposé, how-to, general interest, humor, environmental and profile. "We are always in need of quality gardening articles geared to northern conditions. No articles whose style feigns 'folksiness.' No how-to articles written by people who are not totally familiar with their subject. We feel that in this field simple research does not compensate for lack of long-time personal experience." Buys 10 mss/issue. Query. Length: 500-4,000 words. Pays $150-1,250 but will consider higher rates for major stories.
Photos: State availability of photos with query. Pays $50-250 for 35mm or larger transparencies. Captions required. Buys one-time rights.
Tips: "We have standards of excellence as high as any publication in the country. However, we are by no means a closed market. Much of our material comes from unknown writers. We welcome and give thorough consideration to all freelance submissions. Our magazine is read by Canadians who live in rural areas or who hope to make the urban to rural transition. They want to know as much about the realities of country life as the dreams. They expect quality writing, not folksy clichés."

THE MOTHER EARTH NEWS, 80 5th Ave., New York NY 10011. (212)337-6787. Editor: Alfred Meyer. Managing Editor: John Voelcke. Mostly freelance written. Magazine published 6 times/year. Emphasizes "country living and country skills, for both long-time and would-be ruralites." Circ. 700,000. **Pays on acceptance.** Byline given. Submit seasonal/holiday material 5 months in advance. Computer printout submissions acceptable; prefer letter-quality. No handwritten mss. Reports within 3 months. Publishes ms an average of 6 months after acceptance. Sample copy $3; writer's guidelines for SASE with 2 first class stamps.
Nonfiction: How-to, home business, alternative energy systems, home building, home retrofit and home maintenance, energy-efficient structures, seasonal cooking, gardening and crafts. Buys 100-150 mss/year. Query or send complete ms. "A short, to-the-point paragraph is often enough. If it's a subject we don't need at all, we can answer immediately. If it tickles our imagination, we'll ask to take a look at the whole piece. No phone queries, please." Length: 300-3,000 words.

Photos: Purchased with accompanying ms. Send prints or transparencies. Uses 8 × 10 b&w glossies; any size color transparencies. Include type of film, speed and lighting used. Total purchase price for ms includes payment for photos. Captions and credits required.

Tips: "Probably the best way to break in is to study our magazine, digest our writer's guidelines, and send us a concise article illustrated with color transparencies that we can't resist. When folks query and we give a go-ahead on speculation, we often offer some suggestions. Failure to follow those suggestions can lose the sale for the author. We want articles that tell what real people are doing to take charge of their own lives. Articles should be well-documented and tightly written treatments of topics we haven't already covered. The critical thing is length, and our payment is by space, not word count." No phone queries.

RURAL HERITAGE, Box 516, Albia IA 52531. (515)932-5084. Publisher: D.H. Holle. 98% freelance written. Works with a small number of new/unpublished writers each year. Quarterly magazine covering individuals dedicated to preserving traditional American life. Circ. 10,000. Pays on publication. Publishes ms an average of 1 year after acceptance. Byline given. Buys first North American rights. Submit seasonal/holiday material 1 year in advance. Reports in 2 months. Sample copy $4.50; writer's guidelines #10 SASE.

Nonfiction: Essays; historical/nostalgic; how-to (all types of crafting and farming); interview/profile (especially people using draft animals); photo feature; and travel (emphasizing our theme, "rural heritage"). No articles on *modern* farming. Buys 100 mss/year. Send complete ms. Length: 500-1,500 words. Pays $15-400.

Photos: Send photos with ms. (B&w 5 × 7 or larger.) No negatives. Pays $5-40. Captions, model releases and identification of subjects (if applicable or pertinent) required. Buys one-time rights.

Columns/Departments: Self-Sufficiency (modern people preserving traditional American lifestyle), 500-1,500 words; Drafter's Features (draft horses and mules used for farming, horse shows and pulls—their care), 500-2,000 words; and Crafting (new designs and patterns), 500-1,500 words. Buys 75 mss/year. Send complete ms. Pays $15-125.

Poetry: Traditional. Pays $5-25.

Fillers: Anecdotes and short humor. Pays $15-25.

Tips: "Profiles/articles on draft horses and draft horse shows and pulling events are *very* popular with our readers."

Science

These publications are published for laymen interested in technical and scientific developments and discoveries, applied science and technical or scientific hobbies. Publications of interest to the personal computer owner/user are listed in the Personal Computers section. Journals for scientists and engineers are listed in Trade in various sections.

AD ASTRA, (formerly *Space World*), 922 Pennsylvania Ave. SE, Washington DC 20003. (202)543-3991. FAX: (202)546-4189. Editor-in-Chief: Leonard David. Managing Editor: Kate McMains. 80% freelance written. A monthly magazine covering the space program. "We publish non-technical, lively articles about all aspects of international space programs, from shuttle missions to planetary probes to plans for the future." Estab. 1989. Circ. 24,000. Pays on publication. Byline given. Buys first North American serial rights. Simultaneous, photocopied and previously published submissions OK. Query for electronic submissions. Reports in 6 weeks on queries; 1 month on mss. Sample copy for 9 × 12 SAE; writer's guidelines for #10 SASE.

Nonfiction: Book excerpts, essays, exposé, general interest, historical/nostalgic, interview/profile, opinion, personal experience, photo feature and technical. No science fiction. Query with published clips. Length: 1,200-3,000 words. Pays $150-300 for features.

Photos: State availability of photos with submission. Reviews 4x5 color transparencies and b&w prints. Negotiable payment. Identification of subjects required. Buys one-time rights.

Columns/Departments: Mission Control (news about space from around the world), 100-300 words; Space Ed (information for educators), 700-750 words; Spaceware (reviews of space or astronomy software), 700-750 words; Reviews (reviews of books or other media); Enterprises (commercial space activities); and Touchdown (opinion pieces). Query with published clips. Pay $75-100.

Fillers: Newsbreaks. Length: 100-500 words. Pays $30-50.

ARCHAEOLOGY, Archaeological Institute of America, 15 Park Row, New York NY 10038. (212)732-5154. FAX: (212)732-5707. Editor: Peter A. Young. 5% freelance written. "We generally commission articles from professional archaeologists." Bimonthly magazine on archaeology. "The only magazine of its kind to bring worldwide archaeology to the attention of the general public." Circ. 130,000. Pays on publication. Byline given. Offers kill fee of ⅕ of agreed upon fee. Buys first North American serial rights. Submit seasonal/holiday material 6 months in advance. Simultaneous submissions OK. Free sample copy and writer's guidelines.

Nonfiction: Essays and general interest. Buys 6 mss/year. Length: 1,000-3,000 words. Pays $750 maximum. Sometimes pays expenses of writers on assignment.

Photos: Send photos with submission.

BIOLOGY DIGEST, Plexus Publishing Inc., 143 Old Marlton Pike, Medford NJ 08055. (609)654-6500. Editor: Mary S. Hogan. Monthly abstracts journal covering life sciences. Circ. 2,000. Pays "after publication is returned from printer." Byline given. Not copyrighted.
Nonfiction: Thomas H. Hogan, publisher. Essays. "A list of suggested further readings must accompany each article." Buys 9 mss/year. Send complete ms. Length: 18-25 double-spaced ms pages.
Photos: "A minimum of 5 photos and/or finished drawings are required to go along with the feature article. If drawings are used, there should be at least 2 photos. Photos are a must because the feature article is always depicted on the cover of the issue through the use of a photo."
Tips: "Although *Biology Digest* is intended for students at the high school and college levels, the feature articles published are of a serious nature and contain scientifically accurate material—not conjecture or opinion. Articles should be self-contained; i.e. the author should assume no previous knowledge of the subject area, and scientific terms should be defined. However, avoid 'talking down' to the reader—he or she is probably smarter than you think."

THE ELECTRON, CIE Publishing, 1776 E. 17th St., Cleveland OH 44114-3679. (216)781-9400. Managing Editor: Janice Weaver. 80% freelance written. Bimonthly tabloid on electronics and high technology. Circ. 50,000. Pays on publication. Publishes ms an average of 2 months after acceptance. Byline given. Buys all rights. Simultaneous queries and previously published submissions OK. Reports in 1 month or earlier. Free sample copy and writer's guidelines.
Nonfiction: Technical (tutorial and how-to), technology news and feature, photo feature, career/educational. All submissions must be electronics/technology-related. Query with published clips or send complete ms. Pays $50-1,000. Sometimes pays expenses of writers on assignment.
Photos: State availability of photos. Reviews 8×10 and 5×7 b&w prints. Captions and identification of subjects required.
Tips: "We would like to receive educational electronics/technical articles. They must be written in a manner understandable to the beginning-intermediate electronics student. We are also seeking news/feature-type articles covering timely developments in high technology."

FINAL FRONTIER, The Magazine of Space Exploration, Final Frontier Publishing, P.O. Box 11519, Washington DC 20008 for editorial submissions. FAX: (202)244-0322. 2400 Foshay Tower, Minneapolis MN 55402. (612)332-3001. Editor: Tony Reichardt. 95% freelance written. Bimonthly magazine on space exploration. "We are not a technical journal nor a science fiction magazine. We're looking for well told, factual articles about the people, events and exciting possiblities of the world's space programs." Estab. 1988. Circ. 100,000. **Pays on acceptance.** Byline given. Pays 33% kill fee. Buys first North American serial rights. Submit seasonal/holiday material 6 months in advance. Simultaneous submissions OK. Query for electronic submissions. Reports in 2 months. Sample copy for $3 and a 9×12 SAE with 6 first class stamps. Writer's guidelines for #10 SASE.
Nonfiction: Book excerpts, essays, expose, general interest, historical/nostalgic, humor, interview/profile, new product, personal experience, photo feature. No technical papers, no science fiction or UFOs. Buys 60 mss/year. Query with published clips. Length: 1,000-3,000 words. Pays 30¢/word (or $700-900). Sometimes pays expenses of writers on assignment.
Photos: State availability of photos with submission. Offers no additional payment for photos accepted with ms "except as agreed ahead of time."
Column/Departments: Boundaries (the cutting edge of exploration); The Private Vector (space businesses); Earthly Pursuits (spinoffs of space technology); Global Currents (international space happenings); Reviews (books, films, videos, computer programs), all 800 words; Notes from Earth (miscellaneous short items), 200-250 words. Buys 120 mss/year. Query with published clips. Pays $50-150.
Tips: "Look for fresh approaches to familiar subjects. Rather than simply suggesting a story on the space shuttle or Mars exploration, we need a tie-in to a specific project or personality. Think behind-the-scenes. 'Notes from Earth' is a grab-bag of short, quick stories—no more than 250 words. Send your ideas!"

MODERN ELECTRONICS, For electronics and computer enthusiasts, CQ Communications, 76 N. Broadway, Hicksville NY 11801. (516)681-2922. FAX: (516)681-2926. 90% freelance written. Monthly magazine covering consumer electronics, personal computers, electronic circuitry, construction projects and technology for readers with a technical affinity. Circ. 70,000. **Pays on acceptance.** Publishes ms an average of 3 months after acceptance. Byline given. Offers 25% kill fee. Buys first North American serial rights. Submit seasonal/holiday material minimum 4 months in advance. Prefer floppy disk accompanying ms. Reports in 1 week on queries; 3 weeks on mss. Sample copy for 9×12 SAE and $1; writer's guidelines for #10 SASE.
Nonfiction: General interest (new technology, product buying guides); how-to (construction projects, applications); new product (reviews); opinion (experiences with electronic and computer products); technical (features and tutorials: circuits, applications); includes stereo, video, communications and computer equipment. "Articles must be technically accurate. Writing should be 'loose,' not textbookish." No long computer programs. Buys 75 mss/year. Query. Length: 500-4,000 words. Pays $80-150/published page. Sometimes pays expenses of writers on assignment.

Photos: Send photos with query or ms. Reviews transparencies and 5×7 b&w prints. Captions, model releases, and identification of subjects required. Buys variable rights depending on mss.

Tips: "The writer must have technical or applications acumen and well-researched material. Articles should reflect the latest products and technology. Sharp, interesting photos are helpful, as are rough, clean illustrations for re-drawing. Cover 'hot' subjects (avoid old technology). Areas most open to freelancers include feature articles, technical tutorials, and projects to build. Some writers exhibit problems with longer pieces due to limited technical knowledge and/or poor organization. We can accept more short pieces."

OMNI, 1965 Broadway, New York NY 10023-5965. Editor: Patrice Adcroft. 90% freelance written. Prefers to work with published/established writers; works with a small number of new/unpublished writers each year. Monthly magazine of the future covering science fact, fiction, and fantasy for readers of all ages, backgrounds and interests. Estab. 1978. Circ. 925,436. Average issue includes 2-3 nonfiction feature articles and 1-2 fiction articles; also numerous columns and 2 pictorials. **Pays on acceptance.** Publishes ms an average of 5 months after acceptance. Offers 25% kill fee. Buys exclusive worldwide and exclusive first English rights and rights for *Omni* anthologies. Submit seasonal material 4-6 months in advance. Reports in 6 weeks. Free writer's guidelines with SASE (request fiction or nonfiction).

Nonfiction: "Feature articles for *Omni* cover all branches of science with an emphasis on the future: What will this discovery or technique mean to us next year, in five years, or even by the year 2010? People want to know, want to understand what scientists are doing and how scientific research is affecting their lives and their future. *Omni* publishes articles about science in language that people can understand. We seek very knowledgeable science writers who are ready to work with scientists and futurists to produce articles that can inform, interest and entertain our readers with the opportunity to participate in many ground breaking studies." Send query/proposal. Length: 2,500-3,500 words. Pays $4,500.

Photos: Frank DeVino, graphic director. State availability of photos. Reviews 35mm slides and 4x5 transparencies. Pays the expenses of writers on assignment.

Columns/Departments: Explorations (unusual travel or locations on Earth); Mind (by and about psychiatrists and psychologists); Earth (environment); Space (technology); Arts (theatre, music, film, technology); Interview (of prominent person); Continuum (newsbreaks); Star Tech (new products); Antimatter and UFO Update (unusual newsbreaks, paranormal); Stars (astronomy); First/Last Word (editorial/humor); Artificial Intelligence (computers); The Body (medical). Query with clips of previously published work. Length: 1,500 words maximum. Pays $1,200; $170 for Continuum and Antimatter items.

Fiction: Contact Ellen Datlow. Fantasy and science fiction. Buys 2 mss/issue. Send complete ms. Length: 10,000 words maximum. Pays $1,250-2,000.

Tips: "To get an idea of the kinds of fiction we publish, check recent back issues of the magazine."

POPULAR SCIENCE, 2 Park Ave., New York NY 10016. Editor-in-Chief: Fred Abatemarco. 30% freelance written. Prefers to work with published/established writers. Monthly magazine. For the well-educated adult, interested in science, technology, new products. Circ. 1.8 million. **Pays on acceptance.** Publishes ms an average of 4 months after acceptance. Byline given. Buys all rights. Pays negotiable kill fee. Free guidelines for writers. Any electronic submission OK. Submit seasonal material 4 months in advance. Reports in 3 weeks. Query. Writer's guidelines for #10 SASE.

Nonfiction: "*Popular Science* is devoted to exploring (and explaining) to a nontechnical but knowledgeable readership the technical world around us. We cover the physical sciences, engineering and technology, and above all, products. We are largely a 'thing'-oriented publication: things that fly or travel down a turnpike, or go on or under the sea, or cut wood, or reproduce music, or build buildings, or make pictures. We are especially focused on the new, the ingenious and the useful. We are consumer-oriented and are interested in any product that adds to the enjoyment of the home, yard, car, boat, workshop, outdoor recreation. Some of our 'articles' are only a picture and caption long. Some are a page long. Some occupy 4 or more pages. Contributors should be as alert to the possibility of selling us pictures and short features as they are to major articles. Freelancers should study the magazine to see what we want and avoid irrelevant submissions." Buys several hundred mss/year. Uses mostly color and some b&w photos. Pays expenses of writers on assignment.

Tips: "Probably the easiest way to break in here is by covering a news story in science and technology that we haven't heard about yet. We need people to be acting as scouts for us out there and we are willing to give the most leeway on these performances. We are interested in good, sharply focused ideas in all areas we cover. We prefer a vivid, journalistic style of writing, with the writer taking the reader along with him, showing the reader what he saw, through words. Please query first."

TECHNOLOGY REVIEW, The Association of Alumni and Alumnae of the Massachusetts Institute of Technology, W59-200, Massachusetts Institute of Technology, Cambridge MA 02139. Editor-in-Chief: Jonathan K. Schlefer. 30% freelance written. Emphasizes technology and its implications for scientists, engineers, managers and social scientists. Magazine published 8 times/year. Estab. 1890. Circ. 85,000. Pays on publication. Publishes ms an average of 3-6 months after acceptance. Buys first rights and some exclusive rights. Phone queries OK but *much* prefer written queries. Submit seasonal/holiday material 6 months in advance. Simultaneous submissions OK. Reports in 6 weeks. Sample copy $2.50; writer's guidelines for #10 SASE. "Please send two copies of all submissions and a self-addressed stamped envelope for return of manuscripts. Please double-space everything!"

Nonfiction: General interest, interview, photo feature and technical. Buys 5-10 mss/year. Query. Length: 1,000-6,000 words. Pays $50-750. Sometimes pays the expenses of writers on assignment.

Columns/Departments: Book Reviews; Trend of Affairs; Technology and Economics; and Prospects (guest column). Also special reports on other appropriate subjects. Query. Length: 750-4,000 words. Pays $50-750.

Science Fiction, Fantasy and Horror

Additional science fiction, fantasy and horror markets are in the Literary and "Little" section.

ABORIGINAL SCIENCE FICTION, Absolute Entertainment Inc., P.O. Box 2449, Woburn MA 01888. Editor: Charles C. Ryan. 99% freelance written. A bimonthly science fiction magazine. "We publish short, lively and entertaining science fiction short stories and poems, accompanied by full-color art." Estab. 1985. Circ. 31,000. Pays on publication. Publishes ms an average of 6-8 months after acceptance. Byline given. Buys first North American serial rights, non-exclusive options on other rights. Query for electronic submissions. Sample copy $3.50, 9 × 12 SAE and 90¢ postage; writer's guidelines for #10 SASE.

Fiction: Science fiction of all types. "We do not use fantasy, horror, sword and sorcery or 'Twilight Zone' type stories." Buys 36 mss/year. Send complete ms. Length: 2,000-6,000 words. Pays $250.

Poetry: Science and science fiction. Buys 8-12 poems/year.

Tips: "Read science fiction novels and other science fiction magazines. Do not rely on science fiction movies or TV. We are open to new fiction writers who are making a sincere effort."

AFTER HOURS, When Fantasy Meets the Darkness, P.O. Box 538, Sunset Beach CA 90742. Editor: William G. Raley. 90% freelance written. Quarterly magazine. "All stories *must* take place after dark! No excessive violence. Keep the blood and slime to a minimum." Estab. 1988. Circ. 6,750. **Pays on acceptance.** Publishes ms an average of 6 months after acceptance. Byline given. Buys first North American serial rights. Query for electronic submissions. Reports in 4 months on mss. Sample copy $4. Writer's guidelines for #10 SASE.

Fiction: Fantasy (including S&S), horror, humorous (macabre), mystery and suspense. No science fiction, "typical" crime stories (where the only motive is murder, rape, or robbery). Buys 50 mss/year. Send complete ms. Length: 6,000 words maximum. Pays 1¢/word.

Tips: "I need action (or at least an atmosphere of dread) on *page one*. Good characterization is important. Don't be afraid to be original—if it's too weird or off-the-wall for other magazines, send it here!"

AMAZING® Stories, TSR, Inc., P.O. Box 111, Lake Geneva WI 53147-0111. Editor: Patrick L. Price. 90% freelance written. Bimonthly magazine of science fiction and fantasy short stories. "Audience does not need to be scientifically literate, but the authors must be, where required. *AMAZING* is devoted to the best science fiction and fantasy. There is no formula. We require the writers using scientific concepts be scientifically convincing, and that every story contain believable and interesting characters and some overall point.We accept story manuscripts from both published and new/unpublished writers." Circ. 12,000. **Pays on acceptance.** Publishes ms an average of 18 months after acceptance. Byline given. Buys first worldwide serial rights in the English language only; "single, non-exclusive re-use option (with additional pay)." Reports in 10 weeks. Sample copy for $2.50; writer's guidelines for #10 SASE.

Nonfiction: Historical (about science fiction history and figures); literary and science articles of interest to science fiction audiences; reviews and essays about major science fiction movies written by big names. No "pop pseudo-science trends: The Unified Field Theory Discovered; How I Spoke to the Flying Saucer People; Interpretations of Past Visits by Sentient Beings, as Read in Glacial Scratches on Granite, etc." Buys 4-8 mss/year. Query with or without published clips. Length: 1,000-5,000 words. Pays 10-12¢/word 3,000-5,000 words. Sometimes pays the expenses of writers on assignment.

Fiction: Contemporary and ethnic fantasy; science fiction. "We are looking for hard or speculative science fiction, and fantasy. Horror fiction is OK if it has a science-fictional or fantastic setting. No 'true' experiences, media-derived fiction featuring *Star Wars* (etc.) characters, stories based on UFO reports or standard occultism." Buys 50-60 mss/year. Send complete ms. Length: 500-25,000 words. Pays 8¢/word to 6,000 words; 5¢/word for 12,000 or more words.

Poetry: All types are OK. No prose arranged in columns. Buys 10 poems/year. Submit maximum 3 poems. Length: 30 lines maximum; ideal length, 20 lines or less. Pays $1/line.

Tips: "We are particularly interested in shorter fiction: stories of 7,000 or fewer words. We look for larger pieces by established writers, because their names help sell our product. Don't try to especially tailor one for our 'slant.' We want original concepts, good writing, and well-developed characters. Avoid certain obvious clichés: UFO landings in rural areas, video games which become real (or vice-versa), stories based on contemporary newspaper headlines. 'Hard' science fiction, that is, science fiction which is based on a plausible extrapolation from real science, is increasingly rare and very much in demand. We are moving away from heroic, pseudo-medieval European fantasies, and more toward ethnic (Japanese, Arabian, Central American, etc.) and contemporary fantasies. All sorts of hard, speculative or militaristic science fiction desired."

ANALOG SCIENCE FICTION/SCIENCE FACT, 380 Lexington Ave., New York NY 10017. Editor: Dr. Stanley Schmidt. 100% freelance written. Eager to work with new/unpublished writers. For general future-minded audience. Monthly. Estab. 1930. Buys first North American serial rights and nonexclusive foreign serial rights. **Pays on acceptance.** Publishes ms an average of 6-10 months after acceptance. Byline given. Reports in 1 month. Sample copy $2.50; writer's guidelines for #10 SASE.
Nonfiction: Illustrated technical articles dealing with subjects of not only current but future interest, i.e., topics at the present frontiers of research whose likely future developments have implications of wide interest. Buys about 12 mss/year. Query. Length: 5,000 words. Pays 6¢/word.
Fiction: "Basically, we publish science fiction stories. That is, stories in which some aspect of future science or technology is so integral to the plot that, if that aspect were removed, the story would collapse. The science can be physical, sociological or psychological. The technology can be anything from electronic engineering to biogenetic engineering. But the stories must be strong and realistic, with believable people doing believable things—no matter how fantastic the background might be." Buys 60-100 unsolicited mss/year. Send complete ms on short fiction; query about serials. Length: 2,000-80,000 words. Pays 4¢/word for novels; 5-6¢/word for novelettes; 6-8¢/word for shorts under 7,500 words; $450-550 for intermediate lengths.
Tips: "In query give clear indication of central ideas and themes and general nature of story line—and what is distinctive or unusual about it. We have no hard-and-fast editorial guidelines, because science fiction is such a broad field that I don't want to inhibit a new writer's thinking by imposing 'Thou Shalt Not's.' Besides, a really good story can make an editor swallow his preconceived taboos. I want the best work I can get, regardless of who wrote it—and I need new writers. So I work closely with new writers who show definite promise, but of course it's impossible to do this with *every* new writer. No occult or fantasy."

ISAAC ASIMOV'S SCIENCE FICTION MAGAZINE, Davis Publications, Inc., 380 Lexington Ave., New York NY 10017. (212)557-9100. Editor-in-Chief: Gardner Dozois. 98% freelance written. Works with a small number of new/unpublished writers each year. Emphasizes science fiction. 13 times a year magazine. Circ. 100,000. **Pays on acceptance.** Buys first North American serial rights, nonexclusive foreign serial rights and occasionally reprint rights. No simultaneous submissions. Reports in 6 weeks. Sample copy for 6½ × 9½ SAE and $2; writer's guidelines for #10 SASE.
Nonfiction: Science. Query first.
Fiction: Science fiction primarily. Some fantasy and poetry. "It's best to read a great deal of material in the genre to avoid the use of some *very* old ideas." Buys 10 mss/issue. Submit complete ms. Length: 100-20,000 words. Pays 5-8¢/word except for novel serializations at 4¢/word.
Tips: Query letters not wanted, except for nonfiction.

BEYOND . . ., Science Fiction and Fantasy, Other World Books, P.O. Box 1124, Fair Lawn NJ 07410-1124. (201)791-6721. Editor: Shirley Winston. Managing Editor: Roberta Rogow. 80% freelance written. Eager to work with new/unpublished writers. A science fiction and fantasy magazine published 4 times a year. "Our audience is mostly science fiction fans." Circ. 300. Pays on publication. Publishes ms an average of 6-9 months after acceptance. Byline given. Buys first North American serial rights. Submit seasonal/holiday material 6 months in advance. Query for electronic submissions. Reports in 3 weeks. Sample copy $4.50 and 9 × 12 SAE; writer's guidelines for #10 SASE.
Nonfiction: Essays and humor. Buys 3 mss/year. Send complete ms. Length: 500-1,500 words. Pays $1.25-3.75 and 1 copy.
Columns/Departments: Reviews (of books and periodicals in science fiction and fantasy area), 500-1,500 words. Buys 3 mss/year. Send complete ms. Length: 500-1,500 words. Pays $1.25-3.75.
Fiction: Fantasy and science fiction only. "We enjoy using stories with a humorous aspect. No horror stories, excessive violence or explicit sex; nothing degrading to women or showing prejudice based on race, religion, or planet of origin. No predictions of universal destruction; we prefer an outlook on the future in which the human race survives and progresses." Buys 20 mss/year. Send complete ms. Length: 500-8,000 words; prefers 4,000-5,000 words. Pays $1.25-20 and 1 copy.
Poetry: Free verse, haiku, light verse and traditional. "Poetry should be comprehensible by an educated reader literate in English, take its subject matter from science fiction or fantasy, need not rhyme but should fall musically on the ear." No poetry unrelated to science fiction or fantasy. Buys 18 poems/year. Submit maximum 3 poems. Length: 4-65 words. Pays 2¢/line and 1 copy.
Tips: Fiction and poetry are most open to freelancers.

‡MARION ZIMMER BRADLEY'S FANTASY MAGAZINE, MZB Inc., Box 352, Berkely CA 94701. Editor: Marion Z. Bradley. Managing Editor: Janette Burke. 100% freelance written. Quarterly magazine of fantasy fiction slanted to writers. Estab. 1988. **Pays on acceptance.** Publishes ms an average of 3-6 months after acceptance. Byline given. Offers $25 kill fee. Buys first North American serial rights. Sample copy for $2 and $1 postage.

Nonfiction: Humor, personal experience (writers), technical. "We rarely buy it except on assignment from known writers." Buys 1-2 mss/year. Query with or without published clips, or send complete ms. Length: 5,000 words maximum.

Photos: State availability of photos with submission. Offers no additional payment for photos accepted with ms.

Fiction: Fantasy. No science fiction, very little horror. Buys 55-60 mss/year. Send complete ms. Length: 300-7,500 words. Pays 2-10¢/word.

Tips: "Consult guidelines for fiction. No science fiction or technology, no poetry."

‡FIGMENT, Digest of Fantasy, Horror, & Science Fiction, Figment Press, P.O. Box 3566, Moscow ID 83843-0477. (208)883-8439. Managing Editor: J.P. McLaughlin. 95% freelance written. Quarterly magazine of fiction in the genres of fantasy, horror and science fiction. We look for fiction set apart by solid characterization. Estab. 1989. Circ. 500. **Pays on acceptance.** Publishes ms an average of 4½ months after acceptance. Byline given. Buys first rights. Query on reprints. Submit seasonal/holiday material 6 months in advance. Previously published submissions OK. Query for electronic submissions. Reports in 2 weeks on queries; 2 months on mss. Sample copy $3.95. Writer's guidelines for #10 SAE with 1 first class stamp.

Nonfiction: Barb Hendee. Genre-related essays, general interest, historical/nostalgic, humor, interview/profile, personal experience. No graphic sex and violence. Buys 4 mss/year. Query. Length: 5,000 words maximum. Pays ¼-2¢/word.

Photos: State availability of photos with submission. Reviews contact sheets. Offers no additional payment for photos accepted with ms. Captions required. Buys one-time rights.

Fiction: J.P. McLaughlin–Science Fiction; J.C. Hendee–Fantasy; Barb Hendee–Horror. Experimental, fantasy, horror, humorous, science fiction, slice-of-life-vignette. Never send artwork with stories; we assign artwork *after* a purchase. Buys 50 mss/year. Send complete ms. Length: 500-5,000 words. Pays ¼-2¢/word.

Poetry: J.C. Hendee, poetry editor. Avant-garde, free verse, haiku, light verse, traditional, sonnets, ballads, limericks, folk songs, epics. "We tend to be more formal in style than our competition." Buys 25 poems/year. Submit 3 maximum poems. Pays copy minimum to $5 maximum.

Tips: We look for highly-polished, well-crafted fiction. Strong characterization and a solid plot is a must. Never forget that fiction is by, for and about people. All areas are open to freelancers. We're always looking for new talent. Keep up the hard work–success in this business is a lot of hard work mixed with a bit of luck.

‡GOREZONE, Starlog Communications International, Inc., 475 Park Ave. South, New York NY 10016. (212)689-2830. FAX: (212)889-7933. Editor: Anthony Timpone. Bimonthly magazine on horror movies and horror fiction. "*Gorezone*, like its parent magazine *Fangoria*, covers horror in entertainment–movies, television, etc., but with more of an emphasis on European horror films and independent productions." Estab. 1988. Circ. 225,000. Pays on publication. Publishes ms an average of 4 months after acceptance. Byline given. Offers a kill fee. Buys all rights. Submit seasonal/holiday material 5 months in advance. Reports in 5 weeks on queries; 9 weeks on mss. Sample copy for 8×10 SASE with 5 first class stamps. Writer's guidelines for #10 SASE with 1 first class stamp.

Nonfiction: Essays (reviews of new horror films) and interview/profiles. Buys 25 mss/year. Query with published clips. Length: features 1,800-2,100. Pays $150-200.

Photos: State availability of photos with submission. Reviews transparencies and 8×10 prints. Offers no additional payment for photos accepted with ms. Buys all rights.

Columns/Departments: Movie reviews (reviews of upcoming films during early pre-release screenings. Mostly accepts reviews of independent films. Must be timely and coincide with release dates). Length: 800-1,000 words. Buys 12 mss/year. Query with published clips. Pays $75-100.

Fiction: Horror. "No fantasy, sci-fi, mystery or middle-of-the-road wimpy horror." Buys 6 mss/year. Send complete ms. Length: 1,800-3,000 words. Pays $175-200.

Tips: "Query with SASE. Read magazines (*Gorezone* and *Fangoria*) religiously. See Writer's Fiction Guidelines for tips."

HAUNTS, Nightshade Publications, P.O. Box 3342, Providence RI 02906. (401)781-9438. Editor: Joseph K. Cherkes. 98% freelance written. Prefers to work with published/established writers; works with small number of new/unpublished writers each year. "We are a literary quarterly geared to those fans of the 'pulp' magazines of the 30's, 40's and 50's, with tales of horror, the supernatural, and the bizarre. We are trying to reach those in the 18-35 age group." Estab. 1984. Circ. 1,000. Pays on publication. Publishes ms an average of 8 months after acceptance. Byline given. Buys first North American serial rights. Reports in 3 weeks on queries; 2 months on mss. Sample copy $3.50 and $1.25 postage; writer's guidelines for #10 SASE.

Fiction: Fantasy, horror and suspense. "No fiction involving blow-by-blow dismemberment, explicit sexual scenes or pure adventure." Buys 36 fiction mss/year. Query. Length: 1,500-8,000 words. Pays $5-50.

Poetry: Free verse, light verse and traditional. Buys 4 poems/year. Submit maximum 3 poems. Offers contributor's copies.

Tips: "Market open from June 1 to December 1 inclusive. How the writer handles revisions often is a key to acceptance."

NEW BLOOD MAGAZINE, 1843 E. Venton St., Covina CA 91724. Editor: Chris B. Lacher. 90% freelance written. Quarterly magazine that uses fiction considered too strong or bizarre for ordinary periodicals. *"NB* is an outlet for work that is otherwise unpublishable because of content, view, opinion, or other. We reach all readers—horror, fantasy, sci-fi, mystery/suspense, erotic—because we do not print generic forms of fiction." Estab. 1986. Circ. 15,000. Pays mostly half on acceptance, half on publication; sometimes pays up to 3 months after publication. Publishes ms an average of 6 months after acceptance. Byline given. Offers 50% kill fee. All rights revert to author upon publication. Submit seasonal/holiday material 6 months in advance. Previously published submissions OK. No simultaneous submissions. Reports in 3 weeks. Sample copy $4. Writer's guidelines for #10 SASE.

Nonfiction: Book excerpts (query), essays, exposé, humor, interview/profile, new product, opinion and photo feature. Buys 8-12 mss/year. Query or send complete ms. Length: 500-3,000 words. Pays 3¢/word for assigned articles.

Photos: State availability of photos with submission. Reviews contact sheets. Sometimes offers additional payment for photos accepted with ms. Model releases required. Buys one-time rights.

Columns/Departments: Shelf-Life (book reviews), 100-500 words; Prose & Conversation (novel excerpt/opinion), 1,000-5,000 words. Buys 12-24 mss/year. Query or send complete ms. Pays 1-5¢/word.

Fiction: Adventure, erotica, experimental, fantasy, horror/gore, humorous, mainstream, mystery, novel excerpts, science fiction, slice-of-life vignettes and suspense. Open to all subjects, except libelous fiction, fiction that portrays children in pornographic situations. Buys 50-100 mss/year. Send complete ms. Length: 750-5,000 words. Pays 1-5¢/word; higher for special.

Fillers: Anecdotes, facts, gags to be illustrated by cartoonist, newsbreaks and short humor. Buys 10-25/year. Pays $5 minimum.

Tips: "I support you by answering your submission personally—always, with no exceptions—so I hope you will support me by buying a sample copy of the publication. *NB* was created as an outlet not only for the unpublishable, but also for the beginning or less established author, hence the title. I try not to discourage any contributor—if you're brave enough and dedicated enough to submit your work professionally, I believe you will eventually become successful. Don't get discouraged. I submitted my work for 8 years before I made my first sale, so be persistent."

PANDORA, 2844 Grayson, Ferndale MI 48220. Editors: Meg MacDonald, Polly Vedder (art), Ruth Berman (poetry). 99% freelance written. Works with a number of new/unpublished writers each year. Magazine published 2 times/year covering science fiction and fantasy. Estab. 1978. Circ. 1,000. Pays on publication. Publishes ms an average of 6-12 months after acceptance. Byline given. Buys first North American serial rights and second serial (reprint) rights; one-time rights on some poems. Reports in 6 weeks. Sample copy $5, ($10 overseas); writer's guidelines for #10 SASE.

Columns/Departments: "We buy short reviews of science fiction and fantasy books that a reader feels truly exemplify fine writing and will be of interest and use to other writers. Small press titles as well as major press titles are welcome." Query or send complete ms. Length: under 500 words. Pays $5 and up.

Fiction: Fantasy, science fiction. "No pun stories. Nothing x-rated (no vulgar language or subject matter). No inaccurate science and no horror." Buys 15 mss/year. Send complete ms. Length: 1,000-5,000 words. Longer work must be exceptional. Pays 1-2¢/word.

Poetry: Ruth Berman, poetry editor. 2809 Drew Ave. S., Minneapolis MN 55417. Buys 10-15 poems/year. Payment starts at $14. Length: open. No romance, occult or horror.

Tips: "Send us stories about characters our readers can sympathize with and care about. Then give them convincing, relevant problems they must overcome. Stories about people and their difficulties, victories, and losses are of more interest to us than stories about futuristic gadgets. What impact does the gadget have on society? *That's* what we want to know. Stories must have a point—not just a pun. Happy endings aren't necessary, but we urge authors to leave the reader with a sense that no matter the outcome, something has been accomplished between the first and last pages. Reading our magazine is the best way to determine our needs, and we strongly recommend all contributors read at least one sample. Better yet, subscribe for a while, then start submitting. We like to see whole stories, the shorter the better, and we will make attempts to respond personally with a critique. Stories which support the existance of a higher authority than man are welcome. Foreign contributors, please use two IRCs."

QUANTUM—SCIENCE FICTION AND FANTASY REVIEW, (formerly *Thrust*), Thrust Publications, 8217 Langport Terrace, Gaithersburg MD 20877. (301)948-2514. Editor: D. Douglas Fratz. 20-40% freelance written. Prefers to work with published/established writers; works with small number of new/unpublished writers each year. A quarterly literary review magazine covering science fiction and fantasy literature. *"QUANTUM—Science Fiction and Fantasy Review* is the highly acclaimed, Hugo-Award-nominated magazine about science fiction and fantasy. Since 1973, *QUANTUM* has been featuring in-depth interviews with science fiction's best known authors and artists, articles and columns by the field's most outspoken writers, and reviews of current science fiction books. *QUANTUM* has built its reputation on never failing to take a close look at the most sensitive and controversial issues concerning science fiction and continues to receive the highest praise and most heated comments from professionals and fans in the science fiction field." Estab.

1973. Circ. 1,800. Pays on publication. Publishes ms an average of 6 months after acceptance. Byline given. Buys first North American serial rights, one-time rights and second serial (reprint) rights. Submit seasonal/ holiday material 3-6 months in advance. Simultaneous queries, and simultaneous and previously published submissions OK. Query for electronic submissions. Reports in 2 weeks on queries; 2 months on mss. Sample copy for $3.00 ($3.50 foreign).

Nonfiction: Humor, interview/profile, opinion, personal experience and book reviews. Buys 50-100 mss/year. Query or send complete ms. Length: 200-10,000 words. Pays 1-2¢/word.

Photos: "We publish only photos of writers being interviewed." State availability of photos. Pays $2-15 for smaller than 8×10 b&w prints. Buys one-time rights.

Columns/Departments: Uses science fiction and fantasy book reviews and film reviews. Buys 40-90 mss/ year. Send complete ms. Length: 100-1,000 words. Pays 1¢/word. (Reviews usually paid in subscriptions, not cash.)

Tips: "Reviews are best way to break into *QUANTUM*. Must be on current science fiction and fantasy books. The most frequent mistake made by writers in completing articles for us is writing to a novice audience; *QUANTUM*'s readers are science fiction and fantasy experts."

THE SCREAM FACTORY, The Magazine of Horrors, Past, Present, and Future, Deadline Publications, 145 Tully Rd., San Jose CA 95111. Editors: Clifford Brooks, Peter Enfantino and Joe Lopez. 75% freelance written. Quarterly literary magazine about horror in films and literature. Estab. 1988. Circ. 1,000. **Pays on acceptance.** Publishes ms an average of 6 months after acceptance. Buys first North American serial rights. Submit seasonal/holiday material 6 months in advance. No simultaneous submissions or reprints. Reports in 2 weeks on queries, 1 month on ms. Sample copy $5; writer's guidelines for #10 SASE.

Nonfiction: Book excerpts (from published novelists), essays, historical/nostalgic, interview/profile, new product and personal experience. Buys 10-15 mss/year. Query or send complete ms. Pays 1/2¢/word.

Photos: Send photos with submission. Reviews prints. Offers no additional payment for photos accepted with ms. Captions required. Buys one-time rights.

Columns/Departments: Book reviews of horror novels/collections; Writer's Writing (what horror authors are currently working on); A Tale of Wyrmwood (fiction saga about haunted town). Query or send complete ms. Pays 1/2¢/word.

Fiction: Horror and dark fantasy. No explicit sexual content. Buys 4-10 mss/year. Send complete ms. Pays 1/2¢/word.

Fillers: Facts, newsbreaks. Pays 1/2¢/word.

Tips: "Looking for reviews of horror fiction, especially the lesser known authors. News on the horror genre, interviews with horror authors and strong opinion pieces."

STARLOG MAGAZINE, The Science Fiction Universe, Starlog Group, 475 Park Ave. S., 8th Floor, New York NY 10016. (212)689-2830. FAX: (212) 889-7933. Editor: David McDonnell. 85% freelance written. Very eager to work with new/unpublished writers. Monthly magazine covering "the science fiction-fantasy-adventure genre: its films, TV, books, art and personalities." Estab. 1976. "We concentrate on interviews with actors, directors, screenwriters, producers, special effects technicians and others. Be aware that '*sci-fi*' and 'Trekkie' are seen as derogatory terms by our readers and by us." Pays on publication. Publishes ms an average of 4 months after acceptance. Byline given. Offers kill fee "only to mss *written* or interviews *done*." Buys all rights. Buys second serial (reprint) rights to certain other material. Submit seasonal/holiday material 6 months in advance. Simultaneous queries and submissions OK if noted. Reports in 1 month on queries; 6 weeks on mss. "We provide an assignment sheet and contract to *all* writers with deadline and other info, thus authorizing a queried piece." Sample copy and writer's guidelines for $3.95 and 8½×11 SAE with 3 first class stamps. Writer's guidelines for #10 SASE.

Nonfiction: Interview/profile (actors, directors, screenwriters who've made science fiction films, and science fiction novelists); photo features; special effects how-tos (on filmmaking only); retrospectives of famous SF films and TV series; occasional pieces on science fiction fandom, conventions, etc. "We also sometimes cover animation (especially Disney and WB)." No personal opinion think pieces/essays. *No* first person. "We prefer article format as opposed to Q&A interviews. Buys 150 mss/year. Query first with published clips. "We prefer queries by mail to phone or fax." Length: 500-3,000 words. Pays $35 (500-word pieces); $50-75 (side-bars); $100-225 (1,000-word and up pieces). Avoids articles on horror films/creators and comic book/comic strip creators and creations.

Photos: State availability of photos. Pays $10-25 for slide transparencies and 8×10 b&w prints depending on quality. "No separate payment for photos provided by film studios." Captions, model releases, identification of subjects and credit line on photos required. Photo credit given. Buys all rights.

Columns/Departments: Fan Network (articles on fandom and its aspects—mostly staff-written); Booklog (book reviews, $10 each, by assignment only); Medialog (news of upcoming science fiction films and TV projects and mini-interviews with those involved, $35); Videolog (videocassette and disk releases of genre interest, staff-written). Buys 18-20 mss/year. Query with published clips. Length: 300-500 words. No kill fee.

Tips: "Absolutely *no fiction*. We expect to emphasize literary science fiction much more in 1991 and will need interviews with writers and coverage of science fiction/fantasy literature. We especially *need* writers who know a prospective interviewee's literary work. Additionally, we expect to cover classic science fiction/fantasy TV series and films in much more detail especially with interviews with the guest stars from the original *Star Trek*. A writer can best break in to *Starlog* with short news pieces or by getting an unusual interview or by *out-thinking* us and coming up with something *new* on a current film or book *before* we can think of it. We are always looking for *new* angles on *Star Trek: The Next Generation*, *Star Wars*, the original *Star Trek*, *Doctor Who* and seek features of series that remain very popular: *Starman, Beauty & the Beast, Lost in Space, Space 1999, Battlestar Galactica, The Twilight Zone, The Outer Limits*. Know your subject before you try us. Most full-length major assignments go to freelancers with whom we're already dealing. But if we like your clips and ideas, we'll be happy to give *you* a chance. We're fans of this material—and a prospective writer must be, too—but we were *also* freelancers. And if you love science fiction, we would love to *help* you break in to print as we've done with others in the past."

‡STARSHORE, For the SF Reader, McAlpine Publishing, Suite 116, 800 Seahawk Circle, Virginia Beach VA 23452. (804)468-2969. Editor: Richard Rowand. 99% freelance written. Bimonthly magazine of science fiction. "*Starshore* showcases short science fiction stories with an emphasis on strong plot and characterization aimed at an intelligent, adult reading audience. Some fantasy will be included." Circ. 12,000. **Pays on acceptance.** Publishes ms an average of 4 months after acceptance. Byline given. Buys first North American serial rights. Simultaneous submissions OK. Reports in 3 weeks on queries; 6 weeks on mss. Sample copy $4.50. Writer's guidelines for #10 SAE with 1 first class stamp.
Nonfiction: Interview/profile (SF writers). "No reviews." Buys 4 mss/year. Query. Length: 3,000-5,000 words. Pays 3-5¢/word.
Fiction: Experimental, fantasy and science fiction. Buys 50 mss/year. Send complete ms. Length: 250-10,000 words. 3-5¢/word.
Poetry: Avant-garde, free verse, haiku, light verse and traditional. Buys 20 poems/year. Submit 5 poems maximum. Length: 2-50 lines. Pays $5-25.
Fillers: Cartoons. Buys 6/year. Length: 25-200 words. Pays $5-25.
Tips: "Write the stories you would like to read with both a solid plot and solid characters. Be original . . . we do not print stories based on old television shows. All areas are open to freelancers."

STARWIND, The Starwind Press, P.O. Box 98, Ripley OH 45167. (513)392-4549. Editors: David F. Powell and Susannah C. West. 75% freelance written. Eager to work with new/unpublished writers. A quarterly magazine "for older teenagers and adults who have an interest in science and technology, and who also enjoy reading well-crafted science fiction and fantasy." Estab. 1974. Circ. 2,500. Pays on publication. Publishes ms an average of 1 year after acceptance. Byline given. Rights vary with author and material; negotiated with author. Usually first serial rights and second serial reprint rights (nonfiction). Query for electronic submissions. "In fact, we encourage disposable submissions; easier for us and easier for the author. Just enclose SASE for our response. We prefer non-simultaneous submissions." Reports in 3 months. Sample copy for $3.50 and 9×12 SAE; writer's guidelines for #10 SASE.
Nonfiction: How-to (technological interest, e.g., how to build a robot eye, building your own radio receiver, etc.); interview/profile (of leaders in science and technology fields); and technical ("did you know" articles dealing with development of current technology). "No speculative articles, dealing with topics such as the Abominable Snowman, Bermuda Triangle, etc. At present, most nonfiction is staff-written or reprinted from other sources. We hope to use more freelance written work in the future." Query. Length: 1,000-7,000 words. Pays 1-4¢/word.
Photos: Send photos with accompanying query or ms. Reviews b&w contact sheets and prints. Model releases and identification of subjects required. "If photos are available, we prefer to purchase them as part of the written piece." Buys negotiable rights.
Fiction: Fantasy and science fiction. "No stories whose characters were created by others (e.g. *Lovecraft*, *Star Trek*, *Star Wars* characters, etc.)." Buys 15-20 mss/year. Send complete ms. Length: 2,000-10,000 words. Pays 1-4¢/word. "We prefer previously unpublished fiction." No query necessary. We don't publish horror, poetry, novel excerpts or serialized novels.
Tips: "Our need for nonfiction is greater than for fiction at present. Almost all our fiction and nonfiction is unsolicited. We rarely ask for rewrites, because we've found that rewrites are often disappointing; although the writer may have rewritten it to fix problems, he/she frequently changes parts we liked, too."

2 AM MAGAZINE, P.O. Box 6754, Rockford IL 61125. Editor: Gretta M. Anderson. 100% freelance written. A quarterly magazine of fiction, poetry, articles and art for readers of fantasy, horror and science fiction. Estab. 1986. Circ. 1,000. **Pays on acceptance.** Publishes ms an average of 9 months after acceptance. Byline given. Buys first North American serial rights. Submit seasonal/holiday material 1 year in advance. Reports in 1 month on queries; 3 months on mss. Sample copy $5.95; writer's guidelines for #10 SAE with 1 first class stamp.

Nonfiction: How-to, interview/profile, opinion, also book reviews of horror, fantasy or SF recent releases. "No essays originally written for high school or college courses." Buys 5 mss/year. Query with or without published clips or send complete ms. Length: 500-2,000 words. Pay ½-1¢/word.

Photos: State availability of photos with submission. Offers no additional payment for photos accepted with ms. Identification of subjects required. Buys one-time rights.

Fiction: Fantasy, horror, mystery, science fiction and suspense. Buys 50 mss/year. Send complete ms. Length: 500-5,000 words. Pays ½-1¢/word.

Poetry: Free verse and traditional. "No haiku/zen or short poems without imagery." Buys 20 poems/year. Submit up to 5 poems at one time. Length: 5-100 lines. Pays $1-5.

Tips: "We are looking for taut, imaginative fiction. Please use proper manuscript format; all manuscripts must include a SASE to be considered. We suggest to Canadian and foreign writers that they send disposable manuscripts with one IRC and a #10 SAE for response, if U.S. postage stamps are unavailable to them."

‡VISIONS, the intercollegiate magazine of speculative fiction and fantasy, Visions Magazine, Inc., 409 College Ave., Ithaca NY 14850. (607)272-2000. Editor: Wolfgang Baur. 95% freelance written. Quarterly literary magazine of imaginative fiction by college authors. "Authors must be college students (graduate or undergrad) and write imaginative, speculative fiction for an international audience of fellow students." Estab. 1986. Circ. 8,000 US; 20,000 USSR. Pays on publication. Publishes ms an average of 5 months after acceptance. Byline given. Buys first North American serial rights or first USSR serial rights. Simultaneous submissions. Query for electronic submissions. Reports in 1 month on queries; 3 months on mss. Sample copy $3. Writer's guidelines for #10 SAE with 1 first class stamp.

Fiction: Adventure, experimental, fantasy, horror, novel excerpts, science fiction. "No pulp or space opera (except camp farce), sexist/racist overtones or gritty *New Yorker*-style realism." Buys 50 mss/year. Send complete ms. Pays $6.

Poetry: Charlie Gonzalez, poetry editor. Avant-garde, free verse, haiku, light verse, traditional. "Must be concretely related to SF and fantasy—horror only in Edgar Allen Poe style." Buys 4-8 poems/year. Submit maximum of 4 poems. Length: 5-40 lines. Pays $6.

Tips: "Avoid excessive use of capital letters! Tell human stories about alien conditions rather than the other way around. Know your science and get it right—pseudo science won't make it. Fiction should be snappy and avoid clichés. Grammar and style must be polished, though we do work with authors whose manuscripts can be revised to printable quality. Still looking for U.S. fantasy or magical realism."

Sports

A variety of sports magazines, from general interest to sports medicine, are covered in this section. For the convenience of writers who specialize in one or two areas of sport and outdoor writing, the publications are subcategorized by the sport or subject matter they emphasize. Publications in related categories (for example, Hunting and Fishing; Archery and Bowhunting) often buy similar material. Writers should read through this entire category to become familiar with the subcategories. Publications on horse breeding and hunting dogs are classified in the Animal category, while horse racing is listed here. Publications dealing with automobile or motorcycle racing can be found in the Automotive and Motorcycle category. Markets interested in articles on exercise and fitness are listed in the Health and Fitness section. Outdoor publications that promote the preservation of nature, placing only secondary emphasis on nature as a setting for sport, are in the Nature, Conservation and Ecology category. Regional magazines are frequently interested in sports material with a local angle. Camping publications are classified in the Travel, Camping and Trailer category.

Archery and Bowhunting

BOW AND ARROW HUNTING, Box HH/34249 Camino Capistrano, Capistrano Beach CA 92624. Editorial Director: Roger Combs. 80% freelance written. Eager to work with new/unpublished writers. Bimonthly magazine for bowhunters. **Pays on acceptance.** Publishes ms an average of 6 months after acceptance. Buys first serial rights. Byline given. Reports on submissions in 2 months. Author must have some knowledge of archery terms.

Nonfiction: Articles: bowhunting, techniques used by champs, how to make your own tackle and off-trail hunting tales. Likes a touch of humor in articles. "No dead animals or 'my first hunt.'" Also uses one technical and how-to article per issue. Submit complete ms. Length: 1,500-2,500 words. Pays $150-300.

Photos: Purchased as package with ms; 5 × 7 minimum. Pays $100 for cover chromes, 35mm or larger.

Tips: "Subject matter is more important than style—that's why we have editors and copy pencils. Good b&w photos are of primary importance. Don't submit color prints. We staff-write our shorter pieces."

BOWBENDER, Bill Windsor, 65 McDonald Close, P.O. Box 912, Carstairs, Alberta T0M 0N0 Canada. FAX: (403)337-3460. Editor: Kathleen Windsor. 100% freelance written. Magazine published 5 times a year on archery/bowhunting. "All submissions must concern archery in Canada, especially hunting with the bow and arrow." Estab. 1984. Circ. 47,000. Pays on publication. Publishes ms an average of 6 months after acceptance. Byline given. Buys first North American serial rights. Submit seasonal/holiday material 6-9 months in advance. Reports in 1 week on queries; 3 weeks on mss. Sample copy $2.50 with 9 × 12 SAE and Canadian $1 postage; U.S. $2 in Canadian stamps or (cash). Writer's guidelines for #10 SAE with 39¢ Canadian stamp or 45¢ American postage.

Nonfiction: General interest (archery), how-to (hunting tips), humor (archery), new product (archery), opinion (Canadian bowhunting), personal experience (bowhunting) and technical (bowhunting). Spring—guides directory; Summer—archery dealer directory; Fall—big game summary. "No anti-hunting; American hunts." Buys 40 mss/year. Query. Length: 500-2,500 words. "Does not assign articles." Pays $300 maximum for unsolicited articles. Sometimes pays in other premiums (ad swap).

Photos: Send photos with submission. Reviews 35mm transparencies and 3 × 5 prints. Offers no additional payment for photos accepted with ms. Captions, model releases and identification of subjects preferred, not required. Buys one-time rights.

Columns/Departments: Spotlight On . . . (regular column describing archery personality, club, manufacturer, etc. from Canada), 1,200-1,500 words. Buys 12 mss/year. Send complete ms. Pays $100-150.

Fillers: Anecdotes, facts, gags to be illustrated by cartoonist, newsbreaks and short humor. Pays 10¢/word maximum.

Tips: "Make sure articles(s) is typed. *Please* read the guidelines; that's what they are for. Remember that a quarterly cannot (because of space) accept all manuscripts—this is not a final rejection. Send a cover letter. Guest articles: factual; descriptive but not flowery, add tips for education; enjoy your own story."

BOWHUNTER, The Magazine for the Hunting Archer, Cowles Magazines, 2245 Kohn Rd., Box 8200, Harrisburg PA 17105-8200. (717)540-8192. FAX (717) 657-9526. Editor: M.R. James. Managing Editor: Dave Canfield. 85% freelance written. Bimonthly magazine (with two special issues) on hunting big and small game with bow and arrow. "We are a special interest publication, produced by bowhunters for bowhunters, covering all aspects of the sport. Material included in each issue is designed to entertain and inform readers, making them better bowhunters." Estab. 1971. Circ. 250,000. **Pays on acceptance.** Publishes ms an average of 10-12 months after acceptance. Byline given. Kill fee varies. Buys first North American serial rights and one-time rights. Submit seasonal/holiday material 8 months in advance. Reports in 1 month on queries; 5 weeks on mss. Sample copy $2. Free writer's guidelines.

Nonfiction: General interest, how-to, interview/profile, opinion, personal experience and photo feature. "We publish a special 'Big Game' issue each Fall (September) but need all material by mid-March. Our other annual publication, *Whitetail Bowhunter*, is staff written or by assignment only. We don't want articles that graphically deal with an animal's death. And, please, no articles written from the animal's viewpoint." Buys 100 plus mss/year. Query. Length: 250-2,500 words. Pays $500 maximum for assigned articles; $25-500 for unsolicited articles. Sometimes pays expenses of writers on assignment.

Photos: Send photos with submission. Reviews 35mm and 2¼ × 2¼ transparencies and 5 × 7 and 8 × 10 prints. Offers $35-200 per photo. Captions required. Buys one-time rights.

Columns/Departments: Would You Believe (unusual or offbeat hunting experiences), 250-1,000 words. Buys 6-8 mss/year. Send complete ms. Pays $25-100.

Tips: "A writer must know bowhunting and be willing to share that knowledge. Writers should anticipate *all* questions a reader might ask, then answer them in the article itself or in an appropriate sidebar. Articles should be written with the reader foremost in mind; we won't be impressed by writers seeking to prove how good they are—either as writers or bowhunters. We care about the reader and don't need writers with 'I' trouble. Features are a good bet because most of our material comes from freelancers. The best advice is: Be yourself. Tell your story the same as if sharing the experience around a campfire. Don't try to write like you think a writer writes."

BOWHUNTING WORLD, Ehlert Publishing Group, Suite 101, 319 Barry Ave. S., Wayzata MN 55391. (612)476-2200. Managing Editor: Tim Dehn. 70% freelance written. A magazine published 9 times/year and written for bowhunting and archery enthusiasts who participate in the sport year-round. Estab. 1951. Circ. 250,000. **Pays on acceptance.** Publishes manuscripts an average of 5 months after acceptance. Byline given. Buys first rights. Reports in 3 weeks on queries, 6 weeks on manuscripts. Sample copy for 9 × 12 SAE and $2 postage; free writer's and photographers guidelines.

Nonfiction: Hunting adventure and scouting and hunting how-to features, primarily from a first-person point of view. Also interview/profile pieces, historical articles, humor and assigned product reviews. Buys 60 mss/year. Query or send complete ms. Length: 1,500-3,000 words. Pays from less than $200 to more than $400.

Photos: Send photos with submission. Reviews 35mm transparencies and b&w prints. Captions required. Buys one-time rights. Send for separate photo guidelines.

Tips: "Good writing is paramount. Authors should be bowhunters or, in the case of interviews or profiles, familiar enough with the sport to write well about it. Read bowhunting stories in *Bowhunting World*, *Field & Stream*, *Outdoor Life* and *Sports Afield* for an idea of the level of writing required and the types of subjects most often used. Submit polished manuscripts and support them with a variety of good slides or b&w prints."

INTERNATIONAL BOWHUNTER MAGAZINE, International Bowhunting Publications, Inc., Rt. 1 Box 41E, P.O. Box 67, Pillager MN 56473-0067. (218)746-3333. Editor: Johnny E. Boatner. 95% freelance written. Magazine publishes seven issues per year on bowhunting. "We are interested in any kind of articles that deal with bowhunting. We pride ourselves as a magazine written by hunter/writers, rather than writer/hunters. We are not interested in articles that just fill pages, we like each paragraph to say something." Estab. 1983. Circ. 57,000. Pays on publication. Publishes ms an average of 1 or 2 months after acceptance. Byline sometimes given. Buys first rights. Submit seasonal/holiday material 4 months in advance. Reports in 1 week on queries; 6 weeks on mss. Free sample copy and writer's guidelines.

Nonfiction: Historical/nostalgic, how-to, humor, interview/profile, new product, personal experience, photo feature, technical, travel; bowhunting and archery related. "No commercials of writers' pet products; articles including bad ethics, gory, target archery." Buys 75 mss/year. Send complete ms. Length: 600-3,500 words. Pays $25 minimum for assigned articles; $25-150 for unsolicited articles. Sometimes pays in contributor copies or other premiums (trade ads for articles). Sometimes pays expenses of writers on assignments.

Photos: Send photos with submission. Reviews transparencies and prints. Offers no additional payment for photos accepted with ms. Captions and identification of subjects required. Buys one-time rights.

Fiction: Adventure (bowhunting related) and historical (bowhunting). Send complete ms. Length: 600-3,500 words. Pays $25-150.

Fillers: Anecdotes, facts, gags to be illustrated by cartoonist, newsbreaks and short humor. Buys 10/year. Length: 100-500 words. Pays $10-25.

Tips: "We do mainly first person accounts as long as it relates to hunting with the bow and arrow, If they have a bowhunting story they want to tell, then type it up and send it in. We probably publish more first time writers than any other bowhunting magazine today. Keep the articles clean, entertaining and informative. We do a few how-tos, but mainly want articles about bowhunting and the great outdoors that relate to bowhunting."

Basketball

CALIFORNIA BASKETBALL MAGAZINE, Suite 501, 1330 E. 223rd St., Carson CA 90745-4313. (See *California Football Magazine*).

Bicycling

BICYCLE GUIDE, Raben Publishing Co., 711 Boylston St., Boston MA 02116. (617)236-1885. FAX: (617) 267-1849. Editor: Theodore Costantino. 25% freelance written. "We're equally happy working with established writers and new writers." Magazine published 9 times/year covering "the world of high-performance cycling. We cover racing, touring and mountain biking from an enthusiast's point of view." Estab. 1984. Circ. 200,000. Pays on publication. Publishes ms an average of 4 months after acceptance. Byline given. Offers kill fee. Buys first North American serial rights. Submit seasonal/holiday material 6 months in advance. Simultaneous submissions OK. Reports in 3 weeks on queries; 1 month on mss. Sample copy for 8½ × 11 SAE with 2 first class stamps; writer's guidelines for #10 SASE.

Nonfiction: Humor, interview/profile, new product, opinion, photo feature, technical, and travel (short rides in North America only). Buyers' annual published in April. "We need 'how-to-buy' material by preceding November." No entry-level how-to repairs or projects; long overseas tours; puff pieces on sports medicine; or 'my first ride' articles." Buys 18 mss/year. Query. Length: 900-3,500 words. Pays $200-600. Sometimes pays expenses of writers on assignment.

Photos: Send photos with submissions. Reviews transparencies and 5 × 8 b&w prints. Offers $50-250/photo. Captions, model releases, and identification of subjects required. Buys one-time rights.

Columns/Departments: What's Hot (new product reviews, personalities, events), 100-200 words; Fat Tracks (mountain bike news and events), 100-200 words. Buys 30 mss/year. Query. Pays $25-450.

Tips: "Freelancers should be cyclists with a thorough knowledge of the sport. Areas most open to freelancers are Training Methods (cover specific routines); Rides (75-100-mile loop rides over challenging terrain in continental U.S.); and Technical Pages (covers leading edge, technical innovations, new materials)."

BICYCLING, Rodale Press, Inc., 33 E. Minor St., Emmaus PA 18098. FAX: (215)965-6069. Editor and Publisher: James C. McCullagh. 20-25% freelance written. Prefers to work with published/established writers. Publishes 10 issues/year (7 monthly, 3 bimonthly); 104-250 pages. Estab. 1978. Circ. 350,000. Pays on acceptance or publication. Publishes ms an average of 6 months after acceptance. Byline given. Buys all rights. Submit seasonal/holiday material 5 months in advance. Query for electronic submissions. Writer's guidelines for SASE.

Nonfiction: How-to (on all phases of bicycle touring, bike repair, maintenance, commuting, new products, clothing, riding technique, nutrition for cyclists, conditioning). Fitness is more important than ever. Also travel (bicycling must be central here); photo feature (on cycling events of national significance); and technical (component review – query). "We are strictly a bicycling magazine. We seek readable, clear, well-informed pieces. We rarely run articles that are pure humor or inspiration but a little of either might flavor even our most technical pieces. No poetry or fiction." Buys 1-2 unsolicited mss/issue. Send complete ms. Length: 1,500 words average. Pays $25-1,200. Sometimes pays expenses of writers on assignment.

Photos: State availability of photos with query letter or send photo material with ms. Pays $15-50 for b&w prints and $35-250 for transparencies. Captions preferred; model release required.

Fillers: Anecdotes and news items for Paceline section.

Tips: "We're alway seeking interesting accounts of cycling as a lifestyle."

BIKEOHIO, Peter Wray, Publisher, P.O. Box 141287, Columbus OH 43214. (614)262-1447. Editor: Lynne Barst. 50% freelance written. Monthly tabloid on bicycling in state of Ohio. "All aspects of adult bicycling covering both racing and recreational riding." Estab. 1988. Circ. 35,000. Pays on publication. Byline given. Buys first rights and second serial (reprint) rights. Simultaneous submissions OK. Query for electronic submissions. Sample copy and writer's guidelines for 10 × 13 SAE with 65¢ postage. Writer's guidelines for #10 SASE.

Nonfiction: How-to (athletics), humor (bicycle related), interview/profile (bicycle related), new product (bicycle related), personal experience (bicycle related) and photo feature (bicycle related). Buys 10 mss/year. Query. Length: 500-2,500 words. Pays $25-50. Sometimes pays expenses of writers on assignment.

Photos: Send photos with submission. Reviews contact sheets and 5 × 7 prints. Offers no additional payment for photos accepted with ms. Identification of subjects required. Buys one-time rights.

Tips: "Consult with editor. Looking for reports of racing/riding events, previews, interviews with personalities. Inclusion of art is very important."

BIKEREPORT, Bikecentennial, Inc., The Bicycle Travel Association, Box 8308, Missoula MT 59807. (406)721-1776. Editor: Daniel D'Ambrosio. 75% freelance written. Works with a small number of new/unpublished writers each year. Bimonthly bicycle touring magazine for Bikecentennial members. Circ. 18,000. Pays on publication. Publishes ms an average of 8 months after acceptance. Byline given. Include short bio with manuscript. Buys first serial rights. Submit seasonal/holiday material 3 months in advance. Simultaneous queries OK. Query for electronic submissions. Reports in 2 weeks on queries; 1 month on mss. Sample copy and guidelines for 9 × 12 SAE with $1 postage.

Nonfiction: Historical/nostalgic (interesting spots along bike trails); how-to (bicycle); humor (touring); interview/profile (bicycle industry people); personal experience ("my favorite tour"); photo feature (bicycle); technical (bicycle); travel ("my favorite tour"). Buys 20-25 mss/year. Query with published clips or send complete ms. Length: 800-2,500 words. Pays 3¢/word and up.

Photos: Bicycle, scenery, portraits. State availability of photos. Model releases and identification of subjects required.

Fiction: Adventure, experimental, historical, humorous. Not interested in anything that doesn't involve bicycles. Query with published clips or send complete ms. Length: 800-2,500 words. Pays 3¢/word and up.

Tips: "We don't get many good essays. Consider that a hint. But we are still always interested in travelogs."

CYCLING USA, The Official Publication of the U.S. Cycling Federation, 1750 E. Boulder St., Colorado Springs CO 80909. (719)578-4581. FAX: (719)578-4628. Editor: Kyle Woodlief. 50% freelance written. Monthly magazine covering reportage and commentary on American bicycle racing, personalities and sports physiology, for USCF licensed cyclists. Circ. 32,000. Pays on publication. Publishes ms an average of 2 months after acceptance. Byline given. Simultaneous queries and previously published submissions OK. Reports in 2 weeks. Sample copy for 10 × 12 SAE and 60¢ postage.

Nonfiction: How-to (train, prepare for a bike race); interview/profile; opinion; personal experience; photo feature; technical; and race commentary on major cycling events. No comparative product evaluations. Buys 15 mss/year. Query with published clips. Length: 500-2,000 words. Pays 10¢/word.

Photos: State availability of photos. Pays $10-25 for 5 × 7 b&w prints; $100 for transparencies used as cover. Captions required. Buys one-time rights.

Columns/Departments: Athlete's Kitchen, Nuts & Bolts, Coaches Column.

Tips: "A background in bicycle racing is important because the sport is somewhat insular, technical and complex. Most major articles are generated inhouse. Race reports are most open to freelancers. Be concise, informative and anecdotal. The most frequent mistake made by writers in completing an article for us is that it is too lengthy; our format is more compatible with shorter (500-800-word) articles than longer features."

VELONEWS, A Journal of Bicycle Racing, Suite G, 5595 Arapahoe Ave., Boulder CO 80303. (303)440-0601. FAX: (303)444-6788. Managing Editor: Tim Johnson. 50% freelance written. Monthly tabloid September-February, biweekly March-August covering bicycle racing. Circ. 30,000. Pays on publication. Publishes ms an average of 1 month after acceptance. Byline given. Buys one-time rights. Simultaneous queries and submissions OK. Electronic submissions OK; call first. Reports in 3 weeks. Sample copy for 9 × 12 SAE plus $1.05 postage.
Nonfiction: In addition to race coverage, opportunities for freelancers include reviews (book and videos) and health-and-fitness departments. Buys 30 mss/year. Query. Length: 300-2,000 words. Pays up to 10¢/word.
Photos: State availability of photos. Pays $16.50-34.50 for b&w prints. Pays $100 for color used on cover. Captions and identification of subjects required. Buys one-time rights.

Boating

‡BOAT, Diamandis Communications Inc., 1633 Broadway, New York NY 10019. (212)767-5589. Editor: Charles Plueddeman. Bimonthly magazine covering powerboats. Estab. 1988. Circ. 110,000. Byline given. Offers $250 kill fee. Buys first North American serial rights and all rights. Submit seasonal/holiday material 3 months in advance. Free sample copy. Writer's guidelines for 9 × 12 SAE with $1 postage.
Nonfiction: How-to (care for your boat), new product, technical. "No travel, dangerous boating or safety articles." Buys 3 mss/year. Query with published clips. Length: 500-3,000 words. Pays $300-1,000. Pays expenses of writers on assignment.
Photos: Send photos with submission. Reviews any size transparencies. Offers $10-300 per photo. Buys one-time rights.
Columns/Departments: Engines, Rigged for Fishing, Bilge Rat, Towing. Buys 12 mss/year. Query with published clips. Length: 1,500 words maximum. Pays $300-700.

BOAT JOURNAL, (formerly *Small Boat Journal*), 2100 Powers Ferry Rd., Atlanta GA 30339. (404)955-5656. Editor: Richard Lebovitz. Managing Editor: John Weber. 95% freelance written. Bimonthly magazine covering recreational boating. "*Boat Journal* focuses on the practical and enjoyable aspects of owning and using small boats. *Boat Journal* covers all types of watercraft under 30 feet in length—powerboats, sailboats, rowing boats, sea kayaks and canoes. Topics include cruising areas and adventures, boat evaluations, and helpful tips for building, upgrading and maintaining, and safely handling small boats." Estab. 1979. Circ. 65,000. Pays on publication. Publishes ms an average of 6 months after acceptance. Byline given. Offers 50% kill fee. Buys first rights. Submit seasonal/holiday material 6 months in advance. Simultaneous (as long as author agrees to give first rights to *BJ*) submissions OK. Query for electronic submissions. Reports in 5 weeks on queries; 3 weeks on mss. Sample copy for 8½ × 11 SAE with 7 first class stamps; writer's guidelines for #10 SASE.
Nonfiction: Book excerpts, essays, historical/nostalgic, how-to (boating, maintenance, restoration and improvements), humor, interview/profile, new product, personal experience, photo feature, technical and travel. Plans special issues on electronics, engines, fishing boats and equipment, boatbuilding. Buys 60 mss/year. Query with or without published clips, or send complete ms. Length: 800-3,000 words. Pays $150-600 for assigned articles; pays $75-400 for unsolicited articles. Sometimes pays the expenses of writers on assignment.
Photos: Send photos with submission. Reviews contact sheets, transparencies and prints. Offers $15-200 per photo. Model releases and identification of subjects required. Buys one-time rights.
Columns/Departments: Seamanship (boating safety, piloting and navigation), 1,500 words; Rigs & Rigging (care and improvement of rigging and sails), 1,500 words; Custom Boat (ideas for improving a boat), 1,500 words; Inside Outboards (care and maintenance of outboard engines), 1,500 words. Buys 20 mss/year. Query with published clips. Length: 900-2,500 words. Pays $50-400.
Tips: "Our best stories provide comprehensive, in-depth information about a particular boating subject. *BJ*'s readers are experienced and sophisticated boating enthusiasts—most own more than one type of boat—and expect well-researched articles with a practical, how-to slant. Excellent photos are a must, as are stories with engaging tales drawn from the author's experience." Most open to freelancers are "topics related to seamanship, engine maintenance and repair, boat handling, boat building, hull maintenance and repair, restoration and historical subjects related to small boats."

CANOE MAGAZINE, Canoe Associates, Box 3146, Kirkland WA 98083. (206)827-6363. FAX: (206)827-5177. Managing Editor: Barton Parrott. 80-90% freelance written. A bimonthly magazine on canoeing, whitewater kayaking and sea kayaking. Circ. 60,000. Pays on publication. Publishes ms an average of 2-3 months after acceptance. Byline given. Offers 25% kill fee (rarely needed). Buys right to reprint in annuals; author retains copyright. Submit seasonal/holiday material 4 months in advance. Query for electronic submissions. Reports in 2 months. Free sample copy and writer's guidelines for 9 × 12 SASE.
Nonfiction: Essays, general interest, historical/nostalgic, how-to, humor, interview/profile, new product, opinion, personal experience, photo feature, technical and travel. Plans a special entry-level guide to canoeing and kayaking. No "trip diaries." Buys 60 mss/year. Query with or without published clips, or send complete

ms. Length: 500-3,000 words. Pays $5/column inch. Pays the expenses of writers on assignment.

Photos: State availability of photos with submission or send photos with submission. "Good photos help sell a story." Reviews contact sheets, negatives, transparencies and prints. "Some activities we cover are canoeing, kayaking, canoe fishing, camping, canoe sailing or poling, backpacking (when compatible with the main activity) and occasionally inflatable boats. We are not interested in groups of people in rafts, photos showing disregard for the environment, gasoline-powered, multi-horsepower engines unless appropriate to the discussion, or unskilled persons taking extraordinary risks." Offers $50-150/photo. Model releases and identification of subjects occasionally required. Buys one-time rights.

Columns/Departments: Continuum (essay); Counter Currents (environmental) both 1,500 words; Put-In (short interesting articles); Short Strokes (destinations), 1,000-1,500 words. Buys 60 mss/year. Pays $5/column inch.

Fiction: Uses very little fiction. Buys 5 mss/year.

Fillers: Anecdotes, facts and newsbreaks. Buys 20/year. Length: 500-1,000 words. Pays $5/column inch.

Tips: "Start with Put-In articles (short featurettes) of approximately 500 words, book reviews, or short, unique equipment reviews. Or give us the best, most exciting article we've ever seen—with great photos. Short Strokes is also a good entry forum focusing on short trips on good waterways accessible to lots of people. Focusing more on technique and how-to articles."

CRUISING WORLD, Cruising World Publications, Inc., 5 John Clarke Rd., Newport RI 02840. (401)847-1588. Editor: Bernadette Brennan. 70% freelance written. Monthly magazine for all those who cruise under sail. Circ. 136,000. **Pays on acceptance.** Publishes ms an average of 8 months after acceptance. Offers variable kill fee, $50-150. Buys first North American periodical rights or first world periodical rights. Reports in about 2 months. Query for electronic submissions. Free writer's guidelines.

Nonfiction: Book excerpts, how-to, humor, inspirational, opinion and personal experience. "We are interested in seeing informative articles on the technical and enjoyable aspects of cruising under sail. Also subjects of general interest to seafarers." Buys 135-140 unsolicited mss/year. Submit complete ms. Length: 500-3,500 words. Pays $150-800.

Photos: 35mm slides purchased with accompanying ms. Captions and identification of subjects required. Buys one-time rights.

Columns/Departments: People & Food (recipes for preparation aboard sailboats); Shoreline (sailing news, vignettes); and Workbench (projects for upgrading your boat). Send complete ms. Length: 150-500 words. Pays $25-150.

Tips: "Cruising stories should be first-person narratives. In general, authors must be sailors who read the magazine. Color slides always improve a ms's chances of acceptance. Technical articles should be well-illustrated."

CURRENTS, Voice of the National Organization for River Sports, 314 N. 20th St., Colorado Springs CO 80904. (719)473-2466. Editor: Eric Leaper. Managing Editor: Mary McCurdy. 25% freelance written. Quarterly magazine covering river running (kayaking, rafting, river canoeing). Estab. 1979. Circ. 10,000. Pays on publication. Publishes ms an average of 6 months after acceptance. Byline given. Offers 25% kill fee. Buys first North American serial rights, first rights and one-time rights. Submit seasonal/holiday material 2 months in advance. Simultaneous queries, and simultaneous and previously published submissions OK. Reports in 2 weeks on queries; in 1 month on mss. Sample copy for $1 and 9 × 12 SAE with 3 first class stamps; writer's guidelines for #10 SASE.

Nonfiction: How-to (run rivers and fix equipment); in-depth reporting on river conservation and access issues and problems; humor (related to rivers); interview/profile (any interesting river runner); new product; opinion; personal experience; technical; travel (rivers in other countries). "We tell river runners about river conservation, river access, river equipment, how to do it, when, where, etc." No trip accounts without originality; no stories about "my first river trip." Buys 20 mss/year. Query with or without clips of published work. Length: 500-2,500 words. Pays $12-75.

Photos: State availability of photos. Pays $10-35. Reviews b&w or color prints or slides; b&w preferred. Captions and identification of subjects (if racing) required. Buys one-time rights.

Columns/Departments: Book and film reviews (river-related). Buys 5 mss/year. Query with or without clips of published work or send complete ms. Length: 100-500 words. Pays $5-50.

Fiction: Adventure (river). Buys 2 mss/year. Query. Length: 1,000-2,500 words. Pays $25-75. "Must be well-written, on well-known river and beyond the realm of possibility."

Fillers: Clippings, jokes, gags, anecdotes, short humor, newsbreaks. Buys 5/year. Length: 25-100 words. Pays $5-10.

Tips: "We need more material on river news—proposed dams, wild and scenic river studies, accidents, etc. If you can provide brief (300-500 words) on these subjects, you will have a good chance of being published. Material must be on whitewater rivers. Go to a famous river and investigate it; find out something we don't know—especially about rivers that are *not* in Colorado or adjacent states—we already know about the ones near us."

GREAT LAKES SAILOR, Mid-America's Freshwater Sailing Magazine, Great Lakes Sailor, Inc., 2132 E. 9th St., Cleveland OH 44115. (216)861-1777. Editor: Drew Shippy. 55% freelance written. A monthly magazine on Great Lakes sailing. Estab. 1987. Circ. 24,000. Pays on publication. Byline given. Buys first North America serial rights. Submit seasonal material 3 months in advance. Simultaneous submissions OK. Free sample copy and writer's guidelines. Reports on queries in 1 month; 6 weeks on mss.

Nonfiction: How-to (major and minor sailboat upgrades), humor (sailing oriented), interview/profile (sailing personality), new product (sailboat oriented), personal experience (sailing oriented), photo feature (sail racing), travel (sailing destination). Buys 60 mss/year. Query. Length: 1,000-3,500 words. Pays $50-500.

Photos: Send photos with submissions. Reviews, transparencies and 4×5 or 8×10 prints. Offers no additional payment for photos accepted with ms. Captions required. Buys first North American rights.

Columns/Departments: Yard & Loft (major sailboat upgrades) 1,500-2,000 words; Sailor's Projects (minor sailboat upgrades—under $250) 250-1,000 words; Boat Handling (sailing techniques) 1,500-2,000 words; News (Great Lakes events/developments of interest) 300-500 words. Buys 36 mss/year. Query. Pays $50-250.

HEARTLAND BOATING, Inland Publications, P.O. Box 1067, Martin TN 38237. (901)587-6791. Editor: Molly Lightfoot Blom. 40% freelance written. Bimonthly magazine on boating. "Magazine is devoted to both power and sail boating enthusiasts throughout middle America; houseboats are included. The focus is on the freshwater inland rivers and lakes of the Heartland; primarily the Tennessee, Cumberland, Ohio and Mississippi rivers and the Tennessee-Tombigbee Waterway. No Great Lakes or salt water material wil be considered unless it applies to our area." Estab. 1988. Circ. 11,000. Pays on publication. Publishes ms an average of 3 months after acceptance. Byline given. Buys first North American serial rights and sometimes second serial (reprint) rights. Submit seasonal/holiday material 6 months in advance. Simultaneous submissions OK. Query for electronic submissions. Reports in 1 month. Sample copy $3; free writer's guidelines.

Nonfiction: General interest, historical/nostalgic, how-to, humor, interview/profile, new product, personal experience, photo feature, technical, travel. Buys 20-30 mss/year. Query with or without published clips, or send complete ms. Length: 800-3,000 words. Pays 5-25¢/word.

Photos: Send photos with query. Reviews contact sheets, transparencies. Buys one-time rights.

Columns/Departments: Buys 10 mss/year. Query. Pays 5-25¢/word.

HOT BOAT, LFP Publishing, Suite 300, 9171 Wilshire Blvd., Beverly Hills CA 90210. (213)858-7155. FAX: (213)275-3857. Editor: Kevin Spaise. 50% freelance written. A monthly magazine on performance boating (16-35 feet), water skiing and water sports in general. "We're looking for concise, technically oriented 'how-to' articles on performance modifications; personality features on interesting boating-oriented personalities, and occasional event coverage." Circ. 90,000. Pays 1 month after acceptance. Publishes ms an average of 2 months after acceptance. Byline given. Offers 40% kill fee. Buys all rights; also reprint rights occasionally. Submit seasonal/holiday material 3 months in advance. Reports in 3 weeks on queries; 1 month on mss. Sample copy for $3, and 9×12 SAE with $1.35 postage.

Nonfiction: How-to (increase horsepower, perform simple boat related maintenance), humor, interview/profile (racers and manufacturers), new product, personal experience, photo feature, technical. "Absolutely no sailing—we deal strictly in powerboating." Buys 30 mss/year. Query with published clips. Length: 500-2,000 words. Pays $75-450. Sometimes pays expenses of writers on assignment.

Photos: Send photos with submission. Reviews transparencies. Captions, model releases and identification of subjects required. Buys all rights.

Tips: "We're always open to new writers. If you query with published clips and we like your writing, we can keep you on file even if we reject the particular query. It may be more important to simply establish contact. Once we work together there will be much more work to follow."

‡LAKELAND BOATING, The magazine for Great Lakes boaters, O'Menra-Brown Publications, Suite 500, 1600 Orrington Ave., Evanston IL 60201. (708)869-5400. Editor: Douglas Seibold. 40% freelance written. Monthly magazine covering Great Lakes boating. Estab. 1945. Circ. 60,000. Pays on acceptance. Publishes ms an average of 4 months after acceptance. Byline given. Offers 25% kill fee. Buys first North American serial rights. Query for electronic submissions. Reports in 1 month on queries. Sample copy for $5.50 with 9×12 SAE and 6 first class stamps. Writer's guidelines for #10 SAE with 1 first class stamp.

Nonfiction: Book excerpts, historical/nostalgic, how-to, interview/profile, personal experience, photo feature, technical and travel. No humor, inspirational, religious, exposé or poetry. Must relate to boating in Great Lakes. Buys 20 mss/year. Query. Length: 800-3,500 words. Pays $30-600 for assigned articles. Sometimes pays expenses of writers on assignment.

Photos: State availability of photos. Reviews transparencies. Captions required. Buys one-time rights.

Columns/Departments: Bosin's Locker (technical or how-to pieces on boating), 100-1,000 words. Buys 40 mss/year. Query. Pays $30-100.

MOTORBOAT, Power & Motoryacht Magazine, 1234 Summer St. 5th Fl., Stamford CT 06950. FAX: (203)327-7039. Editor: Richard Thiel. Managing Editor: Catherine Cusmano. 85% freelance written. Magazine will be published 9 times this year; 12 times next year. "This is a how-to magazine about small powerboats. It concentrates on basic skills, product review and technical information." Estab. 1988. Circ. 180,000. **Pays on acceptance.** Publishes ms an average of 3 months after acceptance. Byline given. Offers negotiable kill fee. Buys first North American serial rights. Query for electronic submissions. Sample copy for 9×12 SAE and $1. Prefer submissions on disk accompanied by ms.

Nonfiction: How-to (fishing, boating, maintenance, repair), new product, photo feature and technical. "No reminiscence, ma and pa cruise, fish stories." Buys 45-50 mss/year. Query with published clips. Length: 1,200-1,600 words. Pays $400 and up. Pays expenses of writers on assignment.

Photos: State availability of photos with submission. Captions and model releases required. Buys one-time rights.

‡PLEASURE BOATING MAGAZINE, Graphcom Publishing, Inc., Suite 107, 1995 NE 150th St., N. Miami FL 33181. (305)945-7403. Publisher: Robert Ulrich. Managing Editor: David Swafford. 60% freelance written. Monthly magazine covering boating around Florida and the Caribbean. Estab. 1971. Circ. 25,000. Pays on publication. Publishes ms an average of 2 months after acceptance. Byline given. Kill fee varies. Buys first rights. Reports in 1 month on queries. Free sample copy and writer's guidlines.

Nonfiction: General interest (motor boating), how-to (boating travel, safety and navigation), personal experience (boating adventure), travel (cruising in boat). No silly humor; pornographic stuff. Buys 35-40 mss/year. Query with published clips. Length: 1,200-2,000 words. Pays $200 minimum; maximum amount varies. Sometimes pays the expenses of writers on assignment.

Photos: Send photos with submission. Reviews negatives. Offers no additional payment for photos accepted with ms. Identification of subjects required. Buys one-time rights.

Tips: "Know the region we cover, offer fresh perspectives and be flexible with editors."

‡SAIL, Charlestown Navy Yard, 100 First Ave., Charlestown MA 02129-2097. (617)241-9500. FAX: (617)241-7968. Editor: Patience Wales. Managing Editor: Amy Ullrich. 50% freelance written. Works with a small number of new/unpublished writers each year. Monthly magazine for audience that is "strictly sailors, average age 42, above average education." Estab. 1970. Pays on publication. Publishes ms an average of 10 months after acceptance. Buys first North American rights. Submit seasonal or special material at least 6 months in advance. Reports in 10 weeks. Writer's guidelines for 1 first class stamp.

Nonfiction: Amy Ullrich, managing editor. Wants "articles on sailing: technical, techniques and feature stories." Interested in how-to, personal experience, profiles, historical and new products. "Generally emphasize the excitement of sail and the human, personal aspect. No logs." Special issues: "Cruising issues, chartering issues, fitting-out issues, special race issues (e.g., America's Cup), boat show issues." Buys 100 mss/year (freelance and commissioned). Length: 1,500-2,800 words. Pays $300-800. Sometimes pays the expenses of writers on assignment.

Photos: Offers additional payment for photos. Uses b&w glossy prints or Kodachrome 64 transparencies. Pays $600 if photo is used on the cover.

Tips: Request an articles specification sheet.

SAILING WORLD, N.Y. Times Magazine Group, 5 John Clarke Rd., Newport RI 02840. FAX: (401)848-5048. Editor: John Burnham. 40% freelance written. Magazine published 12 times/year. Estab. 1962. Circ. 57,000. Pays on publication. Publishes ms an average of 4 months after acceptance. Buys first North American serial rights. Byline given. Query for electronic submissions. Sample copy $2.50.

Nonfiction: How-to for racing and performance-oriented sailors, photo feature, profile, regatta reports, and charter. No travelogs. Buys 5-10 unsolicited mss/year. Query. Length: 500-1,500 words. Pays $50 per column of text.

Tips: "Send query with outline and include your experience. The writer may have a better chance of breaking in with short articles and fillers such as regatta news reports from his or her own area."

SANTANA, The So-Cal Sailing Rag, Santana Publications, Inc., #101, 5132 Bolsa, Huntington Beach CA 92649. (714)893-3432. Editor: David Poe. Managing Editor: Kitty James. 50% freelance written. A monthly magazine on sailing. "We publish conversationally written articles of interest to Southern California sailers, including technical, cruising, racing, fiction, etc." Circ. 25,000. Pays on publication. Publishes ms an average of 2 months after acceptance. Byline given. Publication not copyrighted. Buys first North American serial rights or second serial (reprint) rights. Submit seasonal/holiday material 3 months in advance. Previously published submissions OK. Reports in 1 month. Sample copy for 9×12 SAE with 5 first class stamps.

Nonfiction: Essays, general interest, historical/nostalgic, how-to (technical articles), humor, interview/profile, personal experience. Buys 50 mss/year. Query with or without published clips or send complete ms. Length: 1,000-4,000 words. Pays $50-150.

Photos: State availability of photos with submission. Reviews contact sheets, negatives, transparencies (35mm) and prints (5×7 or 8×10). Offers $10/photo. Captions and identification of subjects required. Buys one-time rights.

Fiction: Adventure, humorous. Send complete ms. Length: 1,000-5,000. Pays $50-150.

Tips: "Reading the publication is best as our style tends towards conversational, frequently irreverent, but we are also interested in technical articles. We are also happy to critique submissions with suggestions on how to break in. Virtually the entire range of topics covered is open to freelance submissions. Articles must have Southern California angle."

SEA, The Magazine of Western Boating for 82 years, Duncan McIntosh Co., Inc., Box 1579, Newport Beach CA 92663. FAX: (714)642-8980. Editor and Publisher: Duncan McIntosh Jr. Executive Editor: Linda Yuskaitis. 70% freelance written. A monthly magazine covering recreational power boating, offshore fishing and coastal news of the West Coast, from Alaska to Hawaii. Also includes separate regional sections on Southern California and the Pacific Northwest. Estab. 1908. Circ. 60,000, all regional editions combined. Pays on publication. Publishes ms an average of 4 months after acceptance. Byline given. Buys first North American serial rights or second serial (reprint) rights. Query for electronic submissions. Reports in 1 month on queries; 6 weeks on mss. Free writer's guidelines, deadline schedule and sample copy with 9×12 SASE.

Nonfiction: General interest (on boating and coastal topics); how-to (tips on maintaining a boat, engine, and gear); interview/profile (of a prominent boating personality); travel (West Coast cruising or fishing destination). Buys 150 mss/year. Query with published clips, or send complete ms. Length: 250 (news items) to 2,500 (features) words. Pays $50 (news items) to $275 (features). Some assignment expenses covered if requested in advance.

Photos: Stories accompanied by photos are preferred. Transparencies only; no color negatives or prints. Pays $35 (inside b&w) to $250 (color cover) for photos. Identification of photo subjects required. Buys one-time rights.

Columns/Departments: West Coast Focus (boating and fishing news with color photos); Southern California Focus (boating and fishing news from Ventura to San Diego with b&w photos); Northwest Focus (boating and fishing news in Alaska, Washington and Oregon with b&w photos); Nautical Elegance (feature on a spectacular modern or renovated classic yacht); Fish Hooks (sportfishing tips); Mexico Report (short features on boating and fishing destinations in Mexico).

Tips: "*Sea*'s editorial focus is on West Coast boating and sportfishing. We are not interested in stories about the East Coast, Midwest or foreign countries. First-time contributors should include resume or information about themselves that identifies their knowledge of subject. Written queries required. No first-person 'what happened on our first cruise' stories. No poetry, fiction or cartoons."

SEA KAYAKER, Sea Kayaker, Inc., 6327 Seaview Ave. NW., Seattle WA 98107. (206)789-1326. FAX: (206)789-6392. Editor: Christopher Cunningham. 50% freelance written. Works with small number of new/unpublished writers each year. A quarterly magazine on the sport of sea kayaking. Circ. 12,000. Pays on publication. Publishes ms an average of 6 months after acceptance. Byline sometimes given. Offers 20% kill fee. Buys first North American serial rights or second serial (reprint) rights. Submit seasonal/holiday material 6 months in advance. Previously published submissions OK. Reports in 2 months. Sample copy $4.60; free writer's guidelines.

Nonfiction: Essays, historical/nostalgic, how-to (on making equipment), humor, inspirational, interview/profile, opinion, personal experience, photo feature, technical and travel. Buys 15 mss/year. Query with or without published clips, or send complete ms. Length: 750-4,000 words. Pays 5-10¢/word. Sometimes pays the expenses of writers on assignment.

Photos: Send photos with submission. Reviews contact sheets. Offers $15-35/photo. Captions, model releases, and identification of subjects required. Buys one-time rights.

Columns/Department: History, Safety, Environment, and Humor. Buys 6 mss/year. Length: 750-4,000 words. Pays 5-10¢/word.

Fiction: Adventure, experimental, fantasy, historical, horror, humorous, mainstream, mystery, science fiction, slice-of-life vignettes and suspense. Buys 2 mss/year. Send complete ms. Length: 750-4,000 words. Pays 5-10¢/word.

Tips: "We consider unsolicited mss that include a SASE, but we give greater priority to brief (several paragraphs) descriptions of proposed articles accompanied by at least two samples—published or unpublished—of your writing. Enclose a statement as to why you're qualified to write the piece and indicate whether photographs or illustrations are available to accompany the piece."

‡**SOUTHERN BOATING MAGAZINE,** The South's Largest Boating Magazine, Southern Boating & Yachting, Inc., 1766 Bay Rd., Miami Beach FL 33139. (305)538-0700. Editor: Skip Allen, Sr. Managing Editor: Andree Conrad. 50% freelance written. Monthly magazine on cruising and fishing in the Southeastern U.S. "Our readers are long-time boat owners who spend a good deal of their time on the water. They have an interest in everything from diesel maintenance to one-design sailboat racing. Above all, they are interested in new and accurate information about cruising destinations." Estab. 1973. Circ. 26,000. Pays on publication. Publishes ms an average of 3-6 months after acceptance (depends, some issues have themes). Byline given. Buys first North American serial rights, first rights, or one-time rights. Submit seasonal/holiday material 4 months

in advance. Simultaneous and previously published submissions OK. Query for electronic submissions. Sample copy $4; writer's guidelines with SAE.

Nonfiction: Book excerpts (occasionally), new product, photo feature, technical and travel. "Write for editorial calendar. No personal experience or disasters aboard boats." Buys 50 ms/year. Query with or without published clips, or send complete ms. Length: 750-2,500 words. Pays $100-200 for assigned articles; $75-150 for unsolicited articles. Sometimes pays expenses of writers on assignment.

Photos: Send photos with submission. Reviews transparencies (both slides and larger formats). Offers no additional payment for photos accepted with ms. Captions, model releases, and identification of subjects required. Buys one-time rights.

Tips: "Anyone who has plans to or has already taken a cruise in Southeastern or Carribean waters, and can adequately convey the kind of information other cruising yachtsmen need to decide whether they want to undertake a similar cruise should contact us. We ask for excellent color pictures, preferably slides in Kodachrome or Fujichrome, 35mm or larger. We do not publish stories without photos. Maps are appreciated by all of our readers. Freelancers have the best chance with feature articles. We are also looking for writers with the ability to write technical information on engines, electronics and other sources of interest intelligibly."

TRAILER BOATS MAGAZINE, Poole Publications, Inc., 20700 Belshaw Ave., Carson CA 90746-3510. (213)537-6322. FAX: (213)537-8735. Editor: Chuck Coyne. 30-40% freelance written. Works with a small number of new/unpublished writers each year. Monthly magazine (November/December issue combined). Emphasizes legally trailerable boats and related powerboating activities. Circ. 80,000. Pays on publication. Publishes ms 2-6 months after acceptance. Byline given. Buys all rights. Submit seasonal/holiday material 3 months in advance. Query for electronic submissions. Reports in 1 month. Sample copy $1.25; writer's guidelines for #10 SASE.

Nonfiction: General interest (trailer boating activities); historical (places, events, boats); how-to (repair boats, installation, etc.); humor (almost any boating-related subject); nostalgia (same as historical); personal experience; photo feature; profile; technical; and travel (boating travel on water or highways). No "How I Spent My Summer Vacation" stories, or stories not even remotely connected to trailerable boats and related activities. Buys 18-30 unsolicited mss/year. Query or send complete ms. Length: 500-3,000 words. Pays up to $7/column inch. Pays expenses of writers on assignment.

Photos: Send photos with ms. Pays $10-75 for 8×10 b&w prints; $25-350 for color transparencies. Captions required.

Columns/Departments: Boaters Bookshelf (boating book reviews); Over the Transom (funny or strange boating photos); and Patent Pending (an invention with drawings). Buys 2/issue. Query. Length: 100-500 words. Pays 7¢-10¢/word. Mini-Cruise (short enthusiastic approach to a favorite boating spot). Need map and photographs. Length: 500-750 words. Pays $100. Open to suggestions for new columns/departments.

Fiction: Adventure, experimental, historical, humorous and suspense. "We do not use too many fiction stories but we will consider them if they fit the general editorial guidelines." Query or send complete ms. Length: 500-1,500 words. Pays $50 minimum.

Tips: "Query should contain short general outline of the intended material; what kind of photos; how the photos illustrate the piece. Write with authority covering the subject like an expert. Frequent mistakes are not knowing the subject matter or the audience. Use basic information rather than prose, particularly in travel stories. The writer may have a better chance of breaking in at our publication with short articles and fillers if they are typically hard to find articles. We do most major features inhouse."

WATERWAY GUIDE, Communication Channels, Inc., 6255 Barfield Rd., Atlanta GA 30328. (404)256-9800. FAX: (404)256-3116. Editor: Judith Powers. 90% freelance written. Quarterly magazine on intracoastal waterway travel for recreational boats. "Writer must be knowledgeable about navigation and the areas covered by the guide." Estab. 1947. Circ. 45,000. Pays on publication. Publishes ms an average of 3 months after acceptance. Byline given sometimes. Kill fee varies. Buys all rights. Reports in 2 month on queries; 3 months on mss. Sample copy $25.95 and $3 postage.

Nonfiction: Historical/nostalgic, how-to, photo feature, technical and travel. "No personal boating experiences." Buys 25 mss/year. Query with or without published clips, or send complete ms. Length: 200 words minimum. Pays $50-3,000 for assigned articles. Pays in contributor copies or other premiums for helpful tips and useful information.

Photos: Send photos with submission. Reviews 3×5 prints. Offers $25 per b&w photo, $500 for color photos used on the cover. Identification of subjects required. Buys one-time rights.

Fillers: Facts. Buys 6/year. Length: 250-1,000 words. Pays $50-150.

Tips: "Must have on-the-water experience and be able to provide new and accurate information on geographic areas covered by Waterway Guide."

‡THE WESTERN BOATMAN, For the boating enthusiast west of the Rockies, Poole Publications, 20700 Belshaw Ave., Carson CA 90746. (213)537-6322. Editor: Elyse Mintey. 70% freelance written. Bimonthly magazine covering recreational pleasure boating. "We're a lifestyle/adventure/travel magazine for yachtsmen in the West." Estab. 1983. Circ. 30,000. Pays on publication. Byline given. Pays 25% kill fee. Buys first North

American serial rights and second serial (reprint) rights. Submit seasonal/holiday material 6 months in advance. Query for electronic submissions. Reports in 2 months. Free sample copy and writer's guidelines.

Nonfiction: Book excerpts, historical/nostalgic, how-to (engine maintenance, boat repair, piloting), humor, interview/profile, personal experience, photo feature, technical and travel. Special issues: March/April: fishing; May/June: cruising (travel); Nov./Dec.: Mexico (travel). "No product reviews, book reviews, or disaster stories." Buys 175 ms/year. Query with published clips. Length: 100-2,000 words. Pays $8-10/column inch for assigned articles; $6-7/column inch for unsolicted articles. Sometimes pays expenses of writers on assignment.

Photos: Send photos with submission. Reviews transparencies (35mm) and prints (4×6). Offers $15-250/photo. Identification of subjects required. Buys one-time rights.

Columns/Departments: John Jeffries, associate editor. Explorer (boating/travel/special attractions, historic places/buildings, restaurants on the waterfront), 300-700 words; Fishing with the Pros (how-to catch a specific species with thumbnail biography of a particular fishing guide or pro), 800-900 words; Deck Log (regional news of people, events, and special boats), 50-200 words. Buys 75 ms/year. Send complete ms. Pays $200-300.

Fillers: Anecdotes, facts, and short humor. Buys 20/year. Length: 200-800 words. Pays $6/column inch.

Tips: "We need excellent color photography, authoritative travel and how-to pieces (credentials in field a big help), a thorough knowledge of small boat handling and navigation, a feel for the history and ecology of the maritime states and waterways of the West. Freelancers have the best chance with features. We need tightly written pieces, stories with a lot of human interest, experiential narratives, and well-researched historical stories."

WOODENBOAT MAGAZINE, The Magazine for Wooden Boat Owners, Builders, and Designers, WoodenBoat Publications, Inc., P.O. Box 78, Brooklin ME 04616. (207)359-4651. FAX: (207)359-8920. Editor: Jon Wilson. Executive Editor: Jennifer Elliott. Senior Editor: Mike O'Brien. 50% freelance written. Works with a small number of new/unpublished writers each year. Bimonthly magazine for wooden boat owners, builders, and designers. "We are devoted exclusively to the design, building, care, preservation, and use of wooden boats, both commercial and pleasure, old and new, sail and power. We work to convey quality, integrity, and involvement in the creation and care of these craft, to entertain, to inform, to inspire, and to provide our varied readers with access to individuals who are deeply experienced in the world of wooden boats." Estab. 1974. Circ. 103,000. Pays on publication. Publishes ms an average of 6-12 months after acceptance. Byline given. Offers variable kill fee. Buys first North American serial rights. Simultaneous queries and submissions (with notification) and previously published submissions OK. Query for electronic submissions. Reports in 3 weeks on queries; 4 weeks on mss. Sample copy $4; writer's guidelines for SASE.

Nonfiction: Technical (repair, restoration, maintenance, use, design and building wooden boats). No poetry, fiction. Buys 50 mss/year. Query with published clips. Length: 1,500-5,000 words. Pays $6/column inch. Sometimes pays expenses of writers on assignment.

Photos: Send photos with query. Negatives must be available. Pays $15-75 for b&w; $25-350 for color. Identification of subjects required. Buys one-time rights.

Columns/Departments: On the Waterfront pays for information on wooden boat-related events, projects, boatshop activities, etc. Buys 25/year. "We use the same columnists for each issue." Send complete information. Length: 250-1,000 words. Pays $5-50 for information.

Tips: "We appreciate a detailed, articulate query letter, accompanied by photos, that will give us a clear idea of what the author is proposing. We appreciate samples of previously published work. It is important for a prospective author to become familiar with our magazine first. It is extremely rare for us to make an assignment with a writer with whom we have not worked before. Most work is submitted on speculation. The most common failure is not exploring the subject material in enough depth."

YACHTING, Times-Mirror, 2 Park Ave., New York NY 10016. FAX: (212)725-1035. Publishing Director: Oliver S. Moore III. Managing Editor: Cynthia Taylor. 50% freelance written. "The magazine is written and edited for experienced, knowledgeable yachtsmen." Estab. 1907. Circ. 155,000. Pays on publication. Byline given. Buys first rights. Submit seasonal/holiday material 6 months in advance. Reports in 2 weeks on queries; 1 month on mss.

Nonfiction: Book excerpts, personal experience, photo feature and travel. No cartoons, fiction, poetry. Query with published clips. Length: 250-2,500 words. Pays $250-1,000 for assigned articles. Pays expenses of writers on assignment.

Photos: Send photos with submission. Reviews 35mm transparencies. Offers no additional payment for photos accepted with ms. Captions, model releases and identification of subjects required.

Columns/Departments: Cruising Yachtsman (stories on cruising; contact Cynthia Taylor, managing editor); Racing Yachtsman (stories about sail or power racing; contact Lisa Gosselin); Yacht Yard (how-to and technical pieces on yachts and their systems; contact Charles Barthold, executive editor). Buys 30 mss/year. Send complete ms. Length: 750 words maximum. Pays $250-500.

Tips: "We require considerable expertise in our writing because our audience is experienced and knowledgeable. Vivid descriptions of quaint anchorages and quainter natives are fine, but our readers want to know how the yachtsmen got there, too. They also want to know how their boats work."

Bowling

BOWLERS JOURNAL, 101 E. Erie St., Chicago IL 60611. (312)266-7171. Editor-in-Chief: Mort Luby. Managing Editor: Jim Dressel. 30% freelance written. Prefers to work with published/established writers; works with a small number of new/unpublished writers each year. Emphasizes bowling. Monthly magazine. Circ. 22,000. **Pays on acceptance.** Publishes ms an average of 2 months after acceptance. Buys all rights. Submit seasonal/holiday material 3 months in advance of issue date. Reports in 6 weeks. Sample copy $2.
Nonfiction: General interest (stories on top pros); historical (stories of old-time bowlers or bowling alleys); interview (top pros, men and women); and profile (top pros). "We publish some controversial matter, seek outspoken personalitics. We reject material that is too general; that is, not written for high average bowlers and bowling proprietors who already know basics of playing the game and basics of operating a bowling alley." Buys 15-20 unsolicited mss/year. Query, phone queries OK. Length: 1,200-3,500 words. Pays $75-200.
Photos: State availability of photos with query. Pays $5-15 for 8 × 10 b&w prints; and $15-25 for 35mm or 2¼ × 2¼ color transparencies. Buys one-time rights.

WOMAN BOWLER, 5301 S. 76th St., Greendale WI 53129. (414)421-9000. FAX: (414)421-4420. Editor: Karen Sytsma. 3% freelance written. Works with a small number of new/unpublished writers each year. Published eight times a year with combined March/April, May/June, August/September, November/December issues. Circ. 150,000. Emphasizes bowling for women bowlers, ages 18-90. Buys all rights. **Pays on acceptance.** Publishes ms an average of 3 months after acceptance. Byline given "except on occasion, when freelance article is used as part of a regular magazine department. When this occurs, it is discussed first with the author." Submit seasonal/holiday material 2 months in advance. Previously published submissions OK. Reports in 1 month. Free sample copy and writer's guidelines.
Nonfiction: Interview; profile; and spot news. Buys 25 mss/year. Query. Length: 1,500 words maximum (unless by special assignment). Pays $25-100.
Photos: Purchased with accompanying ms. Query. Pays $25 for b&w glossy prints. Model releases and identification of subjects required.

Football

CALIFORNIA FOOTBALL MAGAZINE, California Team Communications, Inc., Suite 501, 1330 E. 223rd St., Carson CA 90745-4313. (213)513-6232 or (213)835-2000. FAX: (213)835-2451. Editor: David Raatz. 40% freelance written. Bimonthly magazine. "*California Football* and *Basketball* cover all levels of activity in the state, high school through pro, as well as Californians who are excelling in other states. Target audience: 14-24 year-old males and females." Estab. 1986. Circ. 100,000. Pays on publication. Publishes 1½ months after acceptance. Byline given. Buys one-time rights. Simultaneous and previously published submissions OK. Reports in 3 weeks on queries; 2 weeks on mss. Free sample copy and writer's guidelines.
Nonfiction: How-to (training tips), humor, inspirational, new product (sporting goods) and personal experience (athlete's perspective). "Anything unsuitable for family reading is unacceptable." Buys 12 mss/year. Length: 250-3,000 words. Pays $35-250. Sometimes pays expenses of writers on assignment.
Photos: State availability of photos with submission. Reviews 1½ × 1 tranparencies and 8 × 10 prints. Offers $15-150 per photo. Captions, model releases and identification of subjects required. Buys one-time rights.
Columns/Departments: Winning Edge (overcome adversity to gain success), 750-2,000 words; Training Room (performance tips), 750-2,000 words; New Products (sporting goods), 50-500 words; and Extra Points (mini-features with human interest), 50-500 words. Query with published clips. Pays $35-250.
Fillers: Anecdotes, facts, gags to be illustrated by cartoonist, newsbreaks, short humor and statistics. Buys 4/year. Length: 50-750 words. Pays $35-75.
Tips: "Submission of a completed manuscript with a cover letter followed up by a phone call and then a personal interview is the best bet for freelancers. Extra points (or Free Throws for basketball magazine) is the easiest section to get freelance material published. We look for human/general interest stories, with humor or drama being good attributes. This is the off-the-field part of the magazine."

Gambling

THE PLAYER, Nation's Largest Gaming Guide, Player's Intl./ACE Marketing, 2524 Arctic Ave., Atlantic City NJ 08401. (609)344-9000. FAX: (609)345-3239. Editor: Glenn Fine. Managing Editor: Roger Gros. 15% freelance written. Monthly tabloid on gambling. "We cover any issue that would interest the gambler, from casinos to sports betting, to race tracks. Articles should be light, entertaining and give tips on how to win." Estab. 1988. Circ. 210,000. Pays on publication. Byline sometimes given. Buys all rights. Submit seasonal/holiday material 3 months in advance. Sample copy $2 with 9 × 12 SAE and 5 first class stamps.

Nonfiction: How-to (win!) and new product (gaming equipment). "No articles dependent on statistics/no travelogues. No first person gambling stories." Query with published clips. Length: 500-1,000 words. Pays $50-250 for assigned articles; $50-100 for unsolicited articles. Sometimes pays expenses of writers on assignment.
Photos: Send photos with submission. Reviews contact sheets and 5 × 7 prints. Offers $10 per photo. Captions and identification of subjects required. Buys all rights.
Columns/Departments: Table Games (best ways to play, ratings); Slots (new machines, methods, casino policies); Nevada (what's new in state, properties); Tournaments (reports on gaming, tournaments) and Caribbean (gaming in the islands), all 500 words. Buys 2 mss/year. Query with published clips. Pays $50-100.
Fillers: Facts and gags to be illustrated by cartoonist. Buys 10/year. Length: 50-250 words. Pays $25-100.
Tips: "Writer must understand the gambler: why he gambles, what are his motivations. The spread of legalized gaming will be an increasingly important topic in the next year. Write as much to entertain as to inform. We try to give the reader information they will not find elsewhere."

‡**WINNING**, NatCom, Inc., 15115 S. 76th East Ave., Bixby OK 74008. (918)366-4441. FAX: (918)366-6250. Managing Editor: Simon P. McCaffery. 30% freelance written. Monthly magazine covering gaming/travel. How-to-win articles addressing all aspects of gaming-casinos, high-stakes bingo, contests and sweepstakes and so on." Estab. 1976. Circ. 140,000. **Pays on acceptance.** Publishes ms an average of 3 months after acceptance. Byline given. Buys first or second rights. Simultaneous submissions OK. Query for electronic submissions. Reports in 1 week on queries; 1-2 weeks on mss. Sample copy for 9 × 12 SAE with 5 first class stamps. Writer's guidelines for #10 SAE with 1 first class stamp.
Nonfiction: How-to (gaming-casino, etc. bingo, sweepstakes and contests), interview/profile, new product, photo feature, travel. "No negative profiles of casino performers/how-to-cheat gaming articles." Buys 24-30 mss/year. Query. Length: 1,000-3,000 words. Pays $150-400 for assigned articles; $50-400 for unsolicited articles. "Tips section" prizes (merchandise). Sometimes pays expenses of writers on assignment.
Photos: Send photos with submission. Reviews transparencies and prints. Offers $50-250 per photo. Captions, model releases and identification of subjects required. Buys one-time rights.

General Interest

HIGH SCHOOL SPORTS, Suite 2000, 1230 Avenue of the Americas, New York NY 10020. (212)765-3300. FAX: (212)265-7278. Editor: Joe Guise. Assistant Editor: Bob Hill. 80% freelance written. Bimonthly magazine. "We are the only national magazine in America that focuses exclusively on the efforts and achievements of high school athletes. Features are on individuals, teams or issues (steroids, small school basketball)." Estab. 1985. Circ. 500,000. **Pays on acceptance.** Publishes ms an average of 2 months after acceptance. Byline given. Offers 25% kill fee. Buys first rights. Simultaneous and previously published submissions OK. Query for electronic submissions. Sample copy $2 with 8½ × 11 SAE and 90¢ in postage. Writer's guidelines for #10 SASE.
Nonfiction: Buys approximately 35 mss/year. Query with published clips. Length: 1,500-2,000. Pays $400-600. Sometimes pays expenses of writers on assignment.
Photos: State availability of photos with submission. Reviews 35mm transparencies. Most photos are assigned. Buys one-time rights.
Columns/Departments: Dateline: USA (7-page round-up of news in different areas of the country), 250 words; Sports Medicine (nutrition, injuries, etc., single subject, technical); Coach's Clinic (how-to on single subject, i.e., vision training, concentration); Time Out (unusual high school activities); Sneak Previews (a look at the nation's brightest new starts); Retrospect (a high profile sports figure looks back at his/her high school days); Great Rivalries (a look at some of the more emotional, long-running series between teams in a variety of sports). Buys 35 mss/year. Query with published clips. Length 300-750. Pays $75-250.

OUTDOOR CANADA MAGAZINE, Suite 301, 801 York Mills Rd., Don Mills, Ontario M3B 1X7 Canada. (416)443-8888. FAX: (416)443-1869. Editor-in-Chief: Teddi Brown. 70% freelance written. Works with a small number of new/unpublished writers each year. Emphasizes noncompetitive outdoor recreation in Canada *only*. Magazine published 9 times/year. Estab. 1972. Circ. 141,000. Pays on publication. Publishes ms an average of 6-8 months after acceptance. Buys first rights. Submit seasonal/holiday material 1 year in advance of issue date. Byline given. *Enclose SASE or IRCs or material not returned*. Reports in 1 month. Mention *Writer's Market* in request for editorial guidelines.
Nonfiction: Fishing, hunting, adventure, outdoor issues, exploring, outdoor destinations in Canada, some how-to. Buys 35-40 mss/year, usually with photos. Length: 1,000-2,500 words. Pays $100 and up.
Photos: Emphasize people in the outdoors. Pays $35-225 for 35mm transparencies; and $400/cover. Captions and model releases required.
News: Short news pieces. Buys 70-80/year. Length: 200-500 words. Pays $6/printed inch.

OUTSIDE, Mariah Publications Corp., 1165 N. Clark St., Chicago IL 60610. (312)951-0990. Editor: John Rasmus. Managing Editor: Mark Bryant. 90% freelance written. Monthly magazine on outdoor recreation and travel. "*Outside* is a monthly national magazine for active, educated, upscale adults who love the outdoors and are concerned about its preservation." Circ. 325,000. **Pays on acceptance.** Publishes ms an average of 3 months after acceptance. Byline given. Offers 25% kill fee. Buys first North American serial rights. Submit seasonal/holiday material 4-5 months in advance. Electronic submission OK for solicited materials; not unsolicited. Reports in 1 month on queries; 6 weeks on mss. Sample copy $4 with 8½ × 11 SAE and $2.40 postage. Writer's guidelines for SASE.

Nonfiction: Book excerpts, essays, reports on the environment, outdoor sports and expeditions, general interest, how-to, humor, inspirational, interview/profile (major figures associated with sports, travel, environment, outdoor), opinion, personal experience (expeditions; trying out new sports), photo feature (outdoor photography), technical (reviews of equipment; how-to) and travel (adventure, sports-oriented travel). All should pertain to the outdoors: Bike section; Downhill Skiing; Cross-country Skiing; Adventure Travel. Do not want to see articles about sports that we don't cover (basketball, tennis, golf, etc.). Buys 40 mss/year. Query with published clips and SASE. Length: 1,500-4,000 words. Pays 50¢/word. Pays expenses of writers on assignment.

Photos: Send photos with submission. Reviews transparencies. Offers $180 minimum per photo. Captions and identification of subjects required. Buys one-time rights.

Columns/Departments: Dispatches, contact Laura Honhold, (news, events, short profiles relevant to outdoors), 200-1,000 words; Destinations (places to explore, news, and tips for adventure travelers), 250-400 words; Review, contact Dan Ferrara, (evaluations of products), 200-1,500 words. Buys 180 mss/year. Query with published clips. Length: 200-2,000 words. Pays 50¢/word.

Tips: "Prospective writers should study the magazine before querying. Look at the magazine for our style, subject matter and standards." The departments are the best areas for freelancers to break in.

PHILLYSPORT, Lewis Tower Bldg., 15th and Locust Sts., Philadelphia PA 19102. (215)893-4466. FAX: (215)893-4470. Editor: Tim Whitaker. Managing Editor: Linda Belsky Zamost. 100% freelance written. Monthly magazine on professional, collegiate and off-beat sports in Philadelphia. Estab. 1988. Circ. 75,000. **Pays on acceptance.** Publishes ms an average of 2 months after acceptance. Byline given. Offers 20% kill fee. Buys first rights. Submit seasonal/holiday material 4 months in advance. Reports in 3 weeks in queries. Free sample copy and writer's guidelines.

Nonfiction: Book excerpts, historical/nostalgic, humor, interview/profile and personal experience. "We're only interested in Philadelphia sports." Buys 40 mss/year. Query with published clips. Length: 2,000-5,000 words. Pays $100-3,000 for assigned articles; $100-700 for unsolicited articles. Pays expenses of writers on assignment.

Photos: State availability of photos with submission.

Columns/Departments: Books and Media. Buys 24 mss/year. Query with published clips. Length: 1,000-1,500 words. Pays $300-1,000.

REFEREE, Referee Enterprises, Inc., P.O. Box 161, Franksville WI 53126. (414)632-8855. Editor: Tom Hammill. For well-educated, mostly 26- to 50-year-old male sports officials. 20-25% freelance written. Eager to work with new/unpublished writers; works with a small number of new/unpublished writers each year. Monthly magazine. Estab. 1976. Circ. 42,000. Pays on acceptance of completed manuscript. Publishes ms an average of 3-6 months after acceptance. Rights purchased varies. Submit seasonal/holiday material 6 months in advance. Previously published submissions OK. Reports in 2 weeks. Sample copy for 10 × 13 SAE and $1.20 postage; writer's guidelines for #10 SASE.

Nonfiction: How-to, informational, humor, interview, profile, personal experience, photo feature and technical. Buys 54 mss/year. Query. Length: 700-3,000 words. Pays 4-10¢/word. "No general sports articles."

Photos: Purchased with or without accompanying ms or on assignment. Captions preferred. Send contact sheet, prints, negatives or transparencies. Pays $15-25 for each b&w used; $25-40 for each color used; $75-100 for color cover.

Columns/Departments: Arena (bios); Law (legal aspects); Take Care (fitness, medical). Buys 24 mss/year. Query. Length: 200-800 words. Pays 4¢/word up to $100 maximum for Law and Take Care. Arena pays about $15 each, regardless of length.

Fillers: Jokes, gags, anecdotes, puzzles and referee shorts. Query. Length: 50-200 words. Pays 4¢/word in some cases; others offer only author credit lines.

Tips: "Queries with a specific idea appeal most to readers. Generally, we are looking more for feature writers, as we usually do our own shorter/filler-type material. It is helpful to obtain suitable photos to augment a story. Don't send fluff—we need hard-hitting, incisive material tailored just for our audience. Anything smacking of public relations is a no sale. Don't gloss over the material too lightly or fail to go in-depth looking for a quick sale (taking the avenue of least resistance)."

‡SILENT SPORTS, Waupaca Publishing Co., P.O. Box 152, Waupaca WI 54981. (715)258-5546. FAX: (715)258-8162. Editor: Greg Marr. 75% freelance written. Eager to work with new/unpublished writers. Monthly magazine on running, cycling, cross-country skiing, canoeing, camping, backpacking, hiking. A regional publication aimed at people who run, cycle, cross-country ski, canoe, camp and hike in Wisconsin, Minnesota, northern Illinois and portions of Michigan and Iowa. Not a coffee table magazine. "Our readers

Close-up

Joe Guise
Editor
High School Sports

Photo by Sarah Myers

Joe Guise, editor-in-chief of *High School Sports*, knows it's not easy to catch and hold the attention of a high schooler. "All studies show that students are reading less and less, so we have to have something that will appeal to them more effectively, whether it's using more dominant photos, splashier colors in the headlines or shorter, catchier articles."

Since Guise assumed the editorship two years ago, he and a two-person staff have turned the magazine into a more practical, yet graphically-attractive publication that keeps high school students reading.

In 1985, the year *High School Sports* was first published, the magazine emphasized long features on high school athletes from around the country. Guise has shifted to more of an issue-oriented approach, although features still comprise a large part of the magazine. Now the typical four-to six-page feature is complemented by short sidebars, graphs, charts and "tidbits that will be helpful and readable for the kids. We're trying to provide information they can take away with them—we balance out the features with the issues to make it more interesting," he says.

For example, last year the magazine presented a series of award-winning articles on steroid use and its detrimental effects and also featured an article on how alcohol damages the body. Upcoming topics include a two-part series on the recruiting process ("the do's and don'ts for a high school athlete being recruited"), an article on "coping with failure in sports" and another informational piece on how a high school athlete should deal with rehabilitation from an injury.

Guise uses a stable of writers and photographers throughout the U.S. He prefers "an ongoing relationship" with freelancers, and keeps letters and clips from interested writers so he can contact them when he has story ideas in those geographic areas.

"When we have a story in Dubuque, Iowa, I can look up the four or five people who have sent stuff from Dubuque and find out who'd be interested in the story. That's what we encourage. We want people to write in and let us know . . . if they'd do articles within a two-to three-hour radius of them, not only in their own hometown."

Since the magazine is 90% freelance written, Guise says it is imperative for him to receive quality submissions and ideas from new freelancers to maintain originality and freshness. Although he accepts unsolicited submissions, he is continually "shocked" at the poor quality of freelance work sent to him. "I would say that 50-60% of the stuff we receive is unacceptable," says Guise.

"Editing is not a one-way street," Guise says. "It's the give and take between the writer and editor that makes a story successful, not the writer turning in something and hoping the editor molds it into something he wants."

—Brian C. Rushing

are participants from rank amateur weekend athletes to highly competitive racers." Circ. 10,000. Pays on publication. Publishes ms an average of 2 months after acceptance. Byline given. Offers 20% kill fee. Buys one-time rights. Submit seasonal/holiday material 2 months in advance. Simultaneous queries and previously published submissions OK. Reports in 1 month. Sample copy and writer's guidelines for 10×13 SAE and 5 first class stamps.

Nonfiction: General interest, how-to, interview/profile, new product, opinion, technical and travel. First-person articles discouraged. Buys 25 mss/year. Query. Length: 2,500 words maximum. Pays $15-100. Sometimes pays expenses of writers on assignment.

Tips: "Where-to-go, how-to, and personality profiles are areas most open to freelancers. Writers should keep in mind that this is a regional, Midwest-based publication."

SPORTS PARADE, Meridian Publishing Co., Inc., P.O. Box 10010, Ogden UT 84409. (801)394-9446. 65% freelance written. Works with a small number of new/unpublished writers each year. A monthly general interest sports magazine distributed by business and professional firms to employees, customers, clients, etc. Readers are predominantly upscale, mainstream, family oriented. **Pays on acceptance.** Publishes ms an average of 8 months after acceptance. Byline given. Buys first rights, second serial (reprint) rights or nonexclusive reprint rights. Submit seasonal/holiday material 6 months in advance. Simultaneous and previously published submissions OK. Reports in 6 weeks. Sample copy $1 with 9×12 SAE; writer's guidelines for #10 SASE.

Nonfiction: General interest and interview/profile. "General interest articles covering the entire sports spectrum, personality profiles on top flight professional and amateur sports figures." Buys 20 mss/year. Query. Length: 1,200-1,580 words. Pays 15¢/word.

Photos: Send with query or ms. Pays $35 for transparencies; $50 for cover. Captions and model releases required.

Tips: "I will be purchasing more articles based on personalities—today's stars."

WOMEN'S SPORTS AND FITNESS MAGAZINE, Women's Sports and Fitness, Inc., Suite 421, 1919 14th St., Boulder CO 80302. (303)440-5111. Editor: Jane McConnell. 90% freelance written. Works with a small number of new/unpublished writers each year. Magazine published 8 times yearly; 68-125 pages. Emphasizes women's sports, fitness and health. Estab. 1975. Circ. 250,000. Pays on publication. Publishes ms an average of 3 months after acceptance. Buys first North American serial rights. Submit seasonal/holiday material 3 months in advance. Reports in 2 months. Sample copy $2.50 with 9×12 SAE and 2 first class stamps; writer's guidelines for SASE.

Nonfiction: Profile, service piece, interview, how-to, historical, personal experience, personal opinion, new product and sporting event coverage. "All articles should have the latest information from knowledgeable sources. All must be of national interest." Buys 5 mss/issue. Length: 250-2,000 words. Query with published clips. Pays $75-1,000 for features, including expenses.

Photos: State availability of photos. Pays about $25-50 for b&w prints; $50-300 for 35mm color transparencies. Buys one-time rights.

Columns/Departments: Buys 8-10/issue. Query with published clips. Length: 600-1,000 words. Pays $250-2,000.

Fillers: Health, fitness and sporting coverage. Length: about 500 words. Pays $75-150.

Tips: "If the writer doesn't have published clips, best advice for breaking in is to concentrate on columns and fillers (the Living Well and Sporting News departments) first. Query letters should tell why our readers—active women (with an average age in the early thirties) who partake in sports or fitness activities four times a week—would want to read the article. We're especially attracted to articles with a new angle, fresh information, or difficult-to-get information. We go after the latest in health, nutrition and fitness research, or reports about lesser-known women in sports who are on the threshold of greatness. We also present profiles of the best athletes and teams. We want the profiles to give insight into the person as well as the athlete. We have a cadre of writers who we've worked with regularly, we are always looking for new writers."

Golf

GOLF DIGEST, 5520 Park Ave., Trumbull CT 06611. (203)373-7000. Editor: Jerry Tarde. 30% freelance written. Emphasizes golfing. Monthly magazine. Circ. 1.3 million. **Pays on acceptance.** Publishes ms an average of 6 weeks after acceptance. Buys all rights. Byline given. Submit seasonal/holiday material 4 months in advance. Reports in 6 weeks.

Nonfiction: Lisa Sweet, editorial assistant. How-to, informational, historical, humor, inspirational, interview, nostalgia, opinion, profile, travel, new product, personal experience, photo feature and technical; "all on playing and otherwise enjoying the game of golf." Query. Length: 1,000-2,500 words. Pays $150-1,500 depending on length of edited mss.

Photos: Nick DiDio, art director. Purchased without accompanying ms. Pays $75-150 for 5×7 or 8×10 b&w prints; $100-300/35mm transparency. Model release required.

Poetry: Lois Hains, assistant editor. Light verse. Buys 1-2/issue. Length: 4-8 lines. Pays $25.

Fillers: Lois Hains, assistant editor. Jokes, gags, anecdotes and cutlines for cartoons. Buys 1-2/issue. Length: 2-6 lines. Pays $10-25.

GOLF ILLUSTRATED, Family Media, Inc., 3 Park Ave., New York NY 10016. (212)779-6200. Editor-in-Chief: Al Barkow. Executive Editor: David Gould. Managing Editor: Hal Goodman. 50% freelance written. Eager to work with new/unpublished writers. A monthly magazine covering personalities and developments in the sport of golf. Circ. 450,000. Pays on acceptance or publication. Publishes ms an average of 2 months after acceptance. Offers 10% kill fee. Submit seasonal/holiday material 6 months in advance. Query for electronic submissions. Reports in 3 weeks on queries; 6 weeks on manuscripts.

Nonfiction: Essays, historical/nostalgic, how-to, humor, interview/profile, opinion, personal experience, photo feature and travel. Buys 50 mss/year. Query with published clips. Length: 750-1,750 words. Pays $500-1,500 for assigned articles; pays $250-1,000 for unsolicited articles. Sometimes pays the expenses of writers on assignment.

Photos: State availability of photos with submission. Reviews contact sheets and transparencies. Offers $50-500/photo. Captions and identification of subjects required. Buys one-time rights.

Columns/Departments: Health and Fitness, Food and Opinion (all related to golf), approximately 750 words. Query with published clips. Pays $500-1,000.

Fillers: Anecdotes, facts, gags to be illustrated by cartoonist and short humor. Buys 30/year. Length: 100-500 words. Pays $25-300.

Tips: "A freelancer can best break in to our publication by following the personalities—the PGA, LPGA and PGA Senior tour pros and the nature of the game in general."

‡GOLF MAGAZINE, Times-Mirror Magazines, 2 Park Ave., New York NY 10016. (212)779-5000. Editor: George Peper. Senior Editor: David Earl. 40% freelance written. Monthly magazine on golf, professional and amateur. Circ. 1.05 million. **Pays on acceptance.** Publishes ms an average of 2-4 months after acceptance. Byline sometimes given. Offers 20% kill fee. Buys first North American serial rights. Submit seasonal/holiday material 3-4 months in advance. Query for electronic submissions. Reports in 1 month on queries; 2 weeks on mss. Free writer's guidelines.

Nonfiction: General interest, historical/nostalgic, how-to, humor, interview/profile. Buys 10-20 mss/year. Query or query with published clips. Length: 100-2,500 words. Pays $100-2,500. Sometimes pays expenses of writers on assignment.

Photos: State availability of photos with submission or send photos with submission. Offers standard page rate. Captions, model releases and identification of subjects required. Buys one-time rights.

Columns/Departments: See magazines for columns. Buys 5-10 mss/year. Query, query with published clips or send complete ms. Length: 100-1,200 words. Pays $100-1,000.

Fillers: Newsbreaks and short humor. Buys 5-10/year. Length: 50-100 words. Pays $50-100.

Tips: "Be familiar with the magazine and with the game of golf."

Guns

AMERICAN HANDGUNNER, Publishers' Development Corp., Suite 200, 591 Camino de la Reina, San Diego CA 92108. (619)297-5352. FAX: (619)297-5353. Editor: Cameron Hopkins. 90% freelance written. A bi-monthly magazine covering handguns, handgun sports and handgun accessories. "Semi-technical publication for handgun enthusiasts of above-average knowledge/understanding of handguns. Writers must have ability to write about technical designs of handguns as well as ability to write intelligently about the legitimate sporting value of handguns." Circ. 150,000. Pays on publication. Publishes ms an average of 5-9 months after acceptance. Byline given. Offers $50 kill fee. Buys all world rights for text, first North American for photos. Submit seasonal/holiday material 7 months in advance. All submissions must be on computer disk. Reports in 1 week. Free sample copy and writer's guidelines.

Nonfiction: How-to, interview/profile, new product, photo feature, technical and "iconoclastic think pieces." Special issue is the *American Handgunner Annual*. No handgun competition coverage. Buys 60-70 mss/year. Query. Length: 500-3,000 words. Pays $175-600 for assigned articles; pays $100-400 for unsolicited articles. Sometimes pays the expenses of writers on assignment.

Photos: Send photos with submission. Reviews contact sheets, 35mm and 4×5 transparencies and 5×7 b&w prints. Offers no additional payment for b&w photos accepted with ms; offers $50-250/color photo. Captions and identification of subjects required. Buys first North American serial rights.

Tips: "We are always interested in 'round-up' pieces covering a particular product line or mixed bag of different product lines of the same theme. If vacation/travel takes you to an exotic place, we're interested in, say, 'The Guns of Upper Volta.' We are looking more closely at handgun hunting."

GUN DIGEST, HANDLOADER'S DIGEST, DBI Books, Inc., 4092 Commercial Ave., Northbrook IL 60062. (312)272-6310. Editor-in-Chief: Ken Warner. 50% freelance written. Prefers to work with published/established writers and works with a small number of new/unpublished writers each year. Annual journal covering guns and shooting. Estab. 1944. **Pays on acceptance.** Publishes ms an average of 20 months after acceptance. Byline given. Buys all rights. Reports in 1 month.

Nonfiction: Buys 50 mss/issue. Query. Length: 500-5,000 words. Pays $100-600; includes photos or illustration package from author.

Photos: State availability of photos with query letter. Reviews 8 × 10 b&w prints. Payment for photos included in payment for ms. Captions required.

Tips: Award of $1,000 to author of best article (juried) in each issue.

GUN WORLD, 34249 Camino Capistrano, Box HH, Capistrano Beach CA 92624. Editorial Director: Jack Lewis. 50% freelance written. For ages that "range from mid-teens to mid-60s; many professional types who are interested in relaxation of hunting and shooting." Monthly. Circ. 136,000. Buys 80-100 unsolicited mss/year. **Pays on acceptance.** Publishes ms an average of 6 months after acceptance. Buys first rights and sometimes all rights, but rights reassigned on request. Byline given. Submit seasonal material 5 months in advance. Reports in 6 weeks. Copy of editorial requirements for SASE.

Nonfiction and Photos: General subject matter consists of "well-rounded articles—not by amateurs—on shooting techniques, with anecdotes; hunting stories with tips and knowledge integrated. No poems or fiction. We like broad humor in our articles, so long as it does not reflect upon firearms safety. Most arms magazines are pretty deadly, and we feel shooting can be fun. Too much material aimed at pro-gun people. Most of this is staff-written and most shooters don't have to be told of their rights under the Constitution. We want articles on new developments; off-track inventions, novel military uses of arms; police armament and training techniques; do-it-yourself projects in this field." Buys informational, how-to, personal experience and nostalgia articles. Pays up to $300, sometimes more. Purchases photos with mss and captions required. Wants 5 × 7 b&w photos. Sometimes pays the expenses of writers on assignment.

Tips: "The most frequent mistake made by writers in completing an article for us is surface writing with no real knowledge of the subject. To break in, offer an anecdote having to do with proposed copy."

INSIGHTS, NRA News for Young Shooters, National Rifle Association of America, 1600 Rhode Island Ave. NW, Washington DC 20036. (202)828-6075. FAX: (202)223-2691. Editor: John Robbins. 55% freelance written. Monthly magazine covers the shooting sports. "*InSights* is educational yet entertaining. It teaches young shooters and hunters proper and safe shooting techniques and gun handling. Readers are 8-20 years old; 88% are boys." Circ. 35,000. **Pays on acceptance.** Publishes ms an average of 1 month to 1 year after acceptance. Byline given. Buys first North American serial rights and second serial (reprint) rights. Submit seasonal/holiday material 6 months in advance. Reports in 2 months on queries; 3 months on mss. Free sample copy for 9 × 12 SAE with 65¢ postage; writer's guidelines for #10 SASE.

Nonfiction: Historical/nostalgic, how-to, humor, interview/profile, personal experience, technical. "We do not accept manuscripts that are anti-guns or anti-hunting. Nor do we buy articles that describe unsafe or unethical shooting practices." Buys 45 mss/year. Query. Length: 800-1,500 words. Pays $150-300 for assigned articles; $80-300 for unsolicited articles.

Photos: Send photos with submission. Reviews contact sheets and 8 × 10 b&w prints. Offers $10-25 per photo. Captions and identification of subjects required. Buys one-time rights only.

Fiction: Adventure, historical, humorous, western. No unsafe or unethical shooting practices in fiction. Buys 8 mss/year. Query. Length: 800-1,500 words. Pays $80-200.

Tips: "We buy many mss about hunting trips that are unique somehow or teach our young readers about a certain of game. How-to articles like refinishing a gun stock or mounting a scope are purchased as well. Match results or event descriptions for competition shooting are also published; we must receive queries for competition shooting articles."

‡WOMEN & GUNS, SAF Periodicals Group, P.O. Box 488, Station C, Buffalo NY 14209. (716)885-6408. Editor: Sonny Jones. 50% freelance written. Monthly magazine covering "all aspects of women's involvement with firearms, including self-defense, competition, hunting, and target shooting, as well as legal issues." Estab. 1989. Circ. 10,000. Pays within 60 days of publication. Publishes ms an average of 3 months after acceptance. Byline given. Buys first North American serial rights or second serial (reprint) rights. Submit seasonal/holiday material 3 months in advance. Previously published submissions OK. Query for electronic submissions. Reports in 1 month on queries; 2 months on mss. Free sample copy and writer's guidelines.

Nonfiction: How-to, interview/profile, new product, photo feature, and technical. Buys 20-30 mss/year. Query with or without published clips, or send complete ms. Length: 500-2,500 words. Pays $50-100 for assigned articles; $25-50 for unsolicited articles.

Photos: Send photos with submission. Reviews transparencies and 5 × 7 color and b&w prints. Offers no additional payment for photos accepted with ms. Captions, model releases and identification of subjects required. Buys one-time rights.

Columns/Departments: Query. Length: 250-500 words. Pays $10-50.

Fillers: Anecdotes, facts, gags to be illustrated by cartoonist, newsbreaks and short humor. Buys 10/year. Length: 10-100 words. Pays $5-10.

Horse Racing

‡THE BACKSTRETCH, 19363 James Couzens Hwy., Detroit MI 48235. (313)342-6144. FAX: (313)342-6140. Editor: Harriet Randall. Managing Editor: Ruth LeGrove. 40% freelance written. Works with a small number of new/unpublished writers each year. Quarterly magazine. For Thoroughbred horse trainers, owners, breeders, farm managers, track personnel, jockeys, grooms and racing fans who span the age range from very young to very old. Publication of United Thoroughbred Trainers of America, Inc. Estab. 1962. Circ. 25,000. Publishes ms an average of 3 months after acceptance. Sample copy $2.

Nonfiction: "*Backstretch* contains mostly general information. Articles deal with biographical material on trainers, owners, jockeys, horses and their careers on and off the track, historical track articles, etc. Unless writer's material is related to Thoroughbreds and Thoroughbred racing, it should not be submitted. Articles accepted on speculation basis—payment made after material is used. If not suitable, articles are returned. Articles that do not require printing by a specified date are preferred. There is no special length requirement and amount paid depends on material. It is advisable to include photos, if possible. Articles should be original copies and should state whether presented to any other magazine, or whether previously printed in any other magazine. Submit complete ms. We do not buy crossword puzzles, cartoons, newspaper clippings, fiction or poetry."

‡**THE FLORIDA HORSE**, The Florida Horse, Inc., P.O. Box 2106, Ocala FL 32678. (904)237-6444. FAX: (904)237-5610. Editor: F.J. Audette. 25% freelance written. Monthly magazine covering the Florida thoroughbred horse industry. "We seek contemporary coverage and feature material on the Florida breeding, racing and sales scene." Estab. 1958. Circ. 12,000. Pays on publication. Publishes ms an average of 2 months after acceptance. Byline given. Buys first North American serial rights. Reports in 2 weeks. Free sample copy.

Nonfiction: Articles covering horses and people of the Florida thoroughbred industry. Buys 18-24 mss/year. Length: 1,500-3,000 words. Pays $125-200. Sometimes pays expenses of writers on assignment.

Photos: Send photos with ms. Pays $15-25 for sharp, well-composed 8×10 b&w prints. Captions and identification of subjects required. Buys one-time rights.

Columns/Departments: Medically Speaking (veterinarian analysis of equine problems); Legally Speaking (legal analysis of equine legal considerations); and Track Talk (news and features from racetracks—Florida angle only). Buys 24-36 mss/year. Send complete ms. Length: 800-960 words. Pays $35-50.

Tips: "We recommend that writers be at the scene of the action—racetracks, nurseries, provide clean, focused writing from the Florida angle and submit lively, interesting material full of detail and background."

HOOF BEATS, United States Trotting Association, 750 Michigan Ave., Columbus OH 43215. (614)224-2291. FAX: (614)228-1385. Editor: Dean A. Hoffman. 35% freelance written. Works with a small number of new/unpublished writers each year. Monthly magazine covering harness racing for the participants of the sport of harness racing. "We cover all aspects of the sport—racing, breeding, selling, etc." Estab. 1933. Circ. 24,000. Pays on publication. Publishes ms an average of 3 months after acceptance. Byline given. Buys negotiable rights. Submit seasonal/holiday material 3 months in advance. Reports in 3 weeks. Free sample copy, postpaid.

Nonfiction: General interest, historical/nostalgic, humor, inspirational, interview/profile, new product, personal experience, photo feature. Buys 15-20 mss/year. Query. Length: open. Pays $100-400. Pays the expenses of writers on assignment "with approval."

Photos: State availability of photos. Pays variable rates for 35mm transparencies and prints. Identification of subjects required. Buys one-time rights.

Fiction: Historical, humorous, interesting fiction with a harness racing theme. Buys 2-3 mss/year. Query. Length: open. Pays $100-400.

Hunting and Fishing

ALABAMA GAME & FISH, Game & Fish Publications, Inc., Suite 110, 2250 Newmarket Parkway, Marietta GA 30067. (404)953-9222. Editor: Jimmy Jacobs. 90% freelance written. Monthly magazine on in-state outdoor topics of interest to an avid hunting and fishing audience. Circ. 25,000. Pays 75 days prior to cover date of issue. Publishes ms an average of 6 months after acceptance. Byline given. Offers negotiable kill fee. Buys first North American serial rights. Submit seasonal/holiday material 10 months in advance. Editor prefers to hold queries on file until article is assigned or writer informs of prior sale. Reports in 3 months on mss. Sample copy for $2 and 9×12 SAE with 7 first class stamps; writer's guidelines for #10 SASE.

Nonfiction: Send photos with submission. Reviews 2×2 transparencies and 8×10 prints. Offers $25-250 per photo. Captions and identification of subjects required. Buys one-time rights.

Fiction: Gordon Whittington, fiction editor. Humorous (hunting and fishing topics). Buys 12 mss/year. Send complete ms. Length: 2,200-2,500 words. Pays $250-300.

Tips: "We publish hard-core hunting and fishing features for the purpose of informing and entertaining a loyal, state-specific outdoor audience. We do not publish the standard type or outdoor article in quantity. Study our magazine and restrict query ideas to major species in the state."

AMERICAN HUNTER, Suite 1000, 470 Spring Park Pl., Herndon VA 22070. Editor: Tom Fulgham. 90% freelance written. For hunters who are members of the National Rifle Association. Circ. 1.3 million. Buys first North American serial rights. Byline given. Free sample copy for 9×12 SAE with 85¢ postage; writer's guidelines for #10 SASE.

Nonfiction: Factual material on all phases of hunting. Not interested in material on fishing or camping. Prefers queries. Length: 2,000-3,000 words. Pays $250-450.

Photos: No additional payment made for photos used with mss. Pays $25 for b&w photos purchased without accompanying mss. Pays $50-300 for color.

ARKANSAS SPORTSMAN, Game & Fish Publications, Inc., P.O. Box 741, Marietta GA 30061. (404)953-9222. Editor: Jay Langston. 90-95% freelance written. Works with a small number of new/unpublished writers each year. Monthly how-to, where-to and when-to hunting and fishing magazine covering Arkansas. Estab. 1980. Pays 3 months before publication. Byline given. Buys one-time rights. Submit seasonal material 8 months in advance. Simultaneous queries and submissions OK. Reports in 2 months. Sample copy for $2.50 and 10×12 SAE; writer's guidelines for SASE.

Nonfiction: How-to (hunting and fishing *only*); humor (on limited basis); interview/profile (of successful hunter/angler); personal experience (hunting or fishing adventure). No hiking, backpacking or camping. No "my first deer" articles. Buys 60 mss/year. Query with or without published clips. Length: 2,200-2,500 words. Pays $150.

Photos: State availability of photos. Pays $75 for inside color for covers; $250 for covers; $25 for b&w photos not submitted as part of story package. Captions and identification of subjects required. Buys one-time rights.

BASSIN', 15115 S. 76th E. Ave., Bixby OK 74008. (918)366-4441. FAX: (918)366-4436. Managing Editor: Gordon Sprouse. 90% freelance written. Magazine published 8 times/year covering freshwater fishing with emphasis on black bass. Estab. 1985. Circ. 220,000. Publishes ms an average of 8 months after acceptance. Pays within 30 days of acceptance. Byline given. Buys first serial rights. Submit seasonal material 8 months in advance. Prefers queries but will examine mss accompanied by SASE. Query for electronic submissions. Reports in 3 weeks. Sample copy $3; writer's guidelines for #10 SASE.

Nonfiction: How-to and where-to stories on bass fishing. Prefers completed ms. Length: 1,200-1,500 words. Pays $275-400 on acceptance.

Photos: Send photos with ms. Pays $300 for color cover; $100 for color cover inset. Send b&w prints or transparencies. Buys one-time rights. Photo payment on publication.

Tips: "Reduce the common fishing slang terminology when writing for *Bassin'*. This slang is usually regional and confuses anglers in other areas of the country. Good strong features will win me over more quickly than short articles or fillers. Absolutely no poetry. We need stories on fishing tackle and techniques to catch all species of freshwater bass."

BC OUTDOORS, SIP Division, Maclean Hunter Ltd., 202-1132 Hamilton St., Vancouver, British Columbia V6B 2S2 Canada. (604)687-1581. FAX: (604)687-1925. Editor: George Will. 80% freelance written. Works with a small number of new/unpublished writers each year. Outdoor recreation magazine published 7 times/year. *BC Outdoors* covers fishing, camping, hunting, and the environment of outdoor recreation. Estab. 1934. Circ. 55,000. **Pays on acceptance.** Publishes ms an average of 3 months after acceptance. Byline given. Offers negotiable kill fee. Buys first North American serial rights. Query for electronic submissions. Reports in 1 month on queries; 2 months on mss. Sample copy and writer's guidelines for 8×10 SAE with $2 postage.

Nonfiction: How-to (new or innovative articles on outdoor subjects); personal experience (outdoor adventure); and outdoor topics specific to British Columbia. "We would like to receive how-to, where-to features dealing with hunting and fishing in British Columbia and the Yukon." Buys 80-90 mss/year. Query. Length: 1,500-2,000 words. Pays $300-500. Sometimes pays the expenses of writers on assignment.

Photos: State availability of photos with query. Pays $25-75 on publication for 5×7 b&w prints; $35-150 for color contact sheets and 35mm transparencies. Captions and identification of subjects required. Buys one-time rights.

Tips: "More emphasis on saltwater angling and less emphasis on self-propelled activity, like hiking and canoeing will affect the types of freelance material we buy. Subject must be specific to British Columbia. We receive many manuscripts written by people who obviously do not know the magazine or market. The writer has a better chance of breaking in at our publication with short, lesser-paying articles and fillers, because we have a stable of regular writers in constant touch who produce most main features."

CALIFORNIA GAME & FISH, Game & Fish Publications, Inc., Box 741, Marietta GA 30061. Editor: Burt Carey. See *Alabama Game & Fish*.

DAKOTA GAME & FISH, Game & Fish Publications, Inc., Box 741, Marietta GA 30061. (404)953-9222. Editor: Kim Leighton. See *Alabama Game & Fish*.

DEER AND DEER HUNTING, The Stump Sitters, Inc., Box 1117, Appleton WI 54912. (414)734-0009. FAX: (414)734-2919. Editors: Al Hofacker and Rob Wegner. Managing Editor: Randall P. Schwalbach. 80% freelance written. Prefers to work with published/established writers. Magazine (8 issues annually) covers deer hunting for individuals who hunt with bow, gun or camera. Circ. 160,000. **Pays on acceptance**. Publishes ms an average of 6 months after acceptance. Byline given. Offers $50 kill fee. Buys first North American serial rights and second serial (reprint) rights. Submit seasonal/holiday material 8 months in advance. Reports in 2 weeks. Sample copy for 9×12 SAE with 7 first class stamps; writer's guidelines for #10 SASE.
Nonfiction: Historical/nostalgic; how-to (hunting techniques); opinion; personal experience; photo feature; technical. "Our readers desire factual articles of a technical nature that relate deer behavior and habits to hunting methodology. We focus on deer biology, management principles and practices, habitat requirements, natural history of deer, hunting techniques and hunting ethics." No hunting "Hot Spot" or "local" articles. Buys 70 mss/year. Query with clips of published work. Length: 1,000-3,000 words. Pays $50-250.
Photos: Pays $125 for 35mm transparencies; $500 for front cover; $40 for 8×10 b&w prints. Captions and identification of subjects required. Buys one-time rights. Prefers action shots, as opposed to "portraits" of deer. Also need hunter photos.
Columns/Departments: Deer Browse (unusual observations of deer behavior). Buys 20 mss/year. Length: 200-600 words. Pays $10-50.
Fillers: Clippings, anecdotes, newsbreaks. Buys 20/year. Length: 200-800 words. Pays $10-40.
Tips: "Break in by providing material of a technical nature, backed by scientific research, and written in a style understandable to the average deer hunter. We focus primarily on white-tailed deer."

‡MIKE EASTMAN'S OUTDOORSMEN, P.O. Box 68, Jackson Hole WY 83001. (307)856-4055. Editor: Mike Eastman. 75% freelance written. Quarterly magazine on big game hunting in the West. "All readers are avid hunters, wanting helpful information on hunting big game out West. Writers must know the sport of big game hunting." Estab. 1987. Circ. 1,000. Pays on publication. Publishes ms an average of 3 months after acceptance. Byline given. Buys first rights. Submit seasonal/holiday material 3 months in advance. Query for electronic submissions. Reports in 2 months on queries. Sample copy for 9×12 SAE and 4 first class stamps. Writer's guidelines for #10 SASE.
Nonfiction: Exposé, general interest, humor, interview/profile, personal experience, photo feature, technical. Buys 12 mss/year. Send outline ms. Length: 200-1,000 words. Pays 8¢/word maximum for assigned articles; 5¢/word maximum for unsolicited articles.
Photos: Send photos with submission. Reviews 3×4 prints. Captions required. Buys one-time rights.
Columns/Departments: How-To (informative—hunting product use or technique), 500 words; Area Focus (thoroughly researched hot hunting area in a Western state), 200 words. Buys 4-8 mss/year. Length: 200-1,000 words. Pays 8¢/word maximum.
Fillers: Anecdotes, facts, newsbreaks, short humor. Buys 12-16/year. Length: 200-1,000 words. Pays 3¢/word maximum.
Tips: "Send us your qualifications as a writer and a knowledgable person in the hunting field. Give the reader enough information that he feels he has learned something useful he can apply out in the field."

FIELD & STREAM, 2 Park Ave., New York NY 10016. Editor: Duncan Barnes. 50% freelance written. Eager to work with new/unpublished writers. Monthly. Buys first rights. Byline given. Reports in 6 weeks. Query. Writer's guidelines for 8×10 SAE with 1 first class stamp.
Nonfiction and Photos: "This is a broad-based service magazine for the hunter and fisherman. Editorial content ranges from very basic how-to stories detailing a useful technique or a device that sportsmen can make to articles of penetrating depth about national hunting, fishing, and related activities. Also humor and personal essays, nostalgia and 'mood pieces' on the hunting or fishing experience." Prefers color photos to b&w. Query first with photos. Length: 1,000-2,000 words. Payment varies depending on the quality of work, importance of the article. Pays $750 and up for major features. *Field & Stream* also publishes regional sections with feature articles on hunting and fishing in specific areas of the country. The sections are geographically divided into Northeast, Midwest, Far West, West and South, and appear 12 months a year. Usually buys photos with mss. When purchased separately, pays $450 minimum for color. Buys first rights to photos.
Fillers: Buys "how it's done" fillers of 250-750 words. Must be unusual or helpful subjects. Pays $250 on acceptance. Also buys "Field Guide" pieces, short (750-word maximum) articles on natural phenomena as specifically related to hunting and fishing; and "Myths and Misconceptions," short pieces debunking a commonly held belief about hunting and fishing. Pays $500.

The double dagger before a listing indicates that the listing is new in this edition. New markets are often the most receptive to freelance submissions.

THE FISHERMAN, LIF Publishing Corp., 14 Ramsey Rd., Shirley NY 11967-4704. (516)345-5200. FAX: (516)345-5304. Editor: Fred Golofaro. Senior Editor: Pete Barrett. 4 regional editions: *Long Island*, *Metropolitan New York*, Fred Golofaro, editor; *New England*, Tim Coleman, editor; *New Jersey*, Dusty Rhodes, editor; and *Delaware-Maryland-Virginia*, Keith Kaufman, editor. 75% freelance written. A weekly magazine covering fishing with an emphasis on saltwater. Combined circ. 85,000. Pays on publication. Byline given. Offers variable kill fee. Buys all rights. Articles may be run in one or more regional editions by choice of the editors. Submit seasonal/holiday material 2 months in advance. Reports in 3 weeks. Free sample copy and writer's guidelines.
Nonfiction: Send submission to editor of regional edition. General interest, historical/nostalgic, how-to, interview/profile, personal experience, photo feature, technical and travel. Special issues include Trout Fishing (April), Bass Fishing (June), Offshore Fishing (July), Surf Fishing (September), Tackle (October) and Electronics (November). "No 'me and Joe' tales. We stress how, where, when, why." Buys approx. 300 mss/year, each edition. Length: 1,200-2,000 words. Pays $100-150 for unsolicited feature articles.
Photos: Send photos with submission; also buys single photos for cover use. Offers no additional payment for photos accepted with ms. Identification of subjects required.
Tips: "Focus on specific how-to and where-to subjects within each region."

FISHING WORLD, 51 Atlantic Ave., Floral Park NY 11001. FAX: (516)437-6841. Editor: Keith Gardner. 100% freelance written. Bimonthly. Circ. 300,000. Pays on publication. Buys first North American serial rights. Publishes ms an average of 6 months after acceptance. Reports in 2 weeks. Free sample copy; writer's guidelines for #10 SASE.
Nonfiction: "Destination-oriented feature articles range from 2,000-3,000 words with the shorter preferred. A good selection of transparencies must accompany each submission. Subject matter should be a hot fishing site, either freshwater or salt. Where-to articles should be accompanied by sidebars covering how to make reservations and arrange transportation, how to get there, where to stay. Angling methods should be developed in clear detail, with accurate and useful information about tackle and boats. Depending on article length, suitability of photographs and other factors, payment is $200-300 for articles accompanied by suitable photography. Transparencies selected for cover use pay an additional $300. Brief queries accompanied by photos are preferred.
Photos: "Cover shots are purchased separately, rather than selected from those accompanying mss. The editor favors drama rather than serenity in selecting cover shots."
Tips: Looking for "quality photography and more West Coast fishing."

FLORIDA GAME & FISH, Game & Fish Publications, Inc., Box 741, Marietta GA 30061. (404)953-9222. Editor: Jimmy Jacobs. See *Alabama Game & Fish*.

FLORIDA WILDLIFE, Florida Game & Fresh Water Fish Commission, 620 South Meridian St., Tallahassee FL 32399-1600. (904)488-5563. FAX: (904)488-6988. Editor: Andrea H. Blount. About 30% freelance written. Bimonthly state magazine covering hunting, natural history, fishing and wildlife conservation. "In outdoor sporting articles we seek themes of wholesome recreation. In nature articles we seek accuracy and conservation purpose." Estab. 1947. Circ. 29,000. Pays on publication. Publishes ms 2 months to 2 years after acceptance. Byline given. Buys first North American serial rights and occasionally second serial (reprint) rights. Submit seasonal/holiday material 6 months in advance. Simultaneous queries, and simultaneous and previously published submissions OK. "Inform us if it is previously published work." Reports in 6 weeks on queries; variable on mss. Sample copy $1.25; free writer's/photographer's guidelines for SASE.
Nonfiction: General interest (bird watching, hiking, camping, boating); how-to (hunting and fishing); humor (wildlife related; no anthropomorphism); inspirational (conservation oriented); personal experience (wildlife, hunting, fishing, outdoors); photo feature (Florida species: game, nongame, botany); and technical (rarely purchased, but open to experts). "We buy general interest hunting, fishing and nature stories. No stories that humanize animals, or opinionated stories not based on confirmable facts." Buys 30-40 mss/year. Send slides/manuscript. Length: 500-1,500 words. Generally pays $50/published page; including use of photos.
Photos: State availability of photos with story query. Prefer 35mm color slides of hunting, fishing, and natural science series of Florida wildlife species. Pays $20-50 for inside photos; $100 for front cover photos, $50 for back cover. "We like short, specific captions." Buys one-time rights.
Fiction: "We rarely buy fiction, and then only if it is true to life and directly related to good sportsmanship and conservation. No fairy tales, erotica, profanity, or obscenity." Buys 2-3 mss/year. Send complete mss and label "fiction." Length: 500-1,200 words. Generally pays $50/published page.
Tips: "Read and study recent issues for subject matter, style and examples of our viewpoint, philosophy and treatment. We look for wholesome recreation, ethics, safety, and good outdoor experience more than bagging the game in our stories. We usually need well-written hunting and fishing articles that are entertaining and informative and that describe places to hunt and fish in Florida."

FLY FISHERMAN, Cowles Magazines Inc., 2245 Kohn Rd., P.O. Box 8200, Harrisburg PA 17105. (717)657-9555. Editor and Publisher: John Randolph. Associate Editor: Philip Hanyok. 85-90% freelance written. Magazine published 6 times/year on fly fishing. Circ. 140,000. **Pays on acceptance.** Publishes ms an average

10 months after acceptance. Byline given. Buys first North American serial rights and (selectively) all rights. Submit seasonal/holiday material 1 year in advance. Query for electronic submissions. Reports in 6 weeks. Sample copy for 9×12 SAE and 4 first class stamps. Writer's guidelines for #10 SASE.

Nonfiction: Book excerpts, how-to, humor, interview/profile, technical and essays on fly fishing, fly tying, shorts and fishing technique shorts and features. Where-to. No other types of fishing, including spin or bait. Buys 75 mss/year. Length: 50-3,000 words.

Photos: State availability of photos or send photos with query or ms. Captions, model releases and identification of subjects required. Buys one-time rights.

Fillers: Short humor and newsbreaks. Buys 30/year. Length: 25-1,000 words.

Tips: "Our magazine is a tightly focused, technique-intensive special interest magazine. Articles require fly fishing expertise, and writing must be tight and in many instances well researched. The novice fly fisher has little hope of a sale with us, although perhaps 30 percent of our features are entry-level or intermediate-level in nature. Fly-fishing technique pieces that are broadly focused have great appeal. Both features and departments—short features—have the best chance of purchase. Accompany submissions with excellent color slides (35mm), black and white 8×10 prints or line drawing illustrations."

FUR-FISH-GAME, 2878 E. Main, Columbus OH 43209. Editor: Mitch Cox. 65% freelance written. Works with a small number of new/unpublished writers each year. Monthly magazine. For outdoorsmen of all ages who are interested in hunting, fishing, trapping, dogs, camping, conservation and related topics. Estab. 1900. Circ. 180,000. **Pays on acceptance.** Publishes ms an average of 7 months after acceptance. Byline given. Buys first serial rights or all rights. Prefers nonsimultaneous submissions. Reports in 6 weeks. Query. Sample copy for $1 and 8×11 SAE. Writer's guidelines for #10 SASE.

Nonfiction: "We are looking for informative, down-to-earth stories about hunting, fishing, trapping, dogs, camping, boating, conservation and related subjects. Nostalgic articles are also used. Many of our stories are 'how-to' and should appeal to small-town and rural readers who are true outdoorsmen. Some recent articles have told how to train a gun dog, catch big-water catfish, outfit a bowhunter and trap late-season muskrat. We also use personal experience stories and an occasional profile, such as an article about an old-time trapper. 'Where-to' stories are used occasionally if they have broad appeal." Length: 1,500-3,000 words. Pays $75-150 depending upon quality, photo support, and importance to magazine. Short filler stories pay $35-80.

Photos: Send photos with ms. Photos are part of ms package and receive no additional payment. Prefer b&w but color prints or transparencies OK. Prints can be 5×7 or 8×10. Caption information required.

Tips: "We are always looking for quality articles that tell how to hunt or fish for game animals or birds that are popular with everyday outdoorsmen but often overlooked in other publications, such as catfish, bluegill, crappie, squirrel, rabbit, crows, etc. We also use articles on standard seasonal subjects such as deer and pheasant, but like to see a fresh approach or new technique. Trapping articles, especially instructional ones based on personal experience, are useful all year. Articles on gun dogs, ginseng and do-it-yourself projects are also popular with our readers. An assortment of photos and/or sketches greatly enhances any ms, and sidebars, where applicable, can also help."

GEORGIA SPORTSMAN, Game & Fish Publications, Box 741, Marietta GA 30061. (404)953-9222. Editor: Jimmy Jacobs. See *Alabama Game & Fish.*

‡GREAT LAKES FISHERMAN, Outdoor Publishing Co., 1432 Parsons Ave., Columbus OH 43207. Editor: Dan Armitage. 95% freelance written. Eager to work with new/unpublished writers. Monthly magazine covering how, when and where to fish in the Great Lakes region. Estab. 1974. Circ. 50,000. Pays on 15th of month prior to issue date. Publishes ms an average of 8 months after acceptance. Byline given. Offers $40 kill fee. Buys first North American serial rights. Submit seasonal/holiday material 8-12 months in advance. Reports in 5 weeks. Free sample copy and writer's guidelines for 9×12 SAE with 5 first class stamps.

Nonfiction: How-to (where to and when to freshwater fish). "No 'me and Joe' or subject matter outside the Great Lakes region." Buys 84 mss/year. Query with clips of published work. "Letters should be tightly written, but descriptive enough to present no surprises when the ms is received. Prefer b&w photos to be used to illustrate ms with query." Length: 1,000-1,500 words. Pays $135-200. Sometimes pays telephone expenses of writers on assignment.

Photos: Send photos with ms. "Black and white photos are considered part of manuscript package and as such receive no additional payment. We consider b&w photos to be a vital part of a ms package. We look for four types of illustration with each article: scene (a backed off shot of fisherman); result (not the typical meat shot of angler grinning at camera with big stringer but in most cases just a single nice fish with the angler admiring the fish); method (a lure shot or illustration of special rigs mentioned in the text); and action (angler landing a fish, fighting a fish, etc.). Illustrations (line drawings) need not be finished art but should be good enough for our artist to get the idea of what the author is trying to depict." Prefers cover shots to be verticals with fish and fisherman action shots. Pays $200 for 35mm transparencies. Captions, model releases and identification of subjects required. Buys one-time rights.

Tips: "Our feature articles are 95% freelance material. The magazine is circulated in the eight states border-ing the Great Lakes, an area where one-third of the nation's licensed anglers reside. All of our feature content is how, when or where, or a combination of all three covering the species common to the region. Fishing is an age-old sport with countless words printed on the subject each year. A fresh new slant that indicates a desire to share with the reader the author's knowledge is a sale. We expect the freelancer to answer any anticipated questions the reader might have (on accommodations, launch sites, equipment needed, etc.) within the ms. We publish an equal mix each month of both warm- and cold-water species articles."

GULF COAST FISHERMAN, Harold Wells Gulf Coast Fisherman, Inc., 401 W. Main St., Port Lavaca TX 77979. (512)552-8864. Publisher/Editor: Gary M. Ralston. 95% freelance written. A quarterly magazine covering Gulf Coast saltwater fishing. "All editorial material is designed to expand the knowledge of the Gulf Coast angler and promote saltwater fishing in general." Estab. 1979. Circ 15,000. Pays on publication. Publishes ms an average of 2 months after acceptance. Byline given. Buys first North American serial rights. Submit seasonal/holiday material 2 months in advance. Submissions of manuscripts on Macintosh 3½″ disk-ette most preferred. Sample copy and writer's guidelines for 9 × 12 SAE and 5 first class stamps.
Nonfiction: How-to (any aspect relating to saltwater fishing that provides the reader specifics on use of tackle, boats, finding fish, etc.); interview/profile; new product; personal experience; and technical. Buys 25 mss/year. Query with or without published clips, or send complete ms. Length: 900-1,800 words. Pays $100-275.
Photos: State availability of photos with submission. Offers no additional payment for photos accepted with ms. Captions and identification of subjects required. Buys one-time rights.
Tips: "Features are the area of our publication most open to freelancers. Subject matter should concern some aspect of or be in relation to saltwater fishing in coastal bays or offshore."

‡HOOKED ON FISHING MAGAZINE, Southeast Outdoors, Inc., 604 Jefferson, P.O. Box 682, Cape Girardeau MO 63702-0682. (314)651-3638. Editorial Director: Frank Lafentres. Editor: Sheri Robertson. 95% freelance written. Bimonthly magazine covering fishing in: MO, IL, KY, TN, AR, IN, MS. *"Hooked on Fishing* is a family-oriented magazine. 50% of our readers have some college or are college graduates. We emphasize the family aspect of fishing in our region, and our purpose is to educate and entertain." Estab. 1988. Circ. 10,000. Pays on publication. Publishes ms an average of 3-4 months after acceptance. Byline given. Buys first and one-time rights. Submit seasonal/holiday material 4-6 months in advance. Reports in 2 weeks. Sample copy for 9 × 12 SAE with 5 first class stamps. Free writer's guidelines.
Nonfiction: How-to (fishing techniques), humor, interview/profile, new product, opinion, personal experi-ence, photo feature, technical, travel. Special November-December Christmas issue. We are a family-oriented magazine. We do not accept "booze, broads, beards, belles and belt buckles" type of articles (the "good old boy" slant). Buys 30 mss/year. Query with published clips. Length: 1,800-2,500 words. Pays $75-125 for assigned articles; $50-100 for unsolicited articles.
Photos: Send photos with submission. Reviews standard transparencies and 5 × 7 prints. Offers $5-50 per photo. Captions, model releases and identification of subjects required. Buys one-time rights.
Columns/Departments: Buyer's Guide (new fishing gear/products), open length—about 1 column; Club News (for fishing clubs in 7-state area), open; Conservation Dept. (opinion is welcome—ecology, regulations, etc. Also factual information [news]), open. Buys 18 mss/year. Query with published clips. Pays $30-80.
Fiction: Humorous, slice-of-life vignettes on fishing in the 7-state area. No good old boy fiction. Buys 6-10 mss/year. Query with published clips. Length: 1,800-2,500 words. Pays $50-100.
Fillers: Anecdotes, facts, newsbreaks, short humor. Pays $20-30.
Tips: "We are looking for fishing articles that keep a family approach to the sport in mind, but with a certain aesthetic appeal beyond hard facts and technical jargon. Articles *must* have photo or illustrative support and maps if applicable. Ms submissions must include SASE."

ILLINOIS GAME & FISH, Game & Fish Publications, Inc., Box 741, Marietta GA 30061. (404)953-9222. Editor: Jim Low. See *Alabama Game & Fish*.

INDIANA GAME & FISH, Game & Fish Publications, Inc., Box 741, Marietta GA 30061. (404)953-9222. Editor: Jim Low. See *Alabama Game & Fish*.

IOWA GAME & FISH, Game & Fish Publications, Inc., Box 741, Marietta GA 30061. (404)953-9222. Editor: Kim Leighton. See *Alabama Game & Fish*.

KANSAS GAME & FISH, Game & Fish Publications, Inc., Box 741, Marietta GA 30061. (404)953-9222. Editor: Nick Gilmore. See *Alabama Game & Fish*.

KENTUCKY GAME & FISH, Game & Fish Publications, Inc., Box 741, Marietta GA 30061. (404)953-9222. Editor: Bill Hartlage. See *Alabama Game & Fish*.

LOUISIANA GAME & FISH, Game & Fish Publications, Inc., Box 741, Marietta GA 30061. (404)953-9222. Editor: Jay Langston. See *Alabama Game & Fish.*

THE MAINE SPORTSMAN, P.O. Box 365, Augusta ME 04330. Editor: Harry Vanderweide. 100% freelance written. "Eager to work with new/unpublished writers, but because we run over 30 regular columns, it's hard to get into *The Maine Sportsman* as a beginner." Monthly tabloid. Estab. 1972. Circ. 30,000. Pays "during month of publication." Buys first rights. Publishes ms an average of 3 months after acceptance. Byline given. Reports in 1 month.
Nonfiction: "We publish only articles about Maine hunting and fishing activities. Any well-written, researched, knowledgeable article about that subject area is likely to be accepted by us." Exposé, how-to, general interest, interview, nostalgia, personal experience, opinion, profile and technical. Buys 25-40 mss/issue. Submit complete ms. Length: 200-2,000 words. Pays $20-300. Sometimes pays the expenses of writers on assignment.
Photos: "We can have illustrations drawn, but prefer 1-3 b&w photos." Submit photos with accompanying ms. Pays $5-50 for b&w print.
Tips: "It's rewarding finding a writer who has a fresh way of looking at ordinary events. Specific where-to-go about Maine is needed."

MARLIN, The International Sportfishing Magazine, Marlin Magazine, a division of EBSCO Industries, Inc., 21 S. Tarragona St., Pensacola FL 32501. (904)434-5571. FAX: (904)433-6303. Editor: Dave Lear. 90% freelance written. Bimonthly magazine on big game fishing. "*Marlin* covers the sport of big game fishing (billfish, tuna, sharks, dorado and wahoo). Our readers are sophisticated, affluent and serious about their sport—they expect a high-class, well-written magazine that provides information and practical advice." Estab. 1982. Circ. 30,000. **Pays on acceptance.** Publishes ms an average of 3 months after acceptance. Byline given. Offers ⅓ kill fee. Buys first North American serial rights. Submit seasonal/holiday material 2-3 months in advance. Query for electronic submissions. Free sample copy and writer's guidelines.
Nonfiction: General interest, how-to (bait-rigging, tackle maintenance, etc.), new product, personal experience, photo feature, technical and travel. "No freshwater fishing stories. No 'me & Joe went fishing' stories, unless top quality writing." Buys 30-50 mss/year. Query with published clips. Length: 800-2,200 words. Pays $250-500.
Photos: State availability of photos with submission. Reviews negatives, transparencies and prints. Offers $25-300 per photo. $300 is for a cover. Buys one-time rights.
Columns/Departments: Tournament Reports (reports on winners of major big game fishing tournaments), 300-600 words; Blue Water Currents (news features), 300-900 words; and Boats of Interest (reviews of featured fishing boats), 400-500 words. Buys 25 mss/year. Query. Pays $100-250.
Tips: "Tournament reports are a good way to break in to *Marlin.* Make them short but accurate, and provide photos of fishing action (*not* dead fish hanging up at the docks!). We always need how-tos and news items. Our destination pieces (travel stories) emphasize where and when to fish, but include information on where to stay also. For features: crisp, high action stories—nothing flowery or academic. Technical/how-to: concise and informational—specific details. News: Again, concise with good details—watch for legislation affecting big game fishing, outstanding catches, new clubs and organizations, new trends and conservation issues."

MARYLAND-DELAWARE GAME & FISH, Game & Fish Publications, Inc., Box 741, Marietta GA 30061. (404)953-9222. Editor: Ken Freel. See *Alabama Game & Fish.*

MICHIGAN OUT-OF-DOORS, P.O. Box 30235, Lansing MI 48909. (517)371-1041. FAX: (517)371-1505. Editor: Kenneth S. Lowe. 50% freelance written. Works with a small number of new/unpublished writers each year. Emphasizes outdoor recreation, especially hunting and fishing, conservation and environmental affairs. Monthly magazine. Estab. 1947. Circ. 130,000. **Pays on acceptance.** Publishes ms an average of 6 months after acceptance. Byline given. Buys first North American serial rights. Phone queries OK. Submit seasonal/holiday material 6 months in advance. Reports in 1 month. Sample copy $1.50; free writer's guidelines.
Nonfiction: Exposé, historical, how-to, informational, interview, nostalgia, personal experience, personal opinion, photo feature and profile. No humor. "Stories *must* have a Michigan slant unless they treat a subject of universal interest to our readers." Buys 8 mss/issue. Send complete ms. Length: 1,000-3,000 words. Pays $75 minimum for feature stories. Pays expenses of writers on assignment.
Photos: Purchased with or without accompanying ms. Pays $15 minimum for any size b&w glossy prints; $75 maximum for color (for cover). Offers no additional payment for photos accepted with accompanying ms. Buys one-time rights. Captions preferred.
Tips: "Top priority is placed on true accounts of personal adventures in the out-of-doors—well-written tales of very unusual incidents encountered while hunting, fishing, camping, hiking, etc. The most rewarding aspect of working with freelancers is realizing we had a part in their development. But it's annoying to respond to queries that never produce a manuscript."

MICHIGAN SPORTSMAN, Game & Fish Publications, Inc., Box 741, Marietta GA 30061. (404)953-9222. Editor: Jim Schlender. See *Alabama Game & Fish*.

MID WEST OUTDOORS, Mid West Outdoors, Ltd., 111 Shore Drive, Hinsdale (Burr Ridge) IL 60521. (708)887-7722. FAX: (708)887-1958. Editor: Gene Laulunen. Emphasizes fishing, hunting, camping and boating. Monthly tabloid. 100% freelance written. Estab. 1967. Circ. 43,814. Pays on publication. Buys simultaneous rights. Byline given. Submit seasonal material 2 months in advance. Simultaneous and previously published submissions OK. Reports in 3 weeks. Publishes ms an average of 3 months after acceptance. Sample copy $1; free writer's guidelines with #10 SASE.
Nonfiction: How-to (fishing, hunting, camping in the Midwest) and where-to-go (fishing, hunting, camping within 500 miles of Chicago). "We do not want to see any articles on 'my first fishing, hunting or camping experiences,' 'Cleaning My Tackle Box,' 'Tackle Tune-up,' or 'Catch and Release.' " Buys 1,800 unsolicited mss/year. Send complete ms. Length: 1,000-1,500 words. Pays $15-30.
Photos: Offers no additional payment for photos accompanying ms unless used as covers; uses b&w prints. Buys all rights. Captions required.
Columns/Departments: Fishing, Hunting. Open to suggestions for columns/departments. Send complete ms. Pays $25.
Tips: "Break in with a great unknown fishing hole or new technique within 500 miles of Chicago. Where, how, when and why. Know the type of publication you are sending material to."

MINNESOTA SPORTSMAN, Game & Fish Publications, Inc., Box 741, Marietta GA 30061. (404)953-9222. Editor: Jim Schlender. See *Alabama Game & Fish*.

MISSISSIPPI GAME & FISH, Game & Fish Publications, Inc., Box 741, Marietta GA 30061. (404)953-9222. Editor: Jay Langston. See *Alabama Game & Fish*.

MISSOURI GAME & FISH, Game & Fish Publications, Inc., Box 741, Marietta GA 30061. (404)953-9222. Editor: Bill Hartlage. See *Alabama Game & Fish*.

MUSKY HUNTER MAGAZINE, Esox Publishing, Inc., 959 W. Mason St., Green Bay WI 54303. (414)496-0334. Editor: Joe Bucher. 90% freelance written. Magazine published 6 times a year (Feb., May, June, July, Sept. and Dec.) on Musky fishing. "Serves the vertical market of Musky fishing enthusiasts. We're interested in advanced how-to where-to articles." Estab. 1989. Circ. 16,000. Pays on publication. Publishes ms an average of 3 months after acceptance. Byline sometimes given. Buys first rights or one-time rights. Submit seasonal/ holiday material 4 months in advance. Reports in 2 weeks. Sample copy for 9 × 12 SAE with 5 first class stamps. Writer's guidelines for #10 SASE.
Nonfiction: Historical/nostalgic (related only to Musky fishing), how-to (modify lures, boats and tackle for Musky fishing), personal experience (must be Musky fishing experience), technical (fishing equipment) and travel (to lakes and areas for Musky fishing). Buys 50 mss/year. Send complete ms. Length: 1,000-2,000 words. Pays $100-200 for assigned articles; $50-200 for unsolicited articles. Payment of contributor copies or other premiums negotiable.
Photos: Send photos with submission. Reviews 35mm transparencies and 3 × 5 prints. Offers no additional payment for photos accepted with ms. Identification on subjects required. One-time rights.

NEBRASKA GAME & FISH, Game & Fish Publications, Inc., Box 741, Marietta GA 30061. (404)953-9222. Editor: Kim Leighton. See *Alabama Game & Fish*.

NEW ENGLAND GAME & FISH, Game & Fish Publications, Inc., Box 741, Marietta GA 30061. (404)953-9222. Editor: Mike Toth. See *Alabama Game & Fish*.

NEW JERSEY GAME & FISH, Game & Fish Publications, Inc., Box 741, Marietta GA 30061. (404)953-9222. Editor: Ken Freel. See *Alabama Game & Fish*.

NEW YORK GAME & FISH, Game & Fish Publications, Inc., Box 741, Marietta GA 30061. (404)953-9222. Editor: Mike Toth. See *Alabama Game & Fish*.

NORTH AMERICAN FISHERMAN, Official Publication of North American Fishing Club, Suite 260, 12301 Whitewater Dr., Minnetonka MN 55343. (612)936-0555. Editor: Mark LaBarbera. Managing Editor: Steve Pennaz. 45% freelance written. Bimonthly magazine on fresh- and saltwater fishing across North America. Estab. 1988. Circ. 130,000. **Pays on acceptance.** Publishes ms an average of 4 months after acceptance. Offers $150 kill fee. Buys first North American serial rights, one-time rights and all rights. Submit seasonal/holiday material 6 months in advance. Reports in 3 weeks. Sample copy $5 with 9 × 12 SAE and 6 first class stamps.

Nonfiction: How-to (species–specific information on how-to catch fish), news briefs on fishing from various state agencies and travel (where to information on first class fishing lodges). Buys 35-40 mss/year. Query. Length: 700-2,100. Pays $100-325.

Photos: Send photos with submission. Offers no additional payment for photos accepted with ms. Captions and identification of subjects required. Buys one-time rights.

Fillers: Facts and newsbreaks. Buys 60/year. Length: 50-100. Pays $35-50.

Tips: "We are looking for news briefs on important law changes, new lakes, etc. Areas most open for freelancers are: full-length features, cover photos and news briefs. Know what subject you are writing about. Our audience of avid fresh and saltwater anglers know how to fish and will see through weak or dated fishing information. Must be on cutting edge for material to be considered."

NORTH AMERICAN HUNTER, Official Publication of the North American Hunting Club, North American Hunting Club, P.O. Box 3401, Minnetonka MN 55343. (612)936-9333. FAX: (612)944-2687. Publisher: Mark LaBarbera. Editor: Bill Miller. 60% freelance written. A bimonthly magazine for members of the North American Hunting Club covering strictly North American hunting. "The purpose of the NAHC is to enhance the hunting skill and enjoyment of its 215,000 members." Circ. 215,000. **Pays on acceptance.** Publishes ms an average of 6-10 months after acceptance. Byline given. Buys first North American serial rights, first rights, one-time rights, second serial (reprint) rights or all rights. Submit seasonal/holiday material 1 year in advance. Query for electronic submissions. Reports in 3 weeks. Sample copy $5; writer's guidelines for #10 SASE.

Nonfiction: Exposé (on hunting issues); how-to (on hunting); humor; interview/profile; new product; opinion; personal experience; photo feature and where-to-hunt. No fiction or "Me and Joe." Buys 18-24 mss/year. Query. Length: 1,000-2,500 words. Pays $200-325 for assigned articles; pays $25-325 for unsolicited articles.

Photos: Send photos with submissions. Reviews transparencies and 5 × 7 or 8 × 10 prints. Offers no additional payment for photos accepted with ms. Captions and identification of subjects required. Buys one-time rights.

Tips: "Write stories as if they are from one hunting friend to another."

NORTH AMERICAN WHITETAIL, The Magazine Devoted to the Serious Trophy Deer Hunter, Game & Fish Publications, Inc., Suite 110, 2250 Newmarket Parkway, Marietta GA 30067. (404)953-9222. FAX: (404)933-9510. Editor: Gordon Whittington. 70% freelance written. Magazine, published 8 times/year, about hunting trophy-class white-tailed deer in North America, primarily the U.S. "We provide the serious hunter with highly sophisticated information about trophy-class whitetails and how, when and where to hunt them. We are not a general hunting magazine or a magazine for the very occasional deer hunter." Estab. 1975. Pays 75 days prior to cover date of issue. Publishes ms an average of 6 months after acceptance. Byline given. Offers negotiable kill fee. Buys first North American serial rights. Submit seasonal/holiday material 10 months in advance. Reports in 3 months on mss. Editor prefers to keep queries on file, without notification, until the article can be assigned or author informs of prior sale. Sample copy $3 with 9 × 12 SAE and 7 first class stamps. Writer's guidelines for #10 SASE.

Nonfiction: How-to, interview/profile. Buys 50 mss/year. Query. Length: 1,400-3,000 words. Pays $150-400.

Photos: Send photos with submission. Reviews 2 × 2 transparencies and 8 × 10 prints. Offers no additional payment for photos accepted with ms. Captions and identification of subjects required. Buys one-time rights.

Columns/Departments: Trails and Tails (nostalgic, humorous or other entertaining styles of deer-hunting material, fictional or nonfictional), 1,400 words. Buys 8 mss/year. Send complete ms. Pays $150.

Tips: "Our articles are written by persons who are deer hunters first, writers second. Our hard-core hunting audience can see through material produced by non-hunters or those with only marginal deer-hunting expertise. We have a continual need for expert profiles/interviews. Study the magazine to see what type of hunting expert it takes to qualify for our use, and look at how those articles have been directed by the writers. Good photography of the interviewee and his hunting results must accompany such pieces."

NORTH CAROLINA GAME & FISH, Game & Fish Publications, Inc., Box 741, Marietta GA 30061. (404)953-9222. Editor: Aaron Pass. See *Alabama Game & Fish*.

‡OHIO FISHERMAN, Ohio Fisherman Publishing Co., 1432 Parsons Ave., Columbus OH 43207. (614)445-7507. Editor: Dan Armitage. 95% freelance written. Works with a small number of new/unpublished writers each year. Monthly magazine covering the how, when and where of Ohio fishing. Estab. 1974. Circ. 45,000. Pays on 15th of month prior to issue date. Publishes ms an average of 4-6 months after acceptance. Byline given. Offers $40 kill fee. Buys first rights. Submit seasonal/holiday material 6-8 months in advance. Reports in 5 weeks. Sample copy and writer's guidelines for 9 × 12 SAE and 5 first class stamps.

Nonfiction: How-to (also where to and when to fresh water fish). "Our feature articles are 95% freelance material, and all have the same basic theme—sharing fishing knowledge. No 'me and Joe' articles." Buys 84 mss/year. Query with clips of published work. Letters should be "tightly written, but descriptive enough to present no surprises when the ms is received. Prefer b&w photos to be used to illustrate ms with query." Length: 1,000-1,200 words. Pays $135-175.

Photos: "Need cover photos constantly." Pays $200 for 35mm transparencies (cover use); buys b&w prints as part of ms package—"no additional payments." Captions and identification of subjects required. Buys one-time rights.

Tips: "The specialist and regional markets are here to stay. They both offer the freelancer the opportunity for steady income. Fishing is an age-old sport with countless words printed on the subject each year. A fresh new slant that indicates a desire to share with the reader the author's knowledge is a sale. We expect the freelancer to answer any anticipated questions the reader might have (on accommodations, launch sites, equipment needed, etc.) within the ms."

OHIO GAME & FISH, Game & Fish Publications, Inc., Box 741, Marietta GA 30061. (404)953-9222. Editor: Jim Low. See *Alabama Game & Fish*.

OKLAHOMA GAME & FISH, Game & Fish Publications, Box 741, Marietta GA 30061. (404)953-9222. FAX: (404)933-9510. Editor: Nick Gilmore. See *Alabama Game & Fish*.

OUTDOOR LIFE, Times Mirror Magazines, Inc., 2 Park Ave., New York NY 10016. (212)779-5000. Editor: Mr. Clare Conley. Executive Editor: Vin T. Sparano. 95% freelance written. A monthly magazine covering hunting and fishing. Estab. 1890. Circ. 1.5 million. **Pays on acceptance.** Publishes ms an average of 6-12 months after acceptance. Byline given. Buys first North American serial rights. Submit seasonal/holiday material 6 months in advance. Previously published submissions OK on occasion. Reports in 1 month on queries; 2 months on mss. Writer's guidelines for SASE.

Nonfiction: Book excerpts; essays; how-to (must cover hunting, fishing or related outdoor activities); humor; interview/profile; new product; personal experience; photo feature; technical; and travel. Special issues include Bass and Freshwater Fishing Annual (March), Deer and Big Game Annual (Aug.), and Hunting Guns Annual (Sept.). No articles that are too general in scope—need to write specifically. Buys 400 mss/year. Query or send ms—"either way, photos are *very important*." Length: 800-3,000 words. Pays $350-600 for 1,000-word features and regionals; pays $900-1,200 for 2,000-word or longer national features. "We receive and encourage queries over CompuServe."

Photos: Send photos with submission. Reviews 35mm transparencies and 8 × 10 b&w prints. Offers variable payment. Captions and identification of subjects required. Buys one-time rights. "May offer to buy photos after first use if considered good and have potential to be used with other articles in the future (file photos)." Pay for freelance photos is $100 for ¼ page color to $800 for 2-page spread in color; $1,000 for covers. All photos must be stamped with name and address.

Columns/Departments: This Happened to Me (true-to-life, personal outdoor adventure, harrowing experience), approximately 300 words. Buys 12 mss/year. Pays $50.

Fillers: Newsbreaks and do-it-yourself for hunters and fishermen. Buys unlimited number/year. Length: 1,000 words maximum. Payment varies.

Tips: "It is best for freelancers to break in by writing features for one of the regional sections—East, Midwest, South, West. These are where-to-go oriented and run from 800-1,500 words. Writers must send one-page query with photos."

PENNSYLVANIA ANGLER, Pennsylvania Fish Commission, P.O. Box 1673, Harrisburg PA 17105-1673. (717)657-4518. Editor: Art Michaels. 60-80% freelance written. Prefers to work with published/established writers but works with a few unpublished writers every year. A monthly magazine covering fishing and related conservation topics in Pennsylvania. Circ. 55,000. Pays 6-8 weeks after acceptance. Publishes ms an average of 7-9 months after acceptance. Byline given. Rights purchased vary. Submit seasonal/holiday material 8 months in advance. Reports in 2 weeks on queries; 2 months on mss. Sample copy for 9 × 12 SAE with 4 first class stamps; writer's guidelines for #10 SASE.

Nonfiction: Historical/nostalgic, how-to, where-to and technical. No saltwater or hunting material. Buys 120 mss/year. Query. Length: 300-3,000 words. Pays $25-300.

Photos: Send photos with submission. Reviews 35mm and larger transparencies and 8 × 10 b&w prints. Offers no additional payment for photos accepted with ms. Captions, model releases and identification of subjects required.

Tips: "Our mainstays are how-tos, where-tos, and conservation pieces, but we seek more top-quality fiction, first-person stories, humor, reminiscenses and historical articles. These pieces must have a strong, specific Pennsylvania slant."

PENNSYLVANIA GAME & FISH, Game & Fish Publications, Inc., Box 741, Marietta GA 30061. (404)953-9222. Editor: Mike Toth. See *Alabama Game & Fish*.

PENNSYLVANIA SPORTSMAN, Northwoods Publications Inc., Suite 206, 2101 N. Front St., Harrisburg PA 17110. (717)233-4797. Editor: Lou Hoffman. Managing Editor: Sherry Ritchey. 50% freelance written. Magazine appears 8 times a year on region—state of Pennsylvania hunting, fishing sports. Circ. 57,000. **Pays on acceptance.** Publishes ms an average of 4 months after acceptance. Byline given. Buys one-time or first

North American serial rights. Simultaneous submissions OK. Reports in 2 weeks on queries; 3 weeks on mss. Sample copy $2. Free writer's guidelines for #10 SASE.

Nonfiction: How-to, new product, personal experience and photo feature. September—Hunting annual; March—Fishing annual. Buys 80 mss/year. Query. Length: 600-1,800 words. Pays $25-125. Sometimes pays the expenses of writers on assignment.

Photos: Send photos with submissions. Reviews negatives (slides). Offers no additional payment for photos accepted with ms. Captions required. Buys one-time rights.

Fiction: Mainstream and slice-of-life vignettes. Buys 10 mss/year. Query. Length: 600-1,500 words. Pays $25-125.

Fillers: Facts and newsbreaks. Buys 10/year. Length: 300-600 words. Pays $20-50.

ROCKY MOUNTAIN GAME & FISH, Game & Fish Publications, Inc., Box 741, Marietta GA 30061. Editor: Burt Carey. See *Alabama Game & Fish.*

SAFARI MAGAZINE, The Journal of Big Game Hunting, Safari Club International, 4800 W. Gates Pass Rd., Tucson AZ 85745. (602)620-1220. Editor: William R. Quimby. 90% freelance written. Bimonthly club journal covering international big game hunting and wildlife conservation. Circ. 18,000. Pays on publication. Publishes ms an average of 1 year after acceptance. Byline given. Offers $100 kill fee. Buys all rights. Submit seasonal/holiday material 1 year in advance. Reports in 2 weeks on queries; 1 month on mss. Sample copy $3.50; writer's guidelines for SAE.

Nonfiction: Doug Fulton; articles editor. Photo feature (wildlife); and technical (firearms, hunting techniques, etc.). Buys 48 mss/year. Query or send complete ms. Length: 1,500-2,500 words. Pays $200.

Photos: State availability of photos with query or ms, or send photos with query or ms. Payment depends on size in magazine. Pays $35 for b&w; $50-150 color. Captions, model releases and identification of subjects required. Buys one-time rights.

Tips: "Study the magazine. Send manuscripts and photo packages with query. Make it appeal to affluent, knowledgable, world-travelled big game hunters. Features on conservation contributions from big game hunters around the world are most open to freelancers. We have enough stories on first-time African safaris and North American hunting. We need South American and Asian hunting stories, plus stories dealing with hunting and conservation."

SALT WATER SPORTSMAN, 280 Summer St., Boston MA 02210. (617)439-9977. FAX: (617)439-9357. Editor-in-Chief: Barry Gibson. Emphasizes saltwater fishing. 85% freelance written. Works with a small number of new/unpublished writers each year. Monthly magazine. Circ. 150,000. **Pays on acceptance.** Publishes ms an average of 5 months after acceptance. Byline given. Buys first North American serial rights. Offers 100% kill fee. Submit seasonal material 8 months in advance. Reports in 1 month. Sample copy and writer's guidelines for 8½×11 SAE with $1.41 postage.

Nonfiction: How-to, personal experience, technical and travel (to fishing areas). "Readers want solid how-to, where-to information written in an enjoyable, easy-to-read style. Personal anecdotes help the reader identify with the writer." Prefers new slants and specific information. Query. "It is helpful if the writer states experience in salt water fishing and any previous related articles. We want one, possibly two well-explained ideas per query letter—not merely a listing." Buys 100 unsolicited mss/year. Length: 1,200-1,500 words. Pays $350 and up. Sometimes pays the expenses of writers on assignment.

Photos: Purchased with or without accompanying ms. Captions required. Uses 5×7 or 8×10 b&w prints and color slides. Pays $600 minimum for 35mm, 2¼×2¼ or 8×10 transparencies for cover. Offers additional payment for photos accepted with accompanying ms.

Columns: Sportsman's Workbench (how to make fishing or fishing-related boating equipment), 100-300 words.

Tips: "There are a lot of knowledgeable fishermen/budding writers out there who could be valuable to us with a little coaching. Many don't think they can write a story for us, but they'd be surprised. We work with writers. Shorter articles that get to the point which are accompanied by good, sharp photos are hard for us to turn down. Having to delete unnecessary wordage—conversation, clichés, etc.—that writers feel is mandatory is annoying. Often they don't devote enough attention to specific fishing information."

SOUTH CAROLINA GAME & FISH, Game & Fish Publications, Inc., Box 741, Marietta GA 30061. (404)953-9222. Editor: Aaron Pass. See *Alabama Game & Fish.*

SOUTH CAROLINA WILDLIFE, Box 167, Rembert Dennis Bldg., Columbia SC 29202. (803)734-3972. Editor: John Davis. Managing Editor: Linda Renshaw. For South Carolinians interested in wildlife and outdoor activities. 75% freelance written. Bimonthly magazine. Estab. 1954. Circ. 69,000. Byline given. **Pays on acceptance.** Publishes ms an average of 6 months after acceptance. Buys first rights. Free sample copy. Reports in 6 weeks.

Nonfiction and Photos: Articles on outdoor South Carolina with an emphasis on preserving and protecting our natural resources. "Realize that the topic must be of interest to South Carolinians and that we must be able to justify using it in a publication published by the state wildlife department—so if it isn't directly about hunting, fishing, a certain plant or animal, it must be somehow related to the environment and conservation. Readers prefer a broad mix of outdoor related topics (articles that illustrate the beauty of South Carolina's outdoors and those that help the reader get more for his/her time, effort, and money spent in outdoor recreation). These two general areas are the ones we most need. Subjects vary a great deal in topic, area and style, but must all have a common ground in the outdoor resources and heritage of South Carolina. Review back issues and query with a one-page outline citing sources, giving ideas for graphic design, explaining justification and giving an example of the first two paragraphs." Does not need any column material. Generally does not seek photographs. The publisher assumes no responsibility for unsolicited material. Buys 25-30 mss/year. Length: 1,000-3,000 words. Pays an average of $200-400 per article depending upon length and subject matter. Sometimes pays the expenses of writers on assignment.

Tips: "We need more writers in the outdoor field who take pride in the craft of writing and put a real effort toward originality and preciseness in their work. Query on a topic we haven't recently done. The most frequent mistakes made by writers in completing an article are failure to check details and go in-depth on a subject."

SOUTHERN OUTDOORS MAGAZINE, B.A.S.S. Publications, 1 Bell Rd., Montgomery AL 36141. Editor: Larry Teague. Emphasizes Southern outdoor activities, including hunting, fishing, boating, shooting, camping. 90% freelance written. Prefers to work with published/established writers. Published 9 times/year. Estab. 1952. Circ. 240,000. **Pays on acceptance.** Publishes ms an average of 6 months to 1 year after acceptance. Buys all rights. Reports in 2 months. Sample copy for 9×12 SAE, 5 first class stamps, and $2.50.

Nonfiction: Articles should be service-oriented, helping the reader excel in outdoor sports. Emphasis is on techniques, trends and conservation. Some "where-to" stories purchased on Southern destinations with strong fishing or hunting theme. Buys 120 mss/year. Length: 2,000 words maximum. Pays 15¢/word. Sometimes pays the expenses of writers on assignment.

Photos: Usually purchased with manuscripts. Pays $50-75 for 35mm transparencies without ms, and $250-400 for covers.

Fillers: Humorous or thought-provoking pieces (750-1,200 words) appear in each issue's S.O. Essay feature.

Tips: "It's easiest to break in with short features of 500-1,000 words on 'how-to' fishing and hunting topics. We buy very little first-person. Query first and send sample of your writing if we haven't done business before. Stories most likely to sell: bass fishing, deer hunting, other freshwater fishing, inshore saltwater fishing, bird and small-game hunting, shooting, camping and boating. The most frequent mistakes made by writers in completing an article for us are first-person usage; clarity of articles; applicability of topic to the South; lack of quotes from qualified sources."

SPORTS AFIELD, 250 W. 55th St., New York NY 10019. (212)649-4000. Editor: Tom Paugh. Executive Editor: Fred Kesting. 20% freelance written. Eager to work with new/unpublished writers. For people of all ages whose interests are centered around the out-of-doors (hunting and fishing) and related subjects. Monthly magazine. Circ. 518,010. Buys first North American serial rights for features, and all rights for *SA Almanac*. **Pays on acceptance.** Publishes ms an average of 6 months after acceptance. Byline given. "Our magazine is seasonal and material submitted should be in accordance. Fishing in spring and summer; hunting in the fall; camping in summer and fall." Submit seasonal material 6 months in advance. Reports in 1 month. Query or submit complete ms.

Nonfiction and Photos: "Informative how-to articles with emphasis on product and service and personal experiences with good photos on hunting, fishing, camping, boating and subjects such as conservation, environment and some where-to-go related to hunting and fishing. We want first-class writing and reporting." Buys 15-17 unsolicited mss/year. Length: 500-2,500 words. Pays $750 minimum, depending on length and quality. Photos purchased with or without ms. Pays $50 minimum for 8×10 b&w glossy prints. Pays $50 minimum for 35mm or larger transparencies. Sometimes pays the expenses of writers on assignment.

Fiction: Adventure, humor (if related to hunting and fishing).

Fillers: Send to *Almanac* editor. *Almanac* pays $25 and up depending on length, for newsworthy, unusual, how-to and nature items. Payment on publication. Buys all rights.

Tips: "We seldom give assignments to other than staff. Top-quality 35mm slides to illustrate articles a must. Read a recent copy of *Sports Afield* so you know the market you're writing for. Family-oriented features will probably become more important because more and more groups/families are sharing the outdoor experience."

TENNESSEE SPORTSMAN, Game & Fish Publications, Box 741, Marietta GA 30061. (404)953-9222. Editor: Bill Hartlage. See *Alabama Game & Fish*.

TEXAS SPORTSMAN, Game & Fish Publications, Inc., Box 741, Marietta GA 30061. (404)953-9222. Editor: Nick Gilmore. See *Alabama Game & Fish*.

TURKEY CALL, Wild Turkey Center, Box 530, Edgefield SC 29824. (803)637-3106. Editor: Gene Smith. 50-60% freelance written. Eager to work with new/unpublished writers and photographers. An educational publication for members of the National Wild Turkey Federation. Bimonthly magazine. Circ. 65,000. Buys one-time rights. Byline given. **Pays on acceptance.** Publishes ms an average of 6 months after acceptance. Reports in 1 month. No queries necessary. Submit complete package. Wants original ms only. Sample copy $3 with 9 × 12 SAE. Writer's guidelines for #10 SASE.

Nonfiction and Photos: Feature articles dealing with the hunting and management of the American wild turkey. Must be accurate information and must appeal to national readership of turkey hunters and wildlife management experts. No poetry or first-person accounts of unremarkable hunting trips. May use some fiction that educates or entertains in a special way. Length: up to 3,000 words. Pays $35 for items, $65 for short fillers of 600-700 words, $200-350 for illustrated features. "We want quality photos submitted with features." Art illustrations also acceptable. "We are using more and more inside color illustrations." For b&w, prefer 8 × 10 glossies, but 5 × 7s OK. Transparencies of any size are acceptable. No typical hunter-holding-dead-turkey photos or setups using mounted birds or domestic turkeys. Photos with how-to stories must make the techniques clear (example: how to make a turkey call; how to sculpt or carve a bird in wood). Pays $20 minimum for one-time rights on b&w photos and simple art illustrations; up to $75 for inside color, reproduced any size. Covers: Most are donated. Any purchased are negotiated.

Tips: The writer "should simply keep in mind that the audience is 'expert' on wild turkey management, hunting, life history and restoration/conservation history. He/she *must know the subject*. We are buying more third-person, more fiction, more humor—in an attempt to avoid the 'predictability trap' of a single subject magazine."

‡THE TURKEY HUNTER, (formerly *Turkey*), 3941 N. Paradise Rd., Flagstaff AZ 86004. (602)774-6913. Editor: Gerry Blair. 60% freelance written. Works with a small number of new/unpublished writers each year. A monthly magazine covering turkey hunting, biology and conservation of the wild turkey, gear for turkey hunters, where to go, etc. for both novice and experienced wild turkey enthusiasts. "We stress wildlife conservation, ethics, and management of the resource." Circ. 65,000. Pays on publication. Publishes ms an average of 1 year after acceptance. Byline given.

Nonfiction: Book excerpts (turkey related); how-to (turkey-related); and personal experience (turkey hunting). Buys 75-100 mss/year. "The most frequent mistake made by writers in completing an article for us is inadequate photo support." Query. Length: 500-3,000 words. Pay is "competitive."

Photos: Send photos with accompanying query or ms.

Tips: "How-to articles, using fresh ideas, are most open to freelancers."

VIRGINIA GAME & FISH, Game & Fish Publications, Inc., Box 741, Marietta GA 30061. (404)953-9222. Editor: Aaron Pass. See *Alabama Game & Fish*.

WASHINGTON-OREGON GAME & FISH, Game & Fish Publications, Inc., Box 741, Marietta GA 30061. Editor: Burt Carey. See *Alabama Game & Fish*.

WEST VIRGINIA GAME & FISH, Game & Fish Publications, Inc., Box 741, Marietta GA 30061. (404)953-9222. Editor: Ken Freel. See *Alabama Game & Fish*.

WESTERN OUTDOORS, 3197-E Airport Loop, Costa Mesa CA 92626. (714)546-4370. Editor: Jack Brown. 75% freelance written. Works with a small number of new/unpublished writers each year. Emphasizes hunting, fishing, camping, boating for 11 Western states only, Baja California, Canada, Hawaii and Alaska. Publishes 9 issues/year. Estab. 1961. Circ. 138,000. **Pays on acceptance.** Publishes ms an average of 6 months after acceptance. Buys first North American serial rights. Query (in writing). Submit seasonal material 4-6 months in advance. Reports in 6 weeks. Sample copy $1.75; writer's guidelines for #10 SASE.

Nonfiction: Where-to (catch more fish, bag more game, improve equipment, etc.); how-to informational; photo feature. "We do not accept fiction, poetry, cartoons." Buys 70 assigned mss/year. Query. Length: 1,000-1,500 words maximum. Pays $300-500.

Photos: Purchased with ms. Captions required. Uses 8 × 10 b&w glossy prints; prefers Kodachrome II 35mm slides. Offers no additional payment for photos accepted with ms. Pays $200-250 for covers.

Tips: "Provide a complete package of photos, map, trip facts and manuscript written according to our news feature format. Excellence of color photo selections make a sale more likely. The most frequent mistake made by writers in completing an article for us is that they don't follow our style. Our guidelines are quite clear."

WESTERN SPORTSMAN, P.O. Box 737, Regina, Saskatchewan S4P 3A8 Canada. (306)352-2773. FAX: (306)565-2440. Editor: Roger Francis. 90% freelance written. For fishermen, hunters, campers and others interested in outdoor recreation. "Note that our coverage area is Alberta and Saskatchewan." Bimonthly magazine. Estab. 1968. Circ. 31,000. Rights purchased vary with author and material. May buy first North American serial rights or second serial (reprint) rights. Byline given. Pays on publication. Publishes ms an average of 2-12 months after acceptance. "We try to include as much information as possible on all subjects in each edition. Therefore, we usually publish fishing articles in our winter issues along with a variety of winter stories. If material is dated, we would like to receive articles 2 months in advance of our publication date." Reports in 1 month. Sample copy $4; free writer's guidelines.

Nonfiction: "It is necessary that all articles can identify with our coverage area of Alberta and Saskatchewan. We are interested in mss from writers who have experienced an interesting fishing, hunting, camping or other outdoor experience. We also publish how-to and other informational pieces as long as they can relate to our coverage area. We are more interested in articles which tell about the average guy living on beans, guiding his own boat, stalking his game and generally doing his own thing in our part of Western Canada than a story describing a well-to-do outdoorsman traveling by motorhome, staying at an expensive lodge with guides doing everything for him except catching the fish, or shooting the big game animal. The articles that are submitted to us need to be prepared in a knowledgeable way and include more information than the actual fish catch or animal or bird kill. Discuss the terrain, the people involved on the trip, the water or weather conditions, the costs, the planning that went into the trip, the equipment and other data associated with the event in a factual manner. We're always looking for new writers." Buys 60 mss/year. Submit complete ms. Length: 1,500-2,000 words. Pays up to $400. Sometimes pays the expenses of writers on assignment.

Photos: Photos purchased with ms with no additional payment. Also purchased without ms. Pays $30-50/ 5×7 or 8×10 b&w print; $175-250/35mm or larger transparency for front cover.

WISCONSIN SPORTSMAN, Game & Fish Publications, Inc., Box 741, Marietta GA 30061. Editor: Jim Schlender. See *Alabama Game & Fish*.

Martial Arts

BLACK BELT, Rainbow Publications, Inc., 1813 Victory Place, Burbank CA 91504. (818)843-4444. Executive Editor: Jim Coleman. 80-90% freelance written. Works with a small number of new/unpublished writers each year. Emphasizes martial arts for both practitioner and layman. Monthly magazine. Estab. 1961. Circ. 100,000. Pays on publication. Publishes ms an average of 3-5 months after acceptance. Buys first North American serial rights, retains right to republish. Submit seasonal/holiday material 6 months in advance. Reports in 3 weeks.

Nonfiction: Exposé, how-to, informational, interview, new product, personal experience, profile, technical and travel. Buys 8-9 mss/issue. Query or send complete ms. Length: 1,200 words minimum. Pays $10-20/page of manuscript.

Photos: Very seldom buys photos without accompanying mss. Captions required. Total purchase price for ms includes payment for photos. Model releases required.

Fiction: Historical and modern day. Buys 2-3 mss/year. Query. Pays $100-200.

Tips: "We also publish an annual yearbook and special issues periodically. The yearbook includes our annual 'Black Belt Hall of Fame' inductees."

FIGHTING WOMAN NEWS, Martial Arts, Self-Defense, Combative Sports Quarterly, 11438 Cronridge Dr., Owings Mills MD 21117. Editor: Frances Steinberg. Mostly freelance written. Prefers to work with published/established writers. Quarterly magazine. Our audience is composed of adult women actually practicing martial arts with an average experience of 4+ years. Since our audience is also 80+% college grads and 40% holders of advanced degrees we are an action magazine with footnotes. Our material is quite different from what is found in newsstand martial arts publications." Circ. 3,500. Pays on publication. "There is a backlog of poetry and fiction—hence a *very* long wait. A solid factual martial arts article would go out 'next issue' with trumpets and pipes." Byline given. Buys one-time rights. Submit seasonal/holiday material 6 months in advance. Simultaneous queries, simultaneous and previously published submissions OK. "For simultaneous and previously published we *must* be told about it." Query for electronic submissions. Reports as soon as possible. Sample copy $3.50; writer's guidelines for #10 SASE.

Nonfiction: Book excerpts, exposé (e.g. discrimination against women in martial arts governing bodies); historical/nostalgic; how-to (martial arts, self-defense techniques); humor; inspirational (e.g., self-defense success stories); interview/profile ("we have assignments waiting for writers in this field"); new product; opinion; personal experience; photo feature; technical; travel. Buys 6 mss/year. Query. Length: 1,000-3,000 words. Pays in copies, barter or $30 maximum. Some expenses negotiated, but we can't pay major costs such as planes or hotels.

Photos: State availability of photos with query or ms. Reviews "technically competent" b&w contact sheets and 8×10 b&w prints. "We negotiate photos and articles as a package. Sometimes expenses are negotiated. Captions and identification of subjects required. The need for releases depends on the situation."

Columns/Departments: Notes & News (short items relevant to our subject matter); Letters (substantive comment regarding previous issues); Sports Reports; and Reviews (of relevant materials in any medium). Query or send complete ms. Length: 100-1,000 words. Pays in copies or negotiates payment.

Fiction: Adventure, fantasy, historical and science fiction. "Any fiction must feature a woman skilled in martial arts." Buys 0-1 ms/year. Query. Length: 1,000-5,000 words. "We will consider serializing longer stories." Pays in copies or negotiates payment.

Poetry: "We'll look at all types. Must appeal to an audience of martial artists." Buys 3-4 poems/year. Length: open. Pays in copies or negotiates payment.

Tips: "First, read the magazine. Our major reason for rejecting articles is total unsuitability for our publication. A prime example of this is the writer who submitted numerous articles on subjects that we very much wanted to cover, but written in a gosh-gee-wow progress-to-the-abos style that was totally inappropriate. The second most common reason for rejections is vagueness; we need the old Who, What, When, Where, Why and How and if your article doesn't have that save yourself the postage. Several articles returned by *FWN* have later shown up in other martial arts magazines and since they pay a lot more, you're better off trying them first unless an audience of literate, adult, female, martial artists is what you're aiming at."

INSIDE KARATE, The Magazine for Today's Total Martial Artist, Unique Publications, 4201 Vanowen Pl., Burbank CA 91505. (818)845-2656. FAX: (818)845-7761. Editor: John Steven Soet. 90% freelance written. Works with a small number of new/unpublished writers each year. Monthly magazine covering the martial arts. Circ. 120,000. Publishes ms an average of 3 months after acceptance. Byline given. Buys first North American serial rights. Reports in 3 weeks on queries; in 6 weeks on mss. Sample copy $2.50, 9×12 SAE and 5 first class stamps; free writer's guidelines for #10 SASE.

Nonfiction: Book excerpts; exposé (of martial arts); historical/nostalgic; humor; interview/profile (with approval only); opinion; personal experience; photo feature; and technical (with approval only). *Inside Karate* seeks a balance of the following in each issue: tradition, history, glamor, profiles and/or interviews (both by assignment only), technical, philosophical and think pieces. To date, most "how to" pieces have been done inhouse. Buys 70 mss/year. Query. Length: 1,000-2,500 words; prefers 10-12 page mss. Pays $25-125.

Photos: Send photos with ms. Prefers 3×5 bordered b&w. Captions and identification of subjects required. Buys one-time rights.

Tips: "In our publication, writing style and/or expertise is not the determining factor. Beginning writers with martial arts expertise may submit. Trends in magazine publishing that freelance writers should be aware of include the use of less body copy, better (and interesting) photos to be run large with 'story' caps. If the photos are poor and the reader can't grasp the whole story by looking at photos and copy, forget it."

INSIDE KUNG-FU, The Ultimate In Martial Arts Coverage!, Unique Publications, 4201 Vanowen Pl., Burbank CA 91505. (818)845-2656. FAX: (818)845-7761. Editor: Dave Cater. 75% freelance written. Monthly magazine covering martial arts for those with "traditional, modern, athletic and intellectual tastes. The magazine slants toward little-known martial arts, and little-known aspects of established martial arts." Estab. 1973. Circ. 100,000. Pays on publication. Publishes ms an average of 6 months after acceptance. Byline given. Buys first North American serial rights. Submit seasonal/holiday material 4 months in advance. Simultaneous queries and submissions OK. Reports in 3 weeks on queries; 1 month on mss. Sample copy $2.50 with 9×12 SAE and 5 first class stamps; free writer's guidelines for #10 SASE.

Nonfiction: Exposé (topics relating to the martial arts); historical/nostalgic; how-to (primarily technical materials); cultural/philosophical; interview/profile; personal experience; photo feature; and technical. "Articles must be technically or historically accurate." No "sports coverage, first-person articles or articles which constitute personal aggrandizement." Buys 120 mss/year. Query or send complete ms. Length: 8-10 pages, typewritten and double-spaced.

Photos: Send photos with accompanying ms. Reviews b&w contact sheets, b&w negatives and 8×10 b&w prints. "Photos are paid for with payment for ms." Captions and model release required.

Fiction: Adventure, historical, humorous, mystery and suspense. "Fiction must be short (1,000-2,000 words) and relate to the martial arts. We buy very few fiction pieces." Buys 2-3 mss/year.

Tips: "The writer may have a better chance of breaking in at our publication with short articles and fillers since smaller pieces allow us to gauge individual ability, but we're flexible—quality writers get published, period. The most frequent mistakes made by writers in completing an article for us are ignoring photo requirements and model releases (always number one—and who knows why? All requirements are spelled out in writer's guidelines)."

M.A. TRAINING, Rainbow Publications, 1813 Victory Pl., P.O. Box 7728, Burbank CA 91510-7728. (818)843-4444. FAX: (818)953-9244. Contact: Marian K. Castinado. 75% freelance written. Works with a small number of new/unpublished writers each year. Bimonthly magazine about martial arts training. Estab. 1961. Circ. 60,000. Pays on publication. Publishes ms an average of 3-6 months after acceptance. Buys all North American serial rights. Submit seasonal material 4 months in advance, but best to send query letter first. Reports in 6 weeks. Writer's guidelines for SASE.

Nonfiction: How-to: want training related features. Buys 30-40 unsolicited mss/year. Send query or complete ms. Length: 1,000-2,000 words. Pays $50-200.

Photos: State availability of photos. Most ms should be accompanied by photos. Reviews 5×7 and 8×10 b&w and color glossy prints. Can reproduce prints from negatives. Will use illustrations. Offers no additional payment for photos accepted with ms. Model releases required. Buys all rights.

Tips: "I'm looking for how-to, nuts-and-bolts training type stories which are martial arts related. I need stories about developing speed, accuracy, power, etc."

Miscellaneous

BALLOON LIFE, Balloon Life Magazine, Inc., 3381 Pony Express Dr., Sacramento CA 95834. (916)922-9648. Editor: Glen Moyer. 75% freelance written. Monthly magazine for sport of hot air ballooning. Estab. 1986. Circ. 3,500. Pays on publication. Byline given. Offers 50-100% kill fee. Buys first North American serial rights or second serial (reprint) rights. Submit seasonal/holiday material 3-4 months in advance. Previously published submissions OK. Query for electronic submissions. Reports in 3 weeks on queries; 2 weeks on mss. Sample copy for 9×12 SAE with $1.65 postage. Writer's guidelines for letter SASE.

Nonfiction: Book excerpts, general interest, how-to (flying hot air balloons, equipment techniques), interview/profile, new product, letters to the editor, technical. Buys 150 mss/year. Query with or without published or send complete ms. Length: 800-5,000 words. Pays $50-75 for assigned articles; $25-50 for unsolicited articles. Sometimes pays expenses of writers on assignment.

Photos: Send photos with submission. Reviews transparencies and prints. Offers $15-50 per photo. Identification of subjects required. Buys one-time rights.

Columns/Departments: Hangar Flying (real life flying experience that others can learn from), 800-1,500 words; Preflight (a news and information column), 100-500 words; Logbook (recent balloon events—events that have taken place in last 3-4 months), 300-500 words. Buys 60 mss/year. Send complete ms. Pays $15-50.

Fiction: Humorous. Buys 3-5 mss/year. Send complete ms. Length: 800-1,500 words. Pays $50.

Tips: "This magazine slants toward the technical side of ballooning. We are interested in articles that help to educate and provide safety information. Also stories with manufacturers, important individuals and/or of historic events and technological advances important to ballooning. The magazine attempts to present articles that show "how-to" (fly, business opportunities, weather, equipment). Both our Feature Stories section and Logbook section are where most mss are purchased."

BALLS AND STRIKES, Amateur Softball Association, 2801 NE 50th St., Oklahoma City OK 73111. (405)424-5266. Senior Editor: Bill Plummer III. Production/Design Director: Larry Floyd. 20% freelance written. Works with a small number of new/unpublished writers each year. "Only national monthly tabloid covering amateur softball." Circ. 300,000. Pays on publication. Publishes ms an average of 2 months after acceptance. Buys first rights. Byline given. Reports in 3 weeks. Free sample copy.

Nonfiction: General interest, historical/nostalgic, interview/profile and technical. Query. Length: 2-3 pages. Pays $50-65.

Tips: "We generally like shorter features because we try to get as many different features as possible in each issue."

HOCKEY ILLUSTRATED, Lexington Library, Inc., 355 Lexington Ave., New York NY 10017. (212)391-1400. FAX: (212)986-5926. Editor: Stephen Ciacciarelli. 90% freelance written. Published 3 times in season. Magazine covering NHL hockey. "Upbeat stories on NHL superstars—aimed at hockey fans, predominantly a younger audience." **Pays on acceptance.** Publishes ms an average of 1-2 months after acceptance. Byline given. Buys first North American serial rights. Reports in 2 weeks. Sample copy $1.95 with 9×12 SAE with 3 first class stamps.

Nonfiction: Inspirational and interview/profile. Buys 40-50 mss/year. Query with or without published clips, or send complete ms. Length: 1,500-3,000 words. Pays $75-125.

Photos: State availability of photos with submission. Reviews transparencies and prints. Offers no additional payment for photos accepted with ms. Identification of subjects required. Buys one-time rights.

INSIDE TEXAS RUNNING, 9514 Bristlebrook Dr., Houston TX 77083. (713)498-3208. Editor: Joanne Schmidt. 50% freelance written. A monthly tabloid covering running, cycling and triathloning. "Our audience is made up of Texas runners and triathletes who may also be interested in cross training with biking and swimming." Estab. 1977. Circ. 10,000. **Pays on acceptance.** Publishes ms an average of 1-2 months after acceptance. Byline given. Buys first rights, one-time rights, second serial (reprint) rights and all rights. Submit seasonal/holiday material 2 months in advance. Previously published submissions OK. Reports in 1 month on queries; 6 weeks on mss. Sample copy $1.50; writer's guidelines for #10 SASE.

Nonfiction: Book excerpts, exposé, historical/nostalgic, humor, interview/profile, opinion, photo feature, technical and travel. "We would like to receive controversial and detailed news pieces that cover both sides of an issue: for example, how a race director must deal with city government to put on an event. Problems seen by both sides include cost, traffic congestion, red tape, etc." No personal experience such as "Why I

Love to Run," "How I Ran My First Marathon." Buys 18 mss/year. Query with published clips, or send complete ms. Length: 500-2,500 words. Pays $100 maximum for assigned articles; $50 maximum for unsolicited articles. Sometimes pays the expenses of writers on assignment.

Photos: Send photos with submission. Offers $25 maximum/photo. Captions required. Buys one-time rights.

Tips: "We are looking for specific pieces that cite names, places, costs and references to additional information. Writers should be familiar with the sport and understand race strategies, etc. The basic who, what, where, when and how also applies. The best way to break in to our publication is to submit brief (3 or 4 paragraphs) write-ups on road races to be used in the Results section. We also need more cycling articles for new biking section."

INTERNATIONAL GYMNAST, Sundby Sports, Inc., 225 Brooks St., Box G, Oceanside CA 92054. (619)722-0030. Editor: Dwight Normile. 50% freelance written. Monthly magazine on gymnastics. "*IG* is dedicated to serving the gymnastics community with competition reports, personality profiles, training and coaching tips and innovations in the sport." Circ. 25,000. Pays on publication. Publishes ms an average of 3 months after acceptance. Byline given. Buys one-time rights. Submit seasonal/holiday material 3 months in advance. Sample copy $3.25. Writer's guidelines for #10 SASE.

Nonfiction: How-to (coaching/training/ business, i.e. running a club), interview/profile, opinion, photo feature (meets or training sites of interest, etc.), competition reports and technical. "Nothing unsuitable for young readers." Buys 25 mss/year. Send complete ms. Length: 500-2,250 words. Pays $15-25. Pays in contributor copies or other premiums when currency exchange is not feasible i.e., foreign residents.

Photos: Send photos with submission. Reviews transparencies and prints. Offers $5-40 per photo published. Identification of subjects required. Buys one-time rights.

Columns/Departments: Innovations (new moves, new approaches, coaching tips); Nutrition (hints for the competitive gymnast); Dance (ways to improve gymnasts through dance, all types); Club Corner (business hints for club owners/new programs, etc.) and Book Reviews (reviews of new books pertaining to gymnastics). Buys 10 mm/year. Send complete ms. Length: 750-1,000. Pays $15-25.

Fiction: Humorous, anything pertaining to gymnastics, nothing inappropriate for young readers. Buys 1-2 ms/year. Send complete ms. Length: 1,500 words maximum. Pays $15-25.

Tips: "To *IG* readers, a lack of knowledge sticks out like a sore thumb. Writers are generally coaches, ex-gymnasts and 'hardcore' enthusiasts. Most open area would generally be competition reports. Be concise, but details are necessary when covering gymnastics. Again, thorough knowledge of the sport is indispensable."

‡NATIONAL MASTERS RUNNING NEWS, Gain Publications, P.O. Box 2372, Van Nuys CA 91404. (818)785-1895. Editor: Al Sheahen. 50% freelance written. Monthly tabloid. "The only national publication devoted exclusively to runners age 40 and over. We feature results of track meets and road races, profiles, stories, health articles, training advice, etc. for the masters competitive athlete." Estab. 1977. Circ. 5,300. Pays on publication. Byline given. Not copyrighted. Buys one-time rights. Submit seasonal/holiday material 1 month in advance. Simultaneous and previously published submissions OK. Reports in 1 week on queries; 3 weeks on mss. Free sample copy.

Nonfiction: General interest, how-to (training), inspirational, interview/profile, opinion, photo feature. Buys 8 mss/year. Send complete ms. Length: 100-1,500 words. Pays $25-100. Pays writers with contributor copies or other premiums rather than a cash payment by "mutual agreement."

Photos: State availability of photos with submission. Offers $7.50-15 per photo. Identification of subjects required. Buys one-time rights.

Columns/Departments: Health & Fitness (how to keep fit); Training Advice (how to improve performance); Profile (individual profile); Speakers Corner (general interest), all 750-1,000 words. Buys 2 mss/year. Send complete ms. Length: 500-1,500 words. Pays $25-100.

Fillers: Facts, newsbreaks, short humor. Pays $5-25.

NEW YORK RUNNING NEWS, New York Road Runners Club, 9 E. 89th St., New York NY 10128. (212)860-2280. FAX: (212)860-9754. Editor: Raleigh Mayer. 75% freelance written. A bimonthly regional sports magazine covering running, racewalking, nutrition and fitness. Material should be of interest to members of the New York Road Runners Club. Estab. 1958. Circ. 45,000. Pays on publication. Time to publication varies. Byline given. Offers ⅓ kill fee. Buys first North American serial rights. Submit seasonal/holiday material 4 months in advance. Simultaneous and previously published submissions OK. Reports in 1 month. Sample copy for 9×12 SAE with $1.75 postage; writer's guidelines for #10 SASE.

Nonfiction: Running and marathon articles. Special issues include N.Y.C. Marathon (submissions in by August 1). No non-running stories. Buys 25 mss/year. Query. Length: 750-1,750 words. Pays $50-250. Pays documented expenses of writers on assignment.

Photos: Send photos with submission. Reviews 8×10 b&w prints. Offers $35-300/photo. Captions, model releases and identification of subjects required. Buys one-time rights.
Columns/Departments: Essay (running-related topics). Query. Length: 750 words. Pays $50-125.
Fiction: Running stories. Query. Length: 750-1,750 words. Pays $50-150.
Fillers: Anecdotes. Length: 250-500 words. No payment for fillers.
Tips: "Be knowledgeable about the sport of running. Write like a runner."

PRIME TIME SPORTS & FITNESS, GND Prime Time Publishing, P.O. Box 6097, Evanston IL 60204. (312)869-6434. Editor: Dennis A. Dorner. Managing Editor: Nicholas J. Schmitz. 80% freelance written. Eager to work with new/unpublished writers. A monthly magazine covering seasonal pro sports and racquet and health club sports and fitness. Estab. 1974. Circ. 35,000. Pays on publication. Publishes ms an average of 6 months after acceptance. Byline given. Buys all rights; will assign back to author in 85% of cases. Submit seasonal/holiday material 6 months in advance. Simultaneous and previously published submissions OK. Reports in 6 weeks. Sample copy for 9×11 SAE and 7 first class stamps.
Nonfiction: Book excerpts (fitness and health); exposé (in tennis, fitness, racquetball, health clubs, diets); adult (slightly risqué and racy fitness); how-to (expert instructional pieces on any area of coverage); humor (large market for funny pieces on health clubs and fitness); inspirational (on how diet and exercise combine to bring you a better body, self); interview/profile; new product; opinion (only from recognized sources who know what they are talking about); personal experience (definitely—humor); photo feature (on related subjects); technical (on exercise and sport); travel (related to fitness, tennis camps, etc.); news reports (on racquetball, handball, tennis, running events). Special issues: Swimsuit and Resort Issue (March); Baseball Preview (April); Summer Fashion (July); Pro Football Preview (August); Fall Fashion (October); Ski Issue (November); Christmas Gifts and related articles (December). "We love short articles that get to the point. Nationally oriented big events and national championships. No articles on local only tennis and racquetball tournaments without national appeal." Buys 150 mss/year. Length: 2,000 words maximum. Pays $20-150. Sometimes pays the expenses of writers on assignment.
Photos: Randy Lester, photo editor. Specifically looking for fashion photo features. Send photos with ms. Pays $5-75 for b&w prints. Captions, model releases and identification of subjects required. Buys all rights, "but returns 75% of photos to submitter."
Columns/Departments: Nancy Thomas, column/department editor. New Products; Fitness Newsletter; Handball Newsletter; Racquetball Newsletter; Tennis Newsletter; News & Capsule Summaries; Fashion Spot (photos of new fitness and bathing suits and ski equipment); related subjects. Buys 100 mss/year. Send complete ms. Length: 50-250 words ("more if author has good handle to cover complete columns"). Pays $5-25.
Fiction: Judy Johnson, fiction editor. Erotica (if related to fitness club); fantasy (related to subjects); humorous (definite market); religious ("no God-is-my shepherd, but Body-is-God's-temple OK"); romance (related subjects). "Upbeat stories are needed." Buys 20 mss/year. Send complete ms. Length: 500-2,500 words maximum. Pays $20-150.
Poetry: Free verse, haiku, light verse, traditional on related subjects. Length: up to 150 words. Pays $10-25.
Tips: "Looking for articles charting the 1992 Olympics. Send us articles dealing with court club sports, exercise and nutrition that exemplify an upbeat 'you can do it' attitude. Pro sports previews 3-4 months ahead of their seasons are also needed. Good short fiction or humorous articles can break in. Expert knowledge of any related subject can bring assignments; any area is open. A humorous/knowledgeable columnist in pro sports business, aerobics is presently needed. We consider everything as a potential article, but are turned off by credits, past work and degrees. We have a constant demand for well-written articles on instruction, health and trends in both. Other articles needed are professional sports training techniques, fad diets, tennis and fitness resorts, photo features with aerobic routines. A frequent mistake made by writers is length—articles are too long. When we assign an article, we want it newsy if it's news and opinion if opinion."

‡**RUNNER'S WORLD**, Rodale Press, 33 E. Minor St., Emmaus PA 18098. (215)967-5171. Senior Editor: Bob Wischnia. 25% freelance written. Monthly magazine on running, mainly long-distance running. "The magazine for and about distance running, training, health and fitness, injury precaution, race coverage, personalties of the sport." Estab. 1966. Circ. 450,000. Pays on publication. Publishes ms an average of 2-3 months after acceptance. Byline given. Buys one-time rights. Submit seasonal/holiday material 6 months in advance. Query for electronic submissions. Reports in 1 month. Writer's guidelines for #10 SAE with 1 first class stamp.
Nonfiction: How-to (train, prevent injuries), interview/profile, personal experience. No "my first marathon" stories. Buys 30 mss/year. Query. Sometimes pays the expenses of writers on assignment.
Photos: State availability of photos with submission. Identification of subjects required. Buys one-time rights.
Columns/Departments: Christina Negron. Finish Line (personal experience—humor); Training Log (training of well-known runner). Buys 15 mss/year. Query.

SIGNPOST MAGAZINE, Suite 518, 1305 Fourth Ave., Seattle WA 98101. Publisher: Washington Trails Association. Editor: Ann L. Marshall. 10% freelance written. "We will consider working with both previously published and unpublished freelancers." Monthly about hiking, backpacking and similar trail-related activities, mostly from a Pacific Northwest viewpoint. Estab. 1966. Will consider any rights offered by author. Buys 12 mss/year. Pays on publication. Publishes ms an average of 6 months after acceptance. Reports in 6 weeks. Query or submit complete ms. Sample copy and writer's guidelines for SASE.

Nonfiction and Photos: "Most material is donated by subscribers or is staff-written. Payment for purchased material is low, but a good way to break in to print and share your outdoor experiences."

Tips: "We cover only *self-propelled* backcountry sports and won't consider manuscripts about trail bikes, snowmobiles, or power boats. We *are* interested in articles about modified and customized equipment, food and nutrition, and personal experiences in the backcountry (primarily Pacific Northwest, but will consider nation- and world-wide)."

SKYDIVING, Box 1520, DeLand FL 32721. (904)736-9779. Editor: Michael Truffer. 25% freelance written. Works with a small number of new/unpublished writers each year. Monthly tabloid featuring skydiving for sport parachutists, worldwide dealers and equipment manufacturers. Circ. 8,600. Average issue includes 3 feature articles and 3 columns of technical information. Pays on publication. Publishes ms an average of 3 months after acceptance. Byline given. Buys one-time rights. Simultaneous and previously published submissions OK, if so indicated. Query for electronic submissions. Reports in 1 month. Sample copy $2; writer's guidelines with 9×12 SAE and 4 first class stamps.

Nonfiction: "Send us news and information on equipment, techniques, events and outstanding personalities who skydive. We want articles written by people who have a solid knowledge of parachuting." No personal experience or human-interest articles. Query. Length: 500-1,000 words. Pays $25-100. Sometimes pays the expenses of writers on assignment.

Photos: State availability of photos. Reviews 5×7 and larger b&w glossy prints. Offers no additional payment for photos accepted with ms. Captions required.

Fillers: Newsbreaks. Length: 100-200 words. Pays $25 minimum.

Tips: "The most frequent mistake made by writers in completing articles for us is that the writer isn't knowledgeable about the sport of parachuting."

SPORT DETROIT MAGAZINE, Suite 150, 32270 Telegraph, Birmingham MI 48010. (313)433-3162. FAX: (313)645-6645. Editors: Dave Aretha and Michael Halnes. 40% freelance written. Monthly magazine on pro and college sports in Michigan. Estab. 1987. Circ. 50,000. Pays 30 days after publication. Publishes ms an average of 1-2 months after acceptance. Byline given. Offers 30% kill fee. Buys first North American serial rights. Previously published submissions OK. Query for electronic submissions. Reports in 3 weeks. Free sample copy.

Nonfiction: Exposé, general interest and interview/profile; all sports related. "No opinion, personal experience, nostalgia." Buys 75-100. Query with published clips. Length: 250-3,000 words. Pays $40-250 (possible exceptions). Pays writers' expenses on assignment.

Photos: State availability of photos with submission. Reviews contact sheets and transparencies. Offers $25-100 per photo. Captions and identification of subjects required. Buys one-time rights (on-assignment become property of *Sport Detroit*).

Columns/Departments: Short Shorts (short, off-beat features on interesting characters or unusual happenings in the world of sports), 200-500 words. Buys 30-50 mss/year. Query with published clips. Pays $40-60.

Tips: "We're always looking for out-of-state freelancers who can write about Michigan sports celebrities who have fled their state. Interested freelancers should query with published clips of feature stories and/or sports-oriented analytical articles."

‡USA GYMNASTICS, United States Gymnastics Federation, Suite 300, 201 S. Capitol Ave., Pan American Plaza, Indianapolis IN 46225. (317)237-5050. Editor: Luan Peszek. 5% freelance written. Bimonthly magazine covering gymnastics—national and international competitions. Designed to educate readers on fitness, health, safety, technique, current topics, trends and personalities related to the gymnastics/fitness field. Readers are between the ages of 7 and 18, parents and coaches. Estab. 1981. Circ. 63,000. Pays on publication. Publishes ms an average of 3-4 months after acceptance. Byline given. Buys all rights. Submit seasonal/holiday material 4 months in advance. Simultaneous submissions OK. Reports in 1 month. Sample copy $3.

Nonfiction: General interest, how-to (related to fitness, health, gymnastics), inspirational, interview/profile, new product, opinion (Open Floor section), photo feature. Buys 5 mss/year. Query. Length: 2,000 words maximum. Payment to be negotiated. Sometimes pays expenses of writers on assignment.

Photos: Send photos with submission. Offers no additional payment for photos accepted with ms. Identification of subjects required. Buys all rights.

Columns/Departments: Open Floor (opinions—regarding gymnastics/nutrition related topic), up to 1,000 words; Letter to the Editor; New Product, up to 300 words. Buys 2 mss/year. Query or send complete ms. Donated—nonprofit organization.

Tips: "Any articles of interest to gymnasts (men, women and rhythmic gymnastics) coaches, judges and parents, are what we're looking for. This includes nutrition, toning, health, safety, current trends, gymnastics techniques, timing techniques etc. The sections most open to freelancers are Open Floor—opinions on topics related to gymnasts, and features on one of the above mentioned items."

WRESTLING WORLD, Lexington Library Inc., 355 Lexington Ave., New York NY 10017. (212)949-6850. FAX: (212)986-5926. Editor: Stephen Ciacciarelli. 100% freelance written. Magazine published bimonthly. "Professional wrestling fans are our audience. We run profiles of top wrestlers and managers and articles on current topics of interest on the mat scene." Circ. 100,000. **Pays on acceptance.** Byline given. Buys first North American serial rights. Reports in 2 weeks. Sample copy $3.

Nonfiction: Interview/profile and photo feature. "No general think pieces." Buys 100 mss/year. Query with or without published clips or send complete ms. Length: 1,500-2,500 words. Pays $75-125.

Photos: State availability of photos with submision. Reviews 35mm transparencies and prints. Offers $25-50/photo package. Pays $50-150 for transparencies. Identification of subjects required. Buys one-time rights.

Tips: "Anything topical has the best chance of acceptance. Articles on those hard-to-reach wrestlers stand an excellent chance of acceptance."

Skiing and Snow Sports

AMERICAN SKATING WORLD, Independent Publication of the American Ice Skating Community, Business Communications Inc., 2545-47 Brownsville Rd., Pittsburgh PA 15210. (412)885-7600. FAX: (412)885-7617. Editor: Robert A. Mock. Magazine Editor: Doug Graham. 70% freelance written. Eager to work with new/unpublished writers. Monthly tabloid on figure skating. Estab. 1981. Circ. 15,000. Pays on publication. Publishes ms an average of 2-3 months after acceptance. Byline given. Buys first North American serial rights and occasionally second serial rights. Submit seasonal/holiday material 3 months in advance. Reports in 6 weeks. Sample copy and writer's guidelines $2.

Nonfiction: Expose; general interest; historical/nostalgic; how-to (technique in figure skating); humor; inspirational; interview/profile; new product; opinion; personal experience; photo feature; technical and travel. Special issues include recreational (July), classic skaters (August), annual fashion issue (September), adult issue (December). No fiction. AP Style Guidelines are the primary style source. Short, snappy paragraphs desired. Buys 200 mss/year. Send complete ms. "Include phone number; response time longer without it." Length: 600-1,000 words. Pays $25-75.

Photos: Send photos with query or ms. Reviews transparencies and b&w prints. Pays $5 for b&w; $15 for color. Identification of subjects required. Buys all rights for b&w; one-time rights for color.

Columns/Departments: Buys 60 mss/year. Send complete ms. Length: 500-750 words. Pays $25-50.

Fillers: Clippings and anecdotes. No payment for fillers.

Tips: "Event coverage is most open to freelancers; confirm with managing editor to ensure event has not been assigned. Questions are welcome; call managing editor EST, 11 a.m. to 3 p.m., Tuesdays, Wednesdays and Thursdays."

SKATING, United States Figure Skating Association, 20 First St., Colorado Springs CO 80906. (719)635-5200. Editor: Dale Mitch. Published 10 times a year—monthly except August/September. Estab. 1923. Circ. 35,000. Official publication of the USFSA. Pays on publication. Publishes ms an average of 3 months after acceptance. Buys all rights. Byline given.

Nonfiction: Historical; humor; informational; interview; photo feature; historical biographies; profile (background and interests of national-caliber amateur skaters); technical; and competition reports. Buys 4 mss/issue. All work by assignment.

Photos: Photos purchased with or without accompanying ms. Pays $15 for 8×10 or 5×7 b&w glossy prints and $35 for color prints or transparencies. Query.

Columns/Departments: Ice Abroad (competition results and report from outside the U.S.); Book Reviews; People; and Music column (what's new and used for music for skating). Buys 4 mss/issue. All work by assignment. Length: 500-2,000 words.

Tips: "We want sharp, strong, intelligent writing by experienced persons knowledgeable in the technical and artistic aspects of figure skating with a new outlook on the development of the sport. Knowledge and background in technical aspects of figure skating are essential to the quality of writing expected. We would also like to receive articles on former competitive skaters. No professional skater material."

SKI MAGAZINE, 2 Park Ave., New York NY 10016. (212)779-5000. Editor: Dick Needham. Executive Editor: Steve Cohen. 15% freelance written. A monthly magazine on snow skiing. "*Ski* is a ski-lifestyle publication written and edited for recreational skiers. Its content is intended to help them ski better (technique), buy better (equipment and skiwear), and introduce them to new experiences, people and adventures." Estab. 1936. Circ. 430,000. **Pays on acceptance.** Publishes ms an average of 3 months after acceptance. Byline given. Offers 15% kill fee. Buys first North American serial rights. Submit seasonal/holiday material 8 months in advance. Reports in 1 week on queries; 2 weeks on ms. Sample copy for $8\frac{1}{2} \times 11$ SAE and 5 first class stamps.

Nonfiction: Essays, historical/nostalgic, how-to, humor, interview/profile and personal experience. Buys 5-10 mss/year. Send complete ms. Length: 1,000-3,500 words. Pays $500-1,000 for assigned articles; pays $300-700 for unsolicited artiicles. Pays the expenses of writers on assignment.

Photos: Send photos with submission. Offers $75-300/photo. Captions, model releases and identification of subjects required. Buys one-time rights.

Columns/Departments: Ski Life (interesting people, events, oddities in skiing), 150-300 words; Going Places (items on new or unique places, deals or services available to skiers); Discoveries (special products or services available to skiers that are out of the ordinary), 100-200 words; and It Worked for Me (new ideas invented by writer that make his skiing life easier, more convenient, more enjoyable), 50-150 words. Buys 20 mss/year. Send complete ms. Length: 100-300 words. Pays $50-100.

Fillers: Facts and short humor. Buys 10/year. Length: 60-75 words. Pays $50-75.

Tips: "Writers must have an extensive familiarity with the sport and know what concerns, interests and amuses skiers. Ski Life, Discoveries, Going Places and It Worked for Me are most open to freelancers."

SNOW COUNTRY, New York Times Magazine Group, 5520 Park Ave., Trumbull CT 06611. (203)723-7030. FAX: (203)373-7033. Senior Editor: Ron Rudolph. Managing Editor: Bob LaMarche. 50% freelance written. Monthly magazine on sports and leisure activity in North American snow country. "Story ideas should be hooked to a person or people; best market for freelancers are front- and back-of-book pieces which are short—500-700 words." Estab. 1988. Circ. 200,000. Pays on publication. Byline given. Offers ⅓ kill fee. Buys first North American serial rights. Query for electronic submission. Reports in 2 weeks.

Nonfiction: Historical/nostalgic, humor, interview/profile, personal experience, photo feature. Buys 150 mss/year. Query or query with published clips. Length: 200-1,000 words. Pays $150-1,000.

Photos: State availability of photos with submission or send photos with submission. Reviews contact sheets, transparencies and prints. Offers $25-750/photo. Model releases and identification of subjects required. Buys one-time rights.

Columns/Departments: Datebook (events, occasions, anniversaries in snow country; also odd, lively, or poignant quotes from people living in snow country or about snow country) 50 words. Send complete ms. Pays $20-40. Snow Country Store is a department of 150-word takes on artist, artisan, craftsperson, inventor, even cook or songwriter living in snow country who has product that can be purchased locally or by mail. This is not standard mail-order column—no souvenirs, household helps, objects conceived by marketing departments. Interesting people, unique or well-executed products. Query first. $100 minimum payment; extra for 2 pictures—one of person, one of product.

Tips: "We are looking for excellent writing, genuine fondness or interest in the subject. Please query and send clips. Magazine began regular publication in September 1988, 10 times/year and is on newsstands. Most libraries will have, eventually. We do not send copies. No phone queries!"

‡SNOW GOER, For Active Snowmobilers, Ehlert Publishing Group, Inc. 319 Barry Ave., Wayzata, MN 55391. (612)476-2200. Editor: Dick Hendricks. Managing Editor: John Sandberg. Seasonal (Dec-Jan-Feb-March) magazine providing active snowmobilers with more information during the heart of the season. Estab. 1990. Circ. 100,000. Pays on publication. Byline given. Buys first North American serial rights. Submit seasonal/holiday material 2 months in advance. Query for electronic submissions. Reports in 3 weeks. Free writer's guidelines.

Nonfiction: How-to, new product, personal experience, technical, travel. Buys 12 mss/year. Query. Length: 1,000-5,000 words. Pays $100-500. Sometimes pays expenses of writers on assignment.

Photos: Send photos with submission. Reviews 35mm transparencies and 5×7 b&w prints. Offers no additional payment for photos accepted with ms. Captions and identification of subjects required. Buys one-time rights.

SNOWMOBILE MAGAZINE, Ehlert Publishing Group, Inc., Suite 101, 319 Barry Ave., Wayzata MN 55391. (612)476-2200. FAX: (612)476-8065. Editor: Dick Hendricks. 10% freelance written. A seasonal magazine (September, October and December) covering recreational snowmobiling. Estab. 1980. Circ. 500,000. Pays on publication. Byline given. Buys first North American serial rights. Submit seasonal/holiday material 5 months in advance. Reports in 1 month. Sample copy $2.50; free writer's guidelines.

Nonfiction: How-to, interview/profile, new product, photo feature and travel. Buys 5-6 mss/year. Query. Length: 300-1,000 words. Pays $150-500. Sometimes pays the expenses of writers on assignment.

Photos: Send photos with submission. Reviews 35mm transparencies and 3×5 prints. Offers no additional payment for photos accepted with ms. Captions and identification of subjects required. Buys one-time rights.

Tips: The areas most open to freelancers include "travel and tour stories (with photos) on snowmobiling and snowmobile resorts and event coverage (races, winter festivals, etc.)."

Tennis

‡TENNIS, 5520 Park Ave., Trumbull CT 06611. Publisher: Mark Adorney. Editor: Donna Doherty. 10% freelance written. Works with a small number of new/unpublished writers each year. For persons who play tennis and want to play it better and who follow tennis as fans. Monthly magazine. Estab. 1965. Circ. 750,000. Buys all rights. Byline given. Pays on publication. Publishes ms an average of 6 months after acceptance.

Nonfiction and Photos: Emphasis on instructional and reader service articles, but also seeks lively, well-researched features on personalities and other aspects of the game, as well as humor. Query. Length varies. Pays $200 minimum/article, considerably more for major features. Pays $60 and up/8 × 10 b&w glossies; $120 and up/transparencies.

Tips: "When reading our publication the writer should note the depth of the tennis expertise in the stories and should note the conversational, informal writing styles that are used."

WORLD TENNIS, Family Media, 3 Park Ave., New York NY 10016. (212)779-6200. Editor-in-Chief: Bud Collins. Editor: Steve Flink. Managing Editor: Peter M. Coan. Monthly tennis magazine. "We are a magazine catering to the complete tennis player." Circ. 500,000. **Pays on acceptance.** Byline given. Offers 25% kill fee. Buys all rights. Submit seasonal/holiday material 3 months in advance. Query for electronic submissions. Query for electronic submissions. Computer printout submissions OK; no dot-matrix. Reports in 2 weeks on queries; 1 month on manuscripts. Sample copy for 8 × 11 SAE and 5 first class stamps.

Nonfiction: Book excerpts (tennis, fitness, nutrition), essays, interview/profile, new product, personal experience, photo feature, travel (tennis resorts). No instruction, poetry or fiction. Buys 30-40 mss/year. Query with published clips. Length: 750-3,000 words. Pays $100 and up. Sometimes pays expenses of writers on assignment.

Photos: State availability of photos with submission. Reviews contact sheets. Payment varies. Requires captions and identification of subjects. Buys one-time rights.

Columns/Departments: My Ad (personal opinion on hot tennis topics); all 200-1,000 words. Buys 25-30 mss/year. Query with published clips. Pays $100 and up.

Fillers: Anecdotes, facts, people/player news, international tennis news. Buys 10-15/year. Length: 750-1,000 words. Pays $100.

Water Sports

THE DIVER, Diversified Periodicals, P.O. Box 249, Cobalt CT 06414. (203)342-4730. Editor: Bob Taylor. 50% freelance written. Magazine published 6 times/year for divers, coaches and officials. Estab. 1978. Circ. 1,500. Pays on publication. Byline given. Submit material at least 2 months in advance. Simultaneous queries and simultaneous and previously published submissions OK. Reports in 2 weeks on queries; 1 month on mss. Sample copy for 9 × 12 SAE and 85¢ postage.

Nonfiction: Interview/profile (of divers, coaches, officials); results; tournament coverage; any stories connected with platform and springboard diving; photo features and technical. Buys 35 mss/year. Query. Length: 500-2,500 words. Pays $15-40.

Photos: Pays $5-25 for b&w prints. Captions and identification of subjects required. Buys one-time rights.

Tips: "We're very receptive to new writers."

PACIFIC DIVER, Western Outdoors Publications, 3197-E Airport Loop Dr., Costa Mesa CA 92626. (714)546-4370. FAX: (714)662-3486. Editor: John Brumm. Send all mss and queries to Editor, *Pacific Diver*, P.O. Box 6218, Huntington Beach CA 92615. (714)536-7252. 75% freelance written. Bimonthly magazine on scuba diving. "Aimed at scuba diving in the Pacific, covering events, destinations and activities from the Pacific Coast to Hawaii to Mexico and as far as the South Pacific. Aimed at all divers interested in Pacific diving." Estab. 1988. Circ. 25,000. **Pays on acceptance.** Publishes ms an average of 2 months after acceptance. Byline given. Offers $50 kill fee. Buys first North American serial rights and one-time rights. Submit seasonal/holiday material 3 months in advance. Query for electronic submissions. Reports in 3 weeks. Sample copy $2. Free writer's guidelines.

Nonfiction: General interest, historical/nostalgic, how-to, humor, interview/profile, new product, opinion, personal experience, photo feature, technical and travel; all must relate to scuba diving in the Pacific. "No poems, fiction." Buys 60 mss/year. Query or send complete ms. Length: 1,500-2,000. Pays $150-350.

Photos: Send photos with submission. Reviews 35mm transparencies. Offers no additional payment for photos accepted with ms. Captions and identification of subjects required. Buys one-time rights.

SWIM MAGAZINE, Sports Publications, Inc., P.O. Box 45497, Los Angeles CA 90045. (213)674-2120. Editor: Kim A. Hansen. 50% freelance written. Prefers to work with published/selected writers. Bimonthly magazine. "*Swim Magazine* is for adults interested in swimming for fun, fitness and competition. Readers are fitness-oriented adults from varied social and professional backgrounds who share swimming as part of their lifestyle. Readers' ages are evenly distributed from 25 to 90, so articles must appeal to a broad age group." Estab. 1984. Circ. 9,390. Pays approximately 1 month after publication. Publishes ms an average of 4 months after acceptance. Byline given. Submit seasonal/holiday material 4 months in advance. Simultaneous queries OK. Reports in 1 month on queries; 3 months on mss. Sample copy for $2.50 prepaid and 9 × 12 SAE with 11 first class stamps. Free writer's guidelines.

Nonfiction: How-to (training plans and techniques); interview/profile (people associated with fitness and competitive swimming); new product (articles describing new products for fitness and competitive training). "Articles need to be informative as well as interesting. In addition to fitness and health articles, we are interested in exploring fascinating topics dealing with swimming for the adult reader." Send complete ms. Length: 1,000-3,500 words. Pays $3/published column inch. "No payment for articles about personal experiences."

Photos: Send photos with ms. Offers no additional payment for photos accepted with ms. Captions, model releases, and identification of subjects required.

Tips: "Our how-to articles and physiology articles best typify *Swim Magazine*'s projected style for fitness and competitive swimmers. *Swim Magazine* will accept medical guidelines and diet articles only by M.D.s and Ph.Ds."

UNDERCURRENT, Box 1658, Sausalito CA 94966. Managing Editor: Ben Davison. 20-50% freelance written. Works with a small number of new/unpublished writers each year. Monthly consumer-oriented *scuba diving newsletter*. Circ. 15,000. Pays on publication. Publishes ms an average of 2 months after acceptance. Buys first rights. Pays $50 kill fee. Byline given. Simultaneous (if to other than diving publisher), and previously published submissions OK. Reports in 6 weeks. Free sample copy and writer's guidelines; mention *Writer's Market* in request.

Nonfiction: Equipment evaluation, how-to, general interest, new product and travel review. Buys 2 mss/issue. Query with brief outline of story idea and credentials. Will commission. Length: 2,000 words maximum. Pays 10-20¢/word. Sometimes pays the expenses of writers on assignment.

THE WATER SKIER, 799 Overlook Dr., Winter Haven FL 33884. (813)324-4341. FAX: (813)325-8259. Editor: John Baker. Official publication of the American Water Ski Association. 50% freelance written. Published 7 times/year. Estab. 1951. Circ. 25,000. Buys North American serial rights. Byline given. Buys limited amount of freelance material. **Pays on acceptance.** Publishes ms an average of 3 months after acceptance. Reports on submissions within 10 days. Query for electronic submissions. Sample copy for 9 × 12 SAE and 4 first class stamps.

Nonfiction and Photos: Occasionally buys exceptionally offbeat, unusual text/photo features on the sport of water skiing. Emphasis on technique, methods, etc.

Tips: "Freelance writers should be aware of specialization of subject matter; need for more expertise in topic; more professional writing ability."

Teen and Young Adult

The publications in this category are for young people ages 13-19. Publications for college students are listed in Career, College and Alumni. Those for younger children are listed in the Juvenile category.

‡**AMERICAN NEWSPAPER CARRIER**, American Newspaper Press, Box 2225, Kernersville NC 27285. Editor: W.H. Lowry. 50% freelance written. Works with a small number of new/unpublished writers each year. Usually buys all rights but may be released upon request. **Pays on acceptance.** Publishes ms an average of 3 months after acceptance. Reports in 30 days.

Fiction: Uses a limited amount of short fiction written for teen-age newspaper carriers, male and female. It is preferable that stories be written around newspaper carrier characters. Humor, mystery and adventure plots are commonly used. No drugs, sex, fantasy, supernatural, crime or controversial themes. Queries not required. Length: 1,200 words. Pays $25.

Tips: "Fillers are staff-written, usually."

CAMPUS LIFE MAGAZINE, Christianity Today, Inc., 465 Gundersen Dr., Carol Stream IL 60188. FAX: (708)260-0114. Managing Editor: Jim Long. Senior Editor: Chris Lutes. Associate Editor: Diane Eble. Assistant Editor: Kris Bearss. 20-30% freelance written. Prefers to work with published/established writers. For a readership of young adults, high school and college age. "Though our readership is largely Christian, *Campus Life* reflects the interests of all young people—music, bicycling, photography, media and sports." Largely staff-written. "*Campus Life* is a Christian magazine that is *not* overtly religious. The indirect style is intended to create a safety zone with our readers and to reflect our philosophy that God is interested in all of life. Therefore, we publish message stories side by side with general interest, humor, etc." Monthly magazine. Estab. 1942. Circ. 130,000. **Pays on acceptance.** Publishes an average of 3-6 months after acceptance. Buys first serial and one-time rights. Byline given. Submit seasonal/holiday material 6 months in advance. Simultaneous and previously published submissions OK. Query for electronic submissions. Reports in 2 months. Sample copy for 9 × 12 SAE and $2; writer's guidelines for SASE.

Nonfiction: Personal experiences, photo features, unusual sports, humor, short items—how-to, college or career and travel, etc. *Query only.* Length: 500-3,000 words. Pays $100-300. Sometimes pays the expenses of writers on assignment.

Photos: Pays $50 minimum/8×10 b&w glossy print; $90 minimum transparency; $250/cover photo. Buys one-time rights.

Fiction: Stories about problems and experiences kids face. "Trite, simplistic religious stories are not acceptable."

Tips: "The best ms for a freelancer to try to sell us would be a well-written first-person or 'as told to' first-person story (fiction or nonfiction) focusing on a common struggle young people face in any area of life—intellectual, emotional, social, physical or spiritual. Most manuscripts that miss us fail in quality or style. We are always looking for good humor pieces for high school readers. These could be cartoon spreads or other creative humorous pieces that would make kids laugh."

‡CAREERS, The Magazine for Today's Young Achievers, E.M. Guild, Inc., 1001 Avenue of the Americas, New York NY 10018. (212)354-8877. Editor: Mary Dalheim. 75% freelance written. Works with a small number of new/unpublished writers each year. A magazine published 4 times a year covering life-coping skills, career choices, and educational opportunities for high school juniors and seniors. "*Careers* is designed to offer a taste of the working world, new career opportunities, and stories covering the best ways to reach those opportunities—through education, etc." Circ. 600,000. Pays 30 days after acceptance. Publishes ms an average of 2-3 months after acceptance. Byline given. Offers 25% kill fee. Buys first North American serial rights. Submit seasonal/holiday material 6 months in advance. Sometimes accepts previously published submissions. Reports in 2 months on queries. Sample copy $2.50; writer's guidelines for #10 SAE with 1 first class stamp.

Nonfiction: Book excerpts, how-to, interview/profile, photo feature, travel, humor. Buys 25 mss/year. Query with published clips. Length: 1,000-1,500 words. Pays $250. Sometimes pays the expenses of writers on assignment.

Photos: State availability of photos with submission. Reviews contact sheets and transparencies. Offers $100 minimum/photo. Captions, model releases, and identification of subjects required. Buys one-time rights.

Columns/Departments: Money-Wise, College Hotline, Career Watch, Tech Talk, Global Views, High Achievers and Life After High School. Buys 15 mss/year. Length: 1,000-1,500 words. Pays $250.

EXPLORING MAGAZINE, Boy Scouts of America, 1325 W. Walnut Hill Ln., P.O. Box 152079, Irving TX 75015-2079. (214)580-2365. FAX: (214)580-2079. Executive Editor: Scott Daniels. 85% freelance written. Prefers to work with published/established writers. Magazine published 4 times/year—January, March, May, September. Covers the educational teen-age Exploring program of the BSA. Estab. 1970. Circ. 350,000. **Pays on acceptance.** Publishes ms an average of 6 months after acceptance. Byline given. Buys first rights. Submit seasonal/holiday material 6 months in advance. Simultaneous queries OK. Reports in 2 weeks. Sample copy for 9×12 SAE and 4 first class stamps; writer's guidelines for #10 SASE. Write for guidelines and "What is Exploring?" fact sheet.

Nonfiction: General interest, how-to (achieve outdoor skills, organize trips, meetings, etc.); interview/profile (of outstanding Explorer); travel (backpacking or canoeing with Explorers). Buys 15-20 mss/year. Query with clips. Length: 800-1,600 words. Pays $300-450. Pays expenses of writers on assignment.

Photos: Brian Payne, photo editor. State availability of photos with query letter or ms. Reviews b&w contact sheets and 35mm transparencies. Captions required. Buys one-time rights.

Tips: "Contact the local Exploring Director in your area (listed in phone book white pages under Boy Scouts of America). Find out if there are some outstanding post activities going on and then query magazine editor in Irving, Texas. Strive for shorter texts, faster starts and stories that lend themselves to dramatic photographs."

FREEWAY, P.O. Box 632, Glen Ellyn IL 60138. Editor: Kyle L. Olund. For "young Christian adults of high school and college age." 80% freelance written. Eager to work with new/unpublished writers. Weekly. Estab. 1967. Circ. 50,000. Prefers one-time rights but buys some reprints. Purchases 100 mss/year. Byline given. Reports on material accepted for publication in 2 months. Publishes ms an average of 1 year after acceptance. Returns rejected material in 2 months. Free sample copy and writer's guidelines.

Nonfiction: "*FreeWay*'s greatest need is for personal experience stories showing how God has worked in teens' lives. Stories are best written in first-person, 'as told to' author. Incorporate specific details, anecdotes, and dialogue. Show, don't tell, how the subject thought and felt. Weave spiritual conflicts and prayers into entire manuscript; avoid tacked-on sermons and morals. Stories should show how God has helped the person resolve a problem or how God helped save a person from trying circumstances (1,000 words or less). Avoid stories about accident and illness; focus on events and emotions of everyday life. Short-short stories are needed as fillers. We also need self-help or how-to articles with practical Christian advice on daily living, and trend articles addressing secular fads from a Christian perspective. We do not use devotional material, or fictionalized Bible stories." Pays 4-7¢/word. Sometimes pays the expenses of writers on assignment.

Photos: Whenever possible, provide clear 8×10 or 5×7 b&w photos to accompany mss (or any other available photos). Payment is $5-30.

Fiction: "We use little fiction, unless it is allegory, parable, or humor."

Tips: "Study our 'Tips to Writers' pamphlet and sample copy, then query or send complete ms. In your cover letter, include information about who you are, writing qualifications, and experience working with teens. Include SASE."

GUIDE MAGAZINE, 55 W. Oak Ridge Dr., Hagerstown MD 21740. Editor: Jeannette Johnson. 50% freelance written. Works with a small number of new/unpublished writers each year. A journal for junior youth and early teens. "Its content reflects Christian beliefs and standards." Weekly magazine. Estab. 1953. Circ. 40,000. Buys first serial rights, simultaneous rights, and second serial (reprint) rights to material originally published elsewhere. **Pays on acceptance.** Publishes ms an average of 6-9 months after acceptance. Byline given. Submit seasonal/holiday material 6 months in advance. Query for electronic submissions. Reports in 3 weeks. Free sample copy.

Nonfiction: Wants nonfiction stories of character-building and spiritual value. Should emphasize the positive aspects of living, obedience to parents, perseverance, kindness, etc. "We use a number of stories dealing with problems common to today's Christian youth, such as peer pressure, parents' divorce, chemical dependency, etc. We can always use 'drama in real life' stories that show God's protection and seasonal stories—Christmas, Thanksgiving, special holidays. We do not use stories of hunting, fishing, trapping or spiritualism." Buys about 300 mss/year. Send complete ms (include word count and Social Security number). Length: up to 1,200 words. Pays 3-4¢/word.

Tips: "Typical topics we cover in a yearly cycle include choices (music, clothes, friends, diet); friend-making skills; school problems (cheating, peer 'pressure, new school); death; finding and keeping a job; sibling relationships; divorce; step-families; drugs; communication; and suicide. We often buy short fillers, and an author who does not fully understand our needs is more likely to sell with a short-short. Our target age is 10-14. Our most successful writers are those who present stories from the viewpoint of a young teen-ager. Stories that sound like an adult's sentiments passing through a young person's lips are *not* what we're looking for. Use believable dialogue."

IN TOUCH, Wesley Press, P.O. Box 50434, Indianapolis IN 46250-0434. Editor: Rebecca Higgins. 80% freelance written. Eager to work with new/unpublished writers—"quality writing a must, however." A weekly Christian teen magazine. Circ. 14,000. **Pays on acceptance.** Publishes ms an average of 6-18 months after acceptance. Byline given. Offers 30% kill fee. Not copyrighted. Buys first rights or second serial (reprint) rights. Submit seasonal/holiday material 10 months in advance. Simultaneous and previously published submissions OK. Reports in 2 months on manuscripts. Sample copy for 9×12 SAE with 45¢ postage. Writer's guidelines for #10 SASE.

Nonfiction: Book excerpts, essays, how-to, humor, interview/profile, opinion, personal experience, photo feature from Christian perspective. "Our articles are teaching-oriented and contain lots of humor." Also needs true experiences told in fiction style, humorous fiction and allegories. No Sunday "soap." Buys 100 mss/year. Send complete ms. Length: 500-1,000 words. Pays $15-45.

Photos: Send photos with submissions. Pays $15-40/photo. Buys one-time rights.

KEYNOTER, Key Club International, 3636 Woodview Trace, Indianapolis IN 46268. (317)875-8755, ext. 172. Executive Editor: Tamara P. Burley. 65% freelance written. Works with a small number of new/unpublished writers each year, and is eager to work with new/unpublished writers willing to adjust their writing styles to *Keynoter*'s needs. A youth magazine published monthly Oct.-May (Dec./Jan. combined issue), distributed to members of Key Club International, a high school service organization for young men and women. Estab. 1946. Circ. 130,000. **Pays on acceptance.** Publishes ms an average of 5 months after acceptance. Byline given. Buys first North American serial rights. Submit seasonal/holiday material 7 months in advance. Simultaneous queries and submissions (if advised), and previously published submissions OK. Reports in 1 month. Sample copy for 9×12 SAE and 3 first class stamps; writer's guidelines for #10 SASE.

Nonfiction: Book excerpts (may be included in articles but are not accepted alone); general interest (must be geared for intelligent teen audience); historical/nostalgic (generally not accepted); how-to (if it offers advice on how teens can enhance the quality of lives or communities); humor (accepted very infrequently; if adds to story, OK); interview/profile (rarely purchased, "would have to be on/with an irresistible subject"); new product (only if affects teens); photo feature (if subject is right, might consider); technical (if understandable and interesting to teen audience); travel (sometimes OK, but must apply to club travel schedule); subjects that entertain and inform teens on topics that relate directly to their lives. "We would also like to receive self-help and school-related nonfiction on leadership, community service, and teen issues. Please, no first-person confessions, no articles that are written down to our teen readers." Buys 10-15 mss/year. Query. Length: 1,500-2,500 words. Pays $125-250. Sometimes pays the expenses of writers on assignment.

Photos: State availability of photos. Reviews b&w contact sheets and negatives. Identification of subjects required. Buys one-time rights. Payment for photos included in payment for ms.

Tips: "We want to see articles written with attention to style and detail that will enrich the world of teens. Articles must be thoroughly researched and must draw on interviews with nationally and internationally respected sources. Our readers are 13-18, mature and dedicated to community service. We are very committed to working with good writers, and if we see something we like in a well-written query, we'll try to work it through to publication."

‡LIGHTED PATHWAY, Church of God, 922 Montgomery Ave., P.O. Box 2250, Cleveland TN 37320-2250. (615)476-4512. Editor: Lance Colkmire. 5% freelance written. A weekly take-home paper emphasizing Christian living for high schoolers. Estab. 1929. **Pays on acceptance.** Publishes ms an average of 1 year after acceptance. Byline given. Buys first North American serial rights and one-time rights. Submit seasonal/holiday material 1 year in advance. Simultaneous queries, and simultaneous, and previously published submissions OK. Reports in 2 weeks on queries; 1 month on mss. Free sample copy and writer's guidelines for SASE.

Nonfiction: Inspirational, interview/profile, personal experience and travel. "Our primary objective is inspiration, to portray happy, victorious living through faith in God." Buys 2-4 mss/year. Query. Length: 500-1,000 words. Pays 3-5¢/word.

Tips: "Write to evangelical, conservative audience, about current subjects involving young people today." Human interest stories, especially first-person experiences, are most open to freelancers.

THE NEW ERA, 50 E. North Temple, Salt Lake City UT 84150. (801)240-2951. Managing Editor: Richard M. Romney. 60% freelance written. "We work with both established writers and newcomers." Monthly magazine. For young people of the Church of Jesus Christ of Latter-day Saints (Mormon); their church leaders and teachers. Estab. 1971. Circ. 180,000. **Pays on acceptance.** Publishes ms an average of 1 year after acceptance. Byline given. Buys all rights. Submit seasonal material 1 year in advance. Query for electronic submissions. Reports in 1 month. Query preferred. Sample copy $1 and 9×12 SAE; writer's guidelines for SASE.

Nonfiction: Material that shows how the Church of Jesus Christ of Latter-day Saints is relevant in the lives of young people today. Must capture the excitement of being a young Latter-day Saint. Special interest in the experiences of young Mormons in other countries. No general library research or formula pieces without the *New Era* slant and feel. Uses informational, how-to, personal experience, interview, profile, inspirational, humor, historical, think pieces, travel and spot news. Length: 150-3,000 words. Pays 3-12¢/word. *For Your Information* (news of young Mormons around the world). Pays expenses of writers on assignment.

Photos: Uses b&w photos and transparencies with mss. Payment depends on use in magazine, but begins at $10.

Fiction: Adventure, science fiction and humorous. Must relate to young Mormon audience. Pays minimum 3¢/word.

Poetry: Traditional forms, blank verse, free verse, light verse and all other forms. Must relate to editorial viewpoint. Pays minimum 25¢/line.

Tips: "The writer must be able to write from a Mormon point of view. We're especially looking for stories about successful family relationships. We anticipate using more staff-produced material. This means freelance quality will have to improve."

PURPLE COW Newspaper for Teens, Suite 320, 3423 Piedmont Rd. NE, Atlanta GA 30305. (404)239-0642. FAX: (404)261-2214. Editor: Todd Daniel. 5% freelance written. Works with a small number of new/unpublished writers each year. A monthly tabloid circulated to Atlanta area high schools. Estab. 1976. Circ. 59,000. Pays on publication. Buys one-time rights. "Manuscripts are accepted on a 'space-available' basis. If space becomes available, we publish the manuscript under consideration 1-12 months after receiving." Byline given. Submit seasonal/holiday material 2 months in advance. Simultaneous queries and previously published submissions OK. Sample copy for $1 with 9×12 SAE and 2 first class stamps; writer's guidelines for #10 SASE.

Nonfiction: General interest, how-to, humor and anything of interest to teenagers. Especially looking for college and work/career related stories. No opinion or anything which talks down to teens. No fiction. Buys 7-10 mss/year. Send complete ms. Length: 1,000 words maximum. Pays $10-25.

Cartoons and Photos: Must be humorous, teen-related, up-to-date with good illustrations. Buys 12/year. Send photos with ms. Buys one-time rights. Pays $5.

Tips: "A freelancer can best break in to our publication with articles which help teens. Examples might be how to secure financial aid for college or how to survive your freshman year of college."

SCHOLASTIC SCOPE, Scholastic Magazines, Inc., 730 Broadway, New York NY 10003. Senior Editor: Deborah Sussman. 5% freelance written. Works with a small number of new/unpublished writers each year. Published 20 times/year during school session. 4-6th grade reading level; 15-18 age level. Circ. 640,000.

Publishes ms an average of 8 months after acceptance. Buys all rights. Byline given. Reports in 6 weeks. Sample copy for 10x14 SAE with $1.75 postage.
Nonfiction and Photos: Articles with photos about teenagers who have accomplished something against great odds, overcome obstacles, performed heroically, or simply have done something out of the ordinary. Prefers articles about people outside New York area. Length: 400-1,200 words. Pays $125 and up.
Fiction and Drama: Problems of contemporary teenagers (drugs, prejudice, runaways, failure in school, family problems, etc.); relationships between people (interracial, adult-teenage, employer-employee, etc.) in family, job, and school situations. Strive for directness, realism, and action, perhaps carried through dialogue rather than exposition. Try for depth of characterization in at least one character. Avoid too many coincidences and random happenings. Although action stories are wanted, it's not a market for crime fiction. Occasionally uses mysteries and science fiction. Length: 400-1,200 words. Uses plays up to 15,000 words. Pays good rates on acceptance.

SENIOR HIGH I.D., (formerly *Christian Living for Senior Highs*), David C. Cook Publishing Co., 850 N. Grove, Elgin IL 60120. (312)741-2400. Editor: Doug Schmidt. 75% freelance written. Prefers to work with published/established writers and works with a small number of new/unpublished writers each year. Quarterly magazine. "A take-home paper used in senior high Sunday School classes. We encourage Christian teens to write to us." **Pays on acceptance.** Publishes ms an average of 15 months after acceptance. Buys all rights. Reports in 3 months. Sample copy and writer's guidelines for SASE.
Nonfiction: How-to (Sunday School youth projects); humor (from Christian perspective); inspirational and personality (nonpreachy); personal teen experience (Christian); poetry written by teens and photo feature (Christian subject). "Nothing not compatible with a Christian lifestyle." Submit complete ms. Length: 500-1,000 words. Pays $100; $40 for short pieces.
Fiction: Adventure (with religious theme); humorous; and religious. Submit complete ms. Length: 500-1,000 words. Pays $100. "No preachy experiences."
Photos: Brenda Fox, photo editor. Photos purchased with or without accompanying ms or on assignment. Send contact sheets, prints or transparencies. Pays $25-40 for 8½ × 11 b&w photos; $50 minimum for transparencies. "Photo guidelines available."
Tips: "Our demand for manuscripts should increase, but most of these will probably be assigned rather than bought over-the-transom. Our features are always short. A frequent mistake made by writers in completing articles for us is misunderstanding our market. Writing is often not Christian at all, or it's too 'Christian,' i.e. pedantic, condescending and moralistic."

SEVENTEEN, 850 3rd Ave., New York NY 10022. Editor-in-Chief: Midge Turk Richardson. Managing Editor: Mary Anne Baumgold. 80% freelance written. Works with a small number of new/unpublished writers each year. Monthly. Circ. 1.9 million. Buys one-time rights for nonfiction and fiction by adult writers and work by teenagers. Pays 25% kill fee. **Pays on acceptance.** Publishes ms an average of 6 months after acceptance. Byline given. Reports in 6 weeks.
Nonfiction: Roberta Anne Myers, articles editor. Articles and features of general interest to young women who are concerned with the development of their lives and the problems of the world around them; strong emphasis on topicality and helpfulness. Send brief outline and query, including a typical lead paragraph, summing up basic idea of article. Also like to receive articles and features on speculation. Query with tearsheets or copies of published articles. Length: 1,200-2,000 words. Pays $50-150 for articles written by teenagers but more to established adult freelancers. Articles are commissioned after outlines are submitted and approved. Fees for commissioned articles $650-1,500. Sometimes pays the expenses of writers on assignment.
Photos: Kenny Ross, art director. Photos usually by assignment only.
Fiction: Adrian LeBlanc, fiction editor. Thoughtful, well-written stories on subjects of interest to young women between the ages of 12 and 20. Avoid formula stories — "My sainted Granny," "My crush on Brad," etc. — heavy moralizing, condescension of any sort. Humorous stories and mysteries are welcomed. Best lengths are 1,000-3,000 words. Pays $500-1,500.
Poetry: Contact teen features editor. By teenagers only. Pays $15. Submissions are nonreturnable unless accompanied by SASE.
Tips: "Writers have to ask themselves whether or not they feel they can find the right tone for a *Seventeen* article — a tone which is empathetic yet never patronizing; lively yet not superficial. Not all writers feel comfortable with, understand or like teenagers. If you don't like them, *Seventeen* is the wrong market for you. The best way for beginning teenage writers to crack the *Seventeen* lineup is for them to contribute suggestions and short pieces to the New Voices and Views section, a literary format which lends itself to just about every kind of writing: profiles, essays, exposes, reportage, and book reviews."

STRAIGHT, Standard Publishing Co., 8121 Hamilton Ave., Cincinnati OH 45231. (513)931-4050. Editor: Carla J. Crane. 90% freelance written. Estab. 1866 (publishing house). "Teens, age 13-19, from Christian backgrounds generally receive this publication in their Sunday School classes or through subscriptions." Weekly (published quarterly) magazine. **Pays on acceptance.** Publishes ms an average of 1 year after acceptance. Buys first rights, second serial (reprint) rights or simultaneous rights. Byline given. Submit seasonal/ holiday material 1 year in advance. Reports in 6 weeks. Include Social Security number on ms. Free sample copy; writer's guidelines with #10 SASE and 2 first class stamps.

Nonfiction: Religious-oriented topics, teen interest (school, church, family, dating, sports, part-time jobs), humor, inspirational, personal experience. "We want articles that promote Christian values and ideals." No puzzles. Query or submit complete ms. "We're buying more short pieces these days; 12 pages fill up much too quickly." Length: 800-1,500 words.

Fiction: Adventure, humorous, religious and suspense. "All fiction should have some message for the modern Christian teen." Fiction should deal with all subjects in a forthright manner, without being preachy and without talking down to teens. No tasteless manuscripts that promote anything adverse to the Bible's teachings. Submit complete ms. Length: 1,000-1,500 words. Pays 2-3½¢/word; less for reprints.

Photos: May submit photos with ms. Pays $20-25 for 8×10 b&w glossy prints and $100 for color slides. Model releases should be available. Buys one-time rights.

Tips: "Don't be trite. Use unusual settings or problems. Use a lot of illustrations, a good balance of conversation, narration, and action. Style must be clear, fresh—no sermonettes or sickly-sweet fiction. Take a realistic approach to problems. Be willing to submit to editorial policies on doctrine; knowledge of the *Bible* a must. Also, be aware of teens today, and what they do. Language, clothing, and activities included in mss should be contemporary. We are becoming more and more selective about freelance material and the competition seems to be stiffer all the time."

‡**TEEN DREAM**, Starline Publications, 63 Grand Ave., River Edge NJ 07661. (201)487-6124. Editor: Anne Raso. 20% freelance written. Bimonthly magazine of teen entertainment. Estab. 1988. Circ. 180,000. Pays on publication. Byline given. Offers 50% kill fee. Buys all rights. Submit seasonal/holiday material 3 months in advance. Reports in 2 months. Sample copy $3.

Nonfiction: Photo feature. Buys 50 mss/year. Call editor about ms. Length: 500-1,000 words. Pays $50-100 for assigned articles. Sometimes pays expenses of writers on assignment.

Photos: State availability of photos with submission or send photos with submission. Reviews color slides and 8×10 b&w prints. Offers $25-125 per photo. Captions required. Buys one-time rights.

'**TEEN MAGAZINE**, 8490 Sunset Blvd., Hollywood CA 90069. Editor: Roxanne Camron. 20-30% freelance written. Prefers to work with published/established writers. For teenage girls. Monthly magazine. Circ. 1 million. Publishes ms an average of 6 months after acceptance. Buys all rights. Reports in 4 months. Sample copy and writer's guidelines for 8½×11 SAE and $2.50.

Fiction: Dealing specifically with teenage girls and contemporary teen issues. More fiction on emerging alternatives for young women. Suspense, humorous and romance. "Young love is all right, but teens want to read about it in more relevant settings." Length: 2,500-4,000 words. Pays $100. Sometimes pays the expenses of writers on assignment.

Tips: "No fiction with explicit language, casual references to drugs, alcohol, sex, or smoking; no fiction with too depressing outcome."

TQ (TEEN QUEST), The Good News Broadcasting Association, Inc., P.O. Box 82808, Lincoln NE 68501. (402)474-4567. Editor-in-Chief: Warren Wiersbe. Managing Editor: Karen Christianson. 50% freelance written. Works with a small number of new/unpublished writers each year. Monthly magazine emphasizing Christian living for Protestant church-oriented teens, ages 12-17. Circ. 60,000. Buys first serial rights or second serial (reprint) rights. Publishes ms an average of 8 months after acceptance. Byline given. Submit seasonal/holiday material 1 year in advance. Previously published submissions OK. Reports in 2 months. Sample copy and writer's guidelines for 9×12 SAE with 4 first class stamps.

Nonfiction: Interviews with Christian sports personalities and features on teens making unusual achievements or involved in unique pursuits—spiritual emphasis a must. "Articles on issues of particular importance to teens—drugs, pregnancy, school, jobs, recreational activities, etc. Christian element not necessary on morally neutral issues." Buys 1-3 mss/issue. Query or send complete ms. No phone queries. Length: 500-1,800 words. Pays 7-10¢/word for unsolicited mss; 10-15¢ for assigned articles. Sometimes pays expenses of writers on assignment.

Fiction: Needs stories involving problems common to teens (dating, family, alcohol and drugs, peer pressure, school, sex, talking about one's faith to non-believers, standing up for convictions, etc.) in which the resolution (or lack of it) is true to our readers' experiences. "In other words, no happily-ever-after endings, last-page spiritual conversions, or pat answers to complex problems. We are interested in the everyday (though still profound) experiences of teen life. If the story was written just to make a point, or grind the author's favorite axe, we don't want it. Most of our stories feature a protagonist 14-17 years old. The key is the spiritual element—how the protagonist deals with or makes sense of his/her situation in light of Christian spiritual principles and ideals, without being preached to or preaching to another character or to the reader." Buys 30 mss/year. Send complete ms. Length: 800-1,800 words. Pays 7-10¢/word for unsolicited mss; 10-15¢/word for assigned fiction.

Tips: "Articles for *TQ* need to be written in an upbeat style attractive to teens. No preaching. Writers must be familiar with the characteristics of today's teenagers in order to write for them."

‡VISION, A Lifestyles Magazine for Young Adults, Young Calvinist Federation, P.O. Box 7259, Grand Rapids MI 49510. (616)241-5616. FAX: (616)241-5558. Editor: Dale Dieleman. Managing Editor: Judy Blain. 80% freelance written. General interest-lifestyles magazine for singles. Circ. 2,500. **Pays on acceptance.** Publishes ms an average of 3 months after acceptance. Byline given. Offers 50% kill fee. Buys first, one-time, second serial (reprint), and simultaneous rights. Submit seasonal/holiday material 6 months in advance. Simultaneous and previously published submissions OK. Reports in 1 month on queries; 2 months on mss. Sample copy for 9×12 SAE with 3 first class stamps; writer's guidelines for #10 SASE.
Nonfiction: Book excerpts, how-to, inspirational, interview/profile, personal experience, religious. Buys 20 mss/year. Send complete ms. Length: 600-2,000. Pays $25-75 for assigned articles; $25-50 for unsolicited articles. Sometimes pays expenses of writers on assignment.
Photos: Lifestyles, Work World, Creative Christianity, Budget Briefs. Buys 25 mss/year. Send complete ms. Length: 600-1,000 words. Pays $25-35.
Fiction: Humorous, religious, science fiction, slice-of-life vignettes. No formula stories or fictional accounts of biblical characters. Buys 6 mss/year. Send complete ms. Length: 800-2,000. Pays $25-75.
Poetry: Free verse, haiku. Buys 10 poems/year. Submit maximum 6 poems at one time. Length: 4-40 lines. Pays $15-45.
Tips: "We need stories, real-life accounts, how-to tips for better living as single people."

WITH MAGAZINE, Faith and Life Press and Mennonite Publishing House, 722 Main St., Box 347, Newton KS 67114. (316)283-5100. Editor: Susan Janzen. 30% freelance written. Monthly magazine for teenagers. "We approach Christianity from an Anabaptist-Mennonite perspective. Our purpose is to disciple youth within congregations." Circ. 6,500. **Pays on acceptance.** Byline given. Buys one-time rights. Submit seasonal/holiday material 6 months in advance. Simultaneous and previously published submissions OK. Query for electronic submissions. Reports in 6 weeks on queries; 4 months on mss. Sample copy $1.50 with 9×12 SAE and 85¢ postage. Writer's guidelines for #10 SASE.
Nonfiction: Humor, personal experience, religious, youth. "No articles which use religion as a utopian response to conflict." Buys 10 mss/year. Send complete ms. Length: 900-1,500 words. Pays $36-60 for assigned articles; $18-60 for unsolicited articles.
Photos: Sometimes pays the expenses of writers on assignment. Send photos with submission. Reviews 8×10 prints. Offers $10-50 per photo. Identification of subjects required. Buys one-time rights.
Fiction: Humorous, religious, youth. Buys 30 mss/year. Send complete ms. Length: 900-1,500 words. Pays $18-60.
Poetry: Avant-garde, free verse, haiku, light verse, traditional. Buys 30-49 poems. Pays $10-50.
Tips: "Introduce yourself briefly in a cover letter, but don't overdo it. Flowery resumes and pages of credits mean less to me than a well-written story. Fiction is most open to freelancers. When writing for teens, avoid being preachy or talking down to them. Use anecdotes with which they can identify and avoid using jargon which is out of date quickly."

YOUNG SALVATIONIST, The Salvation Army, 799 Bloomfield Ave., Verona NJ 07044. (201)239-0606. Editor: Capt. Robert R. Hostetler. 75% freelance written. Works with a small number of new/unpublished writers each year. Monthly Christian magazine for high school teens. "Only material with a definite Christian emphasis or from a Christian perspective will be considered." Circ. 48,000. **Pays on acceptance.** Publishes ms an average of 10 months after acceptance. Byline given. Buys first North American serial rights, first rights, one-time rights or second serial (reprint) rights. Submit seasonal/holiday material 6 months in advance. Reports in 2 weeks on queries; 1 month on mss. Sample copy for 8½×11 SAE with 3 first class stamps; writer's guidelines for #10 SASE.
Nonfiction: Inspirational, how-to (Bible study, workshop skills), humor, interview/profile, personal experience, photo feature, religious. "Articles should deal with issues of relevance to teens today; avoid 'preachiness' or moralizing." Buys 60 mss/year. Send complete ms. "State whether your submission is for Young Salvationist or The Young Soldier section." Length: 500-1,200 words. Pays 4¢/word for unsolicited mss; 5¢/word for assigned articles.
Columns/Departments: SALSpots (media-related news and human interest from a Christian perspective, book and record reviews). Buys 10-12 mss/year. Send complete ms. Length: 50-200 words. Pays 4-5¢/word.
Fiction: Adventure, fantasy, humorous, religious, romance, science fiction—all from a Christian perspective. Length: 500-1,200 words. Pays 4-5¢/word.
Tips: "Study magazine, familiarize yourself with the unique 'Salvationist' perspective of *Young Salvationist*; learn a little about the Salvation Army; media, sports, sex and dating are strongest appeal."

‡YOUTH FOCUS, Paywoods Communications, Suite 134, 4 Daniels Farm Rd., Trumbull CT 06611. (203)372-1745. Editor: Quentin Plair. 75% freelance written. Monthly teen newsletter for African-American youth ages 12-17. Estab. 1987. Circ. 10,000. Pays on publication. Publishes ms an average of 3 months after acceptance. Byline sometimes given. Buys first rights or one-time rights. Submit seasonal/holiday material 5 months in advance. Simultaneous and previously published submissions OK. Reports in 2 months. Sample copy for $1. Free writer's guidelines.

Nonfiction: Essays, exposé, historical/nostalgic, humor, interview/profile, opinion, personal experience, religious and travel. Buys 2 mss/year. Send complete ms. Length: 10-3,000 words. Pays $15-100.

Photos: Send photos with submission. Offers no additional payment for photos accepted with ms. Captions, model releases and identification of subjects required.

Poetry: Avant-garde, free verse, haiku, light verse and traditional. Buys 7 poems/year. Length 1-200 lines. Pays $10-30.

YOUTH UPDATE, St. Anthony Messenger Press, 1615 Republic St., Cincinnati OH 45210. (513)241-5615. Editor: Carol Ann Morrow. 90% freelance written. Monthly newsletter of faith life for teenagers. Designed to attract, instruct, guide and challenge Catholics of high school age by applying the Gospel to modern problems/situations. Circ. 38,000. **Pays on acceptance.** Publishes ms an average of 6 months after acceptance. Byline given. Reports in 2 months. Sample copy and writer's guidelines for #10 SASE.

Nonfiction: Inspirational, practical self-help and spiritual. Buys 12 mss/year. Query. Length: 2,200-2,300 words. Pays $350. Sometimes pays expenses of writers on assignment.

Travel, Camping and Trailer

Travel magazines give travelers indepth information about destinations, detailing the best places to go, attractions in the area, and sites to see—but they also keep them up-to-date about potential negative aspects of these destinations. Publications in this category tell tourists and campers the where-tos and how-tos of travel. This category is extremely competitive, demanding quality writing, background information and professional photography. Each has its own slant and should be studied carefully before sending submissions.

AAA GOING PLACES, Magazine for Today's Traveler, AAA Florida/Georgia, 1515 No. Westshore Blvd., Tampa FL 33615. (813)289-5923. Editor: Phyllis Zeno. Managing Editor: Janeen Andrews. 50% freelance written. Bimonthly magazine on auto news, driving trips or tips and travel. Circ. 760,000. Pays on publication. Publishes ms an average of 3-6 months after acceptance. Byline given. Buys one-time rights. Submit seasonal/holiday material 9 months in advance. Simultaneous submissions OK. Reports in 2 months. Sample copy for 8 × 10 SAE with $1 postage. Free writer's guidelines.

Nonfiction: Historical/nostalgic, how-to, humor, interview/profile, personal experience, photo feature, travel. Special issues include Cruise Guide and Europe Issue. Buys 15 mss/year. Send complete ms. Length: 500-1,500 words. Pays $15 per printed page.

Photos: State availability of photos with submission. Reviews 2 × 2 transparencies. Offers no additional payment for photos accepted with ms. Captions required.

Columns/Departments: AAAway We Go (local attractions in Florida or Georgia. Bed, breakfast places in Florida or Georgia). Buys 10 ms/year. Send complete ms. Length: 100-200 words. Pays $5.

‡ACCENT, Meridian Publishing Inc., 1720 Washington, P.O. Box 10010, Ogden UT 84409. (801)394-9446. 60-70% freelance written. Works with a small number of new/unpublished writers each year. A monthly inhouse travel magazine distributed by various companies to employees, customers, stockholders, etc. "Readers are predominantly upscale, mainstream, family oriented." Circ. 110,000. **Pays on acceptance.** Publishes ms an average of 8 months after acceptance. Byline given. Buys first rights, second serial (reprint) rights and nonexclusive reprint rights. Simultaneous and previously published submissions OK. Reports in 6 weeks. Sample copy $1 and 9 × 12 SAE; writer's guidelines for #10 SASE.

Nonfiction: "We want upbeat pieces slanted toward the average traveler, but we use some exotic travel. Resorts, cruises, hiking, camping, health retreats, historic sites, sports vacations, national or state forests and parks are all featured. No articles without original color photos, except with travel tips. We also welcome pieces on travel tips and ways to travel." Buys 40 mss/year. Query. Length: 1,200 words. Pays 15¢/word.

Photos: Send photos with ms. Pays $35 for color transparencies; $50 for cover. Captions and model releases required. Buys one-time rights.

Tips: "Write about interesting places. We are inundated with queries for stories on California and the southeastern coast. Excellent color transparencies are essential. Most rejections are because of poor quality photography or the writer didn't study the market. We are using three times as many domestic pieces as foreign because of our readership. Address queries to Attention: Editor."

ADVENTURE ROAD, Condé Nast Publications, 360 Madison Ave., 10th Fl., New York NY 10017. (212)880-2282. Editor: Marilyn Holstein. 100% freelance written. Bimonthly magazine that features domestic, general interest travel articles that stimulate reader to travel. Circ. 1.5 million. **Pays on acceptance.** Publishes ms an average of 4 months after acceptance. Byline given. Offers 25% kill fee. Buys first North American serial rights. Simultaneous and previously published submissions OK. Sample for 9×12 SAE. Writer's guidelines for #10 SASE.

Nonfiction: Travel. "No first-person articles." Buys 21 mss/year. Query with published clips. Length: 800-1,800 words. Pays $300-750. Sometimes pays expenses of writers on assignment.

Photos: State availability of photos with submission. (Do not send unsolicited transparencies). Offers $200 minimum per photo. Captions required. Buys one-time rights.

Columns/Departments: Calendar (events listing, domestic), 90 entries; Weekend Wanderer (3-day trips from a major city), 1,000 words; Motor Talk (automotive tips), 800 words and Certicare Adviser (Q&A from readers), 800 words. Buys 30 mss/year. Query with published clips. Pays $300-450.

AMERICAN WEST, Travel & Life, American West Management Corp., Suite #30, 7000 E. Tanque Verde Rd., Tucson AZ 85715. (602)886-9959. Editor-in-Chief: Sue Giles. Executive Editor: Marjory Vals Maud. 60% freelance written. Bimonthly magazine which covers travel and life in the American West. "We look for relevant subject matter skillfully written to interest our readers who travel or want to travel in the West." Circ. 180,000. **Pays on acceptance.** Byline given. Buys first North American serial rights, second serial rights and anthology rights. Submit seasonal/holiday material 1 year in advance. Reports in 1 month on queries; 2 months on mss. Sample copy $3. Writer's guidelines for #10 SASE.

Nonfiction: General interest, historical/nostalgic, personal experience and travel. Buys 40 mss/year. Query with published clips. Length: 1,000-2,500 words. Pays $100-500.

Columns/Departments: Home Sweet Home (residences, past and present, typical of the West); Westerners (profiles of men and women who have had an impact on the West); The Creative West (an examination of Western arts, crafts and artists); Remembering The Past (human interest photos from the past with brief narratives); Journey's End (unique places to stay in the West); Life in the Old West (history, folklore, yarns and personal experiences); and Western Discoveries (little known treasures—places, events, etc., in the West).

Photos: Generally accepts photos only with submissions. Reviews 35mm or 3×5 transparencies and 5×7 or larger prints. Offers $25 per b&w photo for Remembering the Past. Model releases required. Buys one-time rights.

AMOCO TRAVELER, K.L. Publications, Suite 105, 2001 Killebrew Dr., Bloomington MN 55425. Editor: Mary Lou Brooks. 80% freelance written. A quarterly magazine published for the Amoco Traveler Club. Circ. 65,000. Pays on acceptance by client. Byline given. Buys various rights. "This publication is a mix of original and reprinted material." Previously published submissions OK. Submit seasonal/holiday material 8 months in advance. Simultaneous submissions OK. Reports in 1 month. Sample copy for 9×12 SAE with 3 first class stamps. Writer's guidelines for #10 SASE.

Nonfiction: Focus is on U.S. destinations by car, although occasionally will use a foreign destination. Traveler Roads showcases a North American city or area, its attractions, history and accomodations; Traveler Focus features a romantic, getaway destination for the armchair traveler; Traveler Weekends focuses on an activity-oriented destination. Length: 1,000-1,200 words. Pays $325-425 for originals; $100-150 for reprints.

Columns/Departments: Healthwise (travel-related health tips). Length: 500-600 words. Pays $175.

Photos: Reviews 35mm transparencies. No b&w. Pay varies.

ASU TRAVEL GUIDE, ASU Travel Guide, Inc., 1331 Columbus Ave., San Francisco CA 94133. (415)441-5200. Editor: Christopher Gil. 90% freelance written. Quarterly guidebook covering international travel features and travel discounts for well-traveled airline employees. Estab. 1970. Circ. 60,000. Payment terms negotiable. Publishes ms an average of 18 months after acceptance. Byline given. Buys first North American serial rights, first and second rights to the same material, and second serial (reprint) rights to material originally published elsewhere. Makes work-for-hire assignments. Submit seasonal/holiday material 6 months in advance. Simultaneous queries and simultaneous and previously published submissions OK. Reports in 1 month. Writer's guidelines for #10 SASE.

Nonfiction: International travel articles "similar to those run in consumer magazines." Not interested in amateur efforts from inexperienced travelers or personal experience articles that don't give useful information to other travelers. Buys 17 ms/year. Destination pieces only; no "Tips On Luggage" articles. "We will be accepting fewer manuscripts and relying more on our established group of freelance contributors." Unsolicited mss or queries without SASE will not be acknowledged. No telephone queries. Length: 1,200-1,500 words. Pays $200.

Photos: "Interested in clear, high-contrast photos; we prefer not to receive material without photos." Reviews 5×7 and 8×10 b&w prints. "Payment for photos is included in article price; photos from tourist offices are acceptable."

Tips: "We'll be needing more domestic U.S. destination pieces which combine several cities or areas in a logical manner, e.g., Seattle/Vancouver, Savannah/Atlanta. Query with samples of travel writing and a list of places you've recently visited. We appreciate clean and simple style. Keep verbs in the active tense and involve the reader in what you write. Avoid 'cute' writing, coined words and stale cliches. The most frequent mistakes made by writers in completing an article for us are: 1) Lazy writing—using words to describe a place that could describe any destination such as 'there is so much to do in (fill in destination) that whole guidebooks have been written about it'; 2) Including fare and tour package information – our readers make arrangements through their own airline."

AWAY, c/o ALA, 888 Worcester St., Wellesley MA 02181. (617)237-5200. Editor: Gerard J. Gagnon. For members of the ALA Auto & Travel Club, interested in their autos and in travel. Ages range approximately 20-75. They live primarily in New England. Slanted to seasons. 5-10% freelance written. Quarterly. Circ. 105,000. Buys first serial rights. **Pays on acceptance.** Publishes ms an average of 3 months after acceptance. Submit seasonal material 6 months in advance. Reports "as soon as possible." Although a query is not mandatory, it may be advisable for many articles. Sample copy for 9×12 SAE with 2 first class stamps.
Nonfiction: Articles on "travel, tourist attractions, safety, history, etc., preferably with a New England angle. Also, car care tips and related subjects." Would like a "positive feel to all pieces, but not the chamber of commerce approach." Buys general seasonal travel, specific travel articles, and travel-related articles; outdoor activities, for example, gravestone rubbing; historical articles linked to places to visit. "Would like to see more nonseasonally oriented material. Most material now submitted seems suitable only for our summer issue. Avoid pieces on hunting and about New England's most publicized attractions, such as Old Sturbridge Village and Mystic Seaport." Length: 500-1,200 words, preferably 800-1,000 words. Pays approximately 10¢/word.
Photos: Photos purchased with mss. Captions required. B&w glossy prints. Pays $5-10/b&w photo, payment on publication based upon which photos are used. Not buying color photos at this time.
Tips: "The most frequent mistakes we find in articles submitted to us are spelling, typographical errors and questionable statements of fact, which require additional research by the editorial staff. We are buying very few articles at this time."

‡BACKPACKER, Rodale Press, Inc., 33 E. Minor St., Emmaus PA 18098. (215)967-8296. Editor: John Viehman. Managing Editor: Tom Shealey. 25% freelance written. 8 times/year magazine covering self-propelled wilderness travel. Estab. 1973. Circ. 175,000. Pays on acceptance. Byline given. Offers 25% kill fee. Buys one-time rights or all rights. Reports in 2 months. Sample copy $1. Writer's guidelines for #10 SAE with 1 first class stamp.
Nonfiction: Essays, exposé, historical/nostalgic, how-to (expedition planner), humor, inspirational, interview/profile, new product, opinion, personal experience, technical and travel. No step-by-step accounts of what you did on your summer vacation. Query with published clips and SASE. Length: 750-3,000 words. Pays $400 and up. Sometimes pays (pre-determined) expenses of writers on assignment.
Photos: State availability of photos with submission. Amount varies – depends on size of photo used. Buys one-time rights or all rights.
Columns/Departments: What we want are features that let us and the readers "feel" the place, and experience your wonderment, excitement, disappointment or other emotions encountered "out there." If we feel like we've been there after reading your story, you've succeeded. Footnotes "News From All Over" (adventure, environment, wildlife, trails, techniques, organizations, special interests – well-written, entertaining, short, newsy item) 50-500 words; Geosphere (essay about some biological, psychological or scientific aspect of the natural world, often takes a philosophical approach, should offer the reader a fresh perspective on the natural world), 750-1,200 words; Body Language (health and nutrition column) 750-1,200 words; Weekend Wilderness (brief but detailed guides to wilderness areas, providing thorough trip-planning information, only enough anecdote to give a hint, then the where/when/hows) 500-750 words; Technique (ranging from beginner to expert focus, written by people with solid expertise, details ways to improve performance, how-to-do-it instructions, information on equipment manufacturers and places readers can go), 750-1,500 words; and Backcountry (personal perspectives, quirky and idiosyncratic, humorous critiques, manifestos and misadventures, interesting angle, lesson, revelation or moral), 750-1,200 words. Buys 25-50 mss/year. Query with published clips. Pays $25-350.
Tips: "Our best advice is to read the publication – most freelancers don't know the magazine at all. The best way to break in is with an article for the Backcountry, Weekend Wilderness or Footnotes Department."

BAJA TIMES, Editorial Playas De Rosarito, S.A., P.O. Box 5577, Chula Vista CA 92012-5577. (706)612-1244. Editor: John W. Utley. 90% freelance written. Monthly tourist and travel publication on Baja California, Mexico. "Oriented to the Baja California, Mexico aficionada – the tourist and those Americans who are living in Baja California or have their vacation homes there. Articles should be slanted to Baja." Pays on publication. Publishes ms an average of 8 months after acceptance. Byline given. Buys first rights. Submit

Always check the most recent copy of a magazine for the address and editor's name before you send in a query or manuscript.

seasonal/holiday material 4 months in advance. Sample copy for 9×12 SAE with 4 first class stamps; free writer's guidelines.

Nonfiction: General interest, historical/nostalgic, humor, personal experience, photo feature, travel. All with Baja California slant. "Nothing that describes any negative aspects of Mexico (bribes, bad police, etc.). We are a positive publication." Query with or without published clips, or submit complete ms. Length: 750-2,100 words. Pays $50-100 for assigned articles; $35-50 for unsolicited articles. Sometimes pays expenses of writers on assignment.

Photos: Send photos with submission. Reviews 5×7 prints. Captions and identification of subjects required. Buys one-time rights.

Tips: "Take a chance—send in that Baja California related article. We guarantee to read them all. Over the years we have turned up some real winners from our writers—many who do not have substantial experience. The entire publication is open. We buy an average of 6 freelance each issue. Virtually any subject is acceptable as long as it has a Baja California slant. Remember Tijuana, Mexico (on the border with San Diego, CA) is the busiest border crossing in the world. We are always interested in material relating to Tijuana, Rosarito, Ensenada, San Felipe, LaPaz."

CAMPING & RV MAGAZINE, Camping Voice of Mid-America, Joe Jones Publishing, P.O. Box 337, Iola WI 54945. (715)445-5000. FAX: (715)445-4053. Editor: Deb Lengkeek. 75% freelance written. Monthly magazine on camping in the Midwest and Heartland states. "We accept both casual and technical articles dealing with camping, and destination pieces from our coverage area." Circ. 20,000. Pays on publication. Publishes ms an average of 6 months after acceptance. Byline given. Buys first rights, one-time rights or second serial (reprint) rights. Submit seasonal/holiday material 3 months in advance. Previously published submissions OK. Free sample copy and writer's guidelines.

Nonfiction: General interest, how-to, personal experience, photo feature, technical, and travel. "No articles of destinations out of our coverage area." Buys 60 mss/year. Send complete ms. Length: 1,000-2,000 words. Pays 5¢/word.

Photos: State availability of photos with submission. Reviews prints. Pays $5 per photo. Identification of subjects required. Buys one-time rights.

Columns/Departments: Living on Wheels; Camping Comforts; RV Wife and Care of RV (hints, suggestions, general interest, technical, equipment care), 1,000 words. Buys 50 mss/year. Query. Pays 5¢/word.

Fillers: Anecdotes and facts. Buys 12/year. Length: 500-1,000 words. Pays 3-5¢/word.

Tips: "Write from a campground background—be knowledgeable about how and where to camp as well as camping related activities."

CAMPING CANADA, CRV Publishing Canada Ltd., Suite 202, 2077 Dundas St. East, Mississauga, Ontario L4X 1M2 Canada. (416)624-8218. FAX: (416)624-6764. Editor: Tim Stover. Managing Editor: Norman Rosen. 65-80% freelance written. "We have an established group of writers but are always willing to work with newcomers." A magazine published 7 times/year, covering camping and RVing. Circ. 100,000. Pays on publication. Publishes ms an average of 2-3 months after acceptance. Byline given. Buys first rights. Reports in 2 months. Free sample copy and writer's guidelines.

Nonfiction: Canadian recreational life, especially as it concerns or interests Canadian RV and camping enthusiasts; historical/nostalgic (sometimes); how-to; new product; personal experience; technical; and travel. Will accept occasional material unrelated to Canada. Buys 25-30 mss/year. "Only mss from solicited writers will be considered." Query first. Length: 1,000-2,500 words. Pays $150-300.

Photos: Will buy occasional photos. Query first. Mss must be accompanied by photos, unless otherwise agreed upon.

Tips: "Deep, accurate, thorough research and colorful detail are required for all features. Travel pieces should include places to camp (contact information, if available). We would like to receive profiles of celebrity RVers, preferably Canadians, but will look at celebrities known in the U.S. and Canada."

CAMPING TODAY, Official Publication of National Campers & Hikers Association, 126 Hermitage Rd., Butler PA 16001. (412)283-7401. Editors: DeWayne and June Johnston. 50% freelance written. Prefers to work with published/established writers. The monthly official membership publication of the NCHA, "the largest nonprofit family camping and RV organization in the United States and Canada. Members are heavily oriented toward RV travel, both weekend and extended vacations. A small segment is interested in hiking and backpacking. Concentration is on member activities in chapters. Group is also interested in conservation and wildlife. The majority of members are retired." Circ. 27,500. Pays on publication. Publishes ms an average of 6 months after acceptance. Byline given. Buys one-time rights. Submit seasonal/holiday material 3 months in advance. Simultaneous and previously published submissions OK. Reports in 1 month. Sample copy and guidelines for $1 in stamps or writer's guidelines for #10 SASE.

Nonfiction: Travel (interesting places to visit by RV, camping); humor (camping or travel related, please, no "our first campout stories"); interview/profile (interesting campers); new products and technical (RVs related). Buys 20-30 mss/year. Send complete ms with photos. Length: 750-2,000 words. Pays $50-150.

Photos: Send photos with ms. Need b&w or sharp color prints inside (we can make prints from slides) and vertical transparencies for cover. Captions required.

Tips: "Freelance material on RV travel, RV maintenance/safety, and items of general camping and hiking interest throughout the United States and Canada will receive special attention."

CARIBBEAN TRAVEL AND LIFE, Suite 830, 8403 Colesville Rd., Silver Spring MD 20910. (301)588-2300. Editor: Veronica Gould Stoddart. 90% freelance written. Prefers to work with published/established writers. A bimonthly magazine covering travel to the Caribbean, Bahamas and Bermuda. Estab. 1985. Circ. 100,000. Pays on publication. Publishes ms an average of 3 months after acceptance. Byline given. Offers 25% kill fee. Buys first North American serial rights. Submit seasonal/holiday material 6 months in advance. Reports in 2 months. Sample copy for 9 × 12 SAE with 5 first class stamps; writer's guidelines for #10 SASE.

Nonfiction: General interest, how-to, interview/profile, culture, personal experience and travel. No "guidebook rehashing; superficial destination pieces or critical exposes." Buys 30 mss/year. Query with published clips. Length: 2,000-2,500 words. Pays $550.

Photos: Send photos with submission. Reviews 35mm transparencies. Offers $75-400 per photo. Captions and identification of subjects required. Buys one-time rights.

Columns/Departments: Resort Spotlight (in-depth review of luxury resort); Tradewinds (focus on one particular kind of water sport or sailing/cruising); Island Buys (best shopping for luxury goods, crafts, duty-free); Island Spice (best cuisine and/or restaurant reviews with recipes); all 1,000-1,500 words; Caribbeana (short items on great finds in travel, culture, and special attractions), 500 words. Buys 36 mss/year. Query with published clips or send complete ms. Length: 500-1,250 words. Pays $75-200.

Tips: "We are especially looking for stories with a personal touch and lively, entertaining anecdotes, as well as strong insight into people and places being covered. Also prefers stories with focus on people, i.e, colorful personalities, famous people, etc. Writer should demonstrate why he/she is the best person to do that story based on extensive knowledge of the subject, frequent visits to destination, residence in destination, specialty in field."

‡THE COOL TRAVELER, The Rome Cappucino Review, P.O. Box 11975, Philadelphia PA 19145. (215)440-8257. Editor: Bob Moore. Managing Editor: MaryBeth Feeney. 100% freelance written. Quarterly newsletter covering travel. "Our audience has a zest for travel. Our readers usually have a college education and travel to experience different places and people. We do not emphasize affluence but rather the joy of travel." Estab. 1988. Circ. 750-1,250. Pays on publication. Publishes ms an average of 2-3 months after acceptance. Byline given. Buys one-time rights. Submit seasonal/holiday material 2 months in advance. Simultaneous and previously published submissions OK. Query for electronic submissions. Reports in 2 weeks. Sample copy for #10 SAE with 2 first class stamps. Free writer's guidelines.

Nonfiction: Historical/nostalgic, personal experience, travel, art history. Christmas Issue, International Festival Issue. "We don't want a listing of names and prices but personal experiences and unusual experiences." Buys 20 mss/year. Send complete ms. Length: 2,500 words maximum. Pays $5-20 for unsolicited articles.

Columns/Departments: Seasonal (material pertaining to a certain time of year: like a winter festival or summer carnival), 2,500 words maximum. Pays $5-20.

Poetry: Avant-garde, free verse, haiku, light verse, traditional. No poetry that is too sentimental. Buys 30 poems/year. Submit maximum 10 poems. Length: 5-75 lines. Pays $5-20.

Tips: "Writer should have firsthand knowledge and experience of their topic or topics and be able to give the reader a feeling of being there through cultural, artistic and visual references. All areas of the newsletter are open to freelancers. The same tips apply toward seasonal material. The writer should connote to the reader a feeling of personal experience through the usage of cultural, artistic and visual references."

CRUISE TRAVEL MAGAZINE, World Publishing Co., 990 Grove St., Evanston IL 60201. (708)491-6440. Editor: Robert Meyers. Managing Editor: Charles Doherty. 95% freelance written. A bimonthly magazine on cruise travel. "This is a consumer oriented travel publication covering the world of pleasure cruising on large cruise ships (with some coverage of smaller ships), including ports, travel tips, roundups." Estab. 1979. **Pays on acceptance.** Publishes ms an average of 5 months after acceptance. Byline given. Offers ½ kill fee. Buys first North American serial rights, one-time rights, or second serial (reprint) rights. Simultaneous and previously published submissions OK. Sample copy $3 with 9 × 12 SAE and 5 first class stamps. Writer's guidelines for #10 SASE.

Nonfiction: General interest, historical/nostalgic, interview/profile, personal experience, photo feature, travel. "No daily cruise 'diary'; My First Cruise; etc." Buys 72 mss/year. Query with or without published clips or send complete ms. Length: 500-2,000 words. Pay $75-350.

Photos: Send photos with submission. Reviews transparencies and prints. "Must be color, 35m preferred (other format OK); color prints second choice." Offers no additional payment for photos accepted with ms "but pay more for well-illustrated ms." Captions and identification of subjects required. Buys one-time rights.

Fillers: Anecdotes, facts. Buys 3 mss/year. Length: 300-700 words. Pays $75-200.

Tips: "Do your homework. Know what we do and what sorts of things we publish. Know the cruise industry— we can't use novices. Good, sharp, bright color photography opens the door fast."

DISCOVERY, One Illinois Center, Suite 1700, 111 E. Wacker Dr., Chicago IL 60601. Editor: Scott Powers. 75% freelance written. Prefers to work with published/established writers, and works with a small number of new/unpublished writers each year. A quarterly travel magazine for Allstate Motor Club members. Estab. 1987. Circ. 1.6 million. Buys first North American serial rights. **Pays on acceptance.** Publishes ms an average of 8 months after acceptance. Submit seasonal queries 8-14 months in advance to allow for photo assignment. Reports in 1 month. Sample copy for 9×12 SAE and $1 postage; writer's guidelines for #10 SASE.

Nonfiction: Emphasizes automotive travel, offering a firsthand look at the people and places, trends and activities that help define the world's character. "We're looking for polished magazine articles that are people-oriented and promise insight as well as entertainment—not narratives of peoples' vacations. Destination articles must rely less on the impressions of writers and more on the observations of people who live or work or grew up in the place and have special attachments. We seek ideas for a 'Best of America' department, which is a roundup of particular kinds of places (i.e beaches, national park lodges, space museums) often related to the season." Query. "Submit a thorough proposal suitable for *Discovery*. It must be literate, concise and enthusiastic. Accompany query with relevant published clips and a resume." Buys 12 assigned mss/year. Length: 1,500-2,000 words, plus a 500-word sidebar on other things to see and do. Rates vary, depending on assignment and writer's credentials; usual range is $800-plus. Usually pays the expenses of writers on assignment.

Photography: Transparencies (35mm or larger). Pays day rate. For existing photos, rates depend on use. Photos should work as story; captions required. Send transparencies by registered mail. Buys one-time rights.

Tips: "No personal narratives, mere destination pieces or subjects that are not particularly visual. We have a strong emphasis on photojournalism and our stories reflect this. The most frequent mistakes made by writers in completing an article for us are: not writing to assignment, which results in a weak focus or central theme and poor organization and a lack of development, which diminishes the substance of the story. Word precision frequently is the difference between a dull and an exciting story. Writers will benefit by studying several issues of the publication before sending queries."

ENDLESS VACATION, Endless Vacation Publications, Inc., P.O. 80260, Indianapolis IN 46280. (317)871-9500. Editor: Helen W. O'Guinn. Prefers to work with published/established writers. A 10 times per year magazine covering travel destinations, activities and issues that enhance the lives of vacationers. Estab. 1974. Circ. 700,000. **Pays on acceptance.** Publishes ms an average of 6 months after acceptance. Byline given. Buys first worldwide serial rights. Simultaneous submissions OK. Reports in 1 month on queries and manuscripts. Sample copy $5; writer's guidelines for SAE with 1 first class stamp.

Nonfiction: Contact Manuscript Editor. Travel. Buys 24 mss/year (approx). Most are from established writers already published in *Endless Vacation. Accepts very few unsolicited pieces.* Query with published clips. Length: 1,000-2,000 words. Pays $500-1,000 for assigned articles; pays $250-800 for unsolicited articles. Sometimes pays the expenses of writers on assignment.

Photos: State availability of photos with submissions. Reviews 4×5 transparencies and 35mm slides. Offers $100-500/photo. Model releases and identification of subjects required. Buys one-time rights.

Columns/Departments: Healthy Traveler (vacation health-related topics); Weekender (on domestic weekend vacation travel); Making the Scene (entertainment, nightlife trends); Sporting Life (vacation sports). Query with published clips. Length: 800-1,000 words. Pays $150-300. Sometimes pays the expenses of writers on assignment. Also news items for Hits, Misses and Hot Stuff column on new travel news, products or problems. Length: 100-200 words, $50 per item.

Tips: "We will continue to focus on travel trends and resort and upscale destinations. Articles must be packed with pertinent facts and applicable how-tos. Information—addresses, phone numbers, dates of events, costs—must be current and accurate. We like to see a variety of stylistic approaches, but in all cases the lead must be strong. A writer should realize that we require first-hand knowledge of the subject and plenty of practical information. For further understanding of *Endless Vacations'* direction, the writer should study the magazine and guidelines for writers."

GREAT EXPEDITIONS, P.O. Box 8000-411, Sumas WA 98295; or P.O. Box 8000-411, Abbotsford, British Columbia V2S 6H1 Canada. Editor: Craig Henderson. 90% freelance written. Eager to work with new/unpublished writers. Quarterly magazine covering "off-the-beaten-path" destinations, outdoor recreation, cultural discovery, budget travel, socially-responsible tourism and working abroad. Estab. 1978. Circ. 8,000. Pays on publication. Buys first and second (reprint) rights. Simultaneous queries, and simultaneous and previously published submissions OK. Send SASE for return of article and photos. Reports in 2 months. Sample copy $4; free writer's guidelines.

Nonfiction: Articles range from very adventurous (living with an isolated tribe in the Philippines) to mildly adventurous (Spanish language school vacations in Guatemala and Mexico). We also like to see "how-to" pieces for adventurous travelers (i.e., How to Sail Around the World for Free, Swapping Homes with Residents of Other Countries, How to Get in on an Archaeological Dig). Buys 30 mss/year. Pays $60 maximum. Length 1,000-3,000 words.

Photos: B&w photos, color prints or slides should be sent with article. Captions required.
Tips: "It's best to send for a sample copy for a first-hand look at the style of articles we are looking for. If possible, we appreciate practical information for travelers, either in the form of a sidebar or incorporated into the article, detailing how to get there, where to stay, specific costs, where to write for visas or travel information."

GUIDE TO THE FLORIDA KEYS, Humm's, Crain Communications Inc., P.O. Box 2921, Key Largo FL 33037. (305)451-4429. Editor: Sami Lais. 80% freelance written. A quarterly travel guide to the Florida Keys. Estab. 1972. Circ. 60,000. Pays on publication. Byline given. Buys first rights and second serial (reprint) rights. Submit seasonal/holiday material 6 months in advance. Previously published submissions OK. Reports in 2 weeks on queries; 3 weeks on manuscripts. Free sample copy.
Nonfiction: General interest, historical/nostalgic, personal experience and travel, all for the Florida Keys area. Buys 30-40 mss/year. Send complete ms. Length: 500-1,500 words. Pays $5/column inch. Sometimes pays the expenses of writers on assignment.
Photos: State availability of photos with submission. Reviews negatives, 35mm and $2 \times 2\frac{3}{4}$ transparencies, and 5×7 and 8×10 prints. Offers $40-100/photo. Captions and model releases required. Buys one-time rights.
Columns/Departments: Fishing and Diving (primarily about the Florida Keys), 500-1,500 words. Pays $5/column inch.

THE MATURE TRAVELER, Travel Bonanzas for 49ers-Plus, GEM Publishing Group, Box 50820, Reno NV 89513. (702)786-7419. Editor: Gene E. Malott. 30% freelance written. Monthly newsletter on senior citizen travel. Circ. 1,800. **Pays on acceptance.** Publishes an average of 2 months after acceptance. Byline given. Offers 25% kill fee. Buys one-time rights. Submit seasonal/holiday material 3 months in advance. Simultaneous ("if we know about it") and previously published submissions OK. Query for electronic submissions. Reports in 2 weeks. Sample copy for $1 and #10 SAE with 45¢ postage. Writer's guidelines for SAE with 45¢ postage.
Nonfiction: Travel for seniors. "General travel and destination pieces should be aimed at 49ers +." Query. Length: 200-1,200 words. Pays $20-100.
Photos: State availability of photos with submission. Reviews contact sheets and b&w (only) prints. Captions required. Buys one-time rights.
Fillers: Newsbreaks of interest to senior travelers. Buys 6-10/year. Length: 40-200 words. Pays $5-10.
Tips: "Read the guidelines and write stories to our readers' needs—not the general public."

MEXICO WEST, Mexico West Travel Club, Inc., Suite 107, 3450 Bonita Rd., Chula Vista CA 92010. (619)585-3033. FAX: (619)422-2671. Editor: Shirley Miller. 50% freelance written. Monthly newsletter on Baja California; Mexico as a travel destination. "Yes, our readers are travelers to Mexico, especially Baja California. They are knowledgeable but are always looking for new places to see." Estab. 1975. Circ. 5,000. Pays on publication. Publishes an average of 2 months after acceptance. Byline given. Buys first North American serial rights. Submit seasonal/holiday material 3 months in advance. Previously published submissions OK. Free sample copy. Writer's guidelines for #10 SAE with 2 first class stamps.
Nonfiction: Historical, humor, interview, personal experience and travel. Buys 36-50 mss/year. Send complete ms. Length: 900-1,500 words. Pays $50.
Photos: State availability of photos with submission. Reviews 3x5 prints. Offers no additional payment for photos accepted with ms. Captions required. Buys one-time rights.

MOTORHOME, TL Enterprises, Inc., 29901 Agoura Rd., Agoura CA 91301. (818)991-4980. FAX: (818)991-8102. Editor: Bob Livingston. Managing Editor: Gail Harrington. 60% freelance written. A monthly magazine covering motorhomes. "*MotorHome* is exclusively for motorhome enthusiasts. We feature road tests on new motorhomes, travel locations, controversy concerning motorhomes, how-to and technical articles relating to motorhomes." Estab. 1953. Circ. 150,000. **Pays on acceptance.** Publishes ms an average of 4 months after acceptance. Byline given. Buys first North American serial rights. Submit seasonal/holiday material 8 months in advance. Query for electronic submissions. Reports in 3 weeks on queries; up to 2 months on mss depending on work load. Free sample copy and writer's guidelines.
Nonfiction: General interest; historical/nostalgic; how-to (do it yourself for motorhomes); humor; new product; photo feature; and technical. Buys 80 mss/year. Query with published clips. Length: 1,000-2,000 words. Pays $250-600 for assigned articles; pays $200-500 for unsolicited articles. Sometimes pays expenses of writers and/or photographers on assignment.
Photos: Send photos with submission. Reviews contact sheets and 35mm/120/4 $\times$ 5 transparencies. Offers no additional payment for photos accepted with ms except for use on cover. Captions, model releases and identification of subjects required. Buys first North American serial rights.
Tips: "If a freelancer has an idea for a good article it's best to send a query and include possible photo locations to illustrate the article. We prefer to assign articles and work with the author in developing a piece suitable to our audience. We are in a specialized field with very enthusiastic readers who appreciate articles

by authors who actually enjoy motorhomes. The following areas are most open: Travel—places to go with a motorhome, where to stay, what to see etc.; we prefer not to use travel articles where the motorhome is secondary; and How-to—personal projects on author's motorhomes to make travel easier, etc., unique projects, accessories. Also articles on unique personalities, motorhomes, humorous experiences."

NATIONAL GEOGRAPHIC TRAVELER, National Geographic Society, 17th and M Sts. NW, Washington DC 20036. (202)857-7721. Editorial Director: Richard Busch. 90% freelance written. A bimonthly travel magazine. "*Traveler* highlights mostly U.S. and Canadian subjects, but about 30% of its articles cover other foreign destinations—most often Europe, Mexico, and the Caribbean, occasionally the Pacific." Circ. 775,000. **Pays on acceptance.** Publishes ms an average of 12-15 months after acceptance. Byline given. Offers 50% kill fee. Reports in 2 months. Sample copy $4.50; writer's guidelines for #10 SASE.
Nonfiction: Travel. Buys 50 mss/year. Query with published clips. Length: 1,200-3,500 words. Pays $1/word. Pays expenses of writers on assignment.
Photos: Reviews transparencies and prints.

‡NEW ENGLAND TRAVEL, New England Publishing Group, Inc., 215 Newbury St., Peabody MA 01960. (617)535-4186. Publisher: Thomas J. Parello. 20% freelance written. Works with a small number of new/unpublished writers each year. A monthly magazine covering travel in New England. Estab. 1979. Circ. 40,000. Pays on publication. Publishes ms an average of 3 months after acceptance. Offers kill fee. Buys all rights or makes work-for-hire assignments. Submit seasonal/holiday material 4 months in advance. Query for electronic submissions. Reports in 1 month. Sample copy $5; writer's guidelines for SASE.
Nonfiction: "We are interested in articles that encourage people to see New England, especially those articles that focus on an event that is going on in a town during a specific time period. The writer covers such events, as well as some local points of interest in advance. We then publish the article in the appropriate issue so that readers know the details about the events and sites, and can plan to attend. No nostalgia or general pieces." Query. Length: 500-1,500 words. Pays $100-200 for assigned articles. Sometimes pays expenses of writers on assignment.
Photos: State availability of photos with submission. "Writer is expected to furnish photos once article is assigned." Reviews photos and slides. Offers no additional payment for photos accepted with ms. Captions and model releases required. Buys all rights.
Tips: "Be specific about the area or event you wish to cover. All articles must be information-based—readers want to know the times and places of sites and events, how much they cost, what the hours are, and where they can call for more information. Essentially we want specific articles about what to do and where to go in all of New England. Articles should also include information about mid-week and weekend packages offered by local hotels. Seasonal topics, such as New Year's celebrations or foliage, and New England topics, such as factory outlet shopping or antique shopping, are also acceptable. The best way to see what we want is to write for a sample copy."

NEWSDAY, NEW YORK NEWSDAY, 235 Pinelawn Rd., Melville NY 11747. (516)454-2980. Travel Editor: Marjorie K. Robins. Assistant Travel Editor: Barbara Shea. Travel Writer: Stephen Williams. 20% freelance written. For general readership of Sunday newspaper travel section. Estab. 1940. Circ. 700,000. Buys all rights for New York area only. Buys 45-60 mss/year. Pays on publication, $75-350, depending on space allotment. Fax submissions not encouraged. Prefer typewritten manuscripts. Simultaneous submissions considered if others are being made outside the New York area.
Nonfiction: No assignments to freelancers. No query letters. Only completed manuscripts accepted on spec. All trips must be paid for in full by writer. Proof required. Service stories preferred. Destination pieces must be for the current year. Length: 1,200 words maximum.
Photos: Color slides and black and white photos accepted: $50-250, depending on size of photo used.

NORTHEAST OUTDOORS, Northeast Outdoors, Inc., P.O. Box 2180, Waterbury CT 06722. (203)755-0158. FAX: (203)755-3480. Editor: Jean Wertz. 80% freelance written. Works with a small number of new/unpublished writers each year, and is eager to work with new/unpublished writers. A monthly tabloid covering family camping in the Northeastern U.S. Circ. 14,000. Pays on publication. Publishes ms an average of 8 months after acceptance. Byline given. Buys first rights, one-time rights, and regional rights. Submit seasonal/holiday material 5 months in advance. Query for electronic submissions. Reports in 1 month. Sample copy for 9 × 12 SAE with 6 first class stamps; writer's guidelines for #10 SASE.
Nonfiction: Book excerpts; general interest; historical/nostalgic; how-to (on camping); humor; new product (company and RV releases only); personal experience; photo feature; and travel. "No diaries of trips, dog stories, or anything not camping and RV related." Length: 300-1,500 words. Pays $40-80 for articles with b&w photos; pays $30-75 for articles without art.

Photos: Send photos with submission. Reviews contact sheets and 5 × 7 prints or larger. Captions and identification of subjects required. Buys one-time rights.

Columns/Departments: Mealtime (campground cooking), 300-900 words. Buys 12 mss/year. Query or send complete ms. Length: 750-1,000 words. Pays $25-50.

Fillers: Camping related anecdotes, facts, newsbreaks and short humor. Buys few fillers. Length: 25-200 words. Pays $5-15.

Tips: "We most often need material on private campgrounds and attractions in New England. We are looking for upbeat, first-person stories about where to camp, what to do or see, and how to enjoy camping."

‡ON YOUR WAY, Prestige Publications, Suite 800, 91 Fifth Ave., New York NY 10003. (212)929-5050. FAX: (212)633-1920. Associate Editor: Kate Krader. Managing Editor: Reg Bragonier. 50% freelance written. Annual magazine on travel. "*On Your Way* is for people traveling through any of the 48 contiguous states in the summer." Estab. 1983. Pays on publication. Publishes ms an average of 4-6 months after acceptance. Byline given. Offers 40% kill fee. Buys first North American serial rights. Submit seasonal/holiday material 6 months in advance. Sample copy $4.

Nonfiction: Travel. Buys 15 mss/year. Query with or without published clips, or send complete ms. Length: 1,000 words minimum. Pays $600 minimum for assigned articles. Sometimes pays expenses of writers on assignment.

Photos: State availability of photos with submission. Reviews contact sheets, negatives and transparencies. Model releases required. Buys one-time rights.

RV WEST MAGAZINE, Outdoor Publications, Inc., Suite 226, 2033 Clement Ave., Alameda CA 94501. (415)769-8338. FAX: (415)769-8330. Editor: Dave Preston. 85% freelance written. Works with a small number of new/unpublished writers each year. A monthly magazine for Western recreational vehicle owners. Circ. 30,000. Pays on publication. Publishes ms an average of 6 months after acceptance. Byline given. Buys one-time rights. Submit seasonal/holiday material 6 months in advance. Simultaneous and previously published submissions OK. Query for electronic submissions. Reports in several weeks on queries; several months on mss. Free writer's guidelines.

Nonfiction: Historical/nostalgic; how-to (fix your RV); new product; personal experience (particularly travel); technical; and travel (destinations for RVs). No non-RV travel articles. Buys 36 mss/year. Query with or without published clips. Length: 750-2,000 words. Pays $1.50/inch.

Photos: Send photos with submissions. Reviews contact sheets, negatives, transparencies and prints. Prefers b&w prints. Offers $5 minimum/photo. Identification of subjects required.

Tips: "RV travel/destination stories are most open to freelancers. Include all information of value to RVers, and reasons why they would want to visit the location (12 Western states)."

‡SPA VACATIONS Magazine, BW Inc., 18 Shepard St., Brighton MA 02135. (617)782-1225. Editor: Maria Durell Stone. 40% freelance written. Quarterly magazine covering spas, health, fitness, exercise, beauty. Estab. 1989. Pays on publication. Publishes ms an average of 2-3 months after acceptance. Byline given. Offers $150 kill fee. Buys first rights.

Nonfiction: Interview/profile (if about health/fitness), travel (if to do with fitness/spas, etc.) Buys 50 mss/year. Query with published clips. Length: 1,200-3,500 words. Pays $500 minimum. Depends on writer's experience.

TOURS & RESORTS, The World-Wide Vacation Magazine, World Publishing Co., 990 Grove St., Evanston IL 60201-4370. (312)491-6440. Editor/Associate Publisher: Bob Meyers. Managing Editor: Ray Gudas. 90% freelance written. A bimonthly magazine covering world-wide vacation travel features. Circ. 250,000. **Pays on acceptance.** Byline given. Buys first North American serial rights. Submit seasonal/holiday material 6 months in advance. Previously published submissions acceptable, dependent upon publication—local or regional OK. Reports in 3 weeks on queries; 6 weeks on mss. Sample copy $2.50 with 9 × 12 SASE.

Nonfiction: Primarily destination-oriented travel articles, "Anatomy of a Tour" features, and resort/hotel profiles and roundups, but will consider essays, how-to, humor, company profiles, nostalgia, etc.—if travel-related. "It is best to study current contents and query first." Buys 75 mss/year. Average length: 1,500 words. Pays $150-500.

Photos: Top-quality original color slides preferred. Captions required. Buys one-time rights. Prefers photo feature package (ms plus slides), but will purchase slides only to support a work in progress.

Columns/Departments: Travel Views (travel tips; service articles), and World Shopping (shopping guide). Buys 8-12 mss/year. Query or send complete ms. Length: 800-1,500 words. Pays $125-250.

Tips: "Travel features and the Travel Views department are most open to freelancers. Because we are heavily photo-oriented, superb slides are our foremost concern. The most successful approach is to send 2-3 sheets of slides with the query or complete ms. Include a list of other subjects you can provide as a photo feature package."

‡**TRAILER LIFE**, TL Enterprises, Inc., 29901 Agoura Rd., Agoura CA 91301. (213)991-4980. Editor: Bill Estes. Managing Editor: Merrill Pierson. Editorial Director: Barbara Leonard. 60% freelance written. A monthly magazine covering the RV lifestyle, and RV travel and products. "Readers of *Trailer Life* are owners of recreational vehicles who spend a median 37.8 days traveling on the road. Articles should have a distinctive focus on the needs, entertainment and issues of the RV traveler." Estab. 1941. Circ. 310,000. **Pays on acceptance.** Byline given. Offers 30% kill fee. Buys first North American serial rights. Submit seasonal/holiday material 6 months in advance. Free sample copy and writer's guidelines.

Nonfiction: General interest, historical/nostalgic, how-to, humor, interview/profile, new product, guest editorials, personal experience, photo essay, technical and travel, all with RV focus. Query with or without published clips, or send complete ms. Length: 1,000-2,000 words. Pays $50-500. Sometimes pays the expenses of writers on assignment, under special circumstances.

Photos: Reviews contact sheets, 35mm transparencies (or larger), and 8 × 10 b&w prints. Offers no additional payment for photos accepted with ms, but also buys photos independent of articles. Captions, model releases and identification of subjects required. Buys one-time rights.

Columns/Departments: People on the Move (short RV-related people items with black-and-white photos or 35mm transparencies, can include events, humorous news items), 200-500 words; and RV Bulletin (news items specific to the RV industry/consumer or public lands), 100 words. Send complete ms. Pays $75-150.

Tips: "First-hand experience with recreational vehicles and the RV lifestyle makes the writer's material more appealing. Although the writer need not own an RV, accurate information and a knowledge of the RV lifestyle will lend desired authenticity to article submissions. People on the Move, travel features, how-to articles are areas most open to freelancers. Vehicle evaluations of home-built or home-modified trailers, campers or motorhomes are open to freelancers."

TRANSITIONS ABROAD, 18 Hulst Rd., P.O. Box 344, Amherst MA 01004. (413)256-0373. Editor/Publisher: Prof. Clayton A. Hubbs. 80-90% freelance written. Eager to work with new/unpublished writers. The resource magazine for low-budget international travel with an educational or work component. Bound magazine. Estab. 1977. Circ. 13,000. Pays on publication. Buys first rights and second (reprint) rights to material originally published elsewhere. Byline given. Written queries only. Reports in 2 months. Sample copy $3.50; writer's guidelines and topics schedule for #10 SASE.

Nonfiction: How-to (find courses, inexpensive lodging and travel); interview (information on specific areas and people); personal experience (evaluation of courses, special interest and study tours, economy travel); and travel (what to see and do in specific areas of the world, new learning and travel ideas). Foreign travel only. Few destination ("tourist") pieces. Emphasis on information and on interaction with people in host country. Buys 30 unsolicited mss/issue. Query with credentials. Length: 500-2,000 words. Pays $25-150. Include author's bio with submissions.

Photos: Send photos with ms. Pays $10-25 for 8 × 10 b&w glossy prints, $125 for covers. No color. Additional payment for photos accompanying ms. Photos increase likelihood of acceptance. Buys one-time rights. Captions and ID on photos required.

Columns/Departments: Study/Travel Program Notes (evaluation of courses or programs); Traveler's Advisory/Resources (new information and ideas for offbeat independent travel); Jobnotes (how to find it and what to expect); and Book Reviews (reviews of single books or groups on one area). Buys 8/issue. Send complete ms. Length: 1,000 words maximum. Pays $20-50.

Fillers: Info Exchange (information, preferably first-hand—having to do with travel, particularly offbeat educational travel and work or study abroad). Buys 10/issue. Length: 1,000 words maximum. Pays $20-50.

Tips: "We like nuts and bolts stuff, practical information, especially on how to work, live and cut costs abroad. Our readers want usable information on planning their own travel itinerary. Be specific: names, addresses, current costs. We are particularly interested in educational travel and study abroad for adults and senior citizens. More and more readers want information not only on work but retirement possibilities. We have a new department on exchange programs, homestays, and study/tours for precollege students. *Educational Travel Directory and Travel Planner* published each year in July provides descriptive listings of resources and information sources on work, study, and independent travel abroad along with study/travel programs abroad for adults."

TRAVEL & LEISURE, American Express Publishing Corp., 1120 Avenue of the Americas, New York NY 10036. (212)382-5600. Editor-in-Chief: Ila Stanger. Executive Editor: Susan Crandell. Managing Editor: Maria Shaw. 80% freelance written. Monthly magazine. Circ. 1.2 million. **Pays on acceptance.** Byline given. Offers 25% kill fee. Buys first world and foreign edition rights. Reports in 3 weeks. Sample copy $5. Free writer's guidelines.

Nonfiction: Travel. Buys 200 mss/year. Query. Length open. Payment varies. Pays the expenses of writers on assignment.

Photos: Discourages submission of unsolicited transparencies. Payment varies. Captions required. Buys one-time rights.

Tips: "Read the magazine. Regionals and Taking Off section are best places to start."

TRAVEL SMART, Communications House, Inc., Dobbs Ferry NY 10522. (914)693-4208. Editor/Publisher: H.J. Teison. Managing Editor: Deborah Gaines. Covers information on "good-value travel." Monthly newsletter. Estab. 1976. Pays on publication. Buys all rights. Reports in 6 weeks. Sample copy and writer's guidelines for #10 SAE with 3 first class stamps.

Nonfiction: "Interested primarily in bargains or little-known deals on transportation, lodging, food, unusual destinations that won't break the bank. Also information on trends in industry. No destination stories on major Caribbean islands, London, New York, no travelogs, my vacation, poetry, fillers. No photos or illustrations. Just hard facts. We are not part of 'Rosy fingers of dawn . . .' school." Write for guidelines, then query. Length: 100-1,000 words. Pays "up to $50."

Tips: "When you travel, check out small hotels offering good prices, little known restaurants, and send us brief rundown (with prices, phone numbers, addresses). Information must be current. Include your phone number with submission, because we sometimes make immediate assignments."

TRAVELORE REPORT, Suite #100, 1512 Spruce St., Philadelphia PA 19102. (215)735-3838. Editor: Ted Barkus. For affluent travelers; businessmen, retirees, well-educated readers; interested in specific tips, tours, and bargain opportunities in travel. Monthly newsletter. Estab. 1974. Buys all rights. Pays on publication. Submit seasonal material 2 months in advance. Sample copy $2; writer's guidelines for #10 SASE.

Nonfiction: "Brief insights (25-200 words) with facts, prices, names of hotels and restaurants, etc., on offbeat subjects of interest to people going places. What to do, what not to do. Supply information. We will rewrite if acceptable. We're candid—we tell it like it is with no sugar coating. Avoid telling us about places in United States or abroad without specific recommendations (hotel name, costs, rip-offs, why, how long, etc.). No destination pieces which are general with no specific 'story angle' in mind, or generally available through PR departments." Buys 10-20 mss/year. Pays $5-20.

Tips: "Destinations confronted with political disturbances should be avoided. We'll put more emphasis on travel to North American destinations and Caribbean, and/or South Pacific, while safety exists. We're adding more topics geared to business-related travel and marketing trends in leisure-time industry."

VISTA/USA, P.O. Box 161, Convent Station NJ 07961. (201)538-7600. FAX: (201)538-9509. Editor: Kathleen M. Caccavale. Managing Editor: Martha J. Mendez. 90% freelance written. Will consider ms submissions from *unpublished* writers. Quarterly magazine of Exxon Travel Club. "Our publication uses articles on North American areas. We strive to help our readers gain an in-depth understanding of cities, towns and areas as well as other aspects of American culture that affect the character of the nation." Estab. 1965. Circ. 900,000. **Pays on acceptance.** Publishes ms an average of 1 year after acceptance. Buys first North American serial rights. Query about seasonal subjects 18 months in advance. Reports in 6 weeks. Sample copy for a 9 × 12 or larger SAE with 5 first class stamps; writer's and photographer's guidelines for #10 SASE.

Nonfiction: Geographically oriented articles on North America focused on the character of an area or place; photo essays (recent examples include city lights, Thoreau's Cape Cod, reflections); and some articles dealing with nature, Americana, crafts and collecting. Usually one activity-oriented article per issue. "We buy feature articles on the U.S., Canada, Mexico and the Caribbean that appeal to a national audience and prefer that destination queries have a hook or angle to them that give us a clear, solid argument for covering the average subject 'soon' rather than 'anytime.' " No feature articles that mention driving or follow routes on a map. Uses 7-15 mss/issue. Query with outline and clips of previously published work. Length: 1,200-2,000 words. Pays $450 minimum for features. Pays the expenses of writers on assignment.

Columns/Departments: "MiniTrips are point to point or loop driving tours of from 50 to 350 miles covering a healthy variety of stops along the way. 'Close Focus' covers openings or changing aspects of major attractions, small or limited attractions not appropriate for a feature article (800-1,000 words). 'American Vignettes' covers anything travel related that also reveals a slice of American life, often with a light or humorous touch, such as asking directions from a cranky New Englander, or the phenomenon of vanity plates. 'Information, Please' provides practical information on travel safety, and health trends, tips; a service column."

Photos: Contact: photo researcher. Send photos with ms. Pays $100 minimum for color transparencies. Captions preferred. Buys one-time rights.

Tips: "We are looking for readable pieces with good writing that will interest armchair travelers as much as readers who may want to visit the areas you write about. Queries about well-known destinations should have something new or different to say about them, a specific focus or angle. Articles should have definite themes and should give our readers an insight into the character and flavor of an area or topic. Stories about personal experiences must impart a sense of drama and excitement or have a strong human-interest angle. Stories about areas should communicate a strong sense of what it feels like to be there. Good use of anecdotes and quotes should be included. Study the articles in the magazine to understand how they are organized, how they present their subjects, the range of writing styles, and the specific types of subjects used. Afterwards, query and enclose samples of your best writing. We continue to seek department shorts and inventory articles of a general, nonseasonal nature (1,500 to 1,800 words)."

VOYAGER/SUN SCENE, K.L. Publications, Suite 105, 2001 Killebrew Dr., Bloomington MN 55425. Editor: Mary Lou Brooks. Quarterly magazine published for Gulf Motor Club/Sun Travel Club. 80% freelance written. Estab. 1989. Circ. 114,000. Pays on acceptance by client. Byline given. Considers mostly previously published articles. Submit seasonal/holiday material 6-8 months in advance. Reports in 1 month. Sample copy for 9 × 12 SAE with 3 first class stamps; writer's guidelines for #10 SASE.
Nonfiction: Travel (U.S. destinations by car and some foreign destinations), lifestyle, how-to (travel-related), historical/nostalgic. Length: 500-1,500 words. Pays $75-125.
Photos: Reviews 35mm transparencies. Color only. Pay varies.

‡WESTERN RV NEWS, Suite B, 1350 SW Upland Dr., Portland OR 97221. (503)222-1255. Editor: James E. Hathaway. Managing Editor: Elsie P. Hathaway. 20% freelance written. Magazine published 14 times/year for owners of recreational vehicles. Estab. 1966. Pays on publication. Publishes ms an average of 2-3 months after acceptance. Byline sometimes given. Publication not copyrighted. Buys first North American serial rights. Simultaneous and previously published submissions OK. Reports in 1 month on queries; 2 weeks on mss. Free sample copy and writer's guidelines.
Nonfiction: How-to (RV oriented, purchasing considerations, maintenance), humor (RV experiences), new product (with ancillary interest to RV lifestyle), personal experiences (varying or unique RV lifestyles), technical (RV systems or hardware), and travel. "No articles without an RV slant." Buys 40 mss/year. Submit complete ms. Length: 250-1,500 words. Pays $150 maximum for assigned articles; $15-150 for unsolicited articles.
Photos: Send photos with submission. Reviews 3 × 5 prints. Offers $5-15/photo. Captions, model releases, and identification of subjects required. Buys one-time rights.
Columns/Departments: Jim Schumock, features editor. Tips 'n Techniques (practical advice or specific information about processes or products), 100-250 words. Buys 25-30 mss/ year. Send complete ms. Pays $5-25.
Fillers: Jim Schumock, features editor. Anecdotes, gags to be illustrated by cartoonist, and short humor. Buys 10/year. Length: 50-150 words. Pays $5-25.
Tips: "Highlight the RV lifestyle! Thorough research and a pleasant, informative writing style are paramount. Read other RV publications. All areas are open. No folksy, generic writing. Technical, how-to, and new product writing is primarily what we're looking to publish."

YACHT VACATIONS MAGAZINE, P.O. Box 1657, Palm Harbor FL 34682-1657. (813)785-3101. FAX: (813)786-7969. Editor: Charity Cicardo. 50% freelance written. Prefers to work with published/established writers. "*Yacht Vacations* is a people-oriented yacht charter magazine with a positive approach." Estab. 1984. Circ. 30,000. Pays on publication. Publishes ms an average of 3 months after acceptance. Buys first North American serial rights. Submit seasonal/holiday material at least 5 months in advance. Simultaneous queries and submissions OK. Query for electronic submissions. Reports in 6 weeks. Writer's guidelines for #10 SASE.
Nonfiction: General interest (worldwide, charter boat-oriented travel); historical/nostalgic (charter vacation oriented); how-to (bareboating technique); interview/profile (charter brokers, charter skippers, positive); new product (beach fashion, hair care products, sun screens, etc.); opinion; personal experience (charter boat related, worldwide, positive people-oriented travel); photo feature (charter boat, worldwide, positive, people-oriented travel); travel (charter vacation-oriented); and ancillary topics such as fishing, scuba or underwater photography. Special issues will focus on the Caribbean, diving, and Mediterranean. Buys 30-40 mss/year. Query with published clips. Length: 600-1,500 words. Pays $100 per 600 words. Rarely pays expenses of writers on assignment.
Photos: "We would like to receive quality cover photos reflecting the charter yacht vacation experience, i.e., water, yacht, and people enjoying." State availability of photos or send photos with query or ms. Pays with article for b&w and color negatives, transparencies (35mm), and b&w and color prints (3 × 5 or larger), plus buys cover photos. Requires model releases and identification of subjects. Buys one-time rights.
Tips: "We are happy to look at the work of any established freelancer who may have something appropriate to offer within our scope—travel with a charter vacation orientation. We prefer submissions accompanied by good, professional quality photography. The best first step is a request for editorial guidelines, accompanied by a typed letter and work sample."

Women's

Women have an incredible variety of publications available to them these days—about 50 appear on newsstands in an array of specialties. A number of titles in this area have been redesigned during the past year to compete in the crowded marketplace. Many of the fashion magazines also are following the European trend of putting models in casual minimal settings, especially out-of-doors. Magazines that also use material slanted to women's interests can be found in the following categories: Business and Finance; Child Care and

Parental Guidance; Contemporary Culture; Food and Drink; Health and Fitness; Hobby and Craft; Home and Garden; Relationships; Religious; Romance and Confession; and Sports.

‡**BALANCE, The Lifestyle Magazine for Women Physicians,** Wiesner Publishing, 5951 S. Middlefield Rd., Littleton CO 80123. (303)798-1274. Editor: Jan Shepherd, M.D. Associate Editor: Michelle Gyure. 70% freelance written. Bimonthly magazine. *"Balance* exists to help women physicians balance their lives between their demanding careers, relationships, child rearing, and personal well-being. About half the magazine targets serious women's issues women physicians confront on the job, and half focuses on life outside of work." Estab. 1989. Circ. 50,000. Pays on publication. Publishes ms an average of 1-3 months after acceptance. Byline given. Offers 25% kill fee. Buys first North American serial rights or second serial (reprint) rights, "only when ms was published in a magazine our readers will not have seen." Submit seasonal/holiday material 3-4 months in advance. Simultaneous submissions OK. Query for electronic submissions. Reports in 6 weeks. Sample copy for $1 plus 10×13 SAE with 6 first class stamps; writer's guidelines for #10 SASE.

Nonfiction: Book excerpts, essays, general interest, historical/nostalgic, how-to, inspirational, interview/ profile, opinion, personal experience, photo feature, and travel. "No travelogs or any type of article that does not specifically address our audience. For our highly educated audience, we do not want how-to's by nonprofessionals unless they quote authoritative sources." Buys 56 mss/year. Query with published clips or send complete ms. Length: 1,200-3,500 words. Pays $200-300 for articles. Sometimes pays the expenses of writers on assignment.

Photos: State availability of photos with submission or send photos with submission. Reviews contact sheets, negatives, transparencies and prints. Offers $50-100/photo. Captions, model releases, and identification of subjects required, depending on the situation. Buys one-time rights.

Columns/Departments: In Your Own Time (leisurely pursuits), 1,600 words; Finding Time (focuses on time management issues and techniques to help our extremely busy readers organize their lives), 1,600 words; Personal Worth (a financial column that helps women physicians with their personal finances), 1,600 words; Perspective (an opinion column written by different women physicians), 800 words. Buys 15 mss/year. Query with published clips or send complete ms. Pays $125-200.

Fiction: Ethnic, humorous, mainstream, slice-of-life vignettes. "We will only consider fiction that specifically addresses our readership. None except aforementioned fiction accepted." Buys few mss/year. Send complete ms. Length: 2,000 words maximum. Pays $150-250.

Poetry: Avant-garde, free verse, haiku, light verse, traditional, "we will consider anything. Poetry must be appropriate for our readers. We only accept an occasional poem if it is excellent and appropriate." Submit maximum of 3 poems at one time. Line length: 40 maximum. Pays $25-50.

Tips: "Read our magazine. We look for carefully crafted query letters that not only highlight the interest area, but also demonstrate a knowledge of the subject. Be specific. List your sources and why they are ideal. All areas are open to freelancers. It is more difficult and more valuable to us to explore a trend piece (duo-physician marriages, single women physicians and parenting, women physicians in academia)."

‡**BOSTON WOMAN MAGAZINE,** BW Publishing, 18 Shepard St., Brighton MA 02135. (617)783-8000. Editor: Debra Winograd. Managing Editor: Cara Brown. 50% freelance written. Quarterly magazine of women's lifestyle, issues, interests, regional slant. Readers are ages 24-54, educated, professional women—supportive of women's issues but very mid-stream in approach. Estab. 1986. Circ. 50,000. Pays within 30 days of publication. Publishes ms an average of 6 months after acceptance. Byline given. Offers 10-20% kill fee. Buys first North American serial rights. Submit seasonal/holiday material 4-6 months in advance. Simultaneous submissions OK. Samply copy $3. Writer's guidelines for #10 SASE.

Nonfiction: Essays, exposé, how-to (financing, career, family, etc.), humor, inspirational, interview/profile (with regional slant or tie), new product, opinion (does not mean letters to the editor), personal experience, comic illustrations with female oriented humor. No fiction or poetry. Buys 32 mss/year. Query with or without published clips, or send complete ms. Length: 2,500-3,500 words. Pays $200-500. Sometimes pays expenses of writers on assignment.

Photos: Send photos with submission. Reviews transparencies and 5×7 or 8½×11 prints. Offers no additional payment for photos accepted with ms. Model releases and identificaiton of subjects required. Buys one-time rights.

Columns/Departments: Buys 30 mss/year. Query with pubilshed clips or send complete ms. Length: 1,000-1,500 words. Pays $75-200.

Fillers: Anecdotes, facts, gags to be illustrated by cartoonist, newsbreaks, short humor. Length: 300-400 words. Pays $15-25.

Tips: "We are happy to look at things on spec; write queries that are original, fresh and with some indication of interest for *Boston Woman* readers (vs. other regionals or national women's publications). Writers have the best chance selling us articles for the Body & Soul, Woman About Town, Equal Time and Business Working Woman columns."

BRIDAL GUIDE, The How-To For I Do, Globe Communications Corp., 441 Lexington Ave., New York NY 10017. (212)949-4040. FAX: (212)286-0072. Editor: Deborah Harding. 80% freelance written. Prefers to work with experienced/published writers. A bimonthly magazine covering wedding planning, fashion, beauty, contemporary relationship articles, honeymoon travel and planning for the first home. Sample copy for 9×12 SAE and $2.40 postage (1st class), or $1.50 postage (3rd class); writer's guidelines for #10 SASE.

Nonfiction: The editors prefer queries rather than actual manuscript submissions. All correspondence accompanied by a SASE will be answered (response is usually within 1 month). Length: 800-1,600 words. Pays $200-600 on acceptance. Buys 120 mss/year. Offers 20% kill fee. Buys first North American serial rights. Sample copy for $4.50.

Photos: Jean L. Oberholtzer, design director. Cartoons and photography submissions should be handled through the Art Department.

Columns/Departments: Regular departments include Finance, Sex, Remarriage, and Advice for the Groom.

BRIDAL TRENDS, Meridian Publishing, Inc., Box 10010, Ogden UT 84409. (801)394-9446. 65% freelance written. Monthly magazine with useful articles for today's bride. Circ. 60,000. **Pays on acceptance.** Publishes ms an average of 10 months after acceptance. Byline given. Buys first rights, second serial (reprint) rights and non-exclusive reprint rights. Simultaneous and previously published submissions OK. Reports in 6 weeks. Sample copy for $1 and 9×12 SAE; writer's guidelines for #10 SASE. All requests for sample copies and guidelines should be addressed Attn: Editor.

Nonfiction: "General interest articles about traditional and modern approaches to weddings. Topics include all aspects of ceremony and reception planning; flowers; invitations; catering; wedding apparel and fashion trends for the bride, groom, and other members of the wedding party, etc. Also featured are honeymoon destinations, how to build a relationship and keep romance alive, and adjusting to married life." Buys approximately 15 mss/year. Query. Length: 1,200 words. Pays 15¢/word for first rights plus non-exclusive reprint rights. Payment for second rights is negotiable.

Photos: State availability of photos with query letter. Color transparencies and 5×7 or 8×10 prints are preferred. Pays $35 for inside photo. Captions, model release, and identification of subjects required.

Tips: "We publish articles that detail each aspect of wedding planning: invitations, choosing your flowers, deciding on the style of your wedding, and choosing a photographer and caterer."

BRIDE'S, Conde Nast Bldg., 350 Madison Ave., New York NY 10017. (212)880-8800. Editor-in-Chief: Barbara D. Tober. 40% freelance written. Eager to work with new/unpublished writers. A bimonthly magazine for the first- or second-time bride, her family and friends, the groom and his family and friends. Circ. 479,335. **Pays on acceptance.** Publishes ms an average of 2 months after acceptance. Buys all rights. Also buys first and second serial rights for book excerpts on marriage, communication, finances. Offers 20% kill fee, depending on circumstances. Buys 40 unsolicited mss/year. Byline given. Reports in 2 months. Address mss to Features Department. Writer's guidelines for #10 SASE.

Nonfiction: "We want warm, personal articles, optimistic in tone, with help offered in a clear, specific way. All issues should be handled within the context of marriage. How-to features on all aspects of marriage: communications, in-laws, careers, money, sex, housing, housework, family planning, marriage after having a baby, religion, interfaith marriage, step-parenting, second marriage, reaffirmation of vows; informational articles on the realities of marriage, the changing roles of men and women, the kind of troubles in engagement that are likely to become big issues in marriage; stories from couples or marriage authorities that illustrate marital problems and solutions to men and women; book excerpts on marriage, communication, finances, sex; and how-to features on wedding planning that offer expert advice. Also success stories of marriages of long duration. We use first-person pieces and articles that are well researched, relying on quotes from authorities in the field, and anecdotes and dialogues from real couples. We publish first-person essays on provocative topics unique to marriage." Query or submit complete ms. Article outline preferred. Length: 1,000-3,000 words. Pays $300-800.

Columns/Departments: The Love column accepts reader love poems, for $25 each. The Something New section accepts reader wedding planning and craft ideas; pays $25.

Tips: "Since marriage rates are up and large, traditional weddings are back in style, and since more women work than ever before, do *not* query us on just living together or becoming a stay-at-home wife after marriage. Send us a query or a well-written article that is both easy to read and offers real help for the bride or groom as she/he adjusts to her/his new role. No first-person narratives on wedding and reception planning, home furnishings, cooking, fashion, beauty, travel. We're interested in unusual ideas, experiences, and lifestyles. No 'I used baby pink rose buds' articles."

CHATELAINE, 777 Bay St., Toronto, Ontario M5W 1A7 Canada. Editor-in-Chief: Mildred Istona. 75% freelance written. Prefers to work with published/established writers. Monthly general-interest magazine for Canadian women, from age 20 and up. "*Chatelaine* is read by one woman in three across Canada, a readership that spans almost every age group but is concentrated among those 25 to 45 including homemakers and working women in all walks of life." Circ. over 1 million. **Pays on acceptance.** Publishes ms an average of 3 months after acceptance. Byline given. Reports within 2 weeks. All mss must be accompanied by a SASE (IRCs in lieu of stamps if sent from outside Canada). Sample copy $2 and postage; free writer's guidelines.

Nonfiction: Elizabeth Parr, senior editor, articles. Submit an outline or query first. Full-length major pieces run from 1,500 to 2,500 words. Pays minimum $1,250 for acceptable major article. Buys first North American serial rights in English and French (the latter to cover possible use in *Chatelaine*'s sister French-language edition, edited in Montreal for French Canada). "We look for important national Canadian subjects, examining any and all facets of Canadian life, especially as they concern or interest women. Upfront columns include stories about relationships, health, nutrition, fitness and parents and kids. Submit outline first. Pays $350 for about 500 words. Prefers queries for nonfiction subjects on initial contact plus a resume and writing samples. Also seeks full-length personal experience stories with deep emotional impact. Pays $750. Pays expenses of writers on assignment.

Tips: Features on beauty, food, fashion and home decorating are supplied by staff writers and editors, and unsolicited material is not considered.

‡COMPLETE WOMAN, For All The Women You Are, Associated Publications, Inc., 1165 N. Clark, Chicago IL 60610. (312)266-8680. Editor: Bonnie L. Krueger. Managing Editor: Susan Handy. 90% freelance written. Bimonthly magazine of general interest for women. Areas of concern are love life, health, fitness, emotions, etc. Estab. 1980. Circ. 150,000. Pays on publication. Publishes ms an average of 5 months after acceptance. Byline given. Buys first North American serial rights, second serial (reprint) rights, simultaneous rights. Submit seasonal/holiday material 5 months in advance. Simultaneous submissions OK. Reports in 1 month. Writer's guidelines with SASE.

Nonfiction: Book excerpts, general interest, how-to, humor, inspirational, interview/profile, new product, personal experience, photo feature. No recipes or how to build a closet or sewing! Buys 60-100 mss/year. Query with or without published clips, or send complete ms. Length: 800-2,000 words. Pays $80-400. Sometimes pays expenses of writers on assignment.

Photos: Send photos with submission. Reviews 2¼ or 35mm transparencies and 5×7 prints. Offers $35-75 per photo. Captions, model releases and identification of subjects required. Buys one-time rights.

Poetry: Avant-garde, free verse, light verse, traditional. Nothing over 30 lines. Buys 50 poems/year. Submit maximum 5 poems. Pays $10.

COSMOPOLITAN, The Hearst Corp., 224 W. 57th St., New York NY 10019. Exec. Editor: Roberta Ashley. 90% freelance written. Monthly magazine about 18- to 35-year-old single, married, divorced—all working. **Pays on acceptance.** Byline given. Offers 10% kill fee. Buys all magazine rights and occasionally negotiates first North American rights. Submit seasonal/holiday material 6 months in advance. Previously published submissions in minor publications OK. Reports in 1 week on queries; 3 weeks on mss. Sample copy $2.50. Writer's guidelines for #10 SASE.

Nonfiction: Book excerpts, how-to, humor, opinion, personal experience and anything of interest to young women. Buys 350 mss/year. Query with published clips or send complete ms. Length: 500-3,500 words. Pays expenses of writers on assignment.

Fiction: Betty Kelly. Condensed novels, humorous, novel excerpts, romance and original short stories with romantic plots. Buys 18 mss/year. Query. Length: 750-3,000 words.

Poetry: Free verse and light verse. Buys 30 poems/year. No maximum number. Length: 4-30 lines.

Fillers: Irene Copeland. Facts. Buys 240/year. Length: 300-1,000 words.

COUNTRY WOMAN, Reiman Publications, P.O. Box 643, Milwaukee WI 53201. (414)423-0100. Managing Editor: Kathy Pohl. 75-85% freelance written. Willing to work with new/unpublished writers. Bimonthly magazine on the interests of country women. "*Country Woman* is for contemporary rural women of all ages and backgrounds and from all over the U.S. and Canada. It includes a sampling of the diversity that makes up rural women's lives—love of home, family, farm, ranch, community, hobbies, enduring values, humor, attaining new skills and appreciating present, past and future all within the content of the lifestyle that surrounds country living." Estab. 1970. Circ. 700,000. **Pays on acceptance.** Publishes ms an average of 1 year after acceptance. Byline given. Buys first North American serial rights, one-time rights, and second serial (reprint) rights; makes some work-for-hire assignments. Submit seasonal/holiday material 4-5 months in advance. Previously published (on occasion) submissions OK. Reports in 1 month on queries; 2 months on mss. Sample copy for $2.50; writer's guidelines for #10 SASE.

Nonfiction: General interest, historical/nostalgic, how-to (crafts, community projects, family relations, self-improvement, decorative, antiquing, etc.); humor; inspirational; interview/profile; personal experience; photo/feature packages profiling interesting country women; all pertaining to a rural woman's interest. Articles must be written in a positive, light and entertaining manner. Buys 100 mss/year. Query or send complete ms. Length: 1,000 words maximum.

Photos: Send color photos with query or ms. Reviews 35mm or 2¼ transparencies. Uses only excellent quality color photos. No b&w. "We pay for photo/feature packages." Captions, model releases and identification of subjects required. Buys one-time rights.

Columns/Departments: Why Farm Wives Age Fast (humor), I Remember When (nostalgia), Country Decorating, and Shopping Comparison (new product comparisons). Buys 20 mss (maximum)/year. Query or send complete ms. Length: 500-1,000 words. Pays $75-125.

Fiction: Main character *must* be a country woman. All fiction must have a country setting. Fiction must have a positive, upbeat message. Includes fiction in every issue. Would buy more fiction if stories suitable for our audience were sent our way. Query or send complete ms. Length: 750-1,000 words. Pays $90-125.

Poetry: Traditional and light verse. "Poetry must have rhythm and rhyme! It must be country-related. Always looking for seasonal poetry." Buys 40 poems/year. Submit maximum 6 poems. Length: 5-24 lines. Pays $10-40.

Fillers: Jokes, anecdotes, short humor and consumer news (e.g. safety, tips, etc.). Buys 40/year. Length: 40-250 words. Pays $25-40.

Tips: "We have recently broadened our focus to include 'country' women, not just women on farms and ranches. This allows freelancers a wider scope in material. Write as clearly and with as much zest and enthusiasm as possible. We love good quotes, supporting materials (names, places, etc.) and strong leads and closings. Readers relate strongly to where they live and the lifestyle they've chosen. They want to be informed and entertained, and that's just exactly why they subscribe. Readers are busy—not too busy to read—but when they do sit down, they want good writing, reliable information and something that feels like a reward. How-to, humor, personal experience and nostalgia are areas most open to freelancers. Profiles, to a certain degree, are also open. We are always especially receptive to short items—250 words, 400 words and so on. Be accurate and fresh in approach."

‡ENTREPRENURIAL WOMAN, Entrepreneur Inc., 2392 Morse Ave., Irvine CA 92714. (714)261-2325. Editor: Rieva Lesonsky. Managing Editors: Maria Anton and Maria Johnson. 50% freelance written. Monthly magazine for women business owners. Estab. 1989. Circ. 200,000. **Pays on acceptance.** Publishes ms an average of 5-6 months after acceptance. Byline given. Pays 20% kill fee. Buys first rights or all rights. Submit seasonal/holiday material 6-7 months in advance. Reports in 2 months. Sample copy $3. Writer's guidelines for #10 SASE.

Nonfiction: How-to, interview/profile, or any information to assist women running a business. Buys 75 mss/year. Query with published clips. Length: 500-2,000 words. Pays $250-700. Sometimes pays expenses of writers on assignment.

Photos: State availability of photos with submission or send photos with submission. Reviews transparencies. Payment and rights vary. Identification of subjects required.

Columns/Departments: Who's Hot (short profiles of women entrepreneurs), 500 words; Management Smarts and Building Blocks (how-to advice for running a business), 1,300-1,400 words; Healthy Outlook (specific health-related topics), 1,300 words. Buys 50 mss/year. Query with published clips. Pays $250-400.

Tips: "Submit well-written queries clearly detailing what you'd like to cover in an article. Do not query without reading our guidelines and a sample copy first. The first step to getting an assignment is understanding who the entrepreneurial woman is. We are seeking excellent profile writers and writers who can take deep, psychological issues and see more than one side of the story."

ESSENCE, 1500 Broadway, New York NY 10036. Editor-in-Chief: Susan L. Taylor. Editor: Stephanie Stokes Oliver. Executive Editor: Cheryll Y. Greene. Monthly magazine. Circ. 850,000. **Pays on acceptance.** Makes assignments on work-for-hire basis. 3 month lead time. Pays 25% kill fee. Byline given. Submit seasonal/holiday material 6 months in advance. Reports in 2 months. Sample copy $1.50; free writer's guidelines.

Features: Valerie Wilson Wesley, senior editor. "We're looking for articles that inspire and inform Black women. The topics we include in each issue are provocative. Every article should move the *Essence* woman emotionally and intellectually. We welcome queries from good writers on a wide range of topics; general interest, health and fitness, historical, how-to, humor, self-help, relationships, work, personality interview, personal experience, political issues, business and finances and personal opinion." Buys 200 mss/year. Query only; word length will be given upon assignment. Pays $500 minimum.

Photos: Marlowe Goodson, art director. State availability of photos with query. Pays $100 for b&w page; $300 for color page. Captions and model release required. "We particularly would like to see photographs for our travel section that feature Black travelers."

Columns/Departments: Query department editors: Contemporary Living (home, food, lifestyle, travel, consumer information): Harriette Cole; Arts: Benilde Little; Health & Working: Linda Villarosa; Money: Andrea R. Davis. Query only; word length will be given upon assignment. Pays $100 minimum.

Tips: "Please note that *Essence* no longer accepts unsolicited mss for fiction, poetry or nonfiction, except for the Brothers and Back Talk Interiors columns. So please only send query letters for nonfiction story ideas."

FAIRFIELD COUNTY WOMAN, FCW, Inc., 15 Bank St., Stamford CT 06901. (203)323-3105. Editor: Joan Honig. 90% freelance written. A women's regional monthly tabloid focusing on careers, education, health, relationships and family life. Estab. 1982. Circ. 40,000. Pays 60 days after publications. Byline given. Buys first rights. Submit seasonal/holiday material 3 months in advance. Simultaneous and previously published submissions OK. Query for electronic submissions. Sample copy for 10×13 SAE with $1.25 postage.

Nonfiction: Book excerpts, essays, general interest, how-to, humor, inspirational and local interview/profile. Buys 125 mss/year. Query with published clips. Length: 800-2,000 words. Pays $35-100 for assigned articles; $25-75 for unsolicited articles. Sometimes pays expenses of writers on assignment.

Photos: State availability of photos with submission. Reviews 5 × 7 prints. Offers no additional payment with ms. Buys one-time rights.

Columns/Departments: Health, auto, finance and home. Length: 1,200 words. Buys 50 mss/year. Query with published clips. Pays $25-50.

FAMILY CIRCLE MAGAZINE, 110 Fifth Ave., New York NY 10011. (212)463-1000. Editor-in-Chief: Jacqueline Leo. 70% freelance written. For women. Published 17 times/year. Usually buys all print rights. Offers 20% kill fee. Byline given. **Pays on acceptance.** "We are a national women's magazine which offers advice, fresh information and entertainment to women. Query should stress the unique aspects of an article and expert sources; we want articles that will help our readers." Reports in 1 month.

Nonfiction: Susan Ungaro, executive editor. Women's interest subjects such as family and personal relationships, children, physical and mental health, nutrition, self-improvement and profiles of ordinary women doing extraordinary things for her community or the nation. "We look for well-written, well-reported stories told in terms of people. We want well-researched service journalism on all subjects." Query. Length: 1,000-2,500 words. Pays $1/word.

Tips: Query letters should be "concise and to the point." Also, writers should "keep close tabs on *Family Circle* and other women's magazines to avoid submitting recently run subject matter."

GLAMOUR, Conde Nast, 350 Madison Ave., New York NY 10017. (212)880-8800. Editor-in-Chief: Ruth Whitney. 75% freelance written. Works with a small number of new/unpublished writers each year. For college-educated women, 18-35 years old. Monthly. Estab. 1939. Circ. 2.3 million. **Pays on acceptance.** Offers 20% kill fee. Publishes ms an average of 6-12 months after acceptance. Byline given. Reports in 2 months. Writer's guidelines for #10 SASE.

Nonfiction: Lisa Bain, articles editor. "Editorial approach is 'how-to' with articles that are relevant in the areas of careers, health, psychology, interpersonal relationships, etc. We look for queries that are fresh and include a contemporary, timely angle. Fashion, beauty, decorating, travel, food and entertainment are all staff-written. We use 1,000-word opinion essays for our Viewpoint section. Pays $500. Our His/Hers column features generally stylish essays on relationships or comments on current mores by male and female writers in alternate months." Pays $1,000 for His/Hers mss. Buys first North American serial rights. Buys 10-12 mss/issue. Query "with letter that is detailed, well-focused, well-organized, and documented with surveys, statistics and research, personal essays excepted." Short articles and essays (1,500-2,000 words) pay $1,000 and up; longer mss (2,500-3,000 words) pay $1,500 minimum on acceptance. Sometimes pays the expenses of writers on assignment.

Tips: "We're looking for sharply focused ideas by strong writers and constantly raising our standards. We are interested in getting new writers, and we are approachable, mainly because our range of topics is so broad. We've increased our focus on male-female relationships."

GOOD HOUSEKEEPING, Hearst Corp., 959 8th Ave., New York NY 10019. (212)649-2000. Editor-in-Chief: John Mack Carter. Executive Editor: Mina Mulvey. Managing Editor: Mary Fiore. Prefers to work with published/established writers. Monthly. Circ. 5 million. **Pays on acceptance.** Buys all rights. Pays 25% kill fee. Byline given. Submit seasonal/holiday material 6 months in advance. Reports in 6 weeks. Sample copy $2. Free writer's guidelines with SASE.

Nonfiction: Joan Thursh, articles editor. Medical; informational; investigative stories; inspirational; interview; nostalgia; personal experience; and profile. Buys 4-6 mss/issue. Query. Length: 1,500-2,500 words. Pays $1,500 on acceptance for full articles from new writers. Regional Editor: Shirley Howard. Pays $250-350 for local interest and travel pieces of 2,000 words. Pays the expenses of writers on assignment.

Photos: Herbert Bleiweiss, art director. Photos purchased on assignment mostly. Some short photo features with captions. Pays $100-350 for b&w; $200-400 for color photos. Query. Model releases required.

Columns/Departments: Light Housekeeping & Fillers, edited by Rosemary Leonard. Humorous short-short prose and verse. Jokes, gags, anecdotes. Pays $25-50. The Better Way, edited by Erika Mark. Ideas and in-depth research. Query. Pays $250-500. "Mostly staff written; only outstanding ideas have a chance here."

Fiction: Lee Quarfoot, fiction editor. Uses romance fiction and condensations of novels that can appear in one issue. Looks for reader identification. "We get 1,500 unsolicited mss/month—includes poetry; a freelancer's odds are overwhelming—but we do look at all submissions." Send complete mss. Manuscripts will not be returned. Only responds on acceptance. Length: 1,500 words (short-shorts); novel according to merit of material; average 5,000-word short stories. Pays $1,000 minimum for fiction short-shorts; $1,250 for short stories.

Poetry: Arleen Quarfoot, poetry editor. Light verse and traditional. "Presently overstocked." Poems used as fillers. Pays $5/line for poetry on acceptance.

Tips: "Always send an SASE. We prefer to see a query first. Do not send material on subjects already covered in-house by the Good Housekeeping Institute—these include food, beauty, needlework and crafts."

THE JOYFUL WOMAN, For and About Bible-believing Women Who Want God's Best, The Joyful Woman Ministries, Inc., Business Office: P.O. Box 90028, Chattanooga TN 37412. (615)698-7318. Editor: Elizabeth Handford, 118 Shannon Lake Circle, Greenville SC 29615. 50% freelance written. Works with small number of new/unpublished writers each year. Bimonthly magazine covering the role of women in home and business. *"The Joyful Woman* hopes to encourage, stimulate, teach, and develop the Christian woman to reach the full potential of her womanhood." Estab. 1978. Circ. 12,000. Pays on publication. Publishes ms an average of 4 months after acceptance. Byline given. Buys first rights. Submit seasonal/holiday material 4 months in advance. Reports in 3 months. Sample copy for 9×12 SAE with 4 first class stamps; writer's guidelines for #10 SASE.

Nonfiction: Book excerpts, how-to (housekeeping, childrearing, career management, etc.); inspirational; interview/profile (of Christian women); and personal experience. "We publish material on every facet of the human experience, considering not just a woman's spiritual needs, but her emotional, physical, and intellectual needs and her ministry to others." Buys 80-100 mss/year. Send complete ms. Length: 700-2,500 words. Pays about 2¢/word.

Tips: "The philosophy of the woman's liberation movement tends to minimize the unique and important ministries God has in mind for a woman. We believe that being a woman and a Christian ought to be joyful and fulfilling personally and valuable to God, whatever her situation—career woman, wife, mother, daughter."

LADIES' HOME JOURNAL, Meredith Corporation, 100 Park Ave., New York NY 10017. (212)953-7070. Publishing Director and Editor-in-Chief: Myrna Blyth. Executive Editor: Lynn Langway. 50% freelance written. A monthly magazine focusing on issues of concern to women. *"LHJ* reflects the lives of the contemporary mainstream woman and provides the information she needs and wants to live in today's world." Circ. 5.1 million. **Pays on acceptance.** Publishes ms an average of 3 months after acceptance, but varies according to needs. Byline given. Offers 25% kill fee. Rights bought vary with submission. Submit seasonal/holiday material 6 months in advance. Reports in 6 weeks. Query for sample copy rates. Free writer's guidelines.

Nonfiction: Lynn Langway, executive editor, oversees the entire department and may be queried directly. In addition, submissions may be directed to Janne Farrell, articles editor, and on the following subjects to the editors listed for each: Relationships (senior editor Margery Rosen); medical/health (Nelly Edmondson Gupta); investigative reports or new related features (senior editor Jane Farrell); and celebrities (executive editor Lynn Langway). Travel pieces for Prime Shopper may be sent to Assistant Managing Editor Nina Keilin. Query with published clips. Length: 1,500-3,500 words. Fees vary; average is between $1,000 and $3,500. Pays expenses of writers on assignment.

Photos: State availability of photos with submission. Offers variable payment for photos accepted with ms. Captions, model releases and identification of subjects required. Rights bought vary with submissions.

Columns/Departments: Query the following editors for column ideas. A Woman Today (Pam Guthrie O'Brien, associate editor); Parent News (Mary Mohler, managing editor); and Pet News (Nina Keilin).

Fiction: Sofia Marchant, books and fiction editor. "We consider any short story or novel that is submitted by an agent or publisher that we feel will work for our audience." Buys 12 mss/year. Length: 4,000 words. Fees vary with submission.

LEAR'S, Lear's Publishing, 655 Madison Ave., New York NY 10021. (212)888-0007. Editor: Myra Appleton. Executive Editor: Audreen Ballard. Articles Editor: Nelson W. Aldrich, Jr. Bimonthly magazine for women. Circ. 375,000. **Pays on acceptance.** Byline given. Offers ⅓ kill fee. Buys first North American serial rights and second serial reprint rights. Reports in 6 weeks. Free writer's guidelines.

Nonfiction: Book excerpts, essays, general interest, interview/profile, opinion, personal experience, travel. Query with published clips. Length: 800-1,200 words. Pays $1 per word. Sometimes pays expenses of writers on assignment.

Columns/Departments: Self-Center, Money & Worth, Features, and Pleasures. Query with published clips. Length: 800-1,000 words. Pays $1 per word.

LUTHERAN WOMAN TODAY, Women of the ELCA/Augsburg Publishing House, 8765 West Higgings Rd., Chicago IL 60631. (380)312-2743. Editor: Nancy Stelling. Associate Editor: Sue Edison-Swift. 25% freelance written. Monthly magazine designed for all women of the Evangelical Lutheran Church in American. Estab. 1988. Circ. 300,000. Pays on acceptance or 2 months post due date. Byline given. Buys first rights and one-time rights. Submit seasonal/holiday material 7 months in advance. Reports in 3 months. Sample copy for 6×9 SAE and $1; writer's guidelines for #10 SASE.

Nonfiction: Book excerpts, historical/nostalgic, humor, inspirational, interview/profile, opinion, personal experience, photo feature religious. Buys 24 mss/year. Send complete ms. Length: 350-1,400 words. Pays $50-250.

Photos: State availability of photos or send photos with submission. Reviews contact sheet and prints. Pays variable rate. Captions and identification of subjects required. Buys one-time rights.

Columns/Departments: Devotion, Seasons' Best (essay featuring church year theme); About Women (featuring 3 women of faith); Forum (essay/editorial). Send complete ms. Length: 350-1,000 words. Pays $50-250.

Fiction: Historical humorous, religious, thought-provoking stories. "All with a women's and Christian focus." Buys 5 mss/year. Send complete ms. Length: 350-1,400 words. Pays $50-250.

McCALL'S, 230 Park Ave., New York NY 10169. (212)551-9500. Editor: Anne Smith. Executive Editor: Lisel Eisenheimer. 90% freelance written. "Study recent issues." Our publication "carefully and conscientiously services the needs of the woman reader—concentrating on matters that directly affect her life and offering information and understanding on subjects of personal importance to her." Monthly. Circ. 5 million. **Pays on acceptance.** Publishes ms an average of 6 months after acceptance. Offers 20% kill fee. Byline given. Buys first or exclusive North American rights. Reports in 2 months. Writer's guidelines for SASE.

Nonfiction: Helen Del Monte, managing editor. No subject of wide public or personal interest is out of bounds for *McCall's* so long as it is appropriately treated. The editors are seeking meaningful stories of personal experience, fresh slants for self-help and relationship pieces, and well-researched articles and narratives dealing with social problems concerning readers. *McCall's* buys 200-300 articles/year, many in the 1,000- to 1,500-word length. Pays variable rates for nonfiction. Helen Del Monte and Andrea Thompson are editors of nonfiction books, from which *McCall's* frequently publishes excerpts. These are on subjects of interest to women: personal narratives, celebrity biographies and autobiographies, etc. Almost all features on food, household equipment and management, fashion, beauty, building and decorating are staff-written. Query. "All manuscripts must be submitted on speculation, and *McCall's* accepts no responsibility for unsolicited manuscripts." Sometimes pays the expenses of writers on assignment.

Columns/Departments: Child Care (edited by Maureen Smith Williams); short items that may be humorous, helpful, inspiring and reassuring. Pays $100 and up. Vital Signs (edited by Saralie Falvelson-Neustadt); short items on health and medical news. Pay varies.

Fiction: Jane Ciabattari, department editor. Not considering unsolicited fiction. "Again the editors would remind writers of the contemporary woman's taste and intelligence. Most of all, fiction can awaken a reader's sense of identity, deepen her understanding of herself and others, refresh her with a laugh at herself, etc. *McCall's* looks for stories which will have meaning for an adult reader of some literary sensitivity. *No* stories that are grim, depressing, fragmentary or concerned with themes of abnormality or violence. *McCall's* principal interest is in short stories; but fiction of all lengths is considered." Length: about 3,000 words average. Length for short-shorts: about 2,000 words. Payment begins at $1,500; $2,000 for full-length stories.

Poetry: Jane Ciabattari, poetry editor. Poets with a "very original way of looking at their subjects" are most likely to get her attention. *McCall's* needs poems on love, the family, relationships with friends and relatives, familiar aspects of domestic and suburban life, Americana, and the seasons. Pays $5/line on acceptance for first North American serial rights. Length: no longer than 30 lines.

Tips: "Except for humor, query first. We are interested in holiday-related pieces and personal narratives. We rarely use essays. We don't encourage an idea unless we think we can use it." Preferred length: 750-2,000 words. Address submissions to articles editor unless otherwise specified.

MADEMOISELLE, 350 Madison Ave., New York NY 10017. Articles Editor: Liz Logan. 95% freelance written. Prefers to work with published/established writers. Columns are written by columnists; "sometimes we give new writers a 'chance' on shorter, less complex assignments." Directed to college-educated, unmarried working women 18-34. Circ. 1.1 million. Reports in 1 month. Buys first North American serial rights. Pays on acceptance; rates vary. Publishes ms an average of 1 year after acceptance.

Nonfiction: Particular concentration on articles of interest to the intelligent young woman, including personal relationships, health, careers, trends, and current social problems. Send health queries to Ellen Tien, health editor. Send entertainment queries to Christian Wright, entertainment editor. Query with published clips. Length: 1,500-3,000 words.

Art: Kay Spear, art director. Commissioned work assigned according to needs. Photos of fashion, beauty, travel. Payment ranges from no-charge to an agreed rate of payment per shot, job series or page rate. Buys all rights. Pays on publication for photos.

Fiction: Eileen Schnurr, fiction and books editor. Quality fiction by both established and unknown writers. "We are interested in encouraging and publishing new writers and welcome unsolicited fiction manuscripts. However we are not a market for formula stories, genre fiction, unforgettable character portraits, surprise endings or oblique stream of consciousness sketches. We are looking for well-told stories that speak in fresh and individual voices and help us to understand ourselves and the world we live in. Stories of particular relevance to young women have an especially good chance, but stories need not be by or from the point of view of a woman—we are interested in good fiction on any theme from any point of view." Buys first North American serial rights. Pays $1,500 for short stories (10-25 pages); $1,000 for short shorts (7-10 pages). Allow 3 months for reply. SASE required. In addition to year-round unqualified acceptance of unsolicited fiction manuscripts, *Mademoiselle* conducts a once-a-year fiction contest open to unpublished writers, male and

female, 18-30 years old. First prize is $1,000 plus publication in *Mademoiselle*; second prize, $500 with option to publish. Watch magazine for announcement, usually in January or February issues, or send SASE for rules, after Jan 1.
Tips: "We are looking for timely, well-researched manuscripts."

MODERN BRIDE, 475 Park Ave., South, New York NY 10016. (212)779-1999. Editor: Cele Lalli. Managing Editor: Mary Ann Cavlin. **Pays on acceptance.** Offers 25% kill fee. Buys first periodical rights. Previously published submissions OK. Reports in 1 month.
Nonfiction: Book excerpts, general interest, how-to, personal experience. Buys 70 mss/year. Query with published clips. Length: 500-2,000 words. Pays $600-1,200.
Columns/Departments: Geri Bain, editor. Travel.
Poetry: Free verse, light verse and traditional. Buys very few. Submit maximum 6 poems.

MS. MAGAZINE, Lang Communications, Inc., 1 Times Square, 9th Fl., New York NY 10036. (212)719-9800. Editor: Robin Morgan. Managing Editor: Helen Via. Executive Editor: Mary Thom. 75% freelance written. Monthly magazine on women's issues and news. Circ. 550,000. Pays on publication. Byline given. Offers 20% kill fee. Buys all rights. Submit seasonal/holiday material 6 months in advance. Query for electronic submissions. Reports in 6 weeks. Sample copy $2.25. Writer's guidelines for #10 SASE.
Nonfiction: Book excerpts, essays, exposé, general interest, historical/nostalgic, how-to, humor, interview/profile, opinion, personal experience, photo feature, travel, women's news and sports. "Has special issue on women's health. No fiction, poetry." Buys 150 mss/year. Query with published clips. Length: 300-4,000 words. Pays $150-6,000 for assigned articles; $150-1,000 for unsolicited articles. Pays expenses of writers on assignment.
Photos: State availability of photos with submission. Offers $75-300 per photo. Model releases and identification of subjects required. Buys one-time rights.
Columns/Departments: Our Bodies (women's health), 300-1,000 words; Ms. Adventure (travel), 600-1,000 words; Arts & Books (reviews), 300-750 words; and Technology, 600-750 words. Buys 100 mss/year. Query with published clips. Length: 500-1,000 words. Pays $250-1,000.

NEW WOMAN MAGAZINE, Murdoch Magazines, 215 Lexington Ave., New York NY 10016. (212)685-4790. Editor-in-Chief: Gay Bryant. Managing Editor: Karen Walden. 80% freelance written. Prefers to work with published/established writers, and works with a small number of new/unpublished writers each year. A monthly general interest women's magazine for ages 25-45. "We're especially interested in self-help in relationships and work (career); we also cover food, fashion, beauty, travel, money." Estab. 1970. Circ. 1.4 million. **Pays on acceptance.** Publishes ms an average of 6 months after acceptance. Byline given. Offers 20% kill fee. Buys first North American, British and Australian serial rights. Submit seasonal/holiday material 8 months in advance. Simultaneous and previously published submissions OK. Reports in 2 months. Writer's guidelines for #10 SASE.
Nonfiction: Articles or essays on relationships, psychology, personal experience, travel, health, career advice and money. Does one special section on Money, Careers and/or Health every year. No book or movie reviews, advice columns, fashion, food or beauty material. Buys 75-100 mss/year. Query with published clips or send complete ms. Length: 2,000 words. Pays $500-2,000. Pays the telephone expenses of writers on assignment.
Photos: State availability of photos with submission. Offers no additional payment for photos accepted with ms. Captions, model releases and identification of subjects required. Buys one-time rights.
Fillers: Katherine Lineberger, Briefing section editor. Facts, newsbreaks and newspaper clips (for Briefing section). Buys 3/year. Length: 200-500 words. Pays $10-200.
Tips: "The best approach for breaking in to our publication is a personal letter, with clippings of published work, telling us what you're interested in, what you really like to write about, and your perceptions of *New Woman*. It counts a lot when a writer loves the magazine and responds to it on a personal level. Psychology and relationships articles are most open to freelancers. Best tip: *familiarity with the magazine*. We look for originality, solid research, depth, and a friendly, accessible style."

RADIANCE, The Magazine for Large Women, Box 31703, Oakland CA 94604. (415)482-0680. Editor: Alice Ansfield. 75% freelance written. "A quarterly magazine that encourages and supports women all sizes of large to live fully now, to stop putting their lives on hold until they lose weight." Estab. 1981. Circ. 30,000. Pays on publication. Publishes ms an average of 3 months after acceptance. Byline given. Offers $15 kill fee. Buys one-time and second serial (reprint) rights. Submit seasonal/holiday material 6 months in advance. Simultaneous and previously published submissions OK. Query for electronic submissions. Reports in 1½ months. Sample copy $2.50; writer's guidelines for #10 SASE.
Nonfiction: Book excerpts (related to large women), essays, expose, general interest, historical/nostalgic, how-to (on health/well-being/growth/awareness/fashion/movement, etc.), humor, inspirational, interview/profile, new product, opinion, personal experience, photo feature and travel. Future issues will focus on children and weight, interviews with large men, fashion update, emerging spirituality, women and the arts, and women in the media. "No diet successes or articles condemning people for being fat." Query with

published clips. Length: 1,000-2,000 words. Pays $35-100. Sometimes pays writers with contributor copies or other premiums—"negotiable with writer and us."

Photos: State availability of photos with submission. Offers $15-50 per photo. Captions and identification of subjects preferred. Buys one-time rights.

Columns/Departments: Up Front and Personal (personal profiles of women in all areas of life); Health and Well-Being (physical/emotional well-being, self care, research); Images (designer interviews, color/style/fashion, features); Inner Journeys (spirituality awareness and growth, methods, interviews); Perspectives (cultural and political aspects of being in a larger body). Buys 60 mss/year. Query with published clips. Length: 1,000-2,000 words. Pays $50-100.

Fiction: Condensed novels, ethnic, fantasy, historical, humorous, mainstream, novel excerpts, romance, science fiction, serialized novels and slice-of-life vignettes relating somehow to large women. Buys 15 mss/year. Query with published clips. Length: 800-1,500 words. Pays $35-100.

Poetry: Nothing "too political or jargony." Buys 30 poems/year. Length: 4-45 lines. Pays $20-50.

Tips: "We need talented, sensitive and openminded writers. We profile women from all walks of life who are all sizes of large, of all ages and from all ethnic groups and lifestyles. We welcome writers' ideas on successful and interesting large women from their local areas. We're an open, light-hearted magazine that's working to help women feel good about themselves now, whatever their body size. *Radiance* is one of the major forces working for size acceptance. We want articles to address all areas of vital importance in their lives."

REDBOOK MAGAZINE, 224 W. 57th St., New York NY 10019. (212)649-3450. Editor-in-Chief: Annette Capone. Managing Editor: Jennifer Johnson. Executive Editor: Karen Larson. 80% freelance written. Monthly magazine. Estab. 1903. Circ. 3.9 million. **Pays on acceptance.** Publishes ms an average of 1-2 years after acceptance. Rights purchased vary with author and material. Reports in 3 months. Writer's guidelines for SASE.

Nonfiction: Diane Salvatore, senior editor. Jean Maguire, health editor. "*Redbook* addresses young mothers between the ages of 25 and 44. Most of our readers are married with children under 18; more than half work outside the home. The articles entertain, guide and inspire our readers. A significant percentage of the pieces stress 'how-to,' the ways a woman can solve the problems in her everyday life. Writers are advised to read at least the last *six* issues of the magazine (available in most libraries) to get a better understanding of what we're looking for. We prefer to see queries, not complete manuscripts. Please enclose a sample or two of your writing. Length: articles, 2,500-3,000 words; short articles, 1,000-1,500 words. "We are interested in stories for the Young Mother series offering the dramatic retelling of an experience involving you, your husband or child. Possible topics: how you have handled a child's health or school problem, or conflicts within the family. For each 1,500-2,000 words accepted for publication as Young Mother's Story, we pay $750. Mss accompanied by a 9 × 12 SASE, must be signed, and mailed to: Young Mother's Story, c/o *Redbook Magazine*. Young Mother's reports in 6 months." Pays the expenses of writers on assignment.

Fiction: Dawn Raffel, fiction editor. "Of the 40,000 unsolicited manuscripts that we receive annually, we buy about 36 or more stories/year. We also find many more stories that are not necessarily suited to our needs but are good enough to warrant our encouraging the author to send others. *Redbook* looks for stories by and about men and women, realistic and offbeat stories, humorous or poignant stories, stories about families, couples, or people alone, stories with familiar and exotic settings, love stories and work stories, medical and mystery stories. The elements common to all are high quality of prose and distinctiveness of characters and plots. We also look for stories with emotional resonance. Cool stylistic or intellectually experimental stories are of greater interest, we feel, to readers of literary magazines; all of our stories reflect some aspect of experience, interests, or dreams of our readership. We do not read unsolicited novels." Payment begins at $850 for short shorts; $1,200 for short stories.

Tips: "Shorter, front-of-the-book features are usually easier to develop with first-time contributors. It is very difficult to break into the nonfiction section, although we do buy Young Mother's stories, dramatic personal experience pieces (1,500-2,000 words), from previously unpublished writers. The most frequent mistakes made by writers in completing an article for us are 1) Poor organization. We advise authors to do full outlines before they start writing so they can more easily spot structure problems. 2) Poor or insufficient research. Most *Redbook* articles require solid research and include full, well-developed anecdotes from real people and clear, substantial quotes from established experts in a field; and, when available, additional research such as statistics and other information from reputable studies, surveys, etc."

‡SAVVY WOMAN, Family Media, 3 Park Ave., 37th Floor, New York NY 10016. (212)340-9200. Editor-in-Chief: Martha Nelson. Managing Editor: Curtis Feldman. 90% freelance written. Published 10 times/year. "*Savvy* articles are written for successful women. We try to use as many women as possible for our sources. The age group of our readers falls primarily between 25 and 45 and we address both their home and office lives." Circ. 450,000. Pays 4-6 weeks after due date. Publishes ms an average of 2-5 months after acceptance. Byline given. Offers 15-20% kill fee. Buys first North American serial rights, and reprint rights. Submit seasonal/holiday material 4 months in advance. Free writer's guidelines with SASE.

Nonfiction: Book excerpts, humor, interview/profile, opinion, personal experience and travel. No limit on mss bought/year. Query with published clips. Length: 800-3,000 words ("depends on its position"). Pays $500 minimum. Pays the expenses of writers on assignment.

Columns/Departments: Savvy Money (how to manage, invest and save money), 900-1,000 words; Health (any topics pertaining to health: illnesses, cures, new findings, etc.), 1,000-1,200 words; and Savvy Manager (how to handle career situations, gain ground at work, change jobs, etc.), 900-1,200 words. Query with published clips. Pays $500 minimum. Travel, 1,000-1,200 words; Dining In/Dining Out, 1,000-1,200 words.

Tips: "The best advice is to read the magazine before querying. We have expanded our Savvy Money and Savvy Manager sections to include several shorter pieces."

SELF, Conde Nast, 350 Madison Ave., New York NY 10017. (212)880-8834. FAX: (212)880-8110. Editor-in-Chief: Alexandra Penney. Managing Editor: Linda Rath. 50% freelance written. "We prefer to work with writers—even relatively new ones—with a degree, training or practical experience in specialized areas from psychology to health to nutrition." Monthly magazine emphasizing self improvement of emotional and physical well-being for women of all ages. Estab. 1909. Circ. 1 million. Average issue includes 12-20 feature articles and 4-6 columns. **Pays on acceptance.** Publishes ms an average of 6 months after acceptance. Byline given. Offers 25% kill fee. Buys first North American serial rights. Submit seasonal material 4 months in advance. Simultaneous submissions OK. Reports in 1 month. Writer's guidelines for SASE.

Nonfiction: Well-researched service articles on self improvement, mind, the psychological angle of daily activities, health, careers, nutrition, fitness, fashion and beauty, medicine, male/female relationships and money. "We try to translate major developments and complex information in these areas into practical, personalized articles." Buys 6-10 mss/issue. Query with clips of previously published work. Length: 1,000-2,500 words. Pays $1,000-2,000. "We are always looking for any piece that has a psychological or behavioral side. We rely heavily on freelancers who can take an article on contraceptive research, for example, and add a psychological aspect to it. Everything should relate to the whole person." Pays the expenses of writers on assignment "with prior approval."

Photos: Submit to art director. State availability of photos. Reviews 5×7 b&w glossy prints.

Columns/Departments: Work (800-1,200 words on career topics); and Money (800-1,200 words on finance topics); others, such as Entertaining, Man's View. Buys 4-6 mss/issue. Query. Pays $800-2,000.

Tips: "Original ideas backed up by research open our doors. We almost never risk blowing a major piece on an untried-by-us writer, especially since these ideas are usually staff-conceived. It's usually better for everyone to start small, where there's more time and leeway for re-writes. The most frequent mistakes made by writers in completing an article for us are swiss-cheese research (holes all over it which the writer missed and has to go back and fill in) and/or not personalizing the information by applying it to the reader, but just reporting it."

‡SOUTHERN WOMAN TO WOMAN, BD Publishing, Inc., P.O. Box 306, Mt. Pleasant SC 29465. (803)884-0156. FAX: (803)849-6717. Publisher: Kimberly Young. 70% freelance written. Biweekly magazine "focused on the women of the South along with issues that affect all women." Estab. 1989. Circ. 20,000. Pays on publication. Byline given. Buys one-time rights.

Nonfiction: Interview/profile (with nationally known women), women's issues; general interest articles with a Southern regional slant. Buys 20 mss/year. Query. Length: 1,200 words maximum. Pays $75-150 for assigned articles. Sometimes pays expenses of writers on assignment.

Photos: Send photos with submission. Offers $10 maximum per photo. Captions and identification of subjects required. Buys one-time rights.

Tips: "We are open to good ideas. Our audience is well defined and appreciates well written informative articles that they can relate to."

TODAY'S CHRISTIAN WOMAN, 465 Gundersen Dr., Carol Stream IL 60188. (708)260-6200. FAX: (708)260-0114. Managing Editor: Julie A. Talerico. 25% freelance written. Works with a small number of new/unpublished writers each year. A bimonthly magazine for Christian women of all ages, single and married, homemakers and career women. Estab. 1979. Circ. 190,000. **Pays on acceptance.** Publishes ms an average of 1 year after acceptance. Byline given. Buys first rights only. Submit seasonal/holiday material 9 months in advance. Sample copy $3.50; writer's guidelines for #10 SASE.

Nonfiction: How-to, narrative and inspirational. Query only; no unsolicited mss. "The query should include article summary, purpose and reader value, author's qualifications, suggested length and date to send, availability of photos if applicable." Pays 10-15¢/word.

Tips: "Nature of the articles are: relational, psychological or spiritual. All articles should be highly anecdotal, personal in tone, and universal in appeal."

WOMAN'S DAY, 1633 Broadway, New York NY 10019. (212)767-6000. Articles Editor: Rebecca Greer. 75% or more of articles freelance written. 15 issues/year. Circ. 6 million. Pays negotiable kill fee. Byline given. **Pays on acceptance.** Reports in 1 month on queries; longer on mss. Submit detailed queries.

Nonfiction: Uses articles on all subjects of interest to women—marriage, family life, childrearing, education, homemaking, money management, careers, family health, work and leisure activities. Also interested in fresh, dramatic narratives of women's lives and concerns. "These must be lively and fascinating to read." Length: 500-3,500 words, depending on material. Payment varies depending on length, type, writer, and whether it's for regional or national use, but rates are high. Pays the expenses of writers on confirmed assignment."

Fiction: Eileen Jordan, department editor. Not considering unsolicited fiction.

Fillers: Neighbors and Tips to Share columns also pay $75/each for brief practical suggestions on homemaking, childrearing and relationships. Address to the editor of the appropriate section.

Tips: "Our primary need is for ideas with broad appeal that can be featured on the cover. We're buying more short pieces. Writers should consider Quick section which uses factual pieces of 100-500 words."

WOMAN'S WORLD, The Woman's Weekly, Heinrich Bauer North American, Inc., 270 Sylvan Ave., Englewod Cliffs NJ 07632. Editor-in-Chief: Dena Vane. 95% freelance written. Weekly magazine covering "controversial, dramatic, and human interest women's issues" for women across the nation. **Pays on acceptance.** Publishes ms an average of 4 months after acceptance. Byline given. Offers kill fee. Buys first North American serial rights. Submit seasonal/holiday material 4 months in advance. Simultaneous queries, simultaneous, and previously published submissions OK. Reports in 6 weeks on queries; 2 months on mss. Sample copy $1 and self-addressed mailing label; writer's guidelines for #10 SASE.

Nonfiction: Well-researched material with "a hard-news edge and topics of national scope." Reports of 1,000 words on vital trends and major issues such as women and alcohol or teen suicide; dramatic, personal women's stories; articles on self-improvement, medicine and health topics; and the economics of home, career and daily life. Features include In Real Life (true stories); Turning Point (in a woman's life); Families (highlighting strength of family or how unusual families deal with problems); True Love (tender, beautiful, touching and unusual love stories). Other regular features are Report (1,500-word investigative news features with national scope, statistics, etc.); Scales of Justice (true stories of 1,000-1,200 words on women and crime "if possible, presented with sympathetic" attitude); Between You and Me (600-word humorous and/or poignant slice-of-life essays); and Relationships (800 words on pop psychology or coping). Queries should be addressed to Gerry Hunt, senior editor. We use no fillers, but all the Between You and Me pieces are chosen from mail. Sometimes pays the expenses of writers on assignment.

Fiction: Jeanne Muchnick, fiction editor. Short story, romance and mainstream of 3,600 words and minimysteries of 1,200-2,000 words. "Each of our stories has a light romantic theme with a protagonist no older than forty. Each can be written from either a masculine or feminine point of view. Women characters may be single, married or divorced. Plots must be fast moving with vivid dialogue and action. The problems and dilemmas inherent in them should be contemporary and realistic, handled with warmth and feeling. The stories must have a positive resolution." Not interested in science fiction, fantasy, historical romance or foreign locales. No explicit sex, graphic language or seamy settings. Humor meets with enthusiasm. Specify "short story" on envelope. Always enclose SASE. Reports in 2 months. No phone queries. Pays $1,000 on acceptance for North American serial rights for 6 months. "The mini-mysteries, at a length of 1,600 words, may feature either a 'whodunnit' or 'howdunnit' theme. The mystery may revolve around anything from a theft to a murder. However, we are not interested in sordid or grotesque crimes. Emphasis should be on intricacies of plot rather than gratuitous violence. The story must include a resolution that clearly states the villain is getting his or her come-uppance." Pays $500 on acceptance. Pays approximately 50¢ a published word on acceptance. Buys first North American serial rights. Queries with clips of published work are preferred; accepts complete mss. Specify "mini mystery" on envelope. Enclose SASE. Stories slanted for a particular holiday should be sent at least 6 months in advance. No phone queries.

Photos: State availability of photos. "State photo leads. Photos are assigned to freelance photographers." Buys one-time rights.

Tips: "Come up with good queries. Short queries are best. We have a strong emphasis on well-researched material. Writers must send research with manuscript including book references and phone numbers for double checking. The most frequent mistakes made by writers in completing an article for us are sloppy, incomplete research, not writing to the format, and not studying the magazine carefully enough beforehand."

WOMEN'S CIRCLE, Box 299, Lynnfield MA 01940-0299. Editor: Marjorie Pearl. 100% freelance written. Bimonthly magazine for women of all ages. Buys all rights. **Pays on acceptance.** Byline given. Publishes ms an average of 6 months to 1 year after acceptance. Submit seasonal material 8 months in advance. Reports in 3 months. Sample copy $2. Writer's guidelines for #10 SASE.

Nonfiction: Especially interested in stories about successful, home-based female entrepreneurs with b&w photos or transparencies. Length: 1,000-2,000 words. Also interesting and unusual money-making ideas. Welcomes good quality crafts and how-to directions in any media—crochet, fabric, etc.

‡WOMEN'S HOUSEHOLD, House of White Burches, 306 E. Parr Rd., Berne IN 46711. (219)589-8741. Editor: Allison Ballard. 95% freelance written. Monthly magazine for "pen palling. We publish family oriented articles related to middle-aged and older women trying to juggle busy lives, and pen pal oriented articles." Estab. 1963. Circ. 35,000. Pays on publication. Publishes ms an average of 6-8 months after acceptance. Byline given. Pays 100% kill fee. Buys all rights, "other rights sometimes negotiated," and makes work-for-hire assignments. Submit seasonal/holiday material 8-9 months in advance. Simultaneous submissions OK. Query for electronic submissions. Reports in 6 weeks. Sample copy for $1.50 and 9×12 SAE with 4 first class stamps; free writer's guidelines.

Nonfiction: Essays (short essays on home and family), general interest (regarding home and family), historical/nostalgic (women in history), new product, personal experience, and photo features (especially pen pal events). "No articles dealing with controversial issues." Buys 8 mss/year. Send complete ms. Length: 500-2,000 words. Pays $30-200.

Photos: Send photos with submission. Reviews contact sheets and any size prints. "Does not usually offer additional payment for photos accepted with ms, but negotiable." Captions and identification of subjects required. Buys negotiable rights.

Columns/Departments: Reflections (nostalgic pieces of personal experience), 800-1,000 words; Face to Face (pen pal reunion articles), 500-800 words. Buys 24 mss/year. Send complete ms. Pays $30-50.

Fiction: Adventure, condensed novel, experimental, historical, humorous, mainstream, mystery, novel excerpt, slice-of-life vignettes, and suspense. "No erotic, true confession, heavy romance, or heavy religious." Buys 12 mss/year. Send complete ms. Length: 1,000-2,000 words. Pays $100-200.

Poetry: Free verse, light verse, and traditional. "No long, rambling poems." Buys 50 poems/year. Submit maximum of 5 poems at one time. Line length: 5-20 lines. Pays $5-15.

Fillers: Cartoons. Buys 10-12/year. Pays $10-20.

Tips: "Find out what's going on in the pen pal world and report on it. Freelancers have the best chance with fiction, cover stories, nostalgia, and general features. Make it light, entertaining and appropriate for family-oriented women trying to juggle busy lives."

WORKING MOTHER MAGAZINE, WWT Partnership, 230 Park Ave., New York NY 10169. (212)551-9412. Editor: Judsen Culbreth. Executive Editor: Mary McLaughlin. 90% freelance written. Prefers to work with published/established writers; works with a small number of new/unpublished writers each year. For women who balance a career with the concerns of parenting. Monthly magazine. Circ. 700,000. **Pays on acceptance.** Publishes ms an average of 4 months after acceptance. Byline given. Buys first North American Serial Rights and all rights. Pays 20% kill fee. Submit seasonal/holiday material 6 months in advance. Reports in 6 weeks. Sample copy $1.95; writer's guidelines for SASE.

Nonfiction: Service, humor, child development, material pertinent to the working mother's predicament. "Don't just go out and find some mother who holds a job and describe how she runs her home, manages her children and feels fulfilled. Find a working mother whose story is inherently dramatic." Query. Buys 9-10 mss/issue. Length: 750-2,000 words. Pays $300-1,800. "We pay more to people who write for us regularly." Pays the expenses of writers on assignment.

Tips: "We are looking for pieces that help the reader. In other words, we don't simply report on a trend without discussing how it specifically affects our readers' lives and how they can handle the effects. Where can they look for help if necessary?"

WORKING WOMAN, Working Woman, Inc., 342 Madison Ave., New York NY 10173. (212)309-9800. Editor: Kate White. Executive Editor: Lee Lusardi. Managing Editor: Lisa Higgins. 85% freelance written. Works with a small number of new/unpublished writers each year. Monthly magazine for executive, professional and entrepreneurial women. "Readers are ambitious, educated, affluent managers, executives, and business owners. Median age is 34. Material should be sophisticated, witty, not entry-level, and focus on work-related issues." Circ. 1 million. **Pays on acceptance.** Publishes ms an average of 8 months after acceptance. Byline given. Offers 20% kill fee after attempt at rewrite to make ms acceptable. Buys all rights, first rights for books, and second serial (reprint) rights. Submit seasonal/holiday material 6 months in advance. Sample copy for $2.95 and 8½×12 SAE; writer's guidelines for #10 SASE.

Nonfiction: Lisa Higgins, managing editor, or Jacqueline Johnson, book excerpts editor. Book excerpts; how-to (management skills, small business); humor; interview/profile (high level executive or entrepreneur preferred); new product (office products, computer/high tech); opinion (issues of interest to managerial, professional, entrepreneur women); personal experience; technical (in management or small business field); and other (business). No child-related pieces that don't involve work issues; no entry-level topics; no fiction/poetry. Buys roughly 200 mss/year. Query with clips. Length: 250-3,000 words. Pays $400 and up for most articles. Pays the expenses of writers on assignment.

Photos: State availability of photos with ms.

Columns: Management/Enterprise, Basia Hellwig; Manager's Shoptalk, Laurel Touby; Lifestyle, Food, Lynn Cusack; Fitness, Health, Janette Scandura; Business Trends, Pamela Kruger; Computers, Technology, Anne Russell. Query with clips of published work. Length: 1,200-1,500 words.

Tips: "Be sure to include clips with queries and to make the queries detailed (including writer's expertise in the area, if any). The writer has a better chance of breaking in at our publication with short articles and fillers as we prefer to start new writers out small unless they're very experienced elsewhere. Columns are more open than features. We do not accept phone submissions."

First Bylines

by Glenda Tennant Neff

A writer's first byline may not be the hardest one to obtain, but it frequently is the most memorable. Whether the writer relies on writing as his sole source of income or just writes in his spare time, the first publication of his work instills confidence and frequently leads to more bylines. Some writers, struggling for years on their craft, say their first published work gave them the boost they needed to continue writing.

Following are the "first byline" stories of three writers. One is a fulltime writer and two write part-time. One was published after winning a contest, the others by submitting a query or complete manuscript. They share the background on their first bylines, let you know how they've followed up on that first publication, and offer advice to writers working toward first bylines of their own. Their feelings about writing are summed up by writer Christy Cohen, who says, "No matter how hard it's been, I have never regretted my decision."

Stella Barnes
"First Night Alone" *Boys' Life*

Stella Barnes' first sale was the kind of story she'd consider unbelievable if she read it about somebody else.

Barnes, of Kelowna, British Columbia, began writing about four years ago and began submitting her work about two years ago. "I submitted to a variety of contests at first, mainly to get feedback from any comments the judges made," she says. "First Night Alone" was one of the first stories she wrote, "though it went through a number of metamorphoses" before she entered it in the *Boys' Life* contest for members of the Society of Children's Book Writers.

When the editor phoned to tell her she'd won the $2,000 prize, it was a complete surprise. "In fact, until a contract arrived in the mail, I kept wondering if there'd been a mistake," she says.

There was no mistake. Fiction Editor William Butterworth IV says her story was selected from among 60 entries because "it reflected well on our magazine's content. A suspenseful, action-packed story, it featured a young boy facing great odds—then overcoming them." *Boys' Life* published the story in its March 1990 issue.

Barnes previously taught college part-time and wrote in her spare time. She quit teaching, however, and now spends about 15 to 20 hours per week writing, mostly short stories for the 8-12-year-old age group. She also is revising a novel and has started work on a second one. With three other local writers, she collaborated on a proposal for an anthology of stories for young people. One of the stories from the collection has become the basis for the novel she's currently writing.

Barnes advises writers to research markets before they submit manuscripts. "When you're struggling to find time to write, as many new writers are, it's easy to feel you don't have time for that kind of research," she says. "But it really is important, particularly, I think, when you're writing stories for juveniles. Markets are not that plentiful and are fairly specific in their requirements. Don't overlook conferences that offer writers a chance to meet editors personally, hear them discuss what they're looking for, and ask them questions.

"Secondly, although a writer will usually have a strong personal commitment to whatever he chooses to write, he must also be aware, if he hopes to sell, of what editors and particularly readers want to read."

Richard O. Mann
"A Beginner's Guide to the Secret World of Floppy Disks" *PC Today*

Richard Mann is a certified public accountant who had a life-long ambition to be published. Although he wrote and published science fiction fanzines in high school and college, he didn't write much afterward. Then he was told one Thanksgiving that his brother was quitting his job to be a freelance writer and computer consultant. "It awoke my long-dormant desire to write," he says.

Mann, of Roy, Utah, felt he was "not cut out to write fiction" but found his interest in personal computers was marketable. "As a voracious reader of the personal computer press, I did have expertise in a marketable area," he says. "I just hadn't realized it." Mann began submitting queries on personal computing subjects.

In one day he received two assignments from editors—one for *Management Accounting* and another for *PC Today*. His software review for *Management Accounting* was an unpaid piece, but the *PC Today* cover story netted him $1,250. The printed copies of his first two articles arrived on the same day—within an hour of each other.

Since those twin first publications, Mann has become a contributing editor to *PC Today* and its sister publication *PC Novice*. He's also a software columnist for *Windows Shopper's Guide* and *PC Power Windows Magazine* and has sold more than 30 articles to a variety of computer magazines. Altogether it makes for a busy schedule for Mann, who has sometimes written six articles a month while also working as an internal audit supervisor for The Church of Jesus Christ of Latter-day Saints.

Mann advises nonfiction writers to "find an area where you know something more than the average person. Develop an expertise, even if it comes from just reading thoroughly. Make it a subject for which you have a passion.

"I don't consider myself to have anything but a very rough writing skill right now, but I know that I have the necessary underlying talent. Technique can be learned; I'm working hard to learn it.

"And be aware of what I've discovered: Writing is excruciatingly hard work, much harder than I'd imagined. I'm just relieved to find that it's also as exhilaratingly fun as I'd imagined."

Christy Cohen
"A Test of Love" *Woman's World*

Christy Cohen wrote as a teenager but later gave up her dream to be a novelist while earning her bachelor's degree in psychology. "After graduating college and being miserable at a 9-to-5 job for a few months, however, my husband encouraged me to give my dream of freelance writing a chance," Cohen says. "It was very hard for a while to deal with not making a steady or big salary and to see people's critical and skeptical faces when I told them I worked at home as a writer, but my husband is very supportive and we made a deal that if I could sell anything the first year, I could stick with it."

Cohen, of Palmdale, California, wrote the premise for "A Test of Love" after noticing "how married couples often fall into dull, predictable patterns and lose the passion and romance of their first dates." She thought about the story and the characters for it, then wrote and rewrote it in about three days. She sold it to *Woman's World* on its second submission and was paid $1,000 for it.

Jeanne Muchnick, travel and fiction editor, says she chose the story because "it was truly different. Because our stories are so formatted, I'm always looking for a fresh approach — a male perspective or a more independent woman character.

"Another element I like in her stories, which not all [stories] have, is the element of realism. Her heroes are not always knights in shining armor with chiseled cheeks and strong jawbones. The women aren't perfect either. It's a tough call — especially because our stories are so 'happily-ever-after-like' — but Christy does a super job."

Since that first sale, Cohen has sold three more stories to *Woman's World*, one to *Modern Short Stories* and nonfiction articles to *Modern Bride*, *New Home* and *Bride's* magazine. She writes from 9 a.m. to 3 or 4 p.m. daily and is currently working on a romantic suspense novel and is marketing two mainstream novels.

"With a background in psychology, my passion is people, how they work and think and why they do the strange things they do," she says. "It follows that my favorite type of writing is character-oriented fiction, particularly book-length fiction where the length allows me to delve deeply into a person's emotions and experiences. I am much more comfortable writing about the characters and situation in my imagination than I am interviewing someone for an article, but I do enjoy writing essays and humorous articles."

Other Consumer Publications

The following consumer publications do not have listings in this edition of *Writer's Market*. The majority did not respond to our request to update their listings or return a questionnaire for a new listing. If a reason was given for their exclusion, we have included it in parentheses after the listing name.

A.N.A.L.O.G. Computing
AAA World
Aboard
Aero Art
African Expedition Gazette
Air Destinations
All of Nature
The American Art Journal
American Farriers Journal
American Indian Art Magazine
America's Civil War
Anglofile
Animal Kingdom
Animal World (all writing done in-house)
Animals
The Annals of Saint Anne de Beaupre
Antic Magazine
Apple IIGS Buyer's Guide
Ararat
Arizona Business Gazette
Arizona Living Magazine
Arizona Trend
Arkansas Business
Armed Forces Journal International
Association Executive
Astro Signs (asked to be deleted)
Atari Explorer
Atlantic City Magazine
Baby Talk Magazine
Back to Health Magazine
Badger Sportsman
The Bark Eater
Bassmaster Magazine
Bay & Delta Yachtsman
Beauty Digest
Believers by the Bay
Better Business
Billboard
BMX Plus Magazine
Boat Pennsylvania
Bomb
Bon Appetit (all writing done in-house)
Book Forum
Braniff Magazine (out of business)
Bread
Breaker's Guide
Business Age
Business Month
California Angler
California Baseball Magazine (no longer published)
Calyx (pays in contributor's copies)
The Camper Times
Canadian Dimension
Cape Cod Life

Carrozzeria
Catholic Near East Magazine
Century City Magazine
Champion
Chess Life
Chic Magazine
Chicago's History
Child (asked to be deleted)
Child & Family
Chocolatier
Christian Social Action
The Church Herald
City Guide
City Sports Magazine
C.L.A.S.S. Magazine (complaints)
Class Act
Club Costa Magazine
Coastal Cruising
Colorado Homes & Lifestyles
Comments
Commerce Magazine
Commodore Magazine (no longer published)
Commonweal
Computer Shopper
Compute!'s PC Magazine
Conde Nast's Traveller
Confrontation
Consumer Reports
Coping
Corvette Fever
Czeschin's Mutual Fund Outlook & Recommendations
Daily World
Dallas Life Magazine
Dancscene
Details
The Detroit Free Press Magazine
Directions
Dirt Bike
The Disciple
Drummer
Dungeon Master
El Paso Magazine (no longer published)
Eldritch Tales
Electronics Experimenters Handbook
Elle
Emmy Magazine
The Episcopalian (out of business)
Exhibit
Expressions (new format)
Family Fiction Digest (unable to contact)
Family Motor Coaching
Fathers (out of business)
Fiction Network Magazine (out of business)

The Fighter International
Filmclips (out of business)
Fine Woodworking
First Opportunity
Fishing & Boating Illustrated (out of business)
Fishing & Hunting Journal
Fishing and Hunting News
Flex
Florida Sportsman
Follow Me Gentlemen
Forbes (uses few freelancers)
Fortune
Forum
FQ
Frequent Flyer
Frets Magazine (out of business)
Fundamentalist Journal (out of business)
Funny Business (asked to be deleted)
Games Junior and Games
Garden Design
Gem (publication sold)
Georgia Journal
Gifted Children Monthly
Gig Magazine
Good News
The Gospel Truth
Gourmet
Greater Winnipeg Business
The Guide
Gulf Coast Golfer
Guns Magazine
Hawaii High Tech Journal
Handmade Accents
Hartford Monthly
Harvest Magazine
Health Express (out of business)
HG
Hibiscus (pays with subscription)
Hideaways Guide (mostly staff written)
High Society
Highlights (receiving too many inappropriate submissions)
Home and Studio Recording
Home Magazine
The Home Shop Machinist
Homeworking Mothers
The Horse Digest
Horses All
Horticulture
House Beautiful
Houston Magazine (no longer published)
Inc.
Incider

Indianapolis Monthly
Infantry (does not pay contributors)
Inside Chicago
The International Horse's Mouth
International Medical Advances Now!
International Olympic Lifter
Intimacy/Black Romance
The Italian Times (unable to contact)
The Itinerary Magazine
Jabberwocky
Jackson Town & Country Magazine
Jacksonville Magazine
Jam To-day (suspended publication)
Jewel
Jewish News
Journal of Christian Camping
Junior Scholastic (staff written)
Karate/Kung-Fu Illustrated
Keyboard Magazine
L.A. West
La Red/The Net
Lady's Circle
The Leather Craftsman (unable to contact)
Lector
Letters Magazine
Life
Listen Magazine (unable to contact)
Live Steam
Log Home Living
Lottery! (out of business)
The Lutheran Journal
MacBusiness Journal
The Magazine for Christian Youth!
Magna (investigating payment complaints)
Mainline Modeler
Manhattan
Manhattan, Inc. (merging with M)
Manscape 2
Mature Health (now called Solutions for Better Health, investigating complaints)
Mature Lifestyles
The Mayberry Gazette
Meridian (no longer published)
Metro
Metro Toronto Business Journal
Mexico Magazine
Mexico Today!
Michigan Living
The Michigan Woman
Midstream
Midway Magazine
The Midwest Motorist
The Millitary Engineer
Miniature Collector
The Miraculous Medal
Mississippi Business Journal
Modern Secretary
Money World
Monroe (does not pay

contributors)
The Mountain (uncertain funding for writers)
Movie Collector's World
MTL Magazine, English
Muses Mill (investigating complaints)
NA'AMAT Woman
National Gardening
National Examiner
Nature Friend Magazine
The Nebraska Review (pays in contributor's copies)
Network (not considering freelance submissions)
New Choices (not accepting unsolicited submissions)
New Jersey Living
New Mexico Magazine
New World Outlook
New York Alive
New York Times Magazine
Newservice
Nibble
North Dakota Rec
North Shore
North Texas Golfer
Northwest Living!
Novascope
N.Y. Habitat Magazine
Ocean Realm
Oceans (out of business)
Offshore
Offshore Financial Report
Ohio Business
Oklahoma Home & Lifestyle
Oklahoma Rural News
On Court
On the Scene Magazine
On Video (out of business)
Ontario Motor Coach Review
Ontario Out of Doors
Our Town
Ostomy Quarterly (pays in contributor's copies)
Out West (asked to be deleted)
Outdoor Photographer (unable to contact)
Ovation
Owl Magazine
Paddler
Palm Beach County Magazine
Partisan Review
Passages North
Pennsylvania Game News
Pennywhistle Press
The Pentecostal Messenger
Penthouse
People
People in Action
Petersen's Hunting
Petersen's Photographic Magazine
Pioneer
Pipe Smoker & Tobacciana Trader
Plenty
Polo
Popular Electronics
Popular Electronics Hobbyist's Handbook
Portable 100

A Positive Approach (pays in contributor's copies)
Practical Knowledge
Preferred Traveller
Present Tense
Princeton Alumni Weekly
Proathlete
Prost! (out of business)
The Purdue Alumnus
Quarante
Que Pasa (out of business)
Quilting Today Magazine
Radio-Electronics
Report on Business Magazine
Report on the Americas
Right Here (out of business)
River Runner Magazine
Rock
Rolling Stone (uses selected freelancers)
Running Times
Sacramento Business Journal
Sailing Magazine
St. Louis Magazine
San Diego Home/Garden
San Diego Magazine
San Francisco Focus
Sassy
Score
Seek
Senior Edition and USA/Colorado
Serendipity
Sesame Street Magazine
Schneider Performance Series
Scouting
Shipmate
Shooting Star Review
Signs of the Times
Ski Guide
Skin Diver
Soap Opera Update
Soccer America
Soundings (written in-house)
Soundtrack
Southern Homes
The Southern Jewish Weekly
Southern Saltwater Magazine
Southern Sensations
Southern Tier Images (no longer published)
Southwest Cycling
Southwest Review
Special Reports (asked to be deleted)
Spin-off
Spirit (formerly Southwest Spirit)
Splash
Sporting Classics
Sports Collectors Digest
Sports History (no longer published)
Sports Illustrated (uses selected freelancers)
Spur
ST-Log (no longer published)
Storyboard
Style
Supercuts Style
Surfer
Tampa Bay Magazine (not ac

cepting freelance submissions)
Tavern Sports International
Teenage (no longer published)
Teens Today
Texas Fisherman
Texas Gardener
Texas High Tech Review
3 & 4 Wheel Action
TI Computing
Tiger Beat Magazine (no longer published)
Tiger Beat Star (no longer published)
Time (staff written)
Traditional Quiltworks
Today's Images
Toronto Life Fashion
Town and Country (uses few freelancers)
Trails-A-Way
Treasure
Trip & Tour
Tristate Magazine (no longer published)

Trout
True Story
TV Week Magazine
Twentyone Magazine
II Chronicles Magazine
UFO Review
Uncensored Letters (no longer published)
The Upper Room, Daily Devotional Guide
Upstate Magazine
US
U.S. News and World Report
Vail Magazine
Vanity Fair (uses selected freelancers)
Vermont Business Magazine
Vermont Magazine
Video Choice Magazine (not accepting freelance submissions)
Video Magazine
The Virginian
Visions
Vital Christianity

Vogue
Volleyball Monthly
Walkways (out of business)
Waterfront News (complaints)
West
West Coast Review
Western Canada Outdoors
Western Investor
Whole Life
Wisconsin Trails
Woman Magazine
Woman's Touch
Women of Ohio (out of business)
Women's Household Crochet
The Women's Quarterly
World Trade
Yale Review (ceased publishing)
Yankee
Yankee Homes (ceased publication)
YM

Trade, Technical and Professional Journals

The general term for all publications focusing on a particular occupation or industry is *trade journal*. Other terms used to describe the different types of trade publications are business, technical and professional journals. (Trade magazines are also called "books" by editors and publishers.) "Trade magazines help readers do their jobs better," says one editor. Many technical journals are written for industrial and science trades and publish articles focusing on new technology or research. Professional journals contain articles from practitioners but focus on all aspects of an occupation. Physicians, educators and lawyers have their own professional journals.

Study several trade journals in the field to get a feel for trends and popular topics. "We look for writers who can recognize the cutting-edge of their industry," says an editor of a graphic design magazine. Newspapers are another good source of information. Changes in tax legislation and government regulations may affect several industries. Local news can be expanded into articles for regional, national and special interest magazines.

Although most trade journals have smaller circulations than consumer publications, writing for the trades is similar to writing for consumer magazines in many ways. Trade publication editors, like their consumer counterparts, seek professionally-presented submissions aimed specifically at their readers. An editor of a business journal says, "Our style is down-to-earth and terse. We pack a lot of information into short articles. Our readers are busy executives who want information dispatched quickly and without embroidery."

Most trade articles are shorter than consumer features, however, and trade journals tend to use more fillers, newsbreaks and short pieces. "We're looking for shorter, news-you-can-use articles," says one editor. "The writer should keep it interesting, but at the same time, stay solidly on track," says another.

The Association of Business Publishers (ABP) conducted a survey, reporting that 23% of trade magazines get more than one-half of their copy from freelance writers. The survey reports that editors most often pay freelance writers on acceptance, a practice we are highlighting in the listings beginning this year. The ABP also reported that most publishers pay for expenses incurred by writers on asssignment.

A recent survey conducted by the editors of *Writer's Market* found that 35.1% of trade journals polled buy all rights, and nearly 6% make work-for-hire assignments. This 41% total is significantly higher than the 30% total for consumer magazines polled. The remaining trade journals polled buy mostly one-time rights (35.7%), or first serial rights (26.6%). Only 10.8% buy reprint rights and less than 1% buy first and second serial rights. (The total is more than 100% because some publishers buy more than one type of rights.) For more analysis of these figures, please refer to the Writer's Roundtable discussion.

Photos help increase the value of most stories for trade. If you can provide photos, mention that in your query, or even send photocopies. Like consumer magazines, trade publications are becoming more visual. The availability of computer graphics has also increased the availability of charts, graphs and other explanatory visuals.

Training or experience in a particular field is a definite plus. For some trade publications, it is essential. With others, it may be enough to provide the necessary information from a reliable and knowledgeable source. Access to experts is absolutely required for highly technical information. In fact, many trade journal editors will ask for a list of sources in order to verify information. Keep this in mind when querying—provide names of experts you talked with or plan to contact. Professionals will often consider a co-author arrangement—their expertise, your writing ability. Many professionals are willing interview subjects, eager to talk about trends or important developments in their field.

Query a trade journal as you would a consumer magazine. Most trade editors like to discuss an article idea with a writer first and will sometimes offer names of helpful sources. Some will provide a list of questions they want you to ask an interview subject. Mention any direct experience you may have in the industry in your cover letter. Send a resume; include clips if they show you have some background or related experience in the specific subject area. Don't forget to include a SASE with your query or manuscript. Read the listing carefully for submission guidelines.

One way to break into the trade field and to increase your income at the same time is to rewrite a consumer story to fit a trade publication. While working on a consumer story, you may also uncover a good trade story lead, such as an interesting new business or a manager with innovative ideas about increasing productivity. Remember to be alert for problem-solving material; readers want to know how they can apply this information to their own situations.

A focus on a local company could generate an article for an environmental trade publication or an industry journal. You'll need to dig deeper into different aspects of your original story, but the effort could mean additional sales.

A survey conducted by *Writer's Market* discovered that slightly more than half the trade journals polled do *not* accept electronic submissions (those made by computer disk or modem). However, those that *do* accept them often receive nearly 100% of their submissions electronically. Many trade journals prefer electronic submissions because the editors face shorter deadlines than consumer magazines. Last minute news items can be accommodated more quickly when submitted by disk or modem.

Trade journals responding favorably to electronic submissions most often named ASCii as their files of preference. The ASCii code offers more universal application and greater manipulation of text, editors say. Some publications also scan submissions of hard copy, saving time by eliminating typesetting. Only letter-quality copy can be scanned, however, which is one reason fewer publications accept dot-matrix every day.

New magazines start up almost daily. Writers should watch for new publications. This information can be found in *Publishers Weekly*, *Folio* and *Advertising Age*, as well as several other publications that stay abreast of the publishing industry.

This section contains about 600 listings for trade, technical and professional publications. Another source for trade publications is *The Business Publication Volume*, published by the Standard Rate and Data Service (SRDS). Designed primarily for buyers of ads, the volume provides the names and addresses of thousands of trade journals, listed by subject matter. The volume is updated monthly and should be available at most libraries.

For information on additional trade publications not listed in *Writer's Market*, see Other Trade, Technical and Professional Journals at the end of this section.

Advertising, Marketing and PR

Trade journals for advertising executives, copywriters and marketing and public relations professionals are listed in this category. Those whose main focus are the advertising and marketing of specific products, such as home furnishings, are classified under individual product categories. Journals for sales personnel and general merchandisers can be found in the Selling and Merchandising category.

ADVERTISING AGE, 740 N. Rush, Chicago IL 60611-2590. (312)649-5200. Managing Editor: Valerie Mackie. Special Projects-Director: Robert Goldsborough. Managing Editor/Special Reports; Edward L. Fitch. Executive Editor: Dennis Chase. Deputy Editor: Larry Doherty. New York office: 220 E 42 St., New York NY 10017. (212)210-0100. Editor: Fred Danzig. Currently staff-produced. Includes weekly sections devoted to one topic (i.e. marketing in Southern California, agribusiness/advertising, TV syndication trends). Much of this material is done freelance—on assignment only. Pays kill fee "based on hours spent plus expenses." Byline given "except short articles or contributions to a roundup."

AMERICAN DEMOGRAPHICS, American Demographics, Inc., P.O. Box 68, Ithaca NY 14851. (607)273-6343. Editor-in-Chief: Cheryl Russell. Managing Editor: Caroline Arthur. 25% freelance written. Works with a small number of new/unpublished writers each year. For business executives, market researchers, media and communications people, public policymakers. Monthly magazine. Estab. 1978. Circ. 35,000. Pays on publication. Publishes ms an average of 6 months after acceptance. Buys all rights. Submit seasonal/holiday material 6 months in advance. Query for electronic submissions. Reports in 1 month. Include self-addressed stamped postcard for return word that ms arrived safely. Sample copy for $5 with 9×11 SAE. Writer's guidelines for #10 SASE.
Nonfiction: General interest (on demographic trends, implications of changing demographics, profile of business using demographic data); and how-to (on the use of demographic techniques, psychographics, understand projections, data, apply demography to business and planning). No anecdotal material or humor. Sometimes pays the expenses of writers on assignment.
Tips: "Writer should have clear understanding of specific population trends and their implications for business and planning. The most important thing a freelancer can do is to read the magazine and be familiar with its style and focus."

‡BPME IMAGE, Broadcast Promotion and Marketing Executives, Inc., 1534B Granite Hills Dr., El Cajon CA 92019. (619)588-1368. FAX: (619)588-1568. Editor-in-Chief: Robert P. Rimes. Assistant Editor: Bill Strubbe. 80% freelance written. Works with a large number of new/unpublished writers each year. A trade journal for broadcast advertising and promotion executives, published 10 times/year. "*BPME Image* is a 'how-to' publication that contains editorial material designed to enhance the job performance of broadcast and cable advertising and promotion executives, who constitute the bulk of its readers." Estab. 1979. Circ. 6,000. **Pays on acceptance.** Publishes ms an average of 3 months after acceptance. Byline given. Buys first serial rights. Submit seasonal/holiday material 4 months in advance. Reports in 1 month. Sample copy for $7 with 8×10 SAE and 10 first class stamps postage.
Nonfiction: Essays, how-to, humor, interview/profile, personal experience and photo feature. "Each issue has a theme: outdoor advertising, new advertising technologies, research, etc." Buys 20 mss/year. Query. Length: 800-2,500 words. Pays $300-700 maximum.
Photos: State availability of b&w photos with submission. Offers $400 maximum per photo. Captions, model releases and identification of subjects required. Buys one-time rights.
Columns/Departments: Profile (leader in industry); My Turn (opinion). Buys 12 mss/year. Query with published clips. Length: 800-2,500 words. Pays $700 maximum.
Tips: "We would like to receive queries on any subject having to do with broadcast or cable advertising or promotion—stunts, contests, concepts, successful advertising and promotion campaigns, and marketing management tips. Ours is a specialized audience making it difficult to break into print in our publication. A full knowledge of radio and television and/or advertising will help. The more research that goes into the piece, the better. We favor writers who have something to say rather than lightweight puff pieces that are cleverly written. We especially like articles that are based on speeches or interviews by or with well-known management persons in radio and TV. A copy of a recent issue is the best place to begin your research into our specialized needs."

THE COUNSELOR MAGAZINE, Advertising Specialty Institute, NBS Bldg., 1120 Wheeler Way, Langhorne PA 19047. (215)752-4200. FAX: (215)752-9758. Editor: Daniel B. Cartledge. 25% freelance written. Works with a small number of new/unpublished writers each year. For executives, both distributors and suppliers, in the ad specialty industry. Monthly magazine. Estab. 1954. Circ. 6,000. Pays on publication. Publishes ms an average of 3 months after acceptance. Buys first rights only. No phone queries. Submit seasonal/holiday material 4 months in advance. Simultaneous, and previously published submissions OK. Reports in 3 months. Sample copy for 9×12 SAE with 3 first class stamps.
Nonfiction: Contact managing editor. How-to (promotional case histories); interview (with executives and government figures); profile (of executives); and articles on specific product categories. "Articles almost always have a specialty advertising slant and quotes from specialty advertising practitioners." Buys 30 mss/year. Length: open. Query with samples. Pays according to assigned length. Sometimes pays the expenses of writers on assignment.
Photos: State availability of photos. B&w photos only. Prefers contact sheet(s) and 5×7 prints. Offers some additional payment for original only photos accepted with ms. Captions and model releases required. Buys one-time rights.

Tips: "If a writer shows promise, we can help him or her modify his style to suit our publication and provide leads. Writers must be willing to adapt or rewrite their material for a specific audience. If an article is suitable for 5 or 6 other publications, it's probably not suitable for us. The best way to break in is to write for *Imprint*, a quarterly publication we produce for the clients of ad specialty counselors."

‡IDENTITY For Specifiers and Customers of Sign and Corporate Graphics, ST Publications, 407 Gilbert Ave., Cincinnati OH 45202. (513)421-2050. FAX: (513)421-5144. Editor: Lynn Baxter. 20% freelance written. Quarterly trade magazine on signs: architectural and national (not billboards). "We cover the design and implementation of corporate identity and sign programs for environmental graphics designers, architects and their clients. We stress signage as a part of the total corporate identity program." Estab. 1988. Circ. 12,000. **Pays on acceptance.** Byline given. Offers 30% kill fee. Buys all rights. Query for electronic submission. Reports in 2 weeks. Free sample copy and writer's guidelines.
Nonfiction: How-to, interview/profile, opinion and technical. "No histories or profiles of design firms or manufacturers." Buys 4-10 mss/year. Query with or without published clips, or send complete ms. Length: 1,000-3,000. Pays $250-400. Sometimes pays expenses of writers on assignment.
Photos: Send photos with submission. Reviews 35mm to 4×5 transparencies. "We *sometimes* pay for photo rights from professional photographers." Identification of subjects required. Buys one-time rights.
Tips: "The best approach is a telephone or written query. Ours is a completely 4/color publication geared to graphically sophisticated audience, requiring professional photography and specific information about design solutions, fabrication and management of corporate identity programs. We prefer a case-history approach, but may accept some theoretical articles on the use of corporate identity, the value of signs, etc. Most open are feature stories written for designers (design, fabrication details) or buyers (value, costs, management of national programs). The more specific, the better. The more 'advertorial,' the less likely to be accepted. Unusual design solutions, unusual use of materials and breadth of design scope make stories more of interest."

MORE BUSINESS, 11 Wimbledon Court, Jericho NY 11753. Editor: Trudy Settel. 50% freelance written. "We sell publications material to business for consumer use (incentives, communication, public relations) — look for book ideas and manuscripts." Monthly magazine. Circ. 10,000. **Pays on acceptance.** Publishes ms an average of 1 month after acceptance. Buys all rights. Reports in 1 month.
Nonfiction: General interest, how-to, vocational techniques, nostalgia, photo feature, profile and travel. Reviews new computer software. Buys 10-20 mss/year. Word length varies with article. Payment negotiable. Query. Pays $4,000-7,000 for book mss.

SALES & MARKETING MANAGEMENT IN CANADA, Sanford Evans Communications Ltd., Suite 103, 3500 Dufferin St., Downsview, Ontario M3K 1N2 Canada. (416)633-2020. FAX: (416)633-5725. Editor: Ms. Robin Baytes. Monthly magazine. Estab. 1959. Circ. 13,400. Pays on publication. Byline given. Buy first Canadian rights. Simultaneous queries OK.
Nonfiction: How-to (case histories of successful marketing campaigns). "Canadian articles preferred." Query. Length: 800-1,200 words.
Tips: "Looking for articles on trends in the industry."

SIGNCRAFT, The Magazine for the Sign Artist and Commercial Sign Shop, SignCraft Publishing Co., Inc., P.O. Box 06031, Fort Myers FL 33906. (813)939-4644. Editor: Tom McIltrot. 20% freelance written. Bimonthly magazine of the sign industry. "Like any trade magazine, we need material of direct benefit to our readers. We can't afford space for material of marginal interest." Circ. 20,500. Pays on publication. Publishes ms an average of 9 months after acceptance. Byline given. Offers negotiable kill fee. Buys first North American serial rights or all rights. Previously published submissions OK. Reports in 1 month. Sample copy and writer's guidelines for $2 and 5 first class stamps.
Nonfiction: Interviews and profiles. "All articles should be directly related to quality commercial signs. If you are familiar with the sign trade, we'd like to hear from you." Buys 20 mss/year. Query with or without published clips. Length: 500-2,000 words. Pays up to $150.

SIGNS OF THE TIMES, The Industry Journal Since 1906, ST Publications, 407 Gilbert Ave., Cincinnati OH 45202. (513)421-2050. FAX: (513)421-5144. Editor: Tod Swormstedt. Managing Editor: Wade Swormstedt. 15-30% freelance written. "We are willing to use more freelancers." Magazine published 13 times/year; special buyer's guide between November and December issue. Estab. 1906. Circ. 18,000. Pays on publication. Publishes ms an average of 3 months after acceptance. Byline given. Buys variable rights. Simultaneous queries, and simultaneous and previously published submissions OK. Reports in 3 months. Free sample copy. Writer's guidelines "flexible."
Nonfiction: Historical/nostalgic (regarding the sign industry); how-to (carved signs, goldleaf, etc.); interview/profile (usually on assignment but interested to hear proposed topics); photo feature (query first); and technical (sign engineering, etc.). Nothing "nonspecific on signs, an example being a photo essay on 'signs

I've seen.' We are a trade journal with specific audience interests." Buys 15-20 mss/year. Query with clips. Pays $150-500. Sometimes pays the expenses of writers on assignment.

Photos: Send photos with ms. "Sign industry-related photos only. We sometimes accept photos with funny twists or misspellings."

Fillers: Open to queries; request rates.

VM + SD (Visual Merchandising and Store Design), ST Publications, 407 Gilbert Ave., Cincinnati OH 45202. (513)421-2050. FAX: (513)421-5144. Editor: Ms. P.K. Anderson. Managing Editor: Janet Groeber. 30% freelance written. Emphasizes store design and merchandise presentation. Monthly magazine. Circ. 18,000. Pays on publication. Buys first and second rights to the same material. Simultaneous and previously published submissions OK. Reports in 1 month. Publishes ms an average of 3 months after acceptance. Sample copy for 9×12 SAE with $2.70. Writer's guidelines for #10 SASE.

Nonfiction: How-to (display); informational (store design, construction, merchandise presentation); interview (display directors and store owners, industry personalities); profile (new and remodeled stores); new product; photo feature (window display); and technical (store lighting, carpet, wallcoverings, fixtures). No "advertorials" that tout a single company's product or product line. Buys 24 mss year. Query or submit complete ms. Length: 500-3,000 words. Pays $250-500.

Photos: Purchased with accompanying ms or on assignment.

Tips: "Be fashion and design conscious and reflect that in the article. Submit finished manuscripts with photos or slides always. Look for stories on department and specialty store visual merchandisers and store designers (profiles, methods, views on the industry, sales promotions and new store design or remodels). The size of the publication could very well begin to increase in the year ahead. And with a greater page count, we will need to rely on an increasing number of freelancers."

Art, Design and Collectibles

The businesses of art, art administration, architecture, environmental/package design and antiques/collectibles are covered in these listings. Art-related topics for the general public are located in the Consumer Art and Architecture category. Antiques and collectibles magazines for enthusiasts are listed in Consumer Hobby and Craft. (Listings of markets looking for freelance artists to do art work can be found in *Artist's Market* — see Other Books of Interest).

ANTIQUEWEEK, Mayhill Publications Inc., 27 N. Jefferson St., P.O. Box 90, Knightstown IN 46148. (317)345-5133. Managing Editor: Tom Hoepf. 60% freelance written. Weekly tabloid on antiques, collectibles and genealogy. *AntiqueWeek* publishes two editions: Eastern and Mid-Central. "*AntiqueWeek* has a wide range of readership from dealers and auctioneers to collectors, both advanced and novice. Our readers demand accurate information presented in an entertaining style." Estab. 1968. Circ. 60,000. Pays on publication. Publishes ms an average of 1-2 months after acceptance. Byline given. Buys first and second serial (reprint) rights. Submit seasonal/holiday material 1 month in advance. Reports in 1 month. Free sample copy and writer's guidelines.

Nonfiction: Historical/nostalgic, how-to, interview/profile, opinion, personal experience, photo feature, antique show and auction reports, feature articles on particular types of antiques. Buys 400-500 mss/year. Query with or without published clips, or send complete ms. Length: 1,000-2,000 words. Pays $25-125.

Photos: Send photos with submission. Reviews 3½×5 prints. Offers $10-15 per photo. Identification of subjects required. Buys one-time rights.

Columns/Departments: Insights (opinions on buying, selling and collecting antiques), 500-1,000 words; Your Ancestors (advice, information on locating sources for genealogists), 1,500-2,000 words. Buys 150 mss/ year. Query. Length: 500-1,000 words. Pays $25-50.

Tips: "Writers should know their topic thoroughly to write about it. Feature articles must be well-researched and clearly written. An interview and profile article with a knowledgeable collector might be the break for a first-time contributor. As we move toward the year 2000, there is much more interest in 20th-century collectibles. *Antiqueweek* also seeks articles that reflect the current popularity of Victorian-era antiques."

THE APPRAISERS STANDARD, (formerly *NEAA News*), New England Appraisers Assocation, 5 Gill Terrace, Ludlow VT 05149. (802)228-7444. Editor: Linda L. Tucker. 75% freelance written. Works with a small number of new/unpublished writers each year. Monthly publication on the appraisals of antiques, art, collectibles, jewelry, coins, stamps and real estate. "The writer should be extremely knowledgeable on the subject, and the article should be written with appraisers in mind with prices quoted for objects, good pictures and descriptions of articles being written about." Circ. 1,300. Pays on publication. Publishes ms an average of 2 months after acceptance. Byline given, with short biography to establish writer's credibility. Buys first rights, second serial (reprint) rights, and simultaneous rights. Submit seasonal/holiday material 2 months in advance. Simultaneous and previously published submissions OK. Reports in 1 week on queries; 3 weeks on mss.

Sample copy for 9×12 SAE with 2 first class stamps; writer's guidelines for #10 SASE.

Nonfiction: Interview/profile, personal experience, technical and travel. "All articles must be geared toward professional appraisers." Query with or without published clips, or send complete ms. Length: 700 words. Pays $50.

Photos: Send photos with submission. Reviews negatives and prints. Offers no additional payment for photos accepted with ms. Identification of subjects required. Buys one-time rights.

Tips: "Interviewing members of the Association for articles, reviewing art books, shows and large auctions are all ways for writers who are not in the field to write articles for us."

ART BUSINESS NEWS, Myers Publishing Co., P.O. Box 3837, Stamford CT 06905. (203)356-1745. Editor: Jo Yanow-Schwartz. Managing Editor: Beth Slucher. 25% freelance written. Prefers to work with published/ established writers. Monthly trade tabloid covering news relating to the art and picture framing industry. Circ. 30,000. Pays on publication. Publishes ms an average of 3 months after acceptance. Byline given. Buys first-time rights. Submit seasonal/holiday material 2 months in advance. Simultaneous submissions OK. Reports in 3 months. Sample copy for 12×16 SAE and $4.

Nonfiction: News in art and framing field; interview/marketing profiles (of dealers, publishers in the art industry); new products; articles focusing on small business people—framers, art gallery management, art trends; and how-to (occasional article on "how-to frame" accepted). Buys 8-20 mss/year. Length: 1,000 words maximum. Query first. Pays $75-250. Sometimes pays the expenses of writers on assignment. "Useful if writer can photograph."

ARTS MANAGEMENT, 408 W. 57th St., New York NY 10019. (212)245-3850. Editor: A.H. Reiss. For cultural institutions. Published 5 times/year. 2% freelance written. Estab. 1962. Circ. 6,000. Pays on publication. Byline given. Buys all rights. Mostly staff-written; uses very little outside material. Query. Reports in "several weeks." Writer's guidelines for #10 SASE.

Nonfiction: Short articles, 400-900 words, tightly written, expository, explaining how art administrators solved problems in publicity, fund raising and general administration; actual case histories emphasizing the how-to. Also short articles on the economics and sociology of the arts and important trends in the nonprofit cultural field. Must be fact-filled, well-organized and without rhetoric. Payment is 2-4¢/word. No photographs or pictures.

‡AWARDS & ENGRAVING BUSINESS MAGAZINE, BF Communications Inc., P.O. Box 969, Lake Dallas TX 75065. (817)497-2285. Editor: Kim Wilbanks. 75% freelance written. Bimonthly magazine of engravable awards, gifts and signs. Estab. 1988. Circ. 10,000. Pays on publication. Publishes ms an average of 3 months after acceptance. Byline given. Buys all rights. Submit seasonal/holiday material 4 months in advance. Previously published submissions OK. Reports in 1 month. Sample copy for 9×12 SAE with 6 first class stamps. Writer's guidelines for #10 SASE.

Nonfiction: General interest (business as well as industry related), historical/nostalgic, how-to (engrave various materials, i.e. glass, plastic, metal, etc. Assemble trophies, plaques, awards etc. Also general business how-to, i.e. inventory control, advertising campaigns etc.), interview/profile (retail shops—trophy, sign, jewelry etc., personal experience (business and industry related), technical (computerized engraving digitizing art for logos). Buys 12 mss/year. Query with or without published clips, or send complete ms. Length: 500-1,500 words. Pays $25-250. Sometimes pays expenses of writers on assignment.

Photos: State availability of photos with submission. Reviews 5×7 prints. Offers no additional payment for photos. Identification of subjects required.

Columns/Departments: A&E Storefront (profile of retailers—should offer/incorporate helpful ideas not just story of how they got started), 1,000-1,500 words. Buys 6 mss/year. Query with published clips. Length: 500-1,000 words. Pays $35-100.

Tips: Keep an eye on what types of awards are available. We've pubished articles on the Oscars, Vince Lombardi Trophy (Superbowl) and other famous awards. Slants vary from origin to who designed them, etc. Also way of using awards such as employee recognition awards that are on just about every wall of American fast-food eateries. Use of engraving is also a good source of information from signs at hospitals and businesses to jewelry. Good general and specific business articles are also welcome. Writers have the best chance selling us features. They are the most flexible and can encompass many subjects including natural extensions of the industry such as advertising specialties, signage, jewelry, ribbons, medals, medallions, glassware, gifts and plaques.

The double dagger before a listing indicates that the listing is new in this edition. New markets are often the most receptive to freelance submissions.

‡**CADALYST**, Professional Management of Autocad Systems, CADalyst Publications, Suite 202, 210 W. Broadway, Vancouver, British Columbia V5Y 3W2 Canada. (604)873-0517. Senior Editors: Ralph Grabowski and David Cohn. Managing Editor: Colleen McLaughlin. 50% freelance written. Monthly trade journal covering autocad (computer-aided design). Estab. 1984. Circ. 40,000. Pays on publication. Publishes ms an average of 3-6 months after acceptance. Byline given. Offers $100 kill fee. Buys first North American serial rights. Submit seasonal/holiday 6 months in advance. Previously published submissions OK. Query for electronic submissions. Reports in 2 weeks on queries. Free writer's guidelines.

Nonfiction: Book excerpts (autocad texts), expose, how-to (autocad method articles, short tips), humor (autocad person-in-the-trenches viewpoint), new product (press releases), opinion (guest editorial), personal experience, photo feature (animator and other presentation graphics specific to autocad), and technical (everything is technical; we're a technical journal reviewing hardware and software). "No PR promotional articles on specific products or services." Buys 120 mss/year. Query. Length: 500-2,500 (can be longer for multiple product comparisons). Pays $100-700."

Photos: Send photos with submission. Reviews negatives, transparencies ($2\frac{1}{4} \times 2\frac{1}{4}$), and prints ($8 \times 10$). Offers no additional payment for photos accepted with ms. Captions and identification of subjects required. Buys one-time rights.

Fillers: Anecdotes, facts, gags to be illustrated by cartoonist, newsbreaks, and short humor. Buys 30/year. Length: 50-500 words. Pays $100-300.

Tips: "We are only interested in people with an autocad background in architecture/engineering/industrial design/surveying/construction industry. We are more interested in technical content than style. All areas are open. Please telephone or E-mail us on Compuserve first so we can assign you an article or chat about your story proposals."

CALLIGRAPHY REVIEW, 1624 24th Ave. SW, Norman OK 73072. (405)364-8794. Editor: Karyn L. Gilman. 98% freelance written. Eager to work with new/unpublished writers with calligraphic expertise and language skills. A quarterly magazine on calligraphy and related book arts, both historical and contemporary in nature. Estab. 1985. Circ. 5,500. Pays on publication. Publishes ms an average of 9 months after acceptance. Byline given. Offers 20% kill fee. Buys first rights. Query for electronic submissons. Sample copy for 9×12 SAE with 7 first class stamps; free writer's guidelines.

Nonfiction: Interview/profile, opinion, contemporary and historical. Buys 50 mss/year. Query with or without published clips, or send complete ms. Length: 1,000-2,000 words. Pays $50-200 for assigned articles; pays $25-200 for unsolicited articles. Sometimes pays the expenses of writers on assignment.

Photos: State availability of photos with submission. Reviews contact sheets, negatives, transparencies and prints. Pays agreed upon cost. Captions and identification of subjects required. Buys one-time rights.

Columns/Departments: Book Reviews Viewpoint (critical), 500-1,500 words; Ms. (discussion of manuscripts in collections), 1,000-2,000 words; and Profile (contemporary calligraphic figure), 1,000-2,000 words. Query. Pays $50-200.

Tips: "*Calligraphy Review*'s primary objective is to encourage the exchange of ideas on calligraphy, its past and present as well as trends for the future. Practical and conceptual treatments are welcomed, as are learning and teaching experiences. Third person is preferred, however first person will be considered if appropriate."

THE CRAFTS REPORT, The Newsmonthly of Marketing, Management and Money for Crafts Professionals, The Crafts Report Publishing Co., 87 Wall St., 2nd Floor, Seattle WA 98121. (206)441-3102. FAX: (206)547-7113. Editor: Christine Yarrow. 50% freelance written. A monthly tabloid covering business subjects for crafts professionals. Estab. 1974. Circ. 18,000. Pays on publication. Byline given. Offers $50 kill fee. Buys first rights. Previously published submissions OK. Query for electronic submissions. Reports in 2 weeks. Sample copy $2.50

Nonfiction: Business articles for crafts professionals. No articles on art or crafts techniques. Buys approximately 70 mss/year. Query with published clips. Length: 800-1,200 words. Pays $100-150.

Photos: State availability of photos with submission or send photos with submission. Reviews 5×7 b&w prints, color prints and transparencies. Identification of subjects required. Buys one-time rights.

THE FRONT STRIKER BULLETIN, The Retskin Report, P.O. Box 8101, Alexandria VA 22306-8101. (703)768-1051. FAX: (703)768-4719. Editor: Bill Retskin. 70% freelance written. Quarterly newsletter for matchcover collectors and historical enthusiasts. Estab. 1986. Circ. 500. Pays on publication. Publishes ms an average of 3 months after acceptance. Byline given. Offers 20% kill fee. Buys first North American serial rights. Submit seasonal/holiday material 6 months in advance. Query for electronic submission. Sample copy for 9×12 SAE with 2 first class stamps; writer's guidelines for #10 SASE.

Nonfiction: General interest, historical/nostalgic, how-to (collecting techniques), humor, personal experience and photo feature; all relating to match industry or ephemera. Buys 2 mss/year. Query with published clips. Length: 200-1,200 words. Pays $25-50 for assigned articles; $10-25 for unsolicited articles.

Photos: State availability of photos with submission. Reviews b&w contact sheets and 5×7 prints. Offers $2-5/photo. Captions and identification of subjects required.
Fiction: Historical (match cover related only). Buys 2 mss/year. Query with published clips. Length: 200-1,200 words. Pays $25-50.
Tips: "We are interested in clean, direct style with the collector audience in mind."

GLASS ART, The Magazine for Stained and Decorative Glass, Travin, Inc., P.O. Box 1507, Broomfield CO 80038. (303)465-4965. FAX: (303)465-2821. Editor: Shawn Waggoner. Publisher: Kevin Borgmann. 40% freelance written. Bimonthly magazine. "*Glass Art* magazine covers the spectrum of the glass art industry. We feature national artists and their work as well as provide information on getting commissions, legal issues, safety issues and business issues." Estab. 1985. Circ. 7,000. Byline given. Buys first North American serial rights. Submit seasonal/holiday material 2 months in advance. Simultaneous submissions OK. Reports in 1 month. Writer's guidelines for #10 SASE.
Nonfiction: How-to (any glass process articles are of interest); personal experience (glass artists with experiences of interest to other artists may submit materials); religious (articles relaying crossover between religion and stained glass) and technical (any technical information pertaining to glass and its use as art media). "*Glass Art* rarely accepts freelance material written by persons who are not professional glass artists, engineers, kilnmakers, etc." Query with published clips. Length: 700-2,000 words. Pays $75-250.
Photos: Send photos with submission. Reviews transparencies and slides. Offers no additional payment for photos accepted with ms. Identification of subjects required. Buys one-time rights.
Column/Departments: Hot Glass, Safety, Good Business and Tips & Tricks (technical).
Tips: "Technical information is always needed. If you are a glass artist who can write, simply call with your ideas. Must be well-versed in glass art processes and techniques."

HOW, Ideas and Techniques in Graphic Design, 1507 Dana Ave., Cincinnati OH 45207. (513)531-2222. Editor: Laurel Harper. 75% freelance written. Bimonthly graphic design and illustration business journal. "*HOW* gives a behind-the-scenes look at not only *how* the world's best graphic artists and designers conceive and create their work, but *why* they did it that way. We also focus on the *business* side of design—how to run a profitable studio." Estab. 1985. Circ. 35,000. **Pays on acceptance.** Byline given. Buys first North American serial rights. Query for electronic submission. Reports in 6 weeks. Sample copy for $8.50. Writer's guidelines for #10 SASE.
Nonfiction: Interview/profile, business tips and new products. Special issues—Sept/Oct: Business Annual; Nov/Dec: Self-Promotion Annual. No how-to articles for beginning artists or fine-art-oriented articles. Buys 40 mss/year. Query with published clips and samples of subject's work (artwork or design). Length: 1,200-2,500 words. Pays $250-600. Sometimes pays expenses of writers on assignment.
Photos: State availability of artwork with submission. Reviews 35mm or larger transparencies. May reimburse mechanical photo expenses. Captions are required. Buys one-time rights.
Columns/Departments: Marketplace (focuses on lucrative fields for designers/illustrators); Design Talk (Q&A interviews with top designers); and Production (ins, outs and tips on production). Buys 20 mss/year. Query with published clips. Length: 1,000-1,800 words. Pays $150-400.
Tips: "We look for writers who can recognize graphic designers on the cutting-edge of their industry, both creatively and business-wise. Writers must have an eye for detail, and be able to relay *HOW*'s step-by-step approach in an interesting, concise manner—without omitting any details. Showing you've done your homework on a subject—and that you can go beyond asking 'those same old questions'—will give you a big advantage."

MANHATTAN ARTS MAGAZINE, Renee Phillips Associates, Suite 26L, 200 East 72 St., New York NY 10021. (212) 472-1660. Editor: Renee Phillips. Managing Editor: Michael Jason. 100% freelance written. Monthly magazine covering fine art. Audience is comprised of art professionals, artists and emerging collectors. Educational, informative, easy-to-read style, making art more accessible. Highly promotional of new artists. Estab. 1983. Circ. 50,000. Pays on publication. Publishes ms an average of 1 month after acceptance. Byline given. Makes work for hire assignments. Submit seasonal/holiday material 3 months in advance. Simultaneous submissions OK. Sample copy $1 with 9×12 SAE and 4 first class stamps.
Nonfiction: Book excerpts (art), essays (art world), general interest (collecting art), inspirational (artists success stories), interview/profile (major art leaders), new product (art supplies), technical (art business). Buys 100 mss/year. Query with published clips. Length: 150-750 words. Pays $25-100. New writers receive byline and promotion, art books. Sometimes pays expenses of writers on assignment.
Photos: Send photos with submission. Offers no additional payment for photos accepted with ms. Captions, model releases and identification of subjects required.
Columns/Departments: Reviews/Previews (art critiques of exhibitions in galleries and museums), 150-250 words; Artists/Profiles (features on major art leaders), 400-650 words; The New Collector (collectibles, interviews with dealers, collectors), 150-650 words; Artopia (inspirational features, success stories), 150-650 words; Art Books, Art Services, 150-300 words. Buys 100 mss/year. Query with published clips. Pays $25-100.
Tips: "A knowledge of the current, contemporary art scene is a must. An eye for emerging talent is an asset."

THE MIDATLANTIC ANTIQUES MAGAZINE, Monthly Guide to Antiques, Art, Auctions & Collectibles, The Henderson Daily Dispatch Company, Inc., P.O. Box 908, Henderson NC 27536. (919)492-4001. FAX: (919)430-0125. Editor: Lydia Tucker. 65% freelance written. Monthly tabloid that covers antiques, art, auctions and collectibles. "The *MidAtlantic* is a monthly trade publication that reaches dealers, collectors, antique shows and auction houses primarily on the east coast, but circulation includes 48 states and Europe." Estab. 1984. Circ. 12,000. Pays on publication. Byline given. Buys first rights, second serial (reprint) rights or simultaneous rights (noncompeting markets). Submit seasonal/holiday material 3 months in advance. Simultaneous and previously published submissions OK. Reports in 1 month on queries; 2 months on mss. Free sample copy and writer's guidelines.

Nonfiction: Book excerpts, historical/nostalgic, how-to (choose an antique to collect; how to sell your collection; how to identify market trends), interview/profile, personal experience, photo feature, and technical. Buys 96-120 mss/year. Query. Length: 800-2,000 words. Pays $50-150. Trade for advertising space. Rarely pays expenses of writers on assignment.

Photos: Send photos with submission. Offers no additional payment for photos accepted with ms. Identification of subjects required. Buys one-time rights.

Columns/Departments: Ask An Appraiser, Knock on Wood, Rinker on Collectibles, Lindquist on Antiques and Collecting For Fun (Insights on buying, selling, collecting antiques, art, collectibles, *not* looking for columnists at this time.), 800-2,000 words. Buys 96 mss/year. Query with published clips. Pays $3-50.

Tips: "Please contact by mail first, but a writer may call with specific ideas after initial contact. Looking for writers who have extensive knowledge in specific areas of antiques. Articles should be educational in nature. We are also interested in how-to articles, i.e., how to choose antiques to collect; how to sell your collection and get the most for it; looking for articles that focus on future market trends. We want writers who are active in the antiques business and can predict good investments. (Articles with photographs are given preference.) We are looking for people who are not only knowledgeable, but can write well."

‡MODERN CARTOONING, P.O. Box 1142, Novato CA 94947. Editor: Raymond Moore. Managing Editor: J.A. Moore. 50% freelance written. Monthly trade journal for the professional cartoonist/gagwriter. Buys only from paid subscribers. Estab. 1989. Circ. 250. **Pays on acceptance.** Byline given. Negotiable kill fee. Not copyrighted. Buys second serial (reprint) rights. Submit seasonal/holiday material 3 months in advance. Simultaneous submissions OK. Reports in 1 month on queries. Sample copy $5. Writer's guidelines for #10 SASE.

Nonfiction: Humor, cartoons, comic strips. Buys 12 mss/year. Query with or without published clips, or send complete ms. Pays $10 minimum.

Photos: Send photos with submission. Offers no additional payment for photos accepted with ms. Captions required.

Columns/Departments: Self-bios; Short humor; Promo sheets. Buys 12 ms/year. Query. Pays $10 minimum.

Fillers: Gags to be illustrated by cartoonist, short humor. Buys 12/year. Pays $10 minimum.

Tips: "Obtain sample copy of publication to grasp the slant! Enclose SASE for expected returns."

NEW ENGLAND ANTIQUES JOURNAL, Turley Publications. 4 Church St., Ware MA 01082. (413)967-3505. FAX: (413)967-6009. Editor: Rufus Foshee. 50% freelance written. A monthly newspaper concentrating on antiques for antique dealers, collectors and the general public. Circ. 20,000. Pays on publication. Byline given. Buys first rights.

Nonfiction: Queries advisable, all manuscripts considered. Fees negotiable. "We want original, in-depth articles on all types of antiques, preferably by experts in their fields." Mss under 1,000 words not desirable, no limit on length. Articles must be accompanied by photos.

Tips: "Read our publication; send inquiries first."

TEXAS ARCHITECT, Texas Society of Architects, Suite 1400, 114 W. 7th, Austin TX 78701. (512)478-7386. Editor: Joel Warren Barna. Art Director/Associate Editor: Ray Don Tilley. 30% freelance written. Bimonthly trade journal of architecture and architects of Texas. "*Texas Architect* is a highly visually-oriented look at Texas architecture, design and urban planning. Articles cover varied subtopics within architecture. Readers are mostly architects and related building professionals." Estab. 1951. Circ. 8,000. Pays on publication. Publishes an average of 2 months after acceptance. Byline given. Buys one-time rights, all rights or makes work-for-hire assignments. Submit seasonal/holiday material 4 months in advance. Query for electronic submissions. Reports in 2 weeks. Free sample copy and writer's guidelines.

Nonfiction: Book excerpts, essays, historical/nostalgic, humor, interview/profile, opinion, photo feature and technical. Buys 15 mss/year. Query with or without published clips, or send complete ms. Length: 100-2,000 words. Pays $50-500 for assigned articles; $25-300 for unsolicited articles.

Photos: Send photos with submission. Reviews contact sheets, 35mm or 4 × 5 transparencies and 4 × 5 prints. Offers no additional payment for photos accepted with ms. Identification of subjects required. Buys one-time rights.

Columns: Ray Don Tilley. News (timely reports on architectural issues, projects and people); 100-500 words. Buys 10 mss/year. Query with published clips. Pays $50-100.

Auto and Truck

These publications are geared to automobile, motorcycle and truck dealers; professional truck drivers; service department personnel; or fleet operators. Publications for highway planners and traffic control experts are listed in the Government and Public Service category.

AUTO GLASS JOURNAL, Grawin Publications, Inc., Suite 101, 303 Harvard E., P.O. Box 12099, Seattle WA 98102-0099. (206)322-5120. Editor: Burton Winters. 45% freelance written. Prefers to work with published/established writers. Monthly magazine on auto glass replacement. National publication for the auto glass replacement industry. Includes step-by-step glass replacement procedures for current model cars as well as shop profiles, industry news and trends. Estab. 1953. Circ. 5,500. **Pays on acceptance.** Publishes ms an average of 5 months after acceptance. No byline given. Buys all rights. Query for electronic submissions. Reports in 2 weeks. Sample copy for 6×9 SAE and 3 first class stamps. Writer's guidelines for #10 SASE.
Nonfiction: How-to (install all glass in a current model car); and interview/profile. Buys 22-36 mss/year. Query with published clips. Length: 2,000-3,500 words. Pays $75-250, with photos.
Photos: State availability of photos. Reviews b&w contact sheets and negatives. Payment included with ms. Captions required. Buys all rights.
Tips: "Be willing to visit auto glass replacement shops for installation features."

AUTO LAUNDRY NEWS, Columbia Communications, 370 Lexington Ave., New York NY 10017. (212)532-9290. FAX: (212)779-8345. Publisher: Joe Feldmann. 20% freelance written. Prefers to work with published/established writers. For sophisticated car wash operators. Monthly magazine. Circ. 17,000. Pays on publication. Publishes ms an average of 2 months after acceptance. Buys all rights. Submit seasonal/holiday material 2 months in advance. Query for electronic submissions. Reports in 1 month. Sample copy for 9×12 SAE with 3 first class stamps. Free writer's guidelines.
Nonfiction: How-to, historical, informational, new product, nostalgia, personal experience, technical, interviews, photo features and profiles. Buys 15 mss/year. Query. Length: 1,000-2,000 words. Pays $75-175. Sometimes pays the expenses of writers on assignment.
Tips: "We mainly like to receive car wash profiles. Read the magazine; notice its style and come up with something interesting to the industry. Foremost, the writer has to know the industry."

AUTOMOTIVE EXECUTIVE, Official Publication of National Auto Dealers, NADA Services Corporation. 8400 Westpart Dr., McLean VA 22102. (703)821-7150. FAX: (703)821-7234. Editor-in-Chief: Marc II. Stertz. Managing Editor: Joe Phillips. 80% freelance written. A monthly magazine on the retail new-car and truck business. "We offer a broad view of developments in the nation's $283 billion retail new car and truck market. We seek examples of excellence in sales, service, product, and customer relations." Estab. 1917. Circ. 24,000. Pays on publication. Publishes ms an average of 2 months after acceptance. Byline given. Kill fee negotiable. Buys all rights. Query for electronic submissions. Reports in 1 week on queries; 2 weeks on mss. Free sample copy and writer's guidelines.
Nonfiction: Dealership managament (sales, service, parts, finance, personnel), interview/profile, new product and technical. February—annual convention issue; May—annual dealership design issue; August—annual buyers guide issue; December—annual forecast issue. Buys 50-60 mss/year. Query with published clips. Length: 2,500 words. Pays $200-500 for assigned articles. Pays the expenses of writers on assignment.
Photos: State availability of photos with submission or send photos with submission. Reviews contact sheets. Offers no additional payment for photos accepted with ms. Buys all rights.
Columns/Departments: Column/Department Editor: Joan Mooney. On Track (reports on current auto-industry events /trends and new-car introductions), 100-250 words; pays $50-75. Opinion Page (opinions on current industry controversies/policies) 750-1,000 words; pays $250-300; Showcase (highlights new products related to retail auto market) 750-1,000 words; pays $250-300; Service Department (ideas for efficient servicing of cars/trucks), 750-2,500 words; pays $250-300. Buys 40-50 mss/year. Query with published clips.
Tips: "We're looking for articles dealing with all aspects of retail new car/truck sales/service/customer relations, interviews with manufacturing/import executives, stories on unusual dealers/dealerships and stories from related industry that focus on excellence. We look for current economic and retrail trends in the auto industry and changes in the global economy that may impact dealers (merging car manufacturers, labor relations, trade, etc.)."

BRAKE & FRONT END, 11 S. Forge St., Akron OH 44304. (216)535-6117. FAX: (216)535-0874. Group Publisher: Jack Hone. Editor: Mary DellaValle. 5% freelance written. Works with a small number of new/unpublished writers each year. For owners of automotive repair shops engaged in brake, suspension, driveline exhaust and steering repair, including: specialty shops, general repair shops, new car and truck dealers, gas stations, mass merchandisers and tire stores. Monthly magazine. Estab. 1931. Circ. 28,000. Pays on publication. Publishes ms an average of 3-4 months after acceptance. Byline given. Buys first North American serial rights. Reports immediately. Sample copy and editorial schedule $3; guidelines for SASE.

Nonfiction: Specialty shops taking on new ideas using new merchandising techniques; growth of business, volume; reasons for growth and success. Expansions and unusual brake shops. Prefers no product-oriented material. Query. Length: about 800-1,500 words. Pays 7-9¢/word. Sometimes pays expenses of writers on assignment.

Photos: Pays $8.50 for b&w glossy prints purchased with mss.

‡EASTERN AFTERMARKET JOURNAL, Hubsher Publications, P.O. Box 373, Cedarhurst NY 11516. (516)295-3680. Editor: Stan Hubsher. 100% freelance written. Bimonthly magazine for automotive parts wholesaler buyers at the warehouse and jobber level, on the Eastern seaboard. "Audience operates stores and warehouses that handle replacement parts for automobiles. No technical knowledge necessary. Profiles of owners/buyers, how they operate in highly competitive market that accounts for 40% of the entire country's aftermarket business." Circ. 8,500. Pays on publication. No byline. Buys all rights. Submit material 2 months in advance. Free sample copy and writer's guidelines.

Nonfiction: Buys 6-8 mss/year. Query. Length: 2,000 words. Pays $150 minimum to negotiable maximum. Sometimes pays expenses of writers on assignment.

Photos: Send photos with submission. Offers no additional payments for photos accepted with ms. Captions and identification of subjects required. Buys one-time rights.

HEAVY TRUCK SALESMAN, The Magazine for Truck Sales and Leasing Professionals, Newport Publications, Suite 214, 1045 Taylor Ave., Baltimore MD 21204. (301)828-1092. Editor-in-Chief: David A. Kolman. 15% freelance written. Bimonthly trade magazine on truck sales and leasing industry. "The editorial purpose is to supply timely business and career related articles for those who sell or lease medium and heavy duty trucks. Articles are intended to further sharpen the reader's selling skills and product knowledge in order to sell and lease more trucks." Estab. 1983. Circ. 22,000. Pays on publication. Publishes ms an average of 4 months after acceptance. Byline given. Buys first North American serial rights. Submit seasonal/holiday material 6 months in advance. Query for electronic submissions. Reports in 1 month. Free sample copy.

Nonfiction: How-to (selling, truck engineering), interview/profile (industry personnel), new product, technical (product knowledge, truck engineering). Buys 6 mss/year. Query with or without published clips, or send complete ms. Sometimes pay expenses of writers on assignment.

Photos: Send photo with submission. Reviews contact sheets, negatives, transparencies and prints. Offers $75 minimum per photo. Captions are required. Buys one-time rights.

Tips: "Profiles of successful business and salespeople are most open to freelancers. Find interesting or unique subject that would appeal to *HTS* readers."

MODERN TIRE DEALER, 110 N. Miller Rd., P.O. Box 5417, Akron OH 44313. (216)867-4401. FAX: (216)867-0019. Editor: Lloyd Stoyer. 15-20% freelance written. Prefers to work with published/established writers. For independent tire dealers. Monthly tabloid, plus 2 special emphasis issue magazines. Published 14 times annually. Estab. 1919. Buys all rights. Reports in 1 month. Publishes ms an average of 2 months after acceptance. Sample copy $5. Writer's guidelines for #10 SASE.

Nonfiction: "How independent tire dealers sell tires, accessories and allied services such as brakes, wheel alignment, shocks and mufflers. The emphasis is on merchandising and management. We prefer the writer to zero in on some specific area of interest; avoid shotgun approach." Query. Length: 1,500 words. Pays $300 and up. Sometimes pays the expenses of writers on assignment.

Photos: 8×10, 4×5, 5×7 b&w glossy prints purchased with mss.

Tips: "Changes in the competitive situation among tire manufacturers and/or distributors will affect the types of freelance material we buy. We want articles for or about tire dealers, not generic articles adapted for our publication."

PRO TRUCKER and OVER THE ROAD, Ramp Enterprises, 610 Colonial Park Dr., Roswell GA 30075. (404)587-0311. FAX: (404)642-8874. Associate Editor: Carol Prins. 5-10% freelance written. Monthly magazine on trucking. "*Over the Road* is published the first of each month, *Pro Trucker* the 15th of each month." Estab. 1981. Circ. 75,000 each. **Pays on acceptance.** Publishes ms an average of 2 months after acceptance. Byline given. Buys first rights and second serial (reprint) rights. Submit seasonal/holiday material 3 months in advance. Sample copy for 6×9 SAE with 5 first class stamps.

Nonfiction: Humor, interview/profile and technical. Query. Length: 300-3,000 words. Pays $150-500 for assigned articles. Sometimes pays expenses of writers on assignment.

Photos: State availability of photos with submission. Reviews transparencies and 5×7 prints. Offers no additional payment for photos accepted with ms or may pay—depending on subject. Identification of subjects required. Buys all rights.

Columns/Departments: Puzzler (word search & crossword), 1 page. Query. Pays $50-200.

SOUTHERN MOTOR CARGO, Wallace Witmer Co., 1509 Madison, Memphis TN 38104. (901)276-5424. FAX: (901)276-5400. Editor: Pearce W. Hammond. Managing Editor: Randy Duke. 15% freelance written. Monthly trade journal on heavy-duty truck equipment and safety. Estab. 1944. Circ. 61,000. **Pays on acceptance.** Publishes ms an average of 2 months after acceptance. Byline sometimes given. Buys all rights. Submit seasonal/holiday material 2 months in advance. Free sample copy.
Nonfiction: Interview/profile, new product, technical, trucking industry news and other safety related articles. "We do not want articles about drivers." Buys 10 mss/year. Send complete ms. Length: 500-2,500 words. Pays 10-15¢/word. Pays expenses of writers on assignment.
Photos: Send photos with submission. Reviews contact sheets and negatives. Pays for film and processing. Captions, model releases and identification of subjects required. Buys all rights.
Columns/Departments: Southern Trucking (articles that affect the writer's region. Consists of state news which deals with trucking). Industry News (deals with company expansions, closings, etc.). Send complete ms. Length: 300-1,500 words. Pays 10-15¢/word.
Tips: "We have recently begun publishing *regional* sections. We *need* freelancers in the Atlantic, West South Central, and East South Central regions. These writers will report on truck news in their city and surrounding area."

THE SUCCESSFUL DEALER, Kona-Cal, Inc., 707 Lake Cook Rd., Deerfield IL 60015. (708)498-3180. FAX: (708)498-3187. Editor: David Zaritz. Managing Editor: Denise Rondini. 30% freelance written. "We will consider material from both established writers and new ones." Magazine published 6 times/year covering dealership management of medium and heavy duty trucks, construction equipment, forklift trucks, diesel engines and truck trailers. Estab. 1978. Circ. 19,000. Pays on publication. Byline sometimes given. Buys first serial rights only. Simultaneous queries and submissions OK. Reports in 2 weeks. Publication date "depends on the article; some are contracted for a specific issue, others on an as need basis." Articles must be tailored to heavy truck industry.
Nonfiction: How-to (solve problems within the dealership); interview/profile (concentrating on business, not personality); new product (exceptional only); opinion (by readers—those in industry); personal experience (of readers); photo feature (of major events); and technical (vehicle componentry). Special issues include: March-April: American Truck Dealer Convention. Query. Length: open. Pays $75/page.
Tips: "Phone first, then follow up with a detailed explanation of the proposed article. Allow two weeks for our response. Articles should be based on real problems/solutions encountered by truck or heavy equipment dealership personnel. We are *not* interested in general management tips."

TOW-AGE, Kruza Kaleidoscopix, Inc., Box 389, Franklin MA 02038. Editor: J. Kruza. For readers who run their own towing service business. 5% freelance written. Prefers to work with published/established writers. Published every 6 weeks. Circ. 18,000. Buys all rights; usually reassigns rights. Buys about 18 mss/year. **Pays on acceptance.** Publishes ms an average of 1 month after acceptance. Simultaneous submissions OK. Reports in 1 month. Sample copy $3; writer's guidelines for #10 SASE.
Nonfiction: Articles on business, legal and technical information for the towing industry. "Light reading material; short, with punch." Informational, how-to, personal, interview and profile. Query or submit complete ms. Length: 200-800 words. Pays $50-150. Spot news and successful business operations. Length: 100-800 words. Technical articles. Length: 400-1,000 words. Pays expenses of writers on assignment.
Photos: Buys up to 8×10 b&w photos purchased with or without mss, or on assignment. Pays $25 for first photo; $10 for each additional photo in series. Captions required.

TRUCK WORLD, Truck World Publications Ltd., 3–1610 Kebet Way, Port Coquitvam, British Columbia V3C 5W9 Canada. (604)942-2305. FAX: (604)942-4312. Editor: Rob Robertson. Trade journal on the trucking industry. "*Truck World* is designed to reach people directly or indirectly employed in the Canadian trucking industry. Readers are generally assumed to have an understanding of the industry." We also publish *The Truckers' Almanac* (annual) and *Transport Electronic News* (quarterly). Estab. 1984. Pays on publication. Publishes an average of 2 months after acceptance. Byline given. Buys first North American serial rights. Previously published submissions OK. Query for electronic submissions. Reports in 2 weeks on queries; 1 month on mss. Free sample copy.
Nonfiction: Humor, interview/profile, new product, photo feature and technical. "No personal trucking experiences. Stick to objective reporting on industry issues in Canada and the U.S." Buys 25 mss/year. Query with published clips. Length: 200-2,000 words. Pays $75-800. Pays expenses of writers on assignment.
Photos: State availability of photos with submissions or send photos with submission. Reviews 5×7 color or b&w prints. Offers no additional payment for photos accepted with ms. Captions and identification of subjects required. Buys one-time rights.
Columns/Departments: Finance (general pieces on finance and leasing relating to trucking industry), 500-1,000 words; Maintenance (general tips on trucking maintenance), 50-500 words; and Computers (latest in computer systems for trucking industry), 500-1,000 words. Buys 10 mss/year. Query with published clips. Pays $20-500.

Tips: "Potential contributors must have an awareness of the trucking industry. Do not attempt to write technical articles unless you have substantial knowledge in truck maintenance and operation. We are looking for more contributors from eastern Canada to report on the trucking industry generally. U.S. writers are needed to report on the latest trends in the industry."

WARD'S AUTO WORLD, % 28 W. Adams, Detroit MI 48226. (313)962-4433. FAX: (313)962-4456. Editorial Director: David C. Smith. Editor: Edward K. Miller. 10% freelance written. Prefers to work with published/ established writers; works with a small number of new/unpublished writers each year. For top and middle management in all phases of auto industry. Also includes heavy-duty vehicle coverage. Monthly magazine. Estab. 1924. Circ. 92,000. Pays on publication. Pay varies for kill fee. Byline given. Buys all rights. Phone queries OK. Submit seasonal/holiday material 1 month in advance. Query for electronic submissions. Reports in 2 weeks. Publishes ms an average of 1 month after acceptance. Free sample copy and writer's guidelines.
Nonfiction: Expose, general interest, international automotive news, historical, humor, interview, new product, photo feature and technical. Few consumer type articles. No "nostalgia or personal history stories (like 'My Favorite Car')." Buys 4-8 mss/year. Query. Length: 700-5,000 words. Pays $200-750. Sometimes pays the expenses of writers on assignment.
Photos: "We're heavy on graphics." Submit photo material with query. Pay varies for 8×10 b&w prints or transparencies. Captions required. Buys one-time rights.
Tips: "Don't send poetry, how-to and 'My Favorite Car' stuff. They don't stand a chance. This is a business newsmagazine and operates on a news basis just like any other newsmagazine. We like solid, logical, well-written pieces with *all* holes filled."

Aviation and Space

In this section are journals for aviation business executives, airport operators and aviation technicians. Publications for professional and private pilots can be found in the Consumer Aviation section.

AG-PILOT INTERNATIONAL MAGAZINE, Graphics Plus, 405 Main St., Mt Vernon WA 98273. (206)336-2045. FAX: (206)336-2506. Editor: Tom J. Wood. Executive Editor: Rocky Kemp. Emphasizes agricultural aerial application (crop dusting). "This is intended to be a fun-to-read, technical, as well as humorous, and serious publication for the ag pilot and operator. They are our primary target." 20% freelance written. Monthly magazine. Estab. 1978. Circ. 8,400. Pays on publication. Publishes ms an average of 3 months after acceptance. Buys all rights. Byline given unless writer requests name held. Reports in 2 weeks. Sample copy for 9×12 SAE with 7 first class stamps; writer's guidelines for #10 SASE.
Nonfiction: Expose (of EPA, OSHA, FAA or any government function concerned with this industry); general interest; historical; interview (of well-known ag/aviation person); nostalgia; personal opinion; new product; personal experience; and photo feature. "If we receive an article, in any area we have solicited, it is quite possible this person could contribute intermittently. The international input is what we desire. Industry-related material is a must. *No newspaper clippings.*" Send complete ms. Length: 800-1,500 words. Pays $50-200. Sometimes pays the expenses of writers on assignment.
Photos: "We would like one color or b&w (5×7 preferred) with the manuscript, if applicable—it will help increase your chance of publication." Four color. Offers no additional payment for photos accepted with ms. Captions preferred, model release required.
Columns/Departments: International (of prime interest, crop dusting-related); Embryo Birdman (should be written, or appear to be written, by a beginner spray pilot); The Chopper Hopper (by anyone in the helicopter industry); Trouble Shooter (ag aircraft maintenance tips); and Catchin' The Corner (written by a person obviously skilled in the crop dusting field of experience or other interest-capturing material related to the industry). Send complete ms. Length: 800-1,500 words. Pays $25-100.
Poetry: Interested in all agri-aviation related poetry. Buys 1/issue. Submit no more than 2 at one time. Maximum length: one 20 inch x 48 picas maximum. Pays $10-50.
Fillers: Short jokes, short humor and industry-related newsbreaks. Length: 10-100 words. Pays $5-20.
Tips: "Writers should be witty and knowledgeable about the crop dusting aviation world. Material *must* be agricultural/aviation-oriented. *Crop dusting or nothing!*"

AIR LINE PILOT, Magazine of Professional Flight Crews, Air Line Pilots Association, 535 Herndon Parkway, Box 1169, Herndon VA 22069. (703)689-4176. Editor: Esperison Martinez, Jr. 10% freelance written. Prefers to work with published/established writers. A monthly magazine for airline pilots covering "aviation industry information—economics, avionics, equipment, systems, safety—that affects a pilot's life in professional sense." Also includes information about management/labor relations trends, contract negotiations, etc. Circ. 60,000. **Pays on acceptance.** Publishes ms an average of 6 months after acceptance. Offers 35% kill fee. Buys first serial rights and makes work-for-hire assignments. Submit seasonal/holiday material 6 months in advance. Query for electronic submissions. Reports in 2 months. Sample copy $2 with 9 × 12 SAE; writer's guidelines for #10 SASE.

Nonfiction: Historical/nostalgic, humor, interview/profile, photo feature and technical. "We are backlogged with historical submissions and prefer not to receive unsolicited submissions at this time." Buys 20 mss/year. Query with or without published clips, or send complete ms. Length: 1,000-3,000 words. Pays $100-800 for assigned articles; pays $50-500 for unsolicited articles.

Photos: Send photos with submission. Reviews contact sheets, 35mm transparencies and 8 × 10 prints. Offers $10-25/photo. Identification of subjects required. Buys one-time rights.

Tips: "For our feature section, we seek aviation industry information that affects the life of a professional airline pilot from a career standpoint. We also seek material that affects his life from a job security and work environment standpoint. Historical material that addresses the heritage of the profession or the advancement of the industry is also sought. Any airline pilot featured in an article must be an Air Line Pilots Association member in good standing."

AIRPORT SERVICES MAGAZINE, Lakewood Publications, 50 S. 9th St., Minneapolis MN 55402. (612)333-0471. Managing Editor: Karl Bremer. 33% freelance written. Emphasizes management of airports and airport-based businesses. Monthly magazine. Estab. 1961. Circ. 20,000. **Pays on acceptance.** Publishes ms an average of 3 months after acceptance. Buys one-time rights, exclusive in our industry. Byline given. Phone queries OK. Submit seasonal/holiday material 3 months in advance. Query for electronic submission. Reports in 1 month. Free sample copy and writer's guidelines.

Nonfiction: How-to (manage an airport or aviation service company; work with local governments, etc.); interview (with a successful operator); and technical (how to manage a maintenance shop, snow removal operations, airport terminal, security operations). "No flying, no airport nostalgia or product puff pieces. We don't want pieces on how one company's product solved everyone's problem (how one airport or aviation business solved its problem with a certain product is okay). No descriptions of airport construction projects that don't discuss applications for other airports. Plain 'how-to' story lines, please." Buys 40-50 mss/year, "but at least half are short (750-1,000 words) items for inclusion in one of our monthly departments." Query. Length: 750-3,000 words. Pays $100 for most department articles, $200-400 for features.

Photos: State availability of photos with query. Payment for photos is included in total purchase price. Uses color and b&w photos, charts and line drawings. Uses color only on cover, transparencies 35mm or larger.

Tips: "Writing style should be lively, informal and straightforward, but the *subject matter* must be as functional and as down-to-earth as possible. Trade magazines are *business* magazines that must help readers do their jobs better. Frequent mistakes are using industry vendors/suppliers rather than users and industry officials as *sources*, especially in endorsing products or approaches, and directing articles to pilots or aviation consumers rather than to our specialized audience of aviation business managers and airport managers."

‡JET CARGO NEWS, For Air Shipping Decision-Makers, P.O. Box 920952, #398, Houston TX 77292-0952. (713)681-4760. FAX: (713)682-3871. Editor: Pat Chandler. 50% freelance written. Works with a small number of new/unpublished writers each year. Designed to serve international industry concerned with moving goods by air. "It brings to shippers and manufacturers spot news of airline and aircraft development, air routes, shipping techniques, innovations and rates." Monthly. Estab. 1968. Circ. 25,000. Buys all rights. Buys up to 50 mss/year. Pays on publication. Publishes ms an average of 2 months after acceptance. No simultaneous submissions. Query for electronic submissions. Submit seasonal material 1 month in advance. Reports in 1 month if postage is included. Submit complete ms. Sample copy for 10 × 13 SAE with 5 first class stamps.

Nonfiction: "Direct efforts to the shipper. Tell him about airline service, freight forwarder operations, innovations within the industry, new products, aircraft, packaging, material handling, hazardous materials, computerization of shipping, and pertinent news to the industry. Use a tight newspaper format. The writer must know marketing." Buys informational articles, case studies, how-to's, interviews and coverage of successful business operations. Length: 1,500 words maximum. Pays $4/inch. Sometimes pays the expenses of writers on assignment.

Photos: 8 × 10 b&w glossy prints purchased with and without mss; captions required. Pays $10.

Tips: A frequent mistake is missing target readers and their interests. With short articles and fillers the writer exhibits his/her initiative. "We have moved toward a news orientation since 1988. We hope to generate more case studies of successful shipping solutions and pay a 25 percent premium rate for them. We also hope to see more wrap-ups from a variety of contributors."

WINGS WEST, The Western Aviation Magazine, CAVU Communications, Inc., 89 Sherman St. Denver CO 80203. (303)778-7145. FAX: (303)837-0256. Editor: Babette André. 50% freelance written. Bimonthly magazine on aviation and aerospace in the west. Estab. 1984. Circ. 20,000. Pays on publication. "Writer must bill us." Publishes ms an average of 6 months after acceptance. Byline given. Offers $25 kill fee. Buys all rights. Submit seasonal/holiday material 6 months in advance. Previously published submissions OK. Query for electronic submissions. Sample copy available. Free writer's guidelines.

Nonfiction: General interest, how-to, humor, new product, opinion, mountain flying, photo feature and travel. (July/August—Airshow issue; Nov./Dec.—Holidays.) Buys 18 mss/year. Query with published clips. Length: 800-1,800 words. Pays $50-150.
Fiction: Interested in new ideas. Query.
Photos: Send photos with submission. Reviews contact sheets, transparencies and prints. Offers $25-50. Captions, model releases and identification of subjects required. Buys all rights.
Columns/Departments: Sparky Imeson (personal experiences, seasoned columnist); Medical (aeromedical factors); and Legal (FARS, enforcement), Mountain Flying, Travel and Safety, 800 words. Query with published clips. Pays $25-50.
Fillers: Anecdotes, facts, newsbreaks and short humor. Buys 14/year. Length: 50-150 words. Pays $10-15.
Tips: "Read the past 3 issues as well as a dozen other aviation publications every month. Imagination is the key. We like to do things other aviation publications don't do. Know the national and regional aviation publication market."

Beverages and Bottling

Manufacturers, distributors and retailers of soft drinks and alcoholic beverages read these publications. Publications for bar and tavern operators and managers of restaurants are classified in the Hotels, Motels, Clubs, Resorts and Restaurants category.

‡**AMERICAN BREWER,** P.O. Box 510, Hayward CA 94541. (415)538-9500 (a.m. only). Publisher: Bill Owens. Managing Editor: John Faulkner. 100% freelance written. Quarterly magazine covering micro-breweries. Estab. 1986. Circ. 4,000. Pays on pubilcation. Publishes ms an average of 4 months after acceptance. Byline given. Buys one-time rights. Previously published submissions OK. Query for electronic submissions. Reports in 2 weeks on queries. Sample copy for $5.02.
Nonfiction: Humor, opinion and travel. Query. Length: 1,500-2,500 words. Pays $50-250 for assigned articles.

‡**BEER WHOLESALER,** Beverage Management Associates, Inc., Suite 4, 11460 W. 44th Ave., Wheat Ridge CO 80033. (303)425-4668. Editor: Daniel Morales Brink. 20% freelance written. Bimonthly magazine covering beverage wholesaling. *Beer Wholesaler* is edited for those in the beer distribution field. Editorial covers management, current sales promotions, national conventions, legal news, news on imported beers and various phases of the business activities of interest to the beer wholesaler. Also included are special features on warehouses, truck fleet management, beer consumption trends, computers/data processing systems, and other features pertinent to the beer distributor. *Beer Wholesaler* provides articles on individual wholesale operations as well as interpretive analysis of the industry. Estab. 1968. Circ. 3,217. Pays on acceptance. Byline given. Offers expenses plus 50% kill fee. Buys first North American serial rights. Submit seasonal/holiday material 3 months in advance. Simultaneous and previously published submissions OK. Query for electronic submissions. Reports in 2 weeks. Sample copy for $2. Free writer's guidelines.
Nonfiction: Special upcoming issues: Import issue (May); European Imports Issue (January, 1991); and Transportation Issue (September). Buys 6 mss/year. Query with published clips. Length: 300-3,000 words. Pays $50 minimum for assigned articles; $30-300 for unsolicited articles. Pays expenses of writers on assignment.
Photos: Send photos with submission. Reviews contact sheets and 35mm and 5×7 transparencies. Offers $20-100 per photo. Captions and identification of subjects required. Buys one-time rights.
Columns/Departments: Sales and Marketing Retail (retailer/wholesaler interface). Buys 2 mss/year. Query with published clips. Length: 250-1,500 words. Pays $15-150.
Fillers: Anecdotes, facts, gags to be illustrated by cartoonist, newsbreaks and short humor. Buys 10/year. Length: 10-300 words. Pays $5-50.
Tips: "We appreciate suggestions for possible stories submitted by the writer in his/her areas of expertise or interest. Writers have the best chance breaking in with industry interviews/profiles, emphasis on human interest stories and details of growth in business."

BEVERAGE WORLD, Keller International Publishing Corp., 150 Great Neck Rd., Great Neck NY 11021. (516)829-9210. Editor: Alan Wolf. Monthly magazine on the beverage industry. Circ. 32,000. **Pays on acceptance.** Publishes ms an average of 2 months after acceptance. Byline given. Buys all rights. Submit seasonal/holiday material 2 months in advance. Simultaneous submissions OK. Free sample copy and writer's guidelines.
Nonfiction: How-to (increase profit/sales), interview/profile and technical. Buys 15 mss/year. Query with published clips. Length:1,000-2,500 words. Pays $200-600. Sometimes pays expenses of writers on assignment.
Photos: State availability of photos with submission. Reviews contact sheets. Captions required. Buys one-time rights.
Columns/Departments: Buys 5 mss/year. Query with published clips. Length: 750-1,000 words. Pays $150-400.
Tips: "Requires background in beverage production and marketing. Business and/or technical writing experience *a must.*"

LA BARRIQUE, Kylix Media Inc.. Suite 414, 5165 Sherbrooke St. W., Montreal, Quebec, H4A 1T6 Canada. (514)481-5892. Editor: Nicole Barette-Ryan. 20% freelance written. A magazine on wine published 7 times/year. "The magazine, *written in French*, covers wines of the world specially written for the province of Québec consumers and restaurant trade. It covers wine books, restaurants, vintage reports and European suppliers." Pays on publication. Publishes ms an average of 2 months after acceptance. Byline given. Buys first North American serial rights. Submit seasonal/holiday material 6 months in advance. Simultaneous submissions OK. Reports in 6 weeks on queries.
Nonfiction: General interest, how-to, humor, interview/profile, new product, opinion and travel. Knowledge of wines given primary consideration. Length: 500-1,500 words. Pays $25-100 for unsolicited articles.
Photos: Send photos with submission. Reviews transparencies and prints. Offers $25-100 per photo. Identifiction of subjects required. Buys one-time rights.

MID-CONTINENT BOTTLER, 10741 El Monte, Overland Park KS 66207. (913)341-0020. FAX: (913)341-3025. Publisher: Floyd E. Sageser. 5% freelance written. Prefers to work with published/established writers. For "soft drink bottlers in the 20-state Midwestern area." Bimonthly. Estab. 1970. Not copyrighted. **Pays on acceptance.** Publishes ms an average of 2 months after acceptance. Buys first rights only. Reports "immediately." Sample copy for 9×12 SAE and 10 first class stamps; guidelines for #10 SASE.
Nonfiction: "Items of specific soft drink bottler interest with special emphasis on sales and merchandising techniques. Feature style desired." Buys 2-3 mss/year. Length: 2,000 words. Pays $15-100. Sometimes pays the expenses of writers on assignment.
Photos: Photos purchased with mss.

SOUTHERN BEVERAGE JOURNAL, 13225 SW 88th Ave., Miami FL 33176. (305)233-7230. FAX: (305)252-2580. Senior Editor: Jackie Preston. 60% freelance written. Works with a small number of new/unpublished writers each year, and is eager to work with new/unpublished writers. A monthly magazine for the alcohol beverage industry. Readers are personnel of bars, restaurants, package stores, night clubs, lounges and hotels—owners, managers and salespersons. Estab. 1945. Circ. 30,000. **Pays on acceptance.** Publishes ms an average of 3-4 months after acceptance. Byline given. Buys first rights. Submit seasonal/holiday material 3 months in advance. Query for electronic submissions. Reports in 1 month.
Nonfiction: General interest, historical, personal experience, interview/profile and success stories. Info on legislation (state) affecting alcohol beverage industry. No canned material. Buys 6 mss/year. Send complete ms. Length: 1,000-2,000 words. Pays 10¢/word for assigned articles.
Photos: State availability of photos with submission. Reviews 7×8 or 4×5 transparencies and 3×5 prints. Offers $10 maximum/photo. Identification of subjects required. Buys one-time rights.
Tips: "We are interested in legislation having to do with our industry and also views on trends, drinking and different beverages."

TEA & COFFEE TRADE JOURNAL, Lockwood Book Publishing Co., 130 W. 42nd St., New York NY 10036. (212)661-5980. FAX: (212)827-0945. Editor: Jane Phillips McCabe. 50% freelance written. Prefers to work with published/established writers. A monthly magazine covering the international coffee and tea market. "Tea and coffee trends are analyzed; transportation problems, new equipment for plants and packaging are featured." Circ. 5,000. Pays on publication. Publishes ms an average of 2 months after acceptance. Byline given. Makes work-for-hire assignments. Submit seasonal/holiday material 1 month in advance. Simultaneous submissions OK. Free sample copy.
Nonfiction: Exposé, historical/nostalgic, interview/profile, new product, photo feature and technical. Special issue includes the Coffee Market Forecast and Review (January). "No consumer related submissions. I'm only interested in the trade." Buys 60 mss/year. Query. Length: 750-1,500 words. Pays $5.50/published inch.
Photos: State availability of photos with submission. Reviews contact sheets, negatives, transparencies and prints. Pays $5.50/published inch. Captions and identification of subjects required. Buys one-time rights.
Columns/Departments: Specialties (gourmet trends); and Transportation (shipping lines). Buys 36 mss/year. Query. Pays $5.50/published inch.

VINEYARD & WINERY MANAGEMENT, 103 3rd St., Box 231, Watkins Glen NY 14891. (607)535-7133. FAX: (607)535-2998. Editor: J. William Moffett. 80% freelance written. A bimonthly trade journal on the management of winemaking and grape growing. Circ. 4,500. Pays on publication. Byline given. Buys first North American serial rights and occasionally simultaneous rights. Electronic submissions preferred. Query for formats. Reports in 3 weeks on queries; 1 month on mss. Free sample copy; writer's guidelines for #10 SASE.
Nonfiction: How-to, interview/profile and technical. Buys 30 mss/year. Query. Length: 300-5,000 words. Pays $30-750 for assigned articles; pays $30-500 for unsolicited articles. Pays some expenses of writers on some assignments.
Photos: State availability of photos with submission. Reviews contact sheets, negatives and transparencies. Identification of subjects required. "Black and white often purchased for $20 each to accompany story material; 35mm and/or 4×5 transparencies for $50 and up; 6 per year of vineyard and/or winery scene related to story. Query."

Fiction: Occasional short, humorous fiction related to vineyard/winery operation.
Tips: "We're looking for long term relationships with authors who know the business and write well."

WINES & VINES, 1800 Lincoln Ave., San Rafael CA 94901. FAX: (415)453-2517. Editor: Philip E. Hiaring. 10-20% freelance written. Works with a small number of new/unpublished writers each year. For everyone concerned with the grape and wine industry including winemakers, wine merchants, growers, suppliers, consumers, etc. Monthly magazine. Circ. 4,500. Buy first North American serial rights or simultaneous rights. **Pays on acceptance.** Publishes ms an average of 3 months after acceptance. Submit special material (outlook, January; vineyard, February; Man-of-the-Year, March; Brandy, April; export-import, May; enological, June; statistical, July; merchandising, August; marketing, September; equipment and supplies, November; champagne, December) 3 months in advance. Reports in 2 weeks. Sample copy for 11 × 14 SAE with $2.05 postage; free writer's guidelines.
Nonfiction: Articles of interest to the trade. "These could be on grape growing in unusual areas; new winemaking techniques; wine marketing, retailing, etc." Interview, historical, spot news, merchandising techniques and technical. No stories with a strong consumer orientation as against trade orientation. Author should know the subject matter, i.e., know proper grape growing/winemaking terminology. Buys 3-4 ms/year. Query. Length: 1,000-2,500 words. Pays 5¢/word. Sometimes pays the expenses of writers on assignment.
Photos: Pays $10 for 4 × 5 or 8 × 10 b&w photos purchased with mss. Captions required.
Tips: "Ours is a trade magazine for professionals. Therefore, we do not use 'gee-whiz' wine articles."

Book and Bookstore

Publications for book trade professionals from publishers to bookstore operators are found in this section. Journals for professional writers are classified in the Journalism and Writing category.

THE FEMINIST BOOKSTORE NEWS, P.O. Box 882554, San Francisco CA 94188. (415)626-1556. Editor: Carol Seajay. Managing Editor: Christine Chia. 10% freelance written. Works with a small number of new/unpublished writers each year. A bimonthly magazine covering feminist books and the women-in-print industry. "*Feminist Bookstore News* covers 'everything of interest' to the feminist bookstores, publishers and periodicals, books of interest and provides an overview of feminist publishing by mainstream publishers." Estab. 1976. Circ. 700. Pays on publication. Publishes ms an average of 2 months after acceptance. Byline sometimes given. Buys one-time rights. Simultaneous submissions OK. Reports in 3 weeks. Sample copy $5.
Nonfiction: Essays, exposé, how-to (run a bookstore); new product; opinion; and personal experience (in feminist book trade only). Special issues include Sidelines issue (July) and University Press issue (fall). No submissions that do not directly apply to the feminist book trade. Query with or without published clips, or send complete ms. Length: 250-2,000 words. Pays in copies when appropriate.
Photos: State availability of photos with submission. Model release and identification of subjects required. Buys one-time rights.
Fillers: Anecdotes, facts, newsbreaks and short humor. Length: 100-400 words. Pays $5-15.
Tips: "The writer must have several years experience in the feminist book industry. We publish very little by anyone else."

THE HORN BOOK MAGAZINE, The Horn Book, Inc., 14 Beacon St., Boston MA 02108. (617)227-1555. Editor: Anita Silvey. 25% freelance written. Prefers to work with published/established writers. Bimonthly magazine covering children's literature for librarians, booksellers, professors and students of children's literature. Circ. 22,000. Pays on publication. Publishes ms an average of 4 months after acceptance. Byline given. Buys one-time rights. Submit seasonal/holiday material 6 months in advance. Simultaneous queries, and simultaneous and photocopied submissions OK. Computer printout submissions acceptable; no dot-matrix. Reports in 6 weeks on queries; 2 months on mss. Free sample copy; writer's guidelines for SAE with 1 first class stamp.
Nonfiction: Interview/profile (children's book authors and illustrators). Buys 20 mss/year. Query or send complete ms. Length: 1,000-2,800 words. Pays $25-250.
Tips: "Writers have a better chance of breaking in to our publication with a query letter on a specific article they want to write."

Brick, Glass and Ceramics

These publications are read by manufacturers, dealers and managers of brick, glass and ceramic retail businesses. Other publications related to glass and ceramics are listed in the Consumer Art and Architecture and Consumer Hobby and Craft sections.

AMERICAN GLASS REVIEW, P.O. Box 2147, Clifton NJ 07015. (201)779-1600. FAX: (201)779-3242. Editor-in-Chief: Donald Doctorow. 10% freelance written. Monthly magazine. Pays on publication. Estab. 1888. Byline given. Phone queries OK. Buys first time rights. Submit seasonal/holiday material 2 months in advance of issue date. Reports in 3 weeks. Free sample copy and writer's guidelines; mention *Writer's Market* in request.
Nonfiction: Glass plant and glass manufacturing articles. Buys 3-4 mss/year. Query. Length: 1,500-3,000 words. Pays $200.
Photos: State availability of photos with query. No additional payment for b&w contact sheets. Captions preferred. Buys one-time rights.

‡**PROFESSIONAL STAINED GLASS**, The Edge Publishing Group, Inc., Toretta Lake Rd., P.O. Box 69, Brewster NY 10509. (914)279-7399. Editor: Chris Peterson. 90% freelance written. Monthly trade magazine on decorative glass. "We are a technical journal although freelancers can write by interviewing industry professionals and extrapolating from there. We also run profiles and fillers easily written by freelancers." Estab. 1980. Circ. 15,700. Pays on publication. Publishes ms an average of 2 months after acceptance. Byline given. Offers $25 kill fee. Buys first North American serial rights. Query for electronic submissions. Reports in 2 weeks. Free sample copy and writer's guidelines.
Nonfiction: Technical articles (glassworking techniques) and profiles of successful glass artists doing credible work. "We do not want fluffy newspaper pieces with series of quotes strung together. There is plenty of work here for the freelancer willing to interview, do a modest amount of research and put together a tight article." Buys 60 mss/year. Query. Length: 1,000-3,000 words. Pays $50-175.
Photos: State availability of photos with submission. Reviews contact sheets, 35mm transparencies and prints. Offers no additional payment for photos accepted with ms. Identification of subjects required. Buys one-time rights.
Columns/Departments: Profile (personality profile of industry artists and the work they do), 1,500 words; and Notable Works (brief introduction to unknown artist executing worthy work), 250 words. Buys 12 mss/year. Query.
Tips: "Writers should read our guidelines before writing anything and should discuss their article with an industry professional—not a hobbyist. If that person likes the idea, chances are we will too."

Building Interiors

Owners, managers and sales personnel of floor covering, wall covering and remodeling businesses read the journals listed in this category. Interior design and architecture publications may be found in the Consumer Art, Design and Collectibles category. For journals aimed at other construction trades see the Construction and Contracting section.

ALUMI-NEWS, Work-4 Projects Ltd., Box 400 Victoria Station, Westmount, Québec H3Z 2V8 Canada. (514)489-4941. FAX: (514)489-5505. Publisher: Nachmi Artzy. Exec. Director: Shelley Blidner. 75% freelance written. Home renovation—exterior building products trade journal published 6 times/year. "We are dedicated to the grass roots of the industry: installers, dealers, contractors. We do not play up to our advertisers nor government." Estab. 1976. Circ. 18,000. Pays on publication. Byline usually given. Buys all rights. Simultaneous and previously published submissions OK. Free sample copy.
Nonfiction: Exposé, how-to (pertaining to dealers—profit, production, or management.); new product (exterior building products); technical and survey results (trends or products in our industry). Buys 12-24 mss/year. Query with published clips. Length: 200-2,000 words. Pays 10-20¢/word. Pays in contributor copies or other premiums if mutually suitable. Sometimes pays expenses of writers on assignment.
Photos: State availability of photos with submission. Reviews negatives, transparencies and prints. Pays $300 maximum per photo. Captions and identification of subjects required. Buys all rights.
Columns/Departments: Industry News (company profile: new location, product, personnel), 100-250 words; and Profiles (interviews), 1,000-2,500 words. Query with published clips. Length: 75-300 words. Pays 10-20¢/word.
Fillers: Facts and short humor. Length 5-50 words. Pays 10-20¢/word.
Tips: "Submit articles not found in *every* similar publication. Find a new angle; Canadian content."

REMODELING, Hanley-Wood, Inc., Suite 475, 655 15th St. NW, Washington DC 20005. (202)737-0717. FAX: (202)737-2439. Editor: Wendy Jordan. 5% freelance written. A monthly magazine covering residential and light commercial remodeling. "We cover the best new ideas in remodeling design, business, construction and products." Estab. 1985. Circ. 92,000. Pays on publication. Publishes ms an average of 3 months after acceptance. Byline given. Offers 5¢/word kill fee. Buys first North American serial rights. Query for electronic submissions. Reports in 1 month. Free sample copy and writer's guidelines.

Nonfiction: Interview/profile, new product and technical. Buys 4 mss/year. Query with published clips. Length: 250-1,000 words. Pays 20¢/word. Sometimes pays the expenses of writers on assignment.
Photos: State availability of photos with submission. Reviews slides, 4×5 transparencies, and 8×10 prints. Offers $25-100/photo. Captions, model releases, and identification of subjects required. Buys one-time rights.
Tips: "The areas of our publication most open to freelancers are news and new product news."

WALLS & CEILINGS, 8602 N. 40th St., Tampa FL 33604. (813)989-9300. FAX: (813)980-3982. Managing Editor: Melissa Wells. 10% freelance written. Prefers to work with published/established writers, and works with a small number of new/unpublished writers each year. For contractors involved in lathing and plastering, drywall, acoustics, fireproofing, curtain walls, movable partitions together with manufacturers, dealers, and architects. Monthly magazine. Estab. 1938. Circ. 15,000. Pays on publication. Publishes ms an average of 4-6 months after acceptance. Buys first North American serial rights. Byline given. Phone queries OK. Submit seasonal/holiday material 3 months in advance. Query for electronic submissions. Reports in 3 weeks. Sample copy with 9×12 SAE and $2 postage.
Nonfiction: How-to (drywall and plaster construction and business management); and interview. Buys 12 mss/year. Query. Length: 200-1,500 words. Pays $50-150 maximum. Sometimes pays the expenses of writers on assignment.
Photos: State availability of photos with query. Pays $5 for 8×10 b&w prints. Captions required. Buys one-time rights.
Tips: "We would like to receive wall and ceiling finishing features about unique designs and applications in new buildings (from high-rise to fast food restaurants), fireproofing, and acoustical design with photography (b&w and color)."

Business Management

These publications cover trends, general theory and management practices for business owners and top-level business executives. Publications that use similar material but have a less technical slant are listed in the Consumer Business and Finance section. Journals for middle management, including supervisors and office managers, appear in the Management and Supervision section. Those for industrial plant managers are listed under Industrial Operations and under sections for specific industries, such as Machinery and Metal. Publications for office supply store operators are included in the Office Environment and Equipment section.

CHIEF EXECUTIVE, 233 Park Ave. S., New York NY 10003. (212)979-4810. FAX: (212)979-7431. Editor: J.P. Donlon. Written by and for CEOs. Limited freelance opportunity. Published 9 times/year. Circ. 35,000. **Pays on acceptance.** Publishes ms an average of 2-3 months after acceptance. Byline given. Offers kill fee. Buys world serial rights. Free writer's guidelines. Query required for all departments. Unsolicited manuscripts will not be returned. Pays $300-800. Pays previously agreed upon expenses of writers on assignment.
Photos: State availability of photos with submission. Reviews 4-color transparencies and slides. Offers $100 maximum per photo. Captions required. Buys one-time rights.
Column/Departments: N.B. (profile of CEO/Chairman/President of mid- to large-size company), 400-500 words; Amenities, 1,000-1,500 words; CEO-At-Leisure, 1,000-1,500 words; Business Travel (provides CEOs with *key names* and information on business/government inner network for city/area being visited—who to know to get things done) 1,000-1,500 words.

‡COMMERCE MAGAZINE, 200 N. LaSalle St., Chicago IL 60601. (312)580-6900. Editor: Kelly O'Rourke. For top businessmen and industrial leaders in the greater Chicago area. Monthly magazine. Circ. 10,000. Buys all rights. Buys 30-40 mss/year. **Pays on acceptance.** Query.
Nonfiction: Business articles and pieces of general interest to top business executives. "We select our freelancers and assign topics. Many of our writers are from local newspapers. Considerable freelance material is used but almost exclusively on assignment from Chicago-area specialists within a particular business sector. We do accept story ideas."

COMMUNICATION·BRIEFINGS, Encoders, Inc., 140 S. Broadway, Pitman NJ 08071. (609)589-3503. FAX: (609)582-6572. Executive Editor: Frank Grazian. 15% freelance written. Prefers to work with published/established writers. A monthly newsletter covering business communication and business management. "Most readers are in middle and upper management. They comprise public relations professionals, editors of company publications, marketing and advertising managers, fund raisers, directors of associations and foundations, school and college administrators, human resources professionals, and other middle managers who want to communicate better on the job." Estab. 1980. Circ. 40,000. **Pays on acceptance.** Publishes ms an average of 2-3 months after acceptance. Byline given sometimes on Bonus Items and on other items if idea originates with the writer. Buys one-time rights. Submit seasonal/holiday material 2 months in advance. Previously published submissions OK, "but must be rewritten to conform to our style." Reports in 1 month. Sample copy and writer's guidelines for #10 SAE and 2 first class stamps.

Nonfiction: "Most articles we buy are of the 'how-to' type. They consist of practical ideas, techniques and advice that readers can use to improve business communication and management. Areas covered: writing, speaking, listening, employee communication, human relations, public relations, interpersonal communication, persuasion, conducting meetings, advertising, marketing, fund raising, telephone techniques, teleconferencing, selling, improving publications, handling conflicts, negotiating, etc. Because half of our subscribers are in the nonprofit sector, articles that appeal to both profit and nonprofit organizations are given top priority." *Short Items:* Articles consisting of one or two brief tips that can stand alone. Length: 40-70 words. *Articles:* A collection of tips or ideas that offer a solution to a communication or management problem or that show a better way to communicate or manage. Examples: "How to produce slogans that work," "The wrong way to criticize employees," "Mistakes to avoid when leading a group discussion," and "5 ways to overcome writer's block." Length: 125-150 words. *Bonus Items:* In-depth pieces that probe one area of communication or management and cover it as thoroughly as possible. Examples: "Producing successful special events," "How to evaluate your newsletter," and "How to write to be understood." Length: 1,300 words. Buys 30-50 mss/year. Pays $15-35 for 40- to 150-word pieces; Bonus Items, $200. Pays the expenses of writers on assignment.

Tips: "Our readers are looking for specific and practical ideas and tips that will help them communicate better both within their organizations and with outside publics. Most ideas are rejected because they are too general or too elementary for our audience. Our style is down-to-earth and terse. We pack a lot of useful information into short articles. Our readers are busy executives and managers who want information dispatched quickly and without embroidery. We omit anecdotes, lengthy quotes and long-winded exposition. The writer has a better chance of breaking in at our publication with short articles and fillers since we buy only six major features (bonus items) a year. We require queries on longer items and bonus items. Writers may submit short tips (40-70 words) without querying. The most frequent mistakes made by writers in completing an article for us are failure to master the style of our publication and to understand our readers' needs."

EARLY CHILDHOOD NEWS, Peter Li, Inc. 2451 E. River Rd., Dayton OH 45420. (513)294-5785. FAX: (513)294-7840. Editor: Janet Coburn. 75% freelance written. Bimonthly trade journal on child care centers. "Our publication is a news and service magazine for owners, directors and administrators of child care centers serving children from age 6 weeks to 2nd grade." Estab. 1988. Circ. 30,000. Pays on publication. Publishes ms an average of 3-4 months after acceptance. Copyright pending. Buys first rights. Submit seasonal/holiday material 5-6 months in advance. Query for electronic submissions. Sample copy $4 with 9×12 SAE and 2 first class stamps.

Nonfiction: How-to (how I solved a problem other center directors may face), interview/profile personal experience and business aspects of child care centers. "No articles directed at early childhood teachers or lesson plans." Buys 15 mss/year. Query with or without published clips, or send complete ms. Length: 500-1,500 words. Pays $50-150.

Photos: Send photos with submission if available. Reviews 35mm and 4×5 transparencies and 5×7 prints. Captions, model releases and identification of subjects required. Buys one-time rights.

Fillers: Facts and newsbreaks. Length: 100-250 words. Pays $10-25.

Tips: "Send double-spaced typed mss and pay attention to grammar and punctuation. Enclose SASE for faster reply. No scholarly pieces with footnotes and bibliography. No activities/lesson plans for use with kids. We need short, easy-to-read articles written in popular style that give child care center owners information they can use right away to make their centers better, more effective, more efficient, etc. Feature stories and fillers are most open to freelancers. Be specific and concrete; use examples. Tightly focused topics are better than general 'The Day Care Dilemma' types."

FARM STORE MERCHANDISING, Miller Publishing, P.O. Box 2400, Minneapolis MN 55343. (612)931-0211. FAX: (612)931-0217. Editor: Jan Johnson. 20% freelance written. Eager to work with new/unpublished writers. A monthly magazine for small business owners who sell to farmers. Estab. 1886. Primary business lines are bulk and bagged feed, animal health products, grain storage, agricultural chemicals. Pays on publication. Publishes ms an average of 3 months after acceptance. Byline given. Buys one-time rights. Submit seasonal/holiday material 4 months in advance. Simultaneous and previously published submissions OK. Reports in 2 months. Free sample copy and writer's guidelines.

Nonfiction: How-to (subjects must be business-oriented, credit, taxes, inventory, hiring, firing, etc.); interview/profile (with successful agribusiness dealers or industry leaders); opinion (on controversial industry issues); personal experiences (good or bad ways to run a business); photo features (people-oriented); and technical (how to maintain sprayers, what's the best fertilizer spreader, etc.). Buys 8 mss/year. Query. Length: 500-2,000 words. Pays $100-300 for assigned articles; pays $50-150 for unsolicited articles. Sometimes pays the expenses of writers on assignment.

Photos: State availability of photos with submission. Reviews contact sheets, 2×4 transparencies and 5×7 prints. Offers $10-50 per photo. Identification of subjects required. Buys one-time rights.

Tips: "The area of our publication most open to freelancers is features on successful farm store dealers. Submit two to three black and white photos or color slides. Keep the article under 2,000 words and don't get bogged down in technical details. Tell what sets their business apart and why it works. General business articles also are needed, especially if they have a rural, small-business slant."

FINANCIAL EXECUTIVE, Financial Executives Institute, 10 Madison Ave., Morristown NJ 07962-1938. Editor: Catherine M. Coult. Associate Editor: Robin L. Couch. 5% freelance written. A bimonthly magazine for corporate financial management. "*Financial Executive* is published for senior financial executives of major corporations and explores corporate accounting and treasury related issues without being anti-business." Circ. 18,000. Pays following acceptance. Byline given. Buys first North American serial rights. Reports in 1 month on queries; 2 months on mss. Sample copy $5; writer's guidelines for #10 SASE.

Nonfiction: Analysis, based on interviews, of accounting, finance, and tax developments of interest to financial executives. Buys 3 mss/year. Query with published clips; no unsolicited mss. Length: 1,500-2,500 words. Pays $500-1,000.

Tips: "Most article ideas come from editors, so the query approach is best. (Address correspondence to Robin L. Couch.) We use business or financial articles that follow a Wall Street Journal approach—a fresh idea, with its significance (to financial executives), quotes, anecdotes and an interpretation or evaluation. Our content will follow developments in market volatility, M&A trend, regulatory changes, tax legislation, Congressional hearings/legislation, re business and financial reporting. There is a growing interest in international business and impact of technology, such as exchanges. We have very high journalistic standards."

MAY TRENDS, George S. May International Company. 303 S. Northwest Hwy., Park Ridge IL 60068. (312)825-8806. Editor: John E. McArdle. 20% freelance written. Works with a small number of new/unpublished writers each year. For owners and managers of small and medium-sized businesses, hospitals and nursing homes, trade associations, Better Business Bureaus, educational institutions and newspapers. Magazine published without charge 3 times a year. Estab. 1967. Circ. 30,000. Buys all rights. Byline given. Buys 10-15 mss/year. **Pays on acceptance.** Publishes ms an average of 4-6 months after acceptance. Returns rejected material immediately. Query or submit complete ms. Reports in 2 weeks. Sample copy available on request for 9×12 SAE with 2 first class stamps.

Nonfiction: "We prefer articles dealing with how to solve problems of specific industries (manufacturers, wholesalers, retailers, service businesses, small hospitals and nursing homes) where contact has been made with key executives whose comments regarding their problems may be quoted. We want problem solving articles, *not* success stories that laud an individual company. We like articles that give the business manager concrete suggestions on how to deal with specific problems—i.e., '5 steps to solve . . .,' '6 key questions to ask when . . .,' and '4 tell-tale signs indicating . . .' " Focus is on marketing, economic and technological trends that have an impact on medium- and small-sized businesses, not on the "giants"; automobile dealers coping with existing dull markets; and contractors solving cost-inventory problems. Will consider material on successful business operations and merchandising techniques. Length: 2,000-3,000 words. Pays $150-250.

Tips: Query letter should tell "type of business and problems the article will deal with. We specialize in the problems of small (20-100 employees, $500,000-3,000,000 volume) businesses (manufacturing, wholesale, retail and service), plus medium and small health care facilities. We are now including nationally known writers in each issue—writers like the Vice Chairman of the Federal Reserve Bank, the U.S. Secretary of the Treasury; names like George Bush and Malcolm Baldridge; titles like the Chairman of the Joint Committee on Accreditation of Hospitals; and Canadian Minister of Export. This places extra pressure on freelance writers to submit very good articles. Frequent mistakes: 1) Writing for big business, rather than small, 2) using language that is too academic."

THE MEETING MANAGER, Meeting Planners International, Suite 5018, 1950 Stemmons, Dallas TX 75207. (214)746-5222. FAX: (214)746-5248. Editor: Tina Berres Filipski. 50% freelance written. Monthly magazine on meetings/hospitality/travel. Estab. 1980. Circ. 10,000. **Pays on acceptance.** Publishes ms an average of 2 months after acceptance. Byline given. Query. Reports in 1 month. Free sample and writer's guidelines.

Nonfiction: How-to, trends, humor, inspirational, interview/profile, opinion and personal experience. Query with published clips. Length: 500-2,500 words. Pays $300-400.

Photos: State availability of photos with submission. Reviews contact sheets and transparencies. Offers no additional payment for photos accepted with ms. Captions required.

MEETING NEWS, Facts, News, Ideas For Convention, Meeting and Incentive Planners, Gralla Publications, 1515 Broadway, New York NY 10036. (212)869-1300. FAX: (212)302-6273. Publisher: Peter Johnsmeyer. Editor: Leah Krakinowski. A monthly business travel magazine covering news, facts, ideas and methods in meeting planning and special events; hospitality, industry developments, airline, hotel and business tax legislation, hotel development and acquisitions, new labor contracts, business practices and costs for meeting planners. Estab. 1976. Circ. 75,000. **Pays on acceptance.** Byline given. Buys first rights. Reports in 1 month on queries; 2 weeks on mss. Free sample copy.

Nonfiction: Travel and specifics on how a group improved its meetings or trade shows, saved money or drew more attendees. "Stress is on business and travel articles—facts and figures." Seven special issues covering specific states as meeting destination—Florida/Canada/Texas/California/New York and Arizona. No general or philosophical pieces. Buys 50-75 mss/year. Query with published clips. Length: varies. Pays variable rates.

Tips: "Special issues focusing on certain states as meeting sites are most open. Best suggestion—query in writing, with clips, on any area of expertise about these states that would be of interest to people planning meetings there. Example: food/entertainment, specific sports, group activities, etc."

‡THE MINI-STORAGE MESSENGER, MiniCo Inc.. 2531 W. Dunlap Ave., Phoenix AZ 85021. (800)824-6864. Director of Publishing: Joe Mininni. 65% freelance written. A monthly magazine on the self-service storage industry. "We speak to self-storage owners, operators and managers, as well as those on the industry's fringes such as appraisers and bankers, architects, zoning officials, etc. We strive for balanced multi-source material with solid, practical information." Estab. 1975. Circ. 4,000. Pays within 30 days of acceptance. Publishes ms an average of 2 months after acceptance. Offers 25% kill fee. Buys first rights and second serial (reprint) rights. Reports in 2 weeks. Free sample copy and writer's guidelines.

Nonfiction: How-to (practical information on self-storage and related "storage" industries, i.e. boat, RV storage), interview/profile, new product, photo feature and technical. "One-source, first-person essays accepted." Buys 100 mss/year. Query with published clips. Length: 1,500-2,000 words. Pays $200-350. Pays the expenses of writers' phone bills. State availability of photos with submission. Reviews transparencies (2¼ × 2¼). Offers $50-150 per photo. Identification of subjects required. Buys all rights.

Columns/Departments: Construction (construction issues on self-storage, practical how-to information), 1,000 words; Operations (tips on succssful operating techniques on self-storage), 1,000 words; Managements (tips and trends in mini-storage management), 1,000 words; Marketing (tips and trends in mini-storage marketing), 1,000 words. Buys 50 mss/year. Query with published clips. Length: 1,000-1,200 words. Pays $200.

Tips: "Get to know self-storage industry or dig up something new about the industry or its people. We are very receptive to writers with their own strong ideas. Diligence and original research and sources are ways to impress us. New slants and story ideas will get our attention."

RECOGNITION & PROMOTIONS BUSINESS, DF Publications, 26 Summit St., Box 1230, Brighton MI 48116. (313)227-2614. FAX: (313)229-8230. Editor: James J. Farrell. Managing Editor: Michael J. Davis. 40% freelance written. Prefers to work with published/established writers. A monthly magazine for the recognition and specialty advertising industry, especially awards. "*RPB* is published for retail business owners and owners involved in the recognition/specialty industry. Our aim is to provide solid, down-to-earth information to help them succeed in business, as well as news and ideas about our industry." **Pays on acceptance.** Publishes ms an average of 4 months after acceptance. Buys all rights or makes work-for-hire assignments. Submit seasonal/holiday matcrial 6 months in advance. Previously published submissions OK "if we are so informed." Query for electronic submissions. Reports in 3 weeks. "Sample copy and writer's guidelines sent to those who send us writing samples or query about an article."

Nonfiction: Historical, how-to, interview/profile, new product, photo feature, technical and business and marketing. "Our readers are becoming more involved in the specialty advertising industry. No vague, general articles that could be aimed at any audience. We prefer to receive a query from writers before reviewing a manuscript. Also, a large number of our freelance articles are given to writers on assignment." Buys 20-30 mss/year. Query with clips ("clips do not havc to bc published, but should give us an indication of writer's ability"). Length: depends on subject matter. Pays $50-225.

Photos: Send photos with submission. Reviews 8 × 10 prints. Offers no additional payment for photos accepted with ms, "but we take the photos into consideration when deciding rate of compensation for the assignment." Captions, model releases and identification of subjects required. Buys all rights; "semi-exclusive rights may be purchased, for our industry, depending on subject."

Tips: "The best way to work for *RPB* is to write to us with information about your background and experience (a resume, if possible), and several samples of your writing. We are most interested in receiving business and marketing articles from freelancers. These would provide solid, down-to-earth information for the smaller business owner. For example, recent articles we have included were on tips for writing good business letters; the proper use of titles for awards; legal and practical considerations of setting up a corporation vs. a sole proprietorship. Articles should be written in clear, plain English with examples and anecdotes to add interest to the subject matter."

RECORDS MANAGEMENT QUARTERLY, Association of Records Managers and Administrators, Inc., P.O. Box 4580, Silver Spring MD 20914. Editor: Ira A. Penn, CRM, CSP. 10% freelance written. Eager to work with new/unpublished writers. Quarterly professional journal covering records and information management. Estab. 1967. Circ. 10,000. Pays on publication. Publishes ms an average of 6 months after acceptance. Byline given. Buys all rights. Simultaneous submissions OK. Reports in 1 month on mss. Sample copy $14; free writer's guidelines.

Nonfiction: Professional articles covering theory, case studies, surveys, etc. on any aspect of records and information management. Buys 20-24 mss/year. Send complete ms. Length: 2,500 words minimum. Pays $25-125 "stipend"; no contract.

Photos: Send photos with ms. Does not pay extra for photos. Prefers b&w prints. Captions required.

Tips: "A writer *must* know our magazine. Most work is written by practitioners in the field. We use very little freelance writing, but we have had some and it's been good. A writer must have detailed knowledge of the subject he/she is writing about. Superficiality is not acceptable."

SECURITY DEALER, PTN Security Group, 210 Crossways Park Drive, Woodbury NY 11797. (516)496-8000. Associate Publisher: Thomas S. Kapinos, CPP. Editor: Susan Brady. 25% freelance written. A monthly magazine for electronic alarm dealers; burglary and fire installers, with technical, business, sales and marketing information. Circ. 25,000. Pays 3 weeks after publication. Publishes ms an average of 4 months after acceptance. Byline given sometimes. Buys first North American serial rights. Simultaneous and previously published submissions OK. Prefer computer disk to accompany.

Nonfiction: How-to, interview/profile and technical. No consumer pieces. Query or send complete ms. Length: 1,000-3,000 words. Pays $300 for assigned articles; pays $100-200 for unsolicited articles. Sometimes pays the expenses of writers on assignment.

Photos: State availability of photos with submission. Reviews contact sheets and transparencies. Offers $25 additional payment for photos accepted with ms. Captions and identification of subjects required.

Columns/Departments: Closed Circuit TV, and Access Control (both on application, installation, new products), 500-1,000 words. Buys 25 mss/year. Query. Pays $100-150.

Tips: "The areas of our publication most open to freelancers are technical innovations, trends in the alarm industry and crime patterns as related to the business as well as business finance and management pieces."

SELF-EMPLOYED AMERICA, The News Publication for your Small Business, National Association for the Self-Employed, P.O. Box 612067, DFW Airport TX 75261. FAX: (817)595-5456. Editor: Karen C. Jones. 90% freelance written. Published 6 times/year for association members. "Keep in mind that the self-employed don't need business news tailored to meet needs of what government considers 'small business'. We reach those with few, if any, employees. Our readers are independent business owners going it alone—and in need of information." Estab. 1988. Circ. 230,000. **Pays on acceptance.** Byline given. Offers 10% kill fee. Buys full rights only and makes work-for-hire assignments. Submit seasonal/holiday material 6 months in advance. Query for electronic submissions. Reports in 1 month on queries; 6 weeks on mss. Sample copy for 9 × 12 with 2 first class stamps. Writer's guidelines for #10 SASE.

Nonfiction: Book excerpts, how-to, interview/profile, new product, personal experience and travel (how to save money on travel or how to combine business and personal travel). "No big-business or how to claw your way to the top stuff. Generally my readers are happy as small businesses." Buys 50-60 mss/year. Query with published clips. First article accepted many times on spec only. Length: 150-700 words. Pays $200-350 for assigned articles; $100-250 for unsolicited articles. Sometimes pays expenses of writers on assignment.

Photos: State availability of photos with submission. Reviews 3 × 5 prints. Offers $25-50 per photo. Captions, model releases and identification required. Buys one-time rights.

Columns/Departments: Tax Tips. Send complete ms. Length: 200-300. Pays $50-100. Touch of Success profiles. Pays $70 for 125 words. Tight writing, concise.

Fillers: Anecdotes, facts, newsbreaks and short humor. Buys 50/year. Length: 75-125 words. Pays $25-50.

Tips: "Keep in mind reader demographics show 230,000 people with nothing in common except the desire to be independent."

THE SERVICING DEALER, The Communications Group, Suite 202, 3703 N. Main St., Rockford IL 61103. (815)633-2680. FAX: (815)633-6880. Editor: Craig Wyatt. 15% freelance written. Trade journal, published 10 times/year, on outdoor power equipment retailing and service. "Editorial is basic retail management oriented. Readers are servicing dealers of lawn and other outdoor power equipment. They're good mechanics but not-so-good businessmen." Estab. 1987. Circ. 23,000. Pays on publication. Publishes ms an average of 2 months after acceptance. Byline given. Offers 20% kill fee. Buys one-time rights and exclusive rights within industry. Submit seasonal/holiday material 4 months in advance. Simultaneous and previously published submissions OK. Query for electronic submissions. Sample copy $1 with 9 × 12 SAE and 5 first class stamps. Writer's guidelines for #10 SASE.

Nonfiction: How-to (marketing, personnel management and financial management) and technical (dealing with small air-cooled engines and lawn equipment repair). Buys 6-10 mss/year. Query with published clips. Length: 600-1,200 words. Pays $150-300 for assigned articles; $50-250 for unsolicited articles. Sometimes pays expenses of writers on assignment.

Photos: Send photos with submission. Reviews contact sheets, transparencies and prints. Offers no additional payment for photos accepted with ms. Captions and identification of subjects required.

Columns/Departments: Sales Tips (basic sales methods and suggestions); Out Back (personnel management topics for small business); Greenbacks (financial management) and Ad-Visor (advertising and promotion for small business). Buys 7 mss/year. Query with published clips. Length: 450-675 words. Pays $50-250.

Tips: "Any prior knowledge of the outdoor power equipment industry, retail management topics, small engine repair is a plus. Read our magazine and other industry magazines. Small business management is a plus. Use electronic media to transfer directly into our Mac system. Give readers something they can walk away with and use the minute they put the magazine down."

SIGN BUSINESS, National Business Media Inc., 1008 Depot Hill Rd., P.O. Box 1416, Broomfield CO 80020. (303)469-0424. FAX: (303)469-5730. Editor: Emerson Schwartzkopf. 15% freelance written. Trade journal on the sign industry—electric, commercial, architectural. "This is business-to-business writing; we try to produce news you can use, rather than human interest." Circ. 20,500. Pays on publication. Publishes ms an average of 1-2 months after acceptance. Byline given. Buys first North American serial rights. Submit seasonal/holiday material 4 months in advance. Query for electronic submissions. Reports in 1 week on queries; 2 weeks on mss. Sample copy $2.50. Free writer's guidelines for #10 SASE.

Nonfiction: How-to (sign-painting techniques, new uses for computer cutters, plotters lettering styles); interview/profile (sign company execs, shop owners with *unusual*; work etc.) and other (news on sign codes, legislation, unusual signs, etc.). "No humor, human interest, generic articles with sign replacing another industry, no first person writing, no profiles of a sign shop just because someone nice runs the business." Buys 20 mss/year. Query with published clips. Length: 500-3,000 words. Pays $125-200.

Photos: Send photos with submission. Reviews 3×5 transparencies and 3×5 prints. Offers $5-10 per photo. Identification of subjects required. Buys one-time rights and/or reprint rights.

Tips: "Find a sign shop, or sign company, and take some time to learn the business. The sign business is easily a $5 billion-plus industry every year in the United States, and we treat it like a business, not a hobby. If you see a sign that stops you in your tracks, find out who made it; if it's a one-in-10,000 kind of sign, chances are good we'll want to know more. Writing should be factual and avoid polysyllabic words that waste a reader's time. I'll work with writers who may not know the trade, but can write well."

‡TOBACCO REPORTER, Specialized Agricultural Publications, Inc., Suite 300, 3000 Highwoods Blvd., Raleigh NC 27625. (919)872-5040. Editor/Publisher: Dayton Matlick. Associate Editor: Joe Sokohl. 30% freelance written. Monthly magazine covering the international tobacco industry. "Though we are not aligned with any tobacco manufacturers, we provide the most timely, accurate and interesting coverage of the tobacco industry worldwide. Our readership consists primarily of presidents, VPs, and CEOs of tobacco products manufacturers, leaf processors, and suppliers." Estab. 1873. Circ. 6,000. Pays on publication. Publishes ms an average of 5 months after acceptance. Byline usually given. Offers 25% kill fee on commissioned work. Buys all rights. Submit seasonal/holiday material 4 months in advance. Reports in 1 month on queries; 6 weeks on mss. Sample copy for $5 plus P/H.

Nonfiction: Editorial calendar available on request; we publish features and country profiles each month. We cannot use clippings from major publications; we do not want anything antagonistic to tobacco as an industry, nor do we accept attacks on individual companies. No personal testimonials. Buys 8-15 mss/year. Query with or without published clips, or send complete ms. Length: 500-3,000 words. Pays 72¢ per published line. Sometimes pays expenses of writers on assignment.

Photos: Send photos with submission. Reviews transparencies and 5×7 prints and larger. Offers $25-50 per photo. Captions, model releases and identification of subjects required. Buys one-time rights.

Columns/Departments: International News (crop reports, tobacco/cigarette prices, legislation), 50-300 words; and Top Line (late-breaking news, acquisitions, financial news), 30-100 words. Buys 50 mss/year. Send complete ms. Length: 50-300 words. Pays 72¢ per published line.

Fillers: Anecdotes and newsbreaks. Buys 10/year. Length: 30-100 words. Pays 72¢ per published line.

Tips: "Usually, someone who has had some involvement with the tobacco industry or industry as a whole will be atuned to the needs of our magazine. No antagonistic articles will be accepted. Also, we cannot use material gleaned from USA Today, the WSJ, Time, etc. We would like to see article relating to the international tobacco industry and its issues that we otherwise would not see. The sections most open to freelancers are both International News and our features. Freelancers need to communicate with us to discover what we need in the way of country spotlights, industry issues, news ideas."

WOMEN IN BUSINESS, The ABWA Co., Inc.. 9100 Ward Parkway, Kansas City MO 64114. (816)361-6621. Editor: Wendy Myers. 30% freelance written. A bimonthly magazine for members of the American Business Women's Association. "We publish articles of interest to the American working woman." Circ. 110,000. **Pays on acceptance.** Publishes ms an average of 2 months after acceptance. Byline given. Kill fee negotiable. Buys all rights. Submit seasonal/holiday material 4 months in advance. Reports in 1 week. Sample copy for 9×12 SAE with 4 first class stamps. Writer's guidelines for #10 SASE.

Nonfiction: "We cannot use success stories about individual businesswomen." Buys 30 mss/year. Query with published clips or send complete ms. Length: 1,000-3,000 words. Pays 15¢/word.

Photos: State availability of photos with submission. Offers no additional payment for photos accepted with ms. Identification of subjects required.

Columns/Departments: Bridget Cipolla, column/department editor. Working Capital (personal finance for women), 1,500 words; Health Scope (health topics for women); Moving Up (advice for the up-and-coming woman manager); Business Basics (for women small business owners). Buys 18 mss/year. Query with published clips or send complete ms. Length: 1,000-1,500 words. Pays 15¢/word.

Tips: "It would be very difficult to break into our columns. We have regular contributing freelance writers for those. But we are always on the look out for good feature articles and writers. We are especially interested in writers who provide a fresh, new look to otherwise old topics, such as time management etc."

Church Administration and Ministry

Publications in this section are written for clergy members, church leaders and teachers. Magazines for lay members and the general public are listed in the Consumer Religious section.

CHRISTIAN EDUCATION TODAY: For Teachers, Superintendents and Other Christian Educators, P.O. Box 15337, Denver CO 80215. Editor: James E. Burkett, Jr. Research Editor: Kenneth O. Gangel. 60% freelance written. Works with a small number of new/unpublished writers each year. Quarterly magazine. Pays on publication. Publishes ms an average of 6-9 months after acceptance. Byline given. Buys reprint rights with magazines of different circulations. Reports in 2 months. Sample copy $1 or 9 × 12 SAE with 3 first class stamps. Writer's guidelines for #10 SASE.

Nonfiction: Articles which provide information, instruction and/or inspiration to workers at every level of Christian education. May be slanted to the general area or to specific age-group categories such as preschool, elementary, youth or adult. Simultaneous rights acceptable *only* if offered to magazines that do not have overlapping circulation. Length: 1,000-2,000 words. Payment commensurate with length and value of article to total magazine (5-10¢/word).

Tips: "Often a freelance short article is followed up with a suggestion or firm assignment for more work from that writer."

CHRISTIAN LEADERSHIP, Board of Christian Education of the Church of God, P.O. Box 2458, Anderson IN 46018-2458. (317)642-0257. Editor: Sherrill D. Hayes. 50% freelance written. Works with a small number of new/unpublished writers each year. A bimonthly magazine covering local Sunday school teaching and administrating, youth work, worship, family life and other local church workers. Estab. 1923. Circ. 4,000. Pays on publication. Publishes ms an average of 6 months after acceptance. Byline given. Buys first rights and second serial (reprint) rights. Submit seasonal/holiday material 6 months in advance. Simultaneous queries OK. Reports in 4 months. Sample copy and writer's guidelines for 9 × 12 SAE with 3 first class stamps.

Nonfiction: General interest, how-to, inspirational, personal experience, guidance for carrying out programs for special days, and continuing ministries. No articles that are not specifically related to local church leadership. Buys 20 mss/year. Send complete ms, brief description of present interest in writing for church leaders, background and experience. Length: 300-1,200 words. Pays 2¢/word ($10 minimum).

Photos: Send photos with ms. Pays $15-25 for 5 × 7 b&w photos.

Tips: "How-to articles related to Sunday school teaching, program development and personal teacher enrichment or growth, with illustrations of personal experience of the authors, are most open to freelancers."

‡THE CHRISTIAN MINISTRY, The Christian Century Foundation, Suite 1405, 407 S. Dearborn St., Chicago IL 60605. (312)427-5380. Editor: James M. Wall. Managing Editor: Mark R. Halton. 80% freelance written. Bimonthly magazine for parish clergy. "Most of our articles are written by parish clergy, describing parish situations. Our audience is comprised of mainline church ministers who are looking for practical ideas and insights concerning the ministry. Estab. 1969. Circ. 12,000. Pays on publication. Publishes ms an average of 6 months after acceptance. Byline given. Offers $20 kill fee. Buys all rights. Submit seasonal/holiday material 4 months in advance. Simultaneous submissions OK. Reports in 3 weeks. Sample copy for 9 × 12 SAE with 3 first class stamps. Writer's guidelines for #10 SASE.

Nonfiction: Book excerpts (forthcoming books), essays, how-to (parish subjects), religious and preached sermons. No articles with footnotes or inspirational poetry. Buys 60 mss/year. Send complete ms. Length: 1,000-3,000 words. Pays $50-100 for assigned articles; $40-75 for unsolicited articles. Pays in contributor copies for book reviews.

Photos: State availability of photos with submission. Reviews 8 × 10 prints. Offers $20-50 per photo. Model releases preferred. Buys one-time rights.

Columns/Departments: Reflection on ministry (discusses an instance in which the author reflects on his or her practice of ministry), 2,500 words; From the Pulpit (preached sermons), 2,500 words. Buys 18 mss/year. Send complete ms. Length: 2,000-2,500 words. Pays $50-75.

Fillers: Newsbreaks and short humor. Buys 30/year. Length: 150-300 words. Pays $10.

Tips: "Send us finished manuscripts—not rough drafts. Freelancers have the best chance selling us articles on spec. Issues affecting parish clergy."

‡CHURCH ADMINISTRATION, 127 9th Ave. N., Nashville TN 37234. (615)251-2062. Editor: Gary Hardin. 15% freelance written. Works with a small number of new/unpublished writers each year. Monthly. For Southern Baptist pastors, staff and volunteer church leaders. Uses limited amount of freelance material.

Pays on acceptance. Publishes ms an average of 1 year after acceptance. Byline given. Buys all rights. Free sample copy and writer's guidelines for SAE with 2 first class stamps.
Nonfiction: "Ours is a journal for effectiveness in ministry, including church programming, organizing, and staffing; administrative skills; church financing; church food services; church facilities; communication; and pastoral ministries and community needs." Length: 1,800-2,000 words. Pays 5½¢/word.
Tips: "Send query letter. Writers should be familiar with the organization and policy of Southern Baptist churches. Articles should be practical, how-to articles that meet genuine needs faced by leaders in SBC churches. Type at 54 characters per line, 25 lines per page, double-spaced. Send originals, not copies. Not responsible for manuscripts not accompanied by return postage."

CHURCH EDUCATOR, Creative Resources for Christian Educators, Educational Ministries, Inc., 2861-C Saturn St., Brea CA 92621. (714)961-0622. Editor: Robert G. Davidson. Managing Editor: Linda S. Davidson. 80% freelance written. Works with a small number of new/unpublished writers each year. A monthly magazine covering religious education. Estab. 1976. Circ. 5,200. Pays on publication. Publishes manuscript an average of 4 months after acceptance. Byline given. Buys first rights, second serial (reprint) rights, or all rights. "We prefer all rights." Submit seasonal/holiday material 4 months in advance. Simultaneous submissions OK. Reports in 3 months. Sample copy for 9×12 SAE and 3 first class stamps; free writer's guidelines.
Nonfiction: Book reviews; general interest; how-to (crafts for Church school); inspirational; personal experience; and religious. "Our editorial lines are very middle of the road—mainline Protestant. We are not seeking extreme conservative or liberal theology pieces." No testimonials. Buys 100 mss/year. Send complete ms. Length: 100-2,000 words. Pays 2-4¢/word.
Photos: Send photos with submissions. Reviews 5×7 b&w prints. Offers $5-10/photo. Captions required. Buys one-time rights.
Fiction: Mainstream, religious and slice-of-life vignettes. Buys 15 mss/year. Send complete ms. Length: 100-2,000 words. Pays 2-4¢/word.
Fillers: Anecdotes and short humor. Buys 15/year. Length: 100-700 words. Pays 2-4¢/word.
Tips: "Send the complete manuscript with a cover letter which gives a concise summary of the manuscript. We are looking for how-to articles related to Christian education. That would include most any program held in a church. Be straightforward and to the point—not flowery and wordy. We're especially interested in youth programs. Give steps needed to carry out the program: preparation, starting the program, continuing the program, conclusion. List several discussion questions for each program."

THE CLERGY JOURNAL, Church Management, Inc., P.O. Box 162527, Austin TX 78716. (512)327-8501. Editor: Manfred Holck, Jr. 20% freelance written. Eager to work with new/unpublished writers. Monthly (except June and December) covering religion. Readers are Protestant clergy. Estab. 1924. Circ. 30,000. Pays on publication. Publishes ms an average of 4 months after acceptance. Byline given. Offers 50% kill fee. Buys all rights. Submit seasonal/holiday material 6 months in advance. Reports in 2 weeks on queries; 1 month on mss. Sample copy for $3 and 9×12 SAE with 8 first class stamps.
Nonfiction: How-to (be a more efficient and effective minister/administrator). No devotional, inspirational or sermons. Buys 20 mss/year. Query. Length: 500-1,500 words. Pays $25-40.

DISCIPLESHIP TRAINING, (formerly *Church Training*), 127 9th Ave. N., Nashville TN 37234. (615)251-2843. Editor: Ralph Hodge. 5% freelance written. Works with a small number of new/unpublished writers each year. Monthly. For all workers and leaders in the Church Training program of the Southern Baptist Convention. Estab. 1895. Circ. 30,000. **Pays on acceptance.** Publishes ms an average of 10 months after acceptance. Byline given. Buys all rights. Query for electronic submissions. Reports in 6 weeks. Free sample copy and writer's guidelines.
Nonfiction: Articles that pertain to leadership training in the church; success stories that pertain to Discipleship Training; association articles; informational, how-to's that pertain to discipleship training using Sunday School Board resources and personal testimonies. Buys 15 unsolicited mss/year. Query with rough outline. Length: 500-1,500 words. Pays 5½¢/word. Sometimes pays the expenses of writers on assignment.
Tips: "Write an article that reflects the writer's experience of personal growth through church training or tell how to use BSSB resources to train Christians. Keep in mind the target audience: workers and leaders of Discipleship Training organizations in churches of the Southern Baptist Convention. Often subjects and treatment are too general."

LEADERSHIP, A Practical Journal for Church Leaders, Christianity Today, Inc., 465 Gundersen Dr., Carol Stream IL 60188. (312)260-6200. Editor: Marshall Shelley. 75% freelance written. Works with a small number of new/unpublished writers each year. A quarterly magazine covering church leadership. Writers must have a "knowledge of and sympathy for the unique expectations placed on pastors and local church leaders. Each article must support points by illustrating from real life experiences in local churches." Estab. 1980. Circ. 90,000. **Pays on acceptance.** Publishes ms an average of 6 months after acceptance. Byline given. Buys first North American serial rights. Submit seasonal/holiday material 6 months in advance. Previously published submissions OK. Reports in 6 weeks on queries; 2 months on mss. Sample copy $3; free writer's guidelines.

Nonfiction: How-to, humor and personal experience. "No articles from writers who have never read our journal." Buys 50 mss/year. Send complete ms. Length: 100-5,000 words. Pays $30-300. Sometimes pays the expenses of writers on assignment.

Photos: State availability of photos with submission. Offers no additional payment for photos accepted with ms. Identification of subjects required. Buys one-time rights.

Columns/Departments: People in Print (book reviews with interview of author), 1,500 words. James D. Berkley, editor, To Illustrate (short stories or analogies that illustrate a biblical principle), 100 words. Buys 25 mss/year. Send complete ms. Pays $25-100.

PASTORAL LIFE, Society of St. Paul, Route 224, Canfield OH 44406. Editor: Anthony Chenevey, SSP. 66% freelance written. Eager to work with new/unpublished writers. Emphasizes priests and those interested in pastoral ministry. Monthly magazine. Circ. 3,500. Buys first rights only. Byline given. Pays on publication. Publishes ms an average of 6 months after acceptance. Query with an outline before submitting ms. "New contributors are expected to include, in addition, a few lines of personal data that indicate academic and professional background." Reports within 2 weeks. Free sample copy and writer's guidelines.

Nonfiction: "*Pastoral Life* is a professional review, principally designed to focus attention on current problems, needs, issues and all important activities related to all phases of pastoral work and life." Buys 30 unsolicited mss/year. Length: 2,000-3,400 words. Pays 3¢/word minimum.

THE PREACHER'S MAGAZINE, Nazarene Publishing House, E. 10814 Broadway, Spokane WA 99206. Editor: Randal E. Denny. Assistant Editor: Cindy Osso. 15% freelance written. Works with a small number of new/unpublished writers each year. Quarterly magazine of seasonal/miscellaneous articles. "A resource for ministers; Wesleyan-Arminian in theological persuasion." Circ. 18,000. **Pays on acceptance.** Publishes ms an average of 9 months after acceptance. Byline given. Buys first serial rights, second serial (reprint) rights and simultaneous rights. Submit seasonal/holiday material 9 months in advance. Simultaneous queries OK. Writer's guidelines for #10 SASE.

Nonfiction: How-to, humor, inspirational, opinion and personal experience, all relating to aspects of ministry. No articles that present problems without also presenting answers to them; things not relating to pastoral ministry. Buys 48 mss/year. Send complete ms. Length: 700-2,500 words. Pays 3½¢/word.

Photos: Send photos with ms. Reviews 35mm transparencies and 35mm b&w prints. Pays $25-35. Model release and identification of subjects required. Buys one-time rights.

Columns/Departments: Today's Books for Today's Preacher—book reviews. Buys 24 mss/year. Send complete ms. Length: 300-400 words. Pays $7.50.

Fillers: Anecdotes and short humor. Buys 10/year. Length: 400 words maximum. Pays 3½¢/word.

Tips: "Writers for the *Preacher's Magazine* should have insight into the pastoral ministry, or expertise in a specialized area of ministry. Our magazine is a highly specialized publication aimed at the minister. Our goal is to assist, by both scholarly and practical articles, the modern-day minister in applying Biblical theological truths."

‡PREACHING, Preaching Resources, Inc., 1529 Cesery Blvd., Jacksonville FL 32211. (904)743-5994. Editor: Dr. Michael Duduit. 75% freelance written. Bimonthly magazine for the preaching ministry. "All articles must deal with preaching. Most articles used offer practical assistance in preparation and delivery of sermons, generally from an evangelical stance." Circ. 7,000. Pays on publication. Publishes ms an average of 1 year after acceptance. Byline given. Buys first rights. Submit seasonal/holiday material 1 year in advance. Query for electronic submissions. Reports in 2 months. Sample copy $2.50; writer's guidelines for SASE.

Nonfiction: How-to (preparation and delivery of sermon; worship leadership). Special issues include Personal Computing in Preaching (September-October); materials/resources to assist in preparation of seasonal preaching (November-December, March-April). Buys 18-24 mss/year. Query. Length: 1,000-2,000 words. Pays $35-50.

Photos: Send photos with submission. Reviews prints. Offers no additional payment for photos accepted with ms. Captions, model releases and identification of subjects required. Buys one-time rights.

Fillers: Buys 10-15/year. "Buys only completed cartoons." Art must be related to preaching. Pays $25.

Tips: "Most desirable are practical, 'how-to' articles on preparation and delivery of sermons."

‡YOUR CHURCH, Equipping Pastors for the Business of Ministry, SMS Publications, 1418 Lake St., Evanston IL 60201. (708)328-3386. Managing Editor: Noel Calhoun. 30% freelance written. Bimonthly magazine for the business of today's church. "Articles pertain to the business aspects of ministry pastors are called upon to perform: administration, technology, building, etc." Estab. 1954. Circ. 200,000. Pays on publication. Publishes ms an average of 6 months after acceptance. Byline given. Offers 30% kill fee. Buys one-time rights. Submit seasonal/holiday material 3 months in advance. Simultaneous and previously published submissions OK. Reports in 2 weeks on queries; 2 months on mss. Free sample copy and writer's guidelines.

Nonfiction: How-to, new product and technical. Buys 12 mss/year. Send complete ms. Length: 1,200-1,500 words. Pays 10¢/word. Pays expenses of writers on assignment.
Photos: State availability of photos with submission. Reviews 4×5 transparencies and 5×7 or 8×10 prints. Offers no additional payment for photos accepted with ms. Captions, model releases and identifications of subjects required. Buys one-time rights.
Tips: "The editorial is generally geared toward brief and helpful articles dealing with some form of church business. Concise, bulletted points make a nice-appearing article."

Clothing

‡ATI, America's Textiles International, Billian Publishing Co., 2100 Powers Ferry Rd., Atlanta GA 30339. (404)955-5656. FAX: (404)952-0669. Editor: Monte G. Plott. Associate Editor: Rolf Viertel. 10% freelance written. Monthly magazine covering textiles, apparel, and fibers. "We cover the business of textile, apparel, and fiber industries with considerable technical focus on products and processes. No puff pieces pushing a particular product." Pays on publication. Byline sometimes given. Buys first North American serial rights. Query for electronic submissions.
Nonfiction: Technical, business. "No PR, just straight technical reports." Buys 10 mss/year. Query. Length: 500 words minimum. Pays $100/published page. Sometimes pays expenses of writers on assignment.
Photos: Send photos with submission. Reviews prints. Offers no additional payment for photos accepted with ms. Captions required. Buys one-time rights.

‡BOBBIN, Bobbin Blenheim Media Corp., 1110 Shop Rd., P.O. Box 1986, Columbia SC 29202. (803)771-7500. Publications Director: Sandra B. Staub. 75% freelance written. A monthly magazine for CEO's and top management in apparel companines. Circ. 9,500. Pays on publication. Byline given. Buys all rights. Reports in 6 weeks. Free sample copy and writer's guidelines.
Columns/Departments: Trade law, 807 manufacturing, retail, trade/commerce/policies, company performance, fabric trends, guest editorial.
Tips: "Articles should be written in a style appealing to busy top managers and should in some way foster thought or new ideas, or present solutions/alternatives to common industry problems/concerns. CEOs are most interested in quick read pieces that are also informative and substantive. Articles should not be based on opinions but should be developed through interviews with industry manufacturers, retailers or other experts, etc. Sidebars may be included to expand upon certain aspects within the article. If available, illustrations, graphs/charts, or photographs should accompany the article. Articles focusing on equipment or technical information would not be acceptable for Bobbin but could be considered for our sister publication, *Apparel Manufacturer.*"

SPECIALTY STORE SERVICE, Vanguard Publications, Inc., 6604 W. Saginaw Hwy., Lansing MI 48917. (517)321-0671. FAX: (517)371-1015. Editor: Ralph D. Ward. 70% freelance written. Monthly newsletter for women's independent clothing stores. "The *SSS Bulletin* is a management newsletter geared specifically toward running a women's specialty store business." Estab. 1978. Circ. 1,400. **Pays on acceptance.** Publishes ms an average of 3 months after acceptance. Byline given. Buys first North American serial rights and second serial (reprint) rights. Submit seasonal/holiday material 5 months in advance. Simultaneous submissions OK. Query for electronic submissions. Reports in 2 weeks on queries; 6 weeks on mss. Free sample copy and writer's guidelines for SASE.
Nonfiction: General interest (retail trends), how-to (retail sales, inventory management, retail promotion); Specializing (fresh ideas from various women's specialty retailing areas); Store Money/Your Money (personal/money and lifestyle management for store owners). No color analysis. Buys 60 mss/year. Query with published clips. Length: 350-2,000 words. Pays 75¢/36 character line.
Tips: Writers with retail or fashion experience preferred. Knowledge of industry vital.

WESTERN & ENGLISH FASHIONS, Bell Publishing, 2403 Champa, Denver CO 80205. (303)296-1600. FAX: (303)295-2159. Editor: Larry Bell. Managing Editor: Lee Darrigrand. 90% freelance written. Prefers to work with published/established writers. For "Western and English apparel and equipment retailers, manufacturers and distributors. The magazine features retailing practices such as marketing, merchandising, display techniques, buying and selling to help business grow or improve, etc. Every issue carries feature stories on Western/English/square dance apparel stores throughout the U.S." Monthly magazine. Estab. 1950. Circ. 13,000. Pays on publication. Publishes ms an average of 2 months after acceptance. Not copyrighted. Byline given unless extensive rewriting is required. Phone queries OK. Submit seasonal/holiday material 3 months in advance. Simultaneous (to noncompeting publications) and previously published submissions OK. No fiction or foreign material. Sample copy and writer's guidelines for 9×12 SAE with 6 first class stamps.
Nonfiction: Current trends in fashion of English riding attire, square dance and western; exposé (of government as related to industry or people in industry); general interest (pertaining to Western lifestyle); interview (with Western/English store owners); new product (of interest to Western/English clothing retailers—send

photo); and photo feature. "We will be doing much more fashion-oriented articles and layouts." Buys 20-25 mss/year. Query with outline. Length: 800-3,600 words. Pays $50-150. Sometimes pays the expenses of writers on assignment.

Photos: "We buy photos with manuscripts." State availability of photos. Captions required with "names of people or products and locations." Buys one-time rights.

Tips: "We will be highlighting current fashion trends and continuing to feature retail store operations. We continue to look for material relating to the fashion end of the western and English industry. 'Store stories' are particularly important. Currently we receive *too many* business articles."

Coin-Operated Machines

AMERICAN COIN-OP, 500 N. Dearborn St., Chicago IL 60610. (312)337-7700. FAX: (312)337-8654. Editor: Ben Russell. 30% freelance written. Monthly magazine for owners of coin-operated laundry and dry cleaning stores. Estab. 1960. Circ. 20,100. Rights purchased vary with author and material but are exclusive to the field. Pays two weeks prior to publication. Publishes ms an average of 4 months after acceptance. Byline given for frequent contributors. Reports as soon as possible; usually in 2 weeks. Free sample copy.

Nonfiction: "We emphasize store operation and use features on industry topics: utility use and conservation, maintenance, store management, customer service and advertising. A case study should emphasize how the store operator accomplished whatever he did—in a way that the reader can apply to his own operation. Manuscript should have a no-nonsense, business-like approach." Uses informational, how-to, interview, profile, think pieces and successful business operations articles. Length: 500-3,000 words. Pays 7½¢/word minimum.

Photos: Pays $7.50 minimum for 5×7 b&w glossy photos purchased with mss. (Contact sheets with negatives preferred.)

Fillers: Newsbreaks and clippings. Length: open. Pays $10 minimum.

Tips: "Query about subjects of current interest. Be observant of coin-operated laundries—how they are designed and equipped, how they serve customers and how (if) they advertise and promote their services. Most general articles are turned down because they are not aimed well enough at our audience. Most case histories are turned down because they lack practical purpose (nothing new or worth reporting). A frequent mistake is failure to follow up on an interesting point made by the interviewee—probably due to lack of knowledge about the industry."

PLAY METER MAGAZINE, Skybird Publishing Co., Inc., P.O. Box 24970, New Orleans LA 70184. FAX: (504)488-7083. Publisher: Carol Lally. Editor: Valerie Cognevich. 25% freelance written. "We will work with new writers who are familiar with the amusement industry." Monthly trade magazine for owners/operators of coin-operated amusement machine companies, e.g., pinball machines, video games, arcade pieces, juke-boxes, etc. Estab. 1974. Circ. 6,500. Pays on publication. Publishes ms an average of 2 months after acceptance. Byline given. Buys all rights. Submit seasonal/holiday material 2 months in advance. Previously published submissions OK. Query answered in 2 months. Sample copy $5; free writer's guidelines.

Nonfiction: How-to (get better locations for machines, promote tournaments, evaluate profitability of route, etc.); interview (with industry leaders); new product. "Our readers want to read about how they can make more money from their machines, how they can get better tax breaks, commissions, etc. Also no stories about *playing* pinball or video games. Also, submissions on video-game technology advances; technical pieces on troubleshooting videos, pinballs and novelty machines (all coin-operated); trade-show coverage (query) submissions on the pay-telephone industry. Our readers don't play the games per se; they buy the machines and make money from them." Buys 48 mss/year. Submit complete ms. Length: 250-3,000 words. Pays $30-215. Sometimes pays expenses of writers on assignment.

Photos: "The photography should have news value. We don't want 'stand 'em up-shoot 'em down' group shots." Pays $15 minimum for 5×7 or 8×10 b&w prints. Captions preferred. Buys all rights. Art returned on request.

Tips: "We need feature articles more than small news items or featurettes. Query first. We're interested in writers who either have a few years of reporting/feature-writing experience or who know the coin-operated amusement industry well but are relatively inexperienced writers."

VENDING TIMES, 545 8th Ave., New York NY 10018. Editor: Arthur E. Yohalem. Monthly. For operators of vending machines. Circ. 14,700. Pays on publication. Buys all rights. "We will discuss in detail the story requirements with the writer." Sample copy $3.

Nonfiction: Feature articles and news stories about vending operations; practical and important aspects of the business. "We are always willing to pay for good material." Query.

Confectionery and Snack Foods

These publications focus on the bakery, snack and candy industries. Journals for grocers, wholesalers and other food industry personnel are listed in Groceries and Food Products.

CANDY INDUSTRY, Edgell Communications, Inc., 7500 Old Oak Blvd., Cleveland OH 44130. (216)243-8100. FAX: (216)819-2683. Editor: Susan Tiffany-Jones. 5% freelance written. Monthly. Prefers to work with published/established writers. For confectionery manufacturers. Publishes ms an average of 4 months after acceptance. Buys all rights. Reports in 1 month. Writer's guidelines for #10 SASE.
Nonfiction: "Feature articles of interest to large scale candy manufacturers that deal with activities in the fields of production, packaging (including package design), merchandising; and financial news (sales figures, profits, earnings), advertising campaigns in all media, and promotional methods used to increase the sale or distribution of candy." Length: 1,000-1,250 words. Pays 15¢/word; "special rates on assignments."
Photos: "Good quality glossies with complete and accurate captions, in sizes not smaller than 5×7." Pays $15 b&w; $20 for color.
Fillers: "Short news stories about the trade and anything related to candy and snacks." Pays 5¢/word; $1 for clippings.

PACIFIC BAKERS NEWS, Suite F, 1818, Mt. Diablo Blvd., Walnut Creek CA 94596. (415)932-1256. Publisher: C.W. Soward. 30% freelance written. Eager to work with new/unpublished writers. Monthly business newsletter for commercial bakeries in the western states. Estab. 1961. Pays on publication. No byline given; uses only one-paragraph news items.
Nonfiction: Uses bakery business reports and news about bakers. Buys only brief "boiled-down news items about bakers and bakeries operating only in Alaska, Hawaii, Pacific Coast and Rocky Mountain states. We welcome clippings. We need monthly news reports and clippings about the baking industry and the donut business. No pictures, jokes, poetry or cartoons." Length: 10-200 words. Pays 10¢/word for news and 6¢ for clips (words used).

Construction and Contracting

Builders, architects and contractors learn the latest industry news in these publications. Journals targeted to architects are also included in the Consumer Art and Architecture category. Those for specialists in the interior aspects of construction are listed under Building Interiors.

ACCESS CONTROL, 6255 Barfield Rd., Atlanta GA 30328. (404)256-9800. FAX: (404)256-3116. Editor/Associate Publisher: Steven Lasky. 50% freelance written. Prefers to work with published/established writers. Monthly tabloid for end users and installers of access control equipment. Estab. 1955. Circ. 24,000. Pays on publication. Publishes ms an average of 2 months after acceptance. Buys all rights. Query for electronic submissions. Reports in 3 months. Free sample copy for 8×10 SASE; writer's guidelines for #10 SASE.
Nonfiction: Case histories, large-scale access control "systems approach" equipment installations. A format for these articles has been established. Query for details. Buys 10-12 unsolicited mss/year. Query. Length: 4,500 words maximum.
Columns/Departments: Also take technical or practical application features for following monthly columns dealing with perimeter security fencing and accessories, gate systems, sensor technology card access systems, and CCTV technology. Length: 2,000 words maximum.
Photos: Pays $10 for 5×7 b&w photos purchased with mss. Captions required.
Tips: "We will place more focus on access control installations."

AUTOMATED BUILDER, CMN Associates, Inc., Box 120, Carpinteria CA 93014. (805)684-7659. FAX: (805)684-1765. Editor-in-Chief: Don Carlson. 15% freelance written. Monthly magazine specializing in management for industrialized (manufactured) housing and volume home builders. Circ. 25,000. Pays on acceptance. Publishes ms an average of 3 months after acceptance. Buys first North American serial rights. Phone queries OK. Reports in 2 weeks. Free sample copy and writer's guidelines.
Nonfiction: Case history articles on successful home building companies which may be 1) production (big volume) home builders; 2) mobile home manufacturers; 3) modular home manufacturers; 4) prefabricated home manufacturers; 5) house component manufacturers; or 6) special unit (in-plant commercial building) manufacturers. Also uses interviews, photo features and technical articles. "No architect or plan 'dreams'. Housing projects must be built or under construction." Buys 15 mss/year. Query. Length: 500-1,000 words maximum. Pays $300 minimum.
Photos: Purchased with accompanying ms. Query. No additional payment for 4×5, 5×7 or 8×10 b&w glossies or 35mm or larger color transparencies (35mm preferred). Captions required.
Tips: "Stories often are too long, too loose; we prefer 500 to 750 words. We prefer a phone query on feature articles. If accepted on query, article usually will not be rejected later."

THE CONCRETE TRADER, P.O. Box 660, Dublin OH 43017-0660. (614)793-9711. FAX: (614)793-8380. Editor John D. Cowan. 25% freelance written. Monthly newspaper of business information related to concrete industry. Estab. 1983. Circ. 9,500. Pays on publication. Byline given. Offers $25 kill fee. Buys all rights. Previously published submissions OK. Query for electronic submissions.

Nonfiction: General interest, interview/profile. Buys 5-12 mss/year. Query with published clips. Length: 500-1,000 words.

Photos: State availability of photos with submission. Reviews contact sheets. Offers no additional payment for photos accepted with ms.

Fillers: Length: 50-200 words. Pays $10-50.

CONSTRUCTION COMMENT, Naylor Communications Ltd. 6th Fl., 920 Yonge St., Toronto, Ontario M4W 3C7 Canada. (416)961-1028. FAX: (416)924-4408. Editor: C. Winslow Pettingell. 50% freelance written. Semiannual magazine on construction industry in Ottawa. *"Construction Comment* reaches all members of the Ottawa Construction Association and most senior management of firms relating to the industry." Circ. 3,000. Pays 30 day after deadline. Byline given. Offers ⅓ kill fee. Buys first North American serial rights. Submit seasonal/holiday material 2 months in advance. Simultaneous submissions OK. Query for electronic submissions.

Nonfiction: General interest, historical, interview/profile, new product, photo feature and technical. "We publish a spring/summer issue and a fall/winter issue. Submit correspondingly or inquire two months ahead of these times." Buys 20 mss/year. Query with published clips. Length: 500-2,500 words. Pays 20-25¢/word. Pays expenses of writers on assignment.

Photos: State availability of photos with submission. Send photos with submission. Reviews transparencies and prints. Offers $25-200 per photo. Identification of subjects required.

Tips: "Please send copies of work and a general query. I will respond as promptly as my deadlines allow. Company publications also include *Toronto Construction News* a bimonthly magazine on construction industry inToronto reaching all members of the Toronto Construction Association, and *The Generals,* a quarterly magazine for general contractors in Ontario, reaching all members of the Ontario General Contractors Association."

CONSTRUCTION SPECIFIER, 601 Madison St., Alexandria VA 22314. (703)684-0300. FAX: (703)684-0465. Editor: Kimberly C. Young. 50% freelance written. Works with a small number of new/unpublished writers each year. Monthly professional society magazine for architects, engineers, specification writers and project managers. Monthly. Estab. 1949. Circ. 19,000. Pays on publication. Publishes ms an average of 4 months after acceptance. Deadline: 60 days preceding publication on the 1st of each month. Buys North American serial rights. Query for electronic submissions. "Call or write first." Model release, author copyright transferral requested. Reports in 3 weeks. Sample copy for 9×12 SAE and 6 first class stamps. Writer's guidelines for #10 SASE.

Nonfiction: Articles on selection and specification of products, materials, practices and methods used in commercial (nonresidential) construction projects, specifications as related to construction design, plus legal and management subjects. Query. Length: 3,000-5,000 words maximum. Pays 15¢/published word (negotiable), plus art. Pays minor expenses of writers on assignment, to an agreed upon limit.

Photos: Photos desirable in consideration for publication; line art, sketches, diagrams, charts and graphs also desired. Full color transparencies may be used. 8×10 glossies, 3¼ slides preferred. Payment negotiable.

Tips: "We are increasing in size and will need more good technical articles."

COST CUTS, The Enterprise Foundation, 500 American City Bldg., Columbia MD 21044. (301)964-1230. Editor Cecilia Cassidy. 25% freelance written. Newsletter published 6 times/year on rehabilitation of low-income housing. "As the construction arm of The Enterprise Foundation, the Rehab Work Group, which publishes *Cost Cuts,* seeks ways to reduce the cost of rehabbing and constructing low-income housing. *Cost Cuts* is distributed nationally to rehab specialists, agencies, and others involved in the production of low-income housing." Estab. 1983. Circ. 3,000. Pays on publication. Byline given. Buys one-time rights. Submit seasonal/holiday material 3 months in advance. Previously published submissions OK. Query for electronic submissions. Reports in 1 month. Sample copy for 9×12 SAE with 2 first class stamps. Writer's guidelines for #10 SASE.

Nonfiction: How-to, interview/profile and technical. "No personal experience of do-it-yourselfers in single-family homes. We want articles that contribute to the low cost and high production of low-income housing." Buys 10-15 mss/year. Query with published clips. Length: 100-1,500 words. Pays $50-200 for assigned articles; $200 maximum for unsolicited articles. Sometimes pays expenses of writers on assignment.

Photos: Send photos with submission. Reviews contact sheets and 3×5 and 5×7 prints. Captions and identification of subjects required. Buys one-time rights.

Fillers: Facts and newsbreaks. Buys 20/year. Length: 100-500 words. Pays $25-50.

Tips: "The Foundations's mission is to develop new systems to help poor people help themselves move out of poverty and dependence—into fit and livable housing and self-sufficiency. Freelancers must be conscious of this context. Articles must include case studies of specific projects where costs have been cut. Charts of cost comparisons to show exactly where cuts were made are most helpful."

FINE HOMEBUILDING, The Taunton Press, Inc., 63 S. Main St., P.O. Box 5506, Newtown CT 06470. (203)426-8171. Editor: Mark Feirer. Less than 5% freelance written. Bimonthly magazine covering house building, construction, design for builders, architects and serious amateurs. Estab. 1976. Circ. 245,000. Pays advance, balance on publication. Publishes ms an average of 6-12 months after acceptance. Byline given. Offers negotiable kill fee. Buys first rights and "use in books to be published." Query for electronic submissions. Reports as soon as possible. Free writer's guidelines.

Nonfiction: Technical (techniques in design or construction process). Query. Length: 2,000-3,000 words. Pays $150-1,200.

Columns/Departments: Tools and Materials (products or techniques that are new or unusual); Great Moments in Building History (humorous, embarrassing, or otherwise noteworthy anecdotes); Reviews (short reviews of books on building or design) and Reports and Comment (essays, short reports on construction and architecture trends and developments). Query. Length: 300-1,000 words. Pays $50-250.

HOME BUILDER, Work-4 Projects Ltd., Box 400, Victoria Station, Westmount, Quebec H3Z 2V8 Canada. (514)489-4941. FAX: (514)489-5505. Publisher: Nachmi Artzy. Editor: Rob Bradford. 80% freelance written. Magazine covers new home construction, published 6 times annually. "*Home Builder* reports on builders, architects, mortgage, sub-trades, associations and government. We keep the readers' concerns in the forefront, not the advertisers." Estab. 1976. Circ. 12,000. Pays on publication. Publishes ms an average of 4 months after acceptance. Byline sometimes given. Buys all rights. Simultaneous submissions OK. Reports in 3 weeks on queries. Free sample copy.

Nonfiction: Exposé, how-to (builders, administration, production, etc.), interview/profile, new product and technical. Buys 20-30 mss/year. Query with published clips. Length: 100-500 words. Pays 10-20¢/word. Pays in contributor copies or other premiums "if suitable for both parties." Sometimes pays expenses of writers on assignment.

Photos: Send photos with submission. Reviews transparencies and prints. Offers expense-$300 per photo. Captions and identification of subjects required. Buys all rights.

Columns/Departments: Perspective (general news of importance to audience), 100-300 words; and Industry News (specific company information of relevance—not sales pitch), 75-300 words. Buys 20 mss/year. Query with published clips. Pays 10-20¢/word.

Fillers: Facts and gags. Buys 5/year. Length: 5-50 words. Pays 10¢/word-$25.

Tips: "Keep audience in mind. Give them something that will affect them, not something they will forget five minutes after reading it. Keep in mind Canadian content."

INLAND ARCHITECT, The Midwestern Building Arts Magazine, Inland Architect Press, 10 West Hubbard St., P.O. Box 10394, Chicago IL 60610. (312)321-0583. Editor: Cynthia C. Davidson. 80% freelance written. Prefers to work with published/established writers. Bimonthly magazine covering architecture and urban planning. "*Inland Architect* is a critical journal covering architecture and design in the midwest for an audience primarily of architects. *Inland* is open to all points of view, providing they are intelligently expressed and of relevance to architecture." Estab. 1957. Circ. 7,000. Pays on publication. Publishes ms an average of 2 months after acceptance. Byline given. Offers 60% kill fee. Buys first rights. Reports in 1 month on queries; 2 months on mss. Sample copy $4.95 with 10×13 SAE. Writer's guidelines for #10 SASE.

Nonfiction: Book excerpts, essays, historical/nostalgic, interview/profile, criticism and photo feature of architecture. Every summer *Inland* focuses on a midwestern city, its architecture and urban design. Call to find out 1991 city. No new products, "how to run your office," or technical pieces. Buys 40 mss/year. Query with or without published clips, or send complete ms. Length: 750-3,500 words. Pays $100-300 for assigned articles; pays $75-250 for unsolicited articles. Sometimes pays the expenses of writers on assignment.

Photos: Send photos with submission. Reviews 4×5 transparencies, slides and 8×10 prints. Offers no additional payment for photos accepted with ms. Identification of subjects required. Buys one-time rights.

Columns/Departments: Books (reviews of new publications on architecture, design and, occasionally, art), 250-1,000 words. Buys 10 mss/year. Query. Length: 250-1,000 words. Pays $25-100.

Tips: "Propose to cover a lecture, to interview a certain architect, etc. Articles must be written for an audience primarily consisting of well-educated architects. If an author feels he has a 'hot' timely idea, a phone call is appreciated."

MIDWEST CONTRACTOR MAGAZINE, 3170 Mercier, Box 419766, Kansas City MO 64141. (816)931-2080. FAX: (816)753-1106. 5% freelance written. Biweekly magazine covering the public works and engineering construction industries in Iowa, Nebraska, Kansas and western and northeastern Missouri. Estab. 1901. Circ. 8,426. Pays on publication. Byline given depending on nature of article. Reports in 1 month. Sample copy for 11×15 SAE with 8 first class stamps.

Nonfiction: How-to, photo feature, technical, "nuts and bolts" construction job-site features. "We seek two- to three-page articles on topics of interest to our readership, including marketing trends, tips, and construction job-site stories. Providing concise, accurate and original news stories is another freelance opportunity." Buys 4 mss/year. Query with three published clips. Length: 175 typewritten lines, 35 character count, no maximum. Pays $50/published page.

Tips: "We need writers who can write clearly about our specialized trade area. An engineering/construction background is a plus. The most frequent mistake made by writers is that they do not tailor their article to our specific market—the nonresidential construction market in Nebraska, Iowa, Kansas and Missouri. We are not interested in what happens in New York unless it has a specific impact in the Midwest."

PACIFIC BUILDER & ENGINEER, Vernon Publications Inc.. Suite 200, 3000 Northup Way, Bellevue WA 98004. (206)827-9900. FAX: (206)822-9372. Editor: John M. Watkins. Editorial Director: Michele Dill. 20% freelance written. A biweekly magazine on heavy construction. "We cover non-residential construction in Washington, Oregon, Idaho, Montana and Alaska." Estab. 1902. Circ. 12,000. Pays on publication. Byline given. Buys first North American serial rights. Submit seasonal material 2 months in advance. Reports in 3 weeks on queries; 6 weeks on mss.
Nonfiction: How-to (construction), interview/profile and technical (construction). Buys 10 mss/year. Query with published clips. Length: 1,000-2,500 words. Pays $100-200. Does not pay for unsolicited manuscripts. Sometimes pays the expenses of writers on assignment.
Photos: Send photos with submission. Reviews contact sheets, transparencies (35mm) and prints (8×10). Payment is by the page. Buys North American rights.

ROOFER MAGAZINE, D&H Publications, 10990 Metro Pkwy. SE, Ft. Myers FL 33912. (813)275-7663. Editor: Kaerrie A. Simons. 10% freelance written. Eager to work with new/unpublished writers. Monthly magazine covering the roofing industry for roofing contractors. Estab. 1981. Circ. 16,000. Pays on publication. Publishes ms an average of 5 months after acceptance. Byline given. Buys first serial rights and second serial (reprint) rights. Submit seasonal/holiday material 4 months in advance. Reports in 2 weeks on queries; 1 month on mss. Sample copy and writer's guidelines for SAE and 6 first class stamps.
Nonfiction: Historical/nostalgic; how-to (solve application problems, overcome trying environmental conditions); interview/profile; and technical. "Write articles directed toward areas of specific interest; don't generalize too much." Buys 7 mss/year. Query. Length: 1,500-5,000 words. Pays $125-250.
Photos: Send photos with completed mss; color slides are preferred. Identification of subjects required. Buys all rights. Always searching for photos of unusual roofs or those with a humorous slant.
Tips: "We prefer substantial articles (not short articles and fillers). Slant articles toward roofing contractors. We have little use for generic articles that can appear in any business publication and give little consideration to such material submitted. The tone of articles submitted to us needs to be authoritative but not condescending. We also review material with a humorous slant. Authors of successful freelance articles know the roofing industry."

RSI, Roofing/Siding/Insulation, Edgell Communications, 7500 Old Oak Blvd., Cleveland OH 44130. (216)243-8100. FAX: (216)826-2832. Editor: Michael Russo. 15% freelance written. A monthly magazine about roofing, siding and insulation fields. "Our audience is comprised almost entirely of contractors in the roofing, siding and/or insulation fields. The publication's goal is to help them improve their business, with heavy emphasis on application techniques." Estab. 1945. Circ. 20,000. Pays on publication. Publishes ms an average of 3 months after acceptance. Byline sometimes given. Buys all rights. Free sample copy.
Nonfiction: How-to (application of RSI products), new product, technical (on roofing, siding and/or insulation) and business articles directed at subcontractors. "No consumer-oriented articles. Our readers sell to consumers and building owners." Buys 6 mss/year. Query. Length: 1,000-3,000 words. Pays $100-800 for assigned articles. Pays $50-400 for unsolicited articles. Sometimes pays the expenses of writers on assignment.
Photos: State availability of photos with submission. Reviews transparencies (2¼×2¼) and prints (5×7). Offers no additional payment for photos accepted with ms. Captions and identification of subjects required.

‡SHOPPING CENTER WORLD, Communication Channels Inc., 6255 Barfield Rd., Atlanta GA 30328. (404)256-9800. FAX: (404)256-3116. Managing Editor: Teresa DeFranks. 75% freelance written. Prefers to work with published/established writers. A monthly magazine covering the shopping center industry. "Material is written with the shopping center developer and shopping center tenant in mind." Estab. 1972. Pays on publication. Publishes ms an average of 3 months after acceptance. Byline given. Buys all rights. Submit seasonal/holiday material 3 months in advance. Query for electronic submissions. Reports in 1 month. Sample copy $6.
Nonfiction: Interview/profile, new product, opinion, photo feature, and technical. Especially interested in renovation case studies on shopping centers. Buys 50 mss/year. Query with or without published clips, or send complete ms. Length: 750-3,000 words. Pays $75-500. Sometimes pays expenses of writers on assignment.
Photos: State availability of photos with submission. Reviews 4×5 transparencies and 35mm slides. Offers no additional payment for photos accepted with ms. Model releases and identification of subjects required. Buys one-time rights.
Tips: "We are always looking for talented writers to work on assignment. Send resume and published clips. Writers with real estate writing and business backgrounds have a better chance. Product overviews, renovations, and state reviews are all freelance written on an assignment basis."

SOUTHWEST CONTRACTOR, Akers-Runbeck Publishing, Suite 490, 3101 Central Ave., Phoenix AZ 85012. (602)230-0598. FAX: (602)230-8704. Editor: Elaine M. Beall. 20% freelance written. Monthly magazine about construction industry/engineering. "Problem-solving case histories of projects in Arizona, New Mexico,

Nevada and West Texas emphasizing engineering, equipment, materials and people." Estab. 1938. Circ. 6,200. Pays on publication. Byline given. Buys first rights and makes work-for-hire assignments. Submit seasonal/holiday material 3 months in advance. Previously published submissions OK. Sample $3 with 9 × 12 SAE and 4 first class stamps. Writer's guidelines for #10 SASE.

Nonfiction: Interview/profile and technical. (June – Aggregate/Asphalt; July – Concrete/Ready Mix, and December – Mining.) Buys 12 mss/year. Query. Length: 1,000-3,000 words. Pays $4/column inch at 14 picas wide. Sometimes pays expenses of writers on assignment.

Photos: State availability of photos with submission. Reviews 3x5 prints. Offers $10 maximum per photo. Captions and identification of subjects required. Buys one-time rights.

Columns/Departments: People; Around Southwest (general construction activities), Association News (all associations involved with industry), Manufacturer's News, Legal News (construction only). Contracts awarded (construction only).

Dental

DENTAL ECONOMICS, Penwell Publishing Co., P.O. Box 3408, Tulsa OK 74101. (918)835-3161. FAX: (918)831-9497. Editor: Dick Hale. 50% freelance written. A monthly dental trade journal. "Our readers are actively practicing dentists who look to us for current practice-building, practice-administrative and personal finance assistance." Estab. 1911. Circ. 110,000. **Pays on acceptance.** Publishes ms an average of 3-4 months after acceptance. Byline given. Buys first rights. Submit seasonal/holiday material 6 months in advance. Reports in 3 weeks on queries; 1 month on mss. Free sample copy and writer's guidelines.

Nonfiction: General interest, how-to and new product. "No human interest and consumer-related stories." Buys 40 mss/year. Query. Length: 750-3,500 words. Pays $150-500 for assigned articles; pays $75-350 for unsolicited articles. Sometimes pays the expenses of writers on assignment.

Photos: State availability of photos with submission. Reviews contact sheets. Offers no additional payment for photos accepted with ms. Model releases and identification of subjects required. Buys one-time rights.

Columns/Departments: Ron Combs, editor. Tax Q&A (tax tips for dentists), 1,500 words; Capitolgram (late legislative news – dentistry), 750 words; and Econ Report (national economic outlook), 750 words. Buys 36 mss/year. Pays $50-300.

Tips: "How-to articles on specific subjects such as practice-building, newsletters and collections should be relevant to a busy, solo-practice dentist."

DENTIST, Dental Market Network, Stevens Publishing Corp., 225 N. New Rd., P.O. Box 7573, Waco TX 76714. (817)776-9000. FAX: (817)776-9018. Editor: Mark S. Hartley. 25% freelance written. Will work with new/unpublished writers. A bimonthly trade journal for dentists. Any news or feature story of interest to dentists is considered. Estab. 1985. Circ. 154,860. Pays 60 days after acceptance. Publishes ms an average of 2 months after acceptance. Byline given. Offers 25% kill fee. Buys first North American serial rights. Submit seasonal/holiday material 1 year in advance. Simultaneous submissions OK. Reports in 1 month on queries; 2 months on mss. Sample copy and writer's guidelines for 12½ × 15 SAE with 7 first class stamps.

Nonfiction: How-to, interview/profile, new product and technical. Buys 20 mss/year. Query with or without published clips, or send complete ms. Length: 30 inches of copy. Pays $50-200 for assigned articles. Sometimes pays the expenses of writers on assignment

Photos: Send photos with submission. Reviews contact sheets. Offers $10-100 per photo. Captions and identification of subjects required. Buys one-time rights.

Tips: "Purchased freelance material reflects a knowledgeable, analytical insight into issues concerning the dental profession. Audience is very intelligent and literate; readers can easily spot editorial that is not adequately researched. The emphasis in 1991 will continue to be on obtaining timely, newsworthy editorial pertinent to dentistry: cosmetic dentistry, infection control, periodontics, patient insurance, and alternative methods of patient payment."

GENERAL DENTISTRY, Academy of General Dentistry. Suite 1200, 211 E. Chicago Ave., Chicago IL 60611. (312)440-4344. FAX: (312)440-4315. Managing Editor: Terrance Stanton. 5% freelance written. A bimonthly magazine about dentistry. "Our focus is continuing eduction in dentistry. Our readers are dentists. Articles should be written at a dentist's level of knowledge." Estab. 1955. Circ. 45,000. **Pays on acceptance.** Publishes ms an average of 4 months after acceptance. Offers 50% kill fee. Buys all rights. Simultaneous submissions OK. Reports in 1 month. Sample copy for 9 × 12 SAE with 5 first class stamps; writer's guidelines for #10 SASE.

Nonfiction: Essays, historical/nostalgic, interview/profile, new product and technical. No articles written for dental patients. Buys 10 mss/year. Query with or without published clips, or send complete ms. Pays $125-500 for assigned articles. Pays $125-400 for unsolicited articles. Pays the expenses of writers on assignment.

Photos: State availability of photos with submission. Reviews contact sheets. Offers no additional payment for photos accepted with ms. Captions, model releases and identification of subjects required. All rights for dental market acquired.

Tips: "Understand that our focus is scientific. Any article we buy must be of special interest to the members of our association, which is devoted to fostering continuing education in dentistry. Writers are advised to call or query so that we can assist in developing an idea. Stories that have to do with improvements in clinical practice are the best prospects for our magazine."

PROOFS, The Magazine of Dental Sales and Marketing, P.O. Box 3408, Tulsa OK 74101. (918)835-3161. FAX: (918)831-9497. Publisher: Dick Hale. Editor: Mary Elizabeth Good. 10% freelance written. Magazine published 10 times/year; combined issues July/August, November/December. Pays on publication. Byline given. Reports in 2 weeks. Free sample copy.
Nonfiction: Uses short articles, chiefly on selling to dentists. Must have understanding of dental trade industry and problems of marketing and selling to dentists and dental laboratories. Query. Pays about $75.
Tips: "The most frequent mistakes made by writers are having a lack of familiarity with industry problems and talking down to our audience."

RDH, The National Magazine for Dental Hygiene Professionals, Stevens Publishing Corp., 225 N. New Rd., Waco TX 76714. (817)776-9000. Editor: Laura Albrecht. 65% freelance written. Eager to work with new/unpublished writers. Monthly magazine, covering information relevant to dental hygiene professionals as business-career oriented individuals. "Dental hygienists are highly trained, licensed professionals; most are women. They are concerned with ways to develop rewarding careers, give optimum service to patients and to grow both professionally and personally." Circ. 63,210. Usually pays on publication; sometimes on acceptance. Publishes ms an average of 8 months after acceptance. Byline given. Buys first serial rights. Reports in 2 weeks on queries; 2 months on mss. Sample copy for 9×12 SAE; writer's guidelines for SASE.
Nonfiction: Essays, general interest, interview/profile, personal experience, photo feature and technical. "We are interested in any topic that offers broad reader appeal, especially in the area of personal growth (communication, managing time, balancing career and personal life). No undocumented clinical or technical articles; how-it-feels-to-be-a-patient articles; product-oriented articles (unless in generic terms); anything cutesy-unprofessional." Length: 1,500-3,000 words. Pays $100-350 for assigned articles; pays $50-200 for unsolicited articles. Sometimes pays expenses of writers on assignment.
Photos: Send photos with submission. Reviews 3×5 prints. Model releases required. Buys one-time rights.
Tips: "Freelancers should have a feel for the concerns of today's business-career woman—and address those interests and concerns with practical, meaningful and even motivational messages. We want to see good-quality manuscripts on both personal growth and lifestyle topics. For clinical and/or technical topics, we prefer the writers be members of the dental profession. New approaches to old problems and dilemmas will always get a close look from our editors. *RDH* is also interested in manuscripts for our feature section. Other than clinical information, dental hygienists are interested in all sorts of topics—finances, personal growth, educational opportunities, business management, staff/employer relations, communication and motivation, office rapport and career options. Other than clinical/technical articles, *RDH* maintains an informal tone. Writing style can easily be accommodated to our format."

Drugs, Health Care and Medical Products

THE APOTHECARY, Health Care Marketing Services, #200, 95 First St., P.O. Box AP, Los Altos CA 94023. (415)941-3955. FAX: (415)941-2303. Editor: Jerold Karabensh. Publication Director: Janet Goodman. 100% freelance written. Prefers to work with published/established writers. Quarterly magazine. "*The Apothecary* aims to provide practical information to community retail pharmacists." Estab. 1888. Circ. 60,000. **Pays on acceptance.** Publishes ms an average of 5 months after acceptance. Byline given. Buys all rights. Submit seasonal material 8 months in advance. Simultaneous queries OK. Reports in 6 weeks on queries; 5 months on mss. Sample copy for 9×12 SAE with 4 first class stamps. Writer's guidelines for #10 SASE.
Nonfiction: How-to (e.g., manage a pharmacy); opinion (of registered pharmacists); and health-related feature stories. "We publish only those general health articles with some practical application for the pharmacist as business person. No general articles not geared to our pharmacy readership; no fiction." Buys 4 mss/year. Query with published clips. Length: 750-3,000 words. Pays $100-300.
Columns/Departments: Commentary (views or issues relevant to the subject of pharmacy or to pharmacists). Send complete ms. Length: 750-1,000 words. "This section is unpaid; we will take submissions with byline."
Tips: "Submit material geared to the *pharmacist* as *business person*. Write according to our policy, i.e., business articles with emphasis on practical information for a community pharmacist. We suggest reading several back issues and following general feature story tone, depth, etc. Stay away from condescending use of language. Though our articles are written in simple style, they must reflect knowledge of the subject and reasonable respect for the readers' professionalism and intelligence."

CANADIAN PHARMACEUTICAL JOURNAL, 1785 Alta Vista Dr., Ottawa, Ontario K1G 3Y6 Canada. (613)523-7877. FAX: (613)523-0445. Editor: Jane Dewar. Clinical Editor: Mary MacDonald-LaPrade. News and Features Editor: Diana Gibbs. 40% freelance written. Works with a small number of new/unpublished writers each year. Monthly journal for pharmacists. Estab. 1868. Circ. 12,500. Pays after editing. Publishes ms an average of 3 months after acceptance. Buys first serial rights. Reports in 2 months. Free sample copy and writer's guidelines.

Nonfiction: Relevant to Canadian pharmacy. Publishes exposés (pharmacy practice, education and legislation); how-to (pharmacy business operations); historical (pharmacy practice, Canadian legislation, education). Length: 200-400 words (for news notices); 800-1,500 words (for articles). Query. Payment is contingent on value. Sometimes pays expenses of writers on assignment.

Photos: Color and b&w (5×7) glossies purchased with mss. Captions and model release required.

Tips: "Query with complete description of proposed article, including topic, sources (in general), length, payment requested, suggested submission date, and whether photographs will be included. It is helpful if the writer has read a *recent* (1990) copy of the journal; we are glad to send one if required. References should be included where appropriate (this is vital where medical and scientific information is included). Send 3 copies of each ms. Author's degree and affiliations (if any) and writing background should be listed."

FAHS REVIEW, Suite 308, 1405 N. Pierce St., Little Rock AR 72207. (501)661-9555. FAX: (501)663-4903. Editor: John Herrmann. 10% freelance written. Bimonthly trade journal on health care issues and health care politics (federal and state). "*FAHS Review* publishes news and articles concerning the politics of health care, covers legislative activities and broad grassroots stories involving particular hospitals or organizations and their problems/solutions. Goes to health care managers, executives, to all members of the Congress and key administrative people." Estab. 1967. Circ. 35,000. **Pays on acceptance.** Byline given. Offers $100 kill fee. Buys first North American serial rights and second serial (reprint) rights. Submit seasonal/holiday material 4-5 months in advance. Simultaneous submissions OK. Query for electronic submissions. Reports in 1 week on queries; 1 month on mss. Sample copy for 9×12 SAE with 5 first class stamps.

Nonfiction: Essays, interview/profile, opinion and personal experience. "No articles about health care or medical procedures. No new products pieces. No articles about health care organizations and the stock market." Buys 2 mss/year. Query with published clips. Length: 1,500-3,500 words. Pays $200-750. "Articles by health care leaders, members of Congress and staff and legal columns generally not paid." Pays expenses of writers on assignment.

Photos: Send photo with submission. Reviews contact sheets, transparencies and prints. Offers no additional payment for photos accepted with ms. Captions and identification of subjects required. Buys one-time rights and all rights.

Columns/Departments: Jennifer L. Smith. Health Law Perspectives (analysis of legislative activity; interpretation of laws as they apply to hospitals, etc.), 2,000-3,000 words; Health Care Financing (business issues in health care), 1,500-3,500 words; and Supply Side (health care suppliers news update), 1,500-3,500 words. Buys 2 mss/year. Query with published clips. Pays $100-200.

Tips: "Any specific information on Medicare/Medicaid problems; a good hospital/business story (failure or success story); good contacts with state or federal senators and representatives and/or their staff members for close-ups, profiles. No writing in supply side that sells the supplier or its products but, rather, how it sees current issues from its perspective."

‡JEMS, A Journal of Emergency Medical Services, Jems Publishing Co. Inc., Suite 200, 674 Via de la Valle, P.O. Box 1026, Solana Beach CA 92075. (619)481-1128. FAX: (619)481-2711. Executive Editor: Keith Griffiths. Managing Editor: Nancy Peterson. 25% freelance written. Monthly magazine of emergency medical services—all phases. Our writings are directed to the personnel who service the emergency medicine world: paramedics, EMTs, emergency physicians and nurses, administrators, EMS consultants, etc. Estab. 1980. Circ. 35,000. Pays on publication. Publishes ms an average of 3 months after acceptance. Byline given. Buys first North American serial rights. Submit seasonal/holiday material 6 months in advance. Query for electronic submissions. Reports in 3 weeks on queries; 1 week on mss with acknowledgement letter. Free sample copy and writer's guidelines.

Nonfiction: Essays, general interest, how-to (prehospital care), humor, interview/profile, new product, opinion, photo feature, technical. Buys 18 mss/year. Query. Length: 900-3,600 words. Pays $150-250.

Photos: State availability of photos with submission. Offers no additional payment for photos accepted with ms. Buys one-time rights.

Columns/Departments: Nancy Peterson, managing editor. Teacher Talk (directed toward EMS instructors), 2,400 words; Pediatric Notebook (emergency care of the child), 2,400 words.

Tips: Feature articles are most open to freelancers. We have guidelines available upon request and of course, manuscripts must be geared toward our specific EMS audience.

PHARMACY TIMES, Romaine Pierson Publishers, 80 Shore Rd., Port Washington NY 11050. (516)883-6350. FAX: (516)883-6609. Publisher/Editor-in-Chief: Raymond A. Gosselin, R.Ph. Executive Editor: Joseph Cupolo. 15% freelance written. Monthly magazine on the pharmaceutical industry. Estab. 1897. Circ. 89,076. Pays on publication. Publishes ms an average of 4 months after acceptance. Byline given. Buys one-time rights. Submit seasonal/holiday material 6 months in advance. Query for electronic submissions. Reports in 3 weeks on queries; 6 weeks on mss. Free sample copy and writer's guidelines.

Nonfiction: Interview/profile, new product, opinion, personal experience, photo feature, technical and travel. Buys 12-15 mss/year. Send complete ms. Length: 800-1,500 words. Pays $250-400 for assigned articles; $100-250 for unsolicited articles. Pays in contributor copies or other premiums "per author request or for reprinted material."

Photos: State availability of photos with submission. Reviews negatives and 3×5 prints. Offers no additional payment for photos accepted with ms. Captions, model releases and identification of subjects required. Buys one-time rights.

Education and Counseling

Professional educators, teachers, coaches and counselors—as well as other people involved in training and education—read the journals classified here. Many journals for educators are nonprofit forums for professional advancement; writers contribute articles in return for a byline and contributor's copies. *Writer's Market* includes only educational journals that pay freelancers for articles. Education-related publications for students are included in the Consumer Career, College and Alumni and Teen and Young Adult sections.

ARTS & ACTIVITIES, Publishers' Development Corporation, Suite 200, 591 Camino de la Reina, San Diego CA 92108. (619)297-5352. FAX: (619)297-5353. Editor: Dr. Leven C. Leatherbury. Managing Editor: Maryellen Bridge. 95% freelance written. Eager to work with new/unpublished writers. Monthly (except July and August) art education magazine covering art education at levels from preschool through college for educators and therapists engaged in arts and crafts education and training. Estab. 1932. Circ. 25,433. Pays on publication. Publishes ms an average of 6 months after acceptance. Byline given. Buys first North American rights. Submit seasonal/holiday material 4 months in advance. Reports in 2 months. Sample copy for 9×12 envelope and 8 first class stamps; writer's guidelines for #10 SASE.

Nonfiction: Historical/nostalgic (arts activities history); how-to (classroom art experiences, artists' techniques); interview/profile (of artists); opinion (on arts activities curriculum, ideas on how to do things better); personal experience in the art class room ("this ties in with the how-to, we like it to be *personal*, no recipe style"); and articles on exceptional art programs. Buys 50-80 mss/year. Length: 200-2,000 words. Pays $35-150.

Tips: "Frequently in unsolicited manuscripts, writers obviously have not studied the magazine to see what style of articles we publish. Send for a sample copy to familiarize yourself with our style and needs. The best way to find out if his/her writing style suits our needs is for the author to submit a manuscript on speculation."

CLASSROOM COMPUTER LEARNING, Suite A4, 2169 Francisco Blvd. E., San Rafael CA 94901. FAX: (415)457-4378. Editor-in-Chief: Holly Brady. 50% freelance written. Works with a small number of new/unpublished writers each year. Monthly magazine published during school year emphasizing elementary through high school educational computing topics. Estab. 1980. Circ. 83,000. **Pays on acceptance.** Publishes ms an average of 8 months after acceptance. Buys all rights or first serial rights. Submit seasonal/holiday material 6 months in advance. Reports in 2 months. Writer's guidelines for #10 SASE; sample copy for 8×10 SAE and 6 first class stamps.

Nonfiction: "We publish manuscripts that describe innovative ways of using computers in the classroom as well as articles that discuss controversial issues in computer education." Interviews, brief computer-related activity ideas and longer featurettes describing fully developed and tested classroom ideas. Buys 50 mss/year. Query. Length: 500 words or less for classroom activities; 1,000-1,500 words for classroom activity featurettes; 1,500-2,500 words for major articles. Pays $25 for activities; $150 for featurettes; varying rates for longer articles. Educational Software Reviews: Assigned through editorial offices. "If interested, send a letter telling us of your areas of interest and expertise as well as the microcomputer(s) you have available to you." Pays $150 per review. Sometimes pays expenses of writers on assignment.

Photos: State availability of photos with query.

Tips: "The talent that goes into writing our shorter hands-on pieces is different from that required for features (e.g., interviews, issues pieces, etc.) Write whatever taps your talent best. A frequent mistake is taking too 'novice' or too 'expert' an approach. You need to know our audience well and to understand how much they know about computers. Also, too many manuscripts lack a definite point of view or focus or opinion. We like pieces with clear, strong, well thought out opinions."

COTTONWOOD MONTHLY, Cottonwood Press, Suite 398, 305 W. Magnolia, Ft. Collins CO 80521. (303)493-1286. Editor: Cheryl Thurston. 25% freelance written. Monthly, Sept.-May newsletter for language arts teachers, grades 5 and up. "The *Cottonwood Monthly* publishes ideas, activities, lessons, games and assignments for language arts teachers to use in the classroom. Our emphasis is upon practical materials that a teacher can photocopy and use tomorrow. We also like to use material with a humorous slant." Estab. 1986. Circ. 300. Pays on publication. Publishes ms an average of 3 months after acceptance. Byline sometimes given. Buys all rights. Submit seasonal/holiday material 4 months in advance. Simultaneous submissions OK. Sample copy $1 with SASE.

Nonfiction: How-to (practical ideas on anything that can make a teacher's life easier), humor, (games lessons, activities, assignments for language arts classes grades 5 and up). "Nothing theoretical. We want only practical material teachers can actually *use* in their classrooms." Buys 20 mss/year. Send complete ms. Length: 250-750 words. Pays $20-25 for unsolicited articles.

Columns/Departments: Teacher Tips (practical tips on anything of concern to language arts teachers: discipline, stress management, school programs, motivating students, grading papers, communicating with parents, etc.). Buys 9 mss/year. Send complete ms. Length: 75-200 words. Pays $10.

Tips: "Show us that you know kids, real life kids. If your material will appeal to modern-day students, we are interested and flexible. We don't like to see dry, textbook-like material. We are interested in material that takes a lighter, humorous, even offbeat approach to language arts."

‡DANCE TEACHER NOW, The Practical Magazine of Dance, SMW Communications, Inc., 3020 Beacon Blvd., West Sacramento CA 95691-3436. (916)373-0201. Editor: K.C. Patrick. 80% freelance written. Our readers are professional dance educators, business persons and related professionals. Estab. 1979. Circ. 6,500. Pays on publication. Publishes ms an average of 2-3 months after acceptance. Byline given. Buys all rights and permission to reprint on request. Submit seasonal/holiday material 6 months in advance. Query for electronic submission. Reports in 2 months. Sample copy for $9 × 12$ SAE with 6 first class stamps. Free writer's guidelines.

Nonfiction: Book excerpts, how-to (teach, business), interview/profile, new product, personal experience, photo feature. January—summer programs; March/September—video; May—studio update. November/December—costumes and production preview. No PR or puff pieces. All articles must be well researched. Buys 45 mss/year. Query. Length: 1,000-3,500 words. Pays $100-350 for unsolicited articles.

Photos: Send photos with submission. Reviews contact sheets, negatives transparencies and prints. Limited photo budget.

Columns/Departments: Practical Tips (how-to's or updates, 100-350 words; Free Calendar Listings (auditions/competitions/workshops), 50 words. Pays $25 per pubished tip.

Tips: Read several issues—particularly seasonal. Stay within writers guidelines.

INSTRUCTOR MAGAZINE, Scholastic, Inc., 730 Broadway, New York NY 10003. Editor-in-Chief: John Lent. Executive Editor: Debra Martorelli. Eager to work with new/unpublished writers, "especially teachers." Monthly magazine. Emphasizes elementary education. Circ. 300,000. **Pays on acceptance.** Publishes ms an average of 1 year after acceptance. Byline given. Buys all rights. Submit seasonal/holiday material 6 months in advance. Query for electronic submissions. Reports in 1 month on queries; 2 months on mss. Send a SASE for a free writer's guidelines; mention *Writer's Market* in request.

Nonfiction: How-to articles on elementary classroom practice—practical suggestions and project reports. Occasionally publishes first-person accounts of classroom experiences. Buys 100 mss/year. Query. Length: 400-2,000 words. Pays $15-75 for short items; $125-400 for articles and features. Send all queries to Attention: manuscripts editor.

Photos: Send photos with submission. Reviews $4 × 5$ transparencies and prints. Offers no additional payment for photos accepted with ms. Model releases and identification of subjects required. Buys all rights.

Columns/Departments: Teachers Express (quick teacher tips and ideas); Planner (seasonal activities, bulletin boards and crafts); Whole K Catalog (teaching ideas for primary grades); Partnerships (teacher-initiated school/business partnerships). Buys 100 mss/year. Query with SASE. Length: 50-1,000 words. Pays $30-100.

Fiction: Occasionally buys plays and read-aloud stories for children. Length: 500-2,500 words. Pays $75-200.

Tips: "How-to articles should be kept practical, with concrete examples whenever possible. Writers should keep in mind that our audience is elementary teachers."

JOURNAL OF CAREER PLANNING & EMPLOYMENT, College Placement Council, Inc., 62 Highland Ave., Bethlehem PA 18017. (215)868-1421. FAX: (215)868-0208. Associate Editor: Bill Beebe. 25% freelance written. Published Nov., Jan., March and May. A magazine for career development professionals who counsel and/or hire college students, graduating students, employees and job-changers. Circ. 4,000. **Pays on acceptance.** Publishes ms an average of 4 months after acceptance. Byline given. Buys first rights. Reports in 1 month on queries; 2 months on mss. Free writer's guidelines for #10 SASE.

Nonfiction: Book excerpts, how-to, interview/profile, opinion, photo feature, new techniques/innovative practices and current issues in the field. No articles that speak directly to job candidates. Buys 7-10 mss/year. Query with published clips, or send complete ms. Length: 3,000-4,000 words. Pays $200-400.

Tips: "A freelancer can best break into our publication by sending query with clips of published work, by writing on topics that aim directly at the journal's audience—professionals in the college career planning, placement and recruitment field—and by using an easy-to-read, narrative style rather than a formal, thesis style. The area of our publication most open to freelancers is nonfiction feature articles only. Topics should directly relate to the career planning and employment of the college educated and should go beyond the basics of career planning, job hunting and hiring issues, since journal readers are well-versed in those basics."

LOLLIPOPS, The Magazine for Early Childhood Educators, Good Apple, Inc., 1204 Buchanan, Box 299, Carthage IL 62321. (212)357-3981. Editor: Jerry Aten. 20% freelance written. A magazine published 5 times a year providing easy-to-use, hands-on practical teaching ideas and suggestions for early childhood education. Circ. 20,000. Pays on publication. Months until publication vary. Buys all rights. Submit seasonal/holiday material 6 months in advance. Sample copy for 8 × 12 SAE with 3 first class stamps; writer's guidelines for #10 SAE with 2 first class stamps.
Nonfiction: How-to (on creating usable teaching materials). Buys varying number of mss/year. Query with or without published clips, or send complete ms. Length: 200-1,000 words. Pays $25-100 for assigned articles; pays $10-30 for unsolicited articles. Writer has choice of cash or Good Apple products worth twice the contract value.
Photos: State availability of photos with submission. Reviews contact sheets and transparencies. Offers $10 minimum/photo. Model releases and identification of subjects required. Buys all rights.
Columns/Departments: Accepts material dealing with the solving of problems encountered by early childhood education. Buys varying number of mss/year. Query with published clips. Length: varies. Pays $25-100.
Fiction: Adventure and fantasy (for young children). Query with published clips.
Poetry: Light verse. Buys varying number of poems/year.
Tips: "I'm always looking for something that's new and different—something that works for teachers of young children."

‡**MEDIA & METHODS**, American Society of Educators, 1429 Walnut St., Philadelphia PA 19102. (215)563-3501. Editor/Director: Michele Sokoloff. Bimonthly trade journal published during the school year about educational products, media technologies and programs for schools and universities. Readership: Librarians and media specialists. Estab. 1963. Circ. 40,000. Pays on publication. Publishes ms an average of 3 months after acceptance. Byline given. Buys first North American serial rights. Free smaple copy and writer's guidelines.
Nonfiction: How-to, practical, new product, personal experience, technical. Must send query letter, outline or call editor. Do not send ms. Length: 600-1,200 words. Pays $75-200.
Photos: State availability of photos with submission. Reviews 3 × 5 prints. Offers no additional payment for photos accepted with ms. Captions and identification of subjects required. Buys one-time rights.

MEDIA PROFILES: The Health Sciences Edition, Olympic Media Information, P.O. Box 190, West Park NY 12493-0190. (914)384-6563. Publisher: Walt Carroll. 100% freelance written. For hospital education departments, nursing schools, schools of allied health, paramedical training units, colleges, community colleges, local health organizations. Serial, in magazine format, published every 2 months. Circ. 1,000. Pays on publication. Publishes ms an average of 6 months after acceptance. Buys all rights. Buys 240 mss/year. Electronic submissions OK. "Sample copies and writer's guidelines sent on receipt of resume, background, and mention of audiovisual hardware you have access to. Enclose $5 for writer's guidelines and sample issue. (Refunded with first payment upon publication)." Reports in 1 month. Query.
Nonfiction: "Reviews of all kinds of audiovisual media. We are the only review publication devoted exclusively to evaluation of audiovisual aids for hospital and health training. We have a highly specialized, definite format that must be followed in all cases. Samples should be seen by all means. Our writers should first have a background in health sciences; second, have some experience with audiovisuals; and third, follow our format precisely. Writers with advanced degrees and teaching affiliations with colleges and hospital education departments given preference. We are interested in reviews of media materials for nursing education, in-service education, continuing education, personnel training, patient education, patient care and medical problems. We will assign audiovisual aids to qualified writers and send them these to review for us. Unsolicited mss not welcome." Pays $15/review.

MOMENTUM, National Catholic Educational Association, 1077 30th St. NW, Washington DC 20007. Editor: Patricia Feistritzer. 10% freelance written. Quarterly magazine. For Catholic administrators and teachers, some parents and students, in all levels of education (preschool, elementary, secondary, higher). Estab. 1970. Circ. 25,000. Pays on publication. Buys first serial rights. Reports in 3 months. Free sample copy.
Nonfiction: Articles concerned with educational philosophy, psychology, methodology, innovative programs, teacher training, research, financial and public relations programs and management systems—all applicable to nonpublic schools. Book reviews on educational/religious topics. Avoid general topics or topics applicable *only* to public education. "We look for a straightforward, journalistic style with emphasis on practical examples, as well as scholarly writing and statistics. All references must be footnoted, fully documented. Emphasis is on professionalism." Buys 28-36 mss/year. Query with outline. Length: 1,500-2,000 words. Pays 2¢/word.

‡**THE MUSIC & COMPUTER EDUCATOR**, MCE Publications, Inc., 807 E. Jericho Turnpike, Huntington Station NY 11746. (516)385-7107. Publisher: Nelson Varon. Managing Editor: Lisa Pratt. 75% freelance written. Ten times/year magazine covering technology in music education. Writers must be well versed in music education and technology. Estab. 1989. Circ. 22,000. Pays on publication. Byline given. Buys all rights or makes work-for-hire assignments. Submit seasonal/holiday material 4 months in advance. Query for electronic

submissions. Reports in 6 weeks on queries; 3 months on mss. Sample copy for 10×13 SAE with 5 first class stamps.

Nonfiction: How-to (music applications), interview/profile (music educators), technical (musical instruments). No general overviews. Buys 70 mss/year. Query or query with published clips. Length: 600-1,500 words. Pays $60-150 for assigned articles.

Photos: Send photos with submission. Reviews contact sheets. Offers no additional payment for photos accepted with ms. Captions and identification of subjects required. Buys all rights.

Columns/Departments: Visions (think piece), 1,200 words; Courseware (music class applications), 1,200 words. Buys 20 mss/year. Query with published clips. Length: 900-1,200 words. Pays $90-120.

Tips: "Find a unique local story that may have national appeal. The Profiles department is most open to freelancers."

NATIONAL BEAUTY EDUCATION JOURNAL, Milady Publishing Corp., 220 White Plains Rd., Tarrytown NY 10591. (914)332-4800. Editor: Jacqueline Carlsen. Associate Editor: Catherine Frangie. 75% freelance written. Works with a small number of new/unpublished writers each year. A monthly magazine covering cosmetology education. "Articles must address subjects pertinent to cosmetology education (i.e. articles which will assist the instructor in the classroom or the school owner to run his or her business)." Circ. 4,000 schools. Pays on publication. Publishes ms an average of 2 months after acceptance. Byline given. Buys first rights. Submit seasonal/holiday material 3 months in advance. Simultaneous and previously published submissions OK. Free sample copy with writer's guidelines.

Nonfiction: Book excerpts, essays, historical/nostalgic, how-to (on doing a haircut, teaching a technique) humor, interview/profile, new product, personal experience, photo feature and technical. No articles geared to the salon owner or operator instead of the cosmetology school instructor or owner. Buys 24 mss/year. Query with published clips, or send complete ms. Length: 500-3,000 words. Pays $150 if published.

Photos: Send photos with submissions. Reviews 5×7 b&w prints. Offers no additional payment for photos accepted with ms. Identification of subjects required. Buys first rights; make sure reprint permission is granted.

Columns Departments: Buys 6 mss/year; willing to start new departments. Length: 500-1,000 words. Pays $150.

Fiction: Humorous and slice-of-life vignettes. No fiction relating to anything other than the classroom or the beauty school business. Send complete ms. Length: 500-3,000 words. Pays $150.

Tips: "Talk to school owners and instructors to get a feel for the industry. All areas of our publication are open. Write in clear, simple language."

SCHOOL ARTS MAGAZINE, 50 Portland St., Worcester MA 01608. Editor: Kent Anderson. 85% freelance written. Monthly, except June, July and August. Serves arts and craft education profession, kindergarten-12, higher education and museum education programs. Written by and for art teachers. Estab. 1901. Pays on publication. Publishes ms an average of 3 months "if timely; if less pressing, can be 1 year or more" after acceptance. Buys first serial rights and second serial (reprint) rights. Reports in 3 months. Free sample copy and writer's guidelines.

Nonfiction: Articles, with photos, on art and craft activities in schools. Should include description and photos of activity in progress as well as examples of finished art work. Query or send complete ms. Length: 600-1,400 words. Pays $20-100.

Tips: "We prefer articles on actual art projects or techniques done by students in actual classroom situations. Philosophical and theoretical aspects of art and art education are usually handled by our contributing editors. Our articles are reviewed and accepted on merit and each is tailored to meet our needs. Keep in mind that art teachers want practical tips, above all. Our readers are visually, not verbally, oriented. Write your article with the accompanying photographs in hand." The most frequent mistakes made by writers are "bad visual material (photographs, drawings) submitted with articles, or a lack of complete descriptions of art processes; and no rationale behind programs or activities. It takes a close reading of *School Arts* to understand its function and the needs of its readers. Some writers lack the necessary familiarity with art education."

SCHOOL SHOP/TECH DIRECTIONS, Prakken Publications, Inc., P.O. Box 8623, Ann Arbor MI 48107 FAX: (313)769-8383. Editor: Susanne Peckham. 100% freelance written. Eager to work with new/unpublished writers. A monthly (except June and July) magazine covering issues, trends and projects of interest to industrial, vocational, technical and technology educators at the secondary and postsecondary school levels. Special issue in April deals with varying topics for which mss are solicited. Estab. 1935. Circ. 45,000. Buys all rights. Pays on publication. Publishes ms an average of 8-12 months after acceptance. Byline given. Prefers authors who have direct connection with the field of industrial and/or technical education. Simultaneous queries, and simultaneous and previously published submissions OK. Reports in 6 weeks. Free sample copy and writer's guidelines.

Nonfiction: Uses articles pertinent to the various teaching areas in industrial education (woodwork, electronics, drafting, machine shop, graphic arts, computer training, etc.). "The outlook should be on innovation in educational programs, processes or projects that directly apply to the industrial/technical education area."

Buys general interest, how-to, opinion, personal experience, technical and think pieces, interviews, humor, and coverage of new products. Buys 135 unsolicited mss/year. Length: 200-2,000 words. Pays $25-150.
Photos: Send photos with accompanying query or ms. Reviews b&w and color prints. Payment for photos included in payment for ms.
Columns/Departments: Shop Kinks (brief items which describe short-cuts or special procedures relevant to the industrial arts classroom). Buys 30 mss/year. Send complete ms. Length: 20-100 words. Pays $15 minimum.
Tips: "We are most interested in articles written by industrial, vocational and technical educators about their class projects and their ideas about the field. We need more and more technology-related articles."

TEACHING/K-8, The Professional Magazine, Early Years, Inc., 40 Richards Ave., 7th Fl., Norwalk CT 06854. (203)855-2650. Editor: Allen Raymond. 90% freelance written. "We prefer material from classroom teachers." A monthly magazine covering teaching of kindergarten through eighth grades. Estab. 1970. Pays on publication. Publishes ms an average of 2-7 months after acceptance. Byline given. Buys all rights. Submit seasonal/holiday material 6 months in advance. Reports in 6 weeks. Sample copy $2 with 9 × 12 SASE; writer's guidelines for #10 SASE.
Nonfiction: Patricia Broderick, editorial director. Classroom curriculum material. Send complete ms. Length: 1,200-1,500 words. Pays $35 maximum.
Photos: Offers no additional payment for photos accepted with ms. Model releases and identification of subjects required.
Columns/Departments: Patricia Broderick, editorial director. Send complete ms. Length: 1,100 word maximum. Pays $25 maximum.
Tips: "Manuscripts should be specifically oriented to a successful teaching strategy, idea, project or program. Broad overviews of programs or general theory manuscripts are not usually the type of material we select for publication. Because of the definitive learning level we cover (pre-school through grade eight) we try to avoid presenting general groups of unstructured ideas. We prefer classroom tested ideas and techniques."

TEACHING TODAY, 6112-102 Ave., Edmonton, Alberta T6A 0N4 Canada. (403)465-2990. Editor: Betty Coderre. Managing Editor: Max Coderre. 90% freelance written. Educational magazine published 5 times per year. Estab. 1983. Circ. 16,921. Pays on publication. Publishes ms an average of 6-12 months after acceptance. Byline given. Buys first rights, one-time rights or all rights. Simultaneous and previously published submissions OK. Query for electronic submissions. Free sample and writer's guidelines.
Nonfiction: How-to (related to teaching), humor (related to education), inspirational, interview/profile (publicly visible people's views on education), personal experience (if related to teaching), communication skills and professional development (teacher). Buys 40-50 mss/year. Query with published clips. Length: 150-1,500 words. Pays $20-225 for assigned articles; $15-150 for unsolicited articles. Sometimes pays expenses of writers on assignment.
Photos: Send photos with submission. Reviews 4 × 5 prints. Offers $25-100 per photo. Model releases and identification of subjects required. Buys one-time rights.
Fillers: Anecdotes and gags to be illustrated by cartoonist. Buys 20/year. Length: 20-100 words. Pays $5-25.
Tips: "A freelancer can best break into our magazine with articles, cartoons, fillers related to education. Articles primarily that will *help* educators personally or professionally."

TODAY'S CATHOLIC TEACHER, 2451 E. River Rd., Dayton OH 45439. (513)294-5783. Editor: Stephen Brittan. 40% freelance written. Works with a small number of new/unpublished writers each year. For administrators, teachers and parents concerned with Catholic schools, both parochial and CCD. Estab. 1967. Circ. 60,000. Pays after publication. Publishes ms an average of 3 months after acceptance. Byline given. Buys all rights. Phone queries OK. Submit seasonal/holiday material 3 months in advance. Sample copy $3; writer's guidelines for #10 SASE; mention *Writer's Market* in request.
Nonfiction: How-to (based on experience, particularly in Catholic situations, philosophy with practical applications); interview (of practicing educators, educational leaders); personal experience (classroom happenings); and profile (of educational leader). Buys 40-50 mss/year. Submit complete ms. Length: 800-2,000 words. Pays $15-75.
Photos: State availability of photos with ms. Offers no additional payment for 8 × 10 b&w glossy prints. Buys one-time rights. Captions preferred; model release required.
Tips: "We prefer articles based on the author's own expertise, and/or experience, with a minimum of quotations from other sources. We use many one-page features."

Electronics and Communication

These publications are edited for broadcast and telecommunications technicians and engineers, electrical engineers and electrical contractors. Included are journals for electronic equipment designers and operators who maintain electronic and telecommunication systems. Publications for appliance dealers can be found in Home Furnishings and Household Goods.

‡AMERICAN ELECTRONICS ASSOCIATION UPDATE, The business and management publication for electronics executives, American Electronics Association, 5201 Great America Parkway, Santa Clara CA 95054. (408)987-4200. FAX: (408)970-8565. Editor: April Neilson. 40-50% freelance written. Monthly tabloid covering electronics industry trends, new technologies, finance, marketing, manufacturing, public affairs, task forces and business networking. Pays 10-15 working days after acceptance. U.S. circulation 31,000; mostly executives and managers in large and small electronics companies nationwide.
Nonfiction: Industry event coverage, public policy reporting, international trade, technology education, (company profiles); pays 20-35¢/word for assigned articles. Query with published clips. Buys 30 mss/year. Length: 500-1,500 words. Query for electronic submissions.
Columns/Departments: Public Affairs, Industry Trends, Education and Science Policy, Campus Research Report, Small Business, Management, Regional Councils.
Tips: "We require specialty in writing about the electronics industry and the ability to meet 1 to 1½ week deadlines. Unsolicited work not accepted."

BROADCAST TECHNOLOGY, Box 420, Bolton, Ontario L7E 5T3 Canada. (416)857-6076. FAX: (416)857-6045. Editor-in-Chief: Doug Loney. 50% freelance written. Monthly (except August, December) magazine. Emphasizes broadcast engineering. Estab. 1975. Circ. 9,000. Pays on publication. Byline given. Buys all rights. Phone queries OK.
Nonfiction: Technical articles on developments in broadcast engineering, especially pertaining to Canada. Query. Length: 500-1,500 words. Pays $100-300.
Photos: Purchased with accompanying ms. Black and white or color. Captions required.
Tips: "Most of our outside writing is by regular contributors, usually employed full-time in broadcast engineering. The specialized nature of our magazine requires a specialized knowledge on the part of a writer, as a rule."

BUSINESS RADIO, National Association of Business and Educational Radio, 1501 Duke St., Alexandria VA 22314. (703)739-0300. Editor: Mark C. Huey. Assistant Editor: Diane C. Flaherty. 25% freelance written. Magazine is published 10 times/year on two-way radio communications. "Magazine is for land mobile equipment users, dealers, service shop operators, manufacturers, communications technicians, SMR owners and operators. To acquaint members with the diversity of uses to which land mobile radio can be applied. To identify and discuss new and developing areas of RF technology and their application." Circ. 6,000. **Pays on acceptance.** Publishes ms an average of 3 months after acceptance. Byline given. Buys first rights. Previously published submissions OK. Query for electronic submissions. Reports in 1 month. Sample copy for 9×12 SAE with 5 first class stamps. Writer's guidelines for 9×12 SASE.
Nonfiction: General interest, interview/profile, new product, technical, and general—small business or management articles all related to two-way (land mobile) communications. Buys 5 mss/year. Query with or without published clips, or send complete ms. Length: 2,500-4,000 words. Pays $100-300 for unsolicited articles. Sometimes pays expenses of writers on assignment.
Photos: Send photos with submission. Reviews contact sheets, negatives, transparencies and prints. Offers no additional payment for b&w photos accepted with ms. Offers $200-250 per photo if color used for cover. Captions, model releases and identification of subjects required. Buys one-time rights.
Columns/Departments: Management Notebook (small business, general management), 2,000-3,000 words. Buys 8 mss/year. Query or send complete ms. Pays $50-150.
Tips: "Many people use two-way radios. Any of them could be the subject of a potential article."

‡CABLE COMMUNICATIONS MAGAZINE, Canada's Authoritative International Cable Television Publication, Ter-Sat Media Publications Ltd., 4 Smetana Dr., Kitchener, Ontario N2B 3B8 Canada. (519)744-4111. FAX: (519)744-1261. Editor: Udo Salewsky. 33% freelance written. Prefers to work with published/established writers. Monthly magazine covering the cable television industry. Estab. 1934. Circ. 8,119. **Pays on acceptance.** Publishes ms an average of 2 months after acceptance. Byline given. Buys all rights. Submit seasonal/holiday material 1 month in advance. Query for electronic submissions. Reports in 2 weeks on queries; 1 month on mss. Free writer's guidelines; sample copy for 9×12 SAE and $3.50 in IRCs.
Nonfiction: Expose, how-to, interview/profile, opinion, technical articles, and informed views and comments on topical, industry related issues. Also, problem solving-related articles, new marketing and operating efficiency ideas. No fiction. Buys 50 mss/year. Query with published clips or send complete ms. Length: 1,000-4,000 words. Pays $200-800. Pays expenses of writers on assignment.
Columns/Departments: Buys 48 items/year. Query with published clips or send complete ms. Length: 1,000-1,500 words. Pays $200-300.
Tips: "Forward manuscript and personal resume. We don't need freelance writers for short articles and fillers. Break in with articles related to industry issues, events and new developments; analysis of current issues and events. Be able to interpret the meaning of new developments relative to the cable television

industry and their potential impact on the industry from a growth opportunity as well as a competitive point of view. Material should be well supported by facts and data. Insufficient research and understanding of underlying issues are frequent mistakes."

CABLE MARKETING, The Marketing/Management Magazine for Cable Television Executives, Jobson Publishing, 352 Park Ave. S., New York NY 10010. (212)685-4848. FAX: (212)696-5318. Editor: Les Luchter. Prefers to work with published/established writers. Monthly magazine for cable industry executives. Contains news and features on marketing, promotion and ad sales issues related to cable TV operations, programming and technology. Circ. 15,000. Pays on publication. Publishes ms an average of 2 months after acceptance. Byline given. Buys first North American serial rights. Reports in 1 month. Free sample copy. Query with published clips. Length: 1,500-2,000 words. Pays $500 average. Pays the expenses of writers on assignment.
Tips: "Learn something about the cable TV business before you try to write about it. Have specific story ideas. Have some field of expertise that you can draw upon (e.g., marketing, promotion or advertising). Not interested in reviews of programming. Editorial focus is on the *business* of cable television."

CABLE TV BUSINESS, Cardiff Publishing Co., #650, 6300 S. Syracuse Way, Englewood CO 80111. (303)220-0600. FAX: (303)773-9716. Editor: Chuck Moozakis. 10% freelance written. Prefers writers with telecommunications background. Semimonthly magazine about cable television for CATV system operators and equipment suppliers. Estab. 1964. Circ. 12,000. Pays on publication. Publishes ms an average of 1 month after acceptance. Byline given. Makes work-for-hire assignments. Phone queries OK. Query for electronic submissions. Reports in 2 weeks on queries; 1 month on mss. Free sample copy and writer's guidelines.
Nonfiction: Exposé (of industry corruption and government mismanagement); historical (early days of CATV); interview (of important people in the industry); profiles (of people or companies); how-to (manage or engineer cable systems); new product (description and application); and case history. "We use articles on all aspects of cable television from programming through government regulation to technical pieces. We use both color and b&w photos, charts and graphs. A writer should have some knowledge of cable television, then send a letter with a proposed topic." No first person articles. Buys 5 mss/year. Query. Length: 1,800-3,500 words. Pays $100/page of magazine space. Sometimes pays expenses of writers on assignment.
Photos: State availability of photos. Reviews 35mm color transparencies. Pays $50/page of magazine space for contact sheets. Offers no additional payment for photos accepted with ms. Captions required.
Tips: "The most frequent mistake made by writers in completing an article for us is not being specific enough about what the story topic really means to cable management—i.e., dollars and cents, or operational strategy. Freelancers are only used for major features."

‡ELECTRONIC SERVICING & TECHNOLOGY, Intertec Publishing Corp., P.O. Box 12901, Overland Park KS 66212. (913)888-4664. FAX: (913)541-6697, 6698. Editor: Conrad Persson. Senior Managing Editor: Tom Cook. 90% freelance written. Eager to work with new/unpublished writers. Monthly magazine for professional servicers and electronic enthusiasts who are interested in buying, building, installing and repairing consumer electronic equipment (audio, video, microcomputers, electronic games, etc.) Circ. 45,000. **Pays on acceptance.** Publishes ms an average of 6 months after acceptance. Byline given. Buys all rights. Simultaneous queries OK. Reports in 2 weeks on queries; 1 month on mss. Free sample copy and writer's guidelines.
Nonfiction: How-to (service, build, install and repair home entertainment electronic equipment); personal experience (troubleshooting); and technical (consumer electronic equipment; electronic testing and servicing equipment). "Explain the techniques used carefully so that even hobbyists can understand a how-to article." Buys 36 mss/year. Send complete ms. Length: 1,500 words minimum. Pays $100-300.
Photos: Send photos with ms. Reviews color and b&w transparencies and b&w prints. Captions and identification of subjects required. Buys all rights. Payment included in total ms package.
Columns/Departments: Alisa Carter, associate editor. Troubleshooting Tips. Buys 12 mss/year. Send complete ms. Length: open. Pays $25.
Tips: "In order to write for *ES&T* it is almost essential that a writer have an electronics background: technician, engineer or serious hobbyist. Our readers want nuts-and-bolts information on electronics."

HAM RADIO MAGAZINE, Main St., Greenville NH 03048. (603)878-1441. Publisher: T.H. Tenney, Jr. Editor: Terry Northrup. 75% freelance written. Monthly magazine on amateur radio theory and equipment construction. Estab. 1968. Circ. 40,000. Pays on publication. Publishes ms an average of 6 months after acceptance. Byline given. Buys first rights. Query for electronic submissions. Reports in 1 month. Sample copy $5. Writer's guidelines for #10 SASE.
Nonfiction: Contact: Bob Wilson, consulting technical editor. How-to and technical. "We have four special issues per year: January: Construction Issue; May: Antenna Issue; July: VHF/UHF Issue; and November: Receiver Issue. No human interest stories ('How I Saved the World with my Ham Radio'), or contest information, information on awards. We are a technical publication." Send complete ms. Pays $40 per published page. "We have given subscriptions or books from our bookstore when authors have requested such a payment instead."

Photos: Send photos with submission. Reviews 5 × 7 prints. Offers no additional payment for photos accepted with ms. Captions and identification of subjects required. Buys one-time rights.

Columns/Departments: Ham Notes (Quick fixes for problems with equipment, antennas, etc.). Send complete ms.

Tips: "The best way a writer can 'break in' to our publication is to have a working knowledge of amateur radio and a project of interest to other hams. Our Author's Guide offers tips on how to get started writing for our publication. Authors are welcome to submit feature articles or short pieces for our Ham Notes section."

INFORMATION TODAY, Learned Information Inc., 143 Old Marlton Pike, Medford NJ 08055. (609)654-6266. FAX: (609)654-4309. Publisher: Thomas H. Hogan. Editor: Patricia Lane. 30% freelance written. A tabloid for the users and producers of electronic information services, published 11 times per year. Circ. 10,000. Pays on publication. Publishes ms an average of 1 month after acceptance. Byline given. Buys first North American serial rights. Submit seasonal/holiday material 2 months in advance. Reports in 2 weeks. Free sample copy and writer's guidelines.

Nonfiction: Book reviews; interview/profile and new product; technical (dealing with computerized information services); and articles on library technology, artificial intelligence, database and Videotex services." We also cover software and optical publishing (CD-ROM). More focus on coverage of integrated online library systems." Buys approximately 25 mss/year. Query with published clips or send complete ms on speculation. Length: 500-1,500 words. Pays $90-220.

Photos: State availability of photos with submission.

Tips: "We look for clearly-written, informative articles dealing with the electronic delivery of information. Writing style should not be jargon-laden or heavily technical."

MICROWAVES & RF, 611 Route #46 W., Hasbrouck Heights NJ 07604. (201)393-6285. FAX: (201)393-6297. Associate Publisher/Editor: Michael Kachmar. 50% freelance written. Monthly magazine emphasizing radio frequency design. "Qualified recipients are those individuals actively engaged in microwave and RF research, design, development, production and application engineering, engineering management, administration or purchasing departments in organizations and facilities where application and use of devices, systems and techniques involve frequencies from HF through visible light." Estab. 1964. Circ. 65,000. Pays on publication. Publishes ms an average of 6 months after acceptance. Buys all rights. Phone queries OK. Query for electronic submissions. Reports in 1 month. Free sample copy and writer's guidelines; mention *Writer's Market* in request.

Nonfiction: "We are interested in material on research and development in microwave and RF technology and economic news that affects the industry." How-to (circuit design), new product, opinion, and technical. Buys 100 mss/year. Query. Pays $100.

‡MULTICHANNEL NEWS, Fairchild Publications, 7 E. 12th St., New York NY 10003. (212)741-7825. Editor: Joseph R. Boyle. Managing Editor: Les Luchter. Weekly newspaper tabloid. *"Multichannel News* serves the new electronic media industries of cable TV, pay TV (subscription over-the-air and pay cable), pay-per-view TV, multipoint distribution service, cable TV contractors, consulting firms and investors; broadcasting companies, programming companies, government agencies and others allied to the field." Estab. 1980. Circ. 15,499. Pays on publication. Byline given. Buys all rights. Free sample copy and writer's guidelines.

Nonfiction: General interest, new product, technical. Query. Length: 500 words maximum. Pays $5 minimum.

Photos: State availability of photos with submission. Reviews contact sheets. Offers no additional payment for photos accepted with ms. Captions required. Buys all rights.

OUTSIDE PLANT, Box 183, Cary IL 60013. (312)639-2200. FAX: (312)639-9542. Editor: John S. Saxtan. 50% freelance written. Prefers to work with published/established writers. Trade publication focusing exclusively on the outside plant segment of the telephone industry. Readers are end users and/or specifiers at Bell and independent operating companies, as well as long distance firms whose chief responsibilities are construction, maintenance, OSP planning and engineering. Readership also includes telephone contracting firms. Published an average of 11 issues/year. Circ. 17,000. Buys first rights. Pays on publication. Publishes ms an average of 3 months after acceptance. Reports in 1 month. Free sample copy and guidelines for #10 SASE.

Nonfiction: Must deal specifically with outside plant construction, maintenance, planning and fleet vehicle subjects for the telephone industry. "Case history application articles profiling specific telephone projects are best. Also accepts trend features, tutorials, industry research and seminar presentations. Preferably, features should be by-lined by someone at the telephone company profiled." Pays $35-50/published page, including photographs; pays $35 for cover photos.

Departments: OSP Tips & Advice (short nuts-and-bolts items on new or unusual work methods); and OSP Tommorrow (significant trends in outside plant), 300-600 word items. Pays $5-50. Other departments include new products, literature, vehicles and fiber optics.

Tips: Submissions should include author bio demonstrating expertise in the subject area."

RADIO WORLD NEWSPAPER, Industrial Marketing Advisory Services, Suite 310, 5827 Columbia Pike, Falls Church VA 22041. (703)998-7600. FAX: (703)998-2966. Editor: Judith Gross. News Editor: Alan Carter. 50% freelance written. Bimonthly newspaper on radio station technology and regulatory news. "Articles should be geared toward radio station engineers, producers, technical people and managers wishing to learn more about technical subjects. The approach should be more how-to than theoretical, although emerging technology may be approached in a more abstract way." Estab. 1976. Pays on publication. Publishes ms an average of 1-2 months after acceptance. Byline given. Buys first North American serial rights plus right to publish in monthly international and annual directory supplements. Submit seasonal/holiday material 2 months in advance. Query for electronic submissions. Reports in 2 months. Free sample copy and writer's guidelines.

Nonfiction: Exposé, historical/nostalgic, how-to (radio equipment maintenance and repair), humor, interview/profile, new product, opinion, personal experience, photo feature and technical. "No general financial, or vogue management concept pieces." Buys 24-40 mss/year. Query. Length: 750-1,250 words. Pays $75-200. Pays in contributor copies or other premiums "if they request it, and for one special feature called Great Idea." Sometimes pays expenses of writers on assignment.

Photos: Send photos with submission. Reviews 3×5 or larger prints. Offers no additional payment for photos accepted with ms. Identification of subjects required. Buys one-time rights.

Columns/Departments: Alex Zavistovich, Buyers Guide editor. Buyers Guide User Reports (field reports from engineers on specific pieces of radio station equipment). Buys 100 mss/year. Query. Length: 750-1,250 words. Pays $25-125.

Fillers: Newsbreaks and short humor. Buys 6/year. Length: 500-1,000 words. Pays $25-75.

Tips: "I frequently assign articles by phone. Sometimes just a spark of an idea can lead to a story assignment or publication. The best way is to have some radio station experience and try to think of articles other readers would benefit from reading."

SATELLITE RETAILER, Triple D Publishing, Inc., P.O. Box 2384, Shelby NC 28151. (704)482-9673. FAX: (704)484-8558. Editor: David B. Melton. 75% freelance written. Monthly magazine covering home satellite TV. "We look for technical, how-to, marketing, sales, new products, product testing, and news for the satellite television dealer." Estab. 1981. Circ. 12,000. Pays on publication. Byline given. 30% kill fee. Buys all rights. Submit seasonal/holiday material 3 months in advance. Simultaneous submissions OK. Query for electronic submissions. Free sample copy and writer's guidelines.

Nonfiction: How-to, new product, personal experience, photo feature, technical. Buys 24 mss/year. Query with or without published clips, or send complete ms. Length: 1,800-3,600 words. Pays $150-400. Sometimes pays expenses of writers on assignment.

Photos: Send photos with submission. Reviews contact sheets, transparencies (135 to 4×5). Captions, model releases and identification of subjects required. Buys all rights.

Tips: "Familiarity with electronics and television delivery systems is a definite plus."

SHOPTALK, National Association of Business and Educational Radio, 1501 Duke St., Alexandria VA 22314. (703)739-0300. Editor: Mark C. Huey. Managing Editor: Diane C. Flaherty. 25% freelance written. Monthly newsletter about two-way radios. "Newsletter targeted toward dealers, service shop owners and manufacturers of two-way radio. Newsletter supplies information to help readers manage businesses better." Circ. 1,000. **Pays on acceptance.** Publishes ms an average of 2 months after acceptance. Byline given. Buys first rights. Previously published submissions OK. Query for electronic submissions. Reports in 1 month. Sample copy for #10 SAE with 2 first class stamps. Writer's guidelines for #10 SASE.

Nonfiction: Book excerpts, essays, how-to, new product and technical, all small business or two-way radio related. Buys 9 mss/year. Query with or without published clips, or send complete ms. Length: 1,500-2,500 words. Pays $50-125 for unsolicited articles.

Photos: Send photos with submission. Reviews contact sheets. Offers no additional payment for photos accepted with ms. Captions, model releases and identification of subjects required. Buys one-time rights.

Tips: "All material should be written clearly and simply. Sidebars are helpful."

TECHTALK, National Association of Business and Educational Radio, 1501 Duke St., Alexandria VA 22314. (703)739-0300. Editor: Mark C. Huey. Managing Editor: Diane C. Flaherty. Bimonthly newsletter on two-way radio communications. "Newsletter is for technicians in communications field, especially two-way radio. Material relates to technical changes in the industry, installation procedures, testing and repair methods and self-improvement." Circ. 2,500. **Pays on acceptance.** Publishes ms an average of 2 months after acceptance. Byline given. Buys first rights. Previously published submissions OK. Query for electronic submissions. Reports in 1 month. Sample copy for #10 SAE with 2 first class stamps. Writer's guidelines for #10 SASE.

Nonfiction: Book excerpts, essays, how-to, new product and technical, all dealing with communications. Query with or without published clips, or send complete ms. Length: 1,000-2,500 words. Pays $50-125.

Photos: Send photos with submission. Reviews contact sheets. Offers no additional payment for photos accepted with ms. Captions, model releases and identification of subjects required.

Tips: "Writer needs a technical background such as tech school training and/or experience in communications, especially land-mobile."

TELEVISION BROADCAST, Covering Television Equipment, News, Applications and Technology, P.S.N. Publications, Inc., Suite 1820, 2 Park Ave., New York NY 10016. (212)779-1919. FAX: (212)213-3484. Editor: Elliot Luber. 40% freelance written. Monthly tabloid newsmagazine covering television station technology. "We publish a timely, colorful news tabloid targeted toward managers and engineers at television stations and teleproduction facilities in the U.S. The magazine is a balance between news and technology features." Estab. 1977. Circ. 30,000. Pays on publication. Usually publishes manuscripts the month they are accepted. Byline given. Offers 50% kill fee. Buys all rights. Submit seasonal/holiday material three months in advance. Query for electronic submissions. Free sample copy and writer's guidelines.

Nonfiction: Spot news. How-to (on using technology to improve signal quality, profits or community image), interview/profile, personal experience and technical. No articles that appeal mostly to TV viewers. No product reviews. Buys 100 mss per year. Query with published clips and brief résumé. Length: 500-1,500 words. Pays $100-300 for articles. Sometimes pays expenses of writers on assignment.

Photos: Send photos with submission. Reviews contact sheets. Captions, model releases and identification of subjects required.

Columns/Departments: Opinion, Newsmaker (Q&A interview), Engineering Close-up (quarterly special focus section), ENG/News Technology, Teleproduction, Audio for Video, Post Production, Electronic Graphics, Business/Industrial, Transmission, Product Spotlight (technology close-up), Station Breaks (station news), People & Places, New Products. Columns are 800 words; short features for departments up to 1,200 words.

Fillers: 25-100 word news items regarding television stations. Pays up to $30 each.

Tips: "Every city has a leading TV station and a leading video production company. What technological changes are they experiencing in their businesses, and how have they reacted? What have the consequences been?"

Energy and Utilities

People who supply power to homes, businesses and industry read the publications in this section. This category includes journals covering the electric power, natural gas, petroleum, solar and alternative energy industries.

ALTERNATIVE ENERGY RETAILER, Zackin Publications, Inc., P.O. Box 2180, Waterbury CT 06722. (203)755-0158. FAX: (203)755-3480. Editor: Ed Easley. 20% freelance written. Prefers to work with published/established writers. Monthly magazine on selling alternative energy products—chiefly solid fuel burning appliances. "We seek detailed how-to tips for retailers to improve business. Most freelance material purchased is about retailers and how they succeed." Estab. 1980. Circ. 14,000. Pays on publication. Publishes ms an average of 2 months after acceptance. Buys first North American serial rights. Submit seasonal/holiday material 4 months in advance. Reports in 2 weeks on queries. Sample copy for 9×12 SAE with 4 first class stamps; writer's guidelines for #10 SASE.

Nonfiction: How-to (improve retail profits and business know-how); and interview/profile (of successful retailers in this field). No "general business articles not adapted to this industry." Buys 10-20 mss/year. Query. Length: 1,000 words. Pays $200.

Photos: State availability of photos. Pays $25-125 maximum for 5×7 b&w prints. Reviews color slide transparencies. Identification of subject required. Buys one-time rights.

Tips: "We've redesigned into a more sophisticated, visual format. A freelancer can best break in to our publication with features about readers (retailers). Stick to details about what has made this person a success."

ELECTRICAL APPARATUS, The Magazine of the Electrical Aftermarket, Barks Publications, Inc., 400 N. Michigan Ave., Chicago IL 60611-4198. (312)321-9440. Editorial Director: Elsie Dickson. Managing Editor: Kevin N. Jones. Prefers to work with published/established writers. Uses very little freelance material. A monthly magazine for persons working in electrical maintenance, chiefly in industrial plants, who install and service electrical motors, transformers, generators, and related equipment. Circ. 16,000. **Pays on acceptance.** Publishes ms an average of 2-3 months after acceptance. Byline given. Buys all rights unless other arrangements made. Query for electronic submissions. Reports in 1 week on queries; 1 month on mss. Sample copy $4.

Nonfiction: Technical. Buys very few mss/year. Query essential, along with letter outlining credentials. Length: 1,500-2,500. Pays $250-500 for assigned articles only. Pays the expenses of writers on assignment by advance arrangement. Prefer freelance writers who are interested in becoming regular contributors.

Photos: Send photos with submission. "Photos are important to most articles. We prefer 35mm color slides, but sometimes use color or b&w prints." Offers additional payments, depending on quality and number. Captions and identification of subjects required. Buys one-time rights. "If we reuse photos, we pay residual fee."

Columns/Departments: Electrical Manager (items on managing businesses, people), 150-600 words; and Electropix (photo of interest with electrical slant), brief captions. "We are interested in expanding these departments." Pays $50-100.

Tips: "Queries are essential. Technical expertise is absolutely necessary, preferably an E.E. degree, or practical experience. We are also book publishers and some of the material in *EA* is now in book form, bringing the authors royalties. Also publishes an annual directory, subtitled *ElectroMechanical Bench Reference.*"

ELECTRICAL CONTRACTOR, 7315 Wisconsin Ave., Bethesda MD 20814. (301)657-3110. Managing Editor: Walt Albro. 10% freelance written. Monthly. For electrical contractors. Circ. 67,000. Publishes ms an average of 3 months after acceptance. Buys first serial rights, second serial (reprint) rights or simultaneous rights. Usually reports in 1 month. Byline given. Free sample copy.

Nonfiction: Management articles of interest to the owners of electrical construction and (transmission) line construction companies. Query. Length: 800-2,500 words. Pays $100/printed page, including photos and illustrative material.

Photos: Photos should be sharp, reproducible b&w glossies or color slides.

‡NATIONAL PETROLEUM NEWS, 950 Lee St., Des Plaines IL 60016. (312)296-0770. Editor: Frank Victoria. 3% freelance written. Prefers to work with published/established writers. For businessmen who make their living in the oil marketing industry, either as company employees or through their own business operations. Monthly magazine. Circ. 18,000. Rights purchased vary with author and material. Usually buys all rights. Pays on acceptance if done on assignment. Publishes ms an average of 2 months after acceptance. "The occasional freelance copy we use is done on assignment." Query.

Nonfiction: Material related directly to developments and issues in the oil marketing industry and "how-to" and "what-with" case studies. Informational, and successful business operations. "No unsolicited copy, especially with limited attribution regarding information in story." Buys 3-4 mss/year. Length: 2,000 words maximum. Pays $50-150/printed page. Sometimes pays the expenses of writers on assignment.

Photos: Pays $150/printed page. Payment for b&w photos "depends upon advance understanding."

‡PIPELINE & UNDERGROUND UTILITIES CONSTRUCTION, Oildom Publishing Co. of Texas, Inc., Box 22267, Houston TX 77027. Editor: Chris Homer. 5% freelance written. Prefers to work with published/established writers. Monthly magazine covering oil, gas, water, and sewer pipeline construction for contractors and construction workers who build pipelines. Circ. 19,000. No byline given. Not copyrighted. Buys first North American serial rights. Publishes ms an average of 3 months after acceptance. Simultaneous queries OK. Reports in 2 weeks on queries; 3 weeks on mss. Sample copy for $1 and 9 × 12 SAE.

Nonfiction: How-to. Query with published clips. Length: 1,500-2,500 words. Pays $100/printed page "unless unusual expenses are incurred in getting the story." Sometimes pays the expenses of writers on assignment.

Photos: Send photos with ms. Reviews 5 × 7 and 8 × 10 prints. Captions required. Buys one-time rights.

Tips: "We supply guidelines outlining information we need." The most frequent mistake made by writers in completing articles is unfamiliarity with the field.

PUBLIC POWER, 2301 M St. NW, Washington DC 20037. (202)467-2948. Editor/Publisher: Jeanne Wickline LaBella. 20% freelance written. Prefers to work with published/established writers. Bimonthly. **Pays on acceptance.** Publishes ms an average of 3 months after acceptance. Byline given. Query for electronic submissions. Free sample copy and writer's guidelines.

Nonfiction: Features on municipal and other local publicly owned electric systems. Payment negotiable.

Photos: Uses b&w glossy and color slides.

UTILITY AND TELEPHONE FLEETS, Practical Communications, Inc., 37 W. Main, Box 183, Cary IL 60013. (312)639-2200. FAX: (312)639-9542. Editor: Alan Richter. 5% freelance written. Bimonthly magazine for fleet managers and maintenance supervisors for electric gas and water utilities; telephone, interconnect and cable TV companies and related contractors. "We seek case history/application features covering specific

For explanation of symbols, see the Key to Symbols and Abbreviations on Page 5. For unfamiliar words, see the Glossary.

fleet management and maintenance projects/installations. Instructional/tutorial features are also welcome." Circ. 18,000. Pays on publication. Publishes ms an average of 1 month after acceptance. Byline given. 20% kill fee. Buys all rights. Submit seasonal/holiday material 2 months in advance. Reports in 2 weeks. Free sample copy and writer's guidelines.

Nonfiction: How-to (ways for performing fleet maintenance/improving management skills/vehicle tutorials), technical, case history/application features. No advertorials in which specific product or company is promoted. Buys 2-3 ms/year. Query with published clips. Length: 1,000-2,800 words. Pays $50/page.

Photos: Send photos with submission. Reviews contact sheets, negatives, transparencies (3×5) and prints (3×5). Offers no additional payment for photos accepted with ms. Captions required. Buys one-time rights.

Columns/Departments: Vehicle Management and Maintenance Tips (nuts-and-bolts type items dealing with new or unusual methods for fleet management, maintenance and safety). Buys 2 mss/year. Query with published clips. Length: 100-400 words. Pays $10-20.

Tips: "Working for a utility or telephone company and gathering information about a construction, safety or fleet project is the best approach for a freelancer."

Engineering and Technology

Engineers and professionals with various specialties read the publications in this section. Publications for electrical, electronics and telecommunications engineers are classified separately under Electronics and Communication. Magazines for computer professionals are in the Information Systems section.

AMERICAN MACHINIST & Automated Manufacturing, Penton Publishing, 826 Broadway, 4th Floor, New York NY 10003. (212)477-6420. FAX: (212)477-6457. Editor: Joseph Jablonowski. A monthly magazine about durable-goods manufacturing. Circ. 82,000. **Pays on acceptance.** Publishes ms an average of 4 months after acceptance. Sometimes byline given. Makes work-for-hire assignments. Query for electronic submissions. Reports in 2 months on queries; 3 months on mss. Free sample copy.

Nonfiction: Technical. Query with or without published clips, or send complete ms. Length: 1,500-4,000 words. Pays $300-1,500. Pays the expenses of writers on assignment.

Photos: Send photos with submission. Offers no additional payment for photos accepted with ms. Buys all rights.

Tips: "Articles that are published are probably 85% engineering details. We're interested in feature articles on technology of manufacturing in the metalworking industries (automaking, aircraft, machinery, etc.). Aim at instructing a 45-year-old degreed mechanical engineer in a new method of making, say, a pump housing."

BIONICS, Box 1553, Owosso MI 48867. Editor: Ben Campbell. Managing Editor: Val Kluge. 50% freelance written. Quarterly newsletter on bionics. Estab. 1988. Circ. 1,500. Pay on publication. Buys first North American serial rights, first rights, one-time rights, second serial (reprint) rights and simultaneous rights. Submit seasonal/holiday material 3 months in advance. Simultaneous and previously published submissions OK. Reports in 2 weeks on queries. Sample copy $10. Free writer's guidelines.

Nonfiction: Book excerpts, how-to, interview/profile, new product, opinion, personal experience and technical. Buys 24 mss/year. Query with or without published clips, or send complete ms. Length: 50-5,000 words. Pays 3-5¢/words. Sometimes pays expenses of writers on assignment.

Photos: Send photos with submission. Reviews negatives and 5×8 transparencies. Offers $10-50 per photo. Model releases required. Buys one-time rights.

Columns/Departments: Bionics, Bi-sensors, Bio-Medical and Robotics. Buys 24 mss/year. Send complete ms. Length: 50-1,000 words.

Fiction: Ethnic, experimental and novel excerpts. Buys 12 mss/year. Query. Length: 50-5,000 words.

Fillers: Facts and newsbreaks. Buys 36/year. Length: 50-200 words.

Tips: "Consult with industry experts. Read the latest magazine articles."

CANADIAN LABORATORY, (formerly *Canadian Research*), Sentry Communications, Suite 500, 245 Fairview Mall Dr., Willowdale, Ontario M2J 4T1 Canada. (416)490-0220. FAX: (416)490-0119. Editor: Doug Dingeldein. 60% freelance written. Bimonthly magazine on hard sciences at Ph.D. level. Circ. 28,000. **Pays on acceptance.** Publishes ms an average of 3 months after acceptance. Byline given. Buys first North American serial rights and one-time rights. Query for electronic submissions. Sample copy $4.

Nonfiction: How-to (science techniques), new product, opinion and technical. Buys 50 mss/year. Query. Length: 150-1,500 words. Pays 23¢/word. Sometimes pays expenses of writers on assignment.

Photos: Send photos with submission. Reviews transparencies and prints. Offers $25 per photo. Captions, model releases and identification of subjects required. Buys one-time rights.

Fillers: Facts and newsbreaks. Buys 50/year. Length: 50-200 words. Pays 23¢/word.

Tips: "Tightly written, and *scientifically accurate!*"

HIGH TECHNOLOGY CAREERS, %Writers Connection, Suite 180, 1601 Saratoga-Sunnyvale Rd., Cupertino CA 95014. (408)973-0227. FAX: (408)973-1219. Managing Editor: Meera Lester. 100% freelance written. Monthly tabloid on high technology industries. "Articles must have a high technology tie-in and should be written in a positive and lively manner. The audience includes managers, engineers and other professionals working in the high technology industries." Circ. 348,000. Pays on publication. Publishes ms an average of 3 months after acceptance. Byline given. Offers 25% kill fee. Buys all rights. Query for electronic submissions. Reports in 3 weeks. Free sample copy; writer's guidelines for #10 SASE.

Nonfiction: General interest (with high tech tie-in), technical. No career-oriented material, company or personal profiles. Buys 36 mss/year. Query with or without published clips, or send complete ms. Length: 1,500-2,000 words. Pays 17½¢/word. Sometimes pays expenses of writers on assignment.

Photos: State availability of photo with submission.

LASER FOCUS WORLD MAGAZINE, 1 Technology Park Dr., P.O. Box 989, Westford MA 01886. (508)692-0700. FAX: (508)692-0525. Publisher: Dr. Morris Levitt. Editor-in-Chief: Dr. Lewis M. Holmes. Managing Editor: Barbara Murray. Less than 10% freelance written. A monthly magazine for physicists, scientists and engineers involved in the research and development, design, manufacturing and applications of lasers, laser systems and all other segments of electro-optical technologies. Estab. 1964. Circ. 60,000. Publishes ms an average of 6 months after acceptance. Byline given unless anonymity requested. Retains all rights. Query for electronic submissions. Free sample copy and writer's guidelines.

Nonfiction: Lasers, laser systems, fiberoptics, optics, imaging and other electro-optical materials, components, instrumentation and systems. "Each article should serve our reader's need by either stimulating ideas, increasing technical competence or improving design capabilities in the following areas: natural light and radiation sources, artificial light and radiation sources, light modulators, optical materials and components, image detectors, energy detectors, information displays, image processing, information storage and processing, subsystem and system testing, support equipment and other related areas." No "flighty prose, material not written for our readership, or irrelevant material." Query first "with a clear statement and outline of why the article would be important to our readers." Pay rate negotiable.

Photos: Send photos with ms. Reviews 8 × 10 b&w glossies or 4 × 5 color transparencies. Drawings: Rough drawings acceptable, are finished by staff technical illustrator.

Tips: "The writer has a better chance of breaking in at our publication with short articles because shorter articles are easier to schedule, but must address more carefully our requirements for technical coverage. We use few freelancers that are independent professional writers. Most of our submitted materials come from technical experts in the areas we cover. The most frequent mistake made by writers in completing articles for us is that the articles are too commercial, i.e. emphasize a given product or technology from one company. Also articles are not the right technical depth, too thin or too scientific."

‡MACHINE DESIGN, Penton Publishing Inc., 1100 Superior Ave., Cleveland OH 44114. (216)696-7000. FAX: (216)696-0177. Editor: Ronald Khol. Executive Editor: Richard Beercheck. 1-2% freelance written. Works with a small number of new/unpublished writers each year. A bimonthly magazine covering technical developments in products or purchases of interest to the engineering community. Estab. 1929. Circ. 180,000. Pays on publication. Publishes ms an average of 2 months after acceptance. Byline given. Buys first rights. Reports in 1 month. Free sample copy.

Nonfiction: General interest; how-to (on using new equipment or processes); and new product. No non-technical submissions. Buys 10-15 mss/year. Query. Length and payment for articles must be negotiated in advance. Sometimes pays the expenses of writers on assignment.

Photos: State availability of photos with submission. Offers negotiable payment. Captions, model releases, and identification of subjects required.

Columns/Departments: Design International (international news), captions; Backtalk (technical humor) and Personal Computers in Engineering (use of personal computers), both have negotiable word length. Buys 50-200 items/year. Query. Pays $20 minimum.

Tips: "The departments of our publication most open to freelancers are Back Talk, News Trends and Design International. Those without technical experience almost never send in adequate material."

‡MECHANICAL ENGINEERING, American Society of Mechanical Engineers, 345 E. 47th St., New York NY 10017. (212)705-7782. Editor: Jay O'Leary. Managing Editor: Alexander Wolfe. 30% freelance written. A monthly magazine on mechanical process and design. "We publish general interest articles for graduate mechanical engineers on high-tech topics." Circ. 135,000. **Pays on acceptance.** Sometimes byline given. Kill fee varies. Buys first rights. Submit seasonal material 4 months in advance. Reports in 6 weeks. Free writer's guidelines.

Nonfiction: Historical/nostalgic, interview/profile, new product, photo feature and technical. Buys 25 mss/year. Query with or without published clips, or send complete ms. Length: 1,500-3,500 words. Pays $500-1,500.

Photos: Send photos with submission. Reviews transparencies and prints. Offers no additional payment for photos accepted with ms. Captions and identification of subjects required. Buys one-time rights.

THE MINORITY ENGINEER, An Equal Opportunity Career Publication for Professional and Graduating Minority Engineers, Equal Opportunity Publications, Inc., 44 Broadway, Greenlawn NY 11740. (516)261-8917. FAX: (516)261-8935. Executive Editor: James Schneider. 60% freelance written. Prefers to work with published/established writers. Magazine published 4 times/year covering career guidance for minority engineering students and professional minority engineers. Circ. 16,000. Pays on publication. Publishes ms an average of 3-6 months after acceptance. Byline given. Buys all rights. "Deadline dates: fall, May 1; winter, July 15; spring, October 15; April/May, January 1." Simultaneous and previously published submissions OK. Sample copy and writer's guidelines for 9×12 SAE with 5 first class stamps; writer's guidelines for #10 SASE.

Nonfiction: Book excerpts; articles (on job search techniques, role models); general interest (on specific minority engineering concerns); how-to (land a job, keep a job, etc.); interview/profile (minority engineer role models); new product (new career opportunities); opinion (problems of ethnic minorities); personal experience (student and career experiences); and technical (on career fields offering opportunities for minority engineers). "We're interested in articles dealing with career guidance and job opportunities for minority engineers." Query or send complete ms. Length: 1,000-1,500 words. Sometimes pays the expenses of writers on assignment. Pays 10¢/word.

Photos: Prefers 35mm color slides but will accept b&w. Captions and identification of subjects required. Buys all rights. Pays $15. Cartoons accepted. Pays $25.

Tips: "Articles should focus on career guidance, role model and industry prospects for minority engineers. Prefer articles related to careers, not politically or socially sensitive."

‡NATIONAL DEFENSE, American Defense Preparedness Association, Suite 400, 2101 Wilson Blvd, Arlington VA 22201. (703)522-1820. FAX: (703)522-1885. Editor: D. Ballou. Managing Editor: Vincent P. Grimes. 50% freelance written. A magazine on defense weapons systems published 10 times/year. "This is a nonpolitical magazine for persons who buy or make military weapons systems. We are interested in technology, management, military and defense industry relationships." Estab. 1920. Circ. 45,000. Pays on publication. Publishes ms an average of 3 months after acceptance. Byline given. Buys first rights. Query for electronic submissions. Reports in 3 weeks on queries; 6 weeks on mss. Free sample copy and writer's guidelines.

Nonfiction: New product, opinion, photo feature and technical. Buys 45 mss/year. Query. Length: 1,200-2,000 words. Pays $450-950. Pays expenses of writers on assignment "with prior arrangement." Send photos with submission. Reviews contact sheets, negatives, transparencies and prints. Offers no additional payment for photos accepted with ms. Captions required. Buys one-time rights.

WOMAN ENGINEER, An Equal Opportunity Career Publication for Graduating Women and Experienced Professionals, Equal Opportunity Publications, Inc., 44 Broadway, Greenlawn NY 11740. (516)261-8917. Editor: Anne Kelly. 60% freelance written. Works with a small number of new/unpublished writers each year. Magazine published 4 times/year (fall, winter, spring, April/May) covering career guidance for women engineering students and professional women engineers. Circ. 16,000. Pays on publication. Publishes ms 3-12 months after acceptance. Byline given. Buys all rights. Free sample copy and writer's guidelines.

Nonfiction: "Interested in articles dealing with career guidance and job opportunities for women engineers. Looking for manuscripts showing how to land an engineering position and advance professionally. Wants features on job-search techniques, engineering disciplines offering career opportunities to women, companies with affirmative action and career advancement opportunities for women, problems facing women engineers and how to cope with such problems, in addition to role-model profiles of successful women engineers, especially in government, military and defense-related industries." Query. Length: 1,000-2,500 words. Pays 10¢/word.

Photos: Prefers color slides but will accept b&w. Captions, model release and identification of subjects required. Buys all rights. Pays $15.

Tips: "We will be looking for shorter manuscripts (800-1,000 words) on job-search techniques, and first-person Endpage Essay."

Entertainment and the Arts

The business of the entertainment/amusement industry in arts, film, dance, theater, etc. is covered by these publications. Journals that focus on the people and equipment of various music specialties are listed in the Music section, while art and design business publications can be found in Art, Design and Collectibles. Entertainment publications for the general public can be found in the Consumer Entertainment section.

BOXOFFICE MAGAZINE, RLD Publishing Corp., Suite 710, 1800 N. Highland Ave., Hollywood CA 90028. (213)465-1186. FAX: (213)465-5049. Editor: Harley W. Lond. 5% freelance written. Monthly business magazine about the motion picture industry for members of the film industry: theater owners, film producers, directors, financiers and allied industries. Estab. 1920. Circ. 10,000. Pays on publication. Publishes ms an average of 2-4 months after acceptance. Byline given. Buys one-time rights. Submit seasonal material 2 months in advance. Simultaneous and previously published submissions OK. Reports in 2 months. Sample copy for 9×12 SAE with 6 first class stamps.

Nonfiction: Exposé, interview, profile, new product, photo feature and technical. "We are a general news magazine about the motion picture industry and are looking for stories about trends, developments, problems or opportunities facing the industry. Almost any story will be considered, including corporate profiles, but we don't want gossip or celebrity stuff." Query with published clips. Length: 1,500-2,500 words. Pays $100-150.

Photos: State availability of photos. Pays $10 maximum for 8×10 b&w prints. Captions required.

Tips: "Request a sample copy, indicating you read about *Boxoffice* in *Writer's Market*. Write a clear, comprehensive outline of the proposed story and enclose a resume and clip samples. We welcome new writers but don't want to be a classroom. Know how to write. We look for 'investigative' articles."

THE ELECTRIC WEENIE, Box 2715, Quincy MA 02269. (617)749-6900 ext. 248. FAX: (617)749-3691. Publisher: Jerry Ellis. Editor: James J. Donohue. 80% freelance written. Monthly magazine covering "primarily radio, for 'personalities' worldwide (however, mostly English speaking). We mail flyers mainly to radio people, but obviously no one is excepted if he/she wants a monthly supply of first-rate gags, one liners, zappers, etc." Circ. 1,500. Pays on publication. Publishes ms an average of 2 months after acceptance. No byline given. Buys all rights. Free sample copy and writer's guidelines.

Fillers: Jokes, gags, short humor, one liners, etc. "Short is the bottom line; if it's over two sentences, it's too long." Uses 300/month. Pays $2/gag used—higher price paid for quality material.

Tips: "We like to receive in multiples of 100 if possible; not mandatory, just preferred. And we like a few original 'grossies.' We also publish a tamer version for speakers and toastmasters called '*The Ad-Lib Helper*'."

THE HOLLYWOOD REPORTER, 6715 Sunset Blvd., Hollywood CA 90028. (213)464-7411. Publisher: Tichi Wilkerson Kassel. Editor: Teri Ritzer. Emphasizes entertainment industry, film, TV and theatre and everything to do with financial news in these areas. 15% freelance written. Daily entertainment trade publication: 25-100 pages. Circ. 25,000. Publishes ms an average of 1 month after acceptance. Send queries first. Reports in 1 month. Sample copy $1.

Tips: "Short articles and fillers fit our format best. The most frequent mistake made by writers in completing an article for us is that they are not familiar with our publication."

IDEA TODAY, The Association for Fitness Professionals, Suite 204, 6190 Cornerstone Court E., San Diego CA 92121. (619)535-8979. Editor: Patricia A. Ryan. Senior Editor: Nancy Lee. 70% freelance written. A trade journal published 10 times/year for the dance-exercise and personal training industry. "All articles must be geared to fitness professionals—aerobics instructors, one-to-one trainers and studio and health club owners—covering topics such as aerobics, nutrition, injury prevention, entrepreneurship in fitness, fitness-oriented research and exercise programs." Estab. 1984. Circ. 18,000. **Pays on acceptance.** Publishes ms an average of 4 months after acceptance. Byline given. Buys all rights. Simultaneous submissions OK. Reports in 6 weeks on queries. Sample copy $4.

Nonfiction: How-to, technical. No general information on fitness; our readers are pros who need detailed information. Buys 15 mss/year. Query. Length: 1,000-3,000 words. Pays $100-300.

Photos: State availability of photos with submission. Offers no additional payment for photos with ms. Model releases required. Buys all rights.

Columns/Departments: Exercise Technique (detailed, specific info; must be written by expert), 750-1,500 words; Industry News (short reports on research, programs conferences), 150-300 words; Student Handout (exercise and nutrition info for participants), 750 words; Program Spotlight (detailed explanation of specific exercise program), 1,000-1,500 words. Buys 80 mss/year. Query. Length: 150-1,500 words. Pays $15-150.

Tips: "We don't accept fitness information for the consumer audience on topics such as why exercise is good for you. Industry News (column) is most open to freelancers. We're looking for short reports on fitness-related conferences and conventions, research, innovative exercise programs, trends, news from other countries and reports on aerobics competitions. Writers who have specific knowledge of, or experience working in the fitness industry have an edge."

LOCATION UPDATE, Suite 612, 6922 Hollywood Blvd., Hollywood CA 90028. (213)461-8887. FAX: (213)469-3711. Editor: Jean Drummond. Bimonthly entertainment industry magazine covering all aspects of filming on location. "*Location Update* communicates the issues, trends, problems, solutions and business matters that affect productions working on location. Features include interviews with industry professionals, controversial issues, regional spotlights, hard-to-find or difficult locations, etc. Audience is made up of producers, directors, production managers, location managers—any person who works on location for film, TV, commercials and videos." Estab. 1985. Circ. 30,000. Pays on publication. Publishes ms an average of 2 months after acceptance. Byline given. Offers 50% kill fee. Publication not copyrighted. Buys first North American serial rights. Query for electronic submissions. Reports in 3 weeks. Sample copy for 9×12 SAE with 7 first class stamps; free writer's guidelines.

Nonfiction: Exposé, general interest, historical/nostalgic, interview/profile, new product, opinion, photo feature, technical and features about productions on location. No fluffy or glitzy "Hollywood" slants. Buys 75 mss/year. Query with published clips. Length: 1,000-2,500 words. Pays $100-300 for assigned articles; $50-100 for unsolicited articles. Sometimes pays expenses of writers on assignment.

Photos: State availability of photos with submission. Reviews contact sheets, 35mm, 2¼ × 2¼ transparencies and 8 × 10 prints. Offers no additional payment for photos accepted with ms. Identification of subjects required. Buys one-time rights.

Columns/Departments: Commentary (opinion pieces on issues and problems in film industry), 500-750 words; Locations (hard to find or difficult locations and how to use them), 1,000-1,500 words; Supporting Roles (support services used on location: security companies, catering, etc.), 1,000-1,500 words; Newsreel (short news briefs on location-related issues), 250 words. Buys 25-30 mss/year. Query with published clips. Pays $25-100.

Tips: "The best way to break in is to query with story ideas and to be familiar with film, TV, video and commercials. Know the workings of the entertainment industry and the roles of producers, directors and location managers. Articles about locations are most open to freelance writers. Everything is a possible location for productions. Every state has a film commission that can help with who is where and how to go about using particular locations."

THE LONE STAR COMEDY MONTHLY, Lone Star Publications of Humor, Suite 103, Box 29000, San Antonio TX 78229. Editor: Lauren Barnett. Less than 1% freelance written. Eager to work with new/unpublished writers. Monthly comedy service newsletter for professional humorists—DJs, public speakers, comedians. Includes one-liners and jokes for oral expression. Pays on publication "or before." Publishes ms an average of 4-6 months after acceptance. Byline given if 2 or more jokes are used. Buys all rights, exclusive rights for 6 months from publication date. Submit seasonal/holiday material 1 month in advance. Reports in 3 months. Inquire for update on prices of sample copies. Writer's guidelines for #10 SASE.

Fillers: Jokes, gags and short humor. Buys 20-60/year. Length: 100 words maximum. "We don't use major features in *The Lone Star Comedy Monthly*." Inquire for update on rates. "Submit several (no more than 20) original gags on one or two subjects only."

Tips: "Writers should inquire for an update on our needs before submitting material."

MIDDLE EASTERN DANCER, Mideastern Connection, Inc., P.O. Box 181572, Casselberry FL 32718-1572. (407)831-3402. Editor: Karen Kuzsel. Managing Editor: Tracie Harris. 60% freelance written. Eager to work with new/unpublished writers. A monthly magazine covering Middle Eastern dance and culture (belly dancing). "We provide the most current news and entertainment information available in the world. We focus on the positive, but don't shy away from controversy. All copy and photos must relate to Middle Eastern dance and cultural activities. We do not get into politics." Circ. 2,500. **Pays on acceptance.** Publishes ms an average of 4 months after acceptance, usually sooner, but it depends on type of article and need for that month. Byline given. Buys first rights, simultaneous rights or second serial (reprint) rights. Submit seasonal/holiday material 3 months in advance. Simultaneous and previously published submissions OK, unless printed in another belly dance publication. Reports in 2 weeks on queries; 3 weeks on mss. Sample copy for 9 × 12 SAE with 4 first class stamps; writer's guidelines for #10 SASE.

Nonfiction: Essays; general interest; historical/nostalgic; how-to (on costuming, putting on shows, teaching and exercises); humor; inspirational; interview/profile; personal experience; photo features; travel (to the Middle East or related to dancers); and reviews of seminars, movies, clubs, restaurants and museums. Special issues include costuming (March); and anniversary issue (October). No politics. Buys 60 mss/year. Query. Pays $20 for assigned articles; pays $10 for unsolicited articles. May provide free advertising in trade. Sometimes pays the expenses of writers on assignment.

Photos: Send photos with submission. Offers $5 additional payment for each photo accepted with ms. Identification of subjects required. Buys one-time rights.

Columns/Departments: Critic's Corner (reviews of books, videotapes, records, movies, clubs and restaurants, museums and special events); Helpful Hints (tips for finding accessories and making them easier or for less); Putting on the Ritz (describes costume in detail with photo); and Personal Glimpses (autobiographical) and Profiles (biographical—providing insights of benefit to other dancers). Query.

Fiction: Open to fiction dealing with belly dancers as subject.

Poetry: Avant-garde, free verse, light verse and traditional. Buys 5 poems/year. Submit maximum 3 poems. Pays $5 maximum.

Tips: "It's easy to break in if you stick to belly dancing related information and expect little or no money (advertising instead). Although we are the second largest in the world in this field, we're still small."

OPPORTUNITIES FOR ACTORS & MODELS, A Guide to Working in Cable TV-Radio-Print Advertising, Copy Group, Suite 315, 1900 N. Vine St., Hollywood CA 90068. FAX: (213)465-5161. Editor: Len Miller. 50% freelance written. Works with a small number of new/unpublished writers each year. A monthly newsletter "serving the interests of those people who are (or would like to be) a part of the cable-TV, radio, and print advertising industries." Estab. 1969. Circ. 10,000. **Pays on acceptance.** Publishes ms an average of 3 months after acceptance. Byline given. Buys all rights. Simultaneous queries OK. Reports in 3 weeks. Free sample copy and writer's guidelines for #10 SASE.

Nonfiction: How-to, humor, inspirational, interview/profile, local news, personal experience, photo feature and technical (within cable TV). Coverage should include the model scene, little theatre, drama groups, comedy workshops and other related events and places. "Detailed information about your local cable TV station should be an important part of your coverage. Get to know the station and its creative personnel." Buys 120 mss/year. Query. Length: 100-950 words. Pays $50 maximum.

Photos: State availability of photos. Model release and identification of subjects required. Buys one-time or all rights.

Columns/Departments: "We will consider using your material in a column format with your byline." Buys 60 mss/year. Query. Length: 150-450 words. Pays $50 maximum.

Tips: "Good first person experiences, interviews and articles, all related to modeling, acting, little theatre, photography (model shots) and other interesting items are needed."

TOURIST ATTRACTIONS & PARKS MAGAZINE, Kane Communications, Inc., Suite 210, 7000 Terminal Square, Upper Darby PA 19082. (215)734-2420. FAX: (215)734-2423. Editor: Sandy Meschkow. A bimonthly magazine covering mass entertainment and leisure facilities. Emphasizes management articles. Circ. 19,600. Pays on publication. Buys all rights. Reports in 3 weeks. Sample copy for 9×12 SAE with 6 first class stamps.

Nonfiction: Interview/profile and new product. Buys 10 mss/year. Query. Length: 1,000-2,500 words. Pays $50-250 for assigned articles; sometimes payment arranged individually with publisher. Sometimes pays expenses of writers on assignment.

Photos: State availability of photos with submission. Captions and model releases required.

Tips: "Inquire about covering trade shows for us, such as C.M.A."

UPB MAGAZINE, The Voice of the United Polka Boosters, The United Polka Boosters, P.O. Box 681, Glastonbury CT 06033. (203)568-5343. Editor: Irene Kobelski. 50-60% freelance written. Eager to work with new/unpublished writers. A bimonthly magazine of the polka music industry. "Our readers share a common love for polka music and are dedicated to its preservation. They want information-packed pieces to help them understand and perform better in the polka industry." Estab. 1984. Circ. 1,100. **Pays on acceptance.** Publishes ms an average of 6 months after acceptance. Byline given. Offers 5% kill fee. Buys first or second serial (reprint) rights. Submit seasonal/holiday material 6 months in advance. Simultaneous and previously published submissions OK. Reports in 6 weeks. Sample copy for 9×12 SAE with 4 first class stamps; free writer's guidelines for #10 SASE.

Nonfiction: Historical/nostalgic (polka-related), how-to (have published "How to Make a Polka album," "How to Protect Your Songs," "How to Read Music"), humor (polka-related), interview/profile (polka personalities), opinion (on polka issues), technical and the origins and history of well-known polkas. "No submissions that portray polkas as the dictionary definition 'a Bohemian dance in ¾ time.' Articles should be clearly written and easily understandable. Polka music in the U.S.A. is what we want—not old world music." Buys 15 mss/year. Query with or without published clips, or send complete ms. Length: 300-1,500 words. Pays $10-35 for assigned articles; pays $5-30 for unsolicited articles. Sometimes pays the expenses of writers on assignment.

Photos: State availability of photos with submission; photos required for all profiles/interviews. Reviews 8×10 or 5×7 prints, b&w only. Offers $1-3 per photo. Model releases and identification of subjects required. Buys one-time rights.

Columns/Departments: Behind the Scenes (in-depth report of 'how' and 'why' a polka-related or music-related process is followed), to 1,000 words; Personality Profiles (emphasize the subject's contributions to polka music); 500-1,500 words; Origins of Songs (show dates and facts—pack it with research, tie in a contemporary recording if possible), 300-1,500 words. Buys 16 mss/year. Query or send complete ms. Pays $5-35.

Fillers: Anecdotes, facts, newsbreaks, short humor and puzzles, all *polka* related. Buys 30/year. Length: 150-750 words. Pays $2-20 and contributor copy.

Tips: "We'd love to see some round-up pieces—for example, 'What 10 top bandleaders say about—' or 'Polka fans speak out about—.' Know the polka industry! Articles should be well researched and should reflect the writer's knowledge of the present polka industry. A list of sources should accompany your ms. Our publication serves both industry professionals (musicians, DJs, composers, arrangers and promoters), and polka fans. Articles should be both informative and entertaining. We are very eager to work with freelance writers on a regular basis. We'd like pieces on recording, performing, promoting, composing, dancing—all types of well-written polka-oriented pieces."

Farm

The successful farm writer focuses on the business side of farming. For technical articles, editors feel writers should have a farm background or agricultural training, but there are opportunities for the general freelancer too. The following farm publications are divided into seven categories, each specializing in a different aspect of farming: agricultural equipment; crops and soil management; dairy farming; livestock; management; miscellaneous and regional.

Agricultural Equipment

CUSTOM APPLICATOR, Little Publications, Suite 540, 6263 Poplar Ave., Memphis TN 38119. (901)767-4020. FAX: (901)767-4026. Editor: Rob Wiley. 50% freelance written. Works with a small number of new/unpublished writers each year. For "firms that sell and custom apply agricultural fertilizer and chemicals." Estab. 1957. Circ. 16,100. Pays on publication. Publishes ms an average of 2 months after acceptance. Buys all rights. "Query is best. The editor can help you develop the story line regarding our specific needs." Free sample copy and writer's guidelines.
Nonfiction: "We are looking for articles on custom application firms telling others how to better perform jobs of chemical application, develop new customers, handle credit, etc. Lack of a good idea or usable information will bring a rejection." Length: 1,000-1,200 words "with 3 or 4 b&w glossy prints." Pays 20¢/word.
Photos: Accepts b&w glossy prints. "We will look at color slides for possible cover or inside use."
Tips: "We don't get enough shorter articles, so one that is well-written and informative could catch our eyes. Our readers want pragmatic information to help them run a more efficient business; they can't get that through a story filled with generalities."

Crops and Soil Management

ONION WORLD, Columbia Publishing, 111C S. 7th Ave., P.O. Box 1467, Yakima WA 98907. (509)248-2452. FAX: (509)248-4056. Editor: D. Brent Clement. 90% freelance written. A monthly magazine covering "the world of onion production and marketing" for onion growers and shippers. Estab. 1975. Circ. 5,500. Pays on publication. Publishes ms an average of 1 month after acceptance. Byline given. Not copyrighted. Buys first North American serial rights. Submit seasonal/holiday material 1 month in advance. Simultaneous submissions OK. Reports in several weeks. Sample copy for 9×12 SAE with 4 first class stamps.
Nonfiction: General interest, historical/nostalgic and interview/profile. Buys 60 mss/year. Query. Length: 1,200-1,500 words. Pays $75-150 for assigned articles.
Photos: Send photos with submission. Offers no additional payment for photos accepted with ms unless cover shot. Captions and identification of subjects required. Buys all rights.
Tips: "Writers should be familiar with growing and marketing onions. We use a lot of feature stories on growers, shippers and others in the onion trade—what they are doing, their problems, solutions, marketing plans, etc."

SINSEMILLA TIPS, Domestic Marijuana Journal, New Moon Publishing, 215 SW 2nd, P.O. Box 2046, Corvallis OR 97339. (503)757-8477. FAX: (503)757-0028. Editor: Tom Alexander. 50% freelance written. Eager to work with new/unpublished writers. Quarterly magazine tabloid covering the domestic cultivation of marijuana. Estab. 1980. Circ. 15,000. Pays on publication. Publishes ms an average of 3 months after acceptance. Byline given. "Some writers desire to be anonymous for obvious reasons." Buys first serial rights and second serial (reprint) rights. Submit seasonal/holiday material 2 months in advance. Query for electronic submissions. Reports in 2 months. Sample copy $6; writer's guidelines for #10 SASE.
Nonfiction: Book excerpts and reviews; expose (on political corruption); general interest; how-to; interview/profile; opinion; personal experience; and technical. Send complete ms. Length: 500-2,000 words. Pays 2½¢/word. Sometimes pays the expenses of writers on assignment.
Photos: Send photos with ms. Pays $10-20 for b&w prints; $20-50 color inside print; $50-75 color cover photo. Captions optional; model release required. Buys all rights.
Tips: "Writers have the best chance of publication if article is *specifically* related to the American marijuana industry."

Dairy Farming

BUTTER-FAT, Fraser Valley Milk Producers' Cooperative Association, P.O. Box 9100, Vancouver, British Columbia V6B 4G4 Canada. (604)420-6611. Editor: Grace Chadsey. Managing Editor: Carol A. Paulson. Eager to work with new/unpublished writers. 50% freelance written. Monthly magazine emphasizing this dairy cooperative's processing and marketing operations for dairy farmers and dairy workers in British Columbia. Estab. 1923. Circ. 3,500. **Pays on acceptance.** Publishes ms an average of 4 months after acceptance. Byline given. Buys first rights. Makes work-for-hire assignments. Phone queries preferred. Submit seasonal material 4 months in advance. Simultaneous and previously published submissions OK. Reports in 1 week on queries; 1 month on mss. Free sample copy.

Nonfiction: Interview (character profile with industry leaders); local nostalgia; opinion (of industry leaders); and profile (of association members and employees).
Photos: Reviews 5×7 b&w negatives and contact sheets and color photos. Offers $10/published photo. Captions required. Buys all rights.
Columns/Departments: "We want articles on the people, products, business of producing, processing and marketing dairy foods in this province." Query first. Buys 3 mss/issue. Length: 500-1,500 words. Pays 7¢/word.
Fillers: Jokes, short humor and quotes. Buys 5 mss/issue. Pays $10.
Tips: "Make an appointment to come by and see us!"

‡**THE DAIRYMAN,** Box 819, Corona CA 91718. (714)735-2730. Editor: Dennis Halladay. 10% freelance written. Prefers to work with published/established writers, but also works with a small number of new/ unpublished writers each year. Monthly magazine dealing with large herd commercial dairy industry. Circ. 33,000. Pays on acceptance or publication. Publishes ms an average of 2-3 months after acceptance. Byline given. Buys first North American serial rights. Submit seasonal material 3 months in advance. Reports in 2 weeks. Sample copy for 9×12 SAE with 4 first class stamps.
Nonfiction: Humor, interview/profile, new product, opinion, and industry analysis. Special issues: Computer issue (February); Herd Health issue (August); Feeds and Feeding (May); and Barns and Equipment (November). No religion, nostalgia, politics or 'mom and pop' dairies. Query or send complete ms. Length: 300-5,000 words. Pays $10-200.
Photos: Send photo with query or ms. Reviews b&w contact sheets and 35mm or 2¼×2¼ transparencies. Pays $10-25 for b&w; $25-100 for color. Captions and identification of subjects required. Buys one-time rights.
Columns/Departments: Herd health, computers, economic outlook for dairying. Buys 25/year. Query or send complete ms. Length: 300-2,000 words. Pays $25-200.
Tips: "Pretend you're an editor for a moment; would you want to buy a story without any artwork? Neither would I. Writers often don't know modern commercial dairying and they forget they're writing for an audience of *dairymen*. Publications are becoming more and more specialized. You've really got to know who you're writing for and why they're different."

Livestock

ANGUS JOURNAL, Angus Publications, Inc., 3201 Frederick Blvd., St. Joseph MO 64506. (816)233-0508. FAX: (816)233-0508, ext. 112. Editor: Jerilyn Johnson. 10% freelance written. Monthly (except June/July, which are combined) magazine. "Must be Angus-related or beef cattle with no other breeds mentioned." Circ. 17,000. **Pays on acceptance.** Byline given. Buys first North American serial rights, second serial(reprint) rights, simultaneous rights and makes work-for-hire assignments. Submit seasonal/holiday material 3 months in advance. Simultaneous and previously published submissions OK. Reports in 2 weeks. Samples copy $1.50 wtih 10×13 SAE and 4 first class stamps.
Nonfiction: Historical/nostalgic, how-to, humor, interview/profile and photo feature. Nothing without an Angus slant. Buys 6 mss/year. Send complete ms. Length: 1,000-2,000 words. Pays $225.
Photos: Send photos with submission. Review contact sheets and transparencies. Offers no additional payment for photos accepted with ms. Identification of subjects required. Buys one-time rights.
Columns/Departments: The Grazier (pasture, fencing, range management). Send complete ms. Length: 500-1,000 words. Pays $25-75.
Poetry: Light verse and traditional. Nothing without an Angus or beef cattle slant. Submit up to 4 poems at one time. Length: 4-20 lines. Pays $25.
Tips: Areas most open to freelancers are "farm and ranch profiles—breeder interviews."

BEEF, The Webb Co., 7900 International Dr., Minneapolis MN 55425. (612)851-4668. Editor-in-Chief: Paul D. Andre. Managing Editor: Joe Roybal. 5% freelance written. Prefers to work with published/established writers. Monthly magazine for readers who have the same basic interest—making a living feeding cattle or running a cow herd. Circ. 107,000. **Pays on acceptance.** Publishes ms an average of 4 months after acceptance. Buys all rights. Byline given. Phone queries OK. Submit seasonal material 3 months in advance. Reports in 2 months. Free sample copy and writer's guidelines.
Nonfiction: How-to and informational articles on doing a better job of producing, feeding cattle, market building, managing, and animal health practices. Material must deal with beef cattle only. Buys 8-10 mss/ year. Query. Length: 500-2,000 words. Pays $25-300. Sometimes pays the expenses of writers on assignment.
Photos: B&w glossies (8×10) and color transparencies (35mm or 2¼×2¼) purchased with or without mss. Query or send contact sheet, captions and/or transparencies. Pays $10-50 for b&w; $25-100 for color. Model release required.
Tips: "Be completely knowledgeable about cattle feeding and cowherd operations. Know what makes a story. We want specifics, not a general roundup of an operation. Pick one angle and develop it fully. The most frequent mistake is not following instructions on an angle (or angles) to be developed."

BEEF TODAY, Farm Journal, Inc., 230 W. Washington Sq., Philadelphia PA 19105. (215)829-4700. Editor: Bill Miller. 10% freelance written. Monthly magazine on cattlemen and the beef-cattle industry. "The audience is comprised of larger-scale cattlemen. We emphasize current industry trends, innovative production practices, finances and other business subjects, but also run humor and profiles." Estab. 1985. Circ. 200,000. **Pays on acceptance.** Publishes ms an average of 2 months after acceptance. Byline given. Offers $150 kill fee. Buys all rights. Submit seasonal/holiday material 3 months in advance. Reports in 2 weeks. Sample copy for 9 × 12 SAE with 2 first class stamps; free writer's guidelines.

Nonfiction: How-to (do a better job of running a ranch or feed lot), humor, interview/profile and photo feature. "No articles explaining the cattle industry to the general public." Query with published clips. Length: 500-2,500 words. Pays $300-650 for assigned articles; $150-600 for unsolicited articles. Pays expenses of writers on assignment.

Photos: State availability of photos with submissions or send photos with submissions—preferred. Reviews transparencies. Offers $100-200 per photo. Captions and identification of subjects required. Buys one-time rights.

Tips: "Authors should include details in their queries and mention what sort of expertise they bring to the subject. Most of the unsolicited manuscripts that we've accepted have been on lighter subjects—personality profiles and humor, for instance. But even here, freelance writers should remember that we're a business magazine and that our readers are working cattlemen who already know their business. They (and we) want specifics—numbers, results, problems, etc.—rather than a general introduction. Reports from abroad can be slightly more introductory, though."

THE BRAHMAN JOURNAL, Sagebrush Publishing Co., Inc., P.O. Box 220, Eddy TX 76524. (817)859-5451. Editor: Joe Ed Brockett. 10% freelance written. A monthly magazine covering Brahman cattle. Estab. 1971. Circ. 6,000. Pays on publication. Publishes ms an average of 2 months after acceptance. Byline given. Not copyrighted. Buys first North American serial rights, one-time rights, second serial (reprint) rights and makes work-for-hire assignments. Submit seasonal/holiday material 3 months in advance. Previously published submissions OK. Reports in 1 month. Sample copy for 9 × 12 SAE and 5 first class stamps.

Nonfiction: General interest, historical/nostalgic and interview/profile. Special issues include Herd Bull issue (July) and Texas issue (October). Buys 3-4 mss/year. Query with published clips. Length: 1,200-3,000 words. Pays $100-250 for assigned articles.

Photos: Photos needed for article purchase. Send photos with submission. Reviews 4 × 5 prints. Offers no additional payment for photos accepted with ms. Captions required. Buys one-time rights.

FARM POND HARVEST, Dedicated to successful farm pond planning, construction, management and harvesting, Professional Sportsman's Publishing Company, RR 3, P.O. Box 197, Momence IL 60954. (815)472-2686. Editor: Vic Johnson. Managing Editor: Joan Munyon. 75% freelance written. Quarterly magazine for fisheries. "Mainly informational for pond owners—we have many biologists, university libraries and government agencies on our subscription list." Estab. 1967. Pays on publication. Publishes ms an average of 1-3 months after acceptance. Byline given. Not copyrighted. Buys first rights or second serial (reprint) rights. Submit seasonal/holiday material 2 months in advance. Simultaneous and previously published submissions OK. Free sample copy.

Nonfiction: How-to (fisheries), personal experience, photo feature and technical. Buys 25 mss/year. Query with or without published clips, or send complete ms. Length: 1,300-2,500 words. Pays $50-125 for assigned articles. Sometimes pays in free advertisement.

Photos: State availability of photos with submission. Reviews negatives and 5 × 7 prints. Offers no additional payment for photos accepted with ms. Sometimes pays $5 per photo. Buys one-time rights.

Columns/Departments: What's New (products—news bulletins—magazines—fishery field); Media Net (information pertaining to products/conventions, etc.); Ask Al (answers to questions from readers); and Cutting Bait (subscriber information). Buys 12 mss/year. Send complete ms.

Tips: Most open to freelancers are "how-to on planning, construction, management, fishing in farm ponds or small lakes. Personal experiences—some light-humorous articles accepted; also seasonal stories, winter, spring, summer or fall."

HOG FARM MANAGEMENT, Miller Publishing Co., Suite 160, 12400 Whitewater Dr., Box 2400, Minneapolis MN 55343. (612)931-2900. Editor: Steve Marbery. 25% freelance written. A monthly trade journal on hog production. "Specialized management-oriented features on hog production: feeding, health, finances." Circ. 45,000. Pays on publication. Publishes ms an average of 2 months after acceptance. Byline given. Offers $25 kill fee. Buys all rights. Submit seasonal/holiday material 3 months in advance. Reports in 2 weeks on queries. Sample copy $1; free writer's guidelines.

Nonfiction: General interest, how-to, interview/profile and new product. No humor or excerpts of any kind. Buys 6-8 mss/year. Query with or without published clips, or send complete ms. Length: 200-1,000 words. Pays $150-350.

Photos: State availability of photos with submission. Reviews contact sheets. Offers $10-40 per photo. Model releases and identification of subjects required. Buys all rights.

‡LLAMAS MAGAZINE, The International Camelid Journal, Clay Press, Inc., P.O. Box 100, Herald CA 95638. (916)448-1668. Editor: Cheryl Dal Porto. Magazine published 8 times per year covering llamas, alpacas, camels, vicunas and guanacos. Estab. 1979. Circ. 5,500. **Pays on acceptance.** Publishes ms an average of 4 months after acceptance. Byline given. Buys first rights, second serial (reprint) rights and makes work-for-hire assignments. Submit seasonal/holiday material 6 months in advance. Simultaneous and previously published submissions OK. Reports in 2 weeks. Sample copy for 4 first class stamps; writer's guidelines for #10 SASE.

Nonfiction: How-to (on anything related to raising llamas), humor, interview/profile, opinion, personal experience, photo feature and travel (to countries where there are camelids). "All articles must have a tie in to one of the camelid species." Buys 30 mss/year. Query with published clips. Length: 1,000-5,000 words. Pays $50-300 for assigned articles; pays $50-150 for unsolicited articles. May pay new writers with contributor copies. Sometimes pays the expenses of writers on assignment.

Photos: State availability of photos with submission or send photos with submission. Reviews transparencies and 5×7 prints. Offers $25-100 per photo. Captions, model releases and identification of subjects required. Buys one-time rights.

Fillers: Anecdotes, gags and short humor. Buys 25/year. Length: 100-500 words. Pays $25-50.

Tips: "Get to know the llama folk in your area and query us with an idea. We are open to any and all ideas involving llamas, alpacas and the rest of the camelids. We are always looking for good photos. You must know about camelids to write for us."

‡NATIONAL CATTLEMEN, National Cattlemen's Association, 5420 S. Quebec St., Englewood CO 80155. (303)694-0305. Editor: Scott R. Cooper. 15% freelance written. Monthly trade journal on the beef cattle industry. "We deal extensively with animal health, price outlook, consumer demand for beef, costs of production, emerging technologies, developing export markets, marketing and risk management." Estab. 1985. Circ. 40,000. Pays on publication. Byline given. Buys all rights. Sample copy for 11×15 SAE.

Nonfiction: How-to (cut costs of production, risk management strategies), new product (emerging technologies), opinion, and technical (emerging technologies, animal health, price outlook). Upcoming issue will focus on state of the industry. Buys 10 mss/year. Query with published clips. Length: 1,500-2,000 words. Pays $250-300 for assigned articles. Pays expenses of writers on assignment.

Photos: Send photos with submission. Reviews negatives and transparencies. Identification of subjects required. Buys all rights.

Columns/Departments: My View (opinions dealing with the beef cattle industry), 750 words. Query. Pays $250-300.

‡NATIONAL WOOL GROWER, American Sheep Industry Association, Inc., 6911 S. Yosemite St., Denver CO 80112. (303)771-3500. Editor: Janice Grauberger. 20% freelance written. Monthly trade journal covering sheep industry news. Estab. 1911. Circ. 21,500. Pays on publication. Byline sometimes given. Buys first rights and makes work-for-hire assignments. Submit seasonal/holiday material 3 months in advance. Free sample copy.

Nonfiction: How-to and interview/profile. Buys 15 mss/year. Query with or without published clips, or send complete ms. Length: 1,000-5,000 words. Pays $200-500 for assigned articles; $200-300 for unsolicited articles. Sometimes pays expenses of writers on assignment.

Photos: Send photos with submission. Reviews transparencies and prints. Offers no additional payment for photos accepted with ms. Captions required. Buys one-time rights.

Columns/Departments: Buys 5 mss/year. Query with published clips. Length: 500-1,500 words. Pays $100-300.

POLLED HEREFORD WORLD, 4700 E. 63rd St., Kansas City MO 64130. (816)333-7731. FAX: (816)333-7365. Editor: Ed Bible. 1% freelance written. For "breeders of Polled Hereford cattle—about 80% registered breeders, 5% commercial cattle breeders; remainder are agribusinessmen in related fields." Monthly. Estab. 1947. Circ. 11,500. Not copyrighted. Buys "no unsolicited mss at present." Pays on publication. Publishes ms an average of 2 months after acceptance. Submit seasonal material "as early as possible: 2 months preferred." Reports in 1 month. Query first for reports of events, activities and features. Free sample copy.

Nonfiction: "Features on registered or commercial Polled Hereford breeders. Some on related agricultural subjects (pastures, fences, feeds, buildings, etc.). Mostly technical in nature; some human interest. Our readers make their living with cattle, so write for an informed, mature audience." Buys informational articles, how-to's, personal experience articles, interviews, profiles, historical and think pieces, nostalgia, photo features, coverage of successful business operations, articles on merchandising techniques, and technical articles. Length: "varies with subject and content of feature." Pays about 5¢/word ("usually about 50¢/column inch, but can vary with the value of material").

Photos: Purchased with mss, sometimes purchased without mss, or on assignment; captions required. "Only good quality b&w glossies accepted; any size. Good color prints or transparencies." Pays $2 for b&w, $2-25 for color. Pays $50 for color covers.

SHEEP! MAGAZINE, Rt. 1, Box 78, Helenville WI 53137. (414)593-8385. FAX: (414)593-8384. Editor: Dave Thompson. 50% freelance written. Prefers to work with published/established writers, but works with a small number of new/unpublished writers each year. Monthly magazine. "We're looking for clear, concise, useful information for sheep raisers who have a few sheep to a 1,000 ewe flock." Estab. 1980. Circ. 13,000. Pays on publication. Byline given. Offers $30 kill fee. Buys all rights. Makes work-for-hire assignments. Submit seasonal/holiday material 3 months in advance. Free sample copy and writer's guidelines.

Nonfiction: Book excerpts; information (on personalities and/or political, legal or environmental issues affecting the sheep industry); how-to (on innovative lamb and wool marketing and promotion techniques, efficient record-keeping systems or specific aspects of health and husbandry). Health and husbandry articles should be written by someone with extensive experience or appropriate credentials (i.e., a veterinarian or animal scientist); profiles (on experienced sheep producers who detail the economics and management of their operation); features (on small businesses that promote wool products and stories about local and regional sheep producer's groups and their activities); new products (of value to sheep producers; should be written by someone who has used them); and technical (on genetics, health and nutrition). First person narratives. Buys 80 mss/year. Query with published clips or send complete ms. Length: 750-2,500 words. Pays $45-200. Pays the expenses of writers on assignment.

Photos: "Color—vertical compositions of sheep and/or people—for our cover. Use only b&w inside magazine. B&w, 35mm photos or other visuals improve your chances of a sale." Pays $100 maximum for 35mm color transparencies; $20-50 for 5×7 b&w prints. Identification of subjects required. Buys all rights.

Tips: "Send us your best ideas and photos!"

Management

FARM JOURNAL, 230 W. Washington Square, Philadelphia PA 19105. Contact: Editor. "The business magazine of American agriculture" is published 14 times/year with many regional editions. Material bought for one or more editions depending upon where it fits. Buys all rights. Byline given "except when article is too short or too heavily rewritten to justify one." **Pays on acceptance.** Payment is the same regardless of editions in which the piece is used.

Nonfiction: Timeliness and seasonableness are very important. Material must be highly practical and should be helpful to as many farmers as possible. Farmers' experiences should apply to one or more of these 8 basic commodities: corn, wheat, milo, soybeans, cotton, dairy, beef and hogs. Technical material must be accurate. No farm nostalgia. Query to describe a new idea that farmers can use. Length: 500-1,500 words. Pays 10-20¢/published word.

Photos: Much in demand either separately or with short how-to material in picture stories and as illustrations for articles. Warm human-interest-pix for covers—activities on modern farms. For inside use, shots of homemade and handy ideas to get work done easier and faster, farm news photos, and pictures of farm people with interesting sidelines. In b&w, 8×10 glossies are preferred; color submissions should be 2¼×2¼ for the cover, and 35mm for inside use. Pays $50 and up for b&w shot; $75 and up for color.

Tips: "*Farm Journal* now publishes in hundreds of editions reflecting geographic, demographic and economic sectors of the farm market."

FARM SHOW MAGAZINE, 20088 Kenwood Trail, P.O. Box 1029, Lakeville MN 55044. (612)469-5572. FAX: (612)469-5575. Editor: Mark A. Newhall. 20% freelance written. A bimonthly trade journal covering agriculture. Estab. 1977. Circ. 150,000. **Pays on acceptance.** Publishes ms an average of 4 months after acceptance. Byline sometimes given. Buys one-time and second serial (reprint) rights. Previously published submissions OK. Reports in 1 week. Free sample copy and writer's guidelines.

Nonfiction: How-to and new product. No general interest, historic or nostalgic articles. Buys 90 mss/year. Send complete ms. Length: 100-2,000 words. Pays $50-300.

Photos: Send photos with submission. Reviews any size color or b&w prints. Offers no additional payment for photos accepted with ms. Captions required. Buys one-time rights.

Tips: "We're looking for first-of-its-kind, inventions of the nuts-and-bolts variety for farmers."

FFA NEW HORIZONS, (formerly *The National Future Farmer*), 15160, Alexandria VA 22309. (703)360-3600. Editor-in-Chief: Wilson W. Carnes. 20% freelance written. Prefers to work with published/established writers, but is eager to work with new/unpublished writers. Bimonthly magazine for members of the National FFA Organization who are students of agriculture in high school, ranging in age from 14-21 years; major interest in careers in agriculture/agribusiness and other youth interest subjects. Circ. 422,528. **Pays on acceptance.** Publishes ms an average of 4 months after acceptance. Buys all rights. Byline given. Submit seasonal/holiday material 4 months in advance. Query for electronic submissions. Usually reports in 1 month. Free sample copy and writer's guidelines.

Nonfiction: How-to for youth (outdoor-type such as camping, hunting, fishing); and informational (getting money for college, farming; and other help for youth). Informational, personal experience and interviews are used only if FFA members or former members are involved. "Science-oriented material is being used more extensively as we broaden people's understanding of agriculture." Buys 15 unsolicited mss/year. Query or send complete ms. Length: 1,000 words maximum. Pays 4-6¢/word. Sometimes pays the expenses of writers on assignment.

Photos: Purchased with mss (5×7 or 8×10 b&w glossies; 35mm or larger color transparencies). Pays $15 for b&w; $30-40 for inside color; $100 for cover.

Tips: "Find an FFA member who has done something truly outstanding that will motivate and inspire others, or provide helpful information for a career in farming, ranching or agribusiness. We've increased emphasis on agriscience and marketing. We're accepting manuscripts now that are tighter and more concise. Get straight to the point."

FORD NEW HOLLAND NEWS, P.O. Box 1895, New Holland PA 17557. Editor: Gary Martin. 50% freelance written. Works with a small number of new/unpublished writers each year. Magazine on agriculture; published 8 times/year; designed to entertain and inform farm families. Estab. 1960. **Pays on acceptance.** Publishes ms an average of 9 months after acceptance. Byline given. Offers negotiable kill fee. Buys first North American serial rights, one-time rights and second serial (reprint) rights. Submlt seasonal/holiday material 6 months in advance. Simultaneous queries and previously published submissions OK. Reports in 1 month. Sample copy and writer's guidelines for 9×12 SAE and 2 first class stamps.

Nonfiction: "We need strong photo support for articles of 1,200-1,700 words on farm management and farm human interest." Buys 40 mss/year. Query. Pays $400-600. Sometimes pays the expenses of writers on assignment.

Photos: Send photos with query when possible. Reviews color transparencies. Pays $50-300. Captions, model release and identification of subjects required. Buys one-time rights.

Tips: "We thrive on good article ideas from knowledgeable farm writers. The writer must have an emotional understanding of agriculture and the farm family and must demonstrate in the article an understanding of the unique economics that affect farming in North America. We want to know about the exceptional farm managers, those leading the way in agriculture. We want new efficiencies and technologies presented through the real-life experiences of farmers themselves. Use anecdotes freely. Successful writers keep in touch with the editor as they develop the article."

HIGH PLAINS JOURNAL, The Farmer's Paper, High Plains Publishers, Inc., P.O. Box 760, Dodge City KS 67801. (316)227-7171. Editor: Galen Hubbs. 5-10% freelance written. Weekly tabloid with news, features and photos on all phases of farming and livestock production. Estab. 1884. Circ. 64,000. Pays on publication. Publishes ms an average of 1 month after acceptance. Byline given. Not copyrighted. Buys first serial rights. Submit seasonal/holiday material 1 month in advance. Simultaneous queries OK. Reports in 3 weeks on queries; 1 month on mss. Sample copy for $1.50.

Nonfiction: General interest (agriculture); how-to; interview/profile (farmers or stockmen within the High Plains area); and photo feature (agricultural). No rewrites of USDA, extension or marketing association releases. Buys 10-20 mss/year. Query with published clips. Length: 10-40 inches. Pays $1/column inch. Sometimes pays the expenses of writers on assignment.

Photos: State availability of photos. Pays $5-10 for 4×5 b&w prints. Captions and complete identification of subjects required. Buys one-time rights.

Tips: "Limit submissions to agriculture. Stories should not have a critical time element. Stories should be informative with correct information. Use quotations and bring out the human aspects of the person featured in profiles. Frequently writers do not have a good understanding of the subject. Stories are too long or are too far from our circulation area to be beneficial."

MISSOURI FARM MAGAZINE, Total Concept Small Farming, Gardening, and Rural Living, Missouri Farm Publishing, Ridge Top Ranch, Rt. 1, 3903 W. Ridge Trail Rd., Clark MO 65243. (314)687-3525. Editor: Ron Macher. 60% freelance written. Bimonthly magazine on small farms. "Magazine for small farmers and small-acreage landowners interested in diversification, direct marketing, alternative crops, minor breeds of livestock, exotics, home-based business, gardening, vegetable and small fruit crops, horses, draft horses and small stock." Estab. 1984. Circ. 5,000. Pays on publication. Publishes ms an average of 2 months after acceptance. Byline given. Buys first rights and second serial (reprint) rights to material in our magazine, for use in anthologies. Submit seasonal/holiday material 2-3 months in advance. Reports in 2 weeks on queries; 1 month on mss. Sample copy $2. Writer's guidelines for #10 SASE.

Nonfiction: How-to (small farming, gardening, alternative crops/livestock). "No political opinions, depressing articles." Buys 70 mss/year. Query with or without published clips. Length: 500-2,500 words. Pays $10-75. Pays in contributor copies or other premiums by individual negotiation.

Photos: Send photos with submission. Reviews contact sheets (b&w only), negatives and 3×5 and larger prints. Offers $4-10 per photo. Captions required. Buys one-time rights and nonexclusive reprint rights (for anthologies).

Tips: "We like upbeat, how-to articles on anything pertaining to the small farm. Come up with a good idea that we or competing publications haven't done before, and query. Good black and white photos are also a plus. Probably the best thing for freelancers to do is find people who lives on a small farm and are successful at something (raising hogs, bees, raspberries, etc.), then interview the people and get as much 'how-to' information about their operation as possible. We don't run just profiles: all of our stories have a 'how-to' angle, even if they feature one operation as an example. All mss must be accompanied by a list of sources contacted. Lists of sources for more information (books, associations, etc.) for sidebars are also appreciated. The stories don't have to be about Missouri small farmers, just about successful small farmers."

PROGRESSIVE FARMER, Southern Progress Corp. Suite 2100 Lakeshore Dr., Birmingham AL 35209. (205)877-6401. Editorial Director: Tom Curl. Editor: Jack Odle. 3% freelance written. Monthly agriculture trade journal. Country people, farmers, ranchers are our audience. Estab. 1886. Circ. 865,000. **Pays on acceptance.** Publishes ms an average of 4 months after acceptance. Byline sometimes given. Buys all rights. Reports in 3 weeks. Free sample copy and writer's guidelines.
Nonfiction: How-to (agriculture and country related), humor (farm related) and technical (agriculture). Buys 30-50 mss/year. Query with published clips. Length: 2,000 words maximum. Pays $100 minimum. Sometimes pays expenses of writers on assignment.
Photos: Send photos with submission. Reviews negatives and transparencies. Payment negotiable. Captions and identification of subjects required. Rights depend on assignment.
Columns/Departments: Handy Devices (need photos and short text on shop ideas that make farm work easier and rural living more enjoyable). Buys 70 mss/year Send complete ms. Length: 20-75 words. Pays $50.
Tips: Query with ideas compatible with basic tone of magazine.

‡SUCCESSFUL FARMING, 1716 Locust St., Des Moines IA 50336. (515)284-2897. Managing Editor: Gene Johnston. 3% freelance written. Prefers to work with published/established writers. Magazine for farm families that make farming their business. Published 12 times/year. Estab. 1902. Circ. 500,000. Buys all rights. **Pays on acceptance.** Publishes ms an average of 2 months after acceptance. Reports in 2 weeks. Sample copy for SAE and 5 first class stamps.
Nonfiction: Semitechnical articles on all aspects of farming, including production, business, country living and recreation with emphasis on how to apply this information to one's own farm family. Also articles on interesting farm people and activities. Buys 30 unsolicited mss/year. Query with outline. Length: about 1,000 words maximum. Pays $250-600. Sometimes pays the expenses of writers on assignment.
Photos: Jim Galbraith, art director. Prefers color with transparencies, not prints. Buys exclusive rights. Assignments are given, and sometimes a guarantee, provided the editors can be sure the photography will be acceptable.
Tips: "A frequent mistake made by writers in completing articles is that the focus of the story is not narrow enough and does not include enough facts, examples, dollar signs and a geographic and industry perspective. Greatest need is for short articles and fillers that are specific and to the point."

Miscellaneous

FUR TRADE JOURNAL OF CANADA, Titan Publishing Inc., Unit 5, 24 Hayes Ave., Box 1747, Guelph, Ontario N1H 7A1 Canada. (519)763-5058. 40% freelance written. Monthly magazine on fur ranching and trapping. *"Fur Trade Journal* is a publication dedicated to mink, fox and chinchilla husbandry." Circ. 1,500. Pays on publication. Publishes ms an average of 2 months after acceptance. Byline given. Buys first North American serial rights. Simultaneous and previously published submissions OK. Reports in 6 weeks. Sample copy available for 8×10 SAE with Canadian postage or IRCs.
Nonfiction: How-to (ranching techniques), interview/profile, new product, technical. Buys 25 mss/year. Query with published clips. Length: 100-3,000 words. Pays up to $100.
Photos: State availability of photos with submission. Reviews 5×7 prints. Offers $5 per photo. Identification of subjects required. Buys one-time rights.
Fillers: Facts, short humor. Length: 10-50 words. Pays $10.
Tips: "Read other publications to become familiar with the trade. The sections most open to freelancers are profiles, interviews and summaries of live animal shows."

GLEANINGS IN BEE CULTURE, P.O. Box 706, Medina OH 44258. FAX: (216)725-5624. Editor: Mr. Kim Flottum. 50% freelance written. For beekeepers and those interested in the natural science of honey bees. Publishes environmentally oriented articles relating to honey bees or pollination. Monthly. Estab. 1873. Buys first North American serial rights. Pays on both publication and acceptance. Publishes ms an average of 4 months after acceptance. Reports in 1 month. Sample copy for 9×12 SAE and 5 first class stamps; free writer's guidelines.
Nonfiction: Interested in articles giving new ideas on managing bees. Also looking for articles on honey bee/ environment connections or relationships. Also uses success stories about commercial beekeepers. No "how I began beekeeping" articles. No highly advanced, technical and scientific abstracts or impractical advice. Length: 2,000 word average. Pays $30-50/published page—on negotiation.

Photos: Sharp b&w photos (pertaining to honey bees, honey plants or related to story) purchased with mss. Can be any size, prints or enlargements, but 4×5 or larger preferred. Pays $7-10/picture.

Tips: "Do an interview story on commercial beekeepers who are cooperative enough to furnish accurate, factual information on their operations. Frequent mistakes made by writers in completing articles are that they are too general in nature and lack management knowledge."

‡**UNITED CAPRINE NEWS**, Double Mountain Press, Drawer A, Rotan TX 79546. (915)735-2278. Editor: Kim Pease. Managing Editor: Jeff Klein. 80% freelance written. A monthly tabloid covering dairy pygmy and angora goats. Estab. 1976. Circ. 5,000. Pays on publication. Publishes ms an average of 3 months after acceptance. Byline given. Buys first rights and makes work-for-hire assignments. Reports in 1 month. Sample copy $1.

Nonfiction: Interview/profile, new product, photo feature and technical—articles directed to all phases of goat keeping: management, showing, breeding and products. Buys 50 mss/year. Send complete ms. Length: open. Pays 25¢/column inch.

Photos: Send photos with submission. Reviews 5×7 prints. Offers 25¢/column inch. Captions required. Buys first rights.

Fillers: Facts and newsbreaks. Buys 25/year. Pays 25¢/column inch.

Tips: "We will consider any articles of an informative nature relating to goats that will benefit professional goat breeders. Most acceptable would be features on goat dairies or farms, technical data on health care and state-of-art topics related to breeding and genetics."

Regional

‡**AG ALERT**, California Farm Bureau Federation, 1601 Exposition Blvd., Sacramento CA 95815. (916)924-4140. Editor: Steve Adler. Managing Editor: Don Myrick. 10% freelance written. Weekly farm newspaper covering agriculture. Estab. 1978. Circ. 50,000. **Pays on acceptance.** Publishes ms an average of 1-2 months after acceptance. Byline given. Publication not copyrighted. Buys first North American serial rights. Query for electronic submissions. Reports in 3 weeks on queries; 6 weeks on mss. Free sample copy and writer's guidelines.

Nonfiction: How-to, technical, and news, all farm related. Special issue on irrigation each Sept. Buys 30-40 mss/year. Query. Length: 1,000-1,500 words. Pays $25-300. Sometimes pays expenses of writers on assignment.

Photos: State availability of photos with submission. Reviews contact sheets, negatives and transparencies. Offers no additional payment for photos accepted with ms. Captions required. Buys one-time rights.

Tips: "We need feature articles on farmers who are doing the job better than their neighbors. Articles must be specific to California. Be sure to query before sending mss."

‡**ARKANSAS FARM & COUNTRY, Arkansas' Only Agricultural Journal**, AgCom, Inc., 912 S. Grand, Stuttgart AR 72160. (501)673-3276/673-6283. Editor: Jeffrey Tennant. 20% freelance written. Monthly tabloid covering agriculture. Commercial farmers and ranchers doing business in Arkansas. Estab. 1985. Circ. 11,700. Pays on publication. Byline given. Negotiable kill fee. Buys one-time rights. Submit seasonal/holiday material 1 month in advance. Query for electronic submissions. Reports in 3 weeks on queries; 1 month on mss. Sample copy for 9×13 SAE with 3 first class stamps.

Nonfiction: How-to (farming or ranching only), humor (country or rural oriented), inspirational, interview/profile (farmer, rancher, agribusiness or legislator), new product, technical (farm oriented products or method). No general interest pieces without relevance to farming or country living. Buys 15-20 mss/year. Query with or without published clips, or send complete ms. Length: 125-3,000 words. Pays $1/printed inch.

Photos: State availability of photos with submission. Reviews contact sheets and 3×5 or larger prints. Offers $5-20 per photo. Captions and identification of subjects required. Buys one-time rights.

Tips: Query with good ideas that will be of interest to Arkansas farmers and ranchers. We serve their interests *only*. Keep mss short (15-40 inches maximum). Photos are helpful."

‡**THE FARMER/DAKOTA FARMER**, Webb Division/Intertec Publishing, 7900 International Dr., Minneapolis MN 55425. (612)851-9329. Editor: Tom Doughty. Managing Editor: David Hest. 20% freelance written. Magazine is published 19 times a year about agriculture in the Upper Midwest (MN, ND, SD). *"The Farmer/Dakota Farmer* provides timely indepth information on crop and livestock production, farm business, governmental affairs/policy and farm lifestyle—all tailored to our 3-state area of MN, ND and SD." Estab. 1882. Circ. 115,000. **Pays on acceptance.** Byline given. Buys first rights or one-time rights. Query for electronic submissions. Reports in 3 weeks on mss. Sample copy for 8×10 SAE.

Nonfiction: How-to (make money farming/ranching in the Upper Midwest) and personal experience (success stories on agriculture). Buys 15-25 mss/year. Query. Length: 300-1,200 words. Pays $100-500 for assigned articles; $100-300 for unsolicited articles. Sometimes pays expenses of writers on assignment.

Photos: Send photos with submission. Reviews contact sheets and transparencies. Offers no additional payment for photos accepted with ms. Captions and identification of subjects required. Buys one-time rights.

FARMWEEK, Mayhill Publications, Inc. 27 N. Jefferson, P.O. Box 90, Knightstown IN 46148. (317)345-5133. FAX: (317)345-5133, ext. 198. Editor: Rod Everhart. 5% freelance written. Agriculture newspaper that covers agriculture in Indiana, Ohio and Kentucky. Estab. 1955. Circ. 28,000. Pays on publication. Byline given. Buys first rights or second serial (reprint) rights. Submit seasonal/holiday material 1 month in advance. Simultaneous and previously published submissions OK. Reports in 2 weeks on queries. Free sample copy and writer's guidelines.

Nonfiction: General interest (agriculture), interview/profile (ag leaders), new product, opinion (ag issues) and photo feature (Indiana, Ohio, Kentucky agriculture). "We don't want first person accounts or articles from states outside Indiana, Kentucky, Ohio (unless of general interest to all farmers and agribusiness)." Number of mss/year varies. Query with published clips. Length: 500-1,500 words. Pays $50 maximum. Sometimes pays expenses of writers on assignment.

Photos: State availability of photos with submission. Reviews contact sheets and 4×5 and 5×7 prints. Offers $5 maximum per photo. Identification of subjects required. Buys one-time rights.

Tips: "We want feature stories about farmers and agribusinessmen in Indiana, Ohio and Kentucky. How do they operate their business? Keys to success, etc.? Best thing to do is call us first with idea, or write. Could also be a story about some pressing issue in agriculture nationally that affects farmers everywhere."

FLORIDA GROWER & RANCHER, F.G.R., Inc., 1331 N. Mills Ave., Orlando FL 32803. (407)894-6522. Publisher: Sondra Abrahamson. 10% freelance written. A monthly magazine for Florida farmers. Circ. 28,000. Pays on publication. Byline given. Buys one-time rights. Submit seasonal/holiday material 2 months in advance. Query for electronic submissions. Reports in 2 weeks on queries; 1 month on mss. Sample copy and writer's guidelines for 9×12 SAE and $1 postage.

Nonfiction: General interest, historical/nostalgic, how-to, interview/profile, new product, personal experience, photo feature, technical. Articles should coordinate with editorial calendar, determined 1 year in advance. Query. Length: 500-1,000 words. Pays $5/printed inch.

Photos: Send photos with submission. Reviews transparencies and prints. Pays $10/b&w print, $50/color cover. Identification of subjects required. Buys one-time rights.

MAINE ORGANIC FARMER & GARDENER, Maine Organic Farmers & Gardeners Association, RR 2, Box 595A, Lincolnville ME 04849. (207)622-3118. Editor: Jean English. 40% freelance written. Prefers to work with published/established writers. Bimonthly magazine covering organic farming and gardening for urban and rural farmers and gardeners and nutrition-oriented, environmentally concerned readers. "*MOF&G* promotes and encourages sustainable agriculture and environmentally sound living. Our primary focus is organic farming, gardening and forestry, but we also deal with local, national and international agriculture, food and environmental issues." Circ. 10,000. Pays on publication. Publishes ms an average of 8 months after acceptance. Byline and bio given. Buys first North American serial rights, one-time rights, first serial rights, or second serial (reprint) rights. Submit seasonal/holiday material 9 months in advance. Simultaneous queries, and simultaneous or previously published submissions OK. Reports in 2 months. Sample copy $2; free writer's guidelines.

Nonfiction: Humor; book reviews; how-to information can be handled as first person experience, technical/research report, or interview/profile focusing on farmer, gardener, food plant, forests, livestock, weeds, insects, trees, renewable energy, recycling, nutrition, health, non-toxic pest control, organic farm management. We use profiles of New England organic farmers and gardeners and news reports (500-1,000 words) dealing with U.S./international sustainable ag research and development, rural development, recycling projects, environmental problem solutions, organic farms with broad impact, cooperatives, community projects, American farm crisis and issues, food issues. Buys 30 mss/year. Query with published clips or send complete ms. Length: 1,000-3,000 words. Pays $20-100. Sometimes pays expenses of writers on assignment.

Photos: State availability of photos with query; send photos or proof sheet with manuscript. Prefer b&w but can use color slides or negatives in a pinch. Captions, model releases and identification of subjects required. Buys one-time rights.

Tips: "We are a nonprofit organization. Our publication's primary mission is to inform and educate. Our readers want to know how to, but they also want to enjoy the reading and know the source/expert/writer. We don't want impersonal how-to articles that sound like Extension bulletins or textbooks. As consumers' demand for organically grown food increases, we are increasingly interested in issues about certification of organic food, legislation that affects organic growers, and marketing of organic food."

NEW ENGLAND FARM BULLETIN & GARDEN GAZETTE, Jacob's Meadow, Inc., P.O. Box 147, Cohasset MA 02025. Editor-in-Chief: V.A. Lipsett. Managing Editor: M.S. Maire. 5% freelance written. Works with a small number of new/unpublished writers each year. A biweekly newsletter covering New England farming. Estab. 1976. Circ. 11,000. Pays on publication. Publishes ms an average of 2 months after acceptance. Byline given. Buys first North American serial rights. Submit seasonal/holiday material 6 months in advance. Reports in 1 week. Sample copy and writer's guidelines for #10 SAE and $1.25.

Nonfiction: Essays (farming/agriculture), general interest, historical/nostalgic, how-to, humor, personal experience, and technical. All articles must be related to New England farming. Buys 6-12 mss/year. Query or send complete ms. Length: 500-1,000 words. Pays 10¢/word.

Tips: "We would probably require the writer to live in New England or to have an unmistakable grasp of what New England is like; must also know farmers." Especially interested in general articles on New England crops/livestocks, specific breeds, crop strains and universal agricultural activity in New England.

NEW ENGLAND FARMER, NEF Publishing Co., Box 391, 50 Bay St., St. Johnsbury VT 05819. (802)748-8908. FAX: (802)748-1866. Editors and Publishers: Dan Hurley and Francis Carlet. 40% freelance written. Monthly dairy publication covering New England agriculture for farmers. Circ. 18,000. Pays on publication. Byline given. Buys all rights and makes-work-for-hire assignments. Submit seasonal/holiday material 2 months in advance. Reports in 3 months. Free sample copy.

Nonfiction: How-to, interview/profile, opinion and technical. No romantic views of farming. "We use on-the-farm interviews with good black and white photos that combine technical information with human interest. No poetics!" Buys 150 mss/year. Send complete ms. Pays $75-150. Sometimes pays the expenses of writers on assignment.

Photos: Send photos with ms. Payment for photos is included in payment for articles. Reviews b&w contact sheets and 8 × 10 b&w prints.

Tips: "Good, accurate stories needing minimal editing, with art, of interest to commercial farmers in New England are welcome. A frequent mistake made by writers is sending us items that do not meet our needs; generally, they'll send stories that don't have a New England focus."

THE OHIO FARMER, 1350 W. 5th Ave., Columbus OH 43212. (614)486-9637. Editor: Andrew Stevens. 10% freelance written. "We are backlogged with submissions and prefer not to receive unsolicited submissions at this time." For Ohio farmers and their families. Biweekly magazine. Circ. 81,000. Usually buys all rights. Pays on publication. Publishes ms an average of 2 months after acceptance. Reports in 2 weeks. Query for electronic submissions. Sample copy $1; free writer's guidelines.

Nonfiction: Technical and on-the-farm stories. Buys informational, how-to and personal experience. Buys 5 mss/year. Submit complete ms. Length: 600-700 words. Pays $30.

Photos: Photos purchased with ms with no additional payment, or without ms. Pays $5-25 for b&w; $35-100 for color. 4 × 5 b&w glossies; and transparencies or 8 × 10 color prints.

Tips: "We are now doing more staff-written stories. We buy very little freelance material."

PENNSYLVANIA FARMER, Harcourt Brace Jovanovich Publications, 704 Lisburn Rd., Camp Hill PA 17011. (717)761-6050. Editor: John Vogel. 10% freelance written. A monthly farm business magazine "oriented to providing readers with ideas to help their businesses and personal lives." Estab. 1877. Circ. 68,000. Pays on publication. Publishes ms an average of 3 months after acceptance. Byline sometimes given. Buys first-time rights. Submit seasonal/holiday material 3 months in advance. Simultaneous submissions OK. Reports in 2 weeks. Writer's guidelines for #10 SASE.

Nonfiction: Humor, inspirational and technical. No stories without a strong tie to Mid-Atlantic farming. Buys 15 mss/year. Query. Length: 500-1,000 words. Pays $50-150. Sometimes pays the expenses of writers on assignment.

Photos: Send photos with submission. Reviews contact sheets, 35mm transparencies and 5 × 7 prints. $25-50 for each b&w photo accepted with ms. Captions and identification of subjects required. Buys one-time rights.

WYOMING RURAL ELECTRIC NEWS, P.O. Box 380, Casper WY 82602. (307)234-6152. Editor: Jack Rollison. 10% freelance written. Works with a small number of new/unpublished writers each year. For audience of small town rural people, some farmers and ranchers. Monthly magazine. Circ. 30,000. Not copyrighted. Byline given. Pays on publication. Publishes ms an average of 3 months after acceptance. Buys first serial rights. Will consider simultaneous submissions. Submit seasonal material 2 months in advance. Reports in 1 month. Free sample copy for SAE and 3 first class stamps.

Nonfiction and Fiction: Wants energy-related material, "people" features, historical pieces about Wyoming and the West, and things of interest to Wyoming's rural people. Buys informational, humor, historical, nostalgia and photo mss. Submit complete ms. Buys 12-15 mss/year. Length for nonfiction and fiction: 1,200-1,500 words. Pays $25-50. Buys some experimental, western, humorous and historical fiction. Pays $25-50. Sometimes pays the expenses of writers on assignment.

Photos: Photos purchased with accompanying ms with additional payment, or purchased without ms. Captions required. Pays up to $50 for cover photos. Color only.

Tips: "Study an issue or two of the magazine to become familiar with our focus and the type of freelance material we're using. Submit entire manuscript. Don't submit a regionally set story from some other part of the country and merely change the place names to Wyoming. Photos and illustrations (if appropriate) are always welcomed."

Finance

These magazines deal with banking, investment and financial management. Publications that use similar material but have a less technical slant are listed under the Consumer Business and Finance section.

BANK OPERATIONS REPORT, Warren, Gorham & Lamont, 1 Penn Plaza, New York NY 10119. (212)971-5000. Managing Editor: Pat Durner. 90% freelance written. Prefers to work with published/established writers, but also works with a small number of new/unpublished writers each year. A monthly newsletter covering operations and technology in banking and financial services. Circ. 2,000. Pays on publication. Publishes ms an average of 2 months after acceptance. Buys all rights. Free sample copy.
Nonfiction: How-to articles, case histories, "practical oriented for bank operations managers" and technical. Buys 60 mss/year. Query with published clips. Length: 500-1,000 words. Pays $1.50/line. Sometimes pays the expenses of writers on assignment.

THE BOTTOM LINE, The News and Information Publication for Canada's Financial Professionals, Bottom Line Publications Inc., 75 Clegg Rd., Markham, Ontario L3R 9V6 Canada. (416)474-9532. FAX: (416)474-9803. Editor: Gundi Jeffrey. 35% freelance written. Monthly tabloid on accounting/ finance/ business. "Reaches 80% of all Canadian accountants. Information should be news/commentary/analysis of issues or issues of interest to or about accountants." Estab. 1985. Circ. 48,000. Pays on publication. Publishes ms an average of 2 weeks to 4 months after acceptance. Byline given. Buys first rights. Simultaneous submissions OK. Query for electronic submissions. Reports in 2 weeks. Free sample copy.
Nonfiction: Technical and travel. Buys 12 mss/year. Query. Length: 800-1,200 words. Pays $250-750 for assigned articles.
Photos: State availability of photos with submission. Offers $50 maximum per photo. Buys one-time rights.

‡CHEKLIST, Magazine for Check Cashers, Chek-Mate, 450 Main St., Springfield MA 01105. (413)736-2517. Editor: A.J. Bonavita. 100% freelance written. Quarterly magazine. The majority of our readers are owners of check cashing stores. The rest have an interest in or sell to these stores. They look to the magazine for advice, news, items of interest, advertisements. Estab. 1989. Circ. 3,400. Pays on publication. Publishes ms an average of 1 month after acceptance. Byline given. Buys one-time rights. Submit seasonal/holiday material 3 months in advance. Simultaneous and previously published submissions OK. Query for electronic submissions. Reports in 1 week on queries; 1 months on mss. Sample copy for 9 × 12 SAE with 5 first class stamps. Free writer's guidelines.
Nonfiction: David S. Rosen, marketing director. Book excerpts, exposé, general interest, historical/nostalgic, humor, inspirational, interview/profile, new product, opinion (does not mean letters to the editor), personal experience, photo feature, technical. Buys 20-30 mss/year. Query with or without published clips, or send complete ms. Length: 500 words minimum. Pays $100-300 for assigned articles; $50 minimum for unsolicited articles.
Photos: Send photos with submission. Reviews prints. Offers no additional payment for photos accepted with ms. Identification of subjects required. Buys one-time rights.
Columns/Departments: New Products/Series (generic analysis of new technologies), 500-1,000 words; Profile (person in or near industry), 500-1,500 words. Buys 10-15 mss/year. Query. Pays $100-300.
Fillers: Anecdotes, facts, short humor.
Tips: "Reading really is the best way, but we do our best to outline methods in guidelines. The feature story is the most open. This can range from a phase of the business to a story about related industries or items."

THE FINANCIAL MANAGER, The Magazine for Financial and Accounting Professionals, Warren, Gorham & Lamont, 1 Penn Plaza, 40th Floor, New York NY 10119. (212)971-5280. Editor: Joseph P. Burns. 95% freelance written. Bimonthly magazine for accountants and financial executives in business. "Information for CFOs, VPs of Finance, corporate controllers and treasurers on how to manage their companies' finances, cut costs and increase profit. Estab. 1988. Circ. 30,000. **Pays on acceptance.** Publishes ms an average of 4 months after acceptance. Byline given. Kill fee varies. Reports in 2 months on queries; 4 months on mss. Sample copy for 9 × 12 SAE. Free sample copy and writer's guidelines.
Nonfiction: How-to (articles on managing a medium-sized company's finances), professional experience and technical (accounting terms, regulations and procedures). Buys 60 mss/year. Query. Length: 1,500-3,000 words. Pays $100-1,000 for assigned articles; $50-1,000 for unsolicited articles. Pays expenses of writers on assignment.
Columns/Departments: Richard Stockton, senior technical editor; Vincent Ryan, associate editor. Tax Breaks (tax information for medium-sized companies), 1,500-2,000 words. Financial Reporting Update (financial reporting information for medium-sized companies), 1,500-2,000 words; New Products (new accounting software, books, services), 750-1,500 words; The Prudent Manager (issues in insurance, law, compensation, ERISA and ethics); Management Material (winning management tips and strategies); Career Path

(maximizing your management potential); Financial Resources (dealing with banks and other capital sources); and Capsule Case (how would you handle this?). Buys 30 mss/year. Query. Length: 1,200-1,500 words. Pays $100-500.

FINANCIAL WOMAN TODAY, (formerly *Executive Financial Woman*), Suite 1400, 500 N. Michigan Ave., Chicago IL 60611. (312)661-1700. FAX: (312)661-0769. Managing Editor: Lora Engdahl. 10-15% freelance written. Monthly newspaper for members of *Financial Women International* and paid subscribers covering banking, insurance, financial planning, diversified financials, credit unions, thrifts, investment banking and other industry segments. Circ. 22,000. Publishes ms an average of 2 months after acceptance. Byline given. Buys all rights. Submit seasonal material 2 months in advance. Simultaneous queries OK. Reports in approximately 1 month. Sample copy $1.
Nonfiction: "We are looking for articles in the general areas of financial services, career advancement, businesswomen's issues and management. Because the financial services industry is in a state of flux at present, articles on how to adapt to and benefit from this fact, both personally and professionally, are particularly apt." Query with resume and clips of published work. Length: 500-3,000 words. Pays variable rates.
Photos: "Photos and other graphic material can make an article more attractive to us." Captions and model release required.
Tips: "We're looking for writers who can write effectively about the people who work in the industry and combine that with hard data on how the industry is changing. We're especially interested in how companies are dealing with workforce issues such as childcare, productivity, customer service, pay equity and training."

THE FUTURES AND OPTIONS TRADER, DeLong–Western Publishing Co., 13618 Scenic Crest Dr., Yucaipa CA 92399. (714)797-3532. Editor: Mike Harris. Managing Editor: Jeanne Johnson. 50% freelance written. Monthly newspaper covering futures and options. Publishes "basic descriptions of trading systems or other commodity futures information which would be useful to traders. No hype or sales-related articles." Estab. 1986. Circ. 20,000. **Pays on acceptance.** Publishes ms an average of 1 month after acceptance. Not copyrighted. Buys various rights. Simultaneous submissions OK. Query for electronic submissions. Free sample copy and writer's guidelines.
Nonfiction: Technical and general trading-related articles. Buys 35 mss/year. Send complete ms. Length: 250-1,000 words. Pays $10-100 for unsolicited articles.
Columns/Departments: Options Trader; Spread Trader (futures and options spread and arbitrage trading); Precious Metals Trader; and Index Trader (stock index trading). Buys 35 mss/year. Send complete ms. Length: 250-1,000 words. Pays $10-100.
Tips: "Authors should be active in the markets."

‡FUTURES MAGAZINE, 219 Parkade, Cedar Falls IA 50613. (319)277-6341. Publisher: Merrill Oster. Editor-in-Chief: Darrell Jobman. 20% freelance written. Monthly magazine. For private, individual traders, brokers, exchange members, agribusinessmen, bankers, anyone with an interest in futures or options. Estab. 1972. Circ. 75,000. Buys all rights. Byline given. Pays on publication. Publishes ms an average of 6 months after acceptance. Reports in 1 month. Sample copy for 9×12 SAE with 8 first class stamps.
Nonfiction: Articles analyzing specific commodity futures and options trading strategies; fundamental and technical analysis of individual commodities and markets; interviews, book reviews, "success" stories; and news items. Material on new legislation affecting commodities, trading, any new trading strategy ("results must be able to be substantiated"); and personalities. No "homespun" rules for trading and simplistic approaches to the commodities market. Treatment is always in-depth and broad. Informational, how-to, interview, profile, technical. "Articles should be written for a reader who has traded commodities for one year or more; should not talk down or hypothesize. Relatively complex material is acceptable." No get-rich-quick gimmicks, astrology articles or general, broad topics. "Writers must have solid knowledge of the magazine's specific emphasis and be able to communicate well." Buys 30-40 mss/year. Query or submit complete ms. Length: 1,500 words optimum. Pays $50-1,000, depending upon author's research and writing quality. "Rarely" pays the expenses of writers on assignment.
Tips: "Writers must have a solid understanding and appreciation for futures or options trading. We will have more financial and stock index features as well as new options contracts that will require special knowledge and experience. Trading techniques and corporate strategies involving futures/options will get more emphasis in the coming year."

ILLINOIS BANKER, Illinois Bankers Association, Suite 1111, 111 N. Canal, Chicago IL 60606. (312)876-9900. FAX: (312)876-3826. Vice President, Public Affairs: Martha Rohlfing. Production: Cindy Altman. Communications Assistant: Anne Feeney. 10% freelance written. Monthly magazine about banking for top decision makers and executives, bank officers, title and insurance company executives, elected officials and individual subscribers interested in banking products and services. Estab. 1916. Circ. 3,000. Pays on publication. Publishes ms an average of 4 months after acceptance. Byline given. Buys first serial rights. Phone queries OK. Submit material 6 weeks prior to publication. Simultaneous submissions OK. Free sample copy, writer's guidelines and editorial calendar.

Nonfiction: Interview (ranking government and banking leaders); personal experience (along the lines of customer relations); and technical (specific areas of banking). "The purpose of the publication is to educate, inform and guide its readers on public policy issues affecting banks, new ideas in management and operations, and banking and business trends in the Midwest. Any clear, fresh approach geared to a specific area of banking, such as agricultural bank management, credit, lending, marketing and trust is what we want." Buys 2-3 unsolicited mss/year. Send complete ms. Length: 825-3,000 words. Pays $75-100.

INDEPENDENT BANKER, Independent Bankers Association of America, P.O. Box 267, Sauk Centre MN 56378. (612)352-6546. Editor: Norman Douglas. 15% freelance written. Works with a small number of new/unpublished writers each year. Monthly magazine for the administrators of small, independent banks. Estab. 1950. Circ. 10,000. **Pays on acceptance.** Publishes ms an average of 3 months after acceptance. Byline given. Not copyrighted. Buys all rights. Reports in 1 week. Sample copy and writer's guidelines for 9 × 12 SAE and 5 first class stamps.

Nonfiction: How-to (banking practices and procedures); interview/profile (popular small bankers); technical (bank accounting, automation); and banking trends. "Factual case histories, banker profiles or research pieces of value to bankers in the daily administration of their banks." No material that ridicules banking and finance or puff pieces on products and services. Buys 12 mss/year. Query. Length: 2,000-2,500 words. Pays $300 maximum.

Tips: "In this magazine, the emphasis is on material that will help small banks compete with large banks and large bank holding companies. We look for innovative articles on small bank operations and administration."

OTC REVIEW, OTC Review, Inc., 37 E. 28th St., Suite 706, New York NY 10016. (212)685-6244. Editor: Robert Flaherty. 50% freelance written. A monthly magazine covering publicly owned companies whose stocks trade in the NASDAQ and over-the-counter markets. "We are a financial magazine covering the fastest-growing securities market in the world. We study the management of companies traded over-the-counter and act as critics reviewing their performances. We aspire to be 'The Shareholder's Friend.' " Estab. 1951. Circ. 27,000. Pays on publication. Publishes ms an average of 2 months after acceptance. Byline given. Buys first rights and reprint rights. Sample copy for 9 × 12 SAE with 5 first class stamps.

Nonfiction: New product and technical. Buys 30 mss/year. "We must know the writer first as we are careful about whom we publish. A letter of introduction with résumé and clips is the best way to introduce yourself. Financial writing requires specialized knowledge and a feel for people as well, which can be a tough combination to find." Query with published clips. Length: 300-1,500 words. Pays $150-750 for assigned articles. Offers copies or premiums for guest columns by famous money managers who are not writing for cash payments, but to showcase their ideas and approach. Pays expenses of writers on assignment.

Photos: Send photos with submission. Reviews contact sheets, negatives, transparencies and prints. Offers no additional payment for photos accepted with ms. Identification of subjects required.

Columns/Departments: Pays $25-75 for assigned items only.

Tips: "Anyone who enjoys analyzing a business and telling the story of the people who started it, or run it today, is a potential *OTC Review* contributor. But to protect our readers and ourselves, we are careful about who writes for us. Business writing is an exciting area and our stories reflect that. If a writer relies on numbers and percentages to tell his story, rather than the individuals involved, the result will be numbingly dull."

PENSION WORLD, Communication Channels, Inc., 6255 Barfield Rd., Atlanta GA 30328. (404)256-9800. FAX: (404)256-3116. Editor: Ed LaBorwit. 10% freelance written. Monthly magazine on pension investment and employee benefits. Estab. 1964. Circ. 28,146. Pays on pasteup. Publishes ms an average of 1 month after acceptance. Byline given. Offer 10% kill fee. Buys all rights. Submit seasonal/holiday material 4 months in advance. Reports in 2 weeks on queries; 3 weeks on mss. Free sample copy and writer's guidelines.

Nonfiction: General interest, humor, interview/profile, new product and opinion. Buys 18 mss/year. Query with published clips. Length: 1,500-2,500 words. Pays $300-500 for assigned articles. Pays $250-450 for unsolicited articles. Sometimes pays expenses of writers on assignment.

Photos: State availability of photos with submission. Reviews 3¾ transparencies and 5 × 7 prints. Offers no additional payment for photos accepted with ms. Identification of subjects required. Buys one-time rights.

Tips: "Freelancers should know the major players in the market they are trying to crack, and how those players relate to the market."

RESEARCH MAGAZINE, Ideas for Today's Investors, Research Services, 2201 3rd St., San Francisco CA 94107. (415)621-0220. Editor: Anne Evers. 50% freelance written. Monthly business magazine of corporate profiles and subjects of interest to stockbrokers. Estab. 1979. Circ. 80,000. Pays on publication. Publishes ms an average of 2 months after acceptance. Byline given. Offers 20% kill fee. Buys first North American serial rights or second serial (reprint) rights. Query for electronic submissions. Reports in 1 month. Sample copy for 9 × 12 SAE with 4 first class stamps; writer's guidelines for #10 SASE.

Nonfiction: How-to (sales tips), interview/profile, new product, financial products. Buys approx. 50 mss/year. Query with published clips. Length: 1,000-3,000 words. Pays 300-900. Sometimes pays expenses of writers on assignment.

Tips: "Only submit articles that fit our editorial policy and are appropriate for our audience. *Only the non-corporate profile section is open to freelancers.* We use local freelancers on a regular basis for coporate profiles."

SECONDARY MARKETING EXECUTIVE, LDJ Corporation. P.O. Box 2330, Waterbury CT 06722. (203)755-0158. FAX: (203)755-3480. Editorial Director: John Florian. 60% freelance written. A monthly tabloid on secondary marketing. "The magazine is read monthly by executives in financial institutions who are involved with secondary marketing, which is the buying and selling of mortgage loans and servicing rights. The editorial slant is toward how-to and analysis of trends, rather than spot news." Estab. 1968. Circ. 32,000. **Pays on acceptance.** Publishes ms an average of 1 month after acceptance. Byline given. 30% kill fee. Buys first rights. Submit seasonal/holiday material 4 months in advance. Query for electronic submissions. Reports in 1 week. Free sample copy and writer's guidelines.

Nonfiction: How-to (how to improve secondary marketing operations and profits) and opinion. Buys 40 mss/year. Query. Length: 800-1,200 words. Pays $200-400.

Photos: State availability of photos with submission. Reviews contact sheets. Offers $25 per photo. Captions, model releases and identification of subjects required. Buys one-time rights.

Fishing

PACIFIC FISHING, Salmon Bay Communications, 1515 NW 51st St., Seattle WA 98107. (206)789-5333. FAX: (206)784-5545. Editor: Steve Shapiro. 75% freelance written. Eager to work with new/unpublished writers. Monthly business magazine for commercial fishermen and others in the West Coast commercial fishing industry. *Pacific Fishing* views the fisherman as a small businessman and covers all aspects of the industry, including harvesting, processing and marketing. Estab. 1979. Circ. 10,000. Pays on publication. Publishes ms an average of 2 months after acceptance. Byline given. Offers 10-15% kill fee on assigned articles deemed unsuitable. Buys one-time rights. Queries highly recommended. Reports in 1 month. Free sample copy and writer's guidelines.

Nonfiction: Interview/profile and technical (usually with a business hook or slant). "Articles must be concerned specifically with *commercial* fishing. We view fishermen as small businessmen and professionals who are innovative and success-oriented. To appeal to this reader, *Pacific Fishing* offers four basic features: technical, how-to articles that give fisherman hands-on tips that will make their operation more efficient and profitable; practical, well-researched business articles discussing the dollars and cents of fishing, processing and marketing; profiles of a fisherman, processor or company with emphasis on practical business and technical areas; and in-depth analysis of political, social, fisheries management and resource issues that have a direct bearing on West Coast commercial fishermen." Buys 20 mss/year. Query noting whether photos are available, and enclosing samples of previous work. Length: 1,500-2,500 words. Pays 10-15¢/word. Sometimes pays the expenses of writers on assignment.

Photos: "We need good, high-quality photography, especially color, of West Coast commercial fishing. We prefer 35mm color slides. Our rates are $150 for cover; $50-100 for inside color; $25-50 for b&w and $10 for table of contents."

Tips: "Because of the specialized nature of our audience, the editor strongly recommends that freelance writers query the magazine in writing with a proposal. We enjoy finding a writer who understands our editorial needs and satisfies those needs, a writer willing to work with an editor to make the article just right. Most of our shorter items are staff written. Our freelance budget is such that we get the most benefit by using it for feature material. The most frequent mistakes made by writers are not keeping to specified length and failing to do a complete job on statistics that may be a part of the story."

Florists, Nurseries and Landscaping

Readers of these publications are involved in growing, selling or caring for plants, flowers and trees. Magazines geared to consumers interested in gardening are listed in the Consumer Home and Garden section.

FLORAL & NURSERY TIMES, XXX Publishing Enterprises Ltd., Box 699, Wilmette IL 60091. (708)256-8777. FAX: (708)256-8791. Editor: Barbara Gilbert. 10% freelance written. A bimonthly trade journal covering wholesale and retail horticulture and floriculture. Circ. 17,500. Pays on publication. Byline given. Buys simultaneous rights. Submit seasonal/holiday material 3 months in advance. Simultaneous submissions OK. Reports in 2 weeks. Sample copy for 9×12 SAE and $3; writer's guidelines for #10 SASE.

Nonfiction: General interest and technical. Buys 100 mss/year. Query with or without published clips, or send complete ms. Payment is negotiable.

Photos: State availability of photos with submission. Reviews prints. Offers no additional payment for photos accepted with ms. Captions and identification of subjects required. Buys simultaneous rights.

Columns/Departments: Care & Handling (horticultural products). Query. Payment negotiable.

FLORIST, Florists' Transworld Delivery Association, 29200 Northwestern Hwy., Box 2227, Southfield MI 48037. (313)355-9300. Editor-in-Chief: William P. Golden. Managing Editor: Susan L. Nicholas. 1% freelance written. For retail florists, floriculture growers, wholesalers, researchers and teachers. Monthly magazine. Circ. 28,000. **Pays on acceptance.** Publishes ms an average of 2 months after acceptance. Buys one-time rights. Pays 10-25% kill fee. Byline given "unless the story needs a substantial rewrite." Phone queries OK. Submit seasonal/holiday material 4 months in advance. Simultaneous and previously published submissions OK. Reports in 1 month.

Nonfiction: How-to (more profitably run a retail flower shop, grow and maintain better quality flowers, etc.); general interest (to floriculture and retail floristry); and technical (on flower and plant growing, breeding, etc.). Buys 5 unsolicited mss/year. Query with published clips. Length: 1,200-3,000 words. Pays 20¢/word.

Photos: "We do not like to run stories without photos." State availability of photos with query. Pays $10-25 for 5×7 b&w photos or color transparencies. Buys one-time rights.

Tips: "Send samples of published work with query. Suggest several ideas in query letter."

FLOWER NEWS, 549 W. Randolph St., Chicago IL 60606. (312)236-8648. FAX: (312)236-8891. Editors: M. Karen Barg and Rosemary C. Martin. For retail, wholesale florists, floral suppliers, supply jobbers and growers. Weekly newspaper. Circ. 17,000. **Pays on acceptance.** Byline given. Submit seasonal/holiday material at least 2 months in advance. Previously published submissions OK. Reports "immediately." Sample copy for 10×13 SAE and 10 first class stamps.

Nonfiction: How-to (increase business, set up a new shop, etc.; anything floral related without being an individual shop story); informational (general articles of interest to industry); and technical (grower stories related to industry, but not individual grower stories). Submit complete ms. Length: 3-5 typed pages. Payment varies.

Photos: "We do not buy individual pictures. They may be enclosed with manuscript at regular manuscript rate (b&w only)."

GARDEN SUPPLY RETAILER, Chilton Publishing, 1 Chilton Way, Radnor PA 19089. (215)964-4327. Editor: Jan Brenny. 5% freelance written. Prefers to work with published/established writers but "quality work is more important than experience of the writer." Monthly magazine for lawn and garden retailers. Estab. 1950. Circ. 41,000. Pays on acceptance in most cases. Publishes ms an average of 3-4 months after acceptance. Buys first serial rights, and occasionally second serial (reprint) rights. Previously published submissions "in different fields" OK as long as not in overlapping fields such as hardware, nursery growers, etc. Reports in 1 month on rejections, acceptance may take longer. Sample copy for 9×12 SAE and $1 postage; writer's guidelines for #10 SAE and 2 first class stamps.

Nonfiction: "We aim to provide retailers with management, merchandising, tax planning and computer information. No technical advice on how to care for lawns, plants and lawn mowers. Articles should be of interest to *retailers* of garden supply products. Stories should tell retailers something about the industry that they don't already know; show them how to make more money by better merchandising or management techniques; address a concern or problem directly affecting retailers or the industry." Buys 10-15 mss/year. Send complete ms or rough draft plus clips of previously published work. Length: 800-1,000 words. Pays $150-200.

Photos: Send photos with ms. Reviews color negatives and transparencies, and 5×7 b&w prints. Captions and identification of subjects required.

Tips: "We will not consider manuscripts offered to 'overlapping' publications such as the hardware industry, nursery growers, etc. Query letters outlining an idea should include at least a partial rough draft; lists of titles are uninteresting. We want business-oriented articles specifically relevant to interests and concerns of retailers of lawn and garden products. We seldom use filler material. Freelancers submitting articles to our publication will find it increasingly difficult to get acceptance as we will be soliciting stories from industry experts and will not have much budget for general freelance material."

THE GROWING EDGE, New Moon Publishing Inc., 206 SW Jefferson, P.O. Box 1027, Corvallis OR 97339. (503)757-2511. FAX: (503)757-0028. Editor: Don Parker. 60% freelance written. Eager to work with new or unpublished writers. Quarterly magazine signature covering indoor and outdoor high-tech gardening techniques and tips. Estab. 1980. Circ. 20,000. Pays on publication. Publishes ms an average of 3 months after acceptance. Byline given. Buys first serial rights and reprint rights. Submit seasonal/holiday material at least 6 months in advance. Query for electronic submissions. Sample copy $6.

Nonfiction: Book excerpts and reviews relating to high-tech gardening, general interest, how-to, interview/profile, personal experience and technical. Query first. Length: 500-2,500 words. Pays 7½¢/word.
Photos: Pays $50/color cover photos; $10-30/color inside photo; $10-20/b&w inside photos; $50-150/text/photo package. Pays on publication. Credit line given. Buys first and reprint rights. Simultaneous and previously published submissions OK.
Tips: Looking for information which will give the reader/gardener/farmer the "growing edge" in high-tech gardening and farming on topics such as hydroponics, high intensity grow lights, water conservation, drip irrigation, advanced organic fertilizers, new seed varieties and greenhouse cultivation.

INTERIOR LANDSCAPE INDUSTRY, The Magazine for Designing Minds and Growing Businesses, American Nurseryman Publishing Co., Suite 545, 111 N. Canal St., Chicago IL 60606. (312)782-5505. FAX: (312)782-3232. Editor: Brent C. Marchant. 10% freelance written. Prefers to work with published/established writers. "Willing to work with freelancers as long as they can fulfill the specifics of our requirements." Monthly magazine on business and technical topics for all parties involved in interior plantings, including interior landscapers, growers and allied professionals (landscape architects, architects and interior designers). "We take a professional approach to the material and encourage our writers to emphasize the professionalism of the industry in their writings." Estab. 1984. Circ. 4,500. Pays on publication. Publishes ms an average of 5 months after acceptance. Byline given. Buys all rights. Submit material 2½ months in advance. Query for electronic submissions. Reports in 3 weeks on queries; 2 weeks on mss. Free sample copy and writer's guidelines.
Nonfiction: How-to (technical and business topics related to the audience); interview/profile (companies working in the industry); personal experience (preferably from those who work or have worked in the industry); photo feature (related to interior projects or plant producers); and technical. No shallow, consumer features. Buys 30 mss/year. Query with published clips. Length: 3-15 ms pages double spaced. Pays $2/published inch. Sometimes pays expenses of writers on assignment.
Photos: Send photos with ms. Reviews b&w contact sheet, negatives, and 5×7 prints; standard size or 4×5 color transparencies. Pays $5-10 for b&w; $15 for color. Identification of subjects required. Buys all rights.
Tips: "Demonstrate knowledge of the field—not just interest in it. Features, especially profiles, are most open to freelancers."

TURF MAGAZINE, Box 391, 50 Bay St., St. Johnsbury VT 05819. (802)748-8908. FAX: (802)748-1866. Editors and Publishers: Francis Carlet and Dan Hurley. 40% freelance written. "Primarily focused on the professional turf grass applicators and users: superintendents of grounds for golf courses, cemeteries, athletic fields, parks, recreation fields, lawn care companies, landscape contractors/architects." Circ. 22,000. Pays on publication. Byline given. Buys all rights or makes work-for-hire assignments. Submit seasonal/holiday material 2 months in advance. Reports in 3 months. Free sample copy.
Nonfiction: How to, interview/profile, opinion and technical. We use on-the-job type interviews with good b&w photos that combine technical information with human interest. "No poetics!" Buys 150 mss/year. Send complete ms. Pays $75-150. Sometimes pays the expenses of writers on assignment.
Photos: Send photos with ms. Payment for photos is included in payment for articles. Reviews b&w contact sheets and 8×10 b&w prints.
Tips: "Good, accurate stories needing minimal editing, with art, of interest to commercial applicators east of the Mississippi are welcomed."

Government and Public Service

Listed here are journals for people who provide governmental services at the local, state or federal level or for those who work in franchised utilities. Journals for city managers, politicians, bureaucratic decision makers, civil servants, firefighters, police officers, public administrators, urban transit managers and utilities managers are listed in this section. Those for private citizens interested in government and public affairs are classified in the Consumer Politics and World Affairs category.

THE CALIFORNIA FIRE SERVICE, The Official Publication of the California State Firemen's Association, Suite 1, 2701 K St., Sacramento CA 95816. FAX: (916)325-2560. Editor: Gary Giacomo. 70% freelance written. Monthly fire service trade journal. Estab. 1927. Circ. 31,000. Pays on publication. Publishes ms an average of 2 months after acceptance. Byline given. Buys first North American serial rights. Submit seasonal/holiday material 4 months in advance. Simultaneous submissions OK. Reports in 1 month. Sample copy for $1.50; writer's guidelines for #10 SASE.
Nonfiction: Expose (circumvention of fire regulations), historical/nostalgic (California slant), how-to (fight specific types of fires), interview/profile (innovative chiefs and/or departments and their programs), new product (fire suppression/fire prevention), opinion (current issues related to the fire service), personal experience (fire or rescue related), photo features (large or dramatic fires in California), technical (fire suppression/

fire prevention). Special issues include: January 1991: firefighter's wages survey. For this issue we will be looking for submissions dealing with wages and benefits of firefighters and privitization. "No political submissions." Buys 24 mss/year. Query with or without published clips, or send complete ms. Length: 400-1,200 words. Pays $55-100 for assigned articles; $35-55 for unsolicited articles. Pays in contributor's copies for opinion pieces and book reviews.

Photos: State availability or send photos with submission. Reviews contact sheets, trasparencies and 5×7 prints. Captions and identification of subjects required. Buys one-time rights. Pays $10-15.

Columns/Departments: Opinion (essay related to an issue facing the modern fire service. Some examples: AIDS and emergency medical services; hazardous materials cleanup and cancer) 400-700 words. Buys 9 mss/year. Send complete ms. Pays in contributor's copies.

Fillers: Anecdotes, facts, newsbreaks. Buys 60 fillers/year. Length: 30-180. Pays $2.

Tips: "Send for writer's guidelines, an editorial calendar and sample issue. Study our editorial calendar and submit appropriate articles as early as possible. We are always interested in articles that are accompanied by compelling fire or firefighting photographs. Articles submittted with quality photographs, graphs or other illustrations will receive special consideration. Fire Breaks is a good area to break in. In Fire Breaks we are looking for fire related newsbreaks, facts and anecdotes from around the U.S. and the world. Bear in mind that we only pay for the first submission, because many Fire Breaks submissions are duplicates. Also, if you're a good photojournalist and you submit photographs with complete information there is a good chance you can develop into a regular contributor. Remember that we have readers from all over California — from urban as well as forestry and rural departments."

CANADIAN DEFENCE QUARTERLY, Revue Canadienne de Défense, Baxter Publications Inc., 310 Dupont St., Toronto, Ontario M5R 1V9 Canada. (416)968-7252. FAX: (416)968-2377. Editor: John Marteinson. 90% freelance written. Professional bimonthly journal on strategy, defense policy, military technology, history. "A professional journal for officers of the Canadian Forces and for the academic community working in Canadian foreign and defense affairs. Articles should have Canadian or NATO applicability." Pays on publication. Byline given. Offers $150 kill fee. Buys all rights. Simultaneous submissions OK. Reports in 1 month. Free sample copy and writer's guidelines.

Nonfiction: Historical, new product, opinion, technical and military strategy. Buys 45 mss/year. Query with or without published clips, or send complete ms. Length: 2,500-4,000 words. Pays $150-300.

Photos: State availability of photos with submission. Offers no additional payment for photos accepted with ms. Buys one-time rights.

Tips: "Submit a well-written manuscript in a relevant field that demonstrates an original approach to the subject matter. Manuscripts *must* be double-spaced, with good margins."

CHIEF OF POLICE MAGAZINE, National Association of Chiefs of Police, 1100 NE 125th St., Miami FL 33161. (305)891-9800. FAX: (305)891-1884. Editor: Gerald S. Arenberg. A bimonthly trade journal for law enforcement commanders (command ranks). Circ. 10,000. **Pays on acceptance.** Publishes ms an average of 4-6 months after acceptance. Byline given. Full payment kill fee offered. Buys first rights. Submit seasonal/holiday material 6 months in advance. Simultaneous and previously published submissions OK. Reports in 2 weeks. Sample copy for $3, 9×12 SAE and 5 first class stamps; writer's guidelines for #10 SASE.

Nonfiction: General interest, historical/nostalgic, how-to, humor, inspirational, interview/profile, new product, personal experience, photo feature, religious and technical. "We want stories about interesting police cases and stories on any law enforcement subject or program that is positive in nature. No exposé types. Nothing anti-police." Buys 50 mss/year. Send complete ms. Length: 600-2,000 words. Pays $25-75 for assigned articles; pays $10-50 for unsolicited articles. Sometimes (when pre-requested) pays the expenses of writers on assignment.

Photos: Send photos with submission. Reviews 5×6 prints. Offers $5-75 per photo. Captions required. Buys one-time rights.

Columns/Departments: New Police (police equipment shown and tests), 200-600 words. Buys 6 mss/year. Send complete ms. Pays $5-25.

Fillers: Anecdote and short humor. Buys 100/year. Length: 100-1,600 words. Pays $5-25.

Tips: "Writers need only contact law enforcement officers right in their own areas and we would be delighted. We want to recognize good commanding officers from sergeant and above who are involved with the community. Pictures of the subject or the department are essential and can be snapshots. We are looking for interviews with police chiefs and sheriffs on command level with photos."

FIREHOUSE MAGAZINE, PTN Publishing, 210 Crossways Park Dr., Woodbury NY 11797. (516)496-8000. Executive Editor: Tom Rahilly. 85% freelance written. Works with a small number of new/unpublished writers each year. Monthly magazine covering fire service. "*Firehouse* covers major fires nationwide, controversial issues and trends in the fire service, the latest firefighting equipment and methods of firefighting, historical fires, firefighting history and memorabilia. Fire-related books, firefighters with interesting avocations, fire safety education, hazardous materials incidents and the emergency medical services are also covered." Circ. 110,000. Pays on publication. Byline given. Exclusive submissions only. Query for electronic submissions. Reports ASAP. Sample copy for 8½ × 11 SAE with 7 first class stamps; free writer's guidelines.

Nonfiction: Book excerpts (of recent books on fire, EMS and hazardous materials); historical/nostalgic (great fires in history, fire collectibles, the fire service of yesteryear); how-to (fight certain kinds of fires, buy and maintain equipment, run a fire department); interview/profile (of noteworthy fire leader, centers, commissioners); new product (for firefighting, EMS); personal experience (description of dramatic rescue, helping one's own fire department); photo feature (on unusual apparatus, fire collectibles, a spectacular fire); technical (on almost any phase of firefighting, techniques, equipment, training, administration); and trends (controversies in the fire service). No profiles of people or departments that are not unusual or innovative, reports of nonmajor fires, articles not slanted toward firefighters' interests. Buys 100 mss/year. Query with or without published clips, or send complete ms. Length: 500-3,000 words. Pays $50-400 for assigned articles; pays $50-300 for unsolicited articles. Sometimes pays the expenses of writers on assignment.

Photos: Mike Delia, art director. Send photos with query or ms. Pays $15-45 for 8 × 10 b&w prints; $30-200 for transparencies and 8 × 10 color prints. Captions and identification of subjects required.

Columns/Departments: Command Post (for fire service leaders); Training (effective methods); Book Reviews; Fire Safety (how departments teach fire safety to the public); Communicating (PR, dispatching); Arson (efforts to combat it); Doing Things (profile of a firefighter with an interesting avocation, group projects by firefighters). Buys 50 mss/year. Query or send complete ms. Length: 750-1,000 words. Pays $100-300.

Tips: "Read the magazine to get a full understanding of the subject matter, the writing style and the readers before sending a query or manuscript. Send photos with manuscript or indicate sources for photos. Be sure to focus articles on firefighters."

‡GRASSROOTS FUNDRAISING JOURNAL, Klein & Honig, Partnership, P.O. 11607, Berkeley CA 94601. Editors: Kim Klein and Lisa Honig. A bimonthly newsletter covering grassroots fund raising for small social change and social service nonprofit organizations. Estab. 1981. Circ. 3,000. Pays on publication. Byline given. Buys first serial rights. Submit seasonal/holiday material 2 months in advance. Simultaneous queries, simultaneous and (occasionally) previously published submissions OK. Reports in 2 weeks on queries; 2 months on mss. Sample copy $3.

Nonfiction: Book excerpts; how-to (all fund raising strategies); and personal experience (doing fund raising). Buys 10 mss/year. Query. Length: 2,000-20,000 words. Pays $35 minimum.

LAW AND ORDER, Hendon Co., 1000 Skokie Blvd., Wilmette IL 60091. (312)256-8555. Editor: Bruce W. Cameron. 90% freelance written. Prefers to work with published/established writers. Monthly magazine covering the administration and operation of law enforcement agencies, directed to police chiefs and supervisors. Estab. 1952. Circ. 30,000. Pays on publication. Publishes ms an average of 6 months after acceptance. Byline given. Buys first North American serial rights. Submit seasonal/holiday material 3 months in advance. No simultaneous queries. Query for electronic submissions. Can accept manuscripts via compuserve: #71171, 1344. Reports in 1 month. Sample copy for 9 × 12 SAE; free writer's guidelines.

Nonfiction: General police interest; how-to (do specific police assignments); new product (how applied in police operation); and technical (specific police operation). Special issues include Buyers Guide (January); Communications (February); Training (March); International (April); Administration (May); Small Departments (June); Police Science (July); Equipment (August); Weapons (September); Mobile Patrol (November); and Community Relations (December). No articles dealing with courts (legal field) or convicted prisoners. No nostalgic, financial, travel or recreational material. Buys 100 mss/year. Length: 2,000-3,000 words. Pays 10¢/word.

Photos: Send photos with ms. Reviews transparencies and prints. Identification of subjects required. Buys all rights.

Tips: "*L&O* is a respected magazine that provides up-to-date information that chiefs can use. Writers must know their subject as it applies to this field. Case histories are well received. We are upgrading editorial quality—stories *must* show some understanding of the law enforcement field. A frequent mistake is not getting photographs to accompany article."

PLANNING, American Planning Association, 1313 E. 60th St., Chicago IL 60637. (312)955-9100. Editor: Sylvia Lewis. 25% freelance written. Emphasizes urban planning for adult, college-educated readers who are regional and urban planners in city, state or federal agencies or in private business or university faculty or students. Monthly. Circ. 25,000. Pays on publication. Publishes ms an average of 3 months after acceptance. Buys all rights or first rights. Byline given. Previously published submissions OK. Reports in 2 months. Sample copy and writer's guidelines for 9 × 12 SAE.

Nonfiction: Exposé (on government or business, but on topics related to planning, housing, land use, zoning); general interest (trend stories on cities, land use, government); how-to (successful government or citizen efforts in planning; innovations; concepts that have been applied); and technical (detailed articles on the nitty-gritty of planning, zoning, transportation but no footnotes or mathematical models). Also needs news stories up to 500 words. "It's best to query with a fairly detailed, one-page letter. We'll consider any article that's well written and relevant to our audience. Articles have a better chance if they are timely and related to planning and land use and if they appeal to a national audience. All articles should be written in magazine feature style." Buys 2 features and 1 news story/issue. Length: 500-2,000 words. Pays $50-600. "We pay freelance writers and photographers only, not planners."

Photos: "We prefer that authors supply their own photos, but we sometimes take our own or arrange for them in other ways." State availability of photos. Pays $25 minimum for 8×10 matte or glossy prints and $200 for 4-color cover photos. Caption material required. Buys one-time rights.

POLICE AND SECURITY NEWS, Days Communications, Inc.. 15 Thatcher Rd., Quakertown PA 18951. (215)538-1240. FAX: (215)368-9955. Editor: James Devery. 40% freelance written. A bimonthly tabloid on public law enforcement and private security. "Our publication is designed to provide educational and entertaining information directed toward management level. Technical information written for the expert in a manner that the non-expert can understand." Estab. 1985. Circ. 20,640. Pays on publication. Publishes ms an average of 2 months after acceptance. Byline given. Buys first North American serial rights. Submit seasonal/holiday material 2 months in advance. Simultaneous and previously published submissions OK. Free sample copy and writer's guidelines.

Nonfiction: Al Menear, articles editor. Exposé, historical/nostalgic, how-to, humor, interview/profile, opinion, personal experience, photo feature and technical. Buys 12 mss/year. Query. Length: 200-4,000 words. Pays $50-200. Sometimes pays in trade-out of services.

Photos: State availability of photos with submission. Reviews prints (3×5). Offers $10-50 per photo. Buys one-time rights.

Fillers: Facts, newsbreaks and short humor. Buys 6/year. Length: 200-2,000 words. Pays $50-150.

SUPERINTENDENT'S PROFILE & POCKET EQUIPMENT DIRECTORY, Profile Publications, 220 Central Ave., Box 43, Dunkirk NY 14048. (716)366-4774. Editor: Robert Dyment. 60% freelance written. Prefers to work with published/established writers. Monthly magazine covering "outstanding" town, village, county and city highway superintendents and Department of Public Works Directors throughout New York state only. Circ. 2,600. Publishes ms an average of 4 months after acceptance. Pays within 90 days. Byline given for excellent material. Buys first serial rights. Submit seasonal/holiday material 3 months in advance. Simultaneous queries OK. Reports in 2 weeks on queries; 1 month on mss. Sample copy for 9×12 SAE and 4 first class stamps.

Nonfiction: John Powers, articles editor. Interview/profile (of a highway superintendent or DPW director in NY state who has improved department operations through unique methods or equipment); and technical. Special issues include winter maintenance profiles. No fiction. Buys 20 mss/year. Query. Length: 1,500-2,000 words. Pays $150 for a full-length ms. "Pays more for excellent material. All manuscripts will be edited to fit our format and space limitations." Sometimes pays the expenses of writers on assignment.

Photos: John Powers, photo editor. State availability of photos. Pays $5-10 for b&w contact sheets; reviews 5×7 prints. Captions and identification of subjects required. Buys one-time rights.

Poetry: Buys poetry if it pertains to highway departments. Pays $5-15.

Tips: "We are a widely read and highly respected state-wide magazine, and although we can't pay high rates, we expect quality work. Too many freelance writers are going for the exposé rather than the meat-and-potato type articles that will help readers. We use more major features than fillers. Frequently writers don't read sample copies first. We will be purchasing more material because our page numbers are increasing."

‡TRANSACTION/SOCIETY, Rutgers University, New Brunswick NJ 08903. (201)932-2280, ext. 83. FAX: (201)932-3138. Editor: Irving Louis Horowitz. 10% freelance written. Prefers to work with published/established writers. For social scientists (policymakers with training in sociology, political issues and economics). Published every 2 months. Circ. 45,000. Buys all rights. Byline given. Pays on publication. Publishes ms an average of 6 months after acceptance. No simultaneous submissions. Query for electronic submissions; "manual provided to authors." Reports in 1 month. Query. Sample copy and writer's guidelines for 9×12 SAE and 5 first class stamps.

Nonfiction: Rebecca L. Woolston, managing editor. "Articles of wide interest in areas of specific interest to the social science community. Must have an awareness of problems and issues in education, population and urbanization that are not widely reported. Articles on overpopulation, terrorism, international organizations. No general think pieces." Payment for articles is made only if done on assignment. *No payment for unsolicited articles.*

Photos: Douglas Harper, photo editor. Pays $200 for photographic essays.

Tips: "Submit an article on a thoroughly unique subject, written with good literary quality. Present new ideas and research findings in a readable and useful manner. A frequent mistake is writing to satisfy a journal, rather than the intrinsic requirements of the story itself. Avoid posturing and editorializing."

VICTIMOLOGY: An International Journal, 2333 N. Vernon St., Arlington VA 22207. (703)536-1750. Editor-in-Chief: Emilio C. Viano. "We are the only magazine specifically focusing on the victim, on the dynamics of victimization; for social scientists, criminal justice professionals and practitioners, social workers and volunteer and professional groups engaged in prevention of victimization and in offering assistance to victims of rape, spouse abuse, child abuse, incest, abuse of the elderly, natural disasters, etc." Quarterly magazine.

Circ. 2,500. Pays on publication. Buys all rights. Byline given. Reports in 2 months. Sample copy $5; free writer's guidelines.

Nonfiction: Exposé, historical, how-to, informational, interview, personal experience, profile, research and technical. Buys 10 mss/issue. Query. Length: 500-5,000 words. Pays $50-150.

Photos: Purchased with accompanying ms. Captions required. Send contact sheet. Pays $15-50 for 5×7 or 8×10 b&w glossy prints.

Poetry: Avant-garde, free verse, light verse and traditional. Length: 30 lines maximum. Pays $10-25.

Tips: "Focus on what is being researched and discovered on the victim, the victim/offender relationship, treatment of the offender, the bystander/witness, preventive measures, and what is being done in the areas of service to the victims of rape, spouse abuse, neglect and occupational and environmental hazards and the elderly."

YOUR VIRGINIA STATE TROOPER MAGAZINE, Virginia State Police Association, 6944 Forest Hill Ave., Richmond VA 23225. Editor: Rebecca V. Jackson. 70% freelance written. Triannual magazine covering police topics for troopers (state police), libraries, legislators and medical offices. Estab. 1974. Circ. 10,000. **Pays on acceptance.** Publishes ms an average of 3 months after acceptance. Byline given. Buys first North American serial rights and all rights on assignments. Submit seasonal/holiday material 2 months in advance. Simultaneous submissions OK. Reports in 2 months.

Nonfiction: Exposé (consumer or police-related); general interest; fitness/health; tourist (VA sites); financial planning (tax, estate planning tips); historical/nostalgic; how-to (energy saving); book excerpts/reports (law enforcement related); humor, interview/profile (notable police figures); technical (radar) and other (recreation). Buys 60-65 mss/year. Query with clips or send complete ms. Length: 2,500 words. Pays $250 maximum/article (10¢/word). Sometimes pays expenses of writers on assignment.

Photos: Send photos with ms. Pays $50 maximum for several 5×7 or 8×10 b&w glossy prints to accompany ms. Cutlines and model releases required. Buys one-time rights.

Cartoons: Send copies. Pays $15; $20 if customized per request. Buys one-time rights. Buys 20 cartoons/year.

Fiction: Adventure, humorous, mystery, novel excerpts and suspense. Buys 6 mss/year. Send complete ms. Length: 2,500 words minimum. Pays $250 maximum (10¢/word) on acceptance.

Tips: In addition to items of interest to the VA State Police, general interest is stressed because of large readership by general professionals in VA.

Groceries and Food Products

In this section are publications for grocers, food wholesalers, processors, warehouse owners, caterers, institutional managers and suppliers of grocery store equipment. See the section on Confectionery and Snack Foods for bakery and candy industry magazines.

AUTOMATIC MERCHANDISER, Edgell Communications, 7500 Old Oak Blvd., Cleveland OH 44130. (216)243-8100. FAX: (216)891-2683. Editor: Mark L. Dlugoss. Associate Editor: Elizabeth C. Mezzaros. 10% freelance written. Prefers to work with published/established writers. A monthly trade journal covering vending machines, contract foodservice and office coffee service. "*AM's* readers are owners and managers of these companies; we profile successful companies and report on market trends." Circ. 13,250. **Pays on acceptance.** Publishes ms an average of 3 months after acceptance. Byline sometimes given. Buys first North American serial rights, all rights or makes work-for-hire assignments. Submit seasonal/holiday material 4 months in advance. Reports in 1 month. Free sample copy and writer's guidelines.

Nonfiction: Buys 30 mss/year. Query. Length: 1,000-6,000 words. Pays $150-600. Sometimes pays the expenses of writers on assignment.

Photos: Send photos with submission. Reviews contact sheets, transparencies and prints. Offers $50 maximum per photo. Buys all rights.

CANADIAN GROCER, Maclean-Hunter Ltd., Maclean Hunter Building, 777 Bay St., Toronto, Ontario M5W 1A7 Canada. (416)596-5772. Editor: George H. Condon. 10% freelance written. Prefers to work with published/established writers. Monthly magazine about supermarketing and food retailing for Canadian chain and independent food store managers, owners, buyers, executives, food brokers, food processors and manufacturers. Estab. 1886. Circ 18,500. Pays on publication. Publishes ms an average of 2 months after acceptance. Byline given. Buys first Canadian rights. Phone queries OK. Submit seasonal material 2 months in advance. Previously published submissions OK. Reports in 1 month. Sample copy $5.

Nonfiction: Interview (Canadian trendsetters in marketing, finance or food distribution); technical (store operations, equipment and finance); and news features on supermarkets. "Freelancers should be well versed on the supermarket industry. We don't want unsolicited material. Writers with business and/or finance expertise are preferred. Know the retail food industry and be able to write concisely and accurately on subjects relevant to our readers: food store managers, senior corporate executives, etc. A good example of an article would be 'How a Six Store Chain of Supermarkets Improved Profits 2% and Kept Customers Coming.' " Buys 14 mss/year. Query with clips of previously published work. Pays 25¢/word. Sometimes pays the expenses of writers on assignment.

Photos: State availability of photos. Pays $10-25 for prints or slides. Captions preferred. Buys one-time rights.

Tips: "Suitable writers will be familiar with sales per square foot, merchandising mixes and direct product profitability."

‡**CANDY WHOLESALER,** National Candy Wholesalers Association. Suite 1120, 1120 Vermont Ave. NW, Washington DC 20005. (202)463-2124. Publisher/Editor: Shelley Estersohn. Managing Editor: Kevin Settlage. 35% freelance written. A monthly magazine for distributors of candy/tobacco/snacks/groceries and other convenience-store items. "*Candy Wholesaler* magazine is published to assist the candy/tobacco/snack food distributor in improving his business by providing a variety of relevant operational information. Serves as the voice of the distributor in the candy/tobacco/snack industry." Circ. 11,419. **Pays on acceptance.** Publishes ms an average of 4 months after acceptance. Byline given. Offers $50 kill fee. Buys all rights. Submit seasonal/holiday material 6 months in advance. Query for electronic submissions. Reports in 1 month. Sample copy for 9×12 SAE with 6 first class stamps.

Nonfiction: Historical/nostalgic, how-to (related to distribution), interview/profile, photo feature, technical (data processing) and (profiles of distribution films/or manufacturers). "No simplistic pieces with consumer focus that are financial, tax-related or legal." Buys 30-35 mss/year. Query with or without published clips, or send complete ms. Length: 8-12 double-spaced typewritten pages. Pays $350-600 for assigned articles. Pays $200-400 for unsolicited articles. Sometimes pays copies to industry members who author articles. Pays the expenses of writers on assignment.

Photos: Send photos with submission. Reviews contact sheets, transparencies and prints. Offers $5-10 per photo. Captions and identification of subjects required. Buys all rights.

Fillers: Kevin Settlage, fillers editor. Anecdotes, facts and short humor. Length: 50-200 words. Pays $10-20.

Tips: "Talk to wholesalers about their business—how it works, what their problems are, etc. We need writers who understand this industry. Company profile feature stories are open to freelancers. Get into the nitty gritty of operations and management. Talk to several key people in the company."

CITRUS & VEGETABLE MAGAZINE, and the Florida Farmer, 1819 N. Franklin St. Tampa FL 33602. (813)223-7628. FAX: (813)223-6878. Editor: Sarah Carey. Monthly magazine on the citrus and vegetable industries. Estab. 1938. Circ. 12,000. Pays on publication. Publishes ms an average of 1 month after acceptance. Byline given. Kill fee varies. Buys exclusive first rights. Reports in 2 months on queries. Free sample copy and writer's guidelines.

Nonfiction: Book excerpts (if pertinent to relevant agricultural issues), how-to (grower interest - cultivation practices, etc.), new product (of interest to Florida citrus or vegetable growers), personal experience and photo feature. Buys 50 mss/year. Query with published clips or send complete ms. Length: 3-5 typewritten pages. Pays $4 per column inch.

Photos: Send photos with submission. Reviews 5×7 prints. Offers $15 minimum per photo. Captions and identification of subjects required. Buys first rights.

Columns/Departments: Citrus Summary (news to citrus industry in Florida: market trends, new product lines, anything focusing the competition at home or abroad) and Vegetable Vignettes (new cultivars, anything on trends or developments withing vegetable industry of Florida). Send complete ms. Length: 600 words maximum. Pays $4 per column inch.

Tips: "Show initiative—don't be afraid to call whomever you need to get your information for story together—accurately and with style. Submit ideas and/or completed ms well in advance. Focus on areas that have not been widely written about elsewhere in the press. Looking for fresh copy. Have something to sell and be convinced of its value. Become familiar with the key issues, key players in the citrus industry in Florida. Have a specific idea in mind for a news or feature story and try to submit manuscript at least 1 month in advance of publication."

DELI-DAIRY, Hubsher Publications, P.O. Box 373, Cedarhurst NY 11516. (516)295-3680. Editor Stan Hubsher. 100% freelance written. Bimonthly magazine for deli/dairy buyers in supermarkets. "Audience is volume deli/dairy buyers at chain, supermarket level—how they determine showcase purchases, layout of department, all buying functions as well as training, etc." Estab. 1969. Circ. 8,500. Pays on publication. No byline. Buys all rights. Submit seasonal/holiday material 2 months in advance. Free sample copy and writer's guidelines.

Nonfiction: Buys 6-8 mss/year. Query. Length: 2,000 words. Pays $150 minimum to negotiable maximum. Sometimes pays expenses of writers on assignment.

Photos: Send photos with submission. Offers no additional payment for photos accepted with ms. Captions and identification of subjects required. Buys one-time rights.

FOOD BUSINESS, Putman Publishing Corp., 301 E. Erie St., Chicago IL 60611. (312)644-2020. FAX: (312)644-7870. Editor: Bob Messenger. 33% freelance written. Biweekly magazine on food business. "Everything is written from a *news* slant." Estab. 1988. Circ. 50,000. **Pays on acceptance.** Publishes ms an average of 1 month after acceptance. Byline sometimes given. Buys first rights and second serial (reprint) rights. Query for electronic submissions. Free writer's guidelines.

Nonfiction: Exposé, interview/profile (people/companies/trends), new product and news. Buys 40 mss/year. Send article abstract. Length: 700-2,000 words. Averages $200-500 per feature. Sometimes pays expenses of writers on assignment.

Photos: Send photos with submission—as assigned. Reviews contact sheets, transparencies and prints. Offers no additional payment for photos accepted with ms (with exceptions based on assignment). Identification of subjects required. Buys one-time rights and reprint rights.

Columns/Departments: Packaging (food-related news/trends), New Products (new foods), International (food people/companies) and Finance (performance). Buys 40 mss/year. Query with published clips. Length: 500-1,000 words. Pays average of $250.

FOOD PEOPLE, Olson Publications, Inc., P.O. Box 1208, Woodstock GA 30188. (404)928-8994. Editor: Warren B. Causey. 75% freelance written. Prefers to work with published/established writers, but works with a small number of new/unpublished writers each year. Always willing to consider new writers, but they must have a basic command of their craft. Monthly tabloid covering the retail food industry. Estab. 1981. Circ. 30,000. Pays on publication. Publishes ms an average of 1 month after acceptance. Byline given. Buys all rights. Will reassign subsidiary rights after publication and upon request. Submit seasonal/holiday material 6 weeks in advance. Computer modem submissions encouraged. Reports in 6 weeks. Sample copy for 9 × 12 SAE with 5 first class stamps; writer's guidelines for #10 SASE.

Nonfiction: Interview/profile (of major food industry figures), photo features of ad campaigns, marketing strategies, important new products and services. "We would like to receive feature articles about people and companies that illustrate trends in the food industry. Articles should be informative, tone is upbeat. Do not send recipes or how-to shop articles; we cover food as a business." Buys 250-300 mss/year. Query or send complete ms. Length: 500-1,500 words. Pays $3/published inch minimum. Pays the expenses of writers on assignment.

Photos: "Photos of people. Photos of displays, or store layouts, etc., that illustrate points made in article are good, too. But stay away from storefront shots." State availability of photos with query or send photos with ms. Pays $10 plus expenses for 5 × 7 b&w prints; and $25 plus expenses for color transparencies. Captions required. Buys one-time rights.

Columns/Departments: Company news, People, Organizations, New Products, and Morsels . . . a Smorgasbord of Tidbits in the National Stew. Send complete ms. Pays $3/inch.

Tips: "Begin with an area news event—store openings, new promotions. Write that as news, then go further to examine the consequences. We are staffing more conventions, so writers should concentrate on features about people, companies, trends, new products, innovations in the food industry in their geographic areas and apply these to a national scope when possible. Talk with decision makers to get 'hows' and 'whys.' We now are more feature than news oriented. We look for contributors who work well, quickly and always deliver. We are now buying some international material."

FOODSERVICE DIRECTOR, Bill Communications, 633 3rd Ave., New York NY 10017. (212)984-2356. Editor: Walter J. Schruntek. Managing Editor: Karen Weisberg. 20% freelance written. Monthly tabloid on noncommercial foodservice operations for operators of kitchens and dining halls in schools, colleges, hospitals/health care, office and plant cafeterias, military, airline/transportation, correctional institutions. Estab. 1988. Circ. 45,000. Pays on publication. Byline given sometimes. Offers 25% kill fee. Buys all rights. Submit seasonal/holiday material 2-3 months in advance. Simultaneous submissions OK. Free sample copy.

Nonfiction: How-to, interview/profile. Buys 60-70 mss/year. Query with published clips. Length: 700-900 words. Pays $250-500. Sometimes pays the expenses of writers on assignment.

Photos: Send photos with submission. Reviews transparencies. Offers no additional payment for photos accepted with ms. Identification of subjects required. Buys all rights.

Columns/Departments: Equipment (case studies of kitchen/serving equipment in use), 700-900 words; Food (specific category studies per publication calendar), 750-900 words. Buys 20-30 mss/year. Query. Length: 400-600 words. Pays $150-250.

GOURMET TODAY, Cummins Publishing Company, P.O. Box 1657, Palm Harbor FL 34682-1657. (813)785-3101. FAX: (813)786-7969. Publisher: Andrew J. Cummins. Editor: Charity Cicardo. 25% freelance written. Bimonthly magazine serving specialty food retailers, distributors and manufacturers. A high percentage of our readers are gourmet shop owners; therefore, we look for articles that will help these retailers be more successful. Articles we publish include those concerning industry trends, new products, retailer and manufacturer profiles, "how-tos," hardgoods and features on specific food items, such as chocolates, spices, wines. Estab. 1935. Circ. 20,000. Pays on publication. Byline given. Buys first North American serial rights and first industry rights. Submit queries only. Reports in 1 month on queries. Sample copy for 9 × 12 SAE with 5 first class stamps. Writer's guidelines for #10 SASE.

Nonfiction: Exposé, how-to, interview/profile, new product, personal experience, technical and travel. "Our publication is directed specifically toward retailers, distributors and manufacturers of specialty foods. Any stories that do not directly address these groups are of no use to us." Query with published clips. Length: 800-1,300 words. Pays $100 per 600 words.

Photos: State availability of photos with submission. Reviews negatives, at least 4×5 transparencies and at least 4×5 prints. Model releases and identification of subjects required.

Tips: Prefer writers with knowledge and experience in the specialty food industry.

HEALTH FOODS BUSINESS, Howmark Publishing Corp., 567 Morris Ave., Elizabeth NJ 07208. (201)353-7373. FAX: (201)353-8221. Editor: Gina Geslewitz. 40% freelance written. Eager to work with new/unpublished writers if competent and reliable. For owners and managers of health food stores. Monthly magazine. Circ. 11,000. Pays on publication. Publishes ms an average of 4 months after acceptance. Byline given "if story quality warrants it." Buys first North American serial rights; "also exclusive rights in our trade field." Phone queries OK. "Query us about a good health food store in your area. We use many store profile stories." Simultaneous submissions OK if exclusive to their field. Previously published work OK, but please indicate where and when material appeared previously. Reports in 1 month. Sample copy $3 plus $2 for postage and handling; writer's guidelines for #10 SASE.

Nonfiction: Exposé (government hassling with health food industry); how-to (unique or successful retail operators); informational (how or why a product works; technical aspects must be clear to laymen); historical (natural food use); interview (must be prominent person in industry or closely related to the health food industry or well-known or prominent person in any arena who has undertaken a natural diet/lifestyle); and photo feature (any unusual subject related to the retailer's interests). Buys 1-2 mss/issue. Query for interview and photo features. Will consider complete ms in other categories. Length: long enough to tell the whole story without padding. Pays $50 and up for feature stories, $75 and up for store profiles.

Photos: "Most articles must have photos included;" negatives and contact sheet OK. Captions required. No additional payment.

Tips: "A writer may find that submitting a letter with a sample article he/she believes to be closely related to articles read in our publication is the most of expedient way to determine the appropriateness of his/her skills and expertise."

MINNESOTA GROCER, Official Publication of the Minnesota Grocers Association, Minnesota Grocers Council, Inc., 533 St. Clair Ave., St. Paul MN 55102. (612)228-0973. FAX: (612)228-1949. Editor: Randy Schubring. 25% freelance written. Bimonthly magazine on the retail grocery industry in Minnesota. Estab. 1951. Circ. 4,800. Pays on publication. Publishes ms an average of 1-2 months after acceptance. Byline given. Buys all rights. Submit seasonal/holiday material 3 months in advance. Previously published submissions OK. Reports in 1 month on queries; 2 weeks on mss. Free sample copy and writer's guidelines.

Nonfiction: How-to better market, display and sell food, and other items in a grocery store. How to find new markets. Interview/profile and new products. Special issues: "We do an economic forecast in Jan/Feb. issue." Buys 6 mss/year. Query with published clips. Length: 300-1,500 words. Pays $100-500 for assigned articles. Sometimes pays expenses of writers on assignment.

Photos: State availability of photos with submission. Reviews contact sheets and 5×7 prints. Captions, model releases and identification of subjects required. Buys all rights.

Columns/Departments: Query with published clips.

Tips: "The best way to be considered for a freelance assignment is first and foremost to have a crisp journalistic writing style on clips. Second it is very helpful to have a knowledge of the issues and trends in the grocery industry. Because we are a regional trade publication, it is crucial that articles be localized to Minnesota."

PRODUCE NEWS, 2185 Lemoine Ave., Fort Lee NJ 07024. FAX: (201)592-0809. Editor: Gordon Hochberg. 10-15% freelance written. Works with a small number of new/unpublished writers each year. For commercial growers and shippers, receivers and distributors of fresh fruits and vegetables, including chain store produce buyers and merchandisers. Weekly. Estab. 1897. Circ. 10,000. Pays on publication. Publishes ms an average of 2 weeks after acceptance. Deadline is Tuesday afternoon before Thursday press day. Free sample copy and writer's guidelines.

Nonfiction: News stories (about the produce industry). Buys profiles, spot news, coverage of successful business operations and articles on merchandising techniques. Query. Pays minimum of $1/column inch for original material. Sometimes pays the expenses of writers on assignment.

Photos: B&w glossies. Pays $8-10 for each one used.

Tips: "Stories should be trade-oriented, not consumer-oriented. As our circulation grows in the next year, we are interested in stories and news articles from all fresh fruit-growing areas of the country. Looking especially for writers in southern California and lower Rio Grande Valley of Texas."

QUICK FROZEN FOODS INTERNATIONAL, E.W. Williams Publishing Co., 80 8th Ave., New York NY 10011. (212)989-1101. FAX: (212)242-5991. Editor: John M. Saulnier. 20% freelance written. Works with a small number of new/unpublished writers each year. Quarterly magazine covering frozen foods around the world—

"every phase of frozen food manufacture, retailing, food service, brokerage, transport, warehousing, merchandising. Especially interested in stories from Europe, Asia and emerging nations." Circ. 13,500. Pays on publication. Publishes ms an average of 3 months after acceptance. Byline given. Offers kill fee; "if satisfactory, we will pay promised amount. If bungled, half." Buys all rights, but will relinquish any rights requested. Submit seasonal/holiday material 6 months in advance. Sample copy $5.

Nonfiction: Book excerpts, general interest, historical/nostalgic, interview/profile, new product (from overseas), personal experience, photo feature, technical and travel. No articles peripheral to frozen food industry such as taxes, insurance, government regulation, safety, etc. Buys 20-30 mss/year. Query or send complete ms. Length: 500-4,000 words. Pays 5¢/word or by arrangement. "We will reimburse postage on articles ordered from overseas." Sometimes pays the expenses of writers on assignment.

Photos: "We prefer photos with all articles." State availability of photos or send photos with accompanying ms. Pays $7 for 5 × 7 b&w prints (contact sheet if many shots). Captions and identification of subject required. Buys all rights. Release on request.

Columns/Departments: News or analysis of frozen foods abroad. Buys 20 columns/year. Query. Length: 500-1,500 words. Pays by arrangement.

Fillers: Newsbreaks. Length: 100-500 words. Pays $5-20.

Tips: "We are primarily interested in feature materials, (1,000-3,000 words with pictures). We are now devoting more space to frozen food company developments in Pacific Rim countries. Stories on frozen food merchandising and retailing in foreign supermarket chains in Europe, Japan and Australia/New Zealand are welcome. National frozen food production profiles are also in demand worldwide. A frequent mistake is submitting general interest material instead of specific industry-related stories."

SEAFOOD LEADER, Waterfront Press Co., 1115 NW 45th St., Seattle WA 98107. (206)789-6506. FAX: (206)548-9346. Editor: Peter Redmayne. Managing Editor: Wayne Lee. 20% freelance written. Works with a small number of new/unpublished writers each year. A trade journal on the seafood business published 6 times/year. Circ. 15,000. Pays on publication. Publishes ms an average of 3 months after acceptance. Byline given. Buys first rights and second serial (reprint) rights. Simultaneous and previously published submissions OK. Query for electronic submissions. Reports in 1 month on queries; 2 months on mss. Sample copy $3 with 9 × 12 SAE.

Nonfiction: General seafood interest, marketing/business, historical/nostalgic, interview/profile, opinion and photo feature. Each of *Seafood Leader's* six issues has a slant: Whole Seafood Catalog (Jan/Feb), Buyer's Guide (Mar/Apr), International (May/June), Foodservice/Restaurant (July/Aug), Retail/Aquaculture (Sep/Oct) and Shrimp (Nov/Dec). Each issue also includes stories outside of the particular focus, particularly shorter features and news items. No recreational fishing; no first person articles. Buys 12-15 mss/year. Query with or without published clips, or send complete ms. Length: 1,000-2,500 words. Pay rate is 15-20¢/word published depending upon amount of editing necessary. Sometimes pays the expenses of writers on assignment.

Photos: State availability of photos with submission. Reviews contact sheets and transparencies. Offers $50 per inside color photo, $100 for cover. Buys one-time rights.

Fillers: Newsbreaks. Buys 10-15/year. Length: 100-250 words. Pays $50-100.

Tips: "*Seafood Leader* is steadily increasing in size and has a growing need for full-length feature stories and special sections. Articles on innovative, unique and aggressive people or companies involved in seafood are needed. Writing should be colorful, tight and fact-filled, always emphasizing the subject's formula for increased seafood sales. Readers should feel as if they have learned something applicable to their business."

THE WISCONSIN GROCER, Wisconsin Grocers Association, Suite 203, 802 W. Broadway, Madison WI 53713. (608)222-4515. Editor: Dianne Calgaro. Eager to work with new/unpublished writers. Bimonthly magazine covering grocery industry of Wisconsin. Circ. 1,500. Pays on publication. Publishes ms an average of 3 months after acceptance. Byline given. Not copyrighted. Buys first North American serial rights, second serial (reprint) rights or simultaneous rights. Submit seasonal/holiday material 5 months in advance. Simultaneous and previously published submissions OK. Reports in 2 weeks on queries; 2 months on mss. Sample copy for 9 × 12 SAE with 3 first class stamps.

Nonfiction: How-to (money management, employee training/relations, store design, promotional ideas); interview/profile (of WGA members and Wisconsin politicans only); opinion; technical (store design or equipment). No articles about grocers or companies not affiliated with the WGA. Buys 6 mss/year. Query. Length: 500-2,000 words. Pays $15 minimum. Pays in copies if the writer works for a manufacturer or distributor of goods or services relevant to the grocery industry, or if a political viewpoint is expressed.

Photos: Send photos with submission. Reviews 5 × 7 prints. Offers no additional payment for photos accepted with ms. Identification of subjects required. Buys one-time rights.

Columns/Departments: Security (anti-shoplifting, vendor thefts, employee theft, burglary); Employee Relations (screening, training, management); Customer Relations (better service, corporate-community relations, buying trends); Money Management (DPP programs, bookkeeping, grocery—specific computer applications); Merchandising (promotional or advertising ideas), all 1,000 words. Buys 6 mss/year. Query. Length: 500-1,500 words.

Fillers: Facts and newsbreaks. Buys 6/year. Length: 50-250 words.
Tips: "How-tos are especially strong with our readers. They want to know how to increase sales and cut costs. Cover new management techniques, promotional ideas, customer services and industry trends."

Hardware

Journals for general and specialized hardware wholesalers and retailers are listed in this section. Journals specializing in hardware for a certain trade, such as plumbing or automotive supplies, are classified with other publications for that trade.

CHAIN SAW AGE, 3435 NE Broadway, Portland OR 97232. Editor: Ken Morrison. 1% freelance written. "We will consider any submissions that address pertinent subjects and are well-written." For "chain saw dealers (retailers); small businesses—usually family-owned, typical ages, interests and education." Monthly. Circ. 20,000. Pays on acceptance or publication. Publishes ms an average of 4 months after acceptance. Free sample copy.
Nonfiction: "Must relate to chain saw use, merchandising, adaptation, repair, maintenance, manufacture or display." Buys informational articles, how-to, personal experience, interview, profiles, inspirational, personal opinion, photo feature, coverage of successful business operations, and articles on merchandising techniques. Buys very few mss/year. Query first. Length: 500-1,000 words. Pays $20-50 "5¢/word plus photo fees." Sometimes pays the expenses of writers on assignment.
Photos: Photos purchased with or without mss, or on assignment. For b&w glossies, pay "varies." Captions required.
Tips: "Frequently writers have an inadequate understanding of the subject area."

HARDWARE AGE, Chilton Co., 1 Chilton Way, Radnor PA 19089. (215)964-4275. Editor-in-Chief: Terry Gallagher. Managing Editor: Rick Carter. 2% freelance written. Emphasizes retailing, distribution and merchandising of hardware and building materials. Monthly magazine. Circ. 71,000. Buys first North American serial rights. No guarantee of byline. Simultaneous, and previously published submissions OK, if exclusive in the field. Reports in 2 months. Sample copy for $1; mention *Writer's Market* in request.
Nonfiction: Rick Carter, managing editor. How-to more profitably run a hardware store or a department within a store. "We particularly want stories on local hardware stores and home improvement centers, with photos. Stories should concentrate on one particular aspect of how the retailer in question has been successful." Also wants technical pieces (will consider stories on retail accounting, inventory management and business management by qualified writers). Buys 1-5 unsolicited mss/year. Submit complete ms. Length: 1,500-3,000 words. Pays $75-200.
Photos: "We like store features with b&w photos. Usually use b&w for small freelance features." Send photos with ms. Pays $25 for 4×5 glossy b&w prints. Captions preferred. Buys one-time rights.
Columns/Departments: Retailers' Business Tips; Wholesalers' Business Tips; and Moneysaving Tips. Query or submit complete ms. Length: 1,000-1,250 words. Pays $100-150. Open to suggestions for new columns/departments.

Home Furnishings and Household Goods

Readers rely on these publications to learn more about new products and trends in the home furnishings and appliance trade. Magazines for consumers interested in home furnishings are listed in the Consumer Home and Garden section.

‡APPLIANCE SERVICE NEWS, 110 W. Saint Charles Rd., Box 789, Lombard IL 60148. Editor: William Wingstedt. For professional service people whose main interest is repairing major and/or portable household appliances. Their jobs consist of service shop owner, service manager or service technician. Monthly "newspaper style" publication. Circ. 51,000. Buys all rights. Byline given. Pays on publication. Will consider simultaneous submissions. Reports in about 1 month. Sample copy $2.
Nonfiction: James Hodl, associate editor. "Our main interest is in technical articles about appliances and their repair. Material should be written in a straightforward, easy-to-understand style. It should be crisp and interesting, with high informational content. Our main interest is in the major and portable appliance repair field. We are not interested in retail sales." Query. Length: open. Pays $200-300/feature.
Photos: Pays $20 for b&w photos used with ms. Captions required.

CHINA GLASS & TABLEWARE, Doctorow Communications, Inc., P.O. Box 2147, Clifton NJ 07015. (201)779-1600. FAX: (201)779-3242. Editor-in-Chief: Amy Stavis. 60% freelance written. Works with a small number of new/unpublished writers each year. Monthly magazine for buyers, merchandise managers and specialty store owners who deal in tableware, dinnerware, glassware, flatware and other tabletop accessories. Estab. 1892. Pays on publication. Publishes ms an average of 3-4 months after acceptance. Buys one-time rights. Byline given. Phone queries OK. Submit seasonal/holiday material 3 months in advance. Reports in 3 weeks. Free sample copy for 9×12 SAE and writer's guidelines; mention *Writer's Market* in request.

Nonfiction: General interest (on store successes, reasons for a store's business track record); interview (personalities of store owners, how they cope with industry problems, why they are in tableware); and technical (on the business aspects of retailing china, glassware and flatware). "Bridal registry material always welcomed." No articles on how-to or gift shops. Buys 2-3 mss/issue. Query. Length: 1,500-3,000 words. Pays $50/page. Sometimes pays the expenses of writers on assignment.

Photos: State availability of photos with query. No additional payment for b&w or color contact sheets. Captions required. Buys first serial rights.

Tips: "Show imagination in the query; have a good angle on a story that makes it unique from the competition's coverage and requires less work on the editor's part for rewriting a snappy beginning."

FLOORING MAGAZINE, 7500 Old Oak Blvd., Cleveland OH 44130. FAX: (216)826-2832. Editor: Mark S. Kuhar. 10-20% freelance written. Prefers to work with published/established writers. Monthly magazine for floor covering retailers, wholesalers, contractors, specifiers and designers. Estab. 1931. Circ. 25,000. **Pays on acceptance.** Publishes ms an average of 3 months after acceptance. Byline given. Buys all rights. Query for electronic submissions. "Send letter with writing sample to be placed in our freelance contact file." Editorial calendar available on request. Send #10 SASE.

Nonfiction: "Mostly staff written. Buys a small number of manuscripts throughout the year. Needs writers with 35mm photography skills for local assignments. Study our editorial calender and send a concise query."

GIFT & STATIONERY, 1515 Broadway, New York NY 10036. (212)869-1300. Editor: Joyce Washnik. 10% freelance written. Prefers to work with published/established writers. Monthly for "merchants (department store buyers, specialty shop owners) engaged in the resale of giftware, china and glass, stationery and decorative accessories." Monthly. Circ. 37,500. Buys all rights. Byline given "by request only." Pays on publication. Publishes ms an average of 2 months after acceptance. Query for electronic submissions.

Nonfiction: "Retail store success stories. Describe a single merchandising gimmick. We are a tabloid format—glossy stock. Descriptions of store interiors are less important than sales performance unless display is outstanding. We're interested in articles on aggressive selling tactics. We cannot use material written for the consumer." Buys coverage of successful business operations and merchandising techniques. Query or submit complete ms. Length: 750 words maximum. Sometimes pays the expenses of writers on assignment.

Photos: Purchased with mss and on assignment; captions required. "Individuals are to be identified." Reviews b&w glossy prints (preferred) and color transparencies.

Tips: "All short items are staff produced. The most frequent mistake made by writers is that they don't know the market. As a trade publication, we require a strong business slant, rather than a consumer angle."

GIFTWARE NEWS, Talcott Corp., 112 Adrossan, P.O. Box 5398, Deptford NJ 08096. (609)227-0798. Editor: Anthony DeMasi. 50% freelance written. A monthly magazine covering gifts, collectibles, and tabletops for giftware retailers. Estab. 1976. Circ. 41,000. Pays on publication. Publishes ms an average of 2 months after acceptance. Byline given. Buys all rights. Submit seasonal/holiday material 4 months in advance. Reports in 2 months on mss. Sample copy $1.50.

Nonfiction: How-to (sell, display) and new product. Buys 50 mss/year. Send complete ms. Length: 1,500-2,500 words. Pays $150-250 for assigned articles; pays $75-100 for unsolicited articles.

Photos: Send photos with submission. Reviews 4×5 transparencies and 5×7 prints. Offers no additional payment for photos accepted with ms. Identification of subjects required.

Columns/Departments: Tabletop, Wedding Market and Display—all for the gift retailer. Buys 36 mss/year. Send complete ms. Length: 1,500-2,500 words. Pays $75-200.

Tips: "We are not looking so much for general journalists but rather experts in particular fields who can also write."

HOME LIGHTING & ACCESSORIES, P.O. Box 2147, Clifton NJ 07015. (201)779-1600. FAX: (201)779-3242. Editor: Peter Wulff. 5% freelance written. Prefers to work with published/established writers. For lighting stores/departments. Monthly magazine. Estab. 1923. Circ. 9,000. Pays on publication. Publishes ms an average of 4-6 months after acceptance. Buys all rights. Submit seasonal/holiday material 6 months in advance. Free sample copy.

Nonfiction: Interview (with lighting retailers); personal experience (as a businessperson involved with lighting); profile (of a successful lighting retailer/lamp buyer); and technical (concerning lighting or lighting design). Buys 10 mss/year. Query. Pays $60/published page. Sometimes pays the expenses of writers on assignment.

Photos: State availability of photos with query. Offers no additional payment for 5×7 or 8×10 b&w glossy prints. Pays additional $90 for color transparencies used on cover. Captions required.

Tips: "We don't need fillers—only features."

TILE WORLD, Tradelink Publishing Co.. 320 Kinderkamack Rd., Oradell NJ 07649. (201)599-0136. FAX: (207)599-2378. Editor: Mike Lench. Managing Editor: John Sailer. 25% freelance written. Bimonthly magazine for tile users and specifiers. Circ. 18,000. Pays on publication. Publishes ms an average of 4 months after acceptance. Byline given. Buys first rights and makes work-for-hire assignments. Submit seasonal/holiday material 6 months in advance. Simultaneous and previously published submissions OK. Reports in 1 month on queries; 2 months on mss. Sample copy $5. Free writer's guidelines.

Nonfiction: How-to (install tile), interview/profile, new product, photo feature (architectural design) and technical. Buys 10 mss/year. Query with published clips. Length: 600-2,000 words. Pays $80-240.

Photos: Send photos with submission. Reviews transparencies and prints. Captions and identification of subjects required. Buys one-time rights.

Columns/Departments: News; New Products (new types of tiles); New Equipment (for installing tile); 200 words. Send complete ms. Pays $15-40.

Tips: "Reports on architectural designs using tile are most open to freelancers. Architects are very willing to be quoted and provide good photos. Be sure to include in features all players involved with tile distribution and installation."

Hospitals, Nursing and Nursing Homes

In this section are journals for medical and nonmedical nursing home personnel, clinical and hospital staffs and medical laboratory technicians and managers. Journals publishing technical material on medical research and information for physicians in private practice are listed in the Medical category.

‡CALIFORNIA NURSING REVIEW, 1470 Halford Ave., Santa Clara CA 95051. (408)249-5877. Editor: Cledith A. Rice. Managing Editor: Jeroo Captain. 95% freelance written. Bimonthly trade journal covering trends and ethical issues in nursing. Estab. 1987. Circ. 210,000. Pays on publication. Publishes ms an average of 2 months after acceptance. Byline given. Offers $25 kill fee. Buys first North American serial rights. Query for electronic submissions. Reports in 6 weeks. Sample copy and writer's guidelines for 9×12 SAE and 2 first class stamps.

Nonfiction: Historical/nostalgic (pertaining to nursing), how-to (nursing and clinical), inspirational, interview/profile, personal experience, and technical (continuing education articles). "No articles that do not pertain to nursing." Buys 36 mss/year. Query with published clips. Length: 500-2,000 words. Pays $50-250. Pays expenses of writers on assignment.

Photos: State availability of photos with submission. Reviews prints. Offers $10-50/photo. Captions, model releases, and identification of subjects required. Buys one-time rights.

Columns/Departments: Profile (question/answer interviews with distinguished nurses), 1,000 words; Careers (innovative career paths, entrepreneurs, etc.), 600 words; Keeping Up (new developments in health/nursing), 600 words. Buys 36 mss/year. Query with published clips. Pays $50-100.

Tips: "Offer article ideas rather than asking for assignments. Areas most open to freelancers are profiles of distinguished nurses or nurse advocates in question/answer format."

FLORIDA NURSING NEWS, Landmark Community Newspapers, Inc., Suite 205, 8360 W. Oakland Pk. Blvd., Ft. Lauderdale FL 33351. (305)748-3660. Managing Editor: Steven Ricci. 65% freelance written. Biweekly newspaper on nursing in Florida. "News and feature articles about the nursing profession, especially in Florida." Estab. 1981. Circ. 90,000. Pays on publication. Publishes ms an average of 1-2 months after acceptance. Byline given. Offers $25-50 kill fee. Buys first rights. Submit seasonal/holiday material 3 months in advance. Reports in 3 weeks on queries; 1-2 months on mss. Sample copy for 5×7 SAE with 2 first class stamps. Free writer's guidelines.

Nonfiction: Interview/profile (nursing), opinion (nursing related), personal experience (nursing stories) and technical (nursing). Buys 50 mss/year. Query with published clips. Length: 750-2,500 words. Pays $75-250. Sometimes pays expenses of writers on assignment.

Photos: Send photos with submission. Reviews 5×7 prints. Offers $10 maximum per photo. Captions, model releases and identification of subjects required. Buys one-time rights.

Columns/Departments: Nurses Forum (articles/opinion on or about nursing/by nurses). Buys 10 mss/year. Query. Length: 750-1,000 words. Pays $50 maximum.

Tips: "Cover what's new and different about nursing in Florida! Send stories about outstanding and different Florida nurses."

HOSPITAL SUPERVISOR'S BULLETIN, Bureau of Business Practice, 24 Rope Ferry Rd., Waterford CT 06386. Editor: Michele Dunaj. 40% freelance written. Works with a small number of new/unpublished writers each year. For non-medical hospital supervisors. Semimonthly newsletter. Circ. 3,300. **Pays on acceptance.** Publishes ms an average of 5 months after acceptance. Buys all rights. No byline. Submit seasonal/holiday material 6 months in advance. Reports in 1 month. Sample copy and writer's guidelines for SAE with 2 first class stamps.

Nonfiction: Publishes interviews with non-medical hospital department heads. "You should ask supervisors to pinpoint current problems in supervision, tell how they are trying to solve these problems and what results they're getting—backed up by real examples from daily life." Also publishes interviews on people problems and good methods of management. People problems include the areas of training, planning, evaluating, counseling, discipline, motivation, supervising the undereducated, getting along with the medical staff, dealing with change, layoffs, etc. No material on hospital volunteers. "We prefer six- to eight-page typewritten articles. Articles must be interview-based." Pays 12-15¢/word after editing.

Tips: "Often stories lack concrete examples explaining general principles. I want to stress that freelancers interview supervisors (not high-level managers, doctors, or administrators) of non-medical departments. Interviews should focus on supervisory skills or techniques that would be applicable in any hospital department. The article should be conversational in tone: not stiff or academic. Use the second person to address the supervisor/reader."

‡NURSEWEEK, California's Largest Newspaper and Career Guide for Nurses, California Nursing Review, 1470 Halford Ave., Santa Clara CA 95051. (408)249-5877. Editor: Cledith A. Rice. Managing Editor: Lydia Selling. 90% freelance written. Biweekly trade tabloid on nursing in California. "There is a northern and southern edition of each issue." Estab. 1989. Circ. 119,00. Pays on publication. Byline given. Offers $25 kill fee, which may vary, depending on the situation. Buys all rights. Submit seasonal/holiday material 4 months in advance. Query for electronic submissions. Reports in 6 weeks. Sample copy and writer's guidelines for 9×12 SAE with 2 first class stamps.

Nonfiction: Historical/nostalgic, humor, inspirational, interview/profile, personal experience, technical (continuing education articles), and travel, all nursing related. "Open to new ideas. No articles unrelated to nursing." Buys 120 mss/year. Query with or without published clips, or send complete ms. Length: 300-2,500 words. Pays $100-300 for assigned articles; $75-300 for unsolicited articles. Pays expenses of writers on assignment.

Photos: State availability of photos with submission. Reviews transparencies and 3×5 prints. Offers $20/photo for amateurs; $25-150/photo for professional photographers. Captions, model releases, and identification of subjects required. Buys one-time rights.

Columns/Departments: Adventure (nursing experiences abroad or volunteer experiences within the U.S.), 1,500 words; Unsung Heroes, 700 words; Disease Update (new treatment techniques with a nursing slant), 800 words; Newsmaker (profile of a distinguished nurse), 1,500-2,000 words. Buys 40 mss/year. Query with published clips. Pays $100-300.

Fillers: Clarice Wood, staff editor. Anecdotes, facts, gags to be illustrated by cartoonist, and short humor, all health related. Buys 20/year. Length: 50-650 words. Pays $100-200.

Tips: "Query the editor. Features and news items relevant to registered nurses are the best areas for the freelancer to break in."

NURSING91, Springhouse Corporation, 1111 Bethlehem Pike, Springhouse PA 19477. (215)646-8700. Editor: Maryanne Wagner. Managing Editor: Jane Benner. 100% freelance written. Monthly magazine on the nursing field. "Our articles are written by nurses for nurses; we look for practical advice for the working nurse that reflects the author's experience." Circ. 500,000. Pays on publication. Publishes ms an average of 10-12 months after acceptance. Byline given. Offers 50% kill fee. Buys all rights. Submit seasonal/holiday material 6-8 months in advance. Query for electronic submissions. Reports in 2 weeks on queries; 3 months on mss. Sample copy for $3 with 9×12 SAE. Free writer's guidelines.

Nonfiction: Book excerpts, exposé, how-to (specifically as applies to nursing field), inspirational, new product, opinion, personal experience and photo feature. No articles from patients' point of view; humor articles, poetry, etc. Buys 100 mss/year. Query. Length: 100 words minimum. Pays $50-400.

Photos: State availability of photos with submission. Offers no additional payment for photos accepted with ms. Model releases required. Buys all rights.

SPECIALTY RETAILER, (formerly *Hospital Gift Shop Management*), Creative Age Publications, 7628 Densmore Ave., Van Nuys CA 91406. (818)782-7232. Executive Editor: Barbara Feiner. 50% freelance written. Works with a small number of new/unpublished writers each year. Monthly magazine covering management of specialty stores with "captive" clients: college bookstores, hotel gift stores, hospital gift shops, etc. Circ. 20,000. **Pays on acceptance.** Publishes ms an average of 4 months after acceptance. Byline given. Buys first North American serial rights. Submit seasonal/holiday material 8 months in advance. Reports in 1 month. Sample copy and writer's guidelines for $4 postage.

Nonfiction: How-to and retailing-themed articles. "No fiction, no poetry, no first-person 'I was shopping in a gift shop' kinds of pieces." Buys 12-25 mss/year. Length: 750-2,500 words. Pays $10-100. Query first.

Photos: State availability of photos with query. Reviews 5×7 color or b&w prints; payment depends on photo quality and number used. Captions, model release and identification of subjects required.

Fillers: Cartoons only. Buys 12/year. Pays $20.

Tips: "A freelancer's best bet is to let us know you're out there. We prefer to work on assignment a lot of the time, and we're very receptive to freelancers—especially those in parts of the country to which we have no access. Write—don't phone; let me know you're available. Make your query letter stand out. Convince me that your story is going to be exciting. A boring query usually yields a boring story."

Hotels, Motels, Clubs, Resorts and Restaurants

These publications offer trade tips and advice to hotel, club, resort and restaurant managers, owners and operators. Journals for manufacturers and distributors of bar and beverage supplies are listed in the Beverages and Bottling section.

BARTENDER MAGAZINE, Foley Publishing, Box 158, Liberty Corner NJ 07038. (201)766-6006. FAX: (201)766-6607. Publisher: Raymond P. Foley. Editor: Jaclyn M. Wilson. Emphasizes liquor and bartending for bartenders, tavern owners and owners of restaurants with liquor licenses. 100% freelance written. Prefers to work with published/established writers; eager to work with new/unpublished writers. Magazine published 5 times/year. Circ. 140,000. Pays on publication. Publishes ms an average of 3 months after acceptance. Buys first serial rights, first North American serial rights, one-time rights, second serial (reprint) rights, all rights, and simultaneous U.S. rights. Byline given. Phone queries OK. Submit seasonal/holiday material 3 months in advance. Simultaneous and previously published submissions OK. Reports in 2 months. Sample copies for 9×12 SAE with $2.50 for postage.

Nonfiction: General interest, historical, how-to, humor, interview (with famous bartenders or ex-bartenders); new products, nostalgia, personal experience, unique bars, opinion, new techniques, new drinking trends, photo feature, profile, travel and bar sports or bar magic tricks. Send complete ms. Length: 100-1,000 words. Sometimes pays the expenses of writers on assignment.

Photos: Send photos with ms. Pays $7.50-50 for 8×10 b&w glossy prints; $10-75 for 8×10 color glossy prints. Caption preferred and model release required.

Columns/Departments: Bar of the Month; Bartender of the Month; Drink of the Month; New Drink Ideas; Bar Sports; Quiz; Bar Art; Wine Cellar; Tips from the Top (from prominent figures in the liquor industry); One For The Road (travel); Collectors (bar or liquor-related items); Photo Essays. Query. Length: 200-1,000 words. Pays $50-200.

Fillers: Clippings, jokes, gags, anecdotes, short humor, newsbreaks and anything relating to bartending and the liquor industry. Length: 25-100 words. Pays $5-25.

Tips: "To break in, absolutely make sure that your work will be of interest to all bartenders across the country. Your style of writing should reflect the audience you are addressing. The most frequent mistake made by writers in completing an article for us is using the wrong subject."

FLORIDA HOTEL & MOTEL JOURNAL, The Official Publication of the Florida Hotel & Motel Association, Accommodations, Inc., P.O. Box 1529, Tallahassee FL 32302. (904)224-2888. Editor: Mrs. Jayleen Woods. 10% freelance written. Prefers to work with published/established writers. Monthly magazine for managers in the lodging industry (every licensed hotel, motel and resort in Florida). Estab. 1978. Circ. 6,800. Pays on publication. Publishes ms an average of 2 months after acceptance. Byline given. Offers $50 kill fee. Buys all rights and makes work-for-hire assignments. Submit seasonal/holiday material 3 months in advance. Reports in 1 month. Sample copy for 9×12 SAE and 5 first class stamps; writer's guidelines for #10 SASE.

Nonfiction: General interest (business, finance, taxes); historical/nostalgic (old Florida hotel reminiscences); how-to (improve management, housekeeping procedures, guest services, security and coping with common hotel problems); humor (hotel-related anecdotes); inspirational (succeeding where others have failed); interview/profile (of unusual hotel personalities); new product (industry-related and non brand preferential); photo feature (queries only); technical (emerging patterns of hotel accounting, telephone systems, etc.); travel (transportation and tourism trends only—no scenics or site visits); and property renovations and maintenance techniques. Buys 10-12 mss/year. Query with clips of published work. Length: 750-2,500 words. Pays $75-250 "depending on type of article and amount of research." Sometimes pays the expenses of writers on assignment.

Photos: Send photos with ms. Pays $25-100 for 4×5 color transparencies; $10-15 for 5×7 b&w prints. Captions, model release and identification of subjects required.

Tips: "We prefer feature stories on properties or personalities holding current membership in the Florida Hotel and Motel Association. Membership and/or leadership brochures are available (SASE) on request. We're open to articles showing how hotel management copes with energy systems, repairs, renovations, new guest needs and expectations. The writer may have a better chance of breaking in at our publication with short articles and fillers because the better a writer is at the art of condensation, the better his/her feature articles are likely to be."

FLORIDA RESTAURATEUR, Florida Restaurant Association, 2441 Hollywood Blvd., Hollywood FL 33020. (305)921-6300. FAX: (305)925-6381. Editor: Hugh P. (Mickey) McLinden. 15% freelance written. Monthly magazine for food service and restaurant owners and managers—"deals with trends, legislation, training, sanitation, new products, spot news." Estab. 1946. Circ. 17,142. Pays on publication. Publishes ms an average of 2 months after acceptance. Byline given. Offers $100 kill fee. Buys one-time rights. Submit seasonal/holiday material 3 months in advance. Simultaneous submissions OK. Query for electronic submissions. Reports in 1 week on queries; 2 weeks on mss. Sample copy for 9 × 12 SAE and 3 first class stamps.
Nonfiction: How-to, general interest, interview/profile, new product, personal experience and technical. Query. Length: 500-2,000 words. Pays $200-300 for assigned articles; $150-250 for unsolicited articles.
Photos: State availability of photos with submission. Reviews transparencies and 5 × 7 prints. Offers $50-250 per photo. Model releases and identification of subjects required. Buys one-time rights.

HOTEL AMENITIES IN CANADA, Titan Publishing Inc., Unit 5, 24 Hayes Ave., Box 1747, Guelph, Ontario N1H 7A1 Canada. (519)763-5058. Editor: Jayne Guild. 30% freelance written. Bimonthly magazine covering the lodging hospitality industry. "*Hotel Amenities in Canada* is a publication dedicated to the promotion of amenities and essential supplies and services in the Canadian hospitality industry." Circ. 3,600. Pays on publication. Publishes ms an average of 2 months after acceptance. Byline given. Buys first North American serial rights. Submit seasonal/holiday material 3 months in advance. Simultaneous and previously published submissions OK. Reports in 6 weeks. Sample copy for 8 × 10 SAE with Canadian postage or International Reply Coupon.
Nonfiction: New product, company feature. "*Hotel Amenities in Canada* is aimed primarily at the lodging hospitality industry so we do not need foodservice articles." Buys 12 mss/year. Query with published clips. Length: 500-1,500 words. Pays up to $100.
Photos: State availability of photos with submission. Reviews 5 × 7 prints. Offers $5/photo. Identification of subjects required. Buys one-time rights.
Columns/Departments: Products and Services (new products). Length 50-100 words. Pays up to $10.
Tips: "Research the amenities trend in the hospitality industry."

INNKEEPING WORLD, Box 84108, Seattle WA 98124. Editor/Publisher: Charles Nolte. 75% freelance written. Eager to work with new/unpublished writers. Emphasizes the hotel industry worldwide. Published 10 times a year. Circ. 2,000. **Pays on acceptance.** Publishes ms an average of 4 months after acceptance. Buys all rights. No byline. Submit seasonal/holiday material 1 month in advance. Reports in 1 month. Sample copy and writer's guidelines for 9 × 12 SAE with 3 first class stamps.
Nonfiction: Managing—interviews with successful hotel managers of large and/or famous hotels/resorts (600-1,200 words); Marketing—interviews with hotel marketing executives on successful promotions/case histories (300-1,000 words); Sales Promotion—innovative programs for increasing business (100-600 words); Bill of Fare—outstanding hotel restaurants, menus and merchandising concepts (300-1,000 words); and Guest Relations—guest service programs, management philosophies relative to guests (200-800 words). Pays $100 minimum or 15¢/word (whichever is greater) for main topics. Other topics—advertising, creative packages, cutting expenses, frequent guest profile, guest comfort, hospitality, ideas, public relations, reports and trends, special guestrooms, staff relations. Length: 50-500 words. Pays 15¢/word. "If a writer asks a hotel for a complimentary room, the article will not be accepted, nor will *Innkeeping World* accept future articles from the writer."
Tips: "We need more in-depth reporting on successful case histories—results-oriented information."

LODGING HOSPITALITY MAGAZINE, Penton Publishing, 1100 Superior Ave., Cleveland OH 44114. (216)696-7000. FAX: (216)696-7932. Editor: Edward Watkins. 10% freelance written. Prefers to work with published/established writers. A monthly magazine covering the lodging industry. "Our purpose is to inform lodging management of trends and events which will affect their properties and the way they do business. Audience: owners and managers of hotels, motels, resorts." Estab. 1949. Circ. 50,000. **Pays on acceptance.** Publishes ms an average of 2 months after acceptance. Byline given. Buys first rights. Submit seasonal/holiday material 2 months in advance. Reports in 1 month.
Nonfiction: General interest, how-to, interview/profile and travel. Special issues include technology (January); interior design (April); foodservice (May); investments (June); franchising (July); marketing (September); and state of the industry (December). "We do *not* want personal reviews of hotels visited by writer, or travel pieces. All articles are geared to hotel executives to help them in their business." Buys 25 mss/year. Query. Length: 700-2,000 words. Pays $150-600. Sometimes pays the expenses of writers on assignment.
Photos: State availability of photos with submission. Reviews contact sheets and transparencies. Offers no additional payment for photos accepted with ms. Captions and identification of subjects required. Buys one-time rights.

Columns/Departments: Budget Line, Suite Success, Resort Report, Executive on the Spot, Strategies Marketwatch, Report from Washington, Food for Profit, Technology Update—all one-page reports of 700 words. Buys 25 mss/year. Query. Pays $150-250.

PIZZA TODAY, The Professional Guide To Pizza Profits, ProTech Publishing and Communications, Inc., P.O. Box 114, Santa Claus IN 47579. (812)937-4464. FAX: (812)937-4688. Editor: Paula Werne. 30% freelance written. Prefers to work with published/established writers. A monthly magazine for the pizza industry, covering trends, features of successful pizza operators, business and management advice, etc. Estab. 1983. Circ. 40,000. Pays on publication. Publishes ms an average of 2 months after acceptance. Byline given. Offers 10-30% kill fee. Buys all rights and negotiable rights. Submit seasonal/holiday material 3 months in advance. Simultaneous and previously published submissions OK. Query for electronic submissions. Reports in 2 weeks on queries; 3 weeks on manuscripts. Sample copy and writer's guidelines for 10×13 SAE with 6 first class stamps. No phone calls, please.
Nonfiction: Interview/profile, new product, entrepreneurial slants, time management, pizza delivery and employee training. No fillers, fiction, humor or poetry. Buys 40-60 mss/year. Query with published clips. Length: 750-2,500 words. Pays $50-125/page. Sometimes pays the expenses of writers on assignment.
Photos: Send photos with submission. Reviews contact sheets, negatives, 4×5 transparencies, color slides and 5×7 prints. Offers $5-25/photo. Captions required.
Tips: "We would like to receive nutritional information for low-cal, low-salt, low-fat, etc. pizza. Writers must have strong business and foodservice background."

‡RESTAURANT HOSPITALITY, Penton Publishing, 1100 Superior Ave., Cleveland OH 44114. (216)696-7000. FAX: (216)696-0836. Executive Editor: Michael DeLuca. 30% freelance written. Works exclusively with published/established writers. Monthly magazine covering the foodservice industry for owners and operators of independent restaurants, hotel foodservices, executives of national and regional restaurant chains. Estab. 1919. Circ. 145,000. Average issue includes 5-10 features. **Pays on acceptance.** Publishes ms an average of 3 months after acceptance. Byline given. Buys first North American rights. Reports in 3 weeks. Sample copy for 9×12 SAE and with 10 first class stamps.
Nonfiction: General interest (articles that advise operators how to run their operations profitably and efficiently); interview (with operators); and profile. Stories on psychology, consumer behavior, managerial problems and solutions, design elements and computers in foodservice. No restaurant reviews. Buys 50-60 mss/year. Query with clips of previously published work and a short bio. Length: 500-1,500 words. Pays $125/published page. Pays the expenses of writers on assignment.
Photos: Send color photos with manuscript. Captions required.
Tips: "We would like to receive queries for articles on food trends; shrinking of labor market; ingredient labelling; neo-Prohibitionism; and nutrition. One hard-hitting, investigative piece on the influence of the 'mob' in food service would be welcome. We need new angles on old stories, and we like to see pieces on emerging trends and technologies in the restaurant industry. Our readers don't want to read how to open a restaurant or why John Smith is so successful. We'll be publishing short, snappy profiles—way more than in the past—with fewer major features."

THE SUCCESSFUL HOTEL MARKETER, The Newsletter of Profit-Building Ideas for the Lodging Industry, (incorporating *Motel/Hotel Insider*), Magna Publications, Inc., 2718 Dryden Dr., Madison WI 53704-3006. (608)249-2455. FAX: (608)249-0355. Editor: Bill Merrick. 10% freelance written. "The magazine is a high-priced, semimonthly publication that takes seriously its mission to offer practical, useful, innovative and transferable marketing strategies and success stories to its lodging industry audience. It has no advertising, its articles are brief and targeted. Its checklists, interviews, promotional digests, how-to and perspective pieces are all tightly written to save the reader's valuable time." Estab. 1971. Publishes ms an average of 2 months after acceptance. Byline given. Offers 25% kill fee. Buys first North American serial rights. Submit seasonal material 4 months in advance. Query for electronic submissions. Reports in 3 weeks. Sample copy $6. Writer's guidelines for 6×9 SASE. Query or send complete ms. Length 175-400 words: pays $75-125; 400-650 words: pays $125-200; 650-800 words: Pays $200-300.
Tips: "This newsletter's audience is very knowledgeable about the industry, hungry for fresh marketing ideas and at the same time tends to know all the well-publicized promotional strategies in vogue. It is our mission to find the unpublished ones, by building contacts with creative hotel marketers around the country. Therefore, we welcome sophisticated hotel marketing information: articles, interviews or checklists on new promotional packages, dos and don'ts, marketing for new properties and renovations, successful strategies by B&B's, etc."

VACATION INDUSTRY REVIEW, Worldex Corp., P.O. Box 431920, South Miami FL 33243. (305)285-2200. FAX: (305)665-2546. Managing Editor: George Leposky. 10% freelance written. Prefers to work with published/established writers. A quarterly magazine covering leisure lodgings (timeshare resorts, fractionals, condo hotels, and other types of vacation ownership properties). Estab. 1982. Circ. 10,000. Pays on publication. Publishes ms an average of 3-6 months after acceptance. Byline given. Buys all rights and makes work-for-hire assignments. Submit seasonal/holiday material 6 months advance. "Electronic submissions—query for details." Reports in 1 month. Sample copy $2; writer's guidelines with #10 SASE.

Nonfiction: How-to, interview/profile, new product, opinion, personal experience, technical and travel. No consumer travel or non-vacation real-estate material. Buys 5 mss/year. Query with published clips. Length: 1,000-2,500 words. Pays $75-175. Pays the expenses of writers on assignment, if previously arranged.

Photos: Send photos with submission. Reviews contact sheets, 35mm transparencies, and 5 × 7 prints. Offers no additional payment for photos accepted with ms. Captions and identification of subjects required. Buys one-time rights.

Tips: "We want articles about the business aspects of the vacation industry: entrepreneurship, project financing, design and construction, sales and marketing, operations, management—in short, anything that will help our readers plan, build, sell and run a quality vacation property that satisfies the owners/guests while earning a profit for the proprietor. Our destination pieces are trade-oriented, reporting the status of tourism and the development of various kinds of leisure lodging facilities in a city, region or country. We're interested in homeowners associations at vacation ownership resorts (not residential condos). You can discuss things to see and do in the context of a resort located near an attraction, but that shouldn't be the main focus or reason for the article."

‡**THE WISCONSIN RESTAURATEUR**, Wisconsin Restaurant Association, 125 W. Doty St., Madison WI 53703. (603)251-3663. Editor: Jan La Rue. 10% freelance written. Eager to work with new/unpublished writers. Emphasizes restaurant industry for restaurateurs, hospitals, institutions, food service students, etc. Monthly magazine (December/January combined). Circ. 4,000. **Pays on acceptance.** Publishes ms an average of 3 months after acceptance. Buys all rights or one-time rights. Pays 10% kill fee. Byline given. Phone queries OK. Submit seasonal/holiday material 2-3 months in advance. Previously published submissions OK; "indicate where." Reports in 3 weeks. Sample copy and writer's guidelines with 9 × 12 SASE.

Nonfiction: Exposé, general interest, historical, how-to, humor, inspirational, interview, nostalgia, opinion, profile, travel, new product, personal experience, photo feature and technical articles pertaining to restaurant industry. "Needs more in-depth articles. No features on nonmember restaurants." Buys 1 ms/issue. Query with "copyright clearance information and a note about the writer in general." Length: 700-1,500 words. Pays $10-20.

Photos: Fiction and how-to mss stand a better chance for publication if photos are submitted. State availability of photos. Pays $15 for b&w 8 × 10 glossy prints. Model release required.

Columns/Departments: Spotlight column provides restaurant member profiles. Buys 6/year. Query. Length: 500-1,500 words. Pays $5-10.

Fiction: Experimental, historical and humorous stories related to food service only. Buys 12 mss/year. Query. Length: 1,000-3,000 words. Pays $10-20.

Poetry: Uses all types of poetry, but must have food service as subject. Buys 6-12/year. Submit maximum 5 poems. Length: 10-50 lines. Pays $5-10.

Fillers: Clippings, jokes, gags, anecdotes, newsbreaks and short humor. No puzzles or games. Buys 12/year. Length: 50-500 words. Pays $1.50-7.50.

Industrial Operations

Industrial plant managers, executives, distributors and buyers read these journals. Some industrial management journals are also listed under the names of specific industries. Publications for industrial supervisors are listed in Management and Supervision.

‡**AUTOMATION**, 1100 Superior Ave., Cleveland OH 44114. (216)696-7000. FAX: (216)696-0836. Editor: George Weimer. 50% freelance written. Prefers to work with published/established writers. For "men and women in production engineering—the engineers who plan, design and improve manufacturing operations." Monthly magazine. Estab. 1954. Circ. 95,000. Pays on publication. Publishes ms an average of 6 months after acceptance. Buys exclusive first North American serial rights. Byline given; "if by prior arrangement, an author contributed a segment of a broader article, he might not be bylined." Phone queries OK. Reports in 2 weeks. Free sample copy and writer's guidelines.

Nonfiction: How-to (engineering, data for engineers); personal experience (from *very* senior production or manufacturing engineers only); and technical (technical news or how-to). "We're interested in solid, hard hitting technical articles on the gut issues of manufacturing. Case histories, but no-fat treatments of manufacturing concepts, innovative manufacturing methods, and state-of-the-art procedures. Our readers also enjoy articles that detail a variety of practical solutions to some specific, everyday manufacturing headache." Buys 2-3 mss/issue. Query. Length: 800-3,000 words. Pays $100-300.

Tips: "All manuscripts must include photos, graphs or other visual elements necessary to the story."

CHEMICAL BUSINESS, Schnell Publishing Company, 80 Broad St., New York NY 10004-2203. FAX: (212)248-4901. Editor: J. Robert Warren. Managing Editor: Alan Serchuk. 10% freelance written. A monthly magazine covering chemicals and related process industries such as plastics, paints, some minerals, essential oils, soaps, detergents. Publishes features on the industry, management, financial (Wall Street), marketing, shipping and storage, labor, engineering, environment, research, international and company profiles. Estab. 1875. Circ. 40,000. **Pays on acceptance.** Publishes ms an average of 3 months after acceptance. Byline given. Offers $100 kill fee. Buys all rights. Call before submitting seasonal/holiday material. Previously published book excerpts OK. Free sample copy and writer's guidelines.

Nonfiction: No broad, general industrial submissions on how-to. Buys 10 mss/year. Query. Length: 1,200-1,500 words. Pays $500 for assigned articles. Pays the expenses of writers on assignment.

Photos: Send photos with submission. Reviews contact sheets, negatives and 35mm or 70mm ("almost any size") transparencies. No pay for company photos; offers $10-25/photo taken by writer. Model releases required. Buys all rights.

COMPRESSED AIR, 253 E. Washington Ave., Washington NJ 07882. Editor/Publications Manager: S.M. Parkhill. 75% freelance written. Emphasizes applied technology and industrial management subjects for engineers and managers. Monthly magazine. Estab. 1896. Circ. 150,000. Buys all rights. Publishes ms an average of 3 months after acceptance. Reports in 6 weeks. Free sample copy; mention *Writer's Market* in request.

Nonfiction: "Articles must be reviewed by experts in the field." Buys 48 mss/year. Query with published clips. Pays negotiable fee. Sometimes pays expenses of writers on assignment.

Photos: State availability of photos in query. Payment for slides, transparencies and glossy prints is included in total purchase price. Captions required. Buys all rights.

Tips: "We are presently looking for freelancers with a track record in industrial/technology/management writing. Editorial schedule is developed in the summer before the publication year and relies heavily on article ideas from contributors. Resume and samples help. Writers with access to authorities preferred; and prefer interviews over library research. The magazine's name doesn't reflect its contents. We suggest writers request sample copies."

‡CPI PURCHASING, The Magazine About Buying in the Chemical and Process Industries, Cahners Publishing, 275 Washington St., Newton MA 02158. (617)558-4224. Editor: Kevin R. Fitzgerald. 5% freelance written. A monthly magazine covering the chemical and process industries. Estab. 1983. Circ. 40,000. **Pays on acceptance.** Publishes ms an average of 2 months after acceptance. Byline given. Offers 50% kill fee. Buys all rights. Sample copy $7.

Nonfiction: "We assign stories, usually on chemical market developments. Our readers are buyers of chemicals and related process equipment, packaging, transportation and environmental services. Freelancers should not submit *anything* on spec." Query. Length: 1,000-3,000 words. Pays $300-1,500 for assigned articles. Pays the expenses of writers on assignment.

Photos: State availability of photos.

Tips: "We prefer writers with some background in chemicals or equipment. Houston/Gulf Coast residents are especially welcome, but, please no PR writers."

‡INDUSTRIAL FABRIC PRODUCTS REVIEW, Industrial Fabrics Association, Suite 450, 800 Cedar St., St. Paul MN 55101. (612)222-2508. FAX: (612)222-8215. Editor: Sue Hagen. Director of Publications: Roger Barr. 10% freelance written. Monthly magazine covering industrial textiles and products made from them for company owners, salespersons and researchers in a variety of industrial textile areas. Estab. 1912. Circ. 9,000. Pays on publication. Publishes ms an average of 2 months after acceptance. Byline given. Buys all rights. Simultaneous queries and previously published submissions not in this market OK. Reports in 1 month. Sample copy free "after query and phone conversation."

Nonfiction: Technical, marketing and other topics related to any aspect of industrial fabric industry from fiber to finished fabric product. Special issues include new products, industrial products and equipment. No historical or apparel oriented articles. Buys 30 mss/year. Query with phone number. Length: 1,200-3,000 words. Pays $75/published page. Sometimes pays the expenses of writers on assignment.

Photos: State availability of photos. Reviews 8×10 b&w glossy and color prints. Pay is negotiable. Model release and identification of subjects required. Buys one-time rights.

Tips: "We encourage freelancers to learn our industry and make regular, solicited contributions to the magazine."

MANUFACTURING SYSTEMS, The Management Magazine of Integrated Manufacturing, Hitchcock Publishing Co., 191 S. Gary Ave., Carol Stream IL 60188. (Split office operation between San Jose and Illinois). (708)665-1000. FAX: (708)462-2225 (staff); (408)272-0403 (editor). Editor: Tom Inglesby. Senior Editors: Mary Emrich; Barbara Dutton. 10-15% freelance written. A monthly magazine covering computers/information in manufacturing for upper and middle-level management in manufacturing companies. Estab. 1982. Circ. 115,000. **Pays on acceptance.** Publishes ms an average of 2 months after acceptance. Byline given. Offers 35% kill fee on assignments. Buys all rights. Simultaneous submissions OK. Exclusive submissions do receive more consideration. Query for electronic submissions. Reports in 6 weeks. Free sample copy and writer's guidelines.

Nonfiction: Book excerpts, essays, general interest, interview/profile, new product, opinion, technical, case history — applications of system. "Each issue emphasizes some aspect of manufacturing. Editorial schedule available, usually in September, for next year." Buys 6-8 mss/year. Query with or without published clips, or send complete ms. Length: 500-2,500 words. Pays $150-600 for assigned articles; pays $50/published page for unsolicited articles. Sometimes pays limited, pre-authorized expenses of writers on assignment.

Photos: State availability of photos with submission. Reviews contact sheets, negatives, 2×2 and larger transparencies and 5×7 and larger prints. Offers no additional payment for photos accepted with ms. Captions and identification of subjects required. Buys one-time rights.

Columns/Departments: Forum (VIP-to-VIP, bylined by manufacturing executive), 1,000-1,500 words. Buys 1-2 mss/year. Query. Sometimes pays $100-200. "These are *rarely* paid for but we'd consider ghost written pieces bylined by 'name.' "

Fillers: Anecdotes, facts and newsbreaks. Buys 3-6/year. Length: 25-100 words. Pays $10-50.

Tips: "We are moving more toward personal management issues and away from technical articles — how to manage, not what tools are available. Check out success stories of companies winning against overseas competition in international marketplace. New trends in manufacturing include application of artificial intelligence (expert systems); standards for computer systems, networks, operating systems; computer trends, trade, taxes; movement toward "lights-out" factory (no human workers) in Japan and some U.S. industries; desire to be like Japanese in management style; more computer power in smaller boxes. Features are the most open area. We will be happy to provide market information, reader profile and writer's guidelines on request. We are moving to 'require' submission in electronic form — diskette, MCI-mail. Rekeying ms into our word processing system is more work (and cost)."

PLANT, (formerly *Plant Management & Engineering*), Suite 500, 245 Fairview Mall Dr., Willowdale/Ontario, Ontario M2J 4T1 Canada. FAX: (416)490-0220. Editor: Ron Richardson. 10% freelance written. Prefers to work with published/established writers. For Canadian plant managers and engineers. Monthly magazine. Estab. 1941. Circ. 52,000. **Pays on acceptance.** Publishes ms an average of 2 months after acceptance. Buys first Canadian rights. Reports in 3 weeks. Free sample copy.

Nonfiction: How-to, technical and management technique articles. Must have Canadian slant. No generic articles that appear to be rewritten from textbooks. Buys fewer than 20 unsolicited mss/year. Query. Pays 22¢/word minimum. Sometimes pays the expenses of writers on assignment.

Photos: State availability of photos with query. Pays $25-50 for b&w prints; $50-100 for 2¼×2¼ or 35mm transparencies. Captions required. Buys one-time rights.

Tips: "Increased emphasis on the use of computers and programmable controls in manufacturing will affect the types of freelance material we buy. Read the magazine. Know the Canadian readers' special needs. Case histories and interviews only — no theoretical pieces. We have gone to tabloid-size format, and this means shorter (about 800 word) features."

‡PURCHASING WORLD, Huebcore Communications Inc., 29100 Aurora Rd., Solon OH 44139. (216)248-1125. FAX: (216)248-0187. Editor: James A. Lorincz. 10% freelance written. A monthly magazine on industrial purchasing. "The magazine reaches buyers of industrial firms who purchase products for in-plant use as well as for original equipment manufacturing. Articles should focus on management, governmental, environmental and operations topics." Estab. 1988. Circ. 86,000. Pays on publication. Byline given. Buys first rights. Reports in 2 weeks on queries; 1 week on mss. Free sample copy.

Nonfiction: Ron Stevens, managing editor. General interest and interview/profile. Buys 18 mss/year. Query. Length: 500-2,500 words. Pays $100-300. Sometimes pays the expenses of writers on assignment.

Photos: State availability of photos with submission. Reviews contact sheets, transparencies (35mm) and prints (5×7). Offers $15-50. Captions, model releases and identification of subjects required. Buys one-time rights.

QUALITY CONTROL SUPERVISOR'S BULLETIN, National Foremen's Institute, 24 Rope Ferry Rd., Waterford CT 06386. (800)243-0876. FAX: (203)434-3341. Editor: Steven J. Finn. 80% freelance written. Biweekly newsletter for quality control supervisors. **Pays on acceptance.** No byline given. Buys all rights. Reports in 2 weeks on queries; 1 month on mss. Free sample copy and writer's guidelines.

Nonfiction: Interview and "articles with a strong how-to slant that make use of direct quotes whenever possible." Buys 70 mss/year. Query. Length: 800-1,500 words. Pays 8-15¢/word.

Tips: "Write for our freelancer guidelines and follow them closely. We're looking for steady freelancers we can work with on a regular basis."

WEIGHING & MEASUREMENT, Key Markets Publishing Co., Box 5867, Rockford IL 61125. (815)229-1818. FAX: (815)229-4086. Editor: David M. Mathieu. For users of industrial scales and meters. Bimonthly magazine. Circ. 15,000. **Pays on acceptance.** Buys all rights. Pays 20% kill fee. Byline given. Reports in 2 weeks. Free sample copy.

Nonfiction: Interview (with presidents of companies); personal opinion (guest editorials on government involvement in business, etc.); profile (about users of weighing and measurement equipment); and technical. Buys 25 mss/year. Query on technical articles; submit complete ms for general interest material. Length: 750-1,500 words. Pays $100-175.

Information Systems

These publications give computer professionals more data about their field. Consumer computer publications are listed under Personal Computers.

‡ATUNC NEWSLETTER, Apple Three Users of Northern California, P.O. Box 16427, San Francisco CA 94116. (415)731-0829. Editor: Li Kung Shaw. 50% freelance written. Monthly newsletter of AIII technology, life and stories of all users. Technical and human aspects of AIII and its users in the world. Estab. 1984. Circ. 150. Pays on publication. Buys first rights. Submit seasonal/holiday material 2 months in advance. Simultaneous and previously pubilshed material OK. Query for electronic submissions. Reports in 1 month. Free sample copy.
Nonfiction: Anything related to AIII or its users. Buys 12 mss/ycar. Query. Length: 500-3,000 words. Pays $10-100. Pays in contributor copies or other premiums under mutual agreement.
Photos: Send photos with submission. Reviews contact sheets. Offers no additional payment for photos accepted with ms. Buys one-time rights.
Fiction: "No fiction except those related to AIII and its users."
Poetry: "No poems except those related to AIII or its users."
Fillers: "No fillers except those related to AIII or its users."

‡COMMUNIXATIONS, Uniform Association, Suite 201, 2901 Tasman Dr., Santa Clara CA 95054. (408)986-8840. Editor: Jordan Gold. Managing Editor: Jeffrey Bartlett. 80% freelance writtten. Monthly trade journal covering UNIX. "Writers must have a sound knowledge of the UNIX operating system." Estab. 1981. Circ. 10,000. **Pays on acceptance.** Publishes ms an average of 2 months after acceptance. Byline given. Offers 30% kill fee. Buys all rights. Query for electronic submissions. Reports in 6 weeks. Free sample copy and writer's guidelines.
Nonfiction: Interview/profile, opinion, and technical. Buys 35 mss/year. Query with or without published clips. Length: 1,000-3,500 words. Pays $0-1,200. Sometimes pays in other premiums or contributors copies "when article is written by industry member." Pays expenses of writers on assignment.
Photos: Send photos with submission. "Photos are required with ms, but offers no additional payment." Buys one-time rights.
Columns/Departments: UNIX for Beginners, 700-1,200 words; Programming Tips (technical issues), 700-1,500 words; Career Corner (career tips), 700-800 words; UNIX Abroad (international issues), 800-1,200 words. Buys 12 mss/year. Query. Pays $0-250.

‡DATA BASED ADVISOR, The Database Management Systems Magazine, Data Based Solutions, Inc., Suite 200, 4010 Morena Blvd., San Diego CA 92117. (619)483-6400. Editor: David M. Kalman. Managing Editor: Dian Schaffhauser. 90% freelance written. Monthly magazine covering database management systems for microcomputers. *Data Based Advisor*'s mission is to provide information to users and prospective users of microcomputer database management systems. Estab. 1983. Circ. 39,555. Pays on publication. Publishes ms an average of 4 months after acceptance. Byline given. Offers 25% kill fee. Buys all rights. Query for electronic submissions. Reports in 3 months. Free sample copy and writer's guidelines.
Nonfiction: How-to, interview/profile and technical. "We don't like to see articles that cover database managers superficially. Other computer magazines do this all too well—'What's a database manager?' 'How do you use dBASE?' 'How do you automate your inventory?' Our writers understand their subjects intimately and provide detailed instructions for their products of choice. We also don't like to see queries for software reviews. These are assigned by the editorial staff." Buys 240 mss/year. Query with published clips. Length: 400-3,000 words. Pays $50-650 for assigned articles; $50-350 for unsolicited articles. Sometimes pays expenses of writers on assignment.
Columns/Departments: Fast Takes (reviews of products and books, *always assigned*), 300-1,000 words. Buys 80 mss/year. Query. Pays $25-200.
Tips: "Write a concise query that summarizes who will read the article, why you're the best person to handle the job, and what the article will consist of. Then be *very* patient with us. 'Fast Takes' is a great way to break into the magazine. Query us with your areas of interest and we'll try to make an assignment based on your expertise."

For information on setting your freelance fees, see How Much Should I Charge? in the Business of Writing section.

DG REVIEW, For Data General and Compatible Users, Data Base Publications, Suite 385, 8310 Capital of Texas Hwy., Austin TX 78731. (512)343-9066. FAX: (512)345-1935. Editor: Cynthia Kurkowski. 50% freelance written. Works with a small number of new/unpublished writers each year. A monthly magazine covering Data General computer systems. "*DG Review* is the primary independent source of technical and market-specific information for people who use Data General computer systems or sell to the Data General market." Circ. 25,000. Pays on publication. Publishes ms an average of 3 months after acceptance. Byline given. Buys first North American serial rights and second serial (reprint) rights. Submit seasonal/holiday material 3 months in advance. Query for electronic submissions. Reports in 1 month. Free sample copy and writer's guidelines.

Nonfiction: How-to, new product (computer-related), and technical all specific to Data General systems. No articles which cannot be related to Data General. Buys 25 mss/year. Query with published clips. Length: 1,000-3,500 words. Pays $100-300 for assigned articles.

Photos: State availability of photos with submission. Reviews contact sheets, transparencies and 5 × 7 prints. Offers $0-25/photo. Captions, model releases, and identification of subjects required. Buys first serial rights.

Columns/Departments: Technical columns (instructive articles on Data General computer hardware and software, including reviews by users), 1,000-2,500 words. Query with published clips. Pays $0-300.

Tips: "Feature articles are the area of our publication most open to freelancers."

‡FOCUS, The Magazine of the North American Data General Users Group, Turnkey Publishing, Inc., Suite 3150, 4807 Spicewood Springs Rd., Austin TX 78759. (512)345-5316. Editor: Robin Perry. 80% freelance written. Monthly trade journal covering Data General computers. Technical and practical information specific to the use of Data General computers. Estab. 1985. Circ. 10,000. Pays on publication. Publishes ms an average of 2 months after acceptance. Buys first North American serial rights. Reports in 3 weeks. Free sample copy and writer's guidelines.

Nonfiction: How-to (programming techniques, macros), technical. Query. Length: 1,000-3,000 words. Pays $100 minimum for assigned articles; $50 minimum for unsolicited articles. Pays in contributor copies or other premiums if the writer works for a company that sells hardware or software to the Data General marketplace.

Photos: State availability of photos with submission. Reviews contact sheets, transparencies and prints. Offers no additional payment for photos accepted with ms. Model releases and identification of subjects required. Buys one-time rights.

ID SYSTEMS, The Magazine of Keyless Data Entry, Helmers Publishing, Inc.. 174 Concord St., Peterborough NH 03458. (603)924-9631. FAX: (603)924-7408. Editor: Deborah Navas. Managing Editor: Margaret Ann McCauley. 80% freelance written. A magazine about automatic identification technologies, published 11 times/year. Circ. 48,000. Pays at dummy date of issue. Byline given. Buys all rights. Query for electronic submissions. Reports in 2 months on queries. Free sample copy and writer's guidelines.

Nonfiction: Application stories and technical tutorials. "We want articles we have assigned, not spec articles." Buys 50/year. Query with published clips. Length: 1,500 words. Pays $300.

Photos: Send photos with submission. Reviews contact sheets, transparencies (35mm) and prints. Offers no additional payment for photos accepted with ms. Identification of subjects required. Rights vary article to article.

Tips: "Send letter, resume and clips. If background is appropriate, we will contact writer as needed. We give detailed instructions."

INFORMATION WEEK, CMP Inc., 600 Community Dr., Manhasset NY 11030. (516)365-4600. FAX: (516)562-5474. Contact: Pam Licalei. Assistant Managing Editor: John McCormick. 20% freelance written. Weekly magazine covering strategic use of information systems and telecom. "Our readers are busy executives who want excellent information or thoughtful opinion on making computers and associated equipment improve the competitiveness of their companies." Circ. 145,000. Pays on publication. Publishes ms an average of 1 month after acceptance. Byline given. Offers 25% kill fee. Buys first North American serial rights and second serial (reprint) rights. Submit seasonal/holiday material 2 months in advance. Previously published submissions rarely OK. Query for electronic submissions. Reports in 3 weeks on queries; 2 week on mss. Sample copy for 8 × 11 SAE.

Nonfiction: Book excerpts (information management); exposé (government computing, big vendors); humor (850 word piece reflecting on our information era and its people); and interview/profile (corporate chief information officers). No software reviews, product reviews, no "gee whiz—computers are wonderful" pieces. Buys 20-30 mss/year. Query with or without published clips. Length: 500-3,500 words. Pays $300-1,500. Pays expenses of writers on assignment.

Photos: Send photos with submission. Reviews negatives and transparencies. Pays negotiable rates. Captions, model releases and identification of subjects required. Buys one-time rights.

Columns/Departments: Final Word (a humorous or controversial personal opinion page on high-level computer-oriented business), 850 words; Chiefs (interview, portrait of chief information officer in Fortune 500 Company), 2,000-3,000 words. Buys 100 mss/year. Query. Length: 800-900 words. Pays $100-1,500.

Tips: "We appreciate a *one-paragraph* lead, a headline, a deck and a very brief outline. This evokes the quickest response. Humor is the most difficult thing to create and the one we crave the most. Humor is especially difficult when the subject is management information systems. Good humor is an easy sell with us."

NETWORK WORLD, Network World Publishing, 161 Worcester Rd., Framingham MA 01701. (508)875-6400. FAX: (508)820-3467. Editor: John Gallant. Features Editor: Steve Moore. 25% freelance written. A weekly tabloid covering data, voice and video communications networks (including news and features on communications management, hardware and software, services, education, technology and industry trends) for senior technical managers at large companies. Estab. 1986. Circ. 70,000. **Pays on acceptance.** Byline given. Offers negotiable kill fee. Buys all rights. Submit all material 2 months in advance. Query for electronic submissions. Reports in 3 weeks. Free sample copy and writer's guidelines.
Nonfiction: Exposé, general interest, how-to (build a strong communications staff, evaluate vendors, choose a value-added network service), humor, interview/profile, opinion and technical. Editorial calendar available. "Our readers are users: avoid vendor-oriented material." Buys 100-150 mss/year. Query with published clips. Length: 500-2,500 words. Pays $600 minimum—negotiable maximum for assigned or unsolicited articles.
Photos: Send photos with submission. Reviews 35mm, 2¼ and 4×5 transparencies and b&w prints (prefers 8×10 but can use 5×7). Captions, model releases and identification of subjects required. Buys one-time rights.
Tips: "We look for accessible treatments of technological, managerial or regulatory trends. It's OK to dig into technical issues as long as the article doesn't read like an engineering document. Feature section is most open to freelancers. Be informative, stimulating, controversial and technically accurate."

‡PROGRAMMER'S UPDATE, SDC Communications, 5 Pond Park Rd., Hingham MA 02043. (617)740-2452. FAX: (617)740-2620. Editor: Michael Kei Stewart. Managing Editor: Cheminne Taylor-Smith. 25% freelance written. Monthly magazine of PC programming trends and strategies. Write to enlighten professional software developers, provide perspective on practices and trends; support with concrete examples and useful information. Emphasize *impact* of every subject on programmers. Estab. 1983. Pays on publication. Publishes ms an average of 3 months after acceptance. Byline given. Buys first and second rights. Submit seasonal/holiday material 3 months in advance. Previously published material OK. Query for electronic submissions. Reports in 1 week on queries; 1 month on mss. Free sample copy and writer's guidelines.
Nonfiction: General interest, how-to (programming techniques, tool use and *impact*, user story, interview/profile, new product (if first in category), opinion (industry, technical trends), technical (development strategies and comparisons). No coding techniques, product round ups, how-to's that don't say "why-to" or reviews (unless new category of product). Buys 15-20 mss/year. Query with or without published clips, or send complete ms. Length: 1,000-5,000 words. Pays $1-70/published page. Pays in contributor copies or other premiums if writer works for company that has vested interest in article topic.
Photos: State availability of photos with submission. Offers no additional payment for photos accepted with ms.
Columns/Departments: Daria O'Connor. Outside Insight (perspective from industry analysts, trade publication editors, well-known programmers), 2,000 words. Buy up to 5 mss/year. Query. Length 1,000-2,500 words. Pays $300 maximum.
Fillers: Cartoons. Buys up to 5/year. No payment.
Tips: "Call and get acquainted *if you have a definite idea*. Write a letter with an idea. Send ms with SASE. Writers have the best chance selling us features. Check topic first with us, then make sure tech content is accurate, complete and relevant."

RESELLER MANAGEMENT, Gordon Publications, Inc., P.O. Box 650, Morris Plains NJ 07950-0650. (201)292-5100. Editor: Tom Farre. 50% freelance written. Eager to work with new/unpublished writers if they know the field. Monthly management and technology magazine for computer resellers, including dealers, VARs and systems integrators. Estab. 1978. Circ. 55,000. Pays on publication. Publishes ms an average of 3 months after acceptance. Buys all rights. Query for electronic submissions.
Nonfiction: Management and business issues for resellers. "Writers must know microcomputer hardware and software and be familiar with computer *reselling*—our readers are computer-industry professionals in an extremely competitive field." Buys 3-6 mss/issue. Query with published clips. Length: 400-2,000 words. Pays 5-15¢/word. Sometimes pays the expenses of writers on assignment.
Photos: B&w or color.
Columns/Departments: Solicited by editor. "If the writer has an idea, query by mail to the editor, with clips."
Tips: "We've changed our name to *Reseller Management* from *Computer Dealer*—so all articles must have a heavy managerial slant, while still covering the microcomputer industry for resellers."

‡SOFTWARE MAINTENANCE NEWS, Suite 5F, 141 Saint Mark's Place, Staten Island NY 10301. (718)816-5522. 75% freelance written. Monthly magazine covering software maintenance. Estab. 1983. Circ. 7,000. Pays on publication. Publishes ms an average of 3 months after acceptance. Byline given. Buys one-time rights. Simultaneous submissions OK. Query for electronic submissions. Reports in 1 week. Free sample copy.

Nonfiction: New product, technical. "No how-to or user stories." Buys 36 mss/year. Query or send complete ms. Length: 100-2,400 words. Pays about 4¢/word.

Photos: State availability of photos with submission. Offers no additional payment for photos accepted with ms. Captions required. Buys one-time rights.

Columns/Departments: Bug/People (experiences with software), 600 words. Buys 10 mss/year. Query or send complete ms. Length: 600 words minimum. Pays $35 minimum.

Fiction: We *are* looking for fiction. Must be about software. Buys 1 ms/year. Query or send complete ms. Length: 600-2,400 words. Pays about 4¢/word.

Poetry: Haiku, light verse. Must be about software! Buys 2 poems/year. Pays about 4¢/word.

Tips: "Call first. Show familiarity with field."

SUNTECH JOURNAL, IDGC/Peterborough, 80 Elm St., Peterborough NH 03458. (603)924-9471. Editor-in-chief: John Barry. Managing Editor: Joseph J. Fatton. 75% freelance written. Monthly magazine that covers engineering computers. "*SunTech Journal* covers the technical and application issues relating to scientific and engineering computers and the UNIX operating system." Buys first rights. Simultaneous and previously published submissions OK. Query for electronic submissions. Reports in 2 weeks on queries; 3 weeks on mss. Free sample copy and writer's guidelines.

Nonfiction: How-to (e.g., write a RISC compiler), new product and technical. "Marketing-oriented articles are taboo. Technical audience must be kept in mind." Buys 24-30 mss/year. Query. Length: 2,000-4,000 words. Pays $500-1,000 for assigned articles. Sometimes pays expenses of writers on assignment.

Photos: Send figures, charts and program listings with submission. Offers no additional payment for photos accepted with ms. Captions and identification of subjects required. Buys all rights except advertising.

Columns/Departments: Synergy ("success" story of technical application), 750-1,500 words; and user profile (profile of scientist or engineer using Sun computers), 750-1,500 words. Buys 8 mss/year. Query. Pays $250 maximum.

Tips: "Writers should be technically sophisticated. *SunTech Journal* readers are some of the most technically astute people in the world, which is why their companies/universities give them the powerful computers from Sun to work with. Do not try to fool them with PR-hype. User profiles are the best entry into *SunTech Journal*. Some of the most interesting scientists and engineers in the world use Sun equipment, (e.g., those monitoring Voyager II; those who found the *Titanic*, etc.). This work makes for exciting reading when handled by a fine writer."

SYSTEMS/3X WORLD, Hunter Publishing, 950 Lee St., Des Plaines IL 60016. (708)296-0770. FAX: (708)803-3328. Editor: John Camuso. 10% freelance written. Works with a small number of new/unpublished writers each year. Monthly magazine covering applications of IBM minicomputers (S/34/36/38/ and AS/400) in business. Estab. 1973. Circ. 52,000. Pays on publication. Publishes ms an average of 2 months after acceptance. Byline given. Buys all rights. Submit seasonal/holiday material 4 months in advance. Query for electronic submissions. Reports in 2 weeks on queries. Sample copy for 9 × 12 SAE and 4 first class stamps; writer's guidelines for #10 SASE.

Nonfiction: How-to (use the computer in business); and technical (organization of a data base or file system). "A writer who submits material to us should be an expert in computer applications. No material on large scale computer equipment." No poetry. Buys 8 mss/year. Query. Length: 3,000-4,000 words. Sometimes pays expenses of writers on assignment.

Tips: "Frequent mistakes are not understanding the audience and not having read the magazine (past issues)."

‡UNIX WORLD, McGraw-Hill's Magazine of Open Systems Computing, McGraw Hill Inc., 444 Castro St., Mountain View CA 94041. (415)940-1500. Editor-in-Chief: David L. Flack. 20% freelance written. Mostly freelancers are used for product reviews. Monthly magazine directed to people who use, make or sell UNIX products, particularly in an open systems environment. Readers are employed in management, engineering, and software development. Circ. 60,000. Pays 1 month after publication. Publishes ms an average of 4 months after acceptance. Byline given. Offers kill fee. Buys all rights. Electronic submissions only. Reports in 1 month. Sample copy $3. Writer's guidelines sent. Ask for editorial calendar so query can be tailored to the magazine's need; send SASE with 2 first class stamps.

Nonfiction: Tutorials (technical articles on the Unix system or the C language); new products; technical overviews; and product reviews. Query by phone or with cover letter and published clips. Length: 2,500-3,000 words. Pays $100-1,000. Sometimes pays the expenses of writers on assignment.

Tips: "We are shifting more toward a business and commercial focus and would appreciate knowledge in that area. The best way to get an acceptance on an article is to consult our editorial calendar and tailor a pitch to a particular story."

Insurance

COMPASS, Marine Office of America Corporation (MOAC), 180 Maiden Lane, New York NY 10038. (212)440-7735. Editor: David R. Thompson. 100% freelance written. Prefers to work with published/established writers. Semiannual magazine of the Marine Office of America Corporation. Magazine is distributed in the U.S. and overseas to persons in marine insurance (agents, brokers, risk managers), government authorities and employees. Estab. 1955. Circ. 8,000. Pays half on acceptance, half on publication. Publishes ms an average of 6 months after acceptance. Byline given. Offers $750 kill fee on manuscripts accepted for publication, but subsequently cancelled. Offers $250 kill fee on solicited ms rejected for publication. Not copyrighted. Buys first North American serial rights. Does not accept previously published work, unsolicited mss or works of fiction. Query first. Simultaneous queries OK. Query for electronic submissions. Reports in 1 month on queries. Free sample copy and writer's guidelines.
Nonfiction: General interest, historical/nostalgic and technical. U.S. or overseas locale. "Historical/nostalgia should relate to ships, trains, airplanes, balloons, bridges, sea and land expeditions, marine archeology, seaports and transportation of all types. General interest includes marine and transportation subjects; fishing industry; farming; outdoor occupations; environmental topics such as dams, irrigation projects, water conservations inland waterways; space travel and satellites. Articles must have human interest. Technical articles may cover energy exploration and development—offshore oil and gas drilling, developing new sources of electric power and solar energy; usages of coal, water and wind to generate electric power; special cargo handling such as containerization on land and sea; salvage; shipbuilding; bridge or tunnel construction. Articles must not be overly technical and should have strong reader interest." No book excerpts, first-person, exposes, how-to, or opinion. Buys 8 mss/year. Query with published clips. Length: 1,500-2,000 words. Pays $1,500 maximum. Sometimes pays the expenses of writers on assignment.
Photos: Robert A. Cooney, photo editor. (212)546-2471. State availability of photos. Reviews b&w and transparencies and prints. Captions and identification of subjects required. Buys one-time rights.
Tips: "We want profiles of individuals connected with marine, energy, and transportation fields who are unusual. Send a brief outline of the story idea to editor mentioning also the availability of photographs in b&w and color. All articles must be thoroughly researched and original. Articles should have human interest through the device of interviews. We only publish full-length articles—no fillers."

FLORIDA UNDERWRITER, National Underwriter Company, Suite 115, 1345 S. Missouri Ave., Clearwater FL 34616. (813)442-9189. FAX: (813)443-2479. Editor: James E. Seymour. Managing Editor: Barry Baumgartner. 20-40% freelance written. Monthly magazine about insurance. "*Florida Underwriter* covers insurance for Florida insurance professionals: producers, executives, risk managers, employee benefit administrators. We want material about any insurance line, Life & Health or Property & Casualty, but *must* have a Florida tag—Florida authors preferred." Estab. 1984. Circ. 10,000. Pays on publication. Publishes ms an average of 2-3 months after acceptance. Byline given. Buys all rights. Submit seasonal/holiday material 3 months in advance. Simultaneous and previously published submissions OK (notification of other submission, publications required). Query for electronic submissions. Reports in 3 weeks. Free sample copy and writer's guidelines.
Nonfiction: Essay, exposé, historical/nostalgic, how-to, interview/profile, new product, opinion and technical. "We don't want articles that aren't about insurance for insurance people or those that lack Florida angle. No puff pieces." Buys 6 mss/year. Query with or without published clips, or send complete ms. Length: 500-1,500 words. Pays $50-150 for assigned articles; $25-100 for unsolicited articles. "Industry experts contribute in return for exposure." Sometimes pays expenses of writers on assignment.
Photos: State availability of photos with submission. Send photos with submission. Reviews 5×7 prints. Offers no additional payment for photos accepted with ms. Identification of subjects required.

‡GEICO DIRECT, K.L. Publications, Suite 105, 2001 Killebrew Dr., Bloomington MN 55425. Managing Editor: Eileen Kuehn. 60% freelance written. Semiannual magazine published for the Government Employees Insurance Company (GEICO) policyholders. Circ. 1.5 million. Pays on acceptance by client. Byline given. Buys first North American serial rights. Query for electronic submissions.
Nonfiction: Americana, home and auto safety, and travel. Query with published clips. Length: 1,000 words. Pays $350-600.
Photos: Reviews 35mm transparencies. Payment varies.
Columns/Departments: Moneywise, 50+, Your Car. Query with published clips. Length: 500-600 words. Pays $175-350.
Tips: "We prefer work from published/established writers, especially those with specialized knowledge of the insurance industry, safety issues and automotive topics."

INSURANCE REVIEW, Insurance Information Institute, 110 William St., New York NY 10038. (212)669-9200. Editor: Olga Badillo-Sciortino. Managing Editor: Kenneth M. Coughlin. 100% freelance written. A monthly magazine covering property and casualty insurance for agents, brokers, insurers, risk managers, educators, lawyers, financial analysts and journalists. Estab. 1940. Circ. 70,000. **Pays on acceptance.** Publishes ms an average of 2 months after acceptance. Byline given. Offers 25% kill fee. Buys first North American serial rights; rights returned to author 90 days after publication. "We retain right to reprint." Query for electronic submissions. Reports in 1 month. Free sample copy and writer's guidelines.

Nonfiction: How-to (improve agency business), interview/profile, opinion, industry issues, technical and business articles with insurance information. Buys 75 mss/year. Query with published clips. Length: 750-2,500 words. Pays $350-1,200 for assigned articles. Pays phone and postage expenses.

Photos: Send photos with submission. Reviews contact sheets and transparencies. Captions, model releases and identification of subjects required.

Columns/Departments: By Line (analysis of one line of p/c business, Analysis (financial aspects of p/c industry); Technology (innovative uses for agents or insurers); Agency Profitability; Agency Business. Query. Length: 750-1,200 words. Pays $350-650.

Tips: "Become well-versed in issues facing the insurance industry. Identify provocative topics worthy of in-depth treatment. Profile successful or unusual agents or brokers."

THE LEADER, Fireman's Fund Insurance Co., 777 San Marin Dr., Novato CA 94998. (415)899-2109. FAX: (415)899-2126. Editor: Jim Toland. 50% freelance written. Monthly magazine on insurance. "*The Leader* contains articles and information for Fireman's Fund employees and retirees about the many offices and employees nationwide – emphasizing the business of insurance and the unique people who work for the company." Estab. 1863. **Pays on acceptance.** Publishes ms an average of 1 month after acceptance. Byline given. Buys one-time rights. Simultaneous submissions OK. Reports in 2 weeks on mss. Free sample copy.

Nonfiction: Interview/profile, new products and employees involved in positive activities in the insurance industry and in the communities where company offices are located. Query with published clips. Length: 200-2,500 words. Pays $50-300.

Photos: Reviews contact sheets and prints. Sometimes buys color slides. Offer $25-100 per photo for b&w, more for color. Buys one-time rights.

Tips: "It helps to work in the insurance business and/or know people at Fireman's Fund. Writers with business reporting experience are usually most successful – though we've published many first time writers. Research the local Fireman's Fund branch office (not sales agents who are independents). Look for newsworthy topics. Strong journalism and reporting skills are greatly appreciated."

PROFESSIONAL AGENT MAGAZINE The magazine of the National Association of Professional Insurance Agents, 400 N. Washington St., Alexandria VA 22314. (703)836-9340. FAX: (703)836-1279. Editor: John S. DeMott. 85% freelance written. Monthly magazine covering insurance/small business for independent insurance agents, legislators, regulators and others in the industry. Circ. 30,000. **Pays on acceptance.** Publishes ms an average of 1 month after acceptance. Byline given. Buys exclusive rights in the industry. Prefers electronic submissions. Reports ASAP. Sample copy for SASE.

Nonfiction: Insurance management for small businesses and self-help. Special issues on life insurance and computer interface. Buys 36 mss/year. Query with published clips or send complete ms. Length: 2,000-4,000 words. Pays $800-1,700. Pays the expenses of writers on assignment.

Tips: "We prefer to work with established writers. Query by phone, then send clips or mss. We prefer submissions by modem or disk, with hard copy accompanying by mail."

International Affairs

These publications cover global relations, international trade, economic analysis and philosophy for business executives and government officials involved in foreign affairs. Publications for the general public on related subjects appear in Consumer Politics and World Affairs.

DEFENSE & FOREIGN AFFAIRS, International Media Corporation, Suite 307, 110 North Royal Street, Alexandria VA 22314. (703)684-8455. FAX: (703)684-2207. Editor-In-Chief: Gregory R. Copley. A monthly magazine on defense, strategy and international affairs. Estab. 1972. Circ. 9,400. Pays within 1 month after publication. Publishes ms an average of 1 month after acceptance. Byline given. Buys all rights. Electronic submissions preferred. Reports in 1 week.

Nonfiction: Interview/profile, new product, photo feature, technical. Buys 40 mss/year. Query with or without published clips. Length: 1,500-3,000 words. Pays $150-300. Sometimes pays expense of writers on assignment.

Photos: State availability of photos with submission. Reviews negatives, transparencies and prints. Offers no additional payment for photo accepted with ms. Identification of subjects required. Buys one-time rights.

Columns/Departments: Current estimates: country surveys (political forecasts/assessments, etc.). Length: 1,500 words. Pays $150.

FOREIGN AFFAIRS, 58 E. 68th St., New York NY 10021. (212)734-0400. Editor: William G. Hyland. Primarily freelance written. For academics, businessmen (national and international), government, educational and cultural readers especially interested in international affairs of a political nature. Published 5 times/year. Circ. 100,000. Pays on publication. Byline given. Query for electronic submissions. Reports in 2 months.
Nonfiction: "Articles dealing with international affairs; political, educational, cultural, economic, scientific, philosophical and social sciences. Develop an original idea in depth, with a strong thesis usually leading to policy recommendations. Serious analyses by qualified authors on subjects with international appeal." Buys 25 unsolicited mss/year. Submit complete ms, double-spaced. Length: 5,000 words. Pays approximately $750.
Tips: "We like the writer to include his/her qualifications for writing on the topic in question (educational, past publications, relevant positions or honors), and a clear summation of the article: the argument (or area examined), and the writer's policy conclusions."

‡JOURNAL OF DEFENSE & DIPLOMACY, Defense and Diplomacy, Inc., Suite 200, 6849 Old Dominion Dr., MacLean VA 22101. (703)448-1338. FAX: (703)448-1841. Editor-in-Chief: Alan Capps. 75% freelance written. Eager to work with new/unpublished writers. "Publication credentials not necessary for consideration." Monthly publication covering international affairs and defense. "The *Journal* is a sophisticated, slick publication that analyzes international affairs for decision-makers—heads of state, key government officials, defense industry executives—who have little time to pore through all the details themselves." Estab. 1983. Circ. 20,000. Pays on publication. Publishes ms an average of 2 months after acceptance. Byline given. Offers 10% kill fee. Buys first rights and second serial (reprint) rights. Simultaneous queries, and simultaneous and previously published submissions OK. Reports in 1 month on queries; 2 months on mss. Sample copy $5 (includes postage); writer's guidelines for #10 SASE.
Nonfiction: Book excerpts, general interest (strategy and tactics, diplomacy and defense matters), interview/profile, opinion and photo feature. "Decision-makers are looking for intelligent, straightforward assessments. We want clear, concise writing on articles with international appeal. While we have accepted articles that deal with U.S. decisions, there is always an international aspect to the subject." No articles that focus solely on the United States. Buys 24 mss/year. Send complete ms. Length: 2,000-4,000 words. Pays $900-1,000.
Photos: Reviews color and b&w photos. No additional payment is offered for photos sent with ms.
Columns/Departments: Speaking Out (1,000 to 2,000-word "point of view" piece analyzing any current topic of widespread interest); Materiel (a technical discussion of current and upcoming weapons systems); Books (reviews of books on world politics, history, biography and military matters); interview ("We constantly need interviews with important international figures. We are always looking for the non-U.S. interview."). Buys 12 mss/year. Query with published clips. Length: 1,500-3,000 words. Pays $100-250.
Tips: "We depend on experts in the field for most of the articles that we use. As long as a manuscript demonstrates that the writer knows the subject well, we are willing to consider anyone for publication. The most frequent mistake made by writers in completing an article for us is writing in too technical or too official a style. We want to be very readable. We are looking for writers who are able to digest complex subjects and make them interesting and lively. We need writers who can discuss complicated and technical weapons systems in clear non-technical ways."

Jewelry

‡THE DIAMOND REGISTRY BULLETIN, #806, 580 5th Ave., New York NY 10036. (212)575-0444. FAX: (212)575-0722. Editor-in-Chief: Joseph Schlussel. 15% freelance written. Monthly newsletter. Pays on publication. Buys all rights. Submit seasonal/holiday material 1 month in advance. Simultaneous and previously published submissions OK. Reports in 3 weeks. Sample copy $5.
Nonfiction: Prevention advice (on crimes against jewelers); how-to (ways to increase sales in diamonds, improve security, etc.); and interview (of interest to diamond dealers or jewelers). Submit complete ms. Length: 50-500 words. Pays $10-150.
Tips: "We seek ideas to increase sales of diamonds."

THE ENGRAVERS JOURNAL, P.O. Box 318, 26 Summit St., Brighton MI 48116. (313)229-5725. FAX: (313)229-8320. Co-Publisher and Managing Editor: Michael J. Davis. 15% freelance written. "We are eager to work with published/established writers as well as new/unpublished writers." A bimonthly magazine covering the recognition and identification industry (engraving, marking devices, awards, jewelry, and signage.) "We provide practical information for the education and advancement of our readers, mainly retail business owners." Estab. 1975. **Pays on acceptance.** Publishes ms an average of 1 year after acceptance. Byline given "only if writer is recognized authority." Buys all rights (usually). Query with published clips and resume. Previously published submissions OK. Query for electronic submissions. Reports in 2 weeks. Free writer's guidelines; sample copy to "those who send writing samples with inquiry."
Nonfiction: General interest (industry-related); how-to (small business subjects, increase sales, develop new markets, use new sales techniques, etc.); interview/profile; new product; photo feature (a particularly outstanding signage system); and technical. No general overviews of the industry. Buys 12 mss/year. Query

with writing samples "published or not," or "send samples and resume to be considered for assignments on speculation." Length: 1,000-5,000 words. Pays $75-250, depending on writer's skill and expertise in subject.
Photos: Send photos with query. Reviews 8×10 prints. Pays variable rate. Captions, model release and identification of subjects required.
Tips: "Articles should always be down to earth, practical and thoroughly cover the subject with authority. We do not want the 'textbook' writing approach, vagueness, or theory—our readers look to us for sound practical information."

FASHION ACCESSORIES, S.C.M. Publications, Inc., 65 W. Main St., Bergenfield NJ 07621-1696. (201)384-3336. FAX: (201)384-6776. Managing Editor: Samuel Mendelson. Monthly newspaper covering costume or fashion jewelry. "Serves the manufacturers, manufacturers' sales reps., importers and exporters who sell exclusively through the wholesale level in ladies' fashion jewlery, mens' jewelry, gifts and boutiques and related novelties." Estab. 1951. Circ. 8,000. **Pays on acceptance.** Byline given. Not copyrighted. Buys first rights. Submit seasonal/holiday material 3 months in advance. Sample copy for $2 and 9×12 SAE.
Nonfiction: Essays, general interest, historical/nostalgic, how-to, humor, interview/profile, new product and travel. Buys 20 mss/year. Query with published clips. Length: 1,000-2,000 words. Pays $100-300. Sometimes pays the expenses of writers on assignment.
Photos: Send photos with submission. Reviews 4×5 prints. Offers no additional payment for photos accepted with ms. Identification of subjects required. Buys one-time rights.
Columns/Departments: Fashion Report (interviews and reports of fashion news), 1,000-2,000 words.
Tips: "We are interested in anything that will be of interest to costume jewelry buyers at the wholesale level."

Journalism and Writing

Journalism and writing magazines cover both the business and creative sides of writing. Writing publications offer inspiration and support for professional and beginning writers. Although there are many valuable writing publications that do not pay, we only have space to list those writing publications that pay for articles.

BOOK DEALERS WORLD, American Bookdealers Exchange, Box 2525, La Mesa CA 92041. (619)462-3297. Editorial Director: Al Galasso. Senior Editor: Judy Wiggins. 50% freelance written. Quarterly magazine covering writing, self-publishing and marketing books by mail. Circ. 20,000. Pays on publication. Publishes ms an average of 3 months after acceptance. Byline given. Buys first serial rights and second serial (reprint) rights. Simultaneous and previously published submissions OK. Reports in 1 month. Sample copy for $2.
Nonfiction: Book excerpts (writing, mail order, direct mail, publishing); how-to (home business by mail, advertising); and interview/profile (of successful self-publishers). Positive articles on self-publishing, new writing angles, marketing, etc. Buys 10 mss/year. Send complete ms. Length: 1,000-1,500 words. Pays $25-50.
Columns/Departments: Print Perspective (about new magazines and newsletters); Small Press Scene (news about small press activities); and Self-Publisher Profile (on successful self-publishers and their marketing strategy). Buys 20 mss/year. Send complete ms. Length: 250-1,000 words. Pays $5-20.
Fillers: Fillers concerning writing, publishing or books. Buys 6/year. Length: 100-250 words. Pays $3-10.
Tips: "Query first. Get a sample copy of the magazine."

BRILLIANT IDEAS FOR PUBLISHERS, Creative Brilliance Associates, 4709 Sherwood Rd., P.O. Box 4237, Madison WI 53711. (608)271-6867. Editor: Naomi K. Shapiro. 3% freelance written. A bimonthly magazine covering the newspaper and shopper industry. "We provide business news and ideas to publishers of the daily, weekly, community, surburban newspaper and shopper publishing industry." Estab. 1982. Circ. 17,000. Pays on publication. Publishes ms an average of 4 months after acceptance. Byline given. Buys all rights. Query for electronic submissions. Reports in 3 weeks. Sample copy for 9×12 SAE with 4 first class stamps.
Nonfiction: *Only submit articles related to the newspaper industry*, i.e., sales, marketing or management. General interest, historical/nostalgic, how-to (tips and hints regarding editorial, production, etc.), humor, interview/profile, new product and opinion. *"The writer has to know and understand the industry."* No general writing or editing articles. Buys 3 mss/year. Query. Length: 200 words maximum. Pays $10-50 for unsolicited articles. May pay writers with contributor copies or other premiums if writer requests.
Photos: State availability of photos with submission. Offers no additional payment for photos accepted with ms. Captions, model releases and identification of subjects required. Buys all rights.
Columns/Departments: "Any books or brochures related to sales, marketing, management, etc. can be submitted for consideration for our BIFP Press department." Buys 3 mss/year. Query. Length: 200 words maximum. Pays $10-50.
Tips: "We are interested in working with any writer or researcher who has good, solid, documented pieces of interest to this specific industry."

BYLINE, P.O. Box 130596, Edmond OK 73013. (405)348-3325. Executive Editor/Publisher: Marcia Preston. Managing Editor: Kathryn Fanning. 80-90% freelance written. Eager to work with new/unpublished writers. Monthly magazine for writers and poets. "We stress encouragement of beginning writers." Estab. 1981. Publishes ms an average of 3 months after acceptance. Byline given. Buys first North American serial rights. Reports within 1 month. Sample copy and guidelines for $3.
Nonfiction: How-to, humor, inspirational, personal experience, *all* connected with writing and selling. Read magazine for special departments. Buys approximately 72 mss/year. Prefers queries; will read complete mss. Length: 1,500-2,000 words. Usual rate for features is $50, on acceptance. Needs short humor on writing (400-800 words). Pays $35.
Fiction: General fiction. Writing or literary slant preferred, but not required. Send complete ms: 2,000-3,000 words preferred. Pays $50 on acceptance.
Poetry: Any style, on a writing theme. Preferred length: 4-30 lines. Pays $5-10 on publication plus free issue.

CANADIAN AUTHOR & BOOKMAN, Canadian Authors Association, Suite 104, 121 Avenue Rd., Toronto, Ontario M5R 2G3 Canada. Contact: Editor. 95% freelance written. Prefers to work with published/established writers. "For writers—all ages, all levels of experience." Quarterly magazine. Estab. 1919. Circ. 3,000. Pays on publication. Publishes ms an average of 6 months after acceptance. Buys first Canadian rights. Byline given. Written queries only. Sample copy for $4.50; writer's guidelines for #10 SASE.
Nonfiction: How-to (on writing, selling; the specifics of the different genres—what they are and how to write them); informational (the writing scene—who's who and what's what); interview (on writers, mainly leading ones, but also those with a story that can help others write and sell more often); and opinion. No personal, lightweight writing experiences; no fillers. Query with immediate pinpointing of topic, length (if ms is ready), and writer's background. Length: 1,000-2,500 words. Pays $30/printed page.
Photos: "We're after an interesting-looking magazine, and graphics are a decided help." State availability of photos with query. Offers $10/photo for b&w photos accepted with ms. Buys one-time rights.
Poetry: High quality. "Major poets publish with us—others need to be as good." Buys 60 poems/year. Pays $15.
Tips: "We dislike material that condescends to its reader and articles that advocate an adversarial approach to writer/editor relationships. We agree that there is a time and place for such an approach, but good sense should prevail. If the writer is writing to a Canadian freelance writer, the work will likely fall within our range of interest."

CANADIAN WRITER'S JOURNAL, Gordon M. Smart Publications, P.O. Box 6618, Depot 1, Victoria, British Columbia V8P 5N7 Canada. (604)477-8807. Editor: Gordon M. Smart. Quarterly magazine for writers. Estab. 1985. Circ. 350. 75% freelance written. Will accept well-written articles by inexperienced writers. Pays on publication, an average of 3-6 months after acceptance. Byline given. Sample copy for $3 plus $1 postage; writer's guidelines for #10 SASE.
Nonfiction: How-to articles for writers. Buys 50-55 mss/year. Query optional. Length: 500-1,000 words. Pays about $5 (Canadian) per published magazine page.
Tips: "We prefer short, how-to articles; 1,000 words is our limit and we prefer 700 words. U.S. writers note that U.S. postage cannot be used to mail from Canada. Obtain Canadian stamps, use IRC's or tape coins to a card."

COLUMBIA JOURNALISM REVIEW, 700 Journalism Bldg., Columbia University, New York NY 10027. (212)854-1881. Managing Editor: Gloria Cooper. "We welcome queries concerning media issues and performance. *CJR* also publishes book reviews. We emphasize in-depth reporting, critical analysis and good writing. All queries are read by editors."

THE COMICS JOURNAL, THE Magazine of News and Criticism, Fantagraphics, Inc., 7563 Lake City Way, Seattle WA 98115. (206)524-1967. Managing Editor: Helena G. Harviliez. 90% freelance written. A monthly magazine covering the comic book industry. "Comic books can appeal intellectually and emotionally to an adult audience, and can express ideas that other media are inherently incapable of." Circ. 11,500. Pays on publication. Publishes ms an average of 2 months after acceptance. Byline given. Buys first rights. Submit seasonal/holiday material 5 months in advance. Reports in 2 weeks. Sample copy $3.50.
Nonfiction: Essays, news, exposé, historical, interview/profile, opinion and magazine reviews. Buys 120 mss/year. Send complete ms. Length: 500-3,000 words. Pays 1½¢/word; writers may request trade for merchandise. Pays the expenses of writers on assignment.
Photos: Send photos with submission. Offers additional payment for photos accepted with ms. Identification of subjects required. Buys one-time rights.
Columns/Departments: Opening Shots (brief commentary, often humorous), 1,000 words; Newswatch (in depth reporting on the industry, U.S. and foreign news); The Comics Library (graphic review), and Ethics (examining the ethics of the comic-book industry), both 3,000 words. Buys 60 mss/year. Send complete ms. Pays 1½¢/word; more for news items.
Tips: "Have an intelligent, sophisticated, critical approach to writing about comic books."

EDITOR & PUBLISHER, 11 W. 19th St., New York NY 10011. Editor: Robert U. Brown. Managing Editor: John Consoli. 10% freelance written. Weekly magazine. For newspaper publishers, editors, executives, employees and others in communications, marketing, advertising, etc. Circ. 29,000. Pays on publication. Publishes ms an average of 2 weeks after acceptance. Buys first serial rights. Sample copy $1.
Nonfiction: Uses newspaper business articles and news items; also newspaper personality features and printing technology. Query.
Fillers: "Amusing typographical errors found in newspapers." Pays $5.

THE EDITORIAL EYE, Focusing on Publications Standards and Practices, Editorial Experts, Inc., Suite 200, 66 Canal Center Plaza, Alexandria VA 22314-1578. (703)683-0683. FAX: (703)683-4915. Editor: Ann R. Molpus. 5% freelance written. Prefers to work with published/established writers. Monthly professional newsletter on editorial subjects: writing, editing, proofreading and levels of editing. "Our readers are professional publications people. Use journalistic style. Circ. 3,000. **Pays on acceptance.** Publishes ms an average of 6 months after acceptance. Byline given. Kill fee determined for each assignment. Buys first North American serial rights. "We retain the right to use articles in our training division and in an anthology of collected articles." Reports in 1 month. Sample copy for 6 × 9 SAE and 2 first-class stamps; writer's guidelines for #10 SASE.
Nonfiction: Editorial and production problems, issues, standards, practices and techniques; publication management; publishing technology; style, grammar and usage. No word games, vocabulary building, language puzzles, or jeremiads on how the English language is going to blazes. Buys 12 mss/year. Query. Length: 300-1,200. Pays $25-100.
Tips: "We seek mostly lead articles written by people in the publications field about the practice of publications work. Our style is journalistic with a light touch (not cute). We are interested in submissions on the craft of editing, levels of editing, editing by computer, publications management, indexing, lexicography, usages, proofreading. Our back issue list provides a good idea of the kinds of articles we run."

EDITORS' FORUM, Editors' Forum Publishing Company, P.O. Box 411806, Kansas City MO 64141. (913)236-9235. Managing Editor: William R. Brinton. 50% freelance written. Prefers to work with published/established but works with a small number of new/unpublished writers each year. A monthly newsletter geared toward communicators, particularly those involved in the editing and publication of newsletters and company publications. Circ. 900. Pays on publication. Publishes ms an average of 4 months after acceptance. Byline given. Offers 25% kill fee. Buys first North American serial rights, second serial (reprint) rights and makes work-for-hire assignments. Previously published submissions OK depending on content. Reports in 2 weeks on queries. Sample copy for 9 × 12 SAE and 2 first class stamps. Writer's guidelines for #10 SASE.
Nonfiction: How-to on editing and writing, etc. "With the advent of computer publishing, *EF* is running a regular high tech column on desk top publishing, software, etc. We can use articles on the latest techniques in computer publishing. Not interested in anything that does not have a direct effect on writing and editing newsletters. This is a how-to newsletter." Buys 22 mss/year. Query. Length: 250-1,000 words. Pays $20/page maximum.
Photos: State availability of photos/illustrations with submission. Reviews contact sheets. Offers $5/photo. Captions, model releases and identification of subjects required. Buys one-time rights.
Tips: "We are necessarily interested in articles pertaining to the newsletter business. That would include articles involving writing skills, layout and makeup, the use of pictures and other graphics to brighten up our reader's publication, and an occasional article on how to put out a good publication inexpensively."

FREELANCE WRITER'S REPORT, Cassell Communications Inc., P.O. Box 9844, Fort Lauderdale FL 33310. (305)485-0795. FAX: (305)485-0806. Editor: Dana K. Cassell. 15% freelance written. Prefers to work with published/established writers. Monthly newsletter covering writing and marketing advice for established freelance writers. Estab. 1982. Pays on publication. Publishes ms an average of 6 months after acceptance. Byline given. Buys one-time rights. Submit seasonal/holiday material 2 months in advance. Simultaneous queries, and simultaneous and previously published submissions OK. Reports in 1 month. Sample copy $4. No writer's guidelines; refer to this listing.
Nonfiction: Book excerpts (on writing profession); how-to (market, write, research); interview (of writers or editors); new product (only those pertaining to writers); photojournalism; promotion and administration of a writing business. No humor, fiction or poetry. Buys 36 mss/year. Query or send complete ms. Length: 500 words maximum. Also buys longer material (2,000-2,500 words) for Special Reports; must be timeless and of interest to many writers. Pays 10¢/edited word.
Tips: "Write in terse newsletter style, eliminate flowery adjectives and edit mercilessly. Send something that will help writers increase profits from writing output—must be a proven method. We're targeting to the more established writer, less to the beginner."

GUIDELINES MAGAZINE, Box 608, Pittsburg MO 65724. Editor: Susan Salaki. 97% freelance written. Quarterly at present "but plan to go bi-monthly soon." *GM* is a roundtable forum for writers and editors. "We are interested in what writers on both sides of the desk have to say about the craft of writing." Estab. 1988.

Circ. 1,000. **Pays on acceptance.** Byline given. Rights revert to contributors after publication. Reports in 2 months. Sample copy $4; SASE for writer's guidelines and themes for upcoming issues.

Nonfiction: General interest, historical articles on writers/writing, psychological aspects of being a writer, how-to, interview/profile, personal experience, humor and fillers. "Write to me and present your ideas." Buys 12 mss/year. OK to send in complete mss. Include SASE with all correspondence. Length: 50-1,500 words. Pays up to $50.

Photos: State availability of photos with submission. Reviews b/w glossies. Buys one-time rights on exceptional prints for cover on occasion. Prefers nature scene photos for cover. Pays $2-25 per photo. Captions, model releases and identification of subjects required.

Columns/Departments: Survey questions (questions writers want answers to), 200 words. Buys 6-24 mss/year. Send complete ms. Pays $5 maximum.

Fiction: Only short-short fiction with writing/editing as theme. Can be any genre, but must be good. Buys 3-6 mss/year. Send complete mss. Length: 300 words or less. Pays $5.

Poetry: Short poetry, any form, having to do with writing or editing. Submit minimum of 3 poems. Pays $1 maximum. Length: up to 20 lines "unless it is exceptional."

Fillers: Facts about writing or writers, short humor and cartoons,"wide-open to any facts of interest to writers or editors." No payment for Fillers.

Tips: "If you believe what you have to say about writing or editing has needed to be said for some time now, then I'm interested. If you say it well, I'll buy it. This is a unique publication in that we offer original guidelines for over 300 magazine and book publishers and because of this service, writers and editors are linked in a new and exciting way—as correspondents. Articles that help to bridge the gap which has existed between these two professions have the best chance of being accepted. Publishing background does not matter. Writers should query for theme list. Include a short biography and cover letter with your submissions. All contributors receive a copy of the issue in which their work appears."

HOUSEWIFE-WRITER'S FORUM, Drawer 1518, Lafayette CA 94549. (415)932-1143. Editor: Deborah Haeseler. 90% freelance written. Quarterly newsletter and literary magazine for women writers. "We are a support network and writer's group on paper directed to the unique needs of women who write and juggle home life." Estab. 1988. Circ. 1,200. **Pays on acceptance.** Publishes ms an average of 6-12 months after acceptance. Byline given. Buys one-time rights. Submit seasonal/holiday material 6 months in advance. Simultaneous and previously published submissions OK. Reports in 1 month on queries; 2 months on mss. Sample copy $4; writer's guidelines for #10 SASE.

Nonfiction: Essays, how-to, humor, interview/profile, opinion, personal experience. Buys 60-100 mss/year. Query with or without published clips, or send complete ms. Length: 2,000 words maximum, 400-750 words preferred. Pays ⅛-¼¢ per word.

Columns/Departments: Confessions of Housewife-Writers (essays pertaining to our lives as women, writers, our childhoods, etc.), 25-800 words; Reviews (books, reference texts, products for housewife writers), 50-300 words. Buys 6-20 mss/year. Send complete ms. Length: 25-800 words. Pays $1 maximum.

Fiction: Confession, experimental, fantasy, historical, horror, humorous, mainstream, mystery, romance, science fiction, slice-of-life vignettes, suspense. No pornography. Buys 6-12 mss/year. Send complete ms. Length: 2,000 words maximum. Pays $1-10.

Poetry: Avant-garde, free verse, haiku, light verse, traditional, humorous. Buys 15-20 poems/year. Submit maximum 10 poems at one time. Pays $1 maximum.

Fillers: Anecdotes, facts, short humor, hints on writing and running a home. Length: 25-300 words. Pays $1 maximum.

Tips: "We consider ourselves a beginner's market for women who want to write for the various major women's markets. Like any woman, I like to laugh and I love a good cry. I also like to be educated. More importantly, I want to know about you as a person. My goal is to help each other become the best writers we can be. Everything is open to freelancers."

MAGAZINE ISSUES, Serving Under 500,000 Circulation Publications, Feredonna Communications, Drawer 9808, Knoxville TN 37940. Editor: Michael Ward. 50% freelance written. Quarterly magazine covering magazine publishing. Circulated to approximately 10,000 publishers, editors, ad managers, circulation managers, production managers and art directors of magazines. Estab. 1982. Circ. 10,000. Publishes an average of 2 months after acceptance. Byline given. Submit seasonal/holiday material 6 months in advance. Query for electronic submissions. Reports in 2 months on queries. Sample copy $5. Writer's guidelines available for SASE.

Nonfiction: How-to (write, sell advertising, manage production, manage creative and sales people, etc.); interview/profile (*only* after assignment—must be full of "secrets" of success and how-to detail); personal experiences; new product (no payment); and technical (aspects of magazine publishing). "Features deal with every aspect of publishing, including: creating an effective ad sales team; increasing ad revenue; writing effective direct-mail circulation promotion; improving reproduction quality; planning and implementing ad sales strategies; buying printing; gathering unique information; writing crisp, clear articles with impact; and designing publications with visual impact." No general interest. "Everything must be keyed directly to our typical reader—a 39 year-old publisher/editor producing a trade magazine for 30,000 or more readers." Buys 18-24 mss/year. Query. Length: 900-3,000 words.

Photos: Send photos with ms.

Tips: "Articles must present practical, useful, new information in how-to detail, so readers can do what the articles discuss. Articles that present problems and discuss how they were successfully solved also are welcome. These must carry many specific examples to flesh out general statements. We don't care who you are, just how you write."

NEW WRITER'S MAGAZINE, (formerly *New Writer's Magazette*), Sarasota Bay Publishing, Box 5974, Sarasota FL 34277. (813)953-7903. Editor: George J. Haborak. 95% freelance written. Bimonthly magazine for new writers. "*New Writer's Magazine* believes that *all* writers are *new* writers in that each of us can learn from one another. So, we reach *pro* and non-pro alike." Estab. 1986. Circ. 5,000. Pays on publication. Byline given. Buys first rights. Query for electronic submissions. Reports in 2 weeks on queries; 1 month on mss. Sample copy $2. Writer's guidelines for #10 SASE.

Nonfiction: General interest, how-to (for new writers and desktop publishers), humor, interview/profile, opinion and personal experience (with *pro* writer). Buys 50 mss/year. Send complete ms. Length: 300-1,200 words. Pays $10-35 for assigned articles; $5-25 for unsolicited articles. Pays in contributor copies or other premiums for short items, poetry, fillers, etc.

Photos: Send photos with submission. Reviews 5 × 7 prints. Offers no additional payment for photos accepted with ms. Captions required. Buys one-time rights.

Fiction: Experimental, historical, humorous, mainstream and slice-of-life vignettes. "Again, we do *not* want anything that does not have a tie-in with the writing life or writers in general." Buys 2-6 mss/year. "We offer a special fiction contest held each year with cash prizes." Send complete ms. Length: 750-1,500 words. Pays $5-20.

Poetry: Free verse, light verse and traditional. Does not want anything *not* for writers. Buys 10-20 poems/year. Submit maximum 3 poems. Length: 8-20 lines. Pays $5 maximum.

Fillers: Anecdotes, facts, gags to illustrated by cartoonist, newsbreaks and short humor. Buys 5-15/year. Length: 20-100 words. Pays $5 maximum.

Tips: "Any article *with photos* has a good chance, especially an *up close & personal* interview with an established professional writer offering advice, etc. *Desktop Publishing* section is always in need of good, in-depth articles or interesting columns."

RIGHTING WORDS, The Journal of Language and Editing, Feredonna Communications, Drawer 9808, Knoxville TN 37940. (615)584-1918. Editor: Michael Ward. 80% freelance written. Eager to work with new/unpublished writers. A quarterly magazine on language usage, trends and issues. "Our readers include copy editors, book and magazine editors, and journalism and English teachers—people interested in the changing ways of the language and in ways to improve their editing and writing skills." Estab. 1987. Pays on publication. Publishes ms an average of 1 month after acceptance. Byline given. Buys first North American serial rights. Query for electronic submissions. Reports only on accepted ms. "Allow one month for reply before sending ms elsewhere." Sample copy $5 with 9 × 12 SAE and 3 first class stamps; writer's guidelines for #10 SASE.

Nonfiction: Buys 30 mss/year. Send complete ms. Length: 3,000 words. Pays $100 minimum for assigned articles.

Tips: "Our contributors have included Rudolf Flesch and Willard Espy, but we welcome freelance submissions on editing and language topics that are well-written, contain hard information of value to editors, and that display wit and style. Yes, the editor reads *all* submissions, and often suggests approaches to writers whose material may be good but whose approach is off. No book reviews, please; other than that, all parts of the magazines are open to freelancers."

RISING STAR, 47 Byledge Rd., Manchester NH 03104. (603)623-9796. Editor: Scott E. Green. 50% freelance written. A bimonthly newsletter on science fiction and fantasy markets for writers and artists. Estab. 1980. Circ. 150. Pays on publication. Publishes ms an average of 3 months after acceptance. Byline given. Not copyrighted. Buys first rights. Simultaneous and previously published submissions OK. Reports in 2 weeks on queries. Sample copy $1.50 with #10 SASE; free writer's guidelines.

Nonfiction: Book excerpts, essays, interview/profile and opinion. Buys 8 mss/year. Query. Length: 500-900 words. Pays $3 minimum.

ST. LOUIS JOURNALISM REVIEW, 8380 Olive Blvd., St. Louis MO 63132. (314)991-1699. FAX: (314)997-1898. Editor/Publisher: Charles L. Klotzer. 50% freelance written. Prefers to work with published/established writers. Monthly tabloid newspaper critiquing St. Louis media, print, broadcasting, TV and cable primarily by working journalists and others. Also covers issues not covered adequately by dailies. Occasionally buys articles on national media criticism. Estab. 1962. Circ. 6,500. Buys all rights. Byline given. Sample copy $2.

Nonfiction: "We buy material which analyzes, critically, St. Louis metro area media and, less frequently, national media institutions, personalities or trends." No taboos. Payment depends. Pays the expenses of writers on assignment subject to prior approval.

SCAVENGER'S NEWSLETTER, 519 Ellinwood, Osage City KS 66523. (913)528-3538. Editor: Janet Fox. 25% freelance written. Eager to work with new/unpublished writers. A monthly newsletter covering markets for science fiction/fantasy/horror materials especially with regard to the small press. Estab. 1984. Circ. 1,000. Publishes ms an average of 8 months after acceptance. Byline given. Not copyrighted. Places copyright symbol on title page; rights revert to contributor on publication. Buys one-time rights. Simultaneous and previously published submissions OK. Reports in 2 weeks. Sample copy $1.50; writer's guidelines for #10 SASE.

Nonfiction: Essays; general interest; how-to (write, sell, publish sf/fantasy/horror); humor; interview/profile (writers, artists in the field); and opinion. Buys 12-15 mss/year. Send complete ms. Length: 1,000 words maximum. Pays $4 on acceptance.

Poetry: Avant-garde, free verse, haiku and traditional. All related to science fiction/fantasy/horror genres. Buys 48 poems/year. Submit maximum 3 poems. Length: 10 lines maximum. Pays $2 on acceptance.

Tips: "Because this is a small publication, it has occasional overstocks. We're especially looking for sf/fantasy/horror commentary as opposed to writer's how-to's."

SCIENCE FICTION CHRONICLE, P.O. Box 2730, Brooklyn NY 11202-0036. (718)643-9011. Editor: Andrew Porter. 3% freelance written. Works with a small number of new/unpublished writers each year. Monthly magazine about science fiction, fantasy and horror publishing for readers, editors, writers, et al., who are interested in keeping up with the latest developments and news. Publication also includes market reports, UK news, letters, reviews, columns. Estab. 1963. Circ. 5,600. Buys first serial rights. Pays on publication. Publishes ms an average of 2 months after acceptance. Submit seasonal material 4 months in advance. Reports in 1 month. Sample copy for 9×12 SAE and 5 first class stamps.

Nonfiction: New product and photo feature. No articles about UFOs, or "news we reported six months ago." Buys 10 unsolicited mss/year. Send complete ms. Length: 200-500 words. Pays 3-5¢/word.

Photos: Send photos with ms. Pays $5-15 for 4×5 and 8×10 b&w prints. Captions preferred. Buys one-time rights.

Tips: "News of publishers, booksellers and software related to sf, fantasy and horror is most needed from freelancers. *No fiction.* This is a news magazine, like *Publishers Weekly* or *Time.* (I still get 10-20 story mss a year, which are returned, unread.)"

SMALL PRESS, The Magazine & Book Review of Independent Publishing, Meckler Corporation, 11 Ferry Ln. W., Westport CT 06880. (203)226-6967. FAX: (203)454-5840. Editor: Brenda Mitchell-Powell. 90% freelance written. Bimonthly magazine on independent publishers/independent publishing. "The writers and reviewers of *Small Press,* in cooperation with the publishers, editors, booksellers and trade participants, work to create a periodical that affirms and nurtures independent-press publishing and that epitomizes the ideology and strength of our industry." Estab. 1983. Circ. 5,400. Pays on publication. Publishes ms an average of 2-6 months after acceptance. Byline given. Makes work-for-hire assignments. Submit seasonal/holiday material 3-6 months in advance. "While *Small Press* does, occasionally, reprint articles, we strive to publish only original material; articles of particular relevance to the trade are accepted on other bases with the editor's approval." Query for electronic submissions. Reports in 6 weeks on queries; 2 months on mss. Free sample copy and writer's guidelines.

Nonfiction: Essays, general interest to the trade, how-to (practical applications), interview/profile, new product, technical, use of computers, legal/financial strategies, promotion and marketing. "Interested parties should write for an editorial calendar. Such a calendar is available upon request, and there is no charge. Editorial agenda is fixed to a degree, but certain items are subject to change. NO FICTION!! I prefer not to receive blind submissions. Please inquire before mailing. Articles of a strictly personal nature—not genre-oriented—are discouraged. Articles must relate to the independent-press industry." Buys 10-12 mss/year. Query with published clips or send complete ms. Length: 250-4,000 words. Pays $45-65/page. Book reviewers receive only the title sent for review and a copy of the issue in which the review appears. Sometimes pays expenses of writers on assignment.

Photos: Send photos with submission. Offers no additional payment for photos accepted with ms. Captions, model releases and identification of subjects required.

Columns/Departments: "Columns are assigned to contributing editors. Only practical/advice for trade articles are available to freelance writers at this time." Practical and advisory articles on technical, legal, financial, promotional strategies [e.g., marketing to independent bookstores, tax advice for publishers, non-traditional marketing techniques, implementation of graphics with computer systems, etc.], 250-2,000 words. Buys 30-50 mss/year. Query with published clips. Send complete ms. Pays $45-65/page.

Fillers: Facts and newsbreaks. Buys 6/year. Length: 250-1,500 words. Pays $65 maximum.

Tips: "Please familiarize yourself with the independent-press industry. I neither want nor need writers who have neither knowledge nor appreciation of the industry *Small Press* serves. Writing skills are not sufficient qualification. Genre-oriented articles are sought and preferred. Filler articles on a variety of subjects of practical advice to the trade are the most open to freelance writers. I am amenable to submissions of feature articles relating to publishers, inventories, traditional, and desktop-publishing systems, trade events (London Book Fair, Frankfurt, ABA, etc.), publishing trends, regional pieces (with a direct relationship to the independent-press industry), production issues, business-oriented advice, promotion and marketing strategies, interviews with industry participants."

SMALL PRESS REVIEW, Box 100, Paradise CA 95967. Editor: Len Fulton. Monthly for "people interested in small presses and magazines, current trends and data; many libraries." Circ. 3,500. Byline given. "Query if you're unsure." Reports in 2 months. Free sample copy.
Nonfiction: News, short reviews, photos, short articles on small magazines and presses. Uses how-to, personal experience, interview, profile, spot news, historical, think, photo, and coverage of merchandising techniques. Accepts 50-200 mss/year. Length: 100-200 words.

WDS BOOK AUTHOR'S NEWSLETTER, Writer's Digest School, 1507 Dana Ave., Cincinnati OH 45207. (513)531-2222. Editor: Kirk Polking. Semi-annual newsletter covering writing and marketing information for students of workshops in novel and nonfiction book writing offered by Writer's Digest School. Estab. 1988. Circ. 3,000. **Pays on acceptance.** Publishes ms an average of 6 months after acceptance. Byline given. Pays 25% kill fee. Buys first serial rights and second serial (reprint) rights. Simultaneous and previously published submissions OK. Query for electronic submissions. Reports in 3 weeks. Free sample copy.
Nonfiction: How-to (write or market novels or nonfiction books); and interviews with published authors of novels and books. Buys six mss/year. "Query by mail, please, not phone." Length: 500-1,000 words. Pays $10-25.

WDS FORUM, Writer's Digest School, 1507 Dana Ave., Cincinnati OH 45207. (513)531-2222. Editor: Kirk Polking. 100% freelance written. Quarterly newsletter covering writing techniques and marketing for students of courses in fiction and nonfiction writing offered by Writer's Digest School. Estab. 1970. Circ. 13,000. **Pays on acceptance.** Publishes ms an average of 6 months after acceptance. Byline given. Pays 25% kill fee. Buys first serial rights and second serial (reprint) rights. Submit seasonal/holiday material 4 months in advance. Simultaneous and previously published submissions OK. Query for electronic submissions. Reports in 3 weeks. Free sample copy.
Nonfiction: How-to (write or market short stories or articles, etc.); and interviews (with well-known authors of short stories, or articles). Buys 12 mss/year. "Query by mail, please, not phone." Length: 500-1,000 words. Pays $10-25.

WEST COAST REVIEW OF BOOKS, Rapport Publishing Co., Inc., 5265 Fountain Ave., Upper Terrace #6, Los Angeles CA 90029. (213)660-0433. Editor: D. David Dreis. Bimonthly magazine for book consumers. "Provocative articles based on specific subject matter, books and author retrospectives." Circ. 80,000. Pays on publication. Byline given. Offers kill fee. Buys one-time rights and second serial (reprint) rights to published author interviews. Sample copy $2.
Nonfiction: General interest, historical/nostalgic and profile (author retrospectives). "No individual book reviews." Buys 25 mss/year. Query. Length: open.
Tips: "There must be a reason (current interest, news events, etc.) for any article here. Example: 'The Jew-Haters' was about anti-semitism which was written up in six books; all reviewed and analyzed under that umbrella title. Under no circumstances should articles be submitted unless query has been responded to." No phone calls.

THE WRITER, 120 Boylston St., Boston MA 02116. Editor-in-Chief/Publisher: Sylvia K. Burack. 20-25% freelance written. Prefers to buy work of published/established writers. Monthly. Estab. 1887. **Pays on acceptance.** Publishes ms an average of 6-8 months after acceptance. Buys first serial rights. Uses some freelance material. Sample copy $3.
Nonfiction: Practical articles for writers on how to write for publication, and how and where to market manuscripts in various fields. Will consider all submissions promptly. No assignments. Length: approximately 2,000 words.
Tips: "New types of publications and our continually updated market listings in all fields will determine changes of focus and fact."

WRITER'S DIGEST, 1507 Dana Ave., Cincinnati OH 45207. (513)531-2222. Submissions Editor: Bill Strickland. 90% freelance written. Monthly magazine about writing and publishing. "Our readers write fiction, poetry, nonfiction, plays and all kinds of creative writing. They're interested in improving their writing skills, improving their sales ability, and finding new outlets for their talents." Estab. 1921. Circ. 225,000. **Pays on acceptance.** Publishes ms an average of 1 year after acceptance. Buys first North American serial rights for one-time editorial use, microfilm/microfiche use and magazine promotional use. Pays 20% kill fee. Byline given. Submit seasonal/holiday material 8 months in advance. Previously published submissions OK. Query for electronic submissions. "We're able to use electronic submissions only for accepted pieces/and will discuss details if we buy your work. We'll accept computer printout submissions, of course—but they *must* be readable. We strongly recommend letter-quality. If you don't want your manuscript returned, indicate that on the first page of the manuscript or in a cover letter." Reports in 2 weeks. Sample copy $2.75; writer's guidelines for #10 SASE.

Nonfiction: "Our mainstay is the how-to article—that is, an article telling how to write and sell more of what you write. For instance, how to write compelling leads and conclusions, how to improve your character descriptions, how to become more efficient and productive. We like plenty of examples, anecdotes and $$$ in our articles—so other writers can actually see what's been done successfully by the author of a particular piece. We like our articles to speak directly to the reader through the use of the first-person voice. Don't submit an article on what five book editors say about writing mysteries. Instead, submit an article on how you cracked the mystery market and how our readers can do the same. But don't limit the article to your experiences; include the opinions of those five editors to give your article increased depth and authority." General interest (about writing); how-to (writing and marketing techniques that work); humor (short pieces); inspirational; interview and profile (query first); new product; and personal experience (marketing and free-lancing experiences). "We can always use articles on fiction and nonfiction technique, and solid articles on poetry or scriptwriting are always welcome. No articles titled 'So You Want to Be a Writer,' and no first-person pieces that ramble without giving a lesson or something readers can learn from in the sharing of the story." Buys 90-100 mss/year. Queries are preferred, but complete mss are OK. Length: 500-3,000 words. Pays 10¢/word minimum. Sometimes pays expenses of writers on assignment.

Photos: Used only with interviews and profiles. State availability of photos or send contact sheet with ms. Pays $25 minimum for 5×7 or larger b&w prints. Captions required.

Columns/Departments: Chronicle (first-person narratives about the writing life; length: 1,200-1,500 words; pays 10¢/word); The Writing Life (length: 50-800 words; pays 10¢/word); Tip Sheet (short, unbylined items that offer solutions to writing- and freelance business-related problems that writers commonly face; pays 10¢/word); and My First Sale (an "occasional" department; a first-person account of how a writer broke into print; length: 1,000 words; pays 10¢/word). "For First Sale items, use a narrative, anecdotal style to tell a tale that is both inspirational and instructional. Before you submit a My First Sale item, make certain that your story contains a solid lesson that will benefit other writers." Buys approximately 200 articles/year for Writing Life section, Tip Sheet and shorter pieces. Send complete ms.

Poetry: Light verse about "the writing life"—joys and frustrations of writing. "We are also considering poetry other than short light verse—but related to writing, publishing, other poets and authors, etc." Buys 2-3/issue. Submit poems in batches of 1-8. Length: 2-20 lines. Pays $10-50/poem.

Fillers: Anecdotes and short humor, primarily for use in The Writing Life column. Uses 4/issue. Length: 50-250 words. Pays 10¢/word.

WRITER'S INFO, Box 1870, Hayden ID 83835. (208)772-6184. Editor: Linda Hutton. 90% freelance written. Eager to work with new/unpublished writers. Monthly newsletter on writing. "We provide helpful tips and advice to writers, both beginners and old pros." Circ. 200. **Pays on acceptance.** Publishes ms an average of 6 months after acceptance. Byline given. Buys first North American serial rights and second serial (reprint) rights. Submit seasonal/holiday material 9 months in advance. Simultaneous queries and simultaneous and previously published submissions OK. Reports in 1 month. Sample copy for #10 SAE and 2 first class stamps; writer's guidelines for #10 SASE.

Nonfiction: How-to, humor and personal experience, all related to writing. No interviews or re-hashes of articles published in other writers magazines. Buys 50-75 mss/year. Send complete ms. Length: 300 words. Pays $1-10.

Poetry: Free verse, light verse and traditional. No avant-garde or shaped poetry. Buys 40-50/year. Submit maximum 6 poems. Length: 4-20 lines. Pays $1-10.

Fillers: Jokes, anecdotes and short humor. Buys 3-4/year. Length: 100 words maximum. Pays $1-10.

Tips: "Tell us a system that worked for you to make a sale or inspired you to write. All departments are open to freelancers."

WRITER'S JOURNAL, Minnesota Ink, Inc., P.O. Box 9148, N. St. Paul MN 55109. (612)433-3626. Publisher/Managing Editor: Valerie Hockert. 40% freelance written. Monthly. Circ. 35,000. Pays on publication. Publishes ms an average of 4 months after acceptance. Byline given. Buys first North American serial rights. Submit seasonal/holiday material 6 months in advance. Simultaneous queries OK. Query for electronic submissions. Reports in 1 month on queries; 6 weeks on mss. Sample copy $3; writer's guidelines for #10 SASE.

Nonfiction: How-to (on the business and approach to writing); motivational; interview/profile; opinion. "*Writer's Journal* publishes articles on style, technique, editing methods, copy writing, research, writing of news releases, writing news stories and features, creative writing, grammar reviews, marketing, the business aspects of writing, copyright law and legal advice for writers/editors, independent book publishing, interview techniques, and more." Also articles on the use of computers by writers and a book review section. Buys 30-40 mss/year. Send complete ms. Length: 500-1,500 words. Pays $10-30.

Poetry: Avant-garde, free verse, haiku, light verse and traditional. "The *Writer's Journal* runs two poetry contests each year in the spring and fall: Winner, 2nd, 3rd place and 10 honorable mentions." Buys 20-30 poems/year. Submit maximum 5 poems. Length: 25 lines maximum. Pays $2-7.

Tips: "Articles must be *well* written and slanted toward the business (or commitment) of writing and/or being a writer. Interviews with established writers should be in-depth, particularly reporting interviewee's philosophy on writing, how he or she got started, etc."

THE WRITER'S NOOK NEWS, 38114 3rd St. #181, Willoughby OH 44094-6140. (216)975-8965. Editor: Eugene Ortiz. 100% freelance written. A quarterly newsletter for professional writers. "We don't print fluff, anecdotes or platitudes. Articles must be specific, terse, pithy and contain information readers can put to immediate, practical use. Every article should be the kind you want to cut out and tape to your desk somewhere." Estab. 1985. Circ. 5,000. **Pays on acceptance.** Publishes ms an average of 5 months after acceptance. Byline given. Publication is not copyrighted. Buys first North American serial rights. Submit seasonal/holiday material 5 months in advance. Reports in 6 weeks. Sample copy $3. Writer's guidelines for 9 × 12 SAE with 2 first class stamps.
Nonfiction: How-to and interview/profile (writing and marketing). "No essays, poetry, fiction, ruminations or anecdotes." Buys 100 mss/year. Send complete ms with credits and short bio. Length: 100-400 words. Pays $8-32.
Photos: Send photos with submission. Reviews b&w prints. Offers $5 maximum per photo. Identification of subjects required. Buys one-time rights.
Columns/Departments: Bolton's Book Bench (short reviews of books related to writing), 400 words; Conferences & Klatches (listings of conferences and gatherings), 400-1,200 words; Contests & Awards (listings of contests and awards), 400 words; Writer's Rights (latest information on what's happening on Capital Hill), 400 words; Markets (listings of information on markets for writers), 400 words. Buys 20 mss/year. Query with published clips and short bio. Length: 400 words. Pays $6-64.
Fillers: Facts and newsbreaks. Buys 20/year. Length: 20-100 words. Pays $3.20-$16.
Tips: "Take the writer's guidelines very seriously. 90% of the best submissions are still about 25% fluff. Don't tell me how hard or impossible it is to write anything of worth in only 400 words. This is not a market for beginners. Particularly looking for genre tips. I need more helpful information for established writers, on alternative ways of earning money as a writer, songwriting, playwriting and screenwriting. We also publish a quarterly conference bulletin, contest bulletin and a quarterly markets bulletin."

WRITER'S YEARBOOK, 1507 Dana Ave., Cincinnati OH 45207. Submissions Editor: Bill Strickland. 90% freelance written. Newsstand annual for freelance writers, journalists and teachers of creative writing. "Please note that the *Yearbook* is currently using a 'best of' format. That is, we are reprinting the best of writing about writing published in the last year: articles, fiction, and book excerpts. The *Yearbook* now uses little original material, so do not submit queries or original manuscripts to the *Yearbook*. We will, however, consider already-published material for possible inclusion." Estab. 1929. Buys reprint rights. Pays 20% kill fee. Byline given. **Pays on acceptance.** Publishes ms an average of 6 months after acceptance. "If you don't want your manuscript returned, indicate that on the first page of the manuscript or in a cover letter."
Nonfiction: "In reprints, we want articles that reflect the current state of writing in America. Trends, inside information and money-saving and money-making ideas for the freelance writer. We try to touch on the various facets of writing in each issue of the *Yearbook*—from fiction to poetry to playwriting, and any other endeavor a writer can pursue. How-to articles—that is, articles that explain in detail how to do something— are very important to us. For example, you could explain how to establish mood in fiction, how to improve interviewing techniques, how to write for and sell to specialty magazines, or how to construct and market a good poem. We are also interested in the writer's spare time—what she/he does to retreat occasionally from the writing wars; where and how to refuel and replenish the writing spirit. 'How Beats the Heart of a Writer' features interest us, if written warmly, in the first person, by a writer who has had considerable success. We also want interviews or profiles of well-known bestselling authors, always with good pictures. Articles on writing techniques that are effective today are always welcome. We provide how-to features and information to help our readers become more skilled at writing and successful at selling their writing." Buys 10-15 mss (reprints only)/year. Length: 750-4,500 words. Pays 2½¢/word minimum.
Photos: Interviews and profiles must be accompanied by high-quality photos. Reviews b&w photos only, depending on use; pays $20-50/published photo. Captions required.

Law

While all of these publications deal with topics of interest to attorneys, each has a particular slant. Be sure that your subject is geared to a specific market—lawyers in a single region, law students, paralegals, etc. Publications for law enforcement personnel are listed under Government and Public Service.

ABA JOURNAL, American Bar Association, 750 N. Lake Shore Dr., Chicago IL 60611. (312)988-5000. FAX: (312)988-6014. Editor: Gary A. Hengstler. Managing Editor: Robert Yates. 35% freelance written. Prefers to work with published/established writers. Monthly magazine covering law and laywers. "The content of the

Journal is designed to appeal to the association's diverse membership with emphasis on the general practitioner." Circ. 400,000. **Pays on acceptance.** Publishes ms an average of 2 months after acceptance. Byline given. "Editor works with writer until article is in acceptable form." Buys all rights. Submit seasonal/holiday material 3 months in advance. Simultaneous queries and submissions OK. Query for electronic submissions. Reports in 3 weeks. Free sample copy and writer's guidelines.

Nonfiction: Book excerpts; general interest (legal); how-to (law practice techniques); interview/profile (law firms and prominent individuals); and technical (legal trends). "The emphasis of the *Journal* is on the practical problems faced by lawyers in general practice and how those problems can be overcome. Articles should emphasize the practical rather than the theoretical or esoteric. Writers should avoid the style of law reviews, academic journals or legal briefs and should write in an informal, journalistic style. Short quotations from people and specific examples of your point will improve an article." Special issues have featured women and minorities in the legal profession. Buys 30 mss/year. Query with published clips or send complete ms. Length: 3,000 words. Pays $1,000-2,000. Pays expenses of writers on assignment.

Tips: "Write to us with a specific idea in mind and spell out how the subject would be covered. Full length profiles and feature articles are always needed. We look for practical information. If *The New York Times* or *Wall Street Journal* would like your style, so will we."

THE ALTMAN & WEIL REPORT TO LEGAL MANAGEMENT, Altman & Weil Publications, Inc., P.O. Box 625, Newtown Square PA 19073. (215)359-9900. Editor: Robert I. Weil. 15-20% freelance written. Works with a small number of new/unpublished writers each year. Monthly newsletter covering law office purchases (equipment, insurance services, space, etc.) and technology. Circ. 2,200. Pays on publication. Publishes ms an average of 3-6 months after acceptance. Byline given. Buys all rights; sometimes second serial (reprint) rights. Previously published submissions OK. Query for electronic submissions. Reports in 1 month on queries; 6 weeks on mss. Sample copy for #10 SASE.

Nonfiction: How-to (buy, use, repair), interview/profile and new product. Buys 6 mss/year. Query. Submit a sample of previous writing. Length: 500-2,500 words. Pays $125/published page.

Photos: State availability of photos. Reviews b&w prints; payment is included in payment for ms. Captions and model release required. Buys one-time rights.

‡BARRISTER, American Bar Association Press, 750 N. Lake Shore Dr., Chicago IL 60611. (312)988-6047. Editor: Anthony Monahan. 60% freelance written. Prefers to work with published/established writers. For young lawyers who are members of the American Bar Association concerned about practice of law, improvement of the profession and service to the public. Quarterly magazine. Estab. 1971. Circ. 155,000. **Pays on acceptance.** Publishes ms an average of 3 months after acceptance. Buys all rights, first serial rights or simultaneous rights. Query for electronic submissions. Reports in 6 weeks. Sample copy for 9 × 12 SAE with 4 first class stamps.

Nonfiction: "As a magazine of ideas and opinion, we seek material that will help readers in their interrelated roles of attorney and citizen; major themes in legal and social affairs." Especially needs expository or advocacy articles; position should be defended clearly in good, crisp, journalistic prose. "We would like to see articles on issues such as roles of women and minorities in law, the power and future of multinational corporations; national issues such as gun control; and aspects of the legal profession such as salary comparisons, use of computers in law practice." No humorous court reporter anecdote material or political opinion articles. Buys 15 unsolicited mss/year. Length: 3,000-4,000 words. Query with a working title and outline of topic. "Be specific." Pays $450-850. Sometimes pays the expenses of writers on assignment.

Photos: Donna Tashjian, photo editor. B&w photos and color transparencies purchased without accompanying ms. Pays $35-150.

Tips: "We urge writers to think ahead about new areas of law and social issues: sexual habits, work habits, corporations, etc. We would like to receive sharply-focused, timely profiles of young lawyers (36 or under) doing important, offbeat, innovative or impactful things."

BENCH & BAR OF MINNESOTA, Minnesota State Bar Association, Suite 403, 430 Marquette Ave., Minneapolis MN 55401. (612)333-1183. FAX: (612)333-4927. Editor: Judson Haverkamp. 10% freelance written. A magazine on the law/legal profession published 11 times/year. "Audience is mostly Minnesota lawyers. *Bench & Bar* seeks reportage, analysis, and commentary on developments in the law and the legal profession, especially in Minnesota. Preference to items of practical/human interest to professionals in law." Estab. 1931. Circ. 13,000. **Pays on acceptance.** Publishes ms an average of 3 months after acceptence. Byline given. Buys first North American serial rights and makes work-for-hire assignments. Reports in 1 month. Sample copy for 9 × 12 SAE and 4 first class stamps; free writer's guidelines.

Nonfiction: General interest, historical/nostalgic, how-to (how to handle particular types of legal, ethical problems in office management, representation, etc.), humor, interview/profile and technical/legal. "We do not want one-sided opinion pieces or advertorial." Buys 4-5 mss/year. Query with published clips, or send complete ms. Length: 1,500-4,000 words. Pays $300-800. Sometimes pays expenses of writers on assignment.

Photos: State availability of photos with submission. Reviews 5 × 7 or larger prints. Offers $25-100 per photo upon publication. Model releases and identification of subjects required. Buys one-time rights.

‡CALIFORNIA LAWYER, 1016 Fox Plaza, 1390 Market St., San Francisco CA 94102. (415)558-9888. Editor: Ray Reynolds. Managing Editor: Tom Brom. 80% freelance written. Monthly magazine of law-related articles and general interest subjects of appeal to lawyers and judges. Estab. 1928. Circ. 125,000. **Pays on acceptance.** Publishes ms an average of 3 months after acceptance. Byline given. Buys first rights; publishes only original material. Simultaneous queries and submissions OK. Reports in 2 weeks on queries; 3 weeks on mss. Sample copy and writer's guidelines on request.

Nonfiction: General interest, new and feature articles on law-related topics. "We are interested in concise, well-written and well-researched articles on recent trends in the legal profession, legal aspects of issues of current concern, as well as general interest articles of potential appeal and benefit to the state's lawyers. We would like to see a description or outline of your proposed idea, including a list of possible sources." Buys 36 mss/year. Query with published clips if available. Length: 500-3,000 words. Pays $200-1,500.

Photos: Max Ramirez, director of photography. State availability of photos with query letter or manuscript. Reviews prints. Identification of subjects and releases required.

Columns/Departments: Legal Technology, Law Office Management, Marketing, Ethics, Books. Query with published clips if available. Length: 750-1,500 words. Pays $200-600.

COMPUTER USER'S LEGAL REPORTER, Computer Law Group, Inc., Box 375, Charlottesville VA 22902. (804)977-6343. FAX: (804)977-8570. Editor: Charles P. Lickson. 20% freelance written. Prefers to work with published/established writers or "experts" in fields addressed. Newsletter published 9 times per year featuring legal issues, alternate dispute resolution and considerations facing users of computer and processed data. "The *Computer User's Legal Reporter* is written by a fully qualified legal and technical staff for essentially nonlawyer readers. It features brief summaries on developments in such vital areas as computer contracts, insurance, mediation, arbitration, warranties, crime, proprietary rights and privacy. Each summary is backed by reliable research and sourcework." Circ. 1,000. Pays on publication. Publishes ms an average of 1 month after acceptance. Offers 50% kill fee. Buys first North American serial rights. Simultaneous queries and submissions OK. Reports in 2 weeks. Sample copy for $10 with #10 SAE and 5 first class stamps.

Nonfiction: Book excerpts; expose; how-to (protect ideas, resolve problems); humor (computer law . . . according to Murphy); interview/profile (legal or computer personality); and technical. No articles not related to high-tech and society. Buys 10 mss/year. Query with published clips. Length: 250-1,000 words. Pays $50; $150 for scenes.

Columns/Departments: Computer Law . . . according to Murphy (humorous "laws" relating to computers, definitions, etc.). The editor buys all rights to Murphyisms which may be included in his book, *Computer Law . . . According to Murphy.* Buys 10 mss/year. Length: 25-75 words. Pays $10-50.

Tips: "Send materials with a note on your own background and qualifications to write what you submit. We invite intelligently presented and well-argued controversy within our field. Our audience is non-lawyers. We are looking for new ways to resolve disputes."

THE DOCKET, National Association of Legal Secretaries, Suite 550, 2250 E. 73rd St., Tulsa OK 74136. (918)493-3540. Editor: Debora L. Riggs. 20% freelance written. Bimonthly magazine that covers continuing legal education for legal support staff. "*The Docket* is written and edited for legal secretaries, legal assistants and other non-attorney personnel. Feature articles address general trends and emerging issues in the legal field, provide practical information to achieve proficiency in the delivery of legal services, and offer techniques for career growth and fulfillment." Circ. 20,000. Pays on publication. Publishes ms an average of 3-6 months after acceptance. Byline given. Offers 25-35% of original commission fee as kill fee. Buys first North American serial rights. Simultaneous and previously published submissions OK. Reports in 1 month. Free sample copy and writer's guidelines.

Nonfiction: How-to (enhance the delivery of legal services or any aspect thereof), new product (must be a service or equipment used in a legal office), personal experience (legal related) and technical (legal services and equipment). Buys 20-25 mss/year. Query with or without published clips, or send complete ms. Length: 500-3,000 words. Pays $50-250.

Photos: State availability of photos with submission. Reviews contact sheets, negatives, transparencies and prints. Offers no additional payment for photos accepted with ms. Buys one-time rights.

LAW PRACTICE MANAGEMENT, (formerly *Legal Economics*), A magazine of the section of Law Practice Management of the American Bar Association, P.O. Box 11418, Columbia SC 29211. Managing Editor/Art Director: Delmar L. Roberts. 10% freelance written. For the practicing lawyer and law practice administrator. Magazine published 8 times/year. Estab. 1975. Circ. 23,113 (BPA). Rights purchased vary with author and material. Usually buys all rights. Byline given. Pays on publication. Publishes ms an average of 8 months after acceptance. Query. Free writer's guidelines; sample copy $7 (make check payable to American Bar Association). Returns rejected material in 90 days, if requested.

Nonfiction: "We assist the practicing lawyer in operating and managing his or her office by providing relevant articles and departments written in a readable and informative style. Editorial content is intended to aid the lawyer by conveying management methods that will allow him or her to provide legal services to clients in a prompt and efficient manner at reasonable cost. Typical topics of articles include fees and billing;

client/lawyer relations; computer hardware/software; mergers; retirement/disability; marketing; compensation of partners and associates; legal data base research; and use of paralegals." No elementary articles on a whole field of technology, such as, "why you need computers in the law office." Pays $100-350.

Photos: Pays $50-60 for b&w photos purchased with mss; $50-100 for color; $150-175 for cover transparencies.

Tips: "We have a theme for each issue with two to three articles relating to the theme. We also publish thematic issues occasionally in which an entire issue is devoted to a single topic. The November/December issue each year is devoted to new office technology."

LAWYERS MONTHLY, Lawyers Weekly Publications, Inc., 30 Court Sq., Boston MA 02108. (617)227-6034. Editor: Michelle E. Bates. 50% freelance written. Monthly newspaper feature supplement for 6 law newpapers concerning law, lawyers, law-related events. "We are writing for a highly educated, generally affluent, professional, active national readership, age-range 25-75—busy men and women who are intimately involved with the subjects we cover and who therefore require the best in authority, expertise, timeliness, uniqueness and readability. Circ. 65,000. Pays on publication. Publishes ms an average of 2 months after acceptance. Byline given. Buys first rights. Submit seasonal/holiday material 3 months in advance. Query for electronic submissions. Reports in 4 weeks on queries. Free sample copy.

Nonfiction: National reporting (investigative pieces about important cases, issues or trends), historical/academic (legal history), how-to (concerning law office management and new products), interview/profile (prominent judges and attorneys, or lawyers with serious nonlawyer involvements—professional or hobby) opinion (columns from experts or prominent individuals on current national legal issues and controversies) and book reviews (of practice- or issue-oriented books). Buys 25-50 mss/year. Send complete ms. Length: 1,000-2,500 words. Pays $25-500. Sometimes pays expenses of writers on assignment.

Photos: Send photos or appropriate graphic material with submission. Reviews prints. Payment policy negotiable. Buys one-time rights.

Tips: "Our publication is only open to individuals with an intimate familiarity with the law, either as legal journalists or practitioners of the law. Submissions must be clear, professional, readable, well-researched, timely, crucial, enterprising, original and authoritative."

THE LAWYER'S PC, A Newsletter for Lawyers Using Personal Computers, Shepard's/McGraw-Hill, Inc., P.O. Box 1108, Lexington SC 29072. (803)359-9941. Editor: Robert P. Wilkins. Managing Editor: Daniel E. Harmon. 50% freelance written. A biweekly newsletter covering computerized law firms. "Our readers are lawyers who want to be told how a particular microcomputer program or type of program is being applied to a legal office task, such as timekeeping, litigation support, etc." Estab. 1981. Circ. 4,000. Pays end of the month of publication. Publishes ms an average of 1-2 months after acceptance. Byline given. Buys first North American serial rights and the right to reprint. Submit seasonal/holiday material 5 months in advance. Query for electronic submissions. Computer printout submissions acceptable; prefers letter-quality. Reports in 1 month on queries; 2 months on mss. Sample copy for 9×12 SAE with 3 first class stamps; free writer's guidelines.

Nonfiction: How-to (applications articles on law office computerization) and software reviews written by lawyers who have no compromising interests. No general articles on why lawyers need computers or reviews of products written by public relations representatives or vending consultants. Buys 30-35 mss/year. Query. Length: 500-2,500 words. Pays $25-125. Sometimes pays the expenses of writers on assignment.

Tips: "Most of our writers are lawyers. If you're not a lawyer, you need to at least understand why general business software may not work well in a law firm. If you understand lawyers' specific computer problems, write an article describing how to solve one of those problems, and we'd like to see it."

THE LAWYERS WEEKLY, The Newspaper for the Legal Profession in Canada, Butterworth (Canada) Inc., Suite 201, 423 Queen St. W., Toronto, Ontario M5V 2A5 Canada. (416)598-5211. FAX: (416)598-5659. Editor: D. Michael Fitz-James. 20% freelance written. "We will work with any *talented* writer of whatever experience level." A 48 times/year tabloid covering law and legal affairs for a "sophisticated up-market readership of lawyers and accountants." Circ. 41,000. Pays on publication. Publishes ms an average of 1 month after acceptance. Byline given. Offers 50% kill fee. Usually buys all rights. Submit seasonal/holiday material 6 weeks in advance. Simultaneous queries and submissions OK. Query for electronic submissions. Electronic submissions on PC compatible disks, WordStar or WordPerfect. Printout backup a must. Reports in 1 month. Sample copy $5 Canadian funds and 9×12 SAE.

Nonfiction: Expose; general interest (law); historical/nostalgic; how-to (professional); humor; interview/profile (lawyers and judges); opinion; technical; news; and case comments. "We try to wrap up the week's legal events and issues in a snappy informal package with lots of visual punch. We especially like news stories with photos or illustrations. We are always interested in feature or newsfeature articles involving current legal issues, but contributors should keep in mind our audience is trained in *English/Canadian common law*—not U.S. law. That means most U.S. constitutional or criminal law stories will generally not be accepted. Special Christmas issue. No routine court reporting or fake news stories about commercial products. Buys 200-300 mss/year. Query or send complete ms. Length: 700-1,500 words. Pays $25 minimum, negotiable maximum (have paid up to $500 in the past). Payment in Canadian dollars. Sometimes pays the expenses of writers on assignment.

Photos: State availability of photos with query letter or ms. Reviews b&w and color contact sheets, negatives, and 5×7 prints. Identification of subjects required. Buys one-time rights.

Columns/Departments: Buys 90-100 mss/year. Send complete ms or Wordstar or WordPerfect disk. Length: 500-1,000 words. Pays negotiable rate.

Fillers: Clippings, jokes, gags, anecdotes, short humor and newsbreaks. Cartoon ideas will be drawn by our artists. Length: 50-200 words. Pays $10 minimum.

Tips: "Freelancers can best break into our publication by submitting news, features, and accounts of unusual or bizarre legal events. A frequent mistake made by writers is forgetting that our audience is intelligent and learned in law. They don't need the word 'plaintiff' explained to them." No unsolicited mss returned without SASE (or IRC to U.S. or non Canadian destinations).

LOS ANGELES LAWYER, Los Angeles County Bar Association, P.O. Box 55020, Los Angeles CA 90055. (213)627-2727, ext. 265. Editor: Susan Pettit. 100% freelance written. Prefers to work with published/established writers. Monthly (except for combined July/August issue) magazine covering legal profession with "journalistic and scholarly articles of interest to the legal profession." Circ. 25,000. **Pays on acceptance.** Publishes ms an average of 2 months after acceptance. Byline given. Buys first serial rights only. Submit seasonal/holiday material 4 months in advance. Simultaneous queries OK. Query for electronic submissions. Reports in 1 month on queries; 2 months on mss. Sample copy $1.50; free writer's guidelines.

Nonfiction: How-to (tips for legal practitioners); interview (leading legal figures); opinion (on area of law, lawyer attitudes or group, court decisions, etc.); travel (very occasionally); and consumer-at-law feature articles on topics of interest to lawyers. No first person, nonlegal material. Buys 22 mss/year. Query with published clips. Length: 3,000-4,000 words for feature (cover story); 1,500-2,500 words for consumer article. Pays $500-600 for cover story, $225-300 for consumer article. Sometimes pays the expenses of writers on assignment.

Tips: "Writers should be familiar with the Los Angeles legal community as the magazine has a local focus."

THE PARALEGAL, The Publication for the Paralegal Profession, Paralegal Publishing Corp./National Paralegal Association, Box 406, Solebury PA 18963. (215)297-8333. FAX: (215)297-8358. Editor: William Cameron. 90% freelance written. Works with published/established writers; eager to work with new/unpublished writers. Bimonthly magazine covering the paralegal profession for practicing paralegals, attorneys, paralegal educators, paralegal associations, law librarians and court personnel. Special and controlled circulation includes law libraries, colleges and schools educating paralegals, law schools, law firms and governmental agencies, etc. Circ. 38,000. Byline given. Buys all or limited rights. Simultaneous queries, and simultaneous and previously published submissions OK. Reports in 2 weeks on queries; 1 month on mss. Writer's guidelines and suggested topic sheet for #10 SASE.

Nonfiction: Book excerpts, exposé, general interest, historical/nostalgic, how-to, humor, interview/profile, new product, opinion, personal experience, photo feature, technical and travel. Suggested topics include the paralegal (where do they fit and how do they operate within the law firm in each specialty); the government; the corporation; the trade union; the banking institution; the law library; the legal clinic; the trade or professional association; the educational institution; the court system; the collection agency; the stock brokerage firm; and the insurance company. Articles also wanted on paralegals exploring "Where have they been? Where are they now? Where are they going?" Query or send complete ms. Length: 1,500-3,000 words. Pays variable rates; submissions should state desired fee. Ask amount when submitting ms or other material to be considered. Sometimes pays the expenses of writers on assignment.

Photos: Send photos with query or ms. Captions, model release, and identification of subjects required.

Columns/Departments: Case at Issue (a feature on a current case from a state or federal court which either directly or indirectly affects paralegals and their work with attorneys, the public, private or governmental sector); Humor (cartoons, quips, short humorous stories, anecdotes and one-liners in good taste and germane to the legal profession); and My Position (an actual presentation by a paralegal who wishes to share with others his/her job analysis). Query. Submissions should state desired fee.

Fillers: Clippings, jokes, gags, anecdotes, short humor and newsbreaks.

THE PENNSYLVANIA LAWYER, Pennsylvania Bar Association, 100 South St., Box 186, Harrisburg PA 17108. (717)238-6715. Executive Editor: Marcy Carey Mallory. Managing Editor: Donald C. Sarvey. 25% freelance written. Prefers to work with published/established writers. Magazine published 8 times/year as a service to the legal profession. Circ. 27,000. **Pays on acceptance.** Publishes ms an average of 3-6 months after acceptance. Byline given. Buys negotiable serial rights; generally first rights, occasionally one-time rights or second serial (reprint) rights. Submit seasonal/holiday material 6 months in advance. Simultaneous submissions are discouraged. Reports in 6 weeks. Free sample copy and writer's guidelines.

Nonfiction: General interest, how-to, humor, interview/profile, new product, and personal experience. All features *must* relate in some way to Pennsylvania lawyers or the practice of law in Pennsylvania. Buys 10-12 mss/year. Query. Length: 600-1,500 words. Pays $75-350. Sometimes pays the expenses of writers on assignment.

‡**THE PERFECT LAWYER, A Newsletter for Lawyers Using WordPerfect Products**, Shepard's/McGraw-Hill Inc., P.O. Box 1108, Lexington SC 29072. (803)359-9941. Editor: Robert P. Wilkins. Managing Editor: Daniel E. Harmon. 50% freelance written. Monthly newsletter covering the use of WordPerfect Corporation related products in law offices. Estab. 1990. Circ. 1,000. Pays at end of the month after publication. Publishes ms an average of 2-3 months after acceptance. Byline given. Buys first North American serial rights and the right to reprint. Submit seasonal/holiday material 5 months in advance. Query for electronic submissions. Reports in 1 month on queries; 2 months on mss. Sample copy for 9 × 12 SAE with 4 first class stamps; free writer's guidelines.
Nonfiction: How-to computer articles. Must be law office specific. Occasional reviews of WordPerfect related products for law firms. Buys 25-35 mss/year. Query. Length: 500-2,500 words. Pays $25-200. Sometimes pays expenses of writers on assignment.
Tips: "Writers should understand the specific computer needs of law firms. Our readers are interested in howto solve office automation problems with computers and WordPerfect or related software products."

Leather Goods

SHOE RETAILING TODAY, (formerly *NSRA News*), National Shoe Retailers Association, 9861 Broken Land Pkwy., Columbia MD 21046. (301)381-8282. FAX: (301)381-1167. Editor: Cynthia Emmel. 10% freelance written. Bimonthly newsletter covering footwear/accessory industry. Looks for articles that are "informative, educational, but with wit, interest, and creativity. I hate dry, dusty articles." Estab. 1972. Circ. 4,000-5,000. Byline given. Buys one-time rights. Submit seasonal/holiday material 3 months in advance. Reports in 2 weeks. Free sample copy and writer's guidelines.
Nonfiction: How-to, interview/profile, new product and technical. January and July are shoe show issues. Buys 6 mss/year. Length: 450 words. Pays $125 for assigned articles. Pays up to $200 for "full-fledged research — 1,000 words or more on assigned articles."
Photos: State availability of photos with submission. Offers no additional payment for photos accepted with ms. Buys one-time rights.
Columns/Departments: Query. Pays $50-125.
Tips: "We are a trade magazine/newsletter for the footwear industry. Any information pertaining to our market is helpful: advertising/display/how-tos."

SHOE SERVICE, SSIA Service Corp., 5024 Campbell Blvd., Baltimore MD 21236. (301)256-8100. FAX: (301)529-4612. Editor: Mitchell Lebovic. 50% freelance written. "We want well-written articles, whether they come from new or established writers." Monthly magazine for business people who own and operate small shoe repair shops. Estab. 1921. Circ. 17,000. Pays on publication. Publishes ms an average of 3 months after acceptance. Byline given. Buys first serial rights, first North American serial rights, and one-time rights. Submit seasonal/holiday material 3 months in advance. Simultaneous queries and previously published submissions OK. Reports in 6 weeks. Sample copy $2 and 9 × 12 SAE; free writer's guidelines.
Nonfiction: How-to (run a profitable shop); interview/profile (of an outstanding or unusual person on shoe repair); and business articles (particularly about small business practices in a service/retail shop). Buys 12-24 mss/year. Query with published clips or send complete ms. Length: 500-2,000 words. Pays 5¢/word.
Photos: "Quality photos will help sell an article." State availability of photos. Pays $10-30 for 8 × 10 b&w prints. Uses some color photos, but mostly uses b&w glossies. Captions, model release, and identification of subjects required.
Tips: "Visit some shoe repair shops to get an idea of the kind of person who reads *Shoe Service*. Profiles are the easiest to sell to us if you can find a repairer we think is unusual."

Library Science

Librarians read these journals for advice on promotion and management of libraries, library and book trade issues and information access and transfer. Be aware of current issues such as censorship, declines in funding and government information policies. For journals on the book trade see Book and Bookstore.

AMERICAN LIBRARIES, 50 E. Huron St., Chicago IL 60611. (312)944-6780. Editor: Thomas Gaughan. 5-10% freelance written. Works with a small number of new/unpublished writers each year. Magazine published 11 times/year for librarians. "A highly literate audience. They are for the most part practicing professionals with a down-to-earth interest in people and current trends." Circ. 53,000. Buys first North American serial rights. Publishes ms an average of 4 months after acceptance. Pays negotiable kill fee. Byline given. Submit seasonal material 6 months in advance. Reports in 10 weeks.

Nonfiction: "Material reflecting the special and current interests of the library profession. Nonlibrarians should browse recent journals in the field, available on request in medium-sized and large libraries everywhere. Topic and/or approach must be fresh, vital or highly entertaining. Library memoirs and stereotyped stories about old maids, overdue books, fines, etc., are unacceptable. Our first concern is with the American Library Association's activities and how they relate to the 46,000 reader/members. Tough for an outsider to write on this topic, but not to supplement it with short, offbeat or significant library stories and features." No fillers. Buys 2-6 freelance mss/year. Pays $15 for news tips used, and $25-300 for briefs and articles.

Photos: "Will look at color transparencies and bright color prints for inside and cover use." Pays $50-200 for photos.

Tips: "You can break in with a sparkling, 300-word report on a true, offbeat library event, use of new technology, or with an exciting color photo and caption. Though stories on public libraries are always of interest, we especially need arresting material on academic and school libraries."

CHURCH MEDIA LIBRARY MAGAZINE, 127 9th Ave. N., Nashville TN 37234. (615)251-2752. Editor: Floyd B. Simpson. Quarterly magazine. For adult leaders in church organizations and people interested in library work (especially church library work). Estab. 1891. Circ. 16,000. Pays on publication. Buys all rights, first serial rights and second serial (reprint) rights. Byline given. Phone queries OK. Submit seasonal/holiday material 14 months in advance. Previously published submissions OK. Reports in 1 month. Free sample copy and writer's guidelines.

Nonfiction: "We are primarily interested in articles that relate to the development of church libraries in providing media and services to support the total program of a church and in meeting individual needs. We publish how-to accounts of services provided, promotional ideas, exciting things that have happened as a result of implementing an idea or service; human interest stories that are library-related; and media training (teaching and learning with a media mix). Articles should be practical for church library staffs and for teachers and other leaders of the church." Buys 10-15 mss/issue. Query. Pays 5¢/word.

EMERGENCY LIBRARIAN, Dyad Services, P.O. Box 46258, Stn. G, Vancouver, British Columbia V6R 4G6 Canada. FAX: (604)734-0221. Editor: Ken Haycock. Publishes 5 issues/year. Estab. 1979. Circ. 6,500. Pays on publication. No multiple submissions. Reports in 6 weeks. Free writer's guidelines.

Nonfiction: Emphasis is on improvement of library service for children and young adults in school and public libraries. Also annotated bibliographies. Buys 3 mss/issue. Query. Length: 1,000-3,500 words. Pays $50.

Columns/Departments: Five regular columnists. Also Book Reviews (of professional materials in education, librarianship). Query. Length: 100-300 words. Payment consists of book reviewed.

THE LIBRARY IMAGINATION PAPER, Carol Bryan Imagines, 1000 Byus Dr., Charleston WV 25311. (304)345-2378. 30% freelance written. Quarterly newspaper covering public relations education for librarians. Clip art included in each issue. Estab. 1978. Circ. 3,000. Pays on publication. Publishes ms an average of 6 months after acceptance. Byline given. Buys one-time rights. Submit seasonal/holiday material 3 months in advance. Simultaneous and previously published submissions OK. Reports in 6 weeks on queries; 3 weeks on mss. Sample copy $5; writer's guidelines for SASE.

Nonfiction: How-to (on "all aspects of good library public relations both mental tips and hands-on methods. We need how-to and tips pieces on all aspects of PR, for library subscribers—both school and public libraries. In the past we've featured pieces on taking good photos, promoting an anniversary celebration, working with printers, and producing a slide show.") No articles on "what the library means to me." Buys 4-6 mss/year. Query with or without published clips, or send complete ms. Length: 500-2,200 words. Pays $35.

Photos: Send photos with submission. Reviews 5×7 prints. Offers $5 per photo. Captions required. Buys one-time rights.

Tips: "Someone who has worked in the library field and has first-hand knowledge of library PR needs, methods and processes will do far better with us. Our readers are people who cannot be written down to—but their library training has not always incorporated enough preparation for handling promotion, publicity and the public."

THE NEW LIBRARY SCENE, Library Binding Institute, 8013 Centre Park Dr., Austin TX 78754. (512)836-4141. FAX: (512)836-4849. 50% freelance written. A bimonthly magazine on library book binding and conservation. Circ. 3,000. **Pays on acceptance.** Publishes ms an average of 2 months after acceptance. Byline given. Buys first North American serial rights. Reports in 1 month on queries. Sample copy for 9×12 SAE and 4 first class stamps and writer's guidelines for #10 SASE.

Nonfiction: How-to (libraries, book binding, conservation), interview/profile and technical. Buys 6-10 mss/year. Query. Pays $100.

Photos: State availability of photos with submission. Reviews contact sheets and prints (3×5 or 5×7). Offers no additional payment for photos accepted with ms. Identification of subjects required. Buys one-time rights.

WILSON LIBRARY BULLETIN, 950 University Ave., Bronx NY 10452. (212)588-8400. FAX: (212)538-2716. Editor: Mary Jo Godwin. 80% freelance written. Monthly (September-June) for professional librarians and those interested in the book and library worlds. Estab. 1914. Circ. 14,000. Pays on publication. Publishes ms an average of 2 months after acceptance. Buys first North American serial rights. Sample copies may be seen on request in most libraries. "Manuscript must be original copy, double-spaced; additional photocopy or carbon is appreciated." Deadlines are a minimum 2 months before publication. Reports in 3 months. Free sample copy and writer's guidelines.
Nonfiction: Uses articles "of interest to librarians and information professionals throughout the nation and around the world. Style must be lively, readable and sophisticated, with appeal to modern professionals; facts must be thoroughly researched. Subjects range from the political to the comic in the world of media and libraries, with an emphasis on the human as well as the technical aspects of any story. No condescension: no library stereotypes." Buys 30 mss/year. Send complete ms. Length: 2,500-6,000 words. Pays about $100-400, "depending on the substance of article and its importance to readers." Sometimes pays the expenses of writers on assignment.
Tips: "The best way you can break in is with a first-rate black and white or color photo and caption information on a library, library service or librarian who departs completely from all stereotypes and the commonplace. Libraries have changed. You'd better first discover what is now commonplace."

Lumber

CANADIAN FOREST INDUSTRIES WEST, Southam Communications Ltd., 4285 Canada Way, Burnaby, British Columbia V5G 1H2 Canada. (604)433-6125. Editor: Paul MacDonald. 10% freelance written. Monthly magazine. "*Canadian Forest Industries West* covers all facets of the logging and sawmilling sectors of the forest industry." Estab. 1880. Circ. 22,000. **Pays on acceptance.** Byline given. Buys first rights. Previously published submissions OK. Reports in 6 weeks on queries; 1 month on mss. Free writer's guidelines.
Nonfiction: Humor, interview/profile, new product and technical. "We do not want fiction." Buys 6 mss/year. Query with published clips. Length: 800-1,500 words. Payment varies. Sometimes pays expenses of writers on assignment.
Photos: State availability of photos with submission. Reviews transparencies. Payment varies. Buys one-time rights.

NORTHERN LOGGER AND TIMBER PROCESSOR, Northeastern Loggers' Association, Box 69, Old Forge NY 13420. (315)369-3078. FAX: (315)369-3736. Editor: Eric A. Johnson. 40% freelance written. Monthly magazine of the forest industry in the northern U.S. (Maine to Minnesota and south to Virginia and Missouri). "We are not a purely technical journal, but are more information oriented." Circ. 13,600. Pays on publication. Publishes ms an average of 3 months after acceptance. Byline given. Buys all rights. Submit seasonal/holiday material 3 months in advance. Previously published submissions OK. Reports in 2 weeks. Free sample copy and writer's guidelines.
Nonfiction: Expose, general interest, historical/nostalgic, how-to, interview/profile, new product and opinion. "We only buy feature articles, and those should contain some technical or historical material relating to the forest products industry." Buys 12-15 mss/year. Query. Length: 500-2,500 words. Pays $50-250.
Photos: Send photos with ms. Pays $35 for 35mm color transparencies; $15 for 5×7 b&w prints. Captions and identification of subjects required.
Tips: "We accept most any subject dealing with this part of the country's forest industry, from historical to logging, firewood, and timber processing."

SOUTHERN LUMBERMAN, Greysmith Publishing, Inc., Suite 116, 128 Holiday Ct., Franklin TN 37064. (615)791-1961. FAX: (615)790-6188. Editor: Nanci P. Gregg. 20-30% freelance written. Works with a small number of new/unpublished writers each year. A monthly trade journal for the sawmill industry. Estab. 1881. Circ. 12,000. Pays on publication. Publishes ms an average of 3 months after acceptance. Byline given. Not copyrighted. Buys first North American rights. Submit seasonal/holiday material 6 months in advance. Query for electronic submissions. Reports in 1 month on queries; 2 months on mss. Sample copy $2 with 9×12 SAE and 5 first class stamps; writer's guidelines for #10 SASE.
Nonfiction: How to sawmill better, interview/profile, equipment analysis, technical. Sawmill features. Buys 10-15 mss/year. Query with or without published clips, or send complete ms. Length: 500-2,000 words. Pays $150-350 for assigned articles; pays $100-250 for unsolicited articles. Sometimes pays the expenses of writers on assignment.
Photos: Send photos with submission. Reviews transparencies and 4×5 b&w prints. Offers $10-25 per photo. Captions and identification of subjects required.
Tips: "Like most, we appreciate a clearly-worded query listing merits of suggested story—what it will tell our readers they need/want to know. We want quotes, we want opinions to make others discuss the article. Best hint? Find an interesting sawmill operation owner and start asking questions—I bet a story idea develops. We need b&w photos too. Most open is what we call the Sweethart Mill stories. We publish at least one per

month, and hope to be printing two or more monthly in the immediate future. Find a sawmill operator and ask questions—what's he doing bigger, better, different. We're interested in new facilities, better marketing, improved production."

Machinery and Metal

CANADIAN MACHINERY & METALWORKING, 777 Bay St., Toronto, Ontario M5W 1A7 Canada. (416)596-5714. Editor: James Barnes. 10% freelance written. Monthly. Buys first North American rights. **Pays on acceptance.** Query. Publishes ms an average of 6 weeks after acceptance.
Nonfiction: Technical and semi-technical articles dealing with metalworking operations in Canada and in the U.S., if of particular interest to Canadian readers. Accuracy and service appeal to readers is a must. Pays minimum 30¢ (Canadian)/word.
Photos: Purchased with mss and with captions only. Pays $10 minimum for b&w features.

‡CUTTING TOOL ENGINEERING, 464 Central Ave., Northfield IL 60093. (708)441-7520. Publisher: John William Roberts. Editor: Don Nelson. Prefers to work with published/established writers. For metalworking industry executives and engineers concerned with the metal-cutting/metal and material removal/abrasive machining function in metalworking. Published 9 times yearly. 25% freelance written. Circ. 38,775. Pays on publication. Publishes ms an average of 6 months after acceptance. Byline given. Buys all rights. Query for electronic submissions. Write Don Nelson before querying or submitting ms. Free sample copy.
Nonfiction: "Intelligently written articles on specific applications of all types of metal cutting tools, mills, drills, reamers, etc. Articles must contain all information related to the operation, such as feeds and speeds, materials machined, etc. Should be tersely written, in-depth treatment. In the Annual Diamond/Superabrasive Directory, published in June, we cover the use of diamond/superabrasive cutting tools and diamond/superabrasive grinding wheels." Length: 1,000-2,500 words. Pays "$35/published page, or about 5¢/published word."
Photos: Purchased with mss. 8×10 color or b&w glossies preferred.
Tips: "The most frequent mistake made by writers in submitting an article for us is that they don't know the market."

MODERN MACHINE SHOP, 6600 Clough Pike, Cincinnati OH 45244. FAX: (513)231-2818. Editor: Ken Gettelman. 25% freelance written. Monthly. Estab. 1928. Pays 1 month following acceptance. Publishes ms an average of 6 months after acceptance. Byline given. Query for electronic submissions. Reports in 5 days. Writer's guidelines for #10 SASE.
Nonfiction: Uses articles dealing with all phases of metal working, manufacturing and machine shop work, with photos. No general articles. "Ours is an industrial publication, and contributing authors should have a working knowledge of the metalworking industry." Buys 10 unsolicited mss/year. Query. Length: 1,000-3,500 words. Pays current market rate. Sometimes pays the expenses of writers on assignment.
Tips: "The use of articles relating to computers in manufacturing is growing."

‡NICKEL, The magazine devoted to nickel and its applications, Nickel Development Institute, Suite 402, 15 Toronto St., Toronto, Ontario M5C 2E3 Canada. (416)362-8850. Editor: Desmond M. Chorley. 30% freelance written. Quarterly magazine covering the metal nickel and all of its applications. Estab. 1985. Circ. 30,000. **Pays on acceptance.** Pubishes ms an average of 3 months after acceptance. Byline given. Buys first rights. Free sample copy and writer's guidelines from Nickel Development Institute Librarian.
Nonfiction: Semi technical. Buys 20 mss/year. Query. Length: 50-450 words. Pays competitive rates, by negotiation. Sometimes pays expenses of writers on assignment.
Photos: State availability of photos with submission. Offers competitive rates by negotiation. Captions, model releases and identification of subjects required.
Tips: "Write to Librarian, Nickel Development Institute, for two free copies of *Nickel* and study them. Know something about nickel's 300,000 end uses. Be at home in writing semitechnical material. Then query the Editor with a story IDEA in a one-page letter—no fax queries or phone calls. Complete magazine is open, except Technical Literature column."

Maintenance and Safety

BUILDING SERVICES CONTRACTOR, MacNair Publications Inc., 101 W. 31st St., New York NY 10001. (212)279-4455. Editor: Frank C. Falcetta. 0-5% freelance written. Bimonthly magazine covering building services and maintenance. Estab. 1925. Circ. 8,000. Pays on publication. Publishes ms an average of 2-4 months after acceptance. Byline sometimes given. Buys one-time rights and second serial (reprint) rights. Simultaneous and previously published submissions OK "as long as not published in competitive magazine." Reports in 2 weeks. Writer's guidelines for #10 SASE.

Nonfiction: How-to, humor, interview/profile and technical. Buys 1-5 mss/year. Send material with SASE. Pays $100 minimum.

Photos: State availability of photos with submission. Reviews contact sheets. Offers no additional payment for photos accepted with ms, but "offers higher payment when photos are used." Buys one-time rights.

Tips: "I'd love to do more with freelance, but market and budget make it tough. I do most of it myself."

CLEANING, (formerly *Service Business*), 1512 Western Ave., Seattle WA 98101. (206)622-4241. Publisher: William R. Griffin. Associate Editor: Jim Saunders. 80% freelance written. Quarterly magazine covering technical and management information relating to cleaning and self-employment. "We cater to those who are self-employed in any facet of the cleaning and maintenance industry and seek to be top professionals in their field. Our readership is small but select. We seek concise, factual articles, realistic but definitely upbeat." Circ. 6,000. Pays 1 month after publication. Publishes ms an average of 3 months after acceptance. Byline given. Buys first serial rights, second serial (reprint) rights, and all rights; makes work-for-hire assignments. Submit seasonal/holiday material 4 months in advance. Simultaneous queries and previously published work (rarely) OK. Reports in 3 months. Sample copy for $3, 8 × 10 SAE and 3 first class stamps; writer's guidelines for #10 SASE.

Nonfiction: Exposé (safety/health business practices); how-to (on cleaning, maintenance, small business management); humor (clean jokes, cartoons); interview/profile; new product (must be unusual to rate full article—mostly obtained from manufacturers); opinion; personal experience; and technical. Special issues include "What's New?" in Feb. No "wordy articles written off the top of the head, obviously without research, and needing more editing time than was spent on writing." Buys 40 mss/year. Query with or without published clips. Length: 500-3,000 words. Pays $5-80. ("Pay depends on amount of work, research and polishing put into article much more than on length.") Pays expenses of writers on assignment with prior approval only.

Photos: State availability of photos or send photos with ms. Pays $5-25 for "smallish" b&w prints. Captions, model release, and identification of subjects required. Buys one-time rights and reprint rights. "Magazine size is 7 × 8½—photos need to be proportionate."

Columns/Departments: "Ten regular columnists now sell four columns per year to us. We are interested in adding a Safety & Health column (related to cleaning and maintenance industry). We are also open to other suggestions—send query." Buys 36 columns/year; department information obtained at no cost. Query with or without published clips. Length: 500-1,500 words. Pays $15-85.

Fillers: Jokes, gags, anecdotes, short humor, newsbreaks and cartoons. Buys 40/year. Length: 3-200 words. Pays $1-20.

Tips: "We are constantly seeking quality freelancers from all parts of the country. A freelancer can best break in to our publication with fairly technical articles on how to do specific cleaning/maintenance jobs; interviews with top professionals covering this and how they manage their business; and personal experience. Our readers demand concise, accurate information. Don't ramble. Write only about what you know and/or have researched. Editors don't have time to rewrite your rough draft. Organize and polish before submitting."

CLEANING MANAGEMENT, The Magazine for Today's Building Maintenance Housekeeping Executive, Harris Communications, 15550-D Rockfield Blvd., Irvine CA 92718. (714)770-5008. Editor: R. Daniel Harris Jr. Monthly magazine covering building maintenance/housekeeping operations in large institutions such as hotels, schools, hospitals, etc., as well as commercial and industrial, recreational and religious buildings, stores and markets. For managers with on-staff cleaning operations, contract cleaning service companies, and professional carpet cleaning companies. Circ. 42,000. Pays on publication. Byline given. Offers "full payment, if article has been completed." Buys all rights. Submit seasonal/holiday material 3 months in advance. Simultaneous queries OK. Reports in 1 month. Free sample copy and writer's guidelines.

Nonfiction: How-to (custodial operations); interview/profile (of custodial managers); opinion (of custodial managers); personal experience (on-the-job). Special issues include: March—Carpet Care; April and June—Floor Care; May—Exterior Building Maintenance; September—Office Cleaning. Buys 5-6 mss/year. Query. Length: 1,000-2,000 words. Pays $100-300.

Photos: State availability of photos. Pays $5-15 for 8 × 10 b&w prints; $20-75 for 4 × 5 color transparencies. Captions, model release, and identification of subjects required.

Tips: "We want writers familiar with our field or who can pick it up quickly."

PEST CONTROL MAGAZINE, 7500 Old Oak Blvd., Cleveland OH 44130. (216)243-8100. Editor: Jerry Mix. For professional pest control operators and sanitarians. Monthly magazine. Circ. 15,000. Buys all rights. Buys 12 mss/year. Pays on publication. Submit seasonal material 2 months in advance. Reports in 1 month. Query or submit complete ms.

Nonfiction: Business tips, unique control situations, personal experience (stories about 1-man operations and their problems) articles. Must have trade or business orientation. No general information type of articles desired. Buys 3 unsolicited mss/year. Length: 1,000 words. Pays $150 minimum. Regular columns use material oriented to this profession. Length: 2,000 words.

Photos: No additional payment for photos used with mss. Pays $50-150 for 8 × 10 color or transparencies.

SAFETY COMPLIANCE LETTER, with OSHA Highlights, Bureau of Business Practice, 24 Rope Ferry Rd., Waterford CT 06386. (203)442-4365. Editor: Margot Loomis. Managing Editor: Wayne Muller. 80% freelance written. Bimonthly newsletter covering occupational safety and health. Publishes interview-based 'how-to' and 'success' stories for personnel in charge of safety and health in manufacturing/industrial environments. Estab. 1915. Circ. 8,000. Pays on acceptance after editing. Publishes ms an average of 3-6 months after acceptance. No byline given. Offers 50% kill fee. Buys all rights. Submit seasonal/holiday material 4 months in advance. Reports in 1 week on queries; 1 month on mss. Free sample copy and writer's guidelines.

Nonfiction: How-to (implement an occupational safety/health program), changes in OSHA regulations and examples of safety/health programs. No articles that aren't based on an interview. Buys 24 mss/year. Query. Length: 750-1,200 words. Pays 10¢-15¢/word. Sometimes pays the expenses of writers on assignment.

Management and Supervision

This category includes trade journals for middle management business and industrial managers, including supervisors and office managers. Journals for business executives and owners are classified under Business Management. Those for industrial plant managers are listed in Industrial Operations.

‡**CONSTRUCTION SUPERVISION & SAFETY LETTER,** (CL) Bureau of Business Practice, 24 Rope Ferry Rd., Waterford CT 06386. (203)739-0169. Editor: DeLoris Lidestri. Safety Editor: Winifred Bonney, (203)739-0286. 80% freelance written. "We're willing to work with a few new writers if they're willing to follow guidelines carefully." Semimonthly newsletter. Emphasizes all aspects of construction supervision. Buys all rights. Publishes ms an average of 4 months after acceptance. Phone queries OK. Submit seasonal material at least 4 months in advance. Reports in 6 weeks. Free sample copy and writer's guidelines.

Nonfiction: Publishes solid interviews with construction managers or supervisors on how to improve a single aspect of the supervisor's job. Buys 100 unsolicited mss/year. Length: 360-720 words. Pays 10-15¢/word.

Photos: Purchased with accompanying ms. Pays $10 for head and shoulders photo of person interviewed. Safety interviews do not require photo. Total purchase price for ms includes payment for photo.

Tips: "A writer should call before he or she does anything. We like to spend a few minutes on the phone exchanging information."

EMPLOYEE RELATIONS AND HUMAN RESOURCES BULLETIN, Bureau of Business Practice, 24 Rope Ferry Rd., Waterford CT 06386. Senior Editor: Barbara Kelsey. 75% freelance written. Works with a small number of new/unpublished writers each year. For personnel, human resources and employee relations managers on the executive level. Semimonthly newsletter. Circ. 5,500. **Pays on acceptance.** Publishes ms an average of 3 months after acceptance. Buys all rights. No byline. Phone queries OK. Submit seasonal/holiday material 6 months in advance. Reports in 1 month. Free sample copy and writer's guidelines.

Nonfiction: Interviews about all types of business and industry such as banks, insurance companies, public utilities, airlines, consulting firms, etc. Interviewee should be a high level company officer—general manager, president, industrial relations manager, etc. Writer must get signed release from person interviewed showing that article has been read and approved by him/her, before submission. Some subjects for interviews might be productivity improvement, communications, compensation, labor relations, safety and health, grievance handling, human relations techniques and problems, etc. No general opinions and/or philosophy of good employee relations or general good motivation/morale material. Buys 2 mss/issue. Query is mandatory. Length: 1,500-2,000 words. Pays 8-18¢/word after editing. Sometimes pays the telephone expenses of writers on assignment. Modem transmission available by prior arrangement with editor.

INDUSTRY WEEK, The Industry Management Magazine, Penton Publishing Inc., 1100 Superior Ave., Cleveland OH 44114. (216)696-7000. FAX: (216)696-0836. Editor: Charles R. Day, Jr. Associate Mangaging Editors: Dale W. Sommer, John H. Carson. 10-12% freelance written. Industrial management magazine published on the first and third Monday of each month. "*Industry Week* is designed to help its audience—mid- and upper-level managers in industry—manage and lead their organizations better. Every article should address this editorial mission." Estab. 1921. Circ. 300,200. **Pays on acceptance.** Publishes ms an average of 2-4 months after acceptance. Byline given. Buys first North American serial rights. Free sample copy and writer's guidelines. "An SAE speeds replies."

Nonfiction: Interview/profile. "Any article submitted to *Industry Week* should be consistent with its mission. We suggest authors contacting us before submitting anything." Buys 15-20 mss/year. Query with or without published clips, or send complete ms. Length: 750-2,500 words. Pays $350 minimum. "We pay *routine* expenses; we do *not* pay for travel unless arranged in advance."

Photos: State availability of photos with submission. Send photo with submission. Reviews contact sheets, transparencies and prints. Payment arranged individually. Captions and identification of subjects required. Buys one-time rights.

Tips: "Become familiar with *Industry Week*. We're after articles about managing in industry, period. While we do not use freelancers too often, but do use some. The stories we accept are written with an understanding of our audience, and mission. We prefer multi-source stories that offer lessons for all managers in industry."

MANAGE, 2210 Arbor Blvd., Dayton OH 45439. (513)294-0421. FAX: (513)294-2374. Editor-in-Chief: Douglas E. Shaw. 60% freelance written. Works with a small number of new/unpublished writers each year. Quarterly magazine. For first-line and middle management and scientific/technical managers. Estab. 1925. Circ. 75,000. **Pays on acceptance.** Publishes ms an average of 6 months after acceptance. Buys North American magazine rights with reprint privileges; book rights remain with the author. Reports in 1 month. Free sample copy for 9 × 12 SAE; free writer's guidelines.
Nonfiction: "All material published by *Manage* is in some way management oriented. Most articles concern one or more of the following categories: communications, executive abilities, human relations, job status, leadership, motivation and productivity and professionalism. Articles should be specific and tell the manager how to apply the information to his job immediately. Be sure to include pertinent examples, and back up statements with facts and, where possible, charts and illustrations. *Manage* does not want essays or academic reports, but interesting, well-written and practical articles for and about management." Buys 6 mss/issue. Phone queries OK. Submit complete ms. Length, 600-2,000 words. Pays 5¢/word.
Tips: "Keep current on management subjects; submit timely work."

MIDWEST PURCHASING MANAGEMENT and PURCHASING MANAGEMENT, Meyer Associates, Inc., 14 7th Ave. N., St. Cloud MN 56301. (612)259-4000. FAX: (612)259-4044. Editor: Murdock Johnson. Managing Editor: Peg Meyer. 40% freelance written. Monthly magazines covering all aspects of purchasing and materials management. Estab. 1933. Circ. 12,500. Pays on publication. Publishes ms an average of 6 months after acceptance. Byline given. Negotiable kill fee. Buys first rights. Query for electronic submissions. Reports in 1 month. Sample copy for 9 × 12 SAE with 3 first class stamps. Free writer's guidelines.
Nonfiction: Interview/profile, personal experience, technical. No general interest or general business articles, with single exception of economics. "We prefer 'How to Buy' or 'Ten Tips for Buying' format. Articles should feature a class of products (eg. 'How to Choose Office Equipment) rather than single products ('Ten Tips for Buying a Copier'). Must apply to all levels of buyer—entry level to manager." Buys 6 mss/year. Query with published clips. Length: 1,200-3,000 words. Pays $25-150. Sometimes pays expenses of writers on assignment.
Photos: State availability of photos with submission. Reviews contact sheets, negatives, transparencies and prints. Offers no additional payment for photos accepted with ms. Model releases and identification of subjects required.
Tips: "The best ideas and articles come directly from practitioners in the field. Short interviews, or telephone calls, will yield topic ideas. Go for the unusual, the off-the-beaten-path industry or technique. And send an outline first—let's work together to save time and money. A purchaser or materials manager must be all things to all people. He or she doesn't need more general information. Instead, he or she needs very specific information to help do the job better."

NEW MEXICO BUSINESS JOURNAL, Southwest Publications, Inc., P.O. Box 1788, Albuquerque NM 87103. (505)243-5581. Editor-in-Chief: George Hackler. Managing Editor: Jack Hartsfield. 80% freelance written. A monthly magazine covering the state's business community. Estab. 1976. Circ. 20,000. **Pays on acceptance.** Publishes ms an average of 3 months after acceptance. Byline given. Buys first rights. Submit seasonal/holiday material 4 months in advance. Simultaneous submissions OK. Reports in 3 weeks on queries. Sample copy 9 × 12 SAE with 5 first class stamps; guidelines for #10 SASE.
Nonfiction: How-to interview/profile, trends, technical and general interest (real estate, economic development, finance, mining, construction, etc.). Buys 100 mss/year. Query with published clips or send complete manuscript. Length: 8-5,000 words. Pays $50-500 for assigned articles. Sometimes pays the expenses of writers on assignment.
Tips: "We are interested in well-researched articles of interest to owners and top management of small to medium sized businesses. Include several b&w prints with manuscript if the piece lends itself to illustration. We offer no additional payment for photos accepted with manuscripts. Special emphasis on New Mexico business preferred."

PERSONNEL ADVISORY BULLETIN, Bureau of Business Practice, 24 Rope Ferry Rd., Waterford CT 06386. (203)442-4365, ext. 778. Editor: Jill Whitney. 75% freelance written. Eager to work with new/unpublished writers. Emphasizes all aspects of personnel practices for personnel managers in all types and sizes of companies, both white collar and industrial. Semimonthly newsletter. **Pays on acceptance.** Publishes ms an average of 5 months after acceptance. Buys all rights. Submit seasonal/holiday material 4 months in advance. Reports in 2 weeks. Free sample copy and writer's guidelines for 10 × 13 SAE and 2 first class stamps.
Nonfiction: Interviews with personnel managers or human resource professionals on topics of current interest in the personnel field. Avoid articles on hiring and interviewing, discipline or absenteeism/tardiness control. Buys 30 mss/year. Query with brief, specific outline. Length: 1,500-1,800 words.

Tips: "We're looking for concrete, practical material on how to solve problems. We're providing information about trends and developments in the field. We don't want filler copy. It's very easy to break in. Include your phone number with your query so we can discuss the topic. Send for guidelines first, though, so we can have a coherent conversation."

PERSONNEL JOURNAL, The Management Magazine for Personnel Executives, AC Croft, Inc., 245 Fischer Ave., B-2, Costa Mesa CA 92626. (714)751-1883. FAX: (714)751-4106. Editor: Allan Halcrow. Managing Editor: Stephanie Lawrence. 10% freelance written. Monthly magazine. "*Personnel Journal* is targeted to senior human resources executives in companies with 500 or more employees. The editorial content is aimed at helping readers define and improve corporate policy on personnel issues, as well as to identify trends and issues in the field and provide case examples of successful personnel programs." Estab. 1922. Circ. 30,000. **Pays on acceptance.** Publishes ms an average of 2 months after acceptance. Byline given. Offers kill fee of ½ original fee plus expenses. Buys all rights (can be negotiable). Reports in 3 weeks on queries; 1 month on mss. Free sample copy and writer's guidelines.

Nonfiction: How-to (explanation of a personnel-related program or system), opinion (informed commentary on some aspect of personnel management), personal experience (case study detailing a personnel program's development and implementation) and technical (how to use computers in the personnel department; analysis of recent legislation or court decisions). "We do not want literature surveys (a round-up of all published thought on a topic, such as performance appraisals). We do not want anything written to or for employees." Buys 6-8 mss/year. Query with published clips. Length: 4,000 word minimum. Pays $700-3,000 for assigned articles; $500-2,000 for unsolicited articles. Pays with contributor copies when articles submitted by practitioners (not writers) and when terms are understood up-front. Pays expenses of writers on assignment.

Photos: State availability of photos with submission. Reviews 35mm transparencies. Offers $50-200 per photo. Model releases are required. Buys one-time rights.

Tips: "The best way to get into *Personnel Journal* is to base material in reality. Too many writers present management theory with no evidence it has been tried or write a how-to that does not include examples. Be specific—*why* was a program developed, *how* (step-by-step) was it implemented. Also, it's best to assume readers have some sophistication—they do not need basic techniques defined; they want *new* ideas."

PRODUCTION SUPERVISOR'S BULLETIN, Bureau of Business Practice, 24 Rope Ferry Rd., Waterford CT 06386. (800)243-0876. FAX: (203)434-3341. Editor: Anna Maria Trusky. Managing Editor: Wayne N. Muller. 75% freelance written. Biweekly newsletter. "The audience is primarily first-line production supervisors. Articles are meant to address a common workplace issue faced by such a supervisor, (absenteeism, low productivity, etc.) and explain how interviewee dealt with the problem." Circ. 5,000. **Pays on acceptance.** Publishes ms an average of 4 months after acceptance. Byline not given. Buys all rights. Reports in 2 weeks on queries; 3 weeks on mss. Free sample copy and writer's guidelines.

Nonfiction: How-to (on managing people, solving workplace problems, improving productivity). No high-level articles aimed at upper management. Buys 60-70 mss/year. Query. Length: 800-1,500 words. Pays 9-15¢/word.

Tips: "Freelancers may call me at (800)243-0876 or (203)434-6799. Prospective writers are strongly urged to send for writer's guidelines. Sections of publication most open to freelancers are lead story; inside stories (generally 3 to 4 per issue); and Production Management Clinic (in every other issue). Include concrete, how-to steps for dealing effectively with the topic at hand."

SALES MANAGER'S BULLETIN, The Bureau of Business Practice, 24 Rope Ferry Rd., Waterford CT 06386. Editor: Paulette S. Withers. 33% freelance written. Prefers to work with published/established writers. Newsletter published twice/month. For sales managers and salespeople interested in getting into sales management. Estab. 1917. **Pays on acceptance.** Publishes ms an average of 3-6 months after acceptance. Written queries only except from regulars. Submit seasonal/holiday material 6 months in advance. Original interview-based material only. Buys all rights. Reports in 2 weeks. Sample copy and writer's guidelines only when request is accompanied by SAE with 2 first clas stamps.

Nonfiction: How-to (motivate salespeople, cut costs, create territories, etc.); interview (with working sales managers who use innovative techniques); and technical (marketing stories based on interviews with experts). No articles on territory management, saving fuel in the field, or public speaking skills. Break into this publication by reading the guidelines and sample issue. Follow the directions closely and chances for acceptance go up dramatically. One easy way to start is with an interview article ("Here's what sales executives have to say about . . ."). Query is vital to acceptance: "send a simple postcard explaining briefly the subject matter, the interviewees, slant, length, and date of expected completion, accompanied by a SASE. Does not accept unqueried mss." Length: 800-1,000 words. Pays 10-15¢/word.

Tips: "Freelancers should always request samples and writer's guidelines, accompanied by SASE. Requests without SASE are discarded immediately. Examine the sample, and don't try to improve on our style. Write as we write. Don't 'jump around' from point to point and don't submit articles that are too chatty and with not enough real information. The more time a writer can save the editors, the greater his or her chance of a sale and repeated sales, when queries may not be necessary any longer. We will focus more on selling more product, meeting intense competiton, while spending less money to do it."

SUPERVISOR'S BULLETIN, Bureau of Business Practice, 24 Rope Ferry Rd., Waterford CT 06386. (203)442-4365. FAX: (203)434-3078. Editor: Kelly Donlon. 50-75% freelance written. "We work with both new and established writers, and are always looking for fresh talent." Bimonthly newsletter for manufacturing supervisors wishing to improve their managerial skills. Estab. 1915. **Pays on acceptance.** Publishes ms on average of 2 months after acceptance. No byline given. Buys all rights. Reports in 2 weeks on queries, 6 weeks on mss. Free sample copy and writer's guidelines.

Nonfiction: How-to (solve a supervisory problem on the job); and interview (of top-notch supervisors). Sample topics could include: how-to increase productivity, cut costs, achieve better teamwork." No filler or non-interview based copy. Buys 72 mss/year. Query first. "Strongly urge writers to study guidelines and samples." Length: 750-1,000 words. Pays 8-16¢/word.

Tips: "We need interview-based articles that emphasize direct quotes. Define a problem and show how the supervisor solved it. Write in a light, conversational style, talking directly to supervisors who can benefit from putting the interviewee's tips into practice. We will focus on more safety issues. More articles will cover how supervisors can ensure safety in the workplace."

TRAINING, The Magazine of Human Resources Development, Lakewood Publications, 50 S. Ninth St., Minneapolis MN 55402. (612)333-0471. Editor: Jack Gordon. Managing Editor: Chris Lee. 10% freelance written. A monthly magazine covering training and employee development in the business world. "Our core readers are managers and professionals who specialize in employee training and development (e.g., corporate training directors, VP-human resource development, etc.). We have a large secondary readership among managers of all sorts who are concerned with improving human performance in their organizations. We take a businesslike approach to training and employee education." Estab. 1964. Circ. 52,000. **Pays on acceptance.** Publishes ms an average of 3 months after acceptance. Byline given. Buys first North American serial rights and second serial (reprint) rights. Simultaneous submissions OK. Reports in 2 weeks on queries; 6 weeks on mss. Sample copy for 9×12 SAE with 4 first class stamps. Writer's guidelines for #10 SASE.

Nonfiction: Essay; exposé; how-to (on training, management, sales, productivity improvement, etc.); humor; interview/profile; new product; opinion; photo feature; and technical (use of audiovisual aids, computers, etc.). "No puff, no 'testimonials' or disguised ads in any form, no 'gee-whiz' approaches to the subjects." Buys 10-12 mss/year. Query with or without published clips, or send complete ms. Length: 200-3,000 words. Pays $50-600.

Photos: State availability of photos or send with submission. Reviews contact sheets and prints. Offers no additional payment for photos accepted with ms. Identification of subjects required. Buys one-time rights and reprint rights.

Columns/Departments: Training Today (news briefs, how-to tips, reports on pertinent research, trend analysis, etc.), 200-800 words. Buys 6 mss/year. Query or send complete ms. Pays $50-75.

Tips: "We would like to develop a few freelancers to work with on a regular basis. We almost never give firm assignments to unfamiliar writers, so you have to be willing to hit us with one or two on spec to break in. Short pieces for our Training Today section involve least investment on your part, but also are less likely to convince us to assign you a feature. When studying the magazine, freelancers should look at our staff-written articles for style, approach and tone. Do not concentrate on articles written by people identified as consultants, training directors, etc."

UTILITY SUPERVISION, Bureau of Business Practice, 24 Rope Ferry Rd., Waterford CT 06386. (203)739-0169. Editor: DeLoris Lidestri. 80% freelance written. "We're willing to work with a few new writers if they're willing to follow guidelines carefully." Semimonthly newsletter emphasizing all aspects of utility supervision. **Pays on acceptance.** Publishes ms an average of 4 months after acceptance. Buys all rights. Phone queries OK. Submit seasonal material 4 months in advance. Reports in 6 weeks. Free sample copy and writer's guidelines.

Nonfiction: Publishes how-to (interview on a single aspect of supervision with utility manager/supervisor concentrating on how reader/supervisor can improve in that area). Buys 100 mss/year. Query. Length: 360-750 words. Pays 10-15¢/word.

Photos: Purchased with accompanying ms. Pays $10 for head and shoulders photo of person interviewed. Total purchase price for ms includes payment for photo.

Tips: "A writer should call before he or she does anything. I like to spend a few minutes on the phone exchanging information."

WAREHOUSING SUPERVISOR'S BULLETIN, Bureau of Business Practice, 24 Rope Ferry Rd., Waterford CT 06386. (203)442-4365. FAX: (203)434-3078. Editor: April L. Katz. 75-90% freelance written. "We work with a wide variety of writers, and are always looking for fresh talent." Biweekly newsletter covering traffic, materials handling and distribution for warehouse supervisors "interested in becoming more effective on the job." **Pays on acceptance.** Publishes ms an average of 3 months after acceptance. No byline given. Buys all rights. Reports in 2 weeks on queries; 6 weeks on mss. Free sample copy and writer's guidelines.

Nonfiction: How-to (increase efficiency, control or cut costs, cut absenteeism or tardiness, increase productivity, raise morale); and interview (of warehouse supervisors or managers who have solved problems on the job). No noninterview articles, textbook-like descriptions, union references or advertising of products. Buys 50 mss/year. Query. "A resumé and sample of work are helpful." Length: 1,580-2,900 words. Pays 10-15¢/word. Sometimes pays the expenses of writers on assignment.

Tips: "All articles must be interview-based and emphasize how-to information. They should also include a reference to the interviewee's company (location, size, products, function of the interviewee's department and number of employees under his control). Focus articles on one problem, and get the interviewee to pinpoint the best way to solve it. Write in a light, conversational style, talking directly to warehouse supervisors who can benefit from putting the interviewee's tips into practice."

Marine and Maritime Industries

‡**CANADIAN AQUACULTURE,** Harrison House Publishers, 4611 William Head Rd., Victoria, British Columbia V8X 3W9 Canada. (604)478-9209. FAX: (604)478-1184. Editor: Peter Chettleburgh. 50% freelance written. Works with a small number of new/unpublished writers each year. A bimonthly magazine covering aquaculture in Canada. Estab. 1985. Circ. 3,500. Pays on publication. Publishes ms an average of 3 months after acceptance. Byline given. Buys first North American serial rights. Submit seasonal/holiday material 5 months in advance. Reports in 3 weeks. Free sample copy for 9 × 12 SAE with $2 IRCs.; free writer's guidelines.

Nonfiction: How-to, interview/profile, new product, opinion and photo feature. Buys 20-24 mss/year. Query. Length: 200-1,500 words. Pays 10-20¢/word for assigned articles; pays 10-15¢/word for unsolicited articles. May pay writers with contributor copies if writer requests. Sometimes pays the expenses of writers on assignment.

Photos: Send photos with submission. Reviews 5 × 7 prints. Captions required. Buys one-time rights.

PROCEEDINGS, U.S. Naval Institute, Annapolis MD 21402. (301)268-6110. Editor: Fred H. Rainbow. Managing Editor: John G. Miller. 95% freelance written. Eager to work with new/published writers. Monthly magazine covering naval and maritime subjects. Circ. 100,000. **Pays on acceptance.** Publishes ms an average of 5 months after acceptance. Byline given. Buys all rights. Submit seasonal/holiday material 3 months in advance. Reports in 2 weeks on queries; 1 month on mss. Free sample copy and writer's guidelines.

Nonfiction: Essays, exposé, general interest, historical/nostalgic, how-to (related to sea service professional subjects), humor, interview/profile, new product, opinion, personal experience, photo feature and technical. "*Proceedings* is an unofficial, open forum for the discussion of naval and maritime topics." Special issues include International Navies (March) and Naval Review (May). Buys 250 mss/year. Query or send complete ms. Length: up to 3,500 words. Pays $50-600. Sometimes pays writers with contributor copies or other premiums "if author desires." Sometimes pays the expenses of writers on assignment.

Photos: Send photos with submission. Reviews contact sheets, negatives, transparencies and prints. Offers $10-100 per photo. Buys one-time rights.

Columns/Departments: Book Reviews, Nobody Asked Me About . . ., and Crossword Puzzles (all with naval or maritime slants), all 500-2,000 words. Buys 90 mss/year. Query. Pays $50-200.

Fiction: Adventure, historical and humorous. Buys 4 mss/year. Query. Length: 500-3,000 words. Pays $50-600.

Fillers: Anecdotes. Buys 50/year. Length: 1,000 words maximum. Pays $25-150.

Tips: "Write about something you know about, either from first-hand experience or based on primary source material. Our letters to the editor column is most open to freelancers."

WORKBOAT, P.O. Box 1348, Mandeville LA 70470. (504)626-0298. FAX: (504)624-4801. Editor: Robert Carpenter. Associate Editor: Marilyn Barrett. 60% freelance written. Bimonthly magazine on all working boats: commerical inland and near shore. Target work boat owners, boat captains, operators, service companies and related businesses." Estab. 1943. Pays on acceptance or publication. Publishes ms average of 2 months after acceptance. Byline given. Offers negotiable kill fee. Buys first time rights. Query for electronic submissions. Sample copy for 9 × 12 SAE and $2.50; writer's guidelines for #10 SASE.

Nonfiction: General interest, how-to, interview/profile and technical. Query or query with published clips. Sometimes pays expenses of writers on assignment.

Photos: State availability of photos with submission. Reviews contact sheets and transparencies, prefers color. Pay negotiable. Identification of subjects required. Buys one-time rights.

Tips: "Learn all you can about tugs, barges, supply boats, passenger vessels (excursion and ferry), dredges, fire boats, patrol boats and any vessel doing business on America's inland waterways, harbors and close to shore. Also, familiarity with issues affecting the maritime industry is a plus."

Medical

Through these journals physicians, pharmacists, therapists and mental health professionals learn how other professionals help their patients and manage their medical practices. Publications for nurses, laboratory technicians and other medical personnel are listed in the Hospitals, Nursing and Nursing Home section. Publications for drug store managers and drug wholesalers and retailers, as well as hospital equipment suppliers, are listed with Drugs, Health Care and Medical Products. Publications for consumers that report trends in the medical field are found in the Consumer Health and Fitness categories.

AMERICAN MEDICAL NEWS, American Medical Association, 535 N. Dearborn St., Chicago IL 60610. (312)645-5000. Editor: Dick Walt. Executive Editor: Barbara Bolsen. 5-10% freelance written. "Prefers writers already interested in the health care field—not clinical medicine." Weekly tabloid providing nonclinical information for physicians—information on socio-economic, political and other developments in medicine. "*AMN* is a specialized publication circulating to physicians, covering subjects touching upon their profession, practices and personal lives. This is a well-educated, highly sophisticated audience." Circ. 375,000 physicians. **Pays on acceptance.** Publishes ms an average of 2 months after acceptance. Byline given. Offers variable kill fee. Buys all rights. Rights sometimes returnable on request after publication. Simultaneous queries OK. Reports in 1 month. Sample copy for 9 × 12 SAE and 2 first class stamps. Free writer's guidelines.
Nonfiction: Flora Johnson Skelly, assistant executive editor for outside contributions. Interview/profile (occasional); opinion (mainly from physicians); and news and interpretive features. Special issues include "Year in Review" issue published in January. No clinical articles, general-interest articles physicians would see elsewhere, or recycled versions of articles published elsewhere. Buys 200 mss/year. Query. Length: 200-4,000 words. Pays $400-750 for features; $50-100 for opinions and short news items. "We have limited travel budget for freelancers; we pay minimal local expenses."
Tips: "We are trying to create a group of strong feature writers who will be regular contributors."

THE BEST REPORT, Exploring the World of Quality, Wilton Communications, Inc., 140 E. 45th St., 36th Fl., New York NY 10017. (212)983-4320. Editor: Peter Filichia. 20% freelance written. Monthly magazine. "*The Best Report* is an upscale lifestyle magazine distributed by pharmaceutical companies to doctors nationwide. Articles cover an eclectic mix of luxury goods, services and travel destinations. Our only restriction: everything we write about must be top-of-the-line." Circ. 150,000. **Pays on acceptance.** Publishes ms an average of 3 months after acceptance. No byline, but contributors are listed in masthead under "Contributors to this issue." Offers 25% kill fee. Buys first rights. Submit seasonal/holiday material 4 months in advance. Query for electronic submissions. Reports in 1 month. Free sample copy and writer's guidelines.
Nonfiction: General interest (collectibles, sporting and cultural events, shopping, food, restaurants, roundups—eg. the best places to scuba dive in the world), and other (feature on a classic best—eg. the Jaguar). "We do not want fiction or travel, which is done in-house." Buys about 40 mss/year. Query with published clips. Length: 600-1,400 words. Pays 30¢/word for all articles accepted. Sometimes pays phone and other incidentals of writers on assignment.
Photos: Send photos with submission. Reviews color transparencies and prints. Offers no additional payment for photos accepted with ms. Identification of subjects required.
Columns/Departments: Best Finds (highlights of interesting new gadgets, resorts, restaurants; unusual events), 300-800 words or less. Query with published clips. Pays 30¢/word.
Tips: "In general, articles should be lively, authoritative and concise. Writers should consult with experts and should always include prices, addresses and phone numbers for more information."

CARDIOLOGY WORLD NEWS, Medical Publishing Enterprises, P.O. Box 1548, Marco Island FL 33969. (813)394-0400. Editor: John H. Lavin. 75% freelance written. Prefers to work with published/established writers. Monthly magazine covering cardiology and the cardiovascular system. "We need short news articles *for doctors* on any aspect of our field—diagnosis, treatment, risk factors, etc." Estab. 1985. **Pays on acceptance.** Publishes ms an average of 2 months after acceptance. Byline given "for special reports and feature-length articles." Offers 20% kill fee. Buys first North American serial rights. Query for electronic submissions. Reports in 1 month. Sample copy $1; free writer's guidelines with #10 SASE.
Nonfiction: New product and technical (clinical). No fiction, fillers, profiles of doctors or poetry. Query with published clips. Length: 250-1,500 words. Pays $50-300; $50/column for news articles. Pays expenses of writers on assignment.
Photos: State availability of photos with query. Pays $50/published photo. Rough captions, model release and identification of subjects required. Buys one-time rights.
Tips: "Submit written news articles of 250-500 words on speculation with basic source material (not interview notes) for fact-checking. We demand clinical or writing expertise for full-length feature. Clinical cardiology conventions/symposia are the best source of news and feature articles."

CINCINNATI MEDICINE, Academy of Medicine, 320 Broadway, Cincinnati OH 45202. (513)421-7010. Managing Editor: Vicki L. Black. 40-50% freelance written. Works with a small number of new/unpublished writers each year. Quarterly membership magazine for the Academy of Medicine of Cincinnati. "We cover socio-economic and political factors that affect the practice of medicine in Cincinnati. For example: How will changes in Medicare policies affect local physicians and what will they mean for the quality of care Cincinnati's elderly patients receive. (Ninety-nine percent of our readers are Cincinnati physicians.)" Estab. 1978. Circ. 3,500. **Pays on acceptance.** Publishes ms an average of 3-6 months after acceptance. Byline given. Makes work-for-hire assignments. Simultaneous queries OK. Reports in 6 weeks on queries; 1 month on mss. Sample copy for $3 and 9 × 12 SAE and 7 first class stamps; writer's guidelines for #10 SASE.
Nonfiction: Historical/nostalgic (history of, or reminiscences about, medicine in Cincinnati); interview/profile (of nationally known medical figures or medical leaders in Cincinnati); and opinion (opinion pieces on controversial medico-legal and medico-ethical issues). "We do not want: scientific-research articles, stories that are not based on good journalistic skills (no seat-of-the-pants reporting), or why my 'doc' is the greatest guy in the world stories." Buys 10-12 mss/year. Query with published clips or send complete ms. Length: 800-2,500 words. Pays $125-300. Sometimes pays expenses of writers on assignment.
Photos: State availability of photos with query or ms. Captions and identification of subjects required. Buys one-time rights.
Tips: "Send published clips; do some short features that will help you develop some familiarity with our magazine and our audience; and show initiative to tackle the larger stories. First-time writers often don't realize the emphasis we place on solid reporting. We want accurate, well-balanced reporting or analysis. Our job is to *inform* our readers."

CONSULTANT PHARMACIST, American Society of Consultant Pharmacists, Suite 515, 2300 S. 9th St., Arlington VA 22204. (703)920-8492. FAX: (703)892-2084. Editor: L. Michael Posey. Managing Editor: Joanne Kaldy. 10% freelance written. A monthly magazine on consultant pharmacy. "We do not promote drugs or companies but rather ideas and information." Circ. 10,000. **Pays on acceptance.** Publishes ms an average of 2 months after acceptance. Byline given. Buys first North American serial rights. Query for electronic submissions. Reports in 2 weeks. Sample copy for 9 × 12 SAE with 4 first class stamps. Writer's guidelines for #10 SASE.
Nonfiction: How-to (related to consultant pharmacy), interview/profile, technical. Buys 10 mss/year. Query with published clips. Length: 750-2,000 words. Pays $300-1,200. Sometimes pays expenses of writers on assignment.
Photos: Send photos with submission. Offers $100/per photo session. Captions, model releases, identification of subjects required. Buys one-time rights.
Tips: "This journal is devoted to consultant pharmacy, so articles must relate to this field."

‡DIAGNOSTIC IMAGING, Miller Freeman, 500 Howard St., San Francisco CA 94105. Publisher: Thomas Kemp. Editor: Peter Ogle. 10% freelance written. Monthly news magazine covering radiology, nuclear medicine, magnetic resonance, and ultrasound for physicians in diagnostic imaging professions. Estab. 1902. Circ. 24,000. Average issue includes 4-5 features. **Pays on acceptance.** Publishes ms an average of 2-3 months after acceptance. Byline given. Buys all rights. No phone queries. "Written query should be well-written, concise and contain a brief outline of proposed article and a description of the approach or perspective the author is taking." Submit seasonal material 1 month in advance. Simultaneous submissions OK. Query for electronic submissions. Reports in 2 weeks. Free sample copy.
Nonfiction: "We are interested in topical news features in the areas of radiology, magnetic resonance imaging, nuclear medicine and ultrasound, especially news of state and federal legislation, new products, insurance, regulations, medical literature, professional meetings and symposia and continuing education." Buys 10-12 mss/year. Query with published clips. Length: 1,000-2,000 words. Pays 25¢/word minimum. Sometimes pays the expenses of writers on assignment.
Photos: Reviews 5 × 7 b&w glossy prints and 35mm and larger color transparencies. Offers $20 for photos accepted with ms. Captions required. Buys one-time rights.

DOCTORS SHOPPER, Marketing Communications, Inc., 949 E. 99 St., Brooklyn NY 11236. (718)257-8484. FAX: (718)257-8845. Publisher: Ralph Selitzer. 35% freelance written. Quarterly magazine on medical business, travel, finances, lifestyle articles for doctors. Circ. 211,000. Pays on publication. Byline given. Buys one-time rights. Submit seasonal/holiday material 6 months in advance. Previously published submissions OK. Reports in 1 month. Free sample copy for 9 × 12 SAE and 12 first class stamps. Writer's guidelines for #10 SASE.
Nonfiction: General interest, new product, photo feature, technical, travel and financial. Buys 8 mss/year. Send complete ms. Length: 250-2,000 words. Pays $250-500 for assigned articles; $125-250 for unsolicited articles.
Photos: State availability of photos with submission. Reviews contact sheets and 2 × 2 transparencies. Offers no additional payment for photos accepted with ms. Captions, model releases and identification of subjects required. Buys one-time rights.

Columns/Departments: CME Travel (travel articles for doctors attending continuing education conferences), 500-1,000 words. Buys 4 mss/year. Pays $125-250.

Fillers: Anecdotes, facts, gags to be illustrated by cartoonist, all *medical*. Buys 8/year. Length: 100-500 words. Pays $25-50.

Tips: "Contribute self help articles for physicians on serving patients better, run a more efficient practice, enjoy leisure time, travel, etc. Travel articles, new medical office methods, actual physician case histories are areas most open to freelancers."

EMERGENCY, The Journal of Emergency Services, 6300 Yarrow Drive, Carlsbad CA 92009. (619)438-2511. FAX: (619)931-5809. Editor: Tara C. Regan.100% freelance written. Works with a small number of new/unpublished writers each year. A monthly magazine covering pre-hospital emergency care. "Our readership is primarily composed of EMTs, paramedics and other EMS personnel. We prefer a professional, semi-technical approach to pre-hospital subjects." Estab. 1969. Circ. 25,000. **Pays on acceptance.** Publishes ms an average of 4 months after acceptance. Byline given. Buys all rights, (revert back to author after 90 days). Submit seasonal/holiday material 6 months in advance. Reports in 2 months. Sample copy $3; writer's guidelines for #10 SASE.

Nonfiction: Semi-technical exposé, how-to (on treating pre-hospital emergency patients), interview/profile, new techniques, opinion and photo feature. "We do not publish cartoons, color *print* photos, term papers, product promotions disguised as articles or overly technical manuscripts." Buys 10 mss/year. Query with published clips. Length 1,500-3,000 words. Pays $100-400.

Photos: Send photos with submission. Reviews color transparencies and b&w prints. Offers no additional payment for photos accepted with ms. Offers $30/photo without ms.; $100 for cover photos. Captions and identification of subjects required.

Columns/Departments: Open Forum (opinion page for EMS professionals), 500 words. Trauma Primer (pre-hospital care topics, treatment of injuries, etc.), 1,000-2,000 words. Drug Watch (focus on one particular drug a month). Buys 10 mss/year. Query first. Pays $100-250.

Fillers: Facts and newsbreaks. Buys 10/year. Length: no more than 500 words. Pays $0-75.

Tips: "Writing style for features and departments should be knowledgeable and lively with a clear theme or story line to maintain reader interest and enhance comprehension. The biggest problem we encounter is dull, lifeless term-paper-style writing with nothing to pique reader interest. Keep in mind we are not a textbook. Accompanying photos are a plus.We appreciate a short, one paragraph biography on the author."

‡FACETS, American Medical Association Auxiliary, Inc., 535 N. Dearborn St., Chicago IL 60610. (312)645-4470. FAX: (312)645-4184. Editor: Kathleen T. Jordan. Works with both established and new writers. For physicians' spouses. 30% freelance written. Magazine published 6 times/year. Estab. 1965. Circ. 90,000. **Pays on acceptance.** Publishes ms an average of 6 months after acceptance. Buys first rights. Simultaneous, and previously published submissions OK. Reports in 6 weeks. Free sample copy and writer's guidelines.

Nonfiction: All articles must be related to the experiences of physicians' spouses. Current health issues; financial topics; physicians' family circumstances; business management; volunteer leadership how-to's. Buys 20 mss/year. Query with clear outline of article—what points will be made, what conclusions drawn, what sources will be used. No personal experience or personality stories. Length: 1,000-2,500 words. Pays $300-800. Pays expenses of writers on assignment.

Photos: State availability of photos with query. Uses 8×10 glossy b&w prints and 2¼×2¼ transparencies.

Tips: Uses "articles only on specified topical matter with good sources, not hearsay or personal opinion. Since we use only nonfiction and have a limited readership, we must relate factual material."

FAMILY THERAPY NEWS, American Association for Marriage and Family Therapy, #407, 1717 K St. NW, Washington DC 20006. (202)429-1825. Editor: William C. Nichols. Managing Editor: Kimberly A. Tilley. 10% freelance written. Newspaper for professional organization covering family therapy, family policy, mental health and behavior sciences. *FT News* is a professional newspaper serving marital and family therapists. Writers should be able to reach both doctoral level and graduate student readers. Circ. 16,000. **Pays on acceptance.** Publishes ms an average of 3 months after acceptance. Byline given. Buys first North American serial rights. Submit seasonal/holiday material 6 months in advance. Query for electronic submissions. Reports in 2 weeks. Sample copy and writer's guidelines for 9×12 SAE with 3 first class stamps.

Nonfiction: Only want materials pertaining to the field of family therapy, family policy, family research, mental health and behavioral science for professionals. Query with or without published clips, or send complete ms. Length: 300-1,800 words. Pays $25-200.

Photos: State availability of photos with submission. Reviews 8×10 prints. Payment negotiable. Identification of subjects required. Buys one-time rights.

Columns/Departments: Family Therapy Forum (wide variety of topics and slants on family therapy, education, training, practice, service delivery, the therapists, family therapists in various countries, opinion), to 1,800 words; In Focus (interview with outstanding therapists, other leaders), to 1,500 words. Send complete ms. Length: 600-1,800. Pays $25-100.

Fillers: Facts. Length: 100-300 words. Pays $10-25.

Tips: "The annual conference is a major source of good material for writers, such as those of the American Family Therapy Association. Query editor. Also, we are in need of short, well-written features on current developments in the field. Materials could be developed into columns as well for Family Therapy Forum in some instances, but straight news-based features are the best bet."

FITNESS MANAGEMENT, Issues and solutions for fitness services, Leisure Publications, Inc., Suite 213, 215 S. Highway 101, P.O. Box 1198, Solana Beach CA 92075. (619)481-4155. Editor: Edward H. Pitts. 50% freelance written. Monthly magazine covering commercial, corporate and community fitness centers. "Readers are owners, managers and program directors of physical fitness facilities. *FM* helps them run their enterprises safely, efficiently and profitably. Ethical and professional positions in health, nutrition, sports medicine, management, etc., are consistent with those of established national bodies." Estab. 1985. Circ. 21,000. Pays on publication. Publishes ms an average of 5 months after acceptance. Byline given. Pays 50% kill fee. Buys all rights. Submit seasonal/holiday material 6 months in advance. Query for electronic submissions. Reports in 1 month on queries; 2 months on mss. Writer's guidelines for #10 SASE. Sample copy for $5.

Nonfiction: Book excerpts (prepublication), how-to (manage fitness center and program), new product (no pay), photo feature (facilities/programs), technical and other (news of fitness research and major happenings in fitness industry). No exercise instructions or general ideas without examples of fitness businesses that have used them successfully. Buys 50 mss/year. Query. Length: 750-2,000 words. Pays $60-300 for assigned articles; pays up to $300 for unsolicited articles. Pays expenses of writers on assignment.

Photos: Send photos with submission. Reviews contact sheets, 2 × 2 and 4 × 5 transparencies and 5 × 7 prints. Offers $10 per photo. Captions and model releases required.

Tips: "We seek writers who are expert in a business or science field related to the fitness-service industry or who are experienced in the industry. Be current with the state of the art/science in business and fitness and communicate it in human terms (avoid intimidating academic language; tell the story of how this was learned and/or cite examples of quotes of people who have applied the knowledge successfully)."

GERIATRIC CONSULTANT, Medical Publishing Enterprises, P.O. Box 1548, Marco Island FL 33969. (813)394-0400. Editor: John H. Lavin. 70% freelance written. Prefers to work with published/established writers. Bimonthly magazine for physicians covering medical care of the elderly. "We're a clinical magazine directed to doctors and physician assistants. All articles must *help* these health professionals to help their elderly patients. We're too tough a market for nonmedical beginners." Estab. 1982. Circ. 97,500. **Pays on acceptance.** Publishes ms an average of 3-6 months after acceptance. Byline given. Offers 20% kill fee. Buys first North American serial rights. Simultaneous queries OK. Query for electronic submissions. Reports in 1 month. Sample copy for $1; writer's guidelines for #10 SASE.

Nonfiction: How-to (diagnosis and treatment of health problems of the elderly) and technical/clinical. No fiction or articles directed to a lay audience. Buys 20 mss/year. Query. Length: 750-3,000 words. Pays $200-350 for features; $50-100 for 250 word-plus news articles. Pays expenses of writers on assignment.

Photos: State availability of photos. (Photos are not required.) Model release and identification of subjects required. Buys one-time rights.

Tips: "Many medical meetings are now held in the field of geriatric care. These offer potential sources and subjects for us."

GROUP PRACTICE JOURNAL, American Group Practice Association, 1422 Duke St., Alexandria VA 22314-3430. (703)838-0033. FAX: (703)548-1890. Editor: Charles Honaker. 30% freelance written. Bimonthly magazine on medical group practices. Estab. 1951. Circ. 46,000. Pays on publication. Publishes ms an average of 6 months after acceptance. Byline given. Buys first North American serial rights. Query for electronic submissions. Free sample copy for 11 × 14 SAE and writer's guidelines with #10 SASE.

Nonfiction: How-to, opinion, technical, socio-economic aspects of medical group practices. Buys 10 mss/year. Send complete ms. Length: 1,000-3,000 words. Pays $500-1,000.

Photos: State availability of photos with submissions. Reviews contact sheets, negatives, transparencies, prints. Captions, model releases and identification of subjects required. Buy all rights.

Columns/Departments: Taxes (tax tips); Marketing (medical marketing tips); Legal Forum (law-legislation analysis). Query. Length: 500-1,000 words. Pays $300-500.

Tips: "Call the editor and chat. Discuss story ideas, news needs. Visit a medical group practice and learn what the doctors, CEOs read and want to read."

THE JOURNAL, Addiction Research Foundation of Ontario, 33 Russell St., Toronto, Ontario M5S 2S1 Canada. (416)964-9235. Editor: Anne MacLennan. Managing Editor: Elda Hauschildt. 50% freelance written. Prefers to work with published/established writers. Monthly tabloid covering addictions and related fields around the world. "*The Journal* alerts professionals in the addictions and related fields or disciplines to news events, issues, opinions and developments of potential interest and/or significance to them in their work, and provides them an informed context in which to judge developments in their own specialty/geographical areas." Circ. 10,000. Pays on publication. Publishes ms an average of 3 months after acceptance. Byline

given. Kill fee negotiable. Not copyrighted. Buys first serial rights and second serial (reprint) rights. Reports in 2 months on queries; 3 months on mss. Sample copy and writer's guidelines 9 × 12 SAE.
Nonfiction: Only. Query with published clips or send complete ms. Length: 1,000 words maximum. Pays 22¢/word minimum. Sometimes pays the expenses of writers on assignment.
Photos: Elda Hauschildt, managing editor. State availability of photos. Pays $25 and up for 5 × 7 or 8 × 10 b&w prints. Captions, model release, and identification of subjects required. Buys one-time rights.
Columns/Departments: Under contract.
Tips: "A freelancer can best break in to our publication with six years reporting experience, preferably with medical/science writing background. We rarely use untried writers."

THE NEW PHYSICIAN, 1890 Preston White Dr., Reston VA 22091. Editor: Richard Camer. 30% freelance written. For medical students, interns and residents. Published 9 times/year. Circ. 40,000. Buys first serial rights. Pays on publication. Publishes features an average of 2 months after acceptance. Will consider simultaneous submissions. Reports in 2 months. Sample copy for 10 × 13 SAE with 5 first class stamps; writer's guidelines for SASE.
Nonfiction: Articles on social, political, economic issues in medicine/medical education. "We want skeptical, accurate, professional contributors to do well-researched, comprehensive, incisive reports and offer new perspectives on health care problems. Not interested in highly technical or clinical material. Humorous articles and cartoons welcome." Buys about 12 features/year plus 6 departments. Query or send complete ms. Length: 500-3,500 words. Pays $75-650 with higher fees for selected pieces. Pays expenses of writers on assignment.
Tips: "We need more practically oriented articles for physicians-in-training—how-to's for young doctors starting out. We are not however, *Medical Economics.* They must be authoritative, and from objective sources, not a consultant trying to sell his services. Our magazine demands sophistication on the issues we cover. We are a professional magazine for readers with a progressive view on health care issues and a particular interest in improving the health care system. Freelancers should be willing to look deeply into the issues in question and not be satisfied with a cursory review of those issues."

THE NEW YORK DOCTOR, Chase Communications, Suite 710, 45 John St., New York NY 10038. (212)608-4048. FAX: (212)964-9885. Biweekly news and city magazine for physicians in the five boroughs, Long Island and Westchester. "Our magazine covers AIDS, nursing shortages, malpractice and legislative issues affecting New York-area doctors. Estab. 1985. Circ. 15,000. **Pays on acceptance.** Byline given. No kill fee. Buys first North American serial rights or second rights. Query for electronic submissions. Reports in 1 month on mss. Sample copy for 8 × 10 SAE with 3 first class stamps.
Nonfiction: "We do not want anything too clinical or technical. Buys 35-60 mss/year. Query with published clips. Length: 250-1,500 words. Pays $25-350 for assigned articles.
Photos: State availability of photos with submission. Reviews contact sheets, negatives and prints. Payment varies. Captions and identification of subjects required.
Columns/Departments: Query. Inside-talk (hospitals, government, pharmaceutical companies), Medicare, The Environment/Medical Waste Management, After Hours (New York area physicians' hobbies, life-styles), Recruitment (trends at hospitals, managed-care companies, pharmaceutical companies), Malpractice, Office Labs, Op-Ed (by health-care experts), Research (human-interest behind the effort).

‡**PERINATAL PRESS**, Perinatal Press, Inc., 52nd and F Sts., Sacramento CA 95819. (916)733-1750. Executive Editor: J.M. Schneider, M.D. Managing Editor: K. Mulligan. A newsletter published 6 times per year for perinatal health care providers. Estab. 2,500. Circ. 5,000. Pays on publication. Publishes ms an average of 8 months after acceptance. Byline given. Buys first North American serial rights. Reports in 3 weeks on queries; 6 weeks on mss. Sample copy $3 (guidelines are on inside front cover of each issue).
Nonfiction: How-to, humor, opinion, technical and review articles. Buys 4-6 mss/year. Query. Pays $75-150 for assigned articles. May pay with premiums rather than cash for short pieces, such as book reviews.
Photos: State availability of photos with submission. Reviews 3 × 5 prints. Offers no additional payment for photos accepted with ms. Captions required. Buys one-time rights.
Tips: "Feature articles are most open to freelancers. We have a *professional audience* and need well written articles with nonsexist language, and family-centered care philosophy."

THE PHYSICIAN AND SPORTSMEDICINE, McGraw-Hill, 4530 W. 77th St., Edina MN 55435. (612)835-3222. Acquisitions Manager: Lauren C. Pacelli. Managing Editor: Robin Bodishbaugh. 30% freelance written. Prefers to work with published/established writers. Monthly magazine covering medical aspects of sports and exercise. "We look for feature articles or subjects of practical interest to our physician audience." Circ. 130,000. **Pays on acceptance.** Publishes ms an average of 2 months after acceptance. Byline given. Buys one-time rights. Reports in 1 month. Sample copy for $4; writer's guidelines for #10 SASE.
Nonfiction: Interview (persons active in this field); and technical (new developments in sports medicine). Query. Length: 250-2,500 words. Pays $150-900.
Photos: Ann Harsfe, photo editor. State availability of photos. Buys one-time rights.

PHYSICIAN'S MANAGEMENT, Edgell Communications Health Care Publications, 7500 Old Oak Blvd., Cleveland OH 44130. (216)243-8100. FAX: (216)891-2683. Editor: Bob Feigenbaum. Prefers to work with published/established writers. Monthly magazine emphasizes finances, investments, malpractice, socioeconomic issues, estate and retirement planning, small office administration, practice management, computers, and taxes for primary care physicians in private practice. Estab. 1960. Circ. 110,000. **Pays on acceptance.** Publishes ms an average of 6 months after acceptance. Buys all rights. Submit seasonal or holiday material 5 months in advance. Query for electronic submissions. Reports in 1 month. Sample copy $3.50. Writer's guidelines for #10 SASE.
Nonfiction: *"Physician's Management* is a practice management/economic publication, not a clinical one." Publishes how-to articles (limited to medical practice management); informational (when relevant to audience); and personal experience articles (if written by a physician). No fiction, clinical material or satire that portrays MD in an unfavorable light; or soap opera, "real-life" articles. Length: 2,000-2,500 words. Query with SASE. Pays $125/3-column printed page. Use of charts, tables, graphs, sidebars and photos strongly encouraged. Sometimes pays expenses of writers on assignment.
Tips: "Talk to doctors first about their practices, financial interests, and day-to-day nonclinical problems and then query us. Also, the ability to write a concise, well-structured and well-researched magazine article is essential. Freelancers who think like patients fail with us. Those who can think like MDs are successful. Our magazine is growing significantly. The opportunities for good writers will, therefore, increase greatly."

PODIATRY MANAGEMENT, P.O. Box 50, Island Station NY 10044. (212)355-5216. Publisher: Scott C. Borowsky. Editor: Barry Block, D.P.M. Managing Editor: M.J. Goldberg. Business magazine published 9 times/year for practicing podiatrists. "Aims to help the doctor of podiatric medicine to build a bigger, more successful practice, to conserve and invest his money, to keep him posted on the economic, legal and sociological changes that affect him." Estab. 1982. Circ. 11,000. Pays on publication. Byline given. Buys first North American serial rights and second serial (reprint) rights. Submit seasonal/holiday material 4 months in advance. Simultaneous queries, and simultaneous and previously published submissions OK. Reports in 2 weeks. Sample copy $2 with 9×12 SAE; free writer's guidelines for #10 SASE.
Nonfiction: General interest (taxes, investments, estate planning, recreation, hobbies); how-to (establish and collect fees, practice management, organize office routines, supervise office assistants, handle patient relations); interview/profile about interesting or well-known podiatrists; and personal experience. "These subjects are the mainstay of the magazine, but offbeat articles and humor are always welcome." Buys 25 mss/year. Query. Length: 1,000-2,500 words. Pays $150-350.
Photos: State availability of photos. Pays $15 for b&w contact sheet. Buys one-time rights.

RESCUE, Uniting Rescue and Basic Life Support, (formerly *Response!*), Jems Publishing Co., Inc., P.O. Box 1026, Solana Beach CA 92075. (619)481-1128. FAX: (619)481-2711.Executive Editor: Keith Griffiths. Managing Editor: Lee Reeder. 60% freelance written. Bimonthly magazine covering basic life support and technical areas of interest for providers and administrators of emergency care. Estab. 1980. Circ. 10,000. Pays on publication. Byline given. Offers 20-30% kill fee. Buys first North American serial and one-time rights. Submit seasonal/holiday material 6 months in advance. Query for electronic submissions. Reports in 3 weeks on queries; 2 months on mss. Sample copy and writer's guidelines for $1.41.
Nonfiction: Book excerpts, how-to, humor, new product, opinion, photo feature and technical. Special issues include "Vehicle Extrication, rescue training, mass casualty incidents, water rescue and wilderness rescue. No I was saved by a ranger" articles. Buys 15-20 mss/year. Query with or without published clips, or send complete ms. Length: 1,000-3,000 words. Pays $125-200. Sometimes pays the expenses of writers on assignment.
Photos: Send photos with submission. Reviews contact sheets, negatives, 2×2 transparencies and 5×7 prints. Offers $15-125 per photo. Buys one-time rights.
Tips: "Read our magazine, spend some time with a rescue team. We will begin to focus on all aspects of rescue, including basic life support, vehicle extrication, transport and treatment, in addition to the specialized rescue we have been covering. Emphasis on techniques and new technology, with more color photos as support."

SENIOR PATIENT, McGraw-Hill, 4530 W. 77th St., Edina MN 55435. (612)835-3222. Managing Editor: Terry Monahan. Assistant Managing Editor: Kathleen Kimball-Baker. Monthly magazine covering the health care needs of the elderly. "As the American population ages, doctors need more information to help them better care for the psychosocial — as well as the medical — needs of the elderly." 20-50% freelance written. Estab. 1989. Circ. 135,000. **Pays on acceptance.** Publishes ms an average of 4 months after acceptance. Byline given. (Sometimes byline shared with physician.) Buys limited rights. Send seasonal/holiday material 6 months in advance. Query for electronic submissions. Reports in 6 weeks. Sample copy for $5; writer's guidelines for #10 SASE.
Nonfiction: Articles include journalistic features (Special Reports) on political, economic and social issues of interest to physicians who treat older adults; "not-exactly-medical" features (Features) that share one doctor's experiences about managing senior patients; and short news stories (Currents) with up-to-date

information on Medicare policies, ethical concerns and recent studies that have immediate applicability to our readers' practices. Query. Length: 100-2,500 words. Pays $50-1,000.
Photos: Tina Adamek, photo editor. State availability of photos. Buys one-time rights.

STRATEGIC HEALTH CARE MARKETING, Health Care Communications, 211 Midland Ave., P.O. Box 594, Rye NY 10580. (914)967-6741. Editor: Michele von Dambrowski. 30% freelance written. Prefers to work with published/established writers. "Will only work with unpublished writer on a 'stringer' basis initially." A monthly newsletter covering health care services marketing in a wide range of settings including hospitals and medical group practices, home health services and ambulatory care centers. Emphasizes strategies and techniques employed within the health care field and relevant applications from other service industries. Estab. 1984. Pays on publication. Publishes ms an average of 2 months after acceptance. Byline given. Offers 25% kill fee. Buys first North American serial rights. Reports in 1 month. Sample copy for 9×12 SAE and 3 first class stamps; guidelines sent with sample copy only.
Nonfiction: How-to, interview/profile, new product and technical. Buys 20 mss/year. Query with published clips. No unsolicited mss accepted. Length: 700-2,000 words. Pays $75-350. Sometimes pays the expenses of writers on assignment with prior authorization.
Photos: State availability of photos with submissions. (Photos, unless necessary for subject explanation, are rarely used.) Reviews contact sheets. Offers $10-30/photo. Captions and model releases required. Buys one-time rights.
Tips: "Writers with prior experience on business beat for newspaper or newsletter will do well. This is not a consumer publication—the writer with knowledge of both health care and marketing will excel. Interviews or profiles are most open to freelancers. Absolutely no unsolicited manuscripts; any received will be returned or discarded unread."

Music

Publications for musicians and for the recording industry are listed in this section. Other professional performing arts publications are classified under Entertainment and the Arts. Magazines featuring music industry news for the general public are listed in the Consumer Entertainment and Music sections. (Markets for songwriters can be found in *Songwriter's Market*—see Other Books of Interest).

THE CHURCH MUSICIAN, 127 9th Ave. N., Nashville TN 37234. (615)251-2961. Editor: William Anderson. 30% freelance written. Works with a small number of new/unpublished writers each year; eager to work with new/unpublished writers. Southern Baptist publication for Southern Baptist church music leaders. Quarterly. Circ. 16,000. Buys all rights. **Pays on acceptance.** Publishes ms an average of 1 year after acceptance. No query required. Reports in 2 months. Free sample copy.
Nonfiction: Leadership and how-to features, success stories and articles on Protestant church music. "We reject material when the subject of an article doesn't meet our needs. And they are often poorly written, or contain too many 'glittering generalities' or lack creativity." Length: maximum 1,300 words. Pays up to 5¢/word.
Photos: Purchased with mss; related to mss content only. "We are going to full color in April, 1991."
Fiction: Inspiration, guidance, motivation and morality with Protestant church music slant. Length: to 1,300 words. Pays up to 5¢/word.
Poetry: Church music slant, inspirational. Length: 8-24 lines. Pays $5-15.
Fillers: Short humor. Church music slant. No clippings. Pays $5-15.
Tips: "I'd advise a beginning writer to write about his or her experience with some aspect of church music; the social, musical and spiritual benefits from singing in a choir; a success story about their instrumental group; a testimonial about how they were enlisted in a choir—especially if they were not inclined to be enlisted at first. A writer might speak to hymn singers—what turns them on and what doesn't. Some might include how music has helped them to talk about Jesus as well as sing about Him. We would prefer most of these experiences be related to the church, of course, although we include many articles by freelance writers whose affiliation is other than Baptist. A writer might relate his experience with a choir of blind or deaf members. Some people receive benefits from working with unusual children—retarded, or culturally deprived, emotionally unstable, and so forth."

‡CLAVIER, A Magazine for Pianists and Organists, The Instrumentalist Co., 200 Northfield Rd., Northfield IL 60093. (708)446-5000. FAX: (708)446-6263. Editor: Kingsley Day. 95% freelance written. A magazine published 10/times/year covering keyboard teaching and performance. Estab. 1962. Circ. 20,000. Pays on publication. Publishes ms an average of 1 year after acceptance. Byline given. Buys all rights. Submit seasonal/holiday material 6 months in advance. Reports in 2 weeks on queries; 1 month on manuscripts. Free sample copy and writer's guidelines.

Nonfiction: Essays; historical/nostalgic; how-to (on teaching, keeping a small business running, etc.); humor, interview/profile; personal experience and photo feature. Query with published clips. Length: 1,000-3,000 words. Pays $20-45/printed magazine page.

Photos: Send photos with submission. Reviews contact sheets, negatives, transparencies, and prints. Offers no additional payment for photos accepted with ms; offers $10-20/photo if by major photographers. Captions, model releases and identification of subjects required.

Tips: "Articles should be of interest and direct practical value to our readers, who are studio teachers of piano and organ, church organists, or harpsichordists. Topics may include pedagogy, technique, performance, ensemble playing, and accompanying. Material should be covered clearly and thoroughly but without repetition and unnecessary digressions."

THE INSTRUMENTALIST, Instrumentalist Publishing Company, 200 Northfield Rd., Northfield IL 60093. (708)446-5000. FAX: (708)446-6263. Managing Editor: Judy Nelson. Approximately 95% freelance written. A monthly magazine covering instrumental music education for school band and orchestra directors, as well as performers and students. Estab. 1944. Circ. 22,000. Pays on publication. Publishes ms an average of 6-9 months after acceptance. Byline given. Buys all rights "but willing to permit authors to sell articles again to noncompeting publications." Submit seasonal/holiday material 6 months in advance. Reports in 1 month. Sample copy for 9×12 SAE and $2.50; free writer's guidelines.

Nonfiction: Book excerpts (rarely); essays (on occasion); general interest (on occasion, music); historical/nostalgic (music); how-to (teach, repair instruments); humor (on occasion); interview/profile (performers, conductors, composers); opinion; personal experience; photo feature; and travel. Buys 100 mss/year. Send complete ms. Length: 750-1,750 words. Pays $30-45/published page.

Photos: State availability of photos with submission. Reviews slides and 5×7 prints (photo guidelines available upon request). Payment varies. Captions and identification of subjects required. Buys variable rights.

Columns/Departments: Personal Perspective (opinions on issues facing music educators), 500-750 words; Idea Exchange ('how-tos' from educators), 250-500 words. Send complete ms. Length: 250-500 words. Pays $30-45.

Fillers: Anecdotes and short humor. Buys 5/year. Length: 250 words maximum. Pays $25-45.

Tips: "Know the music education field; specifically band and orchestra. Interviews with performers should focus on the person's contribution to education and opinions about it. We are interested in interviews and features that focus on ideas rather than on personalities. Writers must have a strong educational background in classical music."

INTERNATIONAL BLUEGRASS, International Bluegrass Music Association, 326 St. Elizabeth St., Owensboro KY 42301. (502)684-9025. Editor: Art Menius. All editorial submissions should be directed to Art Menius, Rt. 1, Box 710, Pittsboro NC 27312. (919)542-3997. 30% freelance written. Bimonthly newsletter covering bluegrass music industry. "We are the business publication for the bluegrass music industry. IBMA believes that our music has growth potential. We are interested in hard news and features concerning how to reach that potential and how to conduct business more effectively." Estab. 1985. Circ. 3,000. Pays on publication. Publishes ms an average of 2 months after acceptance. Byline given. Not copyrighted. Buys one-time rights. Submit seasonal/holiday material 4 months in advance. Simultaneous and previously published submissions OK. Query for electronic submissions. Reports in 1 month on queries; 6 weeks on mss. Sample copy for 6×9 SAE and 2 first class stamps.

Nonfiction: Book excerpts, essays, how-to (conduct business effectively within bluegrass music), new product and opinion. No interview/profiles of performers (rare exceptions) or fans. Buys 6 mss/year. Query with or without published clips, or send complete ms. Length: 300-1,200 words. Pays $25 maximum for assigned articles. Pays in contributor's copies unless payment in cash agreed at assignment.

Photos: Send photos with submission. Reviews 5×8 prints. Offers no additional payment for photos accepted with ms. Captions and identification of subjects required. Buys one-time rights.

Columns/Departments: At the Microphone (opinion about the bluegrass music industry). Buys 6 mss/year. Send complete ms. Length: 300-1,200 words. Pays $0-25.

Fillers: Anecdotes, facts and newsbreaks.

Tips: "The easiest break-in is to submit an article about an organizational member of IBMA—such as a bluegrass associate, instrument manufacturer or dealer, or performing venue. We're interested in a slant strongly toward the business end of bluegrass music. At the Microphone is the most open to freelancers. We're especially looking for material dealing with audience development and how to book bluegrass bands outside of the existing market."

OPERA NEWS, 1865 Broadway, New York NY 10023. FAX: (212)664-7653. Editor: Patrick J. Smith. 75% freelance written. Monthly magazine (May-November); biweekly (December-April). For people interested in opera; the opera professional as well as the opera audience. Estab. 1936. Circ. 120,000. Pays on publication. Publishes ms an average of 3 months after acceptance. Buys first serial rights only. Pays negotiable kill fee. Byline given. Sample copy $2.50.

Nonfiction: Most articles are commissioned in advance. Monthly issues feature articles on various aspects of opera; in biweekly issues articles relate to the weekly broadcasts from the Metropolitan Opera. Emphasis is on high quality writing and an intellectual interest to the opera-oriented public. Informational, personal experience, interview, profile, historical, think pieces, personal opinion and opera reviews. Query; no telephone inquiries. Length: 2,500 words maximum. Pays 13¢/word minimum for features; 11¢/word minimum for reviews. Rarely pays the expenses of writers on assignment.

Photos: Pays minimum of $25 for photos purchased on assignment. Captions required.

Office Environment and Equipment

GEYER'S OFFICE DEALER, 51 Madison Ave., New York NY 10010. (212)689-4411. FAX: (212)683-7928. Editor: Robert D. Rauch. 20% freelance written. For independent office equipment and stationery dealers, and special purchasers for store departments handling stationery and office equipment. Monthly. Buys all rights. Byline given. Estab. 1877. Pays on publication. Publishes ms an average of 3 months after acceptance. Reports "immediately."

Nonfiction: Articles on dealer efforts in merchandising and sales promotion; programs of stationery and office equipment dealers. Problem-solving articles related to retailers of office supplies, social stationery items, office furniture and equipment and office machines. Must feature specific stores. Query. Length: 300-1,000 words. Pays $175 minimum but quality of article is real determinant.

Photos: B&w glossies are purchased with accompanying ms with no additional payment.

MODERN OFFICE TECHNOLOGY, Penton Publishing, 1100 Superior Ave., Cleveland OH 44114. (216)696-7000. FAX: (216)696-8765. Associate Publisher and Editorial Director: John Dykeman. Editor: Lura K. Romei. Production Manager: Gina Runyon. 5-10% freelance written. A monthly magazine covering office automation for corporate management and personnel, financial management, administrative and operating management, systems and information management, managers and supervisors of support personnel and purchasing. Estab. 1956. Circ. 160,000. Pays on publication. Publishes ms an average of 6 months after acceptance. Byline given. Buys first and one-time rights. Query for electronic submissions. Reports in 1 month. Sample copy and writer's guidelines for 9×12 SAE and 2 first class stamps.

Nonfiction: New product, opinion and technical. Query with or without published clips, or send complete ms. Length: open. Pays $250-500 for assigned articles; pays $250-400 for unsolicited articles. Pays expenses of writers on assignment.

Photos: Send photos with submission. Reviews contact sheets, 4×5 transparencies and prints. Additional payment for photos accepted with ms. Consult editorial director. Captions and identification of subjects required. Buys one-time rights.

Tips: "Submitted material should alway present topics, ideas, on issues that are clearly and concisely defined. Material should describe problems and solution. Writer should describe benefits to reader in tangible results whenever possible."

Paint

AMERICAN PAINT & COATINGS JOURNAL, American Paint Journal Co., 2911 Washington Ave., St. Louis MO 63103. (314)534-0301. FAX: (314)534-4458. Editor: Chuck Reitter. 10% freelance written. Weekly magazine. For the coatings industry (paint, varnish, lacquer, etc.); manufacturers of coatings, suppliers to coatings industry, educational institutions, salesmen. Circ. 7,300. Pays on publication. Pays kill fee "depending on the work done." Buys all rights. Simultaneous submissions OK. Reports in 3 weeks. Free sample copy and writer's guidelines.

Nonfiction: Informational, historical, interview, new product, technical articles and coatings industry news. Buys 2 mss/issue. Query before sending long articles; submit complete ms for short pieces. Length: 75-1,200 words. Pays $200. Sometimes pays expenses of writers on assignment.

Photos: B&w (5×7) glossies purchased with or without mss or on assignment. Query. Pays $3-10.

Paper

PULP & PAPER CANADA, Southam Information and Communications Group Inc., Suite 410, 3300 Côte Vertu, St. Laurent, Quebec H4R 2B7 Canada. (514)339-1399. FAX: (514)339-1396. Editor: Peter N. Williamson. Managing Editor: Graeme Rodden. 5% freelance written. Prefers to work with published/established writers. Monthly magazine. Estab. 1903. Circ. 9,309. **Pays on acceptance.** Publishes ms "as soon as possible" after acceptance. Byline given. Offers kill fee according to prior agreement. Buys first North American serial rights. Reports in 3 weeks. Free sample copy and writer's guidelines.

Nonfiction: How-to (related to processes and procedures in the industry); interview/profile (of Canadian leaders in pulp and paper industry); and technical (relevant to modern pulp and/or paper industry). No fillers, short industry news items, or product news items. Buys 10 mss/year. Query first with published clips or send complete ms. Articles with photographs (b&w glossy) or other good quality illustrations will get priority review. Length: 1,500-2,000 words (with photos). Pays $150 (Canadian funds)/published page, including photos, graphics, charts, etc. Sometimes pays the expenses of writers on assignment.

Tips: "Any return postage must be in either Canadian stamps or International Reply Coupons *only*."

Pets

Listed here are publications for professionals in the pet industry—pet product wholesalers, manufacturers, suppliers, and retailers, and owners of pet specialty stores, grooming businesses, aquarium retailers and those interested in the pet fish industry. The Veterinary section lists journals for animal health professionals. Publications for pet owners are listed in the Consumer Animal section.

GROOM & BOARD, Incorporating "Groomers Gazette Kennel News," H.H. Backer Associates Inc., Suite 504, 207 S. Wabash Ave., Chicago IL 60604. (312)663-4040. FAX: (312)663-5676. Editor: Karen Long MacLeod. 10% freelance written. Magazine about grooming and boarding pets published 9 times/year. "*Groom & Board* is the only national trade publication for professional pet groomers and boarding kennel operators. It provides news, technical articles and features to help them operate their businesses more successfully." Estab. 1980. Circ. 16,000. **Pays on acceptance.** Publishes ms an average of 6 months after acceptance. Byline given. Buys first North American serial rights, one-time rights, all rights or exclusive to industry. Submit seasonal/holiday material 6 months in advance. Previously published submissions OK (rarely). Query for electronic submissions. Reports in 2 months on queries; 1 month on mss. Sample copy $2.50 plus $3.50 shipping and handling (total $6); writer's guidelines for #10 SASE.

Nonfiction: How-to (groom specific breeds of pets, run business, etc.), interview/profile (successful grooming and/or kennel operations) and technical. "We do not want consumer-oriented articles or stories about a single animal (animal heroes, grief, etc.)." Buys 3-6 mss/year. Query with or without published clips, or send complete ms. Length: 1,000-3,000 words. Pays $90 minimum for assigned articles; $65-200 for unsolicited articles. Sometimes pays expenses of writers on assignment.

Photos: Send photos with submission. Reviews contact sheets, transparencies and prints. Offers $7 per photo. Captions and identification of subjects required. Buys one-time or all rights.

PET AGE, The Largest Circulation Pet Industry Trade Publication, H.H. Backer Associates, Inc., 207 S. Wabash Ave., Chicago IL 60604. (312)663-4040. FAX: (312)663-5676. Editor: Karen Long MacLeod. 20-30% freelance written. Prefers to work with published/established writers. Monthly magazine for pet/pet suppplies retailer, covering the complete pet industry. Estab. 1971. Circ. 17,000. **Pays on acceptance.** Publishes ms an average of 3-6 months after acceptance. Byline given. Buys first North American serial rights, one-time rights, all rights or exclusive industry rights. Submit seasonal/holiday material 6 months in advance. Query for electronic submissions. Reports in 1 month. Sample copy for $2.50 plus $3.50 shipping and hangling (total $6); writer's guidelines for #10 SASE.

Nonfiction: Book excerpts, profile (of a successful, well-run pet retail operation); how-to; interview; photo feature; and technical—all trade-related. Query first with published clips. Buys 6-12 mss/year. "Query as to the name and location of a pet operation you wish to profile and why it would make a good feature. No general retailing articles or consumer-oriented pet articles." Length: 1,000-3,000 words. Pays $75-300 for assigned articles; $50-150 for unsolicited articles. Sometimes pays the expenses of writers on assignment.

Photos: Reviews 5 × 7 b&w glossy prints. Captions and identification of subjects required. Offers $7 (negotiable) for photos. Buys one-time rights or all rights.

Tips: "Our readers already know about general animal care and business practices. This is a business publication for busy people, and must be very informative in easy-to-read, concise style. The type of article we purchase most frequently is the pet shop profile, a story about an interesting/successful pet shop. We need queries on these (we get references on the individual shop from our sources in the industry). We supply typical questions to writers when we answer their queries."

THE PET DEALER, Howmark Publishing Corp., 567 Morris Ave., Elizabeth NJ 07208. (201)353-7373. FAX: (201)353-8221. Editor: Donna Eastman. 35% freelance written. Prefers to work with published/established writers, but is eager to work with new/published writers. "We want writers who are good reporters and clear communicators." Monthly magazine. Emphasizes merchandising, marketing and management for owners and managers of pet specialty stores, departments, and pet groomers and their suppliers. Estab. 1949. Circ. 16,000. Pays on publication. Publication "may be many months between acceptance of a manuscript and publication." Byline given. Phone queries OK. Submit seasonal/holiday material 3 months in advance. Reports in 1 month. Sample copy for 8 × 10 SAE and $5.

Nonfiction: How-to (store operations, administration, merchandising, marketing, management, promotion and purchasing). Consumer pet articles—lost pets, best pets, humane themes—*not* welcome. "We *are* interested in helping—dog, cat, monkey, whatever stories tie in with the human/animal bond." Emphasis is on *trade* merchandising and marketing of pets and supplies. Buys 6-8 unsolicited mss/year. Length: 800-1,500 words. Pays $100-125.

Photos: Submit undeveloped photo material with ms. No additional payment for 5×7 b&w glossy prints. Buys one-time rights. Will give photo credit for photography students.

Fillers: "Will buy some cartoons ($20 each) if they are absolutely hilarious. Will publish poetry (unpaid) as fillers in directory issue."

Tips: "We're interested in store profiles outside the New York, New Jersey, Connecticut and Pennsylvania metro areas. Photos are of key importance. Articles focus on new techniques in merchandising or promotion. Want to see more articles from retailers and veterinarians. Submit query letter first, with writing background summarized; include samples. We seek one-to-one, interview-type features on retail pet store merchandising. Indicate the availability of the proposed article, your willingness to submit on exclusive or first-in-field basis, and whether you are patient enough to await payment on publication."

Photography Trade

Journals for professional photographers are listed in this section. Magazines for the general public interested in photography techniques are in the Consumer Photography section. (For listings of markets for freelance photography use *Photographer's Market*—see Other Books of Interest.)

AMERICAN CINEMATOGRAPHER, A.S.C. Holding Corp., Box 2230, Hollywood CA 90078. (213)876-5080. FAX: (213)876-4973. Editor: George Turner. 50% freelance written. Monthly magazine. An international journal of film and video production techniques "addressed to creative, managerial, and technical people in all aspects of production. Its function is to disseminate practical information about the creative use of film and video equipment, and it strives to maintain a balance between technical sophistication and accessibility." Circ. 31,000. Pays on publication. Publishes ms an average of 3 months after acceptance. Buys all rights. Phone queries OK. Simultaneous submissions OK. Query for electronic submission. Sample copy for 9×12 SAE with $1 postage; writer's guidelines for #10 SASE.

Nonfiction: Jean Turner, associate editor. Descriptions of new equipment and techniques or accounts of specific productions involving unique problems or techniques; historical articles detailing the production of a classic film, the work of a pioneer or legendary cinematographer or the development of a significant technique or type of equipment. Also discussions of the aesthetic principles involved in production techniques. Recent article example: "Chances Are—Bridges the Generation Gap" (April 1989). Length 2,000-2,500 words. Pays according to position and worth. Negotiable. Sometimes pays the expenses of writers on assignment.

Photos: B&w and color purchased with mss. No additional payment.

Tips: "No unsolicited articles. Call first. Doesn't matter whether you are published or new. Queries must describe writer's qualifications and include writing samples. We expect expansion of videography."

PHOTO LAB MANAGEMENT, PLM Publishing, Inc., 1312 Lincoln Blvd., Santa Monica CA 90401. (213)451-1344. FAX: (213)395-9058. Editor: Carolyn Ryan. Associate Editor: Arthur Stern. 75% freelance written. Monthly magazine covering process chemistries and equipment, digital imaging, and marketing/administration for photo lab owners, managers and management personnel. Estab. 1950. Circ. 20,000. Pays on publication. Publishes ms an average of 3 months after acceptance. Byline and brief bio given. Buys first North American serial rights. Query for electronic submissions. Reports on queries in 6 weeks. Free sample copy and writer's guidelines for #10 SASE.

Nonfiction: Personal experience (lab manager); technical; and management or administration. Buys 40-50 mss/year. Query with brief biography. Length: 1,200-1,800 words. Payment negotiable.

Photos: Reviews 35mm color transparencies and 4-color prints suitable for cover. "We're looking for outstanding cover shots of photofinishing images."

Tips: "Our departments are written in-house and we don't use 'fillers'. Send a query if you have some background in the industry or a willingness to dig out information and research for a top quality article that really speaks to our audience. The most frequent mistakes made by writers are on the business management side—taking a generic rather than a photo lab approach. Writers must have photofinishing knowledge."

PHOTO MARKETING, Photo Marketing Association Intl., 3000 Picture Place, Jackson MI 49201. (517)788-8100. Managing Editor: Margaret Hooks. 2% freelance written. A monthly magazine for photo industry retailers, finishers and suppliers. "Articles must be specific to the photo industry and cannot be authored by anyone who writes for other magazines in the photo industry. We provide management information on a variety of topics as well as profiles of successful photo businesses and analyses of current issues in the industry." Circ. 22,000. **Pays on acceptance.** Publishes ms an average of 2 months after acceptance. Byline given. Buys one-time rights and exclusive photo magazine rights. Simultaneous submissions OK. Reports in 2 weeks. Free sample copy and writer's guidelines.

Nonfiction: Interview/profile (anonymous consumer shops for equipment); personal experience (interviews with photo retailers); technical (photofinishing lab equipment); new technology (still electronic video). Buys 5 mss/year. Send complete ms. Length: 1,000-2,300 words. Pays $150-350.

Photos: State availability of photos with submission. Reviews negatives, 5×7 transparencies and prints. Offers $25-35 per photo. Buys one-time rights.

Columns/Departments: Anonymous Consumer (anonymous shopper shops for equipment at photo stores) 1,800 words. Buys 5 mss/year. Query with published clips. Length: 1,800 words. Pays up to $200.

Tips: "All main sections use freelance material: business tips, promotion ideas, employee concerns, advertising, co-op, marketing. But they must be geared to and have direct quotes from members of the association."

PHOTOLETTER, PhotoSource International, Pine Lake Farm, Osceola WI 54020. (715)248-3800. FAX: (715)248-7394. Editor: Lynette Layer. Managing Editor: H.T. White. 10% freelance written. A monthly newsletter on marketing photographs. "The *Photoletter* pairs photobuyers with photographers' collections." Circ. 780. **Pays on acceptance.** Publishes ms an average of 6 months after acceptance. Byline given. Buys one-time rights and simultaneous rights. Submit seasonal/holiday material 3 months in advance. Simultaneous and previously published submissions OK. Query for electronic submissions. Reports in 2 weeks on queries. Sample copy $3; writer's guidelines for #10 SASE.

Nonfiction: How-to market photos and personal experience in marketing photos. "Our readers expect advice in how-to articles." No submissions that do not deal with selling photos. Buys 6 mss/year. Query. Length: 300-850 words. Pays $50-100 for unsolicited articles.

Columns/Departments: Jeri Engh, columns department editor. "We welcome column ideas." Length: 350 words. Pays $45-75.

Fillers: Facts. Buys 20/year. Length: 30-50 words. Pays $10.

Tips: "Columns are most open to freelancers. Bring an *expertise* on marketing photos or some other aspect of aid to small business persons."

PROFESSIONAL PHOTOGRAPHER, The Business Magazine of Professional Photography, Professional Photographers of America, Inc., 1090 Executive Way, Des Plaines IL 60018. (708)299-8161. FAX: (708)299-2685. Editor: Alfred DeBat. 80% freelance written. Monthly magazine of professional portrait, wedding, commercial, corporate and industrial photography. Describes the technical and business sides of professional photography—successful photo techniques, money-making business tips, legal considerations, selling to new markets, and descriptions of tough assignments and how completed. Estab. 1907. Circ. 32,000. Publishes ms an average of 6-9 months after acceptance. Byline given. Buys one-time rights. Submit seasonal/holiday material 6 months in advance. Simultaneous queries and previously published submissions OK. Reports in 2 months. Sample copy $3.25; free writer's guidelines.

Nonfiction: How-to. Professional photographic techniques: How I solved this difficult assignment, How I increased my photo sales, How to buy a studio, run a photo business, etc. Special issues include February: Portrait Photography; April: Wedding Photography; May: Commercial Photography; and August: Industrial Photography. Buys 8-10 ms/issue. Query. Length: 1,000-3,000 words. "We seldom pay, as most writers are PP of A members and want recognition for their professional skills, publicity, etc."

Photos: State availability of photos. Reviews color transparencies and 8×10 unmounted prints. Captions and model release required. Buys one-time rights.

Plumbing, Heating, Air Conditioning and Refrigeration

HEATING, PLUMBING, AIR CONDITIONING, 1450 Don Mills Rd., Don Mills, Ontario M3B 2X7 Canada. (416)445-6641. FAX: (416)442-2077. Editor: Ronald H. Shuker. 20% freelance written. Monthly. For mechanical contractors; plumbers; warm air and hydronic heating, refrigeration, ventilation, air conditioning and insulation contractors; wholesalers; architects; consulting and mechanical engineers who are in key management or specifying positions in the plumbing, heating, air conditioning and refrigeration industries in Canada. Circ. 14,500. Pays on publication. Publishes ms an average of 3 months after acceptance. Reports in 2 months. For a prompt reply, "enclose a sheet on which is typed a statement either approving or rejecting the suggested article which can either be checked off, or a quick answer written in and signed and returned." Free sample copy.

Nonfiction: News, technical, business management and "how-to" articles that will inform, educate, motivate and help readers to be more efficient and profitable who design, manufacture, install, sell, service, maintain or supply all mechanical components and systems in residential, commercial, institutional and industrial installations across Canada. Length: 1,000-1,500 words. Pays 20¢/word. Sometimes pays expenses of writers on assignment.

Photos: Photos purchased with ms. Prefers 4×5 or 5×7 glossies.

Tips: "Topics must relate directly to the day-to-day activities of *HPAC* readers in Canada. Must be detailed, with specific examples, quotes from specific people or authorities—show depth. We specifically want material from other parts of Canada besides southern Ontario. Not really interested in material from U.S. unless specifically related to Canadian readers' concerns. We primarily want articles that show *HPAC* readers how they can increase their sales and business step-by-step based on specific examples of what others have done."

SNIPS MAGAZINE, 407 Mannheim Rd., Bellwood IL 60104. (708)544-3870. FAX: (708)544-3884. Editor: Nick Carter. 2% freelance written. Monthly. For sheet metal, warm air heating, ventilating, air conditioning and roofing contractors. Estab. 1932. Publishes ms an average of 3 months after acceptance. Buys all rights. "Write for detailed list of requirements before submitting any work."

Nonfiction: Material should deal with information about contractors who do sheet metal, warm air heating, air conditioning, ventilation and roofing work; also about successful advertising campaigns conducted by these contractors and the results. Length: "prefers stories to run less than 1,000 words unless on special assignment." Pays 5¢/word for first 500 words, 2¢/word thereafter.

Photos: Pays $5 each for small snapshot pictures, $10 each for usable 8×10 pictures.

Printing

COPY MAGAZINE, The Journal of Imaging and Reproduction, Quoin Communications, Inc., 800 W. Huron St., Chicago IL 60622 (312)226-5600. FAX: (312)226-4640. Managing Editor: Dan Witte. 25% freelance written. Monthly magazine that covers toner-on-paper and other non-impact printing. "*Copy Magazine* seeks to present a technical understanding of the new imaging technologies and the businesses that use them." Estab. 1987. Circ. 20,000. Pays on publication. Byline given. Offers 50% kill fee. Buys all rights. Simultaneous submissions OK. Query for electronic submissions. Reports in 1 month on queries. Sample copy $3 with 9×12 SAE and 3 first class stamps. Writer's guidelines for #10 SASE.

Nonfiction: Book excerpts (DTP, copying), how-to (DTP, copying), interview/profile (industry suppliers), new product (relevant to trade), opinion, personal experience (in industry), photo feature (on DTP) and technical. "We do not want general business stuff (taxes, employee morale, etc.)" Buys 8-10 mss/year. Query. Length: 100-100,000 words. Pays $100-300 for assigned articles; $100-250 for unsolicited articles. Pays in contributor copies or other premiums "if writers request such."

Photos: State availability of photos with submission. Reviews contact sheets. Offers no additional payment for photos accepted with ms. Captions, model releases and identification of subjects required. Buys all rights.

Columns/Departments: Fast Copy (minutiae, trivial news). Buys 40-50 mss/year. Query. Length: 100-1,000 words. Pays $25-75.

PRINT & GRAPHICS, Box 9525, Arlington VA 22209. (703)525-4800. FAX: (703)525-4805. Editor: Ms. Tracy Rammacher. 5% freelance written. Eager to work with new/unpublished writers. Monthly tabloid of the commercial printing industry for owners and executives of graphic arts firms. Circ. 18,000. **Pays on acceptance.** Publishes ms an average of 1 month after acceptance. Byline given. Buys one-time rights. Simultaneous queries, and simultaneous and previously published submissions OK. Electronic submissions OK via standard protocols, but requires hard copy also. Reports in 1 week. Sample copy for $1.50.

Nonfiction: Book excerpts, historical/nostalgic, how-to, interview/profile, new product, opinion, personal experience, photo feature and technical. "All articles should relate to graphic arts management or production." Buys 20 mss/year. Query with published clips. Length: 750-2,000 words. Pays $50-150.

Photos: State availability of photos. Pays $25-75 for 5×7 b&w prints. Captions and identification of subjects required.

PRINTING NEWS MIDWEST, (formerly *Printing Views*), Cahners Publishing Co., 1350 E. Touhy, P.O. Box 5080, Des Plains IL 60017-5080. (708)635-8800. FAX: (708)635-6856. Editor: Ed Schwenn. 10% freelance written. Prefers to work with published/established writers. Monthly tabloid newspaper about printing and graphic arts for Midwest commercial printers, typographers, platemakers, engravers and other trade people. Circ. 15,000. Average issue includes 2-3 features. Pays on publication. Publishes ms an average of 2 months after acceptance. Byline given. Buys one-time rights. Phone queries OK. Reports in 2 weeks. Sample copy $2.

Nonfiction: Interview (possibly with graphic arts personnel); new product (in graphic arts in a Midwest plant); management/sales success in Midwest printing plant; and technical (printing equipment). Buys 6 feature mss/year. Query with clips of previously published work. "We will entertain query letters; no unsolicited manuscripts." Length: 2-9 typed pages. Pays $300 for assigned mss only.

Photos: State availability of photos. Reviews b&w contact sheets. Offers additional payment for photos accepted with ms. Captions preferred. Buys all rights.

QUICK PRINTING, The Information Source for Commercial Copyshops and Printshops, Coast Publishing, 1680 SW Bayshore Blvd., Port St. Lucie FL 34984. (407)879-6666. FAX: (407)879-7388. Publisher: Cyndi Schulman. Editor: Bob Hall. 50% freelance written. A monthly magazine covering the quick printing industry. "Our articles tell quick printers how they can be more profitable. We want figures to illustrate points made." Estab. 1977. Circ. 57,000. **Pays on acceptance.** Publishes ms an average of 4 months after acceptance. Byline given. Buys first North American serial rights, all rights. Submit seasonal/holiday material 6 months in advance. Rarely uses previously published submissions. Query for electronic submissions. Reports in 1 month. Sample copy for $3 and 9 × 12 SAE with 7 first class stamps; writer's guidelines for #10 SASE.
Nonfiction: How-to (on marketing products better or accomplishing more with equipment); new product; opinion (on the quick printing industry); personal experience (from which others can learn); technical (on printing). No generic business articles, or articles on larger printing applications. Buys 75 mss/year. Send complete ms. Length: 1,500-3,000 words. Pays $100 and up.
Photos: State availability of photos with submission. Reviews transparencies and prints. Offers no payment for photos. Captions and identification of subjects required.
Columns/Departments: Viewpoint/Counterpoint (opinion on the industry); QP Profile (shop profiles with a marketing slant); Management (how to handle employees and/or business strategies); and Marketing Impressions, all 500-1,500 words. Buys 10 mss/year. Send complete ms. Pays $75.
Tips: "The use of electronic publishing systems by quick printers is of increasing interest. Show a knowledge of the industry. Try visiting your local quick printer for an afternoon to get to know about us. When your articles make a point, back it up with examples, statistics, and dollar figures. We need good material in all areas, but avoid the shop profile. Technical articles are most needed, but they must be accurate. No puff pieces for a certain industry supplier."

SCREEN PRINTING, 407 Gilbert Ave., Cincinnati OH 45202. (513)421-2050. FAX: (513)421-5144. Editor: Susan Venell. 30% freelance written. Works with a small number of new/unpublished writers each year. Monthly magazine for the screen printing industry, including screen printers (commercial, industrial and captive shops), suppliers and manufacturers, ad agencies and allied professions. Circ. 15,000. Pays on publication. Publishes ms an average of 3-4 months after acceptance. Byline given. Buys all rights. Reporting time varies. Free sample copy and writer's guidelines.
Nonfiction: "Because the screen printing industry covers a broad range of applications and overlaps other fields in the graphic arts, it's necessary that articles be of a significant contribution, preferably to a specific area of screen printing. Subject matter is fairly open, with preference given to articles on administration or technology; trends and developments. We try to give a good sampling of technical business and management articles; articles about unique operations. We also publish special features and issues on important subjects, such as material shortages, new markets and new technology breakthroughs. While most of our material is nitty-gritty, we appreciate a writer who can take an essentially dull subject and encourage the reader to read on through concise, factual, 'flairful' and creative, expressive writing. Interviews are published after consultation with and guidance from the editor." Interested in stories on unique approaches by some shops. No general, promotional treatment of individual companies. Buys 6-10 mss/year. Query. Unsolicited mss not returned. Length: 1,500-3,500 words. Pays minimum of $150 for major features. Sometimes pays the expenses of writers on assignment.
Photos: Cover photos negotiable; b&w or color. Published material becomes the property of the magazine.
Tips: "If the author has a working knowledge of screen printing, assignments are more readily available. General management articles are rarely used."

Real Estate

AREA DEVELOPMENT MAGAZINE, 400 Post Ave., Westbury NY 11590. (516)338-0900. Editor-in-Chief: Tom Bergeron. 50% freelance written. Prefers to work with published/established writers. Emphasizes corporate facility planning and site selection for industrial chief executives worldwide. Monthly magazine. Circ. 33,000. Pays when edited. Publishes ms an average of 2 months after acceptance. Buys first rights only. Byline given. Computer printout submissions acceptable; prefers letter-quality. Reports in 1-3 weeks. Free sample copy. Writer's guidelines for #10 SASE.
Nonfiction: How-to (experiences in site selection and all other aspects of corporate facility planning); historical (if it deals with corporate facility planning); interview (corporate executives and industrial developers); and related areas of site selection and facility planning such as taxes, labor, government, energy, architec-

Always check the most recent copy of a magazine for the address and editor's name before you send in a query or manuscript.

ture and finance. Buys 100 mss/yr. Query. Pays $30-50/ms page; rates for illustrations depend on quality and printed size. Sometimes pays the expenses of writers on assignment.

Photos: State availability of photos with query. Prefer 8×10 or 5×7 b&w glossy prints. Captions preferred.

Tips: "Articles must be accurate, objective (no puffery) and useful to our industrial executive readers. Avoid any discussion of the merits or disadvantages of any particular areas or communities. Writers should realize we serve an intelligent and busy readership—they should avoid 'cute' allegories and get right to the point."

BUSINESS FACILITIES, Group C Communications, Inc., 121 Monmouth St., P.O. Box 2060, Red Bank NJ 07701. (201)842-7433. FAX: (201)758-6634. Editor: Eric Peterson. Managing Editor: James Picerno. 20% freelance written. Prefers to work with published/established writers. A monthly magazine covering economic development and commercial and industrial real estate. "Our audience consists of corporate site selectors and real estate people; our editorial coverage is aimed at providing news and trends on the plant location and corporate expansion field." Estab. 1967. Circ. 32,000. Pays on publication. Publishes ms an average of 3 months after acceptance. Byline given. Buys all rights. Previously published submissions OK. Reports in 2 weeks. Free sample copy and writer's guidelines.

Nonfiction: General interest, how-to, interview/profile and personal experience. No news shorts or clippings; feature material only. Buys 12-15 mss/year. Query. Length: 1,000-3,000 words. Pays $200-1,000 for assigned articles, pays $200-600 for unsolicited articles. Sometimes pays the expenses of writers on assignment.

Photos: State availability of photos with submission. Reviews contact sheets, negatives, transparencies and 8×10 prints. Payment negotiable. Captions and identification of subjects required. Buys one-time rights.

Tips: "First, remember that our reader is a corporate executive responsible for his company's expansion and/or relocation decisions and our writers have to get inside that person's head in order to provide him with something that's helpful in his decision-making process. And second, the biggest turnoff is a telephone query. We're too busy to accept them and must require that all queries be put in writing. Submit major feature articles only; all news departments, fillers, etc., are staff prepared. A writer should be aware that our style is not necessarily dry and business-like. We tend to be more upbeat and a writer should look for that aspect of our approach. We are currently overstocked, however, and for the near future will be accepting fewer pieces."

‡CONDOMINIUM TIMES, Condo Media Corp., Suite 2730, 995 SR 434, Altamonte Springs FL 32714. (407)862-8827. Editor: Charles Martin. 50% freelance written. Biweekly (Oct. through May); monthly (June through Sept.). For condominium and property owner boards of directors. Estab. 1989. Circ. 10,000. Pays on publication. Publishes ms an average of 1 month after acceptance. Byline given. Negotiable kill fee. Buys first, one-time and occasionally second serial (reprint) rights. Query for electronic submisisons. Reports in 2 weeks. Sample copy for 10×13 SAE with 2 first class stamps.

Nonfiction: Essays (condo life, management experiences), exposé (legal cases, scandals), historical/nostalgic (condo history), how-to (management or board-related only), humor, interview/profile, new product, opinion, personal experience, photo feature, technical. Buys 100-200 mss/year. Query with or without published clips, or send complete ms. Length: 450 words minimum. Pays $20 maximum. "Most experts use us simply for the publicity." Sometimes pays expenses of writers on assignment.

Photos: State availability of photos with submission. Reviews contact sheets and any size prints. Offers no additional payment for photos accepted with ms. Captions and identification of subjects required. Buys one-time rights.

Fillers: Anecdotes, facts, newsbreaks, short humor. Length: 100-500 words. Pays $10 maximum

Tips: "First, be knowledgable on our subject—condominium boards of directors and their problems. If you have a background in law, business management, accounting, politics or related fields, understand and/or live in a condominium community *in Florida* and/or have an idea/system that you think would benefit condo board members, we'd like to hear from you! These areas are open: Digging up court records and/or news clips on suits etc. involving condos—we are *always* desperate for this sort of news. Former or current 'motivation' speakers—people who can get you fired lup to do the job, beat apathy, overcome stress, et. al can write for us. We always need tips on how you or some condo board you know solved problems, etc."

FINANCIAL FREEDOM REPORT, 1831 Fort Union Blvd., Salt Lake City UT 84121. (801)943-1280. FAX: (801)942-7489. Chairman of the Board: Mark O. Haroldsen. Managing Editor: Carolyn Tice. 25% freelance written. Eager to work with new/unpublished writers. For "professional and nonprofessional investors and would-be investors in real estate—real estate brokers, insurance companies, investment planners, truck drivers, housewives, doctors, architects, contractors, etc. The magazine's content is presently expanding to interest and inform the readers about other ways to put their money to work for them." Monthly magazine. Estab. 1976. Circ. 50,000. Pays on publication. Publishes ms an average of 3 months after acceptance. Buys all rights. Phone queries OK. Simultaneous submissions OK. Query for electronic submissions. Reports in 2 weeks. Sample copy $3; free writer's guidelines.

Nonfiction: How-to (find real estate bargains, finance property, use of leverage, managing property, developing market trends, goal setting, motivational); and interviews (success stories of those who have relied on own initiative and determination in real estate market or related fields). Buys 25 unsolicited mss/year. Query with clips of published work or submit complete ms. Length: 1,500-3,000 words. "If the topic warranted a two- or three-parter, we would consider it." Pays 5-10¢/word. Sometimes pays the expenses of writers on assignment.

Photos: Send photos with ms. Uses 8×10 b&w or color matte prints. Makes additional payment for photos accepted with ms. Captions required.

Tips: "We would like to find several specialized writers in our field of real estate investments. A writer must have had some hands-on experience in the real estate field."

REAL ESTATE COMPUTING, Real Estate Software Company, Inc., Suite D, 10622 Montwood Dr., El Paso TX 79935. (915)598-2435. Editor: Kevin L. Chestnut. Managing Editor: C. Bryant Crawford. 25% freelance written. Bimonthly tabloid on computers and computerization of/for real estate professionals. Circ. 85,000. Pays on publication. Publishes ms an average of 2 months after acceptance. Byline given. Offers 25% kill fee. Buys first rights, one-time rights, or second serial (reprint) rights. Submit seasonal/holiday material 3 months in advance. Previously published submissions OK. Query for electronic submissions. Reports in 3 weeks on queries.

Nonfiction: Book excerpts, how-to (computerize, increase production with computers), interview/profile (real estate pros, computer experts, opinion (on real estate computerization trends, needs, state of), photo feature, technical and real estate sales and management success secrets. "No articles on competing companies or products or articles which do not involve both computers and real estate. We don't want articles that involve Apple or other non-IBM-compatible computers." Query. Length: 500-1,500 words. Pays $50-150 for assigned articles; $25-100 for unsolicited articles. Sometimes pays expenses of writers on assignment.

Photos: State availability of photos with submission. Reviews contact sheets and prints. Offers $10-35 per photo. Model releases and identification of subjects required. Buys one-time rights.

Tips: "Although originally produced to keep in touch with users of our software products, the strong response from non-users has let us to greatly expand our editorial aim. We now mail to every real estate broker in the USA. Our readers are not technical wizards; they're busy real estate professionals and residential property managers. They look to us for plain-English solutions to their everyday computerization problems. Our publication is colorful and illustrated with graphs, charts and 'button-by-button examples'. We like interviews with agents who've successfully implemented computers into their offices. We expect facts to be researched and well documented."

Resources and Waste Reduction

GROUND WATER AGE, National Trade Publications, 13 Century Hill Dr., Latham NY 12110. (518)783-1281. Editor: Tom Williams. 30% freelance written. Monthly magazine that covers water well drilling and pump installation. "We want good, solid writing, accurate facts and up-to-date information on technical subjects." Estab. 1966. Circ. 20,000. **Pays on acceptance.** Publishes ms an average of 3-4 months after acceptance. Byline given. Buys first North American serial rights. Submit seasonal/holiday material 6 months in advance. Simultaneous and previously published submissions OK. Reports in 2 weeks on queries; 1 month on mss. Sample copy for 9×12 SAE with 5 first class stamps.

Nonfiction: Historical/nostalgic, interview/profile, new product, photo feature and technical. Buys 12-20 mss/year. Query with published clips. Length: 750-3,000 words. Pays $50-350 for assigned articles; $50-250 for unsolicited articles. "Trades articles for advertising, on occasion and when desirable." Sometimes pays expenses of writers on assignment.

Photos: State availability of photos with submission. "We need quality photos of water well drillers, monitoring well contractors or pump installers in action, on the job." Reviews contact sheets, negatives, transparencies and prints. Offers no additional payment for photos accepted with ms. Identification of subjects required. Buys one-time rights.

Columns/Departments: Down the Hole (technical, how-to aspects of water well or monitoring well drilling); Pumps and Water Systems (technical aspects of water well pumps, tanks, valves and piping for domestic well systems); business topics (for improving productivity, marketing, etc.). 300-1,000 words. Buys 6-10 mss/year. Query first by phone or mail. Pays $50-150.

RESOURCE RECYCLING, North America's Recycling Journal, Resource Recycling, Inc., Box 10540, Portland OR 97210. (503)227-1319. FAX: (503)227-6135. Editor-in-Chief: Jerry Powell. Editor: Meg Lynch. 25% freelance written. Eager to work with new/unpublished writers. A trade journal published 12 times/year, covering recycling of paper, plastics, metals and glass. Estab. 1982. Circ. 8,500. Pays on publication. Publishes ms an average of 3-9 months after acceptance. Byline given. Buys first rights. Simultaneous and previously published submissions OK. Query for electronic submissions. Reports in 1 month on queries. Sample copy and writer's guidelines for 9×12 SAE with 5 first class stamps.

Nonfiction: "No non-technical or opinion pieces." Buys 15-20 mss/year. Query with published clips. Length: 1,200-1,800 words. Pays $100-250. Pays with contributor copies "if writers are more interested in professional recognition than financial compensation." Sometimes pays the expenses of writers on assignment.

Close-up

Meg Lynch
Editor
Resource Recycling

Recycling has become a major issue in the past few years. Many people are familiar with curbside collection of recyclable wastes, but few may know about the many products made from recycled goods, commercial recycling, yard wastes, and the disposal of toxins, batteries, tires and the like. There was a time just ten years ago when only a handful of Americans were doing something about recycling at all.

Resource Recycling was the first magazine to tackle these issues. Editor-in-Chief Jerry Powell saw the need to get recycling information into the public sector and launched the publication eight years ago. After consulting and editing articles part-time for the magazine, Meg Lynch signed on as editor three-and-one-half years ago.

"In the years since we've been publishing, other magazines on recycling have started up," says Lynch. While many boast content in favor of recycling, the slick paper they print those articles on is not or cannot be recycled. *Resource Recycling* demonstrates commitment to its subject beyond the writing, Lynch says. "We use 100% recycled paper for our magazine. Always have and always will."

Lynch advises writers seeking publication in *Resource Recycling* to obtain a sample copy of the magazine and study its style and content. She also sends interested freelancers a copy of the magazine's writer's guidelines and its editorial calender. "Then we'll take a look at a query," she says. "We prefer that writers send us an abstract of their proposal."

The writer's experience will determine whether he will write on speculation when publishing in *Resource Recycling* for the first time. "If the writer has experience in the waste management and recycling field, he would not have to write on spec," says Lynch. "If not, the writer probably would have to do it. We look for comprehension of the field."

Lynch considers knowledge of recycling the most important asset a freelancer can offer. "Every field has its own idiosyncrasies and demands," she says. "Of course a writer must be more than competent, but this is probably true of most trade publications: the writer must know the subject thoroughly."

Resource Recycling receives about four queries and manuscripts every week. "Some weeks it seems we get a million ideas," Lynch says. She, Editor-in-Chief Powell and a technical editor read every submission and assign their votes. Lynch then contacts the writers with news of acceptance, rejection or other advice. They buy 12 articles for each issue, half of which are assigned. "We get a lot of manuscripts from people in the business of recycling," she says. "They have a step on those who send us cold inquiries, but again, that's the case for every trade publication.

"We don't usually assign someone something new," says Lynch. The specialization of subject matter in writing for trade magazines creates a particular difficulty for freelance writers, who must keep the article interesting while paying attention to detail. "They have to command a semi-journalistic style to be successful," Lynch says.

— Mark Kissling

Photos: State availability of photos with submission. Reviews contact sheets, negatives and prints. Offers $5-50. Identification of subjects required. Buys one-time rights.

Tips: "Overviews of one recycling aspect in one state (e.g., oil recycling in Alabama) will receive attention. We will increase coverage of yard waste composting."

Selling and Merchandising

Sales personnel and merchandisers interested in how to sell and market products successfully consult these journals. Publications in nearly every category of Trade also buy sales-related material if it is slanted to the product or industry with which they deal.

THE AMERICAN SALESMAN, 424 N. 3rd St., Burlington IA 52601. FAX: (319)752-3421. Publisher: Michael S. Darnall. Editorial Supervisor: Doris J. Ruschill. Editor: Barbara Boeding. 95% freelance written. Prefers to work with published/established writers, but works with a small number of new/unpublished writers each year. Monthly magazine for distribution through company sales representatives. Estab. 1955. Circ. 1,652. Pays on publication. Publishes ms an average of 4 months after acceptance. Buys all rights. Sample copy and writer's guidelines for 8×10 SAE and 2 first class stamps; mention *Writer's Market* in request.

Nonfiction: Sales seminars, customer service and follow-up, closing sales, sales presentations, handling objections, competition, telephone usage and correspondence, managing territory and new innovative sales concepts. No sexist material, illustration written from a salesperson's viewpoint. No ms dealing with supervisory problems. Query. Length: 900-1,200 words. Pays 3¢/word. Uses no advertising. Follow AP Stylebook. Include biography and/or byline with ms submissions. Author photos used.

ART MATERIAL TRADE NEWS, The Journal of All Art, Craft, Engineering and Drafting Supplies, Communication Channels Inc., 6255 Barfield Rd., Atlanta GA 30328. (404)256-9800. Editor: Tom C. Cooper. 15% freelance written. Works with a small number of new/unpublished writers each year. Monthly magazine on art materials. "Our editorial thrust is to bring art materials retailers, distributors and manufacturers information they can use in their everyday operations." Circ. 12,000. Pays on publication. Publishes ms an average of 3 months after acceptance. "All assigned manuscripts are published." Buys first serial rights. Submit seasonal/holiday material 3 months in advance. Reports in 6 weeks. Sample copy for 9×12 SAE and 4 first class stamps. Writer's guidelines for #10 SASE.

Nonfiction: How-to (sell, retail/wholesale employee management, advertising programs); interview/profile (within industry); and technical (commercial art drafting/engineering). "We encourage a strong narrative style where possible. We publish an editorial 'theme' calendar at the beginning of each year." Buys 15-30 mss/year. Query with published clips. Length: 1,000-3,000 words (prefers 2,000 words). Pays $75-300.

Photos: State availability of photos. Pays $10 maximum for b&w contact sheets. Identification of subjects required.

‡ASD/AMD TRADE NEWS, Associated Surplus Dealers/Associated Merchandise Dealers, 1666 Corinth Ave., Los Angeles CA 90025. (213)477-2556. Editor: Jay Hammeran. 75% freelance written. Monthly trade newspaper on trade shows and areas of interest to surplus/merchandise dealers. "Many of our readers have small, family-owned businesses." Estab. 1967. Circ. 70,000. **Pays on acceptance.** Publishes ms an average of 1-2 months after acceptance. Byline given. Negotiable kill fee. Buys all rights. Submit seasonal/holiday material 3 months in advance. Simultaneous submissions OK. Query for electronic submissions. Reports in 2 weeks on queries; 1 month on mss. Free sample copy and writer's guidelines.

Nonfiction: How-to (merchandise a store more effectively), interview/profile (dealers/owners), personal experience (of dealers and merchandisers), photo feature (ASD/AMD trade shows), and general business articles of interest. "Jan. and July are the largest issues of the year. We generally need more freelance material for those two issues. No articles that are solely self-promotion pieces or straight editorials." Buys 100 mss/year. Query with or without published clips, or send complete ms. Length: 500-1,250 words. Pays $50-75. Pays expenses of writers on assignment.

Photos: State availability of photos with submission. Reviews 3½×5 prints. Payment depends on whether photos were assigned or not. Identification of subjects required. Buys all rights.

Columns/Departments: Business & News Briefs (summarizes important news/business news affecting small businesses/merchandisers), 500 words; ASD Profile (interview with successful dealer), 1,000-1,250 words; Merchandising Tips (how to better merchandise a business), 750-1,000. Buys 40 mss/year. Query or send complete ms. Length: 500-1,250 words. Pays $50-75.

Fillers: Facts and newsbreaks. Buys 10/year. Length: 50-300 words. Pays $25-45.

Tips: "Talk to retailers. Find out what their concerns are, and the types of wholesalers/merchandisers they deal with. Talk to those people and learn what they're looking for. Write articles to meet those needs. It's as simple as that. The entire publication is open to freelance writers who can write good articles."

BALLOONS TODAY MAGAZINE, The Original Balloon Magazine of New-Fashioned Ideas, Festivities Publications, 1205 W. Forsyth St., Jacksonville, FL 32204. (904)634-1902. Editor: Debra Paulk. 10% freelance written. Monthly international trade journal for professional party decorators, and for gift delivery businesses. Circ. 12,000. Pays on pubilcation. Publishes ms an average of 3 months after acceptance. Byline given. Buys one-time rights. Submit seasonal/holiday material 6 months in advance. Query for electronic submissions. Reports in 3 weeks on queries; 2 weeks on mss. Sample copy for 9 × 12 SAE with $2 in postage.
Nonfiction: Interview/profile, photo feature, technical, craft. Buys 24 mss/year. Query with or without published clips, or send complete ms. Length: 500-1,500 words. Pays $100-300 assigned articles; $50-200 for unsolicited articles. Sometimes pays expenses of writers on assignment.
Photos: Send photos with submission. Reviews 2 × 2 transparencies and 3 × 5 prints. Pays $25 per photo accepted with manuscript (designs, arrangements, decorations only—no payment for new products). Captions, model releases and identification of subjects required. Buys one-time rights.
Columns/Departments: Great Ideas (craft projects using balloons, large scale decorations), 200-500 words. Send full manuscript with photos. Pays $25 per photo, $20-50.
Tips: "Show unusual, lavish, and outstanding examples of balloon sculpture, design and decorating. Offer specific how-to information. Be positive and motivational in style."

CANADIAN COMPUTER DEALER NEWS, Plesman Publication Ltd., 2005 Sheppard Ave. E., 4th Floor, Willowdale, Ontario M2J 5B1 Canada. (416)497-9562. FAX: (416)497-9427. Editor: Gord Campbell. Managing Editor: Anita Castaldi 10% freelance written. Biweekly newspaper about computers, for retailers. Circ. 9,000. Pays on publication. Publishes ms an average of 1 month after acceptance. Byline given. Offers negotiable kill fee. Buys first North American serial rights. Submit seasonal/holiday material 2 months in advance. Query for electronic submissions. Free sample copy and writer's guidelines.
Nonfiction: Exposé, how-to (market computers effectively, establish advertising budgets or choose a P.R. firm), interview/profile, new product, personal experience (applications) and other. Buys 250 mss/year. Query with or without published clips, or send complete ms. Length: 600-1,000 words. Pays $300-600 for assigned articles. Negotiable payment for unsolicited articles. Sometimes pays expenses of writers on assignment.
Photos: Send photos with submission. Reviews 3 × 5 color prints. Identification of subjects required.
Columns/Departments: Dealer Report (profile of Canadian computer dealer), 800 words; Distribution (profile of Canadian computer distributor), 800 words; VAR Tracks (profile of a Canadian VAR *or* of vendors VAR program), 800 words and Vendor Update (profile of a Canadian computer vendor), 800 words. Buys 50 mss/year. Query with published clips. Pays $300.
Tips: "If freelancer is familiar with the computer industry, he or she might call to discuss story ideas. The writer would then be asked to send a more detailed outline. Managing editor might suggest contacts, sources, if necessary."

CASUAL LIVING, Columbia Communications, 370 Lexington Ave., New York NY 10164. (212)532-9290. FAX: (212)779-8345. Publisher/Editor: Eileen Robinson Smith. A monthly magazine covering outdoor furniture for outdoor furniture specialists, including retailers, mass merchandisers and department store buyers. Estab. 1957. Circ. 14,000. Pays on publication. Buys first North American serial rights. Submit seasonal/holiday material 2 months in advance. Reports in 1 month. Sample copy for 9 × 12 SAE with 2 first class stamps.
Nonfiction: Interview/profile (case histories of retailers in the industry); new product; opinion; and technical. Buys 7-8 mss/year. Query with clips, then follow up with phone call. Length: 1,000 words average. Pays $200-400.
Photos: State availability of photos with query letter or ms. Reviews b&w contact sheets and color prints. Payment for photos usually a package deal with ms. Buys all rights.
Tips: "Know the industry, trades and fashions, and what makes a successful retailer."

EDUCATIONAL DEALER, Fahy-Williams Publishing, Inc. 171 Reed St., Box 1080, Geneva NY 14456. (315)789-0458. Editor: J. Kevin Fahy. 3% freelance written. A publication that covers the educational supply industry, published 5 times per year—January, March, May, August and October. "Slant should be toward educational Supply *dealers, not* teachers or educators, as most commonly happens." Circ. 12,500. Pays on publication. Byline given. Buys one-time rights. Simultaneous and previously published submissions OK. Reports in 3 weeks on queries; 1 month on mss. Sample copies $3.
Nonfiction: New product and technical. Buys 3 mss/year. Query. Length: 1,500 words minimum. Pays $50 minimum.
Photos: Send photos with submission. Reviews contact sheets. Offers no additional payment for photos accepted with ms. Identification of subjects required. Buys one-time rights.
Tips: "Our special features section is most open to freelancers. Become familiar with the educational supply industry, which is growing quickly. While the industry is a large one in terms of dollars spent on school supply products, it's a 'small' one in terms of its players and what they're doing. Everyone knows everyone else; they belong to the same organizations: NSSEA and EDSA."

INCENTIVE, Bill Communications, 633 3rd Ave., New York NY 10017. (212)986-4800. FAX: (212)867-4395. Editor: Bruce Bolger. Managing Editor: Todd Englander. Monthly magazine covering sales promotion and employee motivation: managing and marketing through motivation. Estab. 1905. Circ. 41,000. **Pays on acceptance.** Publishes ms an average of 3 months after acceptance. Byline sometimes given. Buys all rights. Query for electronic submissions. Reports in 1 month on queries; 2 months on mss. Sample copy for 9 × 12 SAE; writer's guidelines for #10 SAE.

Nonfiction: General interest (motivation, demographics), how-to (types of sales promotion, buying product categories, using destinations), interview/profile (sales promotion executives); corporate case studies; and travel (incentive-oriented). Buys up to 48 mss/year. Query with 2 published clips. Length: 500-2,000 words. Pays $250-700 for assigned articles; pays $0-100 for unsolicited articles. Pays expenses of writers on assignment.

Photos: Send photos with submission. Reviews contact sheets and transparencies. Offers no additional payment for photos accepted with ms. Identification of subjects required.

Tips: "Read the publication, then query."

PROFESSIONAL SELLING, 24 Rope Ferry Rd., Waterford CT 06386. (203)442-4365. FAX: (203)434-3078. Editor: Paulette S. Withers. 33% freelance written. Prefers to work with published/established writers, but works with a small number of new/unpublished writers each year. Bimonthly newsletter in two sections for sales professionals covering industrial, wholesale, high-tech and financial services sales. "*Professional Selling* provides field sales personnel with both the basics and current information that can help them better perform the sales function." Estab. 1917. **Pays on acceptance.** Publishes ms an average of 4-6 months after acceptance. No byline given. Buys all rights. Submit seasonal/holiday material 4 months in advance. Reports in 2 weeks. Sample copy and writer's guidelines for #10 SAE and 2 first class stamps.

Nonfiction: How-to (successful sales techniques); and interview/profile (interview-based articles). "We buy only interview-based material." Buys 12-15 mss/year. No unsolicited manuscripts; written queries only. Length: 800-1,000 words.

Tips: "*Professional Selling* includes a 4-page clinic devoted to a single topic of major importance to sales professionals. Only the lead article for each section is open to freelancers. Lead article must be based on an interview with an actual sales professional. Freelancers may occasionally interview sales managers, but the slant must be toward field sales, *not* management."

SOUND MANAGEMENT, Radio Advertising Bureau, 304 Park Ave. S., New York NY 10010. (212)254-4800. FAX: (212)254-8908. Editor-in-Chief: Joan Voukides. Editor: George Swisshelm. 15% freelance written. A monthly magazine covering radio sales and marketing. "We write practical business and how-to stories for the owners and managers of radio stations on topics geared toward increasing ad sales and training salespeople." Estab. 1984. Circ. 10,000. Pays on publication. Publishes ms an average of 4 months after acceptance. Byline given. Buys one-time rights, exclusive rights for the field or makes work-for-hire assignments. Submit seasonal/holiday material 3 months in advance. Previously published submissions OK. Sample copy for 9 × 12 SAE with 3 first class stamps; writer's guidelines for #10 SASE.

Nonfiction: Essays, how-to, interview/profile and personal experience. No articles on disc jockeys or radio programming. Buys 5-10 mss/year. Query with published clips. Length: 400-750 words. Pays $350-650 for assigned articles; $50-150 for unsolicited articles. May pay contributor copies for republished items.

Photos: State availability of photos with submission. Reviews contact sheets, negatives and transparencies. Prefers b&w prints. Captions, model releases, and identification of subjects required. Buys one-time rights.

Tips: "Our cover story is most open to freelancers, but proven experience in writing about media advertising and marketing is necessary, with strong interviewing and critical writing skills."

Sport Trade

Retailers and wholesalers of sports equipment and operators of recreation programs read these journals. Magazines about general and specific sports are classified in the Consumer Sports section.

AMERICAN BICYCLIST, Suite 305, 80 8th Ave., New York NY 10011. (212)206-7230. FAX: (212)633-0079. Editor: Konstantin Doren. 40% freelance written. Prefers to work with published/established writers. Monthly magazine for bicycle sales and service shops. Circ. 11,200. Pays on publication. Publishes ms an average of 4 months after acceptance. Only staff-written articles are bylined, except under special circumstances. Buys all rights.

Nonfiction: Typical story describes (very specifically) unique traffic-builder or merchandising ideas used with success by an actual dealer. Articles may also deal exclusively with moped sales and service operation within conventional bicycle shops. Emphasis on showing other dealers how they can follow similar pattern and increase their business. Articles may also be based entirely on repair shop operation, depicting efficient and profitable service systems and methods. Buys 12 mss/year. Query. Length: 1,000-2,800 words. Pays 11¢/

word, plus bonus for outstanding manuscript. Pays expenses of writers on assignment.

Photos: Reviews relevant b&w photos illustrating principal points in article purchased with ms; 5×7 minimum. Pays $8/photo. Captions required. Buys all rights.

Tips: "A frequent mistake made by writers is writing as if we are a book read by consumers instead of professionals in the bicycle industry."

‡**AMERICAN FIREARMS INDUSTRY**, AFI Communications Group, Inc., 2801 E. Oakland Park Blvd., Ft. Lauderdale FL 33306. 10% freelance written. "Work with writers specifically in the firearms trade." Monthly magazine specializing in the sporting arms trade. Circ. 30,000. Pays on publication. Publishes ms an average of 4 months after acceptance. Buys all rights. Reports in 2 weeks.

Nonfiction: R.A. Lesmeister, articles editor. Publishes informational, technical and new product articles. No general firearms subjects. Query. Length: 900-1,500 words. Pays $100-150. Sometimes pays the expenses of writers on assignment.

Photos: Reviews 8×10 b&w glossy prints. Manuscript price includes payment for photos.

AMERICAN FITNESS, The Official Publication of the Aerobics and Fitness Association of America, Suite 310, 15250 Ventura Blvd., Sherman Oaks CA 91403. (818)905-0040. FAX: (818)990-5468. Editor-at-Large: Peg Jordan, R.N. Managing Editor: Rhonda J. Wilson. 80% freelance written. Eager to work with new/unpublished writers. Bimonthly magazine covering exercise and fitness, health and nutrition. "We need timely, in-depth informative articles on health, fitness, aerobic exercise, sports nutrition, sports medicine and physiology." Circ. 25,100. Pays 4-6 weeks after publication. Publishes ms an average of 6 months after acceptance. Byline given. Buys first North American serial rights and simultaneous rights (in some cases). Submit seasonal/holiday material 4 months in advance. Simultaneous queries and simultaneous and previously published submissions OK. Query for electronic submissions. Reports in 2 weeks. Sample copy for $1 or SAE with 6 first class stamps; writer's guidelines for SAE.

Nonfiction: Book excerpts (fitness book reviews); exposé (on nutritional gimmickry); historical/nostalgic (history of various athletic events); humor (personal fitness profiles); inspirational (sports leader's motivational pieces); interview/profile (fitness figures); new product (plus equipment review); opinion (on clubs); personal experience (successful fitness story); photo feature (on exercise, fitness, new sport); and travel (spas that cater to fitness industry). No articles on unsound nutritional practices, popular trends or unsafe exercise gimmicks. Buys 18-25 mss/year. Query. Length: 800-2,500 words. Pays $80-100. Sometimes pays expenses of writers on assignment.

Photos: Sports, action, fitness, aerobic competitions and exercise classes. Pays $10 for b&w prints; $35 for transparencies. Captions, model release, and identification of subjects required. Buys one-time rights; other rights purchased depend on use of photo.

Columns/Departments: Fitness Industry News (shorts on health, fitness and beauty). Buys 50 mss/year. Query with published clips or send complete ms. Length: 50-150 words. Pays 1¢/word.

Poetry: Buys 2 poems/year. Submit maximum 1 poem. Length: 20-80 lines. Pays $20.

Fillers: Cartoons, clippings, jokes, short humor and newsbreaks. Buys 12/year. Length: 75-200 words. Pays $35.

Tips: "Cover an athletic event, get a unique angle, provide accurate and interesting findings, and write in a lively, intelligent manner. We are looking for new health and fitness reporters and writers. *A&F* is a good place to get started. I have generally been disappointed with short articles and fillers submissions due to their lack of force. Cover a topic with depth."

AMERICAN HOCKEY MAGAZINE, Amateur Hockey Association of the United States, 2997 Broadmoor Valley Rd., Colorado Springs CO 80906. (719)576-4990. FAX: (719)576-4975. Contact: Publisher. Managing Editor: Mike Schroeder. 80% freelance written. Monthly magazine covering hockey in general (with amateur/youth hockey emphasis) for teams, coaches and referees of the Amateur Hockey Association of the U.S., ice facilities in the U.S. and Canada, buyers, schools, colleges, pro teams, and park and recreation departments. Circ. 35,000. Pays on publication. Publishes ms an average of 1 month after acceptance. Byline given. Buys first serial rights; makes work-for-hire assignments. Phone queries OK. Submit seasonal/holiday material 4 months in advance. Previously published submissions OK. Reports in 1 month. Sample copy for 9×12 SAE; writer's guidelines for #10 SASE.

Nonfiction: General interest, profile, new product and technical. Query. Length: 500-3,000 words. Pays $50 minimum.

Photos: Reviews 5×7 b&w glossy prints and color slides. Offers no additional payment for photos accepted with ms. Captions preferred. Buys one-time rights.

Columns/Departments: Rebound Shots (editorial); Americans in the Pros (U.S. players in the NHL); College Notes; Rinks and Arenas (arena news); Equipment/Sports Medicine; Referees Crease; Coaches Playbook; For the Record; and Features (miscellaneous). Query.

‡**ARCHERY BUSINESS**, Ehlert Publishing Group, Suite 101, 319 Barry Ave. S., Waysata MN 55391. Editor: Tim Dehn. 20% freelance written. Bimonthly trade magazine written for dealers, distributors, sales reps and manufacturers of archery and bowhunting equipment. Controlled circulation. Pays on publication. Reports

in 3 weeks on queries; 6 weeks on mss. Free writer's guidelines. Sample copy for 9 × 12 SAE and 10 first class stamps.

Nonfiction: Buys clear and concise articles written to help small retailers improve their profit picture. Articles must be specific to this industry and should use actual examples. Length: 1,500-3,000 words. Pays from less than $200 to more than $400.

BICYCLE BUSINESS JOURNAL, 1904 Wenneca, Box 1570, Fort Worth TX 76101. FAX: (817)332-1619. Editor: Rix Quinn. Works with a small number of new/unpublished writers each year. 10% freelance written. Monthly. Circ. 10,000. **Pays on acceptance.** Publishes ms an average of 3 months after acceptance. Buys all rights. Sample copy for 8 × 10 SAE and 2 first class stamps.

Nonfiction: Stories about dealers who service what they sell, emphasizing progressive, successful sales ideas in the face of rising costs and increased competition. Length: 750 words. Sometimes pays the expenses of writers on assignment.

Photos: B&w or color glossy photo a must; vertical photo preferred. Query.

‡CMAA, The Official Magazine of the Club Managers Association of America, Golf Club Publishing, 16 Forest St., New Canaan CT 06840. (203)972-3892. Editor: John Delves. Managing Editor: Mike Johnson. 80% freelance written. Monthly trade journal covering private club management. Estab. 1989. Circ. 20,000. Pays on publication. Publishes ms an average of 3 months after acceptance. Byline given. Offers ⅓ kill fee. Buys all rights. Submit seasonal/holiday material 4 months in advance. Simultaneous submissions OK. Query for electronic submissions. Reports in 1 month. Sample copy $3; writer's guidelines for #10 SASE.

Nonfiction: Humor, interview/profile, new product, opinion, personal experience, management, current affairs, rennovation, and food service. Buys 36 mss/year. Query with published clips. Length: 300-2,000 words. Pays $50-400 for assigned articles. Sometimes pays expenses of writers on assignment.

Photos: State availability of photos with submission. Reviews transparencies. Offers no additional payment for photos accepted with ms. Captions and identification of subjects required. Buys one-time rights.

Columns/Departments: Query with published clips. Length: 250-500 words. Pays $75-150.

GOLF COURSE MANAGEMENT, Golf Course Superintendents Association of America, 1617 St. Andrews Dr., Lawrence KS 66047. (913)841-2240. FAX: (913)841-2407. Editor: Clay Loyd. 30% freelance written. Eager to work with new/unpublished writers. Monthly magazine covering golf course and turf management. Estab. 1926. Circ. 22,000. Byline given. Buys first-time rights. Submit seasonal/holiday material 6 months in advance. Publishes ms an average of 3 months after acceptance. Simultaneous queries and submissions OK. Reports in 2 weeks on queries; 1 month on mss. Writer's guidelines for #10 SASE; sample copy for $3.

Nonfiction: Book excerpts, historical/nostalgic, interview/profile, personal experience and technical. "All areas that relate to the golf course superintendent—whether features or scholarly pieces related to turf/grass management. We currently lean toward technical mss." Special issues include January "conference issue"—features on convention cities used each year. Buys 50 mss/year. Query with clips of published work. Length: 1,500-3,000 words. Pays $100-300 or more. Sometimes pays the expenses of writers on assignment.

Photos: Send photos with ms. Pays $50-250 for color, slides or transparencies preferred. Captions, model release and identification of subjects required. Buys one-time rights.

Tips: "Call publications department (913)841-2240, offer idea, follow with outline and writing samples. Response from us is immediate."

GOLF SHOP OPERATIONS, 5520 Park Ave., Trumbull CT 06611. (203)373-7232. Editor: Mike Schwanz. 20% freelance written. Works with a small number of new/unpublished writers each year. Magazine published 9 times/year for golf professionals and shop operators at public and private courses, resorts, driving ranges and golf specialty stores. Circ. 14,000. Pays on publication. Publishes ms an average of 2 months after acceptance. Byline given. Submit seasonal material (for Christmas and other holiday sales, or profiles of successful professionals with how-to angle emphasized) 4 months in advance. Reports in 1 month. Sample copy free.

Nonfiction: "We emphasize improving the golf retailer's knowledge of his profession. Articles should describe how pros are buying, promoting, merchandising and displaying wares in their shops that might be of practical value. Must be aimed only at the retailer." How-to, profile, successful business operation and merchandising techniques. Buys 6-8 mss/year. Written queries preferred. Pays $500 maximum for assigned articles. Sometimes pays expenses of writers on assignment.

Columns/Departments: Shop Talk (interesting happenings in the golf market), 250 words; Roaming Range (new and different in the driving range business), 500 words. Buys 4 mss/year. Send complete ms. Pays $50-150.

NSGA RETAIL FOCUS, (formerly *NSGA Sports Retailer*), National Sporting Goods Association, Suite 700, 1699 Wall St., Mt. Prospect IL 60056. (708)439-4000. Publisher: Thomas G. Drake. Managing Editor: Larry Weindruch. 75% freelance written. Works with a small number of new/unpublished writers each year. *NSGA Retail Focus* serves as a monthly trade journal for presidents, CEOs and owners of more than 21,000 retail sporting goods firms. Circ. 9,000. Pays on publication. Publishes ms an average of 1 month after acceptance.

Byline given. Offers 50% kill fee. Buys first and second serial (reprint) rights. Submit seasonal/holiday material 3 months in advance. Query for electronic submissions. Sample copy for 9 × 12 SAE with 5 first class stamps.

Nonfiction: Essays, interview/profile and photo feature. Special issue in December Co-Op Advertising. "No articles written without sporting goods retail businessmen in mind as the audience. In other words, no generic articles sent to several industries." Buys 50 mss/year. Query with published clips. Pays $75-500. Sometimes pays the expenses of writers on assignment.

Photos: State availability of photos with submission. Reviews contact sheets, negatives, transparencies and 5 × 7 prints. Payment negotiable. Buys one-time rights.

Columns/Departments: Personnel Management (succinctt tips on hiring, motivating, firing, etc.); Tax Advisor (simplified explanation of how tax laws affect retailer); Sales Management (in-depth tips to improve sales force performance); Retail Management (detailed explanation of merchandising/inventory control); Advertising (case histories of successful ad campaigns/ad critiques); Legal Advisor; Computers; Store Design; Visual Merchandising; all 1,500 words. Buys 50 mss/year. Query. Length: 1,000-1,500 words. Pays $75-300.

POOL & SPA NEWS, Leisure Publications, 3923 W. 6th St., Los Angeles CA 90020. (213)385-3926. FAX: (213)383-1152. Editor-in-Chief: J. Field. 25-40% freelance written. Semimonthly magazine emphasizing news of the swimming pool and spa industry for pool builders, pool retail stores and pool service firms. Circ. 15,000. Pays on publication. Publishes ms an average of 1-2 months after acceptance. Buys all rights. Query for electronic submissions. Reports in 2 weeks. Sample copy for 9 × 12 SAE and 10 first class stamps; writer's guidelines for #10 SASE.

Nonfiction: Interview, new product, profile and technical. Phone queries OK. Length: 500-2,000 words. Pays 10-12¢/word. Pays expenses of writers on assignment.

Photos: Pays $10 per b&w photo used.

‡PROFESSIONAL BOAT BUILDER MAGAZINE, WoodenBoat Publications Inc., P.O. Box 78, Naskeag Rd., Brooklin ME 04616. (207)359-4651. Chris Cornell. 75% freelance written. Bimonthly magazine on boat building companies, repair yards, naval architects, and marine supervisors. Estab. 1989. Circ. 20,000. Pays 45 days after accetance. Byline given. Offers $200 kill fee. Buys first North American serial rights. Free sample copy and writer's guidelines.

Nonfiction: How-to, new product, opinion, technical. No information better directed to consumers. Buys 20 mss/year. Query with or without published clips or send complete ms. Length: 1,000-6,000 words. Pays 20¢/word. Sometimes pays expenses of writers on assignment.

Photos: State availability of photos with submission. Reviews slide transparencies and 8 × 10 b&w. Offers $15-200 per photo. $350 for color cover. Identification of subjects and full captions required. Buys one-time rights.

Columns/Departments: Barbara Walsh, Assistant editor. Tools of the Trade (new tools/machinery of interest to boat builders), 100-500 words; Work in Progress (new and reconstruction of vessels; 10′-200′ in length—emphasize materials and methods and machinery), 100 words. Buys 12 mss/year. Query with published clips. Pays $25-100.

PRORODEO SPORTS NEWS, Professional Rodeo Cowboys Association, 101 Pro Rodeo Dr., Colorado Springs CO 80919. (719)593-8840. Editor: Timothy C. Bergsten. Biweekly tabloid that covers PRCA Rodeo. "The *Prorodeo Sports News* is the official publication of the PRCA, covering cowboys, stock contractors, contract members and general rodeo-related news about the PRCA membership and PRCA sponsors. We do not print material about any non-sanctioned rodeo event, or other rodeo associations." Circ. 30,000. Pays on publication. Publishes ms 1 month after acceptance. Byline given. Submit seasonal/holiday material 2 months in advance. Sample copy for 8 × 10 SAE and 4 first class stamps; free writer's guidelines.

Nonfiction: Interview/profile and photo feature. Buys 15 mss/year. Query. Length: 1,500 words maximum. Pays $50-100. Sometimes pays expenses of writers on assignment.

Photos: Send photos with submission. Reviews negatives and 5 × 7 and 8 × 10 prints. Offers $10-50 per photo. Identification of subjects required.

Tips: "Feature stories written about PRCA cowboys will always be considered for publication. Along with feature stories on PRCA members, I foresee the *Prorodeo Sports News* printing more articles about rodeo sponsorship and creative rodeo promotions. Like all professional sports, PRCA rodeo is a business. The *Prorodeo Sports News* will reflect the business aspect of professional rodeo, as well as cover the people who make it all happen."

SKI BUSINESS, 537 Post Rd., P.O. Box 1227, Darien CT 06820. FAX: (203)656-0273. Managing Editor: Glen Heitsmith. 70% freelance written. Works with a small number of new/unpublished writers each year. Tabloid magazine published 11 times/year. For ski retailers, both alpine and cross-country. Estab. 1961. Circ. 18,000. Byline given, except on "press releases and round-up articles containing passages from articles submitted by several writers." Pays within 1 month of publication. Buys first rights plus reprint rights for promotional use and republication in special editions. Submit seasonal material 2 months in advance. Query for electronic submissions. Reports in 1 month. Publishes ms an average of 2 months after acceptance. Free sample copy available to qualified writers; writer's guidelines for #10 SAE and 2 first class stamps.

Nonfiction: Will consider ski shop profiles; mss about unique and successful merchandising ideas and equipment rental operations. "All material should be slanted toward usefulness to the ski shop operator. Always interested in in-depth interviews with successful retailers." Uses round-ups of preseason sales and Christmas buying trends across the country from September to December. Would like to see reports on what retailers in major markets are doing. Buys about 100 mss/year. Query first. Pays $50-250. Pays expenses of writers on assignment.

Photos: Photos purchased with accompanying mss. Buys b&w glossies and slides. Pays minimum of $35/photo.

Tips: "We are most interested in retailer profiles of successful ski shop operators, with plenty of advice and examples for our readers."

SPORT STYLE, Fairchild Publication, 7 E. 12th St., New York NY 10003. (212)741-5971. Editor: Dusty Kidd. 10% freelance written. Biweekly tabloid that covers all sports. "Submit material on product technology, business and marketing trends that are helpful for sports *retailers* in selling and running their stores." Circ. 30,000. **Pays on acceptance.** Publishes ms an average of 1 month after acceptance. Byline given. Buys all rights. Submit seasonal/holiday material 1 month in advance. Query for electronic submissions. Free sample copy and writer's guidelines.

Nonfiction: Interview/profile, new product, photo feature, technical and marketing information. Buys 20 mss/year. Query with published clips. Length: 300-1,500 words. Pays $100-500. Sometimes pays expenses of writers on assignment.

Photos: State availability of photos with submission. Reviews contact sheets and negatives. Offers negotiable payment. Identification of subjects required. Buys one-time rights.

Columns/Departments: Sidelines (sports events—unusual first-time marketing oriented), up to 300 words; and Sport Seen (photo essay on trends). Buys 20 mss/year. Query with published clips. Length: 500-1,200 words. Pays $300-500.

THE SPORTING GOODS DEALER, 1212 N. Lindbergh Blvd., St. Louis MO 63132. (314)997-7111. FAX: (314)993-7726. President/CEO: Richard Waters. Editor: Steve Fechter. 20% freelance written. Prefers to work with published/established writers. For members of the sporting goods trade: retailers, manufacturers, wholesalers and representatives. Monthly magazine. Estab. 1899. Circ. 27,000. Buys second serial (reprint) rights. Buys about 15 mss/year. Pays on publication. Publishes ms an average of 3 months after acceptance. Query. Sample copy $4 (refunded with first ms).

Nonfiction: "Articles about specific sporting goods retail stores, their promotions, display techniques, sales ideas, merchandising, timely news of key personnel; expansions, new stores, deaths—all in the sporting goods trade. Specific details on how individual successful sporting goods stores operate and what is new and different. We would also be interested in features dealing with stores doing an outstanding job in retailing of exercise equipment, athletic footwear, athletic apparel, baseball, fishing, golf, tennis, camping, firearms/hunting and allied lines of equipment. Query on these." Successful business operations and merchandising techniques. Does not want to see announcements of doings and engagements. Length: open. Rates negotiated by assignment.

Columns/Departments: Terse Tales of the Trade (store news); Selling Slants (store promotions); and Open for Business (new retail sporting goods stores or sporting goods departments). All material must relate to specific sporting goods stores by name, city and state; general information is not accepted.

Photos: Pays minimum of $3.50 for sharp clear b&w photos; size not important. These are purchased with or without mss. Captions optional, but identification requested.

Fillers: Clippings. These must relate directly to the sporting goods industry. Pays 2¢/published word.

Tips: "The writer has to put himself or herself in our readers' position and ask: Does my style and/or expertise help retailers run their business better?"

TENNIS BUYER'S GUIDE, New York Times Magazine Group, 5520 Park Ave., Trumbull CT 06611. (203)373-7232. FAX: (203)373-7170. Editor: Robert Carney. Managing Editor: Sandra Dolbow. 5% freelance written. A bimonthly tabloid on the tennis industry. "We publish for the tennis retailer. We favor a business angle, providing information that will make our readers better tennis professionals and better business people." Estab. 1985. Circ. 11,000. Pays on publication. Publishes ms an average of 3 months after acceptance. Byline given. Offers 15% kill fee. Buys one-time rights. Submit seasonal/holiday material 6 months in advance. Simultaneous submissions OK. Reports in 6 weeks on queries; 1 month on mss. Free sample copy and writer's guidelines.

Nonfiction: How-to, humor, interview/profile, new product, photo feature, technical and travel. No professional tennis tour articles. Buys 8 mss/year. Send complete ms. Length: 500-2,000 words. Pays $75-300 for assigned articles. Pays $50-300 for unsolicited articles. Sometimes pays the expenses of writers on assignment.

Photos: Reviews transparencies and prints (35mm). Captions, model releases and identification of subjects required. Buys one-time rights.

Tips: "Express an interest and knowledge in tennis or a business management field and an understanding of retail business."

WOODALL'S CAMPGROUND MANAGEMENT, Woodall Publishing Co., 28167 N. Keith Dr., Lake Forest IL 60045. (708)362-6700. Editor: Mike Byrnes. 50% freelance written. Works with a small number of new/unpublished writers each year. A monthly tabloid covering campground management and operation for managers of private and public campgrounds throughout the U.S. Estab. 1970. Circ. 16,000. Pays after publication. Publishes ms an average of 4 months after acceptance. Byline given. Buys all rights. Will reassign rights to author upon written request. Submit seasonal/holiday material 4 months in advance. Simultaneous queries OK. Reports in 1 month on queries; 2 months on mss. Free sample copy and writer's guidelines.

Nonfiction: How-to, interview/profile and technical. "Our articles tell our readers how to maintain their resources, manage personnel and guests, market, develop new campground areas and activities, and interrelate with the major tourism organizations within their areas. 'Improvement' and 'profit' are the two key words." Buys 18 mss/year. Query. Length: 500 words minimum. Pays $50-200. Sometimes pays expenses of writers on assignment.

Photos: Send contact sheets and negatives. "We pay for each photo used."

Tips: "Contact us and give us an idea of your ability to travel and your travel range. We sometimes have assignments in certain areas. The best type of story to break in with is a case history approach about how a campground improved its maintenance, physical plant or profitability."

Stone, Quarry and Mining

‡COAL PEOPLE MAGAZINE, Al Skinner Productions, 629 Virginia St. W., Box 6247, Charleston WV 25362. (304)342-4129. FAX: (304)343-3124. Editor: Al Skinner. Managing Editor: Gary Stuber. 50% freelance written. A monthly magazine with stories about coal people, towns and history. "Most stories are historical — either narrative or biographical about all levels of coal people, past and present — from coal execs down to grass roots miners. Most stories are upbeat — showing warmth of family or success from underground up!" Circ. 10,000. Pays on publication. Publishes ms an average of 3 months after acceptance. Byline given. Buys first rights, second serial (reprint) rights and makes work-for-hire assignments. Submit seasonal/holiday material 2 months in advance. Previously published submissions OK. Reports in 3 months. Sample copy for 9 × 12 SAE and 5 first class stamps.

Nonfiction: Book excerpts (and film if related to coal), historical/nostalgic (coal towns, people, lifestyles), humor (including anecdotes and cartoons), interview/profile (for coal personalities), personal experience (as relates to coal mining), photo feature (on old coal towns, people, past and present). January issue every year is calendar issue for more than 300 annual coal shows, assocation meetings, etc. July issue is always surface mining/reclamation award issue. December issue is Christmas in Coal Country issue. No poetry, no fiction or environmental attacks on the coal industry. Buys 32 mss/year. Query with published clips. Length: 5,000 words. Pays $35.

Photos: Send photos with submission. Reviews contact sheets, transparencies, and 5 × 7 prints. Captions and identification of subjects required. Buys one-time rights and one-time reprint rights.

Columns/Departments: Editorials (anything to do with current coal issues); Mine'ing Our Business (bull pen column — gossip — humorous anecdotes), Coal Show Coverage (freelance photojournalist coverage of any coal function across the U.S.). Buys 10 mss/year. Query. Length: 300-500 words. Pays $5.

Fillers: Anecdotes. Buys 10/year. Length: 300 words. Pays $5.

Tips: "We are looking for good feature articles on coal people, towns, companies — past and present, color slides (for possible cover use) and b/w photos to complement stories. Could also use a few news writers to take photos and do journalistic coverage on coal events across the country."

‡CONCRETE CONSTRUCTION MAGAZINE, The Aberdeen Group, 426 South Westgate, Addison IL 60101. FAX: (708)543-3112. Editorial Director: Ward R. Malisch. Monthly magazine for general and concrete contractors, architects, engineers, concrete producers, cement manufacturers, distributors and dealers in construction equipment and testing labs. Estab. 1956. Circ. 90,000. **Pays on acceptance.** Bylines used only by prearrangement with author. Buys all rights. Reports in 2 months. Free sample copy and writer's guidelines.

Nonfiction: "Our magazine has a major emphasis on cast-in-place and precast concrete. Prestressed concrete is also covered. Our articles deal with tools, techniques and materials that result in better handling, better placing, and ultimately an improved final product. We are particularly firm about not using proprietary names in any of our articles. Manufacturer and product names are rarely mentioned; only the processes or techniques that might be of help to the concrete contractor, the architect or the engineer dealing with the material. We do use reader response cards to relay reader interest to manufacturers." Buys 8-10 mss/year. Submit query with topical outline. Pays $100-200/magazine page. Prefers 1,000-2,000 words with 2-3 illustrations.

Photos: Photos used only as part of complete ms.
Tips: "Condensed, totally factual presentations are preferred."

DIMENSIONAL STONE, Dimensional Stone Institute, Inc., Suite 400, 20335 Ventura Blvd., Woodland Hills CA 91364. (818)704-5555. FAX: (818)704-6500. Editor: Jerry Fisher. 25% freelance written. A bimonthly magazine covering dimensional stone use for managers of producers, importers, contractors, fabricators and specifiers of dimensional stone. Estab. 1979. Circ. 14,986. Pays on publication. Publishes ms an average of 2 months after acceptance. Byline given. Buys first rights or second serial (reprint) rights. Previously published submissions OK. Sample copy for 9×12 SAE and 11 first class stamps; writer's guidelines for #10 SASE.
Nonfiction: Interview/profile and technical, only on users of dimensional stone. Buys 6-7 mss/year. Send complete ms. Length: 1,000-3,000 words. Pays $100 maximum. Sometimes pays the expenses of writers on assignment.
Photos: Send photos with submission. Reviews any size prints. Offers no additional payment for photos accepted with ms. Identification of subjects required.
Tips: "Articles on outstanding uses of dimensional stone are most open to freelancers."

‡**GOLD PROSPECTOR**, Gold Prospectors Association of America, Box 507, Bonsall CA 92003. (619)728-6620. Editor-in-Chief: George Massie. Managing Editor: Perry Massie. Production Editor: Tom Kraak. 60% freelance written. Eager to work with new/unpublished writers. Bimonthly magazine covering gold prospecting and mining. "*Gold Prospector* magazine is the official publication of the Gold Prospectors Association of America. The GPAA is an international organization of more than 25,000 members who are interested in recreational prospecting and mining. Our primary audience is people of all ages who like to take their prospecting gear with them on their weekend camping trips, and fishing and hunting trips. Our readers are interested not only in prospecting, but camping, fishing, hunting, skiing, backpacking, etc. We try to carry stories in each issue pertaining to subjects besides prospecting." Estab. 1965. Circ. 50,000. Pays on publication. Publishes ms an average of 6 months after acceptance. Byline given. Buys first North American serial rights and second serial (reprint) rights. Submit seasonal/holiday material 6 months in advance. Simultaneous queries and previously published submissions OK. Reports in 6 weeks. Sample copy for $2; writer's guidelines for #10 SASE.
Nonfiction: Historical/nostalgic; how-to (prospecting techniques, equipment building, etc.); humor; new product; personal experience; technical; and travel. "One of our publishing beliefs is that our audience would rather experience life than watch it on television—that they would like to take a rough and tumble chance with the sheer adventure of taking gold from the ground or river after it has perhaps lain there for a million years. Even if they don't, they seem to enjoy reading about those who do in the pages of *Gold Prospector* magazine." Buys 75-100 mss/year. Query with or without published clips if available or send complete ms. Length: 1,000-3,000 words. Pays 75¢/column inch (photos and illustrations are measured the same as type).
Photos: State availability of photos with query or ms. Pays 75¢/column inch for photos, transparencies or reflective art. Buys all rights.
Tips: "Articles must be slanted to interest a prospector, miner, or treasure hunter. For example, a first-aid article could address possible mining accidents. Any subject can be so tailored."

STONE REVIEW, National Stone Association, 1415 Elliot Place NW, Washington DC 20007. (202)342-1100. FAX: (202)342-0702. Editor: Frank Atlee. Bimonthly magazine covering quarrying and supplying of crushed stone. "Designed to be a communications forum for the crushed stone industry. Publishes information on industry technology, trends, developments and concerns. Audience are quarry operations/management, and manufacturers of equipment, suppliers of services to the industry." Estab. 1985. Circ. 3,500. Pays on publication. Publishes ms an average of 3 months after acceptance. Byline given. Negotiable kill fee. Buys one-time rights. Simultaneous and previously published submissions OK. Reports in 1 month. Sample copy sent upon request.
Nonfiction: Technical. Query with or without published clips, or send complete ms. Length: 1,000-2,500 words. "Note: We have no budget for freelance material, but I'm willing to secure payment for right material."
Photos: State availability of photos with query, then send photos with submission. Reviews contact sheets, negatives, transparencies and prints. Offers no additional payment for photos accepted with ms. Identification of subjects required. Buys one-time rights.
Tips: "At this point, most features are written by contributors in the industry, but I'd like to open it up. Articles on unique equipment, applications, etc. are good, as are those reporting on trends (e.g., there is a strong push on now for automation of operations). Also interested in stories on family-run operations involving three or more generations."

STONE WORLD, Tradelink Publishing Company, 320 Kinderkamack Rd., Oradell NJ 07649. (201) 599-0136. FAX: (201)599-2378. Editor: Mike Lench. Managing Editor: John Sailer. A monthly magazine on natural building stone for producers and users of granite, marble, limestone, slate, sandstone, onyx and other natural stone products. Circ. 18,000. Pays on publication. Publishes ms an average of 2 months after acceptance. Byline given. Buys first rights or second serial (reprint) rights. Submit seasonal/holiday material 4 months in advance. Previously published submissions OK. Reports in 2 weeks on queries; 1 month on mss. Free sample copy.

Nonfiction: How-to (fabricate and/or install natural building stone), interview/profile, photo feature, technical, architectural design, artistic stone uses, statistics, factory profile, equipment profile and trade show review. Buys 5 mss/year. Query with or without published clips, or send complete ms. Length: 600-3,000 words. Pays $75-150. Pays the expenses of writers on assignment.

Photos: State availability of photos with submission. Reviews transparencies and prints. Offers no additional payment for photos accepted with ms. Captions and identification of subjects required. Buys one-time rights.

Columns/Departments: News (pertaining to stone or design community); New Literature (brochures, catalogs, books, videos, etc. about stone); New Products (stone products); New Equipment (equipment and machinery for working with stone); Calendar (dates and locations of events in stone and design communities). Query or send complete ms. Length: 300-600 words. Pays $25-50.

Tips: "Articles about architectural stone design accompanied by professional photographs and quotes from designing firms are often published, as are articles about new techniques of quarrying and/or fabricating natural building stone."

Toy, Novelty and Hobby

Publications focusing on the toy and hobby industry are listed in this section. For magazines for hobbyists see the Consumer Hobby and Craft section.

MINIATURES DEALER MAGAZINE, 21027 Crossroads Circle, P.O. Box 1612, Waukesha WI 53186. FAX: (414)796-0126. Editor: Geraldine Willems. 50% freelance written. Eager to work with new/unpublished writers. For "retailers in the dollhouse/miniatures trade. Our readers are generally independent, small store owners who don't have time to read anything that does not pertain specifically to their own problems." Monthly magazine. Circ. 1,300. Pays on publication. Publishes ms an average of 3 months after acceptance. Buys all rights. Byline given. Phone queries OK. Submit seasonal/holiday material 4 months in advance. Previously published and simultaneous submissions (if submitted to publications in different fields) OK. Reports in 1 month. Sample copy $1.50; writer's guidelines for SASE.

Nonfiction: How-to (unique articles—e.g., how to finish a dollhouse exterior—are acceptable if they introduce new techniques or ideas; show the retailer how learning this technique will help sell dollhouses); profiles of miniatures shops; and business information pertaining to small store retailers. Buys 2-4 mss/issue. Query or send complete ms. "In query, writer should give clear description of intended article, when he could have it to me plus indication that he has studied the field, and is not making a 'blind' query. Availability of b&w photos should be noted." Pay negotiable.

Photos: "Photos must tie in directly with articles." State availability of photos. Pays $7 for each photo used. Prefers 5×7 b&w glossy prints (reviews contact sheets). Captions and model release preferred.

Tips: "We are interested in articles on full-line miniatures stores. The best way for a freelancer to break in is to study several issues of our magazine, then try to visit a miniatures shop and submit an *MD* Visits . . . article. This is a regular feature that can be written by a sharp freelancer who takes the time to study and follow the formula this feature uses. Also, basic business articles for retailers—inventory control, how to handle bad checks, etc., that are written with miniatures dealers in mind, are always needed. *MD* is extremely interested in good business articles."

PLAYTHINGS, Geyer-McAllister, 51 Madison Ave., New York NY 10010. (212)689-4411. FAX: (212)683-7929. Editor: Frank Reysen, Jr. Senior Editor: Eugene Gilligan. 20-30% freelance written. A monthly merchandising magazine covering toys and hobbies aimed mainly at mass market toy retailers. Estab. 1877. Circ. 15,000. **Pays on acceptance.** Publishes ms an average of 3 months after acceptance. Byline sometimes given. Buys one-time rights. Submit seasonal/holiday material 3 months in advance. Simultaneous submissions OK. Reports in 2 weeks. Free sample copy and writer's guidelines.

Nonfiction: Interview/profile, photo feature and retail profiles of toy and hobby stores and chains. Annual directory published in May. Buys 10 mss/year. Query. Length: 900-2,500 words. Pays $100-350. Sometimes pays the expenses of writers on assignment.

Photos: Send photos with submission. Captions and identification of subjects required. Buys one-time rights.

Columns/Departments: Buys 5 mss/year. Query. Pays $50-100.

SOUVENIRS & NOVELTIES MAGAZINE, Kane Communications, Inc., Suite 210, 7000 Terminal Square, Upper Darby PA 19082. President: Scott Borowsky. Editor: Sandy Meschkow. A magazine published 7 times/year for resort and gift industry. Circ. 21,000. Pays on publication. Byline given. Buys all rights. Reports in 3 weeks. Sample copy for 6×9 SAE with 5 first class stamps.

Nonfiction: Interview/profile and new product. Buys 6 mss/year. Query. Length: 700-1,500 words. Pays $25-175 for assigned articles. Sometimes pays the expenses of writers on assignment.

Photos: State availability of photos with submission. Captions, model releases and identification of subjects required.

THE STAMP WHOLESALER, Box 706, Albany OR 97321. Executive Editor: Dane S. Claussen. 80% freelance written. Newspaper published 28 times/year for philatelic businessmen; many are part-time and/or retired from other work. Circ. 6,000. Pays on publication. Byline given. Buys all rights. Reports in 10 weeks. Free sample copy and writer's guidelines.
Nonfiction: How-to information on how to deal more profitably in postage stamps for collections. Emphasis on merchandising techniques and how to make money. Does not want to see any so-called "humor" items from nonprofessionals. Buys 60 ms/year. Submit complete ms. Length: 1,000-1,500 words. Pays $35 and up/article.
Tips: "Send queries on business stories. Send manuscript on stamp dealer stories. We need stories to help dealers make and save money."

Transportation

These publications are for professional movers and people involved in transportation of goods. For magazines focusing on trucking see also Auto and Truck.

AMERICAN MOVER, American Movers Conference, 2200 Mill Rd., Alexandria VA 22314. (703)838-1938. FAX: (703)838-1925. Editor: Ann S. Dinerman. 10% freelance written. Works with a small number of new/unpublished writers each year. A monthly trade journal on the moving and storage industry for moving company executives. Estab. 1945. Circ. 2,200. Pays on publication. Publishes ms an average of 3 months after acceptance. Byline given. Offers $100 kill fee. Buys first North American serial rights. Submit seasonal/holiday material 3 months in advance. Query for electronic submissions. Reports in 3 weeks on queries. Free sample copy and writer's guidelines.
Nonfiction: How-to, interview/profile, new product, personal experience, photo feature, technical and small business articles. "No fiction or articles geared toward consumers." Buys 6 mss/year. Query with published clips. Length: 1,000-5,000 words. Pays $100-200 for assigned articles. Pays contributor copies at writer's request.
Photos: Send photos with submission. Reviews 5 × 7 prints. Offers no additional payment for photos accepted with ms. Captions required. Buys one-time rights.
Tips: "We have an editorial calendar available that lists topics we'll be covering. Articles on small business are helpful. Feature articles are most open to freelancers. Articles must slant toward moving company presidents on business-related issues. Timely topics are safety, deregulation, drug testing, computers, insurance, tax reform and marketing."

BUS WORLD, Magazine of Buses and Bus Systems, Stauss Publications, P.O. Box 39, Woodland Hills CA 91365. (818)710-0208. Editor: Ed Stauss. 75% freelance written. Quarterly trade journal covering the transit and intercity bus industries. Extensive photographic coverage." Estab. 1978. Circ. 5,000. Pays on publication. Sample copy with writer's guidelines $2.
Photos: "We buy photos with manuscripts under one payment."
Fillers: Cartoons. Buys 4-6/year. Pays $10.
Tips: "No tourist or travelog viewpoints. Be employed in or have a good understanding of the bus industry. Be enthusiastic about buses—their history and future—as well as current events. Acceptable material will be held until used and will not be returned unless requested by sender. Unacceptable and excess material will be returned only if accompanied by suitable SASE."

INBOUND LOGISTICS, Thomas Publishing Co., 5 Penn Plaza, 8th Fl., New York NY 10001. (212)629-1560. FAX: (212)290-7362. Publisher: Keith Biondo. 20% freelance written. Prefers to work with published/established writers. Monthly magazine covering the transportation industry. "*Inbound Logistics* is distributed to people who buy, specify, or recommend inbound freight transportation services and equipment. The editorial matter provides basic explanations of inbound freight transportation, directory listings, how-to technical information, trends and developments affecting inbound freight movements, and expository, case history feature stories." Circ. 43,000. Pays on publication. Publishes ms an average of 3 months after acceptance. Byline given. Buys all rights. Simultaneous queries, and simultaneous submissions OK. Reports in 2 weeks. Sample copy and writer's guidelines for 9 × 12 SAE and 5 first class stamps.
Nonfiction: How-to (basic help for purchasing agents and traffic managers) and interview/profile (purchasing and transportation professionals). Buys 15 mss/year. Query with published clips. Length: 750-1,000 words. Pays $300-1,200. Pays expenses of writers on assignment.
Photos: Michael Ritter, photo editor. State availability of photos with query. Pays $100-500 for b&w contact sheets, negatives, transparencies and prints; $250-500 for color contact sheets, negative transparencies and prints. Captions and identification of subjects required.
Columns/Departments: Viewpoint (discusses current opinions on transportation topics). Query with published clips.
Tips: "Have a sound knowledge of the transportation industry; educational how-to articles get our attention."

SHIPPING DIGEST, The National Shipping Weekly of Export Transportation, Geyer McAllister Publications Inc., 51 Madison Ave., New York NY 10010. (212)689-4411. FAX: (212)683-7929. Editor: Maria Reines. 20% freelance written. Weekly magazine that covers ocean, surface, air transportation, ports, intermodal and EDI. "Read by executives responsible for exporting U.S. goods to foreign markets. Emphasis is on services offered by ocean, surface and air carriers, their development and trends; port developments; trade agreements; government regulation; electronic data interchange." Pays on publication. Publishes ms an average of 1 month after acceptance. Byline given. Offers $150 kill fee. Buys first rights. Reports in 1 week. Free sample copy and writers guidelines.

Nonfiction: Interview/profile. Buys 25 mss/year. Query. Length: 800-1,500 words. Pays $125-300. Sometimes pays expenses of writers on assignment.

Photos: State availability of photos with submission. Reviews contact sheets and 5×7 prints. Offers no payment for photos accepted with ms. Identification of subjects required. Buys one-time rights.

TRUCKS MAGAZINE, Dedicated to the People Behind the Wheel, 765 Churchville Rd., Southampton PA 18966. (215)355-1034. FAX: (215)355-3931. Managing Editor: Michael B. Young. Editor: John Stevens. Publisher: Chris Krieg. 25% freelance written. Magazine covering long haul, heavy-duty trucking. "Dedicated to the health, safety, image and profitability of long haul, heavy-duty truck drivers and their families." Circ. 100,000. Pays within 30 days of publication. Publishes ms an average of 6-10 months after acceptance. Byline given. Buys first rights. Submit seasonal/holiday material 10 months in advance. Reports in 1 week on queries; sample copy for 9×12 SAE with 6 first class stamps.

Nonfiction: Exposé, general interest, how-to, inspirational, new product, personal experience and photo feature. Buys 10 mss/year. Send complete ms. Length: 1,500 words maximum. Pays $50/published page.

Photos: Send photos with submission. Reviews transparencies and prints. Offers no additional payment for photos accepted with ms. Captions, model releases and identification of subjects required. Buys one-time rights.

Travel

Travel professionals read these publications to keep up with trends, tours and changes in transportation. Magazines about vacations and travel for the general public are listed in the Consumer Travel section.

ABC STAR SERVICE, Reed Travel Group, 131 Clarendon St., Boston MA 02116. (617)262-5000. FAX: (617)421-9353. Managing Editor: Steven R. Gordon. Estab. 1960. "Eager to work with new/unpublished writers as well as those working from a home base abroad, planning trips that would allow time for hotel reporting, or living in major ports for cruise ships." Worldwide guide to accommodations and cruise ships founded in 1960 (as *Sloan Travel Agency Reports*) and sold to travel agencies on subscription basis. Pays 15 days after publication. Buys all rights. Query should include details on writer's experience in travel and writing, clips, specific forthcoming travel plans, and how much time would be available for hotel or ship inspections. Buys 5,000 reports/year. Pays $18/report used. Sponsored trips are acceptable. General query statement should precede electronic submission. Writer's guidelines and list of available assignments for #10 SASE.

Nonfiction: Objective, critical evaluations of hotels and cruise ships suitable for international travelers, based on personal inspections. Freelance correspondents ordinarily are assigned to update an entire state or country. "Assignment involves on-site inspections of all hotels we review; revising and updating published reports; and reviewing new properties. Qualities needed are thoroughness, precision, perseverance and keen judgment. Solid research skills and powers of observation are crucial. Travel and travel writing experience are highly desirable. Reviews must be colorful, clear, and documented with hotel's brochure, rate sheet, etc. We accept no hotel advertising or payment for listings, so reviews should dispense praise and criticism where deserved."

Tips: "We may require sample hotel or cruise reports on facilities near freelancer's hometown before giving the first assignment. No byline because of sensitive nature of reviews."

BUS TOURS MAGAZINE, The Magazine of Bus Tours and Long Distance Charters, National Bus Trader, Inc., 9698 W. Judson Rd., Polo IL 61064. (815)946-2341. Editor: Larry Plachno. Editorial Assistant: Ginger Riehle. 80% freelance written. Eager to work with new/unpublished writers. Bimonthly magazine for bus companies and tour brokers who design or sell bus tours. Circ. 9,306. Pays as arranged. Publishes ms an average of 6 months after acceptance. Byline given. Not copyrighted. Buys rights as arranged. Submit seasonal/holiday material 9 months in advance. Simultaneous queries OK. Reports in 1 month. Free sample copy and writer's guidelines.

Nonfiction: Historical/nostalgic, how-to, humor, interview/profile, new product, professional, personal experience and travel; all on bus tours. Buys 10 mss/year. Query. Length: open. Pays negotiable fee.

Photos: State availability of photos. Reviews 35mm transparencies and 6x9 or 8×10 prints. Caption, model release and identification of subjects required.

Columns/Departments: Bus Tour Marketing; and Buses and the Law. Buys 15-20 mss/year. Query. Length: 1-1½ pages.

Tips: "Most of our feature articles are written by freelancers under contract from local convention and tourism bureaus. Specifications sent on request. Writers should query local bureaus regarding their interest. Writer need not have extensive background and knowledge of bus tours."

NATIONAL BUS TRADER, The Magazine of Bus Equipment for the United States and Canada, 9698 W. Judson Rd., Polo IL 61064. (815)946-2341. FAX: (815)946-2347. Editor: Larry Plachno. 25% freelance written. Eager to work with new/unpublished writers. Monthly magazine for manufacturers, dealers and owners of buses and motor coaches. Estab. 1977. Circ. 7,354. Pays on either acceptance or publication. Publishes ms an average of 3 months after acceptance. Byline given. Not copyrighted. Buys rights "as required by writer." Simultaneous queries, and simultaneous and previously published submissions OK. Reports in 1 month. Free sample copy.

Nonfiction: Historical/nostalgic (on old buses); how-to (maintenance repair); new products; photo feature; and technical (aspects of mechanical operation of buses). "We are finding that more and more firms and agencies are hiring freelancers to write articles to our specifications. We are more likely to run them if someone else pays." No material that does *not* pertain to bus tours or bus equipment. Buys 3-5 unsolicited mss/year. Query. Length varies. Pays variable rate. Sometimes pays the expenses of writers on assignment.

Photos: State availability of photos. Reviews 5×7 or 8×10 prints and 35mm transparencies. Captions, model release and identification of subjects required.

Columns/Departments: Bus maintenance; Buses and the Law; Regulations; and Bus of the Month. Buys 20-30 mss/year. Query. Length: 250-400 words. Pays variable rate.

Tips: "We are a very technical publication. Writers should submit qualifications showing extensive background in bus vehicles. We're very interested in well-researched articles on older bus models and manufacturers, or current converted coaches. We would like to receive history of individual bus models prior to 1953 and history of GMC 'new look' models. Write or phone editors with article concept or outline for comments and approval."

RV BUSINESS, TL Enterprises, Inc., 29901 Agoura Rd., Agoura CA 91301. (818)991-4980. FAX: (818)991-8102. Executive Editor: Katherine Sharma. 60% freelance written. Prefers to work with published/established writers. Semi-monthly magazine covering the recreational vehicle and allied industries for people in the RV industry—dealers, manufacturers, suppliers, campground management, and finance experts. Estab. 1950. Circ. 25,000. **Pays on acceptance.** Publishes ms an average of 2 months after acceptance. Byline given. Offers 50% kill fee. Buys first North American serial rights. Submit seasonal/holiday material 6 months in advance. Query for electronic submissions. Reports in 3 weeks on queries; 6 weeks on mss. Sample copy for 9×12 SAE and 3 first class stamps; writer's guidelines for #10 SASE.

Nonfiction: Technical, financial, legal or marketing issues; how-to (deal with any specific aspect of the RV business); interview/profile (persons or companies involved with the industry—legislative, finance, dealerships, manufacturing, supplier); specifics and verification of statistics required—must be factual; and technical (photos required, 4-color preferred). General business articles may be considered. Buys 75 mss/year. Query with published clips. Send complete ms—"but only read on speculation." Length: 1,000-1,500 words. Pays variable rate up to $500. Sometimes pays expenses of writers on assignment.

Photos: State availability of photos with query or send photos with ms. Reviews 35mm transparencies and 8×10 b&w prints. Captions, model release, and identification of subjects required. Buys one-time or all rights; unused photos returned.

Columns/Departments: Guest editorial; News (50-500 words maximum, b&w photos appreciated); and RV People (color photos/4-color transparencies; this section lends itself to fun, upbeat copy). Buys 100-120 mss/year. Query or send complete ms. Pays $10-200 "depending on where used and importance."

Tips: "Query. Phone OK; letter preferable. Send one or several ideas and a few lines letting us know how you plan to treat it/them. We are always looking for good authors knowledgable in the RV industry or related industries. Change of editorial focus requires more articles that are brief, factual, hard hitting, business oriented and in-depth. Will work with promising writers, published or unpublished."

‡TRAVEL LIFE, The magazine for travel professionals, Whittle Communications, L.P., 505 Market St., Knoxville TN 37902. (615)595-5000. Editor: Paula Spencer. 50% freelance written. Bimonthly trade journal for travel agents. "*Travel Life* is a full-color workstyle magazine for front-line sales agents. Though primarily a service book that helps readers become more effective on the job, light features and stress breaking material are an essential part of the editorial mix." Estab. 1988. Publishes ms an average of 2-6 months after acceptance. Offers 25% kill fee. Buys first North American serial rights. Submit seasonal/holiday material 4-6 months in advance. Query for electronic submissions. Reports in 2 months on queries; 2 weeks on mss. Free sample copy and writer's guidelines.

Nonfiction: Book excerpts, how-to, humor, interview/profile (travel agents). Buys 30 mss/year. Query with published clips. Length: 300-2,500 words. Pays 50¢-$1.50/word for assigned articles; 50¢-$1 for unsolicited articles. Pays expenses of writers on assignment.

Photos: State availability of photos with submission. Model releases and identification of subjects required. Buys one-time rights.

TRAVELAGE MIDAMERICA, Official Airlines Guide, Inc., A Dun & Bradstreet Co., Suite 601, 320 N. Michigan, Chicago IL 60601. (312)346-4952. Editor/Publisher: Martin Deutsch. Managing Editor: Karen Goodwin. 15% freelance written. Weekly magazine "for travel agents in the 13 mid America states and in Ontario and Manitoba." Estab. 1975. Circ. 20,000. Pays on publication. Publishes ms an average of 2 months after acceptance. Buys one-time rights and second serial (reprint) rights. Submit seasonal/holiday material 3 months in advance. Simultaneous and previously published submissions OK. Query first. Reports in 2 months. Free sample copy and writer's guidelines with SASE.

Nonfiction: "News on destinations, hotels, operators, rates and other developments in the travel business." Also runs human interest features on retail travel agents in the readership area. No stories that don't contain prices; no queries that don't give detailed story lines. No general destination stories, especially ones on "do-it-yourself" travel. Buys 20 mss/year. Query. Length: 400-1,500 words. Pays $2/column inch.

Photos: State availability of photos with query. Pays $2/column inch for glossy b&w prints.

Tips: "Our major need is for freelance human interest stories with a marketing angle on travel agents in our readership area. Buying freelance destination stories is a much lower priority."

TRAVELAGE WEST, Official Airline Guides, Inc., 100 Grant Ave., San Francisco CA 94108. Managing Editor: Robert Carlsen. 5% freelance written. Prefers to work with published/established writers. Weekly magazine for travel agency sales counselors in the western U.S. and Canada. Circ. 35,000. Pays on publication. Publishes ms an average of 1 month after acceptance. Byline given. Buys all rights. Offers kill fee. Submit seasonal/holiday material 2 months in advance. Query for electronic submissions. Reports in 1 month. Free writer's guidelines.

Nonfiction: Travel. "No promotional approach or any hint of do-it-yourself travel. Emphasis is on news, not description. No static descriptions of places, particularly resort hotels." Buys 40 mss/year. Query. Length: 1,000 words maximum. Pays $2/column inch.

Tips: "Query should be a straightforward description of the proposed story, including (1) an indication of the news angle, no matter how tenuous, and (2) a recognition by the author that we run a trade magazine for travel agents, not a consumer book. I am particularly turned off by letters that try to get me all worked up about the 'beauty' or excitement of some place. Authors planning to travel might discuss with us a proposed angle before they go; otherwise their chances of gathering the right information are slim."

Veterinary

Journals for veterinarians and pet health professionals are located in this section. For publications targeted to pet shop and grooming business managers and the pet supply industry see the Pets section. For magazines for pet owners see the Consumer Animal section.

NEW METHODS, The Journal of Animal Health Technology, P.O. Box 22605, San Francisco CA 94122-0605. (415)664-3469. Managing Editor: Ronald S. Lippert, AHT. *"New Methods* is an educational and informational newsletter about animal health technology." Estab. 1976. Circ. 5,600. Pays on publication. Byline given. Buys simultaneous rights. Submit seasonal/holiday material 2 months in advance. Simultaneous submissions OK. Reports in 2 weeks. Sample copy for $2, #10 SAE and 2 first class stamps; writer's guidelines for #10 SASE.

Nonfiction: How-to (technical), new product and technical. Buys 1 ms/year. Query. Pays in contributor copies or other premiums. Sometimes pays expenses of writers on assignment.

Photos: State availability of photos with submission. Reviews contact sheets. Offers variable payment. Captions, model releases and identification of subjects required. Buys one-time rights.

Columns/Departments: Buys 12 mss/year. Query. Length and payment variable.

Poetry: We do not want unrelated subject matter, very long or abstract poetry. Buys 2 poems/year. Submit maximum 1 poem. Length and payment variable.

Fillers: Facts and newsbreaks. Buys 12/year.

Tips: "Contact *New Methods* in writing with an SASE before writing or submitting any finished material; ideas first."

VETERINARY ECONOMICS MAGAZINE, 9073 Lenexa Dr., Lenexa KS 66215. (913)492-4300. Editor: Rebecca R. Turner. 75% freelance written. Prefers to work with published/established writers but will work with several new/unpublished writers each year. Monthly business magazine for all practicing veterinarians in the U.S. Estab. 1960. Buys exclusive rights in the field. Pays on publication. Publishes ms 3-6 months after acceptance. Free sample copy and writer's guidelines.

Nonfiction: Publishes non-clinical case studies on business and management techniques that will strengthen a veterinarian's private practice. Also interested in articles on financial problems, investments, insurance and similar subjects of particular interest to professionals. "We look for carefully researched articles that are specifically directed to our field." Pays negotiable rates. Pays expenses of writers on assignment.

Tips: "Our stories focus on nuts-and-bolts practice management techniques prescribed by experts in the practice management field. Stories must be useful and appeal to a broad section of our readers."

Other Trade, Technical and Professional Journals

The following trade journals do not have listings in this edition of *Writer's Market*. The majority did not respond to our request to update their listings or return a questionnaire for a new listing. If a reason was given for their exclusion, we have included it in parentheses after the listing name.

Acres U.S.A.
Agri-Times Northwest
Agway Cooperator
American Journal of Nursing
The American School Board Journal
The Amusement Business
ANSOM
Apparel Industry Magazine
Appliance Manufacturer
Asta Agency Management
Atlantic Construction
Automatic Machining
Automotive Booster of California (asked to be deleted)
Bank Personnel Report
Banking Software
The Battery Man
Beauty Age
Boating Industry
Broadcaster
Builder Insider
Bus Ride
CA Magazine
Cablecaster
California Farmer
Canadian Computer Reseller
Canadian Jeweller
Canadian Printer & Publisher
Canadian Shipper
Catering Today
The Cattleman Magazine
Ceramic Scope (unable to contact)
Christian Writer's Newsletter (merged with Cross and Quill; pays in subscriptions and services)
Circuit Rider
Collision
Common Sense
Computers in Education
Computer Language
Contemporary Long-Term Care
Convention South
Cope Magazine
Corporate Health (ceased publication)

Dairy Goat Journal
Data Training
DBMS
Dealer Communicator
Deluxe
Design Management
Directions in Childcare
Distributor
Dixie Contractor
Doctor's Review (asked to be deleted)
Domestic Engineering Magazine
Dr. Dobb's Journal
Entree (ceased publication)
Export
Fair Times
Fancy Food
Farm Futures
Festivity! (asked to be deleted)
The Final Draft (no longer publishing)
Fishing Tackle Retailer
Florida Forum
Florida Grocer
The Flying A (not buying freelance material)
Floor Covering Business
Food & Drug Packaging
Foreign Service Journal
Foundation News Magazine
Glass Magazine
Government Contractor
Hearth & Home
High-Tech Selling
High Technology Business
High Volume Printing
Home Furnishings Reviews (no longer publishing)
Hotel and Motel Management (does not use freelancers)
Human Resource Executive
Hyatt
Ideas
IEEE Software
Info Guide
Inform
Installation News
Insurance Software Review

(publication sold)
International Aviation Mechanics Journal
Jobber Topics
The Journal of Light Construction
Journal of Property Management
Learning 90
Library Journal
Lifting & Transportation International
Looking Fit
Louisiana Contractor
Maintenance Supplies
Management Digest
Management Review (receiving too many inappropriate submissions)
Marriott Portfolio
The Mayo Alumnus
MD Magazine
Meat Plant Magazine
Medical Business Journal (ceased publication)
Medical Meetings
Ministries Today (not accepting freelance submissions)
Motel/Hotel Insider (merged with The Successful Hotel Marketer)
Motor Service (not accepting freelance submissions)
N.D. Rec Magazine
National Utility Contractor
9-1-1- Magazine
NSBE Journal
O and A Marketing News (asked to be deleted)
Occupational Health & Safety Magazine
Ohio Writer
Opportunity Magazine
Outside Business
Paperboard Packaging (receiving too many inappropriate submissions)
Pet Business
The Photo Review

Physicians' Travel & Meeting
  Guide
Police
Police Times
The Private Carrier
Private Practice
Pro
Pro Sound News
Professional Upholsterer
Progressive Architecture
PTN
Publishers Weekly (accepts
  little freelance material)
The Pumper
Purchasing Executive Bulletin
The Rangefinder

Recording Engineer/Producer
Renews (ceased publication)
Restaurant Exchange News
Retailer and Marketing News
Savings Institutions
Se La Vie Writer's Journal
  (does not pay)
Security Management
Sew Business
Silviculture
Small Business Chronicle (pays
  in copies)
Snack Food
Souvenir Magazine
Soybean Digest
Sportcare & Fitness

Studio Photography
Supervision
Swimming Pool/Spa Age
Systems Builder
Systems Integration
Tobacco Reporter
T-Shirt Retailer and Screen
  Printer
Veterinary Practice Manage-
  ment
Video Manager (publication
  sold)
Watersports Business
Writer's Guidelines (no longer
  publishing)
Yard & Garden

Scriptwriting

by Kerry Cox

It isn't necessary for a novelist to know how a printing press is run, or how cover art is designed and produced or how the binding of each book is accomplished. On the other hand, a scriptwriter is well-advised to be thoroughly knowledgable about the techniques and methods used to get a story up on the screen and to have a general idea of the costs involved. Obviously, this kind of knowledge is best gained from hands-on experience, whether it's working as a stagehand at a local theater, a grip at a local television station or by simply shooting a few home movies with a VHS camera. A scriptwriter must be aware of the limitations of the visual medium—and of the freedom it offers, as well.

In scriptwriting, more than perhaps anything but poetry, brevity counts. Keep dialogue short, crisp and purposeful. Action is described in small blocks of copy or the reader's eye tends to skim. Rely on action words; remember, your story is up on the screen or stage, so show, don't tell. Too often—and this is particularly true of business and educational scriptwriters—the infamous "talking heads" are used to convey information or provide exposition when a visual method would be more effective. Talking heads are the easy way out for a scriptwriter, but they also pack a script with about as much visual wallop as your Aunt Estelle's slides of the family vacation.

Short, snappy dialogue and crisp action will enable you to pace your script and inject it with an underlying rhythm that captivates both the reader and eventually the viewer. Frank Pierson, one of the most respected writers in the industry (*Cool Hand Luke*, *Dog Day Afternoon* and many others) says that rhythm is all-important in scriptwriting. As he puts it, "If you can't dance, you can't write scripts." That may be stretching things somewhat, but the point is well-taken—your script must flow naturally from one point to the next, inevitably, but never predictably.

There are a number of markets for scriptwriters, each with its own unique requirements and *modus operandi*. A professional approach to each market requires a comprehensive knowledge of the capabilities of the medium, the procedures and protocol to follow in marketing one's work, and the script format—the actual layout of the page—that each market expects. You wouldn't submit a two-column video script to a movie producer, for example, any more than you would ask a magazine editor to consider a short story you'd written from right to left across the page.

There are many publications that detail the correct format for various scripts, but one of the best ways to learn is to analyze produced scripts. Many production companies develop a format unique to their shows, and it's helpful to be aware of their preferences.

In addition to the markets listed here, stay current with the changing names and needs of potential clients. There are a number of magazines, newsletters and trade publications that track the business side of each marketplace and can keep you "in the know."

Don't just think of Hollywood when you think of scriptwriting. After all, scripts are needed by radio stations, advertising agencies, local and cable television stations, corporations, stand-up comics, public speakers, local theaters, independent video producers and

Kerry Cox is a Los Angeles writer with more than ten years of experience in television, motion picture, theater and business/educational scriptwriting. He is the co-author (with Jurgen Wolff) of Successful Script-writing (*Writer's Digest Books*), and is editor and publisher of Hollywood Scriptwriter, *a newsletter for scriptwriters throughout the U.S. and Canada.*

many other outlets. Gain experience by writing for anyone and everyone you can because the more you practice this unusual, demanding and highly rewarding form of writing, the closer you'll be to writing the script you always knew you had inside.

Business and Educational Writing

Many writers who set their sights on scriptwriting think business and educational writing is glamorless, unattractive or otherwise unappealing. That's probably why there is an elite corps of scriptwriters in every business community who earn good money freelancing for local industry, corporations, ad agencies and independent producers—after all, they don't have a whole lot of competition to worry about. There are plenty of jobs in this field and any number of clients—clients who are extremely loyal to writers who prove they can deliver a quality script on time and within budget.

The misconception writers have about this type of scriptwriting is that it requires little imagination. On the contrary, writers must delve deeply to come up with creative, visually exciting ways to present what may often be somewhat dry, even technical material. Whether the purpose of the script is to inform, advise, train, educate or motivate, it must almost always entertain. Why? Because that's the one surefire way to ensure that the message is seen, heard and understood.

Flexibility is critical in this, as in all forms of scriptwriting. There will very likely be an approval chain of some length, a gamut each script must run prior to production. Scripts for educational use are scrutinized by everyone from the producers to psychologists (especially if the audience is school-aged), while corporate scripts must also satisfy a chain of command. It is the writer's task to willingly incorporate suggested revisions, and whenever possible, to do so without compromising the effectiveness of the script.

To be successful in this area, you must be professional and businesslike. You must be sensitive to budgets. You must hit deadlines without fail. You must also be comfortable dealing with anyone from the warehouse workers to the chairman of the board. You have to be an extremely quick study, able to become an expert overnight, since many times your show will set policy.

Fees vary so much they defy generalization. A good rule of thumb is to base your fee on the expected length of the program, figuring anywhere from $50-200 per minute. Fees should also take into account the amount of research involved, the number of meetings you'll be expected to attend—and they can be numerous—and the number of drafts you are required to provide, usually a first, second and polish.

For more business and education markets, see Other Scriptwriting Markets at the end of the Screenwriting section.

ABS & ASSOCIATES, Box 5127, Evanston IL 60204. (312)982-1414. President: Alan Soell. "We produce material for all levels of corporate, medical, cable, and educational institutions for the purposes of training and development, marketing and meeting presentations. We also are developing programming for the broadcast areas. 75% freelance written. We work with a core of three to five freelance writers from development to final drafts." All scripts published are unagented submissions. Buys all rights. Previously produced material OK. Reports in 2 weeks on queries. Catalog for 8×10 SAE and 6 first class stamps.
Needs: Videotape, 16mm films, silent and sound filmstrips, multimedia kits, overhead transparencies, realia, slides, tapes and cassettes, and television shows/series. Currently interested in "sports instructional series that could be produced for the consumer market on tennis, gymnastics, bowling, golf, aerobics, health and fitness, cross-country skiing and cycling. Also home improvement programs for the novice—for around the house—in a series format. These two areas should be 30 minutes and be timeless in approach for long shelf life." Sports audience, age 25-45; home improvement, 25-65. "Cable TV needs include the two groups of programming detailed here. We are also looking for documentary work on current issues, nuclear power, solar power, urban development, senior citizens—but with a new approach." Query or submit synopsis/outline and resume. Pays by contractual agreement.

Tips: "I am looking for innovative approaches to old problems that just don't go away. The approach should be simple and direct so there is immediate audience identification with the presentation. I also like to see a sense of humor used. Trends in the audiovisual field include interactive video with tape and video disk—for training purposes."

ANIMATION ARTS ASSOCIATES, INC., 1100 E. Hector St., Conshohocken PA 19428. (215)825-8530. Contact: Rozaida Keely. For government, industry, engineers, doctors, scientists, dentists, general public, military. 100% freelance written. Buys average 12 scripts/year.
Needs: Produces 3½-minute 8mm and 16mm film loops; 16mm and 35mm films (ranging from 5-40 minutes); 2¼×2¼ or 4×5 slides; complete film and video productions; and teaching machine programs for training, sales, industry and public relations. Also produces software—motion picture scripts for training sales promotion and recruitment films. Send resume of credits for motion picture and filmstrip productions and software. "The writer should have scriptwriting credits for training, sales, promotion and public relations." Payment dependent on client's budget.
Tips: "Send us a resume listing writing and directing credits for films and sound/slide programs."

ARNOLD AND ASSOCIATES PRODUCTIONS, INC., 2159 Powell St., San Francisco CA 94133. (415)989-3490. President: John Arnold. Executive Producers: James W. Morris and Peter Dutton. Produces material for the general public (entertainment/motion pictures) and for corporate clients (employees/customers/consumers). Buys 10-15 scripts/year. Works with 3 writers/year. Buys all rights. Previously produced material OK. Reports in 1 month.
Needs: Films (35mm) and videotape. Looking for "upscale image and marketing programs. Dramatic writing for "name narrators and post scored original music; and motion picture. $5-6 million dollar budget. Dramatic or horror." Query with samples or submit completed script. Makes outright purchase of $1,000.
Tips: Looking for "upscale writers who understand corporate image production, and motion picture writers who understand story and dialogue."

‡ARZTCO PICTURES, INC., 830 N. Salem Rd., Ridgefield CT 06877. (212)753-1050. President/Producer: Tony Arzt. Produces material for industrial, education, and home viewing audiences (TV specials and documentaries). 80% freelance written. 75% of scripts produced are unagented submissions. Buys 8-10 scripts/year. Buys all rights. Previously produced material OK ("as sample of work only"). SASE, "however, we will only comment in writing on work that interests us." Reports in 3 weeks.
Needs: Business films, sales, training, promotional, educational. "Also interested in low-budget feature film scripts." 16mm and 35mm films, videotapes and cassettes, and software. Submit synopsis/outline or completed script and resume. Pays in accordance with Writers Guild standards.
Tips: "We would like writers to understand that we cannot find time to deal with each individual submission in great detail. If we feel your work is right for us, you will definitely hear from us. We're looking for writers with originality, skill in turning out words, and a sense of humor when appropriate. We prefer to work with writers available in the New York metropolitan area."

A/V CONCEPTS CORP., 30 Montauk Blvd., Oakdale NY 11769. (516)567-7227. Contact: P. Solimene or L. Solimene. Produces material for elementary-high school students, either on grade level or in remedial situations. Estab. 1971. 100% freelance written. Buys 25 scripts/year from unpublished/unproduced writers. Employs filmstrip, book and personal computer media. Reports on outline in 1 month; on final scripts in 6 weeks. Buys all rights.
Needs: Interested in original educational computer (disk-based) software programs for Apple +, 48k. Main concentration in language arts, mathematics and reading. "Manuscripts must be written using our lists of vocabulary words and meet our reading ability formula requirements. Specific guidelines are devised for each level. Length of manuscript and subjects will vary according to grade level for which material is prepared. Basically, we want material that will motivate people to read." Pays $300 and up.
Tips: "Writers must be highly creative and highly disciplined. We are interested in high interest-low readability materials."

SAMUEL R. BLATE ASSOCIATES, 10331 Watkins Mill Dr., Gaithersburg MD 20879-2935. (301)840-2248. President: Samuel R. Blate. Produces audiovisual and educational material for business, education, institutions, state and federal governments. "We work with 2 *local* writers per year on a per project basis—it varies as to business conditions and demand." Buys first rights when possible. Query for electronic submissions. Reports in 1 week on queries; 2 weeks on submissions. SASE for return.
Needs: Filmstrips (silent and sound), multimedia kits, slides, tapes and cassettes. Query with samples. SASE for return. Payment "depends on type of contract with principal client." Pays expenses of writers on assignment.
Tips: "Writers must have a strong track record of technical and aesthetic excellence. Clarity is not next to divinity—it is above it."

LEE CAPLIN PRODUCTIONS, 8274 Grand View Trail, Los Angeles CA 90046. (213)650-1882. Vice President Development: Sonia Mintz. Produces feature films for theatrical audience and TV audience. Buys 2 scripts/year, works with 10 writers/year. Buys all rights. Reports on submissions in 2 months.
Needs: Films (35mm) and videotapes. Feature scripts 100-120 pp. Submit completed script. Pays on a deal by deal basis/some WGA, some not.
Tips: "Don't send derivitive standard material. Emphasis on unique plot and characters, realistic dialogue. *Discourage* period pieces, over-the-top comedy, *graphic* sex/violence. *Encourage* action, action/comedy, thriller, thriller/comedy."

CLEARVUE, INC., 6465 N. Avondale Ave., Chicago IL 60631. (312)775-9433. President: W.O. McDermed. Produces material for educational market—grades kindergarten-12. 90% freelance written. Prefers to work with published/established writers. Buys 20-50 scripts/year from previously unpublished/unproduced writers. Buys all rights. Previously produced material OK. Query for electronic submissions. Reports in 2 weeks on queries; 3 weeks on submissions. Free catalog.
Needs: Videos, filmstrips (sound), multimedia kits, and slides. "Our filmstrips and videos are 35 to 100 frames—8 to 30 minutes for all curriculum areas." Query. Makes outright purchase, $100-5,000. Sometimes pays the expenses of writers on assignment.
Tips: "Our interests are in video for the elementary and high school markets on all subjects."

‡COMPRO PRODUCTIONS, Suite 114, 2080 Peachtree Ind. Ct., Atlanta GA 30341. (404)455-1943. FAX: (404)455-3356. Producers: Nels Anderson and Steve Brinson. Estab. 1977. Audience is general public and specific business audience. Buys 10-25 scripts/year. Buys all rights. No previously produced material. No unsolicited material; submissions will not be returned because "all work is contracted."
Needs: "We solicit writers for corporate films/video in the areas of training, point purchase, sales, how-to, benefit programs, resorts and colleges." Produces 16-35mm films and videotapes. Query with samples. Makes outright purchase or pays cost per minute.

CONTINENTAL FILM PRODUCTIONS CORPORATION, P.O. Box 5126, 4220 Amnicola Hwy., Chattanooga TN 37406. (615)622-1193. FAX: (615)629-0853. Executive Vice President: James L. Webster. Estab. 1951. Produces "AV and video presentations for businesses and non profit organizations for sales, training, public relations, documentation, motivation, etc." Works with many writers annually. Buys all rights. No previously produced material. Unsolicited submissions not returned. Reports in 1 week.
Needs: "We do need new writers of various types. Please contact us by mail with samples and resume. Samples will be returned postpaid." Produces slides, filmstrips, motion pictures, multi-image presentations, and videos. Query with samples and resume. Outright purchase: $250 minimum.
Tips: Looks for writers whose work shows " technical understanding, humor, common sense, practicality, simplicity, creativity, etc. Important for writers to adapt script to available production budget." Suggests writers "increase use of humor in training films." Also seeking scripts on "human behavior in industry."

NICHOLAS DANCY PRODUCTIONS, INC., 333 W. 39th St., New York NY 10018. President: Nicholas Dancy. Produces media material for corporate communications, the health care field, general audiences, employees, members of professional groups, members of associations and special customer groups. 60% freelance written. Prefers to work with published/established writers. Buys 5-10 scripts/year; works with 5-10 writers/year. None of scripts is unagented . Buys all rights. Query for electronic submissions. Reports in 1 month.
Needs: "We use scripts for videotapes or films from 5 minutes to 1 hour for corporate communications, sales, orientation, training, corporate image, medical and documentary." Format: videotape, occasionally 16mm films. Query with résumé. "No unsolicited material. Our field is too specialized." Pays by outright purchase of $800-5,000. Pays expenses of writers on assignment.
Tips: "Writers should have a knowledge of business and industry and professions, an ability to work with clients and communicators, a fresh narrative style, creative use of dialogue, good skills in accomplishing research, and a professional approach to production. New concept trends are important in business. We're looking for new areas. The cautious loosening of FDA processes will create an even sharper need for skilled and talented scriptwriters in the medical field."

EDUCATIONAL IMAGES LTD., Box 3456, Elmira NY 14905. (607)732-1090. Executive Director: Dr. Charles R. Belinky. Produces material (sound filmstrips, multimedia kits and slide sets) for schools, kindergarten through college and graduate school, public libraries, parks, nature centers, etc. Also produces science-related software material. Buys 50 scripts/year. Buys all AV rights. Free catalog.
Needs: Slide sets and filmstrips on science, natural history, anthropology and social studies. "We are looking primarily for complete AV programs; we will consider slide collections to add to our files. This requires high quality, factual text and pictures." Query with a meaningful sample of proposed program. Pays $150 minimum.
Tips: The writer/photographer is given high consideration. "Once we express interest, follow up. Potential contributors lose many sales to us by not following up on initial query. Don't waste our time and yours if you can't deliver. The market seems to be shifting to greater popularity of video and computer software formats."

EDUCATIONAL INSIGHTS, 19560 S. Rancho Way, Dominguez Hills CA 90220. (213)637-2131. FAX: (213)605-5048. VP/Director of Development: Dennis J. Graham. Estab. 1962. Produces material for elementary schools and retail "home-learning" markets. Works with 10 writers/year. Buys all rights. Previously produced material OK. Reports in 2 weeks. Catalog for 9×12 SAE with 2 first class stamps.
Needs: Charts, models, multimedia kits, study prints, tapes and cassettes, and teaching machine programs. Query with samples. Pays varied royalties or makes outright purchase.
Tips: "Keep up-to-date information on educational trends in mind. Study the market before starting to work. We receive 20 manuscripts per week – all reviewed and returned, if rejected."

EDUCATIONAL VIDEO NETWORK, 1401 19th St., Huntsville TX 77340. (409)295-5767. President: Dr. Kenneth L. Russell. Produces material for junior high, senior high, college and university audiences. Buys "perhaps 20 scripts/year." Buys all rights or pays royalty on gross retail and wholesale. Previously produced material OK. Reports in 1 week on queries; in 1 month on submissions. Free catalog.
Needs: "Filmstrips and video for educational purposes." Produces filmstrips with sound and video. "Photographs on 2×2 slides must have good saturation of color." Query. Royalty varies.
Tips: Looks for writers with the "ability to write and illustrate for educational purposes. Schools are asking for more curriculum oriented live-action video. Recent trends include more emphasis on video; less emphasis on filmstrips."

‡EFFECTIVE COMMUNICATION ARTS, INC., 221 W. 57th St., New York NY 10019. (212)333-5656. FAX: (212)333-7748. Vice President: W.J. Comcowich. Estab. 1965. Produces films, videotapes and interactive videodisks for physicians, nurses and medical personnel. Prefers to work with published/established writers. 80% freelance written. Buys approximately 20 scripts/year. Query for electronic submissions. Buys all rights. Reports in 1 month.
Needs: Multimedia kits, 16mm films, television shows/series, videotape presentations and interactive videodisks. Currently producing about 15 films, videotapes for medical audiences; 6 interactive disks for medical audience; 3 interactive disks for point-of-purchase. Submit complete script and resume. Makes outright purchase. Pays expenses of writers on assignment.
Tips: "Videotape scripts on technical subjects are becoming increasingly important. Explain what the film accomplishes – how it is better than the typical."

FIRST RING, 15303 Ventura Blvd., #800, Sherman Oaks CA 91403-3155. Assistant Editor: Phil Potters. Estab. 1987. "Audio material only. Humorous telephone answering machine messages. Intended for use by all persons who utilize telephone answering machines." Buys 20 scripts/year. Buys all rights. Reports in 3 weeks on queries; 4 months on submissions.
Needs: Write for guidelines with SASE. Scripts must not exceed 20 seconds in their finished production; however there is no minimum duration. Produces tapes and cassettes. Query. Outright purchase of $100 upon acceptance.
Tips: Looking for writers with "the ability to write hilarious scripts as set forth in guidelines. All submissions are considered even from writers whose prior work was not accepted."

FLIPTRACK LEARNING SYSTEMS, Division of Mosaic Media, Inc., Suite 200, 999 Main St., Glen Ellyn IL 60137. (708)790-1117. FAX: (708)790-1196. Publisher: F. Lee McFadden. Contact: Patricia Menges. Estab. 1976. Produces training courses for microcomputers and business software. Works with a small number of new/unpublished writers each year. 35% freelance written. Buys 3-5 courses/year; 1-2 from unpublished/unproduced writers. All courses published are unagented submissions. Works with 3-5 writers/year. Buys all rights. Query for electronic submissions. Reports in 3 weeks. Free product literature; sample copy for 9×12 SAE.
Needs: Training courses on how to use personal computers/software, video or audio geared to the adult student in a business setting and usually to the novice user; a few courses at advanced levels. Primarily audio, also some reference manuals, video, and feature articles on personal computers. Query with resume and samples if available. Pays negotiable royalty or makes outright purchase.
Tips: "We prefer to work with Chicago-area writers with strong teaching/training backgrounds and experience with microcomputers. Writers from other regions are also welcome. We also need feature/journalism writers with strong microcomputer interest and experience."

PAUL FRENCH & PARTNERS, INC., 503 Gabbettville Rd., LaGrange GA 30240. (404)882-5581. Contact: Ms. Gene Ballard. 20% freelance written. Buys all rights. Reports in 2 weeks.
Needs: Wants to see multi-screen scripts (all employee-attitude related) and/or multi-screen AV sales meeting scripts or resumes. Produces silent and sound filmstrips, videotapes, cassettes and slides. Query or submit resume. Pays in outright purchase of $500-5,000. Payment is in accordance with Writers Guild standards.

GESSLER PUBLISHING CO., INC., Gessler Educational Software, 55 W. 13th St., New York NY 10011. (212)627-0099. FAX: (212)627-5948. President: Seth C. Levin. Produces material for students learning ESL and foreign languages. 50% freelance written. Eager to work with new/unpublished writers. Buys about 60-

75 scripts/year. 100% of scripts are unagented submissions. Prefers to buy all rights, but will work on royalty basis. Do not send disk submission without documentation. Query for electronic submissions. Reports in 3 weeks on queries; 2 months on submissions.

Needs: Video and filmstrips "to create an interest in learning a foreign language and its usefulness in career objectives; also culturally insightful video/filmstrips on French, German, Italian and Spanish speaking countries." Produces sound filmstrips, multimedia kits, overhead transparencies, games, realia, tapes and cassettes, computer software. Also produces scripts for videos. Submit synopsis/outline or software with complete documentation, introduction, objectives. Makes outright purchase and pays royalties.

Tips: "Be organized in your presentation; be creative but keep in mind that your audience is primarily junior/senior high school teachers. We will be looking for new filmstrips, videotapes, software and videodisks which can be used in foreign language and ESL classes. Also, more of a concentration on hypercard and interactive video projects."

‡GRIFFIN & BOYLE, (formerly Griffin Media Design), 802 Wabash Ave., Chesterton IN 46304. (219)926-8602. Associate Creative Director: H. Karabel. Produces variety of business and industrial programs, specifically for the development of advertising, public relations, training, marketing, conventions, etc. "We may buy as few as 10 to 50 projects per year." Buys all rights. No previously produced material. Reports on queries in 3 weeks. Catalog for 9×12 SAE and 2 first class stamps.

Needs: Films, video multimedia kits, brochures, advertisements, radio spots and cassettes. Query with samples. Makes outright purchase.

Tips: "Potential contributors should make themselves known. It's just as hard for businesses to find good writers as it is for good writers to find work."

BRAD HAGER, Box 18642, Irvine CA 92713. (714)261-7266. Produces material for corporate executives. Buys 10 scripts/year. Buys all rights. No previously produced material. SASE. Reports in 1 month.

Needs: Films, home video market (special interest, dramatic, comedy, kid-vid), videotapes, multimedia kits, slides, tapes and cassettes. Query with samples. Makes outright purchase.

HAYES SCHOOL PUBLISHING CO., INC., 321 Pennwood Ave., Wilkinsburg PA 15221. (412)371-2373. FAX: (800)543-8771. President: Clair N. Hayes, III. Estab. 1940. Produces material for school teachers, principals, elementary through high school. Also produces charts, workbooks, teacher's handbooks, posters, bulletin board material, and reproducible blackline masters (grades kindergarten through 12). 25% freelance written. Prefers to work with published/established writers. Buys 5-10 scripts/year from unpublished/unproduced writers. 100% of scripts produced are unagented submissions. Buys all rights. Query for electronic submissions. Catalog for 3 first class stamps; writer's guidelines for #10 SAE and 2 first class stamps.

Needs: Educational material only. Particularly interested in educational material for elementary school level. Query. Pays $25 minimum.

IMAGE INNOVATIONS, INC., Suite 201, 29 Clyde Rd., Somerset NJ 08873. President: Mark A. Else. Estab. 1974. Produces material for business, education and general audiences. 50% freelance written. "Credentials and reputation important." Buys 15-20 scripts/year from previously unpublished/unproduced writers. All scripts produced are unagented submissions. Reports in 2 weeks. Buys all rights.

Needs: Subject topics include education, sales, public relations and technical. Produces sound/slide, multi-image programs, and hi-image 1″ and ¾″ Betacam video and tapes and cassettes. Query with samples. Pays in outright purchase of $800-5,000. Sometimes pays the expenses of writers on assignment.

‡DAVID JACKSON PRODUCTIONS, 1020 N. Cole St., 3rd Floor, Hollywood CA 90038. (213)465-3810. President: David Jackson. Estab. 1985. We have corporate, commercial and educational audiences. Buys 3-10 scripts/year. Buys all rights. Reports on queries in 1 week; 1 month on submissions.

Needs: Models, phonograph records, tapes and cassettes, videotapes. We are looking for video format—instructional, educational and film format—commercial. Query. Pays in accordance with Writers Guild standards.

Tips: We are interested in both fantasy and real life writings.

JACOBY/STORM PRODUCTIONS INC., 22 Crescent Road, Westport CT 06880. (203)227-2220. Contact: Doris Storm. Produces material for business people, students of all ages, professionals (e.g. medical). Works with 4-6 writers annually. Buys all rights. No previously produced material. Reports in 2 weeks.

Needs: "Short dramatic films on business subjects, educational films and filmstrips on varied subjects, sales and corporate image films." Produces 16mm films, filmstrips (sound), slides, tapes and cassettes, videotapes and videodisks. Query. Makes outright purchase (depends on project).

Tips: "Prefers local people. Look for experience, creativity, dependability, attention to detail, enthusiasm for project, ability to interface with client. Wants more film/video, fewer filmstrips, more emphasis on creative approaches to material."

PAUL S. KARR PRODUCTIONS, 2949 W. Indian School Rd., Box 11711, Phoenix AZ 85017. (602)266-4198. Utah Division: 1024 N. 250 E., Box 1254, Orem UT 84057. (801)226-8209. Produces films and videos for industry, business, education, TV spots and entertainment. *"Do not submit material unless requested."* Works on co-production ventures that have been funded.
Needs: Produces 16mm films and videos. Query. Payment varies.
Tips: "One of the best ways for a writer to become a screenwriter is to come up with a client that requires a film or video. He can take the project to a production company, such as we are, assume the position of an associate producer, work with an experienced professional producer in putting the production into being, and in that way learn about video and filmmaking, chalk up some meaningful credits, and share in the profits. Direct consumer TV spots (that is, 800-number sales spots) have become a big business in the Phoenix market the last few years. Our company is set up to handle all facets of this area of television marketing."

KIMBO EDUCATIONAL-UNITED SOUND ARTS, INC., 10-16 N. 3rd Ave., Box 477, Long Branch NJ 07740. (201)229-4949. Contact: James Kimble or Amy Laufer. Produces materials for the educational market (early childhood, special education, music, physical education, dance, and preschool children 6 months and up). 50% freelance written. Buys approximately 12-15 scripts/year; works with approximately 12-15 writers/year. Buys 5 scripts/year from unpublished/unproduced writers. Most scripts are unagented submissions. Buys all rights or first rights. Previously produced material OK "in some instances." Reports in 1 month. Free catalog.
Needs: "For the next two years we will be concentrating on general early childhood songs and movement oriented products, new albums in the fitness field and more. Each will be an album/cassette with accompanying teacher's manual and, if warranted, manipulatives." Phonograph records and cassettes, "all with accompanying manual or teaching guides." Query with samples and synopsis/outline or completed script. Pays 5-7% royalty on lowest wholesale selling price, and by outright purchase. Both negotiable.
Tips: "We look for creativity first. Having material that is educationally sound is also important. Being organized is certainly helpful. Fitness is growing rapidly in popularity and will always be a necessary thing. Children will always need to be taught the basic fine and gross motor skills. Capturing interest while reaching these goals is the key."

DAVID LANCASTER PRODUCTIONS, 3356 Bennett, Los Angeles CA 90068. (213)874-1415. President: David Lancaster. Buys approximately 5 scripts/year. Buys all rights. Reports in 1 month on queries.
Needs: Feature films (35 mm). Submit completed script. Pays in accordance with Writers Guild standards.
Tips: "Submit clean format per industry—no less than 90 pages, no more than 125."

MARSHFILM ENTERPRISES, INC., P.O. Box 8082, Shawnee Mission KS 66208. (816)523-1059. FAX: (816)333-7421. President: Joan K. Marsh. Estab. 1969. Produces software and video and filmstrips for elementary and junior/senior high school students. 100% freelance written. Works with a small number of new/unpublished writers each year. Buys 8-16 scripts/year. All scripts produced are unagented submissions. Buys all rights.
Needs: 50-frame; 15-minute scripts for video or sound filmstrips. Query only. Pays by outright purchase of $250-500/script.
Tips: "We are seeking generic, curriculum-oriented educational scripts suitable for interactive video disk development."

NYSTROM, 3333 N. Elston Ave., Chicago IL 60618. (312)463-1144. Editorial Director: Darrell A. Coppock. Produces material for school audiences (kindergarten through 12th grade).
Needs: Educational material on social studies, earth and life sciences, career education, reading, language arts and mathematics. Produces charts, sound filmstrips, models, multimedia kits, overhead transparencies and realia. Required credentials depend on topics and subject matter and approach desired. Query. Pays according to circumstances.

OMNI COMMUNICATIONS, Suite 103, 655 W. Carmel Drive, P.O. Box 1703, Carmel IN 46032. (317)844-6664. Vice President: Dr. Sandra M. Long. Estab. 1976. Produces commercial, training, educational and documentary material. Buys all rights. No previously produced material.
Needs: "Educational, documentary, commercial, training, motivational." Produces slides, shows and multi-image videotapes. Query. Makes outright purchase.
Tips: "Must have experience as writer and have examples of work. Examples need to include print copy and finished copy of videotape if possible. A résumé with educational background, general work experience and experience as a writer must be included. Especially interested in documentary-style writing. Writers' payment varies, depending on amount of research needed, complexity of project, length of production and other factors."

OUR SUNDAY VISITOR, INC., Religious Education Dept., 200 Noll Plaza, Huntington IN 46750. (219)356-8400. Estab. 1913. Produces print and video material for students (pre-K through 12th grade), adult religious education groups and teacher trainees. "We are very concerned that the materials we produce meet the needs of today's church." Free catalog.

Needs: "Proposals for projects should be no more than 2 pages in length, in outline form. Programs should display up-to-date audiovisual techniques and cohesiveness. Broadly speaking, material should deal with religious education, including liturgy and daily Christian living, as well as structured catechesis. It must not conflict with sound Catholic doctrine and should reflect modern trends in education." Produces educational books, charts and videos. "Work-for-hire and royalty arrangements possible."

‡**PC ADVISOR**, Mosaic Media Inc., Suite 200, 999 Main St., Glen Ellyn IL 60137. Publisher: F. Lee McFadden. Contact: Al Henderson. Published monthly in a 90-minute audiocassette format for PC users and those who supervise PC users in an office environment. Subscribers have varying degrees of technical expertise and interest, but are in a position to influence the selection of hardware, software, systems and training. Buys all rights. Electronic submissions preferred. Query first.
Needs: 4- to 8-minute scripts on hardware, software, systems and training. Most scripts are distillations of existing print materials, but we will consider original materials from writers with name recognition in the PC field.
Tips: "We prefer to work with writers who are accustomed to writing for a non-technical, business audience. Experience in writing for the ear rather than the eye is preferred. Technical expertise and name recognition are an asset."

PHOTO COMMUNICATION SERVICES, INC., 6410 Knapp NE, Ada MI 49301. (616)676-1499 or (616)676-2429. President: Lynn Jackson. Produces commercial, industrial, sales, training material etc. 95% freelance written. No scripts from unpublished/unproduced writers. 100% of scripts produced are unagented submissions. Buys all rights and first serial rights. Query for electronic submissions. Computer printout submissions acceptable. Reports in 1 month. SASE if you wish to have material returned.
Needs: Multimedia kits, slides, tapes and cassettes, and video presentations. Primarily interested in 35mm multimedia and video. Query with samples or submit completed script and résumé. Pays in outright purchase or by agreement.

PREMIER VIDEO FILM & RECORDING CORP., 3033 Locust, St. Louis MO 63103. (314)531-3555. Secretary/Treasurer: Grace Dalzell. Estab. 1931. Produces material for the corporate community, religious organizations, political arms, and hospital and educational groups. 100% freelance written. Prefers to work with published/established writers. Buys 50-100 scripts/year. All scripts are unagented submissions. Buys all rights; "very occasionally the writer retains rights." Previously produced material OK; "depends upon original purposes and markets." Reports "within a month or as soon as possible."
Needs: "Our work is all custom produced with the needs being known only as required." 35mm film loops, super 8mm and 35mm films, silent and sound filmstrips, multimedia kits, overhead transparencies, phonograph records, slides, and tapes and cassettes. Produces TV, training and educational scripts for video. Submit complete script and resume. Pays in accordance with Writers Guild standards or by outright purchase of $100 or "any appropriate sum." Sometimes pays the expenses of writers on assignment.
Tips: "Always place without fail *occupational pursuit*, name, address and phone number in upper right hand corner of resume. We're looking for writers with creativity, good background and a presentable image."

‡**BILL RASE PRODUCTIONS, INC.**, 955 Venture Ct., Sacramento CA 95825. (916)929-9181. President: Bill Rase. Produces material for business education and mass audience. Buys about 20 scripts/year. Buys all rights. Reports "when an assignment is available."
Needs: Produces multimedia, slides, cassettes and video productions. Submit resume and sample page or two of script, and description of expertise. Pays negotiable rate in 30 days.
Tips: "Call and ask for Bill Rase personally. Must be within 100 miles and thoroughly professional."

RHYTHMS PRODUCTIONS, P.O. Box 34485, Los Angeles CA 90034. President: Ruth White. Estab. 1955. Produces children's educational cassettes/books. Buys all rights. Previously published material OK "if it is suitable for our market and is not now currently on the market. We also look for tapes that have been produced and are ready for publication." Reports on mss in 3 weeks. Catalog for 9 × 12 SAE and 3 first class stamps.
Needs: Phonograph records and tapes and cassettes. "Looking for children's stories with musical treatments. Must have educational content or values." Query with samples. Payment is negotiable.
Tips: "SASE required for return of materials."

ALWAYS submit unsolicited manuscripts or queries with a self-addressed, stamped envelope (SASE) within your country or International Reply Coupons (IRC) purchased from the post office for other countries.

PETER SCHLEGER COMPANY, 200 Central Park S., New York NY 10019. (212)245-4973. President: Peter R. Schleger. Produces material "primarily for employee populations in corporations and non-profit organizations." Buys all rights, "most work is for a one-time use, and that piece may have no life beyond one project." Previously produced material OK. Reports in 1 month. "Typical programs are customized workshops or specific individual programs from subjects such as listening and presentation skills to medical benefits communication. No program is longer than 10 minutes. If they need to be, they become shorter modules."
Needs: Produces sound filmstrips, video and printed manuals and leader's guides. Send completed script and resume. Makes outright purchase; payment "depends on script length."
Tips: "We are looking to receive and keep on file a resume and short, completed script sample of a program not longer than 10 minutes. The shorter the better to get a sense of writing style and the ability to structure a piece. We would also like to know the fees the writer expects for his/her work. Either per-diem, by project budget or by finished script page. We want communicators with a training background or who have written training programs, modules and the like. We want to know of people who have written print material, as well. We do not want to see scripts that have been written and are looking for a producer/director. We will look at queries for possible workshops or new approaches for training, but these must be submitted as longshots only; it is not our primary business."

SPENCER PRODUCTIONS, INC., 234 5th Ave., New York NY 10001. (212)697-5895. General Manager: Bruce Spencer. Executive Producer: Alan Abel. Produces material for high school students, college students and adults. Occasionally uses freelance writers with considerable talent.
Needs: 16mm films, prerecorded tapes and cassettes. Satirical material only. Query. Pay is negotiable.

TALCO PRODUCTIONS, 279 E. 44th St., New York NY 10017. (212)697-4015. President: Alan Lawrence. Vice President: Marty Holberton. Produces variety of material for motion picture theatres, TV, radio, business, trade associations, non-profit organizations, etc. Audiences range from young children to senior citizens. 20-40% freelance written. Buys scripts from published/produced writers only. All scripts produced are un-agented submissions. Buys all rights. No previously published material. Reports in 3 weeks on queries. *Does not accept unsolicited mss.*
Needs: Films (16-35mm), phonograph records, slides, radio tapes and cassettes and videotape. "We maintain a file of writers and call on those with experience in the same general category as the project in production. We do not accept unsolicited manuscripts. We prefer to receive a writer's resume listing credits. If his/her background merits, we will be in touch when a project seems right." Makes outright purchase/project and in accordance with Writer's Guild standards (when appropriate). Sometimes pays the expenses of writers on assignment.
Tips: "In the next year, we will have a greater concentration in TV productions. Production budgets will be tighter. *Productions will be of shorter length to save money.*"

TEL-AIR INTERESTS, INC., 1755 N.E. 149th St., Miami FL 33181. (305)944-3268. President: Grant H. Gravitt. Produces material for groups and theatrical and TV audiences. Buys all rights. Submit resume.
Needs: Documentary films on education, travel and sports. Produces films and videotape. Pays by outright purchase.

TROLL ASSOCIATES, 100 Corporate Dr., Mahwah NJ 07430. (201)529-4000. Contact: M. Schecter. Produces material for elementary and high school students. Buys approximately 200 scripts/year. Buys all rights. Reports in 3 weeks. Free catalog.
Needs: Produces multimedia kits, tapes and cassettes, and (mainly) books. Query or submit outline/synopsis. Pays royalty or by outright purchase.

VISUAL HORIZONS, 180 Metro Park, Rochester NY 14623. (716)424-5300. FAX: (716)424-5313. President: Stanley Feingold. Produces material for general audiences. Buys 5 programs/year. Reports in 5 months. Free catalog.
Needs: Business, medical and general subjects. Produces silent and sound filmstrips, multimedia kits, slide sets and videotapes. Query with samples. Payment negotiable.

Playwriting

The theater represents a genuine refuge for those who wail the universal rallying cry of scriptwriters everywhere: "I can't get no respect!" Traditionally, the stage play is the one avenue where the writer steers the creative juggernaut and oversees the final vision. While changes and rewrites are done constantly, even during the performance run of a play, they are always done with the full participation and cooperation of the writer. This is certainly not the case in writing for movies—and not even close to the case in television writing.

Local theater still represents the best opportunity for aspiring playwrights. While you'll be working for little or no pay, many local theaters are willing to try new material by unproven writers and may even offer the opportunity to act, direct or work in some capacity on the production of your script.

Playwrights must keep a constant watch on the budget demands of their scripts. Local and regional theaters are bound by rigid budget constraints and generally cannot afford to mount elaborate productions. In addition, large casts, multiple sets, special effects (such as weather), exotic props, and highly-demanding action scenes all provide great reasons to have your script rejected. One exception would be children's theater targeted at classroom production since it typically involves a large cast in order to allow as many people as possible to participate. Even here, however, the core of necessary characters should be kept to an absolute minimum, so less populated schools can still produce the play.

Personnel turnover is fairly high at most theaters, so it never hurts to contact current artistic directors about their willingness to review new material. This contact also can give you insight on the types of projects they may be willing to take on.

Keep up with the changing names through trade publications such as the newsletter put out by The Dramatists Guild, 234 W. 44th St., New York NY 10036.

For additional playwriting markets, see Other Scriptwriting Markets at the end of the Screenwriting section.

A.D. PLAYERS, 2710 W. Alabama, Houston TX 77098. (713)526-2721. Artistic Director: Jeannette Clift George. Estab. 1967. Produces 4-6 plays/year. "These are professional productions that are performed either in our mainstage season or on tour. On tour the performance-arenas vary. The full-length road show productions are performed in civic auditoriums, theaters, opera houses. The one-act and revue shows are performed in various settings; churches. Our audiences are primarily family-oriented, a majority come from a church affiliation." Query and synopsis or submit complete ms. Reports in 6 weeks. Pays per performance.
Needs: "We produce one-act and full length plays, any style. As a professional Christian repertory company, we produce shows that express a Christian world view, i.e. God's reality in everyday life. This can range from Biblical to contemporary to anything in between. We produce two children's shows a season and do a lot of touring performances for high school age groups. We are looking for plays that have no more than 14 characters. We have the limitation of a proscenium stage with no fly space."
Tips: "Because of our specific signature as a Christian repertory company we would not be interested in plays that have no reference to the reality of God or man's search for spiritual significance in his world."

‡ACTORS' STOCK COMPANY, 7604 Fair Oaks #1037, Dallas TX 75231. (214)343-9723. Artistic Director: Keith Oncale. Estab. 1988. Produces 3-4 plays/year. We stage semi-professional productions to a young adult to middle-aged general audience. Query and send synopsis. Reports in 3 months. No rights purchased except reading priviliges. Pays royalty.
Needs: 2 and 3 act plays, covering a wide variety of styles, but with fewer than 12 cast members. Our average staging facilities are 100 seat houses or smaller.
Tips: "Trends today reflect a return to comic realism that comments on our society without commenting on the play itself."

ACTORS THEATRE OF LOUISVILLE, 316 W. Main St., Louisville KY 40202. (502)584-1265. Producing Director: Jon Jory. Produces approximately 30 new plays of varying lengths/year. Professional productions are performed for subscription audience from diverse backgrounds. Agented submissions only for full-length plays. Reports in 6-9 months on submissions. Buys production (in Louisville only) rights. Offers variable royalty.
Needs: "No children's shows or musicals. We produce both full-lengths and short one-acts."

‡ALLEY THEATRE, 615 Texas Ave., Houston TX 77002. Artistic Director: Gregory Boyd. A resident professional theatre: large stage seating 824; arena stage seating 296.
Needs: Plays and musicals (script and cassette); plays for young audiences; adaptations and translations. Makes variable royalty arrangements. Send description/synopsis and letter of inquiry. Reports in 6 months. Produces 9-10 plays/year.
Recent Play Production: *Road to Nirvana* by Arthur Kopit.

AMAS REPERTORY THEATRE, INC., 1 E. 104th St., New York NY 10029. (212)369-8000. Artistic Director: Rosetta LeNoire. Produces 3 plays/year. 1 or 2 scripts produced are unagented submissions. "AMAS is a professional, off-off-Broadway showcase theater. We produce three showcase productions of original musicals each season; these are presented for a sophisticated New York theater audience. A number have gone on to commercial productions, the best known of which is *Bubbling Brown Sugar*. We also present one Eubie Blake youth theater and one summer tour for senior citizens in hospitals and centers." Query with synopsis or submit complete script with cassette tape of score or of partial score and SASE. Reports in 2 months. "Be prepared to wait at least two years or more between acceptance and production. Our standard contract calls for a small percentage of gross and royalties to AMAS, should the work be commercially produced within a specified period."

Needs: *"Musicals only*; in addition, all works will be performed by multi-racial casts. Musical biographies are especially welcome. Cast size should be under 13 if possible, including doubling. Because of the physical space, set requirements should be relatively simple."

Tips: "AMAS is dedicated to bringing all people—regardless of race, creed, color or religion—together through the performing arts. In writing for AMAS, an author should keep this overall goal in mind."

AMERICAN STAGE, (formerly American Stage Company), 211 3rd St. So., P.O. Box 1560, St. Petersburg FL 33731. (813)823-1600. Artistic Director: Victoria Holloway. Estab. 1978. Produces 5 plays/year. Plays performed on "our mainstage, in the park (Shakespeare) or on tour in schools." Submit query and synopsis. Reports in 4 months. Payment varies.
Needs: New American plays for small cast. No musicals.

‡AN CLAIDHEAMH SOLUIS/CELTIC ARTS CENTER, 5651 Hollywood Blvd., Hollywood CA 90028. (213)462-6844. Artistic Director: S. Walsh. Estab. 1985. Produces 6 plays/year. Equity waiver. Query and synopsis. Reports in 6 weeks. Rights acquired vary. Pays $25-50.
Needs: Scripts of Celtic interest (Scottish, Welsh, Irish, Cornish, Manx, Breton). "This can apply to writer's background or subject matter. We are particularly concerned with works that relate to the survival of cultures and traditions."

ANGEL'S TOUCH PRODUCTIONS, 7962 Hollywood Way, Sun Valley CA 91352. (818)768-6369. Director of Develpment: Phil Nemy. Professional Broadway productions for all audiences. Send script, query and synopsis. Reports in 6 months. Rights negotiated between production company and author. Payment negotiated.
Needs: All types, all genres, only full-length plays and screenplays—no one-acts or pieces involving homosexuality.
Tips: "Keep in mind the costs involved in mounting a Broadway or regional theater production and try to write accordingly."

ARENA STAGE, 6th and Maine Ave. SW, Washington DC 20024. (202)554-9066. Artistic Director: Zelda Fichandler. Estab. 1950. Produces 8-11 plays/year. Works with 6 commissioned writers through "Stage Four," a series of new plays produced each season. Stages professional productions in Washington for intelligent, educated, sophisticated audiences using resident Equity company. Virtually none of the scripts produced are unagented submissions. Prefers query and synopsis plus the first 10 pages of dialogue, or agented submissions. Reports in 2-3 months.
Needs: Produces classical, contemporary European and American plays; new plays, translations and adaptations without restrictions. Also looking for ethnically diverse plays. No sitcoms, blank verse, pseudo-Shakespearean tragedies, movies-of-the-week or soap operas.
Tips: "We can consider large casts, though big plays are expensive and must justify that expense artistically. Be theatrical. Plays with relevance to the human situation—which cover a multitude of dramatic approaches—are welcome here."

THE ARKANSAS ARTS CENTER CHILDREN'S THEATRE, Box 2137, MacArthur Park, Little Rock AR 72203. (501)372-4000. Artistic Director: Bradley Anderson. Produces 5-6 mainstage plays, 3 tours/year. Mainstage season plays performed at The Arkansas Arts Center for Little Rock and surrounding area; tour season by professional actors throughout Arkansas and surrounding states. Mainstage productions perform to family audiences in public performances; weekday performances for local schools in grades kindergarten through senior high school. Tour audiences generally the same. Accepts unsolicited scripts. Submit complete script. Reports in several months. Buys negotiable rights. Pays $250-1,500 or negotiable commission.
Needs: Original adaptations of classic and contemporary works. Also original scripts. "This theater is defined as a children's theater; this can inspire certain assumptions about the nature of the work. We would be pleased if submissions did not presume to condescend to a particular audience. We are not interested in 'cute' scripts. Submissions should simply strive to be good theater literature."
Tips: "We would welcome scripts open to imaginative production and interpretation. Also, scripts that are mindful that this children's theater casts adults as adults and children as children. Scripts that are not afraid of contemporary issues are welcome."

ARROW ROCK LYCEUM, Main St., Arrow Rock MO 65320. (816)837-3311. Artistic Director: Michael Bollinger. Produces 8 plays/year. "Lyceum has two main projects: a 30-year-old summer season, performing seven plays in repertory in the historic village of Arrow Rock and a Holiday Production, based in a much

larger house in Columbia, MO. The Lyceum is a regional theater, and employs professional actors." Query and synopsis throughout year or submit complete ms with synopsis and résumé for contest subs. Also sponsors the National Playwrights Contest. "Lyceum and original artistic staff to get future credit, and Lyceum to retain 5% of author's gross commissions for first 5 years only. Lyceum either commissions w/separate deals, or simply pays a flat fee to National Playwrights Contest winners, which also receive world premiere."
Needs: The repertory season includes seven diverse plays, including musicals, classic, comedy, drama, world premiere. Generally each season will feature one world premiere, contest winner or a commissioned work. "I would suggest plays with casts not exceeding 12, and one set, or rather open space with various locales."
Tips: "Who knows—if it works, anything can go! However, keeping budgets in mind, etc., works that have a bit of flexibility are best—could be produced with all 20 characters, or could be produced with 6 actors doubling supporting roles. Also, keep in mind set. Generally two or three realistic sets in one play could hinder original chances; one set or open staging could help. I do feel it is important for professional theaters to be 'theatrical creators' as well as mere 'consumers'!"

ART CRAFT PUBLISHING CO., 232 Dows Bldg., Cedar Rapids IA 52406. (319)364-6311. Publisher: C. McMullen. Publishes plays for the junior and senior high school market. Query with synopsis or send complete ms. Reports in 2 months. Acquires amateur rights only. Makes outright purchase or pays royalty.
Needs: One- and three-acts—preferably comedies or mystery comedies. Currently needs plays with a larger number of characters for production within churches and schools. Prefers one-set plays. No "material with the normal 'taboos'—controversial material."

ARTREACH TOURING THEATRE, 3074 Madison Rd., Cincinnati OH 45209. (513)871-2300. Director: Kathryn Schultz Miller. Produces 6 plays/year to be performed nationally in theaters and schools. "We are a professional company. Our audience is primarily young people in schools and their families." Submit complete ms. Reports in 6 weeks. Buys exclusive right to produce for 9 months. Pays $10/show (approximately 1,000 total performances through the year).
Needs: Plays for children and adolescents. Serious, intelligent plays about contemporary life or history/legend. "Limited sets and props. Can use scripts with only 3 actors; 45 minutes long. Should be appropriate for touring." No clichéd approaches, camp or musicals.
Tips: "We look for opportunities to create innovative stage effects using few props, and we like scripts with good acting opportunities."

ASOLO CENTER FOR THE PERFORMING ARTS, (formerly Asolo State Theatre), 5555 N. Tamiami Tr., Sarasota FL 34243. (813)351-9010. Resident Director: Garry Allan Breul. Produces 7 plays/year. 20% freelance written. 100% of scripts produced are unagented submissions. A LORT theater with an intimate performing space. "We play to rather traditional middle-class audiences." Works with 2-4 unpublished/unproduced writers annually. "We do not accept unsolicited scripts. Writers must send us a letter and synopsis with self-addressed stamped postcard." Reports in 8 months. Negotiates rights and payment.
Needs: Play must be *full length*. "We do not restrict ourselves to any particular genre or style—generally we do a good mix of classical and modern works."
Tips: "We have no special approach—we just want well written plays with clear, dramatic throughlines. Don't worry about trends on the stage. Write honestly and write for the stage, not for a publication. We are undertaking to produce more new plays."

AT THE FOOT OF THE MOUNTAIN THEATER, 2000 S. 5th St., Minneapolis MN 55454. (612)375-9487. Executive Director: Nayo Barbara Malcolm Watkins. Estab. 1974. "Put yourself on our newsletter mailing list and watch for when scripts are called for (approximately bi-annually)." No unsolicited scripts are accepted. Submit complete script. Reports in 6 months. Pay $25-30/performance. Submissions returned with SASE.
Needs: All genres: full-length plays, one acts, and musicals by women. Encourages experimental plays. Plays that reflect women's perspectives on the world as it is: multi-cultural, multi-racial, multi-generational, global, personal and political.
Tips: "The theater prefers small casts and simple sets."

AVILA COLLEGE, DEPARTMENT OF THEATRE, (formerly Avila College, Department of Humanities), 11901 Wornall Rd., Kansas City MO 64145. (816)942-8400, Ext. 290. FAX: (816)942-3362. Chairman: Dr. W. Buck Baker. Produces 6-8 plays/year. Possibility of 1-2 scripts produced by unagented submission. Performs collegiate amateur productions (4 main stage, 2-4 studio productions) for Kansas City audiences. Query with synopsis. Reports in 3 months. Buys rights arranged with author. Pay rate arranged with author.
Needs: All genres with wholesome ideas and language—musicals, comedies, dramas. Length 1-2 hours. Small to medium casts (2-8 characters), few props, simple staging.
Tips: Example of play just done: *Towards The Morning*, by John Fenn. Story: "Mentally confused bag lady and 17-year-old egocentric boy discover they need each other; she regains mental stability; he grows up a bit and becomes more responsible. Trends in the American stage freelance writers should be aware of include

(1) point-of-view one step beyond theater of the absurd—theater that makes light of self-pity; and (2) need for witty, energetic social satire done without smut in the style of *Kid Purple*, by Don Wollner."

‡**BAILIWICK REPERTORY**, 3212 N. Broadway, Chicago IL 60657-3515. (312)883-1091. Artistic Director: David Zak. Estab. 1982. Produces 5 full length, 5 late night and 45 one-act in festival plays/year. Our audience is a typical Chicago market. Our plays are highly theatrical and politically aware. Submit complete ms. One acts should be submitted *before* Dec. 1. (One act play fest runs March-April). Reports in 3 months. Pays 4-8% royalty.
Needs: We need daring scripts that break the mold. Large cast or musicals are OK. Creative staging solutions are a must.
Tips: Know the rules, then break them creatively and *boldly*!

BAKER'S PLAY PUBLISHING CO., 100 Chauncy St., Boston MA 02111. Editor: John B. Welch. Estab. 1845. 80% freelance written. Plays performed by amateur groups, high schools, children's theater, churches and community theater groups. "We are the largest publisher of chancel drama in the world." 90% of scripts are unagented submissions. Works with 2-3 unpublished/unproduced writers annually. Submit complete script. Submit complete cassette of music with musical submissions. Publishes 18-25 straight plays and musicals; all originals. Pay varies; outright purchase price to split in production fees. Reports in 4 months.
Needs: "We are finding strong support in our new division—plays for young adults featuring contemporary issue-oriented dramatic pieces for high school production."

‡**BARTER THEATRE**, P.O. Box 867, Abingdon VA 24210. (703)628-2281. Artistic Director: Rex Partington. Estab. 1933. Produces 10 plays/year. Play performed in residency at our two facilities, a 400-seat proscenium theater and a smaller 150-seat thrust theater. "Our plays are intended for diversified audiences of all ages." Submit complete ms. Reports in 6 months. Pays 4-7% royalty.
Needs: "We are looking for good plays, comedies and dramas, that entertain and are relevant; plays that comment on the times and mankind; plays that are universal. We prefer casts of 4-12, single or unit set."
Tips: "No silly, obscene or totally irrelevant material, lacking in wit or humor. Writers should be mindful of, and avoid a lack of the use of good understandable language and resorting to grunts and incomplete phrases."

BERKSHIRE PUBLIC THEATRE, 30 Union St., P.O. Box 860, Pittsfield MA 01202. (413)445-4631. Artistic Director: Frank Bessell. Literary Manager: Linda Austin. Estab. 1976. Produces 10 plays/year. Year-round regional theater. Professional, non-Equity. Special Interests: Contemporary issues; works dealing with ethics and morality; global concerns. Query and synopsis or submit complete ms. Reports in 3 months. Various payment arrangements.

‡**BERKSHIRE THEATRE FESTIVAL, INC.**, E. Main St., Stockbridge MA 01262. Artistic Director: Richard Dunlap. 25% original scripts. Produces 7-8 plays a year (4 are mainstage and 4 are second spaces). Submissions by agents only.

BOARSHEAD THEATER, 425 S. Grand Ave., Lansing MI 48933. (517)484-7800. Artistic Director: John Peakes. Estab. 1966. Produces 7-9 plays/year. Mainstage AEA company; also Youth Theater—touring to schools by our Intern company. Query, synopsis, cast list (with descriptions), 5-10 pages of representative dialogue, SASE postcard. "Reports on query and synopsis in 1 week. Full manuscripts (when requested by us) in 4-8 months." Pays royalty.
Needs: Thrust stage. Cast usually 8 or less; ocassionally up to 12-14. Prefer staging which depends on theatricality rather than multiple sets.

BOSTON POST ROAD STAGE COMPANY, 25 Powers Ct, Westport CT 06880. (203)255-1719. Artistic Director: Douglas Moser. Literary Manager: Burry Fredrik. Produces 6 plays/year. "Small professional (Equity) theater playing to audiences in Fairfield County. Audiences are adult, seniors and interested students." Submit complete ms. Reports in 6 months. Right to produce a 4 week run of the play with an option for several months following conclusion of run to explore further production possibilities. Pays 4-5% royalty.
Needs: Off-Broadway in Connecticut. Emphasis on originality of script. We will take risks if the play is good. We produce a wide range of plays, comedy, drama, musical (small). Budgetary considerations, are our limitations. Maximum eight characters, we prefer less however. We are eligible for grants to develop new plays if something were to strike us which was more expensive than our budget would allow.
Tips: "We're tired of NYC apartment tirades and moot-point 'true' biographies. No obviously large cast or panoramic history plays. The dramatic structure of a play must stimulate an audience. Foul language acceptable only when inherent to the dramatic situation; no headline plays that cannot transcend the ordinary details of everyday life. Even a 'slice-of-life' play must inform us about life, not just illustrate it. Energy, guts, vision and the ability to pull it all together. Those are the well written, stimulating playwrights and plays which will get the most of our attention."

‡**BRISTOL RIVERSIDE THEATRE**, Box 1250, Bristol PA 19007. (215)785-6664. Artistic Director: Susan D. Atkinson. Estab. 1986. Produces 5 mainstage, 3 workshops, and 15 readings plus children's theater/year. "We are a professional regional theater company; we produce new works exclusively in our workshop and reading series. The intention is to develop the works for mainstage productions. Our audience is drawn from Bucks County, Philadelphia, Trenton, Princeton and surrounding New Jersey areas. We also plan a two-show, popular, summer program." Submit complete ms. Reports in 10 months. "Since we are a developmental company and spend a great deal of time on each work selected for reading and/or workshop, we request a percentage of author's revenues for a given period of time and recognition of the theater and key individuals on subsequent productions, after the reading phase of the development is completed." Offers variable royalty.
Needs: "We produce all genres from dramas, comedies to musicals and operas. We also produce one-acts. We would prefer smaller shows with limited costs, but we have never shied away from larger shows. The quality, not the quantity, is the determining factor in all cases."
Tips: "We are not interested in plays that have as their only goal entertainment. We would hope all works would have this quality, but if there is no other value sought, we would not be interested. We are a company in search of the new mainstream of theater in America. We aim to entertain, enlighten and elevate our audience. And we are seeking authors who are interested in developing their works, not just presenting them; we view theater as a process."

CALIFORNIA THEATER CENTER, Box 2007, Sunnyvale CA 94087. (408)245-2978. Literary Manager: Will Huddleston. Produces 12 plays/year. Plays are for young audiences in both our home theater and for tour. Query and synopsis. Reports in 3 months. We negotiate a set fee.
Needs: All plays must be suitable for young audiences, must be under one hour in length. Cast sizes vary. Sets must be able to tour easily.

‡**CENTER STAGE**, 700 N. Calvert St., Baltimore MD 21202. (301)685-3200. Resident dramaturg: Rick Davis. Produces 6-9 plays/year. "Professional LORT 'B' company; audience is both subscription and single-ticket. Wide-ranging audience profile." Query with synopsis and resumé or submit through agent. Reports in 3 months. Rights negotiated. Payment depending on category of production (e.g., mainstage, playwrights series, etc.).
Needs: Produces "dramas and comedies, occasional musicals. No restrictions on topics or styles, though experimental work is encouraged. Casts over 30 would give us pause. Be inventive, theatrical, not precious; we like plays with vigorous language and stage image. Domestic naturalism is discouraged; strong thematic, political, or social interests are encouraged."
Tips: "We are interested in reading adaptations and translations as well as original work."

THE CHANGING SCENE THEATER, 1527½ Champa St., Denver CO 80202. Director: Alfred Brooks. Year-round productions in theater space. Cast may be made up of both professional and amateur actors. For public audience; age varies, but mostly youthful and interested in taking a chance on new and/or experimental works. No limit to subject matter or story themes. Emphasis is on the innovative. "Also, we require that the playwright be present for at least one performance of his work, if not for the entire rehearsal period. We have a small stage area, but are able to convert to round, semi-round or environmental. Prefer to do plays with limited sets and props." one-act, two-act and three-act.
Needs: Produces 8-10 nonmusicals a year; all are originals. 90% freelance written. 65% of scripts produced are unagented submissions. Works with 3-4 unpublished/unproduced writers annually. "We do not pay royalties or sign contracts with playwrights. We function on a performance-share basis of payment. Our theater seats 76; the first 50 seats go to the theater; the balance is divided among the participants in the production. The performance-share process is based on the entire production run and not determined by individual performances. We do not copyright our plays." Send complete script. Reporting time varies; usually several months.
Recent Title: *The Woman, The Man and The Indian*, by Rodney Vance.
Tips: "We are experimental: open to young artists who want to test their talents and open to experienced artists who want to test new ideas/explore new techniques. Dare to write 'strange and wonderful' well-thought-out scripts. We want upbeat ones. Consider that we have a small performance area when submitting."

CHELSEA STAGE, INC./HUDSON GUILD THEATRE, 441 W. 26th St., New York NY 10001. (212)645-4940. Literary Manager: Rebecca Kremen. Produces 5 mainstage plays annually, and conducts readings/workshops. "The plays are performed at the Hudson Guild Theatre. Our audiences (largely subscription) are from the greater New York City area, including parts of New Jersey, Connecticut and all Manhattan boroughs." No unsolicited ms accepted. Send letter of inquiry and synopsis. Enclose SASE for reply. Response time varies from 3-6 months. All rights agreements are worked out individually in production contract negotiations.
Needs: "Our interests are varied and international in scope. Socially and politically aware plays are preferred. We usually limit our casts to no more than 8, although exceptions can be made depending on the project."

‡CHILDREN'S STORY SCRIPTS, Baymax Productions, Suite 130, 2219 W. Olive Ave., Burbank CA 91506. (818)563-6105. Artistic Director: Deedra Bebout. Estab. 1990. Publishes 30 plays/year. "Our audience consists of children, grades K-8 (5-13 year olds)." Query with synopsis or send complete ms. Reports in 1 month. Buys all rights in script form. Pays graduated royalty based on sales.

Needs: We will publish almost any topic. Stories with a purpose, that can be discussed afterwards, work well. Stories that dovetail with classroom studies also work well. Restricted movements allowed. Scripts focus on narration and dialogue. They are not meant to be memorized.

Tips: "No violence. The scripts are not like theatrical scripts. They read like prose. If a writer shows promise, we'll work with him or her. Our most important goal is to benefit children."

CIRCUIT PLAYHOUSE/PLAYHOUSE ON THE SQUARE, 51 S. Cooper, Memphis TN 38104. (901)725-0776. Artistic Director: Jackie Nichols. Produces 16 plays/year. 100% freelance written. Professional plays performed for the Memphis/Mid-South area. Member of the Theatre Communications Group. 100% of scripts are unagented submissions. Works with 1 unpublished/unproduced writer annually. A play contest is held each fall. Submit complete ms. Reports in 3 months. Buys "percentage of royalty rights for 2 years." Pays $500.

Needs: All types; limited to single or unit sets. Cast of 20 or fewer.

Tips: "Each play is read by three readers through the extended length of time a script is kept. Preference is given to scripts for the southeastern region of the U.S."

CITY THEATRE COMPANY, 315 S. Bellefield Ave., Pittsburgh PA 15260. Scott T. Cummings, Resident Dramaturg. Produces 4 full productions and 6 readings/year. "We are a small professional theater, operating under an Equity contract, and committed to twentieth-century American plays. Our seasons are innovative and challenging, both artistically and socially. We perform in a 117-seat thrust stage, playing usually 6 times a week, each production running 5 weeks or more. We have a committed audience following." Query and synopsis or submit through agent. Obtains no rights. Pays 5-6% royalty.

Needs: "No limits on style or subject, but we are most interested in theatrical plays that have something to say about the way we live. No light comedies or TV-issue dramas." Normal cast limit is 8. Plays must be appropriate for small space without flies.

Tips: "Our emphasis is on new and recent American plays. Our staged reading series of 6 plays a year looks for scripts that challenge the dramatic medium and that are asking for further development."

I.E. CLARK, INC., Saint John's Rd., P.O. Box 246, Schulenburg TX 78956. (409)743-3232. Estab. 1956. Publishes 15 plays/year for educational theater, children's theater, religious theater, regional professional theater and amateur community theater. 20% freelance written. 3-4 scripts published/year are unagented submissions. Works with 2-3 unpublished writers annually. Submit complete script. Reports in 6 months. Buys all available rights; "we serve as an agency as well as a publisher." Pays standard book and performance royalty, "the amount and percentages dependent upon type and marketability of play." Catalog for $1.50; writer's guidelines for #10 SASE.

Needs: "We are interested in plays of all types—short or long. Audio tapes of music or videotapes of a performance are requested with submissions of musicals. We prefer that a play have been produced (directed by someone other than the author); photos and reviews of the production are helpful. No limitations in cast, props, staging, etc.; however, the simpler the staging, the larger the market. Plays with more than one set are difficult to sell. So are plays with only one or two characters. We insist on literary quality. We like plays that give new interpretations and understanding of human nature. Correct spelling, punctuation and grammar (befitting the characters, of course) impress our editors."

Tips: "Entertainment value and a sense of moral responsibility seem to be returning as essential qualities of a good play script. The era of glorifying the negative elements of society seems to be fading rapidly. Literary quality, entertainment value and good craftsmanship rank in that order as the characteristics of a good script in our opinion. 'Literary quality' means that the play must—in beautiful, distinctive, and un-trite language—say something; preferably something new and important concerning man's relations with his fellow man; and these 'lessons in living' must be presented in an intelligent, believable and creative manner. Plays for children's theater are tending more toward realism and childhood problems rather than fantasy or dramatization of fairy tales."

THE CLEVELAND PLAY HOUSE, 8500 Euclid Ave., Cleveland OH 44106. (216)795-7010. Artistic Director: Josephine Abady. Produces 12 plays/year. Resident LORT theater. Audience: subscribers and single ticket buyers; three different theaters with different audience needs/requirements: 160-experimental, 499 and 615-mainstage subscription theaters. Agented submissions only. Reports in 6 months. Negotiated rights. Pay negotiable.

Needs: Full length; emphasis on American realism; all styles and topics given full consideration, however. Musicals also welcome.

Tips: "No translations of foreign works. No previously produced works that received national attention."

COLONY STUDIO THEATRE, 1944 Riverside Dr., Los Angeles CA 90039. Managing Director: Barbara Beckley. Produces 5 plays/year. Professional 99-seat theater, (year round) for general audiences. SASE for submission guidelines. Reports in 2 weeks on queries; in 6 months on scripts. Negotiated rights. Pays $25-35 per performance.
Needs: "Produce *full length* (at least 90 minutes) of all genres, topics and styles, but *no musicals*. We cast from a company of resident, professional actors. Extreme casting types could be a problem."
Tips: "Trends are *created* by the skillful writer. An accepted, professional format (such as 'Samuel French's Format Guidelines') to the appearance of a script, helps in the reading process."

COMPANY ONE, 30 Arbor St. S., Hartford CT 06106. (203)233-4588. Artistic Director: Juanita Rockwell. Produces 6-8 plays/year. "One-act plays selected by Company One will be performed as part of our Play With Your Food Lunchtime Theater series. Our audience members are generally downtown employees looking for an entertaining break and thought provoking in their workday. Radio scripts, 5-20 minutes in length, are being sought for two evenings of live staged radio broadcast: *Sounds Scary*, for Halloween Weekend, and *Valentine's Day Massacre* in February. Please submit by September 1 and January 1, for a maximum of four voices plus sound effects and music." Submit complete ms with SASE.
Needs: "Best suited to the Lunchtime format is the 40 minute, 1-4 character, single or multi-purpose set piece. Although a good play can find its way around limitations, Company One tries to keep its casts small (four or less), its sets and props simple, and special effects to a minimum. Each play receives about 12 performances. Radio plays are taped, as well as broadcast live.
Tips: "Company One also welcomes new translations, adaptations from other sources and pieces incorporating music or dance."

CONTEMPORARY DRAMA SERVICE, Meriwether Publishing Ltd., P.O. Box 7710, Colorado Springs CO 80933. (303)594-4422. FAX: (719)594-9916. Editor-in-Chief: Arthur Zapel. Estab. 1969. Publishes 50-60 plays/year. "We publish for the secondary school market and colleges. We also publish for mainline liturgical churches—drama activities for church holidays, youth activities and fundraising entertainments. These may be plays—or drama-related books." Query with synopsis or submit complete ms. Reports in 5 weeks. Obtains either amateur or all rights. Pays 10% royalty or outright negotiated purchase.
Needs: "Most of the plays we publish are one-acts, 15 to 45 minutes in length. We occasionally publish full-length three-act plays. We prefer comedies in the longer plays. Musical plays must have name appeal either by prestige author, prestige title adaptation or performance on Broadway or TV. Comedy sketches, monologues and 2-character plays are welcomed. We prefer simple staging appropriate to high school, college or church performance. We like playwrights who see the world positively and with a sense of humor. Offbeat themes and treatments are accepted if the playwright can sustain a light touch and not take himself or herself too seriously. In documentary or religious plays we look for good research and authenticity. We will be publishing more textbooks on the theatrical arts than trade books."

‡**THE CRICKET THEATRE**, 1407 Nicollet Ave. S., Minneapolis MN 55403. (612)871-3763. Artistic Director: William Partlan. Produces 5 plays/year. Plays performed at the 215-seat Loring Theatre. Submit script or synopsis. Reports in 4-5 months. Obtains variable rights.
Needs: Prefer cast limit of 8. We will consider long one-act plays.
Tips: "*Best submission time* is October through March."

‡**DEEP ELLUM THEATRE GROUP/UNDERMAIN THEATRE**, P.O. Box 141166, Dallas TX 75214. (214)748-3082. Artistic Directors: Raphael Parry and Katherine Owens. Estab. 1983. Produces 5 plays/year. Submit query and synopsis with dialogue sample. Reports in 1 month. Pays 6% royalty.
Needs: "We generally produce plays experimental or avant-garde in style. They are usually under 2 hours in length. We draw an intelligent audience with a wide age range, who seek to be challenged and provoked. We are also drawn to writing poetic or impressionist in style. We work with a resident acting company of 6. We are non-equity. Our stage setup is flexible, thrust proscunium etc. We seat approximately 80."
Tips: "No plays resembling family dramas, soap opera styles, television sit-com styles. The Undermain Company is small and young (under 40). We have great difficulty in casting older parts."

DELAWARE THEATRE COMPANY, P.O. Box 516, Wilmington DE 19899. (302)594-1104. Artistic Director: Cleveland Morris. Estab. 1978. Produces 5 plays/year. 10% freelance written. "Plays are performed as part of a five-play subscription season in a 300-seat auditorium. Professional actors, directors and designers are engaged. The season is intended for a general audience." 10% of scripts are unagented submissions. Works with 1 unpublished/unproduced writer every two years. Query with synopsis. Reports in 6 months. Buys variable rights. Pays 5% (variable) royalty.
Needs: "We present comedies, dramas, tragedies and musicals. All works must be full length and fit in with a season composed of standards and classics. All works have a strong literary element. Plays showing a flair for language and a strong involvement with the interests of classical humanism are of greatest interest. Single-set, small-cast works are likeliest for consideration." Recent trend towards "more economical productions."

DENVER CENTER THEATRE COMPANY, 1050 13th St., Denver CO 80204. (303)893-4200. FAX: (303)893-2860. Artistic Director: Donovan Marley. Estab. 1979. Produces 12 plays/year. "Denver Center Theater Company produces an annual New Plays Festival, entitled US West Theatre Fest. 8-10 new scripts are rehearsed and presented in staged readings. From this festival, 4 are selected for full production in the following DCTC Theatre season." Submit complete ms. Reports in 6 weeks. Theatre Fest submittals must be previously unproduced. DCTC negotiates for production rights on scripts selected for full presentation but does not hold rights on Theatre Fest scripts. Royalty to be negotiated.
Needs: Full-length unproduced scripts. We do not accept one-acts, adaptations, children's plays, or musicals at this time.
Tips: "DCTC is a regional theater, producing new plays as a part of a subscription series that also includes classics. We tend to be interested in plays that explore issues larger than personal growth and comic moments."

‡**DORSET THEATRE FESTIVAL**, Box 519, Dorset VT 05251. (802)867-2223. Artistic Director: Jill Charles. Estab. 1976. Produces 5 plays/year. "Our plays will be performed in the Equity Summer Stock Theatre and are intended for a sophisticated community." Agented submissions only. Reports in 5 weeks. Rights and compensation arranged on an individual basis.
Needs: "We are looking for full length contemporary American drama, 1 comedy, 1 mystery, 1 musical/season. We are limited to a cast of 8."
Tips: "Nothing controversial."

THE DRAMATIC PUBLISHING CO., 311 Washington St., Woodstock IL 60098. (815)338-7170. FAX: (815)338-8981. Estab. 1885. Publishes about 30 new shows per year. 60% freelance written. 40% of scripts published are unagented submissions. "Current growth market is in plays and musicals for children, plays and small-cast musicals for stock and community theater." Also has a large market for plays and musicals for schools and other amateur theater groups. Works with 2-6 unpublished/unproduced writers annually. Reports in 2-6 months. Buys stock and amateur theatrical rights. Pays by usual royalty contract, 10 free scripts and 30% discount on script purchases.
Tips: "Avoid stereotype roles and situations. Submit cassette tapes with musicals whenever possible. Always include SASE if script is to be returned. Only one intermission (if any) in a show running up to two hours."

‡**EAST WEST PLAYERS**, 4424 Santa Monica Blvd., Los Angeles CA 90029. (213)660-0366. Artistic Director: Nobu McCarthy. 90% freelance written. Produces 5-6 plays/year. Professional plays performed in an Equity waiver house for all audiences. Works with 2-3 unpublished/unproduced writers annually. Query with synopsis or submit complete ms. Reports in 5-6 weeks on query and synopsis. "High majority" of scripts produced are unagented submissions. Buys standard Dramatist's Guild contract rights.
Needs: "We prefer plays dealing with Asian-American themes. The majority of the important roles should be playable by Asian-American actors; our acting company is 98 percent Asian." No fluff, TV sitcom-type material.
Tips: "East West Players was founded by a group of Asian-American actors weary of playing stereotypes in theater and film. Submitting writers should bear this in mind and refrain from wallowing in 'exoticism.' There appears to be a minor burgeoning of interest in Asian-American writers and themes—witness David Henry Hwang's success on the East Coast, the continuing success and influence of East West Players on the West Coast and establishment theaters developing Asian American material (e.g., The Mark Taper Forum in Los Angeles working on a stage adaptation of Maxine Hong Kingston's works), etc."

ELDRIDGE PUBLISHING CO., P.O. Box 216, Franklin OH 45005. (513)746-6531. Estab. 1906. Publishes 15-20 plays/year. For middle school, junior high, senior high, church and community audience. Query with synopsis (acceptable) or submit complete ms (preferred). Please send cassette tapes with any operettas. Reports in 2 months. Buys all rights. Pays 35% royalty (three-act royalties approximately $50/$35. Outright purchase from $100-300 or offers 10% of copy sale receipts. Writer's guidelines for #10 SASE.
Needs: "We are always on the lookout for Xmas plays (religious for our church market or secular for the public school market). Also lighthearted one-acts and three-acts. We do like some serious, high caliber plays reflective of today's sophisticated students. Also operettas for jr/sr high school and more limited middle school (fourth grade and above) market. We prefer larger casts for our three-acts and operettas. Staging should be in keeping with school budgets and expertise. We are *not* interested in plays that are highly sexually suggestive or use abusive language."

The double dagger before a listing indicates that the listing is new in this edition. New markets are often the most receptive to freelance submissions.

Tips: "We're especially interested in musicals (large cast) for 1991. Submissions are welcomed at any time but during our fall season, response will definitely take 2 months. Authors are paid royalties twice a year. They receive complimentary copies of their published plays, the annual catalog and 50% discount if buying additional copies."

THE EMPTY SPACE, P.O. Box 1748., Seattle WA 98111-1748. (206)587-3737. Artistic Director: M. Burke Walker. Produces 6 plays/year. 100% freelance written. Professional plays for subscriber base and single ticket Seattle audience. 1 script/year is unagented submission. Works with 5-6 unpublished/unproduced writers annually. Query with synopsis before sending script. Response in 3 months. LOA theater.
Needs: "Other things besides linear, narrative realism, but we are interested in that as well. No restriction on subject matter. Generally we opt for broader, more farcical comedies and harder-edged, uncompromising dramas. We like to go places we've never been before."

‡ENCORE PERFORMANCE PUBLISHING, P.O. Box 692, Orem UT 84057. (801)225-0605. Editor: Michael C. Perry. Estab. 1979. Publishes 8-12 plays/year. "Our audience consists of all ages with emphasis on the family; educational institutions from elementary through college/university, community theaters and professional theaters." Query and synopsis or complete ms. Reports in 3 months. Buys publishing and revival performance rights. Pays 50% royalty.
Needs: "We are looking for plays with strong message about or for families, plays with young actors among cast any length, all genres. We prefer scripts with at least close or equal male/female roles, could lean to more female roles." Plays must have had at least 1 professional or 2 amateur productions.
Tips: "No performance art pieces or plays with overtly sexual themes or language."

RICHARD FICARELLI, P.O. Box 23548, Fort Lauderdale FL 33307-3548. Produces 1-2 plays/year. Plays are Equity productions performed in NY, Broadway and off-Broadway theaters. Regional possibilities. Submit query and synopsis. Reports in 6 weeks. Acquires DGA (standard) rights. Pays standard royalty.
Needs: Situation comedies *only.* Prefers cast of fewer than 14. No dramas.
Tips: "Stronger possibilities for regional and dinner theater productions as well as Broadway and off-Broadway."

THE FIREHOUSE THEATRE, 514 S. 11th St., Omaha NE 68102. (402)346-6009. Artistic Director: Dick Mueller. Produces 7 plays/year. Has produced 4 unagented submissions in 14 years.
Needs: "We produce at the Firehouse Theater in Omaha. Our interest in new scripts is the hope of finding material that can be proven here at our theater and then go on to find its audience." Submit complete ms. Reporting times vary; depends on work load. Buys negotiable rights. Pays $100/week or negotiable rates.
Tips: "We are a small theater. Certainly size and cost are a consideration. Quality is also a consideration. We can't use heavy drama in this theater. We might, however, consider a production if it were a good script and use another theater."

FLORIDA STUDIO THEATRE, 1241 N. Palm Ave., Sarasota FL 34236. (813)366-9017. New plays director: Richard Hopkins. Produces 4 established scripts and 3 new plays/year. "FST is a professional not-for-profit theater." Plays are produced in 165-seat theater for a subscription audience (primarily). FST operates under a small professional theater contract of Actor's Equity. Submit query and synopsis. Reports in 2 months on queries; 7 months on mss. Pays $200 for workshop production of new script.
Needs: Contemporary plays ("courageous and innovative"). Prefers casts of no more than 8, and single sets.

THE FREELANCE PRESS, Box 548, Dover MA 02030. (508)785-1260 or 0068. Artistic Director: Elizabeth H. Bickford. Publishes 4 plays/year. Children/young adults. Query and synopsis. Reports in 2 months. Pays 2-3% royalty. Pays $25 or 10% of the price of each script and score.
Needs: "Publish original musical theater for young people, dealing with issues of importance to them, also adapt 'classics' into musicals for 8-16 year old age groups to perform." Large cast; flexible, simple staging and props.

SAMUEL FRENCH, INC., 45 W. 25th St., New York NY 10010. Editor: Lawrence Harbison. 100% freelance written. "We publish about 80-90 new titles a year. We are the world's largest publisher of plays. 10-20% are unagented submissions. In addition to publishing plays, we occasionally act as agents in the placement of plays for professional production—eventually in New York. Pays on royalty basis. Submit complete ms (bound). Always type your play in the standard, accepted stageplay manuscript format used by all professional playwrights in the U.S. If in doubt, send $3 to the attention of Lawrence Harbison for a copy of 'Guidelines.' We require a minimum of two months to report."
Needs: "We are willing at all times to read the work of freelancers. Our markets prefer simple-to-stage, light, happy romantic comedies or mysteries. If your work does not fall into this category, we would be reading it for consideration for agency representation. No 25-page 'full-length' plays; no children's plays to be performed *by* children; no puppet plays; no adaptations of public domain children's stories; no verse plays;

no large-cast historical (costume) plays; no seasonal and/or religious plays; no television, film or radio scripts; no translations of foreign plays."

GEORGE STREET PLAYHOUSE, 9 Livingston Ave., New Brunswick NJ 08901. (201)846-2895. Producing Director: Gregory Hurst. Literary Manager: Wendy Liscow. Produces 7 plays/year. Professional regional theater (LORT C). Submit synopsis, cast breakdown, dialogue sample, SASE or submit through agent. Reports on inquiry 2 months; scripts 8 months.
Needs: Full-length dramas, comedies and musicals that present a frsh perspective on society and challenge expectations of theatricality. Prefers cast size under 9.
Tips: "We present a series of 6 staged readings each year and an ongoing playwrights' project. We produce at least 2 new plays and one new musical each season. We have a strong interest in receiving work from minority writers."

GEORGETOWN PRODUCTIONS, 7 Park Ave., New York NY 10016. Producers: Gerald van de Vorst and David Singer. Literary Manager: George Greg. Estab. 1972. Produces 1-2 plays/year for a general audience. Works with 2-3 unpublished/unproduced writers annually. Submit complete ms only. Standard Dramatists Guild contract.
Needs: Prefers plays with small casts and not demanding more than one set. Interested in new unconventional scripts dealing with contemporary issues, comedies, mysteries, musicals or dramas. No first drafts, outlines, or one-act plays.
Tips: "The current trend is toward light entertainment, as opposed to meaningful or serious plays."

GUTHRIE THEATER, 725 Vineland Pl., Minneapolis MN 55403. (612)347-1100. Artistic Director: Garland Wright. Produces 8 plays/year at the Guthrie Theater, a professional LORT A Theater; season lasts from May through March. Query and synopsis or submit complete ms (agents). Reports in 3 months. Royalty varies; Advance against performance royalties.
Needs: "We produce full-length plays of consequence in an innovative style on important contemporary issues."
Tips: No One-Acts or Historical Costume Dramas.

HEUER PUBLISHING CO., 233 Dows Bldg., Box 248, Cedar Rapids IA 52406. (319)364-6311. Publishes plays for junior and senior high school and church groups. Query with synopsis or submit complete ms. Reports in 2 months. Purchases amateur rights only. Pays royalty or cash.
Needs: "One- and three-act plays suitable for school production. Preferably comedy or mystery comedy. All material should be of the capabilities of high school actors. We prefer material with one set." No "special day material, material with controversial subject matter."

HONOLULU THEATRE FOR YOUTH, 2846 Ualena St., Honolulu HI 96819. (808)839-9885. Resident Director: Pam Sterling. Produces 6 plays/year. 50% freelance written. Plays are professional productions in Hawaii, primarily for young audiences (aged 2 to 20). 80% of scripts are unagented submissions. Works with 2 unpublished/unproduced writers annually. Reports in 3 months. Buys negotiable rights.
Needs: Contemporary subjects of concern/interest to young people; adaptations of literary classics; fantasy including space, fairy tales, myth and legend. "HTY wants well-written plays, 60-90 minutes in length, that have something worthwhile to say and that will stretch the talents of professional adult actors." Cast not exceeding 8; *no* technical extravaganzas; *no* full-orchestra musicals; simple sets and props, costumes can be elaborate. No plays to be enacted by children or camp versions of popular fairytales. Query with synopsis. Pays $1,000-2,500.
Tips: "Young people are intelligent and perceptive; if anything, more so than lots of adults, and if they are to become fans and eventual supporters of good theater, they must see good theater while they are young. Trends on the American stage that freelance writers should be aware of include a growing awareness that we are living in a world community. We must learn to share and understand other people and other cultures."

WILLIAM E. HUNT, 801 West End Ave., New York NY 10025. Estab. 1947. Interested in reading scripts for stock production, off-Broadway and even Broadway production. "Small cast, youth-oriented, meaningful, technically adventuresome; serious, funny, far-out. Must be about people first, ideas second. No political or social tracts." No one-act, anti-Black, anti-Semitic or anti-gay plays. "I do not want 1920, 1930 or 1940 plays disguised as modern by 'modern' language. I do not want plays with 24 characters, plays with 150 costumes, plays about symbols instead of people. I do not want plays that are really movie or television scripts." Works with 2-3 unpublished/unproduced writers annually. Pays royalties on production. Off-Broadway, 5%; on Broadway, 5%, 7½% and 10%, based on gross. No royalty paid if play is selected for a showcase production. Reports in "a few weeks." Must have SASE or script will not be returned.
Tips: "Production costs and weekly running costs in the legitimate theater are so high today that no play (or it is the very rare play) with more than six characters and more than one set, by a novice playwright, is likely to be produced unless that playwright will either put up or raise the money him or herself for the production."

INVISIBLE THEATRE, 1400 N. 1st Ave., Tucson AZ 85719. (602)882-9721. Artistic Director: Susan Claassen. Literary Manager: Deborah Dickey. Estab. 1971. Produces 5-7 plays/year. 10% freelance written. Semiprofessional regional theater for liberal, college-educated audiences. Plays performed in 78-seat non-Equity theater with small production budget. Works with 1-5 unpublished/unproduced writers annually. Query with synopsis. Reports in 6 months. Buys non-professional rights. Pays 10% royalty.

Needs: "Two-act plays, generally contemporary, some historical, comedies, drama, small musicals, wide range of topics. Limited to plays with small casts of 10 or less, strong female roles, simple sets, minimal props." No large musicals, complex set designs, casts larger than 10.

Tips: "Trends in the American stage that will affect the types of scripts we accept include social issues—social conscience—i.e. South Africa, coming to terms with elderly parents, overcoming effects of disease, family relationships, things that the average person can relate to and think about. Challenges we can all relate to, common experiences, because people enjoy people. Our audiences include some older, somewhat conservative, members (although *not* rigid or dogmatic) as well as younger, more liberal groups. We try to have broad appeal—mixing experimental with comedy and drama throughout the year."

JEWEL BOX THEATRE, 3700 N. Walker, Oklahoma City OK 73118. (405)521-1786. Artistic Director: Charles Tweed. Produces 6 plays/year. Amateur productions. Intended for 2,800 season subscribers and general public. Submit complete ms. Reports in 3 months. "We would like to have first production rights and 'premiere' the play at Jewel Box Theatre." Pays $500 contest prize.

Needs: "Write theater for entry form during September-October. We produce dramas, comedies and musicals. Usually we have two-act plays, but one and three acts are acceptable. Plays usually run two hours. Our theater is in-the-round, so we adapt plays accordingly. We have not used multi-media projections. We do not use excessive profanity. We will dilute dialogue if necessary."

JEWISH REPERTORY THEATRE, 344 E. 14th St., New York NY 10003., (212)674-7200. Artistic Director: Ran Avni. Estab. 1974. Produces 5 plays, 15 readings/year. New York City professional off Broadway production. Submit complete ms. Reports in 1 month. 1st production/option to move to Broadway or off Broadway. Pays royalty.

Needs: Full length only. Straight plays and musicals. Must have some connection to Jewish life, characters, history. Maximum 10 characters. Limited technical facilities.

Tips: No biblical plays.

KUMU KAHUA, 1770 East-West Rd., Honolulu HI 96822. (808)948-7677. Managing Director: Dennis Carroll. Estab. 1971. Produces 4 productions, 4 public readings/year. "Plays performed at various theaters for community audiences." Submit complete ms. Royalty is $25 per performance; usually 10 performances of each production.

Needs: "Plays must have some interest for local audiences, preferably by being set in Hawaii or dealing with some aspect of the Hawaiian experience. Prefer small cast, with simple staging demands. We don't like 'commercial' plays structured and designed for box office success of a Broadway sort. No trivial commercial farces, whodunits, plays like made-for-TV movies or sitcoms."

Tips: "We need time to evaluate, and may hold the script awhile. We're not trendy."

LILLENAS PUBLISHING CO., P.O. Box 419527, Kansas City MO 64141. (816)931-1900. FAX: (816)753-4071. Editor: Paul M. Miller. "We publish on two levels: (1) Program Builders—seasonal and topical collections of recitations, sketches, dialogues and short plays. (2) Drama Resources. These assume more than one format: (a) full length scripts, (b) shorter plays and sketches all by one author, (c) collection of short plays and sketches by various authors. All program and play resources are produced with local church and Christian school in mind. Therefore there are taboos." Queries are encouraged, but synopses and complete manuscripts are read. "First rights are purchased for Program Builder manuscripts. For our line of Drama Resources, we purchase all print rights, but this is negotiable." Writer's guidelines for #10 SASE.

Needs: 98% of Program Builder materials are freelance written. Manuscripts selected for these publications are outright purchases; verse is 25 cents per line, prose (play scripts) are $5 per double-spaced page. Lillenas Drama Resources is a line of play scripts that are, for the most part, written by professionals with experience in production as well as writing. However, while we do read unsolicited manuscripts, more than half of what we publish is written by experienced authors whom we have already published. Drama Resources (whether full-length scripts, one-acts, or sketches) are paid on a 10% royalty. There are no advances.

Tips: "All plays need to be presented in standard play script format. We welcome a summary statement of each play. Purpose statements are always desirable. Approximate playing time, cast and prop lists, etc. are important to include. We are interested in fully scripted traditional plays, reader's theater scripts, choral speaking pieces. Contemporary settings generally have it over Biblical settings. Christmas and Easter scripts must have a bit of a twist. Secular approaches to these seasons (Santas, Easter bunnies, and so on), are not considered. We sell our product in 10,000 Christian bookstores. We are probably in the forefront as a publisher of religious drama resources."

‡**LONG ISLAND STAGE**, P.O. Box 9001, Rockville Centre, NY 11571-9001. (516)456-4600. Artistic Director: Clinton J. Atkinson. Estab. 1974. Produces 6 plays/year. We are a fully professional company, operating under at LORT agreement with all theatrical unions; our audience is a subscription audience of mature adults of conservative bent. Query and synopsis. Reports in 3 months. Pays royalty.
Needs: "We are interested in contemporary materials, small casts, occasional translations, small sets. We have no parameters on materials, etc. The smaller the cast, props, and staging, the better."
Tips: "We rarely do musicals. Writers should write what they feel and want to; let trends take care of themselves."

MAD RIVER THEATER WORKS, Box 248, W. Liberty OH 43357. (513)465-6751. Artistic Director: Jeffrey Hooper. Produces 3 plays/year. "Mad River is a professional company. We present over 150 performances each year at colleges, universities and in small towns, for a broad, multigenerational audience. Our intended audience is primarily rural." Query and synopsis. Reports in 1 month. Buys exclusive production rights for a limited time. Pays negotiable royalty.
Needs: "We primarily produce works that deal with rural themes and/or issues. A small cast is most likely to be accepted. As a touring company, simple technical requirements are also a factor."
Tips: "We reach out to many different kinds of people, particularly audiences in rural areas without other access to professional theater. We seek to challenge, as well as entertain, and present works which can speak to conservative individuals as well as seasoned theatergoers."

MAGNUS THEATRE COMPANY, 137 N. May St., Thunder Bay, Ontario P7C 3N8 Canada. (807)623-5818. Artistic Director: Michael McLaughlin. Produces 6 plays/year. Professional stock theater produced in 197-seat facility, and performed for a demographically diverse general audience.
Needs: "Fairly general in genres, but with a particular emphasis on new plays, must be full-length. Smaller (i.e., up to seven) casts are viewed favorably; some technical limitations. Always, budget limitations. Also produces one-act theater-in-education scripts for all age ranges, with emphasis on socially and curriculum-relevant material."
Tips: "Thunder Bay is a very earthy, working city, and we try to reflect that sensibility in our choice of plays. Beyond that, however, Magnus has gained a national reputation for its commitment to the development and production of new plays, including, where possible, workshops. Scripts should be accessible to Canadian audiences in theme; should be produceable within realistic budget limitations."

MANHATTAN THEATRE CLUB, 453 W. 16th St., New York NY 10011. Director of the Script Department: Kate Loewald. Produces 9 plays/year. All freelance written. A two-theater performing arts complex classified as off-Broadway, using professional actors. No unsolicited scripts. Query with synopsis. Reports in 6 months. Payment is negotiable.
Needs: "We present a wide range of new work, from this country and abroad, to a subscription audience. We want plays about contemporary problems and people. Comedies are welcome. No verse plays or large musicals. Very heavy set shows or multiple detailed sets are discouraged. We present shows with casts of not more than 15. No skits."

MERRIMACK REPERTORY THEATRE, Box 228, Lowell MA 01853. (508)454-6324. Dramaturg/Literary Manager: David Kent. Produces 6 plays/year. Professional LORT D. Agented submissions only. Also sponsors Merrimack Repertory Theatre First Annual Playwriting Contest. Reports in 3-6 months.
Needs: All styles and genres. No avant-garde. "We are a small 300 seat theater—with a modest budget. Plays should appeal to working class/Catholic/and urban-immigrant populations.

MIAMI BEACH COMMUNITY THEATRE, 2231 Prairie Ave., Miami Beach FL 33139. (305)532-4515. Artistic Director: Jay W. Jensen. Produces 5 plays/year. "Amateur productions performed during the year for the Miami Beach community." Send query and synopsis or submit complete ms. Reports in 3 weeks. Pays $35-75/performance (if published work); does not pay for unpublished plays.
Needs: "All types. Interested in Spanish themes—Latin American plots, etc. Interested in new plays dealing with AIDS and short plays dealing wth AIDS that could be used in junior highs and senior highs for motivation—about 30 minutes long. Avoid sex."

MILL, MOUNTAIN THEATRE, Market Square Center in Square, Roanoke VA 24011. (703)342-5730. Executive Director: Jere Lee Hodgin. Produces 10 established plays, 10 new one-acts and 2 new full-length plays/year. "Some of the professional productions will be on the main stage and some in our alternative theater B." Submit complete ms. Reports in 8 months. Payment negotiable on individual play. Writer's guidelines for #10 SASE; do not include loose stamps or money.
Needs: "We are interested in plays with racially mixed casts, but not to the exclusion of others. We are constantly seeking one-act plays for 'Centerpieces', our Lunch Time Program of Script-in-Hand Productions. Playing time should be between 25-35 minutes. Cast limit is 15 for plays and 24 for musicals."

Tips: "Subject matter and character variations are open, but gratuitous language and acts are not acceptable. A play based on large amounts of topical reference or humor has a very short life. Be sure you have written a play and not a film script."

MISE EN SCÈNE THEATRE, 5110 Tujunga #4, North Hollywood CA 91601. (818)763-3101. Artistic Director: Herb Rodgers. Produces 6-16 plays/year at two theaters. For Los Angeles audiences, casting directors, agents and producers. Equity waiver; 99-seat house. Submit complete ms. Reports in 2 months. Payment negotiable.
Needs: "Only original, unproduced, full-lengths and one-acts. Any genre, topic, style." Stage has 28-foot opening, 21-foot depth.
Tips: "No previously produced plays. Our objective is to give playwrights the opportunity to work in production with the directors and actors, to better prepare the play for professional productions. Our plays are reviewed by the *Los Angeles Times, Variety, Hollywood Reporter* and other local papers. Productions are videotaped."

MISSOURI REPERTORY THEATRE, 4949 Cherry St., Kansas City MO 64110. (816)276-2727. Contact: Mary Guaraldi, Director of Second Stage. Estab. 1963. Produces 7 plays/year. Regional professional theater. Query and synopsis. Reports in 2 months. Buys standard Dramatists Guild contract.
Needs: Well-known contemporary American, classics with an emphasis on Shakespeare, and new plays for development.

‡MIXED BLOOD THEATRE COMPANY, 1501 S. 4th St., Minneapolis MN 55454. (612)338-0937. Artistic Director: Jack Reuler. Estab. 1975. Produces 5 plays/year. Equity productions in 200 seat theatre. General audiences. Submit query and synopsis. No unsolicited scripts unless intended for "Mixed Blood Versus America." Annual playwriting contest. SASE.
Needs: In the past we have produced high-tech spectacles, original musicals, wild satires as well as regional and American premieres.
Tips: The best means for submitting new work to our theatre is through our annual playwriting contest Mixed Blood Versus America, a copy of guidelines is available by sending an SASE to our theatre attn: David Kunz, Script Czar. *Otherwise we accept query letters with play synosis ONLY.*

‡NATIONAL MUSIC THEATER CONFERENCE, EUGENE O'NEILL THEATER CENTER, Suite 901, 234 W. 44th St., New York NY 10036. (212)382-2790. Artistic Director: Paulette Haupt. Estab. 1978. Paying audiences drawn from local residents and others. Conference takes place at center in Waterford, CT. Send #10 SASE after September 15 to request application guidelines. Application deadline: February 1, subject to change. Pays stipend plus room and board during conference.
Needs: "We develop new music theater works of all forms, traditional and non-traditional. Singing must play a dominant role. Works are given minimally staged readings, script in hand, no props or lighting, piano only."
Tips: Works not considered eligible are those that have been fully produced by a professional company and adapted works for which rights have not been obtained. Writers and composers must be U.S. citizens or permanent residents.

NECESSARY ANGEL THEATRE, #400, 553 Queen St. W., Toronto, Ontario M5V 2B6 Canada (416)365-0533. Dramaturg: D. D. Kugler. Produces 2 plays/year. Plays are Equity productions in various Toronto theaters and performance spaces for an urban audience between 20-55 years of age. Submit complete ms. Please include SASE (international postal coupon if from the U.S.). Reports in 6 months. Obtains various rights "based on the manuscript (original, translation, adaptation) and the playwright (company member, etc.)." Pays 10% royalty.
Needs: "We are open to new theatrical ideas, environmental pieces, unusual acting styles and large casts. The usual financial constraints exist, but they have never eliminated a work to which we felt a strong commitment." No "TV-influenced sit-coms or melodramas."
Tips: "All submissions are considered for long-term script/playwright development, including one-day readings and one-week workshops, leading to company productions. Playwrights should be aware of our interdisciplinary approach to performance (music, dance and visual arts that support the text)."

THE NEW CONSERVATORY CHILDREN'S THEATRE COMPANY AND SCHOOL, Zephyr Theater Complex, 25 Van Ness, Lower Level, San Francisco CA 94102. (415)861-4814. Artistic Director: Ed Decker. Produces 4-5 plays/year. "The New Conservatory is a children's theater school (ages four to nineteen) and operates year-round. Each year we produce several plays, for which the older students (usually eleven and up) audition. These are presented to the general public at the Zephyr Theatre Complex San Francisco (50-350 seats). Our audience is approximately age 10 to adult." Send query and synopsis. Reports in 1 month. Pays 5% royalty.
Needs: "We emphasize works in which children play *children,* and prefer relevant and controversial subjects, although we also do musicals. We have a commitment to new plays. Examples of our shows are: Mary Gail's *Nobody Home* (world premiere; about latchkey kids); Brian Kral's *Special Class* (about disabled kids), and

The Inner Circle, by Patricia Loughrey (commissioned scripts about AIDS prevention for kids). As we are a non-profit group on limited budget, we tend not to have elaborate staging; however, our staff is inventive—includes choreographer and composer. Write innovative theater that explores topics of concern/interest to young people, that takes risks. We concentrate more on ensemble than individual roles, too. We do *not* want to see fairytales or trite rehashings of things children have seen/heard since the age of two. See theater as education, rather than 'children being cute'."

Tips: "It is important for young people and their families to explore and confront issues relevant to growing up in the '90s. Theatre is a marvelous teaching tool that can educate while it entertains."

NEW PLAYS INCORPORATED, Box 371, Bethel CT 06801. (203)792-4342. Publisher: Patricia Whitton. Publishes an average of 4 plays/year. Publishes plays for producers of plays for young audiences and teachers in college courses on child drama. Query with synopsis. Reports in 2 months. Agent for amateur and semi-professional productions, exclusive agency for script sales. Pays 50% royalty on productions; 10% on script sales. Free catalog.

Needs: Plays for young audiences with something innovative in form and content. Length: usually 45-90 minutes. "Should be suitable for performance by adults for young audiences." No skits, assembly programs, improvisations or unproduced manuscripts.

NEW PLAYWRIGHTS' PROGRAM, THE UNIVERSITY OF ALABAMA, P.O. Box 870239, Tuscaloosa AL 35487-0239. (205)348-9032. Director and Dramaturg: Dr. Paul C. Castagno. Estab. 1982. Produces at least 1 new play/year. University Theatre, The University of Alabama. Submit complete ms. Reports in 1-3 months. Accepts scripts in various forms: New dramaturgy to traditional. Also radio plays.

NEW YORK SHAKESPEARE FESTIVAL/PUBLIC THEATER, 425 Lafayette St., New York NY 10003. (212)598-7100. Producer: Joseph Papp. Director, Script Department: Gail Merrifield. Co-Director: Tom Ross. Estab. 1954. Interested in plays, musicals, translations, adaptations. No restriction as to style, form, subject matter. Produces classics, new American and international works year-round at the Public Theater complex housing 5 theaters (100-300 seat capacity): Newman, Anspacher, Shiva, LuEsther Hall, Martinson. Also at Delacorte 2100-seat amphitheater in Central Park. Transfers to Broadway, film and television. Unsolicited and un-agented submissions accepted. Computer printout manuscripts and electronic submissions via VHS OK with hard copy. All scripts: include cast of characters with age and brief description; musical works: submit cassette with at least 3 songs. Standard options and production agreements. Reports in 2 months.

NEW YORK THEATRE WORKSHOP, 220 W. 42 St., 18th Fl., New York NY 10036. (212)302-7737. Artistic Director: James C. Nicola. Estab. 1979. Produces 6 full productions; approximately 50 readings per year. Plays are performed Off-Broadway, Equity mini-contract theater; Audience: New York theatergoing audience and theater professionals. Query and synopsis or submit complete ms. Reports in 3-5 months. Option to produce commercially; percentage of box office gross from commercial productions within a specified time limit from our original production; percentage of author's net subsidiary rights within specified time limit from our original production. Pays fee because of limited run, with additional royalty payments; for extensions, $1,500-2,000 fee range.

Needs: Full-length plays, one-acts, translations/adaptations, music-theater pieces; proposals for performance projects. Large issues, socially relevant issues, innovative form and language, minority issues. Plays utilizing over eight actors usually require outside funding.

Tips: No overtly commercial, traditional Broadway-type "musicals."

JACKIE NICHOLS, 51 S. Cooper, Memphis TN 38104. Artistic Director: Jackie Nichols. Produces 16 plays/year. Professional productions. Submit complete ms. Reports in 5 months. Pays $500.

Needs: All types. "Small cast, single or unit set."

Tips: "Playwrights from the South will be given preference. South is defined as the following states: Alabama, Florida, Georgia, Kentucky, Louisiana, Mississippi, Missouri, North Carolina, South Carolina, Tennessee, Texas, Virginia and West Virginia. This means we will read all shows and when final decisions are made, if every other aspect of the plays are equal we will choose a Southern author."

NINE O'CLOCK PLAYERS, 1367 N. St. Andrews Pl., Los Angeles CA 90028. (213)469-1973. Artistic Director: Fluff McLean. Estab. 1928. Produces 2 plays/year. "Plays produced at Assistance League Playhouse by resident amateur and semi-professional company. All plays are musical adaptations of classical children's literature. Plays must be appropriate for children ages 4-12." Query and synopsis. Reports in 1 month. Pays negotiable royalty or per performance.

Needs: "Plays must have at least 15 characters and be 1 hour 15 minutes long. Productions are done on a proscenium stage in classical theater style. All plays must have humor, music and good moral values. No audience participation improvisational plays."

NO EMPTY SPACE THEATRE, 568 Metropolitan Ave., Staten Island NY 10301-3431. Artistic Director: James E. Stayoch. Produces 1 play/year. Performed locally on S.I., usually Equity Showcase, intended for NYC audience. Submit complete ms. Reports in 1 month. Buys 1 time production rights. Award - $500. Also sponsors contest beginning again in 1991. Write for more information.

THE NORTH CAROLINA BLACK REPERTORY COMPANY, P.O. Box 2793, Winston-Salem NC 27012. (919)723-7907. Artistic Director: Larry Leon Hamlin. Estab. 1979. Produces 4-6 plays/year. Plays produced primarily in North Carolina, New York City, and possible touring throughout the South. Submit complete ms. Reports in 5 months. Obtains negotiable rights. Negotiable payment.
Needs: "Full-length plays and musicals: mostly African-American with special interest in historical or contemporary *statement* genre. A cast of 10 would be a comfortable limit; we discourage multiple sets."
Tips: "The best time to submit manuscript is between September and February."

ODYSSEY THEATRE ENSEMBLE, 2055 S. Sepulveda Blvd., Los Angeles CA 90025. (213)826-1626. Literary Manager: Jan Lewis. Estab. 1969. Produces 12 plays/year. Plays performed in a 3-theater facility. "All three theaters are Equity 99-seat theater plan. We have a subscription audience of 2,000 who subscribe to a six-play main season and a 3-4 play lab season, and are offered a discount on our remaining non-subscription plays. Remaining seats are sold to the general public." Query with synopsis, cast breakdown and 8-10 pages of sample dialogue. Scripts must be securely bound. Reports in 1 month on queries; 6 months on scripts. Buys negotiable rights. Pays 5-7% royalty or $25-35/performance. "We will *not* return scripts without SASE."
Needs: Full-length plays only with "either an innovative form or extremely provocative subject matter. We desire more theatrical pieces that explore possibilities of the live theater experience. We are seeking full-length musicals. We are not reading one-act plays or light situation comedies. We are seeking Hispanic material for our resident Hispanic Unit."

‡OLD GLOBE THEATRE, P.O. Box 2171, San Diego CA 92112. (619)231-1941. Literary Manager: Mark Hofflund. Produces 12 plays/year. "We are a LORT B professional house with 3 stages: 581-seat thrust, 225-seat arena, 621-seat outdoor. Our plays are produced for a single-ticket and subscription audience of 250,000, a large cross section of southern California, including visitors from the LA area." Submit complete ms through agent only. Send one-page letter or synopsis if not represented. Reports in 6 months. Buys negotiable rights. Royalty varies.
Needs: "We are looking for plays of strong literary and theatrical merit, works that display a mature sense of craft, and works that share a broad and detailed cultural vision. All submissions must be full-length plays or musicals."
Tips: "Get produced wherever and whenever you can. The venues will improve with the work and the experience you accumulate."

OLDCASTLE THEATRE COMPANY, Box 1555, Bennington VT 05201. (802)447-0564. Artistic Director: Eric Peterson. Produces 7 plays/year. Plays are performed in a small (104 seat) theater on a former estate now used by Southern Vermont College, by a professional Equity theater company (in a season from April through October) for general audiences, including residents of a three-state area and tourists during the vacation season. Submit complete ms. Pays "by negotiation with the playwright. A not-for-profit theater company."
Needs: Produces classics, musicals, comedy, drama, most frequently American works. Usual performance time is 2 hours. "With a small stage, we limit to small cast."

EUGENE O'NEILL THEATER CENTER'S NATIONAL PLAYWRIGHTS CONFERENCE/NEW DRAMA FOR TELEVISION PROJECT, Suite 901, 234 W. 44th St., New York NY 10036. (212)382-2790. Artistic Director: Lloyd Richards. Administrator: Peggy Vernieu. Develops staged readings of 10-12 stage plays, 2-3 teleplays/year for a general audience. "We accept unsolicited mss with no prejudice toward either represented or unrepresented writers. Our theater is located in Waterford, Connecticut and we operate under an Equity LORT Contract. We have 3 theaters: Barn-250 seats, Amphitheater-300 seats, Instant Theater-150. Send #10 SASE in the fall for submission guidelines. Complete bound, unproduced, original plays are eligible (no adaptations). Decision by late April. Pays stipend plus room, board and transportation. We accept script submissions from Sept. 15-Dec. 1 of each year. Conference takes place during four weeks in July each summer."
Needs: "We use modular sets for all plays, minimal lighting, minimal props and no costumes. We do script-in-hand readings with professional actors and directors. Our focus is on new play/playwright development."

THE OPEN EYE: NEW STAGINGS, 270 W. 89th St., New York NY 10024. (212)769-4143. Artistic Director: Amie Brockway. Estab. 1972. Produces 3-4 full-length plays/year plus a series of readings and workshop productions of one-acts. "The Open Eye is a professional, Equity LOA and TYA 115-seat, off-off Broadway theater. Our audiences include a broad spectrum of ages and backgrounds." Submit complete ms in clean, bound copy with SASE for its return. Reports in 6 months. Playwright fee for mainstage: $500.

Needs: "New Stagings is particularly interested in one-act and full-length plays that take full advantage of the live performance situation. We tend not to do totally realistic plays. We especially like plays that appeal to young people and adults alike."

OREGON SHAKESPEARE FESTIVAL ASSOCIATION, P.O. Box 158, Ashland OR 97520. (503)482-2111. Literary Manager: Cynthia White. Produces 16 plays/year. The Angus Bowmer Theater has a thrust stage and seats 600. The Black Swan is an experimental space and seats 150; The Elizabethan Outdoor Theatre seats 1,200 (stages almost exclusively Shakespearean productions there—mid-June through September). OSFA also produces a separate five-play season at the Portland Center for The Performing Arts in a 725 seat proscenium theater. Producing director of OSFA Portland Center Stage: Dennis Bigelow. Query and synopsis plus 10 pages of dialogue from unsolicited sources/also resume. Complete scripts from agents only. Reports in 9 months. Negotiates individually for rights with the playwright's agent. "Most plays run within our 10 month season for 6-10 months, so royalties are paid accordingly."
Needs: "A broad range of classic and contemporary scripts. One or two fairly new scripts per season. Also a play readings series which focuses on new work. Plays must fit into our 10-month rotating repertory season. Black Swan shows usually limited to 6 actors." No one-acts or musicals.
Tips: "Send your work through an agent if possible. Send the best examples of your work rather than all of it. Don't become impatient or discouraged if it takes 6 months or more for a response. Don't expect detailed critiques with rejections. As always, I want to see plays with heart and soul, intelligence, humor and wit. I also think theater is a place for the *word*. So, the word first, then spectacle and high-tech effects."

‡PAPER MILL PLAYHOUSE, Brookside Dr., Millburn NJ 07041. (201)379-3636. Literary Advisor: Maryan F. Stephens. Estab. 1934. Produces 4 musicals, 2 plays/year. Paper Mill Playhouse is an artistically oriented nonprofit theatre. Over 370 performances are scheduled annually for nearly 400,000 patrons (including a record 43,000 subscribers). Our audience could be classified as "mainstream." For our mainstage we seat 1,192, proscenium stage with flyloft and orchestra pit. Submit complete ms and include a cassette tape with musicals. Reports in 6 months.
Needs: Paper Mill produces full-length plays (drama, comedy, farce), musicals and operettas. Please do not submit children's plays/musicals or one-acts.
Tips: Playwrights should remember they are writing for the stage, not television or film. We are looking for well crafted new American plays and musicals with strong commercial appeal. Paper Mill Playhouse has a development program, Musical Theatre Project. A series of Staged Readings are given each season, of plays and musicals, with the intention of giving one or more new work full-production. Submissions should have no previous history of professional production.

THE PASSAGE THEATRE COMPANY, P.O. Box 967, Trenton NJ 08605-0967. Artistic Director: Veronica Brady. Produces 4 plays/year. "Passage is a professional theater company. Most of our work is performed at the Mill Hill Playhouse, which is in Trenton NJ. Our work is intended for all audiences, culturally and artistically." Query and synopsis or submit complete ms. Reports in 1 month. Pays royalty.
Needs: "We are committed to producing only new American plays. 1-3 act plays (this is general, based on previous experience) dealing with social, cultural and artistic issues. We also do workshops and readings of plays. We work actively with the writers in developing their work."

PCPA THEATERFEST, P.O. Box 1700, Santa Monica CA 93456. (805)928-7731. Artistic Director: Jack Shouse. Estab. 1967. Produces 14 plays/year. "We have year-round theater: the Marian Theatre seats 500, the Interim Theatre seats 160; Backstage Theatre is 130 seats; the Festival Theatre m Solvang is open-air, seats 750 and is for summer only. Our audience is broad spectrum." Accept only query and synopsis with cast list, production history. No unsolicited scripts. If script is requested, reports within 9 months. Rights negotiaged with each playwright on an individual basis. Pay negotiable.
Needs: All genres. All topics. All styles. Full length only. No children's plays. "We have 2 distinct play series in winter—one for large scale productions, the other for smaller scale, more contemporary/experimental.
Tips: "No formulaic writing or television-style writing. Works *should be theatrical*, using the elements that make theater a distinctive art form. Works should *say* something moving, interesting, thought-provoking and entertaining about the human condition. We want fresh voices. Originality, not repetition is key here. We are looking for top-quality plays with fresh insights/approaches. Musicals should have top-quality music, lyrics and book."

PENNSYLVANIA STAGE COMPANY, 837 Linden St., Allentown PA 18101. (215)437-6110. Artistic Director: Peter Wrenn-Meleck. Estab. 1980. Produces 7 plays and musicals/year. "We are a LORT D theater and our season runs from October through June. The large majority of our audience comes from the Lehigh Valley. Our audience consists largely of adults. We also offer special student and senior citizen matinees." Query and synopsis; also would like a character breakdown and SASE or postcard. Reports in 3 months for scripts; 2 weeks for synopsis. Payment negotiable.

Needs: "The PSC produces full-length plays and musicals that are innovative and imaginative and that broaden our understanding of ourselves and society. Looking for wide range of styles and topics." Prefers 12 characters or fewer (will consider up to 18) for musicals; 8 or fewer for plays.

Tips: "Works presented at the Stage Company have a passion for being presented now, should be entertaining and meaningful to our local community, and perpetuate our theatrical and literary heritage. We do not want to limit our options in achieving this artistic mission. No one-acts and material that contains grossly offensive language. We appreciate also receiving a sample of dialogue with the synopsis. We have a staged reading program where a director, actors and the playwright work together during an intensive 3-day rehearsal period. A discussion with the audience follows the staged reading."

PEOPLE'S LIGHT & THEATRE COMPANY, 39 Conestoga Rd., Malvern PA 19355. (215)647-1900. Producing Director: Danny S. Fruchter. Produces 5 full-length plays/year; no more than 1 new play/year. "LORT D Actors' Equity plays are produced in Malvern 30 miles outside Philadelphia in 350-seat main stage and 150-seat Steinbright Stage. Our audience is mainly suburban, some from Philadelphia." Query with synopsis and cast list. Reports in 10 months. Buys "rights to production in our theater, sometimes for local touring." Pays 2-5% royalty.

Needs: "We will produce anything that interests us." Prefers single set, maximum cast of 12 (for full length), fewer for one act. No musicals, mysteries, domestic comedies.

Tips: "Writers should be aware of trend away from naturalistic family drama and trend toward smaller cast size."

PERSEVERANCE THEATRE, 914 3rd St., Douglas AK 99801. (907)364-2421. Artistic Director: Molly Smith. Produces 5 mainstage, 2-3 second stage plays/year. Professional productions, Southeast Alaska. Primarily Juneau audiences; occasional tours to other places. Submit query and synopsis, no unsolicited mss. Reports in 6 months. Pays $25-50 per performance.

Tips: "We are producing very few original pieces from writers outside of Alaska. Because of that, we are reading few new plays."

PHILADELPHIA FESTIVAL THEATRE FOR NEW PLAYS, 3900 Chestnut St., Philadelphia PA 19104. (215)222-5000. Artistic Director: Dr. Carol Rocamora. Produces 4-6 plays/year. Professional productions (LORT D contract), subscriber series. Submit complete ms with SASE and $5 processing fee. Reports in 6 months.

Needs: A wide variety of new works without previous professional production.

PIER ONE THEATRE, P.O. Box 894, Homer AK 99603. (907)235-7333. Artistic Director: Lance Petersen. Estab. 1973. Produces 5-8 plays/year. "Plays to various audiences for various plays—e.g. children's, senior citizens, adult, family, etc. Plays are produced on Kemai Peninsula." Submit complete ms. Reports in 2 months. Pays $25-125/performance.

Needs: "No restrictions—willing to read *all* genres." No stock reviews, hillbilly or sit-coms.

Tips: "There are slightly increased opportunities for new works. Don't start your play with a telephone conversation. New plays ought to be risky business; they ought to be something the playwright feels is terribly important."

PIONEER DRAMA SERVICE, P.O. Box 22555, Denver CO 80222. (303)759-4297. FAX: (303)759-0475. Publisher: Steven Fendrich. Estab. 1963. 10% freelance written. Plays are performed by high school, junior high and adult groups, colleges, churches and recreation programs for audiences of all ages. "We are one of the largest full-service play publishers in the country in that we handle straight plays, musicals, children's theater and melodrama." Publishes 10 plays/year; 40% musicals and 60% straight plays. Query only; no unsolicited manuscripts. Buys all rights. Outright purchase only with a few exceptions for major musicals. Reports in 2 months.

Needs: "We use the standard two-act format, two-act musicals, religious drama, comedies, mysteries, drama, melodrama and plays for children's theater (plays to be done by adult actors for children)." Length: two-act musicals and two-act comedies up to 90 minutes; and children's theater of 1 hour. Prefer many female roles, one simple set. Currently overstocked on one-act plays.

☐**PLAYERS PRESS, INC.**, Box 1132, Studio City CA 91604. Senior Editor: Robert W. Gordon. "We deal in all areas and handle works for film and television as well as theater. But all works must be in stage play format for publication." Also produces scripts for video, and material for cable television. 80% freelance written. 10-12 scripts/year are unagented submissions. Works with 1-10 unpublished/unproduced writers

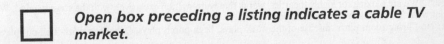

Open box preceding a listing indicates a cable TV market.

annually. Submit query. "Include one #10 SASE, reviews and proof of production. All submissions must have been produced and should include a flyer and/or program with dates of performance." Reports in 3 months. Buys negotiable rights. "We prefer all area rights." Pays variable royalty "according to area; approximately 10-75% of gross receipts." Also pays in outright purchase of $100-25,000 or $5-5,000/performance.
Needs: "We prefer comedies, musicals and children's theater, but are open to all genres. We will rework the ms after acceptance. We are interested in the quality, not the format."
Tips: "Send only material requested. Do not telephone."

PLAYS, The Drama Magazine for Young People, 120 Boylston St., Boston MA 02116. Editor: Sylvia K. Burack. Estab. 1941. Publishes approximately 75 one-act plays and dramatic program material each school year to be performed by junior and senior high, middle grades, lower grades. Mss should follow the general style of *Plays*. Stage directions should not be typed in capital letters or underlined. No incorrect grammar or dialect. Desired lengths for mss are: junior and senior high—18-20 double-spaced ms pages (25 to 30 minutes playing time). Middle grades—10 to 15 pages (15 to 20 minutes playing time). Lower grades—6 to 10 pages (8 to 15 minutes playing time). Pays "good rates on acceptance." Query first for adaptations. Reports in 2-3 weeks. Sample copy $3.50; send SASE for mss specification sheet.
Needs: "Can use comedies, farces, melodramas, skits, mysteries and dramas, plays for holidays and other special occasions, such as Book Week; adaptations of classic stories and fables; historical plays; plays about black history and heroes; puppet plays; folk and fairy tales; creative dramatics; and plays for conservation, ecology or human rights programs."

THE PLAYWRIGHTS' CENTER, 2301 Franklin Ave. E., Minneapolis MN 55406. (612)332-7481. Director of Public Relations: Lisa Stevens. Estab. 1971. "Midwest Playlabs is a 2-week developmental workshop for new plays. The program is held in Minneapolis and is open by script competition. It is an intensive two-week workshop focusing on the development of a script and the playwright. 4-6 new plays are given rehearsed public readings at the site of the workshop." Announcements of playwrights by end of April. Playwrights receive honoraria, travel expenses, room and board.
Needs: "We are interested in playwrights with talent, ambitions for a sustained career in theater and scripts which could benefit from an intensive developmental process involving professional dramaturgs, directors and actors. U.S. citizens, only: no musicals or children's plays. Participants must attend all or part of conference depending on the length of their workshop. Full lengths only. No previously produced materials. Call or write for application. Submission deadline: January 14.
Tips: "We do not buy scripts or produce them. We are a service organization that provides programs for developmental work on scripts for members. Conference: July 28-August 11, 1991."

PLAYWRIGHTS PREVIEW PRODUCTIONS, #304, 1160 5th Ave., New York NY 10029. Artistic Director: Frances Hill. Estab. 1983. Produces 4-6 plays/year. Professional productions Off or Off Off Broadway, 1 production Kennedy Center—throughout the year. General audience. Submit complete ms. Reports in 4 months. If produced, option for six months. Pays royalty.
Needs: Both one-act and full-length; generally one set or styled playing dual. Good imaginative, creative writing. Cast limited to 3-7.
Tips: "We tend to reject 'living-room' plays. We look for imaginative settings. Be creative and interesting with intellectual content."

PLAYWRIGHTS THEATRE OF NEW JERSEY, 33 Green Village Rd., Madison NJ 07940. (201)514-1787. Artistic Director: Buzz McLaughlin. Estab. 1986. Produces 3 productions/6 staged readings/12 sit-down readings/year. "We operate under a small professional theater contract with Actors' Equity Association for all productions and readings." Submit complete ms. Short bio and production history required. Reports in 2 months. "For productions we ask the playwright to sign an agreement that gives us exclusive rights to the play for the production period and for 30 days following. After the 30 days we give the rights back with no strings attached, except for commercial productions. We ask that our developmental work be acknowledged in any other professional productions." Pays $100 for productions and staged readings plus living expenses.
Needs: Any style or length; full-length, one-acts, musicals.
Tips: "No plays that simply reflect the world's chaos. We are interested in developing plays that illuminate the human spirit. We're looking for plays that are in their early stages of development."

PRIMARY STAGES COMPANY, INC., 584 9th Ave., New York NY 10036. (212)333-7471. Artistic Director: Casey Childs. Estab. 1983. Produces 4 plays, 4 workshops, over 100 readings/year. All of the plays are produced professionally off-Broadway at the 45th Street Theatre, 354 West 45th St. Query and synopsis. Reports in 3 months. "If Primary Stages produces the play, we ask for the right to move it for up to six months after the closing performance." Writers paid "same as the actors."
Needs: "We are looking for highly theatrical works that were written exclusively with the stage in mind. We do not want TV scripts or strictly realistic plays."
Tips: No "living room plays, disease-of-the-week plays, back-porch plays, father/son work-it-all-out-plays, etc."

‡**QUAIGH THEATRE**, 808 Lexington Ave., New York NY 10021. (212)223-2547. Artistic Director: Will Lieberson. Estab. 1973. Produces 4 major productions/year. Off-off-Broadway. Query and synopsis. Reports in 2 weeks on queries; 3 months on submissions. Rights differ on each script. Pays variable royalty.
Tips: No plays on familiar subjects done in a familiar way. Plays need action as well as words. Plays are not meant for public reading. If they work as readings they really are rotten plays.

THE QUARTZ THEATRE, P.O. Box 465, Ashland OR 97520. (503)482-8119. Artistic Director: Dr. Robert Spira. Estab. 1973. Produces 5 plays/year. "Semi-professional mini-theater. General audience." Send 3 page dialogue and personal bio. Reports in 2 weeks. Pays 5% royalty after expenses.
Needs: "Any length, any subject, with or without music. We seek playwrights with a flair for language and theatrical imagination."
Tips: "We look at anything. We do not do second productions unless substantial rewriting is involved. Our theatre is a steppingstone to further production. Our playwrights are usually well-read in comparative religion, philosophy, psychology, and have a comprehensive grasp of human problems. We seek the 'self-indulgent' playwright who pleases him/herself first of all."

RADIO REPERTORY COMPANY, INC., P.O. Box 23179, Cincinnati OH 45223. President: Jon C. Hughes. Estab. 1988. Produces 6 plays/year. Public radio. Query before submitting manuscript. Reports in 3 months. Buys first rights. Payment depends on non-profit funding: 1989 authors' honorarium $400.
Needs: Genres: dramatic adaptations of classical and contemporary short stories. Length: 24-27 minutes (about 20 pages). No more than 10 characters.
Tips: "The ms must be in the appropriate format. Request free copy of guidelines and format before submitting ms. Enclose SASE."

THE ROAD COMPANY, P.O. Box 5278 EKS, Johnson City TN 37603. (615)926-7726. Artistic Director: Robert H. Leonard. Literary Manager: Christine Murdock. Estab. 1975. Produces 3 plays/year. "Our professional productions are intended for a general adult audience." Query and synopsis. Reports in 4 months. Pays royalty. "When we do new plays we generally try to have the playwright in residence during rehearsal for 3-4 weeks for about $1,000 plus room and board."
Needs: We like plays that experiment with form, that challenge, inform and entertain. We are a small ensemble based company. We look for smaller cast shows 4-6."
Tips: "We are always looking for 2 character (male/female) plays. We are interested in plays set in the South. We are most interested in new work that deals with new forms. We write our own plays using improvisational techniques which we then tour throughout the Southeast. When funding permits, we include one of our own new plays in our home season."

SEATTLE GROUP THEATRE CO., 3940 Brooklyn Ave. NE, Seattle WA 98105. (206)545-4969. Artistic Director: Ruben Sierra. Estab. 1978. Produces 6 mainstage and Multicultural Playwright's Festival (2 workshops and 4-6 readings). Ethnic Theatre (200 seats) plus Glenn Hughes Playhouse (218 seats) small professional Theatre Contract AEA. Intended for general public. 2,500 subscribers. No unsolicited scripts; synopsis, dialogue sample, resumé and letter of inquiry. Buys licensing for production. Payment negotiated royalties (per performance minimum or % of total box).
Needs: Full length, translations, adaptations. Serious plays with social/cultural issues; satires or comedies with bite. Plays must be suitable for multi-ethnic casts. Cast limit of 10 prefer unit set or simple sets.
Tips: "No non-solicited topics. No fluff."

SHAW FESTIVAL, P.O. Box 774, Niagara-on-the-Lake, Ontario L0S 1J0 Canada. FAX: (416)468-5438. Artistic Director: Christopher Newton. Produces 10 plays/year. "Professional summer festival operating three theaters (Festival: 861 seats, Court House: 370 seats and Royal George: 350 seats). We also host some music and some winter rentals. Mandate is based on the works of G.B. Shaw and his contemporaries." No scripts are unagented submissions. Works with 2 unpublished/unproduced writers annually. Submit complete ms. Reports in 6 months. "We prefer to hold rights for Canada and northeastern U.S., also potential to tour." Pays 5-6% royalty. SASE or SAE and IRCs.
Needs: "We operate an acting ensemble of up to 75 actors, this includes 14 actor/singers and have sophisticated production facilities. We run some winter seasons in Toronto for the production of new works. During the summer season (April-October) the Academy of the Shaw Festival organizes several workshops of new plays."

‡**SHENANDOAH PLAYWRIGHTS RETREAT**, Rt. 5, Box 167F, Staunton VA 24401. (703)248-1868. Program Director: Robert Graham Small. Estab. 1976. Produces in workshop 11 plays/year. Submit complete ms. Obtains no rights. Writers are provided fellowships, room and board to Shenandoah.
Tips: We are looking for *good* material, not derivative; from writers who enjoy exploration with dedicated theatre professionals. Kitchen-sink dramas and sit-coms are self-limiting. Live theatre *must* be theatrical! Consider global issues. Look beyond your personal life-experience and explore connections that will lift your characters/conflicts to a more universal plane.

‡**FRANK SILVERA WRITERS' WORKSHOP**, 317 W. 125th St., Harlem NY 10027. (212)662-8463. Project Director: Pat White. Estab. 1973. Playwrights' development workshop. Reads new plays by new and established writers on Monday evenings from Sept-June. Produces 3 plays annually as well as 3 staged readings. Playwriting seminars conducted by master playwrights on Wednesdays. "All productions, originally read at the Workshop are credited by outside producers. Services primarily African American writers."
Needs: "Full-length plays, one-acts" with universal themes.

‡**THE SNOWMASS ASPEN REPERTORY THEATRE**, (formerly Snowmass Repertory Theatre), P.O. Box 6275, Snowmass Village CO 81615. (303)923-3773. Artistic Director: Gordon Reinhart. Managing Director: Marci Mauller. Estab. 1984. Produces 3 mainstage plays/year and 1 children's play. "Plays performed at The Snowmass Performing Arts Center." Submit synopsis. Reports anywhere from 6 weeks to 6 months. Obtains rights for first professional production. Pays 6-8% royalty.
Needs: "We produce full-length comedies, dramas and musicals. Prefer casts of 3-10 characters with relatively equal numbers of male and female characters and no limitations on minority casting; single or suggestive settings."

SOUTH COAST REPERTORY, P.O. Box 2197, Costa Mesa CA 92628. (714)957-2602. Dramaturg: Jerry Patch. Literary Manager: John Glore. Estab. 1964. Produces 6 plays/year on mainstage, 5 on second stage. A professional non-profit theater; a member of LORT and TCG. "We operate in our own facility which houses a 507-seat mainstage theater and a 161-seat second stage theater. We have a combined subscription audience of 24,000." Submit query and synopsis; manuscripts considered if submitted by agent. Reports in 4 months. Acquires negotiable rights. Pays negotiable royalty.
Needs: "We produce mostly full-lengths but will consider one-acts. Our only-iron-clad restriction is that a play be well written. We prefer plays that address contemporary concerns and are dramaturgically innovative. A play whose cast is larger than 15-20 will need to be extremely compelling and its cast size must be justifiable."
Tips: "We don't look for a writer to write for us—he or she should write for him or herself. We look for honesty and a fresh voice. We're not likely to be interested in writers who are mindful of *any* trends. Originality and craftsmanship are the most important qualities we look for."

SOUTHEAST PLAYWRIGHTS PROJECT, P.O. Box 14252, Atlanta GA 30324. (404)985-8023. Executive Director: Shery Sheppard Kearney. Estab. 1977. Produces approximately 30 readings/workshops/year and provides career development services, including ongoing Writers' Lab, newsletter and workshops. Write (including SASE) for general membership applications. After joining, members may submit full-length script to be considered for Associate or Full membership.
Needs: General membership open to any playwright who lives, or has lived in the Southeast. Associate member must have had public reading of one full-length or two one-act plays. Full Member must have had at least one full production of a full-length play or be Associate Member. Selection is competitive.
Tips: "We aim at becoming a regional type of New Dramatists organization. Selection committee is looking for a distinctive voice, imaginative use of the stage, not just TV movies or sitcoms in play form."

SOUTHERN APPALACHIAN REPERTORY THEATRE (SART), Mars Hill College, P.O. Box 620, Mars Hill NC 28754. (704)689-1384. Artistic Director: James W. Thomas. Estab. 1975. Produces 5 plays/year. "Since 1975 the Southern Appalachian Repertory Theatre has produced 673 performances of 76 plays and played to over 97,000 patrons in the 152-seat Owen Theatre on the Mars Hill College campus. The theater's goals are quality, adventurous programming and integrity, both in artistic form and in the treatment of various aspects of the human condition. SART is a professional summer theater company whose audiences range from students to senior citizens." Also conducts an annual Southern Appalachian Playwrights' Conference in which five playwrights are invited for informal readings of their new scripts. Deadline for submission is Dec. 15 and conference is held the last weekend in January. If script is selected for production during the summer season, an honorarium is paid to the playwright in the amount of $500.
Needs: "Since 1975, one of SART's goals has been to produce at least one original play each summer season. To date, 25 original scripts have been produced. Plays by southern Appalachian playwrights or about southern Appalachia are preferred, but by no means exclusively. Complete new scripts welcomed."

STAGE ONE: The Louisville Children's Theatre, 425 W. Market St., Louisville KY 40202. (502)589-5946. Producing Director: Moses Goldberg. Estab. 1946. Produces 6-7 plays/year. 20% freelance written. 15-20% of scripts produced are unagented submissions (excluding work of playwright-in-residence). Plays performed by an Equity company for young audiences aged 4-18; usually does different plays for different age groups within that range. Submit complete ms. Reports in 4 months. Pays negotiable royalty or $25-50/performance.
Needs: "Good plays for young audiences of all types: adventure, fantasy, realism, serious problem plays about growing up or family entertainment." Cast: ideally, 10 or less. "Honest, visual potentiality, worthwhile story and characters are necessary. An awareness of children and their schooling is a plus. No campy material or anything condescending to children. No musicals unless they are fairly limited in orchestration."

‡**STAGE WEST**, 821 W. Vickery, Fort Worth TX 76104. (812)332-6238. Artistic Director: Jerry Russell. Estab. 1979. Produces 8 plays/year. "We stage professional productions at our own theater for a mixed general audience." Query and synopsis. Reports in 3 months. Rights are negotiable. Pays 7% royalty.
Needs: "We want full-length plays that are accessible to a mainstream audience but possess traits that are highly theatrical. Cast size of 10 or less and single or unit set are desired."

‡**STEPPENWOLF THEATRE COMPANY**, 2851 N. Halsted, Chicago IL 60657. (312)472-4515. Artistic Director: Randall Arney. Estab. 1976. Produces 5 plays/year.
Needs: We look mostly for contemporary comedies.
Tips: No musicals.

CHARLES STILWILL, Managing Director, Community Playhouse, P.O. Box 433, Waterloo IA 50704. (319)235-0367. Estab. 1917. Plays performed by Waterloo Community Playhouse with a volunteer cast. Produces 12 plays (7 adult, 5 children's); 1-2 musicals and 10-12 nonmusicals/year; 1-4 originals. 17% freelance written. Most scripts produced are unagented submissions. Works with 1-4 unpublished/unproduced writers annually. "We are one of few community theaters with a commitment to new scripts. We do at least one and have done as many as four a year. We have 4,300 season members." Average attendance at main stage shows is 3,300; at studio shows 2,000. "We try to fit the play to the theater. We do a wide variety of plays. Our public isn't going to accept nudity, too much sex, too much strong language. We don't have enough Black actors to do all-Black shows." Theatre has done plays with as few as two characters, and as many as 98. "On the main stage, we usually pay between $300 and $500. In our studio, we usually pay between $50 and $500. We also produce children's theater. Send complete script. "Please, no loose pages." "Reports negatively within 1 year, but acceptance sometimes takes longer because we try to fit a wanted script into the balanced season. We sometimes hold a script longer than a year if we like it but cannot immediately find the right slot for it. Next year we will be doing the Midwest premier of *Even in Laughter* and this year we did *Veranda*, which we've had since 1986."
Needs: "We are looking for good adaptations of name children's shows and very good shows that don't necessarily have a name. We produce children's theater with both adult and child actors. We also do a small (2-6 actors) cast show that tours the elementary schools in the spring. This can only be about 45 minutes long."

STOP-GAP, 523 N. Grand, Santa Ana CA 92701. (714)648-0135. Artistic Director: Don Laffoon. Estab. 1979. Produces 3 plays/year. Professional productions for general audiences. Query and synopsis. Reports in 4 months. Buys no rights except directorial syle. Payment for production only. Standard royalty, rates negotiable.
Needs: Full-length plays dealing with topical social issues: substance abuse, AIDS, aging, physical abuse, disabilities, etc. Casts should be small.
Tips: "Plays too individualized to have broader meaning are discouraged. On the other hand we certainly recognize that plays concern individuals and not institutions. Keep stage directions clean and clear. Don't pile too much information and detail on the reader or viewer."

STOREFRONT THEATRE, 213 SW Ash #209, Portland OR 97204. (503)224-9598. Managing Director: Richard Yarnell. Produces 6-8 plays/year. "Productions are professional; we have a 158-seat theater and a 310-seat theater, a subscription audience of around 3,000." Query and synopsis. Reports in 2 months. Pays 6-8% royalty.
Needs: "No Broadway comedies or TV sitcom material, non-mainstream, offbeat, occasional small musicals. Interested in plays that have something to say, but not didactic, heavy."

STREET PLAYERS THEATRE, Box 2687, Norman OK 73070. (405)364-0207. Artistic Director: Thomas C. Lategola. Produces 6 play/year. Professional productions performed for Midwestern university community. One Children's theater piece is toured throughout the region. Submit complete ms. Reports in 6 months. Limited production rights.
Needs: Produces previously unproduced work, with preference given to Oklahoma and Southwest regional writers. Full-length plays preferred; all styles and topics considered. Small cast (5-6), single set preferred. Storefront-type theater, which holds up to 99 people. Fall Festival Contest pays $250, no guarantee of production; deadline: June 30 each year. New Plays Series and Children's 50-minute piece: Negotiated average: $250.

THEATER ARTISTS OF MARIN, P.O. Box 473, San Rafael CA 94915. (415)454-2380. Artistic Director: Charles Brousse. Estab. 1980. Produces 3 plays/year. Professional showcase productions for a general adult audience. Submit complete ms. Reports in 3 months. Pays outright $500. Assists in marketing to other theaters.
Needs: "All types of scripts: comedy, drama, farce. Prefers contemporary setting, with some relevance to current issues in American society. Will also consider 'small musicals,' reviews or plays with music." No children's shows, domestic sitcoms, one-man shows or commercial thrillers.

THEATER LUDICRUM, INC., Suite 83, 64 Charlesgate E., Boston MA 02215. (617)424-6831. Contact: Director. Estab. 1985. Produces 2-3 plays/year. Plays are performed in a small, non-equity theater in Boston. "Our audience includes minority groups (people of color, gays, women)." Submit complete ms. Reports in 2 weeks. Rights revert to author after production. Pays $15-30/performance.
Needs: "As a small theater with a small budget, we look for scripts with minimal sets, costumes, props and expense in general. We are interested in scripts that emphasize the word and acting."

‡**THE THEATER OF NECESSITY**, 11702 Webercrest, Houston TX 77048. (713)733-6042. Artistic Director: Philbert Plumb. Estab. 1981. Produces 4 plays/year. Our plays are produced in a small professional theater. Submis complete ms. Reports in 6 months. Buys performance rights. Pays standard royalties based on size of house for small productions or individual contracts for large productions (average $500/run). We usually keep mss on file unless we are certain we will never use script. Send SASE for script and #10 SASE for response.
Needs: Any play in a recognizable genre must be superlative in form and intensity. Experimental plays are given an easier read. We move to larger venue if the play warrants the expense.
Tips: We are trying to buck some of the trends toward certain hits, and have been taking chances since our founding in 1981. The longer it takes us to respond, the more likely we will be producing your play.

THEATRE CALGARY, 220 9th Ave. SE, Calgary, Alberta T2G 5C4 Canada. (403)294-7440. FAX: (403)294-7493. Artistic Director: Martin Kinch. Estab. 1970. Produces 6-8 plays/year. Professional productions. Reports in 3 months. Buys production rights usually, "but it can vary with specific contracts." Payments and commissions negotiated under individual contracts.
Needs: "Theater Calgary is a major Canadian Regional Theater."
Tips: "Theatre Calgary still accepts unsolicited scripts, but does not have a significant script development program at the present time. We cannot guarantee a quick return time, and we will not return scripts without pre-paid envelopes."

THEATRE DE LA JEUNE LUNE, P.O. Box 25170, Minneapolis MN 55458. (612)332-3968. Artistic Directors: Barbra Berlovitz Desbois, Vincent Garcieux, Robert Rosen, Dominique Serrand. Estab. 1979. Produces 4 plays/year. Professional non-profit company producing September-May for general audience. Query and *synopsis*. Reports in 2 months. Pays royalty or per performance.
Needs: "All subject matter considered, although plays with universal themes are desired; plays that concern people of today. We are constantly looking for plays with large casts. Generally *not* interested in plays with 1-4 characters. No psychological drama or plays that are written alone in a room without the input of outside vitality and life."
Tips: "We are an acting company that takes plays and makes them ours; this could mean cutting a script or not heeding a writer's stage directions. We are committed to the performance in front of the audience as the goal of all the contributing factors; therefore, the actors' voice is extremely important."

THEATRE ON THE MOVE, Box 462, Islington, Ontario M9A 4X4 Canada. (416)234-0717. Artistic Director: Anne Hines. Produces 4 plays/year for families and young audiences—elementary and high schools and special venues (museums, etc.). Uses professional, adult, union actors. Submit query and synopsis or complete ms. Reports in 2 months. Acquires exclusive rights to Ontario, usually for a minimum of 1 year. Pays royalty or commission for works-in-progress.
Needs: Musicals or dramas for small casts (limit 4 actors) which deal with current topics of interest to children and families. Uncomplicated, 'tourable' sets.
Tips: "Our shows have to educate the audience about some aspect of modern life, as well as entertain. The trend is away from fairy tales, etc."

‡**THEATRE PROJECT COMPANY**, 634 N. Grand, #10-H, St. Louis MO 63103. (314)531-1315. FAX: (314)533-3345. Artistic Director: William Freimuth. Estab. 1975. Produces 5 full-length adult plays for adventurous audience, plus one family show in 250-seat theater. Tours with three 50-minute children's plays that tour schools in Illinois and Missouri. Query and synopsis. Reports in 6 weeks. Pays 4-8% royalty.
Needs: "We are leaning toward an overt theatricality. We produce more comedy than drama; Shakespeare to Ionesco to Ludlam; one world premiere per year. We prefer casts of 8 or fewer. No big period costume shows."
Tips: "No 'people sitting around a New York apartment talking,' hopeless angst or historical drama."

‡**THEATRE TESSERACT**, 820 E. Knapp, Milwaukee WI 53202. (414)273-7529. Artistic Director: Sharon McQueen. "Theatre Tesseract produces 4-5 plays per season, extending over a nine-month period from fall to spring. We specialize in presenting contemporary theatre of a Broadway/off-Broadway nature. At this time, we have never produced a piece that has not been given a successful production in another theatrical center."

‡**THEATRE VIRGINIA**, 2800 Grove Ave., Richmond VA 23221-2466. Executive Artistic Director: Terry Burgler. Estab. 1955. Produces 5-8; Publishes 0-2 new plays/year. Query with synopsis and 15 page sample in addition to synopsis. Solicitations in 1 month for initial query—if ms is solicited, 3-8 months. Rights negotiaged. Payment negotiated.
Needs: No one-acts; no children's theater.

THEATREWORKS, University of Colorado, P.O. Box 7150, Colorado Springs CO 80933. (719)593-3232. Producing Director: Whit Andrews. Estab. 1975.Produces 4 full-length plays/year and two new one-acts. "New full-length plays produced on an irregular basis. Casts are semi-professional and plays are produced at the university." Submit query and synopsis. No unsolicited manuscripts. One-act plays are accepted as Playwrights' Forum competition entries—submit complete ms. Deadline: Dec. 1; winners announced March 1. Two one-act competition winners receive full production, cash awards and travel allowances. Acquires exclusive regional option for duration of production. Full rights revert to author upon closing. Pays $300-1,200.
Needs: Full-lengths and one-acts—no restrictions on subject. "Cast size should not exceed 20; stage area is small with limited wing and fly space. Theatreworks is interested in the exploration of new and inventive theatrical work. Points are scored by imaginative use of visual image. Static verbosity and staid conventionalism not encouraged." No melodrama or children's plays.
Tips: "Too often, new plays seem far too derivative of television and film writing. We think theater is a medium which an author must specifically attack. The standard three-act form would appear to be on the way out. Economy, brevity and incisiveness are favorably received."

THEATREWORKS/USA, 890 Broadway, New York NY 10003. (212)677-5959. Artistic Director: Jay Harnick. Literary Manager: Barbara Pasternack. Produces 3 new musical plays/season. Produces professional musicals that primarily tour (TYA contract) but also play at an off-Broadway theater for a young audience. Submit query and synopsis or sample song. Reports in 6 months. Buys all rights. Pays 6% royalty; offers $1,500 advance against future royalties for new, commissioned plays.
Needs: Musicals and plays with music. Historical/biographical themes (ages 8-15), classic literature, fairy tales, and issue-oriented themes suitable for young people ages 5-10. Five person cast, minimal lighting. "We like well-crafted shows with good dramatic structure—a protagonist who wants something specific, an antagonist, a problem to be solved—character development, tension, climax, etc. No Saturday Afternoon Special-type shows, shows with nothing to say or 'kiddie' theater shows."
Tips: "Writing for kids is just like writing for adults—only better (clearer, cleaner). Kids will not sit still for unnecessary exposition and overblown prose. Long monologues, soliloquies and 'I Am' songs and ballads should be avoided. Television, movies and video make the world of entertainment highly competitive. We've noticed lately how well popular children's titles, contemporary and in public domain, sell. We are very interested in acquiring adaptations of this type of material."

TRINITY SQUARE ENSEMBLE, Box 1798, Evanston IL 60204. (312)328-0330. Artistic Director: Karen L. Erickson. Produces 4-6 plays/year. "Professional non-equity company, member of League of Chicago Theatres, ensemble company of artists. We look for scripts adapted from classics suited to our ensemble as well as new works. Writers are encouraged to research our company. We produce new children's pieces—must blend stories with school curriculum." Send query and synopsis. "We do not want full ms submissions. If we request, then we'll return." Reports in 6-18 months. Obtains negotiated percentage of rights, ususally 10%.
Needs: Cast: prefer no more than 10. Set: preferably simple.
Tips: "Our ensemble is 70% women/30% men. Keep this in mind as you develop scripts. No male-dominated, fluffy comedies. Get to know us—write for our performers. Looks for strength in female characters."

UNICORN THEATRE, 3820 Main St., Kansas City MO 64111. (816)531-PLAY. Artistic Director: Cynthia Levin. Produces 8 plays/year. "We are a professional Equity Theatre. Typically, we produce contemporary plays." Query and synopsis. Will not consider unsolicited mss. Reponds in 2 weeks.
Needs: Prefers contemporary (post-1950) scripts. Does not accept musicals, one-acts, or historical plays. When a manuscript is requested, include a brief synopsis, a bio, a character breakdown, SASE if manuscript is to be returned, a SASPC for acknowledgement of receipt is desired. A royalty/prize of $1,000 will be awarded the playwright of any play selected through this process, The National Playwright Award. This script shall receive production as part of the Unicorn's regular season.

UNIVERSITY OF MINNESOTA, DULUTH THEATRE, 10 University Dr., Duluth MN 55812. (218)726-8562. Artistic Director: Ann Bergeron. Produces 12 plays/year. Plays are performed at the University Theatre, American College Theatre Festival and the Minnesota Repertory Theatre (summer). Submit query and synopsis only. Reports in 3 weeks. Acquires performance rights. Pays $35-100/performance.
Needs: All genres. Prefers younger casting requirements and single set or unit setting shows. No previously produced work or one-act plays.
Tips: "We are a very active undergraduate theater program that is very interested in producing new work. We annually produce a new play for the American College Theatre Festival in which there are several major playwriting awards."

VIGILANTE PLAYERS, INC., MSU Media and Theatre Arts, Bozeman MT 59717. (406)994-5884. Artistic Director: John M. Hosking. Estab. 1982. Produces 3-4 plays/year. Plays by professional touring company that does productions by or about people and themes of the Northwest. "Past productions were concerned with homeless people, agriculture, literature by Northwest writers, one-company towns and spouse abuse in rural areas." Submit complete ms. Reports in 6 months. Pays $10-50/performance.

Needs: Produces full-length plays and some one-acts. "Staging suitable for a small touring company and cast limited to four actors (two men, two women). Double casting actors for more play characters is also an option."

Tips: "No musicals requiring orchestras and a chorus line. Although we prefer a script of some thematic substance, the company is very adept at comedy and would prefer the topic to include humor."

WALNUT STREET THEATRE, 9th and Walnut Streets, Philadelphia PA 19107. (215)574-3550. Executive Director: Bernard Havard. Literary Manager: Ernest Tremblay. Produces 5 mainstage and 5 studio plays/ year. "Our plays are performed in our own space. WST has 3 theaters—a proscenium (mainstage), audience capacity: 1,052; 2 studios, audience capacity: 79-99. We have a subscription audience, second largest in the nation." Query with synopsis and 10 pages. Reports in 5 months. Rights negotiated per project. Pays royalty (negotiated per project) or outright purchase.

Needs: "Full-length dramas and comedies, musicals, translations, adaptations and revues. The studio plays must be small cast, simple sets."

Tips: "We will consider anything. Bear in mind that on the mainstage we look for plays with mass appeal, Broadway-style. The studio spaces are our Off-Broadway. No children's plays. Our mainstage audience goes for work that is entertaining and light. Our studio season is when we look for plays that have bite, are more provocative."

WASHINGTON STATE UNIVERSITY THEATRE, Theatre Arts and Drama, Pullman WA 99164-2432. (509)335-3239. FAX: (509)335-3421. Contact: General Manager. Estab. 1889. Produces 10 plays/year. Plays performed in university environment. Submit query and synopsis. Do not send full script. Royalties paid in accordance with standard rates.

WEST COAST ENSEMBLE, Box 38728, Los Angeles CA 90038. (213)871-8673. Artistic Director: Les Hanson. Produces 6 plays/year. Plays will be performed in one of our two theaters in Hollywood in an Equity-waiver situation. Submit complete ms. Reports in 5 months. Obtains the exclusive rights in southern California to present the play for the period specified. All ownership and rights remain with the playwright. Pays $25-45/ performance.

Needs: Prefers a cast of 6-12.

Tips: "Submit the manuscript in acceptable dramatic script format."

‡WESTBETH THEATRE CENTER, INC., 151 Bank St., New York NY 10014. (212)691-2272. Artistic Director: Arnold Engelman. Estab. 1977. Produces 10 readings and 6 productions/year. Professional off-Broadway theater. Query and synopsis, submit complete ms through agent only. Obtains rights to produce as showcase with option to enter into full option agreement.

Needs: "Contemporary full-length plays. Production values (i.e. set, costumes, etc.) should be kept to a minimum." No period pieces. Limit 10 actors; doubling explained.

THE WESTERN STAGE, 156 Homestead Ave., Salinas CA 93901. Dramaturg: Joyce Lower.

Needs: The Steinbeck Playwriting Prize for playwrights whose works are in the spirit of John Steinbeck. One winner will be chosen following staged readings of three finalists to receive a $1,000 cash award, support during the revision process (up to $4,000), a full production and royalties for the production. Submissions accepted Oct. 1-Dec. 31 only. Response by April 15. An application must accompany each submission. For an application and the complete submission guidelines, contact Joyce Lower at The Western Stage.

‡WHOLE THEATRE, 544 Bloomfield Ave., Montclair NJ 07042. (201)744-2996. Aritstic Director: Olympia Dukakis. Estab. 1973. Produces 5 plays/year. Plays performed at Whole Theatre for general audience. Query and synopsis. Rights negotiated. Royalty negotiated.

Needs: Full-length plays, all genres. "Most interested in plays that touch on relevant human, social issues." Average cast size: 6. Usually unit or abstract set.

Tips: "No light commercial fare."

‡THE WOMEN'S PROJECT AND PRODUCTIONS, 220 W. 42nd St., 18th Fl., New York NY 10036. (212)382-2750. Artistic Director: Julia Miles. Estab. 1978. Produces 3 plays/year. Professional off-Broadway productions. Submit query and synopsis. Reports in 3 weeks on queries.

Needs: "We are looking for full length plays, written by women only. No plays by male authors."

WORCESTER FOOTHILLS THEATRE COMPANY, 074 Worcester Center, Worcester MA 01608. (508)754-3314. Artistic Director: Marc P. Smith. Literary Manager: Greg DeJarnett. Estab. 1974. Produces 7 plays/year. Full time professional theater, general audience. Query and synopsis. Reports in 3 weeks. Pays royalty.
Needs: "Produce plays for general audience. No gratuitous violence, sex or language. Prefer cast under 10 and single set. 30' proscenium with apron but no fly space."

YWAM/ACADEMY OF PERFORMING ARTS, P.O. Box 1324, Cambridge, Ontario N1R 7G6 Canada. Artistic Director: Stuart Scadron-Wattles. Estab. 1988. Produces 3 plays/year. Semi-professional productions for a general audience. Send query and synopsis. Reports in 6 months. Pays $50-100/performance.
Needs: "One-act or full-length; comedy or drama; musical or straight; written from a biblical world view." No cast above 10; prefers unit staging.
Tips: Looks for "non-religious writing from a biblical world view for an audience which loves the theater. Avoid current trends toward shorter scenes. Playwrights should be aware that they are writing for the stage—not television."

Screenwriting

Is there anyone, anywhere, who hasn't said at one time or another, "Hey, I've got a great idea for a movie!" Or, "Who wrote that show? I could do better than that!" Everyone has great ideas and everyone can write better than the current crop of sitcoms on the airwaves, right?

So why is it so hard to break into Hollywood?

Probably because screenwriting is a lot harder than it looks, whether it's writing for the big or the small screen. There are very definite rules to follow in terms of structure, story, dialogue, exposition, action and character development, not to mention format and marketing do's and don'ts.

Before you turn your great idea into a screenplay, take some time to study the form. Read some scripts, see some movies, attend some seminars and invest in a few books about screenplay structure and style. Then, put your idea into outline form and see if the basic story will hold up throughout the 90-120 pages of the standard script. See if your turning points are timed correctly, your narrative flows, your characters grow through conscious choices and your scenes generate a forward momentum. If it all checks out to your satisfaction, write the script.

"How about if I write a treatment and try to sell that? Maybe that way someone would pay me to write the script." Not likely. Treatments are used as a shorthand for producers, primarily when developing a story or screening script submissions. They are not used to determine a writer's ability since treatments are generally dry and straightforward, leaving little room for style. To prove your worth as a screenwriter, you have to write a script.

In fact, to approach the movie and television market, you need: 1) A sample script. The best writing you can do. 2) Another script. This one's so good you're not quite sure whether to send out this one instead of your first one. 3) An agent.

You can make submissions to production companies without an agent, but the process takes longer. You'll need a release form, either one sent to you by the production company or a legal "generic" one (an example is in *Successful Scriptwriting* by Writer's Digest Books.) Don't be afraid of this release form. Companies have to protect themselves from nuisance suits when a writer may claim his idea "for this love story between a guy and a girl" was turned into *When Harry Met Sally*. Ask for a form and register your work with the Writers Guild (8955 Beverly Blvd., Los Angeles CA 90048) and send your work in with the signed release form.

Approaching television shows can be more difficult without an agent. The best way to get an agent is with at least two, preferably more, scripts written on speculation for shows currently on the air. The agent will send those scripts around as a calling card demonstrating your talent and then you may be invited in to pitch ideas. If an idea is bought, you usually are assigned at least a first draft. Again, you can approach television shows without an agent simply by writing for a release form and submitting your script. Just be prepared for a longer wait before receiving any response.

Stay current with the industry through trade publications such as *Daily Variety*, (213)856-6600; *Hollywood Reporter*, (213)464-7411; and specialty newsletters such as the *Hollywood Scriptwriter*, (818)991-3096 which specifically targets scriptwriters throughout North America.

Above all, don't stop writing after your first or second script. Most successful screenwriters report that, in looking back, it wasn't until their seventh or eighth script that they started to demonstrate a mastery of their craft.

For additional screenwriting markets, see Other Scriptwriting Markets at the end of the Screenwriting section.

‡AMERICAN MOTION PICTURES, 15108 Trotter Ln., Weldon CA 93283. (619)378-3160. President: Bill Hinchley. Estab. 1983. We have a motion picture/TV audience. Buys 2-3 scripts/year; works with 6-8 writers/year. Buys all rights or first rights. Previously produced material OK. Reports in 1 month.
Needs: Films and film loops (35mm), sound filmstrips, and videotapes. Subjects include action, drama, dark comedy and religious. Submit synopsis/outline, completed script and/or resume. Pays in accordance with Writers Guild standards.
Tips: "More and more the motion picture business is discovering the writer is the key to any project's success."

BLAZING PRODUCTIONS, INC., Suite 125, 4712 Avenue N, Brooklyn NY 11234. Contact: David Aleksander. Estab. 1985. Produces material for "Major and independent studios." Buys 1-3 scripts/year. Buys all rights. No books, no treatments, no articles. ONLY completed movie scripts and television movie scripts. Reports in 6 weeks on queries.
Needs: Commercial, well written, high concept scripts in the drama, comedy, action and thriller genres. No other scripts. Submit a one page synopsis along with a query letter regarding the material. Include SASE. DO NOT SEND ANY SCRIPTS UNLESS REQUESTED.
Tips: "Can always use a GOOD comedy. Writers should be flexible and open to suggestions. Material with interest (in writing) from a known actor/director is a MAJOR PLUS in the consideration of the material."

CAREY-IT-OFF PRODUCTIONS, Suite 4, 14316 Riverside Dr., Sherman Oaks CA 91423. (818)789-0954. President: Kathi Carey. Estab. 1984. Audience is general moviegoers. Works with 3-4 writers/year. Buys all rights. No previously produced material. Reports in 6 weeks on queries; 3 months on mss.
Needs: 35mm films. Wants feature films—strong male and female lead, action/adventure or suspense/thriller or police/action dramas. Do *not* send unsolicited mss. Query with synopsis. All unsolicited mss will be returned. Always enclose SASE. Makes outright purchase in accordance with Writer's Guild standards.
Tips: "Keep in mind that feature films/film packages need stars in the lead roles, and these roles should be written with a star's ego in mind. Also, please do not send articles by registered or certified mail. Do *not* call. You will be notified of any interest in your work."

THE CHICAGO BOARD OF RABBIS BROADCASTING COMMISSION, 1 South Franklin St., Chicago IL 60606. (312)444-2896. Director of Broadcasting: Mindy Soble. "Television scripts are requested for *The Magic Door*, a children's program produced in conjunction with CBS's WBBM-TV 2 in Chicago." 26 scripts are purchased per television season. Buys all rights. Reports in 1 month. Writers guidelines for #10 SASE.
Needs: "*Magic Door* is a weekly series of 26 shows that contain Jewish content and have universal appeal. The program takes place backstage in a theater where a company of actors brings stories to life for a puppet-child, Mazel. (Mazel is a large hand puppet who is worked by a member of the company, Wendy). The company consists of approximately 30 actors and actresses. Most of the programs utilize 3 or 4 of the above, including Wendy." Submit synopsis/outline, resume or a completed script with the right to reject. Outright purchase of $125.
Tips: "A Judaic background is helpful, yet not critical. Writing for children is key. We prefer to use Chicago writers, as script rewrites are paramount and routine."

CINE/DESIGN FILMS, INC., P.O. Box 6495, Denver CO 80205. (303)777-4222. Producer/Director: Jon Husband. Produces educational material for general, sales-training and theatrical audiences. 75% freelance written. 90% of scripts produced are unagented submissions. "Original, solid ideas are encouraged." Rights purchased vary.
Needs: "Motion picture outlines in the theatrical and documentary areas. We are seeking theatrical scripts in the low-budget area that are possible to produce for under $1,000,000. We seek flexibility and personalities who can work well with our clients." Produces 16mm and 35mm films. Send an 8-10 page outline before submitting ms or script. Pays $100-200/screen minute on 16mm productions. Theatrical scripts negotiable.
Tips: "Understand the marketing needs of film production today. Materials will not be returned."

‡**CTS ENTERPRISES,** 1000 Westgate Ave., Los Angeles CA 90049. Artistic Director/President: Mitchell Nestor. Estab. 1985. Buys all rights. Reports in 3 months on submissions.
Needs: 35mm films. We are now starting to work on plays to be made into films. Jackson Pollock is one. Submit synopsis/outline and resume. Payment in accordance with Writers Guild standards.

‡**CUTTING EDGE PRODUCTIONS,** 2026 Federal Ave., Los Angeles CA 90025. (213)478-8700. President: Tom Forsythe. Estab. 1982. We are looking for a network and cable television 2 hour movie and full length feature film scripts and story ideas for theatrical release. We buy 15 scripts/year. Buys film, TV and allied rights. Reports in 3 weeks on submissions.
Needs: Feature films. Television movie material may be in either "treatment" or script format. Treatment means 5-15 double spaced pages laying out the story beats. Subjects should be suitable for network airing, "original" but not too bizarre. Screenplays should be in standard format, approximately 120 pages. Query with synopsis. Pays in accordance with Writers Guild standards.
Tips: "Know that the TV audience is 35 to 55 and conservative. Recognize that film distribution is becoming centralized by the major studios who only buy screenplays that are $20 million ideas. Before starting a script ask yourself: Is this a $20 million idea? Always ask yourself if you would watch the story you're telling. Television is becoming international in market but networks still need to find the story applicable to their core market. The smash hit mentality dominates feature production. Despite films like *Driving Miss Daisy*, hard edged films will continue to be the rule."

‡**HARRY DELIGTER PRODUCTIONS,** 3866 Keeshen Dr., Los Angeles CA 90066. (213)398-4949. President: Harry DeLigter. We have a theatrical motion pictures and television audience. Buys film, TV, worldwide and all media rights. Reports in 1 month.
Needs: Films, scripts, and videotapes. Query with synopsis.
Tips: "Remember we're operating entertainment. Upbeat, uplifting themes inventively presented reach bigger audiences. A sense of humor and good characters are important. Fragmented market means we're competing even more to audiences. Pitch/synopsis should include a simple to grasp one-line hook that might attract audiences in advertisement or in film trailers."

ENTERTAINMENT PRODUCTIONS, INC., 2210 Wilshire Blvd. #744, Santa Monica CA 90403. (213)456-3143. Producer: Edward Coe. Estab. 1971. Produces material for theatrical and television (worldwide) clients. Buys all rights. Reports in 1 month (only if SASE is enclosed for return).
Needs: Films (35mm) and videotapes. Entertainment only material needed. Query with synopsis. Pays outright purchase. Price negotiated on a project-by-project basis.
Tips: "Learn your trade. Be flexible."

‡**ESTEBAN FILMS INC.,** 250 W. 57th St., New York NY 10107. (212)489-1491. Estab. 1988. We have a general audience. Buys all rights. Accepts previously published material. Reports in 1 week on queries; 3 months on submissions. Catalog for #10 SASE.
Needs: 35mm films, tapes and cassettes, and videotapes. We need feature films and music videos. Submit synopsis/outline, completed script and resume. Payment to be discussed personally with writer.

EDWARD D. HANSEN, INC., 437 Harvard Dr., Arcadia CA 91006. (818)447-3168. President: Edward D. Hansen. Estab. 1973. Theatrical, television and home video markets comprise our audience. Buys 3-6 scripts/year. Buys all rights. Reporting time varies.
Needs: Films (35mm) and videotapes. We are looking for feature films, movies of the week, dramatic teleplays of varying lengths and home videos. Query with synopsis. Pays in accordance with Writers Guild standards.
Tips: "What comes around goes around. Don't go with the trends."

INTERNATIONAL HOME ENTERTAINMENT, Suite 350, 1440 Veteran Ave., Los Angeles CA 90024. (213)460-4545. Assistant to the President: Jed Leland, Jr.. Estab. 1976. Buys first rights. Reports in 2 months. Query. Pays in accordance with Writers Guild standards.

☐**LEE MAGID PRODUCTIONS,** Box 532, Malibu CA 90265. (213)463-5998. President: Lee Magid. Produces material for all markets, teenage-adult; commercial—even musicals. 90% freelance written. 70% of scripts produced are unagented submissions. Works with "many" unpublished/unproduced writers. Buys all rights or will negotiate. No previously produced material. Does not return unsolicited material. Query for electronic submissions. Reports in 6 weeks.
Needs: Films, sound filmstrips, phonograph records, television shows/series, videotape presentations. Currently interested in film material, either for video (television) or theatrical. "We deal with cable networks, producers, live-stage productions, etc." Works with musicals for cable TV. Prefers musical forms for video comedy. Submit synopsis/outline and resume. Pays in royalty, in outright purchase, in accordance with Writer's Guild standards, or depending on author.

Tips: "We're interested in comedy material. Forget drug-related scripts."

‡THE WILTON MARKS STUDIO, P.O.Box 30153, Baltimore MD 21270. (301)563-6033. Executive Producer: Timothy Parker. Estab. 1988. Material for all general audiences. Uses 15-20 writers, 80 projects per year. Buys all rights. No previously produced material. Reports in 2 weeks on queries; 1 months on submissions.
Needs: Tapes and cassettes, videotapes. "We need original material for audio and video projects, suitable for general audiences. Also, how-to, sports, etc. of any length." Submit synopsis/outline or completed script. Pays $250-2,500 outright purchse. "Negotiable due to length and content."
Tips: "Creativity and flow of storyline are the most important aspects of good, sound writing. The wildest in imagination are usually the best in results."

‡☐MEDIACOM DEVELOPMENT CORP., P.O. Box 1926, Simi Valley CA 93062. (818)594-4089. Director/Program Development: Felix Girard. Estab. 1978. 80% freelance written. Buys 10-20 scripts annually from unpublished/unproduced writers. 50% of scripts produced are unagented submissions. Query with samples. Reports in 1 month. Buys all rights or first rights.
Needs: Produces charts, sound filmstrips, 16mm films, multimedia kits, overhead transparencies, tapes and cassettes; slides and videotape with programmed instructional print materials, broadcast and cable television programs. Publishes software ("programmed instruction training courses"). Negotiates payment depending on project.
Tips: "Send short samples of work. Especially interested in flexibility to meet clients' demands, creativity in treatment of precise subject matter. We are looking for good, fresh projects (both special and series) for cable and pay television markets. A trend in the audiovisual field that freelance writers should be aware of is the move toward more interactive video disk/computer CRT delivery of training materials for corporate markets."

MERIWETHER PUBLISHING LTD. (Contemporary Drama Service), 885 Elkton Dr., Colorado Springs CO 80907. Editor: Arthur Zapel. Estab. 1969. "We publish how-to materials in book and video formats. We are interested in materials for high school and college level students only. Our contemporary drama division publishes 60-70 plays/year." 80% written by unpublished writers. Buys 40-60 scripts/year from unpublished/unproduced writers. 95% of scripts are unagented submissions. Reports in 1 month on queries; 2 months on full-length submissions. Query should include synopsis/outline, resume of credits, sample of style and SASE. Catalog available for $1 postage. Offers 10% royalty or outright purchase.
Needs: Book mss on theatrical arts subjects. Christian activity book mss also accepted. We will consider elementary level religious materials and plays, but no elementary level children's secular plays. Query. Pays royalty; buys some mss outright.
Tips: "We publish a wide variety of speech contest materials for high school students. We are publishing more reader's theatre scripts and musicals based on classic literature or popular TV shows, provided the writer includes letter of clearance from the copyright owner. Our educational books are sold to teachers and students at college and high school levels. Our religious books are sold to youth activity directors, pastors and choir directors. Our trade books are directed at the pubilc with a sense of humor. Another group of buyers is the professional theater, radio and TV category."

THE MERRYWOOD STUDIO, 137 E. 38th St., New York NY 10016-2650. Creative Director: Raul da Silva. 40% freelance written. Produces animated motion pictures for entertainment audiences. No children's material sought or produced.
Needs: Proprietary material only. Human potential themes woven into highly entertaining drama, high adventure, comedy. This is a new market for animation with only precedent in the illustrated novels published in France and Japan. Cannot handle unsolicited mail/scripts and will not return mail. Open to credit sheets, concepts and synopses only. Profit sharing depending upon value of concept and writer's following. Will pay at least Writer's Guild levels or better, plus expenses.
Tips: "This is not a market for beginning writers. Established, professional work with highly unusual and original themes is sought. If you love writing, it will show and we will recognize it and reward it in every way you can imagine. We are not a 'factory' and work on a very high level of excellence."

NORTHSTAR ENTERTAINMENT GROUP, (formerly Christian Broadcasting Network), 1000 Centerville Turnpike, Virginia Beach VA 23463. (804)424-7777. Head Writer, Producers Group: David Wimbish. Produces material for a general mass audience as well as Christian audiences. "We are looking for family-oriented

☐ **Open box preceding a listing indicates a cable TV market.**

material. Query first and ask for a release form before submitting a short (two-or-three pages) synopsis of your script. Letter-quality please." Reports in 2 months.
Tips: "We are interested in well-written scripts which can attract a family audience. Please, no dramatic retellings of the Second Coming or the Apocalypse. We've seen dozens upon dozens of these!"

‡**NUMAN FILMS,** 11728 Wilshire Blvd., Los Angeles CA 90025. (213)479-7630. Contact: Assistant to Producers. Estab. 1987. Buys 3 scripts/year. Buys all rights. Reports in 1 month.
Needs: Films (35mm). Submit synopsis/outline. Makes outright purchase.
Tips: First 10 pages must demonstrate strong character development. Know where your characters are going. First act (30 pages) must be very clear, and should end at a point in the plot that hurls the audience into the second act."

PACE FILMS, INC., 411 E. 53rd St., PHC, New York NY 10022. (212)755-5486. President: R. Vanderbes. Produces material for a general theatrical audience. Buys all rights. Reports in 2 months.
Needs: Theatrical motion pictures. Produces and distributes 35mm motion pictures for theatrical, TV and videocassettes. Query with synopsis/outline and writing background/credits. Completed scripts should be submitted together with an outline and SASE. Pays in accordance with Writers Guild standards.

‡**PACIFIC WEST ENTERTAINMENT GROUP,** 8489 W. 3rd St., #1006, Los Angeles CA 90048. (213)651-5194. Sr. Vice President of Development: Connie Kingrey. Estab. 1985. Theatrical motion picture professionals make up our audience. 1-2 scripts purchased, 1-2 scripts commissioned per year. Buys all rights. Reports in 1 month on queries; 2 months on submissions.
Needs: 35mm films. Our needs are for theatrical motion pictures, 90-minute screenplays, romantic thrillers (moderate budget). Query with synopsis. Pays upfront fee plus percentage of net profits.

☐ **TOM PARKER MOTION PICTURES,** P.O. Box 15166, Santa Anna CA 92705. (714)556-6636. FAX: (714)545-9775. President: Tom Parker. Produces and distributes feature length motion pictures worldwide (Member AFMA) for theatrical, home video, pay and free TV. Works with 5-10 scripts per year. Previously produced and distributed "Wackiest Wagon Train in the West," (Rated G); "S S Girls," (Rated R); and "Initiation" (Rated R). Will acknowledge receipt of material and report within 90 days. "Follow the instructions herein and do not phone for info or to inquire about your script."
Needs: Completed scripts *only* for low budget (under $1 million) "R" or "PG" rated action/thriller, action/adventure, comedy, adult romance (R), sex comedy (R), family action/adventure to be filmed in 35mm film for the theatrical and home video market (do not send TV movie scripts, series, teleplays, stage plays). *Very limited dialogue.* Scripts should be action oriented and fully described. Screen stories or scripts OK, but no camera angles please. No heavy drama, documentaries, social commentaries, dope stories, weird or horror. Violence or sex OK, but must be well motivated with strong story line. Submit synopsis and description of characters with finished scripts. Outright purchase: $5,000-25,000. Will consider participation, co-production.
Tips: "Absolutely will not return scripts or report on rejected scripts unless accompanied by SASE."

‡**QUICKSILVER PRODUCTIONS,** Suite 311, 1626 N. Wilcox, Hollywood CA 90028. (213)466-9500. Vice President: Bret Carr. Estab. 1986. We have a motion picture audience. 1989: 5 scripts optioned; 8 writers employed per year. Buys all rights. Reports in 3 weeks.
Needs: Filmstrips, sound and videotapes. Submit completed script. Pays in accordance with Writers Guild standards.

‡**SOUTH FORK PRODUCTIONS,** P.O. Box 1935, Santa Monica CA 90406. Producer: Jim Sullivan. Estab. 1979. We have both a theatrical and television audience. Buys 2-3 scripts/year. Buys all rights. Reports in 1 month.
Needs: Feature films. Submit completed script and resume. Pays in accordance with Writers Guild standards.

SPI ENTERTAINMENT, 279 S. Beverly Dr., Beverly Hills CA 90212. (213)827-4229. President/Producer: Michael Sourapas. Estab. 1987. We have a feature film audience. Buys 6-8 scripts/year. Buys all rights or other options. Reports in 2 months
Needs: Feature films. Submit completed script with brief outline only. Pays royalty or makes outright purchase, "depending on the situation."
Tips: "See all movies. Pay attention to grosses and what stays in the theaters. Then pitch finished scripts as though we were going to the movies to see them. Be brief with cast and keep the director in mind. We are looking for entertaining, fast paced, universal themes with a twist."

☐ **TELEVISION PRODUCTION SERVICES CORP.,** Box 1233, Edison NJ 08818. (201)287-3626. Executive Director/Producer: R.S. Burks. Produces video music materials for major market distributor networks, etc. Buys 50-100 scripts/year. Buys all rights. Reports in 2 weeks.

Needs: "We do video music for record companies, MTV, HBO, etc. We use treatments of story ideas from the groups' management. We also do commercials for over-the-air broadcast and cable. We are now doing internal in-house video for display on disco or internally distributed channels, and need good script writers." Submit synopsis/outline or completed script, and resume; include SASE for response or materials will not be returned.

Tips: Looks for rewrite flexibility and availability. "We have the capability of transmission electronically over the phone modem to our printer or directly onto disk for storage."

‡**BOB THOMAS PRODUCTIONS, INC.**, 60 E. 42nd St., New York NY 10165. President: Robert G. Thomas. 100% freelance written. WGA-East & West membership required.

Needs: Scripts of "mass appeal," acceptable for prime-time television audiences. Submit *only* through registered agents.

‡**UNIFILMS, INC.**, 22931 Sycamore Creek Dr., Valencia CA 91354-2050. (805)297-2000. Vice President, Development: Jack Adams. Estab. 1984. We buy 5 scripts/year. Reports in 2 weeks on queries; 2 months on submissions.

Needs: 35mm feature films *only*. We are looking for feature film screenplays, current format, 100-120 pages long; commercial but not stupid, dramatic but not "arty", funny but not puerile. Query with synopsis with SASE.

Tips: "If you've taken classes, read books, attended seminars and writers workshops all concerned with scriptwriting and read hundreds of produced screenplays *prior* to seeing the film and you're still convinced you've got a saleable script, we might want to see it. If you've got someone else in the entertainment industry to recommend your script, we would be more interested in seeing it. But if you waste our time with a project that's not yet ready to be seen, we're not going to react well. Your first draft is not usually the draft you're going to show to the industry. Get a professional opinion first, then rewrite before you submit to us. Very few people care about synopses, outlines or treatments as a starting point. THE SCRIPT is the basic blueprint, and everyone in the country is working on a script. Ideas are a dime a dozen. If you can *execute* that idea well and get people *excited* about that idea, you've got something. But most writers are wanna-bees, who submit scripts that need a lot of work just to get to the "promising" stage. Scripts are *always* rewritten. If you can't convince us your're a *writer*, we don't care. But if you *can* write and you've got a *second* idea we might talk."

‡**UNITY PICTURES CORP.**, Suite 1002, 11661 San Vicente Bl., Los Angeles CA 90049. (213)826-1026. Executive Assistant to Producer: Debra Spalding. Estab. 1981. Our audience is 18 to 35 years old. We buy 1-2 scripts per year. Negotiates on each deal—usually all rights and then we produce film. Reports in 1 month.

Needs: 35mm feature film. We will produce several romantic comedies over the next several years and we are always looking for new writers and possible scripts. Submit completed script. Pays in accordance with Writers Guild standards.

Tips: "Send script with intro letter, give two weeks then call to inquire. Family oriented comedies, reality based, not far fetched."

‡**DIMITRI VILLARD PRODUCTIONS**, 260 S. Beverly Dr. #200, Beverly Hills CA 90212. (213)205-0666. President: Dimitri Villard. Estab. 1980. We have a general audience. We buy 3-4 scripts/year. Buys all rights. Reports in 3 weeks.

Needs: 35mm films and videotapes. We are looking for feature film screenplays. Submit completed script *only*. Payment varies.

Tips: "We particularly like science-fiction."

Other Scriptwriting Markets

The following scriptwriting markets do not have listings in this edition of *Writer's Market*. The majority did not respond to our request to update their listings or return a questionnaire for a new listing. If a reason was given for their exclusion, we have included it in parentheses after the listing name.

A.V. Media Craftsman, Inc.
Admaster, Inc.
Academy Theatre (asked to be deleted)
American Line, The
American Media Inc. (asked to be deleted)
The American Playwright's Theatre (unable to contact)
American Stage Festival
Aran Press (charges fee to publish)
Bachner Productions, Inc.
Barr Films
Berea College Theatre (asked to be deleted)
Cabscott Broadcast Productions, Inc.
Anthony Cardoza Enterprises
Charlotte Repertory Theatre
Cherry St. Films (asked to be deleted)
Circle Repertory Co.
Corman Productions (suspended production)
Creative Productions, Inc.
Crossroads Theatre Company
Dalton Little Theatre New Play Project
Divided Artists (asked to be deleted)
Frederic Defeis
EMC Corp.
Empire State Institute for the

Performing Arts
The Ensemble Studio Theatre
Fire Prevention Through Films (asked to be deleted)
Gaslamp Quarter Theatre Company
The Will Geer Theatricum Botanicum
Geva Theatre
Emmy Gifford Children's Theater
Gloucester Stage Co.
Goodwin, Knab & Company
Hartford Stage Company
Imperial International Learning Corp.
Indiana Repertory Theatre
International Media Services Inc.
Lamb's Players Theatre
The Lamb's Theatre Company
Los Angeles Theatre Center (receiving too many unsolicited mss)
Magnus Films (accepts only Writers Guild submissions)
Manhattan Punch Line
Motivation Media, Inc.
Henry Nason Productions, Inc.
National Jewish Theater
New Mexico Repertory Theatre
New Tuners Theatre
New World Theatre, Inc.

Jackie Nichols
Northlight Theatre
The Organic Theater Company
PAJ Publications
Playwrights Horizon
Playwrights of Philadelphia/ Philadelphia Drama Guild (discontinued project)
Second Stage
Seven Oaks Foundation
The Shazzam Production Company
Spottswood Studios
Tejas Art Press
Theme Song
Translight Media Associates
Transtar Productions, Inc.
Tri Video Teleproduction-Lake Tahoe
University of Wisconsin Stout Teleproduction Center
Miriam Colon Valle (unable to contact)
Victor & Grais Productions
WMC Company (asked to be deleted)
The Ann White Theatre
Williamstown Theatre Festival
Wooly Mammoth Theatre Company
ZM Squared

Syndicates

Syndication is another way to make money with your writing, but the industry is highly competitive and sometimes confusing to writers. This year, columns were syndicated on such specialized topics as home video, travel for seniors and baseball trivia. More general columns on gardening or fashion can usually find a place in newspapers, but the competition is keen. Humor and political commentary columns in newspapers are usually reserved for heavy hitters such as Dave Barry or George Will; however fresh treatments of these areas can get your column a place in the market.

With syndicates, it's always best to start small and build up your clips. Most columnists start with features in local newspapers, compile a good selection of clips and then approach a syndicate. In many cases, the process of acceptance by a syndicate can take several submissions over a period of years. Writers often submit work for consideration, continue to compile clips, and re-submit new work after a year or so.

Most syndicates distribute a variety of columns, cartoons and features. Specialized syndicates—those that deal with a single area such as business—often sell to magazines, trade journals and business publications, as well as to newspapers.

Not only is syndication a competitive field, but it is also challenging. Producing a lively, appealing column on a regular basis requires a certain set of skills and most editors want proof of your ability to produce consistently good work.

Study the popular syndicated columnists to discover how successful columns are structured. For example, most columns are short—from 500 to 750 words—so columnists learn how to make every word count. Don't make the mistake of imitating a well-known columnist—newspapers do not want more of the same. This holds true of subject matter, too. Keep abreast of trends, but make sure you do not submit a column on a subject already covered by that syndicate. The more unique the topic, the greater your chances at syndication, but choose a subject that interests you and one you know well.

Editors look for writers with unique viewpoints on lifestyle or political topics, but they also seek how-to columns and one-shot features on a variety of subjects. One-shot features tend to be longer than columns and can be tied to a news peg or event. Other one-shot items include puzzles, cartoons and graphics.

Most syndicate editors prefer a query letter and about six sample columns or writing samples and a self addressed, stamped envelope. If you have a particular field of expertise, be sure to mention this in your letter and back it up by sending related material. For highly specialized or technical matter you must also provide some credentials to show you are qualified to handle the topic.

In essence, syndicates act as agents or brokers for the material they handle. Writing material is usually sold as a package. The syndicate will promote and market the work and keep careful records of sales. Writers usually receive 40 to 60 percent of gross receipts. Syndicates may also pay a small salary or a flat fee for one-shot items.

Syndicates usually acquire all rights to accepted material, although a few are now offering writers and artists the option of retaining ownership. When selling all rights, writers give up all ownership and future use of their creations. Sale of all rights is not the best deal for the writer and has been one reason writers choose to work with syndicates that buy less restrictive rights. Some choose to self-syndicate their work so they can retain these rights.

Writers who syndicate their own work have all the freedom of a business owner, but must also act as their own managers, marketing team and sales force. Payment is usually negotiated on a case-by-case basis. Small newspapers may offer only $5-10 per column, but larger papers may pay $20 to $30. The number of papers you deal with is only limited by your marketing budget and sales ability.

If you self-syndicate you should be aware that some newspapers are not copyrighted, so you should copyright your own material. It's less expensive to copyright columns as a collection, rather than individually. For more information on copyright procedures see Copyrighting Your Writing in the Business of Writing section.

For information on column writing and syndication see *How to Write & Sell a Column*, by Julie Raskin and Carolyn Males (Writer's Digest Books). Additional information on newspaper markets can be found in *The Gale Directory of Publications* (available in most libraries). *The Editor & Publisher Syndicate Directory* (11 W. 19th St., New York NY 10011) has a list of syndicates, contact names and features; the weekly magazine also has news articles about syndicates and can provide you with information about trends in the industry.

For more information on syndicates not listed in *Writer's Market*, see Other Syndicates at the end of this section.

ADVENTURE FEATURE SYNDICATE, 329 Harvery Dr., Glendale CA 91206. (818)247-1721. Editor: Orpha Harryman Barry. Reports in 1 month. Buys all rights, first North American serial rights and second serial (reprint) rights. Free cartoonist's guidelines.
Needs: Fiction (spies) and fillers (adventure/travel), action/adventure comic strips and graphic novels. Submit complete ms.

‡ALLIED FEATURE SYNDICATE, P.O. Drawer 9127, San Bernardino CA 92427. (714)887-8083. FAX: (714)887-8085. Editor Robert J. Blanset. Estab. 1940. 70% written by writers on contract; 30% freelance by writers on a one-time basis. Works with 36 writers/year. Works with 30-40 previously unpublished writers/year. Syndicates to newspapers (60%); magazines (30%); in-house organs (10%). Submissions will be returned "only on request." Reports in 6 weeks. Buys all rights.
Needs: "We will consider all materials." Buys one-shot features and articles series. Query with clips of published work. Pays 50% author's percentage "after production costs" or 5¢/word. Currently syndicates "A Little Prayer," by Mary Alice Bennett (religious filler); "Murphy's Law of Electronics," by Nic Frising (cartoon panel); "Selling in the Year 2000," by Dick Meza (marketing column).
Tips: "Allied Feature Syndicate is one of very few agencies syndicating electronics manufacturing targeted materials and information."

AMERICA INTERNATIONAL SYNDICATE, (merged with JSA Publications Inc. of Detroit), 1324 N. 3rd St., St. Joseph MO 64501. (816)233-8190. FAX: (816)279-9315. Executive Director: Gerald A. Bennett. Associate Director (London Office): Paul Eisler. 100% freelance written by cartoonists on contract. "We sell to newspapers, trade magazines, puzzle books and comic books." Reports in 6 weeks. Buys all rights.
Needs: Short fictional crime story "You Are The Detective" for magazines, books and comics; also comic strips of adventure, western or family type. Children's features and games also needed. Scientific or unusual features with art and written text needed. Send 6-8 samples with SASE. Pays 50% of gross sales. Currently syndication features: "Alfonso," "Silent Sam," "Tex Benson," "Double Trouble," "Buccaneers," "A.J. Sowell," "Figment," "Adventures in Nature," and "Dad's Place" (comic strips). Panel Features are "Stacey," "Girls," and "The Edge."
Tips: "Keep the art simple and uncluttered as possible: Know your subject and strive for humor."

AMERICAN NEWSPAPER SYNDICATE, 9 Woodrush Dr., Irvine CA 92714. (714)559-8047. Executive Editor: Susan Smith. Estab. 1988. 50% regular columns by writers under contract; 50% freelance articles and series by writers on a one-time basis. Plan to syndicate up to 7 new U.S. and Canadian columnists this year. Plan to buy 20 one-time articles/series per year. Syndicates to U.S. and Canadian medium-to-large general interest and special interest newspapers. Works with previously unpublished and published writers. Pays 50% of net sales, salary on some contracted columns. Buys first North American serial rights. Reports in 3 weeks. Writer's guidelines for SASE.
Needs: Newspaper columns and one-time articles/series on travel, entertainment, how-to, human interest, business, personal finance, lifestyle, health, legal issues. "Practical, money-saving information on everyday needs such as medicine, insurance, automobiles, education, home decoration and repairs, and travel is always in great demand by newspapers." Will not return material without SASE. Columns should be 700 words in length; one-time articles should be 1,500 words.
Tips: "We seek fresh, innovative material that may be overlooked by the other syndicates. Because we know the newspaper syndication market, we feel we can find a place for the previously-unpublished writer if the material is well-executed. Be sure to research your idea thoroughly. Good, solid writing is a must. This is a

very tough business to penetrate—but the rewards can be great for those who are successful."

‡**AP NEWSFEATURES**, 50 Rockefeller Plaza, New York NY 10020. (212)621-1500. Director: Tom Slaughter. **Nonfiction:** Buys column ideas. "We do not buy single features."

ARKIN MAGAZINE SYNDICATE, 1817 NE 164th St., N. Miami Beach FL 33162. Editor: Joseph Arkin. Estab. 1958. 20% freelance written by writers on contract; 70% freelance written by writers on a one-time basis. "We regularly purchase articles from several freelancers for syndication in trade and professional magazines." Previously published submissions OK, "if all rights haven't been sold." Reports in 3 weeks. Buys all North American magazine and newspaper rights.
Needs: Magazine articles (nonfiction, 750-2,200 words), directly relating to business problems common to several different types of businesses); and photos (purchased with written material). "We are in dire need of the 'how-to' business article." Will not consider article series. Submit complete ms; "SASE required with all submissions." Pays 3-10¢/word; $5-10 for photos; "actually, line drawings are preferred instead of photos." **Pays on acceptance.**
Tips: "Study a representative group of trade magazines to learn style, needs and other facets of the field."

ARTHUR'S INTERNATIONAL, Box 10599, Honolulu HI 96816. (808)922-9443. Editor: Marvin C. Arthur. Syndicates to newspapers and magazines. Reports in 1 week. "SASE must be enclosed." Buys all rights.
Needs: Fillers, magazine columns, magazine features, newspaper columns, newspaper features and news items. "We specialize in timely nonfiction and historical stories, and columns, preferably the unusual. We utilize humor. Travel stories utilized in 'World Traveler.' " Buys one-shot features and article series. "Since the majority of what we utilize is column or short story length, it is better to submit the article so as to expedite consideration and reply. Do not send any lengthy manuscripts." Pays 50% of net sales, salary on some contracted work and flat rate on commissioned work. Currently syndicates Marv, by Marvin C. Arthur (informative, humorous, commentary); Humoresque, by Don Alexander (humorous); and World Spotlight, by Don Kampel (commentary).
Tips: "We do not use cartoons but we are open for fine illustrators."

BUDDY BASCH FEATURE SYNDICATE, 771 West End Ave., New York NY 10025-5572. (212)666-2300. Editor/Publisher: Buddy Basch. 10% written by writers on contract; 2% freelance written by writers on a one-time basis. Buys 10 features/year; works with 3-4 previously unpublished writers annually. Syndicates to print media: newspapers, magazines, giveaways, house organs, etc. Reports in 2 weeks. Buys first North American serial rights.
Needs: Magazine features, newspaper features, and one-shot ideas that are really different. "Try to make them unusual, unique, real 'stoppers,' not the usual stuff." Will consider one-shots and article series on travel, entertainment, human interest—"the latter, a wide umbrella that makes people stop and read the piece. Different, unusual and unique are the key words, not what the *writer* thinks is, but that has been done nine million times before." Query. Pays 20-50% commission. Additional payment for photos $10-50. Currently syndicates It Takes a Woman by Frances Scott (woman's feature), Travel Whirl, Scramble Steps (puzzle) and others.
Tips: "Never mind what your mother, fiancé or friend thinks is good. If it has been done before and is old hat, it has no chance. Do some research and see if there are a dozen similar items in the press. Don't just try a very close 'switch' on them. You don't fool anyone with this. There are fewer and fewer newspapers, with more and more people vying for the available space. But there's *always* room for a really good, *different* feature or story. Trouble is few writers (amateurs especially) know a good piece, I'm sorry to say."

BLACK CONSCIENCE SYNDICATION INC., 21 Bedford St., Wyandanch NY 11798. (516)491-7774. President: Clyde Davis. Estab. 1986. 65% of material freelance written. Buys 1,000 features annually. Uses material for magazines, newspapers, radio and television. Reports in 2 weeks. Buys all rights. Writer's guidelines for #10 SASE.
Needs: Magazine columns, magazine features, newspaper columns, newpaper features and news items. Buys single features and article series. Query only. Pays 50% commission.
Tips: "The purpose of Black Conscience Syndication Inc., is to serve God and provide writers who produce material vital to the well-being of the Black community an avenue to have their copy published in Black newspapers and trade publications throughout the world. We are interested in all material that is informative and enlightening: book reviews, interviews, feature articles, cartoons, poetry and travel information. Black Conscience Syndication submits material to 700 publications world-wide; three-fourths of those publications are Black. Black Conscience Syndication is also a weekly cable television program, highlighting material sent to us by writers, poets and illustrators."

BUSINESS FEATURES SYNDICATE, P.O. Box 9844, Ft. Lauderdale FL 33310. (305)485-0795. FAX: (305)485-0806. Editor: Dana K. Cassell. Estab. 1976. 100% freelance written. Buys about 100 features/columns a year. Syndicates to trade journal magazines, business newspapers and tabloids. Buys exclusive rights while being circulated. Writer's guidelines for #10 SASE. Reports in 1 month.

Needs: Buys single features and article series on generic business, how-to, marketing, merchandising, security, management and personnel. Length: 1,000-2,500 words. Complete ms preferred. Pays 50% commission. Currently syndicates Retail Market Clinic and Bookline.
Tips: "We need nonfiction material aimed at the independent retailer or small service business owner. Material must be written for and of value to more than one field, for example: jewelers, drug store owners and sporting goods dealers. We aim at retail trade journals; our material is more how-to business oriented than that bought by other syndicates."

‡CHRONICLE FEATURES, Suite 1009, 870 Market St., San Francisco CA 94102. (415)777-7212. Associate Editor: Jean Q. Arnold. Buys 3 features/year. Syndicates to daily newspapers in the U.S. and Canada with representation overseas. Reports in 1 month. SASE.
Needs: Newspaper columns and features. "In choosing a column subject, the writer should be guided by the concerns and aspirations of today's newspaper reader. We look for originality of expression and, in special fields of interest, exceptional expertise." Preferred length: 500-700 words. Submit complete ms. Pays 50% revenue from syndication. Offers no additional payment for photos or artwork accompanying ms. Currently syndicates Bizarro, by Dan Piraro (cartoon panel); Earthweek, by Steve Newman (planetary diary); Home Entertainment, by Harry Somerfield (audiovisual equipment advice and reviews); Streetwise, by Herb Greenberg (up-to-the-minute business column); and First Person Singular, by Ruthe Stein (singles column).
Tips: "We are seeking features that will be ongoing enterprises, not single articles or news releases. Examples of a proposed feature are more welcome than a query letter describing it."

CONTINENTAL FEATURES/CONTINENTAL NEWS SERVICE, Suite 265, 341 W. Broadway, San Diego CA 92101. (619)492-8696. Editor: Gary P. Salamone. Estab. 1981. 100% written by writers on contract; 30% freelance written by writers on a one-time basis. "Writers who offer the kind and quality of writing we seek stand an equal chance regardless of experience." Syndicates to the print media. Reports in 1 month. Writer's guidelines for #10 SASE.
Needs: Magazine features, newspaper features, "Feature material should fit the equivalent of one-quarter to one-half standard newspaper page, and Continental News considers an ultra-liberal or ultra-conservative slant inappropriate." Query. Pays 70% author's percentage. Currently syndicates News and Comment by Charles Hampton Savage (general news commentary/analysis); Continental Viewpoint, by Staff (political and social commentary); Portfolio, by William F. Pike (cartoon/caricature art); FreedomWatch, by Glen Church; Travelers Checks √√√ and Middle East Cable, by Mike Maggio.
Tips: "Continental News seeks country profiles/background articles that pertain to foreign countries. Writers who possess such specific knowledge/personal experience stand an excellent chance of acceptance, provided they can focus the political, economic and social issues. We welcome them to submit their proposals. We foresee the possibility of diversifying our feature package by representing writers and feature creators on more one-shot projects."

COPLEY NEWS SERVICE, Box 190, San Diego CA 92112. (619)293-1818. Editorial Director: Nanette Wiser. Buys 85% of work from contracted stringers; 15% from freelancers on a one-time basis. Offers 200 features/week. Sells to magazines, newspapers, radio. Reports in 1-2 months. Buys all rights or second serial (reprint) rights (sometimes).
Needs: Fillers, magazine columns, magazine features, newspaper columns and newspaper features. Subjects include interior design, outdoor recreation, fashion, antiques, real estate, pets and gardening. Buys one-shot and articles series. Query with clips of published work. Pays $50-100 flat rate or $400 salary/month.

CREATIVE SYNDICATION SERVICES, P.O. Box 40, Eureka MO 63025. (314)938-9116. FAX: (314)343-0966. Editor: Debra Holly. Estab. 1977. 10% written by writers on contract; 50% freelance written by writers on a one-time basis. Syndicates to magazines, newspapers and radio. Query for electronic submissions. Reports in 1 month. Buys all rights. Currently syndicates The Weekend Workshop, by Ed Baldwin; Woodcrafting, by Ed Baldwin (woodworking) and Classified Clippers, a feature exclusive for the Classified Section of newspapers.

CREATORS SYNDICATE, INC., Suite 700, 5777 W. Century Blvd., Los Angeles CA 90045. (213)337-7003. Columns President: Richard Newcombe. Estab. 1987. Syndicates to newspapers. Reports in 2 months. Buys negotiable rights. Reports in 2 months. Writer's guidelines for SASE.
Needs: Newspaper columns and features. Query with clips of published work or submit complete ms. Author's percentage: 50%. Currently syndicates Ann Landers (advice) B.C. (comic strip) and Herblock (editorial cartoon). Please write "Cartoon Submissions" on lower left of appropriate envelope.
Tips: "Syndication is very competitive. Writing regularly for your local newspaper is a good start."

THE CRICKET LETTER, INC., P.O. Box 527, Ardmore PA 19003. (215)789-2480. Editor: J.D. Krickett. Estab. 1975. 10% written by writers on contract; 10% freelance written by writers on a one-time basis. Works with 2-3 previously unpublished writers annually. Syndicates to trade magazines and newspapers. Reports in 3 weeks. Buys all rights.

Needs: Magazine columns, magazine features, newspaper columns, newspaper features and news items—all tax and financial-oriented (700-1,500 words); newspaper columns, features and news items directed to small business. Query with clips of published work. Pays $50-500. Currently syndicates Hobby/Business, by Mark E. Battersby (tax and financial); Farm Taxes, by various authors; and Small Business Taxes, by Mark E. Battersby.

CROWN SYNDICATE, INC., P.O. Box 99126, Seattle WA 98199. President: L.M. Boyd. Estab. 1967. Buys countless trivia items, cartoons and panel gag lines. Syndicates to newspapers, radio. Reports in 1 month. Buys first North American serial rights. Free writer's guidelines.
Needs: Filler material used weekly, items for trivia column, gaglines for specialty comic strip (format guidelines sent on request). Pays $1-5/item, depending on how it's used, i.e., trivia or filler service or comic strip. Offers no additional payment for photos accompanying ms. Currently syndicates puzzle panels and comic strips.

EDITORIAL CONSULTANT SERVICE, P.O. Box 524, West Hempstead NY 11552. Editorial Director: Arthur A. Ingoglia. Estab. 1964. 40% written by writers on contract; 25% freelance written by writers on a one-time basis. "We work with 75 writers in the U.S. and Canada." Previously published writers only. Adds about 5 new columnists/year. Syndicates material to an average of 60 newspapers, magazines, automotive trade and consumer publications, and radio stations with circulation of 50,000-575,000. Buys all rights. Writer's guidelines for #10 SASE. Reports in 3 weeks.
Needs: Magazine and newspaper columns and features, news items and radio broadcast material. Prefers carefully documented material with automotive slant. Also considers automotive trade features. Will consider article series. No horoscope, child care, lovelorn or pet care. Query. Author's percentage varies; usually averages 50%. Additional payment for 8 × 10 b&w and color photos accepted with ms. Submit 2-3 columns. Currently syndicates Let's Talk About Your Car, by R. Hite.
Tips: "Emphasis is placed on articles and columns with an automotive slant. We prefer consumer-oriented features, how to save money on your car, what every woman should know about her car, how to get more miles per gallon, etc."

FEATURE ENTERPRISES, Suite C, 1827 Arboretum Circle, Birmingham AL 35216. Editor: Maury M. Breecher. Estab. 1979. 10% written by writers on contract; 90% freelance written by writers on a one-time basis. Syndicates 100 mss/year. Works with 10-20 previously unpublished writers/year. Syndicates to magazines and newspapers. Reports in 1 month. Buys first North American serial rights and second serial (reprint) rights. 4-page writer's guidelines for $2.
Needs: Currently syndicates On Health, by Maury Breecher (medicine/health); and Growing Pains by Vivian K. Friedman, Ph.D. Payment on 50/50 standard syndicate split. SASE required for return of material.
Tips: "More intense push on popular psychology and medical breakthroughs."

FOTOPRESS, INDEPENDENT NEWS SERVICE INTERNATIONAL, Box 1268, Station Q, Toronto, Ontario M4T 2P4 Canada. (416)841-4486. FAX: (416)841-5593. 50% written by writers on contract; 25% freelance written by writers on a one-time basis. Works with 30% previously unpublished writers. Syndicates to domestic and international magazines, newspapers, radio, TV stations and motion picture industry. Reports in 6 weeks. Buys variable rights. Writer's guidelines for $3 in IRCs.
Needs: Fillers, magazine columns, magazine features, newspaper columns, newspaper features, news items, radio broadcast material, documentary, the environment, travel and art. Buys one-shot and article series for international politics, scientists, celebrities and religious leaders. Query or submit complete ms. Pays 50-75% author's percentage. Offers $5-150 for accompanying ms.
Tips: "We need all subjects from 500-3,000 words. Photos are purchased with or without features. All writers are regarded respectfully—their success is our success."

(GABRIEL) GRAPHICS NEWS BUREAU, P.O. Box 38, Madison Square Station, New York NY 10010. (212)254-8863. Editor: J. G. Bumberg. 25% freelance written by writers on contract; 50% freelance written by writers on one-time basis. Custom-syndicates for clients to weeklies (selected) and small dailies. Reports in 1 month. Buys all rights for clients, packages. Writer's guidelines for SASE.
Needs: Fillers, magazine features, newspaper columns and features and news items for PR clients custom packages. Pays 15% from client. Also has consulting/conceptualizing services in communications/graphics/management.

Market conditions are constantly changing! If this is 1992 or later, buy the newest edition of Writer's Market at your favorite bookstore or order directly from Writer's Digest Books.

GENERAL NEWS SYNDICATE, 147 W. 42nd St., New York NY 10036. (212)221-0043. 25% written by writers on contract; 12% freelance written by writers on a one-time basis. Works with 12 writers/year; average of 5 previously unpublished writers annually. Syndicates to an average of 12 newspaper and radio outlets averaging 20 million circulation; buys theatre and show business people columns (mostly New York theatre pieces). Reports on *accepted* material in 3 weeks. Buys one-time rights. Writer's guidelines for #10 SASE.
Needs: Entertainment-related material.
Tips: Looking for "short copy (250-500 words)."

HERITAGE FEATURES SYNDICATE, 214 Massachusetts Ave. NE, Washington DC 20002. (202)543-0440. Managing Editor: Andy Seamans. Estab. 1981. 99% written by writers on contract; 1% freelance written by writers on one-time basis. Buys 3 columns/year. Works with 2-3 previously unpublished writers annually. Syndicates to over 170 newspapers with circulations ranging from 2,000 to 630,000. Works with previously published writers. Buys first North American serial rights. Reports in 3 weeks.
Needs: Newspaper columns (practically all material is done by regular columnists). One-shot features. "We purchase 750-800 word columns on political, economic and related subjects." Query. "SASE a must." Pays $50 maximum. Currently syndicates 10 columnists, including A Minority View, by Walter E. Williams; Fed Up, by Don Feder; Main Street U.S.A., by William Murchison.
Tips: "Our material is all op-ed material."

HISPANIC LINK NEWS SERVICE, 1420 N St. NW, Washington DC 20005. (202)234-0280. Publisher: Charles A. Ericksen. Editor: Felix Perez. Estab. 1980. 50% freelance written by writers on contract; 50% freelance written by writers on a one-time basis. Buys 156 columns and features/year. Works with 50 writers/year; 5 previously unpublished writers. Syndicates to 150 newspapers and magazines with circulations ranging from 5,000 to 300,000. Reports in 2 weeks. Buys second serial (reprint) or negotiable rights. Free writer's guidelines.
Needs: Magazine columns, magazine features, newspaper columns and features. One-shot features and article series. "We prefer 650-700 word op/ed or features geared to a general national audience, but focus on issue or subject of particular interest to Hispanic Americans. Some longer pieces accepted occasionally." Query or submit complete ms. Pays $25-100. Currently syndicates Hispanic Link, by various authors (opinion and/or feature columns).
Tips: "This year we would especially like to get topical material and vignettes relating to Hispanic presence and progress in the United States. Provide insights on Hispanic experience geared to a general audience. Eighty-five to 90 percent of the columns we accept are authored by Hispanics; the Link presents Hispanic viewpoints and showcases Hispanic writing talent to its subscribing newspapers and magazines. Copy should be submitted in English. We syndicate in English and Spanish."

HOLLYWOOD INSIDE SYNDICATE, P.O. Box 49957, Los Angeles CA 90049. (714)678-6237. Editor: John Austin. Estab. 1966. 10% written by writers on contract; 40% freelance written by writers on a one-time basis. Purchases entertainment-oriented mss for syndication to newspapers in San Francisco, Philadelphia, Detroit, Montreal, London, Sydney, Manila, South Africa, etc. Works with 2-3 previously unpublished writers annually. Previously published submissions OK, if published in the U.S. and Canada only. Reports in 6 weeks. Negotiates for first rights or second serial (reprint) rights.
Needs: News items (column items concerning entertainment—motion picture—personalities and jet setters for syndicated column; 750-800 words). Also considers series of 1,500-word articles; "suggest descriptive query first. We are also looking for off-beat travel pieces (with pictures) but not on areas covered extensively in the Sunday supplements. We can always use pieces on 'freighter' travel. Not luxury cruise liners but lower cost cruises. We also syndicate nonfiction book subjects—sex, travel, etc., to overseas markets. No fiction. Must have b&w photo with submissions if possible." Also require 1,500 word celebrity profiles on internationally recognized celebrities." Query or submit complete ms. Pay negotiable. Currently syndicates Books of the Week column.
Tips: "Study the entertainment pages of Sunday (and daily) newspapers to see the type of specialized material we deal in. Perhaps we are different from other syndicates, but we deal with celebrities. No 'I' journalism such as 'when I spoke to Cloris Leachman.' Many freelancers submit material from the 'dinner theatre' and summer stock circuit of 'gossip type' items from what they have observed about the 'stars' or featured players in these productions—how they act off stage, who they romance, etc. We use this material."

INTERNATIONAL PHOTO NEWS, Box 2405, West Palm Beach FL 33402. (305)793-3424. Editor: Elliott Kravetz. 10% written by freelance writers under contract. Buys 52 features/year. Works with 25 previously unpublished writers/year. Syndicates to newspapers. Query for electronic submissions. Reports in 1 week. Buys second serial (reprint) rights. Writer's guidelines for SASE.
Needs: Magazine columns and features (celebrity), newspaper columns and features (political or celebrity), news items (political). Buys one-shot features. Query with clips of published work. Pays 50% author's percentage. Pays $5 for photos accepted with ms. Currently syndicates Celebrity Interview, by Jay and Elliott Kravetz.
Tips: "Go after celebrities who are on the cover on major magazines."

INTERPRESS OF LONDON AND NEW YORK, 400 Madison Ave., New York NY 10017. (212)832-2839. Editor: Jeffrey Blyth. Estab. 1971. 50% freelance written by writers on contract; 50% freelance written by writers on a one-time basis. Works with 3-6 previously unpublished writers annually. Buys British and European rights mostly, but can handle world rights. Will consider photocopied submissions. Previously published submissions OK "for overseas." Pays on publication or agreement of sale. Reports immediately or as soon as possible.

Needs: "Unusual nonfiction stories and photos for British and European press. Picture stories, for example, on such 'Americana' as a five-year-old evangelist; the 800-pound 'con-man'; the nude-male calendar; tallest girl in the world; interviews with pop celebrities such as Yoko Ono, Michael Jackson, Bill Cosby, Tom Selleck, Cher, Priscilla Presley, Cheryl Tiegs, Eddie Murphy, Liza Minelli, also news of stars on such shows as 'Dynasty'/'Dallas'; cult subjects such as voodoo, college fads, anything amusing or offbeat. Extracts from books such as Earl Wilson's *Show Business Laid Bare*, inside-Hollywood type series ('Secrets of the Stuntmen'). Real life adventure dramas ('Three Months in an Open Boat,' 'The Air Crash Cannibals of the Andes'). No length limits—short or long, but not too long. Query or submit complete ms. Payment varies; depending on whether material is original, or world rights. Pays top rates, up to several thousand dollars, for exclusive material."

Photos: Purchased with or without features. Captions required. Standard size prints. Pay $50-100, but no limit on exclusive material.

Tips: "Be alert to the unusual story in your area—the sort that interests the American tabloids (and also the European press)."

‡INTERSTATE NEWS SERVICE, 237 S. Clark Ave., St. Louis MO 63135. (314)522-1300. Editor: Michael J. Olds. Estab. 1985. Buys 50% of material from freelancers on a one-time basis. Purchases 1,200 mss/year. "Interstate acts as the local news bureau for newspapers that are too small to operate their own state capital bureau." Buys all rights and makes work-for-hire assignments. Call for information.

Needs: News items. Hard news emphasis, concentrating on local delegations, tax money and local issues. Buys one-shot features. Query with clips of published work. Negotiates with writers under contract.

Tips: "We deal only with freelancers who work with us regularly and in selected states (MO, IL, AR, TX, KS, OH, MD). We do not buy unsolicited mss."

JEWISH TELEGRAPHIC AGENCY, 330 7th Ave., New York NY 10001-5010. (212)643-1890. Editor: Mark Joffe. Managing Editor: Elli Wohlgelernter. 40% written by writers on contract; 40% freelance written by writers on a one-time basis. Buys 40 features/year. Syndicates to newspapers. Query for electronic submissions. Submissions with SASE will not be returned. Reports in 2 months. Buys second serial (reprint) rights.

Needs: Fillers, magazine features, newspaper features and news items. "Anything of Jewish interest, 500-1,000 words. Can be first-person or op-ed; news stories should be balanced." Buys one-shot features and article series. Submit complete ms. Pays $25-50-75 flat rate. Currently syndicates American News Report, by Ben Gallob; and Commentary, by Rabbi Marc Tanenbaum.

Tips: "Simply put, good writing will get published. Anything of Jewish interest, nationally or worldwide, will be considered. I'm looking for good stories on whatever trends are happening in Jewish life."

JSA PUBLICATIONS, P.O. Box 37175, Oak Park MI 48237. (313)546-9123. Director: Joe Ajlouny. Editor: Paul Ammar. Alternative features syndicate and humor/trade book packager; 50% of requirements bought from freelance submissions; 40% from writers and illustrators under contract; 10% self-generated. "Please don't send general/family comic strips. We prefer contemporary and themeatic single panels. Truly unique puzzles only." Always query first with samples and SASE. Reports in 2 months. Buys some rights, prefers licensing agreements. Guidelines for SASE.

Needs: Features capable of book length and other adaptations, such as greeting cards, postcards and booklets. Humorous or clever concepts, articles and illustrations. Will accept magazine articles, nonfiction, only after query with SASE. Pays standard royalties on syndication contracts. Purchases illustrations between $30-700; magazine humor or nonfiction articles between $110-400. Currently syndicated: Party Ranks, The Bob Zone, Future Features, Off the Wall. Packaged: "The Name is Trump," "The Official Handbook of Cold War Nostalgia." Always query first; please enclose SASE.

KING FEATURES SYNDICATE, INC., 235 E. 45th St., New York NY 10017. (212)455-4000. Director of Editorial Projects: Merry Clark. Syndicates material to newspapers. Submit brief cover letter with samples of column or comic proposal. Reports in 2 weeks by letter.

Needs: "We are looking for original ideas for columns and first-rate writing. Check *Editor & Publisher Annual Directory of Syndicated Services* before you submit a column idea."

LOS ANGELES TIMES SYNDICATE, Times Mirror Square, Los Angeles CA 90053. (213)237-3700. Executive Editor: Steven Christenson. Special Articles Editor: Dan O'Toole. Syndicates to U.S. and worldwide markets. Usually buys first North American serial rights and world rights, but rights purchased can vary. Submit seasonal material six weeks in advance. Material ranges from 800-2,000 words.

Needs: Reviews continuing columns and comic strips for U.S. and foreign markets. Send columns and comic strips to Steven Christenson. Also reviews single articles, series, magazine reprints, and book serials. Send these submissions to Dan O'Toole. Send complete mss. Pays 50% commission. Currently syndicates Art Buchwald, Dr. Henry Kissinger, Dr. Jeane Kirkpatrick, William Pfaff, Paul Conrad and Lee Iacocca.
Tips: "We're dealing with fewer undiscovered writers but still do review material."

NATIONAL NEWS BUREAU, 1318 Chancellor St., Philadelphia PA 19107. (215)546-8088. Editor: Harry Jay Katz. "We work with more than 200 writers and buy over 1,000 stories per year." Syndicates to more than 500 publications. Reports in 2 weeks. Buys all rights. Writer's guidelines for 9×12 SAE and 3 first class stamps.
Needs: Newspaper features; "we do many reviews and celebrity interviews. Only original, assigned material." One-shot features and article series; film reviews, etc. Query with clips. Pays $5-200 flat rate. Offers $5-200 additional payment for photos accompanying ms.

NEW YORK TIMES SYNDICATION SALES CORP., 130 5th Ave., New York NY 10011. (212)645-3000. Managing Editor: Barbara Gaynes. Syndicates numerous one-shot articles. Buys first serial rights, first North American serial rights, one-time rights, second serial (reprint) rights, or all rights.
Needs: Magazine and newspaper features. "On syndicated articles, payment to author is varied. We only consider articles that have been previously published. Send tearsheets of articles published." Submit approximately 4 samples of work. Photos are welcome with articles.
Tips: "Topics should cover universal markets and either be by a well-known writer or have an off-beat quality. Quizzes are welcomed if well researched."

‡NEWS FLASH INTERNATIONAL, INC., Division of the Observer Newspapers. 2262 Centre Ave., Bellmore NY 11710. (516)679-9888. Editor: Jackson B. Pokress. 25% written by writers on contract; 25% freelance written by writers on a one-time basis. Supplies material to Observer newspapers and overseas publications. Works with 10-20 previously unpublished writers annually. "Contact editor prior to submission to allow for space if article is newsworthy." Pays on publication.
Nonfiction: "We have been supplying a 'ready-for-camera' sports page (tabloid size) complete with column and current sports photos on a weekly basis to many newspapers on Long Island, as well as pictures and written material to publications in England and Canada. Payment for assignments is based on the article. Payments vary from $20 for a feature of 800 words. Our sports stories feature in-depth reporting as well as book reviews on this subject. We are always in the market for good photos, sharp and clear, action photos of boxing, wrestling, football, baseball and hockey. We cover all major league ball parks during the baseball and football seasons. We are accredited to the Mets, Yanks, Jets and Giants. During the winter we cover basketball and hockey and all sports events at the Nassau Coliseum."
Photos: Purchased on assignment; captions required. Uses "good quality 8×10 b&w glossy prints; good choice of angles and lenses." Pays $7.50 minimum for b&w photos.
Tips: "Submit articles which are fresh in their approach on a regular basis with good quality black and white glossy photos if possible; include samples of work. We prefer well-researched, documented stories with quotes where possible. We are interested in profiles and bios on woman athletes. There is a big interest in this in the foreign market. Women's boxing, volleyball and basketball are major interests."

NEWS USA INC., 1127 National Press Bldg., Washington DC 20045. (202)393-2200. Editor: Jack Landau. 50% written by writers on contract; 50% freelance written by writers on a one-time basis. Buys 75 mss/ month. Works with 50 previously unpublished writers/year. Syndicates to 10,000 U.S. newspapers. Query for electronic submissions. Submissions with SASE will *not* be returned. "Takes staff time." Reports in 1 week. Buys all rights.
Needs: Fillers, newspaper columns, newspaper features, news items and graphics. Buys one-shot features and article series. Health, seniors and consumer. "We consider all features, documents etc." Query with clips of published work or submit complete ms. Pays $50/item flat rate. Pays more for graphics. Currently syndicates Consumer Watch, by Esther Peterson (consumer); Your Medicines, by Todd Dankmyer (health) and The Diet Doctor, by Dr. Herman Frankel (diet).
Tips: "Send resume requesting freelance assignments."

NEWSPAPER ENTERPRISE ASSOCIATION, INC., 200 Park Ave., New York NY 10166. (212)557-5870/ (212)692-3700. Editorial Director: David Hendin. Director, International Newspaper Operations: Sidney Goldberg. Executive Editor: Jim Robinson. Director of Comics: Sarah Gillespie. 100% written by writers on contract. "We provide a comprehensive package of features to mostly small- and medium-sized newspapers." Reports in 6 weeks. Buys all rights.
Needs: "Any column we purchase must fill a need in our feature lineup and must have appeal for a wide variety of people in all parts of the country. We are most interested in lively writing. We are also interested in features that are not merely copies of other features already on the market. The writer must know his or her subject. Any writer who has a feature that meets all of those requirements should send a few copies of

the feature to us, along with his or her plans for the column and some background material on the writer." Current columnists include Bob Walters, Bob Wagman, Chuck Stone, Dr. Peter Gott, Tom Tiede, Ben Wattenberg and William Rusher. Current comics include Born Loser, Frank & Ernest, Eek & Meek, Kit 'n' Carlyle, Bugs Bunny, Berry's World, Arlo and Janis, and Snafu.

Tips: "We get enormous numbers of proposals for first person columns—slice of life material with lots of anecdotes. While many of these columns are big successes in local newspapers, it's been our experience that they are extremely difficult to sell nationally. Most papers seem to prefer to buy this sort of column from a talented local writer."

NORTH AMERICA SYNDICATE, 235 E. 45th St., New York NY 10017. See King Features Syndicate.

ROYAL FEATURES, P.O. Box 58174, Houston TX 77258. (713)280-0777. Executive Director: Fay W. Henry. Estab. 1984. 80% written by writers on contract; 10% freelance written by writers on one-time basis. Syndicates to magazines and newspapers. Reports in 2 months. Buys all rights or first North American serial rights.
Needs: Magazine and newspaper columns and features. Buys one-shot features and article series. Query with or without published clips. Send SASE with unsolicited queries or materials. Pays authors percentage, 40-60%.

SINGER MEDIA CORPORATION, 3164 Tyler Ave., Anaheim CA 92801. (714)527-5650. FAX: (714)527-0268. Editors: Kurt Singer and Dorothy Rosati. Estab. 1940. 25% written by writers on contract; 25% freelance written by writers on a one-time basis. Syndicates to magazines, newspapers, cassettes and book publishers. Reports in 3 weeks. Rights negotiable, world rights preferred. Writer's guidelines for #10 SAE and $1.
Needs: Short stories, crosswords, puzzles, quizzes, interviews, entertainment and psychology features, cartoons, books for serialization and foreign reprints. Syndicates one-shot features and article series on celebrities. Query with clips of published work or submit complete ms. Pays 50% author's percentage. Currently syndicates Solve a Crime, by B. Gordon (mystery puzzle) and Hollywood Gossip, by June Finletter (entertainment).
Tips: "Good interviews with celebrities, men/women relations, business and real estate features have a good chance with us. Aim at world distribution and therefore have a universal approach."

THE SOUTHAM SYNDICATE, 20 Yorks Mills Rd., Toronto, Ontario M2P 2C2 Canada. (416)222-8000. Editor: Jeffrey McBain. Estab. 1986. 70% written by writers on contract; 5% freelance written by writers on a one-time basis. Buys 40 features/year. Works with 3-4 previously unpublished writers/year. Syndicates to newspapers. Query for electronic submissions. Reports in 2 months. Buys Canadian rights.
Needs: Fillers (400-500 words), newspaper columns (700-800 words, self help) and newpaper features (1,000 words). Buys one-shot features and article series. Query with clips of published work. Pays 50% author's percentage. Currently syndicates Claire Hoy, William Johnson, Ben Wicks and David Suzuki.

SPORTS FEATURES SYNDICATE/WORLD FEATURES SYNDICATE, 1005 Mulberry, Marlton NJ 08053. (609)983-7688. Editor: Ronald A. Sataloff. Estab. 1981. 1-5% written by freelance on one-time basis. Nearly all material is syndicated to daily newspapers and the Associated Press's supplemental sports wire. Reports in 2 months. Buys all rights.
Needs: Currently syndicates Sports Lists, by staff; No Kidding?, by Karl Van Asselt; Mr. Music, by Jerry Osborne.
Tips: "No surprise—space is at a premium and one wishing to sell a column is at a disadvantage unless he is an expert in a chosen field and can relate that area of expertise in layman's language. Concentrate on features that take little space and that are helpful to the reader as well as interesting. *USA Today* has revolutionized newspapering in the sense that it is no longer a sin to be brief. That trend is here for a long time, and a writer should be aware of it. Papers are also moving toward more reader-oriented features, and those with an ability to make difficult subjects easy reading have an advantage. No one-shots!"

‡SYNDICATED WRITERS & ARTISTS INC., 2901 Tacoma Ave., Indianapolis IN 46218. (317)924-5143. Contact: Ken Skelton. 99% written by writers on contract; 1% freelance written by writers on a one-time basis. Works with 10 writers annually. Syndicates to newspapers. Reports in 6 weeks. Query for electronic submissions. Buys all rights. Writer's guidelines for SASE.
Needs: Fillers, newspaper columns, newspaper features and news items. 300 words with minority angle. Query with clips of published work. "Three different samples of your work should be submitted (10 cartoon strips or panels). Submissions should also include brief bio of writer/artists. No material is returned without a SASE." Pays author's percentage of 35-40%. Currently syndicates Hobson's House (cartoon) and editorial cartoons by Paul Lang.
Tips: "The kind of writing we seek has a minority angle. More news instead of opinion will be required. Quality requirements."

TEENAGE CORNER, INC., 70-540 Gardenia Ct., Rancho Mirage CA 92270. President: Mrs. David J. Lavin. Buys 122 items/year for use in newspapers. Submit complete ms. Reports in 1 week. Material is not copyrighted.
Needs: 500-word newspaper features. Pays $25.

TRIBUNE MEDIA SERVICES, 64 E. Concord St., Orlando FL 32801. (407)839-5600. President: Robert S. Reed. Editor: Michael Argirion. Estab. 1984. Syndicates to newspapers. Reports in 1 month. Buys all rights, first North American serial rights or second serial (reprint) rights.
Needs: Newspaper columns, comic strips. Query with published clips. Currently syndicates the columns of Mike Royko, Bob Greene, Liz Smith, Andy Rooney and Marilyn Beck; and cartoons of Jeff MacNelly and Don Wright.

UNITED MEDIA, 200 Park Ave., New York NY 10166. (212)692-3700. Columns Editor: Jim Robinson. Executive Editor, Comic Strips: Sarah Gillespie. 100% written by writers on contract. Syndicates to newspapers. Computer printout submission acceptable; prefers letter-quality. Reports in 6 weeks. Writer's guidelines for #10 SASE.
Needs: Newspaper columns and newspaper features. Query with photocopied clips of published work. "Authors under contract have negotiable terms." Currently syndicates Miss Manners, by Judith Martin (etiquette); Dr. Gott, by Peter Gott, M.D. (medical) and Supermarket Shopper, by Martin Sloane (coupon clipping advice), Jack Anderson and Dale van Atta (investigative reporting).
Tips: "We include tips in our guidelines. We buy very few of the hundreds of submissions we see monthly. We are looking for the different feature as opposed to new slants on established columns."

WASHINGTON POST WRITERS GROUP, 1150 15th St. NW, Washington DC 20071. (202)334-6375. Editor/General Manager: William B. Dickinson. Estab. 1973. Currently syndicates 32 features (columns and cartoons). A news syndicate that provides features for newspapers nationwide. Responds in 2 weeks. Buys all rights.
Needs: Newspaper column (editorial, lifestyle, humor), and newspaper features (comic strips, political cartoons). Query with clips of published work. Pays combination of salary and percentage. Currently syndicates George F. Will column (editorial); Ellen Goodman column (editorial).
Tips: "At this time, The Washington Post Writers Group will review editorial page and lifestyle page columns, as well as political cartoons and comic strips. Will not consider games, puzzles, or similar features. Send sample columns to the attention of William Dickinson, general manager. Send sample cartoons or comic strips (photocopies—no original artwork, please) to the attention of Jan Harrod, sales manager. Enclose a SASE for the return and response."

WHITEGATE FEATURES SYNDICATE, 71 Faunce Dr., Providence RI 02906. (401)274-2149. Contact: Eve Green. Editor: Ed Isaac. Estab. 1987. Buys 100% of material from freelance writers. Syndicates to newspapers; planning to begin selling to magazines and radio. Query for electronic submissions. Reports in 3 months. Buys all rights.
Needs: Fiction for Sunday newspaper magazines; magazine columns and features, newspaper columns and features, cartoon strips. Buys one-shots and article series. Query with clips of published work. For cartoon strips, submit samples. Pays 50% author's percentage on columns. Additional payment for photos accepted with ms. Currently syndicates Indoor Gardening, by Jane Adler; Looking Great, by Gloria Lintermans and Strong Style, by Hope Strong; On Marriage and Divorce, by Dr. Melvyn A. Berke.
Tips: "Please aim for a topic that is fresh. Newspapers seem to want short text pieces, 400-800 words. Please include SASE. We like to know a little about author's or cartoonists background. We prefer people who have already been published. Plese send material to Eve Green."

Other Syndicates

The following syndicates do not have listings in this edition of *Writer's Market*. The majority did not respond to our request to update their listings or return a questionnaire for a new listing. If a reason was given for their exclusion, we have included it in parentheses after the listing name.

Continuum Broadcasting Network/Continuum News Features, Inc.
Editors Press Service
Fiction Network (out of business)

Hyde Park Media
Minority Features Syndicate
Pacheco Automotive News Service
San Francisco Style International

The Spelman Syndicate, Inc.
United Cartoonist Syndicate (charges fee to evaluate submissions)
Words By Wire

Greeting Card Publishers

In our fast-paced society, greeting cards have become the new communication method for people too busy to write letters. According to the Greeting Card Association, we buy an average of 33 cards each year per person, totaling 7.3 billion cards and sales of $4.6 billion. The market is highly competitive, and many cards are written by in-house staff, but it's still a good market for quality freelance work.

To submit quality work, it's important to keep up with trends and note style differences between lines of cards. Greeting card companies, always trying to provide consumers with just the right sentiments, have launched many specialized lines. This year cards for African-Americans, for Jewish consumers with Hebrew text and for Hispanics with Spanish text have been popular specialities. In addition, new lines have been launched for the "mature" market, for parents and for businesspeople sending cards to fellow workers. While birthday and "get well" cards will always command their share of the market, non-occasion cards are the fastest-growing segment of the industry.

Keeping aware of these trends requires careful study of the market. A visit to your local card shop is a good first step. Take a look at the card racks, talk to the clerk and watch to see who buys what. Some card companies will provide a market list or catalog of their card lines for a self-addressed, stamped envelope or a small fee. Industry magazines such as *Greetings* also help to keep you informed of changes and happenings within the field.

Although you may spot several new growth areas or trends each year, some factors have remained constant and are important to keep in mind. Women continue to buy the majority of greeting cards. And the three basic card categories—traditional, studio (or contemporary) and alternative—have remained the same for a number of years.

Alternative cards continue to increase in popularity. This category includes cards with offbeat messages or those that celebrate nontraditional events such as a diet, salary raise, divorce or new job. Many smaller card companies have built their businesses on alternative card lines, and these are often good outlets for more adventurous or less conventional card ideas. Sparked by the success of these firms, larger firms also have developed their own lines of nontraditional cards.

For traditional or nontraditional cards, most editorial directors are looking for personal, expressive verse instead of rhymed sentiments. A conversational tone is best—even for traditional cards. In fact many editors say they are looking for fresh expressions of traditional sentiments.

Illustration has always been an important component of greeting cards, but in recent years editors say they've been looking for an even closer relationship between artwork and copy. It is important to think visually—to think of the card as an entire product—even if you are not artistically talented. Although most editors do not want to see artwork unless it is professional, they do appreciate suggestions from writers who have visualized a card as a whole unit. If your verse depends on an illustration to make its point or if you have an idea for a unique card shape or foldout, include a dummy card with your writing samples.

Payment for greeting card verse varies, but most firms pay on a per card or per idea basis; a handful pay small royalties. Some card companies prefer to test a card first and will pay a small fee for a test card idea.

Greeting card companies will also buy ideas for gift products and may plan to use card material for a number of subsequent items. Licensing—the sale of rights to a particular character for a variety of products from mugs to T-shirts—is a growing part of the greetings industry. Because of this, however, note that most card companies buy all rights. Many companies also require writers to provide a release form, guaranteeing the material submitted is original and has not been sold elsewhere. Before signing a release form or a contract to sell all rights, be sure you understand the terms.

Submission requirements may vary slightly from company to company, so send a SASE for writer's guidelines if they are available. To submit conventional card material, type or neatly print your verses or ideas on 8½×11, 4×6 or 3×5 slips of paper or index cards. The usual submission includes from five to 15 cards and an accompanying cover letter. Be sure to include your name and address on the back of each card as well as on the cover letter. For studio cards, or cards with pop-outs or attachments also send a mechanical dummy card. For more help on card submissions see the samples in *The Writer's Digest Guide to Manuscript Formats* (Writer's Digest Books).

Because you will be sending out many samples, you may want to label each sample. Establish a master card for each verse or idea and record where and when each was sent and whether it was rejected or purchased. Keep all cards sent to one company in a batch and give each batch a number. Write this number on the back of your return SASE to help you match up your verses as they are returned.

For information on greeting card companies not included in *Writer's Market*, see Other Greeting Card Publishers at the end of this section.

AMBERLEY GREETING CARD CO., 11510 Goldcoast Dr., Cincinnati OH 45249-1695. (513)489-2775. Editor: Ned Stern. Estab. 1966. 90% freelance written. Bought 250 freelance ideas/samples last year; receives an estimated 25,000 submissions annually. Reports in 1 month. Material copyrighted. Buys all rights. **Pays on acceptance.** Writer's guidelines for #10 SASE. Market list is regularly revised.
Needs: Humorous, informal and studio. No seasonal material or poetry. Prefers unrhymed verses/ideas. Humorous cards sell best. Pays $40/card idea.
Tips: "Amberley publishes specialty lines and humorous studio greeting cards. We accept freelance ideas, including risque and nonrisque. Make it short and to the point. Include SASE (with correct postage) for return of rejects."

‡AMCAL, 1050 Shary Ct., Concord CA 94549. (415)689-9930. Product Development Manager: Jennifer DeCristoforo. 80% of material is freelance written. Buys 6 freelance ideas/samples per year; receives 60 submissions annually. Reports in 3 weeks. Rights negotiable. **Pays on acceptance.** Writer's guidelines/market list for SASE.
Needs: Conventional, informal, sensitivity and soft line. Prefers generally unrhymed. Submit 12 ideas/batch.
Other Product Lines: Calendars and gift books.
Tips: Our target audience is female, ages 20-50. Direct, thoughtful sentiments sell the best. Generally short.

AMERICAN GREETINGS, 10500 American Rd., Cleveland OH 44144. (216)252-7300. Contact: Director-Creative Recruitment. No unsolicited material. "We like to receive a letter of inquiry describing education or experience, or a resume first. We will then screen those applicants and request samples from those that interest us."

‡CAROLYN BEAN PUBLISHING, LTD., 2230 W. Winton Ave., Hayward CA 94545. (415)957-9574. Creative Director: Andrea Axelrod. Estab. 1979. 75% freelance written. Bought 250 freelance ideas/samples last year; receives an estimated 5,000 submissions annually. Submit seasonal/holiday material 18 months in advance. Buys exclusive card rights; negotiates others. **Pays on acceptance.** Reports in 2 months. Writer's guidelines for SAE and 2 first class stamps.
Needs: "Our greatest need is ideas for the cards people send most: birthday and friendship. We are always looking for a new approach—if we like it, we'll try it. We are not tied down to one look, or tone. Alternative cards should be laugh-out-loud funny—not cute. We also do a complete captioned line of traditional cards for all occasions. Copy for traditional cards should be in rhymed verse that scans easily—it should read as you would say it—don't break a line in a strange place just to make it rhyme." Pays $25 but terms are negotiable.

BLUE MOUNTAIN ARTS, INC., Dept. WM, Box 1007, Boulder CO 80306. Contact: Editorial Staff. Buys 50-75 items/year. Reports in 2 months. Pays on publication.

Needs: "Primarily need sensitive and sensible writings about love, friendships, families, philosophies, etc.—written with originality and universal appeal." Also poems and writings for specific holidays (Christmas, Valentine's Day, etc.), and special occasions, such as birthdays, get well, and sympathy. Seasonal writings should be submitted at least 4 months prior to the actual holiday. For worldwide, exclusive rights we pay $200 per poem; for one-time use in anthology, we pay $25.

Other Product Lines: Calendars, gift books and greeting books. Payment varies.

Tips: "Get a feel for the Blue Mountain Arts line prior to submitting material. Our needs differ from other card publishers; we do not use rhymed verse, preferring instead a more honest, person-to-person style. Have a specific person or personal experience in mind as you write. We use unrhymed, sensitive poetry and prose on the deep significance and meaning of life and relationships. A very limited amount of freelance material is selected each year, either for publication on a notecard or in a gift anthology, and the selection prospects are highly competitive. But new material is always welcome and each manuscript is given serious consideration."

BRILLIANT ENTERPRISES, 117 W. Valerio St., Santa Barbara CA 93101. Contact: Editorial Dept. Buys all rights. Submit words and art in black on 3½ × 3⅓ horizontal, thin white paper in batches of no more than 15. Reports "usually in 2 weeks." Catalog and sample set for $2.

Needs: Postcards. Messages should be "of a highly original nature, emphasizing subtlety, simplicity, insight, wit, profundity, beauty and felicity of expression. Accompanying art should be in the nature of oblique commentary or decoration rather than direct illustration. Messages should be of universal appeal, capable of being appreciated by all types of people and of being easily translated into other languages. Because our line of cards is highly unconventional, it is essential that freelancers study it before submitting. No topical references, subjects limited to American culture or puns." Limit of 17 words/card. Pays $50 for "complete ready-to-print word and picture design."

THE CALLIGRAPHY COLLECTION, 2604 NW 74th Place, Gainesville FL 32606. (904)378-0748. Editor: Katy Fischer. Reports in 6 months. Buys all rights. Pays on publication.

Needs: "Ours is a line of framed prints of watercolors with calligraphy." Conventional, humorous, informal, inspirational, sensitivity and soft line. Prefers unrhymed verse, but will consider rhymed. Submit 3 ideas/batch. Pays $50-100/framed print idea.

Other Product Lines: Gift books, greeting books and plaques.

Tips: Sayings for friendship are difficult to get. Bestsellers are humorous, sentimental and inspirational cards—such as wedding sayings, thank you, all occasions, and birthday plaques. "Our audience is women 20 to 50 years of age. Write something they would like to give or receive as a lasting gift."

‡CHIPPENDALES, 929 Pico Blvd., Santa Monica CA 90405. (213)396-4045. FAX: (213)396-9912. Editor: Steve Banerjee. Estab. 1980. 50% of material is freelance written. Submit seasonal/holiday material 1 year in advance. Reports in 1 month. Pays on publication. Free writer's guidelines/market list. Market list is regularly revised.

Needs: Humorous, informal, invitations, sensitivity and soft line. Submit 12 ideas/batch.

Tips: Our target audience requires cards for birthdays, ages 14-40.

COMSTOCK CARDS, Suite 18, 600 S. Rock, Reno NV 89502. FAX: (702)333-9406. Owner: Patti P.Wolf. Art Director: David Delacroix. Estab. 1986. 25% freelance written. Buys 50 freelance ideas/samples per year; receives 500 submissions annually. Submit seasonal/holiday material 1 year in advance. Reports in 5 weeks. Buys all rights. **Pays on acceptance.** Free writer's guidelines/market list. Market list issued one time only.

Needs: Humorous, informal, invitations and "puns, put-downs, put-ons, outrageous humor aimed at a sophisticated, adult female audience. No conventional, soft line or sensitivity hearts and flowers, etc." Prefers to receive 25 cards/batch. Pays $50-75/card idea.

Other Product Lines: Notepads.

Tips: "Always keep holiday occasions in mind and personal me-to-you expressions that relate to today's occurrences. Ideas must be simple and concisely delivered. A combination of strong image and strong gag line make a successful greeting card. Consumers relate to themes of work, sex and friendship combined with current social, political and economic issues."

‡CONTEMPORARY DESIGNS, 213 Main St., Gilbert IA 5C_95. (515)232-5188. Editor: S. Abelson. Estab. 1977. 25% of material is freelance written. Submit seasonal/holiday material 1 year in advance. Reports in 1 month. Buys all rights. **Pays on acceptance.**

Needs: Invitations and memo pads. Prefers unrhymed verse.

Other Product Lines: Activity books, gift books, mugs, totes aprons and pillow cases.

CONTENOVA GIFTS, P.O. Box 69130, Postal Station K, Vancouver, British Columbia V5K 4W4 Canada. (604)253-4444. FAX: (604)253-4014. Editor: Jeff Sinclair. 100% freelance written. Bought over 100 freelance ideas last year; receives an estimated 15,000 submissions annually. Submit ideas on 3 × 5 cards or small mock-ups in batches of 10-15. Buys world rights. **Pays on acceptance.** Current needs list for SAE and IRC.

Needs: Humorous and studio. Both risqué and nonrisqué. "Short gags with good punch work best." Birthday, belated birthday, get well, anniversary, thank you, congratulations, miss you, new job, etc. Seasonal ideas needed for Christmas, Valentine's Day, Mother's Day, Father's Day. Pays $50.

Tips: "Not interested in play-on-words themes. We're leaning toward more 'cute risqué' and no longer using drinking themes. Put together your best ideas and submit them. One great idea sent is much better than 20 poor ideas filling an envelope. We are always searching for new writers who can produce quality work. You need not be previously published. Our audience is 18-65—the full spectrum of studio card readers. We do *not* use poetry."

CREATE-A-CRAFT, P.O. Box 330008, Fort Worth TX 76163-0008. (817)292-1855. Editor: Mitchell Lee. Estab. 1967. 5% freelance written. Buys 2 freelance ideas/samples per year; receives 300 submissions annually. Submit seasonal/holiday material 1 year in advance. Submissions not returned even if accompanied by SASE—"not enough staff to take time to package up returns." Buys all rights. Sample greeting cards are available for $2.50 and a #10 SASE.

Needs: Announcements, conventional, humorous, juvenile and studio. "Payment depends upon the assignment, amount of work involved, and production costs involved in project."

Tips: No unsolicited material. "Send letter of inquiry describing education, experience, or resume with one sample first. We will screen applicants and request samples from those who interest us."

ELDERCARDS, INC., Box 202, Piermont NY 10968. (914)359-7137. Editor: Steve Epstein and Lenore Berkowitz. 10% of material is freelance written. Receives 20 submissions annually. Submit seasonal/holiday material 3 months in advance. Reports in 1 month. Pays royalties.

Needs: Announcements, conventional, humorous, informal, invitations, sensitivity and studio. Prefers unrhymed verse. Submit 24 ideas/batch. Pays $10-200.

Other Product Lines: Calendars ($10-200), post cards ($10-200) and posters ($10-200).

Tips: "Market is contemporary, upbeat, humorous, for 20-50 years old. Writers should be mindful of babies and the baby boom, singles (young and old) but mostly birthdays and anniversaries."

‡**FRAVESSI-LAMONT, INC.,** 11 Edison Place, Springfield NJ 07081. (201)564-7700. Editor: Ruth Golding. 45% of material bought is freelance written. Buys 6 freelance ideas/samples annually; receives 20 submissions annually. Submit seasonal/holiday material 3 months in advance. Reports in 1 week. Buys all rights. **Pays on acceptance.** Free writer's guidelines. Market list available to writers on mailing list basis.

Needs: Conventional, humorous, informal. Submit 10 cards in a batch.

FREEDOM GREETING CARD CO., P.O. Box 715, Bristol PA 19007. (215)945-3300. FAX: (215)547-0248. Editor: J. Levitt. Estab. 1969. 90% freelance written. Submit seasonal/holiday material 1 year in advance. Reports in 2 weeks. **Pays on acceptance.** Free writer's guidelines/market list. Market list available to writer on mailing list basis.

Needs: Announcements, conventional, humorous, inspirational, invitations, juvenile and sensitivity. Payment varies.

Tips: "General and friendly cards sell best. Freedom is looking for a sensitive verse that conveys the special message between family members and friends. We have found that it is becoming more and more difficult to find this type of message in the greeting card stores and we are beginning to target these areas with our prose."

GALLANT GREETINGS, 2654 W. Medill, Chicago IL 60647. Editorial Coordinator: Carolyn McDilda. FAX: (312)489-1860. 90% of material bought is freelance written. Bought 500 freelance ideas/samples last year. Reports in 1 month. Buys world greeting card rights. Pays 60-90 days after acceptance. Writer's guidelines for SASE.

Needs: Announcements, conventional, humorous, informal, inspirational, invitations, juvenile, studio. Submit 20 cards in one batch.

Tips: "Greeting cards should and do move with the times, and sometimes writers don't. Keep aware of what is going on around you."

HALLMARK CARDS, INC., Box 419580, 2501 McGee, Mail Drop 276, Kansas City MO 64141. Contact: Carol King with letter of inquiry only; no sample. Reports in 2 months. Request guidelines if not on current Hallmark freelance roster; include SASE.

Needs: Humorous, studio cards, and conversational prose.

Tips: "Purchasing writing for everyday and seasonal greeting cards. Because Hallmark has an experienced and prolific writing staff, freelance writers must show a high degree of skill and originality to interest editors who are used to reading the very best."

INDUSTRIAL WHIMSY CO., P.O. Box 1330, Cedar Ridge CA 95924. (916)272-5062. Editor: J. Thom. Helsom. Estab. 1988. 75% of material is freelance written. Buys 50 plus freelance ideas/samples per year; receives 1,000 plus submissions monthly. Reports in 3 months. Buys all rights. **Pays on acceptance.** Writer's guidelines for #10 SASE.
Needs: Humorous, informal, Grafitti-style sayings—intellectual or otherwise—unrhymed. Prefers unrhymed verse. Submit 1-10 card ideas/batch.
Other Product Line: Bumper stickers ($10-50), calendars ($10-50), plaques ($10-50), post cards ($10-50) and posters ($10-50).

INNOVISIONS, INC., 445 W. Erie St., #B3, Chicago IL 60610. (312)642-4871. Editor: Jay Blumenfeld. Estab. 1980. 100% of material freelance written. Buys 50 freelance ideas/samples per year; receives 400 submissions annually. Submit seasonal/holiday material 1 year in advance. Reports in 3 weeks. Buys all rights. Pays within 30 days of publication. Market list issued one time only.
Needs: Humorous. Prefers unrhymed verse. Submit any amount/batch.
Tips: Looks for "off-the-wall humor and novelty cards (small 'joke' items that are the punch line)."

KALAN, INC., 97 S. Union Ave., Lansdowne PA 19050. (215)623-1900. Contact: Editor. 80% freelance written. Buys 150 freelance ideas/samples per year; receives 1,000 annually. Submit seasonal/holiday material 10 months in advance. Reports in 1 month. Buys all rights. **Pays on acceptance.** Writer's guidelines for #10 SASE. Foreign submissions must include at least 2 IRC's. Submit ideas on 3×5 cards or small mock-ups. If artwork is necessary for the understanding of the gag, it may be described briefly for our art department.
Needs: Risque and non-risque knock-'em-dead funny messages for birthday, friendship, love, Christmas and Valentine's Day greeting cards. Our x-rated line uses humorous gags with the artwork usually completing the gag. The x-rated line is beyond risqué—very daring! For our key rings and buttons, we seek funny non-risque and risque one-liners about school dating, money, life, sex, etc. Payment is $75/purchased idea. "Put Attn: Editor on submissions envelope."
Other Product Lines: Key rings and buttons. Payment for new product ideas is negotiable.
Tips: "Send for guidelines and samples before submitting. Write for a specific occasion: birthday, celebrating love, good-bye, Christmas, etc. Once you've decided on an occasion, write with a specific person in mind— your best friend, mother, coworker, etc. This tends to produce specific, funny copy able to be sent to many different types of people. The editor is waiting to be impressed by your neatness and creativity."

‡KNOCKOUTS PUBLISHING, INC., Dept. WM, 9030 SW 125th Ave., #E-202, Miami FL 33186. Contact: Sharon Shayne. 75% freelance written. Reports in 1 month. Buys all rights. Pays $60/idea. **Pays on acceptance.**
Needs: Humorous insights and observations about life and the world we live in. Ideas can be sarcastic, irreverent, off-beat, and suggestive (must be in good taste) or warm and cute. Interested in cards for all occasions, mostly birthdays. Non-occasion cards intended to make a lover or friend laugh/smile are heavily needed. Seeking holiday cards also, primarily for Christmas/New Year, Valentines Day, Easter, Mother's and Father's Day. Submit 1 year ahead of holidays. Also, interested in humor for Black, Latin and seniors markets.
Other Product Lines: Stationery, note pads and other paper products. Open to new product ideas.
Tips: We like to create fun visuals to tie in with the message. A concept of a visual to go along with the message is helpful, but not essential.

MAINE LINE CO., P.O. Box 947, Rockland ME 04841. (207)594-9418. Editor: Perri Ardman. Estab. 1979. 95% freelance written. Buys 200-400 freelance ideas/samples per year. Receives approximately 2,500 submissions/year. Submit photocopies (1 idea per page) or index cards. Please send SASE for return of samples. Reports in 2 months. Material copyrighted. Buys greeting card rights. **Pays on acceptance.** Writer's guidelines for #10 SAE and 2 first class stamps. Market list is regularly revised.
Needs: "We use non-humorous, as well as humorous material. We are expanding into 'sensitive language,' and 'inspirational' greeting cards and 'light, cute' greeting cards. Still, we do not want clichés or corny sap. Messages, whether 'light' or 'sensitive', must be real and reflect attitudes and feelings of real people in today's world. Unrhymed material is preferred."
Other Product Lines: Wacky, outrageous humor needed for buttons, mugs, key chains, magnets, tee-shirts, plaques and other novelty items. "We prefer copy that stands on its own humor rather than relies on four-letter words or grossly suggestive material. Material that is *mildly* suggestive is OK. 'Inspirational' material for the above items also requested."

For explanation of symbols, see the Key to Symbols and Abbreviations on Page 5. For unfamiliar words, see the Glossary.

Tips: "Please send for our guidelines. Copy should speak to universal truths that most people will recognize. Writers need not submit any visuals with copy but may suggest visuals. Lack of drawing ability does not decrease chances of having your work accepted; however, we also seek people who can both write and illustrate. Writers who are also illustrators or graphic artists are invited to send samples or tearsheets. Be sure to send an SASE with appropriate postage for return of your material if you want to get it back."

MERLYN GRAPHICS, P.O. Box 9087, Canoga Park CA 91309. (818)349-2775. Editor: Bettie Galling. Estab. 1987. 50% of material bought is freelance written. Bought 50 freelance ideas last year; receives 2,000 submissions annually. Submit seasonal/holiday material 1 year in advance. Reports in 1 month. Buys all rights. Pays on publication. Writer's guidelines for #10 SASE.
Needs: "Humorous everyday cards: birthday, friendship, get well, miss you. The only holiday/occasion cards we are currently publishing are Christmas and Valentine's. We want *very* funny, clever, witty, slightly twisted, belly-busting lines that lend themselves to a very strong visual. We do not want sentimental, 'hearts & flowers,' or cute traditional material. Neither do we want vulgar or 'x-rated' material. Go for clever 'double entendre' and unpredictable punch lines."
Tips: "Please send for and really study our guidelines. Suggested visuals are OK but not required. Only once have we used a writer's suggested visual. However, you must think visually! Remember that you are not writing for 'stand-up comedy.' You should also ask yourself if the card is 'sendable.' Who would you send it to and why? Always remember that most cards (93%) are purchased by women! Our cards are 100% photographic, and almost exclusively photographed in a studio setting. They are 5×7, with the photo on the front and the punchline on the inside, with little or no set-up on the front. Stay away from outlandish 'flying dinosaurs' type concepts. We are not currently accepting outside photography or artwork. We do not guarantee the return of your submissions, so please keep copies. We publish two or three times annually in groups of 36 designs. As a result, when we find material we want to use we may hold it for as long as six months before publishing it. You may write or submit material as often as you wish, but please, no phone calls or certified mail. We provide samples of the finished cards at no charge to the writers, and we give a writer's credit line on the back of the card."

‡MINNEAPOLIS GIFT MART, 10301 Bren Rd. W., Minnetonka MN 55343. (612)932-7200. FAX: (612)932-0847. Editor: Peggy Bradford. Estab. 1953. 15% freelance written. Buys 10 freelance ideas/samples per year; receives 12 submissions annually. Submit seasonal/holiday material 10 months in advance. Reports in 2 months. Material not copyrighted. Pays on publication. Free writer's guidelines/market list. Market list is regularly revised.
Tips: "We purchase magazine articles on trends, color, etc. as it relates to gifts and decorative accessories."

‡NEW BOUNDARY DESIGNS, INC., 1453 Park Rd., Chanhassen MN 55317. (612)474-0924. FAX: (612)474-9525. Estab. 1979. 5% freelance written. Buys 9 freelance ideas/samples per year; receives 100 submissions annually. Submit seasonal/holiday material 1 year in advance. Reports in 2 weeks. Pays on publication.
Needs: Inspirational, juvenile and sensitivity. Prefers unrhymed verse.

NOBLEWORKS, 113 Clinton St., Hoboken NJ 07030. (800)346-6253. Editor: Christopher Noble. Estab. 1982. 35% freelance written. Buys about 25 submissions/year; received about 10,000 last year. Submit seasonal/holiday material 1 year in advance for Christmas; 8-9 months for other holidays. Reports in 3 weeks. Buys greeting card rights only. Pays initial fee no later than publication and a royalty up to a specified amount. Guidelines for SASE. Market list is regularly updated.
Needs: Humorous. Prefers to receive 12-24 card ideas/batch.
Tips: "Through many years of trial and error, we have found that very humorous, silly, irreverent and outrageously humorous cards are what we sell. Our cards are aimed at a sophisticated urban market with humor that is unexpected and off-center (though not sleazy and sexual). Our humor is modern, on the edge and takes risks! A card must be instantly understandable. Though an idea may be clever, it will never fly if the reader must complete the thought in order to get at the gist of the joke. Satire, political and social, is very popular if applied correctly."

OATMEAL STUDIOS, P.O. Box 138W3, Rochester VT 05767. (802)767-3171. Creative Director: Helene Lehrer. Estab. 1979. 85% freelance written. Buys 200-300 greeting card lines/year. **Pays on acceptance.** Reports in 2 weeks. Current market list for self-addressed, #10 SASE.
Needs: Birthday, friendship, anniversary, get well cards, etc. Also Christmas, Chanukah, Mother's Day, Father's Day, Easter, Valentine's Day, etc. Will review concepts. Humorous material (clever and *very* funny) year-round. "Humor, conversational in tone and format, sells best for us." Prefers unrhymed contemporary humor. Current pay schedule available with guidelines.
Other Product Lines: Notepads.
Tips: "The greeting card market has become more competitive with a greater need for creative and original ideas. We are looking for writers who can communicate situations, thoughts, and relationships in a funny way and apply them to a birthday, get well, etc., greeting and we are willing to work with them in targeting

our style. We will be looking for material that says something funny about life in a new way. We tend to see a lot of the same ideas over and over. It's harder to find something different and fresh. Reading card racks is a good way for a writer to stay one step ahead."

OUTREACH PUBLICATIONS, P.O. Box 1010, Siloam Springs AR 72761. (501)524-9381. Editor: Joan Aycock. Estab. 1971. Submit seasonal/holiday material 1 year in advance. Reports in 2 months. **Pays on acceptance.** Guidelines for #10 SASE.
Needs: Calendars, announcements, invitations, all major seasonal and special days, all major everyday cards—birthday, anniversary, get well, friendship, etc. Material must be usable for the Christian market.
Tips: "Study our line, DaySpring Greeting Cards, before submitting. We are looking for sentiments with relational, inspirational messages that minister love and encouragement to the receiver." Prefer unrhymed verse.

PARAMOUNT CARDS INC., 400 Pine St., Pawtucket RI 0286. (401)726-0800. Managing Editor: Elizabeth Gordon. Over 10% of material is freelance written. Buys 300 greeting card ideas/samples per year. Submit seasonal/material at least 6 months in advance. Reports in 1 month. Buys all rights. **Pays on acceptance.** Writer's guidelines for SASE.
Needs: All types of conventional verses. Fresh, inventive humorous verses, especially family birthday cards. Would also like to see lmore conversational prose, especially in family titles such as Mother, Father, Sister, Husband, Wife, etc. Submit in batches of 10-15.

‡POPSHOTS, INC., 472 Riverside Ave., Westport CT 06880. Estab. 1978. 80% freelance written. Buys 20 freelance ideas/samples per year; receives 100 submissions annually. Submit seasonal/holiday material 1 year in advance. Reports in 2 months. Buys all rights. Pays on publication.
Needs: Humorous. Prefers unrhymed verse. Submit 6 ideas/batch.
Tips: "Birthday cards sell best for us. Our target audience is made up of women ages 13-35."

RED FARM STUDIO, 334 Pleasant St., Box 347, Pawtucket RI 02862. (401)728-9300. Art Director: Steven D. Scott. Buys 50 ideas/samples per year. Reports in 2 weeks. Buys all rights. **Pays on acceptance.** Market list for #10 SASE.
Needs: Conventional, inspirational, sensitivity and soft line cards. "We cannot use risqué or insult humor." Submit no more than 10 ideas/samples per batch. Pays $3 per line of copy.
Tips: "Write verses that are direct and honest. Flowery sentiments are not in fashion right now. It is important to show caring and sensitivity, however. Our audience is middle to upper middle class adults of all ages."

ROCKSHOTS, INC., 632 Broadway, New York NY 10012. (212)420-1400. Editor: Bob Vesce. Estab. 1979. "We buy 75 greeting card verse (or gag) lines annually." Submit seasonal/holiday material 1 year in advance. Reports in 2 months. Buys rights for greeting-card use. Writer's guidelines for SASE.
Needs: Humorous ("should be off-the-wall, as outrageous as possible, preferably for sophisticated buyer"); soft line; combination of sexy and humorous come-on type greeting ("sentimental is not our style"); and insult cards ("looking for cute insults"). No sentimental or conventional material. "Card gag can adopt a sentimental style, then take an ironic twist and end on an off-beat note." Submit no more than 10 card ideas/samples per batch. Send to attention: Submissions. Pays $50 per gagline. Prefers gag lines on 8×11 paper with name, address, and phone and social security numbers in right corner, or individually on 3×5 cards.
Tips: "Think of a concept that would normally be too outrageous to use, give it a cute and clever wording to make it drop-dead funny and you will have commercialized a non-commercial message. It's always good to mix sex and humor. Our emphasis is definitely on the erotic. Hard-core eroticism is difficult for the general public to handle on greeting cards. The trend is toward 'light' sexy humor, even cute sexy humor. 'Cute' has always sold cards, and it's a good word to think of even with the most sophisticated, crazy ideas. 80% of our audience is female. Remember that your gag line will be illustrated by a photographer. So try to think visually. If no visual is needed, the gag line *can* stand alone, but we generally prefer some visual representation. It is a very good idea to preview our cards at your local store if this is possible to give you a feeling of our style."

‡SANGAMON, INC., Box 410, Taylorville IL 62568. (217)824-2261. Editor: Michelle Merker. Estab. 1931. 90% freelance written. Submit seasonal/holiday material 18 months in advance. Reports in 6 weeks. Buys all rights. **Pays on acceptance.** Writer's guidelines or market list for SASE. Market list is regularly revised.
Needs: Conventional, humorous, inspirational, juvenile, sensitivity and studio. We offer a balance of many styles. Submit 20 ideas maximum/batch.
Other Product Lines: Calendars and promotions.
Tips: Cute, inspirational and conventional greeting cards sell best.

MARCEL SCHURMAN CO., INC., 2500 North Watney Way, Fairfield CA 94533. Editor: Marshall Berman. 25% freelance written. Buys 50 freelance ideas/samples per year; receives 500 submissions per year. Reports in 1 month. **Pays on acceptance.** Writer's guidelines for #10 SASE.

Needs: Conventional, light humor, informal, invitations, juvenile, sensitivity, soft religious and inspirational; seasonal and everyday categories. Prefers unrhymed verse, but on juvenile cards rhyme is OK. Submit 5-20 cards in one batch.
Tips: "Historically, our nostalgic and art museum cards sell best. However, we are moving towards more contemporary cards. Target market: upscale, professional, well-educated; average age 40; more female."

SCOTT CARDS INC., P.O. Box 906, Newbury Park CA 91319. Editor: Larry Templeman. Estab. 1985. 95% of material is freelance written. Buys 75 freelance ideas/samples per year. Not printing seasonal/holiday cards at present. Reports in 3 months. **Pays on acceptance.** Writer's guidelines/brochure for SAE and 2 first class stamps.
Needs: Conventional, humorous and sensitivity.
Tips: "New ways to say 'I love you' always sell if they aren't corny or too obvious. Humor helps, especially if there is a twist. We are looking for non-traditional sentiments that are sensitive, timely and sophisticated. Our cards have a distinct flavor, so before submitting your work, write for our guidelines and sample brochure."

SILVER VISIONS, Box 49, Newton Highlands MA 02161. (617)244-9504. Editor: B. Kaufman. Submit seasonal/holiday material 9 months to 1 year in advance. Reports in 2 months. Pays on publication. Guidelines are available for SASE.
Needs: Humorous, humorous Jewish, contemporary occasion for photography line. Copy must work with a photograph. Send 10-16 card ideas/batch.

SUNRISE PUBLICATIONS, INC., P.O. Box 2699, Bloomington IN 47402. (812)336-9900. Contact: Editorial Coordinator. Estab. 1973. 75% freelance written. Bought 200 freelance ideas/samples last year; receives an estimated 2,000 submissions annually. Reports in 2 months. Acquires greeting card rights only. **Pays on acceptance.** Free writer's guidelines. Market list is regularly revised.
Needs: Conventional, humorous, informal. No "off-color humor or lengthy poetry." Prefers unrhymed verses/ ideas. "We like short one- or two-line captions, sincere or clever. Our customers prefer this to lengthy rhymed verse. Submit ideas for birthday, get well, friendship, wedding, baby congrats, sympathy, thinking of you, anniversary, belated birthday, thank yous, fun and love. We also have strong seasonal lines that use traditional, humorous and inspirational verses. These seasons include Christmas, Valentine's Day, Easter, Mother's Day, Father's Day, Graduation, Halloween and Thanksgiving." Payment varies.
Tips: "Think always of the sending situation and both the person buying the card and its intended recipient. Most card purchasers are aged between 18 and 45 years, and are female."

‡TRISAR, INC., 2231 Dupont, Anaheim CA 92806. (714)978-1433. FAX. (714)978-3788. Editor: Randy Harris. Estab. 1979. 10% freelance written. Buys 12 freelance ideas/samples per year. Submit seasonal/holiday material 9 months in advance. Reports in 1 month. **Pays on acceptance.**
Needs: Humorous, studio and age-related adult feelings about turning 40, 50, 60. Prefers unrhymed verse.
Other Product Lines: T-shirts and mugs.
Tips: "Our audience is over the hill: Birthdays for adults turning 30, 40, 50 etc. Thoughts on growing older but not wanting to grow up."

VAGABOND CREATIONS, INC., 2560 Lance Dr., Dayton OH 45409. (513)298-1124. Editor: George F. Stanley, Jr. 10% freelance written. Buys 10-15 ideas annually. Submit seasonal/holiday material 6 months in advance. Reports in 1 week. Buys all rights. Ideas sometimes copyrighted. **Pays on acceptance.** Writer's guidelines for #10 SASE. Market list issued one time only.
Needs: Cute, humorous greeting cards (illustrations and copy) often with animated animals or objects in people-situations with short, subtle tie-in message on inside page only. No poetry. Pays $15-25/card idea.

WARNER PRESS, INC., P.O. Box 2499, Anderson IN 46018. (317)644-7721. Product Editor: Cindy Maddox. 60% freelance written. Request guidelines for scheduled reading times. Reports in 5 weeks. Buys all rights. **Pays on acceptance.** Writer's guidelines for #10 SASE. Market list is regularly revised.
Needs: Conventional, informal, inspirational, juvenile, sensitivity and verses of all types with contemporary Christian message and focus. No off-color humor. "Cards with a definite Christian perspective that is subtly stressed, but not preachy, sell best for us." Uses both rhymed and unrhymed verses/ideas "but we're beginning to move away from 'sing-song' rhyme, toward contemporary prose." Pays $15-35 per card idea.
Other Product Lines: Pays $60-150 for calendars; $15-30 for plaques; $15-50 for posters; $20-50 for short meditations; negotiates payment for coloring books.
Tips: "Try to avoid use of 'I' or 'we' on card verses. We purchase for box assortments. An estimated 75% of purchases are Christian in focus; 25% good conventional verses. Our best sellers are short poems or sensitivity verses that are unique, meaningful and appropriate for many people. We do not purchase verses written specifically to one person (such as relative or very close friend) but rather for boxed assortments. *Please* request guidelines before submitting."

‡**WEST GRAPHICS**, 238 Capp St., San Francisco CA 94110. (415)621-4641. FAX: (415)621-8613. Editor: Carol West. Estab. 1980. 60% freelance written. Buys 200 freelance ideas/samples per year; receives 1,000 submissions annually. Reports in 6 weeks. Buys greeting card rights. Pays 30 days past publication. Writer's guidelines/market list for #10 SASE.
Needs: Humorous and studio. Prefers unrhymed verse. Submit 20-40 ideas/batch. Pays $60.
Other Product Lines: Gift books (open) and calendars.
Tips: "The majority of our audience are women in their 30's and 40's and respond to fresh ideas on the cutting edge."

WESTERN GREETING, INC., P.O. Box 81056, Las Vegas NV 89180. Editor: Barbara Jean Sullivan. Estab. 1986. 100% of material is freelance written. Buys 15 freelance ideas/samples per year. Reports in 1 month. Buys all rights. **Pays on acceptance.** Writer's guidelines/market list for #10 SASE.
Needs: Humorous, sensitivity, soft line, Western and Indian and Southwest themes. Considers rhymed and unrhymed verse for birthday, thank you, get well, friendship, anniversary, new baby, Christmas.
Tips: "Our cards are produced from Western and Southwest art. Subjects include the cowboy, mountain man, Indian, cowgirl, western stilllife and landscape. We furnish the art and ask for verse based on this art. We have found that unsolicited material does not fit our cards."

CAROL WILSON FINE ARTS, INC., P.O. Box 17394, Portland OR 97217. FAX: (503)287-2217. Editor: Gary Spector. Estab. 1983. 90% freelance written. Buys 100 freelance ideas/samples per year; receives thousands annually. Submit seasonal/holiday material 1 year in advance. Reports in 6 weeks. Buys negotiable rights. Whether payment is made on acceptance or publication varies, with type of agreement. Writer's guidelines/market list for #10 SASE.
Needs: Humorous and unrhymed. Pays $50-100 per card idea. "Royalties could be considered for a body of work."
Other Product Lines: Postcards.
Tips: "We are looking for laugh-out-loud, unusual and clever ideas for greeting cards. All occasions are needed but most of all birthday cards are needed. It's OK to be outrageous or risque. Cards should be 'personal'—ask yourself—is this a card that someone would buy for a specific person?"

WIZWORKS, P.O. Box 240, Masonville CO 80541-0240. Editor: Tom Cannon. Estab. 1988. 90% of material is freelance written. Submit seasonal/holiday material 6 months in advance. Reports in 2 months. Writer's guidelines/market list for $1 and SASE. Market list available to writer on mailing list basis.
Needs: Conventional, humorous, informal, inspirational, juvenile, sensitivity, soft line, studio, all types non-occasion and holidays, favor orientation to specific market segments rather than generalized. No preference for rhymed or unrhymed; however, no more than 4 lines in rhymed. Submit 10 ideas/batch. Pays royalty on retail sales.
Tips: "We sell to all types of extremely segmented audiences. We want verse ideas specific to age, gender, lifestyle, etc. Our cards are intended to be printed on the retail site by a computer controlled high resolution color printer. Consumers will preview cards on a color CRT before printing. This allows cards to be extremely specific."

Other Greeting Card Publishers

The following greeting card publishers do not have listings in this edition of *Writer's Market*. The majority did not respond to our request to update their listings or return a questionnaire for a new listing. If a reason was given for their exclusion, we have included it in parentheses after the listing name.

Argus Communications
Colortype
Earth Care Paper Inc.
Landmark General Corp. (no
   longer has card line)
Mirage Images, Inc.

Occasions Southwest Greetings
Paper Moon Graphics, Inc.
Paperpotamus Paper Products
   Inc. (asked to be deleted)
Pawprints
Plum Graphics Inc.

Renaissance Greeting Cards
   (asked to be deleted)
Sam Cards (not accepting free-
   lance submissions)
Snafu Designs
Wildwood Design Group

Services & Opportunities

_____ _Author's Agents_

Working with an agent can boost your writing career, but the process of finding an agent can be confusing and the relationship requires trust, good communication and businesslike manners from both sides. Whether you are new in the market or an established freelancer, it's a good idea to become acquainted with the variety of services agents offer, the fees or commissions they charge, and the way they deal with writers and publishers.

In general, agents are a combination of sales representatives and business managers. Agents keep abreast of trends in the industry; in touch with editors and buyers of subsidiary rights; they know where to sell marketable manuscripts and how to negotiate contracts; they help collect payments from publishers and keep accurate records of earnings.

Of course agents don't decide whether or not a manuscript should be published; that's still a job for editors. Agents can only tell you if they believe your manuscript is ready to be submitted to a publisher and where they believe it fits in the current market.

If you've read the Book Publishers section of _Writer's Market_, you know that the publishing industry has become increasingly competitive and cost-conscious. Like any other business, a publishing company that fails to make a profit will not survive. Few publishers can afford to hire a staff of editors or freelance readers to go through hundreds of unsolicited manuscripts; they simply receive too many unpublishable manuscripts for each one that is publishable. For that reason, more and more book publishers will only consider manuscripts submitted through an agent. They rely on agents to do the screening for them and submit only publishable material.

The greater demand for agented submissions has resulted in an increase in the number of literary agencies. In addition to New York-based agents, many agents have settled on the West Coast, primarily to work with film and TV producers. Now more new agencies are opening throughout the U.S., dispensing with the notion that long-distance selling could never be successful.

Commissions and fees

Literary agents have always charged a commission on the manuscripts they place with publishers or producers, in much the same way real estate agents charge a commission. The commission, usually 10-20%, is subtracted from the author's advance and royalty payments from the publisher. Most agents still charge 10%, but a 15% rate is not uncommon these days. Some agents charge established clients 10% and new clients 15%. A 20% rate is not unusual for foreign sales in which the agent deals with a second agent in the foreign country and both receive 10% commission. In any event, a commission arrangement means the writer doesn't pay the agent a commission until the manuscript has been sold. This arrangement provides the best deal for the writer, but it often means that commission agents will accept only referrals from their other clients and queries only from prospective clients. Few can afford to read complete manuscripts without charge.

Agents rarely charge writers for general office overhead like the cost of utilities or secretarial services. Instead, they sometimes ask their clients to pay for specific expenses related to selling that writer's manuscript: photocopying, long distance phone calls, messenger service, etc. They will usually keep a record of these charges and deduct it from the author's earnings; a few will ask the author to pay the costs separately.

Commissions and charges for specific office expenses are regarded as perfectly acceptable in the industry. Additional fees for reading or critiquing manuscripts are becoming more common, although not uniformly accepted. Some agencies charge a reading fee — especially to new writers — in which no comments on improving the manuscript are offered. This is rarely helpful to the writer, who may only receive a rejection without comment. Other agencies charge a criticism fee in which they may provide several pages of detailed suggestions. Because critiques vary widely, you may want to ask for an example to see if this service will be helpful to you. About one-third of the agencies provide some kind of editorial services, ranging from reading fees to writing support, so you'll want to find out early what you can expect with each agency.

Several firms that charge fees regard them as one-time payments; if the writer becomes a client, no more fees will be charged for future manuscripts. Some agencies also reimburse the writer for the original fee when the manuscript is sold.

Understanding fees

Agents' fees continue to be a hotly debated topic. Previous editions of *Writer's Market* sought to protect readers by listing agents who told us they charged only commissions. Since 1987 we have included both commission-only and commission- and fee-charging agents. Why include agents who charge fees? Types of fees vary and services are very difficult to judge. We at *Writer's Market* believe our job is to provide you with the most complete and up-to-date information to allow you to choose an agent. We can't give recommendations or make decisions for you, but we do want to help in your search.

Remember that payment of a reading or criticism fee almost never guarantees that the agency will represent you. You are never obligated to pay a fee or agree to a service just because an agent has expressed interest in your manuscript. Read the individual listings carefully. There is no way to generalize about fee-charging agencies. One of the determining factors you may want to use is a comparison of the agent's percentage of income from fees versus percentage from commission. If the agent makes a significant amount from editorial services, he probably does not feel pressure to make manuscript sales as much as a commission-only agent does.

Likewise, there is no standard when it comes to fees. Some agencies charge criticism fees of $25-75; others charge $200 or more. Reading fees, although less common than criticism fees, are usually less than $75. One fee may apply to a complete manuscript, while another is for an outline and sample chapters. Some agents require fees from unpublished writers only. A few agents charge a marketing, handling or processing fee to all clients. Several agents offer a consultation service, ranging from $15-200 per hour, to advise writers on book contracts they have received without the help of an agent. If you decide to pay a fee, be sure you know *exactly* what you'll receive in return.

How a literary agent works

Agents do many things to earn their commissions, and it's almost impossible to describe what an "average" agent does. Let's begin by considering what literary agents don't do.

An agent can't sell unsalable work or teach you how to write. An agent won't edit your manuscript although his agency may offer editorial support service; editing the manuscript will be an editor's job. An agent can't defend you in a court of law unless he is also an attorney. An agent won't act as your press agent, social secretary or travel agent; you'll have to hire someone else to handle those chores.

As far as what an agent can and will do, each agency is different in the services it offers, the clients it prefers, its contacts in the industry, and the style in which it conducts business. In general, an agent's tasks can be divided into those done before a sale, during a sale and after a sale.

Before the sale, an agent evaluates your manuscript and sometimes make suggestions about revisions. If the agent wants to represent you, you'll usually receive a contract or letter of agreement specifying the agent's commission, fees and the terms of the agreement. If you do not receive a contract, ask for one and review all documents carefully. When that's signed, the agent begins talking to editors and sending your manuscript out. Your agent can tell you about any marketing problems, give you a list of submissions and even send you copies of rejections if you really want them. The agent repeats this sequence until the manuscript sells, you withdraw it or your agreement expires. Some agents also are involved in book packaging or producing work; this activity is noted in individual listings. See the Book Packagers and Producers section introduction for more information.

During the sale the agent negotiates with the publisher for you, offering certain rights to the publisher and perhaps reserving other subsidiary rights for future sale. The agent examines the contract, negotiates clauses for your benefit and tries to get additional rights. Your agent can explain the contract to you and make recommendations, but the final decision is always yours.

After the sale, the agent maintains a separate bank account for you, collects money from the publisher, deducts the appropriate commission and sends you the remainder. The agent examines all royalty statements and requests corrections or an audit when necessary. The agent also checks the publisher's progress on the book and makes sure your copyright has been registered. Sometimes the agent resolves conflicts between a writer and an editor or publisher. If you have retained subsidiary rights to your book, the agent will continue working for additional sales of movie, book club, foreign or video rights, etc.

Do you need an agent?

Not everyone needs an agent. Some writers are perfectly capable of handling the placement of their manuscripts and enjoy being involved in all stages of selling, negotiating and checking production of their books. Other writers have no interest in, or talent for, the business side of writing and feel that their agents are invaluable.

Ask yourself the following questions when evaluating your need for an agent:
- Do you have the skills to handle an agent's usual tasks?
- Can you take care of marketing your book and analyzing your contract?
- Can you afford to pay an agent 10-20% of your royalties?
- Would you like working through a middleman on all aspects of your book's future?
- Will you have more time to write if you have an agent?
- Are you interested in approaching markets that won't accept unagented submissions?

Some book publishers, along with studios and independent producers, won't consider any unagented submissions. Book publishers usually adopt this policy if they have too many submissions to consider, and studios and producers usually return unsolicited material to protect themselves from charges of plagiarism. If you want to submit to these markets, you must work through an agent.

No matter how much you want or need an agent, you'll be wasting time and money if your writing isn't ready for an agent. Try to be objective about whether or not you have truly polished your work and studied the marketplace for your kind of writing. You should also talk to other writers who have agents and read all you can find about working with an agent. It may sound like a lot of work, but if you want an agent to take you seriously, you'll make every effort to obtain some published credits, place in a literary or journalistic contest, and always correspond with an agent in a professional manner.

Making contact

Only about 25% of agents look at unsolicited complete manuscripts. Some will consider queries only if you've been recommended by a client or an editor. But the majority will look at a query and possibly an outline and sample chapters from an unknown writer.

In addition to following the suggestions in each agent's listing, plan your query letter carefully. It should include a brief description of your manuscript, anticipated number of words, whether or not you've been published and your credentials (for nonfiction). It's also important to enclose a self-addressed, stamped envelope (SASE) with all correspondence and manuscripts sent to an agent.

If the agent asks to see more of your work, consider yourself lucky, but don't assume you now have an agent. Just as you need to find out more about the agent, the agent has to know more about you and your writing. Don't expect an immediate response to your query or manuscript. On the other hand, if you receive no response or a negative response to your query, don't be discouraged. Continue to contact other agents. It's fine to send simultaneous queries, but never send a manuscript to more than one agent at a time.

Judging an agent

A bad agent can be worse than no agent at all. We've already discussed the expectations agents have for writers. Now it's time for you to decide what your expectations are for an agent. When an agency indicates an interest in representing your work, don't just assume it's the right one for you. If you want to make a knowledgable decision, you'll need more information—and that means asking questions.

While the answers to many of these questions appear in an agency's individual listing, it's a good idea to ask them again. Policies change and reporting time, commission amounts and fees may vary.

- How soon do you report on queries? On manuscripts?
- Do you charge a reading or critique fee? If yes, how much? What kind of feedback will I receive? If the manuscript is accepted, will my fee be returned? Credited against my marketing expenses? Or is it a nonreturnable charge to cover reading/critiquing expenses?
- Do you charge any other fees?
- How many clients do you represent?
- Will you provide me with a list of recent sales, titles published or clients?
- May I contact any of your clients for referrals? [this is the most valuable information you can get, but some agents regard it as a breach of confidentiality.]
- Who will work with me and what kind of feedback can I expect—regular status reports, good news only, copies of informative letters from editors, etc.?
- Who will negotiate my contracts?
- Which subsidiary rights do you market directly? Which are marketed through sub-agents? Which are handled by the publisher?
- Do you offer any special services—tax/legal consultation, manuscript typing, book promotion or lecture tour coordination, etc.? Which cost extra? Which are covered by commission?
- Do you offer any editorial support? How much?
- Do you offer a written agreement? If yes, how long does it run? What kind of projects are covered? Will (or must) all of my writing be represented? What will your commission be on domestic, foreign and other rights? Which expenses am I responsible for? Are they deducted from earnings, billed directly, or paid by initial deposit? How can the agreement

be terminated? After it terminates, what happens to work already sold, current submissions, etc.?

If the agency doesn't offer a contract or written agreement of any kind, you should write a letter of your own that summarizes your understanding on all these issues. Ask the agent to return a signed copy to you. A few agents prefer informal verbal agreements. No matter how personal a relationship you have with an agent, it's still a business matter. If the agent refuses to sign a simple letter of understanding, you may want to reconsider your choice of agencies.

Additional resources

The search for an agent can be a frustrating and time-consuming task, especially if you don't know what you're looking for. You can learn more about agents by studying several books on the subject. Read *Literary Agents: How to Get and Work with the Right One for You*, by Michael Larsen (Writer's Digest Books) and *Literary Agents: A Writer's Guide*, by Debby Mayer (Poet's & Writer's, Inc., 201 W. 54th St., New York NY 10019). *Literary Agents of North America* (Author Aid/Research Associates International, 340 E. 52nd St., New York NY 10022) is a directory of agents indexed by name, geography, subjects and specialities, size and affiliates. Your library may have a copy of *Literary Market Place*, which includes names, addresses and specialties of agents.

Remember that agents are not required to have any special training or accreditation. Some are members of a number of professional organizations or writers' groups, depending on their special interests. Each of the following three agents' organizations requires its members to subscribe to a code of ethics and standard practices.
- ILAA – Independent Literary Agents Association, Inc., Suite 1205, 432 Park Ave. S., New York NY 10016. Founded in 1977, ILAA is a nationwide association of fulltime literary agents. An informative brochure, list of members and copy of the association's code of ethics are sent on request to writers who enclose #10 SAE with two first class stamps. ILAA does not provide information on specialties of individual members.
- SAR – Society of Author's Representatives, Inc., 10 S. Portland Ave., Brooklyn NY 11217. Founded in 1928, SAR is a voluntary association of New York agents. A brochure and membership list are available for SASE. Members are identified as specializing in literary or dramatic material.
- WGA – Writers Guild of America. Agents and producers in the TV, radio and motion picture industry can become members or signatories of WGA by signing the guild's basic agreement which outlines minimum standards for treatment of writers. If you live east of the Mississippi River, write to WGA East, 555 W. 57th St., New York NY 10019; west of the Mississippi, write WGA West, 8955 Beverly Blvd., Los Angeles CA 90048.

Before *Writer's Market* went to press, we checked affiliations with these agencies to be sure that agents who claimed membership were currently members. This information may change during the year as memberships lapse and others are approved. If membership in a professional organization is important to you, check with the organization to be sure the agent is currently a member.

Like *Writer's Market*, these organizations will not make recommendations of agents but will provide information to help you in your search.

We know that agents are becoming an even more important part of the publishing process as many large publishing houses stop considering unsolicited submissions. For this reason, and so we can provide you with better information, we'd like to hear about your experiences with agents. We'd like to know both the good and bad dealings you've had, from no responses to large contracts with subsidiary deals. We won't be able to acknowledge these letters, but we will keep them on file when considering agents' listings in future editions. Send your correspondence to *Writer's Market*, Agents Listings, 1507 Dana Ave., Cincinnati OH 45207.

See Other Author's Agents for agents not included in this section.

‡CAROLE ABEL LITERARY AGENCY, 160 W. 87th St., New York NY 10024. (212)724-1168. President: Carole Abel. Estab. 1978. Member of ILAA. Represents 45 clients. 25% of clients are new/unpublished authors. Prefers to work with published/established writers; works with a small number of new/unpublished authors. Specializes in contemporary women's novels, biographies, thrillers, health, nutrition, medical nonfiction (diet and exercise) and history.
Will Handle: Nonfiction books, novels. Currently handles 50% nonfiction books and 50% novels. Will read — at no charge — unsolicited queries, outlines and mss. Reports in 2 weeks on queries; 6 weeks on mss.
Terms: Agent receives 15% commission on domestic sales; 15% on dramatic sales; and 20% on foreign sales. Charges for phone, postage, bulk mailing, messenger and photocopying expenses. 100% of income derived from commission on ms sales.
Recent Sales: *Bel Air*, by Katherine Stone (Zebra); *Himmler Equation*, by Bill Kennedy (St. Martin's); and *The Story of Annie D.*, by Susan Chehak (Houghton Mifflin).

DOMINICK ABEL LITERARY AGENCY, INC., Suite 1B, 146 W. 82 St., New York NY 10024. (212)877-0710. President: Dominick Abel. Estab. 1975. Member of ILAA.
Will Handle: Will read — at no charge — unsolicited queries and outlines. Reports in 2 weeks on queries. "Enclose SASE."
Terms: Agent receives 10% commission on domestic sales; 15% on dramatic sales; and 20% on foreign sales.
Fees: Charges for overseas postage, phone and cable expenses.
Recent Sales: *Into the Darkness*, by Barbara Michaels (Simon & Schuster); *Burn Marks*, by Sara Paretsky (Delacorte); *Fade Out*, by Peter Bart (Morrow).

‡ACACIA HOUSE PUBLISHING SERVICES LTD., 51 Acacia Road, Toronto, Ontario M4S 2K6 Canada. (416)484-8356. Contact: Frances Hanna. Estab. 1985. Represents 30 clients. "I prefer that writers be previously published, with at least a few articles to their credit. Strongest consideration will be given to those with, say, three or more published books. However, I *would* take on an unpublished writer of outstanding talent." Works with a small number of new/unpublished authors. Specializes in adult: contemporary fiction — literary or commercial (no horror, occult, or science fiction); nonfiction: all categories but business/economics — in the trade, not textbook area; children's: a few picture books; young adult, mainly fiction.
Will Handle: Nonfiction books, novels and juvenile books. Currently handles 20% nonfiction books; 50% novels and 30% juvenile books. Will read — at no charge — unsolicited queries and outlines. Does not read unsolicited manuscripts. Reports in 3 weeks on queries.
Terms: Agent receives 15% commission on domestic sales; 15% on dramatic sales; and 30% on foreign sales.
Fees: Charges a reading fee on manuscripts over 300 pages (typed, double-spaced) in length; waives reading fee when representing the writer. 4% of income derived from reading fees. Charges $200/300 pages. "If a critique is wanted on a ms under 300 pages in length, then the charge is the same as the reading fee for a longer ms (which incorporates a critique)." 5% of income derived from criticism fees. Critique includes "two-to three-page overall evaluation which will contain any specific points that are thought important enough to detail. Marketing advice is not usually included, since most mss evaluated in this way are not considered to be publishable." Charges writers for photocopying; courier, postage; telephone/fax "if these are excessive."
Recent Sales: *Dear M. . . .*, by Jack Pollock (McClelland & Stewart & Bloomsbury — UK); *Parents' Guide to Daycare*, by Judy Rasminsky and Barbara Kaiser (Little, Brown — Canada); and *By Hate Possessed*, by Maurice Gagnon (Stoddart).

ACTON AND DYSTEL, INC., 928 Broadway, New York NY 10010. (212)473-1700. Contact: Edward Novak. Estab. 1975. Member of ILAA. Represents 150 clients. Works with a small number of new/unpublished authors. Specializes in politics, celebrities, sports, business fiction.
Will Handle: Nonfiction books and novels. Currently handles 60% nonfiction; 40% novels. Will read — at no charge — unsolicited queries and outlines sent with SASE. No unsolicited manuscripts. Reports in 3 weeks on queries.
Terms: Agent receives 15% commission on domestic sales; 15% on dramatic sales; and 19% on foreign sales. Charges for photocopy expenses. 100% of income derived from commission on ms sales.
Recent Sales: *Seconds*, by Lois Wyse (Crown); *China Boy*, by Guslee (NAL); and *Drive*, by Larry Bird and Bob Ryan (Doubleday).

‡AGENTS, INC. FOR MEDICAL AND MENTAL HEALTH PROFESSIONALS, Suite 142, 9400 E. Iliff, Denver CO 80231. (303)745-0775. Director: Sydney H. Harriet, Ph.D. Estab. 1987. Represents 6 clients. "Writer should have education, experience and experience in the medical and mental health professions. Helpful if writer is licensed, but not necessary. Prior book publication not necessary." Works with a small number of new/unpublished authors. Specializes in selling health, medicine, how-to, psychology, self-help, reference, sports medicine, sports psychology, mind-body healing, nutrition and social sciences. Nonfiction trade books and some fiction focused toward the health professions.

Will Handle: Magazine articles, nonfiction books, textbooks. Currently handles 15% magazine articles; 80% nonfiction books; 5% textbooks. Will read—at no charge—unsolicited queries and outlines. Reports in 2 weeks on queries.
Terms: Agent receives 15% commission on domestic sales; 20% or foreign sales.
Fees: "After contract with publisher is signed expenses are negotiated."
Recent Sales: *Not Getting Any Better, (When therapy doesn't work!)*, by Joseph Wolpe, M.D., Tom Giles, Psy, D. (Avery).

‡MAXWELL ALEY ASSOCIATES OF ASPEN, P.O. Box 5098, Aspen CO 81612. (303)925-6500. Managing Editor: William Howell. Estab. 1936. Member of SAR. Represents 15 clients. Prefers to work with published/established authors; works with a small number of new/unpublished authors. Specializes in nonfiction.
Will Handle: Nonfiction books, novels. Handles 95% nonfiction, 5% novels. Will read submissions at no charge, but may charge a criticism fee to unpublished authors or service charge for work performed after the initial reading. Reports in 2 weeks on queries; 3 weeks on mss.
Terms: Agent receives 15% commission on domestic sales; 20% on dramatic sales; 25% on foreign sales.
Fees: Charges a reading fee for unpublished authors who send complete manuscripts. Reading fee will be waived if represents the writer. 5% of income derived from reading fees; charges $35 for a 300-page, typed double-spaced book mss. Charges a criticism fee for unpublished authors. Same charge as reading fee. "Critique by managing editor gives overall view of book, marketing advice, and often line-by-line editing and evaluation. Charges writers for long distance telephone; other charges by mutual agreement." Payment of a fee does not ensure agency will represent writer.
Recent Sales: No information given.

LEE ALLAN AGENCY, Box 18617, Milwaukee WI 53218. (414)357-7708. Agent: Lee A. Matthias. Estab. 1983. Member of WGA, Horror Writers of America, Inc. and Wisconsin Screenwriter's Forum. Represents 20 clients. 80% of clients are new/unpublished writers. "A writer must have a minimum of one (in our judgment) salable work. Credentials are preferred, but we are open to new writers." Specializes in "screenplays for mass film audience, low to medium budget preferred, but of high quality, not exploitation; and novels of high adventure, genre fiction such as mystery and science fiction—no romance, nonfiction, textbooks, or poetry."
Will Handle: Novels (male adventure, mystery, science fiction, literary) and movie scripts (low to medium budget, mass appeal material). Currently handles 50% novels; 50% movie scripts. Will read—at no charge—unsolicited queries and outlines. Does not read unsolicited mss. Must be queried first. Reports in 2 weeks on queries; 6 weeks on mss.
Terms: Agent receives 10% commission on domestic sales; 10% on dramatic sales; and 20% on foreign sales; occasionally higher. Foreign rights handled by Mildred Hird. Charges for photocopying, binding, occasional shipping/postage costs.
Recent Sales: *Valley of the Shadow* (Presidio Press); *Sea Lion* (New American Library); *Barrow*, (Signet/ROC), and episode of *Star Trek: The Next Generation*.

‡JAMES ALLEN, LITERARY AGENT, P.O. Box 278, Milford PA 18337. Agent: James Allen. Estab. 1974. Represents 65 clients. Prefers to work with published/established authors. My quota for first-timers is filled, for the time being. Specializes in SF, fantasy, horror, mystery/suspense, mainstream some historicals.
Will Handle: Novel. Currently handles 5% magazine fiction; 5% nonfiction books; 90% novels. Does not read unsolicited mss. Reports in 1 week on queries.
Terms: Though I rarely do so, I reserve the right to bill authors for photocopying of booklength mss, airmail postage to distribute books for marketing of translation rights abroad, lengthy phone calls on occasion.
Recent Sales: *Torments*, by Lisa W. Cantrell (Tor Books); *The Gulf*, by David C. Poyer (St. Martin's Press); *4-bk SF series*, by Carla J. Mills (Berkley/Ace).
Tips: "I handle mostly genre fiction . . . all genres. To pique my interest, an author must have some previous credits *in the area he wants me to handle*. Someone with six computer books, who wants an agent for a mystery novel is, regardless of his previous sales, a first novelist, and I wouldn't be interested, at this point." When an author approaches me with a query *letter*, containing a 2-3 page synopsis of lthe book's plotline, I may ask to see sample chapters, and require that postage sufficient to cover the return be sent; subsequently, if I like the partial and ask to see the balance of the manuscript, I again require return postage, in case my approbation of the part does not extend to the whole. I absolutely will not answer any queries that do not include an SASE.

MARCIA AMSTERDAM AGENCY, Suite 9A, 41 W. 82nd St., New York NY 10024. (212)873-4945. Contact: Marcia Amsterdam. Estab. 1969. Member of WGA. 20% of clients are new/unpublished writers. Eager to work with new/unpublished writers. Specializes in fiction, nonfiction, young adult, TV and movies.
Will Handle: Nonfiction books, novels, juvenile books (young adult), and movie and TV scripts. Will read—at no charge—unsolicited queries, synopsis and outlines. Reports in 2 weeks on queries; 1 month on mss. "SASE essential."

Terms: Agent receives 15% commission on domestic publication sales; 10% on dramatic sales; and 20% on foreign publication sales.

Fees: Charges for telegraph, cable, phone, and legal fees (when client agrees to them).

Recent Sales: *Ash Ock*, by Christopher Hinz (St. Martin's); *Silvercat*, by Kristopher Franklin (Bantam); and *Face the Dragon*, by Joyce Sweeney (Delacorte).

BART ANDREWS & ASSOCIATES, 1321 N. Stanley Ave., Los Angeles CA 90046. (213)851-8158. FAX: (213)851-9738. Contact: Bart Andrews. Estab. 1982. Represents 50 clients. 10% of clients are new/unpublished writers. Works with small number of new/unpublished writers. Specializes in nonfiction only. "Seventy-five percent of books I represent are in the show business genre—biographies, autobiographies, books about TV, etc."

Will Handle: Nonfiction books. Handles 100% nonfiction books. Will read—at no charge—unsolicited queries and outlines. Reports in 3 weeks on queries.

Terms: Agent receives 15% commission on domestic sales; 10% on dramatic sales; and 25% on foreign sales.

Fees: "New clients are charged $150 marketing fee to offset out-of-pocket costs, i.e. phone, postage, etc." Charges writers for postage, photocopying, long distance phone calls. 95% of income derived from commission on manuscript sales; 5% of income derived from fees.

Recent Sales: *Once Before I Go*, by Wayne Newton with Dick Maurice (William Morrow); *Ringmaster!*, by Kristopher Antekeier (E.P. Dutton); *Film Flubs*, by Bill Givens (Citadel Press).

JOSEPH ANTHONY AGENCY, 8 Locust Ct. Rd. 20, Mays Landing NJ 08330. (609)625-7608. President: Joseph Anthony. Estab. 1964. Member of WGA. Represents 10 clients. 90% of clients are new/unpublished writers. Eager to work with new/unpublished writers. "Specializes in general fiction and nonfiction. Always interested in screenplays."

Will Handle: Magazine fiction, nonfiction books, novels, juvenile books (6-12 years), movie scripts, stage plays and TV scripts. Currently handles 5% magazine articles; 10% magazine fiction; 13% nonfiction books; 60% novels; 2% textbooks; 5% juvenile books; 5% movie scripts; 2% stage plays and 3% syndicated material. Will read—at no charge—unsolicited queries and outlines. Reports in 2 weeks on queries; 1 month on mss. SASE essential.

Terms: Agent receives 15% commission on domestic sales; 15% on dramatic sales; and 20% on foreign sales.

Fees: Charges $75 up to 100,000 words; $125 over 100,000 words for reading fee.

Recent Sales: No information given.

APPLESEEDS MANAGEMENT, Suite 302, 200 E. 30th St., San Bernardino CA 92404. (714)882-1667. Executive Manager: S. James Foiles. Estab. 1988. For screenplays and teleplays only: Suite 560, 1870 North Vermont Avenue, Hollywood, CA 90027. Signatory to Writers Guild of America-Association of Agents Basic Agreement; licensed by the state of California. Represents 25 clients. 40% of our clients are new/unpublished writers.

Will Handle: Specializes in action/adventure, fantasy, horror/occult, mystery and science fiction novels; also in nonfiction, true crime, biography, health/medicine and self-help; also in materials that could be adapted from book to screen; and also in screenplays and teleplays (no unsolicited screenplays and teleplays at this time). 25% nonfiction books; 40% novels; 20% movie scripts; 15% teleplays. Reports in 2 weeks on queries; 2 months on manuscripts.

Terms: Agent receives 10-15% commission on domestic sales; 10-15% on dramatic sales; and 20% on foreign sales. 100% of income derived from sales of writer's work.

AUTHOR AID ASSOCIATES, 340 E. 52nd St., New York NY 10022. (212)758-4213; 697-2419. Editorial Director: Arthur Orrmont. Estab. 1967. Represents 150 clients. 10% of clients are new/unpublished writers. Works with a small number of new/unpublished authors. Publishers of *Literary Agents of North America* (4th edition).

Will Handle: Magazine fiction, nonfiction books, novels, juvenile books, movie scripts, stage plays, TV scripts and poetry collections. Currently handles 5% magazine fiction; 35% nonfiction books; 38% novels; 5% juvenile books (ages 5-8; 9-11; and 12 and up); 5% movie scripts; 2% stage plays; 5% poetry and 5% other. Will read—at no charge—unsolicited queries and outlines. "Queries answered by return mail." Reports within 1 month on mss.

Terms: Agent receives 10-15% commission on domestic sales; 15% on dramatic sales; and 20% on foreign sales.

Fees: Charges a reading fee "to new authors, refundable from commission on sale." Charges for cable, photocopy and messenger express. Offers a consultation service through which writers not represented can get advice on a contract. 15% of income derived from reading fees; 85% of income from sales of writer's work.

Recent Sales: *Waylon: A Biography*, by Sarge Donsoff (St. Martin's Press); *Did Castro Kill Kennedy?*, by Igor YoFimov (S.G. BokFörlag, Swedish, Norwegian, Finnish and Danish editions).

‡THE AUTHORS AND ARTISTS RESOURCE CENTER/TARC LITERARY AGENCY, P.O. Box 64785, Tucson AZ 85740-1785. (602)325-4733. Literary Agents: Adult books—Martha R. Gores; children's books— Diane C. Gore. Estab. 1984. Represents 20 clients. Interested in working with new/unpublished writers. Specializes in adult and children's fiction and nonfiction books.

Will Handle: Nonfiction books, novels and juvenile books. Currently handles 75% nonfiction books; 20% novels and 5% juvenile books. Will read—at no charge—unsolicited queries and outlines. Does not read unsolicited manuscripts. Reports in 2 months.

Terms: Agent receives 15% commission on domestic sales; 20% on dramatic sales and 20% on foreign sales.

Fees: Charges a criticism fee "only if it is requested by the author." No set fee. "Each critique is tailored to the individual needs of the writer. We hire working editors who are employed by book publishers to do critiquing, editing, etc." Charges writers for mailing, photocopying, faxing, telephone calls.

Recent Sales: *Wings of Desire*, by Williamson [Lambert] (Avon); *Grey Pilgrim*, by Hays (Walker); and *Breakthrough*, by McConnell (Harbinger House).

‡AUTHORS MARKETING SERVICES LTD, 217 Degrassi St., Toronto, Ontario M4M 2K8 Canada. (416)463-7200. FAX: (416)469-4494. President: Helene Hoffman. Estab. 1978. Represents 18 clients. While we prefer previously-published writers, we keep our doors open to all. Prefers to work with published/established authors; works with a small number of new/unpublished authors. Specialize in male action fiction, 'woman's' novels, self-help nonfiction.

Will Handle: Currently handles 60% nonfiction; 40% novels. Will read—at no charge—unsolicited queries and outlines. Do not read unsolicited mss. Reports in 2-3 weeks on queries.

Terms: Agent receives 15% commission on domestic sales; 20% on foreign sales.

Fees: We charge only for fiction and only when writer is unpublished. No fees for authors published by reputable houses (i.e., not vanity houses). 5% of income derived from reading fees. Charges $225. Charges a criticism fee. "It is part of our reading fee procedure."

Recent Sales: *Nobody's Child*, by Martyn Kendrick (Macmillan); *Warsaw Concerto*, by Dennis Jones (Macdonald's UK); and *Voyage to the Whales*, by Dr. Hal Whitehead (Chelsea Green).

MALAGA BALDI LITERARY AGENCY, INC., P.O. Box 591, Radio City Station, New York NY 10101. (212)222-1221. President: Malaga Baldi. Estab. 1986. Represents 45 clients. 60% of clients are new/unpublished writers. Eager to work with talented writers, published or unpublished. Specializes in first fiction, literary fiction, a variety of nonfiction work.

Will Handle: Literary novels (non genre); nonfiction proposals. Currently handles 15% magazine articles; 35% nonfiction books and 50% novels. Will read—at no charge—unsolicited queries, outlines and manuscripts. Requires SASE. Reports in 2 months.

Terms: Agent receives 15% commission on domestic sales; 15% on dramatic sales; and 10-20% on foreign sales.

Fees: Charges writers for messenger, overseas mail costs, photocopying costs, cable/telegram/overseas phone calls *to* author, when necessary, lawyer's fees if agreed to prior to signing agent/author agreement.

Recent Sales: *Crossing the River*, by Fenton Johnson (Birch Lane Press/Lyle Stuart/Carol Management); *Waterboys*, by Eric Gabriel (Mercury House); and *The Bed*, by Aleecia Beldegreen (Stewart, Tabori and Chang).

‡BALKIN AGENCY, INC., 850 W. 176th St., New York NY 10033. (212)781-4198. FAX: (212)781-4198. President: R. Balkin. Estab. 1972. Member of ILAA, Authors Guild. Represents 48 clients. Works with a small number of new/unpublished authors. Specializes in adult nonfiction.

Will Handle: Nonfiction books and college textbooks. Currently handles 90% nonfiction books; and 10% textbooks. Will read—at no charge—unsolicited queries and outlines. Does not read unsolicited manuscripts. Reports in 2 weeks.

Terms: Agent receives 15% commission on domestic sales; 20% on foreign sales.

Fees: Charges writers for photocopying and foreign mailing.

Recent Sales: *There Was no Big Bang*, by Lerner (Random House); *Declarations of Independence: Cross-Examining American Idealogies*, by Zinn (Harper and Row); and *George Sanders: An Exhausted Life*, (Madison Books).

MAXIMILIAN BECKER, 115 E. 82nd St., New York NY 10028. (212)988-3887. President: Maximilian Becker. Associate: Aleta Daley. Estab. 1950. Works with a small number of new/unpublished authors.

Will Handle: Nonfiction books, novels and stage plays. Will read—at no charge—unsolicited queries, outlines and mss, but may charge a criticism fee or service charge for work performed after the initial reading if requested. Reports in 2 weeks on queries; 3 weeks on mss.

Terms: Agent receives 15% commission on domestic sales; 20% on foreign sales.

Fees: Charges a criticism fee "if detailed criticism is requested. Writers receive a detailed criticism with suggestions—five to ten pages. No criticism is given if manuscript is hopeless."

Recent Sales: *Goering*, by David Irving (William Morrow); *Enigma*, by David Kahn (Houghton Mifflin); and *Cecile*, by Jamine Boissard (Little, Brown).

MEREDITH BERNSTEIN, 2112 Broadway, Suite 503 A, New York NY 10023. (212)799-1007. FAX: (212)799-1145 (must notify us you are faxing). President: Meredith Bernstein. Estab. 1981. Member of ILAA. Represents about 100 clients. 10% of our clients are new/unpublished writers. Eager to work with new/unpublished writers. Specializes in fiction and nonfiction; contemporary novels, mysteries, child care, business and money, romances, sagas, fashion and beauty, humor, visual books and psychology.

Will Handle: Nonfiction books, novels, and movie scripts. Currently handles 45% nonfiction books; 45% novels; and 10% miscellaneous. Will read unsolicited queries, outlines and mss. Reports in 1 week on queries; 3 weeks on mss.

Terms: Agent receives 15% commission on domestic sales and 20% on foreign sales.

Fees: Charges a reading fee. 5% of income derived from reading fees.

Recent Sales: *Parenting From Scratch*, by Claudette Wassil-Grimm (Pocket); *Bum Steer*, by Nancy Picard (Pocket); and *The Know-It-All's Guide to Life*, by Denis Boyles (Villard).

‡VICKY BIJUR LITERARY AGENCY, 333 West End Ave., New York NY 10023. (212)580-4108. FAX: (212)496-1572. Literary Agent: Vicky Bijur. Estab. 1988. Member of ILAA. Represents 35 clients. "The writer of nonfiction must be able to put together a strong proposal and sample chapters. I sold two books of nonfiction recently by first-time authors. I also represent a few first-time fiction writers." Works with a small number of new/unpublished authors. Specializes in fiction: mostly mysteries; some literary fiction; nonfiction: health/medicine; child care; travel; recovery; biography; food/entertaining; psychology; women's issues; history.

Will Handle: Nonfiction books and novels. Currently handles 2% magazine articles; 4% magazine fiction; 46% nonfiction books; 46% novels and 2% juvenile books. Will read—at no charge—unsolicited queries and outlines. Does not read unsolicited manuscripts. Reports in 2 weeks.

Terms: Agent receives 15% commission on domestic sales; 7½% on dramatic sales (Hollywood co-agent also takes 7½%); and 10% on foreign sales (foreign subagent also takes 10%)

Fees: Charges writers for manuscript photocopying; foreign postage; overseas phone calls.

Recent Sales: *New Orleans Mourning*, by Julie Smith (St. Martin's Press); *Relative Risk: Living with a Family History of Breast Cancer*, by Nancy Baker Jacobs (Viking); and *The Attention Deficit Phenomenon*, by Robert Moss, M.D. and Helen Dunlap (Bantam).

‡DAVID BLACK LITERARY AGENCY, INC., 220 5th Ave., New York NY 10001. (212)689-5154. FAX: (212)684-2606. Assistant: Janice Gordon. Estab. 1990. Member of ILAA. Represents 150 clients. Specializes in sports, politics, novels.

Will Handle: Nonfiction books, novels. Handles 80% nonfiction; 20% novels. Will read—at no charge—unsolicited queries and outlines. Reports in one month on queries.

Terms: Agent receives 15% commission.

Fees: Charges for photocopying manuscripts and for books purchased for sale of foreign rights.

Recent Sales: *Bo*, by Glenn "Bo" Schembechler and Mitch Albom (Warner); *If I Had a Hammer*, by Henry Aaron and Lonnie Wheeler (Harper & Row); and *Birdsong Ascending*, by Sam Harrison (Harcourt Brace Jovanovich).

THE BLAKE GROUP LITERARY AGENCY, Suite 600, One Turtle Creek Village, Dallas TX 75219. (214)520-8562. Director/Agent: Ms. Lee B. Halff. Estab. 1979. Member of Texas Publishers Association (TPA) and Texas Booksellers Association (TBA). Represents 40 clients. Prefers to work with published/established authors; works with a small number of new/unpublished authors.

Will Handle: Fiction and nonfiction books, novels, textbooks and juvenile books. Currently handles 11% fiction; 30% nonfiction books; 40% novels; 2% textbooks; 9% juvenile books; 2% movie scripts; 1% TV scripts; 2% poetry; and 3% science fiction. "Will read at no charge query letter and two sample chapters. Charges criticism fee; $100 for 3-page critique. Reports within 3 months. Pre-stamped return mailer must accompany submissions."

Terms: Agent receives 10% commission on domestic sales; 15% on dramatic sales; and 20% on foreign sales. Sometimes offers a consultation service through which writers not represented can get advice on a contract; charges $50/hour. Income derived from commission on ms sales and critique fees.

For information on author's agents' areas of interest, see the nonfiction and fiction sections in the Author's Agents Subject Index.

Recent Sales: *Captured Corregidor: Diary of an American P.O.W. in WWII*, by John M. Wright, Jr. (McFarland & Co); *Modern Language for Musicians*, by Julie Yarbrough (Pendragon Press); and *Weight Loss for Super Wellness*, by Ted L. Edwards Jr., M.D. (life enhancement).

‡**HARRY BLOOM**, 16272 Via Embeleso, San Diego CA 92128-3219. Estab. 1967. 5% of clients new/unpublished writers. Prefers to work with published/established authors; works with small number of new/unpublished authors. Specializes in mainstream fiction, love, mystery, action/adventure and nonfiction. "No science fiction."
Will Handle: Nonfiction books, novels, movie scripts, syndicated material. Will read—at no charge—unsolicited queries and outlines. Does not read unsolicited mss. Reports in 2 weeks on queries. "If our agency does not respond within 2 weeks to your request to become a client, you may submit requests elsewhere."
Terms: No information given.
Recent Sales: Confidential.

REID BOATES LITERARY AGENCY, P.O. Box 328, Pittstown NJ 08867-0328. (201)730-8523. Contact: Reid Boates. Estab. 1985. Represents 45 clients. 20% of clients are new/unpublished writers. "To be represented writers must have a writing background, though not necessarily in books." Specializes in biography and autobiography; topical nonfiction; wellness and general how-to, business (investigative); fiction: good, clear writing; strong story and character.
Will Handle: Nonfiction books, novels. Currently handles 90% nonfiction books; 10% novels. Will read—at no charge—unsolicited queries and outlines. Does not read unsolicited mss. Reports in 2 weeks.
Terms: Agent receives 15% commission on domestic sales; 15% on dramatic sales; 20% on foreign sales.
Fees: Charges for photocopying over $50.
Recent Sales: *Untitled on the American Night*, by Kevin Coyne (Random House); *Mankind's First Family*, by Donald Johansen and Kevin O'Farrell (Villard); *Honor and Obey*, True Crime by Lawrence Taylor (Morrow).

‡**ALISON M. BOND LTD.**, 171 W. 79th St., New York NY 10024. (212)362-3350. FAX: (212)769-0377. Agents: Alison Bond and Rebecca Gleason. Estab. 1977. Represents 25 clients. No specific qualifications for writers—just good writing and good ideas. Works with a small number of new/unpublished authors. Specializes in literary fiction, high-quality nonfiction. No sci-fi or fantasy.
Will Handle: Magazine articles and magazine fiction (only if we represent author's book-length work as well), nonfiction books and novels. Currently handles 10% magazine fiction; 40% nonfiction books; 40% novels and 10% juvenile books. We prefer to consider an outline and two sample chapters. Does not read unsolicited manuscripts. Reports in 6 weeks.
Terms: Agent receives 10% commission on domestic sales; 10% on dramatic sales; and 15% on foreign sales.
Fees: "We sometimes charge back photocopying expenses for extra-long mss."
Recent Sales: *Behind the Waterfall*, by Chinatsu Nakayama (Atheneum); *In Mysterious Ways*, by Paul Wilkes (Random House); and *The New PLO*, by Scott MacLeod (Knopf).

GEORGES BORCHARDT INC., 136 E. 57th St., New York NY 10022. (212)753-5785. FAX: (212)838-6518. President: Georges Borchardt. Estab. 1967. Member of SAR. Represents 200 clients. 1-2% of our clients are new/unpublished writers. "We do not consider new clients unless highly recommended by someone we trust." Prefers to work with published/established authors; also works with a small number of new/unpublished authors. Specializes in fiction, biography and general nonfiction of unusual interest.
Will Handle: Nonfiction books and novels. Does not read unsolicited mss.
Terms: Agent receives 10% commission on domestic sales; 10% on dramatic sales; and 20% on foreign sales (15% on British).
Fees: Charges for photocopy expenses.
Recent Sales: *If The River Was Whiskey*, by T. Coraghessan Boyle (Viking Press); *Among School Children*, by Tracy Kidder (Houghton Mifflin); and *Jazz Cleopatra*, by Phyllis Rose (Doubleday).

‡**BRANDENBURGH & ASSOCIATES LITERARY AGENCY**, P.O. Box 4073, Palm Desert CA 92261-4073. (619)341-3108. Owner: Don Brandenburgh. Estab. 1986. Represents 30 clients. "We prefer previously published authors, but will evaluate submissions on their own merits." Works with a small number of new/unpublished authors. Specializes in adult nonfiction for the Christian bookstore market; limited fiction for Christian market; very limited children's books also for Christian market.
Will Handle: Nonfiction books, novels and textbooks. Currently handles 70% nonfiction books; 20% novels; and 10% textbooks. Will read—at no charge—unsolicited queries, outlines and manuscripts. Reports in 2 weeks on queries; 3 months on mss.
Terms: Agent receives 10% commission on domestic sales; 20% on dramatic sales; and 20% on foreign sales.
Fees: Charges a $35 mailing/materials fee with signed agency agreement. Payment of criticism fee does not ensure that agency will represent writer.
Recent Sales: *Eve*, by Evelyn Minshull (Harper & Row); *Audeh Rantisi: A Christian Arab in the Occupied West Bank*, by Audeh Rantisi and Ralph Beebe (Zondervan); and *The Throne of Tara*, by John Dejarlais (Crossway).

BRANDT & BRANDT LITERARY AGENTS, INC., 1501 Broadway, New York NY 10036. (212)840-5760. Estab. 1914. Member of SAR. Represents 250 clients. Works with a small number of new/unpublished authors.
Will Handle: Nonfiction books and novels. "We read and answer letters from writers about their work only."
Terms: Agent receives 10% commission on domestic sales; 10% on dramatic sales; and 20% on foreign sales.
Recent Sales: No information given.

RUTH HAGY BROD LITERARY AGENCY, 15 Park Ave., New York NY 10016. (212)683-3232. FAX: (212)269-0313. President: A.T. Brod. Estab. 1975. Represents 10 clients. 10-15% of clients are new/unpublished authors. Prefers to work with published/established authors. Specializes in trade books.
Will Handle: Nonfiction books. Currently handles 95% nonfiction books and 5% novels. Will read submissions at no charge, but may charge a criticism fee or service charge for work performed after the initial reading. Reports in 5 weeks on queries; 2 months on mss.
Terms: Agent receives 15% commission on domestic sales and 20% on foreign sales.
Fees: Charges a reading fee; waives reading fee when representing writer. 5% of income derived from reading fees. Charges a criticism fee. 5% of income derived from criticism fees.
Recent Sales: No information given.

NED BROWN INC., Box 1044, Malibu CA 90265. (213)456-8068. President: Ned Brown. Estab. 1963. Writer must be previously published or have a recommendation from other client or publisher. Prefers to work with published/established authors.
Will Handle: Magazine fiction, nonfiction books, novels, movie scripts, stage plays and TV scripts. Does not read unsolicited mss.
Terms: Agent receives 15% commission on domestic sales; 15% on dramatic sales; and 20% on foreign sales.
Fees: Charges writers for "extraordinary expenses."
Recent Sales: *Lion at the Door*, by Newton Thornsburg (William Morrow); *Back Where the Past Was*, by Charles Champion (Syracuse University Press); and *Humming Birds*, by Robert and Esther Tyrrell (Random House).

ANDREA BROWN, LITERARY AGENCY, Suite 71, 1081 Alameda, Belmont CA 94002. (415)508-8410. FAX: (415) 508-8416. Owner: Andrea Brown. Estab. 1981. Member of ILAA. Number of clients: confidential. 50% of our clients are new/unpublished writers. Specializes in children's books—all ages.
Will Handle: Juvenile books (preschool, ages 6-9 and 8-12). Currently handles 5% adult nonfiction books; 95% juvenile books. "Young adult is dead, so I'm mostly looking for middle-group books." Will read—at no charge—unsolicited queries and outlines. Reports in 2 weeks on queries; 3 months on manuscripts.
Terms: Agent receives 15% commission on domestic sales; 20% on foreign sales.
Recent Sales: *How to Find a Ghost*, by James Deem (Houghton Mifflin); *Harry Newberry and The Raiders of the Red Drink*, by Mel Gilden (Holt); and *Nothing To Fear*, by Jackie French Koller (HBJ).

‡CURTIS BROWN LTD., 10 Astor Pl., New York NY 10003. (212)473-5400. Member of SAR. Prefers to work with published/established authors; works with a small number of new/unpublished authors. Specializes in general fiction and nonfiction.
Will Handle: Nonfiction books, novels and juvenile books. Will read—at no charge—unsolicited queries and outlines accompanied by SASE; does not read unsolicited mss.
Terms: "Will explain to clients when they wish to sign."
Recent Sales: No information given.

PEMA BROWNE LTD., Pine Road HCR Box 104B, Neversink NY 12765. (914)985-2936. FAX: (914)985-7635. President: Pema Browne. Treasurer: Perry J. Browne. Estab. 1966. Represents 40 clients. 25% of clients are new/unpublished writers. "We review only new projects and require that writers have not sent manuscript to publishers or other agents." Specializes in thrillers, mainstream, historical, regencies and contemporary romances; young adult; children's; reference; how-to and other types of nonfiction.
Will Handle: Nonfiction books, novels, juvenile books. Currently handles 25% nonfiction books; 25% novels; 10% juvenile books; and 40% mass-market.
Terms: Agent receives 15% commission on domestic sales; 10% on dramatic sales; and 20% on foreign sales.
Fees: "In some cases, a reading fee."
Recent Sales: *Nellie Lou's Hairdos*, by John Sandford (Warner); *Over the Horizon*, by Kaye Walton (Harlequin); and *Guide*, by Gloria Bledsoe (Carol Publishing).

‡JANE BUTLER, ART AND LITERARY AGENT, 212 Third St., Milford PA 18337. (717)296-2629. Estab. 1981. "Prefers published credits, but all queries are welcome; no SASE, no reply." Specializes in nonfiction (popular natural history, popular soft sciences—anthropology, archaeology; native American and oriental religious history and modern practice; myths and fairy tales; and military history) and fiction (historical, mysteries, science fiction, horror, historical fantasy and fantasy).

Will Handle: Nonfiction books and novels. Currently handles 15% nonfiction books; 80% novels; 5% juvenile books. Will read unsolicited queries. Reports in 2 weeks on queries.

Terms: Agent receives 10% commission on domestic sales; 15% on dramatic sales; and 20% on foreign sales. 100% of income derived from commission on ms sales.

Recent Sales: *Goblin Moon*, by Teresa Edgerton (Berkley Books); *Brother Lowdown*, by S.K. Epperson (St. Martin's Press); and *St. Oswald's Niche*, by Laura Turtledove (Ballantine).

THE MARSHALL CAMERON AGENCY, Rt. 1, Box 125, Lawtey FL 32058. (904)964-7013. FAX: (904)964-9605. Contact: Margo Prescott. California: Box 922101, Sylmar, CA 91392. (818)365-3400. Contact: Wendy Zhorne. Represents 30 clients. "Prefer writers with credits but we are always open to new talent." Specializes in screenplays and teleplays.

Will Handle: Novels and nonfiction, sceenplays, teleplays.

Terms: Agent receives 15% commission on domestic and dramatic sales; 20% on foreign sales.

Fees: Charges $50 reading/evaluation/300 pages (novels, nonfiction); $45 for screenplays. Comprehensive critique is provided at writer's request. Will read queries and synopses at no charge. "We are a 'full service' agency, providing 'hands-on' editing, revising, script doctoring, and typing, for both clients and nonclients.

Recent Sales: "Radical Treatment," (option screenplay).

‡CANADIAN SPEAKERS' AND WRITERS' SERVICE LIMITED, 44 Douglas Crescent, Toronto, Ontario M4W 2L7 Canada. (416)921-4443. President: Matie Molinaro. Estab. 1950. Represents 225 clients. 3% of clients are new/unpublished writers. Prefers to work with published/established authors; works with a small number of new/unpublished authors.

Will Handle: Magazine fiction, nonfiction books, novels, juvenile books, movie scripts, radio scripts, stage plays and TV scripts. Currently handles 70% nonfiction books; 5% novels; 5% movie scripts; 10% radio scripts; 5% stage plays; and 5% TV scripts. Does not read unsolicited mss. Reports in 3 weeks on queries; 1 month on mss. "If our agency does not respond within 1 month to your request to become a client, you may submit requests elsewhere."

Terms: Agent receives 15% commission on domestic sales; 15% on dramatic sales; and 20% on foreign sales. Charges a criticism/reading fee: $50, plus $3/one-thousand words. "Each reading/critique is handled by four people and a composite report is sent out to the writer." Offers a consultation service through which writers not represented can get advice on a contract; charges $160/hour. 5% of income derived from fees; 95% of income derived from commission on manuscript sales. Payment of a criticism fee does not ensure that agency will represent a writer.

Recent Sales: *McLuhan Letter*, (Oxford University Press); *Ben Wicks First Treasury*, by Ben Wicks (Methuen Publishers); and *Medical Survival*, by Dr. Gifford Jones (Methuen).

RUTH CANTOR, LITERARY AGENT, Rm. 1133, 156 5th Ave., New York NY 10010. (212)243-3246. Contact: Ruth Cantor. Estab. 1952. Represents 40 clients. Writer must have "a good, sound track record in the publishing field . . . A skimpy one will sometimes get you a reading if I'm convinced that talent might be lurking in the bulrushes." Prefers to work with published/established authors; works with a small number of new/unpublished authors. Specializes in "any good trade book, fiction of quality, good, competent mysteries with new elements, juvenile books above the age of 8, up through young adult (12-16)."

Will Handle: Nonfiction books, novels and juvenile books. Will read—at no charge—unsolicited queries and outlines. Reports in 1 month on queries; 2 months on mss.

Terms: Agent receives 10% commission on domestic sales; 10% on dramatic sales; and 10% on foreign sales.

Recent Sales: *The Rod of Sybil* (Harcourt); *The Players* (Warner); and *Lady Divine*, by Barbara Sherrod (Warner).

‡MARIA CARVAINIS AGENCY, INC., 235 W. End Ave., New York NY 10023. (212)580-1559. President: Maria Carvainis. Estab. 1977. Member of ILAA, WGA, Authors Guild and Romance Writers of America. Represents 53 clients. Eager to work with new/unpublished writers on a selective basis. Specializes in mainstream fiction, contemporary women's fiction, suspense and mystery, historicals, fantasy, children's and young adult, business and finance, women's issues, medicine, psychology, popular and social sciences, biography.

Will Handle: Nonfiction books, novels and juvenile books. Will read—at no charge—unsolicited queries and outlines accompanied by SASE. Does not read unsolicited mss. Reports in 2 weeks.

Terms: Agent receives 15% commission on domestic sales; 15% on dramatic sales; and 20% on foreign sales. 100% of income derived from commission on ms sales.

Recent Sales: *Workplace 2000*, by Joseph H. Boyette and Henry P. Conn (New American Library); *Easter Weekend*, by David Bottoms (Houghton Mifflin); *Shadow of Seven Moons*, by Nancy V. Berberick (Berkley).

MARTHA CASSELMAN, LITERARY AGENT, P.O. Box 342, Calistoga CA 94515-0342. (707)942-4341. Estab. 1978. Member ILAA. 25% of clients are new/unpublished writers. Works with small number of new/unpublished writers. Specializes in food books, general nonfiction, fiction, small number of children's books.

Will Handle: Nonfiction books; novels, juvenile books. Will read—at no charge—unsolicited queries and outlines. Does not read unsolicited mss. Reports in 6 weeks. "Cannot return long distance query phone calls."
Terms: Agent receives 15% commission on domestic sales.
Fees: Charges for copying, overnight mail or travel made at author's request.
Recent Sales: Confidential.

THE CATALOG™ LITERARY AGENCY, P.O. Box 2964, Vancouver WA 98668. (206)694-8531. Contact: Douglas Storey. Estab. 1986. Represents 27 clients. 50% of clients are new/unpublished writers. Eager to work with new/unpublished writers. Specializes in nonfiction, mainstream fiction, technical, textbooks and juvenile manuscripts.
Will Handle: Popular, professional and textbooks in all subjects (but especially in business, health, money, science and women's interests), how-to and self-help. Will read—at no charge—unsolicited queries, outlines and manuscripts. Reports in 3 weeks on queries. Does not return material unless accompanied by SASE.
Terms: Agent receives 15% commission on domestic sales; 20% on dramatic sales; and 20% on foreign sales.
Fees: Charges a criticism fee "if the writer requests a written evaluation of the submitted manuscript." 2% of income derived from criticism fees. Charges $150/300 pages. Critique is four to six pages and includes overall evaluation with specific examples, marketing advice included—if ms is marketable. Critiques provided by Douglas Storey. Except for recently published authors, charges an upfront handling fee that covers photocopying, postage and telephone expense. 80% of income derived from sales of writers' work; 20% of income derived from criticism services.
Recent Sales: No information given.

‡LINDA CHESTER LITERARY AGENCY, 265 Coast, LaJolla CA 92037. (619)454-3966. Literary Agent: Linda Chester. Estab. 1978. Represents 40 clients. "We prefer writers with previous publishing credits." Works with a small number of new/unpublished authors. Specializes in literary and commercial fiction, psychology/self-help, business/finance, health, biography, history, science, popular culture, arts.
Will Handle Nonfiction books and novels. Currently handles 50% nonfiction books; and 50% novels. Will read—at no charge—unsolicited queries and outlines. We prefer a query or phone call before receiving submission. Will read submissions at no charge, but may charge a criticism fee or service charge for work performed after the initial reading. Reports in 3 weeks.
Terms: Agent receives 15% commission on domestic sales; 15% on dramatic sales; and 30% on foreign sales.
Fees: "If author requests a critique/evaluation; we reserve the right to critique only those mss. which we feel are promising." 2% of income derived from criticism fees. Charges $350/300 pages. Critique includes "overall evaluation of manuscript's strengths and weaknesses, market potential, structure, voice/tone, characterization, plot development. Both Linda Chester and her editorial staff provides the critiques." Charges writers for duplication of ms and legal fees incurred, your consent of author.
Recent Sales: *Leaving the Enchanted Forest*, by Stephanie Covington (Harper & Row); *A Street is Not a Home: Solving America's Homeless Problems*, by Robert Coates (Prometheus Books); and *Night Driving* (Stories), by John Vande Zande (Arbor House/Morrow).

CONNIE CLAUSEN ASSOCIATES, 250 E. 87th St., New York NY 10128. (212)427-6135. Contact: Connie Clausen/Vera Fickey. Estab. 1976. Member ASJA. Represents approximately 90 clients. Prefers to work with published authors who have prior magazine and/or book credits; works with a small number of new authors. Considers recommendations from clients and publishers. Specializes in trade nonfiction of all kinds: self-help, how-to, health, beauty, biographies, true crime and cookbooks, and mainstream and literary fiction for adults and children.
Will Handle: Nonfiction books. No magazine articles, romance or sci-fi novels, screenplays or humor books. Will sell movie rights for books we handle. Currently handles 75% nonfiction; 23% novels; and 2% juvenile. Does not read unsolicited mss. Reports in 6 weeks on full manuscripts, 1 month on proposals.
Terms: Agent receives 15% commission on domestic sales and dramatic sales; and 20% on foreign sales.
Fees: Charges for photocopying and shipping. No reading fees.
Recent Sales: *The "Late Night With David Letterman" Book of Top Ten Lists*, (Pocket Books); *Quitting the Mob: The Yuppie Don and the Billion Dollar Empire He Gave Up for the Woman He Loved*, (Harper & Row); *Back To The Family: Lessons From One Hundred of America's Happiest Families*, (Villard).

RUTH COHEN, INC., P.O. Box 7626, Menlo Park CA 94025. (415)854-2054. President: Ruth Cohen. Estab. 1982. Member of ILAA. Represents 45-60 clients. 30% of clients are new/unpublished writers. Writers must have a book that is well written. Prefers to work with published/established authors; eager to work with new/unpublished writers. Specializes in juvenile fiction, young adult fiction and nonfiction and adult genre books—mystery, western, historical romance, horror and thrillers. No poetry or screenplays.
Will Handle: Fiction and nonfiction books for adults, juvenile books (for ages 3-14) adult and young adult books, and genre novels—mystery, western, mainstream romance, regency romances and historical romance. Currently handles 20% nonfiction books; 30% novels; and 50% juvenile books. Will read—at no charge—

unsolicited queries with 10 opening pages of manuscripts, outlines and partial mss with SASE. "No complete manuscripts unless requested." Reports in 3 weeks on queries; 1 month on mss. "No multiple agency submissions." Must include SASE with all mss on queries.
Terms: Negotiated with each client.
Fees: Charges writers only for photocopying and foreign postage.
Recent Sales: *The Coming of the Bear*, by Lensey Namioka (Harper YA); *Solemn Vows*, by Mary Jo Putney (NAL); and *Jase "The Ace,"* by Joanne Rocklin (Macmillan).

COLLIER ASSOCIATES, 2000 Flat Run Rd., Seaman OH 45679. (513)764-1234. Manager: Oscar Collier. Associate: Carol Cartaino. Estab. 1976. Member of SAR and ILAA. Represents 80 clients. Rarely works with new/unpublished authors. Specializes in fiction trade books (war, crime and historical romances) and nonfiction trade books on business and finance, biographies, math for general audience, politics, exposes, nature and outdoors, history, how-to and consumer reference (Carol Cartaino).
Terms: Agent usually receives 15% on domestic sales; 15% on dramatic sales; and 20% on foreign sales; fee negotiated with well-known authors and celebrities.
Fees: Charges for books ordered from publishers for rights submissions, Express Mail and copying expenses.
Recent Sales: *Memoirs of Vivian Vance*, (National Enquirer); *Deathchain*, by Ken Greenhall (Pocket); and *The Stainbuster's Bible*, by Don Aslett (NAL).

FRANCES COLLIN LITERARY AGENCY, 110 West 40th St., New York NY 10018. (212)840-8664. Contact: Frances Collin. Estab. 1948. Member of SAR. Represents 90 clients. Almost always works only with published/established authors; works with a very small number of new/unpublished authors. Has a "broad general trade list."
Will Handle: Nonfiction books and novels. Currently handles 50% nonfiction books; 50% fiction books. Will read—at no charge—unsolicited queries. Reports in 1 week on queries.
Terms: Agent receives 15% commission on domestic sales; 20% on dramatic sales; and 25% on foreign sales.
Fees: Charges for overseas postage, photocopy and registered mail expenses and copyright registration fees.
Recent Sales: Confidential.

CONNOR LITERARY AGENCY, 640 W. 153rd St., New York NY 10031. (212)491-5233. Owner: Marlene Connor. Estab. 1985. Represents 28 clients. 25% of clients are new/unpublished writers. "Seeking books with strong promotion possibilities; published writers with good track records; new writers with solid credentials." **Will Handle:** Nonfiction: parenting, illustrated books, self-help, beauty, fitness, relationships, how-to, cookbooks, true crime. Fiction: mysteries, horror, espionage, suspense, mainstream. Will read—at no charge— unsolicited queries and outlines. Reports in 2 months on queries. "Material will not be returned without SASE."
Terms: Agent receives 15% commission on domestic sales; and 25% on foreign sales.
Fees: Reading fees $40 for proposals with sample chapter; $65 and up for full ms. Charges for photocopy, postage, telephone and messenger expenses, and special materials for presentation. 2% of income derived from fees; 98% of income derived from commission on ms sales.
Recent Sales: *Venus Unbound: Actualizing the Power of Being Female*, by Dina von Zweck and Jaye Smith (Fireside); *Blindspot*, by Randy Russell (Bantam); *Colorsynergy*, by Dinah Lovett and Patricia George (Fireside).

‡WARREN COOK LITERARY AGENCY, 109 Riverside Drive, New York NY 10024. (212)769-1705. Owner: Warren Cook. Estab. 1983. Represents 23 clients. Works with a small number of new/unpublished authors. Specializes in mysteries, thrillers, adventure, coming of age, humor, literary fiction, true crime, history, biography, politics, ecology, medical, social and scientific issues, self help, young adult fiction and nonfiction, children's books.
Will Handle: Nonfiction books, novels, juvenile books and movie scripts. Currently handles 35% nonfiction books; 35% novels; 15% juvenile books; and 15% movie scripts. Will read—at no charge—unsolicited queries and outlines. Reports in 3 weeks on queries.
Terms: Agent receives 15% commission on domestic sales; 15% on dramatic sales; and 20% on foreign sales.
Fees: Charges a reading fee. "A reading fee is charged to consider for representation the work of writers who have not previously been published by a mainsteam book publisher or national magazine or who have not previously sold a script to a major producer." 2% of income derived from reading fees. $350/300 pages. Charges writers for photocopying manuscripts, messengers and overseas airmail.
Recent Sales: *Client*, by Parnell Hall (Donald T. Fine, Inc.); *The Chase*, by Alejo Carpentier (Farrar Straus & Giroux); and *Harem: The World Behind the Veil*, by Alev Croutier (Abbeville Press).

‡BILL COOPER ASSOC., INC., Suite 411, 224 W. 49th St., New York NY 10019. (212)307-1100. Contact: William Cooper. Estab. 1964. Represents 10 clients. 10% of clients are new/unpublished writers. Prefers to work with published/established authors; works with a small number of new/unpublished authors. Specializes in contemporary fiction.

Will Handle: Novels and movie scripts. Currently handles 90% novels and 10% movie scripts. May charge a reading fee for unpublished writers. Reports in 2 weeks on queries and mss. No unsolicited submissions.
Terms: Agent receives 15% commission on domestic sales; 15% on dramatic sales; and 20% on foreign sales. Payment of a criticism fee does not ensure that agency will represent writer.
Recent Sales: No information given.

CREATIVE CONCEPTS LITERARY AGENCY, P.O. Box 12606, Harrisburg PA 17105-2606. Director: Michele Glance Serwach. Estab. 1987. Represents 20 clients. 80% of clients are new/unpublished writers. "We welcome new/unpublished writers—the only requirement is that you have an outline or manuscript ready to submit." Specializes in how-to books, self-help books, cookbooks, general interest novels, romance novels, mysteries, science fiction, adventure novels. We no longer handle poetry.
Will Handle: Magazine articles, nonfiction books, novels, juvenile books, movie scripts, TV scripts, syndicated material. Currently handles 5% magazine articles; 50% nonfiction books; 20% novels; 5% juvenile books; 5% movie scripts; 5% TV scripts; 5% syndicated material. Will read unsolicited queries and outlines for free. Charges critiquing fee for evaluating a complete manuscript. Reports in 3 weeks on queries; 5 weeks on mss.
Terms: Agent receives 10-12% commission on domestic sales; 12% on dramatic sales; and 12% on foreign sales.
Recent Sales: Confidential.

RICHARD CURTIS ASSOCIATES, INC., Suite 1, 164 E. 64th St., New York NY 10021. (212)371-9481. President: Richard Curtis. Contact: Rob Cohen, Rich Henshaw, associates. Estab. 1969. Member of ILAA. Represents 100 clients. 5% of clients are new/unpublished writers. Writer must have some published work and either a finished novel or proposed nonfiction book. Prefers to work with published/established authors; works with a small number of new/unpublished authors. Specializes in commercial fiction of all genres, mainstream fiction and nonfiction. Especially interested in health, science, how-to, New Age, psychology, biography, social history, women's issues, relationships, business, true crime.
Will Handle: Nonfiction books, novels, movie scripts and juvenile books. Currently handles 1% magazine articles; 1% magazine fiction; 25% nonfiction books; 70% novels; 3% juvenile books. Will read—at no charge—unsolicited queries and outlines. Reports in 2 weeks on queries; 1 month on mss.
Terms: Agent receives 10% commission on domestic fiction, 15% nonfiction sales; 15% on dramatic sales; and 20% on foreign sales.
Fees: Occasionally charges a reading fee; less than 1% of income derived from reading fee. Charges for photocopying, messengers, purchase of books for subsidiary exploitations, cable, air mail and express mail. Offers a consultation service through which writers not represented can get advice on a contract; charges $200/hour.
Recent Sales: *Masquerade*, by Janet Dailey (Little, Brown); *Phases of Gravity*, by Dan Simmons (Bantam); and *Queen of Angels*, by Greg Bear (Warner).

ELAINE DAVIE LITERARY AGENCY, Village Gate Square, 274 North Goodman St., Rochester NY 14607. (716)442-0830. President: Elaine Davie. Estab. 1986. Represents 70 clients. 30% of clients are new/unpublished writers. Works with a small number of new/unpublished authors. Specializes in adult fiction and nonfiction, particularly books by and for women and genre/fiction (romances, historicals, mysteries, horror, westerns, etc.). "We pride ourselves on prompt and personal responses." Please query first with letter and synopsis or brief description of manuscript.
Will Handle: Nonfiction books, novels, juvenile books (no children's books or poetry). Handles 30% nonfiction; 60% novels; 10% juvenile books. Will read—at no charge—unsolicited queries and outlines. Reports in 2 weeks on queries.
Terms: Agent receives 15% commission on domestic sales; 20% on dramatic sales; and 20% on foreign sales.
Recent Sales: *Defiant Captive*, by Christina Skye (Dell); *Acron on a Wine Dark Sea*, by Jessica Dennis (Bantam); and *Night Riders*, by Tony Phillips (Ballentine).

DOROTHY DEERING, LITERARY AGENCY, 1507 Oakmont Dr., Acworth GA 30101. (404)591-2051. Directors: Dorothy Deering and Vicky Richardson. Estab. 1989. Represents 47 clients. 75% of clients are new/unpublished writers.
Will Handle: Historical novels, historical romance, romance, mysteries, horror, sci fi, adventure, short story collections, mainstream, fantasy. Will read—at no charge—unsolicited queries and outlines. Reports in 2 weeks on queries; 6 weeks on manuscripts.
Terms: Agent receives 12% commission on domestic sales; 15% on dramatic sales; 15% on foreign sales; and 18% on movie and dramatic rights.
Fees: Charges a reading fee; provides free critiques. Charges $100 for mss under 100,000 words, $125 over. Charges for postage, packaging and phone calls.
Recent Sales: Confidential.

ANITA DIAMANT, THE WRITER'S WORKSHOP, INC., #1508, 310 Madison Ave., New York NY 10017. (212)687-1122. President: Anita Diamant. Estab. 1917. Member of SAR. Represents 100 clients. 30% of clients are new/unpublished writers. Prefers to work with published/established authors; works with a small number of new/unpublished authors. Specializes in general and commercial fiction (hard and soft cover) such as historical romances, general romances, horror and science fiction; and nonfiction such as health, politics and biography.
Will Handle: Magazine articles, nonfiction books and novels. Currently handles 40% nonfiction books; 40% novels; 10% young adult books; and 10% other. Will read—at no charge—unsolicited queries. Reports in 1 month on queries.
Terms: Agent receives 15% commission on domestic sales—15% on dramatic sales; and 20% on foreign sales.
Fees: Charges for photocopy, messenger, special mailing and telephone expenses.
Recent Sales: *Dawn*, by V.C. Andrews (Pocket); *Play of Words*, by Richard Lederer (Pocket); and *White Rush-Green Fire*, by Mark McGarrity (Morrow).

‡DIAMOND LITERARY AGENCY, INC., 3063 S. Kearney St., Denver CO 80222. (303)759-0291. President: Pat Dalton. Estab. 1982. Represents 20 clients. 15% of clients are new/unpublished writers. Not encouraging submissions from unpublished writers at this time. Specializes in novels, with particular interest in woman's fiction; thrillers, romantic suspense, mysteries, mainstream novels, romance; nonfiction books with a broad appeal; and screenplays.
Will Handle: Nonfiction books, novels, movie scripts, TV scripts. Currently handles 10% nonfiction books; 85% novels; 5% movie scripts. "Do *not* query. Send SASE for guidelines. Then submit first 50-75 pages with cassette tape. Include $15 money order if you have not previously sold the same type of book or script." Reports in 2 weeks on queries; 1 month on manuscripts. "Simultaneous submissions are acceptable as long as indicated as such, and not already under contract to another agent."
Terms: Agent receives 10-15% commission on domestic sales; 15% on dramatic sales; and 20% on foreign sales. Fee is $15 if the writer has not previously sold the same type of project (book or script); fee will be waived if representing the writer. Less than 1% of income derived from fees. "We provide critique if the project is close to being publishable at no additional charge; require that a standard-size cassette tape accompany each submission for possible comments." Charges for foreign air courier only. Over 99% of income derived from writers' work.
Recent Sales: *Critic's Choice*, by Cassie Miles (Crown); *Special Touches*, by Sharon Brondos (Harlequin); and *Close Scrutiny*, by Pat Dalton (Berkley).

SANDRA DIJKSTRA LITERARY AGENCY, Suite 515, 1155 Camino Del Mar, Del Mar CA 92014. (619)755-3115. FAX: (619)792-1494. Contact: Katherine Goodwin. Estab. 1981. Member of ILAA. Represents 80 clients. 60% of clients are new/unpublished writers. "We, of course, prefer to take on established authors, but are happy to represent any writer of brilliance or special ability. Most of our sales are nonfiction, but we are building a quality fiction list."
Will Handle: Nonfiction books (author must have expertise in the field) and quality and commercial fiction. Currently handles 75% nonfiction books; 25% fiction. Will read—at no charge—unsolicited sample chapters and outlines accompanied by a self-addressed, stamped envelope. Reports in 6 weeks on queries.
Terms: Receives 15% commission on domestic sales; 20% on foreign sales.
Fees: Charges a $225 yearly expense fee to cover phone, postage, photocopy costs incurred in marketing ms of authors under contract.
Recent Sales: *The Joy Luck Club*, by Amy Tan (Putnam's); *Leadership is an Art*, by Max DePree (Doubleday); *The Horse Latitudes*, by Robert Ferrigno (William Morrow).

THE JONATHAN DOLGER AGENCY, Suite 9B, 49 E. 96th St., New York NY 10128. (212)427-1853. President: Jonathan Dolger. Estab. 1980. Represents 70 clients. 25% of clients are new/unpublished writers. Writer must have been previously published if submitting fiction. Prefers to work with published/established authors; works with a small number of new/unpublished writers. Specializes in adult trade fiction and nonfiction, and illustrated books.
Will Handle: Nonfiction books, novels and illustrated books. Will read—at no charge—unsolicited queries and outlines with SASE included.
Terms: Agent receives 15% commission on domestic sales; 10% on dramatic sales; and 25-30% on foreign sales.
Fees: Charges for "standard expenses."
Recent Sales: Confidential.

‡THOMAS C. DONLAN, 143 E. 43rd St., New York NY 10017. (212)697-1629. Agent: Thomas C. Donlan. Estab. 1983. Represents 12 clients. "Our agency limits itself to philosophy and theology, mainly, but not exclusively Roman Catholic. No special requirements of earlier publication." Prefers to work with published/established authors. Specializes in philosophical and theological writings, including translations.

Will Handle: Magazine articles, nonfiction books and textbooks. Currently handles 2% magazine articles; 90% nonfiction books and 8% textbooks. Will read—at no charge—unsolicited queries and outlines. Reports in 2 weeks on queries.

Terms: Agent receives 10% commission on domestic sales; 6% on foreign sales.

Recent Sales: *Did Jesus Know He Was God*, by F. Dreyfus (Franciscan Herald); *Duty or Pleasure?—A New Approach to Christian Ethics*, by A. Ple (Paragon House).

‡**DUPREE/MILLER AND ASSOCIATES**, Suite 3, 5518 Dyer St., Dallas TX 75206. (214)692-1388. FAX: (214)987-9654. President: Jan Miller. Literary Associates: Sandra Burrowes/Katherine Hazelwood. Estab. 1979. Represents 62 clients. "We look at material and repersent material by previously published and unpublished authors. We do not specialize per se; at the moment we represent 60% nonfiction to 40% fiction but that varies constantly. We do not limit ourselves to fiction or nonfiction."

Will Handle: Nonfiction books, novels and movie scripts. Currently handles 45% nonfiction books; 45% novels; and 10% movie scripts. Will read for $10 charge, unsolicited queries, outlines and manuscripts. Reports in 2 weeks on queries; 9 weeks on mss.

Terms: Agent receives 15% commission on domestic sales; 15% on dramatic sales; and 15% on foreign sales.

Fees: Charges writers for postage and Federal Express.

Recent Sales: *Unlimited Power*, by Tony Robbins (Simon & Schuster); *Storming Intrepid*, by Payne Harrison (Crown); and *The Great Depression of 1990*, by Dr. Ravi Batra (Simon & Schuster).

DYKEMAN ASSOCIATES, INC., 4115 Rawlins, Dallas TX 75219. (214)528-2991. FAX (214)528-0241. President: Alice Dykeman. Estab. 1974. Represents 15 clients. Prefers to work with published/established authors.

Will Handle: Nonfiction books and some movie scripts. Currently handles 60% nonfiction books (such as celebrity profiles and biographies) and 40% movie scripts. Will read and critique submission for $200 charge.

Terms: Agent receives 15% commission.

Fees: Charges writers for out-of-pocket expenses, photocopies, faxes, long distance.

Recent Sales: "Several in the works; cannot release titles yet."

EDUCATIONAL DESIGN SERVICES, INC., P.O. Box 253, Wantagh NY 11793. (718)539-4107/(516)221-0995. Vice President: Edwin Selzer. President: Bertram Linder. Estab. 1979. Represents 18 clients. 90% of clients are new/unpublished writers. Eager to work with new/unpublished writers in the educational field. Specializes in educational materials aimed at the kindergarten through 12th grade market; primarily textual materials.

Will Handle: Nonfiction books and textbooks. Currently handles 100% textbooks. Reports in 1 month. "You must send SASE."

Terms: Agent receives 15% commission on domestic sales and 25% on foreign sales.

Fees: Charges for phone, postage and delivery expenses, and retyping "if necessary"; charges $50/hour.

Recent Sales: *Money* (Schoolhouse Press); *Nueva Historia de Los Estados Unidos* (Minerva Books); and *U.S. Government* (Minerva Books).

PETER ELEK ASSOCIATES, P.O. Box 223, Canal St. Station, New York NY 10013. (212)431-9368. FAX: (212)966-5768. Associate: Carol Diehl. Assistant: Libby Schmais. Estab. 1979. Also provides book packaging services. Represents 25 clients. 10% of our clients are new/unpublished writers. "An applicant must be, or is clearly intending to be, self-supporting through their writing." Prefers to work with published/established authors; works with a small number of new/unpublished authors. Specializes in illustrated nonfiction, current affairs, self-help (not pop-psych), contemporary biography/autobiography, food, popular culture (all for adults); and preschool and juvenile illustrated fiction, nonfiction and novelties; and contemporary adventure for adults.

Will Handle: Nonfiction books, novels and juvenile books. No category fiction. Currently handles 75% nonfiction books and 25% juvenile books. Will read—at no charge—unsolicited queries and outlines. Reports in 2 weeks on queries.

Terms: Agent receives 15% commission on domestic sales; 20% on dramatic sales; and 20% on foreign sales.

Fees: Charges for manuscript retyping, "if required." 5% of income derived from fees; 30% of income derived from commission on ms sales ("65% derived from sale of finished packaged books").

Recent Sales: *The Fighting Never Stopped*, by Patrick Brogan (Vintage); *The Discovery of the Bismarck*, by Dr. Robert Ballard (Warner); and *Denim: The Iconography of Jeans*, by Ian Finlayson (Simon and Schuster).

ETHAN ELLENBERG, LITERARY AGENT, #5-C, 548 Broadway, New York NY 10012. (212)431-4554. FAX: (212)941-4652. President: Ethan Ellenberg. Estab. 1984. Represents 40 clients. 30% of clients are new/unpublished writers. Eager to work with new/unpublished writers. Specializes in quality fiction and nonfiction, first novels, thriller, glitz, spy, military, history, biography, science fiction.

Will Handle: Nonfiction books, novels, juvenile books. Currently handles 25% nonfiction books; 70% novels; 5% juvenile books. Will read—at no charge—unsolicited queries, outlines and mss. Must include SASE. Reports in 3 weeks on queries; 6 weeks on mss. Prefers outline and first 3 chapters.

Terms: Agent receives 15% commission on domestic sales; 15% on dramatic sales; and 20% on foreign sales.
Fees: Charges for cost of photocopies up to 10 mss for sale, finished copies for submission to foreign markets and Hollywood.
Recent Sales: *Help Yourself to the Golden Years*, by Regina Kessler (Pharos); *Two if by Sea*, by Richard Rosenthal (Pocket); and *Seals*, by T.L. Bosiljevac (Ballantine).

‡**FELICIA ETH LITERARY REPRESENTATION**, Suite 62, 140 University Ave., Palo Alto CA 94301. (415)375-1276. Contact: Felicia Eth. Estab. 1988. Member of ILAA. Represents 25-30 clients. Eager to work with new/unpublished writers, "for nonfiction, established expertise is certainly a plus, as is magazine publication—though not a prerequisite." Specializes in "provocative, intelligent, thoughtful nonfiction on a wide array ofsubjects which are commercial and high-quality fiction; preferably mainstream and contemporary. I am highly selective, but also highly dedicated to those projects I represent."
Will Handle: Nonfiction books, novels. Handles 75% nonfiction, 25% novels. Will read—at no charge—unsolicited queries and outlines. Reports in 2 weeks on queries; 1 month on proposals and sample pages.
Terms: Charges 15% commission on domestic sales; 20% on dramatic sales; and 20% on foreign sales.
Fees: Charges for photocopying, fax, Federal Express service—extraordinary expenses.
Recent Sales: *The Female Hero*, by Kate Noble, Ph.D. (Ballantine); *Forms of Gold: Essays from the Southwest*, by Sherman Russell (Addison-Wesley); and *A Breed Apart: A Journey to the Backside of Racetrack Life*, by Mike Helm (Henry Holt).

EVANS AND ASSOCIATES, 14330 Caves Rd., Novelty OH 44072. (216)338-3264. Agent/Owner: Clyde Evans. Estab. 1987. "This agency will represent any author whose work, based on agency review, is of such quality that it is deemed sellable." Eager to work with new/unpublished writers.
Will Handle: Various types of material. Will read—at no charge—unsolicited queries, outlines and mss. Reports in 3 weeks on queries; 2 months on mss.
Terms: Agent receives 15% commission on domestic sales; 10% on dramatic sales; and 20% total on foreign sales—10% to foreign agent.
Fees: Charges for photocopying over 75 pages, legal advice beyond normal agency services, messenger.
Recent Sales: No information given.

‡**EXECUTIVE EXCELLENCE**, 8 West Center, Provo UT 84601. (801)375-4014. FAX: (801)377-5960. President/Agent: Ken Shelton. Estab. 1984. Represents 20 clients. "Authors must have a manuscript partially completed an annotated outline and a completed synopsis of their book. Services are available to assist authors in the completion of their manuscripts." Specializes in nonfiction trade books (management and personal development)—books with a specialized focus such as ethics in business, managerial effectiveness, organizational productivity."
Will Handle: Magazine articles, nonfiction books and novels. Currently handles 95% nonfiction books; and 5% novels. Will read submissions at no charge, but may charge a criticism fee or service charge for work performed after the initial reading. Reports in 1 month on mss.
Terms: Agent receives 15% commission on domestic sales.
Fees: "We charge a $1 per page ($150 minimum) critical reading and review fee." Waives reading fee if we represent the writer. Charges $300/300/pages. "A $500 deposit is made by the author at the time of signing a contract to cover expenses (calls, mail, etc.). Other fees are charged as listed in the contract. Services may be contracted separately. If expenses exceed $500, the author must approve expenditures." 90% of income derived from sales of writers' work; 10% of income derived from criticism services.
Recent Sales: *Inventing for Profit*, by John Ilich (John Wiley & Sons); and *Straight Talk for Monday Morning*, by Allan Cox (John Wiley & Sons).

JOHN FARQUHARSON LTD., Suite 1007, 250 W. 57th St., New York NY 10107. (212)245-1993. Director: Jane Gelfman. Agent: Deborah Schneider. Estab. 1919 (London); 1980 (New York). Member of SAR and ILAA. Represents 125 clients. Fewer than 5% of clients are new/unpublished writers. Prefers to work with published/established authors; works with a small number of new/unpublished authors. Specializes in general trade fiction and nonfiction. No poetry, short stories or screenplays.
Will Handle: Fiction and nonfiction; handles magazine articles and magazine fiction only for authors already represented. Currently handles 49% nonfiction books; 49% novels; and 2% juvenile books. Will read—at no charge—unsolicited queries and outlines. Reports in 3 weeks on queries. SASE necessary.
Terms: Agent receives 10% commission on domestic sales; 10% on dramatic sales; and 20% on foreign sales.
Fees: Charges for messengers, photocopying and overseas calls.
Recent Sales: *Preventing Miscarriage*, by Johathan Schler, M.D. and Lord Dix (Harper & Row); *Bio of Kay Boyle*, by Joan Miller (Farrar, Straus & Giroux); and *Cosmologists*, by Alan Lightman and Robroh Braner (Harvard University Press).

FARWESTERN CONSULTANTS LITERARY AGENCY, P.O. Box 47786, Phoenix AZ 85068-7786. (602)861-3546. President: Elizabeth "Libbi" Goodman. Estab. 1987. Represents 38 clients. "50% of our clients are new/unpublished writers. We have a strong background in literature, editing; and cover the NY and regional markets. We devote whatever time is needed to help a writer develop his full potential. We believe a dynamic relationship between author and agent is necessary for success." Willing to work with new/unpublished writers if they are ready. "We also work with a number of established authors. We specialize in popular fiction (western, mystery, contemporary/historical romance, espionage, medical thriller, horror, occult and action/adventure), women's fiction and ethnic fiction/nonfiction."
Will Handle: Most book-length nonfiction, contemporary fiction, literary novels, short story collections by established authors. Represents screenplays only for established clients. Does not handle magazine articles, short stories, poetry, juvenile or young adult fiction.
Terms: Receives 15% commission on domestic sales; 15% on dramatic sales; and 20% on foreign sales. Currently handles 70% novels; 25% nonfiction; and 5% screenplays. Prefers query letters, but will read unsolicited queries consisting of a cover letter, outline (nonfiction) or synopsis (fiction), and first 10 pages of manuscript. *No response, to any correspondence, unless SASE is included with submission.* Reports in 2 weeks on queries; 3 months from date of receipt for solicited mss and partials. "No complete manuscripts unless requested. We do not charge a reading fee, therefore, we do not read any requested material that is a multiple submission."
Fees: Charges writers for photocopying and unusual expenses agreed upon in advance.
Recent Sales: *Red Sea, Dead Sea,* by Serita Deborah Stevens (St. Martin's Press); *A Passage of Seasons,* by Douglas Hirt (Doubleday); and *Judas Guns,* by Howard Pelham (Walker Books).

FLORENCE FEILER LITERARY AGENCY, 1524 Sunset Plaza Dr., Los Angeles CA 90069. (659)652-6920/652-0945. Associate: Audrey Rugh. Estab. 1976. Represents 40 clients. No unpublished writers. "Quality is the criterion." Specializes in fiction, nonfiction and screen; very little TV and no short stories.
Will Handle: Textbooks (for special clients), juvenile books, movie scripts. Will read—at no charge—queries and outlines only. Reports in 2 weeks on queries; 10 weeks on mss. "We will not accept simultaneous queries to other agents."
Terms: Agent receives 10% commission on domestic sales; 10% on dramatic sales; and 20% on foreign sales.
Recent Sales: *Babette's Feast* (best foreign film); *Logic of the Heart,* by Patricia Veryan (St. Martine); *Nightwares,* by Collin McDonald (Dutton); and *Midnight Eclacy* (Zebra).

MARJE FIELDS/RITA SCOTT, 165 W. 46th, Room 1205, New York NY 10036. (212)764-5740. Literary Manager: Ray Powers. Estab. 1972. Member ILAA. Represents 50 clients. 50% of clients are new/unpublished writers. Prefers to work with published/established writers, works with a small number of new/unpublished authors. Specializes in novels, nonfiction and plays.
Will Handle: Nonfiction books, novels (including young adult) and stage plays. Currently handles 25% nonfiction books; 75% novels. Reports in 1 week on queries.
Terms: Agent receives 15% commission on domestic sales; 15% on dramatic sales; and 20% on foreign sales.
Recent Sales: *Exit Wounds,* by John Westermann (Soho Press); *Death of a Blue Movie Star,* by Jeff Deaver (Bantam); *Live Free or Die,* by Ernest Hebert (Viking).

FRIEDA FISHBEIN LTD., 2556 Hubbard St., Brooklyn NY 11235. (212)247-4398. President: Janice Fishbein. Estab. 1925. Represents 30 clients. 50% of clients are new/unpublished writers. "We agree to represent a writer solely on the basis of a *complete* work." Eager to work with new/unpublished writers. Specializes in historical romance, historical adventure, male adventure, mysteries, thrillers and family sagas. Books on the environment, how-to, plays and screenplays.
Will Handle: Nonfiction books, novels, young adult, movie scripts, stage plays and TV scripts. No poetry or magazine articles. Currently handles 20% nonfiction books; 30% novels; 5% textbooks; 10% juvenile books; 10% movie scripts; 15% stage plays; and 10% TV scripts. Will read—at no charge—unsolicited queries and brief outlines. Reports in 2 weeks on queries; 1 month on mss.
Terms: Agent receives 10% commission on domestic sales; 10% on dramatic sales; and 20% on foreign sales.
Fees: Charges reading fee; $75/TV script, screenplay or play; $60/50,000 words for manuscripts, $1 for each 1,000 additional words. Only *complete* mss are reviewed. Fee will be returned if representing writer. "Our readers are freelance workers who also serve as editors at magazines and/or publishers. Our reports are always longer for larger manuscripts. The usual reader's report varies between three to five pages, and may or may not include a line-to-line critique, but it always includes an overall evaluation." 20% of income derived from fees; 80% of income derived from commission on ms sales. Payment of a criticism fee does not ensure that agency will represent a writer.
Recent Sales: *Dr. Death,* by Herbert L. Fisher (Berkley Publishing Co.); "Double Cross," by Gary Bohlke (play); and *The Frenchwoman,* by Jeanne Mockin (St. Martin's Press).

JOYCE A. FLAHERTY, LITERARY AGENT, 816 Lynda Court, St. Louis MO 63122. (314)966-3057. Agent: Joyce A. Flaherty. Estab. 1980. Member Romance Writers of America and Mystery Writers of America. Represents 63 clients. 75% of clients are new/unpublished writers. "Most new clients come through referral

by clients and/or editors." Works with small number of new/unpublished authors. Specializes in mainstream women's fiction, general fiction, genre fiction such as horror, historical, romance, family sagas, thrillers, techno-thrillers, mysteries, contemporary romance. General nonfiction, including biographies, cookbooks, true crime, health/science, self-help, how-to, military, Americana, and travel books.
Will Handle: Nonfiction books, novels. Currently handles 40% nonfiction books; 60% novels. Will read—at no charge—unsolicited queries and outlines. "No response without SASE." Reports in 2 months on queries.
Terms: Agent receives 10-15% commission on domestic sales.
Recent Sales: *The World of International Modeling*, by Eve Matheson (Holt); *Defcon-One*, by Joe Weber (Presidio); and *Gentle Pardon*, by Gloria Skinner (Warner).

FLAMING STAR LITERARY ENTERPRISES, 320 Riverside Dr., New York NY 10025-9998. President: Joseph B. Vallely. Estab. 1985. Represents 50 clients. 50% of clients are new/unpublished writers. Eager to work with new/unpublished writers. Specializes in adult commercial and literary fiction and nonfiction.
Will Handle: Nonfiction books and novels. Currently handles 50% nonfiction books and 50% novels. Will read submissions at no charge. Reports in 1 week on queries; 2 weeks on mss. "No phone calls."
Terms: Agent receives 15% commission on domestic sales; 15% on dramatic sales; and 20% on foreign sales. (All rates are for unpublished authors. Commissions are 5% lower for previously published authors.)
Recent Sales: Confidential.

FLANNERY, WHITE & STONE, Suite 110, 180 Cook, Denver CO 80206. (303)399-2264. Literary Agent: Barbara Schoichet. Estab. 1987. Member of International Women's Writer's Guild and Society of Children's Literature. Represents 25 clients. 90% of clients are new/unpublished writers. Specializes in literary fiction, unique nonfiction business books and very interested in screenplays.
Will Handle: Nonfiction books, novels, movie scripts. Currently represents 19% nonfiction; 60% novels; 20% juvenile books; 1% movie scripts. Will read submissions at no charge, but may charge a criticism fee or service charge for work performed after the initial reading. Reports in 2 weeks on queries; 6 weeks on mss.
Terms: Agent receives 15% commission on domestic sales; 15% on dramatic sales; and 20% on foreign sales.
Fees: Usually we don't charge unless a writer wants a written evaluation of his/her work. Charges $1/page of mss for reading/evaluation. Critiques are 3-5 pages of both line-by-line and overall evaluation. Marketing advice is included and the critiques are done by professional editors and/or published authors. 25% of income derived from criticism fees. Charges writers for photocopying unless the author provides copies.
Recent Sales: *Baby Lust*, by Jim Carrier (Zebra); *The Powwow Superhighway*, by David Seals (NAL); and *An Entrepreneur's Guide to Bank Loans*, by Arthur Pulis, III. (Probus).

THE FOLEY AGENCY, 34 E. 38th St., New York NY 10016. (212)686-6930. Partners: Joan and Joseph Foley. Estab. 1956. Represents 30 clients. Works with a small number of new/unpublished authors (1% of new material received).
Will Handle: Nonfiction books and novels. Currently handles 75% nonfiction books and 25% novels. Will read—at no charge—unsolicited queries and outlines if SASE is enclosed. Reports in 2 weeks on queries. Do not submit manuscripts unless requested.
Terms: Agent receives 10% commission on domestic sales; 10-20% on dramatic sales; and 10-20% on foreign sales.
Fees: Charges for occasional messenger fee and special phone expenses.
Recent Sales: "Deals with all major publishers."

‡FORTHWRITE LITERARY SERVICE, P.O. Box 922101, Sylmar CA 91392. (818)365-3400. FAX: (818)362-3443. Agent: Wendy L. Zhorne. Estab. 1988. Represents 20 clients. We prefer writers with credits or professional training, but will look at new works of excellence. Eager to work with new/unpublished writers. Specializes in fiction and nonfiction; scripts of all genres; no occult, religious zealot, new age, explicit sex, or horror accepted.
Will Handle: Nonfiction books, novels, juvenile books, movie scripts and TV scripts. Currently handles 20% nonfiction books; 40% novels, 30% movie scripts; and 10% TV scripts. Will read—at no charge—unsolicited queries and outlines. Reports in 1 month on queries.
Terms: Agent receives 15% commission on domestic sales; 15% on dramatic sales; and 20% on foreign sales.
Fees: Charges a reading fee in the event of no training or previously published work, but has good idea and good query. No reading fee of future work for clients, of course! 25% of income derived from reading fees. Charges $50/300 pages. Charges a criticism fee. In the event the writer needs extensive assistance to bring an idea up to industry standards, we charge a fee which fluctuates based on needs of ms, needs and wants of author. 30% of income derived from criticism fees. Charges varying fees depending on length and genre. Writers receive 8-page critique on separate sheet, covering story, plot, technical execution, characterization, marketability, suggestions for improvement, ideas for additional sub-plots, examples of dialogue, whatever is necessary in however many pages it takes to bring it up to standard. Each client is charged an expense retainer which is fully refundable at close of sale. Payment of criticism fee does not ensure that agency will represent writer.

Recent Sales: Confidential. "An excellent idea is like a lump of clay. It can be sculpted into a work of art, or mixed with mud."

ROBERT A. FREEDMAN DRAMATIC AGENCY, INC., Suite 2310, 1501 Broadway, New York NY 10036. (212)840-5760. President: Robert A. Freedman. Vice President: Selma Luttinger. Estab. 1928. Member of SAR. Prefers to work with established authors; works with a small number of new authors. Specializes in plays, motion picture and television scripts.
Will Handle: Movie scripts, stage plays and TV scripts. Does not read unsolicited mss. Usually reports in 2 weeks on queries; 2 months on mss.
Terms: Agent receives 10% on dramatic sales; "and, as is customary, 20% on amateur rights."
Fees: Charges for photocopying manuscripts.
Recent Sales: "We will speak directly with any prospective client concerning sales that are relevant to his/her specific script."

SAMUEL FRENCH, INC., 45 W. 25th St., New York NY 10010. (212)206-8990. Editor: William Talbot. Assistant Editor: Lawrence Harbison. Estab. 1830. Member of SAR. Represents "hundreds" of clients. Prefers to work with published/established authors; works with a small number of new/unpublished authors. Specializes in plays.
Will Handle: Stage plays. Currently handles 100% stage plays. Will read—at no charge—unsolicited queries and mss. Replies "immediately" on queries; decision in 2-8 months regarding publication. "Enclose SASE."
Terms: Agent receives usually 10% professional production royalties; and 20% amateur production royalties.
Recent Sales: *Mastergate*, by Gelbart.

CANDICE FUHRMAN LITERARY AGENCY, P.O. Box F, Forest Knolls CA 94933. (415)488-0161. President: Candice Fuhrman. Estab. 1987. Represents 30 clients. 75% of clients are new/unpublished writers. Eager to work with new/unpublished writers. Specializes in self-help and how-to nonfiction; adult commercial fiction. No genre or children's books.
Will Handle: Nonfiction and adult fiction novels. Handles 90% nonfiction books; 10% novels. Will read—at no charge—unsolicited queries, outlines and manuscripts. Reports in 2 weeks on queries; 1 months on mss.
Terms: Agent receives 15% commission on domestic sales; 20% on dramatic sales; and 20% on foreign sales.
Fees: Charges for postage and photocopy expenses.
Recent Sales: *Getting Love Right*, by Terry Gorski (Prentice Hall); *A Kiss is Just a Kiss*, by Bruce Velick (Random House); and *1001 Ways to Improve Your Child's Schoolwork*, by Larry Greene (Dell).

JAY GARON-BROOKE ASSOCIATES INC., 17th Floor, 415 Central Park West, New York NY 10025. (212)866-3654. President: Jay Garon. Estab. 1952. Member of ILAA and Authors Guild Inc. Represents 100 clients. 15% of clients are new/unpublished writers. Prefers to work with published/established authors; works with small number of new/unpublished writers.
Will Handle: Nonfiction books, novels, juvenile books (young adult), movie scripts and stage plays. Currently handles 25% nonfiction books; 70% novels; 2% juvenile books; 1% movie scripts; 1% stage plays and 1% TV scripts. Does not read unsolicited material. Submit query letters with bio and SASE. Reports in 1 month.
Terms: Agent receives 15% commission on domestic sales; 10-15% on dramatic sales; and 30% on foreign sales.
Recent Sales: *The Firm*, by John Grisham (Doubleday); *Pandora's Box*, by Elizabeth Gage (Simon & Schuster); *Aces*, by Robert Denny (Donald Fine, Inc.).

MAX GARTENBERG, LITERARY AGENT, Suite 1700, 521 Fifth Ave., New York NY 10175. (212)860-8451. Contact: Max Gartenberg. Estab. 1954. Represents 30 clients. 10% of clients are new/unpublished writers. "The writer must convince me of his or her professional skills, whether through published or unpublished materials he/she has produced." Prefers to work with published/established authors. Specializes in nonfiction and fiction trade books.
Will Handle: Nonfiction books and novels. Currently handles 75% nonfiction books and 25% novels. Will read—at no charge—unsolicited queries and outlines. Reports in 1 week on queries. "SASE required."
Terms: Agent receives 10% commission on domestic sales; 10% on dramatic sales; and 15% on foreign sales.
Recent Sales: *Phantoms*, by Linda Davis (Ticknor & Fields); *The Last Apache*, by David Roberts (Simon & Schuster); and *Encyclopedia of Twentieth Century Wars and Warfare*, by Edwin P. Hoyt (Facts on File).

GELLES-COLE LITERARY ENTERPRISES, Woodstock Towers, Suite 411, 320 E. 42nd St., New York NY 10017. (212)573-9857. President: Sandi Gelles-Cole. Estab. 1983. Represents 50 clients. 25% of clients are new/unpublished writers. "We concentrate on published and unpublished, but we try to avoid writers who seem stuck in mid-list." Specializes in commercial fiction and nonfiction.

Will Handle: Nonfiction books and novels. "We're looking for more nonfiction—fiction has to be complete to submit—publishers buying fewer unfinished novels." Currently handles 50% nonfiction books; 50% novels. Does not read unsolicited mss. Reports in 3 weeks.

Terms: Agent receives 15% commission on domestic sales; 15% on dramatic sales; and 20% on foreign sales.

Fees: Charges reading fee of $75 for proposal; $100, ms under 250 pages; $150, ms over 250 pages. "Our reading fee is for evaluation. Writer receives total evaluation, what is right, what is wrong, is book 'playing' to market, general advice on how to fix." Charges writers for overseas calls, overnight mail, messenger. 5% of income derived from fees charged to writers. 50% of income derived from sales of writer's work; 45% of income derived from editorial service.

Recent Sales: *Legacy*, by Robin Helmsley-Grimes (Berkley); and *The Beyond*, by Barry Harrington (Berkley).

GLADDEN UNLIMITED, P.O. Box 12001, Portland OR 97212. (503)287-9015. Principal: Carolan Gladden. Represents 25 clients. Estab. 1987. 80% of clients are new/unpublished writers. Dedicated to work with new/unpublished writers. Specializes in general interest nonfiction and fiction including mainstream, horror/thriller, action/adventure, sci-fi. "No romance, western, children's poetry or short fiction."

Will Handle: Nonfiction books, novels and screenplays. Currently handles 30% nonfiction books; 60% novels and 10% screenplays. Will read—at no charge—unsolicited queries. SASE required. Reports in 3 weeks on queries.

Terms: Agent receives 15% commission on domestic sales; 20% on dramatic sales; and 20% on foreign sales. Writers Guild of America signatory.

Fees: We charge $100 for a marketability evaluation. This is an in-depth 6-10 page diagnostic appraisal that includes general observations, ideas and specifics to achieve publication. 25% of income derived from criticism fees. Also offers other authors' services and publishes selected books under Diamond Editions imprint.

Recent Sales: Confidential.

LUCIANNE S. GOLDBERG LITERARY AGENTS, INC., Suite 6-A, 255 W. 84th St., New York NY 10024. (212)799-1260. Editorial Director: Sandrine Olm. Estab. 1974. Represents 65 clients. 10% of clients are new/unpublished writers. "Any author we decide to repesent must have a good idea, a good presentation of that idea and writing skill to compete with the market. Representation depends solely on the execution of the work whether writer is published or unpublished." Specializes in nonfiction works, "but will review a limited number of novels."

Will Handle: Nonfiction books and novels. Currently handles 75% nonfiction books and 25% novels. Will read—at no charge—unsolicited queries and outlines. Reports in 2 weeks on queries; 3 weeks on mss. "If our agency does not respond within 1 month to your request to become a client, you may submit requests elsewhere."

Terms: Agent receives 15% commission on domestic sales; 25% on dramatic sales; and 25% on foreign sales. Charges reading fee on unsolicited mss: $150/full-length ms. Criticism is included in reading. 1% of income derived from reading fees. "Our critiques run three to four pages, single-spaced. They deal with the overall evaluation of the work. Three agents within the organization read and then confer. Marketing advice is included." Payment of fee does not ensure the agency will represent a writer. Charges for phone expenses, cable fees, photocopying and messenger service after the work is sold. 80% of income derived from commission on ms sales.

Recent Sales: *Senatorial Privilege*, by Leo Damore (Delacorte-Dell); *Who's Who in Hollywood*, by David Ragan (Facts on File); and *Nina's Journey*, by Nina Markovna (Regnery-Gateway).

IRENE GOODMAN LITERARY AGENCY, 521 5th Ave., 17th Floor, New York NY 10017. (212)682-1978. Contact: Irene Goodman, president. Estab. 1978. Member of ILAA. Represents 100 clients. 20% of clients are new/unpublished writers. Works with a small number of new/unpublished authors. Specializes in women's fiction (mass market, category, and historical romance), popular nonfiction, reference and mysteries.

Will Handle: Novels and nonfiction books. Currently handles 20% nonfiction books; 80% novels. Will read—at no charge—unsolicited queries. Reports in 3 weeks. "No reply without SASE."

Terms: Agent receives 15% commission on domestic sales and 20% on foreign sales. 100% of income from commission on ms sales.

Recent Sales: *Daniel's Bride* (Pocket) and *The Whiskey Man* (Bantam).

CHARLOTTE GORDON AGENCY, 235 E. 22nd St., New York NY 10010. (212)679-5363. Contact: Charlotte Gordon. Estab. 1986. Represents 20 clients. 30% of clients are new/unpublished writers. "I'll work with writers whose work is interesting to me." Specializes in "books (not magazine material, except for my writers, and then only in special situations). My taste is eclectic."

Will Handle: Fiction and nonfiction books, novels and juvenile books (all ages). Currently handles 30% nonfiction books; 30% novels; 30% juvenile and 10% other. Will read—at no charge—unsolicited queries and outlines. Does not read unsolicited manuscripts. Reports in 2 weeks on queries.

Terms: Agent receives 15% commission on domestic sales; 10% on dramatic sales; and 10% on foreign sales.
Fees: Charges writers for photocopying manuscripts.
Recent Sales: *Expert Witness*, by Stockley (Simon & Schuster); *Landing on Marvin Gardens*, by Zable (Bantam); and *Disturbing the Peace*, by Dash (Little Brown).

GRAHAM AGENCY, 311 W. 43rd St., New York NY 10036. (212)489-7730. Owner: Earl Graham. Estab. 1971. Member of SAR. Represents 35 clients. 35% of clients are new/unpublished writers. Willing to work with new/unpublished writers. Specializes in full-length stage plays and musicals.
Will Handle: Stage plays and musicals. Will read—at no charge—unsolicited queries and outlines, "and plays and musicals which we agree to consider on the basis of the letters of inquiry." Reports in 6 weeks on queries.
Terms: Agent receives 10% commission on domestic sales; 10% on dramatic sales; and 10% on foreign sales.
Recent Sales: No information given.

HAROLD R. GREENE, INC., Suite 309, 8455 Beverly Blvd., Los Angeles CA 90048. (213)852-4959. President: Harold Greene. Estab. 1985. Member of WGA and DGA. Represents 12 clients, primarily screenwriters. Specializes in screenplay writing and novels that are adaptable to films or TV movies.
Will Handle: Novels and movie scripts. Currently handles 5% novels and 95% movie scripts. Does not read unsolicited mss.
Terms: Agent receives 10% commission on domestic sales; 10% on dramatic sales; and 10% on foreign sales.
Recent Sales: *The Long Walk*, by George La Fountaine (Putnam); *Lifter*, by Crawford Kilian (Berkeley); and *Forever And a Day*, by Pamela Wallace (Silhouette).

‡**CHARLOTTE GUSAY LITERARY AGENCY**, 10532 Blythe Ave., Los Angeles CA 90064. (213)559-0831. FAX: (213)474-7705. Owner: Charlotte Gusay. Estab. 1988. Represents 14 clients. Specializes in commercial fiction and nonfiction; no plays or poetry.
Will Handle: Nonfiction books, novels, textbooks, juvenile books and movie scripts. Currently handles 30% nonfiction books; 30% novels; 30% juvenile books; 10% movie scripts. Will read—at no charge—unsolicited queries and outlines. Does not read unsolicited manuscripts. Reports in 2 months on queries.
Terms: Agent receives 15% commission on domestic sales; 10% on dramatic sales.
Recent Sales: *A Visit to the Art Galaxy*, by Annie Reiner (Green Tiger Press); *Wearing Dad's Head*, by Barry Yourgran (Peregrine Smith).

ROSE HASS, AGENT, 2020 Ave. V, Apt. 5-C, Brooklyn NY 11229. (718)646-1418 (evenings); (212)529-8900 (days). FAX: (212)529-7399. Contact: Rose Hass. Estab. 1987. Represents 3 clients. To be represented, writer must have published at least three magazine articles. Specializes in selling juvenile fiction and nonfiction, adult fiction and nonfiction, art books (illustrated), some literary criticism.
Will Handle: Nonfiction books, novels and juvenile books (ages 5-12). Currently handles 50% nonfiction books; 25% novels and 25% juvenile books. Will read—at no charge—unsolicited queries and outlines. Does not read unsolicited manuscripts. Reports in 1 month on queries.
Terms: Agent receives 15% commission on domestic sales; 15% on dramatic sales; and 15% on foreign sales.
Fees: "If ms is sent to more than four publishers, writer pays postage."
Recent Sales: *Lovingly Georgia*, by O'Keefe/Pollitzer (Simon & Schuster); *Bernice Abbott: Photographs*, by Bernice Abbott (Smithsonian).

JOHN HAWKINS & ASSOCIATES, INC., Suite 1600, 71 W. 23rd St., New York NY 10010. (212)807-7040. FAX: (212)807-9555. Agents: John Hawkins, William Reiss and Sharon Friedman. Estab. 1893 (Originally Paul R. Reynolds Agency). Member of SAR. Eager to work with new/unpublished writers. Specializes in fiction, nonfiction, children's, young adult, women's fiction and nonfiction, history.
Will Handle: Nonfiction books, novels and juvenile books. Currently handles 40% nonfiction books; 50% novels and 10% juvenile books. Will read—at no charge—unsolicited queries and outlines. Reports in 3 weeks on queries.
Terms: Agent receives 10% commission on domestic sales and 20% on foreign sales.
Recent Sales: No information given.

HEACOCK LITERARY AGENCY, INC., Suite 14, 1523 6th St., Santa Monica CA 90401. (213)393-6227. President: Jim Heacock. Vice President: Rosalie Heacock. Estab. 1978. Member of ILAA and the Association of Talent Agents (writers only). Represents 60 clients. 35% of clients are new/unpublished writers. Works with a small number of new/unpublished authors. Specializes in nonfiction on a wide variety of subjects—health, nutrition, diet, exercise, sports, psychology, crafts, women's studies, business expertise, pregnancy and parenting, alternative health concepts, starting a business and celebrity biographies.
Will Handle: Nonfiction books; novels (by authors who have been previously published by major houses); movie scripts (prefer Writer's Guild members); and TV scripts (prefer Writer's Guild members). Currently handles 85% nonfiction books; 5% novels; 5% movie scripts and 5% TV scripts. "We want to see health

oriented works by professionals with credentials and something original to say. Selected New Age subjects are a growing market at all levels of publishing. Celebrity biographies will continue to sell well if they cover contemporary personalities." Will read—at no charge—unsolicited queries and outlines. Reports in 1 month on queries if SASE is included.

Terms: Agent receives 15% commission on domestic sales; 10% on dramatic sales; 25% on foreign sales (if a foreign agent is used. If we sell direct to a foreign publisher, the commission is 15%).

Fees: Charges writers for postage, phone and photocopying.

Recent Sales: *Inside Paul Horn*, by Paul Horn and Lee Underwood (Harper & Row); *Cory Coleman*; by Larry Dane Brimmer (Henry Holt); and *Oh My Baby Bear*, by Audrey Wood (Harcourt Brace Jovanovich).

THE JEFF HERMAN AGENCY, INC., Suite 501-L, 500 Greenwich St., New York NY 10013. (212)725-4660. President: Jeffrey H. Herman. Estab. 1985. Member ILAA. Represents 65 clients. 40% of clients are new/previously unpublished writers. Willing to work with new/unpublished writers. Specializes in general nonfiction and fiction.

Will Handle: Nonfiction books, novels, textbooks. Currently handles 70% nonfiction; 50% textbooks; 20% general fiction. Will read—at no charge—unsolicited queries. Reports in 2 weeks on queries; 6 weeks on mss.

Terms: Agent receives 15% commission on domestic sales; 15% on foreign sales.

Recent Sales: *Managing the Future*, by Robert Tuckel (Putnam); *Funny Feelings: Explanations for Everyday Sensations*, by Alan Xerakis, M.D. (Villard); and *Embrace an Angry Wind*, by Wiley Sword (Harper Collins).

SUSAN HERNER RIGHTS AGENCY, Suite 1403, 110 W. 40 St., New York NY 10018. (212)221-7515. Contact: Susan Herner or Sue Yuen. Estab. 1987. Represents 50 clients. 25% of clients are new/unpublished writers. Eager to work with new/unpublished writers. Trade expertise in fiction (literary and genre), romance, science fiction, nonfiction.

Will Handle: Nonfiction books and novels. Currently handles 45% nonfiction books; 50% novels; 5% juvenile books (pre-school to age 7). Will read—at no charge—unsolicited queries, outlines and mss. Reports in 1 month on queries; 2 months on mss.

Terms: Agent receives 15% commission on domestic sales; 20% on dramatic sales; and 20% on foreign sales.

Fees: Charges for extraordinary postage and handling, photocopying. "Agency has two divisions: one represents writers on a commission-only basis; the other represents the rights for small publishers and packagers who do not have in-house subsidiary rights representation. Percentage of income derived from each division is currently 50-50."

Recent Sales: *Style is not a Size*, by Hara Marano (Bantam); *Dead Ringers*, by Tim Underwood (NAL); *Dream Lovers*, by Mary and Don Kelly (Simon & Schuster).

FREDERICK HILL ASSOCIATES, 1842 Union St., San Francisco CA 94123. (415)921-2910. FAX: (415)921-2802. Contact: Bonnie Nadell. Estab. 1979. Represents 100 clients. 50% of clients are new/unpublished writers. Specializes in general nonfiction, fiction and young adult fiction.

Will Handle: Nonfiction books and novels.

Terms: Agent receives 15% commission on domestic sales; 15% on dramatic sales; and 20% on foreign sales.

Fees: Charges for overseas airmail (books, proofs only), overseas Telex, cable, domestic Telex. 100% of income derived from commission on ms sales.

Recent Sales: No information given.

ALICE HILTON LITERARY AGENCY, 13131 Welby Way, North Hollywood CA 91606. (818)982-2546. Estab. 1986. Affiliated with Ann Waugh Agency (WGA). Eager to work with new/unpublished writers. Specializes in movie and TV scripts—"Interested in any quality material, although agent's personal taste runs in the genre of 'Cheers,' 'L.A. Law,' 'American Playhouse,' 'Masterpiece Theatre' and Woody Allen vintage humor."

Will Handle: Movie and TV scripts and booklength mss.

Terms: Agent receives 10% commission.

Fees: Charges for phone, postage and photocopy expenses. Charges evaluation fee of $2/1,000 words. Will read movie and TV scripts at no charge if invited. Brochure available. Preliminary phone call appreciated.

Recent Sales: Soap opera comedy, by Kris Meijer to VOO Television (Amsterdam); *Counterparts*, by Kurt Fischel (New Saga) and *The Cradled and the Called*, by Roger Sargeant (New Saga).

‡JOHN L. HOCHMANN BOOKS, 320 E. 58th St., New York NY 10022. (212)319-0505. President: John L. Hochmann. Estab. 1976. Represents 23 clients. Writer must have demonstrable eminence in field or previous publications for nonfiction, and critically and/or commercially successful books for fiction. Prefers to work with published/established authors.

Will Handle: Nonfiction books, textbooks and novels. Currently handles 60% nonfiction, 25% textbooks and 15% fiction. Will read—at no charge—unsolicited queries, outlines and solicited mss. Reports in 1 week on queries; 1 month on mss.

Terms: Agent receives 15% commission on domestic sales; and additional commission on foreign sales. 100% of income derived from commission on ms sales. Include SASE.

Recent Sales: *500 Years of American Clothing*, by Lee Hall (Little, Brown); *Nutrition Challenge for Women*, by Louise Lambert-Lagacé (General Publishing); and *Strategic Communications: How to Make Your Ideas Their Ideas*, by Burton Kaplan (Harper & Row).

‡**HULL HOUSE LITERARY AGENCY**, 240 E. 82nd St., New York NY 10028. (212)988-0725. FAX: (212)439-1777. President: David Stewart Hull. Estab. 1987. Represents 42 clients. Prefers to work with published/ established authors but works with a small number of new/unpublished authors also. Specializes in commercial fiction; nonfiction, particularly biographies, history, military history, books about film and fine arts.
Will Handle: Nonfiction books and novels. Currently handles 50% nonfiction and 50% novels. Does not read unsolicited manuscripts. Reports in 2 weeks on queries submitted with SASE only.
Terms: Agent receives 15% commission on domestic sales; 20% on foreign sales, split with foreign agent.
Fees: Charges writers for copies; Express Mail; overseas telephone if extensive.
Recent Sales: "We do not release this information to the general public."

INTERNATIONAL LITERATURE AND ARTS AGENCY, 50 E. 10th St., New York NY 10003. (212)475-1999. Director: Bonnie R. Crown. Estab. 1977. Represents 10 clients. 10% of clients are new/unpublished writers. Works with a small number of new/unpublished authors; eager to work with new/unpublished writers in area of specialization, and established translators from Asian languages. Specializes in translations of literary works from Asian languages, arts- and literature-related works, and "American writers who have been influenced by some aspect of an Asian culture, for example, a novel set in Japan or India, or nonfiction works about Asia."
Will Handle: Novels, stage plays (related to Asia or Asian American experience), and poetry (translations of Asian classics). Currently handles 50% nonfiction books; 25% novels; and 25% classics from Asian languages. Will read—at no charge—unsolicited queries and brief outlines. Reports in 1 week on queries; 2 weeks on mss. "For details of policy, send query with SASE."
Terms: Agent receives 15% commission on domestic sales; and 20% on foreign sales.
Fees: "We do not do critiques, as such, but do give the writer a brief evaluation of marketing potential based on my reading. There is a processing fee of $25-45. May charge for phone and photocopy expenses." ½% of income derived from fees; 99½% of income is derived from commission on ms sales.
Recent Sales: *Haiku Around the World*, by William Higginson (Simon & Schuster).

INTERNATIONAL PUBLISHER ASSOCIATES, INC., 746 West Shore, Sparta NJ 07871. Executive Vice President: Joe DeRogatis. Estab. 1982. Represents 30 clients. 80% of clients are new/unpublished writers. Eager to work with new/unpublished writers. Specializes in all types of nonfiction.
Will Handle: Nonfiction books and novels. Currently handles 80% nonfiction books and 20% fiction. Will read—at no charge—unsolicited queries and outlines. Reports in 3 weeks on queries.
Terms: Agent receives 15% commission on domestic sales; and 20% on foreign sales. 100% of income derived from commission on ms sales.
Recent Sales: *Under the Clock*, by George Carpozi, Jr. and William Balsam; *Success on the Line*, by Martin Novich (American Management Association); *Venom in the Blood*, by Eric Van Huffmann (Donald I. Fine Inc.).

J&R LITERARY AGENCY, 28 E. 11 St., New York NY 10003. (212)677-4248. Owner: Jean Rosenthal. Estab. 1980. Represents published writers only. Specializes in nonfiction.
Will Handle: Nonfiction books, novels, textbooks, juvenile books. "The lower dollar will cause my focus to switch from European co-productions to some extent, and I shall look for material from U.S. authors and publishers who would like a subsidiary rights agent." Does not read unsolicited mss. Reports in 1 month on queries.
Terms: Agent receives 15% commission on domestic sales; 25% on foreign sales.
Fees: Charges for mailing and telephone. 50% of income derived from commission on ms sales.
Recent Sales: A six volume series of paperback travel books entitled *Off The Beaten Track Italy, France, Switzerland, Spain, Austria, Germany* (Harper and Row); a five-volume *Encyclopedia of Mammals*, by Bernhard Grzimek (McGraw Hill); *The Vineyards of France*, by Don Philpott (Globe Pequot).

SHARON JARVIS AND CO., INC., 260 Willard Ave., Staten Island NY 10314. (718)720-2120. President: Sharon Jarvis. Associate, Joan Winston. Estab. 1985 (previously known as Jarvis, Braff Ltd. Established 1979). Member of ILAA. Represents 80 clients. 20% of clients are new/unpublished writers. Prefers to work with published/established authors; works with a small number of new/unpublished authors. Considers types of genre fiction, commercial fiction and nonfiction. No children's fiction or young adult.

Will Handle: Nonfiction books and novels. Currently handles 20% nonfiction books; 80% novels. Does not read unsolicited mss. Reports in 1 month on queries only.

Terms: Agent receives 15% commission on domestic sales; extra 10% on dramatic sales (splits commission with dramatic agent); and extra 10% on foreign sales. ("We have sub-agents in ten different foreign markets.") "SASE *must* be included."

Fees: Charges reading fee; $50 per manuscript ("fee goes to outside reader; recommended material then read by agency at no extra charge"). Critique is an analysis "aimed toward agency evaluation of author's talent and marketability." Readings and critiques may take up to three months. Charges for photocopying. 100% of income derived from commission on ms sales.

Recent Sales: *Birds of Paradise*, by Elizabeth Lane; *Writers Block*, by Jorja Prover; *Jefferson's War (6 Books)*, by Kevin D. Randle.

JCA LITERARY AGENCY INC., Suite 1103, 27 W. 20th St., New York NY 10011. (212)807-0888. Agents: Jane Cushman, Jeff Gerecke, Tom Cushman and Tony Outhwaite. Estab. 1978. Member SAR. Represents 100 clients. 5% of clients are new/unpublished writers. Specializes in general fiction and nonfiction.

Will Handle: Nonfiction books and novels; no science fiction or juvenile. "We would be interested in adding *high-quality* commerical novelists to our client list." Currently handles 65% nonfiction books; 35% novels. Will read—at no charge—unsolicited queries and outlines accompanied by SASE. Reports in 1 month on queries; 2 months on mss.submit requests elsewhere."

Terms: Agent receives 10% commission on domestic sales; 10% on dramatic sales; 20% on foreign sales.

Fees: Charges for bound galleys and finished books used in subsidiary rights submissions; manuscripts copied for submissions to publishers.

Recent Sales: *Dead Heat: The Race Against the Greenhouse Effect*, by Michael Oppenheimer and Robert H. Boyle (Basic Books, nonfiction); *Woody Allen*, by Eric Lax (Knopf, biography); *Counterattack*, by W.E.B. Griffin (Putnam, military novel).

JET LITERARY ASSOCIATES, INC., 124 E. 84th St., New York NY 10028. (212)879-2578. President: James Trupin. Estab. 1976. Represents 85 clients. 5% of clients are new/unpublished writers. Writer must have published articles or books. Prefers to work with published/established authors. Specializes in nonfiction.

Will Handle: Nonfiction books and novels. Currently handles 50% nonfiction books and 50% novels. Does not read unsolicited mss. Reports in 2 weeks on queries; 1 month on mss.

Terms: Agent receives 15% commission on domestic sales; 15% on dramatic sales; and 25% on foreign sales.

Fees: Charges for phone and postage expenses. 100% of income derived from commission on ms sales.

Recent Sales: *How to Win at Nintendo*, by Jeff Rovin (St. Martin's); *Hoopstats! The Basketball Abstract*, by Josh Trupin (Bantam); *Where in the World*, by David Grambs (Harper & Row).

‡LLOYD JONES LITERARY AGENCY, 4301 Hidden Creek, Arlington TX 76016. (817)483-5103. Owner: Lloyd Jones. Estab. 1987. Represents 22 clients. Prefers to work with published/established authors. Works with a small number of new/unpublished authors. Specializes in nonfiction, business, children, novels and textbooks.

Will Handle: Nonfiction books, novels, textbooks and juvenile books. Currently handles 30% nonfiction books; 50% novels and 20% juvenile books. Will read—at no charge—unsolicited queries and outlines. Reports in 3 weeks on queries.

Terms: Agent receives 15% commission on domestic sales; 10% on dramatic sales; and 10% on foreign sales.

Recent Sales: *The Other Assassin*, by Bill Sloan (Tudor); *Bluebonnet at Dinosaur Valley Park*, by Mary Casad (Pelican); and *The Blood Covenant*, by Dean Shapiro/Rena Chynoweth (Eakin Publications).

‡LAWRENCE JORDAN LITERARY AGENCY, A Division of Morning Star Rising, Inc., Suite 1527, 250 West 57th St., New York NY 10107. (212)690-2748. President: Lawrence Jordan. Estab. 1978. Represents 30 clients. 25% of clients are new/unpublished writers. Works with a small number of new/unpublished authors. Specializes in general adult fiction and nonfiction: religion, inspirational, science, business, computer manuals, history, autobiography, biography, health, self-help and sports.

Will Handle: Magazine articles, magazine fiction, nonfiction books, novels, textbooks, juvenile books, movie scripts and stage plays. Handles 1% magazine articles; 1% magazine fiction; 60% nonfiction; 25% novels; 3% textbooks; 2% juvenile books; 3% movie scripts; 5% stage plays. Will read—at no charge—unsolicited queries and outlines. Reports in 3 weeks on queries; 6 weeks on mss.

Terms: Charges 15% commission on domestic sales; 20% on dramatic sales and 20% on foreign sales.

Fees: Charges long distance calls, photocopying, foreign submission costs, postage, cables and messengers. Makes 1% of income from fees.

Recent Sales: *Great Black Russian*, by John Oliver Killens (Wayne State University Press); *Muhammed Ali's Greatest Fights*, by Dr. Ferdie Pacheco (Birch Lane Press); and *Sippi*, by John Oliver Killens (Thunder's Mouth Press).

LARRY KALTMAN LITERARY AGENCY, 1301 S. Scott St., Arlington VA 22204. (703)920-3771. Director: Larry Kaltman. Estab. 1984. Represents 15 clients. 75% of clients are new/unpublished writers. Works with a small number of new/unpublished authors. Specializes in novels, novellas (mainstream). Sponsors the Washington Prize For Fiction.
Will Handle: Nonfiction books, novels. Currently handles 25% nonfiction books; 75% novels. Reports in 2 weeks.
Terms: Agent receives 15% commission on domestic sales; 15% on dramatic sales; 15% on foreign sales.
Fees: Charges reading fee for all unsolicited mss. Criticism fee automatically included in reading fee. Charges $150/300-page, typed double-spaced book ms. "I don't distinguish between reading fees and criticism fees. Manuscript author receives an approximately 1,000-word letter commenting on writing style, organization and marketability. I write all the critiques." Charges for postage. 80% of income derived from commission on ms sales; 20% derived from fees charged to writers.
Recent Sales: *Rastus on Capitol Hill,* by Samuel Edison (Hunter House); *Anything That's All,* by Shirley Cochrane (Signal Books); and *Wheel of Fortune,* by Larry Kaltman (The Washington Post).

ALEX KAMAROFF ASSOCIATES, Suite 303 East, 200 Park Ave., Pan Am Bldg., New York NY 10166. (212)557-5557. President: Alex Kamaroff. Associate: Josh Behar. Estab. 1985. Represents 86 clients. 25% of clients are new/unpublished writers. Specializes in men's adventure, science fiction, mysteries, horror, category and historical romances, contemporary women's fiction.
Will Handle: Novels. Currently handles 5% nonfiction books; 95% novels. Will read—at no charge—unsolicited queries and outlines; no reply without SASE. Reports in 1 week on queries; 3 weeks on mss.
Fees: Charges $85 reading fee ("includes feedback") refundable upon sale of ms.
Terms: Agent receives 10% commission on domestic sales; 10% on dramatic sales; and 20% on foreign sales.
Recent Sales: *Louis Rukeyser Business Almanac,* by Louis Rukeyser and John Cooney, George Winslow Chief Researcher (Simon & Schuster). *Chapel Hill* (movie to book) (Warner); *Worlds Apart,* by Diana Morgan (Berkley).

J. KELLOCK & ASSOCIATES CO. LTD., 11017 - 80 Avenue, Edmonton Alberta T6G 0R2 Canada. (403)433-0274. President: Joanne Kellock. Estab. 1981. Represents 60 clients. 40% of clients are new/unpublished writers. Specializes in pre-school, juvenile, young adult fiction; literature and all genre fiction; nonfiction trade material. Now acting for illustrators of children's picture books. Requirements: four color slides, photocopies of three/four pencil sketches and/or brochure.
Will Handle: Nonfiction books, novels, juvenile books, movie scripts. Currently handles 45% novels; 5% movie scripts; 50% nonfiction. Will read—at no charge—unsolicited queries and outlines. Reports in 2 weeks on queries.
Terms: Agent receives 15% English language rights; 15% commission on domestic sales; 15% on dramatic sales; and 20% on foreign sales.
Fees: Charges $75 (Canadian) $60 (U.S.) criticism fee for reading three chapters plus brief outline, for all submissions from previously unpublished writers. If I feel style is working with subject the balance of ms will be read free of charge. Always enclose a SASE for possible returns. Charges writers a handling charge; postage for submission to publisher, necessary long distance calls at negotiation of contract with publisher.
Recent Sales: *Dealing with Difficult People,* by Robert Cava (Key Porter Books); *I Spent My Summer Vacation Kidnapped into Space* (Scholastic Inc.); *The Stolen Bride,* by Jo Beverley (Walker and Company).

NATASHA KERN LITERARY AGENCY INC., P.O. Box 2908, Portland OR 97208-2908. (503)226-2221. Contact: Natasha Kern. Estab. 1986. Member ILAA. Represents 55 clients. 35% of clients are new/unpublished writers. Eager to work with new/unpublished writers. Specializes in business, health, New Age, science, psychology, social issues, self-help (on all topics—by authorities only), how-to and cookbooks. Represents mainstream and genre fiction, including romances, historicals, thrillers, mysteries and westerns. For children's books, specialize in middle grade and YA fiction.
Will Handle: Nonfiction books, novels and juvenile books. Currently handles 45% nonfiction books; 45% novels; 10% juvenile books. Will read—at no charge—unsolicited queries. Reports in 2 weeks on queries; 6 weeks on mss.
Terms: Agent receives 15% commission on domestic sales; 15% on dramatic sales; and 20% on foreign sales.
Fees: Charges $35 reading fee for unpublished writers which is credited on sales; no marketing charges except overseas mail and calls and Express Mail. 98% of income derived from sales of writer's work; 2% from reading fees.
Recent Sales: *The Asian Mind Game,* by Chin-ning Chu (Macmillan); *The Surefire Way to Write and Sell Nonfiction,* by Cork Millner (Simon & Schuster); *Conquered Hearts,* by Robin Lee Hatcher (Leisure Books).

The double dagger before a listing indicates that the listing is new in this edition. New markets are often the most receptive to freelance submissions.

‡KIDDE, HOYT AND PICARD LITERARY AGENCY, 335 E. 51st St., New York NY 10022. (212)755-9461. Chief Associate: Katharine Kidde. Estab. 1980. Represents 50 clients. "We require that a writer be published." Works with a small number of new clients. Specializes in mainstream and literary fiction; romantic fiction, some historical, some contemporary; mainstream nonfiction."

Will Handle: Nonfiction books. Will handle magazine articles and magazine fiction for national magazines, if also handling a book-length ms for the author. Currently handles 1% magazine articles; 2% magazine fiction; 22% nonfiction books; 70% novels; and 5% young adult books. Will read submissions—at no charge—if queried first. Reports in 2 weeks on queries; 1 month on mss.

Terms: Agent receives 10% commission on domestic sales; commission on dramatic sales may vary. Sometimes charges for phone, postage and photocopy expenses. 100% of income derived from commission on ms sales.

Recent Sales: *Timeless Towns*, by J.R. Humphreys (St. Martin's); *Beyond Capricorn*, by Frank Sherry (Morrow); and *Twilight Of Innocence*, by Helen Lehr (Sinclair).

DANIEL P. KING, LITERARY AGENT, 5125 N. Cumberland Blvd., Whitefish Bay WI 53217. (414)964-2903. FAX: (414)964-6860. President: Daniel P. King. Estab. 1974. Member of Crime Writer's Association. Represents 125 clients. 25% of clients are new/unpublished writers. Eager to work with new/unpublished writers. Specializes in crime and mystery, science fiction, mainstream fiction, short stories, and books in English for foreign sales. Representative offices in Japan, Mexico City, Zug (Switzerland), England and Spain.

Will Handle: Magazine articles (crime, foreign affairs, economics); magazine fiction (mystery, romance); nonfiction books (crime, politics); novels (mystery, science fiction, romance, mainstream); movie scripts (from California office); TV scripts (from California office); syndicate material (general, politics, economics). Currently handles 5% magazine articles; 10% magazine fiction; 30% nonfiction books; 50% novels; 2% movie scripts; 2% TV scripts; 1% syndicated material. Will read—at no charge—unsolicited queries and outlines. Does not read unsolicited ms. Reports in 1 week.

Terms: Agent receives 10% commission on domestic sales; 10% on dramatic sales; and 20% on foreign sales.

Fees: "Reading and evaluation fees range from $90-175 depending upon the length and complexity of the manuscript submitted. For this fee, we will provide a critique of the work which will address the author's writing skill level, analysis of story line and suggestions for rewriting. Rereadings of revised manuscripts are done without further charge, and telephone consultation is available to assist the author in revisions. Writers having published at least 1 trade book within the last year are exempt from any fees."

Recent Sales: Confidential—available to writers on request.

HARVEY KLINGER, INC., 301 W. 53rd St., New York NY 10019. (212)581-7068. President: Harvey Klinger. Estab. 1977. Represents 100 clients. 25% of our clients are new/unpublished writers. "We seek writers demonstrating great talent, fresh writing and a willingness to listen to editorial criticism and learn." Works with a small number of new/unpublished authors. Specializes in mainstream fiction, (not category romance or mysteries, etc.), nonfiction in the medical, social sciences, autobiography and biography areas.

Will Handle: Nonfiction books and novels. Currently handles 60% nonfiction books and 40% novels. Will read—at no charge—unsolicited queries and outlines. Reports in 2 weeks on queries.

Terms: Agent receives 15% commission on domestic sales; 15% on dramatic sales; and 25% on foreign sales.

Fees: Charges for photocopying expenses. 100% of income derived from commission on ms sales.

Recent Sales: *Butterfly*, by Kathryn Harvey (Villard); *Secrets About Men Every Woman Should Know*, by Barbara DeAngelis (Delacorte); and *Just Desserts*, by Patti Massman and Susan Rosser (Crown).

PAUL KOHNER, INC., 9169 Sunset Blvd., Los Angeles CA 90069. (213)550-1060. FAX: (213)276-1083. Agent: Gary Salt. Estab. 1938. Represents 100 clients. Writer must have sold material in the market or category in which they are seeking representation. Prefers to work with published/established authors. Specializes in film and TV scripts and related material, and dramatic rights for published or soon-to-be published books—both fiction and nonfiction. No plays, poetry or short stories. "We handle dramatic and performing rights only."

Will Handle: Magazine articles and nonfiction books (if they have film or TV potential); novels (only previously published or with publication deals set); movie scripts; and TV scripts. Currently handles 5% magazine articles; 12½% nonfiction books; 12½% novels; 40% movie scripts; and 30% TV scripts. Only queries accompanied by SASE will be answered. *Absolutely no unsolicited material.* Reports in 1 week on queries.

Terms: Agent receives 10% commission on dramatic sales.

Fees: Charges for photocopy and binding expenses.

Recent Sales: *White Lies*, by Jonellen Heckler (Putnam—TV Mini.); *Courtroom Crusaders*, by Mark Litwak (Morrow-TV pilot); *Too Many Crooks*, by Donald Westlake (Playboy—feature).

BARBARA S. KOUTS, (Affiliated with Philip G. Spitzer Literary Agency), 788 9th Ave., New York NY 10019. (212)265-6003. Literary Agent: Barbara S. Kouts. Estab. 1980. Member of ILAA. Represents 50 clients. 50% of clients are new/unpublished writers. Specializes in fiction, nonfiction and children's books.

Close-up

Michael Larsen and Elizabeth Pomada
Michael Larsen/Elizabeth Pomada
Literary Agents

"We weren't the first, but we were the first to survive," recalls Elizabeth Pomada of the Larsen/Pomada Literary Agency. She and partner Michael Larsen began their San Francisco-based business, the oldest in the Bay Area, in 1972 after years in the thick of New York publishing.

Although he'd worked with Elizabeth as a consultant, Michael formally joined the agency after securing a book contract at lightning speed. "Selling a manuscript in four phone calls is definitely a heady experience," he says.

The two met in 1968 at a publisher's party, and it's been nearly 20 years since they moved to the West. Do they feel a handicap in being far from the center of publishing? Elizabeth says the telephone is the equalizer in an agent's work. "The big day comes, the offer is received. This is usually done by phone—not in person, and not at lunch." Perhaps there's a teeny *advantage* with West Coast publishers and film agents? "They're still in Hollywood, and we're still here," she says with a shrug.

Because most editors are in a different time zone, Michael and Elizabeth make some calls as early as 7 a.m. Otherwise, they keep to their own schedule, often staying up until midnight with a promising manuscript.

Visits with Eastern editors occur about twice a year. "We have a map and a schedule, and we often see more people during that time than many agents who live there," Elizabeth explains.

Although they are committed to an international attitude, the two acknowledge New York's continued influence in the market. Savvy agents and authors follow trends by subscriptions to national news and publishing magazines, Michael says. "Some publishers won't believe a new idea until they see it in *The New York Times*," Elizabeth adds.

Notions travel the other way, too. "A lot of trends start in the West," Michael says. "Editors are aware of this." Good editors are always looking for fresh ideas—wherever they originate.

Agents also stay on the lookout for talent, so Elizabeth and Michael appear at conferences regularly to meet up-and-coming writers. They also offer encouragement and practical advice at speaking engagements at which they discuss their "100% Solution," tips on how to transform an idea into a published book.

Members of the Independent Literary Agents Association, the two have handled such diverse topics as New Age psychology, history, business, how-to's and fiction. Michael primarily handles nonfiction for the agency. He suggests that a writer contact him before writing begins—and preferably after reading his book *How to Write a Book Proposal*. Elizabeth manages fiction. She likes to see the first 30 pages and a synopsis of the manuscript. Multiple queries are fine, but multiple submissions are not. The agency does not charge a reading fee.

If an idea seems marketable, the agents and author meet. Although they use a written representation agreement, they emphasize a personal relationship between agent and client. Michael encourages writers to meet their agents, "to see if the chemistry's right. One of the things I recommend is to go to their office, see what they've published." He

Photo by L. Narlesky

also recommends asking how long an agent has been in business and sometimes encourages talking to the agent's other clients.

Elizabeth describes Michael as an agent who "definitely likes to get involved . . . and is very idealistic still." Once, after a publisher handled a client's book in a less than successful fashion, Michael resold it to a publisher who really believed in the concept. "Now the author is doing children's books based on his story. There's a movie coming out," Elizabeth says. Michael interrupts with a modest comment: " . . . and the timing was right."

Michael says Elizabeth is "very businesslike." She believes in her clients, he adds, citing one offer received exactly 10 years after a new novelist signed on. Overnight successes happen too. "There was a first novel that Elizabeth sold for six figures in 10 days."

Elizabeth says of their work: "An agent can be a negotiator, a scout for publishers, an editorial consultant, and a morale booster when that's needed." For a writer approaching the maelstrom of publishing, an agent is a stabilizing influence. Admittedly, it's a complicated business, but Michael says the most important person in the process always is "The writer! Absolutely."

— Lynn Narlesky

66 We weren't the first, but we were the first to survive [in the Bay Area]. 99

— Elizabeth Pomada

Will Handle: Nonfiction books, novels and juvenile books. Currently handles 40% nonfiction books; 30% novels; and 30% juvenile books. Will read—at no charge—unsolicited queries and outlines. Reports in 3 weeks on queries; 2 months on mss.
Terms: Agent receives 10% commission on domestic sales; and 20% on foreign sales.
Fees: Charges writers for photocopy expenses.
Recent Sales: *Short and Shivery*, by Robert San Souci (Doubleday); *Bed and Breakfast, North America*, by Hal Gieseking (Simon & Schuster); *Beethoven's Cat*, by Elisabeth McHugh (Atheneum).

LUCY KROLL AGENCY, 390 W. End Ave., New York NY 10024. (212)877-0627. FAX: (212)769-2832. Agent: Barbara Hogenson. Member of SAR and WGA East and West. Represents 60 clients. 5% of clients are new/unpublished writers. "Recommendations are useful, but good writing is the most important qualification for representation." Specializes in nonfiction, screenplays and plays.
Will Handle: Nonfiction books, novels, movie scripts and stage plays. Currently handles 45% nonfiction books; 15% novels; 15% movie scripts and 25% stage plays. Will read—at no charge—unsolicited queries and outlines "provided SASE is sent." Does not read unsolicited manuscripts. Reports in 1 month.
Terms: Agent receives 10% commission on domestic sales; 10% on dramatic sales; and 20% on foreign sales.
Recent Sales: No information given.

PETER LAMPACK AGENCY, INC., 2015, 551 5th Ave., New York NY 10017. (212)687-9106. FAX: (212)687-9109. President: Peter Lampack. Estab. 1977. Represents 90 clients. 10% of clients are new/unpublished writers. Majority of clients are published/established authors; works with a small number of new/unpublished authors. Specializes in "commercial fiction, particularly contemporary relationships, male-oriented action/adventure, mysteries, horror and historical romance; literary fiction; and upscale, serious nonfiction or general interest nonfiction only from a recognized expert in a given field."
Will Handle: Nonfiction books, novels, movie scripts and TV scripts ("but not for espiodic TV series—must lend itself to movie-of-the-week or mini-series format.") Currently handles 15% nonfiction books; 75% novels; 5% movie scripts; 5% TV scripts. Will read—at no charge—unsolicited queries, outlines and mss. Reports in 2 weeks on queries; 6 weeks on mss.
Terms: Agent receives 15% commission on domestic sales; 15% on dramatic sales; and 20% on foreign sales.
Fees: Charges for photocopy expenses "although we prefer writers supply copies of their work. Writers are required to supply or bear the cost of copies of books for overseas sales."
Recent Sales: *Dragon*, by Clive Cussler (Simon & Schuster); *Age of Iron*, by J.M. Coetree (Random House); *The Glitter and the Gold*, by Fred Mustard Stewart (NAL).

‡RUTH LANGER, Suite 695, 1223 Wilshire Blvd., Santa Monica CA 90403. (213)829-2156. Contact: Ruth Langer. Estab. 1989. Represents 2 clients. Eager to work with new/unpublished writers. Specializes in selling mystery and suspense (especially spy thrillers).
Will Handle: Novels. Will read submissions at no charge, but may charge a criticism fee or service charge for work performed after the initial reading. Reports in 2 weeks on queries; 2 months on mss.
Terms: Agent receives 15% commisison on domestic sales; 15% on dramatic sales; and 20% on foreign sales.
Fees: Charges $45/first three chapters. Waives reading fee when representing the writer. 10% of income derived from reading fees. Charges $150/300 pages. Charges criticism fee. 10% of income derived from criticism fees. Charges $200/300 pages. "3-4 pages of overall evaluation and marketing advice. Ruth Langer and staff provide the critique."

MICHAEL LARSEN/ELIZABETH POMADA LITERARY AGENTS, 1029 Jones St., San Francisco CA 94109. (415)673-0939. Contact: Mike Larsen or Elizabeth Pomada. Estab. 1972. Member of ILAA. Represents 100 clients. 50-55% of clients are new/unpublished writers. Eager to work with new/unpublished writers. "We have very catholic tastes and do not specialize. We handle literary, commercial, and genre fiction, and the full range of nonfiction books."
Will Handle: Adult nonfiction books and novels. Currently handles 75% nonfiction books and 25% novels. Will read—at no charge—unsolicited queries, the first 30 pages and synopsis of completed novels, and nonfiction book proposals. Reports in 8 weeks on queries. Call first. "Always include SASE. Send SASE for brochure."
Terms: Agent receives 15% commission on domestic sales; 15% on dramatic sales; and 20% on foreign sales.
Fees: May charge writer for printing, postage for multiple submissions, foreign mail, foreign phone calls, galleys, books, and legal fees. 100% of income derived from commission on ms sales.
Recent Sales: *Dragon Revenant*, by Katharine Kerr (Foundation/Spectra), and *Chantal*, by Yvone Lenard (Delacorte/Dell); and *Ninety-Minute Hour*, by Jay Levinson (NAL).

THE LAZEAR AGENCY, INCORPORATED, Suite 416, 430 First Ave. N, Minneapolis MN 55401. FAX: (612)332-4648. Contact: Kathy Erickson. Estab. 1984. Represents 240 clients. 30% of clients are new/unpublished writers. Works with a small number of new/unpublished authors. "A full-service entertainment agency."

Will Handle: Nonfiction books, novels, textbooks, juvenile books, movie scripts, radio scripts, TV scripts and syndicated material. Will read—at no charge—unsolicited queries or solicited outlines and manuscripts. Reports in 2 months.

Terms: Agent receives 15% commission on domestic sales; 15% on dramatic sales; and 20% on foreign sales.

Fees: Charges writers for photocopying, overnight mail.

Recent Sales: *Kari*, by Melody Beattie (Prentice Hall Press); *St. Croix Notes*, by Noah Adams (Norton); *Canyon*, by Gary Paulsen (Dell/Delacorte).

L. HARRY LEE LITERARY AGENCY, P.O. Box 203, Rocky Point NY 11778. (516)744-1188. President: L. Harry Lee. Agents: Ralph Schiano (science fiction); Katie Polk (mystery); Patti Roenbeck (science fiction—mainstream); Cami Callirgos (adventure—western); Holli Rouitti (humor—suspense—horror); Lisa Judd (historical/adventure); Colin James (mainstream/horror); Mary Lee Gaylor (West Coast representative). Estab. 1979. Member of WGA. Represents 175 clients. 35% of clients are new/unpublished writers. "Mainly interested in screenwriters." Specializes in movies, TV (episodic, movies-of-the-week and sit-coms) and contemporary novels.

Will Handle: Novels, movie scripts, stage plays, and TV scripts (movies, mini-series, MOW's, episodic, and sit-coms). Currently handles 25% novels; 50% movie scripts; 5% stage plays; 20% TV scripts. Will read—at no charge—unsolicited queries and outlines; does not read material submitted without SASE. Does not consider unsolicited complete mss. No dot-matrix. Reports in 2 weeks on queries; 6 weeks on mss.

Terms: Agent receives 15% commission on domestic sales; 15% on dramatic sales; and 20% on foreign sales. 10% for screenplays/TV.

Fees: Charges a marketing fee. Charges for photocopies, line editing, proofing, typing and postage expenses. 10% of income derived from marketing fees; 90% of income derived from commission on ms sales.

Recent Sales: *The Victorian, Fool's Road, The Gizmo Delicious*.

LEE SHORE AGENCY, 1687 Washington Rd., Pittsburgh PA 15228. (412)831-1299. Owner: Cynthia Semelsberger. Estab. 1988. Represents 26 clients. 50% of clients are new/unpublished writers. "We are always on the lookout for new/unpublished writers that have a strong desire to publish and a serious and professional approach to their work." We prefer to handle nonfiction, health, self-help, how-to, textbooks, new age, quality mainstream fiction and genre (romance, historical, mystery, horror, science fiction, western, etc.) Please do not send children's or poetry.

Will Handle: Young adult and mass market fiction. Currently handles 20% self-help, 20% New Age, 50% novels, 10% young adults. Will read at no charge unsolicited queries and outlines. Reports on query in 1 week; 6 weeks on manuscripts.

Terms: Agent receives 15% commission on domestic sales; 15% on dramatic sales; and 20% on foreign sales.

Fees: Charges a reading fee for proposal and first 100-150 pages; 10% of income derived from reading fees. No additional reading fee once the balance of manuscript is requested. Charges for "standard expenses."

Recent Sales: *Phoenix Cards*, by Susan Sheppard (Inner Traditions); *Medieval Campfire Cookbook*, by Trinette Kern (Tiffany).

‡LEVANT & WALES, LITERARY AGENCY, INC., 108 Hayes St., Seattle WA 98109. (206)284-7114. Agents: Elizabeth Wales and Dan Levant. Estab. 1988. Member of Pacific Northwest Writers' Conference, Book Publishers' Northwest. Represents 15 clients. We are interested in published and not yet published writers. Specializes in nonfiction categories: popular culture, health, lifestyle, psychology, cookbooks, gardening, nature, science, business, biography. Fiction: all mainstream (*no* genre science fiction, romance, or horror).

Will Handle: Nonfiction books and novels. Currently handles 75% nonfiction books; and 25% novels. Will read—at no charge—unsolicited queries, outlines and manuscripts. Reports in 2 weeks on queries; 3 weeks on mss.

Terms: Agent receives 15% commission on domestic sales.

Fees: We make all our income from commissions. We offer editorial help for some of our clients and help some clients with the development of a proposal, but we do not charge for these services. We do charge, after a sale, for express mail, manuscript photocopy costs, foreign postage and outside USA telephone costs.

Recent Sales: *Hot Peppers* by Richard Schweid/New Orleans Cooking School (Tenspeed Press); and *Corporate Rituals* by Bernstein/Rozen (John Wiley & Sons).

ELLEN LEVINE LITERARY AGENCY, INC., Suite 1205, 432 Park Ave. So., New York NY 10016. (212)889-0620. Contact: Diana Finch. Estab. 1980. Member of SAR and ILAA. Represents 100 clients. 10% of clients are new/unpublished writers.

Will Handle: Nonfiction books and novels. Currently handles 45% nonfiction books; 45% novels; and 10% juvenile books. Will read—at no charge—unsolicited queries and outlines. Does not read unsolicited manuscripts. Reports in 2 weeks on queries sent with SASE.

Terms: Agent receives 10% commission on domestic sales; 10% on dramatic sales; and 20% on foreign sales.
Fees: Charges writer for photocopying mss for submissions, overseas calls, and postage incurred in representation of foreign rights, cost of books bought to submit for foreign rights and other subsidiary rights. 100% of income derived from commission on ms sales.
Recent Sales: "We do not release this information except by individual request from prospective clients."

LIGHTHOUSE LITERARY AGENCY, P.O. Box 1000, Edgewater FL 32132-1000. (407)647-2385. Director: Sandra Kangas. Estab. 1988. Represents 46 clients. 50% of clients are new/unpublished writers. "We are interested in working with any new or established writer whose goal is to advance his/her writing career. Some prior success is a plus, but not a requirement." Specializes in nonfiction, novels, movie scripts, juveniles, young adult novels.
Will Handle: Short story collections, nonfiction books, novels, juvenile books, movie scripts, poetry. Currently handles 28% nonfiction books; 50% novels; 16% juvenile books; 2% poetry, 4% scripts. Reports in 2 weeks on queries; 2 months on manuscripts.
Terms: Agent receives 15% commission on domestic sales; 10-15% on dramatic sales; and 20% on foreign sales.
Fees: Reading fee: $45. Reimbursed on acceptance. If rejected we give brief comments. Will do a critique on request, $1/page, $150 min. 95% of income derived from sales of writers' work; 5% of income derived from fees.
Recent Sales: *The Draper Solution*, by Galen C. Dukes (Balantine/Ivy); *Power PR*, by Dennis Cole Hill (Fell Publishers); and *The Goose Got Loose* by Laura Happel (Little, Brown).

‡RAY LINCOLN LITERARY AGENCY, Suite 107-B Elkins Park House, 7900 Old York Rd., Elkins Park PA 19117. (215)635-0827. President: Mrs. Ray Lincoln. Estab. 1974. Represents 30 clients. "I receive many referrals, which I value, but work with new writers, as well." Specializes in book-length fiction and nonfiction for adults and young adults and for middle-grade children. Nonfiction for adults: biography, nature, world affairs, sciences, literature, film history. Fiction: all types.
Will Handle: Nonfiction books, novels, juvenile books and syndicated material. Currently handles 70% adult; 30% juvenile. Will read—at no charge—unsolicited queries and outlines. If interested will then send for full ms. No reading charge Query first. Reports in 3 weeks on queries; 1 month on mss.
Terms: Agent receives 15% commission on domestic sales; 15% on dramatic sales; and 20% on foreign sales.
Fees: Charges writers for overseas telephone calls.
Recent Sales: *Winter in Florida*, by Edward Falco (Soho Press); *Health Freak*, by Joel Schwartz (Dell); and *A Taste for Treason*, by Ora Mendels (Birch Lane).

‡LITERARY AGENCY OF WASHINGTON, P.O. Box 577, Burtonsville MD 20866. (301)421-1261. Director: Fred Reinstein. Estab. 1948. Represents 30 clients. Prefer published writers but do not close the door to the new writer. Works with a small number of new/unpublished authors. We work only in book and magazine fields. Magazines must be national.
Will Handle: Magazine articles, magazine fiction, nonfiction books, novels. Will read—at no charge—unsolicited queries and outlines. Reports in 2 weeks on queries. Include SASE.
Terms: Agent receives 10% commission on domestic sales; 20% on foreign sales.
Fees: Charges a reading fee; waives reading fee when representing the writer. 5% of income derived from reading fees. All fiction is charged a reading fee. Charges $100/300 pages for novel; no fee for nonfiction. Charges a criticism fee for all fiction.
Recent Sales: *Eastern Orthodox Church*, by Paraskevas and Reinstein (El Greco Press); *The Curse of the Black Douglas*, by Thomas B. Flynn (Golf Yearbook); and *Camp David*, by W. Dale Nelson (Madison Books).

‡LITERARY AND CREATIVE ARTISTS AGENCY, 3539 Albemarle St. NW, Washington DC 20008. (202)362-4688. President: Muriel Nellis. Estab. 1982. Member of American Bar Association. Represents 42 clients. "While we prefer published writers, it is not required if the proposed work has great merit." Requires exclusive review of material; no simultaneous submissions. Specializes in nonfiction from health to business, New Age, politics, lifestyle, memoir, how-to, human drama, some cooking, fiction, philosophy.
Will Handle: Nonfiction books, novels, movie scripts and TV scripts. Handles 75% nonfiction books; 20% novels; 1% juvenile books; 2% movie scripts; 2% cookbooks and other one-shots. Will read—at no charge—unsolicited queries and outlines. Does not read unsolicited mss. Reports in 2 weeks on queries.
Terms: Charges 15% commission on domestic sales; 20% on dramatic sales; and 25% on foreign sales.
Fees: Charges for long distance phone and fax; copying and shipping.
Recent Sales: *Quantum Healing*, by Dr. D. Chopra (Bantam); *100 Over 100*, by Heynan/Boyar (Fulcrum); *Ayurvedic Cookbook*, by L. Banchek (Crown/Harmony).

THE LITERARY GROUP, (formerly Victoria Management Co.), Suite 11-1, 262 Central Park West, New York NY 10024. (212)873-0972. FAX: (212)371-1845. President: Frank Weimann. Estab. 1985. Represents 40 clients. Eager to work with new/unpublished writers. Specializes in films, TV scripts, nonfiction, self-help and biography.

Close-up

Eileen Fallon
Literary Agent

The book publishing industry is in a classic good news/bad news state, according to agent Eileen Fallon.

The bad news is the industry is in its worst slump in about nine years, Fallon says, and midlist books are "almost impossible for agents to place with publishers." But there is still good news in the industry. "*All* agents and publishers are eager for manuscripts that suit their needs," she says.

Fallon is a New Jersey native who graduated from Rutgers University. She worked for Jove, an imprint of the Berkley Publishing Group, for three years. In 1982 she joined Lowenstein Associates as a literary agent. Fallon serves as an agent for general fiction, romances and mysteries, as well as nonfiction.

When submitting fiction, Lowenstein Associates wants first to see a query with a self-addressed, stamped envelope. The query should include a description of the novel, the approximate number of words, a brief explanation of the market it's designed for, the author's published credits and a brief summation of the novel. If one of the agents responds favorably to a query, the author is asked to send the first 75 to 100 pages of the novel and a synopsis that covers all the major plot points. The agency also likes to know a little about the status of the novel, including publishers to whom it's already been submitted, if any.

One of Fallon's pet peeves is the use of multiple adjectives touting a novel. "Don't use adjectives," she says. "Don't tell me it's a stunning or marvelous or thoroughly wonderful novel. Let the material speak for itself."

Fallon uses the first 75 to 100 pages, along with the synopsis, to judge if she wishes to consider the complete novel. Frequently, writers lobby for agents to read entire manuscripts on the first submission, but Fallon says few have time to do that. "When you deal with a large number of writers and you give up your night or weekend time to read, you just don't have the time [to read] a complete manuscript for each one—especially before they are even clients," she says.

Lowenstein Associates also handles general nonfiction. For nonfiction, writers should submit query letters that specify their credentials; a summary of the book; information on competitive books and the potential audience for the book; specifications such as length and information about art or photos that will be included; a chapter-by-chapter outline; and a sample chapter. Fallon says the agency works hard with the author to polish this detailed package. "We must be able to give editors something they can consider in one hour," she says, "but which tells them exactly what the finished book will contain."

Although many authors try to make their material flashy to stand out from other submissions, Fallon says this is unnecessary. "I like to see calm competence," she says. "Things are hectic enough in the office and submissions shouldn't be that way too. I want to see professionalism above all."

— Glenda Tennant Neff

Editor's note: After this Close-up was written, Eileen Fallon started her own agency, The Fallon Literary Agency, Suite 108, 2nd Ave., New York NY 10021.

Will Handle: Nonfiction books, novels, movie scripts and syndicated material. Currently handles 60% nonfiction books; 20% novels; and 20% movie scripts. Will read—at no charge—unsolicited queries, outlines and mss. Reports in 2 weeks on queries; 1 month on mss.

Terms: Agent receives 15% commission on domestic sales; 15% on dramatic sales; and 20% on foreign sales.

Recent Sales: *John Wayne*, by Aissa Wayne and Steve Delsahn (Random House); *Tales From a Feminist Lawyer*, by Karen Decrow (NAL); and *Rock 'n' Roll L.O.*, by Art Fein (Faber & Faber).

‡LITERARY MARKETING CONSULTANTS, Suite 701, One Hallidie Plaza, San Francisco CA 94102. (415)585-1698. 11 am-9 pm PST. Associate: K. Allman. Estab. 1984. Represents 20 clients. 15% of clients are new/unpublished writers. Eager to work with new/unpublished writers. Specializes in "nonfiction: religious and scholarly works and magazine articles. Fiction: science fiction, mysteries and romance. Religious fiction is a growing area of interest for us."

Will Handle: Currently handles 10% magazine articles; 20% magazine fiction; 10% nonfiction books; 45% novels; 15% juvenile books. Will read—at no charge—unsolicited queries (letter plus outline/synopsis only first correspondence). Reports in 1 month.

Terms: Agent receives 15% commission on domestic sales; 20% on dramatic sales; and 20% on foreign sales.

Fees: No reading fee. Charges per-ms marketing fee for photocopying, postage and phone for new/unpublished clients. 90% of income derived from commission on ms sales; 10% from fees charged to writers. "We will only take the time to provide a critique if we also have the opportunity to market the work."

Recent Sales: Confidential.

‡LIVING FAITH LITERARY AGENCY, P.O. Box 566427, Atlanta GA 30356. (404)640-0714. Agent: M.L. Jones. Estab. 1988. Represents 10 clients. 20% of clients are new/unpublished writers. Specializes in inspirational/religious books.

Will Handle: Nonfiction and fiction books, poetry, textbooks and children's books. Will read—at no charge—first three chapters and chapter synopsis of remaining chapters.

Terms: Charges 15% commission on domestic sales; 20% on foreign sales.

Fees: Charges for photocopies, postal and delivery expenses, ms retyping "if required" and phone calls.

Recent Sales: Confidential.

NANCY LOVE AGENCY, 250 E. 65th St., New York NY 10021. (212)980-3499. Contact: Nancy Love. Estab. 1984. Member of ILAA. Represents 60 clients. 25% of clients are new/unpublished writers. Prefers to work with published writers. Specializes in adult fiction and nonfiction with the exception of romance novels and science fiction.

Will Handle: Nonfiction books and novels. Curently handles 85% nonfiction books; 15% novels. Will read—at no charge—unsolicited queries, outlines and mss. Reports in 1 month on queries; 6 weeks on mss. "Length of exclusivity negotiated on a per case basis."

Terms: Agent receives 15% commission on domestic sales; 15% TV and movie sales; 20% on foreign sales.

Recent Sales: *Coming Home to the Family Business*, by Marcy Syms (Little, Brown); *Bag of Toys: The True Story of Sex, Drugs and Sadomasochism in Cafe Society*, by David France (Warner Books); and *Cracking the Nutrition Code*, by Artemis Simopoulos, M.D., Victor Herbert, M.D., and Beverly Jacobson (Macmillan).

‡LOWENSTEIN ASSOCIATES, INC., #601, 121 W. 27th St., New York NY 10001. (212)206-1630. President: Barbara Lowenstein. Vice President: Eileen Fallon. Agent: Norman Kurz. Estab. 1976. Member of ILAA. Represents 120 clients. 15% of clients are new/unpublished writers. Specializes in nonfiction—especially science and medical-topic books for the general public—historical and contemporary romance, bigger woman's fiction and general fiction.

Will Handle: Nonfiction books and novels. Currently handles 2% magazine articles; 55% nonfiction books; and 43% novels. Will read—at no charge—query letters. Will not accept unsolicited mss.

Terms: Agent receives 15% commission on domestic sales; 15% on dramatic sales; and 20% on foreign sales. Charges for photocopy, foreign postage and messenger expenses. 100% of income derived from commission on ms, other dramatic and 1st serial sales.

Recent Sales: Confidential.

MARGRET MCBRIDE LITERARY AGENCY, Box 8730, LaJolla CA 92038. (619)459-0559. Contact: Winifred Golden or Sheri Douglas. Estab. 1980. Member of ILAA. Represents 25 clients. 10% of clients are new/unpublished writers. Specializes in historical biographies, literary fiction, mainstream fiction and nonfiction.

Will Handle: Nonfiction books, novels and syndicated material. Will read—at no charge—unsolicited queries and outlines. Does not read unsolicited mss. Reports in 6 weeks on queries. "We are looking for two more novelists to complete our client list."

Terms: Agent receives 15% commission on domestic sales; 10% on dramatic sales; and 25% on foreign sales.
Fees: Charges writers for Federal Express made at author's request. 100% of income derived from commission on ms sales.
Recent Sales: *Barbarian to Bureaucrats*, by Lawrence M. Miller (Clarkson Potter); *The Memoirs of Senator John G. Tower* (Little, Brown); and *Why Men Don't Get Enough Sex And Women Don't Get Enough Love*, by Jonathon Kraner and Diane Dunaway (Pocket).

DONALD MACCAMPBELL INC., 12 E. 41st St., New York NY 10017. (212)683-5580. Editor: Maureen Moran. Estab. 1940. Represents 50 clients. "The agency does not handle unpublished writers." Specializes in women's book-length fiction in all categories.
Will Handle: Novels. Currently handles 100% novels. Does not read unsolicited mss. Reports in 1 week on queries.
Terms: Agent receives 10% commission on domestic sales; and 20% on foreign sales.
Recent Sales: *Love & Smoke*, by Jennifer Blake (Ballantine); *Special Assistant*, by Emilie McGee (Silhouette); *Tycoon's Daughter*, by Lynn Drennan (Doubleday).

RICHARD P. MCDONOUGH, LITERARY AGENT, P.O. Box 1950, Boston MA 02130. (617)522-6388. Estab. 1986. Represents 20 clients. 50% of clients are new/unpublished writers. Works with unpublished and published writers "whose work I think has merit and requires a committed advocate." Specializes in nonfiction for general contract and fiction.
Will Handle: Nonfiction books, novels and syndicated material. Currently handles 80% nonfiction books; 10% novels; and 10% juvenile. Will read—at no charge—unsolicited queries, outlines and mss if accompanied by SASE. Reports in 2 weeks on queries; 5 weeks on mss.
Terms: Agent receives 15% commission on domestic sales; 15% on dramatic sales; 15% on foreign sales.
Fees: Charges for photocopying, phone beyond 300 miles; postage for sold work only.
Recent Sales: *Guide to Museums in N.Y. City*, by R. Garrett (Chelsea Green); *Mystic Lakes*, by D. Musello (Donald Fine); and *Saying Goodbye*, by M.R. Montgomery (Knopf).

‡CAROL MANN AGENCY, 55 Fifth Ave., New York NY 10003. (212)206-5635. FAX: (212)463-8718. Contact: Carol Mann. Estab. 1977. Member of ILAA. Represents 150 clients. Prefers to work with published/established authors. Specializes in nonfiction.
Will Handle: Nonfiction books. Currently handles 90% nonfiction books; 5% novels; and 5% juvenile books. Will read—at no charge—unsolicited queries and outlines. Does not read unsolicited manuscripts.
Terms: Agent receives 15% commission on domestic sales; 15% on dramatic sales; and 20% on foreign sales.
Fees: Charges writers for foreign postage; long distance calls; photocopying, messenger; books etc.
Recent Sales: *Second Chances*, by Judith Wallerstein (Ticknor & Fields); and *In Broad Daylight*, by Harry MacLean (Harper & Row).

JANET WILKENS MANUS LITERARY AGENCY INC., Suite 906, 370 Lexington Ave., New York NY 10017. (212)685-9558. President: Janet Wilkens Manus. Estab. 1981. Member of ILAA. Represents 40 clients. 20% of our clients are new/unpublished writers. Prefers to work with published/established authors; works with a small number of new/unpublished authors. Specializes in general adult trade fiction and nonfiction.
Will Handle: Nonfiction books (trade oriented); novels (adult and young adult); and juvenile books. Currently handles 40% nonfiction books; 45% novels; and 15% juvenile books. Will read—at no charge—unsolicited queries and outlines. Reports in 2 weeks on queries; 5 weeks on manuscripts.
Terms: Agent receives 15% commission on domestic sales; 15% on dramatic sales; and 20% on foreign sales. Charges for photocopying, messenger, overseas phone, and postage expenses.
Recent Sales: *A Cold Killing*, by Deforest Day (Carroll & Graf); *The London Connection*, by Rubin Hunter (William Morrow & Co.); and *Secrets*, by Carlton Stouers (Pocket Books).

MARCH TENTH, INC., 4 Myrtle St., Haworth NJ 07641. (201)387-6551. FAX: (201)387-6552. President: Sandra Choron. Estab. 1982. Represents 40 clients. 5% of clients are new/unpublished writers. "Writers must have professional expertise in the field in which they are writing." Prefers to work with published/established writers.
Will Handle: Nonfiction books. Currently handles 100% nonfiction books. Does not read unsolicited mss. Reports in 1 month.
Terms: Agent receives 15% commission on domestic sales; 20% on dramatic sales; and 20% on foreign sales.
Fees: Charges writers for postage, photocopy and overseas phone expenses. 10% of income is derived from fees; 90% of income derived from commission of ms sales.
Recent Sales: *Sue Finn's Real Life Nutrition Book*, by Sue Finn and Linda Kass Stern (Viking); *The Heart of Rock and Soul*, by Dave Marsh (New American Library); and *Bitch, Bitch, Bitch*, by David Wheeler and Mike Wrenn (Dell).

DENISE MARCIL LITERARY AGENCY, INC., 685 West End Ave., 9C, New York NY 10025. (212)932-3110. President: Denise Marcil. Estab. 1977. Member of ILAA. Represents 80 clients. Works with a small number of new/unpublished authors. Specializes in "solid, informative nonfiction including such areas as money, business, health, child care, parenting, self-help and how-to's and commercial fiction, especially women's fiction; also mysteries, psychological suspense and horror."
Will Handle: Nonfiction books and novels. Currently handles 40% nonfiction books and 60% novels. Will read—at no charge—unsolicited queries and outlines when submitted with an SASE mailer. Reports in 2 weeks on queries; 3 months on mss.
Terms: Agent receives 15% commission on domestic sales; 15% on dramatic sales; and 20% on foreign sales.
Fees: Charges a reading fee: $45/first 3 chapters and outline "only when we request the material." Less than .1% of income derived from reading fees. Charges for disbursements, postage, copying and messenger service. 99.9% of income derived from commission on ms sales. Always send SASE.
Recent Sales: *Belle Epoch*, by Carol Kane (Harper & Row); *Staying on Top When Your World Turns Upside Down*, by Dr. Kathryn Cramer (Viking-Peguin); and *Inside Job: The Looting of American Savings and Loans*, by Steve Pizzo, Mary Fricker, Paul Muolo (McGraw-Hill).

‡**BARBARA MARKOWITZ LITERARY AGENCY**, 117 N. Mansfield Ave., Los Angeles CA 90036. (213)939-5927. Literary Agent/President: Barbara Markowitz. Estab. 1980. Represents 12 clients. Works with a small number of new/unpublished authors. Specializes in children's books, mid-level and young adult only; adult trade fiction and nonfiction.
Will Handle: Nonfiction books, novels and juvenile books. Currently handles 25% nonfiction books; 25% novels; 25% juvenile books and 15% syndicated material. Will read—at no charge—unsolicited queries and outlines. Reports in 3 weeks.
Terms: Agent receives 15% commission on domestic sales; 10% on dramatic sales; and 15% on foreign sales.
Fees: Charges writers for mailing, postage.
Recent Sales: *The Legend of Jimmy Spoon*, by K. Gregory (Harcourt Brace); and *Herald Examiners Guide to Los Angeles Restaurants*, by M. Shindler (Chronicle Books).

BETTY MARKS, Suite 9F, 176 E. 77th St., New York NY 10021. (212)535-8388. Contact: Betty Marks. Estab. 1969. Member of ILAA. Represents 35 clients. Prefers to work with published/established authors; works with a small number of new/unpublished authors. Specializes in journalists' nonfiction.
Will Handle: Nonfiction books, cookbooks and novels. Will read—at no charge—unsolicited queries and outlines. Reports in 1 week on queries; 6 weeks on mss.
Terms: Agent receives 15% commission on domestic sales; and 10% on foreign sales (plus 10% to foreign agent).
Fees: Charges a reading fee for unpublished writers; fee will be waived if representing writer. Charges criticism fee. "Writers receive two-page letter covering storyline, plot, characters, dialogue, language, etc." Written by agent. Charges for "extraordinary" postage, phone and messenger expenses. 95% of income derived from commission on ms sales. Payment of criticism fee does not ensure that agency will represent a writer.
Recent Sales: *Light and Easy Diabetes Cuisine*, by Betty Marks (Price/Stern/Sloan); *The Galapagos*, by Nathan Farb (Rizzoli); and *Manifold Destiny*, by Chris Maynard and William Scheller (Villard).

ELAINE MARKSON LITERARY AGENCY, 44 Greenwich Ave., New York NY 10011. Estab. 1972. Member of ILAA. Represents 200 clients. 10% of clients are new/unpublished writers. Specializes in literary fiction, commercial fiction and trade nonfiction.
Will Handle: Nonfiction books and novels. Currently handles 30% nonfiction books; 40% novels; 20% juvenile books; 5% movie scripts. Will read—at no charge—unsolicited query letters and outlines (must include SASE).
Terms: Agent receives 15% commission on domestic sales; 10% on dramatic sales; and 20% on foreign sales.
Fees: Charges for postage, photocopying, special long distance telephone. 100% of income derived from commission on ms sales.
Recent Sales: No information given.

THE EVAN MARSHALL AGENCY, 228 Watchung Ave., Upper Montclair NJ 07043. (201)744-1661. FAX: (201)744-6312. President: Evan Marshall. Estab. 1987. Member of ILAA and Romance Writers of America. Represents 75 clients. 10% of clients are new/unpublished writers. To be represented, a writer must demonstrate talent as well as knowledge of the market for which he or she is writing. Specializes in adult fiction and nonfiction.
Will Handle: Nonfiction books, novels, movie scripts and TV scripts. Currently handles 45% nonfiction; 45% novels; 5% movie scripts and 5% TV scripts. Does not read unsolicited manuscripts. Reports in 2 weeks on queries.
Terms: Agent receives 15% commission on domestic sales; 20% on dramatic sales; and 20% on foreign sales.
Recent Sales: Confidential.

SCOTT MEREDITH, INC., 845 3rd Ave., New York NY 10022. (212)245-5500. FAX: (212)755-2972. Vice President and Editorial Director: Jack Scovil. Estab. 1946. Represents 2,000 clients. 10% of clients are new/unpublished writers. "We'll represent on a straight commission basis writers who've sold one or more recent books to major publishers, or several (three or four) magazine pieces to major magazines, or a screenplay or teleplay to a major producer. We're a very large agency (staff of 51) and handle all types of material except individual cartoons or drawings, though we will handle collections of these as well."

Will Handle: Magazine articles, magazine fiction, nonfiction books, novels, textbooks, juvenile books, movie scripts, radio scripts, stage plays, TV scripts, syndicated material and poetry. Currently handles 5% magazine articles; 5% magazine fiction; 23% nonfiction books; 23% novels; 5% textbooks; 10% juvenile books; 5% movie scripts; 2% radio scripts; 2% stage plays; 5% TV scripts; 5% syndicated material; and 5% poetry. Will read—at no charge—unsolicited queries, outlines, and manuscripts "if from a writer with track record as described previously; charges a fee if no sales." Reports in 2 weeks.

Terms: Agent receives 10% commission on domestic sales; 10% on dramatic sales; and 20% on foreign sales.

Fees: Charges "a single fee which covers multiple readers, revision assistance or critique as needed. When a script is returned as irreparably unsalable, the accompanying letter of explanation will usually run two single-spaced pages minimum on short stories or articles, or from 4 to 10 single-spaced pages on book-length manuscripts, teleplays, or screenplays. All reports are done by agents on full-time staff. No marketing advice is included, since, if it's salable, we'll market and sell it ourselves." 10% of income derived from fees; 90% of income derived from commission on ms sales.

Recent Sales: *Murder at the Kennedy Center*, by Margaret Truman (Random House); *Rendezvous with Rama II*, by Arthur C. Clarke (Bantam Books); *Stand Up!*, by Roseanne Barr (Harper & Row).

MEWS BOOKS LTD.—**Sidney B. Kramer**, 20 Bluewater Hill, Westport CT 06880. (203)227-1836. FAX: (203)226-6928. Assistant: Fran Pollak. Estab. 1972. Represents 35 clients. Prefers to work with published/established authors; works with small number of new/unpublished authors "producing professional work. No editing services." Specializes in juvenile (pre-school through young adult), cookery, self-help, adult nonfiction and fiction, technical and medical.

Will Handle: Nonfiction books, novels, juvenile books, character merchandising and video use of illustrated published books. Currently handles 20% nonfiction; 20% novels; 50% juvenile books and 10% miscellaneous. Will read unsolicited queries and outlines with character description and a few pages of writing sample.

Terms: Agent receives 10% commission on domestic sales for published authors; 15% for unpublished; total 20% on foreign.

Fees: Charges writers for photocopy and postage expenses and other direct costs. If material is accepted, Agency will ask for $250 circulation fee, from unpublished authors without professional recommendations. Principle agent is an attorney and former publisher. Offers consultation service through which writers can get advice on a contract or on publishing problems.

Recent Sales: No information given.

‡THE PETER MILLER AGENCY, INC., Suite 501, 220 W. 19th St., New York NY 10011. (212)929-1222. FAX: (212)206-0238. President: Peter Miller. Associate Agent: Helen Pfeffer. Estab. 1975. Represents 50 clients. 50% of clients are new/unpublished writers. Eager to work with new/unpublished writers, as well as with published/established authors (especially journalists). Specializes in celebrity books (biographies and self-help), true crime, mysteries, thrillers, historical fiction/family sagas, and "fiction with *real* motion picture potential." Writer's guidelines for 5x8½ SASE and 2 first class stamps.

Will Handle: Nonfiction books, novels and movie scripts. Currently handles 45% nonfiction books; 35% novels; and 20% movie scripts. Will read—at no charge—unsolicited queries and outlines. Reports in 2 weeks on queries; 1 month on mss.

Terms: Agent receives 15% commission on domestic sales; and 20-25% on foreign sales. Charges a criticism fee for unpublished writers. Fee is refunded if book sells. 5% of income derived from criticism fees. "The agency offers a reading evaluation, usually two to four pages in length, which gives a detailed analysis of literary craft, commercial potential and recommendations for improving the work, if necessary." Charges for photocopy expenses.

Recent Sales: *Creole: A Gastronomic History of New Orleans*, by Roy F. Guste, Jr. (Viking Studio Books); *Let's Watch a Movie: 3000 Reviews of Films*, by Ted Sennett (Prentice-Hall Press); and *Fatal Freeway*, by Steven Salerno (Clarkson N. Potter).

‡CLAUDIA MOORE LITERARY AGENCY, Suite 7020, 8306 Wilshire Blvd., Beverly Hills CA 90211. (213)931-7524. FAX: (213)931-7517. President: Claudia Moore. Estab. 1980. Represents 10 clients. "While we prefer the writer have a good track record, we are also interested in seeing demonstrated writing ability and talent even if the track record is meager, provided there is earnest desire to succeed, not just dashing off work." Eager to work with new/unpublished writers. Specializes in selling mainstream fiction—no romances or sci-fi; also movie scripts (which were our specialization until recently).

Will Handle: Novels and movie scripts. Currently handles 65% novels; 35% movie scripts. Will read—at no charge—unsolicited queries and outlines. Does not read unsolicited mss. Reports in 1 month on queries.
Terms: Agent receives 10% commission on domestic sales; 15% on dramatic sales; and 20% on foreign sales.
Fees: "If we've responded positively to query, we will then offer the author the option of a professional reading evaluation, for a fee. Waives reading fee when representing the writer. 1% of income derived from reading fees. Charges $225/300 pages. "The reading fee covers a critique with suggestions on improving the work. Our reading/evaluation is usually 2-4 pages, analyzing the work in detail, as to writing and commercial potential, plus recommendations to author on improvements that could be made to make book more salable. The reading would be done by Claudia Moore or my associate Oliver O'Meara." Charges writers for office expenses (photocopying, shipping, long distance phones).
Recent Sales: No information given.

‡**WILLIAM MORRIS AGENCY**, 1350 Avenue of Americas, New York NY 10019. (212)586-5100. Estab. 1898. Member of SAR. Works with a small number of new/unpublished authors. Specializes in novels/nonfiction.
Will Handle: Nonfiction books and novels. Will read—at no charge—unsolicited queries, outlines and manuscripts. Reports in 6 weeks.
Terms: Agent receives 10% commission on domestic sales; 10% on dramatic sales; and 20% on foreign sales.
Recent Sales: Confidential.

‡**HENRY MORRISON, INC.**, P.O. Box 235, Bedford Hills NY 10507. (914)666-3500. FAX: (914)241-7846. President: Henry Morrison. Estab. 1965. Represents 51 clients. Writer may be totally unpublished, but we prefer to work on book-length material only. Works with a small number of new/unpublished authors. Specializes in novels, some nonfiction, science fiction novels.
Will Handle: Nonfiction books, novels, juvenile books and movie scripts. Currently handles 3% nonfiction books; 95% novels; and 2% movie scripts. Will read—at no charge—unsolicited queries and outlines. Reports in 2 weeks on queries.
Terms: Agent receives 15% commission on domestic sales; 15% on dramatic sales; and 20% on foreign sales.
Fees: Charges writers for making ms copies, ordering galleys and bound books.
Recent Sales: *The Bourne Ultimatum*, by Robert Ludlum (Random House); and *Mollie Pride*, by Beverly S. Martin (Bantam Books).

MULTIMEDIA PRODUCT DEVELOPMENT, INC., Suite 724, 410 S. Michigan Ave., Chicago IL 60605. (312)922-3063. FAX (312)922-1905. President: Jane Jordan Browne. Estab. 1971. Member of ILAA. Represents 100 clients. 10% of clients are new/unpublished authors. Works with a small number of new/unpublished authors. "We are generalists, taking on nonfiction and fiction that we believe will be on target for the market."
Will Handle: Nonfiction books ("new idea" books, how-to, science and biography) and novels (mainstream and genre). Currently handles 68% nonfiction books; 30% novels; and 2% juvenile books. Will read—at no charge—unsolicited queries and outlines. Reports in 3 weeks on queries. "We review manuscripts only if we solicit submission and only as 'exclusives.' "
Terms: Agent receives 15% commission on domestic sales; 15% on dramatic sales; and 20% on foreign sales.
Fees: Charges for photocopying, overseas telegrams and telephone calls, and overseas postage expenses.
Recent Sales: *Time Off From Good Behavior*, by Susan Sussman (Pocket); *Chanel*, by Axel Madsen (Henry Holt); *Echoes*, by Jackie Hyman (William Morrow).

JEAN V. NAGGAR LITERARY AGENCY, 216 #. 75th St., New York NY 10021. (212)794-1082. President: Jean Naggar. Estab. 1978. Member of ILAA and SAR. Represents 80 clients. "If a writer is submitting a first novel, this must be completed and in final draft form before writing to query the agency." Prefers to work with published/established authors; works with small number of new/unpublished authors. Specializes in mainstream fiction and nonfiction—no category romances, no occult.
Will Handle: Nonfiction books, novels and juvenile books. Handles magazine articles and magazine fiction from authors who also write fiction/nonfiction books. Will read—at no charge—unsolicited queries and outlines. Reports in 2 weeks on queries.
Terms: Agent receives 15% commission on domestic sales; 15% on dramatic sales; and 20% on foreign sales.
Fees: Charges writers for photocopying, long distance telephone, cables and overseas postage expenses.
Recent Sales: *The Plains of Passage*, by Jean M. Auel (Crown Publishers); *A Dangerous Woman*, by Mary McGarry Morris (Viking-Penguin); and *The Fatal Crown*, by Ellen Jones (Simon and Schuster).

RUTH NATHAN LITERARY AGENCY, % Cynthia Parzych Publishing, 648 Broadway, New York NY 10012. (212)529-1133. President: Ruth Nathan. Estab. 1987. Member of ILAA. Represents 10 clients. 50% of clients are new/unpublished writers. Works with small number of new/unpublished writers and specialized writers of biography, art history and art. Specializes in nonfiction.

WOULD YOU USE THE SAME CALENDAR YEAR AFTER YEAR?

Of course not! If you scheduled your appointments using last year's calendar, you'd risk missing important meetings and deadlines, so you keep up-to-date with a new calendar each year. Just like your calendar, *Writer's Market*® changes every year, too. Many of the editors move or get promoted, rates of pay increase, and even editorial needs change from the previous year. You can't afford to use an out-of-date book to plan your marketing efforts!

So save yourself the frustration of getting manuscripts returned in the mail, stamped MOVED: ADDRESS UNKNOWN. And of NOT submitting your work to new listings because you don't know they exist. **Make sure you have the most current writing and marketing information by ordering *1992 Writer's Market* today.** All you have to do is complete the attached post card and return it with your payment or charge card information. Order now, and there's one thing that won't change from your *1991 Writer's Market* — the price! That's right, we'll send you the 1992 edition for just $24.95. *1992 Writer's Market* will be published and ready for shipment in September 1991.

Let an old acquaintance be forgot, and toast the new edition of *Writer's Market.* Order today!

(See other side for more new market books to help you get published)

To order, drop this postpaid card in the mail.

☐ **YES!** I want the most current edition of *Writer's Market*.® Please send me the 1992 edition at the 1991 price — $24.95.* (NOTE: *1992 Writer's Market* will be ready for shipment in September 1991.) #10204

Also send me these books to help me get published:

_____ (10191) 1991 Novel & Short Story Writer's Market, $18.95,* paperback (available February 1991)

_____ (10190) 1991 Children's Writer's & Illustrator's Market, $16.95,* paperback (available February 1991)

_____ (10192) 1991 Humor & Cartoon Writer's Market, $16.95,* paperback (available February, 1991)

*Plus postage & handling: $3.00 for one book, $1.00 for each additional book. Ohio residents add 5½% sales tax.

☐ Payment enclosed (Slip this card and your payment into an envelope)
☐ Please charge my: ☐ Visa   ☐ MasterCard

Account # _____ Exp. Date _____

Signature _____

Name _____

Address _____

City _____ State _____ Zip _____

(This offer expires August 1, 1992.)

 1507 Dana Avenue
Cincinnati, OH 45207

5773

GREAT NEWS FOR WRITERS!

3 NEW Market Books to Help You Get Published!

1991 Novel & Short Story Writer's Market (Formerly Fiction Writer's Market)
Edited by Robin Gee

Now in paperback, with all the facts and information you need to get your short stories and novels published. Includes 1,900 detailed listings of commercial books and magazine publishers, small presses, and little/literary magazines, PLUS advice on/listings of agents who handle fiction.
672 pages/$18.95, paperback (available February, 1991)

1991 Children's Writer's & Illustrator's Market

Now in its third year, this annual is even bigger and better with market listings for audiovisual aids, songs, coloring books, comic books, and puzzles. Again includes markets for writing **by** children. Includes a "Business of Writing & Illustrating" article, subject and age-level indexes, and many other features to help you sell in this lucrative market.
256 pages/$16.95, paperback (available February, 1991)

1991 Humor & Cartoon Markets
Edited by Bob Staake

This second edition is filled with 500 listings of magazine, newsletter, greeting card, and comic book publishers, plus articles on the "Business of Humor." You'll find out where and how to sell your gags, cartoons, and funny articles, stories, and songs, and then find yourself laughing all the way to the bank!
256 pages/$16.95, paperback (available February, 1991)

Use coupon on other side to order your copies today!

Will Handle: Nonfiction books. Currently handles 80% nonfiction books; 20% novels. Does not read unsolicited mss. Reports in 1 month on queries.
Terms: Agent receives 15% commission on domestic sales; 10% on foreign sales.
Fees: Charges for long distance phone calls, copying of ms, Fax, and Telex, extra galleys. 100% of income derived from commission on ms sales.
Recent Sales: *Best Revenge*, by Jeannie Sakol (Ballantine); *The Official Guide to Costume Jewelry*, by Harrice Miller (House of Collectibles/Ballantine).

‡**B.K. NELSON LITERARY AGENCY,** 303 Fifth Ave., New York NY 10016. (212)889-0637. President: Bonita K. Nelson. Estab. 1979. Represents 16 clients. Prefers to work with published/established authors. Specializes in nonfiction, how-to, self-help, computer, biography, text books (elementary, high school, college) business, sports.
Will Handle: Nonfiction, novels, textbooks, movie scripts, stage plays and TV scripts. Currently handles 95% nonfiction books; 1% novels; 2% textbooks; 1% movie scripts and 1% TV scripts. Will read — at no charge — unsolicited queries and outlines. Does not read unsolicited manuscripts. Reports in 1 week on queries; 2 weeks on mss.
Terms: Agent receives 15% commission on domestic sales; 15% on dramatic sales; and 15% on foreign sales.
Fees: Charges a reading fee "when evaluation is required." Waives reading fee when representing the writer. .05% of income derived from reading fees. Charges $325/300 pages.
Recent Sales: *How to Buy a House Under $100,000* by Jane White (Wiley); *The Electronic Traveler: Laptop Computer*, by David Rothman (St. Martin's); and *Gertrude Stein*, by Dr. Leon Katz (Ticknor & Fields).

‡**NEW AGE LITERARY AGENCY,** 7815 Hollywood Blvd., Hollywood CA 90046. (213)851-7444. Senior Editor and Vice President: Siv Ohlsson. Estab. 1988. Eager to work with new/unpublished writers. Specializes in physical and behavioral science book publishing and general field of documentary film/video production. "We want new writers with a professional touch and have a strong documentary film message."
Will Handle: Nonfiction books (basic science and behavioral sciences only), movie scripts (documentaries), fiction with a message.
Terms: Agent receives 15-25% commission on domestic sales; 15-20% on foreign sales.
Fees: Charges a $150 evaluation and reading fee for new writers. New agency designed for New Age market for 21st century mentality.

NEW AGE WORLD SERVICES, 62091 Valley View Circle, Joshua Tree CA 92252. (619)366-2833. Owner: Victoria Vandertuin. Estab. 1957. Member of Academy of Science Fiction, Fantasy and Horror Films, New Age Publishing and Retailing Allience, and the Institute of Mentalphysics. Represents 30 clients. 100% of clients are new/unpublished writers. Eager to work with new/unpublished writers. Specializes in all New Age fields: occult, astrology, metaphysical, yoga, U.F.O., ancient continents, para sciences, mystical, magical, health, beauty, political, and all New Age categories in fiction and nonfiction. Writer's guidelines for #10 SAE with four first class stamps.
Will Handle: Nonfiction books, novels and poetry. 40% nonfiction books; 30% novels and 10% poetry. Will read — at no charge — unsolicited queries, outlines and mss; will read submissions at no charge, but may charge a criticism fee or service charge for work performed after the initial reading. Reports in 6 weeks.
Terms: Receives 15% commission on domestic sales; and 20% on foreign sales.
Fees: Charges reading fee of $125 for 300-page, typed, double-spaced ms; reading fee waived if representing writer. Charges criticism fee of $135 for 300-page, typed, double-space ms; 10% of income derived from criticism fees. "I personally read all manuscripts for critique or evaluation, which is typed, double-spaced with about four or more pages, depending on the manuscript and the service for the manuscript the author requests. If requested, marketing advice is included. We charge a representation fee if we represent the author's manuscript." Charges writer for editorial readings, compiling of query letter and synopsis, printing of same, compiling lists and mailings.
Recent Sales: No information given.

NEW ENGLAND PUBLISHING ASSOCIATES, INC., Box 5, Chester CT 06412. New York: (718)788-6641 or Connecticut: (203)345-4976. President: Elizabeth Frost Knappman. Estab. 1983. Represents 45-50 clients. 25% of clients are new/unpublished writers. Specializes in serious nonfiction. "We would like to see mss reflecting long-term research."
Will Handle: Nonfiction books. Currently handles 100% nonfiction books. Will read — at no charge — unsolicited queries and outlines. Phone queries are OK. Reports in 1 month on queries. Simultaneous queries OK.
Terms: Agent receives 15% on domestic sales; and 10% on dramatic and foreign sales (plus 10% to co-agent). 100% of income derived from commission on ms sales.
Recent Sales: *Body Mike*, by Tom Reaner and Joe Cantolupo (Villard); *Lillian Hellman*, by Carl Rollyson (St. Martin's); and *How to Get Your Lover Back*, by Dr. Blase Harris (Dell).

REGULA NOETZLI LITERARY AGENCY, 446 E. 85th St., New York NY 10028. (212)628-1537. FAX: (212)744-3145. Literary Agent: Regula Noetzli. Estab. 1989. Represents 30 clients. Works with a small number of new/unpublished authors. Specializes in literary fiction/nonfiction specifically in the areas of popular science, psychology, history/current affairs; also mysteries.
Will Handle: Nonfiction books and novels. Currently handles 40% novels; 60% textbooks. Will read—at no charge—unsolicited queries and outlines. Reports in 2 weeks on queries.
Terms: Agent receives 15% commission on domestic sales; 15% on dramatic sales; and 20% on foreign sales.
Fees: Charges writers for photocopying of manuscripts/proposals/overseas postage and Federal Express fees.
Recent Sales: Confidential.

THE BETSY NOLAN LITERARY AGENCY, Suite 9 West, 50 W. 29th St., New York NY 10001. (212)779-0700. FAX: (212)689-0376. President: Betsy Nolan. Agents: Donald Lehr and Carla Glasser. Estab. 1980. Represents 50 clients. 50% of clients are new/unpublished writers. Works with a small number of new/unpublished authors.
Will Handle: Nonfiction books and novels. Currently handles 60% nonfiction books and 40% novels. Will read—at no charge—unsolicited queries and outlines. Reports in 2 weeks on queries; 2 months on mss.
Terms: Agent receives 15% commission on domestic sales; and 20% on foreign sales.
Recent Sales: No information given.

THE NORMA-LEWIS AGENCY, 521 5th Ave., New York NY 10175. (212)751-4955. Contact: Norma Liebert. Estab. 1980. 50% of clients are new/unpublished writers. Prefers to work with published/established authors; eager to work with new/unpublished writers. Specializes in young adult and children's books.
Will Handle: Novels, textbooks, juvenile books (pre-school through high school), movie scripts, radio scripts, stage plays and TV scripts. Currently handles 10% nonfiction books; 10% novels; 10% textbooks; 50% juvenile books; 5% movie scripts; 5% radio scripts; 5% stage plays; and 5% TV scripts. Will read—at no charge—unsolicited queries and outlines. Reports in 2 weeks on queries.
Terms: Agent receives 15% commission on domestic sales; 15% on dramatic sales; and 20% on foreign sales.
Recent Sales: No information given.

NUGENT AND ASSOCIATES LITERARY AGENCY, 170 10th Street N., Naples FL 33940. (813)262-3683/7562. President: Ray E. Nugent. Estab. 1976. Represents 41 clients. 50% of clients are new/unpublished writers. Eager to work with new/unpublished writers. Specializes in adult fiction and nonfiction—screenplays.
Will Handle: Nonfiction books, novels, movie scripts, stage plays and TV scripts. Currently handles 55% nonfiction books; 35% novels; 10% movie scripts, stage plays; TV scripts. Will read—at no charge—unsolicited queries and outlines. Reports in 1 month on queries; 2 months on manuscripts.
Terms: Receives 15% commission on domestic sales; 15% on dramatic sales; and 20% on foreign sales.
Fees: Charges writers for long distance phone calls, copies, ms typing, any other extraordinary expenses directly associated with the author's specific material.
Recent Sales: *Disney's World*, by Leonard Mosley (Scarborough House); *How to Retire on the House*, by Andrew McLean (Contemporary Books); and *The Day I Died: The Jay Barbree Story* (New Horizon).

‡OCEANIC PRESS SERVICE, 3164 W. Tyler Ave., Anaheim CA 92801. (714)527-5650. FAX: (714)527-0268. Associate Editor: John J. Kearns. Estab. 1940. Represents 100 clients. Prefers to work with published/established authors; will work with a small number of new/unpublished authors. Specializes in selling features of worldwide interest; romance books, mysteries, biographies, westerns, nonficiton of timeless subjects, reprints of out-of-print titles.
Will Handle: Magazine articles, nonfiction books, novels, juvenile books, syndicated material. Currently handles 20% nonfiction books; 30% novels; 10% juvenile books; 40% syndicated material. Will read—at no charge—unsolicited queries and outlines. Reports in 2 weeks on queries.
Terms: Agent receives 15% commission on domestic sales; 20% on foreign sales. 1% of income derived from reading fees. Charges $250/300 pages. Reading fee includes detailed critique. "We have authors who published many books of their own to do the reading and give a very thorough critique."
Recent Sales: *Sex and Love*, by Dr. Frank Caprio; and *Dictionary of Home Repair*, by K. Singer (Ottenheimer).

FIFI OSCARD ASSOCIATES, 19 W. 44th St., New York NY 10036. (212)764-1100. Contact: Ivy Fischer Stone, Literary Department. Estab. 1956. Member of SAR and WGA. Represents 108 clients. 5% of clients are new/unpublished writers. "Writer must have published articles or books in major markets or have screen credits if movie scripts, etc." Specializes in literary novels, commercial novels, mysteries and nonfiction, especially celebrity biographies and autobiographies.
Will Handle: Nonfiction books, novels, movie scripts and stage plays. Currently handles 40% nonfiction books; 40% novels; 5% movie scripts; 5% stage plays; and 10% TV scripts. Will read—at no charge—unsolicited queries and outlines. Reports in 1 week on queries if SASE enclosed.

Terms: Agent receives 15% commission on domestic sales; 10% on dramatic sales; and 20% on foreign sales.
Fees: Charges for photocopy expenses.
Recent Sales: *TekLords*, by William Shatner (Putnam's) and *Dick Tracy, The Official Biography*, by Jay Maeder (NAL).

THE OTTE COMPANY, 9 Goden St., Belmont MA 02178. (617)484-8505. Contact: Jane H. Otte or L. David Otte. Estab. 1973. Represents 35 clients. 33% of clients are new/unpublished writers. Works with a small number of new/unpublished authors. Specializes in quality adult trade books.
Will Handle: Nonfiction books and novels. Currently handles 40% nonfiction books; and 60% novels. Will consider unsolicited query letters. Reports in 1 week on queries; 1 month on mss.
Terms: Agent receives 15% commission on domestic sales; 7½% on dramatic sales; and 10% on foreign sales plus 10% to foreign agent.
Fees: Charges for photocopy, overseas phone and postage expenses. 100% of income derived from commission on ms sales.
Recent Sales: *The Woman Who Walked Into the Sea*, by Philip Craig (Scribner's); *In Spite of Darkness*, by Robert Begiebing (Algonquin); and *Call Back the Day*, by Olivia Solomon (Houghton Mifflin).

THE PANETTIERI AGENCY, 142 Marcella Rd., Hampton VA 23666. (804)825-1708. President: Eugenia A. Panettieri. Estab. 1988. Member of Romance Writers of America. Represents 36 clients. 70% of clients are new/unpublished writers. Prefers to work with published/established authors. Specializes in romance and women's fiction, young adult, historical, nonfiction (how-to and self-help), mystery, suspense and horror.
Will Handle: Nonfiction books, novels and juvenile books. Currently handles 20% nonfiction books; 70% novels; and 10% juvenile books. Will read—at no charge—unsolicited queries, outlines and manuscripts. Reports in 1 week on queries; 1 month on mss.
Terms: Agent receives 10% commission on domestic sales; 20% on foreign sales.
Recent Sales: *Kindred Spirits*, by Sarah Temple (Silhouette); *The Summoned*, by Steven Ray Fulgham (Berkley); *Love's Masquerade*, by Cynthia Richey (Walker & Co.).

JOHN K. PAYNE LITERARY AGENCY, INC., Box 1003, New York NY 10276. (212)475-6447. President: John K. Payne. Estab. 1923 (as Lenniger Literary Agency). Represents 30 clients. 20% of clients are new/unpublished writers. Prefers writers who have one or two books published. No unsolicited material accepted. Specializes in popular women's fiction, historical romance, biography, sagas.
Will Handle: Nonfiction books, novels, and juvenile books (young adult fiction, nonfiction). Currently publishes 20% nonfiction books and 80% novels.
Terms: Agent receives 10% commission on domestic sales; 10% on dramatic sales; and 20% on foreign sales.
Fees: No fees.
Recent Sales: *All the Wrong Reasons*, by Kathleen Eagle (Silhouette); *Caprock*, by Elmer Kelton (Doubleday); *Sons of Texas*, by Tom Early (Berkley).

PEGASUS INTERNATIONAL, INC., P.O. Box 5470, Winter Park FL 32793-5470. (407)831-1008. Director: Gene Lovitz. Assistant Director/Client Contact: Carole Morling. Estab. 1987. Represents 350 clients. 85% of clients are new/unpublished writers. Specializes in how-to, self-help, technical, business, health, political; mainstream novels, regency, contemporary and historical romance, horror, experimental, sci-fi, mystery.
Will Handle: Nonfiction books, novels, textbooks, juvenile books, movie scripts, TV scripts and video. Currently handles 25% nonfiction books; 45% novels; 5% cookbooks; 5% juvenile books (middle school-high school); 20% film/TV scripts. Will read—at no charge—unsolicited queries and outlines accompanied by SASE. Does not read unsolicited manuscripts. Prompt RSVP by phone. Responds in 2 weeks.
Terms: Agent receives 10% commission on domestic sales; 10% on dramatic sales; 15% on foreign sales.
Fees: Charges reading fee. "We return fee when and if a publishing contract is obtained. No charge for postage or phone expenses." 15% of income derived from reading fees. Charges $200 for up to a 400-page, typed, double-spaced ms. Lower fees for pamphlets, chapbooks, etc. "We charge one fee only (installments acceptable). We term it an 'evaluation' fee which is both a reading fee as well as a criticism fee. We will work with the author as long as necessary to prepare the manuscript for marketing. We do both line-by-line when needed while concentrating on the overall work. Marketing is always a part of the critique. Discuss ways to improve and make the manuscript marketable." 85% of income is derived from commission on mss sales; 15% derived from fees.
Recent Sales: *Crooked Mirror and Other Stories by Anton Chekhov*, by Arnold Hinchliffe (Zebra Books); *Cloudlands*, screenplay by Zohrab Yoncali (River Road Productions); *Beside Still Waters*, novel by Prof. Margaret Hagler (Scholastic Books).

PENMARIN BOOKS, Suite 8, 16 Mary St., San Rafael CA 94901. (415)457-7746. FAX: (415)454-0426. President: Hal Lockwood. Estab. 1987. Represents 20 clients. 80% of clients are new/unpublished writers. "No previous publication is necessary. We do expect authoritative credentials in terms of history, politics, science and the like." Specializes in general trade nonfiction and illustrated books. Have started handling fiction as well.

Will Handle: Nonfiction books. Currently handles 90% nonfiction books, 10% fiction. Will read—at no charge—unsolicited queries and outlines. Will read submissions at no charge, but may charge a criticism fee or service charge for work performed after the initial reading. Reports in 2 weeks on queries; 1 month on mss.

Terms: Agent receives 10% commission on domestic sales; 10% on dramatic sales; and 10% on foreign sales.

Fees: "We normally do not provide extensive criticism as part of our reading but, for a fee, will prepare guidance for editorial development." Charges $200/300 pages. "Our editorial director writes critiques. These may be two to ten pages long. They usually include an overall evaluation and then analysis and recommendations about specific sections, organization, or style."

Recent Sales: *Bank of America Guide to Making the Most of Your Money*, by R. Darden Chambliss, Jr. (Dow Jones-Irwin); *The Picture Fixer: A Problem-Solving Guide to Taking Great Photos with a Point-and-Shoot Camera*, by Jan Blockstom (TAB Books); *The Dinner Party Book*, by Michele Braden (Macmillan).

PERKINS' LITERARY AGENCY, P.O. Box 48, Childs MD 21916. (301)398-2647. Agent/Owner: Esther R. Perkins. Estab. 1979. Represents 35 clients; 75% of clients are new/unpublished authors. Will be adding a few clients, professional or newcomers, in the next year. Specializes in historicals, mysteries, men's adventure, horror, regencies, a few historical/romance and mainstream.

Will Handle: Novels. Currently handles 100% novels. Does not read unsolicited material. Reports in 3 weeks.

Terms: Agent receives 15% commission on domestic sales; 20% on dramatic sales; 20% on foreign sales.

Fees: Charges a reading fee "if writer has not had a book published by a major house in the past two years. Fee refunded if sale made within one year." 5% of income derived from reading fees. Charges $75 for 300-page, typed, double-spaced book ms. "I provide an overall critique of the ms—could be long or short, but not line-by-line. Marketing advice for clients only. I am the only reader." 95% of income is derived from commission on ms sales; 5% from fees.

Recent Sales: *Texas Gamble*, by Vivian Vaughan (Zebra); *Time Spun Rapture*, by Thomasina Ring (Leisure); and *Lady Maryann's Dilemma*, by Karla Hocker (Zebra).

JAMES PETER ASSOCIATES, INC., P.O. Box 772, Tenafly NJ 07670. (201)568-0760. FAX: (201)568-2959. President: Bert Holtje. Estab. 1971. Member of ILAA. Represents 49 clients. "We are especially interested in writers whose backgrounds include psychology, medicine, history, business and politics. Prior publication is important, but not critical." Prefers to work with published/established authors. Specializes in nonfiction only. Psychology, health and related subjects, history, politics,how-to, popular culture, and business—all for general readers.

Will Handle: Nonfiction books. Currently handles 100% nonfiction books. Will read—at no charge—unsolicited queries and outlines. Does not read unsolicited manuscripts. Reports in 1 month on queries.

Terms: Agent receives 15% commission on domestic sales; 20% on foreign sales.

Fees: Charges writers for duplicating proposals.

Recent Sales: *Almanac of the American Revolution*, by L. Edward Purcell (Pharos—World Almanac); *The Ultimate Resumé*, by Dr. David Eyler (Random House); *A Chronicle of the Indian Wars*, by Alan Axelrod (Prentice-Hall).

ALISON PICARD, LITERARY AGENT, Box 2000, Cotuit MA 02635. (508)888-3741. Contact: Alison Picard. Estab. 1985. Represents 40 clients. 30% of clients are new/unpublished writers. "I prefer writers who have been published (at least in magazines) but am willing to consider exceptional new writers." Works with a small number of new/unpublished authors. Specializes in nonfiction. Also handle literary and category fiction, contemporary and historical romances, juvenile/YA books, short stories and articles if suitable for major national magazine.

Will Handle: Magazine articles, magazine fiction, nonfiction books, novels, juvenile books. Currently handles 5% magazine articles; 5% magazine fiction; 30% nonfiction books; 40% novels; and 20% juvenile books. Will read—at no charge—unsolicited queries, outlines and manuscripts. No unsolicited mss or phone queries. Reports in 1 week on queries; 1 month on manuscripts. "Authors *must* send written query first before submitting material."

Terms: Agent receives 15% commission on domestic sales; 15% on dramatic sales; and 15% on foreign sales.

Fees: Charges for copying of ms. 100% of income derived from sales of writers' work.

Recent Sales: *From: The President*, by Bruce Oudes (Harper & Row); *Annabelle Anderson*, by Patricia Beaver (Four Winds Press/Macmillan); and *Secrets for Young Scientists*, by Ray Staszako (Doubleday).

ARTHUR PINE ASSOCIATES, INC., 1780 Broadway, New York NY 10019. (212)265-7330. Contact: Agent. Estab. 1967. Represents 100 clients. 20% of clients are new/unpublished writers. Works with a small number of new/unpublished authors.

Will Handle: Nonfiction books and novels. Currently handles 75% nonfiction books and 25% novels. Does not read unsolicited mss. Reports in 2 weeks on queries.
Terms: Agent receives 15% commission on domestic sales; 15% on dramatic sales; and 15% on foreign sales.
Fees: Charges a reading fee. .1% of income derived from reading fees. Gives 1-3 pages of criticism. Charges for photocopy expenses. 99.9% of income derived from sales of writers' work.
Recent Sales: *Saturday Night*, by Susan Orlean (Simon & Schuster); *Your Erroneous Zones*, by Dr. Wayne W. Dyer; *Gracie*, by George Burns (Putnam).

‡**JULIE POPKIN/NANCY COOKE,** 15340 Albright St., #204, Pacific Palisades CA 90272 (Popkin). (213)459-2834; FAX: (213)459-4128; 236 E. Davie St., Raleigh NC 27601 (Cooke). (919)834-1456. Estab. 1989. Represents 11 clients. 33% of clients are new/unpublished writers. Specializes in selling book-length mss including fiction – all genres – and nonfiction. Especially interested in social issues.
Will Handle: Nonfiction books and novels. Currently handles 50% nonfiction books and 50% novels. Will read submissions at no charge, but may charge a criticism fee or service charge for work performed after the initial reading. Reports in 1 month on queries; 2 months on mss.
Terms: Agent receives 10% commission on domestic sales; 10% on dramatic sales; and 20% on foreign sales.
Fees: Charges writers for photocopying, extraordinary mailing fees.
Recent Sales: *Moments of Light*, by Fred Chappell (New South).

SIDNEY E. PORCELAIN, P.O. Box 1229, Milford PA 18337-1229. (717)296-6420. Manager: Sidney Porcelain. Estab. 1952. Represents 20 clients. 50% of clients are new/unpublished writers. Prefers to work with published/established authors; works with a small number of new/unpublished authors. Specializes in fiction (novels, mysteries, and suspense) and nonfiction (celebrity and exposé).
Will Handle: Magazine articles, magazine fiction, nonfiction books, novels and juvenile books. Currently handles 2% magazine articles; 5% magazine fiction; 5% nonfiction books; 50% novels; 5% juvenile books; 2% movie scripts; 1% TV scripts; and 30% "comments for new writers." Will read – at no charge – unsolicited queries, outlines and mss. Reports in 2 weeks on queries; 3 weeks on mss.
Terms: Agent receives 10% commission on domestic sales; 10% on dramatic sales; and 10% on foreign sales. 50% of income derived from commission on ms sales.
Recent Sales: *No Refills*, by Todd Jenson (Unique); *A House Built on Rock*, by Sidney Porcelain (Hazardous Waste Management); *American Journey*, by Linda Bingham (Unique).

AARON M. PRIEST LITERARY AGENCY, Suite 3902, 122 E. 42nd St., New York NY 10168. (212)818-0344. Contact: Aaron Priest, Molly Friedrich, Robert Colgan and Laurie Liss.
Will Handle: Fiction and nonfiction books. Currently handles 50% nonfiction books and 50% fiction. Will read query letters (must be accompanied by SASE). Unsolicited manuscripts will be returned unread.
Terms: Agent receives 15% commission on domestic sales.
Fees: Charges for photocopy and foreign postage expenses.
Recent Sales: *Disappearing Acts*, by Terry McMillan; *Ordinary Love and Good Will*, by Jane Smiley; *Longing for Darkness*, by China Galland.

‡**PRINTED TREE, INC.,** 2357 Trail Dr., Evansville IN 47711. (812)476-9015. President: Jo Frohbicter-Mueller. Estab. 1983. Represents 26 clients. "Works with authors with credentials and background to write on their subject." Specializes in selling serious nonfiction and textbooks.
Will Handle: Nonfiction books and textbooks. Currently handles 50% nonfiction books; 50% textbooks. Will read – at no charge – unsolicited queries and outlines. Reports in 3 weeks on queries. Does not return material without SASE.
Terms: Agent receives 15% commission on domestic sales; and 15% on foreign sales.
Fees: Charges writers for mailing, phone calls, photocopying and other out-of-pocket expenses.
Recent Sales: *Grow Your Own Mushrooms*, by Mueller (Gardenway); *Practical Stained Glass Crafting*, by Mueller (David & Charles); *Stay Home and Mind Your Own Business*, by Mueller (Betterway).

‡**SUSAN ANN PROTTER LITERARY AGENT,** Suite 1408, 110 W. 40th St., New York NY 10018. (212)840-0480. Contact: Susan Protter. Estab. 1971. Member of ILAA. Represents 50 clients. 10% of clients are new/unpublished writers. Writer must have book-length project or manuscript that is ready to be sold. Works with a small number of new/unpublished authors. Specializes in general nonfiction, self-help, psychology, science, health, medicine, novels, science fiction, mysteries and thrillers.
Will Handle: Nonfiction books and novels. Currently handles 5% magazine articles; 45% nonfiction books; 45% novels; and 5% photography books. Will read – at no charge – unsolicited queries and outlines. "Must include SASE." Reports in 2 weeks on queries; 5 weeks on solicited mss. "Please do not call; mail queries only."
Terms: Agent receives 15% commission on domestic sales; 15% on TV, film and dramatic sales; and 25% on foreign sales. Charges for long distance, photocopying, messenger, express mail and airmail expenses. 100% of income derived from commission on ms sales.

Recent Sales: *Voyage to the Red Planet*, by Terry Bisson (Morrow/Avon); *Parenting Our Schools*, by Jill Bloom (Little, Brown); and *Roosevelt and Hitler*, by Robert E. Herzstein (Paragon House).

‡**ROBERTA PRYOR, INC.**, 24 W. 55th St., New York NY 10019. (212)245-0420. President: Roberta Pryor. Estab. 1985. Member of ILAA. Represents 50 clients. Prefers to work with published/established authors; works with a small number of new/unpublished writers. Specializes in serious nonfiction and (tends toward) literary fiction. Special interest in natural history and good cookbooks.
Will Handle: Nonfiction books, novels, textbooks, juvenile books. Handles 10% magazine fiction; 40% nonfiction books; 40% novels; 10% textbooks; 10% juvenile books. Will read—at no charge—unsolicited quries and outlines. Reports in 10 weeks on queries.
Terms: Charges 10% commission on domestic sales; 10% on dramatic sales; and 20% on foreign sales.
Fees: Charges for photocopying, Federal Express service sometimes.
Recent Sales: *The Bear Flag*, by Cecilia Holland (Houghton Mifflin); *Devices and Desires*, by P.D. James (Knopf); and *Seeing Through Movies*, by Mark C. Miller (Pantheon).

‡**QUICKSILVER BOOKS, INC.**, 50 Wilson St., Hartsdale NY 10530. (914)946-8748. President: Bob Silverstein. Estab. 1973. Represents 40 clients. Works with small number of new/unpublished authors. Specializes in adult full-length quality fiction—literary, sci-fi, suspense, contemporary, "best seller" type novels, etc. Also, nonfiction; self-help; psychology; New Age; healing modes (preferably by M.D.'s or practitioners), spiritual wisdom; true crime; business and professional advice; etc. In short, general *trade* fiction and nonfiction.
Will Handle: Nonfiction books and novels. Film and TV rights. Currently handles 60% nonfiction books and 40% novels. Will read—at no charge—unsolicited queries, outlines and manuscripts (only with SASE). Reports in 2 weeks on queries; 1 month on manuscripts.
Terms: Agent receives 15% commission on domestic sales; 15% on foreign sales.
Recent Sales: *James Baldwin: Artist on Fire*, by W.J. Weatherby (Donald I. Fine); *Walk for Life*, by Deena and David Balboa (Putnam/Perigee); *Beating the College Blues*, by Drs. Grayson and Melman (Facts on File).

D. RADLEY-REGAN & ASSOCIATES, P.O. Box 243, Jamestown NC 27282. (919)454-5040. President and Editor: D. Radley-Regan. Estab. 1987. Eager to work with new/unpublished writers. Specializes in fiction, nonfiction, mystery, thriller.
Will Handle: Nonfiction books, novels, movie scripts and TV scripts. Currently handles 10% nonfiction books; 40% novels; 25% movie scripts; 25% TV scripts. Will read submissions at no charge, but may charge a criticism fee or service charge for work performed after the initial reading. Reports in 2 weeks on queries; 10 weeks on mss.
Terms: Agent receives 15% commission on domestic sales; 15% on dramatic sales; and 15% on foreign sales.
Fees: Charges reading for full mss. Writer receives overall evaluation, marketing advice and agency service. 10% of income derived from commission on mss sales. Payment of criticism fee does not ensure that writer will be represented.
Recent Sales: *Wentworth Place*, and *Return to Wentworth Place*, by D. Radley-Regan.

HELEN REES LITERARY AGENCY, 308 Commonwealth Ave., Boston MA 02116. (617)262-2401. Contact: Catherine Mahar. Estab. 1982. Member of ILAA. Represents 55 clients. 25% of our clients are new/unpublished writers. Writer must have been published or be an authority on a subject. Prefers to work with published/established authors. Specializes in nonfiction—biographies, health and business.
Will Handle: Nonfiction books and novels. Currently handles 90% nonfiction books and 10% novels. Will read—at no charge—unsolicited queries and outlines. Reports in 2 weeks on queries; 3 weeks on mss.
Terms: Agent receives 15% commission on domestic sales and 20% on foreign sales.
Fees: Occasionally charges a reading fee "for clients who are unpublished and want that service. I don't solicit this." Reading fee will be waived if representing the writer. Charges criticism fee of $250; writer receives criticism of characters, dialogue, plot, style and suggestions for reworking areas of weakness.
Recent Sales: *Guilt is The Teacher, Love is The Lesson*, by Dr. Joan Borysenko (Warner); *Quaddafi on The Edge*, by Camelia Sadat (Harper & Row); *In The Falcon's Claw*, by Chet Raymo (Viking).

RHODES LITERARY AGENCY, 140 West End Ave., New York NY 10023. (212)580-1300. Estab. 1971. Member of ILAA.
Will Handle: Nonfiction books, novels (a limited number), and juvenile books. Will read—at no charge—unsolicited queries and outlines. Include SASE. Reports in 2 weeks on queries.
Terms: Agent receives 10% commission on domestic sales; and 20% on foreign sales.
Recent Sales: No information given.

‡**RIGHTS UNLIMITED**, 156 5th Ave., New York NY 10010. (212)741-0404. FAX: (212)691-0546. Agent: B. Kurman. Estab. 1984. Represents 57 clients. Works with a small number of new/unpublished authors. Specializes in fiction and nonfiction.

Will Handle: Nonfiction books, novels and juvenile books. Currently handles 35% novels; 50% textbooks; 15% movie scripts. Will read submissions at no charge, but may charge a criticism fee or service charge for work performed after the initial reading. Reports in 2 weeks on queries; 1 month on manuscripts.
Terms: Agent receives 15% commission on domestic sales; 15% on dramatic sales; and 20% on foreign sales.
Recent Sales: *The Dragon Triangle*, by Charles Berlitz (Wynwood Press); *The Adventures of Taxi Dog*, by D.S. Barracca (The Dial Press); *The Last Ramadan*, by Norman Lang (Harper Paperback).

JOHN R. RIINA LITERARY AGENCY, 5905 Meadowood Rd., Baltimore MD 21212. (301)433-2305. Contact: John R. Riina. Estab. 1977. Works with "authors with credentials to write on their subject." Specializes in college textbooks, professional books and serious nonfiction.
Will Handle: Textbooks. Currently handles 50% nonfiction books and 50% textbooks. Does not read unsolicited mss. Reports in 3 weeks.
Terms: Agent receives 10% commission on domestic sales; 10% on dramatic sales; 15% on foreign sales.
Fees: Charges "exceptional long distance telephone and express of manuscripts." 90% of income is derived from commission on manuscript sales; 10% from fees.
Recent Sales: "Not available for listing."

‡SHERRY ROBB LITERARY PROPERTIES, #102, 7250 Beverly Blvd., Los Angeles CA 90036. (213)965-8780. FAX: (213)965-8784. Mainstream Fiction Agent: Sasha Goodman. Owner: Sherry Robb. Estab. 1982. Represents 250 clients. Works with a small number of new/unpublished authors. Specializes in fiction and nonfiction; TV and film.
Will Handle: Nonfiction books, novels, juvenile books, movie scripts and TV scripts. Currently handles 30% nonfiction books, 30% novels, 20% movie scripts; 20% TV scripts. Will read—at no charge—unsolicited queries and outlines.
Terms: Agent receives 15% commission on domestic sales; 10% on dramatic sales; and 15% on foreign sales.
Fees: Charges writers for copying, postage, phone calls.
Recent Sales: *Finders Keepers*, by Barbara Nickolae (McGraw Hill); *No Easy Place to Be*, by Steven Corbin (Simon and Schuster); *Star Power*, by Jacqueline Stallone (NAL).

THE ROBBINS OFFICE, INC., 866 Second Ave., 12th Floor, New York NY 10017. (212)223-0720. FAX: (212)223-2535. Contact: Kathy P. Robbins and Evelyn Donnelly Rossi. Does not read unsolicited mss. Specializes in selling mainstream nonfiction, commercial and literary fiction.
Will Handle: Nonfiction books, novels and magazine articles for book writers under contract.
Terms: 15% commission on all domestic, dramatic and foreign sales.
Fees: Bills back specific expenses incurred in doing business for a client.

RICHARD H. ROFFMAN ASSOCIATES, Suite 6A, 697 West End Ave., New York NY 10025. (212)749-3647/ 3648. President: Richard H. Roffman. Estab. 1967. 70% of clients are new/unpublished writers. Prefers to work with published/established writers. Specializes in "nonfiction primarily, but other types, too."
Will Handle: Nonfiction books. Currently handles 10% magazine articles; 5% magazine fiction; 5% textbooks; 5% juvenile books; 5% radio scripts; 5% movie scripts; 5% TV scripts; 5% syndicated material; 5% poetry; and 50% other. Does not read unsolicited mss. Reports in 2 weeks. "SASE if written answer requested, please."
Terms: Agent receives 10% commission on domestic sales; 10% on dramatic sales; and 10% on foreign sales.
Fees: "We do not read material (for a fee) actually, only on special occasions. We prefer to refer to other people specializing in that." 10% of income derived from reading fees. "We suggest a moderate montly retainer." Charges for mailings, phone calls, photocopying and messenger service. Offers consultation service through which writers can get advice on a contract. "I am also an attorney at law."
Recent Sales: No information given.

STEPHANIE ROGERS AND ASSOCIATES, 3855 Lankershim Blvd., #218, N. Hollywood CA 91604. (818)509-1010. Owner: Stephanie Rogers. Estab. 1980. Represents 22 clients. 20% of clients are new/unpublished writers. Prefers that the writer has been produced (motion pictures or TV), his/her properties optioned or has references. Prefers to work with published/established authors. Specializes in screenplays—dramas (contemporary), action/adventure, romantic comedies and supsense/thrillers for motion pictures and TV.
Will Handle: Novels (only wishes to see those that have been published and can translate to screen) and movie and TV scripts (must be professional in presentation and not over 125 pages). Currently handles 10% novels; 50% movie scripts and 40% TV scripts. Does not read unsolicited mss.

For information on author's agents' areas of interest, see the nonfiction and fiction sections in the Author's Agents Subject Index.

Terms: Agent receives 10% commission on domestic sales; 10% on dramatic sales; and 20% on foreign sales.
Fees: Charges for phone, photocopying and messenger expenses.
Recent Sales: *Shoot to Kill*, for Touchstone Pictures; *Steel Dawn*, for Vestron; and *South of Picasso*, for Tri-Star.

JANE ROTROSEN AGENCY, 318 East 51st St., New York NY 10022. (212)593-4330. Estab. 1974. Member of ILAA. Represents 100 clients. Works with published and unpublished writers. Specializes in trade fiction and nonfiction.
Will Handle: Nonfiction books, novels and juvenile books. Currently handles 40% nonfiction books and 60% novels. Will read—at no charge—unsolicited queries and short outlines. Reports in 2 weeks.
Terms: Receives 15% commission on domestic sales; 15% on dramatic sales; and 20% on foreign sales.
Fees: Charges writers for photocopies, long-distance/transoceanic telephone, telegraph, Telex, messenger service and foreign postage.
Recent Sales: "Our client list remains confidential."

SANDUM & ASSOCIATES, 144 E. 84th St., New York NY 10028. (212)737-2011. President: Howard E. Sandum. Estab. 1987. Represents 35 clients. 20% of clients are new/unpublished writers. Specializes in general nonfiction—all categories of adult books; commerical and literary fiction.
Will Handle: Nonfiction books and novels. Currently handles 60% nonfiction books and 40% novels. Will read—at no charge—unsolicited queries and outlines. "Do not send full ms unless requested. Include SASE." Reports in 2 weeks on queries.
Terms: Agent receives 15% commission. Agent fee adjustable on dramatic and foreign sales.
Fees: Charges writers for copying, air express, long distance telephone.
Recent Sales: *The Seashell People*, by Martha Horton (M. Evans and Co.); *Judias*, by Chris and Sharon Anderson (Birch Lane); and *Alex Wants to Call It Love*, by Silvia Sanza (Serpent's Tail).

SBC ENTERPRISES, INC., 11 Mabro Dr., Denville NJ 07834-9607. (201)366-3622. Agents: Alec Bernard, Eugenia Cohen. Estab. 1979. 50% of clients are new/unpublished writers. Specializes in trade fiction, nonfiction and screenplays.
Will Handle: Nonfiction books, novels, textbooks, movie scripts, TV scripts. Currently handles 25% nonfiction books; 25% novels; 10% textbooks; 20% movie scripts; 20% TV scripts. Will read—at no charge—unsolicited queries and outlines "provided SASE included." Does not read unsolicited manuscripts. Reports in 2 weeks on queries.
Terms: Agent receives 15% commission on domestic sales for first-time writers up to $15,000, 12½% of the next $10,000, 10% thereafter—all others 10%; 15% on dramatic rights sales; 20% on foreign sales.
Recent Sales: No information given.

SCHLESSINGER-VAN DYCK AGENCY, 2814 PSFS Bldg., 12 S. 12th St., Philadelphia PA 19107. (215)627-4665. FAX: (215)627-0448. Partners: Blanche Schlessinger and Barrie Van Dyck. Estab. 1987. Authors Guild; Philadelphia Writers Organization; Philadelphia Publishers Group; ABA; MABA. Represents 50 clients. 30% of clients are new/unpublished writers. Specializes in mainstream fiction, nonfiction, how-to, mysteries, children's.
Will Handle: Nonfiction books including self-improvement, medical, biography, cookbooks; mainstream fiction, mysteries, suspense; children's books. Handles 60% nonfiction books; 25% novels; 15% children's books. Will read, at no charge, unsolicited queries and proposals. Reports in 2 weeks on queries; 6 weeks on mss. Must include SASE for response.
Terms: Agency receives 15% commission on domestic sales; 15% on dramatic sales; 15% on foreign sales.
Fees: Charges for copying, UPS, long-distance telephone and overseas mailings.
Recent Sales: *The Good Eating, Good Health Cookbook*, by Phyllis Kaufman (Consumer Reports Books); *The Bread Sister of Sinking Creek*, by Robin Moore (Harper & Row); *New Family Traditions*, by Susan Lieberman (Farrar, Straus & Giroux).

THE SUSAN SCHULMAN LITERARY AGENCY, INC., 454 W. 44th St., New York NY 10036. (212)713-1633/4/5. FAX: (212)586-8830. President: Susan Schulman. Estab. 1978. Member of SAR and ILAA. 10-15% of clients are new/unpublished writers. Prefers to work with published/established authors; works with a small number of new/unpublished authors.
Will Handle: Nonfiction, fiction and plays, especially genre fiction such as mysteries. Currently handles 50% nonfiction books; 40% novels; 10% stage plays. Will read—at no charge—unsolicited queries and outlines. Reports in 2 weeks on queries; 6 weeks on mss as long as SASE enclosed.
Terms: Agent receives 15% commission on domestic sales; 10-20% on dramatic sales; and 7½-10% on foreign sales (plus 7½-10% to co-agent).
Fees: Charges a $50 reading fee if detailed analysis requested; fee will be waived if repesenting the writer. Less than 1% of income derived from reading fees. Charges for foreign mail, special messenger or delivery services.

Recent Sales: *Runes*, by Christopher Fowler (Ballantine); *Sweet Narcissus*, by Margaret Kerlstrap (Bantam); and *The Wife-in-Law Trap*, by Ann Crytser (Simon & Schuster).

ARTHUR P. SCHWARTZ, LITERARY AGENT, Box 9132, Christchurch 2, New Zealand. (03)366-4717 or (03)355-8930. New York office: 435 Riverside Dr., New York NY 10025. (212)864-3182. Literary Agent: Arthur P. Schwartz. Estab. 1975. Member of ILAA. Represents 70 clients. 20% of clients are new/unpublished writers. Prefers to work with published/established authors; works with a small number of new/unpublished authors.
Will Handle: Nonfiction books and novels. Currently handles 50% nonfiction books and 50% novels. Reports in 1 month on queries.
Terms: Agent receives 12½% commission on domestic sales; 12½% on dramatic sales and 12½% on foreign sales.
Recent Sales: *Power Speech* by, Roy Alexander (AMAcom); *Angel's Wing*, by Jill Dubois (Ballantine) and *Einstein's Dream*, by Dr. Barry Parker (Plenum).

LAURENS R. SCHWARTZ, ESQUIRE, Suite 15D, 5 E. 22nd St., New York NY 10010-5315. (212)228-2614. Contact: Laurens R. Schwartz. Estab. 1984. Primarily nonfiction, some adult and juvenile fiction. Within nonficiton, half of authors have doctoral and post-doctoral degrees and write for both the academic and crossover (education and trade) markets; other half are general trade (astrology through Zen) and professional/business (real estate, finances, teleconferencing, graphics, etc.). Adult fiction: contemporary; science fiction/fantasy. Juvenile: illustrated; series.
Will Handle: Everything described above, plus ancillaries (from screenplays to calendars). Currently handles 85% nonfiction books; 10% fiction (adult and juvenile); 5% miscellaneous. "Do not like receiving mass mailings sent to all agents. Be selective—do your homework. Do not send *everything* you have ever written. Choose *one* work and promote that. *Always* include an SASE. *Never* send your only copy. *Always* include a background sheet on yourself and a *one*-page synopsis of the work (too many summaries end up being as long as the work)." No longer handle screenplays except as tied in to a book, or unless we solicit the screenwriter directly. Does not read unsolicited mss. Reports in 1 month.
Terms: Agent receives 10% commission on domestic sales; up to 20% on foreign sales.
Fees: "No fees except for photocopies, and that fee is avoided by an author providing necessary copies or, in certain instances, transferring files on diskette. Where necessary to bring a project into publishable form, editorial work and some rewriting provided as part of service. Work with authors on long-term career goals and promotion.

SCRIBE AGENCY, P.O. Box 580393, Houston TX 77258-0393. (713)333-1094. Literary Agent: Marta White or Carl Sinclair. Estab. 1988. Member of Writers Guild of America. Represents 9 clients. 60% of clients are new/unpublished writers. Specializes in book-length literary fiction for adults; film and television rights; motion picture and TV scripts.
Will Handle: Novels, movie scripts, TV scripts. "No horrors/thrillers or other material promoting violence and/or sexual abuse." Currently handles 40% novels; 40% movie scripts; and 20% TV scripts. Will read—at no charge—unsolicited queries and outlines. Submit query with SASE first. Send synopsis with one screenplay/TV script or 3 sample chapters and SASE. Reports in 3 weeks.
Terms: Agent receives 10% commission on domestic sales; 15-20% on foreign sales.
Recent Sales: No information given.

SEBASTIAN AGENCY, Box 1369, San Carlos CA 94070. (415)598-0310. FAX: (415)637-9615. Owner/Agent: Laurie Harper. Estab. 1985. Represents 35 clients. "If previously unpublished, the book must be completed. If previously published but outside of current book's category—book must be complete. If published within same area or category as present book—may contact with proposal and outline plus 3 sample chapters." Works with a small number of new/unpublished authors. Particulary interested in nonfiction: psychology, health, self-help, women's issues, business; fiction: mainstream, adventure, suspense, historical or literary.
Will Handle: Adult nonfiction books and novels. Currently handles 70% nonfiction books and 30% novels. Will read—at no charge—unsolicited queries, outlines and sample chapters. "No submissions during February or September." Reports in 3 weeks on queries; 1 month on sample material.
Terms: Agent receives 15% commission on domestic sales; and 20% on foreign sales.
Fees: "There will be a $100, nonrefundable fee, one time upon contracting with this agency—for previously *unpublished* authors. This is to cover extra costs of marketing a new author." Charges writers for postage after 15 submissions; cable fees; copies of manuscript for submissions.
Recent Sales: *Women Who Shop Too Much*, by Carolyn Wesson (St. Martin's Press); *A Sheaf of Wheat*, by Marjorie Edelson (Ballantine) and *A Funny Thing Happened on the Way to the Bank*, Scott Clark (AMACOM).

‡**LYNN SELIGMAN, LITERARY AGENT,** 400 Highland Ave., Upper Montclair NJ 07043. (201)783-3631. Owner: Lynn Seligman. Estab. 1985. Represents 35 clients. Works with a small number of new/unpublished authors. Specializes in nonfiction in the parenting, psychology, women's issues, health and medicine and science; adult fiction, fantasy and science fiction.
Will Handle: Magazine articles and magazine fiction for clients with books, nonfiction books and novels. Currently handles 25% magazine articles; 60% nonfiction books; 15% novels. Will read—at no charge—unsolicited queries and outlines with SASE. Reports in 2 weeks on queries.
Terms: Agent receives 15% commission on domestic sales; 15% on dramatic sales; and 25% on foreign sales.
Fees: Charges writers for photocopying manuscripts, express mail or unusual calls or mail.
Recent Sales: *Professional Presence*, by Susan Bixler (Putnam); *Congratulations! You've Been Fired*, by Lynne S. Dumas and Emily Koltnow (Ballantine); *The Duke Book of Arthritis*, by Susan Trien (Ballantine).

SHAPIRO-LICHTMAN TALENT AGENCY, 8827 Beverly Blvd., Los Angeles CA 90048. (213)859-8877. FAX: (213)859-7153. Contact: Martin Shapiro. Estab. 1969. Writer must have appropriate academic background and recommendations. Prefers to work with published/established authors.
Will Handle: Movie scripts and TV scripts. Currently handles 90% movie and TV scripts. Does not read unsolicited mss. Reports in 2 weeks on queries.
Terms: Agent receives 10% commission on domestic sales; 10% on dramatic sales; and 20% on foreign sales.
Recent Sales: No information given.

‡**CHARLOTTE SHEEDY LITERARY AGENCY, INC.,** 41 King St., New York NY 10014. (212)633-2288. FAX: (212)633-6261. President: Charlotte Sheedy. Member of ILAA. Represents 250 clients. Specializes in fiction and nonfiction.
Will Handle: Handles 70% nonfiction books, 25% novels, 3% juvenile books and 2% poetry. Will read—at no charge—unsolicited queries, outlines and ms. Reports in 1 week on queries; 3 weeks on mss.
Terms: Charges 15% commission on domestic sales; 15% on dramatic sales; 20% on foreign sales.
Fees: Charges writers for messenger service, Federal Express and overnight courier services, foreign mail, foreign faxes and foreign telephone calls.
Recent Sales: *Current Affairs*, by Barbara Raskin (Random House); *Fear of Falling*, by Barbara Ehrenreich (Pantheon); and *sex, lies and videotape*, by Stephen Soderberg (Harper & Row).

‡**THE SHEPARD AGENCY,** 73 Kingswood Dr., Bethel CT 06801. (203)790-4230. FAX: (203)743-1879. Director: Jean H. Shepard. Estab. 1987. Represents 23 clients. The writer must present quality marketable work—complete fiction or sample and outline for nonfiction. Eager to work with new/unpublished writers. We specialize in nonfiction—business; government; self-help; inspirational; children's; biography.
Will Handle: Nonfiction books, novels, juvenile books. Currently handles 75% nonfiction books; 25% novels. Will read—at no charge—unsolicited queries, outlines and manuscripts. Reports in 3 weeks on queries; 6 weeks on manuscripts.
Terms: Agent receives 10% commission on domestic sales.
Fees: Charges writers for long distance phone, fax and postage. Payment of criticism fee does not ensure that agency will represent writer.
Recent Sales: *Crane's Blue Book*, by Steven Feinberg (Doubleday); *The Competitive Advantage*, by Wm. Seidmann and Steven Skancke (Simon & Schuster).

SHORR STILLE AND ASSOCIATES, Suite 6, 800 S. Robertson Blvd., Los Angeles CA 90035. (213)659-6160. Member of WGA. Writer must have an entertainment industry referral. Works with a small number of new/unpublished authors. Specializes in screenplays, teleplays, high concept action-adventure and romantic comedy.
Will Handle: Movie scripts and TV scripts. Currently handles 50% movie scripts and 50% TV scripts. Will read—at no charge—unsolicited queries. Reports in 1 month on queries; 6 weeks on mss.
Terms: Agent receives 10% commission on domestic sales.
Fees: Charges for photocopy expenses.
Recent Sales: No information given.

BOBBE SIEGEL, LITERARY AGENCY, 41 W. 83rd St., New York NY 10024. (212)877-4985. Estab. 1975. Represents 60 clients. 40% of clients are new/unpublished writers. "The writer must have a good project, have the credentials to be able to write on the subject and must deliver it in proper fashion. In fiction it all depends on whether I like what I read and if I feel I can sell it." Prefers to work with published/established authors. "Prefer track records, but am eager to work with talent." Specializes in literary fiction, detective and suspense fiction, historicals, how-to, health, woman's subjects, fitness, beauty, feminist sports, biographies and crafts.

Will Handle: Nonfiction books and novels. Currently handles 65% nonfiction books and 35% novels. Does not read unsolicited mss. Reports in 2 weeks on queries; 2 months on mss.
Terms: Agent receives 15% commission on domestic sales; 10% on dramatic sales; and 10% on foreign sales.
Fees: "If writer wishes critique, will refer to a freelance editor. Charges for photocopying, telephone, overseas mail, express mail expenses. 70% of income derived from commission on ms sales; 30% comes from foreign representation."
Recent Sales: *North of the Sun*, Fred Hatfield (Birch and Virago); *Calabrinia Falling*, by Diane de Avalle Arce (Crossing Press); and *Go out in Joy*, by Nina H. Donnelley (Ballantine).

SIERRA LITERARY AGENCY, P.O. Box 1090, Janesville CA 96114. (916)253-3250. Owner: Mary Barr. Estab. 1988. Eager to work with new/unpublished writers. Specializes in contemporary women's novels, mainstream fiction and nonfiction, self-help, self-esteem books.
Will Handle: Fiction, nonfiction books and novels. Will read – at no charge – unsolicited queries, outlines and manuscripts. Reports in 2 weeks on queries; 6 weeks on mss.
Terms: Agent receives 10% commission on domestic sales; 15% on dramatic sales; and 20% on foreign sales.
Fees: Charge writers for copying, phone and overseas postage.

EVELYN SINGER LITERARY AGENCY, P.O. Box 594, White Plains NY 10602. Agent: Evelyn Singer. Estab. 1951. Represents 50 clients. To be represented, writer must have $20,000 in past sales of freelance works. Prefers to work with published/established authors. Specializes in fiction and nonfiction books, adult and juvenile (picture books only if writer is also the artist). Enclose SASE.
Will Handle: Nonfiction books (bylined by authority or celebrity); novels (no romances, or pseudo-science, violence or sex); and juvenile books. Currently handles 25% nonfiction books; 25% novels; and 50% juvenile books. Does not read unsolicited mss.
Terms: Agent receives 15% commission on domestic sales; 20% on dramatic sales; and 20% on foreign sales.
Fees: Charges for long distance phone and expenses authorized by the author. 100% of income derived from commission on ms sales.
Recent Sales: *Pursuit of Fear*, by William Beechcroft (Carroll & Graf); *Volcanoes*, by Mary Elting (Simon and Schuster); and *How Things Work*, by Mike and Marcia Folsom (Macmillan).

SINGER MEDIA CORPORATION, INC., 3164 Tyler Ave., Anaheim CA 92801. (714)527-5650. Associate Editor: Dorothy Rosati. Estab. 1940. 10% of clients are new/unpublished writers. Prefers to work with published/established authors; works with a small number of new/unpublished authors. Specializes in contemporary romances, nonfiction and biographies.
Will Handle: Magazine articles and syndicated material (submit tearsheets); nonfiction books (query); and romance novels. Currently handles 5% nonfiction books; 20% novels; 75% syndicated material. Will read – at no charge – unsolicited queries and outlines; but may charge a criticism fee or service charge for work performed after the initial reading. Reports in 2 weeks on queries; 6 weeks on mss.
Terms: Agent receives 15% commission on domestic sales and 20% on foreign sales.
Fees: Charges a reading fee to unpublished writers which will be credited on sales; 5% of income derived from reading fees. Criticism included in reading fee. "A general overall critique averages 3-6 pages. It does not cover spelling or grammar, but the construction of the material. A general marketing critique is also included." 95% of income derived from sales of writers' work; 5% of income derived from criticism services. "Payment of a criticism fee does not ensure that agency will represent a writer. The author may not be satisfied with our reply, or may need help in making the manuscript marketable."
Recent Sales: "Dozens of magazines, W.H. Allen; Mondadori, Pocketbooks Inc."

MICHAEL SNELL LITERARY AGENCY, Bridge and Castle Rd., Truro MA 02666. (508)349-3718. President: Michael Snell. Estab. 1980. Represents 150 clients. 25% of our clients are new/unpublished writers. Eager to work with new/unpublished writers. Specializes in business books (from professional/reference to popular trade how-to); college textbooks (in all subjects, but especially business, science and psychology); and how-to and self-help (on all topics, from diet and exercise to sex and personal finance). All types of computer books: professional and reference, college textbooks, general interest. Increased emphasis on popular and professional science books and science textbooks in all disciplines.
Will Handle: Nonfiction books and textbooks. Currently handles 80% nonfiction books; 10% novels; and 10% textbooks. Will read – at no charge – unsolicited queries and outlines. Reports in 3 weeks on queries. "Will not return rejected material unless accompanied by SASE."
Terms: Agent receives 15% commission on domestic sales; 15% on dramatic sales; and 15% on foreign sales.
Fees: "When a project interests us, we provide a two- to three-page critique and sample editing, a brochure on *How to Write a Book Proposal* and a model book proposal at no charge." Charges collaboration, ghostwriting and developmental editing fee "as an increased percentage of manuscript sale – no cash fee."
Recent Sales: *Green Pages*, by S.J. Bennett (Random House); *The Power of Submissions Selling*, by Corson, et al; (Putnam/Berkley); and *The Shadow Government)*, by Don Axelrod (Wiley).

‡**ELYSE SOMMER, INC.,** P.O. Box E, 110-34 73 Rd., Forest Hills NY 11375. (718)263-2668. President: Elyse Sommer. Estab. 1952. Member of ILAA. Represents 20 clients. Works with a small number of new/ unpublished authors. Specializes in nonfiction: reference books, dictionaries, popular culture.
Will Handle: Novels (some mystery but no sci-fi), juvenile books (no pre-school). Currently handles 90% nonfiction books; 5% novels; 5% juvenile. Will read—at no charge—unsolicited queries and outlines. Reports in 2 weeks on queries.
Terms: Agent receives 15% commission on domestic sales (when advance is under 20,000, 10% over); 20% on dramatic sales; and 20% on foreign sales.
Fees: Charges for photocopying, long distance, express mail, extraordinary expenses.
Recent Sales: The Panel Digest (Annuals), Kids' World Almanac Books and several reference books.

SOUTHERN WRITERS, Suite 1020, 635 Gravier St., New Orleans LA 70130. (504)525-6390. FAX: (504)524-7349. Agent: Pamela G. Ahearn. Estab. 1979. Member Romance Writers of America. Represents 30 clients; 33% of clients are new/unpublished writers. Works with small number of new/unpublished writers. Specializes in fiction or nonfiction with a Southern flavor or background; romances—both contemporary and historical.
Will Handle: Nonfiction books (no autobiographies), novels. Currently handles 30% nonfiction books and 70% novels. Accepts submissions for young adults 12 and up. Will read—at no charge—unsolicited queries and outlines. Reports in 2 weeks on queries; 1 month on mss.
Terms: Agent receives 15% commission on domestic sales; 20% on dramatic sales; 20% on foreign sales.
Fees: Charges reading fee "to unpublished authors and to authors writing in areas other than that of previous publication." 40% of income derived from reading fees; charges $175/300-page, typed, double-spaced book ms. "Criticism fee is charged to unpublished authors who request *only* criticism and not representation." 5% of income derived from criticism fees; charges $300/300-page, typed, double-spaced book ms. Writers receive a letter, usually 3-4 pages long, single-spaced. Includes evaluation of manuscript's writing quality, marketability, and more specific discussion of problems within book (plot, characterization, tone, author's credentials for writing such book, etc.). Specific examples are cited wherever possible. Letter is written by Pamela G. Ahearn. Charges for postage. 55% of income derived from commission on manuscript sales. Payment of fees does not ensure representation.
Recent Sales: *My Gallant Enemy*, by Rexanne Becnel (Dell); *New Orleans in the 40's*, by Mary Lou Widmer (Pelican); and *Surrender a Dream*, by Jill Barnett (Pocket).

F. JOSEPH SPIELER LITERARY AGENCY, 410 W. 24th St., New York NY 10011. (212)757-4439. Contact: Joseph Spieler. Estab. 1983. Represents 53 clients. 7.25% of clients are new/unpublished writers. Specializes in "fiction and nonfiction." No genre books.
Will Handle: Nonfiction books, novels, textbooks, juvenile (all ages) and poetry. Will read—at no charge—unsolicited queries and outlines. Does not read unsolicited mss. "No manuscript will be returned unless accompanied by a stamped envelope suitable for its return." Reports in 1 week.
Terms: Agent receives 15% commission on domestic sales; 15% on dramatic sales; and 20% on foreign sales.
Fees: Charges for bulk and international mail, photocopies, toll and international phone calls and Telexes, etc. 99% of income derived from commission on ms sales.
Recent Sales: *Metaman*, by G. Stock (Simon & Schuster); *When the World Was Whole*, by C. Fengvesi (Vicking); and *A History of Europe*, by W. Laqueur (Viking).

PHILIP G. SPITZER LITERARY AGENCY, 788 9th Ave., New York NY 10019. (212)265-6003. Member of SAR. Represents 50 clients. 10% of clients are new/unpublished writers. Prefers to work with published/established authors; works with a small number of new/unpublished authors. Specializes in general nonfiction (politics, current events, sports, biography) and fiction, including mystery/suspense.
Will Handle: Nonfiction books, novels and movie scripts. Currently handles 50% nonfiction books; 50% fiction. Will read—at no charge—unsolicited queries and outlines. Reports in 2 weeks on queries; 5 weeks on mss.
Terms: Agent receives 15% commission on domestic sales; 15% on dramatic sales; and 20% on foreign sales.
Fees: Charges for photocopying expenses. 100% of income derived from commission on ms sales.
Recent Sales: *My Life and Dr. Joyce Brothers*, by Kelly Cherry (Algonquin); *Stinger*, by Doug Hornig (NAL); *Morning for Flamingos*, by James Lee Burke (Little, Brown).

‡**ELLEN LIVELY STEELE AND ASSOCIATES,** P.O. Drawer 447, Organ NM 88052. (505)382-5449. FAX: (505)382-9821. Contact: Ellen Lively Steele. Estab. 1981. Is signatory agency to Writers Guild of America, West. Represents 18 clients. 75% of clients are new/unpublished writers. Accepts writers on referral only. Prefers to work with published/established writers. Specializes in occult, science fiction, women's fiction, metaphysical, adventure and cookbooks.
Will Handle: Novels, movie scripts, TV scripts and syndicated material. Currently handles 65% novels; 20% movie scripts; 10% TV scripts; 4% syndicated material; and 1% miscellaneous. Does not read unsolicited material. Reports in 3 weeks on queries. "If our agency does not respond within 2 months to your request to become a client, you may submit requests elsewhere."

Terms: Agent receives 10% commission on domestic sales; 10% on dramatic sales; and 5% on foreign sales.
Recent Sales: *New Mexico Cookbook*, by Lynn Nusom (Golden West); *Spoon Desserts*, by Lynn Nusom (Crossing Press); and "The Beast," by Aden and Mary Romine (Tom Tyner Film Production).

LYLE STEELE & COMPANY, Suite 7, 511 E. 73rd St., New York NY 10021. (202)288-2981. President: Lyle Steele. Estab. 1985. Represents 60 clients. To be represented writers "ideally should have published at least one work." Works with small number of new/unpublished writers. Specializes in continuing paperback series and nonfiction.
Will Handle: Nonfiction books, series and novels. Nonfiction books on political, social and true crime issures are especially welcome. Currently handles 50% nonfiction books; 50% novels. Will read—at no charge— unsolicited queries, outlines and manuscripts. Reports in 2 weeks on queries; 1 month on mss.
Terms: Agent receives 15% commission on domestic sales; 15% on dramatic sales; and 15% on foreign sales. 100% of income derived from commission on ms sales.
Recent Sales: *Cracking the Over 50 Job Market*, by J. Robert Connor (NAL); *Aunt Celia*, by Jane Gillespie (St. Martin's Press).

MICHAEL STEINBERG, P.O. Box 274, Glencoe IL 60022. (312)835-8881. Literary Agent/Attorney: Michael Steinberg. Estab. 1980. Represents 15 clients. 40% of clients are new/unpublished writers. "Not currently accepting new writers except by referral from editors or current authors." Specializes in business and general nonfiction, science fiction and mystery.
Will Handle: Nonfiction books and novels. Currently handles 70% nonfiction books and 30% novels. Does not read unsolicited mss.
Terms: Agent receives 15% commission on domestic sales and 20% on foreign sales.
Fees: Charges a reading fee when accepting new material; 4% of income derived from reading fees. Charges writers for postage and phone expenses. Offers a consultation service through which writers not represented can get advice on a contract; charges $75/hour, with a minimum of $125. 95% of income derived from commission on ms sales.
Recent Sales: *Seasonal Futures Spreads*, by Jacob Bernstein (Wiley); *Murder Begins at Home*, by Dale Gilbert (St. Martin's); and *Cycles, Timing and Profits in Stocks*, by Jake Bernstein (Ballinge—Harper & Row).

‡STERLING LORD LITERISTIC, INC., One Madison Ave., New York NY 10010. (212)696-2800. FAX: (212)686-6976. Estab. 1952. Member of SAR. Represents 500 clients. Works only with referred writers.
Will Handle: Magazine fiction, nonfiction books and novels. Does not read unsolicited manuscripts.
Terms: Agent receives 10% commission on domestic sales; 10% on dramatic sales; and 20% on foreign sales.
Fees: Charges writers for photocopying; some foreign mailing.
Recent Sales: No information given.

CHARLES M. STERN ASSOCIATES, P.O. Box 790742, San Antonio TX 78279-0742. (512)349-6141. Owners: Charles M. Stern and Mildred R. Stern. Estab. 1978. 50% of clients are new/unpublished writers. Prefers to work with published/established authors; eager to work with new/unpublished writers. Specializes in historical romances, category romances, how-to, mystery and adventure.
Will Handle: Nonfiction books and novels. Currently handles 50% nonfiction books and 50% novels. Does not read unsolicited mss. Only markets completed mss. Reports in approximately 6 weeks on queries. Writer must supply all copies of ms.
Terms: Agent receives 15% commission on domestic sales; and 20% on foreign sales.
Recent Sales: No information given.

GLORIA STERN, Suite 3, 12535 Chandler Blvd., North Hollywood CA 91607. (818)508-6296. Contact: Gloria Stern. Estab. 1984. Represents 18 clients. 65% of clients are new/unpublished writers. Writer must query with project description or be recommended by qualified reader. Prefers to work with published/established authors; works with a number of new/unpublished authors. Specializes in novels and scripts, some theatrical material, dramas or comedy.
Will Handle: Novels, movie scripts and TV scripts (movie of the week). Currently handles 30% novels; and 70% movie and TV scripts. Will read submissions at charge and may charge a criticism fee or service charge for on-going consultation and editing. Reports in 3 weeks on queries; 6 weeks on mss.
Terms: Agent receives 10-15% commission on domestic sales; 10-15% on dramatic sales; and 18% on foreign sales.
Fees: Occasionally waives fee if representing the writer. Charges criticism fee. "Initial report averages four or five pages with point-by-point recommendation. I will work with the writers I represent to point of accep-tance." Charges for postage, photocopy and long distance phone expenses. Percentage of income derived from commission on ms sales varies with sales.
Recent Sales: Confidential.

GLORIA STERN AGENCY, 1230 Park Ave., New York NY 10128. (212)289-7698. Agent: Gloria Stern. Estab. 1976. Member of ILAA. Represents 30 clients. 2% of our clients are new/unpublished writers. Prefers to work with published/established authors; works with a small number on new/unpublished authors.
Will Handle: Nonfiction books (must have expertise on subject); and novels ("serious mainstream," mysteries, accepts very little fiction). Currently handles 90% nonfiction books and 10% novels. Will read—at no charge—unsolicited queries and outlines (no unsolicited ms). Reports in 1 week on queries; 2 months on manuscripts.
Terms: Agent receives 10-15% commission on domestic sales; and 20% shared with foreign coagent.
Fees: Charges for photocopy expenses. Charges a criticism fee "if the writer requests it and I think that it could be publishable with help. Criticism includes appraisal of style, development of characters and action. Sometimes suggests cutting or building scene. "No guarantee that I can represent finished work." Offers a consultation service ("as a courtesy to some authors") through which writers not represented can get advice on a contract; charges $125. .5% of income derived from fee charged to writers; 99.5% of income derived from commission of manuscript sales.
Recent Sales: *How to Learn Math*, by Sheila Tobias (The College Board); *A Taste of Astrology*, by Lucy Ash (Knopf); and *Parent Power*, by Sherry Ferguson and Lawrence Mazin (Clarkson Potter).

‡JO STEWART AGENCY, 201 E. 66th St., New York NY 10021. (212)879-1301. President and Owner: Jo Stewart. Estab. 1978. Represents 75 clients. We will look at unpublished authors. But query first. Specializes in fiction, nonfiction, any good writing in these areas but no science fiction or fantasy.
Will Handle: Nonfiction books, novels and adult/juvenile books. Will read—at no charge—unsolicited queries and outlines.
Terms: 15% commission on unpubished writers; 10% published for U.S. and Canada; 20% for England, foreign countries; have co-agents in all countries.
Recent Sales: Confidential.

‡H.N. SWANSON, INC., 8523 Sunset Blvd., Los Angeles CA 90069. (213)652-5385. FAX: (213)652-3690. Contact: Ben Kamsler. Estab. 1934. Represents 125 clients. "We require the writer to be published—such as articles if extensive, novels and/or screenplays." Prefers to work with published/established authors. Specializes in contemporary adventure-thriller fiction.
Will Handle: Novels, movie scripts, stage plays and TV scripts. Currently handles 55% novels; 25% movie scripts; 5% stage plays; and 10% TV scripts. Does not read unsolicited mss. Reports in 6 weeks.
Terms: Agent receives 10% commission on domestic sales; 10% on dramatic sales; and 20% on foreign sales. 75% of income derived from commission on ms sales.
Recent Sales: *Kill Shot*, by Elmore Leonard (William Morrow); *Fox on the Run*, by Charles Bennett (Warner Books); and *Desperate Justice*, by Richard Speight (Warner Books).

THE TANTLEFF OFFICE, Suite 700, 375 Greenwich St., New York NY 10013. (212)941-3939. President: Jack Tantleff. Estab. 1986. Member WGA. Represents 30 clients. 20% of clients are new/unpublished writers. Specializes in television, theatre and film.
Will Handle: Movie scripts, stage plays, TV scripts. Currently handles 15% movie scripts; 70% stage plays; 15% TV scripts. Will read—at no charge—unsolicited queries and outlines.
Terms: Agent receives 10% commission on domestic sales; 10% on dramatic sales; and 10% on foreign sales.
Fees: "Charges for unusual expenses agreed upon in advance."
Recent Sales: No information given.

PATRICIA TEAL LITERARY AGENCY, 2036 Vista del Rosa, Fullerton CA 92631. (714)738-8333. Owner: Patricia Teal. Estab. 1978. Member of ILAA and RWA. "Writer must have honed his skills by virtue of educational background, writing classes, previous publications. Any of these *may* qualify him to query." Works with a small number of new/unpublished authors. Limited to category fiction such as mysteries, romances (contemporary and historical), westerns, men's adventure, horror, etc. Also handles nonfiction, limited to self-help and how-to. "Will accept queries on mainstream novels from pubished novelists."
Will Handle: Nonfiction books (self-help and how-to), novels (category only) and mainstream (if published previously). Currently handles 10% nonfiction books and 90% category novels. Will read—at no charge—unsolicited queries and outlines. No response if not accompanied by SASE. Reports in 3 weeks on queries.
Terms: Agent receives 15% commission on domestic sales; 20% on dramatic sales; and 20% on foreign sales.
Fees: Charges for phone, postage and photocopy expenses. 5% of total income derived from fees charged to writers; 95% of income derived from commission on ms sales.
Recent Sales: *Jade*, by Jill Marie Landis (The Berkley Publishing Group); *Thrill Kill*, by B.L. Wilson (Pocket Books); and *The Enchanter*, by Christina Hamlett (M. Evans).

‡JEANNE TOOMEY LITERARY AGENCY, 95 Belden St., Falls Village CT 06031. (203)824-0831. President: Jeanne Toomey. Estab. 1976. Represents 10 clients. Works with a small number of new/unpublished authors. Specializes in nonfiction.

Will Handle: Nonfiction books, novels, how-to, movie scripts and TV scripts. Currently handles 90% nonfiction books and 10% novels. Does not read unsolicited manuscripts. Reports in 3 weeks on queries.
Terms: Agent receives 15% commission on domestic sales; 15% on dramatic sales; and 15% on foreign sales.
Fees: Charges $100, "unless recently published author. The fee I charge of $100 is a reading fee. If the book has merit, I then send it out to at least four publishers. If it is poor work, it is returned to the author."
Recent Sales: While working for Marianne Strong, *A Woman Called Jackie*, by David Heymann (Lyle Stuart); *Mafia Kingfish*, by John H. Davis (McGraw-Hill); *The Owl Hoots Again*, by Cornelius Vanderbilt Whitney (Sunstone Press).

PHYLLIS TORNETTA AGENCY, Box 423, Croton-on-Hudson NY 10521. (914)737-3464. President: Phyllis Tornetta. Estab. 1979. Represents 22 clients. 35% of clients are new/unpublished writers. Specializes in romance, contemporary, mystery.
Will Handle: Novels and juvenile. Currently handles 90% novels and 10% juvenile. Will read—at no charge— unsolicited queries and outlines. Does not read unsolicited mss. Reports in 1 month.
Terms: Agent receives 15% commission on domestic sales and 20% on foreign sales.
Fees: Charges a reading fee "for full manuscripts." Charges $75/300 pages.
Recent Sales: *Intimate Strangers*, by S. Hoover (Harlequin); *Accused* (Silhouette) and *Ride Eagle* (Worldwide).

2M COMMUNICATIONS LTD., Suite 601, 121 West 27th St., New York NY 10001. FAX: (212)691-4460. President: Madeleine Morel. Estab. 1982. Represents 65 clients. 25% of clients are new writers. Specializes in nonfiction, humor, parenting, biographies, lifestyle, pop psychology, health, nutrition, how-to, New Age, cookbooks.
Will Handle: Currently handles 100% nonfiction books. Will read—at no charge—unsolicited queries and outlines. Does not read unsolicited mss. Reports in 2 weeks on queries.
Terms: Agent receives 15% commission on domestic sales and 20% on foreign sales.
Fees: Charges for photocopying, mailing, messengers and fax.
Recent Sales: *Suicide's Other Victims*, by Guinan/Smolin (Prentice Hall); *The New Fish Cookbook*, by Mel and Sheryl London (Prentice Hall); and *What to Do When Your Child Needs Help*, by Doft/Aria (Crown).

SUSAN P. URSTADT, INC., P.O. Box 1676, New Canaan CT 06846. (203)966-6111 or (212)808-9810. President: Susan P. Urstadt. Estab. 1975. Member of ILAA. Represents 50-60 clients. 5% of clients are new/ unpublished writers. Specializes in horse books, decorative arts and antiques, art and architecture, gardening, armchair cookbooks, biography and reference, performing arts, current affairs, lifestyle and current living trends, thoughtful fiction and intelligent nonfiction for juveniles.
Will Handle: Nonfiction books and novels. "We look for serious books of quality with fresh ideas and approaches to current situations and trends from serious dedicated writers." Currently handles 75% nonfiction books; 15% novels; and 10% juvenile books. Query with covering letter, short author bio, chapter outline or proposal, sample chapter and SASE.
Terms: Agent receives 15% commission on domestic sales; 15% on dramatic sales; and 20% on foreign sales.
Fees: Charges phone, photocopying, foreign postage and Express Mail expenses.
Recent Sales: *How to Sell Your Medical Practice*, by Dr. Madeleine P. Cosman (Prentice Hall); *Is It or Isn't It*, by Emyl Jenkins (Crown); and *Environmental Vacations*, by Stephanie Ocko (John Muir).

VAN DER LEUN AND ASSOCIATES, 464 Mill Hill Dr., Southport CT 06490. (203)259-4897. President: Patricia Van Der Leun. Estab. 1985. Represents 30 clients; 50% of clients are new/unpublished writers. Works with small number of new/unpublished authors. Specializes in science, art, fiction.
Will Handle: Nonfiction books and novels. Currently handles 50% nonfiction books; 50% novels. Will read— at no charge—unsolicited queries and outlines "if accompanied by SASE." Reports in 2 weeks on queries; 1 month on mss.
Terms: Agent receives 15% commission on domestic sales; 15% on dramatic sales; and 15% on foreign sales.
Fees: Charges for photocopying.
Recent Sales: *Everything I Really Need To Know I Learned in Kindergarten*, by Robert Fulghum (Villard Books); *Green Rage: Radical Environmentalism and the Unmaking of Civilization*, by Christopher Manes (Little, Brown); *Deep Time: The Journey of a Single Sub-Atomic Particle From The Moment of Creation to the Death of the Universe—And Beyond*, by David Darling (Delacorte Press).

CARLSON WADE, Room K-4, 49 Bokee Ct., Brooklyn NY 11223. (718)743-6983. President: Carlson Wade. Estab. 1949. Represents 40 clients. 50% of clients are new/unpublished writers. Eager to work with new/ unpublished writers. Will consider all types of fiction and nonfiction.
Will Handle: Magazine articles, magazine fiction, nonfiction books and novels. Currently handles 10% magazine articles; 10% magazine fiction; 40% nonfiction books; and 40% novels. Will read submissions at no charge, but may charge a criticism fee or service charge. Reports in 2 weeks.

Terms: Agent receives 10% commission on domestic sales; 10% on dramatic sales; and 10% on foreign sales.
Fees: Charges handling fee: $1/1,000 words on short ms; $50/book. 20% of income derived from reading and handling fees. Charges a criticism fee if ms requires extensive work. 10% of income derived from criticism fees. "Short manuscript receives 5 pages of critique, book receives 15 (single space, page-by-page critique)." 20% of income derived from reading and handling fees; 80% of income derived from commission on ms sales. Payment of a criticism fee does not ensure that agency will represent a writer. "If a writer revises a manuscript properly, then we take it on. Futher help is available at no cost."
Recent Sales: *Eat Away Illness* (Prentice Hall) and *Nutritional Therapy* (Prentice Hall).

BESS WALLACE LITERARY AGENCY, P.O. Box 430, Kamas UT 84036. (801)783-4503. Owner: Bess Wallace. Editor: Penni Wallace, BWALA, 6733 W. Carol Ann Way, Peoria, AZ 85345, (602)486-2389. Estab. 1977. Represents 32 clients. 80% of clients are new/unpublished writers. Eager to work with new/unpublished writers. Specializes in nonfiction.
Will Handle: Nonfiction books and novels. Will read—at no charge—unsolicited queries and outlines. Reports in 3 weeks.
Terms: Agent receives 15% commission on domestic sales; 10% on dramatic sales; and 10% on foreign sales.
Fees: Charges for editing and retyping. 80% of income derived from commission on ms sales; 20% from fees. "Ghostwriters available."
Recent Sales: *Child Abuse, Neglect and Molestation, Terrorism,* and *Our Social Service Agencies,* by M.J. Philippus and Bess Wallace (P.P.I. Publishers); *Language in Tears,* by Robert Thompson (CAP Publishers); and *Children of Alcoholics,* by Bess Wallace and M.J. Philippus, PhD. (P.P.I. Publishers).

THE GERRY B. WALLERSTEIN AGENCY, Suite 12, 2315 Powell Ave., Erie PA 16506. (814)833-5511. President/Owner: Gerry B. Wallerstein. Estab. 1984. Member Author's Guild, Society of Professional Journalists. Represents 40 clients. 23% of clients are new/unpublished writers. "I read/critique works by writers who have sold regularly to major periodicals, or have had a prior book published, or sold a script, on the basis of no reading fee. Works by new writers are read/critiqued on the basis of a reading fee, according to length of ms. I will represent writers of either category. All potential clients should request a brochure." Specializes in adult fiction and nonfiction books, articles, short stories, no poetry or song/lyrics, juvenile material, and scripts for clients only.
Will Handle: Magazine articles and magazine fiction (clients only); nonfiction books; novels. Currently handles 22% magazine articles; 6% magazine fiction; 37% nonfiction books; 35% novels. Will read—at no charge—unsolicited queries and short outlines. Reports in 1 week on queries; 2 months on mss.
Terms: Agent receives 15% commission on domestic sales; 15% on dramatic sales; and 20% on foreign sales.
Fees: Charges reading fee "for writers who have not sold their work regularly to major periodicals, or have not had a prior book published or a script sold to a producer." Reading fees waived after writer becomes a client. 50% of income derived from reading fees. Charges $300 for 300-page typed, double-spaced book ms. "Criticism included in reading fee. Our reading/critique averages 1-2 pages for short material and book proposals; 2-4 pages for book-length manuscripts. I indicate any problem areas, suggest possible ways to solve the problems, and provide marketing advice. Revised ms read at no additional fee. All reading is done by Gerry B. Wallerstein." Charges clients for manuscript typing or copying, copyright fees, attorney's fees (if required, and approved by author), travel fees (if required and approved by author) and a monthly fee of $20 for postage/telephone expenses. 50% of income derived from commission on ms sales. Payment of a reading fee does not ensure that the agency will represent a writer.
Recent Sales: *Strategic Focus,* by Stephen C. Tweed (Frederick Fell Publishers); *How To Customize Your Harley,* by Carl Caiati (Motorbooks International); and *Derailing the Tokyo Express,* by Jack C. Coombe (Stackpole Books).

JOHN A. WARE LITERARY AGENCY, 392 Central Park West, New York NY 10025. (212)866-4733. Contact: John Ware. Estab. 1978. Represents 60 clients. 40% of clients are new/unpublished writers. Writers must have appropriate credentials for authorship of proposal (nonfiction) or manuscript (fiction); no publishing track record required. "Open to good writing and interesting ideas, by 'new' or 'veteran' writers." Specializes in biography; memoirs; investigative journalism; history; health and psychology (academic credentials required); serious and accessible non-category fiction; thrillers and mysteries; current issues and affairs; sports; oral history; Americana and folklore.

ALWAYS submit unsolicited manuscripts or queries with a self-addressed, stamped envelope (SASE) within your country or International Reply Coupons (IRC) purchased from the post office for other countries.

Will Handle: Nonfiction books and novels. Currently handles 75% nonfiction books and 25% novels. Will read unsolicited queries and outlines; does not read unsolicited mss. Reports in 2 weeks on queries.
Terms: Agent receives 10% commission on domestic sales; 10% on dramatic sales; and 20% on foreign sales. Charges for messengering, photocopying and extraordinary expenses.
Recent Sales: *Cycles of Rock and Water: At The Pacific Edge*, by Kenneth Brown (Harper and Row); *Fires In The Sky: A Novel of the Trojan War*, by Phillip Parotti (Ticknor & Fields); *South Pass: A Memoir Along The Oregon Trail*, by Laton McCartney (Doubleday).

JAMES WARREN LITERARY AGENCY, 13131 Welby Way, North Hollywood CA 91606. (818)982-5423. Agent: James Warren. Editors: Sheldon Craig, Bob Carlson. Estab. 1969. Represents 60 clients. 60% of clients are new/unpublished writers. "We are willing to work with select unpublished writers." Specializes in fiction, history, textbooks, professional books, craft books, how-to books, self-improvement books, health books and diet books.
Will Handle: Juvenile books, historical romance novels, movie scripts (especially drama and humor), and TV scripts (drama, humor, documentary). Currently handles 40% nonfiction books; 20% novels; 10% textbooks; 5% juvenile books; 10% movie scripts; and 15% TV scripts and teleplays. Will read — at no charge — unsolicited queries and outlines. Does not read unsolicited mss. Reports in 1 week on queries; 1 month on mss.
Terms: Receives 10% commission on first domestic sales; 20% on foreign sales.
Fees: Charges reading fee of $2 per thousand words. 20% of income derived from reading fees; refunds reading fee if material sells. 20% of total income derived from fees charged to writers; 80% of income derived from commission on ms sales. Payment of fees does not ensure that agency will represent writer.
Recent Sales: *The Woman Inge*, by Audrey R. Langer (New Saga) and *Ashes Under Uricon*, by Audrey R. Langer (New Saga).

WATERSIDE PRODUCTIONS, INC., Suite 2, 832 Camino del Mar, Del Mar CA 92014. (619)481-8335. FAX: (619)481-2433. Estab. 1982. Represents 200 clients. 20% of clients are new/unpublished writers. To be represented "fiction authors must be published in major magazines; nonfiction authors must be recognized experts in their field; computer authors must have superb technical skills." Works with small number of new/unpublished writers. Specializes in computer books and books about new technology; fiction and general nonfiction of exceptional quality. Writer's guidelines for #10 SAE and 2 first class stamps.
Will Handle: Nonfiction books; novels; textbooks. Currently handles 90% nonfiction books; 4% novels; 4% textbooks. Will read — at no charge — unsolicited queries and outlines. Does not read unsolicited mss. Reports in 1 month on queries.
Terms: Agent receives 15% commission on domestic sales; 20% on dramatic sales; and 25% on foreign sales.
Fees: Charges reading fee for "first time novelists or personal nonfiction." Negligible. Charges $300/300-page, typed, double-spaced book ms. 99.9% of income derived from commission on ms sales; .1% derived from fees.
Recent Sales: *Made in America*, by Phillipe Khan (Bantam); *Month of Sundays*, by Melody Martin (Knightsbridge); and *Mastering Wordperfect 5.1*, by Alan Simpson (Sybex).

‡WECKSLER-INCOMCO, 170 West End Ave., New York NY 10023. (212)787-2239. FAX: (212)496-7035. President: Sally Wecksler. Estab. 1971. Represents 20 clients. To be represented writer "must have published articles if not books, or some kind of writing or editing experience." Works with small number of new/unpublished writers. Specializes in nonfiction, topical, nature, how-to and illustrated books.
Will Handle: Nonfiction books. Currently handles 90% nonfiction books; 10% novels. Will read — at no charge — unsolicited queries and outlines. Does not read unsolicited mss. Reports in 2 months on mss.
Terms: Agent receives 12-15% commission on domestic sales; 20% on foreign sales. Sometimes offers consultation service through which writers can get advice on a contract; charges $50/hour. Also represents publishers in sub rights and foreign markets.
Recent Sales: *Do's and Taboos of Hosting International Visitors*, by Roger Axtell (Wiley); *Preserving Porches*, by Renee Kahn (Holt); and *Making Good*, by Loren Singer (Holt).

CHERRY WEINER LITERARY AGENCY, 28 Kipling Way, Manalapan NJ 07726. (201)446-2096. President: Cherry Weiner. Estab. 1980. Represents 50 clients. 20% of clients are new/unpublished writers. To be represented, writer should be recommended by people agency knows. Prefers to work with published/established authors. Specializes in fiction — all genres; some nonfiction, depending on topic.
Will Handle Nonfiction books and novels. Does not read unsolicited manuscripts.
Terms: Agent receives 15% commission on domestic sales; 15% on dramatic sales; and 15% on foreign sales.
Fees: Charges writers for special mailings — overseas phone calls, etc.
Recent Sales: No information given.

RHODA WEYR AGENCY, 151 Bergen St., Brooklyn NY 11217. (718)522-0480. President: Rhoda A. Weyr. Estab. 1983. Member of ILAA. Prefers to work with published/established authors; works with a small number of new/unpublished authors. Specializes in general nonfiction and fiction of high quality.

Will Handle: Nonfiction books and novels. Will read—at no charge—unsolicited queries, outlines and sample chapters sent with SASE.

Terms: Agent receives 15% commission on domestic sales and 20% on foreign sales.

Recent Sales: Confidential.

WINGRA WOODS PRESS/Agenting Division, Suite 3, 33 Witherspoon St., Princeton NJ 08542. (609)683-1218. Agent: Anne Matthews. Estab. 1985. Member of American Booksellers Association and American Book Producers Association. Represents 12 clients. 70% of clients are new/unpublished writers. "Books must be completed, and designed for a distinct market niche." Works with small number of new/unpublished authors.

Will Handle: Currently handles 70% nonfiction books and 30% juvenile books.

Terms: Receives 15% commission on domestic sales; 15% on dramatic sales; and 15% on foreign sales.

Recent Sales: *A Rose for Abby*, by Donna Guthrie (Abingdon); and *The Gone With the Wind Handbook*, by Pauline Bartel (Taylor); *Encore*, by Graciela de Armas (Humbert Books).

RUTH WRESCHNER, AUTHORS' REPRESENTATIVE, 10 W. 74th St., New York NY 10023. (212)877-2605. Agent: Ruth Wreschner. Estab. 1981. Represents 50 clients. 70% of clients are new/unpublished writers. "In fiction, if a client is not published yet, I prefer writers who have written for magazines; in nonfiction, a person well-qualified in his field is acceptable." Prefers to work with published/established authors; works with new/unpublished authors. "I will always pay attention to a writer referred by another client." Specializes in popular medicine, health, how-to books and fiction (no pornography, screenplays or dramatic plays).

Will Handle: Adult and young adult fiction; nonfiction; textbooks; magazine articles (only if appropriate for commercial magazines). Currently handles 5% magazine articles; 80% nonfiction books; 10% novels; 5% textbooks; and 5% juvenile books. Will read—at no charge—unsolicited queries and outlines. Reports in 2 weeks on queries.

Terms: Agent receives 15% commission on domestic sales and 20% on foreign sales.

Fees: Charges for photocopying expenses. "Once a book is placed, I will retain some money from the second advance to cover airmail postage of books, long distance calls, etc. on foreign sales." 100% of income derived from commission on ms sales. "I may consider charging for reviewing contracts in future. In that case I will charge $50/hour plus long distance calls, if any."

Recent Sales: *Off to a Good Start, Advice to Newlyweds*, by Mary Ann Bartusis, M.D.; *Cocaine . . . and Beyond*, by John Flynn, Ph.D. (Birch Lane Press); and *Creative Table Settings*, by Israela Banin (Overlook Press).

ANN WRIGHT REPRESENTATIVES, INC., 136 E. 56th St., 2C, New York NY 10022. (212)832-0110. Head of Literary Department: Dan Wright. Estab. 1963. Member of WGA. Represents 42 clients. 25% of clients are new/unpublished writers. "Writers must be skilled or have superior material for screenplays, stories or novels that can eventually become motion pictures or television properties." Prefers to work with published/established authors; works with a small number of new/unpublished authors. "Eager to work with any author with material that we can effectively market in the motion picture business worldwide." Specializes in themes that make good motion picture projects.

Will Handle: Novels, movie scripts, stage plays and TV scripts. Currently handles 10% novels; 75% movie scripts; and 15% TV scripts. Will read—at no charge—unsolicited queries and outlines; does not read unsolicited mss. Reports in 3 weeks on queries; 2 months on mss. All work must be send with an SASE to ensure its return.

Terms: Agent receives 10% commission on domestic sales; 10% on dramatic sales; 10% on foreign sales; 20% on packaging. Will critique only works of signed clients.

Fees: Charges for photocopying expenses.

Recent Sales: No information given.

‡STEPHEN WRIGHT, P.O. Box 1341, F.D.R. Station, New York NY 10150. Author's Representative: Stephen Wright. Estab. 1984. Prefers to work with pubilshed/established authors. Works with a small number of new/unpublished authors. Specializes in fiction, nonfiction and screenplays.

Will Handle: Magazine articles, magazine fiction, nonfiction books, novels, young adult and juvenile books, movie scripts, radio scripts, stage plays, TV scripts, syndicated material and poetry. Currently handles 20% nonfiction, 40% novels, 20% movie scripts, 20% TV scripts. Reports in 3 weeks on queries.

Terms: Agent receives 10-15% commission on domestic sales; 10-15% on dramatic sales; and 15-20% on foreign sales.

Fees: "When the writer is a beginner or has had no prior sales in the medium for which he or she is writing, we charge a reading criticism fee; does not waive fee when representing the writer." Charges $500/300 pages. We simply do not "read" a manuscript, but give the writer an in-depth criticism. If we very much like what we read, we would represent the writer. Or if the writer revises the ms to meet our professional standards and we believe there is a market for said ms, we would also represent the writer. We tell the writer whether we believe his/her work is marketable. I normally provide the critiques.

Recent Sales: No information given.

WRITER'S CONSULTING GROUP, P.O. Box 492, Burbank CA 91503. (818)841-9294. Director: Jim Barmeier. Estab. 1983. Represents 10 clients. 50% of clients new/unpublished writers. "We prefer to work with established writers unless the author has an unusual true story."
Will Handle: Magazine articles (if written about a true story for which the author has the rights); nonfiction books (educational books, how-to, health, true crime accounts, unusual true stories); novels; movie scripts. Currently handles 40% nonfiction books; 20% novels; and 40% movie scripts. Charges 50¢/page reading fee. Include SASE. Reports in 1 month on queries; 3 months on mss.
Terms: "We will explain our terms to clients when they wish to sign. We receive a 10% commission on domestic sales. Additionally, we offer ghostwriting and editorial services, as well as book publicity services for authors." 100% of income derived from commission on ms sales.
Recent Sales: "We have helped writers sell everything from episodes for children's TV shows ("Smurfs") to move-of-the-week options (including the Craig Smith espionage story)."

WRITERS HOUSE, INC., 21 W. 26 St., New York NY 10010. (212)685-2400. President: Albert Zuckerman. Estab. 1974. Member of ILAA. Represents 200 clients. 20% of clients are new/unpublished writers. Specializes in fiction of all types, adult fiction, juvenile novels, sci-fi and fantasy and nonfiction books on business, parenting, lifestyles, science and rock and pop culture, also history and biography.
Will Handle: Nonfiction books, novels and juvenile books. Currently handles 30% nonfiction books; 40% novels; and 30% juvenile books. Will read—at no charge—unsolicited queries and outlines. Reports in 2 weeks on queries.
Terms: Agent receives 15% commission on sale of adult books, 10% on juvenile and young adult domestic sales; 15% on dramatic sales; and 20% on foreign sales.
Fees: Charges for overseas postage, Telex, messenger, overseas phone and photocopy expenses. 95% of income derived from commission on ms sales; 5% from scouting for foreign publishers.
Recent Sales: *A Time of War*, by Michael Peterson (Pocket); *Garden of Lies*, by Eileen Goudge (Viking); and *Babysitters Club*, by Ann Martin (Scholastic).

WRITERS' PRODUCTIONS, P.O. Box 630, Westport CT 06881. (203)227-8199. Agent: David L. Meth. Estab. 1982. Eager to work with new/unpublished writers. Specializes in "fiction of literary quality and unique, intriguing nonfiction. We are especially interested in works of Asian American writers. Also books on education, health and fitness, and works on a family-oriented theme."
Will Handle: Nonfiction books and novels. Currently handles 50% nonfiction books and 50% novels. Will read—at no charge—unsolicited queries, outlines and mss. Reports in 2 weeks on queries; 1 month on mss. "All correspondence must have a SASE for any response and return of manuscript, due to the large volume of submissions we receive. No phone calls please. We will also work with writers on a fee basis to develop professional book proposals. This is independent of our representation."
Terms: Agent receives 15% commission on domestic sales; 25% on dramatic sales; and 25% on foreign sales. 100% of income derived from commission on ms sales.
Recent Sales: No information given.

WRITERS' REPRESENTATIVES, INC., 25 W. 19th St., New York NY 10011-4202. (212)620-9009. Contact: Glen Hartley or Lynn Chu. Estab. 1985. Represents 35 clients.
Will Handle: Nonfiction books and novels. Journalism handled for our established clients by special arrangement only. Currently handles 66% nonfiction; 33% fiction. Nonfiction submissions should include book proposal, detailed table of contents and sample chapters. For fiction submissions, send sample chapters, not synopses. All submissions should include author bio, publication list, and if available, clips. SASE required. All retained rights (serial, audiovisual, world territories, translation, etc.) handled in-house or through sub-agents.
Terms: Agent receives 15% commission on domestic sales; 20% if sub-agent retained for ancillary rights sales. Charges for out-of-pocket expenses, such as photocopying, long-distance phone calls, etc.
Recent Sales: *The American Religion*, by Harold Bloom (Simon and Schuster); *Pericles*, by Donald Kagan (The Free Press); and *Black Hills, White Justice*, by Edward Lazarus (Harper & Row).

SUSAN ZECKENDORF ASSOCIATES, Suite 11B, 171 W. 57th St., New York NY 10019. (212)245-2928. President: Susan Zeckendorf. Estab. 1979. Member of ILAA. Represents 45 clients. 60% of clients are new writers. Specializes in fiction of all kinds—literary, historical, and commercial women's, mainstream thrillers and mysteries; science, music, self-help and parenting books.
Will Handle: Nonfiction books (by a qualified expert) and novels. Currently handles 40% nonfiction books and 60% novels. Will read—at no charge—unsolicited queries. Reports in 2 weeks on queries; 1 month on mss.
Terms: Agent receives 15% commission on domestic sales; 15% on dramatic (movie or TV) sales; and 20% on foreign sales.
Fees: Charges for phone, photocopy and foreign postage expenses.
Recent Sales: *Enticements*, by Una-Mary Parker (NAL); *Life Itself*, by Boyce Rensberger (Bantam); and *Came a Dead Cat*, by James N. Frey (St. Martin's).

TOM ZELASKY LITERARY AGENCY, 3138 Parkridge Crescent, Chamblee GA 30341. (404)458-0391. Agent: Tom Zelasky. Estab. 1984. Represents 20 clients. 90% of clients are new/unpublished writers. Prefers to work with published/established authors. Handles mainstream fiction or nonfiction, categorical romance, historical romance, historical fiction, westerns, action/detective mysteries, suspense, science fiction.

Will Handle: Nonfiction books, novels, juvenile books, movie scripts, stage plays and TV scripts. Will read— at no charge—unsolicited queries and outlines. "SASE is compulsory; otherwise, manuscript will be in storage and destroyed after 2 years." Reports in 3 weeks on queries; 3 months on mss.

Terms: Agent receives 10-15% commission on domestic sales; 10-15% on dramatic sales; and 15-25% on foreign sales.

Fees: Charges a reading fee; will waive fee if representing the writer. "A critique of one to three pages is mailed to writer when manuscript is rejected. I do reading and critique with assistance from other readers. Critique is a one- to three-page item, single space, citing craft skills, marketability and overall evaluation." Charges writers for phone calls to publishers, writers and postage.

Recent Sales: "Six Western manuscripts sold in 1989."

Other Author's Agents

The following author's agents do not have listings in this edition of *Writer's Market*. The majority did not respond to our request to update their listings or return a questionnaire for a new listing. If a reason was given for their exclusion, we have included it in parentheses after the listing name.

A.M.C. Literary Agents (asked to be deleted)
The Artists Group
The Book Peddlers (not accepting new clients)
Bookstop Literary Agency
The Bradley-Goldstein Agency (not accepting new clients)
James Charlton Associates (asked to be deleted)
Terry Chiz Agency
Diane Cleaver Inc.
Hy Cohen Literary Agency, ·Ltd.
Robert Cornfield Literary Agency
Vicki Eisenberg Literary Agency

The Erikson Literary Agency
Goodman Associates, Literary Agents
Scott Hudson Talent Representation
Asher D. Jason Enterprises, Inc.
Kirchoff/Wohlberg
Wendy Lipkind Agency
Literary/Business Associates
Peter Livingston Associates, Inc.
The Martell Agency
David H. Morgan Literary Agency, Inc.
Charles Neighbors, Inc.
New Writers Literary Project, Ltd. (unable to contact)

Julian Portman & Associates
Raines & Raines
The Sagalyn Agency (unable to contact)
Jack Scagnetti Literary Agency
John Schaffner Associates, Inc. (agency scaled down)
Stepping Stone Literary Agency
Gunther Stuhlman, Author's Representative
A Total Acting Experience
Ralph Vicinanza Ltd. (not accepting new clients)
Sandra Watt & Associates
Weiser & Weiser, Inc.
George Ziegler Literary Agency

Contests and Awards

When selecting a manuscript for publication, quality is not the only factor editors must consider. Timing, tone, length and the publication's image are all considerations that enter into the final decision. A piece might even be rejected simply because it does not fit the editorial mix of a particular issue.

Contests and awards, on the other hand, offer writers the opportunity to have their work judged for quality alone, once entry requirements are met. Writers' works are compared to the work of other writers, whose submissions are subject to identical conditions. Aside from the monetary reward many contests offer, there is the satisfaction of having your work recognized for excellence by established writers and other professionals in the field. Writers often receive the added benefit of having their work published or produced.

Some competitions focus on form, such as a short story or poetry contest, while others reward writers who handle a particular subject well. This year, for example, there are contests listed for the best 10-minute play, the best new children's book and the best Shakespearean sonnet. In addition to contests for poetry, short stories and journalism, we've included competitions for plays, novels, books of nonfiction, film and radio scripts, and even golf writing.

Some contests are free, while others charge entry fees. Not all contests are open to everyone—some are for published authors, others for beginning writers or students. Eligibility may be based on the writer's age, geographic location or whether the work has been previously published or is unpublished. Read contest rules carefully to avoid submitting to contests for which you do not qualify.

If rules are unclear or you are unsure how a particular contest defines terms, send the director a self-addressed, stamped envelope along with a brief letter asking for clarification. It's best to ask a specific question—contest directors have little time to answer lengthy letters.

A number of contests require someone to nominate the work for consideration. If nomination by a publisher is required, just ask—most publishers welcome the opportunity to promote a work in this way. Make the publisher aware of the contest in plenty of time before the deadline.

In addition to contests and awards, we also list grants, scholarships and fellowship programs. Information on funding for writers is available in most large public libraries. See the *Annual Register of Grant Support* (National Register Publishing Co., Inc., 3004 Glenview Road, Wilmette IL 60091); *Foundation Grants to Individuals* (Foundation Center, 79 Fifth Ave., New York NY 10003) and *Grants and Awards Available to American Writers* (PEN American Center, 568 Broadway, New York NY 10012). For more listings of contest and awards for fiction writers see *Novel & Short Story Writer's Market* or for poets see *Poet's Market* (both by Writer's Digest Books). A good source of contests for journalists is the annual Journalism Awards Issue of *Editor & Publisher* magazine, published in the last week of December.

The contests in this section are listed by title, address, contact person, type of competition and deadline. Deadlines that state a range—for example, July to September—will only accept entries within that period. If a contest sounds interesting, send a self-addressed, stamped envelope to the contact person for information, rules and details about prizes.

Don't enter any contest without first seeking this information. For information on contests not included here, see Other Contests and Awards at the end of this section.

HERBERT BAXTER ADAMS PRIZE, Committee Chairman, American Historical Association, 400 A St. SE, Washington DC 20003. European history (first book). Deadline: June 15.

JANE ADDAMS PEACE ASSOCIATION CHILDREN'S BOOK AWARD, Jane Addams Peace Association and Women's International League for Peace and Freedom, 980 Lincoln Pl., Boulder CO 80302. Award Director: Jean Gore. Estab. 1953. Previously published book that promotes peace, social justice, and the equality of the sexes and races. Deadline: April 1.

ADRIATIC AWARD, International Society of Dramatists, Box 1310, Miami FL 33153. (305)674-1831. Award Director: A. Delaplaine. Full-length play either unproduced professionally, *or* with one professional production (using Equity actors). Deadline: Nov. 1. Query.

AIM MAGAZINE SHORT STORY CONTEST, P.O. Box 20554, Chicago IL 60620. (312)874-6184. Publisher: Ruth Apilado. Unpublished short stories (4,000 words maximum) "promoting brotherhood among people and cultures." Deadline: Aug. 15.

AJL MASON REFERENCE BOOK AWARD, Association of Jewish Libraries, YIVO Institute for Jewish Research, 1048 5th Ave., New York NY 10028. (212)535-6700. FAX: (212)879-9763. Contact: Zachary Baker. Outstanding reference book published during the previous year in the field of Jewish studies.

‡ALABAMA ARTISTS FELLOWSHIP AWARDS, Alabama State Council on the Arts, 1 Dexter Ave., Montgomery AL 36130. (205)242-4076. Executive Director: Albert B. Head. Annual fellowship program to encourage the professional development of individual Alabama artists. Deadline: May 1.

‡ALLEGHENY REVIEW LITERARY AWARDS, *Allegheny Review*, Box 32 Allegheny College, Meadville PA 16335. (814)332-6553. Contact: Review's Editors. Unpublished short fiction and poetry. Deadline: February 17.

‡*AMBERGRIS* ANNUAL FICTION CONTEST, *Ambergris* Magazine, P.O. Box 29919, Cincinnati OH 45229. Editor: Mark Kissling. Estab. 1988. Previously unpublished fiction. No simultaneous submissions. Winner is chosen from all works submitted during the year. Writer's guidelines for #10 SASE. Award: $100 and nomination to *The Pushcart Prize*.

AMELIA STUDENT AWARD, *Amelia Magazine*, 329 E St., Bakersfield CA 93304. (805)323-4064. Editor: Frederick A. Raborg, Jr. Previously unpublished poems, essays and short stories by high school students. Deadline: May 15.

‡AMERICAN ASSOCIATION OF UNIVERSITY WOMEN AWARD, NORTH CAROLINA DIVISION, North Carolina Literary and Historical Association, 109 E. Jones St., Raleigh NC 27601-2807. (919)733-7305. Previously published juvenile literature by a North Carolina resident. Deadline: July 15.

AMERICAN SOCIETY OF JOURNALISTS & AUTHORS EXCELLENCE AWARDS, Room 1907, 1501 Broadway, New York NY 10036. (212)997-0947. FAX: (212)768-7414. Executive Director: Alexandra Cantor. Estab. 1948. Author, article and magazine awards. Nominations accepted after February 1 for May 31 deadline each year. Write or call for official nomination forms.

AMERICAN SPEECH-LANGUAGE-HEARING ASSOCIATION (ASHA), NATIONAL MEDIA AWARDS, 10801 Rockville Pike, Rockville MD 20852. (301)897-5700. FAX: (301)571-0457. Estab. 1925. Speech-language pathology and audiology (radio, TV, newspaper, magazine). Deadline: June 30.

AMERICAN-SCANDINAVIAN FOUNDATION/TRANSLATION PRIZE, American-Scandinavian Foundation, 725 Park Ave., New York NY 10021. (212)879-9779. Contact: Publishing Division. Contemporary Scandinavian fiction and poetry translations. Deadline: June 1.

AMWA MEDICAL BOOK AWARDS COMPETITION, American Medical Writers Association, 9650 Rockville Pike, Bethesda MD 20814. (301)493-0003. Contact: Book Awards Committee. Previously published and must have appeared in print previous year. Contest is to honor the best medical book published in the previous year in each of three categories: Books for Physicians, Books for Allied Health Professionals and Trade Books. Deadline April 1. Charges $10 fee.

‡**AMWA VIDEO AND FILM FESTIVAL**, American Medical Writers Association, 9650 Rockville Pike, Bethesda MD 20814. (301)493-0003. Contact: Video and Film Festival Chair. Previously published medical films in professional education, patient education, public information and general information. Deadline: April 30. Charges $75 AMWA member, $125 nonmember.

AMY WRITING AWARDS, The Amy Foundation, P.O. Box 16091, Lansing MI 48901. (517)323-3181. President: James Russell. Articles communicating Biblical truth previously published in the secular media. Deadline: Jan. 31.

THE ANNUAL NISSAN FOCUS AWARDS, Nissan Motor Corporation, 10 E. 34th St., 6th Floor, New York NY 10016. (212)779-0404. Director: Sam Katz. Estab. 1977. Narrative filmmaking; documentary; animation/experimental; screenwriting; sound achievement; film editing; cinematography, Women in Film Foundation Award, Renee Valente Producers Award. Charges $18 fee. Open to student filmmakers and screenwriters enrolled in a U.S. college, university, art institute or film school. Deadline varies annually–late spring.

ANNUAL NORTH AMERICAN ESSAY CONTEST, *The Humanist* magazine, 7 Harwood Dr., P.O. Box 146, Amherst NY 14226. (716)839-5080. Contest/Award Director: Lloyd Morain. Estab. 1941. Unpublished essay by writers age 29 or younger. Deadline: Oct. 15.

‡**ANNUAL POETRY/FICTION/NONFICTION AWARDS**, *Sonora Review*, Department of English, University of Arizona, Tucson AZ 85721. (602)626-8383. For previously unpublished poetry, fiction and nonfiction. Deadlines: April 1, poetry; Nov. 1, fiction and nonfiction. Charges $2 entry fee.

ARIZONA AUTHORS' ASSOCIATION ANNUAL NATIONAL LITERARY CONTEST, Arizona Authors' Association, Suite 117WM, 3509 E. Shea Blvd., Phoenix AZ 85028-3339. (602)996-9706. Contact: Velma Cooper. Previously unpublished poetry, short stories, essays. Deadline: July 29. Charges $4 for poetry; $6 for short stories and essays.

‡**ARTIST ASSISTANCE FELLOWSHIP**, Minnesota State Arts Board, 432 Summit Ave., St. Paul MN 55102. (612)297-2603. FAX: (612)297-4304. Artist Assistance Program Associate: Karen Mueller. Annual fellowships of $6,000 to be used for time, materials, living expenses. Literary categories include prose, poetry and theater arts (playwriting and screenwriting). Minnesota residents only. Deadline: Early January.

ARTIST'S FELLOWSHIPS, New York Foundation for the Arts, Suite 600, 5 Beekman St., New York NY 10038. (212)233-3900. Contact: Penny Dannenberg. New York State resident artists' career awards to be used at the artist's discretion to support their work. Deadlines begin in late summer.

ASPIRATIONS ©, 727 Dodge Ave., Evanston IL 60202. Director: Gail Plunkett. Estab. 1989. Short fiction, nonfiction and essays by unpublished writers.

‡**ASSOCIATION FOR EDUCATION IN JOURNALISM AWARDS**, Magazine Division, School of Journalism, University of Missouri, Columbia MO 65205. Contact: Professor Lee Jolliffe. Awards to enrolled college students for unpublished nonfiction magazine article, research paper on magazine journalism, or magazine design.

VINCENT ASTOR MEMORIAL LEADERSHIP ESSAY CONTEST, U.S. Naval Institute, Preble Hall, U.S. Naval Academy, Annapolis MD 21402. (301)268-6110. Award Director: James A. Barber, Jr. Essays on the topic of leadership (junior officers and officer trainees). Deadline: March 1.

THE ATHENAEUM OF PHILADELPHIA LITERARY AWARD, The Athenaeum of Philadelphia, 219 S. 6th St., Philadelphia PA 19106. (215)925-2688. Award Director: Nathaniel Burt. Estab. 1814. Nominated book by a Philadelphia resident. Deadline: Dec. 31.

AVON FLARE YOUNG ADULT NOVEL COMPETITION, Avon Books, 105 Madison Ave., New York NY 10016. FAX: (212)532-2172. Editorial Director: Ellen Krieger. Unpublished novel written by an author 13-18 years old. Manuscript should be 150-200 pages, and appeal to readers 13-18. Deadline: Jan. 1-Aug. 31. Contest held every other year.

‡**AWP ANNUAL AWARD SERIES**, Associated Writing Programs, Old Dominion University, Norfolk VA 23529-0079. (804)683-3839. Contact: Beth Jarock. Annual award series for book length mss in poetry, short fiction, nonfiction and novel. Deadline: Feb. 28. Charges $10 per ms.

THE MARGARET BARTLE PLAYWRITING AWARD, Community Children's Theatre of Kansas City, 8021 E. 129th Terrace, Grandview MO 64030. (816)761-5775. Award Director: E. Blanche Sellens. Unpublished play for elementary school audiences. Deadline: Jan. 28.

THE ELIZABETH BARTLETT AWARD, 2875 Cowley Way-1302, San Diego CA 92110. (619)276-6199. Contest/ Award Director: Elizabeth Bartlett. For best unpublished 12-tone poem.

‡**GEORGE BENNETT FELLOWSHIP**, Phillips Exeter Academy, Exeter NH 03833. Annual award "to provide time and freedom from material considerations to a person seriously contemplating or pursuing a career as a writer. Applicants should have a manuscript in progress which they intend to complete during the fellowship period." Send SASE for application form and details. Deadline: Dec. 1. Charges $5 fee.

BEST OF *HOUSEWIFE-WRITER'S FORUM*: THE CONTESTED WILLS TO WRITE, *Housewife Writer's Forum*, Drawer 1518, Lafayette CA 94549. (415)932-1143. Contest Director: Deborah Haeseler. Estab. 1988. Unpublished prose and poetry categories. Deadline: April 15. Charges $4 for prose; $2 for poetry.

‡**BEST PRIVATE EYE NOVEL CONTEST**, Private Eye Writers of America and St. Martin's Press, 175 5th Ave., New York NY 10010. Previously unpublished book-length "private eye" novel manuscript. Deadline: September.

ALBERT J. BEVERIDGE AWARD, Committee Chairman, American Historical Association, 400 A St. SE, Washington DC 20003. American history of U.S., Canada and Latin America (book). Deadline: June 15.

THE BEVERLY HILLS THEATRE GUILD-JULIE HARRIS PLAYWRIGHT AWARD COMPETITION, 2815 N. Beachwood Drive, Los Angeles CA 90068. (213)465-2703. Playwright Award Coordinator: Marcella Meharg. Estab. 1978. Original full-length plays, unpublished, unproduced and not currently under option. Application required, available upon request with SASE. Deadline: Nov. 1.

BITTERROOT MAGAZINE POETRY CONTEST, *Bitterroot*, P.O. Box 489, Spring Glen NY 12483. Editor-in-Chief: Menke Katz. Estab. 1962. For information and guidelines include SASE. Sponsors William Kushner Annual Awards and Heershe Dovid-Badonneh Awards for unpublished poetry. Deadline: Dec. 31.

IRMA SIMONTON BLACK AWARD, Bank Street College of Education, 610 W. 112th St., New York NY 10025. (212)222-6700. Award Director: Linda Greengrass. Previously published children's book, for excellence of both text and illustration. Deadline: Jan. 15.

‡**BLACK WARRIOR REVIEW LITERARY AWARDS**, *Black Warrior Review*, Box 2936, Tuscaloosa AL 35486. (205)348-4518. Submit work for possible publication to the appropriate genre editor. Awarded annually to the best poetry and fiction published in the *BWR* the previous volume year. Winners are announced in the Fall/Winter issue.

‡**SUSAN SMITH BLACKBURN PRIZE**, 3239 Avalon Place, Houston TX 77019. (713)654-4484. FAX: (713)654-8184. Director: Emilie S. Kilgore. Annual prize for woman playwright. Deadline: third Monday in September. Nomination by artistic directors or theater professionals only.

HOWARD W. BLAKESLEE AWARDS, American Heart Association, 7320 Greenville Ave., Dallas TX 75231. (214)706-1340. Award Director: Howard L. Lewis. Previously published or broadcast reports on cardiovascular diseases. Deadline: Feb. 1.

BOSTON GLOBE-HORN BOOK AWARDS, *The Boston Globe*, Boston MA 02107. Children's Book Editor: Stephanie Loer. Fiction, nonfiction and illustrated book. Deadline: May 1.

BOWLING WRITING COMPETITION, American Bowling Congress Publications, 5301 S. 76th St., Greendale WI 53129. FAX: (414)421-1194. Director: Rory Gillespie, Publications Manager. Estab. 1935. Feature, editorial and news. Deadline: December 1.

‡**BRITTINGHAM PRIZE IN POETRY**, University of Wisconsin Press, 114 N. Murray, Madison WI 53715. (608)262-6438. Contest Director: Ronald Wallace. Unpublished book-length manuscript of original poetry. Deadline: Submissions must be *received* by the press *during* the month of September (postmark is irrelevant) and must be accompanied by a manuscript-sized unpadded SASE, whether or not the poet wants the ms returned. Charges $10 fee.

BRODY ARTS FUND FELLOWSHIP, California Community Foundation, Suite 1660, 3580 Wilshire Blvd., Los Angeles CA 90010. (213)413-4042. "The Brody Arts Fund is designed to serve the needs of emerging artists and arts organizaitons, especially those rooted in the diverse, multi–cultural communities of Los Angeles. The fellowship program rotates annually between 3 main subsections of the arts. Literary artists will be considered in 1990 (for 1991 awards) and 1993. Applicants must reside in Los Angeles County."

ARLEIGH BURKE ESSAY CONTEST, U.S. Naval Institute, Preble Hall, U.S. Naval Academy, Annapolis MD 21402. (301)268-6110. FAX: (301)269-7940. Award Director: James A. Barber, Jr. Estab. 1873. Essay that advances professional, literary or scientific knowledge of the naval and maritime services. Deadline: Dec. 1.

BUSH ARTIST FELLOWSHIPS, The Bush Foundation, E-900 First Natl. Bank Bldg., 332 Minnesota St., St. Paul MN 55101. (612)227-5222. Contact: Sally F. Dixon. Award for Minnesota, North Dakota, South Dakota, and western Wisconsin residents "to buy 6-18 months of time for the applicant to do his/her own work." Up to 15 fellowships annually. Deadline: Last Friday in October.

BYLINE MAGAZINE Contests, P.O. Box 130596, Edmond OK 73013. (405)348-3325. Publisher: Marcia Preston. Unpublished short stories, poems and other categories. Several categories offered each month. Deadline on annual award, which is for subscribers only, Dec. 1. Charges fee of $5 for short story; $2 for poems on annual award.

CALIFORNIA WRITERS' CLUB CONFERENCE CONTEST, 2214 Derby St., Berkeley CA 94705. (415)841-1217. Unpublished adult fiction, adult nonfiction, juvenile fiction or nonfiction, poetry and scripts. "Our conference is biennial, next being in 1991." Deadline: varies in spring. Charges fee.

CANADIAN AUTHOR & BOOKMAN STUDENT CREATIVE WRITING AWARDS, Canadian Authors Association, 121 Ave. Rd., Toronto, Ontario M5R 2G3 Canada. (416)926-8084. Contact: Editor of Canadian Author & Bookman. Estab. 1919. Contest is to encourage creative writing of unpublished fiction, nonfiction and poetry at the secondary school level. Deadline: Mid-February. Must purchase fall or winter issue of CA&B and use tearsheet entry form. Must be secondary school student and nominated by his/her instructor.

CANADIAN BOOKSELLERS ASSOCIATION AUTHOR OF THE YEAR AWARD, 301 Donlands Ave., Toronto, Ontario M4J 3R8 Canada. Contact: Board of Directors of the Association. Canadian author for body of work over many years. No applications may be made by authors.

CANADIAN FICTION MAGAZINE, Contributor's Prize. P.O. Box 946, Station F, Toronto, Ontario M4Y 2N9 Canada. Contact: Editor-in-Chief. Estab. 1971. Best story of year in French or English. Canadian citizens only. Deadline: Sept. 15.

MELVILLE CANE AWARD, Poetry Society of America, 15 Gramercy Park S., New York NY 10003. (212)254-9268. Contact: Award Director. Published book of poems or prose work on a poet or poetry submitted by the publisher. Deadline: Dec. 31.

‡CAREER OPPORTUNITY GRANTS, Minnesota State Arts Board, 432 Summit Ave., St. Paul MN 55102. (612)297-2603. FAX: (612)297-4304. Artist Assistance Program Associate: Karen Mueller. Award offered quarterly. "Career Opportunity grants ranging from $100 to $1,000 may be used to support unique, concrete opportunities that may significantly enhance an artist's work or career." Applications accepted in fiction, creative nonfiction, poetry, playwrighting, screenwriting. Applicants must be Minnesota residents. Deadline varies.

‡BILL CASEY AWARD, *San José Studies*, San José State University, San José CA 95192. (408)924-4476. Editor: Fauneil J. Rinn. Offered annually. Best published article, short story, poem in previous volume of *San José Studies*. Prize: $100 and full–page notice in spring issue of the following year.

‡CEC NATIONAL CHILDREN'S THEATRE PLAYWRITING CONTEST, Columbia Entertainment Company, 309 Parkade Blvd., Columbia MO 65202. (314)874-5628. Contact: Betsy Phillips. Annual award for "top notch unpublished scripts for theater school use, to challenge and expand the talents of our students, ages 10-15. The entry should be a full length play with speaking roles for 20 to 30 characters of all ages and with at least 10 roles developed in some detail." Deadline: June 30.

RUSSELL L. CECIL ARTHRITIS WRITING AWARDS, Arthritis Foundation, 1314 Spring St. NW, Atlanta GA 30309. (404)872-7100. FAX: (404)872-0457. Contact: Public Relations Department. Estab. 1948. Medical and features (news stories, articles and radio/TV scripts) published or broadcast for general circulation during the previous calendar year. Deadline: Feb. 15.

CELEBRATION OF ONE-ACTS, West Coast Ensemble, P.O. Box 38728, Los Angeles CA 90038. Artistic Director: Les Hanson. Unpublished (in Southern California) one-act plays. Deadline: Oct. 15. "Up to 3 submissions allowed for each playwright." Casts should be no more than 6 and plays no longer than 35 minutes.

PAULETTE CHANDLER AWARD, Council for Wisconsin Writers, P.O. Box 55322, Madison WI 53705. (608)233-0531. Estab. 1964. "For a Wisconsin poet or short story writer based on need and ability." Deadline: Jan. 15. Poets in even years (1992); short story writers in odd years (1991). Applications do not open until November.

‡CHICAGO WOMEN IN PUBLISHING AWARDS, Chicago Women in Publishing, Suite 2400, 2 North Riverside Plaza, Chicago IL 60606. (312)641-6311. FAX: (312)263-0923. Annual award to honor "outstanding publications produced by, for, or about women." Includes 11 categories. Deadline: March. Fee: Charges $20 for CWIP members, $25 for non-members.

THE CHRISTOPHER AWARD, The Christophers, 12 E. 48th St., New York NY 10017. (212)759-4050. Award Director: Peggy Flanagan. Outstanding books published during the calendar year that "affirm the highest values of the human spirit."

CINTAS FELLOWSHIP, Institute of International Education, 809 United Nations Pl., New York NY 10017-3580. (212)984-5564. Contact: Rebecca A. Sayles. "Cintas Fellowships are intended to acknowledge demonstrated creative accomplishment and to encourage the professional development of talented, previously published or unpublished creative artists in the fields of architecture, visual arts, music composition and literature." Deadline: March 1. Eligibility is limited to professionals living outside Cuba, who are of Cuban citizenship or direct lineage and who have completed their academic and technical training. The fellowships are not awarded toward the furtherance of academic study, research on writing, nor to performing artists."

GERTRUDE B. CLAYTOR MEMORIAL AWARD, Poetry Society of America, 15 Gramercy Park S., New York NY 10003. (212)254-9628. Contact: Award Director. Poem in any form on the American scene or character. Deadline: Dec. 31. Members only.

CLEVELAND STATE UNIVERSITY POETRY CENTER PRIZE, Cleveland State University Poetry Center, Cleveland OH 44115. (216)687-3986. FAX: (216)687-9366. Editor: Leonard Trawick. To identify, reward and publish the best unpublished book-length poetry manuscript submitted. Submissions accepted only Dec.-Feb. Deadline: Postmarked on or before March 1. Charges $10 fee. "Submission implies willingness to sign contract for publication if manuscript wins." Two of the other finalist manuscripts are also published for standard royalty (no prize). Send SASE for guidelines and entry form.

COLLEGIATE POETRY CONTEST, *The Lyric,* 307 Dunton Dr. SW, Blacksburg VA 24060. Editor: Leslie Mellichamp. Estab. 1921. Unpublished poems (36 lines or less) by fulltime undergraduates in U.S. or Canadian colleges. Deadline: June 1. Send SASE for rules.

‡COMMONWEALTH OF PENNSYLVANIA COUNCIL ON THE ARTS LITERATURE FELLOWSHIPS, 216 Finance Bldg., Harrisburg PA 17120. (717)787-6883. Award Director: Peter Carnahan. Estab. 1966. Fellowships for Pennsylvania writers of fiction and poetry. Deadline: Oct 1.

COUNCIL FOR WISCONSIN WRITERS, INC. ANNUAL AWARDS COMPETITION, P.O. Box 55322, Madison WI 53705. Contact: Awards committee. Estab. 1964. Book-length fiction, short fiction, short nonfiction, poetry, play, juvenile books, children's picture books and outdoor writing by Wisconsin residents published preceding year. Deadline: Jan. 15. Applications do not open until November.

‡CREATIVE ARTS CONTEST, Woman's National Auxiliary Convention, Free Will Baptists, Box 1088, Nashville TN 37202. Contact: Lorene Miley. Unpublished articles, plays, poetry, programs and art from Auxiliary members. Deadline: March 1.

‡CREATIVE FELLOWSHIPS, Colorado Council on the Arts & Humanities, 750 Pennsylvania St., Denver CO 80203. (303)894-2619. Director: Daniel Salazar. Award offered every three years to "acknowledge outstanding accomplishment among Colorado poets and fiction writers." Deadline: November.

CREATIVITY FELLOWSHIP, Northwood Institute Alden B. Dow Creativity Center, Midland MI 48640-2398. (517)832-4478. Award Director: Carol B. Coppage. Ten-week summer residency for individuals in any field who wish to pursue a new and different creative idea that has the potential of impact in that field. Deadline: Dec. 31.

GUSTAV DAVIDSON MEMORIAL AWARD, Poetry Society of America, 15 Gramercy Park S., New York NY 10003. (212)254-9628. Contact: Award Director. Sonnet or sequence in traditional forms. Deadline: Dec. 31. Members only.

MARY CAROLYN DAVIES MEMORIAL AWARD, Poetry Society of America, 15 Gramercy Park S., New York NY 10003. (212)254-9628. Contact: Award Director. Unpublished poem suitable for setting to music. Deadline: December 31. Members only.

‡DE LA TORRE BUENO PRIZE, Dance Perspectives Foundation, 29 E. 9th St., New York NY 10003. (212)777-1594. Open to writers or their publishers who have published an original book of dance scholarship within the year. Deadline: Dec. 31.

DEEP SOUTH WRITERS CONTEST, Deep South Writers Conference, Box 44691, University of Southwestern Louisiana, Lafayette LA 70504. (318)231-6908. Contact: Contest Clerk. Estab. 1960. Unpublished works of short fiction, nonfiction, novels, poetry, drama and French literature. Deadline: July 15. Charges $25 fee for novels; $15 for full-length plays; $5 for other submissions. No manuscripts are returned except novels and full-length plays if accompanied by SASE.

DELACORTE PRESS PRIZE FOR A FIRST YOUNG ADULT NOVEL, Delacorte Press, 666 5th Ave., New York NY 10103. (212)765-6500. Contest Director: Lisa Oldenburg. Estab. 1963. Previously unpublished contemporary young adult fiction. Submissions: Labor Day through December 31 only.

BILLEE MURRAY DENNY POETRY CONTEST, Lincoln College, 300 Keokuk St., Lincoln IL 62656. (217)732-3155 ext. 201. Contest/Award Director: Valecia Crisafulli. Estab. 1981. Unpublished poetry. Deadline: May 31. Charges $2 fee per poem (limit 3).

MARIE-LOUISE D'ESTERNAUX STUDENT POETRY CONTEST, The Brooklyn Poetry Circle, 2550 Independence Ave., #3V, Bronx NY 10463. Contest Chairman: Ruth Fowler. Poetry by students between 16 and 21 years of age. Deadline: April 15.

ALICE FAY DI CASTAGNOLA AWARD, Poetry Society of America, 15 Gramercy Park S., New York NY 10003. (212)254-9628. Contact: Award Director. Manuscript in progress: poetry, prose (on poetry) or verse-drama. Deadline: Dec. 31. Members only.

EMILY DICKINSON AWARD, Poetry Society of America, 15 Gramercy Park S., New York NY 10003. (212)254-9628. Contact: Award Director. Poem inspired by Emily Dickinson. Deadline: Dec. 31. Members only.

GORDON W. DILLON/RICHARD C. PETERSON MEMORIAL ESSAY PRIZE, American Orchid Society, Inc., 6000 S. Olive Ave., West Palm Beach FL 33405. (407)585-8666. FAX: (407)585-0654. Contact: Dr. Alec M. Pridgeon. Estab. 1932. "To honor the memory of two outstanding former editors of the *American Orchid Society Bulletin*. Annual themes of the essay competitions are announced by the Editor of the *A.O.S. Bulletin* in the May issue. Themes in past years have included Orchid Culture, Orchids in Nature and Orchids in Use. The contest is open to all individuals with the exception of A.O.S. employees and their immediate families."

DISCOVERY/THE NATION, The Poetry Center of the 92nd Street YM-YWHA, 1395 Lexington Ave., New York NY 10128. (212)415-5760. Poetry (unpublished in book form). Deadline: Early February. Write or call for competition guidelines.

‡DIVERSE VISIONS REGIONAL GRANTS PROGRAM, Intermedia Arts, 425 Ontario St. SE, Minneapolis MN 55414. (612)627-4444. Director of Artist Programs: Al Kosters. Regional writers' grants. Deadline: spring

THE DOBIE-PAISANO FELLOWSHIP, Office of Graduate Studies, The University of Texas at Austin, Austin TX 78712. (512)471-7213. FAX: (512)471-7620. Contact: Dr. Audrey N. Slate. Estab. 1967. "The competition offers 2 fellowships per year to creative writers—can be fiction, poetry, playwriting or nonfiction. Provides writers with opportunity to work without distraction for six months at the ranch-retreat of the late Texas writer and folklorist, J. Frank Dobie. The ranch is 256 acres and house is furnished." Deadline: Jan. 21 for 1991. Charges $5 fee. Must be native Texan, living in Texas at time of application, or focus of work is on Texas and Southwest.

DRURY COLLEGE ONE-ACT PLAY CONTEST, Drury College, 900 N. Benton Ave., Springfield MO 65802. (417)865-8731. Contact: Sandy Asher. Contest is offered every two years. Plays must be unpublished and professionally unproduced. One play per playwright. Deadline: Dec. 1. Send SASE for complete guidelines.

DUBUQUE FINE ARTS PLAYERS, 569 S. Grandview Ave., Dubuque IA 52001. (319)582-5558. Contact: Sally T. Ryan. Estab. 1977. Produces 3 one acts, plays/year. Only original material accepted. Obtains first productions rights. Winning plays produced in September. Deadline: Jan. 31. Charges: $5 fee.

JOHN H. DUNNING PRIZE IN AMERICAN HISTORY, Committee Chairman, American Historical Association, 400 A St. SE, Washington DC 20003. Annual award for U.S. history monograph/book. Deadline: June 15.

EATON LITERARY ASSOCIATES LITERARY AWARDS PROGRAM, Box 49795, Sarasota FL 34230-6795. (813)366-6589. Vice President: Richard Lawrence. Previously unpublished short stories and book-length manuscripts. Deadline: March 31 (short story); Aug. 31 (book length).

EDITORS' BOOK AWARD, Pushcart Press, Box 380, Wainscott NY 11975. (516)324-9300. President: Bill Henderson. Unpublished books. Deadline: Aug. 30. "All manuscripts must be nominated by an editor in a publishing house."

EMERGING PLAYWRIGHT AWARD, Playwrights Preview Productions, 1160 5th Ave. #304, New York NY 10029. (212)289-2168. Contact: Thais Fitzsimmons. Submissions required to be unpublished. Awards are announced in the Spring. Submissions accepted year-round.

THE RALPH WALDO EMERSON AWARD, The Phi Beta Kappa Society, 1811 Q St. NW, Washington DC 20009. (202)265-3808. Contact: Administrator, Phi Beta Kappa Book Awards. Studies of the intellectual and cultural condition of man published in the U.S. during the 12-month period preceding the entry deadline, and submitted by the publisher. Deadline: April 30.

LAWRENCE S. EPSTEIN PLAYWRITING AWARD, 280 Park Ave. S., New York NY 10010. (212)979-0865. Contact: Lawrence Epstein. Unpublished submissions. Deadline: October. Published in Dramatist's Guild and other newsletters.

DAVID W. AND BEATRICE C. EVANS BIOGRAPHY AWARD, Mountain West Center for Regional Studies, Utah Sate University, University Hill, Logan UT 84322-0735. (801)750-3630. Contact: F. Ross Peterson or Shannon L. Haskins. Estab. 1986. Submissions to be published or unpublished. To encourage the writing of biography about people who have played a role in Mormon Country. (Not the religion, the country i.e., Intermountain West with parts of Southwestern Canada and Northwestern Mexico.) Deadline: March. Publishers may nominate book. Criteria for consideration: Work must be a biography or autobiography on "Mormon Country"; must be submitted for consideration for publication year's award; new editions or reprints are not eligible; manuscripts are accepted. Submit 5 copies.

‡**EYSTER PRIZE**, *New Delta Review*, % Department of English, Louisiana State University, Baton Rouge LA 70803-5001. (504)336-9638. Editor: Kathleen Fitzpatrick. Semiannual award for best works of poetry and fiction in each issue. Deadline: April 15, spring/summer issue; Oct. 15, fall/winter issue.

JOHN K. FAIRBANK PRIZE IN EAST ASIAN HISTORY, American Historical Association, 400 A St. SE, Washington DC 20003. Contact: Committee Chariman. Book on East Asian history. Deadline: June 15.

‡**FALL FESTIVAL OF PLAYS**, Street Players Theatre, 771 Asp, Norman OK 73069. Contact: Robert R. Woods. Unpublished plays.

NORMA FARBER FIRST BOOK AWARD, Poetry Society of America, 15 Gramercy Park S., New York NY 10003. (212)254-9628. Contact: Award Director. Book of original poetry. Deadline: Dec. 31. Charges $5 entry fee for non-members. Publishers only.

VIRGINIA FAULKNER AWARD FOR EXCELLENCE IN WRITING, *Prairie Schooner*, 201 Andrews, University of Nebraska, Lincoln NE 68588-0334. (402)472-3191. Editor: Hilda Raz. Estab. 1927. All genres eligible for consideration. The winning piece must have been published in *Prairie Schooner* during that calendar year.

‡**FELLOWSHIP AWARDS**, Vermont Council on the Arts, 136 State St., Montpelier VT 05602. (802)828-3291. Annual fellowships for Vermont residents. Deadline: March 15.

‡**FELLOWSHIP/NEW JERSEY STATE COUNCIL ON THE ARTS**, New Jersey State Council on the Arts, CN306, 4 N. Broad St., Trenton NJ 08625. (609)292-6130. Executive Director: Jeffrey Kesper. Annual prose, poetry playwriting in literature awards for New Jersey residents. Deadline: February.

‡**FELLOWSHIPS FOR CREATIVE WRITERS**, Pennsylvania Council on the Arts, 216 Finance Bldg., Harrisburg PA 17120. (717)787-6883. Literature Program Director: Peter M. Carnahan. Annual fellowships for Pennsylvania residents.

‡**FELLOWSHIPS TO ASSIST RESEARCH AND ARTISTIC CREATION**, John Simon Guggenheim Memorial Foundation, 90 Park Ave., New York NY 10016. (212)687-4470. Annual. The fellowships assist scholars and artists to engage in research in any field of knowledge and creation in any of the arts, under the freest possible conditions and irrespective of race, color, or creed. In 1989 the Foundation awarded 198 U.S. and Canadian fellowships.

‡**FEMINIST WRITERS' CONTEST**, Des Plaines/Park Ridge NOW Chapter, P.O. Box 2440, Des Plaines IL 60018. Contact: Clara Johnson for rules; SASE required. Estab. 1990. Categories: Fiction and nonfiction (5,000 or fewer words). Work should reflect feminist perspectives (should not endorse or promote sexism, racism, ageism, anti-lesbianism, etc.) Deadline: Aug. 30. Charge $10 fee. Cash awards.

‡**THE FESTIVAL OF EMERGING AMERICAN THEATRE**, The Phoenix Theatre, 749 N. Park Ave., Indianapolis IN 46202. (317)635-7529. Contact: Bryan Fonseca. Annual playwriting competition. Deadline: April 30.

‡**FESTIVAL OF FIRSTS**, City of Carmel/Sunset Center, Box 5066, Carmel CA 93921. (408)624-3996. Contact: Director. Unpublished plays. Deadline: Aug. 30. $5 registration fee.

FICTION WRITERS CONTEST, *Mademoiselle Magazine*, 350 Madison Ave., New York NY 10017. Contest Director: Eileen Schnurr. Short stories by unpublished writers aged 18-30. Deadline: March 15.

‡**ROBERT L. FISH MEMORIAL AWARD**, Mystery Writers of America, Inc., 236 W. 27th St., New York NY 10001. (212)255-7005. Contact: Priscilla Ridgway. Annual award for the best first mystery or suspense short story pubilshed during the previous year. Deadline: Dec. 1.

WILLIAM FLANAGAN MEMORIAL CREATIVE PERSONS CENTER, Edward F. Albee Foundation, 14 Harrison St., New York NY 10013. (212)226-2020. Annual contest/award. Either previously published or unpublished. One month residency at "The Barn" in Montauk, New York offers writers privacy and a peaceful atmosphere in which to work. Deadline: April 1. Prize: Room only; writers pay for food and travel expenses. Judging by panel of qualified professionals.

FOLIO, Department of Literature, American University, Washington DC 20016. Estab. 1984. Fiction, poetry, essays, interviews and b&w artwork. Published twice a year. Manuscripts read Aug.-April.

CONSUELO FORD AWARD, Poetry Society of America, 15 Gramercy Park S., New York NY 10003. (212)254-9628. Contact: Award Director. Unpublished lyric. Deadline: Dec. 31. Members only.

THE 49th PARALLEL POETRY CONTEST, The Signpost Press Inc., 1007 Queen St., Bellingham WA 98226. (206)734-9781. Contest Director: Knute Skinner. Estab. 1977. Unpublished poetry. Submission period: Sept. 15-Dec. 1.

FOSTER CITY ANNUAL WRITERS CONTEST, Foster City Committee for the Arts, 650 Shell Blvd., Foster City CA 94404. Chairman: Ted Lance. Unpublished fiction, poetry, humor and childrens' stories. $1500 in prizes. Deadline: April 1-Aug. 31. Before submitting, send SASE for contest rules.

GEORGE FREEDLEY MEMORIAL AWARD, Billy Rose Theatre Collection, New York Public Library at Lincoln Center, 111 Amsterdam Ave., New York NY 10023. (212)870-1638. Contact: Award Committee Chair. Published books related to performance in theatre. Deadline: Feb. 1.

‡**DON FREEMAN MEMORIAL GRANT-IN-AID**, Society of Children's Book Writers, P.O. Box 296, Mar Vista, Los Angeles CA 90066. To enable picture-book artists to further their understanding, training and/or work. Members only. Deadline: Feb. 15.

ALWAYS submit unsolicited manuscripts or queries with a self-addressed, stamped envelope (SASE) within your country or International Reply Coupons (IRC) purchased from the post office for other countries.

‡FRENCH-AMERICAN FOUNDATION TRANSLATION PRIZE, 41 E. 72nd St., New York NY 10021. (212)288-4400. Contact: Dana Arifi. Estab. 1986. Previously published French-to-English translation. "We contact publishers to submit entries in the competition." Deadline: April 30.

FULBRIGHT SCHOLAR PROGRAM, Council for International Exchange of Scholars, Suite M-500, 3400 International Dr. NW, Washington DC 20008-3097. (202)686-7877. Estab. 1947. "Approximately 1,000 awards are offered annually in virtually all academic disciplines for university lecturing or research in over 100 countries. The opportunity for multicountry research also exists in many areas. Grant duration ranges from 3 months to an academic year." Deadlines are: June 15 – Australasia, India, Latin America, USSR and Aug. 1 – Africa, Asia, Western Europe, East Europe and the Middle East. Eligibility criteria include U.S. citizenship at the time of application; M.F.A., Ph.D or equivalent professional qualifications; for lecturing awards, university teaching experience.

GALLAUDET JOURNALISM AWARD, Gallaudet University, Public Relations Office, 800 Florida Ave. NE, Washington DC 20002. (202)651-5505. FAX: (202)651-5008. Contact: Muriel Strassler. Previously published "accurate, substantive, and insightful articles that provide the general public with a broad awareness and understanding of the achievements of deaf people, research in the field of deafness and the continuing documentation of deaf expression. Work of reporters and writers employed by U.S. wire services, newspapers or magazines of general circulation may be submitted for consideration. Newsletters or publication written specifically for the deaf community are *not* eligible for this award." Deadline: March 31.

JOHN GASSNER MEMORIAL PLAYWRITING AWARD, The New England Theatre Conference, 50 Exchange St., Waltham MA 02154. (617)893-3120. Estab. 1952. Unpublished one-act plays. Deadline: April 15. Charges $5 fee; free for members of New England Theatre Conference.

THE CHRISTIAN GAUSS AWARD, The Phi Beta Kappa Society, 1811 Q St. NW, Washington DC 20009. (202)265-3808. Contact: Administrator, Phi Beta Kappa Book Awards. Works of literary criticism or scholarship published in the U.S. during the 12-month period preceding the entry deadline, and submitted by the publisher. Deadline: April 30.

GOLDEN GATE ACTORS ENSEMBLE PLAYWRIGHT'S CONTEST, American Theatre Ventures, Inc., 580 Constanzo St., Stanford CA 94305. (415)326-0336. Contact: David Arrow, John Goodman. Estab. 1984. Playwrighting contest held to seek out and develop scripts from previously published or unpublished (cannot be produced previously in an Equity contract) American writers. Its goal is to encourage and stimulate the writing of new and original plays." Contest and dates will vary. For application send SASE.

GOLDEN KITE AWARDS, Society of Children's Book Writers (SCBW), Box 296 Mar Vista Station, Los Angeles CA 90066. (818)347-2849. Coordinator: Sue Alexander. Calendar year published children's fiction, nonfiction and picture illustration books by a SCBW member. Deadline: Dec. 15.

GOLF WRITER'S CONTEST, Golf Course Superintendents Association of America, 1617 St. Andrews Dr., Lawrence KS 66046. Public Relations Manager: Scott Smith. Previously published work pertaining to golf superintendents. Deadline: Jan. 15. Must be a member of GWAA.

GOODMAN AWARD, Thorntree Press, 547 Hawthorn Lane, Winnetka IL 60093. (708)446-8099. Contact: Eloise Bradley Fink or John Dickson. Estab. 1985. Imagery is important. For our $400, $200 and $100 Goodman Awards Jan. 1-Feb. 14, we will be selecting three poets for Troika III. Contestants are asked to submit a stapled group of ten pages of original, unpublished poetry, single or double spaced, photocopied, with a $4 reader's fee. Manuscripts will not be returned. SASE for winners' names.

GOVERNOR GENERAL'S LITERARY AWARDS, Canada Council, Box 1047, Ottawa, Ontario K1P 5V8 Canada. (613)237-3400. Contact: Gwen Hoover. Awards are for best book of the year in categories of fiction, nonfiction, poetry, drama, children's literature (text and illustration) and translation. Canadian writers only.

THE GREAT AMERICAN TENNIS WRITING AWARDS, Tennis Week, 124 E. 40th St., New York NY 10016. (212)808-4750. Publisher: Eugene L. Scott. Category 1: unpublished manuscript by an aspiring journalist with no previous national byline. Category 2: unpublished manuscript by a non-tennis journalist. Category 3: unpublished manuscript by a tennis journalist. Categories 4-6: published articles and one award to a book. Deadline: Nov. 18.

GREAT LAKES COLLEGES ASSOCIATION NEW WRITERS AWARD, English Department, Albion College, Albion MI 49224. (517)629-5511, ext. 271. Director: Paul Loukides. Estab. 1970. Entries must have appeared between February and subsequent January of year submitted. Award given each year to the best *first* book of poetry and fiction submitted by publishers. "To encourage writers of previously published poetry and fiction whose publishers consider their work especially meritorious and to bring those writers together with the students and faculty of the twelve sponsoring colleges of the GLCA to their mutual benefit." Deadline: Feb. 28/29. "Publishers must nominate the works to be considered and may do so by sending *four copies* of the nominated work together with a statement assuring the author will accept the prize under the terms stipulated in the official contest announcement."

‡*THE GREENSBORO REVIEW* LITERARY AWARD IN FICTION AND POETRY, *The Greensboro Review*, English Department, UNCG, Greensboro NC 27412. (919)334-5459. Editor: Jim Clark. Annual award for fiction and poetry; recognizes the best work published in the winter issue of *The Greensboro Review*. Deadline: Sept. 15.

‡GUIDEPOSTS MAGAZINE YOUTH WRITING CONTEST, Guideposts Associates, Inc., 747 3rd Ave., New York NY 10017. Senior Editor: James McDermott. Memorable true experience of 1,200 words, preferably spiritual in nature. Unpublished first person story by high school juniors or seniors or students in equivalent grades overseas. Deadline: Nov. 28.

‡HACKNEY LITERARY AWARDS, Writing Today, Box A-3/Birmingham-Southern College, Birmingham AL 35254. (205)226-4921. Contact: Dr. Myra Crawford. Annual award for unpublished novel, short story and poetry. Deadline: Nov. 24 for novels and Dec. 31 for short stories and poetry.

SARAH JOSEPHA HALE AWARD, Trustees of the Richards Library, 58 N. Main, Newport NH 03773. (603)863-3430. Contact: Director. Estab. 1889. The award is to a New England author for the full body of his/her work. Open only to New England authors.

‡THE HEADLANDS PROJECT, Minnesota State Arts Board, 432 Summit Ave., St. Paul MN 55102. (612)297-2603. FAX: (612)297-4304. Artist Assistance Program Associate: Karen Mueller. Annual award for prose, poetry, theater arts (playwriting and screenwriting) for Minnesota residents. Deadline: January.

‡DRUE HEINZ LITERATURE PRIZE, University of Pittsburgh Press, 127 N. Bellefield Ave., Pittsburgh PA 15260. (412)624-4110. FAX: (412)624-7380. Estab. 1936. Collection of short fiction. Award open to writers who have published a book-length collection of fiction or a minimum of three short stories or novellas in commercial magazines or literary journals of national distribution. Deadline: July-August.

ERNEST HEMINGWAY FOUNDATION AWARD, PEN American Center, 568 Broadway, New York NY 10012. Contact: John Morrone. First-published novel or short story collection by an American author. Submit 3 copies. Deadline: Dec. 31.

CECIL HEMLEY MEMORIAL AWARD, Poetry Society of America, 15 Gramercy Park S., New York NY 10003. (212)254-9628. Contact: Award Director. Unpublished lyric poem on a philosophical theme. Deadline: Dec. 31. Members only.

HIGHLIGHTS FOR CHILDREN FICTION CONTEST, *Highlights for Children*, 803 Church St., Honesdale PA 18431. Editor: Kent L. Brown, Jr. Estab. 1946. Category for 1991 is mystery stories for children ages 2-12. Stories should be limited to 900 words for older readers, 600 words for younger readers. No crime or violence, please. Specify that your manuscript is a contest entry. All entries must be postmarked between Jan. 1 and Feb. 28.

SIDNEY HILLMAN PRIZE AWARD, Sidney Hillman Foundation, Inc., 15 Union Square, New York NY 10003. (212)242-0700. Executive Director: Joyce D. Miller. Social/economic themes related to ideals of Sidney Hillman (daily or periodical journalism, nonfiction, radio and TV). Deadline: Jan. 15.

HOOVER ANNUAL JOURNALISM AWARDS, Herbert Hoover Presidential Library Association, Box 696, West Branch IA 52358. Contact: Tom Walsh. Previously published newspaper and magazine journalism that contributes to public awareness and appreciation of the lives of Herbert and Lou Henry Hoover or is based on research at the Herbert Hoover Presidential Library in West Branch, Iowa. Deadline: Jan. 31.

THE ROY W. HOWARD AWARDS, The Scripps Howard Foundation, P.O. Box 5380, Cincinnati OH 45201. (513)977-3035. Estab. 1962. Public service reporting for newspapers.

‡HTC ONE-ACT PLAYWRITING COMPETITION, Henrico Recreation and Parks, P.O. Box 27032, Richmond VA 23273. (804)672-5100. Contact: J. Larkin Brown. Annual unpublished one-act play or musical.

L. RON HUBBARD'S WRITERS OF THE FUTURE CONTEST, P.O. Box 1630, Los Angeles CA 90078. (213)466-3310. Award Director: Rachel Denk. Estab. 1983. Unpublished science fiction and fantasy.

‡HUTTON FICTION CONTESTS, Hutton Publications, P.O. Box 83835, Hayden ID 83835. (208)772-6184. Contact: Linda Hutton. Quarterly awards for beginning and published writers. Deadline: first or fifteenth. Charges from no fee up to $2.

IDAHO WRITER IN RESIDENCE, Idaho Commission on the Arts, 304 W. State, Boise ID 83720. (208)334-2119. Program Coordinator: Julie Numbers Smith. Previously published works by Idaho writers; award offered every two years.

INDEPENDENT SCHOLARS, LOWELL, MARRARO, SHAUGHNESSY AND MILDENBERGER AWARDS, MLA, 10 Astor Place, New York NY 10003. (212)614-6406. Contact: Richard Brod. Mildenberger Prize: research publication on teaching foreign languages and literatures. Shaughnessy Prize: research publication on teaching English. Lowell Prize: previously published literary, linguistic study or critical edition or biography. Marraro Prize: scholarly book or essay on Italian literature. Independent Scholars: published research in modern languages and literature. Lowell and Marraro awards only open to MLA members in good standing.

‡INDIVIDUAL ARTIST FELLOWSHIP AWARD, Montana Arts Council, 48 N. Last Chance Gulch, Helena MT 59620. (406)444-6430. FAX: (406)442-6179. Contact: Julia Smith. Award made every two years to Montana residents. Deadline: May 1.

‡INDIVIDUAL ARTIST PROGRAM, Wisconsin Arts Board, Suite 301, 131 W. Wilson, Madison WI 53703. (608)266-0190. Annual fellowships and grants for Wisconsin residents. Deadline: Sept. 15.

INTERNATIONAL FILM & FILM LITERATURE AWARDS, International Film & Film Literature Society, P.O. Box 12193, La Jolla CA 92039. Previously published or unpublished. To encourage excellence in films and the literature of film production, pre-production and post-production. Deadline: Dec. 20. Entries postmarked after Dec. 20 automatically entered into next competition.

INTERNATIONAL READING ASSOCIATION PRINT MEDIA AWARD, International Reading Association, 800 Barksdale Rd., P.O. Box 8139, Newark DE 19714-8139. (302)731-1600. FAX: (302)731-1057. Contact: Wendy L. Russ. Estab. 1956. Reports by professional journalists from newspapers, magazines and wire services on reading programs. Deadline: Jan. 15.

‡IOWA ARTS COUNCIL LITERARY AWARDS, Iowa Arts Council, Capitol Complex, Des Moines IA 50319. (515)281-4451. Director: Julie Bailey. Estab. 1967. Unpublished fiction and poetry by Iowa writers (legal residents). Deadline: January 15.

JOSEPH HENRY JACKSON/JAMES D. PHELAN LITERARY AWARDS, The San Francisco Foundation, Suite 910, 685 Market St., San Francisco CA 94105. (415)543-0223. Awards Coordinator: Katherine Brody. Jackson Award: unpublished, work-in-progress—fiction (novel or short story), nonfiction or poetry by author age 20-35, with 3-year consecutive residency in N. California or Nevada prior to submission. Phelan: unpublished, work-in-progress fiction, nonfiction, short story, poetry or drama by California-born author age 20-35. Deadline: Jan. 15.

‡JAMESTOWN PRIZE, Institute of Early American History and Culture, P.O. Box 220, Williamsburg VA 23187. (804)221-1112. Contact: Editor of Publications. Estab. 1943. Book-length scholarly ms on early American history or culture.

1991 JAPAN-U.S. FRIENDSHIP COMMISSION PRIZE FOR THE TRANSLATION OF JAPANESE LITERATURE, Donald Keene Center of Japanese Culture, 407 Kent Hall, Columbia University, New York NY 10027. (212)854-5036/5027. FAX: (212)678-6958. Estab. 1986. Book-length works of any period or genre of Japanese literature by a not widely recognized American translator. Deadline: Dec. 1.

‡JEWEL BOX THEATRE PLAYWRIGHTING COMPETITION, Jewel Box Theatre, 3700 N. Walker, Oklahoma City OK 73118. (405)521-1786. Contact: Charles Tweed. Annual award for unpublished plays. Deadline: Jan. 15.

ANSON JONES AWARD, % Texas Medical Association, 1801 N. Lamar Blvd., Austin TX 78701. (512)477-6704. Health (Texas newspaper,magazine—trade, commercial, association, chamber or company—radio and TV). Deadline: Jan. 15.

THE CHESTER H. JONES NATIONAL POETRY COMPETITION, P.O. Box 498, Chardon OH 44024. Estab. 1982. An annual competition for persons in the U.S., Canada and U.S. citizens living abroad. Winning poems plus others, called "commendations," are published in a chapbook available from the foundation. Deadline: March 31. Charges $1/poem, maximum 10 entries, no more than 32 lines each; must be unpublished.

THE JANET HEIDINGER KAFKA PRIZE, English Department, Susan B. Anthony Center, 538 Lattimore Hall, University of Rochester, Rochester NY 14627. (716)275-8318. Attention: Bonnie G. Smith. Book-length fiction (novel, short story or experimental writing) by U.S. woman citizen submitted by publishers.

‡KANSAS QUARTERLY/KANSAS ARTS COMMISSION AWARDS, SEATON AWARDS, Department of English, Kansas State University, Manhattan KS 66506. (913)532-6716. Editor: Harold Schneideretal. Estab. 1968. *KQ/KAC* awards for poetry and fiction published in *KQ*; Seaton awards for Kansas writers whose poetry, fiction and prose appear in *KQ*.

‡LOUISA KERN AWARD, Padelford Hall, A104, GN-30, University of Washington, Seattle WA 98195. (206)543-9865. Contact: Janie Smith. Annual grant; perference for Northwest writers. Deadline: April 1.

GEORGE R. KERNODLE ONE-ACT PLAYWRITING COMPETITION, University of Arkansas, Department of Drama, 406 Kimpel Hall, Fayetteville AR 72701. (501)575-2953. Contact: Kent R. Brown. Submissions to be unpublished and unproduced (workshop productions acceptable). Deadline: June 1. Charges $3 fee per submission. Three submission limit. Open to entry to all playwrights residing in the United States and Canada.

‡JACK KEROUAC LITERARY PRIZE, Lowell Historic Preservation Commission, Suite 310, 222 Merrimack St., Lowell MA 01852. (508)458-7653. Annual award for unpublished nonfiction, fiction and poetry. Deadline: May 1.

‡DONALD KEYHOE JOURNALISM AWARD, Fund for UFO Research, P.O. Box 277, Mt. Rainier MD 20712. (703)684-6032. Contact: Executive Committee, Fund for UFO Research. Estab. 1979. Annual award for the best article or story published or broadcast in a newspaper, magazine, TV or radio news outlet during the previous calendar year. Also makes unscheduled cash awards for published works on UFO phenomena research or public education.

‡AGA KHAN PRIZE FOR FICTION, *The Paris Review*, 541 E. 72nd St., New York NY 10021. Director: George Plimpton. Estab. 1953. Unpublished fiction less than 10,000 words. Must include self-addressed stamped envelope. Deadline: May 1-June 1.

‡MARC A. KLEIN PLAYWRITING AWARD FOR STUDENTS, Department of Theatre, Case Western Reserve University, 2070 Adelbert Rd., Cleveland OH 44106. (216)368-2858. Chair, Reading Committee: John Orlock. Unpublished, professionally unproduced full-length plays, or substantial one-act play by student in American college or university. Deadline: April 1.

‡KUMU KAHUA/UHM THEATRE DEPARTMENT PLAYWRITING CONTEST, Kumu Kahua/UHM Theatre Dept. 1770 East-West Rd., Honolulu HI 96822. (808)948-7677. Contact: Dennis Carroll. Annual award for unpublished plays in two divisions: one for Hawaiian themes, one for residents of Hawaiian Islands only. Deadline: Jan. 1.

RUTH LAKE MEMORIAL AWARD, Poetry Society of America, 15 Gramercy Park S., New York NY 10003. (212)254-9628. Contact: Award Director. Unpublished poem of retrospection. Deadline: Dec. 31. Charges $5 fee.

LAMONT POETRY SELECTION, Academy of American Poets, 177 E. 87th St., New York NY 10128. (212)427-5665. Award Director: Alex Thorburn. Second book of unpublished poems by an American citizen, submitted by publisher in manuscript form.

THE HAROLD MORTON LANDON TRANSLATION PRIZE, The Academy of American Poets, 177 E. 87th St., New York NY 10128. (212)427-5665. Award Director: Alex Thorburn. Previously published translation of poetry (book) from any language into English by an American translator. Deadline: Dec. 31.

THE PETER I.B. LAVAN YOUNGER POETS AWARD, The Academy of American Poets, 177 East 87th St., New York NY 10128. (212)427-5665. American poets under 40 who have published at least one full-length collection of poetry. Recipients are selected by the Academy's Chancellors. No applications.

LAWRENCE FOUNDATION AWARD, *Prairie Schooner*, 201 Andrews, University of Nebraska, Lincoln NE 68588-0334. (402)472-3191. Editor: Hilda Raz. Short story published in *Prairie Schooner*. Winner announced in the spring issue of the following year.

STEPHEN LEACOCK MEMORIAL AWARD FOR HUMOUR, Stephen Leacock Associates, P.O. Box 854, Orillia, Ontario L3V 6K8 Canada. (705)325-6546. Contest Director: Jean Dickson. Estab. 1947. Previously published book of humor by a Canadian author. Include 10 books each entry and a b&w photo with bio. Deadline: Dec. 31. Charges $25 fee.

LEAGUE OF CANADIAN POETS AWARDS, National Poetry Contest, F.R. Scott Translation Award, Gerald Lampert Memorial Award, and Pat Lowther Memorial Award. 24 Ryerson Ave., Toronto, Ontario M5T 2P3 Canada. (416)363-5047. Submissions to be previously published (awards) in the preceding year or previously unpublished (poetry contest). To promote new Canadian poetry/poets and also to recognize exceptional work in each category. Awards Deadline: Jan. 30. Contest Deadline: Jan. 31. Enquiries from publishers welcome. Charges $5 per poem fee for contest *only*. Open to Canadians living at home and abroad. The candidate must be a Canadian citizen or landed immigrant, although publisher need not be Canadian.

ELIAS LIEBERMAN STUDENT POETRY AWARD, Poetry Society of America, 15 Gramercy Park S., New York NY 10003. (212)254-9628. Contact: Award Director. Unpublished poem by student (grades 9-12). Deadline: Dec. 31. Charges $5 fee.

THE RUTH LILLY POETRY PRIZE, The Modern Poetry Association and The American Council for the Arts, 60 W. Walton St., Chicago IL 60610. (312)413-2210. Contact: Joseph Parisi. Annual prize to poet "whose accomplishments in the field of poetry warrant extraordinary recognition." No applicants or nominations are accepted. Deadline varies.

LINCOLN MEMORIAL ONE-ACT PLAYWRITING CONTEST, International Society of Dramatists, Box 1310, Miami FL 33153. (305)674-1831. Award Director: A. Delaplaine. Unpublished one-act plays, any type, any style. Awards and reading, and possible future production. Deadline: Jan. 15.

LINDEN LANE MAGAZINE ENGLISH-LANGUAGE POETRY CONTEST, Linden Lane Magazine & Press, Inc., P.O. Box 2384, Princeton NJ 08543-2384. (609)921-2833. Editor: Belkis Cuza Male. Unpublished Spanish and English poetry, short story and essay prizes. Deadline: May 15. Charges $12 fee.

JOSEPH W. LIPPINCOTT AWARD, Donated by Joseph W. Lippincott, Jr., Administered by American Library Association, 50 E. Huron, Chicago IL 60611. (312)944-6780. For distinguished service to the profession of librarianship, including notable published professional writing.

LOCKERT LIBRARY OF POETRY IN TRANSLATION, Princeton University Press, 41 William St., Princeton NJ 08540. (609)452-4900. Literature Editor: Robert E. Brown. Book-length poetry translation of a single poet.

LOFT CREATIVE NONFICTION RESIDENCY PROGRAM, The Loft, 2301 E. Franklin Ave., Minneapolis MN 55406. (612)341-0431. Program Director: Lois Vossen. Estab. 1974. Opportunity to work in month-long seminar with resident writer and cash award to six creative nonfiction writers. "Must live close enough to Minneapolis to participate fully." Deadline: April.

LOFT-MCKNIGHT WRITERS AWARD, The Loft, 2301 E. Franklin Ave., Minneapolis MN 55406. (612)341-0431. Program Director: Lois Vossen. Eight awards of $7,500 and two awards of distinction at $10,000 each for Minnesota writers of poetry and creative prose. Deadline: November.

LOFT-MENTOR SERIES, The Loft, 2301 E. Franklin Ave., Minneapolis MN 55406. (612)341-0431. Program Director: Lois Vossen. Estab. 1974. Opportunity to work with four nationally known writers and cash award available to six winning poets and fiction writers. "Must live close enough to Minneapolis to participate fully in the series." Deadline: May.

LOUISIANA LITERARY AWARD, Louisiana Library Association, P.O. Box 3058, Baton Rouge LA 70821. (504)342-4928. Contact: Literary Award Committee. Estab. 1909. Submissions to be previously published. "Must be related to Louisiana. Write for details."

LOUISIANA LITERATURE PRIZE FOR POETRY, Box 792, Southeastern Louisiana University, Hammond LA 70402. Contest Director: Dr. Tim Gautreaux. Unpublished poetry. Deadline: Feb. 15. Write for rules.

MCLEMORE PRIZE, Mississippi Historical Society, P.O. Box 571, Jackson MS 39205. (601)359-1424. FAX: (601)359-6905. Contact: Secretary/Treasurer. Estab. 1902. Scholarly book on a topic in Mississippi history/biography published in the year of competition. Deadline: Jan. 1.

THE LENORE MARSHALL/NATION PRIZE FOR POETRY, The New Hope Foundation and *The Nation* Magazine, 72 5th Ave., New York NY 10011. (212)242-8400. Administrator: Peter Meyer. Book of poems published in the United States during the previous year and nominated by the publisher. Deadline: June 1. Books must be submitted *directly* to judges. Query *The Nation* for addresses of judges.

WALTER RUMSEY MARVIN GRANT, Ohioana Library Association, Room 1105 State Departments Bldg., 65 S. Front St., Columbus OH 43215. (614)466-3831. Director: Linda Hengst. Award given every 2 years, (even years). Applicant must have been born in Ohio or have lived in Ohio for 5 years or more, must be 30 years of age or younger, and not have published a book. Deadline Jan. 31.

JOHN MASEFIELD MEMORIAL AWARD, Poetry Society of America, 15 Gramercy Park S., New York NY 10003. (212)254-9628. Contact: Award Director. Unpublished narrative poem in English. No translations. Deadline: Dec. 31. Charges $5 fee.

‡MASSACHUSETTS ARTISTS FELLOWSHIP PROGRAM, Artists Foundation, 8 Park Plaza, Boston MA 02116. (617)227-2787. Director: Kathleen Brandt. Award offered every two years for fiction, nonfiction, playwriting and poetry for Massachusetts residents. Deadline: first Friday in December. Applications available after October.

THE MAYFLOWER SOCIETY CUP COMPETITION, North Carolina Literary and Historical Association, 109 E. Jones St., Raleigh NC 27601-2807. (919)733-7305. Contact: Award Director. Previously published nonfiction by a North Carolina resident. Deadline: July 15.

LUCILLE MEDWICK MEMORIAL AWARD, Poetry Society of America, 15 Gramercy Park S., New York NY 10003. (212)254-9628. Contact: Award Director. Original poem on a humanitarian theme. Deadline: Dec. 31. Members only.

THE EDWARD J. MEEMAN AWARDS, The Scripps Howard Foundation, P.O. Box 5380, Cincinnati OH 45201. (513)977-3035. Estab. 1962. Environmental reporting for newspapers.

MELCHER BOOK AWARD, Unitarian Universalist Association, 25 Beacon St., Boston MA 02108. Staff Liaison: Judith Meyer. Previously published book on religious liberalism. Deadline: Dec. 31.

MENCKEN AWARDS, Free Press Association, P.O. Box 15548, Columbus OH 43215. FPA Executive Director: Michael Grossberg. Estab. 1987. Defense of human rights and individual liberties; news story or investigative report, feature story, editorial or op-ed column, editorial cartoon; and book published or broadcast during previous year. Entry *must* have been published. *Must* send SASE for entry form, rules. Deadline: April 1. Fee: $3 per entry. Late fee deadline: May 1 (for work published previous year).

‡MIDLAND AUTHORS AWARD, Society of Midland Authors, 220 N. Harvey, Oak Park IL 60302. (708)383-7568. Annual awards for previously published drama, fiction, nonfiction, poetry, biography, children's fiction and children's nonfiction. Authors must reside in the states of Indiana, Iowa, Kansas, Michigan, Minnesota, Missouri, Nebraska, North Dakota, South Dakota, Wisconsin and Ohio. Deadline: Feb. 15.

MIDSOUTH, Circuit Playhouse/Playhouse on the Square, 51 S. Cooper, Memphis TN 38104. (901)725-0776. Contact: Jackie Nichols. Deadline: April 1.

‡MILITARY LIFESTYLE FICTION CONTEST, Military Lifestyle Magazine, 1732 Wisconsin Ave. NW, Washington DC 20007. (202)944-4000. Editor-in-Chief: Hope Daniels. Annual award for previously unpublished writers. Deadline: March 31.

MILL MOUNTAIN THEATRE NEW PLAY COMPETITION, Mill Mountain Theatre, Center in the Square, 1 Market Sq., Roanoke VA 24011. (703)342-5730. Literary Manager: Jo Weinstein. Previously unpublished and unproduced plays for up to 10 cast members. Deadline: Jan. 1.

‡MINNESOTA INK FICTION CONTEST, Minnesota Ink, Inc., P.O. Box 9148, N. St. Paul MN 55109. (612)433-3626. Contact: Valerie Hockert. Previously unpublished fiction. Deadline: Dec. 31. Charges $5 fee.

‡MINNESOTA INK SEMI-ANNUAL POETRY CONTEST, Minnesota Ink, Inc., P.O. Box 9148, N. St. Paul MN 55109. (612)433-3626. Contact: Anthoney Stomski. Offered winter and summer. Unpublished. Deadline: Feb. 28; Aug. 15. Charges $2 for first poem; $1 each poem thereafter.

‡MINNESOTA VOICES PROJECT COMPETITION, New Rivers Press, #910, 420 N. 5th St., Minneapolis MN 55401. (612)339-7114. Editor/Publisher: C.W. Truesdale. Annual award for new and emerging writers of poetry, prose, essays, and memoirs (as well as other forms of creative prose) from Wisconsin, Minnesota, Iowa and the Dakotas, to be published in book form for the first time. Deadline: April 1.

MISSISSIPPI VALLEY POETRY CONTEST, P.O. Box 3188, Rock Island IL 61204. (309)788-8041. Director: Sue Katz. Estab. 1971. Unpublished poetry: adult general, student division, Mississippi Valley, senior citizen, religious, rhyming, humorous, haiku, history, ethnic and traditional jazz. Deadline: Sept. 15. Charges $3 to enter contest. Up to 5 poems may be submitted without line limitation.

MIXED BLOOD VERSUS AMERICA, Mixed Blood Theatre Company, 1501 S. 4th St., Minneapolis MN 55454. (612)338-0984. Contact: David B. Kunz. Estab. 1975. "Mixed Blood Versus America" encourages and seeks out the emerging playwright. Mixed Blood is not necessarily looking for scripts that have multi-racial casts, rather good scripts that will be cast with the best actors available." Open to all playwrights who have had at least one of their works produced or workshopped (either professionally or educationally). Only unpublished unproduced plays are eligible for contest. Limit two submissions per playwright. No translations or adaptations.

FELIX MORLEY MEMORIAL PRIZES, Institute for Humane Studies, George Mason University, 4400 University Dr., Fairfax VA 22030. (703)323-1055. Contact: Marty Zupan or Kurt T. Weber. Awards for "young writers dedicated to individual liberty." Deadline: June 15.

‡MORSE POETRY PRIZE, Northeastern University English Deptment, 406 Holmes Hall, Boston MA 02115. (617)437-2512. Contact: Guy Rotella. Previously published poetry, book-length mss. Charges $10/entry.

‡MOST OUTSTANDING SELF-PUBLISHED BOOK COMPETITION, About Books Inc., 425 Cedar St., P.O. Box 1500, Buena Vista CO 81211. (719)395-2459. FAX: (719)395-8374. Contact: Marilyn Ross. Annual award for previously self-published book "to encourage quality and acknowledge excellence in the field of self-publishing." Send SAE with 2 first class stamps for details. Deadline: Dec. 31. Charges $25 fee.

FRANK LUTHER MOTT-KAPPA TAU ALPHA RESEARCH AWARD IN JOURNALISM, 107 Sondra Ave., Columbia MO 65202. (314)443-3521. Executive Director, Central Office: William H. Taft. For "best researched book in journalism." Deadline: Jan. 15.

MULTICULTURAL PLAYWRIGHTS' FESTIVAL, The Seattle Group Theatre Company, 3940 Brooklyn Ave. NE, Seattle WA 98105. (206)545-4969. One-act and full-length plays by Black, Native American, Hispanic and Asian playwrights. Honorarium, airfare and housing for 2 playwrights plus workshop productions. 4-6 playwrights receive readings. Deadline: Oct. 15.

NATIONAL ARCHIVES ONE-ACT PLAYWRITING COMPETITION, National Archives and Records Administration, Education Branch, NEE-E, Washington DC 20408. Contact: Cynthia A. Hightower. To educate playwrites about the vast resources within the records of the National Archives. Script must be unpublished and based on events, episodes pertaining to the United States' involvement during World War II from 1941 to 1946 such as the homefront, sabotage, O.S.S., Pearl Harbor, propaganda, rationing, WACs, etc. Scripts must be based on records held by the National Archives in Washington, DC and/or its regional archives, and/or any of the presidential libraries. Deadline: Jan. 15. Open to all except the employees of the National Archives and Records Administration, its field branches and the presidential libraries.

NATIONAL BOOK AWARDS, Studio 1002D, 155 Bank St., New York NY 10014. (212)206-0024. Executive Director: Barbara Prete. Fiction and general nonfiction books by American authors. "Publishers must enter the books." Deadline: varies. Charges $100 fee.

NATIONAL ENDOWMENT FOR THE ARTS: ARTS ADMINISTRATION FELLOWS PROGRAM/FELLOWSHIP, National Endowment for the Arts, 1100 Pennsylvania Ave., NW, Washington DC 20506. (202)682-5786. Contact: Anya Nykyforiak. Offered three times each year: Spring, Summer and Fall. "The Arts Administration Fellowships are for arts managers and administrators in the non-profit literary publishing field or writers' centers. Fellows come to the NEA for a 13-week residency to acquire an overview of this Federal agency's operations. Deadline: Jan./April/July. Guidelines may be requested by letter or telephone.

NATIONAL JEWISH BOOK AWARD—AUTOBIOGRAPHY/MEMOIR, Sandra Brand and Arik Weintraub Award, 15 E. 26th St., New York NY 10010. (212)532-4949. Director: Paula G. Gottlieb. Given to an author of an autobiography or a memoir of the life of a Jewish person.

NATIONAL JEWISH BOOK AWARD—CHILDREN'S LITERATURE, Shapolksy Family Award, Jewish Book Council, 15 E. 26th St., New York NY 10010. (212)532-4949. Director: Paula G. Gottlieb. Children's book on Jewish theme. Deadline: Nov. 20.

NATIONAL JEWISH BOOK AWARD—CHILDREN'S PICTURE BOOK, Marcia and Louis Posner Award, Jewish Book Council, 15 E. 26th St., New York NY 10010. (212)532-4949. Director: Paula G. Gottlieb. Author and illustrator of a children's book on a Jewish theme. Deadline: Nov. 20.

NATIONAL JEWISH BOOK AWARD—CONTEMPORARY JEWISH LIFE, Muriel and Phil Berman Award, 15 E. 26th St., New York NY 10010. (212)532-4949. Contact: Paula G. Gottlieb. Nonfiction work dealing with the sociology of modern Jewish life.

NATIONAL JEWISH BOOK AWARD—FICTION, William and Janice Epstein Award, 15 E. 26th St., New York NY 10010. (212)532-4949. Director: Paula G. Gottlieb. Jewish fiction (novel or short story collection). Deadline: Nov. 20.

NATIONAL JEWISH BOOK AWARD—HOLOCAUST, Leon Jolson Award, Jewish Book Council, 15 E. 26th St., New York NY 10010. (212)532-4949. Contact: Paula G. Gottlieb. Nonfiction book concerning the Holocaust. Deadline: Nov. 20.

NATIONAL JEWISH BOOK AWARD—ISRAEL, Morris J. and Betty Kaplun Memorial Award, Jewish Book Council, 15 E. 26th St., New York NY 10010. (212)532-4949. Director: Paula G. Gottlieb. Nonfiction work about the State of Israel. Deadline: Nov. 20.

NATIONAL JEWISH BOOK AWARD—JEWISH HISTORY, Gerrard and Ella Berman Award, Jewish Book Council, 15 E. 26th St., New York NY 10010. (212)532-4949. Director: Paula G. Gottlieb. Book of Jewish history. Deadline: Nov. 20.

NATIONAL JEWISH BOOK AWARD—JEWISH THOUGHT, Jewish Book Council, 15 E. 26th St., New York NY 10010. (212)532-4949. Director: Paula G. Gottlieb. Book dealing with some aspect of Jewish thought, past or present. Deadline: Nov. 20.

NATIONAL JEWISH BOOK AWARD—SCHOLARSHIP, Sarah H. and Julius Kushner Memorial Award, Jewish Book Council, 15 E. 26th St., New York NY 10010. (212)532-4949. Director: Paula G. Gottlieb. Book which makes an original contribution to Jewish learning. Deadline: Nov. 20.

NATIONAL JEWISH BOOK AWARD—VISUAL ARTS, Leon L. Gildesgame Award, Jewish Book Council, 15 E. 26th St., New York NY 10010. (212)532-4949. Director: Paula G. Gottlieb. Book about Jewish art. Deadline: Nov. 20.

‡NATIONAL JOURNALISM AWARDS PROGRAM, Big Brothers/Big Sisters of America, 230 N. 13th St., Philadelphia PA 19107-1510. (215)567-7000. FAX: (215)567-0394. Contact: George L. Beiswinger. Annual award for previously published stories and features about the problems of children from single-parent homes and how they are handled. Deadline: Mar. 15.

NATIONAL ONE-ACT PLAYWRITING COMPETITION, Little Theatre of Alexandria, 600 Wolfe St., Alexandria VA 22314. (703)683-5778. Estab. 1978. To encourage original writing for theatre. Criteria: submissions must be original, unpublished, unproduced one-act stage plays. Deadline: March 31. Send SASE for guidelines.

NATIONAL PLAYWRIGHTS COMPETITION ON THEMES OF "THE AMERICAN DREAM", Arrow Rock Lyceum Theatre, Main St., Arrow Rock MO 65320. Contact: Michael Bollinger. Offered every two years to unpublished full length plays dealing with the reality and myth of "the American dream." Submit between Aug. and Dec.

‡NATIONAL PSYCHOLOGY AWARDS FOR EXCELLENCE IN THE MEDIA, American Psychological Association/Office of Public Affairs, 1200 17th St. NW, Washington DC 20036. (202)955-7710. Newspaper reporting, magazine articles and television (drama/entertainment) television (news/documentary) and radio increasing the public understanding of psychology. Deadline: Apr. 24.

NATIONAL TEN-MINUTE PLAY CONTEST, Actors Theatre of Louisville, 316 W. Main St., Louisville KY 40202. (502)584-1265. Literary Manager: Michael Bigelow Dixon. Previously unproduced (professionally) ten-minute plays (10 pages or less). "Entries must *not* have had an Equity or Equity-waiver production." Deadline: Dec. 1.

THE NEBRASKA REVIEW AWARDS IN FICTION AND POETRY, *The Nebraska Review*, ASH 215, University of Nebraska-Omaha, Omaha NE 68182-0324. (402)554-2771. Contact: Arthur Homer (poetry) and Richard Duggin (fiction). Estab. 1973. Previously unpublished fiction and a poem or group of poems. Deadline: Nov. 30.

NEUSTADT INTERNATIONAL PRIZE FOR LITERATURE, 110 Monnet Hall, Norman OK 73019. (405)325-4531. Director: Dr. Ivar Ivask. Estab. 1927. Previously published fiction, poetry and drama. Nominations are made only by members of the jury, which changes every two years.

‡**ALLAN NEVINS PRIZE**, Society of American Historians, 610 Fayerweather Hall, Columbia University, New York NY 10027. Sec./Treas.: Prof. Kenneth T. Jackson. American history (nominated doctoral dissertations on arts, literature, science and American biographies). Deadline: Dec. 31.

‡**NEW AMERICAN VOICES POETRY/SHORT STORY CONTEST**, Poet Venture Publications, 3591 Quail Lakes Dr., Box 10, Stockton CA 95207. (209)957-2721. Contact: John E. TeSelle. 10 times per year. Submissions must be unpublished. Deadline varies. Charges $3 per poem and $5 per short story.

NEW LETTERS LITERARY AWARDS, University of Missouri-Kansas City, Kansas City MO 64110. Awards Coordinator: Glenda McCrary. Estab. 1986. Unpublished fiction, poetry and essays. Deadline: May 15. Charges $10 fee.

‡**NEW PLAY COMPETITION**, Contemporary Arts Center, P.O. Box 30498, New Orleans LA 70190. (504)523-1216. Contact: Julie Hebert. Writers must be resident of Alabama, Arkansas, Georgia, Louisiana or Mississippi. Only unproduced, unpublished scripts are eligible. Full-length only. Limit two scripts per writer. Deadline: Nov. 1.

NEW PLAY COMPETITION, Theatre Memphis, 630 Perkins Extended, Memphis TN 38117-4799. (901)682-8323. Contact: Martha Graber, Iris Dichtel. Competition offered every three years for unpublished scripts. Deadline: Oct. 1. No musicals. Deadline varies.

NEW PLAYWRIGHTS COMPETITION AND FESTIVAL, The Ann White Theatre, 5266 Gate Lake Road, Ft. Lauderdale FL 33319. (305)722-4371. Director: Ann White. Unpublished full-length play scripts. Award: $500 and production by the Ann White Theatre. Competition opens Aug. 1. Deadline Nov. 15.

‡**NEW YORK STATE HISTORICAL ASSOCIATION MANUSCRIPT AWARD**, P.O. Box 800, Cooperstown NY 13326. (607)547-2508. Director of Publications: Dr. Wendell Tripp. Unpublished book-length monograph on New York State history. Deadline: Feb. 20.

JOHN NEWBERY MEDAL, Association for Library Service to Children/American Library Association, 50 E. Huron St., Chicago IL 60611. (312)944-6780. Award Director: Susan Roman. For children's literature published in the previous year.

NHS BOOK PRIZE, National Historical Society, 2245 Kohn Rd., Box 8200, Harrisburg PA 17105. (717)657-9555. Editor in Chief: William C. Davis. NHS Book Prize for first book published by author. Bell I. Wiley Prize for a distinguished work in the field of Civil War and Reconstruction. Deadline: July 31.

DON AND GEE NICHOLL FELLOWSHIPS IN SCREENWRITING, Academy of Motion Picture Arts & Sciences, 8949 Wilshire Blvd., Beverly Hills CA 90211. (213)278-8990. Director: Greg Beal. Estab. 1927. Unproduced screenplays. Deadline: June 1. Charges $25 fee.

CHARLES H. AND N. MILDRED NILON EXCELLENCE IN MINORITY FICTION AWARD, University of Colorado at Boulder and the Fiction Collective Two, University of Colorado Campus, Box 494, Boulder CO 80309. Contact: Donald Laing. Estab. 1989. Unpublished book-length fiction. Only mss. from minority authors will be considered.

NIMROD, ARTS AND HUMANITIES COUNCIL OF TULSA PRIZES, 2210 South Main, Tulsa OK 74114. (918)584-3333. Editor: Francine Ringold. Unpublished fiction (Katherine Anne Porter prize) and poetry (Pablo Neruda Prize). Deadline: April 1. Fee $10, for which you receive an issue of *Nimrod*. (Writers entering both fiction and poetry contest need only pay once.) Send #10 SASE for complete guidelines.

‡**NMMA DIRECTORS AWARD**, National Marine Manufacturers Association, 353 Lexington Ave., New York NY 10016. (212)684-6622. FAX: (212)683-7074. Contribution to boating and allied water sports through newspaper, magazine, radio, television, film or book as a writer, artist, broadcaster, editor or photographer. Deadline: Nov. 30.

‡**NORTHERN NEW ENGLAND PLAYWRIGHTS AWARD**, Valley Players, Box 441, Waitsfield VT 05673. (802)583-3203. Contact: Howard Chapman. Contest offered annually for unpublished scripts. Non-musical, full length play suitable for production by a community theater group. Any northern New England (Vermont,

New Hampshire, Maine) resident may submit a play (or plays) as long as it has not been produced or published before. Deadline August 1.

‡**NUTS TO US!**, New Hope Press, 304 S. Denton St., Dothan AL 36301. (205)792-2331. Contact: Sue Cronkite. Estab. 1989. Short stories, tales and poems which touch upon peanuts in some way. Deadline: July 31. Charges $12 fee. Prize: $100 first prize in each of the 3 categories-short stories, tales, poems—and publication for winners and runners-up.

O. HENRY FESTIVAL SHORT STORY CONTEST, O. Henry Festival, Inc., P.O. Box 29484, Greensboro NC 27429. Estab. 1985. Contest offered every other year to encourage unpublished writing of literary quality short fiction. No children's stories. Deadline date is variable depending on the festival date. Charges $7 per story.

ELI M. OBOLER MEMORIAL AWARD, American Library Association's Intellectual Freedom Round Table, 50 E. Huron St., Chicago IL 60611. (312)944-6780. Contact: Chairman. "Award offered every two years to previously unpublished author of an article (including a review), a series of thematically connected articles, a book, or a manual published on the local, state or national level, in English or in English translation. The works to be considered must have as their central concern one or more issues, events, questions or controversies in the area of intellectual freedom, including matters of ethical, political, or social concern related to intellectual freedom. The work for which the award is granted must have been published within the *two-year* period ending the December prior to the ALA Annual Conference at which it is granted." Deadline: Dec. 15.

THE FLANNERY O'CONNOR AWARD FOR SHORT FICTION, The University of Georgia Press, Terrell Hall, Athens GA 30602. (404)542-2830. FAX: (404)542-0601. Series Editor: Charles East. Estab. 1938. Submission period: June-July 31. Charges $10 fee. Manuscripts will not be returned.

‡**O'CONNOR PRIZE FOR FICTION**, *Descant*, Texas Christian University, P.O. Box 32872, Fort Worth TX 76129. (817)921-7240. An annual award for the best short story in the *Descant* volume.

SCOTT O'DELL AWARD FOR HISTORICAL FICTION, 1100 E. 57th St., Chicago IL 60637. (312)702-8293. Director: Zena Sutherland. Previously published historical fiction book for children set in the Americas. Entries must have appeared in print during previous year. Deadline: Dec. 31.

OFF-OFF-BROADWAY ORIGINAL SHORT PLAY FESTIVAL, Double Image Theatre, 445 W. 59th St., New York NY 10019. (212)245-2489. Contact: William Talbot. Previously unpublished submissions. "The festival was developed in 1976 to bolster those theatre companies and schools that offer workshops, programs and instruction in playwriting. It proposes to encourage them by offering them and their playwrights the opportunity of having their plays seen by new audiences and critics, and of having them reviewed for publication." Deadline: March/April. "No individual writer may enter on his own initiative. Entries must come from theatre companies, professional schools or colleges that foster playwriting by conducting classes, workshops or similar programs of assistance to playwrights. Nominating companies present their own productions at the Festival."

OGLEBAY INSTITUTE/TOWNGATE THEATRE PLAYWRITING, Oglebay Institute, Oglebay Park, Wheeling WV 26003. (304)242-4200. FAX: (304)242-4203. Contact: Debbie Hynes. Estab. 1976. Deadline: Jan. 1. All full-length *non*-musical plays that have never been professionally produced or published are eligible.

OHIO ARTS COUNCIL INDIVIDUAL ARTISTS FELLOWSHIP, Ohio Arts Council, 727 E. Main St., Columbus OH 43205. (614)466-2613. Contact: Susan Dickson. Estab. 1965. Contest/award offered annually. Intended to recognize and support Ohio's creative artists. Deadline: Jan. 15. Writer should call or write and request guidelines and an application form. SASE is not required. Prize: $5,000 or $10,000. Panel of experts, (writers, critics, editors) judge. Writers must be a residents of the State of Ohio for at least one year prior to the application deadline and the applicant cannot be enrolled in a degree or certificate-granting program of any kind.

OHIOANA BOOK AWARDS, Ohioana Library Association, Room 1105, Ohio Departments Bldg., 65 S. Front St., Columbus OH 43215. (614)466-3831. Director: Linda Hengst. Books published within the past 12 months by Ohioans or about Ohio and Ohioans. Submit two copies of book on publication.

OMMATION PRESS BOOK CONTEST, 5548 N. Sawyer, Chicago IL 60625. (312)539-5745. Contact: Effie Mihopoulos. Estab. 1975. Previously unpublished chapbook manuscripts. Deadline: Dec. 30.

‡**ONES AT EIGHT**, City of Virginia Beach, 800 Monmouth Ln., Virginia Beach VA 23464. (804)495-1892. Contact: Ann Hicks. Annual award for unpublished plays. Deadline: Nov. 15.

THE C.F. ORVIS WRITING CONTEST, The Orvis Company, Inc., Historic Route 7A, Manchester VT 05254. (802)362-3622. Contest/Award Director: Doug Truax. Outdoor writing about upland bird hunting and fly fishing (magazine and newspaper). Deadline: Mar. 15.

‡**THE OTHER SIDE MAGAZINE SHORT FICTION AWARD,** The Other Side Magazine, 300 W. Apsley St., Philadelphia PA 19144. (215)849-2178. Fiction Contest Director: Jeff Schreifels. Annual award for unpublished fiction. Deadline: May 31.

PANHANDLER POETRY CHAPBOOK COMPETITION, *The Panhandler Magazine,* English Dept. University of West Florida, Pensacola FL 32514. (904)474-2923. Editor: Michael Yots. Individual poems may have been published. To honor excellence in the writing of short collections of poetry. Two winning manuscripts are published each year. Submit between Oct. 15 and Jan. 15. Charges $7 (includes copy of winning chapbooks).

‡**THE PAPER BAG SHORT FICTION CONTEST,** The Paper Bag, P.O. Box 268805, Chicago IL 60626-8805. (312)285-7972. Contact: M. Brownstein. Annual award for unpublished short fiction (500 words or less).

‡**WILLIAM PEDEN PRIZE IN FICTION,** *Missouri Review,* 107 Tate Hall, Columbia MO 65211. (314)882-4474. Contact: Greg Michalson. Awarded annually to best piece of fiction published in a given volume year. All work published in *MR* automatically eligible.

PEN CENTER USA WEST AWARDS, PEN Center USA West, 1100 Glendon Ave., Los Angeles CA 90024. (213)824-2041. FAX: (213)824-1679. Estab. 1952. Award offered for previously published work in a calendar year. Deadline: Dec. 31. Open to writers living west of the Mississippi River whose books have been published in the calendar year.

PEN MEDAL FOR TRANSLATION, PEN American Center, 568 Broadway, New York NY 10012. (212)334-1660. Translators nominated by the PEN Translation Committee. Given every 3 years.

PEN PUBLISHER CITATION, PEN American Center, 568 Broadway, New York NY 10012. (212)334-1660. "Awarded every two years to a publisher who has throughout his career, given distinctive and continuous service." Nominated by the PEN Executive Board.

PEN/ROGER KLEIN AWARD FOR EDITING, PEN American Center, 568 Broadway, New York NY 10012. (212)334-1660. "Given every two years to an editor of trade books who has an outstanding record of recognizing talents." Nominated by authors, agents, publishers and editors. Deadline: Oct. 1.

PEN SYNDICATED FICTION PROJECT, P.O. Box 15650, Washington DC 20003. (202)543-6322. Director: Caroline Marshall. Estab. 1982. Syndicates unpublished short fiction (2,500 words maximum) to newspapers and produces radio show. Receives submissions January 1-31 annually.

PEN WRITING AWARDS FOR PRISONERS, PEN American Center, 568 Broadway, New York NY 10012. (212)334-1660. "Awarded to the authors of the best poetry, plays, short fiction and nonfiction received from prison writers in the U.S." Deadline variable.

PEN/BOOK-OF-THE-MONTH CLUB TRANSLATION PRIZE, PEN American Center, 568 Broadway, New York NY 10012. Contact: John Morrone. One award to a literary book-length translation into English. (No technical, scientific or reference.) Deadline: Dec. 31.

PEN/JERARD FUND, PEN American Center, 568 Broadway, New York NY 10012. (212)334-1660. Contact: John Morrone. Estab. 1986. Grant for American woman writer of nonfiction for a booklength work in progress. Deadline: Jan. 15.

‡**PEN/MARTHA ALBRAND AWARD FOR NONFICTION,** PEN American Center, 568 Broadway, New York NY 10012. (212)334-1660. Coordinator: John Morrone. Eligible books must have been published in the calendar year under consideration. Authors must be American citizens or permanent residents. Although there are no restrictions on the subject matter of titles submitted, non-literary books will not be considered. Books should be of adult nonfiction for the general or academic reader. For a first-published book of general nonfiction distinguished by qualities of literary and stylistic excellence. Deadline: Dec. 31. Publishers, agents and authors themselves must submit *three* copies of each eligible title. $1,000 prize.

‡**PEN/REVSON FOUNDATION FELLOWSHIPS,** PEN American Center, 568 Broadway, New York NY 10012. (212)334-1660. Contact: John Morrone. "A candidate for the fellowship will be a writer in 'early-mid career' whose body of work to date (normally no more than two books) has been marked by singular talent but has not been sufficiently recognized by the literary community and the reading public. The Fellowship is intended

to assist the writer at a point in the candidate's career where monetary support and critical encouragement may be particularly needed. Deadline for poetry submissions is Jan. 15, 1991. Deadline for fiction submissions is Jan. 15, 1992. Candidates must be nominated by an editor or a fellow writer. It is strongly recommended that the nominator write a letter of support, describing the literary quality of the candidate's work and explaining in some detail why the candidate's published work has not yet met with the recognition it merits. Three copies of no more than fifty pages of current work, intended as part of a new book, must be submitted."

‡PEN/SPIELVOGEL-DIAMONSTEIN AWARD, PEN American Center, 568 Broadway, New York NY 10012. (212)334-1660. Coordinator: John Morrone. "For the best previously unpublished collection of essays on any subject by an American writer, published in 1990. The $5,000 prize is awarded to preserve the dignity and esteem that the essay form imparts to literature. Authors must be American citizens or permanent residents. The essays included in books submitted may have been previously published in magazines, journals or anthologies, but must not have collectively appeared before in book form. Books will be judged on the basis of the literary character and distinction of the writing. *Three* copies of each eligible title may be submitted by publishers, agents, or the authors themselves. Deadline: Dec. 31.

PERKINS PLAYWRITING CONTEST, International Society of Dramatists, Box 1310, Miami FL 33153. (305)756-8313. Award Director: A. Delaplaine. Unproduced full-length plays, any genre, any style. Awards plus staged reading and possible future production. Travel and expenses. Deadline: Dec. 6.

PHI BETA KAPPA BOOK AWARDS, The Phi Beta Kappa Society, 1811 Q St. NW, Washington DC 20009. (202)265-3808. Contact: Mary Mladinov. Estab. 1776. "Annual award to recognize and honor outstanding scholarly books published in the United States in the fields of the humanities, the social sciences, and the natural sciences and mathematics." Deadline: April 30. "Authors may request information, however it is requested that books be submitted by the publisher." Entries must be the works of authors who are U.S. citizens or residents.

‡PLAYBOY COLLEGE FICTION CONTEST, *Playboy* magazine, 680 North Michigan Ave., Chicago IL 60611. (312)751-8000. Contact: Alice K. Turner. Annual award for unpublished short stories by registered students at a college or university. Deadline: Jan. 1.

PLAYWRIGHTS' CENTER JEROME PLAYWRIGHT-IN-RESIDENCE FELLOWSHIP, The Playwrights' Center, 2301 Franklin Ave. E, Minneapolis MN 55406. (612)332-7481. Estab. 1976. To provide emerging playwrights with funds and services to aid them in the development of their craft. Deadline: March 1. Open to playwrights only—may not have had more than 2 fully staged productions of their works by professional theaters. Must spend fellowship year in Minnesota at Playwrights' Center. U.S. citizens only.

PLAYWRIGHTS' CENTER MCKNIGHT FELLOWSHIP, The Playwrights' Center, 2301 Franklin Ave. E, Minneapolis MN 55406. (612)332-7481. Estab. 1982. Recognition of playwrights whose work has made a significant impact on the contemporary theater. Deadline: Dec. 3. Open to playwrights only. Must have had a minimum of two fully staged productions by professional theaters. Must spend 1 or 2 months at Playwrights' Center. U.S. citizens only.

THE PLAYWRIGHTS' CENTER MIDWEST PLAYLABS, The Playwrights' Center, 2301 Franklin Ave. E, Minneapolis MN 55406. (612)332-7481. Assists in the development of unproduced or unpublished new plays. Deadline: Jan. 14. Playwrights only; no one acts, musicals or childrens plays; and must be available for entire pre-conference and conference.

PLAYWRIGHTS PROJECT, P.O. Box 2068, San Diego CA 92112. (619)232-6188. Contact: Deborah Salzer. Estab. 1985. For Californians under 19 years of age. Every writer receives an individualized script critique: selected scripts receive professional productions. Deadline varies from May to June. Request for poster is sufficient. For California residents under 19 years of age.

‡PLAYWRITING COMPETITION FOR YOUNG AUDIENCES, Indiana University-Purdue University at Indianapolis, Children's Theatre Playwriting Competition, 525 North Blackford St., Indianapolis IN 46202-3120. (317)274-2095. Contact: Literary Manager. Previously unpublished plays for young audiences through high school.

EDGAR ALLAN POE AWARD, Mystery Writers of America, Inc. 236 W. 27th St. #600, New York NY 10001. (212)255-7005. Previously published entries must be copyrighted in the year they are submitted. Deadline: Dec. 1. Entries for the book categories are usually submitted by the publisher but may be submitted by the author or his agent.

POETRY ARTS PROJECT CONTEST, United Resource Press, Suite 388, 4521 Campus Drive, Irvine CA 92715. Director: Charlene B. Brown. Poetry with social commentary. Prizes awarded in US Savings Bonds. Deadline: April 15. Send SASE for entry form. Must sign release. Charges $3 per poem jury fee.

POETRY MAGAZINE POETRY AWARDS, 60 W. Walton St., Chicago IL 60610. (312)280-4870. Editor: Joseph Parisi. All poems published in *Poetry* are automatically considered for prizes.

POETS AND PATRONS, INC. INTERNATIONAL NARRATIVE CONTEST, 1206 Hutchings, Glenview IL 60025. Director: Constance Vogel. Deadline: Sept. 1. Rules available after Mar. 1.

POETS CLUB OF CHICAGO INTERNATIONAL SHAKESPEAREAN SONNET CONTEST, 2930 Franklin St., Highland IN 46332. Chairman: June Shipley. Deadline: Sept. 1. Rules available after Mar. 1.

RENATO POGGIOLI TRANSLATION AWARD, PEN American Center, 568 Broadway, New York NY 10012. (212)334-1660. "Given to encourage a beginning and promising translator who is working on a first book length translation from Italian into English." Deadline: Feb. 1.

***PRAIRIE SCHOONER* BERNICE SLOTE AWARD**, *Prairie Schooner*, 201 Andrews, University of Nebraska, Lincoln NE 68588-0334. (402)472-3191. FAX: (402)472-2410. Editor: Hilda Raz. Estab. 1927. Work by a beginning writer previously published in *Prairie Schooner*. Annual award given for best work by a beginning writer from that year's volume.

***PRAIRIE SCHOONER* STROUSSE AWARD**, *Prairie Schooner*, 201 Andrews, University of Nebraska, Lincoln NE 68588-0334. (402)472-3191. FAX: (402)472-2410. Editor: Hilda Raz. Estab. 1927. Poem or group of poems previously published in *Prairie Schooner*. Annual award given for the best poem or group of poems in that year's volume.

‡PRIX ALVINE-BELISLE, ASTED, 1030 Cherrier, Bureau 505, Montreal, Quebec H2L 1H9 Canada. Agent: Renée Masse Chalifoux. French-Canadian literature for children submitted by the publisher.

PULITZER PRIZES, The Pulitzer Prize Board, 702 Journalism, Columbia University, New York NY 10027. (212)854-3841. Secretary: Robert C. Christopher. Awards for journalism in U.S. newspapers (published daily or weekly), and in literature, drama and music by Americans. Deadline: Feb. 1 (journalism); March 14 (music); March 1 (drama); July 1 and Nov. 1 (letters).

PULP PRESS INTERNATIONAL 3-DAY NOVEL WRITING CONTEST, Pulp Press Book Publishers Ltd., 100-1062 Homer St., Vancouver, British Columbia V6B 2W9 Canada. (604)687-4233. Contact: Brian Lam. Estab. 1972. Best novel written in three days; specifically, over the Labor Day weekend. Entrants return finished novels to Pulp Press for judging. Deadline: Friday before Labor Day weekend. Charges $7 fee.

PURE-BRED DOGS MAGAZINE AWARD. See listing in Consumer Animal section.

ERNIE PYLE AWARD, Scripps Howard Foundation, P.O. Box 5380, Cincinnati OH 45201. (513)977-3035. Estab. 1962. Human-interest reporting for newspaper man and/or woman.

‡QUARTERLY WEST NOVELLA COMPETITION, *Quarterly West*, 317 Olpin Union, University of Utah, Salt Lake City UT 84112 (801)581-3938. Award given every two years for unpublished novellas. Deadline: Dec. 31.

SIR WALTER RALEIGH AWARD, North Carolina Literary and Historical Association, 109 E. Jones St., Raleigh NC 27601-2807. (919)733-7305. Previously published fiction by a North Carolina resident. Deadline: July 15.

***RHYME TIME* CREATIVE WRITING COMPETITION**, *Rhyme Time/Story Time*, Box 1870, Hayden ID 83835. (208)772-6184. Award Director: Linda Hutton. Rhymed poetry, fiction and essays. Deadline: first and fifteenth of each month. Send #10 SASE for entry form.

THE HAROLD U. RIBALOW PRIZE, *Hadassah Magazine*, 50 W. 58th St., New York NY 10019. Executive Editor: Alan M. Tigay. English-language book of fiction on a Jewish theme. Deadline: Feb/March.

MARY ROBERTS RINEHART FUND, English Department, George Mason University, 4400 University Dr., Fairfax VA 22030-4444. (703)323-2396. Contact: Roger Lathbury. Grants by nomination to unpublished creative writers for fiction, poetry, drama, biography, autobiography or history with a strong narrative quality.

Submissions are accepted for fiction and poetry in odd years, and nonfiction and drama in even years. Deadline: Nov. 30.

ROANOKE-CHOWAN AWARD FOR POETRY, North Carolina Literary and Historical Association, 109 E. Jones St., Raleigh NC 27601-2807. (919)733-7305. Previously published poetry by a resident of North Carolina. Deadline: July 15.

FOREST A. ROBERTS PLAYWRITING AWARD, Shiras Institute, Forest A. Roberts Theatre, Northern Michigan University, Marquette MI 49855-5364. (906)227-2553. Award Director: Dr. James A. Panowski. Estab. 1978. Unpublished, unproduced plays. Scripts must be *received* on or before Nov. 16.

ROBERTS WRITING AWARDS, H.G. Roberts Foundation, Inc., P.O. Box 1868, Pittsburg KS 66762. (316)231-2998. Contact: Stephen Meats. Estab. 1988. Competitions in unpublished poetry, short fiction, and informal essays. No limitations on subject matter or form. Deadline: Sept. 1. Charges $5 for 1-5 poems; additional poems $1 each. Short fiction, essays, $5 each. Open to English language works by any writers. SASE for guidelines and entry form.

THE LOIS AND RICHARD ROSENTHAL NEW PLAY PRIZE, Cincinnati Playhouse in the Park, Box 6537, Cincinnati OH 45206. (513)421-5440. Unpublished plays. "Scripts must not have received a full-scale professional production." Deadline: Oct. 15-Jan. 15.

SCHOLASTIC WRITING AWARDS, Scholastic Inc., 730 Broadway, New York NY 10003. (212)505-3000. Fiction, nonfiction, poetry and drama (grades 7-12). Write for complete information. Cash prizes, equipment prizes and scholarships. Deadline: August-December.

THE CHARLES M. SCHULZ AWARD, The Scripps Howard Foundation, P.O. Box 5380, Cincinnati OH 45201. (513)977-3035. Estab. 1962. For a college cartoonist.

‡THE SCIENCE AWARD, The Phi Beta Kappa Society, 1811 Q St. NW, Washington DC 20009. (202)265-3808. Contact: Administrator, Phi Beta Kappa Book Awards. Interpretations of the physical or biological sciences or mathematics published in the U.S. during the 12-month period preceding the entry deadline, and submitted by the publisher. Deadline: April 30.

‡SCIENCE-WRITING AWARD IN PHYSICS AND ASTRONOMY, American Institute of Physics, 335 E. 45th St., New York NY 10017. (212)661-9404. Contact: Pubilc Information Division. Previously published articles, booklets or books "that improve public understanding of physics and astronomy." Deadline: Jan. 10 for professional writers; May 11 for physicists, astronomers or members of AIP member and affiliated soieites; Oct. 10 for articles or books intended for children preschool to 15 years old.

CHARLES E. SCRIPPS AWARD, The Scripps Howard Foundation, P.O. Box 5380, Cincinnati OH 45201. (513)977-3035. Estab. 1962. Combatting illiteracy. For newspapers, television and radio stations.

THE EDWARD WILLIS SCRIPPS AWARD, The Scripps Howard Foundation, P.O. Box 5380, Cincinnati OH 45201. (513)977-3035. Estab. 1962. Service to the First Amendment for newspapers.

SENIOR AWARD, International Society of Dramatists, Box 1310, Miami FL 33153. Award Director: A. Delaplaine. Previously unpublished scripts (any media or length) written by college students. Award plus staged reading and possible future production. Deadline: May 1.

SEVENTEEN MAGAZINE/SMITH CORONA CONNTEST, 850 3rd Ave., New York NY 10022. Estab. 1948. Previously unpublished short stories from writers 13-21 years old. Deadline: Jan. 31.

SFWA NEBULA AWARDS, Science Fiction Writers of America, Inc., P.O. Box 4236, West Columbia SC 29171. Science fiction or fantasy in the categories of novel, novella, novelette and short story recommended by members.

SHELLEY MEMORIAL AWARD, Poetry Society of America, 15 Gramercy Park S., New York NY 10003. (212)254-9628. Contact: Award Director. Deadline: Dec. 31. By nomination only to a living American poet.

‡SHORT STORY CONTEST, *Japanophile,* Box 223, Okemos MI 48864. (517)349-1795. Contact: Earl Snodgrass. Annual award for unpublished fiction "that leads to better kunderstanding of Japanese culture." Entry fee: $5. Deadline: Dec. 31.

SHORT STORY WRITERS COMPETITION, Hemingway Days Festival, P.O. Box 4045, Key West FL 33041. (305)294-4440. Director: Michael Whalton. Estab. 1981. Unpublished short stories. Deadline: early July. Charges $10 fee. Send SASE for rules, specific deadline, and entry form.

SIENA COLLEGE PLAYWRIGHTS' COMPETITION, Siena College Theatre Program, Department of Fine Arts, Loudonville NY 12211. (518)783-2381. Director of Theatre: Mark A. Heckler. Contest offered during even numbered years to recognize unpublished and unproduced works of playwrights, professional and amateur. Winning playwright required to participate in six-week residency on college campus to prepare play for production. Deadline: Feb. 1 - June 30. Next deadlines occur in 1992. $2,000 prize plus $1,000 in living expenses for residency. Write for contest guidelines.

SIERRA REPERTORY THEATRE, P.O. Box 3030, Sonora CA 95370. (209)532-3120. Estab. 1980. Full-length plays. Deadline: May 15.

SILVER GAVEL AWARDS, American Bar Association, 750 N. Lake Shore Dr., Chicago IL 60611. (312)988-6137. Contact: Peggy O'Carroll. Previously published, performed or broadcast works that promote "public understanding of the American system of law and justice." Deadline: Feb. 1.

DOROTHY SILVER PLAYWRITING COMPETITION, (formerly JCC Theatre of Cleveland Playwriting Competition), Jewish Community Center, 3505 Mayfield Rd., Cleveland Heights OH 44118. (216)382-4000, ext. 275. Contact: Elaine Rembrandt. Estab. 1948. All entries must be original works, not previously produced, suitable for a full-length presentation; directly concerned with the Jewish experience. Deadline: Dec. 15.

SMALL PRESS PUBLISHER OF THE YEAR, Quality Books Inc., 918 Sherwood Dr., Lake Bluff IL 60044-2204. (312)295-2010. FAX: (708)295-1556. Contact: Tom Drewes. Estab. 1964. "Each year a publisher is named that publishes titles we stock and has demonstrated ability to produce a timely and topical title, suitable for libraries, and supports their distributor." Title must have been selected for stocking by Quality Books Inc. QBI is the principal nationwide distributor of small press titles to libraries.

C.L. SONNICHSEN BOOK AWARD, Texas Western Press of the University of Texas at El Paso, El Paso TX 79968-0633. (915)747-5688. Press Director: Dale L. Walker. Estab. 1952. Previously unpublished nonfiction manuscript dealing with the history, literature or cultures of the Southwest. Deadline: March 1.

‡SOUTHEASTERN THEATRE CONFERENCE NEW PLAY PROJECT, Department of Performing Arts, Clemson University, Clemson SC 29634. (803)656-3043. FAX: (803)656-0258. Contact: Clifton Egan. Annual contest dedicated to the discovery, development and publicizing of worthy new unproduced plays and playwrights. Submit: Mar. 15-July 31. Prize is $1,000, staged reading at SETC Convention, expenses paid trip to convention, preferred consideration for National Playwrights Conference.

SOUTHERN PLAYWRITING COMPETITION, Festival of Southern Theatre, Dept. of Theatre Arts Univ. of Mississippi, University MS 38677. (601)232-5816. Contact: Scott McCoy. Competiton for unpublished and unproduced original full-length scripts for the theatre by a Southern writer or a work with a markedly Southern theme. Deadline: Dec. 1. Three winners annually are awarded $1,000 each and full professional production.

THE SOUTHERN REVIEW/LOUISIANA STATE UNIVERSITY SHORT FICTION AWARD, Louisiana State University, 43 Allen Hall, Baton Rouge LA 70803. (504)388-5108. Selection Committee Chairman: Veronica Makowsky. First collection of short stories by an American published in the U.S. during previous year. Deadline: Jan. 31. A publisher or an author may submit an entry by mailing two copies of the collection to the *Southern Review* Short Story Award.

‡SOUTHWEST REVIEW AWARDS, Southern Methodist University, 6410 Airline Rd., Dallas TX 75275. (214)373-7440. Annual awards for fiction, nonfiction and poetry published in the magazine. The *John H. McGinnis Memorial Award* is given each year for fiction and nonfiction that has been published in the *Southwest Review* in the previous year. Stories or articles are not submitted directly for the award, but simply for publication in the magazine. From among those published in each two-year period, the judges select the best story for the McGinnis award, $1,000. The *Elizabeth Matchett Stover Award*, an annual prize of $250 is awarded to the author of the best poem published in the magazine during the preceding year.

BRYANT SPANN MEMORIAL PRIZE, History Dept., Indiana State University, Terre Haute IN 47809. Estab. 1963. Social criticism in the tradition of Eugene V. Debs. Deadline: April 30. SASE required.

THE STAND MAGAZINE SHORT STORY COMPETITION, *Stand Magazine* and the Harrogate International Festival, 179 Wingrove Rd., Newcastle on Tyne, NE4 9DA United Kingdom. (091)-2733280. Contact: Editors of *Stand Magazine*. "This competition is an open international contest for unpublished writing in the English

Close-up

Clifton Egan
Head of Department of Performing Arts, Clemson University
Southeastern Theatre Conference New Play Project

Entering its twentieth year, the Southeastern Theatre Conference New Play Project is one of the older contests for playwrights in the country. Clemson University drama professor Clifton Egan hopes the $1,000 cash award that was added two years ago will increase interest in the contest. Coupled with an expense-paid trip to a staged reading at the Southeast Theatre Conference Convention and preferred consideration for the National Playwrights Conference, the New Play Project is also one of the more prestigious drama contests for developing playwrights.

The contest has no theme, length or content guidelines. The playwright must simply provide "a full evening's entertainment," says Egan. The entertainment could either be a series of one-acts or a full-length play. Despite its location in the Southeast, there is no regional restriction for entry; submissions from anywhere in the United States are welcome. Prospective scripts must be unproduced. "They may have had a public reading, but cannot have been given a full production," says Egan.

The conference accepts submissions between the middle of March and the end of July. No individual may submit more than two scripts, but these can have been elsewhere. Unlike many literary contests, there is no problem with simultaneous submissions. "Playwrights do this all the time," Egan says.

The purpose behind the contest is to encourage playwrights with recognition and a cash award. "We see ourselves as players in the early part of a playwright's development," says Egan. Most of the winners are young and have had few if any plays produced. The winners usually continue on the road to success, boosted by the New Play Project's initial recognition.

Apart from the prize money and the opportunity of script development, the playwright receives an extra bonus. The Southeastern Theatre Conference nominates the winning play to the O'Neill National Playwrights Conference. The nomination means special consideration on the part of the national committee.

Egan sees a variety of scripts. Winners from the past four years have set their plays in locations ranging from Victorian England to a post-apocalyptic American metropolis. Egan tends to find that the younger writers prefer to tackle the more serious subjects. "It shouldn't be that way," he says. "Comedies should have an equal chance, but most theater people give greater weight to themes of consequence." If a playwright wants to tackle comedy, however, he should do so with abandon. "Good comedy is rare," according to Egan.

"There are times when it's clear that an issue is steering a play," says Egan, "and this weighs against that play's chances." He advises new and younger writers to remember that plays are about people, not issues. "Don't let issues guide the behavior of your characters or the outcome of the play," says Egan.

— Mark Kissling

language intended to foster a wider interest in the short story as a literary form and to promote and encourage excellent writing in it." Deadline: March 31, 1991. Please note that intending entrants enquiring from outside the U.K. should send International Reply Coupons, not stamps from their own countries. In lieu of an entry fee we ask for a minimum donation of £3 or $6 U.S. per story entered. Editorial inquiries should be made with SASE to: Professor Jack Kingsbury, P.O. Box 1161, Florence AL 35631-1161.

STANLEY DRAMA AWARD, Wagner College, Staten Island NY 10301. (212)390-3256. Estab. 1957. Unpublished and nonprofessionally produced full-length plays, musicals or related one-acts by American playwrights. Submissions must be accompanied by completed application and written recommendation by theatre professional or drama teacher. First prize: $2,000, possibility of production. Deadline: Sept. 1.

THE AGNES LYNCH STARRETT POETRY PRIZE,University of Pittsburgh Press, 127 N. Bellefield Ave., Pittsburgh PA 15260. (412)624-4110. FAX: (412)624-7380. Estab. 1936. First book of poetry for poets who have not had a full-length book published. Deadline: March and April only. Write for complete guidelines for manuscript submission.

‡STEGNER FELLOWSHIP, Stanford Creative Writing Program, Stanford University, Stanford CA 94305-2087. (415)723-2637. Contact: Prof. Nancy Packer. Annual fellowships include all tuition costs and a living stipend (four in fiction and four in poetry) for writers to come to Stanford for a period of two years to attend workshop to develop their particular writing. Deadline: Jan. 1. Charges $20 fee.

‡I.F STONE AWARD FOR STUDENT JOURNALISM, *The Nation,* 72 5th Ave., New York NY 10011. (212)242-8400. Director: Peter Meyer. Annual award "to recognize excellence in student journalism." Deadline: June 30.

THE WALKER STONE AWARDS, The Scripps Howard Foundation, P.O. Box 5380, Cincinnati OH 45201. (513)977-3035. Estab. 1962. Editorial writing for newspaper man and/or woman.

‡ELIZABETH MATCHETT STOVER MEMORIAL AWARD, Southwest Review, 6410 Airline Rd., SMU, Dallas TX 75275. (214)373-7440. For the best poem or group of poems that appeared in the magazine during the previous year.

MARVIN TAYLOR PLAYWRITING AWARD, Sierra Repertory Theatre, P.O. Box 3030, Sonora CA 95370. (209)532-3120. Producing Director: Dennis C. Jones. Full-length plays. Deadline: May 15.

THE TEN BEST "CENSORED" STORIES OF 1990, Project Censored—Sonoma State University, Rohnert Park CA 94928. (707)664-2500. Award Director: Carl Jensen, Ph.D. Estab. 1976. Current published, nonfiction stories of national social significance that have been overlooked or under-reported by the news media. Deadline: Nov. 1.

TEXAS BLUEBONNET AWARD, Texas Association of School Libraries and Children's Round Table, Suite 603, 3355 Bee Cave Rd., Austin TX 78746. (512)328-1518. Contact: Patricia Smith. Published books for children recommended by librarians, teachers and students.

THE THEATRE LIBRARY ASSOCIATION AWARD, Billy Rose Theatre Collection, New York Public Library at Lincoln Center, 111 Amsterdam Ave., New York NY 10023. (212)870-1638. Awards Committee Chair: Stephen M. Vallillo. Book published in the United States in the field of recorded performance, including motion pictures and television. Deadline: Feb. 1.

‡THEATRE MEMPHIS NEW PLAY COMPETITION, Theatre Memphis, 630 Perkins Ext., Memphis TN 38117. (901)682-8323. Co-Chair: Martha Graber, Iris Dichtel. Award offered every 3 years "To promote new playwrights' works and new works by established playwrights." No musicals. Bound scripts only. Deadline: Oct. 1.

TOWSON STATE UNIVERSITY PRIZE FOR LITERATURE, College of Liberal Arts, Towson State University, Towson MD 21204. (301)321-2128. Award Director: Dean Annette Chappell. Estab. 1979. Book or book-length manuscript that has been accepted for publication, written by a Maryland author of no more than 40 years of age. Deadline: May 15.

‡THE JOHN TRAIN HUMOR PRIZE, *The Paris Review,* 541 East 72 St., New York NY 10021. Contest/Award Director: George Plimpton. Estab. 1953. Unpublished humor—fiction, nonfiction or poetry. Deadline: March 31.

THE TRANSLATION CENTER AWARDS, The Translation Center, 412 Dodge, Columbia University, New York NY 10027. (212)854-2305. Executive Director: Frank MacShane. Awards are grants to a translator for an outstanding translation of a substantial part of a book length literary work.

‡THE TURNER TOMORROW AWARD, Turner Publishing, Inc., 1 CNN Center, Atlanta GA 30348. (404)827-3389. FAX (404)827-3665. Managing Director: Tom Guinzburg. Previously unpublished book ms. Deadline: Dec. 31. To receive an entry kit, send a letter of request with the author's name and address.

UCROSS FOUNDATION RESIDENCY, Ucross Rt., Box 19, Ucross WY 82835. (307)737-2291. Contact: Elizabeth Guheen. Four concurrent positions open for artists-in-residence in various disciplines extending from 2 weeks-4 months. No charge for room, board or studio space. Deadline: March 1 for August-December program; Oct. 1 for January-May program.

UNDERGRADUATE ANNUAL PAPER COMPETITION IN CRYPTOLOGY, *Cryptologia*, Rose-Hulman Institute of Technology, Terre Haute IN 47803. Contact: Editor. Unpublished papers on cryptology. Deadline: Jan. 1.

‡UNIVERSITY OF ALABAMA NEW PLAYWRIGHTS PROGRAM, Box 870239, Tuscaloosa AL 35487-0239. (205)348-9032. Artistic Director and Dramaturg: Dr. Paul C. Castagno. Estab. 1982. Full-length plays for mainstage; experimental plays for B stage.

DANIEL VAROUJAN AWARD, New England Poetry Club, Lois Ames, 285 Marbow Rd., Sudbury MA 01776. Contact: Diana DerHovanessian. Unpublished poems in duplicate. Send SASE for rules. Deadline: June 30. Charges $2 per poem; no charge for New England Poetry Club members.

CELIA B. WAGNER AWARD, Poetry Society of America, 15 Gramercy Park St. S., New York NY 10003. (212)254-9628. Contact: Award Director. Unpublished poem. "Poem worthy of the tradition of the art in any style." Deadline: Dec. 31. Charges $5 fee.

EDWARD LEWIS WALLANT BOOK AWARD, Mrs. Irving Waltman, 3 Brighton Rd., West Hartford CT 06117. Published fiction with significance for the American Jew (novel or short stories) by an American writer. Book must have been published during current year. Deadline: Dec. 31.

THEODORE WARD PRIZE FOR PLAYWRITING, Columbia College Theater/Music Center, 72 E 11th St., Chicago IL 60605. Contact: Chuck Smith. Estab. 1985. To uncover and identify new unpublished African American plays that are promising and produceable." Deadline: August 1. All rights for music or biographies must be secured prior to submission. All entrants must be of African American descent and residing within the U.S. Only one completed script per playwright will be accepted.

WAREHOUSE THEATRE ONE-ACT COMPETITION, Warehouse Theatre Company, Stephens College, Columbia MO 65215. (314)876-7194. Contact: Artistic Director. Estab. 1969. Offered annually. Submissions to be unpublished. Deadline: Dec. 31. Varies according to school year. Charges $7.50.

WASHINGTON PRIZE FOR FICTION, Larry Kaltman Literary Agency, 1301 S. Scott St., Arlington VA 22204. (703)920-3771. Contact: Larry Kaltman. Fiction, previously unpublished, of at least 75,000 words. Deadline: Nov. 30. Charges $25 fee.

ARNOLD WEISSBERGER PLAYWRITING AWARD, New Dramatists, 424 W. 44th St., New York NY 10036. (212)757-6960. Contest/Award Director: Beth Nathanson. Unpublished plays; no musicals or children's plays. Accepting applications: Sept. 15-Feb. 1.

WEST COAST ENSEMBLE FULL-PLAY COMPETITION, CELEBRATION OF ONE-ACTS, West Coast Ensemble, P.O. Box 38728, Los Angeles CA 90038. Artistic Director: Les Hanson. Estab. 1982.Unpublished (in Southern California) plays. No musicals or children's plays for full-play competition. No restrictions on subject matter for one-acts. Deadline: Nov. 1; Oct. 15 for one-act plays.

‡WESTERN HERITAGE AWARD, National Cowboy Hall of Fame & Western Heritage Center, 1700 NE 63rd, Oklahoma City OK 73111. (405)478-2250. Contact: Dana Sullivant. Annual award for previously published stories of the American West. Deadline: Dec. 31.

WESTERN STATES BOOK AWARDS, Western States Arts Federation, 236 Montezuma Ave., Santa Fe NM 87501. (505)988-1166. Project Coordinator: Gina Briefs-Elgin. Estab. 1984. Unpublished fiction, poetry or creative nonfiction, that has been accepted for publication in the award year, by a press in a Western States Arts Federation member state. Deadline: spring of the year preceding the award year. Open to authors in Alaska, Arizona, California, Colorado, Hawaii, Idaho, Montana, Nevada, New Mexico, Oregon, Utah, Washington, and Wyoming. Manuscript duplication and return postage fee of $10.

WHITING WRITERS' AWARDS, Mrs. Giles Whiting Foundation, Rm. 3500, 30 Rockefeller Plaza, New York NY 10112. Director: Gerald Freund. For recognized writers, literary scholars and editors. Direct applications and informal nominations are not accepted by the Foundation.

WHITNEY-CARNEGIE AWARD, American Library Association Publishing Services, 40 E. Huron, Chicago IL 60611. (312)944-6780. FAX: (312)440-9374. Contact: Edgar S. McLarin. Submissions to be unpublished. "The grants are awarded to individuals for the preparation of bibliographic aids for research. The aids must be aimed at a scholarly audience but have a general applicability. Products prepared under this project must be offered to ALA Publishing Services for first consideration." Deadline: March 15, Sept. 15.

WICHITA STATE UNIVERSITY PLAYWRITING CONTEST, Wichita State University Theatre, WSU, Box 31, Wichita KS 67208. (316)689-3185. Contest Director: Professor Bela Kiralyfalvi. Estab. 1974. Two or three short, unpublished, unproduced plays or full-length plays by graduate or undergraduate U.S. college students. Deadline: Feb. 15.

LAURA INGALLS WILDER AWARD, Association for Library Service to Children/American Library Association, 50 E. Huron St., Chicago IL 60611. (312)944-6780. Contact: Award Director. Estab. 1954. Awarded every three years to an author or illustrator whose books, published in the United States,have over a period of years made a substantial and lasting contribution to literature for children.

BELL I. WILEY PRIZE, National Historical Society, 2245 Kohn Rd., Box 8200, Harrisburg PA 17105. (717)657-9555. Civil War and Reconstruction nonfiction (book). Biennial award. Deadline: July 31.

WILLIAM CARLOS WILLIAMS AWARD, Poetry Society of America, 15 Gramercy Park S., New York NY 10003. (212)254-9628. Contact: Award Director. Deadline: Dec. 31. Small press, nonprofit, or university press book of poetry submitted by publisher.

H.W. WILSON LIBRARY PERIODICAL AWARD, donated by H.W. Wilson Company, administered by the American Library Association, 50 E. Huron, Chicago IL 60611. (312)944-6780. Periodical published by a local, state or regional library, library group, or association in U.S. or Canada.

L.L. WINSHIP BOOK AWARD, *The Boston Globe*, 135 Morissey Blvd., Boston MA 02107. (617)929-2649. New England-related book. Deadline: June 30.

WISCONSIN ARTS BOARD INDIVIDUAL ARTIST PROGRAM, 131 W. Wilson St., #301, Madison WI 53703. (608)266-0190. Contact: Program Coordinator. Estab. 1973. Literary awards for Wisconsin writers in the categories of poetry, drama, fiction and essay/criticism. Deadline: Sept. 15.

WITTER BYNNER FOUNDATION FOR POETRY, INC. GRANTS, P.O. Box 2188, Santa Fe NM 87504. (505)988-3251. Executive Director: Steven D. Schwartz. Estab. 1972. Grants for poetry and poetry-related projects. Deadline: Feb. 1.

WOODBINE HOUSE AWARD, 5615 Fishers Ln., Rockville MD 20852. (301)468-8800. Editor: Susan Stokes. Unpublished book-length nonfiction. Deadline: Oct. 1.

‡**WORK-IN-PROGRESS GRANT**, Society of Children's Book Writers and Judy Blume, P.O. Box 296 Mar Vista, Los Angeles CA 90066. Write *SCBW* at preceding address. Two grants—one designated specifically for a contemporary novel for young people—to assist SCBW members in the completion of a specific project. Deadline: June 1.

WORLD FANTASY AWARDS, P.O. Box 4236, W. Columbia SC 29171. Contest/Award Director: Peter Dennis Pautz. Previously published work recommended by previous convention attendees in several categories, including life achievement, novel, novella, short story, anthology, collection, artist, special award-pro and special award non-pro. Deadline: July 1. Works are recommended by attendees of previous two years' conventions.

‡**WORLD'S BEST SHORT STORY CONTEST**, English Department, Writing Program, Florida State University, Tallahassee FL 32306. (904)644-4230. Contact: Jerome Stern. Annual award for unpublished short short story (no more than 250 words). Deadline Feb. 15.

Your Guide to Getting Published

Learn to write publishable material and discover the best-paying markets for your work. Subscribe to *Writer's Digest*, the magazine that has instructed, informed and inspired writers since 1920. Every month you'll get:

- Fresh markets for your writing, including the names and addresses of editors, what type of writing they're currently buying, how much they pay, and how to get in touch with them.
- Insights, advice, and how-to information from professional writers and editors.
- In-depth profiles of today's foremost authors and the secrets of their success.
- Monthly expert columns about the writing and selling of fiction, nonfiction, poetry and scripts.

Plus, a $12.00 discount. Subscribe today through this special introductory offer, and receive a full year (12 issues) of *Writer's Digest* for only $18.00—that's a $12.00 savings off the $30 newsstand rate. Enclose payment with your order, and we will add an extra issue to your subscription, absolutely **free**.

Detach postage-free coupon and mail today!

Guarantee: If you are not satisfied with your subscription at any time, you may cancel it and receive a full refund for all unmailed issues due you.

Subscription Savings Certificate
Save $12.00

Yes, I want professional advice on how to write publishable material and sell it to the best-paying markets. Send me 12 issues of *Writer's Digest* for just $18...a $12 discount off the newsstand price. (Outside U.S. add $4 and remit in U.S. funds.)

☐ Payment enclosed (Send me an extra issue free— 13 in all)

☐ Please bill me

Name (please print)

Address   Apt.

City

State   Zip

Basic rate, $24.   VEWM0

Writer's®
DIGEST

How would you like to get:

- up-to-the-minute reports on new markets for your writing
- professional advice from editors and writers about what to write and how to write it to maximize your opportunities for getting published
- in-depth interviews with leading authors who reveal their secrets of success
- expert opinion about writing and selling fiction, nonfiction, poetry and scripts
- ...all at a $12.00 discount?

BUSINESS REPLY MAIL
FIRST CLASS MAIL   PERMIT NO. 76   HARLAN, IOWA

POSTAGE WILL BE PAID BY ADDRESSEE

Writer's®
DIGEST

SUBSCRIBER SERVICE DEPARTMENT
PO BOX 2124
HARLAN IA 51593-2313

‡**WRITER-IN-RESIDENCE PROGRAM,** The Syvenna Foundation, Rt 1, Box 193, Linden TX 75563. (214)835-8252. Contact: Sylva Billue. Opportunity for women writers to have a cottage rent and utilities free for 2 or 3 months to pursue their craft. The amount of time spent in residence depends on the schedule of the recipient. A $300/month stipend is also provided. All types of writing are considered. Deadline: Aug. 1, Oct. 1, Dec. 1., April 1.

WRITERS DIGEST **WRITING COMPETITION,** *Writer's Digest Magazine*, 1507 Dana Ave., Cincinnati OH 45207. (513)531-2222. Contest Director: Bill Strickland. Submissions to be unpublished. Deadline: May 31.

WRITERS' JOURNAL ANNUAL SHORT STORY CONTEST, Minnesota Ink, Inc. Box 9148, N. St. Paul MN 55109. (612)433-3626. Contact: Valerie Hockert. Previously unpublished short stories. Deadline: March 15. Charges $5 per entry.

WRITERS' JOURNAL SEMI-ANNUAL POETRY CONTEST, Minnesota Ink, Inc., Box 9148, N. St. Paul MN 55109. (612)433-3626. Contact: Esther M. Leiper. Previously unpublished poetry. Deadline: Nov. 30 and April 15. Charges fee: $2 first poem; $1 each thereafter.

‡**Y.E.S. NEW PLAY FESTIVAL,** Northern Kentucky University, 227FA, Department of Theatre, Highland Heights KY 41071. (606)572-6303. Artistic director: Joe Conger. Estab. 1981. Deadline: December. Full-length plays, one-acts and musicals.

‡**YOUNG PLAYWRIGHTS PROGRAM,** Very Special Arts, Education Office, John F. Kennedy Center for the Performing Arts, Washington DC 20566. (202)662-8899. FAX: (202)662-8884. Annual award for unpublished play "incorporating some aspect of disability in contemporary society." Deadline: February.

ANNA ZORNIO MEMORIAL THEATRE FOR YOUTH PLAYWRITING AWARD, U of NH Youth Drama Program/TRY, Paul Creative Arts, Durbam NH 03824. (603)862-2150. Contact: Carol Lucha-Burns. To bring quality unpublished plays and musicals (45 minutes-1 hour in length) to young audiences. Deadline: May 31. Production is planned—usually Sept. 1.

Other Contests and Awards

The following contests and awards do not have listings in this edition of *Writer's Market*. The majority did not respond to our request to update their listings or return a questionnaire for a new listing. If a reason was given for their exclusion, we have included it in parentheses after the listing name.

AAAS Prize for Behavioral Science Research

Alberta New Fiction Competition

Annual Journalism Awards Competition

Annual NJ Poetry Contest

Arts Recognition and Talent Search

Award for Literary Translation

Emily Clark Balch Award

Banta Award

George Louis Beer Prize

Best of Blurbs Contest (no longer held)

Biennial Promising Playwright Award

Neltje Blanchan Memorial Award

BMI University Musical Show Competition (no competition in 1991)

Body Story Contest (no competition in 1991)

The Thomas H. Carter Memorial Award for Literary Criticism

Catholic Press Association Journalism Awards

CCLM Editor's Grant Awards (no funding for grant available)

CCLM Seed Grants (no funding for grants available)

Chicano Literary Contest

Children's Science Book Awards

Albert B. Corey Prize in Canadian-American Relations

Dayton Playhouse National Playwriting Competition

The Geraldine R. Dodge Foundation New American Play Award (asked to be deleted)

Dog Writer's Association of America Annual Writing Contest

Frank Nelson Doubleday Memorial Award

FAW Literary Award

Felicity Awards

FIEJ Golden Pen of Freedom

Florida Individual Artist Fellowships

FMCT's Biennial Playwrights Competition (Midwest)

Fourth Estate Award

Lewis Galantiere Prize for Literary Translation

General Electric Foundation Awards for Younger Writers

German Prize for Literary Translation

John Glassco Translation Prize

Darrell Bob Houston Prize

Inner City Culture Center's National Short Play Competition

International Literary Contest (no longer held)

International Reading Association Children's Book Award

Margo Jones Playwriting Competition

Juvenile Book Awards

Robert F. Kennedy Book Award

Robert F. Kennedy Journalism Awards

Lee Korf Playwriting Award

Light and Life Writing Contest

McDonald's Literary Achievement Awards (unable to contact)

Howard R. Marraro Prize in

Italian History
The Merrimack Repertory
Theatre Annual Playwriting
Contest
National Awards for Education
Reporting
National Playwrights' Competi-
tion, Unicorn Theatre (dis-
continued)
National Society of Newspaper
Columnists (unable to
contact)
Nelson Algren Awards
New Day Poetry/Short Story
Contest
Overseas Press Club of
America
Francis Parkman Prize
Playwright's Forum Awards
Playwright's-in-Residence
Grants
Present Tense/Joel H. Cavior

Literary Awards
Prometheus Award/Hall of
Fame
Purgatory Theatre Annual
National Playwrighting
Competition (cancelled)
QRL Poetry Series
Reader Riter Poll
Redbook's Short Story Contest
(discontinued)
Reuben Award
Rhode Island State Council on
the Arts Fellowship
Nicholas Roerich Poetry Prize
Rolling Stone College Journal-
ism Competition
The Carl Sandberg Literary
Arts Awards
Science in Society Journalism
Awards
The Short Story Award, Follow
Me Gentlemen

Charlie May Simon Award
R. Gaines Smith Memorial
Writing Contest
Sovereign Award, Outstanding
News and Feature Stories
Special Libraries Association
Public Relations Award
Spur Awards, Western Writers
of America
Student Grant-in-Aid
Sydney Taylor Book Awards
Harry S Truman Book Prize
Verbatim Essay Competition
World Hunger Media Awards
Writer's Biennial
Writers Guild of America West
Awards
Wyoming Council on the Arts
Literary Fellowships
Xanadu's Annual Poetry
Contest (discontinued)
Peter Zenger Award

Additional New Listings

The following listings were received after the *Writer's Market* original sections were compiled. We are happy to be able to bring you these late arrivals and hope you benefit from the added freelance opportunities they represent. The listings are compiled in alphabetical order according to the major section of the book in which they would appear.

Book Publishers

AMERICAN ASTRONAUTICAL SOCIETY, Univelt, Inc., Publisher, P.O. Box 28130, San Diego CA 92128. (619)746-4005. Editorial Director: H. Jacobs. Estab. 1970. Publishes hardcover originals. Averages 8 titles/year; receives 12-15 submissions annually. 5% of books from first-time authors; 5% of books from unagented writers. Average print order for a writer's first book is 600-2,000. Pays 10% roaylty on actual sales; no advance. Publishes book an average of 4 months after acceptance. Simultaneous submissions OK. Reports in 1 month. Book catalog and ms guidelines for 9×12 SAE and 3 first class stamps.
Nonfiction: Proceedings or monographs in the field of astronautics, including applications of aerospace technology to Earth's problems. "Our books must be space-oriented or space-related. They are meant for technical libraries, research establishments and the aerospace industry worldwide." Submit outline/synopsis and 1-2 sample chapters. Reviews artwork/photos as part of ms package.
Recent Nonfiction Title: *Soviet Space Programs 1980-85*, by N.L. Johnson.

CONSUMER REPORTS BOOKS, Subsidiary of Consumers Union, 51 E. 42nd St., #800, New York NY 10017. (212)983-8250. Contact: Sarah Uman. Estab. 1938. Publishes trade paperback originals and trade paperback reprints. Averages 30-35 titles/year; receives 1,000 submissions annually. Most books from unagented writers. Pays variable royalty on retail price; buys some mss outright. Publishes book an average of 18 months after acceptance. Simultaneous submissions OK. Reports in 6 weeks on queries; 2 months on mss. Free book list and writer's manuscript guidelines on request.
Nonfiction: Cookbook, how-to, reference, self-help and technical. Subjects include finance, cooking and foods, health, music and homeowner guidance. Submit outline/synopsis and 1-2 sample chapters.
Recent Nonfiction Title: *Sleep: Problems and Solutions*, by Quentin Registein, M.D.

CREATIVE ARTS BOOK COMPANY, Donald S. Ellis, San Francisco; Creative Arts Communications Books; 833 Bancroft Way, Berkeley CA 94710. (415)848-4777. Publisher: Donald S. Ellis. Senior Editor: Peg O'Donnell. Publishes hardcover and paperback originals and paperback reprints. Averages 38 titles/year; receives 800-1,000 submissions annually. 10% of books from first-time authors; 20% of books from unagented writers. Pays 5-15% royalty on retail price. Offers minimum $500 advance. Publishes book an average of 12-18 months after acceptance. Simultaneous submissions OK. Reports in 6 weeks. Free book catalog.
Nonfiction: Biographies and essays. Especially interested in music and works on California, health and New Age.
Recent Nonfiction Title: *Russia*, by Nikos Kazantzakis.
Fiction: "Looking for serious literary fiction of broad appeal," especially books by and/or about women and children's books.
Recent Fiction Title: *Driving Under the Cardboard Pines*, by Colleen McElroy.

CREATIVE PUBLISHING CO., The Early West, Box 9292, College Station TX 77840. (409)775-6047. Contact: Theresa Earle. Publishes hardcover originals. Receives 20-40 submissions/year. 50% of books from first-time authors; 100% from unagented writers. Royalty varies on wholesale price. Publishes book an average of 8 months after acceptance. Reports in "several" weeks on queries; "several" months on mss. Free book catalog.
Nonfiction: Biography. Subjects include Americana (western), history. No mss other than 19th century western America. Query. Reviews artwork/photos as part of ms package.
Recent Nonfiction Title: *Garrett & Roosevelt*, by Jack DeMattos.

THE HARVARD COMMON PRESS, 535 Albany St., Boston MA 02118. (617)423-5803. President: Bruce P. Shaw. Publishes hardcover and trade paperback originals and reprints. Averages 6 titles/year. Receives "thousands" of submissions annually. 75% of books from first-time authors; 75% of books from unagented writers. Average print run for a writer's first book is 7,500. Pays royalty; offers average $1,000 advance. Publishes book an average of 9 months after acceptance. Simultaneous submissions OK. Reports in 1 month. Book catalog for 9×12 SAE and 3 first class stamps; ms guidelines for #10 SASE.

Nonfiction: Travel, cookbook, how-to, reference and self-help. Emphasis on travel, family matters and cooking. "We want strong, practical books that help people gain control over a particular area of their lives, whether it's family matters, business or financial matters, health, careers, food or travel. An increasing percentage of our list is made up of books about travel and travel guides; in this area we are looking for authors who are well traveled, and who can offer a different approach to the series guidebooks. We are open to good nonfiction proposals that show evidence of strong organization and writing, and clearly demonstrate a need in the marketplace. First-time authors are welcome." Accepts nonfiction translations. Submit outline/synopsis and 1-3 sample chapters. Reviews artwork/photos as part of ms package.

Recent Nonfiction Title: *Going Places: The Guide to Travel Guides*, by Greg Hayes and Joan Wright.

NEW WORLD LIBRARY, Subsidiary of Whatever Publishing, Inc., P.O. Box 13257, Northgate Station, San Rafael CA 94913. (415)472-2100. Editorial Director: Carol La Russo. Publishes hardcover and trade paperback originals. Averages 10 titles/year. Receives 500 submissions/year. 30% of books from first-time authors; 50% from unagented writers. Pays 12-16% royalty on wholesale price. Offers $5,000-10,000 average advance. Publishes book an average of 1 year after acceptance. Simultaneous submissions OK. Query for electronic submissions. Reports in 6 weeks on queries; 10 weeks on mss. Free book catalog and ms guidelines.

Nonfiction: How-to, self-help (psychology) and inspirational. Subjects include business and economics, government/politics, health/medicine, nature/environment, philosophy, psychology, religion, travel and women's issues/studies. "We are looking for high quality books focusing on self-improvement, with an inspirational style, yet practical and down to earth. Topics can be varied. Nothing too technical, textbook-like, historical or scientific. We aim for an intelligent, aware audience, interested in themselves, the environment and the world." Query with outline/synopsis and sample chapters. Reviews artwork/photos as part of ms package.

Recent Nonfiction Title: *The Eloquence of Living*, Vimala Thakar (philosophical).

Tips: "Most book buyers are women. Therefore, books on women's issues and interests are good sellers, as are books on the environment, global issues, self-improvement and New Age."

OWL CREEK PRESS, 1620 N. 45th St., Seattle WA 98103. Editor: Rich Ives. Estab. 1979. Publishes hardcover, trade paperback and mass market paperback originals, and mass market paperback reprints. Averages 5-10 titles/year. Receives 2,000 submissions/year. 50% of books from first-time authors; 95% from unagented writers. Pays 10-20% royalty on wholesale price (cash or equivalent in copies). If paid in copies, royalty is advanced. Reports in 2 months. Book catalog for #10 SASE.

Nonfiction: Photography. "Our selections are made solely on the basis of lasting artistic quality." No cookbooks, how-to, juvenile, self-help, technical or reference. Submit outline/synopsis and sample chapters.

Recent Nonfiction Title: *The Truth About the Territory*, edited by Rick Ives (anthology of the Northwest).

Fiction: "We seek writing of lasting artistic merit in all areas. Writing genre is irrelevant, although we avoid easy approaches and formula work. We are not interested in writing that attempts to fulfill genre requirements with preconceived notions of mass market appeal. If it's work of lasting quality, we will try to find and build a market for it." Submit outline/synopsis and sample chapters.

Recent Fiction Title: *Sailing to Corinth*, by Irene Wanner.

Poetry: "We publish both full-length and chapbook titles. Selections are based solely on the lasting quality of the manuscripts. No manuscripts where genre category or preconceived ideas of mass market appeal dominate the work." Submit complete ms, unsolicited through contests only.

Recent Poetry Title: *Self Portrait in Unwilling Landscape*, by Laurie Blauer.

Tips: "We attempt to reach the reader with a somewhat discerning taste first. Future plans include further expansion into fiction and translated titles (both poetry and fiction) as well as maintaining a continued series of both full-length and chapbook poetry originals. We are nonprofit, dedicated to the promotion of litereary art."

THE PRESERVATION PRESS, National Trust for Historic Preservation, 1785 Massachusetts Ave. NW, Washington DC 20036. FAX: (202)673-4172. Director: Buckley Jeppson. Estab. 1975. Publishes nonfiction books on historic preservation (saving and reusing the "built environment"). Averages 6 titles/year. Receives 30 submissions/year. 40% of books from first-time authors; 50% from unagented writers. Books are often commissioned by publisher. Publishes book an average of 2 years after acceptance. Query for electronic submissions. Book catalog for 9×12 SASE.

Nonfiction: Subject matter encompasses architecture and architectural history, building restoration and historic preservation. No local history. Looks for "relevance to national preservation-oriented audience; educational or instructional value, depth, uniqueness and need in field." Query. Reviews artwork/photos as part of ms package.

Recent Nonfiction Title: *Lighting for Historic Buildings*, by Roger W. Moss.

Tips: "Writers have the best chance selling us books clearly related to our mission, historic preservation. We need books covering new ideas in a unique and practical fashion."

*UTAH STATE UNIVERSITY PRESS, Utah State University, Logan UT 84322-7800. (801)750-1362. Director: Linda Speth. Publishes hardcover and trade paperback originals and reprints. Averages 6 titles/year. Receives 170 submissions/year. 8% of books from first-time authors. Subsidy publishes 55% of books (45% nonauthor). Pays royalty on net price. Publishes book an average of 18 months after acceptance. Query for electronic submissions. Reports in 2 weeks on queries; 2 months on mss. Free book catalog; ms guidelines for SASE.

Nonfiction: Biography, reference and textbook on folklore, Americana (history and politics). "Particularly interested in book-length scholarly manuscripts dealing with folklore, Western history, Western literature. All submissions must have a scholarly focus." Submit complete ms. Reviews artwork/photos as part of ms package.

Recent Nonfiction Title: *Folk Groups*, by Elliot Oring (folklore).

WESTPORT PUBLISHERS, INC., 4050 Pennsylvania, Kansas City MO 64111. (816)756-1490. FAX: (816)756-0159. Subsidiaries include Test Corporation of America. Managing Editor: Terry Faulkner. Estab. 1983. Publishes hardcover and trade paperback originals. Averages 10-12 titles/year. Receives 100 submissions/year. 50% of books from first-time authors; 100% from unagented writers. Pays royalty. Publishes book an average of 9 months after acceptance. Reports in 1 month on queries; 6 weeks on mss. Manuscript guidelines for #10 SAE and 2 first class stamps.

Nonfiction: Coffee table books, cookbooks and reference works. Subjects include child guidance/parenting, cooking foods and nutrition, psychology, recreation and regional studies. "We will consider all topics except sensationalism." Submit complete ms. Reviews artwork/photos as part of ms package.

Recent Nonfiction Title: *Little People: Guidelines for Commonsense Childrearing*, by Edward R. Christopher-sen (parenting).

Tips: "Books with a well-defined audience have the best chance of succeeding with us. An author must have demonstrated expertise in the field on which he or she is writing."

Small Presses

ECLECTIC PRESS, P.O. Box 566575, Atlanta GA 30356. (404)640-2665. Editor: Robert Tyre. Estab. 1986. Publishes how-to, juvenile, cookbook, diet book, religion, history, biography and philosophy nonfiction; and mainstream fiction.

LONG BEACH PUBLISHING, INC., Box 92829, Long Beach CA 90809. (213)597-5185. Publishers: Louis Palmer and Terry McAlpine. Publishes hardcover and trade paperback originals, specializing in, but not limited to, science fiction and fantasy.

Consumer Publications

Animal

PACIFIC COAST JOURNAL, Pacific Coast Quarter Horse Association, P.O. Box 255847, Sacramento CA 95865. (916)924-7265. Managing Editor: Kate Riordan. 60% freelance written. Monthly magazine covering quarter horses. "We specialize in quarter horse showing and cutting for professionals and serious amateurs with up-to-date information on equine health, training techniques and show trends." Estab. 1947. Circ. 9,000. Pays on publication. Publishes ms an average of 3 months after acceptance. Byline given. Buys first North American serial rights or second serial (reprint) rights. Submit seasonal material 3 months in advance. Previously published submissions OK. Reports in 1 month. Sample copy for 10×13 SAE with 8 first class stamps; free writer's guidelines.

Nonfiction: Historical/nostalgic (some old west), how-to (quarter horse training) and interview/profile (noted quarter horse personalities). "Looking for articles on foals, barns, breeding, apparel and horse trail-ers." Buys 40 mss/year. Send complete ms. Length: 500-8,000 words. Pays $100-350 for assigned articles; $30-150 for unsolicited articles. Sometimes pays expenses of writers on assignment.

Photos: Send photos with submission. Reviews contact sheets, transparencies and prints. Offers $5 maxi-mum/photo. Captions and identification of subjects required. Buys one-time rights.

Business and Finance

EUROPA 1992 The American Business Report on Europe, Wolfe Publishing, Inc., P.O. Box 7599, South Station, Nashua NH 03060. (603)888-0338. Editor: Peter S. Kobs. Managing Editor: Robert J. Wolfegang. 75% freelance written. Monthly business magazine covering economic and political news from Europe. "We give American businesses an inside look at the opportunities and pitfalls of the new European market." Estab. 1989. Circ. 20,000. Pays on publication. Publishes ms an average of 1 month after acceptance. Byline given. Buys first rights. Submit seasonal/holiday material 6 weeks in advance. Simultaneous and previously published submissions OK (depending on where published). Query for electronic submissions. Reports in 2 weeks on queries; 1 month on mss. Free sample copy and writer's guidelines.

Nonfiction: Interview/profile, new product, technical, travel and business/economic. November issue will focus on Portugal. Buys over 100 mss/year. Query with published clips. Length: 1,500-5,000 words. Pays $300-500. Sometimes pays expenses of writers on assignment.

Photos: State availability of photos with submission. Reviews contact sheets and 8 × 10 prints. Offers no additional payment for photos accepted with ms.

Columns/Departments: EC 92 Eye On (focuses on a different European country each month). Length: 1,500-3,000 words. Buys 3-5 mss/year. Query with published clips. Pays $300-500.

Tips: "Call us first to discuss any ideas for an article. We can provide angles and contracts, as well as background information. Then read a back issue to see our style and length. We are always looking for new articles on European regions, countries, companies and markets. We rely heavily on freelancers for such articles."

FLORIDA TREND, Magazine of Florida Business and Finance, Box 611, St. Petersburg FL 33731. (813)821-5800. Editor and Publisher: Paul C. Tash. Managing Editor: Thomas J. Billitteri. Monthly magazine covering business economics and public policy for Florida business people and investors. Circ. 50,000. Pays on final acceptance. Byline given. Buys first North American serial rights. Reports in 1 month. Sample copy $3.50.

Nonfiction: Business and finance. Buys 10-12 mss/year. Query with or without published clips. Length: 1,200-2,500 words.

MOBILE OFFICE, For Business People on the Move, AVCOM Publishing, Ltd., Suite 1600, 21700 Oxnard St., Woodland Hills CA 91367. (818)593-3900. Editor: Michael Meresman. Managing Editor: Peter Otte. 90% freelance written. Bimonthly magazine covering mobile electronics. "We publish applications-oriented articles on personal connectivity and productivity while on the road." Estab. 1990. Circ. 160,000. Pays 1 month after acceptance. Publishes ms an average of 2 months after acceptance. Byline given. Offers 40% kill fee. Makes work-for-hire assignments. Submit seasonal/holiday material 5 months in advance. Simultaneous and previously published submissions OK. Query for electronic submissions. Reports in 3 weeks. Free sample copy and writer's guidelines.

Nonfiction: Interview/profile and new product. Buys 75 mss/year. Query with published clips. Length: 1,300-2,500 words. Pays $400-1,500 for assigned articles; $200-750 for unsolicited articles. Sometimes pays expenses of writers on assignment.

Photos: State availability of photos with submission. Reviews contact sheets, negatives, transparencies and prints. Offers no additional payment for photos accepted with ms. Captions required. Buys one-time rights.

Fillers: Gags to be illustrated by cartoonist. Buys 10/year. Length: 100 words maximum.

Tips: "Gain familiarity with mobile office market. Freelancers have the best chance of breaking into our publication with full-length articles."

Career, College and Alumni

U. THE NATIONAL COLLEGE NEWSPAPER, American Collegiate Network, Suite 104, 3110 Main St., Santa Monica CA 90405. (213)450-2921. Editor: Jacki Hampton. 100% freelance written. Monthly tabloid on college life. "We purchase manuscripts written by college students that have already appeared in college publications." Estab. 1987. Circ. 1.425 million. Pays on publication. Publishes ms an average of 2 months after acceptance. Byline given. Buys second serial (reprint) rights. Submit seasonal/holiday material 3 months in advance. Simultaneous and previously published submissions OK. Reports in 2 weeks. Sample copy for 9 × 12 SAE with 2 first class stamps.

Nonfiction: Essays, general interest, historical/nostalgic, humor, interview/profile (especially of musicians), opinion, personal experience and photo feature (all must relate to college students). Buys 500 mss/year. Send complete ms. Length: 100-2,000 words. Pays $50. Sometimes pays expenses of writers on assignment.

Columns/Departments: Music (reviews of albums and bands), Student Body (sports or health-related topics), Dollars and Sense (business and academic related topics). Length: 100-1,000 words. Buys 30 mss/year. Send complete ms. Pays $50.

Tips: "All of our freelancers must be college students at the time of writing the article. The copy must first appear in a college newspsper. We reprint these. All of our departments are open."

Child Care and Parental Guidance

TALK ABOUT LEARNING, Inquiries into the Nature of Childhood and Learning, 25 Belmede Rd., Portland ME 04101. (207)774-7053. Editor: Earl Stevens. 75% freelance written. Bimonthly magazine on child care and parental guidance. "Our interest is in the discovery of the child apart from the definitions of institutions. We want to find ways in which parents can support the education and healthy development of their children. We think home education is the very best option, but want to speak to families in every educational setting." Estab. 1988. Circ. 700. **Pays on acceptance.** Publishes ms an average of 4 months after acceptance. Byline given. Offers $25 kill fee. Rights negotiable. Submit seasonal/holiday material 4 months in advance. Simultaneous and previously published submissions OK. Query for electronic submissions. Reports in 3 weeks on queries; 5 weeks on mss. Sample copy for $3; free writer's guidelines.

Nonfiction: Book excerpts, essays, humor, inspirational, interview/profile, opinion and personal experience. "Nothing excessively sentimental; no kids as primarily cute, innocent and helpless; no children as as bad until adults make them better; and no academic and financial success as supreme goals." Buys 25-30 mss/year. Query with or without published clips, or send complete ms. Length: 500-3,000 words. Pays $25-50. Sometimes pays expenses of writers on assignment.

Photos: Send photos with submission. Reviews 5×7 black and white prints and contact sheets. Offers $5-15/photo. Captions, model releases and identification of subjects required. Buys one-time rights.

Poetry: Avant-garde, free verse, light verse and traditional. "Wc don't want poems that focus on the good, the sweet and the pure while ignoring the vitality, messiness and ambiguity of everyday life. Buys 12 poems/year. Submit maximum 10 poems. Pays $5-10.

Fillers: Anecdotes, facts. Buys 12-18/year. Length: 100-300 words. Pays $5-15.

Tips: "We are wide open to writers who make an effort to understand the philosophy and intent of the publication. A true respect for children and a genuine interest in their affairs always shines through. With the possible exception of research pieces, there should be room in an article for the author's personality. Send us articles on homeschooling, alternative education, the public schools, the politics of education, new visions of childhood and parenthood, education research, the psychology of childhood, issues of rights and personal freedom, philosophies of education, creativity, little kids, big kids, boys, girls, other cultures, the history of education, unschooling, and many other child-oriented topics and issues that are examined freshly."

Ethnic/Minority

NATIVE PEOPLES MAGAZINE, The Arts and Lifeways, 1833 N. 3rd St., Phoenix AZ 85004. (602)252-2236. FAX: (602)252-6180. Editor: Gary Avey. Quarterly magazine on Native Americans. "The primary purpose of this magazine is to offer a sensitive portrayal of the arts and lifeways of native peoples of the Americas." Estab. 1987. Circ. 25,000. Pays on publication. Byline given. Buys one-time rights. Query for electronic submissions. Reports in 1 month on queries; 2 weeks on mss. Sample copy for 9×12 SAE with 5 first class stamps; free writer's guidelines.

Nonfiction: Book excerpts, historical/nostalgic, interview profile, personal experience and photo feature. Buys 35 mss/year. Query with published clips. Length: 1,400-2,000 words. Pays 25¢/word. Sometimes pays expenses of writers on assignment.

Photos: State availability of photos with submission. Reviews transparencies (all formats). Offers $75-150/page. Identification of subjects required. Buys one-time rights.

General Interest

MAHOGANY & MOLASSES, Family Reader, 3502 Glocca Moora Dr., Apopka FL 32703. (407)862-8056. Editor: Laurie Thoroman. 100% freelance written. Bimonthly magazine for family reading. "The aim of *Mahogany & Molasses* is to provide good, entertaining stories and poetry for all ages to enjoy." Estab. 1989. **Pays on acceptance.** Publishes ms an average of 6 months after acceptance. Bylinc given. Buys first North American serial rights or second serial (reprint) rights. Submit seasonal/holiday material 6 months in advance. Previously published submissions OK. Reports in 2 weeks on queries; 1 month on mss. Sample copy $2; writer's guidelines for #10 SASE.

Nonfiction: Essays, humor and true adventure or nature stories. Buys 2 mss/year. Send complete ms. Length: 100-1,000 words. Pays $2-10.

Fiction: Adventure, historical, humorous, mainstream, romance, science fiction, western and children/teen. No horror or erotica. Buys 20 mss/year. Send complete ms. Length: 100-4,000 words. Pays $2-15.

Poetry: Free verse, haiku, light verse and traditional. Buys 12 poems/year. Submit maximum of 4 poems at one time. Length: 1-50 lines. Pays $1-3.

Tips: "All submissions must be appropriate to a familiy publication. Write in visual terms; employ strong characters who can involve readers emotionally in your story. New writers who follow our guidelines have a good chance of publication here. Remember to enclose an SASE for the return of your mss. Fiction and poetry are most open to freelancers."

SAGACITY MAGAZINE, By, For and About Mature People of Any Age, 560 Lincoln St., P.O. Box 7187-D, Worcester MA 01605. (508)752-0294. Editor: Marcia S. Wilson. 100% freelance written. Bimonthly magazine covering inter-generational relationships and family and personal experiences. Estab. 1989. **Pays on acceptance.** Publishes ms an average of 6 months after acceptance. Byline given. Rights negotiable. Submit seasonal/holiday material 4-6 months in advance. Simultaneous and previously published submissions OK. Reports in 3 months. Sample copy $3.50; writer's guidelines for #10 SASE.

Nonfiction: Essays, nostalgia, humor, opinion, personal experience and inter-generational stories and photos. No health, medical, travel, erotic, fiction, historical or "you know you're getting old when . . . " Buys 100 mss/year. Send complete ms. Length: 1,000 words maximum. Pays $10-60 plus two copies.

Photos: State availability of photos with submission or send photos with submission. Reviews any size prints, color or b&w. Offers $2.50 minimum/photo; $25 for cover photo. Captions, model releases and identification of subjects required. Buys one-time rights.

Columns/Departments: Short Stuff (original quips, comments, opinions, musings and cartoons), 125 words maximum; Reflections (short, thoughtful essay), 350 words maximum; Generations Together (2-page photo section); Keeping Up (coping with changes in everyday life), 50-350 words; I Remember (nostalgia), 250-500 words. Send complete ms. Pays $5-15.

Poetry: Dorothy W. Halleran, 30 Chestnut St., Peabody MA 01960. Free verse, light verse, traditional, sonnets. No erotic, spiritual, religious, no "you're getting old because . . . " or "signs of aging." Buys 50-60 poems/year. Submit maximum 3 poems. Length: 30 lines maximum. Pays $5-10.

Fillers: Facts, short humor (original comments on the passing scene, opinions, original and panel cartoons). Buys 50-60/year. Length: 125 words maximum. Pays $5.

Fillers: "Have a personal connection to your story; tie the past to the present. Use an inter-generational approach when possible. Thoughtful opinion on issues of today, values, relationships, families. Keep a positive attitude. Enclose photos whenever possible. A touch of humor always catches our eye."

Health and Fitness

MASSAGE MAGAZINE, Keeping Those Who Touch—In Touch, Noah Publishing Co., P.O. Box 1500, Davis CA 95617. (916)757-6033. Editor: Robert Calvert. Managing Editor: Melissa Mower. 80% freelance written. Prefers to work with published/established writers, and works with a small number of new/unpublished writers each year. A bimonthly magazine on massage-bodywork and related healing arts. Circ. 35,000. Pays 30 days after publication. Publishes ms an average of 6 months after acceptance. Byline given. Buys first North American rights. Previously published submissions OK. Query for electronic submissions. Reports in 1 month on queries; 2 months on mss. Sample copy $5. Free writer's guidelines.

Nonfiction: Book excerpts, essays, general interest, historical/nostalgic, how-to, humor, inspirational, interview/profile, new product, photo feature, technical and travel. Buys 6-8 mss/year. Query. Length: 600-2,000 words. Pays $50-100 for assigned articles; $25-50 for unsolicited articles. Sometimes pays expenses of writers on assignment.

Photos: Send photos with submission. Offers $5-15/photo. Identification of subjects required. Buys one-time rights.

Columns/Departments: In Sports (massage/bodywork and sports); In Class (how-to technical pieces on aspects of the profession); Touching Tales (foreign travel experience with massage); Table Talk (bits of news). Query. Length: 800-1,200 words. Pays $25-50.

Fillers: Anecdotes, facts, newsbreaks and short humor. Buys 5/year. Length: 100 words. Pays $25 maximum.

Tips: "For first articles accepted, we don't pay much, but as a writer establishes with us, we pay more. Wholesome stories with facts, interviews, and industry insights are welcomed. We're leaning away from a strong emphasis on the touch professions to more consumer touch-related materials."

Hobby and Craft

THE AUTOGRAPH COLLECTOR'S MAGAZINE, P.O. Box 55328, Stockton CA 95205. (209)942-2131. Editor: Joe Kraus. 90% freelance written. 10 times/year magazine covering the hobby of autograph collecting. "The ages of our readers range from 8-100, with all occupations represented." Estab. 1986. Circ. 5,000. Pays on publication. Publishes ms an average of 4 months after acceptance. Byline given. Buys first North American serial rights. Submit seasonal/holiday material 6 months in advance. Simultaneous and previously published submissions OK. Reports in 2 weeks on queries; 1 month on mss. Sample copy $3; free writer's guidelines.

Nonfiction: Book excerpts, essays, expose, historical/nostalgic, how-to, humor, inspirational, interview/profile, new product, opinion, personal experience, photo feature, religious and travel (all on areas of autograph collecting). "No general stories on autograph collecting." Buys 100 mss/year. Query with or without published clips, or send complete ms. Length: 100-2,000 words. Pays $5-100. Pays expenses of writers on assignment.

Photos: Send photos with submission. Offers $10-20/photo. Captions and identification of subjects required. Buys one-time rights.

Columns/Departments: Just for Kids (written by young people age 16 or below on any area of autograph collecting), 1,000 words maximum; Footnotes in History (interesting historical story with autograph involvement), 1,000 words maximum. Buys 20 mss/year. Query or send complete ms. Pays $15-50.

Tips: "We love freelancers and read all material sent in for review. All stories must involve autographs. Everything is open to freelancers. Highly sought are interviews with celebrities and dealers/collectors. Also looking for stories on museums with autographs."

COLLECTOR'S NEWS & THE ANTIQUE REPORTER, 506 2nd St., P.O. Box 156, Grundy Center IA 50638. (319)824-5456. FAX: (319)824-3414. Editor: Linda Kruger. 20% freelance written. Monthly tabloid covering antiques, collectibles and nostalgic memorabilia. Estab. 1960. Circ. 15,000. Byline given. Pays on publication. Publishes ms an average of 1 year after acceptance. Buys first rights and makes work-for-hire assignments. Submit seasonal/holiday material 3 months in advance. Reports in 2 weeks on queries; 6 weeks on mss. Sample copy for $2 and 9×12 SAE; free writer's guidelines.

Nonfiction: General interest, historical/nostalgic, how-to (display, care for, restore, appraise, locate, add to, etc.); interview/profile, technical and travel (shows, seminars, conventions, flea markets, places to visit, etc.); all antique collector and collection related. Special issues include Jan. and June show/flea market issues, and usual seasonal emphases. Buys 100 mss/year. Query with sample of writing. Length: 1,200-1,600 words. Pays 75¢/column inch; $1/column inch for color features.

Photos: Reviews b&w prints and 35mm color slides. Payment for photos included in ms package. Captions required. Buys first rights.

Tips: "Articles most open to freelancers are on celebrity collectors; collectors with unique and/or extensive collections; music, transportation and advertising collectibles; bottles, glass, china and silver; primitives, furniture, toys, political collectibles and movie memorabilia."

JUST ABOUT HORSES, Breyer/Reeves International, Inc., 34 Owens Dr., Wayne NJ 07470. (201)956-9555. Editor: Steven K. Ryan. 98% freelance written. 5 times/year magazine covering model horse collecting. "Our audience is predominantly female 8-16 and over 30. Our magazine deals with model horses semi-exclusively. We consider real horse material if related to models." Estab. 1972. Circ. 9,000. Pays on publication. Publishes ms an average of 3 months after acceptance. Byline given. Buys first North American serial rights. Submit seasonal/holiday material 6 months in advance. Simultaneous submissions OK. Query for electronic submissions. Sample copy for 6×9 SAE and 2 first class stamps.

Nonfiction: How-to, humor, interview/profile and photo feature. "Please, no talking horses or stories about model horses that come alive in the middle of the night and cavort while everyone is sleeping." Buys 25 mss/year. Send complete ms. Length: 2,000 words maximum. Pays $25 maximum. Pays in copies for poetry and fillers.

Photos: Send photos with submission. Reviews contact sheets, transparencies and prints. Offers no additional payment for photos accepted with ms. Captions, model releases and identification of subjects required.

Columns/Departments: How To (tips on model customizing, tackmaking and accessories, must be illustrated); Shelfspace (collecting tips, model restoration, display ideas, judging age and value of a model); Newcomer's Corner (more basic than How To). Buys 15 mss/year. Send complete ms. Length: 500-1,500 words. Pays $25 maximum.

Fiction: Adventure, experimental, humorous and mystery. "No stories about models that come to life, talk and go to dinner parties." Buys 5 mss/year. Send complete ms. Length: 500 words maximum. Pays $25 maximum.

Poetry: Avant-garde, haiku, light verse and traditional. "OK, if a model horse comes to life in a poem, fine. But be unusual." Accepts 5 poems/year. Submit maximum of 5 poems at one time. Line length: 25 maximum. Pays in copies.

Fillers: Anecdotes, facts, newsbreaks and short humor. Length: 25 words maximum. Pays in copies.

Tips: "How-to material should be clear and well-illustrated. Do not condescend. All areas are open. We cannot pay a lot, but we are certainly grateful. Manuscripts are not returned unless accompanied by SASE."

MANUSCRIPTS, The Manuscript Society, Department of History, University of South Carolina, Columbia SC 29208. (803)777-6525. Editor: David R. Chesnutt. 10% freelance written. Quarterly magazine for collectors of autographs and manuscripts. Circ. 1,400. **Pays on acceptance.** Publishes ms an average of 1 year after acceptance. Byline given. Buys all rights. Query for electronic submissions. Reports in 2 weeks on queries; 1 month on mss. Sample for 8×10 SAE and 5 first class stamps.

Nonfiction: Historical, personal experience and photo feature. Buys 4-6 mss/year. Query. Length: 1,500-3,000 words. Pays $50-250 for unsolicited articles.

Photos: State availability of photos with submission. Reviews contact sheets and prints. Pays $15-30/photo. Captions and identification of subjects required. Buys one-time rights.

Tips: "The Society is a mix of autograph collectors, dealers and scholars who are interested in manuscripts. Good illustrations of manuscript material are essential. Unusual documents are most often the basis of articles. Articles about significant collections of documents (or unusual collections) would be welcomed. Please query first."

THE NEW YORK ANTIQUE ALMANAC, The New York Eye Publishing Co. Inc., Box 335, Lawrence NY 11559. (516)371-3300. Editor-in-Chief: Carol Nadel. Tabloid published 10 times/year. Emphasizes antiques, art, investments and nostalgia. 30% freelance written. Circ. 59,000. Pays on publication. Byline given. Buys all rights. Phone queries OK. Submit seasonal/holiday material "whenever available." Previously published submissions OK but must advise. Reports in 6 weeks. Publishes ms an average of 6 months after acceptance. Free sample copy.

Nonfiction: Expose (fraudulent practices); historical (museums, exhibitions, folklore, background of events); how-to (clean, restore, travel, shop, invest); humor (jokes, cartoons, satire); informational; inspirational (essays); interviews (authors, shopkeepers, show managers, appraisers); nostalgia ("The Good Old Days" remembered in various ways); personal experience (anything dealing with antiques, art, investments, nostalgia); opinion; photo feature (antique shows, art shows, fairs, crafts markets, restoration); profile; technical (repairing, purchasing, restoring); travel (shopping guides and tips); and investment (economics, and financial reviews). Buys 9 mss/issue. Query or submit complete ms. Length: 3,000 words maximum. Pays $15-75. "Expenses for accompanying photos will be reimbursed."

Photos: "Occasionally we have photo essays (auctions, shows, street fairs, human interest) and pay $5/photo with caption."

Fillers: Personal experiences, commentaries, anecdotes. "Limited only by author's imagination." Buys 45 mss/year. Pays $5-15.

Tips: "Articles on shows or antique coverage accompanied by photos are definitely preferred."

P-E HOBBYISTS HANDBOOK, Gernsback Publications, 500-B Bi-County Blvd., Farmingdale NY 11735. (516)293-3000. Managing Editor: Carol Laron. 10% freelance written. Annual magazine covering hobby and consumer electronics. Estab. 1989. Circ. 126. **Pays on acceptance.** Byline given. Buys all rights. Query for electronic submissions. Reports in 1 month. Free sample copy and writer's guidelines.

Nonfiction: How-to (build, design and/or use electronics projects or products), new product and technical. Buys 5-6 mss/year. Send complete ms. Length: 1,000-5,000 words. Pays $150-400. Sometimes pays expenses of writers on assignment.

Photos: Send photos with submission. Offers no additional payment for photos accepted with ms. Model releases and identification of subjects required. Buys all rights.

Tips: "Submit complete ms with clear drawings and/or photos. Telephone queries suggested if writer was unsure of our interest in subject area. All areas are open. Request and carefully read our writer's guidelines."

POPULAR ELECTRONICS, Gernsback Publications, 500-B Bi-County Blvd., Farmingdale NY 11735. (516)293-3000. Managing Editor: Carol Laron. 90% freelance written. Monthly magazine covering hobby and consumer electronics. Estab. 1988. Circ. 78,700. **Pays on acceptance.** Publishes ms an average of 6 months after acceptance. Byline given. Buys all rights. Query for electronic submissions. Reports in 1 month. Free sample copy and writer's guidelines.

Nonfiction: How-to (build, design and/or use electronics projects or products), new product and technical. Buys 100 mss/year. Send complete ms. Length: 1,000-10,000 words. Pays $150-400. Sometimes pays expenses of writers on assignment.

Photos: Send photos with submission. Offers no additional payment for photos accepted with ms. Model releases and identification of subjects required. Buys all rights.

Tips: "Submit complete ms with clear drawings and/or photos. Telephone queries suggested if writer was unsure of our interest in subject area. All areas are open. Request and carefully read our writer's guidelines."

RADIO ELECTRONICS, Gernsback Publications, 500-B Bi-County Blvd., Farmingdale NY 11735. (516)293-3000. Editor: Brian D. Fenton. 75% freelance written. Monthly magazine covering electronics technology. Estab. 1948. Circ. 210,779. **Pays on acceptance.** Publishes ms an average of 4 months after acceptance. Byline given. Buys all rights. Submit seasonal/holiday material 6 months in advance. Query for electronic submissions. Reports in 2 months on queries; 4 months on mss. Free sample copy and writer's guidelines.

Nonfiction: How-to (electronics project construction), humor (cartoons), new product and technical. Buys 150-200 mss/year. Send complete ms. Length: 1,000-10,000 words. Pays $100-800.
Photos: Send photos with submission. Offers no additional payment for photos accepted with ms. Captions, model releases and identification of subjects required. Buys all rights.
Tips: "Writers have the best chance selling us construction articles. Send for our writer's guidelines."

R-E EXPERIMENTERS HANDBOOK, Gernsback Publications, 500-B Bi-County Blvd., Farmingdale NY 11735. (516)293-3000. Editor: Brian D. Fenton. 100% freelance written. Annual magazine covering hobby electronics. Estab. 1985. Circ. 150,000. Byline given. Buys all rights. Submit seasonal/holiday material 6 months in advance. Simultaneous submissions OK. Query for electronic submissions. Reports in 2 months. Free sample copy and writer's guidelines.
Nonfiction: How-to (project construction), humor (cartoons), new product and technical. Buys 15-20 mss/year. Send complete ms. Length: 1,000-10,000 words. Pays $100-800.
Photos: Send photos with submission. Offers no additional payment for photos accepted with ms. Captions, model releases and identification of subjects required. Buys all rights.
Tips: "Writers have the best chance selling us construction articles. Send for our writer's guidelines."

Home and Garden

HOME SOURCE, New Venture Publishing, Inc., 2285 University Dr., Boise ID 83702. (208)338-1561. FAX: (208)338-1563. Editor: Mark J. Russell. 75% freelance written. *"The Home Source* is a biannual magazine in several markets with national and regional real estate information for prospective home buyers and sellers. It has a feature/information format to acquaint readers with the ins and outs of real estate and the buying and selling of homes or property." Circ. 200,000. **Pays on acceptance.** Publishes ms an average of 4 months after acceptance. Byline given for major articles. Offers 25% kill fee. Buys first rights, one-time rights or second serial (reprint) rights. Submit seasonal/tax-related material 6 months in advance. Reports in 3 weeks on queries; 2 months on mss. Free sample copy; writer's guidelines for #10 SASE.
Nonfiction: Information on real estate topics; how-to (getting a home ready for sale, selling your home while buying another, tax tips for home owners, finding a good agent). Buys 80-100 mss/year. Query with outlines or complete ms. Length: 800-1,800 words. Pays $300-800.
Photos: State availability of photos with submission.
Tips: "Our readers are either contemplating or in the process of selling or buying a home. They want helpful and practical ideas on getting the best price for their present home, finding a good deal on a new home and how to find the right real estate agent. They also want the latest information available on home financing, new construction, trends in interior design and real estate investments."

Juvenile

BEAR ESSENTIAL NEWS FOR KIDS, Garrett Communications, Inc. P.O. Box 26908, Tempe AZ 85285. (602)345-7323. Executive Editor: Robert Henschen. Senior Editor: Sharon Gee Wong. 25% freelance written. Monthly tabloid covering kids and their interests. "Our readers are aged 6-13. Writers need to think and write on their level." Estab. 1979. Circ. 345,000. Pays on publication. Publishes ms an average of 2 months after acceptance. Byline given. Offers 50% kill fee. Buys all rights. Previously published submissions sometimes OK. Query for electronic submissions. Reports in 2 months. Sample copy $1 with 9×12 SAE and 3 first class stamps. Writer's guidelines for #10 SASE.
Nonfiction: Book excerpts, historical, interview/profile, new product, travel, current events and science. Upcoming issues will feature sports, young careers, computers, wildlife and ecology. Buys 50 mss/year. Query. Length: 350-750 words and variable. Pays $35-75. Sometimes pays expenses of writers on assignment.
Photos: State availability of photos with submission. Reviews contact sheets. Pays $10-35/photo. Captions, model releases and identification of subjects required. Buys all rights.
Columns/Departments: Science; Math; Reading. Current, upbeat, innovative and visual while not preachy. Buys 20 mss/year. Query with published clips. Length: 350-450 words. Pays $35-45.
Fiction and Poetry: Works by juveniles only. Query.
Fillers: Newsbreaks. Buys 10/year. Length: 50-150 words. Pays $5-15.
Tips: "Have a new slant on a current topic; write on a 4th grade wavelength; provide good copy accompanied by visuals. Freelancers have their best chance breaking in with features and insightful columns that are so much fun to read that the learning happens naturally."

Music

THE OPERA COMPANION, 40 Museum Way, San Francisco CA 94114. (415)626-2741. Editor: James Keolker, Ph.D. 25% freelance written. Magazine published 14 times/year covering "opera in particular, music in general. We provide readers with an in depth analysis of 14 operas per year—the personal, philosophical and political content of each composer and his works." Circ. 8,000. **Pays on acceptance.** Publishes ms an average of 2 months after acceptance. Byline given. Buys first rights. Reports in 1 week on queries; 1 month on mss. Sample copy and writer's guidelines for 9×12 SAE and 3 first class stamps.

Nonfiction: Essay, historical/nostalgic, humor and interview/profile (opera composers, singers, producers and designers). No Master's or Doctoral theses. Buys 10 mss/year. Query with published clips. Length: 500-5,000 words. Pays: $50-350.

Fillers: Anecdotes and short humor. Buys 25/year. Length: 150-500 words. Pays $50-250.

Tips: "Be pointed, pithy in statement, accurate in research. Avoid florid, excessive language. Writers must be musically sensitive, interested in opera as a continuing vocal art. Enthusiasm for the subject is important. Contact us for which operaa/composers we will featuring each year. It is those areas of research, anecdote, analysis and humor we will be filling first."

Personal Computers

AMIGAWORLD, Exploring the Amiga, IDGC/P, 80 Elm St., Peterborough NH 03458. (603)924-9471. FAX: (603)924-9384. Editor: Doug Barney. Managing Editor: Swain Pratt. 90% freelance written. Monthly magazine for users of the Amiga computer from Commodore. "We help people understand the inner workings of the machine so that they can better use and enjoy their computer." Circ. 95,000. Pays on publication. Publishes ms an average of 3 months after acceptance. Byline given. Buys all rights. Query for electronic submissions. Reports in 1 month on queries; 2 months on mss. Writer's guidelines for #10 SASE.

Nonfiction: Linda Barrett, articles editor. General interest, how-to, humor (rarely), tutuorials and technical – all related to programming or using the Amiga computer. "No program listings over 20 lines or articles on 'how I got started' or 'why the Amiga computer is so great.'" Buys 50 mss/year. Query with or without published clips, or send complete ms. Length: 2,000-4,000 words. Pays $300-1,500 for assigned articles; $200-800 for unsolicited articles. Sometimes pays expenses of writers on assignment.

Photos: Send photos with submission. Reviews negatives, transparencies and prints. Offers no additional payment for photos accepted with ms. Captions required. Buys all rights.

Columns/Departments: Barbara Gefvert, reviews editor. Reviews (hardware and software). "We assign all reviews and generally do not accept unsolicited review mss. Send one-page biography, areas of expertise, system configuration, writing sample, and list of products you would most like to review. We will contact you." Buys 40 mss/year. Length: 800-1,800 words. Pays $150-350. Reviewer's guidelines for #10 SASE.

Tips: "The author should have a firm knowledge of the Amiga computer and have access to one. Most of our articles are about the computer itself, unique applications and applications tutuorials. If you have an idea for an article, give us a call first. We are more than happy to discuss on the phone and even suggest topics."

ELECTRONIC COMPOSITION AND IMAGING, Youngblood Publishing, 505 Consumers Rd., Willowdale, Ontario M2J 4V8 Canada. (416)492-5777. FAX: (416)492-7595. Editor: Chris Dickman. 70% freelance written. Bimonthly magazine on desktop publishing, computer graphics, video and animation. Estab. 1955. Circ. 25,000. Pays on publication. Publishes ms an average of 2 months after acceptance. Byline given. Offers $100 kill fee. Buys first North American serial rights. Query for electronic submissions. Reports in 1 week on queries; 2 weeks on mss. Free sample copy and writer's guidelines.

Nonfiction: How-to (computers and graphics or publishing), interview/profile, new product, technical. "No humor." Buys 60 mss/year. Query with published clips. Length: 1,000-3,000 words. Pays $200-600.Sometimes pays expenses of writers on assignment.

Photos: State availability of photos with submission. Reviews negatives, 4×5 transparencies and 4×5 prints. Offers $10-50 per photo. Captions required. Buys one-time rights.

Tips: "Call to discuss article ideas, fax query, or mail query. Writers must know their areas of electronic composition and imaging in depth."

Photography

NEW MEXICO PHOTOGRAPHER, Eastern New Mexico University, Box 2582, Portales NM 88130. (505)562-2253. Editor: Wendel Sloan. 50% freelance written. Semiannual magazine of Southwest photography. "We are interested in articles and b&w photos that deal with the Southwest, and/or New Mexico photographers and subjects." Estab. 1989. Circ. 2,000. Pays on publication. Publishes ms an average of 3 months after acceptance. Byline given. Buys first rights. Submit seasonal/holiday material 3 months in advance. Reports in 3 months. Sample copy $5; writer's guidelines for #10 SASE.

Nonfiction: Interview/profile and photo feature. "Nothing technical, and no how-to shoot photographs." Buys 4 mss/year. Send complete ms. Length: 250-500 words. Pays $25-50. Pays with contributor copies "only if requested."

Photos: Send photos with submissions. Reviews any size prints. Offers no additional payment for photos accepted with ms. Captions, model releases and identification of subjects required. Buys one-time rights.
Tips: "We publish b&w photography only. We would like to see articles that deal with Southwestern/New Mexico photographers who are making statements on important social issues, accompanied by candid shots of the photographer and examples of his work. Freelancers have the best chance selling us features. Keep them short (250-500 words) and non-technical."

Politics and World Affairs

CAIRO TODAY, U.S. address: P.O. Box 186, Austin TX 78767. (512)250-3988. Egypt address: 24 Syria Street, Mohandiseen, Cairo, Egypt. (00-202)349-0986. FAX: (00-202)360-1276. Publisher: William W. Harrison. Senior Editor: Mohamed Ragheb. 80% freelance written. Monthly. Estab. 1979. Circ. 25,000. Buys first rights. Pays on publication. Enclose IRCs with submission.
Nonfiction: Culture, politics, business, history, profiles, etc.—all about Egypt and expatriate Egyptians. Features length: 1,000-4,000 words. Reviews length: 750 words. "Reviews of recent books dealing with Egypt, past and present, are welcome."
Photos: State availability of photos for features. Accepts transparencies only. Captions required.
Fiction: "We seldom buy fiction, but will consider anything that has culture shock experienced by a foreigner in Egypt or an Egyptian abroad, as a theme, whether treated in a serious or comic way. Nothing patronizing or racist and no poetry." Length: 4,000 words maximum.

Religious

INNER HORIZONS, A Magazine of Spirituality, Daughters of St. Paul Inc., 50 St. Paul's Ave., Boston MA 02130. (617)522-8911. Editor: Sr. Mary Paula Kolar, FSP. 60% freelance written. Quarterly religious magazine on spiritual life. "*Inner Horizons* is a Catholic magazine of spirituality, geared to bishops, priests and religious lay persons. It reflects Catholic faith and belief." Estab. 1987. Circ. 2,000. Pays on publication. Publishes ms an average of 6 months after acceptance. Byline given. Rights negotiable. Submit seasonal/holiday material 6 months in advance. Simultaneous and previously published submissions OK. Reports in 3 weeks. Free sample copy and writer's guidelines.
Nonfiction: Book excerpts, essays, general interest, how-to (self-help, inspirational art), inspirational, interview/profile, personal experience, religious, witness and scriptural (vocational, priesthood and sisterhood). Nothing non-religious, no fantasy or fiction. Send complete ms. Length: 500-3,000 words. Pays $25-150. Pays with contributor's copies "at author's choice."
Columns/Departments: Self-help (inspirational), Scriptural, Religious (homo psychology). Length: 800-2,000 words. Pays $25-150.

Regional

CHICAGO LIFE, P.O. Box 11311, Chicago Il 60611. (312)549-1523. Articles Editor: J. Wolff. 100% freelance written. Bimonthly lifestyle magazine for contemporary Chicagoans concerned about issues and events shaping their lives. Estab. 1984. Circ. 60,000. **Pays on acceptance.** Publishes ms an average of 4 months after acceptance. Byline given. Buys first rights, one-time rights or second serial (reprint) rights. Previously published submissions OK. Query for electronic submissions. Reports in 2 weeks on queries; 1 month on mss. Sample copy for 9×12 SAE with 7 first class stamps.
Nonfiction: Book excerpts, expose, how-to, new product, photo feature (travel and fashion) and travel. "No personal reminiscence, nostalgia or fiction." Buys 60 mss/year. Send complete ms. Length: 600-3,000 words. Pays $30 maximum. "We could pay writers with contributor copies or other premiums, if requested." Sometimes pays expenses of writers on assignment.
Photos: Send photos with submission. Reviews contact sheets and transparencies. Pays $30 maximum/photo. Buys one-time rights.
Tips: "Writers have the best chance selling us how-to, travel and finance articles."

LANSING CITY MAGAZINE, Smith, Steele and Smith Inc., Suite 206, 5020 Northwind Dr., East Lansing MI 48823. (517)351-2828. Editor: Laura Smith. Managing Editor: Cathy J. Kirvan. 75% freelance written. Monthly magazine on Lansing area people and events. "We prefer people-oriented articles on contemporary topics." Estab. 1987. Circ. 15,000. Pays on middle of month of publication. Publishes ms an average of 4 months after acceptance. Byline given. Offers 100% kill fee. Buys first rights. Submit seasonal/holiday material 6 months in advance. Reports in 6 weeks. Free sample copy and writer's guidelines.
Nonfiction: General interest, historical/nostalgic (about Lansing only) and interview/profile. Special annual features: wedding/bridal (Jan.) and back to school (Aug.). No opinion, religious or technical articles. Buys 60 mss/year. Query with or without published clips. "We will work with new writers." Length: 500-1,200 words. Pays $50-120.

Photos: State availability of photos with submission. Reviews contact sheets and any size transparencies or prints. Pays $5-15. "We rarely buy photos from writers." Captions, model releases and identification of subjects required. Buys one-time rights.

Columns/Departments: Health (current topic), 600-1,000 words; Helping Hands (community or service organization "pat on the back"), 500-750 words; Backwords (humorous or inspirational, only place for personal stories), 600-800 words. Buys 30 mss/years. Query with published clips. Pays $50-100.

Tips: "We prefer to use local writers. Plan your story 4 to 6 months in advance. Send query letters; do not call! Writers have the best chance selling us feature articles on interesting people."

Sports

SCUBA TIMES, The Active Diver's Magazine, 14110 Perdido Key Dr., Pensacola FL 32507. Publisher/Editor: Fred D. Garth. 80% freelance written. Prefers to work with published/established writers. Bimonthly magazine covering scuba diving. "Our reader is the active, affluent scuba diver looking for a more exciting approach to diving than he could find in the other diving magazines." Cir. 40,000. Pays after publication. Byline given. Buys first world serial rights. Sample copy $3. Writer's guidelines for #10 SASE.

Nonfiction: General interest; how-to; interview/profile ("of 'name' people in the sport, especially if they're currently doing something interesting"); new products (how to more effectively use them); personal experience (good underwater photography); and travel (pertaining to diving). No articles without a specific theme. Buys 40 mss/year. Query first with clips of published work. Will not return material unless accompanied with return postage. Pay varies with author. Base rate is $75/published page (30 column inches). Sometimes pays the expenses of writers on assignment.

Photos: Blair Fischrupp, art director. "Underwater photography must be of the highest quality to catch our interest. We can't be responsible for unsolicited photo submissions." Pays $25-150 for 35mm transparencies; reviews 8 × 10 b&w prints. Captions, model releases and identification of subjects required. Buys first world rights. "Enclose 9 × 12 SASE if you want material returned."

Tips: "Our current contributors are among the top writers in the diving field. A newcomer must have a style that captures the inherent adventure of scuba diving, leaves the reader satisfied at the end of it and makes him want to see something else by this same author soon. Writing for diving magazines has become a sophisticated venture. Writers must be able to compete with the best in order to get published. We only use contributors grounded in underwater photojournalism."

Trade, Technical and Professional Journals

Advertising, Marketing and PR

RETAIL STORE IMAGE, Communication Channels, Inc., 6255 Barfield Rd., Atlanta GA 30328. (404)256-9800. Editor: Katherine Field. Managing Editor: Lorna Gentry. 40% freelance written. Bimonthly trade journal covering imaging in a retail store environment. "Our audience includes decision-making, high-ranking retail executives and professional services people (architects, store planners, store designers, etc.). Writers must be familiar with retail marketing and/or design." Estab. 1990. Circ. 25,000. Pays on paste-up. Publishes ms an average of 2 months after acceptance. Byline given. Buys all rights. Submit seasonal/holiday material 6 months in advance. Simultaneous submissions OK. Query for electronic submissions. Reports in 1 month. Sample copy for 9 × 12 SAE with 6 first class stamps.

Nonfiction: Expose, how-to (imaging case history), interview/profile and opinion. "No articles concerning shoplifting, security systems or one specific retail product company." Buys 30-35 mss/year. Query with published clips. Length: 750-2,000 words. Pays $250-1,500. Sometimes pays expenses of writers on assignment.

Photos: State availability of photos with submission. Reviews 4 × 5 transparencies. Offers no additional payment for photos accepted with ms. Identification of subjects required. Buys one-time rights.

Columns/Departments: Image Management (implementation and management of a store identity program; must be written by someone "in the know"); On the Face of It (exterior store materials and appointments); Last Impressions (opinion column: can be controversial; must be relevant to the retail industry). Buys 15 mss/year. Query with published clips or send complete ms. Length: 750-1,000 words. Pays $250-350.

Tips: "The best approach is to submit article ideas and/or spec manuscripts along with clips and a resume. Those knowledgeable in the retail field who also write well are practically shoo-ins. Writers have the best chance selling us feature articles. The writer must be 'retail-smart.' We are very selective in our choice of writers and weed through regularly. Merely adequate journalists need not apply."

Journalism and Writing

SOUTHEAST WRITER'S VOICE, Julian Associates, 8958 Defiance, La Porte TX 77571. (713)930-8551. Editor: Debbie Jordan. 40% freelance written. Monlthly writer's newsletter. Estab. 1989. Circ. 165. Pays on publication. Publishes ms an average of 2 months after acceptance. Byline given. Buys one-time rights. Submit seasonal/holiday material 2 months in advance. Simultaneous and previously published submissions OK. Query for electronic submissions. Reports in 2 weeks. Sample copy for $1.50; writer's guidelines for #10 SASE.

Nonfiction: Essays, how-to, humor and technical (all about writing or surviving as a writer). Buys up to 12 mss/year. Send complete ms. Length: 200-600 words. Pays $1-5.

Columns/Departments: "We currently have 3 regular columnists, but turnover does occur. We would consider a ms sample from a writer who wants to contribute on a regular basis." Buys 36 mss/year, all currently assigned. Send complete ms. Length: 300-600 words. Pays $1-5.

Tips: "We want short, pithy pieces on the art and business of writing and the writer as human being. The tone is friendly, supportive, upbeat and personal — definitely positive. We welcome articles taking a humorous approach to the problems of being a writer. We also want reviews of books on writing."

Scriptwriting

COMPASS FILMS, 921 Jackson Dr., Cleveland WI 53015. Executive Producer: Robert Whittaker. Produces material for educational, industrial and general adult audiences. Specializes in Marine films, stop motion and special effects with a budget; and national/worldwide filming in difficult locations. 60% freelance written. Works with 3 writers/year. Buys 2-4 scripts/year. 100% of scripts are unagented submissions. Buys all rights. Query with samples or submit resume. Reports in 6 weeks.

Needs: Scripts for 5- to 30-minute business films and general documentaries. "We would like to review writers to develop existing film treatments and ideas with strong dialogue." Also needs ghost writers, editors and researchers. Produces 16mm and 35mm films and videotape products. Payment negotiable, depending on experience. Pays expenses of writers on assignment.

Tips: "Writer/photographers receive higher consideration because we could also use them as still photographers on location and they could double-up as rewrite people. Experience in videotape editing supervision an asset. We are producting more high fashion-tech industrial video."

Syndicates

DAVE GOODWIN & ASSOCIATES, Drawer 54-6661, Surfside FL 33154. FAX: (305)531-5490. Editor: Dave Goodwin. 70% written by writers on contract; 10% freelance written by writers on a one-time basis. Buys 25 features/year from freelancers. Rights purchased vary with author and material. Will handle copyrighted material. Query for electronic submissions. Query or submit complete ms. Reports in 3 weeks.

Nonfiction: "Money-saving information for consumers: how to save on home expenses; auto, medical, drug, insurance, boat, business items, etc." Buys article series on brief, practical, down-to-earth items for consumer use or knowledge. Rarely buys single features. Currently handling Insurance for Consumers. Length: 300-5,000 words. Pays 50% on publication. Submit 2-3 columns.

Glossary

Key to symbols and abbreviations is on page 5.

Advance. A sum of money that a publisher pays a writer prior to the publication of a book. It is usually paid in installments, such as one-half on signing the contract; one half on delivery of a complete and satisfactory manuscript. The advance is paid against the royalty money that will be earned by the book.

Advertorial. Advertising presented in such a way as to resemble editorial material. Information may be the same as that contained in an editorial feature, but it is paid for or supplied by an advertiser and the word "advertisement" appears at the top of the page.

All rights. See Rights and the Writer in the Business of Writing article.

Anthology. A collection of selected writings by various authors or a gathering of works by one author.

Assignment. Editor asks a writer to do a specific article for a certain price to be paid upon completion.

Auction. Publishers sometimes bid for the acquisition of a book manuscript that has excellent sales prospects. The bids are for the amount of the author's advance, guaranteed dollar amounts, advertising and promotional expenses, royalty percentage, etc.

B&W. Abbreviation for black and white photographs.

Backlist. A publisher's list of its books that were not published during the current season, but which are still in print.

Belles lettres. A term used to describe fine or literary writing—writing more to entertain than to inform or instruct.

Bimonthly. Every two months. See also *semimonthly*.

Bionote. A sentence or brief paragraph about the writer. Also called a "bio," it can appear at the bottom of the first or last page of a writer's article or short story or on a contributor's page.

Biweekly. Every two weeks.

Boilerplate. A standardized contract. When an editor says "our standard contract," he means the boilerplate with no changes. Writers should be aware that most authors and/ or agents make many changes on the boilerplate.

Book auction. Selling the rights (i.e. paperback, movie, etc.) of a hardback book to the highest bidder. A publisher or agent may initiate the auction.

Book packager. Draws all elements of a book together, from the initial concept to writing and marketing strategies, then sells the book package to a book publisher and/or movie producer. Also known as book producer or book developer.

Business size envelope. Also known as a #10 envelope, it is the standard size used in sending business correspondence.

Byline. Name of the author appearing with the published piece.

Caption. Originally a title or headline over a picture, but now a description of the subject matter of a photograph; includes names of people where appropriate. Also called cut-line.

Category fiction. A term used to include all various labels attached to types of fiction. See also *genre*.

Chapbook. A small booklet, usually paperback, of poetry, ballads or tales.

Clean copy. A manuscript free of errors, cross-outs, wrinkles or smudges.

Clippings. News items of possible interest to trade magazine editors.

Clips. Samples, usually from newspapers or magazines, of your *published* work.

Coffee table book. An oversize book, heavily illustrated, suitable for display on a coffee table.

Column inch. All the type contained in one inch of a typeset column.

Commercial novels. Novels designed to appeal to a broad audience. These are often broken down into categories such as western, mystery and romance. See also *genre*.

Commissioned work. See *assignment*.

Compatible. The condition which allows one type of computer/word processor to share information or communicate with another type of machine.

Concept. A statement that summarizes a screenplay or teleplay—before the outline or treatment is written.

Contributor's copies. Copies of the issues of magazines sent to the author in which the author's work appears.

Cooperative publishing. See *co-publishing*.

Co-publishing. An arrangement in which author and publisher share the publication costs and profits of a book. Also known as *cooperative publishing*. See also *subsidy publisher*.

Copyediting. Editing a manuscript for grammar, punctuation and printing style, not subject content.

Copyright. A means to protect an author's work. See Copyrighting Your Writing in the Business of Writing section.

Cover letter. A brief letter, accompanying a complete manuscript, especially useful if responding to an editor's request for a manuscript. A cover letter may also accompany a book proposal. (A cover letter is *not* a query letter; see Approaching Markets in the Business of Writing section.

Cutline. See *caption*.

Derivative works. A work that has been translated, adapted, abridged, condensed, annotated or otherwise produced by altering a previously created work. Before producing a derivative work, it is necessary to secure the written permission of the author or copyright owner of the original piece.

Desk-top publishing. A publishing system designed for a personal computer. The system is capable of typesetting, some illustration, layout, design and printing—so that the final piece can be distributed and/or sold.

Disk. A round, flat magnetic plate on which computer data may be stored.

Docudrama. A fictional film rendition of recent newsmaking events and people.

Dot-matrix. Printed type where individual characters are composed of a matrix or pattern of tiny dots. Near letter quality (see *NLQ*) dot-matrix submissions are generally acceptable to editors.

Electronic submission. A submission made by modem or computer disk.

El-hi. Elementary to high school.

Epigram. A short, witty sometimes paradoxical saying.

Erotica. Fiction or art that is sexually-oriented.

ESL. Abbreviation for English as a second language.

Fair use. A provision of the copyright law that says short passages from copyrighted material may be used without infringing on the owner's rights.

Fanzine. A noncommercial, small circulation magazine dealing with fantasy or science fiction literature and art.

FAX. A communication system used to transmit documents over telephone lines.

Feature. An article giving the reader information of human interest rather than news. Also used by magazines to indicate a lead article or distinctive department.

Filler. A short item used by an editor to "fill" out a newspaper column or magazine page.

It could be a timeless news item, a joke, an anecdote, some light verse or short humor, puzzle, etc.

First chapter novel. A book for children that is roughly the size of an adult novel's first chapter.

First North American serial rights. See Rights and the Writer in the Business of Writing article.

Formula story. Familiar theme treated in a predictable plot structure—such as boy meets girl, boy loses girl, boy gets girl.

Galleys. The first typeset version of a manuscript that has not yet been divided into pages.

Genre. Refers either to a general classification of writing, such as the novel or the poem, or to the categories within those classifications, such as the problem novel or the sonnet. Genre fiction describes commercial novels, such as mysteries, romances and science fiction. (Also called category fiction.)

Ghostwriter. A writer who puts into literary form an article, speech, story or book based on another person's ideas or knowledge.

Glossy. A black and white photograph with a shiny surface as opposed to one with a non-shiny matte finish.

Gothic novel. A fiction category or genre in which the central character is usually a beautiful young girl, the setting an old mansion or castle, and there is a handsome hero and a real menace, either natural or supernatural.

Graphic novel. A term to describe an adaptation of a novel in graphic form, long comic strip or heavily illustrated story, of 40 pages or more, produced in paperback form.

Hard copy. The printed copy of a computer's output.

Hardware. All the mechanically-integrated components of a computer that are not software. Circuit boards, transistors and the machines that are the actual computer are the hardware.

Honorarium. Token payment—small amount of money, or a byline and copies of the publication.

Illustrations. May be photographs, old engravings, artwork. Usually paid for separately from the manuscript. See also *package sale*.

Imprint. Name applied to a publisher's specific line or lines of books (e.g., Delacorte Press is an imprint of Dell Publishing).

Interactive fiction. Works of fiction in book or computer software format in which the reader determines the path the story will take. The reader chooses from several alternatives at the end of a "chapter," and thus determines the structure of the story. Interactive fiction features multiple plots and endings.

Invasion of privacy. Writing about persons (even though truthfully) without their consent.

Kill fee. Fee for a complete article that was assigned but which was subsequently cancelled.

Letter-quality submission. Computer printout that looks like a typewritten manuscript.

Libel. A false accusation or any published statement or presentation that tends to expose another to public contempt, ridicule, etc. Defenses are truth; fair comment on a matter of public interest; and privileged communication—such as a report of legal proceedings or client's communication to a lawyer.

Little magazine. Publications of limited circulation, usually on literary or political subject matter.

LORT. An acronym for League of Resident Theatres. Letters from A to D follow LORT and designate the size of the theater.

Mainstream fiction. Fiction that transcends popular novel categories such as mystery, romance and science fiction. Using conventional methods, this kind of fiction tells stories about people and their conflicts with greater depth of characterization, background, etc., than the more narrowly focused genre novels.

Mass market. Nonspecialized books of wide appeal directed toward an extremely large audience.

Microcomputer. A small computer system capable of performing various specific tasks with data it receives. Personal computers are microcomputers.

Midlist. Those titles on a publisher's list that are not expected to be big sellers, but are expected to have limited sales. Midlist books are mainstream, not literary, scholarly or genre, and are usually written by new or unknown writers.

Model release. A paper signed by the subject of a photograph (or the subject's guardian, if a juvenile) giving the photographer permission to use the photograph, editorially or for advertising purposes or for some specific purpose as stated.

Modem. A small electrical box that plugs into the serial card of a computer, used to transmit data from one computer to another, usually via telephone lines.

Monograph. Thoroughly detailed and documented scholarly study concerning a singular subject.

MOW. Movie of the week.

Multiple submissions. Sending more than one poem, gag or greeting card idea at the same time. This term is often used synonymously with simultaneous submission.

Mystery Writers of America. Room 600, 236 W. 27 St., New York NY 10001. (212)255-7005. Organization open to professional writers in mystery and other fields, also to students and fans of mystery. The purpose is to enhance the prestige of mystery story and fact crime writing. Also sponsors workshops.

National Writers Union. 13 Astor Place, New York NY 10003. (212)254-0279. Organization for better treatment of freelance writers by publishers. Also negotiates union contracts with publishers, grievance procedures, health insurance and conferences.

Net receipts. A royalty payment based on the amount of money a book publisher receives on the sale of a book after booksellers' discounts, special sales discounts and returned copies.

New Age. A generic term for works linked by a common interest in metaphysical, spiritual, holistic and other alternative approaches to living. It embraces astrology, psychic phenomena, spiritual healing, UFOs, mysticism — anything that deals with reality beyond everyday material perception.

Newsbreak. A brief, late-breaking news story added to the front page of a newspaper at press time or a magazine news item of importance to readers.

NLQ. Near letter-quality print required by some editors for computer printout submissions. See also *dot-matrix*.

Novelette. A short novel, or a long short story; 7,000 to 15,000 words approximately. Also known as a novella.

Novelization. A novel created from the script of a popular movie, usually called movie "tie-ins" and published in paperback.

Offprint. Copies of an author's article taken "out of issue" before a magazine is bound and given to the author in lieu of monetary payment. An offprint could be used by the writer as a published writing sample.

On spec. An editor expresses an interest in a proposed article idea and agrees to consider the finished piece for publication "on speculation." The editor is under no obligation to buy the finished manuscript.

One-time rights. See Rights and the Writer in the Business of Writing article.

Outline. A summary of a book's contents in five to 15 double-spaced pages; often in the form of chapter headings with a descriptive sentence or two under each one to show the scope of the book. A screenplay's or teleplay's outline is a scene-by-scene narrative description of the story (10-15 pages for a ½-hour teleplay; 15-25 pages for a 1-hour teleplay; 25-40 pages for a 90-minute teleplay; 40-60 pages for a 2-hour feature film or teleplay).

Over-the-transom. Unsolicited material submitted by a freelance writer.

Package sale. The editor buys manuscript and photos as a "package" and pays for them with one check.

Page rate. Some magazines pay for material at a fixed rate per published page, rather than per word.

Payment on acceptance. The editor sends you a check for your article, story or poem as soon as he reads it and decides to publish it.

Payment on publication. The editor doesn't send you a check for your material until it is published.

Pen name. The use of a name other than your legal name on articles, stories or books when you wish to remain anonymous. Simply notify your post office and bank that you are using the name so that you'll receive mail and/or checks in that name. Also called a pseudonym.

Photo feature. Feature in which the emphasis is on the photographs rather than on accompanying written material.

Photocopied submissions. Submitting *photocopies* of an original manuscript is acceptable to the majority of editors instead of the author sending the original manuscript. Do not assume that an editor who accepts photocopies will also accept multiple or simultaneous submissions.

Plagiarism. Passing off as one's own the expression of ideas and words of another writer.

Potboiler. Refers to writing projects a freelance writer does to "keep the pot boiling" while working on major articles—quick projects to bring in money with little time or effort. These may be fillers such as anecdotes or how-to tips, but could be short articles or stories.

Proofreading. Close reading and correction of a manuscript's typographical errors.

Prospectus. A preliminary written description of a book or article, usually one page in length.

Pseudonym. See *pen name*.

Public domain. Material that was either never copyrighted or whose copyright term has expired.

Publication not copyrighted. Publication of an author's work in such a publication places it in the public domain and it cannot subsequently be copyrighted. See Copyrighting Your Writing in the Business of Writing article.

Query. A letter to an editor intended to raise interest in an article you propose to write.

Rebus. Stories, quips, puzzles, etc., in juvenile magazines that convey words or syllables with pictures, objects or symbols whose names resemble the sounds of intended words.

Realia. Activities that relate classroom study to real life.

Release. A statement that your idea is original, has never been sold to anyone else and that you are selling the negotiated rights to the idea upon payment.

Remainders. Copies of a book that are slow to sell and can be purchased from the publisher at a reduced price. Depending on the author's book contract, a reduced royalty or no royalty is paid on remainder books.

Reporting time. The time it takes for an editor to report to the author on his/her query or manuscript.

Reprint rights. See Rights and the Writer in the Business of Writing article.

Round-up article. Comments from, or interviews with, a number of celebrities or experts on a single theme.

Royalties, standard hardcover book. 10% of the retail price on the first 5,000 copies sold; 12½% on the next 5,000; 15% thereafter.

Royalties, standard mass paperback book. 4 to 8% of the retail price on the first 150,000 copies sold.

Royalties, trade paperback book. No less than 6% of list price on the first 20,000 copies; 7½% thereafter.

Scanning. A process through which letter quality printed text (see *NLQ*) or artwork is read by a computer scanner and converted into workable data.

Science Fiction Writers of America, SFWA. Box 4236, West Columbia SC 29171. An organization of professional writers, editors, agents, artists and others in the science fiction and fantasy field.

Screenplay. Script for a film intended to be shown in theaters.

Self-publishing. In this arrangement, the author keeps all income derived from the book, but he pays for its manufacturing, production and marketing.

Semimonthly. Twice per month.

Semiweekly. Twice per week.

Serial. Published periodically, such as a newspaper or magazine.

Sidebar. A feature presented as a companion to a straight news report (or main magazine article) giving sidelights on human-interest aspects or sometimes elucidating just one aspect of the story.

Simultaneous submissions. Sending the same article, story or poem to several publishers at the same time. Some publishers refuse to consider such submissions. No simultaneous submissions should be made without stating the fact in your letter.

Slant. The approach or style of a story or article that will appeal to readers of a specific magazine. For example, a magazine may always use stories with an upbeat ending.

Slides. Usually called transparencies by editors looking for color photographs.

Slush pile. The stack of unsolicited or misdirected manuscripts received by an editor or book publisher.

Software. Programs and related documentation for use with a particular computer system.

Speculation. The editor agrees to look at the author's manuscript with no assurance that it will be bought.

Style. The way in which something is written—for example, short, punchy sentences or flowing narrative.

Subsidiary rights. All those rights, other than book publishing rights included in a book contract—such as paperback, book club, movie rights, etc.

Subsidy publisher. A book publisher who charges the author for the cost to typeset and print his book, the jacket, etc. as opposed to a royalty publisher who pays the author.

Syndication rights. See Rights and the Writer in the Business of Writing article.

Synopsis. A brief summary of a story, novel or play. As part of a book proposal, it is a comprehensive summary condensed in a page or page and a half, single-spaced. See also *outline*.

Tabloid. Newspaper format publication on about half the size of the regular newspaper page, such as the *National Enquirer*.

Tagline. A caption for a photo or a comment added to a filler.

Tearsheet. Page from a magazine or newspaper containing your printed story, article, poem or ad.

Trade. Either a hardcover or paperback book; subject matter frequently concerns a special interest. Books are directed toward the layperson rather than the professional.

Transparencies. Positive color slides; not color prints.

Treatment. Synopsis of a television or film script (40-60 pages for a 2-hour feature film or teleplay).

Unsolicited manuscript. A story, article, poem or book that an editor did not specifically ask to see.

User friendly. Easy to handle and use. Refers to computer hardware and software designed with the user in mind.

Vanity Publisher See *subsidy publisher*.

Word processor. A computer that produces typewritten copy via automated typing, text-editing and storage and transmission capabilities.

Work-for-hire. See Copyrighting Your Writing in the Business of Writing article.

YA. Young adult books.

For hundreds of additional definitions and other information of importance to writers see the *Writer's Encyclopedia* (Writer's Digest Books).

Fiction

This index will help you find publishers that consider books on specific subjects—the subjects you choose to write about. Remember that a publisher may be listed here under a general subject category such as Art and Architecture, while the company publishes *only* art history or how-to books. Be sure to consult each company's detailed individual listing, its book catalog and several of its books before you send your query or manuscript.

Adventure. Advocacy Press; Amwell Press, The; Atheneum Children's Books; Avalon Books; Avon Books; Avon Flare Books; Bantam Books; Berkley Publishing Group, The; Bethel Publishing; Branden Publishing Co., Inc.; Breakwater Books; Camelot Books; Carol Publishing; Clarion Books; Davenport, Publishers, May; Dial Books For Young Readers; Dutton Children's Books; English Mountain Publishing Company; Evergreen Communications, Inc.; Fine, Inc., Donald I.; Flying Pencil Publications; Gallaudet University Press; HarperCollins, Inc.; Hendrick-Long Publishing Co., Inc.; Horizon Publishers & Distributors; Kar-Ben Copies Inc.; Knights Press; Library Research Associates, Inc.; Lodestar Books; Mennonite Publishing House, Inc.; Miller Books; Mother Courage Press; Mountaineers Books, The; New Victoria Publishers; Orca Book Publishers Ltd.; Permanent Press/Second Chance Press, The; Pippin Press; Players Press, Inc.; Random House, Inc.; Random House, Inc./Alfred A. Knopf, Inc. Juvenile Books; Scarborough House/Publishers; Soho Press, Inc.; Starburst Publishers; Stevens, Inc., Gareth; Walker and Co.; Wilderness Adventure Books; Woodsong Graphics, Inc.; Yankee Books; Zebra Books.

Confession. Carol Publishing; Permanent Press/Second Chance Press, The; Players Press, Inc.; Random House, Inc.; Zebra Books.

Erotica. Carroll & Graf Publishers, Inc.; Devonshire Publishing Co.; Gay Sunshine Press and Leyland Publications; Knights Press; New Victoria Publishers; Yankee Books; Zebra Books.

Ethnic. African American Images; Atheneum Children's Books; Avon Flare Books; Branden Publishing Co., Inc.; Breakwater Books; City Lights Books; Coteau Books; Cuff Publications Limited, Harry; Faber & Faber, Inc.; Four Walls Eight Windows; Gallaudet University Press; Gay Sunshine Press and Leyland Publications; Gessler Publishing Company, Inc.; Guernica Editions; Hermes House Press; Holloway House Publishing Co.; Interlink Publishing Group, Inc.; Kar-Ben Copies Inc.; Knights Press; Permanent Press/Second Chance Press, The; Players Press, Inc.; Soho Press, Inc.; Thunder's Mouth Press; University of Illinois Press; University of Minnesota Press.

Experimental. Atheneum Children's Books; Blue Dolphin Publishing, Inc.; Breakwater Books; Devonshire Publishing Co.; Faber & Faber, Inc.; Fiddlehead Poetry Books & Goose Lane Editions; Flockophobic Press; Four Walls Eight Windows; Garber Communications, Inc.; Gay Sunshine Press and Leyland Publications; Hermes House Press; Horizon Publishers & Distributors; Knights Press; Permanent Press/Second Chance Press, The; Players Press, Inc.; Porcépic Books; Random House, Inc.; Speech Bin, Inc., The; Thunder's Mouth Press; University of Minnesota Press; Woodsong Graphics, Inc.; York Press Ltd.

Fantasy. Ace Science Fiction; Atheneum Children's Books; Avon Books; Baen Publishing Enterprises; Bantam Books; Bookmakers Guild, Inc.; Breakwater Books; Camelot Books; Carol Publishing; Coteau Books; Crossway Books; Davenport, Publishers, May; DAW Books, Inc.; Del Rey Books; Dial Books For Young Readers; Dutton Children's Books; English Mountain Publishing Company; Fine, Inc., Donald I.; Gallaudet University Press; Green Tiger Press Inc.; HarperCollins, Inc.; Horizon Publishers & Distributors; Imagine, Inc.; Intervarsity Press; Kar-Ben Copies Inc.; Knights Press; Lion Publishing Corporation; Lodestar Books; Mother Courage Press; New Victoria Publishers; Overlook Press, The; Permanent Press/Second Chance Press, The; Pippin Press; Players Press, Inc.; Random House, Inc.; Random House, Inc./Alfred A. Knopf, Inc. Juvenile Books; TOR Books; TSR, Inc.; Woodsong Graphics, Inc.

Feminist. Advocacy Press; Bantam Books; Black Sparrow Press; Blue Dolphin Publishing, Inc.; Breakwater Books; Coteau Books; Firebrand Books; Four Walls Eight Windows; Hermes House Press; Interlink Publishing Group, Inc.; Mercury Press, The; Soho Press, Inc.; Stevens, Inc., Gareth; University of Minnesota Press.

Gay/Lesbian. Alyson Publications, Inc.; Bantam Books; Black Sparrow Press; Carol Publishing; City Lights Books; Cleis Press; Firebrand Books; Gay Sunshine Press and Leyland Publications; Knights Press; Los Hombres Press; Mother Courage Press; Naiad Press, Inc., The; University of Minnesota Press.

Gothic. Atheneum Children's Books; HarperCollins, Inc.; Knights Press; Woodsong Graphics, Inc.; Zebra Books.

Hi-lo. Fearon Education; Peachtree Publishers, Ltd.; Polka-Dot Press; Sunflower University Press.

Historical. Advocacy Press; Atheneum Children's Books; Avalon Books; Avon Books; Bantam Books; Berkley Publishing Group, The; Bradbury Press; Branden Publishing Co., Inc.; Breakwater Books; Capra Press; Carolrhoda Books, Inc.; Cuff Publications Limited, Harry; Devonshire Publishing Co.; Dial Books For Young Readers; Fine, Inc., Donald I.; Gallaudet University Press; Gay Sunshine Press and Leyland Publications; Guernica Editions; HarperCollins, Inc.; Harvest House Publishers; Hendrick-Long Publishing Co., Inc.; Hermes House Press; Houghton Mifflin Co.; Integrated Press; Kar-Ben Copies Inc.; Knights Press; Leisure Books; Library Research Associates, Inc.; Lion Publishing Corporation; Lodestar Books; Mennonite Publishing House, Inc.; Miller Books; Mother Courage Press; Nautical & Aviation Publishing Co., The; New England Press, Inc., The; New Victoria Publishers; Pelican Publishing Company; Permanent Press/Second Chance Press, The; Pineapple Press, Inc.; Pippin Press; Players Press, Inc.; Pocket Books; Random House, Inc.; Random House, Inc./Alfred A. Knopf, Inc. Juvenile Books; Soho Press, Inc.; Stevens, Inc., Gareth; Thunder's Mouth Press; TOR Books; University of Minnesota Press; University of Pittsburgh Press; Wilderness Adventure Books; Winston-Derek Publishers, Inc.; Woodsong Graphics, Inc.; Yankee Books; Zebra Books.

Horror. Atheneum Children's Books; Bantam Books; Carol Publishing; Devonshire Publishing Co.; Fine, Inc., Donald I.; Four Walls Eight Windows; Players Press, Inc.; Random House, Inc.; Random House, Inc./Alfred A. Knopf, Inc. Juvenile Books; TOR Books; TSR, Inc.; Zebra Books.

Humor. Advocacy Press; Atheneum Children's Books; Avon Flare Books; Blue Dolphin Publishing, Inc.; Breakwater Books; Camelot Books; Carol Publishing; Charlesbridge Publishing; Clarion Books; Coteau Books; Cuff Publications Limited, Harry; Dial Books For Young Readers; Down East Books; ECW Press; Fine, Inc., Donald I.; Five Star Publications; Flying Pencil Publications; Gallaudet University Press; Integrated Press; Intervarsity Press; Knights Press; Lodestar Books; Mennonite Publishing House, Inc.; Miller Books; Multnomah Press; New Victoria Publishers; Once Upon a Planet, Inc.; Pelican Publishing Company; Permanent Press/Second Chance Press, The; Pippin

Press; Players Press, Inc.; Pocket Books; Random House, Inc./Alfred A. Knopf, Inc. Juvenile Books; Stevens, Inc., Gareth; Victor Books; Wyrick & Company; Yankee Books; Zebra Books.

Juvenile. African American Images; Archway/Minstrel Books; Atheneum Children's Books; Bantam Books; Blue Heron Publishing; Bookmakers Guild, Inc.; Bradbury Press; Breakwater Books; Camelot Books; Carolrhoda Books, Inc.; Chronicle Books; Concordia Publishing House; Coteau Books; Crossway Books; Denison & Co., Inc., T.S.; Dutton Children's Books; English Mountain Publishing Company; Evergreen Communications, Inc.; Faber & Faber, Inc.; Farrar, Straus and Giroux, Inc.; Fawcett Juniper; Gallaudet University Press; Gessler Publishing Company, Inc.; Green Tiger Press Inc.; Grosset & Dunlap Publishers; Harbinger House, Inc.; Harcourt Brace Jovanovich; Harper Junior Books Group; Hendrick-Long Publishing Co., Inc.; Horizon Publishers & Distributors; Houghton Mifflin Co.; Interlink Publishing Group, Inc.; Knowledge Book Publishers; Lion Publishing Corporation; Lothrop, Lee & Shepard Books; MacMillan Publishing Co.; Morrow Junior Books; Orca Book Publishers Ltd.; Peguis Publishers Limited; Pelican Publishing Company; Pippin Press; St. Paul Books and Media; Scholastic Professional Books (and Instructor Books); Silver Press; Starburst Publishers; Stevens, Inc., Gareth; Thistledown Press; Tidewater Publishers; Trillium Press; Walker and Co.; Western Producer Prairie Books; Winston-Derek Publishers, Inc.; Wyrick & Company.

Literary. Applezaba Press; Bantam Books; Black Sparrow Press; Blue Dolphin Publishing, Inc.; Bookmakers Guild, Inc.; Breakwater Books; Capra Press; Carol Publishing; City Lights Books; Coteau Books; Crossing Press, The; Dembner Books; Fine, Inc., Donald I.; Flockophobic Press; Flying Pencil Publications; Four Walls Eight Windows; Gallaudet University Press; Godine, Publisher, Inc., David R.; Graywolf Press; HarperCollins, Inc.; Houghton Mifflin Co.; Hounslow Press; Integrated Press; Kesend Publishing, Ltd., Michael; Knopf, Inc., Alfred A.; Little, Brown and Co., Inc.; Longstreet Press, Inc.; Longstreet Press, Inc.; Longwood Academic; Louisiana State University Press; Mercury Press, The; NeWest Publishers Ltd.; Orca Book Publishers Ltd.; Overlook Press, The; Peachtree Publishers, Ltd.; Pineapple Press, Inc.; Q.E.D. Press Of Ann Arbor, Inc.; Sandlapper Publishing, Inc.; Scarborough House/Publisherss; Soho Press, Inc.; Stormline Press; Thistledown Press; Three Continents Press; Tuttle Publishing Company, Inc., Charles E.; University of Arkansas Press, The; University of Minnesota Press; University of Pittsburgh Press; Wyrick & Company.

Mainstream/Contemporary. Atheneum Children's Books; Avalon Books; Avon Flare Books; Bantam Books; Berkley Publishing Group, The; Blair, Publisher, John F.; Bradbury Press; Branden Publishing Co., Inc.; Breakwater Books; Camelot Books; Capra Press; Capra Press; Carroll & Graf Publishers, Inc.; Chelsea Green; Child Welfare League Of America; Citadel Press; City Lights Books; Clarion Books; Coteau Books; Crossway Books; Cuff Publications Limited, Harry; Down East Books; E.P. Dutton; Edicones Universal; Eriksson, Publisher, Paul S.; Faber & Faber, Inc.; Fawcett Juniper; Fiddlehead Poetry Books & Goose Lane Editions; Fine, Inc., Donald I.; Flying Pencil Publications; Gallaudet University Press; Hardy—Publisher, Max; Hermes House Press; Houghton Mifflin Co.; International Marine Publishing Co.; International Publishers Co., Inc.; Intervarsity Press; Little, Brown and Co., Inc.; Lodestar Books; Longstreet Press, Inc.; Mercury Press, The; Morrow and Co., William; Norton Co., Inc., W.W.; Orca Book Publishers Ltd.; Peachtree Publishers, Ltd.; Pelican Publishing Company; Permanent Press/Second Chance Press, The; Perspectives Press; Pineapple Press, Inc.; Players Press, Inc.; Porcépic Books; Random House, Inc.; St. Luke's Press; St. Martin's Press; Scarborough House/Publisherss; Simon & Schuster; Soho Press, Inc.; Starburst Publishers; Ticknor & Fields; TSR, Inc.; University of Illinois Press; University of Iowa Press; University of Nevada Press; University Press of Mississippi; Wood-song Graphics, Inc.; Wyrick & Company; Zebra Books.

Mystery. Atheneum Children's Books; Avon Books; Avon Flare Books; Bantam Books; Breakwater Books; Camelot Books; Carol Publishing; Carroll & Graf Publishers, Inc.; Clarion Books; Cliffhanger Press; Countryman Press, Inc., The; Dembner Books; Dial Books For Young Readers; Doubleday & Co., Inc.; English Mountain Publishing Company; Evergreen Communications, Inc.; Fine, Inc., Donald I.; Four Walls Eight Windows; Gallaudet University Press; Gay Sunshine Press and Leyland Publications; Guernica Editions; HarperCollins, Inc.; Harvest House Publishers; Hendrick-Long Publishing Co., Inc.; Horizon Publishers & Distributors; Knights Press; Library Research Associates, Inc.; Lodestar Books; Miller Books; Mother Courage Press; Mysterious Press, The; Overlook Press, The; Permanent Press/Second Chance Press, The; Pippin Press; Players Press, Inc.; Pocket Books; Random House, Inc.; Random House, Inc./Alfred A. Knopf, Inc. Juvenile Books; Scholastic, Inc.; Soho Press, Inc.; Stevens, Inc., Gareth; TOR Books; TSR, Inc.; Walker and Co.; Woodsong Graphics, Inc.

Occult. Berkley Publishing Group, The; TOR Books.

Picture Books. Advocacy Press; Bradbury Press; Breakwater Books; Chronicle Books; Coteau Books; Dutton Children's Books; Five Star Publications; Gallaudet University Press; Gessler Publishing Company, Inc.; Grosset & Dunlap Publishers; Harbinger House, Inc.; Harcourt Brace Jovanovich; Horizon Publishers & Distributors; Interlink Publishing Group, Inc.; Lodestar Books; Lothrop, Lee & Shepard Books; Pippin Press; Random House, Inc./Alfred A. Knopf, Inc. Juvenile Books; Silver Press; Stevens, Inc., Gareth; Yankee Books.

Plays. Breakwater Books; City Lights Books; Coteau Books; Drama Book Publishers; English Mountain Publishing Company; French, Inc., Samuel; Gallaudet University Press; Players Press, Inc.; Playwrights Canada Press.

Poetry. American Studies Press, Inc.; Applezaba Press; Atheneum Children's Books; Blue Dolphin Publishing, Inc.; Breakwater Books; Chatham Press; Christopher Publishing House, The; Cleveland State University Poetry Center; Daniel and Company, Publishers, John; Dante University Of America Press, Inc.; Edicones Universal; English Mountain Publishing Company; Fiddlehead Poetry Books & Goose Lane Editions; Firebrand Books; Flockophobic Press; Guernica Editions; Harper Junior Books Group; Hounslow Press; International Publishers Co., Inc.; Los Hombres Press; Mercury Press, The; Morrow and Co., William; Paragon House Publishers; Sheep Meadow Press, The; Sunstone Press; Thistledown Press; Three Continents Press; Tuttle Publishing Company, Inc., Charles E.; University of Arkansas Press, The; University of California Press; University of Iowa Press; University of Massachusetts Press; University of Pittsburgh Press; University of Utah Press; Vesta Publications, Ltd.; Wake Forest University Press; Wilderness Adventure Books; Winston-Derek Publishers, Inc.; Zebra Books.

Regional. Blair, Publisher, John F.; Borealis Press, Ltd.; Cuff Publications Limited, Harry; Down East Books; English Mountain Publishing Company; Faber & Faber, Inc.; Porcépic Books; Sunstone Press; Texas Christian University Press; Thistledown Press; University of Pittsburgh Press; University of Utah Press.

Religious. Accent Books; Bethany House Publishers; Bethel Publishing; Bookcraft, Inc.; Broadman Press; College Press Publishing Co.; Crossway Books; Devonshire Publishing Co.; Evergreen Communications, Inc.; Harvest House Publishers; Intervarsity Press; Kar-Ben Copies Inc.; Mennonite Publishing House, Inc.; Players Press, Inc.; St. Paul Books and Media; Standard Publishing; Tyndale House Publishers, Inc.; Victor Books; Winston-Derek Publishers, Inc.; Word Books Publisher.

Romance. Atheneum Children's Books; Avalon Books; Avon Books; Avon Flare Books; Bantam Books; Berkley Publishing Group, The; Branden Publishing Co., Inc.; Breakwater Books; Dial Books For Young Readers; Doubleday & Co., Inc.; Evans and Co.,

Inc., M.; Evergreen Communications, Inc.; Knights Press; Leisure Books; Mennonite Publishing House, Inc.; Mother Courage Press; Players Press, Inc.; Pocket Books; Scholastic, Inc.; Silhouette Books; Walker and Co.; Woodsong Graphics, Inc.; Zebra Books.

Science Fiction. Ace Science Fiction; Atheneum Children's Books; Avon Books; Baen Publishing Enterprises; Bantam Books; Blue Dolphin Publishing, Inc.; Breakwater Books; Carol Publishing; Crossway Books; DAW Books, Inc.; Del Rey Books; Devonshire Publishing Co.; Fine, Inc., Donald I.; Four Walls Eight Windows; Gallaudet University Press; Gay Sunshine Press and Leyland Publications; HarperCollins, Inc.; Hermes House Press; Horizon Publishers & Distributors; Imagine, Inc.; Intervarsity Press; Knights Press; Lodestar Books; Mother Courage Press; New Victoria Publishers; Players Press, Inc.; Pocket Books; Porcépic Books; Random House, Inc./Alfred A. Knopf, Inc. Juvenile Books; TOR Books; TSR, Inc.; Woodsong Graphics, Inc.

Short Story Collections. Applezaba Press; Black Sparrow Press; Bookmakers Guild, Inc.; Breakwater Books; Capra Press; Coteau Books; Daniel and Company, Publishers, John; Dutton Children's Books; English Mountain Publishing Company; Faber & Faber, Inc.; Flockophobic Press; Integrated Press; Interlink Publishing Group, Inc.; International Publishers Co., Inc.; Louisiana State University Press; Mercury Press, The; NeWest Publishers Ltd.; NTC Publishing Group; University of Arkansas Press, The.

Spiritual (New Age, etc.). Graywolf Press.

Sports. Starburst Publishers.

Suspense. Atheneum Children's Books; Avon Books; Avon Flare Books; Bantam Books; Berkley Publishing Group, The; Bethel Publishing; Breakwater Books; Carroll & Graf Publishers, Inc.; Clarion Books; Cliffhanger Press; Dembner Books; Dial Books For Young Readers; Doubleday & Co., Inc.; Fine, Inc., Donald I.; Gallaudet University Press; HarperCollins, Inc.; Horizon Publishers & Distributors; Knights Press; Library Research Associates, Inc.; Lodestar Books; Mysterious Press, The; Overlook Press, The; Permanent Press/Second Chance Press, The; Pippin Press; Players Press, Inc.; Pocket Books; Random House, Inc.; Random House, Inc./Alfred A. Knopf, Inc. Juvenile Books; Soho Press, Inc.; Walker and Co.; Winston-Derek Publishers, Inc.; Woodsong Graphics, Inc.; Zebra Books.

TV Scripts. Howell Press, Inc.

Western. Atheneum Children's Books; Avalon Books; Avon Books; Bantam Books; Berkley Publishing Group, The; Evans and Co., Inc., M.; Fine, Inc., Donald I.; HarperCollins, Inc.; Hendrick-Long Publishing Co., Inc.; Horizon Publishers & Distributors; Knights Press; Lodestar Books; Miller Books; New Victoria Publishers; Players Press, Inc.; Pocket Books; Walker and Co.; Woodsong Graphics, Inc.

Young Adult. ABC-CLIO, Inc.; Advocacy Press; African American Images; Archway/Minstrel Books; Atheneum Children's Books; Bale Books; Bantam Books; Barron's Educational Series, Inc.; Berkley Publishing Group, The; Bethel Publishing; Blue Heron Publishing; Breakwater Books; Cliffs Notes, Inc.; College Board, The; Crossway Books; Davenport, Publishers, May; Dial Books For Young Readers; Dillon Press, Inc.; Dutton Children's Books; Education Associates; Enslow Publishers; Evergreen Communications, Inc.; Falcon Press Publishing Co.; Farrar, Straus and Giroux, Inc.; Fawcett Juniper; Fitzhenry & Whiteside, Ltd.; Flying Pencil Publications; Fearon Education; Gallaudet University Press; Gessler Publishing Company, Inc.; Green Tiger Press Inc.; Harcourt Brace Jovanovich; Harper Junior Books Group; Horizon Publishers & Distributors; Houghton Mifflin Co.; Hunter House, Inc., Publishers; Lodestar Books; McElderry Books, Margaret K.; Mennonite Publishing House, Inc.; Pelican Publishing Company; Random House, Inc./Alfred A. Knopf, Inc. Juvenile Books; Rosen Publishing Group, The; St. Paul Books and Media; Scholastic, Inc.; Science Tech Publishers, Inc.;

Silver Burdett Press; Starburst Publishers; Texas Christian University Press; Western Producer Prairie Books; Wilderness Adventure Books

Nonfiction

Agriculture/Horticulture. Between the Lines Inc.; Boxwood Press, The; Camino Books, Inc.; Countrywoman's Press, The; Interstate Publishers, Inc. The; Kumarian Press, The; Lyons & Burford, Publishers, Inc.; Michigan State University Press; Science Tech Publishers, Inc.; Sentinel Books; Stipes Publishing Co.; Stormline Press; Sunflower University Press; Surfside Publishing; University of Alaska Press; University of Minnesota Press; University of Nebraska Press; Western Producer Prairie Books; Westview Press; Woodbridge Press.

Americana. American Studies Press, Inc.; Ancestry Incorporated; Atheneum Children's Books; Auto Book Press; Bantam Books; Bear Flag Books; Blair, Publisher, John F.; Boston Mills Press, The; Bowling Green State University Popular Press; Branden Publishing Co., Inc.; Camino Books, Inc.; Carol Publishing; Caxton Printers, Ltd., The; Cay-Bel Publishing Co.; Christopher Publishing House, The; Clarion Books; Clark Co., Arthur H.; Countrywoman's Press, The; Crown Publishers, Inc.; Denali Press, The; Devin-Adair Publishers, Inc.; Down East Books; Durst Publications Ltd.; Eriksson, Publisher, Paul S.; Faber & Faber, Inc.; Glenbridge Publishing Ltd.; Globe Pequot Press, Inc., The; Godine, Publisher, Inc., David R.; Hancock House Publishers Ltd.; HarperCollins, Inc.; Herald Publishing House; Heyday Books; International Publishers Co., Inc.; International Resources; Interurban Press/Trans Anglo Books; Knowledge Book Publishers; Lexikos; Library Research Associates, Inc.; Longstreet Press, Inc.; Lyons & Burford, Publishers, Inc.; McFarland & Company, Inc., Publishers; Madison Books; Miller Books; Mosaic Press Miniature Books; Mustang Publishing Co.; New England Press, Inc., The; Oregon Historical Society Press; Overlook Press, The; Pacific Books, Publishers; Paragon House Publishers; Pelican Publishing Company; Permanent Press/Second Chance Press, The; Peter Pauper Press, Inc.; Pickering Press, The; Potomac-Pacific Press; Purdue University Press; Scarborough House/Publisherss; Scribner's Sons, Charles; Sentinel Books; Seven Locks Press, Inc.; Shoe String Press, The; Sierra Club Books; Silver Burdett Press; Smith, Publisher, Gibbs; Sterling Publishing; Stevens, Inc., Gareth; Sunflower University Press; Texas Christian University Press; Transaction Books; University of Alaska Press; University of Arizona Press; University of Arkansas Press, The; University of Illinois Press; University of Minnesota Press; University of Nebraska Press; University of North Carolina Press, The; University of Oklahoma Press; University of Pennsylvania Press; University Press of Kentucky; University Press of Mississippi; University Press of New England; Vesta Publications, Ltd.; Washington State University Pess; Westernlore Press; Wilderness Adventure Books; Winston-Derek Publishers, Inc.; Woodbine House; Workman Publishing Company, Inc.; Yankee Books.

Animals. Alpine Publications Inc.; Archway/Minstrel Books; Atheneum Children's Books; Barron's Educational Series, Inc.; Bear Flag Books; Beaver Pond Publishing & Printing; Boxwood Press, The; Canadian Plains Research Center; Capra Press; Capra Press; Carol Publishing; Carolrhoda Books, Inc.; Crown Publishers, Inc.; Dillon Press, Inc.; Dutton Children's Books; Eriksson, Publisher, Paul S.; Faber & Faber, Inc.; Greenhaven Press, Inc.; Half Halt Press, Inc.; HarperCollins, Inc.; Homestead Publishing; Hounslow Press; International Resources; Kesend Publishing, Ltd., Michael; Lone Pine Publishing; Lucent Books; Lyons & Burford, Publishers, Inc.; Miller Books; Mosaic Press Miniature Books; Northland Publishing Co., Inc.; Pineapple Press, Inc.; Pippin Press; Random House, Inc./Alfred A. Knopf, Inc. Juvenile Books; Rocky Top Publications; Sandhill Crane Press, Inc.; Scarborough House/Publisherss; Silver Press; Soules Book Publishers Ltd., Gordon; Southfarm Press; Stormline Press; TAB Books; Tarcher,

Inc. Jeremy P.; University of Alaska Press; Wilderness Adventure Books; Williamson Publishing Co.; Yankee Books.

Anthropology/Archaeology. Inner Traditions International; Kodansha International U.S.A.; Kumarian Press, Inc.; Lone Pine Publishing; Louisiana State University Press; Bantam Books; Beacon Press; Bear Flag Books; Blue Dolphin Publishing, Inc.; Bowling Green State University Popular Press; Cambridge University Press; Center for Thanatology Research; City Lights Books; Dee, Inc., Ivan R.; Denali Press, The; Horizon Publishers & Distributors; Insight Books; International Resources; Johnson Books; Kent State University Press; Milkweed Editions; Northland Publishing Co., Inc.; Noyes Data Corp.; Pennsylvania Historical and Museum Commission; Princeton University Press; Rutgers University Press; Scarborough House/Publisherss; Stanford University Press; Stevens, Inc., Gareth; Sunflower University Press; University of Alabama Press; University of Alaska Press; University of Arizona Press; University of Iowa Press; University of Nevada Press; University of Pennsylvania Press; University of Pittsburgh Press; University of Tennessee Press, The; University of Texas Press; University of Utah Press; University Press of Kentucky; Westernlore Press; Westview Press; White Cliffs Media Company; Wilderness Adventure Books; Wyrick & Company; Yankee Books.

Art/Architecture. ABC-CLIO, Inc.; Abrams, Inc. Harry N.; Architectural Book Publishing Co., Inc.; Art Direction Book Company; Atheneum Children's Books; Barron's Educational Series, Inc.; Beacon Press; Bennett & McKnight Publishing Co.; Bowling Green State University Popular Press; Branden Publishing Co., Inc.; Bucknell University Press; Cambridge University Press; Camino Books, Inc.; C&T Publishing; Capra Press; Carol Publishing; Carolrhoda Books, Inc.; Chelsea Green; Chicago Review Press; Christopher Publishing House, The; Clarkson Potter; Consultant Press, The; Coteau Books; Crown Publishers, Inc.; Davenport, Publishers, May; Davis Publications, Inc.; Dee, Inc., Ivan R.; Dunburn Press Ltd.; Durst Publications Ltd.; Eriksson, Publisher, Paul S.; Fairleigh Dickinson University Press; Family Album, The; Fitzhenry & Whiteside, Ltd.; Flockophobic Press; Forman Publishing; Four Walls Eight Windows; Getty Museum, The J. Paul; Godine, Publisher, Inc., David R.; Guernica Editions; HarperCollins, Inc.; Holmes & Meier Publishers, Inc.; Homestead Publishing; Hounslow Press; Howell Press, Inc.; Hudson Hill Press, Inc.; Inner Traditions International; Insight Books; Interlink Publishing Group, Inc.; International Resources; Intervarsity Press; Iowa State University Press; Kent State University Press; Kodansha International U.S.A.; Lang Publishing, Peter; Learning Publications Inc.; Library Research Associates, Inc.; Lone Pine Publishing; Louisiana State University Press; Loyola University Press; Lyons & Burford, Publishers, Inc.; McFarland & Company, Inc., Publishers; McGraw Hill Ryerson; Meeramma Publications; Mercury Press, The; Milkweed Editions; Morrow and Co., William; Mosaic Press Miniature Books; Museum of Northern Arizona Press; National Book Company; National Gallery of Canada; NeWest Publishers Ltd.; Nichols Publishing; North Light; Northland Publishing Co., Inc.; Noyes Data Corp.; Oregon Historical Society Press; Overlook Press, The; PBC International, Inc.; Pennsylvania Historical and Museum Commission; Pickering Press, The; Prakken Publications, Inc.; Prentice-Hall Canada, Inc.; Prentice Hall Press; Princeton Architectural Press; Princeton University Press; Professional Publications, Inc.; Q.E.D. Press Of Ann Arbor, Inc.; Random House, Inc.; Rosen Publishing Group, The; Rutgers University Press; Sasquatch Books; Sentinel Books; Simon & Schuster; Smith, Publisher, Gibbs; Starrhill Press; Sterling Publishing; Stevens, Inc., Gareth; Stormline Press; Sunstone Press; TAB Books; Tuttle Publishing Company, Inc., Charles E.; Universe Books; University of Alaska Press; University of Alberta Press, The; University of California Press; University of Massachusetts Press; University of Minnesota Press; University of Pittsburgh Press; University of Tennessee Press, The; University of Texas Press; University Press of America, Inc.; University Press of New England; Vesta Publications, Ltd.;

Walch, Publisher, J. Weston; Washington State University Pess; Westgate Press; Whitney Library of Design; Whitson Publishing Co., The; Workman Publishing Company, Inc.; Yankee Books.

Astrology/Psychic/New Age. ACS Publications, Inc.; Aquarian Press, The; Bear and Co., Inc.; Blue Dolphin Publishing, Inc.; Cassandra Press; Delta Books; Garber Communications, Inc.; Humanics Publishing Group; Inner Traditions International; McFarland & Company, Inc., Publishers; Newcastle Publishing Co., Inc.; Prentice Hall Press; Tarcher, Inc. Jeremy P.; Theosophical Publishing House, The; Westgate Press; Wingbow Press.

Audiocassettes. Abingdon Press; Accelerated Development Inc.; Chatham Press; Devin-Adair Publishers, Inc.; Global Business and Trade; Human Kinetics Publishers, Inc.; Humanics Publishing Group; Interstate Publishers, Inc. The; Kar-Ben Copies Inc.; Longman Financial Services Publishing; Metamorphous Press; Muir Publications, John; National Textbook Co.; Peterson's; Potentials Development for Health & Aging Services; Professional Publications, Inc.; Rainbow Books; St. Anthony Messenger Press; Trillium Press; Walch, Publisher, J. Weston; Wilshire Book Co.; Winston-Derek Publishers, Inc.

Autobiography. Berkley Publishing Group, The; Clarkson Potter; Daniel and Company, Publishers, John; Soho Press, Inc.

Bibliographies. Borgo Press, The; Chosen Books Publishing Co.; Family Album, The; Klein Publications, B.; Permanent Press/Second Chance Press, The; Scarecrow Press, Inc.; Vance Bibliographies; Whitson Publishing Co., The.

Biography. Addison-Wesley Publishing Co., Inc.; Advocacy Press; American Atheist Press; Architectural Book Publishing Co., Inc.; Atheneum Children's Books; Avon Books; Baker Book House Company; Bantam Books; Bear Flag Books; Berkley Publishing Group, The; Binford & Mort Publishing; Blair, Publisher, John F.; Blue Dolphin Publishing, Inc.; Bonus Books, Inc.; Borgo Press, The; Bosco Multimedia, Don; Bowling Green State University Popular Press; Boxwood Press, The; Branden Publishing Co., Inc.; Breakwater Books; Camino Books, Inc.; Canadian Plains Research Center; Capra Press; Capra Press; Carol Publishing; Carolrhoda Books, Inc.; Carroll & Graf Publishers, Inc.; Catholic University of America Press; Cay-Bel Publishing Co.; Chelsea Green; Christopher Publishing House, The; Citadel Press; Clarion Books; Clark Co., Arthur H.; Clarkson Potter; Contemporary Books, Inc.; Crown Publishers, Inc.; Cuff Publications Limited, Harry; Daniel and Company, Publishers, John; Dante University Of America Press, Inc.; Dee, Inc., Ivan R.; Delta Books; Dillon Press, Inc.; Dunburn Press Ltd.; Dunburn Press Ltd.; Dutton. E.P.; Edicones Universal; Enslow Publishers; Eriksson, Publisher, Paul S.; Faber & Faber, Inc.; Family Album, The; Fine, Inc., Donald I.; Fitzhenry & Whiteside, Ltd.; Fulcrum, Inc.; Gallaudet University Press; Gardner Press, Inc.; Gaslight Publications; Global Business and Trade; Globe Pequot Press, Inc., The; Godine, Publisher, Inc., David R.; Gospel Publishing House; Great Northwest Publishing and Distributing Company, Inc.; Greenhaven Press, Inc.; Guernica Editions; Hancock House Publishers Ltd.; Harper & Row, San Francisco; HarperCollins, Inc.; Hendrick-Long Publishing Co., Inc.; Here's Life Publishers, Inc.; Hippocrene Books Inc.; Holmes & Meier Publishers, Inc.; Homestead Publishing; Horizon Publishers & Distributors; Houghton Mifflin Co.; Hounslow Press; Huntington House, Inc.; ILR Press; Inner Traditions International; Insight Books; Integrated Press; International Publishers Co., Inc.; International Resources; Iowa State University Press; Kent State University Press; Kesend Publishing, Ltd., Michael; Kodansha International U.S.A.; Lang Publishing, Peter; Lawrence Books, Merloyd; Library Research Associates, Inc.; Little, Brown and Co., Inc.; Lone Pine Publishing; Longstreet Press, Inc.; Louisiana State University Press; Loyola University Press; Lucent Books; McGraw Hill Ryerson; Madison Books; Madison Books; Media Forum International, Ltd.; Mercury Press, The; Morrow and Co.,

William; Mosaic Press Miniature Books; Mother Courage Press; Motorbooks International Publishers & Wholesalers, Inc.; Naval Institute Press; New England Press, Inc., The; New Leaf Press, Inc.; New Victoria Publishers; Noble Press, Incorporated, The; Northland Publishing Co., Inc.; Old Army Press, The; Orca Book Publishers Ltd.; Oregon Historical Society Press; Oregon State University Press; Pacific Press Publishing Association; Paragon House Publishers; Pelican Publishing Company; Permanent Press/ Second Chance Press, The; Pineapple Press, Inc.; Pippin Press; Pocket Books; Polka-Dot Press; Potomac-Pacific Press; Praeger Publishers; Prima Publishing and Communications; Princeton Book Company, Publishers; Princeton University Press; Purdue University Press; Quill; Random House, Inc.; Random House, Inc./Alfred A. Knopf, Inc. Juvenile Books; Rutledge Hill Press; St. Martin's Press; St. Paul Books and Media; San Francisco Press, Inc.; Sandlapper Publishing, Inc.; Scarborough House/Publisherss; Schirmer Books; Science Tech Publishers, Inc.; Scribner's Sons, Charles; Seven Locks Press, Inc.; Shoe String Press, The; Simon & Schuster; Smith, Publisher, Gibbs; Soho Press, Inc.; Stevens, Inc., Gareth; Stormline Press; Sunflower University Press; Tarcher, Inc. Jeremy P.; Thunder's Mouth Press; Times Books; Transaction Books; University of Alabama Press; University of Alaska Press; University of Alberta Press, The; University of Arkansas Press, The; University of Illinois Press; University of Massachusetts Press; University of Nebraska Press; University of Nevada Press; University of Pennsylvania Press; University of Pittsburgh Press; University Press of Kansas; University Press of Kentucky; University Press of Mississippi; University Press of New England; Vanwell Publishing Limited; Vesta Publications, Ltd.; Walker and Co.; Washington State University Pess; Western Producer Prairie Books; Westernlore Press; White Cliffs Media Company; Wilderness Adventure Books; Winston-Derek Publishers, Inc.; Woodbine House; Woodsong Graphics, Inc.; Wyrick & Company; Yankee Books; Zebra Books; Zondervan Corp. The.

Business/Economics. Abbott, Langer & Associates; Adams, Inc., Bob; Addison-Wesley Publishing Co., Inc.; Allen Publishing Co.; Almar Press; Amacom Books; American Business Consultants, Inc.; American Hospital Publishing, Inc.; Atheneum Children's Books; Auto Book Press; Avery Publishing Group; Avon Books; Bantam Books; Barron's Educational Series, Inc.; Benjamin Company, Inc., The; Berkley Publishing Group, The; Between the Lines Inc.; BNA Books; Bonus Books, Inc.; Brevet Press, Inc.; Brick House Publishing Co.; Business & Legal Reports, Inc.; Cambridge University Press; Canadian Plains Research Center; Career Press Inc., The; Carol Publishing; Cassell Publications; Cato Institute; Chilton Book Co.; Christopher Publishing House, The; Cleaning Consultant Services, Inc.; Conari Press; Consultant Press, The; Contemporary Books, Inc.; Dee, Inc., Ivan R.; Devin-Adair Publishers, Inc.; Devonshire Publishing Co.; Durst Publications Ltd.; Eriksson, Publisher, Paul S.; Facts On File, Inc.; Fairchild Books & Visuals; Fairleigh Dickinson University Press; Financial Sourcebooks; Fitzhenry & Whiteside, Ltd.; Forman Publishing; Fraser Institute, The; Free Press, The; Glenbridge Publishing Ltd.; Global Business and Trade; Greenhaven Press, Inc.; Gulf Publishing Co.; HarperCollins, Inc.; Health Administration Press; Holmes & Meier Publishers, Inc.; Horizon Publishers & Distributors; Humanics Publishing Group; ILR Press; In Depth Publishers; Industrial Press, Inc.; Inner Traditions International; Insight Books; Intercultural Press, Inc.; International Foundation Of Employee Benefit Plans; International Publishers Co., Inc.; International Resources; International Self-Counsel Press, Ltd.; Iowa State University Press; Klein Publications, B.; Kodansha International U.S.A.; Kumarian Press, Inc.; Lang Publishing, Peter; Liberty Hall Press; Liberty Publishing Company, Inc.; Library Research Associates, Inc.; Lone Pine Publishing; Longman Financial Services Publishing; Longman Publishing Group; Loompanics Unlimited; Lucent Books; McFarland & Company, Inc., Publishers; McGraw Hill Ryerson; Menasha Ridge Press, Inc.; Mennonite Publishing House, Inc.; Metamorphous Press; MGI Management Institute, Inc., The; Michigan State University Press; Mosaic Press Miniature Books; National Book Company; National Textbook Co.; Nichols Publishing; Noyes Data Corp.; NTC Publishing Group; Overlook Press, The; Pelican Publishing Company; Pilot Books; Potomac-Pacific Press; Praeger Publishers; Prentice Hall Canada, Inc.; Prentice Hall Press; Prima Publishing and Communications; Professional Publications, Inc.; Purdue University Press; R&E Publishers; Random House, Inc.; Ronin Publishing; Ross Books; Roxbury Publishing Co.; Schenkman Books, Inc.; Self-Counsel Press; Seven Locks Press, Inc.; Soules Book Publishers Ltd., Gordon; Starburst Publishers; Sterling Publishing; Stipes Publishing Co.; Sunflower University Press; Synesis Press; TAB Books; Times Books; Transaction Books; Tuttle Publishing Company, Inc., Charles E.; Twin Peaks Press; Union Square Press; University Associates, Inc.; University of Illinois Press; University of Minnesota Press; University of Pennsylvania Press; University of Pittsburgh Press; University Press of America, Inc.; Wadsworth Publishing Company; Walch, Publisher, J. Weston; Walker and Co.; Wall & Emerson, Inc.; Washington State University Pess; Western Producer Prairie Books; Westview Press; Williamson Publishing Co.; Windsor Books; Wordware Publishing, Inc.

Child Guidance/Parenting. Abbey Press; African American Images; ALA Books; Avery Publishing Group; Baker Book House Company; Bantam Books; Barron's Educational Series, Inc.; Bennett & McKnight Publishing Co.; Blue Bird Publishing; Bookmakers Guild, Inc.; Calgre Press; Cambridge Career Products; Camino Books, Inc.; Career Press Inc., The; Carol Publishing; Center for Applied Linguistics; Child Welfare League Of America; College Board, The; Concordia Publishing House; Coventure Press; Delta Books; Evergreen Communications, Inc.; Fisher Books; Gallaudet University Press; Gardner Press, Inc.; Harbinger House, Inc.; Harvest House Publishers; Health Communications, Inc.; Hensley, Inc., Virgil W.; Horizon Publishers & Distributors; Hounslow Press; Inner Traditions International; Interlink Publishing Group, Inc.; Lawrence Books, Merloyd; Lion Publishing Corporation; Mennonite Publishing House, Inc.; Mills & Sanderson, Publishers; Muir Publications, John; R&E Publishers; Scarborough House/Publisherss; Sentinel Books; Sigo Press; Skidmore-Roth Publishing; Starburst Publishers; Tarcher, Inc. Jeremy P.; University of Minnesota Press; Victor Books; Walker and Co.; Williamson Publishing Co.; Yankee Books.

Coffee Table Book. Auto Book Press; Bantam Books; Bentley, Inc., Robert; Bonus Books, Inc.; Breakwater Books; Camino Books, Inc.; Canadian Plains Research Center; C&T Publishing; Capra Press; Caxton Printers, Ltd., The; Dunburn Press Ltd.; E.P. Dutton; Evergreen Communications, Inc.; Fiddlehead Poetry Books & Goose Lane Editions; Flockophobic Press; Four Walls Eight Windows; Gallaudet University Press; Gessler Publishing Company, Inc. Hendrick-Long Publishing Co.; Homestead Publishing; Hounslow Press; Howell Press, Inc.; Imagine, Inc.; Inner Traditions International; Integrated Press; Interlink Publishing Group, Inc.; Knowledge Book Publishers; Lexikos; Library Research Associates, Inc.; Lone Pine Publishing; Longstreet Press, Inc.; Los Hombres Press; Louisiana State University Press; Mennonite Publishing House, Inc.; Mercury Press, The; Multnomah Press; Museum of Northern Arizona Press; Northland Publishing Co., Inc.; Pelican Publishing Company; Pennsylvania Historical and Museum Commission; Princeton Book Company, Publishers; Rutledge Hill Press; Sentinel Books; Surfside Publishing; Tidewater Publishers; Union Square Press; University of Pittsburgh Press; Workman Publishing Company, Inc.; Wyrick & Company; Yankee Books.

Communications. Beacon Press; Longman Publishing Group; TAB Books; Union Square Press; Univelt, Inc.

Community/Public Affairs. Jalmar Press, Inc.; Taylor Publishing Company; University Associates, Inc.; University of Alabama Press.

Computers/Electronics. Addison-Wesley Publishing Co., Inc.; ALA Books; Amacom

Books; Amacom Books; And Books; ARCsoft Publishers; Bantam Books; Boyd & Fraser Publishing Company; Branden Publishing Co., Inc.; Calgre Press; Career Publishing, Inc.; Carol Publishing; Center for Applied Linguistics; Compute! Books; Computer Science Press, Inc.; Digital Press; Entelek; Erlbaum Associates, Inc., Lawrence; Financial Sourcebooks; Gifted Education Press; Grapevine Publications, Inc.; IEEE Press; Industrial Press, Inc.; Lucent Books; MGI Management Institute, Inc., The; Microtrend Books; Nichols Publishing; Osborne/McGraw-Hill; Prentice Hall Canada, Inc.; Princeton University Press; NpsychologyI Research; Q.E.D. Information Sciences, Inc.; Que Corporation; R&E Publishers; Ross Books; San Francisco Press, Inc.; Surfside Publishing; Sybex, Inc.; TAB Books; Teachers College Press; Union Square Press; University of Pennsylvania Press; VGM Career Horizons; Walch, Publisher, J. Weston; Wall & Emerson, Inc.; White Cliffs Media Company; Wordware Publishing, Inc.

Consumer Affairs. Almar Press; And Books; Beacon Press; Brick House Publishing Co.; International Foundation Of Employee Benefit Plans; McGraw Hill Ryerson; Menasha Ridge Press, Inc.; Pharos Books.

Cooking/Foods/Nutrition. Applezaba Press; Atheneum Children's Books; Avery Publishing Group; Bantam Books; Barron's Educational Series, Inc.; Benjamin Company, Inc., The; Better Homes and Gardens Books; Blue Dolphin Publishing, Inc.; Bonus Books, Inc.; Breakwater Books; Briarcliff Press Publishers; Bristol Publishing Enterprises, Inc.; Bull Publishing Co.; Cambridge Career Products; Camino Books, Inc.; Conari Press; Carol Publishing; Cassandra Press; Cay-Bel Publishing Co.; Chicago Review Press; Christopher Publishing House, The; Chronicle Books; Clarkson Potter; Contemporary Books, Inc.; Countryman Press, Inc., The; Countrywoman's Press, The; Crossing Press, The; Crown Publishers, Inc.; Down East Books; Durst Publications Ltd.; E.P. Dutton; Edicones Universal; Eriksson, Publisher, Paul S.; Evans and Co., Inc., M.; Facts On File, Inc.; Fine, Inc., Donald I.; Fisher Books; Five Star Publications; Forman Publishing; Four Walls Eight Windows; Gem Guides Book Company; Globe Pequot Press, Inc., The; Godine, Publisher, Inc., David R.; Golden West Publishers; Hancock House Publishers Ltd.; HarperCollins, Inc.; Hawkes Publishing, Inc.; Horizon Publishers & Distributors; Hounslow Press; Inner Traditions International; Interlink Publishing Group, Inc.; Ishi Press International; Jonathan David Publishers; Liberty Publishing Company, Inc.; Little, Brown and Co., Inc.; Lone Pine Publishing; Longstreet Press, Inc.; Lyons & Burford, Publishers, Inc.; McCutchan Publishing Corporation; McGraw Hill Ryerson; Media Forum International, Ltd.; Mennonite Publishing House, Inc.; Miller Books; Morrow and Co., William; Mosaic Press Miniature Books; Northland Publishing Co., Inc.; Pacific Press Publishing Association; Peachtree Publishers, Ltd.; Pelican Publishing Company; Pennsylvania Historical and Museum Commission; Peter Pauper Press, Inc.; Pocket Books; Prentice-Hall Canada, Inc.; Prentice Hall Press; Prevention Health Books; Prima Publishing and Communications; R&E Publishers; Random House, Inc.; Rutledge Hill Press; Sasquatch Books; Scarborough House/Publisherss; Sentinel Books; Soules Book Publishers Ltd., Gordon; Starburst Publishers; Sterling Publishing; Stevens, Inc., Gareth; Surfside Publishing; Synesis Press; Taylor Publishing Company; Tidewater Publishers; Times Books; Tuttle Publishing Company, Inc., Charles E.; Twin Peaks Press; University of North Carolina Press, The; University of Pittsburgh Press; Vesta Publications, Ltd.; Williamson Publishing Co.; Wine Appreciation Guild, Ltd.; Woodbridge Press; Woodsong Graphics, Inc.; Workman Publishing Company, Inc.; Yankee Books.

Counseling/Career Guidance. Accelerated Development Inc.; Adams, Inc., Bob; Almar Press; Career Publishing, Inc.; Fairchild Books & Visuals; Jist Works, Inc.; National Textbook Co.; Octameron Associates; Peterson's; Pilot Books; Potomac-Pacific Press; Rutgers University Press; Teachers College Press; VGM Career Horizons; Williamson Publishing Co.

Crafts. Barron's Educational Series, Inc.; Better Homes and Gardens Books; Briarcliff Press Publishers; Chilton Book Co.; Davis Publications, Inc.; Down East Books; Naturegraph Publishers, Inc.

Educational. ABC-CLIO, Inc.; Accelerated Development Inc.; Advocacy Press; African American Images; ALA Books; Amacom Books; Amacom Books; American Catholic Press; Barron's Educational Series, Inc.; Benjamin Company, Inc., The; Bennett & McKnight Publishing Co.; Between the Lines Inc.; Blue Bird Publishing; Bookmakers Guild, Inc.; Bosco Multimedia, Don; Breakwater Books; Bull Publishing Co.; Calgre Press; Cambridge Career Products; Canadian Institute of Ukrainian Studies Press; Canadian Plains Research Center; Career Press Inc., The; Cato Institute; Center for Applied Linguistics; Center for Thanatology Research; College Board, The; Dante University Of America Press, Inc.; Denison & Co., Inc., T.S.; Dillon Press, Inc.; Duquesne University Press; Education Associates; EES Publications; English Mountain Publishing Company; Entelek; Erlbaum Associates, Inc., Lawrence; Fairleigh Dickinson University Press; Fearon Education; Five Star Publications; Gallaudet University Press; Gardner Press, Inc.; Garrett Park Press; Gessler Publishing Company, Inc.; Gifted Education Press; Global Business and Trade; Gospel Publishing House; Holmes & Meier Publishers, Inc.; Horizon Publishers & Distributors; Humanics Publishing Group; Insight Books; Intercultural Press, Inc.; Interstate Publishers, Inc. The; Ishiyaku Euroamerica, Inc.; Jalmar Press, Inc.; Kent State University Press; Knopf, Inc., Alfred A.; Lang Publishing, Peter; Learning Publications Inc.; Longman Publishing Group; Longwood Academic; McCutchan Publishing Corporation; Mennonite Publishing House, Inc.; Metamorphous Press; Morehouse Publishing Co.; National Book Company; Naturegraph Publishers, Inc.; Nichols Publishing; Noble Press, Incorporated, The; NTC Publishing Group; Octameron Associates; Open Court Publishing Co.; Peguis Publishers Limited; Peterson's; Pilot Books; Porter Sargent Publishers, Inc.; Praeger Publishers; Prakken Publications, Inc.; Prentice Hall Canada, Inc.; Princeton Book Company, Publishers; Que Corporation; R&E Publishers; Reference Service Press; San Francisco Press, Inc.; Scarborough House/Publisherss; Speech Bin, Inc., The; Standard Publishing; Teachers College Press; Trillium Press; University Associates, Inc.; University of Alaska Press; University of Pittsburgh Press; University Press of America, Inc.; University Press of Colorado; Vanwell Publishing Limited; Walch, Publisher, J. Weston; Wall & Emerson, Inc.; White Cliffs Media Company; Williamson Publishing Co.

Entertainment/Games. Borgo Press, The; Broadway Press; Citadel Press; Delta Books; Dembner Books; Drama Book Publishers; Faber & Faber, Inc.; Fairleigh Dickinson University Press; Focal Press; Holloway House Publishing Co.; Intergalactic Publishing Co.; McFarland & Company, Inc., Publishers; Quill; Speech Bin, Inc., The; Standard Publishing; Sterling Publishing; University of Nevada Press.

Ethnic. African American Images; Bennett & McKnight Publishing Co.; Between the Lines Inc.; Camino Books, Inc.; Canadian Institute of Ukrainian Studies Press; Carol Publishing; Coteau Books; Denali Press, The; Fairleigh Dickinson University Press; Gardner Press, Inc.; Garrett Park Press; Holmes & Meier Publishers, Inc.; Insight Books; International Publishers Co., Inc.; Kar-Ben Copies Inc.; Luramedia; Media Forum International, Ltd.; Mennonite Publishing House, Inc.; NeWest Publishers Ltd.; Noble Press, Incorporated, The; Oregon Historical Society Press; Praeger Publishers; R&E Publishers; Reference Service Press; Scarborough House/Publisherss; Silver Press; Stormline Press; Sunflower University Press; University of Alaska Press; University of Massachusetts Press; University of Nevada Press; University of Oklahoma Press; University of Pittsburgh Press; University of Tennessee Press, The; University of Texas Press; University Press of America, Inc.; University Press of Mississippi; White Cliffs Media Company.

Fashion/Beauty. Fairchild Books & Visuals.

Feminism. Crossing Press, The; Firebrand Books; New Victoria Publishers.

Film/Cinema/Stage. Focal Press; French, Inc., Samuel; Gaslight Publications; Imagine, Inc.; Lone Eagle Publishing Co.; McFarland & Company, Inc., Publishers; Media Forum International, Ltd.; Overlook Press, The; Players Press, Inc.; Prentice Hall Press; Rutgers University Press; Schirmer Books; Southfarm Press; Starrhill Press; TAB Books; Teachers College Press; University of Texas Press; University Press of America, Inc.; Vestal Press, Ltd., The; VGM Career Horizons.

Gardening. Better Homes and Gardens Books; Briarcliff Press Publishers; Camino Books, Inc.; Capra Press; Capra Press; Countrywoman's Press, The; Fisher Books; Globe Pequot Press, Inc., The; Godine, Publisher, Inc., David R.; Horizon Publishers & Distributors; Interlink Publishing Group, Inc.; Kodansha International U.S.A.; Lone Pine Publishing; Longstreet Press, Inc.; Lyons & Burford, Publishers, Inc.; Naturegraph Publishers, Inc.; Prentice Hall Press; Sasquatch Books; Scarborough House/Publisherss; Sentinel Books; Stackpole Books; Surfside Publishing; Timber Press, Inc.; University of North Carolina Press, The; Williamson Publishing Co.; Woodbridge Press; Wyrick & Company.

Gay/Lesbian. Alyson Publications, Inc.; Bantam Books; Between the Lines Inc.; Carol Publishing; City Lights Books; Cleis Press; Crossing Press, The; Firebrand Books; Gardner Press, Inc.; Gay Sunshine Press and Leyland Publications; Knights Press; University of Minnesota Press; Los Hombres Press.

General Nonfiction. American Atheist Press; American Psychiatric Press, Inc., The; Avon Flare Books; Beacon Press; Davis Publishing, Steve; Evans and Co., Inc., M.; Fulcrum, Inc.; Getty Museum, The J. Paul; Johnson Books; Jonathan David Publishers; Kent State University Press; Lothrop, Lee & Shepard Books; Lang Publishing, Peter; Leisure Books; Mercury House Inc.; Mills & Sanderson, Publishers; Morrow and Co., William; Norton Co., Inc., W.W.; Ohio University Press; Pacific Books, Publishers; Peachtree Publishers, Ltd.; Pocket Books; Potentials Development for Health & Aging Services; St. Anthony Messenger Press; St. Martin's Press; Scholastic, Inc.; Shaw Publishers, Harold; Shoe String Press, The; Ticknor & Fields; Time-Life Books Inc.; University of Calgary Press, The; University of Wisconsin Press; Writer's Digest Books.

Government/Politics. ABC-CLIO, Inc.; Addison Wesley Publishing Co., Inc.; American Atheist Press; Avon Books; Bantam Books; Beacon Press; Between the Lines Inc.; Bonus Books, Inc.; Borgo Press, The; Branden Publishing Co., Inc.; Bucknell University Press; Camino Books, Inc.; Canadian Institute of Ukrainian Studies Press; Carol Publishing; Cato Institute; Christopher Publishing House, The; Cleis Press; Crown Publishers, Inc.; Cuff Publications Limited, Harry; Dee, Inc., Ivan R.; Denali Press, The; Devin-Adair Publishers, Inc.; Edicones Universal; Eriksson, Publisher, Paul S.; Fairleigh Dickinson University Press; Financial Sourcebooks; Four Walls Eight Windows; Fraser Institute, The; Glenbridge Publishing Ltd.; Greenhaven Press, Inc.; Guernica Editions; HarperCollins, Inc.; Health Administration Press; Holmes & Meier Publishers, Inc.; Humanities Press International, Inc.; Huntington House, Inc.; Intercultural Press, Inc.; Interlink Publishing Group, Inc.; International Publishers Co., Inc.; Kodansha International U.S.A.; Kumarian Press, Inc.; Lang Publishing, Peter; Library Research Associates, Inc.; Lone Pine Publishing; Longman Publishing Group; Loompanics Unlimited; Louisiana State University Press; Lucent Books; McGraw Hill Ryerson; Mercury Press, The; Michigan State University Press; Milkweed Editions; National Book Company; NeWest Publishers Ltd.; Noble Press, Incorporated, The; Open Court Publishing Co.; Oregon Historical Society Press; Paragon House Publishers; Pelican Publishing Company; Pennsylvania Historical and Museum Commission; Permanent Press/Second Chance Press, The; Plenum Publishing; Potomac-Pacific Press; Praeger Publishers; Prentice-Hall Canada, Inc.; Prima Publishing and Communications; Princeton University Press; R&E Publishers; Regnery/Gateway, Inc.; Riverdale Company, Inc., Publishers, The; St. Martin's Press; San Francisco Press, Inc.; Sasquatch Books; Scarborough House/Publisherss; Schenkman Books, Inc.; Seven Locks Press, Inc.; Shoe String Press, The; Soules Book Publishers Ltd., Gordon; Stanford University Press; Starburst Publishers; Sunflower University Press; Teachers College Press; Thunder's Mouth Press; Transaction Books; Transnational Publishers, Inc.; Tuttle Publishing Company, Inc., Charles E.; University of Alabama Press; University of Alaska Press; University of Alberta Press, The; University of Arkansas Press, The; University of Illinois Press; University of North Carolina Press, The; University of Pittsburgh Press; University Press of Kansas; University Press of Kentucky; University Press of Mississippi; University Press of New England; Vesta Publications, Ltd.; Walch, Publisher, J. Weston; Wall & Emerson, Inc.; Washington State University Pess; Western Producer Prairie Books; Westview Press; Word Books Publisher; Yankee Books.

Health/Medicine. Accelerated Development Inc.; ACS Publications, Inc.; Addison-Wesley Publishing Co., Inc.; Almar Press; American Hospital Publishing, Inc.; Atheneum Children's Books; Avery Publishing Group; Avon Books; Bantam Books; Benjamin Company, Inc., The; Bennett & McKnight Publishing Co.; Berkley Publishing Group, The; Between the Lines Inc.; Blue Dolphin Publishing, Inc.; Bonus Books, Inc.; Bookmakers Guild, Inc.; Boxwood Press, The; Branden Publishing Co., Inc.; Briarcliff Press Publishers; Bull Publishing Co.; Cambridge Career Products; Carol Publishing; Cassandra Press; Cato Institute; Center for Thanatology Research; Christopher Publishing House, The; Cleaning Consultant Services, Inc.; Contemporary Books, Inc.; Coventure Press; Crossing Press, The; Crown Publishers, Inc.; Dee, Inc., Ivan R.; Dembner Books; Devin-Adair Publishers, Inc.; EES Publications; Eriksson, Publisher, Paul S.; Erlbaum Associates, Inc., Lawrence; Evans and Co., Inc., M.; Facts On File, Inc.; Fisher Books; Fitzhenry & Whiteside, Ltd.; Forman Publishing; Gallaudet University Press; Gardner Press, Inc.; Government Institutes, Inc.; Green, Inc., Warren H.; HarperCollins, Inc.; Hawkes Publishing, Inc.; Hazelden Educational Materials; Health Administration Press; Horizon Publishers & Distributors; Houghton Mifflin Co.; Hounslow Press; Human Kinetics Publishers, Inc.; Humanics Publishing Group; Hunter House, Inc., Publishers; Information Resources Press; Inner Traditions International; Insight Books; International Foundation Of Employee Benefit Plans; Iowa State University Press; Ishiyaku Euroamerica, Inc.; Kesend Publishing, Ltd., Michael; Knowledge Book Publishers; Kodansha International U.S.A.; Lawrence Books, Merloyd; Learning Publications Inc.; Leisure Press; Longwood Academic; Luramedia; McFarland & Company, Inc., Publishers; Medical Economics Books; Meeramma Publications; Menasha Ridge Press, Inc.; Mennonite Publishing House, Inc.; Metamorphous Press; Mills & Sanderson, Publishers; Mosaic Press Miniature Books; Mother Courage Press; National Book Company; Naturegraph Publishers, Inc.; Newcastle Publishing Co., Inc.; Pacific Press Publishing Association; Parkside Publishing Coporation; Pelican Publishing Company; Perspectives Press; Potomac-Pacific Press; Praeger Publishers; Prentice-Hall Canada, Inc.; Prevention Health Books; Prima Publishing and Communications; Princeton Book Company, Publishers; R&E Publishers; Random House, Inc.; Rocky Top Publications; Rosen Publishing Group, The; Scarborough House/Publisherss; Science Tech Publishers, Inc.; Scribner's Sons, Charles; Self-Counsel Press; Sierra Club Books; Sigo Press; Skidmore-Roth Publishing; Soules Book Publishers Ltd., Gordon; Speech Bin, Inc., The; Starburst Publishers; Sterling Publishing; Sunflower University Press; Synesis Press; TAB Books; Tarcher, Inc. Jeremy P.; Theosophical Publishing House, The; Times Books; Transaction Books; Twin Peaks Press; Ultralight Publichations, Inc.; University of Alaska Press; University of Minnesota Press; University of Pennsylvania Press; University of Pittsburgh Press; VGM Career Horizons; Walch, Publisher, J. Weston; Walker and Co.; Wall & Emerson, Inc.; Weiser, Inc., Samuel; Westview Press; Williamson Publishing Co.; Wilshire Book Co.; Winston-Derek Publishers, Inc.; Woodbine House;

Woodbridge Press; Word Books Publisher; Workman Publishing Company, Inc.; Zebra Books.

Hi-lo. Cambridge Career Products; Fearon Education; Miller Books; National Textbook Co.; New Readers Press; Rosen Publishing Group, The.

History. ABC-CLIO, Inc.; Academy Chicago; Addison-Wesley Publishing Co., Inc.; African American Images; American Atheist Press; American Studies Press, Inc.; Ancestry Incorporated; Appalachian Mountain Club Books; Architectural Book Publishing Co., Inc.; Atheneum Children's Books; Auto Book Press; Avery Publishing Group; Aviation Book Co.; Avon Books; Beacon Press; Bear Flag Books; Binford & Mort Publishing; Blair, Publisher, John F.; Borgo Press, The; Boston Mills Press, The; Bowling Green State University Popular Press; Boxwood Press, The; Branden Publishing Co., Inc.; Breakwater Books; Brevet Press, Inc.; Bucknell University Press; Camino Books, Inc.; Canadian Institute of Ukrainian Studies Press; Canadian Plains Research Center; Carol Publishing; Carolrhoda Books, Inc.; Carroll & Graf Publishers, Inc.; Catholic University of America Press; Cay-Bel Publishing Co.; Chatham Press; Christopher Publishing House, The; Citadel Press; Clark Co., Arthur H.; Coteau Books; Countryman Press, Inc., The; Crossway Books; Crown Publishers, Inc.; Cuff Publications Limited, Harry; Dee, Inc., Ivan R.; Dembner Books; Denali Press, The; Devin-Adair Publishers, Inc.; Devonshire Publishing Co.; Dillon Press, Inc.; Down East Books; Dunburn Press Ltd.; Eerdmans Publishing Co., William B.; Eriksson, Publisher, Paul S.; Facts On File, Inc.; Fairleigh Dickinson University Press; Family Album, The; Fiddlehead Poetry Books & Goose Lane Editions; Fine, Inc., Donald I.; Fitzhenry & Whiteside, Ltd.; Flores Publications, J.; Flying Pencil Publications; Four Walls Eight Windows; Fulcrum, Inc.; Gallaudet University Press; Gaslight Publications; Getty Museum, The J. Paul; Glenbridge Publishing Ltd.; Globe Pequot Press, Inc., The; Globe Press Books; Godine, Publisher, Inc., David R.; Golden West Publishers; Gospel Publishing House; Greenhaven Press, Inc.; Guernica Editions; Hancock House Publishers Ltd.; HarperCollins, Inc.; Hawkes Publishing, Inc.; Heart Of The Lakes Publishing; Hendrick-Long Publishing Co., Inc.; Herald Publishing House; Heritage Books, Inc.; Heyday Books; Hippocrene Books Inc.; Holmes & Meier Publishers, Inc.; Homestead Publishing; Horizon Publishers & Distributors; Houghton Mifflin Co.; Hounslow Press; Howell Press, Inc.; Humanities Press International, Inc.; ILR Press; Inner Traditions International; Interlink Publishing Group, Inc.; International Publishers Co., Inc.; International Resources; Interurban Press/Trans Anglo Books; Intervarsity Press; Iowa State University Press; Kent State University Press; Kesend Publishing, Ltd., Michael; Kinseeker Publications; Kodansha International U.S.A.; Lang Publishing, Peter; Lexikos; Library Research Associates, Inc.; Little, Brown and Co., Inc.; Lone Pine Publishing; Longman Publishing Group; Longstreet Press, Inc.; Longwood Academic; Louisiana State University Press; Loyola University Press; Lucent Books; McGraw Hill Ryerson; Madison Books; Mennonite Publishing House, Inc.; Mercury Press, The; Michigan State University Press; Milkweed Editions; Miller Books; Morehouse Publishing Co.; Morrow and Co., William; Mosaic Press Miniature Books; Motorbooks International Publishers & Wholesalers, Inc.; National Book Company; Nautical & Aviation Publishing Co., The; Naval Institute Press; New England Press, Inc., The; New Victoria Publishers; NeWest Publishers Ltd.; Noble Press, Incorporated, The; Northern Illinois University Press; Northland Publishing Co., Inc.; Noyes Data Corp.; Oddo Publishing, Inc.; Ohio University Press; Old Army Press, The; Orca Book Publishers Ltd.; Oregon Historical Society Press; Oregon State University Press; Overlook Press, The; Paragon House Publishers; Paragon House Publishers; Peachtree Publishers, Ltd.; Pennsylvania Historical and Museum Commission; Permanent Press/Second Chance Press, The; Pickering Press, The; Pineapple Press, Inc.; Potomac-Pacific Press; Praeger Publishers; Prentice Hall Canada, Inc.; Princeton University Press; Purdue University Press; Quill; R&E Publishers; Random House, Inc.; Riverdale Company, Inc., Publishers, The; Rutgers University Press; St. Martin's Press; San Francisco Press, Inc.; Sandlapper Publishing, Inc.; Sasquatch Books; Scarborough House/Publisherss; Schenkman Books, Inc.; Sentinel Books; Seven Locks Press, Inc.; Shaw Publishers, Harold; Shoe String Press, The; Sierra Club Books; Silver Burdett Press; Silver Press; Simon & Schuster; Smith, Publisher, Gibbs; Soules Book Publishers Ltd., Gordon; Southfarm Press; Stanford University Press; Starburst Publishers; Stevens, Inc., Gareth; Stormline Press; Sunflower University Press; Sunstone Press; Teachers College Press; Texas A&M University Press; Texas Western Press; Three Continents Press; Timber Press, Inc.; Times Books; Transaction Books; Transportation Trails; Tuttle Publishing Company, Inc., Charles E.; Tyndale House Publishers, Inc.; University of Alabama Press; University of Alaska Press; University of Alberta Press, The; University of Arkansas Press, The; University of Illinois Press; University of Iowa Press; University of Massachusetts Press; University of Nebraska Press; University of Nevada Press; University of North Carolina Press, The; University of Oklahoma Press; University of Pennsylvania Press; University of Tennessee Press, The; University of Texas Press; University of Utah Press; University Press of America, Inc.; University Press of Kansas; University Press of Kentucky; University Press of Mississippi; University Press of New England; Vesta Publications, Ltd.; Vestal Press, Ltd., The; Walch, Publisher, J. Weston; Walker and Co.; Wall & Emerson, Inc.; Washington State University Pess; Western Producer Prairie Books; Westernlore Press; Westview Press; Wilderness Adventure Books; Woodbine House; Word Books Publisher; Workman Publishing Company, Inc.; Yankee Books; Zebra Books.

Hobby. Almar Press; Ancestry Incorporated; ARCsoft Publishers; Atheneum Children's Books; Beaver Pond Publishing & Printing; Benjamin Company, Inc., The; C&T Publishing; Carstens Publications, Inc.; Collector Books; Crown Publishers, Inc.; Devonshire Publishing Co.; Dunburn Press Ltd.; Durst Publications Ltd.; Eriksson, Publisher, Paul S.; Facts On File, Inc.; Gem Guides Book Company; Hawkes Publishing, Inc.; Horizon Publishers & Distributors; International Resources; Interurban Press/Trans Anglo Books; Kalmbach Publishing Co.; Kesend Publishing, Ltd., Michael; Klein Publications, B.; Kodansha International U.S.A.; Liberty Publishing Company, Inc.; Menasha Ridge Press, Inc.; Mosaic Press Miniature Books; Mustang Publishing Co.; Polka-Dot Press; Prentice Hall Press; Rocky Top Publications; Scarborough House/Publisherss; Sentinel Books; Silver Press; Stackpole Books; Sterling Publishing; Sunstone Press; Surfside Publishing; TAB Books; Travel Keys; Ultralight Publichations, Inc.; Union Square Press; University of North Carolina Press, The; Vestal Press, Ltd., The; Williamson Publishing Co.; Wilshire Book Co.; Woodbine House; Woodsong Graphics, Inc.; Workman Publishing Company, Inc.

How-to. Abbott, Langer & Associates; ABC-CLIO, Inc.; Accent Books; Addison-Wesley Publishing Co., Inc.; Allen Publishing Co.; Almar Press; Alpine Publications Inc.; Amacom Books; Amacom Books; American Business Consultants, Inc.; Amherst Media; Ancestry Incorporated; Andrews and McMeel; Appalachian Mountain Club Books; Arman Publishing, Inc., M.; Art Direction Book Company; Atheneum Children's Books; Auto Book Press; Avery Publishing Group; Avon Books; Bantam Books; Beaver Pond Publishing & Printing; Benjamin Company, Inc., The; Bentley, Inc., Robert; Berkley Publishing Group, The; Better Homes and Gardens Books; Blue Bird Publishing; Blue Dolphin Publishing, Inc.; Bonus Books, Inc.; Briarcliff Press Publishers; Brick House Publishing Co.; Bull Publishing Co.; Calgre Press; Cambridge Career Products; Camino Books, Inc.; C&T Publishing; Capra Press; Capra Press; Career Press Inc., The; Carol Publishing; Cassandra Press; Cassell Publications; Chicago Review Press; Chilton Book Co.; Chosen Books Publishing Co.; Christopher Publishing House, The; Clarkson Potter; Cleaning Consultant Services, Inc.; College Board, The; Contemporary Books, Inc.; Cornell Maritime Press, Inc.; Countryman Press, Inc., The; Countrywoman's Press,

The; Crossing Press, The; Crown Publishers, Inc.; Dembner Books; Devin-Adair Publishers, Inc.; Durst Publications Ltd.; E.P. Dutton; Education Associates; EES Publications; Eriksson, Publisher, Paul S.; Evergreen Communications, Inc.; Fisher Books; Five Star Publications; Flores Publications, J.; Flying Pencil Publications; Focal Press; Forman Publishing; Gay Sunshine Press and Leyland Publications; Gifted Education Press; Global Business and Trade; Globe Pequot Press, Inc., The; Grapevine Publications, Inc.; Graphic Arts Technical Foundation; Great Northwest Publishing and Distributing Company, Inc.; Hamilton Institute, Alexander; Hancock House Publishers Ltd.; Harper & Row, San Francisco; HarperCollins, Inc.; Harvest House Publishers; Hawkes Publishing, Inc.; Here's Life Publishers, Inc.; Heritage Books, Inc.; Heyday Books; Hippocrene Books Inc.; Holloway House Publishing Co.; Horizon Publishers & Distributors; Hounslow Press; Human Kinetics Publishers, Inc.; Hunter House, Inc., Publishers; Imagine, Inc.; In Depth Publishers; Intercultural Press, Inc.; Interlink Publishing Group, Inc.; International Resources; International Self-Counsel Press, Ltd.; International Wealth Success; Jist Works, Inc.; Kalmbach Publishing Co.; Kesend Publishing, Ltd., Michael; Klein Publications, B.; Knowledge Book Publishers; Leisure Press; Liberty Hall Press; Liberty Publishing Company, Inc.; Library Research Associates, Inc.; Linch Publishing, Inc.; Little, Brown and Co., Inc.; Llewellyn Publications; Lone Eagle Publishing Co.; Lone Pine Publishing; Longman Financial Services Publishing; Loompanics Unlimited; McGraw Hill Ryerson; Menasha Ridge Press, Inc.; Metamorphous Press; MGI Management Institute, Inc., The; Miller Books; Morrow and Co., William; Mother Courage Press; Motorbooks International Publishers & Wholesalers, Inc.; Mountaineers Books, The; Muir Publications, John; Mustang Publishing Co.; Naturegraph Publishers, Inc.; New England Press, Inc., The; Newcastle Publishing Co., Inc.; Noble Press, Incorporated, The; North Light; Northland Publishing Co., Inc.; Overlook Press, The; Pacific Press Publishing Association; Paladin Press; Pelican Publishing Company; Pennsylvania Historical and Museum Commission; Perspectives Press; Pickering Press, The; Pineapple Press, Inc.; Polka-Dot Press; Potomac-Pacific Press; Prevention Health Books; Prima Publishing and Communications; Princeton Book Company, Publishers; NpsychologyI Research; Q.E.D. Press Of Ann Arbor, Inc.; Que Corporation; R&E Publishers; Resource Publications, Inc.; Rocky Top Publications; Ronin Publishing; Ross Books; Scarborough House/Publisherss; Schirmer Books; Self-Counsel Press; Sentinel Books; Sierra Club Books; Soules Book Publishers Ltd., Gordon; Speech Bin, Inc., The; Standard Publishing; Starburst Publishers; Sterling Publishing; Stoeger Publishing Company; Sunstone Press; Surfside Publishing; Synesis Press; TAB Books; Thomas Publications; Tidewater Publishers; Travel Keys; Tuttle Publishing Company, Inc., Charles E.; Twin Peaks Press; Ultralight Publichations, Inc.; Union Square Press; University of Alberta Press, The; Weiser, Inc., Samuel; Wilderness Adventure Books; Wilderness Press; Williamson Publishing Co.; Wilshire Book Co.; Windsor Books; Wine Appreciation Guild, Ltd.; Woodsong Graphics, Inc.; Word Books Publisher; Workman Publishing Company, Inc.; Yankee Books; Zebra Books.

Humanities. Asian Humanities Press; Duquesne University Press; Free Press, The; Plenum Publishing; Riverdale Company, Inc., Publishers, The; Roxbury Publishing Co.; Stanford University Prcss; Whitson Publishing Co., The.

Humor. American Atheist Press; Andrews and McMeel; Atheneum Children's Books; Auto Book Press; Baker Book House Company; Bale Books; Bantam Books; Blue Dolphin Publishing, Inc.; Breakwater Books; C.S.S. Publishing Co.; Camino Books, Inc.; Carol Publishing; CCC Publications; Citadel Press; Clarion Books; Clarkson Potter; Cliffs Notes, Inc.; Contemporary Books, Inc.; Coteau Books; Crown Publishers, Inc.; Cuff Publications Limited, Harry; E.P. Dutton; Edicones Universal; Eriksson, Publisher, Paul S.; Faber & Faber, Inc.; Fine, Inc., Donald I.; Flying Pencil Publications; Fordham University Press; Guernica Editions; HarperCollins, Inc.; Horizon Publishers

& Distributors; Hounslow Press; Inner Traditions International; Jonathan David Publishers; Knowledge Book Publishers; Longstreet Press, Inc.; Media Forum International, Ltd.; Mosaic Press Miniature Books; Mustang Publishing Co.; Once Upon a Planet, Inc.; Paladin Press; Peachtree Publishers, Ltd.; Pelican Publishing Company; Peter Pauper Press, Inc.; Pharos Books; Polka-Dot Press; Potomac-Pacific Press; R&E Publishers; Random House, Inc.; Random House, Inc./Alfred A. Knopf, Inc. Juvenile Books; Ronin Publishing; Rutledge Hill Press; Sandlapper Publishing, Inc.; Sentinel Books; Sterling Publishing; Stormline Press; Synesis Press; Taylor Publishing Company; Tuttle Publishing Company, Inc., Charles E.; University of Arkansas Press, The; Woodsong Graphics, Inc.; Workman Publishing Company, Inc.; Wyrick & Company; Yankee Books.

Illustrated Book. Abrams, Inc. Harry N.; American References Inc.; Atheneum Children's Books; Bantam Books; Bear and Co., Inc.; Bear Flag Books; Boston Mills Press, The; Branden Publishing Co., Inc.; Breakwater Books; Canadian Plains Research Center; Carol Publishing; Chronicle Books; Cleaning Consultant Services, Inc.; Coteau Books; Coventure Press; Davis Publications, Inc.; Dial Books For Young Readers; E.P. Dutton; Five Star Publications; Flockophobic Press; Flores Publications, J.; Gallaudet University Press; Godine, Publisher, Inc., David R.; Graphic Arts Center Publishing Co.; Greenhaven Press, Inc.; Harvest House Publishers; Homestead Publishing; Horizon Publishers & Distributors; Hounslow Press; Howell Press, Inc.; Imagine, Inc.; Inner Traditions International; Interlink Publishing Group, Inc.; International Resources; Kesend Publishing, Ltd., Michael; Lexikos; Longstreet Press, Inc.; Lothrop, Lee & Shepard Books; Metamorphous Press; Milkweed Editions; Mosaic Press Miniature Books; Multnomah Press; New England Press, Inc., The; Noble Press, Incorporated, The; Northland Publishing Co., Inc.; Once Upon a Planet, Inc.; Pelican Publishing Company; Pennsylvania Historical and Museum Commission; Pickering Press, The; Prentice Hall Press; Princeton Architectural Press; R&E Publishers; Random House, Inc.; Random House, Inc./Alfred A. Knopf, Inc. Juvenile Books; Sandlapper Publishing, Inc.; Sentinel Books; Sigo Press; Speech Bin, Inc., The; Stormline Press; Sunflower University Press; Surfside Publishing; Synesis Press; Tidewater Publishers; Tuttle Publishing Company, Inc., Charles E.; Union Square Press; University of Minnesota Press; Westgate Press; Wilderness Adventure Books; Williamson Publishing Co.; Woodsong Graphics, Inc.; Workman Publishing Company, Inc.; Wyrick & Company; Yankee Books.

Juvenile Books. Abingdon Press; Advocacy Press; African American Images; Archway/ Minstrel Books; Atheneum Children's Books; Baker Book House Company; Bantam Books; Barron's Educational Series, Inc.; Beacon Press; Behrman House Inc.; Blue Bird Publishing; Bookmakers Guild, Inc.; Bosco Multimedia, Don; Branden Publishing Co., Inc.; Breakwater Books; Broadman Press; Cambridge Career Products; Camino Books, Inc.; Carolrhoda Books, Inc.; Charlesbridge Publishing; Chronicle Books; Clarion Books; Clarkson Potter; Concordia Publishing House; Coteau Books; Davenport, Publishers, May; Denison & Co., Inc., T.S.; Dial Books For Young Readers; Dillon Press, Inc.; Dunburn Press Ltd.; Dutton Children's Books; Education Associates; English Mountain Publishing Company; Enslow Publishers; Evergreen Communications, Inc.; Fawcett Juniper; Fitzhenry & Whiteside, Ltd.; Gallaudet University Press; Godine, Publisher, Inc., David R.; Greenhaven Press, Inc.; Grosset & Dunlap Publishers; Guernica Editions; Harbinger House, Inc.; Harcourt Brace Jovanovich; Harper Junior Books Group; Harvest House Publishers; Hazelden Educational Materials; Hendrick-Long Publishing Co., Inc.; Homestead Publishing; Horizon Publishers & Distributors; Houghton Mifflin Co.; Huntington House, Inc.; Interlink Publishing Group, Inc.; KarBen Copies Inc.; Knowledge Book Publishers; Lone Pine Publishing; Lothrop, Lee & Shepard Books; Lucent Books; McElderry Books, Margaret K.; MacMillan Publishing

Co.; Mennonite Publishing House, Inc.; Metamorphous Press; Morehouse Publishing Co.; Morrow Junior Books; Multnomah Press; Noble Press, Incorporated, The; Oddo Publishing, Inc.; Orca Book Publishers Ltd.; Oregon Historical Society Press; Pacific Press Publishing Association; Pelican Publishing Company; Perspectives Press; Players Press, Inc.; Random House, Inc./Alfred A. Knopf, Inc. Juvenile Books; Review and Herald Publishing Association; St. Paul Books and Media; Sandlapper Publishing, Inc.; Shaw Publishers, Harold; Shoe String Press, The; Sierra Club Books; Silver Burdett Press; Silver Press; Speech Bin, Inc., The; Standard Publishing; Sterling Publishing; Stevens, Inc., Gareth; Stormline Press; Texas Christian University Press; Tidewater Publishers; Victor Books; Woodbine House; Woodsong Graphics, Inc.; Workman Publishing Company, Inc.; Wyrick & Company; Yankee Books.

Labor/Management. Abbott, Langer & Associates; ALA Books; BNA Books; Drama Book Publishers; Fairchild Books & Visuals; Gulf Publishing Co.; Hamilton Institute, Alexander; ILR Press; International Publishers Co., Inc.; MGI Management Institute, Inc., The; Teachers College Press; University Associates, Inc.

Language and Literature. Asian Humanities Press; Baker Book House Company; Bantam Books; Barron's Educational Series, Inc.; Beacon Press; Black Sparrow Press; Bowling Green State University Popular Press; Breakwater Books; Canadian Institute of Ukrainian Studies Press; Capra Press; Cassell Publications; Catholic University of America Press; Center for Applied Linguistics; Clarion Books; Clarkson Potter; College Board, The; Coteau Books; Crossing Press, The; Daniel and Company, Publishers, John; Dante University Of America Press, Inc.; Dee, Inc., Ivan R.; Dunburn Press Ltd.; Facts On File, Inc.; Family Album, The; Fiddlehead Poetry Books & Goose Lane Editions; Four Walls Eight Windows; Gallaudet University Press; Godine, Publisher, Inc., David R.; Humanities Press International, Inc.; Insight Books; Intervarsity Press; Kent State University Press; Kodansha International U.S.A.; Lang Publishing, Peter; Longstreet Press, Inc.; Longwood Academic; Louisiana State University Press; Mennonite Publishing House, Inc.; Mercury Press, The; Michigan State University Press; Milkweed Editions; Modern Language Association of America; National Textbook Co.; NTC Publishing Group; Ohio University Press; Oregon State University Press; Pippin Press; Prentice Hall Canada, Inc.; Princeton University Press; Purdue University Press; Regnery/Gateway, Inc.; Roxbury Publishing Co.; Sasquatch Books; Scarborough House/Publisherss; Shoe String Press, The; Silver Press; Stanford University Press; Sunflower University Press; Three Continents Press; Tuttle Publishing Company, Inc., Charles E.; University of Alabama Press; University of Alaska Press; University of Arkansas Press, The; University of California Press; University of Illinois Press; University of Iowa Press; University of Nebraska Press; University of Nevada Press; University of North Carolina Press, The; University of Oklahoma Press; University of Pittsburgh Press; University of Texas Press; University Press of America, Inc.; University Press of Mississippi; Wake Forest University Press; Walch, Publisher, J. Weston; Wall & Emerson, Inc.; Wyrick & Company; Yankee Books; York Press Ltd.

Law. And Books; Anderson Publishing Co.; Banks-Baldwin Law Publishing Co.; BNA Books; Copyright Information Services; Davis Publishing Company/Law Enforcement Division; Durst Publications Ltd.; EES Publications; Government Institutes, Inc.; Hamilton Institute, Alexander; International Self-Counsel Press, Ltd.; Liberty Hall Press; Linch Publishing, Inc.; McCutchan Publishing Corporation; Parker-Griffin Publishing Co.; Rutgers University Press; Transaction Books; Transnational Publishers, Inc.; University of North Carolina Press, The; University of Pennsylvania Press; Westview Press.

Literary Criticism. Barron's Educational Series, Inc.; Borgo Press, The; Bucknell University Press; Dunburn Press Ltd.; ECW Press; Fairleigh Dickinson University Press; Firebrand Books; Gaslight Publications; Graywolf Press; Holmes & Meier Publishers, Inc.; Lang Publishing, Peter; Longwood Academic; Mysterious Press, The; Northern

Illinois University Press; Q.E.D. Press Of Ann Arbor, Inc.; Texas Christian University Press; Three Continents Press; University of Alabama Press; University of Massachusetts Press; University of Pennsylvania Press; University of Tennessee Press, The; University Press of Mississippi; York Press Ltd.

Marine Subjects. Binford & Mort Publishing; Cornell Maritime Press, Inc.; Fiddlehead Poetry Books & Goose Lane Editions; Flores Publications, J.; International Marine Publishing Co.; TAB Books; Transportation Trails.

Military/War. ABC-CLIO, Inc.; Avery Publishing Group; Avon Books; Bantam Books; Beau Lac Publishers; Cato Institute; Crown Publishers, Inc.; Dee, Inc., Ivan R.; Fine, Inc., Donald I.; Flores Publications, J.; Global Business and Trade; Howell Press, Inc.; Kodansha International U.S.A.; Louisiana State University Press; Lucent Books; Nautical & Aviation Publishing Co., The; Old Army Press, The; Paladin Press; Praeger Publishers; Prentice Hall Press; Princeton University Press; Reference Service Press; Scarborough House/Publisherss; Shoe String Press, The; Southfarm Press; Stackpole Books; Starburst Publishers; Sterling Publishing; Sunflower University Press; Texas A&M University Press; University of Alaska Press; University Press of Kansas; Vanwell Publishing Limited; Westview Press; Zebra Books; Kodansha International U.S.A.; Louisiana State University Press.

Money/Finance. Allen Publishing Co.; Almar Press; Bale Books; Bantam Books; Better Homes and Gardens Books; Bonus Books, Inc.; Briarcliff Press Publishers; Brick House Publishing Co.; Cambridge Career Products; Career Press Inc., The; Carol Publishing; Cato Institute; Contemporary Books, Inc.; Financial Sourcebooks; Global Business and Trade; Hancock House Publishers Ltd.; Hensley, Inc., Virgil W.; Horizon Publishers & Distributors; Hounslow Press; In Depth Publishers; Insight Books; Intergalactic Publishing Co.; International Resources; International Wealth Success; Liberty Hall Press; Liberty Publishing Company, Inc.; Longman Financial Services Publishing; McGraw Hill Ryerson; Mennonite Publishing House, Inc.; Nichols Publishing; Pilot Books; R&E Publishers; Scarborough House/Publisherss; Self-Counsel Press; Starburst Publishers; Sunflower University Press; Synesis Press; Tuttle Publishing Company, Inc., Charles E.; ULI, The Urban Land Institute; Wilshire Book Co.; Windsor Books.

Music and Dance. American Catholic Press; And Books; Atheneum Children's Books; Bantam Books; Branden Publishing Co., Inc.; Bucknell University Press; Carol Publishing; Carolrhoda Books, Inc.; Dance Horizons; Davenport, Publishers, May; Delta Books; Dembner Books; Drama Book Publishers; Faber & Faber, Inc.; Facts On File, Inc.; Fairleigh Dickinson University Press; Glenbridge Publishing Ltd.; Godine, Publisher, Inc., David R.; Guernica Editions; HarperCollins, Inc.; Holmes & Meier Publishers, Inc.; Horizon Publishers & Distributors; Inner Traditions International; Kodansha International U.S.A.; Lang Publishing, Peter; Longwood Academic; Louisiana State University Press; McFarland & Company, Inc., Publishers; Mercury Press, The; Mosaic Press Miniature Books; National Book Company; Pelican Publishing Company; Pendragon Press; Pippin Press; Prima Publishing and Communications; Princeton Book Company, Publishers; Princeton University Press; Q.E.D. Press Of Ann Arbor, Inc.; Quill; R&E Publishers; Random House, Inc.; Resource Publications, Inc.; Rosen Publishing Group, The; San Francisco Press, Inc.; Scarecrow Press, Inc.; Schirmer Books; Stipes Publishing Co.; Sunflower University Press; TAB Books; Timber Press, Inc.; Transaction Books; University of Illinois Press; University of Minnesota Press; University Press of America, Inc.; Vestal Press, Ltd., The; Wadsworth Publishing Company; Walch, Publisher, J. Weston; Walker and Co.; White Cliffs Media Company; Writer's Digest Books.

Nature and Environment. Abrams, Inc. Harry N.; Amwell Press, The; Appalachian Mountain Club Books; Atheneum Children's Books; Avery Publishing Group; Backcountry Publications; Beacon Press; Bear and Co., Inc.; Bear Flag Books; Beaver Pond

Publishing & Printing; Binford & Mort Publishing; Blue Dolphin Publishing, Inc.; BNA Books; Bookmakers Guild, Inc.; Boxwood Press, The; Breakwater Books; Canadian Plains Research Center; Capra Press; Carol Publishing; Carolrhoda Books, Inc.; Chelsea Green; Clarion Books; Clarkson Potter; Conari Press; Countryman Press, Inc., The; Countrywoman's Press, The; Crown Publishers, Inc.; Devin-Adair Publishers, Inc.; Devonshire Publishing Co.; Down East Books; Dutton Children's Books; Eriksson, Publisher, Paul S.; Facts On File, Inc.; Flying Pencil Publications; Forman Publishing; Four Walls Eight Windows; Fulcrum, Inc.; Gem Guides Book Company; Godine, Publisher, Inc., David R.; Government Institutes, Inc.; Greenhaven Press, Inc.; Grosset & Dunlap Publishers; Hancock House Publishers Ltd.; Harbinger House, Inc.; HarperCollins, Inc.; Heyday Books; Homestead Publishing; Horizon Publishers & Distributors; Houghton Mifflin Co.; Hunter House, Inc., Publishers; Inner Traditions International; Insight Books; Interlink Publishing Group, Inc.; International Resources; Johnson Books; Kesend Publishing, Ltd., Michael; Kodansha International U.S.; Kumarian Press, Inc.; Lawrence Books, Merloyd; Lexikos; Llewellyn Publications; Lone Pine Publishing; Longstreet Press, Inc.; Lucent Books; Lyons & Burford, Publishers, Inc.; Mennonite Publishing House, Inc.; Milkweed Editions; Mosaic Press Miniature Books; Mountaineers Books, The; Muir Publications, John; Museum of Northern Arizona Press; New England Press, Inc., The; Noble Press, Incorporated, The; Northland Publishing Co., Inc.; Noyes Data Corp.; Orca Book Publishers Ltd.; Oregon Historical Society Press; Overlook Press, The; Pacific Press Publishing Association; Pennsylvania Historical and Museum Commission; Pineapple Press, Inc.; Pippin Press; Prentice Hall Press; Princeton University Press; R&E Publishers; Random House, Inc./Alfred A. Knopf, Inc. Juvenile Books; Review and Herald Publishing Association; Rocky Top Publications; Sandhill Crane Press, Inc.; Sasquatch Books; Scribner's Sons, Charles; Sentinel Books; Seven Locks Press, Inc.; Shoe String Press, The; Sierra Club Books; Silver Burdett Press; Soules Book Publishers Ltd., Gordon; Stevens, Inc., Gareth; Sunflower University Press; Texas A&M University Press; Timber Press, Inc.; University of Alaska Press; University of Alberta Press, The; University of Arizona Press; University of Arkansas Press, The; University of California Press; University of Minnesota Press; University of Nebraska Press; University of North Carolina Press, The; University of Pittsburgh Press; University of Texas Press; University Press of Colorado; University Press of Mississippi; University Press of New England; Walker and Co.; Wall & Emerson, Inc.; Washington State University Pess; Western Producer Prairie Books; Westview Press; Wilderness Adventure Books; Williamson Publishing Co.; Woodbridge Press; Workman Publishing Company, Inc.; Yankee Books.

Philosophy. Alba House; American Atheist Press; Aquarian Press, The; Asian Humanities Press; Atheneum Children's Books; Auto Book Press; Baker Book House Company; Bantam Books; Beacon Press; Bucknell University Press; Carol Publishing; Cassandra Press; Catholic University of America Press; Center for Thanatology Research; Christopher Publishing House, The; City Lights Books; Edicones Universal; Eerdmans Publishing Co., William B.; Facts On File, Inc.; Fairleigh Dickinson University Press; Gifted Education Press; Glenbridge Publishing Ltd.; Globe Press Books; Greenhaven Press, Inc.; Guernica Editions; Harper & Row, San Francisco; HarperCollins, Inc.; Humanities Press International, Inc.; Inner Traditions International; Insight Books; Intercultural Press, Inc.; International Publishers Co., Inc.; Intervarsity Press; Kodansha International U.S.A.; Lang Publishing, Peter; Larson Publications/PBPF; Library Research Associates, Inc.; Lone Pine Publishing; Longwood Academic; Loompanics Unlimited; Louisiana State University Press; Meeramma Publications; Michigan State University Press; Miller Books; Noble Press, Incorporated, The; Northern Illinois University Press; Ohio University Press; Open Court Publishing Co.; Paragon House Publishers; Permanent Press/Second Chance Press, The; Praeger Publishers; Princeton University Press;

Purdue University Press; Q.E.D. Press Of Ann Arbor, Inc.; R&E Publishers; Rocky Top Publications; Shoe String Press, The; Sierra Club Books; Simon & Schuster; Synesis Press; Teachers College Press; Theosophical Publishing House, The; Transaction Books; Tuttle Publishing Company, Inc., Charles E.; University of Alabama Press; University of Alberta Press, The; University of Arizona Press; University of Massachusetts Press; University of Minnesota Press; University of Pittsburgh Press; University of Utah Press; University Press of America, Inc.; University Press of Kansas; Vesta Publications, Ltd.; Wadsworth Publishing Company; Wall & Emerson, Inc.; Washington State University Pess; Weiser, Inc., Samuel; Westview Press; Winbow Press; Winston-Derek Publishers, Inc.; Wizards Bookshelf; Woodsong Graphics, Inc.; Word Books Publisher.

Photography. Amherst Media; Atheneum Children's Books; Bear Flag Books; Beaver Pond Publishing & Printing; Black Sparrow Press; Bowling Green State University Popular Press; Branden Publishing Co., Inc.; Breakwater Books; Carstens Publications, Inc.; Clarion Books; Clarkson Potter; Consultant Press, The; Coteau Books; Crown Publishers, Inc.; Cuff Publications Limited, Harry; Fiddlehead Poetry Books & Goose Lane Editions; Focal Press; Godine, Publisher, Inc., David R.; Homestead Publishing; Hounslow Press; Howell Press, Inc.; Hudson Hill Press, Inc.; International Resources; Longstreet Press, Inc.; Louisiana State University Press; Milkweed Editions; Miller Books; Motorbooks International Publishers & Wholesalers, Inc.; Northland Publishing Co., Inc.; NTC Publishing Group; Oregon Historical Society Press; Pennsylvania Historical and Museum Commission; Prentice Hall Press; Purdue University Press; Random House, Inc.; Sasquatch Books; Sentinel Books; Sierra Club Books; Sterling Publishing; Stormline Press; Sunflower University Press; TAB Books; University of Iowa Press; University of Minnesota Press; University of Nebraska Press; Wake Forest University Press; Western Producer Prairie Books; Workman Publishing Company, Inc.; Writer's Digest Books; Wyrick & Company; Yankee Books.

Psychology. Addison-Wesley Publishing Co., Inc.; Advocacy Press; African American Images; Alba House; American Psychiatric Press, Inc., The; And Books; Aquarian Press, The; Atheneum Children's Books; Avon Books; Baker Book House Company; Bantam Books; Beacon Press; Blue Dolphin Publishing, Inc.; Bookmakers Guild, Inc.; Boxwood Press, The; Bucknell University Press; Cambridge University Press; Carol Publishing; Carroll & Graf Publishers, Inc.; Cassandra Press; Center for Thanatology Research; Christopher Publishing House, The; Citadel Press; Conari Press; Contemporary Books, Inc.; Coventure Press; Crown Publishers, Inc.; Dee, Inc., Ivan R.; Devonshire Publishing Co.; Edicones Universal; Education Associates; Eerdmans Publishing Co., William B.; Eriksson, Publisher, Paul S.; Erlbaum Associates, Inc., Lawrence; Facts On File, Inc.; Fairleigh Dickinson University Press; Fisher Books; Forman Publishing; Gallaudet University Press; Gardner Press, Inc.; Gifted Education Press; Glenbridge Publishing Ltd.; Globe Press Books; Guernica Editions; Harbinger House, Inc.; Harper & Row, San Francisco; HarperCollins, Inc.; Hawkes Publishing, Inc.; Health Communications, Inc.; Horizon Publishers & Distributors; Houghton Mifflin Co.; Humanics Publishing Group; Hunter House, Inc., Publishers; Inner Traditions International; Insight Books; Integrated Press; Intercultural Press, Inc.; International Self-Counsel Press, Ltd.; Intervarsity Press; Ishiyaku Euroamerica, Inc.; Kodansha International U.S.A.; Lang Publishing, Peter; Larson Publications/PBPF; Lawrence Books, Merloyd; Libra Publishers, Inc.; Llewellyn Publications; Luramedia; Meeramma Publications; Mennonite Publishing House, Inc.; Metamorphous Press; Mother Courage Press; Newcastle Publishing Co., Inc.; Open Court Publishing Co.; Parkside Publishing Coporation; Perspectives Press; Pickering Press, The; Plenum Publishing; Potomac-Pacific Press; Praeger Publishers; Prentice Hall Press; Prima Publishing and Communications; Quill; R&E Publishers; Riverdale Company, Inc., Publishers, The; Ronin Publishing; St. Paul Books and Media; Scarborough House/Publisherss; Schenkman Books, Inc.; Self-Coun-

Lane Editions; Financial Sourcebooks; Focal Press; Gallaudet University Press; Gardner Press, Inc.; Garrett Park Press; Gaslight Publications; Genealogical Publishing Co., Inc.; Gessler Publishing Company, Inc.; Getty Museum, The J. Paul; Glenbridge Publishing Ltd.; Government Institutes, Inc.; Graphic Arts Technical Foundation; Greenhaven Press, Inc.; Guernica Editions; Gulf Publishing Co.; Harper & Row, San Francisco; HarperCollins, Inc.; Harvest House Publishers; Health Administration Press; Here's Life Publishers, Inc.; Heritage Books, Inc.; Heyday Books; Hippocrene Books Inc.; Holmes & Meier Publishers, Inc.; Homestead Publishing; Human Kinetics Publishers, Inc.; IEEE Press; ILR Press; Imagine, Inc.; Industrial Press, Inc.; Information Resources Press; Intercultural Press, Inc.; International Foundation Of Employee Benefit Plans; International Publishers Co., Inc.; International Resources; International Self-Counsel Press, Ltd.; Ishiyaku Euroamerica, Inc.; Jist Works, Inc.; Jonathan David Publishers; Kinseeker Publications; Klein Publications, B.; Lang Publishing, Peter; Leisure Press; Liberty Publishing Company, Inc.; Libraries Unlimited; Library Research Associates, Inc.; Lone Eagle Publishing Co.; Longman Financial Services Publishing; Longstreet Press, Inc.; Loompanics Unlimited; McFarland & Company, Inc., Publishers; McGraw Hill Ryerson; Madison Books; Media Forum International, Ltd.; Menasha Ridge Press, Inc.; Mennonite Publishing House, Inc.; Metamorphous Press; Michigan State University Press; Modern Language Association of America; Muir Publications, John; Museum of Northern Arizona Press; Mysterious Press, The; National Book Company; Nautical & Aviation Publishing Co., The; Nichols Publishing; Noble Press, Incorporated, The; Octameron Associates; Old Army Press, The; Orca Book Publishers Ltd.; Oregon Historical Society Press; Our Sunday Visitor, Inc.; Overlook Press, The; Pacific Books, Publishers; Paragon House Publishers; Pendragon Press; Pennsylvania Historical and Museum Commission; Pharos Books; Pineapple Press, Inc.; Pocket Books; Porter Sargent Publishers, Inc.; Praeger Publishers; Princeton Book Company, Publishers; Princeton University Press; Professional Publications, Inc.; Que Corporation; Rainbow Books; R&E Publishers; Reference Service Press; Rocky Top Publications; Rosen Publishing Group, The; Rutledge Hill Press; St. Martin's Press; Sandhill Crane Press, Inc.; Sandlapper Publishing, Inc.; Scarborough House/Publisherss; Scarecrow Press, Inc.; Schirmer Books; Science Tech Publishers, Inc.; Self-Counsel Press; Sentinel Books; Seven Locks Press, Inc.; Shaw Publishers, Harold; Shoe String Press, The; Speech Bin, Inc., The; Standard Publishing; Starburst Publishers; Starrhill Press; Sterling Publishing; Stevens, Inc., Gareth; Sunflower University Press; Surfside Publishing; Thomas Publications; Tidewater Publishers; Transaction Books; Transnational Publishers, Inc.; Tuttle Publishing Company, Inc., Charles E.; Twin Peaks Press; Union Square Press; University of Alaska Press; University of Alberta Press, The; University of Illinois Press; University of Minnesota Press; University of Pittsburgh Press; University Press of Kentucky; University Press of New England; Vesta Publications, Ltd.; Victor Books; Walker and Co.; Wall & Emerson, Inc.; Western Producer Prairie Books; Westview Press; Whitson Publishing Co., The; Winbow Press; Woodbine House; Woodsong Graphics, Inc.; Word Books Publisher; Yankee Books; York Press Ltd.; Zondervan Corp. The.

Regional. Abbey Press; Almar Press; Appalachian Mountain Club Books; Bear Flag Books; Binford & Mort Publishing; Blair, Publisher, John F.; Borealis Press, Ltd.; Boston Mills Press, The; Bowling Green State University Popular Press; Boxwood Press, The; Breakwater Books; Camino Books, Inc.; Capra Press; Carol Publishing; Caxton Printers, Ltd., The; Chatham Press; Chicago Review Press; Conari Press; Coteau Books; Countryman Press, Inc., The; Cuff Publications Limited, Harry; Denali Press, The; Dillon Press, Inc.; Down East Books; Dunburn Press Ltd.; ECW Press; Eerdmans Publishing Co., William B.; English Mountain Publishing Company; Faber & Faber, Inc.; Family Album, The; Fiddlehead Poetry Books & Goose Lane Editions; Fitzhenry & Whiteside, Ltd.; Flying Pencil Publications; Gallaudet University Press; Gem Guides

Book Company; Globe Pequot Press, Inc., The; Godine, Publisher, Inc., David R.; Golden West Publishers; Great Northwest Publishing and Distributing Company, Inc.; Guernica Editions; Gulf Publishing Co.; Hancock House Publishers Ltd.; Heart Of The Lakes Publishing; Hendrick-Long Publishing Co., Inc.; Herald Publishing House; Heritage Books, Inc.; Heyday Books; Howell Press, Inc.; Interurban Press/Trans Anglo Books; Johnson Books; Kent State University Press; Lexikos; Longstreet Press, Inc.; McGraw Hill Ryerson; Mennonite Publishing House, Inc.; Milkweed Editions; Museum of Northern Arizona Press; National Gallery of Canada; Northern Illinois University Press; Northland Publishing Co., Inc.; Ohio University Press; Oregon Historical Society Press; Pacific Books, Publishers; Pacific Press Publishing Association; Pennsylvania Historical and Museum Commission; Pickering Press, The; Prentice-Hall Canada, Inc.; Purdue University Press; R&E Publishers; Sandlapper Publishing, Inc.; Sentinel Books; Soules Book Publishers Ltd., Gordon; Stormline Press; Sunflower University Press; Sunstone Press; Syracuse University Press; Texas A&M University Press; Texas Christian University Press; Texas Western Press; Tidewater Publishers; Timber Press, Inc.; Tuttle Publishing Company, Inc., Charles E.; University of Alaska Press; University of Alberta Press, The; University of Arizona Press; University of Minnesota Press; University of Nevada Press; University of Tennessee Press, The; University of Texas Press; University Press of Colorado; University Press of Kansas; University Press of Mississippi; University Press of New England; Vanwell Publishing Limited; Vestal Press, Ltd., The; Washington State University Pess; Westernlore Press; Wilderness Adventure Books; Wordware Publishing, Inc.; Wyrick & Company; Yankee Books.

Religion. Abingdon Press; Accent Books; Aglow Publications; Alba House; Alban Institue, Inc., The; American Atheist Press; American Catholic Press; And Books; Aquarian Press, The; Asian Humanities Press; Atheneum Children's Books; Baker Book House Company; Bantam Books; Beacon Hill Press of Kansas City; Beacon Press; Bear and Co., Inc.; Behrman House Inc.; Berkley Publishing Group, The; Bethany House Publishers; Bethel Publishing; Blue Dolphin Publishing, Inc.; Bookcraft, Inc.; Bosco Multimedia, Don; Bowling Green State University Popular Press; Breakwater Books; Broadman Press; Bucknell University Press; C.S.S. Publishing Co.; Canadian Institute of Ukrainian Studies Press; Cassandra Press; Catholic University of America Press; Center for Thanatology Research; Chosen Books Publishing Co.; Christopher Publishing House, The; Christopher Publishing House, The; College Press Publishing Co.; Concordia Publishing House; Coventure Press; Crossway Books; Dee, Inc., Ivan R.; Devonshire Publishing Co.; Eerdmans Publishing Co., William B.; Evergreen Communications, Inc.; Facts On File, Inc.; Franciscan Herald Press; Fraser Institute, The; Gardner Press, Inc.; Gospel Publishing House; Greenhaven Press, Inc.; Guernica Editions; HarperCollins, Inc.; Harvest House Publishers; Hendrickson Publishers Inc.; Hensley, Inc., Virgil W.; Herald Publishing House; Here's Life Publishers, Inc.; Horizon Publishers & Distributors; Howell Press, Inc.; Human Kinetics Publishers, Inc.; Inner Traditions International; Insight Books; Interlink Publishing Group, Inc.; Intervarsity Press; Jalmar Press, Inc.; Judson Press; Kodansha International U.S.A.; Kumarian Press, Inc.; Lang Publishing, Peter; Larson Publications/PBPF; Lion Publishing Corporation; Longwood Academic; Loyola University Press; Meeramma Publications; Mennonite Publishing House, Inc.; Michigan State University Press; Morehouse Publishing Co.; Morrow and Co., William; Multnomah Press; Nelson Publishers, Thomas; New Leaf Press, Inc.; Newcastle Publishing Co., Inc.; Noble Press, Incorporated, The; Open Court Publishing Co.; Orbis Books; Our Sunday Visitor, Inc.; Pacific Press Publishing Association; Paragon House Publishers; Pelican Publishing Company; Pennsylvania Historical and Museum Commission; Peter Pauper Press, Inc.; Princeton University Press; Purdue University Press; Random House, Inc.; Regal Books; Religious Education Press; Resource Publications, Inc.; Review and Herald Publishing Association; St. Anthony Messenger Press; St. Paul Books and Media; St. Vladimir's Seminary Press; Servant Publications; Seven Locks Press, Inc.; Shoe String Press, The; Sigo Press; Standard Publishing; Starburst Publishers; Sunflower University Press; Theosophical Publishing House, The; Tuttle Publishing Company, Inc., Charles E.; Tyndale House Publishers, Inc.; University of Alabama Press; University of North Carolina Press, The; University of Tennessee Press, The; University Press of America, Inc.; Vesta Publications, Ltd.; Victor Books; Wadsworth Publishing Company; Weiser, Inc., Samuel; Winbow Press; Winston-Derek Publishers, Inc.; Wood Lake Books, Inc.; Word Books Publisher; Workman Publishing Company, Inc.; Yankee Books; Zondervan Corp., The.

Scholarly. Cambridge University Press; Canadian Institute of Ukrainian Studies Press; Getty Museum, The J. Paul; Humanities Press International, Inc.; Longwood Academic; McFarland & Company, Inc., Publishers; Michigan State University Press; Ohio University Press; Oregon State University Press; Pacific Books, Publishers; Princeton University Press; Purdue University Press; Religious Education Press; Riverdale Company, Inc., Publishers, The; Rutgers University Press; St. Vladimir's Seminary Press; Schirmer Books; Stanford University Press; Texas Christian University Press; Texas Western Press; Three Continents Press; Transaction Books; Transnational Publishers, Inc.; University of Alabama Press; University of Alberta Press, The; University of Arizona Press; University of Calgary Press, The; University of California Press; University of Illinois Press; University of North Carolina Press, The; University of Pennsylvania Press; University of Tennessee Press, The; University of Texas Press; University of Utah Press; University of Wisconsin Press; University Press of America, Inc.; University Press of Kansas; University Press of Kentucky; University Press of Mississippi; Washington State University Press; Westernlore Press; Westview Press; Whitson Publishing Co., The; Whitson Publishing Co., The; York Press Ltd.

Science/Technology. Abrams, Inc. Harry N.; Amherst Media; ARCsoft Publishers; Bantam Books; Bear and Co., Inc.; Boxwood Press, The; Cambridge University Press; Carol Publishing; Chicago Review Press; College Board, The; Crown Publishers, Inc.; Delta Books; Dillon Press, Inc.; Dutton Children's Books; Enslow Publishers; Erlbaum Associates, Inc., Lawrence; Focal Press; Four Walls Eight Windows; Gallaudet University Press; Grapevine Publications, Inc.; Green, Inc., Warren H.; Grosset & Dunlap Publishers; Gulf Publishing Co.; HarperCollins, Inc.; Hendrick-Long Publishing Co., Inc.; Houghton Mifflin Co.; IEEE Press; Industrial Press, Inc.; Insight Books; Interstate Publishers, Inc. The; Iowa State University Press; Johnson Books; Knowledge Book Publishers; Kodansha International U.S.A.; Little, Brown and Co., Inc.; Longwood Academic; Lucent Books; Lyons & Burford, Publishers, Inc.; Metamorphous Press; Museum of Northern Arizona Press; National Book Company; Naturegraph Publishers, Inc.; Noyes Data Corp.; Oddo Publishing, Inc.; Oregon State University Press; Pippin Press; Plenum Publishing; Prentice Hall Canada, Inc.; Princeton University Press; Quill; R&E Publishers; Random House, Inc./Alfred A. Knopf, Inc. Juvenile Books; Rocky Top Publications; Ross Books; Rutgers University Press; St. Martin's Press; San Francisco Press, Inc.; Scarborough House/Publisherss; Science Tech Publishers, Inc.; Scribner's Sons, Charles; Sierra Club Books; Silver Burdett Press; Simon & Schuster; Stackpole Books; Stanford University Press; Sunflower University Press; Tarcher, Inc. Jeremy P.; Theosophical Publishing House, The; Times Books; Transaction Books; Union Square Press; Univelt, Inc.; University of Alaska Press; University of Arizona Press; University of Pennsylvania Press; University of Texas Press; University Press of New England; Walker and Co.; Wall & Emerson, Inc.; Westview Press; Woodbine House.

Self-Help. Accent Books; Adams, Inc., Bob; Advocacy Press; African American Images; Aglow Publications; Allen Publishing Co.; Almar Press; Amacom Books; Atheneum Children's Books; Avon Books; Baker Book House Company; Bantam Books; Benjamin

ARE YOU SERIOUS?

About learning to write better? Getting published? Getting paid for what you write? If you're dedicated to your writing, **Writer's Digest School** can put you on the fast track to writing success.

You'll Study With A Professional

Writer's Digest School offers you more than textbooks and assignments. As a student you'll correspond <u>directly with a professional writer</u> who is currently writing **and selling** the kind of material that you want to write. You'll learn from a pro who knows, from personal experience, what it takes to get a manuscript written and published. A writer who can guide you as you work to achieve the same thing. A true mentor.

Work On Your Novel, Short Story, Nonfiction Book, Or Article

Writer's Digest School offers four courses: The Novel Writing Workshop, the Nonfiction Book Workshop, Writing to Sell Fiction (Short Stories), and Writing to Sell Nonfiction (Articles). Each course is described on the reverse side.
If you're serious about your writing, you owe it to yourself to check out **Writer's Digest School.** Mail the coupon below today for FREE information! Or call **1-800-759-0963.** (Outside the U.S., call (513) 531-2222.) Writer's Digest School, 1507 Dana Avenue, Cincinnati, Ohio 45207.

Yes, I'm Serious!

I want to write and sell with the help of the professionals at **Writer's Digest School.** Send me free information about the course I've checked below:

☐ Novel Writing Workshop ☐ Writing to Sell Fiction (Short Stories)
☐ Nonfiction Book Workshop ☐ Writing to Sell Nonfiction (Articles)

Name _____

Address _____

City _____ State _____ Zip _____

Mail this card today! No postage needed.

Or Call **1-800-759-0963** for free information today.

IWMWG1X1

Here are four **Writer's Digest School** courses to help you write better and sell more:

Novel Writing Workshop. A professional novelist helps you iron out your plot, develop your main characters, write the background for your novel, and complete the opening scene and a summary of your novel's complete story. You'll even identify potential publishers, write a query letter, and get practical advice on the submission process.

Nonfiction Book Workshop. You'll work with your mentor to create a book proposal that you can send directly to a publisher. You'll develop and refine your book idea, write a chapter-by-chapter outline of your subject, line up your sources of information, write sample chapters, identify potential publishers, and complete your query letter.

Writing to Sell Fiction. Learn the basics of writing/selling short stories: plotting, characterization, dialogue, theme, conflict, and other elements of a marketable short story. Course includes writing assignments and one complete short story (and its revision).

Writing to Sell Nonfiction. Master the fundamentals of writing/selling nonfiction articles: finding article ideas, conducting interviews, writing effective query letters and attention-getting leads, targeting your articles to the right publication, and other important elements of a salable article. Course includes writing assignments and one complete article manuscript (and its revision).

Mail this card today for **FREE** information!

Company, Inc., The; Blue Dolphin Publishing, Inc.; Bonus Books, Inc.; Bull Publishing Co.; C.S.S. Publishing Co.; Calgre Press; Cambridge Career Products; Career Press Inc., The; Carol Publishing; Cassandra Press; CCC Publications; Center for Thanatology Research; Chosen Books Publishing Co.; Christopher Publishing House, The; Chronicle Books; Clarkson Potter; Cleaning Consultant Services, Inc.; Cliffs Notes, Inc.; College Board, The; Contemporary Books, Inc.; Coventure Press; Crown Publishers, Inc.; E.P. Dutton; Eriksson, Publisher, Paul S.; Evergreen Communications, Inc.; Fine, Inc., Donald I.; Fisher Books; Flores Publications, J.; Forman Publishing; Fulcrum, Inc.; Gallaudet University Press; Gardner Press, Inc.; Global Business and Trade; Globe Press Books; Gospel Publishing House; Grapevine Publications, Inc.; Hancock House Publishers Ltd.; Harbinger House, Inc.; Harper & Row, San Francisco; HarperCollins, Inc.; Harvest House Publishers; Hawkes Publishing, Inc.; Hazelden Educational Materials; Herald Publishing House; Here's Life Publishers, Inc.; Hippocrene Books Inc.; Horizon Publishers & Distributors; Human Kinetics Publishers, Inc.; Humanics Publishing Group; Hunter House, Inc., Publishers; Huntington House, Inc.; Insight Books; Intercultural Press, Inc.; International Resources; International Self-Counsel Press, Ltd.; International Wealth Success; Kesend Publishing, Ltd., Michael; Klein Publications, B.; Liberty Hall Press; Llewellyn Publications; Lone Eagle Publishing Co.; Loompanics Unlimited; Luramedia; McGraw Hill Ryerson; Menasha Ridge Press, Inc.; Mennonite Publishing House, Inc.; Metamorphous Press; Miller Books; Mills & Sanderson, Publishers; Mother Courage Press; Multnomah Press; Mustang Publishing Co.; Nelson Publishers, Thomas; New Leaf Press, Inc.; Newcastle Publishing Co., Inc.; Noble Press, Incorporated, The; Pacific Press Publishing Association; Parkside Publishing Coporation; Pelican Publishing Company; Perspectives Press; Pickering Press, The; Polka-Dot Press; Potomac-Pacific Press; Prentice Hall Press; Prevention Health Books; Prima Publishing and Communications; Princeton Book Company, Publishers; Rainbow Books; R&E Publishers; Random House, Inc.; Rocky Top Publications; Rosen Publishing Group, The; St. Martin's Press; St. Paul Books and Media; Scarborough House/Publisherss; Scribner's Sons, Charles; Self-Counsel Press; Shaw Publishers, Harold; Sigo Press; Skidmore-Roth Publishing; Spinsters/Aunt Lute Books; Starburst Publishers; Sterling Publishing; Surfside Publishing; Synesis Press; Taylor Publishing Company; Theosophical Publishing House, The; Tidewater Publishers; Trillium Press; Twin Peaks Press; Ultralight Publichations, Inc.; Victor Books; Walker and Co.; Weiser, Inc., Samuel; Williamson Publishing Co.; Wilshire Book Co.; Winbow Press; Woodbine House; Woodbridge Press; Woodsong Graphics, Inc.; Word Books Publisher; Workman Publishing Company, Inc.; Yankee Books; Zebra Books; Zondervan Corp., The.

Social Sciences. African American Images; Borgo Press, The; Canadian Plains Research Center; Catholic University of America Press; Chelsea Green; Duquesne University Press; Eerdmans Publishing Co., William B.; Free Press, The; International Publishers Co., Inc.; Longman Publishing Group; Madison Books; Northern Illinois University Press; Prentice Hall Canada, Inc.; Riverdale Company, Inc., Publishers, The; Roxbury Publishing Co.; Stanford University Press; Teachers College Press; University of California Press; Wadsworth Publishing Company; Walch, Publisher, J. Weston; Whitson Publishing Co., The.

Sociology. Alba House; Atheneum Children's Books; Baker Book House Company; Bantam Books; Beacon Press; Bookmakers Guild, Inc.; Bowling Green State University Popular Press; Branden Publishing Co., Inc.; Breakwater Books; Bucknell University Press; Canadian Institute of Ukrainian Studies Press; Canadian Plains Research Center; Capra Press; Capra Press; Cato Institute; Center for Thanatology Research; Child Welfare League Of America; Christopher Publishing House, The; Cleis Press; Cuff Publications Limited, Harry; Dee, Inc., Ivan R.; Dembner Books; Devonshire Publishing Co.; Edicones Universal; Eerdmans Publishing Co., William B.; Enslow Publishers; Eriksson,

Publisher, Paul S.; Faber & Faber, Inc.; Fairleigh Dickinson University Press; Fraser Institute, The; Gallaudet University Press; Gardner Press, Inc.; Glenbridge Publishing Ltd.; Greenhaven Press, Inc.; Harbinger House, Inc.; HarperCollins, Inc.; Health Administration Press; Holmes & Meier Publishers, Inc.; Humanics Publishing Group; Humanities Press International, Inc.; ILR Press; Insight Books; Intercultural Press, Inc.; Intervarsity Press; Kodansha International U.S.A.; Kumarian Press, Inc.; Lang Publishing, Peter; Libra Publishers, Inc.; Longman Publishing Group; McFarland & Company, Inc., Publishers; Madison Books; Mennonite Publishing House, Inc.; Mercury Press, The; Metamorphous Press; Mother Courage Press; Noble Press, Incorporated, The; Pendragon Press; Perspectives Press; Plenum Publishing; Potomac-Pacific Press; Praeger Publishers; Princeton Book Company, Publishers; Princeton University Press; Purdue University Press; R&E Publishers; Random House, Inc.; Riverdale Company, Inc., Publishers, The; Roxbury Publishing Co.; Rutgers University Press; Schenkman Books, Inc.; Seven Locks Press, Inc.; Stanford University Press; Stevens, Inc., Gareth; Sunflower University Press; Tarcher, Inc. Jeremy P.; Teachers College Press; Thomas Publications; Transaction Books; Twin Peaks Press; University of Alberta Press, The; University of Arkansas Press, The; University of Illinois Press; University of Massachusetts Press; University of North Carolina Press, The; University Press of America, Inc.; University Press of Kansas; University Press of Kentucky; University Press of New England; Walch, Publisher, J. Weston; Washington State University Pess; Westview Press; White Cliffs Media Company; Woodbine House; Word Books Publisher.

Software. Anderson Publishing Co.; ARCsoft Publishers; Barron's Educational Series, Inc.; Branden Publishing Co., Inc.; Career Publishing, Inc.; Chronicle Books; Compute! Books; Computer Science Press, Inc.; Devin-Adair Publishers, Inc.; Digital Press; Family Album, The; Gessler Publishing Company, Inc.; Grapevine Publications, Inc.; Heinle & Heinle Publishers, Inc.; Interstate Publishers, Inc. The; Ishi Press International; Jist Works, Inc.; Libraries Unlimited; Michigan State University Press; National Book Company; National Textbook Co.; Osborne/McGraw-Hill; Pacific Press Publishing Association; Que Corporation; R&E Publishers; SAS Institute, SAS Circle Inc.; Sybex, Inc.; TAB Books; Trillium Press; Wadsworth Publishing Company; White Cliffs Media Company; Wine Appreciation Guild, Ltd.; Wordware Publishing, Inc.

Sports. And Books; Archway/Minstrel Books; Atheneum Children's Books; Avon Books; Backcountry Publications; Bantam Books; Benjamin Company, Inc., The; Bentley, Inc., Robert; Bonus Books, Inc.; Bowling Green State University Popular Press; Briarcliff Press Publishers; Bull Publishing Co.; Cambridge Career Products; Carol Publishing; Contemporary Books, Inc.; Crown Publishers, Inc.; Dembner Books; Denali Press, The; Devin-Adair Publishers, Inc.; Eriksson, Publisher, Paul S.; Facts On File, Inc.; Fine, Inc., Donald I.; Fisher Books; Gallaudet University Press; Gardner Press, Inc.; Hancock House Publishers Ltd.; HarperCollins, Inc.; Howell Press, Inc.; Human Kinetics Publishers, Inc.; Jonathan David Publishers; Kesend Publishing, Ltd., Michael; Leisure Press; Liberty Publishing Company, Inc.; Little, Brown and Co., Inc.; Lone Pine Publishing; Longstreet Press, Inc.; Lucent Books; Lyons & Burford, Publishers, Inc.; McFarland & Company, Inc., Publishers; McGraw Hill Ryerson; Menasha Ridge Press, Inc.; Milkweed Editions; Mosaic Press Miniature Books; Motorbooks International Publishers & Wholesalers, Inc.; Mountaineers Books, The; Muir Publications, John; Mustang Publishing Co.; Ohara Publications, Inc.; Orca Book Publishers Ltd.; Pennsylvania Historical and Museum Commission; Polka-Dot Press; Prentice-Hall Canada, Inc.; Prentice Hall Press; Prevention Health Books; Princeton Book Company, Publishers; Random House, Inc.; Random House, Inc./Alfred A. Knopf, Inc. Juvenile Books; Sasquatch Books; Scarborough House/Publisherss; Scribner's Sons, Charles; Sentinel Books; Sierra Club Books; Stackpole Books; Sterling Publishing; Stoeger Publishing Company; Sunflower University Press; Synesis Press; Taylor Publishing Company; Times Books;

Tuttle Publishing Company, Inc., Charles E.; Twin Peaks Press; University of Illinois Press; University of Nebraska Press; Wilderness Adventure Books; Word Books Publisher; Workman Publishing Company, Inc.; Yankee Books.

Technical. Abbott, Langer & Associates; Almar Press; American Hospital Publishing, Inc.; American Psychiatric Press, Inc., The; American Society of Civil Engineers; ARCsoft Publishers; Arman Publishing, Inc., M.; Auto Book Press; Aviation Book Co.; Bentley, Inc., Robert; Boxwood Press, The; Branden Publishing Co., Inc.; Brevet Press, Inc.; Brick House Publishing Co.; Broadway Press; Canadian Plains Research Center; C&T Publishing; Chilton Book Co.; Cleaning Consultant Services, Inc.; Computer Science Press, Inc.; Cornell Maritime Press, Inc.; Cuff Publications Limited, Harry; Devonshire Publishing Co.; Digital Press; EES Publications; Erlbaum Associates, Inc., Lawrence; Financial Sourcebooks; Focal Press; Gallaudet University Press; Government Institutes, Inc.; Grapevine Publications, Inc.; Graphic Arts Technical Foundation; Human Kinetics Publishers, Inc.; IEEE Press; ILR Press; Industrial Press, Inc.; Information Resources Press; Instrument Society of America; International Foundation Of Employee Benefit Plans; Iowa State University Press; Knowledge Book Publishers; Leisure Press; Library Research Associates, Inc.; Lone Eagle Publishing Co.; McFarland & Company, Inc., Publishers; Metamorphous Press; MGI Management Institute, Inc., The; Michigan State University Press; Museum of Northern Arizona Press; National Book Company; Nichols Publishing; Osborne/McGraw-Hill; Pacific Books, Publishers; Parker-Griffin Publishing Co.; Pennsylvania Historical and Museum Commission; Princeton University Press; Professional Publications, Inc.; Q.E.D. Information Sciences, Inc.; Que Corporation; R&E Publishers; Religious Education Press; Riverdale Company, Inc., Publishers, The; Rocky Top Publications; San Francisco Press, Inc.; Sandhill Crane Press, Inc.; SAS Institute, SAS Circle Inc.; Schenkman Books, Inc.; Science Tech Publishers, Inc.; Skidmore-Roth Publishing; Sterling Publishing; Stipes Publishing Co.; Sybex, Inc.; Synesis Press; TAB Books; Texas Western Press; Tidewater Publishers; Transaction Books; ULI, The Urban Land Institute; Ultralight Publichations, Inc.; Union Square Press; Univelt, Inc.; University of Alaska Press; University of Alberta Press, The; University of Minnesota Press; Vestal Press, Ltd., The; White Cliffs Media Company; Windsor Books; Wordware Publishing, Inc.

Textbook. AASLH Press; Abingdon Press; Accelerated Development Inc.; Alba House; Amacom Books; Amacom Books; American Hospital Publishing, Inc.; American Psychiatric Press, Inc., The; Arman Publishing, Inc., M.; Art Direction Book Company; Asian Humanities Press; Avery Publishing Group; Baker Book House Company; Barron's Educational Series, Inc.; Behrman House Inc.; Bennett & McKnight Publishing Co.; Bosco Multimedia, Don; Bowling Green State University Popular Press; Boxwood Press, The; Boyd & Fraser Publishing Company; Branden Publishing Co., Inc.; Breakwater Books; Broadman Press; Cambridge University Press; Canadian Plains Research Center; Career Publishing, Inc.; Charlesbridge Publishing; Christopher Publishing House, The; Cleaning Consultant Services, Inc.; Cliffs Notes, Inc.; College Press Publishing Co.; Computer Science Press, Inc.; Coventure Press; Cuff Publications Limited, Harry; Devonshire Publishing Co.; Drama Book Publishers; Education Associates; Eerdmans Publishing Co., William B.; EES Publications; Erlbaum Associates, Inc., Lawrence; Fairchild Books & Visuals; Financial Sourcebooks; Fitzhenry & Whiteside, Ltd.; Focal Press; Free Press, The; Gallaudet University Press; Gardner Press, Inc.; Gessler Publishing Company, Inc.; Glenbridge Publishing Ltd.; Global Business and Trade; Grapevine Publications, Inc.; Graphic Arts Technical Foundation; Greenhaven Press, Inc.; Guernica Editions; Hardy—Publisher, Max; Hazelden Educational Materials; Health Administration Press; Heinle & Heinle Publishers, Inc.; Hendrick-Long Publishing Co., Inc.; Horizon Publishers & Distributors; Human Kinetics Publishers, Inc.; IEEE Press; ILR Press; Information Resources Press; Inner Traditions International; Intercultural Press, Inc.; International Foundation Of Employee Benefit Plans; International Publishers Co., Inc.; International Resources; Interstate Publishers, Inc. The; Intervarsity Press; Iowa State University Press; Jist Works, Inc.; Learning Publications Inc.; Libraries Unlimited; Longman Financial Services Publishing; Longman Publishing Group; Loyola University Press; McCutchan Publishing Corporation; Mennonite Publishing House, Inc.; Metamorphous Press; Michigan State University Press; Miller Books; National Book Company; National Textbook Co.; Oddo Publishing, Inc.; Pacific Press Publishing Association; Porter Sargent Publishers, Inc.; Praeger Publishers; Prentice Hall Canada, Inc.; Princeton Architectural Press; Princeton Book Company, Publishers; Professional Publications, Inc.; Purdue University Press; Que Corporation; R&E Publishers; Religious Education Press; Rosen Publishing Group, The; Roxbury Publishing Co.; St. Martin's Press; San Francisco Press, Inc.; Sandhill Crane Press, Inc.; Sandlapper Publishing, Inc.; SAS Institute, SAS Circle Inc.; Schenkman Books, Inc.; Schirmer Books; Science Tech Publishers, Inc.; Seven Locks Press, Inc.; Sigo Press; Skidmore-Roth Publishing; Standard Publishing; Stanford University Press; Stipes Publishing Co.; Synesis Press; Thomas Publications; Tidewater Publishers; Transaction Books; Transnational Publishers, Inc.; Trillium Press; University of Alaska Press; University of Alberta Press, The; University of Minnesota Press; University of Pittsburgh Press; University Press of America, Inc.; VGM Career Horizons; Wadsworth Publishing Company; Wall & Emerson, Inc.; White Cliffs Media Company; Word Books Publisher; York Press Ltd.

Translation. Alba House; Alyson Publications, Inc.; Architectural Book Publishing Co., Inc.; ARCsoft Publishers; ARCsoft Publishers; Asian Humanities Press; Barron's Educational Series, Inc.; Blue Dolphin Publishing, Inc.; Bosco Multimedia, Don; Briarcliff Press Publishers; Chatham Press; Citadel Press; City Lights Books; Clarion Books; Clarkson Potter; Cleis Press; Dante University Of America Press, Inc.; Davis Publications, Inc.; Devin-Adair Publishers, Inc.; Drama Book Publishers; Edicones Universal; Enslow Publishers; Free Press, The; Gallaudet University Press; Gardner Press, Inc.; Godine, Publisher, Inc., David R.; Guernica Editions; Holmes & Meier Publishers, Inc.; Hounslow Press; Intercultural Press, Inc.; Iowa State University Press; Johnson Books; Kodansha International U.S.A.; Lang Publishing, Peter; Longwood Academic; Mercury House Inc.; Motorbooks International Publishers & Wholesalers, Inc.; National Gallery of Canada; Northern Illinois University Press; Open Court Publishing Co.; Pacific Books, Publishers; Porter Sargent Publishers, Inc.; Princeton University Press; Resource Publications, Inc.; Ross Books; Sybex, Inc.; TAB Books; Theosophical Publishing House, The; Three Continents Press; Timber Press, Inc.; University of Alabama Press; University of Massachusetts Press; University of Texas Press; University of Utah Press; Vesta Publications, Ltd.; Wake Forest University Press; Western Producer Prairie Books; Wizards Bookshelf.

Transportation. Arman Publishing, Inc., M.; Aviation Book Co.; Bentley, Inc., Robert; Boston Mills Press, The; Carstens Publications, Inc.; Hungness Publishing, Carl; Interurban Press/Trans Anglo Books; Iowa State University Press; McGraw Hill Ryerson; Transportation Trails; Ultralight Publichations, Inc.

Travel. Academy Chicago; Almar Press; Appalachian Mountain Club Books; Atheneum Children's Books; Bantam Books; Barron's Educational Series, Inc.; Bear Flag Books; Binford & Mort Publishing; Briarcliff Press Publishers; Camino Books, Inc.; Canadian Institute of Ukrainian Studies Press; Carol Publishing; Chelsea Green; Chicago Review Press; Christopher Publishing House, The; Countryman Press, Inc., The; Denali Press, The; Devin-Adair Publishers, Inc.; Eerdmans Publishing Co., William B.; Eriksson, Publisher, Paul S.; Falcon Press Publishing Co.; Flying Pencil Publications; Four Walls Eight Windows; Gallaudet University Press; Gem Guides Book Company; Globe Pequot Press, Inc., The; Godine, Publisher, Inc., David R.; Golden West Publishers;

HarperCollins, Inc.; Heyday Books; Hippocrene Books Inc.; Homestead Publishing; Hounslow Press; Inner Traditions International; Intercultural Press, Inc.; Interlink Publishing Group, Inc.; International Resources; Interurban Press/Trans Anglo Books; Johnson Books; Kesend Publishing, Ltd., Michael; Kodansha International U.S.A.; Liberty Publishing Company, Inc.; Library Research Associates, Inc.; Lone Pine Publishing; Loompanics Unlimited; Lyons & Burford, Publishers, Inc.; Marlor Press; Menasha Ridge Press, Inc.; Mennonite Publishing House, Inc.; Mills & Sanderson, Publishers; Moon Publications; Mosaic Press Miniature Books; Mountaineers Books, The; Muir Publications, John; Mustang Publishing Co.; Orca Book Publishers Ltd.; Overlook Press, The; Passport Press; Peachtree Publishers, Ltd.; Pelican Publishing Company; Pennsylvania Historical and Museum Commission; Peterson's; Pilot Books; Prentice-Hall Canada, Inc.; Prentice Hall Press; R&E Publishers; Riverdale Company, Inc., Publishers, The; Sasquatch Books; Scarborough House/Publisherss; Sentinel Books; Sierra Club Books; Soho Press, Inc.; Soules Book Publishers Ltd., Gordon; Taylor Publishing Company; Transportation Trails; Travel Keys; Tuttle Publishing Company, Inc., Charles E.; Twin Peaks Press; Umbrella Books; University of Alaska Press; University of Minnesota Press; Wilderness Adventure Books; Williamson Publishing Co.; Wine Appreciation Guild, Ltd.; Woodbine House; Workman Publishing Company, Inc.; Wyrick & Company.

Womens Issues/Studies. ABC-CLIO, Inc.; Addison-Wesley Publishing Co., Inc.; Advocacy Press; Baker Book House Company; Beacon Press; Between the Lines Inc.; Bonus Books, Inc.; Bowling Green State University Popular Press; C&T Publishing; Carol Publishing; City Lights Books; Cleis Press; Conari Press; Contemporary Books, Inc.; Coteau Books; Coventure Press; Dee, Inc., Ivan R.; Erlbaum Associates, Inc., Lawrence; Evergreen Communications, Inc.; Fairleigh Dickinson University Press; Five Star Publications; Gardner Press, Inc.; Harbinger House, Inc.; Hensley, Inc., Virgil W.; Holmes & Meier Publishers, Inc.; Horizon Publishers & Distributors; Inner Traditions International; Interlink Publishing Group, Inc.; Insight Books; International Publishers Co., Inc.; International Resources; Kumarian Press, Inc.; Learning Publications Inc.; Llewellyn Publications; Longstreet Press, Inc.; Longwood Academic; Louisiana State University Press; Lucent Books; Luramedia; McFarland & Company, Inc., Publishers; Meeramma Publications; Mennonite Publishing House, Inc.; Mercury Press, The; Milkweed Editions; Multnomah Press; Noble Press, Incorporated, The; Oregon Historical Society Press; Praeger Publishers; Princeton Book Company, Publishers; Princeton University Press; R&E Publishers; Reference Service Press; Rutgers University Press; Scarecrow Press, Inc.; Schenkman Books, Inc.; Sigo Press; Spinsters/Aunt Lute Books; Sunflower University Press; Tarcher, Inc. Jeremy P.; Texas A&M University Press; Times Books; Transnational Publishers, Inc.; University of Massachusetts Press; University of Minnesota Press; University of Pittsburgh Press; University of Tennessee Press, The; Victor Books; Westview Press; Winbow Press.

World Affairs. ABC-CLIO, Inc.; Carroll & Graf Publishers, Inc.; Davis Publishing, Steve; Dillon Press, Inc.; Family Album, The; Fraser Institute, The.

Young Adult. ABC-CLIO, Inc.; Archway/Minstrel Books; Atheneum Children's Books; Bale Books; Barron's Educational Series, Inc.; Cliffs Notes, Inc.; College Board, The; Davenport, Publishers, May; Dial Books For Young Readers; Dillon Press, Inc.; Education Associates; Enslow Publishers; Falcon Press Publishing Co.; Fitzhenry & Whiteside, Ltd.; Houghton Mifflin Co.; Hunter House, Inc., Publishers; McElderry Books, Margaret K.; Rosen Publishing Group, The; Silver Burdett Press.

Author's Agents Subject Index

Fiction

This index will help you find agents who consider book manuscripts, articles and scripts on the subjects you write about. Fiction categories are listed before nonfiction categories in the index. Be sure to consult each agent's individual listing for submission information before sending a query or manuscript.

Adventure. Allan Agency, Lee; Appleseeds Management; Authors Marketing Services Ltd; Browne Ltd., Pema; Connor Literary Agency; Cook Literary Agency, Warren; Creative Concepts Literary Agency; Elek Associates, Peter; Ellenberg, Literary Agent, Ethan; Farwestern Consultants, Inc.; Fishbein Ltd., Frieda; Flaherty, Literary Agent, Joyce A.; Gladden Unlimited; Kamaroff Associates, Alex; Lampack Agency, Inc., Peter; Lee, Literary Agency, L. Harry; Perkins' Literary Agency; Sebastian Agency; Steele and Associates, Ellen Lively; Stern Associates, Charles M.; Teal Literary Agency, Patricia; Zelasky Literary Agency, Tom.

Ethnic. Farwestern Consultants, Inc.; Literary Marketing Consultants; Pegasus International, Inc.

Fantasy. Allen, Literary Agent, James; Appleseeds Management; Butler, Art and Literary Agent, Jane; Caravainis Agency, Inc., Maria; Schwartz, Laurens R., Esquire.

Historical. Allen, Literary Agent, James; Butler, Art and Literary Agent, Jane; Caravainis Agency, Inc., Maria; Collier Associates; Deering, Literary Agency, Dorothy; Flaherty, Literary Agent, Joyce A.; Kidde, Hoyt and Picard Literary Agency; Lee Shore Agency; Panettieri Agency, The; Sebastian Agency; Siegel, Literary Agency, Bobbe; Zeckendorf Associates, Susan; Zelasky Literary Agency, Tom.

Horror. Allen, Literary Agent, James; Appleseeds Management; Butler, Art and Literary Agent, Jane; Cohen, Inc., Ruth; Connor Literary Agency; Davie Literary Agency, Elaine; Diamant, The Writer's Workshop, Inc., Anita; Farwestern Consultants, Inc.; Flaherty, Literary Agent, Joyce A.; Gladden Unlimited; Kamaroff Associates, Alex; Lampack Agency, Inc., Peter; Lee, Literary Agency, L. Harry; Lee Shore Agency; Marcil Literary Agency, Inc., Denise; Panettieri Agency, The; Pegasus International, Inc.; Perkins' Literary Agency; Teal Literary Agency, Patricia; Cook Literary Agency, Warren.

Juvenile. Acacia House Publishing Services Ltd.; Anthony Agency, Joseph; Authors and Artists Resource Center/Tarc Literary Agency, The; Bernstein, Meredith; Bijur Literary Agency, Vicky; Blake Group Literary Agency, The; Brown, Literary Agency, Andrea; Brown Ltd., Curtis; Browne Ltd., Pema; Canadian Speakers' and Writers' Service Limited; Cantor, Literary Agent, Ruth; Casselman, Literary Agent, Martha; Catalog Literary Agency, The; Cohen, Inc., Ruth; Cook Literary Agency, Warren; Creative Concepts Literary Agency; Davie Literary Agency, Elaine; Deering, Literary Agency, Dorothy; Elek Associates, Peter; Ellenberg, Literary Agent, Ethan; Farquharson Ltd., John; Feiler Literary Agency, Florence; Forthwrite Literary Service; Gordon Agency, Charlotte; Gusay Literary Agency, Charlotte; Hass, Agent, Rose; Hawkins & Associates, Inc., John; Herner Rights Agency, Susan; J&R Literary Agency; Jones Literary Agency,

Lloyd; Kellock & Associates Co. Ltd., J.; Kern Literary Agency Inc., Natasha; Kouts, Barbara S.; Lazear Agency, Inc., The; Levine Literary Agency, Inc., Ellen; Lighthouse Literary Agency; Lincoln Literary Agency, Ray; McDonough, Literary Agent, Richard P.; Mann Agency, Carol; Manus Literary Agency, Inc., Janet Wilkens; Markowitz Literary Agency, Barbara; Meredith, Inc., Scott; Mews Books Ltd.; Morrison, Inc., Henry; Naggar Literary Agency, Jean V.; Norma-Lewis Agency, The; Nugent and Associates Literary Agency; Oceanic Press Service; Pegasus International, Inc.; Picard, Literary Agent, Alison; Rhodes Literary Agency; Rights Unlimited; Robb Literary Properties, Sherry; Roffman Associates, Richard H.; Rotrosen Agency, Jane; Schlessinger-Van Dyck Agency; Shepard Agency, The; Singer Literary Agency, Evelyn; Sommer, Inc., Elyse; Spieler Literary Agency, F. Joseph; Stewart Agency, Jo; Tornetta Agency, Phyllis; Urstadt, Inc., Susan P.; Warren Literary Agency, James; Wreschner, Authors' Representative, Ruth; Wright, Stephen; Writers House, Inc.

Literary. Allan Agency, Lee; Chester Literary Agency, Linda; Clausen Associates, Connie; Cook Literary Agency, Warren; Flaming Star Literary Enterprises; Flannery, White & Stone; Herner Rights Agency, Susan; Kidde, Hoyt and Picard Literary Agency; Lampack Agency, Inc., Peter; McBride Literary Agency, Margret; Markson Literary Agency, Elaine; Oscard Associates, Fifi; Picard, Literary Agent, Alison; Quicksilver Books, Inc.; Robbins Office, Inc., The; Scribe Agency; Sebastian Agency; Siegel, Literary Agency, Bobbe; Urstadt, Inc., Susan P.; Zeckendorf Associates, Susan.

Magazine Fiction. Allen, Literary Agent, James; Anthony Agency, Joseph; Author Aid Associates; Baldi Literary Agency, Inc., Malaga; Bond Ltd., Alison M.; Brown Inc., Ned; Deering, Literary Agency, Dorothy; Farquharson Ltd., John; Jordan Literary Agency, Lawrence; Kidde, Hoyt and Picard Literary Agency; King, Literary Agent, Daniel P.; Lazear Agency, Inc., The; Literary Marketing Consultants; Manus Literary Agency, Inc., Janet Wilkens; Meredith, Inc., Scott; Naggar Literary Agency, Jean V.; New Age World Services; Picard, Literary Agent, Alison; Roffman Associates, Richard H.; Seligman, Literary Agent, Lynn; Sterling Lord Literistic, Inc.; Wade, Carlson; Wallerstein Agency, The Gerry B.; Wright, Stephen.

Mainstream/Contemporary. Acton and Dystel, Inc.; Browne Ltd., Pema; Cantor, Literary Agent, Ruth; Caravainis Agency, Inc., Maria; Chester Literary Agency, Linda; Clausen Associates, Connie; Connor Literary Agency; Flaherty, Literary Agent, Joyce A.; Gladden Unlimited; Herman Agency, Inc., The Jeff; Hill Associates, Frederick; Kaltman Literary Agency, Larry; Kern Literary Agency Inc., Natasha; Kidde, Hoyt and Picard Literary Agency; King, Literary Agent, Daniel P.; Klinger, Inc., Harvey; Lee, Literary Agency, L. Harry; Lee Shore Agency; Literary Marketing Consultants; McBride Literary Agency, Margret; Multimedia Product Development, Inc.; Naggar Literary Agency, Jean V.; Perkins' Litarary Agency; Quicksilver Books, Inc.; Schlessinger-Van Dyck Agency; Sebastian Agency; Stern Agency, Gloria; Tornetta Agency, Phyllis.

Military/War. Ellenberg, Literary Agent, Ethan.

Movie Scripts. Allan Agency, Lee; Amsterdam Agency, Marcia; Anthony Agency, Joseph; Appleseeds Management; Author Aid Associates; Bernstein, Meredith; Bloom, Harry; Brown Inc., Ned; Canadian Speakers' and Writers' Service Limited; Catalog Literary Agency, The; Cook Literary Agency, Warren; Cooper Assoc., Inc., Bill; Creative Concepts Literary Agency; Curtis Associates, Inc. Richard; Deering, Literary Agency, Dorothy; Diamond Literary Agency, Inc.; Dupree/Miller and Associates; Dykeman Associates, Inc.; Feiler Literary Agency, Florence; Fishbein Ltd., Frieda; Flannery, White & Stone; Forthwrite Literary Service; Freedman Dramatic Agency, Inc., Robert A.; Garon-Brook Associates, Inc., Jay; Gladden Unlimited; Greene, Inc., Harold R.; Gusay Literary Agency, Charlotte; Heacock Literary Agency, Inc.; Hilton Literary Agency, Alice; Kellock & Associates Co. Ltd., J.; King, Literary Agent, Daniel P.; Kohner, Inc., Paul; Kroll Agency, Lucy; Lampack Agency, Inc., Peter; Lazear Agency,

Inc., The; Lee, Literary Agency, L. Harry; Lighthouse Literary Agency; Literary Group, The; McBride Literary Agency, Margret; Marshall Agency, The Evan; Meredith, Inc., Scott; Miller Agency, Inc., The Peter; Moore Literary Agency, Claudia; Morrison, Inc., Henry; Nelson Literary Agency, B.K.; Norma-Lewis Agency, The; Nugent and Associates Literary Agency; Oscard Associates, Fifi; Pegasus International, Inc.; Porcelain, Sidney E.; Radley-Regan & Associates, D.; Rights Unlimited; Robb Literary Properties, Sherry; Roffman Associates, Richard H.; Rogers and Associates, Stephanie; SBC Enterprises, Inc.; Scribe Agency; Shapiro-Lichtman Talent Agency; Shorr Stille and Associates; Spitzer Literary Agency, Philip G.; Steele And Associates, Ellen Lively; Stern, Gloria; Swanson, Inc., H.N.; Tantleff Office, The; Toomey Literary Agency, Jeanne; Warren Literary Agency, James; Wright Representatives, Inc., Ann; Wright, Stephen; Writer's Consulting Group; Zelasky Literary Agency, Tom.

Mystery. Allan Agency, Lee; Allen, Literary Agent, James; Appleseeds Management; Bernstein, Meredith; Butler, Art and Literary Agent, Jane; Cantor, Literary Agent, Ruth; Caravainis Agency, Inc., Maria; Cohen, Inc., Ruth; Connor Literary Agency; Cook Literary Agency, Warren; Creative Concepts Literary Agency; Davie Literary Agency, Elaine; Deering, Literary Agency, Dorothy; Diamond Literary Agency, Inc.; Farwestern Consultants, Inc.; Fishbein Ltd., Frieda; Flaherty, Literary Agent, Joyce A.; Goodman Literary Agency, Irene; Kamaroff Associates, Alex; Kern Literary Agency Inc., Natasha; King, Literary Agent, Daniel P.; Lampack Agency, Inc., Peter; Langer, Ruth; Lee, Literary Agency, L. Harry; Lee Shore Agency; Literary Marketing Consultants; Marcil Literary Agency, Inc., Denise; Noetzli Literary Agency, Regula; Oscard Associates, Fifi; Panettieri Agency, The; Pegasus International, Inc.; Perkins' Literary Agency; Porcelain, Sidney E.; Radley-Regan & Associates, D.; Schlessinger-Van Dyck Agency; Schulman Literary Agency, Inc., The Susan; Sommer, Inc., Elyse; Spitzer Literary Agency, Philip G.; Steinberg, Michael; Stern Associates, Charles M.; Stern, Stern Agency, Gloria; Teal Literary Agency, Patricia; Tornetta Agency, Phyllis; Ware Literary Agency, John A.; Zeckendorf Associates, Susan.

Nostalgia. Bernstein, Meredith; Boates Literary Agency, Reid; Borchardt Inc., Georges; Brown Inc., Ned; Cameron Agency, The Marshall; Cantor, Literary Agent, Ruth; Dykeman Associates, Inc.; Ellenberg, Literary Agent, Ethan; Fields/Rita Scott, Marje; Fishbein Ltd., Frieda; International Literature and Arts Agency; Lighthouse Literary Agency; Nathan Literary Agency, Ruth; Porcelain, Sidney E.; Rees Literary Agency, Helen.

Novels. Abel Literary Agancy, Carole; Abel Literary Agency, Inc., Dominick; Acacia House Publishing Services Ltd.; Acton and Dystel, Inc.; Agents Inc. for Medical and Mental Health Professionals; Aley Associates of Aspen, Maxwell; Allan Agency, Lee; Allen, Literary Agent, James; Amsterdam Agency, Marcia; Author Aid Associates; Authors and Artists Resource Center/Tarc Literary Agency, The; Authors Marketing Services Ltd; Baldi Literary Agency, Inc., Malaga; Becker, Maximilian; Bijur Literary Agency, Vicky; Black Literary Agency, Inc., David; Blake Group Literary Agency, The; Bloom, Harry; Bond Ltd., Alison M.; Brandenburgh and Associates Literary Agency; Brandt & Brandt Literary Agents, Inc.; Brown Ltd., Curtis; Browne Ltd., Pema; Butler, Art and Literary Agent, Jane; Canadian Speakers' and Writers' Service Limited; Cantor, Literary Agent, Ruth; Caravainis Agency, Inc., Maria; Casselman, Literary Agent, Martha; Catalog Literary Agency, The; Chester Literary Agency, Linda; Collin Literary Agency, Frances; Cook Literary Agency, Warren; Cooper Assoc., Inc., Bill; Creative Concepts Literary Agency; Curtis Associates, Inc. Richard; Davie Literary Agency, Elaine; Diamant, The Writer's Workshop, Inc., Anita; Diamond Literary Agency, Inc.; Dijkstra Literary Agency, Sandra; Dolger Agency, The Jonathan; Dupree/Miller and Associates; Eth Literary Representation, Felicia; Evans and Associates; Farquharson Ltd., John; Flaming Star Literary Enterprises; Foley Agency, The; Forthwrite Literary Service; Fuhrman Literary Agency, Candice; Garon-Brook Associates, Inc., Jay; Gartenberg, Literary Agent, Max; Gelles-Cole Literary Enterprises; Gladden Unlimited; Goldberg Literary Agents, Inc., Lucianne S.; Gordon Agency, Charlotte; Greene, Inc., Harold R.; Gusay Literary Agency, Charlotte; Hass, Agent, Rose; Hawkins & Associates, Inc., John; Heacock Literary Agency, Inc.; Herman Agency, Inc., The Jeff; Hochmann Books, John L.; Hull House Literary Agency; International Publisher Associates, Inc.; J&R Literary Agency; Jarvis and Co., Inc., Sharon; JCA Literary Agency Inc.; Jet Literary Associates, Inc.; Jones Literary Agency, Lloyd; Jordan Literary Agency, Lawrence; Kaltman Literary Agency, Larry; Kellock & Associates Co. Ltd., J.; Kern Literary Agency Inc., Natasha; Klinger, Inc., Harvey; Kohner, Inc., Paul; Kouts, Barbara S.; Kroll Agency, Lucy; Lampack Agency, Inc., Peter; Langer, Ruth; Larsen/Elizabeth Pomada Literary Agents, Michael; Lazear Agency, Inc., The; Lee, Literary Agency, L. Harry; Lee Shore Agency; Levine & Wales, Literary Agency, Inc.; Levine Literary Agency, Inc., Ellen; Lincoln Literary Agency, Ray; Literary Agency of Washington; Literary and Creative Artists Agency; Living Faith Literary Agency; Love Agency, Nancy; Lowenstein Associates, Inc.; MacCampbell Inc., Donald; McDonough, Literary Agent, Richard P.; Mann Agency, Carol; Manus Literary Agency, Inc., Janet Wilkens; Markowitz Literary Agency, Barbara; Marks, Betty; Markson Literary Agency, Elaine; Marshall Agency, The Evan; Meredith, Inc., Scott; Miller Agency, Inc., The Peter; Moore Literary Agency, Claudia; Morris Agency, William; Morrison, Inc., Henry; Multimedia Product Development, Inc.; New Age World Services; Noetzli Literary Agency, Regula; Nolan Literary Agency, The Betsy; Nugent and Associates Literary Agency; Oceanic Press Service; Oscard Associates, Fifi; Otte Company, The; Payne Literary Agency, The John K.; Pegasus International, Inc.; Perkins' Litarary Agency; Pine Associates, Inc., Arthur ; Popkin/Nancy Cooke, Julie; Priest Literary Agency, Aaron M.; Printed Tree, Inc.; Protter Literary Agent, Susan Ann; Pryor, Inc., Roberta; Quicksilver Books, Inc.; Rhodes Literary Agency; Rights Unlimited; Robb Literary Properties, Sherry; Robbins Office, Inc., The; Rotrosen Agency, Jane; Sandum & Associates; SBC Enterprises, Inc.; Schulman Literary Agency, Inc., The Susan; Schwartz, Literary Agent, Arthur P.; Seligman, Literary Agent, Lynn; Sheedy Litcrary Agency, Inc., Charlotte; Shepard Agency, The; Siegel, Literary Agency, Bobbe; Sierra Literary Agency; Snell Literary Agency, Michael; Sommer, Inc., Elysc; Steele And Associates, Ellen Lively; Steele & Company, Lyle; Sterling Lord Literistic, Inc.; Stern, Gloria; Stewart Agency, Jo; Swanson, Inc., H.N.; Toomey Literary Agency, Jeanne; Urstadt, Inc., Susan P.; Van Der Leun and Associates; Wade, Carlson; Wallace Literary Agency, Bess; Wallerstein Agency, The Gerry B.; Waterside Productions, Inc.; Wecksler-Incomco; Weiner Literary Agency, Cherry; Weyr Agency, Rhoda; Wreschner, Authors' Representative, Ruth; Wright Representatives, Inc., Ann; Wright, Stephen; Writer's Consulting Group; Writers' Representatives, Inc.

Occult. Farwestern Consultants, Inc.; Literary Marketing Consultants; New Age World Services; Steele And Associates, Ellen Lively.

Picture Books. Kellock & Associates Co. Ltd., J.; Lighthouse Literary Agency; Singer Literary Agency, Evelyn.

Plays. Anthony Agency, Joseph; Appleseeds Management; Author Aid Associates; Becker, Maximilian; Brown Inc., Ned; Cameron Agency, The Marshall; Deering, Literary Agency, Dorothy; Fields/Rita Scott, Marje; Fishbein Ltd., Frieda; Freedman Dramatic Agency, Inc., Robert A.; French, Inc., Samuel; Garon-Brook Associates, Inc., Jay; Graham Agency; International Literature and Arts Agency ; Kroll Agency, Lucy; Lazear Agency, Inc., The; Lee, Literary Agency, L. Harry; Lighthouse Literary Agency; Meredith, Inc., Scott; Nelson Literary Agency, B.K.; Norma-Lewis Agency, The; Nugent and Associates Literary Agency; Oscard Associates, Fifi; Schulman Literary Agency, Inc., The Susan; Swanson, Inc., H.N.; Tantleff Office, The; Wright Representatives, Inc., Ann; Wright, Stephen; Zelasky Literary Agency, Tom.

Poetry. Author Aid Associates; Wright, Stephen.

Radio Scripts. Wright, Stephen.

Religious. Literary Marketing Consultants.

Romance. Bernstein, Meredith; Cohen, Inc., Ruth; Collier Associates; Creative Concepts Literary Agency; Davie Literary Agency, Elaine; Deering, Literary Agency, Dorothy; Diamant, The Writer's Workshop, Inc., Anita; Farwestern Consultants, Inc.; Fishbein Ltd., Frieda; Flaherty, Literary Agent, Joyce A.; Goodman Literary Agency, Irene; Herner Rights Agency, Susan; Kamaroff Associates, Alex; Kern Literary Agency Inc., Natasha; Kidde, Hoyt and Picard Literary Agency; King, Literary Agent, Daniel P.; Lampack Agency, Inc., Peter; Literary Group, The; Literary Marketing Consultants; Panettieri Agency, The; Payne Literary Agency, The John K.; Pegasus International, Inc.; Perkins' Literary Agency; Picard, Literary Agent, Alison; Singer Media Corporation, Inc.; Southern Writers; Stern Associates, Charles M.; Teal Literary Agency, Patricia; Tornetta Agency, Phyllis; Warren Literary Agency, James; Zelasky Literary Agency, Tom.

Science Fiction. Allan Agency, Lee; Allen, Literary Agent, James; Appleseeds Management; Butler, Art and Literary Agent, Jane; Creative Concepts Literary Agency; Deering, Literary Agency, Dorothy; Diamant, The Writer's Workshop, Inc., Anita; Ellenberg, Literary Agent, Ethan; Gladden Unlimited; Herner Rights Agency, Susan; Kamaroff Associates, Alex; King, Literary Agent, Daniel P.; Lee, Literary Agency, L. Harry; Lee Shore Agency; Literary Marketing Consultants; Morrison, Inc., Henry; Pegasus International, Inc.; Quicksilver Books, Inc.; Schwartz, Laurens R., Esquire; Steele And Associates, Ellen Lively; Steinberg, Michael; Writers House, Inc.; Zelasky Literary Agency, Tom.

Short Story Collections. Farwestern Consultants, Inc.; King, Literary Agent, Daniel P.; Lighthouse Literary Agency; Lighthouse Literary Agency.

Spiritual. Heacock Literary Agency, Inc.

Suspense. Caravainis Agency, Inc., Maria; Connor Literary Agency; Diamond Literary Agency, Inc.; Kern Literary Agency Inc., Natasha; Langer, Ruth; Levine & Wales, Literary Agency, Inc.; Marcil Literary Agency, Inc., Denise; Panettieri Agency, The; Porcelain, Sidney E.; Radley-Regan & Associates, D.; Sebastian Agency; Siegel, Literary Agency, Bobbe; Spitzer Literary Agency, Philip G.; Ware Literary Agency, John A.; Zeckendorf Associates, Susan; Zelasky Literary Agency, Tom.

TV Scripts. Amsterdam Agency, Marcia; Anthony Agency, Joseph; Appleseeds Management; Author Aid Associates; Brown Inc., Ned; Canadian Speakers' and Writers' Service Limited; Creative Concepts Literary Agency; Deering, Literary Agency, Dorothy; Dykeman Associates, Inc.; Fishbein Ltd., Frieda; Forthwrite Literary Service; Freedman Dramatic Agency, Inc., Robert A.; Garon-Brook Associates, Inc., Jay; Heacock Literary Agency, Inc.; King, Literary Agent, Daniel P.; Kohner, Inc., Paul; Lampack Agency, Inc., Peter; Lazear Agency, Inc., The; Lee, Literary Agency, L. Harry; Literary and Creative Artists Agency; Literary Group, The; Marshall Agency, The Evan; Meredith, Inc., Scott; Nelson Literary Agency, B.K.; Norma-Lewis Agency, The; Nugent and Associates Literary Agency; Oscard Associates, Fifi; Pegasus International, Inc.; Porcelain, Sidney E.; Radley-Regan & Associates, D.; Robb Literary Properties, Sherry; Roffman Associates, Richard H.; Rogers and Associates, Stephanie; SBC Enterprises, Inc.; Schulman Literary Agency, Inc., The Susan; Scribe Agency; Shapiro-Lichtman Talent Agency; Shorr Stille and Associates; Steele And Associates, Ellen Lively; Stern, Gloria; Swanson, Inc., H.N.; Tantleff Office, The; Toomey Literary Agency, Jeanne; Warren Literary Agency, James; Wright Representatives, Inc., Ann; Wright, Stephen; Zelasky Literary Agency, Tom.

Western. Cohen, Inc., Ruth; Davie Literary Agency, Elaine; Farwestern Consultants, Inc.; Kern Literary Agency Inc., Natasha; Lee, Literary Agency, L. Harry; Lee Shore

Agency; Teal Literary Agency, Patricia; Zelasky Literary Agency, Tom; Zelasky Literary Agency, Tom.

Young Adult. Amsterdam Agency, Marcia; Browne Ltd., Pema; Cantor, Literary Agent, Ruth; Cohen, Inc., Ruth; Cook Literary Agency, Warren; Diamant, The Writer's Workshop, Inc., Anita; Fields/Rita Scott, Marje; Fishbein Ltd., Frieda; Garon-Brook Associates, Inc., Jay; Hill Associates, Frederick; Kellock & Associates Co. Ltd., J.; Kern Literary Agency Inc., Natasha; Lee Shore Agency; Lighthouse Literary Agency; Literary Marketing Consultants; Norma-Lewis Agency, The; Panettieri Agency, The; Payne Literary Agency, The John K.; Picard, Literary Agent, Alison.

Nonfiction

Americana. Butler, Art and Literary Agent, Jane; Ware Literary Agency, John A.

Animals. Urstadt, Inc., Susan P.

Anthropology/Archaeology. Butler, Art and Literary Agent, Jane.

Art/Architecture. Chester Literary Agency, Linda; Hass, Agent, Rose; Nathan Literary Agency, Ruth; Schwartz, Laurens R., Esquire; Urstadt, Inc., Susan P.; Van Der Leun and Associates.

Astrology/Psychic/New Age. Lee Shore Agency; Literary and Creative Artists Agency; New Age World Services; Quicksilver Books, Inc.; Steele And Associates, Ellen Lively; 2-M Communications Ltd.

Audio Cassettes. Creative Concepts Literary Agency; Feiler Literary Agency, Florence; Herman Agency, Inc., The Jeff.

Autobiography. Andrews & Associates, Bart; Boates Literary Agency, Reid; Elek Associates, Peter; Klinger, Inc., Harvey; Oscard Associates, Fifi.

Biography. Andrews & Associates, Bart; Appleseeds Management; Boates Literary Agency, Reid; Borchardt Inc., Georges; Caravainis Agency, Inc., Maria; Chester Literary Agency, Linda; Clausen Associates, Connie; Collier Associates; Diamant, The Writer's Workshop, Inc., Anita; Elek Associates, Peter; Ellenberg, Literary Agent, Ethan; Flaherty, Literary Agent, Joyce A.; Gladden Unlimited; Heacock Literary Agency, Inc.; Hull House Literary Agency; Klinger, Inc., Harvey; Levine & Wales, Literary Agency, Inc.; Lincoln Literary Agency, Ray; Literary Group, The; McBride Literary Agency, Margret; Multimedia Product Development, Inc.; Nathan Literary Agency, Ruth; Oscard Associates, Fifi; Payne Literary Agency, The John K.; Porcelain, Sidney E.; Rees Literary Agency, Helen; Schwartz, Laurens R., Esquire; Shepard Agency, The; Siegel, Literary Agency, Bobbe; Singer Media Corporation, Inc.; Spitzer Literary Agency, Philip G.; 2-M Communications Ltd.; Urstadt, Inc., Susan P.; Ware Literary Agency, John A.

Business/Economics. Acton and Dystel, Inc.; Bernstein, Meredith; Boates Literary Agency, Reid; Caravainis Agency, Inc., Maria; Chester Literary Agency, Linda; Collier Associates; Executive Excellence; Heacock Literary Agency, Inc.; Jones Literary Agency, Lloyd; Jordan Literary Agency, Lawrence; King, Literary Agent, Daniel P.; Levine & Wales, Literary Agency, Inc.; Marcil Literary Agency, Inc., Denise; Pegasus International, Inc.; Peter Associates, Inc., James; Quicksilver Books, Inc.; Rees Literary Agency, Helen; Sebastian Agency; Shepard Agency, The; Snell Literary Agency, Michael; Steinberg, Michael; Writers House, Inc.

Child Guidance/Parenting. Bernstein, Meredith; Connor Literary Agency; Heacock Literary Agency, Inc.; Marcil Literary Agency, Inc., Denise; Seligman, Literary Agent, Lynn; 2-M Communications Ltd.; Writers House, Inc.; Zeckendorf Associates, Susan.

Community/Public Affairs. Noetzli Literary Agency, Regula.

Computers/Electronics. Snell Literary Agency, Michael; Waterside Productions, Inc.; Collier Associates.

Cooking, Foods and Nutrition. Clausen Associates, Connie; Connor Literary Agency;

Creative Concepts Literary Agency; Elek Associates, Peter; Kern Literary Agency Inc., Natasha; Levine & Wales, Literary Agency, Inc.; Literary and Creative Artists Agency; Marks, Betty; Mews Books Ltd.; Pryor, Inc., Roberta; Steele And Associates, Ellen Lively; 2-M Communications Ltd.; Urstadt, Inc., Susan P.; Warren Literary Agency, James.

Crafts. Siegel, Literary Agency, Bobbe; Warren Literary Agency, James.

Entertainment/Games. Andrews & Associates, Bart.

Ethnic. Farwestern Consultants, Inc.; Writers' Production.

Fashion/Beauty. Bernstein, Meredith; Clausen Associates, Connie; Siegel, Literary Agency, Bobbe.

Film/Cinema/Stage. Hull House Literary Agency; Lincoln Literary Agency, Ray.

Gardening. Levine & Wales, Literary Agency, Inc.; Urstadt, Inc., Susan P.

General Nonfiction. Abel Literary Agancy, Carole; Acacia House Publishing Services Ltd.; Acton and Dystel, Inc.; Aley Associates of Aspen, Maxwell; Amsterdam Agency, Marcia; Andrews & Associates, Bart; Anthony Agency, Joseph; Author Aid Associates; Authors and Artists Resource Center/Tarc Literary Agency, The; Baldi Literary Agency, Inc., Malaga; Balkin Agency, Inc.; Becker, Maximilian; Bernstein, Meredith; Black Literary Agency, Inc., David; Blake Group Literary Agency, The; Boates Literary Agency, Reid; Borchardt Inc., Georges; Brandt & Brandt Literary Agents, Inc.; Brod Literary Agency, Ruth Hagy; Brown Inc., Ned; Brown, Literary Agency, Andrea; Browne Ltd., Pema; Cameron Agency, The Marshall; Cantor, Literary Agent, Ruth; Casselman, Literary Agent, Martha; Cohen, Inc., Ruth; Collin Literary Agency, Frances; Davie Literary Agency, Elaine; Deering, Literary Agency, Dorothy; Diamond Literary Agency, Inc.; Dijkstra Literary Agency, Sandra; Dolger Agency, The Jonathan; Dykeman Associates, Inc.; Eth Literary Representation, Felicia; Evans and Associates; Farquharson Ltd., John; Farwestern Consultants, Inc.; Fields/Rita Scott, Marje; Fishbein Ltd., Frieda; Flaming Star Literary Enterprises; Flannery, White & Stone; Foley Agency, The; Garon-Brook Associates, Inc., Jay; Gartenberg, Literary Agent, Max; Gelles-Cole Literary Enterprises; Goldberg Literary Agents, Inc., Lucianne S.; Gordon Agency, Charlotte; Hawkins & Associates, Inc., John; Herman Agency, Inc., The Jeff; Herner Rights Agency, Susan; Hill Associates, Frederick; Hochmann Books, John L.; International Publisher Associates, Inc.; J&R Literary Agency; Jarvis and Co., Inc., Sharon; JCA Literary Agency Inc.; Jet Literary Associates, Inc.; Jordan Literary Agency, Lawrence; Kaltman Literary Agency, Larry; Kamaroff Associates, Alex; Kellock & Associates Co. Ltd., J.; Kern Literary Agency Inc., Natasha; Kohner, Inc., Paul; Kouts, Barbara S.; Kroll Agency, Lucy; Lampack Agency, Inc., Peter; Larsen/Elizabeth Pomada Literary Agents, Michael; Lazear Agency, Inc., The; Lee Shore Agency; Levine Literary Agency, Inc., Ellen ; Lighthouse Literary Agency; Lincoln Literary Agency, Ray; Literary Agency of Washington; Literary and Creative Artists Agency; Love Agency, Nancy; Lowenstein Associates, Inc.; McBride Literary Agency, Margret; McDonough, Literary Agent, Richard P.; Mann Agency, Carol; Manus Literary Agency, Inc., Janet Wilkens; March Tenth, Inc.; Marks, Betty; Markson Literary Agency, Elaine; Marshall Agency, The Evan; Meredith, Inc., Scott; Naggar Literary Agency, Jean V.; New England Publishing Associates, Inc.; Nolan Literary Agency, The Betsy; Nugent and Associates Literary Agency; Otte Company, The; Pine Associates, Inc., Arthur; Popkin/Nancy Cooke, Julie; Priest Literary Agency, Aaron M.; Radley-Regan & Associates, D.; Rhodes Literary Agency; Riina Literary Agency, John, R.; Robbins Office, Inc., The; Rotrosen Agency, Jane; Sandum & Associates; SBC Enterprises, Inc.; Schulman Literary Agency, Inc., The Susan; Schwartz, Literary Agent, Arthur P.; Sheedy Literary Agency, Inc., Charlotte; Singer Literary Agency, Evelyn; Sommer, Inc., Elyse; Steele & Company, Lyle; Steinberg, Michael; Stern Agency, Gloria; Wade, Carlson; Wallace Literary Agency, Bess; Wallerstein Agency, The Gerry B.; Weiner Literary

Agency, Cherry; Weyr Agency, Rhoda; Wingra Woods Press; Zelasky Literary Agency, Tom.

Government/Politics. Acton and Dystel, Inc.; Black Literary Agency, Inc., David; Collier Associates; Diamant, The Writer's Workshop, Inc., Anita; King, Literary Agent, Daniel P.; Literary and Creative Artists Agency; Pegasus International, Inc.; Penmarin Books; Peter Associates, Inc., James; Shepard Agency, The; Spitzer Literary Agency, Philip G.

Health/Medicine. Appleseeds Management; Caravainis Agency, Inc., Maria; Chester Literary Agency, Linda; Clausen Associates, Connie; Diamant, The Writer's Workshop, Inc., Anita; Flaherty, Literary Agent, Joyce A.; Heacock Literary Agency, Inc.; Jordan Literary Agency, Lawrence; Kern Literary Agency Inc., Natasha; Klinger, Inc., Harvey; Lee Shore Agency; Levine & Wales, Literary Agency, Inc.; Marcil Literary Agency, Inc., Denise; Mews Books Ltd.; New Age World Services; Pegasus International, Inc.; Peter Associates, Inc., James; Quicksilver Books, Inc.; Schwartz, Laurens R., Esquire; Sebastian Agency; Seligman, Literary Agent, Lynn; Siegel, Literary Agency, Bobbe; 2-M Communications Ltd.; Ware Literary Agency, John A.; Warren Literary Agency, James; Wreschner, Authors' Representative, Ruth.

History. Chester Literary Agency, Linda; Collier Associates; Cook Literary Agency, Warren; Ellenberg, Literary Agent, Ethan; Fishbein Ltd., Frieda; Hawkins & Associates, Inc., John; Hull House Literary Agency; Jordan Literary Agency, Lawrence; Nathan Literary Agency, Ruth; Noetzli Literary Agency, Regula; Penmarin Books; Peter Associates, Inc., James; Pryor, Inc., Roberta; Ware Literary Agency, John A.; Warren Literary Agency, James.

How-to. Boates Literary Agency, Reid; Browne Ltd., Pema; Catalog Literary Agency, The; Clausen Associates, Connie; Collier Associates; Creative Concepts Literary Agency; Flaherty, Literary Agent, Joyce A.; Fuhrman Literary Agency, Candice; Gladden Unlimited; Kern Literary Agency Inc., Natasha; Lee Shore Agency; Literary and Creative Artists Agency; Marcil Literary Agency, Inc., Denise; Multimedia Product Development, Inc.; Panettieri Agency, The; Pegasus International, Inc.; Peter Associates, Inc., James; Schlessinger-Van Dyck Agency; Siegel, Literary Agency, Bobbe; Snell Literary Agency, Michael; Stern Associates, Charles M.; Teal Literary Agency, Patricia; Toomey Literary Agency, Jeanne; 2-M Communications Ltd.; Warren Literary Agency, James; Wreschner, Authors' Representative, Ruth.

Humanities. Hull House Literary Agency.

Humor. Bernstein, Meredith; 2-M Communications Ltd.

Illustrated Book. Schwartz, Laurens R., Esquire; Connor Literary Agency; Dolger Agency, The Jonathan; Penmarin Books.

Juvenile Books. Amsterdam Agency, Marcia; Author Aid Associates; Bernstein, Meredith; Brown, Literary Agency, Andrea; Browne Ltd., Pema; Cantor, Literary Agent, Ruth; Cohen, Inc., Ruth; Cook Literary Agency, Warren; Curtis Associates, Inc., Richard; Elek Associates, Peter; Ellenberg, Literary Agent, Ethan; Feiler Literary Agency, Florence; Flannery, White & Stone; Gusay Literary Agency, Charlotte; Hass, Agent, Rose; Herner Rights Agency, Susan; Jones Literary Agency, Lloyd; Jordan Literary Agency, Lawrence; Kouts, Barbara S.; Living Faith Literary Agency; Markowitz Literary Agency, Barbara; Mews Books Ltd.; Naggar Literary Agency, Jean V.; Norma-Lewis Agency, The; Nugent and Associates Literary Agency; Pegasus International, Inc.; Pryor, Inc., Roberta; Sheedy Literary Agency, Inc., Charlotte.

Language and Literature. Lincoln Literary Agency, Ray.

Law. Clausen Associates, Connie; Flaherty, Literary Agent, Joyce A.; King, Literary Agent, Daniel P.; Writer's Consulting Group.

Magazine Articles. Agents Inc. for Medical and Mental Health Professionals; Baldi Literary Agency, Inc., Malaga; Bijur Literary Agency, Vicky; Canadian Speakers' and

Writers' Service Limited; Creative Concepts Literary Agency; Deering, Literary Agency, Dorothy; Diamant, The Writer's Workshop, Inc., Anita; Donlan, Thomas C.; Executive Excellence; Farquharson Ltd., John; Jordan Literary Agency, Lawrence; Kidde, Hoyt and Picard Literary Agency; King, Literary Agent, Daniel P.; Kohner, Inc., Paul; Literary Agency of Washington; Literary Marketing Consultants; Lowenstein Associates, Inc.; Manus Literary Agency, Inc., Janet Wilkens; Meredith, Inc., Scott; Naggar Literary Agency, Jean V.; Picard, Literary Agent, Alison; Protter Literary Agent, Susan Ann; Robbins Office, Inc., The; Roffman Associates, Richard H.; Seligman, Literary Agent, Lynn; Singer Media Corporation, Inc.; Wade, Carlson; Wallerstein Agency, The Gerry B.; Wreschner, Authors' Representative, Ruth; Wright, Stephen; Writer's Consulting Group.

Marine Subjects. Jordan Literary Agency, Lawrence; Literary and Creative Artists Agency.

Military. Flaherty, Literary Agent, Joyce A.; Hull House Literary Agency.

Money/Finance. Executive Excellence; Marcil Literary Agency, Inc., Denise.

Music and Dance. Zeckendorf Associates, Susan.

Nature and Environment. Collier Associates; Levine & Wales, Literary Agency, Inc.; Lincoln Literary Agency, Ray; Caravainis Agency, Inc., Maria.

Nonfiction Book. Brown Ltd., Curtis; Butler, Art and Literary Agent, Jane; Cook Literary Agency, Warren; Curtis Associates, Inc. Richard; Donlan, Thomas C.; Dupree/Miller and Associates; Executive Excellence; Forthwrite Literary Service; Gusay Literary Agency, Charlotte; Markowitz Literary Agency, Barbara; Miller Agency, Inc., The Peter; Morris Agency, William; Morrison, Inc., Henry; Nelson Literary Agency, B.K.; Oceanic Press Service; Printed Tree, Inc.; Protter Literary Agent, Susan Ann; Rights Unlimited; Robb Literary Properties, Sherry; Seligman, Literary Agent, Lynn; Shepard Agency, The; Sterling Lord Literistic, Inc.; Stewart Agency, Jo; Toomey Literary Agency, Jeanne; Wecksler-Incomco; Writers' Representatives, Inc.

Philosophy. Literary and Creative Artists Agency.

Photography. Living Faith Literary Agency; Meredith, Inc., Scott; Protter Literary Agent, Susan Ann; Roffman Associates, Richard H.; Spieler Literary Agency, F. Joseph.

Psychology. Bernstein, Meredith; Caravainis Agency, Inc., Maria; Chester Literary Agency, Linda; Kern Literary Agency Inc., Natasha; Levine & Wales, Literary Agency, Inc.; Noetzli Literary Agency, Regula; Peter Associates, Inc., James; Quicksilver Books, Inc.; Sebastian Agency; Seligman, Literary Agent, Lynn; Snell Literary Agency, Michael; 2-M Communications Ltd.; Ware Literary Agency, John A.

Reference. Browne Ltd., Pema; Goodman Literary Agency, Irene; Snell Literary Agency, Michael; Sommer, Inc., Elyse.

Regional. Southern Writers.

Religion. Butler, Art and Literary Agent, Jane; Donlan, Thomas C.; Jordan Literary Agency, Lawrence; Literary Marketing Consultants; Living Faith Literary Agency.

Scholarly. Literary Marketing Consultants; New England Publishing Associates, Inc.

Science/Technology. Catalog Literary Agency, The; Cook Literary Agency, Warren; Jordan Literary Agency, Lawrence; Kern Literary Agency Inc., Natasha; Levine & Wales, Literary Agency, Inc.; Lincoln Literary Agency, Ray; Multimedia Product Development, Inc.; Noetzli Literary Agency, Regula; Penmarin Books; Seligman, Literary Agent, Lynn; Snell Literary Agency, Michael; Van Der Leun and Associates; Waterside Productions, Inc.; Writers House, Inc.; Zeckendorf Associates, Susan.

Self-Help. Appleseeds Management; Authors Marketing Services Ltd; Catalog Literary Agency, The; Chester Literary Agency, Linda; Clausen Associates, Connie; Creative Concepts Literary Agency; Elek Associates, Peter; Flaherty, Literary Agent, Joyce A.; Fuhrman Literary Agency, Candice; Gladden Unlimited; Jordan Literary Agency, Lawrence; Kern Literary Agency Inc., Natasha; Lee Shore Agency; Literary Group, The;

Can't find a listing? Check the end of each section: Book Publishers, page 221; Consumer Publications, pg. 605; Trade Journals, page 756; Scriptwriting Markets, page 797; Syndicates, page 807; Greeting Card Publishers, page 816; Author's Agents, page 876; and Contests, page 905.

Can't find a listing? Check the end of each section: Book Publishers, page 221; Consumer Publications, pg. 605; Trade Journals, page 756; Scriptwriting Markets, page 797; Syndicates, page 807; Greeting Card Publishers, page 816; Author's Agents, page 876; and Contests, page 905.

Can't find a listing? Check the end of each section: Book Publishers, page 221; Consumer Publications, pg. 605; Trade Journals, page 756; Scriptwriting Markets, page 797; Syndicates, page 807; Greeting Card Publishers, page 816; Author's Agents, page 876; and Contests, page 905.

Can't find a listing? Check the end of each section: Book Publishers, page 221; Consumer Publications, pg. 605; Trade Journals, page 756; Scriptwriting Markets, page 797; Syndicates, page 807; Greeting Card Publishers, page 816; Author's Agents, page 876; and Contests, page 905.

Can't find a listing? Check the end of each section: Book Publishers, page 221; Consumer Publications, pg. 605; Trade Journals, page 756; Scriptwriting Markets, page 797; Syndicates, page 807; Greeting Card Publishers, page 816; Author's Agents, page 876; and Contests, page 905.

Can't find a listing? Check the end of each section: Book Publishers, page 221; Consumer Publications, pg. 605; Trade Journals, page 756; Scriptwriting Markets, page 797; Syndicates, page 807; Greeting Card Publishers, page 816; Author's Agents, page 876; and Contests, page 905.

Can't find a listing? Check the end of each section: Book Publishers, page 221; Consumer Publications, pg. 605; Trade Journals, page 756; Scriptwriting Markets, page 797; Syndicates, page 807; Greeting Card Publishers, page 816; Author's Agents, page 876; and Contests, page 905.

Can't find a listing? Check the end of each section: Book Publishers, page 221; Consumer Publications, pg. 605; Trade Journals, page 756; Scriptwriting Markets, page 797; Syndicates, page 807; Greeting Card Publishers, page 816; Author's Agents, page 876; and Contests, page 905.

Can't find a listing? Check the end of each section: Book Publishers, page 221; Consumer Publications, pg. 605; Trade Journals, page 756; Scriptwriting Markets, page 797; Syndicates, page 807; Greeting Card Publishers, page 816; Author's Agents, page 876; and Contests, page 905.

Can't find a listing? Check the end of each section: Book Publishers, page 221; Consumer Publications, pg. 605; Trade Journals, page 756; Scriptwriting Markets, page 797; Syndicates, page 807; Greeting Card Publishers, page 816; Author's Agents, page 876; and Contests, page 905.

Can't find a listing? Check the end of each section: Book Publishers, page 221; Consumer Publications, pg. 605; Trade Journals, page 756; Scriptwriting Markets, page 797; Syndicates, page 807; Greeting Card Publishers, page 816; Author's Agents, page 876; and Contests, page 905.

*Can't find a listing? Check the end of each section: Book
Publishers, page 221; Consumer Publications, pg. 605;
Trade Journals, page 756; Scriptwriting Markets, page 797;
Syndicates, page 807; Greeting Card Publishers, page 816;
Author's Agents, page 876; and Contests, page 905.*

Record of Submissions

DATE SENT	TITLE	MARKET	EDITOR

PIX	DATE RET'D	DATE ACCEPT'D	DATE PUBL'D	COPY RECV'D	EXPENSES	PAYMENT

Record of Submissions

DATE SENT	TITLE	MARKET	EDITOR

PIX	DATE RET'D	DATE ACCEPT'D	DATE PUBL'D	COPY RECV'D	EXPENSES	PAYMENT

Other Books of Interest

Annual Market Books

Artist's Market, edited by Lauri Miller $21.95

Children's Writer's & Illustrator's Market, edited by Lisa Carpenter (paper) $15.95

Humor & Cartoon Markets, by Bob Staake (paper) $15.95

Novel & Short Story Writer's Market, edited by Robin Gee (paper) $18.95

Photographer's Market, edited by Sam Marshall $21.95

Poet's Market, by Judson Jerome $19.95

Songwriter's Market, edited by Mark Garvey $19.95

General Writing Books

Annable's Treasury of Literary Teasers, by H.D. Annable (paper) $10.95

Beginning Writer's Answer Book, edited by Kirk Polking (paper) $13.95

Discovering the Writer Within, by Bruce Ballenger & Barry Lane $16.95

Getting the Words Right: How to Rewrite, Edit and Revise, by Theodore A. Rees Cheney (paper) $12.95

How to Write a Book Proposal, by Michael Larsen (paper) $10.95

Just Open a Vein, edited by William Brohaugh $15.95

Knowing Where to Look: The Ultimate Guide to Research, by Lois Horowitz (paper) $15.95

Make Your Words Work, by Gary Provost $17.95

On Being a Writer, edited by Bill Strickland $19.95

The Story Behind the Word, by Morton S. Freeman (paper) $9.95

12 Keys to Writing Books that Sell, by Kathleen Krull (paper) $12.95

The 29 Most Common Writing Mistakes & How to Avoid Them, by Judy Delton $9.95

The Wordwatcher's Guide to Good Writing & Grammar, by Morton S. Freeman (paper) $15.95

Word Processing Secrets for Writers, by Michael A. Banks & Ansen Dibell (paper) $14.95

Writer's Block & How to Use It, by Victoria Nelson $14.95

The Writer's Digest Guide to Manuscript Formats, by Buchman & Groves $17.95

Nonfiction Writing

Basic Magazine Writing, by Barbara Kevles $16.95

The Complete Guide to Writing Biographies, by Ted Schwarz $19.95

Creative Conversations: The Writer's Guide to Conducting Interviews, by Michael Schumacher $16.95

How to Sell Every Magazine Article You Write, by Lisa Collier Cool (paper) $11.95

How to Write Irresistible Query Letters, by Lisa Collier Cool (paper) $10.95

The Writer's Digest Handbook of Magazine Article Writing, edited by Jean M. Fredette (paper) $11.95

Writing Creative Nonfiction, by Theodore A. Rees Cheney $15.95

Fiction Writing

The Art & Craft of Novel Writing, by Oakley Hall $17.95

Best Stories from New Writers, edited by Linda Sanders $16.95

Characters & Viewpoint, by Orson Scott Card $13.95

The Complete Guide to Writing Fiction, by Barnaby Conrad $17.95

Cosmic Critiques: How & Why 10 Science Fiction Stories Work, edited by Asimov & Greenberg (paper) $12.95

Creating Characters: How To Build Story People, by Dwight V. Swain $16.95

Creating Short Fiction, by Damon Knight (paper) $9.95

Dare to Be a Great Writer: 329 Keys to Powerful Fiction, by Leonard Bishop $16.95

Dialogue, by Lewis Turco $13.95

Fiction Is Folks: How to Create Unforgettable Characters, by Robert Newton Peck (paper) $8.95

Handbook of Short Story Writing: Vol. I, by Dickson and Smythe (paper) $9.95

Handbook of Short Story Writing: Vol. II, edited by Jean M. Fredette $15.95

How to Write & Sell Your First Novel, by Collier & Leighton (paper) $12.95

One Great Way to Write Short Stories, by Ben Nyberg $14.95

Manuscript Submission, by Scott Edelstein $13.95

Plot, by Ansen Dibell $13.95

Revision, by Kit Reed $13.95

Spider Spin Me a Web: Lawrence Block on Writing Fiction, by Lawrence Block $16.95

Storycrafting, by Paul Darcy Boles (paper) $10.95

Theme & Strategy, by Ronald B. Tobias $13.95

Writing the Novel: From Plot to Print, by Lawrence Block (paper) $10.95

Special Interest Writing Books

Armed & Dangerous: A Writer's Guide to Weapons, by Michael Newton (paper) $14.95

The Children's Picture Book: How to Write It, How to Sell It, by Ellen E.M. Roberts (paper) $18.95

Comedy Writing Secrets, by Melvin Helitzer $18.95

The Complete Book of Scriptwriting, by J. Michael Straczynski (paper) $11.95

The Craft of Lyric Writing, by Sheila Davis $19.95

Deadly Doses: A Writer's Guide to Poisons, by Serita Deborah Stevens with Anne Klarner (paper) $16.95

Editing Your Newsletter, by Mark Beach (paper) $18.50

Families Writing, by Peter Stillman $15.95

How to Write a Play, by Raymond Hull (paper) $12.95

How to Write Action/Adventure Novels, by Michael Newton $13.95

How to Write & Sell A Column, by Raskin & Males $10.95

How to Write and Sell Your Personal Experiences, by Lois Duncan (paper) $10.95

How to Write Mysteries, by Shannon OCork $13.95

How to Write Romances, by Phyllis Taylor Pianka $13.95

How To Write Science Fiction & Fantasy, by Orson Scott Card $13.95

How to Write Tales of Horror, Fantasy & Science Fiction, edited by J.N. Williamson $15.95

How to Write the Story of Your Life, by Frank P. Thomas (paper) $11.95

How to Write Western Novels, by Matt Braun $13.95

Mystery Writer's Handbook, by The Mystery Writers of America (paper) $11.95

The Poet's Handbook, by Judson Jerome (paper) $10.95

Successful Lyric Writing (workbook), by Sheila Davis (paper) $18.95

Successful Scriptwriting, by Jurgen Wolff & Kerry Cox $18.95

Travel Writer's Handbook, by Louise Zobel (paper) $11.95

TV Scriptwriter's Handbook, by Alfred Brenner (paper) $10.95

The Writer's Complete Crime Reference Book, by Martin Roth $19.95

Writing for Children & Teenagers, 3rd Edition, by Lee Wyndham & Arnold Madison (paper) $12.95

Writing the Modern Mystery, by Barbara Norville $15.95

Writing to Inspire, edited by William Gentz (paper) $14.95

The Writing Business

A Beginner's Guide to Getting Published, edited by Kirk Polking (paper) $11.95

The Complete Guide to Self-Publishing, by Tom & Marilyn Ross (paper) $16.95

How to Sell & Re-Sell Your Writing, by Duane Newcomb $11.95

How to Write with a Collaborator, by Hal Bennett with Michael Larsen $11.95

How You Can Make $25,000 a Year Writing, by Nancy Edmonds Hanson (paper) $12.95

Is There a Speech Inside You?, by Don Aslett (paper) $9.95

Literary Agents: How to Get & Work with the Right One for You, by Michael Larsen $9.95

Professional Etiquette for Writers, by William Brohaugh $9.95

Time Management for Writers, by Ted Schwarz $10.95

The Writer's Friendly Legal Guide, edited by Kirk Polking $16.95

Writer's Guide to Self-Promotion & Publicity, by Elane Feldman $16.95

A Writer's Guide to Contract Negotiations, by Richard Balkin (paper) $11.95

Writing A to Z, edited by Kirk Polking $19.95

To order directly from the publisher, include $3.00 postage and handling for 1 book and $1.00 for each additional book. Allow 30 days for delivery.

Writer's Digest Books
1507 Dana Avenue, Cincinnati, Ohio 45207
Credit card orders call TOLL-FREE
1-800-289-0963
Prices subject to change without notice.

Write to this same address for information on *Writer's Digest* magazine, *Story* magazine, Writer's Digest Book Club, Writer's Digest School, and Writer's Digest Criticism Service.

Canadian Postage by the Page

The following chart is for the convenience of Canadian writers sending domestic mail and American writers sending an envelope with International Reply Coupons (IRCs) or Canadian stamps for return of a manuscript from a Canadian publisher.

For complete postage assistance, use in conjunction with the U.S. Postage by the Page. Remember that manuscripts returning from the U.S. to Canada will take a U.S. stamped envelope although the original manuscript was sent with Canadian postage. This applies to return envelopes sent by American writers to Canada, too, which must be accompanied with IRCs or Canadian postage.

In a #10 envelope, you can have up to five pages for 39¢ (on manuscripts within Canada) or 45¢ (on manuscripts going to the U.S.). If you enclose a SASE, four pages is the limit. If you use 10×13 envelopes, send one page less than indicated on the chart.

IRC's are worth 45¢ Canadian postage but cost 95¢ to buy in the U.S. (Hint to U.S. writers: If you live near the border or have a friend in Canada, stock up on Canadian stamps. Not only are they more convenient than IRCs, they are cheaper.)

Canada Post has made major changes in designation of types of mail, as follows:

Standard Letter Mail Minimum size: 9cm × 14cm (3⅝″ × 5½″); Maximum size: 14cm × 24.5cm (5½″ × 9⅝″); Maximum thickness: 5mm (³⁄₁₆″)

Oversize Letter Mail Minimum size: 14cm × 24.5cm (5½″ × 9⅝″); Maximum size: 27cm × 38cm (10⅞″ × 15″); Maximum thickness: 2cm (¹³⁄₁₆″)

International Letter Mail Minimum size: 9cm × 14cm (3⅝″ × 5½″); Maximum size: Length + width + depth 90cm (36″) Greatest dimension must not exceed 60cm (24″)

Insurance: To U.S. and within Canada—45¢ for each $100 coverage to a maximum coverage of $1000. International—65¢ for each $100 coverage to a maximum coverage of $1000.

Registered Mail: $3 plus postage (air or surface—any destination). Legal proof of mailing provided.